A DECLENSION GUIDE TO THE *TEXTUS RECEPTUS* GREEK NEW TESTAMENT UNDERLYING THE KING JAMES VERSI

SECOND EDITION

VOLUME TWO

- ACTS to REVELATION -

BY

Park SeungKyu, Ph.D., Th.D.

Ra ChaeWon, Th.M., Ph.D.

Printed in the United States of America
ISBN: 979-8-9896619-8-5
Park SeungKyu
Address:
Bible College of East Africa Tanzania
P. O. Box 15761, Arusha
The United Republic of Tanzania

Telephone: (82) 10 7935 8662; (255) 621 363 522
Website: https://www.youtube.com/@BCEATanzania
https://www.facebook.com/BCEATZ
E-mail: fireinbone@gmail.com

Published by:
THE OLD PATHS PUBLICATIONS, Inc
Web: www.theoldpathspublications.com
Email: TOP@theoldpathspublications.com
March, 2024

All Glory and Praise

to God

The Lord and Everlasting Father

and the Eternal Truth

CONTENTS

ΠΡΑΞΕΙΣ ΤΩΝ ΑΠΟΣΤΟΛΩΝ

1

1 Τὸν art. acc. masc. sg. ὁ ἡ τό the, this, that, he, she, it
μέν conj. μέν indeed, verily, truly, even, so, some
πρῶτον ordinal. adj. acc. neut. sg. πρῶτος first, chief, first of all, chiefest, best
λόγον n. acc. masc. sg. λόγος word, saying, account, speech, thing, matter
περὶ prep. περί (+gen) of, for, concerning, (+acc) about, concerning, in
πάντων adj. gen. neut. pl. πᾶς πᾶσα πᾶν all, every, whosoever, every one, no, whole, any
ὦ interjection. ὦ O
Θεόφιλε n. voc. masc. sg. Θεόφιλος Theophilus
ὧν relative pron. gen. neut. pl. ὅς ἥ ὅ who, which, what, that
ὁ art. nom. masc. sg. ὁ ἡ τό the, this, that, he, she, it
Ἰησοῦς n. nom. masc. sg. Ἰησοῦς Jesus
τε conj. τέ and, both, also
καὶ conj. καί and, even, also, but
2 ἄχρι prep. ἄχρι or ἄχρις (+gen) until, unto, till, even to, as far as, while, into
ἧς relative pron. gen. fem. sg. ὅς ἥ ὅ who, which, what, that
ἡμέρας n. gen. fem. sg. ἡμέρα day, time, year, while, age, day time
τοῖς art. dat. masc. pl. ὁ ἡ τό the, this, that, he, she, it
ἀποστόλοις n. dat. masc. pl. ἀπόστολος apostle, messenger, he that is sent
διὰ prep. διά (+gen) by, through, with, in, of, (+acc) for, because of, for a cause
Πνεύματος n. gen. neut. sg. πνεῦμα spirit, Spirit, Ghost, ghost, life. of the spirit, wind
Ἁγιου adj. gen. neut. sg. ἅγιος Holy, holy, saint, Holy One, holy thing, most holy
οὓς relative pron. acc. masc. pl. ὅς ἥ ὅ who, which, what, that
3 οἷς relative pron. dat. masc. pl. ὅς ἥ ὅ who, which, what, that
καὶ conj. καί and, even, also, but
ἑαυτὸν reflexive pron. acc. masc. 3p. sg. ἑαυτοῦ himself, herself, itself, yourself, ourselves
μετὰ prep. μετά (+gen) with, among, against, (+acc) after
τὸ art. acc. neut. sg. ὁ ἡ τό the, this, that, he, she, it
αὐτὸν pron. acc. masc. 3p. sg. αὐτός ή ό self, of oneself, even, very, the same, he, she, it
ἐν prep. ἐν (+dat) in, by, with, among, at, on, through, to, within, into, of, for
πολλοῖς adj. dat. neut. pl. πολύς many, great, much, long, abundant
τεκμηρίοις n. dat. neut. pl. τεκμήριον infallible proof
δι' prep. διά (+gen) by, through, with, in, of, (+acc) for, because of, for a cause
ἡμερῶν n. gen. fem. pl. ἡμέρα day, time, year, while, age, day time
τεσσαράκοντα num. gen. fem. pl. τεσσαράκοντα forty
αὐτοῖς pron. dat. masc. 3p. pl. αὐτός ή ό self, of oneself, even, very, the same, he, she, it
καὶ conj. καί and, even, also, but
τὰ art. acc. neut. pl. ὁ ἡ τό the, this, that, he, she, it
περὶ prep. περί (+gen) of, for, concerning, (+acc) about, concerning, in
τῆς art. gen. fem. sg. ὁ ἡ τό the, this, that, he, she, it
βασιλείας n. gen. fem. sg. βασιλεία kingdom, reign
τοῦ art. gen. masc. sg. ὁ ἡ τό the, this, that, he, she, it
Θεοῦ n. gen. masc. sg. θεός God, god
4 καὶ conj. καί and, even, also, but
μετ' prep. μετά (+gen) with, among, against, (+acc) after
αὐτῶν pron. gen. masc. 3p. pl. αὐτός ή ό self, of oneself, even, very, the same, he, she, it
αὐτοῖς pron. dat. masc. 3p. pl. αὐτός ή ό self, of oneself, even, very, the same, he, she, it
ἀπὸ prep. ἀπό (+gen) from, of, out of, since, for, off, at, by, in, on
Ἱεροσολύμων n. gen. neut. pl. Ἱεροσόλυμα Jerusalem
μὴ particle of negation. μή not, no, lest, neither, none, nothing, nor, never, without

ἀλλὰ conj. ἀλλά but, yea, yet, nevertheless, howbeit, nay, therefore
τὴν art. acc. fem. sg. ὁ ἡ τό the, this, that, he, she, it
ἐπαγγελίαν n. acc. fem. sg. ἐπαγγελία promise, message
τοῦ art. gen. masc. sg. ὁ ἡ τό the, this, that, he, she, it
πατρὸς n. gen. masc. sg. πατήρ Father, father, parent
ἣν relative pron. acc. fem. sg. ὅς ἥ ὅ who, which, what, that
μου pron. gen. 1p. sg. ἐγώ I
5 ὅτι conj. ὅτι that, for, because, how that, how, because that, for that, though
Ἰωάννης n. nom. masc. sg. Ἰωάννης John
μὲν conj. μέν indeed, verily, truly, even, so, some
ὕδατι n. dat. neut. sg. ὕδωρ water
ὑμεῖς pron. nom. 2p. pl. σύ thou, you
δὲ conj. δέ but, and, now, also, to the contrary, rather, then
ἐν prep. ἐν (+dat) in, by, with, among, at, on, through, to, within, into, of, for
Πνεύματι n. dat. neut. sg. πνεῦμα spirit, Spirit, Ghost, ghost, life. of the spirit, wind
Ἁγίῳ adj. dat. neut. sg. ἅγιος Holy, holy, saint, Holy One, holy thing, most holy
οὐ particle of negation. οὐ οὐκ οὐχ not, no, neither, none, nay, nor, never, nothing
μετὰ prep. μετά (+gen) with, among, against, (+acc) after
πολλὰς adj. acc. fem. pl. πολύς many, great, much, long, abundant
ταύτας demo. pron. acc. fem. pl. οὗτος αὕτη τοῦτο this, the same, this same, he, she, it
ἡμέρας n. acc. fem. pl. ἡμέρα day, time, year, while, age, day time
6 Οἱ art. nom. masc. pl. ὁ ἡ τό the, this, that, he, she, it
μὲν conj. μέν indeed, verily, truly, even, so, some
οὖν conj. οὖν therefore, then, so, and, now, wherefore
αὐτὸν pron. acc. masc. 3p. sg. αὐτός ή ό self, of oneself, even, very, the same, he, she, it
Κύριε n. voc. masc. sg. κύριος Lord, lord, master, sir, LORD, God, Master, owner
εἰ conj. εἰ if, whether, that, though, forasmuch
ἐν prep. ἐν (+dat) in, by, with, among, at, on, through, to, within, into, of, for
τῷ art. dat. masc. sg. ὁ ἡ τό the, this, that, he, she, it
χρόνῳ n. dat. masc. sg. χρόνος time, season, space
τούτῳ demo. pron. dat. masc. sg. οὗτος αὕτη τοῦτο this, the same, this same, he, she, it
τὴν art. acc. fem. sg. ὁ ἡ τό the, this, that, he, she, it
βασιλείαν n. acc. fem. sg. βασιλεία kingdom, reign
τῷ art. dat. masc. sg. ὁ ἡ τό the, this, that, he, she, it
Ἰσραήλ pron. name. masc. inde. Ἰσραήλ Israel
7 δὲ conj. δέ but, and, now, also, to the contrary, rather, then
πρὸς prep. πρός (+gen) for, (+dat) at, (+acc) unto, to, with, for, against
αὐτούς pron. acc. masc. 3p. pl. αὐτός ή ό self, of oneself, even, very, the same, he, she, it
Οὐχ particle of negation. οὐ οὐκ οὐχ not, no, neither, none, nay, nor, never, nothing
ὑμῶν pron. gen. 2p. pl. σύ thou, you
χρόνους n. acc. masc. pl. χρόνος time, season, space
ἢ particle. ἤ or, than, either, nor, or else, and, rather than
καιροὺς n. acc. masc. pl. καιρός time, season, due time, opportunity
οὓς relative pron. acc. masc. pl. ὅς ἥ ὅ who, which, what, that
ὁ art. nom. masc. sg. ὁ ἡ τό the, this, that, he, she, it
πατὴρ n. nom. masc. sg. πατήρ Father, father, parent
ἐν prep. ἐν (+dat) in, by, with, among, at, on, through, to, within, into, of, for
τῇ art. dat. fem. sg. ὁ ἡ τό the, this, that, he, she, it
ἰδίᾳ adj. dat. fem. sg. ἴδιος one's own, one's, privately
ἐξουσίᾳ n. dat. fem. sg. ἐξουσία power, authority, right, strength, jurisdiction
8 ἀλλὰ conj. ἀλλά but, yea, yet, nevertheless, howbeit, nay, therefore
δύναμιν n. acc. fem. sg. δύναμις power, mighty work, miracle, strength, might
τοῦ art. gen. neut. sg. ὁ ἡ τό the, this, that, he, she, it
Ἁγίου adj. gen. neut. sg. ἅγιος Holy, holy, saint, Holy One, holy thing, most holy
Πνεύματος n. gen. neut. sg. πνεῦμα spirit, Spirit, Ghost, ghost, life. of the spirit, wind

ἐφ' prep. ἐπί (+gen) on, in, upon, (+dat) in, at, for, upon, (+acc) on, upon, unto, to, against
ὑμᾶς pron. acc. 2p. pl. σύ thou, you
καὶ conj. καί and, even, also, but
μοι pron. dat. 1p. sg. ἐγώ I
μάρτυρες n. nom. masc. pl. μάρτυς or μάρτυρ witness, martyr, record
ἔν prep. ἐν (+dat) in, by, with, among, at, on, through, to, within, into, of, for
τε conj. τέ and, both, also
Ἱερουσαλήμ pron. name. fem. inde. Ἱερουσαλήμ Jerusalem
καὶ conj. καί and, even, also, but
ἐν prep. ἐν (+dat) in, by, with, among, at, on, through, to, within, into, of, for
πάσῃ adj. dat. fem. sg. πᾶς πᾶσα πᾶν all, every, whosoever, every one, no, whole, any
τῇ art. dat. fem. sg. ὁ ἡ τό the, this, that, he, she, it
Ἰουδαίᾳ n. dat. fem. sg. Ἰουδαία Judaea, Jewry
καὶ conj. καί and, even, also, but
Σαμαρείᾳ n. dat. fem. sg. Σαμάρεια Samaria
καὶ conj. καί and, even, also, but
ἕως conj. ἕως till, until, unto, until when, while, as far as, even, until now
ἐσχάτου adj. gen. neut. sg. ἔσχατος last, lowest, uttermost, uttermost part
τῆς art. gen. fem. sg. ὁ ἡ τό the, this, that, he, she, it
γῆς n. gen. fem. sg. γῆ earth, land, ground, country
9 καὶ conj. καί and, even, also, but
ταῦτα demo. pron. acc. neut. pl. οὗτος αὕτη τοῦτο this, the same, this same, he, she, it
αὐτῶν pron. gen. masc. 3p. pl. αὐτός ή ό self, of oneself, even, very, the same, he, she, it
καὶ conj. καί and, even, also, but
νεφέλη n. nom. fem. sg. νεφέλη cloud
αὐτὸν pron. acc. masc. 3p. sg. αὐτός ή ό self, of oneself, even, very, the same, he, she, it
ἀπὸ prep. ἀπό (+gen) from, of, out of, since, for, off, at, by, in, on
τῶν art. gen. masc. pl. ὁ ἡ τό the, this, that, he, she, it
ὀφθαλμῶν n. gen. masc. pl. ὀφθαλμός eye, sight
αὐτῶν pron. gen. masc. 3p. pl. αὐτός ή ό self, of oneself, even, very, the same, he, she, it
10 καὶ conj. καί and, even, also, but
ὡς adv. ὡς as, when, as it were, how, about, like, as soon as, even as, while
εἰς prep. εἰς (+acc) into, to, unto, for, in, on, toward, against, upon, at, among
τὸν art. acc. masc. sg. ὁ ἡ τό the, this, that, he, she, it
οὐρανὸν n. acc. masc. sg. οὐρανός heaven, air, sky
αὐτοῦ pron. gen. masc. 3p. sg. αὐτός ή ό self, of oneself, even, very, the same, he, she, it
καὶ conj. καί and, even, also, but
ἄνδρες n. nom. masc. pl. ἀνήρ man, husband, sir
δύο num. nom. masc. pl. δύο two, twain, both
αὐτοῖς pron. dat. masc. 3p. pl. αὐτός ή ό self, of oneself, even, very, the same, he, she, it
ἐν prep. ἐν (+dat) in, by, with, among, at, on, through, to, within, into, of, for
ἐσθῆτι n. dat. fem. sg. ἐσθής robe, apparel, clothing, raiment
λευκῇ adj. dat. fem. sg. λευκός white
11 οἳ relative pron. nom. masc. pl. ὅς ἥ ὅ who, which, what, that
καὶ conj. καί and, even, also, but
Ἄνδρες n. voc. masc. pl. ἀνήρ man, husband, sir
Γαλιλαῖοι adj. voc. masc. pl. Γαλιλαῖος Galilean, of Galilee
τί interrog. pron. acc. neut. sg. τίς what, who, why, where, which, how
εἰς prep. εἰς (+acc) into, to, unto, for, in, on, toward, against, upon, at, among
τὸν art. acc. masc. sg. ὁ ἡ τό the, this, that, he, she, it
οὐρανόν n. acc. masc. sg. οὐρανός heaven, air, sky
οὗτος demo. pron. nom. masc. sg. οὗτος αὕτη τοῦτο this, the same, this same, he, she, it
ὁ art. nom. masc. sg. ὁ ἡ τό the, this, that, he, she, it
Ἰησοῦς n. nom. masc. sg. Ἰησοῦς Jesus
ὁ art. nom. masc. sg. ὁ ἡ τό the, this, that, he, she, it

ἀφ' prep. ἀπό (+gen) from, of, out of, since, for, off, at, by, in, on
ὑμῶν pron. gen. 2p. pl. σύ thou, you
εἰς prep. εἰς (+acc) into, to, unto, for, in, on, toward, against, upon, at, among
τὸν art. acc. masc. sg. ὁ ἡ τό the, this, that, he, she, it
οὐρανόν n. acc. masc. sg. οὐρανός heaven, air, sky
οὕτως adv. οὕτω οὕτως so, even so, thus, on this wise, likewise, after this manner
ὃν relative pron. acc. masc. sg. ὅς ἥ ὅ who, which, what, that
τρόπον n. acc. masc. sg. τρόπος as, manner, means, way, conversation
αὐτὸν pron. acc. masc. 3p. sg. αὐτός ή ό self, of oneself, even, very, the same, he, she, it
εἰς prep. εἰς (+acc) into, to, unto, for, in, on, toward, against, upon, at, among
τὸν art. acc. masc. sg. ὁ ἡ τό the, this, that, he, she, it
οὐρανόν n. acc. masc. sg. οὐρανός heaven, air, sky
12 Τότε adv. τότε then, that time
εἰς prep. εἰς (+acc) into, to, unto, for, in, on, toward, against, upon, at, among
Ἰερουσαλήμ pron. name. fem. inde. Ἰερουσαλήμ Jerusalem
ἀπὸ prep. ἀπό (+gen) from, of, out of, since, for, off, at, by, in, on
ὄρους n. gen. neut. sg. ὄρος mountain, mount, hill
τοῦ art. gen. neut. sg. ὁ ἡ τό the, this, that, he, she, it
Ἐλαιῶνος n. gen. masc. sg. ἐλαιών Olivet
ὅ relative pron. nom. neut. sg. ὅς ἥ ὅ who, which, what, that
ἐγγὺς adv. ἐγγύς nigh, at hand, near, nigh at hand, ready, nigh unto
Ἰερουσαλήμ pron. name. fem. inde. Ἰερουσαλήμ Jerusalem
σαββάτου n. gen. neut. sg. σάββατον sabbath day, sabbath, week
ὁδόν n. acc. fem. sg. ὁδός way, journey, highway
13 καὶ conj. καί and, even, also, but
ὅτε adv. ὅτε when, after that, as soon as, while, after
εἰς prep. εἰς (+acc) into, to, unto, for, in, on, toward, against, upon, at, among
τὸ art. acc. neut. sg. ὁ ἡ τό the, this, that, he, she, it
ὑπερῷον n. acc. neut. sg. ὑπερῷον upper room, upper chamber
οὗ adv. οὗ where, whither, wherein
ὅ art. nom. masc. sg. ὁ ἡ τό the, this, that, he, she, it
τε conj. τέ and, both, also
Πέτρος n. nom. masc. sg. Πέτρος Peter
καὶ conj. καί and, even, also, but
Ἰάκωβος n. nom. masc. sg. Ἰάκωβος James
καὶ conj. καί and, even, also, but
Ἰωάννης n. nom. masc. sg. Ἰωάννης John
καὶ conj. καί and, even, also, but
Ἀνδρέας n. nom. masc. sg. Ἀνδρέας Andrew
Φίλιππος n. nom. masc. sg. Φίλιππος Philip, Philippi
καὶ conj. καί and, even, also, but
Θωμᾶς n. nom. masc. sg. Θωμᾶς Thomas
Βαρθολομαῖος n. nom. masc. sg. Βαρθολομαῖος Bartholomew
καὶ conj. καί and, even, also, but
Ματθαῖος n. nom. masc. sg. Ματθαῖος Matthew
Ἰάκωβος n. nom. masc. sg. Ἰάκωβος James
Ἀλφαίου n. gen. masc. sg. Ἀλφαῖος Alphaeus
Ἰάκωβος n. nom. masc. sg. Ἰάκωβος James
Σίμων n. nom. masc. sg. Σίμων Simon
ὁ art. nom. masc. sg. ὁ ἡ τό the, this, that, he, she, it
Ζηλωτὴς n. nom. masc. sg. Ζηλωτής Zelotes
Ἰάκωβος n. nom. masc. sg. Ἰάκωβος James
Ἰούδας n. nom. masc. sg. Ἰούδας Judas, Juda, Judah, Jude
Ἰακώβου n. gen. masc. sg. Ἰάκωβος James
14 οὗτοι demo. pron. nom. masc. pl. οὗτος αὕτη τοῦτο this, the same, this same, he, she, it

πάντες adj. nom. masc. pl. πᾶς πᾶσα πᾶν all, every, whosoever, every one, no, whole, any
ὁμοθυμαδὸν adv. ὁμοθυμαδόν with one accord, with one mind
τῇ art. dat. fem. sg. ὁ ἡ τό the, this, that, he, she, it
προσευχῇ n. dat. fem. sg. προσευχή prayer
καὶ conj. καί and, even, also, but
τῇ art. dat. fem. sg. ὁ ἡ τό the, this, that, he, she, it
δεήσει n. dat. fem. sg. δέησις prayer, supplication, request
σὺν prep. σύν (+dat) with, beside
υναιξὶν n. dat. fem. pl. γυνή woman, wife
καὶ conj. καί and, even, also, but
Μαρίᾳ n. dat. fem. sg. Μαρία Mary
τῇ art. dat. fem. sg. ὁ ἡ τό the, this, that, he, she, it
μητρὶ n. dat. fem. sg. μήτηρ mother
τοῦ art. gen. masc. sg. ὁ ἡ τό the, this, that, he, she, it
Ἰησοῦ n. gen. masc. sg. Ἰησοῦς Jesus
τῇ art. dat. fem. sg. ὁ ἡ τό the, this, that, he, she, it
σὺν prep. σύν (+dat) with, beside
τοῖς art. dat. masc. pl. ὁ ἡ τό the, this, that, he, she, it
ἀδελφοῖς n. dat. masc. pl. ἀδελφός brother
αὐτοῦ pron. gen. masc. 3p. sg. αὐτός ή ό self, of oneself, even, very, the same, he, she, it
15 Καὶ conj. καί and, even, also, but
ἐν prep. ἐν (+dat) in, by, with, among, at, on, through, to, within, into, of, for
ταῖς art. dat. fem. pl. ὁ ἡ τό the, this, that, he, she, it
ἡμέραις n. dat. fem. pl. ἡμέρα day, time, year, while, age, day time
ταύταις demo. pron. dat. fem. pl. οὗτος αὕτη τοῦτο this, the same, this same, he, she, it
Πέτρος n. nom. masc. sg. Πέτρος Peter
ἐν prep. ἐν (+dat) in, by, with, among, at, on, through, to, within, into, of, for
μέσῳ adj. dat. neut. sg. μέσος midst, among, mid, between
τῶν art. gen. masc. pl. ὁ ἡ τό the, this, that, he, she, it
μαθητῶν n. gen. masc. pl. μαθητής disciple
τε conj. τέ and, both, also
ὄχλος n. nom. masc. sg. ὄχλος people, multitude, company, press, number
ὀνομάτων n. gen. neut. pl. ὄνομα name, call, surname
ἐπὶ prep. ἐπί (+gen) on, in, upon, (+dat) in, at, for, upon, (+acc) on, upon, unto, to, against
τὸ art. acc. neut. sg. ὁ ἡ τό the, this, that, he, she, it
αὐτὸ pron. acc. neut. 3p. sg. αὐτός ή ό self, of oneself, even, very, the same, he, she, it
ὡς adv. ὡς as, when, as it were, how, about, like, as soon as, even as, while
ἑκατὸν num. nom. masc. pl. ἑκατόν hundred, hundredfold
εἴκοσιν num. nom. masc. pl. εἴκοσι twenty
16 Ἄνδρες n. voc. masc. pl. ἀνήρ man, husband, sir
ἀδελφοί n. voc. masc. pl. ἀδελφός brother
τὴν art. acc. fem. sg. ὁ ἡ τό the, this, that, he, she, it
γραφὴν n. acc. fem. sg. γραφή scripture
ταύτην demo. pron. acc. fem. sg. οὗτος αὕτη τοῦτο this, the same, this same, he, she, it
ἣν relative pron. acc. fem. sg. ὅς ἥ ὅ who, which, what, that
τὸ art. nom. neut. sg. ὁ ἡ τό the, this, that, he, she, it
Πνεῦμα n. nom. neut. sg. πνεῦμα spirit, Spirit, Ghost, ghost, life. of the spirit, wind
τὸ art. nom. neut. sg. ὁ ἡ τό the, this, that, he, she, it
Ἅγιον adj. nom. neut. sg. ἅγιος Holy, holy, saint, Holy One, holy thing, most holy
διὰ prep. διά (+gen) by, through, with, in, of, (+acc) for, because of, for a cause
στόματος n. gen. neut. sg. στόμα mouth, face, edge
Δαβὶδ n. gen. masc. sg. Δαβίδ David
περὶ prep. περί (+gen) of, for, concerning, (+acc) about, concerning, in
Ἰούδα n. gen. masc. sg. Ἰούδας Judas, Juda, Judah, Jude
τοῦ art. gen. masc. sg. ὁ ἡ τό the, this, that, he, she, it

ὁδηγοῦ n. gen. masc. sg. ὁδηγός leader, guide
τοῖς art. dat. masc. pl. ὁ ἡ τό the, this, that, he, she, it
τὸν art. acc. masc. sg. ὁ ἡ τό the, this, that, he, she, it
Ἰησοῦν n. acc. masc. sg. Ἰησοῦς Jesus
17 ὅτι conj. ὅτι that, for, because, how that, how, because that, for that, though
σὺν prep. σύν (+dat) with, beside
ἡμῖν pron. dat. 1p. pl. ἐγώ I
καὶ conj. καί and, even, also, but
τὸν art. acc. masc. sg. ὁ ἡ τό the, this, that, he, she, it
κλῆρον n. acc. masc. sg. κλῆρος lot, inheritance, part, heritage
τῆς art. gen. fem. sg. ὁ ἡ τό the, this, that, he, she, it
διακονίας n. gen. fem. sg. διακονία ministry, administration, service, office, relief
ταύτης demo. pron. gen. fem. sg. οὗτος αὕτη τοῦτο this, the same, this same, he, she, it
18 οὗτος demo. pron. nom. masc. sg. οὗτος αὕτη τοῦτο this, the same, this same, he, she, it
μέν conj. μέν indeed, verily, truly, even, so, some
οὖν conj. οὖν therefore, then, so, and, now, wherefore
χωρίον n. acc. neut. sg. χωρίον place, field, land, parcel of ground, possession
ἐκ prep. ἐκ ἐξ (+gen) of, from, out of, by, on, with, in, among, through
τοῦ art. gen. masc. sg. ὁ ἡ τό the, this, that, he, she, it
μισθοῦ n. gen. masc. sg. μισθός reward, hire, wage
τῆς art. gen. fem. sg. ὁ ἡ τό the, this, that, he, she, it
ἀδικίας n. gen. fem. sg. ἀδικία iniquity, unrighteousness, unjust, wrong
καὶ conj. καί and, even, also, but
πρηνὴς adj. nom. masc. sg. πρηνής headlong
μέσος adj. nom. masc. sg. μέσος midst, among, mid, between
καὶ conj. καί and, even, also, but
πάντα adj. nom. neut. pl. πᾶς πᾶσα πᾶν all, every, whosoever, every one, no, whole, any
τὰ art. nom. neut. pl. ὁ ἡ τό the, this, that, he, she, it
σπλάγχνα n. nom. neut. pl. σπλάγχνον tender, bowels, inward affection
αὐτοῦ pron. gen. masc. 3p. sg. αὐτός ἡ ὁ self, of oneself, even, very, the same, he, she, it
19 καὶ conj. καί and, even, also, but
γνωστὸν adj. nom. neut. sg. γνωστός acquaintance, known, notable
πᾶσι adj. dat. masc. pl. πᾶς πᾶσα πᾶν all, every, whosoever, every one, no, whole, any
τοῖς art. dat. masc. pl. ὁ ἡ τό the, this, that, he, she, it
Ἱερουσαλήμ pron. name. fem. inde. Ἱερουσαλήμ Jerusalem
ὥστε conj. ὥστε so that, wherefore, insomuch that, therefore, that, so then
τὸ art. acc. neut. sg. ὁ ἡ τό the, this, that, he, she, it
χωρίον n. acc. neut. sg. χωρίον place, field, land, parcel of ground, possession
ἐκεῖνο demo. pron. acc. neut. sg. ἐκεῖνος that, he, the same, that same
τῇ art. dat. fem. sg. ὁ ἡ τό the, this, that, he, she, it
ἰδίᾳ adj. dat. fem. sg. ἴδιος one's own, one's, privately
διαλέκτῳ n. dat. fem. sg. διάλεκτος tongue, language
αὐτῶν pron. gen. masc. 3p. pl. αὐτός ἡ ὁ self, of oneself, even, very, the same, he, she, it
Ἀκελδαμά n. acc. neut. sg. Ἀκελδαμά Aceldama
τοῦτ' demo. pron. nom. neut. sg. οὗτος αὕτη τοῦτο this, the same, this same, he, she, it
Χωρίον n. acc. neut. sg. χωρίον place, field, land, parcel of ground, possession
αἵματος n. gen. neut. sg. αἷμα blood
20 γὰρ conj. γάρ for, and, because, but, indeed
ἐν prep. ἐν (+dat) in, by, with, among, at, on, through, to, within, into, of, for
βίβλῳ n. dat. fem. sg. βίβλος book, record
ψαλμῶν n. gen. masc. pl. ψαλμός Psalm, psalm
ἡ art. nom. fem. sg. ὁ ἡ τό the, this, that, he, she, it
ἔπαυλις n. nom. fem. sg. ἔπαυλις habitation
αὐτοῦ pron. gen. masc. 3p. sg. αὐτός ἡ ὁ self, of oneself, even, very, the same, he, she, it
ἔρημος adj. nom. fem. sg. ἔρημος wilderness, desert

καὶ conj. καί and, even, also, but
μὴ particle of negation. μή not, no, lest, neither, none, nothing, nor, never, without
ὁ art. nom. masc. sg. ὁ ἡ τό the, this, that, he, she, it
ἐν prep. ἐν (+dat) in, by, with, among, at, on, through, to, within, into, of, for
αὐτῇ pron. dat. fem. 3p. sg. αὐτός ή ό self, of oneself, even, very, the same, he, she, it
καὶ conj. καί and, even, also, but
Τὴν art. acc. fem. sg. ὁ ἡ τό the, this, that, he, she, it
ἐπισκοπὴν n. acc. fem. sg. ἐπισκοπή bishoprick, visitation, the office of a bishop
αὐτοῦ pron. gen. masc. 3p. sg. αὐτός ή ό self, of oneself, even, very, the same, he, she, it
ἕτερος adj. nom. masc. sg. ἕτερος another, other, else, strange
21 οὖν conj. οὖν therefore, then, so, and, now, wherefore
τῶν art. gen. masc. pl. ὁ ἡ τό the, this, that, he, she, it
ἡμῖν pron. dat. 1p. pl. ἐγώ I
ἀνδρῶν n. gen. masc. pl. ἀνήρ man, husband, sir
ἐν prep. ἐν (+dat) in, by, with, among, at, on, through, to, within, into, of, for
παντὶ adj. dat. masc. sg. πᾶς πᾶσα πᾶν all, every, whosoever, every one, no, whole, any
χρόνῳ n. dat. masc. sg. χρόνος time, season, space
ἐν prep. ἐν (+dat) in, by, with, among, at, on, through, to, within, into, of, for
ᾧ relative pron. dat. masc. sg. ὅς ἥ ὅ who, which, what, that
καὶ conj. καί and, even, also, but
ἐφ' prep. ἐπί (+gen) on, in, upon, (+dat) in, at, for, upon, (+acc) on, upon, unto, to, against
ἡμᾶς pron. acc. 1p. pl. ἐγώ I
ὁ art. nom. masc. sg. ὁ ἡ τό the, this, that, he, she, it
Κύριος n. nom. masc. sg. κύριος Lord, lord, master, sir, LORD, God, Master, owner
Ἰησοῦς n. nom. masc. sg. Ἰησοῦς Jesus
22 ἀπὸ prep. ἀπό (+gen) from, of, out of, since, for, off, at, by, in, on
τοῦ art. gen. neut. sg. ὁ ἡ τό the, this, that, he, she, it
βαπτίσματος n. gen. neut. sg. βάπτισμα baptism
Ἰωάννου n. gen. masc. sg. Ἰωάννης John
ἕως conj. ἕως till, until, unto, until when, while, as far as, even, until now
τῆς art. gen. fem. sg. ὁ ἡ τό the, this, that, he, she, it
ἡμέρας n. gen. fem. sg. ἡμέρα day, time, year, while, age, day time
ἧς relative pron. gen. fem. sg. ὅς ἥ ὅ who, which, what, that
ἀφ' prep. ἀπό (+gen) from, of, out of, since, for, off, at, by, in, on
ἡμῶν pron. gen. 1p. pl. ἐγώ I
μάρτυρα n. acc. masc. sg. μάρτυς or μάρτυρ witness, martyr, record
τῆς art. gen. fem. sg. ὁ ἡ τό the, this, that, he, she, it
ἀναστάσεως n. gen. fem. sg. ἀνάστασις resurrection, rising again
αὐτοῦ pron. gen. masc. 3p. sg. αὐτός ή ό self, of oneself, even, very, the same, he, she, it
σὺν prep. σύν (+dat) with, beside
ἡμῖν pron. dat. 1p. pl. ἐγώ I
ἕνα num. acc. masc. sg. εἷς or ἕν one, other, some, any, only, a certain
τούτων demo. pron. gen. masc. pl. οὗτος αὕτη τοῦτο this, the same, this same, he, she, it
23 καὶ conj. καί and, even, also, but
δύο num. acc. masc. pl. δύο two, twain, both
Ἰωσὴφ n. acc. masc. sg. Ἰωσήφ Joseph
τὸν art. acc. masc. sg. ὁ ἡ τό the, this, that, he, she, it
Βαρσαβᾶν n. acc. masc. sg. Βαρσαβᾶς Barsabas
ὃς relative pron. nom. masc. sg. ὅς ἥ ὅ who, which, what, that
Ἰοῦστος n. nom. masc. sg. Ἰοῦστος Justus
καὶ conj. καί and, even, also, but
Ματθίαν n. acc. masc. sg. Ματθίας Matthias
24 καὶ conj. καί and, even, also, but
Σὺ pron. nom. 2p. sg. σύ thou, you
Κύριε n. voc. masc. sg. κύριος Lord, lord, master, sir, LORD, God, Master, owner

καρδιογνῶστα n. voc. masc. sg. καρδιογνώστης one which knowest the hearts
πάντων adj. gen. masc. pl. πᾶς πᾶσα πᾶν all, every, whosoever, every one, no, whole, any
ἐκ prep. ἐκ ἐξ (+gen) of, from, out of, by, on, with, in, among, through
τούτων demo. pron. gen. masc. pl. οὗτος αὕτη τοῦτο this, the same, this same, he, she, it
τῶν art. gen. masc. pl. ὁ ἡ τό the, this, that, he, she, it
δύο num. gen. masc. pl. δύο two, twain, both
ὃν relative pron. acc. masc. sg. ὅς ἥ ὅ who, which, what, that
ἕνα num. acc. masc. sg. εἷς or ἕν one, other, some, any, only, a certain
25 τὸν art. acc. masc. sg. ὁ ἡ τό the, this, that, he, she, it
κλῆρον n. acc. masc. sg. κλῆρος lot, inheritance, part, heritage
τῆς art. gen. fem. sg. ὁ ἡ τό the, this, that, he, she, it
διακονίας n. gen. fem. sg. διακονία ministry, administration, service, office, relief
ταύτης demo. pron. gen. fem. sg. οὗτος αὕτη τοῦτο this, the same, this same, he, she, it
καὶ conj. καί and, even, also, but
ἀποστολῆς n. gen. fem. sg. ἀποστολή apostleship
ἐξ prep. ἐκ ἐξ (+gen) of, from, out of, by, on, with, in, among, through
ἧς relative pron. gen. fem. sg. ὅς ἥ ὅ who, which, what, that
Ἰούδας n. nom. masc. sg. Ἰούδας Judas, Juda, Judah, Jude
εἰς prep. εἰς (+acc) into, to, unto, for, in, on, toward, against, upon, at, among
τὸν art. acc. masc. sg. ὁ ἡ τό the, this, that, he, she, it
τόπον n. acc. masc. sg. τόπος place, room, quarter
τὸν art. acc. masc. sg. ὁ ἡ τό the, this, that, he, she, it
ἴδιον adj. acc. masc. sg. ἴδιος one's own, one's, privately
26 καὶ conj. καί and, even, also, but
κλήρους n. acc. masc. pl. κλῆρος lot, inheritance, part, heritage
αὐτῶν pron. gen. masc. 3p. pl. αὐτός ή ό self, of oneself, even, very, the same, he, she, it
καὶ conj. καί and, even, also, but
ὁ art. nom. masc. sg. ὁ ἡ τό the, this, that, he, she, it
κλῆρος n. nom. masc. sg. κλῆρος lot, inheritance, part, heritage
ἐπὶ prep. ἐπί (+gen) on, in, upon, (+dat) in, at, for, upon, (+acc) on, upon, unto, to, against
Ματθίαν n. acc. masc. sg. Ματθίας Matthias
καὶ conj. καί and, even, also, but
μετὰ prep. μετά (+gen) with, among, against, (+acc) after
τῶν art. gen. masc. pl. ὁ ἡ τό the, this, that, he, she, it
ἕνδεκα num. gen. masc. pl. ἕνδεκα eleven
ἀποστόλων n. gen. masc. pl. ἀπόστολος apostle, messenger, he that is sent

2

1 Καὶ conj. καί and, even, also, but
ἐν prep. ἐν (+dat) in, by, with, among, at, on, through, to, within, into, of, for
τῷ art. dat. neut. sg. ὁ ἡ τό the, this, that, he, she, it
τὴν art. acc. fem. sg. ὁ ἡ τό the, this, that, he, she, it
ἡμέραν n. acc. fem. sg. ἡμέρα day, time, year, while, age, day time
τῆς art. gen. fem. sg. ὁ ἡ τό the, this, that, he, she, it
Πεντηκοστῆς n. gen. fem. sg. πεντηκοστή Pentecost
ἅπαντες adj. nom. masc. pl. ἅπας all, whole, all things, every, everyone
ὁμοθυμαδὸν adv. ὁμοθυμαδόν with one accord, with one mind
ἐπὶ prep. ἐπί (+gen) on, in, upon, (+dat) in, at, for, upon, (+acc) on, upon, unto, to, against
τὸ art. acc. neut. sg. ὁ ἡ τό the, this, that, he, she, it
αὐτό adj. acc. neut. sg. αὐτός ή ό self, of oneself, even, very, the same, he, she, it
2 καὶ conj. καί and, even, also, but
ἄφνω adv. ἄφνω suddenly
ἐκ prep. ἐκ ἐξ (+gen) of, from, out of, by, on, with, in, among, through
τοῦ art. gen. masc. sg. ὁ ἡ τό the, this, that, he, she, it

οὐρανοῦ n. gen. masc. sg. οὐρανός heaven, air, sky
ἦχος n. nom. neut. sg. ἦχος fame, sound
ὥσπερ conj. ὥσπερ as, even as, like as
πνοῆς n. gen. fem. sg. πνοή wind, breath
βιαίας adj. gen. fem. sg. βίαιος mighty
καὶ conj. καί and, even, also, but
ὅλον adj. acc. masc. sg. ὅλος all, whole, every whit, altogether
τὸν art. acc. masc. sg. ὁ ἡ τό the, this, that, he, she, it
οἶκον n. acc. masc. sg. οἶκος house, home, household
οὗ adv. οὗ where, whither, wherein
3 καὶ conj. καί and, even, also, but
αὐτοῖς pron. dat. masc. 3p. pl. αὐτός ή ό self, of oneself, even, very, the same, he, she, it
γλῶσσαι n. nom. fem. pl. γλῶσσα tongue
ὡσεὶ adv. ὡσεί about, as, like, as it had been, as it were, like as
πυρὸς n. gen. neut. sg. πῦρ fire, fiery
τε conj. τέ and, both, also
ἐφ' prep. ἐπί (+gen) on, in, upon, (+dat) in, at, for, upon, (+acc) on, upon, unto, to, against
ἕνα num. acc. masc. sg. εἶς or ἕν one, other, some, any, only, a certain
ἕκαστον adj. acc. masc. sg. ἕκαστος every man, every, every one, any man, each
αὐτῶν pron. gen. masc. 3p. pl. αὐτός ή ό self, of oneself, even, very, the same, he, she, it
4 καὶ conj. καί and, even, also, but
ἅπαντες adj. nom. masc. pl. ἅπας all, whole, all things, every, everyone
Πνεύματος n. gen. neut. sg. πνεῦμα spirit, Spirit, Ghost, ghost, life. of the spirit, wind
Ἁγίου adj. gen. neut. sg. ἅγιος Holy, holy, saint, Holy One, holy thing, most holy
καὶ conj. καί and, even, also, but
ἑτέραις adj. dat. fem. pl. ἕτερος another, other, else, strange
γλώσσαις n. dat. fem. pl. γλῶσσα tongue
καθὼς adv. καθώς as, even as, according as, according to
τὸ art. nom. neut. sg. ὁ ἡ τό the, this, that, he, she, it
Πνεῦμα n. nom. neut. sg. πνεῦμα spirit, Spirit, Ghost, ghost, life. of the spirit, wind
αὐτοῖς pron. dat. masc. 3p. pl. αὐτός ή ό self, of oneself, even, very, the same, he, she, it
5 δὲ conj. δέ but, and, now, also, to the contrary, rather, then
ἐν prep. ἐν (+dat) in, by, with, among, at, on, through, to, within, into, of, for
Ἰερουσαλὴμ pron. name. fem. inde. Ἰερουσαλήμ Jerusalem
Ἰουδαῖοι adj. nom. masc. pl. Ἰουδαῖος Jew, Jewess
ἄνδρες n. nom. masc. pl. ἀνήρ man, husband, sir
εὐλαβεῖς adj. nom. masc. pl. εὐλαβής devout
ἀπὸ prep. ἀπό (+gen) from, of, out of, since, for, off, at, by, in, on
παντὸς adj. gen. neut. sg. πᾶς πᾶσα πᾶν all, every, whosoever, every one, no, whole, any
ἔθνους n. gen. neut. sg. ἔθνος Gentile, nation, heathen, people
τῶν art. gen. neut. pl. ὁ ἡ τό the, this, that, he, she, it
ὑπὸ prep. ὑπό (+gen) of, by, with, from, among, (+acc) under
τὸν art. acc. masc. sg. ὁ ἡ τό the, this, that, he, she, it
οὐρανόν n. acc. masc. sg. οὐρανός heaven, air, sky
6 δὲ conj. δέ but, and, now, also, to the contrary, rather, then
τῆς art. gen. fem. sg. ὁ ἡ τό the, this, that, he, she, it
φωνῆς n. gen. fem. sg. φωνή voice, sound, noise
ταύτης demo. pron. gen. fem. sg. οὗτος αὕτη τοῦτο this, the same, this same, he, she, it
τὸ art. nom. neut. sg. ὁ ἡ τό the, this, that, he, she, it
πλῆθος n. nom. neut. sg. πλῆθος multitude, bundle, company
καὶ conj. καί and, even, also, but
ὅτι conj. ὅτι that, for, because, how that, how, because that, for that, though
εἷς num. nom. masc. sg. εἷς or ἕν one, other, some, any, only, a certain
ἕκαστος adj. nom. masc. sg. ἕκαστος every man, every, every one, any man, each
τῇ art. dat. fem. sg. ὁ ἡ τό the, this, that, he, she, it

ἰδίᾳ adj. dat. fem. sg. ἴδιος one's own, one's, privately
διαλέκτῳ n. dat. fem. sg. διάλεκτος tongue, language
αὐτῶν pron. gen. masc. 3p. pl. αὐτός ή ό self, of oneself, even, very, the same, he, she, it
7 δὲ conj. δέ but, and, now, also, to the contrary, rather, then
πάντες adj. nom. masc. pl. πᾶς πᾶσα πᾶν all, every, whosoever, every one, no, whole, any
καὶ conj. καί and, even, also, but
πρὸς prep. πρός (+gen) for, (+dat) at, (+acc) unto, to, with, for, against
ἀλλήλους pron. acc. masc. 3p. pl. ἀλλήλων one another, themselves, together, mutual
Οὐχ particle of negation. οὐ οὐκ οὐχ not, no, neither, none, nay, nor, never, nothing
πάντες adj. nom. masc. pl. πᾶς πᾶσα πᾶν all, every, whosoever, every one, no, whole, any
οὗτοί demo. pron. nom. masc. pl. οὗτος αὕτη τοῦτο this, the same, this same, he, she, it
οἱ art. nom. masc. pl. ὁ ἡ τό the, this, that, he, she, it
Γαλιλαῖοι adj. nom. masc. pl. Γαλιλαῖος Galilean, of Galilee
8 καὶ conj. καί and, even, also, but
πῶς adv. πῶς how, by what means, after what manner
ἡμεῖς pron. nom. 1p. pl. ἐγώ I
ἕκαστος adj. nom. masc. sg. ἕκαστος every man, every, every one, any man, each
τῇ art. dat. fem. sg. ὁ ἡ τό the, this, that, he, she, it
ἰδίᾳ adj. dat. fem. sg. ἴδιος one's own, one's, privately
διαλέκτῳ n. dat. fem. sg. διάλεκτος tongue, language
ἡμῶν pron. gen. 1p. pl. ἐγώ I
ἐν prep. ἐν (+dat) in, by, with, among, at, on, through, to, within, into, of, for
ᾗ relative pron. dat. fem. sg. ὅς ἥ ὅ who, which, what, that
9 Πάρθοι n. nom. masc. pl. Πάρθος Parthian
καὶ conj. καί and, even, also, but
Μῆδοι n. nom. masc. pl. Μῆδος Medes
καὶ conj. καί and, even, also, but
Ἐλαμῖται n. nom. masc. pl. Ἐλαμίτης Elamite
καὶ conj. καί and, even, also, but
οἱ art. nom. masc. pl. ὁ ἡ τό the, this, that, he, she, it
τὴν art. acc. fem. sg. ὁ ἡ τό the, this, that, he, she, it
Μεσοποταμίαν n. acc. fem. sg. Μεσοποταμία Mesopotamia
Ἰουδαίαν n. acc. fem. sg. Ἰουδαία Judaea, Jewry
τε conj. τέ and, both, also
καὶ conj. καί and, even, also, but
Καππαδοκίαν n. acc. fem. sg. Καππαδοκία Cappadocia
Πόντον n. acc. masc. sg. Πόντος Pontus
καὶ conj. καί and, even, also, but
τὴν art. acc. fem. sg. ὁ ἡ τό the, this, that, he, she, it
Ἀσίαν n. acc. fem. sg. Ἀσία Asia
10 Φρυγίαν n. acc. fem. sg. Φρυγία Phrygia
τε conj. τέ and, both, also
καὶ conj. καί and, even, also, but
Παμφυλίαν n. acc. fem. sg. Παμφυλία Pamphylia
Αἴγυπτον n. acc. fem. sg. Αἴγυπτος Egypt
καὶ conj. καί and, even, also, but
τὰ art. acc. neut. pl. ὁ ἡ τό the, this, that, he, she, it
μέρη n. acc. neut. pl. μέρος part, coast, portion, behalf, respect, piece, side
τῆς art. gen. fem. sg. ὁ ἡ τό the, this, that, he, she, it
Λιβύης n. gen. fem. sg. Λιβύη Libya
τῆς art. gen. fem. sg. ὁ ἡ τό the, this, that, he, she, it
κατὰ prep. κατά (+gen) against, by, throughout, down, (+acc) according to, after, with
Κυρήνην n. acc. fem. sg. Κυρήνη Cyrene
καὶ conj. καί and, even, also, but
οἱ art. nom. masc. pl. ὁ ἡ τό the, this, that, he, she, it

Ῥωμαῖοι adj. nom. masc. pl. Ῥωμαῖος Roman, Rome
11 Ἰουδαῖοί adj. nom. masc. pl. Ἰουδαῖος Jew, Jewess
τε conj. τέ and, both, also
καὶ conj. καί and, even, also, but
προσήλυτοι n. nom. masc. pl. προσήλυτος proselyte
Κρῆτες n. nom. masc. pl. Κρής (pl.) Cretes, Cretians
καὶ conj. καί and, even, also, but
Ἄραβες n. nom. masc. pl. Ἄραψ Arabian
αὐτῶν pron. gen. masc. 3p. pl. αὐτός ή ό self, of oneself, even, very, the same, he, she, it
ταῖς art. dat. fem. pl. ὁ ἡ τό the, this, that, he, she, it
ἡμετέραις poss. pron. dat. fem. 1p. pl. ἡμέτερος our
γλώσσαις n. dat. fem. pl. γλῶσσα tongue
τὰ art. acc. neut. pl. ὁ ἡ τό the, this, that, he, she, it
μεγαλεῖα adj. acc. neut. pl. μεγαλεῖος wonderful work, great thing
τοῦ art. gen. masc. sg. ὁ ἡ τό the, this, that, he, she, it
Θεοῦ n. gen. masc. sg. θεός God, god
12 δὲ conj. δέ but, and, now, also, to the contrary, rather, then
πάντες adj. nom. masc. pl. πᾶς πᾶσα πᾶν all, every, whosoever, every one, no, whole, any
καὶ conj. καί and, even, also, but
ἄλλος adj. nom. masc. sg. ἄλλος other, another, some, one, more, otherwise
πρὸς prep. πρός (+gen) for, (+dat) at, (+acc) unto, to, with, for, against
ἄλλον adj. acc. masc. sg. ἄλλος other, another, some, one, more, otherwise
Τί interrog. pron. nom. neut. sg. τίς what, who, why, where, which, how
ἂν particle. ἄν Indicating contingency. No English translation.
τοῦτο demo. pron. nom. neut. sg. οὗτος αὕτη τοῦτο this, the same, this same, he, she, it
13 ἕτεροι adj. nom. masc. pl. ἕτερος another, other, else, strange
δὲ conj. δέ but, and, now, also, to the contrary, rather, then
ὅτι conj. ὅτι that, for, because, how that, how, because that, for that, though
Γλεύκους n. gen. neut. sg. γλεῦκος new wine
14 δὲ conj. δέ but, and, now, also, to the contrary, rather, then
Πέτρος n. nom. masc. sg. Πέτρος Peter
σὺν prep. σύν (+dat) with, beside
τοῖς art. dat. masc. pl. ὁ ἡ τό the, this, that, he, she, it
ἕνδεκα num. dat. masc. pl. ἕνδεκα eleven
τὴν art. acc. fem. sg. ὁ ἡ τό the, this, that, he, she, it
φωνὴν n. acc. fem. sg. φωνή voice, sound, noise
αὐτοῦ pron. gen. masc. 3p. sg. αὐτός ή ό self, of oneself, even, very, the same, he, she, it
καὶ conj. καί and, even, also, but
αὐτοῖς pron. dat. masc. 3p. pl. αὐτός ή ό self, of oneself, even, very, the same, he, she, it
Ἄνδρες n. voc. masc. pl. ἀνήρ man, husband, sir
Ἰουδαῖοι adj. voc. masc. pl. Ἰουδαῖος Jew, Jewess
καὶ conj. καί and, even, also, but
οἱ art. nom. masc. pl. ὁ ἡ τό the, this, that, he, she, it
Ἱερουσαλὴμ pron. name. fem. inde. Ἱερουσαλήμ Jerusalem
ἅπαντες adj. nom. masc. pl. ἅπας all, whole, all things, every, everyone
τοῦτο demo. pron. nom. neut. sg. οὗτος αὕτη τοῦτο this, the same, this same, he, she, it
ὑμῖν pron. dat. 2p. pl. σύ thou, you
γνωστὸν adj. nom. neut. sg. γνωστός acquaintance, known, notable
καὶ conj. καί and, even, also, but
τὰ art. acc. neut. pl. ὁ ἡ τό the, this, that, he, she, it
ῥήματά n. acc. neut. pl. ῥῆμα word, saying, thing
μου pron. gen. 1p. sg. ἐγώ I
15 οὐ particle of negation. οὐ οὐκ οὐχ not, no, neither, none, nay, nor, never, nothing
γὰρ conj. γάρ for, and, because, but, indeed
ὡς adv. ὡς as, when, as it were, how, about, like, as soon as, even as, while

ὑμεῖς pron. nom. 2p. pl. σύ thou, you
οὗτοι demo. pron. nom. masc. pl. οὗτος αὕτη τοῦτο this, the same, this same, he, she, it
γὰρ conj. γάρ for, and, because, but, indeed
ὥρα n. nom. fem. sg. ὥρα hour, time, season
τρίτη ordinal. adj. nom. fem. sg. τρίτος third
τῆς art. gen. fem. sg. ὁ ἡ τό the, this, that, he, she, it
ἡμέρας n. gen. fem. sg. ἡμέρα day, time, year, while, age, day time
16 ἀλλὰ conj. ἀλλά but, yea, yet, nevertheless, howbeit, nay, therefore
τοῦτό demo. pron. nom. neut. sg. οὗτος αὕτη τοῦτο this, the same, this same, he, she, it
τὸ art. nom. neut. sg. ὁ ἡ τό the, this, that, he, she, it
διὰ prep. διά (+gen) by, through, with, in, of, (+acc) for, because of, for a cause
τοῦ art. gen. masc. sg. ὁ ἡ τό the, this, that, he, she, it
προφήτου n. gen. masc. sg. προφήτης prophet
Ἰωήλ n. gen. masc. sg. Ἰωήλ Joel
17 Καὶ conj. καί and, even, also, but
ἐν prep. ἐν (+dat) in, by, with, among, at, on, through, to, within, into, of, for
ταῖς art. dat. fem. pl. ὁ ἡ τό the, this, that, he, she, it
ἐσχάταις adj. dat. fem. pl. ἔσχατος last, lowest, uttermost, uttermost part
ἡμέραις n. dat. fem. pl. ἡμέρα day, time, year, while, age, day time
ὁ art. nom. masc. sg. ὁ ἡ τό the, this, that, he, she, it
Θεός n. nom. masc. sg. θεός God, god
ἀπὸ prep. ἀπό (+gen) from, of, out of, since, for, off, at, by, in, on
τοῦ art. gen. neut. sg. ὁ ἡ τό the, this, that, he, she, it
πνεύματός n. gen. neut. sg. πνεῦμα spirit, Spirit, Ghost, ghost, life. of the spirit, wind
μου pron. gen. 1p. sg. ἐγώ I
ἐπὶ prep. ἐπί (+gen) on, in, upon, (+dat) in, at, for, upon, (+acc) on, upon, unto, to, against
πᾶσαν adj. acc. fem. sg. πᾶς πᾶσα πᾶν all, every, whosoever, every one, no, whole, any
σάρκα n. acc. fem. sg. σάρξ flesh, carnal
καὶ conj. καί and, even, also, but
οἱ art. nom. masc. pl. ὁ ἡ τό the, this, that, he, she, it
υἱοὶ n. nom. masc. pl. υἱός son, child, descendant, offspring, heir
ὑμῶν pron. gen. 2p. pl. σύ thou, you
καὶ conj. καί and, even, also, but
αἱ art. nom. fem. pl. ὁ ἡ τό the, this, that, he, she, it
θυγατέρες n. nom. fem. pl. θυγάτηρ daughter
ὑμῶν pron. gen. 2p. pl. σύ thou, you
καὶ conj. καί and, even, also, but
οἱ art. nom. masc. pl. ὁ ἡ τό the, this, that, he, she, it
νεανίσκοι n. nom. masc. pl. νεανίσκος young man
ὑμῶν pron. gen. 2p. pl. σύ thou, you
ὁράσεις n. acc. fem. pl. ὅρασις vision, to look upon, in sight
καὶ conj. καί and, even, also, but
οἱ art. nom. masc. pl. ὁ ἡ τό the, this, that, he, she, it
πρεσβύτεροι compar. adj. nom. masc. pl. πρεσβύτερος elder, elder woman, eldest, old man
ὑμῶν pron. gen. 2p. pl. σύ thou, you
ἐνύπνια n. dat. neut. pl. ἐνύπνιον dream
18 καί conj. καί and, even, also, but
γε particle. γέ yet, and beside, at least, doubtless
ἐπὶ prep. ἐπί (+gen) on, in, upon, (+dat) in, at, for, upon, (+acc) on, upon, unto, to, against
τοὺς art. acc. masc. pl. ὁ ἡ τό the, this, that, he, she, it
δούλους n. acc. masc. pl. δοῦλος servant, bondman, bond, slave
μου pron. gen. 1p. sg. ἐγώ I
καί conj. καί and, even, also, but
ἐπὶ prep. ἐπί (+gen) on, in, upon, (+dat) in, at, for, upon, (+acc) on, upon, unto, to, against
τὰς art. acc. fem. pl. ὁ ἡ τό the, this, that, he, she, it

δούλας n. acc. fem. pl. δούλη handmaid, handmaiden
μου pron. gen. 1p. sg. ἐγώ I
ἐν prep. ἐν (+dat) in, by, with, among, at, on, through, to, within, into, of, for
ταῖς art. dat. fem. pl. ὁ ἡ τό the, this, that, he, she, it
ἡμέραις n. dat. fem. pl. ἡμέρα day, time, year, while, age, day time
ἐκείναις demo. pron. dat. fem. pl. ἐκεῖνος that, he, the same, that same
ἀπὸ prep. ἀπό (+gen) from, of, out of, since, for, off, at, by, in, on
τοῦ art. gen. neut. sg. ὁ ἡ τό the, this, that, he, she, it
πνεύματός n. gen. neut. sg. πνεῦμα spirit, Spirit, Ghost, ghost, life. of the spirit, wind
μου pron. gen. 1p. sg. ἐγώ I
καί conj. καί and, even, also, but
19 καὶ conj. καί and, even, also, but
τέρατα n. acc. neut. pl. τέρας wonder
ἐν prep. ἐν (+dat) in, by, with, among, at, on, through, to, within, into, of, for
τῷ art. dat. masc. sg. ὁ ἡ τό the, this, that, he, she, it
οὐρανῷ n. dat. masc. sg. οὐρανός heaven, air, sky
ἄνω adv. ἄνω above, up, high, the brim
καί conj. καί and, even, also, but
σημεῖα n. acc. neut. pl. σημεῖον sign, miracle, wonder, token
ἐπὶ prep. ἐπί (+gen) on, in, upon, (+dat) in, at, for, upon, (+acc) on, upon, unto, to, against
τῆς art. gen. fem. sg. ὁ ἡ τό the, this, that, he, she, it
γῆς n. gen. fem. sg. γῆ earth, land, ground, country
κάτω adv. κάτω under, down, beneath, bottom
αἷμα n. acc. neut. sg. αἷμα blood
καί conj. καί and, even, also, but
πῦρ n. acc. neut. sg. πῦρ fire, fiery
καί conj. καί and, even, also, but
ἀτμίδα n. acc. fem. sg. ἀτμίς vapour
καπνοῦ n. gen. masc. sg. καπνός smoke
20 ὁ art. nom. masc. sg. ὁ ἡ τό the, this, that, he, she, it
ἥλιος n. nom. masc. sg. ἥλιος sun, east
εἰς prep. εἰς (+acc) into, to, unto, for, in, on, toward, against, upon, at, among
σκότος n. acc. neut. sg. σκότος darkness
καὶ conj. καί and, even, also, but
ἡ art. nom. fem. sg. ὁ ἡ τό the, this, that, he, she, it
σελήνη n. nom. fem. sg. σελήνη moon
εἰς prep. εἰς (+acc) into, to, unto, for, in, on, toward, against, upon, at, among
αἷμα n. acc. neut. sg. αἷμα blood
πρὶν conj. πρίν before, ere
ἢ particle. ἤ or, than, either, nor, or else, and, rather than
τὴν art. acc. fem. sg. ὁ ἡ τό the, this, that, he, she, it
ἡμέραν n. acc. fem. sg. ἡμέρα day, time, year, while, age, day time
Κυρίου n. gen. masc. sg. κύριος Lord, lord, master, sir, LORD, God, Master, owner
τὴν art. acc. fem. sg. ὁ ἡ τό the, this, that, he, she, it
μεγάλην adj. acc. fem. sg. μέγας great, loud, greatest, high, large, mighty, strong
καὶ conj. καί and, even, also, but
ἐπιφανῆ adj. acc. fem. sg. ἐπιφανής notable
21 καὶ conj. καί and, even, also, but
πᾶς adj. nom. masc. sg. πᾶς πᾶσα πᾶν all, every, whosoever, every one, no, whole, any
ὃς relative pron. nom. masc. sg. ὅς ἥ ὅ who, which, what, that
ἂν particle. ἄν Indicating contingency. No English translation.
τὸ art. acc. neut. sg. ὁ ἡ τό the, this, that, he, she, it
ὄνομα n. acc. neut. sg. ὄνομα name, call, surname
Κυρίου n. gen. masc. sg. κύριος Lord, lord, master, sir, LORD, God, Master, owner
22 Ἄνδρες n. voc. masc. pl. ἀνήρ man, husband, sir

Ἰσραηλῖται n. voc. masc. pl. Ἰσραηλίτης Israelite, Israel
τοὺς art. acc. masc. pl. ὁ ἡ τό the, this, that, he, she, it
λόγους n. acc. masc. pl. λόγος word, saying, account, speech, thing, matter
τούτους demo. pron. acc. masc. pl. οὗτος αὕτη τοῦτο this, the same, this same, he, she, it
Ἰησοῦν n. acc. masc. sg. Ἰησοῦς Jesus
τὸν art. acc. masc. sg. ὁ ἡ τό the, this, that, he, she, it
Ναζωραῖον n. acc. masc. sg. Ναζωραῖος Nazareth, Nazarene
ἄνδρα n. acc. masc. sg. ἀνήρ man, husband, sir
ἀπὸ prep. ἀπό (+gen) from, of, out of, since, for, off, at, by, in, on
τοῦ art. gen. masc. sg. ὁ ἡ τό the, this, that, he, she, it
Θεοῦ n. gen. masc. sg. θεός God, god
εἰς prep. εἰς (+acc) into, to, unto, for, in, on, toward, against, upon, at, among
ὑμᾶς pron. acc. 2p. pl. σύ thou, you
δυνάμεσι n. dat. fem. pl. δύναμις power, mighty work, miracle, strength, might
καὶ conj. καί and, even, also, but
τέρασι n. dat. neut. pl. τέρας wonder
καὶ conj. καί and, even, also, but
σημείοις n. dat. neut. pl. σημεῖον sign, miracle, wonder, token
οἷς relative pron. dat. neut. pl. ὅς ἥ ὅ who, which, what, that
δι' prep. διά (+gen) by, through, with, in, of, (+acc) for, because of, for a cause
αὐτοῦ pron. gen. masc. 3p. sg. αὐτός ή ό self, of oneself, even, very, the same, he, she, it
ὁ art. nom. masc. sg. ὁ ἡ τό the, this, that, he, she, it
Θεὸς n. nom. masc. sg. θεός God, god
ἐν prep. ἐν (+dat) in, by, with, among, at, on, through, to, within, into, of, for
μέσῳ adj. dat. neut. sg. μέσος midst, among, mid, between
ὑμῶν pron. gen. 2p. pl. σύ thou, you
καθὼς adv. καθώς as, even as, according as, according to
καὶ conj. καί and, even, also, but
αὐτοὶ pron. nom. masc. 2p. pl. αὐτός ή ό self, of oneself, even, very, the same, he, she, it
23 τοῦτον demo. pron. acc. masc. sg. οὗτος αὕτη τοῦτο this, the same, this same, he, she, it
τῇ art. dat. fem. sg. ὁ ἡ τό the, this, that, he, she, it
βουλῇ n. dat. fem. sg. βουλή counsel, advise, will
καὶ conj. καί and, even, also, but
προγνώσει n. dat. fem. sg. πρόγνωσις foreknowledge
τοῦ art. gen. masc. sg. ὁ ἡ τό the, this, that, he, she, it
Θεοῦ n. gen. masc. sg. θεός God, god
ἔκδοτον adj. acc. masc. sg. ἔκδοτος delivered
διὰ prep. διά (+gen) by, through, with, in, of, (+acc) for, because of, for a cause
χειρῶν n. gen. fem. pl. χείρ hand
ἀνόμων adj. gen. masc. pl. ἄνομος without law, transgressor, wicked, lawless, unlawful
24 ὃν relative pron. acc. masc. sg. ὅς ἥ ὅ who, which, what, that
ὁ art. nom. masc. sg. ὁ ἡ τό the, this, that, he, she, it
Θεὸς n. nom. masc. sg. θεός God, god
τὰς art. acc. fem. pl. ὁ ἡ τό the, this, that, he, she, it
ὠδῖνας n. acc. fem. pl. ὠδίν sorrow, pain, travail
τοῦ art. gen. masc. sg. ὁ ἡ τό the, this, that, he, she, it
θανάτου n. gen. masc. sg. θάνατος death
καθότι conj. καθότι because, according as, as, because that, forasmuch as
οὐκ particle of negation. οὐ οὐκ οὐχ not, no, neither, none, nay, nor, never, nothing
δυνατὸν adj. nom. neut. sg. δυνατός able, possible, mighty, strong
αὐτὸν pron. acc. masc. 3p. sg. αὐτός ή ό self, of oneself, even, very, the same, he, she, it
ὑπ' prep. ὑπό (+gen) of, by, with, from, among, (+acc) under
αὐτοῦ pron. gen. masc. 3p. sg. αὐτός ή ό self, of oneself, even, very, the same, he, she, it
25 Δαβὶδ n. nom. masc. sg. Δαβίδ David
γὰρ conj. γάρ for, and, because, but, indeed

εἰς prep. εἰς (+acc) into, to, unto, for, in, on, toward, against, upon, at, among
αὐτόν pron. acc. masc. 3p. sg. αὐτός ἡ ὁ self, of oneself, even, very, the same, he, she, it
τὸν art. acc. masc. sg. ὁ ἡ τό the, this, that, he, she, it
Κύριον n. acc. masc. sg. κύριος Lord, lord, master, sir, LORD, God, Master, owner
ἐνώπιον adv. ἐνώπιον before, in the sight of, in the presence of
μου pron. gen. 1p. sg. ἐγώ I
διὰ prep. διά (+gen) by, through, with, in, of, (+acc) for, because of, for a cause
παντός adj. gen. neut. sg. πᾶς πᾶσα πᾶν all, every, whosoever, every one, no, whole, any
ὅτι conj. ὅτι that, for, because, how that, how, because that, for that, though
ἐκ prep. ἐκ ἐξ (+gen) of, from, out of, by, on, with, in, among, through
δεξιῶν adj. gen. neut. pl. δεξιός right, right hand, right side
μου pron. gen. 1p. sg. ἐγώ I
ἵνα conj. ἵνα that, to, lest, for to, so that, albeit, because, for, so as
μὴ particle of negation. μή not, no, lest, neither, none, nothing, nor, never, without
26 διὰ prep. διά (+gen) by, through, with, in, of, (+acc) for, because of, for a cause
τοῦτο demo. pron. acc. neut. sg. οὗτος αὕτη τοῦτο this, the same, this same, he, she, it
ἡ art. nom. fem. sg. ὁ ἡ τό the, this, that, he, she, it
καρδία n. nom. fem. sg. καρδία heart
μου pron. gen. 1p. sg. ἐγώ I
καὶ conj. καί and, even, also, but
ἡ art. nom. fem. sg. ὁ ἡ τό the, this, that, he, she, it
γλῶσσά n. nom. fem. sg. γλῶσσα tongue
μου pron. gen. 1p. sg. ἐγώ I
ἔτι adv. ἔτι yet, more, any more, further, still, moreover
δὲ conj. δέ but, and, now, also, to the contrary, rather, then
καὶ conj. καί and, even, also, but
ἡ art. nom. fem. sg. ὁ ἡ τό the, this, that, he, she, it
σάρξ n. nom. fem. sg. σάρξ flesh, carnal
μου pron. gen. 1p. sg. ἐγώ I
ἐπ' prep. ἐπί (+gen) on, in, upon, (+dat) in, at, for, upon, (+acc) on, upon, unto, to, against
ἐλπίδι n. dat. fem. sg. ἐλπίς hope, faith
27 ὅτι conj. ὅτι that, for, because, how that, how, because that, for that, though
οὐκ particle of negation. οὐ οὐκ οὐχ not, no, neither, none, nay, nor, never, nothing
τὴν art. acc. fem. sg. ὁ ἡ τό the, this, that, he, she, it
ψυχήν n. acc. fem. sg. ψυχή life, soul, mind, heart
μου pron. gen. 1p. sg. ἐγώ I
εἰς prep. εἰς (+acc) into, to, unto, for, in, on, toward, against, upon, at, among
ᾄδου n. gen. masc. sg. ᾄδης hell, grave
οὐδὲ conj. οὐδέ neither, nor, not, no, not even, never, not yet
τὸν art. acc. masc. sg. ὁ ἡ τό the, this, that, he, she, it
ὅσιόν adj. acc. masc. sg. ὅσιος holy, Holy, mercy
σου pron. gen. 2p. sg. σύ thou, you
διαφθοράν n. acc. fem. sg. διαφθορά corruption
28 μοι pron. dat. 1p. sg. ἐγώ I
ὁδοὺς n. acc. fem. pl. ὁδός way, journey, highway
ζωῆς n. gen. fem. sg. ζωή life, lifetime
με pron. acc. 1p. sg. ἐγώ I
εὐφροσύνης n. gen. fem. sg. εὐφροσύνη joy, gladness
μετὰ prep. μετά (+gen) with, among, against, (+acc) after
τοῦ art. gen. neut. sg. ὁ ἡ τό the, this, that, he, she, it
προσώπου n. gen. neut. sg. πρόσωπον face, presence, person, countenance
σου pron. gen. 2p. sg. σύ thou, you
29 Ἄνδρες n. voc. masc. pl. ἀνήρ man, husband, sir
ἀδελφοί n. voc. masc. pl. ἀδελφός brother
μετὰ prep. μετά (+gen) with, among, against, (+acc) after

παρρησίας n. gen. fem. sg. παρρησία boldness, confidence, openly, plainly, freely
πρὸς prep. πρός (+gen) for, (+dat) at, (+acc) unto, to, with, for, against
ὑμᾶς pron. acc. 2p. pl. σύ thou, you
περὶ prep. περί (+gen) of, for, concerning, (+acc) about, concerning, in
τοῦ art. gen. masc. sg. ὁ ἡ τό the, this, that, he, she, it
πατριάρχου n. gen. masc. sg. πατριάρχης patriarch
Δαβὶδ n. gen. masc. sg. Δαβίδ David
ὅτι conj. ὅτι that, for, because, how that, how, because that, for that, though
καὶ conj. καί and, even, also, but
καὶ conj. καί and, even, also, but
καὶ conj. καί and, even, also, but
τὸ art. nom. neut. sg. ὁ ἡ τό the, this, that, he, she, it
μνῆμα n. nom. neut. sg. μνῆμα sepulchre, tomb, grave
αὐτοῦ pron. gen. masc. 3p. sg. αὐτός ή ό self, of oneself, even, very, the same, he, she, it
ἐν prep. ἐν (+dat) in, by, with, among, at, on, through, to, within, into, of, for
ἡμῖν pron. dat. 1p. pl. ἐγώ I
ἄχρι prep. ἄχρι or ἄχρις (+gen) until, unto, till, even to, as far as, while, into
τῆς art. gen. fem. sg. ὁ ἡ τό the, this, that, he, she, it
ἡμέρας n. gen. fem. sg. ἡμέρα day, time, year, while, age, day time
ταύτης demo. pron. gen. fem. sg. οὗτος αὕτη τοῦτο this, the same, this same, he, she, it
30 προφήτης n. nom. masc. sg. προφήτης prophet
οὖν conj. οὖν therefore, then, so, and, now, wherefore
καὶ conj. καί and, even, also, but
ὅτι conj. ὅτι that, for, because, how that, how, because that, for that, though
ὅρκῳ n. dat. masc. sg. ὅρκος oath
αὐτῷ pron. dat. masc. 3p. sg. αὐτός ή ό self, of oneself, even, very, the same, he, she, it
ὁ art. nom. masc. sg. ὁ ἡ τό the, this, that, he, she, it
Θεὸς n. nom. masc. sg. θεός God, god
ἐκ prep. ἐκ ἐξ (+gen) of, from, out of, by, on, with, in, among, through
καρποῦ n. gen. masc. sg. καρπός fruit
τῆς art. gen. fem. sg. ὁ ἡ τό the, this, that, he, she, it
ὀσφύος n. gen. fem. sg. ὀσφύς loins
αὐτοῦ pron. gen. masc. 3p. sg. αὐτός ή ό self, of oneself, even, very, the same, he, she, it
τὸ art. acc. neut. sg. ὁ ἡ τό the, this, that, he, she, it
κατὰ prep. κατά (+gen) against, by, throughout, down, (+acc) according to, after, with
σάρκα n. acc. fem. sg. σάρξ flesh, carnal
τὸν art. acc. masc. sg. ὁ ἡ τό the, this, that, he, she, it
Χριστόν n. acc. masc. sg. Χριστός Christ
ἐπὶ prep. ἐπί (+gen) on, in, upon, (+dat) in, at, for, upon, (+acc) on, upon, unto, to, against
τοῦ art. gen. neut. sg. ὁ ἡ τό the, this, that, he, she, it
θρόνου n. gen. masc. sg. θρόνος throne, seat
αὐτοῦ pron. gen. masc. 3p. sg. αὐτός ή ό self, of oneself, even, very, the same, he, she, it
31 περὶ prep. περί (+gen) of, for, concerning, (+acc) about, concerning, in
τῆς art. gen. fem. sg. ὁ ἡ τό the, this, that, he, she, it
ἀναστάσεως n. gen. fem. sg. ἀνάστασις resurrection, rising again
τοῦ art. gen. masc. sg. ὁ ἡ τό the, this, that, he, she, it
Χριστοῦ n. gen. masc. sg. Χριστός Christ
ὅτι conj. ὅτι that, for, because, how that, how, because that, for that, though
οὐ particle of negation. οὐ οὐκ οὐχ not, no, neither, none, nay, nor, never, nothing
ἡ art. nom. fem. sg. ὁ ἡ τό the, this, that, he, she, it
ψυχὴ n. nom. fem. sg. ψυχή life, soul, mind, heart
αὐτοῦ pron. gen. masc. 3p. sg. αὐτός ή ό self, of oneself, even, very, the same, he, she, it
εἰς prep. εἰς (+acc) into, to, unto, for, in, on, toward, against, upon, at, among
ᾅδου n. gen. masc. sg. ᾅδης hell, grave
οὐδὲ adv. οὐδέ neither, nor, not, no, not even, never, not yet

ἡ art. nom. fem. sg. ὁ ἡ τό the, this, that, he, she, it
σὰρξ n. nom. fem. sg. σάρξ flesh, carnal
αὐτοῦ pron. gen. masc. 3p. sg. αὐτός ἡ ὁ self, of oneself, even, very, the same, he, she, it
διαφθοράν n. acc. fem. sg. διαφθορά corruption
32 τοῦτον demo. pron. acc. masc. sg. οὗτος αὕτη τοῦτο this, the same, this same, he, she, it
τὸν art. acc. masc. sg. ὁ ἡ τό the, this, that, he, she, it
Ἰησοῦν n. acc. masc. sg. Ἰησοῦς Jesus
ὁ art. nom. masc. sg. ὁ ἡ τό the, this, that, he, she, it
Θεός n. nom. masc. sg. θεός God, god
οὗ relative pron. gen. masc. sg. ὅς ἥ ὅ who, which, what, that
πάντες adj. nom. masc. pl. πᾶς πᾶσα πᾶν all, every, whosoever, every one, no, whole, any
ἡμεῖς pron. nom. 1p. pl. ἐγώ I
μάρτυρες n. nom. masc. pl. μάρτυς or μάρτυρ witness, martyr, record
33 τῇ art. dat. fem. sg. ὁ ἡ τό the, this, that, he, she, it
δεξιᾷ adj. dat. fem. sg. δεξιός right, right hand, right side
οὖν conj. οὖν therefore, then, so, and, now, wherefore
τοῦ art. gen. masc. sg. ὁ ἡ τό the, this, that, he, she, it
Θεοῦ n. gen. masc. sg. θεός God, god
τήν art. acc. fem. sg. ὁ ἡ τό the, this, that, he, she, it
τε conj. τέ and, both, also
ἐπαγγελίαν n. acc. fem. sg. ἐπαγγελία promise, message
τοῦ art. gen. neut. sg. ὁ ἡ τό the, this, that, he, she, it
Ἁγίου adj. gen. neut. sg. ἅγιος Holy, holy, saint, Holy One, holy thing, most holy
Πνεύματος n. gen. neut. sg. πνεῦμα spirit, Spirit, Ghost, ghost, life. of the spirit, wind
παρὰ prep. παρά (+gen) of, from, (+dat) with, for, (+acc) beside, at, by, above, against
τοῦ art. gen. masc. sg. ὁ ἡ τό the, this, that, he, she, it
πατρός n. gen. masc. sg. πατήρ Father, father, parent
τοῦτο demo. pron. acc. neut. sg. οὗτος αὕτη τοῦτο this, the same, this same, he, she, it
ὃ relative pron. acc. neut. sg. ὅς ἥ ὅ who, which, what, that
νῦν adv. νῦν now, henceforth, present, this time
ὑμεῖς pron. nom. 2p. pl. σύ thou, you
καὶ conj. καί and, even, also, but
34 οὐ particle of negation. οὐ οὐκ οὐχ not, no, neither, none, nay, nor, never, nothing
γὰρ conj. γάρ for, and, because, but, indeed
Δαβὶδ n. nom. masc. sg. Δαβίδ David
εἰς prep. εἰς (+acc) into, to, unto, for, in, on, toward, against, upon, at, among
τοὺς art. acc. masc. pl. ὁ ἡ τό the, this, that, he, she, it
οὐρανούς n. acc. masc. pl. οὐρανός heaven, air, sky
δὲ conj. δέ but, and, now, also, to the contrary, rather, then
αὐτός pron. nom. masc. 3p. sg. αὐτός ἡ ὁ self, of oneself, even, very, the same, he, she, it
ὁ art. nom. masc. sg. ὁ ἡ τό the, this, that, he, she, it
Κύριος n. nom. masc. sg. κύριος Lord, lord, master, sir, LORD, God, Master, owner
τῷ art. dat. masc. sg. ὁ ἡ τό the, this, that, he, she, it
Κυρίῳ n. dat. masc. sg. κύριος Lord, lord, master, sir, LORD, God, Master, owner
μου pron. gen. 1p. sg. ἐγώ I
ἐκ prep. ἐκ ἐξ (+gen) of, from, out of, by, on, with, in, among, through
δεξιῶν adj. gen. neut. pl. δεξιός right, right hand, right side
μου pron. gen. 1p. sg. ἐγώ I
35 ἕως conj. ἕως till, until, unto, until when, while, as far as, even, until now
ἂν particle. ἄν Indicating contingency. No English translation.
τοὺς art. acc. masc. pl. ὁ ἡ τό the, this, that, he, she, it
ἐχθρούς adj. acc. masc. pl. ἐχθρός enemy, foe
σου pron. gen. 2p. sg. σύ thou, you
ὑποπόδιον n. acc. neut. sg. ὑποπόδιον footstool
τῶν art. gen. masc. pl. ὁ ἡ τό the, this, that, he, she, it

ποδῶν n. gen. masc. pl. πούς foot
σου pron. gen. 2p. sg. σύ thou, you
36 ἀσφαλῶς adv. ἀσφαλῶς safely, assuredly
οὖν conj. οὖν therefore, then, so, and, now, wherefore
πᾶς adj. nom. masc. sg. πᾶς πᾶσα πᾶν all, every, whosoever, every one, no, whole, any
οἶκος n. nom. masc. sg. οἶκος house, home, household
Ἰσραήλ pron. name. masc. inde. Ἰσραήλ Israel
ὅτι conj. ὅτι that, for, because, how that, how, because that, for that, though
καὶ conj. καί and, even, also, but
Κύριον n. acc. masc. sg. κύριος Lord, lord, master, sir, LORD, God, Master, owner
καὶ conj. καί and, even, also, but
Χριστὸν n. acc. masc. sg. Χριστός Christ
αὐτὸν pron. acc. masc. 3p. sg. αὐτός ή ό self, of oneself, even, very, the same, he, she, it
ὁ art. nom. masc. sg. ὁ ἡ τό the, this, that, he, she, it
Θεός n. nom. masc. sg. θεός God, god
τοῦτον demo. pron. acc. masc. sg. οὗτος αὕτη τοῦτο this, the same, this same, he, she, it
τὸν art. acc. masc. sg. ὁ ἡ τό the, this, that, he, she, it
Ἰησοῦν n. acc. masc. sg. Ἰησοῦς Jesus
ὃν relative pron. acc. masc. sg. ὅς ἥ ὅ who, which, what, that
ὑμεῖς pron. nom. 2p. pl. σύ thou, you
37 δὲ conj. δέ but, and, now, also, to the contrary, rather, then
τῇ art. dat. fem. sg. ὁ ἡ τό the, this, that, he, she, it
καρδίᾳ n. dat. fem. sg. καρδία heart
τε conj. τέ and, both, also
πρὸς prep. πρός (+gen) for, (+dat) at, (+acc) unto, to, with, for, against
τὸν art. acc. masc. sg. ὁ ἡ τό the, this, that, he, she, it
Πέτρον n. acc. masc. sg. Πέτρος Peter
καὶ conj. καί and, even, also, but
τοὺς art. acc. masc. pl. ὁ ἡ τό the, this, that, he, she, it
λοιποὺς adj. acc. masc. pl. λοιπός other, rest, remnant, residue, which remain
ἀποστόλους n. acc. masc. pl. ἀπόστολος apostle, messenger, he that is sent
Τί interrog. pron. acc. neut. sg. τίς what, who, why, where, which, how
ἄνδρες n. voc. masc. pl. ἀνήρ man, husband, sir
ἀδελφοί n. voc. masc. pl. ἀδελφός brother
38 Πέτρος n. nom. masc. sg. Πέτρος Peter
δὲ conj. δέ but, and, now, also, to the contrary, rather, then
πρὸς prep. πρός (+gen) for, (+dat) at, (+acc) unto, to, with, for, against
αὐτούς pron. acc. masc. 3p. pl. αὐτός ή ό self, of oneself, even, very, the same, he, she, it
καὶ conj. καί and, even, also, but
ἕκαστος adj. nom. masc. sg. ἕκαστος every man, every, every one, any man, each
ὑμῶν pron. gen. 2p. pl. σύ thou, you
ἐπὶ prep. ἐπί (+gen) on, in, upon, (+dat) in, at, for, upon, (+acc) on, upon, unto, to, against
τῷ art. dat. neut. sg. ὁ ἡ τό the, this, that, he, she, it
ὀνόματι n. dat. neut. sg. ὄνομα name, call, surname
Ἰησοῦ n. gen. masc. sg. Ἰησοῦς Jesus
Χριστοῦ n. gen. masc. sg. Χριστός Christ
εἰς prep. εἰς (+acc) into, to, unto, for, in, on, toward, against, upon, at, among
ἄφεσιν n. acc. fem. sg. ἄφεσις remission, forgiveness, deliverance, liberty
ἁμαρτιῶν n. gen. fem. pl. ἁμαρτία sin, offence, sinful
καὶ conj. καί and, even, also, but
τὴν art. acc. fem. sg. ὁ ἡ τό the, this, that, he, she, it
δωρεὰν n. acc. fem. sg. δωρεά gift
τοῦ art. gen. neut. sg. ὁ ἡ τό the, this, that, he, she, it
Ἁγίου adj. gen. neut. sg. ἅγιος Holy, holy, saint, Holy One, holy thing, most holy
Πνεύματος n. gen. neut. sg. πνεῦμα spirit, Spirit, Ghost, ghost, life. of the spirit, wind

39 ὑμῖν pron. dat. 2p. pl. σύ thou, you
γάρ conj. γάρ for, and, because, but, indeed
ἡ art. nom. fem. sg. ὁ ἡ τό the, this, that, he, she, it
ἐπαγγελία n. nom. fem. sg. ἐπαγγελία promise, message
καὶ conj. καί and, even, also, but
τοῖς art. dat. neut. pl. ὁ ἡ τό the, this, that, he, she, it
τέκνοις n. dat. neut. pl. τέκνον child, son, daughter
ὑμῶν pron. gen. 2p. pl. σύ thou, you
καὶ conj. καί and, even, also, but
πᾶσι adj. dat. masc. pl. πᾶς πᾶσα πᾶν all, every, whosoever, every one, no, whole, any
τοῖς art. dat. masc. pl. ὁ ἡ τό the, this, that, he, she, it
εἰς prep. εἰς (+acc) into, to, unto, for, in, on, toward, against, upon, at, among
μακράν adj. acc. fem. sg. μακρός far, long
ὅσους relative pron. acc. masc. pl. ὅσος as many as, whatsoever, that, as long as, how much
ἂν particle. ἄν Indicating contingency. No English translation.
Κύριος n. nom. masc. sg. κύριος Lord, lord, master, sir, LORD, God, Master, owner
ὁ art. nom. masc. sg. ὁ ἡ τό the, this, that, he, she, it
Θεὸς n. nom. masc. sg. θεός God, god
ἡμῶν pron. gen. 1p. pl. ἐγώ I
40 ἑτέροις adj. dat. masc. pl. ἕτερος another, other, else, strange
τε conj. τέ and, both, also
λόγοις n. dat. masc. pl. λόγος word, saying, account, speech, thing, matter
πλείοσι compar. adj. dat. masc. pl. πολύς many, great, much, long, abundant
καὶ conj. καί and, even, also, but
ἀπὸ prep. ἀπό (+gen) from, of, out of, since, for, off, at, by, in, on
τῆς art. gen. fem. sg. ὁ ἡ τό the, this, that, he, she, it
γενεᾶς n. gen. fem. sg. γενεά generation, age, time, nation
τῆς art. gen. fem. sg. ὁ ἡ τό the, this, that, he, she, it
σκολιᾶς adj. gen. fem. sg. σκολιός crooked, froward, untoward
ταύτης demo. pron. gen. fem. sg. οὗτος αὕτη τοῦτο this, the same, this same, he, she, it
41 οἱ art. nom. masc. pl. ὁ ἡ τό the, this, that, he, she, it
μέν conj. μέν indeed, verily, truly, even, so, some
οὖν conj. οὖν therefore, then, so, and, now, wherefore
ἀσμένως adv. ἀσμένως gladly
τὸν art. acc. masc. sg. ὁ ἡ τό the, this, that, he, she, it
λόγον n. acc. masc. sg. λόγος word, saying, account, speech, thing, matter
αὐτοῦ pron. gen. masc. 3p. sg. αὐτός ἡ ό self, of oneself, even, very, the same, he, she, it
καὶ conj. καί and, even, also, but
τῇ art. dat. fem. sg. ὁ ἡ τό the, this, that, he, she, it
ἡμέρᾳ n. dat. fem. sg. ἡμέρα day, time, year, while, age, day time
ἐκείνῃ demo. pron. dat. fem. sg. ἐκεῖνος that, he, the same, that same
ψυχαὶ n. nom. fem. pl. ψυχή life, soul, mind, heart
ὡσεὶ adv. ὡσεί about, as, like, as it had been, as it were, like as
τρισχίλιαι num. nom. fem. pl. τρισχίλιοι three thousand
42 δὲ conj. δέ but, and, now, also, to the contrary, rather, then
τῇ art. dat. fem. sg. ὁ ἡ τό the, this, that, he, she, it
διδαχῇ n. dat. fem. sg. διδαχή doctrine, teaching
τῶν art. gen. masc. pl. ὁ ἡ τό the, this, that, he, she, it
ἀποστόλων n. gen. masc. pl. ἀπόστολος apostle, messenger, he that is sent
καὶ conj. καί and, even, also, but
τῇ art. dat. fem. sg. ὁ ἡ τό the, this, that, he, she, it
κοινωνίᾳ n. dat. fem. sg. κοινωνία fellowship, communion, contribution, distribution
καὶ conj. καί and, even, also, but
τῇ art. dat. fem. sg. ὁ ἡ τό the, this, that, he, she, it
κλάσει n. dat. fem. sg. κλάσις breaking

τοῦ art. gen. masc. sg. ὁ ἡ τό the, this, that, he, she, it
ἄρτου n. gen. masc. sg. ἄρτος bread, loaf
καὶ conj. καί and, even, also, but
ταῖς art. dat. fem. pl. ὁ ἡ τό the, this, that, he, she, it
προσευχαῖς n. dat. fem. pl. προσευχή prayer
43 δὲ conj. δέ but, and, now, also, to the contrary, rather, then
πάσῃ adj. dat. fem. sg. πᾶς πᾶσα πᾶν all, every, whosoever, every one, no, whole, any
ψυχῇ n. dat. fem. sg. ψυχή life, soul, mind, heart
φόβος n. nom. masc. sg. φόβος fear, terror, sore afraid
πολλά adj. nom. neut. pl. πολύς many, great, much, long, abundant
τε conj. τέ and, both, also
τέρατα n. nom. neut. pl. τέρας wonder
καὶ conj. καί and, even, also, but
σημεῖα n. nom. neut. pl. σημεῖον sign, miracle, wonder, token
διὰ prep. διά (+gen) by, through, with, in, of, (+acc) for, because of, for a cause
τῶν art. gen. masc. pl. ὁ ἡ τό the, this, that, he, she, it
ἀποστόλων n. gen. masc. pl. ἀπόστολος apostle, messenger, he that is sent
44 πάντες adj. nom. masc. pl. πᾶς πᾶσα πᾶν all, every, whosoever, every one, no, whole, any
δὲ conj. δέ but, and, now, also, to the contrary, rather, then
οἱ art. nom. masc. pl. ὁ ἡ τό the, this, that, he, she, it
ἐπὶ prep. ἐπί (+gen) on, in, upon, (+dat) in, at, for, upon, (+acc) on, upon, unto, to, against
τὸ art. acc. neut. sg. ὁ ἡ τό the, this, that, he, she, it
αὐτὸ pron. acc. neut. 3p. sg. αὐτός ή ό self, of oneself, even, very, the same, he, she, it
καὶ conj. καί and, even, also, but
ἅπαντα adj. acc. neut. pl. ἅπας all, whole, all things, every, everyone
κοινὰ adj. acc. neut. pl. κοινός common, unclean, defiled, unholy
45 καὶ conj. καί and, even, also, but
τὰ art. acc. neut. pl. ὁ ἡ τό the, this, that, he, she, it
κτήματα n. acc. neut. pl. κτῆμα possession
καὶ conj. καί and, even, also, but
τὰς art. acc. fem. pl. ὁ ἡ τό the, this, that, he, she, it
ὑπάρξεις n. acc. fem. pl. ὕπαρξις goods, substance
καὶ conj. καί and, even, also, but
αὐτὰ pron. acc. neut. 3p. pl. αὐτός ή ό self, of oneself, even, very, the same, he, she, it
πᾶσι adj. dat. masc. pl. πᾶς πᾶσα πᾶν all, every, whosoever, every one, no, whole, any
καθότι conj. καθότι because, according as, as, because that, forasmuch as
ἄν particle. ἄν Indicating contingency. No English translation.
τις indefinite pron. nom. masc. sg. τὶς certain, some, any man, one, any thing
χρείαν n. acc. fem. sg. χρεία need, necessity, lack, want
46 καθ' prep. κατά (+gen) against, by, throughout, down, (+acc) according to, after, with
ἡμέραν n. acc. fem. sg. ἡμέρα day, time, year, while, age, day time
τε conj. τέ and, both, also
ὁμοθυμαδὸν adv. ὁμοθυμαδόν with one accord, with one mind
ἐν prep. ἐν (+dat) in, by, with, among, at, on, through, to, within, into, of, for
τῷ art. dat. neut. sg. ὁ ἡ τό the, this, that, he, she, it
ἱερῷ n. dat. neut. sg. ἱερόν temple
τε conj. τέ and, both, also
κατ' prep. κατά (+gen) against, by, throughout, down, (+acc) according to, after, with
οἶκον n. acc. masc. sg. οἶκος house, home, household
ἄρτον n. acc. masc. sg. ἄρτος bread, loaf
τροφῆς n. gen. fem. sg. τροφή meat, food
ἐν prep. ἐν (+dat) in, by, with, among, at, on, through, to, within, into, of, for
ἀγαλλιάσει n. dat. fem. sg. ἀγαλλίασις gladness, exceeding joy, joy
καὶ conj. καί and, even, also, but
ἀφελότητι n. dat. fem. sg. ἀφελότης singleness

καρδίας n. gen. fem. sg. καρδία heart
47 τὸν art. acc. masc. sg. ὁ ἡ τό the, this, that, he, she, it
Θεὸν n. acc. masc. sg. θεός God, god
καὶ conj. καί and, even, also, but
χάριν n. acc. fem. sg. χάρις grace, thank, favour, pleasure
πρὸς prep. πρός (+gen) for, (+dat) at, (+acc) unto, to, with, for, against
ὅλον adj. acc. masc. sg. ὅλος all, whole, every whit, altogether
τὸν art. acc. masc. sg. ὁ ἡ τό the, this, that, he, she, it
λαόν n. acc. masc. sg. λαός people
ὁ art. nom. masc. sg. ὁ ἡ τό the, this, that, he, she, it
δὲ conj. δέ but, and, now, also, to the contrary, rather, then
Κύριος n. nom. masc. sg. κύριος Lord, lord, master, sir, LORD, God, Master, owner
τοὺς art. acc. masc. pl. ὁ ἡ τό the, this, that, he, she, it
καθ' prep. κατά (+gen) against, by, throughout, down, (+acc) according to, after, with
ἡμέραν n. acc. fem. sg. ἡμέρα day, time, year, while, age, day time
τῇ art. dat. fem. sg. ὁ ἡ τό the, this, that, he, she, it
ἐκκλησίᾳ n. dat. fem. sg. ἐκκλησία church, assembly

3

1 Ἐπὶ prep. ἐπί (+gen) on, in, upon, (+dat) in, at, for, upon, (+acc) on, upon, unto, to, against
τὸ art. acc. neut. sg. ὁ ἡ τό the, this, that, he, she, it
αὐτὸ pron. acc. neut. 3p. sg. αὐτός ή ό self, of oneself, even, very, the same, he, she, it
δὲ conj. δέ but, and, now, also, to the contrary, rather, then
Πέτρος n. nom. masc. sg. Πέτρος Peter
καὶ conj. καί and, even, also, but
Ἰωάννης n. nom. masc. sg. Ἰωάννης John
εἰς prep. εἰς (+acc) into, to, unto, for, in, on, toward, against, upon, at, among
τὸ art. acc. neut. sg. ὁ ἡ τό the, this, that, he, she, it
ἱερὸν n. acc. neut. sg. ἱερόν temple
ἐπὶ prep. ἐπί (+gen) on, in, upon, (+dat) in, at, for, upon, (+acc) on, upon, unto, to, against
τὴν art. acc. fem. sg. ὁ ἡ τό the, this, that, he, she, it
ὥραν n. acc. fem. sg. ὥρα hour, time, season
τῆς art. gen. fem. sg. ὁ ἡ τό the, this, that, he, she, it
προσευχῆς n. gen. fem. sg. προσευχή prayer
τὴν art. acc. fem. sg. ὁ ἡ τό the, this, that, he, she, it
ἐννάτην ordinal. adj. acc. fem. sg. ἔννατος ninth
2 καί conj. καί and, even, also, but
τις indefinite pron. nom. masc. sg. τὶς certain, some, any man, one, any thing
ἀνὴρ n. nom. masc. sg. ἀνήρ man, husband, sir
χωλὸς adj. nom. masc. sg. χωλός lame, halt, cripple
ἐκ prep. ἐκ ἐξ (+gen) of, from, out of, by, on, with, in, among, through
κοιλίας n. gen. fem. sg. κοιλία belly, womb
μητρὸς n. gen. fem. sg. μήτηρ mother
αὐτοῦ pron. gen. masc. 3p. sg. αὐτός ή ό self, of oneself, even, very, the same, he, she, it
ὃν relative pron. acc. masc. sg. ὅς ἥ ὅ who, which, what, that
καθ' prep. κατά (+gen) against, by, throughout, down, (+acc) according to, after, with
ἡμέραν n. acc. fem. sg. ἡμέρα day, time, year, while, age, day time
πρὸς prep. πρός (+gen) for, (+dat) at, (+acc) unto, to, with, for, against
τὴν art. acc. fem. sg. ὁ ἡ τό the, this, that, he, she, it
θύραν n. acc. fem. sg. θύρα door, gate
τοῦ art. gen. neut. sg. ὁ ἡ τό the, this, that, he, she, it
ἱεροῦ n. gen. neut. sg. ἱερόν temple
τὴν art. acc. fem. sg. ὁ ἡ τό the, this, that, he, she, it
Ὡραίαν adj. acc. fem. sg. ὡραῖος beautiful

τοῦ art. gen. neut. sg. ὁ ἡ τό the, this, that, he, she, it
ἐλεημοσύνην n. acc. fem. sg. ἐλεημοσύνη alms, almsdeed
παρὰ prep. παρά (+gen) of, from, (+dat) with, for, (+acc) beside, at, by, above, against
τῶν art. gen. masc. pl. ὁ ἡ τό the, this, that, he, she, it
εἰς prep. εἰς (+acc) into, to, unto, for, in, on, toward, against, upon, at, among
τὸ art. acc. neut. sg. ὁ ἡ τό the, this, that, he, she, it
ἱερόν n. acc. neut. sg. ἱερόν temple
3 ὃς relative pron. nom. masc. sg. ὅς ἥ ὅ who, which, what, that
Πέτρον n. acc. masc. sg. Πέτρος Peter
καὶ conj. καί and, even, also, but
Ἰωάννην n. acc. masc. sg. Ἰωάννης John
εἰς prep. εἰς (+acc) into, to, unto, for, in, on, toward, against, upon, at, among
τὸ art. acc. neut. sg. ὁ ἡ τό the, this, that, he, she, it
ἱερόν n. acc. neut. sg. ἱερόν temple
ἐλεημοσύνην n. acc. fem. sg. ἐλεημοσύνη alms, almsdeed
4 δὲ conj. δέ but, and, now, also, to the contrary, rather, then
Πέτρος n. nom. masc. sg. Πέτρος Peter
εἰς prep. εἰς (+acc) into, to, unto, for, in, on, toward, against, upon, at, among
αὐτὸν pron. acc. masc. 3p. sg. αὐτός ή ό self, of oneself, even, very, the same, he, she, it
σὺν prep. σύν (+dat) with, beside
τῷ art. dat. masc. sg. ὁ ἡ τό the, this, that, he, she, it
Ἰωάννῃ n. dat. masc. sg. Ἰωάννης John
εἰς prep. εἰς (+acc) into, to, unto, for, in, on, toward, against, upon, at, among
ἡμᾶς pron. acc. 1p. pl. ἐγώ I
5 ὁ art. nom. masc. sg. ὁ ἡ τό the, this, that, he, she, it
δὲ conj. δέ but, and, now, also, to the contrary, rather, then
αὐτοῖς pron. dat. masc. 3p. pl. αὐτός ή ό self, of oneself, even, very, the same, he, she, it
τι indefinite pron. acc. neut. sg. τὶς certain, some, any man, one, any thing
παρ' prep. παρά (+gen) of, from, (+dat) with, for, (+acc) beside, at, by, above, against
αὐτῶν pron. gen. masc. 3p. pl. αὐτός ή ό self, of oneself, even, very, the same, he, she, it
6 δὲ conj. δέ but, and, now, also, to the contrary, rather, then
Πέτρος n. nom. masc. sg. Πέτρος Peter
Ἀργύριον n. nom. neut. sg. ἀργύριον money, piece of silver, silver
καὶ conj. καί and, even, also, but
χρυσίον n. nom. neut. sg. χρυσίον gold
οὐχ particle of negation. οὐ οὐκ οὐχ not, no, neither, none, nay, nor, never, nothing
μοι pron. dat. 1p. sg. ἐγώ I
ὃ relative pron. acc. neut. sg. ὅς ἥ ὅ who, which, what, that
δὲ conj. δέ but, and, now, also, to the contrary, rather, then
τοῦτό demo. pron. acc. neut. sg. οὗτος αὕτη τοῦτο this, the same, this same, he, she, it
σοι pron. dat. 2p. sg. σύ thou, you
ἐν prep. ἐν (+dat) in, by, with, among, at, on, through, to, within, into, of, for
τῷ art. dat. neut. sg. ὁ ἡ τό the, this, that, he, she, it
ὀνόματι n. dat. neut. sg. ὄνομα name, call, surname
Ἰησοῦ n. gen. masc. sg. Ἰησοῦς Jesus
Χριστοῦ n. gen. masc. sg. Χριστός Christ
τοῦ art. gen. masc. sg. ὁ ἡ τό the, this, that, he, she, it
Ναζωραίου n. gen. masc. sg. Ναζωραῖος Nazareth, Nazarene
καὶ conj. καί and, even, also, but
7 καὶ conj. καί and, even, also, but
αὐτὸν pron. acc. masc. 3p. sg. αὐτός ή ό self, of oneself, even, very, the same, he, she, it
τῆς art. gen. fem. sg. ὁ ἡ τό the, this, that, he, she, it
δεξιᾶς adj. gen. fem. sg. δεξιός right, right hand, right side
χειρὸς n. gen. fem. sg. χείρ hand
παραχρῆμα adv. παραχρῆμα immediately, straightway, forthwith, presently, soon

δὲ conj. δέ but, and, now, also, to the contrary, rather, then
αὐτοῦ pron. gen. masc. 3p. sg. αὐτός ή ό self, of oneself, even, very, the same, he, she, it
αἱ art. nom. fem. pl. ὁ ἡ τό the, this, that, he, she, it
βάσεις n. nom. fem. pl. βάσις feet
καὶ conj. καί and, even, also, but
τὰ art. nom. neut. pl. ὁ ἡ τό the, this, that, he, she, it
σφυρά n. nom. neut. pl. σφυρόν ankle bone
8 καὶ conj. καί and, even, also, but
καὶ conj. καί and, even, also, but
καὶ conj. καί and, even, also, but
σὺν prep. σύν (+dat) with, beside
αὐτοῖς pron. dat. masc. 3p. pl. αὐτός ή ό self, of oneself, even, very, the same, he, she, it
εἰς prep. εἰς (+acc) into, to, unto, for, in, on, toward, against, upon, at, among
τὸ art. acc. neut. sg. ὁ ἡ τό the, this, that, he, she, it
ἱερὸν n. acc. neut. sg. ἱερόν temple
καὶ conj. καί and, even, also, but
καὶ conj. καί and, even, also, but
τὸν art. acc. masc. sg. ὁ ἡ τό the, this, that, he, she, it
Θεόν n. acc. masc. sg. θεός God, god
9 καὶ conj. καί and, even, also, but
αὐτὸν pron. acc. masc. 3p. sg. αὐτός ή ό self, of oneself, even, very, the same, he, she, it
πᾶς adj. nom. masc. sg. πᾶς πᾶσα πᾶν all, every, whosoever, every one, no, whole, any
ὁ art. nom. masc. sg. ὁ ἡ τό the, this, that, he, she, it
λαὸς n. nom. masc. sg. λαός people
καὶ conj. καί and, even, also, but
τὸν art. acc. masc. sg. ὁ ἡ τό the, this, that, he, she, it
Θεόν n. acc. masc. sg. θεός God, god
10 τε conj. τέ and, both, also
αὐτὸν pron. acc. masc. 3p. sg. αὐτός ή ό self, of oneself, even, very, the same, he, she, it
ὅτι conj. ὅτι that, for, because, how that, how, because that, for that, though
οὗτος demo. pron. nom. masc. sg. οὗτος αὕτη τοῦτο this, the same, this same, he, she, it
ὁ art. nom. masc. sg. ὁ ἡ τό the, this, that, he, she, it
πρὸς prep. πρός (+gen) for, (+dat) at, (+acc) unto, to, with, for, against
τὴν art. acc. fem. sg. ὁ ἡ τό the, this, that, he, she, it
ἐλεημοσύνην n. acc. fem. sg. ἐλεημοσύνη alms, almsdeed
ἐπὶ prep. ἐπί (+gen) on, in, upon, (+dat) in, at, for, upon, (+acc) on, upon, unto, to, against
τῇ art. dat. fem. sg. ὁ ἡ τό the, this, that, he, she, it
Ὡραίᾳ adj. dat. fem. sg. ὡραῖος beautiful
πύλῃ n. dat. fem. sg. πύλη gate
τοῦ art. gen. neut. sg. ὁ ἡ τό the, this, that, he, she, it
ἱεροῦ n. gen. neut. sg. ἱερόν temple
καὶ conj. καί and, even, also, but
θάμβους n. gen. neut. sg. θάμβος amazement, astonishment, wonder
καὶ conj. καί and, even, also, but
ἐκστάσεως n. gen. fem. sg. ἔκστασις trance, astonishment, amazement, amazed
ἐπὶ prep. ἐπί (+gen) on, in, upon, (+dat) in, at, for, upon, (+acc) on, upon, unto, to, against
τῷ art. dat. neut. sg. ὁ ἡ τό the, this, that, he, she, it
αὐτῷ pron. dat. masc. 3p. sg. αὐτός ή ό self, of oneself, even, very, the same, he, she, it
11 δὲ conj. δέ but, and, now, also, to the contrary, rather, then
τοῦ art. gen. masc. sg. ὁ ἡ τό the, this, that, he, she, it
χωλοῦ adj. gen. masc. sg. χωλός lame, halt, cripple
τὸν art. acc. masc. sg. ὁ ἡ τό the, this, that, he, she, it
Πέτρον n. acc. masc. sg. Πέτρος Peter
καὶ conj. καί and, even, also, but
Ἰωάννην n. acc. masc. sg. Ἰωάννης John

πρὸς prep. πρός (+gen) for, (+dat) at, (+acc) unto, to, with, for, against
αὐτοὺς pron. acc. masc. 3p. pl. αὐτός ή ό self, of oneself, even, very, the same, he, she, it
πᾶς adj. nom. masc. sg. πᾶς πᾶσα πᾶν all, every, whosoever, every one, no, whole, any
ὁ art. nom. masc. sg. ὁ ἡ τό the, this, that, he, she, it
λαὸς n. nom. masc. sg. λαός people
ἐπὶ prep. ἐπί (+gen) on, in, upon, (+dat) in, at, for, upon, (+acc) on, upon, unto, to, against
τῇ art. dat. fem. sg. ὁ ἡ τό the, this, that, he, she, it
στοᾷ n. dat. fem. sg. στοά porch
τῇ art. dat. fem. sg. ὁ ἡ τό the, this, that, he, she, it
Σολομῶντος n. gen. masc. sg. Σολομών Solomon
ἔκθαμβοι adj. nom. masc. pl. ἔκθαμβος greatly wondering
12 δὲ conj. δέ but, and, now, also, to the contrary, rather, then
Πέτρος n. nom. masc. sg. Πέτρος Peter
πρὸς prep. πρός (+gen) for, (+dat) at, (+acc) unto, to, with, for, against
τὸν art. acc. masc. sg. ὁ ἡ τό the, this, that, he, she, it
λαόν n. acc. masc. sg. λαός people
Ἄνδρες n. voc. masc. pl. ἀνήρ man, husband, sir
Ἰσραηλῖται n. voc. masc. pl. Ἰσραηλίτης Israelite, Israel
τί interrog. pron. acc. neut. sg. τίς what, who, why, where, which, how
ἐπὶ prep. ἐπί (+gen) on, in, upon, (+dat) in, at, for, upon, (+acc) on, upon, unto, to, against
τούτῳ demo. pron. dat. neut. sg. οὗτος αὕτη τοῦτο this, the same, this same, he, she, it
ἢ particle. ἤ or, than, either, nor, or else, and, rather than
ἡμῖν pron. dat. 1p. pl. ἐγώ I
τί interrog. pron. acc. neut. sg. τίς what, who, why, where, which, how
ὡς adv. ὡς as, when, as it were, how, about, like, as soon as, even as, while
ἰδίᾳ adj. dat. fem. sg. ἴδιος one's own, one's, privately
δυνάμει n. dat. fem. sg. δύναμις power, mighty work, miracle, strength, might
ἢ particle. ἤ or, than, either, nor, or else, and, rather than
εὐσεβείᾳ n. dat. fem. sg. εὐσέβεια godliness, holiness
τοῦ art. gen. neut. sg. ὁ ἡ τό the, this, that, he, she, it
αὐτόν pron. acc. masc. 3p. sg. αὐτός ή ό self, of oneself, even, very, the same, he, she, it
13 ὁ art. nom. masc. sg. ὁ ἡ τό the, this, that, he, she, it
Θεὸς n. nom. masc. sg. θεός God, god
Ἀβραὰμ n. gen. masc. sg. Ἀβραάμ Abraham
καὶ conj. καί and, even, also, but
Ἰσαὰκ n. gen. masc. sg. Ἰσαάκ Isaac
καὶ conj. καί and, even, also, but
Ἰακώβ n. gen. masc. sg. Ἰακώβ Jacob
ὁ art. nom. masc. sg. ὁ ἡ τό the, this, that, he, she, it
Θεὸς n. nom. masc. sg. θεός God, god
τῶν art. gen. masc. pl. ὁ ἡ τό the, this, that, he, she, it
πατέρων n. gen. masc. pl. πατήρ Father, father, parent
ἡμῶν pron. gen. 1p. pl. ἐγώ I
τὸν art. acc. masc. sg. ὁ ἡ τό the, this, that, he, she, it
παῖδα n. acc. masc. sg. παῖς servant, child, son, maid, young man, manservant
αὐτοῦ pron. gen. masc. 3p. sg. αὐτός ή ό self, of oneself, even, very, the same, he, she, it
Ἰησοῦν n. acc. masc. sg. Ἰησοῦς Jesus
ὃν relative pron. acc. masc. sg. ὅς ἥ ὅ who, which, what, that
ὑμεῖς pron. nom. 2p. pl. σύ thou, you
καὶ conj. καί and, even, also, but
αὐτόν pron. acc. masc. 3p. sg. αὐτός ή ό self, of oneself, even, very, the same, he, she, it
κατὰ prep. κατά (+gen) against, by, throughout, down, (+acc) according to, after, with
πρόσωπον n. acc. neut. sg. πρόσωπον face, presence, person, countenance
Πιλάτου n. gen. masc. sg. Πιλᾶτος Pilate
ἐκείνου demo. pron. gen. masc. sg. ἐκεῖνος that, he, the same, that same

14 ὑμεῖς pron. nom. 2p. pl. σύ thou, you
δὲ conj. δέ but, and, now, also, to the contrary, rather, then
τὸν art. acc. masc. sg. ὁ ἡ τό the, this, that, he, she, it
ἅγιον adj. acc. masc. sg. ἅγιος Holy, holy, saint, Holy One, holy thing, most holy
καὶ conj. καί and, even, also, but
δίκαιον adj. acc. masc. sg. δίκαιος righteous, just, meet, right
καὶ conj. καί and, even, also, but
ἄνδρα n. acc. masc. sg. ἀνήρ man, husband, sir
φονέα n. acc. masc. sg. φονεύς murderer
ὑμῖν pron. dat. 2p. pl. σύ thou, you
15 τὸν art. acc. masc. sg. ὁ ἡ τό the, this, that, he, she, it
δὲ conj. δέ but, and, now, also, to the contrary, rather, then
ἀρχηγὸν n. acc. masc. sg. ἀρχηγός Prince, author, captain
τῆς art. gen. fem. sg. ὁ ἡ τό the, this, that, he, she, it
ζωῆς n. gen. fem. sg. ζωή life, lifetime
ὃν relative pron. acc. masc. sg. ὅς ἥ ὅ who, which, what, that
ὁ art. nom. masc. sg. ὁ ἡ τό the, this, that, he, she, it
Θεὸς n. nom. masc. sg. θεός God, god
ἐκ prep. ἐκ ἐξ (+gen) of, from, out of, by, on, with, in, among, through
νεκρῶν adj. gen. masc. pl. νεκρός dead
οὗ relative pron. gen. neut. sg. ὅς ἥ ὅ who, which, what, that
ἡμεῖς pron. nom. 1p. pl. ἐγώ I
μάρτυρές n. nom. masc. pl. μάρτυς or μάρτυρ witness, martyr, record
16 καὶ conj. καί and, even, also, but
ἐπὶ prep. ἐπί (+gen) on, in, upon, (+dat) in, at, for, upon, (+acc) on, upon, unto, to, against
τῇ art. dat. fem. sg. ὁ ἡ τό the, this, that, he, she, it
πίστει n. dat. fem. sg. πίστις faith, assurance, belief, fidelity
τοῦ art. gen. neut. sg. ὁ ἡ τό the, this, that, he, she, it
ὀνόματος n. gen. neut. sg. ὄνομα name, call, surname
αὐτοῦ pron. gen. masc. 3p. sg. αὐτός ή ό self, of oneself, even, very, the same, he, she, it
τοῦτον demo. pron. acc. masc. sg. οὗτος αὕτη τοῦτο this, the same, this same, he, she, it
ὃν relative pron. acc. masc. sg. ὅς ἥ ὅ who, which, what, that
καὶ conj. καί and, even, also, but
τὸ art. nom. neut. sg. ὁ ἡ τό the, this, that, he, she, it
ὄνομα n. nom. neut. sg. ὄνομα name, call, surname
αὐτοῦ pron. gen. masc. 3p. sg. αὐτός ή ό self, of oneself, even, very, the same, he, she, it
καὶ conj. καί and, even, also, but
ἡ art. nom. fem. sg. ὁ ἡ τό the, this, that, he, she, it
πίστις n. nom. fem. sg. πίστις faith, assurance, belief, fidelity
ἡ art. nom. fem. sg. ὁ ἡ τό the, this, that, he, she, it
δι' prep. διά (+gen) by, through, with, in, of, (+acc) for, because of, for a cause
αὐτοῦ pron. gen. masc. 3p. sg. αὐτός ή ό self, of oneself, even, very, the same, he, she, it
αὐτῷ pron. dat. masc. 3p. sg. αὐτός ή ό self, of oneself, even, very, the same, he, she, it
τὴν art. acc. fem. sg. ὁ ἡ τό the, this, that, he, she, it
ὁλοκληρίαν n. acc. fem. sg. ὁλοκληρία perfect soundness
ταύτην demo. pron. acc. fem. sg. οὗτος αὕτη τοῦτο this, the same, this same, he, she, it
ἀπέναντι prep. ἀπέναντι before, over against, contrary, in the presence
πάντων adj. gen. masc. pl. πᾶς πᾶσα πᾶν all, every, whosoever, every one, no, whole, any
ὑμῶν pron. gen. 2p. pl. σύ thou, you
17 καὶ conj. καί and, even, also, but
νῦν adv. νῦν now, henceforth, present, this time
ἀδελφοί n. voc. masc. pl. ἀδελφός brother
ὅτι conj. ὅτι that, for, because, how that, how, because that, for that, though
κατὰ prep. κατά (+gen) against, by, throughout, down, (+acc) according to, after, with
ἄγνοιαν n. acc. fem. sg. ἄγνοια ignorance

ὥσπερ conj. ὥσπερ as, even as, like as
καὶ conj. καί and, even, also, but
οἱ art. nom. masc. pl. ὁ ἡ τό the, this, that, he, she, it
ἄρχοντες n. nom. masc. pl. ἄρχων ruler, prince, chief, magistrate, chief ruler
ὑμῶν pron. gen. 2p. pl. σύ thou, you
18 ὁ art. nom. masc. sg. ὁ ἡ τό the, this, that, he, she, it
δὲ conj. δέ but, and, now, also, to the contrary, rather, then
Θεός n. nom. masc. sg. θεός God, god
ἃ relative pron. acc. neut. pl. ὅς ἥ ὅ who, which, what, that
διὰ prep. διά (+gen) by, through, with, in, of, (+acc) for, because of, for a cause
στόματος n. gen. neut. sg. στόμα mouth, face, edge
πάντων adj. gen. masc. pl. πᾶς πᾶσα πᾶν all, every, whosoever, every one, no, whole, any
τῶν art. gen. masc. pl. ὁ ἡ τό the, this, that, he, she, it
προφητῶν n. gen. masc. pl. προφήτης prophet
αὐτοῦ pron. gen. masc. 3p. sg. αὐτός ή ό self, of oneself, even, very, the same, he, she, it
τὸν art. acc. masc. sg. ὁ ἡ τό the, this, that, he, she, it
Χριστὸν n. acc. masc. sg. Χριστός Christ
οὕτω adv. οὕτω οὕτως so, even so, thus, on this wise, likewise, after this manner
19 οὖν conj. οὖν therefore, then, so, and, now, wherefore
καὶ conj. καί and, even, also, but
εἰς prep. εἰς (+acc) into, to, unto, for, in, on, toward, against, upon, at, among
τὸ art. acc. neut. sg. ὁ ἡ τό the, this, that, he, she, it
ὑμῶν pron. gen. 2p. pl. σύ thou, you
τὰς art. acc. fem. pl. ὁ ἡ τό the, this, that, he, she, it
ἁμαρτίας n. acc. fem. pl. ἁμαρτία sin, offence, sinful
ὅπως adv. ὅπως that, how, to, because, so that, when
ἂν particle. ἄν Indicating contingency. No English translation.
καιροὶ n. nom. masc. pl. καιρός time, season, due time, opportunity
ἀναψύξεως n. gen. fem. sg. ἀνάψυξις refreshing
ἀπὸ prep. ἀπό (+gen) from, of, out of, since, for, off, at, by, in, on
προσώπου n. gen. neut. sg. πρόσωπον face, presence, person, countenance
τοῦ art. gen. masc. sg. ὁ ἡ τό the, this, that, he, she, it
Κυρίου n. gen. masc. sg. κύριος Lord, lord, master, sir, LORD, God, Master, owner
20 καὶ conj. καί and, even, also, but
τὸν art. acc. masc. sg. ὁ ἡ τό the, this, that, he, she, it
ὑμῖν pron. dat. 2p. pl. σύ thou, you
Ἰησοῦν n. acc. masc. sg. Ἰησοῦς Jesus
Χριστὸν n. acc. masc. sg. Χριστός Christ
21 ὃν relative pron. acc. masc. sg. ὅς ἥ ὅ who, which, what, that
οὐρανὸν n. acc. masc. sg. οὐρανός heaven, air, sky
μέν conj. μέν indeed, verily, truly, even, so, some
ἄχρι prep. ἄχρι or ἄχρις (+gen) until, unto, till, even to, as far as, while, into
χρόνων n. gen. masc. pl. χρόνος time, season, space
ἀποκαταστάσεως n. gen. fem. sg. ἀποκατάστασις restitution
πάντων adj. gen. neut. pl. πᾶς πᾶσα πᾶν all, every, whosoever, every one, no, whole, any
ὧν relative pron. gen. neut. pl. ὅς ἥ ὅ who, which, what, that
ὁ art. nom. masc. sg. ὁ ἡ τό the, this, that, he, she, it
Θεὸς n. nom. masc. sg. θεός God, god
διὰ prep. διά (+gen) by, through, with, in, of, (+acc) for, because of, for a cause
στόματος n. gen. neut. sg. στόμα mouth, face, edge
πάντων adj. gen. masc. pl. πᾶς πᾶσα πᾶν all, every, whosoever, every one, no, whole, any
ἁγίων adj. gen. masc. pl. ἅγιος Holy, holy, saint, Holy One, holy thing, most holy
αὐτοῦ pron. gen. masc. 3p. sg. αὐτός ή ό self, of oneself, even, very, the same, he, she, it
προφητῶν n. gen. masc. pl. προφήτης prophet
ἀπ' prep. ἀπό (+gen) from, of, out of, since, for, off, at, by, in, on

αἰῶνος n. gen. masc. sg. αἰών ever, ever and ever, evermore, age, eternal, world
22 Μωσῆς n. nom. masc. sg. Μωσῆς Moses
μέν conj. μέν indeed, verily, truly, even, so, some
γὰρ conj. γάρ for, and, because, but, indeed
πρὸς prep. πρός (+gen) for, (+dat) at, (+acc) unto, to, with, for, against
τοὺς art. acc. masc. pl. ὁ ἡ τό the, this, that, he, she, it
πατέρας n. acc. masc. pl. πατήρ Father, father, parent
ὅτι conj. ὅτι that, for, because, how that, how, because that, for that, though
Προφήτην n. acc. masc. sg. προφήτης prophet
ὑμῖν pron. dat. 2p. pl. σύ thou, you
Κύριος n. nom. masc. sg. κύριος Lord, lord, master, sir, LORD, God, Master, owner
ὁ art. nom. masc. sg. ὁ ἡ τό the, this, that, he, she, it
Θεὸς n. nom. masc. sg. θεός God, god
ὑμῶν pron. gen. 2p. pl. σύ thou, you
ἐκ prep. ἐκ ἐξ (+gen) of, from, out of, by, on, with, in, among, through
τῶν art. gen. masc. pl. ὁ ἡ τό the, this, that, he, she, it
ἀδελφῶν n. gen. masc. pl. ἀδελφός brother
ὑμῶν pron. gen. 2p. pl. σύ thou, you
ὡς adv. ὡς as, when, as it were, how, about, like, as soon as, even as, while
ἐμέ pron. acc. 1p. sg. ἐγώ I
αὐτοῦ pron. gen. masc. 3p. sg. αὐτός ή ό self, of oneself, even, very, the same, he, she, it
κατὰ prep. κατά (+gen) against, by, throughout, down, (+acc) according to, after, with
πάντα adj. acc. neut. pl. πᾶς πᾶσα πᾶν all, every, whosoever, every one, no, whole, any
ὅσα relative pron. acc. neut. pl. ὅσος as many as, whatsoever, that, as long as, how much
ἂν particle. ἄν Indicating contingency. No English translation.
πρὸς prep. πρός (+gen) for, (+dat) at, (+acc) unto, to, with, for, against
ὑμᾶς pron. acc. 2p. pl. σύ thou, you
23 δὲ conj. δέ but, and, now, also, to the contrary, rather, then
πᾶσα adj. nom. fem. sg. πᾶς πᾶσα πᾶν all, every, whosoever, every one, no, whole, any
ψυχὴ n. nom. fem. sg. ψυχή life, soul, mind, heart
ἥτις relative pron. nom. fem. sg. ὅστις which, who, whosoever, that, whatsoever
ἂν particle. ἄν Indicating contingency. No English translation.
μὴ particle of negation. μή not, no, lest, neither, none, nothing, nor, never, without
τοῦ art. gen. masc. sg. ὁ ἡ τό the, this, that, he, she, it
προφήτου n. gen. masc. sg. προφήτης prophet
ἐκείνου demo. pron. gen. masc. sg. ἐκεῖνος that, he, the same, that same
ἐκ prep. ἐκ ἐξ (+gen) of, from, out of, by, on, with, in, among, through
τοῦ art. gen. masc. sg. ὁ ἡ τό the, this, that, he, she, it
λαοῦ n. gen. masc. sg. λαός people
24 καὶ conj. καί and, even, also, but
πάντες adj. nom. masc. pl. πᾶς πᾶσα πᾶν all, every, whosoever, every one, no, whole, any
δὲ conj. δέ but, and, now, also, to the contrary, rather, then
οἱ art. nom. masc. pl. ὁ ἡ τό the, this, that, he, she, it
προφῆται n. nom. masc. pl. προφήτης prophet
ἀπὸ prep. ἀπό (+gen) from, of, out of, since, for, off, at, by, in, on
Σαμουὴλ n. gen. masc. sg. Σαμουήλ Samuel
καὶ conj. καί and, even, also, but
τῶν art. gen. masc. pl. ὁ ἡ τό the, this, that, he, she, it
καθεξῆς adv. καθεξῆς in order, after, afterward, by order
ὅσοι relative pron. nom. masc. pl. ὅσος as many as, whatsoever, that, as long as, how much
καὶ conj. καί and, even, also, but
τὰς art. acc. fem. pl. ὁ ἡ τό the, this, that, he, she, it
ἡμέρας n. acc. fem. pl. ἡμέρα day, time, year, while, age, day time
ταύτας demo. pron. acc. fem. pl. οὗτος αὕτη τοῦτο this, the same, this same, he, she, it
25 ὑμεῖς pron. nom. 2p. pl. σύ thou, you

υἱοὶ n. nom. masc. pl. υἱός son, child, descendant, offspring, heir
τῶν art. gen. masc. pl. ὁ ἡ τό the, this, that, he, she, it
προφητῶν n. gen. masc. pl. προφήτης prophet
καὶ conj. καί and, even, also, but
τῆς art. gen. fem. sg. ὁ ἡ τό the, this, that, he, she, it
διαθήκης n. gen. fem. sg. διαθήκη testament, covenant
ἧς relative pron. gen. fem. sg. ὅς ἥ ὅ who, which, what, that
ὁ art. nom. masc. sg. ὁ ἡ τό the, this, that, he, she, it
Θεὸς n. nom. masc. sg. θεός God, god
πρὸς prep. πρός (+gen) for, (+dat) at, (+acc) unto, to, with, for, against
τοὺς art. acc. masc. pl. ὁ ἡ τό the, this, that, he, she, it
πατέρας n. acc. masc. pl. πατήρ Father, father, parent
ἡμῶν pron. gen. 1p. pl. ἐγώ I
πρὸς prep. πρός (+gen) for, (+dat) at, (+acc) unto, to, with, for, against
'Αβραάμ n. acc. masc. sg. 'Αβραάμ Abraham
Καὶ conj. καί and, even, also, but
τῷ art. dat. neut. sg. ὁ ἡ τό the, this, that, he, she, it
σπέρματί n. dat. neut. sg. σπέρμα seed, issue
σου pron. gen. 2p. sg. σύ thou, you
πᾶσαι adj. nom. fem. pl. πᾶς πᾶσα πᾶν all, every, whosoever, every one, no, whole, any
αἱ art. nom. fem. pl. ὁ ἡ τό the, this, that, he, she, it
πατριαὶ n. nom. fem. pl. πατριά lineage, family, kindred
τῆς art. gen. fem. sg. ὁ ἡ τό the, this, that, he, she, it
γῆς n. gen. fem. sg. γῆ earth, land, ground, country
26 ὑμῖν pron. dat. 2p. pl. σύ thou, you
πρῶτον ordinal. adj. acc. neut. sg. πρῶτος first, chief, first of all, chiefest, best
ὁ art. nom. masc. sg. ὁ ἡ τό the, this, that, he, she, it
Θεὸς n. nom. masc. sg. θεός God, god
τὸν art. acc. masc. sg. ὁ ἡ τό the, this, that, he, she, it
παῖδα n. acc. masc. sg. παῖς servant, child, son, maid, young man, manservant
αὐτοῦ pron. gen. masc. 3p. sg. αὐτός ἡ ὁ self, of oneself, even, very, the same, he, she, it
'Ιησοῦν n. acc. masc. sg. 'Ιησοῦς Jesus
αὐτὸν pron. acc. masc. 3p. sg. αὐτός ἡ ὁ self, of oneself, even, very, the same, he, she, it
ὑμᾶς pron. acc. 2p. pl. σύ thou, you
ἐν prep. ἐν (+dat) in, by, with, among, at, on, through, to, within, into, of, for
τῷ art. dat. neut. sg. ὁ ἡ τό the, this, that, he, she, it
ἕκαστον adj. acc. masc. sg. ἕκαστος every man, every, every one, any man, each
ἀπὸ prep. ἀπό (+gen) from, of, out of, since, for, off, at, by, in, on
τῶν art. gen. fem. pl. ὁ ἡ τό the, this, that, he, she, it
πονηριῶν n. gen. fem. pl. πονηρία wickedness, iniquity
ὑμῶν pron. gen. 2p. pl. σύ thou, you

4

1 δὲ conj. δέ but, and, now, also, to the contrary, rather, then
αὐτῶν pron. gen. masc. 3p. pl. αὐτός ἡ ὁ self, of oneself, even, very, the same, he, she, it
πρὸς prep. πρός (+gen) for, (+dat) at, (+acc) unto, to, with, for, against
τὸν art. acc. masc. sg. ὁ ἡ τό the, this, that, he, she, it
λαὸν n. acc. masc. sg. λαός people
αὐτοῖς pron. dat. masc. 3p. pl. αὐτός ἡ ὁ self, of oneself, even, very, the same, he, she, it
οἱ art. nom. masc. pl. ὁ ἡ τό the, this, that, he, she, it
ἱερεῖς n. nom. masc. pl. ἱερεύς priest
καὶ conj. καί and, even, also, but
ὁ art. nom. masc. sg. ὁ ἡ τό the, this, that, he, she, it
στρατηγὸς n. nom. masc. sg. στρατηγός captain, magistrate

τοῦ art. gen. neut. sg. ὁ ἡ τό the, this, that, he, she, it
ἱεροῦ n. gen. neut. sg. ἱερόν temple
καὶ conj. καί and, even, also, but
οἱ art. nom. masc. pl. ὁ ἡ τό the, this, that, he, she, it
Σαδδουκαῖοι n. nom. masc. pl. Σαδδουκαῖος Sadducee
2 διὰ prep. διά (+gen) by, through, with, in, of, (+acc) for, because of, for a cause
τὸ art. acc. neut. sg. ὁ ἡ τό the, this, that, he, she, it
αὐτοὺς pron. acc. masc. 3p. pl. αὐτός ή ὁ self, of oneself, even, very, the same, he, she, it
τὸν art. acc. masc. sg. ὁ ἡ τό the, this, that, he, she, it
λαὸν n. acc. masc. sg. λαός people
καὶ conj. καί and, even, also, but
ἐν prep. ἐν (+dat) in, by, with, among, at, on, through, to, within, into, of, for
τῷ art. dat. masc. sg. ὁ ἡ τό the, this, that, he, she, it
Ἰησοῦ n. dat. masc. sg. Ἰησοῦς Jesus
τὴν art. acc. fem. sg. ὁ ἡ τό the, this, that, he, she, it
ἀνάστασιν n. acc. fem. sg. ἀνάστασις resurrection, rising again
τὴν art. acc. fem. sg. ὁ ἡ τό the, this, that, he, she, it
ἐκ prep. ἐκ ἐξ (+gen) of, from, out of, by, on, with, in, among, through
νεκρῶν adj. gen. masc. pl. νεκρός dead
3 καὶ conj. καί and, even, also, but
αὐτοῖς pron. dat. masc. 3p. pl. αὐτός ή ὁ self, of oneself, even, very, the same, he, she, it
τὰς art. acc. fem. pl. ὁ ἡ τό the, this, that, he, she, it
χεῖρας n. acc. fem. pl. χείρ hand
καὶ conj. καί and, even, also, but
εἰς prep. εἰς (+acc) into, to, unto, for, in, on, toward, against, upon, at, among
τήρησιν n. acc. fem. sg. τήρησις hold, keeping, prison
εἰς prep. εἰς (+acc) into, to, unto, for, in, on, toward, against, upon, at, among
τὴν art. acc. fem. sg. ὁ ἡ τό the, this, that, he, she, it
αὔριον adv. αὔριον tomorrow, morrow, next day
γὰρ conj. γάρ for, and, because, but, indeed
ἑσπέρα n. nom. fem. sg. ἑσπέρα evening, eventide
ἤδη adv. ἤδη now, already, yet, by this time, even now, now already
4 πολλοὶ adj. nom. masc. pl. πολύς many, great, much, long, abundant
δὲ conj. δέ but, and, now, also, to the contrary, rather, then
τῶν art. gen. masc. pl. ὁ ἡ τό the, this, that, he, she, it
τὸν art. acc. masc. sg. ὁ ἡ τό the, this, that, he, she, it
λόγον n. acc. masc. sg. λόγος word, saying, account, speech, thing, matter
καὶ conj. καί and, even, also, but
ὁ art. nom. masc. sg. ὁ ἡ τό the, this, that, he, she, it
ἀριθμὸς n. nom. masc. sg. ἀριθμός number
τῶν art. gen. masc. pl. ὁ ἡ τό the, this, that, he, she, it
ἀνδρῶν n. gen. masc. pl. ἀνήρ man, husband, sir
ὡσεὶ adv. ὡσεί about, as, like, as it had been, as it were, like as
χιλιάδες n. nom. fem. pl. χιλιάς thousand
πέντε num. nom. fem. pl. πέντε five
5 δὲ conj. δέ but, and, now, also, to the contrary, rather, then
ἐπὶ prep. ἐπί (+gen) on, in, upon, (+dat) in, at, for, upon, (+acc) on, upon, unto, to, against
τὴν art. acc. fem. sg. ὁ ἡ τό the, this, that, he, she, it
αὔριον adv. αὔριον tomorrow, morrow, next day
αὐτῶν pron. gen. masc. 3p. pl. αὐτός ή ὁ self, of oneself, even, very, the same, he, she, it
τοὺς art. acc. masc. pl. ὁ ἡ τό the, this, that, he, she, it
ἄρχοντας n. acc. masc. pl. ἄρχων ruler, prince, chief, magistrate, chief ruler
καὶ conj. καί and, even, also, but
πρεσβυτέρους adj. acc. masc. pl. πρεσβύτερος elder, elder woman, eldest, old man
καὶ conj. καί and, even, also, but

γραμματεῖς n. acc. masc. pl. γραμματεύς scribe, townclerk
εἰς prep. εἰς (+acc) into, to, unto, for, in, on, toward, against, upon, at, among
Ἱερουσαλήμ pron. name. fem. inde. Ἱερουσαλήμ Jerusalem
6 καὶ conj. καί and, even, also, but
Ἄνναν n. acc. masc. sg. Ἄννας Annas
τὸν art. acc. masc. sg. ὁ ἡ τό the, this, that, he, she, it
ἀρχιερέα n. acc. masc. sg. ἀρχιερεύς chief priest, high priest
καὶ conj. καί and, even, also, but
Καϊάφαν n. acc. masc. sg. Καϊάφας Caiaphas
καὶ conj. καί and, even, also, but
Ἰωάννην n. nom. masc. sg. Ἰωάννης John
καὶ conj. καί and, even, also, but
Ἀλέξανδρον n. nom. masc. sg. Ἀλέξανδρος Alexander
καὶ conj. καί and, even, also, but
ὅσοι relative pron. nom. masc. pl. ὅσος as many as, whatsoever, that, as long as, how much
ἐκ prep. ἐκ ἐξ (+gen) of, from, out of, by, on, with, in, among, through
γένους n. gen. neut. sg. γένος kind, kindred, offspring, nation, countrymen
ἀρχιερατικοῦ adj. gen. neut. sg. ἀρχιερατικός of the high priest
7 καὶ conj. καί and, even, also, but
αὐτοὺς pron. acc. masc. 3p. pl. αὐτός ή ό self, of oneself, even, very, the same, he, she, it
ἐν prep. ἐν (+dat) in, by, with, among, at, on, through, to, within, into, of, for
τῷ art. dat. neut. sg. ὁ ἡ τό the, this, that, he, she, it
μέσῳ adj. dat. neut. sg. μέσος midst, among, mid, between
Ἐν prep. ἐν (+dat) in, by, with, among, at, on, through, to, within, into, of, for
ποίᾳ interrog. pron. dat. fem. sg. ποῖος what, which, what manner of
δυνάμει n. dat. fem. sg. δύναμις power, mighty work, miracle, strength, might
ἢ particle. ἤ or, than, either, nor, or else, and, rather than
ἐν prep. ἐν (+dat) in, by, with, among, at, on, through, to, within, into, of, for
ποίῳ interrog. pron. dat. neut. sg. ποῖος what, which, what manner of
ὀνόματι n. dat. neut. sg. ὄνομα name, call, surname
τοῦτο demo. pron. acc. neut. sg. οὗτος αὕτη τοῦτο this, the same, this same, he, she, it
ὑμεῖς pron. nom. 2p. pl. σύ thou, you
8 τότε adv. τότε then, that time
Πέτρος n. nom. masc. sg. Πέτρος Peter
Πνεύματος n. gen. neut. sg. πνεῦμα spirit, Spirit, Ghost, ghost, life. of the spirit, wind
Ἁγίου adj. gen. neut. sg. ἅγιος Holy, holy, saint, Holy One, holy thing, most holy
πρὸς prep. πρός (+gen) for, (+dat) at, (+acc) unto, to, with, for, against
αὐτούς pron. acc. masc. 3p. pl. αὐτός ή ό self, of oneself, even, very, the same, he, she, it
Ἄρχοντες n. voc. masc. pl. ἄρχων ruler, prince, chief, magistrate, chief ruler
τοῦ art. gen. masc. sg. ὁ ἡ τό the, this, that, he, she, it
λαοῦ n. gen. masc. sg. λαός people
καὶ conj. καί and, even, also, but
πρεσβύτεροι adj. voc. masc. pl. πρεσβύτερος elder, elder woman, eldest, old man
τοῦ art. gen. masc. sg. ὁ ἡ τό the, this, that, he, she, it
Ἰσραήλ pron. name. masc. inde. Ἰσραήλ Israel
9 εἰ conj. εἰ if, whether, that, though, forasmuch
ἡμεῖς pron. nom. 1p. pl. ἐγώ I
σήμερον adv. σήμερον this day, today
ἐπὶ prep. ἐπί (+gen) on, in, upon, (+dat) in, at, for, upon, (+acc) on, upon, unto, to, against
εὐεργεσίᾳ n. dat. fem. sg. εὐεργεσία good deed done, benefit
ἀνθρώπου n. gen. masc. sg. ἄνθρωπος man, human being, person, one, certain
ἀσθενοῦς adj. gen. masc. sg. ἀσθενής weak, sick, impotent, more feeble
ἐν prep. ἐν (+dat) in, by, with, among, at, on, through, to, within, into, of, for
τίνι interrog. pron. dat. neut. sg. τίς what, who, why, where, which, how
οὗτος demo. pron. nom. masc. sg. οὗτος αὕτη τοῦτο this, the same, this same, he, she, it

10 γνωστὸν adj. nom. neut. sg. γνωστός acquaintance, known, notable
πᾶσιν adj. dat. masc. pl. πᾶς πᾶσα πᾶν all, every, whosoever, every one, no, whole, any
ὑμῖν pron. dat. 2p. pl. σύ thou, you
καὶ conj. καί and, even, also, but
παντὶ adj. dat. masc. sg. πᾶς πᾶσα πᾶν all, every, whosoever, every one, no, whole, any
τῷ art. dat. masc. sg. ὁ ἡ τό the, this, that, he, she, it
λαῷ n. dat. masc. sg. λαός people
Ἰσραήλ pron. name. masc. inde. Ἰσραήλ Israel
ὅτι conj. ὅτι that, for, because, how that, how, because that, for that, though
ἐν prep. ἐν (+dat) in, by, with, among, at, on, through, to, within, into, of, for
τῷ art. dat. neut. sg. ὁ ἡ τό the, this, that, he, she, it
ὀνόματι n. dat. neut. sg. ὄνομα name, call, surname
Ἰησοῦ n. gen. masc. sg. Ἰησοῦς Jesus
Χριστοῦ n. gen. masc. sg. Χριστός Christ
τοῦ art. gen. masc. sg. ὁ ἡ τό the, this, that, he, she, it
Ναζωραίου n. gen. masc. sg. Ναζωραῖος Nazareth, Nazarene
ὃν relative pron. acc. masc. sg. ὅς ἥ ὅ who, which, what, that
ὑμεῖς pron. nom. 2p. pl. σύ thou, you
ὃν relative pron. acc. masc. sg. ὅς ἥ ὅ who, which, what, that
ὁ art. nom. masc. sg. ὁ ἡ τό the, this, that, he, she, it
Θεὸς n. nom. masc. sg. θεός God, god
ἐκ prep. ἐκ ἐξ (+gen) of, from, out of, by, on, with, in, among, through
νεκρῶν adj. gen. masc. pl. νεκρός dead
ἐν prep. ἐν (+dat) in, by, with, among, at, on, through, to, within, into, of, for
τούτῳ demo. pron. dat. neut. sg. οὗτος αὕτη τοῦτο this, the same, this same, he, she, it
οὗτος demo. pron. nom. masc. sg. οὗτος αὕτη τοῦτο this, the same, this same, he, she, it
ἐνώπιον adv. ἐνώπιον before, in the sight of, in the presence of
ὑμῶν pron. gen. 2p. pl. σύ thou, you
ὑγιής adj. nom. masc. sg. ὑγιής whole, sound
11 οὗτός demo. pron. nom. masc. sg. οὗτος αὕτη τοῦτο this, the same, this same, he, she, it
ὁ art. nom. masc. sg. ὁ ἡ τό the, this, that, he, she, it
λίθος n. nom. masc. sg. λίθος stone
ὁ art. nom. masc. sg. ὁ ἡ τό the, this, that, he, she, it
ὑφ' prep. ὑπό (+gen) of, by, with, from, among, (+acc) under
ὑμῶν pron. gen. 2p. pl. σύ thou, you
τῶν art. gen. masc. pl. ὁ ἡ τό the, this, that, he, she, it
ὁ art. nom. masc. sg. ὁ ἡ τό the, this, that, he, she, it
εἰς prep. εἰς (+acc) into, to, unto, for, in, on, toward, against, upon, at, among
κεφαλὴν n. acc. fem. sg. κεφαλή head
γωνίας n. gen. fem. sg. γωνία corner, quarter
12 καὶ conj. καί and, even, also, but
οὐκ particle of negation. οὐ οὐκ οὐχ not, no, neither, none, nay, nor, never, nothing
ἐν prep. ἐν (+dat) in, by, with, among, at, on, through, to, within, into, of, for
ἄλλῳ adj. dat. masc. sg. ἄλλος other, another, some, one, more, otherwise
οὐδενὶ num. dat. masc. sg. οὐδείς no man, nothing, no, none, neither, not, nought
ἡ art. nom. fem. sg. ὁ ἡ τό the, this, that, he, she, it
σωτηρία n. nom. fem. sg. σωτηρία salvation, deliver, health, saving
οὔτε conj. οὔτε neither, nor, nor yet, no, none
γὰρ conj. γάρ for, and, because, but, indeed
ὄνομά n. nom. neut. sg. ὄνομα name, call, surname
ἕτερον adj. nom. neut. sg. ἕτερος another, other, else, strange
ὑπὸ prep. ὑπό (+gen) of, by, with, from, among, (+acc) under
τὸν art. acc. masc. sg. ὁ ἡ τό the, this, that, he, she, it
οὐρανὸν n. acc. masc. sg. οὐρανός heaven, air, sky
τὸ art. nom. neut. sg. ὁ ἡ τό the, this, that, he, she, it

ἐν prep. ἐν (+dat) in, by, with, among, at, on, through, to, within, into, of, for
ἀνθρώποις n. dat. masc. pl. ἄνθρωπος man, human being, person, one, certain
ἐν prep. ἐν (+dat) in, by, with, among, at, on, through, to, within, into, of, for
ᾧ relative pron. dat. neut. sg. ὅς ἥ ὅ who, which, what, that
ἡμᾶς pron. acc. 1p. pl. ἐγώ I
13 δὲ conj. δέ but, and, now, also, to the contrary, rather, then
τὴν art. acc. fem. sg. ὁ ἡ τό the, this, that, he, she, it
τοῦ art. gen. masc. sg. ὁ ἡ τό the, this, that, he, she, it
Πέτρου n. gen. masc. sg. Πέτρος Peter
παρρησίαν n. acc. fem. sg. παρρησία boldness, confidence, openly, plainly, freely
καὶ conj. καί and, even, also, but
Ἰωάννου n. gen. masc. sg. Ἰωάννης John
καὶ conj. καί and, even, also, but
ὅτι conj. ὅτι that, for, because, how that, how, because that, for that, though
ἄνθρωποι n. nom. masc. pl. ἄνθρωπος man, human being, person, one, certain
ἀγράμματοί adj. nom. masc. pl. ἀγράμματος unlearned
καὶ conj. καί and, even, also, but
ἰδιῶται n. nom. masc. pl. ἰδιώτης ignorant, unlearned, rude
τε conj. τέ and, both, also
αὐτοὺς pron. acc. masc. 3p. pl. αὐτός ἡ ὁ self, of oneself, even, very, the same, he, she, it
ὅτι conj. ὅτι that, for, because, how that, how, because that, for that, though
σὺν prep. σύν (+dat) with, beside
τῷ art. dat. masc. sg. ὁ ἡ τό the, this, that, he, she, it
Ἰησοῦ n. dat. masc. sg. Ἰησοῦς Jesus
14 τόν art. acc. masc. sg. ὁ ἡ τό the, this, that, he, she, it
δὲ conj. δέ but, and, now, also, to the contrary, rather, then
ἄνθρωπον n. acc. masc. sg. ἄνθρωπος man, human being, person, one, certain
σὺν prep. σύν (+dat) with, beside
αὐτοῖς pron. dat. masc. 3p. pl. αὐτός ἡ ὁ self, of oneself, even, very, the same, he, she, it
τόν art. acc. masc. sg. ὁ ἡ τό the, this, that, he, she, it
οὐδὲν adj. acc. neut. sg. οὐδείς no man, nothing, no, none, neither, not, nought
15 δὲ conj. δέ but, and, now, also, to the contrary, rather, then
αὐτοὺς pron. acc. masc. 3p. pl. αὐτός ἡ ὁ self, of oneself, even, very, the same, he, she, it
ἔξω adv. ἔξω out, without, out of, forth, away, outward
τοῦ art. gen. neut. sg. ὁ ἡ τό the, this, that, he, she, it
συνεδρίου n. gen. neut. sg. συνέδριον council
πρὸς prep. πρός (+gen) for, (+dat) at, (+acc) unto, to, with, for, against
ἀλλήλους pron. acc. masc. 3p. pl. ἀλλήλων one another, themselves, together, mutual
16 Τί interrog. pron. acc. neut. sg. τίς what, who, why, where, which, how
τοῖς art. dat. masc. pl. ὁ ἡ τό the, this, that, he, she, it
ἀνθρώποις n. dat. masc. pl. ἄνθρωπος man, human being, person, one, certain
τούτοις demo. pron. dat. masc. pl. οὗτος αὕτη τοῦτο this, the same, this same, he, she, it
ὅτι conj. ὅτι that, for, because, how that, how, because that, for that, though
μέν conj. μέν indeed, verily, truly, even, so, some
γὰρ conj. γάρ for, and, because, but, indeed
γνωστὸν adj. nom. neut. sg. γνωστός acquaintance, known, notable
σημεῖον n. nom. neut. sg. σημεῖον sign, miracle, wonder, token
δι' prep. διά (+gen) by, through, with, in, of, (+acc) for, because of, for a cause
αὐτῶν pron. gen. masc. 3p. pl. αὐτός ἡ ὁ self, of oneself, even, very, the same, he, she, it
πᾶσι adj. dat. masc. pl. πᾶς πᾶσα πᾶν all, every, whosoever, every one, no, whole, any
τοῖς art. dat. masc. pl. ὁ ἡ τό the, this, that, he, she, it
Ἱερουσαλὴμ pron. name. fem. inde. Ἱερουσαλήμ Jerusalem
φανερὸν adj. nom. neut. sg. φανερός manifest, abroad, open, known, outward, appear
καὶ conj. καί and, even, also, but
οὐ particle of negation. οὐ οὐκ οὐχ not, no, neither, none, nay, nor, never, nothing

17 ἀλλ' conj. ἀλλά but, yea, yet, nevertheless, howbeit, nay, therefore
ἵνα conj. ἵνα that, to, lest, for to, so that, albeit, because, for, so as
μὴ particle of negation. μή not, no, lest, neither, none, nothing, nor, never, without
ἐπὶ prep. ἐπί (+gen) on, in, upon, (+dat) in, at, for, upon, (+acc) on, upon, unto, to, against
πλεῖον compar. adj. acc. neut. sg. πολύς many, great, much, long, abundant
εἰς prep. εἰς (+acc) into, to, unto, for, in, on, toward, against, upon, at, among
τὸν art. acc. masc. sg. ὁ ἡ τό the, this, that, he, she, it
λαὸν n. acc. masc. sg. λαός people
ἀπειλῇ n. dat. fem. sg. ἀπειλή threatening
αὐτοῖς pron. dat. masc. 3p. pl. αὐτός ή ό self, of oneself, even, very, the same, he, she, it
μηκέτι adv. μηκέτι no more, no longer, not any more, not henceforth, not henceforward
ἐπὶ prep. ἐπί (+gen) on, in, upon, (+dat) in, at, for, upon, (+acc) on, upon, unto, to, against
τῷ art. dat. neut. sg. ὁ ἡ τό the, this, that, he, she, it
ὀνόματι n. dat. neut. sg. ὄνομα name, call, surname
τούτῳ demo. pron. dat. neut. sg. οὗτος αὕτη τοῦτο this, the same, this same, he, she, it
μηδενὶ num. dat. masc. sg. μηδείς μηδεμία μηδέν no man, nothing, no, none, not at all
ἀνθρώπων n. gen. masc. pl. ἄνθρωπος man, human being, person, one, certain
18 καὶ conj. καί and, even, also, but
αὐτοὺς pron. acc. masc. 3p. pl. αὐτός ή ό self, of oneself, even, very, the same, he, she, it
αὐτοῖς pron. dat. masc. 3p. pl. αὐτός ή ό self, of oneself, even, very, the same, he, she, it
τὸ art. acc. neut. sg. ὁ ἡ τό the, this, that, he, she, it
καθόλου adv. καθόλου at all
μὴ particle of negation. μή not, no, lest, neither, none, nothing, nor, never, without
μηδὲ conj. μηδέ neither, nor, not, no not, nor yet, not once, not so much as
ἐπὶ prep. ἐπί (+gen) on, in, upon, (+dat) in, at, for, upon, (+acc) on, upon, unto, to, against
τῷ art. dat. neut. sg. ὁ ἡ τό the, this, that, he, she, it
ὀνόματι n. dat. neut. sg. ὄνομα name, call, surname
τοῦ art. gen. masc. sg. ὁ ἡ τό the, this, that, he, she, it
Ἰησοῦ n. gen. masc. sg. Ἰησοῦς Jesus
19 ὁ art. nom. masc. sg. ὁ ἡ τό the, this, that, he, she, it
δὲ conj. δέ but, and, now, also, to the contrary, rather, then
Πέτρος n. nom. masc. sg. Πέτρος Peter
καὶ conj. καί and, even, also, but
Ἰωάννης n. nom. masc. sg. Ἰωάννης John
πρὸς prep. πρός (+gen) for, (+dat) at, (+acc) unto, to, with, for, against
αὐτούς pron. acc. masc. 3p. pl. αὐτός ή ό self, of oneself, even, very, the same, he, she, it
Εἰ conj. εἰ if, whether, that, though, forasmuch
δίκαιόν adj. nom. neut. sg. δίκαιος righteous, just, meet, right
ἐνώπιον adv. ἐνώπιον before, in the sight of, in the presence of
τοῦ art. gen. masc. sg. ὁ ἡ τό the, this, that, he, she, it
Θεοῦ n. gen. masc. sg. θεός God, god
ὑμῶν pron. gen. 2p. pl. σύ thou, you
μᾶλλον compar. adv. μᾶλλον rather, more, more and more, better, much, much the more
ἢ particle. ἤ or, than, either, nor, or else, and, rather than
τοῦ art. gen. masc. sg. ὁ ἡ τό the, this, that, he, she, it
Θεοῦ n. gen. masc. sg. θεός God, god
20 οὐ particle of negation. οὐ οὐκ οὐχ not, no, neither, none, nay, nor, never, nothing
γὰρ conj. γάρ for, and, because, but, indeed
ἡμεῖς pron. nom. 1p. pl. ἐγώ I
ἃ relative pron. acc. neut. pl. ὅς ἥ ὅ who, which, what, that
καὶ conj. καί and, even, also, but
μὴ particle of negation. μή not, no, lest, neither, none, nothing, nor, never, without
21 οἱ art. nom. masc. pl. ὁ ἡ τό the, this, that, he, she, it
δὲ conj. δέ but, and, now, also, to the contrary, rather, then
αὐτούς pron. acc. masc. 3p. pl. αὐτός ή ό self, of oneself, even, very, the same, he, she, it

μηδὲν adj. acc. neut. sg. μηδείς μηδεμία μηδέν no man, nothing, no, none, not at all
τὸ art. acc. neut. sg. ὁ ἡ τό the, this, that, he, she, it
πῶς adv. πῶς how, by what means, after what manner
αὐτούς pron. acc. masc. 3p. pl. αὐτός ή ὁ self, of oneself, even, very, the same, he, she, it
διὰ prep. διά (+gen) by, through, with, in, of, (+acc) for, because of, for a cause
τὸν art. acc. masc. sg. ὁ ἡ τό the, this, that, he, she, it
λαόν n. acc. masc. sg. λαός people
ὅτι conj. ὅτι that, for, because, how that, how, because that, for that, though
πάντες adj. nom. masc. pl. πᾶς πᾶσα πᾶν all, every, whosoever, every one, no, whole, any
τὸν art. acc. masc. sg. ὁ ἡ τό the, this, that, he, she, it
Θεὸν n. acc. masc. sg. θεός God, god
ἐπὶ prep. ἐπί (+gen) on, in, upon, (+dat) in, at, for, upon, (+acc) on, upon, unto, to, against
τῷ art. dat. neut. sg. ὁ ἡ τό the, this, that, he, she, it
22 ἐτῶν n. gen. neut. pl. ἔτος year
γὰρ conj. γάρ for, and, because, but, indeed
πλειόνων compar. adj. gen. neut. pl. πολύς many, great, much, long, abundant
τεσσαράκοντα num. gen. neut. pl. τεσσαράκοντα forty
ὁ art. nom. masc. sg. ὁ ἡ τό the, this, that, he, she, it
ἄνθρωπος n. nom. masc. sg. ἄνθρωπος man, human being, person, one, certain
ἐφ' prep. ἐπί (+gen) on, in, upon, (+dat) in, at, for, upon, (+acc) on, upon, unto, to, against
ὃν relative pron. acc. masc. sg. ὅς ἥ ὅ who, which, what, that
τὸ art. nom. neut. sg. ὁ ἡ τό the, this, that, he, she, it
σημεῖον n. nom. neut. sg. σημεῖον sign, miracle, wonder, token
τοῦτο demo. pron. nom. neut. sg. οὗτος αὕτη τοῦτο this, the same, this same, he, she, it
τῆς art. gen. fem. sg. ὁ ἡ τό the, this, that, he, she, it
ἰάσεως n. gen. fem. sg. ἴασις cure, healing, heal
23 δὲ conj. δέ but, and, now, also, to the contrary, rather, then
πρὸς prep. πρός (+gen) for, (+dat) at, (+acc) unto, to, with, for, against
τοὺς art. acc. masc. pl. ὁ ἡ τό the, this, that, he, she, it
ἰδίους adj. acc. masc. pl. ἴδιος one's own, one's, privately
καὶ conj. καί and, even, also, but
ὅσα relative pron. acc. neut. pl. ὅσος as many as, whatsoever, that, as long as, how much
πρὸς prep. πρός (+gen) for, (+dat) at, (+acc) unto, to, with, for, against
αὐτοὺς pron. acc. masc. 3p. pl. αὐτός ή ὁ self, of oneself, even, very, the same, he, she, it
οἱ art. nom. masc. pl. ὁ ἡ τό the, this, that, he, she, it
ἀρχιερεῖς n. nom. masc. pl. ἀρχιερεύς chief priest, high priest
καὶ conj. καί and, even, also, but
οἱ art. nom. masc. pl. ὁ ἡ τό the, this, that, he, she, it
πρεσβύτεροι adj. nom. masc. pl. πρεσβύτερος elder, elder woman, eldest, old man
24 οἱ art. nom. masc. pl. ὁ ἡ τό the, this, that, he, she, it
δὲ conj. δέ but, and, now, also, to the contrary, rather, then
ὁμοθυμαδὸν adv. ὁμοθυμαδόν with one accord, with one mind
φωνὴν n. acc. fem. sg. φωνή voice, sound, noise
πρὸς prep. πρός (+gen) for, (+dat) at, (+acc) unto, to, with, for, against
τὸν art. acc. masc. sg. ὁ ἡ τό the, this, that, he, she, it
Θεὸν n. acc. masc. sg. θεός God, god
καὶ conj. καί and, even, also, but
Δέσποτα n. voc. masc. sg. δεσπότης Lord, master
σὺ pron. nom. 2p. sg. σύ thou, you
ὁ art. nom. masc. sg. ὁ ἡ τό the, this, that, he, she, it
Θεὸς n. nom. masc. sg. θεός God, god
ὁ art. nom. masc. sg. ὁ ἡ τό the, this, that, he, she, it
τὸν art. acc. masc. sg. ὁ ἡ τό the, this, that, he, she, it
οὐρανὸν n. acc. masc. sg. οὐρανός heaven, air, sky
καὶ conj. καί and, even, also, but

τὴν art. acc. fem. sg. ὁ ἡ τό the, this, that, he, she, it
γῆν n. acc. fem. sg. γῆ earth, land, ground, country
καὶ conj. καί and, even, also, but
τὴν art. acc. fem. sg. ὁ ἡ τό the, this, that, he, she, it
θάλασσαν n. acc. fem. sg. θάλασσα sea
καὶ conj. καί and, even, also, but
πάντα adj. acc. neut. pl. πᾶς πᾶσα πᾶν all, every, whosoever, every one, no, whole, any
τὰ art. acc. neut. pl. ὁ ἡ τό the, this, that, he, she, it
ἐν prep. ἐν (+dat) in, by, with, among, at, on, through, to, within, into, of, for
αὐτοῖς pron. dat. neut. 3p. pl. αὐτός ἡ ὁ self, of oneself, even, very, the same, he, she, it
25 ὁ art. nom. masc. sg. ὁ ἡ τό the, this, that, he, she, it
διὰ prep. διά (+gen) by, through, with, in, of, (+acc) for, because of, for a cause
στόματος n. gen. neut. sg. στόμα mouth, face, edge
Δαβὶδ n. gen. masc. sg. Δαβίδ David
τοῦ art. gen. masc. sg. ὁ ἡ τό the, this, that, he, she, it
παιδός n. gen. masc. sg. παῖς servant, child, son, maid, young man, manservant
σου pron. gen. 2p. sg. σύ thou, you
Ἱνατί adv. ἱνατί or ἵνα τί why, wherefore
ἔθνη n. nom. neut. pl. ἔθνος Gentile, nation, heathen, people
καὶ conj. καί and, even, also, but
λαοὶ n. nom. masc. pl. λαός people
κενά adj. acc. neut. pl. κενός empty, vain, in vain
26 οἱ art. nom. masc. pl. ὁ ἡ τό the, this, that, he, she, it
βασιλεῖς n. nom. masc. pl. βασιλεύς king
τῆς art. gen. fem. sg. ὁ ἡ τό the, this, that, he, she, it
γῆς n. gen. fem. sg. γῆ earth, land, ground, country
καὶ conj. καί and, even, also, but
οἱ art. nom. masc. pl. ὁ ἡ τό the, this, that, he, she, it
ἄρχοντες n. nom. masc. pl. ἄρχων ruler, prince, chief, magistrate, chief ruler
ἐπὶ prep. ἐπί (+gen) on, in, upon, (+dat) in, at, for, upon, (+acc) on, upon, unto, to, against
τὸ art. acc. neut. sg. ὁ ἡ τό the, this, that, he, she, it
αὐτὸ pron. acc. neut. 3p. sg. αὐτός ἡ ὁ self, of oneself, even, very, the same, he, she, it
κατὰ prep. κατά (+gen) against, by, throughout, down, (+acc) according to, after, with
τοῦ art. gen. masc. sg. ὁ ἡ τό the, this, that, he, she, it
Κυρίου n. gen. masc. sg. κύριος Lord, lord, master, sir, LORD, God, Master, owner
καὶ conj. καί and, even, also, but
τοῦ art. gen. masc. sg. ὁ ἡ τό the, this, that, he, she, it
Χριστοῦ n. gen. masc. sg. Χριστός Christ
αὐτοῦ pron. gen. masc. 3p. sg. αὐτός ἡ ὁ self, of oneself, even, very, the same, he, she, it
27 γὰρ conj. γάρ for, and, because, but, indeed
ἐπ' prep. ἐπί (+gen) on, in, upon, (+dat) in, at, for, upon, (+acc) on, upon, unto, to, against
ἀληθείας n. gen. fem. sg. ἀλήθεια truth, verity
ἐπὶ prep. ἐπί (+gen) on, in, upon, (+dat) in, at, for, upon, (+acc) on, upon, unto, to, against
τὸν art. acc. masc. sg. ὁ ἡ τό the, this, that, he, she, it
ἅγιον adj. acc. masc. sg. ἅγιος Holy, holy, saint, Holy One, holy thing, most holy
παῖδά n. acc. masc. sg. παῖς servant, child, son, maid, young man, manservant
σου pron. gen. 2p. sg. σύ thou, you
Ἰησοῦν n. acc. masc. sg. Ἰησοῦς Jesus
ὃν relative pron. acc. masc. sg. ὅς ἥ ὅ who, which, what, that
Ἡρώδης n. nom. masc. sg. Ἡρῴδης Herod
τε conj. τέ and, both, also
καὶ conj. καί and, even, also, but
Πόντιος n. nom. masc. sg. Πόντιος Pontius
Πιλᾶτος n. nom. masc. sg. Πιλᾶτος Pilate
σὺν prep. σύν (+dat) with, beside

ἔθνεσιν n. dat. neut. pl. ἔθνος Gentile, nation, heathen, people
καὶ conj. καί and, even, also, but
λαοῖς n. dat. masc. pl. λαός people
Ἰσραήλ pron. name. masc. inde. Ἰσραήλ Israel
28 ὅσα relative pron. acc. neut. pl. ὅσος as many as, whatsoever, that, as long as, how much
ἡ art. nom. fem. sg. ὁ ἡ τό the, this, that, he, she, it
χείρ n. nom. fem. sg. χείρ hand
σου pron. gen. 2p. sg. σύ thou, you
καὶ conj. καί and, even, also, but
ἡ art. nom. fem. sg. ὁ ἡ τό the, this, that, he, she, it
βουλή n. nom. fem. sg. βουλή counsel, advise, will
σου pron. gen. 2p. sg. σύ thou, you
29 καὶ conj. καί and, even, also, but
τὰ art. acc. neut. pl. ὁ ἡ τό the, this, that, he, she, it
νῦν adv. νῦν now, henceforth, present, this time
Κύριε n. voc. masc. sg. κύριος Lord, lord, master, sir, LORD, God, Master, owner
ἐπὶ prep. ἐπί (+gen) on, in, upon, (+dat) in, at, for, upon, (+acc) on, upon, unto, to, against
τὰς art. acc. fem. pl. ὁ ἡ τό the, this, that, he, she, it
ἀπειλὰς n. acc. fem. pl. ἀπειλή threatening
αὐτῶν pron. gen. masc. 3p. pl. αὐτός ή ό self, of oneself, even, very, the same, he, she, it
καὶ conj. καί and, even, also, but
τοῖς art. dat. masc. pl. ὁ ἡ τό the, this, that, he, she, it
δούλοις n. dat. masc. pl. δοῦλος servant, bondman, bond, slave
σου pron. gen. 2p. sg. σύ thou, you
μετὰ prep. μετά (+gen) with, among, against, (+acc) after
παρρησίας n. gen. fem. sg. παρρησία boldness, confidence, openly, plainly, freely
πάσης adj. gen. fem. sg. πᾶς πᾶσα πᾶν all, every, whosoever, every one, no, whole, any
τὸν art. acc. masc. sg. ὁ ἡ τό the, this, that, he, she, it
λόγον n. acc. masc. sg. λόγος word, saying, account, speech, thing, matter
σου pron. gen. 2p. sg. σύ thou, you
30 ἐν prep. ἐν (+dat) in, by, with, among, at, on, through, to, within, into, of, for
τῷ art. dat. neut. sg. ὁ ἡ τό the, this, that, he, she, it
τὴν art. acc. fem. sg. ὁ ἡ τό the, this, that, he, she, it
χεῖρά n. acc. fem. sg. χείρ hand
σου pron. gen. 2p. sg. σύ thou, you
σε pron. acc. 2p. sg. σύ thou, you
εἰς prep. εἰς (+acc) into, to, unto, for, in, on, toward, against, upon, at, among
ἴασιν n. acc. fem. sg. ἴασις cure, healing, heal
καὶ conj. καί and, even, also, but
σημεῖα n. acc. neut. pl. σημεῖον sign, miracle, wonder, token
καὶ conj. καί and, even, also, but
τέρατα n. acc. neut. pl. τέρας wonder
διὰ prep. διά (+gen) by, through, with, in, of, (+acc) for, because of, for a cause
τοῦ art. gen. neut. sg. ὁ ἡ τό the, this, that, he, she, it
ὀνόματος n. gen. neut. sg. ὄνομα name, call, surname
τοῦ art. gen. masc. sg. ὁ ἡ τό the, this, that, he, she, it
ἁγίου adj. gen. masc. sg. ἅγιος Holy, holy, saint, Holy One, holy thing, most holy
παιδός n. gen. masc. sg. παῖς servant, child, son, maid, young man, manservant
σου pron. gen. 2p. sg. σύ thou, you
Ἰησοῦ n. gen. masc. sg. Ἰησοῦς Jesus
31 καὶ conj. καί and, even, also, but
αὐτῶν pron. gen. masc. 3p. pl. αὐτός ή ό self, of oneself, even, very, the same, he, she, it
ὁ art. nom. masc. sg. ὁ ἡ τό the, this, that, he, she, it
τόπος n. nom. masc. sg. τόπος place, room, quarter
ἐν prep. ἐν (+dat) in, by, with, among, at, on, through, to, within, into, of, for

ᾧ relative pron. dat. masc. sg. ὅς ἥ ὅ who, which, what, that
καὶ conj. καί and, even, also, but
ἅπαντες adj. nom. masc. pl. ἅπας all, whole, all things, every, everyone
Πνεύματος n. gen. neut. sg. πνεῦμα spirit, Spirit, Ghost, ghost, life. of the spirit, wind
Ἁγίου adj. gen. neut. sg. ἅγιος Holy, holy, saint, Holy One, holy thing, most holy
καὶ conj. καί and, even, also, but
τὸν art. acc. masc. sg. ὁ ἡ τό the, this, that, he, she, it
λόγον n. acc. masc. sg. λόγος word, saying, account, speech, thing, matter
τοῦ art. gen. masc. sg. ὁ ἡ τό the, this, that, he, she, it
Θεοῦ n. gen. masc. sg. θεός God, god
μετὰ prep. μετά (+gen) with, among, against, (+acc) after
παρρησίας n. gen. fem. sg. παρρησία boldness, confidence, openly, plainly, freely
32 Τοῦ art. gen. neut. sg. ὁ ἡ τό the, this, that, he, she, it
δὲ conj. δέ but, and, now, also, to the contrary, rather, then
πλήθους n. gen. neut. sg. πλῆθος multitude, bundle, company
τῶν art. gen. masc. pl. ὁ ἡ τό the, this, that, he, she, it
ἡ art. nom. fem. sg. ὁ ἡ τό the, this, that, he, she, it
καρδία n. nom. fem. sg. καρδία heart
καὶ conj. καί and, even, also, but
ἡ art. nom. fem. sg. ὁ ἡ τό the, this, that, he, she, it
ψυχὴ n. nom. fem. sg. ψυχή life, soul, mind, heart
μία num. nom. fem. sg. εἷς or ἕν one, other, some, any, only, a certain
καὶ conj. καί and, even, also, but
οὐδ' adv. οὐδέ neither, nor, not, no, not even, never, not yet
εἷς num. nom. masc. sg. εἷς or ἕν one, other, some, any, only, a certain
τι indefinite pron. acc. neut. sg. τὶς certain, some, any man, one, any thing
τῶν art. gen. neut. pl. ὁ ἡ τό the, this, that, he, she, it
αὐτῷ pron. dat. masc. 3p. sg. αὐτός ἡ ὁ self, of oneself, even, very, the same, he, she, it
ἴδιον adj. acc. neut. sg. ἴδιος one's own, one's, privately
ἀλλ' conj. ἀλλά but, yea, yet, nevertheless, howbeit, nay, therefore
αὐτοῖς pron. dat. masc. 3p. pl. αὐτός ἡ ὁ self, of oneself, even, very, the same, he, she, it
ἅπαντα adj. nom. neut. pl. ἅπας all, whole, all things, every, everyone
κοινά adj. nom. neut. pl. κοινός common, unclean, defiled, unholy
33 καὶ conj. καί and, even, also, but
μεγάλῃ adj. dat. fem. sg. μέγας great, loud, greatest, high, large, mighty, strong
δυνάμει n. dat. fem. sg. δύναμις power, mighty work, miracle, strength, might
τὸ art. acc. neut. sg. ὁ ἡ τό the, this, that, he, she, it
μαρτύριον n. acc. neut. sg. μαρτύριον testimony, witness
οἱ art. nom. masc. pl. ὁ ἡ τό the, this, that, he, she, it
ἀπόστολοι n. nom. masc. pl. ἀπόστολος apostle, messenger, he that is sent
τῆς art. gen. fem. sg. ὁ ἡ τό the, this, that, he, she, it
ἀναστάσεως n. gen. fem. sg. ἀνάστασις resurrection, rising again
τοῦ art. gen. masc. sg. ὁ ἡ τό the, this, that, he, she, it
Κυρίου n. gen. masc. sg. κύριος Lord, lord, master, sir, LORD, God, Master, owner
Ἰησοῦ n. gen. masc. sg. Ἰησοῦς Jesus
χάρις n. nom. fem. sg. χάρις grace, thank, favour, pleasure
τε conj. τέ and, both, also
μεγάλη adj. nom. fem. sg. μέγας great, loud, greatest, high, large, mighty, strong
ἐπὶ prep. ἐπί (+gen) on, in, upon, (+dat) in, at, for, upon, (+acc) on, upon, unto, to, against
πάντας adj. acc. masc. pl. πᾶς πᾶσα πᾶν all, every, whosoever, every one, no, whole, any
αὐτούς pron. acc. masc. 3p. pl. αὐτός ἡ ὁ self, of oneself, even, very, the same, he, she, it
34 οὐδὲ adv. οὐδέ neither, nor, not, no, not even, never, not yet
γὰρ conj. γάρ for, and, because, but, indeed
ἐνδεής adj. nom. masc. sg. ἐνδεής lacked, needy
τις indefinite pron. nom. masc. sg. τὶς certain, some, any man, one, any thing

ἐν prep. ἐν (+dat) in, by, with, among, at, on, through, to, within, into, of, for
αὐτοῖς pron. dat. masc. 3p. pl. αὐτός ή ό self, of oneself, even, very, the same, he, she, it
ὅσοι relative pron. nom. masc. pl. ὅσος as many as, whatsoever, that, as long as, how much
γὰρ conj. γάρ for, and, because, but, indeed
κτήτορες n. nom. masc. pl. κτήτωρ possessors
χωρίων n. gen. neut. pl. χωρίον place, field, land, parcel of ground, possession
ἢ particle. ἤ or, than, either, nor, or else, and, rather than
οἰκιῶν n. gen. fem. pl. οἰκία house, home, household
τὰς art. acc. fem. pl. ὁ ἡ τό the, this, that, he, she, it
τιμὰς n. acc. fem. pl. τιμή honour, price, preciousness, sum
τῶν art. gen. neut. pl. ὁ ἡ τό the, this, that, he, she, it
35 καὶ conj. καί and, even, also, but
παρὰ prep. παρά (+gen) of, from, (+dat) with, for, (+acc) beside, at, by, above, against
τοὺς art. acc. masc. pl. ὁ ἡ τό the, this, that, he, she, it
πόδας n. acc. masc. pl. πούς foot
τῶν art. gen. masc. pl. ὁ ἡ τό the, this, that, he, she, it
ἀποστόλων n. gen. masc. pl. ἀπόστολος apostle, messenger, he that is sent
δὲ conj. δέ but, and, now, also, to the contrary, rather, then
ἑκάστῳ adj. dat. masc. sg. ἕκαστος every man, every, every one, any man, each
καθότι conj. καθότι because, according as, as, because that, forasmuch as
ἄν particle. ἄν Indicating contingency. No English translation.
τις indefinite pron. nom. masc. sg. τὶς certain, some, any man, one, any thing
χρείαν n. acc. fem. sg. χρεία need, necessity, lack, want
36 Ἰωσῆς n. nom. masc. sg. Ἰωσῆς Joses, Jose
δὲ conj. δέ but, and, now, also, to the contrary, rather, then
ὁ art. nom. masc. sg. ὁ ἡ τό the, this, that, he, she, it
Βαρνάβας n. nom. masc. sg. Βαρναβᾶς Barnabas
ὑπὸ prep. ὑπό (+gen) of, by, with, from, among, (+acc) under
ἀπὸ prep. ἀπό (+gen) from, of, out of, since, for, off, at, by, in, on
τῶν art. gen. masc. pl. ὁ ἡ τό the, this, that, he, she, it
ἀποστόλων n. gen. masc. pl. ἀπόστολος apostle, messenger, he that is sent
ὅ relative pron. nom. neut. sg. ὅς ἥ ὅ who, which, what, that
υἱὸς n. nom. masc. sg. υἱός son, child, descendant, offspring, heir
παρακλήσεως n. gen. fem. sg. παράκλησις consolation, exhortation, comfort
Λευΐτης n. nom. masc. sg. Λευΐτης Levite
Κύπριος n. nom. masc. sg. Κύπριος Cypriot, inhabitant of Cyprus
τῷ art. dat. neut. sg. ὁ ἡ τό the, this, that, he, she, it
γένει n. dat. neut. sg. γένος kind, kindred, offspring, nation, countrymen
37 αὐτῷ pron. dat. masc. 3p. sg. αὐτός ή ό self, of oneself, even, very, the same, he, she, it
ἀγροῦ n. gen. masc. sg. ἀγρός field, country, land, farm, piece of ground
τὸ art. acc. neut. sg. ὁ ἡ τό the, this, that, he, she, it
χρῆμα n. acc. neut. sg. χρῆμα riches, money
καὶ conj. καί and, even, also, but
παρὰ prep. παρά (+gen) of, from, (+dat) with, for, (+acc) beside, at, by, above, against
τοὺς art. acc. masc. pl. ὁ ἡ τό the, this, that, he, she, it
πόδας n. acc. masc. pl. πούς foot
τῶν art. gen. masc. pl. ὁ ἡ τό the, this, that, he, she, it
ἀποστόλων n. gen. masc. pl. ἀπόστολος apostle, messenger, he that is sent

5

1 Ἀνὴρ n. nom. masc. sg. ἀνήρ man, husband, sir
δὲ conj. δέ but, and, now, also, to the contrary, rather, then
τις indefinite pron. nom. masc. sg. τὶς certain, some, any man, one, any thing
Ἀνανίας n. nom. masc. sg. Ἀνανίας Ananias

ὀνόματι n. dat. neut. sg. ὄνομα name, call, surname
σὺν prep. σύν (+dat) with, beside
Σαπφείρῃ n. dat. fem. sg. Σαπφείρη Sapphira
τῇ art. dat. fem. sg. ὁ ἡ τό the, this, that, he, she, it
γυναικὶ n. dat. fem. sg. γυνή woman, wife
αὐτοῦ pron. gen. masc. 3p. sg. αὐτός ή ό self, of oneself, even, very, the same, he, she, it
κτῆμα n. acc. neut. sg. κτῆμα possession
2 καὶ conj. καί and, even, also, but
ἀπὸ prep. ἀπό (+gen) from, of, out of, since, for, off, at, by, in, on
τῆς art. gen. fem. sg. ὁ ἡ τό the, this, that, he, she, it
τιμῆς n. gen. fem. sg. τιμή honour, price, preciousness, sum
καὶ conj. καί and, even, also, but
τῆς art. gen. fem. sg. ὁ ἡ τό the, this, that, he, she, it
γυναικός n. gen. fem. sg. γυνή woman, wife
αὐτοῦ pron. gen. masc. 3p. sg. αὐτός ή ό self, of oneself, even, very, the same, he, she, it
καὶ conj. καί and, even, also, but
μέρος n. acc. neut. sg. μέρος part, coast, portion, behalf, respect, piece, side
τι indefinite pron. acc. neut. sg. τὶς certain, some, any man, one, any thing
παρὰ prep. παρά (+gen) of, from, (+dat) with, for, (+acc) beside, at, by, above, against
τοὺς art. acc. masc. pl. ὁ ἡ τό the, this, that, he, she, it
πόδας n. acc. masc. pl. πούς foot
τῶν art. gen. masc. pl. ὁ ἡ τό the, this, that, he, she, it
ἀποστόλων n. gen. masc. pl. ἀπόστολος apostle, messenger, he that is sent
3 δὲ conj. δέ but, and, now, also, to the contrary, rather, then
Πέτρος n. nom. masc. sg. Πέτρος Peter
Ἀνανία n. voc. masc. sg. Ἀνανίας Ananias
διατί adv. διατί why, for what, wherefore
ὁ art. nom. masc. sg. ὁ ἡ τό the, this, that, he, she, it
Σατανᾶς n. nom. masc. sg. Σατανᾶς Satan
τὴν art. acc. fem. sg. ὁ ἡ τό the, this, that, he, she, it
καρδίαν n. acc. fem. sg. καρδία heart
σου pron. gen. 2p. sg. σύ thou, you
σε pron. acc. 2p. sg. σύ thou, you
τὸ art. acc. neut. sg. ὁ ἡ τό the, this, that, he, she, it
Πνεῦμα n. acc. neut. sg. πνεῦμα spirit, Spirit, Ghost, ghost, life. of the spirit, wind
τὸ art. acc. neut. sg. ὁ ἡ τό the, this, that, he, she, it
Ἅγιον adj. acc. neut. sg. ἅγιος Holy, holy, saint, Holy One, holy thing, most holy
καὶ conj. καί and, even, also, but
ἀπὸ prep. ἀπό (+gen) from, of, out of, since, for, off, at, by, in, on
τῆς art. gen. fem. sg. ὁ ἡ τό the, this, that, he, she, it
τιμῆς n. gen. fem. sg. τιμή honour, price, preciousness, sum
τοῦ art. gen. neut. sg. ὁ ἡ τό the, this, that, he, she, it
χωρίου n. gen. neut. sg. χωρίον place, field, land, parcel of ground, possession
4 οὐχὶ adv. οὐχί not, nay
σοὶ pron. dat. 2p. sg. σύ thou, you
καὶ conj. καί and, even, also, but
ἐν prep. ἐν (+dat) in, by, with, among, at, on, through, to, within, into, of, for
τῇ art. dat. fem. sg. ὁ ἡ τό the, this, that, he, she, it
σῇ poss. pron. dat. fem. 2p. sg. σός thy, thine, thine own
ἐξουσίᾳ n. dat. fem. sg. ἐξουσία power, authority, right, strength, jurisdiction
τί interrog. pron. acc. neut. sg. τίς what, who, why, where, which, how
ὅτι conj. ὅτι that, for, because, how that, how, because that, for that, though
ἐν prep. ἐν (+dat) in, by, with, among, at, on, through, to, within, into, of, for
τῇ art. dat. fem. sg. ὁ ἡ τό the, this, that, he, she, it
καρδίᾳ n. dat. fem. sg. καρδία heart

σου pron. gen. 2p. sg. σύ thou, you
τὸ art. acc. neut. sg. ὁ ἡ τό the, this, that, he, she, it
πρᾶγμα n. acc. neut. sg. πρᾶγμα thing, matter, business, work
τοῦτο demo. pron. acc. neut. sg. οὗτος αὕτη τοῦτο this, the same, this same, he, she, it
οὐκ particle of negation. οὐ οὐκ οὐχ not, no, neither, none, nay, nor, never, nothing
ἀνθρώποις n. dat. masc. pl. ἄνθρωπος man, human being, person, one, certain
ἀλλὰ conj. ἀλλά but, yea, yet, nevertheless, howbeit, nay, therefore
τῷ art. dat. masc. sg. ὁ ἡ τό the, this, that, he, she, it
Θεῷ n. dat. masc. sg. θεός God, god
5 δὲ conj. δέ but, and, now, also, to the contrary, rather, then
Ἀνανίας n. nom. masc. sg. Ἀνανίας Ananias
τοὺς art. acc. masc. pl. ὁ ἡ τό the, this, that, he, she, it
λόγους n. acc. masc. pl. λόγος word, saying, account, speech, thing, matter
τούτους demo. pron. acc. masc. pl. οὗτος αὕτη τοῦτο this, the same, this same, he, she, it
καὶ conj. καί and, even, also, but
φόβος n. nom. masc. sg. φόβος fear, terror, sore afraid
μέγας adj. nom. masc. sg. μέγας great, loud, greatest, high, large, mighty, strong
ἐπὶ prep. ἐπί (+gen) on, in, upon, (+dat) in, at, for, upon, (+acc) on, upon, unto, to, against
πάντας adj. acc. masc. pl. πᾶς πᾶσα πᾶν all, every, whosoever, every one, no, whole, any
τοὺς art. acc. masc. pl. ὁ ἡ τό the, this, that, he, she, it
ταῦτα demo. pron. acc. neut. pl. οὗτος αὕτη τοῦτο this, the same, this same, he, she, it
6 δὲ conj. δέ but, and, now, also, to the contrary, rather, then
οἱ art. nom. masc. pl. ὁ ἡ τό the, this, that, he, she, it
νεώτεροι compar. adj. nom. masc. pl. νέος new
αὐτὸν pron. acc. masc. 3p. sg. αὐτός ἡ ὁ self, of oneself, even, very, the same, he, she, it
καὶ conj. καί and, even, also, but
7 δὲ conj. δέ but, and, now, also, to the contrary, rather, then
ὡς adv. ὡς as, when, as it were, how, about, like, as soon as, even as, while
ὡρῶν n. gen. fem. pl. ὥρα hour, time, season
τριῶν num. gen. fem. pl. τρεῖς three
διάστημα n. nom. neut. sg. διάστημα space
καὶ conj. καί and, even, also, but
ἡ art. nom. fem. sg. ὁ ἡ τό the, this, that, he, she, it
γυνὴ n. nom. fem. sg. γυνή woman, wife
αὐτοῦ pron. gen. masc. 3p. sg. αὐτός ἡ ὁ self, of oneself, even, very, the same, he, she, it
μὴ particle of negation. μή not, no, lest, neither, none, nothing, nor, never, without
τὸ art. acc. neut. sg. ὁ ἡ τό the, this, that, he, she, it
8 δὲ conj. δέ but, and, now, also, to the contrary, rather, then
αὐτῇ pron. dat. fem. 3p. sg. αὐτός ἡ ὁ self, of oneself, even, very, the same, he, she, it
ὁ art. nom. masc. sg. ὁ ἡ τό the, this, that, he, she, it
Πέτρος n. nom. masc. sg. Πέτρος Peter
μοι pron. dat. 1p. sg. ἐγώ I
εἰ conj. εἰ if, whether, that, though, forasmuch
τοσούτου demo. pron. gen. neut. sg. τοσοῦτος so much, so great, so many, so long
τὸ art. acc. neut. sg. ὁ ἡ τό the, this, that, he, she, it
χωρίον n. acc. neut. sg. χωρίον place, field, land, parcel of ground, possession
ἡ art. nom. fem. sg. ὁ ἡ τό the, this, that, he, she, it
δὲ conj. δέ but, and, now, also, to the contrary, rather, then
Ναί particle. ναί yea, even so, yes, surely, truth, verily
τοσούτου demo. pron. gen. neut. sg. τοσοῦτος so much, so great, so many, so long
9 ὁ art. nom. masc. sg. ὁ ἡ τό the, this, that, he, she, it
δὲ conj. δέ but, and, now, also, to the contrary, rather, then
Πέτρος n. nom. masc. sg. Πέτρος Peter
πρὸς prep. πρός (+gen) for, (+dat) at, (+acc) unto, to, with, for, against
αὐτήν pron. acc. fem. 3p. sg. αὐτός ἡ ὁ self, of oneself, even, very, the same, he, she, it

Τί interrog. pron. nom. neut. sg. τίς what, who, why, where, which, how
ὅτι conj. ὅτι that, for, because, how that, how, because that, for that, though
ὑμῖν pron. dat. 2p. pl. σύ thou, you
τὸ art. acc. neut. sg. ὁ ἡ τό the, this, that, he, she, it
Πνεῦμα n. acc. neut. sg. πνεῦμα spirit, Spirit, Ghost, ghost, life. of the spirit, wind
Κυρίου n. gen. masc. sg. κύριος Lord, lord, master, sir, LORD, God, Master, owner
οἱ art. nom. masc. pl. ὁ ἡ τό the, this, that, he, she, it
πόδες n. nom. masc. pl. πούς foot
τῶν art. gen. masc. pl. ὁ ἡ τό the, this, that, he, she, it
τὸν art. acc. masc. sg. ὁ ἡ τό the, this, that, he, she, it
ἄνδρα n. acc. masc. sg. ἀνήρ man, husband, sir
σου pron. gen. 2p. sg. σύ thou, you
ἐπὶ prep. ἐπί (+gen) on, in, upon, (+dat) in, at, for, upon, (+acc) on, upon, unto, to, against
τῇ art. dat. fem. sg. ὁ ἡ τό the, this, that, he, she, it
θύρᾳ n. dat. fem. sg. θύρα door, gate
καὶ conj. καί and, even, also, but
σε pron. acc. 2p. sg. σύ thou, you
10 δὲ conj. δέ but, and, now, also, to the contrary, rather, then
παραχρῆμα adv. παραχρῆμα immediately, straightway, forthwith, presently, soon
παρὰ prep. παρά (+gen) of, from, (+dat) with, for, (+acc) beside, at, by, above, against
τοὺς art. acc. masc. pl. ὁ ἡ τό the, this, that, he, she, it
πόδας n. acc. masc. pl. πούς foot
αὐτοῦ pron. gen. masc. 3p. sg. αὐτός ή ό self, of oneself, even, very, the same, he, she, it
καὶ conj. καί and, even, also, but
δὲ conj. δέ but, and, now, also, to the contrary, rather, then
οἱ art. nom. masc. pl. ὁ ἡ τό the, this, that, he, she, it
νεανίσκοι n. nom. masc. pl. νεανίσκος young man
αὐτὴν pron. acc. fem. 3p. sg. αὐτός ή ό self, of oneself, even, very, the same, he, she, it
νεκρὰν adj. acc. fem. sg. νεκρός dead
καὶ conj. καί and, even, also, but
πρὸς prep. πρός (+gen) for, (+dat) at, (+acc) unto, to, with, for, against
τὸν art. acc. masc. sg. ὁ ἡ τό the, this, that, he, she, it
ἄνδρα n. acc. masc. sg. ἀνήρ man, husband, sir
αὐτῆς pron. gen. fem. 3p. sg. αὐτός ή ό self, of oneself, even, very, the same, he, she, it
11 καὶ conj. καί and, even, also, but
φόβος n. nom. masc. sg. φόβος fear, terror, sore afraid
μέγας adj. nom. masc. sg. μέγας great, loud, greatest, high, large, mighty, strong
ἐφ' prep. ἐπί (+gen) on, in, upon, (+dat) in, at, for, upon, (+acc) on, upon, unto, to, against
ὅλην adj. acc. fem. sg. ὅλος all, whole, every whit, altogether
τὴν art. acc. fem. sg. ὁ ἡ τό the, this, that, he, she, it
ἐκκλησίαν n. acc. fem. sg. ἐκκλησία church, assembly
καὶ conj. καί and, even, also, but
ἐπὶ prep. ἐπί (+gen) on, in, upon, (+dat) in, at, for, upon, (+acc) on, upon, unto, to, against
πάντας adj. acc. masc. pl. πᾶς πᾶσα πᾶν all, every, whosoever, every one, no, whole, any
τοὺς art. acc. masc. pl. ὁ ἡ τό the, this, that, he, she, it
ταῦτα demo. pron. acc. neut. pl. οὗτος αὕτη τοῦτο this, the same, this same, he, she, it
12 Διὰ prep. διά (+gen) by, through, with, in, of, (+acc) for, because of, for a cause
δὲ conj. δέ but, and, now, also, to the contrary, rather, then
τῶν art. gen. fem. pl. ὁ ἡ τό the, this, that, he, she, it
χειρῶν n. gen. fem. pl. χείρ hand
τῶν art. gen. fem. pl. ὁ ἡ τό the, this, that, he, she, it
ἀποστόλων n. gen. masc. pl. ἀπόστολος apostle, messenger, he that is sent
σημεῖα n. nom. neut. pl. σημεῖον sign, miracle, wonder, token
καὶ conj. καί and, even, also, but
τέρατα n. nom. neut. pl. τέρας wonder

ἐν prep. ἐν (+dat) in, by, with, among, at, on, through, to, within, into, of, for
τῷ art. dat. masc. sg. ὁ ἡ τό the, this, that, he, she, it
λαῷ n. dat. masc. sg. λαός people
πολλὰ adj. nom. neut. pl. πολύς many, great, much, long, abundant
καὶ conj. καί and, even, also, but
ὁμοθυμαδὸν adv. ὁμοθυμαδόν with one accord, with one mind
ἅπαντες adj. nom. masc. pl. ἅπας all, whole, all things, every, everyone
ἐν prep. ἐν (+dat) in, by, with, among, at, on, through, to, within, into, of, for
τῇ art. dat. fem. sg. ὁ ἡ τό the, this, that, he, she, it
στοᾷ n. dat. fem. sg. στοά porch
Σολομῶντος n. gen. masc. sg. Σολομών Solomon
13 τῶν art. gen. masc. pl. ὁ ἡ τό the, this, that, he, she, it
δὲ conj. δέ but, and, now, also, to the contrary, rather, then
λοιπῶν adj. gen. masc. pl. λοιπός other, rest, remnant, residue, which remain
οὐδεὶς num. nom. masc. sg. οὐδείς no man, nothing, no, none, neither, not, nought
αὐτοῖς pron. dat. masc. 3p. pl. αὐτός ή ό self, of oneself, even, very, the same, he, she, it
ἀλλ' conj. ἀλλά but, yea, yet, nevertheless, howbeit, nay, therefore
αὐτοὺς pron. acc. masc. 3p. pl. αὐτός ή ό self, of oneself, even, very, the same, he, she, it
ὁ art. nom. masc. sg. ὁ ἡ τό the, this, that, he, she, it
λαός n. nom. masc. sg. λαός people
14 μᾶλλον compar. adv. μᾶλλον rather, more, more and more, better, much, much the more
δὲ conj. δέ but, and, now, also, to the contrary, rather, then
τῷ art. dat. masc. sg. ὁ ἡ τό the, this, that, he, she, it
Κυρίῳ n. dat. masc. sg. κύριος Lord, lord, master, sir, LORD, God, Master, owner
πλήθη n. nom. neut. pl. πλῆθος multitude, bundle, company
ἀνδρῶν n. gen. masc. pl. ἀνήρ man, husband, sir
τε conj. τέ and, both, also
καὶ conj. καί and, even, also, but
γυναικῶν n. gen. fem. pl. γυνή woman, wife
15 ὥστε conj. ὥστε so that, wherefore, insomuch that, therefore, that, so then
κατὰ prep. κατά (+gen) against, by, throughout, down, (+acc) according to, after, with
τὰς art. acc. fem. pl. ὁ ἡ τό the, this, that, he, she, it
πλατείας adj. acc. fem. pl. πλατύς wide, broad
τοὺς art. acc. masc. pl. ὁ ἡ τό the, this, that, he, she, it
ἀσθενεῖς adj. acc. masc. pl. ἀσθενής weak, sick, impotent, more feeble
καὶ conj. καί and, even, also, but
ἐπὶ prep. ἐπί (+gen) on, in, upon, (+dat) in, at, for, upon, (+acc) on, upon, unto, to, against
κλινῶν n. gen. neut. pl. κλίνη bed, table
καὶ conj. καί and, even, also, but
κραββάτων n. gen. masc. pl. κράββατος bed, couch
ἵνα conj. ἵνα that, to, lest, for to, so that, albeit, because, for, so as
Πέτρου n. gen. masc. sg. Πέτρος Peter
κἂν adv. κἄν though, and if, if but, also if, and if so much, at the least, yet as
ἡ art. nom. fem. sg. ὁ ἡ τό the, this, that, he, she, it
σκιὰ n. nom. fem. sg. σκιά shadow
τινὶ indefinite pron. dat. masc. sg. τὶς certain, some, any man, one, any thing
αὐτῶν pron. gen. masc. 3p. pl. αὐτός ή ό self, of oneself, even, very, the same, he, she, it
16 δὲ conj. δέ but, and, now, also, to the contrary, rather, then
καὶ conj. καί and, even, also, but
τὸ art. nom. neut. sg. ὁ ἡ τό the, this, that, he, she, it
πλῆθος n. nom. neut. sg. πλῆθος multitude, bundle, company
τῶν art. gen. fem. pl. ὁ ἡ τό the, this, that, he, she, it
πέριξ adv. πέριξ round about
πόλεων n. gen. fem. pl. πόλις city
εἰς prep. εἰς (+acc) into, to, unto, for, in, on, toward, against, upon, at, among

Ἰερουσαλήμ pron. name. fem. inde. Ἰερουσαλήμ Jerusalem
ἀσθενεῖς adj. acc. masc. pl. ἀσθενής weak, sick, impotent, more feeble
καὶ conj. καί and, even, also, but
ὑπὸ prep. ὑπό (+gen) of, by, with, from, among, (+acc) under
πνευμάτων n. gen. neut. pl. πνεῦμα spirit, Spirit, Ghost, ghost, life. of the spirit, wind
ἀκαθάρτων adj. gen. neut. pl. ἀκάθαρτος unclean, foul
οἵτινες relative pron. nom. masc. pl. ὅστις which, who, whosoever, that, whatsoever
ἅπαντες adj. nom. masc. pl. ἅπας all, whole, all things, every, everyone
17 δὲ conj. δέ but, and, now, also, to the contrary, rather, then
ὁ art. nom. masc. sg. ὁ ἡ τό the, this, that, he, she, it
ἀρχιερεὺς n. nom. masc. sg. ἀρχιερεύς chief priest, high priest
καὶ conj. καί and, even, also, but
πάντες adj. nom. masc. pl. πᾶς πᾶσα πᾶν all, every, whosoever, every one, no, whole, any
οἱ art. nom. masc. pl. ὁ ἡ τό the, this, that, he, she, it
σὺν prep. σύν (+dat) with, beside
αὐτῷ pron. dat. masc. 3p. sg. αὐτός ή ό self, of oneself, even, very, the same, he, she, it
ἡ art. nom. fem. sg. ὁ ἡ τό the, this, that, he, she, it
αἵρεσις n. nom. fem. sg. αἵρεσις sect, heresy
τῶν art. gen. masc. pl. ὁ ἡ τό the, this, that, he, she, it
Σαδδουκαίων n. gen. masc. pl. Σαδδουκαῖος Sadducee
ζήλου n. gen. masc. sg. ζῆλος zeal, envying, indignation, emulation, jealousy
18 καὶ conj. καί and, even, also, but
τὰς art. acc. fem. pl. ὁ ἡ τό the, this, that, he, she, it
χεῖρας n. acc. fem. pl. χείρ hand
αὐτῶν pron. gen. masc. 3p. pl. αὐτός ή ό self, of oneself, even, very, the same, he, she, it
ἐπὶ prep. ἐπί (+gen) on, in, upon, (+dat) in, at, for, upon, (+acc) on, upon, unto, to, against
τοὺς art. acc. masc. pl. ὁ ἡ τό the, this, that, he, she, it
ἀποστόλους n. acc. masc. pl. ἀπόστολος apostle, messenger, he that is sent
καὶ conj. καί and, even, also, but
αὐτοὺς pron. acc. masc. 3p. pl. αὐτός ή ό self, of oneself, even, very, the same, he, she, it
ἐν prep. ἐν (+dat) in, by, with, among, at, on, through, to, within, into, of, for
τηρήσει n. dat. fem. sg. τήρησις hold, keeping, prison
δημοσίᾳ adv. |adj. dat. fem. sg. δημόσιος common
19 ἄγγελος n. nom. masc. sg. ἄγγελος angel, messenger
δὲ conj. δέ but, and, now, also, to the contrary, rather, then
Κυρίου n. gen. masc. sg. κύριος Lord, lord, master, sir, LORD, God, Master, owner
διὰ prep. διά (+gen) by, through, with, in, of, (+acc) for, because of, for a cause
τῆς art. gen. fem. sg. ὁ ἡ τό the, this, that, he, she, it
νυκτὸς n. gen. fem. sg. νύξ night
τὰς art. acc. fem. pl. ὁ ἡ τό the, this, that, he, she, it
θύρας n. acc. fem. pl. θύρα door, gate
τῆς art. gen. fem. sg. ὁ ἡ τό the, this, that, he, she, it
φυλακῆς n. gen. fem. sg. φυλακή prison, watch, imprisonment, cage, hold, ward
τε conj. τέ and, both, also
αὐτοὺς pron. acc. masc. 3p. pl. αὐτός ή ό self, of oneself, even, very, the same, he, she, it
20 καὶ conj. καί and, even, also, but
ἐν prep. ἐν (+dat) in, by, with, among, at, on, through, to, within, into, of, for
τῷ art. dat. neut. sg. ὁ ἡ τό the, this, that, he, she, it
ἱερῷ n. dat. neut. sg. ἱερόν temple
τῷ art. dat. masc. sg. ὁ ἡ τό the, this, that, he, she, it
λαῷ n. dat. masc. sg. λαός people
πάντα adj. acc. neut. pl. πᾶς πᾶσα πᾶν all, every, whosoever, every one, no, whole, any
τὰ art. acc. neut. pl. ὁ ἡ τό the, this, that, he, she, it
ῥήματα n. acc. neut. pl. ῥῆμα word, saying, thing
τῆς art. gen. fem. sg. ὁ ἡ τό the, this, that, he, she, it

ζωῆς n. gen. fem. sg. ζωή life, lifetime
ταύτης demo. pron. gen. fem. sg. οὗτος αὕτη τοῦτο this, the same, this same, he, she, it
21 δὲ conj. δέ but, and, now, also, to the contrary, rather, then
ὑπὸ prep. ὑπό (+gen) of, by, with, from, among, (+acc) under
τὸν art. acc. masc. sg. ὁ ἡ τό the, this, that, he, she, it
ὄρθρον n. acc. masc. sg. ὄρθρος early in the morning
εἰς prep. εἰς (+acc) into, to, unto, for, in, on, toward, against, upon, at, among
τὸ art. acc. neut. sg. ὁ ἡ τό the, this, that, he, she, it
ἱερὸν n. acc. neut. sg. ἱερόν temple
καὶ conj. καί and, even, also, but
δὲ conj. δέ but, and, now, also, to the contrary, rather, then
ὁ art. nom. masc. sg. ὁ ἡ τό the, this, that, he, she, it
ἀρχιερεὺς n. nom. masc. sg. ἀρχιερεύς chief priest, high priest
καὶ conj. καί and, even, also, but
οἱ art. nom. masc. pl. ὁ ἡ τό the, this, that, he, she, it
σὺν prep. σύν (+dat) with, beside
αὐτῷ pron. dat. masc. 3p. sg. αὐτός ή ό self, of oneself, even, very, the same, he, she, it
τὸ art. acc. neut. sg. ὁ ἡ τό the, this, that, he, she, it
συνέδριον n. acc. neut. sg. συνέδριον council
καὶ conj. καί and, even, also, but
πᾶσαν adj. acc. fem. sg. πᾶς πᾶσα πᾶν all, every, whosoever, every one, no, whole, any
τὴν art. acc. fem. sg. ὁ ἡ τό the, this, that, he, she, it
γερουσίαν n. acc. fem. sg. γερουσία senate
τῶν art. gen. masc. pl. ὁ ἡ τό the, this, that, he, she, it
υἱῶν n. gen. masc. pl. υἱός son, child, descendant, offspring, heir
Ἰσραήλ pron. name. masc. inde. Ἰσραήλ Israel
καὶ conj. καί and, even, also, but
εἰς prep. εἰς (+acc) into, to, unto, for, in, on, toward, against, upon, at, among
τὸ art. acc. neut. sg. ὁ ἡ τό the, this, that, he, she, it
δεσμωτήριον n. acc. neut. sg. δεσμωτήριον prison
αὐτούς pron. acc. masc. 3p. pl. αὐτός ή ό self, of oneself, even, very, the same, he, she, it
22 οἱ art. nom. masc. pl. ὁ ἡ τό the, this, that, he, she, it
δὲ conj. δέ but, and, now, also, to the contrary, rather, then
ὑπηρέται n. nom. masc. pl. ὑπηρέτης officer, minister, servant
οὐχ particle of negation. οὐ οὐκ οὐχ not, no, neither, none, nay, nor, never, nothing
αὐτοὺς pron. acc. masc. 3p. pl. αὐτός ή ό self, of oneself, even, very, the same, he, she, it
ἐν prep. ἐν (+dat) in, by, with, among, at, on, through, to, within, into, of, for
τῇ art. dat. fem. sg. ὁ ἡ τό the, this, that, he, she, it
φυλακῇ n. dat. fem. sg. φυλακή prison, watch, imprisonment, cage, hold, ward
δὲ conj. δέ but, and, now, also, to the contrary, rather, then
23 ὅτι conj. ὅτι that, for, because, how that, how, because that, for that, though
Τὸ art. acc. neut. sg. ὁ ἡ τό the, this, that, he, she, it
μὲν conj. μέν indeed, verily, truly, even, so, some
δεσμωτήριον n. acc. neut. sg. δεσμωτήριον prison
ἐν prep. ἐν (+dat) in, by, with, among, at, on, through, to, within, into, of, for
πάσῃ adj. dat. fem. sg. πᾶς πᾶσα πᾶν all, every, whosoever, every one, no, whole, any
ἀσφαλείᾳ n. dat. fem. sg. ἀσφάλεια certainty, safety
καὶ conj. καί and, even, also, but
τοὺς art. acc. masc. pl. ὁ ἡ τό the, this, that, he, she, it
φύλακας n. acc. masc. pl. φύλαξ keeper
ἔξω adv. ἔξω out, without, out of, forth, away, outward
πρὸ prep. πρό (+gen) before, above
τῶν art. gen. fem. pl. ὁ ἡ τό the, this, that, he, she, it
θυρῶν n. gen. fem. pl. θύρα door, gate
δὲ conj. δέ but, and, now, also, to the contrary, rather, then

ἔσω adv. ἔσω within, in, inner, into, inward
οὐδένα num. acc. masc. sg. οὐδείς no man, nothing, no, none, neither, not, nought
24 ὡς adv. ὡς as, when, as it were, how, about, like, as soon as, even as, while
δὲ conj. δέ but, and, now, also, to the contrary, rather, then
τοὺς art. acc. masc. pl. ὁ ἡ τό the, this, that, he, she, it
λόγους n. acc. masc. pl. λόγος word, saying, account, speech, thing, matter
τούτους demo. pron. acc. masc. pl. οὗτος αὕτη τοῦτο this, the same, this same, he, she, it
ὅ art. nom. masc. sg. ὁ ἡ τό the, this, that, he, she, it
τε conj. τέ and, both, also
ἱερεὺς n. nom. masc. sg. ἱερεύς priest
καὶ conj. καί and, even, also, but
ὁ art. nom. masc. sg. ὁ ἡ τό the, this, that, he, she, it
στρατηγὸς n. nom. masc. sg. στρατηγός captain, magistrate
τοῦ art. gen. neut. sg. ὁ ἡ τό the, this, that, he, she, it
ἱεροῦ n. gen. neut. sg. ἱερόν temple
καὶ conj. καί and, even, also, but
οἱ art. nom. masc. pl. ὁ ἡ τό the, this, that, he, she, it
ἀρχιερεῖς n. nom. masc. pl. ἀρχιερεύς chief priest, high priest
περὶ prep. περί (+gen) of, for, concerning, (+acc) about, concerning, in
αὐτῶν pron. gen. masc. 3p. pl. αὐτός ή ό self, of oneself, even, very, the same, he, she, it
τί interrog. pron. nom. neut. sg. τίς what, who, why, where, which, how
ἂν particle. ἄν Indicating contingency. No English translation.
τοῦτο demo. pron. nom. neut. sg. οὗτος αὕτη τοῦτο this, the same, this same, he, she, it
25 δὲ conj. δέ but, and, now, also, to the contrary, rather, then
τις indefinite pron. nom. masc. sg. τὶς certain, some, any man, one, any thing
αὐτοῖς pron. dat. masc. 3p. pl. αὐτός ή ό self, of oneself, even, very, the same, he, she, it
ὅτι conj. ὅτι that, for, because, how that, how, because that, for that, though
οἱ art. nom. masc. pl. ὁ ἡ τό the, this, that, he, she, it
ἄνδρες n. nom. masc. pl. ἀνήρ man, husband, sir
οὓς relative pron. acc. masc. pl. ὅς ἥ ὅ who, which, what, that
ἐν prep. ἐν (+dat) in, by, with, among, at, on, through, to, within, into, of, for
τῇ art. dat. fem. sg. ὁ ἡ τό the, this, that, he, she, it
φυλακῇ n. dat. fem. sg. φυλακή prison, watch, imprisonment, cage, hold, ward
ἐν prep. ἐν (+dat) in, by, with, among, at, on, through, to, within, into, of, for
τῷ art. dat. neut. sg. ὁ ἡ τό the, this, that, he, she, it
ἱερῷ n. dat. neut. sg. ἱερόν temple
καὶ conj. καί and, even, also, but
τὸν art. acc. masc. sg. ὁ ἡ τό the, this, that, he, she, it
λαόν n. acc. masc. sg. λαός people
26 τότε adv. τότε then, that time
ὁ art. nom. masc. sg. ὁ ἡ τό the, this, that, he, she, it
στρατηγὸς n. nom. masc. sg. στρατηγός captain, magistrate
σὺν prep. σύν (+dat) with, beside
τοῖς art. dat. masc. pl. ὁ ἡ τό the, this, that, he, she, it
ὑπηρέταις n. dat. masc. pl. ὑπηρέτης officer, minister, servant
αὐτοὺς pron. acc. masc. 3p. pl. αὐτός ή ό self, of oneself, even, very, the same, he, she, it
οὐ particle of negation. οὐ οὐκ οὐχ not, no, neither, none, nay, nor, never, nothing
μετὰ prep. μετά (+gen) with, among, against, (+acc) after
βίας n. gen. fem. sg. βία violence
γὰρ conj. γάρ for, and, because, but, indeed
τὸν art. acc. masc. sg. ὁ ἡ τό the, this, that, he, she, it
λαὸν n. acc. masc. sg. λαός people
ἵνα conj. ἵνα that, to, lest, for to, so that, albeit, because, for, so as
μὴ particle of negation. μή not, no, lest, neither, none, nothing, nor, never, without
27 δὲ conj. δέ but, and, now, also, to the contrary, rather, then

αὐτοὺς pron. acc. masc. 3p. pl. αὐτός ἡ ὁ self, of oneself, even, very, the same, he, she, it
ἐν prep. ἐν (+dat) in, by, with, among, at, on, through, to, within, into, of, for
τῷ art. dat. neut. sg. ὁ ἡ τό the, this, that, he, she, it
συνεδρίῳ n. dat. neut. sg. συνέδριον council
καὶ conj. καί and, even, also, but
αὐτοὺς pron. acc. masc. 3p. pl. αὐτός ἡ ὁ self, of oneself, even, very, the same, he, she, it
ὁ art. nom. masc. sg. ὁ ἡ τό the, this, that, he, she, it
ἀρχιερεὺς n. nom. masc. sg. ἀρχιερεύς chief priest, high priest
28 Οὐ particle of negation. οὐ οὐκ οὐχ not, no, neither, none, nay, nor, never, nothing
παραγγελίᾳ n. dat. fem. sg. παραγγελία charge, commandment
ὑμῖν pron. dat. 2p. pl. σύ thou, you
μὴ particle of negation. μή not, no, lest, neither, none, nothing, nor, never, without
ἐπὶ prep. ἐπί (+gen) on, in, upon, (+dat) in, at, for, upon, (+acc) on, upon, unto, to, against
τῷ art. dat. neut. sg. ὁ ἡ τό the, this, that, he, she, it
ὀνόματι n. dat. neut. sg. ὄνομα name, call, surname
τούτῳ demo. pron. dat. neut. sg. οὗτος αὕτη τοῦτο this, the same, this same, he, she, it
καὶ conj. καί and, even, also, but
τὴν art. acc. fem. sg. ὁ ἡ τό the, this, that, he, she, it
Ἰερουσαλὴμ pron. name. fem. inde. Ἰερουσαλήμ Jerusalem
τῆς art. gen. fem. sg. ὁ ἡ τό the, this, that, he, she, it
διδαχῆς n. gen. fem. sg. διδαχή doctrine, teaching
ὑμῶν pron. gen. 2p. pl. σύ thou, you
καὶ conj. καί and, even, also, but
ἐφ' prep. ἐπί (+gen) on, in, upon, (+dat) in, at, for, upon, (+acc) on, upon, unto, to, against
ἡμᾶς pron. acc. 1p. pl. ἐγώ I
τὸ art. acc. neut. sg. ὁ ἡ τό the, this, that, he, she, it
αἷμα n. acc. neut. sg. αἷμα blood
τοῦ art. gen. masc. sg. ὁ ἡ τό the, this, that, he, she, it
ἀνθρώπου n. gen. masc. sg. ἄνθρωπος man, human being, person, one, certain
τούτου demo. pron. gen. masc. sg. οὗτος αὕτη τοῦτο this, the same, this same, he, she, it
29 δὲ conj. δέ but, and, now, also, to the contrary, rather, then
ὁ art. nom. masc. sg. ὁ ἡ τό the, this, that, he, she, it
Πέτρος n. nom. masc. sg. Πέτρος Peter
καὶ conj. καί and, even, also, but
οἱ art. nom. masc. pl. ὁ ἡ τό the, this, that, he, she, it
ἀπόστολοι n. nom. masc. pl. ἀπόστολος apostle, messenger, he that is sent
Θεῷ n. dat. masc. sg. θεός God, god
μᾶλλον compar. adv. μᾶλλον rather, more, more and more, better, much, much the more
ἢ particle. ἤ or, than, either, nor, or else, and, rather than
ἀνθρώποις n. dat. masc. pl. ἄνθρωπος man, human being, person, one, certain
30 ὁ art. nom. masc. sg. ὁ ἡ τό the, this, that, he, she, it
Θεὸς n. nom. masc. sg. θεός God, god
τῶν art. gen. masc. pl. ὁ ἡ τό the, this, that, he, she, it
πατέρων n. gen. masc. pl. πατήρ Father, father, parent
ἡμῶν pron. gen. 1p. pl. ἐγώ I
Ἰησοῦν n. acc. masc. sg. Ἰησοῦς Jesus
ὃν relative pron. acc. masc. sg. ὅς ἥ ὅ who, which, what, that
ὑμεῖς pron. nom. 2p. pl. σύ thou, you
ἐπὶ prep. ἐπί (+gen) on, in, upon, (+dat) in, at, for, upon, (+acc) on, upon, unto, to, against
ξύλου n. gen. neut. sg. ξύλον tree, stave, wood, the stocks
31 τοῦτον demo. pron. acc. masc. sg. οὗτος αὕτη τοῦτο this, the same, this same, he, she, it
ὁ art. nom. masc. sg. ὁ ἡ τό the, this, that, he, she, it
Θεὸς n. nom. masc. sg. θεός God, god
ἀρχηγὸν n. acc. masc. sg. ἀρχηγός Prince, author, captain
καὶ conj. καί and, even, also, but

σωτῆρα n. acc. masc. sg. σωτήρ Saviour, saviour
τῇ art. dat. fem. sg. ὁ ἡ τό the, this, that, he, she, it
δεξιᾷ adj. dat. fem. sg. δεξιός right, right hand, right side
αὐτοῦ pron. gen. masc. 3p. sg. αὐτός ή ό self, of oneself, even, very, the same, he, she, it
μετάνοιαν n. acc. fem. sg. μετάνοια repentance
τῷ art. dat. masc. sg. ὁ ἡ τό the, this, that, he, she, it
Ἰσραὴλ pron. name. masc. inde. Ἰσραήλ Israel
καὶ conj. καί and, even, also, but
ἄφεσιν n. acc. fem. sg. ἄφεσις remission, forgiveness, deliverance, liberty
ἁμαρτιῶν n. gen. fem. pl. ἁμαρτία sin, offence, sinful
32 καὶ conj. καί and, even, also, but
ἡμεῖς pron. nom. 1p. pl. ἐγώ I
αὐτοῦ pron. gen. masc. 3p. sg. αὐτός ή ό self, of oneself, even, very, the same, he, she, it
μάρτυρες n. nom. masc. pl. μάρτυς or μάρτυρ witness, martyr, record
τῶν art. gen. neut. pl. ὁ ἡ τό the, this, that, he, she, it
ῥημάτων n. gen. neut. pl. ῥῆμα word, saying, thing
τούτων demo. pron. gen. neut. pl. οὗτος αὕτη τοῦτο this, the same, this same, he, she, it
καὶ conj. καί and, even, also, but
τὸ art. nom. neut. sg. ὁ ἡ τό the, this, that, he, she, it
Πνεῦμα n. nom. neut. sg. πνεῦμα spirit, Spirit, Ghost, ghost, life. of the spirit, wind
δὲ conj. δέ but, and, now, also, to the contrary, rather, then
τὸ art. nom. neut. sg. ὁ ἡ τό the, this, that, he, she, it
Ἅγιον adj. nom. neut. sg. ἅγιος Holy, holy, saint, Holy One, holy thing, most holy
ὃ relative pron. acc. neut. sg. ὅς ἥ ὅ who, which, what, that
ὁ art. nom. masc. sg. ὁ ἡ τό the, this, that, he, she, it
Θεὸς n. nom. masc. sg. θεός God, god
τοῖς art. dat. masc. pl. ὁ ἡ τό the, this, that, he, she, it
αὐτῷ pron. dat. masc. 3p. sg. αὐτός ή ό self, of oneself, even, very, the same, he, she, it
33 Οἱ art. nom. masc. pl. ὁ ἡ τό the, this, that, he, she, it
δὲ conj. δέ but, and, now, also, to the contrary, rather, then
καὶ conj. καί and, even, also, but
αὐτούς pron. acc. masc. 3p. pl. αὐτός ή ό self, of oneself, even, very, the same, he, she, it
34 δὲ conj. δέ but, and, now, also, to the contrary, rather, then
τις indefinite pron. nom. masc. sg. τὶς certain, some, any man, one, any thing
ἐν prep. ἐν (+dat) in, by, with, among, at, on, through, to, within, into, of, for
τῷ art. dat. neut. sg. ὁ ἡ τό the, this, that, he, she, it
συνεδρίῳ n. dat. neut. sg. συνέδριον council
Φαρισαῖος n. nom. masc. sg. Φαρισαῖος Pharisee
ὀνόματι n. dat. neut. sg. ὄνομα name, call, surname
Γαμαλιήλ n. nom. masc. sg. Γαμαλιήλ Gamaliel
νομοδιδάσκαλος n. nom. masc. sg. νομοδιδάσκαλος doctor of the law, teacher of the law
τίμιος adj. nom. masc. sg. τίμιος precious, dear, has in reputation, honourable
παντὶ adj. dat. masc. sg. πᾶς πᾶsα πᾶν all, every, whosoever, every one, no, whole, any
τῷ art. dat. masc. sg. ὁ ἡ τό the, this, that, he, she, it
λαῷ n. dat. masc. sg. λαός people
ἔξω adv. ἔξω out, without, out of, forth, away, outward
βραχὺ adv. βραχύς little while, little, few words, little space
τι indefinite pron. acc. neut. sg. τὶς certain, some, any man, one, any thing
τοὺς art. acc. masc. pl. ὁ ἡ τό the, this, that, he, she, it
ἀποστόλους n. acc. masc. pl. ἀπόστολος apostle, messenger, he that is sent
35 τε conj. τέ and, both, also
πρὸς prep. πρός (+gen) for, (+dat) at, (+acc) unto, to, with, for, against
αὐτούς pron. acc. masc. 3p. pl. αὐτός ή ό self, of oneself, even, very, the same, he, she, it
Ἄνδρες n. voc. masc. pl. ἀνήρ man, husband, sir
Ἰσραηλῖται n. voc. masc. pl. Ἰσραηλίτης Israelite, Israel

ἑαυτοῖς reflexive pron. dat. masc. 3p. pl. ἑαυτοῦ himself, herself, itself, yourself, ourselves
ἐπὶ prep. ἐπί (+gen) on, in, upon, (+dat) in, at, for, upon, (+acc) on, upon, unto, to, against
τοῖς art. dat. masc. pl. ὁ ἡ τό the, this, that, he, she, it
ἀνθρώποις n. dat. masc. pl. ἄνθρωπος man, human being, person, one, certain
τούτοις demo. pron. dat. masc. pl. οὗτος αὕτη τοῦτο this, the same, this same, he, she, it
τί interrog. pron. acc. neut. sg. τίς what, who, why, where, which, how
36 πρὸ prep. πρό (+gen) before, above
γὰρ conj. γάρ for, and, because, but, indeed
τούτων demo. pron. gen. fem. pl. οὗτος αὕτη τοῦτο this, the same, this same, he, she, it
τῶν art. gen. fem. pl. ὁ ἡ τό the, this, that, he, she, it
ἡμερῶν n. gen. fem. pl. ἡμέρα day, time, year, while, age, day time
Θευδᾶς n. nom. masc. sg. Θευδᾶς Theudas
τινα indefinite pron. acc. masc. sg. τὶς certain, some, any man, one, any thing
ἑαυτόν reflexive pron. acc. masc. 3p. sg. ἑαυτοῦ himself, herself, itself, yourself, ourselves
ᾧ relative pron. dat. masc. sg. ὅς ἥ ὅ who, which, what, that
ἀριθμὸς n. nom. masc. sg. ἀριθμός number
ἀνδρῶν n. gen. masc. pl. ἀνήρ man, husband, sir
ὡσεὶ adv. ὡσεί about, as, like, as it had been, as it were, like as
τετρακοσίων num. gen. masc. pl. τετρακόσιοι four hundred
ὃς relative pron. nom. masc. sg. ὅς ἥ ὅ who, which, what, that
καὶ conj. καί and, even, also, but
πάντες adj. nom. masc. pl. πᾶς πᾶσα πᾶν all, every, whosoever, every one, no, whole, any
ὅσοι relative pron. nom. masc. pl. ὅσος as many as, whatsoever, that, as long as, how much
αὐτῷ pron. dat. masc. 3p. sg. αὐτός ή ό self, of oneself, even, very, the same, he, she, it
καὶ conj. καί and, even, also, but
εἰς prep. εἰς (+acc) into, to, unto, for, in, on, toward, against, upon, at, among
οὐδέν adj. acc. neut. sg. οὐδείς no man, nothing, no, none, neither, not, nought
37 μετὰ prep. μετά (+gen) with, among, against, (+acc) after
τοῦτον demo. pron. acc. masc. sg. οὗτος αὕτη τοῦτο this, the same, this same, he, she, it
Ἰούδας n. nom. masc. sg. Ἰούδας Judas, Juda, Judah, Jude
ὁ art. nom. masc. sg. ὁ ἡ τό the, this, that, he, she, it
Γαλιλαῖος adj. nom. masc. sg. Γαλιλαῖος Galilean, of Galilee
ἐν prep. ἐν (+dat) in, by, with, among, at, on, through, to, within, into, of, for
ταῖς art. dat. fem. pl. ὁ ἡ τό the, this, that, he, she, it
ἡμέραις n. dat. fem. pl. ἡμέρα day, time, year, while, age, day time
τῆς art. gen. fem. sg. ὁ ἡ τό the, this, that, he, she, it
ἀπογραφῆς n. gen. fem. sg. ἀπογραφή taxing
καὶ conj. καί and, even, also, but
λαὸν n. acc. masc. sg. λαός people
ἱκανὸν adj. acc. masc. sg. ἱκανός many, much, long, worthy, sufficient, great, able
ὀπίσω prep. ὀπίσω (+gen) after. (adv.) back, behind
αὐτοῦ pron. gen. masc. 3p. sg. αὐτός ή ό self, of oneself, even, very, the same, he, she, it
κἀκεῖνος demo. pron. nom. masc. sg. κἀκεῖνος and he, he also, and the other, even he
καὶ conj. καί and, even, also, but
πάντες adj. nom. masc. pl. πᾶς πᾶσα πᾶν all, every, whosoever, every one, no, whole, any
ὅσοι relative pron. nom. masc. pl. ὅσος as many as, whatsoever, that, as long as, how much
αὐτῷ pron. dat. masc. 3p. sg. αὐτός ή ό self, of oneself, even, very, the same, he, she, it
38 καὶ conj. καί and, even, also, but
τὰ art. acc. neut. pl. ὁ ἡ τό the, this, that, he, she, it
νῦν adv. νῦν now, henceforth, present, this time
ὑμῖν pron. dat. 2p. pl. σύ thou, you
ἀπὸ prep. ἀπό (+gen) from, of, out of, since, for, off, at, by, in, on
τῶν art. gen. masc. pl. ὁ ἡ τό the, this, that, he, she, it
ἀνθρώπων n. gen. masc. pl. ἄνθρωπος man, human being, person, one, certain
τούτων demo. pron. gen. masc. pl. οὗτος αὕτη τοῦτο this, the same, this same, he, she, it

καὶ conj. καί and, even, also, but
αὐτούς pron. acc. masc. 3p. pl. αὐτός ή ό self, of oneself, even, very, the same, he, she, it
ὅτι conj. ὅτι that, for, because, how that, how, because that, for that, though
ἐὰν conj. ἐάν if, soever, except, though, and if, but, whether, if so, so
ἐξ prep. ἐκ ἐξ (+gen) of, from, out of, by, on, with, in, among, through
ἀνθρώπων n. gen. masc. pl. ἄνθρωπος man, human being, person, one, certain
ἡ art. nom. fem. sg. ὁ ἡ τό the, this, that, he, she, it
βουλὴ n. nom. fem. sg. βουλή counsel, advise, will
αὕτη demo. pron. nom. fem. sg. οὗτος αὕτη τοῦτο this, the same, this same, he, she, it
ἢ particle. ἤ or, than, either, nor, or else, and, rather than
τὸ art. nom. neut. sg. ὁ ἡ τό the, this, that, he, she, it
ἔργον n. nom. neut. sg. ἔργον work, deed, doing labour
τοῦτο demo. pron. nom. neut. sg. οὗτος αὕτη τοῦτο this, the same, this same, he, she, it
39 εἰ conj. εἰ if, whether, that, though, forasmuch
δὲ conj. δέ but, and, now, also, to the contrary, rather, then
ἐκ prep. ἐκ ἐξ (+gen) of, from, out of, by, on, with, in, among, through
Θεοῦ n. gen. masc. sg. θεός God, god
οὐ particle of negation. οὐ οὐκ οὐχ not, no, neither, none, nay, nor, never, nothing
αὐτό pron. acc. neut. 3p. sg. αὐτός ή ό self, of oneself, even, very, the same, he, she, it
μήποτε conj. μήποτε lest, lest at any time, lest haply
καὶ conj. καί and, even, also, but
θεομάχοι adj. nom. masc. pl. θεομάχος to fight against God
δὲ conj. δέ but, and, now, also, to the contrary, rather, then
αὐτῷ pron. dat. masc. 3p. sg. αὐτός ή ό self, of oneself, even, very, the same, he, she, it
40 καὶ conj. καί and, even, also, but
τοὺς art. acc. masc. pl. ὁ ἡ τό the, this, that, he, she, it
ἀποστόλους n. acc. masc. pl. ἀπόστολος apostle, messenger, he that is sent
μὴ particle of negation. μή not, no, lest, neither, none, nothing, nor, never, without
ἐπὶ prep. ἐπί (+gen) on, in, upon, (+dat) in, at, for, upon, (+acc) on, upon, unto, to, against
τῷ art. dat. neut. sg. ὁ ἡ τό the, this, that, he, she, it
ὀνόματι n. dat. neut. sg. ὄνομα name, call, surname
τοῦ art. gen. masc. sg. ὁ ἡ τό the, this, that, he, she, it
Ἰησοῦ n. gen. masc. sg. Ἰησοῦς Jesus
καὶ conj. καί and, even, also, but
αὐτούς pron. acc. masc. 3p. pl. αὐτός ή ό self, of oneself, even, very, the same, he, she, it
41 οἱ art. nom. masc. pl. ὁ ἡ τό the, this, that, he, she, it
μέν conj. μέν indeed, verily, truly, even, so, some
οὖν conj. οὖν therefore, then, so, and, now, wherefore
ἀπὸ prep. ἀπό (+gen) from, of, out of, since, for, off, at, by, in, on
προσώπου n. gen. neut. sg. πρόσωπον face, presence, person, countenance
τοῦ art. gen. neut. sg. ὁ ἡ τό the, this, that, he, she, it
συνεδρίου n. gen. neut. sg. συνέδριον council
ὅτι conj. ὅτι that, for, because, how that, how, because that, for that, though
ὑπὲρ prep. ὑπέρ (+gen) for, of, for the sake of, (+acc) above, more than
τοῦ art. gen. neut. sg. ὁ ἡ τό the, this, that, he, she, it
ὀνόματος n. gen. neut. sg. ὄνομα name, call, surname
αὐτοῦ pron. gen. masc. 3p. sg. αὐτός ή ό self, of oneself, even, very, the same, he, she, it
42 πᾶσάν adj. acc. fem. sg. πᾶς πᾶσα πᾶν all, every, whosoever, every one, no, whole, any
τε conj. τέ and, both, also
ἡμέραν n. acc. fem. sg. ἡμέρα day, time, year, while, age, day time
ἐν prep. ἐν (+dat) in, by, with, among, at, on, through, to, within, into, of, for
τῷ art. dat. neut. sg. ὁ ἡ τό the, this, that, he, she, it
ἱερῷ n. dat. neut. sg. ἱερόν temple
καὶ conj. καί and, even, also, but
κατ' prep. κατά (+gen) against, by, throughout, down, (+acc) according to, after, with

οἶκον n. acc. masc. sg. οἶκος house, home, household
οὐκ particle of negation. οὐ οὐκ οὐχ not, no, neither, none, nay, nor, never, nothing
καὶ conj. καί and, even, also, but
Ἰησοῦν n. acc. masc. sg. Ἰησοῦς Jesus
τὸν art. acc. masc. sg. ὁ ἡ τό the, this, that, he, she, it
Χριστόν n. acc. masc. sg. Χριστός Christ

6

1 Ἐν prep. ἐν (+dat) in, by, with, among, at, on, through, to, within, into, of, for
δὲ conj. δέ but, and, now, also, to the contrary, rather, then
ταῖς art. dat. fem. pl. ὁ ἡ τό the, this, that, he, she, it
ἡμέραις n. dat. fem. pl. ἡμέρα day, time, year, while, age, day time
ταύταις demo. pron. dat. fem. pl. οὗτος αὕτη τοῦτο this, the same, this same, he, she, it
τῶν art. gen. masc. pl. ὁ ἡ τό the, this, that, he, she, it
μαθητῶν n. gen. masc. pl. μαθητής disciple
γογγυσμὸς n. nom. masc. sg. γογγυσμός murmuring, grudging
τῶν art. gen. masc. pl. ὁ ἡ τό the, this, that, he, she, it
Ἑλληνιστῶν n. gen. masc. pl. Ἑλληνιστής Grecian
πρὸς prep. πρός (+gen) for, (+dat) at, (+acc) unto, to, with, for, against
τοὺς art. acc. masc. pl. ὁ ἡ τό the, this, that, he, she, it
Ἑβραίους n. acc. masc. pl. Ἑβραῖος Hebrew
ὅτι conj. ὅτι that, for, because, how that, how, because that, for that, though
ἐν prep. ἐν (+dat) in, by, with, among, at, on, through, to, within, into, of, for
τῇ art. dat. fem. sg. ὁ ἡ τό the, this, that, he, she, it
διακονίᾳ n. dat. fem. sg. διακονία ministry, administration, service, office, relief
τῇ art. dat. fem. sg. ὁ ἡ τό the, this, that, he, she, it
καθημερινῇ adj. dat. fem. sg. καθημερινός daily
αἱ art. nom. fem. pl. ὁ ἡ τό the, this, that, he, she, it
χῆραι n. nom. fem. pl. χήρα widow
αὐτῶν pron. gen. masc. 3p. pl. αὐτός ή ό self, of oneself, even, very, the same, he, she, it
2 δὲ conj. δέ but, and, now, also, to the contrary, rather, then
οἱ art. nom. masc. pl. ὁ ἡ τό the, this, that, he, she, it
δώδεκα num. nom. masc. pl. δώδεκα twelve
τὸ art. acc. neut. sg. ὁ ἡ τό the, this, that, he, she, it
πλῆθος n. acc. neut. sg. πλῆθος multitude, bundle, company
τῶν art. gen. masc. pl. ὁ ἡ τό the, this, that, he, she, it
μαθητῶν n. gen. masc. pl. μαθητής disciple
Οὐκ particle of negation. οὐ οὐκ οὐχ not, no, neither, none, nay, nor, never, nothing
ἀρεστόν adj. nom. neut. sg. ἀρεστός thing that please, please, reason
ἡμᾶς pron. acc. 1p. pl. ἐγώ I
τὸν art. acc. masc. sg. ὁ ἡ τό the, this, that, he, she, it
λόγον n. acc. masc. sg. λόγος word, saying, account, speech, thing, matter
τοῦ art. gen. masc. sg. ὁ ἡ τό the, this, that, he, she, it
Θεοῦ n. gen. masc. sg. θεός God, god
τραπέζαις n. dat. fem. pl. τράπεζα table
3 οὖν conj. οὖν therefore, then, so, and, now, wherefore
ἀδελφοί n. voc. masc. pl. ἀδελφός brother
ἄνδρας n. acc. masc. pl. ἀνήρ man, husband, sir
ἐξ prep. ἐκ ἐξ (+gen) of, from, out of, by, on, with, in, among, through
ὑμῶν pron. gen. 2p. pl. σύ thou, you
ἑπτά num. acc. masc. pl. ἑπτά seven, seventh
πλήρεις adj. acc. masc. pl. πλήρης full
Πνεύματος n. gen. neut. sg. πνεῦμα spirit, Spirit, Ghost, ghost, life. of the spirit, wind
Ἁγίου adj. gen. neut. sg. ἅγιος Holy, holy, saint, Holy One, holy thing, most holy

καὶ conj. καί and, even, also, but
σοφίας n. gen. fem. sg. σοφία wisdom
οὓς relative pron. acc. masc. pl. ὅς ἥ ὅ who, which, what, that
ἐπὶ prep. ἐπί (+gen) on, in, upon, (+dat) in, at, for, upon, (+acc) on, upon, unto, to, against
τῆς art. gen. fem. sg. ὁ ἡ τό the, this, that, he, she, it
χρείας n. gen. fem. sg. χρεία need, necessity, lack, want
ταύτης demo. pron. gen. fem. sg. οὗτος αὕτη τοῦτο this, the same, this same, he, she, it
4 ἡμεῖς pron. nom. 1p. pl. ἐγώ I
δὲ conj. δέ but, and, now, also, to the contrary, rather, then
τῇ art. dat. fem. sg. ὁ ἡ τό the, this, that, he, she, it
προσευχῇ n. dat. fem. sg. προσευχή prayer
καὶ conj. καί and, even, also, but
τῇ art. dat. fem. sg. ὁ ἡ τό the, this, that, he, she, it
διακονίᾳ n. dat. fem. sg. διακονία ministry, administration, service, office, relief
τοῦ art. gen. masc. sg. ὁ ἡ τό the, this, that, he, she, it
λόγου n. gen. masc. sg. λόγος word, saying, account, speech, thing, matter
5 καὶ conj. καί and, even, also, but
ὁ art. nom. masc. sg. ὁ ἡ τό the, this, that, he, she, it
λόγος n. nom. masc. sg. λόγος word, saying, account, speech, thing, matter
ἐνώπιον adv. ἐνώπιον before, in the sight of, in the presence of
παντὸς adj. gen. neut. sg. πᾶς πᾶσα πᾶν all, every, whosoever, every one, no, whole, any
τοῦ art. gen. neut. sg. ὁ ἡ τό the, this, that, he, she, it
πλήθους n. gen. neut. sg. πλῆθος multitude, bundle, company
καὶ conj. καί and, even, also, but
Στέφανον n. acc. masc. sg. Στέφανος Stephen
ἄνδρα n. acc. masc. sg. ἀνήρ man, husband, sir
πλήρη adj. acc. masc. sg. πλήρης full
πίστεως n. gen. fem. sg. πίστις faith, assurance, belief, fidelity
καὶ conj. καί and, even, also, but
Πνεύματος n. gen. neut. sg. πνεῦμα spirit, Spirit, Ghost, ghost, life. of the spirit, wind
Ἁγίου adj. gen. neut. sg. ἅγιος Holy, holy, saint, Holy One, holy thing, most holy
καὶ conj. καί and, even, also, but
Φίλιππον n. acc. masc. sg. Φίλιππος Philip, Philippi
καὶ conj. καί and, even, also, but
Πρόχορον n. acc. masc. sg. Πρόχορος Prochorus
καὶ conj. καί and, even, also, but
Νικάνορα n. acc. masc. sg. Νικάνωρ Nicanor
καὶ conj. καί and, even, also, but
Τίμωνα n. acc. masc. sg. Τίμων Timon
καὶ conj. καί and, even, also, but
Παρμενᾶν n. acc. masc. sg. Παρμενᾶς Parmenas
καὶ conj. καί and, even, also, but
Νικόλαον n. acc. masc. sg. Νικόλαος Nicolas
προσήλυτον n. acc. masc. sg. προσήλυτος proselyte
Ἀντιοχέα n. acc. masc. sg. Ἀντιοχεύς of Antioch
6 οὓς relative pron. acc. masc. pl. ὅς ἥ ὅ who, which, what, that
ἐνώπιον adv. ἐνώπιον before, in the sight of, in the presence of
τῶν art. gen. masc. pl. ὁ ἡ τό the, this, that, he, she, it
ἀποστόλων n. gen. masc. pl. ἀπόστολος apostle, messenger, he that is sent
καὶ conj. καί and, even, also, but
αὐτοῖς pron. dat. masc. 3p. pl. αὐτός ή ό self, of oneself, even, very, the same, he, she, it
τὰς art. acc. fem. pl. ὁ ἡ τό the, this, that, he, she, it
χεῖρας n. acc. fem. pl. χείρ hand
7 Καὶ conj. καί and, even, also, but
ὁ art. nom. masc. sg. ὁ ἡ τό the, this, that, he, she, it

λόγος n. nom. masc. sg. λόγος word, saying, account, speech, thing, matter
τοῦ art. gen. masc. sg. ὁ ἡ τό the, this, that, he, she, it
Θεοῦ n. gen. masc. sg. θεός God, god
καὶ conj. καί and, even, also, but
ὁ art. nom. masc. sg. ὁ ἡ τό the, this, that, he, she, it
ἀριθμὸς n. nom. masc. sg. ἀριθμός number
τῶν art. gen. masc. pl. ὁ ἡ τό the, this, that, he, she, it
μαθητῶν n. gen. masc. pl. μαθητής disciple
ἐν prep. ἐν (+dat) in, by, with, among, at, on, through, to, within, into, of, for
Ἰερουσαλὴμ pron. name. fem. inde. Ἰερουσαλήμ Jerusalem
σφόδρα adv. σφόδρα exceeding, very, greatly, exceedingly, sore
πολύς adj. nom. masc. sg. πολύς many, great, much, long, abundant
τε conj. τέ and, both, also
ὄχλος n. nom. masc. sg. ὄχλος people, multitude, company, press, number
τῶν art. gen. masc. pl. ὁ ἡ τό the, this, that, he, she, it
ἱερέων n. gen. masc. pl. ἱερεύς priest
τῇ art. dat. fem. sg. ὁ ἡ τό the, this, that, he, she, it
πίστει n. dat. fem. sg. πίστις faith, assurance, belief, fidelity
8 Στέφανος n. nom. masc. sg. Στέφανος Stephen
δὲ conj. δέ but, and, now, also, to the contrary, rather, then
πλήρης adj. nom. masc. sg. πλήρης full
πίστεως n. gen. fem. sg. πίστις faith, assurance, belief, fidelity
καὶ conj. καί and, even, also, but
δυνάμεως n. gen. fem. sg. δύναμις power, mighty work, miracle, strength, might
τέρατα n. acc. neut. pl. τέρας wonder
καὶ conj. καί and, even, also, but
σημεῖα n. acc. neut. pl. σημεῖον sign, miracle, wonder, token
μεγάλα adj. acc. neut. pl. μέγας great, loud, greatest, high, large, mighty, strong
ἐν prep. ἐν (+dat) in, by, with, among, at, on, through, to, within, into, of, for
τῷ art. dat. masc. sg. ὁ ἡ τό the, this, that, he, she, it
λαῷ. n. dat. masc. sg. λαός people
9 δὲ conj. δέ but, and, now, also, to the contrary, rather, then
τινες indefinite pron. nom. masc. pl. τὶς certain, some, any man, one, any thing
τῶν art. gen. masc. pl. ὁ ἡ τό the, this, that, he, she, it
ἐκ prep. ἐκ ἐξ (+gen) of, from, out of, by, on, with, in, among, through
τῆς art. gen. fem. sg. ὁ ἡ τό the, this, that, he, she, it
συναγωγῆς n. gen. fem. sg. συναγωγή synagogue, assembly, congregation
τῆς art. gen. fem. sg. ὁ ἡ τό the, this, that, he, she, it
Λιβερτίνων n. gen. masc. pl. Λιβερτῖνος Libertine
καὶ conj. καί and, even, also, but
Κυρηναίων n. gen. masc. pl. Κυρηναῖος Cyrene, Cyrenian
καὶ conj. καί and, even, also, but
'Αλεξανδρέων n. gen. masc. pl. 'Αλεξανδρεύς Alexandrian
καὶ conj. καί and, even, also, but
τῶν art. gen. masc. pl. ὁ ἡ τό the, this, that, he, she, it
ἀπὸ prep. ἀπό (+gen) from, of, out of, since, for, off, at, by, in, on
Κιλικίας n. gen. fem. sg. Κιλικία Cilicia
καὶ conj. καί and, even, also, but
'Ασίας n. gen. fem. sg. 'Ασία Asia
τῷ art. dat. masc. sg. ὁ ἡ τό the, this, that, he, she, it
Στεφάνῳ n. dat. masc. sg. Στέφανος Stephen
10 καὶ conj. καί and, even, also, but
οὐκ particle of negation. οὐ οὐκ οὐχ not, no, neither, none, nay, nor, never, nothing
τῇ art. dat. fem. sg. ὁ ἡ τό the, this, that, he, she, it
σοφίᾳ n. dat. fem. sg. σοφία wisdom

καὶ conj. καί and, even, also, but
τῷ art. dat. neut. sg. ὁ ἡ τό the, this, that, he, she, it
πνεύματι n. dat. neut. sg. πνεῦμα spirit, Spirit, Ghost, ghost, life. of the spirit, wind
ᾧ relative pron. dat. neut. sg. ὅς ἥ ὅ who, which, what, that
11 τότε adv. τότε then, that time
ἄνδρας n. acc. masc. pl. ἀνήρ man, husband, sir
ὅτι conj. ὅτι that, for, because, how that, how, because that, for that, though
αὐτοῦ pron. gen. masc. 3p. sg. αὐτός ή ό self, of oneself, even, very, the same, he, she, it
ῥήματα n. acc. neut. pl. ῥῆμα word, saying, thing
βλάσφημα adj. acc. neut. pl. βλάσφημος blasphemous, blasphemer, railing
εἰς prep. εἰς (+acc) into, to, unto, for, in, on, toward, against, upon, at, among
Μωσῆν n. acc. masc. sg. Μωσῆς Moses
καὶ conj. καί and, even, also, but
τὸν art. acc. masc. sg. ὁ ἡ τό the, this, that, he, she, it
Θεόν n. acc. masc. sg. θεός God, god
12 τε conj. τέ and, both, also
τὸν art. acc. masc. sg. ὁ ἡ τό the, this, that, he, she, it
λαὸν n. acc. masc. sg. λαός people
καὶ conj. καί and, even, also, but
τοὺς art. acc. masc. pl. ὁ ἡ τό the, this, that, he, she, it
πρεσβυτέρους adj. acc. masc. pl. πρεσβύτερος elder, elder woman, eldest, old man
καὶ conj. καί and, even, also, but
τοὺς art. acc. masc. pl. ὁ ἡ τό the, this, that, he, she, it
γραμματεῖς n. acc. masc. pl. γραμματεύς scribe, townclerk
καὶ conj. καί and, even, also, but
αὐτὸν pron. acc. masc. 3p. sg. αὐτός ή ό self, of oneself, even, very, the same, he, she, it
καὶ conj. καί and, even, also, but
εἰς prep. εἰς (+acc) into, to, unto, for, in, on, toward, against, upon, at, among
τὸ art. acc. neut. sg. ὁ ἡ τό the, this, that, he, she, it
συνέδριον n. acc. neut. sg. συνέδριον council
13 τε conj. τέ and, both, also
μάρτυρας n. acc. masc. pl. μάρτυς or μάρτυρ witness, martyr, record
ψευδεῖς adj. acc. masc. pl. ψευδής false, liar
Ὁ art. nom. masc. sg. ὁ ἡ τό the, this, that, he, she, it
ἄνθρωπος n. nom. masc. sg. ἄνθρωπος man, human being, person, one, certain
οὗτος demo. pron. nom. masc. sg. οὗτος αὕτη τοῦτο this, the same, this same, he, she, it
οὐ particle of negation. οὐ οὐκ οὐχ not, no, neither, none, nay, nor, never, nothing
ῥήματα n. acc. neut. pl. ῥῆμα word, saying, thing
βλάσφημα adj. acc. neut. pl. βλάσφημος blasphemous, blasphemer, railing
κατὰ prep. κατά (+gen) against, by, throughout, down, (+acc) according to, after, with
τοῦ art. gen. masc. sg. ὁ ἡ τό the, this, that, he, she, it
τόπου n. gen. masc. sg. τόπος place, room, quarter
τοῦ art. gen. masc. sg. ὁ ἡ τό the, this, that, he, she, it
ἁγίου adj. gen. masc. sg. ἅγιος Holy, holy, saint, Holy One, holy thing, most holy
τούτου demo. pron. gen. masc. sg. οὗτος αὕτη τοῦτο this, the same, this same, he, she, it
καὶ conj. καί and, even, also, but
τοῦ art. gen. masc. sg. ὁ ἡ τό the, this, that, he, she, it
νόμου n. gen. masc. sg. νόμος law, the law
14 γὰρ conj. γάρ for, and, because, but, indeed
αὐτοῦ pron. gen. masc. 3p. sg. αὐτός ή ό self, of oneself, even, very, the same, he, she, it
ὅτι conj. ὅτι that, for, because, how that, how, because that, for that, though
Ἰησοῦς n. nom. masc. sg. Ἰησοῦς Jesus
ὁ art. nom. masc. sg. ὁ ἡ τό the, this, that, he, she, it
Ναζωραῖος n. nom. masc. sg. Ναζωραῖος Nazareth, Nazarene
οὗτος demo. pron. nom. masc. sg. οὗτος αὕτη τοῦτο this, the same, this same, he, she, it

τὸν art. acc. masc. sg. ὁ ἡ τό the, this, that, he, she, it
τόπον n. acc. masc. sg. τόπος place, room, quarter
τοῦτον demo. pron. acc. masc. sg. οὗτος αὕτη τοῦτο this, the same, this same, he, she, it
καὶ conj. καί and, even, also, but
τὰ art. acc. neut. pl. ὁ ἡ τό the, this, that, he, she, it
ἔθη n. acc. neut. pl. ἔθος custom, manner, be wont
ἃ relative pron. acc. neut. pl. ὅς ἥ ὅ who, which, what, that
ἡμῖν pron. dat. 1p. pl. ἐγώ I
Μωϋσῆς n. nom. masc. sg. Μωϋσῆς Moses
15 καὶ conj. καί and, even, also, but
εἰς prep. εἰς (+acc) into, to, unto, for, in, on, toward, against, upon, at, among
αὐτὸν pron. acc. masc. 3p. sg. αὐτός ή ό self, of oneself, even, very, the same, he, she, it
ἅπαντες adj. nom. masc. pl. ἅπας all, whole, all things, every, everyone
οἱ art. nom. masc. pl. ὁ ἡ τό the, this, that, he, she, it
ἐν prep. ἐν (+dat) in, by, with, among, at, on, through, to, within, into, of, for
τῷ art. dat. neut. sg. ὁ ἡ τό the, this, that, he, she, it
συνεδρίῳ n. dat. neut. sg. συνέδριον council
τὸ art. acc. neut. sg. ὁ ἡ τό the, this, that, he, she, it
πρόσωπον n. acc. neut. sg. πρόσωπον face, presence, person, countenance
αὐτοῦ pron. gen. masc. 3p. sg. αὐτός ή ό self, of oneself, even, very, the same, he, she, it
ὡσεὶ adv. ὡσεί about, as, like, as it had been, as it were, like as
πρόσωπον n. acc. neut. sg. πρόσωπον face, presence, person, countenance
ἀγγέλου n. gen. masc. sg. ἄγγελος angel, messenger

7

1 δὲ conj. δέ but, and, now, also, to the contrary, rather, then
ὁ art. nom. masc. sg. ὁ ἡ τό the, this, that, he, she, it
ἀρχιερεύς n. nom. masc. sg. ἀρχιερεύς chief priest, high priest
Εἰ conj. εἰ if, whether, that, though, forasmuch
ἄρα conj. ἄρα then, therefore, haply, wherefore, perhaps, manner, no doubt, truly
ταῦτα demo. pron. nom. neut. pl. οὗτος αὕτη τοῦτο this, the same, this same, he, she, it
οὕτως adv. οὕτω οὕτως so, even so, thus, on this wise, likewise, after this manner
2 ὁ art. nom. masc. sg. ὁ ἡ τό the, this, that, he, she, it
δὲ conj. δέ but, and, now, also, to the contrary, rather, then
Ἄνδρες n. voc. masc. pl. ἀνήρ man, husband, sir
ἀδελφοὶ n. voc. masc. pl. ἀδελφός brother
καὶ conj. καί and, even, also, but
πατέρες n. voc. masc. pl. πατήρ Father, father, parent
ὁ art. nom. masc. sg. ὁ ἡ τό the, this, that, he, she, it
Θεὸς n. nom. masc. sg. θεός God, god
τῆς art. gen. fem. sg. ὁ ἡ τό the, this, that, he, she, it
δόξης n. gen. fem. sg. δόξα glory, honour, praise, dignity, worship
τῷ art. dat. masc. sg. ὁ ἡ τό the, this, that, he, she, it
πατρὶ n. dat. masc. sg. πατήρ Father, father, parent
ἡμῶν pron. gen. 1p. pl. ἐγώ I
Ἀβραὰμ n. dat. masc. sg. Ἀβραάμ Abraham
ἐν prep. ἐν (+dat) in, by, with, among, at, on, through, to, within, into, of, for
τῇ art. dat. fem. sg. ὁ ἡ τό the, this, that, he, she, it
Μεσοποταμίᾳ n. dat. fem. sg. Μεσοποταμία Mesopotamia
πρὶν adv. πρίν before, ere
ἢ particle. ἤ or, than, either, nor, or else, and, rather than
αὐτὸν pron. acc. masc. 3p. sg. αὐτός ή ό self, of oneself, even, very, the same, he, she, it
ἐν prep. ἐν (+dat) in, by, with, among, at, on, through, to, within, into, of, for
Χαρρὰν n. dat. fem. sg. Χαρράν Charran

3 καὶ conj. καί and, even, also, but
πρὸς prep. πρός (+gen) for, (+dat) at, (+acc) unto, to, with, for, against
αὐτόν pron. acc. masc. 3p. sg. αὐτός ή ό self, of oneself, even, very, the same, he, she, it
ἐκ prep. ἐκ ἐξ (+gen) of, from, out of, by, on, with, in, among, through
τῆς art. gen. fem. sg. ὁ ἡ τό the, this, that, he, she, it
γῆς n. gen. fem. sg. γῆ earth, land, ground, country
σου pron. gen. 2p. sg. σύ thou, you
καὶ conj. καί and, even, also, but
ἐκ prep. ἐκ ἐξ (+gen) of, from, out of, by, on, with, in, among, through
τῆς art. gen. fem. sg. ὁ ἡ τό the, this, that, he, she, it
συγγενείας n. gen. fem. sg. συγγένεια kindred
σου pron. gen. 2p. sg. σύ thou, you
καὶ conj. καί and, even, also, but
δεῦρο adv. δεῦρο come, come hither
εἰς prep. εἰς (+acc) into, to, unto, for, in, on, toward, against, upon, at, among
γῆν n. acc. fem. sg. γῆ earth, land, ground, country
ἣν relative pron. acc. fem. sg. ὅς ἥ ὅ who, which, what, that
ἄν particle. ἄν Indicating contingency. No English translation.
σοι pron. dat. 2p. sg. σύ thou, you
4 τότε adv. τότε then, that time
ἐκ prep. ἐκ ἐξ (+gen) of, from, out of, by, on, with, in, among, through
γῆς n. gen. fem. sg. γῆ earth, land, ground, country
Χαλδαίων n. gen. masc. pl. Χαλδαῖος Chaldaean
ἐν prep. ἐν (+dat) in, by, with, among, at, on, through, to, within, into, of, for
Χαρράν n. dat. fem. sg. Χαρράν Charran
κἀκεῖθεν adv. κἀκεῖθεν and from thence, and thence, and afterward, thence also
μετὰ prep. μετά (+gen) with, among, against, (+acc) after
τὸ art. acc. neut. sg. ὁ ἡ τό the, this, that, he, she, it
τὸν art. acc. masc. sg. ὁ ἡ τό the, this, that, he, she, it
πατέρα n. acc. masc. sg. πατήρ Father, father, parent
αὐτοῦ pron. gen. masc. 3p. sg. αὐτός ή ό self, of oneself, even, very, the same, he, she, it
αὐτὸν pron. acc. masc. 3p. sg. αὐτός ή ό self, of oneself, even, very, the same, he, she, it
εἰς prep. εἰς (+acc) into, to, unto, for, in, on, toward, against, upon, at, among
τὴν art. acc. fem. sg. ὁ ἡ τό the, this, that, he, she, it
γῆν n. acc. fem. sg. γῆ earth, land, ground, country
ταύτην demo. pron. acc. fem. sg. οὗτος αὕτη τοῦτο this, the same, this same, he, she, it
εἰς prep. εἰς (+acc) into, to, unto, for, in, on, toward, against, upon, at, among
ἣν relative pron. acc. fem. sg. ὅς ἥ ὅ who, which, what, that
ὑμεῖς pron. nom. 2p. pl. σύ thou, you
νῦν adv. νῦν now, henceforth, present, this time
5 καὶ conj. καί and, even, also, but
οὐκ particle of negation. οὐ οὐκ οὐχ not, no, neither, none, nay, nor, never, nothing
αὐτῷ pron. dat. masc. 3p. sg. αὐτός ή ό self, of oneself, even, very, the same, he, she, it
κληρονομίαν n. acc. fem. sg. κληρονομία inheritance
ἐν prep. ἐν (+dat) in, by, with, among, at, on, through, to, within, into, of, for
αὐτῇ pron. dat. fem. 3p. sg. αὐτός ή ό self, of oneself, even, very, the same, he, she, it
οὐδὲ adv. οὐδέ neither, nor, not, no, not even, never, not yet
βῆμα n. acc. neut. sg. βῆμα judgment seat, throne
ποδὸς n. gen. masc. sg. πούς foot
καὶ conj. καί and, even, also, but
αὐτῷ pron. dat. masc. 3p. sg. αὐτός ή ό self, of oneself, even, very, the same, he, she, it
εἰς prep. εἰς (+acc) into, to, unto, for, in, on, toward, against, upon, at, among
κατάσχεσιν n. acc. fem. sg. κατάσχεσις possession
αὐτὴν pron. acc. fem. 3p. sg. αὐτός ή ό self, of oneself, even, very, the same, he, she, it
καὶ conj. καί and, even, also, but

τῷ art. dat. neut. sg. ὁ ἡ τό the, this, that, he, she, it
σπέρματι n. dat. neut. sg. σπέρμα seed, issue
αὐτοῦ pron. gen. masc. 3p. sg. αὐτός ή ό self, of oneself, even, very, the same, he, she, it
μετ' prep. μετά (+gen) with, among, against, (+acc) after
αὐτόν pron. acc. masc. 3p. sg. αὐτός ή ό self, of oneself, even, very, the same, he, she, it
οὐκ particle of negation. οὐ οὐκ οὐχ not, no, neither, none, nay, nor, never, nothing
αὐτῷ pron. dat. masc. 3p. sg. αὐτός ή ό self, of oneself, even, very, the same, he, she, it
τέκνου n. gen. neut. sg. τέκνον child, son, daughter
6 δὲ conj. δέ but, and, now, also, to the contrary, rather, then
οὕτως adv. οὕτω οὕτως so, even so, thus, on this wise, likewise, after this manner
ὁ art. nom. masc. sg. ὁ ἡ τό the, this, that, he, she, it
Θεὸς n. nom. masc. sg. θεός God, god
ὅτι conj. ὅτι that, for, because, how that, how, because that, for that, though
τὸ art. nom. neut. sg. ὁ ἡ τό the, this, that, he, she, it
σπέρμα n. nom. neut. sg. σπέρμα seed, issue
αὐτοῦ pron. gen. masc. 3p. sg. αὐτός ή ό self, of oneself, even, very, the same, he, she, it
πάροικον adj. nom. neut. sg. πάροικος sojourn, stranger, foreigner
ἐν prep. ἐν (+dat) in, by, with, among, at, on, through, to, within, into, of, for
γῇ n. dat. fem. sg. γῆ earth, land, ground, country
ἀλλοτρίᾳ adj. dat. fem. sg. ἀλλότριος stranger, another man, alien, strange
καὶ conj. καί and, even, also, but
αὐτὸ pron. acc. neut. 3p. sg. αὐτός ή ό self, of oneself, even, very, the same, he, she, it
καὶ conj. καί and, even, also, but
ἔτη n. acc. neut. pl. ἔτος year
τετρακόσια num. acc. neut. pl. τετρακόσιοι four hundred
7 καὶ conj. καί and, even, also, but
τὸ art. acc. neut. sg. ὁ ἡ τό the, this, that, he, she, it
ἔθνος n. acc. neut. sg. ἔθνος Gentile, nation, heathen, people
ᾧ relative pron. dat. neut. sg. ὅς ἥ ὅ who, which, what, that
ἐὰν particle. ἐάν if, soever, except, though, and if, but, whether, if so, so
ἐγώ pron. nom. 1p. sg. ἐγώ I
ὁ art. nom. masc. sg. ὁ ἡ τό the, this, that, he, she, it
Θεὸς n. nom. masc. sg. θεός God, god
καὶ conj. καί and, even, also, but
μετὰ prep. μετά (+gen) with, among, against, (+acc) after
ταῦτα demo. pron. acc. neut. pl. οὗτος αὕτη τοῦτο this, the same, this same, he, she, it
καὶ conj. καί and, even, also, but
μοι pron. dat. 1p. sg. ἐγώ I
ἐν prep. ἐν (+dat) in, by, with, among, at, on, through, to, within, into, of, for
τῷ art. dat. masc. sg. ὁ ἡ τό the, this, that, he, she, it
τόπῳ n. dat. masc. sg. τόπος place, room, quarter
τούτῳ demo. pron. dat. masc. sg. οὗτος αὕτη τοῦτο this, the same, this same, he, she, it
8 καὶ conj. καί and, even, also, but
αὐτῷ pron. dat. masc. 3p. sg. αὐτός ή ό self, of oneself, even, very, the same, he, she, it
διαθήκην n. acc. fem. sg. διαθήκη testament, covenant
περιτομῆς n. gen. fem. sg. περιτομή circumcision
καὶ conj. καί and, even, also, but
οὕτως adv. οὕτω οὕτως so, even so, thus, on this wise, likewise, after this manner
τὸν art. acc. masc. sg. ὁ ἡ τό the, this, that, he, she, it
Ἰσαὰκ n. acc. masc. sg. Ἰσαάκ Isaac
καὶ conj. καί and, even, also, but
αὐτὸν pron. acc. masc. 3p. sg. αὐτός ή ό self, of oneself, even, very, the same, he, she, it
τῇ art. dat. fem. sg. ὁ ἡ τό the, this, that, he, she, it
ἡμέρᾳ n. dat. fem. sg. ἡμέρα day, time, year, while, age, day time
τῇ art. dat. fem. sg. ὁ ἡ τό the, this, that, he, she, it

ὀγδόῃ ordinal. adj. dat. fem. sg. ὄγδοος eighth
καὶ conj. καί and, even, also, but
ὁ art. nom. masc. sg. ὁ ἡ τό the, this, that, he, she, it
Ἰσαὰκ n. nom. masc. sg. Ἰσαάκ Isaac
τὸν art. acc. masc. sg. ὁ ἡ τό the, this, that, he, she, it
Ἰακώβ n. acc. masc. sg. Ἰακώβ Jacob
καὶ conj. καί and, even, also, but
ὁ art. nom. masc. sg. ὁ ἡ τό the, this, that, he, she, it
Ἰακὼβ n. nom. masc. sg. Ἰακώβ Jacob
τοὺς art. acc. masc. pl. ὁ ἡ τό the, this, that, he, she, it
δώδεκα num. acc. masc. pl. δώδεκα twelve
πατριάρχας n. acc. masc. pl. πατριάρχης patriarch
9 καὶ conj. καί and, even, also, but
οἱ art. nom. masc. pl. ὁ ἡ τό the, this, that, he, she, it
πατριάρχαι n. nom. masc. pl. πατριάρχης patriarch
τὸν art. acc. masc. sg. ὁ ἡ τό the, this, that, he, she, it
Ἰωσὴφ n. acc. masc. sg. Ἰωσήφ Joseph
εἰς prep. εἰς (+acc) into, to, unto, for, in, on, toward, against, upon, at, among
Αἴγυπτον n. acc. fem. sg. Αἴγυπτος Egypt
καὶ conj. καί and, even, also, but
ὁ art. nom. masc. sg. ὁ ἡ τό the, this, that, he, she, it
Θεὸς n. nom. masc. sg. θεός God, god
μετ' prep. μετά (+gen) with, among, against, (+acc) after
αὐτοῦ pron. gen. masc. 3p. sg. αὐτός ή ό self, of oneself, even, very, the same, he, she, it
10 καὶ conj. καί and, even, also, but
αὐτὸν pron. acc. masc. 3p. sg. αὐτός ή ό self, of oneself, even, very, the same, he, she, it
ἐκ prep. ἐκ ἐξ (+gen) of, from, out of, by, on, with, in, among, through
πασῶν adj. gen. fem. pl. πᾶς πᾶσα πᾶν all, every, whosoever, every one, no, whole, any
τῶν art. gen. fem. pl. ὁ ἡ τό the, this, that, he, she, it
θλίψεων n. gen. fem. pl. θλῖψις tribulation, affliction, anguish, persecution
αὐτοῦ pron. gen. masc. 3p. sg. αὐτός ή ό self, of oneself, even, very, the same, he, she, it
καὶ conj. καί and, even, also, but
αὐτῷ pron. dat. masc. 3p. sg. αὐτός ή ό self, of oneself, even, very, the same, he, she, it
χάριν n. acc. fem. sg. χάρις grace, thank, favour, pleasure
καὶ conj. καί and, even, also, but
σοφίαν n. acc. fem. sg. σοφία wisdom
ἐναντίον adv. ἐναντίον before, in the sight of
Φαραὼ n. gen. masc. sg. Φαραώ Pharaoh
βασιλέως n. gen. masc. sg. βασιλεύς king
Αἰγύπτου n. gen. fem. sg. Αἴγυπτος Egypt
καὶ conj. καί and, even, also, but
αὐτὸν pron. acc. masc. 3p. sg. αὐτός ή ό self, of oneself, even, very, the same, he, she, it
ἐπ' prep. ἐπί (+gen) on, in, upon, (+dat) in, at, for, upon, (+acc) on, upon, unto, to, against
Αἴγυπτον n. acc. fem. sg. Αἴγυπτος Egypt
καὶ conj. καί and, even, also, but
ὅλον adj. acc. masc. sg. ὅλος all, whole, every whit, altogether
τὸν art. acc. masc. sg. ὁ ἡ τό the, this, that, he, she, it
οἶκον n. acc. masc. sg. οἶκος house, home, household
αὐτοῦ pron. gen. masc. 3p. sg. αὐτός ή ό self, of oneself, even, very, the same, he, she, it
11 δὲ conj. δέ but, and, now, also, to the contrary, rather, then
λιμὸς n. nom. masc. sg. λιμός famine, hunger, dearth
ἐφ' prep. ἐπί (+gen) on, in, upon, (+dat) in, at, for, upon, (+acc) on, upon, unto, to, against
ὅλην adj. acc. fem. sg. ὅλος all, whole, every whit, altogether
τὴν art. acc. fem. sg. ὁ ἡ τό the, this, that, he, she, it
γῆν n. acc. fem. sg. γῆ earth, land, ground, country

Αἰγύπτου n. gen. fem. sg. Αἴγυπτος Egypt
καὶ conj. καί and, even, also, but
Χανάαν n. acc. fem. sg. Χανάαν Chanaan
καὶ conj. καί and, even, also, but
θλῖψις n. nom. fem. sg. θλῖψις tribulation, affliction, anguish, persecution
μεγάλη adj. nom. fem. sg. μέγας great, loud, greatest, high, large, mighty, strong
καὶ conj. καί and, even, also, but
οὐχ particle of negation. οὐ οὐκ οὐχ not, no, neither, none, nay, nor, never, nothing
χορτάσματα n. acc. neut. pl. χόρτασμα sustenance
οἱ art. nom. masc. pl. ὁ ἡ τό the, this, that, he, she, it
πατέρες n. nom. masc. pl. πατήρ Father, father, parent
ἡμῶν pron. gen. 1p. pl. ἐγώ I
12 δὲ conj. δέ but, and, now, also, to the contrary, rather, then
Ἰακὼβ n. nom. masc. sg. Ἰακώβ Jacob
σῖτα n. acc. masc. pl. σῖτος wheat, corn
ἐν prep. ἐν (+dat) in, by, with, among, at, on, through, to, within, into, of, for
Αἰγύπτῳ n. dat. fem. sg. Αἴγυπτος Egypt
τοὺς art. acc. masc. pl. ὁ ἡ τό the, this, that, he, she, it
πατέρας n. acc. masc. pl. πατήρ Father, father, parent
ἡμῶν pron. gen. 1p. pl. ἐγώ I
πρῶτον ordinal. adj. acc. neut. sg. πρῶτος first, chief, first of all, chiefest, best
13 καὶ conj. καί and, even, also, but
ἐν prep. ἐν (+dat) in, by, with, among, at, on, through, to, within, into, of, for
τῷ art. dat. neut. sg. ὁ ἡ τό the, this, that, he, she, it
δευτέρῳ ordinal. adj. dat. neut. sg. δεύτερος second, second time, again, afterward
Ἰωσὴφ n. nom. masc. sg. Ἰωσήφ Joseph
τοῖς art. dat. masc. pl. ὁ ἡ τό the, this, that, he, she, it
ἀδελφοῖς n. dat. masc. pl. ἀδελφός brother
αὐτοῦ pron. gen. masc. 3p. sg. αὐτός ή ό self, of oneself, even, very, the same, he, she, it
καὶ conj. καί and, even, also, but
φανερὸν adj. nom. neut. sg. φανερός manifest, abroad, open, known, outward, appear
τῷ art. dat. masc. sg. ὁ ἡ τό the, this, that, he, she, it
Φαραὼ n. dat. masc. sg. Φαραώ Pharaoh
τὸ art. nom. neut. sg. ὁ ἡ τό the, this, that, he, she, it
γένος n. nom. neut. sg. γένος kind, kindred, offspring, nation, countrymen
τοῦ art. gen. masc. sg. ὁ ἡ τό the, this, that, he, she, it
Ιωσήφ n. gen. masc. sg. Ἰωσήφ Joseph
14 δὲ conj. δέ but, and, now, also, to the contrary, rather, then
Ἰωσὴφ n. nom. masc. sg. Ἰωσήφ Joseph
τὸν art. acc. masc. sg. ὁ ἡ τό the, this, that, he, she, it
πατέρα n. acc. masc. sg. πατήρ Father, father, parent
αὐτοῦ pron. gen. masc. 3p. sg. αὐτός ή ό self, of oneself, even, very, the same, he, she, it
Ἰακὼβ n. acc. masc. sg. Ἰακώβ Jacob
καὶ conj. καί and, even, also, but
πᾶσαν adj. acc. fem. sg. πᾶς πᾶςα πᾶν all, every, whosoever, every one, no, whole, any
τὴν art. acc. fem. sg. ὁ ἡ τό the, this, that, he, she, it
συγγένειαν n. acc. fem. sg. συγγένεια kindred
αὐτοῦ pron. gen. masc. 3p. sg. αὐτός ή ό self, of oneself, even, very, the same, he, she, it
ἐν prep. ἐν (+dat) in, by, with, among, at, on, through, to, within, into, of, for
ψυχαῖς n. dat. fem. pl. ψυχή life, soul, mind, heart
ἑβδομήκοντα num. dat. fem. pl. ἑβδομήκοντα seventy, threescore and ten
πέντε num. dat. fem. pl. πέντε five
15 δὲ conj. δέ but, and, now, also, to the contrary, rather, then
Ἰακὼβ n. nom. masc. sg. Ἰακώβ Jacob
εἰς prep. εἰς (+acc) into, to, unto, for, in, on, toward, against, upon, at, among

Αἴγυπτον n. acc. fem. sg. Αἴγυπτος Egypt
καὶ conj. καί and, even, also, but
αὐτὸς pron. nom. masc. 3p. sg. αὐτός ή ό self, of oneself, even, very, the same, he, she, it
καὶ conj. καί and, even, also, but
οἱ art. nom. masc. pl. ὁ ἡ τό the, this, that, he, she, it
πατέρες n. nom. masc. pl. πατήρ Father, father, parent
ἡμῶν pron. gen. 1p. pl. ἐγώ I
16 καὶ conj. καί and, even, also, but
εἰς prep. εἰς (+acc) into, to, unto, for, in, on, toward, against, upon, at, among
Σιχέμ n. acc. fem. sg. Σιχέμ Sychem
καί and, even, also, but
ἐν prep. ἐν (+dat) in, by, with, among, at, on, through, to, within, into, of, for
τῷ art. dat. neut. sg. ὁ ἡ τό the, this, that, he, she, it
μνήματι n. dat. neut. sg. μνῆμα sepulchre, tomb, grave
ὃ relative pron. acc. neut. sg. ὅς ἥ ὅ who, which, what, that
Ἀβραὰμ n. nom. masc. sg. Ἀβραάμ Abraham
τιμῆς n. gen. fem. sg. τιμή honour, price, preciousness, sum
ἀργυρίου n. gen. neut. sg. ἀργύριον money, piece of silver, silver
παρὰ prep. παρά (+gen) of, from, (+dat) with, for, (+acc) beside, at, by, above, against
τῶν art. gen. masc. pl. ὁ ἡ τό the, this, that, he, she, it
υἱῶν n. gen. masc. pl. υἱός son, child, descendant, offspring, heir
Ἐμὸρ n. gen. masc. sg. Ἐμόρ Emmor
τοῦ art. gen. neut. sg. ὁ ἡ τό the, this, that, he, she, it
Σιχέμ n. dat. fem. sg. Σιχέμ Sychem
17 καθὼς adv. καθώς as, even as, according as, according to
δὲ conj. δέ but, and, now, also, to the contrary, rather, then
ὁ art. nom. masc. sg. ὁ ἡ τό the, this, that, he, she, it
χρόνος n. nom. masc. sg. χρόνος time, season, space
τῆς art. gen. fem. sg. ὁ ἡ τό the, this, that, he, she, it
ἐπαγγελίας n. gen. fem. sg. ἐπαγγελία promise, message
ἧς relative pron. gen. fem. sg. ὅς ἥ ὅ who, which, what, that
ὁ art. nom. masc. sg. ὁ ἡ τό the, this, that, he, she, it
Θεὸς n. nom. masc. sg. θεός God, god
τῷ art. dat. masc. sg. ὁ ἡ τό the, this, that, he, she, it
Ἀβραάμ n. dat. masc. sg. Ἀβραάμ Abraham
ὁ art. nom. masc. sg. ὁ ἡ τό the, this, that, he, she, it
λαὸς n. nom. masc. sg. λαός people
καὶ conj. καί and, even, also, but
ἐν prep. ἐν (+dat) in, by, with, among, at, on, through, to, within, into, of, for
Αἰγύπτῳ n. dat. fem. sg. Αἴγυπτος Egypt
18 ἄχρις prep. ἄχρι or ἄχρις (+gen) until, unto, till, even to, as far as, while, into
οὗ relative pron. gen. masc. sg. ὅς ἥ ὅ who, which, what, that
βασιλεὺς n. nom. masc. sg. βασιλεύς king
ἕτερος adj. nom. masc. sg. ἕτερος another, other, else, strange
ὃς relative pron. nom. masc. sg. ὅς ἥ ὅ who, which, what, that
οὐκ particle of negation. οὐ οὐκ οὐχ not, no, neither, none, nay, nor, never, nothing
τὸν art. acc. masc. sg. ὁ ἡ τό the, this, that, he, she, it
Ἰωσήφ n. acc. masc. sg. Ἰωσήφ Joseph
19 οὗτος demo. pron. nom. masc. sg. οὗτος αὕτη τοῦτο this, the same, this same, he, she, it
τὸ art. acc. neut. sg. ὁ ἡ τό the, this, that, he, she, it
γένος n. acc. neut. sg. γένος kind, kindred, offspring, nation, countrymen
ἡμῶν pron. gen. 1p. pl. ἐγώ I
τοὺς art. acc. masc. pl. ὁ ἡ τό the, this, that, he, she, it
πατέρας n. acc. masc. pl. πατήρ Father, father, parent
ἡμῶν pron. gen. 1p. pl. ἐγώ I

τοῦ art. gen. neut. sg. ὁ ἡ τό the, this, that, he, she, it
ἔκθετα adj. acc. neut. pl. ἔκθετος cast out, exposed, abandoned
τὰ art. acc. neut. pl. ὁ ἡ τό the, this, that, he, she, it
βρέφη n. acc. neut. pl. βρέφος babe, child, infant, young child
αὐτῶν pron. gen. masc. 3p. pl. αὐτός ή ό self, of oneself, even, very, the same, he, she, it
εἰς prep. εἰς (+acc) into, to, unto, for, in, on, toward, against, upon, at, among
τὸ art. acc. neut. sg. ὁ ἡ τό the, this, that, he, she, it
μὴ particle of negation. μή not, no, lest, neither, none, nothing, nor, never, without
20 ἐν prep. ἐν (+dat) in, by, with, among, at, on, through, to, within, into, of, for
ᾧ relative pron. dat. masc. sg. ὅς ἥ ὅ who, which, what, that
καιρῷ n. dat. masc. sg. καιρός time, season, due time, opportunity
Μωσῆς n. nom. masc. sg. Μωσῆς Moses
καὶ conj. καί and, even, also, but
ἀστεῖος adj. nom. masc. sg. ἀστεῖος fair, proper
τῷ art. dat. masc. sg. ὁ ἡ τό the, this, that, he, she, it
Θεῷ n. dat. masc. sg. θεός God, god
ὃς relative pron. nom. masc. sg. ὅς ἥ ὅ who, which, what, that
μῆνας n. acc. masc. pl. μήν month
τρεῖς num. acc. masc. pl. τρεῖς three
ἐν prep. ἐν (+dat) in, by, with, among, at, on, through, to, within, into, of, for
τῷ art. dat. masc. sg. ὁ ἡ τό the, this, that, he, she, it
οἴκῳ n. dat. masc. sg. οἶκος house, home, household
τοῦ art. gen. masc. sg. ὁ ἡ τό the, this, that, he, she, it
πατρός n. gen. masc. sg. πατήρ Father, father, parent
αὐτοῦ pron. gen. masc. 3p. sg. αὐτός ή ό self, of oneself, even, very, the same, he, she, it
21 δὲ conj. δέ but, and, now, also, to the contrary, rather, then
αὐτὸν pron. acc. masc. 3p. sg. αὐτός ή ό self, of oneself, even, very, the same, he, she, it
αὐτὸν pron. acc. masc. 3p. sg. αὐτός ή ό self, of oneself, even, very, the same, he, she, it
ἡ art. nom. fem. sg. ὁ ἡ τό the, this, that, he, she, it
θυγάτηρ n. nom. fem. sg. θυγάτηρ daughter
Φαραὼ n. gen. masc. sg. Φαραώ Pharaoh
καὶ conj. καί and, even, also, but
αὐτὸν pron. acc. masc. 3p. sg. αὐτός ή ό self, of oneself, even, very, the same, he, she, it
ἑαυτῇ reflexive pron. dat. fem. 3p. sg. ἑαυτοῦ himself, herself, itself, yourself, ourselves
εἰς prep. εἰς (+acc) into, to, unto, for, in, on, toward, against, upon, at, among
υἱόν n. acc. masc. sg. υἱός son, child, descendant, offspring, heir
22 καὶ conj. καί and, even, also, but
Μωσῆς n. nom. masc. sg. Μωσῆς Moses
πάσῃ adj. dat. fem. sg. πᾶς πᾶσα πᾶν all, every, whosoever, every one, no, whole, any
σοφίᾳ n. dat. fem. sg. σοφία wisdom
Αἰγυπτίων adj. gen. masc. pl. Αἰγύπτιος Egyptian
δὲ conj. δέ but, and, now, also, to the contrary, rather, then
δυνατὸς adj. nom. masc. sg. δυνατός able, possible, mighty, strong
ἐν prep. ἐν (+dat) in, by, with, among, at, on, through, to, within, into, of, for
λόγοις n. dat. masc. pl. λόγος word, saying, account, speech, thing, matter
καὶ conj. καί and, even, also, but
ἐν prep. ἐν (+dat) in, by, with, among, at, on, through, to, within, into, of, for
ἔργοις n. dat. neut. pl. ἔργον work, deed, doing labour
23 ὡς adv. ὡς as, when, as it were, how, about, like, as soon as, even as, while
δὲ conj. δέ but, and, now, also, to the contrary, rather, then
αὐτῷ pron. dat. masc. 3p. sg. αὐτός ή ό self, of oneself, even, very, the same, he, she, it
τεσσαρακονταετὴς adj. nom. masc. sg. τεσσαρακονταετής of forty years
χρόνος n. nom. masc. sg. χρόνος time, season, space
ἐπὶ prep. ἐπί (+gen) on, in, upon, (+dat) in, at, for, upon, (+acc) on, upon, unto, to, against
τὴν art. acc. fem. sg. ὁ ἡ τό the, this, that, he, she, it

καρδίαν n. acc. fem. sg. καρδία heart
αὐτοῦ pron. gen. masc. 3p. sg. αὐτός ή ό self, of oneself, even, very, the same, he, she, it
τοὺς art. acc. masc. pl. ὁ ἡ τό the, this, that, he, she, it
ἀδελφοὺς n. acc. masc. pl. ἀδελφός brother
αὐτοῦ pron. gen. masc. 3p. sg. αὐτός ή ό self, of oneself, even, very, the same, he, she, it
τοὺς art. acc. masc. pl. ὁ ἡ τό the, this, that, he, she, it
υἱοὺς n. acc. masc. pl. υἱός son, child, descendant, offspring, heir
Ἰσραήλ pron. name. masc. inde. Ἰσραήλ Israel
24 καὶ conj. καί and, even, also, but
τινα indefinite pron. acc. masc. sg. τὶς certain, some, any man, one, any thing
καὶ conj. καί and, even, also, but
ἐκδίκησιν n. acc. fem. sg. ἐκδίκησις vengeance, punishment, revenge
τῷ art. dat. masc. sg. ὁ ἡ τό the, this, that, he, she, it
τὸν art. acc. masc. sg. ὁ ἡ τό the, this, that, he, she, it
Αἰγύπτιον adj. acc. masc. sg. Αἰγύπτιος Egyptian
25 δὲ conj. δέ but, and, now, also, to the contrary, rather, then
τοὺς art. acc. masc. pl. ὁ ἡ τό the, this, that, he, she, it
ἀδελφοὺς n. acc. masc. pl. ἀδελφός brother
αὐτοῦ pron. gen. masc. 3p. sg. αὐτός ή ό self, of oneself, even, very, the same, he, she, it
ὅτι conj. ὅτι that, for, because, how that, how, because that, for that, though
ὁ art. nom. masc. sg. ὁ ἡ τό the, this, that, he, she, it
Θεὸς n. nom. masc. sg. θεός God, god
διὰ prep. διά (+gen) by, through, with, in, of, (+acc) for, because of, for a cause
χειρὸς n. gen. fem. sg. χείρ hand
αὐτοῦ pron. gen. masc. 3p. sg. αὐτός ή ό self, of oneself, even, very, the same, he, she, it
αὐτοῖς pron. dat. masc. 3p. pl. αὐτός ή ό self, of oneself, even, very, the same, he, she, it
σωτηρίαν n. acc. fem. sg. σωτηρία salvation, deliver, health, saving
οἱ art. nom. masc. pl. ὁ ἡ τό the, this, that, he, she, it
δὲ conj. δέ but, and, now, also, to the contrary, rather, then
οὐ particle of negation. οὐ οὐκ οὐχ not, no, neither, none, nay, nor, never, nothing
26 τῇ art. dat. fem. sg. ὁ ἡ τό the, this, that, he, she, it
δὲ conj. δέ but, and, now, also, to the contrary, rather, then
ἡμέρᾳ n. dat. fem. sg. ἡμέρα day, time, year, while, age, day time
αὐτοῖς pron. dat. masc. 3p. pl. αὐτός ή ό self, of oneself, even, very, the same, he, she, it
καὶ conj. καί and, even, also, but
αὐτοὺς pron. acc. masc. 3p. pl. αὐτός ή ό self, of oneself, even, very, the same, he, she, it
εἰς prep. εἰς (+acc) into, to, unto, for, in, on, toward, against, upon, at, among
εἰρήνην n. acc. fem. sg. εἰρήνη peace, quietness, rest
Ἄνδρες n. voc. masc. pl. ἀνήρ man, husband, sir
ἀδελφοί n. nom. masc. pl. ἀδελφός brother
ὑμεῖς pron. nom. 2p. pl. σύ thou, you
ἱνατί adv. ἱνατί or ἵνα τί why, wherefore
ἀλλήλους pron. acc. masc. 2p. pl. ἀλλήλων one another, themselves, together, mutual
27 ὁ art. nom. masc. sg. ὁ ἡ τό the, this, that, he, she, it
δὲ conj. δέ but, and, now, also, to the contrary, rather, then
τὸν art. acc. masc. sg. ὁ ἡ τό the, this, that, he, she, it
πλησίον adv. πλησίον neighbour, near
αὐτὸν pron. acc. masc. 3p. sg. αὐτός ή ό self, of oneself, even, very, the same, he, she, it
Τίς interrog. pron. nom. masc. sg. τίς what, who, why, where, which, how
σε pron. acc. 2p. sg. σύ thou, you
ἄρχοντα n. acc. masc. sg. ἄρχων ruler, prince, chief, magistrate, chief ruler
καὶ conj. καί and, even, also, but
δικαστὴν n. acc. masc. sg. δικαστής judge
ἐφ' prep. ἐπί (+gen) on, in, upon, (+dat) in, at, for, upon, (+acc) on, upon, unto, to, against
ἡμᾶς pron. acc. 1p. pl. ἐγώ I

28 μὴ particle of negation. μή not, no, lest, neither, none, nothing, nor, never, without
μϵ pron. acc. 1p. sg. ἐγώ I
σὺ pron. nom. 2p. sg. σύ thou, you
ὃν relative pron. acc. masc. sg. ὅς ἥ ὅ who, which, what, that
τρόπον n. acc. masc. sg. τρόπος as, manner, means, way, conversation
χθὲς adv. χθές yesterday
τὸν art. acc. masc. sg. ὁ ἡ τό the, this, that, he, she, it
Αἰγύπτιον adj. acc. masc. sg. Αἰγύπτιος Egyptian
29 δὲ conj. δέ but, and, now, also, to the contrary, rather, then
Μωσῆς n. nom. masc. sg. Μωσῆς Moses
ἐν prep. ἐν (+dat) in, by, with, among, at, on, through, to, within, into, of, for
τῷ art. dat. masc. sg. ὁ ἡ τό the, this, that, he, she, it
λόγῳ n. dat. masc. sg. λόγος word, saying, account, speech, thing, matter
τούτῳ demo. pron. dat. masc. sg. οὗτος αὕτη τοῦτο this, the same, this same, he, she, it
καὶ conj. καί and, even, also, but
πάροικος adj. nom. masc. sg. πάροικος sojourn, stranger, foreigner
ἐν prep. ἐν (+dat) in, by, with, among, at, on, through, to, within, into, of, for
γῇ n. dat. fem. sg. γῆ earth, land, ground, country
Μαδιάμ n. gen. masc. sg. Μαδιάμ Madian
οὗ adv. οὗ where, whither, wherein
υἱοὺς n. acc. masc. pl. υἱός son, child, descendant, offspring, heir
δύο num. acc. masc. pl. δύο two, twain, both
30 καὶ conj. καί and, even, also, but
ἐτῶν n. gen. neut. pl. ἔτος year
τεσσαράκοντα num. gen. neut. pl. τεσσαράκοντα forty
αὐτῷ pron. dat. masc. 3p. sg. αὐτός ή ό self, of oneself, even, very, the same, he, she, it
ἐν prep. ἐν (+dat) in, by, with, among, at, on, through, to, within, into, of, for
τῇ art. dat. fem. sg. ὁ ἡ τό the, this, that, he, she, it
ἐρήμῳ adj. dat. fem. sg. ἔρημος wilderness, desert
τοῦ art. gen. neut. sg. ὁ ἡ τό the, this, that, he, she, it
ὄρους n. gen. neut. sg. ὄρος mountain, mount, hill
Σινᾶ n. gen. neut. sg. Σινᾶ Sina, Sinai
ἄγγελος n. nom. masc. sg. ἄγγελος angel, messenger
Κυρίου n. gen. masc. sg. κύριος Lord, lord, master, sir, LORD, God, Master, owner
ἐν prep. ἐν (+dat) in, by, with, among, at, on, through, to, within, into, of, for
φλογὶ n. dat. fem. sg. φλόξ flame, flaming
πυρὸς n. gen. neut. sg. πῦρ fire, fiery
βάτου n. gen. fem. sg. βάτος bush, bramble bush
31 ὁ art. nom. masc. sg. ὁ ἡ τό the, this, that, he, she, it
δὲ conj. δέ but, and, now, also, to the contrary, rather, then
Μωσῆς n. nom. masc. sg. Μωσῆς Moses
τὸ art. acc. neut. sg. ὁ ἡ τό the, this, that, he, she, it
ὅραμα n. acc. neut. sg. ὅραμα vision, sight
δὲ conj. δέ but, and, now, also, to the contrary, rather, then
αὐτοῦ pron. gen. masc. 3p. sg. αὐτός ή ό self, of oneself, even, very, the same, he, she, it
φωνὴ n. nom. fem. sg. φωνή voice, sound, noise
Κυρίου n. gen. masc. sg. κύριος Lord, lord, master, sir, LORD, God, Master, owner
πρὸς prep. πρός (+gen) for, (+dat) at, (+acc) unto, to, with, for, against
αὐτόν pron. acc. masc. 3p. sg. αὐτός ή ό self, of oneself, even, very, the same, he, she, it
32 Ἐγὼ pron. nom. 1p. sg. ἐγώ I
ὁ art. nom. masc. sg. ὁ ἡ τό the, this, that, he, she, it
Θεὸς n. nom. masc. sg. θεός God, god
τῶν art. gen. masc. pl. ὁ ἡ τό the, this, that, he, she, it
πατέρων n. gen. masc. pl. πατήρ Father, father, parent
σου pron. gen. 2p. sg. σύ thou, you

ὁ art. nom. masc. sg. ὁ ἡ τό the, this, that, he, she, it
Θεὸς n. nom. masc. sg. θεός God, god
Ἀβραὰμ n. gen. masc. sg. Ἀβραάμ Abraham
καὶ conj. καί and, even, also, but
ὁ art. nom. masc. sg. ὁ ἡ τό the, this, that, he, she, it
Θεὸς n. nom. masc. sg. θεός God, god
Ἰσαὰκ n. gen. masc. sg. Ἰσαάκ Isaac
καὶ conj. καί and, even, also, but
ὁ art. nom. masc. sg. ὁ ἡ τό the, this, that, he, she, it
Θεὸς n. nom. masc. sg. θεός God, god
Ἰακώβ n. gen. masc. sg. Ἰακώβ Jacob
ἔντρομος adj. nom. masc. sg. ἔντρομος trembling, quaking
δὲ conj. δέ but, and, now, also, to the contrary, rather, then
Μωσῆς n. nom. masc. sg. Μωσῆς Moses
οὐκ particle of negation. οὐ οὐκ οὐχ not, no, neither, none, nay, nor, never, nothing
33 δὲ conj. δέ but, and, now, also, to the contrary, rather, then
αὐτῷ pron. dat. masc. 3p. sg. αὐτός ή ὁ self, of oneself, even, very, the same, he, she, it
ὁ art. nom. masc. sg. ὁ ἡ τό the, this, that, he, she, it
Κύριος n. nom. masc. sg. κύριος Lord, lord, master, sir, LORD, God, Master, owner
τὸ art. acc. neut. sg. ὁ ἡ τό the, this, that, he, she, it
ὑπόδημα n. acc. neut. sg. ὑπόδημα shoe
τῶν art. gen. masc. pl. ὁ ἡ τό the, this, that, he, she, it
ποδῶν n. gen. masc. pl. πούς foot
σου pron. gen. 2p. sg. σύ thou, you
ὁ art. nom. masc. sg. ὁ ἡ τό the, this, that, he, she, it
γὰρ conj. γάρ for, and, because, but, indeed
τόπος n. nom. masc. sg. τόπος place, room, quarter
ἐν prep. ἐν (+dat) in, by, with, among, at, on, through, to, within, into, of, for
ᾧ relative pron. dat. masc. sg. ὅς ἥ ὅ who, which, what, that
γῆ n. nom. fem. sg. γῆ earth, land, ground, country
ἁγία adj. nom. fem. sg. ἅγιος Holy, holy, saint, Holy One, holy thing, most holy
34 τὴν art. acc. fem. sg. ὁ ἡ τό the, this, that, he, she, it
κάκωσιν n. acc. fem. sg. κάκωσις affliction
τοῦ art. gen. masc. sg. ὁ ἡ τό the, this, that, he, she, it
λαοῦ n. gen. masc. sg. λαός people
μου pron. gen. 1p. sg. ἐγώ I
τοῦ art. gen. masc. sg. ὁ ἡ τό the, this, that, he, she, it
ἐν prep. ἐν (+dat) in, by, with, among, at, on, through, to, within, into, of, for
Αἰγύπτῳ n. dat. fem. sg. Αἴγυπτος Egypt
καὶ conj. καί and, even, also, but
τοῦ art. gen. masc. sg. ὁ ἡ τό the, this, that, he, she, it
στεναγμοῦ n. gen. masc. sg. στεναγμός groaning
αὐτῶν pron. gen. masc. 3p. pl. αὐτός ή ὁ self, of oneself, even, very, the same, he, she, it
καὶ conj. καί and, even, also, but
αὐτούς pron. acc. masc. 3p. pl. αὐτός ή ὁ self, of oneself, even, very, the same, he, she, it
καὶ conj. καί and, even, also, but
νῦν adv. νῦν now, henceforth, present, this time
δεῦρο adv. δεῦρο come, come hither
σε pron. acc. 2p. sg. σύ thou, you
εἰς prep. εἰς (+acc) into, to, unto, for, in, on, toward, against, upon, at, among
Αἴγυπτον n. acc. fem. sg. Αἴγυπτος Egypt
35 τοῦτον demo. pron. acc. masc. sg. οὗτος αὕτη τοῦτο this, the same, this same, he, she, it
τὸν art. acc. masc. sg. ὁ ἡ τό the, this, that, he, she, it
Μωϋσῆν n. acc. masc. sg. Μωϋσῆς Moses
ὃν relative pron. acc. masc. sg. ὅς ἥ ὅ who, which, what, that

Τίς interrog. pron. nom. masc. sg. τίς what, who, why, where, which, how
σε pron. acc. 2p. sg. σύ thou, you
ἄρχοντα n. acc. masc. sg. ἄρχων ruler, prince, chief, magistrate, chief ruler
καὶ conj. καί and, even, also, but
δικαστήν n. acc. masc. sg. δικαστής judge
τοῦτον demo. pron. acc. masc. sg. οὗτος αὕτη τοῦτο this, the same, this same, he, she, it
ὁ art. nom. masc. sg. ὁ ἡ τό the, this, that, he, she, it
Θεὸς n. nom. masc. sg. θεός God, god
ἄρχοντα n. acc. masc. sg. ἄρχων ruler, prince, chief, magistrate, chief ruler
καὶ conj. καί and, even, also, but
λυτρωτὴν n. acc. masc. sg. λυτρωτής deliverer
ἐν prep. ἐν (+dat) in, by, with, among, at, on, through, to, within, into, of, for
χειρὶ n. dat. fem. sg. χείρ hand
ἀγγέλου n. gen. masc. sg. ἄγγελος angel, messenger
τοῦ art. gen. masc. sg. ὁ ἡ τό the, this, that, he, she, it
αὐτῷ pron. dat. masc. 3p. sg. αὐτός ἡ ὁ self, of oneself, even, very, the same, he, she, it
ἐν prep. ἐν (+dat) in, by, with, among, at, on, through, to, within, into, of, for
τῇ art. dat. fem. sg. ὁ ἡ τό the, this, that, he, she, it
βάτῳ n. dat. fem. sg. βάτος bush, bramble bush
36 οὗτος demo. pron. nom. masc. sg. οὗτος αὕτη τοῦτο this, the same, this same, he, she, it
αὐτοὺς pron. acc. masc. 3p. pl. αὐτός ἡ ὁ self, of oneself, even, very, the same, he, she, it
τέρατα n. acc. neut. pl. τέρας wonder
καὶ conj. καί and, even, also, but
σημεῖα n. acc. neut. pl. σημεῖον sign, miracle, wonder, token
ἐν prep. ἐν (+dat) in, by, with, among, at, on, through, to, within, into, of, for
γῇ n. dat. fem. sg. γῆ earth, land, ground, country
Αἰγύπτου n. gen. fem. sg. Αἴγυπτος Egypt
καὶ conj. καί and, even, also, but
ἐν prep. ἐν (+dat) in, by, with, among, at, on, through, to, within, into, of, for
Ἐρυθρᾷ adj. dat. fem. sg. ἐρυθρός Red
θαλάσσῃ n. dat. fem. sg. θάλασσα sea
καὶ conj. καί and, even, also, but
ἐν prep. ἐν (+dat) in, by, with, among, at, on, through, to, within, into, of, for
τῇ art. dat. fem. sg. ὁ ἡ τό the, this, that, he, she, it
ἐρήμῳ adj. dat. fem. sg. ἔρημος wilderness, desert
ἔτη n. acc. neut. pl. ἔτος year
τεσσαράκοντα num. acc. neut. pl. τεσσαράκοντα forty
37 οὗτός demo. pron. nom. masc. sg. οὗτος αὕτη τοῦτο this, the same, this same, he, she, it
ὁ art. nom. masc. sg. ὁ ἡ τό the, this, that, he, she, it
Μωϋσῆς n. nom. masc. sg. Μωϋσῆς Moses
ὁ art. nom. masc. sg. ὁ ἡ τό the, this, that, he, she, it
τοῖς art. dat. masc. pl. ὁ ἡ τό the, this, that, he, she, it
υἱοῖς n. dat. masc. pl. υἱός son, child, descendant, offspring, heir
Ἰσραήλ pron. name. masc. inde. Ἰσραήλ Israel
Προφήτην n. acc. masc. sg. προφήτης prophet
ὑμῖν pron. dat. 2p. pl. σύ thou, you
Κύριος n. nom. masc. sg. κύριος Lord, lord, master, sir, LORD, God, Master, owner
ὁ art. nom. masc. sg. ὁ ἡ τό the, this, that, he, she, it
Θεὸς n. nom. masc. sg. θεός God, god
ὑμῶν pron. gen. 2p. pl. σύ thou, you
ἐκ prep. ἐκ ἐξ (+gen) of, from, out of, by, on, with, in, among, through
τῶν art. gen. masc. pl. ὁ ἡ τό the, this, that, he, she, it
ἀδελφῶν n. gen. masc. pl. ἀδελφός brother
ὑμῶν pron. gen. 2p. pl. σύ thou, you
ὡς adv. ὡς as, when, as it were, how, about, like, as soon as, even as, while

ἐμέ pron. acc. 1p. sg. ἐγώ I
αὐτοῦ pron. gen. masc. 3p. sg. αὐτός ή ό self, of oneself, even, very, the same, he, she, it
38 οὗτός demo. pron. nom. masc. sg. οὗτος αὕτη τοῦτο this, the same, this same, he, she, it
ὁ art. nom. masc. sg. ὁ ἡ τό the, this, that, he, she, it
ἐν prep. ἐν (+dat) in, by, with, among, at, on, through, to, within, into, of, for
τῇ art. dat. fem. sg. ὁ ἡ τό the, this, that, he, she, it
ἐκκλησίᾳ n. dat. fem. sg. ἐκκλησία church, assembly
ἐν prep. ἐν (+dat) in, by, with, among, at, on, through, to, within, into, of, for
τῇ art. dat. fem. sg. ὁ ἡ τό the, this, that, he, she, it
ἐρήμῳ adj. dat. fem. sg. ἔρημος wilderness, desert
μετὰ prep. μετά (+gen) with, among, against, (+acc) after
τοῦ art. gen. masc. sg. ὁ ἡ τό the, this, that, he, she, it
ἀγγέλου n. gen. masc. sg. ἄγγελος angel, messenger
τοῦ art. gen. masc. sg. ὁ ἡ τό the, this, that, he, she, it
αὐτῷ pron. dat. masc. 3p. sg. αὐτός ή ό self, of oneself, even, very, the same, he, she, it
ἐν prep. ἐν (+dat) in, by, with, among, at, on, through, to, within, into, of, for
τῷ art. dat. neut. sg. ὁ ἡ τό the, this, that, he, she, it
ὄρει n. dat. neut. sg. ὄρος mountain, mount, hill
Σινᾶ n. dat. neut. sg. Σινᾶ Sina, Sinai
καὶ conj. καί and, even, also, but
τῶν art. gen. masc. pl. ὁ ἡ τό the, this, that, he, she, it
πατέρων n. gen. masc. pl. πατήρ Father, father, parent
ἡμῶν pron. gen. 1p. pl. ἐγώ I
ὃς relative pron. nom. masc. sg. ὅς ἥ ὅ who, which, what, that
λόγια n. acc. neut. pl. λόγιον oracle
ἡμῖν pron. dat. 1p. pl. ἐγώ I
39 ᾧ relative pron. dat. masc. sg. ὅς ἥ ὅ who, which, what, that
οὐκ particle of negation. οὐ οὐκ οὐχ not, no, neither, none, nay, nor, never, nothing
ὑπήκοοι adj. nom. masc. pl. ὑπήκοος obedient
οἱ art. nom. masc. pl. ὁ ἡ τό the, this, that, he, she, it
πατέρες n. nom. masc. pl. πατήρ Father, father, parent
ἡμῶν pron. gen. 1p. pl. ἐγώ I
ἀλλ' conj. ἀλλά but, yea, yet, nevertheless, howbeit, nay, therefore
καὶ conj. καί and, even, also, but
ταῖς art. dat. fem. pl. ὁ ἡ τό the, this, that, he, she, it
καρδίαις n. dat. fem. pl. καρδία heart
αὐτῶν pron. gen. masc. 3p. pl. αὐτός ή ό self, of oneself, even, very, the same, he, she, it
εἰς prep. εἰς (+acc) into, to, unto, for, in, on, toward, against, upon, at, among
Αἴγυπτον n. acc. fem. sg. Αἴγυπτος Egypt
40 τῷ art. dat. masc. sg. ὁ ἡ τό the, this, that, he, she, it
Ἀαρών n. dat. masc. sg. Ἀαρών Aaron
ἡμῖν pron. dat. 1p. pl. ἐγώ I
θεοὺς n. acc. masc. pl. θεός God, god
οἳ relative pron. nom. masc. pl. ὅς ἥ ὅ who, which, what, that
ἡμῶν pron. gen. 1p. pl. ἐγώ I
ὁ art. nom. masc. sg. ὁ ἡ τό the, this, that, he, she, it
γὰρ conj. γάρ for, and, because, but, indeed
Μωσῆς n. nom. masc. sg. Μωσῆς Moses
οὗτος demo. pron. nom. masc. sg. οὗτος αὕτη τοῦτο this, the same, this same, he, she, it
ὃς relative pron. nom. masc. sg. ὅς ἥ ὅ who, which, what, that
ἡμᾶς pron. acc. 1p. pl. ἐγώ I
ἐκ prep. ἐκ ἐξ (+gen) of, from, out of, by, on, with, in, among, through
γῆς n. gen. fem. sg. γῆ earth, land, ground, country
Αἰγύπτου n. gen. fem. sg. Αἴγυπτος Egypt
οὐκ particle of negation. οὐ οὐκ οὐχ not, no, neither, none, nay, nor, never, nothing

τί interrog. pron. nom. neut. sg. τίς what, who, why, where, which, how
αὐτῷ pron. dat. masc. 3p. sg. αὐτός ἡ ὁ self, of oneself, even, very, the same, he, she, it
41 καὶ conj. καί and, even, also, but
ἐν prep. ἐν (+dat) in, by, with, among, at, on, through, to, within, into, of, for
ταῖς art. dat. fem. pl. ὁ ἡ τό the, this, that, he, she, it
ἡμέραις n. dat. fem. pl. ἡμέρα day, time, year, while, age, day time
ἐκείναις demo. pron. dat. fem. pl. ἐκεῖνος that, he, the same, that same
καὶ conj. καί and, even, also, but
θυσίαν n. acc. fem. sg. θυσία sacrifice
τῷ art. dat. neut. sg. ὁ ἡ τό the, this, that, he, she, it
εἰδώλῳ n. dat. neut. sg. εἴδωλον idol
καὶ conj. καί and, even, also, but
ἐν prep. ἐν (+dat) in, by, with, among, at, on, through, to, within, into, of, for
τοῖς art. dat. neut. pl. ὁ ἡ τό the, this, that, he, she, it
ἔργοις n. dat. neut. pl. ἔργον work, deed, doing labour
τῶν art. gen. fem. pl. ὁ ἡ τό the, this, that, he, she, it
χειρῶν n. gen. fem. pl. χείρ hand
αὐτῶν pron. gen. masc. 3p. pl. αὐτός ἡ ὁ self, of oneself, even, very, the same, he, she, it
42 δὲ conj. δέ but, and, now, also, to the contrary, rather, then
ὁ art. nom. masc. sg. ὁ ἡ τό the, this, that, he, she, it
Θεὸς n. nom. masc. sg. θεός God, god
καὶ conj. καί and, even, also, but
αὐτοὺς pron. acc. masc. 3p. pl. αὐτός ἡ ὁ self, of oneself, even, very, the same, he, she, it
τῇ art. dat. fem. sg. ὁ ἡ τό the, this, that, he, she, it
στρατιᾷ n. dat. fem. sg. στρατιά host
τοῦ art. gen. masc. sg. ὁ ἡ τό the, this, that, he, she, it
οὐρανοῦ n. gen. masc. sg. οὐρανός heaven, air, sky
καθὼς adv. καθώς as, even as, according as, according to
ἐν prep. ἐν (+dat) in, by, with, among, at, on, through, to, within, into, of, for
βίβλῳ n. dat. fem. sg. βίβλος book, record
τῶν art. gen. masc. pl. ὁ ἡ τό the, this, that, he, she, it
προφητῶν n. gen. masc. pl. προφήτης prophet
Μὴ particle of negation. μή not, no, lest, neither, none, nothing, nor, never, without
σφάγια n. acc. neut. pl. σφάγιον slain beast
καὶ conj. καί and, even, also, but
θυσίας n. acc. fem. pl. θυσία sacrifice
μοι pron. dat. 1p. sg. ἐγώ I
ἔτη n. acc. neut. pl. ἔτος year
τεσσαράκοντα num. acc. neut. pl. τεσσαράκοντα forty
ἐν prep. ἐν (+dat) in, by, with, among, at, on, through, to, within, into, of, for
τῇ art. dat. fem. sg. ὁ ἡ τό the, this, that, he, she, it
ἐρήμῳ adj. dat. fem. sg. ἔρημος wilderness, desert
οἶκος n. voc. masc. sg. οἶκος house, home, household
Ἰσραήλ pron. name. masc. inde. Ἰσραήλ Israel
43 καὶ conj. καί and, even, also, but
τὴν art. acc. fem. sg. ὁ ἡ τό the, this, that, he, she, it
σκηνὴν n. acc. fem. sg. σκηνή tabernacle, habitation
τοῦ art. gen. masc. sg. ὁ ἡ τό the, this, that, he, she, it
Μόλοχ n. gen. masc. sg. Μολόχ Moloch
καὶ conj. καί and, even, also, but
τὸ art. acc. neut. sg. ὁ ἡ τό the, this, that, he, she, it
ἄστρον n. acc. neut. sg. ἄστρον star
τοῦ art. gen. masc. sg. ὁ ἡ τό the, this, that, he, she, it
Θεοῦ n. gen. masc. sg. θεός God, god
ὑμῶν pron. gen. 2p. pl. σύ thou, you

Ῥεμφάν n. gen. masc. sg. Ῥεμφὰν Remphan
τοὺς art. acc. masc. pl. ὁ ἡ τό the, this, that, he, she, it
τύπους n. acc. masc. pl. τύπος ensample, example, pattern, print, figure, fashion
οὓς relative pron. acc. masc. pl. ὅς ἥ ὅ who, which, what, that
αὐτοῖς pron. dat. masc. 3p. pl. αὐτός ή ό self, of oneself, even, very, the same, he, she, it
καὶ conj. καί and, even, also, but
ὑμᾶς pron. acc. 2p. pl. σύ thou, you
ἐπέκεινα adv. ἐπέκεινα beyond
Βαβυλῶνος n. gen. fem. sg. Βαβυλών Babylon
44 ἡ art. nom. fem. sg. ὁ ἡ τό the, this, that, he, she, it
σκηνὴ n. nom. fem. sg. σκηνή tabernacle, habitation
τοῦ art. gen. neut. sg. ὁ ἡ τό the, this, that, he, she, it
μαρτυρίου n. gen. neut. sg. μαρτύριον testimony, witness
τοῖς art. dat. masc. pl. ὁ ἡ τό the, this, that, he, she, it
πατράσιν n. dat. masc. pl. πατήρ Father, father, parent
ἡμῶν pron. gen. 1p. pl. ἐγώ I
ἐν prep. ἐν (+dat) in, by, with, among, at, on, through, to, within, into, of, for
τῇ art. dat. fem. sg. ὁ ἡ τό the, this, that, he, she, it
ἐρήμῳ adj. dat. fem. sg. ἔρημος wilderness, desert
καθὼς adv. καθώς as, even as, according as, according to
ὁ art. nom. masc. sg. ὁ ἡ τό the, this, that, he, she, it
τῷ art. dat. masc. sg. ὁ ἡ τό the, this, that, he, she, it
Μωσῇ n. dat. masc. sg. Μωσῆς Moses
αὐτὴν pron. acc. fem. 3p. sg. αὐτός ή ό self, of oneself, even, very, the same, he, she, it
κατὰ prep. κατά (+gen) against, by, throughout, down, (+acc) according to, after, with
τὸν art. acc. masc. sg. ὁ ἡ τό the, this, that, he, she, it
τύπον n. acc. masc. sg. τύπος ensample, example, pattern, print, figure, fashion
ὃν relative pron. acc. masc. sg. ὅς ἥ ὅ who, which, what, that
45 ἣν relative pron. acc. fem. sg. ὅς ἥ ὅ who, which, what, that
καὶ conj. καί and, even, also, but
οἱ art. nom. masc. pl. ὁ ἡ τό the, this, that, he, she, it
πατέρες n. nom. masc. pl. πατήρ Father, father, parent
ἡμῶν pron. gen. 1p. pl. ἐγώ I
μετὰ prep. μετά (+gen) with, among, against, (+acc) after
Ἰησοῦ n. gen. masc. sg. Ἰησοῦς Jesus, Joshua
ἐν prep. ἐν (+dat) in, by, with, among, at, on, through, to, within, into, of, for
τῇ art. dat. fem. sg. ὁ ἡ τό the, this, that, he, she, it
κατασχέσει n. dat. fem. sg. κατάσχεσις possession
τῶν art. gen. neut. pl. ὁ ἡ τό the, this, that, he, she, it
ἐθνῶν n. gen. neut. pl. ἔθνος Gentile, nation, heathen, people
ὧν relative pron. gen. neut. pl. ὅς ἥ ὅ who, which, what, that
ὁ art. nom. masc. sg. ὁ ἡ τό the, this, that, he, she, it
Θεὸς n. nom. masc. sg. θεός God, god
ἀπὸ prep. ἀπό (+gen) from, of, out of, since, for, off, at, by, in, on
προσώπου n. gen. neut. sg. πρόσωπον face, presence, person, countenance
τῶν art. gen. masc. pl. ὁ ἡ τό the, this, that, he, she, it
πατέρων n. gen. masc. pl. πατήρ Father, father, parent
ἡμῶν pron. gen. 1p. pl. ἐγώ I
ἕως conj. ἕως till, until, unto, until when, while, as far as, even, until now
τῶν art. gen. fem. pl. ὁ ἡ τό the, this, that, he, she, it
ἡμερῶν n. gen. fem. pl. ἡμέρα day, time, year, while, age, day time
Δαβίδ n. gen. masc. sg. Δαβίδ David
46 ὃς relative pron. nom. masc. sg. ὅς ἥ ὅ who, which, what, that
χάριν n. acc. fem. sg. χάρις grace, thank, favour, pleasure
ἐνώπιον adv. ἐνώπιον before, in the sight of, in the presence of

τοῦ art. gen. masc. sg. ὁ ἡ τό the, this, that, he, she, it
Θεοῦ n. gen. masc. sg. θεός God, god
καὶ conj. καί and, even, also, but
σκήνωμα n. acc. neut. sg. σκήνωμα tabernacle
τῷ art. dat. masc. sg. ὁ ἡ τό the, this, that, he, she, it
Θεῷ n. dat. masc. sg. θεός God, god
Ἰακώβ n. gen. masc. sg. Ἰακώβ Jacob
47 Σολομῶν n. nom. masc. sg. Σολομών Solomon
δὲ conj. δέ but, and, now, also, to the contrary, rather, then
αὐτῷ pron. dat. masc. 3p. sg. αὐτός ή ό self, of oneself, even, very, the same, he, she, it
οἶκον n. acc. masc. sg. οἶκος house, home, household
48 ἀλλ' conj. ἀλλά but, yea, yet, nevertheless, howbeit, nay, therefore
οὐχ particle of negation. οὐ οὐκ οὐχ not, no, neither, none, nay, nor, never, nothing
ὁ art. nom. masc. sg. ὁ ἡ τό the, this, that, he, she, it
ὕψιστος superl. adj. nom. masc. sg. ὕψιστος highest, Highest, most high, most High
ἐν prep. ἐν (+dat) in, by, with, among, at, on, through, to, within, into, of, for
χειροποιήτοις adj. dat. masc. pl. χειροποίητος made with hands, made by hands
ναοῖς n. dat. masc. pl. ναός temple, shrine
καθὼς adv. καθώς as, even as, according as, according to
ὁ art. nom. masc. sg. ὁ ἡ τό the, this, that, he, she, it
προφήτης n. nom. masc. sg. προφήτης prophet
49 Ὁ art. nom. masc. sg. ὁ ἡ τό the, this, that, he, she, it
οὐρανός n. nom. masc. sg. οὐρανός heaven, air, sky
μοι pron. dat. 1p. sg. ἐγώ I
θρόνος n. nom. masc. sg. θρόνος throne, seat
ἡ art. nom. fem. sg. ὁ ἡ τό the, this, that, he, she, it
δὲ conj. δέ but, and, now, also, to the contrary, rather, then
γῆ n. nom. fem. sg. γῆ earth, land, ground, country
ὑποπόδιον n. nom. neut. sg. ὑποπόδιον footstool
τῶν art. gen. masc. pl. ὁ ἡ τό the, this, that, he, she, it
ποδῶν n. gen. masc. pl. πούς foot
μου pron. gen. 1p. sg. ἐγώ I
ποῖον interrog. pron. acc. masc. sg. ποῖος what, which, what manner of
οἶκον n. acc. masc. sg. οἶκος house, home, household
μοι pron. dat. 1p. sg. ἐγώ I
Κύριος n. nom. masc. sg. κύριος Lord, lord, master, sir, LORD, God, Master, owner
ἢ particle. ἤ or, than, either, nor, or else, and, rather than
τίς interrog. pron. nom. masc. sg. τίς what, who, why, where, which, how
τόπος n. nom. masc. sg. τόπος place, room, quarter
τῆς art. gen. fem. sg. ὁ ἡ τό the, this, that, he, she, it
καταπαύσεώς n. gen. fem. sg. κατάπαυσις rest
50 οὐχὶ adv. οὐχί not, nay
ἡ art. nom. fem. sg. ὁ ἡ τό the, this, that, he, she, it
χείρ n. nom. fem. sg. χείρ hand
μου pron. gen. 1p. sg. ἐγώ I
ταῦτα demo. pron. acc. neut. pl. οὗτος αὕτη τοῦτο this, the same, this same, he, she, it
πάντα adj. acc. neut. pl. πᾶς πᾶσα πᾶν all, every, whosoever, every one, no, whole, any
51 Σκληροτράχηλοι adj. voc. masc. pl. σκληροτράχηλος stiffnecked
καὶ conj. καί and, even, also, but
ἀπερίτμητοι adj. voc. masc. pl. ἀπερίτμητος uncircumcised
τῇ art. dat. fem. sg. ὁ ἡ τό the, this, that, he, she, it
καρδίᾳ n. dat. fem. sg. καρδία heart
καὶ conj. καί and, even, also, but
τοῖς art. dat. neut. pl. ὁ ἡ τό the, this, that, he, she, it
ὠσίν n. dat. neut. pl. οὖς ear

ὑμεῖς pron. nom. 2p. pl. σύ thou, you
ἀεὶ adv. ἀεί always, always, ever
τῷ art. dat. neut. sg. ὁ ἡ τό the, this, that, he, she, it
Πνεύματι n. dat. neut. sg. πνεῦμα spirit, Spirit, Ghost, ghost, life. of the spirit, wind
τῷ art. dat. neut. sg. ὁ ἡ τό the, this, that, he, she, it
Ἁγίῳ adj. dat. neut. sg. ἅγιος Holy, holy, saint, Holy One, holy thing, most holy
ὡς adv. ὡς as, when, as it were, how, about, like, as soon as, even as, while
οἱ art. nom. masc. pl. ὁ ἡ τό the, this, that, he, she, it
πατέρες n. nom. masc. pl. πατήρ Father, father, parent
ὑμῶν pron. gen. 2p. pl. σύ thou, you
καὶ conj. καί and, even, also, but
ὑμεῖς pron. nom. 2p. pl. σύ thou, you
52 τίνα interrog. pron. acc. masc. sg. τίς what, who, why, where, which, how
τῶν art. gen. masc. pl. ὁ ἡ τό the, this, that, he, she, it
προφητῶν n. gen. masc. pl. προφήτης prophet
οὐκ particle of negation. οὐ οὐκ οὐχ not, no, neither, none, nay, nor, never, nothing
οἱ art. nom. masc. pl. ὁ ἡ τό the, this, that, he, she, it
πατέρες n. nom. masc. pl. πατήρ Father, father, parent
ὑμῶν pron. gen. 2p. pl. σύ thou, you
καὶ conj. καί and, even, also, but
τοὺς art. acc. masc. pl. ὁ ἡ τό the, this, that, he, she, it
περὶ prep. περί (+gen) of, for, concerning, (+acc) about, concerning, in
τῆς art. gen. fem. sg. ὁ ἡ τό the, this, that, he, she, it
ἐλεύσεως n. gen. fem. sg. ἔλευσις coming
τοῦ art. gen. masc. sg. ὁ ἡ τό the, this, that, he, she, it
δικαίου adj. gen. masc. sg. δίκαιος righteous, just, meet, right
οὗ relative pron. gen. masc. sg. ὅς ἥ ὅ who, which, what, that
νῦν adv. νῦν now, henceforth, present, this time
ὑμεῖς pron. nom. 2p. pl. σύ thou, you
προδόται n. nom. masc. pl. προδότης traitor, betrayer
καὶ conj. καί and, even, also, but
φονεῖς n. nom. masc. pl. φονεύς murderer
53 οἵτινες relative pron. nom. masc. pl. ὅστις which, who, whosoever, that, whatsoever
τὸν art. acc. masc. sg. ὁ ἡ τό the, this, that, he, she, it
νόμον n. acc. masc. sg. νόμος law, the law
εἰς prep. εἰς (+acc) into, to, unto, for, in, on, toward, against, upon, at, among
διαταγὰς n. acc. fem. pl. διαταγή disposition, ordinance
ἀγγέλων n. gen. masc. pl. ἄγγελος angel, messenger
καὶ conj. καί and, even, also, but
οὐκ particle of negation. οὐ οὐκ οὐχ not, no, neither, none, nay, nor, never, nothing
54 δὲ conj. δέ but, and, now, also, to the contrary, rather, then
ταῦτα demo. pron. acc. neut. pl. οὗτος αὕτη τοῦτο this, the same, this same, he, she, it
ταῖς art. dat. fem. pl. ὁ ἡ τό the, this, that, he, she, it
καρδίαις n. dat. fem. pl. καρδία heart
αὐτῶν pron. gen. masc. 3p. pl. αὐτός ἡ ὁ self, of oneself, even, very, the same, he, she, it
καὶ conj. καί and, even, also, but
τοὺς art. acc. masc. pl. ὁ ἡ τό the, this, that, he, she, it
ὀδόντας n. acc. masc. pl. ὀδούς tooth
ἐπ' prep. ἐπί (+gen) on, in, upon, (+dat) in, at, for, upon, (+acc) on, upon, unto, to, against
αὐτόν pron. acc. masc. 3p. sg. αὐτός ἡ ὁ self, of oneself, even, very, the same, he, she, it
55 δὲ conj. δέ but, and, now, also, to the contrary, rather, then
πλήρης adj. nom. masc. sg. πλήρης full
Πνεύματος n. gen. neut. sg. πνεῦμα spirit, Spirit, Ghost, ghost, life. of the spirit, wind
Ἁγίου adj. gen. neut. sg. ἅγιος Holy, holy, saint, Holy One, holy thing, most holy
εἰς prep. εἰς (+acc) into, to, unto, for, in, on, toward, against, upon, at, among

τὸν art. acc. masc. sg. ὁ ἡ τό the, this, that, he, she, it
οὐρανὸν n. acc. masc. sg. οὐρανός heaven, air, sky
δόξαν n. acc. fem. sg. δόξα glory, honour, praise, dignity, worship
Θεοῦ n. gen. masc. sg. θεός God, god
καὶ conj. καί and, even, also, but
Ἰησοῦν n. acc. masc. sg. Ἰησοῦς Jesus
ἐκ prep. ἐκ ἐξ (+gen) of, from, out of, by, on, with, in, among, through
δεξιῶν adj. gen. neut. pl. δεξιός right, right hand, right side
τοῦ art. gen. masc. sg. ὁ ἡ τό the, this, that, he, she, it
Θεοῦ n. gen. masc. sg. θεός God, god
56 καὶ conj. καί and, even, also, but
τοὺς art. acc. masc. pl. ὁ ἡ τό the, this, that, he, she, it
οὐρανοὺς n. acc. masc. pl. οὐρανός heaven, air, sky
καὶ conj. καί and, even, also, but
τὸν art. acc. masc. sg. ὁ ἡ τό the, this, that, he, she, it
υἱὸν n. acc. masc. sg. υἱός son, child, descendant, offspring, heir
τοῦ art. gen. masc. sg. ὁ ἡ τό the, this, that, he, she, it
ἀνθρώπου n. gen. masc. sg. ἄνθρωπος man, human being, person, one, certain
ἐκ prep. ἐκ ἐξ (+gen) of, from, out of, by, on, with, in, among, through
δεξιῶν adj. gen. neut. pl. δεξιός right, right hand, right side
τοῦ art. gen. masc. sg. ὁ ἡ τό the, this, that, he, she, it
Θεοῦ n. gen. masc. sg. θεός God, god
57 δὲ conj. δέ but, and, now, also, to the contrary, rather, then
φωνῇ n. dat. fem. sg. φωνή voice, sound, noise
μεγάλῃ adj. dat. fem. sg. μέγας great, loud, greatest, high, large, mighty, strong
τὰ art. acc. neut. pl. ὁ ἡ τό the, this, that, he, she, it
ὦτα n. acc. neut. pl. οὖς ear
αὐτῶν pron. gen. masc. 3p. pl. αὐτός ἡ ὁ self, of oneself, even, very, the same, he, she, it
καὶ conj. καί and, even, also, but
ὁμοθυμαδὸν adv. ὁμοθυμαδόν with one accord, with one mind
ἐπ' prep. ἐπί (+gen) on, in, upon, (+dat) in, at, for, upon, (+acc) on, upon, unto, to, against
αὐτὸν pron. acc. masc. 3p. sg. αὐτός ἡ ὁ self, of oneself, even, very, the same, he, she, it
58 καὶ conj. καί and, even, also, but
ἔξω adv. ἔξω out, without, out of, forth, away, outward
τῆς art. gen. fem. sg. ὁ ἡ τό the, this, that, he, she, it
πόλεως n. gen. fem. sg. πόλις city
καὶ conj. καί and, even, also, but
οἱ art. nom. masc. pl. ὁ ἡ τό the, this, that, he, she, it
μάρτυρες n. nom. masc. pl. μάρτυς or μάρτυρ witness, martyr, record
τὰ art. acc. neut. pl. ὁ ἡ τό the, this, that, he, she, it
ἱμάτια n. acc. neut. pl. ἱμάτιον cloke, garment, clothes, raiment, robe, vesture
αὐτῶν pron. gen. masc. 3p. pl. αὐτός ἡ ὁ self, of oneself, even, very, the same, he, she, it
παρὰ prep. παρά (+gen) of, from, (+dat) with, for, (+acc) beside, at, by, above, against
τοὺς art. acc. masc. pl. ὁ ἡ τό the, this, that, he, she, it
πόδας n. acc. masc. pl. πούς foot
νεανίου n. gen. masc. sg. νεανίας young man
Σαύλου n. gen. masc. sg. Σαῦλος Saul
59 καὶ conj. καί and, even, also, but
τὸν art. acc. masc. sg. ὁ ἡ τό the, this, that, he, she, it
Στέφανον n. acc. masc. sg. Στέφανος Stephen
καὶ conj. καί and, even, also, but
Κύριε n. voc. masc. sg. κύριος Lord, lord, master, sir, LORD, God, Master, owner
Ἰησοῦ n. voc. masc. sg. Ἰησοῦς Jesus
τὸ art. acc. neut. sg. ὁ ἡ τό the, this, that, he, she, it
πνεῦμά n. acc. neut. sg. πνεῦμα spirit, Spirit, Ghost, ghost, life. of the spirit, wind

μου pron. gen. 1p. sg. ἐγώ I
60 δὲ conj. δέ but, and, now, also, to the contrary, rather, then
τὰ art. acc. neut. pl. ὁ ἡ τό the, this, that, he, she, it
γόνατα n. acc. neut. pl. γόνυ knee, kneel
φωνῇ n. dat. fem. sg. φωνή voice, sound, noise
μεγάλῃ adj. dat. fem. sg. μέγας great, loud, greatest, high, large, mighty, strong
Κύριε n. voc. masc. sg. κύριος Lord, lord, master, sir, LORD, God, Master, owner
μὴ particle of negation. μή not, no, lest, neither, none, nothing, nor, never, without
αὐτοῖς pron. dat. masc. 3p. pl. αὐτός ἡ ὁ self, of oneself, even, very, the same, he, she, it
τὴν art. acc. fem. sg. ὁ ἡ τό the, this, that, he, she, it
ἁμαρτίαν n. acc. fem. sg. ἁμαρτία sin, offence, sinful
ταύτην demo. pron. acc. fem. sg. οὗτος αὕτη τοῦτο this, the same, this same, he, she, it
καὶ conj. καί and, even, also, but
τοῦτο demo. pron. acc. neut. sg. οὗτος αὕτη τοῦτο this, the same, this same, he, she, it

8

1 Σαῦλος n. nom. masc. sg. Σαῦλος Saul
δὲ conj. δέ but, and, now, also, to the contrary, rather, then
τῇ art. dat. fem. sg. ὁ ἡ τό the, this, that, he, she, it
ἀναιρέσει n. dat. fem. sg. ἀναίρεσις death
αὐτοῦ pron. gen. masc. 3p. sg. αὐτός ἡ ὁ self, of oneself, even, very, the same, he, she, it
δὲ conj. δέ but, and, now, also, to the contrary, rather, then
ἐν prep. ἐν (+dat) in, by, with, among, at, on, through, to, within, into, of, for
ἐκείνῃ demo. pron. dat. fem. sg. ἐκεῖνος that, he, the same, that same
ἡμέρᾳ n. dat. fem. sg. ἡμέρα day, time, year, while, age, day time
διωγμὸς n. nom. masc. sg. διωγμός persecution
μέγας adj. nom. masc. sg. μέγας great, loud, greatest, high, large, mighty, strong
ἐπὶ prep. ἐπί (+gen) on, in, upon, (+dat) in, at, for, upon, (+acc) on, upon, unto, to, against
τὴν art. acc. fem. sg. ὁ ἡ τό the, this, that, he, she, it
ἐκκλησίαν n. acc. fem. sg. ἐκκλησία church, assembly
τὴν art. acc. fem. sg. ὁ ἡ τό the, this, that, he, she, it
ἐν prep. ἐν (+dat) in, by, with, among, at, on, through, to, within, into, of, for
Ἱεροσολύμοις n. dat. neut. pl. Ἱεροσόλυμα Jerusalem
πάντες adj. nom. masc. pl. πᾶς πᾶσα πᾶν all, every, whosoever, every one, no, whole, any
τε conj. τέ and, both, also
κατὰ prep. κατά (+gen) against, by, throughout, down, (+acc) according to, after, with
τὰς art. acc. fem. pl. ὁ ἡ τό the, this, that, he, she, it
χώρας n. acc. fem. pl. χώρα country, region, land, field, coast, ground
τῆς art. gen. fem. sg. ὁ ἡ τό the, this, that, he, she, it
Ἰουδαίας n. gen. fem. sg. Ἰουδαία Judaea, Jewry
καὶ conj. καί and, even, also, but
Σαμαρείας n. gen. fem. sg. Σαμάρεια Samaria
πλὴν prep. πλήν but, nevertheless, but rather, notwithstanding, except, than
τῶν art. gen. masc. pl. ὁ ἡ τό the, this, that, he, she, it
ἀποστόλων n. gen. masc. pl. ἀπόστολος apostle, messenger, he that is sent
2 δὲ conj. δέ but, and, now, also, to the contrary, rather, then
τὸν art. acc. masc. sg. ὁ ἡ τό the, this, that, he, she, it
Στέφανον n. acc. masc. sg. Στέφανος Stephen
ἄνδρες n. nom. masc. pl. ἀνήρ man, husband, sir
εὐλαβεῖς adj. nom. masc. pl. εὐλαβής devout
καὶ conj. καί and, even, also, but
κοπετὸν n. acc. masc. sg. κοπετός lamentation
μέγαν adj. acc. masc. sg. μέγας great, loud, greatest, high, large, mighty, strong
ἐπ' prep. ἐπί (+gen) on, in, upon, (+dat) in, at, for, upon, (+acc) on, upon, unto, to, against

αὐτῷ pron. dat. masc. 3p. sg. αὐτός ή ό self, of oneself, even, very, the same, he, she, it
3 Σαῦλος n. nom. masc. sg. Σαῦλος Saul
δὲ conj. δέ but, and, now, also, to the contrary, rather, then
τὴν art. acc. fem. sg. ὁ ἡ τό the, this, that, he, she, it
ἐκκλησίαν n. acc. fem. sg. ἐκκλησία church, assembly
κατὰ prep. κατά (+gen) against, by, throughout, down, (+acc) according to, after, with
τοὺς art. acc. masc. pl. ὁ ἡ τό the, this, that, he, she, it
οἴκους n. acc. masc. pl. οἶκος house, home, household
τε conj. τέ and, both, also
ἄνδρας n. acc. masc. pl. ἀνήρ man, husband, sir
καὶ conj. καί and, even, also, but
γυναῖκας n. acc. fem. pl. γυνή woman, wife
εἰς prep. εἰς (+acc) into, to, unto, for, in, on, toward, against, upon, at, among
φυλακήν n. acc. fem. sg. φυλακή prison, watch, imprisonment, cage, hold, ward
4 Οἱ art. nom. masc. pl. ὁ ἡ τό the, this, that, he, she, it
μέν conj. μέν indeed, verily, truly, even, so, some
οὖν conj. οὖν therefore, then, so, and, now, wherefore
τὸν art. acc. masc. sg. ὁ ἡ τό the, this, that, he, she, it
λόγον n. acc. masc. sg. λόγος word, saying, account, speech, thing, matter
5 Φίλιππος n. nom. masc. sg. Φίλιππος Philip, Philippi
δὲ conj. δέ but, and, now, also, to the contrary, rather, then
εἰς prep. εἰς (+acc) into, to, unto, for, in, on, toward, against, upon, at, among
πόλιν n. acc. fem. sg. πόλις city
τῆς art. gen. fem. sg. ὁ ἡ τό the, this, that, he, she, it
Σαμαρείας n. gen. fem. sg. Σαμάρεια Samaria
αὐτοῖς pron. dat. masc. 3p. pl. αὐτός ή ό self, of oneself, even, very, the same, he, she, it
τὸν art. acc. masc. sg. ὁ ἡ τό the, this, that, he, she, it
Χριστόν n. acc. masc. sg. Χριστός Christ
6 τε conj. τέ and, both, also
οἱ art. nom. masc. pl. ὁ ἡ τό the, this, that, he, she, it
ὄχλοι n. nom. masc. pl. ὄχλος people, multitude, company, press, number
τοῖς art. dat. neut. pl. ὁ ἡ τό the, this, that, he, she, it
ὑπὸ prep. ὑπό (+gen) of, by, with, from, among, (+acc) under
τοῦ art. gen. masc. sg. ὁ ἡ τό the, this, that, he, she, it
Φιλίππου n. gen. masc. sg. Φίλιππος Philip, Philippi
ὁμοθυμαδὸν adv. ὁμοθυμαδόν with one accord, with one mind
ἐν prep. ἐν (+dat) in, by, with, among, at, on, through, to, within, into, of, for
τῷ art. dat. neut. sg. ὁ ἡ τό the, this, that, he, she, it
αὐτοὺς pron. acc. masc. 3p. pl. αὐτός ή ό self, of oneself, even, very, the same, he, she, it
καὶ conj. καί and, even, also, but
τὰ art. acc. neut. pl. ὁ ἡ τό the, this, that, he, she, it
σημεῖα n. acc. neut. pl. σημεῖον sign, miracle, wonder, token
ἃ relative pron. acc. neut. pl. ὅς ἥ ὅ who, which, what, that
7 πολλῶν adj. gen. masc. pl. πολύς many, great, much, long, abundant
γὰρ conj. γάρ for, and, because, but, indeed
τῶν art. gen. masc. pl. ὁ ἡ τό the, this, that, he, she, it
πνεύματα n. acc. neut. pl. πνεῦμα spirit, Spirit, Ghost, ghost, life. of the spirit, wind
ἀκάθαρτα adj. acc. neut. pl. ἀκάθαρτος unclean, foul
μεγάλῃ adj. dat. fem. sg. μέγας great, loud, greatest, high, large, mighty, strong
φωνῇ n. dat. fem. sg. φωνή voice, sound, noise
πολλοὶ adj. nom. masc. pl. πολύς many, great, much, long, abundant
δὲ conj. δέ but, and, now, also, to the contrary, rather, then
καὶ conj. καί and, even, also, but
χωλοὶ adj. nom. masc. pl. χωλός lame, halt, cripple
8 καὶ conj. καί and, even, also, but

χαρὰ n. nom. fem. sg. χαρά joy, gladness, joyfulness
μεγάλη adj. nom. fem. sg. μέγας great, loud, greatest, high, large, mighty, strong
ἐν prep. ἐν (+dat) in, by, with, among, at, on, through, to, within, into, of, for
τῇ art. dat. fem. sg. ὁ ἡ τό the, this, that, he, she, it
πόλει n. dat. fem. sg. πόλις city
ἐκείνῃ demo. pron. dat. fem. sg. ἐκεῖνος that, he, the same, that same
9 Ἀνὴρ n. nom. masc. sg. ἀνήρ man, husband, sir
δὲ conj. δέ but, and, now, also, to the contrary, rather, then
τις indefinite pron. nom. masc. sg. τὶς certain, some, any man, one, any thing
ὀνόματι n. dat. neut. sg. ὄνομα name, call, surname
Σίμων n. nom. masc. sg. Σίμων Simon
ἐν prep. ἐν (+dat) in, by, with, among, at, on, through, to, within, into, of, for
τῇ art. dat. fem. sg. ὁ ἡ τό the, this, that, he, she, it
πόλει n. dat. fem. sg. πόλις city
καὶ conj. καί and, even, also, but
τὸ art. acc. neut. sg. ὁ ἡ τό the, this, that, he, she, it
ἔθνος n. acc. neut. sg. ἔθνος Gentile, nation, heathen, people
τῆς art. gen. fem. sg. ὁ ἡ τό the, this, that, he, she, it
Σαμαρείας n. gen. fem. sg. Σαμάρεια Samaria
τινα indefinite pron. acc. masc. sg. τὶς certain, some, any man, one, any thing
ἑαυτὸν reflexive pron. acc. masc. 3p. sg. ἑαυτοῦ himself, herself, itself, yourself, ourselves
μέγαν adj. acc. masc. sg. μέγας great, loud, greatest, high, large, mighty, strong
10 ᾧ relative pron. dat. masc. sg. ὅς ἥ ὅ who, which, what, that
πάντες adj. nom. masc. pl. πᾶς πᾶσα πᾶν all, every, whosoever, every one, no, whole, any
ἀπὸ prep. ἀπό (+gen) from, of, out of, since, for, off, at, by, in, on
μικροῦ adj. gen. masc. sg. μικρός little, small, least, less
ἕως conj. ἕως till, until, unto, until when, while, as far as, even, until now
μεγάλου adj. gen. masc. sg. μέγας great, loud, greatest, high, large, mighty, strong
Οὗτός demo. pron. nom. masc. sg. οὗτος αὕτη τοῦτο this, the same, this same, he, she, it
ἡ art. nom. fem. sg. ὁ ἡ τό the, this, that, he, she, it
δύναμις n. nom. fem. sg. δύναμις power, mighty work, miracle, strength, might
τοῦ art. gen. masc. sg. ὁ ἡ τό the, this, that, he, she, it
Θεοῦ n. gen. masc. sg. θεός God, god
ἡ art. nom. fem. sg. ὁ ἡ τό the, this, that, he, she, it
μεγάλη adj. nom. fem. sg. μέγας great, loud, greatest, high, large, mighty, strong
11 δὲ conj. δέ but, and, now, also, to the contrary, rather, then
αὐτῷ pron. dat. masc. 3p. sg. αὐτός ἡ ὁ self, of oneself, even, very, the same, he, she, it
διὰ prep. διά (+gen) by, through, with, in, of, (+acc) for, because of, for a cause
τὸ art. acc. neut. sg. ὁ ἡ τό the, this, that, he, she, it
ἱκανῷ adj. dat. masc. sg. ἱκανός many, much, long, worthy, sufficient, great, able
χρόνῳ n. dat. masc. sg. χρόνος time, season, space
ταῖς art. dat. fem. pl. ὁ ἡ τό the, this, that, he, she, it
μαγείαις n. dat. fem. pl. μαγεία sorcery
αὐτούς pron. acc. masc. 3p. pl. αὐτός ἡ ὁ self, of oneself, even, very, the same, he, she, it
12 ὅτε adv. ὅτε when, after that, as soon as, while, after
δὲ conj. δέ but, and, now, also, to the contrary, rather, then
τῷ art. dat. masc. sg. ὁ ἡ τό the, this, that, he, she, it
Φιλίππῳ n. dat. masc. sg. Φίλιππος Philip, Philippi
τὰ art. acc. neut. pl. ὁ ἡ τό the, this, that, he, she, it
περὶ prep. περί (+gen) of, for, concerning, (+acc) about, concerning, in
τῆς art. gen. fem. sg. ὁ ἡ τό the, this, that, he, she, it
βασιλείας n. gen. fem. sg. βασιλεία kingdom, reign
τοῦ art. gen. masc. sg. ὁ ἡ τό the, this, that, he, she, it
Θεοῦ n. gen. masc. sg. θεός God, god
καὶ conj. καί and, even, also, but

τοῦ art. gen. neut. sg. ὁ ἡ τό the, this, that, he, she, it
ὀνόματος n. gen. neut. sg. ὄνομα name, call, surname
τοῦ art. gen. neut. sg. ὁ ἡ τό the, this, that, he, she, it
Ἰησοῦ n. gen. masc. sg. Ἰησοῦς Jesus
Χριστοῦ n. gen. masc. sg. Χριστός Christ
ἄνδρες n. nom. masc. pl. ἀνήρ man, husband, sir
τε conj. τέ and, both, also
καὶ conj. καί and, even, also, but
γυναῖκες n. nom. fem. pl. γυνή woman, wife
13 ὁ art. nom. masc. sg. ὁ ἡ τό the, this, that, he, she, it
δὲ conj. δέ but, and, now, also, to the contrary, rather, then
Σίμων n. nom. masc. sg. Σίμων Simon
καὶ conj. καί and, even, also, but
αὐτὸς pron. nom. masc. 3p. sg. αὐτός ή ό self, of oneself, even, very, the same, he, she, it
καὶ conj. καί and, even, also, but
τῷ art. dat. masc. sg. ὁ ἡ τό the, this, that, he, she, it
Φιλίππῳ n. dat. masc. sg. Φίλιππος Philip, Philippi
τε conj. τέ and, both, also
δυνάμεις n. acc. fem. pl. δύναμις power, mighty work, miracle, strength, might
καὶ conj. καί and, even, also, but
σημεῖα n. acc. neut. pl. σημεῖον sign, miracle, wonder, token
14 δὲ conj. δέ but, and, now, also, to the contrary, rather, then
οἱ art. nom. masc. pl. ὁ ἡ τό the, this, that, he, she, it
ἐν prep. ἐν (+dat) in, by, with, among, at, on, through, to, within, into, of, for
Ἱεροσολύμοις n. dat. neut. pl. Ἱεροσόλυμα Jerusalem
ἀπόστολοι n. nom. masc. pl. ἀπόστολος apostle, messenger, he that is sent
ὅτι conj. ὅτι that, for, because, how that, how, because that, for that, though
ἡ art. nom. fem. sg. ὁ ἡ τό the, this, that, he, she, it
Σαμάρεια n. nom. fem. sg. Σαμάρεια Samaria
τὸν art. acc. masc. sg. ὁ ἡ τό the, this, that, he, she, it
λόγον n. acc. masc. sg. λόγος word, saying, account, speech, thing, matter
τοῦ art. gen. masc. sg. ὁ ἡ τό the, this, that, he, she, it
Θεοῦ n. gen. masc. sg. θεός God, god
πρὸς prep. πρός (+gen) for, (+dat) at, (+acc) unto, to, with, for, against
αὐτοὺς pron. acc. masc. 3p. pl. αὐτός ή ό self, of oneself, even, very, the same, he, she, it
τὸν art. acc. masc. sg. ὁ ἡ τό the, this, that, he, she, it
Πέτρον n. acc. masc. sg. Πέτρος Peter
καὶ conj. καί and, even, also, but
Ἰωάννην n. acc. masc. sg. Ἰωάννης John
15 οἵτινες relative pron. nom. masc. pl. ὅστις which, who, whosoever, that, whatsoever
περὶ prep. περί (+gen) of, for, concerning, (+acc) about, concerning, in
αὐτῶν pron. gen. masc. 3p. pl. αὐτός ή ό self, of oneself, even, very, the same, he, she, it
ὅπως adv. ὅπως that, how, to, because, so that, when
Πνεῦμα n. acc. neut. sg. πνεῦμα spirit, Spirit, Ghost, ghost, life. of the spirit, wind
Ἅγιον adj. acc. neut. sg. ἅγιος Holy, holy, saint, Holy One, holy thing, most holy
16 οὔπω adv. οὔπω not yet
γὰρ conj. γάρ for, and, because, but, indeed
ἐπ' prep. ἐπί (+gen) on, in, upon, (+dat) in, at, for, upon, (+acc) on, upon, unto, to, against
οὐδενὶ num. dat. masc. sg. οὐδείς no man, nothing, no, none, neither, not, nought
αὐτῶν pron. gen. masc. 3p. pl. αὐτός ή ό self, of oneself, even, very, the same, he, she, it
μόνον adv. μόνος only, alone, by oneself
δὲ conj. δέ but, and, now, also, to the contrary, rather, then
εἰς prep. εἰς (+acc) into, to, unto, for, in, on, toward, against, upon, at, among
τὸ art. acc. neut. sg. ὁ ἡ τό the, this, that, he, she, it
ὄνομα n. acc. neut. sg. ὄνομα name, call, surname

τοῦ art. gen. masc. sg. ὁ ἡ τό the, this, that, he, she, it
Κυρίου n. gen. masc. sg. κύριος Lord, lord, master, sir, LORD, God, Master, owner
Ἰησοῦ n. gen. masc. sg. Ἰησοῦς Jesus
17 τότε adv. τότε then, that time
τὰς art. acc. fem. pl. ὁ ἡ τό the, this, that, he, she, it
χεῖρας n. acc. fem. pl. χείρ hand
ἐπ' prep. ἐπί (+gen) on, in, upon, (+dat) in, at, for, upon, (+acc) on, upon, unto, to, against
αὐτοὺς pron. acc. masc. 3p. pl. αὐτός ή ό self, of oneself, even, very, the same, he, she, it
καὶ conj. καί and, even, also, but
Πνεῦμα n. acc. neut. sg. πνεῦμα spirit, Spirit, Ghost, ghost, life. of the spirit, wind
Ἅγιον adj. acc. neut. sg. ἅγιος Holy, holy, saint, Holy One, holy thing, most holy
18 δὲ conj. δέ but, and, now, also, to the contrary, rather, then
ὁ art. nom. masc. sg. ὁ ἡ τό the, this, that, he, she, it
Σίμων n. nom. masc. sg. Σίμων Simon
ὅτι conj. ὅτι that, for, because, how that, how, because that, for that, though
διὰ prep. διά (+gen) by, through, with, in, of, (+acc) for, because of, for a cause
τῆς art. gen. fem. sg. ὁ ἡ τό the, this, that, he, she, it
ἐπιθέσεως n. gen. fem. sg. ἐπίθεσις putting on, laying on
τῶν art. gen. fem. pl. ὁ ἡ τό the, this, that, he, she, it
χειρῶν n. gen. fem. pl. χείρ hand
τῶν art. gen. fem. pl. ὁ ἡ τό the, this, that, he, she, it
ἀποστόλων n. gen. masc. pl. ἀπόστολος apostle, messenger, he that is sent
τὸ art. acc. neut. sg. ὁ ἡ τό the, this, that, he, she, it
Πνεῦμα n. acc. neut. sg. πνεῦμα spirit, Spirit, Ghost, ghost, life. of the spirit, wind
τὸ art. acc. neut. sg. ὁ ἡ τό the, this, that, he, she, it
Ἅγιον adj. acc. neut. sg. ἅγιος Holy, holy, saint, Holy One, holy thing, most holy
αὐτοῖς pron. dat. masc. 3p. pl. αὐτός ή ό self, of oneself, even, very, the same, he, she, it
χρήματα n. acc. neut. pl. χρῆμα riches, money
19 κἀμοὶ crasis for καὶ ἐμοί κἀγώ and I, I also, so I, even as I
τὴν art. acc. fem. sg. ὁ ἡ τό the, this, that, he, she, it
ἐξουσίαν n. acc. fem. sg. ἐξουσία power, authority, right, strength, jurisdiction
ταύτην demo. pron. acc. fem. sg. οὗτος αὕτη τοῦτο this, the same, this same, he, she, it
ἵνα conj. ἵνα that, to, lest, for to, so that, albeit, because, for, so as
ᾧ relative pron. dat. masc. sg. ὅς ἥ ὅ who, which, what, that
ἐὰν particle. ἐάν if, soever, except, though, and if, but, whether, if so, so
τὰς art. acc. fem. pl. ὁ ἡ τό the, this, that, he, she, it
χεῖρας n. acc. fem. pl. χείρ hand
Πνεῦμα n. acc. neut. sg. πνεῦμα spirit, Spirit, Ghost, ghost, life. of the spirit, wind
Ἅγιον adj. acc. neut. sg. ἅγιος Holy, holy, saint, Holy One, holy thing, most holy
20 Πέτρος n. nom. masc. sg. Πέτρος Peter
δὲ conj. δέ but, and, now, also, to the contrary, rather, then
πρὸς prep. πρός (+gen) for, (+dat) at, (+acc) unto, to, with, for, against
αὐτόν pron. acc. masc. 3p. sg. αὐτός ή ό self, of oneself, even, very, the same, he, she, it
Τὸ art. nom. neut. sg. ὁ ἡ τό the, this, that, he, she, it
ἀργύριόν n. nom. neut. sg. ἀργύριον money, piece of silver, silver
σου pron. gen. 2p. sg. σύ thou, you
σὺν prep. σύν (+dat) with, beside
σοὶ pron. dat. 2p. sg. σύ thou, you
εἰς prep. εἰς (+acc) into, to, unto, for, in, on, toward, against, upon, at, among
ἀπώλειαν n. acc. fem. sg. ἀπώλεια destruction, perdition, waste, damnation
ὅτι conj. ὅτι that, for, because, how that, how, because that, for that, though
τὴν art. acc. fem. sg. ὁ ἡ τό the, this, that, he, she, it
δωρεὰν n. acc. fem. sg. δωρεά gift
τοῦ art. gen. masc. sg. ὁ ἡ τό the, this, that, he, she, it
Θεοῦ n. gen. masc. sg. θεός God, god

διὰ prep. διά (+gen) by, through, with, in, of, (+acc) for, because of, for a cause
χρημάτων n. gen. neut. pl. χρῆμα riches, money
21 οὐκ particle of negation. οὐ οὐκ οὐχ not, no, neither, none, nay, nor, never, nothing
σοι pron. dat. 2p. sg. σύ thou, you
μερὶς n. nom. fem. sg. μερίς part, share
οὐδὲ conj. οὐδέ neither, nor, not, no, not even, never, not yet
κλῆρος n. nom. masc. sg. κλῆρος lot, inheritance, part, heritage
ἐν prep. ἐν (+dat) in, by, with, among, at, on, through, to, within, into, of, for
τῷ art. dat. masc. sg. ὁ ἡ τό the, this, that, he, she, it
λόγῳ n. dat. masc. sg. λόγος word, saying, account, speech, thing, matter
τούτῳ demo. pron. dat. masc. sg. οὗτος αὕτη τοῦτο this, the same, this same, he, she, it
ἡ art. nom. fem. sg. ὁ ἡ τό the, this, that, he, she, it
γὰρ conj. γάρ for, and, because, but, indeed
καρδία n. nom. fem. sg. καρδία heart
σου pron. gen. 2p. sg. σύ thou, you
οὐκ particle of negation. οὐ οὐκ οὐχ not, no, neither, none, nay, nor, never, nothing
εὐθεῖα adj. nom. fem. sg. εὐθύς straight, right
ἐνώπιον adv. ἐνώπιον before, in the sight of, in the presence of
τοῦ art. gen. masc. sg. ὁ ἡ τό the, this, that, he, she, it
Θεοῦ n. gen. masc. sg. θεός God, god
22 οὖν conj. οὖν therefore, then, so, and, now, wherefore
ἀπὸ prep. ἀπό (+gen) from, of, out of, since, for, off, at, by, in, on
τῆς art. gen. fem. sg. ὁ ἡ τό the, this, that, he, she, it
κακίας n. gen. fem. sg. κακία malice, maliciousness, evil, naughtiness, wickedness
σου pron. gen. 2p. sg. σύ thou, you
ταύτης demo. pron. gen. fem. sg. οὗτος αὕτη τοῦτο this, the same, this same, he, she, it
καὶ conj. καί and, even, also, but
τοῦ art. gen. masc. sg. ὁ ἡ τό the, this, that, he, she, it
Θεοῦ n. gen. masc. sg. θεός God, god
εἰ conj. εἰ if, whether, that, though, forasmuch
ἄρα conj. ἄρα then, therefore, haply, wherefore, perhaps, manner, no doubt, truly
σοι pron. dat. 2p. sg. σύ thou, you
ἡ art. nom. fem. sg. ὁ ἡ τό the, this, that, he, she, it
ἐπίνοια n. nom. fem. sg. ἐπίνοια thought
τῆς art. gen. fem. sg. ὁ ἡ τό the, this, that, he, she, it
κακίας n. gen. fem. sg. κακία malice, maliciousness, evil, naughtiness, wickedness
σου pron. gen. 2p. sg. σύ thou, you
23 εἰς prep. εἰς (+acc) into, to, unto, for, in, on, toward, against, upon, at, among
γὰρ conj. γάρ for, and, because, but, indeed
χολὴν n. acc. fem. sg. χολή gall
πικρίας n. gen. fem. sg. πικρία bitterness
καὶ conj. καί and, even, also, but
σύνδεσμον n. acc. masc. sg. σύνδεσμος bond, band
ἀδικίας n. gen. fem. sg. ἀδικία iniquity, unrighteousness, unjust, wrong
σε pron. acc. 2p. sg. σύ thou, you
24 δὲ conj. δέ but, and, now, also, to the contrary, rather, then
ὁ art. nom. masc. sg. ὁ ἡ τό the, this, that, he, she, it
Σίμων n. nom. masc. sg. Σίμων Simon
ὑμεῖς pron. nom. 2p. pl. σύ thou, you
ὑπὲρ prep. ὑπέρ (+gen) for, of, for the sake of, (+acc) above, more than
ἐμοῦ pron. gen. 1p. sg. ἐγώ I
πρὸς prep. πρός (+gen) for, (+dat) at, (+acc) unto, to, with, for, against
τὸν art. acc. masc. sg. ὁ ἡ τό the, this, that, he, she, it
Κύριον n. acc. masc. sg. κύριος Lord, lord, master, sir, LORD, God, Master, owner
ὅπως adv. ὅπως that, how, to, because, so that, when

μηδὲν num. nom. neut. sg. μηδείς μηδεμία μηδέν no man, nothing, no, none, not at all
ἐπ' prep. ἐπί (+gen) on, in, upon, (+dat) in, at, for, upon, (+acc) on, upon, unto, to, against
ἐμὲ pron. acc. 1p. sg. ἐγώ I
ὧν relative pron. gen. neut. pl. ὅς ἥ ὅ who, which, what, that
25 Οἱ art. nom. masc. pl. ὁ ἡ τό the, this, that, he, she, it
μέν conj. μέν indeed, verily, truly, even, so, some
οὖν conj. οὖν therefore, then, so, and, now, wherefore
καὶ conj. καί and, even, also, but
τὸν art. acc. masc. sg. ὁ ἡ τό the, this, that, he, she, it
λόγον n. acc. masc. sg. λόγος word, saying, account, speech, thing, matter
τοῦ art. gen. masc. sg. ὁ ἡ τό the, this, that, he, she, it
Κυρίου n. gen. masc. sg. κύριος Lord, lord, master, sir, LORD, God, Master, owner
εἰς prep. εἰς (+acc) into, to, unto, for, in, on, toward, against, upon, at, among
Ἱερουσαλήμ pron. name. fem. inde. Ἱερουσαλήμ Jerusalem
πολλάς adj. acc. fem. pl. πολύς many, great, much, long, abundant
τε conj. τέ and, both, also
κώμας n. acc. fem. pl. κώμη village, town
τῶν art. gen. masc. pl. ὁ ἡ τό the, this, that, he, she, it
Σαμαρειτῶν n. gen. masc. pl. Σαμαρείτης Samaritan
26 Ἄγγελος n. nom. masc. sg. ἄγγελος angel, messenger
δὲ conj. δέ but, and, now, also, to the contrary, rather, then
Κυρίου n. gen. masc. sg. κύριος Lord, lord, master, sir, LORD, God, Master, owner
πρὸς prep. πρός (+gen) for, (+dat) at, (+acc) unto, to, with, for, against
Φίλιππον n. acc. masc. sg. Φίλιππος Philip, Philippi
καὶ conj. καί and, even, also, but
κατὰ prep. κατά (+gen) against, by, throughout, down, (+acc) according to, after, with
μεσημβρίαν n. acc. fem. sg. μεσημβρία south, noon
ἐπὶ prep. ἐπί (+gen) on, in, upon, (+dat) in, at, for, upon, (+acc) on, upon, unto, to, against
τὴν art. acc. fem. sg. ὁ ἡ τό the, this, that, he, she, it
ὁδὸν n. acc. fem. sg. ὁδός way, journey, highway
τὴν art. acc. fem. sg. ὁ ἡ τό the, this, that, he, she, it
ἀπὸ prep. ἀπό (+gen) from, of, out of, since, for, off, at, by, in, on
Ἱερουσαλὴμ pron. name. fem. inde. Ἱερουσαλήμ Jerusalem
εἰς prep. εἰς (+acc) into, to, unto, for, in, on, toward, against, upon, at, among
Γάζαν n. acc. fem. sg. Γάζα Gaza
αὕτη demo. pron. nom. fem. sg. οὗτος αὕτη τοῦτο this, the same, this same, he, she, it
ἔρημος adj. nom. fem. sg. ἔρημος wilderness, desert
27 καὶ conj. καί and, even, also, but
καὶ conj. καί and, even, also, but
ἀνὴρ n. nom. masc. sg. ἀνήρ man, husband, sir
Αἰθίοψ n. nom. masc. sg. Αἰθίοψ Ethiopia, Ethiopian
εὐνοῦχος n. nom. masc. sg. εὐνοῦχος eunuch
δυνάστης n. nom. masc. sg. δυνάστης mighty, of great authority, Potentate
Κανδάκης n. gen. fem. sg. Κανδάκη Candace
τῆς art. gen. fem. sg. ὁ ἡ τό the, this, that, he, she, it
βασιλίσσης n. gen. fem. sg. βασίλισσα queen
Αἰθιόπων n. gen. masc. pl. Αἰθίοψ Ethiopia, Ethiopian
ὃς relative pron. nom. masc. sg. ὅς ἥ ὅ who, which, what, that
ἐπὶ prep. ἐπί (+gen) on, in, upon, (+dat) in, at, for, upon, (+acc) on, upon, unto, to, against
πάσης adj. gen. fem. sg. πᾶς πᾶσα πᾶν all, every, whosoever, every one, no, whole, any
τῆς art. gen. fem. sg. ὁ ἡ τό the, this, that, he, she, it
γάζης n. gen. fem. sg. γάζα treasure
αὐτῆς pron. gen. fem. 3p. sg. αὐτός ή ό self, of oneself, even, very, the same, he, she, it
ὃς relative pron. nom. masc. sg. ὅς ἥ ὅ who, which, what, that
εἰς prep. εἰς (+acc) into, to, unto, for, in, on, toward, against, upon, at, among

Ἱερουσαλήμ pron. name. fem. inde. Ἱερουσαλήμ Jerusalem
28 τε conj. τέ and, both, also
καὶ conj. καί and, even, also, but
ἐπὶ prep. ἐπί (+gen) on, in, upon, (+dat) in, at, for, upon, (+acc) on, upon, unto, to, against
τοῦ art. gen. neut. sg. ὁ ἡ τό the, this, that, he, she, it
ἅρματος n. gen. neut. sg. ἅρμα chariot
αὐτοῦ pron. gen. masc. 3p. sg. αὐτός ή ό self, of oneself, even, very, the same, he, she, it
τὸν art. acc. masc. sg. ὁ ἡ τό the, this, that, he, she, it
προφήτην n. acc. masc. sg. προφήτης prophet
Ἠσαΐαν n. acc. masc. sg. Ἠσαΐας Esaias, Isaiah
29 δὲ conj. δέ but, and, now, also, to the contrary, rather, then
τὸ art. nom. neut. sg. ὁ ἡ τό the, this, that, he, she, it
Πνεῦμα n. nom. neut. sg. πνεῦμα spirit, Spirit, Ghost, ghost, life. of the spirit, wind
τῷ art. dat. masc. sg. ὁ ἡ τό the, this, that, he, she, it
Φιλίππῳ n. dat. masc. sg. Φίλιππος Philip, Philippi
καὶ conj. καί and, even, also, but
τῷ art. dat. neut. sg. ὁ ἡ τό the, this, that, he, she, it
ἅρματι n. dat. neut. sg. ἅρμα chariot
τούτῳ demo. pron. dat. neut. sg. οὗτος αὕτη τοῦτο this, the same, this same, he, she, it
30 δὲ conj. δέ but, and, now, also, to the contrary, rather, then
ὁ art. nom. masc. sg. ὁ ἡ τό the, this, that, he, she, it
Φίλιππος n. nom. masc. sg. Φίλιππος Philip, Philippi
αὐτοῦ pron. gen. masc. 3p. sg. αὐτός ή ό self, of oneself, even, very, the same, he, she, it
τὸν art. acc. masc. sg. ὁ ἡ τό the, this, that, he, she, it
προφήτην n. acc. masc. sg. προφήτης prophet
Ἠσαΐαν n. acc. masc. sg. Ἠσαΐας Esaias, Isaiah
καὶ conj. καί and, even, also, but
Ἆρά adv. ἆρα therefore
γε particle. γέ yet, and beside, at least, doubtless
ἃ relative pron. acc. neut. pl. ὅς ἥ ὅ who, which, what, that
31 ὁ art. nom. masc. sg. ὁ ἡ τό the, this, that, he, she, it
δὲ conj. δέ but, and, now, also, to the contrary, rather, then
Πῶς adv. πῶς how, by what means, after what manner
γὰρ particle. γάρ for, and, because, but, indeed
ἂν particle. ἄν Indicating contingency. No English translation.
ἐὰν conj. ἐάν if, soever, except, though, and if, but, whether, if so, so
μή particle of negation. μή not, no, lest, neither, none, nothing, nor, never, without
τις indefinite pron. nom. masc. sg. τὶς certain, some, any man, one, any thing
με pron. acc. 1p. sg. ἐγώ I
τε conj. τέ and, both, also
τὸν art. acc. masc. sg. ὁ ἡ τό the, this, that, he, she, it
Φίλιππον n. acc. masc. sg. Φίλιππος Philip, Philippi
σὺν prep. σύν (+dat) with, beside
αὐτῷ pron. dat. masc. 3p. sg. αὐτός ή ό self, of oneself, even, very, the same, he, she, it
32 ἡ art. nom. fem. sg. ὁ ἡ τό the, this, that, he, she, it
δὲ conj. δέ but, and, now, also, to the contrary, rather, then
περιοχὴ n. nom. fem. sg. περιοχή place, context
τῆς art. gen. fem. sg. ὁ ἡ τό the, this, that, he, she, it
γραφῆς n. gen. fem. sg. γραφή scripture
ἣν relative pron. acc. fem. sg. ὅς ἥ ὅ who, which, what, that
αὕτη demo. pron. nom. fem. sg. οὗτος αὕτη τοῦτο this, the same, this same, he, she, it
Ὡς conj. ὡς as, when, as it were, how, about, like, as soon as, even as, while
πρόβατον n. nom. neut. sg. πρόβατον sheep
ἐπὶ prep. ἐπί (+gen) on, in, upon, (+dat) in, at, for, upon, (+acc) on, upon, unto, to, against
σφαγὴν n. acc. fem. sg. σφαγή slaughter

καὶ conj. καί and, even, also, but
ὡς adv. ὡς as, when, as it were, how, about, like, as soon as, even as, while
ἀμνὸς n. nom. masc. sg. ἀμνός lamb, Lamb
ἐναντίον adv. ἐναντίον before, in the sight of
τοῦ art. gen. masc. sg. ὁ ἡ τό the, this, that, he, she, it
αὐτὸν pron. acc. masc. 3p. sg. αὐτός ἡ ό self, of oneself, even, very, the same, he, she, it
ἄφωνος adj. nom. masc. sg. ἄφωνος dumb, without signification
οὕτως adv. οὕτω οὕτως so, even so, thus, on this wise, likewise, after this manner
οὐκ particle of negation. οὐ οὐκ οὐχ not, no, neither, none, nay, nor, never, nothing
τὸ art. acc. neut. sg. ὁ ἡ τό the, this, that, he, she, it
στόμα n. acc. neut. sg. στόμα mouth, face, edge
αὐτοῦ pron. gen. masc. 3p. sg. αὐτός ἡ ό self, of oneself, even, very, the same, he, she, it
33 ἐν prep. ἐν ἐν (+dat) in, by, with, among, at, on, through, to, within, into, of, for
τῇ art. dat. fem. sg. ὁ ἡ τό the, this, that, he, she, it
ταπεινώσει n. dat. fem. sg. ταπείνωσις low estate, humiliation, that is made low
αὐτοῦ pron. gen. masc. 3p. sg. αὐτός ἡ ό self, of oneself, even, very, the same, he, she, it
ἡ art. nom. fem. sg. ὁ ἡ τό the, this, that, he, she, it
κρίσις n. nom. fem. sg. κρίσις judgment, damnation, accusation, condemnation
αὐτοῦ pron. gen. masc. 3p. sg. αὐτός ἡ ό self, of oneself, even, very, the same, he, she, it
τὴν art. acc. fem. sg. ὁ ἡ τό the, this, that, he, she, it
δὲ conj. δέ but, and, now, also, to the contrary, rather, then
γενεὰν n. acc. fem. sg. γενεά generation, age, time, nation
αὐτοῦ pron. gen. masc. 3p. sg. αὐτός ἡ ό self, of oneself, even, very, the same, he, she, it
τίς interrog. pron. nom. masc. sg. τίς what, who, why, where, which, how
ὅτι conj. ὅτι that, for, because, how that, how, because that, for that, though
ἀπὸ prep. ἀπό (+gen) from, of, out of, since, for, off, at, by, in, on
τῆς art. gen. fem. sg. ὁ ἡ τό the, this, that, he, she, it
γῆς n. gen. fem. sg. γῆ earth, land, ground, country
ἡ art. nom. fem. sg. ὁ ἡ τό the, this, that, he, she, it
ζωὴ n. nom. fem. sg. ζωή life, lifetime
αὐτοῦ pron. gen. masc. 3p. sg. αὐτός ἡ ό self, of oneself, even, very, the same, he, she, it
34 δὲ conj. δέ but, and, now, also, to the contrary, rather, then
ὁ art. nom. masc. sg. ὁ ἡ τό the, this, that, he, she, it
εὐνοῦχος n. nom. masc. sg. εὐνοῦχος eunuch
τῷ art. dat. masc. sg. ὁ ἡ τό the, this, that, he, she, it
Φιλίππῳ n. dat. masc. sg. Φίλιππος Philip, Philippi
σου pron. gen. 2p. sg. σύ thou, you
περὶ prep. περί (+gen) of, for, concerning, (+acc) about, concerning, in
τίνος interrog. pron. gen. masc. sg. τίς what, who, why, where, which, how
ὁ art. nom. masc. sg. ὁ ἡ τό the, this, that, he, she, it
προφήτης n. nom. masc. sg. προφήτης prophet
τοῦτο demo. pron. acc. neut. sg. οὗτος αὕτη τοῦτο this, the same, this same, he, she, it
περὶ prep. περί (+gen) of, for, concerning, (+acc) about, concerning, in
ἑαυτοῦ reflexive pron. gen. masc. 3p. sg. ἑαυτοῦ himself, herself, itself, yourself, ourselves
ἢ particle. ἤ or, than, either, nor, or else, and, rather than
περὶ prep. περί (+gen) of, for, concerning, (+acc) about, concerning, in
ἑτέρου adj. gen. masc. sg. ἕτερος another, other, else, strange
τινός indefinite pron. gen. masc. sg. τὶς certain, some, any man, one, any thing
35 δὲ conj. δέ but, and, now, also, to the contrary, rather, then
ὁ art. nom. masc. sg. ὁ ἡ τό the, this, that, he, she, it
Φίλιππος n. nom. masc. sg. Φίλιππος Philip, Philippi
τὸ art. acc. neut. sg. ὁ ἡ τό the, this, that, he, she, it
στόμα n. acc. neut. sg. στόμα mouth, face, edge
αὐτοῦ pron. gen. masc. 3p. sg. αὐτός ἡ ό self, of oneself, even, very, the same, he, she, it
καὶ conj. καί and, even, also, but

ἀπὸ prep. ἀπό (+gen) from, of, out of, since, for, off, at, by, in, on
τῆς art. gen. fem. sg. ὁ ἡ τό the, this, that, he, she, it
γραφῆς n. gen. fem. sg. γραφή scripture
ταύτης demo. pron. gen. fem. sg. οὗτος αὕτη τοῦτο this, the same, this same, he, she, it
αὐτῷ pron. dat. masc. 3p. sg. αὐτός ἡ ὁ self, of oneself, even, very, the same, he, she, it
τὸν art. acc. masc. sg. ὁ ἡ τό the, this, that, he, she, it
Ἰησοῦν n. acc. masc. sg. Ἰησοῦς Jesus
36 ὡς adv. ὡς as, when, as it were, how, about, like, as soon as, even as, while
δὲ conj. δέ but, and, now, also, to the contrary, rather, then
κατὰ prep. κατά (+gen) against, by, throughout, down, (+acc) according to, after, with
τὴν art. acc. fem. sg. ὁ ἡ τό the, this, that, he, she, it
ὁδόν n. acc. fem. sg. ὁδός way, journey, highway
ἐπί prep. ἐπί (+gen) on, in, upon, (+dat) in, at, for, upon, (+acc) on, upon, unto, to, against
τι indefinite pron. acc. neut. sg. τὶς certain, some, any man, one, any thing
ὕδωρ n. acc. neut. sg. ὕδωρ water
καί conj. καί and, even, also, but
ὁ art. nom. masc. sg. ὁ ἡ τό the, this, that, he, she, it
εὐνοῦχος n. nom. masc. sg. εὐνοῦχος eunuch
ὕδωρ n. nom. neut. sg. ὕδωρ water
τί interrog. pron. nom. neut. sg. τίς what, who, why, where, which, how
με pron. acc. 1p. sg. ἐγώ I
37 δὲ conj. δέ but, and, now, also, to the contrary, rather, then
ὁ art. nom. masc. sg. ὁ ἡ τό the, this, that, he, she, it
Φίλιππος n. nom. masc. sg. Φίλιππος Philip, Philippi
Εἰ conj. εἰ if, whether, that, though, forasmuch
ἐξ prep. ἐκ ἐξ (+gen) of, from, out of, by, on, with, in, among, through
ὅλης adj. gen. fem. sg. ὅλος all, whole, every whit, altogether
τῆς art. gen. fem. sg. ὁ ἡ τό the, this, that, he, she, it
καρδίας n. gen. fem. sg. καρδία heart
δὲ conj. δέ but, and, now, also, to the contrary, rather, then
τὸν art. acc. masc. sg. ὁ ἡ τό the, this, that, he, she, it
υἱὸν n. acc. masc. sg. υἱός son, child, descendant, offspring, heir
τοῦ art. gen. masc. sg. ὁ ἡ τό the, this, that, he, she, it
Θεοῦ n. gen. masc. sg. θεός God, god
τὸν art. acc. masc. sg. ὁ ἡ τό the, this, that, he, she, it
Ἰησοῦν n. acc. masc. sg. Ἰησοῦς Jesus
Χριστόν n. acc. masc. sg. Χριστός Christ
38 καὶ conj. καί and, even, also, but
τὸ art. acc. neut. sg. ὁ ἡ τό the, this, that, he, she, it
ἅρμα n. acc. neut. sg. ἅρμα chariot
καὶ conj. καί and, even, also, but
ἀμφότεροι adj. nom. masc. pl. ἀμφότερος both
εἰς prep. εἰς (+acc) into, to, unto, for, in, on, toward, against, upon, at, among
τὸ art. acc. neut. sg. ὁ ἡ τό the, this, that, he, she, it
ὕδωρ n. acc. neut. sg. ὕδωρ water
ὅ art. nom. masc. sg. ὁ ἡ τό the, this, that, he, she, it
τε conj. τέ and, both, also
Φίλιππος n. nom. masc. sg. Φίλιππος Philip, Philippi
καὶ conj. καί and, even, also, but
ὁ art. nom. masc. sg. ὁ ἡ τό the, this, that, he, she, it
εὐνοῦχος n. nom. masc. sg. εὐνοῦχος eunuch
καὶ conj. καί and, even, also, but
αὐτόν pron. acc. masc. 3p. sg. αὐτός ἡ ὁ self, of oneself, even, very, the same, he, she, it
39 ὅτε adv. ὅτε when, after that, as soon as, while, after
δὲ conj. δέ but, and, now, also, to the contrary, rather, then

ἐκ prep. ἐκ ἐξ (+gen) of, from, out of, by, on, with, in, among, through
τοῦ art. gen. neut. sg. ὁ ἡ τό the, this, that, he, she, it
ὕδατος n. gen. neut. sg. ὕδωρ water
Πνεῦμα n. nom. neut. sg. πνεῦμα spirit, Spirit, Ghost, ghost, life. of the spirit, wind
Κυρίου n. gen. masc. sg. κύριος Lord, lord, master, sir, LORD, God, Master, owner
τὸν art. acc. masc. sg. ὁ ἡ τό the, this, that, he, she, it
Φίλιππον n. acc. masc. sg. Φίλιππος Philip, Philippi
καὶ conj. καί and, even, also, but
οὐκ particle of negation. οὐ οὐκ οὐχ not, no, neither, none, nay, nor, never, nothing
αὐτὸν pron. acc. masc. 3p. sg. αὐτός ἡ ὁ self, of oneself, even, very, the same, he, she, it
οὐκέτι adv. οὐκέτι or οὐκ ἔτι no more, no longer, not any more
ὁ art. nom. masc. sg. ὁ ἡ τό the, this, that, he, she, it
εὐνοῦχος n. nom. masc. sg. εὐνοῦχος eunuch
γὰρ conj. γάρ for, and, because, but, indeed
τὴν art. acc. fem. sg. ὁ ἡ τό the, this, that, he, she, it
ὁδὸν n. acc. fem. sg. ὁδός way, journey, highway
αὐτοῦ pron. gen. masc. 3p. sg. αὐτός ἡ ὁ self, of oneself, even, very, the same, he, she, it
40 Φίλιππος n. nom. masc. sg. Φίλιππος Philip, Philippi
δὲ conj. δέ but, and, now, also, to the contrary, rather, then
εἰς prep. εἰς (+acc) into, to, unto, for, in, on, toward, against, upon, at, among
Ἄζωτον n. acc. fem. sg. Ἄζωτος Azotus
καὶ conj. καί and, even, also, but
τὰς art. acc. fem. pl. ὁ ἡ τό the, this, that, he, she, it
πόλεις n. acc. fem. pl. πόλις city
πάσας adj. acc. fem. pl. πᾶς πᾶσα πᾶν all, every, whosoever, every one, no, whole, any
ἕως conj. ἕως till, until, unto, until when, while, as far as, even, until now
τοῦ art. gen. neut. sg. ὁ ἡ τό the, this, that, he, she, it
αὐτὸν pron. acc. masc. 3p. sg. αὐτός ἡ ὁ self, of oneself, even, very, the same, he, she, it
εἰς prep. εἰς (+acc) into, to, unto, for, in, on, toward, against, upon, at, among
Καισάρειαν n. acc. fem. sg. Καισάρεια Caesarea

9

1 Ὁ art. nom. masc. sg. ὁ ἡ τό the, this, that, he, she, it
δὲ conj. δέ but, and, now, also, to the contrary, rather, then
Σαῦλος n. nom. masc. sg. Σαῦλος Saul
ἔτι adv. ἔτι yet, more, any more, further, still, moreover
ἀπειλῆς n. gen. fem. sg. ἀπειλή threatening
καὶ conj. καί and, even, also, but
φόνου n. gen. masc. sg. φόνος murder, slaughter
εἰς prep. εἰς (+acc) into, to, unto, for, in, on, toward, against, upon, at, among
τοὺς art. acc. masc. pl. ὁ ἡ τό the, this, that, he, she, it
μαθητὰς n. acc. masc. pl. μαθητής disciple
τοῦ art. gen. masc. sg. ὁ ἡ τό the, this, that, he, she, it
Κυρίου n. gen. masc. sg. κύριος Lord, lord, master, sir, LORD, God, Master, owner
τῷ art. dat. masc. sg. ὁ ἡ τό the, this, that, he, she, it
ἀρχιερεῖ n. dat. masc. sg. ἀρχιερεύς chief priest, high priest
2 παρ' prep. παρά (+gen) of, from, (+dat) with, for, (+acc) beside, at, by, above, against
αὐτοῦ pron. gen. masc. 3p. sg. αὐτός ἡ ὁ self, of oneself, even, very, the same, he, she, it
ἐπιστολὰς n. acc. fem. pl. ἐπιστολή letter, epistle
εἰς prep. εἰς (+acc) into, to, unto, for, in, on, toward, against, upon, at, among
Δαμασκὸν n. acc. fem. sg. Δαμασκός Damascus
πρὸς prep. πρός (+gen) for, (+dat) at, (+acc) unto, to, with, for, against
τὰς art. acc. fem. pl. ὁ ἡ τό the, this, that, he, she, it
συναγωγάς n. acc. fem. pl. συναγωγή synagogue, assembly, congregation

ὅπως adv. ὅπως that, how, to, because, so that, when
ἐάν conj. ἐάν if, soever, except, though, and if, but, whether, if so, so
τινας indefinite pron. acc. masc. pl. τὶς certain, some, any man, one, any thing
τῆς art. gen. fem. sg. ὁ ἡ τό the, this, that, he, she, it
ὁδοῦ n. gen. fem. sg. ὁδός way, journey, highway
ἄνδρας n. acc. masc. pl. ἀνήρ man, husband, sir
τε conj. τέ and, both, also
καὶ conj. καί and, even, also, but
γυναῖκας n. acc. fem. pl. γυνή woman, wife
εἰς prep. εἰς (+acc) into, to, unto, for, in, on, toward, against, upon, at, among
Ἰερουσαλήμ pron. name. fem. inde. Ἰερουσαλήμ Jerusalem
3 ἐν prep. ἐν (+dat) in, by, with, among, at, on, through, to, within, into, of, for
δὲ conj. δέ but, and, now, also, to the contrary, rather, then
τῷ art. dat. neut. sg. ὁ ἡ τό the, this, that, he, she, it
αὐτὸν pron. acc. masc. 3p. sg. αὐτός ή ό self, of oneself, even, very, the same, he, she, it
τῇ art. dat. fem. sg. ὁ ἡ τό the, this, that, he, she, it
Δαμασκῷ n. dat. fem. sg. Δαμασκός Damascus
καὶ conj. καί and, even, also, but
ἐξαίφνης adv. ἐξαίφνης suddenly
αὐτὸν pron. acc. masc. 3p. sg. αὐτός ή ό self, of oneself, even, very, the same, he, she, it
φῶς n. nom. neut. sg. φῶς light, fire
ἀπὸ prep. ἀπό (+gen) from, of, out of, since, for, off, at, by, in, on
τοῦ art. gen. masc. sg. ὁ ἡ τό the, this, that, he, she, it
οὐρανοῦ n. gen. masc. sg. οὐρανός heaven, air, sky
4 καὶ conj. καί and, even, also, but
ἐπὶ prep. ἐπί (+gen) on, in, upon, (+dat) in, at, for, upon, (+acc) on, upon, unto, to, against
τὴν art. acc. fem. sg. ὁ ἡ τό the, this, that, he, she, it
γῆν n. acc. fem. sg. γῆ earth, land, ground, country
φωνὴν n. acc. fem. sg. φωνή voice, sound, noise
αὐτῷ pron. dat. masc. 3p. sg. αὐτός ή ό self, of oneself, even, very, the same, he, she, it
Σαούλ n. voc. masc. sg. Σαούλ Saul
Σαούλ n. voc. masc. sg. Σαούλ Saul
τί interrog. pron. acc. neut. sg. τίς what, who, why, where, which, how
με pron. acc. 1p. sg. ἐγώ I
5 δέ conj. δέ but, and, now, also, to the contrary, rather, then
Τίς interrog. pron. nom. masc. sg. τίς what, who, why, where, which, how
Κύριε n. voc. masc. sg. κύριος Lord, lord, master, sir, LORD, God, Master, owner
ὁ art. nom. masc. sg. ὁ ἡ τό the, this, that, he, she, it
δέ conj. δέ but, and, now, also, to the contrary, rather, then
Κύριος n. nom. masc. sg. κύριος Lord, lord, master, sir, LORD, God, Master, owner
Ἐγώ pron. nom. 1p. sg. ἐγώ I
Ἰησοῦς n. nom. masc. sg. Ἰησοῦς Jesus
ὃν relative pron. acc. masc. sg. ὅς ἥ ὅ who, which, what, that
σὺ pron. nom. 2p. sg. σύ thou, you
σκληρόν adj. nom. neut. sg. σκληρός hard, fierce
σοι pron. dat. 2p. sg. σύ thou, you
πρὸς prep. πρός (+gen) for, (+dat) at, (+acc) unto, to, with, for, against
κέντρα n. acc. neut. pl. κέντρον sting, prick
6 τε conj. τέ and, both, also
καὶ conj. καί and, even, also, but
Κύριε n. voc. masc. sg. κύριος Lord, lord, master, sir, LORD, God, Master, owner
τί interrog. pron. nom. neut. sg. τίς what, who, why, where, which, how
με pron. acc. 1p. sg. ἐγώ I
καὶ conj. καί and, even, also, but
ὁ art. nom. masc. sg. ὁ ἡ τό the, this, that, he, she, it

Κύριος n. nom. masc. sg. κύριος Lord, lord, master, sir, LORD, God, Master, owner
πρὸς prep. πρός (+gen) for, (+dat) at, (+acc) unto, to, with, for, against
αὐτόν pron. acc. masc. 3p. sg. αὐτός ή ό self, of oneself, even, very, the same, he, she, it
καὶ conj. καί and, even, also, but
εἰς prep. εἰς (+acc) into, to, unto, for, in, on, toward, against, upon, at, among
τὴν art. acc. fem. sg. ὁ ἡ τό the, this, that, he, she, it
πόλιν n. acc. fem. sg. πόλις city
καὶ conj. καί and, even, also, but
σοι pron. dat. 2p. sg. σύ thou, you
τί interrog. pron. nom. neut. sg. τίς what, who, why, where, which, how
σε pron. acc. 2p. sg. σύ thou, you
7 οἱ art. nom. masc. pl. ὁ ἡ τό the, this, that, he, she, it
δὲ conj. δέ but, and, now, also, to the contrary, rather, then
ἄνδρες n. nom. masc. pl. ἀνήρ man, husband, sir
οἱ art. nom. masc. pl. ὁ ἡ τό the, this, that, he, she, it
αὐτῷ pron. dat. masc. 3p. sg. αὐτός ή ό self, of oneself, even, very, the same, he, she, it
ἐννεοί adj. nom. masc. pl. ἐννεός speechless
μέν conj. μέν indeed, verily, truly, even, so, some
τῆς art. gen. fem. sg. ὁ ἡ τό the, this, that, he, she, it
φωνῆς n. gen. fem. sg. φωνή voice, sound, noise
μηδένα num. acc. masc. sg. μηδείς μηδεμία μηδέν no man, nothing, no, none, not at all
δὲ conj. δέ but, and, now, also, to the contrary, rather, then
8 δὲ conj. δέ but, and, now, also, to the contrary, rather, then
ὁ art. nom. masc. sg. ὁ ἡ τό the, this, that, he, she, it
Σαῦλος n. nom. masc. sg. Σαῦλος Saul
ἀπὸ prep. ἀπό (+gen) from, of, out of, since, for, off, at, by, in, on
τῆς art. gen. fem. sg. ὁ ἡ τό the, this, that, he, she, it
γῆς n. gen. fem. sg. γῆ earth, land, ground, country
δὲ conj. δέ but, and, now, also, to the contrary, rather, then
τῶν art. gen. masc. pl. ὁ ἡ τό the, this, that, he, she, it
ὀφθαλμῶν n. gen. masc. pl. ὀφθαλμός eye, sight
αὐτοῦ pron. gen. masc. 3p. sg. αὐτός ή ό self, of oneself, even, very, the same, he, she, it
οὐδένα num. acc. masc. sg. οὐδείς no man, nothing, no, none, neither, not, nought
δὲ conj. δέ but, and, now, also, to the contrary, rather, then
αὐτὸν pron. acc. masc. 3p. sg. αὐτός ή ό self, of oneself, even, very, the same, he, she, it
εἰς prep. εἰς (+acc) into, to, unto, for, in, on, toward, against, upon, at, among
Δαμασκόν n. acc. fem. sg. Δαμασκός Damascus
9 καὶ conj. καί and, even, also, but
ἡμέρας n. acc. fem. pl. ἡμέρα day, time, year, while, age, day time
τρεῖς num. acc. fem. pl. τρεῖς three
μὴ particle of negation. μή not, no, lest, neither, none, nothing, nor, never, without
καὶ conj. καί and, even, also, but
οὐκ particle of negation. οὐ οὐκ οὐχ not, no, neither, none, nay, nor, never, nothing
οὐδὲ conj. οὐδέ neither, nor, not, no, not even, never, not yet
10 δὲ conj. δέ but, and, now, also, to the contrary, rather, then
τις indefinite pron. nom. masc. sg. τὶς certain, some, any man, one, any thing
μαθητὴς n. nom. masc. sg. μαθητής disciple
ἐν prep. ἐν (+dat) in, by, with, among, at, on, through, to, within, into, of, for
Δαμασκῷ n. dat. fem. sg. Δαμασκός Damascus
ὀνόματι n. dat. neut. sg. ὄνομα name, call, surname
Ἀνανίας n. nom. masc. sg. Ἀνανίας Ananias
καὶ conj. καί and, even, also, but
πρὸς prep. πρός (+gen) for, (+dat) at, (+acc) unto, to, with, for, against
αὐτὸν pron. acc. masc. 3p. sg. αὐτός ή ό self, of oneself, even, very, the same, he, she, it
ὁ art. nom. masc. sg. ὁ ἡ τό the, this, that, he, she, it

Κύριος n. nom. masc. sg. κύριος Lord, lord, master, sir, LORD, God, Master, owner
ἐν prep. ἐν (+dat) in, by, with, among, at, on, through, to, within, into, of, for
ὁράματι n. dat. neut. sg. ὅραμα vision, sight
'Ανανία n. voc. masc. sg. 'Ανανίας Ananias
ὁ art. nom. masc. sg. ὁ ἡ τό the, this, that, he, she, it
δὲ conj. δέ but, and, now, also, to the contrary, rather, then
ἐγώ pron. nom. 1p. sg. ἐγώ I
Κύριε n. voc. masc. sg. κύριος Lord, lord, master, sir, LORD, God, Master, owner
11 ὁ art. nom. masc. sg. ὁ ἡ τό the, this, that, he, she, it
δὲ conj. δέ but, and, now, also, to the contrary, rather, then
Κύριος n. nom. masc. sg. κύριος Lord, lord, master, sir, LORD, God, Master, owner
πρὸς prep. πρός (+gen) for, (+dat) at, (+acc) unto, to, with, for, against
αὐτόν pron. acc. masc. 3p. sg. αὐτός ή ό self, of oneself, even, very, the same, he, she, it
ἐπὶ prep. ἐπί (+gen) on, in, upon, (+dat) in, at, for, upon, (+acc) on, upon, unto, to, against
τὴν art. acc. fem. sg. ὁ ἡ τό the, this, that, he, she, it
ῥύμην n. acc. fem. sg. ῥύμη street, lane
τὴν art. acc. fem. sg. ὁ ἡ τό the, this, that, he, she, it
Εὐθεῖαν adj. acc. fem. sg. εὐθύς straight, right
καὶ conj. καί and, even, also, but
ἐν prep. ἐν (+dat) in, by, with, among, at, on, through, to, within, into, of, for
οἰκίᾳ n. dat. fem. sg. οἰκία house, home, household
'Ιούδα n. gen. masc. sg. 'Ιούδας Judas, Juda, Judah, Jude
Σαῦλον n. acc. masc. sg. Σαῦλος Saul
ὀνόματι n. dat. neut. sg. ὄνομα name, call, surname
Ταρσέα n. acc. masc. sg. Ταρσεύς of Tarsus
γὰρ conj. γάρ for, and, because, but, indeed
12 καὶ conj. καί and, even, also, but
ἐν prep. ἐν (+dat) in, by, with, among, at, on, through, to, within, into, of, for
ὁράματι n. dat. neut. sg. ὅραμα vision, sight
ἄνδρα n. acc. masc. sg. ἀνήρ man, husband, sir
ὀνόματι n. dat. neut. sg. ὄνομα name, call, surname
'Ανανίαν n. acc. masc. sg. 'Ανανίας Ananias
καὶ conj. καί and, even, also, but
αὐτῷ pron. dat. masc. 3p. sg. αὐτός ή ό self, of oneself, even, very, the same, he, she, it
χεῖρα n. acc. fem. sg. χείρ hand
ὅπως adv. ὅπως that, how, to, because, so that, when
13 δὲ conj. δέ but, and, now, also, to the contrary, rather, then
ὁ art. nom. masc. sg. ὁ ἡ τό the, this, that, he, she, it
'Ανανίας n. nom. masc. sg. 'Ανανίας Ananias
Κύριε n. voc. masc. sg. κύριος Lord, lord, master, sir, LORD, God, Master, owner
ἀπὸ prep. ἀπό (+gen) from, of, out of, since, for, off, at, by, in, on
πολλῶν adj. gen. masc. pl. πολύς many, great, much, long, abundant
περὶ prep. περί (+gen) of, for, concerning, (+acc) about, concerning, in
τοῦ art. gen. masc. sg. ὁ ἡ τό the, this, that, he, she, it
ἀνδρὸς n. gen. masc. sg. ἀνήρ man, husband, sir
τούτου demo. pron. gen. masc. sg. οὗτος αὕτη τοῦτο this, the same, this same, he, she, it
ὅσα relative pron. acc. neut. pl. ὅσος as many as, whatsoever, that, as long as, how much
κακὰ adj. acc. neut. pl. κακός evil, evil thing, noisome, wicked
τοῖς art. dat. masc. pl. ὁ ἡ τό the, this, that, he, she, it
ἁγίοις adj. dat. masc. pl. ἅγιος Holy, holy, saint, Holy One, holy thing, most holy
σου pron. gen. 2p. sg. σύ thou, you
ἐν prep. ἐν (+dat) in, by, with, among, at, on, through, to, within, into, of, for
'Ιερουσαλήμ pron. name. fem. inde. 'Ιερουσαλήμ Jerusalem
14 καὶ conj. καί and, even, also, but
ὧδε adv. ὧδε here, hither, in this place, there, this place

ἐξουσίαν n. acc. fem. sg. ἐξουσία power, authority, right, strength, jurisdiction
παρὰ prep. παρά (+gen) of, from, (+dat) with, for, (+acc) beside, at, by, above, against
τῶν art. gen. masc. pl. ὁ ἡ τό the, this, that, he, she, it
ἀρχιερέων n. gen. masc. pl. ἀρχιερεύς chief priest, high priest
πάντας adj. acc. masc. pl. πᾶς πᾶσα πᾶν all, every, whosoever, every one, no, whole, any
τοὺς art. acc. masc. pl. ὁ ἡ τό the, this, that, he, she, it
τὸ art. acc. neut. sg. ὁ ἡ τό the, this, that, he, she, it
ὄνομά n. acc. neut. sg. ὄνομα name, call, surname
σου pron. gen. 2p. sg. σύ thou, you
15 δὲ conj. δέ but, and, now, also, to the contrary, rather, then
πρὸς prep. πρός (+gen) for, (+dat) at, (+acc) unto, to, with, for, against
αὐτὸν pron. acc. masc. 3p. sg. αὐτός ή ό self, of oneself, even, very, the same, he, she, it
ὁ art. nom. masc. sg. ὁ ἡ τό the, this, that, he, she, it
Κύριος n. nom. masc. sg. κύριος Lord, lord, master, sir, LORD, God, Master, owner
ὅτι conj. ὅτι that, for, because, how that, how, because that, for that, though
σκεῦος n. nom. neut. sg. σκεῦος vessel, good, sail, stuff
ἐκλογῆς n. gen. fem. sg. ἐκλογή election, chosen
μοι pron. dat. 1p. sg. ἐγώ I
οὗτος demo. pron. nom. masc. sg. οὗτος αὕτη τοῦτο this, the same, this same, he, she, it
τοῦ art. gen. neut. sg. ὁ ἡ τό the, this, that, he, she, it
τὸ art. acc. neut. sg. ὁ ἡ τό the, this, that, he, she, it
ὄνομά n. acc. neut. sg. ὄνομα name, call, surname
μου pron. gen. 1p. sg. ἐγώ I
ἐνώπιον adv. ἐνώπιον before, in the sight of, in the presence of
ἐθνῶν n. gen. neut. pl. ἔθνος Gentile, nation, heathen, people
καὶ conj. καί and, even, also, but
βασιλέων n. gen. masc. pl. βασιλεύς king
υἱῶν n. gen. masc. pl. υἱός son, child, descendant, offspring, heir
τε conj. τέ and, both, also
Ἰσραήλ pron. name. masc. inde. Ἰσραήλ Israel
16 ἐγὼ pron. nom. 1p. sg. ἐγώ I
γὰρ conj. γάρ for, and, because, but, indeed
αὐτῷ pron. dat. masc. 3p. sg. αὐτός ή ό self, of oneself, even, very, the same, he, she, it
ὅσα relative pron. acc. neut. pl. ὅσος as many as, whatsoever, that, as long as, how much
αὐτὸν pron. acc. masc. 3p. sg. αὐτός ή ό self, of oneself, even, very, the same, he, she, it
ὑπὲρ prep. ὑπέρ (+gen) for, of, for the sake of, (+acc) above, more than
τοῦ art. gen. neut. sg. ὁ ἡ τό the, this, that, he, she, it
ὀνόματός n. gen. neut. sg. ὄνομα name, call, surname
μου pron. gen. 1p. sg. ἐγώ I
17 δὲ conj. δέ but, and, now, also, to the contrary, rather, then
Ἀνανίας n. nom. masc. sg. Ἀνανίας Ananias
καὶ conj. καί and, even, also, but
εἰς prep. εἰς (+acc) into, to, unto, for, in, on, toward, against, upon, at, among
τὴν art. acc. fem. sg. ὁ ἡ τό the, this, that, he, she, it
οἰκίαν n. acc. fem. sg. οἰκία house, home, household
καὶ conj. καί and, even, also, but
ἐπ' prep. ἐπί (+gen) on, in, upon, (+dat) in, at, for, upon, (+acc) on, upon, unto, to, against
αὐτὸν pron. acc. masc. 3p. sg. αὐτός ή ό self, of oneself, even, very, the same, he, she, it
τὰς art. acc. fem. pl. ὁ ἡ τό the, this, that, he, she, it
χεῖρας n. acc. fem. pl. χείρ hand
Σαοὺλ n. voc. masc. sg. Σαούλ Saul
ἀδελφέ n. voc. masc. sg. ἀδελφός brother
ὁ art. nom. masc. sg. ὁ ἡ τό the, this, that, he, she, it
Κύριος n. nom. masc. sg. κύριος Lord, lord, master, sir, LORD, God, Master, owner
με pron. acc. 1p. sg. ἐγώ I

Ἰησοῦς n. nom. masc. sg. Ἰησοῦς Jesus
ὁ art. nom. masc. sg. ὁ ἡ τό the, this, that, he, she, it
σοι pron. dat. 2p. sg. σύ thou, you
ἐν prep. ἐν (+dat) in, by, with, among, at, on, through, to, within, into, of, for
τῇ art. dat. fem. sg. ὁ ἡ τό the, this, that, he, she, it
ὁδῷ n. dat. fem. sg. ὁδός way, journey, highway
ᾗ relative pron. dat. fem. sg. ὅς ἥ ὅ who, which, what, that
ὅπως adv. ὅπως that, how, to, because, so that, when
καὶ conj. καί and, even, also, but
Πνεύματος n. gen. neut. sg. πνεῦμα spirit, Spirit, Ghost, ghost, life. of the spirit, wind
Ἁγινου adj. gen. neut. sg. ἅγιος Holy, holy, saint, Holy One, holy thing, most holy
18 καὶ conj. καί and, even, also, but
εὐθέως adv. εὐθέως immediately, straightway, forthwith, as soon as, by and by, shortly
ἀπὸ prep. ἀπό (+gen) from, of, out of, since, for, off, at, by, in, on
τῶν art. gen. masc. pl. ὁ ἡ τό the, this, that, he, she, it
ὀφθαλμῶν n. gen. masc. pl. ὀφθαλμός eye, sight
αὐτοῦ pron. gen. masc. 3p. sg. αὐτός ή ό self, of oneself, even, very, the same, he, she, it
ὡσεὶ adv. ὡσεί about, as, like, as it had been, as it were, like as
λεπίδες n. nom. fem. pl. λεπίς scale
τε conj. τέ and, both, also
παραχρῆμα adv. παραχρῆμα immediately, straightway, forthwith, presently, soon
καὶ conj. καί and, even, also, but
19 καὶ conj. καί and, even, also, but
τροφὴν n. acc. fem. sg. τροφή meat, food
δὲ conj. δέ but, and, now, also, to the contrary, rather, then
ὁ art. nom. masc. sg. ὁ ἡ τό the, this, that, he, she, it
Σαῦλος n. nom. masc. sg. Σαῦλος Saul
μετὰ prep. μετά (+gen) with, among, against, (+acc) after
τῶν art. gen. masc. pl. ὁ ἡ τό the, this, that, he, she, it
ἐν prep. ἐν (+dat) in, by, with, among, at, on, through, to, within, into, of, for
Δαμασκῷ n. dat. fem. sg. Δαμασκός Damascus
μαθητῶν n. gen. masc. pl. μαθητής disciple
ἡμέρας n. acc. fem. pl. ἡμέρα day, time, year, while, age, day time
τινὰς indefinite pron. acc. fem. pl. τὶς certain, some, any man, one, any thing
20 καὶ conj. καί and, even, also, but
εὐθέως adv. εὐθέως immediately, straightway, forthwith, as soon as, by and by, shortly
ἐν prep. ἐν (+dat) in, by, with, among, at, on, through, to, within, into, of, for
ταῖς art. dat. fem. pl. ὁ ἡ τό the, this, that, he, she, it
συναγωγαῖς n. dat. fem. pl. συναγωγή synagogue, assembly, congregation
τὸν art. acc. masc. sg. ὁ ἡ τό the, this, that, he, she, it
Χριστόν n. acc. masc. sg. Χριστός Christ
ὅτι conj. ὅτι that, for, because, how that, how, because that, for that, though
οὗτός demo. pron. nom. masc. sg. οὗτος αὕτη τοῦτο this, the same, this same, he, she, it
ὁ art. nom. masc. sg. ὁ ἡ τό the, this, that, he, she, it
υἱὸς n. nom. masc. sg. υἱός son, child, descendant, offspring, heir
τοῦ art. gen. masc. sg. ὁ ἡ τό the, this, that, he, she, it
Θεοῦ n. gen. masc. sg. θεός God, god
21 δὲ conj. δέ but, and, now, also, to the contrary, rather, then
πάντες adj. nom. masc. pl. πᾶς πᾶσα πᾶν all, every, whosoever, every one, no, whole, any
οἱ art. nom. masc. pl. ὁ ἡ τό the, this, that, he, she, it
καὶ conj. καί and, even, also, but
Οὐχ particle of negation. οὐ οὐκ οὐχ not, no, neither, none, nay, nor, never, nothing
οὗτός demo. pron. nom. masc. sg. οὗτος αὕτη τοῦτο this, the same, this same, he, she, it
ὁ art. nom. masc. sg. ὁ ἡ τό the, this, that, he, she, it
ἐν prep. ἐν (+dat) in, by, with, among, at, on, through, to, within, into, of, for

Ἰερουσαλὴμ pron. name. fem. inde. Ἰερουσαλήμ Jerusalem
τοὺς art. acc. masc. pl. ὁ ἡ τό the, this, that, he, she, it
τὸ art. acc. neut. sg. ὁ ἡ τό the, this, that, he, she, it
ὄνομα n. acc. neut. sg. ὄνομα name, call, surname
τοῦτο demo. pron. acc. neut. sg. οὗτος αὕτη τοῦτο this, the same, this same, he, she, it
καὶ conj. καί and, even, also, but
ὧδε adv. ὧδε here, hither, in this place, there, this place
εἰς prep. εἰς (+acc) into, to, unto, for, in, on, toward, against, upon, at, among
τοῦτο demo. pron. acc. neut. sg. οὗτος αὕτη τοῦτο this, the same, this same, he, she, it
ἵνα conj. ἵνα that, to, lest, for to, so that, albeit, because, for, so as
αὐτοὺς pron. acc. masc. 3p. pl. αὐτός ἡ ὁ self, of oneself, even, very, the same, he, she, it
ἐπὶ prep. ἐπί (+gen) on, in, upon, (+dat) in, at, for, upon, (+acc) on, upon, unto, to, against
τοὺς art. acc. masc. pl. ὁ ἡ τό the, this, that, he, she, it
ἀρχιερεῖς n. acc. masc. pl. ἀρχιερεύς chief priest, high priest
22 Σαῦλος n. nom. masc. sg. Σαῦλος Saul
δὲ conj. δέ but, and, now, also, to the contrary, rather, then
μᾶλλον compar. adv. μᾶλλον rather, more, more and more, better, much, much the more
καὶ conj. καί and, even, also, but
τοὺς art. acc. masc. pl. ὁ ἡ τό the, this, that, he, she, it
Ἰουδαίους adj. acc. masc. pl. Ἰουδαῖος Jew, Jewess
τοὺς art. acc. masc. pl. ὁ ἡ τό the, this, that, he, she, it
ἐν prep. ἐν (+dat) in, by, with, among, at, on, through, to, within, into, of, for
Δαμασκῷ n. dat. fem. sg. Δαμασκός Damascus
ὅτι conj. ὅτι that, for, because, how that, how, because that, for that, though
οὗτός demo. pron. nom. masc. sg. οὗτος αὕτη τοῦτο this, the same, this same, he, she, it
ὁ art. nom. masc. sg. ὁ ἡ τό the, this, that, he, she, it
Χριστός n. nom. masc. sg. Χριστός Christ
23 Ὡς conj. ὡς as, when, as it were, how, about, like, as soon as, even as, while
δὲ conj. δέ but, and, now, also, to the contrary, rather, then
ἡμέραι n. nom. fem. pl. ἡμέρα day, time, year, while, age, day time
ἱκαναί adj. nom. fem. pl. ἱκανός many, much, long, worthy, sufficient, great, able
οἱ art. nom. masc. pl. ὁ ἡ τό the, this, that, he, she, it
Ἰουδαῖοι adj. nom. masc. pl. Ἰουδαῖος Jew, Jewess
αὐτόν pron. acc. masc. 3p. sg. αὐτός ἡ ὁ self, of oneself, even, very, the same, he, she, it
24 δὲ conj. δέ but, and, now, also, to the contrary, rather, then
τῷ art. dat. masc. sg. ὁ ἡ τό the, this, that, he, she, it
Σαύλῳ n. dat. masc. sg. Σαῦλος Saul
ἡ art. nom. fem. sg. ὁ ἡ τό the, this, that, he, she, it
ἐπιβουλὴ n. nom. fem. sg. ἐπιβουλή laying await, lying in wait
αὐτῶν pron. gen. masc. 3p. pl. αὐτός ἡ ὁ self, of oneself, even, very, the same, he, she, it
τε conj. τέ and, both, also
τὰς art. acc. fem. pl. ὁ ἡ τό the, this, that, he, she, it
πύλας n. acc. fem. pl. πύλη gate
ἡμέρας n. gen. fem. sg. ἡμέρα day, time, year, while, age, day time
τε conj. τέ and, both, also
καὶ conj. καί and, even, also, but
νυκτὸς n. gen. fem. sg. νύξ night
ὅπως adv. ὅπως that, how, to, because, so that, when
αὐτὸν pron. acc. masc. 3p. sg. αὐτός ἡ ὁ self, of oneself, even, very, the same, he, she, it
25 δὲ conj. δέ but, and, now, also, to the contrary, rather, then
αὐτὸν pron. acc. masc. 3p. sg. αὐτός ἡ ὁ self, of oneself, even, very, the same, he, she, it
οἱ art. nom. masc. pl. ὁ ἡ τό the, this, that, he, she, it
μαθηταὶ n. nom. masc. pl. μαθητής disciple
νυκτὸς n. gen. fem. sg. νύξ night
διὰ prep. διά (+gen) by, through, with, in, of, (+acc) for, because of, for a cause

τοῦ art. gen. neut. sg. ὁ ἡ τό the, this, that, he, she, it
τείχους n. gen. neut. sg. τεῖχος wall
ἐν prep. ἐν (+dat) in, by, with, among, at, on, through, to, within, into, of, for
σπυρίδι n. dat. fem. sg. σπυρίς basket
26 δὲ conj. δέ but, and, now, also, to the contrary, rather, then
ὁ art. nom. masc. sg. ὁ ἡ τό the, this, that, he, she, it
Σαῦλος n. nom. masc. sg. Σαῦλος Saul
εἰς prep. εἰς (+acc) into, to, unto, for, in, on, toward, against, upon, at, among
Ἱερουσαλὴμ pron. name. fem. inde. Ἱερουσαλήμ Jerusalem
τοῖς art. dat. masc. pl. ὁ ἡ τό the, this, that, he, she, it
μαθηταῖς n. dat. masc. pl. μαθητής disciple
καὶ conj. καί and, even, also, but
πάντες adj. nom. masc. pl. πᾶς πᾶσα πᾶν all, every, whosoever, every one, no, whole, any
αὐτὸν pron. acc. masc. 3p. sg. αὐτός ή ό self, of oneself, even, very, the same, he, she, it
μὴ particle of negation. μή not, no, lest, neither, none, nothing, nor, never, without
ὅτι conj. ὅτι that, for, because, how that, how, because that, for that, though
μαθητής n. nom. masc. sg. μαθητής disciple
27 Βαρναβᾶς n. nom. masc. sg. Βαρναβᾶς Barnabas
δὲ conj. δέ but, and, now, also, to the contrary, rather, then
αὐτὸν pron. acc. masc. 3p. sg. αὐτός ή ό self, of oneself, even, very, the same, he, she, it
πρὸς prep. πρός (+gen) for, (+dat) at, (+acc) unto, to, with, for, against
τοὺς art. acc. masc. pl. ὁ ἡ τό the, this, that, he, she, it
ἀποστόλους n. acc. masc. pl. ἀπόστολος apostle, messenger, he that is sent
καὶ conj. καί and, even, also, but
αὐτοῖς pron. dat. masc. 3p. pl. αὐτός ή ό self, of oneself, even, very, the same, he, she, it
πῶς adv. πῶς how, by what means, after what manner
ἐν prep. ἐν (+dat) in, by, with, among, at, on, through, to, within, into, of, for
τῇ art. dat. fem. sg. ὁ ἡ τό the, this, that, he, she, it
ὁδῷ n. dat. fem. sg. ὁδός way, journey, highway
τὸν art. acc. masc. sg. ὁ ἡ τό the, this, that, he, she, it
Κύριον n. acc. masc. sg. κύριος Lord, lord, master, sir, LORD, God, Master, owner
καὶ conj. καί and, even, also, but
ὅτι conj. ὅτι that, for, because, how that, how, because that, for that, though
αὐτῷ pron. dat. masc. 3p. sg. αὐτός ή ό self, of oneself, even, very, the same, he, she, it
καὶ conj. καί and, even, also, but
πῶς adv. πῶς how, by what means, after what manner
ἐν prep. ἐν (+dat) in, by, with, among, at, on, through, to, within, into, of, for
Δαμασκῷ n. dat. fem. sg. Δαμασκός Damascus
ἐν prep. ἐν (+dat) in, by, with, among, at, on, through, to, within, into, of, for
τῷ art. dat. neut. sg. ὁ ἡ τό the, this, that, he, she, it
ὀνόματι n. dat. neut. sg. ὄνομα name, call, surname
τοῦ art. gen. masc. sg. ὁ ἡ τό the, this, that, he, she, it
Ἰησοῦ n. gen. masc. sg. Ἰησοῦς Jesus
28 καὶ conj. καί and, even, also, but
μετ' prep. μετά (+gen) with, among, against, (+acc) after
αὐτῶν pron. gen. masc. 3p. pl. αὐτός ή ό self, of oneself, even, very, the same, he, she, it
καὶ conj. καί and, even, also, but
ἐν prep. ἐν (+dat) in, by, with, among, at, on, through, to, within, into, of, for
Ἱερουσαλήμ pron. name. fem. inde. Ἱερουσαλήμ Jerusalem
29 καὶ conj. καί and, even, also, but
ἐν prep. ἐν (+dat) in, by, with, among, at, on, through, to, within, into, of, for
τῷ art. dat. neut. sg. ὁ ἡ τό the, this, that, he, she, it
ὀνόματι n. dat. neut. sg. ὄνομα name, call, surname
τοῦ art. gen. masc. sg. ὁ ἡ τό the, this, that, he, she, it
Κυρίου n. gen. masc. sg. κύριος Lord, lord, master, sir, LORD, God, Master, owner

Ἰησοῦ n. gen. masc. sg. Ἰησοῦς Jesus
τε conj. τέ and, both, also
καὶ conj. καί and, even, also, but
πρὸς prep. πρός (+gen) for, (+dat) at, (+acc) unto, to, with, for, against
τοὺς art. acc. masc. pl. ὁ ἡ τό the, this, that, he, she, it
Ἑλληνιστάς n. acc. masc. pl. Ἑλληνιστής Grecian
οἱ art. nom. masc. pl. ὁ ἡ τό the, this, that, he, she, it
δὲ conj. δέ but, and, now, also, to the contrary, rather, then
αὐτόν pron. acc. masc. 3p. sg. αὐτός ἡ ὁ self, of oneself, even, very, the same, he, she, it
30 δὲ conj. δέ but, and, now, also, to the contrary, rather, then
οἱ art. nom. masc. pl. ὁ ἡ τό the, this, that, he, she, it
ἀδελφοὶ n. nom. masc. pl. ἀδελφός brother
αὐτὸν pron. acc. masc. 3p. sg. αὐτός ἡ ὁ self, of oneself, even, very, the same, he, she, it
εἰς prep. εἰς (+acc) into, to, unto, for, in, on, toward, against, upon, at, among
Καισάρειαν n. acc. fem. sg. Καισάρεια Caesarea
καὶ conj. καί and, even, also, but
αὐτὸν pron. acc. masc. 3p. sg. αὐτός ἡ ὁ self, of oneself, even, very, the same, he, she, it
εἰς prep. εἰς (+acc) into, to, unto, for, in, on, toward, against, upon, at, among
Ταρσόν n. acc. fem. sg. Ταρσός Tarsus
31 Αἱ art. nom. fem. pl. ὁ ἡ τό the, this, that, he, she, it
μέν conj. μέν indeed, verily, truly, even, so, some
οὖν conj. οὖν therefore, then, so, and, now, wherefore
ἐκκλησίαι n. nom. fem. pl. ἐκκλησία church, assembly
καθ' prep. κατά (+gen) against, by, throughout, down, (+acc) according to, after, with
ὅλης adj. gen. fem. sg. ὅλος all, whole, every whit, altogether
τῆς art. gen. fem. sg. ὁ ἡ τό the, this, that, he, she, it
Ἰουδαίας n. gen. fem. sg. Ἰουδαία Judaea, Jewry
καὶ conj. καί and, even, also, but
Γαλιλαίας n. gen. fem. sg. Γαλιλαία Galilee
καὶ conj. καί and, even, also, but
Σαμαρείας n. gen. fem. sg. Σαμάρεια Samaria
εἰρήνην n. acc. fem. sg. εἰρήνη peace, quietness, rest
καὶ conj. καί and, even, also, but
τῷ art. dat. masc. sg. ὁ ἡ τό the, this, that, he, she, it
φόβῳ n. dat. masc. sg. φόβος fear, terror, sore afraid
τοῦ art. gen. masc. sg. ὁ ἡ τό the, this, that, he, she, it
Κυρίου n. gen. masc. sg. κύριος Lord, lord, master, sir, LORD, God, Master, owner
καὶ conj. καί and, even, also, but
τῇ art. dat. fem. sg. ὁ ἡ τό the, this, that, he, she, it
παρακλήσει n. dat. fem. sg. παράκλησις consolation, exhortation, comfort
τοῦ art. gen. neut. sg. ὁ ἡ τό the, this, that, he, she, it
Ἁγίου adj. gen. neut. sg. ἅγιος Holy, holy, saint, Holy One, holy thing, most holy
Πνεύματος n. gen. neut. sg. πνεῦμα spirit, Spirit, Ghost, ghost, life. of the spirit, wind
32 δὲ conj. δέ but, and, now, also, to the contrary, rather, then
Πέτρον n. acc. masc. sg. Πέτρος Peter
διὰ prep. διά (+gen) by, through, with, in, of, (+acc) for, because of, for a cause
πάντων adj. gen. neut. pl. πᾶς πᾶσα πᾶν all, every, whosoever, every one, no, whole, any
καὶ conj. καί and, even, also, but
πρὸς prep. πρός (+gen) for, (+dat) at, (+acc) unto, to, with, for, against
τοὺς art. acc. masc. pl. ὁ ἡ τό the, this, that, he, she, it
ἁγίους adj. acc. masc. pl. ἅγιος Holy, holy, saint, Holy One, holy thing, most holy
τοὺς art. acc. masc. pl. ὁ ἡ τό the, this, that, he, she, it
Λύδδαν n. acc. fem. sg. Λύδδα Lydda
33 δὲ conj. δέ but, and, now, also, to the contrary, rather, then
ἐκεῖ adv. ἐκεῖ there, thither, thitherward, yonder, yonder place

ἄνθρωπόν n. acc. masc. sg. ἄνθρωπος man, human being, person, one, certain
τινα indefinite pron. acc. masc. sg. τὶς certain, some, any man, one, any thing
Αἰνέαν n. acc. masc. sg. Αἰνέας Aeneas
ὀνόματι n. dat. neut. sg. ὄνομα name, call, surname
ἐξ prep. ἐκ ἐξ (+gen) of, from, out of, by, on, with, in, among, through
ἐτῶν n. gen. neut. pl. ἔτος year
ὀκτὼ num. gen. neut. pl. ὀκτώ eight
ἐπὶ prep. ἐπί (+gen) on, in, upon, (+dat) in, at, for, upon, (+acc) on, upon, unto, to, against
κραββάτῳ n. dat. masc. sg. κράββατος bed, couch
ὃς relative pron. nom. masc. sg. ὅς ἥ ὅ who, which, what, that
34 καὶ conj. καί and, even, also, but
αὐτῷ pron. dat. masc. 3p. sg. αὐτός ή ό self, of oneself, even, very, the same, he, she, it
ὁ art. nom. masc. sg. ὁ ἡ τό the, this, that, he, she, it
Πέτρος n. nom. masc. sg. Πέτρος Peter
Αἰνέα n. voc. masc. sg. Αἰνέας Aeneas
σε pron. acc. 2p. sg. σύ thou, you
Ἰησοῦς n. nom. masc. sg. Ἰησοῦς Jesus
ὁ art. nom. masc. sg. ὁ ἡ τό the, this, that, he, she, it
Χριστός n. nom. masc. sg. Χριστός Christ
καὶ conj. καί and, even, also, but
σεαυτῷ pron. dat. masc. 2p. sg. σεαυτοῦ σεαυτῷ σεαυτόν thyself, thine own self
καὶ conj. καί and, even, also, but
εὐθέως adv. εὐθέως immediately, straightway, forthwith, as soon as, by and by, shortly
35 καὶ conj. καί and, even, also, but
αὐτὸν pron. acc. masc. 3p. sg. αὐτός ή ό self, of oneself, even, very, the same, he, she, it
πάντες adj. nom. masc. pl. πᾶς πᾶσα πᾶν all, every, whosoever, every one, no, whole, any
οἱ art. nom. masc. pl. ὁ ἡ τό the, this, that, he, she, it
Λύδδαν n. acc. fem. sg. Λύδδα Lydda
καὶ conj. καί and, even, also, but
τὸν art. acc. masc. sg. ὁ ἡ τό the, this, that, he, she, it
Σαρῶνα n. acc. masc. sg. Σαρών Saron
οἵτινες relative pron. nom. masc. pl. ὅστις which, who, whosoever, that, whatsoever
ἐπὶ prep. ἐπί (+gen) on, in, upon, (+dat) in, at, for, upon, (+acc) on, upon, unto, to, against
τὸν art. acc. masc. sg. ὁ ἡ τό the, this, that, he, she, it
Κύριον n. acc. masc. sg. κύριος Lord, lord, master, sir, LORD, God, Master, owner
36 Ἐν prep. ἐν (+dat) in, by, with, among, at, on, through, to, within, into, of, for
Ἰόππῃ n. dat. fem. sg. Ἰόππη Joppa
δὲ conj. δέ but, and, now, also, to the contrary, rather, then
τις indefinite pron. nom. fem. sg. τὶς certain, some, any man, one, any thing
μαθήτρια n. nom. fem. sg. μαθήτρια female disciple
ὀνόματι n. dat. neut. sg. ὄνομα name, call, surname
Ταβιθά n. nom. fem. sg. Ταβιθά Tabitha
ἣ relative pron. nom. fem. sg. ὅς ἥ ὅ who, which, what, that
Δορκάς n. nom. fem. sg. Δορκάς Dorcas, gazelle, antelope
αὕτη demo. pron. nom. fem. sg. οὗτος αὕτη τοῦτο this, the same, this same, he, she, it
πλήρης adj. nom. fem. sg. πλήρης full
ἀγαθῶν adj. gen. neut. pl. ἀγαθός good, good thing, that which is good, well
ἔργων n. gen. neut. pl. ἔργον work, deed, doing labour
καὶ conj. καί and, even, also, but
ἐλεημοσυνῶν n. gen. fem. pl. ἐλεημοσύνη alms, almsdeed
ὧν relative pron. gen. fem. pl. ὅς ἥ ὅ who, which, what, that
37 δὲ conj. δέ but, and, now, also, to the contrary, rather, then
ἐν prep. ἐν (+dat) in, by, with, among, at, on, through, to, within, into, of, for
ταῖς art. dat. fem. pl. ὁ ἡ τό the, this, that, he, she, it
ἡμέραις n. dat. fem. pl. ἡμέρα day, time, year, while, age, day time

ἐκείναις demo. pron. dat. fem. pl. ἐκεῖνος that, he, the same, that same
αὐτὴν pron. acc. fem. 3p. sg. αὐτός ή ό self, of oneself, even, very, the same, he, she, it
δὲ conj. δέ but, and, now, also, to the contrary, rather, then
αὐτὴν pron. acc. fem. 3p. sg. αὐτός ή ό self, of oneself, even, very, the same, he, she, it
ἐν prep. ἐν (+dat) in, by, with, among, at, on, through, to, within, into, of, for
ὑπερῴῳ. n. dat. neut. sg. ὑπερῷον upper room, upper chamber
38 ἐγγὺς adv. ἐγγύς nigh, at hand, near, nigh at hand, ready, nigh unto
δὲ conj. δέ but, and, now, also, to the contrary, rather, then
Λύδδας n. gen. fem. sg. Λύδδα Lydda
τῇ art. dat. fem. sg. ὁ ἡ τό the, this, that, he, she, it
Ἰόππῃ n. dat. fem. sg. Ἰόππη Joppa
οἱ art. nom. masc. pl. ὁ ἡ τό the, this, that, he, she, it
μαθηταὶ n. nom. masc. pl. μαθητής disciple
ὅτι conj. ὅτι that, for, because, how that, how, because that, for that, though
Πέτρος n. nom. masc. sg. Πέτρος Peter
ἐν prep. ἐν (+dat) in, by, with, among, at, on, through, to, within, into, of, for
αὐτῇ pron. dat. fem. 3p. sg. αὐτός ή ό self, of oneself, even, very, the same, he, she, it
δύο num. acc. masc. pl. δύο two, twain, both
ἄνδρας n. acc. masc. pl. ἀνήρ man, husband, sir
πρὸς prep. πρός (+gen) for, (+dat) at, (+acc) unto, to, with, for, against
αὐτὸν pron. acc. masc. 3p. sg. αὐτός ή ό self, of oneself, even, very, the same, he, she, it
μὴ particle of negation. μή not, no, lest, neither, none, nothing, nor, never, without
ἕως conj. ἕως till, until, unto, until when, while, as far as, even, until now
αὐτῶν pron. gen. fem. 3p. pl. αὐτός ή ό self, of oneself, even, very, the same, he, she, it
39 δὲ conj. δέ but, and, now, also, to the contrary, rather, then
Πέτρος n. nom. masc. sg. Πέτρος Peter
αὐτοῖς pron. dat. masc. 3p. pl. αὐτός ή ό self, of oneself, even, very, the same, he, she, it
ὃν relative pron. acc. masc. sg. ὅς ἥ ὅ who, which, what, that
εἰς prep. εἰς (+acc) into, to, unto, for, in, on, toward, against, upon, at, among
τὸ art. acc. neut. sg. ὁ ἡ τό the, this, that, he, she, it
ὑπερῷον n. acc. neut. sg. ὑπερῷον upper room, upper chamber
καὶ conj. καί and, even, also, but
αὐτῷ pron. dat. masc. 3p. sg. αὐτός ή ό self, of oneself, even, very, the same, he, she, it
πᾶσαι adj. nom. fem. pl. πᾶς πᾶσα πᾶν all, every, whosoever, every one, no, whole, any
αἱ art. nom. fem. pl. ὁ ἡ τό the, this, that, he, she, it
χῆραι n. nom. fem. pl. χήρα widow
καὶ conj. καί and, even, also, but
χιτῶνας n. acc. masc. pl. χιτών coat, clothes, garment
καὶ conj. καί and, even, also, but
ἱμάτια n. acc. neut. pl. ἱμάτιον cloke, garment, clothes, raiment, robe, vesture
ὅσα relative pron. acc. neut. pl. ὅσος as many as, whatsoever, that, as long as, how much
μετ᾽ prep. μετά (+gen) with, among, against, (+acc) after
αὐτῶν pron. gen. fem. 3p. pl. αὐτός ή ό self, of oneself, even, very, the same, he, she, it
ἡ art. nom. fem. sg. ὁ ἡ τό the, this, that, he, she, it
Δορκάς n. nom. fem. sg. Δορκάς Dorcas, gazelle, antelope
40 δὲ conj. δέ but, and, now, also, to the contrary, rather, then
ἔξω adv. ἔξω out, without, out of, forth, away, outward
πάντας adj. acc. masc. pl. πᾶς πᾶσα πᾶν all, every, whosoever, every one, no, whole, any
ὁ art. nom. masc. sg. ὁ ἡ τό the, this, that, he, she, it
Πέτρος n. nom. masc. sg. Πέτρος Peter
τὰ art. acc. neut. pl. ὁ ἡ τό the, this, that, he, she, it
γόνατα n. acc. neut. pl. γόνυ knee, kneel
καὶ conj. καί and, even, also, but
πρὸς prep. πρός (+gen) for, (+dat) at, (+acc) unto, to, with, for, against
τὸ art. acc. neut. sg. ὁ ἡ τό the, this, that, he, she, it

σῶμα n. acc. neut. sg. σῶμα body, bodily, slave
Ταβιθά n. voc. fem. sg. Ταβιθά Tabitha
ἡ art. nom. fem. sg. ὁ ἡ τό the, this, that, he, she, it
δὲ conj. δέ but, and, now, also, to the contrary, rather, then
τοὺς art. acc. masc. pl. ὁ ἡ τό the, this, that, he, she, it
ὀφθαλμοὺς n. acc. masc. pl. ὀφθαλμός eye, sight
αὐτῆς pron. gen. fem. 3p. sg. αὐτός ή ό self, of oneself, even, very, the same, he, she, it
καὶ conj. καί and, even, also, but
τὸν art. acc. masc. sg. ὁ ἡ τό the, this, that, he, she, it
Πέτρον n. acc. masc. sg. Πέτρος Peter
41 δὲ conj. δέ but, and, now, also, to the contrary, rather, then
αὐτῇ pron. dat. fem. 3p. sg. αὐτός ή ό self, of oneself, even, very, the same, he, she, it
χεῖρα n. acc. fem. sg. χείρ hand
αὐτήν pron. acc. fem. 3p. sg. αὐτός ή ό self, of oneself, even, very, the same, he, she, it
δὲ conj. δέ but, and, now, also, to the contrary, rather, then
τοὺς art. acc. masc. pl. ὁ ἡ τό the, this, that, he, she, it
ἁγίους adj. acc. masc. pl. ἅγιος Holy, holy, saint, Holy One, holy thing, most holy
καὶ conj. καί and, even, also, but
τὰς art. acc. fem. pl. ὁ ἡ τό the, this, that, he, she, it
χήρας adj. acc. fem. pl. χήρα widow
αὐτήν pron. acc. fem. 3p. sg. αὐτός ή ό self, of oneself, even, very, the same, he, she, it
42 γνωστὸν adj. nom. neut. sg. γνωστός acquaintance, known, notable
δὲ conj. δέ but, and, now, also, to the contrary, rather, then
καθ' prep. κατά (+gen) against, by, throughout, down, (+acc) according to, after, with
ὅλης adj. gen. fem. sg. ὅλος all, whole, every whit, altogether
τῆς art. gen. fem. sg. ὁ ἡ τό the, this, that, he, she, it
Ἰόππης n. gen. fem. sg. Ἰόππη Joppa
καὶ conj. καί and, even, also, but
πολλοὶ adj. nom. masc. pl. πολύς many, great, much, long, abundant
ἐπὶ prep. ἐπί (+gen) on, in, upon, (+dat) in, at, for, upon, (+acc) on, upon, unto, to, against
τὸν art. acc. masc. sg. ὁ ἡ τό the, this, that, he, she, it
Κύριον n. acc. masc. sg. κύριος Lord, lord, master, sir, LORD, God, Master, owner
43 δὲ conj. δέ but, and, now, also, to the contrary, rather, then
ἡμέρας n. acc. fem. pl. ἡμέρα day, time, year, while, age, day time
ἱκανὰς adj. acc. fem. pl. ἱκανός many, much, long, worthy, sufficient, great, able
αὐτὸν pron. acc. masc. 3p. sg. αὐτός ή ό self, of oneself, even, very, the same, he, she, it
ἐν prep. ἐν (+dat) in, by, with, among, at, on, through, to, within, into, of, for
Ἰόππῃ n. dat. fem. sg. Ἰόππη Joppa
παρά prep. παρά (+gen) of, from, (+dat) with, for, (+acc) beside, at, by, above, against
τινι indefinite pron. dat. masc. sg. τὶς certain, some, any man, one, any thing
Σίμωνι n. dat. masc. sg. Σίμων Simon
βυρσεῖ n. dat. masc. sg. βυρσεύς tanner

10

1 Ἀνὴρ n. nom. masc. sg. ἀνήρ man, husband, sir
δὲ conj. δέ but, and, now, also, to the contrary, rather, then
τις indefinite pron. nom. masc. sg. τὶς certain, some, any man, one, any thing
ἐν prep. ἐν (+dat) in, by, with, among, at, on, through, to, within, into, of, for
Καισαρείᾳ n. dat. fem. sg. Καισάρεια Caesarea
ὀνόματι n. dat. neut. sg. ὄνομα name, call, surname
Κορνήλιος n. nom. masc. sg. Κορνήλιος Cornelius
ἑκατοντάρχης n. nom. masc. sg. ἑκατοντάρχης centurion
ἐκ prep. ἐκ ἐξ (+gen) of, from, out of, by, on, with, in, among, through
σπείρης n. gen. fem. sg. σπεῖρα band

τῆς art. gen. fem. sg. ὁ ἡ τό the, this, that, he, she, it
Ἰταλικῆς adj. gen. fem. sg. Ἰταλικός Italian
2 εὐσεβὴς adj. nom. masc. sg. εὐσεβής devout, godly
καὶ conj. καί and, even, also, but
τὸν art. acc. masc. sg. ὁ ἡ τό the, this, that, he, she, it
Θεὸν n. acc. masc. sg. θεός God, god
σὺν prep. σύν (+dat) with, beside
παντὶ adj. dat. masc. sg. πᾶς πᾶσα πᾶν all, every, whosoever, every one, no, whole, any
τῷ art. dat. masc. sg. ὁ ἡ τό the, this, that, he, she, it
οἴκῳ n. dat. masc. sg. οἶκος house, home, household
αὐτοῦ pron. gen. masc. 3p. sg. αὐτός ή ό self, of oneself, even, very, the same, he, she, it
τε conj. τέ and, both, also
ἐλεημοσύνας n. acc. fem. pl. ἐλεημοσύνη alms, almsdeed
πολλὰς adj. acc. fem. pl. πολύς many, great, much, long, abundant
τῷ art. dat. masc. sg. ὁ ἡ τό the, this, that, he, she, it
λαῷ n. dat. masc. sg. λαός people
καὶ conj. καί and, even, also, but
τοῦ art. gen. masc. sg. ὁ ἡ τό the, this, that, he, she, it
Θεοῦ n. gen. masc. sg. θεός God, god
διὰ prep. διά (+gen) by, through, with, in, of, (+acc) for, because of, for a cause
παντός adj. gen. neut. sg. πᾶς πᾶσα πᾶν all, every, whosoever, every one, no, whole, any
3 ἐν prep. ἐν (+dat) in, by, with, among, at, on, through, to, within, into, of, for
ὁράματι n. dat. neut. sg. ὅραμα vision, sight
φανερῶς adv. φανερῶς openly, evidently
ὡσεὶ adv. ὡσεί about, as, like, as it had been, as it were, like as
ὥραν n. acc. fem. sg. ὥρα hour, time, season
ἐννάτην ordinal. adj. acc. fem. sg. ἔννατος ninth
τῆς art. gen. fem. sg. ὁ ἡ τό the, this, that, he, she, it
ἡμέρας n. gen. fem. sg. ἡμέρα day, time, year, while, age, day time
ἄγγελον n. acc. masc. sg. ἄγγελος angel, messenger
τοῦ art. gen. masc. sg. ὁ ἡ τό the, this, that, he, she, it
Θεοῦ n. gen. masc. sg. θεός God, god
πρὸς prep. πρός (+gen) for, (+dat) at, (+acc) unto, to, with, for, against
αὐτὸν pron. acc. masc. 3p. sg. αὐτός ή ό self, of oneself, even, very, the same, he, she, it
καὶ conj. καί and, even, also, but
αὐτῷ pron. dat. masc. 3p. sg. αὐτός ή ό self, of oneself, even, very, the same, he, she, it
Κορνήλιε n. voc. masc. sg. Κορνήλιος Cornelius
4 ὁ art. nom. masc. sg. ὁ ἡ τό the, this, that, he, she, it
δὲ conj. δέ but, and, now, also, to the contrary, rather, then
αὐτῷ pron. dat. masc. 3p. sg. αὐτός ή ό self, of oneself, even, very, the same, he, she, it
καὶ conj. καί and, even, also, but
ἔμφοβος adj. nom. masc. sg. ἔμφοβος afraid, affrighted, tremble
Τί interrog. pron. nom. neut. sg. τίς what, who, why, where, which, how
Κύριε n. voc. masc. sg. κύριος Lord, lord, master, sir, LORD, God, Master, owner
δὲ conj. δέ but, and, now, also, to the contrary, rather, then
αὐτῷ pron. dat. masc. 3p. sg. αὐτός ή ό self, of oneself, even, very, the same, he, she, it
Αἱ art. nom. fem. pl. ὁ ἡ τό the, this, that, he, she, it
προσευχαί n. nom. fem. pl. προσευχή prayer
σου pron. gen. 2p. sg. σύ thou, you
καὶ conj. καί and, even, also, but
αἱ art. nom. fem. pl. ὁ ἡ τό the, this, that, he, she, it
ἐλεημοσύναι n. nom. fem. pl. ἐλεημοσύνη alms, almsdeed
σου pron. gen. 2p. sg. σύ thou, you
εἰς prep. εἰς (+acc) into, to, unto, for, in, on, toward, against, upon, at, among
μνημόσυνον n. acc. neut. sg. μνημόσυνον memorial

ἐνώπιον adv. ἐνώπιον before, in the sight of, in the presence of
τοῦ art. gen. masc. sg. ὁ ἡ τό the, this, that, he, she, it
Θεοῦ n. gen. masc. sg. θεός God, god
5 καὶ conj. καί and, even, also, but
νῦν adv. νῦν now, henceforth, present, this time
εἰς prep. εἰς (+acc) into, to, unto, for, in, on, toward, against, upon, at, among
Ἰόππην n. acc. fem. sg. Ἰόππη Joppa
ἄνδρας n. acc. masc. pl. ἀνήρ man, husband, sir
καὶ conj. καί and, even, also, but
Σίμωνά n. acc. masc. sg. Σίμων Simon
ὅς relative pron. nom. masc. sg. ὅς ἥ ὅ who, which, what, that
Πέτρος n. nom. masc. sg. Πέτρος Peter
6 οὗτος demo. pron. nom. masc. sg. οὗτος αὕτη τοῦτο this, the same, this same, he, she, it
παρά prep. παρά (+gen) of, from, (+dat) with, for, (+acc) beside, at, by, above, against
τινι indefinite pron. dat. masc. sg. τὶς certain, some, any man, one, any thing
Σίμωνι n. dat. masc. sg. Σίμων Simon
βυρσεῖ n. dat. masc. sg. βυρσεύς tanner
ᾧ relative pron. dat. masc. sg. ὅς ἥ ὅ who, which, what, that
οἰκία n. nom. fem. sg. οἰκία house, home, household
παρὰ prep. παρά (+gen) of, from, (+dat) with, for, (+acc) beside, at, by, above, against
θάλασσαν n. acc. fem. sg. θάλασσα sea
οὗτος demo. pron. nom. masc. sg. οὗτος αὕτη τοῦτο this, the same, this same, he, she, it
σοι pron. dat. 2p. sg. σύ thou, you
τί interrog. pron. acc. neut. sg. τίς what, who, why, where, which, how
σε pron. acc. 2p. sg. σύ thou, you
7 ὡς adv. ὡς as, when, as it were, how, about, like, as soon as, even as, while
δὲ conj. δέ but, and, now, also, to the contrary, rather, then
ὁ art. nom. masc. sg. ὁ ἡ τό the, this, that, he, she, it
ἄγγελος n. nom. masc. sg. ἄγγελος angel, messenger
ὁ art. nom. masc. sg. ὁ ἡ τό the, this, that, he, she, it
τῷ art. dat. masc. sg. ὁ ἡ τό the, this, that, he, she, it
Κορνηλίῳ n. dat. masc. sg. Κορνήλιος Cornelius
δύο num. acc. masc. pl. δύο two, twain, both
τῶν art. gen. masc. pl. ὁ ἡ τό the, this, that, he, she, it
οἰκετῶν n. gen. masc. pl. οἰκέτης servant, household servant
αὐτοῦ pron. gen. masc. 3p. sg. αὐτός ή ό self, of oneself, even, very, the same, he, she, it
καὶ conj. καί and, even, also, but
στρατιώτην n. acc. masc. sg. στρατιώτης soldier
εὐσεβῆ adj. acc. masc. sg. εὐσεβής devout, godly
τῶν art. gen. masc. pl. ὁ ἡ τό the, this, that, he, she, it
αὐτῷ pron. dat. masc. 3p. sg. αὐτός ή ό self, of oneself, even, very, the same, he, she, it
8 καὶ conj. καί and, even, also, but
αὐτοῖς pron. dat. masc. 3p. pl. αὐτός ή ό self, of oneself, even, very, the same, he, she, it
ἅπαντα adj. acc. neut. pl. ἅπας all, whole, all things, every, everyone
αὐτοὺς pron. acc. masc. 3p. pl. αὐτός ή ό self, of oneself, even, very, the same, he, she, it
εἰς prep. εἰς (+acc) into, to, unto, for, in, on, toward, against, upon, at, among
τὴν art. acc. fem. sg. ὁ ἡ τό the, this, that, he, she, it
Ἰόππην n. acc. fem. sg. Ἰόππη Joppa
9 Τῇ art. dat. fem. sg. ὁ ἡ τό the, this, that, he, she, it
δὲ conj. δέ but, and, now, also, to the contrary, rather, then
ἐπαύριον adv. ἐπαύριον next day, morrow, day following, nest day after
ἐκείνων demo. pron. gen. masc. pl. ἐκεῖνος that, he, the same, that same
καὶ conj. καί and, even, also, but
τῇ art. dat. fem. sg. ὁ ἡ τό the, this, that, he, she, it
πόλει n. dat. fem. sg. πόλις city

Πέτρος n. nom. masc. sg. Πέτρος Peter
ἐπὶ prep. ἐπί (+gen) on, in, upon, (+dat) in, at, for, upon, (+acc) on, upon, unto, to, against
τὸ art. acc. neut. sg. ὁ ἡ τό the, this, that, he, she, it
δῶμα n. acc. neut. sg. δῶμα housetop
περὶ prep. περί (+gen) of, for, concerning, (+acc) about, concerning, in
ὥραν n. acc. fem. sg. ὥρα hour, time, season
ἕκτην ordinal. adj. acc. fem. sg. ἕκτος sixth
10 δὲ conj. δέ but, and, now, also, to the contrary, rather, then
πρόσπεινος adj. nom. masc. sg. πρόσπεινος very hungry
καὶ conj. καί and, even, also, but
δὲ conj. δέ but, and, now, also, to the contrary, rather, then
ἐκείνων demo. pron. gen. masc. pl. ἐκεῖνος that, he, the same, that same
ἐπ' prep. ἐπί (+gen) on, in, upon, (+dat) in, at, for, upon, (+acc) on, upon, unto, to, against
αὐτὸν pron. acc. masc. 3p. sg. αὐτός ή ό self, of oneself, even, very, the same, he, she, it
ἔκστασις n. nom. fem. sg. ἔκστασις trance, astonishment, amazement, amazed
11 καὶ conj. καί and, even, also, but
τὸν art. acc. masc. sg. ὁ ἡ τό the, this, that, he, she, it
οὐρανὸν n. acc. masc. sg. οὐρανός heaven, air, sky
καὶ conj. καί and, even, also, but
ἐπ' prep. ἐπί (+gen) on, in, upon, (+dat) in, at, for, upon, (+acc) on, upon, unto, to, against
αὐτὸν pron. acc. masc. 3p. sg. αὐτός ή ό self, of oneself, even, very, the same, he, she, it
σκεῦός n. acc. neut. sg. σκεῦος vessel, good, sail, stuff
τι indefinite pron. acc. neut. sg. τὶς certain, some, any man, one, any thing
ὡς adv. ὡς as, when, as it were, how, about, like, as soon as, even as, while
ὀθόνην n. acc. fem. sg. ὀθόνη sheet
μεγάλην adj. acc. fem. sg. μέγας great, loud, greatest, high, large, mighty, strong
τέσσαρσιν num. dat. fem. pl. τέσσαρες four
ἀρχαῖς n. dat. fem. pl. ἀρχή beginning, principality, corner, first, magistrate, rule
καὶ conj. καί and, even, also, but
ἐπὶ prep. ἐπί (+gen) on, in, upon, (+dat) in, at, for, upon, (+acc) on, upon, unto, to, against
τῆς art. gen. fem. sg. ὁ ἡ τό the, this, that, he, she, it
γῆς n. gen. fem. sg. γῆ earth, land, ground, country
12 ἐν prep. ἐν (+dat) in, by, with, among, at, on, through, to, within, into, of, for
ᾧ relative pron. dat. neut. sg. ὅς ἥ ὅ who, which, what, that
πάντα adj. nom. neut. pl. πᾶς πᾶσα πᾶν all, every, whosoever, every one, no, whole, any
τὰ art. nom. neut. pl. ὁ ἡ τό the, this, that, he, she, it
τετράποδα adj. nom. neut. pl. τετράπους fourfooted beast
τῆς art. gen. fem. sg. ὁ ἡ τό the, this, that, he, she, it
γῆς n. gen. fem. sg. γῆ earth, land, ground, country
καὶ conj. καί and, even, also, but
τὰ art. nom. neut. pl. ὁ ἡ τό the, this, that, he, she, it
θηρία n. acc. neut. pl. θηρίον beast, wild beast, venomous beast
καὶ conj. καί and, even, also, but
τὰ art. nom. neut. pl. ὁ ἡ τό the, this, that, he, she, it
ἑρπετὰ n. nom. neut. pl. ἑρπετόν creeping thing, serpent
καὶ conj. καί and, even, also, but
τὰ art. nom. neut. pl. ὁ ἡ τό the, this, that, he, she, it
πετεινὰ adj. nom. neut. pl. πετεινόν fowl, bird
τοῦ art. gen. masc. sg. ὁ ἡ τό the, this, that, he, she, it
οὐρανοῦ n. gen. masc. sg. οὐρανός heaven, air, sky
13 καὶ conj. καί and, even, also, but
φωνὴ n. nom. fem. sg. φωνή voice, sound, noise
πρὸς prep. πρός (+gen) for, (+dat) at, (+acc) unto, to, with, for, against
αὐτόν pron. acc. masc. 3p. sg. αὐτός ή ό self, of oneself, even, very, the same, he, she, it
Πέτρε n. voc. masc. sg. Πέτρος Peter

καὶ conj. καί and, even, also, but
14 ὁ art. nom. masc. sg. ὁ ἡ τό the, this, that, he, she, it
δὲ conj. δέ but, and, now, also, to the contrary, rather, then
Πέτρος n. nom. masc. sg. Πέτρος Peter
Μηδαμῶς adv. μηδαμῶς not so
Κύριε n. voc. masc. sg. κύριος Lord, lord, master, sir, LORD, God, Master, owner
ὅτι conj. ὅτι that, for, because, how that, how, because that, for that, though
οὐδέποτε adv. οὐδέποτε never, neither at any time, no at any time
πᾶν adj. acc. neut. sg. πᾶς πᾶσα πᾶν all, every, whosoever, every one, no, whole, any
κοινὸν adj. acc. neut. sg. κοινός common, unclean, defiled, unholy
ἢ particle. ἤ or, than, either, nor, or else, and, rather than
ἀκάθαρτον adj. acc. neut. sg. ἀκάθαρτος unclean, foul
15 καὶ conj. καί and, even, also, but
φωνὴ n. nom. fem. sg. φωνή voice, sound, noise
πάλιν adv. πάλιν again
ἐκ prep. ἐκ ἐξ (+gen) of, from, out of, by, on, with, in, among, through
δευτέρου ordinal. adj. gen. neut. sg. δεύτερος second, second time, again, afterward
πρὸς prep. πρός (+gen) for, (+dat) at, (+acc) unto, to, with, for, against
αὐτόν pron. acc. masc. 3p. sg. αὐτός ή ό self, of oneself, even, very, the same, he, she, it
Ἃ relative pron. acc. neut. pl. ὅς ἥ ὅ who, which, what, that
ὁ art. nom. masc. sg. ὁ ἡ τό the, this, that, he, she, it
Θεὸς n. nom. masc. sg. θεός God, god
σὺ pron. nom. 2p. sg. σύ thou, you
μὴ particle of negation. μή not, no, lest, neither, none, nothing, nor, never, without
16 τοῦτο demo. pron. nom. neut. sg. οὗτος αὕτη τοῦτο this, the same, this same, he, she, it
δὲ conj. δέ but, and, now, also, to the contrary, rather, then
ἐπὶ prep. ἐπί (+gen) on, in, upon, (+dat) in, at, for, upon, (+acc) on, upon, unto, to, against
τρίς adv. τρίς thrice, three times
καὶ conj. καί and, even, also, but
πάλιν adv. πάλιν again
τὸ art. nom. neut. sg. ὁ ἡ τό the, this, that, he, she, it
σκεῦος n. nom. neut. sg. σκεῦος vessel, good, sail, stuff
εἰς prep. εἰς (+acc) into, to, unto, for, in, on, toward, against, upon, at, among
τὸν art. acc. masc. sg. ὁ ἡ τό the, this, that, he, she, it
οὐρανόν n. acc. masc. sg. οὐρανός heaven, air, sky
17 Ὡς conj. ὡς as, when, as it were, how, about, like, as soon as, even as, while
δὲ conj. δέ but, and, now, also, to the contrary, rather, then
ἐν prep. ἐν (+dat) in, by, with, among, at, on, through, to, within, into, of, for
ἑαυτῷ reflexive pron. dat. masc. 3p. sg. ἑαυτοῦ himself, herself, itself, yourself, ourselves
ὁ art. nom. masc. sg. ὁ ἡ τό the, this, that, he, she, it
Πέτρος n. nom. masc. sg. Πέτρος Peter
τί interrog. pron. nom. neut. sg. τίς what, who, why, where, which, how
ἂν particle. ἄν Indicating contingency. No English translation.
τὸ art. nom. neut. sg. ὁ ἡ τό the, this, that, he, she, it
ὅραμα n. nom. neut. sg. ὅραμα vision, sight
ὃ relative pron. acc. neut. sg. ὅς ἥ ὅ who, which, what, that
καὶ conj. καί and, even, also, but
οἱ art. nom. masc. pl. ὁ ἡ τό the, this, that, he, she, it
ἄνδρες n. nom. masc. pl. ἀνήρ man, husband, sir
οἱ art. nom. masc. pl. ὁ ἡ τό the, this, that, he, she, it
ἀπὸ prep. ἀπό (+gen) from, of, out of, since, for, off, at, by, in, on
τοῦ art. gen. masc. sg. ὁ ἡ τό the, this, that, he, she, it
Κορνηλίου n. gen. masc. sg. Κορνήλιος Cornelius
τὴν art. acc. fem. sg. ὁ ἡ τό the, this, that, he, she, it
οἰκίαν n. acc. fem. sg. οἰκία house, home, household

Σίμωνος n. gen. masc. sg. Σίμων Simon
ἐπὶ prep. ἐπί (+gen) on, in, upon, (+dat) in, at, for, upon, (+acc) on, upon, unto, to, against
τὸν art. acc. masc. sg. ὁ ἡ τό the, this, that, he, she, it
πυλῶνα n. acc. masc. sg. πυλών gate, porch
18 καὶ conj. καί and, even, also, but
εἰ conj. εἰ if, whether, that, though, forasmuch
Σίμων n. nom. masc. sg. Σίμων Simon
ὁ art. nom. masc. sg. ὁ ἡ τό the, this, that, he, she, it
Πέτρος n. nom. masc. sg. Πέτρος Peter
ἐνθάδε adv. ἐνθάδε here, there, hither
19 τοῦ art. gen. masc. sg. ὁ ἡ τό the, this, that, he, she, it
δὲ conj. δέ but, and, now, also, to the contrary, rather, then
Πέτρου n. gen. masc. sg. Πέτρος Peter
περὶ prep. περί (+gen) of, for, concerning, (+acc) about, concerning, in
τοῦ art. gen. neut. sg. ὁ ἡ τό the, this, that, he, she, it
ὁράματος n. gen. neut. sg. ὅραμα vision, sight
αὐτῷ pron. dat. masc. 3p. sg. αὐτός ἡ ὁ self, of oneself, even, very, the same, he, she, it
τὸ art. nom. neut. sg. ὁ ἡ τό the, this, that, he, she, it
Πνεῦμα n. nom. neut. sg. πνεῦμα spirit, Spirit, Ghost, ghost, life. of the spirit, wind
ἄνδρες n. nom. masc. pl. ἀνήρ man, husband, sir
τρεῖς num. nom. masc. pl. τρεῖς three
σε pron. acc. 2p. sg. σύ thou, you
20 ἀλλὰ conj. ἀλλά but, yea, yet, nevertheless, howbeit, nay, therefore
καὶ conj. καί and, even, also, but
σὺν prep. σύν (+dat) with, beside
αὐτοῖς pron. dat. masc. 3p. pl. αὐτός ἡ ὁ self, of oneself, even, very, the same, he, she, it
μηδὲν adj. acc. neut. sg. μηδείς μηδεμία μηδέν no man, nothing, no, none, not at all
διότι conj. διότι for, because, because that, therefore
ἐγὼ pron. nom. 1p. sg. ἐγώ I
αὐτούς pron. acc. masc. 3p. pl. αὐτός ἡ ὁ self, of oneself, even, very, the same, he, she, it
21 δὲ conj. δέ but, and, now, also, to the contrary, rather, then
Πέτρος n. nom. masc. sg. Πέτρος Peter
πρὸς prep. πρός (+gen) for, (+dat) at, (+acc) unto, to, with, for, against
τοὺς art. acc. masc. pl. ὁ ἡ τό the, this, that, he, she, it
ἄνδρας n. acc. masc. pl. ἀνήρ man, husband, sir
τοὺς art. acc. masc. pl. ὁ ἡ τό the, this, that, he, she, it
ἀπὸ prep. ἀπό (+gen) from, of, out of, since, for, off, at, by, in, on
τοῦ art. gen. masc. sg. ὁ ἡ τό the, this, that, he, she, it
Κορνηλίου n. gen. masc. sg. Κορνήλιος Cornelius
πρὸς prep. πρός (+gen) for, (+dat) at, (+acc) unto, to, with, for, against
αὐτόν pron. acc. masc. 3p. sg. αὐτός ἡ ὁ self, of oneself, even, very, the same, he, she, it
ἐγώ pron. nom. 1p. sg. ἐγώ I
ὃν relative pron. acc. masc. sg. ὅς ἥ ὅ who, which, what, that
τίς interrog. pron. nom. fem. sg. τίς what, who, why, where, which, how
ἡ art. nom. fem. sg. ὁ ἡ τό the, this, that, he, she, it
αἰτία n. nom. fem. sg. αἰτία cause, reason, accusation, fault
δι' prep. διά (+gen) by, through, with, in, of, (+acc) for, because of, for a cause
ἣν relative pron. acc. fem. sg. ὅς ἥ ὅ who, which, what, that
22 οἱ art. nom. masc. pl. ὁ ἡ τό the, this, that, he, she, it
δὲ conj. δέ but, and, now, also, to the contrary, rather, then
Κορνήλιος n. nom. masc. sg. Κορνήλιος Cornelius
ἑκατοντάρχης n. nom. masc. sg. ἑκατοντάρχης centurion
ἀνὴρ n. nom. masc. sg. ἀνήρ man, husband, sir
δίκαιος adj. nom. masc. sg. δίκαιος righteous, just, meet, right
καὶ conj. καί and, even, also, but

τὸν art. acc. masc. sg. ὁ ἡ τό the, this, that, he, she, it
Θεόν n. acc. masc. sg. θεός God, god
τε conj. τέ and, both, also
ὑπὸ prep. ὑπό (+gen) of, by, with, from, among, (+acc) under
ὅλου adj. gen. neut. sg. ὅλος all, whole, every whit, altogether
τοῦ art. gen. neut. sg. ὁ ἡ τό the, this, that, he, she, it
ἔθνους n. gen. neut. sg. ἔθνος Gentile, nation, heathen, people
τῶν art. gen. masc. pl. ὁ ἡ τό the, this, that, he, she, it
Ἰουδαίων adj. gen. masc. pl. Ἰουδαῖος Jew, Jewess
ὑπὸ prep. ὑπό (+gen) of, by, with, from, among, (+acc) under
ἀγγέλου n. gen. masc. sg. ἄγγελος angel, messenger
ἁγίου adj. gen. masc. sg. ἅγιος Holy, holy, saint, Holy One, holy thing, most holy
σε pron. acc. 2p. sg. σύ thou, you
εἰς prep. εἰς (+acc) into, to, unto, for, in, on, toward, against, upon, at, among
τὸν art. acc. masc. sg. ὁ ἡ τό the, this, that, he, she, it
οἶκον n. acc. masc. sg. οἶκος house, home, household
αὐτοῦ pron. gen. masc. 3p. sg. αὐτός ή ό self, of oneself, even, very, the same, he, she, it
καὶ conj. καί and, even, also, but
ῥήματα n. acc. neut. pl. ῥῆμα word, saying, thing
παρὰ prep. παρά (+gen) of, from, (+dat) with, for, (+acc) beside, at, by, above, against
σοῦ pron. gen. 2p. sg. σύ thou, you
23 οὖν conj. οὖν therefore, then, so, and, now, wherefore
αὐτοὺς pron. acc. masc. 3p. pl. αὐτός ή ό self, of oneself, even, very, the same, he, she, it
Τῇ art. dat. fem. sg. ὁ ἡ τό the, this, that, he, she, it
δὲ conj. δέ but, and, now, also, to the contrary, rather, then
ἐπαύριον adv. ἐπαύριον next day, morrow, day following, nest day after
ὁ art. nom. masc. sg. ὁ ἡ τό the, this, that, he, she, it
Πέτρος n. nom. masc. sg. Πέτρος Peter
σὺν prep. σύν (+dat) with, beside
αὐτοῖς pron. dat. masc. 3p. pl. αὐτός ή ό self, of oneself, even, very, the same, he, she, it
καί conj. καί and, even, also, but
τινες indefinite pron. nom. masc. pl. τὶς certain, some, any man, one, any thing
τῶν art. gen. masc. pl. ὁ ἡ τό the, this, that, he, she, it
ἀδελφῶν n. gen. masc. pl. ἀδελφός brother
τῶν art. gen. masc. pl. ὁ ἡ τό the, this, that, he, she, it
ἀπὸ prep. ἀπό (+gen) from, of, out of, since, for, off, at, by, in, on
τῆς art. gen. fem. sg. ὁ ἡ τό the, this, that, he, she, it
Ἰόππης n. gen. fem. sg. Ἰόππη Joppa
αὐτῷ pron. dat. masc. 3p. sg. αὐτός ή ό self, of oneself, even, very, the same, he, she, it
24 καί conj. καί and, even, also, but
τῇ art. dat. fem. sg. ὁ ἡ τό the, this, that, he, she, it
ἐπαύριον adv. ἐπαύριον next day, morrow, day following, nest day after
εἰς prep. εἰς (+acc) into, to, unto, for, in, on, toward, against, upon, at, among
τὴν art. acc. fem. sg. ὁ ἡ τό the, this, that, he, she, it
Καισάρειαν n. acc. fem. sg. Καισάρεια Caesarea
ὁ art. nom. masc. sg. ὁ ἡ τό the, this, that, he, she, it
δὲ conj. δέ but, and, now, also, to the contrary, rather, then
Κορνήλιος n. nom. masc. sg. Κορνήλιος Cornelius
αὐτοὺς pron. acc. masc. 3p. pl. αὐτός ή ό self, of oneself, even, very, the same, he, she, it
τοὺς art. acc. masc. pl. ὁ ἡ τό the, this, that, he, she, it
συγγενεῖς adj. acc. masc. pl. συγγενής kinsman, cousin, kinsfolk, kin
αὐτοῦ pron. gen. masc. 3p. sg. αὐτός ή ό self, of oneself, even, very, the same, he, she, it
καί conj. καί and, even, also, but
τοὺς art. acc. masc. pl. ὁ ἡ τό the, this, that, he, she, it
ἀναγκαίους adj. acc. masc. pl. ἀναγκαῖος near, necessary, more needful, of necessity

φίλους adj. acc. masc. pl. φίλος friend
25 ὡς adv. ὡς as, when, as it were, how, about, like, as soon as, even as, while
δὲ conj. δέ but, and, now, also, to the contrary, rather, then
τὸν art. acc. masc. sg. ὁ ἡ τό the, this, that, he, she, it
Πέτρον n. acc. masc. sg. Πέτρος Peter
αὐτῷ pron. dat. masc. 3p. sg. αὐτός ἡ ὁ self, of oneself, even, very, the same, he, she, it
ὁ art. nom. masc. sg. ὁ ἡ τό the, this, that, he, she, it
Κορνήλιος n. nom. masc. sg. Κορνήλιος Cornelius
ἐπὶ prep. ἐπί (+gen) on, in, upon, (+dat) in, at, for, upon, (+acc) on, upon, unto, to, against
τοὺς art. acc. masc. pl. ὁ ἡ τό the, this, that, he, she, it
πόδας n. acc. masc. pl. πούς foot
26 ὁ art. nom. masc. sg. ὁ ἡ τό the, this, that, he, she, it
δὲ conj. δέ but, and, now, also, to the contrary, rather, then
Πέτρος n. nom. masc. sg. Πέτρος Peter
αὐτὸν pron. acc. masc. 3p. sg. αὐτός ἡ ὁ self, of oneself, even, very, the same, he, she, it
κἀγὼ pron. nom. 1p. σγ. κἀγώ and I, I also, so I, even as I
αὐτὸς pron. nom. masc. 3p. sg. αὐτός ἡ ὁ self, of oneself, even, very, the same, he, she, it
ἄνθρωπός n. nom. masc. sg. ἄνθρωπος man, human being, person, one, certain
27 καὶ conj. καί and, even, also, but
αὐτῷ pron. dat. masc. 3p. sg. αὐτός ἡ ὁ self, of oneself, even, very, the same, he, she, it
καὶ conj. καί and, even, also, but
πολλούς adj. acc. masc. pl. πολύς many, great, much, long, abundant
28 τε conj. τέ and, both, also
πρὸς prep. πρός (+gen) for, (+dat) at, (+acc) unto, to, with, for, against
αὐτούς pron. acc. masc. 3p. pl. αὐτός ἡ ὁ self, of oneself, even, very, the same, he, she, it
Ὑμεῖς pron. nom. 2p. pl. σύ thou, you
ὡς adv. ὡς as, when, as it were, how, about, like, as soon as, even as, while
ἀθέμιτόν adj. nom. neut. sg. ἀθέμιτος unlawful thing, abominable
ἀνδρὶ n. dat. masc. sg. ἀνήρ man, husband, sir
Ἰουδαίῳ adj. dat. masc. sg. Ἰουδαῖος Jew, Jewess
ἢ particle. ἤ or, than, either, nor, or else, and, rather than
ἀλλοφύλῳ adj. dat. masc. sg. ἀλλόφυλος one of another nation
καὶ conj. καί and, even, also, but
ἐμοὶ pron. dat. 1p. sg. ἐγώ I
ὁ art. nom. masc. sg. ὁ ἡ τό the, this, that, he, she, it
Θεὸς n. nom. masc. sg. θεός God, god
μηδένα num. acc. masc. sg. μηδείς μηδεμία μηδέν no man, nothing, no, none, not at all
κοινὸν adj. acc. masc. sg. κοινός common, unclean, defiled, unholy
ἢ particle. ἤ or, than, either, nor, or else, and, rather than
ἀκάθαρτον adj. acc. masc. sg. ἀκάθαρτος unclean, foul
ἄνθρωπον n. acc. masc. sg. ἄνθρωπος man, human being, person, one, certain
29 διὸ conj. διό wherefore, therefore, for which cause
καὶ conj. καί and, even, also, but
ἀναντιρρήτως adv. ἀναντιρρήτως without gainsaying
οὖν conj. οὖν therefore, then, so, and, now, wherefore
τίνι interrog. pron. dat. masc. sg. τίς what, who, why, where, which, how
λόγῳ n. dat. masc. sg. λόγος word, saying, account, speech, thing, matter
με pron. acc. 1p. sg. ἐγώ I
30 καὶ conj. καί and, even, also, but
ὁ art. nom. masc. sg. ὁ ἡ τό the, this, that, he, she, it
Κορνήλιος n. nom. masc. sg. Κορνήλιος Cornelius
Ἀπὸ prep. ἀπό (+gen) from, of, out of, since, for, off, at, by, in, on
τετάρτης ordinal. adj. gen. fem. sg. τέταρτος fourth, four
ἡμέρας n. gen. fem. sg. ἡμέρα day, time, year, while, age, day time
μέχρι prep. μέχρι until, unto, till, to

ταύτης demo. pron. gen. fem. sg. οὗτος αὕτη τοῦτο this, the same, this same, he, she, it
τῆς art. gen. fem. sg. ὁ ἡ τό the, this, that, he, she, it
ὥρας n. gen. fem. sg. ὥρα hour, time, season
καὶ conj. καί and, even, also, but
τὴν art. acc. fem. sg. ὁ ἡ τό the, this, that, he, she, it
ἐννάτην ordinal. adj. acc. fem. sg. ἔννατος ninth
ὥραν n. acc. fem. sg. ὥρα hour, time, season
ἐν prep. ἐν (+dat) in, by, with, among, at, on, through, to, within, into, of, for
τῷ art. dat. masc. sg. ὁ ἡ τό the, this, that, he, she, it
οἴκῳ n. dat. masc. sg. οἶκος house, home, household
μου pron. gen. 1p. sg. ἐγώ I
καὶ conj. καί and, even, also, but
ἀνὴρ n. nom. masc. sg. ἀνήρ man, husband, sir
ἐνώπιον adv. ἐνώπιον before, in the sight of, in the presence of
μου pron. gen. 1p. sg. ἐγώ I
ἐν prep. ἐν (+dat) in, by, with, among, at, on, through, to, within, into, of, for
ἐσθῆτι n. dat. fem. sg. ἐσθής robe, apparel, clothing, raiment
λαμπρᾷ adj. dat. fem. sg. λαμπρός gorgeous, bright, goodly, white, clear
31 καὶ conj. καί and, even, also, but
Κορνήλιε n. voc. masc. sg. Κορνήλιος Cornelius
σου pron. gen. 2p. sg. σύ thou, you
ἡ art. nom. fem. sg. ὁ ἡ τό the, this, that, he, she, it
προσευχὴ n. nom. fem. sg. προσευχή prayer
καὶ conj. καί and, even, also, but
αἱ art. nom. fem. pl. ὁ ἡ τό the, this, that, he, she, it
ἐλεημοσύναι n. nom. fem. pl. ἐλεημοσύνη alms, almsdeed
σου pron. gen. 2p. sg. σύ thou, you
ἐνώπιον adv. ἐνώπιον before, in the sight of, in the presence of
τοῦ art. gen. masc. sg. ὁ ἡ τό the, this, that, he, she, it
Θεοῦ n. gen. masc. sg. θεός God, god
32 οὖν conj. οὖν therefore, then, so, and, now, wherefore
εἰς prep. εἰς (+acc) into, to, unto, for, in, on, toward, against, upon, at, among
Ἰόππην n. acc. fem. sg. Ἰόππη Joppa
καὶ conj. καί and, even, also, but
Σίμωνα n. acc. masc. sg. Σίμων Simon
ὃς relative pron. nom. masc. sg. ὅς ἥ ὅ who, which, what, that
Πέτρος n. nom. masc. sg. Πέτρος Peter
οὗτος demo. pron. nom. masc. sg. οὗτος αὕτη τοῦτο this, the same, this same, he, she, it
ἐν prep. ἐν (+dat) in, by, with, among, at, on, through, to, within, into, of, for
οἰκίᾳ n. dat. fem. sg. οἰκία house, home, household
Σίμωνος n. gen. masc. sg. Σίμων Simon
βυρσέως n. gen. masc. sg. βυρσεύς tanner
παρὰ prep. παρά (+gen) of, from, (+dat) with, for, (+acc) beside, at, by, above, against
θάλασσαν n. acc. fem. sg. θάλασσα sea
ὃς relative pron. nom. masc. sg. ὅς ἥ ὅ who, which, what, that
σοι pron. dat. 2p. sg. σύ thou, you
33 Ἐξαυτῆς adv. ἐξαυτῆς immediately, by and by, presently, straightway
οὖν conj. οὖν therefore, then, so, and, now, wherefore
πρὸς prep. πρός (+gen) for, (+dat) at, (+acc) unto, to, with, for, against
σέ pron. acc. 2p. sg. σύ thou, you
σύ pron. nom. 2p. sg. σύ thou, you
τε conj. τέ and, both, also
καλῶς adv. καλῶς good, well, full well
νῦν adv. νῦν now, henceforth, present, this time
οὖν conj. οὖν therefore, then, so, and, now, wherefore

πάντες adj. nom. masc. pl. πᾶς πᾶσα πᾶν all, every, whosoever, every one, no, whole, any
ἡμεῖς pron. nom. 1p. pl. ἐγώ I
ἐνώπιον adv. ἐνώπιον before, in the sight of, in the presence of
τοῦ art. gen. masc. sg. ὁ ἡ τό the, this, that, he, she, it
Θεοῦ n. gen. masc. sg. θεός God, god
πάντα adj. acc. neut. pl. πᾶς πᾶσα πᾶν all, every, whosoever, every one, no, whole, any
τὰ art. acc. neut. pl. ὁ ἡ τό the, this, that, he, she, it
σοι pron. dat. 2p. sg. σύ thou, you
ὑπὸ prep. ὑπό (+gen) of, by, with, from, among, (+acc) under
τοῦ art. gen. masc. sg. ὁ ἡ τό the, this, that, he, she, it
Θεοῦ n. gen. masc. sg. θεός God, god
34 δὲ conj. δέ but, and, now, also, to the contrary, rather, then
Πέτρος n. nom. masc. sg. Πέτρος Peter
τὸ art. acc. neut. sg. ὁ ἡ τό the, this, that, he, she, it
στόμα n. acc. neut. sg. στόμα mouth, face, edge
Ἐπ' prep. ἐπί (+gen) on, in, upon, (+dat) in, at, for, upon, (+acc) on, upon, unto, to, against
ἀληθείας n. gen. fem. sg. ἀλήθεια truth, verity
ὅτι conj. ὅτι that, for, because, how that, how, because that, for that, though
οὐκ particle of negation. οὐ οὐκ οὐχ not, no, neither, none, nay, nor, never, nothing
προσωπολήπτης n. nom. masc. sg. προσωπολήπτης respecter of persons
ὁ art. nom. masc. sg. ὁ ἡ τό the, this, that, he, she, it
Θεός n. nom. masc. sg. θεός God, god
35 ἀλλ' conj. ἀλλά but, yea, yet, nevertheless, howbeit, nay, therefore
ἐν prep. ἐν (+dat) in, by, with, among, at, on, through, to, within, into, of, for
παντὶ adj. dat. neut. sg. πᾶς πᾶσα πᾶν all, every, whosoever, every one, no, whole, any
ἔθνει n. dat. neut. sg. ἔθνος Gentile, nation, heathen, people
ὁ art. nom. masc. sg. ὁ ἡ τό the, this, that, he, she, it
αὐτὸν pron. acc. masc. 3p. sg. αὐτός ἡ ὁ self, of oneself, even, very, the same, he, she, it
καὶ conj. καί and, even, also, but
δικαιοσύνην n. acc. fem. sg. δικαιοσύνη righteousness
δεκτὸς adj. nom. masc. sg. δεκτός acceptable, accepted
αὐτῷ pron. dat. masc. 3p. sg. αὐτός ἡ ὁ self, of oneself, even, very, the same, he, she, it
36 τὸν art. acc. masc. sg. ὁ ἡ τό the, this, that, he, she, it
λόγον n. acc. masc. sg. λόγος word, saying, account, speech, thing, matter
ὃν relative pron. acc. masc. sg. ὅς ἥ ὅ who, which, what, that
τοῖς art. dat. masc. pl. ὁ ἡ τό the, this, that, he, she, it
υἱοῖς n. dat. masc. pl. υἱός son, child, descendant, offspring, heir
Ἰσραήλ pron. name. masc. inde. Ἰσραήλ Israel
εἰρήνην n. acc. fem. sg. εἰρήνη peace, quietness, rest
διὰ prep. διά (+gen) by, through, with, in, of, (+acc) for, because of, for a cause
Ἰησοῦ n. gen. masc. sg. Ἰησοῦς Jesus
Χριστοῦ n. gen. masc. sg. Χριστός Christ
οὗτός demo. pron. nom. masc. sg. οὗτος αὕτη τοῦτο this, the same, this same, he, she, it
πάντων adj. gen. masc. pl. πᾶς πᾶσα πᾶν all, every, whosoever, every one, no, whole, any
Κύριος n. nom. masc. sg. κύριος Lord, lord, master, sir, LORD, God, Master, owner
37 ὑμεῖς pron. nom. 2p. pl. σύ thou, you
τὸ art. acc. neut. sg. ὁ ἡ τό the, this, that, he, she, it
ῥῆμα n. acc. neut. sg. ῥῆμα word, saying, thing
καθ' prep. κατά (+gen) against, by, throughout, down, (+acc) according to, after, with
ὅλης adj. gen. fem. sg. ὅλος all, whole, every whit, altogether
τῆς art. gen. fem. sg. ὁ ἡ τό the, this, that, he, she, it
Ἰουδαίας n. gen. fem. sg. Ἰουδαία Judaea, Jewry
ἀπὸ prep. ἀπό (+gen) from, of, out of, since, for, off, at, by, in, on
τῆς art. gen. fem. sg. ὁ ἡ τό the, this, that, he, she, it
Γαλιλαίας n. gen. fem. sg. Γαλιλαία Galilee

μετὰ prep. μετά (+gen) with, among, against, (+acc) after
τὸ art. acc. neut. sg. ὁ ἡ τό the, this, that, he, she, it
βάπτισμα n. acc. neut. sg. βάπτισμα baptism
ὃ relative pron. acc. neut. sg. ὅς ἥ ὅ who, which, what, that
Ἰωάννης n. nom. masc. sg. Ἰωάννης John
38 Ἰησοῦν n. acc. masc. sg. Ἰησοῦς Jesus
τὸν art. acc. masc. sg. ὁ ἡ τό the, this, that, he, she, it
ἀπὸ prep. ἀπό (+gen) from, of, out of, since, for, off, at, by, in, on
Ναζαρέθ n. gen. fem. sg. Ναζαρέθ Nazareth
ὡς adv. ὡς as, when, as it were, how, about, like, as soon as, even as, while
αὐτὸν pron. acc. masc. 3p. sg. αὐτός ἡ ὁ self, of oneself, even, very, the same, he, she, it
ὁ art. nom. masc. sg. ὁ ἡ τό the, this, that, he, she, it
Θεὸς n. nom. masc. sg. θεός God, god
Πνεύματι n. dat. neut. sg. πνεῦμα spirit, Spirit, Ghost, ghost, life. of the spirit, wind
Ἁγίῳ adj. dat. neut. sg. ἅγιος Holy, holy, saint, Holy One, holy thing, most holy
καὶ conj. καί and, even, also, but
δυνάμει n. dat. fem. sg. δύναμις power, mighty work, miracle, strength, might
ὃς relative pron. nom. masc. sg. ὅς ἥ ὅ who, which, what, that
καὶ conj. καί and, even, also, but
πάντας adj. acc. masc. pl. πᾶς πᾶσα πᾶν all, every, whosoever, every one, no, whole, any
τοὺς art. acc. masc. pl. ὁ ἡ τό the, this, that, he, she, it
ὑπὸ prep. ὑπό (+gen) of, by, with, from, among, (+acc) under
τοῦ art. gen. masc. sg. ὁ ἡ τό the, this, that, he, she, it
διαβόλου adj. gen. masc. sg. διάβολος devil, false accuser, Devil, slanderer
ὅτι conj. ὅτι that, for, because, how that, how, because that, for that, though
ὁ art. nom. masc. sg. ὁ ἡ τό the, this, that, he, she, it
Θεὸς n. nom. masc. sg. θεός God, god
μετ' prep. μετά (+gen) with, among, against, (+acc) after
αὐτοῦ pron. gen. masc. 3p. sg. αὐτός ἡ ὁ self, of oneself, even, very, the same, he, she, it
39 καὶ conj. καί and, even, also, but
ἡμεῖς pron. nom. 1p. pl. ἐγώ I
μάρτυρες n. nom. masc. pl. μάρτυς or μάρτυρ witness, martyr, record
πάντων adj. gen. neut. pl. πᾶς πᾶσα πᾶν all, every, whosoever, every one, no, whole, any
ὧν relative pron. gen. neut. pl. ὅς ἥ ὅ who, which, what, that
ἔν prep. ἐν (+dat) in, by, with, among, at, on, through, to, within, into, of, for
τε conj. τέ and, both, also
τῇ art. dat. fem. sg. ὁ ἡ τό the, this, that, he, she, it
χώρᾳ n. dat. fem. sg. χώρα country, region, land, field, coast, ground
τῶν art. gen. masc. pl. ὁ ἡ τό the, this, that, he, she, it
Ἰουδαίων adj. gen. masc. pl. Ἰουδαῖος Jew, Jewess
καὶ conj. καί and, even, also, but
ἐν prep. ἐν (+dat) in, by, with, among, at, on, through, to, within, into, of, for
Ἱερουσαλήμ pron. name. fem. inde. Ἱερουσαλήμ Jerusalem
ὃν relative pron. acc. masc. sg. ὅς ἥ ὅ who, which, what, that
ἐπὶ prep. ἐπί (+gen) on, in, upon, (+dat) in, at, for, upon, (+acc) on, upon, unto, to, against
ξύλου n. gen. neut. sg. ξύλον tree, stave, wood, the stocks
40 τοῦτον demo. pron. acc. masc. sg. οὗτος αὕτη τοῦτο this, the same, this same, he, she, it
ὁ art. nom. masc. sg. ὁ ἡ τό the, this, that, he, she, it
Θεὸς n. nom. masc. sg. θεός God, god
τῇ art. dat. fem. sg. ὁ ἡ τό the, this, that, he, she, it
τρίτῃ ordinal. adj. dat. fem. sg. τρίτος third
ἡμέρᾳ n. dat. fem. sg. ἡμέρα day, time, year, while, age, day time
καὶ conj. καί and, even, also, but
αὐτὸν pron. acc. masc. 3p. sg. αὐτός ἡ ὁ self, of oneself, even, very, the same, he, she, it
ἐμφανῆ adj. acc. masc. sg. ἐμφανής openly, manifest

41 οὐ particle of negation. οὐ οὐκ οὐχ not, no, neither, none, nay, nor, never, nothing
παντὶ adj. dat. masc. sg. πᾶς πᾶσα πᾶν all, every, whosoever, every one, no, whole, any
τῷ art. dat. masc. sg. ὁ ἡ τό the, this, that, he, she, it
λαῷ n. dat. masc. sg. λαός people
ἀλλὰ conj. ἀλλά but, yea, yet, nevertheless, howbeit, nay, therefore
μάρτυσι n. dat. masc. pl. μάρτυς or μάρτυρ witness, martyr, record
τοῖς art. dat. masc. pl. ὁ ἡ τό the, this, that, he, she, it
ὑπὸ prep. ὑπό (+gen) of, by, with, from, among, (+acc) under
τοῦ art. gen. masc. sg. ὁ ἡ τό the, this, that, he, she, it
Θεοῦ n. gen. masc. sg. θεός God, god
ἡμῖν pron. dat. 1p. pl. ἐγώ I
οἵτινες relative pron. nom. masc. pl. ὅστις which, who, whosoever, that, whatsoever
καὶ conj. καί and, even, also, but
αὐτῷ pron. dat. masc. 3p. sg. αὐτός ἡ ὁ self, of oneself, even, very, the same, he, she, it
μετὰ prep. μετά (+gen) with, among, against, (+acc) after
τὸ art. acc. neut. sg. ὁ ἡ τό the, this, that, he, she, it
αὐτὸν pron. acc. masc. 3p. sg. αὐτός ἡ ὁ self, of oneself, even, very, the same, he, she, it
ἐκ prep. ἐκ ἐξ (+gen) of, from, out of, by, on, with, in, among, through
νεκρῶν adj. gen. masc. pl. νεκρός dead
42 καὶ conj. καί and, even, also, but
ἡμῖν pron. dat. 1p. pl. ἐγώ I
τῷ art. dat. masc. sg. ὁ ἡ τό the, this, that, he, she, it
λαῷ n. dat. masc. sg. λαός people
καὶ conj. καί and, even, also, but
ὅτι conj. ὅτι that, for, because, how that, how, because that, for that, though
αὐτός pron. nom. masc. 3p. sg. αὐτός ἡ ὁ self, of oneself, even, very, the same, he, she, it
ὁ art. nom. masc. sg. ὁ ἡ τό the, this, that, he, she, it
ὑπὸ prep. ὑπό (+gen) of, by, with, from, among, (+acc) under
τοῦ art. gen. masc. sg. ὁ ἡ τό the, this, that, he, she, it
Θεοῦ n. gen. masc. sg. θεός God, god
κριτὴς n. nom. masc. sg. κριτής judge
καὶ conj. καί and, even, also, but
νεκρῶν adj. gen. masc. pl. νεκρός dead
43 τούτῳ demo. pron. dat. masc. sg. οὗτος αὕτη τοῦτο this, the same, this same, he, she, it
πάντες adj. nom. masc. pl. πᾶς πᾶσα πᾶν all, every, whosoever, every one, no, whole, any
οἱ art. nom. masc. pl. ὁ ἡ τό the, this, that, he, she, it
προφῆται n. nom. masc. pl. προφήτης prophet
ἄφεσιν n. acc. fem. sg. ἄφεσις remission, forgiveness, deliverance, liberty
ἁμαρτιῶν n. gen. fem. pl. ἁμαρτία sin, offence, sinful
διὰ prep. διά (+gen) by, through, with, in, of, (+acc) for, because of, for a cause
τοῦ art. gen. neut. sg. ὁ ἡ τό the, this, that, he, she, it
ὀνόματος n. gen. neut. sg. ὄνομα name, call, surname
αὐτοῦ pron. gen. masc. 3p. sg. αὐτός ἡ ὁ self, of oneself, even, very, the same, he, she, it
πάντα adj. acc. masc. sg. πᾶς πᾶσα πᾶν all, every, whosoever, every one, no, whole, any
τὸν art. acc. masc. sg. ὁ ἡ τό the, this, that, he, she, it
εἰς prep. εἰς (+acc) into, to, unto, for, in, on, toward, against, upon, at, among
αὐτόν pron. acc. masc. 3p. sg. αὐτός ἡ ὁ self, of oneself, even, very, the same, he, she, it
44 Ἔτι adv. ἔτι yet, more, any more, further, still, moreover
τοῦ art. gen. masc. sg. ὁ ἡ τό the, this, that, he, she, it
Πέτρου n. gen. masc. sg. Πέτρος Peter
τὰ art. acc. neut. pl. ὁ ἡ τό the, this, that, he, she, it
ῥήματα n. acc. neut. pl. ῥῆμα word, saying, thing
ταῦτα demo. pron. acc. neut. pl. οὗτος αὕτη τοῦτο this, the same, this same, he, she, it
τὸ art. nom. neut. sg. ὁ ἡ τό the, this, that, he, she, it
Πνεῦμα n. nom. neut. sg. πνεῦμα spirit, Spirit, Ghost, ghost, life. of the spirit, wind

τὸ art. nom. neut. sg. ὁ ἡ τό the, this, that, he, she, it
Ἅγιον adj. nom. neut. sg. ἅγιος Holy, holy, saint, Holy One, holy thing, most holy
ἐπὶ prep. ἐπί (+gen) on, in, upon, (+dat) in, at, for, upon, (+acc) on, upon, unto, to, against
πάντας adj. acc. masc. pl. πᾶς πᾶσα πᾶν all, every, whosoever, every one, no, whole, any
τοὺς art. acc. masc. pl. ὁ ἡ τό the, this, that, he, she, it
τὸν art. acc. masc. sg. ὁ ἡ τό the, this, that, he, she, it
λόγον n. acc. masc. sg. λόγος word, saying, account, speech, thing, matter
45 καὶ conj. καί and, even, also, but
οἱ art. nom. masc. pl. ὁ ἡ τό the, this, that, he, she, it
ἐκ prep. ἐκ ἐξ (+gen) of, from, out of, by, on, with, in, among, through
περιτομῆς n. gen. fem. sg. περιτομή circumcision
πιστοὶ adj. nom. masc. pl. πιστός faithful, believing, true, sure
ὅσοι relative pron. nom. masc. pl. ὅσος as many as, whatsoever, that, as long as, how much
τῷ art. dat. masc. sg. ὁ ἡ τό the, this, that, he, she, it
Πέτρῳ n. dat. masc. sg. Πέτρος Peter
ὅτι conj. ὅτι that, for, because, how that, how, because that, for that, though
καὶ conj. καί and, even, also, but
ἐπὶ prep. ἐπί (+gen) on, in, upon, (+dat) in, at, for, upon, (+acc) on, upon, unto, to, against
τὰ art. acc. neut. pl. ὁ ἡ τό the, this, that, he, she, it
ἔθνη n. acc. neut. pl. ἔθνος Gentile, nation, heathen, people
ἡ art. nom. fem. sg. ὁ ἡ τό the, this, that, he, she, it
δωρεὰ n. nom. fem. sg. δωρεά gift
τοῦ art. gen. neut. sg. ὁ ἡ τό the, this, that, he, she, it
Ἁγίου adj. gen. neut. sg. ἅγιος Holy, holy, saint, Holy One, holy thing, most holy
Πνεύματος n. gen. neut. sg. πνεῦμα spirit, Spirit, Ghost, ghost, life. of the spirit, wind
46 γὰρ conj. γάρ for, and, because, but, indeed
αὐτῶν pron. gen. masc. 3p. pl. αὐτός ή ό self, of oneself, even, very, the same, he, she, it
γλώσσαις n. dat. fem. pl. γλῶσσα tongue
καὶ conj. καί and, even, also, but
τὸν art. acc. masc. sg. ὁ ἡ τό the, this, that, he, she, it
Θεόν n. acc. masc. sg. θεός God, god
τότε adv. τότε then, that time
ὁ art. nom. masc. sg. ὁ ἡ τό the, this, that, he, she, it
Πέτρος n. nom. masc. sg. Πέτρος Peter
47 Μήτι interrog. particle of negation. μήτι not, how much more
τὸ art. acc. neut. sg. ὁ ἡ τό the, this, that, he, she, it
ὕδωρ n. acc. neut. sg. ὕδωρ water
τις indefinite pron. nom. masc. sg. τὶς certain, some, any man, one, any thing
τοῦ art. gen. neut. sg. ὁ ἡ τό the, this, that, he, she, it
μὴ particle of negation. μή not, no, lest, neither, none, nothing, nor, never, without
τούτους demo. pron. acc. masc. pl. οὗτος αὕτη τοῦτο this, the same, this same, he, she, it
οἵτινες relative pron. nom. masc. pl. ὅστις which, who, whosoever, that, whatsoever
τὸ art. acc. neut. sg. ὁ ἡ τό the, this, that, he, she, it
Πνεῦμα n. acc. neut. sg. πνεῦμα spirit, Spirit, Ghost, ghost, life. of the spirit, wind
τὸ art. acc. neut. sg. ὁ ἡ τό the, this, that, he, she, it
Ἅγιον adj. acc. neut. sg. ἅγιος Holy, holy, saint, Holy One, holy thing, most holy
καθὼς adv. καθώς as, even as, according as, according to
καὶ conj. καί and, even, also, but
ἡμεῖς pron. nom. 1p. pl. ἐγώ I
48 τε conj. τέ and, both, also
αὐτοὺς pron. acc. masc. 3p. pl. αὐτός ή ό self, of oneself, even, very, the same, he, she, it
ἐν prep. ἐν (+dat) in, by, with, among, at, on, through, to, within, into, of, for
τῷ art. dat. neut. sg. ὁ ἡ τό the, this, that, he, she, it
ὀνόματι n. dat. neut. sg. ὄνομα name, call, surname
τοῦ art. gen. masc. sg. ὁ ἡ τό the, this, that, he, she, it

Κυρίου n. gen. masc. sg. κύριος Lord, lord, master, sir, LORD, God, Master, owner
τότε adv. τότε then, that time
αὐτὸν pron. acc. masc. 3p. sg. αὐτός ή ό self, of oneself, even, very, the same, he, she, it
ἡμέρας n. acc. fem. pl. ἡμέρα day, time, year, while, age, day time
τινάς indefinite pron. acc. fem. pl. τὶς certain, some, any man, one, any thing

11

1 δὲ conj. δέ but, and, now, also, to the contrary, rather, then
οἱ art. nom. masc. pl. ὁ ἡ τό the, this, that, he, she, it
ἀπόστολοι n. nom. masc. pl. ἀπόστολος apostle, messenger, he that is sent
καὶ conj. καί and, even, also, but
οἱ art. nom. masc. pl. ὁ ἡ τό the, this, that, he, she, it
ἀδελφοὶ n. nom. masc. pl. ἀδελφός brother
οἱ art. nom. masc. pl. ὁ ἡ τό the, this, that, he, she, it
κατὰ prep. κατά (+gen) against, by, throughout, down, (+acc) according to, after, with
τὴν art. acc. fem. sg. ὁ ἡ τό the, this, that, he, she, it
Ἰουδαίαν n. acc. fem. sg. Ἰουδαία Judaea, Jewry
ὅτι conj. ὅτι that, for, because, how that, how, because that, for that, though
καὶ conj. καί and, even, also, but
τὰ art. nom. neut. pl. ὁ ἡ τό the, this, that, he, she, it
ἔθνη n. nom. neut. pl. ἔθνος Gentile, nation, heathen, people
τὸν art. acc. masc. sg. ὁ ἡ τό the, this, that, he, she, it
λόγον n. acc. masc. sg. λόγος word, saying, account, speech, thing, matter
τοῦ art. gen. masc. sg. ὁ ἡ τό the, this, that, he, she, it
Θεοῦ n. gen. masc. sg. θεός God, god
2 καὶ conj. καί and, even, also, but
ὅτε adv. ὅτε when, after that, as soon as, while, after
Πέτρος n. nom. masc. sg. Πέτρος Peter
εἰς prep. εἰς (+acc) into, to, unto, for, in, on, toward, against, upon, at, among
Ἱεροσόλυμα n. acc. neut. sg. Ἱεροσόλυμα Jerusalem
πρὸς prep. πρός (+gen) for, (+dat) at, (+acc) unto, to, with, for, against
αὐτὸν pron. acc. masc. 3p. sg. αὐτός ή ό self, of oneself, even, very, the same, he, she, it
οἱ art. nom. masc. pl. ὁ ἡ τό the, this, that, he, she, it
ἐκ prep. ἐκ ἐξ (+gen) of, from, out of, by, on, with, in, among, through
περιτομῆς n. gen. fem. sg. περιτομή circumcision
3 ὅτι conj. ὅτι that, for, because, how that, how, because that, for that, though
πρὸς prep. πρός (+gen) for, (+dat) at, (+acc) unto, to, with, for, against
ἄνδρας n. acc. masc. pl. ἀνήρ man, husband, sir
ἀκροβυστίαν n. acc. fem. sg. ἀκροβυστία uncircumcised, uncircumcision
καὶ conj. καί and, even, also, but
αὐτοῖς pron. dat. masc. 3p. pl. αὐτός ή ό self, of oneself, even, very, the same, he, she, it
4 δὲ conj. δέ but, and, now, also, to the contrary, rather, then
ὁ art. nom. masc. sg. ὁ ἡ τό the, this, that, he, she, it
Πέτρος n. nom. masc. sg. Πέτρος Peter
αὐτοῖς pron. dat. masc. 3p. pl. αὐτός ή ό self, of oneself, even, very, the same, he, she, it
καθεξῆς adv. καθεξῆς in order, after, afterward, by order
5 Ἐγὼ pron. nom. 1p. sg. ἐγώ I
ἐν prep. ἐν (+dat) in, by, with, among, at, on, through, to, within, into, of, for
πόλει n. dat. fem. sg. πόλις city
Ἰόππῃ n. dat. fem. sg. Ἰόππη Joppa
καὶ conj. καί and, even, also, but
ἐκστάσει n. dat. fem. sg. ἔκστασις trance, astonishment, amazement, amazed
ὅραμα n. acc. neut. sg. ὅραμα vision, sight
σκεῦός n. acc. neut. sg. σκεῦος vessel, good, sail, stuff

τι indefinite pron. acc. neut. sg. τὶς certain, some, any man, one, any thing
ὡς adv. ὡς as, when, as it were, how, about, like, as soon as, even as, while
ὀθόνην n. acc. fem. sg. ὀθόνη sheet
μεγάλην adj. acc. fem. sg. μέγας great, loud, greatest, high, large, mighty, strong
τέσσαρσιν num. dat. fem. pl. τέσσαρες four
ἀρχαῖς n. dat. fem. pl. ἀρχή beginning, principality, corner, first, magistrate, rule
ἐκ prep. ἐκ ἐξ (+gen) of, from, out of, by, on, with, in, among, through
τοῦ art. gen. masc. sg. ὁ ἡ τό the, this, that, he, she, it
οὐρανοῦ n. gen. masc. sg. οὐρανός heaven, air, sky
καὶ conj. καί and, even, also, but
ἄχρις prep. ἄχρι or ἄχρις (+gen) until, unto, till, even to, as far as, while, into
ἐμοῦ pron. gen. 1p. sg. ἐγώ I
6 εἰς prep. εἰς (+acc) into, to, unto, for, in, on, toward, against, upon, at, among
ἣν relative pron. acc. fem. sg. ὅς ἥ ὅ who, which, what, that
καὶ conj. καί and, even, also, but
τὰ art. acc. neut. pl. ὁ ἡ τό the, this, that, he, she, it
τετράποδα adj. acc. neut. pl. τετράπους fourfooted beast
τῆς art. gen. fem. sg. ὁ ἡ τό the, this, that, he, she, it
γῆς n. gen. fem. sg. γῆ earth, land, ground, country
καὶ conj. καί and, even, also, but
τὰ art. acc. neut. pl. ὁ ἡ τό the, this, that, he, she, it
θηρία n. acc. neut. pl. θηρίον beast, wild beast, venomous beast
καὶ conj. καί and, even, also, but
τὰ art. acc. neut. pl. ὁ ἡ τό the, this, that, he, she, it
ἑρπετὰ n. acc. neut. pl. ἑρπετόν creeping thing, serpent
καὶ conj. καί and, even, also, but
τὰ art. acc. neut. pl. ὁ ἡ τό the, this, that, he, she, it
πετεινὰ adj. acc. neut. pl. πετεινόν fowl, bird
τοῦ art. gen. masc. sg. ὁ ἡ τό the, this, that, he, she, it
οὐρανοῦ n. gen. masc. sg. οὐρανός heaven, air, sky
7 δὲ conj. δέ but, and, now, also, to the contrary, rather, then
φωνῆς n. gen. fem. sg. φωνή voice, sound, noise
μοι pron. dat. 1p. sg. ἐγώ I
Πέτρε n. voc. masc. sg. Πέτρος Peter
καὶ conj. καί and, even, also, but
8 δὲ conj. δέ but, and, now, also, to the contrary, rather, then
Μηδαμῶς adv. μηδαμῶς not so
Κύριε n. voc. masc. sg. κύριος Lord, lord, master, sir, LORD, God, Master, owner
ὅτι conj. ὅτι that, for, because, how that, how, because that, for that, though
πᾶν adj. acc. neut. sg. πᾶς πᾶsa πᾶν all, every, whosoever, every one, no, whole, any
κοινὸν adj. nom. neut. sg. κοινός common, unclean, defiled, unholy
ἢ particle. ἤ or, than, either, nor, or else, and, rather than
ἀκάθαρτον adj. nom. neut. sg. ἀκάθαρτος unclean, foul
οὐδέποτε adv. οὐδέποτε never, neither at any time, no at any time
εἰς prep. εἰς (+acc) into, to, unto, for, in, on, toward, against, upon, at, among
τὸ art. acc. neut. sg. ὁ ἡ τό the, this, that, he, she, it
στόμα n. acc. neut. sg. στόμα mouth, face, edge
μου pron. gen. 1p. sg. ἐγώ I
9 δὲ conj. δέ but, and, now, also, to the contrary, rather, then
μοι pron. dat. 1p. sg. ἐγώ I
φωνὴ n. nom. fem. sg. φωνή voice, sound, noise
ἐκ prep. ἐκ ἐξ (+gen) of, from, out of, by, on, with, in, among, through
δευτέρου ordinal. adj. gen. neut. sg. δεύτερος second, second time, again, afterward
ἐκ prep. ἐκ ἐξ (+gen) of, from, out of, by, on, with, in, among, through
τοῦ art. gen. masc. sg. ὁ ἡ τό the, this, that, he, she, it

οὐρανοῦ n. gen. masc. sg. οὐρανός heaven, air, sky
Ἅ relative pron. acc. neut. pl. ὅς ἥ ὅ who, which, what, that
ὁ art. nom. masc. sg. ὁ ἡ τό the, this, that, he, she, it
Θεὸς n. nom. masc. sg. θεός God, god
σὺ pron. nom. 2p. sg. σύ thou, you
μὴ particle of negation. μή not, no, lest, neither, none, nothing, nor, never, without
10 τοῦτο demo. pron. nom. neut. sg. οὗτος αὕτη τοῦτο this, the same, this same, he, she, it
δὲ conj. δέ but, and, now, also, to the contrary, rather, then
ἐπὶ prep. ἐπί (+gen) on, in, upon, (+dat) in, at, for, upon, (+acc) on, upon, unto, to, against
τρίς adv. τρίς thrice, three times
καὶ conj. καί and, even, also, but
πάλιν adv. πάλιν again
ἅπαντα adj. nom. neut. pl. ἅπας all, whole, all things, every, everyone
εἰς prep. εἰς (+acc) into, to, unto, for, in, on, toward, against, upon, at, among
τὸν art. acc. masc. sg. ὁ ἡ τό the, this, that, he, she, it
οὐρανόν n. acc. masc. sg. οὐρανός heaven, air, sky
11 καὶ conj. καί and, even, also, but
ἐξαυτῆς adv. ἐξαυτῆς immediately, by and by, presently, straightway
τρεῖς num. nom. masc. pl. τρεῖς three
ἄνδρες n. nom. masc. pl. ἀνήρ man, husband, sir
ἐπὶ prep. ἐπί (+gen) on, in, upon, (+dat) in, at, for, upon, (+acc) on, upon, unto, to, against
τὴν art. acc. fem. sg. ὁ ἡ τό the, this, that, he, she, it
οἰκίαν n. acc. fem. sg. οἰκία house, home, household
ἐν prep. ἐν (+dat) in, by, with, among, at, on, through, to, within, into, of, for
ᾗ relative pron. dat. fem. sg. ὅς ἥ ὅ who, which, what, that
ἀπὸ prep. ἀπό (+gen) from, of, out of, since, for, off, at, by, in, on
Καισαρείας n. gen. fem. sg. Καισάρεια Caesarea
πρός prep. πρός (+gen) for, (+dat) at, (+acc) unto, to, with, for, against
με pron. acc. 1p. sg. ἐγώ I
12 δὲ conj. δέ but, and, now, also, to the contrary, rather, then
μοι pron. dat. 1p. sg. ἐγώ I
τὸ art. nom. neut. sg. ὁ ἡ τό the, this, that, he, she, it
Πνεῦμά n. nom. neut. sg. πνεῦμα spirit, Spirit, Ghost, ghost, life. of the spirit, wind
αὐτοῖς pron. dat. masc. 3p. pl. αὐτός ή ό self, of oneself, even, very, the same, he, she, it
μηδὲν adj. acc. neut. sg. μηδείς μηδεμία μηδέν no man, nothing, no, none, not at all
δὲ conj. δέ but, and, now, also, to the contrary, rather, then
σὺν prep. σύν (+dat) with, beside
ἐμοὶ pron. dat. 1p. sg. ἐγώ I
καὶ conj. καί and, even, also, but
οἱ art. nom. masc. pl. ὁ ἡ τό the, this, that, he, she, it
ἓξ num. nom. masc. pl. ἕξ six
ἀδελφοὶ n. nom. masc. pl. ἀδελφός brother
οὗτοι demo. pron. nom. masc. pl. οὗτος αὕτη τοῦτο this, the same, this same, he, she, it
καὶ conj. καί and, even, also, but
εἰς prep. εἰς (+acc) into, to, unto, for, in, on, toward, against, upon, at, among
τὸν art. acc. masc. sg. ὁ ἡ τό the, this, that, he, she, it
οἶκον n. acc. masc. sg. οἶκος house, home, household
τοῦ art. gen. masc. sg. ὁ ἡ τό the, this, that, he, she, it
ἀνδρός n. gen. masc. sg. ἀνήρ man, husband, sir
13 τε conj. τέ and, both, also
ἡμῖν pron. dat. 1p. pl. ἐγώ I
πῶς adv. πῶς how, by what means, after what manner
τὸν art. acc. masc. sg. ὁ ἡ τό the, this, that, he, she, it
ἄγγελον n. acc. masc. sg. ἄγγελος angel, messenger
ἐν prep. ἐν (+dat) in, by, with, among, at, on, through, to, within, into, of, for

τῷ art. dat. masc. sg. ὁ ἡ τό the, this, that, he, she, it
οἴκῳ n. dat. masc. sg. οἶκος house, home, household
αὐτοῦ pron. gen. masc. 3p. sg. αὐτός ἡ ὁ self, of oneself, even, very, the same, he, she, it
καὶ conj. καί and, even, also, but
αὐτῷ pron. dat. masc. 3p. sg. αὐτός ἡ ὁ self, of oneself, even, very, the same, he, she, it
εἰς prep. εἰς (+acc) into, to, unto, for, in, on, toward, against, upon, at, among
Ἰόππην n. acc. fem. sg. Ἰόππη Joppa
ἄνδρας n. acc. masc. pl. ἀνήρ man, husband, sir
καὶ conj. καί and, even, also, but
Σίμωνα n. acc. masc. sg. Σίμων Simon
τὸν art. acc. masc. sg. ὁ ἡ τό the, this, that, he, she, it
Πέτρον n. acc. masc. sg. Πέτρος Peter
14 ὃς relative pron. nom. masc. sg. ὅς ἥ ὅ who, which, what, that
ῥήματα n. acc. neut. pl. ῥῆμα word, saying, thing
πρὸς prep. πρός (+gen) for, (+dat) at, (+acc) unto, to, with, for, against
σὲ pron. acc. 2p. sg. σύ thou, you
ἐν prep. ἐν (+dat) in, by, with, among, at, on, through, to, within, into, of, for
οἷς relative pron. dat. neut. pl. ὅς ἥ ὅ who, which, what, that
σὺ pron. nom. 2p. sg. σύ thou, you
καὶ conj. καί and, even, also, but
πᾶς adj. nom. masc. sg. πᾶς πᾶσα πᾶν all, every, whosoever, every one, no, whole, any
ὁ art. nom. masc. sg. ὁ ἡ τό the, this, that, he, she, it
οἶκός n. nom. masc. sg. οἶκος house, home, household
σου pron. gen. 2p. sg. σύ thou, you
15 ἐν prep. ἐν (+dat) in, by, with, among, at, on, through, to, within, into, of, for
δὲ conj. δέ but, and, now, also, to the contrary, rather, then
τῷ art. dat. neut. sg. ὁ ἡ τό the, this, that, he, she, it
με pron. acc. 1p. sg. ἐγώ I
τὸ art. nom. neut. sg. ὁ ἡ τό the, this, that, he, she, it
Πνεῦμα n. nom. neut. sg. πνεῦμα spirit, Spirit, Ghost, ghost, life. of the spirit, wind
τὸ art. nom. neut. sg. ὁ ἡ τό the, this, that, he, she, it
Ἅγιον adj. nom. neut. sg. ἅγιος Holy, holy, saint, Holy One, holy thing, most holy
ἐπ' prep. ἐπί (+gen) on, in, upon, (+dat) in, at, for, upon, (+acc) on, upon, unto, to, against
αὐτοὺς pron. acc. masc. 3p. pl. αὐτός ἡ ὁ self, of oneself, even, very, the same, he, she, it
ὥσπερ conj. ὥσπερ as, even as, like as
καὶ conj. καί and, even, also, but
ἐφ' prep. ἐπί (+gen) on, in, upon, (+dat) in, at, for, upon, (+acc) on, upon, unto, to, against
ἡμᾶς pron. acc. 1p. pl. ἐγώ I
ἐν prep. ἐν (+dat) in, by, with, among, at, on, through, to, within, into, of, for
ἀρχῇ n. dat. fem. sg. ἀρχή beginning, principality, corner, first, magistrate, rule
16 δὲ conj. δέ but, and, now, also, to the contrary, rather, then
τοῦ art. gen. neut. sg. ὁ ἡ τό the, this, that, he, she, it
ῥήματος n. gen. neut. sg. ῥῆμα word, saying, thing
Κυρίου n. gen. masc. sg. κύριος Lord, lord, master, sir, LORD, God, Master, owner
ὡς adv. ὡς as, when, as it were, how, about, like, as soon as, even as, while
Ἰωάννης n. nom. masc. sg. Ἰωάννης John
μέν conj. μέν indeed, verily, truly, even, so, some
ὕδατι n. dat. neut. sg. ὕδωρ water
ὑμεῖς pron. nom. 2p. pl. σύ thou, you
δὲ conj. δέ but, and, now, also, to the contrary, rather, then
ἐν prep. ἐν (+dat) in, by, with, among, at, on, through, to, within, into, of, for
Πνεύματι n. dat. neut. sg. πνεῦμα spirit, Spirit, Ghost, ghost, life. of the spirit, wind
Ἁγίῳ adj. dat. neut. sg. ἅγιος Holy, holy, saint, Holy One, holy thing, most holy
17 εἰ conj. εἰ if, whether, that, though, forasmuch
οὖν conj. οὖν therefore, then, so, and, now, wherefore

τὴν art. acc. fem. sg. ὁ ἡ τό the, this, that, he, she, it
ἴσην adj. acc. fem. sg. ἴσος equal, as much, like
δωρεὰν n. acc. fem. sg. δωρεά gift
αὐτοῖς pron. dat. masc. 3p. pl. αὐτός ή ό self, of oneself, even, very, the same, he, she, it
ὁ art. nom. masc. sg. ὁ ἡ τό the, this, that, he, she, it
Θεὸς n. nom. masc. sg. θεός God, god
ὡς adv. ὡς as, when, as it were, how, about, like, as soon as, even as, while
καὶ conj. καί and, even, also, but
ἡμῖν pron. dat. 1p. pl. ἐγώ I
ἐπὶ prep. ἐπί (+gen) on, in, upon, (+dat) in, at, for, upon, (+acc) on, upon, unto, to, against
τὸν art. acc. masc. sg. ὁ ἡ τό the, this, that, he, she, it
Κύριον n. acc. masc. sg. κύριος Lord, lord, master, sir, LORD, God, Master, owner
Ἰησοῦν n. acc. masc. sg. Ἰησοῦς Jesus
Χριστόν n. acc. masc. sg. Χριστός Christ
ἐγὼ pron. nom. 1p. sg. ἐγώ I
δὲ conj. δέ but, and, now, also, to the contrary, rather, then
τίς indefinite pron. nom. masc. sg. τίς what, who, why, where, which, how
δυνατὸς adj. nom. masc. sg. δυνατός able, possible, mighty, strong
τὸν art. acc. masc. sg. ὁ ἡ τό the, this, that, he, she, it
Θεόν n. acc. masc. sg. θεός God, god
18 δὲ conj. δέ but, and, now, also, to the contrary, rather, then
ταῦτα demo. pron. acc. neut. pl. οὗτος αὕτη τοῦτο this, the same, this same, he, she, it
καὶ conj. καί and, even, also, but
τὸν art. acc. masc. sg. ὁ ἡ τό the, this, that, he, she, it
Θεὸν n. acc. masc. sg. θεός God, god
Ἄραγε particle. ἄραγε then, surely, so then, wherefore
καὶ conj. καί and, even, also, but
τοῖς art. dat. neut. pl. ὁ ἡ τό the, this, that, he, she, it
ἔθνεσιν n. dat. neut. pl. ἔθνος Gentile, nation, heathen, people
ὁ art. nom. masc. sg. ὁ ἡ τό the, this, that, he, she, it
Θεὸς n. nom. masc. sg. θεός God, god
τὴν art. acc. fem. sg. ὁ ἡ τό the, this, that, he, she, it
μετάνοιαν n. acc. fem. sg. μετάνοια repentance
εἰς prep. εἰς (+acc) into, to, unto, for, in, on, toward, against, upon, at, among
ζωὴν n. acc. fem. sg. ζωή life, lifetime
19 Οἱ art. nom. masc. pl. ὁ ἡ τό the, this, that, he, she, it
μέν conj. μέν indeed, verily, truly, even, so, some
οὖν conj. οὖν therefore, then, so, and, now, wherefore
ἀπὸ prep. ἀπό (+gen) from, of, out of, since, for, off, at, by, in, on
τῆς art. gen. fem. sg. ὁ ἡ τό the, this, that, he, she, it
θλίψεως n. gen. fem. sg. θλῖψις tribulation, affliction, anguish, persecution
τῆς art. gen. fem. sg. ὁ ἡ τό the, this, that, he, she, it
ἐπὶ prep. ἐπί (+gen) on, in, upon, (+dat) in, at, for, upon, (+acc) on, upon, unto, to, against
Στεφάνῳ n. dat. masc. sg. Στέφανος Stephen
ἕως conj. ἕως till, until, unto, until when, while, as far as, even, until now
Φοινίκης n. gen. fem. sg. Φοινίκη Phenice, Phenicia
καὶ conj. καί and, even, also, but
Κύπρου n. gen. fem. sg. Κύπρος Cyprus
καὶ conj. καί and, even, also, but
Ἀντιοχείας n. gen. fem. sg. Ἀντιόχεια Antioch
μηδενὶ num. dat. masc. sg. μηδείς μηδεμία μηδέν no man, nothing, no, none, not at all
τὸν art. acc. masc. sg. ὁ ἡ τό the, this, that, he, she, it
λόγον n. acc. masc. sg. λόγος word, saying, account, speech, thing, matter
εἰ conj. εἰ if, whether, that, though, forasmuch
μὴ particle of negation. μή not, no, lest, neither, none, nothing, nor, never, without

μόνον adv. μόνος only, alone, by oneself
Ἰουδαίοις adj. dat. masc. pl. Ἰουδαῖος Jew, Jewess
20 δὲ conj. δέ but, and, now, also, to the contrary, rather, then
τινες indefinite pron. nom. masc. pl. τὶς certain, some, any man, one, any thing
ἐξ prep. ἐκ ἐξ (+gen) of, from, out of, by, on, with, in, among, through
αὐτῶν pron. gen. masc. 3p. pl. αὐτός ή ό self, of oneself, even, very, the same, he, she, it
ἄνδρες n. nom. masc. pl. ἀνήρ man, husband, sir
Κύπριοι n. nom. masc. pl. Κύπριος Cypriot, inhabitant of Cyprus
καὶ conj. καί and, even, also, but
Κυρηναῖοι n. nom. masc. pl. Κυρηναῖος Cyrene, Cyrenian
οἵτινες relative pron. nom. masc. pl. ὅστις which, who, whosoever, that, whatsoever
εἰς prep. εἰς (+acc) into, to, unto, for, in, on, toward, against, upon, at, among
Ἀντιόχειαν n. acc. fem. sg. Ἀντιόχεια Antioch
πρὸς prep. πρός (+gen) for, (+dat) at, (+acc) unto, to, with, for, against
τοὺς art. acc. masc. pl. ὁ ἡ τό the, this, that, he, she, it
Ἑλληνιστὰς n. acc. masc. pl. Ἑλληνιστής Grecian
τὸν art. acc. masc. sg. ὁ ἡ τό the, this, that, he, she, it
Κύριον n. acc. masc. sg. κύριος Lord, lord, master, sir, LORD, God, Master, owner
Ἰησοῦν n. acc. masc. sg. Ἰησοῦς Jesus
21 καὶ conj. καί and, even, also, but
χεὶρ n. nom. fem. sg. χείρ hand
Κυρίου n. gen. masc. sg. κύριος Lord, lord, master, sir, LORD, God, Master, owner
μετ' prep. μετά (+gen) with, among, against, (+acc) after
αὐτῶν pron. gen. masc. 3p. pl. αὐτός ή ό self, of oneself, even, very, the same, he, she, it
πολύς adj. nom. masc. sg. πολύς many, great, much, long, abundant
τε conj. τέ and, both, also
ἀριθμὸς n. nom. masc. sg. ἀριθμός number
ἐπὶ prep. ἐπί (+gen) on, in, upon, (+dat) in, at, for, upon, (+acc) on, upon, unto, to, against
τὸν art. acc. masc. sg. ὁ ἡ τό the, this, that, he, she, it
Κύριον n. acc. masc. sg. κύριος Lord, lord, master, sir, LORD, God, Master, owner
22 δὲ conj. δέ but, and, now, also, to the contrary, rather, then
ὁ art. nom. masc. sg. ὁ ἡ τό the, this, that, he, she, it
λόγος n. nom. masc. sg. λόγος word, saying, account, speech, thing, matter
εἰς prep. εἰς (+acc) into, to, unto, for, in, on, toward, against, upon, at, among
τὰ art. acc. neut. pl. ὁ ἡ τό the, this, that, he, she, it
ὦτα n. acc. neut. pl. οὖς ear
τῆς art. gen. fem. sg. ὁ ἡ τό the, this, that, he, she, it
ἐκκλησίας n. gen. fem. sg. ἐκκλησία church, assembly
τῆς art. gen. fem. sg. ὁ ἡ τό the, this, that, he, she, it
ἐν prep. ἐν (+dat) in, by, with, among, at, on, through, to, within, into, of, for
Ἱεροσολύμοις n. dat. neut. pl. Ἱεροσόλυμα Jerusalem
περὶ prep. περί (+gen) of, for, concerning, (+acc) about, concerning, in
αὐτῶν pron. gen. masc. 3p. pl. αὐτός ή ό self, of oneself, even, very, the same, he, she, it
καὶ conj. καί and, even, also, but
Βαρναβᾶν n. acc. masc. sg. Βαρναβᾶς Barnabas
ἕως conj. ἕως till, until, unto, until when, while, as far as, even, until now
Ἀντιοχείας n. gen. fem. sg. Ἀντιόχεια Antioch
23 ὃς relative pron. nom. masc. sg. ὅς ἥ ὅ who, which, what, that
καὶ conj. καί and, even, also, but
τὴν art. acc. fem. sg. ὁ ἡ τό the, this, that, he, she, it
χάριν n. acc. fem. sg. χάρις grace, thank, favour, pleasure
τοῦ art. gen. masc. sg. ὁ ἡ τό the, this, that, he, she, it
Θεοῦ n. gen. masc. sg. θεός God, god
καὶ conj. καί and, even, also, but
πάντας adj. acc. masc. pl. πᾶς πᾶσα πᾶν all, every, whosoever, every one, no, whole, any

τῇ art. dat. fem. sg. ὁ ἡ τό the, this, that, he, she, it
προθέσει n. dat. fem. sg. πρόθεσις purpose, shew, shewbread
τῆς art. gen. fem. sg. ὁ ἡ τό the, this, that, he, she, it
καρδίας n. gen. fem. sg. καρδία heart
τῷ art. dat. masc. sg. ὁ ἡ τό the, this, that, he, she, it
Κυρίῳ n. dat. masc. sg. κύριος Lord, lord, master, sir, LORD, God, Master, owner
24 ὅτι conj. ὅτι that, for, because, how that, how, because that, for that, though
ἀνὴρ n. nom. masc. sg. ἀνήρ man, husband, sir
ἀγαθὸς adj. nom. masc. sg. ἀγαθός good, good thing, that which is good, well
καὶ conj. καί and, even, also, but
πλήρης adj. nom. masc. sg. πλήρης full
Πνεύματος n. gen. neut. sg. πνεῦμα spirit, Spirit, Ghost, ghost, life. of the spirit, wind
Ἁγίου adj. gen. neut. sg. ἅγιος Holy, holy, saint, Holy One, holy thing, most holy
καὶ conj. καί and, even, also, but
πίστεως n. gen. fem. sg. πίστις faith, assurance, belief, fidelity
καὶ conj. καί and, even, also, but
ὄχλος n. nom. masc. sg. ὄχλος people, multitude, company, press, number
ἱκανὸς adj. nom. masc. sg. ἱκανός many, much, long, worthy, sufficient, great, able
τῷ art. dat. masc. sg. ὁ ἡ τό the, this, that, he, she, it
Κυρίῳ n. dat. masc. sg. κύριος Lord, lord, master, sir, LORD, God, Master, owner
25 δὲ conj. δέ but, and, now, also, to the contrary, rather, then
εἰς prep. εἰς (+acc) into, to, unto, for, in, on, toward, against, upon, at, among
Ταρσὸν n. acc. fem. sg. Ταρσός Tarsus
ὁ art. nom. masc. sg. ὁ ἡ τό the, this, that, he, she, it
Βαρνάβας n. nom. masc. sg. Βαρναβᾶς Barnabas
Σαῦλον n. acc. masc. sg. Σαῦλος Saul
26 καὶ conj. καί and, even, also, but
αὐτὸν pron. acc. masc. 3p. sg. αὐτός ἡ ὁ self, of oneself, even, very, the same, he, she, it
αὐτὸν pron. acc. masc. 3p. sg. αὐτός ἡ ὁ self, of oneself, even, very, the same, he, she, it
εἰς prep. εἰς (+acc) into, to, unto, for, in, on, toward, against, upon, at, among
Ἀντιόχειαν n. acc. fem. sg. Ἀντιόχεια Antioch
δὲ conj. δέ but, and, now, also, to the contrary, rather, then
αὐτοὺς pron. acc. masc. 3p. pl. αὐτός ἡ ὁ self, of oneself, even, very, the same, he, she, it
ἐνιαυτὸν n. acc. masc. sg. ἐνιαυτός year
ὅλον adj. acc. masc. sg. ὅλος all, whole, every whit, altogether
ἐν prep. ἐν (+dat) in, by, with, among, at, on, through, to, within, into, of, for
τῇ art. dat. fem. sg. ὁ ἡ τό the, this, that, he, she, it
ἐκκλησίᾳ n. dat. fem. sg. ἐκκλησία church, assembly
καὶ conj. καί and, even, also, but
ὄχλον n. acc. masc. sg. ὄχλος people, multitude, company, press, number
ἱκανόν adj. acc. masc. sg. ἱκανός many, much, long, worthy, sufficient, great, able
τε conj. τέ and, both, also
πρῶτον ordinal. adj. acc. neut. sg. πρῶτος first, chief, first of all, chiefest, best
ἐν prep. ἐν (+dat) in, by, with, among, at, on, through, to, within, into, of, for
Ἀντιοχείᾳ n. dat. fem. sg. Ἀντιόχεια Antioch
τοὺς art. acc. masc. pl. ὁ ἡ τό the, this, that, he, she, it
μαθητὰς n. acc. masc. pl. μαθητής disciple
Χριστιανούς n. acc. masc. pl. Χριστιανός Christian
27 Ἐν prep. ἐν (+dat) in, by, with, among, at, on, through, to, within, into, of, for
ταύταις demo. pron. dat. fem. pl. οὗτος αὕτη τοῦτο this, the same, this same, he, she, it
δὲ conj. δέ but, and, now, also, to the contrary, rather, then
ταῖς art. dat. fem. pl. ὁ ἡ τό the, this, that, he, she, it
ἡμέραις n. dat. fem. pl. ἡμέρα day, time, year, while, age, day time
ἀπὸ prep. ἀπό (+gen) from, of, out of, since, for, off, at, by, in, on
Ἱεροσολύμων n. gen. neut. pl. Ἱεροσόλυμα Jerusalem

προφῆται n. nom. masc. pl. προφήτης prophet
εἰς prep. εἰς (+acc) into, to, unto, for, in, on, toward, against, upon, at, among
'Αντιόχειαν n. acc. fem. sg. 'Αντιόχεια Antioch
28 δὲ conj. δέ but, and, now, also, to the contrary, rather, then
εἷς num. nom. masc. sg. εἷς or ἕν one, other, some, any, only, a certain
ἐξ prep. ἐκ ἐξ (+gen) of, from, out of, by, on, with, in, among, through
αὐτῶν pron. gen. masc. 3p. pl. αὐτός ή ό self, of oneself, even, very, the same, he, she, it
ὀνόματι n. dat. neut. sg. ὄνομα name, call, surname
῞Αγαβος n. nom. masc. sg. ῞Αγαβος Agabus
διὰ prep. διά (+gen) by, through, with, in, of, (+acc) for, because of, for a cause
τοῦ art. gen. neut. sg. ό ἡ τό the, this, that, he, she, it
Πνεύματος n. gen. neut. sg. πνεῦμα spirit, Spirit, Ghost, ghost, life. of the spirit, wind
λιμὸν n. acc. fem. sg. λιμός famine, hunger, dearth
μεγάν adj. acc. masc. sg. μέγας great, loud, greatest, high, large, mighty, strong
ἐφ' prep. ἐπί (+gen) on, in, upon, (+dat) in, at, for, upon, (+acc) on, upon, unto, to, against
ὅλην adj. acc. fem. sg. ὅλος all, whole, every whit, altogether
τὴν art. acc. fem. sg. ό ἡ τό the, this, that, he, she, it
οἰκουμένην n. acc. fem. sg. οἰκουμένη world, earth
ὅστις relative pron. nom. masc. sg. ὅστις which, who, whosoever, that, whatsoever
καὶ conj. καί and, even, also, but
ἐπὶ prep. ἐπί (+gen) on, in, upon, (+dat) in, at, for, upon, (+acc) on, upon, unto, to, against
Κλαυδίου n. gen. masc. sg. Κλαύδιος Claudius
Καίσαρος n. gen. masc. sg. Καῖσαρ Caesar
29 τῶν art. gen. masc. pl. ό ἡ τό the, this, that, he, she, it
δὲ conj. δέ but, and, now, also, to the contrary, rather, then
μαθητῶν n. gen. masc. pl. μαθητής disciple
καθὼς adv. καθώς as, even as, according as, according to
τις indefinite pron. nom. masc. sg. τὶς certain, some, any man, one, any thing
ἕκαστος adj. nom. masc. sg. ἕκαστος every man, every, every one, any man, each
αὐτῶν pron. gen. masc. 3p. pl. αὐτός ή ό self, of oneself, even, very, the same, he, she, it
εἰς prep. εἰς (+acc) into, to, unto, for, in, on, toward, against, upon, at, among
διακονίαν n. acc. fem. sg. διακονία ministry, administration, service, office, relief
τοῖς art. dat. masc. pl. ό ἡ τό the, this, that, he, she, it
ἐν prep. ἐν (+dat) in, by, with, among, at, on, through, to, within, into, of, for
τῇ art. dat. fem. sg. ό ἡ τό the, this, that, he, she, it
'Ιουδαίᾳ n. dat. fem. sg. 'Ιουδαία Judaea, Jewry
ἀδελφοῖς n. dat. masc. pl. ἀδελφός brother
30 ὃ relative pron. acc. neut. sg. ὅς ἥ ὅ who, which, what, that
καὶ conj. καί and, even, also, but
πρὸς prep. πρός (+gen) for, (+dat) at, (+acc) unto, to, with, for, against
τοὺς art. acc. masc. pl. ό ἡ τό the, this, that, he, she, it
πρεσβυτέρους adj. acc. masc. pl. πρεσβύτερος elder, elder woman, eldest, old man
διὰ prep. διά (+gen) by, through, with, in, of, (+acc) for, because of, for a cause
χειρὸς n. gen. fem. sg. χείρ hand
Βαρνάβα n. gen. masc. sg. Βαρναβᾶς Barnabas
καὶ conj. καί and, even, also, but
Σαύλου n. gen. masc. sg. Σαῦλος Saul

12

1 Κατ' prep. κατά (+gen) against, by, throughout, down, (+acc) according to, after, with
ἐκεῖνον demo. pron. acc. masc. sg. ἐκεῖνος that, he, the same, that same
δὲ conj. δέ but, and, now, also, to the contrary, rather, then
τὸν art. acc. masc. sg. ό ἡ τό the, this, that, he, she, it
καιρὸν n. acc. masc. sg. καιρός time, season, due time, opportunity

Ἡρώδης n. nom. masc. sg. Ἡρῴδης Herod
ὁ art. nom. masc. sg. ὁ ἡ τό the, this, that, he, she, it
βασιλεὺς n. nom. masc. sg. βασιλεύς king
τὰς art. acc. fem. pl. ὁ ἡ τό the, this, that, he, she, it
χεῖρας n. acc. fem. pl. χείρ hand
τινας indefinite pron. acc. masc. pl. τὶς certain, some, any man, one, any thing
τῶν art. gen. masc. pl. ὁ ἡ τό the, this, that, he, she, it
ἀπὸ prep. ἀπό (+gen) from, of, out of, since, for, off, at, by, in, on
τῆς art. gen. fem. sg. ὁ ἡ τό the, this, that, he, she, it
ἐκκλησίας n. gen. fem. sg. ἐκκλησία church, assembly
2 δὲ conj. δέ but, and, now, also, to the contrary, rather, then
Ἰάκωβον n. acc. masc. sg. Ἰάκωβος James
τὸν art. acc. masc. sg. ὁ ἡ τό the, this, that, he, she, it
ἀδελφὸν n. acc. masc. sg. ἀδελφός brother
Ἰωάννου n. gen. masc. sg. Ἰωάννης John
μαχαίρᾳ n. dat. fem. sg. μάχαιρα sword
3 καὶ conj. καί and, even, also, but
ὅτι conj. ὅτι that, for, because, how that, how, because that, for that, though
ἀρεστόν adj. nom. neut. sg. ἀρεστός thing that please, please, reason
τοῖς art. dat. masc. pl. ὁ ἡ τό the, this, that, he, she, it
Ἰουδαίοις adj. dat. masc. pl. Ἰουδαῖος Jew, Jewess
καὶ conj. καί and, even, also, but
Πέτρον n. acc. masc. sg. Πέτρος Peter
δὲ conj. δέ but, and, now, also, to the contrary, rather, then
ἡμέραι n. nom. fem. pl. ἡμέρα day, time, year, while, age, day time
τῶν art. gen. neut. pl. ὁ ἡ τό the, this, that, he, she, it
ἀζύμων adj. gen. neut. pl. ἄζυμος unleavened bread, unleavened
4 ὃν relative pron. acc. masc. sg. ὅς ἥ ὅ who, which, what, that
καὶ conj. καί and, even, also, but
εἰς prep. εἰς (+acc) into, to, unto, for, in, on, toward, against, upon, at, among
φυλακὴν n. acc. fem. sg. φυλακή prison, watch, imprisonment, cage, hold, ward
τέσσαρσι num. dat. neut. pl. τέσσαρες four
τετραδίοις n. dat. neut. pl. τετράδιον quaternion
στρατιωτῶν n. gen. masc. pl. στρατιώτης soldier
αὐτόν pron. acc. masc. 3p. sg. αὐτός ή ό self, of oneself, even, very, the same, he, she, it
μετὰ prep. μετά (+gen) with, among, against, (+acc) after
τὸ art. acc. neut. sg. ὁ ἡ τό the, this, that, he, she, it
πάσχα n. acc. neut. sg. πάσχα passover, Easter
αὐτόν pron. acc. masc. 3p. sg. αὐτός ή ό self, of oneself, even, very, the same, he, she, it
τῷ art. dat. masc. sg. ὁ ἡ τό the, this, that, he, she, it
λαῷ n. dat. masc. sg. λαός people
5 ὁ art. nom. masc. sg. ὁ ἡ τό the, this, that, he, she, it
μέν conj. μέν indeed, verily, truly, even, so, some
οὖν conj. οὖν therefore, then, so, and, now, wherefore
Πέτρος n. nom. masc. sg. Πέτρος Peter
ἐν prep. ἐν (+dat) in, by, with, among, at, on, through, to, within, into, of, for
τῇ art. dat. fem. sg. ὁ ἡ τό the, this, that, he, she, it
φυλακῇ n. dat. fem. sg. φυλακή prison, watch, imprisonment, cage, hold, ward
προσευχὴ n. nom. fem. sg. προσευχή prayer
δὲ conj. δέ but, and, now, also, to the contrary, rather, then
ἐκτενὴς adj. nom. fem. sg. ἐκτενής fervent, without ceasing, intense
ὑπὸ prep. ὑπό (+gen) of, by, with, from, among, (+acc) under
τῆς art. gen. fem. sg. ὁ ἡ τό the, this, that, he, she, it
ἐκκλησίας n. gen. fem. sg. ἐκκλησία church, assembly
πρὸς prep. πρός (+gen) for, (+dat) at, (+acc) unto, to, with, for, against

τὸν art. acc. masc. sg. ὁ ἡ τό the, this, that, he, she, it
Θεὸν n. acc. masc. sg. θεός God, god
ὑπὲρ prep. ὑπέρ (+gen) for, of, for the sake of, (+acc) above, more than
αὐτοῦ pron. gen. masc. 3p. sg. αὐτός ή ό self, of oneself, even, very, the same, he, she, it
6 ὅτε adv. ὅτε when, after that, as soon as, while, after
δὲ conj. δέ but, and, now, also, to the contrary, rather, then
αὐτὸν pron. acc. masc. 3p. sg. αὐτός ή ό self, of oneself, even, very, the same, he, she, it
ὁ art. nom. masc. sg. ὁ ἡ τό the, this, that, he, she, it
Ἡρώδης n. nom. masc. sg. Ἡρῴδης Herod
τῇ art. dat. fem. sg. ὁ ἡ τό the, this, that, he, she, it
νυκτὶ n. dat. fem. sg. νύξ night
ἐκείνῃ demo. pron. dat. fem. sg. ἐκεῖνος that, he, the same, that same
ὁ art. nom. masc. sg. ὁ ἡ τό the, this, that, he, she, it
Πέτρος n. nom. masc. sg. Πέτρος Peter
μεταξὺ adv. μεταξύ between
δύο num. gen. masc. pl. δύο two, twain, both
στρατιωτῶν n. gen. masc. pl. στρατιώτης soldier
ἁλύσεσι n. dat. fem. pl. ἅλυσις chain, bond
δυσὶ num. dat. fem. pl. δύο two, twain, both
φύλακές n. nom. masc. pl. φύλαξ keeper
τε conj. τέ and, both, also
πρὸ prep. πρό (+gen) before, above
τῆς art. gen. fem. sg. ὁ ἡ τό the, this, that, he, she, it
θύρας n. gen. fem. sg. θύρα door, gate
τὴν art. acc. fem. sg. ὁ ἡ τό the, this, that, he, she, it
φυλακήν n. acc. fem. sg. φυλακή prison, watch, imprisonment, cage, hold, ward
7 καὶ conj. |conj. καί and, even, also, but
ἄγγελος n. nom. masc. sg. ἄγγελος angel, messenger
Κυρίου n. gen. masc. sg. κύριος Lord, lord, master, sir, LORD, God, Master, owner
καὶ conj. |conj. καί and, even, also, but
φῶς n. nom. neut. sg. φῶς light, fire
ἐν prep. ἐν (+dat) in, by, with, among, at, on, through, to, within, into, of, for
τῷ art. dat. neut. sg. ὁ ἡ τό the, this, that, he, she, it
οἰκήματι n. dat. neut. sg. οἴκημα prison
δὲ conj. δέ but, and, now, also, to the contrary, rather, then
τὴν art. acc. fem. sg. ὁ ἡ τό the, this, that, he, she, it
πλευρὰν n. acc. fem. sg. πλευρά side
τοῦ art. gen. masc. sg. ὁ ἡ τό the, this, that, he, she, it
Πέτρου n. gen. masc. sg. Πέτρος Peter
αὐτὸν pron. acc. masc. 3p. sg. αὐτός ή ό self, of oneself, even, very, the same, he, she, it
ἐν prep. ἐν (+dat) in, by, with, among, at, on, through, to, within, into, of, for
τάχει n. dat. neut. sg. τάχος speedily, short, quick
καὶ conj. |conj. καί and, even, also, but
αὐτοῦ pron. gen. masc. 3p. sg. αὐτός ή ό self, of oneself, even, very, the same, he, she, it
αἱ art. nom. fem. pl. ὁ ἡ τό the, this, that, he, she, it
ἁλύσεις n. nom. fem. pl. ἅλυσις chain, bond
ἐκ prep. ἐκ ἐξ (+gen) of, from, out of, by, on, with, in, among, through
τῶν art. gen. fem. pl. ὁ ἡ τό the, this, that, he, she, it
χειρῶν n. gen. fem. pl. χείρ hand
8 τε conj. τέ and, both, also
ὁ art. nom. masc. sg. ὁ ἡ τό the, this, that, he, she, it
ἄγγελος n. nom. masc. sg. ἄγγελος angel, messenger
πρὸς prep. πρός (+gen) for, (+dat) at, (+acc) unto, to, with, for, against
αὐτόν pron. acc. masc. 3p. sg. αὐτός ή ό self, of oneself, even, very, the same, he, she, it
καὶ conj. καί and, even, also, but

τὰ art. acc. neut. pl. ὁ ἡ τό the, this, that, he, she, it
σανδάλιά n. acc. neut. pl. σανδάλιον sandal
σου pron. gen. 2p. sg. σύ thou, you
δὲ conj. δέ but, and, now, also, to the contrary, rather, then
οὕτω adv. οὕτω οὕτως so, even so, thus, on this wise, likewise, after this manner
καὶ conj. καί and, even, also, but
αὐτῷ pron. dat. masc. 3p. sg. αὐτός ή ό self, of oneself, even, very, the same, he, she, it
τὸ art. acc. neut. sg. ὁ ἡ τό the, this, that, he, she, it
ἱμάτιόν n. acc. neut. sg. ἱμάτιον cloke, garment, clothes, raiment, robe, vesture
σου pron. gen. 2p. sg. σύ thou, you
καὶ conj. καί and, even, also, but
μοι pron. dat. 1p. sg. ἐγώ I
9 καὶ conj. καί and, even, also, but
αὐτῷ pron. dat. masc. 3p. sg. αὐτός ή ό self, of oneself, even, very, the same, he, she, it
καὶ conj. καί and, even, also, but
οὐκ particle of negation. οὐ οὐκ οὐχ not, no, neither, none, nay, nor, never, nothing
ὅτι conj. ὅτι that, for, because, how that, how, because that, for that, though
ἀληθές adj. nom. neut. sg. ἀληθής true, truly, truth
τὸ art. nom. neut. sg. ὁ ἡ τό the, this, that, he, she, it
διὰ prep. διά (+gen) by, through, with, in, of, (+acc) for, because of, for a cause
τοῦ art. gen. masc. sg. ὁ ἡ τό the, this, that, he, she, it
ἀγγέλου n. gen. masc. sg. ἄγγελος angel, messenger
δὲ conj. δέ but, and, now, also, to the contrary, rather, then
ὅραμα n. acc. neut. sg. ὅραμα vision, sight
10 δὲ conj. δέ but, and, now, also, to the contrary, rather, then
πρώτην ordinal. adj. acc. fem. sg. πρῶτος first, chief, first of all, chiefest, best
φυλακὴν n. acc. fem. sg. φυλακή prison, watch, imprisonment, cage, hold, ward
καὶ conj. καί and, even, also, but
δευτέραν ordinal. adj. acc. fem. sg. δεύτερος second, second time, again, afterward
ἐπὶ prep. ἐπί (+gen) on, in, upon, (+dat) in, at, for, upon, (+acc) on, upon, unto, to, against
τὴν art. acc. fem. sg. ὁ ἡ τό the, this, that, he, she, it
πύλην n. acc. fem. sg. πύλη gate
τὴν art. acc. fem. sg. ὁ ἡ τό the, this, that, he, she, it
σιδηρᾶν adj. acc. fem. sg. σιδήρεος iron, of iron
τὴν art. acc. fem. sg. ὁ ἡ τό the, this, that, he, she, it
εἰς prep. εἰς (+acc) into, to, unto, for, in, on, toward, against, upon, at, among
τὴν art. acc. fem. sg. ὁ ἡ τό the, this, that, he, she, it
πόλιν n. acc. fem. sg. πόλις city
ἥτις relative pron. nom. fem. sg. ὅστις which, who, whosoever, that, whatsoever
αὐτομάτη adj. nom. fem. sg. αὐτόματος self, herself, of own accord
αὐτοῖς pron. dat. masc. 3p. pl. αὐτός ή ό self, of oneself, even, very, the same, he, she, it
καὶ conj. καί and, even, also, but
ῥύμην n. acc. fem. sg. ῥύμη street, lane
μίαν num. acc. fem. sg. εἷς or ἕν one, other, some, any, only, a certain
καὶ conj. καί and, even, also, but
εὐθέως adv. εὐθέως immediately, straightway, forthwith, as soon as, by and by, shortly
ὁ art. nom. masc. sg. ὁ ἡ τό the, this, that, he, she, it
ἄγγελος n. nom. masc. sg. ἄγγελος angel, messenger
ἀπ' prep. ἀπό (+gen) from, of, out of, since, for, off, at, by, in, on
αὐτοῦ pron. gen. masc. 3p. sg. αὐτός ή ό self, of oneself, even, very, the same, he, she, it
11 καὶ conj. καί and, even, also, but
ὁ art. nom. masc. sg. ὁ ἡ τό the, this, that, he, she, it
Πέτρος n. nom. masc. sg. Πέτρος Peter
ἐν prep. ἐν (+dat) in, by, with, among, at, on, through, to, within, into, of, for
ἑαυτῷ reflexive pron. dat. masc. 3p. sg. ἑαυτοῦ himself, herself, itself, yourself, ourselves

Νῦν adv. νῦν now, henceforth, present, this time
ἀληθῶς adv. ἀληθῶς indeed, of a truth, surely, truly, in truth, of a surety, verily, very
ὅτι conj. ὅτι that, for, because, how that, how, because that, for that, though
Κύριος n. nom. masc. sg. κύριος Lord, lord, master, sir, LORD, God, Master, owner
τὸν art. acc. masc. sg. ὁ ἡ τό the, this, that, he, she, it
ἄγγελον n. acc. masc. sg. ἄγγελος angel, messenger
αὐτοῦ pron. gen. masc. 3p. sg. αὐτός ή ό self, of oneself, even, very, the same, he, she, it
καὶ conj. καί and, even, also, but
με pron. acc. 1p. sg. ἐγώ I
ἐκ prep. ἐκ ἐξ (+gen) of, from, out of, by, on, with, in, among, through
χειρὸς n. gen. fem. sg. χείρ hand
Ἡρώδου n. gen. masc. sg. Ἡρῴδης Herod
καὶ conj. καί and, even, also, but
πάσης adj. gen. fem. sg. πᾶς πᾶσα πᾶν all, every, whosoever, every one, no, whole, any
τῆς art. gen. fem. sg. ὁ ἡ τό the, this, that, he, she, it
προσδοκίας n. gen. fem. sg. προσδοκία looking after, expectation
τοῦ art. gen. masc. sg. ὁ ἡ τό the, this, that, he, she, it
λαοῦ n. gen. masc. sg. λαός people
τῶν art. gen. masc. pl. ὁ ἡ τό the, this, that, he, she, it
Ἰουδαίων adj. gen. masc. pl. Ἰουδαῖος Jew, Jewess
12 τε conj. τέ and, both, also
ἐπὶ prep. ἐπί (+gen) on, in, upon, (+dat) in, at, for, upon, (+acc) on, upon, unto, to, against
τὴν art. acc. fem. sg. ὁ ἡ τό the, this, that, he, she, it
οἰκίαν n. acc. fem. sg. οἰκία house, home, household
Μαρίας n. gen. fem. sg. Μαρία Mary
τῆς art. gen. fem. sg. ὁ ἡ τό the, this, that, he, she, it
μητρὸς n. gen. fem. sg. μήτηρ mother
Ἰωάννου n. gen. masc. sg. Ἰωάννης John
τοῦ art. gen. masc. sg. ὁ ἡ τό the, this, that, he, she, it
Μάρκου n. gen. masc. sg. Μᾶρκος Mark, Marcus
οὗ adv. οὗ where, whither, wherein
ἱκανοὶ adj. nom. masc. pl. ἱκανός many, much, long, worthy, sufficient, great, able
καὶ conj. καί and, even, also, but
13 δὲ conj. δέ but, and, now, also, to the contrary, rather, then
τοῦ art. gen. masc. sg. ὁ ἡ τό the, this, that, he, she, it
Πέτρου n. gen. masc. sg. Πέτρος Peter
τὴν art. acc. fem. sg. ὁ ἡ τό the, this, that, he, she, it
θύραν n. acc. fem. sg. θύρα door, gate
τοῦ art. gen. masc. sg. ὁ ἡ τό the, this, that, he, she, it
πυλῶνος n. gen. masc. sg. πυλών gate, porch
παιδίσκη n. nom. fem. sg. παιδίσκη damsel, bondwoman, maid, bondmaid, maiden
ὀνόματι n. dat. neut. sg. ὄνομα name, call, surname
Ῥόδη n. nom. fem. sg. Ῥόδη Rhoda
14 καὶ conj. καί and, even, also, but
τὴν art. acc. fem. sg. ὁ ἡ τό the, this, that, he, she, it
φωνὴν n. acc. fem. sg. φωνή voice, sound, noise
τοῦ art. gen. masc. sg. ὁ ἡ τό the, this, that, he, she, it
Πέτρου n. gen. masc. sg. Πέτρος Peter
ἀπὸ prep. ἀπό (+gen) from, of, out of, since, for, off, at, by, in, on
τῆς art. gen. fem. sg. ὁ ἡ τό the, this, that, he, she, it
χαρᾶς n. gen. fem. sg. χαρά joy, gladness, joyfulness
οὐκ particle of negation. οὐ οὐκ οὐχ not, no, neither, none, nay, nor, never, nothing
τὸν art. acc. masc. sg. ὁ ἡ τό the, this, that, he, she, it
πυλῶνα n. acc. masc. sg. πυλών gate, porch
δὲ conj. δέ but, and, now, also, to the contrary, rather, then

τὸν art. acc. masc. sg. ὁ ἡ τό the, this, that, he, she, it
Πέτρον n. acc. masc. sg. Πέτρος Peter
πρὸ prep. πρό (+gen) before, above
τοῦ art. gen. masc. sg. ὁ ἡ τό the, this, that, he, she, it
πυλῶνος n. gen. masc. sg. πυλών gate, porch
15 οἱ art. nom. masc. pl. ὁ ἡ τό the, this, that, he, she, it
δὲ conj. δέ but, and, now, also, to the contrary, rather, then
πρὸς prep. πρός (+gen) for, (+dat) at, (+acc) unto, to, with, for, against
αὐτὴν pron. acc. fem. 3p. sg. αὐτός ή ὁ self, of oneself, even, very, the same, he, she, it
ἡ art. nom. fem. sg. ὁ ἡ τό the, this, that, he, she, it
δὲ conj. δέ but, and, now, also, to the contrary, rather, then
οὕτως adv. οὕτω οὕτως so, even so, thus, on this wise, likewise, after this manner
οἱ art. nom. masc. pl. ὁ ἡ τό the, this, that, he, she, it
δ' conj. δέ but, and, now, also, to the contrary, rather, then
Ὁ art. nom. masc. sg. ὁ ἡ τό the, this, that, he, she, it
ἄγγελός n. nom. masc. sg. ἄγγελος angel, messenger
αὐτοῦ pron. gen. masc. 3p. sg. αὐτός ή ὁ self, of oneself, even, very, the same, he, she, it
16 ὁ art. nom. masc. sg. ὁ ἡ τό the, this, that, he, she, it
δὲ conj. δέ but, and, now, also, to the contrary, rather, then
Πέτρος n. nom. masc. sg. Πέτρος Peter
δὲ conj. δέ but, and, now, also, to the contrary, rather, then
αὐτὸν pron. acc. masc. 3p. sg. αὐτός ή ὁ self, of oneself, even, very, the same, he, she, it
καὶ conj. καί and, even, also, but
17 δὲ conj. δέ but, and, now, also, to the contrary, rather, then
αὐτοῖς pron. dat. masc. 3p. pl. αὐτός ή ὁ self, of oneself, even, very, the same, he, she, it
τῇ art. dat. fem. sg. ὁ ἡ τό the, this, that, he, she, it
χειρὶ n. dat. fem. sg. χείρ hand
αὐτοῖς pron. dat. masc. 3p. pl. αὐτός ή ὁ self, of oneself, even, very, the same, he, she, it
πῶς adv. πῶς how, by what means, after what manner
ὁ art. nom. masc. sg. ὁ ἡ τό the, this, that, he, she, it
Κύριος n. nom. masc. sg. κύριος Lord, lord, master, sir, LORD, God, Master, owner
αὐτὸν pron. acc. masc. 3p. sg. αὐτός ή ὁ self, of oneself, even, very, the same, he, she, it
ἐκ prep. ἐκ ἐξ (+gen) of, from, out of, by, on, with, in, among, through
τῆς art. gen. fem. sg. ὁ ἡ τό the, this, that, he, she, it
φυλακῆς n. gen. fem. sg. φυλακή prison, watch, imprisonment, cage, hold, ward
δὲ conj. δέ but, and, now, also, to the contrary, rather, then
Ἰακώβῳ n. dat. masc. sg. Ἰάκωβος James
καὶ conj. καί and, even, also, but
τοῖς art. dat. masc. pl. ὁ ἡ τό the, this, that, he, she, it
ἀδελφοῖς n. dat. masc. pl. ἀδελφός brother
ταῦτα demo. pron. acc. neut. pl. οὗτος αὕτη τοῦτο this, the same, this same, he, she, it
καὶ conj. καί and, even, also, but
εἰς prep. εἰς (+acc) into, to, unto, for, in, on, toward, against, upon, at, among
ἕτερον adj. acc. masc. sg. ἕτερος another, other, else, strange
τόπον n. acc. masc. sg. τόπος place, room, quarter
18 δὲ conj. δέ but, and, now, also, to the contrary, rather, then
ἡμέρας n. gen. fem. sg. ἡμέρα day, time, year, while, age, day time
τάραχος n. nom. masc. sg. τάραχος stir
οὐκ particle of negation. οὐ οὐκ οὐχ not, no, neither, none, nay, nor, never, nothing
ὀλίγος adj. nom. masc. sg. ὀλίγος few, little, small, a while, brief, short, short space
ἐν prep. ἐν (+dat) in, by, with, among, at, on, through, to, within, into, of, for
τοῖς art. dat. masc. pl. ὁ ἡ τό the, this, that, he, she, it
στρατιώταις n. dat. masc. pl. στρατιώτης soldier
τί interrog. pron. nom. neut. sg. τίς what, who, why, where, which, how
ἄρα conj. ἄρα then, therefore, haply, wherefore, perhaps, manner, no doubt, truly

ὁ art. nom. masc. sg. ὁ ἡ τό the, this, that, he, she, it
Πέτρος n. nom. masc. sg. Πέτρος Peter
19 Ἡρώδης n. nom. masc. sg. Ἡρῴδης Herod
δὲ conj. δέ but, and, now, also, to the contrary, rather, then
αὐτὸν pron. acc. masc. 3p. sg. αὐτός ή ό self, of oneself, even, very, the same, he, she, it
καὶ conj. καί and, even, also, but
μὴ particle of negation. μή not, no, lest, neither, none, nothing, nor, never, without
τοὺς art. acc. masc. pl. ὁ ἡ τό the, this, that, he, she, it
φύλακας n. acc. masc. pl. φύλαξ keeper
καὶ conj. καί and, even, also, but
ἀπὸ prep. ἀπό (+gen) from, of, out of, since, for, off, at, by, in, on
τῆς art. gen. fem. sg. ὁ ἡ τό the, this, that, he, she, it
Ἰουδαίας n. gen. fem. sg. Ἰουδαία Judaea, Jewry
εἰς prep. εἰς (+acc) into, to, unto, for, in, on, toward, against, upon, at, among
τὴν art. acc. fem. sg. ὁ ἡ τό the, this, that, he, she, it
Καισάρειαν n. acc. fem. sg. Καισάρεια Caesarea
20 δὲ conj. δέ but, and, now, also, to the contrary, rather, then
ὁ art. nom. masc. sg. ὁ ἡ τό the, this, that, he, she, it
Ἡρώδης n. nom. masc. sg. Ἡρῴδης Herod
Τυρίοις n. dat. masc. pl. Τύριος of Tyre
καὶ conj. καί and, even, also, but
Σιδωνίοις adj. dat. masc. pl. Σιδώνιος of Sidon
ὁμοθυμαδὸν adv. ὁμοθυμαδόν with one accord, with one mind
δὲ conj. δέ but, and, now, also, to the contrary, rather, then
πρὸς prep. πρός (+gen) for, (+dat) at, (+acc) unto, to, with, for, against
αὐτὸν pron. acc. masc. 3p. sg. αὐτός ή ό self, of oneself, even, very, the same, he, she, it
καὶ conj. καί and, even, also, but
Βλάστον n. acc. masc. sg. Βλάστος Blastus
τὸν art. acc. masc. sg. ὁ ἡ τό the, this, that, he, she, it
ἐπὶ prep. ἐπί (+gen) on, in, upon, (+dat) in, at, for, upon, (+acc) on, upon, unto, to, against
τοῦ art. gen. masc. sg. ὁ ἡ τό the, this, that, he, she, it
κοιτῶνος n. gen. masc. sg. κοιτών chamberlain, bedchamber
τοῦ art. gen. masc. sg. ὁ ἡ τό the, this, that, he, she, it
βασιλέως n. gen. masc. sg. βασιλεύς king
εἰρήνην n. acc. fem. sg. εἰρήνη peace, quietness, rest
διὰ prep. διά (+gen) by, through, with, in, of, (+acc) for, because of, for a cause
τὸ art. acc. neut. sg. ὁ ἡ τό the, this, that, he, she, it
αὐτῶν pron. gen. masc. 3p. pl. αὐτός ή ό self, of oneself, even, very, the same, he, she, it
τὴν art. acc. fem. sg. ὁ ἡ τό the, this, that, he, she, it
χώραν n. acc. fem. sg. χώρα country, region, land, field, coast, ground
ἀπὸ prep. ἀπό (+gen) from, of, out of, since, for, off, at, by, in, on
τῆς art. gen. fem. sg. ὁ ἡ τό the, this, that, he, she, it
βασιλικῆς adj. gen. fem. sg. βασιλικός nobleman, royal, king
21 τακτῇ adj. dat. fem. sg. τακτός set
δὲ conj. δέ but, and, now, also, to the contrary, rather, then
ἡμέρᾳ n. dat. fem. sg. ἡμέρα day, time, year, while, age, day time
ὁ art. nom. masc. sg. ὁ ἡ τό the, this, that, he, she, it
Ἡρώδης n. nom. masc. sg. Ἡρῴδης Herod
ἐσθῆτα n. acc. fem. sg. ἐσθής robe, apparel, clothing, raiment
βασιλικὴν adj. acc. fem. sg. βασιλικός nobleman, royal, king
καὶ conj. καί and, even, also, but
ἐπὶ prep. ἐπί (+gen) on, in, upon, (+dat) in, at, for, upon, (+acc) on, upon, unto, to, against
τοῦ art. gen. neut. sg. ὁ ἡ τό the, this, that, he, she, it
βήματος n. gen. neut. sg. βῆμα judgment seat, throne
πρὸς prep. πρός (+gen) for, (+dat) at, (+acc) unto, to, with, for, against

αὐτούς pron. acc. masc. 3p. pl. αὐτός ή ό self, of oneself, even, very, the same, he, she, it
22 ὁ art. nom. masc. sg. ὁ ἡ τό the, this, that, he, she, it
δὲ conj. δέ but, and, now, also, to the contrary, rather, then
δῆμος n. nom. masc. sg. δῆμος people
Θεοῦ n. gen. masc. sg. θεός God, god
φωνὴ n. nom. fem. sg. φωνή voice, sound, noise
καὶ conj. καί and, even, also, but
οὐκ particle of negation. οὐ οὐκ οὐχ not, no, neither, none, nay, nor, never, nothing
ἀνθρώπου n. gen. masc. sg. ἄνθρωπος man, human being, person, one, certain
23 παραχρῆμα adv. παραχρῆμα immediately, straightway, forthwith, presently, soon
δὲ conj. δέ but, and, now, also, to the contrary, rather, then
αὐτὸν pron. acc. masc. 3p. sg. αὐτός ή ό self, of oneself, even, very, the same, he, she, it
ἄγγελος n. nom. masc. sg. ἄγγελος angel, messenger
Κυρίου n. gen. masc. sg. κύριος Lord, lord, master, sir, LORD, God, Master, owner
ἀνθ' prep. ἀντί (+gen) for, because, in the room
ὧν relative pron. gen. neut. pl. ὅς ἥ ὅ who, which, what, that
οὐκ particle of negation. οὐ οὐκ οὐχ not, no, neither, none, nay, nor, never, nothing
τὴν art. acc. fem. sg. ὁ ἡ τό the, this, that, he, she, it
δόξαν n. acc. fem. sg. δόξα glory, honour, praise, dignity, worship
τῷ art. dat. masc. sg. ὁ ἡ τό the, this, that, he, she, it
Θεῷ n. dat. masc. sg. θεός God, god
καὶ conj. καί and, even, also, but
σκωληκόβρωτος adj. nom. masc. sg. σκωληκόβρωτος eaten of worms
24 Ὁ art. nom. masc. sg. ὁ ἡ τό the, this, that, he, she, it
δὲ conj. δέ but, and, now, also, to the contrary, rather, then
λόγος n. nom. masc. sg. λόγος word, saying, account, speech, thing, matter
τοῦ art. gen. masc. sg. ὁ ἡ τό the, this, that, he, she, it
Θεοῦ n. gen. masc. sg. θεός God, god
καὶ conj. καί and, even, also, but
25 Βαρναβᾶς n. nom. masc. sg. Βαρναβᾶς Barnabas
δὲ conj. δέ but, and, now, also, to the contrary, rather, then
καὶ conj. καί and, even, also, but
Σαῦλος n. nom. masc. sg. Σαῦλος Saul
ἐξ prep. ἐκ ἐξ (+gen) of, from, out of, by, on, with, in, among, through
Ἱερουσαλὴμ pron. name. fem. inde. Ἱερουσαλήμ Jerusalem
τὴν art. acc. fem. sg. ὁ ἡ τό the, this, that, he, she, it
διακονίαν n. acc. fem. sg. διακονία ministry, administration, service, office, relief
καὶ conj. καί and, even, also, but
Ἰωάννην n. acc. masc. sg. Ἰωάννης John
τὸν art. acc. masc. sg. ὁ ἡ τό the, this, that, he, she, it
Μᾶρκον n. acc. masc. sg. Μᾶρκος Mark, Marcus

13

1 δὲ conj. δέ but, and, now, also, to the contrary, rather, then
τινες indefinite pron. nom. masc. pl. τὶς certain, some, any man, one, any thing
ἐν prep. ἐν (+dat) in, by, with, among, at, on, through, to, within, into, of, for
Ἀντιοχείᾳ n. dat. fem. sg. Ἀντιόχεια Antioch
κατὰ prep. κατά (+gen) against, by, throughout, down, (+acc) according to, after, with
τὴν art. acc. fem. sg. ὁ ἡ τό the, this, that, he, she, it
ἐκκλησίαν n. acc. fem. sg. ἐκκλησία church, assembly
προφῆται n. nom. masc. pl. προφήτης prophet
καὶ conj. καί and, even, also, but
διδάσκαλοι n. nom. masc. pl. διδάσκαλος teacher, master, doctor
ὅ art. nom. masc. sg. ὁ ἡ τό the, this, that, he, she, it

τε conj. τέ and, both, also
Βαρναβᾶς n. nom. masc. sg. Βαρναβᾶς Barnabas
καὶ conj. καί and, even, also, but
Συμεὼν n. nom. masc. sg. Συμεών Simeon, Simon
ὁ art. nom. masc. sg. ὁ ἡ τό the, this, that, he, she, it
Νίγερ n. nom. masc. sg. Νίγερ Niger, black
ὁ art. nom. masc. sg. ὁ ἡ τό the, this, that, he, she, it
Λούκιος n. nom. masc. sg. Λούκιος Lucius
ὁ art. nom. masc. sg. ὁ ἡ τό the, this, that, he, she, it
Κυρηναῖος n. nom. masc. sg. Κυρηναῖος Cyrene, Cyrenian
Μαναήν n. nom. masc. sg. Μαναήν Manaen
τε conj. τέ and, both, also
Ἡρώδου n. gen. masc. sg. Ἡρῴδης Herod
τοῦ art. gen. masc. sg. ὁ ἡ τό the, this, that, he, she, it
τετράρχου n. gen. masc. sg. τετράρχης tetrarch
σύντροφος adj. nom. masc. sg. σύντροφος which had been brought up with
καὶ conj. καί and, even, also, but
Σαῦλος n. nom. masc. sg. Σαῦλος Saul
2 δὲ conj. δέ but, and, now, also, to the contrary, rather, then
αὐτῶν pron. gen. masc. 3p. pl. αὐτός ή ό self, of oneself, even, very, the same, he, she, it
τῷ art. dat. masc. sg. ὁ ἡ τό the, this, that, he, she, it
Κυρίῳ n. dat. masc. sg. κύριος Lord, lord, master, sir, LORD, God, Master, owner
καὶ conj. καί and, even, also, but
τὸ art. nom. neut. sg. ὁ ἡ τό the, this, that, he, she, it
Πνεῦμα n. nom. neut. sg. πνεῦμα spirit, Spirit, Ghost, ghost, life. of the spirit, wind
τὸ art. nom. neut. sg. ὁ ἡ τό the, this, that, he, she, it
Ἅγιον adj. nom. neut. sg. ἅγιος Holy, holy, saint, Holy One, holy thing, most holy
δή particle. δή also, and, doubtless, now, therefore
μοι pron. dat. 1p. sg. ἐγώ I
τὸν art. acc. masc. sg. ὁ ἡ τό the, this, that, he, she, it
τε conj. τέ and, both, also
Βαρναβᾶν n. acc. masc. sg. Βαρναβᾶς Barnabas
καὶ conj. καί and, even, also, but
τὸν art. acc. masc. sg. ὁ ἡ τό the, this, that, he, she, it
Σαῦλον n. acc. masc. sg. Σαῦλος Saul
εἰς prep. εἰς (+acc) into, to, unto, for, in, on, toward, against, upon, at, among
τὸ art. acc. neut. sg. ὁ ἡ τό the, this, that, he, she, it
ἔργον n. acc. neut. sg. ἔργον work, deed, doing labour
ὃ relative pron. acc. neut. sg. ὅς ἥ ὅ who, which, what, that
αὐτούς pron. acc. masc. 3p. pl. αὐτός ή ό self, of oneself, even, very, the same, he, she, it
3 τότε adv. τότε then, that time
καὶ conj. καί and, even, also, but
τὰς art. acc. fem. pl. ὁ ἡ τό the, this, that, he, she, it
χεῖρας n. acc. fem. pl. χείρ hand
αὐτοῖς pron. dat. masc. 3p. pl. αὐτός ή ό self, of oneself, even, very, the same, he, she, it
4 Οὗτοι demo. pron. nom. masc. pl. οὗτος αὕτη τοῦτο this, the same, this same, he, she, it
μέν conj. μέν indeed, verily, truly, even, so, some
οὖν conj. οὖν therefore, then, so, and, now, wherefore
ὑπὸ prep. ὑπό (+gen) of, by, with, from, among, (+acc) under
τοῦ art. gen. neut. sg. ὁ ἡ τό the, this, that, he, she, it
Πνεύματος n. gen. neut. sg. πνεῦμα spirit, Spirit, Ghost, ghost, life. of the spirit, wind
τοῦ art. gen. neut. sg. ὁ ἡ τό the, this, that, he, she, it
Ἁγίου adj. gen. neut. sg. ἅγιος Holy, holy, saint, Holy One, holy thing, most holy
εἰς prep. εἰς (+acc) into, to, unto, for, in, on, toward, against, upon, at, among
τὴν art. acc. fem. sg. ὁ ἡ τό the, this, that, he, she, it

Σελεύκειαν n. acc. fem. sg. Σελεύκεια Seleucia
ἐκεῖθέν adv. ἐκεῖθεν thence, from thence, from that place
τε conj. τέ and, both, also
εἰς prep. εἰς (+acc) into, to, unto, for, in, on, toward, against, upon, at, among
τὴν art. acc. fem. sg. ὁ ἡ τό the, this, that, he, she, it
Κύπρον n. acc. fem. sg. Κύπρος Cyprus
5 καὶ conj. καί and, even, also, but
ἐν prep. ἐν (+dat) in, by, with, among, at, on, through, to, within, into, of, for
Σαλαμῖνι n. dat. fem. sg. Σαλαμίς Salamis
τὸν art. acc. masc. sg. ὁ ἡ τό the, this, that, he, she, it
λόγον n. acc. masc. sg. λόγος word, saying, account, speech, thing, matter
τοῦ art. gen. masc. sg. ὁ ἡ τό the, this, that, he, she, it
Θεοῦ n. gen. masc. sg. θεός God, god
ἐν prep. ἐν (+dat) in, by, with, among, at, on, through, to, within, into, of, for
ταῖς art. dat. fem. pl. ὁ ἡ τό the, this, that, he, she, it
συναγωγαῖς n. dat. fem. pl. συναγωγή synagogue, assembly, congregation
τῶν art. gen. masc. pl. ὁ ἡ τό the, this, that, he, she, it
Ἰουδαίων adj. gen. masc. pl. Ἰουδαῖος Jew, Jewess
δὲ conj. δέ but, and, now, also, to the contrary, rather, then
καὶ conj. καί and, even, also, but
Ἰωάννην n. acc. masc. sg. Ἰωάννης John
ὑπηρέτην n. acc. masc. sg. ὑπηρέτης officer, minister, servant
6 δὲ conj. δέ but, and, now, also, to the contrary, rather, then
τὴν art. acc. fem. sg. ὁ ἡ τό the, this, that, he, she, it
νῆσον n. acc. fem. sg. νῆσος isle, island
ἄχρι prep. ἄχρι or ἄχρις (+gen) until, unto, till, even to, as far as, while, into
Πάφου n. gen. fem. sg. Πάφος Paphos
τινὰ indefinite pron. acc. masc. sg. τὶς certain, some, any man, one, any thing
μάγον n. acc. masc. sg. μάγος wise men, sorcerer
ψευδοπροφήτην n. acc. masc. sg. ψευδοπροφήτης false prophet
Ἰουδαῖον adj. acc. masc. sg. Ἰουδαῖος Jew, Jewess
ᾧ relative pron. dat. masc. sg. ὅς ἥ ὅ who, which, what, that
ὄνομα n. nom. neut. sg. ὄνομα name, call, surname
Βαριησοῦ n. gen. masc. sg. Βαριησοῦς Barjesus
7 ὃς relative pron. nom. masc. sg. ὅς ἥ ὅ who, which, what, that
σὺν prep. σύν (+dat) with, beside
τῷ art. dat. masc. sg. ὁ ἡ τό the, this, that, he, she, it
ἀνθυπάτῳ n. dat. masc. sg. ἀνθύπατος deputy
Σεργίῳ n. dat. masc. sg. Σέργιος Sergius
Παύλῳ n. dat. masc. sg. Παῦλος Paulus, Paul
ἀνδρὶ n. dat. masc. sg. ἀνήρ man, husband, sir
συνετῷ adj. dat. masc. sg. συνετός prudent
οὗτος demo. pron. nom. masc. sg. οὗτος αὕτη τοῦτο this, the same, this same, he, she, it
Βαρναβᾶν n. acc. masc. sg. Βαρναβᾶς Barnabas
καὶ conj. καί and, even, also, but
Σαῦλον n. acc. masc. sg. Σαῦλος Saul
τὸν art. acc. masc. sg. ὁ ἡ τό the, this, that, he, she, it
λόγον n. acc. masc. sg. λόγος word, saying, account, speech, thing, matter
τοῦ art. gen. masc. sg. ὁ ἡ τό the, this, that, he, she, it
Θεοῦ n. gen. masc. sg. θεός God, god
8 δὲ conj. δέ but, and, now, also, to the contrary, rather, then
αὐτοῖς pron. dat. masc. 3p. pl. αὐτός ή ό self, of oneself, even, very, the same, he, she, it
Ἐλύμας n. nom. masc. sg. Ἐλύμας Elymas
ὁ art. nom. masc. sg. ὁ ἡ τό the, this, that, he, she, it
μάγος n. nom. masc. sg. μάγος wise men, sorcerer

οὕτω adv. οὕτω οὕτως so, even so, thus, on this wise, likewise, after this manner
γὰρ conj. γάρ for, and, because, but, indeed
τὸ art. nom. neut. sg. ὁ ἡ τό the, this, that, he, she, it
ὄνομα n. nom. neut. sg. ὄνομα name, call, surname
αὐτοῦ pron. gen. masc. 3p. sg. αὐτός ή ό self, of oneself, even, very, the same, he, she, it
τὸν art. acc. masc. sg. ὁ ἡ τό the, this, that, he, she, it
ἀνθύπατον n. acc. masc. sg. ἀνθύπατος deputy
ἀπὸ prep. ἀπό (+gen) from, of, out of, since, for, off, at, by, in, on
τῆς art. gen. fem. sg. ὁ ἡ τό the, this, that, he, she, it
πίστεως n. gen. fem. sg. πίστις faith, assurance, belief, fidelity
9 Σαῦλος n. nom. masc. sg. Σαῦλος Saul
δέ conj. δέ but, and, now, also, to the contrary, rather, then
ὁ art. nom. masc. sg. ὁ ἡ τό the, this, that, he, she, it
καὶ conj. καί and, even, also, but
Παῦλος n. nom. masc. sg. Παῦλος Paul, Paulus
Πνεύματος n. gen. neut. sg. πνεῦμα spirit, Spirit, Ghost, ghost, life. of the spirit, wind
Ἁγίου adj. gen. neut. sg. ἅγιος Holy, holy, saint, Holy One, holy thing, most holy
καὶ conj. καί and, even, also, but
εἰς prep. εἰς (+acc) into, to, unto, for, in, on, toward, against, upon, at, among
αὐτὸν pron. acc. masc. 3p. sg. αὐτός ή ό self, of oneself, even, very, the same, he, she, it
10 Ὦ interjection. ὦ O
πλήρης adj. voc. masc. sg. πλήρης full
παντὸς adj. gen. masc. sg. πᾶς πᾶσα πᾶν all, every, whosoever, every one, no, whole, any
δόλου n. gen. masc. sg. δόλος guile, deceit, subtilty, craft
καὶ conj. καί and, even, also, but
πάσης adj. gen. fem. sg. πᾶς πᾶσα πᾶν all, every, whosoever, every one, no, whole, any
ῥᾳδιουργίας n. gen. fem. sg. ῥᾳδιουργία mischief
υἱὲ n. voc. masc. sg. υἱός son, child, descendant, offspring, heir
διαβόλου adj. gen. masc. sg. διάβολος devil, false accuser, Devil, slanderer
ἐχθρὲ adj. voc. masc. sg. ἐχθρός enemy, foe
πάσης adj. gen. fem. sg. πᾶς πᾶσα πᾶν all, every, whosoever, every one, no, whole, any
δικαιοσύνης n. gen. fem. sg. δικαιοσύνη righteousness
οὐ particle of negation. οὐ οὐκ οὐχ not, no, neither, none, nay, nor, never, nothing
τὰς art. acc. fem. pl. ὁ ἡ τό the, this, that, he, she, it
ὁδοὺς n. acc. fem. pl. ὁδός way, journey, highway
Κυρίου n. gen. masc. sg. κύριος Lord, lord, master, sir, LORD, God, Master, owner
τὰς art. acc. fem. pl. ὁ ἡ τό the, this, that, he, she, it
εὐθείας adj. acc. fem. pl. εὐθύς straight, right
11 καὶ conj. καί and, even, also, but
νῦν adv. νῦν now, henceforth, present, this time
χεὶρ n. nom. fem. sg. χείρ hand
τοῦ art. gen. masc. sg. ὁ ἡ τό the, this, that, he, she, it
Κυρίου n. gen. masc. sg. κύριος Lord, lord, master, sir, LORD, God, Master, owner
ἐπὶ prep. ἐπί (+gen) on, in, upon, (+dat) in, at, for, upon, (+acc) on, upon, unto, to, against
σὲ pron. acc. 2p. sg. σύ thou, you
καὶ conj. καί and, even, also, but
τυφλὸς adj. nom. masc. sg. τυφλός blind
μὴ particle of negation. μή not, no, lest, neither, none, nothing, nor, never, without
τὸν art. acc. masc. sg. ὁ ἡ τό the, this, that, he, she, it
ἥλιον n. acc. masc. sg. ἥλιος sun, east
ἄχρι prep. ἄχρι or ἄχρις (+gen) until, unto, till, even to, as far as, while, into
καιροῦ n. gen. masc. sg. καιρός time, season, due time, opportunity
παραχρῆμά adv. παραχρῆμα immediately, straightway, forthwith, presently, soon
δέ conj. δέ but, and, now, also, to the contrary, rather, then
ἐπ' prep. ἐπί (+gen) on, in, upon, (+dat) in, at, for, upon, (+acc) on, upon, unto, to, against

αὐτὸν pron. acc. masc. 3p. sg. αὐτός ἡ ό self, of oneself, even, very, the same, he, she, it
ἀχλὺς n. nom. fem. sg. ἀχλύς mist
καὶ conj. καί and, even, also, but
σκότος n. nom. neut. sg. σκότος darkness
καὶ conj. καί and, even, also, but
χειραγωγούς n. acc. masc. pl. χειραγωγός one to lead by the hand
12 τότε adv. τότε then, that time
ὁ art. nom. masc. sg. ὁ ἡ τό the, this, that, he, she, it
ἀνθύπατος n. nom. masc. sg. ἀνθύπατος deputy
τὸ art. acc. neut. sg. ὁ ἡ τό the, this, that, he, she, it
ἐπὶ prep. ἐπί (+gen) on, in, upon, (+dat) in, at, for, upon, (+acc) on, upon, unto, to, against
τῇ art. dat. fem. sg. ὁ ἡ τό the, this, that, he, she, it
διδαχῇ n. dat. fem. sg. διδαχή doctrine, teaching
τοῦ art. gen. masc. sg. ὁ ἡ τό the, this, that, he, she, it
Κυρίου n. gen. masc. sg. κύριος Lord, lord, master, sir, LORD, God, Master, owner
13 δὲ conj. δέ but, and, now, also, to the contrary, rather, then
ἀπὸ prep. ἀπό (+gen) from, of, out of, since, for, off, at, by, in, on
τῆς art. gen. fem. sg. ὁ ἡ τό the, this, that, he, she, it
Πάφου n. gen. fem. sg. Πάφος Paphos
οἱ art. nom. masc. pl. ὁ ἡ τό the, this, that, he, she, it
περὶ prep. περί (+gen) of, for, concerning, (+acc) about, concerning, in
τὸν art. acc. masc. sg. ὁ ἡ τό the, this, that, he, she, it
Παῦλον n. acc. masc. sg. Παῦλος Paul, Paulus
εἰς prep. εἰς (+acc) into, to, unto, for, in, on, toward, against, upon, at, among
Πέργην n. acc. fem. sg. Πέργη Perga
τῆς art. gen. fem. sg. ὁ ἡ τό the, this, that, he, she, it
Παμφυλίας n. gen. fem. sg. Παμφυλία Pamphylia
Ἰωάννης n. nom. masc. sg. Ἰωάννης John
δὲ conj. δέ but, and, now, also, to the contrary, rather, then
ἀπ' prep. ἀπό (+gen) from, of, out of, since, for, off, at, by, in, on
αὐτῶν pron. gen. masc. 3p. pl. αὐτός ἡ ό self, of oneself, even, very, the same, he, she, it
εἰς prep. εἰς (+acc) into, to, unto, for, in, on, toward, against, upon, at, among
Ἱεροσόλυμα n. acc. neut. sg. Ἱεροσόλυμα Jerusalem
14 αὐτοὶ pron. nom. masc. 3p. pl. αὐτός ἡ ό self, of oneself, even, very, the same, he, she, it
δὲ conj. δέ but, and, now, also, to the contrary, rather, then
ἀπὸ prep. ἀπό (+gen) from, of, out of, since, for, off, at, by, in, on
τῆς art. gen. fem. sg. ὁ ἡ τό the, this, that, he, she, it
Πέργης n. gen. fem. sg. Πέργη Perga
εἰς prep. εἰς (+acc) into, to, unto, for, in, on, toward, against, upon, at, among
Ἀντιόχειαν n. acc. fem. sg. Ἀντιόχεια Antioch
τῆς art. gen. fem. sg. ὁ ἡ τό the, this, that, he, she, it
Πισιδίας adj. gen. fem. sg. Πισιδία Pisidia
καὶ conj. καί and, even, also, but
εἰς prep. εἰς (+acc) into, to, unto, for, in, on, toward, against, upon, at, among
τὴν art. acc. fem. sg. ὁ ἡ τό the, this, that, he, she, it
συναγωγὴν n. acc. fem. sg. συναγωγή synagogue, assembly, congregation
τῇ art. dat. fem. sg. ὁ ἡ τό the, this, that, he, she, it
ἡμέρᾳ n. dat. fem. sg. ἡμέρα day, time, year, while, age, day time
τῶν art. gen. neut. pl. ὁ ἡ τό the, this, that, he, she, it
σαββάτων n. gen. neut. pl. σάββατον sabbath day, sabbath, week
15 μετὰ prep. μετά (+gen) with, among, against, (+acc) after
δὲ conj. δέ but, and, now, also, to the contrary, rather, then
τὴν art. acc. fem. sg. ὁ ἡ τό the, this, that, he, she, it
ἀνάγνωσιν n. acc. fem. sg. ἀνάγνωσις reading
τοῦ art. gen. masc. sg. ὁ ἡ τό the, this, that, he, she, it

νόμου n. gen. masc. sg. νόμος law, the law
καὶ conj. καί and, even, also, but
τῶν art. gen. masc. pl. ὁ ἡ τό the, this, that, he, she, it
προφητῶν n. gen. masc. pl. προφήτης prophet
οἱ art. nom. masc. pl. ὁ ἡ τό the, this, that, he, she, it
ἀρχισυνάγωγοι n. nom. masc. pl. ἀρχισυνάγωγος ruler of the synagogue
πρὸς prep. πρός (+gen) for, (+dat) at, (+acc) unto, to, with, for, against
αὐτοὺς pron. acc. masc. 3p. pl. αὐτός ή ό self, of oneself, even, very, the same, he, she, it
Ἄνδρες n. voc. masc. pl. ἀνήρ man, husband, sir
ἀδελφοί n. voc. masc. pl. ἀδελφός brother
εἰ conj. εἰ if, whether, that, though, forasmuch
λόγος n. nom. masc. sg. λόγος word, saying, account, speech, thing, matter
ἐν prep. ἐν (+dat) in, by, with, among, at, on, through, to, within, into, of, for
ὑμῖν pron. dat. 2p. pl. σύ thou, you
παρακλήσεως n. gen. fem. sg. παράκλησις consolation, exhortation, comfort
πρὸς prep. πρός (+gen) for, (+dat) at, (+acc) unto, to, with, for, against
τὸν art. acc. masc. sg. ὁ ἡ τό the, this, that, he, she, it
λαόν n. acc. masc. sg. λαός people
16 δὲ conj. δέ but, and, now, also, to the contrary, rather, then
Παῦλος n. nom. masc. sg. Παῦλος Paul, Paulus
καὶ conj. καί and, even, also, but
τῇ art. dat. fem. sg. ὁ ἡ τό the, this, that, he, she, it
χειρὶ n. dat. fem. sg. χείρ hand
Ἄνδρες n. voc. masc. pl. ἀνήρ man, husband, sir
Ἰσραηλῖται n. voc. masc. pl. Ἰσραηλίτης Israelite, Israel
καὶ conj. καί and, even, also, but
οἱ art. voc. masc. pl. ὁ ἡ τό the, this, that, he, she, it
τὸν art. acc. masc. sg. ὁ ἡ τό the, this, that, he, she, it
Θεόν n. acc. masc. sg. θεός God, god
17 ὁ art. nom. masc. sg. ὁ ἡ τό the, this, that, he, she, it
Θεὸς n. nom. masc. sg. θεός God, god
τοῦ art. gen. masc. sg. ὁ ἡ τό the, this, that, he, she, it
λαοῦ n. gen. masc. sg. λαός people
τούτου demo. pron. gen. masc. sg. οὗτος αὕτη τοῦτο this, the same, this same, he, she, it
Ἰσραὴλ pron. name. masc. inde. Ἰσραήλ Israel
τοὺς art. acc. masc. pl. ὁ ἡ τό the, this, that, he, she, it
πατέρας n. acc. masc. pl. πατήρ Father, father, parent
ἡμῶν pron. gen. 1p. pl. ἐγώ I
καὶ conj. καί and, even, also, but
τὸν art. acc. masc. sg. ὁ ἡ τό the, this, that, he, she, it
λαὸν n. acc. masc. sg. λαός people
ἐν prep. ἐν (+dat) in, by, with, among, at, on, through, to, within, into, of, for
τῇ art. dat. fem. sg. ὁ ἡ τό the, this, that, he, she, it
παροικίᾳ n. dat. fem. sg. παροικία sojourning
ἐν prep. ἐν (+dat) in, by, with, among, at, on, through, to, within, into, of, for
γῇ n. dat. fem. sg. γῆ earth, land, ground, country
Αἰγύπτῳ n. dat. fem. sg. Αἴγυπτος Egypt
καὶ conj. καί and, even, also, but
μετὰ prep. μετά (+gen) with, among, against, (+acc) after
βραχίονος n. gen. masc. sg. βραχίων arm
ὑψηλοῦ adj. gen. masc. sg. ὑψηλός high, higher, highly esteemed
αὐτοὺς pron. acc. masc. 3p. pl. αὐτός ή ό self, of oneself, even, very, the same, he, she, it
ἐξ prep. ἐκ ἐξ (+gen) of, from, out of, by, on, with, in, among, through
αὐτῆς pron. gen. fem. 3p. sg. αὐτός ή ό self, of oneself, even, very, the same, he, she, it
18 καὶ conj. καί and, even, also, but

ὡς adv. ὡς as, when, as it were, how, about, like, as soon as, even as, while
τεσσαρακονταετῆ adj. acc. masc. sg. τεσσαρακονταετής of forty years
χρόνον n. acc. masc. sg. χρόνος time, season, space
αὐτοὺς pron. acc. masc. 3p. pl. αὐτός ή ό self, of oneself, even, very, the same, he, she, it
ἐν prep. ἐν (+dat) in, by, with, among, at, on, through, to, within, into, of, for
τῇ art. dat. fem. sg. ὁ ἡ τό the, this, that, he, she, it
ἐρήμῳ adj. dat. fem. sg. ἔρημος wilderness, desert
19 καὶ conj. καί and, even, also, but
ἔθνη n. acc. neut. pl. ἔθνος Gentile, nation, heathen, people
ἑπτὰ num. acc. neut. pl. ἑπτά seven, seventh
ἐν prep. ἐν (+dat) in, by, with, among, at, on, through, to, within, into, of, for
γῇ n. dat. fem. sg. γῆ earth, land, ground, country
Χανάαν n. gen. fem. sg. Χανάαν Chanaan
αὐτοῖς pron. dat. masc. 3p. pl. αὐτός ή ό self, of oneself, even, very, the same, he, she, it
τὴν art. acc. fem. sg. ὁ ἡ τό the, this, that, he, she, it
γῆν n. acc. fem. sg. γῆ earth, land, ground, country
αὐτῶν pron. gen. neut. 3p. pl. αὐτός ή ό self, of oneself, even, very, the same, he, she, it
20 καὶ conj. καί and, even, also, but
μετὰ prep. μετά (+gen) with, among, against, (+acc) after
ταῦτα demo. pron. acc. neut. pl. οὗτος αὕτη τοῦτο this, the same, this same, he, she, it
ὡς adv. ὡς as, when, as it were, how, about, like, as soon as, even as, while
ἔτεσι n. dat. neut. pl. ἔτος year
τετρακοσίοις num. dat. neut. pl. τετρακόσιοι four hundred
καὶ conj. καί and, even, also, but
πεντήκοντα num. dat. neut. pl. πεντήκοντα fifty
κριτὰς n. acc. masc. pl. κριτής judge
ἕως conj. ἕως till, until, unto, until when, while, as far as, even, until now
Σαμουὴλ n. gen. masc. sg. Σαμουήλ Samuel
τοῦ art. gen. masc. sg. ὁ ἡ τό the, this, that, he, she, it
προφήτου n. gen. masc. sg. προφήτης prophet
21 κἀκεῖθεν adv. κἀκεῖθεν and from thence, and thence, and afterward, thence also
βασιλέα n. acc. masc. sg. βασιλεύς king
καὶ conj. καί and, even, also, but
αὐτοῖς pron. dat. masc. 3p. pl. αὐτός ή ό self, of oneself, even, very, the same, he, she, it
ὁ art. nom. masc. sg. ὁ ἡ τό the, this, that, he, she, it
Θεὸς n. nom. masc. sg. θεός God, god
τὸν art. acc. masc. sg. ὁ ἡ τό the, this, that, he, she, it
Σαοὺλ n. acc. masc. sg. Σαούλ Saul
υἱὸν n. acc. masc. sg. υἱός son, child, descendant, offspring, heir
Κίς n. gen. masc. sg. Κίς Cis
ἄνδρα n. acc. masc. sg. ἀνήρ man, husband, sir
ἐκ prep. ἐκ ἐξ (+gen) of, from, out of, by, on, with, in, among, through
φυλῆς n. gen. fem. sg. φυλή tribe, kindred
Βενιαμίν n. gen. masc. sg. Βενιαμίν Benjamin
ἔτη n. acc. neut. pl. ἔτος year
τεσσαράκοντα num. acc. neut. pl. τεσσαράκοντα forty
22 καὶ conj. καί and, even, also, but
αὐτὸν pron. acc. masc. 3p. sg. αὐτός ή ό self, of oneself, even, very, the same, he, she, it
αὐτοῖς pron. dat. masc. 3p. pl. αὐτός ή ό self, of oneself, even, very, the same, he, she, it
τὸν art. acc. masc. sg. ὁ ἡ τό the, this, that, he, she, it
Δαβὶδ n. acc. masc. sg. Δαβίδ David
εἰς prep. εἰς (+acc) into, to, unto, for, in, on, toward, against, upon, at, among
βασιλέα n. acc. masc. sg. βασιλεύς king
ᾧ relative pron. dat. masc. sg. ὅς ἥ ὅ who, which, what, that
καὶ conj. καί and, even, also, but

Δαβὶδ n. acc. masc. sg. Δαβίδ David
τὸν art. acc. masc. sg. ὁ ἡ τό the, this, that, he, she, it
τοῦ art. gen. masc. sg. ὁ ἡ τό the, this, that, he, she, it
Ἰεσσαί n. gen. masc. sg. Ἰεσσαί Jesse
ἄνδρα n. acc. masc. sg. ἀνήρ man, husband, sir
κατὰ prep. κατά (+gen) against, by, throughout, down, (+acc) according to, after, with
τὴν art. acc. fem. sg. ὁ ἡ τό the, this, that, he, she, it
καρδίαν n. acc. fem. sg. καρδία heart
μου pron. gen. 1p. sg. ἐγώ I
ὃς relative pron. nom. masc. sg. ὅς ἥ ὅ who, which, what, that
πάντα adj. acc. neut. pl. πᾶς πᾶσα πᾶν all, every, whosoever, every one, no, whole, any
τὰ art. acc. neut. pl. ὁ ἡ τό the, this, that, he, she, it
θελήματά n. acc. neut. pl. θέλημα will, desire, pleasure
μου pron. gen. 1p. sg. ἐγώ I
23 τούτου demo. pron. gen. masc. sg. οὗτος αὕτη τοῦτο this, the same, this same, he, she, it
ὁ art. nom. masc. sg. ὁ ἡ τό the, this, that, he, she, it
Θεὸς n. nom. masc. sg. θεός God, god
ἀπὸ prep. ἀπό (+gen) from, of, out of, since, for, off, at, by, in, on
τοῦ art. gen. neut. sg. ὁ ἡ τό the, this, that, he, she, it
σπέρματος n. gen. neut. sg. σπέρμα seed, issue
κατ' prep. κατά (+gen) against, by, throughout, down, (+acc) according to, after, with
ἐπαγγελίαν n. acc. fem. sg. ἐπαγγελία promise, message
τῷ art. dat. masc. sg. ὁ ἡ τό the, this, that, he, she, it
Ἰσραὴλ pron. name. masc. inde. Ἰσραήλ Israel
σωτῆρα n. acc. masc. sg. σωτήρ Saviour, saviour
Ἰησοῦν n. acc. masc. sg. Ἰησοῦς Jesus
24 Ἰωάννου n. gen. masc. sg. Ἰωάννης John
πρὸ prep. πρό (+gen) before, above
προσώπου n. gen. neut. sg. πρόσωπον face, presence, person, countenance
τῆς art. gen. fem. sg. ὁ ἡ τό the, this, that, he, she, it
εἰσόδου n. gen. fem. sg. εἴσοδος coming, entrance into, entering in
αὐτοῦ pron. gen. masc. 3p. sg. αὐτός ή ό self, of oneself, even, very, the same, he, she, it
βάπτισμα n. acc. neut. sg. βάπτισμα baptism
μετανοίας n. gen. fem. sg. μετάνοια repentance
παντὶ adj. dat. masc. sg. πᾶς πᾶσα πᾶν all, every, whosoever, every one, no, whole, any
τῷ art. dat. masc. sg. ὁ ἡ τό the, this, that, he, she, it
λαῷ n. dat. masc. sg. λαός people
Ἰσραήλ pron. name. masc. inde. Ἰσραήλ Israel
25 ὡς adv. ὡς as, when, as it were, how, about, like, as soon as, even as, while
δὲ conj. δέ but, and, now, also, to the contrary, rather, then
ὁ art. nom. masc. sg. ὁ ἡ τό the, this, that, he, she, it
Ἰωάννης n. nom. masc. sg. Ἰωάννης John
τὸν art. acc. masc. sg. ὁ ἡ τό the, this, that, he, she, it
δρόμον n. acc. masc. sg. δρόμος course
Τίνα interrog. pron. acc. masc. sg. τίς what, who, why, where, which, how
με pron. acc. 1p. sg. ἐγώ I
οὐκ particle of negation. οὐ οὐκ οὐχ not, no, neither, none, nay, nor, never, nothing
ἐγώ pron. nom. 1p. sg. ἐγώ I
ἀλλ' conj. ἀλλά but, yea, yet, nevertheless, howbeit, nay, therefore
μετ' prep. μετά (+gen) with, among, against, (+acc) after
ἐμὲ pron. acc. 1p. sg. ἐγώ I
οὗ relative pron. gen. masc. sg. ὅς ἥ ὅ who, which, what, that
οὐκ particle of negation. οὐ οὐκ οὐχ not, no, neither, none, nay, nor, never, nothing
ἄξιος adj. nom. masc. sg. ἄξιος worthy, meet, due reward
τὸ art. acc. neut. sg. ὁ ἡ τό the, this, that, he, she, it

ὑπόδημα n. acc. neut. sg. ὑπόδημα shoe
τῶν art. gen. masc. pl. ὁ ἡ τό the, this, that, he, she, it
ποδῶν n. gen. masc. pl. πούς foot
26 ἄνδρες n. voc. masc. pl. ἀνήρ man, husband, sir
ἀδελφοί n. voc. masc. pl. ἀδελφός brother
υἱοὶ n. voc. masc. pl. υἱός son, child, descendant, offspring, heir
γένους n. gen. neut. sg. γένος kind, kindred, offspring, nation, countrymen
Ἀβραὰμ n. gen. masc. sg. Ἀβραάμ Abraham
καὶ conj. καί and, even, also, but
οἱ art. voc. masc. pl. ὁ ἡ τό the, this, that, he, she, it
ἐν prep. ἐν (+dat) in, by, with, among, at, on, through, to, within, into, of, for
ὑμῖν pron. dat. 2p. pl. σύ thou, you
τὸν art. acc. masc. sg. ὁ ἡ τό the, this, that, he, she, it
Θεόν n. acc. masc. sg. θεός God, god
ὑμῖν pron. dat. 2p. pl. σύ thou, you
ὁ art. nom. masc. sg. ὁ ἡ τό the, this, that, he, she, it
λόγος n. nom. masc. sg. λόγος word, saying, account, speech, thing, matter
τῆς art. gen. fem. sg. ὁ ἡ τό the, this, that, he, she, it
σωτηρίας n. gen. fem. sg. σωτηρία salvation, deliver, health, saving
ταύτης demo. pron. gen. fem. sg. οὗτος αὕτη τοῦτο this, the same, this same, he, she, it
27 οἱ art. nom. masc. pl. ὁ ἡ τό the, this, that, he, she, it
γὰρ conj. γάρ for, and, because, but, indeed
ἐν prep. ἐν (+dat) in, by, with, among, at, on, through, to, within, into, of, for
Ἱερουσαλήμ pron. name. fem. inde. Ἱερουσαλήμ Jerusalem
καὶ conj. καί and, even, also, but
οἱ art. nom. masc. pl. ὁ ἡ τό the, this, that, he, she, it
ἄρχοντες n. nom. masc. pl. ἄρχων ruler, prince, chief, magistrate, chief ruler
αὐτῶν pron. gen. masc. 3p. pl. αὐτός ή ό self, of oneself, even, very, the same, he, she, it
τοῦτον demo. pron. acc. masc. sg. οὗτος αὕτη τοῦτο this, the same, this same, he, she, it
καὶ conj. καί and, even, also, but
τὰς art. acc. fem. pl. ὁ ἡ τό the, this, that, he, she, it
φωνὰς n. acc. fem. pl. φωνή voice, sound, noise
τῶν art. gen. masc. pl. ὁ ἡ τό the, this, that, he, she, it
προφητῶν n. gen. masc. pl. προφήτης prophet
τὰς art. acc. fem. pl. ὁ ἡ τό the, this, that, he, she, it
κατὰ prep. κατά (+gen) against, by, throughout, down, (+acc) according to, after, with
πᾶν adj. acc. neut. sg. πᾶς πᾶσα πᾶν all, every, whosoever, every one, no, whole, any
σάββατον n. acc. neut. sg. σάββατον sabbath day, sabbath, week
28 καὶ conj. καί and, even, also, but
μηδεμίαν num. acc. fem. sg. μηδείς μηδεμία μηδέν no man, nothing, no, none, not at all
αἰτίαν n. acc. fem. sg. αἰτία cause, reason, accusation, fault
θανάτου n. gen. masc. sg. θάνατος death
Πιλᾶτον n. acc. masc. sg. Πιλᾶτος Pilate
αὐτόν pron. acc. masc. 3p. sg. αὐτός ή ό self, of oneself, even, very, the same, he, she, it
29 ὡς adv. ὡς as, when, as it were, how, about, like, as soon as, even as, while
δὲ conj. δέ but, and, now, also, to the contrary, rather, then
ἅπαντα adj. acc. neut. pl. ἅπας all, whole, all things, every, everyone
τὰ art. acc. neut. pl. ὁ ἡ τό the, this, that, he, she, it
περὶ prep. περί (+gen) of, for, concerning, (+acc) about, concerning, in
αὐτοῦ pron. gen. masc. 3p. sg. αὐτός ή ό self, of oneself, even, very, the same, he, she, it
ἀπὸ prep. ἀπό (+gen) from, of, out of, since, for, off, at, by, in, on
τοῦ art. gen. neut. sg. ὁ ἡ τό the, this, that, he, she, it
ξύλου n. gen. neut. sg. ξύλον tree, stave, wood, the stocks
εἰς prep. εἰς (+acc) into, to, unto, for, in, on, toward, against, upon, at, among
μνημεῖον n. acc. neut. sg. μνημεῖον sepulchre, grave, tomb

30 ὁ art. nom. masc. sg. ὁ ἡ τό the, this, that, he, she, it
δὲ conj. δέ but, and, now, also, to the contrary, rather, then
Θεὸς n. nom. masc. sg. θεός God, god
αὐτὸν pron. acc. masc. 3p. sg. αὐτός ή ό self, of oneself, even, very, the same, he, she, it
ἐκ prep. ἐκ ἐξ (+gen) of, from, out of, by, on, with, in, among, through
νεκρῶν adj. gen. masc. pl. νεκρός dead
31 ὃς relative pron. nom. masc. sg. ὅς ἥ ὅ who, which, what, that
ἐπὶ prep. ἐπί (+gen) on, in, upon, (+dat) in, at, for, upon, (+acc) on, upon, unto, to, against
ἡμέρας n. acc. fem. pl. ἡμέρα day, time, year, while, age, day time
πλείους compar. adj. acc. fem. pl. πλείων more, many, greater, further, more part
τοῖς art. dat. masc. pl. ὁ ἡ τό the, this, that, he, she, it
αὐτῷ pron. dat. masc. 3p. sg. αὐτός ή ό self, of oneself, even, very, the same, he, she, it
ἀπὸ prep. ἀπό (+gen) from, of, out of, since, for, off, at, by, in, on
τῆς art. gen. fem. sg. ὁ ἡ τό the, this, that, he, she, it
Γαλιλαίας n. gen. fem. sg. Γαλιλαία Galilee
εἰς prep. εἰς (+acc) into, to, unto, for, in, on, toward, against, upon, at, among
Ἰερουσαλήμ pron. name. fem. inde. Ἰερουσαλήμ Jerusalem
οἵτινες relative pron. nom. masc. pl. ὅστις which, who, whosoever, that, whatsoever
μάρτυρες n. nom. masc. pl. μάρτυς or μάρτυρ witness, martyr, record
αὐτοῦ pron. gen. masc. 3p. sg. αὐτός ή ό self, of oneself, even, very, the same, he, she, it
πρὸς prep. πρός (+gen) for, (+dat) at, (+acc) unto, to, with, for, against
τὸν art. acc. masc. sg. ὁ ἡ τό the, this, that, he, she, it
λαόν n. acc. masc. sg. λαός people
32 καὶ conj. καί and, even, also, but
ἡμεῖς pron. nom. 1p. pl. ἐγώ I
ὑμᾶς pron. acc. 2p. pl. σύ thou, you
τὴν art. acc. fem. sg. ὁ ἡ τό the, this, that, he, she, it
πρὸς prep. πρός (+gen) for, (+dat) at, (+acc) unto, to, with, for, against
τοὺς art. acc. masc. pl. ὁ ἡ τό the, this, that, he, she, it
πατέρας n. acc. masc. pl. πατήρ Father, father, parent
ἐπαγγελίαν n. acc. fem. sg. ἐπαγγελία promise, message
33 ὅτι conj. ὅτι that, for, because, how that, how, because that, for that, though
ταύτην demo. pron. acc. fem. sg. οὗτος αὕτη τοῦτο this, the same, this same, he, she, it
ὁ art. nom. masc. sg. ὁ ἡ τό the, this, that, he, she, it
Θεὸς n. nom. masc. sg. θεός God, god
τοῖς art. dat. neut. pl. ὁ ἡ τό the, this, that, he, she, it
τέκνοις n. dat. neut. pl. τέκνον child, son, daughter
αὐτῶν pron. gen. masc. 3p. pl. αὐτός ή ό self, of oneself, even, very, the same, he, she, it
ἡμῖν pron. dat. 1p. pl. ἐγώ I
Ἰησοῦν n. acc. masc. sg. Ἰησοῦς Jesus
ὡς adv. ὡς as, when, as it were, how, about, like, as soon as, even as, while
καὶ conj. καί and, even, also, but
ἐν prep. ἐν (+dat) in, by, with, among, at, on, through, to, within, into, of, for
τῷ art. dat. masc. sg. ὁ ἡ τό the, this, that, he, she, it
ψαλμῷ n. dat. masc. sg. ψαλμός Psalm, psalm
τῷ art. dat. masc. sg. ὁ ἡ τό the, this, that, he, she, it
δευτέρῳ ordinal. adj. dat. masc. sg. δεύτερος second, second time, again, afterward
Υἱός n. nom. masc. sg. υἱός son, child, descendant, offspring, heir
μου pron. gen. 1p. sg. ἐγώ I
σύ pron. nom. 2p. sg. σύ thou, you
ἐγὼ pron. nom. 1p. sg. ἐγώ I
σήμερον adv. σήμερον this day, today
σε pron. acc. 2p. sg. σύ thou, you
34 ὅτι conj. ὅτι that, for, because, how that, how, because that, for that, though
δὲ conj. δέ but, and, now, also, to the contrary, rather, then

αὐτὸν pron. acc. masc. 3p. sg. αὐτός ή ό self, of oneself, even, very, the same, he, she, it
ἐκ prep. ἐκ ἐξ (+gen) of, from, out of, by, on, with, in, among, through
νεκρῶν adj. gen. masc. pl. νεκρός dead
μηκέτι adv. μηκέτι no more, no longer, not any more, not henceforth, not henceforward
εἰς prep. εἰς (+acc) into, to, unto, for, in, on, toward, against, upon, at, among
διαφθοράν n. acc. fem. sg. διαφθορά corruption
οὕτως adv. οὕτω οὕτως so, even so, thus, on this wise, likewise, after this manner
ὅτι conj. ὅτι that, for, because, how that, how, because that, for that, though
ὑμῖν pron. dat. 2p. pl. σύ thou, you
τὰ art. acc. neut. pl. ὁ ἡ τό the, this, that, he, she, it
ὅσια adj. acc. neut. pl. ὅσιος holy, Holy, mercy
Δαβὶδ n. gen. masc. sg. Δαβίδ David
τὰ art. acc. neut. pl. ὁ ἡ τό the, this, that, he, she, it
πιστά adj. acc. neut. pl. πιστός faithful, believing, true, sure
35 διὸ conj. διό wherefore, therefore, for which cause
καὶ conj. καί and, even, also, but
ἐν prep. ἐν (+dat) in, by, with, among, at, on, through, to, within, into, of, for
ἑτέρῳ adj. dat. masc. sg. ἕτερος another, other, else, strange
Οὐ particle of negation. οὐ οὐκ οὐχ not, no, neither, none, nay, nor, never, nothing
τὸν art. acc. masc. sg. ὁ ἡ τό the, this, that, he, she, it
ὅσιόν adj. acc. masc. sg. ὅσιος holy, Holy, mercy
σου pron. gen. 2p. sg. σύ thou, you
διαφθοράν n. acc. fem. sg. διαφθορά corruption
36 Δαβὶδ n. nom. masc. sg. Δαβίδ David
μέν conj. μέν indeed, verily, truly, even, so, some
γὰρ conj. γάρ for, and, because, but, indeed
ἰδίᾳ adj. dat. fem. sg. ἴδιος one's own, one's, privately
γενεᾷ n. dat. fem. sg. γενεά generation, age, time, nation
τῇ art. dat. fem. sg. ὁ ἡ τό the, this, that, he, she, it
τοῦ art. gen. masc. sg. ὁ ἡ τό the, this, that, he, she, it
Θεοῦ n. gen. masc. sg. θεός God, god
βουλῇ n. dat. fem. sg. βουλή counsel, advise, will
καὶ conj. καί and, even, also, but
πρὸς prep. πρός (+gen) for, (+dat) at, (+acc) unto, to, with, for, against
τοὺς art. acc. masc. pl. ὁ ἡ τό the, this, that, he, she, it
πατέρας n. acc. masc. pl. πατήρ Father, father, parent
αὐτοῦ pron. gen. masc. 3p. sg. αὐτός ή ό self, of oneself, even, very, the same, he, she, it
καὶ conj. καί and, even, also, but
διαφθοράν n. acc. fem. sg. διαφθορά corruption
37 ὃν relative pron. acc. masc. sg. ὅς ἥ ὅ who, which, what, that
δὲ conj. δέ but, and, now, also, to the contrary, rather, then
ὁ art. nom. masc. sg. ὁ ἡ τό the, this, that, he, she, it
Θεὸς n. nom. masc. sg. θεός God, god
οὐκ particle of negation. οὐ οὐκ οὐχ not, no, neither, none, nay, nor, never, nothing
διαφθοράν n. acc. fem. sg. διαφθορά corruption
38 γνωστὸν adj. nom. neut. sg. γνωστός acquaintance, known, notable
οὖν conj. οὖν therefore, then, so, and, now, wherefore
ὑμῖν pron. dat. 2p. pl. σύ thou, you
ἄνδρες n. voc. masc. pl. ἀνήρ man, husband, sir
ἀδελφοί n. voc. masc. pl. ἀδελφός brother
ὅτι conj. ὅτι that, for, because, how that, how, because that, for that, though
διὰ prep. διά (+gen) by, through, with, in, of, (+acc) for, because of, for a cause
τούτου demo. pron. gen. masc. sg. οὗτος αὕτη τοῦτο this, the same, this same, he, she, it
ὑμῖν pron. dat. 2p. pl. σύ thou, you
ἄφεσις n. nom. fem. sg. ἄφεσις remission, forgiveness, deliverance, liberty

ἁμαρτιῶν n. gen. fem. pl. ἁμαρτία sin, offence, sinful
39 καὶ conj. καί and, even, also, but
ἀπὸ prep. ἀπό (+gen) from, of, out of, since, for, off, at, by, in, on
πάντων adj. gen. neut. pl. πᾶς πᾶσα πᾶν all, every, whosoever, every one, no, whole, any
ὧν relative pron. gen. neut. pl. ὅς ἥ ὅ who, which, what, that
οὐκ particle of negation. οὐ οὐκ οὐχ not, no, neither, none, nay, nor, never, nothing
ἐν prep. ἐν (+dat) in, by, with, among, at, on, through, to, within, into, of, for
τῷ art. dat. masc. sg. ὁ ἡ τό the, this, that, he, she, it
νόμῳ n. dat. masc. sg. νόμος law, the law
Μωσέως n. gen. masc. sg. Μωσῆς Moses
ἐν prep. ἐν (+dat) in, by, with, among, at, on, through, to, within, into, of, for
τούτῳ demo. pron. dat. masc. sg. οὗτος αὕτη τοῦτο this, the same, this same, he, she, it
πᾶς adj. nom. masc. sg. πᾶς πᾶσα πᾶν all, every, whosoever, every one, no, whole, any
ὁ art. nom. masc. sg. ὁ ἡ τό the, this, that, he, she, it
40 οὖν conj. οὖν therefore, then, so, and, now, wherefore
μὴ particle of negation. μή not, no, lest, neither, none, nothing, nor, never, without
ἐφ' prep. ἐπί (+gen) on, in, upon, (+dat) in, at, for, upon, (+acc) on, upon, unto, to, against
ὑμᾶς pron. acc. 2p. pl. σύ thou, you
τὸ art. nom. neut. sg. ὁ ἡ τό the, this, that, he, she, it
ἐν prep. ἐν (+dat) in, by, with, among, at, on, through, to, within, into, of, for
τοῖς art. dat. masc. pl. ὁ ἡ τό the, this, that, he, she, it
προφήταις n. dat. masc. pl. προφήτης prophet
41 οἱ art. voc. masc. pl. ὁ ἡ τό the, this, that, he, she, it
καταφρονηταί n. voc. masc. pl. καταφρονητής despiser
καὶ conj. καί and, even, also, but
καὶ conj. καί and, even, also, but
ὅτι conj. ὅτι that, for, because, how that, how, because that, for that, though
ἔργον n. acc. neut. sg. ἔργον work, deed, doing labour
ἐγὼ pron. nom. 1p. sg. ἐγώ I
ἐν prep. ἐν (+dat) in, by, with, among, at, on, through, to, within, into, of, for
ταῖς art. dat. fem. pl. ὁ ἡ τό the, this, that, he, she, it
ἡμέραις n. dat. fem. pl. ἡμέρα day, time, year, while, age, day time
ὑμῶν pron. gen. 2p. pl. σύ thou, you
ἔργον n. acc. neut. sg. ἔργον work, deed, doing labour
ᾧ relative pron. dat. neut. sg. ὅς ἥ ὅ who, which, what, that
οὐ particle of negation. οὐ οὐκ οὐχ not, no, neither, none, nay, nor, never, nothing
μὴ particle of negation. μή not, no, lest, neither, none, nothing, nor, never, without
ἐάν conj. ἐάν if, soever, except, though, and if, but, whether, if so, so
τις indefinite pron. nom. masc. sg. τὶς certain, some, any man, one, any thing
ὑμῖν pron. dat. 2p. pl. σύ thou, you
42 δὲ conj. δέ but, and, now, also, to the contrary, rather, then
ἐκ prep. ἐκ ἐξ (+gen) of, from, out of, by, on, with, in, among, through
τῆς art. gen. fem. sg. ὁ ἡ τό the, this, that, he, she, it
συναγωγῆς n. gen. fem. sg. συναγωγή synagogue, assembly, congregation
τῶν art. gen. masc. pl. ὁ ἡ τό the, this, that, he, she, it
Ἰουδαίων adj. gen. masc. pl. Ἰουδαῖος Jew, Jewess
τὰ art. nom. neut. pl. ὁ ἡ τό the, this, that, he, she, it
ἔθνη n. nom. neut. pl. ἔθνος Gentile, nation, heathen, people
εἰς prep. εἰς (+acc) into, to, unto, for, in, on, toward, against, upon, at, among
τὸ art. acc. neut. sg. ὁ ἡ τό the, this, that, he, she, it
μεταξὺ adv. μεταξύ between
σάββατον n. acc. neut. sg. σάββατον sabbath day, sabbath, week
αὐτοῖς pron. dat. masc. 3p. pl. αὐτός ἡ ὁ self, of oneself, even, very, the same, he, she, it
τὰ art. acc. neut. pl. ὁ ἡ τό the, this, that, he, she, it
ῥήματα n. acc. neut. pl. ῥῆμα word, saying, thing

ταῦτα demo. pron. acc. neut. pl. οὗτος αὕτη τοῦτο this, the same, this same, he, she, it
43 δὲ conj. δέ but, and, now, also, to the contrary, rather, then
τῆς art. gen. fem. sg. ὁ ἡ τό the, this, that, he, she, it
συναγωγῆς n. gen. fem. sg. συναγωγή synagogue, assembly, congregation
πολλοὶ adj. nom. masc. pl. πολύς many, great, much, long, abundant
τῶν art. gen. masc. pl. ὁ ἡ τό the, this, that, he, she, it
Ἰουδαίων adj. gen. masc. pl. Ἰουδαῖος Jew, Jewess
καὶ conj. καί and, even, also, but
τῶν art. gen. masc. pl. ὁ ἡ τό the, this, that, he, she, it
προσηλύτων n. gen. masc. pl. προσήλυτος proselyte
τῷ art. dat. masc. sg. ὁ ἡ τό the, this, that, he, she, it
Παύλῳ n. dat. masc. sg. Παῦλος Paul, Paulus
καὶ conj. καί and, even, also, but
τῷ art. dat. masc. sg. ὁ ἡ τό the, this, that, he, she, it
Βαρναβᾷ n. dat. masc. sg. Βαρναβᾶς Barnabas
οἵτινες relative pron. nom. masc. pl. ὅστις which, who, whosoever, that, whatsoever
αὐτοῖς pron. dat. masc. 3p. pl. αὐτός ή ό self, of oneself, even, very, the same, he, she, it
αὐτοὺς pron. acc. masc. 3p. pl. αὐτός ή ό self, of oneself, even, very, the same, he, she, it
τῇ art. dat. fem. sg. ὁ ἡ τό the, this, that, he, she, it
χάριτι n. dat. fem. sg. χάρις grace, thank, favour, pleasure
τοῦ art. gen. masc. sg. ὁ ἡ τό the, this, that, he, she, it
Θεοῦ n. gen. masc. sg. θεός God, god
44 Τῷ art. dat. neut. sg. ὁ ἡ τό the, this, that, he, she, it
δὲ conj. δέ but, and, now, also, to the contrary, rather, then
σαββάτῳ n. dat. neut. sg. σάββατον sabbath day, sabbath, week
σχεδὸν adv. σχεδόν almost
πᾶσα adj. nom. fem. sg. πᾶς πᾶσα πᾶν all, every, whosoever, every one, no, whole, any
ἡ art. nom. fem. sg. ὁ ἡ τό the, this, that, he, she, it
πόλις n. nom. fem. sg. πόλις city
τὸν art. acc. masc. sg. ὁ ἡ τό the, this, that, he, she, it
λόγον n. acc. masc. sg. λόγος word, saying, account, speech, thing, matter
τοῦ art. gen. masc. sg. ὁ ἡ τό the, this, that, he, she, it
Θεοῦ n. gen. masc. sg. θεός God, god
45 δὲ conj. δέ but, and, now, also, to the contrary, rather, then
οἱ art. nom. masc. pl. ὁ ἡ τό the, this, that, he, she, it
Ἰουδαῖοι adj. nom. masc. pl. Ἰουδαῖος Jew, Jewess
τοὺς art. acc. masc. pl. ὁ ἡ τό the, this, that, he, she, it
ὄχλους n. acc. masc. pl. ὄχλος people, multitude, company, press, number
ζήλου n. gen. masc. sg. ζῆλος zeal, envying, indignation, emulation, jealousy
καὶ conj. καί and, even, also, but
τοῖς art. dat. neut. pl. ὁ ἡ τό the, this, that, he, she, it
ὑπὸ prep. ὑπό (+gen) of, by, with, from, among, (+acc) under
τοῦ art. gen. masc. sg. ὁ ἡ τό the, this, that, he, she, it
Παύλου n. gen. masc. sg. Παῦλος Paul, Paulus
καὶ conj. καί and, even, also, but
46 δὲ conj. δέ but, and, now, also, to the contrary, rather, then
ὁ art. nom. masc. sg. ὁ ἡ τό the, this, that, he, she, it
Παῦλος n. nom. masc. sg. Παῦλος Paul, Paulus
καὶ conj. καί and, even, also, but
ὁ art. nom. masc. sg. ὁ ἡ τό the, this, that, he, she, it
Βαρναβᾶς n. nom. masc. sg. Βαρναβᾶς Barnabas
Ὑμῖν pron. dat. 2p. pl. σύ thou, you
ἀναγκαῖον adj. nom. neut. sg. ἀναγκαῖος near, necessary, more needful, of necessity
πρῶτον ordinal. adj. acc. neut. sg. πρῶτος first, chief, first of all, chiefest, best
τὸν art. acc. masc. sg. ὁ ἡ τό the, this, that, he, she, it

λόγον n. acc. masc. sg. λόγος word, saying, account, speech, thing, matter
τοῦ art. gen. masc. sg. ὁ ἡ τό the, this, that, he, she, it
Θεοῦ n. gen. masc. sg. θεός God, god
ἐπειδὴ conj. ἐπειδή because, for, after that, for that, for as much as, since
δὲ conj. δέ but, and, now, also, to the contrary, rather, then
αὐτὸν pron. acc. masc. 3p. sg. αὐτός ή ό self, of oneself, even, very, the same, he, she, it
καὶ conj. καί and, even, also, but
οὐκ particle of negation. οὐ οὐκ οὐχ not, no, neither, none, nay, nor, never, nothing
ἀξίους adj. acc. masc. pl. ἄξιος worthy, meet, due reward
ἑαυτοὺς reflexive pron. acc. masc. 3p. pl. ἑαυτοῦ himself, herself, itself, yourself, ourselves
τῆς art. gen. fem. sg. ὁ ἡ τό the, this, that, he, she, it
αἰωνίου adj. gen. fem. sg. αἰώνιος eternal, everlasting, world, for ever
ζωῆς n. gen. fem. sg. ζωή life, lifetime
εἰς prep. εἰς (+acc) into, to, unto, for, in, on, toward, against, upon, at, among
τὰ art. acc. neut. pl. ὁ ἡ τό the, this, that, he, she, it
ἔθνη n. acc. neut. pl. ἔθνος Gentile, nation, heathen, people
47 οὕτω adv. οὕτω οὕτως so, even so, thus, on this wise, likewise, after this manner
γὰρ conj. γάρ for, and, because, but, indeed
ἡμῖν pron. dat. 1p. pl. ἐγώ I
ὁ art. nom. masc. sg. ὁ ἡ τό the, this, that, he, she, it
Κύριος n. nom. masc. sg. κύριος Lord, lord, master, sir, LORD, God, Master, owner
σε pron. acc. 2p. sg. σύ thou, you
εἰς prep. εἰς (+acc) into, to, unto, for, in, on, toward, against, upon, at, among
φῶς n. acc. neut. sg. φῶς light, fire
ἐθνῶν n. gen. neut. pl. ἔθνος Gentile, nation, heathen, people
τοῦ art. gen. neut. sg. ὁ ἡ τό the, this, that, he, she, it
σε pron. acc. 2p. sg. σύ thou, you
εἰς prep. εἰς (+acc) into, to, unto, for, in, on, toward, against, upon, at, among
σωτηρίαν n. acc. fem. sg. σωτηρία salvation, deliver, health, saving
ἕως conj. ἕως till, until, unto, until when, while, as far as, even, until now
ἐσχάτου adj. gen. neut. sg. ἔσχατος last, lowest, uttermost, uttermost part
τῆς art. gen. fem. sg. ὁ ἡ τό the, this, that, he, she, it
γῆς n. gen. fem. sg. γῆ earth, land, ground, country
48 δὲ conj. δέ but, and, now, also, to the contrary, rather, then
τὰ art. nom. neut. pl. ὁ ἡ τό the, this, that, he, she, it
ἔθνη n. nom. neut. pl. ἔθνος Gentile, nation, heathen, people
καὶ conj. καί and, even, also, but
τὸν art. acc. masc. sg. ὁ ἡ τό the, this, that, he, she, it
λόγον n. acc. masc. sg. λόγος word, saying, account, speech, thing, matter
τοῦ art. gen. masc. sg. ὁ ἡ τό the, this, that, he, she, it
Κυρίου n. gen. masc. sg. κύριος Lord, lord, master, sir, LORD, God, Master, owner
καὶ conj. καί and, even, also, but
ὅσοι relative pron. nom. masc. pl. ὅσος as many as, whatsoever, that, as long as, how much
εἰς prep. εἰς (+acc) into, to, unto, for, in, on, toward, against, upon, at, among
ζωὴν n. acc. fem. sg. ζωή life, lifetime
αἰώνιον adj. acc. fem. sg. αἰώνιος eternal, everlasting, world, for ever
49 δὲ conj. δέ but, and, now, also, to the contrary, rather, then
ὁ art. nom. masc. sg. ὁ ἡ τό the, this, that, he, she, it
λόγος n. nom. masc. sg. λόγος word, saying, account, speech, thing, matter
τοῦ art. gen. masc. sg. ὁ ἡ τό the, this, that, he, she, it
Κυρίου n. gen. masc. sg. κύριος Lord, lord, master, sir, LORD, God, Master, owner
δι' prep. διά (+gen) by, through, with, in, of, (+acc) for, because of, for a cause
ὅλης adj. gen. fem. sg. ὅλος all, whole, every whit, altogether
τῆς art. gen. fem. sg. ὁ ἡ τό the, this, that, he, she, it
χώρας n. gen. fem. sg. χώρα country, region, land, field, coast, ground

50 οἱ art. nom. masc. pl. ὁ ἡ τό the, this, that, he, she, it
δὲ conj. δέ but, and, now, also, to the contrary, rather, then
Ἰουδαῖοι adj. nom. masc. pl. Ἰουδαῖος Jew, Jewess
τὰς art. acc. fem. pl. ὁ ἡ τό the, this, that, he, she, it
γυναῖκας n. acc. fem. pl. γυνή woman, wife
καὶ conj. καί and, even, also, but
τὰς art. acc. fem. pl. ὁ ἡ τό the, this, that, he, she, it
εὐσχήμονας adj. acc. fem. pl. εὐσχήμων honourable, comely
καὶ conj. καί and, even, also, but
τοὺς art. acc. masc. pl. ὁ ἡ τό the, this, that, he, she, it
πρώτους ordinal. adj. acc. masc. pl. πρῶτος first, chief, first of all, chiefest, best
τῆς art. gen. fem. sg. ὁ ἡ τό the, this, that, he, she, it
πόλεως n. gen. fem. sg. πόλις city
καὶ conj. καί and, even, also, but
διωγμὸν n. acc. masc. sg. διωγμός persecution
ἐπὶ prep. ἐπί (+gen) on, in, upon, (+dat) in, at, for, upon, (+acc) on, upon, unto, to, against
τὸν art. acc. masc. sg. ὁ ἡ τό the, this, that, he, she, it
Παῦλον n. acc. masc. sg. Παῦλος Paul, Paulus
καὶ conj. καί and, even, also, but
τὸν art. acc. masc. sg. ὁ ἡ τό the, this, that, he, she, it
Βαρναβᾶν n. acc. masc. sg. Βαρναβᾶς Barnabas
καὶ conj. καί and, even, also, but
αὐτοὺς pron. acc. masc. 3p. pl. αὐτός ή ό self, of oneself, even, very, the same, he, she, it
ἀπὸ prep. ἀπό (+gen) from, of, out of, since, for, off, at, by, in, on
τῶν art. gen. neut. pl. ὁ ἡ τό the, this, that, he, she, it
ὁρίων n. gen. neut. pl. ὅριον coast, border
αὐτῶν pron. gen. masc. 3p. pl. αὐτός ή ό self, of oneself, even, very, the same, he, she, it
51 οἱ art. nom. masc. pl. ὁ ἡ τό the, this, that, he, she, it
δὲ conj. δέ but, and, now, also, to the contrary, rather, then
τὸν art. acc. masc. sg. ὁ ἡ τό the, this, that, he, she, it
κονιορτὸν n. acc. masc. sg. κονιορτός dust
τῶν art. gen. masc. pl. ὁ ἡ τό the, this, that, he, she, it
ποδῶν n. gen. masc. pl. πούς foot
αὐτῶν pron. gen. masc. 3p. pl. αὐτός ή ό self, of oneself, even, very, the same, he, she, it
ἐπ' prep. ἐπί (+gen) on, in, upon, (+dat) in, at, for, upon, (+acc) on, upon, unto, to, against
αὐτοὺς pron. acc. masc. 3p. pl. αὐτός ή ό self, of oneself, even, very, the same, he, she, it
εἰς prep. εἰς (+acc) into, to, unto, for, in, on, toward, against, upon, at, among
Ἰκόνιον n. acc. neut. sg. Ἰκόνιον Iconium
52 οἱ art. nom. masc. pl. ὁ ἡ τό the, this, that, he, she, it
δὲ conj. δέ but, and, now, also, to the contrary, rather, then
μαθηταὶ n. nom. masc. pl. μαθητής disciple
χαρᾶς n. gen. fem. sg. χαρά joy, gladness, joyfulness
καὶ conj. καί and, even, also, but
Πνεύματος n. gen. neut. sg. πνεῦμα spirit, Spirit, Ghost, ghost, life. of the spirit, wind
Ἁγίου adj. gen. neut. sg. ἅγιος Holy, holy, saint, Holy One, holy thing, most holy

14

1 δὲ conj. δέ but, and, now, also, to the contrary, rather, then
ἐν prep. ἐν (+dat) in, by, with, among, at, on, through, to, within, into, of, for
Ἰκονίῳ n. dat. neut. sg. Ἰκόνιον Iconium
κατὰ prep. κατά (+gen) against, by, throughout, down, (+acc) according to, after, with
τὸ art. acc. neut. sg. ὁ ἡ τό the, this, that, he, she, it
αὐτὸ adj. acc. neut. sg. αὐτός ή ό self, of oneself, even, very, the same, he, she, it
αὐτοὺς pron. acc. masc. 3p. pl. αὐτός ή ό self, of oneself, even, very, the same, he, she, it

εἰς prep. εἰς (+acc) into, to, unto, for, in, on, toward, against, upon, at, among
τὴν art. acc. fem. sg. ὁ ἡ τό the, this, that, he, she, it
συναγωγὴν n. acc. fem. sg. συναγωγή synagogue, assembly, congregation
τῶν art. gen. masc. pl. ὁ ἡ τό the, this, that, he, she, it
Ἰουδαίων adj. gen. masc. pl. Ἰουδαῖος Jew, Jewess
καὶ conj. καί and, even, also, but
οὕτως adv. οὕτω οὕτως so, even so, thus, on this wise, likewise, after this manner
ὥστε conj. ὥστε so that, wherefore, insomuch that, therefore, that, so then
Ἰουδαίων adj. gen. masc. pl. Ἰουδαῖος Jew, Jewess
τε conj. τέ and, both, also
καὶ conj. καί and, even, also, but
Ἑλλήνων n. gen. masc. pl. Ἕλλην Greek, Gentile
πολὺ adj. acc. neut. sg. πολύς many, great, much, long, abundant
πλῆθος n. acc. neut. sg. πλῆθος multitude, bundle, company
2 οἱ art. nom. masc. pl. ὁ ἡ τό the, this, that, he, she, it
δὲ conj. δέ but, and, now, also, to the contrary, rather, then
Ἰουδαῖοι adj. nom. masc. pl. Ἰουδαῖος Jew, Jewess
καὶ conj. καί and, even, also, but
τὰς art. acc. fem. pl. ὁ ἡ τό the, this, that, he, she, it
ψυχὰς n. acc. fem. pl. ψυχή life, soul, mind, heart
τῶν art. gen. neut. pl. ὁ ἡ τό the, this, that, he, she, it
ἐθνῶν n. gen. neut. pl. ἔθνος Gentile, nation, heathen, people
κατὰ prep. κατά (+gen) against, by, throughout, down, (+acc) according to, after, with
τῶν art. gen. masc. pl. ὁ ἡ τό the, this, that, he, she, it
ἀδελφῶν n. gen. masc. pl. ἀδελφός brother
3 ἱκανὸν adj. acc. masc. sg. ἱκανός many, much, long, worthy, sufficient, great, able
μέν conj. μέν indeed, verily, truly, even, so, some
οὖν conj. οὖν therefore, then, so, and, now, wherefore
χρόνον n. acc. masc. sg. χρόνος time, season, space
ἐπὶ prep. ἐπί (+gen) on, in, upon, (+dat) in, at, for, upon, (+acc) on, upon, unto, to, against
τῷ art. dat. masc. sg. ὁ ἡ τό the, this, that, he, she, it
Κυρίῳ n. dat. masc. sg. κύριος Lord, lord, master, sir, LORD, God, Master, owner
τῷ art. dat. masc. sg. ὁ ἡ τό the, this, that, he, she, it
τῷ art. dat. masc. sg. ὁ ἡ τό the, this, that, he, she, it
λόγῳ n. dat. masc. sg. λόγος word, saying, account, speech, thing, matter
τῆς art. gen. fem. sg. ὁ ἡ τό the, this, that, he, she, it
χάριτος n. gen. fem. sg. χάρις grace, thank, favour, pleasure
αὐτοῦ pron. gen. masc. 3p. sg. αὐτός ή ό self, of oneself, even, very, the same, he, she, it
καὶ conj. καί and, even, also, but
σημεῖα n. acc. neut. pl. σημεῖον sign, miracle, wonder, token
καὶ conj. καί and, even, also, but
τέρατα n. acc. neut. pl. τέρας wonder
διὰ prep. διά (+gen) by, through, with, in, of, (+acc) for, because of, for a cause
τῶν art. gen. fem. pl. ὁ ἡ τό the, this, that, he, she, it
χειρῶν n. gen. fem. pl. χείρ hand
αὐτῶν pron. gen. masc. 3p. pl. αὐτός ή ό self, of oneself, even, very, the same, he, she, it
4 δὲ conj. δέ but, and, now, also, to the contrary, rather, then
τὸ art. nom. neut. sg. ὁ ἡ τό the, this, that, he, she, it
πλῆθος n. nom. neut. sg. πλῆθος multitude, bundle, company
τῆς art. gen. fem. sg. ὁ ἡ τό the, this, that, he, she, it
πόλεως n. gen. fem. sg. πόλις city
καὶ conj. καί and, even, also, but
οἱ art. nom. masc. pl. ὁ ἡ τό the, this, that, he, she, it
μέν conj. μέν indeed, verily, truly, even, so, some
σὺν prep. σύν (+dat) with, beside

τοῖς art. dat. masc. pl. ὁ ἡ τό the, this, that, he, she, it
Ἰουδαίοις adj. dat. masc. pl. Ἰουδαῖος Jew, Jewess
οἱ art. nom. masc. pl. ὁ ἡ τό the, this, that, he, she, it
δὲ conj. δέ but, and, now, also, to the contrary, rather, then
σὺν prep. σύν (+dat) with, beside
τοῖς art. dat. masc. pl. ὁ ἡ τό the, this, that, he, she, it
ἀποστόλοις n. dat. masc. pl. ἀπόστολος apostle, messenger, he that is sent
5 ὡς adv. ὡς as, when, as it were, how, about, like, as soon as, even as, while
δὲ conj. δέ but, and, now, also, to the contrary, rather, then
ὁρμὴ n. nom. fem. sg. ὁρμή assault, impulse
τῶν art. gen. neut. pl. ὁ ἡ τό the, this, that, he, she, it
ἐθνῶν n. gen. neut. pl. ἔθνος Gentile, nation, heathen, people
τε conj. τέ and, both, also
καὶ conj. καί and, even, also, but
Ἰουδαίων adj. gen. masc. pl. Ἰουδαῖος Jew, Jewess
σὺν prep. σύν (+dat) with, beside
τοῖς art. dat. masc. pl. ὁ ἡ τό the, this, that, he, she, it
ἄρχουσιν n. dat. masc. pl. ἄρχων ruler, prince, chief, magistrate, chief ruler
αὐτῶν pron. gen. masc. 3p. pl. αὐτός ή ό self, of oneself, even, very, the same, he, she, it
καὶ conj. καί and, even, also, but
αὐτούς pron. acc. masc. 3p. pl. αὐτός ή ό self, of oneself, even, very, the same, he, she, it
6 εἰς prep. εἰς (+acc) into, to, unto, for, in, on, toward, against, upon, at, among
τὰς art. acc. fem. pl. ὁ ἡ τό the, this, that, he, she, it
πόλεις n. acc. fem. pl. πόλις city
τῆς art. gen. fem. sg. ὁ ἡ τό the, this, that, he, she, it
Λυκαονίας n. gen. fem. sg. Λυκαονία Lycaonia
Λύστραν n. acc. fem. sg. Λύστρα Lystra
καὶ conj. καί and, even, also, but
Δέρβην n. acc. fem. sg. Δέρβη Derbe
καὶ conj. καί and, even, also, but
τὴν art. acc. fem. sg. ὁ ἡ τό the, this, that, he, she, it
περίχωρον adj. acc. fem. sg. περίχωρος region round about, country round about
7 κἀκεῖ adv. κἀκεῖ and there, there also, thither also
8 Καί conj. καί and, even, also, but
τις indefinite pron. nom. masc. sg. τὶς certain, some, any man, one, any thing
ἀνὴρ n. nom. masc. sg. ἀνήρ man, husband, sir
ἐν prep. ἐν (+dat) in, by, with, among, at, on, through, to, within, into, of, for
Λύστροις n. dat. neut. pl. Λύστρα Lystra
ἀδύνατος adj. nom. masc. sg. ἀδύνατος impossible, not possible, cannot do
τοῖς art. dat. masc. pl. ὁ ἡ τό the, this, that, he, she, it
ποσὶν n. dat. masc. pl. πούς foot
χωλὸς adj. nom. masc. sg. χωλός lame, halt, cripple
ἐκ prep. ἐκ ἐξ (+gen) of, from, out of, by, on, with, in, among, through
κοιλίας n. gen. fem. sg. κοιλία belly, womb
μητρὸς n. gen. fem. sg. μήτηρ mother
αὐτοῦ pron. gen. masc. 3p. sg. αὐτός ή ό self, of oneself, even, very, the same, he, she, it
ὃς relative pron. nom. masc. sg. ὅς ἥ ὅ who, which, what, that
οὐδέποτε adv. οὐδέποτε never, neither at any time, no at any time
9 οὗτος demo. pron. nom. masc. sg. οὗτος αὕτη τοῦτο this, the same, this same, he, she, it
τοῦ art. gen. masc. sg. ὁ ἡ τό the, this, that, he, she, it
Παύλου n. gen. masc. sg. Παῦλος Paul, Paulus
ὃς relative pron. nom. masc. sg. ὅς ἥ ὅ who, which, what, that
αὐτῷ pron. dat. masc. 3p. sg. αὐτός ή ό self, of oneself, even, very, the same, he, she, it
καὶ conj. καί and, even, also, but
ὅτι conj. ὅτι that, for, because, how that, how, because that, for that, though

πίστιν n. acc. fem. sg. πίστις faith, assurance, belief, fidelity
τοῦ art. gen. neut. sg. ὁ ἡ τό the, this, that, he, she, it
10 μεγάλῃ adj. dat. fem. sg. μέγας great, loud, greatest, high, large, mighty, strong
τῇ art. dat. fem. sg. ὁ ἡ τό the, this, that, he, she, it
φωνῇ n. dat. fem. sg. φωνή voice, sound, noise
ἐπὶ prep. ἐπί (+gen) on, in, upon, (+dat) in, at, for, upon, (+acc) on, upon, unto, to, against
τοὺς art. acc. masc. pl. ὁ ἡ τό the, this, that, he, she, it
πόδας n. acc. masc. pl. πούς foot
σου pron. gen. 2p. sg. σύ thou, you
ὀρθός adj. nom. masc. sg. ὀρθός upright, straight
καὶ conj. καί and, even, also, but
καὶ conj. καί and, even, also, but
11 οἱ art. nom. masc. pl. ὁ ἡ τό the, this, that, he, she, it
δὲ conj. δέ but, and, now, also, to the contrary, rather, then
ὄχλοι n. nom. masc. pl. ὄχλος people, multitude, company, press, number
ὃ relative pron. acc. neut. sg. ὅς ἥ ὅ who, which, what, that
ὁ art. nom. masc. sg. ὁ ἡ τό the, this, that, he, she, it
Παῦλος n. nom. masc. sg. Παῦλος Paul, Paulus
τὴν art. acc. fem. sg. ὁ ἡ τό the, this, that, he, she, it
φωνὴν n. acc. fem. sg. φωνή voice, sound, noise
αὐτῶν pron. gen. masc. 3p. pl. αὐτός ἡ ὁ self, of oneself, even, very, the same, he, she, it
Λυκαονιστὶ adv. Λυκαονιστί speech of Lycaonia
Οἱ art. nom. masc. pl. ὁ ἡ τό the, this, that, he, she, it
θεοὶ n. nom. masc. pl. θεός God, god
ἀνθρώποις n. dat. masc. pl. ἄνθρωπος man, human being, person, one, certain
πρὸς prep. πρός (+gen) for, (+dat) at, (+acc) unto, to, with, for, against
ἡμᾶς pron. acc. 1p. pl. ἐγώ I
12 τε conj. τέ and, both, also
τὸν art. acc. masc. sg. ὁ ἡ τό the, this, that, he, she, it
μὲν conj. μέν indeed, verily, truly, even, so, some
Βαρναβᾶν n. acc. masc. sg. Βαρναβᾶς Barnabas
Δία n. acc. masc. sg. Ζεύς Jupiter, Zeus
τὸν art. acc. masc. sg. ὁ ἡ τό the, this, that, he, she, it
δὲ conj. δέ but, and, now, also, to the contrary, rather, then
Παῦλον n. acc. masc. sg. Παῦλος Paul, Paulus
Ἑρμῆν n. acc. masc. sg. Ἑρμῆς Mercurius, Hermes
ἐπειδὴ conj. ἐπειδή because, for, after that, for that, for as much as, since
αὐτὸς pron. nom. masc. 3p. sg. αὐτός ἡ ὁ self, of oneself, even, very, the same, he, she, it
ὁ art. nom. masc. sg. ὁ ἡ τό the, this, that, he, she, it
τοῦ art. gen. masc. sg. ὁ ἡ τό the, this, that, he, she, it
λόγου n. gen. masc. sg. λόγος word, saying, account, speech, thing, matter
13 ὁ art. nom. masc. sg. ὁ ἡ τό the, this, that, he, she, it
δὲ conj. δέ but, and, now, also, to the contrary, rather, then
ἱερεὺς n. nom. masc. sg. ἱερεύς priest
τοῦ art. gen. masc. sg. ὁ ἡ τό the, this, that, he, she, it
Διὸς n. gen. masc. sg. Ζεύς Jupiter, Zeus
τοῦ art. gen. masc. sg. ὁ ἡ τό the, this, that, he, she, it
πρὸ prep. πρό (+gen) before, above
τῆς art. gen. fem. sg. ὁ ἡ τό the, this, that, he, she, it
πόλεως n. gen. fem. sg. πόλις city
αὐτῶν pron. gen. masc. 3p. pl. αὐτός ἡ ὁ self, of oneself, even, very, the same, he, she, it
ταύρους n. acc. masc. pl. ταῦρος oxen, bull
καὶ conj. καί and, even, also, but
στέμματα n. acc. neut. pl. στέμμα garland
ἐπὶ prep. ἐπί (+gen) on, in, upon, (+dat) in, at, for, upon, (+acc) on, upon, unto, to, against

τοὺς art. acc. masc. pl. ὁ ἡ τό the, this, that, he, she, it
πυλῶνας n. acc. masc. pl. πυλών gate, porch
σὺν prep. σύν (+dat) with, beside
τοῖς art. dat. masc. pl. ὁ ἡ τό the, this, that, he, she, it
ὄχλοις n. dat. masc. pl. ὄχλος people, multitude, company, press, number
14 δὲ conj. δέ but, and, now, also, to the contrary, rather, then
οἱ art. nom. masc. pl. ὁ ἡ τό the, this, that, he, she, it
ἀπόστολοι n. nom. masc. pl. ἀπόστολος apostle, messenger, he that is sent
Βαρναβᾶς n. nom. masc. sg. Βαρναβᾶς Barnabas
καὶ conj. καί and, even, also, but
Παῦλος n. nom. masc. sg. Παῦλος Paul, Paulus
τὰ art. acc. neut. pl. ὁ ἡ τό the, this, that, he, she, it
ἱμάτια n. acc. neut. pl. ἱμάτιον cloke, garment, clothes, raiment, robe, vesture
αὐτῶν pron. gen. masc. 3p. pl. αὐτός ἡ ὁ self, of oneself, even, very, the same, he, she, it
εἰς prep. εἰς (+acc) into, to, unto, for, in, on, toward, against, upon, at, among
τὸν art. acc. masc. sg. ὁ ἡ τό the, this, that, he, she, it
ὄχλον n. acc. masc. sg. ὄχλος people, multitude, company, press, number
15 καὶ conj. καί and, even, also, but
Ἄνδρες n. voc. masc. pl. ἀνήρ man, husband, sir
τί interrog. pron. acc. neut. sg. τίς what, who, why, where, which, how
ταῦτα demo. pron. acc. neut. pl. οὗτος αὕτη τοῦτο this, the same, this same, he, she, it
καὶ conj. καί and, even, also, but
ἡμεῖς pron. nom. 1p. pl. ἐγώ I
ὁμοιοπαθεῖς adj. nom. masc. pl. ὁμοιοπαθής of like passion, subject to like passion
ὑμῖν pron. dat. 2p. pl. σύ thou, you
ἄνθρωποι n. nom. masc. pl. ἄνθρωπος man, human being, person, one, certain
ὑμᾶς pron. acc. 2p. pl. σύ thou, you
ἀπὸ prep. ἀπό (+gen) from, of, out of, since, for, off, at, by, in, on
τούτων demo. pron. gen. neut. pl. οὗτος αὕτη τοῦτο this, the same, this same, he, she, it
τῶν art. gen. neut. pl. ὁ ἡ τό the, this, that, he, she, it
ματαίων adj. gen. neut. pl. μάταιος vanity, vain
ἐπὶ prep. ἐπί (+gen) on, in, upon, (+dat) in, at, for, upon, (+acc) on, upon, unto, to, against
τὸν art. acc. masc. sg. ὁ ἡ τό the, this, that, he, she, it
Θεὸν n. acc. masc. sg. θεός God, god
τὸν art. acc. masc. sg. ὁ ἡ τό the, this, that, he, she, it
ὃς relative pron. nom. masc. sg. ὅς ἥ ὅ who, which, what, that
τὸν art. acc. masc. sg. ὁ ἡ τό the, this, that, he, she, it
οὐρανὸν n. acc. masc. sg. οὐρανός heaven, air, sky
καὶ conj. καί and, even, also, but
τὴν art. acc. fem. sg. ὁ ἡ τό the, this, that, he, she, it
γῆν n. acc. fem. sg. γῆ earth, land, ground, country
καὶ conj. καί and, even, also, but
τὴν art. acc. fem. sg. ὁ ἡ τό the, this, that, he, she, it
θάλασσαν n. acc. fem. sg. θάλασσα sea
καὶ conj. καί and, even, also, but
πάντα adj. acc. neut. pl. πᾶς πᾶσα πᾶν all, every, whosoever, every one, no, whole, any
τὰ art. acc. neut. pl. ὁ ἡ τό the, this, that, he, she, it
ἐν prep. ἐν (+dat) in, by, with, among, at, on, through, to, within, into, of, for
αὐτοῖς pron. dat. neut. 3p. pl. αὐτός ἡ ὁ self, of oneself, even, very, the same, he, she, it
16 ὃς relative pron. nom. masc. sg. ὅς ἥ ὅ who, which, what, that
ἐν prep. ἐν (+dat) in, by, with, among, at, on, through, to, within, into, of, for
ταῖς art. dat. fem. pl. ὁ ἡ τό the, this, that, he, she, it
γενεαῖς n. dat. fem. pl. γενεά generation, age, time, nation
πάντα adj. acc. neut. pl. πᾶς πᾶσα πᾶν all, every, whosoever, every one, no, whole, any
τὰ art. acc. neut. pl. ὁ ἡ τό the, this, that, he, she, it

ἔθνη n. acc. neut. pl. ἔθνος Gentile, nation, heathen, people
ταῖς art. dat. fem. pl. ὁ ἡ τό the, this, that, he, she, it
ὁδοῖς n. dat. fem. pl. ὁδός way, journey, highway
αὐτῶν pron. gen. neut. 3p. pl. αὐτός ἡ ό self, of oneself, even, very, the same, he, she, it
17 καίτοιγε conj. καίτοιγε though, nevertheless
οὐκ particle of negation. οὐ οὐκ οὐχ not, no, neither, none, nay, nor, never, nothing
ἀμάρτυρον adj. acc. masc. sg. ἀμάρτυρος without witness
ἑαυτὸν reflexive pron. acc. masc. 3p. sg. ἑαυτοῦ himself, herself, itself, yourself, ourselves
οὐρανόθεν adv. οὐρανόθεν from heaven
ἡμῖν pron. dat. 1p. pl. ἐγώ I
ὑετοὺς n. acc. masc. pl. ὑετός rain
καὶ conj. καί and, even, also, but
καιροὺς n. acc. masc. pl. καιρός time, season, due time, opportunity
καρποφόρους adj. acc. masc. pl. καρποφόρος fruitful
τροφῆς n. gen. fem. sg. τροφή meat, food
καὶ conj. καί and, even, also, but
εὐφροσύνης n. gen. fem. sg. εὐφροσύνη joy, gladness
τὰς art. acc. fem. pl. ὁ ἡ τό the, this, that, he, she, it
καρδίας n. acc. fem. pl. καρδία heart
ἡμῶν pron. gen. 1p. pl. ἐγώ I
18 καὶ conj. καί and, even, also, but
ταῦτα demo. pron. acc. neut. pl. οὗτος αὕτη τοῦτο this, the same, this same, he, she, it
μόλις adv. μόλις scarce, with difficulty, scarcely, hardly
τοὺς art. acc. masc. pl. ὁ ἡ τό the, this, that, he, she, it
ὄχλους n. acc. masc. pl. ὄχλος people, multitude, company, press, number
τοῦ art. gen. neut. sg. ὁ ἡ τό the, this, that, he, she, it
μὴ particle of negation. μή not, no, lest, neither, none, nothing, nor, never, without
αὐτοῖς pron. dat. masc. 3p. pl. αὐτός ἡ ό self, of oneself, even, very, the same, he, she, it
19 δὲ conj. δέ but, and, now, also, to the contrary, rather, then
ἀπὸ prep. ἀπό (+gen) from, of, out of, since, for, off, at, by, in, on
Ἀντιοχείας n. gen. fem. sg. Ἀντιόχεια Antioch
καὶ conj. καί and, even, also, but
Ἰκονίου n. gen. neut. sg. Ἰκόνιον Iconium
Ἰουδαῖοι adj. nom. masc. pl. Ἰουδαῖος Jew, Jewess
καὶ conj. καί and, even, also, but
τοὺς art. acc. masc. pl. ὁ ἡ τό the, this, that, he, she, it
ὄχλους n. acc. masc. pl. ὄχλος people, multitude, company, press, number
καὶ conj. καί and, even, also, but
τὸν art. acc. masc. sg. ὁ ἡ τό the, this, that, he, she, it
Παῦλον n. acc. masc. sg. Παῦλος Paul, Paulus
ἔξω adv. ἔξω out, without, out of, forth, away, outward
τῆς art. gen. fem. sg. ὁ ἡ τό the, this, that, he, she, it
πόλεως n. gen. fem. sg. πόλις city
αὐτὸν pron. acc. masc. 3p. sg. αὐτός ἡ ό self, of oneself, even, very, the same, he, she, it
20 δὲ conj. δέ but, and, now, also, to the contrary, rather, then
αὐτὸν pron. acc. masc. 3p. sg. αὐτός ἡ ό self, of oneself, even, very, the same, he, she, it
τῶν art. gen. masc. pl. ὁ ἡ τό the, this, that, he, she, it
μαθητῶν n. gen. masc. pl. μαθητής disciple
εἰς prep. εἰς (+acc) into, to, unto, for, in, on, toward, against, upon, at, among
τὴν art. acc. fem. sg. ὁ ἡ τό the, this, that, he, she, it
πόλιν n. acc. fem. sg. πόλις city
καὶ conj. καί and, even, also, but
τῇ art. dat. fem. sg. ὁ ἡ τό the, this, that, he, she, it
ἐπαύριον adv. ἐπαύριον next day, morrow, day following, nest day after
σὺν prep. σύν (+dat) with, beside

τῷ art. dat. masc. sg. ὁ ἡ τό the, this, that, he, she, it
Βαρναβᾷ n. dat. masc. sg. Βαρναβᾶς Barnabas
εἰς prep. εἰς (+acc) into, to, unto, for, in, on, toward, against, upon, at, among
Δέρβην n. acc. fem. sg. Δέρβη Derbe
21 τε conj. τέ and, both, also
τὴν art. acc. fem. sg. ὁ ἡ τό the, this, that, he, she, it
πόλιν n. acc. fem. sg. πόλις city
ἐκείνην demo. pron. acc. fem. sg. ἐκεῖνος that, he, the same, that same
καὶ conj. καί and, even, also, but
ἱκανοὺς adj. acc. masc. pl. ἱκανός many, much, long, worthy, sufficient, great, able
εἰς prep. εἰς (+acc) into, to, unto, for, in, on, toward, against, upon, at, among
τὴν art. acc. fem. sg. ὁ ἡ τό the, this, that, he, she, it
Λύστραν n. acc. fem. sg. Λύστρα Lystra
καὶ conj. καί and, even, also, but
Ἰκόνιον n. acc. neut. sg. Ἰκόνιον Iconium
καὶ conj. καί and, even, also, but
Ἀντιόχειαν n. acc. fem. sg. Ἀντιόχεια Antioch
22 τὰς art. acc. fem. pl. ὁ ἡ τό the, this, that, he, she, it
ψυχὰς n. acc. fem. pl. ψυχή life, soul, mind, heart
τῶν art. gen. masc. pl. ὁ ἡ τό the, this, that, he, she, it
μαθητῶν n. gen. masc. pl. μαθητής disciple
τῇ art. dat. fem. sg. ὁ ἡ τό the, this, that, he, she, it
πίστει n. dat. fem. sg. πίστις faith, assurance, belief, fidelity
καὶ conj. καί and, even, also, but
ὅτι conj. ὅτι that, for, because, how that, how, because that, for that, though
διὰ prep. διά (+gen) by, through, with, in, of, (+acc) for, because of, for a cause
πολλῶν adj. gen. fem. pl. πολύς many, great, much, long, abundant
θλίψεων n. gen. fem. pl. θλῖψις tribulation, affliction, anguish, persecution
ἡμᾶς pron. acc. 1p. pl. ἐγώ I
εἰς prep. εἰς (+acc) into, to, unto, for, in, on, toward, against, upon, at, among
τὴν art. acc. fem. sg. ὁ ἡ τό the, this, that, he, she, it
βασιλείαν n. acc. fem. sg. βασιλεία kingdom, reign
τοῦ art. gen. masc. sg. ὁ ἡ τό the, this, that, he, she, it
Θεοῦ n. gen. masc. sg. θεός God, god
23 δὲ conj. δέ but, and, now, also, to the contrary, rather, then
αὐτοῖς pron. dat. masc. 3p. pl. αὐτός ή ό self, of oneself, even, very, the same, he, she, it
πρεσβυτέρους adj. acc. masc. pl. πρεσβύτερος elder, elder woman, eldest, old man
κατ’ prep. κατά (+gen) against, by, throughout, down, (+acc) according to, after, with
ἐκκλησίαν n. acc. fem. sg. ἐκκλησία church, assembly
μετὰ prep. μετά (+gen) with, among, against, (+acc) after
νηστειῶν n. gen. fem. pl. νηστεία fasting, fast
αὐτοὺς pron. acc. masc. 3p. pl. αὐτός ή ό self, of oneself, even, very, the same, he, she, it
τῷ art. dat. masc. sg. ὁ ἡ τό the, this, that, he, she, it
Κυρίῳ n. dat. masc. sg. κύριος Lord, lord, master, sir, LORD, God, Master, owner
εἰς prep. εἰς (+acc) into, to, unto, for, in, on, toward, against, upon, at, among
ὃν relative pron. acc. masc. sg. ὅς ἥ ὅ who, which, what, that
24 καὶ conj. καί and, even, also, but
τὴν art. acc. fem. sg. ὁ ἡ τό the, this, that, he, she, it
Πισιδίαν n. acc. fem. sg. Πισιδία Pisidia
εἰς prep. εἰς (+acc) into, to, unto, for, in, on, toward, against, upon, at, among
Παμφυλίαν n. acc. fem. sg. Παμφυλία Pamphylia
25 καὶ conj. καί and, even, also, but
ἐν prep. ἐν (+dat) in, by, with, among, at, on, through, to, within, into, of, for
Πέργῃ n. dat. fem. sg. Πέργη Perga
τὸν art. acc. masc. sg. ὁ ἡ τό the, this, that, he, she, it

λόγον n. acc. masc. sg. λόγος word, saying, account, speech, thing, matter
εἰς prep. εἰς (+acc) into, to, unto, for, in, on, toward, against, upon, at, among
Ἀττάλειαν n. acc. fem. sg. Ἀττάλεια Attalia
26 κἀκεῖθεν adv. κἀκεῖθεν and from thence, and thence, and afterward, thence also
εἰς prep. εἰς (+acc) into, to, unto, for, in, on, toward, against, upon, at, among
Ἀντιόχειαν n. acc. fem. sg. Ἀντιόχεια Antioch
ὅθεν adv. ὅθεν wherefore, from whence, whereupon, where, from thence, whence
τῇ art. dat. fem. sg. ὁ ἡ τό the, this, that, he, she, it
χάριτι n. dat. fem. sg. χάρις grace, thank, favour, pleasure
τοῦ art. gen. masc. sg. ὁ ἡ τό the, this, that, he, she, it
Θεοῦ n. gen. masc. sg. θεός God, god
εἰς prep. εἰς (+acc) into, to, unto, for, in, on, toward, against, upon, at, among
τὸ art. acc. neut. sg. ὁ ἡ τό the, this, that, he, she, it
ἔργον n. acc. neut. sg. ἔργον work, deed, doing labour
ὃ relative pron. acc. neut. sg. ὅς ἥ ὅ who, which, what, that
27 δὲ conj. δέ but, and, now, also, to the contrary, rather, then
καὶ conj. καί and, even, also, but
τὴν art. acc. fem. sg. ὁ ἡ τό the, this, that, he, she, it
ἐκκλησίαν n. acc. fem. sg. ἐκκλησία church, assembly
ὅσα relative pron. acc. neut. pl. ὅσος as many as, whatsoever, that, as long as, how much
ὁ art. nom. masc. sg. ὁ ἡ τό the, this, that, he, she, it
Θεὸς n. nom. masc. sg. θεός God, god
μετ' prep. μετά (+gen) with, among, against, (+acc) after
αὐτῶν pron. gen. masc. 3p. pl. αὐτός ή ό self, of oneself, even, very, the same, he, she, it
καὶ conj. καί and, even, also, but
ὅτι conj. ὅτι that, for, because, how that, how, because that, for that, though
τοῖς art. dat. neut. pl. ὁ ἡ τό the, this, that, he, she, it
ἔθνεσιν n. dat. neut. pl. ἔθνος Gentile, nation, heathen, people
θύραν n. acc. fem. sg. θύρα door, gate
πίστεως n. gen. fem. sg. πίστις faith, assurance, belief, fidelity
28 δὲ conj. δέ but, and, now, also, to the contrary, rather, then
ἐκεῖ adv. ἐκεῖ there, thither, thitherward, yonder, yonder place
χρόνον n. acc. masc. sg. χρόνος time, season, space
οὐκ particle of negation. οὐ οὐκ οὐχ not, no, neither, none, nay, nor, never, nothing
ὀλίγον adj. acc. masc. sg. ὀλίγος few, little, small, a while, brief, short, short space
σὺν prep. σύν (+dat) with, beside
τοῖς art. dat. masc. pl. ὁ ἡ τό the, this, that, he, she, it
μαθηταῖς n. dat. masc. pl. μαθητής disciple

15

1 Καί conj. καί and, even, also, but
τινες indefinite pron. nom. masc. pl. τὶς certain, some, any man, one, any thing
ἀπὸ prep. ἀπό (+gen) from, of, out of, since, for, off, at, by, in, on
τῆς art. gen. fem. sg. ὁ ἡ τό the, this, that, he, she, it
Ἰουδαίας n. gen. fem. sg. Ἰουδαία Judaea, Jewry
τοὺς art. acc. masc. pl. ὁ ἡ τό the, this, that, he, she, it
ἀδελφοὺς n. acc. masc. pl. ἀδελφός brother
ὅτι conj. ὅτι that, for, because, how that, how, because that, for that, though
Ἐὰν conj. ἐάν if, soever, except, though, and if, but, whether, if so, so
μὴ particle of negation. μή not, no, lest, neither, none, nothing, nor, never, without
τῷ art. dat. neut. sg. ὁ ἡ τό the, this, that, he, she, it
ἔθει n. dat. neut. sg. ἔθος custom, manner, be wont
Μωϋσέως n. gen. masc. sg. Μωϋσεύς Moses
οὐ particle of negation. οὐ οὐκ οὐχ not, no, neither, none, nay, nor, never, nothing

2 οὖν conj. οὖν therefore, then, so, and, now, wherefore
στάσεως n. gen. fem. sg. στάσις dissension, sedition, insurrection, standing, uproar
καὶ conj. καί and, even, also, but
συζητήσεως n. gen. fem. sg. συζήτησις disputation, disputing, reasoning
οὐκ particle of negation. οὐ οὐκ οὐχ not, no, neither, none, nay, nor, never, nothing
ὀλίγης adj. gen. fem. sg. ὀλίγος few, little, small, a while, brief, short, short space
τῷ art. dat. masc. sg. ὁ ἡ τό the, this, that, he, she, it
Παύλῳ n. dat. masc. sg. Παῦλος Paul, Paulus
καὶ conj. καί and, even, also, but
τῷ art. dat. masc. sg. ὁ ἡ τό the, this, that, he, she, it
Βαρναβᾷ n. dat. masc. sg. Βαρναβᾶς Barnabas
πρὸς prep. πρός (+gen) for, (+dat) at, (+acc) unto, to, with, for, against
αὐτούς pron. acc. masc. 3p. pl. αὐτός ή ό self, of oneself, even, very, the same, he, she, it
Παῦλον n. acc. masc. sg. Παῦλος Paul, Paulus
καὶ conj. καί and, even, also, but
Βαρναβᾶν n. acc. masc. sg. Βαρναβᾶς Barnabas
καὶ conj. καί and, even, also, but
τινας indefinite pron. acc. masc. pl. τὶς certain, some, any man, one, any thing
ἄλλους adj. acc. masc. pl. ἄλλος other, another, some, one, more, otherwise
ἐξ prep. ἐκ ἐξ (+gen) of, from, out of, by, on, with, in, among, through
αὐτῶν pron. gen. masc. 3p. pl. αὐτός ή ό self, of oneself, even, very, the same, he, she, it
πρὸς prep. πρός (+gen) for, (+dat) at, (+acc) unto, to, with, for, against
τοὺς art. acc. masc. pl. ὁ ἡ τό the, this, that, he, she, it
ἀποστόλους n. acc. masc. pl. ἀπόστολος apostle, messenger, he that is sent
πρὸς prep. πρός (+gen) for, (+dat) at, (+acc) unto, to, with, for, against
πρεσβυτέρους adj. acc. masc. pl. πρεσβύτερος elder, elder woman, eldest, old man
εἰς prep. εἰς (+acc) into, to, unto, for, in, on, toward, against, upon, at, among
Ἰερουσαλήμ pron. name. fem. inde. Ἰερουσαλήμ Jerusalem
περὶ prep. περί (+gen) of, for, concerning, (+acc) about, concerning, in
τοῦ art. gen. neut. sg. ὁ ἡ τό the, this, that, he, she, it
ζητήματος n. gen. neut. sg. ζήτημα question
τούτου demo. pron. gen. neut. sg. οὗτος αὕτη τοῦτο this, the same, this same, he, she, it
3 οἱ art. nom. masc. pl. ὁ ἡ τό the, this, that, he, she, it
μέν conj. μέν indeed, verily, truly, even, so, some
οὖν conj. οὖν therefore, then, so, and, now, wherefore
ὑπὸ prep. ὑπό (+gen) of, by, with, from, among, (+acc) under
τῆς art. gen. fem. sg. ὁ ἡ τό the, this, that, he, she, it
ἐκκλησίας n. gen. fem. sg. ἐκκλησία church, assembly
τήν art. acc. fem. sg. ὁ ἡ τό the, this, that, he, she, it
Φοινίκην n. acc. fem. sg. Φοινίκη Phenice, Phenicia
καὶ conj. καί and, even, also, but
Σαμάρειαν n. acc. fem. sg. Σαμάρεια Samaria
τήν art. acc. fem. sg. ὁ ἡ τό the, this, that, he, she, it
ἐπιστροφὴν n. acc. fem. sg. ἐπιστροφή conversion
τῶν art. gen. neut. pl. ὁ ἡ τό the, this, that, he, she, it
ἐθνῶν n. gen. neut. pl. ἔθνος Gentile, nation, heathen, people
καὶ conj. καί and, even, also, but
χαρὰν n. acc. fem. sg. χαρά joy, gladness, joyfulness
μεγάλην adj. acc. fem. sg. μέγας great, loud, greatest, high, large, mighty, strong
πᾶσι adj. dat. masc. pl. πᾶς πᾶσα πᾶν all, every, whosoever, every one, no, whole, any
τοῖς art. dat. masc. pl. ὁ ἡ τό the, this, that, he, she, it
ἀδελφοῖς n. dat. masc. pl. ἀδελφός brother
4 δὲ conj. δέ but, and, now, also, to the contrary, rather, then
εἰς prep. εἰς (+acc) into, to, unto, for, in, on, toward, against, upon, at, among
Ἰερουσαλήμ pron. name. fem. inde. Ἰερουσαλήμ Jerusalem

ὑπὸ prep. ὑπό (+gen) of, by, with, from, among, (+acc) under
τῆς art. gen. fem. sg. ὁ ἡ τό the, this, that, he, she, it
ἐκκλησίας n. gen. fem. sg. ἐκκλησία church, assembly
καὶ conj. καί and, even, also, but
τῶν art. gen. masc. pl. ὁ ἡ τό the, this, that, he, she, it
ἀποστόλων n. gen. masc. pl. ἀπόστολος apostle, messenger, he that is sent
καὶ conj. καί and, even, also, but
τῶν art. gen. masc. pl. ὁ ἡ τό the, this, that, he, she, it
πρεσβυτέρων adj. gen. masc. pl. πρεσβύτερος elder, elder woman, eldest, old man
τε conj. τέ and, both, also
ὅσα relative pron. acc. neut. pl. ὅσος as many as, whatsoever, that, as long as, how much
ὁ art. nom. masc. sg. ὁ ἡ τό the, this, that, he, she, it
Θεὸς n. nom. masc. sg. θεός God, god
μετ' prep. μετά (+gen) with, among, against, (+acc) after
αὐτῶν pron. gen. masc. 3p. pl. αὐτός ἡ ὁ self, of oneself, even, very, the same, he, she, it
5 δὲ conj. δέ but, and, now, also, to the contrary, rather, then
τινες indefinite pron. nom. masc. pl. τὶς certain, some, any man, one, any thing
τῶν art. gen. masc. pl. ὁ ἡ τό the, this, that, he, she, it
ἀπὸ prep. ἀπό (+gen) from, of, out of, since, for, off, at, by, in, on
τῆς art. gen. fem. sg. ὁ ἡ τό the, this, that, he, she, it
αἱρέσεως n. gen. fem. sg. αἵρεσις sect, heresy
τῶν art. gen. masc. pl. ὁ ἡ τό the, this, that, he, she, it
Φαρισαίων n. gen. masc. pl. Φαρισαῖος Pharisee
ὅτι conj. ὅτι that, for, because, how that, how, because that, for that, though
αὐτοὺς pron. acc. masc. 3p. pl. αὐτός ἡ ὁ self, of oneself, even, very, the same, he, she, it
τε conj. τέ and, both, also
τὸν art. acc. masc. sg. ὁ ἡ τό the, this, that, he, she, it
νόμον n. acc. masc. sg. νόμος law, the law
Μωϋσέως n. gen. masc. sg. Μωϋσεύς Moses
6 δὲ conj. δέ but, and, now, also, to the contrary, rather, then
οἱ art. nom. masc. pl. ὁ ἡ τό the, this, that, he, she, it
ἀπόστολοι n. nom. masc. pl. ἀπόστολος apostle, messenger, he that is sent
καὶ conj. καί and, even, also, but
οἱ art. nom. masc. pl. ὁ ἡ τό the, this, that, he, she, it
πρεσβύτεροι adj. nom. masc. pl. πρεσβύτερος elder, elder woman, eldest, old man
περὶ prep. περί (+gen) of, for, concerning, (+acc) about, concerning, in
τοῦ art. gen. masc. sg. ὁ ἡ τό the, this, that, he, she, it
λόγου n. gen. masc. sg. λόγος word, saying, account, speech, thing, matter
τούτου demo. pron. gen. masc. sg. οὗτος αὕτη τοῦτο this, the same, this same, he, she, it
7 πολλῆς adj. gen. fem. sg. πολύς many, great, much, long, abundant
δὲ conj. δέ but, and, now, also, to the contrary, rather, then
συζητήσεως n. gen. fem. sg. συζήτησις disputation, disputing, reasoning
Πέτρος n. nom. masc. sg. Πέτρος Peter
πρὸς prep. πρός (+gen) for, (+dat) at, (+acc) unto, to, with, for, against
αὐτούς pron. acc. masc. 3p. pl. αὐτός ἡ ὁ self, of oneself, even, very, the same, he, she, it
Ἄνδρες n. voc. masc. pl. ἀνήρ man, husband, sir
ἀδελφοί n. voc. masc. pl. ἀδελφός brother
ὑμεῖς pron. nom. 2p. pl. σύ thou, you
ὅτι conj. ὅτι that, for, because, how that, how, because that, for that, though
ἀφ' prep. ἀπό (+gen) from, of, out of, since, for, off, at, by, in, on
ἡμερῶν n. gen. fem. pl. ἡμέρα day, time, year, while, age, day time
ἀρχαίων adj. gen. fem. pl. ἀρχαῖος old, one of old time
ὁ art. nom. masc. sg. ὁ ἡ τό the, this, that, he, she, it
Θεὸς n. nom. masc. sg. θεός God, god
ἐν prep. ἐν (+dat) in, by, with, among, at, on, through, to, within, into, of, for

ὑμῖν pron. dat. 2p. pl. σύ thou, you
διὰ prep. διά (+gen) by, through, with, in, of, (+acc) for, because of, for a cause
τοῦ art. gen. neut. sg. ὁ ἡ τό the, this, that, he, she, it
στόματός n. gen. neut. sg. στόμα mouth, face, edge
μου pron. gen. 1p. sg. ἐγώ I
τὰ art. acc. neut. pl. ὁ ἡ τό the, this, that, he, she, it
ἔθνη n. acc. neut. pl. ἔθνος Gentile, nation, heathen, people
τὸν art. acc. masc. sg. ὁ ἡ τό the, this, that, he, she, it
λόγον n. acc. masc. sg. λόγος word, saying, account, speech, thing, matter
τοῦ art. gen. neut. sg. ὁ ἡ τό the, this, that, he, she, it
εὐαγγελίου n. gen. neut. sg. εὐαγγέλιον gospel
καὶ conj. καί and, even, also, but
8 καὶ conj. καί and, even, also, but
ὁ art. nom. masc. sg. ὁ ἡ τό the, this, that, he, she, it
καρδιογνώστης n. nom. masc. sg. καρδιογνώστης one which knowest the hearts
Θεὸς n. nom. masc. sg. θεός God, god
αὐτοῖς pron. dat. masc. 3p. pl. αὐτός ή ό self, of oneself, even, very, the same, he, she, it
αὐτοῖς pron. dat. masc. 3p. pl. αὐτός ή ό self, of oneself, even, very, the same, he, she, it
τὸ art. acc. neut. sg. ὁ ἡ τό the, this, that, he, she, it
Πνεῦμα n. acc. neut. sg. πνεῦμα spirit, Spirit, Ghost, ghost, life. of the spirit, wind
τὸ art. acc. neut. sg. ὁ ἡ τό the, this, that, he, she, it
Ἅγιον adj. acc. neut. sg. ἅγιος Holy, holy, saint, Holy One, holy thing, most holy
καθὼς adv. καθώς as, even as, according as, according to
καὶ conj. καί and, even, also, but
ἡμῖν pron. dat. 1p. pl. ἐγώ I
9 καὶ conj. καί and, even, also, but
οὐδὲν adj. acc. neut. sg. οὐδείς no man, nothing, no, none, neither, not, nought
μεταξὺ adv. μεταξύ between
ἡμῶν pron. gen. 1p. pl. ἐγώ I
τε conj. τέ and, both, also
καὶ conj. καί and, even, also, but
αὐτῶν pron. gen. masc. 3p. pl. αὐτός ή ό self, of oneself, even, very, the same, he, she, it
τῇ art. dat. fem. sg. ὁ ἡ τό the, this, that, he, she, it
πίστει n. dat. fem. sg. πίστις faith, assurance, belief, fidelity
τὰς art. acc. fem. pl. ὁ ἡ τό the, this, that, he, she, it
καρδίας n. acc. fem. pl. καρδία heart
αὐτῶν pron. gen. masc. 3p. pl. αὐτός ή ό self, of oneself, even, very, the same, he, she, it
10 νῦν adv. νῦν now, henceforth, present, this time
οὖν conj. οὖν therefore, then, so, and, now, wherefore
τί interrog. pron. acc. neut. sg. τίς what, who, why, where, which, how
τὸν art. acc. masc. sg. ὁ ἡ τό the, this, that, he, she, it
Θεὸν n. acc. masc. sg. θεός God, god
ζυγὸν n. acc. masc. sg. ζυγός yoke, pair of balances
ἐπὶ prep. ἐπί (+gen) on, in, upon, (+dat) in, at, for, upon, (+acc) on, upon, unto, to, against
τὸν art. acc. masc. sg. ὁ ἡ τό the, this, that, he, she, it
τράχηλον n. acc. masc. sg. τράχηλος neck
τῶν art. gen. masc. pl. ὁ ἡ τό the, this, that, he, she, it
μαθητῶν n. gen. masc. pl. μαθητής disciple
ὃν relative pron. acc. masc. sg. ὅς ἥ ὅ who, which, what, that
οὔτε conj. οὔτε neither, nor, nor yet, no, none
οἱ art. nom. masc. pl. ὁ ἡ τό the, this, that, he, she, it
πατέρες n. nom. masc. pl. πατήρ Father, father, parent
ἡμῶν pron. gen. 1p. pl. ἐγώ I
οὔτε conj. οὔτε neither, nor, nor yet, no, none
ἡμεῖς pron. nom. 1p. pl. ἐγώ I

11 ἀλλὰ conj. ἀλλά but, yea, yet, nevertheless, howbeit, nay, therefore
διὰ prep. διά (+gen) by, through, with, in, of, (+acc) for, because of, for a cause
τῆς art. gen. fem. sg. ὁ ἡ τό the, this, that, he, she, it
χάριτος n. gen. fem. sg. χάρις grace, thank, favour, pleasure
Κυρίου n. gen. masc. sg. κύριος Lord, lord, master, sir, LORD, God, Master, owner
Ἰησοῦ n. gen. masc. sg. Ἰησοῦς Jesus
Χριστοῦ n. gen. masc. sg. Χριστός Christ
καθ' prep. κατά (+gen) against, by, throughout, down, (+acc) according to, after, with
ὃν relative pron. acc. masc. sg. ὅς ἥ ὅ who, which, what, that
τρόπον n. acc. masc. sg. τρόπος as, manner, means, way, conversation
κἀκεῖνοι demo. pron. nom. masc. pl. κἀκεῖνος and he, he also, and the other, even he
12 δὲ conj. δέ but, and, now, also, to the contrary, rather, then
πᾶν adj. nom. neut. sg. πᾶς πᾶσα πᾶν all, every, whosoever, every one, no, whole, any
τὸ art. nom. neut. sg. ὁ ἡ τό the, this, that, he, she, it
πλῆθος n. nom. neut. sg. πλῆθος multitude, bundle, company
καὶ conj. καί and, even, also, but
Βαρναβᾶ n. gen. masc. sg. Βαρναβᾶς Barnabas
καὶ conj. καί and, even, also, but
Παύλου n. gen. masc. sg. Παῦλος Paul, Paulus
ὅσα relative pron. acc. neut. pl. ὅσος as many as, whatsoever, that, as long as, how much
ὁ art. nom. masc. sg. ὁ ἡ τό the, this, that, he, she, it
Θεὸς n. nom. masc. sg. θεός God, god
σημεῖα n. acc. neut. pl. σημεῖον sign, miracle, wonder, token
καὶ conj. καί and, even, also, but
τέρατα n. acc. neut. pl. τέρας wonder
ἐν prep. ἐν (+dat) in, by, with, among, at, on, through, to, within, into, of, for
τοῖς art. dat. neut. pl. ὁ ἡ τό the, this, that, he, she, it
ἔθνεσιν n. dat. neut. pl. ἔθνος Gentile, nation, heathen, people
δι' prep. διά (+gen) by, through, with, in, of, (+acc) for, because of, for a cause
αὐτῶν pron. gen. masc. 3p. pl. αὐτός ή ό self, of oneself, even, very, the same, he, she, it
13 μετὰ prep. μετά (+gen) with, among, against, (+acc) after
δὲ conj. δέ but, and, now, also, to the contrary, rather, then
τὸ art. acc. neut. sg. ὁ ἡ τό the, this, that, he, she, it
αὐτοὺς pron. acc. masc. 3p. pl. αὐτός ή ό self, of oneself, even, very, the same, he, she, it
Ἰάκωβος n. nom. masc. sg. Ἰάκωβος James
Ἄνδρες n. voc. masc. pl. ἀνήρ man, husband, sir
ἀδελφοί n. voc. masc. pl. ἀδελφός brother
μου pron. gen. 1p. sg. ἐγώ I
14 Συμεὼν n. nom. masc. sg. Συμεών Simeon, Simon
καθὼς adv. καθώς as, even as, according as, according to
πρῶτον ordinal. adj. acc. neut. sg. πρῶτος first, chief, first of all, chiefest, best
ὁ art. nom. masc. sg. ὁ ἡ τό the, this, that, he, she, it
Θὸς n. nom. masc. sg. θεός God, god
ἐξ prep. ἐκ ἐξ (+gen) of, from, out of, by, on, with, in, among, through
ἐθνῶν n. gen. neut. pl. ἔθνος Gentile, nation, heathen, people
λαὸν n. acc. masc. sg. λαός people
ἐπὶ prep. ἐπί (+gen) on, in, upon, (+dat) in, at, for, upon, (+acc) on, upon, unto, to, against
τῷ art. dat. neut. sg. ὁ ἡ τό the, this, that, he, she, it
ὀνόματι n. dat. neut. sg. ὄνομα name, call, surname
αὐτοῦ pron. gen. masc. 3p. sg. αὐτός ή ό self, of oneself, even, very, the same, he, she, it
15 καὶ conj. καί and, even, also, but
τούτῳ demo. pron. dat. neut. sg. οὗτος αὕτη τοῦτο this, the same, this same, he, she, it
οἱ art. nom. masc. pl. ὁ ἡ τό the, this, that, he, she, it
λόγοι n. nom. masc. pl. λόγος word, saying, account, speech, thing, matter
τῶν art. gen. masc. pl. ὁ ἡ τό the, this, that, he, she, it

προφητῶν n. gen. masc. pl. προφήτης prophet
καθὼς adv. καθώς as, even as, according as, according to
16 Μετὰ prep. μετά (+gen) with, among, against, (+acc) after
ταῦτα demo. pron. acc. neut. pl. οὗτος αὕτη τοῦτο this, the same, this same, he, she, it
καὶ conj. καί and, even, also, but
τὴν art. acc. fem. sg. ὁ ἡ τό the, this, that, he, she, it
σκηνὴν n. acc. fem. sg. σκηνή tabernacle, habitation
Δαβὶδ n. gen. masc. sg. Δαβίδ David
τὴν art. acc. fem. sg. ὁ ἡ τό the, this, that, he, she, it
καὶ conj. καί and, even, also, but
τὰ art. acc. neut. pl. ὁ ἡ τό the, this, that, he, she, it
αὐτῆς pron. gen. fem. 3p. sg. αὐτός ή ό self, of oneself, even, very, the same, he, she, it
καὶ conj. καί and, even, also, but
αὐτήν pron. acc. fem. 3p. sg. αὐτός ή ό self, of oneself, even, very, the same, he, she, it
17 ὅπως adv. ὅπως that, how, to, because, so that, when
ἂν particle. ἄν Indicating contingency. No English translation.
οἱ art. nom. masc. pl. ὁ ἡ τό the, this, that, he, she, it
κατάλοιποι adj. nom. masc. pl. κατάλοιπος residue
τῶν art. gen. masc. pl. ὁ ἡ τό the, this, that, he, she, it
ἀνθρώπων n. gen. masc. pl. ἄνθρωπος man, human being, person, one, certain
τὸν art. acc. masc. sg. ὁ ἡ τό the, this, that, he, she, it
Κύριον n. acc. masc. sg. κύριος Lord, lord, master, sir, LORD, God, Master, owner
καὶ conj. καί and, even, also, but
πάντα adj. nom. neut. pl. πᾶς πᾶσα πᾶν all, every, whosoever, every one, no, whole, any
τὰ art. nom. neut. pl. ὁ ἡ τό the, this, that, he, she, it
ἔθνη n. nom. neut. pl. ἔθνος Gentile, nation, heathen, people
ἐφ' prep. ἐπί (+gen) on, in, upon, (+dat) in, at, for, upon, (+acc) on, upon, unto, to, against
οὓς relative pron. acc. masc. pl. ὅς ἥ ὅ who, which, what, that
τὸ art. nom. neut. sg. ὁ ἡ τό the, this, that, he, she, it
ὄνομά n. nom. neut. sg. ὄνομα name, call, surname
μου pron. gen. 1p. sg. ἐγώ I
ἐπ' prep. ἐπί (+gen) on, in, upon, (+dat) in, at, for, upon, (+acc) on, upon, unto, to, against
αὐτούς pron. acc. masc. 3p. pl. αὐτός ή ό self, of oneself, even, very, the same, he, she, it
Κύριος n. nom. masc. sg. κύριος Lord, lord, master, sir, LORD, God, Master, owner
ὁ art. nom. masc. sg. ὁ ἡ τό the, this, that, he, she, it
ταῦτα demo. pron. acc. neut. pl. οὗτος αὕτη τοῦτο this, the same, this same, he, she, it
πάντα adj. acc. neut. pl. πᾶς πᾶσα πᾶν all, every, whosoever, every one, no, whole, any
18 γνωστὰ adj. acc. neut. pl. γνωστός acquaintance, known, notable
ἀπ' prep. ἀπό (+gen) from, of, out of, since, for, off, at, by, in, on
αἰῶνος n. gen. masc. sg. αἰών ever, ever and ever, evermore, age, eternal, world
τῷ art. dat. masc. sg. ὁ ἡ τό the, this, that, he, she, it
Θεῷ n. dat. masc. sg. θεός God, god
πάντα adj. nom. neut. pl. πᾶς πᾶσα πᾶν all, every, whosoever, every one, no, whole, any
τὰ art. nom. neut. pl. ὁ ἡ τό the, this, that, he, she, it
ἔργα n. nom. neut. pl. ἔργον work, deed, doing labour
αὐτοῦ pron. gen. masc. 3p. sg. αὐτός ή ό self, of oneself, even, very, the same, he, she, it
19 διὸ conj. διό wherefore, therefore, for which cause
ἐγὼ pron. nom. 1p. sg. ἐγώ I
μὴ particle of negation. μή not, no, lest, neither, none, nothing, nor, never, without
τοῖς art. dat. masc. pl. ὁ ἡ τό the, this, that, he, she, it
ἀπὸ prep. ἀπό (+gen) from, of, out of, since, for, off, at, by, in, on
τῶν art. gen. neut. pl. ὁ ἡ τό the, this, that, he, she, it
ἐθνῶν n. gen. neut. pl. ἔθνος Gentile, nation, heathen, people
ἐπὶ prep. ἐπί (+gen) on, in, upon, (+dat) in, at, for, upon, (+acc) on, upon, unto, to, against
τὸν art. acc. masc. sg. ὁ ἡ τό the, this, that, he, she, it

Θεόν n. acc. masc. sg. θεός God, god
20 ἀλλὰ conj. ἀλλά but, yea, yet, nevertheless, howbeit, nay, therefore
αὐτοῖς pron. dat. masc. 3p. pl. αὐτός ή ό self, of oneself, even, very, the same, he, she, it
τοῦ art. gen. neut. sg. ὁ ἡ τό the, this, that, he, she, it
ἀπὸ prep. ἀπό (+gen) from, of, out of, since, for, off, at, by, in, on
τῶν art. gen. neut. pl. ὁ ἡ τό the, this, that, he, she, it
ἀλισγημάτων n. gen. neut. pl. ἀλίσγημα pollution
τῶν art. gen. neut. pl. ὁ ἡ τό the, this, that, he, she, it
εἰδώλων n. gen. neut. pl. εἴδωλον idol
καὶ conj. καί and, even, also, but
τῆς art. gen. fem. sg. ὁ ἡ τό the, this, that, he, she, it
πορνείας n. gen. fem. sg. πορνεία fornication
καὶ conj. καί and, even, also, but
τοῦ art. gen. neut. sg. ὁ ἡ τό the, this, that, he, she, it
πνικτοῦ adj. gen. neut. sg. πνικτός strangled
καὶ conj. καί and, even, also, but
τοῦ art. gen. neut. sg. ὁ ἡ τό the, this, that, he, she, it
αἵματος n. gen. neut. sg. αἷμα blood
21 Μωσῆς n. nom. masc. sg. Μωσῆς Moses
γὰρ conj. γάρ for, and, because, but, indeed
ἐκ prep. ἐκ ἐξ (+gen) of, from, out of, by, on, with, in, among, through
γενεῶν n. gen. fem. pl. γενεά generation, age, time, nation
ἀρχαίων adj. gen. fem. pl. ἀρχαῖος old, one of old time
κατὰ prep. κατά (+gen) against, by, throughout, down, (+acc) according to, after, with
πόλιν n. acc. fem. sg. πόλις city
τοὺς art. acc. masc. pl. ὁ ἡ τό the, this, that, he, she, it
αὐτὸν pron. acc. masc. 3p. sg. αὐτός ή ό self, of oneself, even, very, the same, he, she, it
ἐν prep. ἐν (+dat) in, by, with, among, at, on, through, to, within, into, of, for
ταῖς art. dat. fem. pl. ὁ ἡ τό the, this, that, he, she, it
συναγωγαῖς n. dat. fem. pl. συναγωγή synagogue, assembly, congregation
κατὰ prep. κατά (+gen) against, by, throughout, down, (+acc) according to, after, with
πᾶν adj. acc. neut. sg. πᾶς πᾶσα πᾶν all, every, whosoever, every one, no, whole, any
σάββατον n. acc. neut. sg. σάββατον sabbath day, sabbath, week
22 Τότε adv. τότε then, that time
τοῖς art. dat. masc. pl. ὁ ἡ τό the, this, that, he, she, it
ἀποστόλοις n. dat. masc. pl. ἀπόστολος apostle, messenger, he that is sent
καὶ conj. καί and, even, also, but
τοῖς art. dat. masc. pl. ὁ ἡ τό the, this, that, he, she, it
πρεσβυτέροις adj. dat. masc. pl. πρεσβύτερος elder, elder woman, eldest, old man
σὺν prep. σύν (+dat) with, beside
ὅλῃ adj. dat. fem. sg. ὅλος all, whole, every whit, altogether
τῇ art. dat. fem. sg. ὁ ἡ τό the, this, that, he, she, it
ἐκκλησίᾳ n. dat. fem. sg. ἐκκλησία church, assembly
ἄνδρας n. acc. masc. pl. ἀνήρ man, husband, sir
ἐξ prep. ἐκ ἐξ (+gen) of, from, out of, by, on, with, in, among, through
αὐτῶν pron. gen. masc. 3p. pl. αὐτός ή ό self, of oneself, even, very, the same, he, she, it
εἰς prep. εἰς (+acc) into, to, unto, for, in, on, toward, against, upon, at, among
'Αντιόχειαν n. acc. fem. sg. 'Αντιόχεια Antioch
σὺν prep. σύν (+dat) with, beside
τῷ art. dat. masc. sg. ὁ ἡ τό the, this, that, he, she, it
Παύλῳ n. dat. masc. sg. Παῦλος Paul, Paulus
καὶ conj. καί and, even, also, but
Βαρναβᾷ n. dat. masc. sg. Βαρναβᾶς Barnabas
'Ιούδαν n. acc. masc. sg. 'Ιούδας Judas, Juda, Judah, Jude
τὸν art. acc. masc. sg. ὁ ἡ τό the, this, that, he, she, it

Βαρσαβᾶν n. acc. masc. sg. Βαρσαβᾶς Barsabas
καὶ conj. καί and, even, also, but
Σιλᾶν n. acc. masc. sg. Σιλᾶς Silas
ἄνδρας n. acc. masc. pl. ἀνήρ man, husband, sir
ἐν prep. ἐν (+dat) in, by, with, among, at, on, through, to, within, into, of, for
τοῖς art. dat. masc. pl. ὁ ἡ τό the, this, that, he, she, it
ἀδελφοῖς n. dat. masc. pl. ἀδελφός brother
23 διὰ prep. διά (+gen) by, through, with, in, of, (+acc) for, because of, for a cause
χειρὸς n. gen. fem. sg. χείρ hand
αὐτῶν pron. gen. masc. 3p. pl. αὐτός ή ό self, of oneself, even, very, the same, he, she, it
τάδε demo. pron. acc. neut. pl. ὅδε ἥδε τόδε this, he, she, such, thus
Οἱ art. nom. masc. pl. ὁ ἡ τό the, this, that, he, she, it
ἀπόστολοι n. nom. masc. pl. ἀπόστολος apostle, messenger, he that is sent
καὶ conj. καί and, even, also, but
οἱ art. nom. masc. pl. ὁ ἡ τό the, this, that, he, she, it
πρεσβύτεροι compar. adj. nom. masc. pl. πρεσβύτερος elder, elder woman, eldest, old man
καὶ conj. καί and, even, also, but
οἱ art. nom. masc. pl. ὁ ἡ τό the, this, that, he, she, it
ἀδελφοὶ n. nom. masc. pl. ἀδελφός brother
τοῖς art. dat. masc. pl. ὁ ἡ τό the, this, that, he, she, it
κατὰ prep. κατά (+gen) against, by, throughout, down, (+acc) according to, after, with
τὴν art. acc. fem. sg. ὁ ἡ τό the, this, that, he, she, it
Ἀντιόχειαν n. acc. fem. sg. Ἀντιόχεια Antioch
καὶ conj. καί and, even, also, but
Συρίαν n. acc. fem. sg. Συρία Syria
καὶ conj. καί and, even, also, but
Κιλικίαν n. acc. fem. sg. Κιλικία Cilicia
ἀδελφοῖς n. dat. masc. pl. ἀδελφός brother
τοῖς art. dat. masc. pl. ὁ ἡ τό the, this, that, he, she, it
ἐξ prep. ἐκ ἐξ (+gen) of, from, out of, by, on, with, in, among, through
ἐθνῶν n. gen. neut. pl. ἔθνος Gentile, nation, heathen, people
24 ἐπειδὴ conj. ἐπειδή because, for, after that, for that, for as much as, since
ὅτι conj. ὅτι that, for, because, how that, how, because that, for that, though
τινὲς indefinite pron. nom. masc. pl. τὶς certain, some, any man, one, any thing
ἐξ prep. ἐκ ἐξ (+gen) of, from, out of, by, on, with, in, among, through
ἡμῶν pron. gen. 1p. pl. ἐγώ I
ὑμᾶς pron. acc. 2p. pl. σύ thou, you
λόγοις n. dat. masc. pl. λόγος word, saying, account, speech, thing, matter
τὰς art. acc. fem. pl. ὁ ἡ τό the, this, that, he, she, it
ψυχὰς n. acc. fem. pl. ψυχή life, soul, mind, heart
ὑμῶν pron. gen. 2p. pl. σύ thou, you
καὶ conj. καί and, even, also, but
τὸν art. acc. masc. sg. ὁ ἡ τό the, this, that, he, she, it
νόμον n. acc. masc. sg. νόμος law, the law
οἷς relative pron. dat. masc. pl. ὅς ἥ ὅ who, which, what, that
οὐ particle of negation. οὐ οὐκ οὐχ not, no, neither, none, nay, nor, never, nothing
25 ἡμῖν pron. dat. 1p. pl. ἐγώ I
ὁμοθυμαδὸν adv. ὁμοθυμαδόν with one accord, with one mind
ἄνδρας n. acc. masc. pl. ἀνήρ man, husband, sir
πρὸς prep. πρός (+gen) for, (+dat) at, (+acc) unto, to, with, for, against
ὑμᾶς pron. acc. 2p. pl. σύ thou, you
σὺν prep. σύν (+dat) with, beside
τοῖς art. dat. masc. pl. ὁ ἡ τό the, this, that, he, she, it
ἀγαπητοῖς adj. dat. masc. pl. ἀγαπητός beloved, dearly beloved, dear, wellbeloved
ἡμῶν pron. gen. 1p. pl. ἐγώ I

Βαρναβᾷ n. dat. masc. sg. Βαρναβᾶς Barnabas
καὶ conj. καί and, even, also, but
Παύλῳ n. dat. masc. sg. Παῦλος Paul, Paulus
26 ἀνθρώποις n. dat. masc. pl. ἄνθρωπος man, human being, person, one, certain
τὰς art. acc. fem. pl. ὁ ἡ τό the, this, that, he, she, it
ψυχὰς n. acc. fem. pl. ψυχή life, soul, mind, heart
αὐτῶν pron. gen. masc. 3p. pl. αὐτός ή ό self, of oneself, even, very, the same, he, she, it
ὑπὲρ prep. ὑπέρ (+gen) for, of, for the sake of, (+acc) above, more than
τοῦ art. gen. neut. sg. ὁ ἡ τό the, this, that, he, she, it
ὀνόματος n. gen. neut. sg. ὄνομα name, call, surname
τοῦ art. gen. masc. sg. ὁ ἡ τό the, this, that, he, she, it
Κυρίου n. gen. masc. sg. κύριος Lord, lord, master, sir, LORD, God, Master, owner
ἡμῶν pron. gen. 1p. pl. ἐγώ I
Ἰησοῦ n. gen. masc. sg. Ἰησοῦς Jesus
Χριστοῦ n. gen. masc. sg. Χριστός Christ
27 οὖν conj. οὖν therefore, then, so, and, now, wherefore
Ἰούδαν n. acc. masc. sg. Ἰούδας Judas, Juda, Judah, Jude
καὶ conj. καί and, even, also, but
Σιλᾶν n. acc. masc. sg. Σιλᾶς Silas
καὶ conj. καί and, even, also, but
αὐτοὺς pron. acc. masc. 3p. pl. αὐτός ή ό self, of oneself, even, very, the same, he, she, it
διὰ prep. διά (+gen) by, through, with, in, of, (+acc) for, because of, for a cause
λόγου n. gen. masc. sg. λόγος word, saying, account, speech, thing, matter
τὰ art. acc. neut. pl. ὁ ἡ τό the, this, that, he, she, it
αὐτά adj. acc. neut. pl. αὐτός ή ό self, of oneself, even, very, the same, he, she, it
28 γὰρ conj. γάρ for, and, because, but, indeed
τῷ art. dat. neut. sg. ὁ ἡ τό the, this, that, he, she, it
Ἁγίῳ adj. dat. neut. sg. ἅγιος Holy, holy, saint, Holy One, holy thing, most holy
Πνεύματι n. dat. neut. sg. πνεῦμα spirit, Spirit, Ghost, ghost, life. of the spirit, wind
καὶ conj. καί and, even, also, but
ἡμῖν pron. dat. 1p. pl. ἐγώ I
μηδὲν num. acc. neut. sg. μηδείς μηδεμία μηδέν no man, nothing, no, none, not at all
πλέον compar. adj. acc. neut. sg. πολύς many, great, much, long, abundant
ὑμῖν pron. dat. 2p. pl. σύ thou, you
βάρος n. acc. neut. sg. βάρος burden, burdensome, weight
πλὴν prep. πλήν but, nevertheless, but rather, notwithstanding, except, than
τῶν art. gen. neut. pl. ὁ ἡ τό the, this, that, he, she, it
ἐπάναγκες adv. ἐπάναγκες necessary
τούτων demo. pron. gen. neut. pl. οὗτος αὕτη τοῦτο this, the same, this same, he, she, it
29 εἰδωλοθύτων adj. gen. neut. pl. εἰδωλόθυτον meat offered to idols
καὶ conj. καί and, even, also, but
αἵματος n. gen. neut. sg. αἷμα blood
καὶ conj. καί and, even, also, but
πνικτοῦ adj. gen. neut. sg. πνικτός strangled
καὶ conj. καί and, even, also, but
πορνείας n. gen. fem. sg. πορνεία fornication
ἐξ prep. ἐκ ἐξ (+gen) of, from, out of, by, on, with, in, among, through
ὧν relative pron. gen. neut. pl. ὅς ἥ ὅ who, which, what, that
ἑαυτοὺς reflexive pron. acc. masc. 3p. pl. ἑαυτοῦ himself, herself, itself, yourself, ourselves
εὖ adv. εὖ well, well done, good
30 Οἱ art. nom. masc. pl. ὁ ἡ τό the, this, that, he, she, it
μέν conj. μέν indeed, verily, truly, even, so, some
οὖν conj. οὖν therefore, then, so, and, now, wherefore
εἰς prep. εἰς (+acc) into, to, unto, for, in, on, toward, against, upon, at, among
Ἀντιόχειαν n. acc. fem. sg. Ἀντιόχεια Antioch

καὶ conj. καί and, even, also, but
τὸ art. acc. neut. sg. ὁ ἡ τό the, this, that, he, she, it
πλῆθος n. acc. neut. sg. πλῆθος multitude, bundle, company
τὴν art. acc. fem. sg. ὁ ἡ τό the, this, that, he, she, it
ἐπιστολήν n. acc. fem. sg. ἐπιστολή letter, epistle
31 δὲ conj. δέ but, and, now, also, to the contrary, rather, then
ἐπὶ prep. ἐπί (+gen) on, in, upon, (+dat) in, at, for, upon, (+acc) on, upon, unto, to, against
τῇ art. dat. fem. sg. ὁ ἡ τό the, this, that, he, she, it
παρακλήσει n. dat. fem. sg. παράκλησις consolation, exhortation, comfort
32 Ἰούδας n. nom. masc. sg. Ἰούδας Judas, Juda, Judah, Jude
δὲ conj. δέ but, and, now, also, to the contrary, rather, then
καὶ conj. καί and, even, also, but
Σιλᾶς n. nom. masc. sg. Σιλᾶς Silas
καὶ conj. καί and, even, also, but
αὐτοὶ pron. nom. masc. 3p. pl. αὐτός ἡ ὁ self, of oneself, even, very, the same, he, she, it
προφῆται n. nom. masc. pl. προφήτης prophet
διὰ prep. διά (+gen) by, through, with, in, of, (+acc) for, because of, for a cause
λόγου n. gen. masc. sg. λόγος word, saying, account, speech, thing, matter
πολλοῦ adj. gen. masc. sg. πολύς many, great, much, long, abundant
τοὺς art. acc. masc. pl. ὁ ἡ τό the, this, that, he, she, it
ἀδελφοὺς n. acc. masc. pl. ἀδελφός brother
καὶ conj. καί and, even, also, but
33 δὲ conj. δέ but, and, now, also, to the contrary, rather, then
χρόνον n. acc. masc. sg. χρόνος time, season, space
μετ' prep. μετά (+gen) with, among, against, (+acc) after
εἰρήνης n. gen. fem. sg. εἰρήνη peace, quietness, rest
ἀπὸ prep. ἀπό (+gen) from, of, out of, since, for, off, at, by, in, on
τῶν art. gen. masc. pl. ὁ ἡ τό the, this, that, he, she, it
ἀδελφῶν n. gen. masc. pl. ἀδελφός brother
πρὸς prep. πρός (+gen) for, (+dat) at, (+acc) unto, to, with, for, against
τοὺς art. acc. masc. pl. ὁ ἡ τό the, this, that, he, she, it
ἀποστόλους n. acc. masc. pl. ἀπόστολος apostle, messenger, he that is sent
34 δὲ conj. δέ but, and, now, also, to the contrary, rather, then
τῷ art. dat. masc. sg. ὁ ἡ τό the, this, that, he, she, it
Σίλᾳ n. dat. masc. sg. Σιλᾶς Silas
αὐτοῦ adv. αὐτοῦ here, there
35 Παῦλος n. nom. masc. sg. Παῦλος Paul, Paulus
δὲ conj. δέ but, and, now, also, to the contrary, rather, then
καὶ conj. καί and, even, also, but
Βαρναβᾶς n. nom. masc. sg. Βαρναβᾶς Barnabas
ἐν prep. ἐν (+dat) in, by, with, among, at, on, through, to, within, into, of, for
Ἀντιοχείᾳ n. dat. fem. sg. Ἀντιόχεια Antioch
καὶ conj. καί and, even, also, but
μετὰ prep. μετά (+gen) with, among, against, (+acc) after
καὶ conj. καί and, even, also, but
ἑτέρων adj. gen. masc. pl. ἕτερος another, other, else, strange
πολλῶν adj. gen. masc. pl. πολύς many, great, much, long, abundant
τὸν art. acc. masc. sg. ὁ ἡ τό the, this, that, he, she, it
λόγον n. acc. masc. sg. λόγος word, saying, account, speech, thing, matter
τοῦ art. gen. masc. sg. ὁ ἡ τό the, this, that, he, she, it
Κυρίου n. gen. masc. sg. κύριος Lord, lord, master, sir, LORD, God, Master, owner
36 Μετὰ prep. μετά (+gen) with, among, against, (+acc) after
δὲ conj. δέ but, and, now, also, to the contrary, rather, then
τινας indefinite pron. acc. fem. pl. τὶς certain, some, any man, one, any thing
ἡμέρας n. acc. fem. pl. ἡμέρα day, time, year, while, age, day time

Παῦλος n. nom. masc. sg. Παῦλος Paul, Paulus
πρὸς prep. πρός (+gen) for, (+dat) at, (+acc) unto, to, with, for, against
Βαρναβᾶν n. acc. masc. sg. Βαρναβᾶς Barnabas
δή particle. δή also, and, doubtless, now, therefore
τοὺς art. acc. masc. pl. ὁ ἡ τό the, this, that, he, she, it
ἀδελφοὺς n. acc. masc. pl. ἀδελφός brother
ἡμῶν pron. gen. 1p. pl. ἐγώ I
κατὰ prep. κατά (+gen) against, by, throughout, down, (+acc) according to, after, with
πᾶσαν adj. acc. fem. sg. πᾶς πᾶσα πᾶν all, every, whosoever, every one, no, whole, any
πόλιν n. acc. fem. sg. πόλις city
ἐν prep. ἐν (+dat) in, by, with, among, at, on, through, to, within, into, of, for
αἷς relative pron. dat. fem. pl. ὅς ἥ ὅ who, which, what, that
τὸν art. acc. masc. sg. ὁ ἡ τό the, this, that, he, she, it
λόγον n. acc. masc. sg. λόγος word, saying, account, speech, thing, matter
τοῦ art. gen. masc. sg. ὁ ἡ τό the, this, that, he, she, it
Κυρίου n. gen. masc. sg. κύριος Lord, lord, master, sir, LORD, God, Master, owner
πῶς adv. πῶς how, by what means, after what manner
37 Βαρναβᾶς n. nom. masc. sg. Βαρναβᾶς Barnabas
δὲ conj. δέ but, and, now, also, to the contrary, rather, then
τὸν art. acc. masc. sg. ὁ ἡ τό the, this, that, he, she, it
Ἰωάννην n. acc. masc. sg. Ἰωάννης John
τὸν art. acc. masc. sg. ὁ ἡ τό the, this, that, he, she, it
Μᾶρκον n. acc. masc. sg. Μᾶρκος Mark, Marcus
38 Παῦλος n. nom. masc. sg. Παῦλος Paul, Paulus
δὲ conj. δέ but, and, now, also, to the contrary, rather, then
τὸν art. acc. masc. sg. ὁ ἡ τό the, this, that, he, she, it
ἀπ' prep. ἀπό (+gen) from, of, out of, since, for, off, at, by, in, on
αὐτῶν pron. gen. masc. 3p. pl. αὐτός ή ό self, of oneself, even, very, the same, he, she, it
ἀπὸ prep. ἀπό (+gen) from, of, out of, since, for, off, at, by, in, on
Παμφυλίας n. gen. fem. sg. Παμφυλία Pamphylia
καὶ conj. καί and, even, also, but
μὴ particle of negation. μή not, no, lest, neither, none, nothing, nor, never, without
αὐτοῖς pron. dat. masc. 3p. pl. αὐτός ή ό self, of oneself, even, very, the same, he, she, it
εἰς prep. εἰς (+acc) into, to, unto, for, in, on, toward, against, upon, at, among
τὸ art. acc. neut. sg. ὁ ἡ τό the, this, that, he, she, it
ἔργον n. acc. neut. sg. ἔργον work, deed, doing labour
μὴ particle of negation. μή not, no, lest, neither, none, nothing, nor, never, without
τοῦτον demo. pron. acc. masc. sg. οὗτος αὕτη τοῦτο this, the same, this same, he, she, it
39 οὖν conj. οὖν therefore, then, so, and, now, wherefore
παροξυσμὸς n. nom. masc. sg. παροξυσμός contention so sharp, to provoke unto
ὥστε conj. ὥστε so that, wherefore, insomuch that, therefore, that, so then
αὐτοὺς pron. acc. masc. 3p. pl. αὐτός ή ό self, of oneself, even, very, the same, he, she, it
ἀπ' prep. ἀπό (+gen) from, of, out of, since, for, off, at, by, in, on
ἀλλήλων pron. gen. masc. pl. ἀλλήλων one another, themselves, together, mutual
τόν art. acc. masc. sg. ὁ ἡ τό the, this, that, he, she, it
τε conj. τέ and, both, also
Βαρναβᾶν n. acc. masc. sg. Βαρναβᾶς Barnabas
τόν art. acc. masc. sg. ὁ ἡ τό the, this, that, he, she, it
Μᾶρκον n. acc. masc. sg. Μᾶρκος Mark, Marcus
εἰς prep. εἰς (+acc) into, to, unto, for, in, on, toward, against, upon, at, among
Κύπρον n. acc. fem. sg. Κύπρος Cyprus
40 Παῦλος n. nom. masc. sg. Παῦλος Paul, Paulus
δὲ conj. δέ but, and, now, also, to the contrary, rather, then
Σιλᾶν n. acc. masc. sg. Σιλᾶς Silas
τῇ art. dat. fem. sg. ὁ ἡ τό the, this, that, he, she, it

χάριτι n. dat. fem. sg. χάρις grace, thank, favour, pleasure
τοῦ art. gen. masc. sg. ὁ ἡ τό the, this, that, he, she, it
Θεοῦ n. gen. masc. sg. θεός God, god
ὑπὸ prep. ὑπό (+gen) of, by, with, from, among, (+acc) under
τῶν art. gen. masc. pl. ὁ ἡ τό the, this, that, he, she, it
ἀδελφῶν n. gen. masc. pl. ἀδελφός brother
41 δὲ conj. δέ but, and, now, also, to the contrary, rather, then
τὴν art. acc. fem. sg. ὁ ἡ τό the, this, that, he, she, it
Συρίαν n. acc. fem. sg. Συρία Syria
καὶ conj. καί and, even, also, but
Κιλικίαν n. acc. fem. sg. Κιλικία Cilicia
τὰς art. acc. fem. pl. ὁ ἡ τό the, this, that, he, she, it
ἐκκλησίας n. acc. fem. pl. ἐκκλησία church, assembly

16

1 δὲ conj. δέ but, and, now, also, to the contrary, rather, then
εἰς prep. εἰς (+acc) into, to, unto, for, in, on, toward, against, upon, at, among
Δέρβην n. acc. fem. sg. Δέρβη Derbe
καὶ conj. καί and, even, also, but
Λύστραν n. acc. fem. sg. Λύστρα Lystra
καὶ conj. καί and, even, also, but
μαθητής n. nom. masc. sg. μαθητής disciple
τις indefinite pron. nom. masc. sg. τὶς certain, some, any man, one, any thing
ἐκεῖ adv. ἐκεῖ there, thither, thitherward, yonder, yonder place
ὀνόματι n. dat. neut. sg. ὄνομα name, call, surname
Τιμόθεος n. nom. masc. sg. Τιμόθεος Timotheus, Timothy
υἱὸς n. nom. masc. sg. υἱός son, child, descendant, offspring, heir
γυναικὸς n. gen. fem. sg. γυνή woman, wife
τινος indefinite pron. gen. fem. sg. τὶς certain, some, any man, one, any thing
Ἰουδαίας adj. gen. fem. sg. Ἰουδαῖος Jew, Jewess
πιστῆς adj. gen. fem. sg. πιστός faithful, believing, true, sure
πατρὸς n. gen. masc. sg. πατήρ Father, father, parent
δὲ conj. δέ but, and, now, also, to the contrary, rather, then
Ἕλληνος n. gen. masc. sg. Ἕλλην Greek, Gentile
2 ὃς relative pron. nom. masc. sg. ὅς ἥ ὅ who, which, what, that
ὑπὸ prep. ὑπό (+gen) of, by, with, from, among, (+acc) under
τῶν art. gen. masc. pl. ὁ ἡ τό the, this, that, he, she, it
ἐν prep. ἐν (+dat) in, by, with, among, at, on, through, to, within, into, of, for
Λύστροις n. dat. neut. pl. Λύστρα Lystra
καὶ conj. καί and, even, also, but
Ἰκονίῳ n. dat. neut. sg. Ἰκόνιον Iconium
ἀδελφῶν n. gen. masc. pl. ἀδελφός brother
3 τοῦτον demo. pron. acc. masc. sg. οὗτος αὕτη τοῦτο this, the same, this same, he, she, it
ὁ art. nom. masc. sg. ὁ ἡ τό the, this, that, he, she, it
Παῦλος n. nom. masc. sg. Παῦλος Paul, Paulus
σὺν prep. σύν (+dat) with, beside
αὐτῷ pron. dat. masc. 3p. sg. αὐτός ή ό self, of oneself, even, very, the same, he, she, it
καὶ conj. καί and, even, also, but
αὐτὸν pron. acc. masc. 3p. sg. αὐτός ή ό self, of oneself, even, very, the same, he, she, it
διὰ prep. διά (+gen) by, through, with, in, of, (+acc) for, because of, for a cause
τοὺς art. acc. masc. pl. ὁ ἡ τό the, this, that, he, she, it
Ἰουδαίους adj. acc. masc. pl. Ἰουδαῖος Jew, Jewess
τοὺς art. acc. masc. pl. ὁ ἡ τό the, this, that, he, she, it
ἐν prep. ἐν (+dat) in, by, with, among, at, on, through, to, within, into, of, for

τοῖς art. dat. masc. pl. ὁ ἡ τό the, this, that, he, she, it
τόποις n. dat. masc. pl. τόπος place, room, quarter
ἐκείνοις demo. pron. dat. masc. pl. ἐκεῖνος that, he, the same, that same
γὰρ conj. γάρ for, and, because, but, indeed
ἅπαντες adj. nom. masc. pl. ἅπας all, whole, all things, every, everyone
τὸν art. acc. masc. sg. ὁ ἡ τό the, this, that, he, she, it
πατέρα n. acc. masc. sg. πατήρ Father, father, parent
αὐτοῦ pron. gen. masc. 3p. sg. αὐτός ή ό self, of oneself, even, very, the same, he, she, it
ὅτι conj. ὅτι that, for, because, how that, how, because that, for that, though
Ἕλλην n. nom. masc. sg. Ἕλλην Greek, Gentile
4 ὡς adv. ὡς as, when, as it were, how, about, like, as soon as, even as, while
δὲ conj. δέ but, and, now, also, to the contrary, rather, then
τὰς art. acc. fem. pl. ὁ ἡ τό the, this, that, he, she, it
πόλεις n. acc. fem. pl. πόλις city
αὐτοῖς pron. dat. masc. 3p. pl. αὐτός ή ό self, of oneself, even, very, the same, he, she, it
τὰ art. acc. neut. pl. ὁ ἡ τό the, this, that, he, she, it
δόγματα n. acc. neut. pl. δόγμα decree, ordinance
τὰ art. acc. neut. pl. ὁ ἡ τό the, this, that, he, she, it
ὑπὸ prep. ὑπό (+gen) of, by, with, from, among, (+acc) under
τῶν art. gen. masc. pl. ὁ ἡ τό the, this, that, he, she, it
ἀποστόλων n. gen. masc. pl. ἀπόστολος apostle, messenger, he that is sent
καὶ conj. καί and, even, also, but
τῶν art. gen. masc. pl. ὁ ἡ τό the, this, that, he, she, it
πρεσβυτέρων adj. gen. masc. pl. πρεσβύτερος elder, elder woman, eldest, old man
τῶν art. gen. masc. pl. ὁ ἡ τό the, this, that, he, she, it
ἐν prep. ἐν (+dat) in, by, with, among, at, on, through, to, within, into, of, for
Ἰερουσαλὴμ pron. name. fem. inde. Ἰερουσαλήμ Jerusalem
5 αἱ art. nom. fem. pl. ὁ ἡ τό the, this, that, he, she, it
μέν conj. μέν indeed, verily, truly, even, so, some
οὖν conj. οὖν therefore, then, so, and, now, wherefore
ἐκκλησίαι n. nom. fem. pl. ἐκκλησία church, assembly
τῇ art. dat. fem. sg. ὁ ἡ τό the, this, that, he, she, it
πίστει n. dat. fem. sg. πίστις faith, assurance, belief, fidelity
καὶ conj. καί and, even, also, but
τῷ art. dat. masc. sg. ὁ ἡ τό the, this, that, he, she, it
ἀριθμῷ n. dat. masc. sg. ἀριθμός number
καθ' prep. κατά (+gen) against, by, throughout, down, (+acc) according to, after, with
ἡμέραν n. acc. fem. sg. ἡμέρα day, time, year, while, age, day time
6 δὲ conj. δέ but, and, now, also, to the contrary, rather, then
τὴν art. acc. fem. sg. ὁ ἡ τό the, this, that, he, she, it
Φρυγίαν n. acc. fem. sg. Φρυγία Phrygia
καὶ conj. καί and, even, also, but
τὴν art. acc. fem. sg. ὁ ἡ τό the, this, that, he, she, it
Γαλατικὴν adj. acc. fem. sg. Γαλατικός of Galatia
χώραν n. acc. fem. sg. χώρα country, region, land, field, coast, ground
ὑπὸ prep. ὑπό (+gen) of, by, with, from, among, (+acc) under
τοῦ art. gen. neut. sg. ὁ ἡ τό the, this, that, he, she, it
Ἁγίου adj. gen. neut. sg. ἅγιος Holy, holy, saint, Holy One, holy thing, most holy
Πνεύματος n. gen. neut. sg. πνεῦμα spirit, Spirit, Ghost, ghost, life. of the spirit, wind
τὸν art. acc. masc. sg. ὁ ἡ τό the, this, that, he, she, it
λόγον n. acc. masc. sg. λόγος word, saying, account, speech, thing, matter
ἐν prep. ἐν (+dat) in, by, with, among, at, on, through, to, within, into, of, for
τῇ art. dat. fem. sg. ὁ ἡ τό the, this, that, he, she, it
Ἀσίᾳ n. dat. fem. sg. Ἀσία Asia
7 κατὰ prep. κατά (+gen) against, by, throughout, down, (+acc) according to, after, with

τὴν art. acc. fem. sg. ὁ ἡ τό the, this, that, he, she, it
Μυσίαν n. acc. fem. sg. Μυσία Mysia
κατὰ prep. κατά (+gen) against, by, throughout, down, (+acc) according to, after, with
τὴν art. acc. fem. sg. ὁ ἡ τό the, this, that, he, she, it
Βιθυνίαν n. acc. fem. sg. Βιθυνία Bithynia
καὶ conj. καί and, even, also, but
οὐκ particle of negation. οὐ οὐκ οὐχ not, no, neither, none, nay, nor, never, nothing
αὐτοὺς pron. acc. masc. 3p. pl. αὐτός ή ό self, of oneself, even, very, the same, he, she, it
τὸ art. nom. neut. sg. ὁ ἡ τό the, this, that, he, she, it
Πνεῦμα n. nom. neut. sg. πνεῦμα spirit, Spirit, Ghost, ghost, life. of the spirit, wind
8 δὲ conj. δέ but, and, now, also, to the contrary, rather, then
τὴν art. acc. fem. sg. ὁ ἡ τό the, this, that, he, she, it
Μυσίαν n. acc. fem. sg. Μυσία Mysia
εἰς prep. εἰς (+acc) into, to, unto, for, in, on, toward, against, upon, at, among
Τρῳάδα n. acc. fem. sg. Τρῳάς Troas
9 καὶ conj. καί and, even, also, but
ὅραμα n. nom. neut. sg. ὅραμα vision, sight
διὰ prep. διά (+gen) by, through, with, in, of, (+acc) for, because of, for a cause
τῆς art. gen. fem. sg. ὁ ἡ τό the, this, that, he, she, it
νυκτὸς n. gen. fem. sg. νύξ night
τῷ art. dat. masc. sg. ὁ ἡ τό the, this, that, he, she, it
Παύλῳ n. dat. masc. sg. Παῦλος Paul, Paulus
ἀνὴρ n. nom. masc. sg. ἀνήρ man, husband, sir
τις indefinite pron. nom. masc. sg. τὶς certain, some, any man, one, any thing
Μακεδών n. nom. masc. sg. Μακεδών of Macedonia, Macedonian
αὐτὸν pron. acc. masc. 3p. sg. αὐτός ή ό self, of oneself, even, very, the same, he, she, it
καὶ conj. καί and, even, also, but
εἰς prep. εἰς (+acc) into, to, unto, for, in, on, toward, against, upon, at, among
Μακεδονίαν n. acc. fem. sg. Μακεδονία Macedonia
ἡμῖν pron. dat. 1p. pl. ἐγώ I
10 ὡς adv. ὡς as, when, as it were, how, about, like, as soon as, even as, while
δὲ conj. δέ but, and, now, also, to the contrary, rather, then
τὸ art. acc. neut. sg. ὁ ἡ τό the, this, that, he, she, it
ὅραμα n. acc. neut. sg. ὅραμα vision, sight
εὐθέως adv. εὐθέως immediately, straightway, forthwith, as soon as, by and by, shortly
εἰς prep. εἰς (+acc) into, to, unto, for, in, on, toward, against, upon, at, among
τὴν art. acc. fem. sg. ὁ ἡ τό the, this, that, he, she, it
Μακεδονίαν n. acc. fem. sg. Μακεδονία Macedonia
ὅτι conj. ὅτι that, for, because, how that, how, because that, for that, though
ἡμᾶς pron. acc. 1p. pl. ἐγώ I
ὁ art. nom. masc. sg. ὁ ἡ τό the, this, that, he, she, it
Κύριος n. nom. masc. sg. κύριος Lord, lord, master, sir, LORD, God, Master, owner
αὐτούς pron. acc. masc. 3p. pl. αὐτός ή ό self, of oneself, even, very, the same, he, she, it
11 οὖν conj. οὖν therefore, then, so, and, now, wherefore
ἀπὸ prep. ἀπό (+gen) from, of, out of, since, for, off, at, by, in, on
τῆς art. gen. fem. sg. ὁ ἡ τό the, this, that, he, she, it
Τρῳάδος n. gen. fem. sg. Τρῳάς Troas
εἰς prep. εἰς (+acc) into, to, unto, for, in, on, toward, against, upon, at, among
Σαμοθρᾴκην n. acc. fem. sg. Σαμοθρᾴκη Samothracia
τῇ art. dat. fem. sg. ὁ ἡ τό the, this, that, he, she, it
τε conj. τέ and, both, also
εἰς prep. εἰς (+acc) into, to, unto, for, in, on, toward, against, upon, at, among
Νεάπολιν n. acc. fem. sg. Νεάπολις Neapolis
12 ἐκεῖθέν adv. ἐκεῖθεν thence, from thence, from that place
τε conj. τέ and, both, also

εἰς prep. εἰς (+acc) into, to, unto, for, in, on, toward, against, upon, at, among
Φιλίππους n. acc. masc. pl. Φίλιπποι Philippi
ἥτις relative pron. nom. fem. sg. ὅστις which, who, whosoever, that, whatsoever
πρώτη ordinal. adj. nom. fem. sg. πρῶτος first, chief, first of all, chiefest, best
τῆς art. gen. fem. sg. ὁ ἡ τό the, this, that, he, she, it
μερίδος n. gen. fem. sg. μερίς part, share
τῆς art. gen. fem. sg. ὁ ἡ τό the, this, that, he, she, it
Μακεδονίας n. gen. fem. sg. Μακεδονία Macedonia
πόλις n. nom. fem. sg. πόλις city
κολωνία n. nom. fem. sg. κολωνία colony
δὲ conj. δέ but, and, now, also, to the contrary, rather, then
ἐν prep. ἐν (+dat) in, by, with, among, at, on, through, to, within, into, of, for
ταύτῃ demo. pron. dat. fem. sg. οὗτος αὕτη τοῦτο this, the same, this same, he, she, it
τῇ art. dat. fem. sg. ὁ ἡ τό the, this, that, he, she, it
πόλει n. dat. fem. sg. πόλις city
ἡμέρας n. acc. fem. pl. ἡμέρα day, time, year, while, age, day time
τινάς indefinite pron. acc. fem. pl. τὶς certain, some, any man, one, any thing
13 τῇ art. dat. fem. sg. ὁ ἡ τό the, this, that, he, she, it
τε conj. τέ and, both, also
ἡμέρᾳ n. dat. fem. sg. ἡμέρα day, time, year, while, age, day time
τῶν art. gen. neut. pl. ὁ ἡ τό the, this, that, he, she, it
σαββάτων n. gen. neut. pl. σάββατον sabbath day, sabbath, week
ἔξω adv. ἔξω out, without, out of, forth, away, outward
τῆς art. gen. fem. sg. ὁ ἡ τό the, this, that, he, she, it
πόλεως n. gen. fem. sg. πόλις city
παρὰ prep. παρά (+gen) of, from, (+dat) with, for, (+acc) beside, at, by, above, against
ποταμὸν n. acc. masc. sg. ποταμός river, flood , stream, water
οὗ adv. οὗ where, whither, wherein
προσευχὴ n. nom. fem. sg. προσευχή prayer
καὶ conj. καί and, even, also, but
ταῖς art. dat. fem. pl. ὁ ἡ τό the, this, that, he, she, it
γυναιξί n. dat. fem. pl. γυνή woman, wife
14 καί conj. καί and, even, also, but
τις indefinite pron. nom. fem. sg. τὶς certain, some, any man, one, any thing
γυνὴ n. nom. fem. sg. γυνή woman, wife
ὀνόματι n. dat. neut. sg. ὄνομα name, call, surname
Λυδία n. nom. fem. sg. Λυδία Lydia
πορφυρόπωλις n. nom. fem. sg. πορφυρόπωλις seller of purple
πόλεως n. gen. fem. sg. πόλις city
Θυατείρων n. gen. neut. pl. Θυάτειρα Thyatira
τὸν art. acc. masc. sg. ὁ ἡ τό the, this, that, he, she, it
Θεόν n. acc. masc. sg. θεός God, god
ἧς relative pron. gen. fem. sg. ὅς ἥ ὅ who, which, what, that
ὁ art. nom. masc. sg. ὁ ἡ τό the, this, that, he, she, it
Κύριος n. nom. masc. sg. κύριος Lord, lord, master, sir, LORD, God, Master, owner
τὴν art. acc. fem. sg. ὁ ἡ τό the, this, that, he, she, it
καρδίαν n. acc. fem. sg. καρδία heart
τοῖς art. dat. neut. pl. ὁ ἡ τό the, this, that, he, she, it
ὑπὸ prep. ὑπό (+gen) of, by, with, from, among, (+acc) under
τοῦ art. gen. masc. sg. ὁ ἡ τό the, this, that, he, she, it
Παύλου n. gen. masc. sg. Παῦλος Paul, Paulus
15 ὡς adv. ὡς as, when, as it were, how, about, like, as soon as, even as, while
δὲ conj. δέ but, and, now, also, to the contrary, rather, then
καὶ conj. καί and, even, also, but
ὁ art. nom. masc. sg. ὁ ἡ τό the, this, that, he, she, it

οἶκος n. nom. masc. sg. οἶκος house, home, household
αὐτῆς pron. gen. fem. 3p. sg. αὐτός ἡ ὁ self, of oneself, even, very, the same, he, she, it
Εἰ conj. εἰ if, whether, that, though, forasmuch
με pron. acc. 1p. sg. ἐγώ I
πιστὴν adj. acc. fem. sg. πιστός faithful, believing, true, sure
τῷ art. dat. masc. sg. ὁ ἡ τό the, this, that, he, she, it
Κυρίῳ n. dat. masc. sg. κύριος Lord, lord, master, sir, LORD, God, Master, owner
εἰς prep. εἰς (+acc) into, to, unto, for, in, on, toward, against, upon, at, among
τὸν art. acc. masc. sg. ὁ ἡ τό the, this, that, he, she, it
οἶκόν n. acc. masc. sg. οἶκος house, home, household
μου pron. gen. 1p. sg. ἐγώ I
καὶ conj. καί and, even, also, but
ἡμᾶς pron. acc. 1p. pl. ἐγώ I
16 δὲ conj. δέ but, and, now, also, to the contrary, rather, then
ἡμῶν pron. gen. 1p. pl. ἐγώ I
εἰς prep. εἰς (+acc) into, to, unto, for, in, on, toward, against, upon, at, among
προσευχὴν n. acc. fem. sg. προσευχή prayer
παιδίσκην n. acc. fem. sg. παιδίσκη damsel, bondwoman, maid, bondmaid, maiden
τινὰ indefinite pron. acc. fem. sg. τὶς certain, some, any man, one, any thing
πνεῦμα n. acc. neut. sg. πνεῦμα spirit, Spirit, Ghost, ghost, life. of the spirit, wind
Πύθωνος n. gen. masc. sg. πύθων divination
ἡμῖν pron. dat. 1p. pl. ἐγώ I
ἥτις relative pron. nom. fem. sg. ὅστις which, who, whosoever, that, whatsoever
ἐργασίαν n. acc. fem. sg. ἐργασία diligence, working, gain, craft
πολλὴν adj. acc. fem. sg. πολύς many, great, much, long, abundant
τοῖς art. dat. masc. pl. ὁ ἡ τό the, this, that, he, she, it
κυρίοις n. dat. masc. pl. κύριος Lord, lord, master, sir, LORD, God, Master, owner
αὐτῆς pron. gen. fem. 3p. sg. αὐτός ἡ ὁ self, of oneself, even, very, the same, he, she, it
17 αὕτη demo. pron. nom. fem. sg. οὗτος αὕτη τοῦτο this, the same, this same, he, she, it
τῷ art. dat. masc. sg. ὁ ἡ τό the, this, that, he, she, it
Παύλῳ n. dat. masc. sg. Παῦλος Paul, Paulus
καὶ conj. καί and, even, also, but
ἡμῖν pron. dat. 1p. pl. ἐγώ I
Οὗτοι demo. pron. nom. masc. pl. οὗτος αὕτη τοῦτο this, the same, this same, he, she, it
οἱ art. nom. masc. pl. ὁ ἡ τό the, this, that, he, she, it
ἄνθρωποι n. nom. masc. pl. ἄνθρωπος man, human being, person, one, certain
δοῦλοι n. nom. masc. pl. δοῦλος servant, bondman, bond, slave
τοῦ art. gen. masc. sg. ὁ ἡ τό the, this, that, he, she, it
Θεοῦ n. gen. masc. sg. θεός God, god
τοῦ art. gen. masc. sg. ὁ ἡ τό the, this, that, he, she, it
ὑψίστου superl. adj. gen. masc. sg. ὕψιστος highest, Highest, most high, most High
οἵτινες relative pron. nom. masc. pl. ὅστις which, who, whosoever, that, whatsoever
ἡμῖν pron. dat. 1p. pl. ἐγώ I
ὁδὸν n. acc. fem. sg. ὁδός way, journey, highway
σωτηρίας n. gen. fem. sg. σωτηρία salvation, deliver, health, saving
18 τοῦτο demo. pron. acc. neut. sg. οὗτος αὕτη τοῦτο this, the same, this same, he, she, it
δὲ conj. δέ but, and, now, also, to the contrary, rather, then
ἐπὶ prep. ἐπί (+gen) on, in, upon, (+dat) in, at, for, upon, (+acc) on, upon, unto, to, against
πολλὰς adj. acc. fem. pl. πολύς many, great, much, long, abundant
ἡμέρας n. acc. fem. pl. ἡμέρα day, time, year, while, age, day time
δὲ conj. δέ but, and, now, also, to the contrary, rather, then
ὁ art. nom. masc. sg. ὁ ἡ τό the, this, that, he, she, it
Παῦλος n. nom. masc. sg. Παῦλος Paul, Paulus
καὶ conj. καί and, even, also, but
τῷ art. dat. neut. sg. ὁ ἡ τό the, this, that, he, she, it

πνεύματι n. dat. neut. sg. πνεῦμα spirit, Spirit, Ghost, ghost, life. of the spirit, wind
σοι pron. dat. 2p. sg. σύ thou, you
ἐν prep. ἐν (+dat) in, by, with, among, at, on, through, to, within, into, of, for
τῷ art. dat. neut. sg. ὁ ἡ τό the, this, that, he, she, it
ὀνόματι n. dat. neut. sg. ὄνομα name, call, surname
Ἰησοῦ n. gen. masc. sg. Ἰησοῦς Jesus
Χριστοῦ n. gen. masc. sg. Χριστός Christ
ἀπ' prep. ἀπό (+gen) from, of, out of, since, for, off, at, by, in, on
αὐτῆς pron. gen. fem. 3p. sg. αὐτός ή ό self, of oneself, even, very, the same, he, she, it
καὶ conj. καί and, even, also, but
αὐτῇ pron. dat. fem. 3p. sg. αὐτός ή ό self, of oneself, even, very, the same, he, she, it
τῇ art. dat. fem. sg. ὁ ἡ τό the, this, that, he, she, it
ὥρᾳ n. dat. fem. sg. ὥρα hour, time, season
19 δὲ conj. δέ but, and, now, also, to the contrary, rather, then
οἱ art. nom. masc. pl. ὁ ἡ τό the, this, that, he, she, it
κύριοι n. nom. masc. pl. κύριος Lord, lord, master, sir, LORD, God, Master, owner
αὐτῆς pron. gen. fem. 3p. sg. αὐτός ή ό self, of oneself, even, very, the same, he, she, it
ὅτι conj. ὅτι that, for, because, how that, how, because that, for that, though
ἡ art. nom. fem. sg. ὁ ἡ τό the, this, that, he, she, it
ἐλπὶς n. nom. fem. sg. ἐλπίς hope, faith
τῆς art. gen. fem. sg. ὁ ἡ τό the, this, that, he, she, it
ἐργασίας n. gen. fem. sg. ἐργασία diligence, working, gain, craft
αὐτῶν pron. gen. masc. 3p. pl. αὐτός ή ό self, of oneself, even, very, the same, he, she, it
τὸν art. acc. masc. sg. ὁ ἡ τό the, this, that, he, she, it
Παῦλον n. acc. masc. sg. Παῦλος Paul, Paulus
καὶ conj. καί and, even, also, but
τὸν art. acc. masc. sg. ὁ ἡ τό the, this, that, he, she, it
Σιλᾶν n. acc. masc. sg. Σιλᾶς Silas
εἰς prep. εἰς (+acc) into, to, unto, for, in, on, toward, against, upon, at, among
τὴν art. acc. fem. sg. ὁ ἡ τό the, this, that, he, she, it
ἀγορὰν n. acc. fem. sg. ἀγορά market, marketplace, street
ἐπὶ prep. ἐπί (+gen) on, in, upon, (+dat) in, at, for, upon, (+acc) on, upon, unto, to, against
τοὺς art. acc. masc. pl. ὁ ἡ τό the, this, that, he, she, it
ἄρχοντας n. acc. masc. pl. ἄρχων ruler, prince, chief, magistrate, chief ruler
20 καὶ conj. καί and, even, also, but
αὐτοὺς pron. acc. masc. 3p. pl. αὐτός ή ό self, of oneself, even, very, the same, he, she, it
τοῖς art. dat. masc. pl. ὁ ἡ τό the, this, that, he, she, it
στρατηγοῖς n. dat. masc. pl. στρατηγός captain, magistrate
Οὗτοι demo. pron. nom. masc. pl. οὗτος αὕτη τοῦτο this, the same, this same, he, she, it
οἱ art. nom. masc. pl. ὁ ἡ τό the, this, that, he, she, it
ἄνθρωποι n. nom. masc. pl. ἄνθρωπος man, human being, person, one, certain
ἡμῶν pron. gen. 1p. pl. ἐγώ I
τὴν art. acc. fem. sg. ὁ ἡ τό the, this, that, he, she, it
πόλιν n. acc. fem. sg. πόλις city
Ἰουδαῖοι adj. nom. masc. pl. Ἰουδαῖος Jew, Jewess
21 καὶ conj. καί and, even, also, but
ἔθη n. acc. neut. pl. ἔθος custom, manner, be wont
ἃ relative pron. acc. neut. pl. ὅς ἥ ὅ who, which, what, that
οὐκ particle of negation. οὐ οὐκ οὐχ not, no, neither, none, nay, nor, never, nothing
ἡμῖν pron. dat. 1p. pl. ἐγώ I
οὐδὲ conj. οὐδέ neither, nor, not, no, not even, never, not yet
Ῥωμαίοις adj. dat. masc. pl. Ῥωμαῖος Roman, Rome
22 καὶ conj. καί and, even, also, but
ὁ art. nom. masc. sg. ὁ ἡ τό the, this, that, he, she, it
ὄχλος n. nom. masc. sg. ὄχλος people, multitude, company, press, number

κατ' prep. κατά (+gen) against, by, throughout, down, (+acc) according to, after, with
αὐτῶν pron. gen. masc. 3p. pl. αὐτός ή ό self, of oneself, even, very, the same, he, she, it
καὶ conj. καί and, even, also, but
οἱ art. nom. masc. pl. ὁ ἡ τό the, this, that, he, she, it
στρατηγοὶ n. nom. masc. pl. στρατηγός captain, magistrate
αὐτῶν pron. gen. masc. 3p. pl. αὐτός ή ό self, of oneself, even, very, the same, he, she, it
τὰ art. acc. neut. pl. ὁ ἡ τό the, this, that, he, she, it
ἱμάτια n. acc. neut. pl. ἱμάτιον cloke, garment, clothes, raiment, robe, vesture
23 πολλάς adj. acc. fem. pl. πολύς many, great, much, long, abundant
τε conj. τέ and, both, also
αὐτοῖς pron. dat. masc. 3p. pl. αὐτός ή ό self, of oneself, even, very, the same, he, she, it
πληγὰς n. acc. fem. pl. πληγή wound, plague, stripe
εἰς prep. εἰς (+acc) into, to, unto, for, in, on, toward, against, upon, at, among
φυλακὴν n. acc. fem. sg. φυλακή prison, watch, imprisonment, cage, hold, ward
τῷ art. dat. masc. sg. ὁ ἡ τό the, this, that, he, she, it
δεσμοφύλακι n. dat. masc. sg. δεσμοφύλαξ jailor, keeper of the prison
ἀσφαλῶς adv. ἀσφαλῶς safely, assuredly
αὐτούς pron. acc. masc. 3p. pl. αὐτός ή ό self, of oneself, even, very, the same, he, she, it
24 ὃς relative pron. nom. masc. sg. ὅς ἥ ὅ who, which, what, that
παραγγελίαν n. acc. fem. sg. παραγγελία charge, commandment
τοιαύτην demo. pron. acc. fem. sg. τοιοῦτος such, like
αὐτοὺς pron. acc. masc. 3p. pl. αὐτός ή ό self, of oneself, even, very, the same, he, she, it
εἰς prep. εἰς (+acc) into, to, unto, for, in, on, toward, against, upon, at, among
τὴν art. acc. fem. sg. ὁ ἡ τό the, this, that, he, she, it
ἐσωτέραν compar. adj. acc. fem. sg. ἐσώτερος inner, within
φυλακὴν n. acc. fem. sg. φυλακή prison, watch, imprisonment, cage, hold, ward
καὶ conj. καί and, even, also, but
τοὺς art. acc. masc. pl. ὁ ἡ τό the, this, that, he, she, it
πόδας n. acc. masc. pl. πούς foot
αὐτῶν pron. gen. masc. 3p. pl. αὐτός ή ό self, of oneself, even, very, the same, he, she, it
εἰς prep. εἰς (+acc) into, to, unto, for, in, on, toward, against, upon, at, among
τὸ art. acc. neut. sg. ὁ ἡ τό the, this, that, he, she, it
ξύλον n. acc. neut. sg. ξύλον tree, stave, wood, the stocks
25 κατὰ prep. κατά (+gen) against, by, throughout, down, (+acc) according to, after, with
δὲ conj. δέ but, and, now, also, to the contrary, rather, then
τὸ art. acc. neut. sg. ὁ ἡ τό the, this, that, he, she, it
μεσονύκτιον n. acc. neut. sg. μεσονύκτιον midnight
Παῦλος n. nom. masc. sg. Παῦλος Paul, Paulus
καὶ conj. καί and, even, also, but
Σιλᾶς n. nom. masc. sg. Σιλᾶς Silas
τὸν art. acc. masc. sg. ὁ ἡ τό the, this, that, he, she, it
Θεόν n. acc. masc. sg. θεός God, god
δὲ conj. δέ but, and, now, also, to the contrary, rather, then
αὐτῶν pron. gen. masc. 3p. pl. αὐτός ή ό self, of oneself, even, very, the same, he, she, it
οἱ art. nom. masc. pl. ὁ ἡ τό the, this, that, he, she, it
δέσμιοι n. nom. masc. pl. δέσμιος prisoner, in bonds, that is in bond
26 ἄφνω adv. ἄφνω suddenly
δὲ conj. δέ but, and, now, also, to the contrary, rather, then
σεισμὸς n. nom. masc. sg. σεισμός earthquake, tempest
μέγας adj. nom. masc. sg. μέγας great, loud, greatest, high, large, mighty, strong
ὥστε conj. ὥστε so that, wherefore, insomuch that, therefore, that, so then
τὰ art. acc. neut. pl. ὁ ἡ τό the, this, that, he, she, it
θεμέλια n. acc. neut. pl. θεμέλιος foundation
τοῦ art. gen. neut. sg. ὁ ἡ τό the, this, that, he, she, it
δεσμωτηρίου n. gen. neut. sg. δεσμωτήριον prison

τε conj. τέ and, both, also
παραχρῆμα adv. παραχρῆμα immediately, straightway, forthwith, presently, soon
αἱ art. nom. fem. pl. ὁ ἡ τό the, this, that, he, she, it
θύραι n. nom. fem. pl. θύρα door, gate
πᾶσαι adj. nom. fem. pl. πᾶς πᾶσα πᾶν all, every, whosoever, every one, no, whole, any
καὶ conj. καί and, even, also, but
πάντων adj. gen. masc. pl. πᾶς πᾶσα πᾶν all, every, whosoever, every one, no, whole, any
τὰ art. nom. neut. pl. ὁ ἡ τό the, this, that, he, she, it
δεσμὰ n. nom. neut. pl. δεσμός bond, band, chain, string
27 ἔξυπνος adj. nom. masc. sg. ἔξυπνος awake out of his sleep
δὲ conj. δέ but, and, now, also, to the contrary, rather, then
ὁ art. nom. masc. sg. ὁ ἡ τό the, this, that, he, she, it
δεσμοφύλαξ n. nom. masc. sg. δεσμοφύλαξ jailor, keeper of the prison
καὶ conj. καί and, even, also, but
τὰς art. acc. fem. pl. ὁ ἡ τό the, this, that, he, she, it
θύρας n. acc. fem. pl. θύρα door, gate
τῆς art. gen. fem. sg. ὁ ἡ τό the, this, that, he, she, it
φυλακῆς n. gen. fem. sg. φυλακή prison, watch, imprisonment, cage, hold, ward
μάχαιραν n. acc. fem. sg. μάχαιρα sword
ἑαυτὸν reflexive pron. acc. masc. 3p. sg. ἑαυτοῦ himself, herself, itself, yourself, ourselves
τοὺς art. acc. masc. pl. ὁ ἡ τό the, this, that, he, she, it
δεσμίους n. acc. masc. pl. δέσμιος prisoner, in bonds, that is in bond
28 δὲ conj. δέ but, and, now, also, to the contrary, rather, then
φωνῇ n. dat. fem. sg. φωνή voice, sound, noise
μεγάλῃ adj. dat. fem. sg. μέγας great, loud, greatest, high, large, mighty, strong
ὁ art. nom. masc. sg. ὁ ἡ τό the, this, that, he, she, it
Παῦλος n. nom. masc. sg. Παῦλος Paul, Paulus
Μηδὲν adj. acc. neut. sg. μηδείς μηδεμία μηδέν no man, nothing, no, none, not at all
σεαυτῷ pron. dat. masc. 2p. sg. σεαυτοῦ σεαυτῷ σεαυτόν thyself, thine own self
κακόν adj. acc. neut. sg. κακός evil, evil thing, noisome, wicked
ἅπαντες adj. nom. masc. pl. ἅπας all, whole, all things, every, everyone
γάρ conj. γάρ for, and, because, but, indeed
ἐνθάδε adv. ἐνθάδε here, there, hither
29 δὲ conj. δέ but, and, now, also, to the contrary, rather, then
φῶτα n. acc. neut. pl. φῶς light, fire
καὶ conj. καί and, even, also, but
ἔντρομος adj. nom. masc. sg. ἔντρομος trembling, quaking
τῷ art. dat. masc. sg. ὁ ἡ τό the, this, that, he, she, it
Παύλῳ n. dat. masc. sg. Παῦλος Paul, Paulus
καὶ conj. καί and, even, also, but
τῷ art. dat. masc. sg. ὁ ἡ τό the, this, that, he, she, it
Σιλᾷ n. dat. masc. sg. Σιλᾶς Silas
30 καὶ conj. καί and, even, also, but
αὐτοὺς pron. acc. masc. 3p. pl. αὐτός ἡ ό self, of oneself, even, very, the same, he, she, it
ἔξω adv. ἔξω out, without, out of, forth, away, outward
Κύριοι n. voc. masc. pl. κύριος Lord, lord, master, sir, LORD, God, Master, owner
τί interrog. pron. acc. neut. sg. τίς what, who, why, where, which, how
με pron. acc. 1p. sg. ἐγώ I
ἵνα conj. ἵνα that, to, lest, for to, so that, albeit, because, for, so as
31 οἱ art. nom. masc. pl. ὁ ἡ τό the, this, that, he, she, it
δὲ conj. δέ but, and, now, also, to the contrary, rather, then
ἐπὶ prep. ἐπί (+gen) on, in, upon, (+dat) in, at, for, upon, (+acc) on, upon, unto, to, against
τὸν art. acc. masc. sg. ὁ ἡ τό the, this, that, he, she, it
Κύριον n. acc. masc. sg. κύριος Lord, lord, master, sir, LORD, God, Master, owner
Ἰησοῦν n. acc. masc. sg. Ἰησοῦς Jesus

Χριστόν n. acc. masc. sg. Χριστός Christ
καὶ conj. καί and, even, also, but
σὺ pron. nom. 2p. sg. σύ thou, you
καὶ conj. καί and, even, also, but
ὁ art. nom. masc. sg. ὁ ἡ τό the, this, that, he, she, it
οἶκός n. nom. masc. sg. οἶκος house, home, household
σου pron. gen. 2p. sg. σύ thou, you
32 καὶ conj. καί and, even, also, but
αὐτῷ pron. dat. masc. 3p. sg. αὐτός ἡ ὁ self, of oneself, even, very, the same, he, she, it
τὸν art. acc. masc. sg. ὁ ἡ τό the, this, that, he, she, it
λόγον n. acc. masc. sg. λόγος word, saying, account, speech, thing, matter
τοῦ art. gen. masc. sg. ὁ ἡ τό the, this, that, he, she, it
Κυρίου n. gen. masc. sg. κύριος Lord, lord, master, sir, LORD, God, Master, owner
καὶ conj. καί and, even, also, but
πᾶσι adj. dat. masc. pl. πᾶς πᾶσα πᾶν all, every, whosoever, every one, no, whole, any
τοῖς art. dat. masc. pl. ὁ ἡ τό the, this, that, he, she, it
ἐν prep. ἐν (+dat) in, by, with, among, at, on, through, to, within, into, of, for
τῇ art. dat. fem. sg. ὁ ἡ τό the, this, that, he, she, it
οἰκίᾳ n. dat. fem. sg. οἰκία house, home, household
αὐτοῦ pron. gen. masc. 3p. sg. αὐτός ἡ ὁ self, of oneself, even, very, the same, he, she, it
33 καὶ conj. καί and, even, also, but
αὐτοὺς pron. acc. masc. 3p. pl. αὐτός ἡ ὁ self, of oneself, even, very, the same, he, she, it
ἐν prep. ἐν (+dat) in, by, with, among, at, on, through, to, within, into, of, for
ἐκείνῃ demo. pron. dat. fem. sg. ἐκεῖνος that, he, the same, that same
τῇ art. dat. fem. sg. ὁ ἡ τό the, this, that, he, she, it
ὥρᾳ n. dat. fem. sg. ὥρα hour, time, season
τῆς art. gen. fem. sg. ὁ ἡ τό the, this, that, he, she, it
νυκτὸς n. gen. fem. sg. νύξ night
ἀπὸ prep. ἀπό (+gen) from, of, out of, since, for, off, at, by, in, on
τῶν art. gen. fem. pl. ὁ ἡ τό the, this, that, he, she, it
πληγῶν n. gen. fem. pl. πληγή wound, plague, stripe
καὶ conj. καί and, even, also, but
αὐτὸς pron. nom. masc. 3p. sg. αὐτός ἡ ὁ self, of oneself, even, very, the same, he, she, it
καὶ conj. καί and, even, also, but
οἱ art. nom. masc. pl. ὁ ἡ τό the, this, that, he, she, it
αὐτοῦ pron. gen. masc. 3p. sg. αὐτός ἡ ὁ self, of oneself, even, very, the same, he, she, it
πάντες adj. nom. masc. pl. πᾶς πᾶσα πᾶν all, every, whosoever, every one, no, whole, any
παραχρῆμα adv. παραχρῆμα immediately, straightway, forthwith, presently, soon
34 τε conj. τέ and, both, also
αὐτοὺς pron. acc. masc. 3p. pl. αὐτός ἡ ὁ self, of oneself, even, very, the same, he, she, it
εἰς prep. εἰς (+acc) into, to, unto, for, in, on, toward, against, upon, at, among
τὸν art. acc. masc. sg. ὁ ἡ τό the, this, that, he, she, it
οἶκον n. acc. masc. sg. οἶκος house, home, household
αὐτοῦ pron. gen. masc. 3p. sg. αὐτός ἡ ὁ self, of oneself, even, very, the same, he, she, it
τράπεζαν n. acc. fem. sg. τράπεζα table
καὶ conj. καί and, even, also, but
πανοικεὶ adv. πανοικί with all one's house
τῷ art. dat. masc. sg. ὁ ἡ τό the, this, that, he, she, it
Θεῷ n. dat. masc. sg. θεός God, god
35 Ἡμέρας n. gen. fem. sg. ἡμέρα day, time, year, while, age, day time
δὲ conj. δέ but, and, now, also, to the contrary, rather, then
οἱ art. nom. masc. pl. ὁ ἡ τό the, this, that, he, she, it
στρατηγοὶ n. nom. masc. pl. στρατηγός captain, magistrate
τοὺς art. acc. masc. pl. ὁ ἡ τό the, this, that, he, she, it
ῥαβδούχους n. acc. masc. pl. ῥαβδοῦχος serjeant

τοὺς art. acc. masc. pl. ὁ ἡ τό the, this, that, he, she, it
ἀνθρώπους n. acc. masc. pl. ἄνθρωπος man, human being, person, one, certain
ἐκείνους demo. pron. acc. masc. pl. ἐκεῖνος that, he, the same, that same
36 δὲ conj. δέ but, and, now, also, to the contrary, rather, then
ὁ art. nom. masc. sg. ὁ ἡ τό the, this, that, he, she, it
δεσμοφύλαξ n. nom. masc. sg. δεσμοφύλαξ jailor, keeper of the prison
τοὺς art. acc. masc. pl. ὁ ἡ τό the, this, that, he, she, it
λόγους n. acc. masc. pl. λόγος word, saying, account, speech, thing, matter
τούτους demo. pron. acc. masc. pl. οὗτος αὕτη τοῦτο this, the same, this same, he, she, it
πρὸς prep. πρός (+gen) for, (+dat) at, (+acc) unto, to, with, for, against
τὸν art. acc. masc. sg. ὁ ἡ τό the, this, that, he, she, it
Παῦλον n. acc. masc. sg. Παῦλος Paul, Paulus
ὅτι conj. ὅτι that, for, because, how that, how, because that, for that, though
οἱ art. nom. masc. pl. ὁ ἡ τό the, this, that, he, she, it
στρατηγοὶ n. nom. masc. pl. στρατηγός captain, magistrate
ἵνα conj. ἵνα that, to, lest, for to, so that, albeit, because, for, so as
νῦν adv. νῦν now, henceforth, present, this time
οὖν conj. οὖν therefore, then, so, and, now, wherefore
ἐν prep. ἐν (+dat) in, by, with, among, at, on, through, to, within, into, of, for
εἰρήνῃ n. dat. fem. sg. εἰρήνη peace, quietness, rest
37 ὁ art. nom. masc. sg. ὁ ἡ τό the, this, that, he, she, it
δὲ conj. δέ but, and, now, also, to the contrary, rather, then
Παῦλος n. nom. masc. sg. Παῦλος Paul, Paulus
πρὸς prep. πρός (+gen) for, (+dat) at, (+acc) unto, to, with, for, against
αὐτούς pron. acc. masc. 3p. pl. αὐτός ή ό self, of oneself, even, very, the same, he, she, it
ἡμᾶς pron. acc. 1p. pl. ἐγώ I
δημοσίᾳ adv. δημόσιος common, publicly, openly
ἀκατακρίτους adj. acc. masc. pl. ἀκατάκριτος uncondemned
ἀνθρώπους n. acc. masc. pl. ἄνθρωπος man, human being, person, one, certain
Ῥωμαίους adj. acc. masc. pl. Ῥωμαῖος Roman, Rome
εἰς prep. εἰς (+acc) into, to, unto, for, in, on, toward, against, upon, at, among
φυλακήν n. acc. fem. sg. φυλακή prison, watch, imprisonment, cage, hold, ward
καὶ conj. καί and, even, also, but
νῦν adv. νῦν now, henceforth, present, this time
λάθρᾳ adv. λάθρα privily, secretly
ἡμᾶς pron. acc. 1p. pl. ἐγώ I
οὐ particle of negation. οὐ οὐκ οὐχ not, no, neither, none, nay, nor, never, nothing
γάρ particle. γάρ for, and, because, but, indeed
ἀλλὰ conj. ἀλλά but, yea, yet, nevertheless, howbeit, nay, therefore
αὐτοὶ pron. nom. masc. 3p. pl. αὐτός ή ό self, of oneself, even, very, the same, he, she, it
ἡμᾶς pron. acc. 1p. pl. ἐγώ I
38 δὲ conj. δέ but, and, now, also, to the contrary, rather, then
τοῖς art. dat. masc. pl. ὁ ἡ τό the, this, that, he, she, it
στρατηγοῖς n. dat. masc. pl. στρατηγός captain, magistrate
οἱ art. nom. masc. pl. ὁ ἡ τό the, this, that, he, she, it
ῥαβδοῦχοι n. nom. masc. pl. ῥαβδοῦχος serjeant
τὰ art. acc. neut. pl. ὁ ἡ τό the, this, that, he, she, it
ῥήματα n. acc. neut. pl. ῥῆμα word, saying, thing
ταῦτα demo. pron. acc. neut. pl. οὗτος αὕτη τοῦτο this, the same, this same, he, she, it
καὶ conj. καί and, even, also, but
ὅτι conj. ὅτι that, for, because, how that, how, because that, for that, though
Ῥωμαῖοί adj. nom. masc. pl. Ῥωμαῖος Roman, Rome
39 καὶ conj. καί and, even, also, but
αὐτοὺς pron. acc. masc. 3p. pl. αὐτός ή ό self, of oneself, even, very, the same, he, she, it
καὶ conj. καί and, even, also, but

τῆς art. gen. fem. sg. ὁ ἡ τό the, this, that, he, she, it
πόλεως n. gen. fem. sg. πόλις city
40 δὲ conj. δέ but, and, now, also, to the contrary, rather, then
ἐκ prep. ἐκ ἐξ (+gen) of, from, out of, by, on, with, in, among, through
τῆς art. gen. fem. sg. ὁ ἡ τό the, this, that, he, she, it
φυλακῆς n. gen. fem. sg. φυλακή prison, watch, imprisonment, cage, hold, ward
εἰς prep. εἰς (+acc) into, to, unto, for, in, on, toward, against, upon, at, among
τὴν art. acc. fem. sg. ὁ ἡ τό the, this, that, he, she, it
Λυδίαν n. acc. fem. sg. Λυδία Lydia
καὶ conj. καί and, even, also, but
τοὺς art. acc. masc. pl. ὁ ἡ τό the, this, that, he, she, it
ἀδελφοὺς n. acc. masc. pl. ἀδελφός brother
αὐτούς pron. acc. masc. 3p. pl. αὐτός ή ό self, of oneself, even, very, the same, he, she, it
καὶ conj. καί and, even, also, but

17

1 δὲ conj. δέ but, and, now, also, to the contrary, rather, then
τὴν art. acc. fem. sg. ὁ ἡ τό the, this, that, he, she, it
'Αμφίπολιν n. acc. fem. sg. 'Αμφίπολις Amphipolis
καὶ conj. καί and, even, also, but
'Απολλωνίαν n. acc. fem. sg. 'Απολλωνία Apollonia
εἰς prep. εἰς (+acc) into, to, unto, for, in, on, toward, against, upon, at, among
Θεσσαλονίκην n. acc. fem. sg. Θεσσαλονίκη Thessalonica
ὅπου adv. ὅπου where, whither, whereas, in what place, wheresoever
ἡ art. nom. fem. sg. ὁ ἡ τό the, this, that, he, she, it
συναγωγὴ n. nom. fem. sg. συναγωγή synagogue, assembly, congregation
τῶν art. gen. masc. pl. ὁ ἡ τό the, this, that, he, she, it
'Ιουδαίων adj. gen. masc. pl. 'Ιουδαῖος Jew, Jewess
2 κατὰ prep. κατά (+gen) against, by, throughout, down, (+acc) according to, after, with
δὲ conj. δέ but, and, now, also, to the contrary, rather, then
τὸ art. acc. neut. sg. ὁ ἡ τό the, this, that, he, she, it
τῷ art. dat. masc. sg. ὁ ἡ τό the, this, that, he, she, it
Παύλῳ n. dat. masc. sg. Παῦλος Paul, Paulus
πρὸς prep. πρός (+gen) for, (+dat) at, (+acc) unto, to, with, for, against
αὐτοὺς pron. acc. masc. 3p. pl. αὐτός ή ό self, of oneself, even, very, the same, he, she, it
καὶ conj. καί and, even, also, but
ἐπὶ prep. ἐπί (+gen) on, in, upon, (+dat) in, at, for, upon, (+acc) on, upon, unto, to, against
σάββατα n. acc. neut. pl. σάββατον sabbath day, sabbath, week
τρία num. acc. neut. pl. τρεῖς three
αὐτοῖς pron. dat. masc. 3p. pl. αὐτός ή ό self, of oneself, even, very, the same, he, she, it
ἀπὸ prep. ἀπό (+gen) from, of, out of, since, for, off, at, by, in, on
τῶν art. gen. fem. pl. ὁ ἡ τό the, this, that, he, she, it
γραφῶν n. gen. fem. pl. γραφή scripture
3 καὶ conj. καί and, even, also, but
ὅτι conj. ὅτι that, for, because, how that, how, because that, for that, though
τὸν art. acc. masc. sg. ὁ ἡ τό the, this, that, he, she, it
Χριστὸν n. acc. masc. sg. Χριστός Christ
καὶ conj. καί and, even, also, but
ἐκ prep. ἐκ ἐξ (+gen) of, from, out of, by, on, with, in, among, through
νεκρῶν adj. gen. masc. pl. νεκρός dead
καὶ conj. καί and, even, also, but
ὅτι conj. ὅτι that, for, because, how that, how, because that, for that, though
οὗτός demo. pron. nom. masc. sg. οὗτος αὕτη τοῦτο this, the same, this same, he, she, it
ὁ art. nom. masc. sg. ὁ ἡ τό the, this, that, he, she, it

Χριστὸς n. nom. masc. sg. Χριστός Christ
Ἰησοῦς n. nom. masc. sg. Ἰησοῦς Jesus
ὃν relative pron. acc. masc. sg. ὅς ἥ ὅ who, which, what, that
ἐγὼ pron. nom. 1p. sg. ἐγώ I
ὑμῖν pron. dat. 2p. pl. σύ thou, you
4 καί conj. καί and, even, also, but
τινες indefinite pron. nom. masc. pl. τὶς certain, some, any man, one, any thing
ἐξ prep. ἐκ ἐξ (+gen) of, from, out of, by, on, with, in, among, through
αὐτῶν pron. gen. masc. 3p. pl. αὐτός ή ό self, of oneself, even, very, the same, he, she, it
καί conj. καί and, even, also, but
τῷ art. dat. masc. sg. ὁ ἡ τό the, this, that, he, she, it
Παύλῳ n. dat. masc. sg. Παῦλος Paul, Paulus
καί conj. καί and, even, also, but
τῷ art. dat. masc. sg. ὁ ἡ τό the, this, that, he, she, it
Σιλᾷ n. dat. masc. sg. Σιλᾶς Silas
τῶν art. gen. masc. pl. ὁ ἡ τό the, this, that, he, she, it
τε conj. τέ and, both, also
Ἑλλήνων n. gen. masc. pl. Ἕλλην Greek, Gentile
πολὺ adj. nom. neut. sg. πολύς many, great, much, long, abundant
πλῆθος n. nom. neut. sg. πλῆθος multitude, bundle, company
γυναικῶν n. gen. fem. pl. γυνή woman, wife
τε conj. τέ and, both, also
τῶν art. gen. fem. pl. ὁ ἡ τό the, this, that, he, she, it
πρώτων ordinal. adj. gen. fem. pl. πρῶτος first, chief, first of all, chiefest, best
οὐκ particle of negation. οὐ οὐκ οὐχ not, no, neither, none, nay, nor, never, nothing
ὀλίγαι adj. nom. fem. pl. ὀλίγος few, little, small, a while, brief, short, short space
5 δὲ conj. δέ but, and, now, also, to the contrary, rather, then
οἱ art. nom. masc. pl. ὁ ἡ τό the, this, that, he, she, it
Ἰουδαῖοι adj. nom. masc. pl. Ἰουδαῖος Jew, Jewess
καὶ conj. καί and, even, also, but
τῶν art. gen. masc. pl. ὁ ἡ τό the, this, that, he, she, it
ἀγοραίων adj. gen. masc. pl. ἀγοραῖος of the baser sort, from the market, law, judicial
τινὰς indefinite pron. acc. masc. pl. τὶς certain, some, any man, one, any thing
ἄνδρας n. acc. masc. pl. ἀνήρ man, husband, sir
πονηροὺς adj. acc. masc. pl. πονηρός evil, wicked, bad
καὶ conj. καί and, even, also, but
τὴν art. acc. fem. sg. ὁ ἡ τό the, this, that, he, she, it
πόλιν n. acc. fem. sg. πόλις city
τε conj. τέ and, both, also
τῇ art. dat. fem. sg. ὁ ἡ τό the, this, that, he, she, it
οἰκίᾳ n. dat. fem. sg. οἰκία house, home, household
Ἰάσονος n. gen. masc. sg. Ἰάσων Jason
αὐτοὺς pron. acc. masc. 3p. pl. αὐτός ή ό self, of oneself, even, very, the same, he, she, it
εἰς prep. εἰς (+acc) into, to, unto, for, in, on, toward, against, upon, at, among
τὸν art. acc. masc. sg. ὁ ἡ τό the, this, that, he, she, it
δῆμον n. acc. masc. sg. δῆμος people
6 μὴ particle of negation. μή not, no, lest, neither, none, nothing, nor, never, without
δὲ conj. δέ but, and, now, also, to the contrary, rather, then
αὐτοὺς pron. acc. masc. 3p. pl. αὐτός ή ό self, of oneself, even, very, the same, he, she, it
τὸν art. acc. masc. sg. ὁ ἡ τό the, this, that, he, she, it
Ἰάσονα n. acc. masc. sg. Ἰάσων Jason
καί conj. καί and, even, also, but
τινας indefinite pron. acc. masc. pl. τὶς certain, some, any man, one, any thing
ἀδελφοὺς n. acc. masc. pl. ἀδελφός brother
ἐπὶ prep. ἐπί (+gen) on, in, upon, (+dat) in, at, for, upon, (+acc) on, upon, unto, to, against

τοὺς art. acc. masc. pl. ὁ ἡ τό the, this, that, he, she, it
πολιτάρχας n. acc. masc. pl. πολιτάρχης ruler of the city
ὅτι conj. ὅτι that, for, because, how that, how, because that, for that, though
Οἱ art. nom. masc. pl. ὁ ἡ τό the, this, that, he, she, it
τὴν art. acc. fem. sg. ὁ ἡ τό the, this, that, he, she, it
οἰκουμένην n. acc. fem. sg. οἰκουμένη world, earth
οὗτοι demo. pron. nom. masc. pl. οὗτος αὕτη τοῦτο this, the same, this same, he, she, it
καί conj. καί and, even, also, but
ἐνθάδε adv. ἐνθάδε here, there, hither
7 οὓς relative pron. acc. masc. pl. ὅς ἥ ὅ who, which, what, that
Ἰάσων n. nom. masc. sg. Ἰάσων Jason
καὶ conj. καί and, even, also, but
οὗτοι demo. pron. nom. masc. pl. οὗτος αὕτη τοῦτο this, the same, this same, he, she, it
πάντες adj. nom. masc. pl. πᾶς πᾶσα πᾶν all, every, whosoever, every one, no, whole, any
ἀπέναντι prep. ἀπέναντι before, over against, contrary, in the presence
τῶν art. gen. neut. pl. ὁ ἡ τό the, this, that, he, she, it
δογμάτων n. gen. neut. pl. δόγμα decree, ordinance
Καίσαρος n. gen. masc. sg. Καῖσαρ Caesar
βασιλέα n. acc. masc. sg. βασιλεύς king
ἕτερον adj. acc. masc. sg. ἕτερος another, other, else, strange
Ἰησοῦν n. acc. masc. sg. Ἰησοῦς Jesus
8 δὲ conj. δέ but, and, now, also, to the contrary, rather, then
τὸν art. acc. masc. sg. ὁ ἡ τό the, this, that, he, she, it
ὄχλον n. acc. masc. sg. ὄχλος people, multitude, company, press, number
καὶ conj. καί and, even, also, but
τοὺς art. acc. masc. pl. ὁ ἡ τό the, this, that, he, she, it
πολιτάρχας n. acc. masc. pl. πολιτάρχης ruler of the city
ταῦτα demo. pron. acc. neut. pl. οὗτος αὕτη τοῦτο this, the same, this same, he, she, it
9 καὶ conj. καί and, even, also, but
τὸ art. acc. neut. sg. ὁ ἡ τό the, this, that, he, she, it
ἱκανὸν adj. acc. neut. sg. ἱκανός many, much, long, worthy, sufficient, great, able
παρὰ prep. παρά (+gen) of, from, (+dat) with, for, (+acc) beside, at, by, above, against
τοῦ art. gen. masc. sg. ὁ ἡ τό the, this, that, he, she, it
Ἰάσονος n. gen. masc. sg. Ἰάσων Jason
καὶ conj. καί and, even, also, but
τῶν art. gen. masc. pl. ὁ ἡ τό the, this, that, he, she, it
λοιπῶν adj. gen. masc. pl. λοιπός other, rest, remnant, residue, which remain
αὐτούς pron. acc. masc. 3p. pl. αὐτός ή ό self, of oneself, even, very, the same, he, she, it
10 Οἱ art. nom. masc. pl. ὁ ἡ τό the, this, that, he, she, it
δὲ conj. δέ but, and, now, also, to the contrary, rather, then
ἀδελφοὶ n. nom. masc. pl. ἀδελφός brother
εὐθέως adv. εὐθέως immediately, straightway, forthwith, as soon as, by and by, shortly
διὰ prep. διά (+gen) by, through, with, in, of, (+acc) for, because of, for a cause
τῆς art. gen. fem. sg. ὁ ἡ τό the, this, that, he, she, it
νυκτὸς n. gen. fem. sg. νύξ night
τόν art. acc. masc. sg. ὁ ἡ τό the, this, that, he, she, it
τε conj. τέ and, both, also
Παῦλον n. acc. masc. sg. Παῦλος Paul, Paulus
καὶ conj. καί and, even, also, but
τὸν art. acc. masc. sg. ὁ ἡ τό the, this, that, he, she, it
Σιλᾶν n. acc. masc. sg. Σιλᾶς Silas
εἰς prep. εἰς (+acc) into, to, unto, for, in, on, toward, against, upon, at, among
Βέροιαν n. acc. fem. sg. Βέροια Berea
οἵτινες relative pron. nom. masc. pl. ὅστις which, who, whosoever, that, whatsoever
εἰς prep. εἰς (+acc) into, to, unto, for, in, on, toward, against, upon, at, among

τὴν art. acc. fem. sg. ὁ ἡ τό the, this, that, he, she, it
συναγωγὴν n. acc. fem. sg. συναγωγή synagogue, assembly, congregation
τῶν art. gen. masc. pl. ὁ ἡ τό the, this, that, he, she, it
'Ιουδαίων adj. gen. masc. pl. 'Ιουδαῖος Jew, Jewess
11 οὗτοι demo. pron. nom. masc. pl. οὗτος αὕτη τοῦτο this, the same, this same, he, she, it
δὲ conj. δέ but, and, now, also, to the contrary, rather, then
εὐγενέστεροι compar. adj. nom. masc. pl. εὐγενής noble, more noble
τῶν art. gen. masc. pl. ὁ ἡ τό the, this, that, he, she, it
ἐν prep. ἐν (+dat) in, by, with, among, at, on, through, to, within, into, of, for
Θεσσαλονίκῃ n. dat. fem. sg. Θεσσαλονίκη Thessalonica
οἵτινες relative pron. nom. masc. pl. ὅστις which, who, whosoever, that, whatsoever
τὸν art. acc. masc. sg. ὁ ἡ τό the, this, that, he, she, it
λόγον n. acc. masc. sg. λόγος word, saying, account, speech, thing, matter
μετὰ prep. μετά (+gen) with, among, against, (+acc) after
πάσης adj. gen. fem. sg. πᾶς πᾶσα πᾶν all, every, whosoever, every one, no, whole, any
προθυμίας n. gen. fem. sg. προθυμία readiness of mind, forwardness of mind
τὸ art. acc. neut. sg. ὁ ἡ τό the, this, that, he, she, it
καθ' prep. κατά (+gen) against, by, throughout, down, (+acc) according to, after, with
ἡμέραν n. acc. fem. sg. ἡμέρα day, time, year, while, age, day time
τὰς art. acc. fem. pl. ὁ ἡ τό the, this, that, he, she, it
γραφὰς n. acc. fem. pl. γραφή scripture
εἰ conj. εἰ if, whether, that, though, forasmuch
ταῦτα demo. pron. nom. neut. pl. οὗτος αὕτη τοῦτο this, the same, this same, he, she, it
οὕτως adv. οὕτω οὕτως so, even so, thus, on this wise, likewise, after this manner
12 πολλοὶ adj. nom. masc. pl. πολύς many, great, much, long, abundant
μέν conj. μέν indeed, verily, truly, even, so, some
οὖν conj. οὖν therefore, then, so, and, now, wherefore
ἐξ prep. ἐκ ἐξ (+gen) of, from, out of, by, on, with, in, among, through
αὐτῶν pron. gen. masc. 3p. pl. αὐτός ή ό self, of oneself, even, very, the same, he, she, it
καὶ conj. καί and, even, also, but
τῶν art. gen. fem. pl. ὁ ἡ τό the, this, that, he, she, it
Ἑλληνίδων n. gen. fem. pl. Ἑλληνίς Greek
γυναικῶν n. gen. fem. pl. γυνή woman, wife
τῶν art. gen. fem. pl. ὁ ἡ τό the, this, that, he, she, it
εὐσχημόνων adj. gen. fem. pl. εὐσχήμων honourable, comely
καὶ conj. καί and, even, also, but
ἀνδρῶν n. gen. masc. pl. ἀνήρ man, husband, sir
οὐκ particle of negation. οὐ οὐκ οὐχ not, no, neither, none, nay, nor, never, nothing
ὀλίγοι adj. nom. masc. pl. ὀλίγος few, little, small, a while, brief, short, short space
13 ὡς adv. ὡς as, when, as it were, how, about, like, as soon as, even as, while
δὲ conj. δέ but, and, now, also, to the contrary, rather, then
οἱ art. nom. masc. pl. ὁ ἡ τό the, this, that, he, she, it
ἀπὸ prep. ἀπό (+gen) from, of, out of, since, for, off, at, by, in, on
τῆς art. gen. fem. sg. ὁ ἡ τό the, this, that, he, she, it
Θεσσαλονίκης n. gen. fem. sg. Θεσσαλονίκη Thessalonica
'Ιουδαῖοι adj. nom. masc. pl. 'Ιουδαῖος Jew, Jewess
ὅτι conj. ὅτι that, for, because, how that, how, because that, for that, though
καὶ conj. καί and, even, also, but
ἐν prep. ἐν (+dat) in, by, with, among, at, on, through, to, within, into, of, for
τῇ art. dat. fem. sg. ὁ ἡ τό the, this, that, he, she, it
Βεροίᾳ n. dat. fem. sg. Βέροια Berea
ὑπὸ prep. ὑπό (+gen) of, by, with, from, among, (+acc) under
τοῦ art. gen. masc. sg. ὁ ἡ τό the, this, that, he, she, it
Παύλου n. gen. masc. sg. Παῦλος Paul, Paulus
ὁ art. nom. masc. sg. ὁ ἡ τό the, this, that, he, she, it

λόγος n. nom. masc. sg. λόγος word, saying, account, speech, thing, matter
τοῦ art. gen. masc. sg. ὁ ἡ τό the, this, that, he, she, it
Θεοῦ n. gen. masc. sg. θεός God, god
κἀκεῖ adv. κἀκεῖ and there, there also, thither also
τοὺς art. acc. masc. pl. ὁ ἡ τό the, this, that, he, she, it
ὄχλους n. acc. masc. pl. ὄχλος people, multitude, company, press, number
14 εὐθέως adv. εὐθέως immediately, straightway, forthwith, as soon as, by and by, shortly
δὲ conj. δέ but, and, now, also, to the contrary, rather, then
τότε adv. τότε then, that time
τὸν art. acc. masc. sg. ὁ ἡ τό the, this, that, he, she, it
Παῦλον n. acc. masc. sg. Παῦλος Paul, Paulus
οἱ art. nom. masc. pl. ὁ ἡ τό the, this, that, he, she, it
ἀδελφοὶ n. nom. masc. pl. ἀδελφός brother
ὡς adv. ὡς as, when, as it were, how, about, like, as soon as, even as, while
ἐπὶ prep. ἐπί (+gen) on, in, upon, (+dat) in, at, for, upon, (+acc) on, upon, unto, to, against
τὴν art. acc. fem. sg. ὁ ἡ τό the, this, that, he, she, it
θάλασσαν n. acc. fem. sg. θάλασσα sea
δὲ conj. δέ but, and, now, also, to the contrary, rather, then
ὅ art. nom. masc. sg. ὁ ἡ τό the, this, that, he, she, it
τε conj. τέ and, both, also
Σιλᾶς n. nom. masc. sg. Σιλᾶς Silas
καὶ conj. καί and, even, also, but
ὁ art. nom. masc. sg. ὁ ἡ τό the, this, that, he, she, it
Τιμόθεος n. nom. masc. sg. Τιμόθεος Timotheus, Timothy
ἐκεῖ adv. ἐκεῖ there, thither, thitherward, yonder, yonder place
15 οἱ art. nom. masc. pl. ὁ ἡ τό the, this, that, he, she, it
δὲ conj. δέ but, and, now, also, to the contrary, rather, then
τὸν art. acc. masc. sg. ὁ ἡ τό the, this, that, he, she, it
Παῦλον n. acc. masc. sg. Παῦλος Paul, Paulus
αὐτὸν pron. acc. masc. 3p. sg. αὐτός ἡ ὁ self, of oneself, even, very, the same, he, she, it
ἕως conj. ἕως till, until, unto, until when, while, as far as, even, until now
Ἀθηνῶν n. gen. fem. pl. Ἀθῆναι Athens
καὶ conj. καί and, even, also, but
ἐντολὴν n. acc. fem. sg. ἐντολή commandment, precept
πρὸς prep. πρός (+gen) for, (+dat) at, (+acc) unto, to, with, for, against
τὸν art. acc. masc. sg. ὁ ἡ τό the, this, that, he, she, it
Σιλᾶν n. acc. masc. sg. Σιλᾶς Silas
καὶ conj. καί and, even, also, but
Τιμόθεον n. acc. masc. sg. Τιμόθεος Timotheus, Timothy
ἵνα conj. ἵνα that, to, lest, for to, so that, albeit, because, for, so as
ὡς adv. ὡς as, when, as it were, how, about, like, as soon as, even as, while
τάχιστα adv. τάχιστα with all speed, as soon, most quickly, most speedily
πρὸς prep. πρός (+gen) for, (+dat) at, (+acc) unto, to, with, for, against
αὐτὸν pron. acc. masc. 3p. sg. αὐτός ἡ ὁ self, of oneself, even, very, the same, he, she, it
16 Ἐν prep. ἐν (+dat) in, by, with, among, at, on, through, to, within, into, of, for
δὲ conj. δέ but, and, now, also, to the contrary, rather, then
ταῖς art. dat. fem. pl. ὁ ἡ τό the, this, that, he, she, it
Ἀθήναις n. dat. fem. pl. Ἀθῆναι Athens
αὐτοὺς pron. acc. masc. 3p. pl. αὐτός ἡ ὁ self, of oneself, even, very, the same, he, she, it
τοῦ art. gen. masc. sg. ὁ ἡ τό the, this, that, he, she, it
Παύλου n. gen. masc. sg. Παῦλος Paul, Paulus
τὸ art. nom. neut. sg. ὁ ἡ τό the, this, that, he, she, it
πνεῦμα n. nom. neut. sg. πνεῦμα spirit, Spirit, Ghost, ghost, life. of the spirit, wind
αὐτοῦ pron. gen. masc. 3p. sg. αὐτός ἡ ὁ self, of oneself, even, very, the same, he, she, it
ἐν prep. ἐν (+dat) in, by, with, among, at, on, through, to, within, into, of, for

αὐτῷ pron. dat. masc. 3p. sg. αὐτός ή ό self, of oneself, even, very, the same, he, she, it
κατείδωλον adj. acc. fem. sg. κατείδωλος wholly given to idolatry
τὴν art. acc. fem. sg. ό ή τό the, this, that, he, she, it
πόλιν n. acc. fem. sg. πόλις city
17 μέν conj. μέν indeed, verily, truly, even, so, some
οὖν conj. οὖν therefore, then, so, and, now, wherefore
ἐν prep. ἐν (+dat) in, by, with, among, at, on, through, to, within, into, of, for
τῇ art. dat. fem. sg. ό ή τό the, this, that, he, she, it
συναγωγῇ n. dat. fem. sg. συναγωγή synagogue, assembly, congregation
τοῖς art. dat. masc. pl. ό ή τό the, this, that, he, she, it
Ἰουδαίοις adj. dat. masc. pl. Ἰουδαῖος Jew, Jewess
καὶ conj. καί and, even, also, but
τοῖς art. dat. masc. pl. ό ή τό the, this, that, he, she, it
καὶ conj. καί and, even, also, but
ἐν prep. ἐν (+dat) in, by, with, among, at, on, through, to, within, into, of, for
τῇ art. dat. fem. sg. ό ή τό the, this, that, he, she, it
ἀγορᾷ n. dat. fem. sg. ἀγορά market, marketplace, street
κατὰ prep. κατά (+gen) against, by, throughout, down, (+acc) according to, after, with
πᾶσαν adj. acc. fem. sg. πᾶς πᾶσα πᾶν all, every, whosoever, every one, no, whole, any
ἡμέραν n. acc. fem. sg. ἡμέρα day, time, year, while, age, day time
πρὸς prep. πρός (+gen) for, (+dat) at, (+acc) unto, to, with, for, against
τοὺς art. acc. masc. pl. ό ή τό the, this, that, he, she, it
18 τινὲς indefinite pron. nom. masc. pl. τὶς certain, some, any man, one, any thing
δὲ conj. δέ but, and, now, also, to the contrary, rather, then
τῶν art. gen. masc. pl. ό ή τό the, this, that, he, she, it
Ἐπικουρείων n. gen. masc. pl. Ἐπικούρειος Epicurean
καὶ conj. καί and, even, also, but
τῶν art. gen. masc. pl. ό ή τό the, this, that, he, she, it
Στοϊκῶν adj. gen. masc. pl. Στωϊκός Stoick
φιλοσόφων n. gen. masc. pl. φιλόσοφος philosopher
αὐτῷ pron. dat. masc. 3p. sg. αὐτός ή ό self, of oneself, even, very, the same, he, she, it
καὶ conj. καί and, even, also, but
τινὲς indefinite pron. nom. masc. pl. τὶς certain, some, any man, one, any thing
Τί interrog. pron. acc. neut. sg. τίς what, who, why, where, which, how
ἂν particle. ἄν Indicating contingency. No English translation.
ὁ art. nom. masc. sg. ό ή τό the, this, that, he, she, it
σπερμολόγος adj. nom. masc. sg. σπερμολόγος babbler
οὗτος demo. pron. nom. masc. sg. οὗτος αὕτη τοῦτο this, the same, this same, he, she, it
οἱ art. nom. masc. pl. ό ή τό the, this, that, he, she, it
δὲ conj. δέ but, and, now, also, to the contrary, rather, then
Ξένων adj. gen. neut. pl. ξένος stranger, strange, host
δαιμονίων n. gen. neut. pl. δαιμόνιον devil, demon, god
καταγγελεὺς n. nom. masc. sg. καταγγελεύς setter forth
ὅτι conj. ὅτι that, for, because, how that, how, because that, for that, though
τὸν art. acc. masc. sg. ό ή τό the, this, that, he, she, it
Ἰησοῦν n. acc. masc. sg. Ἰησοῦς Jesus
καὶ conj. καί and, even, also, but
τὴν art. acc. fem. sg. ό ή τό the, this, that, he, she, it
ἀνάστασιν n. acc. fem. sg. ἀνάστασις resurrection, rising again
αὐτοῖς pron. dat. masc. 3p. pl. αὐτός ή ό self, of oneself, even, very, the same, he, she, it
19 τε conj. τέ and, both, also
αὐτοῦ pron. gen. masc. 3p. sg. αὐτός ή ό self, of oneself, even, very, the same, he, she, it
ἐπὶ prep. ἐπί (+gen) on, in, upon, (+dat) in, at, for, upon, (+acc) on, upon, unto, to, against
τὸν art. acc. masc. sg. ό ή τό the, this, that, he, she, it
Ἄρειον adj. acc. masc. sg. Ἄρειος Areo, of Mars

πάγον n. acc. masc. sg. πάγος pagus, hill
τίς interrog. pron. nom. fem. sg. τίς what, who, why, where, which, how
ἡ art. nom. fem. sg. ὁ ἡ τό the, this, that, he, she, it
καινὴ adj. nom. fem. sg. καινός new
αὕτη demo. pron. nom. fem. sg. οὗτος αὕτη τοῦτο this, the same, this same, he, she, it
ἡ art. nom. fem. sg. ὁ ἡ τό the, this, that, he, she, it
ὑπὸ prep. ὑπό (+gen) of, by, with, from, among, (+acc) under
σοῦ pron. gen. 2p. sg. σύ thou, you
διδαχή n. nom. fem. sg. διδαχή doctrine, teaching
20 γάρ conj. γάρ for, and, because, but, indeed
τινα indefinite pron. acc. neut. pl. τὶς certain, some, any man, one, any thing
εἰς prep. εἰς (+acc) into, to, unto, for, in, on, toward, against, upon, at, among
τὰς art. acc. fem. pl. ὁ ἡ τό the, this, that, he, she, it
ἀκοὰς n. acc. fem. pl. ἀκοή hearing, ear, fame, report, rumour, which one heard
ἡμῶν pron. gen. 1p. pl. ἐγώ I
οὖν conj. οὖν therefore, then, so, and, now, wherefore
τί interrog. pron. acc. neut. sg. τίς what, who, why, where, which, how
ἂν particle. ἄν Indicating contingency. No English translation.
ταῦτα demo. pron. nom. neut. pl. οὗτος αὕτη τοῦτο this, the same, this same, he, she, it
21 Ἀθηναῖοι adj. nom. masc. pl. Ἀθηναῖος Athenian, of Athens
δὲ conj. δέ but, and, now, also, to the contrary, rather, then
πάντες adj. nom. masc. pl. πᾶς πᾶσα πᾶν all, every, whosoever, every one, no, whole, any
καὶ conj. καί and, even, also, but
οἱ art. nom. masc. pl. ὁ ἡ τό the, this, that, he, she, it
ξένοι adj. nom. masc. pl. ξένος stranger, strange, host
εἰς prep. εἰς (+acc) into, to, unto, for, in, on, toward, against, upon, at, among
οὐδὲν adj. acc. neut. sg. οὐδείς no man, nothing, no, none, neither, not, nought
ἕτερον adj. acc. neut. sg. ἕτερος another, other, else, strange
ἢ particle. ἤ or, than, either, nor, or else, and, rather than
τι indefinite pron. acc. neut. sg. τὶς certain, some, any man, one, any thing
καὶ conj. καί and, even, also, but
καινότερον compar. adj. acc. neut. sg. καινός new
22 δὲ conj. δέ but, and, now, also, to the contrary, rather, then
ὁ art. nom. masc. sg. ὁ ἡ τό the, this, that, he, she, it
Παῦλος n. nom. masc. sg. Παῦλος Paul, Paulus
ἐν prep. ἐν (+dat) in, by, with, among, at, on, through, to, within, into, of, for
μέσῳ adj. dat. neut. sg. μέσος midst, among, mid, between
τοῦ art. gen. masc. sg. ὁ ἡ τό the, this, that, he, she, it
Ἀρείου n. gen. masc. sg. Ἄρειος Areo, of Mars
πάγου n. gen. masc. sg. πάγος pagus, hill
Ἄνδρες n. voc. masc. pl. ἀνήρ man, husband, sir
Ἀθηναῖοι adj. voc. masc. pl. Ἀθηναῖος Athenian, of Athens
κατὰ prep. κατά (+gen) against, by, throughout, down, (+acc) according to, after, with
πάντα adj. acc. neut. pl. πᾶς πᾶσα πᾶν all, every, whosoever, every one, no, whole, any
ὡς adv. ὡς as, when, as it were, how, about, like, as soon as, even as, while
δεισιδαιμονεστέρους compar. adj. acc. masc. pl. δεισιδαιμονέστερος too superstitious
ὑμᾶς pron. acc. 2p. pl. σύ thou, you
23 γὰρ conj. γάρ for, and, because, but, indeed
καὶ conj. καί and, even, also, but
τὰ art. acc. neut. pl. ὁ ἡ τό the, this, that, he, she, it
σεβάσματα n. acc. neut. pl. σέβασμα devotion, that is worshipped
ὑμῶν pron. gen. 2p. pl. σύ thou, you
καὶ conj. καί and, even, also, but
βωμὸν n. acc. masc. sg. βωμός altar
ἐν prep. ἐν (+dat) in, by, with, among, at, on, through, to, within, into, of, for

ᾧ relative pron. dat. masc. sg. ὅς ἥ ὅ who, which, what, that
Ἀγνώστῳ adj. dat. masc. sg. ἄγνωστος unknown
Θεῷ n. dat. masc. sg. θεός God, god
ὃν relative pron. acc. masc. sg. ὅς ἥ ὅ who, which, what, that
οὖν conj. οὖν therefore, then, so, and, now, wherefore
τοῦτον demo. pron. acc. masc. sg. οὗτος αὕτη τοῦτο this, the same, this same, he, she, it
ἐγὼ pron. nom. 1p. sg. ἐγώ I
ὑμῖν pron. dat. 2p. pl. σύ thou, you
24 ὁ art. nom. masc. sg. ὁ ἡ τό the, this, that, he, she, it
Θεὸς n. nom. masc. sg. θεός God, god
ὁ art. nom. masc. sg. ὁ ἡ τό the, this, that, he, she, it
τὸν art. acc. masc. sg. ὁ ἡ τό the, this, that, he, she, it
κόσμον n. acc. masc. sg. κόσμος world, adorning
καὶ conj. καί and, even, also, but
πάντα adj. acc. neut. pl. πᾶς πᾶσα πᾶν all, every, whosoever, every one, no, whole, any
τὰ art. acc. neut. pl. ὁ ἡ τό the, this, that, he, she, it
ἐν prep. ἐν (+dat) in, by, with, among, at, on, through, to, within, into, of, for
αὐτῷ pron. dat. masc. 3p. sg. αὐτός ἡ ὁ self, of oneself, even, very, the same, he, she, it
οὗτος demo. pron. nom. masc. sg. οὗτος αὕτη τοῦτο this, the same, this same, he, she, it
οὐρανοῦ n. gen. masc. sg. οὐρανός heaven, air, sky
καὶ conj. καί and, even, also, but
γῆς n. gen. fem. sg. γῆ earth, land, ground, country
κύριος n. nom. masc. sg. κύριος Lord, lord, master, sir, LORD, God, Master, owner
οὐκ particle of negation. οὐ οὐκ οὐχ not, no, neither, none, nay, nor, never, nothing
ἐν prep. ἐν (+dat) in, by, with, among, at, on, through, to, within, into, of, for
χειροποιήτοις adj. dat. masc. pl. χειροποίητος made with hands, made by hands
ναοῖς n. dat. masc. pl. ναός temple, shrine
25 οὐδὲ conj. οὐδέ neither, nor, not, no, not even, never, not yet
ὑπὸ prep. ὑπό (+gen) of, by, with, from, among, (+acc) under
χειρῶν n. gen. fem. pl. χείρ hand
ἀνθρώπων n. gen. masc. pl. ἄνθρωπος man, human being, person, one, certain
τινος indefinite pron. gen. neut. sg. τὶς certain, some, any man, one, any thing
αὐτὸς pron. nom. masc. 3p. sg. αὐτός ἡ ὁ self, of oneself, even, very, the same, he, she, it
πᾶσι adj. dat. masc. pl. πᾶς πᾶσα πᾶν all, every, whosoever, every one, no, whole, any
ζωὴν n. acc. fem. sg. ζωή life, lifetime
καὶ conj. καί and, even, also, but
πνοὴν n. acc. fem. sg. πνοή wind, breath
καὶ conj. καί and, even, also, but
τὰ art. acc. neut. pl. ὁ ἡ τό the, this, that, he, she, it
πάντα adj. acc. neut. pl. πᾶς πᾶσα πᾶν all, every, whosoever, every one, no, whole, any
26 τε conj. τέ and, both, also
ἐξ prep. ἐκ ἐξ (+gen) of, from, out of, by, on, with, in, among, through
ἑνὸς num. gen. masc. sg. εἷς or ἕν one, other, some, any, only, a certain
αἵματος n. gen. neut. sg. αἷμα blood
πᾶν adj. acc. neut. sg. πᾶς πᾶσα πᾶν all, every, whosoever, every one, no, whole, any
ἔθνος n. acc. neut. sg. ἔθνος Gentile, nation, heathen, people
ἀνθρώπων n. gen. masc. pl. ἄνθρωπος man, human being, person, one, certain
ἐπὶ prep. ἐπί (+gen) on, in, upon, (+dat) in, at, for, upon, (+acc) on, upon, unto, to, against
πᾶν adj. acc. neut. sg. πᾶς πᾶσα πᾶν all, every, whosoever, every one, no, whole, any
τὸ art. acc. neut. sg. ὁ ἡ τό the, this, that, he, she, it
πρόσωπόν n. acc. neut. sg. πρόσωπον face, presence, person, countenance
τῆς art. gen. fem. sg. ὁ ἡ τό the, this, that, he, she, it
γῆς n. gen. fem. sg. γῆ earth, land, ground, country
καιροὺς n. acc. masc. pl. καιρός time, season, due time, opportunity
καὶ conj. καί and, even, also, but

τὰς art. acc. fem. pl. ὁ ἡ τό the, this, that, he, she, it
ὁροθεσίας n. acc. fem. pl. ὁροθεσία bound
τῆς art. gen. fem. sg. ὁ ἡ τό the, this, that, he, she, it
κατοικίας n. gen. fem. sg. κατοικία habitation
αὐτῶν pron. gen. masc. 3p. pl. αὐτός ἡ ὁ self, of oneself, even, very, the same, he, she, it
27 τὸν art. acc. masc. sg. ὁ ἡ τό the, this, that, he, she, it
Κύριον n. acc. masc. sg. κύριος Lord, lord, master, sir, LORD, God, Master, owner
εἰ conj. εἰ if, whether, that, though, forasmuch
ἄραγε particle. ἄραγε then, surely, so then, wherefore
αὐτὸν pron. acc. masc. 3p. sg. αὐτός ἡ ὁ self, of oneself, even, very, the same, he, she, it
καὶ conj. καί and, even, also, but
καίτοιγε conj. καίτοιγε though, nevertheless
οὐ particle of negation. οὐ οὐκ οὐχ not, no, neither, none, nay, nor, never, nothing
μακρὰν adv. μακράν far, afar off, far off, good way off, great way off
ἀπὸ prep. ἀπό (+gen) from, of, out of, since, for, off, at, by, in, on
ἑνὸς num. gen. masc. sg. εἷς or ἕν one, other, some, any, only, a certain
ἑκάστου adj. gen. masc. sg. ἕκαστος every man, every, every one, any man, each
ἡμῶν pron. gen. 1p. pl. ἐγώ I
28 ἐν prep. ἐν (+dat) in, by, with, among, at, on, through, to, within, into, of, for
αὐτῷ pron. dat. masc. 3p. sg. αὐτός ἡ ὁ self, of oneself, even, very, the same, he, she, it
γὰρ conj. γάρ for, and, because, but, indeed
καὶ conj. καί and, even, also, but
καὶ conj. καί and, even, also, but
ὡς adv. ὡς as, when, as it were, how, about, like, as soon as, even as, while
καὶ conj. καί and, even, also, but
τινες indefinite pron. nom. masc. pl. τὶς certain, some, any man, one, any thing
τῶν art. gen. masc. pl. ὁ ἡ τό the, this, that, he, she, it
καθ' prep. κατά (+gen) against, by, throughout, down, (+acc) according to, after, with
ὑμᾶς pron. acc. 2p. pl. σύ thou, you
ποιητῶν n. gen. masc. pl. ποιητής doer, poet
Τοῦ art. gen. masc. sg. ὁ ἡ τό the, this, that, he, she, it
γὰρ conj. γάρ for, and, because, but, indeed
καὶ conj. καί and, even, also, but
γένος n. nom. neut. sg. γένος kind, kindred, offspring, nation, countrymen
29 γένος n. nom. neut. sg. γένος kind, kindred, offspring, nation, countrymen
οὖν conj. οὖν therefore, then, so, and, now, wherefore
τοῦ art. gen. masc. sg. ὁ ἡ τό the, this, that, he, she, it
Θεοῦ n. gen. masc. sg. θεός God, god
οὐκ particle of negation. οὐ οὐκ οὐχ not, no, neither, none, nay, nor, never, nothing
χρυσῷ n. dat. masc. sg. χρυσός gold
ἢ particle. ἤ or, than, either, nor, or else, and, rather than
ἀργύρῳ n. dat. masc. sg. ἄργυρος silver
ἢ particle. ἤ or, than, either, nor, or else, and, rather than
λίθῳ n. dat. masc. sg. λίθος stone
χαράγματι n. dat. neut. sg. χάραγμα mark, graven
τέχνης n. gen. fem. sg. τέχνη art, craft, occupation
καὶ conj. καί and, even, also, but
ἐνθυμήσεως n. gen. fem. sg. ἐνθύμησις thought, device
ἀνθρώπου n. gen. masc. sg. ἄνθρωπος man, human being, person, one, certain
τὸ art. acc. neut. sg. ὁ ἡ τό the, this, that, he, she, it
θεῖον adj. acc. neut. sg. θεῖον brimstone
ὅμοιον adj. acc. neut. sg. ὅμοιος like
30 τοὺς art. acc. masc. pl. ὁ ἡ τό the, this, that, he, she, it
μέν conj. μέν indeed, verily, truly, even, so, some
οὖν conj. οὖν therefore, then, so, and, now, wherefore

χρόνους n. acc. masc. pl. χρόνος time, season, space
τῆς art. gen. fem. sg. ὁ ἡ τό the, this, that, he, she, it
ἀγνοίας n. gen. fem. sg. ἄγνοια ignorance
ὁ art. nom. masc. sg. ὁ ἡ τό the, this, that, he, she, it
Θεός n. nom. masc. sg. θεός God, god
τὰ art. acc. neut. pl. ὁ ἡ τό the, this, that, he, she, it
νῦν adv. νῦν now, henceforth, present, this time
τοῖς art. dat. masc. pl. ὁ ἡ τό the, this, that, he, she, it
ἀνθρώποις n. dat. masc. pl. ἄνθρωπος man, human being, person, one, certain
πᾶσι adj. dat. masc. pl. πᾶς πᾶσα πᾶν all, every, whosoever, every one, no, whole, any
πανταχοῦ adv. πανταχοῦ every where, in all places
31 διότι conj. διότι for, because, because that, therefore
ἡμέραν n. acc. fem. sg. ἡμέρα day, time, year, while, age, day time
ἐν prep. ἐν (+dat) in, by, with, among, at, on, through, to, within, into, of, for
ᾗ relative pron. dat. fem. sg. ὅς ἥ ὅ who, which, what, that
τὴν art. acc. fem. sg. ὁ ἡ τό the, this, that, he, she, it
οἰκουμένην n. acc. fem. sg. οἰκουμένη world, earth
ἐν prep. ἐν (+dat) in, by, with, among, at, on, through, to, within, into, of, for
δικαιοσύνῃ n. dat. fem. sg. δικαιοσύνη righteousness
ἐν prep. ἐν (+dat) in, by, with, among, at, on, through, to, within, into, of, for
ἀνδρὶ n. dat. masc. sg. ἀνήρ man, husband, sir
ᾧ relative pron. dat. masc. sg. ὅς ἥ ὅ who, which, what, that
πίστιν n. acc. fem. sg. πίστις faith, assurance, belief, fidelity
πᾶσιν adj. dat. masc. pl. πᾶς πᾶσα πᾶν all, every, whosoever, every one, no, whole, any
αὐτὸν pron. acc. masc. 3p. sg. αὐτός ἡ ὁ self, of oneself, even, very, the same, he, she, it
ἐκ prep. ἐκ ἐξ (+gen) of, from, out of, by, on, with, in, among, through
νεκρῶν adj. gen. masc. pl. νεκρός dead
32 δὲ conj. δέ but, and, now, also, to the contrary, rather, then
ἀνάστασιν n. acc. fem. sg. ἀνάστασις resurrection, rising again
νεκρῶν adj. gen. masc. pl. νεκρός dead
οἱ art. nom. masc. pl. ὁ ἡ τό the, this, that, he, she, it
μέν conj. μέν indeed, verily, truly, even, so, some
οἱ art. nom. masc. pl. ὁ ἡ τό the, this, that, he, she, it
δὲ conj. δέ but, and, now, also, to the contrary, rather, then
σου pron. gen. 2p. sg. σύ thou, you
πάλιν adv. πάλιν again
περὶ prep. περί (+gen) of, for, concerning, (+acc) about, concerning, in
τούτου demo. pron. gen. neut. sg. οὗτος αὕτη τοῦτο this, the same, this same, he, she, it
33 καὶ conj. καί and, even, also, but
οὕτως adv. οὕτω οὕτως so, even so, thus, on this wise, likewise, after this manner
ὁ art. nom. masc. sg. ὁ ἡ τό the, this, that, he, she, it
Παῦλος n. nom. masc. sg. Παῦλος Paul, Paulus
ἐκ prep. ἐκ ἐξ (+gen) of, from, out of, by, on, with, in, among, through
μέσου adj. gen. neut. sg. μέσος midst, among, mid, between
αὐτῶν pron. gen. masc. 3p. pl. αὐτός ἡ ὁ self, of oneself, even, very, the same, he, she, it
34 τινὲς indefinite pron. nom. masc. pl. τὶς certain, some, any man, one, any thing
δὲ conj. δέ but, and, now, also, to the contrary, rather, then
ἄνδρες n. nom. masc. pl. ἀνήρ man, husband, sir
αὐτῷ pron. dat. masc. 3p. sg. αὐτός ἡ ὁ self, of oneself, even, very, the same, he, she, it
ἐν prep. ἐν (+dat) in, by, with, among, at, on, through, to, within, into, of, for
οἷς relative pron. dat. masc. pl. ὅς ἥ ὅ who, which, what, that
καὶ conj. καί and, even, also, but
Διονύσιος n. nom. masc. sg. Διονύσιος Dionysius
ὁ art. nom. masc. sg. ὁ ἡ τό the, this, that, he, she, it
'Αρεοπαγίτης n. nom. masc. sg. 'Αρεοπαγίτης Areopagite

καὶ conj. καί and, even, also, but
γυνὴ n. nom. fem. sg. γυνή woman, wife
ὀνόματι n. dat. neut. sg. ὄνομα name, call, surname
Δάμαρις n. nom. fem. sg. Δάμαρις Damaris
καὶ conj. καί and, even, also, but
ἕτεροι adj. nom. masc. pl. ἕτερος another, other, else, strange
σὺν prep. σύν (+dat) with, beside
αὐτοῖς pron. dat. masc. 3p. pl. αὐτός ή ό self, of oneself, even, very, the same, he, she, it

18

1 Μετὰ prep. μετά (+gen) with, among, against, (+acc) after
δὲ conj. δέ but, and, now, also, to the contrary, rather, then
ταῦτα demo. pron. acc. neut. pl. οὗτος αὕτη τοῦτο this, the same, this same, he, she, it
ὁ art. nom. masc. sg. ὁ ἡ τό the, this, that, he, she, it
Παῦλος n. nom. masc. sg. Παῦλος Paul, Paulus
ἐκ prep. ἐκ ἐξ (+gen) of, from, out of, by, on, with, in, among, through
τῶν art. gen. fem. pl. ὁ ἡ τό the, this, that, he, she, it
᾿Αθηνῶν n. gen. fem. pl. ᾿Αθῆναι Athens
εἰς prep. εἰς (+acc) into, to, unto, for, in, on, toward, against, upon, at, among
Κόρινθον n. acc. fem. sg. Κόρινθος Corinth
2 καὶ conj. καί and, even, also, but
τινα indefinite pron. acc. masc. sg. τὶς certain, some, any man, one, any thing
᾿Ιουδαῖον adj. acc. masc. sg. ᾿Ιουδαῖος Jew, Jewess
ὀνόματι n. dat. neut. sg. ὄνομα name, call, surname
᾿Ακύλαν n. acc. masc. sg. ᾿Ακύλας Aquila
Ποντικὸν adj. acc. masc. sg. Ποντικός belonging to Pontus, inhabitant of Pontus
τῷ art. dat. neut. sg. ὁ ἡ τό the, this, that, he, she, it
γένει n. dat. neut. sg. γένος kind, kindred, offspring, nation, countrymen
προσφάτως adv. προσφάτως lately
ἀπὸ prep. ἀπό (+gen) from, of, out of, since, for, off, at, by, in, on
τῆς art. gen. fem. sg. ὁ ἡ τό the, this, that, he, she, it
᾿Ιταλίας n. gen. fem. sg. ᾿Ιταλία Italy
καὶ conj. καί and, even, also, but
Πρίσκιλλαν n. acc. fem. sg. Πρίσκιλλα Priscilla
γυναῖκα n. acc. fem. sg. γυνή woman, wife
αὐτοῦ pron. gen. masc. 3p. sg. αὐτός ή ό self, of oneself, even, very, the same, he, she, it
διὰ prep. διά (+gen) by, through, with, in, of, (+acc) for, because of, for a cause
τὸ art. acc. neut. sg. ὁ ἡ τό the, this, that, he, she, it
Κλαύδιον n. acc. masc. sg. Κλαύδιος Claudius
πάντας adj. acc. masc. pl. πᾶς πᾶσα πᾶν all, every, whosoever, every one, no, whole, any
τοὺς art. acc. masc. pl. ὁ ἡ τό the, this, that, he, she, it
᾿Ιουδαίους adj. acc. masc. pl. ᾿Ιουδαῖος Jew, Jewess
ἐκ prep. ἐκ ἐξ (+gen) of, from, out of, by, on, with, in, among, through
τῆς art. gen. fem. sg. ὁ ἡ τό the, this, that, he, she, it
῾Ρώμης n. gen. fem. sg. ῾Ρώμη Rome
αὐτοῖς pron. dat. masc. 3p. pl. αὐτός ή ό self, of oneself, even, very, the same, he, she, it
3 καὶ conj. καί and, even, also, but
διὰ prep. διά (+gen) by, through, with, in, of, (+acc) for, because of, for a cause
τὸ art. acc. neut. sg. ὁ ἡ τό the, this, that, he, she, it
ὁμότεχνον adj. acc. masc. sg. ὁμότεχνος of the same craft
παρ' prep. παρά (+gen) of, from, (+dat) with, for, (+acc) beside, at, by, above, against
αὐτοῖς pron. dat. masc. 3p. pl. αὐτός ή ό self, of oneself, even, very, the same, he, she, it
καὶ conj. καί and, even, also, but
γὰρ conj. γάρ for, and, because, but, indeed

σκηνοποιοὶ n. nom. masc. pl. σκηνοποιός tentmaker
τὴν art. acc. fem. sg. ὁ ἡ τό the, this, that, he, she, it
τέχνην n. acc. fem. sg. τέχνη art, craft, occupation
4 δὲ conj. δέ but, and, now, also, to the contrary, rather, then
ἐν prep. ἐν (+dat) in, by, with, among, at, on, through, to, within, into, of, for
τῇ art. dat. fem. sg. ὁ ἡ τό the, this, that, he, she, it
συναγωγῇ n. dat. fem. sg. συναγωγή synagogue, assembly, congregation
κατὰ prep. κατά (+gen) against, by, throughout, down, (+acc) according to, after, with
πᾶν adj. acc. neut. sg. πᾶς πᾶσα πᾶν all, every, whosoever, every one, no, whole, any
σάββατον n. acc. neut. sg. σάββατον sabbath day, sabbath, week
τε conj. τέ and, both, also
Ἰουδαίους adj. acc. masc. pl. Ἰουδαῖος Jew, Jewess
καὶ conj. καί and, even, also, but
Ἕλληνας n. acc. masc. pl. Ἕλλην Greek, Gentile
5 Ὡς conj. ὡς as, when, as it were, how, about, like, as soon as, even as, while
δὲ conj. δέ but, and, now, also, to the contrary, rather, then
ἀπὸ prep. ἀπό (+gen) from, of, out of, since, for, off, at, by, in, on
τῆς art. gen. fem. sg. ὁ ἡ τό the, this, that, he, she, it
Μακεδονίας n. gen. fem. sg. Μακεδονία Macedonia
ὅ art. nom. masc. sg. ὁ ἡ τό the, this, that, he, she, it
τε conj. τέ and, both, also
Σιλᾶς n. nom. masc. sg. Σιλᾶς Silas
καὶ conj. καί and, even, also, but
ὁ art. nom. masc. sg. ὁ ἡ τό the, this, that, he, she, it
Τιμόθεος n. nom. masc. sg. Τιμόθεος Timotheus, Timothy
τῷ art. dat. masc. sg. ὁ ἡ τό the, this, that, he, she, it
πνεύματι n. dat. neut. sg. πνεῦμα spirit, Spirit, Ghost, ghost, life. of the spirit, wind
ὁ art. nom. masc. sg. ὁ ἡ τό the, this, that, he, she, it
Παῦλος n. nom. masc. sg. Παῦλος Paul, Paulus
τοῖς art. dat. masc. pl. ὁ ἡ τό the, this, that, he, she, it
Ἰουδαίοις adj. dat. masc. pl. Ἰουδαῖος Jew, Jewess
τὸν art. acc. masc. sg. ὁ ἡ τό the, this, that, he, she, it
Χριστὸν n. acc. masc. sg. Χριστός Christ
Ἰησοῦν n. acc. masc. sg. Ἰησοῦς Jesus
6 δὲ conj. δέ but, and, now, also, to the contrary, rather, then
αὐτῶν pron. gen. masc. 3p. pl. αὐτός ή ό self, of oneself, even, very, the same, he, she, it
καὶ conj. καί and, even, also, but
τὰ art. acc. neut. pl. ὁ ἡ τό the, this, that, he, she, it
ἱμάτια n. acc. neut. pl. ἱμάτιον cloke, garment, clothes, raiment, robe, vesture
πρὸς prep. πρός (+gen) for, (+dat) at, (+acc) unto, to, with, for, against
αὐτούς pron. acc. masc. 3p. pl. αὐτός ή ό self, of oneself, even, very, the same, he, she, it
Τὸ art. nom. neut. sg. ὁ ἡ τό the, this, that, he, she, it
αἷμα n. nom. neut. sg. αἷμα blood
ὑμῶν pron. gen. 2p. pl. σύ thou, you
ἐπὶ prep. ἐπί (+gen) on, in, upon, (+dat) in, at, for, upon, (+acc) on, upon, unto, to, against
τὴν art. acc. fem. sg. ὁ ἡ τό the, this, that, he, she, it
κεφαλὴν n. acc. fem. sg. κεφαλή head
ὑμῶν pron. gen. 2p. pl. σύ thou, you
καθαρὸς adj. nom. masc. sg. καθαρός pure, clean, clear
ἐγὼ pron. nom. 1p. sg. ἐγώ I
ἀπὸ prep. ἀπό (+gen) from, of, out of, since, for, off, at, by, in, on
τοῦ art. gen. masc. sg. ὁ ἡ τό the, this, that, he, she, it
νῦν adv. νῦν now, henceforth, present, this time
εἰς prep. εἰς (+acc) into, to, unto, for, in, on, toward, against, upon, at, among
τὰ art. acc. neut. pl. ὁ ἡ τό the, this, that, he, she, it

ἔθνη n. acc. neut. pl. ἔθνος Gentile, nation, heathen, people
7 καὶ conj. καί and, even, also, but
ἐκεῖθεν adv. ἐκεῖθεν thence, from thence, from that place
εἰς prep. εἰς (+acc) into, to, unto, for, in, on, toward, against, upon, at, among
οἰκίαν n. acc. fem. sg. οἰκία house, home, household
τινὸς indefinite pron. gen. masc. sg. τὶς certain, some, any man, one, any thing
ὀνόματι n. dat. neut. sg. ὄνομα name, call, surname
Ἰούστου n. gen. masc. sg. Ἰοῦστος Justus
τὸν art. acc. masc. sg. ὁ ἡ τό the, this, that, he, she, it
Θεόν n. acc. masc. sg. θεός God, god
οὗ relative pron. gen. masc. sg. ὅς ἥ ὅ who, which, what, that
ἡ art. nom. fem. sg. ὁ ἡ τό the, this, that, he, she, it
οἰκία n. nom. fem. sg. οἰκία house, home, household
τῇ art. dat. fem. sg. ὁ ἡ τό the, this, that, he, she, it
συναγωγῇ n. dat. fem. sg. συναγωγή synagogue, assembly, congregation
8 Κρίσπος n. nom. masc. sg. Κρίσπος Crispus
δὲ conj. δέ but, and, now, also, to the contrary, rather, then
ὁ art. nom. masc. sg. ὁ ἡ τό the, this, that, he, she, it
ἀρχισυνάγωγος n. nom. masc. sg. ἀρχισυνάγωγος ruler of the synagogue
τῷ art. dat. masc. sg. ὁ ἡ τό the, this, that, he, she, it
Κυρίῳ n. dat. masc. sg. κύριος Lord, lord, master, sir, LORD, God, Master, owner
σὺν prep. σύν (+dat) with, beside
ὅλῳ adj. dat. masc. sg. ὅλος all, whole, every whit, altogether
τῷ art. dat. masc. sg. ὁ ἡ τό the, this, that, he, she, it
οἴκῳ n. dat. masc. sg. οἶκος house, home, household
αὐτοῦ pron. gen. masc. 3p. sg. αὐτός ἡ ὁ self, of oneself, even, very, the same, he, she, it
καὶ conj. καί and, even, also, but
πολλοὶ adj. nom. masc. pl. πολύς many, great, much, long, abundant
τῶν art. gen. masc. pl. ὁ ἡ τό the, this, that, he, she, it
Κορινθίων n. gen. masc. pl. Κορίνθιος Corinthian
καὶ conj. καί and, even, also, but
9 δὲ conj. δέ but, and, now, also, to the contrary, rather, then
ὁ art. nom. masc. sg. ὁ ἡ τό the, this, that, he, she, it
Κύριος n. nom. masc. sg. κύριος Lord, lord, master, sir, LORD, God, Master, owner
δι' prep. διά (+gen) by, through, with, in, of, (+acc) for, because of, for a cause
ὁράματος n. gen. neut. sg. ὅραμα vision, sight
ἐν prep. ἐν (+dat) in, by, with, among, at, on, through, to, within, into, of, for
νυκτὶ n. dat. fem. sg. νύξ night
τῷ art. dat. masc. sg. ὁ ἡ τό the, this, that, he, she, it
Παύλῳ n. dat. masc. sg. Παῦλος Paul, Paulus
Μὴ particle of negation. μή not, no, lest, neither, none, nothing, nor, never, without
ἀλλὰ conj. ἀλλά but, yea, yet, nevertheless, howbeit, nay, therefore
καὶ conj. καί and, even, also, but
μὴ particle of negation. μή not, no, lest, neither, none, nothing, nor, never, without
10 διότι conj. διότι for, because, because that, therefore
ἐγώ pron. nom. 1p. sg. ἐγώ I
μετὰ prep. μετά (+gen) with, among, against, (+acc) after
σοῦ pron. gen. 2p. sg. σύ thou, you
καὶ conj. καί and, even, also, but
οὐδεὶς num. nom. masc. sg. οὐδείς no man, nothing, no, none, neither, not, nought
σοι pron. dat. 2p. sg. σύ thou, you
τοῦ art. gen. neut. sg. ὁ ἡ τό the, this, that, he, she, it
σε pron. acc. 2p. sg. σύ thou, you
διότι conj. διότι for, because, because that, therefore
λαός n. nom. masc. sg. λαός people

μοι pron. dat. 1p. sg. ἐγώ I
πολὺς adj. nom. masc. sg. πολύς many, great, much, long, abundant
ἐν prep. ἐν (+dat) in, by, with, among, at, on, through, to, within, into, of, for
τῇ art. dat. fem. sg. ὁ ἡ τό the, this, that, he, she, it
πόλει n. dat. fem. sg. πόλις city
ταύτῃ demo. pron. dat. fem. sg. οὗτος αὕτη τοῦτο this, the same, this same, he, she, it
11 τε conj. τέ and, both, also
ἐνιαυτὸν n. acc. masc. sg. ἐνιαυτός year
καὶ conj. καί and, even, also, but
μῆνας n. acc. masc. pl. μήν month
ἕξ num. acc. masc. pl. ἕξ six
ἐν prep. ἐν (+dat) in, by, with, among, at, on, through, to, within, into, of, for
αὐτοῖς pron. dat. masc. 3p. pl. αὐτός ή ό self, of oneself, even, very, the same, he, she, it
τὸν art. acc. masc. sg. ὁ ἡ τό the, this, that, he, she, it
λόγον n. acc. masc. sg. λόγος word, saying, account, speech, thing, matter
τοῦ art. gen. masc. sg. ὁ ἡ τό the, this, that, he, she, it
Θεοῦ n. gen. masc. sg. θεός God, god
12 Γαλλίωνος n. gen. masc. sg. Γαλλίων Gallio
δὲ conj. δέ but, and, now, also, to the contrary, rather, then
τῆς art. gen. fem. sg. ὁ ἡ τό the, this, that, he, she, it
Ἀχαΐας n. gen. fem. sg. Ἀχαΐα Achaia
ὁμοθυμαδὸν adv. ὁμοθυμαδόν with one accord, with one mind
οἱ art. nom. masc. pl. ὁ ἡ τό the, this, that, he, she, it
Ἰουδαῖοι adj. nom. masc. pl. Ἰουδαῖος Jew, Jewess
τῷ art. dat. masc. sg. ὁ ἡ τό the, this, that, he, she, it
Παύλῳ n. dat. masc. sg. Παῦλος Paul, Paulus
καὶ conj. καί and, even, also, but
αὐτὸν pron. acc. masc. 3p. sg. αὐτός ή ό self, of oneself, even, very, the same, he, she, it
ἐπὶ prep. ἐπί (+gen) on, in, upon, (+dat) in, at, for, upon, (+acc) on, upon, unto, to, against
τὸ art. acc. neut. sg. ὁ ἡ τό the, this, that, he, she, it
βῆμα n. acc. neut. sg. βῆμα judgment seat, throne
13 ὅτι conj. ὅτι that, for, because, how that, how, because that, for that, though
Παρὰ prep. παρά (+gen) of, from, (+dat) with, for, (+acc) beside, at, by, above, against
τὸν art. acc. masc. sg. ὁ ἡ τό the, this, that, he, she, it
νόμον n. acc. masc. sg. νόμος law, the law
οὗτος demo. pron. nom. masc. sg. οὗτος αὕτη τοῦτο this, the same, this same, he, she, it
τοὺς art. acc. masc. pl. ὁ ἡ τό the, this, that, he, she, it
ἀνθρώπους n. acc. masc. pl. ἄνθρωπος man, human being, person, one, certain
τὸν art. acc. masc. sg. ὁ ἡ τό the, this, that, he, she, it
Θεόν n. acc. masc. sg. θεός God, god
14 δὲ conj. δέ but, and, now, also, to the contrary, rather, then
τοῦ art. gen. masc. sg. ὁ ἡ τό the, this, that, he, she, it
Παύλου n. gen. masc. sg. Παῦλος Paul, Paulus
τὸ art. acc. neut. sg. ὁ ἡ τό the, this, that, he, she, it
στόμα n. acc. neut. sg. στόμα mouth, face, edge
ὁ art. nom. masc. sg. ὁ ἡ τό the, this, that, he, she, it
Γαλλίων n. nom. masc. sg. Γαλλίων Gallio
πρὸς prep. πρός (+gen) for, (+dat) at, (+acc) unto, to, with, for, against
τοὺς art. acc. masc. pl. ὁ ἡ τό the, this, that, he, she, it
Ἰουδαίους adj. acc. masc. pl. Ἰουδαῖος Jew, Jewess
Εἰ conj. εἰ if, whether, that, though, forasmuch
μέν conj. μέν indeed, verily, truly, even, so, some
οὖν conj. οὖν therefore, then, so, and, now, wherefore
ἀδίκημά n. nom. neut. sg. ἀδίκημα matter of wrong, evil doing, iniquity
τι indefinite pron. nom. neut. sg. τὶς certain, some, any man, one, any thing

ἢ particle. ἤ or, than, either, nor, or else, and, rather than
ῥᾳδιούργημα n. nom. neut. sg. ῥᾳδιούργημα lewdness
πονηρόν adj. nom. neut. sg. πονηρός evil, wicked, bad
ὦ interjection. ὦ O
Ἰουδαῖοι adj. voc. masc. pl. Ἰουδαῖος Jew, Jewess
κατὰ prep. κατά (+gen) against, by, throughout, down, (+acc) according to, after, with
λόγον n. acc. masc. sg. λόλόγος word, saying, account, speech, thing, matterγος
ἂν particle. ἄν Indicating contingency. No English translation.
ὑμῶν pron. gen. 2p. pl. σύ thou, you
15 εἰ conj. εἰ if, whether, that, though, forasmuch
δὲ conj. δέ but, and, now, also, to the contrary, rather, then
ζήτημά n. nom. neut. sg. ζήτημα question
περὶ prep. περί (+gen) of, for, concerning, (+acc) about, concerning, in
λόγου n. gen. masc. sg. λόγος word, saying, account, speech, thing, matter
καὶ conj. καί and, even, also, but
ὀνομάτων n. gen. neut. pl. ὄνομα name, call, surname
καὶ conj. καί and, even, also, but
νόμου n. gen. masc. sg. νόμος law, the law
τοῦ art. gen. masc. sg. ὁ ἡ τό the, this, that, he, she, it
καθ' prep. κατά (+gen) against, by, throughout, down, (+acc) according to, after, with
ὑμᾶς pron. acc. 2p. pl. σύ thou, you
αὐτοί pron. nom. masc. 2p. pl. αὐτός ή ό self, of oneself, even, very, the same, he, she, it
κριτὴς n. nom. masc. sg. κριτής judge
γὰρ conj. γάρ for, and, because, but, indeed
ἐγὼ pron. nom. 1p. sg. ἐγώ I
τούτων demo. pron. gen. neut. pl. οὗτος αὕτη τοῦτο this, the same, this same, he, she, it
οὐ particle of negation. οὐ οὐκ οὐχ not, no, neither, none, nay, nor, never, nothing
16 καὶ conj. καί and, even, also, but
αὐτοὺς pron. acc. masc. 3p. pl. αὐτός ή ό self, of oneself, even, very, the same, he, she, it
ἀπὸ prep. ἀπό (+gen) from, of, out of, since, for, off, at, by, in, on
τοῦ art. gen. neut. sg. ὁ ἡ τό the, this, that, he, she, it
βήματος n. gen. neut. sg. βῆμα judgment seat, throne
17 δὲ conj. δέ but, and, now, also, to the contrary, rather, then
πάντες adj. nom. masc. pl. πᾶς πᾶσα πᾶν all, every, whosoever, every one, no, whole, any
οἱ art. nom. masc. pl. ὁ ἡ τό the, this, that, he, she, it
Ἕλληνες n. nom. masc. pl. Ἕλλην Greek, Gentile
Σωσθένην n. acc. fem. sg. Σωσθένης Sosthenes
τὸν art. acc. masc. sg. ὁ ἡ τό the, this, that, he, she, it
ἀρχισυνάγωγον n. acc. masc. sg. ἀρχισυνάγωγος ruler of the synagogue
ἔμπροσθεν prep. ἔμπροσθεν (+gen) before, in the sight of, in the presence of
τοῦ art. gen. neut. sg. ὁ ἡ τό the, this, that, he, she, it
βήματος n. gen. neut. sg. βῆμα judgment seat, throne
καὶ conj. καί and, even, also, but
οὐδὲν num. nom. neut. sg. οὐδείς no man, nothing, no, none, neither, not, nought
τούτων demo. pron. gen. neut. pl. οὗτος αὕτη τοῦτο this, the same, this same, he, she, it
τῷ art. dat. masc. sg. ὁ ἡ τό the, this, that, he, she, it
Γαλλίωνι n. dat. masc. sg. Γαλλίων Gallio
18 Ὁ art. nom. masc. sg. ὁ ἡ τό the, this, that, he, she, it
δὲ conj. δέ but, and, now, also, to the contrary, rather, then
Παῦλος n. nom. masc. sg. Παῦλος Paul, Paulus
ἔτι adv. ἔτι yet, more, any more, further, still, moreover
ἡμέρας n. acc. fem. pl. ἡμέρα day, time, year, while, age, day time
ἱκανὰς adj. acc. fem. pl. ἱκανός many, much, long, worthy, sufficient, great, able
τοῖς art. dat. masc. pl. ὁ ἡ τό the, this, that, he, she, it
ἀδελφοῖς n. dat. masc. pl. ἀδελφός brother

εἰς prep. εἰς (+acc) into, to, unto, for, in, on, toward, against, upon, at, among
τὴν art. acc. fem. sg. ὁ ἡ τό the, this, that, he, she, it
Συρίαν n. acc. fem. sg. Συρία Syria
καὶ conj. καί and, even, also, but
σὺν prep. σύν (+dat) with, beside
αὐτῷ pron. dat. masc. 3p. sg. αὐτός ή ό self, of oneself, even, very, the same, he, she, it
Πρίσκιλλα n. nom. fem. sg. Πρίσκιλλα Priscilla
καὶ conj. καί and, even, also, but
᾽Ακύλας n. nom. masc. sg. ᾽Ακύλας Aquila
τὴν art. acc. fem. sg. ὁ ἡ τό the, this, that, he, she, it
κεφαλήν n. acc. fem. sg. κεφαλή head
ἐν prep. ἐν (+dat) in, by, with, among, at, on, through, to, within, into, of, for
Κεγχρεαῖς n. dat. fem. pl. Κεγχρεαί Cenchrea
γὰρ conj. γάρ for, and, because, but, indeed
εὐχήν n. acc. fem. sg. εὐχή vow, prayer
19 δὲ conj. δέ but, and, now, also, to the contrary, rather, then
εἰς prep. εἰς (+acc) into, to, unto, for, in, on, toward, against, upon, at, among
Ἔφεσον n. acc. fem. sg. Ἔφεσος Ephesus
κἀκείνους demo. pron. acc. masc. pl. κἀκεῖνος and he, he also, and the other, even he
αὐτοῦ adv. αὐτοῦ here, there
αὐτὸς pron. nom. masc. 3p. sg. αὐτός ή ό self, of oneself, even, very, the same, he, she, it
δὲ conj. δέ but, and, now, also, to the contrary, rather, then
εἰς prep. εἰς (+acc) into, to, unto, for, in, on, toward, against, upon, at, among
τὴν art. acc. fem. sg. ὁ ἡ τό the, this, that, he, she, it
συναγωγὴν n. acc. fem. sg. συναγωγή synagogue, assembly, congregation
τοῖς art. dat. masc. pl. ὁ ἡ τό the, this, that, he, she, it
᾽Ιουδαίοις adj. dat. masc. pl. ᾽Ιουδαῖος Jew, Jewess
20 δὲ conj. δέ but, and, now, also, to the contrary, rather, then
αὐτῶν pron. gen. masc. 3p. pl. αὐτός ή ό self, of oneself, even, very, the same, he, she, it
ἐπὶ prep. ἐπί (+gen) on, in, upon, (+dat) in, at, for, upon, (+acc) on, upon, unto, to, against
πλείονα compar. adj. acc. masc. sg. πολύς many, great, much, long, abundant
χρόνον n. acc. masc. sg. χρόνος time, season, space
παρ᾽ prep. παρά (+gen) of, from, (+dat) with, for, (+acc) beside, at, by, above, against
αὐτοῖς pron. dat. masc. 3p. pl. αὐτός ή ό self, of oneself, even, very, the same, he, she, it
οὐκ particle of negation. οὐ οὐκ οὐχ not, no, neither, none, nay, nor, never, nothing
21 ἀλλ᾽ conj. ἀλλά but, yea, yet, nevertheless, howbeit, nay, therefore
αὐτοῖς pron. dat. masc. 3p. pl. αὐτός ή ό self, of oneself, even, very, the same, he, she, it
με pron. acc. 1p. sg. ἐγώ I
πάντως adv. πάντως surely, altogether, by all means, at all, needs, no doubt
τὴν art. acc. fem. sg. ὁ ἡ τό the, this, that, he, she, it
ἑορτὴν n. acc. fem. sg. ἑορτή feast, holyday
τὴν art. acc. fem. sg. ὁ ἡ τό the, this, that, he, she, it
εἰς prep. εἰς (+acc) into, to, unto, for, in, on, toward, against, upon, at, among
῾Ιεροσόλυμα n. acc. neut. sg. ῾Ιεροσόλυμα Jerusalem
πάλιν adv. πάλιν again
δὲ conj. δέ but, and, now, also, to the contrary, rather, then
πρὸς prep. πρός (+gen) for, (+dat) at, (+acc) unto, to, with, for, against
ὑμᾶς pron. acc. 2p. pl. σύ thou, you
τοῦ art. gen. masc. sg. ὁ ἡ τό the, this, that, he, she, it
Θεοῦ n. gen. masc. sg. θεός God, god
καὶ conj. καί and, even, also, but
ἀπὸ prep. ἀπό (+gen) from, of, out of, since, for, off, at, by, in, on
τῆς art. gen. fem. sg. ὁ ἡ τό the, this, that, he, she, it
᾽Εφέσου n. gen. fem. sg. Ἔφεσος Ephesus
22 καὶ conj. καί and, even, also, but

εἰς prep. εἰς (+acc) into, to, unto, for, in, on, toward, against, upon, at, among
Καισάρειαν n. acc. fem. sg. Καισάρεια Caesarea
καὶ conj. καί and, even, also, but
τὴν art. acc. fem. sg. ὁ ἡ τό the, this, that, he, she, it
ἐκκλησίαν n. acc. fem. sg. ἐκκλησία church, assembly
εἰς prep. εἰς (+acc) into, to, unto, for, in, on, toward, against, upon, at, among
Ἀντιόχειαν n. acc. fem. sg. Ἀντιόχεια Antioch
23 καὶ conj. καί and, even, also, but
χρόνον n. acc. masc. sg. χρόνος time, season, space
τινὰ indefinite pron. acc. masc. sg. τὶς certain, some, any man, one, any thing
καθεξῆς adv. καθεξῆς in order, after, afterward, by order
τὴν art. acc. fem. sg. ὁ ἡ τό the, this, that, he, she, it
Γαλατικὴν adj. acc. fem. sg. Γαλατικός of Galatia
χώραν n. acc. fem. sg. χώρα country, region, land, field, coast, ground
καὶ conj. καί and, even, also, but
Φρυγίαν n. acc. fem. sg. Φρυγία Phrygia
πάντας adj. acc. masc. pl. πᾶς πᾶσα πᾶν all, every, whosoever, every one, no, whole, any
τοὺς art. acc. masc. pl. ὁ ἡ τό the, this, that, he, she, it
μαθητάς n. acc. masc. pl. μαθητής disciple
24 Ἰουδαῖος adj. nom. masc. sg. Ἰουδαῖος Jew, Jewess
δέ conj. δέ but, and, now, also, to the contrary, rather, then
τις indefinite pron. nom. masc. sg. τὶς certain, some, any man, one, any thing
Ἀπολλῶς n. nom. masc. sg. Ἀπολλῶς Apollos
ὀνόματι n. dat. neut. sg. ὄνομα name, call, surname
Ἀλεξανδρεὺς n. nom. masc. sg. Ἀλεξανδρεύς Alexandrian
τῷ art. dat. neut. sg. ὁ ἡ τό the, this, that, he, she, it
γένει n. dat. neut. sg. γένος kind, kindred, offspring, nation, countrymen
ἀνὴρ n. nom. masc. sg. ἀνήρ man, husband, sir
λόγιος adj. nom. masc. sg. λόγιος eloquent
εἰς prep. εἰς (+acc) into, to, unto, for, in, on, toward, against, upon, at, among
Ἔφεσον n. acc. fem. sg. Ἔφεσος Ephesus
δυνατὸς adj. nom. masc. sg. δυνατός able, possible, mighty, strong
ἐν prep. ἐν (+dat) in, by, with, among, at, on, through, to, within, into, of, for
ταῖς art. dat. fem. pl. ὁ ἡ τό the, this, that, he, she, it
γραφαῖς n. dat. fem. pl. γραφή scripture
25 οὗτος demo. pron. nom. masc. sg. οὗτος αὕτη τοῦτο this, the same, this same, he, she, it
τὴν art. acc. fem. sg. ὁ ἡ τό the, this, that, he, she, it
ὁδὸν n. acc. fem. sg. ὁδός way, journey, highway
τοῦ art. gen. masc. sg. ὁ ἡ τό the, this, that, he, she, it
Κυρίου n. gen. masc. sg. κύριος Lord, lord, master, sir, LORD, God, Master, owner
καὶ conj. καί and, even, also, but
τῷ art. dat. neut. sg. ὁ ἡ τό the, this, that, he, she, it
πνεύματι n. dat. neut. sg. πνεῦμα spirit, Spirit, Ghost, ghost, life. of the spirit, wind
καὶ conj. καί and, even, also, but
ἀκριβῶς adv. ἀκριβῶς diligently, circumspectly, perfect, perfectly
τὰ art. acc. neut. pl. ὁ ἡ τό the, this, that, he, she, it
περὶ prep. περί (+gen) of, for, concerning, (+acc) about, concerning, in
τοῦ art. gen. masc. sg. ὁ ἡ τό the, this, that, he, she, it
Κυρίου n. gen. masc. sg. κύριος Lord, lord, master, sir, LORD, God, Master, owner
μόνον adv. μόνος only, alone, by oneself
τὸ art. acc. neut. sg. ὁ ἡ τό the, this, that, he, she, it
βάπτισμα n. acc. neut. sg. βάπτισμα baptism
Ἰωάννου n. gen. masc. sg. Ἰωάννης John
26 οὗτός demo. pron. nom. masc. sg. οὗτος αὕτη τοῦτο this, the same, this same, he, she, it
τε conj. τέ and, both, also

ἐν prep. ἐν (+dat) in, by, with, among, at, on, through, to, within, into, of, for
τῇ art. dat. fem. sg. ὁ ἡ τό the, this, that, he, she, it
συναγωγῇ n. dat. fem. sg. συναγωγή synagogue, assembly, congregation
δὲ conj. δέ but, and, now, also, to the contrary, rather, then
αὐτοῦ pron. gen. masc. 3p. sg. αὐτός ή ό self, of oneself, even, very, the same, he, she, it
'Ακύλας n. nom. masc. sg. 'Ακύλας Aquila
καὶ conj. καί and, even, also, but
Πρίσκιλλα n. nom. fem. sg. Πρίσκιλλα Priscilla
αὐτὸν pron. acc. masc. 3p. sg. αὐτός ή ό self, of oneself, even, very, the same, he, she, it
καὶ conj. καί and, even, also, but
ἀκριβέστερον compar. adv. ἀκριβέστερον more perfectly, more perfect
αὐτῷ pron. dat. masc. 3p. sg. αὐτός ή ό self, of oneself, even, very, the same, he, she, it
τὴν art. acc. fem. sg. ὁ ἡ τό the, this, that, he, she, it
τοῦ art. gen. masc. sg. ὁ ἡ τό the, this, that, he, she, it
Θεοῦ n. gen. masc. sg. θεός God, god
ὁδὸν n. acc. fem. sg. ὁδός way, journey, highway
27 δὲ conj. δέ but, and, now, also, to the contrary, rather, then
αὐτοῦ pron. gen. masc. 3p. sg. αὐτός ή ό self, of oneself, even, very, the same, he, she, it
εἰς prep. εἰς (+acc) into, to, unto, for, in, on, toward, against, upon, at, among
τὴν art. acc. fem. sg. ὁ ἡ τό the, this, that, he, she, it
'Αχαΐαν n. acc. fem. sg. 'Αχαΐα Achaia
οἱ art. nom. masc. pl. ὁ ἡ τό the, this, that, he, she, it
ἀδελφοὶ n. nom. masc. pl. ἀδελφός brother
τοῖς art. dat. masc. pl. ὁ ἡ τό the, this, that, he, she, it
μαθηταῖς n. dat. masc. pl. μαθητής disciple
αὐτόν pron. acc. masc. 3p. sg. αὐτός ή ό self, of oneself, even, very, the same, he, she, it
ὃς relative pron. nom. masc. sg. ὅς ἥ ὅ who, which, what, that
πολὺ adv. πολύς many, great, much, long, abundant
τοῖς art. dat. masc. pl. ὁ ἡ τό the, this, that, he, she, it
διὰ prep. διά (+gen) by, through, with, in, of, (+acc) for, because of, for a cause
τῆς art. gen. fem. sg. ὁ ἡ τό the, this, that, he, she, it
χάριτος n. gen. fem. sg. χάρις grace, thank, favour, pleasure
28 εὐτόνως adv. εὐτόνως vehemently, mightly
γὰρ conj. γάρ for, and, because, but, indeed
τοῖς art. dat. masc. pl. ὁ ἡ τό the, this, that, he, she, it
'Ιουδαίοις adj. dat. masc. pl. 'Ιουδαῖος Jew, Jewess
δημοσίᾳ adv. δημόσιος common, publicly, openly
διὰ prep. διά (+gen) by, through, with, in, of, (+acc) for, because of, for a cause
τῶν art. gen. fem. pl. ὁ ἡ τό the, this, that, he, she, it
γραφῶν n. gen. fem. pl. γραφή scripture
τὸν art. acc. masc. sg. ὁ ἡ τό the, this, that, he, she, it
Χριστὸν n. acc. masc. sg. Χριστός Christ
'Ιησοῦν n. acc. masc. sg. 'Ιησοῦς Jesus

19

1 δὲ conj. δέ but, and, now, also, to the contrary, rather, then
ἐν prep. ἐν (+dat) in, by, with, among, at, on, through, to, within, into, of, for
τῷ art. dat. neut. sg. ὁ ἡ τό the, this, that, he, she, it
τὸν art. acc. masc. sg. ὁ ἡ τό the, this, that, he, she, it
'Απολλῶ n. acc. masc. sg. 'Απολλῶς Apollos
ἐν prep. ἐν (+dat) in, by, with, among, at, on, through, to, within, into, of, for
Κορίνθῳ n. dat. fem. sg. Κόρινθος Corinth
Παῦλον n. acc. masc. sg. Παῦλος Paul, Paulus
τὰ art. acc. neut. pl. ὁ ἡ τό the, this, that, he, she, it

ἀνωτερικὰ adj. acc. neut. pl. ἀνωτερικός upper
μέρη n. acc. neut. pl. μέρος part, coast, portion, behalf, respect, piece, side
εἰς prep. εἰς (+acc) into, to, unto, for, in, on, toward, against, upon, at, among
Ἔφεσον n. acc. fem. sg. Ἔφεσος Ephesus
καὶ conj. καί and, even, also, but
τινας indefinite pron. acc. masc. pl. τὶς certain, some, any man, one, any thing
μαθητὰς n. acc. masc. pl. μαθητής disciple
2 πρὸς prep. πρός (+gen) for, (+dat) at, (+acc) unto, to, with, for, against
αὐτούς pron. acc. masc. 3p. pl. αὐτός ἡ ὁ self, of oneself, even, very, the same, he, she, it
Εἰ conj. εἰ if, whether, that, though, forasmuch
Πνεῦμα n. acc. neut. sg. πνεῦμα spirit, Spirit, Ghost, ghost, life. of the spirit, wind
Ἅγιον adj. acc. neut. sg. ἅγιος Holy, holy, saint, Holy One, holy thing, most holy
οἱ art. nom. masc. pl. ὁ ἡ τό the, this, that, he, she, it
δὲ conj. δέ but, and, now, also, to the contrary, rather, then
πρὸς prep. πρός (+gen) for, (+dat) at, (+acc) unto, to, with, for, against
αὐτόν pron. acc. masc. 3p. sg. αὐτός ἡ ὁ self, of oneself, even, very, the same, he, she, it
Ἀλλ' conj. ἀλλά but, yea, yet, nevertheless, howbeit, nay, therefore
οὐδὲ adv. οὐδέ neither, nor, not, no, not even, never, not yet
εἰ conj. εἰ if, whether, that, though, forasmuch
Πνεῦμα n. acc. neut. sg. πνεῦμα spirit, Spirit, Ghost, ghost, life. of the spirit, wind
Ἅγιον adj. acc. neut. sg. ἅγιος Holy, holy, saint, Holy One, holy thing, most holy
3 τε conj. τέ and, both, also
πρὸς prep. πρός (+gen) for, (+dat) at, (+acc) unto, to, with, for, against
αὐτούς pron. acc. masc. 3p. pl. αὐτός ἡ ὁ self, of oneself, even, very, the same, he, she, it
Εἰς prep. εἰς (+acc) into, to, unto, for, in, on, toward, against, upon, at, among
τί interrog. pron. acc. neut. sg. τίς what, who, why, where, which, how
οὖν conj. οὖν therefore, then, so, and, now, wherefore
οἱ art. nom. masc. pl. ὁ ἡ τό the, this, that, he, she, it
δὲ conj. δέ but, and, now, also, to the contrary, rather, then
Εἰς prep. εἰς (+acc) into, to, unto, for, in, on, toward, against, upon, at, among
τὸ art. acc. neut. sg. ὁ ἡ τό the, this, that, he, she, it
Ἰωάννου n. gen. masc. sg. Ἰωάννης John
βάπτισμα n. acc. neut. sg. βάπτισμα baptism
4 δὲ conj. δέ but, and, now, also, to the contrary, rather, then
Παῦλος n. nom. masc. sg. Παῦλος Paul, Paulus
Ἰωάννης n. nom. masc. sg. Ἰωάννης John
μὲν conj. μέν indeed, verily, truly, even, so, some
βάπτισμα n. acc. neut. sg. βάπτισμα baptism
μετανοίας n. gen. fem. sg. μετάνοια repentance
τῷ art. dat. masc. sg. ὁ ἡ τό the, this, that, he, she, it
λαῷ n. dat. masc. sg. λαός people
εἰς prep. εἰς (+acc) into, to, unto, for, in, on, toward, against, upon, at, among
τὸν art. acc. masc. sg. ὁ ἡ τό the, this, that, he, she, it
μετ' prep. μετά (+gen) with, among, against, (+acc) after
αὐτὸν pron. acc. masc. 3p. sg. αὐτός ἡ ὁ self, of oneself, even, very, the same, he, she, it
ἵνα conj. ἵνα that, to, lest, for to, so that, albeit, because, for, so as
τοῦτ' demo. pron. nom. neut. sg. οὗτος αὕτη τοῦτο this, the same, this same, he, she, it
εἰς prep. εἰς (+acc) into, to, unto, for, in, on, toward, against, upon, at, among
τὸν art. acc. masc. sg. ὁ ἡ τό the, this, that, he, she, it
Χριστὸν n. acc. masc. sg. Χριστός Christ
Ἰησοῦν n. acc. masc. sg. Ἰησοῦς Jesus
5 δὲ conj. δέ but, and, now, also, to the contrary, rather, then
εἰς prep. εἰς (+acc) into, to, unto, for, in, on, toward, against, upon, at, among
τὸ art. acc. neut. sg. ὁ ἡ τό the, this, that, he, she, it
ὄνομα n. acc. neut. sg. ὄνομα name, call, surname

τοῦ art. gen. masc. sg. ὁ ἡ τό the, this, that, he, she, it
Κυρίου n. gen. masc. sg. κύριος Lord, lord, master, sir, LORD, God, Master, owner
Ἰησοῦ n. gen. masc. sg. Ἰησοῦς Jesus
6 καὶ conj. καί and, even, also, but
αὐτοῖς pron. dat. masc. 3p. pl. αὐτός ἡ ό self, of oneself, even, very, the same, he, she, it
τοῦ art. gen. masc. sg. ὁ ἡ τό the, this, that, he, she, it
Παύλου n. gen. masc. sg. Παῦλος Paul, Paulus
τὰς art. acc. fem. pl. ὁ ἡ τό the, this, that, he, she, it
χεῖρας n. acc. fem. pl. χείρ hand
τὸ art. nom. neut. sg. ὁ ἡ τό the, this, that, he, she, it
Πνεῦμα n. nom. neut. sg. πνεῦμα spirit, Spirit, Ghost, ghost, life. of the spirit, wind
τὸ art. nom. neut. sg. ὁ ἡ τό the, this, that, he, she, it
Ἅγιον adj. nom. neut. sg. ἅγιος Holy, holy, saint, Holy One, holy thing, most holy
ἐπ' prep. ἐπί (+gen) on, in, upon, (+dat) in, at, for, upon, (+acc) on, upon, unto, to, against
αὐτούς pron. acc. masc. 3p. pl. αὐτός ἡ ό self, of oneself, even, very, the same, he, she, it
τε conj. τέ and, both, also
γλώσσαις n. dat. fem. pl. γλῶσσα tongue
καὶ conj. καί and, even, also, but
7 δὲ conj. δέ but, and, now, also, to the contrary, rather, then
οἱ art. nom. masc. pl. ὁ ἡ τό the, this, that, he, she, it
πάντες adj. nom. masc. pl. πᾶς πᾶσα πᾶν all, every, whosoever, every one, no, whole, any
ἄνδρες n. nom. masc. pl. ἀνήρ man, husband, sir
ὡσεὶ adv. ὡσεί about, as, like, as it had been, as it were, like as
δεκαδύο num. nom. masc. pl. δεκαδύο twelve, ten and two
8 δὲ conj. δέ but, and, now, also, to the contrary, rather, then
εἰς prep. εἰς (+acc) into, to, unto, for, in, on, toward, against, upon, at, among
τὴν art. acc. fem. sg. ὁ ἡ τό the, this, that, he, she, it
συναγωγὴν n. acc. fem. sg. συναγωγή synagogue, assembly, congregation
ἐπὶ prep. ἐπί (+gen) on, in, upon, (+dat) in, at, for, upon, (+acc) on, upon, unto, to, against
μῆνας n. acc. masc. pl. μήν month
τρεῖς num. acc. masc. pl. τρεῖς three
καὶ conj. καί and, even, also, but
τὰ art. acc. neut. pl. ὁ ἡ τό the, this, that, he, she, it
περὶ prep. περί (+gen) of, for, concerning, (+acc) about, concerning, in
τῆς art. gen. fem. sg. ὁ ἡ τό the, this, that, he, she, it
βασιλείας n. gen. fem. sg. βασιλεία kingdom, reign
τοῦ art. gen. masc. sg. ὁ ἡ τό the, this, that, he, she, it
Θεοῦ n. gen. masc. sg. θεός God, god
9 ὡς adv. ὡς as, when, as it were, how, about, like, as soon as, even as, while
δέ conj. δέ but, and, now, also, to the contrary, rather, then
τινες indefinite pron. nom. masc. pl. τὶς certain, some, any man, one, any thing
καὶ conj. καί and, even, also, but
τὴν art. acc. fem. sg. ὁ ἡ τό the, this, that, he, she, it
ὁδὸν n. acc. fem. sg. ὁδός way, journey, highway
ἐνώπιον adv. ἐνώπιον before, in the sight of, in the presence of
τοῦ art. gen. neut. sg. ὁ ἡ τό the, this, that, he, she, it
πλήθους n. gen. neut. sg. πλῆθος multitude, bundle, company
ἀπ' prep. ἀπό (+gen) from, of, out of, since, for, off, at, by, in, on
αὐτῶν pron. gen. masc. 3p. pl. αὐτός ἡ ό self, of oneself, even, very, the same, he, she, it
τοὺς art. acc. masc. pl. ὁ ἡ τό the, this, that, he, she, it
μαθητὰς n. acc. masc. pl. μαθητής disciple
καθ' prep. κατά (+gen) against, by, throughout, down, (+acc) according to, after, with
ἡμέραν n. acc. fem. sg. ἡμέρα day, time, year, while, age, day time
ἐν prep. ἐν (+dat) in, by, with, among, at, on, through, to, within, into, of, for
τῇ art. dat. fem. sg. ὁ ἡ τό the, this, that, he, she, it

σχολῇ n. dat. fem. sg. σχολή school
Τυράννου n. gen. masc. sg. Τύραννος Tyrannus
τινός indefinite pron. gen. masc. sg. τὶς certain, some, any man, one, any thing
10 τοῦτο demo. pron. nom. neut. sg. οὗτος αὕτη τοῦτο this, the same, this same, he, she, it
δὲ conj. δέ but, and, now, also, to the contrary, rather, then
ἐπὶ prep. ἐπί (+gen) on, in, upon, (+dat) in, at, for, upon, (+acc) on, upon, unto, to, against
ἔτη n. acc. neut. pl. ἔτος year
δύο num. acc. neut. pl. δύο two, twain, both
ὥστε conj. ὥστε so that, wherefore, insomuch that, therefore, that, so then
πάντας adj. acc. masc. pl. πᾶς πᾶσα πᾶν all, every, whosoever, every one, no, whole, any
τοὺς art. acc. masc. pl. ὁ ἡ τό the, this, that, he, she, it
τὴν art. acc. fem. sg. ὁ ἡ τό the, this, that, he, she, it
'Ασίαν n. acc. fem. sg. 'Ασία Asia
τὸν art. acc. masc. sg. ὁ ἡ τό the, this, that, he, she, it
λόγον n. acc. masc. sg. λόγος word, saying, account, speech, thing, matter
τοῦ art. gen. masc. sg. ὁ ἡ τό the, this, that, he, she, it
Κυρίου n. gen. masc. sg. κύριος Lord, lord, master, sir, LORD, God, Master, owner
'Ιησοῦ n. gen. masc. sg. 'Ιησοῦς Jesus
'Ιουδαίους adj. acc. masc. pl. 'Ιουδαῖος Jew, Jewess
τε conj. τέ and, both, also
καὶ conj. καί and, even, also, but
Ἕλληνας n. acc. masc. pl. Ἕλλην Greek, Gentile
11 δυνάμεις n. acc. fem. pl. δύναμις power, mighty work, miracle, strength, might
τε conj. τέ and, both, also
οὐ particle of negation. οὐ οὐκ οὐχ not, no, neither, none, nay, nor, never, nothing
τὰς art. acc. fem. pl. ὁ ἡ τό the, this, that, he, she, it
ὁ art. nom. masc. sg. ὁ ἡ τό the, this, that, he, she, it
Θεὸς n. nom. masc. sg. θεός God, god
διὰ prep. διά (+gen) by, through, with, in, of, (+acc) for, because of, for a cause
τῶν art. gen. fem. pl. ὁ ἡ τό the, this, that, he, she, it
χειρῶν n. gen. fem. pl. χείρ hand
Παύλου n. gen. masc. sg. Παῦλος Paul, Paulus
12 ὥστε conj. ὥστε so that, wherefore, insomuch that, therefore, that, so then
καὶ conj. καί and, even, also, but
ἐπὶ prep. ἐπί (+gen) on, in, upon, (+dat) in, at, for, upon, (+acc) on, upon, unto, to, against
τοὺς art. acc. masc. pl. ὁ ἡ τό the, this, that, he, she, it
ἀπὸ prep. ἀπό (+gen) from, of, out of, since, for, off, at, by, in, on
τοῦ art. gen. masc. sg. ὁ ἡ τό the, this, that, he, she, it
χρωτὸς n. gen. masc. sg. χρώς body
αὐτοῦ pron. gen. masc. 3p. sg. αὐτός ἡ ὁ self, of oneself, even, very, the same, he, she, it
σουδάρια n. acc. neut. pl. σουδάριον napkin, handkerchief
ἢ particle. ἤ or, than, either, nor, or else, and, rather than
σιμικίνθια n. acc. neut. pl. σιμικίνθιον apron
καὶ conj. καί and, even, also, but
ἀπ' prep. ἀπό (+gen) from, of, out of, since, for, off, at, by, in, on
αὐτῶν pron. gen. masc. 3p. pl. αὐτός ἡ ὁ self, of oneself, even, very, the same, he, she, it
τὰς art. acc. fem. pl. ὁ ἡ τό the, this, that, he, she, it
νόσους n. acc. fem. pl. νόσος sickness, disease, infirmity
τά art. acc. neut. pl. ὁ ἡ τό the, this, that, he, she, it
τε conj. τέ and, both, also
πνεύματα n. acc. neut. pl. πνεῦμα spirit, Spirit, Ghost, ghost, life. of the spirit, wind
τά art. acc. neut. pl. ὁ ἡ τό the, this, that, he, she, it
πονηρὰ adj. acc. neut. pl. πονηρός evil, wicked, bad
ἀπ' prep. ἀπό (+gen) from, of, out of, since, for, off, at, by, in, on
αὐτῶν pron. gen. masc. 3p. pl. αὐτός ἡ ὁ self, of oneself, even, very, the same, he, she, it

13 δέ conj. δέ but, and, now, also, to the contrary, rather, then
τινες indefinite pron. nom. masc. pl. τὶς certain, some, any man, one, any thing
ἀπὸ prep. ἀπό (+gen) from, of, out of, since, for, off, at, by, in, on
τῶν art. gen. masc. pl. ὁ ἡ τό the, this, that, he, she, it
Ἰουδαίων adj. gen. masc. pl. Ἰουδαῖος Jew, Jewess
ἐξορκιστῶν n. gen. masc. pl. ἐξορκιστής exorcist
ἐπὶ prep. ἐπί (+gen) on, in, upon, (+dat) in, at, for, upon, (+acc) on, upon, unto, to, against
τοὺς art. acc. masc. pl. ὁ ἡ τό the, this, that, he, she, it
τὰ art. acc. neut. pl. ὁ ἡ τό the, this, that, he, she, it
πνεύματα n. acc. neut. pl. πνεῦμα spirit, Spirit, Ghost, ghost, life. of the spirit, wind
τὰ art. acc. neut. pl. ὁ ἡ τό the, this, that, he, she, it
πονηρὰ adj. acc. neut. pl. πονηρός evil, wicked, bad
τὸ art. acc. neut. sg. ὁ ἡ τό the, this, that, he, she, it
ὄνομα n. acc. neut. sg. ὄνομα name, call, surname
τοῦ art. gen. masc. sg. ὁ ἡ τό the, this, that, he, she, it
Κυρίου n. gen. masc. sg. κύριος Lord, lord, master, sir, LORD, God, Master, owner
Ἰησοῦ n. gen. masc. sg. Ἰησοῦς Jesus
ὑμᾶς pron. acc. 2p. pl. σύ thou, you
τὸν art. acc. masc. sg. ὁ ἡ τό the, this, that, he, she, it
Ἰησοῦν n. acc. masc. sg. Ἰησοῦς Jesus
ὃν relative pron. acc. masc. sg. ὅς ἥ ὅ who, which, what, that
ὁ art. nom. masc. sg. ὁ ἡ τό the, this, that, he, she, it
Παῦλος n. nom. masc. sg. Παῦλος Paul, Paulus
14 δέ conj. δέ but, and, now, also, to the contrary, rather, then
τινες indefinite pron. nom. masc. pl. τὶς certain, some, any man, one, any thing
υἱοὶ n. nom. masc. pl. υἱός son, child, descendant, offspring, heir
Σκευᾶ n. gen. masc. sg. Σκευᾶς Sceva
Ἰουδαίου adj. gen. masc. sg. Ἰουδαῖος Jew, Jewess
ἀρχιερέως n. gen. masc. sg. ἀρχιερεύς chief priest, high priest
ἑπτὰ num. nom. masc. pl. ἑπτά seven, seventh
οἱ art. nom. masc. pl. ὁ ἡ τό the, this, that, he, she, it
τοῦτο demo. pron. acc. neut. sg. οὗτος αὕτη τοῦτο this, the same, this same, he, she, it
15 δὲ conj. δέ but, and, now, also, to the contrary, rather, then
τὸ art. nom. neut. sg. ὁ ἡ τό the, this, that, he, she, it
πνεῦμα n. nom. neut. sg. πνεῦμα spirit, Spirit, Ghost, ghost, life. of the spirit, wind
τὸ art. nom. neut. sg. ὁ ἡ τό the, this, that, he, she, it
πονηρὸν adj. nom. neut. sg. πονηρός evil, wicked, bad
Τὸν art. acc. masc. sg. ὁ ἡ τό the, this, that, he, she, it
Ἰησοῦν n. acc. masc. sg. Ἰησοῦς Jesus
καὶ conj. καί and, even, also, but
τὸν art. acc. masc. sg. ὁ ἡ τό the, this, that, he, she, it
Παῦλον n. acc. masc. sg. Παῦλος Paul, Paulus
ὑμεῖς pron. nom. 2p. pl. σύ thou, you
δὲ conj. δέ but, and, now, also, to the contrary, rather, then
τίνες interrog. pron. nom. masc. pl. τίς what, who, why, where, which, how
16 καὶ conj. καί and, even, also, but
ἐπ' prep. ἐπί (+gen) on, in, upon, (+dat) in, at, for, upon, (+acc) on, upon, unto, to, against
αὐτοὺς pron. acc. masc. 3p. pl. αὐτός ή ό self, of oneself, even, very, the same, he, she, it
ὁ art. nom. masc. sg. ὁ ἡ τό the, this, that, he, she, it
ἄνθρωπος n. nom. masc. sg. ἄνθρωπος man, human being, person, one, certain
ἐν prep. ἐν (+dat) in, by, with, among, at, on, through, to, within, into, of, for
ᾧ relative pron. dat. masc. sg. ὅς ἥ ὅ who, which, what, that
τὸ art. nom. neut. sg. ὁ ἡ τό the, this, that, he, she, it
πνεῦμα n. nom. neut. sg. πνεῦμα spirit, Spirit, Ghost, ghost, life. of the spirit, wind
τὸ art. nom. neut. sg. ὁ ἡ τό the, this, that, he, she, it

πονηρόν adj. nom. neut. sg. πονηρός evil, wicked, bad
καὶ conj. καί and, even, also, but
αὐτῶν pron. gen. masc. 3p. pl. αὐτός ή ό self, of oneself, even, very, the same, he, she, it
κατ' prep. κατά (+gen) against, by, throughout, down, (+acc) according to, after, with
αὐτῶν pron. gen. masc. 3p. pl. αὐτός ή ό self, of oneself, even, very, the same, he, she, it
ὥστε conj. ὥστε so that, wherefore, insomuch that, therefore, that, so then
γυμνοὺς adj. acc. masc. pl. γυμνός naked, bare
καὶ conj. καί and, even, also, but
ἐκ prep. ἐκ ἐξ (+gen) of, from, out of, by, on, with, in, among, through
τοῦ art. gen. masc. sg. ὁ ἡ τό the, this, that, he, she, it
οἴκου n. gen. masc. sg. οἶκος house, home, household
ἐκείνου demo. pron. gen. masc. sg. ἐκεῖνος that, he, the same, that same
17 τοῦτο demo. pron. nom. neut. sg. οὗτος αὕτη τοῦτο this, the same, this same, he, she, it
δὲ conj. δέ but, and, now, also, to the contrary, rather, then
γνωστὸν adj. nom. neut. sg. γνωστός acquaintance, known, notable
πᾶσιν adj. dat. masc. pl. πᾶς πᾶσα πᾶν all, every, whosoever, every one, no, whole, any
Ἰουδαίοις adj. dat. masc. pl. Ἰουδαῖος Jew, Jewess
τε conj. τέ and, both, also
καὶ conj. καί and, even, also, but
Ἕλλησιν n. dat. masc. pl. Ἕλλην Greek, Gentile
τοῖς art. dat. masc. pl. ὁ ἡ τό the, this, that, he, she, it
τὴν art. acc. fem. sg. ὁ ἡ τό the, this, that, he, she, it
Ἔφεσον n. acc. fem. sg. Ἔφεσος Ephesus
καὶ conj. καί and, even, also, but
φόβος n. nom. masc. sg. φόβος fear, terror, sore afraid
ἐπὶ prep. ἐπί (+gen) on, in, upon, (+dat) in, at, for, upon, (+acc) on, upon, unto, to, against
πάντας adj. acc. masc. pl. πᾶς πᾶσα πᾶν all, every, whosoever, every one, no, whole, any
αὐτοὺς pron. acc. masc. 3p. pl. αὐτός ή ό self, of oneself, even, very, the same, he, she, it
καὶ conj. καί and, even, also, but
τὸ art. nom. neut. sg. ὁ ἡ τό the, this, that, he, she, it
ὄνομα n. nom. neut. sg. ὄνομα name, call, surname
τοῦ art. gen. masc. sg. ὁ ἡ τό the, this, that, he, she, it
Κυρίου n. gen. masc. sg. κύριος Lord, lord, master, sir, LORD, God, Master, owner
Ἰησοῦ n. gen. masc. sg. Ἰησοῦς Jesus
18 πολλοί adj. nom. masc. pl. πολύς many, great, much, long, abundant
τε conj. τέ and, both, also
τῶν art. gen. masc. pl. ὁ ἡ τό the, this, that, he, she, it
καὶ conj. καί and, even, also, but
τὰς art. acc. fem. pl. ὁ ἡ τό the, this, that, he, she, it
πράξεις n. acc. fem. pl. πρᾶξις deed, office, acting
αὐτῶν pron. gen. masc. 3p. pl. αὐτός ή ό self, of oneself, even, very, the same, he, she, it
19 ἱκανοὶ adj. nom. masc. pl. ἱκανός many, much, long, worthy, sufficient, great, able
δὲ conj. δέ but, and, now, also, to the contrary, rather, then
τῶν art. gen. masc. pl. ὁ ἡ τό the, this, that, he, she, it
τὰ art. acc. neut. pl. ὁ ἡ τό the, this, that, he, she, it
περίεργα adj. acc. neut. pl. περίεργος curious, busy, sorcery
τὰς art. acc. fem. pl. ὁ ἡ τό the, this, that, he, she, it
βίβλους n. acc. fem. pl. βίβλος book, record
ἐνώπιον adv. ἐνώπιον before, in the sight of, in the presence of
πάντων adj. gen. masc. pl. πᾶς πᾶσα πᾶν all, every, whosoever, every one, no, whole, any
καὶ conj. καί and, even, also, but
τὰς art. acc. fem. pl. ὁ ἡ τό the, this, that, he, she, it
τιμὰς n. acc. fem. pl. τιμή honour, price, preciousness, sum
αὐτῶν pron. gen. fem. 3p. pl. αὐτός ή ό self, of oneself, even, very, the same, he, she, it
καὶ conj. καί and, even, also, but

ἀργυρίου n. gen. neut. sg. ἀργύριον money, piece of silver, silver
μυριάδας n. acc. fem. pl. μυριάς ten thousand, myriad, innumerable company
πέντε num. acc. fem. pl. πέντε five
20 οὕτω adv. οὕτω οὕτως so, even so, thus, on this wise, likewise, after this manner
κατὰ prep. κατά (+gen) against, by, throughout, down, (+acc) according to, after, with
κράτος n. acc. neut. sg. κράτος power, dominion, might, strength
ὁ art. nom. masc. sg. ὁ ἡ τό the, this, that, he, she, it
λόγος n. nom. masc. sg. λόγος word, saying, account, speech, thing, matter
τοῦ art. gen. masc. sg. ὁ ἡ τό the, this, that, he, she, it
Κυρίου n. gen. masc. sg. κύριος Lord, lord, master, sir, LORD, God, Master, owner
καὶ conj. καί and, even, also, but
21 Ὡς conj. ὡς as, when, as it were, how, about, like, as soon as, even as, while
δὲ conj. δέ but, and, now, also, to the contrary, rather, then
ταῦτα demo. pron. nom. neut. pl. οὗτος αὕτη τοῦτο this, the same, this same, he, she, it
ὁ art. nom. masc. sg. ὁ ἡ τό the, this, that, he, she, it
Παῦλος n. nom. masc. sg. Παῦλος Paul, Paulus
ἐν prep. ἐν (+dat) in, by, with, among, at, on, through, to, within, into, of, for
τῷ art. dat. neut. sg. ὁ ἡ τό the, this, that, he, she, it
πνεύματι n. dat. neut. sg. πνεῦμα spirit, Spirit, Ghost, ghost, life. of the spirit, wind
τὴν art. acc. fem. sg. ὁ ἡ τό the, this, that, he, she, it
Μακεδονίαν n. acc. fem. sg. Μακεδονία Macedonia
καὶ conj. καί and, even, also, but
Ἀχαΐαν n. acc. fem. sg. Ἀχαΐα Achaia
εἰς prep. εἰς (+acc) into, to, unto, for, in, on, toward, against, upon, at, among
Ἱερουσαλὴμ pron. name. fem. inde. Ἱερουσαλήμ Jerusalem
ὅτι conj. ὅτι that, for, because, how that, how, because that, for that, though
Μετὰ prep. μετά (+gen) with, among, against, (+acc) after
τὸ art. acc. neut. sg. ὁ ἡ τό the, this, that, he, she, it
με pron. acc. 1p. sg. ἐγώ I
ἐκεῖ adv. ἐκεῖ there, thither, thitherward, yonder, yonder place
με pron. acc. 1p. sg. ἐγώ I
καὶ conj. καί and, even, also, but
Ῥώμην n. acc. fem. sg. Ῥώμη Rome
22 δὲ conj. δέ but, and, now, also, to the contrary, rather, then
εἰς prep. εἰς (+acc) into, to, unto, for, in, on, toward, against, upon, at, among
τὴν art. acc. fem. sg. ὁ ἡ τό the, this, that, he, she, it
Μακεδονίαν n. acc. fem. sg. Μακεδονία Macedonia
δύο num. acc. masc. pl. δύο two, twain, both
τῶν art. gen. masc. pl. ὁ ἡ τό the, this, that, he, she, it
αὐτῷ pron. dat. masc. 3p. sg. αὐτός ἡ ὁ self, of oneself, even, very, the same, he, she, it
Τιμόθεον n. acc. masc. sg. Τιμόθεος Timotheus, Timothy
καὶ conj. καί and, even, also, but
Ἔραστον n. acc. masc. sg. Ἔραστος Erastus
αὐτὸς pron. nom. masc. 3p. sg. αὐτός ἡ ὁ self, of oneself, even, very, the same, he, she, it
χρόνον n. acc. masc. sg. χρόνος time, season, space
εἰς prep. εἰς (+acc) into, to, unto, for, in, on, toward, against, upon, at, among
τὴν art. acc. fem. sg. ὁ ἡ τό the, this, that, he, she, it
Ἀσίαν n. acc. fem. sg. Ἀσία Asia
23 δὲ conj. δέ but, and, now, also, to the contrary, rather, then
κατὰ prep. κατά (+gen) against, by, throughout, down, (+acc) according to, after, with
τὸν art. acc. masc. sg. ὁ ἡ τό the, this, that, he, she, it
καιρὸν n. acc. masc. sg. καιρός time, season, due time, opportunity
ἐκεῖνον demo. pron. acc. masc. sg. ἐκεῖνος that, he, the same, that same
τάραχος n. nom. masc. sg. τάραχος stir
οὐκ particle of negation. οὐ οὐκ οὐχ not, no, neither, none, nay, nor, never, nothing

ὀλίγος adj. nom. masc. sg. ὀλίγος few, little, small, a while, brief, short, short space
περὶ prep. περί (+gen) of, for, concerning, (+acc) about, concerning, in
τῆς art. gen. fem. sg. ὁ ἡ τό the, this, that, he, she, it
ὁδοῦ n. gen. fem. sg. ὁδός way, journey, highway
24 Δημήτριος n. nom. masc. sg. Δημήτριος Demetrius
γάρ conj. γάρ for, and, because, but, indeed
τις indefinite pron. nom. masc. sg. τὶς certain, some, any man, one, any thing
ὀνόματι n. dat. neut. sg. ὄνομα name, call, surname
ἀργυροκόπος n. nom. masc. sg. ἀργυροκόπος silversmith
ναοὺς n. acc. masc. pl. ναός temple, shrine
ἀργυροῦς adj. acc. masc. pl. ἀργύρεος of silver
Ἀρτέμιδος n. gen. fem. sg. Ἄρτεμις Diana, Artemis
τοῖς art. dat. masc. pl. ὁ ἡ τό the, this, that, he, she, it
τεχνίταις n. dat. masc. pl. τεχνίτης craftsmen, builder
ἐργασίαν n. acc. fem. sg. ἐργασία diligence, working, gain, craft
οὐκ particle of negation. οὐ οὐκ οὐχ not, no, neither, none, nay, nor, never, nothing
ὀλίγην adj. acc. fem. sg. ὀλίγος few, little, small, a while, brief, short, short space
25 οὓς relative pron. acc. masc. pl. ὅς ἥ ὅ who, which, what, that
καὶ conj. καί and, even, also, but
τοὺς art. acc. masc. pl. ὁ ἡ τό the, this, that, he, she, it
περὶ prep. περί (+gen) of, for, concerning, (+acc) about, concerning, in
τὰ art. acc. neut. pl. ὁ ἡ τό the, this, that, he, she, it
τοιαῦτα demo. pron. acc. neut. pl. τοιοῦτος such, like
ἐργάτας n. acc. masc. pl. ἐργάτης labourer, worker, workman
Ἄνδρες n. voc. masc. pl. ἀνήρ man, husband, sir
ὅτι conj. ὅτι that, for, because, how that, how, because that, for that, though
ἐκ prep. ἐκ ἐξ (+gen) of, from, out of, by, on, with, in, among, through
ταύτης demo. pron. gen. fem. sg. οὗτος αὕτη τοῦτο this, the same, this same, he, she, it
τῆς art. gen. fem. sg. ὁ ἡ τό the, this, that, he, she, it
ἐργασίας n. gen. fem. sg. ἐργασία diligence, working, gain, craft
ἡ art. nom. fem. sg. ὁ ἡ τό the, this, that, he, she, it
εὐπορία n. nom. fem. sg. εὐπορία wealth
ἡμῶν pron. gen. 1p. pl. ἐγώ I
26 καὶ conj. καί and, even, also, but
καὶ conj. καί and, even, also, but
ὅτι conj. ὅτι that, for, because, how that, how, because that, for that, though
οὐ particle of negation. οὐ οὐκ οὐχ not, no, neither, none, nay, nor, never, nothing
μόνον adv. μόνος only, alone, by oneself
Ἐφέσου n. gen. fem. sg. Ἔφεσος Ephesus
ἀλλὰ conj. ἀλλά but, yea, yet, nevertheless, howbeit, nay, therefore
σχεδὸν adv. σχεδόν almost
πάσης adj. gen. fem. sg. πᾶς πᾶσα πᾶν all, every, whosoever, every one, no, whole, any
τῆς art. gen. fem. sg. ὁ ἡ τό the, this, that, he, she, it
Ἀσίας n. gen. fem. sg. Ἀσία Asia
ὁ art. nom. masc. sg. ὁ ἡ τό the, this, that, he, she, it
Παῦλος n. nom. masc. sg. Παῦλος Paul, Paulus
οὗτος demo. pron. nom. masc. sg. οὗτος αὕτη τοῦτο this, the same, this same, he, she, it
ἱκανὸν adj. acc. masc. sg. ἱκανός many, much, long, worthy, sufficient, great, able
ὄχλον n. acc. masc. sg. ὄχλος people, multitude, company, press, number
ὅτι conj. ὅτι that, for, because, how that, how, because that, for that, though
οὐκ particle of negation. οὐ οὐκ οὐχ not, no, neither, none, nay, nor, never, nothing
θεοὶ n. nom. masc. pl. θεός God, god
οἱ art. nom. masc. pl. ὁ ἡ τό the, this, that, he, she, it
διὰ prep. διά (+gen) by, through, with, in, of, (+acc) for, because of, for a cause
χειρῶν n. gen. fem. pl. χείρ hand

27 οὐ particle of negation. οὐ οὐκ οὐχ not, no, neither, none, nay, nor, never, nothing
μόνον adv. μόνος only, alone, by oneself
δὲ conj. δέ but, and, now, also, to the contrary, rather, then
τοῦτο demo. pron. acc. neut. sg. οὗτος αὕτη τοῦτο this, the same, this same, he, she, it
ἡμῖν pron. dat. 1p. pl. ἐγώ I
τὸ art. acc. neut. sg. ὁ ἡ τό the, this, that, he, she, it
μέρος n. acc. neut. sg. μέρος part, coast, portion, behalf, respect, piece, side
εἰς prep. εἰς (+acc) into, to, unto, for, in, on, toward, against, upon, at, among
ἀπελεγμὸν n. acc. masc. sg. ἀπελεγμός nought
ἀλλὰ conj. ἀλλά but, yea, yet, nevertheless, howbeit, nay, therefore
καὶ conj. καί and, even, also, but
τὸ art. acc. neut. sg. ὁ ἡ τό the, this, that, he, she, it
τῆς art. gen. fem. sg. ὁ ἡ τό the, this, that, he, she, it
μεγάλης adj. gen. fem. sg. μέγας great, loud, greatest, high, large, mighty, strong
θεᾶς n. gen. fem. sg. θεά goddess
Ἀρτέμιδος n. gen. fem. sg. Ἄρτεμις Diana, Artemis
ἱερὸν n. acc. neut. sg. ἱερόν temple
εἰς prep. εἰς (+acc) into, to, unto, for, in, on, toward, against, upon, at, among
οὐδὲν adj. acc. neut. sg. οὐδείς no man, nothing, no, none, neither, not, nought
τε conj. τέ and, both, also
καὶ conj. καί and, even, also, but
τὴν art. acc. fem. sg. ὁ ἡ τό the, this, that, he, she, it
μεγαλειότητα n. acc. fem. sg. μεγαλειότης mighty power, magnificence, majesty
αὐτῆς pron. gen. fem. 3p. sg. αὐτός ή ό self, of oneself, even, very, the same, he, she, it
ἣν relative pron. acc. fem. sg. ὅς ἥ ὅ who, which, what, that
ὅλη adj. nom. fem. sg. ὅλος all, whole, every whit, altogether
ἡ art. nom. fem. sg. ὁ ἡ τό the, this, that, he, she, it
Ἀσία n. nom. fem. sg. Ἀσία Asia
καὶ conj. καί and, even, also, but
ἡ art. nom. fem. sg. ὁ ἡ τό the, this, that, he, she, it
οἰκουμένη n. nom. fem. sg. οἰκουμένη world, earth
28 δὲ conj. δέ but, and, now, also, to the contrary, rather, then
καὶ conj. καί and, even, also, but
πλήρεις adj. nom. masc. pl. πλήρης full
θυμοῦ n. gen. masc. sg. θυμός wrath, fierceness, indignation
Μεγάλη adj. nom. fem. sg. μέγας great, loud, greatest, high, large, mighty, strong
ἡ art. nom. fem. sg. ὁ ἡ τό the, this, that, he, she, it
Ἄρτεμις n. nom. fem. sg. Ἄρτεμις Diana, Artemis
Ἐφεσίων adj. gen. masc. pl. Ἐφέσιος Ephesian, of Ephesus
29 καὶ conj. καί and, even, also, but
ἡ art. nom. fem. sg. ὁ ἡ τό the, this, that, he, she, it
πόλις n. nom. fem. sg. πόλις city
ὅλη adj. nom. fem. sg. ὅλος all, whole, every whit, altogether
συγχύσεως n. gen. fem. sg. σύγχυσις confusion
τε conj. τέ and, both, also
ὁμοθυμαδὸν adv. ὁμοθυμαδόν with one accord, with one mind
εἰς prep. εἰς (+acc) into, to, unto, for, in, on, toward, against, upon, at, among
τὸ art. acc. neut. sg. ὁ ἡ τό the, this, that, he, she, it
θέατρον n. acc. neut. sg. θέατρον theatre, spectacle
Γάϊον n. acc. masc. sg. Γάϊος Gaius
καὶ conj. καί and, even, also, but
Ἀρίσταρχον n. acc. masc. sg. Ἀρίσταρχος Aristarchus
Μακεδόνας n. acc. masc. pl. Μακεδών of Macedonia, Macedonian
συνεκδήμους n. acc. masc. pl. συνέκδημος companion in travel, travel with
τοῦ art. gen. masc. sg. ὁ ἡ τό the, this, that, he, she, it

Παύλου n. gen. masc. sg. Παῦλος Paul, Paulus
30 τοῦ art. gen. masc. sg. ὁ ἡ τό the, this, that, he, she, it
δὲ conj. δέ but, and, now, also, to the contrary, rather, then
Παύλου n. gen. masc. sg. Παῦλος Paul, Paulus
εἰς prep. εἰς (+acc) into, to, unto, for, in, on, toward, against, upon, at, among
τὸν art. acc. masc. sg. ὁ ἡ τό the, this, that, he, she, it
δῆμον n. acc. masc. sg. δῆμος people
οὐκ particle of negation. οὐ οὐκ οὐχ not, no, neither, none, nay, nor, never, nothing
αὐτὸν pron. acc. masc. 3p. sg. αὐτός ἡ ὁ self, of oneself, even, very, the same, he, she, it
οἱ art. nom. masc. pl. ὁ ἡ τό the, this, that, he, she, it
μαθηταί n. nom. masc. pl. μαθητής disciple
31 τινὲς indefinite pron. nom. masc. pl. τὶς certain, some, any man, one, any thing
δὲ conj. δέ but, and, now, also, to the contrary, rather, then
καὶ conj. καί and, even, also, but
τῶν art. gen. masc. pl. ὁ ἡ τό the, this, that, he, she, it
'Ασιαρχῶν n. gen. masc. pl. 'Ασιάρχης chief of Asia
αὐτῷ pron. dat. masc. 3p. sg. αὐτός ἡ ὁ self, of oneself, even, very, the same, he, she, it
φίλοι adj. nom. masc. pl. φίλος friend
πρὸς prep. πρός (+gen) for, (+dat) at, (+acc) unto, to, with, for, against
αὐτὸν pron. acc. masc. 3p. sg. αὐτός ἡ ὁ self, of oneself, even, very, the same, he, she, it
μὴ particle of negation. μή not, no, lest, neither, none, nothing, nor, never, without
ἑαυτὸν reflexive pron. acc. masc. 3p. sg. ἑαυτοῦ himself, herself, itself, yourself, ourselves
εἰς prep. εἰς (+acc) into, to, unto, for, in, on, toward, against, upon, at, among
τὸ art. acc. neut. sg. ὁ ἡ τό the, this, that, he, she, it
θέατρον n. acc. neut. sg. θέατρον theatre, spectacle
32 ἄλλοι adj. nom. masc. pl. ἄλλος other, another, some, one, more, otherwise
μέν conj. μέν indeed, verily, truly, even, so, some
οὖν conj. οὖν therefore, then, so, and, now, wherefore
ἄλλο adj. acc. neut. sg. ἄλλος other, another, some, one, more, otherwise
τι indefinite pron. acc. neut. sg. τὶς certain, some, any man, one, any thing
γὰρ conj. γάρ for, and, because, but, indeed
ἡ art. nom. fem. sg. ὁ ἡ τό the, this, that, he, she, it
ἐκκλησία n. nom. fem. sg. ἐκκλησία church, assembly
καὶ conj. καί and, even, also, but
οἱ art. nom. masc. pl. ὁ ἡ τό the, this, that, he, she, it
πλείους compar. adj. nom. masc. pl. πλείων more, many, greater, further, more part
οὐκ particle of negation. οὐ οὐκ οὐχ not, no, neither, none, nay, nor, never, nothing
τίνος interrog. pron. gen. neut. sg. τίς what, who, why, where, which, how
ἕνεκεν prep. ἕνεκα, ἕνεκεν or εἵνεκεν (+gen) for the sake, for a cause, for, by reason of
33 ἐκ prep. ἐκ ἐξ (+gen) of, from, out of, by, on, with, in, among, through
δὲ conj. δέ but, and, now, also, to the contrary, rather, then
τοῦ art. gen. masc. sg. ὁ ἡ τό the, this, that, he, she, it
ὄχλου n. gen. masc. sg. ὄχλος people, multitude, company, press, number
'Αλέξανδρον n. acc. masc. sg. 'Αλέξανδρος Alexander
αὐτὸν pron. acc. masc. 3p. sg. αὐτός ἡ ὁ self, of oneself, even, very, the same, he, she, it
τῶν art. gen. masc. pl. ὁ ἡ τό the, this, that, he, she, it
'Ιουδαίων adj. gen. masc. pl. 'Ιουδαῖος Jew, Jewess
ὁ art. nom. masc. sg. ὁ ἡ τό the, this, that, he, she, it
δὲ conj. δέ but, and, now, also, to the contrary, rather, then
'Αλέξανδρος n. nom. masc. sg. 'Αλέξανδρος Alexander
τὴν art. acc. fem. sg. ὁ ἡ τό the, this, that, he, she, it
χεῖρα n. acc. fem. sg. χείρ hand
τῷ art. dat. masc. sg. ὁ ἡ τό the, this, that, he, she, it
δήμῳ n. dat. masc. sg. δῆμος people
34 δὲ conj. δέ but, and, now, also, to the contrary, rather, then

ὅτι conj. ὅτι that, for, because, how that, how, because that, for that, though
Ἰουδαῖός adj. nom. masc. sg. Ἰουδαῖος Jew, Jewess
φωνὴ n. nom. fem. sg. φωνή voice, sound, noise
μία num. nom. fem. sg. εἷς or ἕν one, other, some, any, only, a certain
ἐκ prep. ἐκ ἐξ (+gen) of, from, out of, by, on, with, in, among, through
πάντων adj. gen. masc. pl. πᾶς πᾶσα πᾶν all, every, whosoever, every one, no, whole, any
ὡς adv. ὡς as, when, as it were, how, about, like, as soon as, even as, while
ἐπὶ prep. ἐπί (+gen) on, in, upon, (+dat) in, at, for, upon, (+acc) on, upon, unto, to, against
ὥρας n. acc. fem. pl. ὥρα hour, time, season
δύο num. acc. fem. pl. δύο two, twain, both
Μεγάλη adj. nom. fem. sg. μέγας great, loud, greatest, high, large, mighty, strong
ἡ art. nom. fem. sg. ὁ ἡ τό the, this, that, he, she, it
Ἄρτεμις n. nom. fem. sg. Ἄρτεμις Diana, Artemis
Ἐφεσίων adj. gen. masc. pl. Ἐφέσιος Ephesian, of Ephesus
35 δὲ conj. δέ but, and, now, also, to the contrary, rather, then
ὁ art. nom. masc. sg. ὁ ἡ τό the, this, that, he, she, it
γραμματεὺς n. nom. masc. sg. γραμματεύς townclerk, scribe
τὸν art. acc. masc. sg. ὁ ἡ τό the, this, that, he, she, it
ὄχλον n. acc. masc. sg. ὄχλος people, multitude, company, press, number
Ἄνδρες n. voc. masc. pl. ἀνήρ man, husband, sir
Ἐφέσιοι adj. voc. masc. pl. Ἐφέσιος Ephesian, of Ephesus
τίς interrog. pron. nom. masc. sg. τίς what, who, why, where, which, how
γάρ particle. γάρ for, and, because, but, indeed
ἄνθρωπος n. nom. masc. pl. ἄνθρωπος man, human being, person, one, certain
ὃς relative pron. nom. masc. sg. ὅς ἥ ὅ who, which, what, that
οὐ particle of negation. οὐ οὐκ οὐχ not, no, neither, none, nay, nor, never, nothing
τὴν art. acc. fem. sg. ὁ ἡ τό the, this, that, he, she, it
Ἐφεσίων adj. gen. masc. pl. Ἐφέσιος Ephesian, of Ephesus
πόλιν n. acc. fem. sg. πόλις city
νεωκόρον n. acc. masc. sg. νεωκόρος worshipper, temple-keeper
τῆς art. gen. fem. sg. ὁ ἡ τό the, this, that, he, she, it
μεγάλης adj. gen. fem. sg. μέγας great, loud, greatest, high, large, mighty, strong
θεᾶς n. gen. fem. sg. θεά goddess
Ἀρτέμιδος n. gen. fem. sg. Ἄρτεμις Diana, Artemis
καὶ conj. καί and, even, also, but
τοῦ art. gen. neut. sg. ὁ ἡ τό the, this, that, he, she, it
Διοπετοῦς adj. gen. neut. sg. διοπετής fell down from Jupiter
36 ἀναντιρρήτων adj. gen. neut. pl. ἀναντίρρητος cannot be spoken against
οὖν conj. οὖν therefore, then, so, and, now, wherefore
τούτων demo. pron. gen. neut. pl. οὗτος αὕτη τοῦτο this, the same, this same, he, she, it
ὑμᾶς pron. acc. 2p. pl. σύ thou, you
καὶ conj. καί and, even, also, but
μηδὲν adj. acc. neut. sg. μηδείς μηδεμία μηδέν no man, nothing, no, none, not at all
προπετὲς adj. acc. neut. sg. προπετής rashly, heady
37 γὰρ conj. γάρ for, and, because, but, indeed
τοὺς art. acc. masc. pl. ὁ ἡ τό the, this, that, he, she, it
ἄνδρας n. acc. masc. pl. ἀνήρ man, husband, sir
τούτους demo. pron. acc. masc. pl. οὗτος αὕτη τοῦτο this, the same, this same, he, she, it
οὔτε conj. οὔτε neither, nor, nor yet, no, none
ἱεροσύλους adj. acc. masc. pl. ἱερόσυλος robbers of temples
οὔτε conj. οὔτε neither, nor, nor yet, no, none
τὴν art. acc. fem. sg. ὁ ἡ τό the, this, that, he, she, it
θεὰν n. acc. fem. sg. θεά goddess
ἡμῶν pron. gen. 1p. pl. ἐγώ I
38 εἰ conj. εἰ if, whether, that, though, forasmuch

μέν conj. μέν indeed, verily, truly, even, so, some
οὖν conj. οὖν therefore, then, so, and, now, wherefore
Δημήτριος n. nom. masc. sg. Δημήτριος Demetrius
καὶ conj. καί and, even, also, but
οἱ art. nom. masc. pl. ὁ ἡ τό the, this, that, he, she, it
σὺν prep. σύν (+dat) with, beside
αὐτῷ pron. dat. masc. 3p. sg. αὐτός ή ό self, of oneself, even, very, the same, he, she, it
τεχνῖται n. nom. masc. pl. τεχνίτης craftsmen, builder
πρός prep. πρός (+gen) for, (+dat) at, (+acc) unto, to, with, for, against
τινα indefinite pron. acc. masc. sg. τὶς certain, some, any man, one, any thing
λόγον n. acc. masc. sg. λόγος word, saying, account, speech, thing, matter
ἀγοραῖοι adj. nom. fem. pl. ἀγοραῖος of the baser sort, from the market, law, judicial
καὶ conj. καί and, even, also, but
ἀνθύπατοί n. nom. masc. pl. ἀνθύπατος deputy
ἀλλήλοις pron. dat. masc. 3p. pl. ἀλλήλων one another, themselves, together, mutual
39 εἰ conj. εἰ if, whether, that, though, forasmuch
δέ conj. δέ but, and, now, also, to the contrary, rather, then
τι indefinite pron. acc. neut. sg. τὶς certain, some, any man, one, any thing
περὶ prep. περί (+gen) of, for, concerning, (+acc) about, concerning, in
ἑτέρων adj. gen. neut. pl. ἕτερος another, other, else, strange
ἐν prep. ἐν (+dat) in, by, with, among, at, on, through, to, within, into, of, for
τῇ art. dat. fem. sg. ὁ ἡ τό the, this, that, he, she, it
ἐννόμῳ adj. dat. fem. sg. ἔννομος lawful, under law
ἐκκλησίᾳ n. dat. fem. sg. ἐκκλησία church, assembly
40 καὶ conj. καί and, even, also, but
γὰρ conj. γάρ for, and, because, but, indeed
στάσεως n. gen. fem. sg. στάσις dissension, sedition, insurrection, standing, uproar
περὶ prep. περί (+gen) of, for, concerning, (+acc) about, concerning, in
τῆς art. gen. fem. sg. ὁ ἡ τό the, this, that, he, she, it
σήμερον adv. σήμερον this day, today
μηδενὸς num. gen. neut. sg. μηδείς μηδεμία μηδέν no man, nothing, no, none, not at all
αἰτίου adj. gen. neut. sg. αἴτιος cause, fault, author
περὶ prep. περί (+gen) of, for, concerning, (+acc) about, concerning, in
οὗ relative pron. gen. neut. sg. ὅς ἥ ὅ who, which, what, that
λόγον n. acc. masc. sg. λόγος word, saying, account, speech, thing, matter
τῆς art. gen. fem. sg. ὁ ἡ τό the, this, that, he, she, it
συστροφῆς n. gen. fem. sg. συστροφή concourse, band together, combination
ταύτης demo. pron. gen. fem. sg. οὗτος αὕτη τοῦτο this, the same, this same, he, she, it
41 καὶ conj. καί and, even, also, but
ταῦτα demo. pron. acc. neut. pl. οὗτος αὕτη τοῦτο this, the same, this same, he, she, it
τὴν art. acc. fem. sg. ὁ ἡ τό the, this, that, he, she, it
ἐκκλησίαν n. acc. fem. sg. ἐκκλησία church, assembly

20

1 Μετὰ prep. μετά (+gen) with, among, against, (+acc) after
δὲ conj. δέ but, and, now, also, to the contrary, rather, then
τὸ art. acc. neut. sg. ὁ ἡ τό the, this, that, he, she, it
τὸν art. acc. masc. sg. ὁ ἡ τό the, this, that, he, she, it
θόρυβον n. acc. masc. sg. θόρυβος tumult, uproar
ὁ art. nom. masc. sg. ὁ ἡ τό the, this, that, he, she, it
Παῦλος n. nom. masc. sg. Παῦλος Paul, Paulus
τοὺς art. acc. masc. pl. ὁ ἡ τό the, this, that, he, she, it
μαθητὰς n. acc. masc. pl. μαθητής disciple
καὶ conj. καί and, even, also, but

εἰς prep. εἰς (+acc) into, to, unto, for, in, on, toward, against, upon, at, among
τὴν art. acc. fem. sg. ὁ ἡ τό the, this, that, he, she, it
Μακεδονίαν n. acc. fem. sg. Μακεδονία Macedonia
2 δὲ conj. δέ but, and, now, also, to the contrary, rather, then
τὰ art. acc. neut. pl. ὁ ἡ τό the, this, that, he, she, it
μέρη n. acc. neut. pl. μέρος part, coast, portion, behalf, respect, piece, side
ἐκεῖνα demo. pron. acc. neut. pl. ἐκεῖνος that, he, the same, that same
καὶ conj. καί and, even, also, but
αὐτοὺς pron. acc. masc. 3p. pl. αὐτός ἡ ὁ self, of oneself, even, very, the same, he, she, it
λόγῳ n. dat. masc. sg. λόγος word, saying, account, speech, thing, matter
πολλῷ adj. dat. masc. sg. πολύς many, great, much, long, abundant
εἰς prep. εἰς (+acc) into, to, unto, for, in, on, toward, against, upon, at, among
τὴν art. acc. fem. sg. ὁ ἡ τό the, this, that, he, she, it
Ἑλλάδα n. acc. fem. sg. Ἑλλάς Greece
3 τε conj. τέ and, both, also
μῆνας n. acc. masc. pl. μήν month
τρεῖς num. acc. masc. pl. τρεῖς three
αὐτῷ pron. dat. masc. 3p. sg. αὐτός ἡ ὁ self, of oneself, even, very, the same, he, she, it
ἐπιβουλῆς n. gen. fem. sg. ἐπιβουλή laying await, lying in wait
ὑπὸ prep. ὑπό (+gen) of, by, with, from, among, (+acc) under
τῶν art. gen. masc. pl. ὁ ἡ τό the, this, that, he, she, it
Ἰουδαίων adj. gen. masc. pl. Ἰουδαῖος Jew, Jewess
εἰς prep. εἰς (+acc) into, to, unto, for, in, on, toward, against, upon, at, among
τὴν art. acc. fem. sg. ὁ ἡ τό the, this, that, he, she, it
Συρίαν n. acc. fem. sg. Συρία Syria
γνώμη n. nom. fem. sg. γνώμη judgement, mind, advice, purpose, will
τοῦ art. gen. neut. sg. ὁ ἡ τό the, this, that, he, she, it
διὰ prep. διά (+gen) by, through, with, in, of, (+acc) for, because of, for a cause
Μακεδονίας n. gen. fem. sg. Μακεδονία Macedonia
4 δὲ conj. δέ but, and, now, also, to the contrary, rather, then
αὐτῷ pron. dat. masc. 3p. sg. αὐτός ἡ ὁ self, of oneself, even, very, the same, he, she, it
ἄχρι prep. ἄχρι or ἄχρις (+gen) until, unto, till, even to, as far as, while, into
τῆς art. gen. fem. sg. ὁ ἡ τό the, this, that, he, she, it
Ἀσίας n. gen. fem. sg. Ἀσία Asia
Σώπατρος n. nom. masc. sg. Σώπατρος Sopater
Βεροιαῖος adj. nom. masc. sg. Βεροιαῖος of Berea
Θεσσαλονικέων n. gen. masc. pl. Θεσσαλονικεύς Thessalonian, of Thessalonica
Ἀρίσταρχος n. nom. masc. sg. Ἀρίσταρχος Aristarchus
καὶ conj. καί and, even, also, but
Σεκοῦνδος n. nom. masc. sg. Σεκοῦνδος Secundus
Γάϊος n. nom. masc. sg. Γάϊος Gaius
Δερβαῖος adj. nom. masc. sg. Δερβαῖος of Derbe
Τιμόθεος n. nom. masc. sg. Τιμόθεος Timotheus, Timothy
Ἀσιανοὶ n. nom. masc. pl. Ἀσιανός of Asia
Τύχικος n. nom. masc. sg. Τυχικός Tychicus
Τρόφιμος n. nom. masc. sg. Τρόφιμος Trophimus
5 οὗτοι demo. pron. nom. masc. pl. οὗτος αὕτη τοῦτο this, the same, this same, he, she, it
ἡμᾶς pron. acc. 1p. pl. ἐγώ I
ἐν prep. ἐν (+dat) in, by, with, among, at, on, through, to, within, into, of, for
Τρῳάδι n. dat. fem. sg. Τρῳάς Troas
6 ἡμεῖς pron. nom. 1p. pl. ἐγώ I
δὲ conj. δέ but, and, now, also, to the contrary, rather, then
μετὰ prep. μετά (+gen) with, among, against, (+acc) after
τὰς art. acc. fem. pl. ὁ ἡ τό the, this, that, he, she, it
ἡμέρας n. acc. fem. pl. ἡμέρα day, time, year, while, age, day time

τῶν art. gen. neut. pl. ὁ ἡ τό the, this, that, he, she, it
ἀζύμων adj. gen. neut. pl. ἄζυμος unleavened bread, unleavened
ἀπὸ prep. ἀπό (+gen) from, of, out of, since, for, off, at, by, in, on
Φιλίππων n. gen. masc. pl. Φίλιπποι Philippi
καὶ conj. καί and, even, also, but
πρὸς prep. πρός (+gen) for, (+dat) at, (+acc) unto, to, with, for, against
αὐτοὺς pron. acc. masc. 3p. pl. αὐτός ή ό self, of oneself, even, very, the same, he, she, it
εἰς prep. εἰς (+acc) into, to, unto, for, in, on, toward, against, upon, at, among
τὴν art. acc. fem. sg. ὁ ἡ τό the, this, that, he, she, it
Τρῳάδα n. acc. fem. sg. Τρῳάς Troas
ἄχρις prep. ἄχρι or ἄχρις (+gen) until, unto, till, even to, as far as, while, into
ἡμερῶν n. gen. fem. pl. ἡμέρα day, time, year, while, age, day time
πέντε num. gen. fem. pl. πέντε five
οὗ adv. οὗ where, whither, wherein
ἡμέρας n. acc. fem. pl. ἡμέρα day, time, year, while, age, day time
ἑπτά num. acc. fem. pl. ἑπτά seven, seventh
7 Ἐν prep. ἐν (+dat) in, by, with, among, at, on, through, to, within, into, of, for
δὲ conj. δέ but, and, now, also, to the contrary, rather, then
τῇ art. dat. fem. sg. ὁ ἡ τό the, this, that, he, she, it
μιᾷ num. dat. fem. sg. εἷς or ἕν one, other, some, any, only, a certain
τῶν art. gen. neut. pl. ὁ ἡ τό the, this, that, he, she, it
σαββάτων n. gen. neut. pl. σάββατον sabbath day, sabbath, week
τῶν art. gen. masc. pl. ὁ ἡ τό the, this, that, he, she, it
μαθητῶν n. gen. masc. pl. μαθητής disciple
τοῦ art. gen. masc. sg. ὁ ἡ τό the, this, that, he, she, it
ἄρτον n. acc. masc. sg. ἄρτος bread, loaf
ὁ art. nom. masc. sg. ὁ ἡ τό the, this, that, he, she, it
Παῦλος n. nom. masc. sg. Παῦλος Paul, Paulus
αὐτοῖς pron. dat. masc. 3p. pl. αὐτός ή ό self, of oneself, even, very, the same, he, she, it
τῇ art. dat. fem. sg. ὁ ἡ τό the, this, that, he, she, it
ἐπαύριον adv. ἐπαύριον next day, morrow, day following, nest day after
τε conj. τέ and, both, also
τὸν art. acc. masc. sg. ὁ ἡ τό the, this, that, he, she, it
λόγον n. acc. masc. sg. λόγος word, saying, account, speech, thing, matter
μέχρι prep. μέχρι until, unto, till, to
μεσονυκτίου n. gen. neut. sg. μεσονύκτιον midnight
8 δὲ conj. δέ but, and, now, also, to the contrary, rather, then
λαμπάδες n. nom. fem. pl. λαμπάς lamp, light, torch
ἱκαναὶ adj. nom. fem. pl. ἱκανός many, much, long, worthy, sufficient, great, able
ἐν prep. ἐν (+dat) in, by, with, among, at, on, through, to, within, into, of, for
τῷ art. dat. neut. sg. ὁ ἡ τό the, this, that, he, she, it
ὑπερῴῳ n. dat. neut. sg. ὑπερῷον upper room, upper chamber
οὗ adv. οὗ where, whither, wherein
9 δέ conj. δέ but, and, now, also, to the contrary, rather, then
τις indefinite pron. nom. masc. sg. τὶς certain, some, any man, one, any thing
νεανίας n. nom. masc. sg. νεανίας young man
ὀνόματι n. dat. neut. sg. ὄνομα name, call, surname
Εὔτυχος n. nom. masc. sg. Εὔτυχος Eutychus
ἐπὶ prep. ἐπί (+gen) on, in, upon, (+dat) in, at, for, upon, (+acc) on, upon, unto, to, against
τῆς art. gen. fem. sg. ὁ ἡ τό the, this, that, he, she, it
θυρίδος n. gen. fem. sg. θυρίς window
ὕπνῳ n. dat. masc. sg. ὕπνος sleep
βαθεῖ adj. dat. masc. sg. βαθύς deep, very early
τοῦ art. gen. masc. sg. ὁ ἡ τό the, this, that, he, she, it
Παύλου n. gen. masc. sg. Παῦλος Paul, Paulus

ἐπὶ prep. ἐπί (+gen) on, in, upon, (+dat) in, at, for, upon, (+acc) on, upon, unto, to, against
πλεῖον compar. adj. acc. neut. sg. πολύς many, great, much, long, abundant
ἀπὸ prep. ἀπό (+gen) from, of, out of, since, for, off, at, by, in, on
τοῦ art. gen. masc. sg. ὁ ἡ τό the, this, that, he, she, it
ὕπνου n. gen. masc. sg. ὕπνος sleep
ἀπὸ prep. ἀπό (+gen) from, of, out of, since, for, off, at, by, in, on
τοῦ art. gen. neut. sg. ὁ ἡ τό the, this, that, he, she, it
τριστέγου n. gen. neut. sg. τρίστεγον third loft, upper storey
κάτω adv. κάτω under, down, beneath, bottom
καὶ conj. καί and, even, also, but
νεκρός adj. nom. masc. sg. νεκρός dead
10 δὲ conj. δέ but, and, now, also, to the contrary, rather, then
ὁ art. nom. masc. sg. ὁ ἡ τό the, this, that, he, she, it
Παῦλος n. nom. masc. sg. Παῦλος Paul, Paulus
αὐτῷ pron. dat. masc. 3p. sg. αὐτός ἡ ὁ self, of oneself, even, very, the same, he, she, it
καὶ conj. καί and, even, also, but
Μὴ particle of negation. μή not, no, lest, neither, none, nothing, nor, never, without
ἡ art. nom. fem. sg. ὁ ἡ τό the, this, that, he, she, it
γὰρ conj. γάρ for, and, because, but, indeed
ψυχὴ n. nom. fem. sg. ψυχή life, soul, mind, heart
αὐτοῦ pron. gen. masc. 3p. sg. αὐτός ἡ ὁ self, of oneself, even, very, the same, he, she, it
ἐν prep. ἐν (+dat) in, by, with, among, at, on, through, to, within, into, of, for
αὐτῷ pron. dat. masc. 3p. sg. αὐτός ἡ ὁ self, of oneself, even, very, the same, he, she, it
11 δὲ conj. δέ but, and, now, also, to the contrary, rather, then
καὶ conj. καί and, even, also, but
ἄρτον n. acc. masc. sg. ἄρτος bread, loaf
καὶ conj. καί and, even, also, but
ἐφ' prep. ἐπί (+gen) on, in, upon, (+dat) in, at, for, upon, (+acc) on, upon, unto, to, against
ἱκανόν adj. acc. masc. sg. ἱκανός many, much, long, worthy, sufficient, great, able
τε conj. τέ and, both, also
ἄχρις prep. ἄχρι or ἄχρις (+gen) until, unto, till, even to, as far as, while, into
αὐγῆς n. gen. fem. sg. αὐγή break of day
οὕτως adv. οὕτω οὕτως so, even so, thus, on this wise, likewise, after this manner
12 δὲ conj. δέ but, and, now, also, to the contrary, rather, then
τὸν art. acc. masc. sg. ὁ ἡ τό the, this, that, he, she, it
παῖδα n. acc. masc. sg. παῖς servant, child, son, maid, young man, manservant
καὶ conj. καί and, even, also, but
οὐ particle of negation. οὐ οὐκ οὐχ not, no, neither, none, nay, nor, never, nothing
μετρίως adv. μετρίως a little
13 Ἡμεῖς pron. nom. 1p. pl. ἐγώ I
δὲ conj. δέ but, and, now, also, to the contrary, rather, then
ἐπὶ prep. ἐπί (+gen) on, in, upon, (+dat) in, at, for, upon, (+acc) on, upon, unto, to, against
τὸ art. acc. neut. sg. ὁ ἡ τό the, this, that, he, she, it
πλοῖον n. acc. neut. sg. πλοῖον ship, boat
εἰς prep. εἰς (+acc) into, to, unto, for, in, on, toward, against, upon, at, among
τὴν art. acc. fem. sg. ὁ ἡ τό the, this, that, he, she, it
Ἄσσον n. acc. fem. sg. Ἄσσος Assos
ἐκεῖθεν adv. ἐκεῖθεν thence, from thence, from that place
τὸν art. acc. masc. sg. ὁ ἡ τό the, this, that, he, she, it
Παῦλον n. acc. masc. sg. Παῦλος Paul, Paulus
οὕτω adv. οὕτω οὕτως so, even so, thus, on this wise, likewise, after this manner
γὰρ conj. γάρ for, and, because, but, indeed
αὐτὸς pron. nom. masc. 3p. sg. αὐτός ἡ ὁ self, of oneself, even, very, the same, he, she, it
14 ὡς adv. ὡς as, when, as it were, how, about, like, as soon as, even as, while
δὲ conj. δέ but, and, now, also, to the contrary, rather, then

ἡμῖν pron. dat. 1p. pl. ἐγώ I
εἰς prep. εἰς (+acc) into, to, unto, for, in, on, toward, against, upon, at, among
τὴν art. acc. fem. sg. ὁ ἡ τό the, this, that, he, she, it
Ἄσσον n. acc. fem. sg. Ἄσσος Assos
αὐτὸν pron. acc. masc. 3p. sg. αὐτός ἡ ὁ self, of oneself, even, very, the same, he, she, it
εἰς prep. εἰς (+acc) into, to, unto, for, in, on, toward, against, upon, at, among
Μιτυλήνην n. acc. fem. sg. Μιτυλήνη Mitylene
15 κἀκεῖθεν adv. κἀκεῖθεν and from thence, and thence, and afterward, thence also
τῇ art. dat. fem. sg. ὁ ἡ τό the, this, that, he, she, it
ἀντικρὺ adv. ἀντικρύ over against
Χίου n. gen. fem. sg. Χίος Chios
τῇ art. dat. fem. sg. ὁ ἡ τό the, this, that, he, she, it
δὲ conj. δέ but, and, now, also, to the contrary, rather, then
ἑτέρᾳ adj. dat. fem. sg. ἕτερος another, other, else, strange
εἰς prep. εἰς (+acc) into, to, unto, for, in, on, toward, against, upon, at, among
Σάμον n. acc. fem. sg. Σάμος Samos
καὶ conj. καί and, even, also, but
ἐν prep. ἐν (+dat) in, by, with, among, at, on, through, to, within, into, of, for
Τρωγυλλίῳ n. dat. neut. sg. Τρωγύλλιον Trogyllium
τῇ art. dat. fem. sg. ὁ ἡ τό the, this, that, he, she, it
εἰς prep. εἰς (+acc) into, to, unto, for, in, on, toward, against, upon, at, among
Μίλητον n. acc. fem. sg. Μίλητος Miletus, Miletum
16 γὰρ conj. γάρ for, and, because, but, indeed
ὁ art. nom. masc. sg. ὁ ἡ τό the, this, that, he, she, it
Παῦλος n. nom. masc. sg. Παῦλος Paul, Paulus
τὴν art. acc. fem. sg. ὁ ἡ τό the, this, that, he, she, it
Ἔφεσον n. acc. fem. sg. Ἔφεσος Ephesus
ὅπως adv. ὅπως that, how, to, because, so that, when
μὴ particle of negation. μή not, no, lest, neither, none, nothing, nor, never, without
αὐτῷ pron. dat. masc. 3p. sg. αὐτός ἡ ὁ self, of oneself, even, very, the same, he, she, it
ἐν prep. ἐν (+dat) in, by, with, among, at, on, through, to, within, into, of, for
τῇ art. dat. fem. sg. ὁ ἡ τό the, this, that, he, she, it
Ἀσίᾳ n. dat. fem. sg. Ἀσία Asia
γὰρ conj. γάρ for, and, because, but, indeed
εἰ conj. εἰ if, whether, that, though, forasmuch
δυνατὸν adj. nom. neut. sg. δυνατός able, possible, mighty, strong
αὐτῷ pron. dat. masc. 3p. sg. αὐτός ἡ ὁ self, of oneself, even, very, the same, he, she, it
τὴν art. acc. fem. sg. ὁ ἡ τό the, this, that, he, she, it
ἡμέραν n. acc. fem. sg. ἡμέρα day, time, year, while, age, day time
τῆς art. gen. fem. sg. ὁ ἡ τό the, this, that, he, she, it
Πντηκοστῆς n. gen. fem. sg. πεντηκοστή Pentecost
εἰς prep. εἰς (+acc) into, to, unto, for, in, on, toward, against, upon, at, among
Ἱεροσόλυμα n. acc. neut. sg. Ἱεροσόλυμα Jerusalem
17 Ἀπὸ prep. ἀπό (+gen) from, of, out of, since, for, off, at, by, in, on
δὲ conj. δέ but, and, now, also, to the contrary, rather, then
τῆς art. gen. fem. sg. ὁ ἡ τό the, this, that, he, she, it
Μιλήτου n. gen. fem. sg. Μίλητος Miletus, Miletum
εἰς prep. εἰς (+acc) into, to, unto, for, in, on, toward, against, upon, at, among
Ἔφεσον n. acc. fem. sg. Ἔφεσος Ephesus
τοὺς art. acc. masc. pl. ὁ ἡ τό the, this, that, he, she, it
πρεσβυτέρους adj. acc. masc. pl. πρεσβύτερος elder, elder woman, eldest, old man
τῆς art. gen. fem. sg. ὁ ἡ τό the, this, that, he, she, it
ἐκκλησίας n. gen. fem. sg. ἐκκλησία church, assembly
18 ὡς adv. ὡς as, when, as it were, how, about, like, as soon as, even as, while
δὲ conj. δέ but, and, now, also, to the contrary, rather, then

πρὸς prep. πρός (+gen) for, (+dat) at, (+acc) unto, to, with, for, against
αὐτὸν pron. acc. masc. 3p. sg. αὐτός ή ό self, of oneself, even, very, the same, he, she, it
αὐτοῖς pron. dat. masc. 3p. pl. αὐτός ή ό self, of oneself, even, very, the same, he, she, it
Ὑμεῖς pron. nom. 2p. pl. σύ thou, you
ἀπὸ prep. ἀπό (+gen) from, of, out of, since, for, off, at, by, in, on
πρώτης ordinal. adj. gen. fem. sg. πρῶτος first, chief, first of all, chiefest, best
ἡμέρας n. gen. fem. sg. ἡμέρα day, time, year, while, age, day time
ἀφ' prep. ἀπό (+gen) from, of, out of, since, for, off, at, by, in, on
ἧς relative pron. gen. fem. sg. ὅς ἥ ὅ who, which, what, that
εἰς prep. εἰς (+acc) into, to, unto, for, in, on, toward, against, upon, at, among
τὴν art. acc. fem. sg. ὁ ἡ τό the, this, that, he, she, it
Ἀσίαν n. acc. fem. sg. Ἀσία Asia
πῶς adv. πῶς how, by what means, after what manner
μεθ' prep. μετά (+gen) with, among, against, (+acc) after
ὑμῶν pron. gen. 2p. pl. σύ thou, you
τὸν art. acc. masc. sg. ὁ ἡ τό the, this, that, he, she, it
πάντα adj. acc. masc. sg. πᾶς πᾶσα πᾶν all, every, whosoever, every one, no, whole, any
χρόνον n. acc. masc. sg. χρόνος time, season, space
19 τῷ art. dat. masc. sg. ὁ ἡ τό the, this, that, he, she, it
Κυρίῳ n. dat. masc. sg. κύριος Lord, lord, master, sir, LORD, God, Master, owner
μετὰ prep. μετά (+gen) with, among, against, (+acc) after
πάσης adj. gen. fem. sg. πᾶς πᾶσα πᾶν all, every, whosoever, every one, no, whole, any
ταπεινοφροσύνης n. gen. fem. sg. ταπεινοφροσύνη humility of mind, humility, lowliness
καὶ conj. καί and, even, also, but
πολλῶν adj. gen. neut. pl. πολύς many, great, much, long, abundant
δακρύων n. gen. neut. pl. δάκρυον tears
καὶ conj. καί and, even, also, but
πειρασμῶν n. gen. masc. pl. πειρασμός temptation, trial
τῶν art. gen. masc. pl. ὁ ἡ τό the, this, that, he, she, it
μοι pron. dat. 1p. sg. ἐγώ I
ἐν prep. ἐν (+dat) in, by, with, among, at, on, through, to, within, into, of, for
ταῖς art. dat. fem. pl. ὁ ἡ τό the, this, that, he, she, it
ἐπιβουλαῖς n. dat. fem. pl. ἐπιβουλή laying await, lying in wait
τῶν art. gen. masc. pl. ὁ ἡ τό the, this, that, he, she, it
Ἰουδαίων adj. gen. masc. pl. Ἰουδαῖος Jew, Jewess
20 ὡς adv. ὡς as, when, as it were, how, about, like, as soon as, even as, while
οὐδὲν adj. acc. neut. sg. οὐδείς no man, nothing, no, none, neither, not, nought
τῶν art. gen. neut. pl. ὁ ἡ τό the, this, that, he, she, it
τοῦ art. gen. neut. sg. ὁ ἡ τό the, this, that, he, she, it
μὴ particle of negation. μή not, no, lest, neither, none, nothing, nor, never, without
ὑμῖν pron. dat. 2p. pl. σύ thou, you
καὶ conj. καί and, even, also, but
ὑμᾶς pron. acc. 2p. pl. σύ thou, you
δημοσίᾳ adv. δημόσιος common, publicly, openly
καὶ conj. καί and, even, also, but
κατ' prep. κατά (+gen) against, by, throughout, down, (+acc) according to, after, with
οἴκους n. acc. masc. pl. οἶκος house, home, household
21 Ἰουδαίοις adj. dat. masc. pl. Ἰουδαῖος Jew, Jewess
τε conj. τέ and, both, also
καὶ conj. καί and, even, also, but
Ἕλλησι n. dat. masc. pl. Ἕλλην Greek, Gentile
τὴν art. acc. fem. sg. ὁ ἡ τό the, this, that, he, she, it
εἰς prep. εἰς (+acc) into, to, unto, for, in, on, toward, against, upon, at, among
τὸν art. acc. masc. sg. ὁ ἡ τό the, this, that, he, she, it
Θεὸν n. acc. masc. sg. θεός God, god

μετάνοιαν n. acc. fem. sg. μετάνοια repentance
καὶ conj. καί and, even, also, but
πίστιν n. acc. fem. sg. πίστις faith, assurance, belief, fidelity
τὴν art. acc. fem. sg. ὁ ἡ τό the, this, that, he, she, it
εἰς prep. εἰς (+acc) into, to, unto, for, in, on, toward, against, upon, at, among
τὸν art. acc. masc. sg. ὁ ἡ τό the, this, that, he, she, it
Κύριον n. acc. masc. sg. κύριος Lord, lord, master, sir, LORD, God, Master, owner
ἡμῶν pron. gen. 1p. pl. ἐγώ I
Ἰησοῦν n. acc. masc. sg. Ἰησοῦς Jesus
Χριστόν n. acc. masc. sg. Χριστός Christ
22 καὶ conj. καί and, even, also, but
νῦν adv. νῦν now, henceforth, present, this time
ἐγὼ pron. nom. 1p. sg. ἐγώ I
τῷ art. dat. neut. sg. ὁ ἡ τό the, this, that, he, she, it
πνεύματι n. dat. neut. sg. πνεῦμα spirit, Spirit, Ghost, ghost, life. of the spirit, wind
εἰς prep. εἰς (+acc) into, to, unto, for, in, on, toward, against, upon, at, among
Ἱερουσαλήμ pron. name. fem. inde. Ἱερουσαλήμ Jerusalem
τὰ art. acc. neut. pl. ὁ ἡ τό the, this, that, he, she, it
ἐν prep. ἐν (+dat) in, by, with, among, at, on, through, to, within, into, of, for
αὐτῇ pron. dat. fem. 3p. sg. αὐτός ἡ ὁ self, of oneself, even, very, the same, he, she, it
μοι pron. dat. 1p. sg. ἐγώ I
μὴ particle of negation. μή not, no, lest, neither, none, nothing, nor, never, without
23 πλὴν conj. πλήν but, nevertheless, but rather, notwithstanding, except, than
ὅτι conj. ὅτι that, for, because, how that, how, because that, for that, though
τὸ art. nom. neut. sg. ὁ ἡ τό the, this, that, he, she, it
Πνεῦμα n. nom. neut. sg. πνεῦμα spirit, Spirit, Ghost, ghost, life. of the spirit, wind
τὸ art. nom. neut. sg. ὁ ἡ τό the, this, that, he, she, it
Ἅγιον adj. nom. neut. sg. ἅγιος Holy, holy, saint, Holy One, holy thing, most holy
κατὰ prep. κατά (+gen) against, by, throughout, down, (+acc) according to, after, with
πόλιν n. acc. fem. sg. πόλις city
ὅτι conj. ὅτι that, for, because, how that, how, because that, for that, though
δεσμὰ n. nom. neut. pl. δεσμός bond, band, chain, string
με pron. acc. 1p. sg. ἐγώ I
καὶ conj. καί and, even, also, but
θλίψεις n. nom. fem. pl. θλῖψις tribulation, affliction, anguish, persecution
24 ἀλλ' conj. ἀλλά but, yea, yet, nevertheless, howbeit, nay, therefore
οὐδενὸς num. gen. neut. sg. οὐδείς no man, nothing, no, none, neither, not, nought
λόγον n. acc. masc. sg. λόγος word, saying, account, speech, thing, matter
οὐδὲ conj. οὐδέ neither, nor, not, no, not even, never, not yet
τὴν art. acc. fem. sg. ὁ ἡ τό the, this, that, he, she, it
ψυχὴν n. acc. fem. sg. ψυχή life, soul, mind, heart
μου pron. gen. 1p. sg. ἐγώ I
τιμίαν adj. acc. fem. sg. τίμιος precious, dear, has in reputation, honourable
ἐμαυτῷ pron. dat. masc. 1p. sg. ἐμαυτοῦ myself, me
ὡς adv. ὡς as, when, as it were, how, about, like, as soon as, even as, while
τὸν art. acc. masc. sg. ὁ ἡ τό the, this, that, he, she, it
δρόμον n. acc. masc. sg. δρόμος course
μου pron. gen. 1p. sg. ἐγώ I
μετὰ prep. μετά (+gen) with, among, against, (+acc) after
χαρᾶς n. gen. fem. sg. χαρά joy, gladness, joyfulness
καὶ conj. καί and, even, also, but
τὴν art. acc. fem. sg. ὁ ἡ τό the, this, that, he, she, it
διακονίαν n. acc. fem. sg. διακονία ministry, administration, service, office, relief
ἣν relative pron. acc. fem. sg. ὅς ἥ ὅ who, which, what, that
παρὰ prep. παρά (+gen) of, from, (+dat) with, for, (+acc) beside, at, by, above, against

τοῦ art. gen. masc. sg. ὁ ἡ τό the, this, that, he, she, it
Κυρίου n. gen. masc. sg. κύριος Lord, lord, master, sir, LORD, God, Master, owner
Ἰησοῦ n. gen. masc. sg. Ἰησοῦς Jesus
τὸ art. acc. neut. sg. ὁ ἡ τό the, this, that, he, she, it
εὐαγγέλιον n. acc. neut. sg. εὐαγγέλιον gospel
τῆς art. gen. fem. sg. ὁ ἡ τό the, this, that, he, she, it
χάριτος n. gen. fem. sg. χάρις grace, thank, favour, pleasure
τοῦ art. gen. masc. sg. ὁ ἡ τό the, this, that, he, she, it
Θεοῦ n. gen. masc. sg. θεός God, god
25 καὶ conj. καί and, even, also, but
νῦν adv. νῦν now, henceforth, present, this time
ἐγὼ pron. nom. 1p. sg. ἐγώ I
ὅτι conj. ὅτι that, for, because, how that, how, because that, for that, though
οὐκέτι adv. οὐκέτι or οὐκ ἔτι no more, no longer, not any more
τὸ art. acc. neut. sg. ὁ ἡ τό the, this, that, he, she, it
πρόσωπόν n. acc. neut. sg. πρόσωπον face, presence, person, countenance
μου pron. gen. 1p. sg. ἐγώ I
ὑμεῖς pron. nom. 2p. pl. σύ thou, you
πάντες adj. nom. masc. pl. πᾶς πᾶσα πᾶν all, every, whosoever, every one, no, whole, any
ἐν prep. ἐν (+dat) in, by, with, among, at, on, through, to, within, into, of, for
οἷς relative pron. dat. masc. pl. ὅς ἥ ὅ who, which, what, that
τὴν art. acc. fem. sg. ὁ ἡ τό the, this, that, he, she, it
βασιλείαν n. acc. fem. sg. βασιλεία kingdom, reign
τοῦ art. gen. masc. sg. ὁ ἡ τό the, this, that, he, she, it
Θεοῦ n. gen. masc. sg. θεός God, god
26 διὸ conj. διό wherefore, therefore, for which cause
ὑμῖν pron. dat. 2p. pl. σύ thou, you
ἐν prep. ἐν (+dat) in, by, with, among, at, on, through, to, within, into, of, for
τῇ art. dat. fem. sg. ὁ ἡ τό the, this, that, he, she, it
σήμερον adv. σήμερον this day, today
ἡμέρᾳ n. dat. fem. sg. ἡμέρα day, time, year, while, age, day time
ὅτι conj. ὅτι that, for, because, how that, how, because that, for that, though
καθαρός adj. nom. masc. sg. καθαρός pure, clean, clear
ἐγὼ pron. nom. 1p. sg. ἐγώ I
ἀπὸ prep. ἀπό (+gen) from, of, out of, since, for, off, at, by, in, on
τοῦ art. gen. neut. sg. ὁ ἡ τό the, this, that, he, she, it
αἵματος n. gen. neut. sg. αἷμα blood
πάντων adj. gen. masc. pl. πᾶς πᾶσα πᾶν all, every, whosoever, every one, no, whole, any
27 οὐ particle of negation. οὐ οὐκ οὐχ not, no, neither, none, nay, nor, never, nothing
γὰρ conj. γάρ for, and, because, but, indeed
τοῦ art. gen. neut. sg. ὁ ἡ τό the, this, that, he, she, it
μὴ particle of negation. μή not, no, lest, neither, none, nothing, nor, never, without
ὑμῖν pron. dat. 2p. pl. σύ thou, you
πᾶσαν adj. acc. fem. sg. πᾶς πᾶσα πᾶν all, every, whosoever, every one, no, whole, any
τὴν art. acc. fem. sg. ὁ ἡ τό the, this, that, he, she, it
βουλὴν n. acc. fem. sg. βουλή counsel, advise, will
τοῦ art. gen. masc. sg. ὁ ἡ τό the, this, that, he, she, it
Θεοῦ n. gen. masc. sg. θεός God, god
28 οὖν conj. οὖν therefore, then, so, and, now, wherefore
ἑαυτοῖς reflexive pron. dat. masc. 3p. pl. ἑαυτοῦ himself, herself, itself, yourself, ourselves
καὶ conj. καί and, even, also, but
παντὶ adj. dat. neut. sg. πᾶς πᾶσα πᾶν all, every, whosoever, every one, no, whole, any
τῷ art. dat. neut. sg. ὁ ἡ τό the, this, that, he, she, it
ποιμνίῳ n. dat. neut. sg. ποίμνιον flock
ἐν prep. ἐν (+dat) in, by, with, among, at, on, through, to, within, into, of, for

ᾧ relative pron. dat. neut. sg. ὅς ἥ ὅ who, which, what, that
ὑμᾶς pron. acc. 2p. pl. σύ thou, you
τὸ art. nom. neut. sg. ὁ ἡ τό the, this, that, he, she, it
Πνεῦμα n. nom. neut. sg. πνεῦμα spirit, Spirit, Ghost, ghost, life. of the spirit, wind
τὸ art. nom. neut. sg. ὁ ἡ τό the, this, that, he, she, it
Ἅγιον adj. nom. neut. sg. ἅγιος Holy, holy, saint, Holy One, holy thing, most holy
ἐπισκόπους n. acc. masc. pl. ἐπίσκοπος overseer, bishop
τὴν art. acc. fem. sg. ὁ ἡ τό the, this, that, he, she, it
ἐκκλησίαν n. acc. fem. sg. ἐκκλησία church, assembly
τοῦ art. gen. masc. sg. ὁ ἡ τό the, this, that, he, she, it
Θεοῦ n. gen. masc. sg. θεός God, god
ἣν relative pron. acc. fem. sg. ὅς ἥ ὅ who, which, what, that
διὰ prep. διά (+gen) by, through, with, in, of, (+acc) for, because of, for a cause
τοῦ art. gen. neut. sg. ὁ ἡ τό the, this, that, he, she, it
ἰδίου adj. gen. neut. sg. ἴδιος one's own, one's, privately
αἵματος n. gen. neut. sg. αἷμα blood
29 ἐγὼ pron. nom. 1p. sg. ἐγώ I
γὰρ conj. γάρ for, and, because, but, indeed
τοῦτο demo. pron. acc. neut. sg. οὗτος αὕτη τοῦτο this, the same, this same, he, she, it
ὅτι conj. ὅτι that, for, because, how that, how, because that, for that, though
μετὰ prep. μετά (+gen) with, among, against, (+acc) after
τὴν art. acc. fem. sg. ὁ ἡ τό the, this, that, he, she, it
ἄφιξίν n. acc. fem. sg. ἄφιξις departing
μου pron. gen. 1p. sg. ἐγώ I
λύκοι n. nom. masc. pl. λύκος wolf
βαρεῖς adj. nom. masc. pl. βαρύς grievous, heavy, weightier, weighty
εἰς prep. εἰς (+acc) into, to, unto, for, in, on, toward, against, upon, at, among
ὑμᾶς pron. acc. 2p. pl. σύ thou, you
μὴ particle of negation. μή not, no, lest, neither, none, nothing, nor, never, without
τοῦ art. gen. neut. sg. ὁ ἡ τό the, this, that, he, she, it
ποιμνίου n. gen. neut. sg. ποίμνιον flock
30 καὶ conj. καί and, even, also, but
ἐξ prep. ἐκ ἐξ (+gen) of, from, out of, by, on, with, in, among, through
ὑμῶν pron. gen. 2p. pl. σύ thou, you
αὐτῶν pron. gen. masc. 3p. pl. αὐτός ή ό self, of oneself, even, very, the same, he, she, it
ἄνδρες n. nom. masc. pl. ἀνήρ man, husband, sir
τοῦ art. gen. neut. sg. ὁ ἡ τό the, this, that, he, she, it
τοὺς art. acc. masc. pl. ὁ ἡ τό the, this, that, he, she, it
μαθητὰς n. acc. masc. pl. μαθητής disciple
ὀπίσω prep. ὀπίσω (+gen) after. (adv.) back, behind
αὐτῶν pron. gen. masc. 3p. pl. αὐτός ή ό self, of oneself, even, very, the same, he, she, it
31 διὸ conj. διό wherefore, therefore, for which cause
ὅτι conj. ὅτι that, for, because, how that, how, because that, for that, though
τριετίαν n. acc. fem. sg. τριετία space of three years
νύκτα n. acc. fem. sg. νύξ night
καὶ conj. καί and, even, also, but
ἡμέραν n. acc. fem. sg. ἡμέρα day, time, year, while, age, day time
οὐκ particle of negation. οὐ οὐκ οὐχ not, no, neither, none, nay, nor, never, nothing
μετὰ prep. μετά (+gen) with, among, against, (+acc) after
δακρύων n. gen. neut. pl. δάκρυον tears
ἕνα num. acc. masc. sg. εἷς or ἕν one, other, some, any, only, a certain
ἕκαστον adj. acc. masc. sg. ἕκαστος every man, every, every one, any man, each
32 καὶ conj. καί and, even, also, but
τὰ art. acc. neut. pl. ὁ ἡ τό the, this, that, he, she, it
νῦν adv. νῦν now, henceforth, present, this time

ὑμᾶς pron. acc. 2p. pl. σύ thou, you
ἀδελφοί n. voc. masc. pl. ἀδελφός brother
τῷ art. dat. masc. sg. ὁ ἡ τό the, this, that, he, she, it
Θεῷ n. dat. masc. sg. θεός God, god
καὶ conj. καί and, even, also, but
τῷ art. dat. masc. sg. ὁ ἡ τό the, this, that, he, she, it
λόγῳ n. dat. masc. sg. λόγος word, saying, account, speech, thing, matter
τῆς art. gen. fem. sg. ὁ ἡ τό the, this, that, he, she, it
χάριτος n. gen. fem. sg. χάρις grace, thank, favour, pleasure
αὐτοῦ pron. gen. masc. 3p. sg. αὐτός ἡ ὁ self, of oneself, even, very, the same, he, she, it
τῷ art. dat. masc. sg. ὁ ἡ τό the, this, that, he, she, it
καὶ conj. καί and, even, also, but
ὑμῖν pron. dat. 2p. pl. σύ thou, you
κληρονομίαν n. acc. fem. sg. κληρονομία inheritance
ἐν prep. ἐν (+dat) in, by, with, among, at, on, through, to, within, into, of, for
τοῖς art. dat. masc. pl. ὁ ἡ τό the, this, that, he, she, it
πᾶσιν adj. dat. masc. pl. πᾶς πᾶσα πᾶν all, every, whosoever, every one, no, whole, any
33 ἀργυρίου n. gen. neut. sg. ἀργύριον money, piece of silver, silver
ἢ particle. ἤ or, than, either, nor, or else, and, rather than
χρυσίου n. gen. neut. sg. χρυσίον gold
ἢ particle. ἤ or, than, either, nor, or else, and, rather than
ἱματισμοῦ n. gen. masc. sg. ἱματισμός apparel, array, raiment, vesture
οὐδενὸς num. gen. masc. sg. οὐδείς no man, nothing, no, none, neither, not, nought
34 αὐτοὶ pron. nom. masc. 2p. pl. αὐτός ἡ ὁ self, of oneself, even, very, the same, he, she, it
δὲ conj. δέ but, and, now, also, to the contrary, rather, then
ὅτι conj. ὅτι that, for, because, how that, how, because that, for that, though
ταῖς art. dat. fem. pl. ὁ ἡ τό the, this, that, he, she, it
χρείαις n. dat. fem. pl. χρεία need, necessity, lack, want
μου pron. gen. 1p. sg. ἐγώ I
καὶ conj. καί and, even, also, but
τοῖς art. dat. masc. pl. ὁ ἡ τό the, this, that, he, she, it
μετ' prep. μετά (+gen) with, among, against, (+acc) after
ἐμοῦ pron. gen. 1p. sg. ἐγώ I
αἱ art. nom. fem. pl. ὁ ἡ τό the, this, that, he, she, it
χεῖρες n. nom. fem. pl. χείρ hand
αὗται demo. pron. nom. fem. pl. οὗτος αὕτη τοῦτο this, the same, this same, he, she, it
35 πάντα adj. acc. neut. pl. πᾶς πᾶσα πᾶν all, every, whosoever, every one, no, whole, any
ὑμῖν pron. dat. 2p. pl. σύ thou, you
ὅτι conj. ὅτι that, for, because, how that, how, because that, for that, though
οὕτω adv. οὕτω οὕτως so, even so, thus, on this wise, likewise, after this manner
τῶν art. gen. masc. pl. ὁ ἡ τό the, this, that, he, she, it
τε conj. τέ and, both, also
τῶν art. gen. masc. pl. ὁ ἡ τό the, this, that, he, she, it
λόγων n. gen. masc. pl. λόγος word, saying, account, speech, thing, matter
τοῦ art. gen. masc. sg. ὁ ἡ τό the, this, that, he, she, it
Κυρίου n. gen. masc. sg. κύριος Lord, lord, master, sir, LORD, God, Master, owner
Ἰησοῦ n. gen. masc. sg. Ἰησοῦς Jesus
ὅτι conj. ὅτι that, for, because, how that, how, because that, for that, though
αὐτὸς pron. nom. masc. 3p. sg. αὐτός ἡ ὁ self, of oneself, even, very, the same, he, she, it
Μακάριόν adj. nom. neut. sg. μακάριος blessed, happy
μᾶλλον compar. adv. μᾶλλον rather, more, more and more, better, much, much the more
ἢ particle. ἤ or, than, either, nor, or else, and, rather than
36 Καὶ conj. καί and, even, also, but
ταῦτα demo. pron. acc. neut. pl. οὗτος αὕτη τοῦτο this, the same, this same, he, she, it
τὰ art. acc. neut. pl. ὁ ἡ τό the, this, that, he, she, it

γόνατα n. acc. neut. pl. γόνυ knee, kneel
αὐτοῦ pron. gen. masc. 3p. sg. αὐτός ἡ ὁ self, of oneself, even, very, the same, he, she, it
σὺν prep. σύν (+dat) with, beside
πᾶσιν adj. dat. masc. pl. πᾶς πᾶσα πᾶν all, every, whosoever, every one, no, whole, any
αὐτοῖς pron. dat. masc. 3p. pl. αὐτός ἡ ὁ self, of oneself, even, very, the same, he, she, it
37 ἱκανὸς adj. nom. masc. sg. ἱκανός many, much, long, worthy, sufficient, great, able
δὲ conj. δέ but, and, now, also, to the contrary, rather, then
κλαυθμὸς n. nom. masc. sg. κλαυθμός weeping, wailing, great weeping
πάντων adj. gen. masc. pl. πᾶς πᾶσα πᾶν all, every, whosoever, every one, no, whole, any
καὶ conj. καί and, even, also, but
ἐπὶ prep. ἐπί (+gen) on, in, upon, (+dat) in, at, for, upon, (+acc) on, upon, unto, to, against
τὸν art. acc. masc. sg. ὁ ἡ τό the, this, that, he, she, it
τράχηλον n. acc. masc. sg. τράχηλος neck
τοῦ art. gen. masc. sg. ὁ ἡ τό the, this, that, he, she, it
Παύλου n. gen. masc. sg. Παῦλος Paul, Paulus
αὐτόν pron. acc. masc. 3p. sg. αὐτός ἡ ὁ self, of oneself, even, very, the same, he, she, it
38 μάλιστα adv. μάλιστα specially, especially, chiefly, most of all
ἐπὶ prep. ἐπί (+gen) on, in, upon, (+dat) in, at, for, upon, (+acc) on, upon, unto, to, against
τῷ art. dat. masc. sg. ὁ ἡ τό the, this, that, he, she, it
λόγῳ n. dat. masc. sg. λόγος word, saying, account, speech, thing, matter
ᾧ relative pron. dat. masc. sg. ὅς ἥ ὅ who, which, what, that
ὅτι conj. ὅτι that, for, because, how that, how, because that, for that, though
οὐκέτι adv. οὐκέτι or οὐκ ἔτι no more, no longer, not any more
τὸ art. acc. neut. sg. ὁ ἡ τό the, this, that, he, she, it
πρόσωπον n. acc. neut. sg. πρόσωπον face, presence, person, countenance
αὐτοῦ pron. gen. masc. 3p. sg. αὐτός ἡ ὁ self, of oneself, even, very, the same, he, she, it
δὲ conj. δέ but, and, now, also, to the contrary, rather, then
αὐτὸν pron. acc. masc. 3p. sg. αὐτός ἡ ὁ self, of oneself, even, very, the same, he, she, it
εἰς prep. εἰς (+acc) into, to, unto, for, in, on, toward, against, upon, at, among
τὸ art. acc. neut. sg. ὁ ἡ τό the, this, that, he, she, it
πλοῖον n. acc. neut. sg. πλοῖον ship, boat

21

1 Ὡς conj. ὡς as, when, as it were, how, about, like, as soon as, even as, while
δὲ conj. δέ but, and, now, also, to the contrary, rather, then
ἡμᾶς pron. acc. 1p. pl. ἐγώ I
ἀπ' prep. ἀπό (+gen) from, of, out of, since, for, off, at, by, in, on
αὐτῶν pron. gen. masc. 3p. pl. αὐτός ἡ ὁ self, of oneself, even, very, the same, he, she, it
εἰς prep. εἰς (+acc) into, to, unto, for, in, on, toward, against, upon, at, among
τὴν art. acc. fem. sg. ὁ ἡ τό the, this, that, he, she, it
Κῶν n. acc. fem. sg. Κῶς Coos
τῇ art. dat. fem. sg. ὁ ἡ τό the, this, that, he, she, it
δὲ conj. δέ but, and, now, also, to the contrary, rather, then
ἑξῆς adv. ἑξῆς the after, the next, following, on the morrow
εἰς prep. εἰς (+acc) into, to, unto, for, in, on, toward, against, upon, at, among
τὴν art. acc. fem. sg. ὁ ἡ τό the, this, that, he, she, it
Ῥόδον n. acc. fem. sg. Ῥόδος Rhodes
κἀκεῖθεν adv. κἀκεῖθεν and from thence, and thence, and afterward, thence also
εἰς prep. εἰς (+acc) into, to, unto, for, in, on, toward, against, upon, at, among
Πάταρα n. acc. neut. pl. Πάταρα Patara
2 καὶ conj. καί and, even, also, but
πλοῖον n. acc. neut. sg. πλοῖον ship, boat
εἰς prep. εἰς (+acc) into, to, unto, for, in, on, toward, against, upon, at, among
Φοινίκην n. acc. fem. sg. Φοινίκη Phenice, Phenicia

3 δὲ conj. δέ but, and, now, also, to the contrary, rather, then
τὴν art. acc. fem. sg. ὁ ἡ τό the, this, that, he, she, it
Κύπρον n. acc. fem. sg. Κύπρος Cyprus
καὶ conj. καί and, even, also, but
αὐτὴν pron. acc. fem. 3p. sg. αὐτός ἡ ὁ self, of oneself, even, very, the same, he, she, it
εὐώνυμον adj. acc. fem. sg. εὐώνυμος left
εἰς prep. εἰς (+acc) into, to, unto, for, in, on, toward, against, upon, at, among
Συρίαν n. acc. fem. sg. Συρία Syria
καὶ conj. καί and, even, also, but
εἰς prep. εἰς (+acc) into, to, unto, for, in, on, toward, against, upon, at, among
Τύρον n. acc. fem. sg. Τύρος Tyre
ἐκεῖσε adv. ἐκεῖσε there
γὰρ conj. γάρ for, and, because, but, indeed
τὸ art. nom. neut. sg. ὁ ἡ τό the, this, that, he, she, it
πλοῖον n. nom. neut. sg. πλοῖον ship, boat
τὸν art. acc. masc. sg. ὁ ἡ τό the, this, that, he, she, it
γόμον n. acc. masc. sg. γόμος burden, merchandise
4 καὶ conj. καί and, even, also, but
μαθητὰς n. acc. masc. pl. μαθητής disciple
αὐτοῦ adv. αὐτοῦ here, there
ἡμέρας n. acc. fem. pl. ἡμέρα day, time, year, while, age, day time
ἑπτά num. acc. fem. pl. ἑπτά seven, seventh
οἵτινες relative pron. nom. masc. pl. ὅστις which, who, whosoever, that, whatsoever
τῷ art. dat. masc. sg. ὁ ἡ τό the, this, that, he, she, it
Παύλῳ n. dat. masc. sg. Παῦλος Paul, Paulus
διὰ prep. διά (+gen) by, through, with, in, of, (+acc) for, because of, for a cause
τοῦ art. gen. neut. sg. ὁ ἡ τό the, this, that, he, she, it
Πνεύματος n. gen. neut. sg. πνεῦμα spirit, Spirit, Ghost, ghost, life. of the spirit, wind
μὴ particle of negation. μή not, no, lest, neither, none, nothing, nor, never, without
εἰς prep. εἰς (+acc) into, to, unto, for, in, on, toward, against, upon, at, among
Ἱερουσαλήμ pron. name. fem. inde. Ἱερουσαλήμ Jerusalem
5 ὅτε adv. ὅτε when, after that, as soon as, while, after
δὲ conj. δέ but, and, now, also, to the contrary, rather, then
ἡμᾶς pron. acc. 1p. pl. ἐγώ I
τὰς art. acc. fem. pl. ὁ ἡ τό the, this, that, he, she, it
ἡμέρας n. acc. fem. pl. ἡμέρα day, time, year, while, age, day time
ἡμᾶς pron. acc. 1p. pl. ἐγώ I
πάντων adj. gen. masc. pl. πᾶς πᾶσα πᾶν all, every, whosoever, every one, no, whole, any
σὺν prep. σύν (+dat) with, beside
γυναιξὶ n. dat. fem. pl. γυνή woman, wife
καὶ conj. καί and, even, also, but
τέκνοις n. dat. neut. pl. τέκνον child, son, daughter
ἕως conj. ἕως till, until, unto, until when, while, as far as, even, until now
ἔξω adv. ἔξω out, without, out of, forth, away, outward
τῆς art. gen. fem. sg. ὁ ἡ τό the, this, that, he, she, it
πόλεως n. gen. fem. sg. πόλις city
καὶ conj. καί and, even, also, but
τὰ art. acc. neut. pl. ὁ ἡ τό the, this, that, he, she, it
γόνατα n. acc. neut. pl. γόνυ knee, kneel
ἐπὶ prep. ἐπί (+gen) on, in, upon, (+dat) in, at, for, upon, (+acc) on, upon, unto, to, against
τὸν art. acc. masc. sg. ὁ ἡ τό the, this, that, he, she, it
αἰγιαλὸν n. acc. masc. sg. αἰγιαλός shore
6 καὶ conj. καί and, even, also, but
ἀλλήλους pron. acc. masc. 3p. pl. ἀλλήλων one another, themselves, together, mutual
εἰς prep. εἰς (+acc) into, to, unto, for, in, on, toward, against, upon, at, among

τὸ art. acc. neut. sg. ὁ ἡ τό the, this, that, he, she, it
πλοῖον n. acc. neut. sg. πλοῖον ship, boat
ἐκεῖνοι demo. pron. nom. masc. pl. ἐκεῖνος that, he, the same, that same
δὲ conj. δέ but, and, now, also, to the contrary, rather, then
εἰς prep. εἰς (+acc) into, to, unto, for, in, on, toward, against, upon, at, among
τὰ art. acc. neut. pl. ὁ ἡ τό the, this, that, he, she, it
ἴδια adj. acc. neut. pl. ἴδιος one's own, one's, privately
7 Ἡμεῖς pron. nom. 1p. pl. ἐγώ I
δὲ conj. δέ but, and, now, also, to the contrary, rather, then
τὸν art. acc. masc. sg. ὁ ἡ τό the, this, that, he, she, it
πλοῦν n. acc. masc. sg. πλόος course, voyage, sailing
ἀπὸ prep. ἀπό (+gen) from, of, out of, since, for, off, at, by, in, on
Τύρου n. gen. fem. sg. Τύρος Tyre
εἰς prep. εἰς (+acc) into, to, unto, for, in, on, toward, against, upon, at, among
Πτολεμαΐδα n. acc. fem. sg. Πτολεμαΐς Ptolemais
καὶ conj. καί and, even, also, but
τοὺς art. acc. masc. pl. ὁ ἡ τό the, this, that, he, she, it
ἀδελφοὺς n. acc. masc. pl. ἀδελφός brother
ἡμέραν n. acc. fem. sg. ἡμέρα day, time, year, while, age, day time
μίαν num. acc. fem. sg. εἷς or ἕν one, other, some, any, only, a certain
παρ' prep. παρά (+gen) of, from, (+dat) with, for, (+acc) beside, at, by, above, against
αὐτοῖς pron. dat. masc. 3p. pl. αὐτός ή ό self, of oneself, even, very, the same, he, she, it
8 τῇ art. dat. fem. sg. ὁ ἡ τό the, this, that, he, she, it
δὲ conj. δέ but, and, now, also, to the contrary, rather, then
ἐπαύριον adv. ἐπαύριον next day, morrow, day following, nest day after
οἱ art. nom. masc. pl. ὁ ἡ τό the, this, that, he, she, it
περὶ prep. περί (+gen) of, for, concerning, (+acc) about, concerning, in
τὸν art. acc. masc. sg. ὁ ἡ τό the, this, that, he, she, it
Παῦλον n. acc. masc. sg. Παῦλος Paul, Paulus
εἰς prep. εἰς (+acc) into, to, unto, for, in, on, toward, against, upon, at, among
Καισάρειαν n. acc. fem. sg. Καισάρεια Caesarea
καὶ conj. καί and, even, also, but
εἰς prep. εἰς (+acc) into, to, unto, for, in, on, toward, against, upon, at, among
τὸν art. acc. masc. sg. ὁ ἡ τό the, this, that, he, she, it
οἶκον n. acc. masc. sg. οἶκος house, home, household
Φιλίππου n. gen. masc. sg. Φίλιππος Philip, Philippi
τοῦ art. gen. masc. sg. ὁ ἡ τό the, this, that, he, she, it
εὐαγγελιστοῦ n. gen. masc. sg. εὐαγγελιστής evangelist
τοῦ art. gen. masc. sg. ὁ ἡ τό the, this, that, he, she, it
ἐκ prep. ἐκ ἐξ (+gen) of, from, out of, by, on, with, in, among, through
τῶν art. gen. masc. pl. ὁ ἡ τό the, this, that, he, she, it
ἑπτά num. gen. masc. pl. ἑπτά seven, seventh
παρ' prep. παρά (+gen) of, from, (+dat) with, for, (+acc) beside, at, by, above, against
αὐτῷ pron. dat. masc. 3p. sg. αὐτός ή ό self, of oneself, even, very, the same, he, she, it
9 τούτῳ demo. pron. dat. masc. sg. οὗτος αὕτη τοῦτο this, the same, this same, he, she, it
δὲ conj. δέ but, and, now, also, to the contrary, rather, then
θυγατέρες n. nom. fem. pl. θυγάτηρ daughter
παρθένοι n. nom. fem. pl. παρθένος virgin
τέσσαρες num. nom. fem. pl. τέσσαρες four
10 δὲ conj. δέ but, and, now, also, to the contrary, rather, then
ἡμῶν pron. gen. 1p. pl. ἐγώ I
ἡμέρας n. acc. fem. pl. ἡμέρα day, time, year, while, age, day time
πλείους compar. adj. acc. fem. pl. πλείων more, many, greater, further, more part
τις indefinite pron. nom. masc. sg. τὶς certain, some, any man, one, any thing
ἀπὸ prep. ἀπό (+gen) from, of, out of, since, for, off, at, by, in, on

τῆς art. gen. fem. sg. ὁ ἡ τό the, this, that, he, she, it
Ἰουδαίας n. gen. fem. sg. Ἰουδαία Judaea, Jewry
προφήτης n. nom. masc. sg. προφήτης prophet
ὀνόματι n. dat. neut. sg. ὄνομα name, call, surname
Ἄγαβος n. nom. masc. sg. Ἄγαβος Agabus
11 καὶ conj. καί and, even, also, but
πρὸς prep. πρός (+gen) for, (+dat) at, (+acc) unto, to, with, for, against
ἡμᾶς pron. acc. 1p. pl. ἐγώ I
καὶ conj. καί and, even, also, but
τὴν art. acc. fem. sg. ὁ ἡ τό the, this, that, he, she, it
ζώνην n. acc. fem. sg. ζώνη girdle, purse
τοῦ art. gen. masc. sg. ὁ ἡ τό the, this, that, he, she, it
Παύλου n. gen. masc. sg. Παῦλος Paul, Paulus
τε conj. τέ and, both, also
αὐτοῦ pron. gen. masc. 3p. sg. αὐτός ή ό self, of oneself, even, very, the same, he, she, it
τὰς art. acc. fem. pl. ὁ ἡ τό the, this, that, he, she, it
χεῖρας n. acc. fem. pl. χείρ hand
καὶ conj. καί and, even, also, but
τοὺς art. acc. masc. pl. ὁ ἡ τό the, this, that, he, she, it
πόδας n. acc. masc. pl. πούς foot
Τάδε demo. pron. acc. neut. pl. ὅδε ἥδε τόδε this, he, she, such, thus
τὸ art. nom. neut. sg. ὁ ἡ τό the, this, that, he, she, it
Πνεῦμα n. nom. neut. sg. πνεῦμα spirit, Spirit, Ghost, ghost, life. of the spirit, wind
τὸ art. nom. neut. sg. ὁ ἡ τό the, this, that, he, she, it
Ἅγιον adj. nom. neut. sg. ἅγιος Holy, holy, saint, Holy One, holy thing, most holy
Τὸν art. acc. masc. sg. ὁ ἡ τό the, this, that, he, she, it
ἄνδρα n. acc. masc. sg. ἀνήρ man, husband, sir
οὗ relative pron. gen. masc. sg. ὅς ἥ ὅ who, which, what, that
ἡ art. nom. fem. sg. ὁ ἡ τό the, this, that, he, she, it
ζώνη n. nom. fem. sg. ζώνη girdle, purse
αὕτη demo. pron. nom. fem. sg. οὗτος αὕτη τοῦτο this, the same, this same, he, she, it
οὕτω adv. οὕτω οὕτως so, even so, thus, on this wise, likewise, after this manner
ἐν prep. ἐν (+dat) in, by, with, among, at, on, through, to, within, into, of, for
Ἱερουσαλὴμ pron. name. fem. inde. Ἱερουσαλήμ Jerusalem
οἱ art. nom. masc. pl. ὁ ἡ τό the, this, that, he, she, it
Ἰουδαῖοι adj. nom. masc. pl. Ἰουδαῖος Jew, Jewess
καὶ conj. καί and, even, also, but
εἰς prep. εἰς (+acc) into, to, unto, for, in, on, toward, against, upon, at, among
χεῖρας n. acc. fem. pl. χείρ hand
ἐθνῶν n. gen. neut. pl. ἔθνος Gentile, nation, heathen, people
12 ὡς adv. ὡς as, when, as it were, how, about, like, as soon as, even as, while
δὲ conj. δέ but, and, now, also, to the contrary, rather, then
ταῦτα demo. pron. acc. neut. pl. οὗτος αὕτη τοῦτο this, the same, this same, he, she, it
ἡμεῖς pron. nom. 1p. pl. ἐγώ I
τε conj. τέ and, both, also
καὶ conj. καί and, even, also, but
οἱ art. nom. masc. pl. ὁ ἡ τό the, this, that, he, she, it
ἐντόπιοι adj. nom. masc. pl. ἐντόπιος
τοῦ art. gen. neut. sg. ὁ ἡ τό the, this, that, he, she, it
μὴ particle of negation. μή not, no, lest, neither, none, nothing, nor, never, without
αὐτὸν pron. acc. masc. 3p. sg. αὐτός ή ό self, of oneself, even, very, the same, he, she, it
εἰς prep. εἰς (+acc) into, to, unto, for, in, on, toward, against, upon, at, among
Ἱερουσαλὴμ pron. name. fem. inde. Ἱερουσαλήμ Jerusalem
13 δὲ conj. δέ but, and, now, also, to the contrary, rather, then
ὁ art. nom. masc. sg. ὁ ἡ τό the, this, that, he, she, it

Παῦλος n. nom. masc. sg. Παῦλος Paul, Paulus
Τί interrog. pron. acc. neut. sg. τίς what, who, why, where, which, how
καὶ conj. καί and, even, also, but
μου pron. gen. 1p. sg. ἐγώ I
τὴν art. acc. fem. sg. ὁ ἡ τό the, this, that, he, she, it
καρδίαν n. acc. fem. sg. καρδία heart
ἐγὼ pron. nom. 1p. sg. ἐγώ I
γὰρ conj. γάρ for, and, because, but, indeed
οὐ particle of negation. οὐ οὐκ οὐχ not, no, neither, none, nay, nor, never, nothing
μόνον adv. μόνος only, alone, by oneself
ἀλλὰ conj. ἀλλά but, yea, yet, nevertheless, howbeit, nay, therefore
καὶ conj. καί and, even, also, but
εἰς prep. εἰς (+acc) into, to, unto, for, in, on, toward, against, upon, at, among
Ἱερουσαλὴμ pron. name. fem. inde. Ἱερουσαλήμ Jerusalem
ἑτοίμως adv. ἑτοίμως ready
ὑπὲρ prep. ὑπέρ (+gen) for, of, for the sake of, (+acc) above, more than
τοῦ art. gen. neut. sg. ὁ ἡ τό the, this, that, he, she, it
ὀνόματος n. gen. neut. sg. ὄνομα name, call, surname
τοῦ art. gen. masc. sg. ὁ ἡ τό the, this, that, he, she, it
Κυρίου n. gen. masc. sg. κύριος Lord, lord, master, sir, LORD, God, Master, owner
Ἰησοῦ n. gen. masc. sg. Ἰησοῦς Jesus
14 μὴ particle of negation. μή not, no, lest, neither, none, nothing, nor, never, without
δὲ conj. δέ but, and, now, also, to the contrary, rather, then
αὐτοῦ pron. gen. masc. 3p. sg. αὐτός ή ό self, of oneself, even, very, the same, he, she, it
Τὸ art. nom. neut. sg. ὁ ἡ τό the, this, that, he, she, it
θέλημα n. nom. neut. sg. θέλημα will, desire, pleasure
τοῦ art. gen. masc. sg. ὁ ἡ τό the, this, that, he, she, it
Κυρίου n. gen. masc. sg. κύριος Lord, lord, master, sir, LORD, God, Master, owner
15 Μετὰ prep. μετά (+gen) with, among, against, (+acc) after
δὲ conj. δέ but, and, now, also, to the contrary, rather, then
τὰς art. acc. fem. pl. ὁ ἡ τό the, this, that, he, she, it
ἡμέρας n. acc. fem. pl. ἡμέρα day, time, year, while, age, day time
ταύτας demo. pron. acc. fem. pl. οὗτος αὕτη τοῦτο this, the same, this same, he, she, it
εἰς prep. εἰς (+acc) into, to, unto, for, in, on, toward, against, upon, at, among
Ἱερουσαλήμ pron. name. fem. inde. Ἱερουσαλήμ Jerusalem
16 δὲ conj. δέ but, and, now, also, to the contrary, rather, then
καὶ conj. καί and, even, also, but
τῶν art. gen. masc. pl. ὁ ἡ τό the, this, that, he, she, it
μαθητῶν n. gen. masc. pl. μαθητής disciple
ἀπὸ prep. ἀπό (+gen) from, of, out of, since, for, off, at, by, in, on
Καισαρείας n. gen. fem. sg. Καισάρεια Caesarea
σὺν prep. σύν (+dat) with, beside
ἡμῖν pron. dat. 1p. pl. ἐγώ I
παρ' prep. παρά (+gen) of, from, (+dat) with, for, (+acc) beside, at, by, above, against
ᾧ relative pron. dat. masc. sg. ὅς ἥ ὅ who, which, what, that
Μνάσωνί n. dat. masc. sg. Μνάσων Mnason
τινι indefinite pron. dat. masc. sg. τὶς certain, some, any man, one, any thing
Κυπρίῳ n. dat. masc. sg. Κύπριος Cypriot, inhabitant of Cyprus
ἀρχαίῳ adj. dat. masc. sg. ἀρχαῖος old, one of old time
μαθητῇ n. dat. masc. sg. μαθητής disciple
17 δὲ conj. δέ but, and, now, also, to the contrary, rather, then
ἡμῶν pron. gen. 1p. pl. ἐγώ I
εἰς prep. εἰς (+acc) into, to, unto, for, in, on, toward, against, upon, at, among
Ἱεροσόλυμα n. acc. neut. sg. Ἱεροσόλυμα Jerusalem
ἀσμένως adv. ἀσμένως gladly

ἡμᾶς pron. acc. 1p. pl. ἐγώ I
οἱ art. nom. masc. pl. ὁ ἡ τό the, this, that, he, she, it
ἀδελφοί n. nom. masc. pl. ἀδελφός brother
18 τῇ art. dat. fem. sg. ὁ ἡ τό the, this, that, he, she, it
δὲ conj. δέ but, and, now, also, to the contrary, rather, then
ὁ art. nom. masc. sg. ὁ ἡ τό the, this, that, he, she, it
Παῦλος n. nom. masc. sg. Παῦλος Paul, Paulus
σὺν prep. σύν (+dat) with, beside
ἡμῖν pron. dat. 1p. pl. ἐγώ I
πρὸς prep. πρός (+gen) for, (+dat) at, (+acc) unto, to, with, for, against
Ἰάκωβον n. acc. masc. sg. Ἰάκωβος James
πάντες adj. nom. masc. pl. πᾶς πᾶσα πᾶν all, every, whosoever, every one, no, whole, any
τε conj. τέ and, both, also
οἱ art. nom. masc. pl. ὁ ἡ τό the, this, that, he, she, it
πρεσβύτεροι adj. nom. masc. pl. πρεσβύτερος elder, elder woman, eldest, old man
19 καὶ conj. καί and, even, also, but
αὐτοὺς pron. acc. masc. 3p. pl. αὐτός ἡ ὁ self, of oneself, even, very, the same, he, she, it
καθ' prep. κατά (+gen) against, by, throughout, down, (+acc) according to, after, with
ἓν num. acc. neut. sg. εἷς or ἕν one, other, some, any, only, a certain
ἕκαστον adj. acc. neut. sg. ἕκαστος every man, every, every one, any man, each
ὧν relative pron. gen. neut. pl. ὅς ἥ ὅ who, which, what, that
ὁ art. nom. masc. sg. ὁ ἡ τό the, this, that, he, she, it
Θεὸς n. nom. masc. sg. θεός God, god
ἐν prep. ἐν (+dat) in, by, with, among, at, on, through, to, within, into, of, for
τοῖς art. dat. neut. pl. ὁ ἡ τό the, this, that, he, she, it
ἔθνεσιν n. dat. neut. pl. ἔθνος Gentile, nation, heathen, people
διὰ prep. διά (+gen) by, through, with, in, of, (+acc) for, because of, for a cause
τῆς art. gen. fem. sg. ὁ ἡ τό the, this, that, he, she, it
διακονίας n. gen. fem. sg. διακονία ministry, administration, service, office, relief
αὐτοῦ pron. gen. masc. 3p. sg. αὐτός ἡ ὁ self, of oneself, even, very, the same, he, she, it
20 οἱ art. nom. masc. pl. ὁ ἡ τό the, this, that, he, she, it
δὲ conj. δέ but, and, now, also, to the contrary, rather, then
τὸν art. acc. masc. sg. ὁ ἡ τό the, this, that, he, she, it
Κύριον n. acc. masc. sg. κύριος Lord, lord, master, sir, LORD, God, Master, owner
τε conj. τέ and, both, also
αὐτῷ pron. dat. masc. 3p. sg. αὐτός ἡ ὁ self, of oneself, even, very, the same, he, she, it
ἀδελφέ n. voc. masc. sg. ἀδελφός brother
πόσαι interrog. pron. nom. fem. pl. πόσος how much, how many, how great, how long
μυριάδες n. nom. fem. pl. μυριάς innumerable multitude, myriad, innumerable company
Ἰουδαίων adj. gen. masc. pl. Ἰουδαῖος Jew, Jewess
τῶν art. gen. masc. pl. ὁ ἡ τό the, this, that, he, she, it
καὶ conj. καί and, even, also, but
πάντες adj. nom. masc. pl. πᾶς πᾶσα πᾶν all, every, whosoever, every one, no, whole, any
ζηλωταὶ n. nom. masc. pl. ζηλωτής zealous
τοῦ art. gen. masc. sg. ὁ ἡ τό the, this, that, he, she, it
νόμου n. gen. masc. sg. νόμος law, the law
21 δὲ conj. δέ but, and, now, also, to the contrary, rather, then
περὶ prep. περί (+gen) of, for, concerning, (+acc) about, concerning, in
σοῦ pron. gen. 2p. sg. σύ thou, you
ὅτι conj. ὅτι that, for, because, how that, how, because that, for that, though
ἀποστασίαν n. acc. fem. sg. ἀποστασία forsake, falling away, apostasy
ἀπὸ prep. ἀπό (+gen) from, of, out of, since, for, off, at, by, in, on
Μωσέως n. gen. masc. sg. Μωσῆς Moses
τοὺς art. acc. masc. pl. ὁ ἡ τό the, this, that, he, she, it
κατὰ prep. κατά (+gen) against, by, throughout, down, (+acc) according to, after, with

τὰ art. acc. neut. pl. ὁ ἡ τό the, this, that, he, she, it
ἔθνη n. acc. neut. pl. ἔθνος Gentile, nation, heathen, people
πάντας adj. acc. masc. pl. πᾶς πᾶσα πᾶν all, every, whosoever, every one, no, whole, any
Ἰουδαίους adj. acc. masc. pl. Ἰουδαῖος Jew, Jewess
μὴ particle of negation. μή not, no, lest, neither, none, nothing, nor, never, without
αὐτοὺς pron. acc. masc. 3p. pl. αὐτός ή ό self, of oneself, even, very, the same, he, she, it
τὰ art. acc. neut. pl. ὁ ἡ τό the, this, that, he, she, it
τέκνα n. acc. neut. pl. τέκνον child, son, daughter
μηδὲ conj. μηδέ neither, nor, not, no not, nor yet, not once, not so much as
τοῖς art. dat. neut. pl. ὁ ἡ τό the, this, that, he, she, it
ἔθεσιν n. dat. neut. pl. ἔθος custom, manner, be wont
22 τί interrog. pron. nom. neut. sg. τίς what, who, why, where, which, how
οὖν conj. οὖν therefore, then, so, and, now, wherefore
πάντως adv. πάντως surely, altogether, by all means, at all, needs, no doubt
πλῆθος n. nom. neut. sg. πλῆθος multitude, bundle, company
γὰρ conj. γάρ for, and, because, but, indeed
ὅτι conj. ὅτι that, for, because, how that, how, because that, for that, though
23 τοῦτο demo. pron. acc. neut. sg. οὗτος αὕτη τοῦτο this, the same, this same, he, she, it
οὖν conj. οὖν therefore, then, so, and, now, wherefore
ὅ relative pron. acc. neut. sg. ὅς ἥ ὅ who, which, what, that
σοι pron. dat. 2p. sg. σύ thou, you
ἡμῖν pron. dat. 1p. pl. ἐγώ I
ἄνδρες n. nom. masc. pl. ἀνήρ man, husband, sir
τέσσαρες num. nom. masc. pl. τέσσαρες four
εὐχὴν n. acc. fem. sg. εὐχή vow, prayer
ἐφ' prep. ἐπί (+gen) on, in, upon, (+dat) in, at, for, upon, (+acc) on, upon, unto, to, against
ἑαυτῶν reflexive pron. gen. masc. 3p. pl. ἑαυτοῦ himself, herself, itself, yourself, ourselves
24 τούτους demo. pron. acc. masc. pl. οὗτος αὕτη τοῦτο this, the same, this same, he, she, it
σὺν prep. σύν (+dat) with, beside
αὐτοῖς pron. dat. masc. 3p. pl. αὐτός ή ό self, of oneself, even, very, the same, he, she, it
καὶ conj. καί and, even, also, but
ἐπ' prep. ἐπί (+gen) on, in, upon, (+dat) in, at, for, upon, (+acc) on, upon, unto, to, against
αὐτοῖς pron. dat. masc. 3p. pl. αὐτός ή ό self, of oneself, even, very, the same, he, she, it
ἵνα conj. ἵνα that, to, lest, for to, so that, albeit, because, for, so as
τὴν art. acc. fem. sg. ὁ ἡ τό the, this, that, he, she, it
κεφαλήν n. acc. fem. sg. κεφαλή head
καὶ conj. καί and, even, also, but
πάντες adj. nom. masc. pl. πᾶς πᾶσα πᾶν all, every, whosoever, every one, no, whole, any
ὅτι conj. ὅτι that, for, because, how that, how, because that, for that, though
ὧν relative pron. gen. neut. pl. ὅς ἥ ὅ who, which, what, that
περὶ prep. περί (+gen) of, for, concerning, (+acc) about, concerning, in
σοῦ pron. gen. 2p. sg. σύ thou, you
οὐδέν num. nom. neut. sg. οὐδείς no man, nothing, no, none, neither, not, nought
ἀλλὰ conj. ἀλλά but, yea, yet, nevertheless, howbeit, nay, therefore
καὶ conj. καί and, even, also, but
αὐτὸς pron. nom. masc. 3p. sg. αὐτός ή ό self, of oneself, even, very, the same, he, she, it
τὸν art. acc. masc. sg. ὁ ἡ τό the, this, that, he, she, it
νόμον n. acc. masc. sg. νόμος law, the law
25 περὶ prep. περί (+gen) of, for, concerning, (+acc) about, concerning, in
δὲ conj. δέ but, and, now, also, to the contrary, rather, then
τῶν art. gen. neut. pl. ὁ ἡ τό the, this, that, he, she, it
ἐθνῶν n. gen. neut. pl. ἔθνος Gentile, nation, heathen, people
ἡμεῖς pron. nom. 1p. pl. ἐγώ I
μηδὲν num. acc. neut. sg. μηδείς μηδεμία μηδέν no man, nothing, no, none, not at all
τοιοῦτον demo. pron. acc. neut. sg. τοιοῦτος such, like

αὐτοὺς pron. acc. masc. 3p. pl. αὐτός ή ό self, of oneself, even, very, the same, he, she, it
εἰ conj. εἰ if, whether, that, though, forasmuch
μὴ particle of negation. μή not, no, lest, neither, none, nothing, nor, never, without
αὐτοὺς pron. acc. masc. 3p. pl. αὐτός ή ό self, of oneself, even, very, the same, he, she, it
τό art. acc. neut. sg. ὁ ἡ τό the, this, that, he, she, it
τε conj. τέ and, both, also
εἰδωλόθυτον adj. acc. neut. sg. εἰδωλόθυτον offered to idols
καὶ conj. καί and, even, also, but
τό art. acc. neut. sg. ὁ ἡ τό the, this, that, he, she, it
αἷμα n. acc. neut. sg. αἷμα blood
καὶ conj. καί and, even, also, but
πνικτὸν adj. acc. neut. sg. πνικτός strangled
καὶ conj. καί and, even, also, but
πορνείαν n. acc. fem. sg. πορνεία fornication
26 τότε adv. τότε then, that time
ὁ art. nom. masc. sg. ὁ ἡ τό the, this, that, he, she, it
Παῦλος n. nom. masc. sg. Παῦλος Paul, Paulus
τοὺς art. acc. masc. pl. ὁ ἡ τό the, this, that, he, she, it
ἄνδρας n. acc. masc. pl. ἀνήρ man, husband, sir
τῇ art. dat. fem. sg. ὁ ἡ τό the, this, that, he, she, it
ἡμέρᾳ n. dat. fem. sg. ἡμέρα day, time, year, while, age, day time
σὺν prep. σύν (+dat) with, beside
αὐτοῖς pron. dat. masc. 3p. pl. αὐτός ή ό self, of oneself, even, very, the same, he, she, it
εἰς prep. εἰς (+acc) into, to, unto, for, in, on, toward, against, upon, at, among
τὸ art. acc. neut. sg. ὁ ἡ τό the, this, that, he, she, it
ἱερὸν n. acc. neut. sg. ἱερόν temple
τὴν art. acc. fem. sg. ὁ ἡ τό the, this, that, he, she, it
ἐκπλήρωσιν n. acc. fem. sg. ἐκπλήρωσις accomplishment
τῶν art. gen. fem. pl. ὁ ἡ τό the, this, that, he, she, it
ἡμερῶν n. gen. fem. pl. ἡμέρα day, time, year, while, age, day time
τοῦ art. gen. masc. sg. ὁ ἡ τό the, this, that, he, she, it
ἁγνισμοῦ n. gen. masc. sg. ἁγνισμός purification
ἕως conj. ἕως till, until, unto, until when, while, as far as, even, until now
οὗ relative pron. gen. masc. sg. ὅς ἥ ὅ who, which, what, that
ὑπὲρ prep. ὑπέρ (+gen) for, of, for the sake of, (+acc) above, more than
ἑνὸς num. gen. masc. sg. εἷς or ἕν one, other, some, any, only, a certain
ἑκάστου adj. gen. masc. sg. ἕκαστος every man, every, every one, any man, each
αὐτῶν pron. gen. masc. 3p. pl. αὐτός ή ό self, of oneself, even, very, the same, he, she, it
ἡ art. nom. fem. sg. ὁ ἡ τό the, this, that, he, she, it
προσφορά n. nom. fem. sg. προσφορά offering, offering up
27 Ὡς conj. ὡς as, when, as it were, how, about, like, as soon as, even as, while
δὲ conj. δέ but, and, now, also, to the contrary, rather, then
αἱ art. nom. fem. pl. ὁ ἡ τό the, this, that, he, she, it
ἑπτὰ num. nom. fem. pl. ἑπτά seven, seventh
ἡμέραι n. nom. fem. pl. ἡμέρα day, time, year, while, age, day time
οἱ art. nom. masc. pl. ὁ ἡ τό the, this, that, he, she, it
ἀπὸ prep. ἀπό (+gen) from, of, out of, since, for, off, at, by, in, on
τῆς art. gen. fem. sg. ὁ ἡ τό the, this, that, he, she, it
Ἀσίας n. gen. fem. sg. Ἀσία Asia
Ἰουδαῖοι adj. nom. masc. pl. Ἰουδαῖος Jew, Jewess
αὐτὸν pron. acc. masc. 3p. sg. αὐτός ή ό self, of oneself, even, very, the same, he, she, it
ἐν prep. ἐν (+dat) in, by, with, among, at, on, through, to, within, into, of, for
τῷ art. dat. neut. sg. ὁ ἡ τό the, this, that, he, she, it
ἱερῷ n. dat. neut. sg. ἱερόν temple
πάντα adj. acc. masc. sg. πᾶς πᾶσα πᾶν all, every, whosoever, every one, no, whole, any

τὸν art. acc. masc. sg. ὁ ἡ τό the, this, that, he, she, it
ὄχλον n. acc. masc. sg. ὄχλος people, multitude, company, press, number
καὶ conj. καί and, even, also, but
τὰς art. acc. fem. pl. ὁ ἡ τό the, this, that, he, she, it
χεῖρας n. acc. fem. pl. χείρ hand
ἐπ' prep. ἐπί (+gen) on, in, upon, (+dat) in, at, for, upon, (+acc) on, upon, unto, to, against
αὐτὸν pron. acc. masc. 3p. sg. αὐτός ή ό self, of oneself, even, very, the same, he, she, it
28 Ἄνδρες n. voc. masc. pl. ἀνήρ man, husband, sir
Ἰσραηλῖται n. voc. masc. pl. Ἰσραηλίτης Israelite, Israel
οὗτός demo. pron. nom. masc. sg. οὗτος αὕτη τοῦτο this, the same, this same, he, she, it
ὁ art. nom. masc. sg. ὁ ἡ τό the, this, that, he, she, it
ἄνθρωπος n. nom. masc. sg. ἄνθρωπος man, human being, person, one, certain
ὁ art. nom. masc. sg. ὁ ἡ τό the, this, that, he, she, it
κατὰ prep. κατά (+gen) against, by, throughout, down, (+acc) according to, after, with
τοῦ art. gen. masc. sg. ὁ ἡ τό the, this, that, he, she, it
λαοῦ n. gen. masc. sg. λαός people
καὶ conj. καί and, even, also, but
τοῦ art. gen. masc. sg. ὁ ἡ τό the, this, that, he, she, it
νόμου n. gen. masc. sg. νόμος law, the law
καὶ conj. καί and, even, also, but
τοῦ art. gen. masc. sg. ὁ ἡ τό the, this, that, he, she, it
τόπου n. gen. masc. sg. τόπος place, room, quarter
τούτου demo. pron. gen. masc. sg. οὗτος αὕτη τοῦτο this, the same, this same, he, she, it
πάντας adj. acc. masc. pl. πᾶς πᾶσα πᾶν all, every, whosoever, every one, no, whole, any
πανταχοῦ adv. πανταχοῦ every where, in all places
ἔτι adv. ἔτι yet, more, any more, further, still, moreover
τε conj. τέ and, both, also
καὶ conj. καί and, even, also, but
Ἕλληνας n. acc. masc. pl. Ἕλλην Greek, Gentile
εἰς prep. εἰς (+acc) into, to, unto, for, in, on, toward, against, upon, at, among
τὸ art. acc. neut. sg. ὁ ἡ τό the, this, that, he, she, it
ἱερὸν n. acc. neut. sg. ἱερόν temple
καὶ conj. καί and, even, also, but
τὸν art. acc. masc. sg. ὁ ἡ τό the, this, that, he, she, it
ἅγιον adj. acc. masc. sg. ἅγιος Holy, holy, saint, Holy One, holy thing, most holy
τόπον n. acc. masc. sg. τόπος place, room, quarter
τοῦτον demo. pron. acc. masc. sg. οὗτος αὕτη τοῦτο this, the same, this same, he, she, it
29 γὰρ conj. γάρ for, and, because, but, indeed
Τρόφιμον n. acc. masc. sg. Τρόφιμος Trophimus
τὸν art. acc. masc. sg. ὁ ἡ τό the, this, that, he, she, it
Ἐφέσιον adj. acc. masc. sg. Ἐφέσιος Ephesian, of Ephesus
ἐν prep. ἐν (+dat) in, by, with, among, at, on, through, to, within, into, of, for
τῇ art. dat. fem. sg. ὁ ἡ τό the, this, that, he, she, it
πόλει n. dat. fem. sg. πόλις city
σὺν prep. σύν (+dat) with, beside
αὐτῷ pron. dat. masc. 3p. sg. αὐτός ή ό self, of oneself, even, very, the same, he, she, it
ὃν relative pron. acc. masc. sg. ὅς ἥ ὅ who, which, what, that
ὅτι conj. ὅτι that, for, because, how that, how, because that, for that, though
εἰς prep. εἰς (+acc) into, to, unto, for, in, on, toward, against, upon, at, among
τὸ art. acc. neut. sg. ὁ ἡ τό the, this, that, he, she, it
ἱερὸν n. acc. neut. sg. ἱερόν temple
ὁ art. nom. masc. sg. ὁ ἡ τό the, this, that, he, she, it
Παῦλος n. nom. masc. sg. Παῦλος Paul, Paulus
30 τε conj. τέ and, both, also
ἡ art. nom. fem. sg. ὁ ἡ τό the, this, that, he, she, it

πόλις n. nom. fem. sg. πόλις city
ὅλη adj. nom. fem. sg. ὅλος all, whole, every whit, altogether
καὶ conj. καί and, even, also, but
συνδρομὴ n. nom. fem. sg. συνδρομή run together, concourse
τοῦ art. gen. masc. sg. ὁ ἡ τό the, this, that, he, she, it
λαοῦ n. gen. masc. sg. λαός people
καὶ conj. καί and, even, also, but
τοῦ art. gen. masc. sg. ὁ ἡ τό the, this, that, he, she, it
Παύλου n. gen. masc. sg. Παῦλος Paul, Paulus
αὐτὸν pron. acc. masc. 3p. sg. αὐτός ἡ ὁ self, of oneself, even, very, the same, he, she, it
ἔξω adv. ἔξω out, without, out of, forth, away, outward
τοῦ art. gen. neut. sg. ὁ ἡ τό the, this, that, he, she, it
ἱεροῦ n. gen. neut. sg. ἱερόν temple
καὶ conj. καί and, even, also, but
εὐθέως adv. εὐθέως immediately, straightway, forthwith, as soon as, by and by, shortly
αἱ art. nom. fem. pl. ὁ ἡ τό the, this, that, he, she, it
θύραι n. nom. fem. pl. θύρα door, gate
31 δὲ conj. δέ but, and, now, also, to the contrary, rather, then
αὐτὸν pron. acc. masc. 3p. sg. αὐτός ἡ ὁ self, of oneself, even, very, the same, he, she, it
φάσις n. nom. fem. sg. φάσις tiding
τῷ art. dat. masc. sg. ὁ ἡ τό the, this, that, he, she, it
χιλιάρχῳ n. dat. masc. sg. χιλίαρχος high captain, chief captain, captain
τῆς art. gen. fem. sg. ὁ ἡ τό the, this, that, he, she, it
σπείρης n. gen. fem. sg. σπεῖρα band
ὅτι conj. ὅτι that, for, because, how that, how, because that, for that, though
ὅλη adj. nom. fem. sg. ὅλος all, whole, every whit, altogether
Ἱερουσαλήμ pron. name. fem. inde. Ἱερουσαλήμ Jerusalem
32 ὃς relative pron. nom. masc. sg. ὅς ἥ ὅ who, which, what, that
ἐξαυτῆς adv. ἐξαυτῆς immediately, by and by, presently, straightway
στρατιώτας n. acc. masc. pl. στρατιώτης soldier
καὶ conj. καί and, even, also, but
ἑκατοντάρχους n. acc. masc. pl. ἑκατοντάρχος centurion
ἐπ' prep. ἐπί (+gen) on, in, upon, (+dat) in, at, for, upon, (+acc) on, upon, unto, to, against
αὐτούς pron. acc. masc. 3p. pl. αὐτός ἡ ὁ self, of oneself, even, very, the same, he, she, it
οἱ art. nom. masc. pl. ὁ ἡ τό the, this, that, he, she, it
δὲ conj. δέ but, and, now, also, to the contrary, rather, then
τὸν art. acc. masc. sg. ὁ ἡ τό the, this, that, he, she, it
χιλίαρχον n. acc. masc. sg. χιλίαρχος high captain, chief captain, captain
καὶ conj. καί and, even, also, but
τοὺς art. acc. masc. pl. ὁ ἡ τό the, this, that, he, she, it
στρατιώτας n. acc. masc. pl. στρατιώτης soldier
τὸν art. acc. masc. sg. ὁ ἡ τό the, this, that, he, she, it
Παῦλον n. acc. masc. sg. Παῦλος Paul, Paulus
33 τότε adv. τότε then, that time
ὁ art. nom. masc. sg. ὁ ἡ τό the, this, that, he, she, it
χιλίαρχος n. nom. masc. sg. χιλίαρχος high captain, chief captain, captain
αὐτοῦ pron. gen. masc. 3p. sg. αὐτός ἡ ὁ self, of oneself, even, very, the same, he, she, it
καὶ conj. καί and, even, also, but
ἁλύσεσι n. dat. fem. pl. ἅλυσις chain, bond
δυσί num. dat. fem. pl. δύο two, twain, both
καὶ conj. καί and, even, also, but
τίς interrog. pron. nom. masc. sg. τίς what, who, why, where, which, how
ἂν particle. ἄν Indicating contingency. No English translation.
καὶ conj. καί and, even, also, but
τί interrog. pron. acc. neut. sg. τίς what, who, why, where, which, how

34 ἄλλοι adj. nom. masc. pl. ἄλλος other, another, some, one, more, otherwise
δὲ conj. δέ but, and, now, also, to the contrary, rather, then
ἄλλο adj. acc. neut. sg. ἄλλος other, another, some, one, more, otherwise
τι indefinite pron. acc. neut. sg. τὶς certain, some, any man, one, any thing
ἐν prep. ἐν (+dat) in, by, with, among, at, on, through, to, within, into, of, for
τῷ art. dat. masc. sg. ὁ ἡ τό the, this, that, he, she, it
ὄχλῳ n. dat. masc. sg. ὄχλος people, multitude, company, press, number
μὴ particle of negation. μή not, no, lest, neither, none, nothing, nor, never, without
δὲ conj. δέ but, and, now, also, to the contrary, rather, then
τὸ art. acc. neut. sg. ὁ ἡ τό the, this, that, he, she, it
ἀσφαλὲς adj. acc. neut. sg. ἀσφαλής certainty, certain, safe, sure
διὰ prep. διά (+gen) by, through, with, in, of, (+acc) for, because of, for a cause
τὸν art. acc. masc. sg. ὁ ἡ τό the, this, that, he, she, it
θόρυβον n. acc. masc. sg. θόρυβος tumult, uproar
αὐτὸν pron. acc. masc. 3p. sg. αὐτός ἡ ὁ self, of oneself, even, very, the same, he, she, it
εἰς prep. εἰς (+acc) into, to, unto, for, in, on, toward, against, upon, at, among
τὴν art. acc. fem. sg. ὁ ἡ τό the, this, that, he, she, it
παρεμβολήν n. acc. fem. sg. παρεμβολή castle, camp, army
35 ὅτε adv. ὅτε when, after that, as soon as, while, after
δὲ conj. δέ but, and, now, also, to the contrary, rather, then
ἐπὶ prep. ἐπί (+gen) on, in, upon, (+dat) in, at, for, upon, (+acc) on, upon, unto, to, against
τοὺς art. acc. masc. pl. ὁ ἡ τό the, this, that, he, she, it
ἀναβαθμούς n. acc. masc. pl. ἀναβαθμός stair
αὐτὸν pron. acc. masc. 3p. sg. αὐτός ἡ ὁ self, of oneself, even, very, the same, he, she, it
ὑπὸ prep. ὑπό (+gen) of, by, with, from, among, (+acc) under
τῶν art. gen. masc. pl. ὁ ἡ τό the, this, that, he, she, it
στρατιωτῶν n. gen. masc. pl. στρατιώτης soldier
διὰ prep. διά (+gen) by, through, with, in, of, (+acc) for, because of, for a cause
τὴν art. acc. fem. sg. ὁ ἡ τό the, this, that, he, she, it
βίαν n. acc. fem. sg. βία violence
τοῦ art. gen. masc. sg. ὁ ἡ τό the, this, that, he, she, it
ὄχλου n. gen. masc. sg. ὄχλος people, multitude, company, press, number
36 γὰρ conj. γάρ for, and, because, but, indeed
τὸ art. nom. neut. sg. ὁ ἡ τό the, this, that, he, she, it
πλῆθος n. nom. neut. sg. πλῆθος multitude, bundle, company
τοῦ art. gen. masc. sg. ὁ ἡ τό the, this, that, he, she, it
λαοῦ n. gen. masc. sg. λαός people
αὐτόν pron. acc. masc. 3p. sg. αὐτός ἡ ὁ self, of oneself, even, very, the same, he, she, it
37 τε conj. τέ and, both, also
εἰς prep. εἰς (+acc) into, to, unto, for, in, on, toward, against, upon, at, among
τὴν art. acc. fem. sg. ὁ ἡ τό the, this, that, he, she, it
παρεμβολὴν n. acc. fem. sg. παρεμβολή castle, camp, army
ὁ art. nom. masc. sg. ὁ ἡ τό the, this, that, he, she, it
Παῦλος n. nom. masc. sg. Παῦλος Paul, Paulus
τῷ art. dat. masc. sg. ὁ ἡ τό the, this, that, he, she, it
χιλιάρχῳ n. dat. masc. sg. χιλίαρχος high captain, chief captain, captain
Εἰ conj. εἰ if, whether, that, though, forasmuch
μοι pron. dat. 1p. sg. ἐγώ I
τι indefinite pron. acc. neut. sg. τὶς certain, some, any man, one, any thing
πρὸς prep. πρός (+gen) for, (+dat) at, (+acc) unto, to, with, for, against
σέ pron. acc. 2p. sg. σύ thou, you
ὁ art. nom. masc. sg. ὁ ἡ τό the, this, that, he, she, it
δὲ conj. δέ but, and, now, also, to the contrary, rather, then
Ἑλληνιστὶ adv. Ἑλληνιστί Greek
38 οὐκ particle of negation. οὐ οὐκ οὐχ not, no, neither, none, nay, nor, never, nothing

ἄρα conj. ἄρα then, therefore, haply, wherefore, perhaps, manner, no doubt, truly
σὺ pron. nom. 2p. sg. σύ thou, you
ὁ art. nom. masc. sg. ὁ ἡ τό the, this, that, he, she, it
Αἰγύπτιος adj. nom. masc. sg. Αἰγύπτιος Egyptian
ὁ art. nom. masc. sg. ὁ ἡ τό the, this, that, he, she, it
πρὸ prep. πρό (+gen) before, above
τούτων demo. pron. gen. fem. pl. οὗτος αὕτη τοῦτο this, the same, this same, he, she, it
τῶν art. gen. fem. pl. ὁ ἡ τό the, this, that, he, she, it
ἡμερῶν n. gen. fem. pl. ἡμέρα day, time, year, while, age, day time
καὶ conj. καί and, even, also, but
εἰς prep. εἰς (+acc) into, to, unto, for, in, on, toward, against, upon, at, among
τὴν art. acc. fem. sg. ὁ ἡ τό the, this, that, he, she, it
ἔρημον adj. acc. fem. sg. ἔρημος wilderness, desert
τοὺς art. acc. masc. pl. ὁ ἡ τό the, this, that, he, she, it
τετρακισχιλίους num. acc. masc. pl. τετρακισχίλιοι four thousand
ἄνδρας n. acc. masc. pl. ἀνήρ man, husband, sir
τῶν art. gen. masc. pl. ὁ ἡ τό the, this, that, he, she, it
σικαρίων n. gen. masc. pl. σικάριος murderer
39 δὲ conj. δέ but, and, now, also, to the contrary, rather, then
ὁ art. nom. masc. sg. ὁ ἡ τό the, this, that, he, she, it
Παῦλος n. nom. masc. sg. Παῦλος Paul, Paulus
Ἐγὼ pron. nom. 1p. sg. ἐγώ I
ἄνθρωπος n. nom. masc. sg. ἄνθρωπος man, human being, person, one, certain
μέν conj. μέν indeed, verily, truly, even, so, some
Ἰουδαῖος adj. nom. masc. sg. Ἰουδαῖος Jew, Jewess
Ταρσεὺς n. nom. masc. sg. Ταρσεύς of Tarsus
τῆς art. gen. fem. sg. ὁ ἡ τό the, this, that, he, she, it
Κιλικίας n. gen. fem. sg. Κιλικία Cilicia
οὐκ particle of negation. οὐ οὐκ οὐχ not, no, neither, none, nay, nor, never, nothing
ἀσήμου adj. gen. fem. sg. ἄσημος mean
πόλεως n. gen. fem. sg. πόλις city
πολίτης n. nom. masc. sg. πολίτης citizen
δὲ conj. δέ but, and, now, also, to the contrary, rather, then
σου pron. gen. 2p. sg. σύ thou, you
μοι pron. dat. 1p. sg. ἐγώ I
πρὸς prep. πρός (+gen) for, (+dat) at, (+acc) unto, to, with, for, against
τὸν art. acc. masc. sg. ὁ ἡ τό the, this, that, he, she, it
λαόν n. acc. masc. sg. λαός people
40 δὲ conj. δέ but, and, now, also, to the contrary, rather, then
αὐτοῦ pron. gen. masc. 3p. sg. αὐτός ἡ ὁ self, of oneself, even, very, the same, he, she, it
ὁ art. nom. masc. sg. ὁ ἡ τό the, this, that, he, she, it
Παῦλος n. nom. masc. sg. Παῦλος Paul, Paulus
ἐπὶ prep. ἐπί (+gen) on, in, upon, (+dat) in, at, for, upon, (+acc) on, upon, unto, to, against
τῶν art. gen. masc. pl. ὁ ἡ τό the, this, that, he, she, it
ἀναβαθμῶν n. gen. masc. pl. ἀναβαθμός stair
τῇ art. dat. fem. sg. ὁ ἡ τό the, this, that, he, she, it
χειρὶ n. dat. fem. sg. χείρ hand
τῷ art. dat. masc. sg. ὁ ἡ τό the, this, that, he, she, it
λαῷ n. dat. masc. sg. λαός people
πολλῆς adj. gen. fem. sg. πολύς many, great, much, long, abundant
δὲ conj. δέ but, and, now, also, to the contrary, rather, then
σιγῆς n. gen. fem. sg. σιγή silence
τῇ art. dat. fem. sg. ὁ ἡ τό the, this, that, he, she, it
Ἑβραΐδι adj. dat. fem. sg. Ἑβραΐς Hebrew
διαλέκτῳ n. dat. fem. sg. διάλεκτος tongue, language

22

1 Ἄνδρες n. voc. masc. pl. ἀνήρ man, husband, sir
ἀδελφοὶ n. voc. masc. pl. ἀδελφός brother
καὶ conj. καί and, even, also, but
πατέρες n. voc. masc. pl. πατήρ Father, father, parent
μου pron. gen. 1p. sg. ἐγώ I
τῆς art. gen. fem. sg. ὁ ἡ τό the, this, that, he, she, it
πρὸς prep. πρός (+gen) for, (+dat) at, (+acc) unto, to, with, for, against
ὑμᾶς pron. acc. 2p. pl. σύ thou, you
νῦν adv. νῦν now, henceforth, present, this time
ἀπολογίας n. gen. fem. sg. ἀπολογία defence, answer, answer for oneself, clear oneself
2 δὲ conj. δέ but, and, now, also, to the contrary, rather, then
ὅτι conj. ὅτι that, for, because, how that, how, because that, for that, though
τῇ art. dat. fem. sg. ὁ ἡ τό the, this, that, he, she, it
Ἑβραΐδι adj. dat. fem. sg. Ἑβραΐς Hebrew
διαλέκτῳ n. dat. fem. sg. διάλεκτος tongue, language
αὐτοῖς pron. dat. masc. 3p. pl. αὐτός ἡ ὁ self, of oneself, even, very, the same, he, she, it
μᾶλλον compar. adv. μᾶλλον rather, more, more and more, better, much, much the more
ἡσυχίαν n. acc. fem. sg. ἡσυχία silence, quietness
καὶ conj. καί and, even, also, but
3 Ἐγώ pron. nom. 1p. sg. ἐγώ I
μὲν conj. μέν indeed, verily, truly, even, so, some
ἀνὴρ n. nom. masc. sg. ἀνήρ man, husband, sir
Ἰουδαῖος adj. nom. masc. sg. Ἰουδαῖος Jew, Jewess
ἐν prep. ἐν (+dat) in, by, with, among, at, on, through, to, within, into, of, for
Ταρσῷ n. dat. fem. sg. Ταρσός Tarsus
τῆς art. gen. fem. sg. ὁ ἡ τό the, this, that, he, she, it
Κιλικίας n. gen. fem. sg. Κιλικία Cilicia
δὲ conj. δέ but, and, now, also, to the contrary, rather, then
ἐν prep. ἐν (+dat) in, by, with, among, at, on, through, to, within, into, of, for
τῇ art. dat. fem. sg. ὁ ἡ τό the, this, that, he, she, it
πόλει n. dat. fem. sg. πόλις city
ταύτῃ demo. pron. dat. fem. sg. οὗτος αὕτη τοῦτο this, the same, this same, he, she, it
παρὰ prep. παρά (+gen) of, from, (+dat) with, for, (+acc) beside, at, by, above, against
τοὺς art. acc. masc. pl. ὁ ἡ τό the, this, that, he, she, it
πόδας n. acc. masc. pl. πούς foot
Γαμαλιὴλ n. gen. masc. sg. Γαμαλιήλ Gamaliel
κατὰ prep. κατά (+gen) against, by, throughout, down, (+acc) according to, after, with
ἀκρίβειαν n. acc. fem. sg. ἀκρίβεια perfect manner
τοῦ art. gen. masc. sg. ὁ ἡ τό the, this, that, he, she, it
πατρῴου adj. gen. masc. sg. πατρῷος of fathers
νόμου n. gen. masc. sg. νόμος law, the law
ζηλωτὴς n. nom. masc. sg. ζηλωτής zealous
τοῦ art. gen. masc. sg. ὁ ἡ τό the, this, that, he, she, it
Θεοῦ n. gen. masc. sg. θεός God, god
καθὼς adv. καθώς as, even as, according as, according to
πάντες adj. nom. masc. pl. πᾶς πᾶσα πᾶν all, every, whosoever, every one, no, whole, any
ὑμεῖς pron. nom. 2p. pl. σύ thou, you
σήμερον adv. σήμερον this day, today
4 ὃς relative pron. nom. masc. sg. ὅς ἥ ὅ who, which, what, that
ταύτην demo. pron. acc. fem. sg. οὗτος αὕτη τοῦτο this, the same, this same, he, she, it
τὴν art. acc. fem. sg. ὁ ἡ τό the, this, that, he, she, it
ὁδὸν n. acc. fem. sg. ὁδός way, journey, highway

ἄχρι prep. ἄχρι or ἄχρις (+gen) until, unto, till, even to, as far as, while, into
θανάτου n. gen. masc. sg. θάνατος death
καὶ conj. καί and, even, also, but
εἰς prep. εἰς (+acc) into, to, unto, for, in, on, toward, against, upon, at, among
φυλακὰς n. acc. fem. pl. φυλακή prison, watch, imprisonment, cage, hold, ward
ἄνδρας n. acc. masc. pl. ἀνήρ man, husband, sir
τε conj. τέ and, both, also
καὶ conj. καί and, even, also, but
γυναῖκας n. acc. fem. pl. γυνή woman, wife
5 ὡς adv. ὡς as, when, as it were, how, about, like, as soon as, even as, while
καὶ conj. καί and, even, also, but
ὁ art. nom. masc. sg. ὁ ἡ τό the, this, that, he, she, it
ἀρχιερεὺς n. nom. masc. sg. ἀρχιερεύς chief priest, high priest
μοι pron. dat. 1p. sg. ἐγώ I
καὶ conj. καί and, even, also, but
πᾶν adj. nom. neut. sg. πᾶς πᾶσα πᾶν all, every, whosoever, every one, no, whole, any
τὸ art. nom. neut. sg. ὁ ἡ τό the, this, that, he, she, it
πρεσβυτέριον n. nom. neut. sg. πρεσβυτέριον elder, estate of an elder, presbytery
παρ' prep. παρά (+gen) of, from, (+dat) with, for, (+acc) beside, at, by, above, against
ὧν relative pron. gen. masc. pl. ὅς ἥ ὅ who, which, what, that
καὶ conj. καί and, even, also, but
ἐπιστολὰς n. acc. fem. pl. ἐπιστολή letter, epistle
πρὸς prep. πρός (+gen) for, (+dat) at, (+acc) unto, to, with, for, against
τοὺς art. acc. masc. pl. ὁ ἡ τό the, this, that, he, she, it
ἀδελφοὺς n. acc. masc. pl. ἀδελφός brother
εἰς prep. εἰς (+acc) into, to, unto, for, in, on, toward, against, upon, at, among
Δαμασκὸν n. acc. fem. sg. Δαμασκός Damascus
καὶ conj. καί and, even, also, but
τοὺς art. acc. masc. pl. ὁ ἡ τό the, this, that, he, she, it
ἐκεῖσε adv. ἐκεῖσε there
εἰς prep. εἰς (+acc) into, to, unto, for, in, on, toward, against, upon, at, among
Ἰερουσαλὴμ pron. name. fem. inde. Ἰερουσαλήμ Jerusalem
ἵνα conj. ἵνα that, to, lest, for to, so that, albeit, because, for, so as
6 δέ conj. δέ but, and, now, also, to the contrary, rather, then
μοι pron. dat. 1p. sg. ἐγώ I
καὶ conj. καί and, even, also, but
τῇ art. dat. fem. sg. ὁ ἡ τό the, this, that, he, she, it
Δαμασκῷ n. dat. fem. sg. Δαμασκός Damascus
περὶ prep. περί (+gen) of, for, concerning, (+acc) about, concerning, in
μεσημβρίαν n. acc. fem. sg. μεσημβρία south, noon
ἐξαίφνης adv. ἐξαίφνης suddenly
ἐκ prep. ἐκ ἐξ (+gen) of, from, out of, by, on, with, in, among, through
τοῦ art. gen. masc. sg. ὁ ἡ τό the, this, that, he, she, it
οὐρανοῦ n. gen. masc. sg. οὐρανός heaven, air, sky
φῶς n. acc. neut. sg. φῶς light, fire
ἱκανὸν adj. acc. neut. sg. ἱκανός many, much, long, worthy, sufficient, great, able
περὶ prep. περί (+gen) of, for, concerning, (+acc) about, concerning, in
ἐμέ pron. acc. 1p. sg. ἐγώ I
7 τε conj. τέ and, both, also
εἰς prep. εἰς (+acc) into, to, unto, for, in, on, toward, against, upon, at, among
τὸ art. acc. neut. sg. ὁ ἡ τό the, this, that, he, she, it
ἔδαφος n. acc. neut. sg. ἔδαφος ground
καὶ conj. καί and, even, also, but
φωνῆς n. gen. fem. sg. φωνή voice, sound, noise
μοι pron. dat. 1p. sg. ἐγώ I

Σαούλ n. voc. masc. sg. Σαούλ Saul
Σαούλ n. voc. masc. sg. Σαούλ Saul
τί interrog. pron. acc. neut. sg. τίς what, who, why, where, which, how
με pron. acc. 1p. sg. ἐγώ I
8 ἐγὼ pron. nom. 1p. sg. ἐγώ I
δὲ conj. δέ but, and, now, also, to the contrary, rather, then
Τίς interrog. pron. nom. masc. sg. τίς what, who, why, where, which, how
Κύριε n. voc. masc. sg. κύριος Lord, lord, master, sir, LORD, God, Master, owner
τε conj. τέ and, both, also
πρός prep. πρός (+gen) for, (+dat) at, (+acc) unto, to, with, for, against
με pron. acc. 1p. sg. ἐγώ I
Ἐγὼ pron. nom. 1p. sg. ἐγώ I
Ἰησοῦς n. nom. masc. sg. Ἰησοῦς Jesus
ὁ art. nom. masc. sg. ὁ ἡ τό the, this, that, he, she, it
Ναζωραῖος n. nom. masc. sg. Ναζωραῖος Nazareth, Nazarene
ὃν relative pron. acc. masc. sg. ὅς ἥ ὅ who, which, what, that
σὺ pron. nom. 2p. sg. σύ thou, you
9 οἱ art. nom. masc. pl. ὁ ἡ τό the, this, that, he, she, it
δὲ conj. δέ but, and, now, also, to the contrary, rather, then
σὺν prep. σύν (+dat) with, beside
ἐμοὶ pron. dat. 1p. sg. ἐγώ I
τὸ art. acc. neut. sg. ὁ ἡ τό the, this, that, he, she, it
μέν conj. μέν indeed, verily, truly, even, so, some
φῶς n. acc. neut. sg. φῶς light, fire
καὶ conj. καί and, even, also, but
ἔμφοβοι adj. nom. masc. pl. ἔμφοβος afraid, affrighted, tremble
τὴν art. acc. fem. sg. ὁ ἡ τό the, this, that, he, she, it
δὲ conj. δέ but, and, now, also, to the contrary, rather, then
φωνὴν n. acc. fem. sg. φωνή voice, sound, noise
οὐκ particle of negation. οὐ οὐκ οὐχ not, no, neither, none, nay, nor, never, nothing
τοῦ art. gen. masc. sg. ὁ ἡ τό the, this, that, he, she, it
μοι pron. dat. 1p. sg. ἐγώ I
10 δέ conj. δέ but, and, now, also, to the contrary, rather, then
Τί interrog. pron. acc. neut. sg. τίς what, who, why, where, which, how
Κύριε n. voc. masc. sg. κύριος Lord, lord, master, sir, LORD, God, Master, owner
ὁ art. nom. masc. sg. ὁ ἡ τό the, this, that, he, she, it
δὲ conj. δέ but, and, now, also, to the contrary, rather, then
Κύριος n. nom. masc. sg. κύριος Lord, lord, master, sir, LORD, God, Master, owner
πρός prep. πρός (+gen) for, (+dat) at, (+acc) unto, to, with, for, against
με pron. acc. 1p. sg. ἐγώ I
εἰς prep. εἰς (+acc) into, to, unto, for, in, on, toward, against, upon, at, among
Δαμασκὸν n. acc. fem. sg. Δαμασκός Damascus
κἀκεῖ adv. κἀκεῖ and there, there also, thither also
σοι pron. dat. 2p. sg. σύ thou, you
περὶ prep. περί (+gen) of, for, concerning, (+acc) about, concerning, in
πάντων adj. gen. neut. pl. πᾶς πᾶσα πᾶν all, every, whosoever, every one, no, whole, any
ὧν relative pron. gen. neut. pl. ὅς ἥ ὅ who, which, what, that
σοι pron. dat. 2p. sg. σύ thou, you
11 ὡς adv. ὡς as, when, as it were, how, about, like, as soon as, even as, while
δὲ conj. δέ but, and, now, also, to the contrary, rather, then
οὐκ particle of negation. οὐ οὐκ οὐχ not, no, neither, none, nay, nor, never, nothing
ἀπὸ prep. ἀπό (+gen) from, of, out of, since, for, off, at, by, in, on
τῆς art. gen. fem. sg. ὁ ἡ τό the, this, that, he, she, it
δόξης n. gen. fem. sg. δόξα glory, honour, praise, dignity, worship
τοῦ art. gen. neut. sg. ὁ ἡ τό the, this, that, he, she, it

φωτὸς n. gen. neut. sg. φῶς light, fire
ἐκείνου demo. pron. gen. neut. sg. ἐκεῖνος that, he, the same, that same
ὑπὸ prep. ὑπό (+gen) of, by, with, from, among, (+acc) under
τῶν art. gen. masc. pl. ὁ ἡ τό the, this, that, he, she, it
μοι pron. dat. 1p. sg. ἐγώ I
εἰς prep. εἰς (+acc) into, to, unto, for, in, on, toward, against, upon, at, among
Δαμασκόν n. acc. fem. sg. Δαμασκός Damascus
12 Ἀνανίας n. nom. masc. sg. Ἀνανίας Ananias
δέ conj. δέ but, and, now, also, to the contrary, rather, then
τις indefinite pron. nom. masc. sg. τὶς certain, some, any man, one, any thing
ἀνὴρ n. nom. masc. sg. ἀνήρ man, husband, sir
εὐσεβὴς adj. nom. masc. sg. εὐσεβής devout, godly
κατὰ prep. κατά (+gen) against, by, throughout, down, (+acc) according to, after, with
τὸν art. acc. masc. sg. ὁ ἡ τό the, this, that, he, she, it
νόμον n. acc. masc. sg. νόμος law, the law
ὑπὸ prep. ὑπό (+gen) of, by, with, from, among, (+acc) under
πάντων adj. gen. masc. pl. πᾶς πᾶσα πᾶν all, every, whosoever, every one, no, whole, any
τῶν art. gen. masc. pl. ὁ ἡ τό the, this, that, he, she, it
Ἰουδαίων adj. gen. masc. pl. Ἰουδαῖος Jew, Jewess
13 πρός prep. πρός (+gen) for, (+dat) at, (+acc) unto, to, with, for, against
με pron. acc. 1p. sg. ἐγώ I
καὶ conj. καί and, even, also, but
μοι pron. dat. 1p. sg. ἐγώ I
Σαοὺλ n. voc. masc. sg. Σαούλ Saul
ἀδελφε n. voc. masc. sg. ἀδελφός brother
κἀγὼ pron. nom. 1p. σγ. κἀγώ and I, I also, so I, even as I
αὐτῇ pron. dat. fem. 3p. sg. αὐτός ή ό self, of oneself, even, very, the same, he, she, it
τῇ art. dat. fem. sg. ὁ ἡ τό the, this, that, he, she, it
ὥρᾳ n. dat. fem. sg. ὥρα hour, time, season
εἰς prep. εἰς (+acc) into, to, unto, for, in, on, toward, against, upon, at, among
αὐτόν pron. acc. masc. 3p. sg. αὐτός ή ό self, of oneself, even, very, the same, he, she, it
14 ὁ art. nom. masc. sg. ὁ ἡ τό the, this, that, he, she, it
δὲ conj. δέ but, and, now, also, to the contrary, rather, then
Ὁ art. nom. masc. sg. ὁ ἡ τό the, this, that, he, she, it
Θεὸς n. nom. masc. sg. θεός God, god
τῶν art. gen. masc. pl. ὁ ἡ τό the, this, that, he, she, it
πατέρων n. gen. masc. pl. πατήρ Father, father, parent
ἡμῶν pron. gen. 1p. pl. ἐγώ I
σε pron. acc. 2p. sg. σύ thou, you
τὸ art. acc. neut. sg. ὁ ἡ τό the, this, that, he, she, it
θέλημα n. acc. neut. sg. θέλημα will, desire, pleasure
αὐτοῦ pron. gen. masc. 3p. sg. αὐτός ή ό self, of oneself, even, very, the same, he, she, it
καὶ conj. καί and, even, also, but
τὸν art. acc. masc. sg. ὁ ἡ τό the, this, that, he, she, it
δίκαιον adj. acc. masc. sg. δίκαιος righteous, just, meet, right
καὶ conj. καί and, even, also, but
φωνὴν n. acc. fem. sg. φωνή voice, sound, noise
ἐκ prep. ἐκ ἐξ (+gen) of, from, out of, by, on, with, in, among, through
τοῦ art. gen. neut. sg. ὁ ἡ τό the, this, that, he, she, it
στόματος n. gen. neut. sg. στόμα mouth, face, edge
αὐτοῦ pron. gen. masc. 3p. sg. αὐτός ή ό self, of oneself, even, very, the same, he, she, it
15 ὅτι conj. ὅτι that, for, because, how that, how, because that, for that, though
μάρτυς n. nom. masc. sg. μάρτυς or μάρτυρ witness, martyr, record
αὐτῷ pron. dat. masc. 3p. sg. αὐτός ή ό self, of oneself, even, very, the same, he, she, it
πρὸς prep. πρός (+gen) for, (+dat) at, (+acc) unto, to, with, for, against

πάντας adj. acc. masc. pl. πᾶς πᾶσα πᾶν all, every, whosoever, every one, no, whole, any
ἀνθρώπους n. acc. masc. pl. ἄνθρωπος man, human being, person, one, certain
ὧν relative pron. gen. neut. pl. ὅς ἥ ὅ who, which, what, that
καὶ conj. καί and, even, also, but
16 καὶ conj. καί and, even, also, but
νῦν adv. νῦν now, henceforth, present, this time
τί interrog. pron. acc. neut. sg. τίς what, who, why, where, which, how
καὶ conj. καί and, even, also, but
τὰς art. acc. fem. pl. ὁ ἡ τό the, this, that, he, she, it
ἁμαρτίας n. acc. fem. pl. ἁμαρτία sin, offence, sinful
σου pron. gen. 2p. sg. σύ thou, you
τὸ art. acc. neut. sg. ὁ ἡ τό the, this, that, he, she, it
ὄνομα n. acc. neut. sg. ὄνομα name, call, surname
τοῦ art. gen. masc. sg. ὁ ἡ τό the, this, that, he, she, it
Κυρίου n. gen. masc. sg. κύριος Lord, lord, master, sir, LORD, God, Master, owner
17 δέ conj. δέ but, and, now, also, to the contrary, rather, then
μοι pron. dat. 1p. sg. ἐγώ I
εἰς prep. εἰς (+acc) into, to, unto, for, in, on, toward, against, upon, at, among
Ἱερουσαλήμ pron. name. fem. inde. Ἱερουσαλήμ Jerusalem
καὶ conj. καί and, even, also, but
μου pron. gen. 1p. sg. ἐγώ I
ἐν prep. ἐν (+dat) in, by, with, among, at, on, through, to, within, into, of, for
τῷ art. dat. neut. sg. ὁ ἡ τό the, this, that, he, she, it
ἱερῷ n. dat. neut. sg. ἱερόν temple
με pron. acc. 1p. sg. ἐγώ I
ἐν prep. ἐν (+dat) in, by, with, among, at, on, through, to, within, into, of, for
ἐκστάσει n. dat. fem. sg. ἔκστασις trance, astonishment, amazement, amazed
18 καὶ conj. καί and, even, also, but
αὐτὸν pron. acc. masc. 3p. sg. αὐτός ἡ ὁ self, of oneself, even, very, the same, he, she, it
μοι pron. dat. 1p. sg. ἐγώ I
καὶ conj. καί and, even, also, but
ἐν prep. ἐν (+dat) in, by, with, among, at, on, through, to, within, into, of, for
τάχει n. dat. neut. sg. τάχος speedily, short, quick
ἐξ prep. ἐκ ἐξ (+gen) of, from, out of, by, on, with, in, among, through
Ἱερουσαλήμ pron. name. fem. inde. Ἱερουσαλήμ Jerusalem
διότι conj. διότι for, because, because that, therefore
οὐ particle of negation. οὐ οὐκ οὐχ not, no, neither, none, nay, nor, never, nothing
σου pron. gen. 2p. sg. σύ thou, you
τὴν art. acc. fem. sg. ὁ ἡ τό the, this, that, he, she, it
μαρτυρίαν n. acc. fem. sg. μαρτυρία testimony, witness, record, report
περὶ prep. περί (+gen) of, for, concerning, (+acc) about, concerning, in
ἐμοῦ pron. gen. 1p. sg. ἐγώ I
19 κἀγὼ pron. nom. 1p. σγ. κἀγώ and I, I also, so I, even as I
Κύριε n. voc. masc. sg. κύριος Lord, lord, master, sir, LORD, God, Master, owner
αὐτοὶ pron. nom. masc. 3p. pl. αὐτός ἡ ὁ self, of oneself, even, very, the same, he, she, it
ὅτι conj. ὅτι that, for, because, how that, how, because that, for that, though
ἐγὼ pron. nom. 1p. sg. ἐγώ I
καὶ conj. καί and, even, also, but
κατὰ prep. κατά (+gen) against, by, throughout, down, (+acc) according to, after, with
τὰς art. acc. fem. pl. ὁ ἡ τό the, this, that, he, she, it
συναγωγὰς n. acc. fem. pl. συναγωγή synagogue, assembly, congregation
τοὺς art. acc. masc. pl. ὁ ἡ τό the, this, that, he, she, it
ἐπὶ prep. ἐπί (+gen) on, in, upon, (+dat) in, at, for, upon, (+acc) on, upon, unto, to, against
σέ pron. acc. 2p. sg. σύ thou, you
20 καὶ conj. καί and, even, also, but

ὅτε adv. ὅτε when, after that, as soon as, while, after
τὸ art. nom. neut. sg. ὁ ἡ τό the, this, that, he, she, it
αἷμα n. nom. neut. sg. αἷμα blood
Στεφάνου n. gen. masc. sg. Στέφανος Stephen
τοῦ art. gen. masc. sg. ὁ ἡ τό the, this, that, he, she, it
μάρτυρός n. gen. masc. sg. μάρτυς or μάρτυρ witness, martyr, record
σου pron. gen. 2p. sg. σύ thou, you
καὶ conj. καί and, even, also, but
αὐτὸς pron. nom. masc. 3p. sg. αὐτός ή ὁ self, of oneself, even, very, the same, he, she, it
καὶ conj. καί and, even, also, but
τῇ art. dat. fem. sg. ὁ ἡ τό the, this, that, he, she, it
ἀναιρέσει n. dat. fem. sg. ἀναίρεσις death
αὐτοῦ pron. gen. masc. 3p. sg. αὐτός ή ὁ self, of oneself, even, very, the same, he, she, it
καὶ conj. καί and, even, also, but
τὰ art. acc. neut. pl. ὁ ἡ τό the, this, that, he, she, it
ἱμάτια n. acc. neut. pl. ἱμάτιον cloke, garment, clothes, raiment, robe, vesture
τῶν art. gen. masc. pl. ὁ ἡ τό the, this, that, he, she, it
αὐτόν pron. acc. masc. 3p. sg. αὐτός ή ὁ self, of oneself, even, very, the same, he, she, it
21 καὶ conj. καί and, even, also, but
πρός prep. πρός (+gen) for, (+dat) at, (+acc) unto, to, with, for, against
με pron. acc. 1p. sg. ἐγώ I
ὅτι conj. ὅτι that, for, because, how that, how, because that, for that, though
ἐγὼ pron. nom. 1p. sg. ἐγώ I
εἰς prep. εἰς (+acc) into, to, unto, for, in, on, toward, against, upon, at, among
ἔθνη n. acc. neut. pl. ἔθνος Gentile, nation, heathen, people
μακρὰν adv. μακράν far, afar off, far off, good way off, great way off
σε pron. acc. 2p. sg. σύ thou, you
22 δὲ conj. δέ but, and, now, also, to the contrary, rather, then
αὐτοῦ pron. gen. masc. 3p. sg. αὐτός ή ὁ self, of oneself, even, very, the same, he, she, it
ἄχρι prep. ἄχρι or ἄχρις (+gen) until, unto, till, even to, as far as, while, into
τούτου demo. pron. gen. masc. sg. οὗτος αὕτη τοῦτο this, the same, this same, he, she, it
τοῦ art. gen. masc. sg. ὁ ἡ τό the, this, that, he, she, it
λόγου n. gen. masc. sg. λόγος word, saying, account, speech, thing, matter
καὶ conj. καί and, even, also, but
τὴν art. acc. fem. sg. ὁ ἡ τό the, this, that, he, she, it
φωνὴν n. acc. fem. sg. φωνή voice, sound, noise
αὐτῶν pron. gen. masc. 3p. pl. αὐτός ή ὁ self, of oneself, even, very, the same, he, she, it
ἀπὸ prep. ἀπό (+gen) from, of, out of, since, for, off, at, by, in, on
τῆς art. gen. fem. sg. ὁ ἡ τό the, this, that, he, she, it
γῆς n. gen. fem. sg. γῆ earth, land, ground, country
τὸν art. acc. masc. sg. ὁ ἡ τό the, this, that, he, she, it
τοιοῦτον demo. pron. acc. masc. sg. τοιοῦτος such, like
οὐ particle of negation. οὐ οὐκ οὐχ not, no, neither, none, nay, nor, never, nothing
γὰρ conj. γάρ for, and, because, but, indeed
αὐτὸν pron. acc. masc. 3p. sg. αὐτός ή ὁ self, of oneself, even, very, the same, he, she, it
23 δέ conj. δέ but, and, now, also, to the contrary, rather, then
αὐτῶν pron. gen. masc. 3p. pl. αὐτός ή ὁ self, of oneself, even, very, the same, he, she, it
καὶ conj. καί and, even, also, but
τὰ art. acc. neut. pl. ὁ ἡ τό the, this, that, he, she, it
ἱμάτια n. acc. neut. pl. ἱμάτιον cloke, garment, clothes, raiment, robe, vesture
καὶ conj. καί and, even, also, but
κονιορτὸν n. acc. masc. sg. κονιορτός dust
εἰς prep. εἰς (+acc) into, to, unto, for, in, on, toward, against, upon, at, among
τὸν art. acc. masc. sg. ὁ ἡ τό the, this, that, he, she, it
ἀέρα n. acc. masc. sg. ἀήρ air

24 αὐτὸν pron. acc. masc. 3p. sg. αὐτός ή ό self, of oneself, even, very, the same, he, she, it
ὁ art. nom. masc. sg. ὁ ἡ τό the, this, that, he, she, it
χιλίαρχος n. nom. masc. sg. χιλίαρχος high captain, chief captain, captain
εἰς prep. εἰς (+acc) into, to, unto, for, in, on, toward, against, upon, at, among
τὴν art. acc. fem. sg. ὁ ἡ τό the, this, that, he, she, it
παρεμβολήν n. acc. fem. sg. παρεμβολή castle, camp, army
μάστιξιν n. dat. fem. pl. μάστιξ plague, scourging
αὐτὸν pron. acc. masc. 3p. sg. αὐτός ή ό self, of oneself, even, very, the same, he, she, it
ἵνα conj. ἵνα that, to, lest, for to, so that, albeit, because, for, so as
δι' prep. διά (+gen) by, through, with, in, of, (+acc) for, because of, for a cause
ἣν relative pron. acc. fem. sg. ὅς ἥ ὅ who, which, what, that
αἰτίαν n. acc. fem. sg. αἰτία cause, reason, accusation, fault
οὕτως adv. οὕτω οὕτως so, even so, thus, on this wise, likewise, after this manner
αὐτῷ pron. dat. masc. 3p. sg. αὐτός ή ό self, of oneself, even, very, the same, he, she, it
25 ὡς adv. ὡς as, when, as it were, how, about, like, as soon as, even as, while
δὲ conj. δέ but, and, now, also, to the contrary, rather, then
αὐτὸν pron. acc. masc. 3p. sg. αὐτός ή ό self, of oneself, even, very, the same, he, she, it
τοῖς art. dat. masc. pl. ὁ ἡ τό the, this, that, he, she, it
ἱμᾶσιν n. dat. masc. pl. ἱμάς latchet, thong
πρὸς prep. πρός (+gen) for, (+dat) at, (+acc) unto, to, with, for, against
τὸν art. acc. masc. sg. ὁ ἡ τό the, this, that, he, she, it
ἑκατόνταρχον n. acc. masc. sg. ἑκατοντάρχος centurion
ὁ art. nom. masc. sg. ὁ ἡ τό the, this, that, he, she, it
Παῦλος n. nom. masc. sg. Παῦλος Paul, Paulus
Εἰ conj. εἰ if, whether, that, though, forasmuch
ἄνθρωπον n. acc. masc. sg. ἄνθρωπος man, human being, person, one, certain
Ῥωμαῖον adj. acc. masc. sg. Ῥωμαῖος Roman, Rome
καὶ conj. καί and, even, also, but
ἀκατάκριτον adj. acc. masc. sg. ἀκατάκριτος uncondemned
ὑμῖν pron. dat. 2p. pl. σύ thou, you
26 δὲ conj. δέ but, and, now, also, to the contrary, rather, then
ὁ art. nom. masc. sg. ὁ ἡ τό the, this, that, he, she, it
ἑκατόνταρχος n. nom. masc. sg. ἑκατόνταρχος centurion
τῷ art. dat. masc. sg. ὁ ἡ τό the, this, that, he, she, it
χιλιάρχῳ n. dat. masc. sg. χιλίαρχος high captain, chief captain, captain
τί interrog. pron. acc. neut. sg. τίς what, who, why, where, which, how
ὁ art. nom. masc. sg. ὁ ἡ τό the, this, that, he, she, it
γὰρ conj. γάρ for, and, because, but, indeed
ἄνθρωπος n. nom. masc. sg. ἄνθρωπος man, human being, person, one, certain
οὗτος demo. pron. nom. masc. sg. οὗτος αὕτη τοῦτο this, the same, this same, he, she, it
Ῥωμαῖός adj. nom. masc. sg. Ῥωμαῖος Roman, Rome
27 δὲ conj. δέ but, and, now, also, to the contrary, rather, then
ὁ art. nom. masc. sg. ὁ ἡ τό the, this, that, he, she, it
χιλίαρχος n. nom. masc. sg. χιλίαρχος high captain, chief captain, captain
αὐτῷ pron. dat. masc. 3p. sg. αὐτός ή ό self, of oneself, even, very, the same, he, she, it
μοι pron. dat. 1p. sg. ἐγώ I
εἰ conj. εἰ if, whether, that, though, forasmuch
σὺ pron. nom. 2p. sg. σύ thou, you
Ῥωμαῖος adj. nom. masc. sg. Ῥωμαῖος Roman, Rome
ὁ art. nom. masc. sg. ὁ ἡ τό the, this, that, he, she, it
δὲ conj. δέ but, and, now, also, to the contrary, rather, then
Ναί particle. ναί yea, even so, yes, surely, truth, verily
28 τε conj. τέ and, both, also
ὁ art. nom. masc. sg. ὁ ἡ τό the, this, that, he, she, it
χιλίαρχος n. nom. masc. sg. χιλίαρχος high captain, chief captain, captain

Ἐγὼ pron. nom. 1p. sg. ἐγώ I
πολλοῦ adj. gen. neut. sg. πολύς many, great, much, long, abundant
κεφαλαίου n. gen. neut. sg. κεφάλαιον sum
τὴν art. acc. fem. sg. ὁ ἡ τό the, this, that, he, she, it
πολιτείαν n. acc. fem. sg. πολιτεία freedom, citizenship, commonwealth, polity
ταύτην demo. pron. acc. fem. sg. οὗτος αὕτη τοῦτο this, the same, this same, he, she, it
ὁ art. nom. masc. sg. ὁ ἡ τό the, this, that, he, she, it
δὲ conj. δέ but, and, now, also, to the contrary, rather, then
Παῦλος n. nom. masc. sg. Παῦλος Paul, Paulus
Ἐγὼ pron. nom. 1p. sg. ἐγώ I
δὲ conj. δέ but, and, now, also, to the contrary, rather, then
καὶ conj. καί and, even, also, but
29 εὐθέως adv. εὐθέως immediately, straightway, forthwith, as soon as, by and by, shortly
οὖν conj. οὖν therefore, then, so, and, now, wherefore
ἀπ' prep. ἀπό (+gen) from, of, out of, since, for, off, at, by, in, on
αὐτοῦ pron. gen. masc. 3p. sg. αὐτός ή ό self, of oneself, even, very, the same, he, she, it
οἱ art. nom. masc. pl. ὁ ἡ τό the, this, that, he, she, it
αὐτὸν pron. acc. masc. 3p. sg. αὐτός ή ό self, of oneself, even, very, the same, he, she, it
καὶ conj. καί and, even, also, but
ὁ art. nom. masc. sg. ὁ ἡ τό the, this, that, he, she, it
χιλίαρχος n. nom. masc. sg. χιλίαρχος high captain, chief captain, captain
δὲ conj. δέ but, and, now, also, to the contrary, rather, then
ὅτι conj. ὅτι that, for, because, how that, how, because that, for that, though
Ῥωμαῖός adj. nom. masc. sg. Ῥωμαῖος Roman, Rome
καὶ conj. καί and, even, also, but
ὅτι conj. ὅτι that, for, because, how that, how, because that, for that, though
αὐτὸν pron. acc. masc. 3p. sg. αὐτός ή ό self, of oneself, even, very, the same, he, she, it
30 Τῇ art. dat. fem. sg. ὁ ἡ τό the, this, that, he, she, it
δὲ conj. δέ but, and, now, also, to the contrary, rather, then
ἐπαύριον adv. ἐπαύριον next day, morrow, day following, nest day after
τὸ art. acc. neut. sg. ὁ ἡ τό the, this, that, he, she, it
ἀσφαλές adj. acc. neut. sg. ἀσφαλής certainty, certain, safe, sure
τὸ art. acc. neut. sg. ὁ ἡ τό the, this, that, he, she, it
τί interrog. pron. acc. neut. sg. τίς what, who, why, where, which, how
παρὰ prep. παρά (+gen) of, from, (+dat) with, for, (+acc) beside, at, by, above, against
τῶν art. gen. masc. pl. ὁ ἡ τό the, this, that, he, she, it
Ἰουδαίων adj. gen. masc. pl. Ἰουδαῖος Jew, Jewess
αὐτὸν pron. acc. masc. 3p. sg. αὐτός ή ό self, of oneself, even, very, the same, he, she, it
ἀπὸ prep. ἀπό (+gen) from, of, out of, since, for, off, at, by, in, on
τῶν art. gen. neut. pl. ὁ ἡ τό the, this, that, he, she, it
δεσμῶν n. gen. neut. pl. δεσμός bond, band, chain, string
καὶ conj. καί and, even, also, but
τοὺς art. acc. masc. pl. ὁ ἡ τό the, this, that, he, she, it
ἀρχιερεῖς n. acc. masc. pl. ἀρχιερεύς chief priest, high priest
καὶ conj. καί and, even, also, but
ὅλον adj. acc. neut. sg. ὅλος all, whole, every whit, altogether
τὸ art. acc. neut. sg. ὁ ἡ τό the, this, that, he, she, it
συνέδριον n. acc. neut. sg. συνέδριον council
αὐτῶν pron. gen. masc. 3p. pl. αὐτός ή ό self, of oneself, even, very, the same, he, she, it
καὶ conj. καί and, even, also, but
τὸν art. acc. masc. sg. ὁ ἡ τό the, this, that, he, she, it
Παῦλον n. acc. masc. sg. Παῦλος Paul, Paulus
εἰς prep. εἰς (+acc) into, to, unto, for, in, on, toward, against, upon, at, among
αὐτούς pron. acc. masc. 3p. pl. αὐτός ή ό self, of oneself, even, very, the same, he, she, it

23

1 δὲ conj. δέ but, and, now, also, to the contrary, rather, then
ὁ art. nom. masc. sg. ὁ ἡ τό the, this, that, he, she, it
Παῦλος n. nom. masc. sg. Παῦλος Paul, Paulus
τῷ art. dat. neut. sg. ὁ ἡ τό the, this, that, he, she, it
συνεδρίῳ n. dat. neut. sg. συνέδριον council
"Ανδρες n. voc. masc. pl. ἀνήρ man, husband, sir
ἀδελφοί n. voc. masc. pl. ἀδελφός brother
ἐγὼ pron. nom. 1p. sg. ἐγώ I
πάσῃ adj. dat. fem. sg. πᾶς πᾶσα πᾶν all, every, whosoever, every one, no, whole, any
συνειδήσει n. dat. fem. sg. συνείδησις conscience
ἀγαθῇ adj. dat. fem. sg. ἀγαθός good, good thing, that which is good, well
τῷ art. dat. masc. sg. ὁ ἡ τό the, this, that, he, she, it
Θεῷ n. dat. masc. sg. θεός God, god
ἄχρι prep. ἄχρι or ἄχρις (+gen) until, unto, till, even to, as far as, while, into
ταύτης demo. pron. gen. fem. sg. οὗτος αὕτη τοῦτο this, the same, this same, he, she, it
τῆς art. gen. fem. sg. ὁ ἡ τό the, this, that, he, she, it
ἡμέρας n. gen. fem. sg. ἡμέρα day, time, year, while, age, day time
2 ὁ art. nom. masc. sg. ὁ ἡ τό the, this, that, he, she, it
δὲ conj. δέ but, and, now, also, to the contrary, rather, then
ἀρχιερεὺς n. nom. masc. sg. ἀρχιερεύς chief priest, high priest
'Ανανίας n. nom. masc. sg. 'Ανανίας Ananias
τοῖς art. dat. masc. pl. ὁ ἡ τό the, this, that, he, she, it
αὐτῷ pron. dat. masc. 3p. sg. αὐτός ή ό self, of oneself, even, very, the same, he, she, it
αὐτοῦ pron. gen. masc. 3p. sg. αὐτός ή ό self, of oneself, even, very, the same, he, she, it
τὸ art. acc. neut. sg. ὁ ἡ τό the, this, that, he, she, it
στόμα n. acc. neut. sg. στόμα mouth, face, edge
3 τότε adv. τότε then, that time
ὁ art. nom. masc. sg. ὁ ἡ τό the, this, that, he, she, it
Παῦλος n. nom. masc. sg. Παῦλος Paul, Paulus
πρὸς prep. πρός (+gen) for, (+dat) at, (+acc) unto, to, with, for, against
αὐτὸν pron. acc. masc. 3p. sg. αὐτός ή ό self, of oneself, even, very, the same, he, she, it
σε pron. acc. 2p. sg. σύ thou, you
ὁ art. nom. masc. sg. ὁ ἡ τό the, this, that, he, she, it
Θεός n. nom. masc. sg. θεός God, god
τοῖχε n. voc. masc. sg. τοῖχος wall
καὶ conj. καί and, even, also, but
σὺ pron. nom. 2p. sg. σύ thou, you
με pron. acc. 1p. sg. ἐγώ I
κατὰ prep. κατά (+gen) against, by, throughout, down, (+acc) according to, after, with
τὸν art. acc. masc. sg. ὁ ἡ τό the, this, that, he, she, it
νόμον n. acc. masc. sg. νόμος law, the law
καὶ conj. καί and, even, also, but
με pron. acc. 1p. sg. ἐγώ I
4 οἱ art. nom. masc. pl. ὁ ἡ τό the, this, that, he, she, it
δὲ conj. δέ but, and, now, also, to the contrary, rather, then
Τὸν art. acc. masc. sg. ὁ ἡ τό the, this, that, he, she, it
ἀρχιερέα n. acc. masc. sg. ἀρχιερεύς chief priest, high priest
τοῦ art. gen. masc. sg. ὁ ἡ τό the, this, that, he, she, it
Θεοῦ n. gen. masc. sg. θεός God, god
5 τε conj. τέ and, both, also
ὁ art. nom. masc. sg. ὁ ἡ τό the, this, that, he, she, it
Παῦλος n. nom. masc. sg. Παῦλος Paul, Paulus
Οὐκ particle of negation. οὐ οὐκ οὐχ not, no, neither, none, nay, nor, never, nothing

ἀδελφοί n. voc. masc. pl. ἀδελφός brother
ὅτι conj. ὅτι that, for, because, how that, how, because that, for that, though
ἀρχιερεύς n. nom. masc. sg. ἀρχιερεύς chief priest, high priest
γὰρ conj. γάρ for, and, because, but, indeed
Ἄρχοντα n. acc. masc. sg. ἄρχων ruler, prince, chief, magistrate, chief ruler
τοῦ art. gen. masc. sg. ὁ ἡ τό the, this, that, he, she, it
λαοῦ n. gen. masc. sg. λαός people
σου pron. gen. 2p. sg. σύ thou, you
οὐκ particle of negation. οὐ οὐκ οὐχ not, no, neither, none, nay, nor, never, nothing
κακῶς adv. κακῶς sick, diseased, evil, amiss, grievously, miserably, sore
6 δὲ conj. δέ but, and, now, also, to the contrary, rather, then
ὁ art. nom. masc. sg. ὁ ἡ τό the, this, that, he, she, it
Παῦλος n. nom. masc. sg. Παῦλος Paul, Paulus
ὅτι conj. ὅτι that, for, because, how that, how, because that, for that, though
τὸ art. nom. neut. sg. ὁ ἡ τό the, this, that, he, she, it
ἓν num. nom. neut. sg. εἷς or ἕν one, other, some, any, only, a certain
μέρος n. nom. neut. sg. μέρος part, coast, portion, behalf, respect, piece, side
Σαδδουκαίων n. gen. masc. pl. Σαδδουκαῖος Sadducee
τὸ art. nom. neut. sg. ὁ ἡ τό the, this, that, he, she, it
δὲ conj. δέ but, and, now, also, to the contrary, rather, then
ἕτερον adj. nom. neut. sg. ἕτερος another, other, else, strange
Φαρισαίων n. gen. masc. pl. Φαρισαῖος Pharisee
ἐν prep. ἐν (+dat) in, by, with, among, at, on, through, to, within, into, of, for
τῷ art. dat. neut. sg. ὁ ἡ τό the, this, that, he, she, it
συνεδρίῳ n. dat. neut. sg. συνέδριον council
Ἄνδρες n. voc. masc. pl. ἀνήρ man, husband, sir
ἀδελφοί n. voc. masc. pl. ἀδελφός brother
ἐγὼ pron. nom. 1p. sg. ἐγώ I
Φαρισαῖός n. nom. masc. sg. Φαρισαῖος Pharisee
υἱὸς n. nom. masc. sg. υἱός son, child, descendant, offspring, heir
Φαρισαίου n. gen. masc. sg. Φαρισαῖος Pharisee
περὶ prep. περί (+gen) of, for, concerning, (+acc) about, concerning, in
ἐλπίδος n. gen. fem. sg. ἐλπίς hope, faith
καὶ conj. καί and, even, also, but
ἀναστάσεως n. gen. fem. sg. ἀνάστασις resurrection, rising again
νεκρῶν adj. gen. masc. pl. νεκρός dead
ἐγὼ pron. nom. 1p. sg. ἐγώ I
7 τοῦτο demo. pron. acc. neut. sg. οὗτος αὕτη τοῦτο this, the same, this same, he, she, it
δὲ conj. δέ but, and, now, also, to the contrary, rather, then
αὐτοῦ pron. gen. masc. 3p. sg. αὐτός ἡ ὁ self, of oneself, even, very, the same, he, she, it
στάσις n. nom. fem. sg. στάσις dissension, sedition, insurrection, standing, uproar
τῶν art. gen. masc. pl. ὁ ἡ τό the, this, that, he, she, it
Φαρισαίων n. gen. masc. pl. Φαρισαῖος Pharisee
καὶ conj. καί and, even, also, but
τῶν art. gen. masc. pl. ὁ ἡ τό the, this, that, he, she, it
Σαδδουκαίων n. gen. masc. pl. Σαδδουκαῖος Sadducee
καὶ conj. καί and, even, also, but
τὸ art. nom. neut. sg. ὁ ἡ τό the, this, that, he, she, it
πλῆθος n. nom. neut. sg. πλῆθος multitude, bundle, company
8 Σαδδουκαῖοι n. nom. masc. pl. Σαδδουκαῖος Sadducee
μέν conj. μέν indeed, verily, truly, even, so, some
γὰρ conj. γάρ for, and, because, but, indeed
μὴ particle of negation. μή not, no, lest, neither, none, nothing, nor, never, without
ἀνάστασιν n. acc. fem. sg. ἀνάστασις resurrection, rising again
μηδὲ conj. μηδέ neither, nor, not, no not, nor yet, not once, not so much as

ἄγγελον n. acc. masc. sg. ἄγγελος angel, messenger
μήτε conj. μήτε neither, nor, so much as, or
πνεῦμα n. acc. neut. sg. πνεῦμα spirit, Spirit, Ghost, ghost, life. of the spirit, wind
Φαρισαῖοι n. nom. masc. pl. Φαρισαῖος Pharisee
δὲ conj. δέ but, and, now, also, to the contrary, rather, then
τὰ art. acc. neut. pl. ὁ ἡ τό the, this, that, he, she, it
ἀμφότερα adj. acc. neut. pl. ἀμφότερος both
9 δὲ conj. δέ but, and, now, also, to the contrary, rather, then
κραυγὴ n. nom. fem. sg. κραυγή cry, crying, clamour
μεγάλη adj. nom. fem. sg. μέγας great, loud, greatest, high, large, mighty, strong
καὶ conj. καί and, even, also, but
οἱ art. nom. masc. pl. ὁ ἡ τό the, this, that, he, she, it
γραμματεῖς n. nom. masc. pl. γραμματεύς scribe, townclerk
τοῦ art. gen. neut. sg. ὁ ἡ τό the, this, that, he, she, it
μέρους n. gen. neut. sg. μέρος part, coast, portion, behalf, respect, piece, side
τῶν art. gen. masc. pl. ὁ ἡ τό the, this, that, he, she, it
Φαρισαίων n. gen. masc. pl. Φαρισαῖος Pharisee
Οὐδὲν num. acc. neut. sg. οὐδείς no man, nothing, no, none, neither, not, nought
κακὸν adj. acc. neut. sg. κακός evil, evil thing, noisome, wicked
ἐν prep. ἐν (+dat) in, by, with, among, at, on, through, to, within, into, of, for
τῷ art. dat. masc. sg. ὁ ἡ τό the, this, that, he, she, it
ἀνθρώπῳ n. dat. masc. sg. ἄνθρωπος man, human being, person, one, certain
τούτῳ demo. pron. dat. masc. sg. οὗτος αὕτη τοῦτο this, the same, this same, he, she, it
εἰ conj. εἰ if, whether, that, though, forasmuch
δὲ conj. δέ but, and, now, also, to the contrary, rather, then
πνεῦμα n. nom. neut. sg. πνεῦμα spirit, Spirit, Ghost, ghost, life. of the spirit, wind
αὐτῷ pron. dat. masc. 3p. sg. αὐτός ἡ ὁ self, of oneself, even, very, the same, he, she, it
ἢ particle. ἤ or, than, either, nor, or else, and, rather than
ἄγγελος n. nom. masc. sg. ἄγγελος angel, messenger
μὴ particle of negation. μή not, no, lest, neither, none, nothing, nor, never, without
10 Πολλῆς adj. gen. fem. sg. πολύς many, great, much, long, abundant
δὲ conj. δέ but, and, now, also, to the contrary, rather, then
στάσεως n. gen. fem. sg. στάσις dissension, sedition, insurrection, standing, uproar
ὁ art. nom. masc. sg. ὁ ἡ τό the, this, that, he, she, it
χιλίαρχος n. nom. masc. sg. χιλίαρχος high captain, chief captain, captain
μὴ particle of negation. μή not, no, lest, neither, none, nothing, nor, never, without
ὁ art. nom. masc. sg. ὁ ἡ τό the, this, that, he, she, it
Παῦλος n. nom. masc. sg. Παῦλος Paul, Paulus
ὑπ' prep. ὑπό (+gen) of, by, with, from, among, (+acc) under
αὐτῶν pron. gen. masc. 3p. pl. αὐτός ἡ ὁ self, of oneself, even, very, the same, he, she, it
τὸ art. acc. neut. sg. ὁ ἡ τό the, this, that, he, she, it
στράτευμα n. acc. neut. sg. στράτευμα army, man of war, soldier
αὐτὸν pron. acc. masc. 3p. sg. αὐτός ἡ ὁ self, of oneself, even, very, the same, he, she, it
ἐκ prep. ἐκ ἐξ (+gen) of, from, out of, by, on, with, in, among, through
μέσου adj. gen. neut. sg. μέσος midst, among, mid, between
αὐτῶν pron. gen. masc. 3p. pl. αὐτός ἡ ὁ self, of oneself, even, very, the same, he, she, it
τε conj. τέ and, both, also
εἰς prep. εἰς (+acc) into, to, unto, for, in, on, toward, against, upon, at, among
τὴν art. acc. fem. sg. ὁ ἡ τό the, this, that, he, she, it
παρεμβολήν n. acc. fem. sg. παρεμβολή castle, camp, army
11 Τῇ art. dat. fem. sg. ὁ ἡ τό the, this, that, he, she, it
δὲ conj. δέ but, and, now, also, to the contrary, rather, then
νυκτὶ n. dat. fem. sg. νύξ night
αὐτῷ pron. dat. masc. 3p. sg. αὐτός ἡ ὁ self, of oneself, even, very, the same, he, she, it
ὁ art. nom. masc. sg. ὁ ἡ τό the, this, that, he, she, it

Κύριος n. nom. masc. sg. κύριος Lord, lord, master, sir, LORD, God, Master, owner
Παῦλε n. voc. masc. sg. Παῦλος Paul, Paulus
ὡς adv. ὡς as, when, as it were, how, about, like, as soon as, even as, while
γὰρ conj. γάρ for, and, because, but, indeed
τὰ art. acc. neut. pl. ὁ ἡ τό the, this, that, he, she, it
περὶ prep. περί (+gen) of, for, concerning, (+acc) about, concerning, in
ἐμοῦ pron. gen. 1p. sg. ἐγώ I
εἰς prep. εἰς (+acc) into, to, unto, for, in, on, toward, against, upon, at, among
Ἰερουσαλὴμ pron. name. fem. inde. Ἰερουσαλήμ Jerusalem
οὕτω adv. οὕτω οὕτως so, even so, thus, on this wise, likewise, after this manner
σε pron. acc. 2p. sg. σύ thou, you
καὶ conj. καί and, even, also, but
εἰς prep. εἰς (+acc) into, to, unto, for, in, on, toward, against, upon, at, among
Ῥώμην n. acc. fem. sg. Ῥώμη Rome
12 δὲ conj. δέ but, and, now, also, to the contrary, rather, then
ἡμέρας n. gen. fem. sg. ἡμέρα day, time, year, while, age, day time
τινες indefinite pron. nom. masc. pl. τὶς certain, some, any man, one, any thing
τῶν art. gen. masc. pl. ὁ ἡ τό the, this, that, he, she, it
Ἰουδαίων adj. gen. masc. pl. Ἰουδαῖος Jew, Jewess
συστροφὴν n. acc. fem. sg. συστροφή concourse, band together, combination
ἑαυτοὺς reflexive pron. acc. masc. 3p. pl. ἑαυτοῦ himself, herself, itself, yourself, ourselves
μήτε conj. μήτε neither, nor, so much as, or
ἕως conj. ἕως till, until, unto, until when, while, as far as, even, until now
οὗ relative pron. gen. masc. sg. ὅς ἥ ὅ who, which, what, that
τὸν art. acc. masc. sg. ὁ ἡ τό the, this, that, he, she, it
Παῦλον n. acc. masc. sg. Παῦλος Paul, Paulus
13 δὲ conj. δέ but, and, now, also, to the contrary, rather, then
πλείους compar. adj. nom. masc. pl. πλείων more, many, greater, further, more part
τεσσαράκοντα num. gen. masc. pl. τεσσαράκοντα forty
οἱ art. nom. masc. pl. ὁ ἡ τό the, this, that, he, she, it
ταύτην demo. pron. acc. fem. sg. οὗτος αὕτη τοῦτο this, the same, this same, he, she, it
τὴν art. acc. fem. sg. ὁ ἡ τό the, this, that, he, she, it
συνωμοσίαν n. acc. fem. sg. συνωμοσία conspiracy
14 οἵτινες relative pron. nom. masc. pl. ὅστις which, who, whosoever, that, whatsoever
τοῖς art. dat. masc. pl. ὁ ἡ τό the, this, that, he, she, it
ἀρχιερεῦσιν n. dat. masc. pl. ἀρχιερεύς chief priest, high priest
καὶ conj. καί and, even, also, but
τοῖς art. dat. masc. pl. ὁ ἡ τό the, this, that, he, she, it
πρεσβυτέροις adj. dat. masc. pl. πρεσβύτερος elder, elder woman, eldest, old man
Ἀναθέματι n. dat. neut. sg. ἀνάθεμα accursed, Anathema, great course
ἑαυτοὺς reflexive pron. acc. masc. 3p. pl. ἑαυτοῦ himself, herself, itself, yourself, ourselves
μηδενὸς num. gen. neut. sg. μηδείς μηδεμία μηδέν no man, nothing, no, none, not at all
ἕως conj. ἕως till, until, unto, until when, while, as far as, even, until now
οὗ relative pron. gen. masc. sg. ὅς ἥ ὅ who, which, what, that
τὸν art. acc. masc. sg. ὁ ἡ τό the, this, that, he, she, it
Παῦλον n. acc. masc. sg. Παῦλος Paul, Paulus
15 νῦν adv. νῦν now, henceforth, present, this time
οὖν conj. οὖν therefore, then, so, and, now, wherefore
ὑμεῖς pron. nom. 2p. pl. σύ thou, you
τῷ art. dat. masc. sg. ὁ ἡ τό the, this, that, he, she, it
χιλιάρχῳ n. dat. masc. sg. χιλίαρχος high captain, chief captain, captain
σὺν prep. σύν (+dat) with, beside
τῷ art. dat. neut. sg. ὁ ἡ τό the, this, that, he, she, it
συνεδρίῳ n. dat. neut. sg. συνέδριον council
ὅπως adv. ὅπως that, how, to, because, so that, when

αὔριον adv. αὔριον tomorrow, morrow, next day
αὐτὸν pron. acc. masc. 3p. sg. αὐτός ή ό self, of oneself, even, very, the same, he, she, it
πρὸς prep. πρός (+gen) for, (+dat) at, (+acc) unto, to, with, for, against
ὑμᾶς pron. acc. 2p. pl. σύ thou, you
ὡς adv. ὡς as, when, as it were, how, about, like, as soon as, even as, while
ἀκριβέστερον compar. adv. ἀκριβέστερον more perfectly, more perfect
τὰ art. acc. neut. pl. ὁ ἡ τό the, this, that, he, she, it
περὶ prep. περί (+gen) of, for, concerning, (+acc) about, concerning, in
αὐτοῦ pron. gen. masc. 3p. sg. αὐτός ή ό self, of oneself, even, very, the same, he, she, it
ἡμεῖς pron. nom. 1p. pl. ἐγώ I
δὲ conj. δέ but, and, now, also, to the contrary, rather, then
πρὸ prep. πρό (+gen) before, above
τοῦ art. gen. neut. sg. ὁ ἡ τό the, this, that, he, she, it
αὐτὸν pron. acc. masc. 3p. sg. αὐτός ή ό self, of oneself, even, very, the same, he, she, it
ἕτοιμοί adj. nom. masc. pl. ἕτοιμος ready, prepared, readiness
τοῦ art. gen. neut. sg. ὁ ἡ τό the, this, that, he, she, it
αὐτὸν pron. acc. masc. 3p. sg. αὐτός ή ό self, of oneself, even, very, the same, he, she, it
16 δὲ conj. δέ but, and, now, also, to the contrary, rather, then
ὁ art. nom. masc. sg. ὁ ἡ τό the, this, that, he, she, it
υἱὸς n. nom. masc. sg. υἱός son, child, descendant, offspring, heir
τῆς art. gen. fem. sg. ὁ ἡ τό the, this, that, he, she, it
ἀδελφῆς n. gen. fem. sg. ἀδελφή sister
Παύλου n. gen. masc. sg. Παῦλος Paul, Paulus
τὴν art. acc. fem. sg. ὁ ἡ τό the, this, that, he, she, it
ἐνέδραν n. acc. fem. sg. ἐνέδρα lying in wait
καὶ conj. καί and, even, also, but
εἰς prep. εἰς (+acc) into, to, unto, for, in, on, toward, against, upon, at, among
τὴν art. acc. fem. sg. ὁ ἡ τό the, this, that, he, she, it
παρεμβολὴν n. acc. fem. sg. παρεμβολή castle, camp, army
τῷ art. dat. masc. sg. ὁ ἡ τό the, this, that, he, she, it
Παύλῳ n. dat. masc. sg. Παῦλος Paul, Paulus
17 δὲ conj. δέ but, and, now, also, to the contrary, rather, then
ὁ art. nom. masc. sg. ὁ ἡ τό the, this, that, he, she, it
Παῦλος n. nom. masc. sg. Παῦλος Paul, Paulus
ἕνα num. acc. masc. sg. εἷς or ἕν one, other, some, any, only, a certain
τῶν art. gen. masc. pl. ὁ ἡ τό the, this, that, he, she, it
ἑκατονταρχῶν n. gen. masc. pl. ἑκατοντάρχης centurion
Τὸν art. acc. masc. sg. ὁ ἡ τό the, this, that, he, she, it
νεανίαν n. acc. masc. sg. νεανίας young man
τοῦτον demo. pron. acc. masc. sg. οὗτος αὕτη τοῦτο this, the same, this same, he, she, it
πρὸς prep. πρός (+gen) for, (+dat) at, (+acc) unto, to, with, for, against
τὸν art. acc. masc. sg. ὁ ἡ τό the, this, that, he, she, it
χιλίαρχον n. acc. masc. sg. χιλίαρχος high captain, chief captain, captain
γὰρ conj. γάρ for, and, because, but, indeed
τι indefinite pron. acc. neut. sg. τὶς certain, some, any man, one, any thing
αὐτῷ pron. dat. masc. 3p. sg. αὐτός ή ό self, of oneself, even, very, the same, he, she, it
18 ὁ art. nom. masc. sg. ὁ ἡ τό the, this, that, he, she, it
μὲν conj. μέν indeed, verily, truly, even, so, some
οὖν conj. οὖν therefore, then, so, and, now, wherefore
αὐτὸν pron. acc. masc. 3p. sg. αὐτός ή ό self, of oneself, even, very, the same, he, she, it
πρὸς prep. πρός (+gen) for, (+dat) at, (+acc) unto, to, with, for, against
τὸν art. acc. masc. sg. ὁ ἡ τό the, this, that, he, she, it
χιλίαρχον n. acc. masc. sg. χιλίαρχος high captain, chief captain, captain
καὶ conj. καί and, even, also, but
Ὁ art. nom. masc. sg. ὁ ἡ τό the, this, that, he, she, it

δέσμιος n. nom. masc. sg. δέσμιος prisoner, in bonds, that is in bond
Παῦλος n. nom. masc. sg. Παῦλος Paul, Paulus
με pron. acc. 1p. sg. ἐγώ I
τοῦτον demo. pron. acc. masc. sg. οὗτος αὕτη τοῦτο this, the same, this same, he, she, it
τὸν art. acc. masc. sg. ὁ ἡ τό the, this, that, he, she, it
νεανίαν n. acc. masc. sg. νεανίας young man
πρὸς prep. πρός (+gen) for, (+dat) at, (+acc) unto, to, with, for, against
σὲ pron. acc. 2p. sg. σύ thou, you
τι indefinite pron. acc. neut. sg. τὶς certain, some, any man, one, any thing
σοι pron. dat. 2p. sg. σύ thou, you
19 δὲ conj. δέ but, and, now, also, to the contrary, rather, then
τῆς art. gen. fem. sg. ὁ ἡ τό the, this, that, he, she, it
χειρὸς n. gen. fem. sg. χείρ hand
αὐτοῦ pron. gen. masc. 3p. sg. αὐτός ή ό self, of oneself, even, very, the same, he, she, it
ὁ art. nom. masc. sg. ὁ ἡ τό the, this, that, he, she, it
χιλίαρχος n. nom. masc. sg. χιλίαρχος high captain, chief captain, captain
καὶ conj. καί and, even, also, but
κατ' prep. κατά (+gen) against, by, throughout, down, (+acc) according to, after, with
ἰδίαν adj. acc. fem. sg. ἴδιος one's own, one's, privately
Τί interrog. pron. nom. neut. sg. τίς what, who, why, where, which, how
ὃ relative pron. acc. neut. sg. ὅς ἥ ὅ who, which, what, that
μοι pron. dat. 1p. sg. ἐγώ I
20 δὲ conj. δέ but, and, now, also, to the contrary, rather, then
ὅτι conj. ὅτι that, for, because, how that, how, because that, for that, though
Οἱ art. nom. masc. pl. ὁ ἡ τό the, this, that, he, she, it
Ἰουδαῖοι adj. nom. masc. pl. Ἰουδαῖος Jew, Jewess
τοῦ art. gen. neut. sg. ὁ ἡ τό the, this, that, he, she, it
σε pron. acc. 2p. sg. σύ thou, you
ὅπως adv. ὅπως that, how, to, because, so that, when
αὔριον adv. αὔριον tomorrow, morrow, next day
εἰς prep. εἰς (+acc) into, to, unto, for, in, on, toward, against, upon, at, among
τὸ art. acc. neut. sg. ὁ ἡ τό the, this, that, he, she, it
συνέδριον n. acc. neut. sg. συνέδριον council
τὸν art. acc. masc. sg. ὁ ἡ τό the, this, that, he, she, it
Παῦλον n. acc. masc. sg. Παῦλος Paul, Paulus
ὡς adv. ὡς as, when, as it were, how, about, like, as soon as, even as, while
τι indefinite pron. acc. neut. sg. τὶς certain, some, any man, one, any thing
ἀκριβέστερον compar. adj. acc. neut. sg. ἀκριβέστερον more perfectly, more perfect
περὶ prep. περί (+gen) of, for, concerning, (+acc) about, concerning, in
αὐτοῦ pron. gen. masc. 3p. sg. αὐτός ή ό self, of oneself, even, very, the same, he, she, it
21 σὺ pron. nom. 2p. sg. σύ thou, you
οὖν conj. οὖν therefore, then, so, and, now, wherefore
μὴ particle of negation. μή not, no, lest, neither, none, nothing, nor, never, without
αὐτοῖς pron. dat. masc. 3p. pl. αὐτός ή ό self, of oneself, even, very, the same, he, she, it
γὰρ conj. γάρ for, and, because, but, indeed
αὐτὸν pron. acc. masc. 3p. sg. αὐτός ή ό self, of oneself, even, very, the same, he, she, it
ἐξ prep. ἐκ ἐξ (+gen) of, from, out of, by, on, with, in, among, through
αὐτῶν pron. gen. masc. 3p. pl. αὐτός ή ό self, of oneself, even, very, the same, he, she, it
ἄνδρες n. nom. masc. pl. ἀνήρ man, husband, sir
πλείους compar. adj. nom. masc. pl. πλείων more, many, greater, further, more part
τεσσαράκοντα num. gen. masc. pl. τεσσαράκοντα forty
οἵτινες relative pron. nom. masc. pl. ὅστις which, who, whosoever, that, whatsoever
ἑαυτοὺς reflexive pron. acc. masc. 3p. pl. ἑαυτοῦ himself, herself, itself, yourself, ourselves
μήτε conj. μήτε neither, nor, so much as, or
ἕως conj. ἕως till, until, unto, until when, while, as far as, even, until now

οὗ relative pron. gen. masc. sg. ὅς ἥ ὅ who, which, what, that
αὐτὸν pron. acc. masc. 3p. sg. αὐτός ἡ ὁ self, of oneself, even, very, the same, he, she, it
καὶ conj. καί and, even, also, but
νῦν adv. νῦν now, henceforth, present, this time
ἕτοιμοι adj. nom. masc. pl. ἕτοιμος ready, prepared, readiness
τὴν art. acc. fem. sg. ὁ ἡ τό the, this, that, he, she, it
ἀπὸ prep. ἀπό (+gen) from, of, out of, since, for, off, at, by, in, on
σοῦ pron. gen. 2p. sg. σύ thou, you
ἐπαγγελίαν n. acc. fem. sg. ἐπαγγελία promise, message
22 ὁ art. nom. masc. sg. ὁ ἡ τό the, this, that, he, she, it
μέν conj. μέν indeed, verily, truly, even, so, some
οὖν conj. οὖν therefore, then, so, and, now, wherefore
χιλίαρχος n. nom. masc. sg. χιλίαρχος high captain, chief captain, captain
τὸν art. acc. masc. sg. ὁ ἡ τό the, this, that, he, she, it
νεανίαν n. acc. masc. sg. νεανίας young man
μηδενὶ num. dat. masc. sg. μηδείς μηδεμία μηδέν no man, nothing, no, none, not at all
ὅτι conj. ὅτι that, for, because, how that, how, because that, for that, though
ταῦτα demo. pron. acc. neut. pl. οὗτος αὕτη τοῦτο this, the same, this same, he, she, it
πρός prep. πρός (+gen) for, (+dat) at, (+acc) unto, to, with, for, against
με pron. acc. 1p. sg. ἐγώ I
23 καὶ conj. καί and, even, also, but
δύο num. acc. masc. pl. δύο two, twain, both
τινὰς indefinite pron. acc. masc. pl. τὶς certain, some, any man, one, any thing
τῶν art. gen. masc. pl. ὁ ἡ τό the, this, that, he, she, it
ἑκατονταρχῶν n. gen. masc. pl. ἑκατοντάρχης centurion
στρατιώτας n. acc. masc. pl. στρατιώτης soldier
διακοσίους num. acc. masc. pl. διακόσιοι two hundred
ὅπως adv. ὅπως that, how, to, because, so that, when
ἕως conj. ἕως till, until, unto, until when, while, as far as, even, until now
Καισαρείας n. gen. fem. sg. Καισάρεια Caesarea
καὶ conj. καί and, even, also, but
ἱππεῖς n. acc. masc. pl. ἱππεύς horseman
ἑβδομήκοντα num. acc. masc. pl. ἑβδομήκοντα seventy, threescore and ten
καὶ conj. καί and, even, also, but
δεξιολάβους n. acc. masc. pl. δεξιολάβος spearman
διακοσίους num. acc. masc. pl. διακόσιοι two hundred
ἀπὸ prep. ἀπό (+gen) from, of, out of, since, for, off, at, by, in, on
τρίτης ordinal. adj. gen. fem. sg. τρίτος third
ὥρας n. gen. fem. sg. ὥρα hour, time, season
τῆς art. gen. fem. sg. ὁ ἡ τό the, this, that, he, she, it
νυκτός n. gen. fem. sg. νύξ night
24 κτήνη n. acc. neut. pl. κτῆνος beast
τε conj. τέ and, both, also
ἵνα conj. ἵνα that, to, lest, for to, so that, albeit, because, for, so as
τὸν art. acc. masc. sg. ὁ ἡ τό the, this, that, he, she, it
Παῦλον n. acc. masc. sg. Παῦλος Paul, Paulus
πρὸς prep. πρός (+gen) for, (+dat) at, (+acc) unto, to, with, for, against
Φήλικα n. acc. masc. sg. Φῆλιξ Felix
τὸν art. acc. masc. sg. ὁ ἡ τό the, this, that, he, she, it
ἡγεμόνα n. acc. masc. sg. ἡγεμών governor, ruler, prince
25 ἐπιστολὴν n. acc. fem. sg. ἐπιστολή letter, epistle
τὸν art. acc. masc. sg. ὁ ἡ τό the, this, that, he, she, it
τύπον n. acc. masc. sg. τύπος ensample, example, pattern, print, figure, fashion
τοῦτον demo. pron. acc. masc. sg. οὗτος αὕτη τοῦτο this, the same, this same, he, she, it
26 Κλαύδιος n. nom. masc. sg. Κλαύδιος Claudius

Λυσίας n. nom. masc. sg. Λυσίας Lysias
τῷ art. dat. masc. sg. ὁ ἡ τό the, this, that, he, she, it
κρατίστῳ superl. adj. dat. masc. sg. κράτιστος most excellent, most noble
ἡγεμόνι n. dat. masc. sg. ἡγεμών governor, ruler, prince
Φήλικι n. dat. masc. sg. Φῆλιξ Felix
27 τὸν art. acc. masc. sg. ὁ ἡ τό the, this, that, he, she, it
ἄνδρα n. acc. masc. sg. ἀνήρ man, husband, sir
τοῦτον demo. pron. acc. masc. sg. οὗτος αὕτη τοῦτο this, the same, this same, he, she, it
ὑπὸ prep. ὑπό (+gen) of, by, with, from, among, (+acc) under
τῶν art. gen. masc. pl. ὁ ἡ τό the, this, that, he, she, it
Ἰουδαίων adj. gen. masc. pl. Ἰουδαῖος Jew, Jewess
καὶ conj. καί and, even, also, but
ὑπ' prep. ὑπό (+gen) of, by, with, from, among, (+acc) under
αὐτῶν pron. gen. masc. 3p. pl. αὐτός ἡ ὁ self, of oneself, even, very, the same, he, she, it
σὺν prep. σύν (+dat) with, beside
τῷ art. dat. neut. sg. ὁ ἡ τό the, this, that, he, she, it
στρατεύματι n. dat. neut. sg. στράτευμα army, man of war, soldier
αὐτὸν pron. acc. masc. 3p. sg. αὐτός ἡ ὁ self, of oneself, even, very, the same, he, she, it
ὅτι conj. ὅτι that, for, because, how that, how, because that, for that, though
Ῥωμαῖός adj. nom. masc. sg. Ῥωμαῖος Roman, Rome
28 δὲ conj. δέ but, and, now, also, to the contrary, rather, then
τὴν art. acc. fem. sg. ὁ ἡ τό the, this, that, he, she, it
αἰτίαν n. acc. fem. sg. αἰτία cause, reason, accusation, fault
δι' prep. διά (+gen) by, through, with, in, of, (+acc) for, because of, for a cause
ἣν relative pron. acc. fem. sg. ὅς ἥ ὅ who, which, what, that
αὐτῷ pron. dat. masc. 3p. sg. αὐτός ἡ ὁ self, of oneself, even, very, the same, he, she, it
αὐτὸν pron. acc. masc. 3p. sg. αὐτός ἡ ὁ self, of oneself, even, very, the same, he, she, it
εἰς prep. εἰς (+acc) into, to, unto, for, in, on, toward, against, upon, at, among
τὸ art. acc. neut. sg. ὁ ἡ τό the, this, that, he, she, it
συνέδριον n. acc. neut. sg. συνέδριον council
αὐτῶν pron. gen. masc. 3p. pl. αὐτός ἡ ὁ self, of oneself, even, very, the same, he, she, it
29 ὃν relative pron. acc. masc. sg. ὅς ἥ ὅ who, which, what, that
περὶ prep. περί (+gen) of, for, concerning, (+acc) about, concerning, in
ζητημάτων n. gen. neut. pl. ζήτημα question
τοῦ art. gen. masc. sg. ὁ ἡ τό the, this, that, he, she, it
νόμου n. gen. masc. sg. νόμος law, the law
αὐτῶν pron. gen. masc. 3p. pl. αὐτός ἡ ὁ self, of oneself, even, very, the same, he, she, it
μηδὲν num. acc. neut. sg. μηδείς μηδεμία μηδέν no man, nothing, no, none, not at all
δὲ conj. δέ but, and, now, also, to the contrary, rather, then
ἄξιον adj. acc. neut. sg. ἄξιος worthy, meet, due reward
θανάτου n. gen. masc. sg. θάνατος death
ἢ particle. ἤ or, than, either, nor, or else, and, rather than
δεσμῶν n. gen. masc. pl. δεσμός bond, band, chain, string
ἔγκλημα n. acc. neut. sg. ἔγκλημα lay to charge, crime laid against
30 δέ conj. δέ but, and, now, also, to the contrary, rather, then
μοι pron. dat. 1p. sg. ἐγώ I
ἐπιβουλῆς n. gen. fem. sg. ἐπιβουλή laying await, lying in wait
εἰς prep. εἰς (+acc) into, to, unto, for, in, on, toward, against, upon, at, among
τὸν art. acc. masc. sg. ὁ ἡ τό the, this, that, he, she, it
ἄνδρα n. acc. masc. sg. ἀνήρ man, husband, sir
ὑπὸ prep. ὑπό (+gen) of, by, with, from, among, (+acc) under
τῶν art. gen. masc. pl. ὁ ἡ τό the, this, that, he, she, it
Ἰουδαίων adj. gen. masc. pl. Ἰουδαῖος Jew, Jewess
ἐξαυτῆς adv. ἐξαυτῆς immediately, by and by, presently, straightway
πρὸς prep. πρός (+gen) for, (+dat) at, (+acc) unto, to, with, for, against

σὲ pron. acc. 2p. sg. σύ thou, you
καὶ conj. καί and, even, also, but
τοῖς art. dat. masc. pl. ὁ ἡ τό the, this, that, he, she, it
κατηγόροις n. dat. masc. pl. κατήγορος accuser
τὰ art. acc. neut. pl. ὁ ἡ τό the, this, that, he, she, it
πρὸς prep. πρός (+gen) for, (+dat) at, (+acc) unto, to, with, for, against
αὐτὸν pron. acc. masc. 3p. sg. αὐτός ἡ ὁ self, of oneself, even, very, the same, he, she, it
ἐπὶ prep. ἐπί (+gen) on, in, upon, (+dat) in, at, for, upon, (+acc) on, upon, unto, to, against
σοῦ pron. gen. 2p. sg. σύ thou, you
31 Οἱ art. nom. masc. pl. ὁ ἡ τό the, this, that, he, she, it
μὲν conj. μέν indeed, verily, truly, even, so, some
οὖν conj. οὖν therefore, then, so, and, now, wherefore
στρατιῶται n. nom. masc. pl. στρατιώτης soldier
κατὰ prep. κατά (+gen) against, by, throughout, down, (+acc) according to, after, with
τὸ art. acc. neut. sg. ὁ ἡ τό the, this, that, he, she, it
αὐτοῖς pron. dat. masc. 3p. pl. αὐτός ἡ ὁ self, of oneself, even, very, the same, he, she, it
τὸν art. acc. masc. sg. ὁ ἡ τό the, this, that, he, she, it
Παῦλον n. acc. masc. sg. Παῦλος Paul, Paulus
διὰ prep. διά (+gen) by, through, with, in, of, (+acc) for, because of, for a cause
τῆς art. gen. fem. sg. ὁ ἡ τό the, this, that, he, she, it
νυκτὸς n. gen. fem. sg. νύξ night
εἰς prep. εἰς (+acc) into, to, unto, for, in, on, toward, against, upon, at, among
τὴν art. acc. fem. sg. ὁ ἡ τό the, this, that, he, she, it
Ἀντιπατρίδα n. acc. fem. sg. Ἀντιπατρίς Antipatris
32 τῇ art. dat. fem. sg. ὁ ἡ τό the, this, that, he, she, it
δὲ conj. δέ but, and, now, also, to the contrary, rather, then
ἐπαύριον adv. ἐπαύριον next day, morrow, day following, nest day after
τοὺς art. acc. masc. pl. ὁ ἡ τό the, this, that, he, she, it
ἱππεῖς n. acc. masc. pl. ἱππεύς horseman
σὺν prep. σύν (+dat) with, beside
αὐτῷ pron. dat. masc. 3p. sg. αὐτός ἡ ὁ self, of oneself, even, very, the same, he, she, it
εἰς prep. εἰς (+acc) into, to, unto, for, in, on, toward, against, upon, at, among
τὴν art. acc. fem. sg. ὁ ἡ τό the, this, that, he, she, it
παρεμβολήν n. acc. fem. sg. παρεμβολή castle, camp, army
33 οἵτινες relative pron. nom. masc. pl. ὅστις which, who, whosoever, that, whatsoever
εἰς prep. εἰς (+acc) into, to, unto, for, in, on, toward, against, upon, at, among
τὴν art. acc. fem. sg. ὁ ἡ τό the, this, that, he, she, it
Καισάρειαν n. acc. fem. sg. Καισάρεια Caesarea
καὶ conj. καί and, even, also, but
τὴν art. acc. fem. sg. ὁ ἡ τό the, this, that, he, she, it
ἐπιστολὴν n. acc. fem. sg. ἐπιστολή letter, epistle
τῷ art. dat. masc. sg. ὁ ἡ τό the, this, that, he, she, it
ἡγεμόνι n. dat. masc. sg. ἡγεμών governor, ruler, prince
καὶ conj. καί and, even, also, but
τὸν art. acc. masc. sg. ὁ ἡ τό the, this, that, he, she, it
Παῦλον n. acc. masc. sg. Παῦλος Paul, Paulus
αὐτῷ pron. dat. masc. 3p. sg. αὐτός ἡ ὁ self, of oneself, even, very, the same, he, she, it
34 δὲ conj. δέ but, and, now, also, to the contrary, rather, then
ὁ art. nom. masc. sg. ὁ ἡ τό the, this, that, he, she, it
ἡγεμών n. nom. masc. sg. ἡγεμών governor, ruler, prince
καὶ conj. καί and, even, also, but
ἐκ prep. ἐκ ἐξ (+gen) of, from, out of, by, on, with, in, among, through
ποίας interrog. pron. gen. fem. sg. ποῖος what, which, what manner of
ἐπαρχείας n. gen. fem. sg. ἐπαρχία province
καὶ conj. καί and, even, also, but

ὅτι conj. ὅτι that, for, because, how that, how, because that, for that, though
ἀπὸ prep. ἀπό (+gen) from, of, out of, since, for, off, at, by, in, on
Κιλικίας n. gen. fem. sg. Κιλικία Cilicia
35 σου pron. gen. 2p. sg. σύ thou, you
ὅταν conj. ὅταν when, as soon as, as long as, that, whensoever, while
καὶ conj. καί and, even, also, but
οἱ art. nom. masc. pl. ὁ ἡ τό the, this, that, he, she, it
κατήγοροί n. nom. masc. pl. κατήγορος accuser
σου pron. gen. 2p. sg. σύ thou, you
τε conj. τέ and, both, also
αὐτὸν pron. acc. masc. 3p. sg. αὐτός ή ό self, of oneself, even, very, the same, he, she, it
ἐν prep. ἐν (+dat) in, by, with, among, at, on, through, to, within, into, of, for
τῷ art. dat. neut. sg. ὁ ἡ τό the, this, that, he, she, it
πραιτωρίῳ n. dat. neut. sg. πραιτώριον judgement hall, common hall, palace, Praetorium
τοῦ art. gen. masc. sg. ὁ ἡ τό the, this, that, he, she, it
Ἡρώδου n. gen. masc. sg. Ἡρῴδης Herod

24

1 Μετὰ prep. μετά (+gen) with, among, against, (+acc) after
δὲ conj. δέ but, and, now, also, to the contrary, rather, then
πέντε num. acc. fem. pl. πέντε five
ἡμέρας n. acc. fem. pl. ἡμέρα day, time, year, while, age, day time
ὁ art. nom. masc. sg. ὁ ἡ τό the, this, that, he, she, it
ἀρχιερεὺς n. nom. masc. sg. ἀρχιερεύς chief priest, high priest
Ἀνανίας n. nom. masc. sg. Ἀνανίας Ananias
μετὰ prep. μετά (+gen) with, among, against, (+acc) after
τῶν art. gen. masc. pl. ὁ ἡ τό the, this, that, he, she, it
πρεσβυτέρων adj. gen. masc. pl. πρεσβύτερος elder, elder woman, eldest, old man
καὶ conj. καί and, even, also, but
ῥήτορος n. gen. masc. sg. ῥήτωρ orator
Τερτύλλου n. gen. masc. sg. Τέρτυλλος Tertullus
τινός indefinite pron. gen. masc. sg. τὶς certain, some, any man, one, any thing
οἵτινες relative pron. nom. masc. pl. ὅστις which, who, whosoever, that, whatsoever
τῷ art. dat. masc. sg. ὁ ἡ τό the, this, that, he, she, it
ἡγεμόνι n. dat. masc. sg. ἡγεμών governor, ruler, prince
κατὰ prep. κατά (+gen) against, by, throughout, down, (+acc) according to, after, with
τοῦ art. gen. masc. sg. ὁ ἡ τό the, this, that, he, she, it
Παύλου n. gen. masc. sg. Παῦλος Paul, Paulus
2 δὲ conj. δέ but, and, now, also, to the contrary, rather, then
αὐτοῦ pron. gen. masc. 3p. sg. αὐτός ή ό self, of oneself, even, very, the same, he, she, it
ὁ art. nom. masc. sg. ὁ ἡ τό the, this, that, he, she, it
Τέρτυλλος n. nom. masc. sg. Τέρτυλλος Tertullus
Πολλῆς adj. gen. fem. sg. πολύς many, great, much, long, abundant
εἰρήνης n. gen. fem. sg. εἰρήνη peace, quietness, rest
διὰ prep. διά (+gen) by, through, with, in, of, (+acc) for, because of, for a cause
σοῦ pron. gen. 2p. sg. σύ thou, you
καὶ conj. καί and, even, also, but
κατορθωμάτων n. gen. neut. pl. κατόρθωμα very worthy deed
τῷ art. dat. neut. sg. ὁ ἡ τό the, this, that, he, she, it
ἔθνει n. dat. neut. sg. ἔθνος Gentile, nation, heathen, people
τούτῳ demo. pron. dat. neut. sg. οὗτος αὕτη τοῦτο this, the same, this same, he, she, it
διὰ prep. διά (+gen) by, through, with, in, of, (+acc) for, because of, for a cause
τῆς art. gen. fem. sg. ὁ ἡ τό the, this, that, he, she, it
σῆς poss. pron. gen. fem. 2p. sg. σός thy, thine, thine own

προνοίας n. gen. fem. sg. πρόνοια providence, provision for
3 πάντῃ adv. πάντῃ always
τε conj. τέ and, both, also
καὶ conj. καί and, even, also, but
πανταχοῦ adv. πανταχοῦ every where, in all places
κράτιστε superl. adj. voc. masc. sg. κράτιστος most excellent, most noble
Φῆλιξ n. voc. masc. sg. Φῆλιξ Felix
μετὰ prep. μετά (+gen) with, among, against, (+acc) after
πάσης adj. gen. fem. sg. πᾶς πᾶσα πᾶν all, every, whosoever, every one, no, whole, any
εὐχαριστίας n. gen. fem. sg. εὐχαριστία thankfulness, thanksgiving, giving of thanks
4 ἵνα conj. ἵνα that, to, lest, for to, so that, albeit, because, for, so as
δὲ conj. δέ but, and, now, also, to the contrary, rather, then
μὴ particle of negation. μή not, no, lest, neither, none, nothing, nor, never, without
ἐπὶ prep. ἐπί (+gen) on, in, upon, (+dat) in, at, for, upon, (+acc) on, upon, unto, to, against
πλεῖόν compar. adj. acc. neut. sg. πολύς many, great, much, long, abundant
σε pron. acc. 2p. sg. σύ thou, you
σε pron. acc. 2p. sg. σύ thou, you
ἡμῶν pron. gen. 1p. pl. ἐγώ I
συντόμως adv. συντόμως a few words, concisely
τῇ art. dat. fem. sg. ὁ ἡ τό the, this, that, he, she, it
σῇ poss. pron. dat. fem. 2p. sg. σός thy, thine, thine own
ἐπιεικείᾳ n. dat. fem. sg. ἐπιείκεια clemency, gentleness
5 γὰρ conj. γάρ for, and, because, but, indeed
τὸν art. acc. masc. sg. ὁ ἡ τό the, this, that, he, she, it
ἄνδρα n. acc. masc. sg. ἀνήρ man, husband, sir
τοῦτον demo. pron. acc. masc. sg. οὗτος αὕτη τοῦτο this, the same, this same, he, she, it
λοιμὸν adj. acc. masc. sg. λοιμός pestilence, plague, pestilent fellow
καὶ conj. καί and, even, also, but
στάσιν n. acc. fem. sg. στάσις dissension, sedition, insurrection, standing, uproar
πᾶσι adj. dat. masc. pl. πᾶς πᾶσα πᾶν all, every, whosoever, every one, no, whole, any
τοῖς art. dat. masc. pl. ὁ ἡ τό the, this, that, he, she, it
Ἰουδαίοις adj. dat. masc. pl. Ἰουδαῖος Jew, Jewess
τοῖς art. dat. masc. pl. ὁ ἡ τό the, this, that, he, she, it
κατὰ prep. κατά (+gen) against, by, throughout, down, (+acc) according to, after, with
τὴν art. acc. fem. sg. ὁ ἡ τό the, this, that, he, she, it
οἰκουμένην n. acc. fem. sg. οἰκουμένη world, earth
πρωτοστάτην n. acc. masc. sg. πρωτοστάτης ringleader
τε conj. τέ and, both, also
τῆς art. gen. fem. sg. ὁ ἡ τό the, this, that, he, she, it
τῶν art. gen. masc. pl. ὁ ἡ τό the, this, that, he, she, it
Ναζωραίων n. gen. masc. pl. Ναζωραῖος Nazareth, Nazarene
αἱρέσεως n. gen. fem. sg. αἵρεσις sect, heresy
6 ὃς relative pron. nom. masc. sg. ὅς ἥ ὅ who, which, what, that
καὶ conj. καί and, even, also, but
τὸ art. acc. neut. sg. ὁ ἡ τό the, this, that, he, she, it
ἱερὸν n. acc. neut. sg. ἱερόν temple
ὃν relative pron. acc. masc. sg. ὅς ἥ ὅ who, which, what, that
καὶ conj. καί and, even, also, but
καὶ conj. καί and, even, also, but
κατὰ prep. κατά (+gen) against, by, throughout, down, (+acc) according to, after, with
τὸν art. acc. masc. sg. ὁ ἡ τό the, this, that, he, she, it
ἡμέτερον poss. pron. acc. masc. 1p. sg. ἡμέτερος our
νόμον n. acc. masc. sg. νόμος law, the law
7 δὲ conj. δέ but, and, now, also, to the contrary, rather, then
Λυσίας n. nom. masc. sg. Λυσίας Lysias

ὁ art. nom. masc. sg. ὁ ἡ τό the, this, that, he, she, it
χιλίαρχος n. nom. masc. sg. χιλίαρχος high captain, chief captain, captain
μετὰ prep. μετά (+gen) with, among, against, (+acc) after
πολλῆς adj. gen. fem. sg. πολύς many, great, much, long, abundant
βίας n. gen. fem. sg. βία violence
ἐκ prep. ἐκ ἐξ (+gen) of, from, out of, by, on, with, in, among, through
τῶν art. gen. fem. pl. ὁ ἡ τό the, this, that, he, she, it
χειρῶν n. gen. fem. pl. χείρ hand
ἡμῶν pron. gen. 1p. pl. ἐγώ I
8 τοὺς art. acc. masc. pl. ὁ ἡ τό the, this, that, he, she, it
κατηγόρους n. acc. masc. pl. κατήγορος accuser
αὐτοῦ pron. gen. masc. 3p. sg. αὐτός ή ό self, of oneself, even, very, the same, he, she, it
ἐπὶ prep. ἐπί (+gen) on, in, upon, (+dat) in, at, for, upon, (+acc) on, upon, unto, to, against
σέ pron. acc. 2p. sg. σύ thou, you
παρ' prep. παρά (+gen) of, from, (+dat) with, for, (+acc) beside, at, by, above, against
οὗ relative pron. gen. masc. sg. ὅς ἥ ὅ who, which, what, that
αὐτὸς pron. nom. masc. 3p. sg. αὐτός ή ό self, of oneself, even, very, the same, he, she, it
περὶ prep. περί (+gen) of, for, concerning, (+acc) about, concerning, in
πάντων adj. gen. neut. pl. πᾶς πᾶσα πᾶν all, every, whosoever, every one, no, whole, any
τούτων demo. pron. gen. neut. pl. οὗτος αὕτη τοῦτο this, the same, this same, he, she, it
ὧν relative pron. gen. neut. pl. ὅς ἥ ὅ who, which, what, that
ἡμεῖς pron. nom. 1p. pl. ἐγώ I
αὐτοῦ pron. gen. masc. 3p. sg. αὐτός ή ό self, of oneself, even, very, the same, he, she, it
9 δὲ conj. δέ but, and, now, also, to the contrary, rather, then
καὶ conj. καί and, even, also, but
οἱ art. nom. masc. pl. ὁ ἡ τό the, this, that, he, she, it
Ἰουδαῖοι adj. nom. masc. pl. Ἰουδαῖος Jew, Jewess
ταῦτα demo. pron. acc. neut. pl. οὗτος αὕτη τοῦτο this, the same, this same, he, she, it
οὕτως adv. οὕτω οὕτως so, even so, thus, on this wise, likewise, after this manner
10 δὲ conj. δέ but, and, now, also, to the contrary, rather, then
ὁ art. nom. masc. sg. ὁ ἡ τό the, this, that, he, she, it
Παῦλος n. nom. masc. sg. Παῦλος Paul, Paulus
αὐτῷ pron. dat. masc. 3p. sg. αὐτός ή ό self, of oneself, even, very, the same, he, she, it
τοῦ art. gen. masc. sg. ὁ ἡ τό the, this, that, he, she, it
ἡγεμόνος n. gen. masc. sg. ἡγεμών governor, ruler, prince
Ἐκ prep. ἐκ ἐξ (+gen) of, from, out of, by, on, with, in, among, through
πολλῶν adj. gen. neut. pl. πολύς many, great, much, long, abundant
ἐτῶν n. gen. neut. pl. ἔτος year
σε pron. acc. 2p. sg. σύ thou, you
κριτὴν n. acc. masc. sg. κριτής judge
τῷ art. dat. neut. sg. ὁ ἡ τό the, this, that, he, she, it
ἔθνει n. dat. neut. sg. ἔθνος Gentile, nation, heathen, people
τούτῳ demo. pron. dat. neut. sg. οὗτος αὕτη τοῦτο this, the same, this same, he, she, it
εὐθυμότερον adv. εὐθυμότερον more cheerfully
τὰ art. acc. neut. pl. ὁ ἡ τό the, this, that, he, she, it
περὶ prep. περί (+gen) of, for, concerning, (+acc) about, concerning, in
ἐμαυτοῦ pron. gen. masc. 1p. sg. ἐμαυτοῦ myself, me
11 σου pron. gen. 2p. sg. σύ thou, you
ὅτι conj. ὅτι that, for, because, how that, how, because that, for that, though
οὐ particle of negation. οὐ οὐκ οὐχ not, no, neither, none, nay, nor, never, nothing
πλείους compar. adj. nom. fem. pl. πλείων more, many, greater, further, more part
μοι pron. dat. 1p. sg. ἐγώ I
ἡμέραι n. nom. fem. pl. ἡμέρα day, time, year, while, age, day time
ἢ particle. ἤ or, than, either, nor, or else, and, rather than
δεκαδύο num. nom. fem. pl. δεκαδύο twelve, ten and two

ἀφ' prep. ἀπό (+gen) from, of, out of, since, for, off, at, by, in, on
ἧς relative pron. gen. fem. sg. ὅς ἥ ὅ who, which, what, that
ἐν prep. ἐν (+dat) in, by, with, among, at, on, through, to, within, into, of, for
Ἰερουσαλήμ pron. name. fem. inde. Ἰερουσαλήμ Jerusalem
12 καὶ conj. καί and, even, also, but
οὔτε conj. οὔτε neither, nor, nor yet, no, none
ἐν prep. ἐν (+dat) in, by, with, among, at, on, through, to, within, into, of, for
τῷ art. dat. neut. sg. ὁ ἡ τό the, this, that, he, she, it
ἱερῷ n. dat. neut. sg. ἱερόν temple
με pron. acc. 1p. sg. ἐγώ I
πρός prep. πρός (+gen) for, (+dat) at, (+acc) unto, to, with, for, against
τινα indefinite pron. acc. masc. sg. τὶς certain, some, any man, one, any thing
ἢ particle. ἤ or, than, either, nor, or else, and, rather than
ἐπισύστασιν n. acc. fem. sg. ἐπισύστασις raising up the people, that which comes upon
ὄχλου n. gen. masc. sg. ὄχλος people, multitude, company, press, number
οὔτε conj. οὔτε neither, nor, nor yet, no, none
ἐν prep. ἐν (+dat) in, by, with, among, at, on, through, to, within, into, of, for
ταῖς art. dat. fem. pl. ὁ ἡ τό the, this, that, he, she, it
συναγωγαῖς n. dat. fem. pl. συναγωγή synagogue, assembly, congregation
οὔτε conj. οὔτε neither, nor, nor yet, no, none
κατὰ prep. κατά (+gen) against, by, throughout, down, (+acc) according to, after, with
τὴν art. acc. fem. sg. ὁ ἡ τό the, this, that, he, she, it
πόλιν n. acc. fem. sg. πόλις city
13 οὔτε conj. οὔτε neither, nor, nor yet, no, none
περὶ prep. περί (+gen) of, for, concerning, (+acc) about, concerning, in
ὧν relative pron. gen. neut. pl. ὅς ἥ ὅ who, which, what, that
νῦν adv. νῦν now, henceforth, present, this time
μου pron. gen. 1p. sg. ἐγώ I
14 δὲ conj. δέ but, and, now, also, to the contrary, rather, then
τοῦτό demo. pron. acc. neut. sg. οὗτος αὕτη τοῦτο this, the same, this same, he, she, it
σοι pron. dat. 2p. sg. σύ thou, you
ὅτι conj. ὅτι that, for, because, how that, how, because that, for that, though
κατὰ prep. κατά (+gen) against, by, throughout, down, (+acc) according to, after, with
τὴν art. acc. fem. sg. ὁ ἡ τό the, this, that, he, she, it
ὁδὸν n. acc. fem. sg. ὁδός way, journey, highway
ἣν relative pron. acc. fem. sg. ὅς ἥ ὅ who, which, what, that
αἵρεσιν n. acc. fem. sg. αἵρεσις sect, heresy
οὕτω adv. οὕτω οὕτως so, even so, thus, on this wise, likewise, after this manner
τῷ art. dat. masc. sg. ὁ ἡ τό the, this, that, he, she, it
πατρῴῳ adj. dat. masc. sg. πατρῷος of fathers
Θεῷ n. dat. masc. sg. θεός God, god
πᾶσι adj. dat. neut. pl. πᾶς πᾶσα πᾶν all, every, whosoever, every one, no, whole, any
τοῖς art. dat. neut. pl. ὁ ἡ τό the, this, that, he, she, it
κατὰ prep. κατά (+gen) against, by, throughout, down, (+acc) according to, after, with
τὸν art. acc. masc. sg. ὁ ἡ τό the, this, that, he, she, it
νόμον n. acc. masc. sg. νόμος law, the law
καὶ conj. καί and, even, also, but
τοῖς art. dat. masc. pl. ὁ ἡ τό the, this, that, he, she, it
προφήταις n. dat. masc. pl. προφήτης prophet
15 ἐλπίδα n. acc. fem. sg. ἐλπίς hope, faith
εἰς prep. εἰς (+acc) into, to, unto, for, in, on, toward, against, upon, at, among
τὸν art. acc. masc. sg. ὁ ἡ τό the, this, that, he, she, it
Θεὸν n. acc. masc. sg. θεός God, god
ἣν relative pron. acc. fem. sg. ὅς ἥ ὅ who, which, what, that
καὶ conj. καί and, even, also, but

αὐτοὶ pron. nom. masc. 3p. pl. αὐτός ἡ ὁ self, of oneself, even, very, the same, he, she, it
οὗτοι demo. pron. nom. masc. pl. οὗτος αὕτη τοῦτο this, the same, this same, he, she, it
ἀνάστασιν n. acc. fem. sg. ἀνάστασις resurrection, rising again
νεκρῶν adj. gen. masc. pl. νεκρός dead
δικαίων adj. gen. masc. pl. δίκαιος righteous, just, meet, right
τε conj. τέ and, both, also
καὶ conj. καί and, even, also, but
ἀδίκων adj. gen. masc. pl. ἄδικος unjust, unrighteous
16 ἐν prep. ἐν (+dat) in, by, with, among, at, on, through, to, within, into, of, for
τούτῳ demo. pron. dat. neut. sg. οὗτος αὕτη τοῦτο this, the same, this same, he, she, it
δὲ conj. δέ but, and, now, also, to the contrary, rather, then
αὐτὸς pron. nom. masc. 3p. sg. αὐτός ἡ ὁ self, of oneself, even, very, the same, he, she, it
ἀπρόσκοπον adj. acc. fem. sg. ἀπρόσκοπος void of offence, none offence
συνείδησιν n. acc. fem. sg. συνείδησις conscience
πρὸς prep. πρός (+gen) for, (+dat) at, (+acc) unto, to, with, for, against
τὸν art. acc. masc. sg. ὁ ἡ τό the, this, that, he, she, it
Θεὸν n. acc. masc. sg. θεός God, god
καὶ conj. καί and, even, also, but
τοὺς art. acc. masc. pl. ὁ ἡ τό the, this, that, he, she, it
ἀνθρώπους n. acc. masc. pl. ἄνθρωπος man, human being, person, one, certain
διὰ prep. διά (+gen) by, through, with, in, of, (+acc) for, because of, for a cause
παντός adj. gen. neut. sg. πᾶς πᾶσα πᾶν all, every, whosoever, every one, no, whole, any
17 δι' prep. διά (+gen) by, through, with, in, of, (+acc) for, because of, for a cause
ἐτῶν n. gen. neut. pl. ἔτος year
δὲ conj. δέ but, and, now, also, to the contrary, rather, then
πλειόνων compar. adj. gen. neut. pl. πολύς many, great, much, long, abundant
ἐλεημοσύνας n. acc. fem. pl. ἐλεημοσύνη alms, almsdeed
εἰς prep. εἰς (+acc) into, to, unto, for, in, on, toward, against, upon, at, among
τὸ art. acc. neut. sg. ὁ ἡ τό the, this, that, he, she, it
ἔθνος n. acc. neut. sg. ἔθνος Gentile, nation, heathen, people
μου pron. gen. 1p. sg. ἐγώ I
καὶ conj. καί and, even, also, but
προσφοράς n. acc. fem. pl. προσφορά offering, offering up
18 ἐν prep. ἐν (+dat) in, by, with, among, at, on, through, to, within, into, of, for
οἷς relative pron. dat. neut. pl. ὅς ἥ ὅ who, which, what, that
με pron. acc. 1p. sg. ἐγώ I
ἐν prep. ἐν (+dat) in, by, with, among, at, on, through, to, within, into, of, for
τῷ art. dat. neut. sg. ὁ ἡ τό the, this, that, he, she, it
ἱερῷ n. dat. neut. sg. ἱερόν temple
οὐ particle of negation. οὐ οὐκ οὐχ not, no, neither, none, nay, nor, never, nothing
μετὰ prep. μετά (+gen) with, among, against, (+acc) after
ὄχλου n. gen. masc. sg. ὄχλος people, multitude, company, press, number
οὐδὲ conj. οὐδέ neither, nor, not, no, not even, never, not yet
μετὰ prep. μετά (+gen) with, among, against, (+acc) after
θορύβου n. gen. masc. sg. θόρυβος tumult, uproar
τινὲς indefinite pron. nom. masc. pl. τὶς certain, some, any man, one, any thing
ἀπὸ prep. ἀπό (+gen) from, of, out of, since, for, off, at, by, in, on
τῆς art. gen. fem. sg. ὁ ἡ τό the, this, that, he, she, it
'Ασίας n. gen. fem. sg. 'Ασία Asia
'Ιουδαῖοι adj. nom. masc. pl. 'Ιουδαῖος Jew, Jewess
19 οὓς relative pron. acc. masc. pl. ὅς ἥ ὅ who, which, what, that
ἐπὶ prep. ἐπί (+gen) on, in, upon, (+dat) in, at, for, upon, (+acc) on, upon, unto, to, against
σοῦ pron. gen. 2p. sg. σύ thou, you
καὶ conj. καί and, even, also, but
εἴ conj. εἰ if, whether, that, though, forasmuch

τι indefinite pron. acc. neut. sg. τὶς certain, some, any man, one, any thing
πρὸς prep. πρός (+gen) for, (+dat) at, (+acc) unto, to, with, for, against
με pron. acc. 1p. sg. ἐγώ I
20 ἢ particle. ἤ or, than, either, nor, or else, and, rather than
αὐτοὶ pron. nom. masc. 3p. pl. αὐτός ή ό self, of oneself, even, very, the same, he, she, it
οὗτοι demo. pron. nom. masc. pl. οὗτος αὕτη τοῦτο this, the same, this same, he, she, it
εἴ conj. εἰ if, whether, that, though, forasmuch
τι interrog. pron. acc. neut. sg. τίς what, who, why, where, which, how
ἐν prep. ἐν (+dat) in, by, with, among, at, on, through, to, within, into, of, for
ἐμοὶ pron. dat. 1p. sg. ἐγώ I
ἀδίκημα n. acc. neut. sg. ἀδίκημα matter of wrong, evil doing, iniquity
μου pron. gen. 1p. sg. ἐγώ I
ἐπὶ prep. ἐπί (+gen) on, in, upon, (+dat) in, at, for, upon, (+acc) on, upon, unto, to, against
τοῦ art. gen. neut. sg. ὁ ἡ τό the, this, that, he, she, it
συνεδρίου n. gen. neut. sg. συνέδριον council
21 ἢ particle. ἤ or, than, either, nor, or else, and, rather than
περὶ prep. περί (+gen) of, for, concerning, (+acc) about, concerning, in
μιᾶς num. gen. fem. sg. εἷς or ἕν one, other, some, any, only, a certain
ταύτης demo. pron. gen. fem. sg. οὗτος αὕτη τοῦτο this, the same, this same, he, she, it
φωνῆς n. gen. fem. sg. φωνή voice, sound, noise
ἧς relative pron. gen. fem. sg. ὅς ἥ ὅ who, which, what, that
ἐν prep. ἐν (+dat) in, by, with, among, at, on, through, to, within, into, of, for
αὐτοῖς pron. dat. masc. 3p. pl. αὐτός ή ό self, of oneself, even, very, the same, he, she, it
ὅτι conj. ὅτι that, for, because, how that, how, because that, for that, though
Περὶ prep. περί (+gen) of, for, concerning, (+acc) about, concerning, in
ἀναστάσεως n. gen. fem. sg. ἀνάστασις resurrection, rising again
νεκρῶν adj. gen. masc. pl. νεκρός dead
ἐγὼ pron. nom. 1p. sg. ἐγώ I
σήμερον adv. σήμερον this day, today
ὑφ' prep. ὑπό (+gen) of, by, with, from, among, (+acc) under
ὑμῶν pron. gen. 2p. pl. σύ thou, you
22 δὲ conj. δέ but, and, now, also, to the contrary, rather, then
ταῦτα demo. pron. acc. neut. pl. οὗτος αὕτη τοῦτο this, the same, this same, he, she, it
ὁ art. nom. masc. sg. ὁ ἡ τό the, this, that, he, she, it
Φῆλιξ n. nom. masc. sg. Φῆλιξ Felix
αὐτοὺς pron. acc. masc. 3p. pl. αὐτός ή ό self, of oneself, even, very, the same, he, she, it
ἀκριβέστερον compar. adv. ἀκριβέστερον more perfectly, more perfect
τὰ art. acc. neut. pl. ὁ ἡ τό the, this, that, he, she, it
περὶ prep. περί (+gen) of, for, concerning, (+acc) about, concerning, in
τῆς art. gen. fem. sg. ὁ ἡ τό the, this, that, he, she, it
ὁδοῦ n. gen. fem. sg. ὁδός way, journey, highway
Ὅταν conj. ὅταν when, as soon as, as long as, that, whensoever, while
Λυσίας n. nom. masc. sg. Λυσίας Lysias
ὁ art. nom. masc. sg. ὁ ἡ τό the, this, that, he, she, it
χιλίαρχος n. nom. masc. sg. χιλίαρχος high captain, chief captain, captain
τὰ art. acc. neut. pl. ὁ ἡ τό the, this, that, he, she, it
καθ' prep. κατά (+gen) against, by, throughout, down, (+acc) according to, after, with
ὑμᾶς pron. acc. 2p. pl. σύ thou, you
23 τε conj. τέ and, both, also
τῷ art. dat. masc. sg. ὁ ἡ τό the, this, that, he, she, it
ἑκατοντάρχῃ n. dat. masc. sg. ἑκατοντάρχης centurion
τὸν art. acc. masc. sg. ὁ ἡ τό the, this, that, he, she, it
Παῦλον n. acc. masc. sg. Παῦλος Paul, Paulus
τε conj. τέ and, both, also
ἄνεσιν n. acc. fem. sg. ἄνεσις liberty, rest, eased

καὶ conj. καί and, even, also, but
μηδένα num. acc. masc. sg. μηδείς μηδεμία μηδέν no man, nothing, no, none, not at all
τῶν art. gen. masc. pl. ὁ ἡ τό the, this, that, he, she, it
ἰδίων adj. gen. masc. pl. ἴδιος one's own, one's, privately
αὐτοῦ pron. gen. masc. 3p. sg. αὐτός ή ό self, of oneself, even, very, the same, he, she, it
ἢ particle. ἤ or, than, either, nor, or else, and, rather than
αὐτῷ pron. dat. masc. 3p. sg. αὐτός ή ό self, of oneself, even, very, the same, he, she, it
24 Μετὰ prep. μετά (+gen) with, among, against, (+acc) after
δὲ conj. δέ but, and, now, also, to the contrary, rather, then
ἡμέρας n. acc. fem. pl. ἡμέρα day, time, year, while, age, day time
τινὰς indefinite pron. acc. fem. pl. τὶς certain, some, any man, one, any thing
ὁ art. nom. masc. sg. ὁ ἡ τό the, this, that, he, she, it
Φῆλιξ n. nom. masc. sg. Φῆλιξ Felix
σὺν prep. σύν (+dat) with, beside
Δρουσίλλῃ n. dat. fem. sg. Δρούσιλλα Drusilla
τῇ art. dat. fem. sg. ὁ ἡ τό the, this, that, he, she, it
γυναικὶ n. dat. fem. sg. γυνή woman, wife
αὐτοῦ pron. gen. masc. 3p. sg. αὐτός ή ό self, of oneself, even, very, the same, he, she, it
Ἰουδαίᾳ adj. dat. fem. sg. Ἰουδαῖος Jew, Jewess
τὸν art. acc. masc. sg. ὁ ἡ τό the, this, that, he, she, it
Παῦλον n. acc. masc. sg. Παῦλος Paul, Paulus
καὶ conj. καί and, even, also, but
αὐτοῦ pron. gen. masc. 3p. sg. αὐτός ή ό self, of oneself, even, very, the same, he, she, it
περὶ prep. περί (+gen) of, for, concerning, (+acc) about, concerning, in
τῆς art. gen. fem. sg. ὁ ἡ τό the, this, that, he, she, it
εἰς prep. εἰς (+acc) into, to, unto, for, in, on, toward, against, upon, at, among
Χριστὸν n. acc. masc. sg. Χριστός Christ
πίστεως n. gen. fem. sg. πίστις faith, assurance, belief, fidelity
25 δὲ conj. δέ but, and, now, also, to the contrary, rather, then
αὐτοῦ pron. gen. masc. 3p. sg. αὐτός ή ό self, of oneself, even, very, the same, he, she, it
περὶ prep. περί (+gen) of, for, concerning, (+acc) about, concerning, in
δικαιοσύνης n. gen. fem. sg. δικαιοσύνη righteousness
καὶ conj. καί and, even, also, but
ἐγκρατείας n. gen. fem. sg. ἐγκράτεια temperance
καὶ conj. καί and, even, also, but
τοῦ art. gen. neut. sg. ὁ ἡ τό the, this, that, he, she, it
κρίματος n. gen. neut. sg. κρίμα judgment, damnation, condemnation
τοῦ art. gen. neut. sg. ὁ ἡ τό the, this, that, he, she, it
ἔμφοβος adj. nom. masc. sg. ἔμφοβος afraid, affrighted, tremble
ὁ art. nom. masc. sg. ὁ ἡ τό the, this, that, he, she, it
Φῆλιξ n. nom. masc. sg. Φῆλιξ Felix
Τὸ art. acc. neut. sg. ὁ ἡ τό the, this, that, he, she, it
νῦν adv. νῦν now, henceforth, present, this time
καιρὸν n. acc. masc. sg. καιρός time, season, due time, opportunity
δὲ conj. δέ but, and, now, also, to the contrary, rather, then
σε pron. acc. 2p. sg. σύ thou, you
26 ἅμα prep. ἅμα (+dat) together, with, also. (adv.) at the same time, together
δὲ conj. δέ but, and, now, also, to the contrary, rather, then
καὶ conj. καί and, even, also, but
ὅτι conj. ὅτι that, for, because, how that, how, because that, for that, though
χρήματα n. nom. neut. pl. χρῆμα riches, money
αὐτῷ pron. dat. masc. 3p. sg. αὐτός ή ό self, of oneself, even, very, the same, he, she, it
ὑπὸ prep. ὑπό (+gen) of, by, with, from, among, (+acc) under
τοῦ art. gen. masc. sg. ὁ ἡ τό the, this, that, he, she, it
Παύλου n. gen. masc. sg. Παῦλος Paul, Paulus

ὅπως adv. ὅπως that, how, to, because, so that, when
αὐτόν pron. acc. masc. 3p. sg. αὐτός ή ό self, of oneself, even, very, the same, he, she, it
διὸ conj. διό wherefore, therefore, for which cause
καὶ conj. καί and, even, also, but
πυκνότερον compar. adv. πυκνός often, frequently
αὐτόν pron. acc. masc. 3p. sg. αὐτός ή ό self, of oneself, even, very, the same, he, she, it
αὐτῷ pron. dat. masc. 3p. sg. αὐτός ή ό self, of oneself, even, very, the same, he, she, it
27 διετίας n. gen. fem. sg. διετία two years
δὲ conj. δέ but, and, now, also, to the contrary, rather, then
διάδοχον n. acc. masc. sg. διάδοχος room
ὁ art. nom. masc. sg. ὁ ἡ τό the, this, that, he, she, it
Φῆλιξ n. nom. masc. sg. Φῆλιξ Felix
Πόρκιον n. acc. masc. sg. Πόρκιος Porcius
Φῆστον n. acc. masc. sg. Φῆστος Festus
τε conj. τέ and, both, also
χάριτας n. acc. fem. pl. χάρις grace, thank, favour, pleasure
τοῖς art. dat. masc. pl. ὁ ἡ τό the, this, that, he, she, it
Ἰουδαίοις adj. dat. masc. pl. Ἰουδαῖος Jew, Jewess
ὁ art. nom. masc. sg. ὁ ἡ τό the, this, that, he, she, it
Φῆλιξ n. nom. masc. sg. Φῆλιξ Felix
τὸν art. acc. masc. sg. ὁ ἡ τό the, this, that, he, she, it
Παῦλον n. acc. masc. sg. Παῦλος Paul, Paulus

25

1 Φῆστος n. nom. masc. sg. Φῆστος Festus
οὖν conj. οὖν therefore, then, so, and, now, wherefore
τῇ art. dat. fem. sg. ὁ ἡ τό the, this, that, he, she, it
ἐπαρχίᾳ n. dat. fem. sg. ἐπαρχία province
μετὰ prep. μετά (+gen) with, among, against, (+acc) after
τρεῖς num. acc. fem. pl. τρεῖς three
ἡμέρας n. acc. fem. pl. ἡμέρα day, time, year, while, age, day time
εἰς prep. εἰς (+acc) into, to, unto, for, in, on, toward, against, upon, at, among
Ἱεροσόλυμα n. acc. neut. sg. Ἱεροσόλυμα Jerusalem
ἀπὸ prep. ἀπό (+gen) from, of, out of, since, for, off, at, by, in, on
Καισαρείας n. gen. fem. sg. Καισάρεια Caesarea
2 δὲ conj. δέ but, and, now, also, to the contrary, rather, then
αὐτῷ pron. dat. masc. 3p. sg. αὐτός ή ό self, of oneself, even, very, the same, he, she, it
ὁ art. nom. masc. sg. ὁ ἡ τό the, this, that, he, she, it
ἀρχιερεὺς n. nom. masc. sg. ἀρχιερεύς chief priest, high priest
καὶ conj. καί and, even, also, but
οἱ art. nom. masc. pl. ὁ ἡ τό the, this, that, he, she, it
πρῶτοι ordinal. adj. nom. masc. pl. πρῶτος first, chief, first of all, chiefest, best
τῶν art. gen. masc. pl. ὁ ἡ τό the, this, that, he, she, it
Ἰουδαίων adj. gen. masc. pl. Ἰουδαῖος Jew, Jewess
κατὰ prep. κατά (+gen) against, by, throughout, down, (+acc) according to, after, with
τοῦ art. gen. masc. sg. ὁ ἡ τό the, this, that, he, she, it
Παύλου n. gen. masc. sg. Παῦλος Paul, Paulus
καὶ conj. καί and, even, also, but
αὐτὸν pron. acc. masc. 3p. sg. αὐτός ή ό self, of oneself, even, very, the same, he, she, it
3 χάριν n. acc. fem. sg. χάρις grace, thank, favour, pleasure
κατ' prep. κατά (+gen) against, by, throughout, down, (+acc) according to, after, with
αὐτοῦ pron. gen. masc. 3p. sg. αὐτός ή ό self, of oneself, even, very, the same, he, she, it
ὅπως adv. ὅπως that, how, to, because, so that, when
αὐτὸν pron. acc. masc. 3p. sg. αὐτός ή ό self, of oneself, even, very, the same, he, she, it

εἰς prep. εἰς (+acc) into, to, unto, for, in, on, toward, against, upon, at, among
Ἱερουσαλήμ pron. name. fem. inde. Ἱερουσαλήμ Jerusalem
ἐνέδραν n. acc. fem. sg. ἐνέδρα lying in wait
αὐτὸν pron. acc. masc. 3p. sg. αὐτός ἡ ὁ self, of oneself, even, very, the same, he, she, it
κατὰ prep. κατά (+gen) against, by, throughout, down, (+acc) according to, after, with
τὴν art. acc. fem. sg. ὁ ἡ τό the, this, that, he, she, it
ὁδόν n. acc. fem. sg. ὁδός way, journey, highway
4 ὁ art. nom. masc. sg. ὁ ἡ τό the, this, that, he, she, it
μέν conj. μέν indeed, verily, truly, even, so, some
οὖν conj. οὖν therefore, then, so, and, now, wherefore
Φῆστος n. nom. masc. sg. Φῆστος Festus
τὸν art. acc. masc. sg. ὁ ἡ τό the, this, that, he, she, it
Παῦλον n. acc. masc. sg. Παῦλος Paul, Paulus
ἐν prep. ἐν (+dat) in, by, with, among, at, on, through, to, within, into, of, for
Καισαρείᾳ n. dat. fem. sg. Καισάρεια Caesarea
ἑαυτὸν reflexive pron. acc. masc. 3p. sg. ἑαυτοῦ himself, herself, itself, yourself, ourselves
δὲ conj. δέ but, and, now, also, to the contrary, rather, then
ἐν prep. ἐν (+dat) in, by, with, among, at, on, through, to, within, into, of, for
τάχει n. dat. neut. sg. τάχος speedily, short, quick
5 οἱ art. nom. masc. pl. ὁ ἡ τό the, this, that, he, she, it
οὖν conj. οὖν therefore, then, so, and, now, wherefore
δυνατοὶ adj. nom. masc. pl. δυνατός able, possible, mighty, strong
ἐν prep. ἐν (+dat) in, by, with, among, at, on, through, to, within, into, of, for
ὑμῖν pron. dat. 2p. pl. σύ thou, you
εἴ conj. εἰ if, whether, that, though, forasmuch
τι indefinite pron. nom. neut. sg. τὶς certain, some, any man, one, any thing
ἄτοπον adj. nom. neut. sg. ἄτοπος amiss, harm, unreasonable
ἐν prep. ἐν (+dat) in, by, with, among, at, on, through, to, within, into, of, for
τῷ art. dat. masc. sg. ὁ ἡ τό the, this, that, he, she, it
ἀνδρὶ n. dat. masc. sg. ἀνήρ man, husband, sir
τούτῳ demo. pron. dat. masc. sg. οὗτος αὕτη τοῦτο this, the same, this same, he, she, it
αὐτοῦ pron. gen. masc. 3p. sg. αὐτός ἡ ὁ self, of oneself, even, very, the same, he, she, it
6 δὲ conj. δέ but, and, now, also, to the contrary, rather, then
ἐν prep. ἐν (+dat) in, by, with, among, at, on, through, to, within, into, of, for
αὐτοῖς pron. dat. masc. 3p. pl. αὐτός ἡ ὁ self, of oneself, even, very, the same, he, she, it
ἡμέρας n. acc. fem. pl. ἡμέρα day, time, year, while, age, day time
πλείους compar. adj. acc. fem. pl. πλείων more, many, greater, further, more part
ἢ particle. ἤ or, than, either, nor, or else, and, rather than
δέκα num. gen. fem. pl. δέκα ten
εἰς prep. εἰς (+acc) into, to, unto, for, in, on, toward, against, upon, at, among
Καισάρειαν n. acc. fem. sg. Καισάρεια Caesarea
τῇ art. dat. fem. sg. ὁ ἡ τό the, this, that, he, she, it
ἐπαύριον adv. ἐπαύριον next day, morrow, day following, nest day after
ἐπὶ prep. ἐπί (+gen) on, in, upon, (+dat) in, at, for, upon, (+acc) on, upon, unto, to, against
τοῦ art. gen. neut. sg. ὁ ἡ τό the, this, that, he, she, it
βήματος n. gen. neut. sg. βῆμα judgment seat, throne
τὸν art. acc. masc. sg. ὁ ἡ τό the, this, that, he, she, it
Παῦλον n. acc. masc. sg. Παῦλος Paul, Paulus
7 δὲ conj. δέ but, and, now, also, to the contrary, rather, then
αὐτοῦ pron. gen. masc. 3p. sg. αὐτός ἡ ὁ self, of oneself, even, very, the same, he, she, it
οἱ art. nom. masc. pl. ὁ ἡ τό the, this, that, he, she, it
ἀπὸ prep. ἀπό (+gen) from, of, out of, since, for, off, at, by, in, on
Ἱεροσολύμων n. gen. neut. pl. Ἱεροσόλυμα Jerusalem
Ἰουδαῖοι adj. nom. masc. pl. Ἰουδαῖος Jew, Jewess
πολλὰ adj. acc. neut. pl. πολύς many, great, much, long, abundant

καὶ conj. καί and, even, also, but
βαρέα adj. acc. neut. pl. βαρύς grievous, heavy, weightier, weighty
αἰτιάματα n. acc. neut. pl. αἰτίαμα complaint
κατὰ prep. κατά (+gen) against, by, throughout, down, (+acc) according to, after, with
τοῦ art. gen. masc. sg. ὁ ἡ τό the, this, that, he, she, it
Παύλου n. gen. masc. sg. Παῦλος Paul, Paulus
ἃ relative pron. acc. neut. pl. ὅς ἥ ὅ who, which, what, that
οὐκ particle of negation. οὐ οὐκ οὐχ not, no, neither, none, nay, nor, never, nothing
8 αὐτοῦ pron. gen. masc. 3p. sg. αὐτός ή ό self, of oneself, even, very, the same, he, she, it
ὅτι conj. ὅτι that, for, because, how that, how, because that, for that, though
Οὔτε conj. οὔτε neither, nor, nor yet, no, none
εἰς prep. εἰς (+acc) into, to, unto, for, in, on, toward, against, upon, at, among
τὸν art. acc. masc. sg. ὁ ἡ τό the, this, that, he, she, it
νόμον n. acc. masc. sg. νόμος law, the law
τῶν art. gen. masc. pl. ὁ ἡ τό the, this, that, he, she, it
Ἰουδαίων adj. gen. masc. pl. Ἰουδαῖος Jew, Jewess
οὔτε conj. οὔτε neither, nor, nor yet, no, none
εἰς prep. εἰς (+acc) into, to, unto, for, in, on, toward, against, upon, at, among
τὸ art. acc. neut. sg. ὁ ἡ τό the, this, that, he, she, it
ἱερὸν n. acc. neut. sg. ἱερόν temple
οὔτε conj. οὔτε neither, nor, nor yet, no, none
εἰς prep. εἰς (+acc) into, to, unto, for, in, on, toward, against, upon, at, among
Καίσαρά n. acc. masc. sg. Καῖσαρ Caesar
τι indefinite pron. acc. neut. sg. τὶς certain, some, any man, one, any thing
9 ὁ art. nom. masc. sg. ὁ ἡ τό the, this, that, he, she, it
Φῆστος n. nom. masc. sg. Φῆστος Festus
δὲ conj. δέ but, and, now, also, to the contrary, rather, then
τοῖς art. dat. masc. pl. ὁ ἡ τό the, this, that, he, she, it
Ἰουδαίοις adj. dat. masc. pl. Ἰουδαῖος Jew, Jewess
χάριν n. acc. fem. sg. χάρις grace, thank, favour, pleasure
τῷ art. dat. masc. sg. ὁ ἡ τό the, this, that, he, she, it
Παύλῳ n. dat. masc. sg. Παῦλος Paul, Paulus
εἰς prep. εἰς (+acc) into, to, unto, for, in, on, toward, against, upon, at, among
Ἱεροσόλυμα n. acc. neut. sg. Ἱεροσόλυμα Jerusalem
ἐκεῖ adv. ἐκεῖ there, thither, thitherward, yonder, yonder place
περὶ prep. περί (+gen) of, for, concerning, (+acc) about, concerning, in
τούτων demo. pron. gen. neut. pl. οὗτος αὕτη τοῦτο this, the same, this same, he, she, it
ἐπ' prep. ἐπί (+gen) on, in, upon, (+dat) in, at, for, upon, (+acc) on, upon, unto, to, against
ἐμοῦ pron. gen. 1p. sg. ἐγώ I
10 δὲ conj. δέ but, and, now, also, to the contrary, rather, then
ὁ art. nom. masc. sg. ὁ ἡ τό the, this, that, he, she, it
Παῦλος n. nom. masc. sg. Παῦλος Paul, Paulus
Ἐπὶ prep. ἐπί (+gen) on, in, upon, (+dat) in, at, for, upon, (+acc) on, upon, unto, to, against
τοῦ art. gen. neut. sg. ὁ ἡ τό the, this, that, he, she, it
βήματος n. gen. neut. sg. βῆμα judgment seat, throne
Καίσαρος n. gen. masc. sg. Καῖσαρ Caesar
οὗ adv. οὗ where, whither, wherein
με pron. acc. 1p. sg. ἐγώ I
Ἰουδαίους adj. acc. masc. pl. Ἰουδαῖος Jew, Jewess
οὐδὲν adj. acc. neut. sg. οὐδείς no man, nothing, no, none, neither, not, nought
ὡς adv. ὡς as, when, as it were, how, about, like, as soon as, even as, while
καὶ conj. καί and, even, also, but
σὺ pron. nom. 2p. sg. σύ thou, you
κάλλιον compar. adv. καλός good, better, goodly, meet, honest, fair, well, worthy
11 εἰ conj. εἰ if, whether, that, though, forasmuch

μέν conj. μέν indeed, verily, truly, even, so, some
γὰρ conj. γάρ for, and, because, but, indeed
καὶ conj. καί and, even, also, but
ἄξιον adj. acc. neut. sg. ἄξιος worthy, meet, due reward
θανάτου n. gen. masc. sg. θάνατος death
τι indefinite pron. acc. neut. sg. τὶς certain, some, any man, one, any thing
οὐ particle of negation. οὐ οὐκ οὐχ not, no, neither, none, nay, nor, never, nothing
τὸ art. acc. neut. sg. ὁ ἡ τό the, this, that, he, she, it
εἰ conj. εἰ if, whether, that, though, forasmuch
δὲ conj. δέ but, and, now, also, to the contrary, rather, then
οὐδέν num. nom. neut. sg. οὐδείς no man, nothing, no, none, neither, not, nought
ὧν relative pron. gen. neut. pl. ὅς ἥ ὅ who, which, what, that
οὗτοι demo. pron. nom. masc. pl. οὗτος αὕτη τοῦτο this, the same, this same, he, she, it
μου pron. gen. 1p. sg. ἐγώ I
οὐδείς num. nom. masc. sg. οὐδείς no man, nothing, no, none, neither, not, nought
με pron. acc. 1p. sg. ἐγώ I
αὐτοῖς pron. dat. masc. 3p. pl. αὐτός ή ὁ self, of oneself, even, very, the same, he, she, it
Καίσαρα n. acc. masc. sg. Καῖσαρ Caesar
12 τότε adv. τότε then, that time
ὁ art. nom. masc. sg. ὁ ἡ τό the, this, that, he, she, it
Φῆστος n. nom. masc. sg. Φῆστος Festus
μετὰ prep. μετά (+gen) with, among, against, (+acc) after
τοῦ art. gen. neut. sg. ὁ ἡ τό the, this, that, he, she, it
συμβουλίου n. gen. neut. sg. συμβούλιον counsel, council, consultation
Καίσαρα n. acc. masc. sg. Καῖσαρ Caesar
ἐπὶ prep. ἐπί (+gen) on, in, upon, (+dat) in, at, for, upon, (+acc) on, upon, unto, to, against
Καίσαρα n. acc. masc. sg. Καῖσαρ Caesar
13 Ἡμερῶν n. gen. fem. pl. ἡμέρα day, time, year, while, age, day time
δὲ conj. δέ but, and, now, also, to the contrary, rather, then
τινῶν indefinite pron. gen. fem. pl. τὶς certain, some, any man, one, any thing
Ἀγρίππας n. nom. masc. sg. Ἀγρίππας Agrippa
ὁ art. nom. masc. sg. ὁ ἡ τό the, this, that, he, she, it
βασιλεὺς n. nom. masc. sg. βασιλεύς king
καὶ conj. καί and, even, also, but
Βερνίκη n. nom. fem. sg. Βερνίκη Bernice
εἰς prep. εἰς (+acc) into, to, unto, for, in, on, toward, against, upon, at, among
Καισάρειαν n. acc. fem. sg. Καισάρεια Caesarea
τὸν art. acc. masc. sg. ὁ ἡ τό the, this, that, he, she, it
Φῆστον n. acc. masc. sg. Φῆστος Festus
14 ὡς adv. ὡς as, when, as it were, how, about, like, as soon as, even as, while
δὲ conj. δέ but, and, now, also, to the contrary, rather, then
πλείους compar. adj. acc. fem. pl. πλείων more, many, greater, further, more part
ἡμέρας n. acc. fem. pl. ἡμέρα day, time, year, while, age, day time
ἐκεῖ adv. ἐκεῖ there, thither, thitherward, yonder, yonder place
ὁ art. nom. masc. sg. ὁ ἡ τό the, this, that, he, she, it
Φῆστος n. nom. masc. sg. Φῆστος Festus
τῷ art. dat. masc. sg. ὁ ἡ τό the, this, that, he, she, it
βασιλεῖ n. dat. masc. sg. βασιλεύς king
τὰ art. acc. neut. pl. ὁ ἡ τό the, this, that, he, she, it
κατὰ prep. κατά (+gen) against, by, throughout, down, (+acc) according to, after, with
τὸν art. acc. masc. sg. ὁ ἡ τό the, this, that, he, she, it
Παῦλον n. acc. masc. sg. Παῦλος Paul, Paulus
Ἀνήρ n. nom. masc. sg. ἀνήρ man, husband, sir
τίς indefinite pron. nom. masc. sg. τίς what, who, why, where, which, how
ὑπὸ prep. ὑπό (+gen) of, by, with, from, among, (+acc) under

Φήλικος n. gen. masc. sg. Φῆλιξ Felix
δέσμιος n. nom. masc. sg. δέσμιος prisoner, in bonds, that is in bond
15 περὶ prep. περί (+gen) of, for, concerning, (+acc) about, concerning, in
οὗ relative pron. gen. masc. sg. ὅς ἥ ὅ who, which, what, that
μου pron. gen. 1p. sg. ἐγώ I
εἰς prep. εἰς (+acc) into, to, unto, for, in, on, toward, against, upon, at, among
Ἱεροσόλυμα n. acc. neut. sg. Ἱεροσόλυμα Jerusalem
οἱ art. nom. masc. pl. ὁ ἡ τό the, this, that, he, she, it
ἀρχιερεῖς n. nom. masc. pl. ἀρχιερεύς chief priest, high priest
καὶ conj. καί and, even, also, but
οἱ art. nom. masc. pl. ὁ ἡ τό the, this, that, he, she, it
πρεσβύτεροι adj. nom. masc. pl. πρεσβύτερος elder, elder woman, eldest, old man
τῶν art. gen. masc. pl. ὁ ἡ τό the, this, that, he, she, it
Ἰουδαίων adj. gen. masc. pl. Ἰουδαῖος Jew, Jewess
κατ' prep. κατά (+gen) against, by, throughout, down, (+acc) according to, after, with
αὐτοῦ pron. gen. masc. 3p. sg. αὐτός ή ό self, of oneself, even, very, the same, he, she, it
δίκην n. acc. fem. sg. δίκη judgment, vengeance, punish
16 πρὸς prep. πρός (+gen) for, (+dat) at, (+acc) unto, to, with, for, against
οὓς relative pron. acc. masc. pl. ὅς ἥ ὅ who, which, what, that
ὅτι conj. ὅτι that, for, because, how that, how, because that, for that, though
οὐκ particle of negation. οὐ οὐκ οὐχ not, no, neither, none, nay, nor, never, nothing
ἔθος n. nom. neut. sg. ἔθος custom, manner, be wont
Ῥωμαίοις adj. dat. masc. pl. Ῥωμαῖος Roman, Rome
τινα indefinite pron. acc. masc. sg. τὶς certain, some, any man, one, any thing
ἄνθρωπον n. acc. masc. sg. ἄνθρωπος man, human being, person, one, certain
εἰς prep. εἰς (+acc) into, to, unto, for, in, on, toward, against, upon, at, among
ἀπώλειαν n. acc. fem. sg. ἀπώλεια destruction, perdition, waste, damnation
πρὶν adv. πρίν before, ere
ἢ particle. ἤ or, than, either, nor, or else, and, rather than
ὁ art. nom. masc. sg. ὁ ἡ τό the, this, that, he, she, it
κατὰ prep. κατά (+gen) against, by, throughout, down, (+acc) according to, after, with
πρόσωπον n. acc. neut. sg. πρόσωπον face, presence, person, countenance
τοὺς art. acc. masc. pl. ὁ ἡ τό the, this, that, he, she, it
κατηγόρους n. acc. masc. pl. κατήγορος accuser
τόπον n. acc. masc. sg. τόπος place, room, quarter
τε conj. τέ and, both, also
ἀπολογίας n. gen. fem. sg. ἀπολογία defence, answer, answer for oneself, clear oneself
περὶ prep. περί (+gen) of, for, concerning, (+acc) about, concerning, in
τοῦ art. gen. neut. sg. ὁ ἡ τό the, this, that, he, she, it
ἐγκλήματος n. gen. neut. sg. ἔγκλημα lay to charge, crime laid against
17 οὖν conj. οὖν therefore, then, so, and, now, wherefore
αὐτῶν pron. gen. masc. 3p. pl. αὐτός ή ό self, of oneself, even, very, the same, he, she, it
ἐνθάδε adv. ἐνθάδε here, there, hither
ἀναβολὴν n. acc. fem. sg. ἀναβολή delay
μηδεμίαν num. acc. fem. sg. μηδείς μηδεμία μηδέν no man, nothing, no, none, not at all
τῇ art. dat. fem. sg. ὁ ἡ τό the, this, that, he, she, it
ἑξῆς adv. ἑξῆς the after, the next, following, on the morrow
ἐπὶ prep. ἐπί (+gen) on, in, upon, (+dat) in, at, for, upon, (+acc) on, upon, unto, to, against
τοῦ art. gen. neut. sg. ὁ ἡ τό the, this, that, he, she, it
βήματος n. gen. neut. sg. βῆμα judgment seat, throne
τὸν art. acc. masc. sg. ὁ ἡ τό the, this, that, he, she, it
ἄνδρα n. acc. masc. sg. ἀνήρ man, husband, sir
18 περὶ prep. περί (+gen) of, for, concerning, (+acc) about, concerning, in
οὗ relative pron. gen. masc. sg. ὅς ἥ ὅ who, which, what, that
οἱ art. nom. masc. pl. ὁ ἡ τό the, this, that, he, she, it

κατήγοροι n. nom. masc. pl. κατήγορος accuser
οὐδεμίαν num. acc. fem. sg. οὐδείς no man, nothing, no, none, neither, not, nought
αἰτίαν n. acc. fem. sg. αἰτία cause, reason, accusation, fault
ὧν relative pron. gen. neut. pl. ὅς ἥ ὅ who, which, what, that
ἐγὼ pron. nom. 1p. sg. ἐγώ I
19 ζητήματα n. acc. neut. pl. ζήτημα question
δέ conj. δέ but, and, now, also, to the contrary, rather, then
τινα indefinite pron. acc. neut. pl. τὶς certain, some, any man, one, any thing
περὶ prep. περί (+gen) of, for, concerning, (+acc) about, concerning, in
τῆς art. gen. fem. sg. ὁ ἡ τό the, this, that, he, she, it
ἰδίας adj. gen. fem. sg. ἴδιος one's own, one's, privately
δεισιδαιμονίας n. gen. fem. sg. δεισιδαιμονία superstition
πρὸς prep. πρός (+gen) for, (+dat) at, (+acc) unto, to, with, for, against
αὐτὸν pron. acc. masc. 3p. sg. αὐτός ή ό self, of oneself, even, very, the same, he, she, it
καὶ conj. καί and, even, also, but
περί prep. περί (+gen) of, for, concerning, (+acc) about, concerning, in
τινος indefinite pron. gen. masc. sg. τὶς certain, some, any man, one, any thing
Ἰησοῦ n. gen. masc. sg. Ἰησοῦς Jesus
ὃν relative pron. acc. masc. sg. ὅς ἥ ὅ who, which, what, that
ὁ art. nom. masc. sg. ὁ ἡ τό the, this, that, he, she, it
Παῦλος n. nom. masc. sg. Παῦλος Paul, Paulus
20 δὲ conj. δέ but, and, now, also, to the contrary, rather, then
ἐγὼ pron. nom. 1p. sg. ἐγώ I
εἰς prep. εἰς (+acc) into, to, unto, for, in, on, toward, against, upon, at, among
τὴν art. acc. fem. sg. ὁ ἡ τό the, this, that, he, she, it
περὶ prep. περί (+gen) of, for, concerning, (+acc) about, concerning, in
τούτου demo. pron. gen. masc. sg. οὗτος αὕτη τοῦτο this, the same, this same, he, she, it
ζήτησιν n. acc. fem. sg. ζήτησις question
εἰ conj. εἰ if, whether, that, though, forasmuch
εἰς prep. εἰς (+acc) into, to, unto, for, in, on, toward, against, upon, at, among
Ἱερουσαλήμ pron. name. fem. inde. Ἱερουσαλήμ Jerusalem
κἀκεῖ adv. κἀκεῖ and there, there also, thither also
περὶ prep. περί (+gen) of, for, concerning, (+acc) about, concerning, in
τούτων demo. pron. gen. neut. pl. οὗτος αὕτη τοῦτο this, the same, this same, he, she, it
21 τοῦ art. gen. masc. sg. ὁ ἡ τό the, this, that, he, she, it
δὲ conj. δέ but, and, now, also, to the contrary, rather, then
Παύλου n. gen. masc. sg. Παῦλος Paul, Paulus
αὐτὸν pron. acc. masc. 3p. sg. αὐτός ή ό self, of oneself, even, very, the same, he, she, it
εἰς prep. εἰς (+acc) into, to, unto, for, in, on, toward, against, upon, at, among
τὴν art. acc. fem. sg. ὁ ἡ τό the, this, that, he, she, it
τοῦ art. gen. masc. sg. ὁ ἡ τό the, this, that, he, she, it
Σεβαστοῦ adj. gen. masc. sg. Σεβαστός Augustus
διάγνωσιν n. acc. fem. sg. διάγνωσις hearing
αὐτὸν pron. acc. masc. 3p. sg. αὐτός ή ό self, of oneself, even, very, the same, he, she, it
ἕως conj. ἕως till, until, unto, until when, while, as far as, even, until now
οὗ relative pron. gen. masc. sg. ὅς ἥ ὅ who, which, what, that
αὐτὸν pron. acc. masc. 3p. sg. αὐτός ή ό self, of oneself, even, very, the same, he, she, it
πρὸς prep. πρός (+gen) for, (+dat) at, (+acc) unto, to, with, for, against
Καίσαρα n. acc. masc. sg. Καῖσαρ Caesar
22 Ἀγρίππας n. nom. masc. sg. Ἀγρίππας Agrippa
δὲ conj. δέ but, and, now, also, to the contrary, rather, then
πρὸς prep. πρός (+gen) for, (+dat) at, (+acc) unto, to, with, for, against
τὸν art. acc. masc. sg. ὁ ἡ τό the, this, that, he, she, it
Φῆστον n. acc. masc. sg. Φῆστος Festus
καὶ conj. καί and, even, also, but

αὐτὸς pron. nom. masc. 3p. sg. αὐτός ή ό self, of oneself, even, very, the same, he, she, it
τοῦ art. gen. masc. sg. ὁ ἡ τό the, this, that, he, she, it
ἀνθρώπου n. gen. masc. sg. ἄνθρωπος man, human being, person, one, certain
ὁ art. nom. masc. sg. ὁ ἡ τό the, this, that, he, she, it
δὲ conj. δέ but, and, now, also, to the contrary, rather, then
Αὔριον adv. αὔριον tomorrow, morrow, next day
αὐτοῦ pron. gen. masc. 3p. sg. αὐτός ή ό self, of oneself, even, very, the same, he, she, it
23 Τῇ art. dat. fem. sg. ὁ ἡ τό the, this, that, he, she, it
οὖν conj. οὖν therefore, then, so, and, now, wherefore
ἐπαύριον adv. ἐπαύριον next day, morrow, day following, nest day after
τοῦ art. gen. masc. sg. ὁ ἡ τό the, this, that, he, she, it
᾿Αγρίππα n. gen. masc. sg. ᾿Αγρίππας Agrippa
καὶ conj. καί and, even, also, but
τῆς art. gen. fem. sg. ὁ ἡ τό the, this, that, he, she, it
Βερνίκης n. gen. fem. sg. Βερνίκη Bernice
μετὰ prep. μετά (+gen) with, among, against, (+acc) after
πολλῆς adj. gen. fem. sg. πολύς many, great, much, long, abundant
φαντασίας n. gen. fem. sg. φαντασία pomp
καὶ conj. καί and, even, also, but
εἰς prep. εἰς (+acc) into, to, unto, for, in, on, toward, against, upon, at, among
τὸ art. acc. neut. sg. ὁ ἡ τό the, this, that, he, she, it
ἀκροατήριον n. acc. neut. sg. ἀκροατήριον place of hearing
σύν prep. σύν (+dat) with, beside
τε conj. τέ and, both, also
τοῖς art. dat. masc. pl. ὁ ἡ τό the, this, that, he, she, it
χιλιάρχοις n. dat. masc. pl. χιλίαρχος high captain, chief captain, captain
καὶ conj. καί and, even, also, but
ἀνδράσι n. dat. masc. pl. ἀνήρ man, husband, sir
τοῖς art. dat. masc. pl. ὁ ἡ τό the, this, that, he, she, it
κατ' prep. κατά (+gen) against, by, throughout, down, (+acc) according to, after, with
ἐξοχὴν n. acc. fem. sg. ἐξοχή principal, eminence
τῆς art. gen. fem. sg. ὁ ἡ τό the, this, that, he, she, it
πόλεως n. gen. fem. sg. πόλις city
καὶ conj. καί and, even, also, but
τοῦ art. gen. masc. sg. ὁ ἡ τό the, this, that, he, she, it
Φήστου n. gen. masc. sg. Φῆστος Festus
ὁ art. nom. masc. sg. ὁ ἡ τό the, this, that, he, she, it
Παῦλος n. nom. masc. sg. Παῦλος Paul, Paulus
24 καί conj. καί and, even, also, but
ὁ art. nom. masc. sg. ὁ ἡ τό the, this, that, he, she, it
Φῆστος n. nom. masc. sg. Φῆστος Festus
᾿Αγρίππα n. voc. masc. sg. ᾿Αγρίππας Agrippa
βασιλεῦ n. voc. masc. sg. βασιλεύς king
καί conj. καί and, even, also, but
πάντες adj. voc. masc. pl. πᾶς πᾶσα πᾶν all, every, whosoever, every one, no, whole, any
οἱ art. voc. masc. pl. ὁ ἡ τό the, this, that, he, she, it
ἡμῖν pron. dat. 1p. pl. ἐγώ I
ἄνδρες n. voc. masc. pl. ἀνήρ man, husband, sir
τοῦτον demo. pron. acc. masc. sg. οὗτος αὕτη τοῦτο this, the same, this same, he, she, it
περὶ prep. περί (+gen) of, for, concerning, (+acc) about, concerning, in
οὗ relative pron. gen. masc. sg. ὅς ἥ ὅ who, which, what, that
πᾶν adj. nom. neut. sg. πᾶς πᾶσα πᾶν all, every, whosoever, every one, no, whole, any
τὸ art. nom. neut. sg. ὁ ἡ τό the, this, that, he, she, it
πλῆθος n. nom. neut. sg. πλῆθος multitude, bundle, company
τῶν art. gen. masc. pl. ὁ ἡ τό the, this, that, he, she, it

Ἰουδαίων adj. gen. masc. pl. Ἰουδαῖος Jew, Jewess
μοι pron. dat. 1p. sg. ἐγώ I
ἔν prep. ἐν (+dat) in, by, with, among, at, on, through, to, within, into, of, for
τε conj. τέ and, both, also
Ἱεροσολύμοις n. dat. neut. pl. Ἱεροσόλυμα Jerusalem
καί conj. καί and, even, also, but
ἐνθάδε adv. ἐνθάδε here, there, hither
μὴ particle of negation. μή not, no, lest, neither, none, nothing, nor, never, without
αὐτὸν pron. acc. masc. 3p. sg. αὐτός ή ό self, of oneself, even, very, the same, he, she, it
μηκέτι adv. μηκέτι no more, no longer, not any more, not henceforth, not henceforward
25 ἐγὼ pron. nom. 1p. sg. ἐγώ I
δὲ conj. δέ but, and, now, also, to the contrary, rather, then
μηδὲν adj. acc. neut. sg. μηδείς μηδεμία μηδέν no man, nothing, no, none, not at all
ἄξιον adj. acc. neut. sg. ἄξιος worthy, meet, due reward
θανάτου n. gen. masc. sg. θάνατος death
αὐτὸν pron. acc. masc. 3p. sg. αὐτός ή ό self, of oneself, even, very, the same, he, she, it
καί conj. καί and, even, also, but
αὐτοῦ pron. gen. masc. 3p. sg. αὐτός ή ό self, of oneself, even, very, the same, he, she, it
δὲ conj. δέ but, and, now, also, to the contrary, rather, then
τούτου demo. pron. gen. masc. sg. οὗτος αὕτη τοῦτο this, the same, this same, he, she, it
τὸν art. acc. masc. sg. ὁ ἡ τό the, this, that, he, she, it
Σεβαστὸν adj. acc. masc. sg. Σεβαστός Augustus
αὐτὸν pron. acc. masc. 3p. sg. αὐτός ή ό self, of oneself, even, very, the same, he, she, it
26 περὶ prep. περί (+gen) of, for, concerning, (+acc) about, concerning, in
οὗ relative pron. gen. masc. sg. ὅς ἥ ὅ who, which, what, that
ἀσφαλές adj. acc. neut. sg. ἀσφαλής certainty, certain, safe, sure
τι indefinite pron. acc. neut. sg. τὶς certain, some, any man, one, any thing
τῷ art. dat. masc. sg. ὁ ἡ τό the, this, that, he, she, it
κυρίῳ n. dat. masc. sg. κύριος Lord, lord, master, sir, LORD, God, Master, owner
οὐκ particle of negation. οὐ οὐκ οὐχ not, no, neither, none, nay, nor, never, nothing
διὸ conj. διό wherefore, therefore, for which cause
αὐτὸν pron. acc. masc. 3p. sg. αὐτός ή ό self, of oneself, even, very, the same, he, she, it
ἐφ' prep. ἐπί (+gen) on, in, upon, (+dat) in, at, for, upon, (+acc) on, upon, unto, to, against
ὑμῶν pron. gen. 2p. pl. σύ thou, you
καὶ conj. καί and, even, also, but
μάλιστα adv. μάλιστα specially, especially, chiefly, most of all
ἐπὶ prep. ἐπί (+gen) on, in, upon, (+dat) in, at, for, upon, (+acc) on, upon, unto, to, against
σοῦ pron. gen. 2p. sg. σύ thou, you
βασιλεῦ n. voc. masc. sg. βασιλεύς king
Ἀγρίππα n. voc. masc. sg. Ἀγρίππας Agrippa
ὅπως adv. ὅπως that, how, to, because, so that, when
τῆς art. gen. fem. sg. ὁ ἡ τό the, this, that, he, she, it
ἀνακρίσεως n. gen. fem. sg. ἀνάκρισις examination
τί interrog. pron. acc. neut. sg. τίς what, who, why, where, which, how
27 ἄλογον adj. nom. neut. sg. ἄλογος unreasonable, brute
γάρ conj. γάρ for, and, because, but, indeed
μοι pron. dat. 1p. sg. ἐγώ I
δέσμιον n. acc. masc. sg. δέσμιος prisoner, in bonds, that is in bond
μὴ particle of negation. μή not, no, lest, neither, none, nothing, nor, never, without
καὶ conj. καί and, even, also, but
τὰς art. acc. fem. pl. ὁ ἡ τό the, this, that, he, she, it
κατ' prep. κατά (+gen) against, by, throughout, down, (+acc) according to, after, with
αὐτοῦ pron. gen. masc. 3p. sg. αὐτός ή ό self, of oneself, even, very, the same, he, she, it
αἰτίας n. acc. fem. pl. αἰτία cause, reason, accusation, fault

26

1 Ἀγρίππας n. nom. masc. sg. Ἀγρίππας Agrippa
δὲ conj. δέ but, and, now, also, to the contrary, rather, then
πρὸς prep. πρός (+gen) for, (+dat) at, (+acc) unto, to, with, for, against
τὸν art. acc. masc. sg. ὁ ἡ τό the, this, that, he, she, it
Παῦλον n. acc. masc. sg. Παῦλος Paul, Paulus
σοι pron. dat. 2p. sg. σύ thou, you
ὑπὲρ prep. ὑπέρ (+gen) for, of, for the sake of, (+acc) above, more than
σεαυτοῦ pron. gen. masc. 2p. sg. σεαυτοῦ σεαυτῷ σεαυτόν thyself, thine own self
τότε adv. τότε then, that time
ὁ art. nom. masc. sg. ὁ ἡ τό the, this, that, he, she, it
Παῦλος n. nom. masc. sg. Παῦλος Paul, Paulus
τὴν art. acc. fem. sg. ὁ ἡ τό the, this, that, he, she, it
χεῖρα n. acc. fem. sg. χείρ hand
2 Περὶ prep. περί (+gen) of, for, concerning, (+acc) about, concerning, in
πάντων adj. gen. neut. pl. πᾶς πᾶσα πᾶν all, every, whosoever, every one, no, whole, any
ὧν relative pron. gen. neut. pl. ὅς ἥ ὅ who, which, what, that
ὑπὸ prep. ὑπό (+gen) of, by, with, from, among, (+acc) under
Ἰουδαίων adj. gen. masc. pl. Ἰουδαῖος Jew, Jewess
βασιλεῦ n. voc. masc. sg. βασιλεύς king
Ἀγρίππα n. voc. masc. sg. Ἀγρίππας Agrippa
ἐμαυτὸν pron. acc. masc. 1p. sg. ἐμαυτοῦ myself, me
μακάριον adj. acc. masc. sg. μακάριος blessed, happy
ἐπὶ prep. ἐπί (+gen) on, in, upon, (+dat) in, at, for, upon, (+acc) on, upon, unto, to, against
σοῦ pron. gen. 2p. sg. σύ thou, you
σήμερον adv. σήμερον this day, today
3 μάλιστα adv. μάλιστα specially, especially, chiefly, most of all
γνώστην n. acc. masc. sg. γνώστης expert
σε pron. acc. 2p. sg. σύ thou, you
πάντων adj. gen. neut. pl. πᾶς πᾶσα πᾶν all, every, whosoever, every one, no, whole, any
τῶν art. gen. neut. pl. ὁ ἡ τό the, this, that, he, she, it
κατὰ prep. κατά (+gen) against, by, throughout, down, (+acc) according to, after, with
Ἰουδαίους adj. acc. masc. pl. Ἰουδαῖος Jew, Jewess
ἐθῶν n. gen. neut. pl. ἔθος custom, manner, be wont
τε conj. τέ and, both, also
καὶ conj. καί and, even, also, but
ζητημάτων n. gen. neut. pl. ζήτημα question
διὸ conj. διό wherefore, therefore, for which cause
σου pron. gen. 2p. sg. σύ thou, you
μακροθύμως adv. μακροθύμως patiently
μου pron. gen. 1p. sg. ἐγώ I
4 τὴν art. acc. fem. sg. ὁ ἡ τό the, this, that, he, she, it
μέν conj. μέν indeed, verily, truly, even, so, some
οὖν conj. οὖν therefore, then, so, and, now, wherefore
βίωσίν n. acc. fem. sg. βίωσις manner of life
μου pron. gen. 1p. sg. ἐγώ I
τὴν art. acc. fem. sg. ὁ ἡ τό the, this, that, he, she, it
ἐκ prep. ἐκ ἐξ (+gen) of, from, out of, by, on, with, in, among, through
νεότητος n. gen. fem. sg. νεότης youth
τὴν art. acc. fem. sg. ὁ ἡ τό the, this, that, he, she, it
ἀπ' prep. ἀπό (+gen) from, of, out of, since, for, off, at, by, in, on
ἀρχῆς n. gen. fem. sg. ἀρχή beginning, principality, corner, first, magistrate, rule
ἐν prep. ἐν (+dat) in, by, with, among, at, on, through, to, within, into, of, for
τῷ art. dat. neut. sg. ὁ ἡ τό the, this, that, he, she, it

ἔθνει n. dat. neut. sg. ἔθνος Gentile, nation, heathen, people
μου pron. gen. 1p. sg. ἐγώ I
ἐν prep. ἐν (+dat) in, by, with, among, at, on, through, to, within, into, of, for
Ἱεροσολύμοις n. dat. neut. pl. Ἱεροσόλυμα Jerusalem
πάντες adj. nom. masc. pl. πᾶς πᾶσα πᾶν all, every, whosoever, every one, no, whole, any
οἱ art. nom. masc. pl. ὁ ἡ τό the, this, that, he, she, it
Ἰουδαῖοι adj. nom. masc. pl. Ἰουδαῖος Jew, Jewess
5 με pron. acc. 1p. sg. ἐγώ I
ἄνωθεν adv. ἄνωθεν from above, again, the top, from the beginning, from the very first
ἐὰν conj. ἐάν if, soever, except, though, and if, but, whether, if so, so
ὅτι conj. ὅτι that, for, because, how that, how, because that, for that, though
κατὰ prep. κατά (+gen) against, by, throughout, down, (+acc) according to, after, with
τὴν art. acc. fem. sg. ὁ ἡ τό the, this, that, he, she, it
ἀκριβεστάτην superl. adj. acc. fem. sg. ἀκριβέστατος most straitest
αἵρεσιν n. acc. fem. sg. αἵρεσις sect, heresy
τῆς art. gen. fem. sg. ὁ ἡ τό the, this, that, he, she, it
ἡμετέρας poss. pron. gen. fem. 1p. sg. ἡμέτερος our
θρησκείας n. gen. fem. sg. θρησκεία religion, worshipping
Φαρισαῖος n. nom. masc. sg. Φαρισαῖος Pharisee
6 καὶ conj. καί and, even, also, but
νῦν adv. νῦν now, henceforth, present, this time
ἐπ' prep. ἐπί (+gen) on, in, upon, (+dat) in, at, for, upon, (+acc) on, upon, unto, to, against
ἐλπίδι n. dat. fem. sg. ἐλπίς hope, faith
τῆς art. gen. fem. sg. ὁ ἡ τό the, this, that, he, she, it
πρὸς prep. πρός (+gen) for, (+dat) at, (+acc) unto, to, with, for, against
τοὺς art. acc. masc. pl. ὁ ἡ τό the, this, that, he, she, it
πατέρας n. acc. masc. pl. πατήρ Father, father, parent
ἐπαγγελίας n. gen. fem. sg. ἐπαγγελία promise, message
ὑπὸ prep. ὑπό (+gen) of, by, with, from, among, (+acc) under
τοῦ art. gen. masc. sg. ὁ ἡ τό the, this, that, he, she, it
Θεοῦ n. gen. masc. sg. θεός God, god
7 εἰς prep. εἰς (+acc) into, to, unto, for, in, on, toward, against, upon, at, among
ἣν relative pron. acc. fem. sg. ὅς ἥ ὅ who, which, what, that
τὸ art. nom. neut. sg. ὁ ἡ τό the, this, that, he, she, it
δωδεκάφυλον n. nom. neut. sg. δωδεκάφυλον twelve tribes
ἡμῶν pron. gen. 1p. pl. ἐγώ I
ἐν prep. ἐν (+dat) in, by, with, among, at, on, through, to, within, into, of, for
ἐκτενείᾳ n. dat. fem. sg. ἐκτένεια instantly, assiduously
νύκτα n. acc. fem. sg. νύξ night
καὶ conj. καί and, even, also, but
ἡμέραν n. acc. fem. sg. ἡμέρα day, time, year, while, age, day time
περὶ prep. περί (+gen) of, for, concerning, (+acc) about, concerning, in
ἧς relative pron. gen. fem. sg. ὅς ἥ ὅ who, which, what, that
ἐλπίδος n. gen. fem. sg. ἐλπίς hope, faith
βασιλεῦ n. voc. masc. sg. βασιλεύς king
Ἀγρίππα n. voc. masc. sg. Ἀγρίππας Agrippa
ὑπὸ prep. ὑπό (+gen) of, by, with, from, among, (+acc) under
τῶν art. gen. masc. pl. ὁ ἡ τό the, this, that, he, she, it
Ἰουδαίων adj. gen. masc. pl. Ἰουδαῖος Jew, Jewess
8 τί interrog. pron. acc. neut. sg. τίς what, who, why, where, which, how
ἄπιστον adj. nom. neut. sg. ἄπιστος faithless, unbelieving, infidel, thing incredible
παρ' prep. παρά (+gen) of, from, (+dat) with, for, (+acc) beside, at, by, above, against
ὑμῖν pron. dat. 2p. pl. σύ thou, you
εἰ conj. εἰ if, whether, that, though, forasmuch
ὁ art. nom. masc. sg. ὁ ἡ τό the, this, that, he, she, it

Θεὸς n. nom. masc. sg. θεός God, god
νεκροὺς adj. acc. masc. pl. νεκρός dead
9 ἐγὼ pron. nom. 1p. sg. ἐγώ I
μέν conj. μέν indeed, verily, truly, even, so, some
οὖν conj. οὖν therefore, then, so, and, now, wherefore
ἐμαυτῷ pron. dat. masc. 1p. sg. ἐμαυτοῦ myself, me
πρὸς prep. πρός (+gen) for, (+dat) at, (+acc) unto, to, with, for, against
τὸ art. acc. neut. sg. ὁ ἡ τό the, this, that, he, she, it
ὄνομα n. acc. neut. sg. ὄνομα name, call, surname
Ἰησοῦ n. gen. masc. sg. Ἰησοῦς Jesus
τοῦ art. gen. masc. sg. ὁ ἡ τό the, this, that, he, she, it
Ναζωραίου n. gen. masc. sg. Ναζωραῖος Nazareth, Nazarene
πολλὰ adj. acc. neut. pl. πολύς many, great, much, long, abundant
ἐναντία adj. acc. neut. pl. ἐναντίος contrary, against, over against
10 ὃ relative pron. acc. neut. sg. ὅς ἥ ὅ who, which, what, that
καὶ conj. καί and, even, also, but
ἐν prep. ἐν (+dat) in, by, with, among, at, on, through, to, within, into, of, for
Ἱεροσολύμοις n. dat. neut. sg. Ἱεροσόλυμα Jerusalem
καὶ conj. καί and, even, also, but
πολλούς adj. acc. masc. pl. πολύς many, great, much, long, abundant
τῶν art. gen. masc. pl. ὁ ἡ τό the, this, that, he, she, it
ἁγίων adj. gen. masc. pl. ἅγιος Holy, holy, saint, Holy One, holy thing, most holy
ἐγὼ pron. nom. 1p. sg. ἐγώ I
φυλακαῖς n. dat. fem. pl. φυλακή prison, watch, imprisonment, cage, hold, ward
τὴν art. acc. fem. sg. ὁ ἡ τό the, this, that, he, she, it
παρὰ prep. παρά (+gen) of, from, (+dat) with, for, (+acc) beside, at, by, above, against
τῶν art. gen. masc. pl. ὁ ἡ τό the, this, that, he, she, it
ἀρχιερέων n. gen. masc. pl. ἀρχιερεύς chief priest, high priest
ἐξουσίαν n. acc. fem. sg. ἐξουσία power, authority, right, strength, jurisdiction
τε conj. τέ and, both, also
αὐτῶν pron. gen. masc. 3p. pl. αὐτός ή ό self, of oneself, even, very, the same, he, she, it
ψῆφον n. acc. fem. sg. ψῆφος voice, pebble of voting, stone
11 καὶ conj. καί and, even, also, but
κατὰ prep. κατά (+gen) against, by, throughout, down, (+acc) according to, after, with
πάσας adj. acc. fem. pl. πᾶς πᾶσα πᾶν all, every, whosoever, every one, no, whole, any
τὰς art. acc. fem. pl. ὁ ἡ τό the, this, that, he, she, it
συναγωγὰς n. acc. fem. pl. συναγωγή synagogue, assembly, congregation
πολλάκις adv. πολλάκις often, ofttimes, oft
αὐτοὺς pron. acc. masc. 3p. pl. αὐτός ή ό self, of oneself, even, very, the same, he, she, it
περισσῶς adv. περισσῶς exceedingly, out of measure, the more
τε conj. τέ and, both, also
αὐτοῖς pron. dat. masc. 3p. pl. αὐτός ή ό self, of oneself, even, very, the same, he, she, it
ἕως conj. ἕως till, until, unto, until when, while, as far as, even, until now
καὶ conj. καί and, even, also, but
εἰς prep. εἰς (+acc) into, to, unto, for, in, on, toward, against, upon, at, among
τὰς art. acc. fem. pl. ὁ ἡ τό the, this, that, he, she, it
ἔξω adv. ἔξω out, without, out of, forth, away, outward
πόλεις n. acc. fem. pl. πόλις city
12 ἐν prep. ἐν (+dat) in, by, with, among, at, on, through, to, within, into, of, for
οἷς relative pron. dat. neut. pl. ὅς ἥ ὅ who, which, what, that
καὶ conj. καί and, even, also, but
εἰς prep. εἰς (+acc) into, to, unto, for, in, on, toward, against, upon, at, among
τὴν art. acc. fem. sg. ὁ ἡ τό the, this, that, he, she, it
Δαμασκὸν n. acc. fem. sg. Δαμασκός Damascus
μετ' prep. μετά (+gen) with, among, against, (+acc) after

ἐξουσίας n. gen. fem. sg. ἐξουσία power, authority, right, strength, jurisdiction
καὶ conj. καί and, even, also, but
ἐπιτροπῆς n. gen. fem. sg. ἐπιτροπή commission
τῆς art. gen. fem. sg. ὁ ἡ τό the, this, that, he, she, it
παρὰ prep. παρά (+gen) of, from, (+dat) with, for, (+acc) beside, at, by, above, against
τῶν art. gen. masc. pl. ὁ ἡ τό the, this, that, he, she, it
ἀρχιερέων n. gen. masc. pl. ἀρχιερεύς chief priest, high priest
13 ἡμέρας n. gen. fem. sg. ἡμέρα day, time, year, while, age, day time
μέσης adj. gen. fem. sg. μέσος midst, among, mid, between
κατὰ prep. κατά (+gen) against, by, throughout, down, (+acc) according to, after, with
τὴν art. acc. fem. sg. ὁ ἡ τό the, this, that, he, she, it
ὁδὸν n. acc. fem. sg. ὁδός way, journey, highway
βασιλεῦ n. voc. masc. sg. βασιλεύς king
οὐρανόθεν adv. οὐρανόθεν from heaven
ὑπὲρ prep. ὑπέρ (+gen) for, of, for the sake of, (+acc) above, more than
τὴν art. acc. fem. sg. ὁ ἡ τό the, this, that, he, she, it
λαμπρότητα n. acc. fem. sg. λαμπρότης brightness
τοῦ art. gen. masc. sg. ὁ ἡ τό the, this, that, he, she, it
ἡλίου n. gen. masc. sg. ἥλιος sun, east
με pron. acc. 1p. sg. ἐγώ I
φῶς n. acc. neut. sg. φῶς light, fire
καὶ conj. καί and, even, also, but
τοὺς art. acc. masc. pl. ὁ ἡ τό the, this, that, he, she, it
σὺν prep. σύν (+dat) with, beside
ἐμοὶ pron. dat. 1p. sg. ἐγώ I
14 πάντων adj. gen. masc. pl. πᾶς πᾶσα πᾶν all, every, whosoever, every one, no, whole, any
δὲ conj. δέ but, and, now, also, to the contrary, rather, then
ἡμῶν pron. gen. 1p. pl. ἐγώ I
εἰς prep. εἰς (+acc) into, to, unto, for, in, on, toward, against, upon, at, among
τὴν art. acc. fem. sg. ὁ ἡ τό the, this, that, he, she, it
γῆν n. acc. fem. sg. γῆ earth, land, ground, country
φωνὴν n. acc. fem. sg. φωνή voice, sound, noise
πρός prep. πρός (+gen) for, (+dat) at, (+acc) unto, to, with, for, against
με pron. acc. 1p. sg. ἐγώ I
καὶ conj. καί and, even, also, but
τῇ art. dat. fem. sg. ὁ ἡ τό the, this, that, he, she, it
Ἑβραΐδι adj. dat. fem. sg. Ἑβραΐς Hebrew
διαλέκτῳ n. dat. fem. sg. διάλεκτος tongue, language
Σαούλ n. voc. masc. sg. Σαούλ Saul
Σαούλ n. voc. masc. sg. Σαούλ Saul
τί interrog. pron. acc. neut. sg. τίς what, who, why, where, which, how
με pron. acc. 1p. sg. ἐγώ I
σκληρόν adj. nom. neut. sg. σκληρός hard, fierce
σοι pron. dat. 2p. sg. σύ thou, you
πρὸς prep. πρός (+gen) for, (+dat) at, (+acc) unto, to, with, for, against
κέντρα n. acc. neut. pl. κέντρον sting, prick
15 ἐγὼ pron. nom. 1p. sg. ἐγώ I
δὲ conj. δέ but, and, now, also, to the contrary, rather, then
Τίς interrog. pron. nom. masc. sg. τίς what, who, why, where, which, how
Κύριε n. voc. masc. sg. κύριος Lord, lord, master, sir, LORD, God, Master, owner
ὁ art. nom. masc. sg. ὁ ἡ τό the, this, that, he, she, it
δὲ conj. δέ but, and, now, also, to the contrary, rather, then
Ἐγώ pron. nom. 1p. sg. ἐγώ I
Ἰησοῦς n. nom. masc. sg. Ἰησοῦς Jesus
ὃν relative pron. acc. masc. sg. ὅς ἥ ὅ who, which, what, that

σὺ pron. nom. 2p. sg. σύ thou, you
16 ἀλλὰ conj. ἀλλά but, yea, yet, nevertheless, howbeit, nay, therefore
καὶ conj. καί and, even, also, but
ἐπὶ prep. ἐπί (+gen) on, in, upon, (+dat) in, at, for, upon, (+acc) on, upon, unto, to, against
τοὺς art. acc. masc. pl. ὁ ἡ τό the, this, that, he, she, it
πόδας n. acc. masc. pl. πούς foot
σου pron. gen. 2p. sg. σύ thou, you
εἰς prep. εἰς (+acc) into, to, unto, for, in, on, toward, against, upon, at, among
τοῦτο demo. pron. acc. neut. sg. οὗτος αὕτη τοῦτο this, the same, this same, he, she, it
γὰρ conj. γάρ for, and, because, but, indeed
σοι pron. dat. 2p. sg. σύ thou, you
σε pron. acc. 2p. sg. σύ thou, you
ὑπηρέτην n. acc. masc. sg. ὑπηρέτης officer, minister, servant
καὶ conj. καί and, even, also, but
μάρτυρα n. acc. masc. sg. μάρτυς or μάρτυρ witness, martyr, record
ὧν relative pron. gen. neut. pl. ὅς ἥ ὅ who, which, what, that
τε conj. τέ and, both, also
ὧν relative pron. gen. neut. pl. ὅς ἥ ὅ who, which, what, that
τε conj. τέ and, both, also
σοι pron. dat. 2p. sg. σύ thou, you
17 σε pron. acc. 2p. sg. σύ thou, you
ἐκ prep. ἐκ ἐξ (+gen) of, from, out of, by, on, with, in, among, through
τοῦ art. gen. masc. sg. ὁ ἡ τό the, this, that, he, she, it
λαοῦ n. gen. masc. sg. λαός people
καὶ conj. καί and, even, also, but
τῶν art. gen. neut. pl. ὁ ἡ τό the, this, that, he, she, it
ἐθνῶν n. gen. neut. pl. ἔθνος Gentile, nation, heathen, people
εἰς prep. εἰς (+acc) into, to, unto, for, in, on, toward, against, upon, at, among
οὓς relative pron. acc. masc. pl. ὅς ἥ ὅ who, which, what, that
νῦν adv. νῦν now, henceforth, present, this time
σε pron. acc. 2p. sg. σύ thou, you
18 ὀφθαλμοὺς n. acc. masc. pl. ὀφθαλμός eye, sight
αὐτῶν pron. gen. masc. 3p. pl. αὐτός ἡ ὁ self, of oneself, even, very, the same, he, she, it
καὶ conj. καί and, even, also, but
ἀπὸ prep. ἀπό (+gen) from, of, out of, since, for, off, at, by, in, on
σκότους n. gen. neut. sg. σκότος darkness
εἰς prep. εἰς (+acc) into, to, unto, for, in, on, toward, against, upon, at, among
φῶς n. acc. neut. sg. φῶς light, fire
καὶ conj. καί and, even, also, but
τῆς art. gen. fem. sg. ὁ ἡ τό the, this, that, he, she, it
ἐξουσίας n. gen. fem. sg. ἐξουσία power, authority, right, strength, jurisdiction
τοῦ art. gen. masc. sg. ὁ ἡ τό the, this, that, he, she, it
Σατανᾶ n. gen. masc. sg. Σατανᾶς Satan
ἐπὶ prep. ἐπί (+gen) on, in, upon, (+dat) in, at, for, upon, (+acc) on, upon, unto, to, against
τὸν art. acc. masc. sg. ὁ ἡ τό the, this, that, he, she, it
Θεόν n. acc. masc. sg. θεός God, god
τοῦ art. gen. neut. sg. ὁ ἡ τό the, this, that, he, she, it
αὐτοὺς pron. acc. masc. 3p. pl. αὐτός ἡ ὁ self, of oneself, even, very, the same, he, she, it
ἄφεσιν n. acc. fem. sg. ἄφεσις remission, forgiveness, deliverance, liberty
ἁμαρτιῶν n. gen. fem. pl. ἁμαρτία sin, offence, sinful
καὶ conj. καί and, even, also, but
κλῆρον n. acc. masc. sg. κλῆρος lot, inheritance, part, heritage
ἐν prep. ἐν (+dat) in, by, with, among, at, on, through, to, within, into, of, for
τοῖς art. dat. masc. pl. ὁ ἡ τό the, this, that, he, she, it
πίστει n. dat. fem. sg. πίστις faith, assurance, belief, fidelity

τῇ art. dat. fem. sg. ὁ ἡ τό the, this, that, he, she, it
εἰς prep. εἰς (+acc) into, to, unto, for, in, on, toward, against, upon, at, among
ἐμέ pron. acc. 1p. sg. ἐγώ I
19 ὅθεν adv. ὅθεν wherefore, from whence, whereupon, where, from thence, whence
βασιλεῦ n. voc. masc. sg. βασιλεύς king
Ἀγρίππα n. voc. masc. sg. Ἀγρίππας Agrippa
οὐκ particle of negation. οὐ οὐκ οὐχ not, no, neither, none, nay, nor, never, nothing
ἀπειθὴς adj. nom. masc. sg. ἀπειθής disobedient
τῇ art. dat. fem. sg. ὁ ἡ τό the, this, that, he, she, it
οὐρανίῳ adj. dat. fem. sg. οὐράνιος heavenly
ὀπτασίᾳ n. dat. fem. sg. ὀπτασία vision
20 ἀλλὰ conj. ἀλλά but, yea, yet, nevertheless, howbeit, nay, therefore
τοῖς art. dat. masc. pl. ὁ ἡ τό the, this, that, he, she, it
ἐν prep. ἐν (+dat) in, by, with, among, at, on, through, to, within, into, of, for
Δαμασκῷ n. dat. fem. sg. Δαμασκός Damascus
πρῶτον ordinal. adj. acc. neut. sg. πρῶτος first, chief, first of all, chiefest, best
καὶ conj. καί and, even, also, but
Ἱεροσολύμοις n. dat. neut. pl. Ἱεροσόλυμα Jerusalem
εἰς prep. εἰς (+acc) into, to, unto, for, in, on, toward, against, upon, at, among
πᾶσάν adj. acc. fem. sg. πᾶς πᾶσα πᾶν all, every, whosoever, every one, no, whole, any
τε conj. τέ and, both, also
τὴν art. acc. fem. sg. ὁ ἡ τό the, this, that, he, she, it
χώραν n. acc. fem. sg. χώρα country, region, land, field, coast, ground
τῆς art. gen. fem. sg. ὁ ἡ τό the, this, that, he, she, it
Ἰουδαίας n. gen. fem. sg. Ἰουδαία Judaea, Jewry
καὶ conj. καί and, even, also, but
τοῖς art. dat. neut. pl. ὁ ἡ τό the, this, that, he, she, it
ἔθνεσιν n. dat. neut. pl. ἔθνος Gentile, nation, heathen, people
καὶ conj. καί and, even, also, but
ἐπὶ prep. ἐπί (+gen) on, in, upon, (+dat) in, at, for, upon, (+acc) on, upon, unto, to, against
τὸν art. acc. masc. sg. ὁ ἡ τό the, this, that, he, she, it
Θεόν n. acc. masc. sg. θεός God, god
ἄξια adj. acc. neut. pl. ἄξιος worthy, meet, due reward
τῆς art. gen. fem. sg. ὁ ἡ τό the, this, that, he, she, it
μετανοίας n. gen. fem. sg. μετάνοια repentance
ἔργα n. acc. neut. pl. ἔργον work, deed, doing labour
21 ἕνεκεν prep. ἕνεκα, ἕνεκεν or εἵνεκεν (+gen) for the sake, for a cause, for, by reason of
τούτων demo. pron. gen. neut. pl. οὗτος αὕτη τοῦτο this, the same, this same, he, she, it
με pron. acc. 1p. sg. ἐγώ I
οἱ art. nom. masc. pl. ὁ ἡ τό the, this, that, he, she, it
Ἰουδαῖοι adj. nom. masc. pl. Ἰουδαῖος Jew, Jewess
ἐν prep. ἐν (+dat) in, by, with, among, at, on, through, to, within, into, of, for
τῷ art. dat. neut. sg. ὁ ἡ τό the, this, that, he, she, it
ἱερῷ n. dat. neut. sg. ἱερόν temple
22 ἐπικουρίας n. gen. fem. sg. ἐπικουρία help
οὖν conj. οὖν therefore, then, so, and, now, wherefore
τῆς art. gen. fem. sg. ὁ ἡ τό the, this, that, he, she, it
παρὰ prep. παρά (+gen) of, from, (+dat) with, for, (+acc) beside, at, by, above, against
τοῦ art. gen. masc. sg. ὁ ἡ τό the, this, that, he, she, it
Θεοῦ n. gen. masc. sg. θεός God, god
ἄχρι prep. ἄχρι or ἄχρις (+gen) until, unto, till, even to, as far as, while, into
τῆς art. gen. fem. sg. ὁ ἡ τό the, this, that, he, she, it
ἡμέρας n. gen. fem. sg. ἡμέρα day, time, year, while, age, day time
ταύτης demo. pron. gen. fem. sg. οὗτος αὕτη τοῦτο this, the same, this same, he, she, it
μικρῷ adj. dat. masc. sg. μικρός little, small, least, less

τε conj. τέ and, both, also
καὶ conj. καί and, even, also, but
μεγάλῳ adj. dat. masc. sg. μέγας great, loud, greatest, high, large, mighty, strong
οὐδὲν adj. acc. neut. sg. οὐδείς no man, nothing, no, none, neither, not, nought
ἐκτὸς prep. ἐκτός except, out of, other than, outside, unless, without
ὧν relative pron. gen. neut. pl. ὅς ἥ ὅ who, which, what, that
τε conj. τέ and, both, also
οἱ art. nom. masc. pl. ὁ ἡ τό the, this, that, he, she, it
προφῆται n. nom. masc. pl. προφήτης prophet
καὶ conj. καί and, even, also, but
Μωσῆς n. nom. masc. sg. Μωσῆς Moses
23 εἰ conj. εἰ if, whether, that, though, forasmuch
παθητὸς adj. nom. masc. sg. παθητός suffer
ὁ art. nom. masc. sg. ὁ ἡ τό the, this, that, he, she, it
Χριστός n. nom. masc. sg. Χριστός Christ
εἰ conj. εἰ if, whether, that, though, forasmuch
πρῶτος ordinal. adj. nom. masc. sg. πρῶτος first, chief, first of all, chiefest, best
ἐξ prep. ἐκ ἐξ (+gen) of, from, out of, by, on, with, in, among, through
ἀναστάσεως n. gen. fem. sg. ἀνάστασις resurrection, rising again
νεκρῶν adj. gen. masc. pl. νεκρός dead
φῶς n. acc. neut. sg. φῶς light, fire
τῷ art. dat. masc. sg. ὁ ἡ τό the, this, that, he, she, it
λαῷ n. dat. masc. sg. λαός people
καὶ conj. καί and, even, also, but
τοῖς art. dat. neut. pl. ὁ ἡ τό the, this, that, he, she, it
ἔθνεσι n. dat. neut. pl. ἔθνος Gentile, nation, heathen, people
24 Ταῦτα demo. pron. acc. neut. pl. οὗτος αὕτη τοῦτο this, the same, this same, he, she, it
δὲ conj. δέ but, and, now, also, to the contrary, rather, then
αὐτοῦ pron. gen. masc. 3p. sg. αὐτός ἡ ὁ self, of oneself, even, very, the same, he, she, it
ὁ art. nom. masc. sg. ὁ ἡ τό the, this, that, he, she, it
Φῆστος n. nom. masc. sg. Φῆστος Festus
μεγάλῃ adj. dat. fem. sg. μέγας great, loud, greatest, high, large, mighty, strong
τῇ art. dat. fem. sg. ὁ ἡ τό the, this, that, he, she, it
φωνῇ n. dat. fem. sg. φωνή voice, sound, noise
Παῦλε n. voc. masc. sg. Παῦλος Paul, Paulus
τὰ art. nom. neut. pl. ὁ ἡ τό the, this, that, he, she, it
πολλά adj. nom. neut. pl. πολύς many, great, much, long, abundant
σε pron. acc. 2p. sg. σύ thou, you
γράμματα n. nom. neut. pl. γράμμα letter, bill, learning, scripture, writing
εἰς prep. εἰς (+acc) into, to, unto, for, in, on, toward, against, upon, at, among
μανίαν n. acc. fem. sg. μανία mad, madness
25 ὁ art. nom. masc. sg. ὁ ἡ τό the, this, that, he, she, it
δὲ conj. δέ but, and, now, also, to the contrary, rather, then
Οὐ particle of negation. οὐ οὐκ οὐχ not, no, neither, none, nay, nor, never, nothing
κράτιστε superl. adj. voc. masc. sg. κράτιστος most excellent, most noble
Φῆστε n. voc. masc. sg. Φῆστος Festus
ἀλλ' conj. ἀλλά but, yea, yet, nevertheless, howbeit, nay, therefore
ἀληθείας n. gen. fem. sg. ἀλήθεια truth, verity
καὶ conj. καί and, even, also, but
σωφροσύνης n. gen. fem. sg. σωφροσύνη soberness, sobriety
ῥήματα n. acc. neut. pl. ῥῆμα word, saying, thing
26 γὰρ conj. γάρ for, and, because, but, indeed
περὶ prep. περί (+gen) of, for, concerning, (+acc) about, concerning, in
τούτων demo. pron. gen. neut. pl. οὗτος αὕτη τοῦτο this, the same, this same, he, she, it
ὁ art. nom. masc. sg. ὁ ἡ τό the, this, that, he, she, it

βασιλεὺς n. nom. masc. sg. βασιλεύς king
πρὸς prep. πρός (+gen) for, (+dat) at, (+acc) unto, to, with, for, against
ὃν relative pron. acc. masc. sg. ὅς ἥ ὅ who, which, what, that
καὶ conj. καί and, even, also, but
γὰρ conj. γάρ for, and, because, but, indeed
αὐτόν pron. acc. masc. 3p. sg. αὐτός ή ό self, of oneself, even, very, the same, he, she, it
τι indefinite pron. acc. neut. sg. τὶς certain, some, any man, one, any thing
τούτων demo. pron. gen. neut. pl. οὗτος αὕτη τοῦτο this, the same, this same, he, she, it
οὐ particle of negation. οὐ οὐκ οὐχ not, no, neither, none, nay, nor, never, nothing
οὐδέν num. acc. neut. sg. οὐδείς no man, nothing, no, none, neither, not, nought
οὐ particle of negation. οὐ οὐκ οὐχ not, no, neither, none, nay, nor, never, nothing
γὰρ conj. γάρ for, and, because, but, indeed
ἐν prep. ἐν (+dat) in, by, with, among, at, on, through, to, within, into, of, for
γωνίᾳ n. dat. fem. sg. γωνία corner, quarter
τοῦτο demo. pron. nom. neut. sg. οὗτος αὕτη τοῦτο this, the same, this same, he, she, it
27 βασιλεῦ n. voc. masc. sg. βασιλεύς king
Ἀγρίππα n. voc. masc. sg. Ἀγρίππας Agrippa
τοῖς art. dat. masc. pl. ὁ ἡ τό the, this, that, he, she, it
προφήταις n. dat. masc. pl. προφήτης prophet
ὅτι conj. ὅτι that, for, because, how that, how, because that, for that, though
28 ὁ art. nom. masc. sg. ὁ ἡ τό the, this, that, he, she, it
δὲ conj. δέ but, and, now, also, to the contrary, rather, then
Ἀγρίππας n. nom. masc. sg. Ἀγρίππας Agrippa
πρὸς prep. πρός (+gen) for, (+dat) at, (+acc) unto, to, with, for, against
τὸν art. acc. masc. sg. ὁ ἡ τό the, this, that, he, she, it
Παῦλον n. acc. masc. sg. Παῦλος Paul, Paulus
Ἐν prep. ἐν (+dat) in, by, with, among, at, on, through, to, within, into, of, for
ὀλίγῳ adj. dat. neut. sg. ὀλίγος few, little, small, a while, brief, short, short space
με pron. acc. 1p. sg. ἐγώ I
Χριστιανὸν n. acc. masc. sg. Χριστιανός Christian
29 ὁ art. nom. masc. sg. ὁ ἡ τό the, this, that, he, she, it
δὲ conj. δέ but, and, now, also, to the contrary, rather, then
Παῦλος n. nom. masc. sg. Παῦλος Paul, Paulus
ἂν particle. ἄν Indicating contingency. No English translation.
τῷ art. dat. masc. sg. ὁ ἡ τό the, this, that, he, she, it
Θεῷ n. dat. masc. sg. θεός God, god
καὶ conj. καί and, even, also, but
ἐν prep. ἐν (+dat) in, by, with, among, at, on, through, to, within, into, of, for
ὀλίγῳ adj. dat. neut. sg. ὀλίγος few, little, small, a while, brief, short, short space
καὶ conj. καί and, even, also, but
ἐν prep. ἐν (+dat) in, by, with, among, at, on, through, to, within, into, of, for
πολλῷ adj. dat. neut. sg. πολύς many, great, much, long, abundant
οὐ particle of negation. οὐ οὐκ οὐχ not, no, neither, none, nay, nor, never, nothing
μόνον adv. μόνος only, alone, by oneself
σὲ pron. acc. 2p. sg. σύ thou, you
ἀλλὰ conj. ἀλλά but, yea, yet, nevertheless, howbeit, nay, therefore
καὶ conj. καί and, even, also, but
πάντας adj. acc. masc. pl. πᾶς πᾶσα πᾶν all, every, whosoever, every one, no, whole, any
τοὺς art. acc. masc. pl. ὁ ἡ τό the, this, that, he, she, it
μου pron. gen. 1p. sg. ἐγώ I
σήμερον adv. σήμερον this day, today
τοιούτους demo. pron. acc. masc. pl. τοιοῦτος such, like
ὁποῖος adj. nom. masc. sg. ὁποῖος what manner of, as, of what sort, whatsoever
κἀγώ pron. nom. 1p. σγ. κἀγώ and I, I also, so I, even as I
παρεκτὸς prep. παρεκτός (+gen) except, saving. (adv.) without, besides

τῶν art. gen. neut. pl. ὁ ἡ τό the, this, that, he, she, it
δεσμῶν n. gen. neut. pl. δεσμός bond, band, chain, string
τούτων demo. pron. gen. neut. pl. οὗτος αὕτη τοῦτο this, the same, this same, he, she, it
30 Καὶ conj. καί and, even, also, but
ταῦτα demo. pron. acc. neut. pl. οὗτος αὕτη τοῦτο this, the same, this same, he, she, it
αὐτοῦ pron. gen. masc. 3p. sg. αὐτός ή ὁ self, of oneself, even, very, the same, he, she, it
ὁ art. nom. masc. sg. ὁ ἡ τό the, this, that, he, she, it
βασιλεὺς n. nom. masc. sg. βασιλεύς king
καὶ conj. καί and, even, also, but
ὁ art. nom. masc. sg. ὁ ἡ τό the, this, that, he, she, it
ἡγεμὼν n. nom. masc. sg. ἡγεμών governor, ruler, prince
ἥ art. nom. fem. sg. ὁ ἡ τό the, this, that, he, she, it
τε conj. τέ and, both, also
Βερνίκη n. nom. fem. sg. Βερνίκη Bernice
καὶ conj. καί and, even, also, but
οἱ art. nom. masc. pl. ὁ ἡ τό the, this, that, he, she, it
αὐτοῖς pron. dat. masc. 3p. pl. αὐτός ή ὁ self, of oneself, even, very, the same, he, she, it
31 καὶ conj. καί and, even, also, but
πρὸς prep. πρός (+gen) for, (+dat) at, (+acc) unto, to, with, for, against
ἀλλήλους pron. acc. masc. 3p. pl. ἀλλήλων one another, themselves, together, mutual
ὅτι conj. ὅτι that, for, because, how that, how, because that, for that, though
Οὐδὲν adj. acc. neut. sg. οὐδείς no man, nothing, no, none, neither, not, nought
θανάτου n. gen. masc. sg. θάνατος death
ἄξιόν adj. acc. neut. sg. ἄξιος worthy, meet, due reward
ἢ particle. ἤ or, than, either, nor, or else, and, rather than
δεσμῶν n. gen. neut. pl. δεσμός bond, band, chain, string
ὁ art. nom. masc. sg. ὁ ἡ τό the, this, that, he, she, it
ἄνθρωπος n. nom. masc. sg. ἄνθρωπος man, human being, person, one, certain
οὗτος demo. pron. nom. masc. sg. οὗτος αὕτη τοῦτο this, the same, this same, he, she, it
32 Ἀγρίππας n. nom. masc. sg. Ἀγρίππας Agrippa
δὲ conj. δέ but, and, now, also, to the contrary, rather, then
τῷ art. dat. masc. sg. ὁ ἡ τό the, this, that, he, she, it
Φήστῳ n. dat. masc. sg. Φῆστος Festus
ὁ art. nom. masc. sg. ὁ ἡ τό the, this, that, he, she, it
ἄνθρωπος n. nom. masc. sg. ἄνθρωπος man, human being, person, one, certain
οὗτος demo. pron. nom. masc. sg. οὗτος αὕτη τοῦτο this, the same, this same, he, she, it
εἰ conj. εἰ if, whether, that, though, forasmuch
μὴ particle of negation. μή not, no, lest, neither, none, nothing, nor, never, without
Καίσαρα n. acc. masc. sg. Καῖσαρ Caesar

27

1 Ὡς conj. ὡς as, when, as it were, how, about, like, as soon as, even as, while
δὲ conj. δέ but, and, now, also, to the contrary, rather, then
τοῦ art. gen. neut. sg. ὁ ἡ τό the, this, that, he, she, it
ἡμᾶς pron. acc. 1p. pl. ἐγώ I
εἰς prep. εἰς (+acc) into, to, unto, for, in, on, toward, against, upon, at, among
τὴν art. acc. fem. sg. ὁ ἡ τό the, this, that, he, she, it
Ἰταλίαν n. acc. fem. sg. Ἰταλία Italy
τόν art. acc. masc. sg. ὁ ἡ τό the, this, that, he, she, it
τε conj. τέ and, both, also
Παῦλον n. acc. masc. sg. Παῦλος Paul, Paulus
καί conj. καί and, even, also, but
τινας indefinite pron. acc. masc. pl. τὶς certain, some, any man, one, any thing
ἑτέρους adj. acc. masc. pl. ἕτερος another, other, else, strange

δεσμώτας n. acc. masc. pl. δεσμώτης prisoner
ἑκατοντάρχῃ n. dat. masc. sg. ἑκατοντάρχης centurion
ὀνόματι n. dat. neut. sg. ὄνομα name, call, surname
Ἰουλίῳ n. dat. masc. sg. Ἰούλιος Julius
σπείρης n. gen. fem. sg. σπεῖρα band
Σεβαστῆς adj. gen. fem. sg. Σεβαστός Augustus
2 δὲ conj. δέ but, and, now, also, to the contrary, rather, then
πλοίῳ n. dat. neut. sg. πλοῖον ship, boat
Ἀδραμυττηνῷ adj. dat. neut. sg. Ἀδραμυττηνός of Adramyttium
τοὺς art. acc. masc. pl. ὁ ἡ τό the, this, that, he, she, it
κατὰ prep. κατά (+gen) against, by, throughout, down, (+acc) according to, after, with
τὴν art. acc. fem. sg. ὁ ἡ τό the, this, that, he, she, it
Ἀσίαν n. acc. fem. sg. Ἀσία Asia
τόπους n. acc. masc. pl. τόπος place, room, quarter
σὺν prep. σύν (+dat) with, beside
ἡμῖν pron. dat. 1p. pl. ἐγώ I
Ἀριστάρχου n. gen. masc. sg. Ἀρίσταρχος Aristarchus
Μακεδόνος n. gen. masc. sg. Μακεδών of Macedonia, Macedonian
Θεσσαλονικέως n. gen. masc. sg. Θεσσαλονικεύς Thessalonian, of Thessalonica
3 τῇ art. dat. fem. sg. ὁ ἡ τό the, this, that, he, she, it
τε conj. τέ and, both, also
ἑτέρᾳ adj. dat. fem. sg. ἕτερος another, other, else, strange
εἰς prep. εἰς (+acc) into, to, unto, for, in, on, toward, against, upon, at, among
Σιδῶνα n. acc. fem. sg. Σιδών Sidon
φιλανθρώπως adv. φιλανθρώπως courteously
τε conj. τέ and, both, also
ὁ art. nom. masc. sg. ὁ ἡ τό the, this, that, he, she, it
Ἰούλιος n. nom. masc. sg. Ἰούλιος Julius
τῷ art. dat. masc. sg. ὁ ἡ τό the, this, that, he, she, it
Παύλῳ n. dat. masc. sg. Παῦλος Paul, Paulus
πρὸς prep. πρός (+gen) for, (+dat) at, (+acc) unto, to, with, for, against
τοὺς art. acc. masc. pl. ὁ ἡ τό the, this, that, he, she, it
φίλους adj. acc. masc. pl. φίλος friend
ἐπιμελείας n. gen. fem. sg. ἐπιμέλεια refresh, care
4 κἀκεῖθεν adv. κἀκεῖθεν and from thence, and thence, and afterward, thence also
τὴν art. acc. fem. sg. ὁ ἡ τό the, this, that, he, she, it
Κύπρον n. acc. fem. sg. Κύπρος Cyprus
διὰ prep. διά (+gen) by, through, with, in, of, (+acc) for, because of, for a cause
τὸ art. acc. neut. sg. ὁ ἡ τό the, this, that, he, she, it
τοὺς art. acc. masc. pl. ὁ ἡ τό the, this, that, he, she, it
ἀνέμους n. acc. masc. pl. ἄνεμος wind
ἐναντίους adj. acc. masc. pl. ἐναντίος contrary, against, over against
5 τό art. acc. neut. sg. ὁ ἡ τό the, this, that, he, she, it
τε conj. τέ and, both, also
πέλαγος n. acc. neut. sg. πέλαγος depth, sea
τό art. acc. neut. sg. ὁ ἡ τό the, this, that, he, she, it
κατὰ prep. κατά (+gen) against, by, throughout, down, (+acc) according to, after, with
τὴν art. acc. fem. sg. ὁ ἡ τό the, this, that, he, she, it
Κιλικίαν n. acc. fem. sg. Κιλικία Cilicia
καὶ conj. καί and, even, also, but
Παμφυλίαν n. acc. fem. sg. Παμφυλία Pamphylia
εἰς prep. εἰς (+acc) into, to, unto, for, in, on, toward, against, upon, at, among
Μύρα n. acc. neut. pl. Μύρα Myra
τῆς art. gen. fem. sg. ὁ ἡ τό the, this, that, he, she, it
Λυκίας n. gen. fem. sg. Λυκία Lycia

6 κἀκεῖ adv. κἀκεῖ and there, there also, thither also
ὁ art. nom. masc. sg. ὁ ἡ τό the, this, that, he, she, it
ἑκατόνταρχος n. nom. masc. sg. ἑκατόνταρχος centurion
πλοῖον n. acc. neut. sg. πλοῖον ship, boat
Ἀλεξανδρῖνον adj. acc. neut. sg. Ἀλεξανδρῖνος of Alexandria
εἰς prep. εἰς (+acc) into, to, unto, for, in, on, toward, against, upon, at, among
τὴν art. acc. fem. sg. ὁ ἡ τό the, this, that, he, she, it
Ἰταλίαν n. acc. fem. sg. Ἰταλία Italy
ἡμᾶς pron. acc. 1p. pl. ἐγώ I
εἰς prep. εἰς (+acc) into, to, unto, for, in, on, toward, against, upon, at, among
αὐτό pron. acc. neut. 3p. sg. αὐτός ἡ ὁ self, of oneself, even, very, the same, he, she, it
7 ἐν prep. ἐν (+dat) in, by, with, among, at, on, through, to, within, into, of, for
ἱκαναῖς adj. dat. fem. pl. ἱκανός many, much, long, worthy, sufficient, great, able
δὲ conj. δέ but, and, now, also, to the contrary, rather, then
ἡμέραις n. dat. fem. pl. ἡμέρα day, time, year, while, age, day time
καὶ conj. καί and, even, also, but
μόλις adv. μόλις scarce, with difficulty, scarcely, hardly
κατὰ prep. κατά (+gen) against, by, throughout, down, (+acc) according to, after, with
τὴν art. acc. fem. sg. ὁ ἡ τό the, this, that, he, she, it
Κνίδον n. acc. fem. sg. Κνίδος Cnidus
μὴ particle of negation. μή not, no, lest, neither, none, nothing, nor, never, without
ἡμᾶς pron. acc. 1p. pl. ἐγώ I
τοῦ art. gen. masc. sg. ὁ ἡ τό the, this, that, he, she, it
ἀνέμου n. gen. masc. sg. ἄνεμος wind
τὴν art. acc. fem. sg. ὁ ἡ τό the, this, that, he, she, it
Κρήτην n. acc. fem. sg. Κρήτη Crete
κατὰ prep. κατά (+gen) against, by, throughout, down, (+acc) according to, after, with
Σαλμώνην n. acc. fem. sg. Σαλμώνη Salmone
8 μόλις adv. μόλις scarce, with difficulty, scarcely, hardly
τε conj. τέ and, both, also
αὐτὴν pron. acc. fem. 3p. sg. αὐτός ἡ ὁ self, of oneself, even, very, the same, he, she, it
εἰς prep. εἰς (+acc) into, to, unto, for, in, on, toward, against, upon, at, among
τόπον n. acc. masc. sg. τόπος place, room, quarter
τινὰ indefinite pron. acc. masc. sg. τὶς certain, some, any man, one, any thing
Καλοὺς adj. acc. masc. pl. καλός good, better, goodly, meet, honest, fair, well, worthy
Λιμένας n. acc. masc. pl. λιμήν haven
ᾧ relative pron. dat. masc. sg. ὅς ἥ ὅ who, which, what, that
ἐγγὺς adv. ἐγγύς nigh, at hand, near, nigh at hand, ready, nigh unto
πόλις n. nom. fem. sg. πόλις city
Λασαία n. nom. fem. sg. Λασαία Lasea
9 Ἱκανοῦ adj. gen. masc. sg. ἱκανός many, much, long, worthy, sufficient, great, able
δὲ conj. δέ but, and, now, also, to the contrary, rather, then
χρόνου n. gen. masc. sg. χρόνος time, season, space
καὶ conj. καί and, even, also, but
ἤδη adv. ἤδη now, already, yet, by this time, even now, now already
ἐπισφαλοῦς adj. gen. masc. sg. ἐπισφαλής dangerous
τοῦ art. gen. masc. sg. ὁ ἡ τό the, this, that, he, she, it
πλοὸς n. gen. masc. sg. πλόος course, voyage, sailing
διὰ prep. διά (+gen) by, through, with, in, of, (+acc) for, because of, for a cause
τὸ art. acc. neut. sg. ὁ ἡ τό the, this, that, he, she, it
καὶ conj. καί and, even, also, but
τὴν art. acc. fem. sg. ὁ ἡ τό the, this, that, he, she, it
νηστείαν n. acc. fem. sg. νηστεία fasting, fast
ἤδη adv. ἤδη now, already, yet, by this time, even now, now already
ὁ art. nom. masc. sg. ὁ ἡ τό the, this, that, he, she, it

Παῦλος n. nom. masc. sg. Παῦλος Paul, Paulus
10 αὐτοῖς pron. dat. masc. 3p. pl. αὐτός ἡ ὁ self, of oneself, even, very, the same, he, she, it
Ἄνδρες n. voc. masc. pl. ἀνήρ man, husband, sir
ὅτι conj. ὅτι that, for, because, how that, how, because that, for that, though
μετὰ prep. μετά (+gen) with, among, against, (+acc) after
ὕβρεως n. gen. fem. sg. ὕβρις hurt, harm, reproach
καὶ conj. καί and, even, also, but
πολλῆς adj. gen. fem. sg. πολύς many, great, much, long, abundant
ζημίας n. gen. fem. sg. ζημία damage, loss
οὐ particle of negation. οὐ οὐκ οὐχ not, no, neither, none, nay, nor, never, nothing
μόνον adv. μόνος only, alone, by oneself
τοῦ art. gen. masc. sg. ὁ ἡ τό the, this, that, he, she, it
φόρτου n. gen. masc. sg. φόρτος lading, cargo
καὶ conj. καί and, even, also, but
τοῦ art. gen. masc. sg. ὁ ἡ τό the, this, that, he, she, it
πλοίου n. gen. neut. sg. πλοῖον ship, boat
ἀλλὰ conj. ἀλλά but, yea, yet, nevertheless, howbeit, nay, therefore
καὶ conj. καί and, even, also, but
τῶν art. gen. fem. pl. ὁ ἡ τό the, this, that, he, she, it
ψυχῶν n. gen. fem. pl. ψυχή life, soul, mind, heart
ἡμῶν pron. gen. 1p. pl. ἐγώ I
τὸν art. acc. masc. sg. ὁ ἡ τό the, this, that, he, she, it
πλοῦν n. acc. masc. sg. πλόος course, voyage, sailing
11 ὁ art. nom. masc. sg. ὁ ἡ τό the, this, that, he, she, it
δὲ conj. δέ but, and, now, also, to the contrary, rather, then
ἑκατόνταρχος n. nom. masc. sg. ἑκατόνταρχος centurion
τῷ art. dat. masc. sg. ὁ ἡ τό the, this, that, he, she, it
κυβερνήτῃ n. dat. masc. sg. κυβερνήτης master, shipmaster
καὶ conj. καί and, even, also, but
τῷ art. dat. masc. sg. ὁ ἡ τό the, this, that, he, she, it
ναυκλήρῳ n. dat. masc. sg. ναύκληρος owner of the ship
μᾶλλον compar. adv. μᾶλλον rather, more, more and more, better, much, much the more
ἢ particle. ἤ or, than, either, nor, or else, and, rather than
τοῖς art. dat. neut. pl. ὁ ἡ τό the, this, that, he, she, it
ὑπὸ prep. ὑπό (+gen) of, by, with, from, among, (+acc) under
τοῦ art. gen. masc. sg. ὁ ἡ τό the, this, that, he, she, it
Παύλου n. gen. masc. sg. Παῦλος Paul, Paulus
12 ἀνευθέτου adj. gen. masc. sg. ἀνεύθετος not commodious, not suitable
δὲ conj. δέ but, and, now, also, to the contrary, rather, then
τοῦ art. gen. masc. sg. ὁ ἡ τό the, this, that, he, she, it
λιμένος n. gen. masc. sg. λιμήν haven
πρὸς prep. πρός (+gen) for, (+dat) at, (+acc) unto, to, with, for, against
παραχειμασίαν n. acc. fem. sg. παραχειμασία winter in
οἱ art. nom. masc. pl. ὁ ἡ τό the, this, that, he, she, it
πλείους compar. adj. nom. masc. pl. πλείων more, many, greater, further, more part
βουλὴν n. acc. fem. sg. βουλή counsel, advise, will
κἀκεῖθεν adv. κἀκεῖθεν and from thence, and thence, and afterward, thence also
εἴπως conj. εἴπως if by any means
εἰς prep. εἰς (+acc) into, to, unto, for, in, on, toward, against, upon, at, among
Φοίνικα n. acc. masc. sg. Φοίνιξ Phenice
λιμένα n. acc. masc. sg. λιμήν haven
τῆς art. gen. fem. sg. ὁ ἡ τό the, this, that, he, she, it
Κρήτης n. gen. fem. sg. Κρήτη Crete
κατὰ prep. κατά (+gen) against, by, throughout, down, (+acc) according to, after, with
λίβα n. acc. masc. sg. λίψ south west

καὶ conj. καί and, even, also, but
κατὰ prep. κατά (+gen) against, by, throughout, down, (+acc) according to, after, with
χῶρον n. acc. masc. sg. χῶρος north west
13 δὲ conj. δέ but, and, now, also, to the contrary, rather, then
νότου n. gen. masc. sg. νότος south, south wind
τῆς art. gen. fem. sg. ὁ ἡ τό the, this, that, he, she, it
προθέσεως n. gen. fem. sg. πρόθεσις purpose, shew, shewbread
ἆσσον compar. adv. ἆσσον close
τὴν art. acc. fem. sg. ὁ ἡ τό the, this, that, he, she, it
Κρήτην n. acc. fem. sg. Κρήτη Crete
14 μετ' prep. μετά (+gen) with, among, against, (+acc) after
οὐ particle of negation. οὐ οὐκ οὐχ not, no, neither, none, nay, nor, never, nothing
πολὺ adj. acc. neut. sg. πολύς many, great, much, long, abundant
δὲ conj. δέ but, and, now, also, to the contrary, rather, then
κατ' prep. κατά (+gen) against, by, throughout, down, (+acc) according to, after, with
αὐτῆς pron. gen. fem. 3p. sg. αὐτός ἡ ὁ self, of oneself, even, very, the same, he, she, it
ἄνεμος n. nom. masc. sg. ἄνεμος wind
τυφωνικὸς adj. nom. masc. sg. τυφωνικός tempestuous
ὁ art. nom. masc. sg. ὁ ἡ τό the, this, that, he, she, it
Εὐροκλύδων n. nom. masc. sg. Εὐροκλύδων Euroclydon
15 δὲ conj. δέ but, and, now, also, to the contrary, rather, then
τοῦ art. gen. neut. sg. ὁ ἡ τό the, this, that, he, she, it
πλοίου n. gen. neut. sg. πλοῖον ship, boat
καὶ conj. καί and, even, also, but
μὴ particle of negation. μή not, no, lest, neither, none, nothing, nor, never, without
τῷ art. dat. masc. sg. ὁ ἡ τό the, this, that, he, she, it
ἀνέμῳ n. dat. masc. sg. ἄνεμος wind
16 νησίον n. acc. neut. sg. νησίον island
δέ conj. δέ but, and, now, also, to the contrary, rather, then
τι indefinite pron. acc. neut. sg. τὶς certain, some, any man, one, any thing
Κλαύδην n. acc. neut. sg. Κλαύδη Clauda
μόλις adv. μόλις scarce, with difficulty, scarcely, hardly
περικρατεῖς adj. nom. masc. pl. περικρατής to come by, master
τῆς art. gen. fem. sg. ὁ ἡ τό the, this, that, he, she, it
σκάφης n. gen. fem. sg. σκάφη boat
17 ἣν relative pron. acc. fem. sg. ὅς ἥ ὅ who, which, what, that
βοηθείαις n. dat. fem. pl. βοήθεια help, need
τὸ art. acc. neut. sg. ὁ ἡ τό the, this, that, he, she, it
πλοῖον n. acc. neut. sg. πλοῖον ship, boat
τε conj. τέ and, both, also
μὴ particle of negation. μή not, no, lest, neither, none, nothing, nor, never, without
εἰς prep. εἰς (+acc) into, to, unto, for, in, on, toward, against, upon, at, among
τὴν art. acc. fem. sg. ὁ ἡ τό the, this, that, he, she, it
σύρτιν n. acc. fem. sg. σύρτις quicksand
τὸ art. acc. neut. sg. ὁ ἡ τό the, this, that, he, she, it
σκεῦος n. acc. neut. sg. σκεῦος vessel, good, sail, stuff
οὕτως adv. οὕτω οὕτως so, even so, thus, on this wise, likewise, after this manner
18 σφοδρῶς adv. σφοδρῶς exceedingly
δὲ conj. δέ but, and, now, also, to the contrary, rather, then
ἡμῶν pron. gen. 1p. pl. ἐγώ I
τῇ art. dat. fem. sg. ὁ ἡ τό the, this, that, he, she, it
ἑξῆς adv. ἑξῆς the after, the next, following, on the morrow
ἐκβολὴν n. acc. fem. sg. ἐκβολή casting out
19 καὶ conj. καί and, even, also, but
τῇ art. dat. fem. sg. ὁ ἡ τό the, this, that, he, she, it

τρίτῃ ordinal. adj. dat. fem. sg. τρίτος third
αὐτόχειρες adj. nom. masc. pl. αὐτόχειρ own hand
τὴν art. acc. fem. sg. ὁ ἡ τό the, this, that, he, she, it
σκευὴν n. acc. fem. sg. σκευή tackling
τοῦ art. gen. neut. sg. ὁ ἡ τό the, this, that, he, she, it
πλοίου n. gen. neut. sg. πλοῖον ship, boat
20 μήτε conj. μήτε neither, nor, so much as, or
δὲ conj. δέ but, and, now, also, to the contrary, rather, then
ἡλίου n. gen. masc. sg. ἥλιος sun, east
μήτε conj. μήτε neither, nor, so much as, or
ἄστρων n. gen. neut. pl. ἄστρον star
ἐπὶ prep. ἐπί (+gen) on, in, upon, (+dat) in, at, for, upon, (+acc) on, upon, unto, to, against
πλείονας compar. adj. acc. fem. pl. πολύς many, great, much, long, abundant
ἡμέρας n. acc. fem. pl. ἡμέρα day, time, year, while, age, day time
χειμῶνός n. gen. masc. sg. χειμών foul weather, winter, tempest
τε conj. τέ and, both, also
οὐκ particle of negation. οὐ οὐκ οὐχ not, no, neither, none, nay, nor, never, nothing
ὀλίγου adj. gen. masc. sg. ὀλίγος few, little, small, a while, brief, short, short space
λοιπὸν adv. λοιπόν finally, henceforth, now, besides, furthermore, moreover, then
πᾶσα adj. nom. fem. sg. πᾶς πᾶσα πᾶν all, every, whosoever, every one, no, whole, any
ἐλπὶς n. nom. fem. sg. ἐλπίς hope, faith
τοῦ art. gen. neut. sg. ὁ ἡ τό the, this, that, he, she, it
ἡμᾶς pron. acc. 1p. pl. ἐγώ I
21 πολλῆς adj. gen. fem. sg. πολύς many, great, much, long, abundant
δὲ conj. δέ but, and, now, also, to the contrary, rather, then
ἀσιτίας n. gen. fem. sg. ἀσιτία abstinence
τότε adv. τότε then, that time
ὁ art. nom. masc. sg. ὁ ἡ τό the, this, that, he, she, it
Παῦλος n. nom. masc. sg. Παῦλος Paul, Paulus
ἐν prep. ἐν (+dat) in, by, with, among, at, on, through, to, within, into, of, for
μέσῳ adj. dat. neut. sg. μέσος midst, among, mid, between
αὐτῶν pron. gen. masc. 3p. pl. αὐτός ἡ ό self, of oneself, even, very, the same, he, she, it
μέν conj. μέν indeed, verily, truly, even, so, some
ὦ interjection. ὦ O
ἄνδρες n. voc. masc. pl. ἀνήρ man, husband, sir
μοι pron. dat. 1p. sg. ἐγώ I
μὴ particle of negation. μή not, no, lest, neither, none, nothing, nor, never, without
ἀπὸ prep. ἀπό (+gen) from, of, out of, since, for, off, at, by, in, on
τῆς art. gen. fem. sg. ὁ ἡ τό the, this, that, he, she, it
Κρήτης n. gen. fem. sg. Κρήτη Crete
τε conj. τέ and, both, also
τὴν art. acc. fem. sg. ὁ ἡ τό the, this, that, he, she, it
ὕβριν n. acc. fem. sg. ὕβρις hurt, harm, reproach
ταύτην demo. pron. acc. fem. sg. οὗτος αὕτη τοῦτο this, the same, this same, he, she, it
καὶ conj. καί and, even, also, but
τὴν art. acc. fem. sg. ὁ ἡ τό the, this, that, he, she, it
ζημίαν n. acc. fem. sg. ζημία damage, loss
22 καὶ conj. καί and, even, also, but
τὰ art. acc. neut. pl. ὁ ἡ τό the, this, that, he, she, it
νῦν adv. νῦν now, henceforth, present, this time
ὑμᾶς pron. acc. 2p. pl. σύ thou, you
ἀποβολὴ n. nom. fem. sg. ἀποβολή loss, cast away
γὰρ conj. γάρ for, and, because, but, indeed
ψυχῆς n. gen. fem. sg. ψυχή life, soul, mind, heart
οὐδεμία num. nom. fem. sg. οὐδείς no man, nothing, no, none, neither, not, nought

ἐξ prep. ἐκ ἐξ (+gen) of, from, out of, by, on, with, in, among, through
ὑμῶν pron. gen. 2p. pl. σύ thou, you
πλὴν prep. πλήν but, nevertheless, but rather, notwithstanding, except, than
τοῦ art. gen. neut. sg. ὁ ἡ τό the, this, that, he, she, it
πλοίου n. gen. neut. sg. πλοῖον ship, boat
23 γάρ conj. γάρ for, and, because, but, indeed
μοι pron. dat. 1p. sg. ἐγώ I
τῇ art. dat. fem. sg. ὁ ἡ τό the, this, that, he, she, it
νυκτὶ n. dat. fem. sg. νύξ night
ταύτῃ demo. pron. dat. fem. sg. οὗτος αὕτη τοῦτο this, the same, this same, he, she, it
ἄγγελος n. nom. masc. sg. ἄγγελος angel, messenger
τοῦ art. gen. masc. sg. ὁ ἡ τό the, this, that, he, she, it
Θεοῦ n. gen. masc. sg. θεός God, god
οὗ relative pron. gen. masc. sg. ὅς ἥ ὅ who, which, what, that
ᾧ relative pron. dat. masc. sg. ὅς ἥ ὅ who, which, what, that
καὶ conj. καί and, even, also, but
24 Μὴ particle of negation. μή not, no, lest, neither, none, nothing, nor, never, without
Παῦλε n. voc. masc. sg. Παῦλος Paul, Paulus
Καίσαρί n. dat. masc. sg. Καῖσαρ Caesar
σε pron. acc. 2p. sg. σύ thou, you
καὶ conj. καί and, even, also, but
σοι pron. dat. 2p. sg. σύ thou, you
ὁ art. nom. masc. sg. ὁ ἡ τό the, this, that, he, she, it
Θεὸς n. nom. masc. sg. θεός God, god
πάντας adj. acc. masc. pl. πᾶς πᾶσα πᾶν all, every, whosoever, every one, no, whole, any
τοὺς art. acc. masc. pl. ὁ ἡ τό the, this, that, he, she, it
μετὰ prep. μετά (+gen) with, among, against, (+acc) after
σοῦ pron. gen. 2p. sg. σύ thou, you
25 διὸ conj. διό wherefore, therefore, for which cause
ἄνδρες n. voc. masc. pl. ἀνήρ man, husband, sir
γὰρ conj. γάρ for, and, because, but, indeed
τῷ art. dat. masc. sg. ὁ ἡ τό the, this, that, he, she, it
Θεῷ n. dat. masc. sg. θεός God, god
ὅτι conj. ὅτι that, for, because, how that, how, because that, for that, though
οὕτως adv. οὕτω οὕτως so, even so, thus, on this wise, likewise, after this manner
καθ' prep. κατά (+gen) against, by, throughout, down, (+acc) according to, after, with
ὃν relative pron. acc. masc. sg. ὅς ἥ ὅ who, which, what, that
τρόπον n. acc. masc. sg. τρόπος as, manner, means, way, conversation
μοι pron. dat. 1p. sg. ἐγώ I
26 εἰς prep. εἰς (+acc) into, to, unto, for, in, on, toward, against, upon, at, among
νῆσον n. acc. fem. sg. νῆσος isle, island
δέ conj. δέ but, and, now, also, to the contrary, rather, then
τινα indefinite pron. acc. fem. sg. τὶς certain, some, any man, one, any thing
ἡμᾶς pron. acc. 1p. pl. ἐγώ I
27 Ὡς conj. ὡς as, when, as it were, how, about, like, as soon as, even as, while
δὲ conj. δέ but, and, now, also, to the contrary, rather, then
τεσσαρεσκαιδεκάτη ordinal. adj. nom. fem. sg. τεσσαρεσκαιδέκατος fourteenth
νὺξ n. nom. fem. sg. νύξ night
ἡμῶν pron. gen. 1p. pl. ἐγώ I
ἐν prep. ἐν (+dat) in, by, with, among, at, on, through, to, within, into, of, for
τῷ art. dat. masc. sg. ὁ ἡ τό the, this, that, he, she, it
'Αδρίᾳ n. dat. masc. sg. 'Αδρίας Adria
κατὰ prep. κατά (+gen) against, by, throughout, down, (+acc) according to, after, with
μέσον adj. acc. neut. sg. μέσος midst, among, mid, between
τῆς art. gen. fem. sg. ὁ ἡ τό the, this, that, he, she, it

νυκτὸς n. gen. fem. sg. νύξ night
οἱ art. nom. masc. pl. ὁ ἡ τό the, this, that, he, she, it
ναῦται n. nom. masc. pl. ναύτης shipman, sailor
τινὰ indefinite pron. acc. fem. sg. τὶς certain, some, any man, one, any thing
αὐτοῖς pron. dat. masc. 3p. pl. αὐτός ή ό self, of oneself, even, very, the same, he, she, it
χώραν n. acc. fem. sg. χώρα country, region, land, field, coast, ground
28 καὶ conj. καί and, even, also, but
ὀργυιὰς n. acc. fem. pl. ὀργυιά fathom
εἴκοσι num. acc. fem. pl. εἴκοσι twenty
βραχὺ adv. βραχύς little while, little, few words, little space
δὲ conj. δέ but, and, now, also, to the contrary, rather, then
καὶ conj. καί and, even, also, but
πάλιν adv. πάλιν again
ὀργυιὰς n. acc. fem. pl. ὀργυιά fathom
δεκαπέντε num. acc. fem. pl. δεκαπέντε fifteen
29 τε conj. τέ and, both, also
μήπως conj. μήπως lest, lest by any means, lest by some means, lest haply
εἰς prep. εἰς (+acc) into, to, unto, for, in, on, toward, against, upon, at, among
τραχεῖς adj. acc. masc. pl. τραχύς rough, rock, rough place
τόπους n. acc. masc. pl. τόπος place, room, quarter
ἐκ prep. ἐκ ἐξ (+gen) of, from, out of, by, on, with, in, among, through
πρύμνης n. gen. fem. sg. πρύμνα hinder part of the ship, hinder part, stern
ἀγκύρας n. acc. fem. pl. ἄγκυρα anchor
τέσσαρας num. acc. fem. pl. τέσσαρες four
ἡμέραν n. acc. fem. sg. ἡμέρα day, time, year, while, age, day time
30 τῶν art. gen. masc. pl. ὁ ἡ τό the, this, that, he, she, it
δὲ conj. δέ but, and, now, also, to the contrary, rather, then
ναυτῶν n. gen. masc. pl. ναύτης shipman, sailor
ἐκ prep. ἐκ ἐξ (+gen) of, from, out of, by, on, with, in, among, through
τοῦ art. gen. neut. sg. ὁ ἡ τό the, this, that, he, she, it
πλοίου n. gen. neut. sg. πλοῖον ship, boat
καὶ conj. καί and, even, also, but
τὴν art. acc. fem. sg. ὁ ἡ τό the, this, that, he, she, it
σκάφην n. acc. fem. sg. σκάφη boat
εἰς prep. εἰς (+acc) into, to, unto, for, in, on, toward, against, upon, at, among
τὴν art. acc. fem. sg. ὁ ἡ τό the, this, that, he, she, it
θάλασσαν n. acc. fem. sg. θάλασσα sea
προφάσει n. dat. fem. sg. πρόφασις pretence, cloke, colour, show
ὡς adv. ὡς as, when, as it were, how, about, like, as soon as, even as, while
ἐκ prep. ἐκ ἐξ (+gen) of, from, out of, by, on, with, in, among, through
πρώρας n. gen. fem. sg. πρῶρα foreship, forepart
ἀγκύρας n. acc. fem. pl. ἄγκυρα anchor
31 ὁ art. nom. masc. sg. ὁ ἡ τό the, this, that, he, she, it
Παῦλος n. nom. masc. sg. Παῦλος Paul, Paulus
τῷ art. dat. masc. sg. ὁ ἡ τό the, this, that, he, she, it
ἑκατοντάρχῃ n. dat. masc. sg. ἑκατοντάρχης centurion
καὶ conj. καί and, even, also, but
τοῖς art. dat. masc. pl. ὁ ἡ τό the, this, that, he, she, it
στρατιώταις n. dat. masc. pl. στρατιώτης soldier
Ἐὰν conj. ἐάν if, soever, except, though, and if, but, whether, if so, so
μὴ particle of negation. μή not, no, lest, neither, none, nothing, nor, never, without
οὗτοι demo. pron. nom. masc. pl. οὗτος αὕτη τοῦτο this, the same, this same, he, she, it
ἐν prep. ἐν (+dat) in, by, with, among, at, on, through, to, within, into, of, for
τῷ art. dat. neut. sg. ὁ ἡ τό the, this, that, he, she, it
πλοίῳ n. dat. neut. sg. πλοῖον ship, boat

ὑμεῖς pron. nom. 2p. pl. σύ thou, you
οὐ particle of negation. οὐ οὐκ οὐχ not, no, neither, none, nay, nor, never, nothing
32 τότε adv. τότε then, that time
οἱ art. nom. masc. pl. ὁ ἡ τό the, this, that, he, she, it
στρατιῶται n. nom. masc. pl. στρατιώτης soldier
τὰ art. acc. neut. pl. ὁ ἡ τό the, this, that, he, she, it
σχοινία n. acc. neut. pl. σχοινίον small cord, rope
τῆς art. gen. fem. sg. ὁ ἡ τό the, this, that, he, she, it
σκάφης n. gen. fem. sg. σκάφη boat
καὶ conj. καί and, even, also, but
αὐτὴν pron. acc. fem. 3p. sg. αὐτός ἡ ὁ self, of oneself, even, very, the same, he, she, it
33 ἄχρι prep. ἄχρι or ἄχρις (+gen) until, unto, till, even to, as far as, while, into
δὲ conj. δέ but, and, now, also, to the contrary, rather, then
οὗ relative pron. gen. masc. sg. ὅς ἥ ὅ who, which, what, that
ἡμέρα n. nom. fem. sg. ἡμέρα day, time, year, while, age, day time
ὁ art. nom. masc. sg. ὁ ἡ τό the, this, that, he, she, it
Παῦλος n. nom. masc. sg. Παῦλος Paul, Paulus
ἅπαντας adj. acc. masc. pl. ἅπας all, whole, all things, every, everyone
τροφῆς n. gen. fem. sg. τροφή meat, food
Τεσσαρεσκαιδεκάτην ordinal. adj. acc. fem. sg. τεσσαρεσκαιδέκατος fourteenth
σήμερον adv. σήμερον this day, today
ἡμέραν n. acc. fem. sg. ἡμέρα day, time, year, while, age, day time
ἄσιτοι adj. nom. masc. pl. ἄσιτος fasting
μηδὲν adj. acc. neut. sg. μηδείς μηδεμία μηδέν no man, nothing, no, none, not at all
34 διὸ conj. διό wherefore, therefore, for which cause
ὑμᾶς pron. acc. 2p. pl. σύ thou, you
τροφῆς n. gen. fem. sg. τροφή meat, food
τοῦτο demo. pron. nom. neut. sg. οὗτος αὕτη τοῦτο this, the same, this same, he, she, it
γὰρ conj. γάρ for, and, because, but, indeed
πρὸς prep. πρός (+gen) for, (+dat) at, (+acc) unto, to, with, for, against
τῆς art. gen. fem. sg. ὁ ἡ τό the, this, that, he, she, it
ὑμετέρας poss. pron. gen. fem. 2p. sg. ὑμέτερος your, yours, your own
σωτηρίας n. gen. fem. sg. σωτηρία salvation, deliver, health, saving
οὐδενὸς num. gen. masc. sg. οὐδείς no man, nothing, no, none, neither, not, nought
γὰρ conj. γάρ for, and, because, but, indeed
ὑμῶν pron. gen. 2p. pl. σύ thou, you
θρὶξ n. nom. fem. sg. θρίξ hair
ἐκ prep. ἐκ ἐξ (+gen) of, from, out of, by, on, with, in, among, through
τῆς art. gen. fem. sg. ὁ ἡ τό the, this, that, he, she, it
κεφαλῆς n. gen. fem. sg. κεφαλή head
35 δὲ conj. δέ but, and, now, also, to the contrary, rather, then
ταῦτα demo. pron. acc. neut. pl. οὗτος αὕτη τοῦτο this, the same, this same, he, she, it
καὶ conj. καί and, even, also, but
ἄρτον n. acc. masc. sg. ἄρτος bread, loaf
τῷ art. dat. masc. sg. ὁ ἡ τό the, this, that, he, she, it
Θεῷ n. dat. masc. sg. θεός God, god
ἐνώπιον adv. ἐνώπιον before, in the sight of, in the presence of
πάντων adj. gen. masc. pl. πᾶς πᾶσα πᾶν all, every, whosoever, every one, no, whole, any
καὶ conj. καί and, even, also, but
36 εὔθυμοι adj. nom. masc. pl. εὔθυμος of good cheer
δὲ conj. δέ but, and, now, also, to the contrary, rather, then
πάντες adj. nom. masc. pl. πᾶς πᾶσα πᾶν all, every, whosoever, every one, no, whole, any
καὶ conj. καί and, even, also, but
αὐτοὶ pron. nom. masc. 3p. pl. αὐτός ἡ ὁ self, of oneself, even, very, the same, he, she, it
τροφῆς n. gen. fem. sg. τροφή meat, food

37 δὲ conj. δέ but, and, now, also, to the contrary, rather, then
ἐν prep. ἐν (+dat) in, by, with, among, at, on, through, to, within, into, of, for
τῷ art. dat. neut. sg. ὁ ἡ τό the, this, that, he, she, it
πλοίῳ n. dat. neut. sg. πλοῖον ship, boat
αἱ art. nom. fem. pl. ὁ ἡ τό the, this, that, he, she, it
πᾶσαι adj. nom. fem. pl. πᾶς πᾶσα πᾶν all, every, whosoever, every one, no, whole, any
ψυχαὶ n. nom. fem. pl. ψυχή life, soul, mind, heart
διακόσιαι num. nom. fem. pl. διακόσιοι two hundred
ἑβδομηκονταέξ num. nom. fem. pl. ἑβδομηκονταέξ seventy six
38 δὲ conj. δέ but, and, now, also, to the contrary, rather, then
τροφῆς n. gen. fem. sg. τροφή meat, food
τὸ art. acc. neut. sg. ὁ ἡ τό the, this, that, he, she, it
πλοῖον n. acc. neut. sg. πλοῖον ship, boat
τὸν art. acc. masc. sg. ὁ ἡ τό the, this, that, he, she, it
σῖτον n. acc. masc. sg. σῖτος wheat, corn
εἰς prep. εἰς (+acc) into, to, unto, for, in, on, toward, against, upon, at, among
τὴν art. acc. fem. sg. ὁ ἡ τό the, this, that, he, she, it
θάλασσαν n. acc. fem. sg. θάλασσα sea
39 ὅτε adv. ὅτε when, after that, as soon as, while, after
δὲ conj. δέ but, and, now, also, to the contrary, rather, then
ἡμέρα n. nom. fem. sg. ἡμέρα day, time, year, while, age, day time
τὴν art. acc. fem. sg. ὁ ἡ τό the, this, that, he, she, it
γῆν n. acc. fem. sg. γῆ earth, land, ground, country
οὐκ particle of negation. οὐ οὐκ οὐχ not, no, neither, none, nay, nor, never, nothing
κόλπον n. acc. masc. sg. κόλπος bosom, creek
δέ conj. δέ but, and, now, also, to the contrary, rather, then
τινα indefinite pron. acc. masc. sg. τὶς certain, some, any man, one, any thing
αἰγιαλὸν n. acc. masc. sg. αἰγιαλός shore
εἰς prep. εἰς (+acc) into, to, unto, for, in, on, toward, against, upon, at, among
ὃν relative pron. acc. masc. sg. ὅς ἥ ὅ who, which, what, that
εἰ conj. εἰ if, whether, that, though, forasmuch
τὸ art. acc. neut. sg. ὁ ἡ τό the, this, that, he, she, it
πλοῖον n. acc. neut. sg. πλοῖον ship, boat
40 καὶ conj. καί and, even, also, but
τὰς art. acc. fem. pl. ὁ ἡ τό the, this, that, he, she, it
ἀγκύρας n. acc. fem. pl. ἄγκυρα anchor
εἰς prep. εἰς (+acc) into, to, unto, for, in, on, toward, against, upon, at, among
τὴν art. acc. fem. sg. ὁ ἡ τό the, this, that, he, she, it
θάλασσαν n. acc. fem. sg. θάλασσα sea
ἅμα prep. ἅμα (+dat) together, with, also. (adv.) at the same time, together
τὰς art. acc. fem. pl. ὁ ἡ τό the, this, that, he, she, it
ζευκτηρίας n. acc. fem. pl. ζευκτηρία band
τῶν art. gen. neut. pl. ὁ ἡ τό the, this, that, he, she, it
πηδαλίων n. gen. neut. pl. πηδάλιον rudder, helm
καὶ conj. καί and, even, also, but
τὸν art. acc. masc. sg. ὁ ἡ τό the, this, that, he, she, it
ἀρτέμονα n. acc. masc. sg. ἀρτέμων mainsail
τῇ art. dat. fem. sg. ὁ ἡ τό the, this, that, he, she, it
εἰς prep. εἰς (+acc) into, to, unto, for, in, on, toward, against, upon, at, among
τὸν art. acc. masc. sg. ὁ ἡ τό the, this, that, he, she, it
αἰγιαλόν n. acc. masc. sg. αἰγιαλός shore
41 δὲ conj. δέ but, and, now, also, to the contrary, rather, then
εἰς prep. εἰς (+acc) into, to, unto, for, in, on, toward, against, upon, at, among
τόπον n. acc. masc. sg. τόπος place, room, quarter
διθάλασσον adj. acc. masc. sg. διθάλασσος where two seas met

τὴν art. acc. fem. sg. ὁ ἡ τό the, this, that, he, she, it
ναῦν n. acc. fem. sg. ναῦς ship
καὶ conj. καί and, even, also, but
ἡ art. nom. fem. sg. ὁ ἡ τό the, this, that, he, she, it
μέν conj. μέν indeed, verily, truly, even, so, some
πρῷρα n. nom. fem. sg. πρῷρα foreship, forepart
ἀσάλευτος adj. nom. fem. sg. ἀσάλευτος unmoveable, which cannot be moved
ἡ art. nom. fem. sg. ὁ ἡ τό the, this, that, he, she, it
δὲ conj. δέ but, and, now, also, to the contrary, rather, then
πρύμνα n. nom. fem. sg. πρύμνα hinder part of the ship, hinder part, stern
ὑπὸ prep. ὑπό (+gen) of, by, with, from, among, (+acc) under
τῆς art. gen. fem. sg. ὁ ἡ τό the, this, that, he, she, it
βίας n. gen. fem. sg. βία violence
τῶν art. gen. neut. pl. ὁ ἡ τό the, this, that, he, she, it
κυμάτων n. gen. neut. pl. κῦμα wave
42 τῶν art. gen. masc. pl. ὁ ἡ τό the, this, that, he, she, it
δὲ conj. δέ but, and, now, also, to the contrary, rather, then
στρατιωτῶν n. gen. masc. pl. στρατιώτης soldier
βουλὴ n. nom. fem. sg. βουλή counsel, advise, will
ἵνα conj. ἵνα that, to, lest, for to, so that, albeit, because, for, so as
τοὺς art. acc. masc. pl. ὁ ἡ τό the, this, that, he, she, it
δεσμώτας n. acc. masc. pl. δεσμώτης prisoner
μήτις interrog. pron. nom. masc. sg. μήτις or μή τις any, any man
43 ὁ art. nom. masc. sg. ὁ ἡ τό the, this, that, he, she, it
δὲ conj. δέ but, and, now, also, to the contrary, rather, then
ἑκατόνταρχος n. nom. masc. sg. ἑκατόνταρχος centurion
τὸν art. acc. masc. sg. ὁ ἡ τό the, this, that, he, she, it
Παῦλον n. acc. masc. sg. Παῦλος Paul, Paulus
αὐτοὺς pron. acc. masc. 3p. pl. αὐτός ή ό self, of oneself, even, very, the same, he, she, it
τοῦ art. gen. neut. sg. ὁ ἡ τό the, this, that, he, she, it
βουλήματος n. gen. neut. sg. βούλημα purpose, will
τε conj. τέ and, both, also
τοὺς art. acc. masc. pl. ὁ ἡ τό the, this, that, he, she, it
πρώτους ordinal. adj. acc. masc. pl. πρῶτος first, chief, first of all, chiefest, best
ἐπὶ prep. ἐπί (+gen) on, in, upon, (+dat) in, at, for, upon, (+acc) on, upon, unto, to, against
τὴν art. acc. fem. sg. ὁ ἡ τό the, this, that, he, she, it
γῆν n. acc. fem. sg. γῆ earth, land, ground, country
44 καὶ conj. καί and, even, also, but
τοὺς art. acc. masc. pl. ὁ ἡ τό the, this, that, he, she, it
λοιποὺς adj. acc. masc. pl. λοιπός other, rest, remnant, residue, which remain
οὓς relative pron. acc. masc. pl. ὅς ἥ ὅ who, which, what, that
μέν conj. μέν indeed, verily, truly, even, so, some
ἐπὶ prep. ἐπί (+gen) on, in, upon, (+dat) in, at, for, upon, (+acc) on, upon, unto, to, against
σανίσιν n. dat. fem. pl. σανίς board
οὓς relative pron. acc. masc. pl. ὅς ἥ ὅ who, which, what, that
δὲ conj. δέ but, and, now, also, to the contrary, rather, then
ἐπὶ prep. ἐπί (+gen) on, in, upon, (+dat) in, at, for, upon, (+acc) on, upon, unto, to, against
τινων indefinite pron. gen. neut. pl. τὶς certain, some, any man, one, any thing
τῶν art. gen. neut. pl. ὁ ἡ τό the, this, that, he, she, it
ἀπὸ prep. ἀπό (+gen) from, of, out of, since, for, off, at, by, in, on
τοῦ art. gen. neut. sg. ὁ ἡ τό the, this, that, he, she, it
πλοίου n. gen. neut. sg. πλοῖον ship, boat
καὶ conj. καί and, even, also, but
οὕτως adv. οὕτω οὕτως so, even so, thus, on this wise, likewise, after this manner
πάντας adj. acc. masc. pl. πᾶς πᾶσα πᾶν all, every, whosoever, every one, no, whole, any

ἐπὶ prep. ἐπί (+gen) on, in, upon, (+dat) in, at, for, upon, (+acc) on, upon, unto, to, against
τὴν art. acc. fem. sg. ὁ ἡ τό the, this, that, he, she, it
γῆν n. acc. fem. sg. γῆ earth, land, ground, country

28

1 Καὶ conj. καί and, even, also, but
τότε adv. τότε then, that time
ὅτι conj. ὅτι that, for, because, how that, how, because that, for that, though
Μελίτη n. nom. fem. sg. Μελίτη Melita
ἡ art. nom. fem. sg. ὁ ἡ τό the, this, that, he, she, it
νῆσος n. nom. fem. sg. νῆσος isle, island
2 οἱ art. nom. masc. pl. ὁ ἡ τό the, this, that, he, she, it
δὲ conj. δέ but, and, now, also, to the contrary, rather, then
βάρβαροι adj. nom. masc. pl. βάρβαρος barbarous, barbarian
οὐ particle of negation. οὐ οὐκ οὐχ not, no, neither, none, nay, nor, never, nothing
τὴν art. acc. fem. sg. ὁ ἡ τό the, this, that, he, she, it
φιλανθρωπίαν n. acc. fem. sg. φιλανθρωπία kindness, love toward man
ἡμῖν pron. dat. 1p. pl. ἐγώ I
γὰρ conj. γάρ for, and, because, but, indeed
πυρὰν n. acc. fem. sg. πυρά fire
πάντας adj. acc. masc. pl. πᾶς πᾶσα πᾶν all, every, whosoever, every one, no, whole, any
ἡμᾶς pron. acc. 1p. pl. ἐγώ I
διὰ prep. διά (+gen) by, through, with, in, of, (+acc) for, because of, for a cause
τὸν art. acc. masc. sg. ὁ ἡ τό the, this, that, he, she, it
ὑετὸν n. acc. masc. sg. ὑετός rain
τὸν art. acc. masc. sg. ὁ ἡ τό the, this, that, he, she, it
καὶ conj. καί and, even, also, but
διὰ prep. διά (+gen) by, through, with, in, of, (+acc) for, because of, for a cause
τὸ art. acc. neut. sg. ὁ ἡ τό the, this, that, he, she, it
ψύχος n. acc. neut. sg. ψύχος cold
3 δὲ conj. δέ but, and, now, also, to the contrary, rather, then
τοῦ art. gen. masc. sg. ὁ ἡ τό the, this, that, he, she, it
Παύλου n. gen. masc. sg. Παῦλος Paul, Paulus
φρυγάνων n. gen. neut. pl. φρύγανον stick
πλῆθος n. acc. neut. sg. πλῆθος multitude, bundle, company
καὶ conj. καί and, even, also, but
ἐπὶ prep. ἐπί (+gen) on, in, upon, (+dat) in, at, for, upon, (+acc) on, upon, unto, to, against
τὴν art. acc. fem. sg. ὁ ἡ τό the, this, that, he, she, it
πυράν n. acc. fem. sg. πυρά fire
ἔχιδνα n. nom. fem. sg. ἔχιδνα viper
ἐκ prep. ἐκ ἐξ (+gen) of, from, out of, by, on, with, in, among, through
τῆς art. gen. fem. sg. ὁ ἡ τό the, this, that, he, she, it
θέρμης n. gen. fem. sg. θέρμη heat
τῆς art. gen. fem. sg. ὁ ἡ τό the, this, that, he, she, it
χειρὸς n. gen. fem. sg. χείρ hand
αὐτοῦ pron. gen. masc. 3p. sg. αὐτός ἡ ὁ self, of oneself, even, very, the same, he, she, it
4 ὡς adv. ὡς as, when, as it were, how, about, like, as soon as, even as, while
δὲ conj. δέ but, and, now, also, to the contrary, rather, then
οἱ art. nom. masc. pl. ὁ ἡ τό the, this, that, he, she, it
βάρβαροι adj. nom. masc. pl. βάρβαρος barbarous, barbarian
τὸ art. acc. neut. sg. ὁ ἡ τό the, this, that, he, she, it
θηρίον n. acc. neut. sg. θηρίον beast, wild beast, venomous beast
ἐκ prep. ἐκ ἐξ (+gen) of, from, out of, by, on, with, in, among, through
τῆς art. gen. fem. sg. ὁ ἡ τό the, this, that, he, she, it

χειρὸς n. gen. fem. sg. χείρ hand
αὐτοῦ pron. gen. masc. 3p. sg. αὐτός ή ό self, of oneself, even, very, the same, he, she, it
πρὸς prep. πρός (+gen) for, (+dat) at, (+acc) unto, to, with, for, against
ἀλλήλους pron. acc. masc. 3p. pl. ἀλλήλων one another, themselves, together, mutual
Πάντως adv. πάντως surely, altogether, by all means, at all, needs, no doubt
φονεύς n. nom. masc. sg. φονεύς murderer
ὁ art. nom. masc. sg. ὁ ἡ τό the, this, that, he, she, it
ἄνθρωπος n. nom. masc. sg. ἄνθρωπος man, human being, person, one, certain
οὗτος demo. pron. nom. masc. sg. οὗτος αὕτη τοῦτο this, the same, this same, he, she, it
ὃν relative pron. acc. masc. sg. ὅς ἥ ὅ who, which, what, that
ἐκ prep. ἐκ ἐξ (+gen) of, from, out of, by, on, with, in, among, through
τῆς art. gen. fem. sg. ὁ ἡ τό the, this, that, he, she, it
θαλάσσης n. gen. fem. sg. θάλασσα sea
ἡ art. nom. fem. sg. ὁ ἡ τό the, this, that, he, she, it
Δίκη n. nom. fem. sg. δίκη judgment, vengeance, punish
οὐκ particle of negation. οὐ οὐκ οὐχ not, no, neither, none, nay, nor, never, nothing
5 ὁ art. nom. masc. sg. ὁ ἡ τό the, this, that, he, she, it
μέν conj. μέν indeed, verily, truly, even, so, some
οὖν conj. οὖν therefore, then, so, and, now, wherefore
τὸ art. acc. neut. sg. ὁ ἡ τό the, this, that, he, she, it
θηρίον n. acc. neut. sg. θηρίον beast, wild beast, venomous beast
εἰς prep. εἰς (+acc) into, to, unto, for, in, on, toward, against, upon, at, among
τὸ art. acc. neut. sg. ὁ ἡ τό the, this, that, he, she, it
πῦρ n. acc. neut. sg. πῦρ fire, fiery
οὐδὲν num. acc. neut. sg. οὐδείς no man, nothing, no, none, neither, not, nought
κακόν adj. acc. neut. sg. κακός evil, evil thing, noisome, wicked
6 οἱ art. nom. masc. pl. ὁ ἡ τό the, this, that, he, she, it
δὲ conj. δέ but, and, now, also, to the contrary, rather, then
αὐτὸν pron. acc. masc. 3p. sg. αὐτός ή ό self, of oneself, even, very, the same, he, she, it
ἢ particle. ἤ or, than, either, nor, or else, and, rather than
ἄφνω adv. ἄφνω suddenly
νεκρόν adj. acc. masc. sg. νεκρός dead
ἐπὶ prep. ἐπί (+gen) on, in, upon, (+dat) in, at, for, upon, (+acc) on, upon, unto, to, against
πολὺ adj. acc. neut. sg. πολύς many, great, much, long, abundant
δὲ conj. δέ but, and, now, also, to the contrary, rather, then
αὐτῶν pron. gen. masc. 3p. pl. αὐτός ή ό self, of oneself, even, very, the same, he, she, it
καὶ conj. καί and, even, also, but
μηδὲν adj. acc. neut. sg. μηδείς μηδεμία μηδέν no man, nothing, no, none, not at all
ἄτοπον adj. acc. neut. sg. ἄτοπος amiss, harm, unreasonable
εἰς prep. εἰς (+acc) into, to, unto, for, in, on, toward, against, upon, at, among
αὐτὸν pron. acc. masc. 3p. sg. αὐτός ή ό self, of oneself, even, very, the same, he, she, it
θεόν n. acc. masc. sg. θεός God, god
αὐτὸν pron. acc. masc. 3p. sg. αὐτός ή ό self, of oneself, even, very, the same, he, she, it
7 Ἐν prep. ἐν (+dat) in, by, with, among, at, on, through, to, within, into, of, for
δὲ conj. δέ but, and, now, also, to the contrary, rather, then
τοῖς art. dat. neut. pl. ὁ ἡ τό the, this, that, he, she, it
περὶ prep. περί (+gen) of, for, concerning, (+acc) about, concerning, in
τὸν art. acc. masc. sg. ὁ ἡ τό the, this, that, he, she, it
τόπον n. acc. masc. sg. τόπος place, room, quarter
ἐκεῖνον demo. pron. acc. masc. sg. ἐκεῖνος that, he, the same, that same
χωρία n. nom. neut. pl. χωρίον place, field, land, parcel of ground, possession
τῷ art. dat. masc. sg. ὁ ἡ τό the, this, that, he, she, it
πρώτῳ ordinal. adj. dat. masc. sg. πρῶτος first, chief, first of all, chiefest, best
τῆς art. gen. fem. sg. ὁ ἡ τό the, this, that, he, she, it
νήσου n. gen. fem. sg. νῆσος isle, island

ὀνόματι n. dat. neut. sg. ὄνομα name, call, surname
Ποπλίῳ n. dat. masc. sg. Πόπλιος Publius
ὃς relative pron. nom. masc. sg. ὅς ἥ ὅ who, which, what, that
ἡμᾶς pron. acc. 1p. pl. ἐγώ I
τρεῖς num. acc. fem. pl. τρεῖς three
ἡμέρας n. acc. fem. pl. ἡμέρα day, time, year, while, age, day time
φιλοφρόνως adv. φιλοφρόνως courteously
8 δὲ conj. δέ but, and, now, also, to the contrary, rather, then
τὸν art. acc. masc. sg. ὁ ἡ τό the, this, that, he, she, it
πατέρα n. acc. masc. sg. πατήρ Father, father, parent
τοῦ art. gen. masc. sg. ὁ ἡ τό the, this, that, he, she, it
Ποπλίου n. gen. masc. sg. Πόπλιος Publius
πυρετοῖς n. dat. masc. pl. πυρετός fever
καὶ conj. καί and, even, also, but
δυσεντερίᾳ n. dat. neut. sg. δυσεντερίᾳ bloody flux, dysentery
πρὸς prep. πρός (+gen) for, (+dat) at, (+acc) unto, to, with, for, against
ὃν relative pron. acc. masc. sg. ὅς ἥ ὅ who, which, what, that
ὁ art. nom. masc. sg. ὁ ἡ τό the, this, that, he, she, it
Παῦλος n. nom. masc. sg. Παῦλος Paul, Paulus
καὶ conj. καί and, even, also, but
τὰς art. acc. fem. pl. ὁ ἡ τό the, this, that, he, she, it
χεῖρας n. acc. fem. pl. χείρ hand
αὐτῷ pron. dat. masc. 3p. sg. αὐτός ἡ ὁ self, of oneself, even, very, the same, he, she, it
αὐτόν pron. acc. masc. 3p. sg. αὐτός ἡ ὁ self, of oneself, even, very, the same, he, she, it
9 τούτου demo. pron. gen. neut. sg. οὗτος αὕτη τοῦτο this, the same, this same, he, she, it
οὖν conj. οὖν therefore, then, so, and, now, wherefore
καὶ conj. καί and, even, also, but
οἱ art. nom. masc. pl. ὁ ἡ τό the, this, that, he, she, it
λοιποὶ adj. nom. masc. pl. λοιπός other, rest, remnant, residue, which remain
οἱ art. nom. masc. pl. ὁ ἡ τό the, this, that, he, she, it
ἀσθενείας n. acc. fem. pl. ἀσθένεια infirmity, weakness, disease, sickness
ἐν prep. ἐν (+dat) in, by, with, among, at, on, through, to, within, into, of, for
τῇ art. dat. fem. sg. ὁ ἡ τό the, this, that, he, she, it
νήσῳ n. dat. fem. sg. νῆσος isle, island
καὶ conj. καί and, even, also, but
10 οἳ relative pron. nom. masc. pl. ὅς ἥ ὅ who, which, what, that
καὶ conj. καί and, even, also, but
πολλαῖς adj. dat. fem. pl. πολύς many, great, much, long, abundant
τιμαῖς n. dat. fem. pl. τιμή honour, price, preciousness, sum
ἡμᾶς pron. acc. 1p. pl. ἐγώ I
καὶ conj. καί and, even, also, but
τὰ art. acc. neut. pl. ὁ ἡ τό the, this, that, he, she, it
πρὸς prep. πρός (+gen) for, (+dat) at, (+acc) unto, to, with, for, against
τὴν art. acc. fem. sg. ὁ ἡ τό the, this, that, he, she, it
χρείαν n. acc. fem. sg. χρεία need, necessity, lack, want
11 Μετὰ prep. μετά (+gen) with, among, against, (+acc) after
δὲ conj. δέ but, and, now, also, to the contrary, rather, then
τρεῖς num. acc. masc. pl. τρεῖς three
μῆνας n. acc. masc. pl. μήν month
ἐν prep. ἐν (+dat) in, by, with, among, at, on, through, to, within, into, of, for
πλοίῳ n. dat. neut. sg. πλοῖον ship, boat
ἐν prep. ἐν (+dat) in, by, with, among, at, on, through, to, within, into, of, for
τῇ art. dat. fem. sg. ὁ ἡ τό the, this, that, he, she, it
νήσῳ n. dat. fem. sg. νῆσος isle, island
Ἀλεξανδρίνῳ adj. dat. neut. sg. Ἀλεξανδρῖνος of Alexandria

παρασήμῳ adj. dat. neut. sg. παράσημος whose sign is
Διοσκούροις n. dat. masc. pl. Διόσκουροι Castor and Pollux, Dioscuri
12 καὶ conj. καί and, even, also, but
εἰς prep. εἰς (+acc) into, to, unto, for, in, on, toward, against, upon, at, among
Συρακούσας n. acc. fem. pl. Συράκουσαι Syracuse
ἡμέρας n. acc. fem. pl. ἡμέρα day, time, year, while, age, day time
τρεῖς num. acc. fem. pl. τρεῖς three
13 ὅθεν adv. ὅθεν wherefore, from whence, whereupon, where, from thence, whence
εἰς prep. εἰς (+acc) into, to, unto, for, in, on, toward, against, upon, at, among
Ῥήγιον n. acc. neut. sg. Ῥήγιον Rhegium
καὶ conj. καί and, even, also, but
μετὰ prep. μετά (+gen) with, among, against, (+acc) after
μίαν num. acc. fem. sg. εἶς or ἕν one, other, some, any, only, a certain
ἡμέραν n. acc. fem. sg. ἡμέρα day, time, year, while, age, day time
νότου n. gen. masc. sg. νότος south, south wind
δευτεραῖοι adj. nom. masc. pl. δευτεραῖος next day
εἰς prep. εἰς (+acc) into, to, unto, for, in, on, toward, against, upon, at, among
Ποτιόλους n. acc. masc. pl. Ποτίολοι Puteoli
14 οὗ adv. οὗ where, whither, wherein
ἀδελφοὺς n. acc. masc. pl. ἀδελφός brother
ἐπ' prep. ἐπί (+gen) on, in, upon, (+dat) in, at, for, upon, (+acc) on, upon, unto, to, against
αὐτοῖς pron. dat. masc. 3p. pl. αὐτός ἡ ὁ self, of oneself, even, very, the same, he, she, it
ἡμέρας n. acc. fem. pl. ἡμέρα day, time, year, while, age, day time
ἑπτά num. acc. fem. pl. ἑπτά seven, seventh
καὶ conj. καί and, even, also, but
οὕτως adv. οὕτω οὕτως so, even so, thus, on this wise, likewise, after this manner
εἰς prep. εἰς (+acc) into, to, unto, for, in, on, toward, against, upon, at, among
τὴν art. acc. fem. sg. ὁ ἡ τό the, this, that, he, she, it
Ῥώμην n. acc. fem. sg. Ῥώμη Rome
15 κἀκεῖθεν adv. κἀκεῖθεν and from thence, and thence, and afterward, thence also
οἱ art. nom. masc. pl. ὁ ἡ τό the, this, that, he, she, it
ἀδελφοὶ n. nom. masc. pl. ἀδελφός brother
τὰ art. acc. neut. pl. ὁ ἡ τό the, this, that, he, she, it
περὶ prep. περί (+gen) of, for, concerning, (+acc) about, concerning, in
ἡμῶν pron. gen. 1p. pl. ἐγώ I
εἰς prep. εἰς (+acc) into, to, unto, for, in, on, toward, against, upon, at, among
ἀπάντησιν n. acc. fem. sg. ἀπάντησις meet, encounter
ἡμῖν pron. dat. 1p. pl. ἐγώ I
ἄχρις prep. ἄχρι or ἄχρις (+gen) until, unto, till, even to, as far as, while, into
Ἀππίου n. gen. masc. sg. Ἀππίος Appii, Appius
Φόρου n. gen. neut. sg. Φόρον Forum, marketplace
καὶ conj. καί and, even, also, but
Τριῶν num. gen. fem. pl. Τρεῖς Three
Ταβερνῶν n. gen. fem. pl. Ταβέρναι Tavern
οὓς relative pron. acc. masc. pl. ὅς ἥ ὅ who, which, what, that
ὁ art. nom. masc. sg. ὁ ἡ τό the, this, that, he, she, it
Παῦλος n. nom. masc. sg. Παῦλος Paul, Paulus
τῷ art. dat. masc. sg. ὁ ἡ τό the, this, that, he, she, it
Θεῷ n. dat. masc. sg. θεός God, god
θάρσος n. acc. neut. sg. θάρσος courage
16 Ὅτε conj. ὅτε when, after that, as soon as, while, after
δὲ conj. δέ but, and, now, also, to the contrary, rather, then
εἰς prep. εἰς (+acc) into, to, unto, for, in, on, toward, against, upon, at, among
Ῥώμην n. acc. fem. sg. Ῥώμη Rome
ὁ art. nom. masc. sg. ὁ ἡ τό the, this, that, he, she, it

ἑκατόνταρχος n. nom. masc. sg. ἑκατόνταρχος centurion
τοὺς art. acc. masc. pl. ὁ ἡ τό the, this, that, he, she, it
δεσμίους n. acc. masc. pl. δέσμιος prisoner, in bonds, that is in bond
τῷ art. dat. masc. sg. ὁ ἡ τό the, this, that, he, she, it
στρατοπεδάρχῃ n. dat. masc. sg. στρατοπεδάρχης captain of the guard
τῷ art. dat. masc. sg. ὁ ἡ τό the, this, that, he, she, it
δὲ conj. δέ but, and, now, also, to the contrary, rather, then
Παύλῳ n. dat. masc. sg. Παῦλος Paul, Paulus
καθ' prep. κατά (+gen) against, by, throughout, down, (+acc) according to, after, with
ἑαυτὸν reflexive pron. acc. masc. 3p. sg. ἑαυτοῦ himself, herself, itself, yourself, ourselves
σὺν prep. σύν (+dat) with, beside
τῷ art. dat. masc. sg. ὁ ἡ τό the, this, that, he, she, it
αὐτὸν pron. acc. masc. 3p. sg. αὐτός ἡ ὁ self, of oneself, even, very, the same, he, she, it
στρατιώτῃ n. dat. masc. sg. στρατιώτης soldier
17 δὲ conj. δέ but, and, now, also, to the contrary, rather, then
μετὰ prep. μετά (+gen) with, among, against, (+acc) after
ἡμέρας n. acc. fem. pl. ἡμέρα day, time, year, while, age, day time
τρεῖς num. acc. fem. pl. τρεῖς three
τὸν art. acc. masc. sg. ὁ ἡ τό the, this, that, he, she, it
Παῦλον n. acc. masc. sg. Παῦλος Paul, Paulus
τοὺς art. acc. masc. pl. ὁ ἡ τό the, this, that, he, she, it
τῶν art. gen. masc. pl. ὁ ἡ τό the, this, that, he, she, it
Ἰουδαίων adj. gen. masc. pl. Ἰουδαῖος Jew, Jewess
πρώτους ordinal. adj. acc. masc. pl. πρῶτος first, chief, first of all, chiefest, best
δὲ conj. δέ but, and, now, also, to the contrary, rather, then
αὐτῶν pron. gen. masc. 3p. pl. αὐτός ἡ ὁ self, of oneself, even, very, the same, he, she, it
πρὸς prep. πρός (+gen) for, (+dat) at, (+acc) unto, to, with, for, against
αὐτούς pron. acc. masc. 3p. pl. αὐτός ἡ ὁ self, of oneself, even, very, the same, he, she, it
Ἄνδρες n. voc. masc. pl. ἀνήρ man, husband, sir
ἀδελφοί n. voc. masc. pl. ἀδελφός brother
ἐγὼ p pron. nom. 1p. sg. ἐγώ I
οὐδὲν adj. acc. neut. sg. οὐδείς no man, nothing, no, none, neither, not, nought
ἐναντίον adj. acc. neut. sg. ἐναντίος contrary, against, over against
τῷ art. dat. masc. sg. ὁ ἡ τό the, this, that, he, she, it
λαῷ n. dat. masc. sg. λαός people
ἢ particle. ἤ or, than, either, nor, or else, and, rather than
τοῖς art. dat. neut. pl. ὁ ἡ τό the, this, that, he, she, it
ἔθεσι n. dat. neut. pl. ἔθος custom, manner, be wont
τοῖς art. dat. neut. pl. ὁ ἡ τό the, this, that, he, she, it
πατρῴοις adj. dat. neut. pl. πατρῷος of fathers
δέσμιος n. nom. masc. sg. δέσμιος prisoner, in bonds, that is in bond
ἐξ prep. ἐκ ἐξ (+gen) of, from, out of, by, on, with, in, among, through
Ἱεροσολύμων n. gen. neut. pl. Ἱεροσόλυμα Jerusalem
εἰς prep. εἰς (+acc) into, to, unto, for, in, on, toward, against, upon, at, among
τὰς art. acc. fem. pl. ὁ ἡ τό the, this, that, he, she, it
χεῖρας n. acc. fem. pl. χείρ hand
τῶν art. gen. masc. pl. ὁ ἡ τό the, this, that, he, she, it
Ῥωμαίων adj. gen. masc. pl. Ῥωμαῖος Roman, Rome
18 οἵτινες relative pron. nom. masc. pl. ὅστις which, who, whosoever, that, whatsoever
με pron. acc. 1p. sg. ἐγώ I
διὰ prep. διά (+gen) by, through, with, in, of, (+acc) for, because of, for a cause
τὸ art. acc. neut. sg. ὁ ἡ τό the, this, that, he, she, it
μηδεμίαν num. acc. fem. sg. μηδείς μηδεμία μηδέν no man, nothing, no, none, not at all
αἰτίαν n. acc. fem. sg. αἰτία cause, reason, accusation, fault
θανάτου n. gen. masc. sg. θάνατος death

ἐν prep. ἐν (+dat) in, by, with, among, at, on, through, to, within, into, of, for
ἐμοί pron. dat. 1p. sg. ἐγώ I
19 δὲ conj. δέ but, and, now, also, to the contrary, rather, then
τῶν art. gen. masc. pl. ὁ ἡ τό the, this, that, he, she, it
Ἰουδαίων adj. gen. masc. pl. Ἰουδαῖος Jew, Jewess
Καίσαρα n. acc. masc. sg. Καῖσαρ Caesar
οὐχ particle of negation. οὐ οὐκ οὐχ not, no, neither, none, nay, nor, never, nothing
ὡς adv. ὡς as, when, as it were, how, about, like, as soon as, even as, while
τοῦ art. gen. neut. sg. ὁ ἡ τό the, this, that, he, she, it
ἔθνους n. gen. neut. sg. ἔθνος Gentile, nation, heathen, people
μου pron. gen. 1p. sg. ἐγώ I
τι indefinite pron. acc. neut. sg. τὶς certain, some, any man, one, any thing
20 διὰ prep. διά (+gen) by, through, with, in, of, (+acc) for, because of, for a cause
ταύτην demo. pron. acc. fem. sg. οὗτος αὕτη τοῦτο this, the same, this same, he, she, it
οὖν conj. οὖν therefore, then, so, and, now, wherefore
τὴν art. acc. fem. sg. ὁ ἡ τό the, this, that, he, she, it
αἰτίαν n. acc. fem. sg. αἰτία cause, reason, accusation, fault
ὑμᾶς pron. acc. 2p. pl. σύ thou, you
καὶ conj. καί and, even, also, but
ἕνεκεν prep. ἕνεκα, ἕνεκεν or εἵνεκεν (+gen) for the sake, for a cause, for, by reason of
γὰρ conj. γάρ for, and, because, but, indeed
τῆς art. gen. fem. sg. ὁ ἡ τό the, this, that, he, she, it
ἐλπίδος n. gen. fem. sg. ἐλπίς hope, faith
τοῦ art. gen. masc. sg. ὁ ἡ τό the, this, that, he, she, it
Ἰσραὴλ pron. name. masc. inde. Ἰσραήλ Israel
τὴν art. acc. fem. sg. ὁ ἡ τό the, this, that, he, she, it
ἅλυσιν n. acc. fem. sg. ἅλυσις chain, bond
ταύτην demo. pron. acc. fem. sg. οὗτος αὕτη τοῦτο this, the same, this same, he, she, it
21 οἱ art. nom. masc. pl. ὁ ἡ τό the, this, that, he, she, it
δὲ conj. δέ but, and, now, also, to the contrary, rather, then
πρὸς prep. πρός (+gen) for, (+dat) at, (+acc) unto, to, with, for, against
αὐτὸν pron. acc. masc. 3p. sg. αὐτός ἡ ὁ self, of oneself, even, very, the same, he, she, it
Ἡμεῖς pron. nom. 1p. pl. ἐγώ I
οὔτε conj. οὔτε neither, nor, nor yet, no, none
γράμματα n. acc. neut. pl. γράμμα letter, bill, learning, scripture, writing
περὶ prep. περί (+gen) of, for, concerning, (+acc) about, concerning, in
σοῦ pron. gen. 2p. sg. σύ thou, you
ἀπὸ prep. ἀπό (+gen) from, of, out of, since, for, off, at, by, in, on
τῆς art. gen. fem. sg. ὁ ἡ τό the, this, that, he, she, it
Ἰουδαίας n. gen. fem. sg. Ἰουδαία Judaea, Jewry
οὔτε conj. οὔτε neither, nor, nor yet, no, none
τις indefinite pron. nom. masc. sg. τὶς certain, some, any man, one, any thing
τῶν art. gen. masc. pl. ὁ ἡ τό the, this, that, he, she, it
ἀδελφῶν n. gen. masc. pl. ἀδελφός brother
ἢ particle. ἤ or, than, either, nor, or else, and, rather than
τι indefinite pron. acc. neut. sg. τὶς certain, some, any man, one, any thing
περὶ prep. περί (+gen) of, for, concerning, (+acc) about, concerning, in
σοῦ pron. gen. 2p. sg. σύ thou, you
πονηρόν adj. acc. neut. sg. πονηρός evil, wicked, bad
22 δὲ conj. δέ but, and, now, also, to the contrary, rather, then
παρὰ prep. παρά (+gen) of, from, (+dat) with, for, (+acc) beside, at, by, above, against
σοῦ pron. gen. 2p. sg. σύ thou, you
ἃ relative pron. acc. neut. pl. ὅς ἥ ὅ who, which, what, that
περὶ prep. περί (+gen) of, for, concerning, (+acc) about, concerning, in
μέν conj. μέν indeed, verily, truly, even, so, some

γὰρ conj. γάρ for, and, because, but, indeed
τῆς art. gen. fem. sg. ὁ ἡ τό the, this, that, he, she, it
αἱρέσεως n. gen. fem. sg. αἵρεσις sect, heresy
ταύτης demo. pron. gen. fem. sg. οὗτος αὕτη τοῦτο this, the same, this same, he, she, it
γνωστὸν adj. nom. neut. sg. γνωστός acquaintance, known, notable
ἡμῖν pron. dat. 1p. pl. ἐγώ I
ὅτι conj. ὅτι that, for, because, how that, how, because that, for that, though
πανταχοῦ adv. πανταχοῦ every where, in all places
23 δὲ conj. δέ but, and, now, also, to the contrary, rather, then
αὐτῷ pron. dat. masc. 3p. sg. αὐτός ή ὁ self, of oneself, even, very, the same, he, she, it
ἡμέραν n. acc. fem. sg. ἡμέρα day, time, year, while, age, day time
πρὸς prep. πρός (+gen) for, (+dat) at, (+acc) unto, to, with, for, against
αὐτὸν pron. acc. masc. 3p. sg. αὐτός ή ὁ self, of oneself, even, very, the same, he, she, it
εἰς prep. εἰς (+acc) into, to, unto, for, in, on, toward, against, upon, at, among
τὴν art. acc. fem. sg. ὁ ἡ τό the, this, that, he, she, it
ξενίαν n. acc. fem. sg. ξενία lodging
πλείονες compar. adj. nom. masc. pl. πολύς many, great, much, long, abundant
οἷς relative pron. dat. masc. pl. ὅς ἥ ὅ who, which, what, that
τὴν art. acc. fem. sg. ὁ ἡ τό the, this, that, he, she, it
βασιλείαν n. acc. fem. sg. βασιλεία kingdom, reign
τοῦ art. gen. masc. sg. ὁ ἡ τό the, this, that, he, she, it
Θεοῦ n. gen. masc. sg. θεός God, god
τε conj. τέ and, both, also
αὐτοὺς pron. acc. masc. 3p. pl. αὐτός ή ὁ self, of oneself, even, very, the same, he, she, it
τὰ art. acc. neut. pl. ὁ ἡ τό the, this, that, he, she, it
περὶ prep. περί (+gen) of, for, concerning, (+acc) about, concerning, in
τοῦ art. gen. masc. sg. ὁ ἡ τό the, this, that, he, she, it
Ἰησοῦ n. gen. masc. sg. Ἰησοῦς Jesus
ἀπό prep. ἀπό (+gen) from, of, out of, since, for, off, at, by, in, on
τε conj. τέ and, both, also
τοῦ art. gen. masc. sg. ὁ ἡ τό the, this, that, he, she, it
νόμου n. gen. masc. sg. νόμος law, the law
Μωσέως n. gen. masc. sg. Μωσῆς Moses
καὶ conj. καί and, even, also, but
τῶν art. gen. masc. pl. ὁ ἡ τό the, this, that, he, she, it
προφητῶν n. gen. masc. pl. προφήτης prophet
ἀπό prep. ἀπό (+gen) from, of, out of, since, for, off, at, by, in, on
πρωῒ adv. πρωΐ in the morning, early, early in the morning
ἕως conj. ἕως till, until, unto, until when, while, as far as, even, until now
ἑσπέρας n. gen. fem. sg. ἑσπέρα evening, eventide
24 καὶ conj. καί and, even, also, but
οἱ art. nom. masc. pl. ὁ ἡ τό the, this, that, he, she, it
μέν conj. μέν indeed, verily, truly, even, so, some
τοῖς art. dat. neut. pl. ὁ ἡ τό the, this, that, he, she, it
οἱ art. nom. masc. pl. ὁ ἡ τό the, this, that, he, she, it
δὲ conj. δέ but, and, now, also, to the contrary, rather, then
25 ἀσύμφωνοι adj. nom. masc. pl. ἀσύμφωνος agreed not
δὲ conj. δέ but, and, now, also, to the contrary, rather, then
πρὸς prep. πρός (+gen) for, (+dat) at, (+acc) unto, to, with, for, against
ἀλλήλους pron. acc. masc. 3p. pl. ἀλλήλων one another, themselves, together, mutual
τοῦ art. gen. masc. sg. ὁ ἡ τό the, this, that, he, she, it
Παύλου n. gen. masc. sg. Παῦλος Paul, Paulus
ῥῆμα n. acc. neut. sg. ῥῆμα word, saying, thing
ἓν num. acc. neut. sg. εἷς or ἓν one, other, some, any, only, a certain
ὅτι conj. ὅτι that, for, because, how that, how, because that, for that, though

Καλῶς adv. καλῶς good, well, full well
τὸ art. nom. neut. sg. ὁ ἡ τό the, this, that, he, she, it
Πνεῦμα n. nom. neut. sg. πνεῦμα spirit, Spirit, Ghost, ghost, life. of the spirit, wind
τὸ art. nom. neut. sg. ὁ ἡ τό the, this, that, he, she, it
Ἅγιον adj. nom. neut. sg. ἅγιος Holy, holy, saint, Holy One, holy thing, most holy
διὰ prep. διά (+gen) by, through, with, in, of, (+acc) for, because of, for a cause
Ἠσαΐου n. gen. masc. sg. Ἠσαΐας Esaias, Isaiah
τοῦ art. gen. masc. sg. ὁ ἡ τό the, this, that, he, she, it
προφήτου n. gen. masc. sg. προφήτης prophet
πρὸς prep. πρός (+gen) for, (+dat) at, (+acc) unto, to, with, for, against
τοὺς art. acc. masc. pl. ὁ ἡ τό the, this, that, he, she, it
πατέρας n. acc. masc. pl. πατήρ Father, father, parent
ἡμῶν pron. gen. 1p. pl. ἐγώ I
26 πρὸς prep. πρός (+gen) for, (+dat) at, (+acc) unto, to, with, for, against
τὸν art. acc. masc. sg. ὁ ἡ τό the, this, that, he, she, it
λαὸν n. acc. masc. sg. λαός people
τοῦτον demo. pron. acc. masc. sg. οὗτος αὕτη τοῦτο this, the same, this same, he, she, it
καὶ conj. καί and, even, also, but
Ἀκοῇ n. dat. fem. sg. ἀκοή hearing, ear, fame, report, rumour, which one heard
καὶ conj. καί and, even, also, but
οὐ particle of negation. οὐ οὐκ οὐχ not, no, neither, none, nay, nor, never, nothing
μὴ particle of negation. μή not, no, lest, neither, none, nothing, nor, never, without
καὶ conj. καί and, even, also, but
καὶ conj. καί and, even, also, but
οὐ particle of negation. οὐ οὐκ οὐχ not, no, neither, none, nay, nor, never, nothing
μὴ particle of negation. μή not, no, lest, neither, none, nothing, nor, never, without
27 γὰρ conj. γάρ for, and, because, but, indeed
ἡ art. nom. fem. sg. ὁ ἡ τό the, this, that, he, she, it
καρδία n. nom. fem. sg. καρδία heart
τοῦ art. gen. masc. sg. ὁ ἡ τό the, this, that, he, she, it
λαοῦ n. gen. masc. sg. λαός people
τούτου demo. pron. gen. masc. sg. οὗτος αὕτη τοῦτο this, the same, this same, he, she, it
καὶ conj. καί and, even, also, but
τοῖς art. dat. neut. pl. ὁ ἡ τό the, this, that, he, she, it
ὠσὶ n. dat. neut. pl. οὖς ear
βαρέως adv. βαρέως dull
καὶ conj. καί and, even, also, but
τοὺς art. acc. masc. pl. ὁ ἡ τό the, this, that, he, she, it
ὀφθαλμοὺς n. acc. masc. pl. ὀφθαλμός eye, sight
αὐτῶν pron. gen. masc. 3p. pl. αὐτός ἡ ὁ self, of oneself, even, very, the same, he, she, it
μήποτε conj. μήποτε lest, lest at any time, lest haply
τοῖς art. dat. masc. pl. ὁ ἡ τό the, this, that, he, she, it
ὀφθαλμοῖς n. dat. masc. pl. ὀφθαλμός eye, sight
καὶ conj. καί and, even, also, but
τοῖς art. dat. neut. pl. ὁ ἡ τό the, this, that, he, she, it
ὠσὶν n. dat. neut. pl. οὖς ear
καὶ conj. καί and, even, also, but
τῇ art. dat. fem. sg. ὁ ἡ τό the, this, that, he, she, it
καρδίᾳ n. dat. fem. sg. καρδία heart
καὶ conj. καί and, even, also, but
καὶ conj. καί and, even, also, but
αὐτούς pron. acc. masc. 3p. pl. αὐτός ἡ ὁ self, of oneself, even, very, the same, he, she, it
28 γνωστὸν adj. nom. neut. sg. γνωστός acquaintance, known, notable
οὖν conj. οὖν therefore, then, so, and, now, wherefore
ὑμῖν pron. dat. 2p. pl. σύ thou, you

ὅτι conj. ὅτι that, for, because, how that, how, because that, for that, though
τοῖς art. dat. neut. pl. ὁ ἡ τό the, this, that, he, she, it
ἔθνεσιν n. dat. neut. pl. ἔθνος Gentile, nation, heathen, people
τὸ art. nom. neut. sg. ὁ ἡ τό the, this, that, he, she, it
σωτήριον adj. nom. neut. sg. σωτήριον salvation
τοῦ art. gen. masc. sg. ὁ ἡ τό the, this, that, he, she, it
Θεοῦ n. gen. masc. sg. θεός God, god
αὐτοὶ pron. nom. masc. 3p. pl. αὐτός ή ό self, of oneself, even, very, the same, he, she, it
καὶ conj. καί and, even, also, but
29 καὶ conj. καί and, even, also, but
ταῦτα demo. pron. acc. neut. pl. οὗτος αὕτη τοῦτο this, the same, this same, he, she, it
αὐτοῦ pron. gen. masc. 3p. sg. αὐτός ή ό self, of oneself, even, very, the same, he, she, it
οἱ art. nom. masc. pl. ὁ ἡ τό the, this, that, he, she, it
'Ιουδαῖοι adj. nom. masc. pl. 'Ιουδαῖος Jew, Jewess
πολλὴν adj. acc. fem. sg. πολύς many, great, much, long, abundant
ἐν prep. ἐν (+dat) in, by, with, among, at, on, through, to, within, into, of, for
ἑαυτοῖς reflexive pron. dat. masc. 3p. pl. ἑαυτοῦ himself, herself, itself, yourself, ourselves
συζήτησιν n. acc. fem. sg. συζήτησις disputation, disputing, reasoning
30 δὲ conj. δέ but, and, now, also, to the contrary, rather, then
ὁ art. nom. masc. sg. ὁ ἡ τό the, this, that, he, she, it
Παῦλος n. nom. masc. sg. Παῦλος Paul, Paulus
διετίαν n. acc. fem. sg. διετία two years
ὅλην adj. acc. fem. sg. ὅλος all, whole, every whit, altogether
ἐν prep. ἐν (+dat) in, by, with, among, at, on, through, to, within, into, of, for
ἰδίῳ adj. dat. neut. sg. ἴδιος one's own, one's, privately
μισθώματι n. dat. neut. sg. μίσθωμα hired house
καὶ conj. καί and, even, also, but
πάντας adj. acc. masc. pl. πᾶς πᾶσα πᾶν all, every, whosoever, every one, no, whole, any
τοὺς art. acc. masc. pl. ὁ ἡ τό the, this, that, he, she, it
πρὸς prep. πρός (+gen) for, (+dat) at, (+acc) unto, to, with, for, against
αὐτόν pron. acc. masc. 3p. sg. αὐτός ή ό self, of oneself, even, very, the same, he, she, it
31 τὴν art. acc. fem. sg. ὁ ἡ τό the, this, that, he, she, it
βασιλείαν n. acc. fem. sg. βασιλεία kingdom, reign
τοῦ art. gen. masc. sg. ὁ ἡ τό the, this, that, he, she, it
Θεοῦ n. gen. masc. sg. θεός God, god
καὶ conj. καί and, even, also, but
τὰ art. acc. neut. pl. ὁ ἡ τό the, this, that, he, she, it
περὶ prep. περί (+gen) of, for, concerning, (+acc) about, concerning, in
τοῦ art. gen. masc. sg. ὁ ἡ τό the, this, that, he, she, it
Κυρίου n. gen. masc. sg. κύριος Lord, lord, master, sir, LORD, God, Master, owner
'Ιησοῦ n. gen. masc. sg. 'Ιησοῦς Jesus
Χριστοῦ n. gen. masc. sg. Χριστός Christ
μετὰ prep. μετά (+gen) with, among, against, (+acc) after
πάσης adj. gen. fem. sg. πᾶς πᾶσα πᾶν all, every, whosoever, every one, no, whole, any
παρρησίας n. gen. fem. sg. παρρησία boldness, confidence, openly, plainly, freely
ἀκωλύτως adv. ἀκωλύτως no man forbidding him, without hindrance, freely

ΠΑΥΛΟΥ ΤΟΥ ΑΠΟΣΤΟΛΟΥ
Η ΠΡΟΣ
ΡΩΜΑΙΟΥΣ ΕΠΙΣΤΟΛΗ

1

1 Παῦλος n. nom. masc. sg. Παῦλος Paul, Paulus
δοῦλος n. nom. masc. sg. δοῦλος servant, bondman, bond, slave
Ἰησοῦ n. gen. masc. sg. Ἰησοῦς Jesus
Χριστοῦ n. gen. masc. sg. Χριστός Christ
κλητὸς adj. nom. masc. sg. κλητός called
ἀπόστολος n. nom. masc. sg. ἀπόστολος apostle, messenger, he that is sent
εἰς prep. εἰς (+acc) into, to, unto, for, in, on, toward, against, upon, at, among
εὐαγγέλιον n. acc. neut. sg. εὐαγγέλιον gospel
Θεοῦ n. gen. masc. sg. θεός God, god
2 ὃ relative pron. acc. neut. sg. ὅς ἥ ὅ who, which, what, that
διὰ prep. διά (+gen) by, through, with, in, of, (+acc) for, because of, for a cause
τῶν art. gen. masc. pl. ὁ ἡ τό the, this, that, he, she, it
προφητῶν n. gen. masc. pl. προφήτης prophet
αὐτοῦ pron. gen. masc. 3p. sg. αὐτός ή ό self, of oneself, even, very, the same, he, she, it
ἐν prep. ἐν (+dat) in, by, with, among, at, on, through, to, within, into, of, for
γραφαῖς n. dat. fem. pl. γραφή scripture
ἁγίαις adj. dat. fem. pl. ἅγιος Holy, holy, saint, Holy One, holy thing, most holy
3 περὶ prep. περί (+gen) of, for, concerning, (+acc) about, concerning, in
τοῦ art. gen. masc. sg. ὁ ἡ τό the, this, that, he, she, it
υἱοῦ n. gen. masc. sg. υἱός son, child, descendant, offspring, heir
αὐτοῦ pron. gen. masc. 3p. sg. αὐτός ή ό self, of oneself, even, very, the same, he, she, it
τοῦ art. gen. masc. sg. ὁ ἡ τό the, this, that, he, she, it
ἐκ prep. ἐκ ἐξ (+gen) of, from, out of, by, on, with, in, among, through
σπέρματος n. gen. neut. sg. σπέρμα seed, issue
Δαβὶδ n. gen. masc. sg. Δαβίδ David
κατὰ prep. κατά (+gen) against, by, throughout, down, (+acc) according to, after, with
σάρκα n. acc. fem. sg. σάρξ flesh, carnal
4 τοῦ art. gen. masc. sg. ὁ ἡ τό the, this, that, he, she, it
υἱοῦ n. gen. masc. sg. υἱός son, child, descendant, offspring, heir
Θεοῦ n. gen. masc. sg. θεός God, god
ἐν prep. ἐν (+dat) in, by, with, among, at, on, through, to, within, into, of, for
δυνάμει n. dat. fem. sg. δύναμις power, mighty work, miracle, strength, might
κατὰ prep. κατά (+gen) against, by, throughout, down, (+acc) according to, after, with
πνεῦμα n. acc. neut. sg. πνεῦμα spirit, Spirit, Ghost, ghost, life. of the spirit, wind
ἁγιωσύνης n. gen. fem. sg. ἁγιωσύνη holiness
ἐξ prep. ἐκ ἐξ (+gen) of, from, out of, by, on, with, in, among, through
ἀναστάσεως n. gen. fem. sg. ἀνάστασις resurrection, rising again
νεκρῶν adj. gen. masc. pl. νεκρός dead
Ἰησοῦ n. gen. masc. sg. Ἰησοῦς Jesus
Χριστοῦ n. gen. masc. sg. Χριστός Christ
τοῦ art. gen. masc. sg. ὁ ἡ τό the, this, that, he, she, it
Κυρίου n. gen. masc. sg. κύριος Lord, lord, master, sir, LORD, God, Master, owner
ἡμῶν pron. gen. 1p. pl. ἐγώ I
5 δι' prep. διά (+gen) by, through, with, in, of, (+acc) for, because of, for a cause
οὗ relative pron. gen. masc. sg. ὅς ἥ ὅ who, which, what, that
χάριν n. acc. fem. sg. χάρις grace, thank, favour, pleasure
καὶ conj. καί and, even, also, but

ἀποστολὴν n. acc. fem. sg. ἀποστολή apostleship
εἰς prep. εἰς (+acc) into, to, unto, for, in, on, toward, against, upon, at, among
ὑπακοὴν n. acc. fem. sg. ὑπακοή obedience, obey, make obedient, obedient
πίστεως n. gen. fem. sg. πίστις faith, assurance, belief, fidelity
ἐν prep. ἐν (+dat) in, by, with, among, at, on, through, to, within, into, of, for
πᾶσι adj. dat. neut. pl. πᾶς πᾶσα πᾶν all, every, whosoever, every one, no, whole, any
τοῖς art. dat. neut. pl. ὁ ἡ τό the, this, that, he, she, it
ἔθνεσιν n. dat. neut. pl. ἔθνος Gentile, nation, heathen, people
ὑπὲρ prep. ὑπέρ (+gen) for, of, for the sake of, (+acc) above, more than
τοῦ art. gen. neut. sg. ὁ ἡ τό the, this, that, he, she, it
ὀνόματος n. gen. neut. sg. ὄνομα name, call, surname
αὐτοῦ pron. gen. masc. 3p. sg. αὐτός ἡ ὁ self, of oneself, even, very, the same, he, she, it
6 ἐν prep. ἐν (+dat) in, by, with, among, at, on, through, to, within, into, of, for
οἷς relative pron. dat. neut. pl. ὅς ἥ ὅ who, which, what, that
καὶ conj. καί and, even, also, but
ὑμεῖς pron. nom. 2p. pl. σύ thou, you
κλητοὶ adj. nom. masc. pl. κλητός called
Ἰησοῦ n. gen. masc. sg. Ἰησοῦς Jesus
Χριστοῦ n. gen. masc. sg. Χριστός Christ
7 πᾶσι adj. dat. masc. pl. πᾶς πᾶσα πᾶν all, every, whosoever, every one, no, whole, any
τοῖς art. dat. masc. pl. ὁ ἡ τό the, this, that, he, she, it
ἐν prep. ἐν (+dat) in, by, with, among, at, on, through, to, within, into, of, for
Ῥώμῃ n. dat. fem. sg. Ῥώμη Rome
ἀγαπητοῖς adj. dat. masc. pl. ἀγαπητός beloved, dearly beloved, dear, wellbeloved
Θεοῦ n. gen. masc. sg. θεός God, god
κλητοῖς adj. dat. masc. pl. κλητός called
ἁγίοις adj. dat. masc. pl. ἅγιος Holy, holy, saint, Holy One, holy thing, most holy
χάρις n. nom. fem. sg. χάρις grace, thank, favour, pleasure
ὑμῖν pron. dat. 2p. pl. σύ thou, you
καὶ conj. καί and, even, also, but
εἰρήνη n. nom. fem. sg. εἰρήνη peace, quietness, rest
ἀπὸ prep. ἀπό (+gen) from, of, out of, since, for, off, at, by, in, on
Θεοῦ n. gen. masc. sg. θεός God, god
πατρὸς n. gen. masc. sg. πατήρ Father, father, parent
ἡμῶν pron. gen. 1p. pl. ἐγώ I
καὶ conj. καί and, even, also, but
Κυρίου n. gen. masc. sg. κύριος Lord, lord, master, sir, LORD, God, Master, owner
Ἰησοῦ n. gen. masc. sg. Ἰησοῦς Jesus
Χριστοῦ n. gen. masc. sg. Χριστός Christ
8 Πρῶτον adv. πρῶτον first, at the first, first of all, at first, at the beginning, before, chiefly
μὲν conj. μέν indeed, verily, truly, even, so, some
τῷ art. dat. masc. sg. ὁ ἡ τό the, this, that, he, she, it
Θεῷ n. dat. masc. sg. θεός God, god
μου pron. gen. 1p. sg. ἐγώ I
διὰ prep. διά (+gen) by, through, with, in, of, (+acc) for, because of, for a cause
Ἰησοῦ n. gen. masc. sg. Ἰησοῦς Jesus
Χριστοῦ n. gen. masc. sg. Χριστός Christ
ὑπὲρ prep. ὑπέρ (+gen) for, of, for the sake of, (+acc) above, more than
πάντων adj. gen. masc. pl. πᾶς πᾶσα πᾶν all, every, whosoever, every one, no, whole, any
ὑμῶν pron. gen. 2p. pl. σύ thou, you
ὅτι conj. ὅτι that, for, because, how that, how, because that, for that, though
ἡ art. nom. fem. sg. ὁ ἡ τό the, this, that, he, she, it
πίστις n. nom. fem. sg. πίστις faith, assurance, belief, fidelity
ὑμῶν pron. gen. 2p. pl. σύ thou, you
ἐν prep. ἐν (+dat) in, by, with, among, at, on, through, to, within, into, of, for

ὅλῳ adj. dat. masc. sg. ὅλος all, whole, every whit, altogether
τῷ art. dat. masc. sg. ὁ ἡ τό the, this, that, he, she, it
κόσμῳ n. dat. masc. sg. κόσμος world, adorning
9 μάρτυς n. nom. masc. sg. μάρτυς or μάρτυρ witness, martyr, record
γάρ conj. γάρ for, and, because, but, indeed
μού pron. gen. 1p. sg. ἐγώ I
ὁ art. nom. masc. sg. ὁ ἡ τό the, this, that, he, she, it
Θεός n. nom. masc. sg. θεός God, god
ᾧ relative pron. dat. masc. sg. ὅς ἥ ὅ who, which, what, that
ἐν prep. ἐν (+dat) in, by, with, among, at, on, through, to, within, into, of, for
τῷ art. dat. neut. sg. ὁ ἡ τό the, this, that, he, she, it
πνεύματί n. dat. neut. sg. πνεῦμα spirit, Spirit, Ghost, ghost, life. of the spirit, wind
μου pron. gen. 1p. sg. ἐγώ I
ἐν prep. ἐν (+dat) in, by, with, among, at, on, through, to, within, into, of, for
τῷ art. dat. neut. sg. ὁ ἡ τό the, this, that, he, she, it
εὐαγγελίῳ n. dat. neut. sg. εὐαγγέλιον gospel
τοῦ art. gen. masc. sg. ὁ ἡ τό the, this, that, he, she, it
υἱοῦ n. gen. masc. sg. υἱός son, child, descendant, offspring, heir
αὐτοῦ pron. gen. masc. 3p. sg. αὐτός ή ό self, of oneself, even, very, the same, he, she, it
ὡς adv. ὡς as, when, as it were, how, about, like, as soon as, even as, while
ἀδιαλείπτως adv. ἀδιαλείπτως without ceasing
μνείαν n. acc. fem. sg. μνεία mention, remembrance
ὑμῶν pron. gen. 2p. pl. σύ thou, you
10 πάντοτε adv. πάντοτε always, ever, always, evermore
ἐπὶ prep. ἐπί (+gen) on, in, upon, (+dat) in, at, for, upon, (+acc) on, upon, unto, to, against
τῶν art. gen. fem. pl. ὁ ἡ τό the, this, that, he, she, it
προσευχῶν n. gen. fem. pl. προσευχή prayer
μου pron. gen. 1p. sg. ἐγώ I
εἴπως conj. εἴπως if by any means
ἤδη adv. ἤδη now, already, yet, by this time, even now, now already
ποτὲ adv. ποτέ in time past, at any time, sometimes, in old time, once, when
ἐν prep. ἐν (+dat) in, by, with, among, at, on, through, to, within, into, of, for
τῷ art. dat. neut. sg. ὁ ἡ τό the, this, that, he, she, it
θελήματι n. dat. neut. sg. θέλημα will, desire, pleasure
τοῦ art. gen. masc. sg. ὁ ἡ τό the, this, that, he, she, it
Θεοῦ n. gen. masc. sg. θεός God, god
πρὸς prep. πρός (+gen) for, (+dat) at, (+acc) unto, to, with, for, against
ὑμᾶς pron. acc. 2p. pl. σύ thou, you
11 γὰρ conj. γάρ for, and, because, but, indeed
ὑμᾶς pron. acc. 2p. pl. σύ thou, you
ἵνα conj. ἵνα that, to, lest, for to, so that, albeit, because, for, so as
τι indefinite pron. acc. neut. sg. τὶς certain, some, any man, one, any thing
χάρισμα n. acc. neut. sg. χάρισμα gift, free gift
ὑμῖν pron. dat. 2p. pl. σύ thou, you
πνευματικὸν adj. acc. neut. sg. πνευματικός spiritual
εἰς prep. εἰς (+acc) into, to, unto, for, in, on, toward, against, upon, at, among
τὸ art. acc. neut. sg. ὁ ἡ τό the, this, that, he, she, it
ὑμᾶς pron. acc. 2p. pl. σύ thou, you
12 τοῦτο demo. pron. nom. neut. sg. οὗτος αὕτη τοῦτο this, the same, this same, he, she, it
δέ conj. δέ but, and, now, also, to the contrary, rather, then
ἐν prep. ἐν (+dat) in, by, with, among, at, on, through, to, within, into, of, for
ὑμῖν pron. dat. 2p. pl. σύ thou, you
διὰ prep. διά (+gen) by, through, with, in, of, (+acc) for, because of, for a cause
τῆς art. gen. fem. sg. ὁ ἡ τό the, this, that, he, she, it
ἐν prep. ἐν (+dat) in, by, with, among, at, on, through, to, within, into, of, for

ἀλλήλοις pron. dat. masc. 1p. pl. ἀλλήλων one another, themselves, together, mutual
πίστεως n. gen. fem. sg. πίστις faith, assurance, belief, fidelity
ὑμῶν pron. gen. 2p. pl. σύ thou, you
τε conj. τέ and, both, also
καὶ conj. καί and, even, also, but
ἐμοῦ pron. gen. 1p. sg. ἐγώ I
13 οὐ particle of negation. οὐ οὐκ οὐχ not, no, neither, none, nay, nor, never, nothing
δὲ conj. δέ but, and, now, also, to the contrary, rather, then
ὑμᾶς pron. acc. 2p. pl. σύ thou, you
ἀδελφοί n. voc. masc. pl. ἀδελφός brother
ὅτι conj. ὅτι that, for, because, how that, how, because that, for that, though
πολλάκις adv. πολλάκις often, ofttimes, oft
πρὸς prep. πρός (+gen) for, (+dat) at, (+acc) unto, to, with, for, against
ὑμᾶς pron. acc. 2p. pl. σύ thou, you
καὶ conj. καί and, even, also, but
ἄχρι prep. ἄχρι or ἄχρις (+gen) until, unto, till, even to, as far as, while, into
τοῦ art. gen. masc. sg. ὁ ἡ τό the, this, that, he, she, it
δεῦρο adv. δεῦρο come, come hither
ἵνα conj. ἵνα that, to, lest, for to, so that, albeit, because, for, so as
καρπὸν n. acc. masc. sg. καρπός fruit
τινα indefinite pron. acc. masc. sg. τὶς certain, some, any man, one, any thing
καὶ conj. καί and, even, also, but
ἐν prep. ἐν (+dat) in, by, with, among, at, on, through, to, within, into, of, for
ὑμῖν pron. dat. 2p. pl. σύ thou, you
καθὼς adv. καθώς as, even as, according as, according to
καὶ conj. καί and, even, also, but
ἐν prep. ἐν (+dat) in, by, with, among, at, on, through, to, within, into, of, for
τοῖς art. dat. neut. pl. ὁ ἡ τό the, this, that, he, she, it
λοιποῖς adj. dat. neut. pl. λοιπός other, rest, remnant, residue, which remain
ἔθνεσιν n. dat. neut. pl. ἔθνος Gentile, nation, heathen, people
14 Ἕλλησί n. dat. masc. pl. Ἕλλην Greek, Gentile
τε conj. τέ and, both, also
καὶ conj. καί and, even, also, but
βαρβάροις adj. dat. masc. pl. βάρβαρος barbarous, barbarian
σοφοῖς adj. dat. masc. pl. σοφός wise, wiser
τε conj. τέ and, both, also
καὶ conj. καί and, even, also, but
ἀνοήτοις adj. dat. masc. pl. ἀνόητος fool, foolish, unwise
ὀφειλέτης n. nom. masc. sg. ὀφειλέτης debtor, sinner, owe
15 οὕτω adv. οὕτω οὕτως so, even so, thus, on this wise, likewise, after this manner
τὸ art. nom. neut. sg. ὁ ἡ τό the, this, that, he, she, it
κατ᾽ prep. κατά (+gen) against, by, throughout, down, (+acc) according to, after, with
ἐμὲ pron. acc. 1p. sg. ἐγώ I
πρόθυμον adj. nom. neut. sg. πρόθυμος willing, ready
καὶ conj. καί and, even, also, but
ὑμῖν pron. dat. 2p. pl. σύ thou, you
τοῖς art. dat. masc. pl. ὁ ἡ τό the, this, that, he, she, it
ἐν prep. ἐν (+dat) in, by, with, among, at, on, through, to, within, into, of, for
Ῥώμῃ n. dat. fem. sg. Ῥώμη Rome
16 οὐ particle of negation. οὐ οὐκ οὐχ not, no, neither, none, nay, nor, never, nothing
γὰρ conj. γάρ for, and, because, but, indeed
τὸ art. acc. neut. sg. ὁ ἡ τό the, this, that, he, she, it
εὐαγγέλιον n. acc. neut. sg. εὐαγγέλιον gospel
τοῦ art. gen. masc. sg. ὁ ἡ τό the, this, that, he, she, it
Χριστοῦ n. gen. masc. sg. Χριστός Christ

δύναμις n. nom. fem. sg. δύναμις power, mighty work, miracle, strength, might
γὰρ conj. γάρ for, and, because, but, indeed
Θεοῦ n. gen. masc. sg. θεός God, god
εἰς prep. εἰς (+acc) into, to, unto, for, in, on, toward, against, upon, at, among
σωτηρίαν n. acc. fem. sg. σωτηρία salvation, deliver, health, saving
παντὶ adj. dat. masc. sg. πᾶς πᾶσα πᾶν all, every, whosoever, every one, no, whole, any
τῷ art. dat. masc. sg. ὁ ἡ τό the, this, that, he, she, it
Ἰουδαίῳ adj. dat. masc. sg. Ἰουδαῖος Jew, Jewess
τε conj. τέ and, both, also
πρῶτον adv. πρῶτον first, at the first, first of all, at first, at the beginning, before, chiefly
καὶ conj. καί and, even, also, but
Ἕλληνι n. dat. masc. sg. Ἕλλην Greek, Gentile
17 δικαιοσύνη n. nom. fem. sg. δικαιοσύνη righteousness
γὰρ conj. γάρ for, and, because, but, indeed
Θεοῦ n. gen. masc. sg. θεός God, god
ἐν prep. ἐν (+dat) in, by, with, among, at, on, through, to, within, into, of, for
αὐτῷ pron. dat. neut. 3p. sg. αὐτός ή ό self, of oneself, even, very, the same, he, she, it
ἐκ prep. ἐκ ἐξ (+gen) of, from, out of, by, on, with, in, among, through
πίστεως n. gen. fem. sg. πίστις faith, assurance, belief, fidelity
εἰς prep. εἰς (+acc) into, to, unto, for, in, on, toward, against, upon, at, among
πίστιν n. acc. fem. sg. πίστις faith, assurance, belief, fidelity
καθὼς adv. καθώς as, even as, according as, according to
Ὁ art. nom. masc. sg. ὁ ἡ τό the, this, that, he, she, it
δὲ conj. δέ but, and, now, also, to the contrary, rather, then
δίκαιος adj. nom. masc. sg. δίκαιος righteous, just, meet, right
ἐκ prep. ἐκ ἐξ (+gen) of, from, out of, by, on, with, in, among, through
πίστεως n. gen. fem. sg. πίστις faith, assurance, belief, fidelity
18 γὰρ conj. γάρ for, and, because, but, indeed
ὀργὴ n. nom. fem. sg. ὀργή wrath, anger, indignation, vengeance
Θεοῦ n. gen. masc. sg. θεός God, god
ἀπ' prep. ἀπό (+gen) from, of, out of, since, for, off, at, by, in, on
οὐρανοῦ n. gen. masc. sg. οὐρανός heaven, air, sky
ἐπὶ prep. ἐπί (+gen) on, in, upon, (+dat) in, at, for, upon, (+acc) on, upon, unto, to, against
πᾶσαν adj. acc. fem. sg. πᾶς πᾶσα πᾶν all, every, whosoever, every one, no, whole, any
ἀσέβειαν n. acc. fem. sg. ἀσέβεια ungodliness, ungodly
καὶ conj. καί and, even, also, but
ἀδικίαν n. acc. fem. sg. ἀδικία iniquity, unrighteousness, unjust, wrong
ἀνθρώπων n. gen. masc. pl. ἄνθρωπος man, human being, person, one, certain
τῶν art. gen. masc. pl. ὁ ἡ τό the, this, that, he, she, it
τὴν art. acc. fem. sg. ὁ ἡ τό the, this, that, he, she, it
ἀλήθειαν n. acc. fem. sg. ἀλήθεια truth, verity
ἐν prep. ἐν (+dat) in, by, with, among, at, on, through, to, within, into, of, for
ἀδικίᾳ n. dat. fem. sg. ἀδικία iniquity, unrighteousness, unjust, wrong
19 διότι conj. διότι for, because, because that, therefore
τὸ art. nom. neut. sg. ὁ ἡ τό the, this, that, he, she, it
γνωστὸν adj. nom. neut. sg. γνωστός acquaintance, known, notable
τοῦ art. gen. masc. sg. ὁ ἡ τό the, this, that, he, she, it
Θεοῦ n. gen. masc. sg. θεός God, god
φανερόν adj. nom. neut. sg. φανερός manifest, abroad, open, known, outward, appear
ἐν prep. ἐν (+dat) in, by, with, among, at, on, through, to, within, into, of, for
αὐτοῖς pron. dat. masc. 3p. pl. αὐτός ή ό self, of oneself, even, very, the same, he, she, it
ὁ art. nom. masc. sg. ὁ ἡ τό the, this, that, he, she, it
γὰρ conj. γάρ for, and, because, but, indeed
Θεὸς n. nom. masc. sg. θεός God, god
αὐτοῖς pron. dat. masc. 3p. pl. αὐτός ή ό self, of oneself, even, very, the same, he, she, it

20 τὰ art. nom. neut. pl. ὁ ἡ τό the, this, that, he, she, it
γὰρ conj. γάρ for, and, because, but, indeed
ἀόρατα adj. nom. neut. pl. ἀόρατος invisible, invisible thing
αὐτοῦ pron. gen. masc. 3p. sg. αὐτός ἡ ὁ self, of oneself, even, very, the same, he, she, it
ἀπὸ prep. ἀπό (+gen) from, of, out of, since, for, off, at, by, in, on
κτίσεως n. gen. fem. sg. κτίσις creature, creation, building, ordinance
κόσμου n. gen. masc. sg. κόσμος world, adorning
τοῖς art. dat. neut. pl. ὁ ἡ τό the, this, that, he, she, it
ποιήμασιν n. dat. neut. pl. ποίημα thing that are made, workmanship
ἥ art. nom. fem. sg. ὁ ἡ τό the, this, that, he, she, it
τε conj. τέ and, both, also
ἀΐδιος adj. nom. fem. sg. ἀΐδιος eternal, everlasting
αὐτοῦ pron. gen. masc. 3p. sg. αὐτός ἡ ὁ self, of oneself, even, very, the same, he, she, it
δύναμις n. nom. fem. sg. δύναμις power, mighty work, miracle, strength, might
καὶ conj. καί and, even, also, but
θειότης n. nom. fem. sg. θειότης Godhead
εἰς prep. εἰς (+acc) into, to, unto, for, in, on, toward, against, upon, at, among
τὸ art. acc. neut. sg. ὁ ἡ τό the, this, that, he, she, it
αὐτοὺς pron. acc. masc. 3p. pl. αὐτός ἡ ὁ self, of oneself, even, very, the same, he, she, it
ἀναπολογήτους adj. acc. masc. pl. ἀναπολόγητος without excuse, inexcusable
21 διότι conj. διότι for, because, because that, therefore
τὸν art. acc. masc. sg. ὁ ἡ τό the, this, that, he, she, it
Θεὸν n. acc. masc. sg. θεός God, god
οὐχ particle of negation. οὐ οὐκ οὐχ not, no, neither, none, nay, nor, never, nothing
ὡς adv. ὡς as, when, as it were, how, about, like, as soon as, even as, while
Θεὸν n. acc. masc. sg. θεός God, god
ἢ particle. ἢ or, than, either, nor, or else, and, rather than
ἀλλ' conj. ἀλλά but, yea, yet, nevertheless, howbeit, nay, therefore
ἐν prep. ἐν (+dat) in, by, with, among, at, on, through, to, within, into, of, for
τοῖς art. dat. masc. pl. ὁ ἡ τό the, this, that, he, she, it
διαλογισμοῖς n. dat. masc. pl. διαλογισμός thought, reasoning, imagination, disputing
αὐτῶν pron. gen. masc. 3p. pl. αὐτός ἡ ὁ self, of oneself, even, very, the same, he, she, it
καὶ conj. καί and, even, also, but
ἡ art. nom. fem. sg. ὁ ἡ τό the, this, that, he, she, it
ἀσύνετος adj. nom. fem. sg. ἀσύνετος without understanding, foolish
αὐτῶν pron. gen. masc. 3p. pl. αὐτός ἡ ὁ self, of oneself, even, very, the same, he, she, it
καρδία n. nom. fem. sg. καρδία heart
22 σοφοὶ adj. nom. masc. pl. σοφός wise, wiser
23 καὶ conj. καί and, even, also, but
τὴν art. acc. fem. sg. ὁ ἡ τό the, this, that, he, she, it
δόξαν n. acc. fem. sg. δόξα glory, honour, praise, dignity, worship
τοῦ art. gen. masc. sg. ὁ ἡ τό the, this, that, he, she, it
ἀφθάρτου adj. gen. masc. sg. ἄφθαρτος uncorruptible, incorruptible, immortal, not corruptible
Θεοῦ n. gen. masc. sg. θεός God, god
ἐν prep. ἐν (+dat) in, by, with, among, at, on, through, to, within, into, of, for
ὁμοιώματι n. dat. neut. sg. ὁμοίωμα likeness, made like to, shape, similitude
εἰκόνος n. gen. fem. sg. εἰκών image
φθαρτοῦ adj. gen. masc. sg. φθαρτός corruptible
ἀνθρώπου n. gen. masc. sg. ἄνθρωπος man, human being, person, one, certain
καὶ conj. καί and, even, also, but
πετεινῶν adj. gen. neut. pl. πετεινόν fowl, bird
καὶ conj. καί and, even, also, but
τετραπόδων adj. gen. neut. pl. τετράπους fourfooted beast
καὶ conj. καί and, even, also, but
ἑρπετῶν n. gen. neut. pl. ἑρπετόν creeping thing, serpent

24 Διὸ conj. διό wherefore, therefore, for which cause
καὶ conj. καί and, even, also, but
αὐτοὺς pron. acc. masc. 3p. pl. αὐτός ή ό self, of oneself, even, very, the same, he, she, it
ὁ art. nom. masc. sg. ὁ ἡ τό the, this, that, he, she, it
Θεὸς n. nom. masc. sg. θεός God, god
ἐν prep. ἐν (+dat) in, by, with, among, at, on, through, to, within, into, of, for
ταῖς art. dat. fem. pl. ὁ ἡ τό the, this, that, he, she, it
ἐπιθυμίαις n. dat. fem. pl. ἐπιθυμία lust, concupiscence, desire
τῶν art. gen. fem. pl. ὁ ἡ τό the, this, that, he, she, it
καρδιῶν n. gen. fem. pl. καρδία heart
αὐτῶν pron. gen. masc. 3p. pl. αὐτός ή ό self, of oneself, even, very, the same, he, she, it
εἰς prep. εἰς (+acc) into, to, unto, for, in, on, toward, against, upon, at, among
ἀκαθαρσίαν n. acc. fem. sg. ἀκαθαρσία uncleanness
τοῦ art. gen. neut. sg. ὁ ἡ τό the, this, that, he, she, it
τὰ art. acc. neut. pl. ὁ ἡ τό the, this, that, he, she, it
σώματα n. acc. neut. pl. σῶμα body, bodily, slave
αὐτῶν pron. gen. masc. 3p. pl. αὐτός ή ό self, of oneself, even, very, the same, he, she, it
ἐν prep. ἐν (+dat) in, by, with, among, at, on, through, to, within, into, of, for
ἑαυτοῖς reflexive pron. dat. masc. 3p. pl. ἑαυτοῦ himself, herself, itself, yourself, ourselves
25 οἵτινες relative pron. nom. masc. pl. ὅστις which, who, whosoever, that, whatsoever
τὴν art. acc. fem. sg. ὁ ἡ τό the, this, that, he, she, it
ἀλήθειαν n. acc. fem. sg. ἀλήθεια truth, verity
τοῦ art. gen. masc. sg. ὁ ἡ τό the, this, that, he, she, it
Θεοῦ n. gen. masc. sg. θεός God, god
ἐν prep. ἐν (+dat) in, by, with, among, at, on, through, to, within, into, of, for
τῷ art. dat. neut. sg. ὁ ἡ τό the, this, that, he, she, it
ψεύδει n. dat. neut. sg. ψεῦδος lie, lying
καὶ conj. καί and, even, also, but
τῇ art. dat. fem. sg. ὁ ἡ τό the, this, that, he, she, it
κτίσει n. dat. fem. sg. κτίσις creature, creation, building, ordinance
παρὰ prep. παρά (+gen) of, from, (+dat) with, for, (+acc) beside, at, by, above, against
τὸν art. acc. masc. sg. ὁ ἡ τό the, this, that, he, she, it
ὅς relative pron. nom. masc. sg. ὅς ἥ ὅ who, which, what, that
εὐλογητὸς adj. nom. masc. sg. εὐλογητός blessed
εἰς prep. εἰς (+acc) into, to, unto, for, in, on, toward, against, upon, at, among
τοὺς art. acc. masc. pl. ὁ ἡ τό the, this, that, he, she, it
αἰῶνας n. acc. masc. pl. αἰών ever, ever and ever, evermore, age, eternal, world
ἀμήν particle. ἀμήν amen, verily
26 Διὰ prep. διά (+gen) by, through, with, in, of, (+acc) for, because of, for a cause
τοῦτο demo. pron. acc. neut. sg. οὗτος αὕτη τοῦτο this, the same, this same, he, she, it
αὐτοὺς pron. acc. masc. 3p. pl. αὐτός ή ό self, of oneself, even, very, the same, he, she, it
ὁ art. nom. masc. sg. ὁ ἡ τό the, this, that, he, she, it
Θεὸς n. nom. masc. sg. θεός God, god
εἰς prep. εἰς (+acc) into, to, unto, for, in, on, toward, against, upon, at, among
πάθη n. acc. neut. pl. πάθος affection, inordinate affection, lust
ἀτιμίας n. gen. fem. sg. ἀτιμία vile, dishonour, reproach, shame
αἵ art. nom. fem. pl. ὁ ἡ τό the, this, that, he, she, it
τε conj. τέ and, both, also
γὰρ conj. γάρ for, and, because, but, indeed
θήλειαι adj. nom. fem. pl. θῆλυς female
αὐτῶν pron. gen. masc. 3p. pl. αὐτός ή ό self, of oneself, even, very, the same, he, she, it
τὴν art. acc. fem. sg. ὁ ἡ τό the, this, that, he, she, it
φυσικὴν adj. acc. fem. sg. φυσικός natural
χρῆσιν n. acc. fem. sg. χρῆσις use
εἰς prep. εἰς (+acc) into, to, unto, for, in, on, toward, against, upon, at, among

τὴν art. acc. fem. sg. ὁ ἡ τό the, this, that, he, she, it
παρὰ prep. παρά (+gen) of, from, (+dat) with, for, (+acc) beside, at, by, above, against
φύσιν n. acc. fem. sg. φύσις nature
27 ὁμοίως adv. ὁμοίως likewise, so
τε conj. τέ and, both, also
καὶ conj. καί and, even, also, but
οἱ art. nom. masc. pl. ὁ ἡ τό the, this, that, he, she, it
ἄρσενες adj. nom. masc. pl. ἄρρην man, male
τὴν art. acc. fem. sg. ὁ ἡ τό the, this, that, he, she, it
φυσικὴν adj. acc. fem. sg. φυσικός natural
χρῆσιν n. acc. fem. sg. χρῆσις use
τῆς art. gen. fem. sg. ὁ ἡ τό the, this, that, he, she, it
θηλείας adj. gen. fem. sg. θῆλυς female
ἐν prep. ἐν (+dat) in, by, with, among, at, on, through, to, within, into, of, for
τῇ art. dat. fem. sg. ὁ ἡ τό the, this, that, he, she, it
ὀρέξει n. dat. fem. sg. ὄρεξις lust
αὐτῶν pron. gen. masc. 3p. pl. αὐτός ή ό self, of oneself, even, very, the same, he, she, it
εἰς prep. εἰς (+acc) into, to, unto, for, in, on, toward, against, upon, at, among
ἀλλήλους pron. acc. masc. 3p. pl. ἀλλήλων one another, themselves, together, mutual
ἄρσενες adj. nom. masc. pl. ἄρρην man, male
ἐν prep. ἐν (+dat) in, by, with, among, at, on, through, to, within, into, of, for
ἄρσεσι adj. dat. masc. pl. ἄρρην man, male
τὴν art. acc. fem. sg. ὁ ἡ τό the, this, that, he, she, it
ἀσχημοσύνην n. acc. fem. sg. ἀσχημοσύνη that which is unseemly, shame
καὶ conj. καί and, even, also, but
τὴν art. acc. fem. sg. ὁ ἡ τό the, this, that, he, she, it
ἀντιμισθίαν n. acc. fem. sg. ἀντιμισθία recompence
ἣν relative pron. acc. fem. sg. ὅς ἥ ὅ who, which, what, that
τῆς art. gen. fem. sg. ὁ ἡ τό the, this, that, he, she, it
πλάνης n. gen. fem. sg. πλάνη error, deception, deceit, delusion
αὐτῶν pron. gen. masc. 3p. pl. αὐτός ή ό self, of oneself, even, very, the same, he, she, it
ἐν prep. ἐν (+dat) in, by, with, among, at, on, through, to, within, into, of, for
ἑαυτοῖς reflexive pron. dat. masc. 3p. pl. ἑαυτοῦ himself, herself, itself, yourself, ourselves
28 Καὶ conj. καί and, even, also, but
καθὼς adv. καθώς as, even as, according as, according to
οὐκ particle of negation. οὐ οὐκ οὐχ not, no, neither, none, nay, nor, never, nothing
τὸν art. acc. masc. sg. ὁ ἡ τό the, this, that, he, she, it
Θεὸν n. acc. masc. sg. θεός God, god
ἐν prep. ἐν (+dat) in, by, with, among, at, on, through, to, within, into, of, for
ἐπιγνώσει n. dat. fem. sg. ἐπίγνωσις knowledge, acknowledging, acknowledgement
αὐτοὺς pron. acc. masc. 3p. pl. αὐτός ή ό self, of oneself, even, very, the same, he, she, it
ὁ art. nom. masc. sg. ὁ ἡ τό the, this, that, he, she, it
Θεὸς n. nom. masc. sg. θεός God, god
εἰς prep. εἰς (+acc) into, to, unto, for, in, on, toward, against, upon, at, among
ἀδόκιμον adj. acc. masc. sg. ἀδόκιμος reprobate, castaway, rejected
νοῦν n. acc. masc. sg. νοῦς understanding, mind
τὰ art. acc. neut. pl. ὁ ἡ τό the, this, that, he, she, it
μὴ particle of negation. μή not, no, lest, neither, none, nothing, nor, never, without
29 πάσῃ adj. dat. fem. sg. πᾶς πᾶςα πᾶν all, every, whosoever, every one, no, whole, any
ἀδικίᾳ n. dat. fem. sg. ἀδικία iniquity, unrighteousness, unjust, wrong
πορνείᾳ n. dat. fem. sg. πορνεία fornication
πονηρίᾳ n. dat. fem. sg. πονηρία wickedness, iniquity
πλεονεξίᾳ n. dat. fem. sg. πλεονεξία covetousness, covetous practice, greediness
κακίᾳ n. dat. fem. sg. κακία malice, maliciousness, evil, naughtiness, wickedness
μεστοὺς adj. acc. masc. pl. μεστός full

φθόνου n. gen. masc. sg. φθόνος envy, envying
φόνου n. gen. masc. sg. φόνος murder, slaughter
ἔριδος n. gen. fem. sg. ἔρις debate, strife, contention, variance
δόλου n. gen. masc. sg. δόλος guile, deceit, subtilty, craft
κακοηθείας n. gen. fem. sg. κακοήθεια malignity
ψιθυριστάς n. acc. masc. pl. ψιθυριστής whisperer
30 καταλάλους adj. acc. masc. pl. κατάλαλος backbiter
θεοστυγεῖς adj. acc. masc. pl. θεοστυγής hater of God
ὑβριστὰς n. acc. masc. pl. ὑβριστής despiteful, injurious
ὑπερηφάνους adj. acc. masc. pl. ὑπερήφανος proud
ἀλαζόνας n. acc. masc. pl. ἀλαζών boaster
ἐφευρετὰς n. acc. masc. pl. ἐφευρετής inventor
κακῶν adj. gen. neut. pl. κακός evil, evil thing, noisome, wicked
γονεῦσιν n. dat. masc. pl. γονεύς father, (pl.) parents
ἀπειθεῖς adj. acc. masc. pl. ἀπειθής disobedient
31 ἀσυνέτους adj. acc. masc. pl. ἀσύνετος without understanding, foolish
ἀσυνθέτους adj. acc. masc. pl. ἀσύνθετος covenantbreaker
ἀστόργους adj. acc. masc. pl. ἄστοργος without natural affection
ἀσπόνδους adj. acc. masc. pl. ἄσπονδος implacable, trucebreaker
ἀνελεήμονας adj. acc. masc. pl. ἀνελεήμων unmerciful
32 οἵτινες relative pron. nom. masc. pl. ὅστις which, who, whosoever, that, whatsoever
τὸ art. acc. neut. sg. ὁ ἡ τό the, this, that, he, she, it
δικαίωμα n. acc. neut. sg. δικαίωμα ordinance, righteousness, judgement, justification
τοῦ art. gen. masc. sg. ὁ ἡ τό the, this, that, he, she, it
Θεοῦ n. gen. masc. sg. θεός God, god
ὅτι conj. ὅτι that, for, because, how that, how, because that, for that, though
οἱ art. nom. masc. pl. ὁ ἡ τό the, this, that, he, she, it
τὰ art. acc. neut. pl. ὁ ἡ τό the, this, that, he, she, it
τοιαῦτα demo. pron. acc. neut. pl. τοιοῦτος such, like
ἄξιοι adj. nom. masc. pl. ἄξιος worthy, meet, due reward
θανάτου n. gen. masc. sg. θάνατος death
οὐ particle of negation. οὐ οὐκ οὐχ not, no, neither, none, nay, nor, never, nothing
μόνον adv. μόνος only, alone, by oneself
αὐτὰ pron. acc. neut. 3p. pl. αὐτός ἡ ὁ self, of oneself, even, very, the same, he, she, it
ἀλλὰ conj. ἀλλά but, yea, yet, nevertheless, howbeit, nay, therefore
καὶ conj. καί and, even, also, but
τοῖς art. dat. masc. pl. ὁ ἡ τό the, this, that, he, she, it

2

1 Διὸ conj. διό wherefore, therefore, for which cause
ἀναπολόγητος adj. nom. masc. sg. ἀναπολόγητος without excuse, inexcusable
ὦ interjection. ὦ O
ἄνθρωπε n. voc. masc. sg. ἄνθρωπος man, human being, person, one, certain
πᾶς adj. nom. masc. sg. πᾶς πᾶσα πᾶν all, every, whosoever, every one, no, whole, any
ὁ art. nom. masc. sg. ὁ ἡ τό the, this, that, he, she, it
ἐν prep. ἐν (+dat) in, by, with, among, at, on, through, to, within, into, of, for
ᾧ relative pron. dat. neut. sg. ὅς ἥ ὅ who, which, what, that
γὰρ conj. γάρ for, and, because, but, indeed
τὸν art. acc. masc. sg. ὁ ἡ τό the, this, that, he, she, it
ἕτερον adj. acc. masc. sg. ἕτερος another, other, else, strange
σεαυτὸν pron. acc. masc. 2p. sg. σεαυτοῦ σεαυτῷ σεαυτόν thyself, thine own self
τὰ art. acc. neut. pl. ὁ ἡ τό the, this, that, he, she, it
γὰρ conj. γάρ for, and, because, but, indeed
αὐτὰ adj. acc. neut. pl. αὐτός ἡ ὁ self, of oneself, even, very, the same, he, she, it

ὁ art. nom. masc. sg. ὁ ἡ τό the, this, that, he, she, it
2 δὲ conj. δέ but, and, now, also, to the contrary, rather, then
ὅτι conj. ὅτι that, for, because, how that, how, because that, for that, though
τὸ art. nom. neut. sg. ὁ ἡ τό the, this, that, he, she, it
κρίμα n. nom. neut. sg. κρίμα judgment, damnation, condemnation
τοῦ art. gen. masc. sg. ὁ ἡ τό the, this, that, he, she, it
Θεοῦ n. gen. masc. sg. θεός God, god
κατὰ prep. κατά (+gen) against, by, throughout, down, (+acc) according to, after, with
ἀλήθειαν n. acc. fem. sg. ἀλήθεια truth, verity
ἐπὶ prep. ἐπί (+gen) on, in, upon, (+dat) in, at, for, upon, (+acc) on, upon, unto, to, against
τοὺς art. acc. masc. pl. ὁ ἡ τό the, this, that, he, she, it
τὰ art. acc. neut. pl. ὁ ἡ τό the, this, that, he, she, it
τοιαῦτα demo. pron. acc. neut. pl. τοιοῦτος such, like
3 δὲ conj. δέ but, and, now, also, to the contrary, rather, then
τοῦτο demo. pron. acc. neut. sg. οὗτος αὕτη τοῦτο this, the same, this same, he, she, it
ὦ interjection. ὦ O
ἄνθρωπε n. voc. masc. sg. ἄνθρωπος man, human being, person, one, certain
ὁ art. nom. masc. sg. ὁ ἡ τό the, this, that, he, she, it
τοὺς art. acc. masc. pl. ὁ ἡ τό the, this, that, he, she, it
τὰ art. acc. neut. pl. ὁ ἡ τό the, this, that, he, she, it
τοιαῦτα demo. pron. acc. neut. pl. τοιοῦτος such, like
καὶ conj. καί and, even, also, but
αὐτά pron. acc. neut. 3p. pl. αὐτός ή ό self, of oneself, even, very, the same, he, she, it
ὅτι conj. ὅτι that, for, because, how that, how, because that, for that, though
σὺ pron. nom. 2p. sg. σύ thou, you
τὸ art. acc. neut. sg. ὁ ἡ τό the, this, that, he, she, it
κρίμα n. acc. neut. sg. κρίμα judgment, damnation, condemnation
τοῦ art. gen. masc. sg. ὁ ἡ τό the, this, that, he, she, it
Θεοῦ n. gen. masc. sg. θεός God, god
4 ἢ particle. ἤ or, than, either, nor, or else, and, rather than
τοῦ art. gen. masc. sg. ὁ ἡ τό the, this, that, he, she, it
πλούτου n. gen. masc. sg. πλοῦτος riches
τῆς art. gen. fem. sg. ὁ ἡ τό the, this, that, he, she, it
χρηστότητος n. gen. fem. sg. χρηστότης goodness, kindness, gentleness, good
αὐτοῦ pron. gen. masc. 3p. sg. αὐτός ή ό self, of oneself, even, very, the same, he, she, it
καὶ conj. καί and, even, also, but
τῆς art. gen. fem. sg. ὁ ἡ τό the, this, that, he, she, it
ἀνοχῆς n. gen. fem. sg. ἀνοχή forbearance
καὶ conj. καί and, even, also, but
τῆς art. gen. fem. sg. ὁ ἡ τό the, this, that, he, she, it
μακροθυμίας n. gen. fem. sg. μακροθυμία longsuffering, patience
ὅτι conj. ὅτι that, for, because, how that, how, because that, for that, though
τὸ art. nom. neut. sg. ὁ ἡ τό the, this, that, he, she, it
χρηστὸν adj. nom. neut. sg. χρηστός easy, kind, better, good, gracious, goodness
τοῦ art. gen. masc. sg. ὁ ἡ τό the, this, that, he, she, it
Θεοῦ n. gen. masc. sg. θεός God, god
εἰς prep. εἰς (+acc) into, to, unto, for, in, on, toward, against, upon, at, among
μετάνοιάν n. acc. fem. sg. μετάνοια repentance
σε pron. acc. 2p. sg. σύ thou, you
5 κατὰ prep. κατά (+gen) against, by, throughout, down, (+acc) according to, after, with
δὲ conj. δέ but, and, now, also, to the contrary, rather, then
τὴν art. acc. fem. sg. ὁ ἡ τό the, this, that, he, she, it
σκληρότητά n. acc. fem. sg. σκληρότης hardness
σου pron. gen. 2p. sg. σύ thou, you
καὶ conj. καί and, even, also, but

ἀμετανόητον adj. acc. fem. sg. ἀμετανόητος impenitent
καρδίαν n. acc. fem. sg. καρδία heart
σεαυτῷ pron. dat. masc. 2p. sg. σεαυτοῦ σεαυτῷ σεαυτόν thyself, thine own self
ὀργὴν n. acc. fem. sg. ὀργή wrath, anger, indignation, vengeance
ἐν prep. ἐν (+dat) in, by, with, among, at, on, through, to, within, into, of, for
ἡμέρᾳ n. dat. fem. sg. ἡμέρα day, time, year, while, age, day time
ὀργῆς n. gen. fem. sg. ὀργή wrath, anger, indignation, vengeance
καὶ conj. καί and, even, also, but
ἀποκαλύψεως n. gen. fem. sg. ἀποκάλυψις revelation, appearing, coming, manifestation
δικαιοκρισίας n. gen. fem. sg. δικαιοκρισία righteous judgment
τοῦ art. gen. masc. sg. ὁ ἡ τό the, this, that, he, she, it
Θεοῦ n. gen. masc. sg. θεός God, god
6 ὃς relative pron. nom. masc. sg. ὅς ἥ ὅ who, which, what, that
ἑκάστῳ adj. dat. masc. sg. ἕκαστος every man, every, every one, any man, each
κατὰ prep. κατά (+gen) against, by, throughout, down, (+acc) according to, after, with
τὰ art. acc. neut. pl. ὁ ἡ τό the, this, that, he, she, it
ἔργα n. acc. neut. pl. ἔργον work, deed, doing labour
αὐτοῦ pron. gen. masc. 3p. sg. αὐτός ή ό self, of oneself, even, very, the same, he, she, it
7 τοῖς art. dat. masc. pl. ὁ ἡ τό the, this, that, he, she, it
μὲν conj. μέν indeed, verily, truly, even, so, some
καθ' prep. κατά (+gen) against, by, throughout, down, (+acc) according to, after, with
ὑπομονὴν n. acc. fem. sg. ὑπομονή patience, enduring
ἔργου n. gen. neut. sg. ἔργον work, deed, doing labour
ἀγαθοῦ adj. gen. neut. sg. ἀγαθός good, good thing, that which is good, well
δόξαν n. acc. fem. sg. δόξα glory, honour, praise, dignity, worship
καὶ conj. καί and, even, also, but
τιμὴν n. acc. fem. sg. τιμή honour, price, preciousness, sum
καὶ conj. καί and, even, also, but
ἀφθαρσίαν n. acc. fem. sg. ἀφθαρσία immortality, incorruption, sincerity
ζωὴν n. acc. fem. sg. ζωή life, lifetime
αἰώνιον adj. acc. fem. sg. αἰώνιος eternal, everlasting, world, for ever
8 τοῖς art. dat. masc. pl. ὁ ἡ τό the, this, that, he, she, it
δὲ conj. δέ but, and, now, also, to the contrary, rather, then
ἐξ prep. ἐκ ἐξ (+gen) of, from, out of, by, on, with, in, among, through
ἐριθείας n. gen. fem. sg. ἐριθεία strife, contention, contentious
καὶ conj. καί and, even, also, but
μὲν conj. μέν indeed, verily, truly, even, so, some
τῇ art. dat. fem. sg. ὁ ἡ τό the, this, that, he, she, it
ἀληθείᾳ n. dat. fem. sg. ἀλήθεια truth, verity
δὲ conj. δέ but, and, now, also, to the contrary, rather, then
τῇ art. dat. fem. sg. ὁ ἡ τό the, this, that, he, she, it
ἀδικίᾳ n. dat. fem. sg. ἀδικία iniquity, unrighteousness, unjust, wrong
θυμός n. nom. masc. sg. θυμός wrath, fierceness, indignation
καὶ conj. καί and, even, also, but
ὀργὴ n. nom. fem. sg. ὀργή wrath, anger, indignation, vengeance
9 θλῖψις n. nom. fem. sg. θλῖψις tribulation, affliction, anguish, persecution
καὶ conj. καί and, even, also, but
στενοχωρία n. nom. fem. sg. στενοχωρία anguish, distress
ἐπὶ prep. ἐπί (+gen) on, in, upon, (+dat) in, at, for, upon, (+acc) on, upon, unto, to, against
πᾶσαν adj. acc. fem. sg. πᾶς πᾶσa πᾶν all, every, whosoever, every one, no, whole, any
ψυχὴν n. acc. fem. sg. ψυχή life, soul, mind, heart
ἀνθρώπου n. gen. masc. sg. ἄνθρωπος man, human being, person, one, certain
τοῦ art. gen. masc. sg. ὁ ἡ τό the, this, that, he, she, it
τὸ art. acc. neut. sg. ὁ ἡ τό the, this, that, he, she, it
κακόν adj. acc. neut. sg. κακός evil, evil thing, noisome, wicked

Ἰουδαίου adj. gen. masc. sg. Ἰουδαῖος Jew, Jewess
τε conj. τέ and, both, also
πρῶτον adv. πρῶτον first, at the first, first of all, at first, at the beginning, before, chiefly
καὶ conj. καί and, even, also, but
Ἕλληνος n. gen. masc. sg. Ἕλλην Greek, Gentile
10 δόξα n. nom. fem. sg. δόξα glory, honour, praise, dignity, worship
δὲ conj. δέ but, and, now, also, to the contrary, rather, then
καὶ conj. καί and, even, also, but
τιμὴ n. nom. fem. sg. τιμή honour, price, preciousness, sum
καὶ conj. καί and, even, also, but
εἰρήνη n. nom. fem. sg. εἰρήνη peace, quietness, rest
παντὶ adj. dat. masc. sg. πᾶς πᾶσα πᾶν all, every, whosoever, every one, no, whole, any
τῷ art. dat. masc. sg. ὁ ἡ τό the, this, that, he, she, it
τὸ art. acc. neut. sg. ὁ ἡ τό the, this, that, he, she, it
ἀγαθόν adj. acc. neut. sg. ἀγαθός good, good thing, that which is good, well
Ἰουδαίῳ adj. dat. masc. sg. Ἰουδαῖος Jew, Jewess
τε conj. τέ and, both, also
πρῶτον adv. πρῶτον first, at the first, first of all, at first, at the beginning, before, chiefly
καὶ conj. καί and, even, also, but
Ἕλληνι n. dat. masc. sg. Ἕλλην Greek, Gentile
11 οὐ particle of negation. οὐ οὐκ οὐχ not, no, neither, none, nay, nor, never, nothing
γάρ conj. γάρ for, and, because, but, indeed
προσωποληψία n. nom. fem. sg. προσωποληψία respect of persons
παρὰ prep. παρά (+gen) of, from, (+dat) with, for, (+acc) beside, at, by, above, against
τῷ art. dat. masc. sg. ὁ ἡ τό the, this, that, he, she, it
Θεῷ n. dat. masc. sg. θεός God, god
12 ὅσοι relative pron. nom. masc. pl. ὅσος as many as, whatsoever, that, as long as, how much
γὰρ conj. γάρ for, and, because, but, indeed
ἀνόμως adv. ἀνόμως without law
ἀνόμως adv. ἀνόμως without law
καὶ conj. καί and, even, also, but
καὶ conj. καί and, even, also, but
ὅσοι relative pron. nom. masc. pl. ὅσος as many as, whatsoever, that, as long as, how much
ἐν prep. ἐν (+dat) in, by, with, among, at, on, through, to, within, into, of, for
νόμῳ n. dat. masc. sg. νόμος law, the law
διὰ prep. διά (+gen) by, through, with, in, of, (+acc) for, because of, for a cause
νόμου n. gen. masc. sg. νόμος law, the law
13 οὐ particle of negation. οὐ οὐκ οὐχ not, no, neither, none, nay, nor, never, nothing
γὰρ conj. γάρ for, and, because, but, indeed
οἱ art. nom. masc. pl. ὁ ἡ τό the, this, that, he, she, it
ἀκροαταὶ n. nom. masc. pl. ἀκροατής hearer
τοῦ art. gen. masc. sg. ὁ ἡ τό the, this, that, he, she, it
νόμου n. gen. masc. sg. νόμος law, the law
δίκαιοι adj. nom. masc. pl. δίκαιος righteous, just, meet, right
παρὰ prep. παρά (+gen) of, from, (+dat) with, for, (+acc) beside, at, by, above, against
τῷ art. dat. masc. sg. ὁ ἡ τό the, this, that, he, she, it
Θεῷ n. dat. masc. sg. θεός God, god
ἀλλ' conj. ἀλλά but, yea, yet, nevertheless, howbeit, nay, therefore
οἱ art. nom. masc. pl. ὁ ἡ τό the, this, that, he, she, it
ποιηταὶ n. nom. masc. pl. ποιητής doer, poet
τοῦ art. gen. masc. sg. ὁ ἡ τό the, this, that, he, she, it
νόμου n. gen. masc. sg. νόμος law, the law
14 ὅταν conj. ὅταν when, as soon as, as long as, that, whensoever, while
γὰρ conj. γάρ for, and, because, but, indeed
ἔθνη n. nom. neut. pl. ἔθνος Gentile, nation, heathen, people

τὰ art. nom. neut. pl. ὁ ἡ τό the, this, that, he, she, it
μὴ particle of negation. μή not, no, lest, neither, none, nothing, nor, never, without
νόμον n. acc. masc. sg. νόμος law, the law
φύσει n. dat. fem. sg. φύσις nature
τὰ art. acc. neut. pl. ὁ ἡ τό the, this, that, he, she, it
τοῦ art. gen. masc. sg. ὁ ἡ τό the, this, that, he, she, it
νόμου n. gen. masc. sg. νόμος law, the law
οὗτοι demo. pron. nom. masc. pl. οὗτος αὕτη τοῦτο this, the same, this same, he, she, it
νόμον n. acc. masc. sg. νόμος law, the law
μὴ particle of negation. μή not, no, lest, neither, none, nothing, nor, never, without
ἑαυτοῖς reflexive pron. dat. masc. 3p. pl. ἑαυτοῦ himself, herself, itself, yourself, ourselves
νόμος n. nom. masc. sg. νόμος law, the law
15 οἵτινες relative pron. nom. masc. pl. ὅστις which, who, whosoever, that, whatsoever
τὸ art. acc. neut. sg. ὁ ἡ τό the, this, that, he, she, it
ἔργον n. acc. neut. sg. ἔργον work, deed, doing labour
τοῦ art. gen. masc. sg. ὁ ἡ τό the, this, that, he, she, it
νόμου n. gen. masc. sg. νόμος law, the law
γραπτὸν adj. acc. neut. sg. γραπτός written
ἐν prep. ἐν (+dat) in, by, with, among, at, on, through, to, within, into, of, for
ταῖς art. dat. fem. pl. ὁ ἡ τό the, this, that, he, she, it
καρδίαις n. dat. fem. pl. καρδία heart
αὐτῶν pron. gen. masc. 3p. pl. αὐτός ή ό self, of oneself, even, very, the same, he, she, it
τῆς art. gen. fem. sg. ὁ ἡ τό the, this, that, he, she, it
συνειδήσεως n. gen. fem. sg. συνείδησις conscience
καὶ conj. καί and, even, also, but
μεταξὺ adv. μεταξύ between
ἀλλήλων pron. gen. masc. pl. ἀλλήλων one another, themselves, together, mutual
τῶν art. gen. masc. pl. ὁ ἡ τό the, this, that, he, she, it
λογισμῶν n. gen. masc. pl. λογισμός thought, imagination
ἢ particle. ἤ or, than, either, nor, or else, and, rather than
καὶ conj. καί and, even, also, but
16 ἐν prep. ἐν (+dat) in, by, with, among, at, on, through, to, within, into, of, for
ἡμέρᾳ n. dat. fem. sg. ἡμέρα day, time, year, while, age, day time
ὅτε adv. ὅτε when, after that, as soon as, while, after
ὁ art. nom. masc. sg. ὁ ἡ τό the, this, that, he, she, it
Θεὸς n. nom. masc. sg. θεός God, god
τὰ art. acc. neut. pl. ὁ ἡ τό the, this, that, he, she, it
κρυπτὰ adj. acc. neut. pl. κρυπτός secret, hid, hidden, inwardly
τῶν art. gen. masc. pl. ὁ ἡ τό the, this, that, he, she, it
ἀνθρώπων n. gen. masc. pl. ἄνθρωπος man, human being, person, one, certain
κατὰ prep. κατά (+gen) against, by, throughout, down, (+acc) according to, after, with
τὸ art. acc. neut. sg. ὁ ἡ τό the, this, that, he, she, it
εὐαγγέλιόν n. acc. neut. sg. εὐαγγέλιον gospel
μου pron. gen. 1p. sg. ἐγώ I
διὰ prep. διά (+gen) by, through, with, in, of, (+acc) for, because of, for a cause
Ἰησοῦ n. gen. masc. sg. Ἰησοῦς Jesus
Χριστοῦ n. gen. masc. sg. Χριστός Christ
17 σὺ pron. nom. 2p. sg. σύ thou, you
Ἰουδαῖος adj. nom. masc. sg. Ἰουδαῖος Jew, Jewess
καὶ conj. καί and, even, also, but
τῷ art. dat. masc. sg. ὁ ἡ τό the, this, that, he, she, it
νόμῳ n. dat. masc. sg. νόμος law, the law
καὶ conj. καί and, even, also, but
ἐν prep. ἐν (+dat) in, by, with, among, at, on, through, to, within, into, of, for
Θεῷ n. dat. masc. sg. θεός God, god

18 καὶ conj. καί and, even, also, but
τὸ art. acc. neut. sg. ὁ ἡ τό the, this, that, he, she, it
θέλημα n. acc. neut. sg. θέλημα will, desire, pleasure
καὶ conj. καί and, even, also, but
τὰ art. acc. neut. pl. ὁ ἡ τό the, this, that, he, she, it
ἐκ prep. ἐκ ἐξ (+gen) of, from, out of, by, on, with, in, among, through
τοῦ art. gen. masc. sg. ὁ ἡ τό the, this, that, he, she, it
νόμου n. gen. masc. sg. νόμος law, the law
19 τε conj. τέ and, both, also
σεαυτὸν pron. acc. masc. 2p. sg. σεαυτοῦ σεαυτῷ σεαυτόν thyself, thine own self
ὁδηγὸν n. acc. masc. sg. ὁδηγός leader, guide
τυφλῶν adj. gen. masc. pl. τυφλός blind
φῶς n. acc. neut. sg. φῶς light, fire
τῶν art. gen. masc. pl. ὁ ἡ τό the, this, that, he, she, it
ἐν prep. ἐν (+dat) in, by, with, among, at, on, through, to, within, into, of, for
σκότει n. dat. neut. sg. σκότος darkness
20 παιδευτὴν n. acc. masc. sg. παιδευτής instructor, correct
ἀφρόνων adj. gen. masc. pl. ἄφρων fool, foolish, unwise
διδάσκαλον n. acc. masc. sg. διδάσκαλος teacher, master, doctor
νηπίων adj. gen. masc. pl. νήπιος babe, child, childish
τὴν art. acc. fem. sg. ὁ ἡ τό the, this, that, he, she, it
μόρφωσιν n. acc. fem. sg. μόρφωσις form
τῆς art. gen. fem. sg. ὁ ἡ τό the, this, that, he, she, it
γνώσεως n. gen. fem. sg. γνῶσις knowledge, science
καὶ conj. καί and, even, also, but
τῆς art. gen. fem. sg. ὁ ἡ τό the, this, that, he, she, it
ἀληθείας n. gen. fem. sg. ἀλήθεια truth, verity
ἐν prep. ἐν (+dat) in, by, with, among, at, on, through, to, within, into, of, for
τῷ art. dat. masc. sg. ὁ ἡ τό the, this, that, he, she, it
νόμῳ n. dat. masc. sg. νόμος law, the law
21 ὁ art. nom. masc. sg. ὁ ἡ τό the, this, that, he, she, it
οὖν conj. οὖν therefore, then, so, and, now, wherefore
ἕτερον adj. acc. masc. sg. ἕτερος another, other, else, strange
σεαυτὸν pron. acc. masc. 2p. sg. σεαυτοῦ σεαυτῷ σεαυτόν thyself, thine own self
οὐ particle of negation. οὐ οὐκ οὐχ not, no, neither, none, nay, nor, never, nothing
ὁ art. nom. masc. sg. ὁ ἡ τό the, this, that, he, she, it
μὴ particle of negation. μή not, no, lest, neither, none, nothing, nor, never, without
22 ὁ art. nom. masc. sg. ὁ ἡ τό the, this, that, he, she, it
μὴ particle of negation. μή not, no, lest, neither, none, nothing, nor, never, without
ὁ art. nom. masc. sg. ὁ ἡ τό the, this, that, he, she, it
τὰ art. acc. neut. pl. ὁ ἡ τό the, this, that, he, she, it
εἴδωλα n. acc. neut. pl. εἴδωλον idol
23 ὃς relative pron. nom. masc. sg. ὅς ἥ ὅ who, which, what, that
ἐν prep. ἐν (+dat) in, by, with, among, at, on, through, to, within, into, of, for
νόμῳ n. dat. masc. sg. νόμος law, the law
διὰ prep. διά (+gen) by, through, with, in, of, (+acc) for, because of, for a cause
τῆς art. gen. fem. sg. ὁ ἡ τό the, this, that, he, she, it
παραβάσεως n. gen. fem. sg. παράβασις breaking, transgression
τοῦ art. gen. masc. sg. ὁ ἡ τό the, this, that, he, she, it
νόμου n. gen. masc. sg. νόμος law, the law
τὸν art. acc. masc. sg. ὁ ἡ τό the, this, that, he, she, it
Θεὸν n. acc. masc. sg. θεός God, god
24 τὸ art. nom. neut. sg. ὁ ἡ τό the, this, that, he, she, it
γὰρ conj. γάρ for, and, because, but, indeed
ὄνομα n. nom. neut. sg. ὄνομα name, call, surname

τοῦ art. gen. masc. sg. ὁ ἡ τό the, this, that, he, she, it
Θεοῦ n. gen. masc. sg. θεός God, god
δι' prep. διά (+gen) by, through, with, in, of, (+acc) for, because of, for a cause
ὑμᾶς pron. acc. 2p. pl. σύ thou, you
ἐν prep. ἐν (+dat) in, by, with, among, at, on, through, to, within, into, of, for
τοῖς art. dat. neut. pl. ὁ ἡ τό the, this, that, he, she, it
ἔθνεσι n. dat. neut. pl. ἔθνος Gentile, nation, heathen, people
καθὼς adv. καθώς as, even as, according as, according to
25 περιτομὴ n. nom. fem. sg. περιτομή circumcision
μὲν conj. μέν indeed, verily, truly, even, so, some
γὰρ conj. γάρ for, and, because, but, indeed
ἐὰν conj. ἐάν if, soever, except, though, and if, but, whether, if so, so
νόμον n. acc. masc. sg. νόμος law, the law
ἐὰν conj. ἐάν if, soever, except, though, and if, but, whether, if so, so
δὲ conj. δέ but, and, now, also, to the contrary, rather, then
παραβάτης n. nom. masc. sg. παραβάτης breaker, transgressor
νόμου n. gen. masc. sg. νόμος law, the law
ἡ art. nom. fem. sg. ὁ ἡ τό the, this, that, he, she, it
περιτομή n. nom. fem. sg. περιτομή circumcision
σου pron. gen. 2p. sg. σύ thou, you
ἀκροβυστία n. nom. fem. sg. ἀκροβυστία uncircumcised, uncircumcision
26 ἐὰν conj. ἐάν if, soever, except, though, and if, but, whether, if so, so
οὖν conj. οὖν therefore, then, so, and, now, wherefore
ἡ art. nom. fem. sg. ὁ ἡ τό the, this, that, he, she, it
ἀκροβυστία n. nom. fem. sg. ἀκροβυστία uncircumcised, uncircumcision
τὰ art. acc. neut. pl. ὁ ἡ τό the, this, that, he, she, it
δικαιώματα n. acc. neut. pl. δικαίωμα ordinance, righteousness, judgement, justification
τοῦ art. gen. masc. sg. ὁ ἡ τό the, this, that, he, she, it
νόμου n. gen. masc. sg. νόμος law, the law
οὐχὶ adv. οὐχί not, nay
ἡ art. nom. fem. sg. ὁ ἡ τό the, this, that, he, she, it
ἀκροβυστία n. nom. fem. sg. ἀκροβυστία uncircumcised, uncircumcision
αὐτοῦ pron. gen. masc. 3p. sg. αὐτός ή ό self, of oneself, even, very, the same, he, she, it
εἰς prep. εἰς (+acc) into, to, unto, for, in, on, toward, against, upon, at, among
περιτομὴν n. acc. fem. sg. περιτομή circumcision
27 καὶ conj. καί and, even, also, but
ἡ art. nom. fem. sg. ὁ ἡ τό the, this, that, he, she, it
ἐκ prep. ἐκ ἐξ (+gen) of, from, out of, by, on, with, in, among, through
φύσεως n. gen. fem. sg. φύσις nature
ἀκροβυστία n. nom. fem. sg. ἀκροβυστία uncircumcised, uncircumcision
τὸν art. acc. masc. sg. ὁ ἡ τό the, this, that, he, she, it
νόμον n. acc. masc. sg. νόμος law, the law
σὲ pron. acc. 2p. sg. σύ thou, you
τὸν art. acc. masc. sg. ὁ ἡ τό the, this, that, he, she, it
διὰ prep. διά (+gen) by, through, with, in, of, (+acc) for, because of, for a cause
γράμματος n. gen. neut. sg. γράμμα letter, bill, learning, scripture, writing
καὶ conj. καί and, even, also, but
περιτομῆς n. gen. fem. sg. περιτομή circumcision
παραβάτην n. acc. masc. sg. παραβάτης breaker, transgressor
νόμου n. gen. masc. sg. νόμος law, the law
28 οὐ particle of negation. οὐ οὐκ οὐχ not, no, neither, none, nay, nor, never, nothing
γὰρ conj. γάρ for, and, because, but, indeed
ὁ art. nom. masc. sg. ὁ ἡ τό the, this, that, he, she, it
ἐν prep. ἐν (+dat) in, by, with, among, at, on, through, to, within, into, of, for
τῷ art. dat. neut. sg. ὁ ἡ τό the, this, that, he, she, it

φανερῷ adj. dat. neut. sg. φανερός manifest, abroad, open, known, outward, appear
Ἰουδαῖός adj. nom. masc. sg. Ἰουδαῖος Jew, Jewess
οὐδὲ conj. οὐδέ neither, nor, not, no, not even, never, not yet
ἡ art. nom. fem. sg. ὁ ἡ τό the, this, that, he, she, it
ἐν prep. ἐν (+dat) in, by, with, among, at, on, through, to, within, into, of, for
τῷ art. dat. neut. sg. ὁ ἡ τό the, this, that, he, she, it
φανερῷ adj. dat. neut. sg. φανερός manifest, abroad, open, known, outward, appear
ἐν prep. ἐν (+dat) in, by, with, among, at, on, through, to, within, into, of, for
σαρκὶ n. dat. fem. sg. σάρξ flesh, carnal
περιτομή n. nom. fem. sg. περιτομή circumcision
29 ἀλλ' conj. ἀλλά but, yea, yet, nevertheless, howbeit, nay, therefore
ὁ art. nom. masc. sg. ὁ ἡ τό the, this, that, he, she, it
ἐν prep. ἐν (+dat) in, by, with, among, at, on, through, to, within, into, of, for
τῷ art. dat. neut. sg. ὁ ἡ τό the, this, that, he, she, it
κρυπτῷ adj. dat. neut. sg. κρυπτός secret, hid, hidden, inwardly
Ἰουδαῖος adj. nom. masc. sg. Ἰουδαῖος Jew, Jewess
καὶ conj. καί and, even, also, but
περιτομὴ n. nom. fem. sg. περιτομή circumcision
καρδίας n. gen. fem. sg. καρδία heart
ἐν prep. ἐν (+dat) in, by, with, among, at, on, through, to, within, into, of, for
πνεύματι n. dat. neut. sg. πνεῦμα spirit, Spirit, Ghost, ghost, life. of the spirit, wind
οὐ particle of negation. οὐ οὐκ οὐχ not, no, neither, none, nay, nor, never, nothing
γράμματι n. dat. neut. sg. γράμμα letter, bill, learning, scripture, writing
οὗ relative pron. gen. masc. sg. ὅς ἥ ὅ who, which, what, that
ὁ art. nom. masc. sg. ὁ ἡ τό the, this, that, he, she, it
ἔπαινος n. nom. masc. sg. ἔπαινος praise
οὐκ particle of negation. οὐ οὐκ οὐχ not, no, neither, none, nay, nor, never, nothing
ἐξ prep. ἐκ ἐξ (+gen) of, from, out of, by, on, with, in, among, through
ἀνθρώπων n. gen. masc. pl. ἄνθρωπος man, human being, person, one, certain
ἀλλ' conj. ἀλλά but, yea, yet, nevertheless, howbeit, nay, therefore
ἐκ prep. ἐκ ἐξ (+gen) of, from, out of, by, on, with, in, among, through
τοῦ art. gen. masc. sg. ὁ ἡ τό the, this, that, he, she, it
Θεοῦ n. gen. masc. sg. θεός God, god

3

1 Τί interrog. pron. nom. neut. sg. τίς what, who, why, where, which, how
οὖν conj. οὖν therefore, then, so, and, now, wherefore
τὸ art. nom. neut. sg. ὁ ἡ τό the, this, that, he, she, it
περισσὸν adj. nom. neut. sg. περισσός more, beyond measure, advantage, exceedingly
τοῦ art. gen. masc. sg. ὁ ἡ τό the, this, that, he, she, it
Ἰουδαίου adj. gen. masc. sg. Ἰουδαῖος Jew, Jewess
ἢ particle. ἤ or, than, either, nor, or else, and, rather than
τίς interrog. pron. nom. fem. sg. τίς what, who, why, where, which, how
ἡ art. nom. fem. sg. ὁ ἡ τό the, this, that, he, she, it
ὠφέλεια n. nom. fem. sg. ὠφέλεια profit, advantage
τῆς art. gen. fem. sg. ὁ ἡ τό the, this, that, he, she, it
περιτομῆς n. gen. fem. sg. περιτομή circumcision
2 πολὺ adj. nom. neut. sg. πολύς many, great, much, long, abundant
κατὰ prep. κατά (+gen) against, by, throughout, down, (+acc) according to, after, with
πάντα adj. acc. masc. sg. πᾶς πᾶσα πᾶν all, every, whosoever, every one, no, whole, any
τρόπον n. acc. masc. sg. τρόπος as, manner, means, way, conversation
πρῶτον adv. πρῶτον first, at the first, first of all, at first, at the beginning, before, chiefly
μὲν conj. μέν indeed, verily, truly, even, so, some
γὰρ conj. γάρ for, and, because, but, indeed

ὅτι conj. ὅτι that, for, because, how that, how, because that, for that, though
τὰ art. acc. neut. pl. ὁ ἡ τό the, this, that, he, she, it
λόγια n. acc. neut. pl. λόγιον oracle
τοῦ art. gen. masc. sg. ὁ ἡ τό the, this, that, he, she, it
Θεοῦ n. gen. masc. sg. θεός God, god
3 τί interrog. pron. nom. neut. sg. τίς what, who, why, where, which, how
γάρ conj. γάρ for, and, because, but, indeed
εἰ conj. εἰ if, whether, that, though, forasmuch
τινες indefinite pron. nom. masc. pl. τὶς certain, some, any man, one, any thing
μὴ particle of negation. μή not, no, lest, neither, none, nothing, nor, never, without
ἡ art. nom. fem. sg. ὁ ἡ τό the, this, that, he, she, it
ἀπιστία n. nom. fem. sg. ἀπιστία unbelief
αὐτῶν pron. gen. masc. 3p. pl. αὐτός ἡ ὁ self, of oneself, even, very, the same, he, she, it
τὴν art. acc. fem. sg. ὁ ἡ τό the, this, that, he, she, it
πίστιν n. acc. fem. sg. πίστις faith, assurance, belief, fidelity
τοῦ art. gen. masc. sg. ὁ ἡ τό the, this, that, he, she, it
Θεοῦ n. gen. masc. sg. θεός God, god
4 μὴ particle of negation. μή not, no, lest, neither, none, nothing, nor, never, without
δὲ conj. δέ but, and, now, also, to the contrary, rather, then
ὁ art. nom. masc. sg. ὁ ἡ τό the, this, that, he, she, it
Θεὸς n. nom. masc. sg. θεός God, god
ἀληθής adj. nom. masc. sg. ἀληθής true, truly, truth
πᾶς adj. nom. masc. sg. πᾶς πᾶσa πᾶν all, every, whosoever, every one, no, whole, any
δὲ conj. δέ but, and, now, also, to the contrary, rather, then
ἄνθρωπος n. nom. masc. sg. ἄνθρωπος man, human being, person, one, certain
ψεύστης n. nom. masc. sg. ψεύστης liar
καθὼς adv. καθώς as, even as, according as, according to
Ὅπως adv. ὅπως that, how, to, because, so that, when
ἂν particle. ἄν Indicating contingency. No English translation.
ἐν prep. ἐν (+dat) in, by, with, among, at, on, through, to, within, into, of, for
τοῖς art. dat. masc. pl. ὁ ἡ τό the, this, that, he, she, it
λόγοις n. dat. masc. pl. λόγος word, saying, account, speech, thing, matter
σου pron. gen. 2p. sg. σύ thou, you
καὶ conj. καί and, even, also, but
ἐν prep. ἐν (+dat) in, by, with, among, at, on, through, to, within, into, of, for
τῷ art. dat. neut. sg. ὁ ἡ τό the, this, that, he, she, it
σε pron. acc. 2p. sg. σύ thou, you
5 εἰ conj. εἰ if, whether, that, though, forasmuch
δὲ conj. δέ but, and, now, also, to the contrary, rather, then
ἡ art. nom. fem. sg. ὁ ἡ τό the, this, that, he, she, it
ἀδικία n. nom. fem. sg. ἀδικία iniquity, unrighteousness, unjust, wrong
ἡμῶν pron. gen. 1p. pl. ἐγώ I
Θεοῦ n. gen. masc. sg. θεός God, god
δικαιοσύνην n. acc. fem. sg. δικαιοσύνη righteousness
τί interrog. pron. acc. neut. sg. τίς what, who, why, where, which, how
μὴ particle of negation. μή not, no, lest, neither, none, nothing, nor, never, without
ἄδικος adj. nom. masc. sg. ἄδικος unjust, unrighteous
ὁ art. nom. masc. sg. ὁ ἡ τό the, this, that, he, she, it
Θεὸς n. nom. masc. sg. θεός God, god
ὁ art. nom. masc. sg. ὁ ἡ τό the, this, that, he, she, it
τὴν art. acc. fem. sg. ὁ ἡ τό the, this, that, he, she, it
ὀργήν n. acc. fem. sg. ὀργή wrath, anger, indignation, vengeance
κατὰ prep. κατά (+gen) against, by, throughout, down, (+acc) according to, after, with
ἄνθρωπον n. acc. masc. sg. ἄνθρωπος man, human being, person, one, certain
6 μὴ particle of negation. μή not, no, lest, neither, none, nothing, nor, never, without

ἐπεὶ conj. ἐπεί because, otherwise, seeing, else, for then, for as much as, for, since
πῶς adv. πῶς how, by what means, after what manner
ὁ art. nom. masc. sg. ὁ ἡ τό the, this, that, he, she, it
Θεὸς n. nom. masc. sg. θεός God, god
τὸν art. acc. masc. sg. ὁ ἡ τό the, this, that, he, she, it
κόσμον n. acc. masc. sg. κόσμος world, adorning
7 εἰ conj. εἰ if, whether, that, though, forasmuch
γὰρ conj. γάρ for, and, because, but, indeed
ἡ art. nom. fem. sg. ὁ ἡ τό the, this, that, he, she, it
ἀλήθεια n. nom. fem. sg. ἀλήθεια truth, verity
τοῦ art. gen. masc. sg. ὁ ἡ τό the, this, that, he, she, it
Θεοῦ n. gen. masc. sg. θεός God, god
ἐν prep. ἐν (+dat) in, by, with, among, at, on, through, to, within, into, of, for
τῷ art. dat. neut. sg. ὁ ἡ τό the, this, that, he, she, it
ἐμῷ poss. pron. dat. neut. 1p. sg. ἐμός my, mine, mine own, of me
ψεύσματι n. dat. neut. sg. ψεῦσμα lie
εἰς prep. εἰς (+acc) into, to, unto, for, in, on, toward, against, upon, at, among
τὴν art. acc. fem. sg. ὁ ἡ τό the, this, that, he, she, it
δόξαν n. acc. fem. sg. δόξα glory, honour, praise, dignity, worship
αὐτοῦ pron. gen. masc. 3p. sg. αὐτός ή ό self, of oneself, even, very, the same, he, she, it
τί interrog. pron. acc. neut. sg. τίς what, who, why, where, which, how
ἔτι adv. ἔτι yet, more, any more, further, still, moreover
κἀγὼ pron. nom. 1p. sg. κἀγώ and I, I also, so I, even as I
ὡς adv. ὡς as, when, as it were, how, about, like, as soon as, even as, while
ἁμαρτωλὸς adj. nom. masc. sg. ἁμαρτωλός sinner, sinful
8 καὶ conj. καί and, even, also, but
μὴ particle of negation. μή not, no, lest, neither, none, nothing, nor, never, without
καθὼς adv. καθώς as, even as, according as, according to
καὶ conj. καί and, even, also, but
καθὼς adv. καθώς as, even as, according as, according to
τινες indefinite pron. nom. masc. pl. τὶς certain, some, any man, one, any thing
ἡμᾶς pron. acc. 1p. pl. ἐγώ I
ὅτι conj. ὅτι that, for, because, how that, how, because that, for that, though
τὰ art. acc. neut. pl. ὁ ἡ τό the, this, that, he, she, it
κακά adj. acc. neut. pl. κακός evil, evil thing, noisome, wicked
ἵνα conj. ἵνα that, to, lest, for to, so that, albeit, because, for, so as
τὰ art. nom. neut. pl. ὁ ἡ τό the, this, that, he, she, it
ἀγαθά adj. nom. neut. pl. ἀγαθός good, good thing, that which is good, well
ὧν relative pron. gen. masc. pl. ὅς ἥ ὅ who, which, what, that
τὸ art. nom. neut. sg. ὁ ἡ τό the, this, that, he, she, it
κρίμα n. nom. neut. sg. κρίμα judgment, damnation, condemnation
ἔνδικόν adj. nom. neut. sg. ἔνδικος just
9 Τί interrog. pron. acc. neut. sg. τίς what, who, why, where, which, how
οὖν conj. οὖν therefore, then, so, and, now, wherefore
οὐ particle of negation. οὐ οὐκ οὐχ not, no, neither, none, nay, nor, never, nothing
πάντως adv. πάντως surely, altogether, by all means, at all, needs, no doubt
γὰρ conj. γάρ for, and, because, but, indeed
Ἰουδαίους adj. acc. masc. pl. Ἰουδαῖος Jew, Jewess
τε conj. τέ and, both, also
καὶ conj. καί and, even, also, but
Ἕλληνας n. acc. masc. pl. Ἕλλην Greek, Gentile
πάντας adj. acc. masc. pl. πᾶς πᾶσα πᾶν all, every, whosoever, every one, no, whole, any
ὑφ' prep. ὑπό (+gen) of, by, with, from, among, (+acc) under
ἁμαρτίαν n. acc. fem. sg. ἁμαρτία sin, offence, sinful
10 καθὼς adv. καθώς as, even as, according as, according to

ὅτι conj. ὅτι that, for, because, how that, how, because that, for that, though
Οὐκ particle of negation. οὐ οὐκ οὐχ not, no, neither, none, nay, nor, never, nothing
δίκαιος adj. nom. masc. sg. δίκαιος righteous, just, meet, right
οὐδὲ adv. οὐδέ neither, nor, not, no, not even, never, not yet
εἷς num. nom. masc. sg. εἷς or ἕν one, other, some, any, only, a certain
11 οὐκ particle of negation. οὐ οὐκ οὐχ not, no, neither, none, nay, nor, never, nothing
ὁ art. nom. masc. sg. ὁ ἡ τό the, this, that, he, she, it
οὐκ particle of negation. οὐ οὐκ οὐχ not, no, neither, none, nay, nor, never, nothing
ὁ art. nom. masc. sg. ὁ ἡ τό the, this, that, he, she, it
τὸν art. acc. masc. sg. ὁ ἡ τό the, this, that, he, she, it
Θεόν n. acc. masc. sg. θεός God, god
12 πάντες adj. nom. masc. pl. πᾶς πᾶσα πᾶν all, every, whosoever, every one, no, whole, any
ἅμα adv. ἅμα (+dat) together, with, also. (adv.) at the same time, together
οὐκ particle of negation. οὐ οὐκ οὐχ not, no, neither, none, nay, nor, never, nothing
ὁ art. nom. masc. sg. ὁ ἡ τό the, this, that, he, she, it
χρηστότητα n. acc. fem. sg. χρηστότης goodness, kindness, gentleness, good
οὐκ particle of negation. οὐ οὐκ οὐχ not, no, neither, none, nay, nor, never, nothing
ἕως conj. ἕως till, until, unto, until when, while, as far as, even, until now
ἑνός num. gen. masc. sg. εἷς or ἕν one, other, some, any, only, a certain
13 τάφος n. nom. masc. sg. τάφος sepulchre, tomb
ὁ art. nom. masc. sg. ὁ ἡ τό the, this, that, he, she, it
λάρυγξ n. nom. masc. sg. λάρυγξ throat
αὐτῶν pron. gen. masc. 3p. pl. αὐτός ἡ ὁ self, of oneself, even, very, the same, he, she, it
ταῖς art. dat. fem. pl. ὁ ἡ τό the, this, that, he, she, it
γλώσσαις n. dat. fem. pl. γλῶσσα tongue
αὐτῶν pron. gen. masc. 3p. pl. αὐτός ἡ ὁ self, of oneself, even, very, the same, he, she, it
ἰὸς n. nom. masc. sg. ἰός poison, rust
ἀσπίδων n. gen. fem. pl. ἀσπίς asp
ὑπὸ prep. ὑπό (+gen) of, by, with, from, among, (+acc) under
τὰ art. acc. neut. pl. ὁ ἡ τό the, this, that, he, she, it
χείλη n. acc. neut. pl. χεῖλος lip, shore
αὐτῶν pron. gen. masc. 3p. pl. αὐτός ἡ ὁ self, of oneself, even, very, the same, he, she, it
14 ὧν relative pron. gen. masc. pl. ὅς ἥ ὅ who, which, what, that
τὸ art. nom. neut. sg. ὁ ἡ τό the, this, that, he, she, it
στόμα n. nom. neut. sg. στόμα mouth, face, edge
ἀρᾶς n. gen. fem. sg. ἀρά cursing
καὶ conj. καί and, even, also, but
πικρίας n. gen. fem. sg. πικρία bitterness
15 ὀξεῖς adj. nom. masc. pl. ὀξύς swift, sharp
οἱ art. nom. masc. pl. ὁ ἡ τό the, this, that, he, she, it
πόδες n. nom. masc. pl. πούς foot
αὐτῶν pron. gen. masc. 3p. pl. αὐτός ἡ ὁ self, of oneself, even, very, the same, he, she, it
αἷμα n. acc. neut. sg. αἷμα blood
16 σύντριμμα n. nom. neut. sg. σύντριμμα destruction
καὶ conj. καί and, even, also, but
ταλαιπωρία n. nom. fem. sg. ταλαιπωρία misery
ἐν prep. ἐν (+dat) in, by, with, among, at, on, through, to, within, into, of, for
ταῖς art. dat. fem. pl. ὁ ἡ τό the, this, that, he, she, it
ὁδοῖς n. dat. fem. pl. ὁδός way, journey, highway
αὐτῶν pron. gen. masc. 3p. pl. αὐτός ἡ ὁ self, of oneself, even, very, the same, he, she, it
17 καὶ conj. καί and, even, also, but
ὁδὸν n. acc. fem. sg. ὁδός way, journey, highway
εἰρήνης n. gen. fem. sg. εἰρήνη peace, quietness, rest
οὐκ particle of negation. οὐ οὐκ οὐχ not, no, neither, none, nay, nor, never, nothing
18 οὐκ particle of negation. οὐ οὐκ οὐχ not, no, neither, none, nay, nor, never, nothing

φόβος n. nom. masc. sg. φόβος fear, terror, sore afraid
Θεοῦ n. gen. masc. sg. θεός God, god
ἀπέναντι prep. ἀπέναντι before, over against, contrary, in the presence
τῶν art. gen. masc. pl. ὁ ἡ τό the, this, that, he, she, it
ὀφθαλμῶν n. gen. masc. pl. ὀφθαλμός eye, sight
αὐτῶν pron. gen. masc. 3p. pl. αὐτός ἡ ὁ self, of oneself, even, very, the same, he, she, it
19 δὲ conj. δέ but, and, now, also, to the contrary, rather, then
ὅτι conj. ὅτι that, for, because, how that, how, because that, for that, though
ὅσα relative pron. acc. neut. pl. ὅσος as many as, whatsoever, that, as long as, how much
ὁ art. nom. masc. sg. ὁ ἡ τό the, this, that, he, she, it
νόμος n. nom. masc. sg. νόμος law, the law
τοῖς art. dat. masc. pl. ὁ ἡ τό the, this, that, he, she, it
ἐν prep. ἐν (+dat) in, by, with, among, at, on, through, to, within, into, of, for
τῷ art. dat. masc. sg. ὁ ἡ τό the, this, that, he, she, it
νόμῳ n. dat. masc. sg. νόμος law, the law
ἵνα conj. ἵνα that, to, lest, for to, so that, albeit, because, for, so as
πᾶν adj. nom. neut. sg. πᾶς πᾶσα πᾶν all, every, whosoever, every one, no, whole, any
στόμα n. nom. neut. sg. στόμα mouth, face, edge
καὶ conj. καί and, even, also, but
ὑπόδικος adj. nom. masc. sg. ὑπόδικος guilty
πᾶς adj. nom. masc. sg. πᾶς πᾶσα πᾶν all, every, whosoever, every one, no, whole, any
ὁ art. nom. masc. sg. ὁ ἡ τό the, this, that, he, she, it
κόσμος n. nom. masc. sg. κόσμος world, adorning
τῷ art. dat. masc. sg. ὁ ἡ τό the, this, that, he, she, it
Θεῷ n. dat. masc. sg. θεός God, god
20 διότι conj. διότι for, because, because that, therefore
ἐξ prep. ἐκ ἐξ (+gen) of, from, out of, by, on, with, in, among, through
ἔργων n. gen. neut. pl. ἔργον work, deed, doing labour
νόμου n. gen. masc. sg. νόμος law, the law
οὐ particle of negation. οὐ οὐκ οὐχ not, no, neither, none, nay, nor, never, nothing
πᾶσα adj. nom. fem. sg. πᾶς πᾶσα πᾶν all, every, whosoever, every one, no, whole, any
σὰρξ n. nom. fem. sg. σάρξ flesh, carnal
ἐνώπιον prep. ἐνώπιον (+gen) before, in the sight of, in the presence of. (adv.) before
αὐτοῦ pron. gen. masc. 3p. sg. αὐτός ἡ ὁ self, of oneself, even, very, the same, he, she, it
διὰ prep. διά (+gen) by, through, with, in, of, (+acc) for, because of, for a cause
γὰρ conj. γάρ for, and, because, but, indeed
νόμου n. gen. masc. sg. νόμος law, the law
ἐπίγνωσις n. nom. fem. sg. ἐπίγνωσις knowledge, acknowledging, acknowledgement
ἁμαρτίας n. gen. fem. sg. ἁμαρτία sin, offence, sinful
21 νυνὶ adv. νυνί now
δὲ conj. δέ but, and, now, also, to the contrary, rather, then
χωρὶς prep. χωρίς (+gen) without, beside. (adv.) by itself, apart, separately
νόμου n. gen. masc. sg. νόμος law, the law
δικαιοσύνη n. nom. fem. sg. δικαιοσύνη righteousness
Θεοῦ n. gen. masc. sg. θεός God, god
ὑπὸ prep. ὑπό (+gen) of, by, with, from, among, (+acc) under
τοῦ art. gen. masc. sg. ὁ ἡ τό the, this, that, he, she, it
νόμου n. gen. masc. sg. νόμος law, the law
καὶ conj. καί and, even, also, but
τῶν art. gen. masc. pl. ὁ ἡ τό the, this, that, he, she, it
προφητῶν n. gen. masc. pl. προφήτης prophet
22 δικαιοσύνη n. nom. fem. sg. δικαιοσύνη righteousness
δὲ conj. δέ but, and, now, also, to the contrary, rather, then
Θεοῦ n. gen. masc. sg. θεός God, god
διὰ prep. διά (+gen) by, through, with, in, of, (+acc) for, because of, for a cause

πίστεως n. gen. fem. sg. πίστις faith, assurance, belief, fidelity
Ἰησοῦ n. gen. masc. sg. Ἰησοῦς Jesus
Χριστοῦ n. gen. masc. sg. Χριστός Christ
εἰς prep. εἰς (+acc) into, to, unto, for, in, on, toward, against, upon, at, among
πάντας adj. acc. masc. pl. πᾶς πᾶσα πᾶν all, every, whosoever, every one, no, whole, any
καὶ conj. καί and, even, also, but
ἐπὶ prep. ἐπί (+gen) on, in, upon, (+dat) in, at, for, upon, (+acc) on, upon, unto, to, against
πάντας adj. acc. masc. pl. πᾶς πᾶσα πᾶν all, every, whosoever, every one, no, whole, any
τοὺς art. acc. masc. pl. ὁ ἡ τό the, this, that, he, she, it
οὐ particle of negation. οὐ οὐκ οὐχ not, no, neither, none, nay, nor, never, nothing
γάρ conj. γάρ for, and, because, but, indeed
διαστολή n. nom. fem. sg. διαστολή difference, distinction
23 πάντες adj. nom. masc. pl. πᾶς πᾶσα πᾶν all, every, whosoever, every one, no, whole, any
γὰρ conj. γάρ for, and, because, but, indeed
καὶ conj. καί and, even, also, but
τῆς art. gen. fem. sg. ὁ ἡ τό the, this, that, he, she, it
δόξης n. gen. fem. sg. δόξα glory, honour, praise, dignity, worship
τοῦ art. gen. masc. sg. ὁ ἡ τό the, this, that, he, she, it
Θεοῦ n. gen. masc. sg. θεός God, god
24 δωρεὰν adv. δωρεάν freely, for nought, in vain, without a cause
τῇ art. dat. fem. sg. ὁ ἡ τό the, this, that, he, she, it
αὐτοῦ pron. gen. masc. 3p. sg. αὐτός ή ό self, of oneself, even, very, the same, he, she, it
χάριτι n. dat. fem. sg. χάρις grace, thank, favour, pleasure
διὰ prep. διά (+gen) by, through, with, in, of, (+acc) for, because of, for a cause
τῆς art. gen. fem. sg. ὁ ἡ τό the, this, that, he, she, it
ἀπολυτρώσεως n. gen. fem. sg. ἀπολύτρωσις redemption, deliverance
τῆς art. gen. fem. sg. ὁ ἡ τό the, this, that, he, she, it
ἐν prep. ἐν (+dat) in, by, with, among, at, on, through, to, within, into, of, for
Χριστῷ n. dat. masc. sg. Χριστός Christ
Ἰησοῦ n. dat. masc. sg. Ἰησοῦς Jesus
25 ὃν relative pron. acc. masc. sg. ὅς ἥ ὅ who, which, what, that
ὁ art. nom. masc. sg. ὁ ἡ τό the, this, that, he, she, it
Θεὸς n. nom. masc. sg. θεός God, god
ἱλαστήριον adj. acc. neut. sg. ἱλαστήριον propitiation, mercyseat
διὰ prep. διά (+gen) by, through, with, in, of, (+acc) for, because of, for a cause
τῆς art. gen. fem. sg. ὁ ἡ τό the, this, that, he, she, it
πίστεως n. gen. fem. sg. πίστις faith, assurance, belief, fidelity
ἐν prep. ἐν (+dat) in, by, with, among, at, on, through, to, within, into, of, for
τῷ art. dat. neut. sg. ὁ ἡ τό the, this, that, he, she, it
αὐτοῦ pron. gen. masc. 3p. sg. αὐτός ή ό self, of oneself, even, very, the same, he, she, it
αἵματι n. dat. neut. sg. αἷμα blood
εἰς prep. εἰς (+acc) into, to, unto, for, in, on, toward, against, upon, at, among
ἔνδειξιν n. acc. fem. sg. ἔνδειξις declare, evident token, proof
τῆς art. gen. fem. sg. ὁ ἡ τό the, this, that, he, she, it
δικαιοσύνης n. gen. fem. sg. δικαιοσύνη righteousness
αὐτοῦ pron. gen. masc. 3p. sg. αὐτός ή ό self, of oneself, even, very, the same, he, she, it
διὰ prep. διά (+gen) by, through, with, in, of, (+acc) for, because of, for a cause
τὴν art. acc. fem. sg. ὁ ἡ τό the, this, that, he, she, it
πάρεσιν n. acc. fem. sg. πάρεσις remission
τῶν art. gen. neut. pl. ὁ ἡ τό the, this, that, he, she, it
ἁμαρτημάτων n. gen. neut. pl. ἁμάρτημα sin
26 ἐν prep. ἐν (+dat) in, by, with, among, at, on, through, to, within, into, of, for
τῇ art. dat. fem. sg. ὁ ἡ τό the, this, that, he, she, it
ἀνοχῇ n. dat. fem. sg. ἀνοχή forbearance
τοῦ art. gen. masc. sg. ὁ ἡ τό the, this, that, he, she, it

Θεοῦ n. gen. masc. sg. θεός God, god
πρὸς prep. πρός (+gen) for, (+dat) at, (+acc) unto, to, with, for, against
ἔνδειξιν n. acc. fem. sg. ἔνδειξις declare, evident token, proof
τῆς art. gen. fem. sg. ὁ ἡ τό the, this, that, he, she, it
δικαιοσύνης n. gen. fem. sg. δικαιοσύνη righteousness
αὐτοῦ pron. gen. masc. 3p. sg. αὐτός ή ό self, of oneself, even, very, the same, he, she, it
ἐν prep. ἐν (+dat) in, by, with, among, at, on, through, to, within, into, of, for
τῷ art. dat. masc. sg. ὁ ἡ τό the, this, that, he, she, it
νῦν adv. νῦν now, henceforth, present, this time
καιρῷ n. dat. masc. sg. καιρός time, season, due time, opportunity
εἰς prep. εἰς (+acc) into, to, unto, for, in, on, toward, against, upon, at, among
τὸ art. acc. neut. sg. ὁ ἡ τό the, this, that, he, she, it
αὐτὸν pron. acc. masc. 3p. sg. αὐτός ή ό self, of oneself, even, very, the same, he, she, it
δίκαιον adj. acc. masc. sg. δίκαιος righteous, just, meet, right
καὶ conj. καί and, even, also, but
τὸν art. acc. masc. sg. ὁ ἡ τό the, this, that, he, she, it
ἐκ prep. ἐκ ἐξ (+gen) of, from, out of, by, on, with, in, among, through
πίστεως n. gen. fem. sg. πίστις faith, assurance, belief, fidelity
Ἰησοῦ n. gen. masc. sg. Ἰησοῦς Jesus
27 ποῦ particle of place. ποῦ where, whither
οὖν conj. οὖν therefore, then, so, and, now, wherefore
ἡ art. nom. fem. sg. ὁ ἡ τό the, this, that, he, she, it
καύχησις n. nom. fem. sg. καύχησις boasting, rejoicing, glorying
διὰ prep. διά (+gen) by, through, with, in, of, (+acc) for, because of, for a cause
ποίου interrog. pron. gen. masc. sg. ποῖος what, which, what manner of
νόμου n. gen. masc. sg. νόμος law, the law
τῶν art. gen. neut. pl. ὁ ἡ τό the, this, that, he, she, it
ἔργων n. gen. neut. pl. ἔργον work, deed, doing labour
οὐχί adv. οὐχί not, nay
ἀλλὰ conj. ἀλλά but, yea, yet, nevertheless, howbeit, nay, therefore
διὰ prep. διά (+gen) by, through, with, in, of, (+acc) for, because of, for a cause
νόμου n. gen. masc. sg. νόμος law, the law
πίστεως n. gen. fem. sg. πίστις faith, assurance, belief, fidelity
28 οὖν conj. οὖν therefore, then, so, and, now, wherefore
πίστει n. dat. fem. sg. πίστις faith, assurance, belief, fidelity
ἄνθρωπον n. acc. masc. sg. ἄνθρωπος man, human being, person, one, certain
χωρὶς prep. χωρίς (+gen) without, beside. (adv.) by itself, apart, separately
ἔργων n. gen. neut. pl. ἔργον work, deed, doing labour
νόμου n. gen. masc. sg. νόμος law, the law
29 ἢ particle. ἤ or, than, either, nor, or else, and, rather than
Ἰουδαίων adj. gen. masc. pl. Ἰουδαῖος Jew, Jewess
ὁ art. nom. masc. sg. ὁ ἡ τό the, this, that, he, she, it
Θεὸς n. nom. masc. sg. θεός God, god
μόνον adv. μόνος only, alone, by oneself
οὐχὶ adv. οὐχί not, nay
δὲ conj. δέ but, and, now, also, to the contrary, rather, then
καὶ conj. καί and, even, also, but
ἐθνῶν n. gen. neut. pl. ἔθνος Gentile, nation, heathen, people
ναὶ particle. ναί yea, even so, yes, surely, truth, verily
καὶ conj. καί and, even, also, but
ἐθνῶν n. gen. neut. pl. ἔθνος Gentile, nation, heathen, people
30 ἐπείπερ conj. ἐπείπερ seeing, since indeed
εἷς num. nom. masc. sg. εἷς or ἕν one, other, some, any, only, a certain
ὁ art. nom. masc. sg. ὁ ἡ τό the, this, that, he, she, it
Θεὸς n. nom. masc. sg. θεός God, god

ὃς relative pron. nom. masc. sg. ὅς ἥ ὅ who, which, what, that
περιτομὴν n. acc. fem. sg. περιτομή circumcision
ἐκ prep. ἐκ ἐξ (+gen) of, from, out of, by, on, with, in, among, through
πίστεως n. gen. fem. sg. πίστις faith, assurance, belief, fidelity
καὶ conj. καί and, even, also, but
ἀκροβυστίαν n. acc. fem. sg. ἀκροβυστία uncircumcised, uncircumcision
διὰ prep. διά (+gen) by, through, with, in, of, (+acc) for, because of, for a cause
τῆς art. gen. fem. sg. ὁ ἡ τό the, this, that, he, she, it
πίστεως n. gen. fem. sg. πίστις faith, assurance, belief, fidelity
31 νόμον n. acc. masc. sg. νόμος law, the law
οὖν conj. οὖν therefore, then, so, and, now, wherefore
διὰ prep. διά (+gen) by, through, with, in, of, (+acc) for, because of, for a cause
τῆς art. gen. fem. sg. ὁ ἡ τό the, this, that, he, she, it
πίστεως n. gen. fem. sg. πίστις faith, assurance, belief, fidelity
μὴ particle of negation. μή not, no, lest, neither, none, nothing, nor, never, without
ἀλλὰ conj. ἀλλά but, yea, yet, nevertheless, howbeit, nay, therefore
νόμον n. acc. masc. sg. νόμος law, the law

4

1 Τί interrog. pron. acc. neut. sg. τίς what, who, why, where, which, how
οὖν conj. οὖν therefore, then, so, and, now, wherefore
Ἀβραὰμ n. acc. masc. sg. Ἀβραάμ Abraham
τὸν art. acc. masc. sg. ὁ ἡ τό the, this, that, he, she, it
πατέρα n. acc. masc. sg. πατήρ Father, father, parent
ἡμῶν pron. gen. 1p. pl. ἐγώ I
κατὰ prep. κατά (+gen) against, by, throughout, down, (+acc) according to, after, with
σάρκα n. acc. fem. sg. σάρξ flesh, carnal
2 εἰ conj. εἰ if, whether, that, though, forasmuch
γὰρ conj. γάρ for, and, because, but, indeed
Ἀβραὰμ n. nom. masc. sg. Ἀβραάμ Abraham
ἐξ prep. ἐκ ἐξ (+gen) of, from, out of, by, on, with, in, among, through
ἔργων n. gen. neut. pl. ἔργον work, deed, doing labour
καύχημα n. acc. neut. sg. καύχημα whereof to glory, rejoicing, glorying, boasting
ἀλλ' conj. ἀλλά but, yea, yet, nevertheless, howbeit, nay, therefore
οὐ particle of negation. οὐ οὐκ οὐχ not, no, neither, none, nay, nor, never, nothing
πρὸς prep. πρός (+gen) for, (+dat) at, (+acc) unto, to, with, for, against
τὸν art. acc. masc. sg. ὁ ἡ τό the, this, that, he, she, it
Θεόν n. acc. masc. sg. θεός God, god
3 τί interrog. pron. acc. neut. sg. τίς what, who, why, where, which, how
γὰρ conj. γάρ for, and, because, but, indeed
ἡ art. nom. fem. sg. ὁ ἡ τό the, this, that, he, she, it
γραφὴ n. nom. fem. sg. γραφή scripture
δὲ conj. δέ but, and, now, also, to the contrary, rather, then
Ἀβραὰμ n. nom. masc. sg. Ἀβραάμ Abraham
τῷ art. dat. masc. sg. ὁ ἡ τό the, this, that, he, she, it
Θεῷ n. dat. masc. sg. θεός God, god
καὶ conj. καί and, even, also, but
αὐτῷ pron. dat. masc. 3p. sg. αὐτός ἡ ὁ self, of oneself, even, very, the same, he, she, it
εἰς prep. εἰς (+acc) into, to, unto, for, in, on, toward, against, upon, at, among
δικαιοσύνην n. acc. fem. sg. δικαιοσύνη righteousness
4 τῷ art. dat. masc. sg. ὁ ἡ τό the, this, that, he, she, it
δὲ conj. δέ but, and, now, also, to the contrary, rather, then
ὁ art. nom. masc. sg. ὁ ἡ τό the, this, that, he, she, it
μισθὸς n. nom. masc. sg. μισθός reward, hire, wage

οὐ particle of negation. οὐ οὐκ οὐχ not, no, neither, none, nay, nor, never, nothing
κατὰ prep. κατά (+gen) against, by, throughout, down, (+acc) according to, after, with
χάριν n. acc. fem. sg. χάρις grace, thank, favour, pleasure
ἀλλὰ conj. ἀλλά but, yea, yet, nevertheless, howbeit, nay, therefore
κατὰ prep. κατά (+gen) against, by, throughout, down, (+acc) according to, after, with
τὸ art. acc. neut. sg. ὁ ἡ τό the, this, that, he, she, it
ὀφείλημα n. acc. neut. sg. ὀφείλημα debt
5 τῷ art. dat. masc. sg. ὁ ἡ τό the, this, that, he, she, it
δὲ conj. δέ but, and, now, also, to the contrary, rather, then
μὴ particle of negation. μή not, no, lest, neither, none, nothing, nor, never, without
δὲ conj. δέ but, and, now, also, to the contrary, rather, then
ἐπὶ prep. ἐπί (+gen) on, in, upon, (+dat) in, at, for, upon, (+acc) on, upon, unto, to, against
τὸν art. acc. masc. sg. ὁ ἡ τό the, this, that, he, she, it
τὸν art. acc. masc. sg. ὁ ἡ τό the, this, that, he, she, it
ἀσεβῆ adj. acc. masc. sg. ἀσεβής ungodly, ungodly man
ἡ art. nom. fem. sg. ὁ ἡ τό the, this, that, he, she, it
πίστις n. nom. fem. sg. πίστις faith, assurance, belief, fidelity
αὐτοῦ pron. gen. masc. 3p. sg. αὐτός ἡ ὁ self, of oneself, even, very, the same, he, she, it
εἰς prep. εἰς (+acc) into, to, unto, for, in, on, toward, against, upon, at, among
δικαιοσύνην n. acc. fem. sg. δικαιοσύνη righteousness
6 καθάπερ adv. καθάπερ even as, as, as well as
καὶ conj. καί and, even, also, but
Δαβὶδ n. nom. masc. sg. Δαβίδ David
τὸν art. acc. masc. sg. ὁ ἡ τό the, this, that, he, she, it
μακαρισμὸν n. acc. masc. sg. μακαρισμός blessedness
τοῦ art. gen. masc. sg. ὁ ἡ τό the, this, that, he, she, it
ἀνθρώπου n. gen. masc. sg. ἄνθρωπος man, human being, person, one, certain
ᾧ relative pron. dat. masc. sg. ὅς ἥ ὅ who, which, what, that
ὁ art. nom. masc. sg. ὁ ἡ τό the, this, that, he, she, it
Θεὸς n. nom. masc. sg. θεός God, god
δικαιοσύνην n. acc. fem. sg. δικαιοσύνη righteousness
χωρὶς prep. χωρίς (+gen) without, beside. (adv.) by itself, apart, separately
ἔργων n. gen. neut. pl. ἔργον work, deed, doing labour
7 Μακάριοι adj. nom. masc. pl. μακάριος blessed, happy
ὧν relative pron. gen. masc. pl. ὅς ἥ ὅ who, which, what, that
αἱ art. nom. fem. pl. ὁ ἡ τό the, this, that, he, she, it
ἀνομίαι n. nom. fem. pl. ἀνομία iniquity, transgression of the law, lawlessness
καὶ conj. καί and, even, also, but
ὧν relative pron. gen. masc. pl. ὅς ἥ ὅ who, which, what, that
αἱ art. nom. fem. pl. ὁ ἡ τό the, this, that, he, she, it
ἁμαρτίαι n. nom. fem. pl. ἁμαρτία sin, offence, sinful
8 μακάριος adj. nom. masc. sg. μακάριος blessed, happy
ἀνὴρ n. nom. masc. sg. ἀνήρ man, husband, sir
ᾧ relative pron. dat. masc. sg. ὅς ἥ ὅ who, which, what, that
οὐ particle of negation. οὐ οὐκ οὐχ not, no, neither, none, nay, nor, never, nothing
μὴ particle of negation. μή not, no, lest, neither, none, nothing, nor, never, without
Κύριος n. nom. masc. sg. κύριος Lord, lord, master, sir, LORD, God, Master, owner
ἁμαρτίαν n. acc. fem. sg. ἁμαρτία sin, offence, sinful
9 ὁ art. nom. masc. sg. ὁ ἡ τό the, this, that, he, she, it
μακαρισμὸς n. nom. masc. sg. μακαρισμός blessedness
οὖν conj. οὖν therefore, then, so, and, now, wherefore
οὗτος demo. pron. nom. masc. sg. οὗτος αὕτη τοῦτο this, the same, this same, he, she, it
ἐπὶ prep. ἐπί (+gen) on, in, upon, (+dat) in, at, for, upon, (+acc) on, upon, unto, to, against
τὴν art. acc. fem. sg. ὁ ἡ τό the, this, that, he, she, it
περιτομὴν n. acc. fem. sg. περιτομή circumcision

ἢ particle. ἤ or, than, either, nor, or else, and, rather than
καὶ conj. καί and, even, also, but
ἐπὶ prep. ἐπί (+gen) on, in, upon, (+dat) in, at, for, upon, (+acc) on, upon, unto, to, against
τὴν art. acc. fem. sg. ὁ ἡ τό the, this, that, he, she, it
ἀκροβυστίαν n. acc. fem. sg. ἀκροβυστία uncircumcised, uncircumcision
γάρ conj. γάρ for, and, because, but, indeed
ὅτι conj. ὅτι that, for, because, how that, how, because that, for that, though
τῷ art. dat. masc. sg. ὁ ἡ τό the, this, that, he, she, it
Ἀβραὰμ n. dat. masc. sg. Ἀβραάμ Abraham
ἡ art. nom. fem. sg. ὁ ἡ τό the, this, that, he, she, it
πίστις n. nom. fem. sg. πίστις faith, assurance, belief, fidelity
εἰς prep. εἰς (+acc) into, to, unto, for, in, on, toward, against, upon, at, among
δικαιοσύνην n. acc. fem. sg. δικαιοσύνη righteousness
10 πῶς adv. πῶς how, by what means, after what manner
οὖν conj. οὖν therefore, then, so, and, now, wherefore
ἐν prep. ἐν (+dat) in, by, with, among, at, on, through, to, within, into, of, for
περιτομῇ n. dat. fem. sg. περιτομή circumcision
ἢ particle. ἤ or, than, either, nor, or else, and, rather than
ἐν prep. ἐν (+dat) in, by, with, among, at, on, through, to, within, into, of, for
ἀκροβυστίᾳ n. dat. fem. sg. ἀκροβυστία uncircumcised, uncircumcision
οὐκ particle of negation. οὐ οὐκ οὐχ not, no, neither, none, nay, nor, never, nothing
ἐν prep. ἐν (+dat) in, by, with, among, at, on, through, to, within, into, of, for
περιτομῇ n. dat. fem. sg. περιτομή circumcision
ἀλλ' conj. ἀλλά but, yea, yet, nevertheless, howbeit, nay, therefore
ἐν prep. ἐν (+dat) in, by, with, among, at, on, through, to, within, into, of, for
ἀκροβυστίᾳ n. dat. fem. sg. ἀκροβυστία uncircumcised, uncircumcision
11 καὶ conj. καί and, even, also, but
σημεῖον n. acc. neut. sg. σημεῖον sign, miracle, wonder, token
περιτομῆς n. gen. fem. sg. περιτομή circumcision
σφραγῖδα n. acc. fem. sg. σφραγίς seal
τῆς art. gen. fem. sg. ὁ ἡ τό the, this, that, he, she, it
δικαιοσύνης n. gen. fem. sg. δικαιοσύνη righteousness
τῆς art. gen. fem. sg. ὁ ἡ τό the, this, that, he, she, it
πίστεως n. gen. fem. sg. πίστις faith, assurance, belief, fidelity
τῆς art. gen. fem. sg. ὁ ἡ τό the, this, that, he, she, it
ἐν prep. ἐν (+dat) in, by, with, among, at, on, through, to, within, into, of, for
τῇ art. dat. fem. sg. ὁ ἡ τό the, this, that, he, she, it
ἀκροβυστίᾳ n. dat. fem. sg. ἀκροβυστία uncircumcised, uncircumcision
εἰς prep. εἰς (+acc) into, to, unto, for, in, on, toward, against, upon, at, among
τὸ art. acc. neut. sg. ὁ ἡ τό the, this, that, he, she, it
αὐτὸν pron. acc. masc. 3p. sg. αὐτός ἡ ὁ self, of oneself, even, very, the same, he, she, it
πατέρα n. acc. masc. sg. πατήρ Father, father, parent
πάντων adj. gen. masc. pl. πᾶς πᾶσα πᾶν all, every, whosoever, every one, no, whole, any
τῶν art. gen. masc. pl. ὁ ἡ τό the, this, that, he, she, it
δι' prep. διά (+gen) by, through, with, in, of, (+acc) for, because of, for a cause
ἀκροβυστίας n. gen. fem. sg. ἀκροβυστία uncircumcised, uncircumcision
εἰς prep. εἰς (+acc) into, to, unto, for, in, on, toward, against, upon, at, among
τὸ art. acc. neut. sg. ὁ ἡ τό the, this, that, he, she, it
καὶ conj. καί and, even, also, but
αὐτοῖς pron. dat. masc. 3p. pl. αὐτός ἡ ὁ self, of oneself, even, very, the same, he, she, it
τὴν art. acc. fem. sg. ὁ ἡ τό the, this, that, he, she, it
δικαιοσύνην n. acc. fem. sg. δικαιοσύνη righteousness
12 καὶ conj. καί and, even, also, but
πατέρα n. acc. masc. sg. πατήρ Father, father, parent
περιτομῆς n. gen. fem. sg. περιτομή circumcision

τοῖς art. dat. masc. pl. ὁ ἡ τό the, this, that, he, she, it
οὐκ particle of negation. οὐ οὐκ οὐχ not, no, neither, none, nay, nor, never, nothing
ἐκ prep. ἐκ ἐξ (+gen) of, from, out of, by, on, with, in, among, through
περιτομῆς n. gen. fem. sg. περιτομή circumcision
μόνον adv. μόνος only, alone, by oneself
ἀλλὰ conj. ἀλλά but, yea, yet, nevertheless, howbeit, nay, therefore
καὶ conj. καί and, even, also, but
τοῖς art. dat. neut. pl. ὁ ἡ τό the, this, that, he, she, it
τοῖς art. dat. neut. pl. ὁ ἡ τό the, this, that, he, she, it
ἴχνεσιν n. dat. neut. pl. ἴχνος step
τῆς art. gen. fem. sg. ὁ ἡ τό the, this, that, he, she, it
ἐν prep. ἐν (+dat) in, by, with, among, at, on, through, to, within, into, of, for
τῇ art. dat. fem. sg. ὁ ἡ τό the, this, that, he, she, it
ἀκροβυστίᾳ n. dat. fem. sg. ἀκροβυστία uncircumcised, uncircumcision
πίστεως n. gen. fem. sg. πίστις faith, assurance, belief, fidelity
τοῦ art. gen. masc. sg. ὁ ἡ τό the, this, that, he, she, it
πατρὸς n. gen. masc. sg. πατήρ Father, father, parent
ἡμῶν pron. gen. 1p. pl. ἐγώ I
᾿Αβραάμ n. gen. masc. sg. ᾿Αβραάμ Abraham
13 οὐ particle of negation. οὐ οὐκ οὐχ not, no, neither, none, nay, nor, never, nothing
γὰρ conj. γάρ for, and, because, but, indeed
διὰ prep. διά (+gen) by, through, with, in, of, (+acc) for, because of, for a cause
νόμου n. gen. masc. sg. νόμος law, the law
ἡ art. nom. fem. sg. ὁ ἡ τό the, this, that, he, she, it
ἐπαγγελία n. nom. fem. sg. ἐπαγγελία promise, message
τῷ art. dat. masc. sg. ὁ ἡ τό the, this, that, he, she, it
᾿Αβραὰμ n. dat. masc. sg. ᾿Αβραάμ Abraham
ἢ particle. ἤ or, than, either, nor, or else, and, rather than
τῷ art. dat. neut. sg. ὁ ἡ τό the, this, that, he, she, it
σπέρματι n. dat. neut. sg. σπέρμα seed, issue
αὐτοῦ pron. gen. masc. 3p. sg. αὐτός ή ό self, of oneself, even, very, the same, he, she, it
τὸ art. nom. neut. sg. ὁ ἡ τό the, this, that, he, she, it
κληρονόμον n. acc. masc. sg. κληρονόμος heir
αὐτὸν pron. acc. masc. 3p. sg. αὐτός ή ό self, of oneself, even, very, the same, he, she, it
τοῦ art. gen. masc. sg. ὁ ἡ τό the, this, that, he, she, it
κόσμου n. gen. masc. sg. κόσμος world, adorning
ἀλλὰ conj. ἀλλά but, yea, yet, nevertheless, howbeit, nay, therefore
διὰ prep. διά (+gen) by, through, with, in, of, (+acc) for, because of, for a cause
δικαιοσύνης n. gen. fem. sg. δικαιοσύνη righteousness
πίστεως n. gen. fem. sg. πίστις faith, assurance, belief, fidelity
14 εἰ conj. εἰ if, whether, that, though, forasmuch
γὰρ conj. γάρ for, and, because, but, indeed
οἱ art. nom. masc. pl. ὁ ἡ τό the, this, that, he, she, it
ἐκ prep. ἐκ ἐξ (+gen) of, from, out of, by, on, with, in, among, through
νόμου n. gen. masc. sg. νόμος law, the law
κληρονόμοι n. nom. masc. pl. κληρονόμος heir
ἡ art. nom. fem. sg. ὁ ἡ τό the, this, that, he, she, it
πίστις n. nom. fem. sg. πίστις faith, assurance, belief, fidelity
καὶ conj. καί and, even, also, but
ἡ art. nom. fem. sg. ὁ ἡ τό the, this, that, he, she, it
ἐπαγγελία n. nom. fem. sg. ἐπαγγελία promise, message
15 ὁ art. nom. masc. sg. ὁ ἡ τό the, this, that, he, she, it
γὰρ conj. γάρ for, and, because, but, indeed
νόμος n. nom. masc. sg. νόμος law, the law
ὀργὴν n. acc. fem. sg. ὀργή wrath, anger, indignation, vengeance

οὗ adv. οὗ where, whither, wherein
γὰρ conj. γάρ for, and, because, but, indeed
οὐκ particle of negation. οὐ οὐκ οὐχ not, no, neither, none, nay, nor, never, nothing
νόμος n. nom. masc. sg. νόμος law, the law
οὐδὲ adv. οὐδέ neither, nor, not, no, not even, never, not yet
παράβασις n. nom. fem. sg. παράβασις breaking, transgression
16 διὰ prep. διά (+gen) by, through, with, in, of, (+acc) for, because of, for a cause
τοῦτο demo. pron. acc. neut. sg. οὗτος αὕτη τοῦτο this, the same, this same, he, she, it
ἐκ prep. ἐκ ἐξ (+gen) of, from, out of, by, on, with, in, among, through
πίστεως n. gen. fem. sg. πίστις faith, assurance, belief, fidelity
ἵνα conj. ἵνα that, to, lest, for to, so that, albeit, because, for, so as
κατὰ prep. κατά (+gen) against, by, throughout, down, (+acc) according to, after, with
χάριν n. acc. fem. sg. χάρις grace, thank, favour, pleasure
εἰς prep. εἰς (+acc) into, to, unto, for, in, on, toward, against, upon, at, among
τὸ art. acc. neut. sg. ὁ ἡ τό the, this, that, he, she, it
βεβαίαν adj. acc. fem. sg. βέβαιος sure, stedfast, firm, more sure, of force
τὴν art. acc. fem. sg. ὁ ἡ τό the, this, that, he, she, it
ἐπαγγελίαν n. acc. fem. sg. ἐπαγγελία promise, message
παντὶ adj. dat. neut. sg. πᾶς πᾶσα πᾶν all, every, whosoever, every one, no, whole, any
τῷ art. dat. neut. sg. ὁ ἡ τό the, this, that, he, she, it
σπέρματι n. dat. neut. sg. σπέρμα seed, issue
οὐ particle of negation. οὐ οὐκ οὐχ not, no, neither, none, nay, nor, never, nothing
τῷ art. dat. neut. sg. ὁ ἡ τό the, this, that, he, she, it
ἐκ prep. ἐκ ἐξ (+gen) of, from, out of, by, on, with, in, among, through
τοῦ art. gen. masc. sg. ὁ ἡ τό the, this, that, he, she, it
νόμου n. gen. masc. sg. νόμος law, the law
μόνον adv. μόνος only, alone, by oneself
ἀλλὰ conj. ἀλλά but, yea, yet, nevertheless, howbeit, nay, therefore
καὶ conj. καί and, even, also, but
τῷ art. dat. neut. sg. ὁ ἡ τό the, this, that, he, she, it
ἐκ prep. ἐκ ἐξ (+gen) of, from, out of, by, on, with, in, among, through
πίστεως n. gen. fem. sg. πίστις faith, assurance, belief, fidelity
᾿Αβραάμ n. gen. masc. sg. ᾿Αβραάμ Abraham
ὅς relative pron. nom. masc. sg. ὅς ἥ ὅ who, which, what, that
πατὴρ n. nom. masc. sg. πατήρ Father, father, parent
πάντων adj. gen. masc. pl. πᾶς πᾶσα πᾶν all, every, whosoever, every one, no, whole, any
ἡμῶν pron. gen. 1p. pl. ἐγώ I
17 καθὼς adv. καθώς as, even as, according as, according to
ὅτι conj. ὅτι that, for, because, how that, how, because that, for that, though
Πατέρα n. acc. masc. sg. πατήρ Father, father, parent
πολλῶν adj. gen. neut. pl. πολύς many, great, much, long, abundant
ἐθνῶν n. gen. neut. pl. ἔθνος Gentile, nation, heathen, people
σε pron. acc. 2p. sg. σύ thou, you
κατέναντι adv. κατέναντι over against, before
οὗ relative pron. gen. masc. sg. ὅς ἥ ὅ who, which, what, that
Θεοῦ n. gen. masc. sg. θεός God, god
τοῦ art. gen. masc. sg. ὁ ἡ τό the, this, that, he, she, it
τοὺς art. acc. masc. pl. ὁ ἡ τό the, this, that, he, she, it
νεκροὺς adj. acc. masc. pl. νεκρός dead
καὶ conj. καί and, even, also, but
τὰ art. acc. neut. pl. ὁ ἡ τό the, this, that, he, she, it
μὴ particle of negation. μή not, no, lest, neither, none, nothing, nor, never, without
ὡς adv. ὡς as, when, as it were, how, about, like, as soon as, even as, while
18 ὃς relative pron. nom. masc. sg. ὅς ἥ ὅ who, which, what, that
παρ᾿ prep. παρά (+gen) of, from, (+dat) with, for, (+acc) beside, at, by, above, against

ἐλπίδα n. acc. fem. sg. ἐλπίς hope, faith
ἐπ' prep. ἐπί (+gen) on, in, upon, (+dat) in, at, for, upon, (+acc) on, upon, unto, to, against
ἐλπίδι n. dat. fem. sg. ἐλπίς hope, faith
εἰς prep. εἰς (+acc) into, to, unto, for, in, on, toward, against, upon, at, among
τὸ art. acc. neut. sg. ὁ ἡ τό the, this, that, he, she, it
αὐτὸν pron. acc. masc. 3p. sg. αὐτός ή ό self, of oneself, even, very, the same, he, she, it
πατέρα n. acc. masc. sg. πατήρ Father, father, parent
πολλῶν adj. gen. neut. pl. πολύς many, great, much, long, abundant
ἐθνῶν n. gen. neut. pl. ἔθνος Gentile, nation, heathen, people
κατὰ prep. κατά (+gen) against, by, throughout, down, (+acc) according to, after, with
τὸ art. acc. neut. sg. ὁ ἡ τό the, this, that, he, she, it
Οὕτως adv. οὕτω οὕτως so, even so, thus, on this wise, likewise, after this manner
τὸ art. nom. neut. sg. ὁ ἡ τό the, this, that, he, she, it
σπέρμα n. nom. neut. sg. σπέρμα seed, issue
σου pron. gen. 2p. sg. σύ thou, you
19 καὶ conj. καί and, even, also, but
μὴ particle of negation. μή not, no, lest, neither, none, nothing, nor, never, without
τῇ art. dat. fem. sg. ὁ ἡ τό the, this, that, he, she, it
πίστει n. dat. fem. sg. πίστις faith, assurance, belief, fidelity
οὐ particle of negation. οὐ οὐκ οὐχ not, no, neither, none, nay, nor, never, nothing
τὸ art. acc. neut. sg. ὁ ἡ τό the, this, that, he, she, it
ἑαυτοῦ reflexive pron. gen. masc. 3p. sg. ἑαυτοῦ himself, herself, itself, yourself, ourselves
σῶμα n. acc. neut. sg. σῶμα body, bodily, slave
ἤδη adv. ἤδη now, already, yet, by this time, even now, now already
ἑκατονταετής adj. nom. masc. sg. ἑκατονταετής hundred years old
που particle. πού about, in a certain place
καὶ conj. καί and, even, also, but
τὴν art. acc. fem. sg. ὁ ἡ τό the, this, that, he, she, it
νέκρωσιν n. acc. fem. sg. νέκρωσις deadness, dying
τῆς art. gen. fem. sg. ὁ ἡ τό the, this, that, he, she, it
μήτρας n. gen. fem. sg. μήτρα womb
Σάρρας n. gen. fem. sg. Σάρρα Sara, Sarah
20 εἰς prep. εἰς (+acc) into, to, unto, for, in, on, toward, against, upon, at, among
δὲ conj. δέ but, and, now, also, to the contrary, rather, then
τὴν art. acc. fem. sg. ὁ ἡ τό the, this, that, he, she, it
ἐπαγγελίαν n. acc. fem. sg. ἐπαγγελία promise, message
τοῦ art. gen. masc. sg. ὁ ἡ τό the, this, that, he, she, it
Θεοῦ n. gen. masc. sg. θεός God, god
οὐ particle of negation. οὐ οὐκ οὐχ not, no, neither, none, nay, nor, never, nothing
τῇ art. dat. fem. sg. ὁ ἡ τό the, this, that, he, she, it
ἀπιστίᾳ n. dat. fem. sg. ἀπιστία unbelief
ἀλλ' conj. ἀλλά but, yea, yet, nevertheless, howbeit, nay, therefore
τῇ art. dat. fem. sg. ὁ ἡ τό the, this, that, he, she, it
πίστει n. dat. fem. sg. πίστις faith, assurance, belief, fidelity
δόξαν n. acc. fem. sg. δόξα glory, honour, praise, dignity, worship
τῷ art. dat. masc. sg. ὁ ἡ τό the, this, that, he, she, it
Θεῷ n. dat. masc. sg. θεός God, god
21 καὶ conj. καί and, even, also, but
ὅτι conj. ὅτι that, for, because, how that, how, because that, for that, though
ὃ relative pron. acc. neut. sg. ὅς ἥ ὅ who, which, what, that
δυνατός adj. nom. masc. sg. δυνατός able, possible, mighty, strong
καὶ conj. καί and, even, also, but
22 διὸ conj. διό wherefore, therefore, for which cause
καὶ conj. καί and, even, also, but
αὐτῷ pron. dat. masc. 3p. sg. αὐτός ή ό self, of oneself, even, very, the same, he, she, it

εἰς prep. εἰς (+acc) into, to, unto, for, in, on, toward, against, upon, at, among
δικαιοσύνην n. acc. fem. sg. δικαιοσύνη righteousness
23 οὐκ particle of negation. οὐ οὐκ οὐχ not, no, neither, none, nay, nor, never, nothing
δὲ conj. δέ but, and, now, also, to the contrary, rather, then
δι' prep. διά (+gen) by, through, with, in, of, (+acc) for, because of, for a cause
αὐτὸν pron. acc. masc. 3p. sg. αὐτός ή ό self, of oneself, even, very, the same, he, she, it
μόνον adj. acc. masc. sg. μόνος only, alone, by oneself
ὅτι conj. ὅτι that, for, because, how that, how, because that, for that, though
αὐτῷ pron. dat. masc. 3p. sg. αὐτός ή ό self, of oneself, even, very, the same, he, she, it
24 ἀλλὰ conj. ἀλλά but, yea, yet, nevertheless, howbeit, nay, therefore
καὶ conj. καί and, even, also, but
δι' prep. διά (+gen) by, through, with, in, of, (+acc) for, because of, for a cause
ἡμᾶς pron. acc. 1p. pl. ἐγώ I
οἷς relative pron. dat. masc. pl. ὅς ἥ ὅ who, which, what, that
τοῖς art. dat. masc. pl. ὁ ἡ τό the, this, that, he, she, it
ἐπὶ prep. ἐπί (+gen) on, in, upon, (+dat) in, at, for, upon, (+acc) on, upon, unto, to, against
τὸν art. acc. masc. sg. ὁ ἡ τό the, this, that, he, she, it
Ἰησοῦν n. acc. masc. sg. Ἰησοῦς Jesus
τὸν art. acc. masc. sg. ὁ ἡ τό the, this, that, he, she, it
Κύριον n. acc. masc. sg. κύριος Lord, lord, master, sir, LORD, God, Master, owner
ἡμῶν pron. gen. 1p. pl. ἐγώ I
ἐκ prep. ἐκ ἐξ (+gen) of, from, out of, by, on, with, in, among, through
νεκρῶν adj. gen. masc. pl. νεκρός dead
25 ὃς relative pron. nom. masc. sg. ὅς ἥ ὅ who, which, what, that
διὰ prep. διά (+gen) by, through, with, in, of, (+acc) for, because of, for a cause
τὰ art. acc. neut. pl. ὁ ἡ τό the, this, that, he, she, it
παραπτώματα n. acc. neut. pl. παράπτωμα trespass, offence, sin, fall, fault
ἡμῶν pron. gen. 1p. pl. ἐγώ I
καὶ conj. καί and, even, also, but
διὰ prep. διά (+gen) by, through, with, in, of, (+acc) for, because of, for a cause
τὴν art. acc. fem. sg. ὁ ἡ τό the, this, that, he, she, it
δικαίωσιν n. acc. fem. sg. δικαίωσις justification
ἡμῶν pron. gen. 1p. pl. ἐγώ I

5

1 οὖν conj. οὖν therefore, then, so, and, now, wherefore
ἐκ prep. ἐκ ἐξ (+gen) of, from, out of, by, on, with, in, among, through
πίστεως n. gen. fem. sg. πίστις faith, assurance, belief, fidelity
εἰρήνην n. acc. fem. sg. εἰρήνη peace, quietness, rest
πρὸς prep. πρός (+gen) for, (+dat) at, (+acc) unto, to, with, for, against
τὸν art. acc. masc. sg. ὁ ἡ τό the, this, that, he, she, it
Θεὸν n. acc. masc. sg. θεός God, god
διὰ prep. διά (+gen) by, through, with, in, of, (+acc) for, because of, for a cause
τοῦ art. gen. masc. sg. ὁ ἡ τό the, this, that, he, she, it
Κυρίου n. gen. masc. sg. κύριος Lord, lord, master, sir, LORD, God, Master, owner
ἡμῶν pron. gen. 1p. pl. ἐγώ I
Ἰησοῦ n. gen. masc. sg. Ἰησοῦς Jesus
Χριστοῦ n. gen. masc. sg. Χριστός Christ
2 δι' prep. διά (+gen) by, through, with, in, of, (+acc) for, because of, for a cause
οὗ relative pron. gen. masc. sg. ὅς ἥ ὅ who, which, what, that
καὶ conj. καί and, even, also, but
τὴν art. acc. fem. sg. ὁ ἡ τό the, this, that, he, she, it
προσαγωγὴν n. acc. fem. sg. προσαγωγή access
τῇ art. dat. fem. sg. ὁ ἡ τό the, this, that, he, she, it

πίστει n. dat. fem. sg. πίστις faith, assurance, belief, fidelity
εἰς prep. εἰς (+acc) into, to, unto, for, in, on, toward, against, upon, at, among
τὴν art. acc. fem. sg. ὁ ἡ τό the, this, that, he, she, it
χάριν n. acc. fem. sg. χάρις grace, thank, favour, pleasure
ταύτην demo. pron. acc. fem. sg. οὗτος αὕτη τοῦτο this, the same, this same, he, she, it
ἐν prep. ἐν (+dat) in, by, with, among, at, on, through, to, within, into, of, for
ᾗ relative pron. dat. fem. sg. ὅς ἥ ὅ who, which, what, that
καὶ conj. καί and, even, also, but
ἐπ' prep. ἐπί (+gen) on, in, upon, (+dat) in, at, for, upon, (+acc) on, upon, unto, to, against
ἐλπίδι n. dat. fem. sg. ἐλπίς hope, faith
τῆς art. gen. fem. sg. ὁ ἡ τό the, this, that, he, she, it
δόξης n. gen. fem. sg. δόξα glory, honour, praise, dignity, worship
τοῦ art. gen. masc. sg. ὁ ἡ τό the, this, that, he, she, it
Θεοῦ n. gen. masc. sg. θεός God, god
3 οὐ particle of negation. οὐ οὐκ οὐχ not, no, neither, none, nay, nor, never, nothing
μόνον adv. μόνος only, alone, by oneself
δέ conj. δέ but, and, now, also, to the contrary, rather, then
ἀλλὰ conj. ἀλλά but, yea, yet, nevertheless, howbeit, nay, therefore
καὶ conj. καί and, even, also, but
ἐν prep. ἐν (+dat) in, by, with, among, at, on, through, to, within, into, of, for
ταῖς art. dat. fem. pl. ὁ ἡ τό the, this, that, he, she, it
θλίψεσιν n. dat. fem. pl. θλῖψις tribulation, affliction, anguish, persecution
ὅτι conj. ὅτι that, for, because, how that, how, because that, for that, though
ἡ art. nom. fem. sg. ὁ ἡ τό the, this, that, he, she, it
θλῖψις n. nom. fem. sg. θλῖψις tribulation, affliction, anguish, persecution
ὑπομονὴν n. acc. fem. sg. ὑπομονή patience, enduring
4 ἡ art. nom. fem. sg. ὁ ἡ τό the, this, that, he, she, it
δὲ conj. δέ but, and, now, also, to the contrary, rather, then
ὑπομονὴ n. nom. fem. sg. ὑπομονή patience, enduring
δοκιμήν n. acc. fem. sg. δοκιμή experience, proof, experiment, trial
ἡ art. nom. fem. sg. ὁ ἡ τό the, this, that, he, she, it
δὲ conj. δέ but, and, now, also, to the contrary, rather, then
δοκιμὴ n. nom. fem. sg. δοκιμή experience, proof, experiment, trial
ἐλπίδα n. acc. fem. sg. ἐλπίς hope, faith
5 ἡ art. nom. fem. sg. ὁ ἡ τό the, this, that, he, she, it
δὲ conj. δέ but, and, now, also, to the contrary, rather, then
ἐλπὶς n. nom. fem. sg. ἐλπίς hope, faith
οὐ particle of negation. οὐ οὐκ οὐχ not, no, neither, none, nay, nor, never, nothing
ὅτι conj. ὅτι that, for, because, how that, how, because that, for that, though
ἡ art. nom. fem. sg. ὁ ἡ τό the, this, that, he, she, it
ἀγάπη n. nom. fem. sg. ἀγάπη love, charity, feast of charity
τοῦ art. gen. masc. sg. ὁ ἡ τό the, this, that, he, she, it
Θεοῦ n. gen. masc. sg. θεός God, god
ἐν prep. ἐν (+dat) in, by, with, among, at, on, through, to, within, into, of, for
ταῖς art. dat. fem. pl. ὁ ἡ τό the, this, that, he, she, it
καρδίαις n. dat. fem. pl. καρδία heart
ἡμῶν pron. gen. 1p. pl. ἐγώ I
διὰ prep. διά (+gen) by, through, with, in, of, (+acc) for, because of, for a cause
Πνεύματος n. gen. neut. sg. πνεῦμα spirit, Spirit, Ghost, ghost, life. of the spirit, wind
Ἁγίου adj. gen. neut. sg. ἅγιος Holy, holy, saint, Holy One, holy thing, most holy
τοῦ art. gen. neut. sg. ὁ ἡ τό the, this, that, he, she, it
ἡμῖν pron. dat. 1p. pl. ἐγώ I
6 ἔτι adv. ἔτι yet, more, any more, further, still, moreover
γὰρ conj. γάρ for, and, because, but, indeed
Χριστὸς n. nom. masc. sg. Χριστός Christ

ἡμῶν pron. gen. 1p. pl. ἐγώ I
ἀσθενῶν adj. gen. masc. pl. ἀσθενής weak, sick, impotent, more feeble
κατὰ prep. κατά (+gen) against, by, throughout, down, (+acc) according to, after, with
καιρὸν n. acc. masc. sg. καιρός time, season, due time, opportunity
ὑπὲρ prep. ὑπέρ (+gen) for, of, for the sake of, (+acc) above, more than
ἀσεβῶν adj. gen. masc. pl. ἀσεβής ungodly, ungodly man
7 μόλις adv. μόλις scarce, with difficulty, scarcely, hardly
γὰρ conj. γάρ for, and, because, but, indeed
ὑπὲρ prep. ὑπέρ (+gen) for, of, for the sake of, (+acc) above, more than
δικαίου adj. gen. masc. sg. δίκαιος righteous, just, meet, right
τις indefinite pron. nom. masc. sg. τὶς certain, some, any man, one, any thing
ὑπὲρ prep. ὑπέρ (+gen) for, of, for the sake of, (+acc) above, more than
γὰρ conj. γάρ for, and, because, but, indeed
τοῦ art. gen. masc. sg. ὁ ἡ τό the, this, that, he, she, it
ἀγαθοῦ adj. gen. masc. sg. ἀγαθός good, good thing, that which is good, well
τάχα adv. τάχα peradventure, perhaps
τις indefinite pron. nom. masc. sg. τὶς certain, some, any man, one, any thing
καὶ conj. καί and, even, also, but
8 δὲ conj. δέ but, and, now, also, to the contrary, rather, then
τὴν art. acc. fem. sg. ὁ ἡ τό the, this, that, he, she, it
ἑαυτοῦ reflexive pron. gen. masc. 3p. sg. ἑαυτοῦ himself, herself, itself, yourself, ourselves
ἀγάπην n. acc. fem. sg. ἀγάπη love, charity, feast of charity
εἰς prep. εἰς (+acc) into, to, unto, for, in, on, toward, against, upon, at, among
ἡμᾶς pron. acc. 1p. pl. ἐγώ I
ὁ art. nom. masc. sg. ὁ ἡ τό the, this, that, he, she, it
Θεός n. nom. masc. sg. θεός God, god
ὅτι conj. ὅτι that, for, because, how that, how, because that, for that, though
ἔτι adv. ἔτι yet, more, any more, further, still, moreover
ἁμαρτωλῶν adj. gen. masc. pl. ἁμαρτωλός sinner, sinful
ἡμῶν pron. gen. 1p. pl. ἐγώ I
Χριστὸς n. nom. masc. sg. Χριστός Christ
ὑπὲρ prep. ὑπέρ (+gen) for, of, for the sake of, (+acc) above, more than
ἡμῶν pron. gen. 1p. pl. ἐγώ I
9 πολλῷ adj. dat. neut. sg. πολύς many, great, much, long, abundant
οὖν conj. οὖν therefore, then, so, and, now, wherefore
μᾶλλον adv. μᾶλλον rather, more, more and more, better, much, much the more
νῦν adv. νῦν now, henceforth, present, this time
ἐν prep. ἐν (+dat) in, by, with, among, at, on, through, to, within, into, of, for
τῷ art. dat. neut. sg. ὁ ἡ τό the, this, that, he, she, it
αἵματι n. dat. neut. sg. αἷμα blood
αὐτοῦ pron. gen. masc. 3p. sg. αὐτός ή ό self, of oneself, even, very, the same, he, she, it
δι' prep. διά (+gen) by, through, with, in, of, (+acc) for, because of, for a cause
αὐτοῦ pron. gen. masc. 3p. sg. αὐτός ή ό self, of oneself, even, very, the same, he, she, it
ἀπὸ prep. ἀπό (+gen) from, of, out of, since, for, off, at, by, in, on
τῆς art. gen. fem. sg. ὁ ἡ τό the, this, that, he, she, it
ὀργῆς n. gen. fem. sg. ὀργή wrath, anger, indignation, vengeance
10 εἰ conj. εἰ if, whether, that, though, forasmuch
γὰρ conj. γάρ for, and, because, but, indeed
ἐχθροὶ adj. nom. masc. pl. ἐχθρός enemy, foe
τῷ art. dat. masc. sg. ὁ ἡ τό the, this, that, he, she, it
Θεῷ n. dat. masc. sg. θεός God, god
διὰ prep. διά (+gen) by, through, with, in, of, (+acc) for, because of, for a cause
τοῦ art. gen. masc. sg. ὁ ἡ τό the, this, that, he, she, it
θανάτου n. gen. masc. sg. θάνατος death
τοῦ art. gen. masc. sg. ὁ ἡ τό the, this, that, he, she, it

υἱοῦ n. gen. masc. sg. υἱός son, child, descendant, offspring, heir
αὐτοῦ pron. gen. masc. 3p. sg. αὐτός ἡ ὁ self, of oneself, even, very, the same, he, she, it
πολλῷ adj. dat. neut. sg. πολύς many, great, much, long, abundant
μᾶλλον adv. μᾶλλον rather, more, more and more, better, much, much the more
ἐν prep. ἐν (+dat) in, by, with, among, at, on, through, to, within, into, of, for
τῇ art. dat. fem. sg. ὁ ἡ τό the, this, that, he, she, it
ζωῇ n. dat. fem. sg. ζωή life, lifetime
αὐτοῦ pron. gen. masc. 3p. sg. αὐτός ἡ ὁ self, of oneself, even, very, the same, he, she, it
11 οὐ particle of negation. οὐ οὐκ οὐχ not, no, neither, none, nay, nor, never, nothing
μόνον adv. μόνος only, alone, by oneself
δέ conj. δέ but, and, now, also, to the contrary, rather, then
ἀλλὰ conj. ἀλλά but, yea, yet, nevertheless, howbeit, nay, therefore
καὶ conj. καί and, even, also, but
ἐν prep. ἐν (+dat) in, by, with, among, at, on, through, to, within, into, of, for
τῷ art. dat. masc. sg. ὁ ἡ τό the, this, that, he, she, it
Θεῷ n. dat. masc. sg. θεός God, god
διὰ prep. διά (+gen) by, through, with, in, of, (+acc) for, because of, for a cause
τοῦ art. gen. masc. sg. ὁ ἡ τό the, this, that, he, she, it
Κυρίου n. gen. masc. sg. κύριος Lord, lord, master, sir, LORD, God, Master, owner
ἡμῶν pron. gen. 1p. pl. ἐγώ I
Ἰησοῦ n. gen. masc. sg. Ἰησοῦς Jesus
Χριστοῦ n. gen. masc. sg. Χριστός Christ
δι' prep. διά (+gen) by, through, with, in, of, (+acc) for, because of, for a cause
οὗ relative pron. gen. masc. sg. ὅς ἥ ὅ who, which, what, that
νῦν adv. νῦν now, henceforth, present, this time
τὴν art. acc. fem. sg. ὁ ἡ τό the, this, that, he, she, it
καταλλαγὴν n. acc. fem. sg. καταλλαγή reconciliation, atonement, reconciling
12 Διὰ prep. διά (+gen) by, through, with, in, of, (+acc) for, because of, for a cause
τοῦτο demo. pron. acc. neut. sg. οὗτος αὕτη τοῦτο this, the same, this same, he, she, it
ὥσπερ adv. ὥσπερ as, even as, like as
δι' prep. διά (+gen) by, through, with, in, of, (+acc) for, because of, for a cause
ἑνὸς num. gen. masc. sg. εἷς or ἕν one, other, some, any, only, a certain
ἀνθρώπου n. gen. masc. sg. ἄνθρωπος man, human being, person, one, certain
ἡ art. nom. fem. sg. ὁ ἡ τό the, this, that, he, she, it
ἁμαρτία n. nom. fem. sg. ἁμαρτία sin, offence, sinful
εἰς prep. εἰς (+acc) into, to, unto, for, in, on, toward, against, upon, at, among
τὸν art. acc. masc. sg. ὁ ἡ τό the, this, that, he, she, it
κόσμον n. acc. masc. sg. κόσμος world, adorning
καὶ conj. καί and, even, also, but
διὰ prep. διά (+gen) by, through, with, in, of, (+acc) for, because of, for a cause
τῆς art. gen. fem. sg. ὁ ἡ τό the, this, that, he, she, it
ἁμαρτίας n. gen. fem. sg. ἁμαρτία sin, offence, sinful
ὁ art. nom. masc. sg. ὁ ἡ τό the, this, that, he, she, it
θάνατος n. nom. masc. sg. θάνατος death
καὶ conj. καί and, even, also, but
οὕτως adv. οὕτω οὕτως so, even so, thus, on this wise, likewise, after this manner
εἰς prep. εἰς (+acc) into, to, unto, for, in, on, toward, against, upon, at, among
πάντας adj. acc. masc. pl. πᾶς πᾶσα πᾶν all, every, whosoever, every one, no, whole, any
ἀνθρώπους n. acc. masc. pl. ἄνθρωπος man, human being, person, one, certain
ὁ art. nom. masc. sg. ὁ ἡ τό the, this, that, he, she, it
θάνατος n. nom. masc. sg. θάνατος death
ἐφ' prep. ἐπί (+gen) on, in, upon, (+dat) in, at, for, upon, (+acc) on, upon, unto, to, against
ᾧ relative pron. dat. neut. sg. ὅς ἥ ὅ who, which, what, that
πάντες adj. nom. masc. pl. πᾶς πᾶσα πᾶν all, every, whosoever, every one, no, whole, any
13 ἄχρι prep. ἄχρι or ἄχρις (+gen) until, unto, till, even to, as far as, while, into

γὰρ conj. γάρ for, and, because, but, indeed
νόμου n. gen. masc. sg. νόμος law, the law
ἁμαρτία n. nom. fem. sg. ἁμαρτία sin, offence, sinful
ἐν prep. ἐν (+dat) in, by, with, among, at, on, through, to, within, into, of, for
κόσμῳ n. dat. masc. sg. κόσμος world, adorning
ἁμαρτία n. nom. fem. sg. ἁμαρτία sin, offence, sinful
δὲ conj. δέ but, and, now, also, to the contrary, rather, then
οὐκ particle of negation. οὐ οὐκ οὐχ not, no, neither, none, nay, nor, never, nothing
μὴ particle of negation. μή not, no, lest, neither, none, nothing, nor, never, without
νόμου n. gen. masc. sg. νόμος law, the law
14 ἀλλὰ conj. ἀλλά but, yea, yet, nevertheless, howbeit, nay, therefore
ὁ art. nom. masc. sg. ὁ ἡ τό the, this, that, he, she, it
θάνατος n. nom. masc. sg. θάνατος death
ἀπὸ prep. ἀπό (+gen) from, of, out of, since, for, off, at, by, in, on
'Αδὰμ n. gen. masc. sg. 'Αδάμ Adam
μέχρι prep. μέχρι until, unto, till, to
Μωσέως n. gen. masc. sg. Μωσῆς Moses
καὶ conj. καί and, even, also, but
ἐπὶ prep. ἐπί (+gen) on, in, upon, (+dat) in, at, for, upon, (+acc) on, upon, unto, to, against
τοὺς art. acc. masc. pl. ὁ ἡ τό the, this, that, he, she, it
μὴ particle of negation. μή not, no, lest, neither, none, nothing, nor, never, without
ἐπὶ prep. ἐπί (+gen) on, in, upon, (+dat) in, at, for, upon, (+acc) on, upon, unto, to, against
τῷ art. dat. neut. sg. ὁ ἡ τό the, this, that, he, she, it
ὁμοιώματι n. dat. neut. sg. ὁμοίωμα likeness, made like to, shape, similitude
τῆς art. gen. fem. sg. ὁ ἡ τό the, this, that, he, she, it
παραβάσεως n. gen. fem. sg. παράβασις breaking, transgression
'Αδὰμ n. gen. masc. sg. 'Αδάμ Adam
ὅς relative pron. nom. masc. sg. ὅς ἥ ὅ who, which, what, that
τύπος n. nom. masc. sg. τύπος ensample, example, pattern, print, figure, fashion
τοῦ art. gen. masc. sg. ὁ ἡ τό the, this, that, he, she, it
15 ἀλλ' conj. ἀλλά but, yea, yet, nevertheless, howbeit, nay, therefore
οὐχ particle of negation. οὐ οὐκ οὐχ not, no, neither, none, nay, nor, never, nothing
ὡς adv. ὡς as, when, as it were, how, about, like, as soon as, even as, while
τὸ art. nom. neut. sg. ὁ ἡ τό the, this, that, he, she, it
παράπτωμα n. nom. neut. sg. παράπτωμα trespass, offence, sin, fall, fault
οὕτω adv. οὕτω οὕτως so, even so, thus, on this wise, likewise, after this manner
καὶ conj. καί and, even, also, but
τὸ art. nom. neut. sg. ὁ ἡ τό the, this, that, he, she, it
χάρισμα n. nom. neut. sg. χάρισμα gift, free gift
εἰ conj. εἰ if, whether, that, though, forasmuch
γὰρ conj. γάρ for, and, because, but, indeed
τῷ art. dat. neut. sg. ὁ ἡ τό the, this, that, he, she, it
τοῦ art. gen. masc. sg. ὁ ἡ τό the, this, that, he, she, it
ἑνὸς num. gen. masc. sg. εἷς or ἕν one, other, some, any, only, a certain
παραπτώματι n. dat. neut. sg. παράπτωμα trespass, offence, sin, fall, fault
οἱ art. nom. masc. pl. ὁ ἡ τό the, this, that, he, she, it
πολλοὶ adj. nom. masc. pl. πολύς many, great, much, long, abundant
πολλῷ adj. dat. neut. sg. πολύς many, great, much, long, abundant
μᾶλλον adv. μᾶλλον rather, more, more and more, better, much, much the more
ἡ art. nom. fem. sg. ὁ ἡ τό the, this, that, he, she, it
χάρις n. nom. fem. sg. χάρις grace, thank, favour, pleasure
τοῦ art. gen. masc. sg. ὁ ἡ τό the, this, that, he, she, it
Θεοῦ n. gen. masc. sg. θεός God, god
καὶ conj. καί and, even, also, but
ἡ art. nom. fem. sg. ὁ ἡ τό the, this, that, he, she, it

δωρεὰ n. nom. fem. sg. δωρεά gift
ἐν prep. ἐν (+dat) in, by, with, among, at, on, through, to, within, into, of, for
χάριτι n. dat. fem. sg. χάρις grace, thank, favour, pleasure
τῇ art. dat. fem. sg. ὁ ἡ τό the, this, that, he, she, it
τοῦ art. gen. masc. sg. ὁ ἡ τό the, this, that, he, she, it
ἑνὸς num. gen. masc. sg. εἷς or ἕν one, other, some, any, only, a certain
ἀνθρώπου n. gen. masc. sg. ἄνθρωπος man, human being, person, one, certain
Ἰησοῦ n. gen. masc. sg. Ἰησοῦς Jesus
Χριστοῦ n. gen. masc. sg. Χριστός Christ
εἰς prep. εἰς (+acc) into, to, unto, for, in, on, toward, against, upon, at, among
τοὺς art. acc. masc. pl. ὁ ἡ τό the, this, that, he, she, it
πολλοὺς adj. acc. masc. pl. πολύς many, great, much, long, abundant
16 καὶ conj. καί and, even, also, but
οὐχ particle of negation. οὐ οὐκ οὐχ not, no, neither, none, nay, nor, never, nothing
ὡς adv. ὡς as, when, as it were, how, about, like, as soon as, even as, while
δι᾽ prep. διά (+gen) by, through, with, in, of, (+acc) for, because of, for a cause
ἑνὸς num. gen. masc. sg. εἷς or ἕν one, other, some, any, only, a certain
τὸ art. nom. neut. sg. ὁ ἡ τό the, this, that, he, she, it
δώρημα n. nom. neut. sg. δώρημα gift
τὸ art. nom. neut. sg. ὁ ἡ τό the, this, that, he, she, it
μὲν conj. μέν indeed, verily, truly, even, so, some
γὰρ conj. γάρ for, and, because, but, indeed
κρίμα n. nom. neut. sg. κρίμα judgment, damnation, condemnation
ἐξ prep. ἐκ ἐξ (+gen) of, from, out of, by, on, with, in, among, through
ἑνὸς num. gen. masc. sg. εἷς or ἕν one, other, some, any, only, a certain
εἰς prep. εἰς (+acc) into, to, unto, for, in, on, toward, against, upon, at, among
κατάκριμα n. acc. neut. sg. κατάκριμα condemnation
τὸ art. nom. neut. sg. ὁ ἡ τό the, this, that, he, she, it
δὲ conj. δέ but, and, now, also, to the contrary, rather, then
χάρισμα n. nom. neut. sg. χάρισμα gift, free gift
ἐκ prep. ἐκ ἐξ (+gen) of, from, out of, by, on, with, in, among, through
πολλῶν adj. gen. neut. pl. πολύς many, great, much, long, abundant
παραπτωμάτων n. gen. neut. pl. παράπτωμα trespass, offence, sin, fall, fault
εἰς prep. εἰς (+acc) into, to, unto, for, in, on, toward, against, upon, at, among
δικαίωμα n. acc. neut. sg. δικαίωμα ordinance, righteousness, judgement, justification
17 εἰ conj. εἰ if, whether, that, though, forasmuch
γὰρ conj. γάρ for, and, because, but, indeed
τῷ art. dat. neut. sg. ὁ ἡ τό the, this, that, he, she, it
τοῦ art. gen. masc. sg. ὁ ἡ τό the, this, that, he, she, it
ἑνὸς num. gen. masc. sg. εἷς or ἕν one, other, some, any, only, a certain
παραπτώματι n. dat. neut. sg. παράπτωμα trespass, offence, sin, fall, fault
ὁ art. nom. masc. sg. ὁ ἡ τό the, this, that, he, she, it
θάνατος n. nom. masc. sg. θάνατος death
διὰ prep. διά (+gen) by, through, with, in, of, (+acc) for, because of, for a cause
τοῦ art. gen. masc. sg. ὁ ἡ τό the, this, that, he, she, it
ἑνὸς num. gen. masc. sg. εἷς or ἕν one, other, some, any, only, a certain
πολλῷ adj. dat. neut. sg. πολύς many, great, much, long, abundant
μᾶλλον adv. μᾶλλον rather, more, more and more, better, much, much the more
οἱ art. nom. masc. pl. ὁ ἡ τό the, this, that, he, she, it
τὴν art. acc. fem. sg. ὁ ἡ τό the, this, that, he, she, it
περισσείαν n. acc. fem. sg. περισσεία abundance, abundant, superfluity
τῆς art. gen. fem. sg. ὁ ἡ τό the, this, that, he, she, it
χάριτος n. gen. fem. sg. χάρις grace, thank, favour, pleasure
καὶ conj. καί and, even, also, but
τῆς art. gen. fem. sg. ὁ ἡ τό the, this, that, he, she, it

δωρεᾶς n. gen. fem. sg. δωρεά gift
τῆς art. gen. fem. sg. ὁ ἡ τό the, this, that, he, she, it
δικαιοσύνης n. gen. fem. sg. δικαιοσύνη righteousness
ἐν prep. ἐν (+dat) in, by, with, among, at, on, through, to, within, into, of, for
ζωῇ n. dat. fem. sg. ζωή life, lifetime
διὰ prep. διά (+gen) by, through, with, in, of, (+acc) for, because of, for a cause
τοῦ art. gen. masc. sg. ὁ ἡ τό the, this, that, he, she, it
ἑνὸς num. gen. masc. sg. εἷς or ἕν one, other, some, any, only, a certain
Ἰησοῦ n. gen. masc. sg. Ἰησοῦς Jesus
Χριστοῦ n. gen. masc. sg. Χριστός Christ
18 ἄρα conj. ἄρα then, therefore, haply, wherefore, perhaps, manner, no doubt, truly
οὖν conj. οὖν therefore, then, so, and, now, wherefore
ὡς adv. ὡς as, when, as it were, how, about, like, as soon as, even as, while
δι' prep. διά (+gen) by, through, with, in, of, (+acc) for, because of, for a cause
ἑνὸς num. gen. masc. sg. εἷς or ἕν one, other, some, any, only, a certain
παραπτώματος n. gen. neut. sg. παράπτωμα trespass, offence, sin, fall, fault
εἰς prep. εἰς (+acc) into, to, unto, for, in, on, toward, against, upon, at, among
πάντας adj. acc. masc. pl. πᾶς πᾶσα πᾶν all, every, whosoever, every one, no, whole, any
ἀνθρώπους n. acc. masc. pl. ἄνθρωπος man, human being, person, one, certain
εἰς prep. εἰς (+acc) into, to, unto, for, in, on, toward, against, upon, at, among
κατάκριμα n. acc. neut. sg. κατάκριμα condemnation
οὕτω adv. οὕτω οὕτως so, even so, thus, on this wise, likewise, after this manner
καὶ conj. καί and, even, also, but
δι' prep. διά (+gen) by, through, with, in, of, (+acc) for, because of, for a cause
ἑνὸς num. gen. masc. sg. εἷς or ἕν one, other, some, any, only, a certain
δικαιώματος n. gen. neut. sg. δικαίωμα ordinance, righteousness, judgement, justification
εἰς prep. εἰς (+acc) into, to, unto, for, in, on, toward, against, upon, at, among
πάντας adj. acc. masc. pl. πᾶς πᾶσα πᾶν all, every, whosoever, every one, no, whole, any
ἀνθρώπους n. acc. masc. pl. ἄνθρωπος man, human being, person, one, certain
εἰς prep. εἰς (+acc) into, to, unto, for, in, on, toward, against, upon, at, among
δικαίωσιν n. acc. fem. sg. δικαίωσις justification
ζωῆς n. gen. fem. sg. ζωή life, lifetime
19 ὥσπερ adv. ὥσπερ as, even as, like as
γὰρ conj. γάρ for, and, because, but, indeed
διὰ prep. διά (+gen) by, through, with, in, of, (+acc) for, because of, for a cause
τῆς art. gen. fem. sg. ὁ ἡ τό the, this, that, he, she, it
παρακοῆς n. gen. fem. sg. παρακοή disobedience
τοῦ art. gen. masc. sg. ὁ ἡ τό the, this, that, he, she, it
ἑνὸς num. gen. masc. sg. εἷς or ἕν one, other, some, any, only, a certain
ἀνθρώπου n. gen. masc. sg. ἄνθρωπος man, human being, person, one, certain
ἁμαρτωλοὶ adj. nom. masc. pl. ἁμαρτωλός sinner, sinful
οἱ art. nom. masc. pl. ὁ ἡ τό the, this, that, he, she, it
πολλοί adj. nom. masc. pl. πολύς many, great, much, long, abundant
οὕτω adv. οὕτω οὕτως so, even so, thus, on this wise, likewise, after this manner
καὶ conj. καί and, even, also, but
διὰ prep. διά (+gen) by, through, with, in, of, (+acc) for, because of, for a cause
τῆς art. gen. fem. sg. ὁ ἡ τό the, this, that, he, she, it
ὑπακοῆς n. gen. fem. sg. ὑπακοή obedience, obey, make obedient, obedient
τοῦ art. gen. masc. sg. ὁ ἡ τό the, this, that, he, she, it
ἑνὸς num. gen. masc. sg. εἷς or ἕν one, other, some, any, only, a certain
δίκαιοι adj. nom. masc. pl. δίκαιος righteous, just, meet, right
οἱ art. nom. masc. pl. ὁ ἡ τό the, this, that, he, she, it
πολλοί adj. nom. masc. pl. πολύς many, great, much, long, abundant
20 νόμος n. nom. masc. sg. νόμος law, the law
δὲ conj. δέ but, and, now, also, to the contrary, rather, then

ἵνα conj. ἵνα that, to, lest, for to, so that, albeit, because, for, so as
τὸ art. nom. neut. sg. ὁ ἡ τό the, this, that, he, she, it
παράπτωμα n. nom. neut. sg. παράπτωμα trespass, offence, sin, fall, fault
οὗ adv. οὗ where, whither, wherein
δὲ conj. δέ but, and, now, also, to the contrary, rather, then
ἡ art. nom. fem. sg. ὁ ἡ τό the, this, that, he, she, it
ἁμαρτία n. nom. fem. sg. ἁμαρτία sin, offence, sinful
ἡ art. nom. fem. sg. ὁ ἡ τό the, this, that, he, she, it
χάρις n. nom. fem. sg. χάρις grace, thank, favour, pleasure
21 ἵνα conj. ἵνα that, to, lest, for to, so that, albeit, because, for, so as
ὥσπερ adv. ὥσπερ as, even as, like as
ἡ art. nom. fem. sg. ὁ ἡ τό the, this, that, he, she, it
ἁμαρτία n. nom. fem. sg. ἁμαρτία sin, offence, sinful
ἐν prep. ἐν (+dat) in, by, with, among, at, on, through, to, within, into, of, for
τῷ art. dat. masc. sg. ὁ ἡ τό the, this, that, he, she, it
θανάτῳ n. dat. masc. sg. θάνατος death
οὕτω adv. οὕτω οὕτως so, even so, thus, on this wise, likewise, after this manner
καὶ conj. καί and, even, also, but
ἡ art. nom. fem. sg. ὁ ἡ τό the, this, that, he, she, it
χάρις n. nom. fem. sg. χάρις grace, thank, favour, pleasure
διὰ prep. διά (+gen) by, through, with, in, of, (+acc) for, because of, for a cause
δικαιοσύνης n. gen. fem. sg. δικαιοσύνη righteousness
εἰς prep. εἰς (+acc) into, to, unto, for, in, on, toward, against, upon, at, among
ζωὴν n. acc. fem. sg. ζωή life, lifetime
αἰώνιον adj. acc. fem. sg. αἰώνιος eternal, everlasting, world, for ever
διὰ prep. διά (+gen) by, through, with, in, of, (+acc) for, because of, for a cause
Ἰησοῦ n. gen. masc. sg. Ἰησοῦς Jesus
Χριστοῦ n. gen. masc. sg. Χριστός Christ
τοῦ art. gen. masc. sg. ὁ ἡ τό the, this, that, he, she, it
Κυρίου n. gen. masc. sg. κύριος Lord, lord, master, sir, LORD, God, Master, owner
ἡμῶν pron. gen. 1p. pl. ἐγώ I

6

1 Τί interrog. pron. acc. neut. sg. τίς what, who, why, where, which, how
οὖν conj. οὖν therefore, then, so, and, now, wherefore
τῇ art. dat. fem. sg. ὁ ἡ τό the, this, that, he, she, it
ἁμαρτίᾳ n. dat. fem. sg. ἁμαρτία sin, offence, sinful
ἵνα conj. ἵνα that, to, lest, for to, so that, albeit, because, for, so as
ἡ art. nom. fem. sg. ὁ ἡ τό the, this, that, he, she, it
χάρις n. nom. fem. sg. χάρις grace, thank, favour, pleasure
2 μὴ particle of negation. μή not, no, lest, neither, none, nothing, nor, never, without
οἵτινες relative pron. nom. masc. pl. ὅστις which, who, whosoever, that, whatsoever
τῇ art. dat. fem. sg. ὁ ἡ τό the, this, that, he, she, it
ἁμαρτίᾳ n. dat. fem. sg. ἁμαρτία sin, offence, sinful
πῶς adv. πῶς how, by what means, after what manner
ἔτι adv. ἔτι yet, more, any more, further, still, moreover
ἐν prep. ἐν (+dat) in, by, with, among, at, on, through, to, within, into, of, for
αὐτῇ pron. dat. fem. 3p. sg. αὐτός ἡ ὁ self, of oneself, even, very, the same, he, she, it
3 ἢ particle. ἤ or, than, either, nor, or else, and, rather than
ὅτι conj. ὅτι that, for, because, how that, how, because that, for that, though
ὅσοι relative pron. nom. masc. pl. ὅσος as many as, whatsoever, that, as long as, how much
εἰς prep. εἰς (+acc) into, to, unto, for, in, on, toward, against, upon, at, among
Χριστὸν n. acc. masc. sg. Χριστός Christ
Ἰησοῦν n. acc. masc. sg. Ἰησοῦς Jesus

εἰς prep. εἰς (+acc) into, to, unto, for, in, on, toward, against, upon, at, among
τὸν art. acc. masc. sg. ὁ ἡ τό the, this, that, he, she, it
θάνατον n. acc. masc. sg. θάνατος death
αὐτοῦ pron. gen. masc. 3p. sg. αὐτός ή ό self, of oneself, even, very, the same, he, she, it
4 οὖν conj. οὖν therefore, then, so, and, now, wherefore
αὐτῷ pron. dat. masc. 3p. sg. αὐτός ή ό self, of oneself, even, very, the same, he, she, it
διὰ prep. διά (+gen) by, through, with, in, of, (+acc) for, because of, for a cause
τοῦ art. gen. neut. sg. ὁ ἡ τό the, this, that, he, she, it
βαπτίσματος n. gen. neut. sg. βάπτισμα baptism
εἰς prep. εἰς (+acc) into, to, unto, for, in, on, toward, against, upon, at, among
τὸν art. acc. masc. sg. ὁ ἡ τό the, this, that, he, she, it
θάνατον n. acc. masc. sg. θάνατος death
ἵνα conj. ἵνα that, to, lest, for to, so that, albeit, because, for, so as
ὥσπερ adv. ὥσπερ as, even as, like as
Χριστὸς n. nom. masc. sg. Χριστός Christ
ἐκ prep. ἐκ ἐξ (+gen) of, from, out of, by, on, with, in, among, through
νεκρῶν adj. gen. masc. pl. νεκρός dead
διὰ prep. διά (+gen) by, through, with, in, of, (+acc) for, because of, for a cause
τῆς art. gen. fem. sg. ὁ ἡ τό the, this, that, he, she, it
δόξης n. gen. fem. sg. δόξα glory, honour, praise, dignity, worship
τοῦ art. gen. masc. sg. ὁ ἡ τό the, this, that, he, she, it
πατρός n. gen. masc. sg. πατήρ Father, father, parent
οὕτω adv. οὕτω οὕτως so, even so, thus, on this wise, likewise, after this manner
καὶ conj. καί and, even, also, but
ἡμεῖς pron. nom. 1p. pl. ἐγώ I
ἐν prep. ἐν (+dat) in, by, with, among, at, on, through, to, within, into, of, for
καινότητι n. dat. fem. sg. καινότης newness
ζωῆς n. gen. fem. sg. ζωή life, lifetime
5 εἰ conj. εἰ if, whether, that, though, forasmuch
γὰρ conj. γάρ for, and, because, but, indeed
σύμφυτοι adj. nom. masc. pl. σύμφυτος plant together
τῷ art. dat. neut. sg. ὁ ἡ τό the, this, that, he, she, it
ὁμοιώματι n. dat. neut. sg. ὁμοίωμα likeness, made like to, shape, similitude
τοῦ art. gen. masc. sg. ὁ ἡ τό the, this, that, he, she, it
θανάτου n. gen. masc. sg. θάνατος death
αὐτοῦ pron. gen. masc. 3p. sg. αὐτός ή ό self, of oneself, even, very, the same, he, she, it
ἀλλὰ conj. ἀλλά but, yea, yet, nevertheless, howbeit, nay, therefore
καὶ conj. καί and, even, also, but
τῆς art. gen. fem. sg. ὁ ἡ τό the, this, that, he, she, it
ἀναστάσεως n. gen. fem. sg. ἀνάστασις resurrection, rising again
6 τοῦτο demo. pron. acc. neut. sg. οὗτος αὕτη τοῦτο this, the same, this same, he, she, it
ὅτι conj. ὅτι that, for, because, how that, how, because that, for that, though
ὁ art. nom. masc. sg. ὁ ἡ τό the, this, that, he, she, it
παλαιὸς adj. nom. masc. sg. παλαιός old
ἡμῶν pron. gen. 1p. pl. ἐγώ I
ἄνθρωπος n. nom. masc. sg. ἄνθρωπος man, human being, person, one, certain
ἵνα conj. ἵνα that, to, lest, for to, so that, albeit, because, for, so as
τὸ art. nom. neut. sg. ὁ ἡ τό the, this, that, he, she, it
σῶμα n. nom. neut. sg. σῶμα body, bodily, slave
τῆς art. gen. fem. sg. ὁ ἡ τό the, this, that, he, she, it
ἁμαρτίας n. gen. fem. sg. ἁμαρτία sin, offence, sinful
τοῦ art. gen. neut. sg. ὁ ἡ τό the, this, that, he, she, it
μηκέτι adv. μηκέτι no more, no longer, not any more, not henceforth, not henceforward
ἡμᾶς pron. acc. 1p. pl. ἐγώ I
τῇ art. dat. fem. sg. ὁ ἡ τό the, this, that, he, she, it

ἁμαρτίᾳ n. dat. fem. sg. ἁμαρτία sin, offence, sinful
7 ὁ art. nom. masc. sg. ὁ ἡ τό the, this, that, he, she, it
γὰρ conj. γάρ for, and, because, but, indeed
ἀπὸ prep. ἀπό (+gen) from, of, out of, since, for, off, at, by, in, on
τῆς art. gen. fem. sg. ὁ ἡ τό the, this, that, he, she, it
ἁμαρτίας n. gen. fem. sg. ἁμαρτία sin, offence, sinful
8 εἰ conj. εἰ if, whether, that, though, forasmuch
δὲ conj. δέ but, and, now, also, to the contrary, rather, then
σὺν prep. σύν (+dat) with, beside
Χριστῷ n. dat. masc. sg. Χριστός Christ
ὅτι conj. ὅτι that, for, because, how that, how, because that, for that, though
καὶ conj. καί and, even, also, but
αὐτῷ pron. dat. masc. 3p. sg. αὐτός ή ό self, of oneself, even, very, the same, he, she, it
9 ὅτι conj. ὅτι that, for, because, how that, how, because that, for that, though
Χριστὸς n. nom. masc. sg. Χριστός Christ
ἐκ prep. ἐκ ἐξ (+gen) of, from, out of, by, on, with, in, among, through
νεκρῶν adj. gen. masc. pl. νεκρός dead
οὐκέτι adv. οὐκέτι or οὐκ ἔτι no more, no longer, not any more
θάνατος n. nom. masc. sg. θάνατος death
αὐτοῦ pron. gen. masc. 3p. sg. αὐτός ή ό self, of oneself, even, very, the same, he, she, it
οὐκέτι adv. οὐκέτι or οὐκ ἔτι no more, no longer, not any more
10 ὃ relative pron. acc. neut. sg. ὅς ἥ ὅ who, which, what, that
γὰρ conj. γάρ for, and, because, but, indeed
τῇ art. dat. fem. sg. ὁ ἡ τό the, this, that, he, she, it
ἁμαρτίᾳ n. dat. fem. sg. ἁμαρτία sin, offence, sinful
ἐφάπαξ adv. ἐφάπαξ once, once for all
ὃ relative pron. acc. neut. sg. ὅς ἥ ὅ who, which, what, that
δὲ conj. δέ but, and, now, also, to the contrary, rather, then
τῷ art. dat. masc. sg. ὁ ἡ τό the, this, that, he, she, it
Θεῷ n. dat. masc. sg. θεός God, god
11 οὕτω adv. οὕτω οὕτως so, even so, thus, on this wise, likewise, after this manner
καὶ conj. καί and, even, also, but
ὑμεῖς pron. nom. 2p. pl. σύ thou, you
ἑαυτοὺς reflexive pron. acc. masc. 3p. pl. ἑαυτοῦ himself, herself, itself, yourself, ourselves
νεκροὺς adj. acc. masc. pl. νεκρός dead
μὲν conj. μέν indeed, verily, truly, even, so, some
τῇ art. dat. fem. sg. ὁ ἡ τό the, this, that, he, she, it
ἁμαρτίᾳ n. dat. fem. sg. ἁμαρτία sin, offence, sinful
δὲ conj. δέ but, and, now, also, to the contrary, rather, then
τῷ art. dat. masc. sg. ὁ ἡ τό the, this, that, he, she, it
Θεῷ n. dat. masc. sg. θεός God, god
ἐν prep. ἐν (+dat) in, by, with, among, at, on, through, to, within, into, of, for
Χριστῷ n. dat. masc. sg. Χριστός Christ
Ἰησοῦ n. dat. masc. sg. Ἰησοῦς Jesus
τῷ art. dat. masc. sg. ὁ ἡ τό the, this, that, he, she, it
Κυρίῳ n. dat. masc. sg. κύριος Lord, lord, master, sir, LORD, God, Master, owner
ἡμῶν pron. gen. 1p. pl. ἐγώ I
12 Μὴ particle of negation. μή not, no, lest, neither, none, nothing, nor, never, without
οὖν conj. οὖν therefore, then, so, and, now, wherefore
ἡ art. nom. fem. sg. ὁ ἡ τό the, this, that, he, she, it
ἁμαρτία n. nom. fem. sg. ἁμαρτία sin, offence, sinful
ἐν prep. ἐν (+dat) in, by, with, among, at, on, through, to, within, into, of, for
τῷ art. dat. neut. sg. ὁ ἡ τό the, this, that, he, she, it
θνητῷ adj. dat. neut. sg. θνητός mortal, mortality
ὑμῶν pron. gen. 2p. pl. σύ thou, you

σώματι n. dat. neut. sg. σῶμα body, bodily, slave
εἰς prep. εἰς (+acc) into, to, unto, for, in, on, toward, against, upon, at, among
τὸ art. acc. neut. sg. ὁ ἡ τό the, this, that, he, she, it
αὐτῇ pron. dat. fem. 3p. sg. αὐτός ή ὁ self, of oneself, even, very, the same, he, she, it
ἐν prep. ἐν (+dat) in, by, with, among, at, on, through, to, within, into, of, for
ταῖς art. dat. fem. pl. ὁ ἡ τό the, this, that, he, she, it
ἐπιθυμίαις n. dat. fem. pl. ἐπιθυμία lust, concupiscence, desire
αὐτοῦ pron. gen. neut. 3p. sg. αὐτός ή ὁ self, of oneself, even, very, the same, he, she, it
13 μηδὲ conj. μηδέ neither, nor, not, no not, nor yet, not once, not so much as
τὰ art. acc. neut. pl. ὁ ἡ τό the, this, that, he, she, it
μέλη n. acc. neut. pl. μέλος member
ὑμῶν pron. gen. 2p. pl. σύ thou, you
ὅπλα n. acc. neut. pl. ὅπλον instrument, armour, weapon
ἀδικίας n. gen. fem. sg. ἀδικία iniquity, unrighteousness, unjust, wrong
τῇ art. dat. fem. sg. ὁ ἡ τό the, this, that, he, she, it
ἁμαρτίᾳ n. dat. fem. sg. ἁμαρτία sin, offence, sinful
ἀλλὰ conj. ἀλλά but, yea, yet, nevertheless, howbeit, nay, therefore
ἑαυτοὺς reflexive pron. acc. masc. 3p. pl. ἑαυτοῦ himself, herself, itself, yourself, ourselves
τῷ art. dat. masc. sg. ὁ ἡ τό the, this, that, he, she, it
Θεῷ n. dat. masc. sg. θεός God, god
ὡς adv. ὡς as, when, as it were, how, about, like, as soon as, even as, while
ἐκ prep. ἐκ ἐξ (+gen) of, from, out of, by, on, with, in, among, through
νεκρῶν adj. gen. masc. pl. νεκρός dead
καὶ conj. καί and, even, also, but
τὰ art. acc. neut. pl. ὁ ἡ τό the, this, that, he, she, it
μέλη n. acc. neut. pl. μέλος member
ὑμῶν pron. gen. 2p. pl. σύ thou, you
ὅπλα n. acc. neut. pl. ὅπλον instrument, armour, weapon
δικαιοσύνης n. gen. fem. sg. δικαιοσύνη righteousness
τῷ art. dat. masc. sg. ὁ ἡ τό the, this, that, he, she, it
Θεῷ n. dat. masc. sg. θεός God, god
14 ἁμαρτία n. nom. fem. sg. ἁμαρτία sin, offence, sinful
γὰρ conj. γάρ for, and, because, but, indeed
ὑμῶν pron. gen. 2p. pl. σύ thou, you
οὐ particle of negation. οὐ οὐκ οὐχ not, no, neither, none, nay, nor, never, nothing
οὐ particle of negation. οὐ οὐκ οὐχ not, no, neither, none, nay, nor, never, nothing
γὰρ conj. γάρ for, and, because, but, indeed
ὑπὸ prep. ὑπό (+gen) of, by, with, from, among, (+acc) under
νόμον n. acc. masc. sg. νόμος law, the law
ἀλλ' conj. ἀλλά but, yea, yet, nevertheless, howbeit, nay, therefore
ὑπὸ prep. ὑπό (+gen) of, by, with, from, among, (+acc) under
χάριν n. acc. fem. sg. χάρις grace, thank, favour, pleasure
15 Τί interrog. pron. acc. neut. sg. τίς what, who, why, where, which, how
οὖν conj. οὖν therefore, then, so, and, now, wherefore
ὅτι conj. ὅτι that, for, because, how that, how, because that, for that, though
οὐκ particle of negation. οὐ οὐκ οὐχ not, no, neither, none, nay, nor, never, nothing
ὑπὸ prep. ὑπό (+gen) of, by, with, from, among, (+acc) under
νόμον n. acc. masc. sg. νόμος law, the law
ἀλλ' conj. ἀλλά but, yea, yet, nevertheless, howbeit, nay, therefore
ὑπὸ prep. ὑπό (+gen) of, by, with, from, among, (+acc) under
χάριν n. acc. fem. sg. χάρις grace, thank, favour, pleasure
μὴ particle of negation. μή not, no, lest, neither, none, nothing, nor, never, without
16 οὐκ particle of negation. οὐ οὐκ οὐχ not, no, neither, none, nay, nor, never, nothing
ὅτι conj. ὅτι that, for, because, how that, how, because that, for that, though
ᾧ relative pron. dat. masc. sg. ὅς ἥ ὅ who, which, what, that

ἑαυτοὺς reflexive pron. acc. masc. 3p. pl. ἑαυτοῦ himself, herself, itself, yourself, ourselves
δούλους n. acc. masc. pl. δοῦλος servant, bondman, bond, slave
εἰς prep. εἰς (+acc) into, to, unto, for, in, on, toward, against, upon, at, among
ὑπακοήν n. acc. fem. sg. ὑπακοή obedience, obey, make obedient, obedient
δοῦλοί n. nom. masc. pl. δοῦλος servant, bondman, bond, slave
ᾧ relative pron. dat. masc. sg. ὅς ἥ ὅ who, which, what, that
ἤτοι conj. ἤτοι whether
ἁμαρτίας n. gen. fem. sg. ἁμαρτία sin, offence, sinful
εἰς prep. εἰς (+acc) into, to, unto, for, in, on, toward, against, upon, at, among
θάνατον n. acc. masc. sg. θάνατος death
ἢ particle. ἤ or, than, either, nor, or else, and, rather than
ὑπακοῆς n. gen. fem. sg. ὑπακοή obedience, obey, make obedient, obedient
εἰς prep. εἰς (+acc) into, to, unto, for, in, on, toward, against, upon, at, among
δικαιοσύνην n. acc. fem. sg. δικαιοσύνη righteousness
17 χάρις n. nom. fem. sg. χάρις grace, thank, favour, pleasure
δὲ conj. δέ but, and, now, also, to the contrary, rather, then
τῷ art. dat. masc. sg. ὁ ἡ τό the, this, that, he, she, it
Θεῷ n. dat. masc. sg. θεός God, god
ὅτι conj. ὅτι that, for, because, how that, how, because that, for that, though
δοῦλοι n. nom. masc. pl. δοῦλος servant, bondman, bond, slave
τῆς art. gen. fem. sg. ὁ ἡ τό the, this, that, he, she, it
ἁμαρτίας n. gen. fem. sg. ἁμαρτία sin, offence, sinful
δὲ conj. δέ but, and, now, also, to the contrary, rather, then
ἐκ prep. ἐκ ἐξ (+gen) of, from, out of, by, on, with, in, among, through
καρδίας n. gen. fem. sg. καρδία heart
εἰς prep. εἰς (+acc) into, to, unto, for, in, on, toward, against, upon, at, among
ὃν relative pron. acc. masc. sg. ὅς ἥ ὅ who, which, what, that
τύπον n. acc. masc. sg. τύπος ensample, example, pattern, print, figure, fashion
διδαχῆς n. gen. fem. sg. διδαχή doctrine, teaching
18 δὲ conj. δέ but, and, now, also, to the contrary, rather, then
ἀπὸ prep. ἀπό (+gen) from, of, out of, since, for, off, at, by, in, on
τῆς art. gen. fem. sg. ὁ ἡ τό the, this, that, he, she, it
ἁμαρτίας n. gen. fem. sg. ἁμαρτία sin, offence, sinful
τῇ art. dat. fem. sg. ὁ ἡ τό the, this, that, he, she, it
δικαιοσύνῃ n. dat. fem. sg. δικαιοσύνη righteousness
19 ἀνθρώπινον adv. ἀνθρώπινος after the manner of men man, common to man
διὰ prep. διά (+gen) by, through, with, in, of, (+acc) for, because of, for a cause
τὴν art. acc. fem. sg. ὁ ἡ τό the, this, that, he, she, it
ἀσθένειαν n. acc. fem. sg. ἀσθένεια infirmity, weakness, disease, sickness
τῆς art. gen. fem. sg. ὁ ἡ τό the, this, that, he, she, it
σαρκὸς n. gen. fem. sg. σάρξ flesh, carnal
ὑμῶν pron. gen. 2p. pl. σύ thou, you
ὥσπερ adv. ὥσπερ as, even as, like as
γὰρ conj. γάρ for, and, because, but, indeed
τὰ art. acc. neut. pl. ὁ ἡ τό the, this, that, he, she, it
μέλη n. acc. neut. pl. μέλος member
ὑμῶν pron. gen. 2p. pl. σύ thou, you
δοῦλα adj. acc. neut. pl. δοῦλος servant, bondman, bond, slave
τῇ art. dat. fem. sg. ὁ ἡ τό the, this, that, he, she, it
ἀκαθαρσίᾳ n. dat. fem. sg. ἀκαθαρσία uncleanness
καὶ conj. καί and, even, also, but
τῇ art. dat. fem. sg. ὁ ἡ τό the, this, that, he, she, it
ἀνομίᾳ n. dat. fem. sg. ἀνομία iniquity, transgression of the law, lawlessness
εἰς prep. εἰς (+acc) into, to, unto, for, in, on, toward, against, upon, at, among
τὴν art. acc. fem. sg. ὁ ἡ τό the, this, that, he, she, it

ἀνομίαν n. acc. fem. sg. ἀνομία iniquity, transgression of the law, lawlessness
οὕτω adv. οὕτω οὕτως so, even so, thus, on this wise, likewise, after this manner
νῦν adv. νῦν now, henceforth, present, this time
τὰ art. acc. neut. pl. ὁ ἡ τό the, this, that, he, she, it
μέλη n. acc. neut. pl. μέλος member
ὑμῶν pron. gen. 2p. pl. σύ thou, you
δοῦλα adj. acc. neut. pl. δοῦλος servant, bondman, bond, slave
τῇ art. dat. fem. sg. ὁ ἡ τό the, this, that, he, she, it
δικαιοσύνῃ n. dat. fem. sg. δικαιοσύνη righteousness
εἰς prep. εἰς (+acc) into, to, unto, for, in, on, toward, against, upon, at, among
ἁγιασμόν n. acc. masc. sg. ἁγιασμός holiness, sanctification
20 ὅτε adv. ὅτε when, after that, as soon as, while, after
γὰρ conj. γάρ for, and, because, but, indeed
δοῦλοι n. nom. masc. pl. δοῦλος servant, bondman, bond, slave
τῆς art. gen. fem. sg. ὁ ἡ τό the, this, that, he, she, it
ἁμαρτίας n. gen. fem. sg. ἁμαρτία sin, offence, sinful
ἐλεύθεροι adj. nom. masc. pl. ἐλεύθερος free, freewoman, at liberty, freeman
τῇ art. dat. fem. sg. ὁ ἡ τό the, this, that, he, she, it
δικαιοσύνῃ n. dat. fem. sg. δικαιοσύνη righteousness
21 τίνα interrog. pron. acc. masc. sg. τίς what, who, why, where, which, how
οὖν conj. οὖν therefore, then, so, and, now, wherefore
καρπὸν n. acc. masc. sg. καρπός fruit
τότε adv. τότε then, that time
ἐφ' prep. ἐπί (+gen) on, in, upon, (+dat) in, at, for, upon, (+acc) on, upon, unto, to, against
οἷς relative pron. dat. neut. pl. ὅς ἥ ὅ who, which, what, that
νῦν adv. νῦν now, henceforth, present, this time
τὸ art. nom. neut. sg. ὁ ἡ τό the, this, that, he, she, it
γὰρ conj. γάρ for, and, because, but, indeed
τέλος n. nom. neut. sg. τέλος end, custom, ending, finally, uttermost
ἐκείνων demo. pron. gen. masc. pl. ἐκεῖνος that, he, the same, that same
θάνατος n. nom. masc. sg. θάνατος death
22 νυνὶ adv. νυνί now
δὲ conj. δέ but, and, now, also, to the contrary, rather, then
ἀπὸ prep. ἀπό (+gen) from, of, out of, since, for, off, at, by, in, on
τῆς art. gen. fem. sg. ὁ ἡ τό the, this, that, he, she, it
ἁμαρτίας n. gen. fem. sg. ἁμαρτία sin, offence, sinful
δὲ conj. δέ but, and, now, also, to the contrary, rather, then
τῷ art. dat. masc. sg. ὁ ἡ τό the, this, that, he, she, it
Θεῷ n. dat. masc. sg. θεός God, god
τὸν art. acc. masc. sg. ὁ ἡ τό the, this, that, he, she, it
καρπὸν n. acc. masc. sg. καρπός fruit
ὑμῶν pron. gen. 2p. pl. σύ thou, you
εἰς prep. εἰς (+acc) into, to, unto, for, in, on, toward, against, upon, at, among
ἁγιασμόν n. acc. masc. sg. ἁγιασμός holiness, sanctification
τὸ art. acc. neut. sg. ὁ ἡ τό the, this, that, he, she, it
δὲ conj. δέ but, and, now, also, to the contrary, rather, then
τέλος n. acc. neut. sg. τέλος end, custom, ending, finally, uttermost
ζωὴν n. acc. fem. sg. ζωή life, lifetime
αἰώνιον adj. acc. fem. sg. αἰώνιος eternal, everlasting, world, for ever
23 τὰ art. nom. neut. pl. ὁ ἡ τό the, this, that, he, she, it
γὰρ conj. γάρ for, and, because, but, indeed
ὀψώνια n. nom. neut. pl. ὀψώνιον wage, charge
τῆς art. gen. fem. sg. ὁ ἡ τό the, this, that, he, she, it
ἁμαρτίας n. gen. fem. sg. ἁμαρτία sin, offence, sinful
θάνατος n. nom. masc. sg. θάνατος death

τὸ art. nom. neut. sg. ὁ ἡ τό the, this, that, he, she, it
δὲ conj. δέ but, and, now, also, to the contrary, rather, then
χάρισμα n. nom. neut. sg. χάρισμα gift, free gift
τοῦ art. gen. masc. sg. ὁ ἡ τό the, this, that, he, she, it
Θεοῦ n. gen. masc. sg. θεός God, god
ζωὴ n. nom. fem. sg. ζωή life, lifetime
αἰώνιος adj. nom. fem. sg. αἰώνιος eternal, everlasting, world, for ever
ἐν prep. ἐν (+dat) in, by, with, among, at, on, through, to, within, into, of, for
Χριστῷ n. dat. masc. sg. Χριστός Christ
Ἰησοῦ n. dat. masc. sg. Ἰησοῦς Jesus
τῷ art. dat. masc. sg. ὁ ἡ τό the, this, that, he, she, it
Κυρίῳ n. dat. masc. sg. κύριος Lord, lord, master, sir, LORD, God, Master, owner
ἡμῶν pron. gen. 1p. pl. ἐγώ I

7

1 Ἢ conj. ἤ or, than, either, nor, or else, and, rather than
ἀδελφοί n. voc. masc. pl. ἀδελφός brother
γὰρ conj. γάρ for, and, because, but, indeed
νόμον n. acc. masc. sg. νόμος law, the law
ὅτι conj. ὅτι that, for, because, how that, how, because that, for that, though
ὁ art. nom. masc. sg. ὁ ἡ τό the, this, that, he, she, it
νόμος n. nom. masc. sg. νόμος law, the law
τοῦ art. gen. masc. sg. ὁ ἡ τό the, this, that, he, she, it
ἀνθρώπου n. gen. masc. sg. ἄνθρωπος man, human being, person, one, certain
ἐφ' prep. ἐπί (+gen) on, in, upon, (+dat) in, at, for, upon, (+acc) on, upon, unto, to, against
ὅσον relative pron. acc. masc. sg. ὅσος as many as, whatsoever, that, as long as, how much
χρόνον n. acc. masc. sg. χρόνος time, season, space
2 ἡ art. nom. fem. sg. ὁ ἡ τό the, this, that, he, she, it
γὰρ conj. γάρ for, and, because, but, indeed
ὕπανδρος adj. nom. fem. sg. ὕπανδρος which has an husband
γυνὴ n. nom. fem. sg. γυνή woman, wife
τῷ art. dat. masc. sg. ὁ ἡ τό the, this, that, he, she, it
ἀνδρὶ n. dat. masc. sg. ἀνήρ man, husband, sir
νόμῳ n. dat. masc. sg. νόμος law, the law
ἐὰν conj. ἐάν if, soever, except, though, and if, but, whether, if so, so
δὲ conj. δέ but, and, now, also, to the contrary, rather, then
ὁ art. nom. masc. sg. ὁ ἡ τό the, this, that, he, she, it
ἀνήρ n. nom. masc. sg. ἀνήρ man, husband, sir
ἀπὸ prep. ἀπό (+gen) from, of, out of, since, for, off, at, by, in, on
τοῦ art. gen. masc. sg. ὁ ἡ τό the, this, that, he, she, it
νόμου n. gen. masc. sg. νόμος law, the law
τοῦ art. gen. masc. sg. ὁ ἡ τό the, this, that, he, she, it
ἀνδρός n. gen. masc. sg. ἀνήρ man, husband, sir
3 ἄρα conj. ἄρα then, therefore, haply, wherefore, perhaps, manner, no doubt, truly
οὖν conj. οὖν therefore, then, so, and, now, wherefore
τοῦ art. gen. masc. sg. ὁ ἡ τό the, this, that, he, she, it
ἀνδρὸς n. gen. masc. sg. ἀνήρ man, husband, sir
μοιχαλὶς adj. nom. fem. sg. μοιχαλίς adulterous, adulteress, adultery
ἐὰν conj. ἐάν if, soever, except, though, and if, but, whether, if so, so
ἀνδρὶ n. dat. masc. sg. ἀνήρ man, husband, sir
ἑτέρῳ adj. dat. masc. sg. ἕτερος another, other, else, strange
ἐὰν conj. ἐάν if, soever, except, though, and if, but, whether, if so, so
δὲ conj. δέ but, and, now, also, to the contrary, rather, then
ὁ art. nom. masc. sg. ὁ ἡ τό the, this, that, he, she, it

ἀνήρ n. nom. masc. sg. ἀνήρ man, husband, sir
ἐλευθέρα adj. nom. fem. sg. ἐλεύθερος free, freewoman, at liberty, freeman
ἀπὸ prep. ἀπό (+gen) from, of, out of, since, for, off, at, by, in, on
τοῦ art. gen. masc. sg. ὁ ἡ τό the, this, that, he, she, it
νόμου n. gen. masc. sg. νόμος law, the law
τοῦ art. gen. neut. sg. ὁ ἡ τό the, this, that, he, she, it
μὴ particle of negation. μή not, no, lest, neither, none, nothing, nor, never, without
αὐτὴν pron. acc. fem. 3p. sg. αὐτός ἡ ὁ self, of oneself, even, very, the same, he, she, it
μοιχαλίδα adj. acc. fem. sg. μοιχαλίς adulterous, adulteress, adultery
ἀνδρὶ n. dat. masc. sg. ἀνήρ man, husband, sir
ἑτέρῳ adj. dat. masc. sg. ἕτερος another, other, else, strange
4 ὥστε conj. ὥστε so that, wherefore, insomuch that, therefore, that, so then
ἀδελφοί n. voc. masc. pl. ἀδελφός brother
μου pron. gen. 1p. sg. ἐγώ I
καὶ conj. καί and, even, also, but
ὑμεῖς pron. nom. 2p. pl. σύ thou, you
τῷ art. dat. masc. sg. ὁ ἡ τό the, this, that, he, she, it
νόμῳ n. dat. masc. sg. νόμος law, the law
διὰ prep. διά (+gen) by, through, with, in, of, (+acc) for, because of, for a cause
τοῦ art. gen. neut. sg. ὁ ἡ τό the, this, that, he, she, it
σώματος n. gen. neut. sg. σῶμα body, bodily, slave
τοῦ art. gen. masc. sg. ὁ ἡ τό the, this, that, he, she, it
Χριστοῦ n. gen. masc. sg. Χριστός Christ
εἰς prep. εἰς (+acc) into, to, unto, for, in, on, toward, against, upon, at, among
τὸ art. acc. neut. sg. ὁ ἡ τό the, this, that, he, she, it
ὑμᾶς pron. acc. 2p. pl. σύ thou, you
ἑτέρῳ adj. dat. masc. sg. ἕτερος another, other, else, strange
τῷ art. dat. masc. sg. ὁ ἡ τό the, this, that, he, she, it
ἐκ prep. ἐκ ἐξ (+gen) of, from, out of, by, on, with, in, among, through
νεκρῶν adj. gen. masc. pl. νεκρός dead
ἵνα conj. ἵνα that, to, lest, for to, so that, albeit, because, for, so as
τῷ art. dat. masc. sg. ὁ ἡ τό the, this, that, he, she, it
Θεῷ n. dat. masc. sg. θεός God, god
5 ὅτε adv. ὅτε when, after that, as soon as, while, after
γὰρ conj. γάρ for, and, because, but, indeed
ἐν prep. ἐν (+dat) in, by, with, among, at, on, through, to, within, into, of, for
τῇ art. dat. fem. sg. ὁ ἡ τό the, this, that, he, she, it
σαρκί n. dat. fem. sg. σάρξ flesh, carnal
τὰ art. nom. neut. pl. ὁ ἡ τό the, this, that, he, she, it
παθήματα n. nom. neut. pl. πάθημα suffering, affliction, affection, motion
τῶν art. gen. fem. pl. ὁ ἡ τό the, this, that, he, she, it
ἁμαρτιῶν n. gen. fem. pl. ἁμαρτία sin, offence, sinful
τὰ art. nom. neut. pl. ὁ ἡ τό the, this, that, he, she, it
διὰ prep. διά (+gen) by, through, with, in, of, (+acc) for, because of, for a cause
τοῦ art. gen. masc. sg. ὁ ἡ τό the, this, that, he, she, it
νόμου n. gen. masc. sg. νόμος law, the law
ἐν prep. ἐν (+dat) in, by, with, among, at, on, through, to, within, into, of, for
τοῖς art. dat. neut. pl. ὁ ἡ τό the, this, that, he, she, it
μέλεσιν n. dat. neut. pl. μέλος member
ἡμῶν pron. gen. 1p. pl. ἐγώ I
εἰς prep. εἰς (+acc) into, to, unto, for, in, on, toward, against, upon, at, among
τὸ art. acc. neut. sg. ὁ ἡ τό the, this, that, he, she, it
τῷ art. dat. masc. sg. ὁ ἡ τό the, this, that, he, she, it
θανάτῳ n. dat. masc. sg. θάνατος death
6 νυνὶ adv. νυνί now

δὲ conj. δέ but, and, now, also, to the contrary, rather, then
ἀπὸ prep. ἀπό (+gen) from, of, out of, since, for, off, at, by, in, on
τοῦ art. gen. masc. sg. ὁ ἡ τό the, this, that, he, she, it
νόμου n. gen. masc. sg. νόμος law, the law
ἐν prep. ἐν (+dat) in, by, with, among, at, on, through, to, within, into, of, for
ᾧ relative pron. dat. masc. sg. ὅς ἥ ὅ who, which, what, that
ὥστε conj. ὥστε so that, wherefore, insomuch that, therefore, that, so then
ἡμᾶς pron. acc. 1p. pl. ἐγώ I
ἐν prep. ἐν (+dat) in, by, with, among, at, on, through, to, within, into, of, for
καινότητι n. dat. fem. sg. καινότης newness
πνεύματος n. gen. neut. sg. πνεῦμα spirit, Spirit, Ghost, ghost, life. of the spirit, wind
καὶ conj. καί and, even, also, but
οὐ particle of negation. οὐ οὐκ οὐχ not, no, neither, none, nay, nor, never, nothing
παλαιότητι n. dat. fem. sg. παλαιότης oldness
γράμματος n. gen. neut. sg. γράμμα letter, bill, learning, scripture, writing
7 Τί interrog. pron. acc. neut. sg. τίς what, who, why, where, which, how
οὖν conj. οὖν therefore, then, so, and, now, wherefore
ὁ art. nom. masc. sg. ὁ ἡ τό the, this, that, he, she, it
νόμος n. nom. masc. sg. νόμος law, the law
ἁμαρτία n. nom. fem. sg. ἁμαρτία sin, offence, sinful
μὴ particle of negation. μή not, no, lest, neither, none, nothing, nor, never, without
ἀλλὰ conj. ἀλλά but, yea, yet, nevertheless, howbeit, nay, therefore
τὴν art. acc. fem. sg. ὁ ἡ τό the, this, that, he, she, it
ἁμαρτίαν n. acc. fem. sg. ἁμαρτία sin, offence, sinful
οὐκ particle of negation. οὐ οὐκ οὐχ not, no, neither, none, nay, nor, never, nothing
εἰ conj. εἰ if, whether, that, though, forasmuch
μὴ particle of negation. μή not, no, lest, neither, none, nothing, nor, never, without
διὰ prep. διά (+gen) by, through, with, in, of, (+acc) for, because of, for a cause
νόμου n. gen. masc. sg. νόμος law, the law
τήν art. acc. fem. sg. ὁ ἡ τό the, this, that, he, she, it
τε conj. τέ and, both, also
γὰρ conj. γάρ for, and, because, but, indeed
ἐπιθυμίαν n. acc. fem. sg. ἐπιθυμία lust, concupiscence, desire
οὐκ particle of negation. οὐ οὐκ οὐχ not, no, neither, none, nay, nor, never, nothing
εἰ conj. εἰ if, whether, that, though, forasmuch
μὴ particle of negation. μή not, no, lest, neither, none, nothing, nor, never, without
ὁ art. nom. masc. sg. ὁ ἡ τό the, this, that, he, she, it
νόμος n. nom. masc. sg. νόμος law, the law
Οὐκ particle of negation. οὐ οὐκ οὐχ not, no, neither, none, nay, nor, never, nothing
8 ἀφορμὴν n. acc. fem. sg. ἀφορμή occasion
δὲ conj. δέ but, and, now, also, to the contrary, rather, then
ἡ art. nom. fem. sg. ὁ ἡ τό the, this, that, he, she, it
ἁμαρτία n. nom. fem. sg. ἁμαρτία sin, offence, sinful
διὰ prep. διά (+gen) by, through, with, in, of, (+acc) for, because of, for a cause
τῆς art. gen. fem. sg. ὁ ἡ τό the, this, that, he, she, it
ἐντολῆς n. gen. fem. sg. ἐντολή commandment, precept
ἐν prep. ἐν (+dat) in, by, with, among, at, on, through, to, within, into, of, for
ἐμοὶ pron. dat. 1p. sg. ἐγώ I
πᾶσαν adj. acc. fem. sg. πᾶς πᾶσα πᾶν all, every, whosoever, every one, no, whole, any
ἐπιθυμίαν n. acc. fem. sg. ἐπιθυμία lust, concupiscence, desire
χωρὶς prep. χωρίς (+gen) without, beside. (adv.) by itself, apart, separately
γὰρ conj. γάρ for, and, because, but, indeed
νόμου n. gen. masc. sg. νόμος law, the law
ἁμαρτία n. nom. fem. sg. ἁμαρτία sin, offence, sinful
νεκρά adj. nom. fem. sg. νεκρός dead

9 ἐγὼ pron. nom. 1p. sg. ἐγώ I
δὲ conj. δέ but, and, now, also, to the contrary, rather, then
χωρὶς prep. χωρίς (+gen) without, beside. (adv.) by itself, apart, separately
νόμου n. gen. masc. sg. νόμος law, the law
ποτέ adv. ποτέ in time past, at any time, sometimes, in old time, once, when
δὲ conj. δέ but, and, now, also, to the contrary, rather, then
τῆς art. gen. fem. sg. ὁ ἡ τό the, this, that, he, she, it
ἐντολῆς n. gen. fem. sg. ἐντολή commandment, precept
ἡ art. nom. fem. sg. ὁ ἡ τό the, this, that, he, she, it
ἁμαρτία n. nom. fem. sg. ἁμαρτία sin, offence, sinful
10 ἐγὼ pron. nom. 1p. sg. ἐγώ I
δὲ conj. δέ but, and, now, also, to the contrary, rather, then
καὶ conj. καί and, even, also, but
μοι pron. dat. 1p. sg. ἐγώ I
ἡ art. nom. fem. sg. ὁ ἡ τό the, this, that, he, she, it
ἐντολὴ n. nom. fem. sg. ἐντολή commandment, precept
ἡ art. nom. fem. sg. ὁ ἡ τό the, this, that, he, she, it
εἰς prep. εἰς (+acc) into, to, unto, for, in, on, toward, against, upon, at, among
ζωὴν n. acc. fem. sg. ζωή life, lifetime
αὕτη demo. pron. nom. fem. sg. οὗτος αὕτη τοῦτο this, the same, this same, he, she, it
εἰς prep. εἰς (+acc) into, to, unto, for, in, on, toward, against, upon, at, among
θάνατον n. acc. masc. sg. θάνατος death
11 ἡ art. nom. fem. sg. ὁ ἡ τό the, this, that, he, she, it
γὰρ conj. γάρ for, and, because, but, indeed
ἁμαρτία n. nom. fem. sg. ἁμαρτία sin, offence, sinful
ἀφορμὴν n. acc. fem. sg. ἀφορμή occasion
διὰ prep. διά (+gen) by, through, with, in, of, (+acc) for, because of, for a cause
τῆς art. gen. fem. sg. ὁ ἡ τό the, this, that, he, she, it
ἐντολῆς n. gen. fem. sg. ἐντολή commandment, precept
με pron. acc. 1p. sg. ἐγώ I
καὶ conj. καί and, even, also, but
δι᾽ prep. διά (+gen) by, through, with, in, of, (+acc) for, because of, for a cause
αὐτῆς pron. gen. fem. 3p. sg. αὐτός ἡ ό self, of oneself, even, very, the same, he, she, it
12 ὥστε conj. ὥστε so that, wherefore, insomuch that, therefore, that, so then
ὁ art. nom. masc. sg. ὁ ἡ τό the, this, that, he, she, it
μὲν conj. μέν indeed, verily, truly, even, so, some
νόμος n. nom. masc. sg. νόμος law, the law
ἅγιος adj. nom. masc. sg. ἅγιος Holy, holy, saint, Holy One, holy thing, most holy
καὶ conj. καί and, even, also, but
ἡ art. nom. fem. sg. ὁ ἡ τό the, this, that, he, she, it
ἐντολὴ n. nom. fem. sg. ἐντολή commandment, precept
ἁγία adj. nom. fem. sg. ἅγιος Holy, holy, saint, Holy One, holy thing, most holy
καὶ conj. καί and, even, also, but
δικαία adj. nom. fem. sg. δίκαιος righteous, just, meet, right
καὶ conj. καί and, even, also, but
ἀγαθή adj. nom. fem. sg. ἀγαθός good, good thing, that which is good, well
13 τὸ art. nom. neut. sg. ὁ ἡ τό the, this, that, he, she, it
οὖν conj. οὖν therefore, then, so, and, now, wherefore
ἀγαθὸν adj. nom. neut. sg. ἀγαθός good, good thing, that which is good, well
ἐμοὶ pron. dat. 1p. sg. ἐγώ I
θάνατος n. nom. masc. sg. θάνατος death
μὴ particle of negation. μή not, no, lest, neither, none, nothing, nor, never, without
ἀλλὰ conj. ἀλλά but, yea, yet, nevertheless, howbeit, nay, therefore
ἡ art. nom. fem. sg. ὁ ἡ τό the, this, that, he, she, it
ἁμαρτία n. nom. fem. sg. ἁμαρτία sin, offence, sinful

ἵνα conj. ἵνα that, to, lest, for to, so that, albeit, because, for, so as
ἁμαρτία n. nom. fem. sg. ἁμαρτία sin, offence, sinful
διὰ prep. διά (+gen) by, through, with, in, of, (+acc) for, because of, for a cause
τοῦ art. gen. neut. sg. ὁ ἡ τό the, this, that, he, she, it
ἀγαθοῦ adj. gen. neut. sg. ἀγαθός good, good thing, that which is good, well
μοι pron. dat. 1p. sg. ἐγώ I
θάνατον n. acc. masc. sg. θάνατος death
ἵνα conj. ἵνα that, to, lest, for to, so that, albeit, because, for, so as
καθ' prep. κατά (+gen) against, by, throughout, down, (+acc) according to, after, with
ὑπερβολὴν n. acc. fem. sg. ὑπερβολή abundance, beyond measure, exceeding, excellency
ἁμαρτωλὸς adj. nom. fem. sg. ἁμαρτωλός sinner, sinful
ἡ art. nom. fem. sg. ὁ ἡ τό the, this, that, he, she, it
ἁμαρτία n. nom. fem. sg. ἁμαρτία sin, offence, sinful
διὰ prep. διά (+gen) by, through, with, in, of, (+acc) for, because of, for a cause
τῆς art. gen. fem. sg. ὁ ἡ τό the, this, that, he, she, it
ἐντολῆς n. gen. fem. sg. ἐντολή commandment, precept
14 γὰρ conj. γάρ for, and, because, but, indeed
ὅτι conj. ὅτι that, for, because, how that, how, because that, for that, though
ὁ art. nom. masc. sg. ὁ ἡ τό the, this, that, he, she, it
νόμος n. nom. masc. sg. νόμος law, the law
πνευματικός adj. nom. masc. sg. πνευματικός spiritual
ἐγὼ pron. nom. 1p. sg. ἐγώ I
δὲ conj. δέ but, and, now, also, to the contrary, rather, then
σαρκικός adj. nom. masc. sg. σαρκιός carnal, fleshly
ὑπὸ prep. ὑπό (+gen) of, by, with, from, among, (+acc) under
τὴν art. acc. fem. sg. ὁ ἡ τό the, this, that, he, she, it
ἁμαρτίαν n. acc. fem. sg. ἁμαρτία sin, offence, sinful
15 ὃ relative pron. acc. neut. sg. ὅς ἥ ὅ who, which, what, that
γὰρ conj. γάρ for, and, because, but, indeed
οὐ particle of negation. οὐ οὐκ οὐχ not, no, neither, none, nay, nor, never, nothing
οὐ particle of negation. οὐ οὐκ οὐχ not, no, neither, none, nay, nor, never, nothing
γὰρ conj. γάρ for, and, because, but, indeed
ὃ relative pron. acc. neut. sg. ὅς ἥ ὅ who, which, what, that
τοῦτο demo. pron. acc. neut. sg. οὗτος αὕτη τοῦτο this, the same, this same, he, she, it
ἀλλ' conj. ἀλλά but, yea, yet, nevertheless, howbeit, nay, therefore
ὃ relative pron. acc. neut. sg. ὅς ἥ ὅ who, which, what, that
τοῦτο demo. pron. acc. neut. sg. οὗτος αὕτη τοῦτο this, the same, this same, he, she, it
16 εἰ conj. εἰ if, whether, that, though, forasmuch
δὲ conj. δέ but, and, now, also, to the contrary, rather, then
ὃ relative pron. acc. neut. sg. ὅς ἥ ὅ who, which, what, that
οὐ particle of negation. οὐ οὐκ οὐχ not, no, neither, none, nay, nor, never, nothing
τοῦτο demo. pron. acc. neut. sg. οὗτος αὕτη τοῦτο this, the same, this same, he, she, it
τῷ art. dat. masc. sg. ὁ ἡ τό the, this, that, he, she, it
νόμῳ n. dat. masc. sg. νόμος law, the law
ὅτι conj. ὅτι that, for, because, how that, how, because that, for that, though
καλός adj. nom. masc. sg. καλός good, better, goodly, meet, honest, fair, well, worthy
17 νυνὶ adv. νυνί now
δὲ conj. δέ but, and, now, also, to the contrary, rather, then
οὐκέτι adv. οὐκέτι or οὐκ ἔτι no more, no longer, not any more
ἐγὼ pron. nom. 1p. sg. ἐγώ I
αὐτὸ pron. acc. neut. 3p. sg. αὐτός ή ό self, of oneself, even, very, the same, he, she, it
ἀλλ' conj. ἀλλά but, yea, yet, nevertheless, howbeit, nay, therefore
ἡ art. nom. fem. sg. ὁ ἡ τό the, this, that, he, she, it
ἐν prep. ἐν (+dat) in, by, with, among, at, on, through, to, within, into, of, for
ἐμοὶ pron. dat. 1p. sg. ἐγώ I

ἁμαρτία n. nom. fem. sg. ἁμαρτία sin, offence, sinful
18 γὰρ conj. γάρ for, and, because, but, indeed
ὅτι conj. ὅτι that, for, because, how that, how, because that, for that, though
οὐκ particle of negation. οὐ οὐκ οὐχ not, no, neither, none, nay, nor, never, nothing
ἐν prep. ἐν (+dat) in, by, with, among, at, on, through, to, within, into, of, for
ἐμοί pron. dat. 1p. sg. ἐγώ I
τοῦτ' demo. pron. nom. neut. sg. οὗτος αὕτη τοῦτο this, the same, this same, he, she, it
ἐν prep. ἐν (+dat) in, by, with, among, at, on, through, to, within, into, of, for
τῇ art. dat. fem. sg. ὁ ἡ τό the, this, that, he, she, it
σαρκί n. dat. fem. sg. σάρξ flesh, carnal
μου pron. gen. 1p. sg. ἐγώ I
ἀγαθόν adj. nom. neut. sg. ἀγαθός good, good thing, that which is good, well
τὸ art. nom. neut. sg. ὁ ἡ τό the, this, that, he, she, it
γὰρ conj. γάρ for, and, because, but, indeed
μοι pron. dat. 1p. sg. ἐγώ I
τὸ art. nom. neut. sg. ὁ ἡ τό the, this, that, he, she, it
δὲ conj. δέ but, and, now, also, to the contrary, rather, then
τὸ art. acc. neut. sg. ὁ ἡ τό the, this, that, he, she, it
καλὸν adj. acc. neut. sg. καλός good, better, goodly, meet, honest, fair, well, worthy
οὐχ particle of negation. οὐ οὐκ οὐχ not, no, neither, none, nay, nor, never, nothing
19 οὐ particle of negation. οὐ οὐκ οὐχ not, no, neither, none, nay, nor, never, nothing
γὰρ conj. γάρ for, and, because, but, indeed
ὃ relative pron. acc. neut. sg. ὅς ἥ ὅ who, which, what, that
ἀγαθόν adj. acc. neut. sg. ἀγαθός good, good thing, that which is good, well
ἀλλ' conj. ἀλλά but, yea, yet, nevertheless, howbeit, nay, therefore
ὃ relative pron. acc. neut. sg. ὅς ἥ ὅ who, which, what, that
οὐ particle of negation. οὐ οὐκ οὐχ not, no, neither, none, nay, nor, never, nothing
κακὸν adj. acc. neut. sg. κακός evil, evil thing, noisome, wicked
τοῦτο demo. pron. acc. neut. sg. οὗτος αὕτη τοῦτο this, the same, this same, he, she, it
20 εἰ conj. εἰ if, whether, that, though, forasmuch
δὲ conj. δέ but, and, now, also, to the contrary, rather, then
ὃ relative pron. acc. neut. sg. ὅς ἥ ὅ who, which, what, that
οὐ particle of negation. οὐ οὐκ οὐχ not, no, neither, none, nay, nor, never, nothing
ἐγὼ pron. nom. 1p. sg. ἐγώ I
τοῦτο demo. pron. acc. neut. sg. οὗτος αὕτη τοῦτο this, the same, this same, he, she, it
οὐκέτι adv. οὐκέτι or οὐκ ἔτι no more, no longer, not any more
ἐγὼ pron. nom. 1p. sg. ἐγώ I
αὐτὸ pron. acc. neut. 3p. sg. αὐτός ή ó self, of oneself, even, very, the same, he, she, it
ἀλλ' conj. ἀλλά but, yea, yet, nevertheless, howbeit, nay, therefore
ἡ art. nom. fem. sg. ὁ ἡ τό the, this, that, he, she, it
ἐν prep. ἐν (+dat) in, by, with, among, at, on, through, to, within, into, of, for
ἐμοὶ pron. dat. 1p. sg. ἐγώ I
ἁμαρτία n. nom. fem. sg. ἁμαρτία sin, offence, sinful
21 ἄρα conj. ἄρα then, therefore, haply, wherefore, perhaps, manner, no doubt, truly
τὸν art. acc. masc. sg. ὁ ἡ τό the, this, that, he, she, it
νόμον n. acc. masc. sg. νόμος law, the law
τῷ art. dat. masc. sg. ὁ ἡ τό the, this, that, he, she, it
ἐμοὶ pron. dat. 1p. sg. ἐγώ I
τὸ art. acc. neut. sg. ὁ ἡ τό the, this, that, he, she, it
καλόν adj. acc. neut. sg. καλός good, better, goodly, meet, honest, fair, well, worthy
ὅτι conj. ὅτι that, for, because, how that, how, because that, for that, though
ἐμοὶ pron. dat. 1p. sg. ἐγώ I
τὸ art. nom. neut. sg. ὁ ἡ τό the, this, that, he, she, it
κακὸν adj. nom. neut. sg. κακός evil, evil thing, noisome, wicked
22 γὰρ conj. γάρ for, and, because, but, indeed

τῷ art. dat. masc. sg. ὁ ἡ τό the, this, that, he, she, it
νόμῳ n. dat. masc. sg. νόμος law, the law
τοῦ art. gen. masc. sg. ὁ ἡ τό the, this, that, he, she, it
Θεοῦ n. gen. masc. sg. θεός God, god
κατὰ prep. κατά (+gen) against, by, throughout, down, (+acc) according to, after, with
τὸν art. acc. masc. sg. ὁ ἡ τό the, this, that, he, she, it
ἔσω adv. ἔσω within, in, inner, into, inward
ἄνθρωπον n. acc. masc. sg. ἄνθρωπος man, human being, person, one, certain
23 δὲ conj. δέ but, and, now, also, to the contrary, rather, then
ἕτερον adj. acc. masc. sg. ἕτερος another, other, else, strange
νόμον n. acc. masc. sg. νόμος law, the law
ἐν prep. ἐν (+dat) in, by, with, among, at, on, through, to, within, into, of, for
τοῖς art. dat. neut. pl. ὁ ἡ τό the, this, that, he, she, it
μέλεσί n. dat. neut. pl. μέλος member
μου pron. gen. 1p. sg. ἐγώ I
τῷ art. dat. masc. sg. ὁ ἡ τό the, this, that, he, she, it
νόμῳ n. dat. masc. sg. νόμος law, the law
τοῦ art. gen. masc. sg. ὁ ἡ τό the, this, that, he, she, it
νοός n. gen. masc. sg. νοῦς understanding, mind
μου pron. gen. 1p. sg. ἐγώ I
καὶ conj. καί and, even, also, but
με pron. acc. 1p. sg. ἐγώ I
τῷ art. dat. masc. sg. ὁ ἡ τό the, this, that, he, she, it
νόμῳ n. dat. masc. sg. νόμος law, the law
τῆς art. gen. fem. sg. ὁ ἡ τό the, this, that, he, she, it
ἁμαρτίας n. gen. fem. sg. ἁμαρτία sin, offence, sinful
τῷ art. dat. masc. sg. ὁ ἡ τό the, this, that, he, she, it
ἐν prep. ἐν (+dat) in, by, with, among, at, on, through, to, within, into, of, for
τοῖς art. dat. neut. pl. ὁ ἡ τό the, this, that, he, she, it
μέλεσί n. dat. neut. pl. μέλος member
μου pron. gen. 1p. sg. ἐγώ I
24 ταλαίπωρος adj. nom. masc. sg. ταλαίπωρος wretched
ἐγὼ pron. nom. 1p. sg. ἐγώ I
ἄνθρωπος n. nom. masc. sg. ἄνθρωπος man, human being, person, one, certain
τίς interrog. pron. nom. masc. sg. τίς what, who, why, where, which, how
με pron. acc. 1p. sg. ἐγώ I
ἐκ prep. ἐκ ἐξ (+gen) of, from, out of, by, on, with, in, among, through
τοῦ art. gen. neut. sg. ὁ ἡ τό the, this, that, he, she, it
σώματος n. gen. neut. sg. σῶμα body, bodily, slave
τοῦ art. gen. masc. sg. ὁ ἡ τό the, this, that, he, she, it
θανάτου n. gen. masc. sg. θάνατος death
τούτου demo. pron. gen. masc. sg. οὗτος αὕτη τοῦτο this, the same, this same, he, she, it
25 τῷ art. dat. masc. sg. ὁ ἡ τό the, this, that, he, she, it
Θεῷ n. dat. masc. sg. θεός God, god
διὰ prep. διά (+gen) by, through, with, in, of, (+acc) for, because of, for a cause
Ἰησοῦ n. gen. masc. sg. Ἰησοῦς Jesus
Χριστοῦ n. gen. masc. sg. Χριστός Christ
τοῦ art. gen. masc. sg. ὁ ἡ τό the, this, that, he, she, it
Κυρίου n. gen. masc. sg. κύριος Lord, lord, master, sir, LORD, God, Master, owner
ἡμῶν pron. gen. 1p. pl. ἐγώ I
ἄρα conj. ἄρα then, therefore, haply, wherefore, perhaps, manner, no doubt, truly
οὖν conj. οὖν therefore, then, so, and, now, wherefore
αὐτὸς pron. nom. masc. 3p. sg. αὐτός ή ό self, of oneself, even, very, the same, he, she, it
ἐγὼ pron. nom. 1p. sg. ἐγώ I
τῷ art. dat. masc. sg. ὁ ἡ τό the, this, that, he, she, it

μὲν conj. μέν indeed, verily, truly, even, so, some
νοΐ n. dat. masc. sg. νοῦς understanding, mind
νόμῳ n. dat. masc. sg. νόμος law, the law
Θεοῦ n. gen. masc. sg. θεός God, god
τῇ art. dat. fem. sg. ὁ ἡ τό the, this, that, he, she, it
δὲ conj. δέ but, and, now, also, to the contrary, rather, then
σαρκὶ n. dat. fem. sg. σάρξ flesh, carnal
νόμῳ n. dat. masc. sg. νόμος law, the law
ἁμαρτίας n. gen. fem. sg. ἁμαρτία sin, offence, sinful

8

1 Οὐδὲν num. nom. neut. sg. οὐδείς no man, nothing, no, none, neither, not, nought
ἄρα conj. ἄρα then, therefore, haply, wherefore, perhaps, manner, no doubt, truly
νῦν adv. νῦν now, henceforth, present, this time
κατάκριμα n. nom. neut. sg. κατάκριμα condemnation
τοῖς art. dat. masc. pl. ὁ ἡ τό the, this, that, he, she, it
ἐν prep. ἐν (+dat) in, by, with, among, at, on, through, to, within, into, of, for
Χριστῷ n. dat. masc. sg. Χριστός Christ
Ἰησοῦ n. dat. masc. sg. Ἰησοῦς Jesus
μὴ particle of negation. μή not, no, lest, neither, none, nothing, nor, never, without
κατὰ prep. κατά (+gen) against, by, throughout, down, (+acc) according to, after, with
σάρκα n. acc. fem. sg. σάρξ flesh, carnal
ἀλλὰ conj. ἀλλά but, yea, yet, nevertheless, howbeit, nay, therefore
κατὰ prep. κατά (+gen) against, by, throughout, down, (+acc) according to, after, with
πνεῦμα n. acc. neut. sg. πνεῦμα spirit, Spirit, Ghost, ghost, life. of the spirit, wind
2 ὁ art. nom. masc. sg. ὁ ἡ τό the, this, that, he, she, it
γὰρ conj. γάρ for, and, because, but, indeed
νόμος n. nom. masc. sg. νόμος law, the law
τοῦ art. gen. neut. sg. ὁ ἡ τό the, this, that, he, she, it
πνεύματος n. gen. neut. sg. πνεῦμα spirit, Spirit, Ghost, ghost, life. of the spirit, wind
τῆς art. gen. fem. sg. ὁ ἡ τό the, this, that, he, she, it
ζωῆς n. gen. fem. sg. ζωή life, lifetime
ἐν prep. ἐν (+dat) in, by, with, among, at, on, through, to, within, into, of, for
Χριστῷ n. dat. masc. sg. Χριστός Christ
Ἰησοῦ n. dat. masc. sg. Ἰησοῦς Jesus
με pron. acc. 1p. sg. ἐγώ I
ἀπὸ prep. ἀπό (+gen) from, of, out of, since, for, off, at, by, in, on
τοῦ art. gen. masc. sg. ὁ ἡ τό the, this, that, he, she, it
νόμου n. gen. masc. sg. νόμος law, the law
τῆς art. gen. fem. sg. ὁ ἡ τό the, this, that, he, she, it
ἁμαρτίας n. gen. fem. sg. ἁμαρτία sin, offence, sinful
καὶ conj. καί and, even, also, but
τοῦ art. gen. masc. sg. ὁ ἡ τό the, this, that, he, she, it
θανάτου n. gen. masc. sg. θάνατος death
3 τὸ art. acc. neut. sg. ὁ ἡ τό the, this, that, he, she, it
γὰρ conj. γάρ for, and, because, but, indeed
ἀδύνατον adj. acc. neut. sg. ἀδύνατος impossible, not possible, cannot do
τοῦ art. gen. masc. sg. ὁ ἡ τό the, this, that, he, she, it
νόμου n. gen. masc. sg. νόμος law, the law
ἐν prep. ἐν (+dat) in, by, with, among, at, on, through, to, within, into, of, for
ᾧ relative pron. dat. neut. sg. ὅς ἥ ὅ who, which, what, that
διὰ prep. διά (+gen) by, through, with, in, of, (+acc) for, because of, for a cause
τῆς art. gen. fem. sg. ὁ ἡ τό the, this, that, he, she, it
σαρκός n. gen. fem. sg. σάρξ flesh, carnal

ὁ art. nom. masc. sg. ὁ ἡ τό the, this, that, he, she, it
Θεὸς n. nom. masc. sg. θεός God, god
τὸν art. acc. masc. sg. ὁ ἡ τό the, this, that, he, she, it
ἑαυτοῦ reflexive pron. gen. masc. 3p. sg. ἑαυτοῦ himself, herself, itself, yourself, ourselves
υἱὸν n. acc. masc. sg. υἱός son, child, descendant, offspring, heir
ἐν prep. ἐν (+dat) in, by, with, among, at, on, through, to, within, into, of, for
ὁμοιώματι n. dat. neut. sg. ὁμοίωμα likeness, made like to, shape, similitude
σαρκὸς n. gen. fem. sg. σάρξ flesh, carnal
ἁμαρτίας n. gen. fem. sg. ἁμαρτία sin, offence, sinful
καὶ conj. καί and, even, also, but
περὶ prep. περί (+gen) of, for, concerning, (+acc) about, concerning, in
ἁμαρτίας n. gen. fem. sg. ἁμαρτία sin, offence, sinful
τὴν art. acc. fem. sg. ὁ ἡ τό the, this, that, he, she, it
ἁμαρτίαν n. acc. fem. sg. ἁμαρτία sin, offence, sinful
ἐν prep. ἐν (+dat) in, by, with, among, at, on, through, to, within, into, of, for
τῇ art. dat. fem. sg. ὁ ἡ τό the, this, that, he, she, it
σαρκί n. dat. fem. sg. σάρξ flesh, carnal
4 ἵνα conj. ἵνα that, to, lest, for to, so that, albeit, because, for, so as
τὸ art. nom. neut. sg. ὁ ἡ τό the, this, that, he, she, it
δικαίωμα n. nom. neut. sg. δικαίωμα ordinance, righteousness, judgement, justification
τοῦ art. gen. masc. sg. ὁ ἡ τό the, this, that, he, she, it
νόμου n. gen. masc. sg. νόμος law, the law
ἐν prep. ἐν (+dat) in, by, with, among, at, on, through, to, within, into, of, for
ἡμῖν pron. dat. 1p. pl. ἐγώ I
τοῖς art. dat. masc. pl. ὁ ἡ τό the, this, that, he, she, it
μὴ particle of negation. μή not, no, lest, neither, none, nothing, nor, never, without
κατὰ prep. κατά (+gen) against, by, throughout, down, (+acc) according to, after, with
σάρκα n. acc. fem. sg. σάρξ flesh, carnal
ἀλλὰ conj. ἀλλά but, yea, yet, nevertheless, howbeit, nay, therefore
κατὰ prep. κατά (+gen) against, by, throughout, down, (+acc) according to, after, with
πνεῦμα n. acc. neut. sg. πνεῦμα spirit, Spirit, Ghost, ghost, life. of the spirit, wind
5 οἱ art. nom. masc. pl. ὁ ἡ τό the, this, that, he, she, it
γὰρ conj. γάρ for, and, because, but, indeed
κατὰ prep. κατά (+gen) against, by, throughout, down, (+acc) according to, after, with
σάρκα n. acc. fem. sg. σάρξ flesh, carnal
τὰ art. acc. neut. pl. ὁ ἡ τό the, this, that, he, she, it
τῆς art. gen. fem. sg. ὁ ἡ τό the, this, that, he, she, it
σαρκὸς n. gen. fem. sg. σάρξ flesh, carnal
οἱ art. nom. masc. pl. ὁ ἡ τό the, this, that, he, she, it
δὲ conj. δέ but, and, now, also, to the contrary, rather, then
κατὰ prep. κατά (+gen) against, by, throughout, down, (+acc) according to, after, with
πνεῦμα n. acc. neut. sg. πνεῦμα spirit, Spirit, Ghost, ghost, life. of the spirit, wind
τὰ art. acc. neut. pl. ὁ ἡ τό the, this, that, he, she, it
τοῦ art. gen. neut. sg. ὁ ἡ τό the, this, that, he, she, it
πνεύματος n. gen. neut. sg. πνεῦμα spirit, Spirit, Ghost, ghost, life. of the spirit, wind
6 τὸ art. nom. neut. sg. ὁ ἡ τό the, this, that, he, she, it
γὰρ conj. γάρ for, and, because, but, indeed
φρόνημα n. nom. neut. sg. φρόνημα mind
τῆς art. gen. fem. sg. ὁ ἡ τό the, this, that, he, she, it
σαρκὸς n. gen. fem. sg. σάρξ flesh, carnal
θάνατος n. nom. masc. sg. θάνατος death
τὸ art. nom. neut. sg. ὁ ἡ τό the, this, that, he, she, it
δὲ conj. δέ but, and, now, also, to the contrary, rather, then
φρόνημα n. nom. neut. sg. φρόνημα mind
τοῦ art. gen. neut. sg. ὁ ἡ τό the, this, that, he, she, it

πνεύματος n. gen. neut. sg. πνεῦμα spirit, Spirit, Ghost, ghost, life. of the spirit, wind
ζωὴ n. nom. fem. sg. ζωή life, lifetime
καὶ conj. καί and, even, also, but
εἰρήνη n. nom. fem. sg. εἰρήνη peace, quietness, rest
7 διότι conj. διότι for, because, because that, therefore
τὸ art. nom. neut. sg. ὁ ἡ τό the, this, that, he, she, it
φρόνημα n. nom. neut. sg. φρόνημα mind
τῆς art. gen. fem. sg. ὁ ἡ τό the, this, that, he, she, it
σαρκὸς n. gen. fem. sg. σάρξ flesh, carnal
ἔχθρα n. nom. fem. sg. ἔχθρα enmity, hatred
εἰς prep. εἰς (+acc) into, to, unto, for, in, on, toward, against, upon, at, among
Θεόν n. acc. masc. sg. θεός God, god
τῷ art. dat. masc. sg. ὁ ἡ τό the, this, that, he, she, it
γὰρ conj. γάρ for, and, because, but, indeed
νόμῳ n. dat. masc. sg. νόμος law, the law
τοῦ art. gen. masc. sg. ὁ ἡ τό the, this, that, he, she, it
Θεοῦ n. gen. masc. sg. θεός God, god
οὐχ particle of negation. οὐ οὐκ οὐχ not, no, neither, none, nay, nor, never, nothing
οὐδὲ adv. οὐδέ neither, nor, not, no, not even, never, not yet
γὰρ conj. γάρ for, and, because, but, indeed
8 οἱ art. nom. masc. pl. ὁ ἡ τό the, this, that, he, she, it
δὲ conj. δέ but, and, now, also, to the contrary, rather, then
ἐν prep. ἐν (+dat) in, by, with, among, at, on, through, to, within, into, of, for
σαρκὶ n. dat. fem. sg. σάρξ flesh, carnal
Θεῷ n. dat. masc. sg. θεός God, god
οὐ particle of negation. οὐ οὐκ οὐχ not, no, neither, none, nay, nor, never, nothing
9 ὑμεῖς pron. nom. 2p. pl. σύ thou, you
δὲ conj. δέ but, and, now, also, to the contrary, rather, then
οὐκ particle of negation. οὐ οὐκ οὐχ not, no, neither, none, nay, nor, never, nothing
ἐν prep. ἐν (+dat) in, by, with, among, at, on, through, to, within, into, of, for
σαρκὶ n. dat. fem. sg. σάρξ flesh, carnal
ἀλλ' conj. ἀλλά but, yea, yet, nevertheless, howbeit, nay, therefore
ἐν prep. ἐν (+dat) in, by, with, among, at, on, through, to, within, into, of, for
πνεύματι n. dat. neut. sg. πνεῦμα spirit, Spirit, Ghost, ghost, life. of the spirit, wind
εἴπερ conj. εἴπερ if it be so that, if indeed, since indeed, since, although indeed
Πνεῦμα n. nom. neut. sg. πνεῦμα spirit, Spirit, Ghost, ghost, life. of the spirit, wind
Θεοῦ n. gen. masc. sg. θεός God, god
ἐν prep. ἐν (+dat) in, by, with, among, at, on, through, to, within, into, of, for
ὑμῖν pron. dat. 2p. pl. σύ thou, you
εἰ conj. εἰ if, whether, that, though, forasmuch
δὲ conj. δέ but, and, now, also, to the contrary, rather, then
τις indefinite pron. nom. masc. sg. τὶς certain, some, any man, one, any thing
Πνεῦμα n. acc. neut. sg. πνεῦμα spirit, Spirit, Ghost, ghost, life. of the spirit, wind
Χριστοῦ n. gen. masc. sg. Χριστός Christ
οὐκ particle of negation. οὐ οὐκ οὐχ not, no, neither, none, nay, nor, never, nothing
οὗτος demo. pron. nom. masc. sg. οὗτος αὕτη τοῦτο this, the same, this same, he, she, it
οὐκ particle of negation. οὐ οὐκ οὐχ not, no, neither, none, nay, nor, never, nothing
αὐτοῦ pron. gen. masc. 3p. sg. αὐτός ή ό self, of oneself, even, very, the same, he, she, it
10 εἰ conj. εἰ if, whether, that, though, forasmuch
δὲ conj. δέ but, and, now, also, to the contrary, rather, then
Χριστὸς n. nom. masc. sg. Χριστός Christ
ἐν prep. ἐν (+dat) in, by, with, among, at, on, through, to, within, into, of, for
ὑμῖν pron. dat. 2p. pl. σύ thou, you
τὸ art. nom. neut. sg. ὁ ἡ τό the, this, that, he, she, it
μὲν conj. μέν indeed, verily, truly, even, so, some

σῶμα n. nom. neut. sg. σῶμα body, bodily, slave
νεκρὸν adj. nom. neut. sg. νεκρός dead
δι' prep. διά (+gen) by, through, with, in, of, (+acc) for, because of, for a cause
ἁμαρτίαν n. acc. fem. sg. ἁμαρτία sin, offence, sinful
τὸ art. nom. neut. sg. ὁ ἡ τό the, this, that, he, she, it
δὲ conj. δέ but, and, now, also, to the contrary, rather, then
πνεῦμα n. nom. neut. sg. πνεῦμα spirit, Spirit, Ghost, ghost, life. of the spirit, wind
ζωὴ n. nom. fem. sg. ζωή life, lifetime
διὰ prep. διά (+gen) by, through, with, in, of, (+acc) for, because of, for a cause
δικαιοσύνην n. acc. fem. sg. δικαιοσύνη righteousness
11 εἰ conj. εἰ if, whether, that, though, forasmuch
δὲ conj. δέ but, and, now, also, to the contrary, rather, then
τὸ art. nom. neut. sg. ὁ ἡ τό the, this, that, he, she, it
Πνεῦμα n. nom. neut. sg. πνεῦμα spirit, Spirit, Ghost, ghost, life. of the spirit, wind
τοῦ art. gen. masc. sg. ὁ ἡ τό the, this, that, he, she, it
Ἰησοῦν n. acc. masc. sg. Ἰησοῦς Jesus
ἐκ prep. ἐκ ἐξ (+gen) of, from, out of, by, on, with, in, among, through
νεκρῶν adj. gen. masc. pl. νεκρός dead
ἐν prep. ἐν (+dat) in, by, with, among, at, on, through, to, within, into, of, for
ὑμῖν pron. dat. 2p. pl. σύ thou, you
ὁ art. nom. masc. sg. ὁ ἡ τό the, this, that, he, she, it
τὸν art. acc. masc. sg. ὁ ἡ τό the, this, that, he, she, it
Χριστὸν n. acc. masc. sg. Χριστός Christ
ἐκ prep. ἐκ ἐξ (+gen) of, from, out of, by, on, with, in, among, through
νεκρῶν adj. gen. masc. pl. νεκρός dead
καὶ conj. καί and, even, also, but
τὰ art. acc. neut. pl. ὁ ἡ τό the, this, that, he, she, it
θνητὰ adj. acc. neut. pl. θνητός mortal, mortality
σώματα n. acc. neut. pl. σῶμα body, bodily, slave
ὑμῶν pron. gen. 2p. pl. σύ thou, you
διὰ prep. διά (+gen) by, through, with, in, of, (+acc) for, because of, for a cause
τοῦ art. gen. neut. sg. ὁ ἡ τό the, this, that, he, she, it
αὐτοῦ pron. gen. masc. 3p. sg. αὐτός ή ό self, of oneself, even, very, the same, he, she, it
Πνεύματος n. gen. neut. sg. πνεῦμα spirit, Spirit, Ghost, ghost, life. of the spirit, wind
ἐν prep. ἐν (+dat) in, by, with, among, at, on, through, to, within, into, of, for
ὑμῖν pron. dat. 2p. pl. σύ thou, you
12 Ἄρα conj. ἄρα then, therefore, haply, wherefore, perhaps, manner, no doubt, truly
οὖν conj. οὖν therefore, then, so, and, now, wherefore
ἀδελφοί n. voc. masc. pl. ἀδελφός brother
ὀφειλέται n. nom. masc. pl. ὀφειλέτης debtor, sinner, owe
οὐ particle of negation. οὐ οὐκ οὐχ not, no, neither, none, nay, nor, never, nothing
τῇ art. dat. fem. sg. ὁ ἡ τό the, this, that, he, she, it
σαρκὶ n. dat. fem. sg. σάρξ flesh, carnal
τοῦ art. gen. neut. sg. ὁ ἡ τό the, this, that, he, she, it
κατὰ prep. κατά (+gen) against, by, throughout, down, (+acc) according to, after, with
σάρκα n. acc. fem. sg. σάρξ flesh, carnal
13 εἰ conj. εἰ if, whether, that, though, forasmuch
γὰρ conj. γάρ for, and, because, but, indeed
κατὰ prep. κατά (+gen) against, by, throughout, down, (+acc) according to, after, with
σάρκα n. acc. fem. sg. σάρξ flesh, carnal
εἰ conj. εἰ if, whether, that, though, forasmuch
δὲ conj. δέ but, and, now, also, to the contrary, rather, then
πνεύματι n. dat. neut. sg. πνεῦμα spirit, Spirit, Ghost, ghost, life. of the spirit, wind
τὰς art. acc. fem. pl. ὁ ἡ τό the, this, that, he, she, it
πράξεις n. acc. fem. pl. πρᾶξις deed, office, acting

τοῦ art. gen. neut. sg. ὁ ἡ τό the, this, that, he, she, it
σώματος n. gen. neut. sg. σῶμα body, bodily, slave
14 ὅσοι relative pron. nom. masc. pl. ὅσος as many as, whatsoever, that, as long as, how much
γὰρ conj. γάρ for, and, because, but, indeed
Πνεύματι n. dat. neut. sg. πνεῦμα spirit, Spirit, Ghost, ghost, life. of the spirit, wind
Θεοῦ n. gen. masc. sg. θεός God, god
οὗτοι demo. pron. nom. masc. pl. οὗτος αὕτη τοῦτο this, the same, this same, he, she, it
υἱοὶ n. nom. masc. pl. υἱός son, child, descendant, offspring, heir
Θεοῦ n. gen. masc. sg. θεός God, god
15 οὐ particle of negation. οὐ οὐκ οὐχ not, no, neither, none, nay, nor, never, nothing
γὰρ conj. γάρ for, and, because, but, indeed
πνεῦμα n. acc. neut. sg. πνεῦμα spirit, Spirit, Ghost, ghost, life. of the spirit, wind
δουλείας n. gen. fem. sg. δουλεία bondage
πάλιν adv. πάλιν again
εἰς prep. εἰς (+acc) into, to, unto, for, in, on, toward, against, upon, at, among
φόβον n. acc. masc. sg. φόβος fear, terror, sore afraid
ἀλλ' conj. ἀλλά but, yea, yet, nevertheless, howbeit, nay, therefore
πνεῦμα n. acc. neut. sg. πνεῦμα spirit, Spirit, Ghost, ghost, life. of the spirit, wind
υἱοθεσίας n. gen. fem. sg. υἱοθεσία adoption, adoption of children, adoption of sons
ἐν prep. ἐν (+dat) in, by, with, among, at, on, through, to, within, into, of, for
ᾧ relative pron. dat. neut. sg. ὅς ἥ ὅ who, which, what, that
'Αββᾶ n. voc. masc. sg. 'Αββᾶ Abba
ὁ art. nom. masc. sg. ὁ ἡ τό the, this, that, he, she, it
πατήρ n. nom. masc. sg. πατήρ Father, father, parent
16 αὐτὸ pron. nom. neut. 3p. sg. αὐτός ή ό self, of oneself, even, very, the same, he, she, it
τὸ art. nom. neut. sg. ὁ ἡ τό the, this, that, he, she, it
Πνεῦμα n. nom. neut. sg. πνεῦμα spirit, Spirit, Ghost, ghost, life. of the spirit, wind
τῷ art. dat. neut. sg. ὁ ἡ τό the, this, that, he, she, it
πνεύματι n. dat. neut. sg. πνεῦμα spirit, Spirit, Ghost, ghost, life. of the spirit, wind
ἡμῶν pron. gen. 1p. pl. ἐγώ I
ὅτι conj. ὅτι that, for, because, how that, how, because that, for that, though
τέκνα n. nom. neut. pl. τέκνον child, son, daughter
Θεοῦ n. gen. masc. sg. θεός God, god
17 εἰ conj. εἰ if, whether, that, though, forasmuch
δὲ conj. δέ but, and, now, also, to the contrary, rather, then
τέκνα n. nom. neut. pl. τέκνον child, son, daughter
καὶ conj. καί and, even, also, but
κληρονόμοι n. nom. masc. pl. κληρονόμος heir
κληρονόμοι n. nom. masc. pl. κληρονόμος heir
μὲν conj. μέν indeed, verily, truly, even, so, some
Θεοῦ n. gen. masc. sg. θεός God, god
συγκληρονόμοι adj. nom. masc. pl. συγκληρονόμος joint-heir, fellowheir, heir together
δὲ conj. δέ but, and, now, also, to the contrary, rather, then
Χριστοῦ n. gen. masc. sg. Χριστός Christ
εἴπερ conj. εἴπερ if it be so that, if indeed, since indeed, since, although indeed
ἵνα conj. ἵνα that, to, lest, for to, so that, albeit, because, for, so as
καὶ conj. καί and, even, also, but
18 γὰρ conj. γάρ for, and, because, but, indeed
ὅτι conj. ὅτι that, for, because, how that, how, because that, for that, though
οὐκ particle of negation. οὐ οὐκ οὐχ not, no, neither, none, nay, nor, never, nothing
ἄξια adj. nom. neut. pl. ἄξιος worthy, meet, due reward
τὰ art. nom. neut. pl. ὁ ἡ τό the, this, that, he, she, it
παθήματα n. nom. neut. pl. πάθημα suffering, affliction, affection, motion
τοῦ art. gen. masc. sg. ὁ ἡ τό the, this, that, he, she, it
νῦν adv. νῦν now, henceforth, present, this time

καιροῦ n. gen. masc. sg. καιρός time, season, due time, opportunity
πρὸς prep. πρός (+gen) for, (+dat) at, (+acc) unto, to, with, for, against
τὴν art. acc. fem. sg. ὁ ἡ τό the, this, that, he, she, it
δόξαν n. acc. fem. sg. δόξα glory, honour, praise, dignity, worship
εἰς prep. εἰς (+acc) into, to, unto, for, in, on, toward, against, upon, at, among
ἡμᾶς pron. acc. 1p. pl. ἐγώ I
19 ἡ art. nom. fem. sg. ὁ ἡ τό the, this, that, he, she, it
γὰρ conj. γάρ for, and, because, but, indeed
ἀποκαραδοκία n. nom. fem. sg. ἀποκαραδοκία earnest expectation
τῆς art. gen. fem. sg. ὁ ἡ τό the, this, that, he, she, it
κτίσεως n. gen. fem. sg. κτίσις creature, creation, building, ordinance
τὴν art. acc. fem. sg. ὁ ἡ τό the, this, that, he, she, it
ἀποκάλυψιν n. acc. fem. sg. ἀποκάλυψις revelation, appearing, coming, manifestation
τῶν art. gen. masc. pl. ὁ ἡ τό the, this, that, he, she, it
υἱῶν n. gen. masc. pl. υἱός son, child, descendant, offspring, heir
τοῦ art. gen. masc. sg. ὁ ἡ τό the, this, that, he, she, it
Θεοῦ n. gen. masc. sg. θεός God, god
20 τῇ art. dat. fem. sg. ὁ ἡ τό the, this, that, he, she, it
γὰρ conj. γάρ for, and, because, but, indeed
ματαιότητι n. dat. fem. sg. ματαιότης vanity
ἡ art. nom. fem. sg. ὁ ἡ τό the, this, that, he, she, it
κτίσις n. nom. fem. sg. κτίσις creature, creation, building, ordinance
οὐχ particle of negation. οὐ οὐκ οὐχ not, no, neither, none, nay, nor, never, nothing
ἑκοῦσα adj. nom. fem. sg. ἑκών willingly, willing
ἀλλὰ conj. ἀλλά but, yea, yet, nevertheless, howbeit, nay, therefore
διὰ prep. διά (+gen) by, through, with, in, of, (+acc) for, because of, for a cause
τὸν art. acc. masc. sg. ὁ ἡ τό the, this, that, he, she, it
ἐπ' prep. ἐπί (+gen) on, in, upon, (+dat) in, at, for, upon, (+acc) on, upon, unto, to, against
ἐλπίδι n. dat. fem. sg. ἐλπίς hope, faith
21 ὅτι conj. ὅτι that, for, because, how that, how, because that, for that, though
καὶ conj. καί and, even, also, but
αὐτὴ pron. nom. fem. 3p. sg. αὐτός ἡ ὁ self, of oneself, even, very, the same, he, she, it
ἡ art. nom. fem. sg. ὁ ἡ τό the, this, that, he, she, it
κτίσις n. nom. fem. sg. κτίσις creature, creation, building, ordinance
ἀπὸ prep. ἀπό (+gen) from, of, out of, since, for, off, at, by, in, on
τῆς art. gen. fem. sg. ὁ ἡ τό the, this, that, he, she, it
δουλείας n. gen. fem. sg. δουλεία bondage
τῆς art. gen. fem. sg. ὁ ἡ τό the, this, that, he, she, it
φθορᾶς n. gen. fem. sg. φθορά corruption, destroy, perish
εἰς prep. εἰς (+acc) into, to, unto, for, in, on, toward, against, upon, at, among
τὴν art. acc. fem. sg. ὁ ἡ τό the, this, that, he, she, it
ἐλευθερίαν n. acc. fem. sg. ἐλευθερία liberty
τῆς art. gen. fem. sg. ὁ ἡ τό the, this, that, he, she, it
δόξης n. gen. fem. sg. δόξα glory, honour, praise, dignity, worship
τῶν art. gen. neut. pl. ὁ ἡ τό the, this, that, he, she, it
τέκνων n. gen. neut. pl. τέκνον child, son, daughter
τοῦ art. gen. masc. sg. ὁ ἡ τό the, this, that, he, she, it
Θεοῦ n. gen. masc. sg. θεός God, god
22 γὰρ conj. γάρ for, and, because, but, indeed
ὅτι conj. ὅτι that, for, because, how that, how, because that, for that, though
πᾶσα adj. nom. fem. sg. πᾶς πᾶσα πᾶν all, every, whosoever, every one, no, whole, any
ἡ art. nom. fem. sg. ὁ ἡ τό the, this, that, he, she, it
κτίσις n. nom. fem. sg. κτίσις creature, creation, building, ordinance
καὶ conj. καί and, even, also, but
ἄχρι prep. ἄχρι or ἄχρις (+gen) until, unto, till, even to, as far as, while, into

τοῦ art. gen. masc. sg. ὁ ἡ τό the, this, that, he, she, it
νῦν adv. νῦν now, henceforth, present, this time
23 οὐ particle of negation. οὐ οὐκ οὐχ not, no, neither, none, nay, nor, never, nothing
μόνον adv. μόνος only, alone, by oneself
δέ conj. δέ but, and, now, also, to the contrary, rather, then
ἀλλὰ conj. ἀλλά but, yea, yet, nevertheless, howbeit, nay, therefore
καὶ conj. καί and, even, also, but
αὐτοὶ pron. nom. masc. 3p. pl. αὐτός ή ό self, of oneself, even, very, the same, he, she, it
τὴν art. acc. fem. sg. ὁ ἡ τό the, this, that, he, she, it
ἀπαρχὴν n. acc. fem. sg. ἀπαρχή firstfruit
τοῦ art. gen. neut. sg. ὁ ἡ τό the, this, that, he, she, it
Πνεύματος n. gen. neut. sg. πνεῦμα spirit, Spirit, Ghost, ghost, life. of the spirit, wind
καὶ conj. καί and, even, also, but
ἡμεῖς pron. nom. 1p. pl. ἐγώ I
αὐτοὶ pron. nom. masc. 3p. pl. αὐτός ή ό self, of oneself, even, very, the same, he, she, it
ἐν prep. ἐν (+dat) in, by, with, among, at, on, through, to, within, into, of, for
ἑαυτοῖς reflexive pron. dat. masc. 3p. pl. ἑαυτοῦ himself, herself, itself, yourself, ourselves
υἱοθεσίαν n. acc. fem. sg. υἱοθεσία adoption, adoption of children, adoption of sons
τὴν art. acc. fem. sg. ὁ ἡ τό the, this, that, he, she, it
ἀπολύτρωσιν n. acc. fem. sg. ἀπολύτρωσις redemption, deliverance
τοῦ art. gen. neut. sg. ὁ ἡ τό the, this, that, he, she, it
σώματος n. gen. neut. sg. σῶμα body, bodily, slave
ἡμῶν pron. gen. 1p. pl. ἐγώ I
24 τῇ art. dat. fem. sg. ὁ ἡ τό the, this, that, he, she, it
γὰρ conj. γάρ for, and, because, but, indeed
ἐλπίδι n. dat. fem. sg. ἐλπίς hope, faith
ἐλπὶς n. nom. fem. sg. ἐλπίς hope, faith
δὲ conj. δέ but, and, now, also, to the contrary, rather, then
οὐκ particle of negation. οὐ οὐκ οὐχ not, no, neither, none, nay, nor, never, nothing
ἐλπίς n. nom. fem. sg. ἐλπίς hope, faith
ὃ relative pron. acc. neut. sg. ὅς ἥ ὅ who, which, what, that
γὰρ conj. γάρ for, and, because, but, indeed
τις indefinite pron. nom. masc. sg. τὶς certain, some, any man, one, any thing
τί interrog. pron. acc. neut. sg. τίς what, who, why, where, which, how
καὶ conj. καί and, even, also, but
25 εἰ conj. εἰ if, whether, that, though, forasmuch
δὲ conj. δέ but, and, now, also, to the contrary, rather, then
ὃ relative pron. acc. neut. sg. ὅς ἥ ὅ who, which, what, that
οὐ particle of negation. οὐ οὐκ οὐχ not, no, neither, none, nay, nor, never, nothing
δι' prep. διά (+gen) by, through, with, in, of, (+acc) for, because of, for a cause
ὑπομονῆς n. gen. fem. sg. ὑπομονή patience, enduring
26 Ὡσαύτως adv. ὡσαύτως likewise, in like manner, after the same manner, even so
δὲ conj. δέ but, and, now, also, to the contrary, rather, then
καὶ conj. καί and, even, also, but
τὸ art. nom. neut. sg. ὁ ἡ τό the, this, that, he, she, it
Πνεῦμα n. nom. neut. sg. πνεῦμα spirit, Spirit, Ghost, ghost, life. of the spirit, wind
ταῖς art. dat. fem. pl. ὁ ἡ τό the, this, that, he, she, it
ἀσθενείαις n. dat. fem. pl. ἀσθένεια infirmity, weakness, disease, sickness
ἡμῶν pron. gen. 1p. pl. ἐγώ I
τὸ art. acc. neut. sg. ὁ ἡ τό the, this, that, he, she, it
γὰρ conj. γάρ for, and, because, but, indeed
τί interrog. pron. acc. neut. sg. τίς what, who, why, where, which, how
καθὸ adv. καθό as, according to that, inasmuch as
οὐκ particle of negation. οὐ οὐκ οὐχ not, no, neither, none, nay, nor, never, nothing
ἀλλ' conj. ἀλλά but, yea, yet, nevertheless, howbeit, nay, therefore

αὐτὸ pron. nom. neut. 3p. sg. αὐτός ή ό self, of oneself, even, very, the same, he, she, it
τὸ art. nom. neut. sg. ὁ ἡ τό the, this, that, he, she, it
Πνεῦμα n. nom. neut. sg. πνεῦμα spirit, Spirit, Ghost, ghost, life. of the spirit, wind
ὑπὲρ prep. ὑπέρ (+gen) for, of, for the sake of, (+acc) above, more than
ἡμῶν pron. gen. 1p. pl. ἐγώ I
στεναγμοῖς n. dat. masc. pl. στεναγμός groaning
ἀλαλήτοις adj. dat. masc. pl. ἀλάλητος which cannot be uttered
27 ὁ art. nom. masc. sg. ὁ ἡ τό the, this, that, he, she, it
δὲ conj. δέ but, and, now, also, to the contrary, rather, then
τὰς art. acc. fem. pl. ὁ ἡ τό the, this, that, he, she, it
καρδίας n. acc. fem. pl. καρδία heart
τί interrog. pron. acc. neut. sg. τίς what, who, why, where, which, how
τὸ art. nom. neut. sg. ὁ ἡ τό the, this, that, he, she, it
φρόνημα n. nom. neut. sg. φρόνημα mind
τοῦ art. gen. neut. sg. ὁ ἡ τό the, this, that, he, she, it
Πνεύματος n. gen. neut. sg. πνεῦμα spirit, Spirit, Ghost, ghost, life. of the spirit, wind
ὅτι conj. ὅτι that, for, because, how that, how, because that, for that, though
κατὰ prep. κατά (+gen) against, by, throughout, down, (+acc) according to, after, with
Θεὸν n. acc. masc. sg. θεός God, god
ὑπὲρ prep. ὑπέρ (+gen) for, of, for the sake of, (+acc) above, more than
ἁγίων adj. gen. masc. pl. ἅγιος Holy, holy, saint, Holy One, holy thing, most holy
28 δὲ conj. δέ but, and, now, also, to the contrary, rather, then
ὅτι conj. ὅτι that, for, because, how that, how, because that, for that, though
τοῖς art. dat. masc. pl. ὁ ἡ τό the, this, that, he, she, it
τὸν art. acc. masc. sg. ὁ ἡ τό the, this, that, he, she, it
Θεὸν n. acc. masc. sg. θεός God, god
πάντα adj. nom. neut. pl. πᾶς πᾶσα πᾶν all, every, whosoever, every one, no, whole, any
εἰς prep. εἰς (+acc) into, to, unto, for, in, on, toward, against, upon, at, among
ἀγαθόν adj. acc. neut. sg. ἀγαθός good, good thing, that which is good, well
τοῖς art. dat. masc. pl. ὁ ἡ τό the, this, that, he, she, it
κατὰ prep. κατά (+gen) against, by, throughout, down, (+acc) according to, after, with
πρόθεσιν n. acc. fem. sg. πρόθεσις purpose, shew, shewbread
κλητοῖς adj. dat. masc. pl. κλητός called
29 ὅτι conj. ὅτι that, for, because, how that, how, because that, for that, though
οὓς relative pron. acc. masc. pl. ὅς ἥ ὅ who, which, what, that
καὶ conj. καί and, even, also, but
συμμόρφους adj. acc. masc. pl. σύμμορφος conformed to, fashioned like unto
τῆς art. gen. fem. sg. ὁ ἡ τό the, this, that, he, she, it
εἰκόνος n. gen. fem. sg. εἰκών image
τοῦ art. gen. masc. sg. ὁ ἡ τό the, this, that, he, she, it
υἱοῦ n. gen. masc. sg. υἱός son, child, descendant, offspring, heir
αὐτοῦ pron. gen. masc. 3p. sg. αὐτός ή ό self, of oneself, even, very, the same, he, she, it
εἰς prep. εἰς (+acc) into, to, unto, for, in, on, toward, against, upon, at, among
τὸ art. acc. neut. sg. ὁ ἡ τό the, this, that, he, she, it
αὐτὸν pron. acc. masc. 3p. sg. αὐτός ή ό self, of oneself, even, very, the same, he, she, it
πρωτότοκον adj. acc. masc. sg. πρωτότοκος firstborn, first begotten
ἐν prep. ἐν (+dat) in, by, with, among, at, on, through, to, within, into, of, for
πολλοῖς adj. dat. masc. pl. πολύς many, great, much, long, abundant
ἀδελφοῖς n. dat. masc. pl. ἀδελφός brother
30 οὓς relative pron. acc. masc. pl. ὅς ἥ ὅ who, which, what, that
δὲ conj. δέ but, and, now, also, to the contrary, rather, then
τούτους demo. pron. acc. masc. pl. οὗτος αὕτη τοῦτο this, the same, this same, he, she, it
καὶ conj. καί and, even, also, but
καὶ conj. καί and, even, also, but
οὓς relative pron. acc. masc. pl. ὅς ἥ ὅ who, which, what, that

τούτους demo. pron. acc. masc. pl. οὗτος αὕτη τοῦτο this, the same, this same, he, she, it
καὶ conj. καί and, even, also, but
οὓς relative pron. acc. masc. pl. ὅς ἥ ὅ who, which, what, that
δὲ conj. δέ but, and, now, also, to the contrary, rather, then
τούτους demo. pron. acc. masc. pl. οὗτος αὕτη τοῦτο this, the same, this same, he, she, it
καὶ conj. καί and, even, also, but
31 Τί interrog. pron. acc. neut. sg. τίς what, who, why, where, which, how
οὖν conj. οὖν therefore, then, so, and, now, wherefore
πρὸς prep. πρός (+gen) for, (+dat) at, (+acc) unto, to, with, for, against
ταῦτα demo. pron. acc. neut. pl. οὗτος αὕτη τοῦτο this, the same, this same, he, she, it
εἰ conj. εἰ if, whether, that, though, forasmuch
ὁ art. nom. masc. sg. ὁ ἡ τό the, this, that, he, she, it
Θεὸς n. nom. masc. sg. θεός God, god
ὑπὲρ prep. ὑπέρ (+gen) for, of, for the sake of, (+acc) above, more than
ἡμῶν pron. gen. 1p. pl. ἐγώ I
τίς interrog. pron. nom. masc. sg. τίς what, who, why, where, which, how
καθ' prep. κατά (+gen) against, by, throughout, down, (+acc) according to, after, with
ἡμῶν pron. gen. 1p. pl. ἐγώ I
32 ὅς relative pron. nom. masc. sg. ὅς ἥ ὅ who, which, what, that
γε particle. γέ yet, and beside, at least, doubtless
τοῦ art. gen. masc. sg. ὁ ἡ τό the, this, that, he, she, it
ἰδίου adj. gen. masc. sg. ἴδιος one's own, one's, privately
υἱοῦ n. gen. masc. sg. υἱός son, child, descendant, offspring, heir
οὐκ particle of negation. οὐ οὐκ οὐχ not, no, neither, none, nay, nor, never, nothing
ἀλλ' conj. ἀλλά but, yea, yet, nevertheless, howbeit, nay, therefore
ὑπὲρ prep. ὑπέρ (+gen) for, of, for the sake of, (+acc) above, more than
ἡμῶν pron. gen. 1p. pl. ἐγώ I
πάντων adj. gen. masc. pl. πᾶς πᾶσα πᾶν all, every, whosoever, every one, no, whole, any
αὐτόν pron. acc. masc. 3p. sg. αὐτός ή ό self, of oneself, even, very, the same, he, she, it
πῶς adv. πῶς how, by what means, after what manner
οὐχὶ adv. οὐχί not, nay
καὶ conj. καί and, even, also, but
σὺν prep. σύν (+dat) with, beside
αὐτῷ pron. dat. masc. 3p. sg. αὐτός ή ό self, of oneself, even, very, the same, he, she, it
τὰ art. acc. neut. pl. ὁ ἡ τό the, this, that, he, she, it
πάντα adj. acc. neut. pl. πᾶς πᾶσα πᾶν all, every, whosoever, every one, no, whole, any
ἡμῖν pron. dat. 1p. pl. ἐγώ I
33 τίς interrog. pron. nom. masc. sg. τίς what, who, why, where, which, how
κατὰ prep. κατά (+gen) against, by, throughout, down, (+acc) according to, after, with
ἐκλεκτῶν adj. gen. masc. pl. ἐκλεκτός elect, chosen
Θεοῦ n. gen. masc. sg. θεός God, god
Θεὸς n. nom. masc. sg. θεός God, god
ὁ art. nom. masc. sg. ὁ ἡ τό the, this, that, he, she, it
34 τίς interrog. pron. nom. masc. sg. τίς what, who, why, where, which, how
ὁ art. nom. masc. sg. ὁ ἡ τό the, this, that, he, she, it
Χριστὸς n. nom. masc. sg. Χριστός Christ
ὁ art. nom. masc. sg. ὁ ἡ τό the, this, that, he, she, it
μᾶλλον adv. μᾶλλον rather, more, more and more, better, much, much the more
δὲ conj. δέ but, and, now, also, to the contrary, rather, then
καὶ conj. καί and, even, also, but
ὃς relative pron. nom. masc. sg. ὅς ἥ ὅ who, which, what, that
καὶ conj. καί and, even, also, but
ἐν prep. ἐν (+dat) in, by, with, among, at, on, through, to, within, into, of, for
δεξιᾷ adj. dat. fem. sg. δεξιός right, right hand, right side
τοῦ art. gen. masc. sg. ὁ ἡ τό the, this, that, he, she, it

Θεοῦ n. gen. masc. sg. θεός God, god
ὃς relative pron. nom. masc. sg. ὅς ἥ ὅ who, which, what, that
καὶ conj. καί and, even, also, but
ὑπὲρ prep. ὑπέρ (+gen) for, of, for the sake of, (+acc) above, more than
ἡμῶν pron. gen. 1p. pl. ἐγώ I
35 τίς interrog. pron. nom. masc. sg. τίς what, who, why, where, which, how
ἡμᾶς pron. acc. 1p. pl. ἐγώ I
ἀπὸ prep. ἀπό (+gen) from, of, out of, since, for, off, at, by, in, on
τῆς art. gen. fem. sg. ὁ ἡ τό the, this, that, he, she, it
ἀγάπης n. gen. fem. sg. ἀγάπη love, charity, feast of charity
τοῦ art. gen. masc. sg. ὁ ἡ τό the, this, that, he, she, it
Χριστοῦ n. gen. masc. sg. Χριστός Christ
θλῖψις n. nom. fem. sg. θλῖψις tribulation, affliction, anguish, persecution
ἢ particle. ἤ or, than, either, nor, or else, and, rather than
στενοχωρία n. nom. fem. sg. στενοχωρία anguish, distress
ἢ particle. ἤ or, than, either, nor, or else, and, rather than
διωγμὸς n. nom. masc. sg. διωγμός persecution
ἢ particle. ἤ or, than, either, nor, or else, and, rather than
λιμὸς n. nom. masc. sg. λιμός famine, hunger, dearth
ἢ particle. ἤ or, than, either, nor, or else, and, rather than
γυμνότης n. nom. fem. sg. γυμνότης nakedness
ἢ particle. ἤ or, than, either, nor, or else, and, rather than
κίνδυνος n. nom. masc. sg. κίνδυνος peril
ἢ particle. ἤ or, than, either, nor, or else, and, rather than
μάχαιρα n. nom. fem. sg. μάχαιρα sword
36 καθὼς adv. καθώς as, even as, according as, according to
ὅτι conj. ὅτι that, for, because, how that, how, because that, for that, though
Ἕνεκά prep. ἕνεκα, ἕνεκεν or εἵνεκεν (+gen) for the sake, for a cause, for, by reason of
σοῦ pron. gen. 2p. sg. σύ thou, you
ὅλην adj. acc. fem. sg. ὅλος all, whole, every whit, altogether
τὴν art. acc. fem. sg. ὁ ἡ τό the, this, that, he, she, it
ἡμέραν n. acc. fem. sg. ἡμέρα day, time, year, while, age, day time
ὡς adv. ὡς as, when, as it were, how, about, like, as soon as, even as, while
πρόβατα n. nom. neut. pl. πρόβατον sheep
σφαγῆς n. gen. fem. sg. σφαγή slaughter
37 ἀλλ' conj. ἀλλά but, yea, yet, nevertheless, howbeit, nay, therefore
ἐν prep. ἐν (+dat) in, by, with, among, at, on, through, to, within, into, of, for
τούτοις demo. pron. dat. neut. pl. οὗτος αὕτη τοῦτο this, the same, this same, he, she, it
πᾶσιν adj. dat. neut. pl. πᾶς πᾶσα πᾶν all, every, whosoever, every one, no, whole, any
διὰ prep. διά (+gen) by, through, with, in, of, (+acc) for, because of, for a cause
τοῦ art. gen. masc. sg. ὁ ἡ τό the, this, that, he, she, it
ἡμᾶς pron. acc. 1p. pl. ἐγώ I
38 γὰρ conj. γάρ for, and, because, but, indeed
ὅτι conj. ὅτι that, for, because, how that, how, because that, for that, though
οὔτε conj. οὔτε neither, nor, nor yet, no, none
θάνατος n. nom. masc. sg. θάνατος death
οὔτε conj. οὔτε neither, nor, nor yet, no, none
ζωὴ n. nom. fem. sg. ζωή life, lifetime
οὔτε conj. οὔτε neither, nor, nor yet, no, none
ἄγγελοι n. nom. masc. pl. ἄγγελος angel, messenger
οὔτε conj. οὔτε neither, nor, nor yet, no, none
ἀρχαὶ n. nom. fem. pl. ἀρχή beginning, principality, corner, first, magistrate, rule
οὔτε conj. οὔτε neither, nor, nor yet, no, none
δυνάμεις n. nom. fem. pl. δύναμις power, mighty work, miracle, strength, might
οὔτε conj. οὔτε neither, nor, nor yet, no, none

οὔτε conj. οὔτε neither, nor, nor yet, no, none
39 οὔτε conj. οὔτε neither, nor, nor yet, no, none
ὕψωμα n. nom. neut. sg. ὕψωμα height, high thing
οὔτε conj. οὔτε neither, nor, nor yet, no, none
βάθος n. nom. neut. sg. βάθος deepness, depth, deep, deep thing
οὔτε conj. οὔτε neither, nor, nor yet, no, none
τις indefinite pron. nom. fem. sg. τὶς certain, some, any man, one, any thing
κτίσις n. nom. fem. sg. κτίσις creature, creation, building, ordinance
ἑτέρα adj. nom. fem. sg. ἕτερος another, other, else, strange
ἡμᾶς pron. acc. 1p. pl. ἐγώ I
ἀπὸ prep. ἀπό (+gen) from, of, out of, since, for, off, at, by, in, on
τῆς art. gen. fem. sg. ὁ ἡ τό the, this, that, he, she, it
ἀγάπης n. gen. fem. sg. ἀγάπη love, charity, feast of charity
τοῦ art. gen. masc. sg. ὁ ἡ τό the, this, that, he, she, it
Θεοῦ n. gen. masc. sg. θεός God, god
τῆς art. gen. fem. sg. ὁ ἡ τό the, this, that, he, she, it
ἐν prep. ἐν (+dat) in, by, with, among, at, on, through, to, within, into, of, for
Χριστῷ n. dat. masc. sg. Χριστός Christ
Ἰησοῦ n. dat. masc. sg. Ἰησοῦς Jesus
τῷ art. dat. masc. sg. ὁ ἡ τό the, this, that, he, she, it
Κυρίῳ n. dat. masc. sg. κύριος Lord, lord, master, sir, LORD, God, Master, owner
ἡμῶν pron. gen. 1p. pl. ἐγώ I

9

1 Ἀλήθειαν n. acc. fem. sg. ἀλήθεια truth, verity
ἐν prep. ἐν (+dat) in, by, with, among, at, on, through, to, within, into, of, for
Χριστῷ n. dat. masc. sg. Χριστός Christ
οὐ particle of negation. οὐ οὐκ οὐχ not, no, neither, none, nay, nor, never, nothing
μοι pron. dat. 1p. sg. ἐγώ I
τῆς art. gen. fem. sg. ὁ ἡ τό the, this, that, he, she, it
συνειδήσεώς n. gen. fem. sg. συνείδησις conscience
μου pron. gen. 1p. sg. ἐγώ I
ἐν prep. ἐν (+dat) in, by, with, among, at, on, through, to, within, into, of, for
Πνεύματι n. dat. neut. sg. πνεῦμα spirit, Spirit, Ghost, ghost, life. of the spirit, wind
Ἁγίῳ adj. dat. neut. sg. ἅγιος Holy, holy, saint, Holy One, holy thing, most holy
2 ὅτι conj. ὅτι that, for, because, how that, how, because that, for that, though
λύπη n. nom. fem. sg. λύπη sorrow, heaviness, grief, grievous, grudgingly
μοί pron. dat. 1p. sg. ἐγώ I
μεγάλη adj. nom. fem. sg. μέγας great, loud, greatest, high, large, mighty, strong
καὶ conj. καί and, even, also, but
ἀδιάλειπτος adj. nom. fem. sg. ἀδιάλειπτος without ceasing, continual
ὀδύνη n. nom. fem. sg. ὀδύνη sorrow
τῇ art. dat. fem. sg. ὁ ἡ τό the, this, that, he, she, it
καρδίᾳ n. dat. fem. sg. καρδία heart
μου pron. gen. 1p. sg. ἐγώ I
3 γὰρ conj. γάρ for, and, because, but, indeed
αὐτὸς pron. nom. masc. 3p. sg. αὐτός ἡ ὁ self, of oneself, even, very, the same, he, she, it
ἐγὼ pron. nom. 1p. sg. ἐγώ I
ἀνάθεμα n. nom. neut. sg. ἀνάθεμα accursed, Anathema, great course
ἀπὸ prep. ἀπό (+gen) from, of, out of, since, for, off, at, by, in, on
τοῦ art. gen. masc. sg. ὁ ἡ τό the, this, that, he, she, it
Χριστοῦ n. gen. masc. sg. Χριστός Christ
ὑπὲρ prep. ὑπέρ (+gen) for, of, for the sake of, (+acc) above, more than
τῶν art. gen. masc. pl. ὁ ἡ τό the, this, that, he, she, it

ἀδελφῶν n. gen. masc. pl. ἀδελφός brother
μου pron. gen. 1p. sg. ἐγώ I
τῶν art. gen. masc. pl. ὁ ἡ τό the, this, that, he, she, it
συγγενῶν adj. gen. masc. pl. συγγενής kinsman, cousin, kinsfolk, kin
μου pron. gen. 1p. sg. ἐγώ I
κατὰ prep. κατά (+gen) against, by, throughout, down, (+acc) according to, after, with
σάρκα n. acc. fem. sg. σάρξ flesh, carnal
4 οἵτινες relative pron. nom. masc. pl. ὅστις which, who, whosoever, that, whatsoever
Ἰσραηλῖται n. nom. masc. pl. Ἰσραηλίτης Israelite, Israel
ὧν relative pron. gen. masc. pl. ὅς ἥ ὅ who, which, what, that
ἡ art. nom. fem. sg. ὁ ἡ τό the, this, that, he, she, it
υἱοθεσία n. nom. fem. sg. υἱοθεσία adoption, adoption of children, adoption of sons
καὶ conj. καί and, even, also, but
ἡ art. nom. fem. sg. ὁ ἡ τό the, this, that, he, she, it
δόξα n. nom. fem. sg. δόξα glory, honour, praise, dignity, worship
καὶ conj. καί and, even, also, but
αἱ art. nom. fem. pl. ὁ ἡ τό the, this, that, he, she, it
διαθῆκαι n. nom. fem. pl. διαθήκη testament, covenant
καὶ conj. καί and, even, also, but
ἡ art. nom. fem. sg. ὁ ἡ τό the, this, that, he, she, it
νομοθεσία n. nom. fem. sg. νομοθεσία giving of the law
καὶ conj. καί and, even, also, but
ἡ art. nom. fem. sg. ὁ ἡ τό the, this, that, he, she, it
λατρεία n. nom. fem. sg. λατρεία service, divine service
καὶ conj. καί and, even, also, but
αἱ art. nom. fem. pl. ὁ ἡ τό the, this, that, he, she, it
ἐπαγγελίαι n. nom. fem. pl. ἐπαγγελία promise, message
5 ὧν relative pron. gen. masc. pl. ὅς ἥ ὅ who, which, what, that
οἱ art. nom. masc. pl. ὁ ἡ τό the, this, that, he, she, it
πατέρες n. nom. masc. pl. πατήρ Father, father, parent
καὶ conj. καί and, even, also, but
ἐξ prep. ἐκ ἐξ (+gen) of, from, out of, by, on, with, in, among, through
ὧν relative pron. gen. masc. pl. ὅς ἥ ὅ who, which, what, that
ὁ art. nom. masc. sg. ὁ ἡ τό the, this, that, he, she, it
Χριστὸς n. nom. masc. sg. Χριστός Christ
τὸ art. acc. neut. sg. ὁ ἡ τό the, this, that, he, she, it
κατὰ prep. κατά (+gen) against, by, throughout, down, (+acc) according to, after, with
σάρκα n. acc. fem. sg. σάρξ flesh, carnal
ὁ art. nom. masc. sg. ὁ ἡ τό the, this, that, he, she, it
ἐπὶ prep. ἐπί (+gen) on, in, upon, (+dat) in, at, for, upon, (+acc) on, upon, unto, to, against
πάντων adj. gen. neut. pl. πᾶς πᾶσα πᾶν all, every, whosoever, every one, no, whole, any
Θεὸς n. nom. masc. sg. θεός God, god
εὐλογητὸς adj. nom. masc. sg. εὐλογητός blessed
εἰς prep. εἰς (+acc) into, to, unto, for, in, on, toward, against, upon, at, among
τοὺς art. acc. masc. pl. ὁ ἡ τό the, this, that, he, she, it
αἰῶνας n. acc. masc. pl. αἰών ever, ever and ever, evermore, age, eternal, world
ἀμήν particle. ἀμήν amen, verily
6 οὐχ particle of negation. οὐ οὐκ οὐχ not, no, neither, none, nay, nor, never, nothing
οἷον relative pron. nom. neut. sg. οἷος what manner of, such as, as, which, what, so as
δὲ conj. δέ but, and, now, also, to the contrary, rather, then
ὅτι conj. ὅτι that, for, because, how that, how, because that, for that, though
ὁ art. nom. masc. sg. ὁ ἡ τό the, this, that, he, she, it
λόγος n. nom. masc. sg. λόγος word, saying, account, speech, thing, matter
τοῦ art. gen. masc. sg. ὁ ἡ τό the, this, that, he, she, it
Θεοῦ n. gen. masc. sg. θεός God, god

οὐ particle of negation. οὐ οὐκ οὐχ not, no, neither, none, nay, nor, never, nothing
γὰρ conj. γάρ for, and, because, but, indeed
πάντες adj. nom. masc. pl. πᾶς πᾶσα πᾶν all, every, whosoever, every one, no, whole, any
οἱ art. nom. masc. pl. ὁ ἡ τό the, this, that, he, she, it
ἐξ prep. ἐκ ἐξ (+gen) of, from, out of, by, on, with, in, among, through
Ἰσραὴλ pron. name. masc. inde. Ἰσραήλ Israel
οὗτοι demo. pron. nom. masc. pl. οὗτος αὕτη τοῦτο this, the same, this same, he, she, it
Ἰσραήλ pron. name. masc. inde. Ἰσραήλ Israel
7 οὐδ' adv. οὐδέ neither, nor, not, no, not even, never, not yet
ὅτι conj. ὅτι that, for, because, how that, how, because that, for that, though
σπέρμα n. nom. neut. sg. σπέρμα seed, issue
Ἀβραὰμ n. gen. masc. sg. Ἀβραάμ Abraham
πάντες adj. nom. masc. pl. πᾶς πᾶσα πᾶν all, every, whosoever, every one, no, whole, any
τέκνα n. nom. neut. pl. τέκνον child, son, daughter
ἀλλ' conj. ἀλλά but, yea, yet, nevertheless, howbeit, nay, therefore
Ἐν prep. ἐν (+dat) in, by, with, among, at, on, through, to, within, into, of, for
Ἰσαὰκ n. dat. masc. sg. Ἰσαάκ Isaac
σοι pron. dat. 2p. sg. σύ thou, you
σπέρμα n. nom. neut. sg. σπέρμα seed, issue
8 τοῦτ' demo. pron. nom. neut. sg. οὗτος αὕτη τοῦτο this, the same, this same, he, she, it
οὐ particle of negation. οὐ οὐκ οὐχ not, no, neither, none, nay, nor, never, nothing
τὰ art. nom. neut. pl. ὁ ἡ τό the, this, that, he, she, it
τέκνα n. nom. neut. pl. τέκνον child, son, daughter
τῆς art. gen. fem. sg. ὁ ἡ τό the, this, that, he, she, it
σαρκὸς n. gen. fem. sg. σάρξ flesh, carnal
ταῦτα demo. pron. nom. neut. pl. οὗτος αὕτη τοῦτο this, the same, this same, he, she, it
τέκνα n. nom. neut. pl. τέκνον child, son, daughter
τοῦ art. gen. masc. sg. ὁ ἡ τό the, this, that, he, she, it
Θεοῦ n. gen. masc. sg. θεός God, god
ἀλλὰ conj. ἀλλά but, yea, yet, nevertheless, howbeit, nay, therefore
τὰ art. nom. neut. pl. ὁ ἡ τό the, this, that, he, she, it
τέκνα n. nom. neut. pl. τέκνον child, son, daughter
τῆς art. gen. fem. sg. ὁ ἡ τό the, this, that, he, she, it
ἐπαγγελίας n. gen. fem. sg. ἐπαγγελία promise, message
εἰς prep. εἰς (+acc) into, to, unto, for, in, on, toward, against, upon, at, among
σπέρμα n. acc. neut. sg. σπέρμα seed, issue
9 ἐπαγγελίας n. gen. fem. sg. ἐπαγγελία promise, message
γὰρ conj. γάρ for, and, because, but, indeed
ὁ art. nom. masc. sg. ὁ ἡ τό the, this, that, he, she, it
λόγος n. nom. masc. sg. λόγος word, saying, account, speech, thing, matter
οὗτος demo. pron. nom. masc. sg. οὗτος αὕτη τοῦτο this, the same, this same, he, she, it
Κατὰ prep. κατά (+gen) against, by, throughout, down, (+acc) according to, after, with
τὸν art. acc. masc. sg. ὁ ἡ τό the, this, that, he, she, it
καιρὸν n. acc. masc. sg. καιρός time, season, due time, opportunity
τοῦτον demo. pron. acc. masc. sg. οὗτος αὕτη τοῦτο this, the same, this same, he, she, it
καὶ conj. καί and, even, also, but
τῇ art. dat. fem. sg. ὁ ἡ τό the, this, that, he, she, it
Σάρρᾳ n. dat. fem. sg. Σάρρα Sara, Sarah
υἱός n. nom. masc. sg. υἱός son, child, descendant, offspring, heir
10 οὐ particle of negation. οὐ οὐκ οὐχ not, no, neither, none, nay, nor, never, nothing
μόνον adv. μόνος only, alone, by oneself
δέ conj. δέ but, and, now, also, to the contrary, rather, then
ἀλλὰ conj. ἀλλά but, yea, yet, nevertheless, howbeit, nay, therefore
καὶ conj. καί and, even, also, but
Ῥεβέκκα n. nom. fem. sg. Ῥεβέκκα Rebecca

ἐξ prep. ἐκ ἐξ (+gen) of, from, out of, by, on, with, in, among, through
ἑνὸς num. gen. masc. sg. εἷς or ἕν one, other, some, any, only, a certain
κοίτην n. acc. fem. sg. κοίτη bed, chambering
Ἰσαὰκ n. gen. masc. sg. Ἰσαάκ Isaac
τοῦ art. gen. masc. sg. ὁ ἡ τό the, this, that, he, she, it
πατρὸς n. gen. masc. sg. πατήρ Father, father, parent
ἡμῶν pron. gen. 1p. pl. ἐγώ I
11 μήπω adv. μήπω not yet
γὰρ conj. γάρ for, and, because, but, indeed
μηδὲ conj. μηδέ neither, nor, not, no not, nor yet, not once, not so much as
τι indefinite pron. acc. neut. sg. τὶς certain, some, any man, one, any thing
ἀγαθὸν adj. acc. neut. sg. ἀγαθός good, good thing, that which is good, well
ἢ particle. ἤ or, than, either, nor, or else, and, rather than
κακόν adj. acc. neut. sg. κακός evil, evil thing, noisome, wicked
ἵνα conj. ἵνα that, to, lest, for to, so that, albeit, because, for, so as
ἡ art. nom. fem. sg. ὁ ἡ τό the, this, that, he, she, it
κατ' prep. κατά (+gen) against, by, throughout, down, (+acc) according to, after, with
ἐκλογὴν n. acc. fem. sg. ἐκλογή election, chosen
τοῦ art. gen. masc. sg. ὁ ἡ τό the, this, that, he, she, it
Θεοῦ n. gen. masc. sg. θεός God, god
πρόθεσις n. nom. fem. sg. πρόθεσις purpose, shew, shewbread
οὐκ particle of negation. οὐ οὐκ οὐχ not, no, neither, none, nay, nor, never, nothing
ἐξ prep. ἐκ ἐξ (+gen) of, from, out of, by, on, with, in, among, through
ἔργων n. gen. neut. pl. ἔργον work, deed, doing labour
ἀλλ' conj. ἀλλά but, yea, yet, nevertheless, howbeit, nay, therefore
ἐκ prep. ἐκ ἐξ (+gen) of, from, out of, by, on, with, in, among, through
τοῦ art. gen. masc. sg. ὁ ἡ τό the, this, that, he, she, it
12 αὐτῇ pron. dat. fem. 3p. sg. αὐτός ἡ ὁ self, of oneself, even, very, the same, he, she, it
ὅτι conj. ὅτι that, for, because, how that, how, because that, for that, though
Ὁ art. nom. masc. sg. ὁ ἡ τό the, this, that, he, she, it
μείζων compar. adj. nom. masc. sg. μέγας great, loud, greatest, high, large, mighty, strong
τῷ art. dat. masc. sg. ὁ ἡ τό the, this, that, he, she, it
ἐλάσσονι compar. adj. dat. masc. sg. ἐλάσσων worse, younger
13 καθὼς adv. καθώς as, even as, according as, according to
Τὸν art. acc. masc. sg. ὁ ἡ τό the, this, that, he, she, it
Ἰακὼβ n. acc. masc. sg. Ἰακώβ Jacob
τὸν art. acc. masc. sg. ὁ ἡ τό the, this, that, he, she, it
δὲ conj. δέ but, and, now, also, to the contrary, rather, then
Ἠσαῦ n. acc. masc. sg. Ἠσαῦ Esau
14 Τί interrog. pron. acc. neut. sg. τίς what, who, why, where, which, how
οὖν conj. οὖν therefore, then, so, and, now, wherefore
μὴ particle of negation. μή not, no, lest, neither, none, nothing, nor, never, without
ἀδικία n. nom. fem. sg. ἀδικία iniquity, unrighteousness, unjust, wrong
παρὰ prep. παρά (+gen) of, from, (+dat) with, for, (+acc) beside, at, by, above, against
τῷ art. dat. masc. sg. ὁ ἡ τό the, this, that, he, she, it
Θεῷ n. dat. masc. sg. θεός God, god
μὴ particle of negation. μή not, no, lest, neither, none, nothing, nor, never, without
15 τῷ art. dat. masc. sg. ὁ ἡ τό the, this, that, he, she, it
γὰρ conj. γάρ for, and, because, but, indeed
Μωσῇ n. dat. masc. sg. Μωσῆς Moses
ὃν relative pron. acc. masc. sg. ὅς ἥ ὅ who, which, what, that
ἂν particle. ἄν Indicating contingency. No English translation.
καὶ conj. καί and, even, also, but
ὃν relative pron. acc. masc. sg. ὅς ἥ ὅ who, which, what, that
ἂν particle. ἄν Indicating contingency. No English translation.

16 ἄρα conj. ἄρα then, therefore, haply, wherefore, perhaps, manner, no doubt, truly
οὖν conj. οὖν therefore, then, so, and, now, wherefore
οὐ particle of negation. οὐ οὐκ οὐχ not, no, neither, none, nay, nor, never, nothing
τοῦ art. gen. masc. sg. ὁ ἡ τό the, this, that, he, she, it
οὐδὲ adv. οὐδέ neither, nor, not, no, not even, never, not yet
τοῦ art. gen. masc. sg. ὁ ἡ τό the, this, that, he, she, it
ἀλλὰ conj. ἀλλά but, yea, yet, nevertheless, howbeit, nay, therefore
τοῦ art. gen. masc. sg. ὁ ἡ τό the, this, that, he, she, it
Θεοῦ n. gen. masc. sg. θεός God, god
17 γὰρ conj. γάρ for, and, because, but, indeed
ἡ art. nom. fem. sg. ὁ ἡ τό the, this, that, he, she, it
γραφὴ n. nom. fem. sg. γραφή scripture
τῷ art. dat. masc. sg. ὁ ἡ τό the, this, that, he, she, it
Φαραὼ n. dat. masc. sg. Φαραώ Pharaoh
ὅτι conj. ὅτι that, for, because, how that, how, because that, for that, though
Εἰς prep. εἰς (+acc) into, to, unto, for, in, on, toward, against, upon, at, among
αὐτὸ pron. acc. neut. 3p. sg. αὐτός ή ό self, of oneself, even, very, the same, he, she, it
τοῦτο demo. pron. acc. neut. sg. οὗτος αὕτη τοῦτο this, the same, this same, he, she, it
σε pron. acc. 2p. sg. σύ thou, you
ὅπως adv. ὅπως that, how, to, because, so that, when
ἐν prep. ἐν (+dat) in, by, with, among, at, on, through, to, within, into, of, for
σοὶ pron. dat. 2p. sg. σύ thou, you
τὴν art. acc. fem. sg. ὁ ἡ τό the, this, that, he, she, it
δύναμίν n. acc. fem. sg. δύναμις power, mighty work, miracle, strength, might
μου pron. gen. 1p. sg. ἐγώ I
καὶ conj. καί and, even, also, but
ὅπως adv. ὅπως that, how, to, because, so that, when
τὸ art. acc. neut. sg. ὁ ἡ τό the, this, that, he, she, it
ὄνομά n. acc. neut. sg. ὄνομα name, call, surname
μου pron. gen. 1p. sg. ἐγώ I
ἐν prep. ἐν (+dat) in, by, with, among, at, on, through, to, within, into, of, for
πάσῃ adj. dat. fem. sg. πᾶς πᾶσα πᾶν all, every, whosoever, every one, no, whole, any
τῇ art. dat. fem. sg. ὁ ἡ τό the, this, that, he, she, it
γῇ n. dat. fem. sg. γῆ earth, land, ground, country
18 ἄρα conj. ἄρα then, therefore, haply, wherefore, perhaps, manner, no doubt, truly
οὖν conj. οὖν therefore, then, so, and, now, wherefore
ὃν relative pron. acc. masc. sg. ὅς ἥ ὅ who, which, what, that
ὃν relative pron. acc. masc. sg. ὅς ἥ ὅ who, which, what, that
δὲ conj. δέ but, and, now, also, to the contrary, rather, then
19 οὖν conj. οὖν therefore, then, so, and, now, wherefore
μοι pron. dat. 1p. sg. ἐγώ I
Τί interrog. pron. acc. neut. sg. τίς what, who, why, where, which, how
ἔτι adv. ἔτι yet, more, any more, further, still, moreover
τῷ art. dat. neut. sg. ὁ ἡ τό the, this, that, he, she, it
γὰρ conj. γάρ for, and, because, but, indeed
βουλήματι n. dat. neut. sg. βούλημα purpose, will
αὐτοῦ pron. gen. masc. 3p. sg. αὐτός ή ό self, of oneself, even, very, the same, he, she, it
τίς interrog. pron. nom. masc. sg. τίς what, who, why, where, which, how
20 μενοῦνγε particle. μενοῦνγε yea rather, nay but, yea doubtless
ὦ interjection. ὦ O
ἄνθρωπε n. voc. masc. sg. ἄνθρωπος man, human being, person, one, certain
σὺ pron. nom. 2p. sg. σύ thou, you
τίς interrog. pron. nom. masc. sg. τίς what, who, why, where, which, how
ὁ art. nom. masc. sg. ὁ ἡ τό the, this, that, he, she, it
τῷ art. dat. masc. sg. ὁ ἡ τό the, this, that, he, she, it

Θεῷ n. dat. masc. sg. θεός God, god
μὴ particle of negation. μή not, no, lest, neither, none, nothing, nor, never, without
τὸ art. nom. neut. sg. ὁ ἡ τό the, this, that, he, she, it
πλάσμα n. nom. neut. sg. πλάσμα thing formed
τῷ art. dat. masc. sg. ὁ ἡ τό the, this, that, he, she, it
Τί interrog. pron. acc. neut. sg. τίς what, who, why, where, which, how
με pron. acc. 1p. sg. ἐγώ I
οὕτως adv. οὕτω οὕτως so, even so, thus, on this wise, likewise, after this manner
21 ἢ particle. ἤ or, than, either, nor, or else, and, rather than
οὐκ particle of negation. οὐ οὐκ οὐχ not, no, neither, none, nay, nor, never, nothing
ἐξουσίαν n. acc. fem. sg. ἐξουσία power, authority, right, strength, jurisdiction
ὁ art. nom. masc. sg. ὁ ἡ τό the, this, that, he, she, it
κεραμεὺς n. nom. masc. sg. κεραμεύς potter
τοῦ art. gen. masc. sg. ὁ ἡ τό the, this, that, he, she, it
πηλοῦ n. gen. masc. sg. πηλός clay
ἐκ prep. ἐκ ἐξ (+gen) of, from, out of, by, on, with, in, among, through
τοῦ art. gen. neut. sg. ὁ ἡ τό the, this, that, he, she, it
αὐτοῦ pron. gen. masc. 3p. sg. αὐτός ή ό self, of oneself, even, very, the same, he, she, it
φυράματος n. gen. neut. sg. φύραμα lump
ὃ relative pron. acc. neut. sg. ὅς ἥ ὅ who, which, what, that
μὲν conj. μέν indeed, verily, truly, even, so, some
εἰς prep. εἰς (+acc) into, to, unto, for, in, on, toward, against, upon, at, among
τιμὴν n. acc. fem. sg. τιμή honour, price, preciousness, sum
σκεῦος n. acc. neut. sg. σκεῦος vessel, good, sail, stuff
ὃ relative pron. acc. neut. sg. ὅς ἥ ὅ who, which, what, that
δὲ conj. δέ but, and, now, also, to the contrary, rather, then
εἰς prep. εἰς (+acc) into, to, unto, for, in, on, toward, against, upon, at, among
ἀτιμίαν n. acc. fem. sg. ἀτιμία vile, dishonour, reproach, shame
22 εἰ conj. εἰ if, whether, that, though, forasmuch
δὲ conj. δέ but, and, now, also, to the contrary, rather, then
ὁ art. nom. masc. sg. ὁ ἡ τό the, this, that, he, she, it
Θεὸς n. nom. masc. sg. θεός God, god
τὴν art. acc. fem. sg. ὁ ἡ τό the, this, that, he, she, it
ὀργὴν n. acc. fem. sg. ὀργή wrath, anger, indignation, vengeance
καὶ conj. καί and, even, also, but
τὸ art. acc. neut. sg. ὁ ἡ τό the, this, that, he, she, it
δυνατὸν adj. acc. neut. sg. δυνατός able, possible, mighty, strong
αὐτοῦ pron. gen. masc. 3p. sg. αὐτός ή ό self, of oneself, even, very, the same, he, she, it
ἐν prep. ἐν (+dat) in, by, with, among, at, on, through, to, within, into, of, for
πολλῇ adj. dat. fem. sg. πολύς many, great, much, long, abundant
μακροθυμίᾳ n. dat. fem. sg. μακροθυμία longsuffering, patience
σκεύη n. acc. neut. pl. σκεῦος vessel, good, sail, stuff
ὀργῆς n. gen. fem. sg. ὀργή wrath, anger, indignation, vengeance
εἰς prep. εἰς (+acc) into, to, unto, for, in, on, toward, against, upon, at, among
ἀπώλειαν n. acc. fem. sg. ἀπώλεια destruction, perdition, waste, damnation
23 καὶ conj. καί and, even, also, but
ἵνα conj. ἵνα that, to, lest, for to, so that, albeit, because, for, so as
τὸν art. acc. masc. sg. ὁ ἡ τό the, this, that, he, she, it
πλοῦτον n. acc. masc. sg. πλοῦτος riches
τῆς art. gen. fem. sg. ὁ ἡ τό the, this, that, he, she, it
δόξης n. gen. fem. sg. δόξα glory, honour, praise, dignity, worship
αὐτοῦ pron. gen. masc. 3p. sg. αὐτός ή ό self, of oneself, even, very, the same, he, she, it
ἐπὶ prep. ἐπί (+gen) on, in, upon, (+dat) in, at, for, upon, (+acc) on, upon, unto, to, against
σκεύη n. acc. neut. pl. σκεῦος vessel, good, sail, stuff
ἐλέους n. gen. neut. sg. ἔλεος mercy

ἃ relative pron. acc. neut. pl. ὅς ἥ ὅ who, which, what, that
εἰς prep. εἰς (+acc) into, to, unto, for, in, on, toward, against, upon, at, among
δόξαν n. acc. fem. sg. δόξα glory, honour, praise, dignity, worship
24 οὓς relative pron. acc. masc. pl. ὅς ἥ ὅ who, which, what, that
καὶ conj. καί and, even, also, but
ἡμᾶς pron. acc. 1p. pl. ἐγώ I
οὐ particle of negation. οὐ οὐκ οὐχ not, no, neither, none, nay, nor, never, nothing
μόνον adv. μόνος only, alone, by oneself
ἐξ prep. ἐκ ἐξ (+gen) of, from, out of, by, on, with, in, among, through
Ἰουδαίων adj. gen. masc. pl. Ἰουδαῖος Jew, Jewess
ἀλλὰ conj. ἀλλά but, yea, yet, nevertheless, howbeit, nay, therefore
καὶ conj. καί and, even, also, but
ἐξ prep. ἐκ ἐξ (+gen) of, from, out of, by, on, with, in, among, through
ἐθνῶν n. gen. neut. pl. ἔθνος Gentile, nation, heathen, people
25 ὡς adv. ὡς as, when, as it were, how, about, like, as soon as, even as, while
καὶ conj. καί and, even, also, but
ἐν prep. ἐν (+dat) in, by, with, among, at, on, through, to, within, into, of, for
τῷ art. dat. masc. sg. ὁ ἡ τό the, this, that, he, she, it
Ὡσηὲ n. dat. masc. sg. Ὡσηέ Osee, Hosea
τὸν art. acc. masc. sg. ὁ ἡ τό the, this, that, he, she, it
οὐ particle of negation. οὐ οὐκ οὐχ not, no, neither, none, nay, nor, never, nothing
λαόν n. acc. masc. sg. λαός people
μου pron. gen. 1p. sg. ἐγώ I
λαόν n. acc. masc. sg. λαός people
μου pron. gen. 1p. sg. ἐγώ I
καὶ conj. καί and, even, also, but
τὴν art. acc. fem. sg. ὁ ἡ τό the, this, that, he, she, it
οὐκ particle of negation. οὐ οὐκ οὐχ not, no, neither, none, nay, nor, never, nothing
26 καὶ conj. καί and, even, also, but
ἐν prep. ἐν (+dat) in, by, with, among, at, on, through, to, within, into, of, for
τῷ art. dat. masc. sg. ὁ ἡ τό the, this, that, he, she, it
τόπῳ n. dat. masc. sg. τόπος place, room, quarter
οὗ relative pron. gen. masc. sg. ὅς ἥ ὅ who, which, what, that
αὐτοῖς pron. dat. masc. 3p. pl. αὐτός ή ό self, of oneself, even, very, the same, he, she, it
Οὐ particle of negation. οὐ οὐκ οὐχ not, no, neither, none, nay, nor, never, nothing
λαός n. nom. masc. sg. λαός people
μου pron. gen. 1p. sg. ἐγώ I
ὑμεῖς pron. nom. 2p. pl. σύ thou, you
ἐκεῖ adv. ἐκεῖ there, thither, thitherward, yonder, yonder place
υἱοὶ n. nom. masc. pl. υἱός son, child, descendant, offspring, heir
Θεοῦ n. gen. masc. sg. θεός God, god
27 Ἠσαΐας n. nom. masc. sg. Ἠσαΐας Esaias, Isaiah
δὲ conj. δέ but, and, now, also, to the contrary, rather, then
ὑπὲρ prep. ὑπέρ (+gen) for, of, for the sake of, (+acc) above, more than
τοῦ art. gen. masc. sg. ὁ ἡ τό the, this, that, he, she, it
Ἰσραήλ pron. name. masc. inde. Ἰσραήλ Israel
Ἐὰν conj. ἐάν if, soever, except, though, and if, but, whether, if so, so
ὁ art. nom. masc. sg. ὁ ἡ τό the, this, that, he, she, it
ἀριθμὸς n. nom. masc. sg. ἀριθμός number
τῶν art. gen. masc. pl. ὁ ἡ τό the, this, that, he, she, it
υἱῶν n. gen. masc. pl. υἱός son, child, descendant, offspring, heir
Ἰσραὴλ pron. name. masc. inde. Ἰσραήλ Israel
ὡς adv. ὡς as, when, as it were, how, about, like, as soon as, even as, while
ἡ art. nom. fem. sg. ὁ ἡ τό the, this, that, he, she, it
ἄμμος n. nom. fem. sg. ἄμμος sand

τῆς art. gen. fem. sg. ὁ ἡ τό the, this, that, he, she, it
θαλάσσης n. gen. fem. sg. θάλασσα sea
τὸ art. nom. neut. sg. ὁ ἡ τό the, this, that, he, she, it
κατάλειμμα n. nom. neut. sg. κατάλειμμα remnant
28 λόγον n. acc. masc. sg. λόγος word, saying, account, speech, thing, matter
γὰρ conj. γάρ for, and, because, but, indeed
καὶ conj. καί and, even, also, but
ἐν prep. ἐν (+dat) in, by, with, among, at, on, through, to, within, into, of, for
δικαιοσύνῃ n. dat. fem. sg. δικαιοσύνη righteousness
ὅτι conj. ὅτι that, for, because, how that, how, because that, for that, though
λόγον n. acc. masc. sg. λόγος word, saying, account, speech, thing, matter
Κύριος n. nom. masc. sg. κύριος Lord, lord, master, sir, LORD, God, Master, owner
ἐπὶ prep. ἐπί (+gen) on, in, upon, (+dat) in, at, for, upon, (+acc) on, upon, unto, to, against
τῆς art. gen. fem. sg. ὁ ἡ τό the, this, that, he, she, it
γῆς n. gen. fem. sg. γῆ earth, land, ground, country
29 καὶ conj. καί and, even, also, but
καθὼς adv. καθώς as, even as, according as, according to
Ἡσαΐας n. nom. masc. sg. Ἡσαΐας Esaias, Isaiah
Εἰ conj. εἰ if, whether, that, though, forasmuch
μὴ particle of negation. μή not, no, lest, neither, none, nothing, nor, never, without
Κύριος n. nom. masc. sg. κύριος Lord, lord, master, sir, LORD, God, Master, owner
Σαβαὼθ n. gen. masc. pl. Σαβαώθ Sabaoth
ἡμῖν pron. dat. 1p. pl. ἐγώ I
σπέρμα n. acc. neut. sg. σπέρμα seed, issue
ὡς adv. ὡς as, when, as it were, how, about, like, as soon as, even as, while
Σόδομα n. nom. neut. pl. Σόδομα Sodom, Sodoma
ἂν particle. ἄν Indicating contingency. No English translation.
καὶ conj. καί and, even, also, but
ὡς adv. ὡς as, when, as it were, how, about, like, as soon as, even as, while
Γόμορρα n. nom. neut. pl. Γόμορρα Gomorrha
ἂν particle. ἄν Indicating contingency. No English translation.
30 Τί interrog. pron. acc. neut. sg. τίς what, who, why, where, which, how
οὖν conj. οὖν therefore, then, so, and, now, wherefore
ὅτι conj. ὅτι that, for, because, how that, how, because that, for that, though
ἔθνη n. nom. neut. pl. ἔθνος Gentile, nation, heathen, people
τὰ art. nom. neut. pl. ὁ ἡ τό the, this, that, he, she, it
μὴ particle of negation. μή not, no, lest, neither, none, nothing, nor, never, without
δικαιοσύνην n. acc. fem. sg. δικαιοσύνη righteousness
δικαιοσύνην n. acc. fem. sg. δικαιοσύνη righteousness
δικαιοσύνην n. acc. fem. sg. δικαιοσύνη righteousness
δὲ conj. δέ but, and, now, also, to the contrary, rather, then
τὴν art. acc. fem. sg. ὁ ἡ τό the, this, that, he, she, it
ἐκ prep. ἐκ ἐξ (+gen) of, from, out of, by, on, with, in, among, through
πίστεως n. gen. fem. sg. πίστις faith, assurance, belief, fidelity
31 Ἰσραὴλ pron. name. masc. inde. Ἰσραήλ Israel
δὲ conj. δέ but, and, now, also, to the contrary, rather, then
νόμον n. acc. masc. sg. νόμος law, the law
δικαιοσύνης n. gen. fem. sg. δικαιοσύνη righteousness
εἰς prep. εἰς (+acc) into, to, unto, for, in, on, toward, against, upon, at, among
νόμον n. acc. masc. sg. νόμος law, the law
δικαιοσύνης n. gen. fem. sg. δικαιοσύνη righteousness
οὐκ particle of negation. οὐ οὐκ οὐχ not, no, neither, none, nay, nor, never, nothing
32 διατί adv. διατί why, for what, wherefore
ὅτι conj. ὅτι that, for, because, how that, how, because that, for that, though
οὐκ particle of negation. οὐ οὐκ οὐχ not, no, neither, none, nay, nor, never, nothing

ἐκ prep. ἐκ ἐξ (+gen) of, from, out of, by, on, with, in, among, through
πίστεως n. gen. fem. sg. πίστις faith, assurance, belief, fidelity
ἀλλ' conj. ἀλλά but, yea, yet, nevertheless, howbeit, nay, therefore
ὡς adv. ὡς as, when, as it were, how, about, like, as soon as, even as, while
ἐξ prep. ἐκ ἐξ (+gen) of, from, out of, by, on, with, in, among, through
ἔργων n. gen. neut. pl. ἔργον work, deed, doing labour
νόμου n. gen. masc. sg. νόμος law, the law
γὰρ conj. γάρ for, and, because, but, indeed
τῷ art. dat. masc. sg. ὁ ἡ τό the, this, that, he, she, it
λίθῳ n. dat. masc. sg. λίθος stone
τοῦ art. gen. neut. sg. ὁ ἡ τό the, this, that, he, she, it
προσκόμματος n. gen. neut. sg. πρόσκομμα stumbling, offence
33 καθὼς adv. καθώς as, even as, according as, according to
ἐν prep. ἐν (+dat) in, by, with, among, at, on, through, to, within, into, of, for
Σιὼν n. dat. fem. sg. Σιών Sion
λίθον n. acc. masc. sg. λίθος stone
προσκόμματος n. gen. neut. sg. πρόσκομμα stumbling, offence
καὶ conj. καί and, even, also, but
πέτραν n. acc. fem. sg. πέτρα rock
σκανδάλου n. gen. neut. sg. σκάνδαλον offence, stumblingblock, thing that offend
καὶ conj. καί and, even, also, but
πᾶς adj. nom. masc. sg. πᾶς πᾶσα πᾶν all, every, whosoever, every one, no, whole, any
ὁ art. nom. masc. sg. ὁ ἡ τό the, this, that, he, she, it
ἐπ' prep. ἐπί (+gen) on, in, upon, (+dat) in, at, for, upon, (+acc) on, upon, unto, to, against
αὐτῷ pron. dat. masc. 3p. sg. αὐτός ή ό self, of oneself, even, very, the same, he, she, it
οὐ particle of negation. οὐ οὐκ οὐχ not, no, neither, none, nay, nor, never, nothing

10

1 'Αδελφοί n. voc. masc. pl. ἀδελφός brother
ἡ art. nom. fem. sg. ὁ ἡ τό the, this, that, he, she, it
μὲν conj. μέν indeed, verily, truly, even, so, some
εὐδοκία n. nom. fem. sg. εὐδοκία good pleasure, good will, desire
τῆς art. gen. fem. sg. ὁ ἡ τό the, this, that, he, she, it
ἐμῆς poss. pron. gen. fem. 1p. sg. ἐμός my, mine, mine own, of me
καρδίας n. gen. fem. sg. καρδία heart
καὶ conj. καί and, even, also, but
ἡ art. nom. fem. sg. ὁ ἡ τό the, this, that, he, she, it
δέησις n. nom. fem. sg. δέησις prayer, supplication, request
ἡ art. nom. fem. sg. ὁ ἡ τό the, this, that, he, she, it
πρὸς prep. πρός (+gen) for, (+dat) at, (+acc) unto, to, with, for, against
τὸν art. acc. masc. sg. ὁ ἡ τό the, this, that, he, she, it
Θεὸν n. acc. masc. sg. θεός God, god
ὑπὲρ prep. ὑπέρ (+gen) for, of, for the sake of, (+acc) above, more than
τοῦ art. gen. masc. sg. ὁ ἡ τό the, this, that, he, she, it
'Ισραήλ pron. name. masc. inde. 'Ισραήλ Israel
εἰς prep. εἰς (+acc) into, to, unto, for, in, on, toward, against, upon, at, among
σωτηρίαν n. acc. fem. sg. σωτηρία salvation, deliver, health, saving
2 γὰρ conj. γάρ for, and, because, but, indeed
αὐτοῖς pron. dat. masc. 3p. pl. αὐτός ή ό self, of oneself, even, very, the same, he, she, it
ὅτι conj. ὅτι that, for, because, how that, how, because that, for that, though
ζῆλον n. acc. masc. sg. ζῆλος zeal, envying, indignation, emulation, jealousy
Θεοῦ n. gen. masc. sg. θεός God, god
ἀλλ' conj. ἀλλά but, yea, yet, nevertheless, howbeit, nay, therefore
οὐ particle of negation. οὐ οὐκ οὐχ not, no, neither, none, nay, nor, never, nothing

κατ' prep. κατά (+gen) against, by, throughout, down, (+acc) according to, after, with
ἐπίγνωσιν n. acc. fem. sg. ἐπίγνωσις knowledge, acknowledging, acknowledgement
3 γὰρ conj. γάρ for, and, because, but, indeed
τὴν art. acc. fem. sg. ὁ ἡ τό the, this, that, he, she, it
τοῦ art. gen. masc. sg. ὁ ἡ τό the, this, that, he, she, it
Θεοῦ n. gen. masc. sg. θεός God, god
δικαιοσύνην n. acc. fem. sg. δικαιοσύνη righteousness
καὶ conj. καί and, even, also, but
τὴν art. acc. fem. sg. ὁ ἡ τό the, this, that, he, she, it
ἰδίαν adj. acc. fem. sg. ἴδιος one's own, one's, privately
δικαιοσύνην n. acc. fem. sg. δικαιοσύνη righteousness
τῇ art. dat. fem. sg. ὁ ἡ τό the, this, that, he, she, it
δικαιοσύνῃ n. dat. fem. sg. δικαιοσύνη righteousness
τοῦ art. gen. masc. sg. ὁ ἡ τό the, this, that, he, she, it
Θεοῦ n. gen. masc. sg. θεός God, god
οὐχ particle of negation. οὐ οὐκ οὐχ not, no, neither, none, nay, nor, never, nothing
4 τέλος n. nom. neut. sg. τέλος end, custom, ending, finally, uttermost
γὰρ conj. γάρ for, and, because, but, indeed
νόμου n. gen. masc. sg. νόμος law, the law
Χριστὸς n. nom. masc. sg. Χριστός Christ
εἰς prep. εἰς (+acc) into, to, unto, for, in, on, toward, against, upon, at, among
δικαιοσύνην n. acc. fem. sg. δικαιοσύνη righteousness
παντὶ adj. dat. masc. sg. πᾶς πᾶσα πᾶν all, every, whosoever, every one, no, whole, any
τῷ art. dat. masc. sg. ὁ ἡ τό the, this, that, he, she, it
5 Μωσῆς n. nom. masc. sg. Μωσῆς Moses
γὰρ conj. γάρ for, and, because, but, indeed
τὴν art. acc. fem. sg. ὁ ἡ τό the, this, that, he, she, it
δικαιοσύνην n. acc. fem. sg. δικαιοσύνη righteousness
τὴν art. acc. fem. sg. ὁ ἡ τό the, this, that, he, she, it
ἐκ prep. ἐκ ἐξ (+gen) of, from, out of, by, on, with, in, among, through
τοῦ art. gen. masc. sg. ὁ ἡ τό the, this, that, he, she, it
νόμου n. gen. masc. sg. νόμος law, the law
ὅτι conj. ὅτι that, for, because, how that, how, because that, for that, though
ὁ art. nom. masc. sg. ὁ ἡ τό the, this, that, he, she, it
αὐτὰ pron. acc. neut. 3p. pl. αὐτός ή ό self, of oneself, even, very, the same, he, she, it
ἄνθρωπος n. nom. masc. sg. ἄνθρωπος man, human being, person, one, certain
ἐν prep. ἐν (+dat) in, by, with, among, at, on, through, to, within, into, of, for
αὐτοῖς pron. dat. masc. 3p. pl. αὐτός ή ό self, of oneself, even, very, the same, he, she, it
6 ἡ art. nom. fem. sg. ὁ ἡ τό the, this, that, he, she, it
δὲ conj. δέ but, and, now, also, to the contrary, rather, then
ἐκ prep. ἐκ ἐξ (+gen) of, from, out of, by, on, with, in, among, through
πίστεως n. gen. fem. sg. πίστις faith, assurance, belief, fidelity
δικαιοσύνη n. nom. fem. sg. δικαιοσύνη righteousness
οὕτω adv. οὕτω οὕτως so, even so, thus, on this wise, likewise, after this manner
Μὴ particle of negation. μή not, no, lest, neither, none, nothing, nor, never, without
ἐν prep. ἐν (+dat) in, by, with, among, at, on, through, to, within, into, of, for
τῇ art. dat. fem. sg. ὁ ἡ τό the, this, that, he, she, it
καρδίᾳ n. dat. fem. sg. καρδία heart
σου pron. gen. 2p. sg. σύ thou, you
Τίς interrog. pron. nom. masc. sg. τίς what, who, why, where, which, how
εἰς prep. εἰς (+acc) into, to, unto, for, in, on, toward, against, upon, at, among
τὸν art. acc. masc. sg. ὁ ἡ τό the, this, that, he, she, it
οὐρανόν n. acc. masc. sg. οὐρανός heaven, air, sky
τοῦτ' demo. pron. nom. neut. sg. οὗτος αὕτη τοῦτο this, the same, this same, he, she, it
Χριστὸν n. acc. masc. sg. Χριστός Christ

7 ἢ conj. ἤ or, than, either, nor, or else, and, rather than
Τίς interrog. pron. nom. masc. sg. τίς what, who, why, where, which, how
εἰς prep. εἰς (+acc) into, to, unto, for, in, on, toward, against, upon, at, among
τὴν art. acc. fem. sg. ὁ ἡ τό the, this, that, he, she, it
ἄβυσσον n. acc. fem. sg. ἄβυσσος deep, abyss, bottomless pit, bottomless
τοῦτ' demo. pron. nom. neut. sg. οὗτος αὕτη τοῦτο this, the same, this same, he, she, it
Χριστὸν n. acc. masc. sg. Χριστός Christ
ἐκ prep. ἐκ ἐξ (+gen) of, from, out of, by, on, with, in, among, through
νεκρῶν adj. gen. masc. pl. νεκρός dead
8 ἀλλὰ conj. ἀλλά but, yea, yet, nevertheless, howbeit, nay, therefore
τί interrog. pron. acc. neut. sg. τίς what, who, why, where, which, how
Ἐγγύς adv. ἐγγύς nigh, at hand, near, nigh at hand, ready, nigh unto
σου pron. gen. 2p. sg. σύ thou, you
τὸ art. nom. neut. sg. ὁ ἡ τό the, this, that, he, she, it
ῥῆμά n. nom. neut. sg. ῥῆμα word, saying, thing
ἐν prep. ἐν (+dat) in, by, with, among, at, on, through, to, within, into, of, for
τῷ art. dat. neut. sg. ὁ ἡ τό the, this, that, he, she, it
στόματί n. dat. neut. sg. στόμα mouth, face, edge
σου pron. gen. 2p. sg. σύ thou, you
καὶ conj. καί and, even, also, but
ἐν prep. ἐν (+dat) in, by, with, among, at, on, through, to, within, into, of, for
τῇ art. dat. fem. sg. ὁ ἡ τό the, this, that, he, she, it
καρδίᾳ n. dat. fem. sg. καρδία heart
σου pron. gen. 2p. sg. σύ thou, you
τοῦτ' demo. pron. nom. neut. sg. οὗτος αὕτη τοῦτο this, the same, this same, he, she, it
τὸ art. nom. neut. sg. ὁ ἡ τό the, this, that, he, she, it
ῥῆμά n. nom. neut. sg. ῥῆμα word, saying, thing
τῆς art. gen. fem. sg. ὁ ἡ τό the, this, that, he, she, it
πίστεως n. gen. fem. sg. πίστις faith, assurance, belief, fidelity
ὃ relative pron. acc. neut. sg. ὅς ἥ ὅ who, which, what, that
9 ὅτι conj. ὅτι that, for, because, how that, how, because that, for that, though
ἐὰν conj. ἐάν if, soever, except, though, and if, but, whether, if so, so
ἐν prep. ἐν (+dat) in, by, with, among, at, on, through, to, within, into, of, for
τῷ art. dat. neut. sg. ὁ ἡ τό the, this, that, he, she, it
στόματί n. dat. neut. sg. στόμα mouth, face, edge
σου pron. gen. 2p. sg. σύ thou, you
Κύριον n. acc. masc. sg. κύριος Lord, lord, master, sir, LORD, God, Master, owner
Ἰησοῦν n. acc. masc. sg. Ἰησοῦς Jesus
καὶ conj. καί and, even, also, but
ἐν prep. ἐν (+dat) in, by, with, among, at, on, through, to, within, into, of, for
τῇ art. dat. fem. sg. ὁ ἡ τό the, this, that, he, she, it
καρδίᾳ n. dat. fem. sg. καρδία heart
σου pron. gen. 2p. sg. σύ thou, you
ὅτι conj. ὅτι that, for, because, how that, how, because that, for that, though
ὁ art. nom. masc. sg. ὁ ἡ τό the, this, that, he, she, it
Θεὸς n. nom. masc. sg. θεός God, god
αὐτὸν pron. acc. masc. 3p. sg. αὐτός ή ό self, of oneself, even, very, the same, he, she, it
ἐκ prep. ἐκ ἐξ (+gen) of, from, out of, by, on, with, in, among, through
νεκρῶν adj. gen. masc. pl. νεκρός dead
10 καρδίᾳ n. dat. fem. sg. καρδία heart
γὰρ conj. γάρ for, and, because, but, indeed
εἰς prep. εἰς (+acc) into, to, unto, for, in, on, toward, against, upon, at, among
δικαιοσύνην n. acc. fem. sg. δικαιοσύνη righteousness
στόματι n. dat. neut. sg. στόμα mouth, face, edge
δὲ conj. δέ but, and, now, also, to the contrary, rather, then

εἰς prep. εἰς (+acc) into, to, unto, for, in, on, toward, against, upon, at, among
σωτηρίαν n. acc. fem. sg. σωτηρία salvation, deliver, health, saving
11 γὰρ conj. γάρ for, and, because, but, indeed
ἡ art. nom. fem. sg. ὁ ἡ τό the, this, that, he, she, it
γραφή n. nom. fem. sg. γραφή scripture
Πᾶς adj. nom. masc. sg. πᾶς πᾶσα πᾶν all, every, whosoever, every one, no, whole, any
ὁ art. nom. masc. sg. ὁ ἡ τό the, this, that, he, she, it
ἐπ' prep. ἐπί (+gen) on, in, upon, (+dat) in, at, for, upon, (+acc) on, upon, unto, to, against
αὐτῷ pron. dat. masc. 3p. sg. αὐτός ή ό self, of oneself, even, very, the same, he, she, it
οὐ particle of negation. οὐ οὐκ οὐχ not, no, neither, none, nay, nor, never, nothing
12 οὐ particle of negation. οὐ οὐκ οὐχ not, no, neither, none, nay, nor, never, nothing
γάρ conj. γάρ for, and, because, but, indeed
διαστολὴ n. nom. fem. sg. διαστολή difference, distinction
Ἰουδαίου adj. gen. masc. sg. Ἰουδαῖος Jew, Jewess
τε conj. τέ and, both, also
καὶ conj. καί and, even, also, but
Ἕλληνος n. gen. masc. sg. Ἕλλην Greek, Gentile
ὁ art. nom. masc. sg. ὁ ἡ τό the, this, that, he, she, it
γάρ conj. γάρ for, and, because, but, indeed
αὐτὸς pron. nom. masc. 3p. sg. αὐτός ή ό self, of oneself, even, very, the same, he, she, it
Κύριος n. nom. masc. sg. κύριος Lord, lord, master, sir, LORD, God, Master, owner
πάντων adj. gen. masc. pl. πᾶς πᾶσα πᾶν all, every, whosoever, every one, no, whole, any
εἰς prep. εἰς (+acc) into, to, unto, for, in, on, toward, against, upon, at, among
πάντας adj. acc. masc. pl. πᾶς πᾶσα πᾶν all, every, whosoever, every one, no, whole, any
τοὺς art. acc. masc. pl. ὁ ἡ τό the, this, that, he, she, it
αὐτόν pron. acc. masc. 3p. sg. αὐτός ή ό self, of oneself, even, very, the same, he, she, it
13 πᾶς adj. nom. masc. sg. πᾶς πᾶσα πᾶν all, every, whosoever, every one, no, whole, any
γὰρ conj. γάρ for, and, because, but, indeed
ὃς relative pron. nom. masc. sg. ὅς ἥ ὅ who, which, what, that
ἂν particle. ἄν Indicating contingency. No English translation.
τὸ art. acc. neut. sg. ὁ ἡ τό the, this, that, he, she, it
ὄνομα n. acc. neut. sg. ὄνομα name, call, surname
Κυρίου n. gen. masc. sg. κύριος Lord, lord, master, sir, LORD, God, Master, owner
14 πῶς adv. πῶς how, by what means, after what manner
οὖν conj. οὖν therefore, then, so, and, now, wherefore
εἰς prep. εἰς (+acc) into, to, unto, for, in, on, toward, against, upon, at, among
ὃν relative pron. acc. masc. sg. ὅς ἥ ὅ who, which, what, that
οὐκ particle of negation. οὐ οὐκ οὐχ not, no, neither, none, nay, nor, never, nothing
πῶς adv. πῶς how, by what means, after what manner
δὲ conj. δέ but, and, now, also, to the contrary, rather, then
οὗ relative pron. gen. masc. sg. ὅς ἥ ὅ who, which, what, that
οὐκ particle of negation. οὐ οὐκ οὐχ not, no, neither, none, nay, nor, never, nothing
πῶς adv. πῶς how, by what means, after what manner
δὲ conj. δέ but, and, now, also, to the contrary, rather, then
χωρὶς prep. χωρίς (+gen) without, beside. (adv.) by itself, apart, separately
15 πῶς adv. πῶς how, by what means, after what manner
δὲ conj. δέ but, and, now, also, to the contrary, rather, then
ἐὰν conj. ἐάν if, soever, except, though, and if, but, whether, if so, so
μὴ particle of negation. μή not, no, lest, neither, none, nothing, nor, never, without
καθὼς adv. καθώς as, even as, according as, according to
Ὡς adv. ὡς as, when, as it were, how, about, like, as soon as, even as, while
ὡραῖοι adj. nom. masc. pl. ὡραῖος beautiful
οἱ art. nom. masc. pl. ὁ ἡ τό the, this, that, he, she, it
πόδες n. nom. masc. pl. πούς foot
τῶν art. gen. masc. pl. ὁ ἡ τό the, this, that, he, she, it

εἰρήνην n. acc. fem. sg. εἰρήνη peace, quietness, rest
τῶν art. gen. masc. pl. ὁ ἡ τό the, this, that, he, she, it
τὰ art. acc. neut. pl. ὁ ἡ τό the, this, that, he, she, it
ἀγαθά adj. acc. neut. pl. ἀγαθός good, good thing, that which is good, well
16 'Αλλ' conj. ἀλλά but, yea, yet, nevertheless, howbeit, nay, therefore
οὐ particle of negation. οὐ οὐκ οὐχ not, no, neither, none, nay, nor, never, nothing
πάντες adj. nom. masc. pl. πᾶς πᾶσα πᾶν all, every, whosoever, every one, no, whole, any
τῷ art. dat. neut. sg. ὁ ἡ τό the, this, that, he, she, it
εὐαγγελίῳ n. dat. neut. sg. εὐαγγέλιον gospel
'Ησαΐας n. nom. masc. sg. 'Ησαΐας Esaias, Isaiah
γὰρ conj. γάρ for, and, because, but, indeed
Κύριε n. voc. masc. sg. κύριος Lord, lord, master, sir, LORD, God, Master, owner
τίς interrog. pron. nom. masc. sg. τίς what, who, why, where, which, how
τῇ art. dat. fem. sg. ὁ ἡ τό the, this, that, he, she, it
ἀκοῇ n. dat. fem. sg. ἀκοή hearing, ear, fame, report, rumour, which one heard
ἡμῶν pron. gen. 1p. pl. ἐγώ I
17 ἄρα conj. ἄρα then, therefore, haply, wherefore, perhaps, manner, no doubt, truly
ἡ art. nom. fem. sg. ὁ ἡ τό the, this, that, he, she, it
πίστις n. nom. fem. sg. πίστις faith, assurance, belief, fidelity
ἐξ prep. ἐκ ἐξ (+gen) of, from, out of, by, on, with, in, among, through
ἀκοῆς n. gen. fem. sg. ἀκοή hearing, ear, fame, report, rumour, which one heard
ἡ art. nom. fem. sg. ὁ ἡ τό the, this, that, he, she, it
δὲ conj. δέ but, and, now, also, to the contrary, rather, then
ἀκοὴ n. nom. fem. sg. ἀκοή hearing, ear, fame, report, rumour, which one heard
διὰ prep. διά (+gen) by, through, with, in, of, (+acc) for, because of, for a cause
ῥήματος n. gen. neut. sg. ῥῆμα word, saying, thing
Θεοῦ n. gen. masc. sg. θεός God, god
18 ἀλλὰ conj. ἀλλά but, yea, yet, nevertheless, howbeit, nay, therefore
Μὴ particle of negation. μή not, no, lest, neither, none, nothing, nor, never, without
οὐκ particle of negation. οὐ οὐκ οὐχ not, no, neither, none, nay, nor, never, nothing
μενοῦνγε particle. μενοῦνγε yea rather, nay but, yea doubtless
εἰς prep. εἰς (+acc) into, to, unto, for, in, on, toward, against, upon, at, among
πᾶσαν adj. acc. fem. sg. πᾶς πᾶσα πᾶν all, every, whosoever, every one, no, whole, any
τὴν art. acc. fem. sg. ὁ ἡ τό the, this, that, he, she, it
γῆν n. acc. fem. sg. γῆ earth, land, ground, country
ὁ art. nom. masc. sg. ὁ ἡ τό the, this, that, he, she, it
φθόγγος n. nom. masc. sg. φθόγγος sound
αὐτῶν pron. gen. masc. 3p. pl. αὐτός ἡ ὁ self, of oneself, even, very, the same, he, she, it
καὶ conj. καί and, even, also, but
εἰς prep. εἰς (+acc) into, to, unto, for, in, on, toward, against, upon, at, among
τὰ art. acc. neut. pl. ὁ ἡ τό the, this, that, he, she, it
πέρατα n. acc. neut. pl. πέρας uttermost parts, utmost part, end
τῆς art. gen. fem. sg. ὁ ἡ τό the, this, that, he, she, it
οἰκουμένης n. gen. fem. sg. οἰκουμένη world, earth
τὰ art. nom. neut. pl. ὁ ἡ τό the, this, that, he, she, it
ῥήματα n. nom. neut. pl. ῥῆμα word, saying, thing
αὐτῶν pron. gen. masc. 3p. pl. αὐτός ἡ ὁ self, of oneself, even, very, the same, he, she, it
19 ἀλλὰ conj. ἀλλά but, yea, yet, nevertheless, howbeit, nay, therefore
Μὴ particle of negation. μή not, no, lest, neither, none, nothing, nor, never, without
οὐκ particle of negation. οὐ οὐκ οὐχ not, no, neither, none, nay, nor, never, nothing
'Ισραὴλ pron. name. masc. inde. 'Ισραήλ Israel
πρῶτος ordinal. adj. nom. masc. sg. πρῶτος first, chief, first of all, chiefest, best
Μωσῆς n. nom. masc. sg. Μωσῆς Moses
'Εγὼ pron. nom. 1p. sg. ἐγώ I
ὑμᾶς pron. acc. 2p. pl. σύ thou, you

ἐπ' prep. ἐπί (+gen) on, in, upon, (+dat) in, at, for, upon, (+acc) on, upon, unto, to, against
οὐκ particle of negation. οὐ οὐκ οὐχ not, no, neither, none, nay, nor, never, nothing
ἔθνει n. dat. neut. sg. ἔθνος Gentile, nation, heathen, people
ἐπὶ prep. ἐπί (+gen) on, in, upon, (+dat) in, at, for, upon, (+acc) on, upon, unto, to, against
ἔθνει n. dat. neut. sg. ἔθνος Gentile, nation, heathen, people
ἀσυνέτῳ adj. dat. neut. sg. ἀσύνετος without understanding, foolish
ὑμᾶς pron. acc. 2p. pl. σύ thou, you
20 Ἠσαΐας n. nom. masc. sg. Ἠσαΐας Esaias, Isaiah
δὲ conj. δέ but, and, now, also, to the contrary, rather, then
καὶ conj. καί and, even, also, but
τοῖς art. dat. masc. pl. ὁ ἡ τό the, this, that, he, she, it
ἐμὲ pron. acc. 1p. sg. ἐγώ I
μὴ particle of negation. μή not, no, lest, neither, none, nothing, nor, never, without
ἐμφανὴς adj. nom. masc. sg. ἐμφανής openly, manifest
τοῖς art. dat. masc. pl. ὁ ἡ τό the, this, that, he, she, it
ἐμὲ pron. acc. 1p. sg. ἐγώ I
μὴ particle of negation. μή not, no, lest, neither, none, nothing, nor, never, without
21 πρὸς prep. πρός (+gen) for, (+dat) at, (+acc) unto, to, with, for, against
δὲ conj. δέ but, and, now, also, to the contrary, rather, then
τὸν art. acc. masc. sg. ὁ ἡ τό the, this, that, he, she, it
Ἰσραὴλ pron. name. masc. inde. Ἰσραήλ Israel
Ὅλην adj. acc. fem. sg. ὅλος all, whole, every whit, altogether
τὴν art. acc. fem. sg. ὁ ἡ τό the, this, that, he, she, it
ἡμέραν n. acc. fem. sg. ἡμέρα day, time, year, while, age, day time
τὰς art. acc. fem. pl. ὁ ἡ τό the, this, that, he, she, it
χεῖράς n. acc. fem. pl. χείρ hand
μου pron. gen. 1p. sg. ἐγώ I
πρὸς prep. πρός (+gen) for, (+dat) at, (+acc) unto, to, with, for, against
λαὸν n. acc. masc. sg. λαός people
καὶ conj. καί and, even, also, but

11

1 οὖν conj. οὖν therefore, then, so, and, now, wherefore
Μὴ particle of negation. μή not, no, lest, neither, none, nothing, nor, never, without
ὁ art. nom. masc. sg. ὁ ἡ τό the, this, that, he, she, it
Θεὸς n. nom. masc. sg. θεός God, god
τὸν art. acc. masc. sg. ὁ ἡ τό the, this, that, he, she, it
λαὸν n. acc. masc. sg. λαός people
αὐτοῦ pron. gen. masc. 3p. sg. αὐτός ή ό self, of oneself, even, very, the same, he, she, it
μὴ particle of negation. μή not, no, lest, neither, none, nothing, nor, never, without
καὶ conj. καί and, even, also, but
γὰρ conj. γάρ for, and, because, but, indeed
ἐγὼ pron. nom. 1p. sg. ἐγώ I
Ἰσραηλίτης n. nom. masc. sg. Ἰσραηλίτης Israelite, Israel
ἐκ prep. ἐκ ἐξ (+gen) of, from, out of, by, on, with, in, among, through
σπέρματος n. gen. neut. sg. σπέρμα seed, issue
Ἀβραάμ n. gen. masc. sg. Ἀβραάμ Abraham
φυλῆς n. gen. fem. sg. φυλή tribe, kindred
Βενϊαμίν n. gen. masc. sg. Βενιαμίν Benjamin
2 οὐκ particle of negation. οὐ οὐκ οὐχ not, no, neither, none, nay, nor, never, nothing
ὁ art. nom. masc. sg. ὁ ἡ τό the, this, that, he, she, it
Θεὸς n. nom. masc. sg. θεός God, god
τὸν art. acc. masc. sg. ὁ ἡ τό the, this, that, he, she, it
λαὸν n. acc. masc. sg. λαός people

αὐτοῦ pron. gen. masc. 3p. sg. αὐτός ἡ ὁ self, of oneself, even, very, the same, he, she, it
ὃν relative pron. acc. masc. sg. ὅς ἥ ὅ who, which, what, that
ἢ particle. ἤ or, than, either, nor, or else, and, rather than
οὐκ particle of negation. οὐ οὐκ οὐχ not, no, neither, none, nay, nor, never, nothing
ἐν prep. ἐν (+dat) in, by, with, among, at, on, through, to, within, into, of, for
Ἠλίᾳ n. dat. masc. sg. Ἠλίας Elias, Elijah
τί interrog. pron. acc. neut. sg. τίς what, who, why, where, which, how
ἡ art. nom. fem. sg. ὁ ἡ τό the, this, that, he, she, it
γραφή n. nom. fem. sg. γραφή scripture
ὡς adv. ὡς as, when, as it were, how, about, like, as soon as, even as, while
τῷ art. dat. masc. sg. ὁ ἡ τό the, this, that, he, she, it
Θεῷ n. dat. masc. sg. θεός God, god
κατὰ prep. κατά (+gen) against, by, throughout, down, (+acc) according to, after, with
τοῦ art. gen. masc. sg. ὁ ἡ τό the, this, that, he, she, it
Ἰσραήλ pron. name. masc. inde. Ἰσραήλ Israel
3 Κύριε n. voc. masc. sg. κύριος Lord, lord, master, sir, LORD, God, Master, owner
τοὺς art. acc. masc. pl. ὁ ἡ τό the, this, that, he, she, it
προφήτας n. acc. masc. pl. προφήτης prophet
σου pron. gen. 2p. sg. σύ thou, you
καὶ conj. καί and, even, also, but
τὰ art. acc. neut. pl. ὁ ἡ τό the, this, that, he, she, it
θυσιαστήριά n. acc. neut. pl. θυσιαστήριον altar
σου pron. gen. 2p. sg. σύ thou, you
κἀγὼ pron. nom. 1p. sg. κἀγώ and I, I also, so I, even as I
μόνος adj. nom. masc. sg. μόνος only, alone, by oneself
καὶ conj. καί and, even, also, but
τὴν art. acc. fem. sg. ὁ ἡ τό the, this, that, he, she, it
ψυχήν n. acc. fem. sg. ψυχή life, soul, mind, heart
μου pron. gen. 1p. sg. ἐγώ I
4 ἀλλὰ conj. ἀλλά but, yea, yet, nevertheless, howbeit, nay, therefore
τί interrog. pron. acc. neut. sg. τίς what, who, why, where, which, how
αὐτῷ pron. dat. masc. 3p. sg. αὐτός ἡ ὁ self, of oneself, even, very, the same, he, she, it
ὁ art. nom. masc. sg. ὁ ἡ τό the, this, that, he, she, it
χρηματισμός n. nom. masc. sg. χρηματισμός answer of God
ἐμαυτῷ pron. dat. masc. 1p. sg. ἐμαυτοῦ myself, me
ἑπτακισχιλίους num. acc. masc. pl. ἑπτακισχίλιοι seven thousand
ἄνδρας n. acc. masc. pl. ἀνήρ man, husband, sir
οἵτινες relative pron. nom. masc. pl. ὅστις which, who, whosoever, that, whatsoever
οὐκ particle of negation. οὐ οὐκ οὐχ not, no, neither, none, nay, nor, never, nothing
γόνυ n. acc. neut. sg. γόνυ knee, kneel
τῇ art. dat. fem. sg. ὁ ἡ τό the, this, that, he, she, it
Βάαλ n. gen. masc. sg. Βάαλ Baal
5 οὕτως adv. οὕτω οὕτως so, even so, thus, on this wise, likewise, after this manner
οὖν conj. οὖν therefore, then, so, and, now, wherefore
καὶ conj. καί and, even, also, but
ἐν prep. ἐν (+dat) in, by, with, among, at, on, through, to, within, into, of, for
τῷ art. dat. masc. sg. ὁ ἡ τό the, this, that, he, she, it
νῦν adv. νῦν now, henceforth, present, this time
καιρῷ n. dat. masc. sg. καιρός time, season, due time, opportunity
λεῖμμα n. nom. neut. sg. λεῖμμα remnant
κατ᾽ prep. κατά (+gen) against, by, throughout, down, (+acc) according to, after, with
ἐκλογὴν n. acc. fem. sg. ἐκλογή election, chosen
χάριτος n. gen. fem. sg. χάρις grace, thank, favour, pleasure
6 εἰ conj. εἰ if, whether, that, though, forasmuch
δὲ conj. δέ but, and, now, also, to the contrary, rather, then

χάριτι n. dat. fem. sg. χάρις grace, thank, favour, pleasure
οὐκέτι adv. οὐκέτι or οὐκ ἔτι no more, no longer, not any more
ἐξ prep. ἐκ ἐξ (+gen) of, from, out of, by, on, with, in, among, through
ἔργων n. gen. neut. pl. ἔργον work, deed, doing labour
ἐπεὶ conj. ἐπεί because, otherwise, seeing, else, for then, for as much as, for, since
ἡ art. nom. fem. sg. ὁ ἡ τό the, this, that, he, she, it
χάρις n. nom. fem. sg. χάρις grace, thank, favour, pleasure
οὐκέτι adv. οὐκέτι or οὐκ ἔτι no more, no longer, not any more
χάρις n. nom. fem. sg. χάρις grace, thank, favour, pleasure
εἰ conj. εἰ if, whether, that, though, forasmuch
δὲ conj. δέ but, and, now, also, to the contrary, rather, then
ἐξ prep. ἐκ ἐξ (+gen) of, from, out of, by, on, with, in, among, through
ἔργων n. gen. neut. pl. ἔργον work, deed, doing labour
οὐκέτι adv. οὐκέτι or οὐκ ἔτι no more, no longer, not any more
χάρις n. nom. fem. sg. χάρις grace, thank, favour, pleasure
ἐπεὶ conj. ἐπεί because, otherwise, seeing, else, for then, for as much as, for, since
τὸ art. nom. neut. sg. ὁ ἡ τό the, this, that, he, she, it
ἔργον n. nom. neut. sg. ἔργον work, deed, doing labour
οὐκέτι adv. οὐκέτι or οὐκ ἔτι no more, no longer, not any more
ἔργον n. nom. neut. sg. ἔργον work, deed, doing labour
7 τί interrog. pron. acc. neut. sg. τίς what, who, why, where, which, how
οὖν conj. οὖν therefore, then, so, and, now, wherefore
ὃ relative pron. acc. neut. sg. ὅς ἥ ὅ who, which, what, that
Ἰσραήλ pron. name. masc. inde. Ἰσραήλ Israel
τούτου demo. pron. gen. neut. sg. οὗτος αὕτη τοῦτο this, the same, this same, he, she, it
οὐκ particle of negation. οὐ οὐκ οὐχ not, no, neither, none, nay, nor, never, nothing
ἡ art. nom. fem. sg. ὁ ἡ τό the, this, that, he, she, it
δὲ conj. δέ but, and, now, also, to the contrary, rather, then
ἐκλογὴ n. nom. fem. sg. ἐκλογή election, chosen
οἱ art. nom. masc. pl. ὁ ἡ τό the, this, that, he, she, it
δὲ conj. δέ but, and, now, also, to the contrary, rather, then
λοιποὶ adj. nom. masc. pl. λοιπός other, rest, remnant, residue, which remain
8 καθὼς adv. καθώς as, even as, according as, according to
αὐτοῖς pron. dat. masc. 3p. pl. αὐτός ἡ ὁ self, of oneself, even, very, the same, he, she, it
ὁ art. nom. masc. sg. ὁ ἡ τό the, this, that, he, she, it
Θεὸς n. nom. masc. sg. θεός God, god
πνεῦμα n. acc. neut. sg. πνεῦμα spirit, Spirit, Ghost, ghost, life. of the spirit, wind
κατανύξεως n. gen. fem. sg. κατάνυξις slumber
ὀφθαλμοὺς n. acc. masc. pl. ὀφθαλμός eye, sight
τοῦ art. gen. neut. sg. ὁ ἡ τό the, this, that, he, she, it
μὴ particle of negation. μή not, no, lest, neither, none, nothing, nor, never, without
καὶ conj. καί and, even, also, but
ὦτα n. acc. neut. pl. οὖς ear
τοῦ art. gen. neut. sg. ὁ ἡ τό the, this, that, he, she, it
μὴ particle of negation. μή not, no, lest, neither, none, nothing, nor, never, without
ἕως conj. ἕως till, until, unto, until when, while, as far as, even, until now
τῆς art. gen. fem. sg. ὁ ἡ τό the, this, that, he, she, it
σήμερον adv. σήμερον this day, today
ἡμέρας n. gen. fem. sg. ἡμέρα day, time, year, while, age, day time
9 καὶ conj. καί and, even, also, but
Δαβὶδ n. nom. masc. sg. Δαβίδ David
ἡ art. nom. fem. sg. ὁ ἡ τό the, this, that, he, she, it
τράπεζα n. nom. fem. sg. τράπεζα table
αὐτῶν pron. gen. masc. 3p. pl. αὐτός ἡ ὁ self, of oneself, even, very, the same, he, she, it
εἰς prep. εἰς (+acc) into, to, unto, for, in, on, toward, against, upon, at, among

παγίδα n. acc. fem. sg. παγίς snare
καὶ conj. καί and, even, also, but
εἰς prep. εἰς (+acc) into, to, unto, for, in, on, toward, against, upon, at, among
θήραν n. acc. fem. sg. θήρα trap
καὶ conj. καί and, even, also, but
εἰς prep. εἰς (+acc) into, to, unto, for, in, on, toward, against, upon, at, among
σκάνδαλον n. acc. neut. sg. σκάνδαλον offence, stumblingblock, thing that offend
καὶ conj. καί and, even, also, but
εἰς prep. εἰς (+acc) into, to, unto, for, in, on, toward, against, upon, at, among
ἀνταπόδομα n. acc. neut. sg. ἀνταπόδομα recompence
αὐτοῖς pron. dat. masc. 3p. pl. αὐτός ή ό self, of oneself, even, very, the same, he, she, it
10 οἱ art. nom. masc. pl. ὁ ἡ τό the, this, that, he, she, it
ὀφθαλμοὶ n. nom. masc. pl. ὀφθαλμός eye, sight
αὐτῶν pron. gen. masc. 3p. pl. αὐτός ή ό self, of oneself, even, very, the same, he, she, it
τοῦ art. gen. neut. sg. ὁ ἡ τό the, this, that, he, she, it
μὴ particle of negation. μή not, no, lest, neither, none, nothing, nor, never, without
καὶ conj. καί and, even, also, but
τὸν art. acc. masc. sg. ὁ ἡ τό the, this, that, he, she, it
νῶτον n. acc. masc. sg. νῶτος back
αὐτῶν pron. gen. masc. 3p. pl. αὐτός ή ό self, of oneself, even, very, the same, he, she, it
διὰ prep. διά (+gen) by, through, with, in, of, (+acc) for, because of, for a cause
παντὸς adj. gen. neut. sg. πᾶς πᾶσα πᾶν all, every, whosoever, every one, no, whole, any
11 οὖν conj. οὖν therefore, then, so, and, now, wherefore
μὴ particle of negation. μή not, no, lest, neither, none, nothing, nor, never, without
ἵνα conj. ἵνα that, to, lest, for to, so that, albeit, because, for, so as
μὴ particle of negation. μή not, no, lest, neither, none, nothing, nor, never, without
ἀλλὰ conj. ἀλλά but, yea, yet, nevertheless, howbeit, nay, therefore
τῷ art. dat. neut. sg. ὁ ἡ τό the, this, that, he, she, it
αὐτῶν pron. gen. masc. 3p. pl. αὐτός ή ό self, of oneself, even, very, the same, he, she, it
παραπτώματι n. dat. neut. sg. παράπτωμα trespass, offence, sin, fall, fault
ἡ art. nom. fem. sg. ὁ ἡ τό the, this, that, he, she, it
σωτηρία n. nom. fem. sg. σωτηρία salvation, deliver, health, saving
τοῖς art. dat. neut. pl. ὁ ἡ τό the, this, that, he, she, it
ἔθνεσιν n. dat. neut. pl. ἔθνος Gentile, nation, heathen, people
εἰς prep. εἰς (+acc) into, to, unto, for, in, on, toward, against, upon, at, among
τὸ art. acc. neut. sg. ὁ ἡ τό the, this, that, he, she, it
αὐτούς pron. acc. masc. 3p. pl. αὐτός ή ό self, of oneself, even, very, the same, he, she, it
12 εἰ conj. εἰ if, whether, that, though, forasmuch
δὲ conj. δέ but, and, now, also, to the contrary, rather, then
τὸ art. nom. neut. sg. ὁ ἡ τό the, this, that, he, she, it
παράπτωμα n. nom. neut. sg. παράπτωμα trespass, offence, sin, fall, fault
αὐτῶν pron. gen. masc. 3p. pl. αὐτός ή ό self, of oneself, even, very, the same, he, she, it
πλοῦτος n. nom. masc. sg. πλοῦτος riches
κόσμου n. gen. masc. sg. κόσμος world, adorning
καὶ conj. καί and, even, also, but
τὸ art. nom. neut. sg. ὁ ἡ τό the, this, that, he, she, it
ἥττημα n. nom. neut. sg. ἥττημα diminishing, fault
αὐτῶν pron. gen. masc. 3p. pl. αὐτός ή ό self, of oneself, even, very, the same, he, she, it
πλοῦτος n. nom. masc. sg. πλοῦτος riches
ἐθνῶν n. gen. neut. pl. ἔθνος Gentile, nation, heathen, people
πόσῳ interrog. pron. dat. neut. sg. πόσος how much, how many, how great, how long
μᾶλλον adv. μᾶλλον rather, more, more and more, better, much, much the more
τὸ art. nom. neut. sg. ὁ ἡ τό the, this, that, he, she, it
πλήρωμα n. nom. neut. sg. πλήρωμα fullness, fulfilling, full
αὐτῶν pron. gen. masc. 3p. pl. αὐτός ή ό self, of oneself, even, very, the same, he, she, it

13 Ὑμῖν pron. dat. 2p. pl. σύ thou, you
γὰρ conj. γάρ for, and, because, but, indeed
τοῖς art. dat. neut. pl. ὁ ἡ τό the, this, that, he, she, it
ἔθνεσιν n. dat. neut. pl. ἔθνος Gentile, nation, heathen, people
ἐφ' prep. ἐπί (+gen) on, in, upon, (+dat) in, at, for, upon, (+acc) on, upon, unto, to, against
ὅσον relative pron. acc. neut. sg. ὅσος as many as, whatsoever, that, as long as, how much
μὲν conj. μέν indeed, verily, truly, even, so, some
ἐγὼ pron. nom. 1p. sg. ἐγώ I
ἐθνῶν n. gen. neut. pl. ἔθνος Gentile, nation, heathen, people
ἀπόστολος n. nom. masc. sg. ἀπόστολος apostle, messenger, he that is sent
τὴν art. acc. fem. sg. ὁ ἡ τό the, this, that, he, she, it
διακονίαν n. acc. fem. sg. διακονία ministry, administration, service, office, relief
μου pron. gen. 1p. sg. ἐγώ I
14 εἴ conj. εἰ if, whether, that, though, forasmuch
πως particle. πώς by any means, by some means, haply, perhaps
μου pron. gen. 1p. sg. ἐγώ I
τὴν art. acc. fem. sg. ὁ ἡ τό the, this, that, he, she, it
σάρκα n. acc. fem. sg. σάρξ flesh, carnal
καὶ conj. καί and, even, also, but
τινὰς indefinite pron. acc. masc. pl. τὶς certain, some, any man, one, any thing
ἐξ prep. ἐκ ἐξ (+gen) of, from, out of, by, on, with, in, among, through
αὐτῶν pron. gen. masc. 3p. pl. αὐτός ή ό self, of oneself, even, very, the same, he, she, it
15 εἰ conj. εἰ if, whether, that, though, forasmuch
γὰρ conj. γάρ for, and, because, but, indeed
ἡ art. nom. fem. sg. ὁ ἡ τό the, this, that, he, she, it
ἀποβολὴ n. nom. fem. sg. ἀποβολή loss, cast away
αὐτῶν pron. gen. masc. 3p. pl. αὐτός ή ό self, of oneself, even, very, the same, he, she, it
καταλλαγὴ n. nom. fem. sg. καταλλαγή reconciliation, atonement, reconciling
κόσμου n. gen. masc. sg. κόσμος world, adorning
τίς interrog. pron. nom. fem. sg. τίς what, who, why, where, which, how
ἡ art. nom. fem. sg. ὁ ἡ τό the, this, that, he, she, it
πρόσληψις n. nom. fem. sg. πρόσληπσις receiving
εἰ conj. εἰ if, whether, that, though, forasmuch
μὴ particle of negation. μή not, no, lest, neither, none, nothing, nor, never, without
ζωὴ n. nom. fem. sg. ζωή life, lifetime
ἐκ prep. ἐκ ἐξ (+gen) of, from, out of, by, on, with, in, among, through
νεκρῶν adj. gen. masc. pl. νεκρός dead
16 εἰ conj. εἰ if, whether, that, though, forasmuch
δὲ conj. δέ but, and, now, also, to the contrary, rather, then
ἡ art. nom. fem. sg. ὁ ἡ τό the, this, that, he, she, it
ἀπαρχὴ n. nom. fem. sg. ἀπαρχή firstfruit
ἁγία adj. nom. fem. sg. ἅγιος Holy, holy, saint, Holy One, holy thing, most holy
καὶ conj. καί and, even, also, but
τὸ art. nom. neut. sg. ὁ ἡ τό the, this, that, he, she, it
φύραμα n. nom. neut. sg. φύραμα lump
καὶ conj. καί and, even, also, but
εἰ conj. εἰ if, whether, that, though, forasmuch
ἡ art. nom. fem. sg. ὁ ἡ τό the, this, that, he, she, it
ῥίζα n. nom. fem. sg. ῥίζα root
ἁγία adj. nom. fem. sg. ἅγιος Holy, holy, saint, Holy One, holy thing, most holy
καὶ conj. καί and, even, also, but
οἱ art. nom. masc. pl. ὁ ἡ τό the, this, that, he, she, it
κλάδοι n. nom. masc. pl. κλάδος branch
17 εἰ conj. εἰ if, whether, that, though, forasmuch
δέ conj. δέ but, and, now, also, to the contrary, rather, then

τινες indefinite pron. nom. masc. pl. τὶς certain, some, any man, one, any thing
τῶν art. gen. masc. pl. ὁ ἡ τό the, this, that, he, she, it
κλάδων n. gen. masc. pl. κλάδος branch
σὺ pron. nom. 2p. sg. σύ thou, you
δέ conj. δέ but, and, now, also, to the contrary, rather, then
ἀγριέλαιος n. nom. fem. sg. ἀγριέλαιος wild olive tree, olive tree which is wild
ἐν prep. ἐν (+dat) in, by, with, among, at, on, through, to, within, into, of, for
αὐτοῖς pron. dat. masc. 3p. pl. αὐτός ἡ ὁ self, of oneself, even, very, the same, he, she, it
καὶ conj. καί and, even, also, but
συγκοινωνὸς n. nom. masc. sg. συγκοινωνός companion, partake with, partaker
τῆς art. gen. fem. sg. ὁ ἡ τό the, this, that, he, she, it
ῥίζης n. gen. fem. sg. ῥίζα root
καὶ conj. καί and, even, also, but
τῆς art. gen. fem. sg. ὁ ἡ τό the, this, that, he, she, it
πιότητος n. gen. fem. sg. πιότης fatness
τῆς art. gen. fem. sg. ὁ ἡ τό the, this, that, he, she, it
ἐλαίας n. gen. fem. sg. ἐλαία Olives, olive tree, olive berry
18 μὴ particle of negation. μή not, no, lest, neither, none, nothing, nor, never, without
τῶν art. gen. masc. pl. ὁ ἡ τό the, this, that, he, she, it
κλάδων n. gen. masc. pl. κλάδος branch
εἰ conj. εἰ if, whether, that, though, forasmuch
δὲ conj. δέ but, and, now, also, to the contrary, rather, then
οὐ particle of negation. οὐ οὐκ οὐχ not, no, neither, none, nay, nor, never, nothing
σὺ pron. nom. 2p. sg. σύ thou, you
τὴν art. acc. fem. sg. ὁ ἡ τό the, this, that, he, she, it
ῥίζαν n. acc. fem. sg. ῥίζα root
ἀλλ' conj. ἀλλά but, yea, yet, nevertheless, howbeit, nay, therefore
ἡ art. nom. fem. sg. ὁ ἡ τό the, this, that, he, she, it
ῥίζα n. nom. fem. sg. ῥίζα root
σέ pron. acc. 2p. sg. σύ thou, you
19 οὖν conj. οὖν therefore, then, so, and, now, wherefore
οἱ art. nom. masc. pl. ὁ ἡ τό the, this, that, he, she, it
κλάδοι n. nom. masc. pl. κλάδος branch
ἵνα conj. ἵνα that, to, lest, for to, so that, albeit, because, for, so as
ἐγὼ pron. nom. 1p. sg. ἐγώ I
20 καλῶς adv. καλῶς good, well, full well
τῇ art. dat. fem. sg. ὁ ἡ τό the, this, that, he, she, it
ἀπιστίᾳ n. dat. fem. sg. ἀπιστία unbelief
σὺ pron. nom. 2p. sg. σύ thou, you
δὲ conj. δέ but, and, now, also, to the contrary, rather, then
τῇ art. dat. fem. sg. ὁ ἡ τό the, this, that, he, she, it
πίστει n. dat. fem. sg. πίστις faith, assurance, belief, fidelity
μὴ particle of negation. μή not, no, lest, neither, none, nothing, nor, never, without
ἀλλὰ conj. ἀλλά but, yea, yet, nevertheless, howbeit, nay, therefore
21 εἰ conj. εἰ if, whether, that, though, forasmuch
γὰρ conj. γάρ for, and, because, but, indeed
ὁ art. nom. masc. sg. ὁ ἡ τό the, this, that, he, she, it
Θεὸς n. nom. masc. sg. θεός God, god
τῶν art. gen. masc. pl. ὁ ἡ τό the, this, that, he, she, it
κατὰ prep. κατά (+gen) against, by, throughout, down, (+acc) according to, after, with
φύσιν n. acc. fem. sg. φύσις nature
κλάδων n. gen. masc. pl. κλάδος branch
οὐκ particle of negation. οὐ οὐκ οὐχ not, no, neither, none, nay, nor, never, nothing
μήπως conj. μήπως lest, lest by any means, lest by some means, lest haply
οὐδὲ adv. οὐδέ neither, nor, not, no, not even, never, not yet

σοῦ pron. gen. 2p. sg. σύ thou, you
22 οὖν conj. οὖν therefore, then, so, and, now, wherefore
χρηστότητα n. acc. fem. sg. χρηστότης goodness, kindness, gentleness, good
καὶ conj. καί and, even, also, but
ἀποτομίαν n. acc. fem. sg. ἀποτομία severity
Θεοῦ n. gen. masc. sg. θεός God, god
ἐπὶ prep. ἐπί (+gen) on, in, upon, (+dat) in, at, for, upon, (+acc) on, upon, unto, to, against
μὲν conj. μέν indeed, verily, truly, even, so, some
τοὺς art. acc. masc. pl. ὁ ἡ τό the, this, that, he, she, it
ἀποτομίαν n. acc. fem. sg. ἀποτομία severity
ἐπὶ prep. ἐπί (+gen) on, in, upon, (+dat) in, at, for, upon, (+acc) on, upon, unto, to, against
δέ conj. δέ but, and, now, also, to the contrary, rather, then
σε pron. acc. 2p. sg. σύ thou, you
χρηστότητα n. acc. fem. sg. χρηστότης goodness, kindness, gentleness, good
ἐὰν conj. ἐάν if, soever, except, though, and if, but, whether, if so, so
τῇ art. dat. fem. sg. ὁ ἡ τό the, this, that, he, she, it
χρηστότητι n. dat. fem. sg. χρηστότης goodness, kindness, gentleness, good
ἐπεὶ conj. ἐπεί because, otherwise, seeing, else, for then, for as much as, for, since
καὶ conj. καί and, even, also, but
σὺ pron. nom. 2p. sg. σύ thou, you
23 καὶ conj. καί and, even, also, but
ἐκεῖνοι demo. pron. nom. masc. pl. ἐκεῖνος that, he, the same, that same
δέ conj. δέ but, and, now, also, to the contrary, rather, then
ἐὰν conj. ἐάν if, soever, except, though, and if, but, whether, if so, so
μὴ particle of negation. μή not, no, lest, neither, none, nothing, nor, never, without
τῇ art. dat. fem. sg. ὁ ἡ τό the, this, that, he, she, it
ἀπιστίᾳ n. dat. fem. sg. ἀπιστία unbelief
δυνατὸς adj. nom. masc. sg. δυνατός able, possible, mighty, strong
γάρ conj. γάρ for, and, because, but, indeed
ὁ art. nom. masc. sg. ὁ ἡ τό the, this, that, he, she, it
Θεὸς n. nom. masc. sg. θεός God, god
πάλιν adv. πάλιν again
αὐτούς pron. acc. masc. 3p. pl. αὐτός ἡ ὁ self, of oneself, even, very, the same, he, she, it
24 εἰ conj. εἰ if, whether, that, though, forasmuch
γὰρ conj. γάρ for, and, because, but, indeed
σὺ pron. nom. 2p. sg. σύ thou, you
ἐκ prep. ἐκ ἐξ (+gen) of, from, out of, by, on, with, in, among, through
τῆς art. gen. fem. sg. ὁ ἡ τό the, this, that, he, she, it
κατὰ prep. κατά (+gen) against, by, throughout, down, (+acc) according to, after, with
φύσιν n. acc. fem. sg. φύσις nature
ἀγριελαίου n. gen. fem. sg. ἀγριέλαιος wild olive tree, olive tree which is wild
καὶ conj. καί and, even, also, but
παρὰ prep. παρά (+gen) of, from, (+dat) with, for, (+acc) beside, at, by, above, against
φύσιν n. acc. fem. sg. φύσις nature
εἰς prep. εἰς (+acc) into, to, unto, for, in, on, toward, against, upon, at, among
καλλιέλαιον n. acc. fem. sg. καλλιέλαιος good olive tree
πόσῳ interrog. pron. dat. neut. sg. πόσος how much, how many, how great, how long
μᾶλλον adv. μᾶλλον rather, more, more and more, better, much, much the more
οὗτοι demo. pron. nom. masc. pl. οὗτος αὕτη τοῦτο this, the same, this same, he, she, it
οἱ art. nom. masc. pl. ὁ ἡ τό the, this, that, he, she, it
κατὰ prep. κατά (+gen) against, by, throughout, down, (+acc) according to, after, with
φύσιν n. acc. fem. sg. φύσις nature
τῇ art. dat. fem. sg. ὁ ἡ τό the, this, that, he, she, it
ἰδίᾳ adj. dat. fem. sg. ἴδιος one's own, one's, privately
ἐλαίᾳ n. dat. fem. sg. ἐλαία Olives, olive tree, olive berry

25 Οὐ particle of negation. οὐ οὐκ οὐχ not, no, neither, none, nay, nor, never, nothing
γὰρ conj. γάρ for, and, because, but, indeed
ὑμᾶς pron. acc. 2p. pl. σύ thou, you
ἀδελφοί n. voc. masc. pl. ἀδελφός brother
τὸ art. acc. neut. sg. ὁ ἡ τό the, this, that, he, she, it
μυστήριον n. acc. neut. sg. μυστήριον mystery
τοῦτο demo. pron. acc. neut. sg. οὗτος αὕτη τοῦτο this, the same, this same, he, she, it
ἵνα conj. ἵνα that, to, lest, for to, so that, albeit, because, for, so as
μὴ particle of negation. μή not, no, lest, neither, none, nothing, nor, never, without
παῤ prep. παρά (+gen) of, from, (+dat) with, for, (+acc) beside, at, by, above, against
ἑαυτοῖς reflexive pron. dat. masc. 3p. pl. ἑαυτοῦ himself, herself, itself, yourself, ourselves
φρόνιμοι adj. nom. masc. pl. φρόνιμος wise, wiser
ὅτι conj. ὅτι that, for, because, how that, how, because that, for that, though
πώρωσις n. nom. fem. sg. πώρωσις hardness, blindness
ἀπὸ prep. ἀπό (+gen) from, of, out of, since, for, off, at, by, in, on
μέρους n. gen. neut. sg. μέρος part, coast, portion, behalf, respect, piece, side
τῷ art. dat. masc. sg. ὁ ἡ τό the, this, that, he, she, it
Ἰσραὴλ pron. name. masc. inde. Ἰσραήλ Israel
ἄχρις prep. ἄχρι or ἄχρις (+gen) until, unto, till, even to, as far as, while, into
οὗ relative pron. gen. masc. sg. ὅς ἥ ὅ who, which, what, that
τὸ art. nom. neut. sg. ὁ ἡ τό the, this, that, he, she, it
πλήρωμα n. nom. neut. sg. πλήρωμα fullness, fulfilling, full
τῶν art. gen. neut. pl. ὁ ἡ τό the, this, that, he, she, it
ἐθνῶν n. gen. neut. pl. ἔθνος Gentile, nation, heathen, people
26 καὶ conj. καί and, even, also, but
οὕτω adv. οὕτω οὕτως so, even so, thus, on this wise, likewise, after this manner
πᾶς adj. nom. masc. sg. πᾶς πᾶσα πᾶν all, every, whosoever, every one, no, whole, any
Ἰσραὴλ pron. name. masc. inde. Ἰσραήλ Israel
καθὼς adv. καθώς as, even as, according as, according to
ἐκ prep. ἐκ ἐξ (+gen) of, from, out of, by, on, with, in, among, through
Σιὼν n. gen. fem. sg. Σιών Sion
ὁ art. nom. masc. sg. ὁ ἡ τό the, this, that, he, she, it
καὶ conj. καί and, even, also, but
ἀσεβείας n. acc. fem. pl. ἀσέβεια ungodliness, ungodly
ἀπὸ prep. ἀπό (+gen) from, of, out of, since, for, off, at, by, in, on
Ἰακώβ n. gen. masc. sg. Ἰακώβ Jacob
27 καὶ conj. καί and, even, also, but
αὕτη demo. pron. nom. fem. sg. οὗτος αὕτη τοῦτο this, the same, this same, he, she, it
αὐτοῖς pron. dat. masc. 3p. pl. αὐτός ή ό self, of oneself, even, very, the same, he, she, it
ἡ art. nom. fem. sg. ὁ ἡ τό the, this, that, he, she, it
παρ' prep. παρά (+gen) of, from, (+dat) with, for, (+acc) beside, at, by, above, against
ἐμοῦ pron. gen. 1p. sg. ἐγώ I
διαθήκη n. nom. fem. sg. διαθήκη testament, covenant
ὅταν conj. ὅταν when, as soon as, as long as, that, whensoever, while
τὰς art. acc. fem. pl. ὁ ἡ τό the, this, that, he, she, it
ἁμαρτίας n. acc. fem. pl. ἁμαρτία sin, offence, sinful
αὐτῶν pron. gen. masc. 3p. pl. αὐτός ή ό self, of oneself, even, very, the same, he, she, it
28 κατὰ prep. κατά (+gen) against, by, throughout, down, (+acc) according to, after, with
μὲν conj. μέν indeed, verily, truly, even, so, some
τὸ art. acc. neut. sg. ὁ ἡ τό the, this, that, he, she, it
εὐαγγέλιον n. acc. neut. sg. εὐαγγέλιον gospel
ἐχθροὶ adj. nom. masc. pl. ἐχθρός enemy, foe
δι' prep. διά (+gen) by, through, with, in, of, (+acc) for, because of, for a cause
ὑμᾶς pron. acc. 2p. pl. σύ thou, you
κατὰ prep. κατά (+gen) against, by, throughout, down, (+acc) according to, after, with

δὲ conj. δέ but, and, now, also, to the contrary, rather, then
τὴν art. acc. fem. sg. ὁ ἡ τό the, this, that, he, she, it
ἐκλογὴν n. acc. fem. sg. ἐκλογή election, chosen
ἀγαπητοὶ adj. nom. masc. pl. ἀγαπητός beloved, dearly beloved, dear, wellbeloved
διὰ prep. διά (+gen) by, through, with, in, of, (+acc) for, because of, for a cause
τοὺς art. acc. masc. pl. ὁ ἡ τό the, this, that, he, she, it
πατέρας n. acc. masc. pl. πατήρ Father, father, parent
29 ἀμεταμέλητα adj. nom. neut. pl. ἀμεταμέλητος without repentance, not to be repented of
γὰρ conj. γάρ for, and, because, but, indeed
τὰ art. nom. neut. pl. ὁ ἡ τό the, this, that, he, she, it
χαρίσματα n. nom. neut. pl. χάρισμα gift, free gift
καὶ conj. καί and, even, also, but
ἡ art. nom. fem. sg. ὁ ἡ τό the, this, that, he, she, it
κλῆσις n. nom. fem. sg. κλῆσις calling, vocation
τοῦ art. gen. masc. sg. ὁ ἡ τό the, this, that, he, she, it
Θεοῦ n. gen. masc. sg. θεός God, god
30 ὥσπερ adv. ὥσπερ as, even as, like as
γὰρ conj. γάρ for, and, because, but, indeed
καὶ conj. καί and, even, also, but
ὑμεῖς pron. nom. 2p. pl. σύ thou, you
ποτε adv. ποτέ in time past, at any time, sometimes, in old time, once, when
τῷ art. dat. masc. sg. ὁ ἡ τό the, this, that, he, she, it
Θεῷ n. dat. masc. sg. θεός God, god
νῦν adv. νῦν now, henceforth, present, this time
δὲ conj. δέ but, and, now, also, to the contrary, rather, then
τῇ art. dat. fem. sg. ὁ ἡ τό the, this, that, he, she, it
τούτων demo. pron. gen. masc. pl. οὗτος αὕτη τοῦτο this, the same, this same, he, she, it
ἀπειθείᾳ n. dat. fem. sg. ἀπείθεια unbelief, disobedience
31 οὕτω adv. οὕτω οὕτως so, even so, thus, on this wise, likewise, after this manner
καὶ conj. καί and, even, also, but
οὗτοι demo. pron. nom. masc. pl. οὗτος αὕτη τοῦτο this, the same, this same, he, she, it
νῦν adv. νῦν now, henceforth, present, this time
τῷ art. dat. neut. sg. ὁ ἡ τό the, this, that, he, she, it
ὑμετέρῳ poss. pron. dat. neut. 2p. sg. ὑμέτερος your, yours, your own
ἐλέει n. dat. neut. sg. ἔλεος mercy
ἵνα conj. ἵνα that, to, lest, for to, so that, albeit, because, for, so as
καὶ conj. καί and, even, also, but
αὐτοὶ pron. nom. masc. 3p. pl. αὐτός ή ό self, of oneself, even, very, the same, he, she, it
32 γὰρ conj. γάρ for, and, because, but, indeed
ὁ art. nom. masc. sg. ὁ ἡ τό the, this, that, he, she, it
Θεὸς n. nom. masc. sg. θεός God, god
τοὺς art. acc. masc. pl. ὁ ἡ τό the, this, that, he, she, it
πάντας adj. acc. masc. pl. πᾶς πᾶσα πᾶν all, every, whosoever, every one, no, whole, any
εἰς prep. εἰς (+acc) into, to, unto, for, in, on, toward, against, upon, at, among
ἀπείθειαν n. acc. fem. sg. ἀπείθεια unbelief, disobedience
ἵνα conj. ἵνα that, to, lest, for to, so that, albeit, because, for, so as
τοὺς art. acc. masc. pl. ὁ ἡ τό the, this, that, he, she, it
πάντας adj. acc. masc. pl. πᾶς πᾶσα πᾶν all, every, whosoever, every one, no, whole, any
33 Ὦ interjection. ὦ O
βάθος n. nom. neut. sg. βάθος deepness, depth, deep, deep thing
πλούτου n. gen. masc. sg. πλοῦτος riches
καὶ conj. καί and, even, also, but
σοφίας n. gen. fem. sg. σοφία wisdom
καὶ conj. καί and, even, also, but
γνώσεως n. gen. fem. sg. γνῶσις knowledge, science

Θεοῦ n. gen. masc. sg. θεός God, god
ὡς adv. ὡς as, when, as it were, how, about, like, as soon as, even as, while
ἀνεξερεύνητα adj. nom. neut. pl. ἀνεξερεύνητος unsearchable
τὰ art. nom. neut. pl. ὁ ἡ τό the, this, that, he, she, it
κρίματα n. nom. neut. pl. κρίμα judgment, damnation, condemnation
αὐτοῦ pron. gen. masc. 3p. sg. αὐτός ή ό self, of oneself, even, very, the same, he, she, it
καὶ conj. καί and, even, also, but
ἀνεξιχνίαστοι adj. nom. fem. pl. ἀνεξιχνίαστος past finding out, unsearchable
αἱ art. nom. fem. pl. ὁ ἡ τό the, this, that, he, she, it
ὁδοὶ n. nom. fem. pl. ὁδός way, journey, highway
αὐτοῦ pron. gen. masc. 3p. sg. αὐτός ή ό self, of oneself, even, very, the same, he, she, it
34 τίς interrog. pron. nom. masc. sg. τίς what, who, why, where, which, how
γὰρ conj. γάρ for, and, because, but, indeed
νοῦν n. acc. masc. sg. νοῦς understanding, mind
Κυρίου n. gen. masc. sg. κύριος Lord, lord, master, sir, LORD, God, Master, owner
ἢ particle. ἤ or, than, either, nor, or else, and, rather than
τίς interrog. pron. nom. masc. sg. τίς what, who, why, where, which, how
σύμβουλος n. nom. masc. sg. σύμβουλος counsellor
αὐτοῦ pron. gen. masc. 3p. sg. αὐτός ή ό self, of oneself, even, very, the same, he, she, it
35 ἢ particle. ἤ or, than, either, nor, or else, and, rather than
τίς interrog. pron. nom. masc. sg. τίς what, who, why, where, which, how
αὐτῷ pron. dat. masc. 3p. sg. αὐτός ή ό self, of oneself, even, very, the same, he, she, it
καὶ conj. καί and, even, also, but
αὐτῷ pron. dat. masc. 3p. sg. αὐτός ή ό self, of oneself, even, very, the same, he, she, it
36 ὅτι conj. ὅτι that, for, because, how that, how, because that, for that, though
ἐξ prep. ἐκ ἐξ (+gen) of, from, out of, by, on, with, in, among, through
αὐτοῦ pron. gen. masc. 3p. sg. αὐτός ή ό self, of oneself, even, very, the same, he, she, it
καὶ conj. καί and, even, also, but
δι' prep. διά (+gen) by, through, with, in, of, (+acc) for, because of, for a cause
αὐτοῦ pron. gen. masc. 3p. sg. αὐτός ή ό self, of oneself, even, very, the same, he, she, it
καὶ conj. καί and, even, also, but
εἰς prep. εἰς (+acc) into, to, unto, for, in, on, toward, against, upon, at, among
αὐτὸν pron. acc. masc. 3p. sg. αὐτός ή ό self, of oneself, even, very, the same, he, she, it
τὰ art. nom. neut. pl. ὁ ἡ τό the, this, that, he, she, it
πάντα adj. nom. neut. pl. πᾶς πᾶσα πᾶν all, every, whosoever, every one, no, whole, any
αὐτῷ pron. dat. masc. 3p. sg. αὐτός ή ό self, of oneself, even, very, the same, he, she, it
ἡ art. nom. fem. sg. ὁ ἡ τό the, this, that, he, she, it
δόξα n. nom. fem. sg. δόξα glory, honour, praise, dignity, worship
εἰς prep. εἰς (+acc) into, to, unto, for, in, on, toward, against, upon, at, among
τοὺς art. acc. masc. pl. ὁ ἡ τό the, this, that, he, she, it
αἰῶνας n. acc. masc. pl. αἰών ever, ever and ever, evermore, age, eternal, world
ἀμήν particle. ἀμήν amen, verily

12

1 οὖν conj. οὖν therefore, then, so, and, now, wherefore
ὑμᾶς pron. acc. 2p. pl. σύ thou, you
ἀδελφοί n. voc. masc. pl. ἀδελφός brother
διὰ prep. διά (+gen) by, through, with, in, of, (+acc) for, because of, for a cause
τῶν art. gen. masc. pl. ὁ ἡ τό the, this, that, he, she, it
οἰκτιρμῶν n. gen. masc. pl. οἰκτιρμός mercy
τοῦ art. gen. masc. sg. ὁ ἡ τό the, this, that, he, she, it
Θεοῦ n. gen. masc. sg. θεός God, god
τὰ art. acc. neut. pl. ὁ ἡ τό the, this, that, he, she, it
σώματα n. acc. neut. pl. σῶμα body, bodily, slave

ὑμῶν pron. gen. 2p. pl. σύ thou, you
θυσίαν n. acc. fem. sg. θυσία sacrifice
ἁγίαν adj. acc. fem. sg. ἅγιος Holy, holy, saint, Holy One, holy thing, most holy
εὐάρεστον adj. acc. fem. sg. εὐάρεστος acceptable, wellpleasing, accepted, please well
τῷ art. dat. masc. sg. ὁ ἡ τό the, this, that, he, she, it
Θεῷ n. dat. masc. sg. θεός God, god
τὴν art. acc. fem. sg. ὁ ἡ τό the, this, that, he, she, it
λογικὴν adj. acc. fem. sg. λογικός reasonable, of the word
λατρείαν n. acc. fem. sg. λατρεία service, divine service
ὑμῶν pron. gen. 2p. pl. σύ thou, you
2 καὶ conj. καί and, even, also, but
μὴ particle of negation. μή not, no, lest, neither, none, nothing, nor, never, without
τῷ art. dat. masc. sg. ὁ ἡ τό the, this, that, he, she, it
αἰῶνι n. dat. masc. sg. αἰών ever, ever and ever, evermore, age, eternal, world
τούτῳ demo. pron. dat. masc. sg. οὗτος αὕτη τοῦτο this, the same, this same, he, she, it
ἀλλὰ conj. ἀλλά but, yea, yet, nevertheless, howbeit, nay, therefore
τῇ art. dat. fem. sg. ὁ ἡ τό the, this, that, he, she, it
ἀνακαινώσει n. dat. fem. sg. ἀνακαίνωσις renewing
τοῦ art. gen. masc. sg. ὁ ἡ τό the, this, that, he, she, it
νοὸς n. gen. masc. sg. νοῦς understanding, mind
ὑμῶν pron. gen. 2p. pl. σύ thou, you
εἰς prep. εἰς (+acc) into, to, unto, for, in, on, toward, against, upon, at, among
τὸ art. acc. neut. sg. ὁ ἡ τό the, this, that, he, she, it
ὑμᾶς pron. acc. 2p. pl. σύ thou, you
τί interrog. pron. nom. neut. sg. τίς what, who, why, where, which, how
τὸ art. nom. neut. sg. ὁ ἡ τό the, this, that, he, she, it
θέλημα n. nom. neut. sg. θέλημα will, desire, pleasure
τοῦ art. gen. masc. sg. ὁ ἡ τό the, this, that, he, she, it
Θεοῦ n. gen. masc. sg. θεός God, god
τὸ art. nom. neut. sg. ὁ ἡ τό the, this, that, he, she, it
ἀγαθὸν adj. nom. neut. sg. ἀγαθός good, good thing, that which is good, well
καὶ conj. καί and, even, also, but
εὐάρεστον adj. nom. neut. sg. εὐάρεστος acceptable, wellpleasing, accepted, please well
καὶ conj. καί and, even, also, but
τέλειον adj. nom. neut. sg. τέλειος perfect, of full age
3 γὰρ conj. γάρ for, and, because, but, indeed
διὰ prep. διά (+gen) by, through, with, in, of, (+acc) for, because of, for a cause
τῆς art. gen. fem. sg. ὁ ἡ τό the, this, that, he, she, it
χάριτος n. gen. fem. sg. χάρις grace, thank, favour, pleasure
τῆς art. gen. fem. sg. ὁ ἡ τό the, this, that, he, she, it
μοι pron. dat. 1p. sg. ἐγώ I
παντὶ adj. dat. masc. sg. πᾶς πᾶσα πᾶν all, every, whosoever, every one, no, whole, any
τῷ art. dat. masc. sg. ὁ ἡ τό the, this, that, he, she, it
ἐν prep. ἐν (+dat) in, by, with, among, at, on, through, to, within, into, of, for
ὑμῖν pron. dat. 2p. pl. σύ thou, you
μὴ particle of negation. μή not, no, lest, neither, none, nothing, nor, never, without
παρ' prep. παρά (+gen) of, from, (+dat) with, for, (+acc) beside, at, by, above, against
ὃ relative pron. acc. neut. sg. ὅς ἥ ὅ who, which, what, that
ἀλλὰ conj. ἀλλά but, yea, yet, nevertheless, howbeit, nay, therefore
εἰς prep. εἰς (+acc) into, to, unto, for, in, on, toward, against, upon, at, among
τὸ art. acc. neut. sg. ὁ ἡ τό the, this, that, he, she, it
ἑκάστῳ adj. dat. masc. sg. ἕκαστος every man, every, every one, any man, each
ὡς adv. ὡς as, when, as it were, how, about, like, as soon as, even as, while
ὁ art. nom. masc. sg. ὁ ἡ τό the, this, that, he, she, it
Θεὸς n. nom. masc. sg. θεός God, god

μέτρον n. acc. neut. sg. μέτρον measure
πίστεως n. gen. fem. sg. πίστις faith, assurance, belief, fidelity
4 καθάπερ adv. καθάπερ even as, as, as well as
γὰρ conj. γάρ for, and, because, but, indeed
ἐν prep. ἐν (+dat) in, by, with, among, at, on, through, to, within, into, of, for
ἑνὶ num. dat. neut. sg. εἷς or ἕν one, other, some, any, only, a certain
σώματι n. dat. neut. sg. σῶμα body, bodily, slave
μέλη n. acc. neut. pl. μέλος member
πολλὰ adj. acc. neut. pl. πολύς many, great, much, long, abundant
τὰ art. nom. neut. pl. ὁ ἡ τό the, this, that, he, she, it
δὲ conj. δέ but, and, now, also, to the contrary, rather, then
μέλη n. nom. neut. pl. μέλος member
πάντα adj. nom. neut. pl. πᾶς πᾶσα πᾶν all, every, whosoever, every one, no, whole, any
οὐ particle of negation. οὐ οὐκ οὐχ not, no, neither, none, nay, nor, never, nothing
τὴν art. acc. fem. sg. ὁ ἡ τό the, this, that, he, she, it
αὐτὴν pron. acc. fem. 3p. sg. αὐτός ἡ ό self, of oneself, even, very, the same, he, she, it
πρᾶξιν n. acc. fem. sg. πρᾶξις deed, office, acting
5 οὕτως adv. οὕτω οὕτως so, even so, thus, on this wise, likewise, after this manner
οἱ art. nom. masc. pl. ὁ ἡ τό the, this, that, he, she, it
πολλοὶ adj. nom. masc. pl. πολύς many, great, much, long, abundant
ἕν num. nom. neut. sg. εἷς or ἕν one, other, some, any, only, a certain
σῶμά n. nom. neut. sg. σῶμα body, bodily, slave
ἐν prep. ἐν (+dat) in, by, with, among, at, on, through, to, within, into, of, for
Χριστῷ n. dat. masc. sg. Χριστός Christ
ὁ art. nom. masc. sg. ὁ ἡ τό the, this, that, he, she, it
δὲ conj. δέ but, and, now, also, to the contrary, rather, then
καθ' prep. κατά (+gen) against, by, throughout, down, (+acc) according to, after, with
εἷς num. nom. masc. sg. εἷς or ἕν one, other, some, any, only, a certain
ἀλλήλων pron. gen. masc. pl. ἀλλήλων one another, themselves, together, mutual
μέλη n. nom. neut. pl. μέλος member
6 δὲ conj. δέ but, and, now, also, to the contrary, rather, then
χαρίσματα n. acc. neut. pl. χάρισμα gift, free gift
κατὰ prep. κατά (+gen) against, by, throughout, down, (+acc) according to, after, with
τὴν art. acc. fem. sg. ὁ ἡ τό the, this, that, he, she, it
χάριν n. acc. fem. sg. χάρις grace, thank, favour, pleasure
τὴν art. acc. fem. sg. ὁ ἡ τό the, this, that, he, she, it
ἡμῖν pron. dat. 1p. pl. ἐγώ I
διάφορα adj. acc. neut. pl. διάφορος differing, more excellent, divers
εἴτε conj. εἴτε whether
προφητείαν n. acc. fem. sg. προφητεία prophecy, prophesying
κατὰ prep. κατά (+gen) against, by, throughout, down, (+acc) according to, after, with
τὴν art. acc. fem. sg. ὁ ἡ τό the, this, that, he, she, it
ἀναλογίαν n. acc. fem. sg. ἀναλογία proportion
τῆς art. gen. fem. sg. ὁ ἡ τό the, this, that, he, she, it
πίστεως n. gen. fem. sg. πίστις faith, assurance, belief, fidelity
7 εἴτε conj. εἴτε whether
διακονίαν n. acc. fem. sg. διακονία ministry, administration, service, office, relief
ἐν prep. ἐν (+dat) in, by, with, among, at, on, through, to, within, into, of, for
τῇ art. dat. fem. sg. ὁ ἡ τό the, this, that, he, she, it
διακονίᾳ n. dat. fem. sg. διακονία ministry, administration, service, office, relief
εἴτε conj. εἴτε whether
ὁ art. nom. masc. sg. ὁ ἡ τό the, this, that, he, she, it
ἐν prep. ἐν (+dat) in, by, with, among, at, on, through, to, within, into, of, for
τῇ art. dat. fem. sg. ὁ ἡ τό the, this, that, he, she, it
διδασκαλίᾳ n. dat. fem. sg. διδασκαλία doctrine, learning, teaching

8 εἴτε conj. εἴτε whether
ὁ art. nom. masc. sg. ὁ ἡ τό the, this, that, he, she, it
ἐν prep. ἐν (+dat) in, by, with, among, at, on, through, to, within, into, of, for
τῇ art. dat. fem. sg. ὁ ἡ τό the, this, that, he, she, it
παρακλήσει n. dat. fem. sg. παράκλησις consolation, exhortation, comfort
ὁ art. nom. masc. sg. ὁ ἡ τό the, this, that, he, she, it
ἐν prep. ἐν (+dat) in, by, with, among, at, on, through, to, within, into, of, for
ἁπλότητι n. dat. fem. sg. ἁπλότης simplicity, singleness, bountifulness, liberal, liberality
ὁ art. nom. masc. sg. ὁ ἡ τό the, this, that, he, she, it
ἐν prep. ἐν (+dat) in, by, with, among, at, on, through, to, within, into, of, for
σπουδῇ n. dat. fem. sg. σπουδή diligence, haste, business, care, carefulness
ὁ art. nom. masc. sg. ὁ ἡ τό the, this, that, he, she, it
ἐν prep. ἐν (+dat) in, by, with, among, at, on, through, to, within, into, of, for
ἱλαρότητι n. dat. fem. sg. ἱλαρότης cheerfulness
9 ἡ art. nom. fem. sg. ὁ ἡ τό the, this, that, he, she, it
ἀγάπη n. nom. fem. sg. ἀγάπη love, charity, feast of charity
ἀνυπόκριτος adj. nom. fem. sg. ἀνυπόκριτος unfeigned, without dissimulation
τὸ art. acc. neut. sg. ὁ ἡ τό the, this, that, he, she, it
πονηρόν adj. acc. neut. sg. πονηρός evil, wicked, bad
τῷ art. dat. neut. sg. ὁ ἡ τό the, this, that, he, she, it
ἀγαθῷ adj. dat. neut. sg. ἀγαθός good, good thing, that which is good, well
10 τῇ art. dat. fem. sg. ὁ ἡ τό the, this, that, he, she, it
φιλαδελφίᾳ n. dat. fem. sg. φιλαδελφία brotherly love, brotherly kindness
εἰς prep. εἰς (+acc) into, to, unto, for, in, on, toward, against, upon, at, among
ἀλλήλους pron. acc. masc. 2p. pl. ἀλλήλων one another, themselves, together, mutual
φιλόστοργοι adj. nom. masc. pl. φιλόστοργος kindly affectioned
τῇ art. dat. fem. sg. ὁ ἡ τό the, this, that, he, she, it
τιμῇ n. dat. fem. sg. τιμή honour, price, preciousness, sum
ἀλλήλους pron. acc. masc. 2p. pl. ἀλλήλων one another, themselves, together, mutual
11 τῇ art. dat. fem. sg. ὁ ἡ τό the, this, that, he, she, it
σπουδῇ n. dat. fem. sg. σπουδή diligence, haste, business, care, carefulness
μὴ particle of negation. μή not, no, lest, neither, none, nothing, nor, never, without
ὀκνηροί adj. nom. masc. pl. ὀκνηρός slothful, grievous
τῷ art. dat. neut. sg. ὁ ἡ τό the, this, that, he, she, it
πνεύματι n. dat. neut. sg. πνεῦμα spirit, Spirit, Ghost, ghost, life. of the spirit, wind
τῷ art. dat. neut. sg. ὁ ἡ τό the, this, that, he, she, it
Κυρίῳ n. dat. masc. sg. κύριος Lord, lord, master, sir, LORD, God, Master, owner
12 τῇ art. dat. fem. sg. ὁ ἡ τό the, this, that, he, she, it
ἐλπίδι n. dat. fem. sg. ἐλπίς hope, faith
τῇ art. dat. fem. sg. ὁ ἡ τό the, this, that, he, she, it
θλίψει n. dat. fem. sg. θλῖψις tribulation, affliction, anguish, persecution
τῇ art. dat. fem. sg. ὁ ἡ τό the, this, that, he, she, it
προσευχῇ n. dat. fem. sg. προσευχή prayer
13 ταῖς art. dat. fem. pl. ὁ ἡ τό the, this, that, he, she, it
χρείαις n. dat. fem. pl. χρεία need, necessity, lack, want
τῶν art. gen. masc. pl. ὁ ἡ τό the, this, that, he, she, it
ἁγίων adj. gen. masc. pl. ἅγιος Holy, holy, saint, Holy One, holy thing, most holy
τὴν art. acc. fem. sg. ὁ ἡ τό the, this, that, he, she, it
φιλοξενίαν n. acc. fem. sg. φιλοξενία hospitality
14 τοὺς art. acc. masc. pl. ὁ ἡ τό the, this, that, he, she, it
ὑμᾶς pron. acc. 2p. pl. σύ thou, you
καὶ conj. καί and, even, also, but
μὴ particle of negation. μή not, no, lest, neither, none, nothing, nor, never, without
15 μετὰ prep. μετά (+gen) with, among, against, (+acc) after
καὶ conj. καί and, even, also, but

μετὰ prep. μετά (+gen) with, among, against, (+acc) after
16 τὸ art. acc. neut. sg. ὁ ἡ τό the, this, that, he, she, it
αὐτὸ pron. acc. neut. 3p. sg. αὐτός ἡ ὁ self, of oneself, even, very, the same, he, she, it
εἰς prep. εἰς (+acc) into, to, unto, for, in, on, toward, against, upon, at, among
ἀλλήλους pron. acc. masc. 2p. pl. ἀλλήλων one another, themselves, together, mutual
μὴ particle of negation. μή not, no, lest, neither, none, nothing, nor, never, without
τὰ art. acc. neut. pl. ὁ ἡ τό the, this, that, he, she, it
ὑψηλὰ adj. acc. neut. pl. ὑψηλός high, higher, highly esteemed
ἀλλὰ conj. ἀλλά but, yea, yet, nevertheless, howbeit, nay, therefore
τοῖς art. dat. masc. pl. ὁ ἡ τό the, this, that, he, she, it
ταπεινοῖς adj. dat. masc. pl. ταπεινός humble, of low degree, base, cast down, lowly
μὴ particle of negation. μή not, no, lest, neither, none, nothing, nor, never, without
φρόνιμοι adj. nom. masc. pl. φρόνιμος wise, wiser
παρ' prep. παρά (+gen) of, from, (+dat) with, for, (+acc) beside, at, by, above, against
ἑαυτοῖς reflexive pron. dat. masc. 3p. pl. ἑαυτοῦ himself, herself, itself, yourself, ourselves
17 μηδενὶ num. dat. masc. sg. μηδείς μηδεμία μηδέν no man, nothing, no, none, not at all
κακὸν adj. acc. neut. sg. κακός evil, evil thing, noisome, wicked
ἀντὶ prep. ἀντί (+gen) for, because, in the room
κακοῦ adj. gen. neut. sg. κακός evil, evil thing, noisome, wicked
καλὰ adj. acc. neut. pl. καλός good, better, goodly, meet, honest, fair, well, worthy
ἐνώπιον prep. ἐνώπιον (+gen) before, in the sight of, in the presence of. (adv.) before
πάντων adj. gen. masc. pl. πᾶς πᾶσα πᾶν all, every, whosoever, every one, no, whole, any
ἀνθρώπων n. gen. masc. pl. ἄνθρωπος man, human being, person, one, certain
18 εἰ conj. εἰ if, whether, that, though, forasmuch
δυνατὸν adj. nom. neut. sg. δυνατός able, possible, mighty, strong
τὸ art. acc. neut. sg. ὁ ἡ τό the, this, that, he, she, it
ἐξ prep. ἐκ ἐξ (+gen) of, from, out of, by, on, with, in, among, through
ὑμῶν pron. gen. 2p. pl. σύ thou, you
μετὰ prep. μετά (+gen) with, among, against, (+acc) after
πάντων adj. gen. masc. pl. πᾶς πᾶσα πᾶν all, every, whosoever, every one, no, whole, any
ἀνθρώπων n. gen. masc. pl. ἄνθρωπος man, human being, person, one, certain
19 μὴ particle of negation. μή not, no, lest, neither, none, nothing, nor, never, without
ἑαυτοὺς reflexive pron. acc. masc. 3p. pl. ἑαυτοῦ himself, herself, itself, yourself, ourselves
ἀγαπητοί adj. voc. masc. pl. ἀγαπητός beloved, dearly beloved, dear, wellbeloved
ἀλλὰ conj. ἀλλά but, yea, yet, nevertheless, howbeit, nay, therefore
τόπον n. acc. masc. sg. τόπος place, room, quarter
τῇ art. dat. fem. sg. ὁ ἡ τό the, this, that, he, she, it
ὀργῇ n. dat. fem. sg. ὀργή wrath, anger, indignation, vengeance
γάρ conj. γάρ for, and, because, but, indeed
Ἐμοὶ pron. dat. 1p. sg. ἐγώ I
ἐκδίκησις n. nom. fem. sg. ἐκδίκησις vengeance, punishment, revenge
ἐγὼ pron. nom. 1p. sg. ἐγώ I
Κύριος n. nom. masc. sg. κύριος Lord, lord, master, sir, LORD, God, Master, owner
20 ἐὰν conj. ἐάν if, soever, except, though, and if, but, whether, if so, so
οὖν conj. οὖν therefore, then, so, and, now, wherefore
ὁ art. nom. masc. sg. ὁ ἡ τό the, this, that, he, she, it
ἐχθρός adj. nom. masc. sg. ἐχθρός enemy, foe
σου pron. gen. 2p. sg. σύ thou, you
αὐτόν pron. acc. masc. 3p. sg. αὐτός ἡ ὁ self, of oneself, even, very, the same, he, she, it
ἐὰν conj. ἐάν if, soever, except, though, and if, but, whether, if so, so
αὐτόν pron. acc. masc. 3p. sg. αὐτός ἡ ὁ self, of oneself, even, very, the same, he, she, it
τοῦτο demo. pron. acc. neut. sg. οὗτος αὕτη τοῦτο this, the same, this same, he, she, it
γὰρ conj. γάρ for, and, because, but, indeed
ἄνθρακας n. acc. masc. pl. ἄνθραξ coal
πυρὸς n. gen. neut. sg. πῦρ fire, fiery

ἐπὶ prep. ἐπί (+gen) on, in, upon, (+dat) in, at, for, upon, (+acc) on, upon, unto, to, against
τὴν art. acc. fem. sg. ὁ ἡ τό the, this, that, he, she, it
κεφαλὴν n. acc. fem. sg. κεφαλή head
αὐτοῦ pron. gen. masc. 3p. sg. αὐτός ή ό self, of oneself, even, very, the same, he, she, it
21 μὴ particle of negation. μή not, no, lest, neither, none, nothing, nor, never, without
ὑπὸ prep. ὑπό (+gen) of, by, with, from, among, (+acc) under
τοῦ art. gen. neut. sg. ὁ ἡ τό the, this, that, he, she, it
κακοῦ adj. gen. neut. sg. κακός evil, evil thing, noisome, wicked
ἀλλὰ conj. ἀλλά but, yea, yet, nevertheless, howbeit, nay, therefore
ἐν prep. ἐν (+dat) in, by, with, among, at, on, through, to, within, into, of, for
τῷ art. dat. neut. sg. ὁ ἡ τό the, this, that, he, she, it
ἀγαθῷ adj. dat. neut. sg. ἀγαθός good, good thing, that which is good, well
τὸ art. acc. neut. sg. ὁ ἡ τό the, this, that, he, she, it
κακόν adj. acc. neut. sg. κακός evil, evil thing, noisome, wicked

13

1 Πᾶσα adj. nom. fem. sg. πᾶς πᾶσα πᾶν all, every, whosoever, every one, no, whole, any
ψυχὴ n. nom. fem. sg. ψυχή life, soul, mind, heart
ἐξουσίαις n. dat. fem. pl. ἐξουσία power, authority, right, strength, jurisdiction
οὐ particle of negation. οὐ οὐκ οὐχ not, no, neither, none, nay, nor, never, nothing
γὰρ conj. γάρ for, and, because, but, indeed
ἐξουσία n. nom. fem. sg. ἐξουσία power, authority, right, strength, jurisdiction
εἰ conj. εἰ if, whether, that, though, forasmuch
μὴ particle of negation. μή not, no, lest, neither, none, nothing, nor, never, without
ἀπὸ prep. ἀπό (+gen) from, of, out of, since, for, off, at, by, in, on
Θεοῦ n. gen. masc. sg. θεός God, god
αἱ art. nom. fem. pl. ὁ ἡ τό the, this, that, he, she, it
δὲ conj. δέ but, and, now, also, to the contrary, rather, then
ἐξουσίαι n. nom. fem. pl. ἐξουσία power, authority, right, strength, jurisdiction
ὑπὸ prep. ὑπό (+gen) of, by, with, from, among, (+acc) under
τοῦ art. gen. masc. sg. ὁ ἡ τό the, this, that, he, she, it
Θεοῦ n. gen. masc. sg. θεός God, god
2 ὥστε conj. ὥστε so that, wherefore, insomuch that, therefore, that, so then
ὁ art. nom. masc. sg. ὁ ἡ τό the, this, that, he, she, it
τῇ art. dat. fem. sg. ὁ ἡ τό the, this, that, he, she, it
ἐξουσίᾳ n. dat. fem. sg. ἐξουσία power, authority, right, strength, jurisdiction
τῇ art. dat. fem. sg. ὁ ἡ τό the, this, that, he, she, it
τοῦ art. gen. masc. sg. ὁ ἡ τό the, this, that, he, she, it
Θεοῦ n. gen. masc. sg. θεός God, god
διαταγῇ n. dat. fem. sg. διαταγή disposition, ordinance
οἱ art. nom. masc. pl. ὁ ἡ τό the, this, that, he, she, it
δὲ conj. δέ but, and, now, also, to the contrary, rather, then
ἑαυτοῖς reflexive pron. dat. masc. 3p. pl. ἑαυτοῦ himself, herself, itself, yourself, ourselves
κρίμα n. acc. neut. sg. κρίμα judgment, damnation, condemnation
3 οἱ art. nom. masc. pl. ὁ ἡ τό the, this, that, he, she, it
γὰρ conj. γάρ for, and, because, but, indeed
ἄρχοντες n. nom. masc. pl. ἄρχων ruler, prince, chief, magistrate, chief ruler
οὐκ particle of negation. οὐ οὐκ οὐχ not, no, neither, none, nay, nor, never, nothing
φόβος n. nom. masc. sg. φόβος fear, terror, sore afraid
τῶν art. gen. neut. pl. ὁ ἡ τό the, this, that, he, she, it
ἀγαθῶν adj. gen. neut. pl. ἀγαθός good, good thing, that which is good, well
ἔργων n. gen. neut. pl. ἔργον work, deed, doing labour
ἀλλὰ conj. ἀλλά but, yea, yet, nevertheless, howbeit, nay, therefore
τῶν art. gen. neut. pl. ὁ ἡ τό the, this, that, he, she, it

κακῶν adj. gen. neut. pl. κακός evil, evil thing, noisome, wicked
δὲ conj. δέ but, and, now, also, to the contrary, rather, then
μὴ particle of negation. μή not, no, lest, neither, none, nothing, nor, never, without
τὴν art. acc. fem. sg. ὁ ἡ τό the, this, that, he, she, it
ἐξουσίαν n. acc. fem. sg. ἐξουσία power, authority, right, strength, jurisdiction
τὸ art. acc. neut. sg. ὁ ἡ τό the, this, that, he, she, it
ἀγαθὸν adj. acc. neut. sg. ἀγαθός good, good thing, that which is good, well
καὶ conj. καί and, even, also, but
ἔπαινον n. acc. masc. sg. ἔπαινος praise
ἐξ prep. ἐκ ἐξ (+gen) of, from, out of, by, on, with, in, among, through
αὐτῆς pron. gen. fem. 3p. sg. αὐτός ή ό self, of oneself, even, very, the same, he, she, it
4 Θεοῦ n. gen. masc. sg. θεός God, god
γὰρ conj. γάρ for, and, because, but, indeed
διάκονός n. nom. masc. sg. διάκονος minister, servant, deacon
σοὶ pron. dat. 2p. sg. σύ thou, you
εἰς prep. εἰς (+acc) into, to, unto, for, in, on, toward, against, upon, at, among
τὸ art. acc. neut. sg. ὁ ἡ τό the, this, that, he, she, it
ἀγαθόν adj. acc. neut. sg. ἀγαθός good, good thing, that which is good, well
ἐὰν conj. ἐάν if, soever, except, though, and if, but, whether, if so, so
δὲ conj. δέ but, and, now, also, to the contrary, rather, then
τὸ art. acc. neut. sg. ὁ ἡ τό the, this, that, he, she, it
κακὸν adj. acc. neut. sg. κακός evil, evil thing, noisome, wicked
οὐ particle of negation. οὐ οὐκ οὐχ not, no, neither, none, nay, nor, never, nothing
γὰρ conj. γάρ for, and, because, but, indeed
εἰκῆ adv. εἰκῆ in vain, vainly, without a cause
τὴν art. acc. fem. sg. ὁ ἡ τό the, this, that, he, she, it
μάχαιραν n. acc. fem. sg. μάχαιρα sword
Θεοῦ n. gen. masc. sg. θεός God, god
γὰρ conj. γάρ for, and, because, but, indeed
διάκονός n. nom. masc. sg. διάκονος minister, servant, deacon
ἔκδικος adj. nom. masc. sg. ἔκδικος revenger, avenger
εἰς prep. εἰς (+acc) into, to, unto, for, in, on, toward, against, upon, at, among
ὀργὴν n. acc. fem. sg. ὀργή wrath, anger, indignation, vengeance
τῷ art. dat. masc. sg. ὁ ἡ τό the, this, that, he, she, it
τὸ art. acc. neut. sg. ὁ ἡ τό the, this, that, he, she, it
κακὸν adj. acc. neut. sg. κακός evil, evil thing, noisome, wicked
5 διὸ conj. διό wherefore, therefore, for which cause
ἀνάγκη n. nom. fem. sg. ἀνάγκη must needs, necessity, distress, inevitable
οὐ particle of negation. οὐ οὐκ οὐχ not, no, neither, none, nay, nor, never, nothing
μόνον adv. μόνος only, alone, by oneself
διὰ prep. διά (+gen) by, through, with, in, of, (+acc) for, because of, for a cause
τὴν art. acc. fem. sg. ὁ ἡ τό the, this, that, he, she, it
ὀργὴν n. acc. fem. sg. ὀργή wrath, anger, indignation, vengeance
ἀλλὰ conj. ἀλλά but, yea, yet, nevertheless, howbeit, nay, therefore
καὶ conj. καί and, even, also, but
διὰ prep. διά (+gen) by, through, with, in, of, (+acc) for, because of, for a cause
τὴν art. acc. fem. sg. ὁ ἡ τό the, this, that, he, she, it
συνείδησιν n. acc. fem. sg. συνείδησις conscience
6 διὰ prep. διά (+gen) by, through, with, in, of, (+acc) for, because of, for a cause
τοῦτο demo. pron. acc. neut. sg. οὗτος αὕτη τοῦτο this, the same, this same, he, she, it
γὰρ conj. γάρ for, and, because, but, indeed
καὶ conj. καί and, even, also, but
φόρους n. acc. masc. pl. φόρος tribute
λειτουργοὶ n. nom. masc. pl. λειτουργός minister, he that minister
γὰρ conj. γάρ for, and, because, but, indeed

Θεοῦ n. gen. masc. sg. θεός God, god
εἰς prep. εἰς (+acc) into, to, unto, for, in, on, toward, against, upon, at, among
αὐτὸ pron. acc. neut. 3p. sg. αὐτός ή ὁ self, of oneself, even, very, the same, he, she, it
τοῦτο demo. pron. acc. neut. sg. οὗτος αὕτη τοῦτο this, the same, this same, he, she, it
7 οὖν conj. οὖν therefore, then, so, and, now, wherefore
πᾶσι adj. dat. masc. pl. πᾶς πᾶσα πᾶν all, every, whosoever, every one, no, whole, any
τὰς art. acc. fem. pl. ὁ ἡ τό the, this, that, he, she, it
ὀφειλάς n. acc. fem. pl. ὀφειλή debt, due
τῷ art. dat. masc. sg. ὁ ἡ τό the, this, that, he, she, it
τὸν art. acc. masc. sg. ὁ ἡ τό the, this, that, he, she, it
φόρον n. acc. masc. sg. φόρος tribute
τὸν art. acc. masc. sg. ὁ ἡ τό the, this, that, he, she, it
φόρον n. acc. masc. sg. φόρος tribute
τῷ art. dat. masc. sg. ὁ ἡ τό the, this, that, he, she, it
τὸ art. acc. neut. sg. ὁ ἡ τό the, this, that, he, she, it
τέλος n. acc. neut. sg. τέλος end, custom, ending, finally, uttermost
τὸ art. acc. neut. sg. ὁ ἡ τό the, this, that, he, she, it
τέλος n. acc. neut. sg. τέλος end, custom, ending, finally, uttermost
τῷ art. dat. masc. sg. ὁ ἡ τό the, this, that, he, she, it
τὸν art. acc. masc. sg. ὁ ἡ τό the, this, that, he, she, it
φόβον n. acc. masc. sg. φόβος fear, terror, sore afraid
τὸν art. acc. masc. sg. ὁ ἡ τό the, this, that, he, she, it
φόβον n. acc. masc. sg. φόβος fear, terror, sore afraid
τῷ art. dat. masc. sg. ὁ ἡ τό the, this, that, he, she, it
τὴν art. acc. fem. sg. ὁ ἡ τό the, this, that, he, she, it
τιμὴν n. acc. fem. sg. τιμή honour, price, preciousness, sum
τὴν art. acc. fem. sg. ὁ ἡ τό the, this, that, he, she, it
τιμὴν n. acc. fem. sg. τιμή honour, price, preciousness, sum
8 Μηδενὶ num. dat. masc. sg. μηδείς μηδεμία μηδέν no man, nothing, no, none, not at all
μηδὲν num. acc. neut. sg. μηδείς μηδεμία μηδέν no man, nothing, no, none, not at all
εἰ conj. εἰ if, whether, that, though, forasmuch
μὴ particle of negation. μή not, no, lest, neither, none, nothing, nor, never, withoutv
τὸ art. acc. neut. sg. ὁ ἡ τό the, this, that, he, she, it
ἀλλήλους pron. acc. masc. 2p. pl. ἀλλήλων one another, themselves, together, mutual
ὁ art. nom. masc. sg. ὁ ἡ τό the, this, that, he, she, it
γὰρ conj. γάρ for, and, because, but, indeed
τὸν art. acc. masc. sg. ὁ ἡ τό the, this, that, he, she, it
ἕτερον adj. acc. masc. sg. ἕτερος another, other, else, strange
νόμον n. acc. masc. sg. νόμος law, the law
9 τὸ art. nom. neut. sg. ὁ ἡ τό the, this, that, he, she, it
γὰρ conj. γάρ for, and, because, but, indeed
Οὐ particle of negation. οὐ οὐκ οὐχ not, no, neither, none, nay, nor, never, nothing
οὐ particle of negation. οὐ οὐκ οὐχ not, no, neither, none, nay, nor, never, nothing
οὐ particle of negation. οὐ οὐκ οὐχ not, no, neither, none, nay, nor, never, nothing
οὐ particle of negation. οὐ οὐκ οὐχ not, no, neither, none, nay, nor, never, nothing
Οὐκ particle of negation. οὐ οὐκ οὐχ not, no, neither, none, nay, nor, never, nothing
καὶ conj. καί and, even, also, but
εἴ conj. εἰ if, whether, that, though, forasmuch
τις indefinite pron. nom. fem. sg. τὶς certain, some, any man, one, any thing
ἑτέρα adj. nom. fem. sg. ἕτερος another, other, else, strange
ἐντολή n. nom. fem. sg. ἐντολή commandment, precept
ἐν prep. ἐν (+dat) in, by, with, among, at, on, through, to, within, into, of, for
τούτῳ demo. pron. dat. masc. sg. οὗτος αὕτη τοῦτο this, the same, this same, he, she, it
τῷ art. dat. masc. sg. ὁ ἡ τό the, this, that, he, she, it
λόγῳ n. dat. masc. sg. λόγος word, saying, account, speech, thing, matter

ἐν prep. ἐν (+dat) in, by, with, among, at, on, through, to, within, into, of, for
τῷ art. dat. masc. sg. ὁ ἡ τό the, this, that, he, she, it
τὸν art. acc. masc. sg. ὁ ἡ τό the, this, that, he, she, it
πλησίον adv. πλησίον neighbour, near
σου pron. gen. 2p. sg. σύ thou, you
ὡς adv. ὡς as, when, as it were, how, about, like, as soon as, even as, while
ἑαυτόν reflexive pron. acc. masc. 3p. sg. ἑαυτοῦ himself, herself, itself, yourself, ourselves
10 ἡ art. nom. fem. sg. ὁ ἡ τό the, this, that, he, she, it
ἀγάπη n. nom. fem. sg. ἀγάπη love, charity, feast of charity
τῷ art. dat. masc. sg. ὁ ἡ τό the, this, that, he, she, it
πλησίον adv. πλησίον neighbour, near
κακὸν adj. acc. neut. sg. κακός evil, evil thing, noisome, wicked
οὐκ particle of negation. οὐ οὐκ οὐχ not, no, neither, none, nay, nor, never, nothing
πλήρωμα n. nom. neut. sg. πλήρωμα fullness, fulfilling, full
οὖν conj. οὖν therefore, then, so, and, now, wherefore
νόμου n. gen. masc. sg. νόμος law, the law
ἡ art. nom. fem. sg. ὁ ἡ τό the, this, that, he, she, it
ἀγάπη n. nom. fem. sg. ἀγάπη love, charity, feast of charity
11 Καὶ conj. καί and, even, also, but
τοῦτο demo. pron. acc. neut. sg. οὗτος αὕτη τοῦτο this, the same, this same, he, she, it
τὸν art. acc. masc. sg. ὁ ἡ τό the, this, that, he, she, it
καιρόν n. acc. masc. sg. καιρός time, season, due time, opportunity
ὅτι conj. ὅτι that, for, because, how that, how, because that, for that, though
ὥρα n. nom. fem. sg. ὥρα hour, time, season
ὑμᾶς pron. acc. 2p. pl. σύ thou, you
ἤδη adv. ἤδη now, already, yet, by this time, even now, now already
ἐξ prep. ἐκ ἐξ (+gen) of, from, out of, by, on, with, in, among, through
ὕπνου n. gen. masc. sg. ὕπνος sleep
νῦν adv. νῦν now, henceforth, present, this time
γὰρ conj. γάρ for, and, because, but, indeed
ἐγγύτερον compar. adv. ἐγγύς nigh, at hand, near, nigh at hand, ready, nigh unto
ἡμῶν pron. gen. 1p. pl. ἐγώ I
ἡ art. nom. fem. sg. ὁ ἡ τό the, this, that, he, she, it
σωτηρία n. nom. fem. sg. σωτηρία salvation, deliver, health, saving
ἢ particle. ἤ or, than, either, nor, or else, and, rather than
ὅτε adv. ὅτε when, after that, as soon as, while, after
12 ἡ art. nom. fem. sg. ὁ ἡ τό the, this, that, he, she, it
νὺξ n. nom. fem. sg. νύξ night
ἡ art. nom. fem. sg. ὁ ἡ τό the, this, that, he, she, it
δὲ conj. δέ but, and, now, also, to the contrary, rather, then
ἡμέρα n. nom. fem. sg. ἡμέρα day, time, year, while, age, day time
οὖν conj. οὖν therefore, then, so, and, now, wherefore
τὰ art. acc. neut. pl. ὁ ἡ τό the, this, that, he, she, it
ἔργα n. acc. neut. pl. ἔργον work, deed, doing labour
τοῦ art. gen. neut. sg. ὁ ἡ τό the, this, that, he, she, it
σκότους n. gen. neut. sg. σκότος darkness
καὶ conj. καί and, even, also, but
τὰ art. acc. neut. pl. ὁ ἡ τό the, this, that, he, she, it
ὅπλα n. acc. neut. pl. ὅπλον instrument, armour, weapon
τοῦ art. gen. neut. sg. ὁ ἡ τό the, this, that, he, she, it
φωτός n. gen. neut. sg. φῶς light, fire
13 ὡς adv. ὡς as, when, as it were, how, about, like, as soon as, even as, while
ἐν prep. ἐν (+dat) in, by, with, among, at, on, through, to, within, into, of, for
ἡμέρᾳ n. dat. fem. sg. ἡμέρα day, time, year, while, age, day time
εὐσχημόνως adv. εὐσχημόνως honestly, decently

μὴ particle of negation. μή not, no, lest, neither, none, nothing, nor, never, without
κώμοις n. dat. masc. pl. κῶμος rioting, revelling
καὶ conj. καί and, even, also, but
μέθαις n. dat. fem. pl. μέθη drunkenness
μὴ particle of negation. μή not, no, lest, neither, none, nothing, nor, never, without
κοίταις n. dat. fem. pl. κοίτη bed, chambering
καὶ conj. καί and, even, also, but
ἀσελγείαις n. dat. fem. pl. ἀσέλγεια lasciviousness, wantonness, filthy
μὴ particle of negation. μή not, no, lest, neither, none, nothing, nor, never, without
ἔριδι n. dat. fem. sg. ἔρις debate, strife, contention, variance
καὶ conj. καί and, even, also, but
ζήλῳ n. dat. masc. sg. ζῆλος zeal, envying, indignation, emulation, jealousy
14 ἀλλ' conj. ἀλλά but, yea, yet, nevertheless, howbeit, nay, therefore
τὸν art. acc. masc. sg. ὁ ἡ τό the, this, that, he, she, it
Κύριον n. acc. masc. sg. κύριος Lord, lord, master, sir, LORD, God, Master, owner
Ἰησοῦν n. acc. masc. sg. Ἰησοῦς Jesus
Χριστὸν n. acc. masc. sg. Χριστός Christ
καὶ conj. καί and, even, also, but
τῆς art. gen. fem. sg. ὁ ἡ τό the, this, that, he, she, it
σαρκὸς n. gen. fem. sg. σάρξ flesh, carnal
πρόνοιαν n. acc. fem. sg. πρόνοια providence, provision for
μὴ particle of negation. μή not, no, lest, neither, none, nothing, nor, never, without
εἰς prep. εἰς (+acc) into, to, unto, for, in, on, toward, against, upon, at, among
ἐπιθυμίας n. acc. fem. pl. ἐπιθυμία lust, concupiscence, desire

14

1 Τὸν art. acc. masc. sg. ὁ ἡ τό the, this, that, he, she, it
δὲ conj. δέ but, and, now, also, to the contrary, rather, then
τῇ art. dat. fem. sg. ὁ ἡ τό the, this, that, he, she, it
πίστει n. dat. fem. sg. πίστις faith, assurance, belief, fidelity
μὴ particle of negation. μή not, no, lest, neither, none, nothing, nor, never, without
εἰς prep. εἰς (+acc) into, to, unto, for, in, on, toward, against, upon, at, among
διακρίσεις n. acc. fem. pl. διάκρισις disputations, discern, discerning
διαλογισμῶν n. gen. masc. pl. διαλογισμός thought, reasoning, imagination, disputing
2 ὃς relative pron. nom. masc. sg. ὅς ἥ ὅ who, which, what, that
μὲν conj. μέν indeed, verily, truly, even, so, some
πάντα adj. acc. neut. pl. πᾶς πᾶσα πᾶν all, every, whosoever, every one, no, whole, any
ὁ art. nom. masc. sg. ὁ ἡ τό the, this, that, he, she, it
δὲ conj. δέ but, and, now, also, to the contrary, rather, then
λάχανα n. acc. neut. pl. λάχανον herb
3 ὁ art. nom. masc. sg. ὁ ἡ τό the, this, that, he, she, it
τὸν art. acc. masc. sg. ὁ ἡ τό the, this, that, he, she, it
μὴ particle of negation. μή not, no, lest, neither, none, nothing, nor, never, without
μὴ particle of negation. μή not, no, lest, neither, none, nothing, nor, never, without
καὶ conj. καί and, even, also, but
ὁ art. nom. masc. sg. ὁ ἡ τό the, this, that, he, she, it
μὴ particle of negation. μή not, no, lest, neither, none, nothing, nor, never, without
τὸν art. acc. masc. sg. ὁ ἡ τό the, this, that, he, she, it
μὴ particle of negation. μή not, no, lest, neither, none, nothing, nor, never, without
ὁ art. nom. masc. sg. ὁ ἡ τό the, this, that, he, she, it
Θεὸς n. nom. masc. sg. θεός God, god
γὰρ conj. γάρ for, and, because, but, indeed
αὐτὸν pron. acc. masc. 3p. sg. αὐτός ἡ ὁ self, of oneself, even, very, the same, he, she, it
4 σὺ pron. nom. 2p. sg. σύ thou, you

τίς interrog. pron. nom. masc. sg. τίς what, who, why, where, which, how
ὁ art. nom. masc. sg. ὁ ἡ τό the, this, that, he, she, it
ἀλλότριον adj. acc. masc. sg. ἀλλότριος stranger, another man, alien, strange
οἰκέτην n. acc. masc. sg. οἰκέτης servant, household servant
τῷ art. dat. masc. sg. ὁ ἡ τό the, this, that, he, she, it
ἰδίῳ adj. dat. masc. sg. ἴδιος one's own, one's, privately
κυρίῳ n. dat. masc. sg. κύριος Lord, lord, master, sir, LORD, God, Master, owner
ἢ particle. ἤ or, than, either, nor, or else, and, rather than
δέ conj. δέ but, and, now, also, to the contrary, rather, then
δυνατὸς adj. nom. masc. sg. δυνατός able, possible, mighty, strong
γὰρ conj. γάρ for, and, because, but, indeed
ὁ art. nom. masc. sg. ὁ ἡ τό the, this, that, he, she, it
Θεὸς n. nom. masc. sg. θεός God, god
αὐτόν pron. acc. masc. 3p. sg. αὐτός ἡ ὁ self, of oneself, even, very, the same, he, she, it
5 ὃς relative pron. nom. masc. sg. ὅς ἥ ὅ who, which, what, that
μὲν conj. μέν indeed, verily, truly, even, so, some
ἡμέραν n. acc. fem. sg. ἡμέρα day, time, year, while, age, day time
παρ' prep. παρά (+gen) of, from, (+dat) with, for, (+acc) beside, at, by, above, against
ἡμέραν n. acc. fem. sg. ἡμέρα day, time, year, while, age, day time
ὃς relative pron. nom. masc. sg. ὅς ἥ ὅ who, which, what, that
δὲ conj. δέ but, and, now, also, to the contrary, rather, then
πᾶσαν adj. acc. fem. sg. πᾶς πᾶσα πᾶν all, every, whosoever, every one, no, whole, any
ἡμέραν n. acc. fem. sg. ἡμέρα day, time, year, while, age, day time
ἕκαστος adj. nom. masc. sg. ἕκαστος every man, every, every one, any man, each
ἐν prep. ἐν (+dat) in, by, with, among, at, on, through, to, within, into, of, for
τῷ art. dat. masc. sg. ὁ ἡ τό the, this, that, he, she, it
ἰδίῳ adj. dat. masc. sg. ἴδιος one's own, one's, privately
νοῒ n. dat. masc. sg. νοῦς understanding, mind
6 ὁ art. nom. masc. sg. ὁ ἡ τό the, this, that, he, she, it
τὴν art. acc. fem. sg. ὁ ἡ τό the, this, that, he, she, it
ἡμέραν n. acc. fem. sg. ἡμέρα day, time, year, while, age, day time
Κυρίῳ n. dat. masc. sg. κύριος Lord, lord, master, sir, LORD, God, Master, owner
καὶ conj. καί and, even, also, but
ὁ art. nom. masc. sg. ὁ ἡ τό the, this, that, he, she, it
μὴ particle of negation. μή not, no, lest, neither, none, nothing, nor, never, without
τὴν art. acc. fem. sg. ὁ ἡ τό the, this, that, he, she, it
ἡμέραν n. acc. fem. sg. ἡμέρα day, time, year, while, age, day time
Κυρίῳ n. dat. masc. sg. κύριος Lord, lord, master, sir, LORD, God, Master, owner
οὐ particle of negation. οὐ οὐκ οὐχ not, no, neither, none, nay, nor, never, nothing
ὁ art. nom. masc. sg. ὁ ἡ τό the, this, that, he, she, it
Κυρίῳ n. dat. masc. sg. κύριος Lord, lord, master, sir, LORD, God, Master, owner
γὰρ conj. γάρ for, and, because, but, indeed
τῷ art. dat. masc. sg. ὁ ἡ τό the, this, that, he, she, it
Θεῷ n. dat. masc. sg. θεός God, god
καὶ conj. καί and, even, also, but
ὁ art. nom. masc. sg. ὁ ἡ τό the, this, that, he, she, it
μὴ particle of negation. μή not, no, lest, neither, none, nothing, nor, never, without
Κυρίῳ n. dat. masc. sg. κύριος Lord, lord, master, sir, LORD, God, Master, owner
οὐκ particle of negation. οὐ οὐκ οὐχ not, no, neither, none, nay, nor, never, nothing
καὶ conj. καί and, even, also, but
τῷ art. dat. masc. sg. ὁ ἡ τό the, this, that, he, she, it
Θεῷ n. dat. masc. sg. θεός God, god
7 οὐδεὶς num. nom. masc. sg. οὐδείς no man, nothing, no, none, neither, not, nought
γὰρ conj. γάρ for, and, because, but, indeed
ἡμῶν pron. gen. 1p. pl. ἐγώ I

ἑαυτῷ reflexive pron. dat. masc. 3p. sg. ἑαυτοῦ himself, herself, itself, yourself, ourselves
καὶ conj. καί and, even, also, but
οὐδεὶς num. nom. masc. sg. οὐδείς no man, nothing, no, none, neither, not, nought
ἑαυτῷ reflexive pron. dat. masc. 3p. sg. ἑαυτοῦ himself, herself, itself, yourself, ourselves
8 ἐάν conj. ἐάν if, soever, except, though, and if, but, whether, if so, so
τε conj. τέ and, both, also
γὰρ conj. γάρ for, and, because, but, indeed
τῷ art. dat. masc. sg. ὁ ἡ τό the, this, that, he, she, it
Κυρίῳ n. dat. masc. sg. κύριος Lord, lord, master, sir, LORD, God, Master, owner
ἐάν conj. ἐάν if, soever, except, though, and if, but, whether, if so, so
τε conj. τέ and, both, also
τῷ art. dat. masc. sg. ὁ ἡ τό the, this, that, he, she, it
Κυρίῳ n. dat. masc. sg. κύριος Lord, lord, master, sir, LORD, God, Master, owner
ἐάν conj. ἐάν if, soever, except, though, and if, but, whether, if so, so
τε conj. τέ and, both, also
οὖν conj. οὖν therefore, then, so, and, now, wherefore
ἐάν conj. ἐάν if, soever, except, though, and if, but, whether, if so, so
τε conj. τέ and, both, also
τοῦ art. gen. masc. sg. ὁ ἡ τό the, this, that, he, she, it
Κυρίου n. gen. masc. sg. κύριος Lord, lord, master, sir, LORD, God, Master, owner
9 εἰς prep. εἰς (+acc) into, to, unto, for, in, on, toward, against, upon, at, among
τοῦτο demo. pron. acc. neut. sg. οὗτος αὕτη τοῦτο this, the same, this same, he, she, it
γὰρ conj. γάρ for, and, because, but, indeed
Χριστὸς n. nom. masc. sg. Χριστός Christ
καὶ conj. καί and, even, also, but
καὶ conj. καί and, even, also, but
καὶ conj. καί and, even, also, but
ἵνα conj. ἵνα that, to, lest, for to, so that, albeit, because, for, so as
καὶ conj. καί and, even, also, but
νεκρῶν adj. gen. masc. pl. νεκρός dead
καὶ conj. καί and, even, also, but
10 σὺ pron. nom. 2p. sg. σύ thou, you
δὲ conj. δέ but, and, now, also, to the contrary, rather, then
τί interrog. pron. acc. neut. sg. τίς what, who, why, where, which, how
τὸν art. acc. masc. sg. ὁ ἡ τό the, this, that, he, she, it
ἀδελφόν n. acc. masc. sg. ἀδελφός brother
σου pron. gen. 2p. sg. σύ thou, you
ἢ particle. ἤ or, than, either, nor, or else, and, rather than
καὶ conj. καί and, even, also, but
σὺ pron. nom. 2p. sg. σύ thou, you
τί interrog. pron. acc. neut. sg. τίς what, who, why, where, which, how
τὸν art. acc. masc. sg. ὁ ἡ τό the, this, that, he, she, it
ἀδελφόν n. acc. masc. sg. ἀδελφός brother
σου pron. gen. 2p. sg. σύ thou, you
πάντες adj. nom. masc. pl. πᾶς πᾶσα πᾶν all, every, whosoever, every one, no, whole, any
γὰρ conj. γάρ for, and, because, but, indeed
τῷ art. dat. neut. sg. ὁ ἡ τό the, this, that, he, she, it
βήματι n. dat. neut. sg. βῆμα judgment seat, throne
τοῦ art. gen. masc. sg. ὁ ἡ τό the, this, that, he, she, it
Χριστοῦ n. gen. masc. sg. Χριστός Christ
11 γάρ conj. γάρ for, and, because, but, indeed
ἐγώ pron. nom. 1p. sg. ἐγώ I
Κύριος n. nom. masc. sg. κύριος Lord, lord, master, sir, LORD, God, Master, owner
ὅτι conj. ὅτι that, for, because, how that, how, because that, for that, though
ἐμοὶ pron. dat. 1p. sg. ἐγώ I

πᾶν adj. nom. neut. sg. πᾶς πᾶσα πᾶν all, every, whosoever, every one, no, whole, any
γόνυ n. nom. neut. sg. γόνυ knee, kneel
καὶ conj. καί and, even, also, but
πᾶσα adj. nom. fem. sg. πᾶς πᾶσα πᾶν all, every, whosoever, every one, no, whole, any
γλῶσσα n. nom. fem. sg. γλῶσσα tongue
τῷ art. dat. masc. sg. ὁ ἡ τό the, this, that, he, she, it
Θεῷ n. dat. masc. sg. θεός God, god
12 ἄρα conj. ἄρα then, therefore, haply, wherefore, perhaps, manner, no doubt, truly
οὖν conj. οὖν therefore, then, so, and, now, wherefore
ἕκαστος adj. nom. masc. sg. ἕκαστος every man, every, every one, any man, each
ἡμῶν pron. gen. 1p. pl. ἐγώ I
περὶ prep. περί (+gen) of, for, concerning, (+acc) about, concerning, in
ἑαυτοῦ reflexive pron. gen. masc. 3p. sg. ἑαυτοῦ himself, herself, itself, yourself, ourselves
λόγον n. acc. masc. sg. λόγος word, saying, account, speech, thing, matter
τῷ art. dat. masc. sg. ὁ ἡ τό the, this, that, he, she, it
Θεῷ n. dat. masc. sg. θεός God, god
13 Μηκέτι adv. μηκέτι no more, no longer, not any more, not henceforth, not henceforward
οὖν conj. οὖν therefore, then, so, and, now, wherefore
ἀλλήλους pron. acc. masc. 1p. pl. ἀλλήλων one another, themselves, together, mutual
ἀλλὰ conj. ἀλλά but, yea, yet, nevertheless, howbeit, nay, therefore
τοῦτο demo. pron. acc. neut. sg. οὗτος αὕτη τοῦτο this, the same, this same, he, she, it
μᾶλλον adv. μᾶλλον rather, more, more and more, better, much, much the more
τὸ art. acc. neut. sg. ὁ ἡ τό the, this, that, he, she, it
μὴ particle of negation. μή not, no, lest, neither, none, nothing, nor, never, without
πρόσκομμα n. acc. neut. sg. πρόσκομμα stumbling, offence
τῷ art. dat. masc. sg. ὁ ἡ τό the, this, that, he, she, it
ἀδελφῷ n. dat. masc. sg. ἀδελφός brother
ἢ particle. ἤ or, than, either, nor, or else, and, rather than
σκάνδαλον n. acc. neut. sg. σκάνδαλον offence, stumblingblock, thing that offend
14 καὶ conj. καί and, even, also, but
ἐν prep. ἐν (+dat) in, by, with, among, at, on, through, to, within, into, of, for
Κυρίῳ n. dat. masc. sg. κύριος Lord, lord, master, sir, LORD, God, Master, owner
Ἰησοῦ n. dat. masc. sg. Ἰησοῦς Jesus
ὅτι conj. ὅτι that, for, because, how that, how, because that, for that, though
οὐδὲν num. nom. neut. sg. οὐδείς no man, nothing, no, none, neither, not, nought
κοινὸν adj. nom. neut. sg. κοινός common, unclean, defiled, unholy
δι' prep. διά (+gen) by, through, with, in, of, (+acc) for, because of, for a cause
ἑαυτοῦ reflexive pron. gen. neut. 3p. sg. ἑαυτοῦ himself, herself, itself, yourself, ourselves
εἰ conj. εἰ if, whether, that, though, forasmuch
μὴ particle of negation. μή not, no, lest, neither, none, nothing, nor, never, without
τῷ art. dat. masc. sg. ὁ ἡ τό the, this, that, he, she, it
τι indefinite pron. acc. neut. sg. τὶς certain, some, any man, one, any thing
κοινὸν adj. acc. neut. sg. κοινός common, unclean, defiled, unholy
ἐκείνῳ demo. pron. dat. masc. sg. ἐκεῖνος that, he, the same, that same
κοινὸν adj. nom. neut. sg. κοινός common, unclean, defiled, unholy
15 εἰ conj. εἰ if, whether, that, though, forasmuch
δὲ conj. δέ but, and, now, also, to the contrary, rather, then
διὰ prep. διά (+gen) by, through, with, in, of, (+acc) for, because of, for a cause
βρῶμα n. acc. neut. sg. βρῶμα victual, meat, food
ὁ art. nom. masc. sg. ὁ ἡ τό the, this, that, he, she, it
ἀδελφός n. nom. masc. sg. ἀδελφός brother
σου pron. gen. 2p. sg. σύ thou, you
οὐκέτι adv. οὐκέτι or οὐκ έτι no more, no longer, not any more
κατὰ prep. κατά (+gen) against, by, throughout, down, (+acc) according to, after, with
ἀγάπην n. acc. fem. sg. ἀγάπη love, charity, feast of charity

μὴ particle of negation. μή not, no, lest, neither, none, nothing, nor, never, without
τῷ art. dat. neut. sg. ὁ ἡ τό the, this, that, he, she, it
βρώματί n. dat. neut. sg. βρῶμα victual, meat, food
σου pron. gen. 2p. sg. σύ thou, you
ἐκεῖνον demo. pron. acc. masc. sg. ἐκεῖνος that, he, the same, that same
ὑπὲρ prep. ὑπέρ (+gen) for, of, for the sake of, (+acc) above, more than
οὗ relative pron. gen. masc. sg. ὅς ἥ ὅ who, which, what, that
Χριστὸς n. nom. masc. sg. Χριστός Christ
16 μὴ particle of negation. μή not, no, lest, neither, none, nothing, nor, never, without
οὖν conj. οὖν therefore, then, so, and, now, wherefore
ὑμῶν pron. gen. 2p. pl. σύ thou, you
τὸ art. nom. neut. sg. ὁ ἡ τό the, this, that, he, she, it
ἀγαθόν adj. nom. neut. sg. ἀγαθός good, good thing, that which is good, well
17 οὐ particle of negation. οὐ οὐκ οὐχ not, no, neither, none, nay, nor, never, nothing
γάρ conj. γάρ for, and, because, but, indeed
ἡ art. nom. fem. sg. ὁ ἡ τό the, this, that, he, she, it
βασιλεία n. nom. fem. sg. βασιλεία kingdom, reign
τοῦ art. gen. masc. sg. ὁ ἡ τό the, this, that, he, she, it
Θεοῦ n. gen. masc. sg. θεός God, god
βρῶσις n. nom. fem. sg. βρῶσις rust, meat, eating, food, morsel of meat
καὶ conj. καί and, even, also, but
πόσις n. nom. fem. sg. πόσις drink
ἀλλὰ conj. ἀλλά but, yea, yet, nevertheless, howbeit, nay, therefore
δικαιοσύνη n. nom. fem. sg. δικαιοσύνη righteousness
καὶ conj. καί and, even, also, but
εἰρήνη n. nom. fem. sg. εἰρήνη peace, quietness, rest
καὶ conj. καί and, even, also, but
χαρὰ n. nom. fem. sg. χαρά joy, gladness, joyfulness
ἐν prep. ἐν (+dat) in, by, with, among, at, on, through, to, within, into, of, for
Πνεύματι n. dat. neut. sg. πνεῦμα spirit, Spirit, Ghost, ghost, life. of the spirit, wind
Ἁγίῳ adj. dat. neut. sg. ἅγιος Holy, holy, saint, Holy One, holy thing, most holy
18 ὁ art. nom. masc. sg. ὁ ἡ τό the, this, that, he, she, it
γὰρ conj. γάρ for, and, because, but, indeed
ἐν prep. ἐν (+dat) in, by, with, among, at, on, through, to, within, into, of, for
τούτοις demo. pron. dat. neut. pl. οὗτος αὕτη τοῦτο this, the same, this same, he, she, it
τῷ art. dat. masc. sg. ὁ ἡ τό the, this, that, he, she, it
Χριστῷ n. dat. masc. sg. Χριστός Christ
εὐάρεστος adj. nom. masc. sg. εὐάρεστος acceptable, wellpleasing, accepted, please well
τῷ art. dat. masc. sg. ὁ ἡ τό the, this, that, he, she, it
Θεῷ n. dat. masc. sg. θεός God, god
καὶ conj. καί and, even, also, but
δόκιμος adj. nom. masc. sg. δόκιμος approved, tried
τοῖς art. dat. masc. pl. ὁ ἡ τό the, this, that, he, she, it
ἀνθρώποις n. dat. masc. pl. ἄνθρωπος man, human being, person, one, certain
19 ἄρα conj. ἄρα then, therefore, haply, wherefore, perhaps, manner, no doubt, truly
οὖν conj. οὖν therefore, then, so, and, now, wherefore
τὰ art. acc. neut. pl. ὁ ἡ τό the, this, that, he, she, it
τῆς art. gen. fem. sg. ὁ ἡ τό the, this, that, he, she, it
εἰρήνης n. gen. fem. sg. εἰρήνη peace, quietness, rest
καὶ conj. καί and, even, also, but
τὰ art. acc. neut. pl. ὁ ἡ τό the, this, that, he, she, it
τῆς art. gen. fem. sg. ὁ ἡ τό the, this, that, he, she, it
οἰκοδομῆς n. gen. fem. sg. οἰκοδομή building, edifying, edification
τῆς art. gen. fem. sg. ὁ ἡ τό the, this, that, he, she, it
εἰς prep. εἰς (+acc) into, to, unto, for, in, on, toward, against, upon, at, among

ἀλλήλους pron. acc. masc. 1p. pl. ἀλλήλων one another, themselves, together, mutual
20 μὴ particle of negation. μή not, no, lest, neither, none, nothing, nor, never, without
ἕνεκεν prep. ἕνεκα, ἕνεκεν or εἵνεκεν (+gen) for the sake, for a cause, for, by reason of
βρώματος n. gen. neut. sg. βρῶμα victual, meat, food
τὸ art. acc. neut. sg. ὁ ἡ τό the, this, that, he, she, it
ἔργον n. acc. neut. sg. ἔργον work, deed, doing labour
τοῦ art. gen. masc. sg. ὁ ἡ τό the, this, that, he, she, it
Θεοῦ n. gen. masc. sg. θεός God, god
πάντα adj. nom. neut. pl. πᾶς πᾶσα πᾶν all, every, whosoever, every one, no, whole, any
μὲν conj. μέν indeed, verily, truly, even, so, some
καθαρά adj. nom. neut. pl. καθαρός pure, clean, clear
ἀλλὰ conj. ἀλλά but, yea, yet, nevertheless, howbeit, nay, therefore
κακὸν adj. nom. neut. sg. κακός evil, evil thing, noisome, wicked
τῷ art. dat. masc. sg. ὁ ἡ τό the, this, that, he, she, it
ἀνθρώπῳ n. dat. masc. sg. ἄνθρωπος man, human being, person, one, certain
τῷ art. dat. masc. sg. ὁ ἡ τό the, this, that, he, she, it
διὰ prep. διά (+gen) by, through, with, in, of, (+acc) for, because of, for a cause
προσκόμματος n. gen. neut. sg. πρόσκομμα stumbling, offence
21 καλὸν adj. nom. neut. sg. καλός good, better, goodly, meet, honest, fair, well, worthy
τὸ art. nom. neut. sg. ὁ ἡ τό the, this, that, he, she, it
μὴ particle of negation. μή not, no, lest, neither, none, nothing, nor, never, without
κρέα n. acc. neut. pl. κρέας flesh
μηδὲ conj. μηδέ neither, nor, not, no not, nor yet, not once, not so much as
οἶνον n. acc. masc. sg. οἶνος wine
μηδὲ conj. μηδέ neither, nor, not, no not, nor yet, not once, not so much as
ἐν prep. ἐν (+dat) in, by, with, among, at, on, through, to, within, into, of, for
ᾧ relative pron. dat. neut. sg. ὅς ἥ ὅ who, which, what, that
ὁ art. nom. masc. sg. ὁ ἡ τό the, this, that, he, she, it
ἀδελφός n. nom. masc. sg. ἀδελφός brother
σου pron. gen. 2p. sg. σύ thou, you
ἢ particle. ἤ or, than, either, nor, or else, and, rather than
ἢ particle. ἤ or, than, either, nor, or else, and, rather than
22 σὺ pron. nom. 2p. sg. σύ thou, you
πίστιν n. acc. fem. sg. πίστις faith, assurance, belief, fidelity
κατὰ prep. κατά (+gen) against, by, throughout, down, (+acc) according to, after, with
σαυτὸν pron. acc. masc. 2p. sg. σεαυτοῦ σεαυτῷ σεαυτόν thyself, thine own self
ἐνώπιον prep. ἐνώπιον (+gen) before, in the sight of, in the presence of. (adv.) before
τοῦ art. gen. masc. sg. ὁ ἡ τό the, this, that, he, she, it
Θεοῦ n. gen. masc. sg. θεός God, god
μακάριος adj. nom. masc. sg. μακάριος blessed, happy
ὁ art. nom. masc. sg. ὁ ἡ τό the, this, that, he, she, it
μὴ particle of negation. μή not, no, lest, neither, none, nothing, nor, never, without
ἑαυτὸν reflexive pron. acc. masc. 3p. sg. ἑαυτοῦ himself, herself, itself, yourself, ourselves
ἐν prep. ἐν (+dat) in, by, with, among, at, on, through, to, within, into, of, for
ᾧ relative pron. dat. neut. sg. ὅς ἥ ὅ who, which, what, that
23 ὁ art. nom. masc. sg. ὁ ἡ τό the, this, that, he, she, it
δὲ conj. δέ but, and, now, also, to the contrary, rather, then
ἐὰν conj. ἐάν if, soever, except, though, and if, but, whether, if so, so
ὅτι conj. ὅτι that, for, because, how that, how, because that, for that, though
οὐκ particle of negation. οὐ οὐκ οὐχ not, no, neither, none, nay, nor, never, nothing
ἐκ prep. ἐκ ἐξ (+gen) of, from, out of, by, on, with, in, among, through
πίστεως n. gen. fem. sg. πίστις faith, assurance, belief, fidelity
πᾶν adj. nom. neut. sg. πᾶς πᾶσα πᾶν all, every, whosoever, every one, no, whole, any
δὲ conj. δέ but, and, now, also, to the contrary, rather, then
ὃ relative pron. nom. neut. sg. ὅς ἥ ὅ who, which, what, that

οὐκ particle of negation. οὐ οὐκ οὐχ not, no, neither, none, nay, nor, never, nothing
ἐκ prep. ἐκ ἐξ (+gen) of, from, out of, by, on, with, in, among, through
πίστεως n. gen. fem. sg. πίστις faith, assurance, belief, fidelity
ἁμαρτία n. nom. fem. sg. ἁμαρτία sin, offence, sinful

15

1 δὲ conj. δέ but, and, now, also, to the contrary, rather, then
ἡμεῖς pron. nom. 1p. pl. ἐγώ I
οἱ art. nom. masc. pl. ὁ ἡ τό the, this, that, he, she, it
δυνατοὶ adj. nom. masc. pl. δυνατός able, possible, mighty, strong
τὰ art. acc. neut. pl. ὁ ἡ τό the, this, that, he, she, it
ἀσθενήματα n. acc. neut. pl. ἀσθένημα infirmity
τῶν art. gen. masc. pl. ὁ ἡ τό the, this, that, he, she, it
ἀδυνάτων adj. gen. masc. pl. ἀδύνατος impossible, not possible, cannot do
καὶ conj. καί and, even, also, but
μὴ particle of negation. μή not, no, lest, neither, none, nothing, nor, never, without
ἑαυτοῖς reflexive pron. dat. masc. 3p. pl. ἑαυτοῦ himself, herself, itself, yourself, ourselves
2 ἕκαστος adj. nom. masc. sg. ἕκαστος every man, every, every one, any man, each
γὰρ conj. γάρ for, and, because, but, indeed
ἡμῶν pron. gen. 1p. pl. ἐγώ I
τῷ art. dat. masc. sg. ὁ ἡ τό the, this, that, he, she, it
πλησίον adv. πλησίον neighbour, near
εἰς prep. εἰς (+acc) into, to, unto, for, in, on, toward, against, upon, at, among
τὸ art. acc. neut. sg. ὁ ἡ τό the, this, that, he, she, it
ἀγαθὸν adj. acc. neut. sg. ἀγαθός good, good thing, that which is good, well
πρὸς prep. πρός (+gen) for, (+dat) at, (+acc) unto, to, with, for, against
οἰκοδομήν n. acc. fem. sg. οἰκοδομή building, edifying, edification
3 καὶ conj. καί and, even, also, but
γὰρ conj. γάρ for, and, because, but, indeed
ὁ art. nom. masc. sg. ὁ ἡ τό the, this, that, he, she, it
Χριστὸς n. nom. masc. sg. Χριστός Christ
οὐχ particle of negation. οὐ οὐκ οὐχ not, no, neither, none, nay, nor, never, nothing
ἑαυτῷ reflexive pron. dat. masc. 3p. sg. ἑαυτοῦ himself, herself, itself, yourself, ourselves
ἀλλὰ conj. ἀλλά but, yea, yet, nevertheless, howbeit, nay, therefore
καθὼς adv. καθώς as, even as, according as, according to
Οἱ art. nom. masc. pl. ὁ ἡ τό the, this, that, he, she, it
ὀνειδισμοὶ n. nom. masc. pl. ὀνειδισμός reproach
τῶν art. gen. masc. pl. ὁ ἡ τό the, this, that, he, she, it
σε pron. acc. 2p. sg. σύ thou, you
ἐπ' prep. ἐπί (+gen) on, in, upon, (+dat) in, at, for, upon, (+acc) on, upon, unto, to, against
ἐμέ pron. acc. 1p. sg. ἐγώ I
4 ὅσα relative pron. nom. neut. pl. ὅσος as many as, whatsoever, that, as long as, how much
γὰρ conj. γάρ for, and, because, but, indeed
εἰς prep. εἰς (+acc) into, to, unto, for, in, on, toward, against, upon, at, among
τὴν art. acc. fem. sg. ὁ ἡ τό the, this, that, he, she, it
ἡμετέραν poss. pron. acc. fem. 1p. sg. ἡμέτερος our
διδασκαλίαν n. acc. fem. sg. διδασκαλία doctrine, learning, teaching
ἵνα conj. ἵνα that, to, lest, for to, so that, albeit, because, for, so as
διὰ prep. διά (+gen) by, through, with, in, of, (+acc) for, because of, for a cause
τῆς art. gen. fem. sg. ὁ ἡ τό the, this, that, he, she, it
ὑπομονῆς n. gen. fem. sg. ὑπομονή patience, enduring
καὶ conj. καί and, even, also, but
τῆς art. gen. fem. sg. ὁ ἡ τό the, this, that, he, she, it
παρακλήσεως n. gen. fem. sg. παράκλησις consolation, exhortation, comfort

τῶν art. gen. fem. pl. ὁ ἡ τό the, this, that, he, she, it
γραφῶν n. gen. fem. pl. γραφή scripture
τὴν art. acc. fem. sg. ὁ ἡ τό the, this, that, he, she, it
ἐλπίδα n. acc. fem. sg. ἐλπίς hope, faith
5 ὁ art. nom. masc. sg. ὁ ἡ τό the, this, that, he, she, it
δὲ conj. δέ but, and, now, also, to the contrary, rather, then
Θεὸς n. nom. masc. sg. θεός God, god
τῆς art. gen. fem. sg. ὁ ἡ τό the, this, that, he, she, it
ὑπομονῆς n. gen. fem. sg. ὑπομονή patience, enduring
καὶ conj. καί and, even, also, but
τῆς art. gen. fem. sg. ὁ ἡ τό the, this, that, he, she, it
παρακλήσεως n. gen. fem. sg. παράκλησις consolation, exhortation, comfort
ὑμῖν pron. dat. 2p. pl. σύ thou, you
τὸ art. acc. neut. sg. ὁ ἡ τό the, this, that, he, she, it
αὐτὸ pron. acc. neut. 3p. sg. αὐτός ή ό self, of oneself, even, very, the same, he, she, it
ἐν prep. ἐν (+dat) in, by, with, among, at, on, through, to, within, into, of, for
ἀλλήλοις pron. dat. masc. 2p. pl. ἀλλήλων one another, themselves, together, mutual
κατὰ prep. κατά (+gen) against, by, throughout, down, (+acc) according to, after, with
Χριστὸν n. acc. masc. sg. Χριστός Christ
Ἰησοῦν n. acc. masc. sg. Ἰησοῦς Jesus
6 ἵνα conj. ἵνα that, to, lest, for to, so that, albeit, because, for, so as
ὁμοθυμαδὸν adv. ὁμοθυμαδόν with one accord, with one mind
ἐν prep. ἐν (+dat) in, by, with, among, at, on, through, to, within, into, of, for
ἑνὶ num. dat. neut. sg. εἷς or ἕν one, other, some, any, only, a certain
στόματι n. dat. neut. sg. στόμα mouth, face, edge
τὸν art. acc. masc. sg. ὁ ἡ τό the, this, that, he, she, it
Θεὸν n. acc. masc. sg. θεός God, god
καὶ conj. καί and, even, also, but
πατέρα n. acc. masc. sg. πατήρ Father, father, parent
τοῦ art. gen. masc. sg. ὁ ἡ τό the, this, that, he, she, it
Κυρίου n. gen. masc. sg. κύριος Lord, lord, master, sir, LORD, God, Master, owner
ἡμῶν pron. gen. 1p. pl. ἐγώ I
Ἰησοῦ n. gen. masc. sg. Ἰησοῦς Jesus
Χριστοῦ n. gen. masc. sg. Χριστός Christ
7 διὸ conj. διό wherefore, therefore, for which cause
ἀλλήλους pron. acc. masc. 2p. pl. ἀλλήλων one another, themselves, together, mutual
καθὼς adv. καθώς as, even as, according as, according to
καὶ conj. καί and, even, also, but
ὁ art. nom. masc. sg. ὁ ἡ τό the, this, that, he, she, it
Χριστὸς n. nom. masc. sg. Χριστός Christ
ἡμᾶς pron. acc. 1p. pl. ἐγώ I
εἰς prep. εἰς (+acc) into, to, unto, for, in, on, toward, against, upon, at, among
δόξαν n. acc. fem. sg. δόξα glory, honour, praise, dignity, worship
Θεοῦ n. gen. masc. sg. θεός God, god
8 δὲ conj. δέ but, and, now, also, to the contrary, rather, then
Ἰησοῦν n. acc. masc. sg. Ἰησοῦς Jesus
Χριστὸν n. acc. masc. sg. Χριστός Christ
διάκονον n. acc. masc. sg. διάκονος minister, servant, deacon
περιτομῆς n. gen. fem. sg. περιτομή circumcision
ὑπὲρ prep. ὑπέρ (+gen) for, of, for the sake of, (+acc) above, more than
ἀληθείας n. gen. fem. sg. ἀλήθεια truth, verity
Θεοῦ n. gen. masc. sg. θεός God, god
εἰς prep. εἰς (+acc) into, to, unto, for, in, on, toward, against, upon, at, among
τὸ art. acc. neut. sg. ὁ ἡ τό the, this, that, he, she, it
τὰς art. acc. fem. pl. ὁ ἡ τό the, this, that, he, she, it

ἐπαγγελίας n. acc. fem. pl. ἐπαγγελία promise, message
τῶν art. gen. masc. pl. ὁ ἡ τό the, this, that, he, she, it
πατέρων n. gen. masc. pl. πατήρ Father, father, parent
9 τὰ art. acc. neut. pl. ὁ ἡ τό the, this, that, he, she, it
δὲ conj. δέ but, and, now, also, to the contrary, rather, then
ἔθνη n. acc. neut. pl. ἔθνος Gentile, nation, heathen, people
ὑπὲρ prep. ὑπέρ (+gen) for, of, for the sake of, (+acc) above, more than
ἐλέους n. gen. neut. sg. ἔλεος mercy
τὸν art. acc. masc. sg. ὁ ἡ τό the, this, that, he, she, it
Θεόν n. acc. masc. sg. θεός God, god
καθὼς adv. καθώς as, even as, according as, according to
Διὰ prep. διά (+gen) by, through, with, in, of, (+acc) for, because of, for a cause
τοῦτο demo. pron. acc. neut. sg. οὗτος αὕτη τοῦτο this, the same, this same, he, she, it
σοι pron. dat. 2p. sg. σύ thou, you
ἐν prep. ἐν (+dat) in, by, with, among, at, on, through, to, within, into, of, for
ἔθνεσι n. dat. neut. pl. ἔθνος Gentile, nation, heathen, people
καὶ conj. καί and, even, also, but
τῷ art. dat. neut. sg. ὁ ἡ τό the, this, that, he, she, it
ὀνοματί n. dat. neut. sg. ὄνομα name, call, surname
σου pron. gen. 2p. sg. σύ thou, you
10 καὶ conj. καί and, even, also, but
πάλιν adv. πάλιν again
ἔθνη n. voc. neut. pl. ἔθνος Gentile, nation, heathen, people
μετὰ prep. μετά (+gen) with, among, against, (+acc) after
τοῦ art. gen. masc. sg. ὁ ἡ τό the, this, that, he, she, it
λαοῦ n. gen. masc. sg. λαός people
αὐτοῦ pron. gen. masc. 3p. sg. αὐτός ή ό self, of oneself, even, very, the same, he, she, it
11 καὶ conj. καί and, even, also, but
πάλιν adv. πάλιν again
τὸν art. acc. masc. sg. ὁ ἡ τό the, this, that, he, she, it
Κύριον n. acc. masc. sg. κύριος Lord, lord, master, sir, LORD, God, Master, owner
πάντα adj. nom. neut. pl. πᾶς πᾶσα πᾶν all, every, whosoever, every one, no, whole, any
τὰ art. nom. neut. pl. ὁ ἡ τό the, this, that, he, she, it
ἔθνη n. nom. neut. pl. ἔθνος Gentile, nation, heathen, people
καὶ conj. καί and, even, also, but
αὐτὸν pron. acc. masc. 3p. sg. αὐτός ή ό self, of oneself, even, very, the same, he, she, it
πάντες adj. nom. masc. pl. πᾶς πᾶσα πᾶν all, every, whosoever, every one, no, whole, any
οἱ art. nom. masc. pl. ὁ ἡ τό the, this, that, he, she, it
λαοί n. nom. masc. pl. λαός people
12 καὶ conj. καί and, even, also, but
πάλιν adv. πάλιν again
Ἠσαΐας n. nom. masc. sg. Ἠσαΐας Esaias, Isaiah
ἡ art. nom. fem. sg. ὁ ἡ τό the, this, that, he, she, it
ῥίζα n. nom. fem. sg. ῥίζα root
τοῦ art. gen. masc. sg. ὁ ἡ τό the, this, that, he, she, it
Ἰεσσαὶ n. gen. masc. sg. Ἰεσσαί Jesse
καὶ conj. καί and, even, also, but
ὁ art. nom. masc. sg. ὁ ἡ τό the, this, that, he, she, it
ἐθνῶν n. gen. neut. pl. ἔθνος Gentile, nation, heathen, people
ἐπ' prep. ἐπί (+gen) on, in, upon, (+dat) in, at, for, upon, (+acc) on, upon, unto, to, against
αὐτῷ pron. dat. masc. 3p. sg. αὐτός ή ό self, of oneself, even, very, the same, he, she, it
ἔθνη n. nom. neut. pl. ἔθνος Gentile, nation, heathen, people
13 ὁ art. nom. masc. sg. ὁ ἡ τό the, this, that, he, she, it
δὲ conj. δέ but, and, now, also, to the contrary, rather, then
Θεὸς n. nom. masc. sg. θεός God, god

τῆς art. gen. fem. sg. ὁ ἡ τό the, this, that, he, she, it
ἐλπίδος n. gen. fem. sg. ἐλπίς hope, faith
ὑμᾶς pron. acc. 2p. pl. σύ thou, you
πάσης adj. gen. fem. sg. πᾶς πᾶσα πᾶν all, every, whosoever, every one, no, whole, any
χαρᾶς n. gen. fem. sg. χαρά joy, gladness, joyfulness
καὶ conj. καί and, even, also, but
εἰρήνης n. gen. fem. sg. εἰρήνη peace, quietness, rest
ἐν prep. ἐν (+dat) in, by, with, among, at, on, through, to, within, into, of, for
τῷ art. dat. neut. sg. ὁ ἡ τό the, this, that, he, she, it
εἰς prep. εἰς (+acc) into, to, unto, for, in, on, toward, against, upon, at, among
τὸ art. acc. neut. sg. ὁ ἡ τό the, this, that, he, she, it
ὑμᾶς pron. acc. 2p. pl. σύ thou, you
ἐν prep. ἐν (+dat) in, by, with, among, at, on, through, to, within, into, of, for
τῇ art. dat. fem. sg. ὁ ἡ τό the, this, that, he, she, it
ἐλπίδι n. dat. fem. sg. ἐλπίς hope, faith
ἐν prep. ἐν (+dat) in, by, with, among, at, on, through, to, within, into, of, for
δυνάμει n. dat. fem. sg. δύναμις power, mighty work, miracle, strength, might
Πνεύματος n. gen. neut. sg. πνεῦμα spirit, Spirit, Ghost, ghost, life. of the spirit, wind
Ἁγίου adj. gen. neut. sg. ἅγιος Holy, holy, saint, Holy One, holy thing, most holy
14 δέ conj. δέ but, and, now, also, to the contrary, rather, then
ἀδελφοί n. voc. masc. pl. ἀδελφός brother
μου pron. gen. 1p. sg. ἐγώ I
καὶ conj. καί and, even, also, but
αὐτὸς pron. nom. masc. 3p. sg. αὐτός ή ό self, of oneself, even, very, the same, he, she, it
ἐγὼ pron. nom. 1p. sg. ἐγώ I
περὶ prep. περί (+gen) of, for, concerning, (+acc) about, concerning, in
ὑμῶν pron. gen. 2p. pl. σύ thou, you
ὅτι conj. ὅτι that, for, because, how that, how, because that, for that, though
καὶ conj. καί and, even, also, but
αὐτοὶ pron. nom. masc. 2p. pl. αὐτός ή ό self, of oneself, even, very, the same, he, she, it
μεστοί adj. nom. masc. pl. μεστός full
ἀγαθωσύνης n. gen. fem. sg. ἀγαθωσύνη goodness
πάσης adj. gen. fem. sg. πᾶς πᾶσα πᾶν all, every, whosoever, every one, no, whole, any
γνώσεως n. gen. fem. sg. γνῶσις knowledge, science
καὶ conj. καί and, even, also, but
ἀλλήλους pron. acc. masc. 2p. pl. ἀλλήλων one another, themselves, together, mutual
15 τολμηρότερον adv. τολμηρότερον more boldly
δὲ conj. δέ but, and, now, also, to the contrary, rather, then
ὑμῖν pron. dat. 2p. pl. σύ thou, you
ἀδελφοί n. voc. masc. pl. ἀδελφός brother
ἀπὸ prep. ἀπό (+gen) from, of, out of, since, for, off, at, by, in, on
μέρους n. gen. neut. sg. μέρος part, coast, portion, behalf, respect, piece, side
ὡς adv. ὡς as, when, as it were, how, about, like, as soon as, even as, while
ὑμᾶς pron. acc. 2p. pl. σύ thou, you
διὰ prep. διά (+gen) by, through, with, in, of, (+acc) for, because of, for a cause
τὴν art. acc. fem. sg. ὁ ἡ τό the, this, that, he, she, it
χάριν n. acc. fem. sg. χάρις grace, thank, favour, pleasure
τὴν art. acc. fem. sg. ὁ ἡ τό the, this, that, he, she, it
μοι pron. dat. 1p. sg. ἐγώ I
ὑπὸ prep. ὑπό (+gen) of, by, with, from, among, (+acc) under
τοῦ art. gen. masc. sg. ὁ ἡ τό the, this, that, he, she, it
Θεοῦ n. gen. masc. sg. θεός God, god
16 εἰς prep. εἰς (+acc) into, to, unto, for, in, on, toward, against, upon, at, among
τὸ art. acc. neut. sg. ὁ ἡ τό the, this, that, he, she, it
με pron. acc. 1p. sg. ἐγώ I

λειτουργὸν n. acc. masc. sg. λειτουργός minister, he that minister
Ἰησοῦ n. gen. masc. sg. Ἰησοῦς Jesus
Χριστοῦ n. gen. masc. sg. Χριστός Christ
εἰς prep. εἰς (+acc) into, to, unto, for, in, on, toward, against, upon, at, among
τὰ art. acc. neut. pl. ὁ ἡ τό the, this, that, he, she, it
ἔθνη n. acc. neut. pl. ἔθνος Gentile, nation, heathen, people
τὸ art. acc. neut. sg. ὁ ἡ τό the, this, that, he, she, it
εὐαγγέλιον n. acc. neut. sg. εὐαγγέλιον gospel
τοῦ art. gen. masc. sg. ὁ ἡ τό the, this, that, he, she, it
Θεοῦ n. gen. masc. sg. θεός God, god
ἵνα conj. ἵνα that, to, lest, for to, so that, albeit, because, for, so as
ἡ art. nom. fem. sg. ὁ ἡ τό the, this, that, he, she, it
προσφορὰ n. nom. fem. sg. προσφορά offering, offering up
τῶν art. gen. neut. pl. ὁ ἡ τό the, this, that, he, she, it
ἐθνῶν n. gen. neut. pl. ἔθνος Gentile, nation, heathen, people
εὐπρόσδεκτος adj. nom. fem. sg. εὐπρόσδεκτος acceptable, accepted
ἐν prep. ἐν (+dat) in, by, with, among, at, on, through, to, within, into, of, for
Πνεύματι n. dat. neut. sg. πνεῦμα spirit, Spirit, Ghost, ghost, life. of the spirit, wind
Ἁγίῳ adj. dat. neut. sg. ἅγιος Holy, holy, saint, Holy One, holy thing, most holy
17 οὖν conj. οὖν therefore, then, so, and, now, wherefore
καύχησιν n. acc. fem. sg. καύχησις boasting, rejoicing, glorying
ἐν prep. ἐν (+dat) in, by, with, among, at, on, through, to, within, into, of, for
Χριστῷ n. dat. masc. sg. Χριστός Christ
Ἰησοῦ n. dat. masc. sg. Ἰησοῦς Jesus
τὰ art. acc. neut. pl. ὁ ἡ τό the, this, that, he, she, it
πρὸς prep. πρός (+gen) for, (+dat) at, (+acc) unto, to, with, for, against
Θεόν n. acc. masc. sg. θεός God, god
18 οὐ particle of negation. οὐ οὐκ οὐχ not, no, neither, none, nay, nor, never, nothing
γὰρ conj. γάρ for, and, because, but, indeed
τι indefinite pron. acc. neut. sg. τὶς certain, some, any man, one, any thing
ὧν relative pron. gen. neut. pl. ὅς ἥ ὅ who, which, what, that
οὐ particle of negation. οὐ οὐκ οὐχ not, no, neither, none, nay, nor, never, nothing
Χριστὸς n. nom. masc. sg. Χριστός Christ
δι' prep. διά (+gen) by, through, with, in, of, (+acc) for, because of, for a cause
ἐμοῦ pron. gen. 1p. sg. ἐγώ I
εἰς prep. εἰς (+acc) into, to, unto, for, in, on, toward, against, upon, at, among
ὑπακοὴν n. acc. fem. sg. ὑπακοή obedience, obey, make obedient, obedient
ἐθνῶν n. gen. neut. pl. ἔθνος Gentile, nation, heathen, people
λόγῳ n. dat. masc. sg. λόγος word, saying, account, speech, thing, matter
καὶ conj. καί and, even, also, but
ἔργῳ n. dat. neut. sg. ἔργον work, deed, doing labour
19 ἐν prep. ἐν (+dat) in, by, with, among, at, on, through, to, within, into, of, for
δυνάμει n. dat. fem. sg. δύναμις power, mighty work, miracle, strength, might
σημείων n. gen. neut. pl. σημεῖον sign, miracle, wonder, token
καὶ conj. καί and, even, also, but
τεράτων n. gen. neut. pl. τέρας wonder
ἐν prep. ἐν (+dat) in, by, with, among, at, on, through, to, within, into, of, for
δυνάμει n. dat. fem. sg. δύναμις power, mighty work, miracle, strength, might
Πνεύματος n. gen. neut. sg. πνεῦμα spirit, Spirit, Ghost, ghost, life. of the spirit, wind
Θεοῦ n. gen. masc. sg. θεός God, god
ὥστε conj. ὥστε so that, wherefore, insomuch that, therefore, that, so then
με pron. acc. 1p. sg. ἐγώ I
ἀπὸ prep. ἀπό (+gen) from, of, out of, since, for, off, at, by, in, on
Ἱερουσαλὴμ pron. name. fem. inde. Ἱερουσαλήμ Jerusalem
καὶ conj. καί and, even, also, but

κύκλῳ adv. κύκλῳ round about, round
μέχρι prep. μέχρι until, unto, till, to
τοῦ art. gen. neut. sg. ὁ ἡ τό the, this, that, he, she, it
Ἰλλυρικοῦ n. gen. neut. sg. Ἰλλυρικόν Illyricum
τὸ art. acc. neut. sg. ὁ ἡ τό the, this, that, he, she, it
εὐαγγέλιον n. acc. neut. sg. εὐαγγέλιον gospel
τοῦ art. gen. masc. sg. ὁ ἡ τό the, this, that, he, she, it
Χριστοῦ n. gen. masc. sg. Χριστός Christ
20 οὕτω adv. οὕτω οὕτως so, even so, thus, on this wise, likewise, after this manner
δὲ conj. δέ but, and, now, also, to the contrary, rather, then
οὐχ particle of negation. οὐ οὐκ οὐχ not, no, neither, none, nay, nor, never, nothing
ὅπου adv. ὅπου where, whither, whereas, in what place, wheresoever
Χριστός n. nom. masc. sg. Χριστός Christ
ἵνα conj. ἵνα that, to, lest, for to, so that, albeit, because, for, so as
μὴ particle of negation. μή not, no, lest, neither, none, nothing, nor, never, without
ἐπ' prep. ἐπί (+gen) on, in, upon, (+dat) in, at, for, upon, (+acc) on, upon, unto, to, against
ἀλλότριον adj. acc. masc. sg. ἀλλότριος stranger, another man, alien, strange
θεμέλιον n. acc. masc. sg. θεμέλιος foundation
21 ἀλλὰ conj. ἀλλά but, yea, yet, nevertheless, howbeit, nay, therefore
καθὼς adv. καθώς as, even as, according as, according to
Οἷς relative pron. dat. masc. pl. ὅς ἥ ὅ who, which, what, that
οὐκ particle of negation. οὐ οὐκ οὐχ not, no, neither, none, nay, nor, never, nothing
περὶ prep. περί (+gen) of, for, concerning, (+acc) about, concerning, in
αὐτοῦ pron. gen. masc. 3p. sg. αὐτός ή ό self, of oneself, even, very, the same, he, she, it
καὶ conj. καί and, even, also, but
οἳ relative pron. nom. masc. pl. ὅς ἥ ὅ who, which, what, that
οὐκ particle of negation. οὐ οὐκ οὐχ not, no, neither, none, nay, nor, never, nothing
22 Διὸ conj. διό wherefore, therefore, for which cause
καὶ conj. καί and, even, also, but
τὰ art. acc. neut. pl. ὁ ἡ τό the, this, that, he, she, it
πολλὰ adj. acc. neut. pl. πολύς many, great, much, long, abundant
τοῦ art. gen. neut. sg. ὁ ἡ τό the, this, that, he, she, it
πρὸς prep. πρός (+gen) for, (+dat) at, (+acc) unto, to, with, for, against
ὑμᾶς pron. acc. 2p. pl. σύ thou, you
23 νυνὶ adv. νυνί now
δὲ conj. δέ but, and, now, also, to the contrary, rather, then
μηκέτι adv. μηκέτι no more, no longer, not any more, not henceforth, not henceforward
τόπον n. acc. masc. sg. τόπος place, room, quarter
ἐν prep. ἐν (+dat) in, by, with, among, at, on, through, to, within, into, of, for
τοῖς art. dat. neut. pl. ὁ ἡ τό the, this, that, he, she, it
κλίμασι n. dat. neut. pl. κλίμα region, part
τούτοις demo. pron. dat. neut. pl. οὗτος αὕτη τοῦτο this, the same, this same, he, she, it
ἐπιποθίαν n. acc. fem. sg. ἐπιποθία great desire
δὲ conj. δέ but, and, now, also, to the contrary, rather, then
τοῦ art. gen. neut. sg. ὁ ἡ τό the, this, that, he, she, it
πρὸς prep. πρός (+gen) for, (+dat) at, (+acc) unto, to, with, for, against
ὑμᾶς pron. acc. 2p. pl. σύ thou, you
ἀπὸ prep. ἀπό (+gen) from, of, out of, since, for, off, at, by, in, on
πολλῶν adj. gen. neut. pl. πολύς many, great, much, long, abundant
ἐτῶν n. gen. neut. pl. ἔτος year
24 ὡς adv. ὡς as, when, as it were, how, about, like, as soon as, even as, while
ἐὰν conj. ἐάν if, soever, except, though, and if, but, whether, if so, so
εἰς prep. εἰς (+acc) into, to, unto, for, in, on, toward, against, upon, at, among
τὴν art. acc. fem. sg. ὁ ἡ τό the, this, that, he, she, it
Σπανίαν n. acc. fem. sg. Σπανία Spain

πρὸς prep. πρός (+gen) for, (+dat) at, (+acc) unto, to, with, for, against
ὑμᾶς pron. acc. 2p. pl. σύ thou, you
γὰρ conj. γάρ for, and, because, but, indeed
ὑμᾶς pron. acc. 2p. pl. σύ thou, you
καὶ conj. καί and, even, also, but
ὑφ' prep. ὑπό (+gen) of, by, with, from, among, (+acc) under
ὑμῶν pron. gen. 2p. pl. σύ thou, you
ἐκεῖ adv. ἐκεῖ there, thither, thitherward, yonder, yonder place
ἐὰν conj. ἐάν if, soever, except, though, and if, but, whether, if so, so
ὑμῶν pron. gen. 2p. pl. σύ thou, you
πρῶτον adv. πρῶτον first, at the first, first of all, at first, at the beginning, before, chiefly
ἀπὸ prep. ἀπό (+gen) from, of, out of, since, for, off, at, by, in, on
μέρους n. gen. neut. sg. μέρος part, coast, portion, behalf, respect, piece, side
25 νυνὶ adv. νυνί now
δὲ conj. δέ but, and, now, also, to the contrary, rather, then
εἰς prep. εἰς (+acc) into, to, unto, for, in, on, toward, against, upon, at, among
Ἱερουσαλὴμ pron. name. fem. inde. Ἱερουσαλήμ Jerusalem
τοῖς art. dat. masc. pl. ὁ ἡ τό the, this, that, he, she, it
ἁγίοις adj. dat. masc. pl. ἅγιος Holy, holy, saint, Holy One, holy thing, most holy
26 γὰρ conj. γάρ for, and, because, but, indeed
Μακεδονία n. nom. fem. sg. Μακεδονία Macedonia
καὶ conj. καί and, even, also, but
Ἀχαΐα n. nom. fem. sg. Ἀχαΐα Achaia
κοινωνίαν n. acc. fem. sg. κοινωνία fellowship, communion, contribution, distribution
τινὰ indefinite pron. acc. fem. sg. τὶς certain, some, any man, one, any thing
εἰς prep. εἰς (+acc) into, to, unto, for, in, on, toward, against, upon, at, among
τοὺς art. acc. masc. pl. ὁ ἡ τό the, this, that, he, she, it
πτωχοὺς adj. acc. masc. pl. πτωχός poor, beggar, beggarly
τῶν art. gen. masc. pl. ὁ ἡ τό the, this, that, he, she, it
ἁγίων adj. gen. masc. pl. ἅγιος Holy, holy, saint, Holy One, holy thing, most holy
τῶν art. gen. masc. pl. ὁ ἡ τό the, this, that, he, she, it
ἐν prep. ἐν (+dat) in, by, with, among, at, on, through, to, within, into, of, for
Ἱερουσαλὴμ pron. name. fem. inde. Ἱερουσαλήμ Jerusalem
27 γὰρ conj. γάρ for, and, because, but, indeed
καὶ conj. καί and, even, also, but
ὀφειλέται n. nom. masc. pl. ὀφειλέτης debtor, sinner, owe
αὐτῶν pron. gen. masc. 3p. pl. αὐτός ἡ ὁ self, of oneself, even, very, the same, he, she, it
εἰ conj. εἰ if, whether, that, though, forasmuch
γὰρ conj. γάρ for, and, because, but, indeed
τοῖς art. dat. neut. pl. ὁ ἡ τό the, this, that, he, she, it
πνευματικοῖς adj. dat. neut. pl. πνευματικός spiritual
αὐτῶν pron. gen. masc. 3p. pl. αὐτός ἡ ὁ self, of oneself, even, very, the same, he, she, it
τὰ art. nom. neut. pl. ὁ ἡ τό the, this, that, he, she, it
ἔθνη n. nom. neut. pl. ἔθνος Gentile, nation, heathen, people
καὶ conj. καί and, even, also, but
ἐν prep. ἐν (+dat) in, by, with, among, at, on, through, to, within, into, of, for
τοῖς art. dat. neut. pl. ὁ ἡ τό the, this, that, he, she, it
σαρκικοῖς adj. dat. neut. pl. σαρκικός carnal, fleshly
αὐτοῖς pron. dat. masc. 3p. pl. αὐτός ἡ ὁ self, of oneself, even, very, the same, he, she, it
28 τοῦτο demo. pron. acc. neut. sg. οὗτος αὕτη τοῦτο this, the same, this same, he, she, it
οὖν conj. οὖν therefore, then, so, and, now, wherefore
καὶ conj. καί and, even, also, but
αὐτοῖς pron. dat. masc. 3p. pl. αὐτός ἡ ὁ self, of oneself, even, very, the same, he, she, it
τὸν art. acc. masc. sg. ὁ ἡ τό the, this, that, he, she, it
καρπὸν n. acc. masc. sg. καρπός fruit

τοῦτον demo. pron. acc. masc. sg. οὗτος αὕτη τοῦτο this, the same, this same, he, she, it
δι' prep. διά (+gen) by, through, with, in, of, (+acc) for, because of, for a cause
ὑμῶν pron. gen. 2p. pl. σύ thou, you
εἰς prep. εἰς (+acc) into, to, unto, for, in, on, toward, against, upon, at, among
τὴν art. acc. fem. sg. ὁ ἡ τό the, this, that, he, she, it
Σπανίαν n. acc. fem. sg. Σπανία Spain
29 δὲ conj. δέ but, and, now, also, to the contrary, rather, then
ὅτι conj. ὅτι that, for, because, how that, how, because that, for that, though
πρὸς prep. πρός (+gen) for, (+dat) at, (+acc) unto, to, with, for, against
ὑμᾶς pron. acc. 2p. pl. σύ thou, you
ἐν prep. ἐν (+dat) in, by, with, among, at, on, through, to, within, into, of, for
πληρώματι n. dat. neut. sg. πλήρωμα fullness, fulfilling, full
εὐλογίας n. gen. fem. sg. εὐλογία blessing, bounty, matter of bounty, fair speech
τοῦ art. gen. neut. sg. ὁ ἡ τό the, this, that, he, she, it
εὐαγγελίου n. gen. neut. sg. εὐαγγέλιον gospel
τοῦ art. gen. masc. sg. ὁ ἡ τό the, this, that, he, she, it
Χριστοῦ n. gen. masc. sg. Χριστός Christ
30 δὲ conj. δέ but, and, now, also, to the contrary, rather, then
ὑμᾶς pron. acc. 2p. pl. σύ thou, you
ἀδελφοί n. voc. masc. pl. ἀδελφός brother
διὰ prep. διά (+gen) by, through, with, in, of, (+acc) for, because of, for a cause
τοῦ art. gen. masc. sg. ὁ ἡ τό the, this, that, he, she, it
Κυρίου n. gen. masc. sg. κύριος Lord, lord, master, sir, LORD, God, Master, owner
ἡμῶν pron. gen. 1p. pl. ἐγώ I
Ἰησοῦ n. gen. masc. sg. Ἰησοῦς Jesus
Χριστοῦ n. gen. masc. sg. Χριστός Christ
καὶ conj. καί and, even, also, but
διὰ prep. διά (+gen) by, through, with, in, of, (+acc) for, because of, for a cause
τῆς art. gen. fem. sg. ὁ ἡ τό the, this, that, he, she, it
ἀγάπης n. gen. fem. sg. ἀγάπη love, charity, feast of charity
τοῦ art. gen. neut. sg. ὁ ἡ τό the, this, that, he, she, it
Πνεύματος n. gen. neut. sg. πνεῦμα spirit, Spirit, Ghost, ghost, life. of the spirit, wind
μοι pron. dat. 1p. sg. ἐγώ I
ἐν prep. ἐν (+dat) in, by, with, among, at, on, through, to, within, into, of, for
ταῖς art. dat. fem. pl. ὁ ἡ τό the, this, that, he, she, it
προσευχαῖς n. dat. fem. pl. προσευχή prayer
ὑπὲρ prep. ὑπέρ (+gen) for, of, for the sake of, (+acc) above, more than
ἐμοῦ pron. gen. 1p. sg. ἐγώ I
πρὸς prep. πρός (+gen) for, (+dat) at, (+acc) unto, to, with, for, against
τὸν art. acc. masc. sg. ὁ ἡ τό the, this, that, he, she, it
Θεόν n. acc. masc. sg. θεός God, god
31 ἵνα conj. ἵνα that, to, lest, for to, so that, albeit, because, for, so as
ἀπὸ prep. ἀπό (+gen) from, of, out of, since, for, off, at, by, in, on
τῶν art. gen. masc. pl. ὁ ἡ τό the, this, that, he, she, it
ἐν prep. ἐν (+dat) in, by, with, among, at, on, through, to, within, into, of, for
τῇ art. dat. fem. sg. ὁ ἡ τό the, this, that, he, she, it
Ἰουδαίᾳ n. dat. fem. sg. Ἰουδαία Judaea, Jewry
καὶ conj. καί and, even, also, but
ἵνα conj. ἵνα that, to, lest, for to, so that, albeit, because, for, so as
ἡ art. nom. fem. sg. ὁ ἡ τό the, this, that, he, she, it
διακονία n. nom. fem. sg. διακονία ministry, administration, service, office, relief
μου pron. gen. 1p. sg. ἐγώ I
ἡ art. nom. fem. sg. ὁ ἡ τό the, this, that, he, she, it
εἰς prep. εἰς (+acc) into, to, unto, for, in, on, toward, against, upon, at, among
Ἱερουσαλήμ pron. name. fem. inde. Ἱερουσαλήμ Jerusalem

εὐπρόσδεκτος adj. nom. fem. sg. εὐπρόσδεκτος acceptable, accepted
τοῖς art. dat. masc. pl. ὁ ἡ τό the, this, that, he, she, it
ἁγίοις adj. dat. masc. pl. ἅγιος Holy, holy, saint, Holy One, holy thing, most holy
32 ἵνα conj. ἵνα that, to, lest, for to, so that, albeit, because, for, so as
ἐν prep. ἐν (+dat) in, by, with, among, at, on, through, to, within, into, of, for
χαρᾷ n. dat. fem. sg. χαρά joy, gladness, joyfulness
πρὸς prep. πρός (+gen) for, (+dat) at, (+acc) unto, to, with, for, against
ὑμᾶς pron. acc. 2p. pl. σύ thou, you
διὰ prep. διά (+gen) by, through, with, in, of, (+acc) for, because of, for a cause
θελήματος n. gen. neut. sg. θέλημα will, desire, pleasure
Θεοῦ n. gen. masc. sg. θεός God, god
καὶ conj. καί and, even, also, but
ὑμῖν pron. dat. 2p. pl. σύ thou, you
33 ὁ art. nom. masc. sg. ὁ ἡ τό the, this, that, he, she, it
δὲ conj. δέ but, and, now, also, to the contrary, rather, then
Θεὸς n. nom. masc. sg. θεός God, god
τῆς art. gen. fem. sg. ὁ ἡ τό the, this, that, he, she, it
εἰρήνης n. gen. fem. sg. εἰρήνη peace, quietness, rest
μετὰ prep. μετά (+gen) with, among, against, (+acc) after
πάντων adj. gen. masc. pl. πᾶς πᾶσα πᾶν all, every, whosoever, every one, no, whole, any
ὑμῶν pron. gen. 2p. pl. σύ thou, you
ἀμήν particle. ἀμήν amen, verily

16

1 δὲ conj. δέ but, and, now, also, to the contrary, rather, then
ὑμῖν pron. dat. 2p. pl. σύ thou, you
Φοίβην n. acc. fem. sg. Φοίβη Phebe
τὴν art. acc. fem. sg. ὁ ἡ τό the, this, that, he, she, it
ἀδελφὴν n. acc. fem. sg. ἀδελφή sister
ἡμῶν pron. gen. 1p. pl. ἐγώ I
διάκονον n. acc. fem. sg. διάκονος minister, servant, deacon
τῆς art. gen. fem. sg. ὁ ἡ τό the, this, that, he, she, it
ἐκκλησίας n. gen. fem. sg. ἐκκλησία church, assembly
ἐν prep. ἐν (+dat) in, by, with, among, at, on, through, to, within, into, of, for
τῆς art. gen. fem. sg. ὁ ἡ τό the, this, that, he, she, it
Κεγχρεαῖς n. dat. fem. pl. Κεγχρεαί Cenchrea
2 ἵνα conj. ἵνα that, to, lest, for to, so that, albeit, because, for, so as
αὐτὴν pron. acc. fem. 3p. sg. αὐτός ἡ ὁ self, of oneself, even, very, the same, he, she, it
ἐν prep. ἐν (+dat) in, by, with, among, at, on, through, to, within, into, of, for
Κυρίῳ n. dat. masc. sg. κύριος Lord, lord, master, sir, LORD, God, Master, owner
ἀξίως adv. ἀξίως worthy, as become, after a godly sort
τῶν art. gen. masc. pl. ὁ ἡ τό the, this, that, he, she, it
ἁγίων adj. gen. masc. pl. ἅγιος Holy, holy, saint, Holy One, holy thing, most holy
καὶ conj. καί and, even, also, but
αὐτῇ pron. dat. fem. 3p. sg. αὐτός ἡ ὁ self, of oneself, even, very, the same, he, she, it
ἐν prep. ἐν (+dat) in, by, with, among, at, on, through, to, within, into, of, for
ᾧ relative pron. dat. neut. sg. ὅς ἥ ὅ who, which, what, that
ἂν particle. ἄν Indicating contingency. No English translation.
ὑμῶν pron. gen. 2p. pl. σύ thou, you
πράγματι n. dat. neut. sg. πρᾶγμα thing, matter, business, work
καὶ conj. καί and, even, also, but
γὰρ conj. γάρ for, and, because, but, indeed
αὕτη demo. pron. nom. fem. sg. οὗτος αὕτη τοῦτο this, the same, this same, he, she, it
προστάτις n. nom. fem. sg. προστάτις succourer, helper

πολλῶν adj. gen. masc. pl. πολύς many, great, much, long, abundant
καὶ conj. καί and, even, also, but
αὐτοῦ pron. gen. masc. 3p. sg. αὐτός ή ό self, of oneself, even, very, the same, he, she, it
ἐμοῦ pron. gen. 1p. sg. ἐγώ I
3 Πρίσκιλλαν n. acc. fem. sg. Πρίσκιλλα Priscilla
καὶ conj. καί and, even, also, but
'Ακύλαν n. acc. masc. sg. 'Ακύλας Aquila
τοὺς art. acc. masc. pl. ὁ ἡ τό the, this, that, he, she, it
συνεργούς adj. acc. masc. pl. συνεργός fellowlabourer, fellowhelper, fellowworker
μου pron. gen. 1p. sg. ἐγώ I
ἐν prep. ἐν (+dat) in, by, with, among, at, on, through, to, within, into, of, for
Χριστῷ n. dat. masc. sg. Χριστός Christ
'Ιησοῦ n. dat. masc. sg. 'Ιησοῦς Jesus
4 οἵτινες relative pron. nom. masc. pl. ὅστις which, who, whosoever, that, whatsoever
ὑπὲρ prep. ὑπέρ (+gen) for, of, for the sake of, (+acc) above, more than
τῆς art. gen. fem. sg. ὁ ἡ τό the, this, that, he, she, it
ψυχῆς n. gen. fem. sg. ψυχή life, soul, mind, heart
μου pron. gen. 1p. sg. ἐγώ I
τὸν art. acc. masc. sg. ὁ ἡ τό the, this, that, he, she, it
ἑαυτῶν reflexive pron. gen. masc. 3p. pl. ἑαυτοῦ himself, herself, itself, yourself, ourselves
τράχηλον n. acc. masc. sg. τράχηλος neck
οἷς relative pron. dat. masc. pl. ὅς ἥ ὅ who, which, what, that
οὐκ particle of negation. οὐ οὐκ οὐχ not, no, neither, none, nay, nor, never, nothing
ἐγὼ pron. nom. 1p. sg. ἐγώ I
μόνος adj. nom. masc. sg. μόνος only, alone, by oneself
ἀλλὰ conj. ἀλλά but, yea, yet, nevertheless, howbeit, nay, therefore
καὶ conj. καί and, even, also, but
πᾶσαι adj. nom. fem. pl. πᾶς πᾶσα πᾶν all, every, whosoever, every one, no, whole, any
αἱ art. nom. fem. pl. ὁ ἡ τό the, this, that, he, she, it
ἐκκλησίαι n. nom. fem. pl. ἐκκλησία church, assembly
τῶν art. gen. neut. pl. ὁ ἡ τό the, this, that, he, she, it
ἐθνῶν n. gen. neut. pl. ἔθνος Gentile, nation, heathen, people
5 καὶ conj. καί and, even, also, but
τὴν art. acc. fem. sg. ὁ ἡ τό the, this, that, he, she, it
κατ' prep. κατά (+gen) against, by, throughout, down, (+acc) according to, after, with
οἶκον n. acc. masc. sg. οἶκος house, home, household
αὐτῶν pron. gen. masc. 3p. pl. αὐτός ή ό self, of oneself, even, very, the same, he, she, it
ἐκκλησίαν n. acc. fem. sg. ἐκκλησία church, assembly
'Επαίνετον n. acc. masc. sg. 'Επαίνετος Epaenetus
τὸν art. acc. masc. sg. ὁ ἡ τό the, this, that, he, she, it
ἀγαπητόν adj. acc. masc. sg. ἀγαπητός beloved, dearly beloved, dear, wellbeloved
μου pron. gen. 1p. sg. ἐγώ I
ὅς relative pron. nom. masc. sg. ὅς ἥ ὅ who, which, what, that
ἀπαρχὴ n. nom. fem. sg. ἀπαρχή firstfruit
τῆς art. gen. fem. sg. ὁ ἡ τό the, this, that, he, she, it
'Αχαΐας n. gen. fem. sg. 'Αχαΐα Achaia
εἰς prep. εἰς (+acc) into, to, unto, for, in, on, toward, against, upon, at, among
Χριστόν n. acc. masc. sg. Χριστός Christ
6 Μαρίαμ n. acc. fem. sg. Μαρίαμ Mary
ἥτις relative pron. nom. fem. sg. ὅστις which, who, whosoever, that, whatsoever
πολλὰ adj. acc. neut. pl. πολύς many, great, much, long, abundant
εἰς prep. εἰς (+acc) into, to, unto, for, in, on, toward, against, upon, at, among
ἡμᾶς pron. acc. 1p. pl. ἐγώ I
7 'Ανδρόνικον n. acc. masc. sg. 'Ανδρόνικος Andronicus
καὶ conj. καί and, even, also, but

Ἰουνιᾶν n. acc. masc. sg. Ἰουνιᾶς Junia
τοὺς art. acc. masc. pl. ὁ ἡ τό the, this, that, he, she, it
συγγενεῖς adj. acc. masc. pl. συγγενής kinsman, cousin, kinsfolk, kin
μου pron. gen. 1p. sg. ἐγώ I
καὶ conj. καί and, even, also, but
συναιχμαλώτους n. acc. masc. pl. συναιχμάλωτος fellowprisoner
μου pron. gen. 1p. sg. ἐγώ I
οἵτινες relative pron. nom. masc. pl. ὅστις which, who, whosoever, that, whatsoever
ἐπίσημοι adj. nom. masc. pl. ἐπίσημος notable, of note
ἐν prep. ἐν (+dat) in, by, with, among, at, on, through, to, within, into, of, for
τοῖς art. dat. masc. pl. ὁ ἡ τό the, this, that, he, she, it
ἀποστόλοις n. dat. masc. pl. ἀπόστολος apostle, messenger, he that is sent
οἳ relative pron. nom. masc. pl. ὅς ἥ ὅ who, which, what, that
καὶ conj. καί and, even, also, but
πρὸ prep. πρό (+gen) before, above
ἐμοῦ pron. gen. 1p. sg. ἐγώ I
ἐν prep. ἐν (+dat) in, by, with, among, at, on, through, to, within, into, of, for
Χριστῷ n. dat. masc. sg. Χριστός Christ
8 Ἀμπλίαν n. acc. masc. sg. Ἀμπλίας Amplias
τὸν art. acc. masc. sg. ὁ ἡ τό the, this, that, he, she, it
ἀγαπητόν adj. acc. masc. sg. ἀγαπητός beloved, dearly beloved, dear, wellbeloved
μου pron. gen. 1p. sg. ἐγώ I
ἐν prep. ἐν (+dat) in, by, with, among, at, on, through, to, within, into, of, for
Κυρίῳ n. dat. masc. sg. κύριος Lord, lord, master, sir, LORD, God, Master, owner
9 Οὐρβανὸν n. acc. masc. sg. Οὐρβανός Urbane
τὸν art. acc. masc. sg. ὁ ἡ τό the, this, that, he, she, it
συνεργὸν adj. acc. masc. sg. συνεργός fellowlabourer, fellowhelper, fellowworker
ἡμῶν pron. gen. 1p. pl. ἐγώ I
ἐν prep. ἐν (+dat) in, by, with, among, at, on, through, to, within, into, of, for
Χριστῷ n. dat. masc. sg. Χριστός Christ
καὶ conj. καί and, even, also, but
Στάχυν n. acc. masc. sg. Στάχυς Stachys
τὸν art. acc. masc. sg. ὁ ἡ τό the, this, that, he, she, it
ἀγαπητόν adj. acc. masc. sg. ἀγαπητός beloved, dearly beloved, dear, wellbeloved
μου pron. gen. 1p. sg. ἐγώ I
10 Ἀπελλῆν n. acc. masc. sg. Ἀπελλῆς Apelles
τὸν art. acc. masc. sg. ὁ ἡ τό the, this, that, he, she, it
δόκιμον adj. acc. masc. sg. δόκιμος approved, tried
ἐν prep. ἐν (+dat) in, by, with, among, at, on, through, to, within, into, of, for
Χριστῷ n. dat. masc. sg. Χριστός Christ
τοὺς art. acc. masc. pl. ὁ ἡ τό the, this, that, he, she, it
ἐκ prep. ἐκ ἐξ (+gen) of, from, out of, by, on, with, in, among, through
τῶν art. gen. masc. pl. ὁ ἡ τό the, this, that, he, she, it
Ἀριστοβούλου n. gen. masc. sg. Ἀριστόβουλος Aristobulus
11 Ἡρωδίωνα n. acc. masc. sg. Ἡρῳδίων Herodion
τὸν art. acc. masc. sg. ὁ ἡ τό the, this, that, he, she, it
συγγενῆ adj. acc. masc. sg. συγγενής kinsman, cousin, kinsfolk, kin
μου pron. gen. 1p. sg. ἐγώ I
τοὺς art. acc. masc. pl. ὁ ἡ τό the, this, that, he, she, it
ἐκ prep. ἐκ ἐξ (+gen) of, from, out of, by, on, with, in, among, through
τῶν art. gen. masc. pl. ὁ ἡ τό the, this, that, he, she, it
Ναρκίσσου n. gen. masc. sg. Νάρκισσος Narcissus
τοὺς art. acc. masc. pl. ὁ ἡ τό the, this, that, he, she, it
ἐν prep. ἐν (+dat) in, by, with, among, at, on, through, to, within, into, of, for
Κυρίῳ n. dat. masc. sg. κύριος Lord, lord, master, sir, LORD, God, Master, owner

12 Τρύφαιναν n. acc. fem. sg. Τρύφαινα Tryphena
καὶ conj. καί and, even, also, but
Τρυφῶσαν n. acc. fem. sg. Τρυφῶσα Tryphosa
τὰς art. acc. fem. pl. ὁ ἡ τό the, this, that, he, she, it
ἐν prep. ἐν (+dat) in, by, with, among, at, on, through, to, within, into, of, for
Κυρίῳ n. dat. masc. sg. κύριος Lord, lord, master, sir, LORD, God, Master, owner
Περσίδα n. acc. fem. sg. Περσίς Persis
τὴν art. acc. fem. sg. ὁ ἡ τό the, this, that, he, she, it
ἀγαπητήν adj. acc. fem. sg. ἀγαπητός beloved, dearly beloved, dear, wellbeloved
ἥτις relative pron. nom. fem. sg. ὅστις which, who, whosoever, that, whatsoever
πολλὰ adj. acc. neut. pl. πολύς many, great, much, long, abundant
ἐν prep. ἐν (+dat) in, by, with, among, at, on, through, to, within, into, of, for
Κυρίῳ n. dat. masc. sg. κύριος Lord, lord, master, sir, LORD, God, Master, owner
13 Ῥοῦφον n. acc. masc. sg. Ῥοῦφος Rufus
τὸν art. acc. masc. sg. ὁ ἡ τό the, this, that, he, she, it
ἐκλεκτὸν adj. acc. masc. sg. ἐκλεκτός elect, chosen
ἐν prep. ἐν (+dat) in, by, with, among, at, on, through, to, within, into, of, for
Κυρίῳ n. dat. masc. sg. κύριος Lord, lord, master, sir, LORD, God, Master, owner
καὶ conj. καί and, even, also, but
τὴν art. acc. fem. sg. ὁ ἡ τό the, this, that, he, she, it
μητέρα n. acc. fem. sg. μήτηρ mother
αὐτοῦ pron. gen. masc. 3p. sg. αὐτός ή ό self, of oneself, even, very, the same, he, she, it
καὶ conj. καί and, even, also, but
ἐμοῦ pron. gen. 1p. sg. ἐγώ I
14 Ἀσύγκριτον n. acc. masc. sg. Ἀσύγκριτος Asyncritus
Φλέγοντα n. acc. masc. sg. Φλέγων Phlegon
Ἑρμᾶν n. acc. masc. sg. Ἑρμᾶς Hermas
Πατροβᾶν n. acc. masc. sg. Πατροβᾶς Patrobas
Ἑρμῆν n. acc. masc. sg. Ἑρμῆς Hermes
καὶ conj. καί and, even, also, but
τοὺς art. acc. masc. pl. ὁ ἡ τό the, this, that, he, she, it
σὺν prep. σύν (+dat) with, beside
αὐτοῖς pron. dat. masc. 3p. pl. αὐτός ή ό self, of oneself, even, very, the same, he, she, it
ἀδελφούς n. acc. masc. pl. ἀδελφός brother
15 Φιλόλογον n. acc. masc. sg. Φιλόλογος Philologus
καὶ conj. καί and, even, also, but
Ἰουλίαν n. acc. fem. sg. Ἰουλία Julia
Νηρέα n. acc. masc. sg. Νηρεύς Nereus
καὶ conj. καί and, even, also, but
τὴν art. acc. fem. sg. ὁ ἡ τό the, this, that, he, she, it
ἀδελφὴν n. acc. fem. sg. ἀδελφή sister
αὐτοῦ pron. gen. masc. 3p. sg. αὐτός ή ό self, of oneself, even, very, the same, he, she, it
καὶ conj. καί and, even, also, but
Ὀλυμπᾶν n. acc. masc. sg. Ὀλυμπᾶς Olympas
καὶ conj. καί and, even, also, but
τοὺς art. acc. masc. pl. ὁ ἡ τό the, this, that, he, she, it
σὺν prep. σύν (+dat) with, beside
αὐτοῖς pron. dat. masc. 3p. pl. αὐτός ή ό self, of oneself, even, very, the same, he, she, it
πάντας adj. acc. masc. pl. πᾶς πᾶσα πᾶν all, every, whosoever, every one, no, whole, any
ἁγίους adj. acc. masc. pl. ἅγιος Holy, holy, saint, Holy One, holy thing, most holy
16 ἀλλήλους pron. acc. masc. 2p. pl. ἀλλήλων one another, themselves, together, mutual
ἐν prep. ἐν (+dat) in, by, with, among, at, on, through, to, within, into, of, for
φιλήματι n. dat. neut. sg. φίλημα kiss
ἁγίῳ adj. dat. neut. sg. ἅγιος Holy, holy, saint, Holy One, holy thing, most holy
ὑμᾶς pron. acc. 2p. pl. σύ thou, you

αἱ art. nom. fem. pl. ὁ ἡ τό the, this, that, he, she, it
ἐκκλησίαι n. nom. fem. pl. ἐκκλησία church, assembly
τοῦ art. gen. masc. sg. ὁ ἡ τό the, this, that, he, she, it
Χριστοῦ n. gen. masc. sg. Χριστός Christ
17 δὲ conj. δέ but, and, now, also, to the contrary, rather, then
ὑμᾶς pron. acc. 2p. pl. σύ thou, you
ἀδελφοί n. voc. masc. pl. ἀδελφός brother
τοὺς art. acc. masc. pl. ὁ ἡ τό the, this, that, he, she, it
τὰς art. acc. fem. pl. ὁ ἡ τό the, this, that, he, she, it
διχοστασίας n. acc. fem. pl. διχοστασία division, sedition
καὶ conj. καί and, even, also, but
τὰ art. acc. neut. pl. ὁ ἡ τό the, this, that, he, she, it
σκάνδαλα n. acc. neut. pl. σκάνδαλον offence, stumblingblock, thing that offend
παρὰ prep. παρά (+gen) of, from, (+dat) with, for, (+acc) beside, at, by, above, against
τὴν art. acc. fem. sg. ὁ ἡ τό the, this, that, he, she, it
διδαχὴν n. acc. fem. sg. διδαχή doctrine, teaching
ἣν relative pron. acc. fem. sg. ὅς ἥ ὅ who, which, what, that
ὑμεῖς pron. nom. 2p. pl. σύ thou, you
καὶ conj. καί and, even, also, but
ἀπ' prep. ἀπό (+gen) from, of, out of, since, for, off, at, by, in, on
αὐτῶν pron. gen. masc. 3p. pl. αὐτός ἡ ὁ self, of oneself, even, very, the same, he, she, it
18 οἱ art. nom. masc. pl. ὁ ἡ τό the, this, that, he, she, it
γὰρ conj. γάρ for, and, because, but, indeed
τοιοῦτοι demo. pron. nom. masc. pl. τοιοῦτος such, like
τῷ art. dat. masc. sg. ὁ ἡ τό the, this, that, he, she, it
Κυρίῳ n. dat. masc. sg. κύριος Lord, lord, master, sir, LORD, God, Master, owner
ἡμῶν pron. gen. 1p. pl. ἐγώ I
Ἰησοῦ n. dat. masc. sg. Ἰησοῦς Jesus
Χριστῷ n. dat. masc. sg. Χριστός Christ
οὐ particle of negation. οὐ οὐκ οὐχ not, no, neither, none, nay, nor, never, nothing
ἀλλὰ conj. ἀλλά but, yea, yet, nevertheless, howbeit, nay, therefore
τῇ art. dat. fem. sg. ὁ ἡ τό the, this, that, he, she, it
ἑαυτῶν reflexive pron. gen. masc. 3p. pl. ἑαυτοῦ himself, herself, itself, yourself, ourselves
κοιλίᾳ n. dat. fem. sg. κοιλία belly, womb
καὶ conj. καί and, even, also, but
διὰ prep. διά (+gen) by, through, with, in, of, (+acc) for, because of, for a cause
τῆς art. gen. fem. sg. ὁ ἡ τό the, this, that, he, she, it
χρηστολογίας n. gen. fem. sg. χρηστολογία good word
καὶ conj. καί and, even, also, but
εὐλογίας n. gen. fem. sg. εὐλογία blessing, bounty, matter of bounty, fair speech
τὰς art. acc. fem. pl. ὁ ἡ τό the, this, that, he, she, it
καρδίας n. acc. fem. pl. καρδία heart
τῶν art. gen. masc. pl. ὁ ἡ τό the, this, that, he, she, it
ἀκάκων adj. gen. masc. pl. ἄκακος simple, harmless
19 ἡ art. nom. fem. sg. ὁ ἡ τό the, this, that, he, she, it
γὰρ conj. γάρ for, and, because, but, indeed
ὑμῶν pron. gen. 2p. pl. σύ thou, you
ὑπακοὴ n. nom. fem. sg. ὑπακοή obedience, obey, make obedient, obedient
εἰς prep. εἰς (+acc) into, to, unto, for, in, on, toward, against, upon, at, among
πάντας adj. acc. masc. pl. πᾶς πᾶσα πᾶν all, every, whosoever, every one, no, whole, any
οὖν conj. οὖν therefore, then, so, and, now, wherefore
τὸ art. acc. neut. sg. ὁ ἡ τό the, this, that, he, she, it
ἐφ' prep. ἐπί (+gen) on, in, upon, (+dat) in, at, for, upon, (+acc) on, upon, unto, to, against
ὑμῖν pron. dat. 2p. pl. σύ thou, you
δὲ conj. δέ but, and, now, also, to the contrary, rather, then

ὑμᾶς pron. acc. 2p. pl. σύ thou, you
σοφοὺς adj. acc. masc. pl. σοφός wise, wiser
μὲν conj. μέν indeed, verily, truly, even, so, some
εἰς prep. εἰς (+acc) into, to, unto, for, in, on, toward, against, upon, at, among
τὸ art. acc. neut. sg. ὁ ἡ τό the, this, that, he, she, it
ἀγαθόν adj. acc. neut. sg. ἀγαθός good, good thing, that which is good, well
ἀκεραίους adj. acc. masc. pl. ἀκέραιος harmless, innocent, simple
δὲ conj. δέ but, and, now, also, to the contrary, rather, then
εἰς prep. εἰς (+acc) into, to, unto, for, in, on, toward, against, upon, at, among
τὸ art. acc. neut. sg. ὁ ἡ τό the, this, that, he, she, it
κακόν adj. acc. neut. sg. κακός evil, evil thing, noisome, wicked
20 ὁ art. nom. masc. sg. ὁ ἡ τό the, this, that, he, she, it
δὲ conj. δέ but, and, now, also, to the contrary, rather, then
Θεὸς n. nom. masc. sg. θεός God, god
τῆς art. gen. fem. sg. ὁ ἡ τό the, this, that, he, she, it
εἰρήνης n. gen. fem. sg. εἰρήνη peace, quietness, rest
τὸν art. acc. masc. sg. ὁ ἡ τό the, this, that, he, she, it
Σατανᾶν n. acc. masc. sg. Σατανᾶς Satan
ὑπὸ prep. ὑπό (+gen) of, by, with, from, among, (+acc) under
τοὺς art. acc. masc. pl. ὁ ἡ τό the, this, that, he, she, it
πόδας n. acc. masc. pl. πούς foot
ὑμῶν pron. gen. 2p. pl. σύ thou, you
ἐν prep. ἐν (+dat) in, by, with, among, at, on, through, to, within, into, of, for
τάχει n. dat. neut. sg. τάχος speedily, short, quick
Ἡ art. nom. fem. sg. ὁ ἡ τό the, this, that, he, she, it
χάρις n. nom. fem. sg. χάρις grace, thank, favour, pleasure
τοῦ art. gen. masc. sg. ὁ ἡ τό the, this, that, he, she, it
Κυρίου n. gen. masc. sg. κύριος Lord, lord, master, sir, LORD, God, Master, owner
ἡμῶν pron. gen. 1p. pl. ἐγώ I
Ἰησοῦ n. gen. masc. sg. Ἰησοῦς Jesus
Χριστοῦ n. gen. masc. sg. Χριστός Christ
μεθ’ prep. μετά (+gen) with, among, against, (+acc) after
ὑμῶν pron. gen. 2p. pl. σύ thou, you
ἀμήν particle. ἀμήν amen, verily
21 ὑμᾶς pron. acc. 2p. pl. σύ thou, you
Τιμόθεος n. nom. masc. sg. Τιμόθεος Timotheus, Timothy
ὁ art. nom. masc. sg. ὁ ἡ τό the, this, that, he, she, it
συνεργός adj. nom. masc. sg. συνεργός fellowlabourer, fellowhelper, fellowworker
μου pron. gen. 1p. sg. ἐγώ I
καὶ conj. καί and, even, also, but
Λούκιος n. nom. masc. sg. Λούκιος Lucius
καὶ conj. καί and, even, also, but
Ἰάσων n. nom. masc. sg. Ἰάσων Jason
καὶ conj. καί and, even, also, but
Σωσίπατρος n. nom. masc. sg. Σωσίπατρος Sosipater
οἱ art. nom. masc. pl. ὁ ἡ τό the, this, that, he, she, it
συγγενεῖς adj. nom. masc. pl. συγγενής kinsman, cousin, kinsfolk, kin
μου pron. gen. 1p. sg. ἐγώ I
22 ὑμᾶς pron. acc. 2p. pl. σύ thou, you
ἐγὼ pron. nom. 1p. sg. ἐγώ I
Τέρτιος n. nom. masc. sg. Τέρτιος Tertius
ὁ art. nom. masc. sg. ὁ ἡ τό the, this, that, he, she, it
τὴν art. acc. fem. sg. ὁ ἡ τό the, this, that, he, she, it
ἐπιστολὴν n. acc. fem. sg. ἐπιστολή letter, epistle
ἐν prep. ἐν (+dat) in, by, with, among, at, on, through, to, within, into, of, for

Κυρίῳ n. dat. masc. sg. κύριος Lord, lord, master, sir, LORD, God, Master, owner
23 ὑμᾶς pron. acc. 2p. pl. σύ thou, you
Γάϊος n. nom. masc. sg. Γάϊος Gaius
ὁ art. nom. masc. sg. ὁ ἡ τό the, this, that, he, she, it
ξένος adj. nom. masc. sg. ξένος stranger, strange, host
μου pron. gen. 1p. sg. ἐγώ I
καὶ conj. καί and, even, also, but
τῆς art. gen. fem. sg. ὁ ἡ τό the, this, that, he, she, it
ἐκκλησίας n. gen. fem. sg. ἐκκλησία church, assembly
ὅλης adj. gen. fem. sg. ὅλος all, whole, every whit, altogether
ὑμᾶς pron. acc. 2p. pl. σύ thou, you
Ἔραστος n. nom. masc. sg. Ἔραστος Erastus
ὁ art. nom. masc. sg. ὁ ἡ τό the, this, that, he, she, it
οἰκονόμος n. nom. masc. sg. οἰκονόμος steward, chamberlain, governor
τῆς art. gen. fem. sg. ὁ ἡ τό the, this, that, he, she, it
πόλεως n. gen. fem. sg. πόλις city
καὶ conj. καί and, even, also, but
Κούαρτος n. nom. masc. sg. Κούαρτος Quartus
ὁ art. nom. masc. sg. ὁ ἡ τό the, this, that, he, she, it
ἀδελφός n. nom. masc. sg. ἀδελφός brother
24 Ἡ art. nom. fem. sg. ὁ ἡ τό the, this, that, he, she, it
χάρις n. nom. fem. sg. χάρις grace, thank, favour, pleasure
τοῦ art. gen. masc. sg. ὁ ἡ τό the, this, that, he, she, it
Κυρίου n. gen. masc. sg. κύριος Lord, lord, master, sir, LORD, God, Master, owner
ἡμῶν pron. gen. 1p. pl. ἐγώ I
Ἰησοῦ n. gen. masc. sg. Ἰησοῦς Jesus
Χριστοῦ n. gen. masc. sg. Χριστός Christ
μετὰ prep. μετά (+gen) with, among, against, (+acc) after
πάντων adj. gen. masc. pl. πᾶς πᾶσα πᾶν all, every, whosoever, every one, no, whole, any
ὑμῶν pron. gen. 2p. pl. σύ thou, you
ἀμήν particle. ἀμήν amen, verily
25 Τῷ art. dat. masc. sg. ὁ ἡ τό the, this, that, he, she, it
δὲ conj. δέ but, and, now, also, to the contrary, rather, then
ὑμᾶς pron. acc. 2p. pl. σύ thou, you
κατὰ prep. κατά (+gen) against, by, throughout, down, (+acc) according to, after, with
τὸ art. acc. neut. sg. ὁ ἡ τό the, this, that, he, she, it
εὐαγγέλιόν n. acc. neut. sg. εὐαγγέλιον gospel
μου pron. gen. 1p. sg. ἐγώ I
καὶ conj. καί and, even, also, but
τὸ art. acc. neut. sg. ὁ ἡ τό the, this, that, he, she, it
κήρυγμα n. acc. neut. sg. κήρυγμα preaching
Ἰησοῦ n. gen. masc. sg. Ἰησοῦς Jesus
Χριστοῦ n. gen. masc. sg. Χριστός Christ
κατὰ prep. κατά (+gen) against, by, throughout, down, (+acc) according to, after, with
ἀποκάλυψιν n. acc. fem. sg. ἀποκάλυψις revelation, appearing, coming, manifestation
μυστηρίου n. gen. neut. sg. μυστήριον mystery
χρόνοις n. dat. masc. pl. χρόνος time, season, space
αἰωνίοις adj. dat. masc. pl. αἰώνιος eternal, everlasting, world, for ever
26 δὲ conj. δέ but, and, now, also, to the contrary, rather, then
νῦν adv. νῦν now, henceforth, present, this time
διά prep. διά (+gen) by, through, with, in, of, (+acc) for, because of, for a cause
τε conj. τέ and, both, also
γραφῶν n. gen. fem. pl. γραφή scripture
προφητικῶν adj. gen. fem. pl. προφητικός of the prophets, of prophecy
κατ' prep. κατά (+gen) against, by, throughout, down, (+acc) according to, after, with

ἐπιταγὴν n. acc. fem. sg. ἐπιταγή commandment, authority
τοῦ art. gen. masc. sg. ὁ ἡ τό the, this, that, he, she, it
αἰωνίου adj. gen. masc. sg. αἰώνιος eternal, everlasting, world, for ever
Θεοῦ n. gen. masc. sg. θεός God, god
εἰς prep. εἰς (+acc) into, to, unto, for, in, on, toward, against, upon, at, among
ὑπακοὴν n. acc. fem. sg. ὑπακοή obedience, obey, make obedient, obedient
πίστεως n. gen. fem. sg. πίστις faith, assurance, belief, fidelity
εἰς prep. εἰς (+acc) into, to, unto, for, in, on, toward, against, upon, at, among
πάντα adj. acc. neut. pl. πᾶς πᾶσα πᾶν all, every, whosoever, every one, no, whole, any
τὰ art. acc. neut. pl. ὁ ἡ τό the, this, that, he, she, it
ἔθνη n. acc. neut. pl. ἔθνος Gentile, nation, heathen, people
27 μόνῳ adj. dat. masc. sg. μόνος only, alone, by oneself
σοφῷ adj. dat. masc. sg. σοφός wise, wiser
Θεῷ n. dat. masc. sg. θεός God, god
διὰ prep. διά (+gen) by, through, with, in, of, (+acc) for, because of, for a cause
Ἰησοῦ n. gen. masc. sg. Ἰησοῦς Jesus
Χριστοῦ n. gen. masc. sg. Χριστός Christ
ᾧ relative pron. dat. masc. sg. ὅς ἥ ὅ who, which, what, that
ἡ art. nom. fem. sg. ὁ ἡ τό the, this, that, he, she, it
δόξα n. nom. fem. sg. δόξα glory, honour, praise, dignity, worship
εἰς prep. εἰς (+acc) into, to, unto, for, in, on, toward, against, upon, at, among
τοὺς art. acc. masc. pl. ὁ ἡ τό the, this, that, he, she, it
αἰῶνας n. acc. masc. pl. αἰών ever, ever and ever, evermore, age, eternal, world
ἀμήν particle. ἀμήν amen, verily

ΠΑΥΛΟΥ ΤΟΥ ΑΠΟΣΤΟΛΟΥ
Η ΠΡΟΣ
ΚΟΡΙΝΘΙΟΥΣ
ΕΠΙΣΤΟΛΗ ΠΡΩΤΗ

1

1 Παῦλος n. nom. masc. sg. Παῦλος Paul, Paulus
κλητὸς adj. nom. masc. sg. κλητός called
ἀπόστολος n. nom. masc. sg. ἀπόστολος apostle, messenger, he that is sent
Ἰησοῦ n. gen. masc. sg. Ἰησοῦς Jesus
Χριστοῦ n. gen. masc. sg. Χριστός Christ
διὰ prep. διά (+gen) by, through, with, in, of, (+acc) for, because of, for a cause
θελήματος n. gen. neut. sg. θέλημα will, desire, pleasure
Θεοῦ n. gen. masc. sg. θεός God, god
καὶ conj. καί and, even, also, but
Σωσθένης n. nom. masc. sg. Σωσθένης Sosthenes
ὁ art. nom. masc. sg. ὁ ἡ τό the, this, that, he, she, it
ἀδελφὸς n. nom. masc. sg. ἀδελφός brother
2 τῇ art. dat. fem. sg. ὁ ἡ τό the, this, that, he, she, it
ἐκκλησίᾳ n. dat. fem. sg. ἐκκλησία church, assembly
τοῦ art. gen. masc. sg. ὁ ἡ τό the, this, that, he, she, it
Θεοῦ n. gen. masc. sg. θεός God, god
τῇ art. dat. fem. sg. ὁ ἡ τό the, this, that, he, she, it
ἐν prep. ἐν (+dat) in, by, with, among, at, on, through, to, within, into, of, for
Κορίνθῳ n. dat. fem. sg. Κόρινθος Corinth
ἐν prep. ἐν (+dat) in, by, with, among, at, on, through, to, within, into, of, for
Χριστῷ n. dat. masc. sg. Χριστός Christ
Ἰησοῦ n. dat. masc. sg. Ἰησοῦς Jesus
κλητοῖς adj. dat. masc. pl. κλητός called
ἁγίοις adj. dat. masc. pl. ἅγιος Holy, holy, saint, Holy One, holy thing, most holy
σὺν prep. σύν (+dat) with, beside
πᾶσι adj. dat. masc. pl. πᾶς πᾶσα πᾶν all, every, whosoever, every one, no, whole, any
τοῖς art. dat. masc. pl. ὁ ἡ τό the, this, that, he, she, it
τὸ art. acc. neut. sg. ὁ ἡ τό the, this, that, he, she, it
ὄνομα n. acc. neut. sg. ὄνομα name, call, surname
Κυρίου n. gen. masc. sg. κύριος Lord, lord, master, sir, LORD, God, Master, owner
ἡμῶν pron. gen. 1p. pl. ἐγώ I
Ἰησοῦ n. gen. masc. sg. Ἰησοῦς Jesus
Χριστοῦ n. gen. masc. sg. Χριστός Christ
ἐν prep. ἐν (+dat) in, by, with, among, at, on, through, to, within, into, of, for
παντὶ adj. dat. masc. sg. πᾶς πᾶσα πᾶν all, every, whosoever, every one, no, whole, any
τόπῳ n. dat. masc. sg. τόπος place, room, quarter
αὐτῶν pron. gen. masc. 3p. pl. αὐτός ἡ ὁ self, of oneself, even, very, the same, he, she, it
τε conj. τέ and, both, also
καὶ conj. καί and, even, also, but
ἡμῶν pron. gen. 1p. pl. ἐγώ I
3 χάρις n. nom. fem. sg. χάρις grace, thank, favour, pleasure
ὑμῖν pron. dat. 2p. pl. σύ thou, you
καὶ conj. καί and, even, also, but
εἰρήνη n. nom. fem. sg. εἰρήνη peace, quietness, rest
ἀπὸ prep. ἀπό (+gen) from, of, out of, since, for, off, at, by, in, on
Θεοῦ n. gen. masc. sg. θεός God, god

πατρὸς n. gen. masc. sg. πατήρ Father, father, parent
ἡμῶν pron. gen. 1p. pl. ἐγώ I
καὶ conj. καί and, even, also, but
Κυρίου n. gen. masc. sg. κύριος Lord, lord, master, sir, LORD, God, Master, owner
Ἰησοῦ n. gen. masc. sg. Ἰησοῦς Jesus
Χριστοῦ n. gen. masc. sg. Χριστός Christ
4 τῷ art. dat. masc. sg. ὁ ἡ τό the, this, that, he, she, it
Θεῷ n. dat. masc. sg. θεός God, god
μου pron. gen. 1p. sg. ἐγώ I
πάντοτε adv. πάντοτε always, ever, always, evermore
περὶ prep. περί (+gen) of, for, concerning, (+acc) about, concerning, in
ὑμῶν pron. gen. 2p. pl. σύ thou, you
ἐπὶ prep. ἐπί (+gen) on, in, upon, (+dat) in, at, for, upon, (+acc) on, upon, unto, to, against
τῇ art. dat. fem. sg. ὁ ἡ τό the, this, that, he, she, it
χάριτι n. dat. fem. sg. χάρις grace, thank, favour, pleasure
τοῦ art. gen. masc. sg. ὁ ἡ τό the, this, that, he, she, it
Θεοῦ n. gen. masc. sg. θεός God, god
τῇ art. dat. fem. sg. ὁ ἡ τό the, this, that, he, she, it
ὑμῖν pron. dat. 2p. pl. σύ thou, you
ἐν prep. ἐν (+dat) in, by, with, among, at, on, through, to, within, into, of, for
Χριστῷ n. dat. masc. sg. Χριστός Christ
Ἰησοῦ n. dat. masc. sg. Ἰησοῦς Jesus
5 ὅτι conj. ὅτι that, for, because, how that, how, because that, for that, though
ἐν prep. ἐν (+dat) in, by, with, among, at, on, through, to, within, into, of, for
παντὶ adj. dat. neut. sg. πᾶς πᾶσα πᾶν all, every, whosoever, every one, no, whole, any
ἐν prep. ἐν (+dat) in, by, with, among, at, on, through, to, within, into, of, for
αὐτῷ pron. dat. masc. 3p. sg. αὐτός ή ό self, of oneself, even, very, the same, he, she, it
ἐν prep. ἐν (+dat) in, by, with, among, at, on, through, to, within, into, of, for
παντὶ adj. dat. masc. sg. πᾶς πᾶσα πᾶν all, every, whosoever, every one, no, whole, any
λόγῳ n. dat. masc. sg. λόγος word, saying, account, speech, thing, matter
καὶ conj. καί and, even, also, but
πάσῃ adj. dat. fem. sg. πᾶς πᾶσα πᾶν all, every, whosoever, every one, no, whole, any
γνώσει n. dat. fem. sg. γνῶσις knowledge, science
6 καθὼς adv. καθώς as, even as, according as, according to
τὸ art. nom. neut. sg. ὁ ἡ τό the, this, that, he, she, it
μαρτύριον n. nom. neut. sg. μαρτύριον testimony, witness
τοῦ art. gen. masc. sg. ὁ ἡ τό the, this, that, he, she, it
Χριστοῦ n. gen. masc. sg. Χριστός Christ
ἐν prep. ἐν (+dat) in, by, with, among, at, on, through, to, within, into, of, for
ὑμῖν pron. dat. 2p. pl. σύ thou, you
7 ὥστε conj. ὥστε so that, wherefore, insomuch that, therefore, that, so then
ὑμᾶς pron. acc. 2p. pl. σύ thou, you
μὴ particle of negation. μή not, no, lest, neither, none, nothing, nor, never, without
ἐν prep. ἐν (+dat) in, by, with, among, at, on, through, to, within, into, of, for
μηδενὶ num. dat. neut. sg. μηδείς μηδεμία μηδέν no man, nothing, no, none, not at all
χαρίσματι n. dat. neut. pl. χάρισμα gift, free gift
τὴν art. acc. fem. sg. ὁ ἡ τό the, this, that, he, she, it
ἀποκάλυψιν n. acc. fem. sg. ἀποκάλυψις revelation, appearing, coming, manifestation
τοῦ art. gen. masc. sg. ὁ ἡ τό the, this, that, he, she, it
Κυρίου n. gen. masc. sg. κύριος Lord, lord, master, sir, LORD, God, Master, owner
ἡμῶν pron. gen. 1p. pl. ἐγώ I
Ἰησοῦ n. gen. masc. sg. Ἰησοῦς Jesus
Χριστοῦ n. gen. masc. sg. Χριστός Christ
8 ὃς relative pron. nom. masc. sg. ὅς ἥ ὅ who, which, what, that
καὶ conj. καί and, even, also, but

ὑμᾶς pron. acc. 2p. pl. σύ thou, you
ἕως conj. ἕως till, until, unto, until when, while, as far as, even, until now
τέλους n. gen. neut. sg. τέλος end, custom, ending, finally, uttermost
ἀνεγκλήτους adj. acc. masc. pl. ἀνέγκλητος blameless, unreprovable
ἐν prep. ἐν (+dat) in, by, with, among, at, on, through, to, within, into, of, for
τῇ art. dat. fem. sg. ὁ ἡ τό the, this, that, he, she, it
ἡμέρᾳ n. dat. fem. sg. ἡμέρα day, time, year, while, age, day time
τοῦ art. gen. masc. sg. ὁ ἡ τό the, this, that, he, she, it
Κυρίου n. gen. masc. sg. κύριος Lord, lord, master, sir, LORD, God, Master, owner
ἡμῶν pron. gen. 1p. pl. ἐγώ I
Ἰησοῦ n. gen. masc. sg. Ἰησοῦς Jesus
Χριστοῦ n. gen. masc. sg. Χριστός Christ
9 πιστὸς adj. nom. masc. sg. πιστός faithful, believing, true, sure
ὁ art. nom. masc. sg. ὁ ἡ τό the, this, that, he, she, it
Θεός n. nom. masc. sg. θεός God, god
δι' prep. διά (+gen) by, through, with, in, of, (+acc) for, because of, for a cause
οὗ relative pron. gen. masc. sg. ὅς ἥ ὅ who, which, what, that
εἰς prep. εἰς (+acc) into, to, unto, for, in, on, toward, against, upon, at, among
κοινωνίαν n. acc. fem. sg. κοινωνία fellowship, communion, contribution, distribution
τοῦ art. gen. masc. sg. ὁ ἡ τό the, this, that, he, she, it
υἱοῦ n. gen. masc. sg. υἱός son, child, descendant, offspring, heir
αὐτοῦ pron. gen. masc. 3p. sg. αὐτός ἡ ὁ self, of oneself, even, very, the same, he, she, it
Ἰησοῦ n. gen. masc. sg. Ἰησοῦς Jesus
Χριστοῦ n. gen. masc. sg. Χριστός Christ
τοῦ art. gen. masc. sg. ὁ ἡ τό the, this, that, he, she, it
Κυρίου n. gen. masc. sg. κύριος Lord, lord, master, sir, LORD, God, Master, owner
ἡμῶν pron. gen. 1p. pl. ἐγώ I
10 δὲ conj. δέ but, and, now, also, to the contrary, rather, then
ὑμᾶς pron. acc. 2p. pl. σύ thou, you
ἀδελφοί n. voc. masc. pl. ἀδελφός brother
διὰ prep. διά (+gen) by, through, with, in, of, (+acc) for, because of, for a cause
τοῦ art. gen. neut. sg. ὁ ἡ τό the, this, that, he, she, it
ὀνόματος n. gen. neut. sg. ὄνομα name, call, surname
τοῦ art. gen. masc. sg. ὁ ἡ τό the, this, that, he, she, it
Κυρίου n. gen. masc. sg. κύριος Lord, lord, master, sir, LORD, God, Master, owner
ἡμῶν pron. gen. 1p. pl. ἐγώ I
Ἰησοῦ n. gen. masc. sg. Ἰησοῦς Jesus
Χριστοῦ n. gen. masc. sg. Χριστός Christ
ἵνα conj. ἵνα that, to, lest, for to, so that, albeit, because, for, so as
τὸ art. acc. neut. sg. ὁ ἡ τό the, this, that, he, she, it
αὐτὸ pron. acc. neut. 3p. sg. αὐτός ἡ ὁ self, of oneself, even, very, the same, he, she, it
πάντες adj. nom. masc. pl. πᾶς πᾶσα πᾶν all, every, whosoever, every one, no, whole, any
καὶ conj. καί and, even, also, but
μὴ particle of negation. μή not, no, lest, neither, none, nothing, nor, never, without
ἐν prep. ἐν (+dat) in, by, with, among, at, on, through, to, within, into, of, for
ὑμῖν pron. dat. 2p. pl. σύ thou, you
σχίσματα n. nom. neut. pl. σχίσμα rent, division, schism
δὲ conj. δέ but, and, now, also, to the contrary, rather, then
ἐν prep. ἐν (+dat) in, by, with, among, at, on, through, to, within, into, of, for
τῷ art. dat. masc. sg. ὁ ἡ τό the, this, that, he, she, it
αὐτῷ adj. dat. masc. sg. αὐτός ἡ ὁ self, of oneself, even, very, the same, he, she, it
νοΐ n. dat. masc. sg. νοῦς understanding, mind
καὶ conj. καί and, even, also, but
ἐν prep. ἐν (+dat) in, by, with, among, at, on, through, to, within, into, of, for
τῇ art. dat. fem. sg. ὁ ἡ τό the, this, that, he, she, it

αὐτῇ adj. dat. fem. sg. αὐτός ή ό self, of oneself, even, very, the same, he, she, it
γνώμῃ n. dat. fem. sg. γνώμη judgement, mind, advice, purpose, will
11 γάρ conj. γάρ for, and, because, but, indeed
μοι pron. dat. 1p. sg. ἐγώ I
περὶ prep. περί (+gen) of, for, concerning, (+acc) about, concerning, in
ὑμῶν pron. gen. 2p. pl. σύ thou, you
ἀδελφοί n. voc. masc. pl. ἀδελφός brother
μου pron. gen. 1p. sg. ἐγώ I
ὑπὸ prep. ὑπό (+gen) of, by, with, from, among, (+acc) under
τῶν art. gen. masc. pl. ὁ ἡ τό the, this, that, he, she, it
Χλόης n. gen. fem. sg. Χλόη Chloe
ὅτι conj. ὅτι that, for, because, how that, how, because that, for that, though
ἔριδες n. nom. fem. pl. ἔρις debate, strife, contention, variance
ἐν prep. ἐν (+dat) in, by, with, among, at, on, through, to, within, into, of, for
ὑμῖν pron. dat. 2p. pl. σύ thou, you
12 δὲ conj. δέ but, and, now, also, to the contrary, rather, then
τοῦτο demo. pron. acc. neut. sg. οὗτος αὕτη τοῦτο this, the same, this same, he, she, it
ὅτι conj. ὅτι that, for, because, how that, how, because that, for that, though
ἕκαστος adj. nom. masc. sg. ἕκαστος every man, every, every one, any man, each
ὑμῶν pron. gen. 2p. pl. σύ thou, you
Ἐγὼ pron. nom. 1p. sg. ἐγώ I
μέν conj. μέν indeed, verily, truly, even, so, some
Παύλου n. gen. masc. sg. Παῦλος Paul, Paulus
Ἐγὼ pron. nom. 1p. sg. ἐγώ I
δὲ conj. δέ but, and, now, also, to the contrary, rather, then
Ἀπολλῶ n. gen. masc. sg. Ἀπολλώς Apollos
Ἐγὼ pron. nom. 1p. sg. ἐγώ I
δὲ conj. δέ but, and, now, also, to the contrary, rather, then
Κηφᾶ n. gen. masc. sg. Κηφᾶς Cephas
Ἐγὼ pron. nom. 1p. sg. ἐγώ I
δὲ conj. δέ but, and, now, also, to the contrary, rather, then
Χριστοῦ n. gen. masc. sg. Χριστός Christ
13 ὁ art. nom. masc. sg. ὁ ἡ τό the, this, that, he, she, it
Χριστός n. nom. masc. sg. Χριστός Christ
μὴ particle of negation. μή not, no, lest, neither, none, nothing, nor, never, without
Παῦλος n. nom. masc. sg. Παῦλος Paul, Paulus
ὑπὲρ prep. ὑπέρ (+gen) for, of, for the sake of, (+acc) above, more than
ὑμῶν pron. gen. 2p. pl. σύ thou, you
ἢ particle. ἤ or, than, either, nor, or else, and, rather than
εἰς prep. εἰς (+acc) into, to, unto, for, in, on, toward, against, upon, at, among
τὸ art. acc. neut. sg. ὁ ἡ τό the, this, that, he, she, it
ὄνομα n. acc. neut. sg. ὄνομα name, call, surname
Παύλου n. gen. masc. sg. Παῦλος Paul, Paulus
14 τῷ art. dat. masc. sg. ὁ ἡ τό the, this, that, he, she, it
Θεῷ n. dat. masc. sg. θεός God, god
ὅτι conj. ὅτι that, for, because, how that, how, because that, for that, though
οὐδένα num. acc. masc. sg. οὐδείς no man, nothing, no, none, neither, not, nought
ὑμῶν pron. gen. 2p. pl. σύ thou, you
εἰ conj. εἰ if, whether, that, though, forasmuch
μὴ particle of negation. μή not, no, lest, neither, none, nothing, nor, never, without
Κρίσπον n. acc. masc. sg. Κρίσπος Crispus
καὶ conj. καί and, even, also, but
Γάϊον n. acc. masc. sg. Γάϊος Gaius
15 ἵνα conj. ἵνα that, to, lest, for to, so that, albeit, because, for, so as
μή particle of negation. μή not, no, lest, neither, none, nothing, nor, never, without

τις indefinite pron. nom. masc. sg. τὶς certain, some, any man, one, any thing
ὅτι conj. ὅτι that, for, because, how that, how, because that, for that, though
εἰς prep. εἰς (+acc) into, to, unto, for, in, on, toward, against, upon, at, among
τὸ art. acc. neut. sg. ὁ ἡ τό the, this, that, he, she, it
ἐμὸν poss. pron. acc. neut. 1p. sg. ἐμός my, mine, mine own, of me
ὄνομα n. acc. neut. sg. ὄνομα name, call, surname
16 δὲ conj. δέ but, and, now, also, to the contrary, rather, then
καὶ conj. καί and, even, also, but
τὸν art. acc. masc. sg. ὁ ἡ τό the, this, that, he, she, it
Στεφανᾶ n. gen. masc. sg. Στεφανᾶς Stephanas
οἶκον n. acc. masc. sg. οἶκος house, home, household
λοιπὸν adv. λοιπόν finally, henceforth, now, besides, furthermore, moreover, then
οὐκ particle of negation. οὐ οὐκ οὐχ not, no, neither, none, nay, nor, never, nothing
εἴ conj. εἰ if, whether, that, though, forasmuch
τινα indefinite pron. acc. masc. sg. τὶς certain, some, any man, one, any thing
ἄλλον adj. acc. masc. sg. ἄλλος other, another, some, one, more, otherwise
17 οὐ particle of negation. οὐ οὐκ οὐχ not, no, neither, none, nay, nor, never, nothing
γὰρ conj. γάρ for, and, because, but, indeed
με pron. acc. 1p. sg. ἐγώ I
Χριστὸς n. nom. masc. sg. Χριστός Christ
ἀλλ' conj. ἀλλά but, yea, yet, nevertheless, howbeit, nay, therefore
οὐκ particle of negation. οὐ οὐκ οὐχ not, no, neither, none, nay, nor, never, nothing
ἐν prep. ἐν (+dat) in, by, with, among, at, on, through, to, within, into, of, for
σοφίᾳ n. dat. fem. sg. σοφία wisdom
λόγου n. gen. masc. sg. λόγος word, saying, account, speech, thing, matter
ἵνα conj. ἵνα that, to, lest, for to, so that, albeit, because, for, so as
μὴ particle of negation. μή not, no, lest, neither, none, nothing, nor, never, without
ὁ art. nom. masc. sg. ὁ ἡ τό the, this, that, he, she, it
σταυρὸς n. nom. masc. sg. σταυρός cross
τοῦ art. gen. masc. sg. ὁ ἡ τό the, this, that, he, she, it
Χριστοῦ n. gen. masc. sg. Χριστός Christ
18 Ὁ art. nom. masc. sg. ὁ ἡ τό the, this, that, he, she, it
λόγος n. nom. masc. sg. λόγος word, saying, account, speech, thing, matter
γὰρ conj. γάρ for, and, because, but, indeed
ὁ art. nom. masc. sg. ὁ ἡ τό the, this, that, he, she, it
τοῦ art. gen. masc. sg. ὁ ἡ τό the, this, that, he, she, it
σταυροῦ n. gen. masc. sg. σταυρός cross
τοῖς art. dat. masc. pl. ὁ ἡ τό the, this, that, he, she, it
μὲν conj. μέν indeed, verily, truly, even, so, some
μωρία n. nom. fem. sg. μωρία foolishness
τοῖς art. dat. masc. pl. ὁ ἡ τό the, this, that, he, she, it
δὲ conj. δέ but, and, now, also, to the contrary, rather, then
ἡμῖν pron. dat. 1p. pl. ἐγώ I
δύναμις n. nom. fem. sg. δύναμις power, mighty work, miracle, strength, might
Θεοῦ n. gen. masc. sg. θεός God, god
19 γάρ conj. γάρ for, and, because, but, indeed
τὴν art. acc. fem. sg. ὁ ἡ τό the, this, that, he, she, it
σοφίαν n. acc. fem. sg. σοφία wisdom
τῶν art. gen. masc. pl. ὁ ἡ τό the, this, that, he, she, it
σοφῶν adj. gen. masc. pl. σοφός wise, wiser
καὶ conj. καί and, even, also, but
τὴν art. acc. fem. sg. ὁ ἡ τό the, this, that, he, she, it
σύνεσιν n. acc. fem. sg. σύνεσις understanding, knowledge
τῶν art. gen. masc. pl. ὁ ἡ τό the, this, that, he, she, it
συνετῶν adj. gen. masc. pl. συνετός prudent

20 ποῦ particle of place. ποῦ where, whither
σοφός adj. nom. masc. sg. σοφός wise, wiser
ποῦ particle of place. ποῦ where, whither
γραμματεύς n. nom. masc. sg. γραμματεύς scribe, townclerk
ποῦ particle of place. ποῦ where, whither
συζητητὴς n. nom. masc. sg. συζητητής
τοῦ art. gen. masc. sg. ὁ ἡ τό the, this, that, he, she, it
αἰῶνος n. gen. masc. sg. αἰών ever, ever and ever, evermore, age, eternal, world
τούτου demo. pron. gen. masc. sg. οὗτος αὕτη τοῦτο this, the same, this same, he, she, it
οὐχὶ adv. οὐχί not, nay
ὁ art. nom. masc. sg. ὁ ἡ τό the, this, that, he, she, it
Θεὸς n. nom. masc. sg. θεός God, god
τὴν art. acc. fem. sg. ὁ ἡ τό the, this, that, he, she, it
σοφίαν n. acc. fem. sg. σοφία wisdom
τοῦ art. gen. masc. sg. ὁ ἡ τό the, this, that, he, she, it
κόσμου n. gen. masc. sg. κόσμος world, adorning
τούτου demo. pron. gen. masc. sg. οὗτος αὕτη τοῦτο this, the same, this same, he, she, it
21 ἐπειδὴ conj. ἐπειδή because, for, after that, for that, for as much as, since
γὰρ conj. γάρ for, and, because, but, indeed
ἐν prep. ἐν (+dat) in, by, with, among, at, on, through, to, within, into, of, for
τῇ art. dat. fem. sg. ὁ ἡ τό the, this, that, he, she, it
σοφίᾳ n. dat. fem. sg. σοφία wisdom
τοῦ art. gen. masc. sg. ὁ ἡ τό the, this, that, he, she, it
Θεοῦ n. gen. masc. sg. θεός God, god
οὐκ particle of negation. οὐ οὐκ οὐχ not, no, neither, none, nay, nor, never, nothing
ὁ art. nom. masc. sg. ὁ ἡ τό the, this, that, he, she, it
κόσμος n. nom. masc. sg. κόσμος world, adorning
διὰ prep. διά (+gen) by, through, with, in, of, (+acc) for, because of, for a cause
τῆς art. gen. fem. sg. ὁ ἡ τό the, this, that, he, she, it
σοφίας n. gen. fem. sg. σοφία wisdom
τὸν art. acc. masc. sg. ὁ ἡ τό the, this, that, he, she, it
Θεόν n. acc. masc. sg. θεός God, god
ὁ art. nom. masc. sg. ὁ ἡ τό the, this, that, he, she, it
Θεὸς n. nom. masc. sg. θεός God, god
διὰ prep. διά (+gen) by, through, with, in, of, (+acc) for, because of, for a cause
τῆς art. gen. fem. sg. ὁ ἡ τό the, this, that, he, she, it
μωρίας n. gen. fem. sg. μωρία foolishness
τοῦ art. gen. neut. sg. ὁ ἡ τό the, this, that, he, she, it
κηρύγματος n. gen. neut. sg. κήρυγμα preaching
τοὺς art. acc. masc. pl. ὁ ἡ τό the, this, that, he, she, it
22 ἐπειδὴ conj. ἐπειδή because, for, after that, for that, for as much as, since
καὶ conj. καί and, even, also, but
Ἰουδαῖοι adj. nom. masc. pl. Ἰουδαῖος Jew, Jewess
σημεῖον n. nom. neut. sg. σημεῖον sign, miracle, wonder, token
καὶ conj. καί and, even, also, but
Ἕλληνες n. nom. masc. pl. Ἕλλην Greek, Gentile
σοφίαν n. acc. fem. sg. σοφία wisdom
23 ἡμεῖς pron. nom. 1p. pl. ἐγώ I
δὲ conj. δέ but, and, now, also, to the contrary, rather, then
Χριστὸν n. acc. masc. sg. Χριστός Christ
Ἰουδαίοις adj. dat. masc. pl. Ἰουδαῖος Jew, Jewess
μὲν conj. μέν indeed, verily, truly, even, so, some
σκάνδαλον n. acc. neut. sg. σκάνδαλον offence, stumblingblock, thing that offend
Ἕλλησι n. dat. masc. pl. Ἕλλην Greek, Gentile
δὲ conj. δέ but, and, now, also, to the contrary, rather, then

μωρίαν n. acc. fem. sg. μωρία foolishness
24 αὐτοῖς pron. dat. masc. 3p. pl. αὐτός ή ό self, of oneself, even, very, the same, he, she, it
δὲ conj. δέ but, and, now, also, to the contrary, rather, then
τοῖς art. dat. masc. pl. ὁ ἡ τό the, this, that, he, she, it
κλητοῖς adj. dat. masc. pl. κλητός called
Ἰουδαίοις adj. dat. masc. pl. Ἰουδαῖος Jew, Jewess
τε conj. τέ and, both, also
καὶ conj. καί and, even, also, but
Ἕλλησι n. dat. masc. pl. Ἕλλην Greek, Gentile
Χριστὸν n. acc. masc. sg. Χριστός Christ
Θεοῦ n. gen. masc. sg. θεός God, god
δύναμιν n. acc. fem. sg. δύναμις power, mighty work, miracle, strength, might
καὶ conj. καί and, even, also, but
Θεοῦ n. gen. masc. sg. θεός God, god
σοφίαν n. acc. fem. sg. σοφία wisdom
25 ὅτι conj. ὅτι that, for, because, how that, how, because that, for that, though
τὸ art. nom. neut. sg. ὁ ἡ τό the, this, that, he, she, it
μωρὸν adj. nom. neut. sg. μωρός fool, foolish
τοῦ art. gen. masc. sg. ὁ ἡ τό the, this, that, he, she, it
Θεοῦ n. gen. masc. sg. θεός God, god
σοφώτερον compar. adj. nom. neut. sg. σοφός wise, wiser
τῶν art. gen. masc. pl. ὁ ἡ τό the, this, that, he, she, it
ἀνθρώπων n. gen. masc. pl. ἄνθρωπος man, human being, person, one, certain
καὶ conj. καί and, even, also, but
τὸ art. nom. neut. sg. ὁ ἡ τό the, this, that, he, she, it
ἀσθενὲς adj. nom. neut. sg. ἀσθενής weak, sick, impotent, more feeble
τοῦ art. gen. masc. sg. ὁ ἡ τό the, this, that, he, she, it
Θεοῦ n. gen. masc. sg. θεός God, god
ἰσχυρότερον compar. adj. nom. neut. sg. ἰσχυρός mighty, strong, mightier, stronger
τῶν art. gen. masc. pl. ὁ ἡ τό the, this, that, he, she, it
ἀνθρώπων n. gen. masc. pl. ἄνθρωπος man, human being, person, one, certain
26 γὰρ conj. γάρ for, and, because, but, indeed
τὴν art. acc. fem. sg. ὁ ἡ τό the, this, that, he, she, it
κλῆσιν n. acc. fem. sg. κλῆσις calling, vocation
ὑμῶν pron. gen. 2p. pl. σύ thou, you
ἀδελφοί n. voc. masc. pl. ἀδελφός brother
ὅτι conj. ὅτι that, for, because, how that, how, because that, for that, though
οὐ particle of negation. οὐ οὐκ οὐχ not, no, neither, none, nay, nor, never, nothing
πολλοὶ adj. nom. masc. pl. πολύς many, great, much, long, abundant
σοφοὶ adj. nom. masc. pl. σοφός wise, wiser
κατὰ prep. κατά (+gen) against, by, throughout, down, (+acc) according to, after, with
σάρκα n. acc. fem. sg. σάρξ flesh, carnal
οὐ particle of negation. οὐ οὐκ οὐχ not, no, neither, none, nay, nor, never, nothing
πολλοὶ adj. nom. masc. pl. πολύς many, great, much, long, abundant
δυνατοί adj. nom. masc. pl. δυνατός able, possible, mighty, strong
οὐ particle of negation. οὐ οὐκ οὐχ not, no, neither, none, nay, nor, never, nothing
πολλοὶ adj. nom. masc. pl. πολύς many, great, much, long, abundant
εὐγενεῖς adj. nom. masc. pl. εὐγενής noble, more noble
27 ἀλλὰ conj. ἀλλά but, yea, yet, nevertheless, howbeit, nay, therefore
τὰ art. acc. neut. pl. ὁ ἡ τό the, this, that, he, she, it
μωρὰ adj. acc. neut. pl. μωρός fool, foolish
τοῦ art. gen. masc. sg. ὁ ἡ τό the, this, that, he, she, it
κόσμου n. gen. masc. sg. κόσμος world, adorning
ὁ art. nom. masc. sg. ὁ ἡ τό the, this, that, he, she, it
Θεός n. nom. masc. sg. θεός God, god

ἵνα conj. ἵνα that, to, lest, for to, so that, albeit, because, for, so as
τοὺς art. acc. masc. pl. ὁ ἡ τό the, this, that, he, she, it
σοφούς adj. acc. masc. pl. σοφός wise, wiser
καὶ conj. καί and, even, also, but
τὰ art. acc. neut. pl. ὁ ἡ τό the, this, that, he, she, it
ἀσθενῆ adj. acc. neut. pl. ἀσθενής weak, sick, impotent, more feeble
τοῦ art. gen. masc. sg. ὁ ἡ τό the, this, that, he, she, it
κόσμου n. gen. masc. sg. κόσμος world, adorning
ὁ art. nom. masc. sg. ὁ ἡ τό the, this, that, he, she, it
Θεός n. nom. masc. sg. θεός God, god
ἵνα conj. ἵνα that, to, lest, for to, so that, albeit, because, for, so as
τὰ art. acc. neut. pl. ὁ ἡ τό the, this, that, he, she, it
ἰσχυρά adj. acc. neut. pl. ἰσχυρός mighty, strong, mightier, stronger
28 καὶ conj. καί and, even, also, but
τὰ art. acc. neut. pl. ὁ ἡ τό the, this, that, he, she, it
ἀγενῆ adj. acc. neut. pl. ἀγενής base thing
τοῦ art. gen. masc. sg. ὁ ἡ τό the, this, that, he, she, it
κόσμου n. gen. masc. sg. κόσμος world, adorning
καὶ conj. καί and, even, also, but
τὰ art. acc. neut. pl. ὁ ἡ τό the, this, that, he, she, it
ὁ art. nom. masc. sg. ὁ ἡ τό the, this, that, he, she, it
Θεός n. nom. masc. sg. θεός God, god
καὶ conj. καί and, even, also, but
τὰ art. acc. neut. pl. ὁ ἡ τό the, this, that, he, she, it
μὴ particle of negation. μή not, no, lest, neither, none, nothing, nor, never, without
ἵνα conj. ἵνα that, to, lest, for to, so that, albeit, because, for, so as
τὰ art. acc. neut. pl. ὁ ἡ τό the, this, that, he, she, it
29 ὅπως adv. ὅπως that, how, to, because, so that, when
μὴ particle of negation. μή not, no, lest, neither, none, nothing, nor, never, without
πᾶσα adj. nom. fem. sg. πᾶς πᾶσα πᾶν all, every, whosoever, every one, no, whole, any
σὰρξ n. nom. fem. sg. σάρξ flesh, carnal
ἐνώπιον prep. ἐνώπιον (+gen) before, in the sight of, in the presence of. (adv.) before
αὐτοῦ pron. gen. masc. 3p. sg. αὐτός ή ό self, of oneself, even, very, the same, he, she, it
30 ἐξ prep. ἐκ ἐξ (+gen) of, from, out of, by, on, with, in, among, through
αὐτοῦ pron. gen. masc. 3p. sg. αὐτός ή ό self, of oneself, even, very, the same, he, she, it
δὲ conj. δέ but, and, now, also, to the contrary, rather, then
ὑμεῖς pron. nom. 2p. pl. σύ thou, you
ἐν prep. ἐν (+dat) in, by, with, among, at, on, through, to, within, into, of, for
Χριστῷ n. dat. masc. sg. Χριστός Christ
Ἰησοῦ n. dat. masc. sg. Ἰησοῦς Jesus
ὃς relative pron. nom. masc. sg. ὅς ἥ ὅ who, which, what, that
ἡμῖν pron. dat. 1p. pl. ἐγώ I
σοφία n. nom. fem. sg. σοφία wisdom
ἀπὸ prep. ἀπό (+gen) from, of, out of, since, for, off, at, by, in, on
Θεοῦ n. gen. masc. sg. θεός God, god
δικαιοσύνη n. nom. fem. sg. δικαιοσύνη righteousness
τε conj. τέ and, both, also
καὶ conj. καί and, even, also, but
ἁγιασμὸς n. nom. masc. sg. ἁγιασμός holiness, sanctification
καὶ conj. καί and, even, also, but
ἀπολύτρωσις n. nom. fem. sg. ἀπολύτρωσις redemption, deliverance
31 ἵνα conj. ἵνα that, to, lest, for to, so that, albeit, because, for, so as
καθὼς adv. καθώς as, even as, according as, according to
Ὁ art. nom. masc. sg. ὁ ἡ τό the, this, that, he, she, it
ἐν prep. ἐν (+dat) in, by, with, among, at, on, through, to, within, into, of, for

Κυρίῳ n. dat. masc. sg. κύριος Lord, lord, master, sir, LORD, God, Master, owner

2

1 Κἀγὼ pron. nom. 1p. sg. κἀγώ and I, I also, so I, even as I
πρὸς prep. πρός (+gen) for, (+dat) at, (+acc) unto, to, with, for, against
ὑμᾶς pron. acc. 2p. pl. σύ thou, you
ἀδελφοί n. voc. masc. pl. ἀδελφός brother
οὐ particle of negation. οὐ οὐκ οὐχ not, no, neither, none, nay, nor, never, nothing
καθ' prep. κατά (+gen) against, by, throughout, down, (+acc) according to, after, with
ὑπεροχὴν n. acc. fem. sg. ὑπεροχή excellency, authority
λόγου n. gen. masc. sg. λόγος word, saying, account, speech, thing, matter
ἢ particle. ἤ or, than, either, nor, or else, and, rather than
σοφίας n. gen. fem. sg. σοφία wisdom
ὑμῖν pron. dat. 2p. pl. σύ thou, you
τὸ art. acc. neut. sg. ὁ ἡ τό the, this, that, he, she, it
μαρτύριον n. acc. neut. sg. μαρτύριον testimony, witness
τοῦ art. gen. masc. sg. ὁ ἡ τό the, this, that, he, she, it
Θεοῦ n. gen. masc. sg. θεός God, god
2 οὐ particle of negation. οὐ οὐκ οὐχ not, no, neither, none, nay, nor, never, nothing
γὰρ conj. γάρ for, and, because, but, indeed
τοῦ art. gen. masc. sg. ὁ ἡ τό the, this, that, he, she, it
τι indefinite pron. acc. neut. sg. τὶς certain, some, any man, one, any thing
ἐν prep. ἐν (+dat) in, by, with, among, at, on, through, to, within, into, of, for
ὑμῖν pron. dat. 2p. pl. σύ thou, you
εἰ conj. εἰ if, whether, that, though, forasmuch
μὴ particle of negation. μή not, no, lest, neither, none, nothing, nor, never, without
Ἰησοῦν n. acc. masc. sg. Ἰησοῦς Jesus
Χριστὸν n. acc. masc. sg. Χριστός Christ
καὶ conj. καί and, even, also, but
τοῦτον demo. pron. acc. masc. sg. οὗτος αὕτη τοῦτο this, the same, this same, he, she, it
3 καὶ conj. καί and, even, also, but
ἐγὼ pron. nom. 1p. sg. ἐγώ I
ἐν prep. ἐν (+dat) in, by, with, among, at, on, through, to, within, into, of, for
ἀσθενείᾳ n. dat. fem. sg. ἀσθένεια infirmity, weakness, disease, sickness
καὶ conj. καί and, even, also, but
ἐν prep. ἐν (+dat) in, by, with, among, at, on, through, to, within, into, of, for
φόβῳ n. dat. masc. sg. φόβος fear, terror, sore afraid
καὶ conj. καί and, even, also, but
ἐν prep. ἐν (+dat) in, by, with, among, at, on, through, to, within, into, of, for
τρόμῳ n. dat. masc. sg. τρόμος trembling, tremble
πολλῷ adj. dat. masc. sg. πολύς many, great, much, long, abundant
πρὸς prep. πρός (+gen) for, (+dat) at, (+acc) unto, to, with, for, against
ὑμᾶς pron. acc. 2p. pl. σύ thou, you
4 καὶ conj. καί and, even, also, but
ὁ art. nom. masc. sg. ὁ ἡ τό the, this, that, he, she, it
λόγος n. nom. masc. sg. λόγος word, saying, account, speech, thing, matter
μου pron. gen. 1p. sg. ἐγώ I
καὶ conj. καί and, even, also, but
τὸ art. nom. neut. sg. ὁ ἡ τό the, this, that, he, she, it
κήρυγμά n. nom. neut. sg. κήρυγμα preaching
μου pron. gen. 1p. sg. ἐγώ I
οὐκ particle of negation. οὐ οὐκ οὐχ not, no, neither, none, nay, nor, never, nothing
ἐν prep. ἐν (+dat) in, by, with, among, at, on, through, to, within, into, of, for
πειθοῖς adj. dat. masc. pl. πειθός enticing

ἀνθρωπίνης adj. gen. fem. sg. ἀνθρώπινος man, after the manner of men man
σοφίας n. gen. fem. sg. σοφία wisdom
λόγοις n. dat. masc. pl. λόγος word, saying, account, speech, thing, matter
ἀλλ' conj. ἀλλά but, yea, yet, nevertheless, howbeit, nay, therefore
ἐν prep. ἐν (+dat) in, by, with, among, at, on, through, to, within, into, of, for
ἀποδείξει n. dat. fem. sg. ἀπόδειξις demonstration
πνεύματος n. gen. neut. sg. πνεῦμα spirit, Spirit, Ghost, ghost, life. of the spirit, wind
καὶ conj. καί and, even, also, but
δυνάμεως n. gen. fem. sg. δύναμις power, mighty work, miracle, strength, might
5 ἵνα conj. ἵνα that, to, lest, for to, so that, albeit, because, for, so as
ἡ art. nom. fem. sg. ὁ ἡ τό the, this, that, he, she, it
πίστις n. nom. fem. sg. πίστις faith, assurance, belief, fidelity
ὑμῶν pron. gen. 2p. pl. σύ thou, you
μὴ particle of negation. μή not, no, lest, neither, none, nothing, nor, never, without
ἐν prep. ἐν (+dat) in, by, with, among, at, on, through, to, within, into, of, for
σοφίᾳ n. dat. fem. sg. σοφία wisdom
ἀνθρώπων n. gen. masc. pl. ἄνθρωπος man, human being, person, one, certain
ἀλλ' conj. ἀλλά but, yea, yet, nevertheless, howbeit, nay, therefore
ἐν prep. ἐν (+dat) in, by, with, among, at, on, through, to, within, into, of, for
δυνάμει n. dat. fem. sg. δύναμις power, mighty work, miracle, strength, might
Θεοῦ n. gen. masc. sg. θεός God, god
6 Σοφίαν n. acc. fem. sg. σοφία wisdom
δὲ conj. δέ but, and, now, also, to the contrary, rather, then
ἐν prep. ἐν (+dat) in, by, with, among, at, on, through, to, within, into, of, for
τοῖς art. dat. masc. pl. ὁ ἡ τό the, this, that, he, she, it
τελείοις adj. dat. masc. pl. τέλειος perfect, of full age
σοφίαν n. acc. fem. sg. σοφία wisdom
δὲ conj. δέ but, and, now, also, to the contrary, rather, then
οὐ particle of negation. οὐ οὐκ οὐχ not, no, neither, none, nay, nor, never, nothing
τοῦ art. gen. masc. sg. ὁ ἡ τό the, this, that, he, she, it
αἰῶνος n. gen. masc. sg. αἰών ever, ever and ever, evermore, age, eternal, world
τούτου demo. pron. gen. masc. sg. οὗτος αὕτη τοῦτο this, the same, this same, he, she, it
οὐδὲ adv. οὐδέ neither, nor, not, no, not even, never, not yet
τῶν art. gen. masc. pl. ὁ ἡ τό the, this, that, he, she, it
ἀρχόντων n. gen. masc. pl. ἄρχων ruler, prince, chief, magistrate, chief ruler
τοῦ art. gen. masc. sg. ὁ ἡ τό the, this, that, he, she, it
αἰῶνος n. gen. masc. sg. αἰών ever, ever and ever, evermore, age, eternal, world
τούτου demo. pron. gen. masc. sg. οὗτος αὕτη τοῦτο this, the same, this same, he, she, it
τῶν art. gen. masc. pl. ὁ ἡ τό the, this, that, he, she, it
7 ἀλλὰ conj. ἀλλά but, yea, yet, nevertheless, howbeit, nay, therefore
σοφίαν n. acc. fem. sg. σοφία wisdom
Θεοῦ n. gen. masc. sg. θεός God, god
ἐν prep. ἐν (+dat) in, by, with, among, at, on, through, to, within, into, of, for
μυστηρίῳ n. dat. neut. sg. μυστήριον mystery
τὴν art. acc. fem. sg. ὁ ἡ τό the, this, that, he, she, it
ἣν relative pron. acc. fem. sg. ὅς ἥ ὅ who, which, what, that
ὁ art. nom. masc. sg. ὁ ἡ τό the, this, that, he, she, it
Θεὸς n. nom. masc. sg. θεός God, god
πρὸ prep. πρό (+gen) before, above
τῶν art. gen. masc. pl. ὁ ἡ τό the, this, that, he, she, it
αἰώνων n. gen. masc. pl. αἰών ever, ever and ever, evermore, age, eternal, world
εἰς prep. εἰς (+acc) into, to, unto, for, in, on, toward, against, upon, at, among
δόξαν n. acc. fem. sg. δόξα glory, honour, praise, dignity, worship
ἡμῶν pron. gen. 1p. pl. ἐγώ I
8 ἣν relative pron. acc. fem. sg. ὅς ἥ ὅ who, which, what, that

οὐδεὶς num. nom. masc. sg. οὐδείς no man, nothing, no, none, neither, not, nought
τῶν art. gen. masc. pl. ὁ ἡ τό the, this, that, he, she, it
ἀρχόντων n. gen. masc. pl. ἄρχων ruler, prince, chief, magistrate, chief ruler
τοῦ art. gen. masc. sg. ὁ ἡ τό the, this, that, he, she, it
αἰῶνος n. gen. masc. sg. αἰών ever, ever and ever, evermore, age, eternal, world
τούτου demo. pron. gen. masc. sg. οὗτος αὕτη τοῦτο this, the same, this same, he, she, it
εἰ conj. εἰ if, whether, that, though, forasmuch
γὰρ conj. γάρ for, and, because, but, indeed
οὐκ particle of negation. οὐ οὐκ οὐχ not, no, neither, none, nay, nor, never, nothing
ἂν particle. ἄν Indicating contingency. No English translation.
τὸν art. acc. masc. sg. ὁ ἡ τό the, this, that, he, she, it
Κύριον n. acc. masc. sg. κύριος Lord, lord, master, sir, LORD, God, Master, owner
τῆς art. gen. fem. sg. ὁ ἡ τό the, this, that, he, she, it
δόξης n. gen. fem. sg. δόξα glory, honour, praise, dignity, worship
9 ἀλλὰ conj. ἀλλά but, yea, yet, nevertheless, howbeit, nay, therefore
καθὼς adv. καθώς as, even as, according as, according to
"Α relative pron. acc. neut. pl. ὅς ἥ ὅ who, which, what, that
ὀφθαλμὸς n. nom. masc. sg. ὀφθαλμός eye, sight
οὐκ particle of negation. οὐ οὐκ οὐχ not, no, neither, none, nay, nor, never, nothing
καὶ conj. καί and, even, also, but
οὖς n. nom. neut. sg. οὖς ear
οὐκ particle of negation. οὐ οὐκ οὐχ not, no, neither, none, nay, nor, never, nothing
καὶ conj. καί and, even, also, but
ἐπὶ prep. ἐπί (+gen) on, in, upon, (+dat) in, at, for, upon, (+acc) on, upon, unto, to, against
καρδίαν n. acc. fem. sg. καρδία heart
ἀνθρώπου n. gen. masc. sg. ἄνθρωπος man, human being, person, one, certain
οὐκ particle of negation. οὐ οὐκ οὐχ not, no, neither, none, nay, nor, never, nothing
ἃ relative pron. acc. neut. pl. ὅς ἥ ὅ who, which, what, that
ὁ art. nom. masc. sg. ὁ ἡ τό the, this, that, he, she, it
Θεὸς n. nom. masc. sg. θεός God, god
τοῖς art. dat. masc. pl. ὁ ἡ τό the, this, that, he, she, it
αὐτόν pron. acc. masc. 3p. sg. αὐτός ἡ ὁ self, of oneself, even, very, the same, he, she, it
10 ἡμῖν pron. dat. 1p. pl. ἐγώ I
δὲ conj. δέ but, and, now, also, to the contrary, rather, then
ὁ art. nom. masc. sg. ὁ ἡ τό the, this, that, he, she, it
Θεὸς n. nom. masc. sg. θεός God, god
διὰ prep. διά (+gen) by, through, with, in, of, (+acc) for, because of, for a cause
τοῦ art. gen. neut. sg. ὁ ἡ τό the, this, that, he, she, it
πνεύματος n. gen. neut. sg. πνεῦμα spirit, Spirit, Ghost, ghost, life. of the spirit, wind
αὐτοῦ pron. gen. masc. 3p. sg. αὐτός ἡ ὁ self, of oneself, even, very, the same, he, she, it
τὸ art. nom. neut. sg. ὁ ἡ τό the, this, that, he, she, it
γὰρ conj. γάρ for, and, because, but, indeed
πνεῦμα n. nom. neut. sg. πνεῦμα spirit, Spirit, Ghost, ghost, life. of the spirit, wind
πάντα adj. acc. neut. pl. πᾶς πᾶσα πᾶν all, every, whosoever, every one, no, whole, any
καὶ conj. καί and, even, also, but
τὰ art. acc. neut. pl. ὁ ἡ τό the, this, that, he, she, it
βάθη n. acc. neut. pl. βάθος deepness, depth, deep, deep thing
τοῦ art. gen. masc. sg. ὁ ἡ τό the, this, that, he, she, it
Θεοῦ n. gen. masc. sg. θεός God, god
11 τίς interrog. pron. nom. masc. sg. τίς what, who, why, where, which, how
γὰρ conj. γάρ for, and, because, but, indeed
ἀνθρώπων n. gen. masc. pl. ἄνθρωπος man, human being, person, one, certain
τὰ art. acc. neut. pl. ὁ ἡ τό the, this, that, he, she, it
τοῦ art. gen. masc. sg. ὁ ἡ τό the, this, that, he, she, it
ἀνθρώπου n. gen. masc. sg. ἄνθρωπος man, human being, person, one, certain

εἰ conj. εἰ if, whether, that, though, forasmuch
μὴ particle of negation. μή not, no, lest, neither, none, nothing, nor, never, without
τὸ art. nom. neut. sg. ὁ ἡ τό the, this, that, he, she, it
πνεῦμα n. nom. neut. sg. πνεῦμα spirit, Spirit, Ghost, ghost, life. of the spirit, wind
τοῦ art. gen. masc. sg. ὁ ἡ τό the, this, that, he, she, it
ἀνθρώπου n. gen. masc. sg. ἄνθρωπος man, human being, person, one, certain
τὸ art. nom. neut. sg. ὁ ἡ τό the, this, that, he, she, it
ἐν prep. ἐν (+dat) in, by, with, among, at, on, through, to, within, into, of, for
αὐτῷ pron. dat. masc. 3p. sg. αὐτός ἡ ὁ self, of oneself, even, very, the same, he, she, it
οὕτω adv. οὕτω οὕτως so, even so, thus, on this wise, likewise, after this manner
καὶ conj. καί and, even, also, but
τὰ art. acc. neut. pl. ὁ ἡ τό the, this, that, he, she, it
τοῦ art. gen. masc. sg. ὁ ἡ τό the, this, that, he, she, it
Θεοῦ n. gen. masc. sg. θεός God, god
οὐδεὶς num. nom. masc. sg. οὐδείς no man, nothing, no, none, neither, not, nought
εἰ conj. εἰ if, whether, that, though, forasmuch
μὴ particle of negation. μή not, no, lest, neither, none, nothing, nor, never, without
τὸ art. nom. neut. sg. ὁ ἡ τό the, this, that, he, she, it
πνεῦμα n. nom. neut. sg. πνεῦμα spirit, Spirit, Ghost, ghost, life. of the spirit, wind
τοῦ art. gen. masc. sg. ὁ ἡ τό the, this, that, he, she, it
Θεοῦ n. gen. masc. sg. θεός God, god
12 ἡμεῖς pron. nom. 1p. pl. ἐγώ I
δὲ conj. δέ but, and, now, also, to the contrary, rather, then
οὐ particle of negation. οὐ οὐκ οὐχ not, no, neither, none, nay, nor, never, nothing
τὸ art. acc. neut. sg. ὁ ἡ τό the, this, that, he, she, it
πνεῦμα n. acc. neut. sg. πνεῦμα spirit, Spirit, Ghost, ghost, life. of the spirit, wind
τοῦ art. gen. masc. sg. ὁ ἡ τό the, this, that, he, she, it
κόσμου n. gen. masc. sg. κόσμος world, adorning
ἀλλὰ conj. ἀλλά but, yea, yet, nevertheless, howbeit, nay, therefore
τὸ art. acc. neut. sg. ὁ ἡ τό the, this, that, he, she, it
πνεῦμα n. acc. neut. sg. πνεῦμα spirit, Spirit, Ghost, ghost, life. of the spirit, wind
τὸ art. acc. neut. sg. ὁ ἡ τό the, this, that, he, she, it
ἐκ prep. ἐκ ἐξ (+gen) of, from, out of, by, on, with, in, among, through
τοῦ art. gen. masc. sg. ὁ ἡ τό the, this, that, he, she, it
Θεοῦ n. gen. masc. sg. θεός God, god
ἵνα conj. ἵνα that, to, lest, for to, so that, albeit, because, for, so as
τὰ art. acc. neut. pl. ὁ ἡ τό the, this, that, he, she, it
ὑπὸ prep. ὑπό (+gen) of, by, with, from, among, (+acc) under
τοῦ art. gen. masc. sg. ὁ ἡ τό the, this, that, he, she, it
Θεοῦ n. gen. masc. sg. θεός God, god
ἡμῖν pron. dat. 1p. pl. ἐγώ I
13 ἃ relative pron. acc. neut. pl. ὅς ἥ ὅ who, which, what, that
καὶ conj. καί and, even, also, but
οὐκ particle of negation. οὐ οὐκ οὐχ not, no, neither, none, nay, nor, never, nothing
ἐν prep. ἐν (+dat) in, by, with, among, at, on, through, to, within, into, of, for
διδακτοῖς adj. dat. masc. pl. διδακτός taught, which teach
ἀνθρωπίνης adj. gen. fem. sg. ἀνθρώπινος man, after the manner of men man
σοφίας n. gen. fem. sg. σοφία wisdom
λόγοις n. dat. masc. pl. λόγος word, saying, account, speech, thing, matter
ἀλλ' conj. ἀλλά but, yea, yet, nevertheless, howbeit, nay, therefore
ἐν prep. ἐν (+dat) in, by, with, among, at, on, through, to, within, into, of, for
διδακτοῖς adj. dat. masc. pl. διδακτός taught, which teach
Πνεύματος n. gen. neut. sg. πνεῦμα spirit, Spirit, Ghost, ghost, life. of the spirit, wind
Ἁγίου adj. gen. neut. sg. ἅγιος Holy, holy, saint, Holy One, holy thing, most holy
πνευματικοῖς adj. dat. neut. pl. πνευματικός spiritual

πνευματικὰ adj. acc. neut. pl. πνευματικός spiritual
14 ψυχικὸς adj. nom. masc. sg. ψυχικός natural, sensual
δὲ conj. δέ but, and, now, also, to the contrary, rather, then
ἄνθρωπος n. nom. masc. sg. ἄνθρωπος man, human being, person, one, certain
οὐ particle of negation. οὐ οὐκ οὐχ not, no, neither, none, nay, nor, never, nothing
τὰ art. acc. neut. pl. ὁ ἡ τό the, this, that, he, she, it
τοῦ art. gen. neut. sg. ὁ ἡ τό the, this, that, he, she, it
Πνεύματος n. gen. neut. sg. πνεῦμα spirit, Spirit, Ghost, ghost, life. of the spirit, wind
τοῦ art. gen. masc. sg. ὁ ἡ τό the, this, that, he, she, it
Θεοῦ n. gen. masc. sg. θεός God, god
μωρία n. nom. fem. sg. μωρία foolishness
γὰρ conj. γάρ for, and, because, but, indeed
αὐτῷ pron. dat. masc. 3p. sg. αὐτός ή ό self, of oneself, even, very, the same, he, she, it
καὶ conj. καί and, even, also, but
οὐ particle of negation. οὐ οὐκ οὐχ not, no, neither, none, nay, nor, never, nothing
ὅτι conj. ὅτι that, for, because, how that, how, because that, for that, though
πνευματικῶς adv. πνευματικῶς spiritually
15 ὁ art. nom. masc. sg. ὁ ἡ τό the, this, that, he, she, it
δὲ conj. δέ but, and, now, also, to the contrary, rather, then
πνευματικὸς adj. nom. masc. sg. πνευματικός spiritual
μὲν conj. μέν indeed, verily, truly, even, so, some
πάντα adj. acc. neut. pl. πᾶς πᾶsα πᾶν all, every, whosoever, every one, no, whole, any
αὐτὸς pron. nom. masc. 3p. sg. αὐτός ή ό self, of oneself, even, very, the same, he, she, it
δὲ conj. δέ but, and, now, also, to the contrary, rather, then
ὑπ' prep. ὑπό (+gen) of, by, with, from, among, (+acc) under
οὐδενὸς num. gen. masc. sg. οὐδείς no man, nothing, no, none, neither, not, nought
16 τίς interrog. pron. nom. masc. sg. τίς what, who, why, where, which, how
γὰρ conj. γάρ for, and, because, but, indeed
νοῦν n. acc. masc. sg. νοῦς understanding, mind
Κυρίου n. gen. masc. sg. κύριος Lord, lord, master, sir, LORD, God, Master, owner
ὃς relative pron. nom. masc. sg. ὅς ἥ ὅ who, which, what, that
αὐτόν pron. acc. masc. 3p. sg. αὐτός ή ό self, of oneself, even, very, the same, he, she, it
ἡμεῖς pron. nom. 1p. pl. ἐγώ I
δὲ conj. δέ but, and, now, also, to the contrary, rather, then
νοῦν n. acc. masc. sg. νοῦς understanding, mind
Χριστοῦ n. gen. masc. sg. Χριστός Christ

3

1 Καὶ conj. καί and, even, also, but
ἐγώ pron. nom. 1p. sg. ἐγώ I
ἀδελφοί n. voc. masc. pl. ἀδελφός brother
οὐκ particle of negation. οὐ οὐκ οὐχ not, no, neither, none, nay, nor, never, nothing
ὑμῖν pron. dat. 2p. pl. σύ thou, you
ὡς adv. ὡς as, when, as it were, how, about, like, as soon as, even as, while
πνευματικοῖς adj. dat. masc. pl. πνευματικός spiritual
ἀλλ' conj. ἀλλά but, yea, yet, nevertheless, howbeit, nay, therefore
ὡς adv. ὡς as, when, as it were, how, about, like, as soon as, even as, while
σαρκικοῖς adj. dat. masc. pl. σαρκικός carnal, fleshly
ὡς adv. ὡς as, when, as it were, how, about, like, as soon as, even as, while
νηπίοις adj. dat. masc. pl. νήπιος babe, child, childish
ἐν prep. ἐν (+dat) in, by, with, among, at, on, through, to, within, into, of, for
Χριστῷ n. dat. masc. sg. Χριστός Christ
2 γάλα n. acc. neut. sg. γάλα milk
ὑμᾶς pron. acc. 2p. pl. σύ thou, you

καὶ conj. καί and, even, also, but
οὐ particle of negation. οὐ οὐκ οὐχ not, no, neither, none, nay, nor, never, nothing
βρῶμα n. acc. neut. sg. βρῶμα victual, meat, food
οὔπω adv. οὔπω not yet
γὰρ conj. γάρ for, and, because, but, indeed
ἀλλ' conj. ἀλλά but, yea, yet, nevertheless, howbeit, nay, therefore
οὔτε conj. οὔτε neither, nor, nor yet, no, none
ἔτι adv. ἔτι yet, more, any more, further, still, moreover
νῦν adv. νῦν now, henceforth, present, this time
3 ἔτι adv. ἔτι yet, more, any more, further, still, moreover
γὰρ conj. γάρ for, and, because, but, indeed
σαρκικοί adj. nom. masc. pl. σαρκικός carnal, fleshly
ὅπου adv. ὅπου where, whither, whereas, in what place, wheresoever
γὰρ conj. γάρ for, and, because, but, indeed
ἐν prep. ἐν (+dat) in, by, with, among, at, on, through, to, within, into, of, for
ὑμῖν pron. dat. 2p. pl. σύ thou, you
ζῆλος n. nom. masc. sg. ζῆλος zeal, envying, indignation, emulation, jealousy
καὶ conj. καί and, even, also, but
ἔρις n. nom. fem. sg. ἔρις debate, strife, contention, variance
καὶ conj. καί and, even, also, but
διχοστασίαι n. nom. fem. pl. διχοστασία division, sedition
οὐχὶ adv. οὐχί not, nay
σαρκικοί adj. nom. masc. pl. σαρκικός carnal, fleshly
καὶ conj. καί and, even, also, but
κατὰ prep. κατά (+gen) against, by, throughout, down, (+acc) according to, after, with
ἄνθρωπον n. acc. masc. sg. ἄνθρωπος man, human being, person, one, certain
4 ὅταν conj. ὅταν when, as soon as, as long as, that, whensoever, while
γὰρ conj. γάρ for, and, because, but, indeed
τις indefinite pron. nom. masc. sg. τὶς certain, some, any man, one, any thing
Ἐγὼ pron. nom. 1p. sg. ἐγώ I
μέν conj. μέν indeed, verily, truly, even, so, some
Παύλου n. gen. masc. sg. Παῦλος Paul, Paulus
ἕτερος adj. nom. masc. sg. ἕτερος another, other, else, strange
δέ conj. δέ but, and, now, also, to the contrary, rather, then
Ἐγὼ pron. nom. 1p. sg. ἐγώ I
Ἀπολλῶ n. gen. masc. sg. Ἀπολλῶς Apollos
οὐχὶ adv. οὐχί not, nay
σαρκικοί adj. nom. masc. pl. σαρκικός carnal, fleshly
5 τίς interrog. pron. nom. masc. sg. τίς what, who, why, where, which, how
οὖν conj. οὖν therefore, then, so, and, now, wherefore
Παῦλος n. nom. masc. sg. Παῦλος Paul, Paulus
τίς interrog. pron. nom. masc. sg. τίς what, who, why, where, which, how
δέ conj. δέ but, and, now, also, to the contrary, rather, then
Ἀπολλῶς n. nom. masc. sg. Ἀπολλῶς Apollos
ἀλλ' conj. ἀλλά but, yea, yet, nevertheless, howbeit, nay, therefore
ἢ particle. ἤ or, than, either, nor, or else, and, rather than
διάκονοι n. nom. masc. pl. διάκονος minister, servant, deacon
δι' prep. διά (+gen) by, through, with, in, of, (+acc) for, because of, for a cause
ὧν relative pron. gen. masc. pl. ὅς ἥ ὅ who, which, what, that
καὶ conj. καί and, even, also, but
ἑκάστῳ adj. dat. masc. sg. ἕκαστος every man, every, every one, any man, each
ὡς adv. ὡς as, when, as it were, how, about, like, as soon as, even as, while
ὁ art. nom. masc. sg. ὁ ἡ τό the, this, that, he, she, it
Κύριος n. nom. masc. sg. κύριος Lord, lord, master, sir, LORD, God, Master, owner
6 ἐγὼ pron. nom. 1p. sg. ἐγώ I

'Απολλῶς n. nom. masc. sg. 'Απολλῶς Apollos
ἀλλ' conj. ἀλλά but, yea, yet, nevertheless, howbeit, nay, therefore
ὁ art. nom. masc. sg. ὁ ἡ τό the, this, that, he, she, it
Θεὸς n. nom. masc. sg. θεός God, god
7 ὥστε conj. ὥστε so that, wherefore, insomuch that, therefore, that, so then
οὔτε conj. οὔτε neither, nor, nor yet, no, none
ὁ art. nom. masc. sg. ὁ ἡ τό the, this, that, he, she, it
τι indefinite pron. nom. neut. sg. τὶς certain, some, any man, one, any thing
οὔτε conj. οὔτε neither, nor, nor yet, no, none
ὁ art. nom. masc. sg. ὁ ἡ τό the, this, that, he, she, it
ἀλλ' conj. ἀλλά but, yea, yet, nevertheless, howbeit, nay, therefore
ὁ art. nom. masc. sg. ὁ ἡ τό the, this, that, he, she, it
Θεός n. nom. masc. sg. θεός God, god
8 ὁ art. nom. masc. sg. ὁ ἡ τό the, this, that, he, she, it
δὲ conj. δέ but, and, now, also, to the contrary, rather, then
καὶ conj. καί and, even, also, but
ὁ art. nom. masc. sg. ὁ ἡ τό the, this, that, he, she, it
ἕν num. nom. neut. sg. εἷς or ἕν one, other, some, any, only, a certain
ἕκαστος adj. nom. masc. sg. ἕκαστος every man, every, every one, any man, each
δὲ conj. δέ but, and, now, also, to the contrary, rather, then
τὸν art. acc. masc. sg. ὁ ἡ τό the, this, that, he, she, it
ἴδιον adj. acc. masc. sg. ἴδιος one's own, one's, privately
μισθὸν n. acc. masc. sg. μισθός reward, hire, wage
κατὰ prep. κατά (+gen) against, by, throughout, down, (+acc) according to, after, with
τὸν art. acc. masc. sg. ὁ ἡ τό the, this, that, he, she, it
ἴδιον adj. acc. masc. sg. ἴδιος one's own, one's, privately
κόπον n. acc. masc. sg. κόπος labour, trouble, weariness
9 Θεοῦ n. gen. masc. sg. θεός God, god
γάρ conj. γάρ for, and, because, but, indeed
συνεργοί adj. nom. masc. pl. συνεργός fellowlabourer, fellowhelper, fellowworker
Θεοῦ n. gen. masc. sg. θεός God, god
γεώργιον n. nom. neut. sg. γεώργιον husbandry
Θεοῦ n. gen. masc. sg. θεός God, god
οἰκοδομή n. nom. fem. sg. οἰκοδομή building, edifying, edification
10 Κατὰ prep. κατά (+gen) against, by, throughout, down, (+acc) according to, after, with
τὴν art. acc. fem. sg. ὁ ἡ τό the, this, that, he, she, it
χάριν n. acc. fem. sg. χάρις grace, thank, favour, pleasure
τοῦ art. gen. masc. sg. ὁ ἡ τό the, this, that, he, she, it
Θεοῦ n. gen. masc. sg. θεός God, god
τὴν art. acc. fem. sg. ὁ ἡ τό the, this, that, he, she, it
μοι pron. dat. 1p. sg. ἐγώ I
ὡς adv. ὡς as, when, as it were, how, about, like, as soon as, even as, while
σοφὸς adj. nom. masc. sg. σοφός wise, wiser
ἀρχιτέκτων n. nom. masc. sg. ἀρχιτέκτων masterbuilder
θεμέλιον n. acc. masc. sg. θεμέλιος foundation
ἄλλος adj. nom. masc. sg. ἄλλος other, another, some, one, more, otherwise
δὲ conj. δέ but, and, now, also, to the contrary, rather, then
ἕκαστος adj. nom. masc. sg. ἕκαστος every man, every, every one, any man, each
δὲ conj. δέ but, and, now, also, to the contrary, rather, then
πῶς adv. πῶς how, by what means, after what manner
11 θεμέλιον n. acc. masc. sg. θεμέλιος foundation
γὰρ conj. γάρ for, and, because, but, indeed
ἄλλον adj. acc. masc. sg. ἄλλος other, another, some, one, more, otherwise
οὐδεὶς num. nom. masc. sg. οὐδείς no man, nothing, no, none, neither, not, nought
παρὰ prep. παρά (+gen) of, from, (+dat) with, for, (+acc) beside, at, by, above, against

τὸν art. acc. masc. sg. ὁ ἡ τό the, this, that, he, she, it
ὅς relative pron. nom. masc. sg. ὅς ἥ ὅ who, which, what, that
Ἰησοῦς n. nom. masc. sg. Ἰησοῦς Jesus
ὁ art. nom. masc. sg. ὁ ἡ τό the, this, that, he, she, it
Χριστός n. nom. masc. sg. Χριστός Christ
12 εἰ conj. εἰ if, whether, that, though, forasmuch
δέ conj. δέ but, and, now, also, to the contrary, rather, then
τις indefinite pron. nom. masc. sg. τὶς certain, some, any man, one, any thing
ἐπὶ prep. ἐπί (+gen) on, in, upon, (+dat) in, at, for, upon, (+acc) on, upon, unto, to, against
τὸν art. acc. masc. sg. ὁ ἡ τό the, this, that, he, she, it
θεμέλιον n. acc. masc. sg. θεμέλιος foundation
τοῦτον demo. pron. acc. masc. sg. οὗτος αὕτη τοῦτο this, the same, this same, he, she, it
χρυσόν n. acc. masc. sg. χρυσός gold
ἄργυρον n. acc. masc. sg. ἄργυρος silver
λίθους n. acc. masc. pl. λίθος stone
τιμίους adj. acc. masc. pl. τίμιος precious, dear, has in reputation, honourable
ξύλα n. acc. neut. pl. ξύλον tree, stave, wood, the stocks
χόρτον n. acc. masc. sg. χόρτος grass, blade, hay
καλάμην n. acc. fem. sg. καλάμη stubble
13 ἑκάστου adj. gen. masc. sg. ἕκαστος every man, every, every one, any man, each
τὸ art. nom. neut. sg. ὁ ἡ τό the, this, that, he, she, it
ἔργον n. nom. neut. sg. ἔργον work, deed, doing labour
φανερὸν adj. nom. neut. sg. φανερός manifest, abroad, open, known, outward, appear
ἡ art. nom. fem. sg. ὁ ἡ τό the, this, that, he, she, it
γὰρ conj. γάρ for, and, because, but, indeed
ἡμέρα n. nom. fem. sg. ἡμέρα day, time, year, while, age, day time
ὅτι conj. ὅτι that, for, because, how that, how, because that, for that, though
ἐν prep. ἐν (+dat) in, by, with, among, at, on, through, to, within, into, of, for
πυρὶ n. dat. neut. sg. πῦρ fire, fiery
καὶ conj. καί and, even, also, but
ἑκάστου adj. gen. masc. sg. ἕκαστος every man, every, every one, any man, each
τὸ art. nom. neut. sg. ὁ ἡ τό the, this, that, he, she, it
ἔργον n. nom. neut. sg. ἔργον work, deed, doing labour
ὁποῖόν adj. nom. neut. sg. ὁποῖος what manner of, as, of what sort, whatsoever
τὸ art. nom. neut. sg. ὁ ἡ τό the, this, that, he, she, it
πῦρ n. nom. neut. sg. πῦρ fire, fiery
14 εἴ conj. εἰ if, whether, that, though, forasmuch
τινος indefinite pron. gen. masc. sg. τὶς certain, some, any man, one, any thing
τὸ art. nom. neut. sg. ὁ ἡ τό the, this, that, he, she, it
ἔργον n. nom. neut. sg. ἔργον work, deed, doing labour
ὃ relative pron. acc. neut. sg. ὅς ἥ ὅ who, which, what, that
μισθὸν n. acc. masc. sg. μισθός reward, hire, wage
15 εἴ conj. εἰ if, whether, that, though, forasmuch
τινος indefinite pron. gen. masc. sg. τὶς certain, some, any man, one, any thing
τὸ art. nom. neut. sg. ὁ ἡ τό the, this, that, he, she, it
ἔργον n. nom. neut. sg. ἔργον work, deed, doing labour
αὐτὸς pron. nom. masc. 3p. sg. αὐτός ἡ ὁ self, of oneself, even, very, the same, he, she, it
δὲ conj. δέ but, and, now, also, to the contrary, rather, then
οὕτω adv. οὕτω οὕτως so, even so, thus, on this wise, likewise, after this manner
δὲ conj. δέ but, and, now, also, to the contrary, rather, then
ὡς adv. ὡς as, when, as it were, how, about, like, as soon as, even as, while
διὰ prep. διά (+gen) by, through, with, in, of, (+acc) for, because of, for a cause
πυρός n. gen. neut. sg. πῦρ fire, fiery
16 Οὐκ particle of negation. οὐ οὐκ οὐχ not, no, neither, none, nay, nor, never, nothing
ὅτι conj. ὅτι that, for, because, how that, how, because that, for that, though

ναὸς n. nom. masc. sg. ναός temple, shrine
Θεοῦ n. gen. masc. sg. θεός God, god
καὶ conj. καί and, even, also, but
τὸ art. nom. neut. sg. ὁ ἡ τό the, this, that, he, she, it
Πνεῦμα n. nom. neut. sg. πνεῦμα spirit, Spirit, Ghost, ghost, life. of the spirit, wind
τοῦ art. gen. masc. sg. ὁ ἡ τό the, this, that, he, she, it
Θεοῦ n. gen. masc. sg. θεός God, god
ἐν prep. ἐν (+dat) in, by, with, among, at, on, through, to, within, into, of, for
ὑμῖν pron. dat. 2p. pl. σύ thou, you
17 εἴ conj. εἰ if, whether, that, though, forasmuch
τις indefinite pron. nom. masc. sg. τὶς certain, some, any man, one, any thing
τὸν art. acc. masc. sg. ὁ ἡ τό the, this, that, he, she, it
ναὸν n. acc. masc. sg. ναός temple, shrine
τοῦ art. gen. masc. sg. ὁ ἡ τό the, this, that, he, she, it
Θεοῦ n. gen. masc. sg. θεός God, god
τοῦτον demo. pron. acc. masc. sg. οὗτος αὕτη τοῦτο this, the same, this same, he, she, it
ὁ art. nom. masc. sg. ὁ ἡ τό the, this, that, he, she, it
Θεός n. nom. masc. sg. θεός God, god
ὁ art. nom. masc. sg. ὁ ἡ τό the, this, that, he, she, it
γὰρ conj. γάρ for, and, because, but, indeed
ναὸς n. nom. masc. sg. ναός temple, shrine
τοῦ art. gen. masc. sg. ὁ ἡ τό the, this, that, he, she, it
Θεοῦ n. gen. masc. sg. θεός God, god
ἅγιός adj. nom. masc. sg. ἅγιος Holy, holy, saint, Holy One, holy thing, most holy
οἵτινες relative pron. nom. masc. pl. ὅστις which, who, whosoever, that, whatsoever
ὑμεῖς pron. nom. 2p. pl. σύ thou, you
18 Μηδεὶς num. nom. masc. sg. μηδείς μηδεμία μηδέν no man, nothing, no, none, not at all
ἑαυτὸν reflexive pron. acc. masc. 3p. sg. ἑαυτοῦ himself, herself, itself, yourself, ourselves
εἴ conj. εἰ if, whether, that, though, forasmuch
τις indefinite pron. nom. masc. sg. τὶς certain, some, any man, one, any thing
σοφὸς adj. nom. masc. sg. σοφός wise, wiser
ἐν prep. ἐν (+dat) in, by, with, among, at, on, through, to, within, into, of, for
ὑμῖν pron. dat. 2p. pl. σύ thou, you
ἐν prep. ἐν (+dat) in, by, with, among, at, on, through, to, within, into, of, for
τῷ art. dat. masc. sg. ὁ ἡ τό the, this, that, he, she, it
αἰῶνι n. dat. masc. sg. αἰών ever, ever and ever, evermore, age, eternal, world
τούτῳ demo. pron. dat. masc. sg. οὗτος αὕτη τοῦτο this, the same, this same, he, she, it
μωρὸς adj. nom. masc. sg. μωρός fool, foolish
ἵνα conj. ἵνα that, to, lest, for to, so that, albeit, because, for, so as
σοφὸς adj. nom. masc. sg. σοφός wise, wiser
19 ἡ art. nom. fem. sg. ὁ ἡ τό the, this, that, he, she, it
γὰρ conj. γάρ for, and, because, but, indeed
σοφία n. nom. fem. sg. σοφία wisdom
τοῦ art. gen. masc. sg. ὁ ἡ τό the, this, that, he, she, it
κόσμου n. gen. masc. sg. κόσμος world, adorning
τούτου demo. pron. gen. masc. sg. οὗτος αὕτη τοῦτο this, the same, this same, he, she, it
μωρία n. nom. fem. sg. μωρία foolishness
παρὰ prep. παρά (+gen) of, from, (+dat) with, for, (+acc) beside, at, by, above, against
τῷ art. dat. masc. sg. ὁ ἡ τό the, this, that, he, she, it
Θεῷ n. dat. masc. sg. θεός God, god
γὰρ conj. γάρ for, and, because, but, indeed
Ὁ art. nom. masc. sg. ὁ ἡ τό the, this, that, he, she, it
τοὺς art. acc. masc. pl. ὁ ἡ τό the, this, that, he, she, it
σοφοὺς adj. acc. masc. pl. σοφός wise, wiser
ἐν prep. ἐν (+dat) in, by, with, among, at, on, through, to, within, into, of, for

τῇ art. dat. fem. sg. ὁ ἡ τό the, this, that, he, she, it
πανουργίᾳ n. dat. fem. sg. πανουργία craftiness, cunning craftiness, subtilty
αὐτῶν pron. gen. masc. 3p. pl. αὐτός ή ό self, of oneself, even, very, the same, he, she, it
20 καὶ conj. καί and, even, also, but
πάλιν adv. πάλιν again
Κύριος n. nom. masc. sg. κύριος Lord, lord, master, sir, LORD, God, Master, owner
τοὺς art. acc. masc. pl. ὁ ἡ τό the, this, that, he, she, it
διαλογισμοὺς n. acc. masc. pl. διαλογισμός thought, reasoning, imagination, disputing
τῶν art. gen. masc. pl. ὁ ἡ τό the, this, that, he, she, it
σοφῶν adj. gen. masc. pl. σοφός wise, wiser
ὅτι conj. ὅτι that, for, because, how that, how, because that, for that, though
μάταιοι adj. nom. masc. pl. μάταιος vanity, vain
21 ὥστε conj. ὥστε so that, wherefore, insomuch that, therefore, that, so then
μηδεὶς num. nom. masc. sg. μηδείς μηδεμία μηδέν no man, nothing, no, none, not at all
ἐν prep. ἐν (+dat) in, by, with, among, at, on, through, to, within, into, of, for
ἀνθρώποις n. dat. masc. pl. ἄνθρωπος man, human being, person, one, certain
πάντα adj. nom. neut. pl. πᾶς πᾶσα πᾶν all, every, whosoever, every one, no, whole, any
γὰρ conj. γάρ for, and, because, but, indeed
ὑμῶν pron. gen. 2p. pl. σύ thou, you
22 εἴτε conj. εἴτε whether
Παῦλος n. nom. masc. sg. Παῦλος Paul, Paulus
εἴτε conj. εἴτε whether
'Απολλῶς n. nom. masc. sg. 'Απολλώς Apollos
εἴτε conj. εἴτε whether
Κηφᾶς n. nom. masc. sg. Κηφᾶς Cephas
εἴτε conj. εἴτε whether
κόσμος n. nom. masc. sg. κόσμος world, adorning
εἴτε conj. εἴτε whether
ζωὴ n. nom. fem. sg. ζωή life, lifetime
εἴτε conj. εἴτε whether
θάνατος n. nom. masc. sg. θάνατος death
εἴτε conj. εἴτε whether
εἴτε conj. εἴτε whether
πάντα adj. nom. neut. pl. πᾶς πᾶσα πᾶν all, every, whosoever, every one, no, whole, any
ὑμῶν pron. gen. 2p. pl. σύ thou, you
23 ὑμεῖς pron. nom. 2p. pl. σύ thou, you
δὲ conj. δέ but, and, now, also, to the contrary, rather, then
Χριστοῦ n. gen. masc. sg. Χριστός Christ
Χριστὸς n. nom. masc. sg. Χριστός Christ
δὲ conj. δέ but, and, now, also, to the contrary, rather, then
Θεοῦ n. gen. masc. sg. θεός God, god

4

1 Οὕτως adv. οὕτω οὕτως so, even so, thus, on this wise, likewise, after this manner
ἡμᾶς pron. acc. 1p. pl. ἐγώ I
ἄνθρωπος n. nom. masc. sg. ἄνθρωπος man, human being, person, one, certain
ὡς adv. ὡς as, when, as it were, how, about, like, as soon as, even as, while
ὑπηρέτας n. acc. masc. pl. ὑπηρέτης officer, minister, servant
Χριστοῦ n. gen. masc. sg. Χριστός Christ
καὶ conj. καί and, even, also, but
οἰκονόμους n. acc. masc. pl. οἰκονόμος steward, chamberlain, governor
μυστηρίων n. gen. neut. pl. μυστήριον mystery
Θεοῦ n. gen. masc. sg. θεός God, god
2 ὃ relative pron. acc. neut. sg. ὅς ἥ ὅ who, which, what, that

δὲ conj. δέ but, and, now, also, to the contrary, rather, then
λοιπὸν adv. λοιπόν finally, henceforth, now, besides, furthermore, moreover, then
ἐν prep. ἐν (+dat) in, by, with, among, at, on, through, to, within, into, of, for
τοῖς art. dat. masc. pl. ὁ ἡ τό the, this, that, he, she, it
οἰκονόμοις n. dat. masc. pl. οἰκονόμος steward, chamberlain, governor
ἵνα conj. ἵνα that, to, lest, for to, so that, albeit, because, for, so as
πιστός adj. nom. masc. sg. πιστός faithful, believing, true, sure
τις indefinite pron. nom. masc. sg. τὶς certain, some, any man, one, any thing
3 ἐμοὶ pron. dat. 1p. sg. ἐγώ I
δὲ conj. δέ but, and, now, also, to the contrary, rather, then
εἰς prep. εἰς (+acc) into, to, unto, for, in, on, toward, against, upon, at, among
ἐλάχιστόν superl. adj. acc. neut. sg. ἐλάχιστος least, very small, smallest, very little
ἵνα conj. ἵνα that, to, lest, for to, so that, albeit, because, for, so as
ὑφ' prep. ὑπό (+gen) of, by, with, from, among, (+acc) under
ὑμῶν pron. gen. 2p. pl. σύ thou, you
ἢ particle. ἤ or, than, either, nor, or else, and, rather than
ὑπὸ prep. ὑπό (+gen) of, by, with, from, among, (+acc) under
ἀνθρωπίνης adj. gen. fem. sg. ἀνθρώπινος man, after the manner of men man
ἡμέρας n. gen. fem. sg. ἡμέρα day, time, year, while, age, day time
ἀλλ' conj. ἀλλά but, yea, yet, nevertheless, howbeit, nay, therefore
οὐδὲ adv. οὐδέ neither, nor, not, no, not even, never, not yet
ἐμαυτὸν pron. acc. masc. 1p. sg. ἐμαυτοῦ myself, me
4 οὐδὲν num. acc. neut. sg. οὐδείς no man, nothing, no, none, neither, not, nought
γὰρ conj. γάρ for, and, because, but, indeed
ἐμαυτῷ pron. dat. masc. 1p. sg. ἐμαυτοῦ myself, me
ἀλλ' conj. ἀλλά but, yea, yet, nevertheless, howbeit, nay, therefore
οὐκ particle of negation. οὐ οὐκ οὐχ not, no, neither, none, nay, nor, never, nothing
ἐν prep. ἐν (+dat) in, by, with, among, at, on, through, to, within, into, of, for
τούτῳ demo. pron. dat. neut. sg. οὗτος αὕτη τοῦτο this, the same, this same, he, she, it
ὁ art. nom. masc. sg. ὁ ἡ τό the, this, that, he, she, it
δὲ conj. δέ but, and, now, also, to the contrary, rather, then
με pron. acc. 1p. sg. ἐγώ I
Κύριός n. nom. masc. sg. κύριος Lord, lord, master, sir, LORD, God, Master, owner
5 ὥστε conj. ὥστε so that, wherefore, insomuch that, therefore, that, so then
μὴ particle of negation. μή not, no, lest, neither, none, nothing, nor, never, without
πρὸ prep. πρό (+gen) before, above
καιροῦ n. gen. masc. sg. καιρός time, season, due time, opportunity
τι indefinite pron. acc. neut. sg. τὶς certain, some, any man, one, any thing
ἕως conj. ἕως till, until, unto, until when, while, as far as, even, until now
ἂν particle. ἄν Indicating contingency. No English translation.
ὁ art. nom. masc. sg. ὁ ἡ τό the, this, that, he, she, it
Κύριος n. nom. masc. sg. κύριος Lord, lord, master, sir, LORD, God, Master, owner
ὃς relative pron. nom. masc. sg. ὅς ἥ ὅ who, which, what, that
καὶ conj. καί and, even, also, but
τὰ art. acc. neut. pl. ὁ ἡ τό the, this, that, he, she, it
κρυπτὰ adj. acc. neut. pl. κρυπτός secret, hid, hidden, inwardly
τοῦ art. gen. neut. sg. ὁ ἡ τό the, this, that, he, she, it
σκότους n. gen. neut. sg. σκότος darkness
καὶ conj. καί and, even, also, but
τὰς art. acc. fem. pl. ὁ ἡ τό the, this, that, he, she, it
βουλὰς n. acc. fem. pl. βουλή counsel, advise, will
τῶν art. gen. fem. pl. ὁ ἡ τό the, this, that, he, she, it
καρδιῶν n. gen. fem. pl. καρδία heart
καὶ conj. καί and, even, also, but
τότε adv. τότε then, that time

ὁ art. nom. masc. sg. ὁ ἡ τό the, this, that, he, she, it
ἔπαινος n. nom. masc. sg. ἔπαινος praise
ἑκάστῳ adj. dat. masc. sg. ἕκαστος every man, every, every one, any man, each
ἀπὸ prep. ἀπό (+gen) from, of, out of, since, for, off, at, by, in, on
τοῦ art. gen. masc. sg. ὁ ἡ τό the, this, that, he, she, it
Θεοῦ n. gen. masc. sg. θεός God, god
6 Ταῦτα demo. pron. acc. neut. pl. οὗτος αὕτη τοῦτο this, the same, this same, he, she, it
δέ conj. δέ but, and, now, also, to the contrary, rather, then
ἀδελφοί n. voc. masc. pl. ἀδελφός brother
εἰς prep. εἰς (+acc) into, to, unto, for, in, on, toward, against, upon, at, among
ἐμαυτὸν pron. acc. masc. 1p. sg. ἐμαυτοῦ myself, me
καὶ conj. καί and, even, also, but
Ἀπολλῶ n. acc. masc. sg. Ἀπολλώς Apollos
δι' prep. διά (+gen) by, through, with, in, of, (+acc) for, because of, for a cause
ὑμᾶς pron. acc. 2p. pl. σύ thou, you
ἵνα conj. ἵνα that, to, lest, for to, so that, albeit, because, for, so as
ἐν prep. ἐν (+dat) in, by, with, among, at, on, through, to, within, into, of, for
ἡμῖν pron. dat. 1p. pl. ἐγώ I
τὸ art. acc. neut. sg. ὁ ἡ τό the, this, that, he, she, it
μὴ particle of negation. μή not, no, lest, neither, none, nothing, nor, never, without
ὑπὲρ prep. ὑπέρ (+gen) for, of, for the sake of, (+acc) above, more than
ὅ relative pron. acc. neut. sg. ὅς ἥ ὅ who, which, what, that
ἵνα conj. ἵνα that, to, lest, for to, so that, albeit, because, for, so as
μὴ particle of negation. μή not, no, lest, neither, none, nothing, nor, never, without
εἷς num. nom. masc. sg. εἷς or ἕν one, other, some, any, only, a certain
ὑπὲρ prep. ὑπέρ (+gen) for, of, for the sake of, (+acc) above, more than
τοῦ art. gen. masc. sg. ὁ ἡ τό the, this, that, he, she, it
ἑνὸς num. gen. masc. sg. εἷς or ἕν one, other, some, any, only, a certain
κατὰ prep. κατά (+gen) against, by, throughout, down, (+acc) according to, after, with
τοῦ art. gen. masc. sg. ὁ ἡ τό the, this, that, he, she, it
ἑτέρου adj. gen. masc. sg. ἕτερος another, other, else, strange
7 τίς interrog. pron. nom. masc. sg. τίς what, who, why, where, which, how
γάρ conj. γάρ for, and, because, but, indeed
σε pron. acc. 2p. sg. σύ thou, you
τί interrog. pron. acc. neut. sg. τίς what, who, why, where, which, how
δὲ conj. δέ but, and, now, also, to the contrary, rather, then
ὃ relative pron. acc. neut. sg. ὅς ἥ ὅ who, which, what, that
οὐκ particle of negation. οὐ οὐκ οὐχ not, no, neither, none, nay, nor, never, nothing
εἰ conj. εἰ if, whether, that, though, forasmuch
δὲ conj. δέ but, and, now, also, to the contrary, rather, then
καὶ conj. καί and, even, also, but
τί interrog. pron. acc. neut. sg. τίς what, who, why, where, which, how
ὡς adv. ὡς as, when, as it were, how, about, like, as soon as, even as, while
μὴ particle of negation. μή not, no, lest, neither, none, nothing, nor, never, without
8 ἤδη adv. ἤδη now, already, yet, by this time, even now, now already
ἤδη adv. ἤδη now, already, yet, by this time, even now, now already
χωρὶς prep. χωρίς (+gen) without, beside. (adv.) by itself, apart, separately
ἡμῶν pron. gen. 1p. pl. ἐγώ I
καὶ conj. καί and, even, also, but
ὄφελόν interj. ὄφελον O that! Would that!
γε particle. γέ yet, and beside, at least, doubtless
ἵνα conj. ἵνα that, to, lest, for to, so that, albeit, because, for, so as
καὶ conj. καί and, even, also, but
ἡμεῖς pron. nom. 1p. pl. ἐγώ I
ὑμῖν pron. dat. 2p. pl. σύ thou, you

9 γάρ conj. γάρ for, and, because, but, indeed
ὅτι conj. ὅτι that, for, because, how that, how, because that, for that, though
ὁ art. nom. masc. sg. ὁ ἡ τό the, this, that, he, she, it
Θεὸς n. nom. masc. sg. θεός God, god
ἡμᾶς pron. acc. 1p. pl. ἐγώ I
τοὺς art. acc. masc. pl. ὁ ἡ τό the, this, that, he, she, it
ἀποστόλους n. acc. masc. pl. ἀπόστολος apostle, messenger, he that is sent
ἐσχάτους adj. acc. masc. pl. ἔσχατος last, lowest, uttermost, uttermost part
ὡς adv. ὡς as, when, as it were, how, about, like, as soon as, even as, while
ἐπιθανατίους adj. acc. masc. pl. ἐπιθανάτιος appointed to death
ὅτι conj. ὅτι that, for, because, how that, how, because that, for that, though
θέατρον n. nom. neut. sg. θέατρον theatre, spectacle
τῷ art. dat. masc. sg. ὁ ἡ τό the, this, that, he, she, it
κόσμῳ n. dat. masc. sg. κόσμος world, adorning
καὶ conj. καί and, even, also, but
ἀγγέλοις n. dat. masc. pl. ἄγγελος angel, messenger
καὶ conj. καί and, even, also, but
ἀνθρώποις n. dat. masc. pl. ἄνθρωπος man, human being, person, one, certain
10 ἡμεῖς pron. nom. 1p. pl. ἐγώ I
μωροὶ adj. nom. masc. pl. μωρός fool, foolish
διὰ prep. διά (+gen) by, through, with, in, of, (+acc) for, because of, for a cause
Χριστόν n. acc. masc. sg. Χριστός Christ
ὑμεῖς pron. nom. 2p. pl. σύ thou, you
δὲ conj. δέ but, and, now, also, to the contrary, rather, then
φρόνιμοι adj. nom. masc. pl. φρόνιμος wise, wiser
ἐν prep. ἐν (+dat) in, by, with, among, at, on, through, to, within, into, of, for
Χριστῷ n. dat. masc. sg. Χριστός Christ
ἡμεῖς pron. nom. 1p. pl. ἐγώ I
ἀσθενεῖς adj. nom. masc. pl. ἀσθενής weak, sick, impotent, more feeble
ὑμεῖς pron. nom. 2p. pl. σύ thou, you
δὲ conj. δέ but, and, now, also, to the contrary, rather, then
ἰσχυροί adj. nom. masc. pl. ἰσχυρός mighty, strong, mightier, stronger
ὑμεῖς pron. nom. 2p. pl. σύ thou, you
ἔνδοξοι adj. nom. masc. pl. ἔνδοξος glorious, gorgeously, honourably
ἡμεῖς pron. nom. 1p. pl. ἐγώ I
δὲ conj. δέ but, and, now, also, to the contrary, rather, then
ἄτιμοι adj. nom. masc. pl. ἄτιμος without honour, despised, less honourable
11 ἄχρι prep. ἄχρι or ἄχρις (+gen) until, unto, till, even to, as far as, while, into
τῆς art. gen. fem. sg. ὁ ἡ τό the, this, that, he, she, it
ἄρτι adv. ἄρτι now, hence, here, hither, even now, present
ὥρας n. gen. fem. sg. ὥρα hour, time, season
καὶ conj. καί and, even, also, but
καὶ conj. καί and, even, also, but
καὶ conj. καί and, even, also, but
καὶ conj. καί and, even, also, but
καὶ conj. καί and, even, also, but
12 καὶ conj. καί and, even, also, but
ταῖς art. dat. fem. pl. ὁ ἡ τό the, this, that, he, she, it
ἰδίαις adj. dat. fem. pl. ἴδιος one's own, one's, privately
χερσί n. dat. fem. pl. χείρ hand
13 ὡς adv. ὡς as, when, as it were, how, about, like, as soon as, even as, while
περικαθάρματα n. nom. neut. pl. περικάθαρμα filth
τοῦ art. gen. masc. sg. ὁ ἡ τό the, this, that, he, she, it
κόσμου n. gen. masc. sg. κόσμος world, adorning
πάντων adj. gen. neut. pl. πᾶς πᾶσα πᾶν all, every, whosoever, every one, no, whole, any

περίψημα n. nom. neut. sg. περίψημα offscouring
ἕως conj. ἕως till, until, unto, until when, while, as far as, even, until now
ἄρτι adv. ἄρτι now, hence, here, hither, even now, present
14 Οὐκ particle of negation. οὐ οὐκ οὐχ not, no, neither, none, nay, nor, never, nothing
ὑμᾶς pron. acc. 2p. pl. σύ thou, you
ταῦτα demo. pron. acc. neut. pl. οὗτος αὕτη τοῦτο this, the same, this same, he, she, it
ἀλλ' conj. ἀλλά but, yea, yet, nevertheless, howbeit, nay, therefore
ὡς adv. ὡς as, when, as it were, how, about, like, as soon as, even as, while
τέκνα n. acc. neut. pl. τέκνον child, son, daughter
μου pron. gen. 1p. sg. ἐγώ I
ἀγαπητὰ adj. acc. neut. pl. ἀγαπητός beloved, dearly beloved, dear, wellbeloved
15 ἐὰν conj. ἐάν if, soever, except, though, and if, but, whether, if so, so
γὰρ conj. γάρ for, and, because, but, indeed
μυρίους adj. acc. masc. pl. μύριοι ten thousand
παιδαγωγοὺς n. acc. masc. pl. παιδαγωγός schoolmaster, instructor
ἐν prep. ἐν (+dat) in, by, with, among, at, on, through, to, within, into, of, for
Χριστῷ n. dat. masc. sg. Χριστός Christ
ἀλλ' conj. ἀλλά but, yea, yet, nevertheless, howbeit, nay, therefore
οὐ particle of negation. οὐ οὐκ οὐχ not, no, neither, none, nay, nor, never, nothing
πολλοὺς adj. acc. masc. pl. πολύς many, great, much, long, abundant
πατέρας n. acc. masc. pl. πατήρ Father, father, parent
ἐν prep. ἐν (+dat) in, by, with, among, at, on, through, to, within, into, of, for
γὰρ conj. γάρ for, and, because, but, indeed
Χριστῷ n. dat. masc. sg. Χριστός Christ
Ἰησοῦ n. dat. masc. sg. Ἰησοῦς Jesus
διὰ prep. διά (+gen) by, through, with, in, of, (+acc) for, because of, for a cause
τοῦ art. gen. neut. sg. ὁ ἡ τό the, this, that, he, she, it
εὐαγγελίου n. gen. neut. sg. εὐαγγέλιον gospel
ἐγὼ pron. nom. 1p. sg. ἐγώ I
ὑμᾶς pron. acc. 2p. pl. σύ thou, you
16 οὖν conj. οὖν therefore, then, so, and, now, wherefore
ὑμᾶς pron. acc. 2p. pl. σύ thou, you
μιμηταί n. nom. masc. pl. μιμητής follower
μου pron. gen. 1p. sg. ἐγώ I
17 διὰ prep. διά (+gen) by, through, with, in, of, (+acc) for, because of, for a cause
τοῦτο demo. pron. acc. neut. sg. οὗτος αὕτη τοῦτο this, the same, this same, he, she, it
ὑμῖν pron. dat. 2p. pl. σύ thou, you
Τιμόθεον n. acc. masc. sg. Τιμόθεος Timotheus, Timothy
ὅς relative pron. nom. masc. sg. ὅς ἥ ὅ who, which, what, that
τέκνον n. nom. neut. sg. τέκνον child, son, daughter
μου pron. gen. 1p. sg. ἐγώ I
ἀγαπητὸν adj. nom. neut. sg. ἀγαπητός beloved, dearly beloved, dear, wellbeloved
καὶ conj. καί and, even, also, but
πιστὸν adj. nom. neut. sg. πιστός faithful, believing, true, sure
ἐν prep. ἐν (+dat) in, by, with, among, at, on, through, to, within, into, of, for
Κυρίῳ n. dat. masc. sg. κύριος Lord, lord, master, sir, LORD, God, Master, owner
ὃς relative pron. nom. masc. sg. ὅς ἥ ὅ who, which, what, that
ὑμᾶς pron. acc. 2p. pl. σύ thou, you
τὰς art. acc. fem. pl. ὁ ἡ τό the, this, that, he, she, it
ὁδούς n. acc. fem. pl. ὁδός way, journey, highway
Χριστῷ n. dat. masc. sg. Χριστός Christ
μου pron. gen. 1p. sg. ἐγώ I
τὰς art. acc. fem. pl. ὁ ἡ τό the, this, that, he, she, it
ἐν prep. ἐν (+dat) in, by, with, among, at, on, through, to, within, into, of, for
Χριστῷ n. dat. masc. sg. Χριστός Christ

καθὼς adv. καθώς as, even as, according as, according to
πανταχοῦ adv. πανταχοῦ every where, in all places
ἐν prep. ἐν (+dat) in, by, with, among, at, on, through, to, within, into, of, for
πάσῃ adj. dat. fem. sg. πᾶς πᾶσα πᾶν all, every, whosoever, every one, no, whole, any
ἐκκλησίᾳ n. dat. fem. sg. ἐκκλησία church, assembly
18 ὡς adv. ὡς as, when, as it were, how, about, like, as soon as, even as, while
μὴ particle of negation. μή not, no, lest, neither, none, nothing, nor, never, without
δέ conj. δέ but, and, now, also, to the contrary, rather, then
μου pron. gen. 1p. sg. ἐγώ I
πρὸς prep. πρός (+gen) for, (+dat) at, (+acc) unto, to, with, for, against
ὑμᾶς pron. acc. 2p. pl. σύ thou, you
τινες indefinite pron. nom. masc. pl. τὶς certain, some, any man, one, any thing
19 δὲ conj. δέ but, and, now, also, to the contrary, rather, then
ταχέως adv. ταχέως sortly, quickly, soon, hastily, suddenly
πρὸς prep. πρός (+gen) for, (+dat) at, (+acc) unto, to, with, for, against
ὑμᾶς pron. acc. 2p. pl. σύ thou, you
ἐὰν conj. ἐάν if, soever, except, though, and if, but, whether, if so, so
ὁ art. nom. masc. sg. ὁ ἡ τό the, this, that, he, she, it
Κύριος n. nom. masc. sg. κύριος Lord, lord, master, sir, LORD, God, Master, owner
καὶ conj. καί and, even, also, but
οὐ particle of negation. οὐ οὐκ οὐχ not, no, neither, none, nay, nor, never, nothing
τὸν art. acc. masc. sg. ὁ ἡ τό the, this, that, he, she, it
λόγον n. acc. masc. sg. λόγος word, saying, account, speech, thing, matter
τῶν art. gen. masc. pl. ὁ ἡ τό the, this, that, he, she, it
ἀλλὰ conj. ἀλλά but, yea, yet, nevertheless, howbeit, nay, therefore
τὴν art. acc. fem. sg. ὁ ἡ τό the, this, that, he, she, it
δύναμιν n. acc. fem. sg. δύναμις power, mighty work, miracle, strength, might
20 οὐ particle of negation. οὐ οὐκ οὐχ not, no, neither, none, nay, nor, never, nothing
γὰρ conj. γάρ for, and, because, but, indeed
ἐν prep. ἐν (+dat) in, by, with, among, at, on, through, to, within, into, of, for
λόγῳ n. dat. masc. sg. λόγος word, saying, account, speech, thing, matter
ἡ art. nom. fem. sg. ὁ ἡ τό the, this, that, he, she, it
βασιλεία n. nom. fem. sg. βασιλεία kingdom, reign
τοῦ art. gen. masc. sg. ὁ ἡ τό the, this, that, he, she, it
Θεοῦ n. gen. masc. sg. θεός God, god
ἀλλ' conj. ἀλλά but, yea, yet, nevertheless, howbeit, nay, therefore
ἐν prep. ἐν (+dat) in, by, with, among, at, on, through, to, within, into, of, for
δυνάμει n. dat. fem. sg. δύναμις power, mighty work, miracle, strength, might
21 τί interrog. pron. acc. neut. sg. τίς what, who, why, where, which, how
ἐν prep. ἐν (+dat) in, by, with, among, at, on, through, to, within, into, of, for
ῥάβδῳ n. dat. fem. sg. ῥάβδος rod, sceptre, stave, staff
πρὸς prep. πρός (+gen) for, (+dat) at, (+acc) unto, to, with, for, against
ὑμᾶς pron. acc. 2p. pl. σύ thou, you
ἢ particle. ἤ or, than, either, nor, or else, and, rather than
ἐν prep. ἐν (+dat) in, by, with, among, at, on, through, to, within, into, of, for
ἀγάπῃ n. dat. fem. sg. ἀγάπη love, charity, feast of charity
πνεύματί n. dat. neut. sg. πνεῦμα spirit, Spirit, Ghost, ghost, life. of the spirit, wind
τε conj. τέ and, both, also
πρᾳότητος n. gen. fem. sg. πρᾳότης meekness

5

1 Ὅλως adv. ὅλως at all, commonly, utterly
ἐν prep. ἐν (+dat) in, by, with, among, at, on, through, to, within, into, of, for
ὑμῖν pron. dat. 2p. pl. σύ thou, you

πορνεία n. nom. fem. sg. πορνεία fornication
καὶ conj. καί and, even, also, but
τοιαύτη demo. pron. nom. fem. sg. τοιοῦτος such, like
πορνεία n. nom. fem. sg. πορνεία fornication
ἥτις relative pron. nom. fem. sg. ὅστις which, who, whosoever, that, whatsoever
οὐδὲ adv. οὐδέ neither, nor, not, no, not even, never, not yet
ἐν prep. ἐν (+dat) in, by, with, among, at, on, through, to, within, into, of, for
τοῖς art. dat. neut. pl. ὁ ἡ τό the, this, that, he, she, it
ἔθνεσιν n. dat. neut. pl. ἔθνος Gentile, nation, heathen, people
ὥστε conj. ὥστε so that, wherefore, insomuch that, therefore, that, so then
γυναῖκά n. acc. fem. sg. γυνή woman, wife
τινα indefinite pron. acc. masc. sg. τὶς certain, some, any man, one, any thing
τοῦ art. gen. masc. sg. ὁ ἡ τό the, this, that, he, she, it
πατρὸς n. gen. masc. sg. πατήρ Father, father, parent
2 καὶ conj. καί and, even, also, but
ὑμεῖς pron. nom. 2p. pl. σύ thou, you
καὶ conj. καί and, even, also, but
οὐχὶ adv. οὐχί not, nay
μᾶλλον adv. μᾶλλον rather, more, more and more, better, much, much the more
ἵνα conj. ἵνα that, to, lest, for to, so that, albeit, because, for, so as
ἐκ prep. ἐκ ἐξ (+gen) of, from, out of, by, on, with, in, among, through
μέσου adj. gen. neut. sg. μέσος midst, among, mid, between
ὑμῶν pron. gen. 2p. pl. σύ thou, you
ὁ art. nom. masc. sg. ὁ ἡ τό the, this, that, he, she, it
τὸ art. acc. neut. sg. ὁ ἡ τό the, this, that, he, she, it
ἔργον n. acc. neut. sg. ἔργον work, deed, doing labour
τοῦτο demo. pron. acc. neut. sg. οὗτος αὕτη τοῦτο this, the same, this same, he, she, it
3 ἐγὼ pron. nom. 1p. sg. ἐγώ I
μὲν conj. μέν indeed, verily, truly, even, so, some
γάρ conj. γάρ for, and, because, but, indeed
ὡς adv. ὡς as, when, as it were, how, about, like, as soon as, even as, while
τῷ art. dat. neut. sg. ὁ ἡ τό the, this, that, he, she, it
σώματι n. dat. neut. sg. σῶμα body, bodily, slave
δὲ conj. δέ but, and, now, also, to the contrary, rather, then
τῷ art. dat. neut. sg. ὁ ἡ τό the, this, that, he, she, it
πνεύματι n. dat. neut. sg. πνεῦμα spirit, Spirit, Ghost, ghost, life. of the spirit, wind
ἤδη adv. ἤδη now, already, yet, by this time, even now, now already
ὡς adv. ὡς as, when, as it were, how, about, like, as soon as, even as, while
τὸν art. acc. masc. sg. ὁ ἡ τό the, this, that, he, she, it
οὕτω adv. οὕτω οὕτως so, even so, thus, on this wise, likewise, after this manner
τοῦτο demo. pron. acc. neut. sg. οὗτος αὕτη τοῦτο this, the same, this same, he, she, it
4 ἐν prep. ἐν (+dat) in, by, with, among, at, on, through, to, within, into, of, for
τῷ art. dat. neut. sg. ὁ ἡ τό the, this, that, he, she, it
ὀνόματι n. dat. neut. sg. ὄνομα name, call, surname
τοῦ art. gen. masc. sg. ὁ ἡ τό the, this, that, he, she, it
Κυρίου n. gen. masc. sg. κύριος Lord, lord, master, sir, LORD, God, Master, owner
ἡμῶν pron. gen. 1p. pl. ἐγώ I
Ἰησοῦ n. gen. masc. sg. Ἰησοῦς Jesus
Χριστοῦ n. gen. masc. sg. Χριστός Christ
ὑμῶν pron. gen. 2p. pl. σύ thou, you
καὶ conj. καί and, even, also, but
τοῦ art. gen. neut. sg. ὁ ἡ τό the, this, that, he, she, it
ἐμοῦ poss. pron. gen. neut. 1p. sg. ἐμός my, mine, mine own, of me
πνεύματος n. gen. neut. sg. πνεῦμα spirit, Spirit, Ghost, ghost, life. of the spirit, wind
σὺν prep. σύν (+dat) with, beside

τῇ art. dat. fem. sg. ὁ ἡ τό the, this, that, he, she, it
δυνάμει n. dat. fem. sg. δύναμις power, mighty work, miracle, strength, might
τοῦ art. gen. masc. sg. ὁ ἡ τό the, this, that, he, she, it
Κυρίου n. gen. masc. sg. κύριος Lord, lord, master, sir, LORD, God, Master, owner
ἡμῶν pron. gen. 1p. pl. ἐγώ I
Ἰησοῦ n. gen. masc. sg. Ἰησοῦς Jesus
Χριστοῦ n. gen. masc. sg. Χριστός Christ
5 τὸν art. acc. masc. sg. ὁ ἡ τό the, this, that, he, she, it
τοιοῦτον demo. pron. acc. masc. sg. τοιοῦτος such, like
τῷ art. dat. masc. sg. ὁ ἡ τό the, this, that, he, she, it
Σατανᾷ n. dat. masc. sg. Σατανᾶς Satan
εἰς prep. εἰς (+acc) into, to, unto, for, in, on, toward, against, upon, at, among
ὄλεθρον n. acc. masc. sg. ὄλεθρος destruction
τῆς art. gen. fem. sg. ὁ ἡ τό the, this, that, he, she, it
σαρκός n. gen. fem. sg. σάρξ flesh, carnal
ἵνα conj. ἵνα that, to, lest, for to, so that, albeit, because, for, so as
τὸ art. nom. neut. sg. ὁ ἡ τό the, this, that, he, she, it
πνεῦμα n. nom. neut. sg. πνεῦμα spirit, Spirit, Ghost, ghost, life. of the spirit, wind
ἐν prep. ἐν (+dat) in, by, with, among, at, on, through, to, within, into, of, for
τῇ art. dat. fem. sg. ὁ ἡ τό the, this, that, he, she, it
ἡμέρᾳ n. dat. fem. sg. ἡμέρα day, time, year, while, age, day time
τοῦ art. gen. masc. sg. ὁ ἡ τό the, this, that, he, she, it
Κυρίου n. gen. masc. sg. κύριος Lord, lord, master, sir, LORD, God, Master, owner
Ἰησοῦ n. gen. masc. sg. Ἰησοῦς Jesus
6 οὐ particle of negation. οὐ οὐκ οὐχ not, no, neither, none, nay, nor, never, nothing
καλὸν adj. nom. neut. sg. καλός good, better, goodly, meet, honest, fair, well, worthy
τὸ art. nom. neut. sg. ὁ ἡ τό the, this, that, he, she, it
καύχημα n. nom. neut. sg. καύχημα whereof to glory, rejoicing, glorying, boasting
ὑμῶν pron. gen. 2p. pl. σύ thou, you
οὐκ particle of negation. οὐ οὐκ οὐχ not, no, neither, none, nay, nor, never, nothing
ὅτι conj. ὅτι that, for, because, how that, how, because that, for that, though
μικρὰ adj. nom. fem. sg. μικρός little, small, least, less
ζύμη n. nom. fem. sg. ζύμη leaven
ὅλον adj. acc. neut. sg. ὅλος all, whole, every whit, altogether
τὸ art. acc. neut. sg. ὁ ἡ τό the, this, that, he, she, it
φύραμα n. acc. neut. sg. φύραμα lump
7 οὖν conj. οὖν therefore, then, so, and, now, wherefore
τὴν art. acc. fem. sg. ὁ ἡ τό the, this, that, he, she, it
παλαιὰν adj. acc. fem. sg. παλαιός old
ζύμην n. acc. fem. sg. ζύμη leaven
ἵνα conj. ἵνα that, to, lest, for to, so that, albeit, because, for, so as
νέον adj. nom. neut. sg. νέος new
φύραμα n. nom. neut. sg. φύραμα lump
καθώς adv. καθώς as, even as, according as, according to
ἄζυμοι adj. nom. masc. pl. ἄζυμος unleavened bread, unleavened
καὶ conj. καί and, even, also, but
γὰρ conj. γάρ for, and, because, but, indeed
τὸ art. nom. neut. sg. ὁ ἡ τό the, this, that, he, she, it
πάσχα n. nom. neut. sg. πάσχα passover, Easter
ἡμῶν pron. gen. 1p. pl. ἐγώ I
ὑπὲρ prep. ὑπέρ (+gen) for, of, for the sake of, (+acc) above, more than
ἡμῶν pron. gen. 1p. pl. ἐγώ I
Χριστός n. nom. masc. sg. Χριστός Christ
8 ὥστε conj. ὥστε so that, wherefore, insomuch that, therefore, that, so then
μὴ particle of negation. μή not, no, lest, neither, none, nothing, nor, never, without

ἐν prep. ἐν (+dat) in, by, with, among, at, on, through, to, within, into, of, for
ζύμῃ n. dat. fem. sg. ζύμη leaven
παλαιᾷ adj. dat. fem. sg. παλαιός old
μηδὲ conj. δέ but, and, now, also, to the contrary, rather, then
ἐν prep. ἐν (+dat) in, by, with, among, at, on, through, to, within, into, of, for
ζύμῃ n. dat. fem. sg. ζύμη leaven
κακίας n. gen. fem. sg. κακία malice, maliciousness, evil, naughtiness, wickedness
καὶ conj. καί and, even, also, but
πονηρίας n. gen. fem. sg. πονηρία wickedness, iniquity
ἀλλ' conj. ἀλλά but, yea, yet, nevertheless, howbeit, nay, therefore
ἐν prep. ἐν (+dat) in, by, with, among, at, on, through, to, within, into, of, for
ἀζύμοις adj. dat. neut. pl. ἄζυμος unleavened bread, unleavened
εἰλικρινείας n. gen. fem. sg. εἰλικρίνεια sincerity
καὶ conj. καί and, even, also, but
ἀληθείας n. gen. fem. sg. ἀλήθεια truth, verity
9 ὑμῖν pron. dat. 2p. pl. σύ thou, you
ἐν prep. ἐν (+dat) in, by, with, among, at, on, through, to, within, into, of, for
τῇ art. dat. fem. sg. ὁ ἡ τό the, this, that, he, she, it
ἐπιστολῇ n. dat. fem. sg. ἐπιστολή letter, epistle
μὴ particle of negation. μή not, no, lest, neither, none, nothing, nor, never, without
πόρνοις n. dat. masc. pl. πόρνος fornicator
10 καὶ conj. καί and, even, also, but
οὐ particle of negation. οὐ οὐκ οὐχ not, no, neither, none, nay, nor, never, nothing
πάντως adv. πάντως surely, altogether, by all means, at all, needs, no doubt
τοῖς art. dat. masc. pl. ὁ ἡ τό the, this, that, he, she, it
πόρνοις n. dat. masc. pl. πόρνος fornicator
τοῦ art. gen. masc. sg. ὁ ἡ τό the, this, that, he, she, it
κόσμου n. gen. masc. sg. κόσμος world, adorning
τούτου demo. pron. gen. masc. sg. οὗτος αὕτη τοῦτο this, the same, this same, he, she, it
ἢ particle. ἤ or, than, either, nor, or else, and, rather than
τοῖς art. dat. masc. pl. ὁ ἡ τό the, this, that, he, she, it
πλεονέκταις n. dat. masc. pl. πλεονέκτης covetous
ἢ particle. ἤ or, than, either, nor, or else, and, rather than
ἅρπαξιν adj. dat. masc. pl. ἅρπαξ extortioner, ravening
ἢ particle. ἤ or, than, either, nor, or else, and, rather than
εἰδωλολάτραις n. dat. masc. pl. εἰδωλολάτρης idolater
ἐπεὶ conj. ἐπεί because, otherwise, seeing, else, for then, for as much as, for, since
ἄρα conj. ἄρα then, therefore, haply, wherefore, perhaps, manner, no doubt, truly
ἐκ prep. ἐκ ἐξ (+gen) of, from, out of, by, on, with, in, among, through
τοῦ art. gen. masc. sg. ὁ ἡ τό the, this, that, he, she, it
κόσμου n. gen. masc. sg. κόσμος world, adorning
11 νυνὶ adv. νυνί now
δὲ conj. δέ but, and, now, also, to the contrary, rather, then
ὑμῖν pron. dat. 2p. pl. σύ thou, you
μὴ particle of negation. μή not, no, lest, neither, none, nothing, nor, never, without
ἐάν conj. ἐάν if, soever, except, though, and if, but, whether, if so, so
τις indefinite pron. nom. masc. sg. τὶς certain, some, any man, one, any thing
ἀδελφὸς n. nom. masc. sg. ἀδελφός brother
πόρνος n. nom. masc. sg. πόρνος fornicator
ἢ particle. ἤ or, than, either, nor, or else, and, rather than
πλεονέκτης n. nom. masc. sg. πλεονέκτης covetous
ἢ particle. ἤ or, than, either, nor, or else, and, rather than
εἰδωλολάτρης n. nom. masc. sg. εἰδωλολάτρης idolater
ἢ particle. ἤ or, than, either, nor, or else, and, rather than
λοίδορος n. nom. masc. sg. λοίδορος railer, reviler

ἢ particle. ἤ or, than, either, nor, or else, and, rather than
μέθυσος n. nom. masc. sg. μέθυσος drunkard
ἢ particle. ἤ or, than, either, nor, or else, and, rather than
ἅρπαξ adj. nom. masc. sg. ἅρπαξ extortioner, ravening
τῷ art. dat. masc. sg. ὁ ἡ τό the, this, that, he, she, it
τοιούτῳ demo. pron. dat. masc. sg. τοιοῦτος such, like
μηδὲ adv. μηδέ neither, nor, not, no not, nor yet, not once, not so much as
12 τί interrog. pron. nom. neut. sg. τίς what, who, why, where, which, how
γάρ conj. γάρ for, and, because, but, indeed
μοι pron. dat. 1p. sg. ἐγώ I
καὶ conj. καί and, even, also, but
τοὺς art. acc. masc. pl. ὁ ἡ τό the, this, that, he, she, it
ἔξω adv. ἔξω out, without, out of, forth, away, outward
οὐχὶ adv. οὐχί not, nay
τοὺς art. acc. masc. pl. ὁ ἡ τό the, this, that, he, she, it
ἔσω adv. ἔσω within, in, inner, into, inward
ὑμεῖς pron. nom. 2p. pl. σύ thou, you
13 τοὺς art. acc. masc. pl. ὁ ἡ τό the, this, that, he, she, it
δὲ conj. δέ but, and, now, also, to the contrary, rather, then
ἔξω adv. ἔξω out, without, out of, forth, away, outward
ὁ art. nom. masc. sg. ὁ ἡ τό the, this, that, he, she, it
Θεὸς n. nom. masc. sg. θεός God, god
καὶ conj. καί and, even, also, but
τὸν art. acc. masc. sg. ὁ ἡ τό the, this, that, he, she, it
πονηρὸν adj. acc. masc. sg. πονηρός evil, wicked, bad
ἐξ prep. ἐκ ἐξ (+gen) of, from, out of, by, on, with, in, among, through
ὑμῶν pron. gen. 2p. pl. σύ thou, you
αὐτῶν pron. gen. masc. 3p. pl. αὐτός ή ό self, of oneself, even, very, the same, he, she, it

6

1 τις indefinite pron. nom. masc. sg. τὶς certain, some, any man, one, any thing
ὑμῶν pron. gen. 2p. pl. σύ thou, you
πρᾶγμα n. acc. neut. sg. πρᾶγμα thing, matter, business, work
πρὸς prep. πρός (+gen) for, (+dat) at, (+acc) unto, to, with, for, against
τὸν art. acc. masc. sg. ὁ ἡ τό the, this, that, he, she, it
ἕτερον adj. acc. masc. sg. ἕτερος another, other, else, strange
ἐπὶ prep. ἐπί (+gen) on, in, upon, (+dat) in, at, for, upon, (+acc) on, upon, unto, to, against
τῶν art. gen. masc. pl. ὁ ἡ τό the, this, that, he, she, it
ἀδίκων adj. gen. masc. pl. ἄδικος unjust, unrighteous
καὶ conj. καί and, even, also, but
οὐχὶ adv. οὐχί not, nay
ἐπὶ prep. ἐπί (+gen) on, in, upon, (+dat) in, at, for, upon, (+acc) on, upon, unto, to, against
τῶν art. gen. masc. pl. ὁ ἡ τό the, this, that, he, she, it
ἁγίων adj. gen. masc. pl. ἅγιος Holy, holy, saint, Holy One, holy thing, most holy
2 οὐκ particle of negation. οὐ οὐκ οὐχ not, no, neither, none, nay, nor, never, nothing
ὅτι conj. ὅτι that, for, because, how that, how, because that, for that, though
οἱ art. nom. masc. pl. ὁ ἡ τό the, this, that, he, she, it
ἅγιοι adj. nom. masc. pl. ἅγιος Holy, holy, saint, Holy One, holy thing, most holy
τὸν art. acc. masc. sg. ὁ ἡ τό the, this, that, he, she, it
κόσμον n. acc. masc. sg. κόσμος world, adorning
καὶ conj. καί and, even, also, but
εἰ conj. εἰ if, whether, that, though, forasmuch
ἐν prep. ἐν (+dat) in, by, with, among, at, on, through, to, within, into, of, for
ὑμῖν pron. dat. 2p. pl. σύ thou, you

ὁ art. nom. masc. sg. ὁ ἡ τό the, this, that, he, she, it
κόσμος n. nom. masc. sg. κόσμος world, adorning
ἀνάξιοί adj. nom. masc. pl. ἀνάξιος unworthy
κριτηρίων n. gen. neut. pl. κριτήριον judge, judgement, judgement seat
ἐλαχίστων superl. adj. gen. neut. pl. ἐλάχιστος least, very small, smallest, very little
3 οὐκ particle of negation. οὐ οὐκ οὐχ not, no, neither, none, nay, nor, never, nothing
ὅτι conj. ὅτι that, for, because, how that, how, because that, for that, though
ἀγγέλους n. acc. masc. pl. ἄγγελος angel, messenger
μήτι interrog. particle of negation. μήτι not, how much more
γε particle. γέ yet, and beside, at least, doubtless
βιωτικά adj. acc. neut. pl. βιωτικός of this life, thing that pertain to this life
4 βιωτικὰ adj. acc. neut. pl. βιωτικός of this life, thing that pertain to this life
μὲν conj. μέν indeed, verily, truly, even, so, some
οὖν conj. οὖν therefore, then, so, and, now, wherefore
κριτήρια n. acc. neut. pl. κριτήριον judge, judgement, judgement seat
ἐὰν conj. ἐάν if, soever, except, though, and if, but, whether, if so, so
τοὺς art. acc. masc. pl. ὁ ἡ τό the, this, that, he, she, it
ἐν prep. ἐν (+dat) in, by, with, among, at, on, through, to, within, into, of, for
τῇ art. dat. fem. sg. ὁ ἡ τό the, this, that, he, she, it
ἐκκλησίᾳ n. dat. fem. sg. ἐκκλησία church, assembly
τούτους demo. pron. acc. masc. pl. οὗτος αὕτη τοῦτο this, the same, this same, he, she, it
5 πρὸς prep. πρός (+gen) for, (+dat) at, (+acc) unto, to, with, for, against
ἐντροπὴν n. acc. fem. sg. ἐντροπή shame
ὑμῖν pron. dat. 2p. pl. σύ thou, you
οὕτως adv. οὕτω οὕτως so, even so, thus, on this wise, likewise, after this manner
οὐκ particle of negation. οὐ οὐκ οὐχ not, no, neither, none, nay, nor, never, nothing
ἐν prep. ἐν (+dat) in, by, with, among, at, on, through, to, within, into, of, for
ὑμῖν pron. dat. 2p. pl. σύ thou, you
σοφός adj. nom. masc. sg. σοφός wise, wiser
οὐδὲ adv. οὐδέ neither, nor, not, no, not even, never, not yet
εἷς num. nom. masc. sg. εἷς or ἕν one, other, some, any, only, a certain
ὃς relative pron. nom. masc. sg. ὅς ἥ ὅ who, which, what, that
ἀνὰ prep. ἀνά (+acc) by, in, through, among, between. (adv.) apiece, every man, each
μέσον adj. acc. neut. sg. μέσος midst, among, mid, between
τοῦ art. gen. masc. sg. ὁ ἡ τό the, this, that, he, she, it
ἀδελφοῦ n. gen. masc. sg. ἀδελφός brother
αὐτοῦ pron. gen. masc. 3p. sg. αὐτός ή ό self, of oneself, even, very, the same, he, she, it
6 ἀλλὰ conj. ἀλλά but, yea, yet, nevertheless, howbeit, nay, therefore
ἀδελφὸς n. nom. masc. sg. ἀδελφός brother
μετὰ prep. μετά (+gen) with, among, against, (+acc) after
ἀδελφοῦ n. gen. masc. sg. ἀδελφός brother
καὶ conj. καί and, even, also, but
τοῦτο demo. pron. nom. neut. sg. οὗτος αὕτη τοῦτο this, the same, this same, he, she, it
ἐπὶ prep. ἐπί (+gen) on, in, upon, (+dat) in, at, for, upon, (+acc) on, upon, unto, to, against
ἀπίστων adj. gen. masc. pl. ἄπιστος faithless, unbelieving, infidel, thing incredible
7 ἤδη adv. ἤδη now, already, yet, by this time, even now, now already
μὲν conj. μέν indeed, verily, truly, even, so, some
οὖν conj. οὖν therefore, then, so, and, now, wherefore
ὅλως adv. ὅλως at all, commonly, utterly
ἥττημα n. nom. neut. sg. ἥττημα diminishing, fault
ἐν prep. ἐν (+dat) in, by, with, among, at, on, through, to, within, into, of, for
ὑμῖν pron. dat. 2p. pl. σύ thou, you
ὅτι conj. ὅτι that, for, because, how that, how, because that, for that, though
κρίματα n. acc. neut. pl. κρίμα judgment, damnation, condemnation
μεθ' prep. μετά (+gen) with, among, against, (+acc) after

ἑαυτῶν reflexive pron. gen. masc. 3p. pl. ἑαυτοῦ himself, herself, itself, yourself, ourselves
διατί adv. διατί why, for what, wherefore
οὐχὶ adv. οὐχί not, nay
μᾶλλον adv. μᾶλλον rather, more, more and more, better, much, much the more
διατί adv. διατί why, for what, wherefore
οὐχὶ adv. οὐχί not, nay
μᾶλλον adv. μᾶλλον rather, more, more and more, better, much, much the more
8 ἀλλὰ conj. ἀλλά but, yea, yet, nevertheless, howbeit, nay, therefore
ὑμεῖς pron. nom. 2p. pl. σύ thou, you
καὶ conj. καί and, even, also, but
καὶ conj. καί and, even, also, but
ταῦτα demo. pron. nom. neut. pl. οὗτος αὕτη τοῦτο this, the same, this same, he, she, it
ἀδελφούς n. acc. masc. pl. ἀδελφός brother
9 ἢ particle. ἤ or, than, either, nor, or else, and, rather than
οὐκ particle of negation. οὐ οὐκ οὐχ not, no, neither, none, nay, nor, never, nothing
ὅτι conj. ὅτι that, for, because, how that, how, because that, for that, though
ἄδικοι adj. nom. masc. pl. ἄδικος unjust, unrighteous
βασιλείαν n. acc. fem. sg. βασιλεία kingdom, reign
Θεοῦ n. gen. masc. sg. θεός God, god
οὐ particle of negation. οὐ οὐκ οὐχ not, no, neither, none, nay, nor, never, nothing
μὴ particle of negation. μή not, no, lest, neither, none, nothing, nor, never, without
οὔτε conj. οὔτε neither, nor, nor yet, no, none
πόρνοι n. nom. masc. pl. πόρνος fornicator
οὔτε conj. οὔτε neither, nor, nor yet, no, none
εἰδωλολάτραι n. nom. masc. pl. εἰδωλολάτρης idolater
οὔτε conj. οὔτε neither, nor, nor yet, no, none
μοιχοὶ n. nom. masc. pl. μοιχός adulterer
οὔτε conj. οὔτε neither, nor, nor yet, no, none
μαλακοὶ adj. nom. masc. pl. μαλακός soft, effeminate
οὔτε conj. οὔτε neither, nor, nor yet, no, none
ἀρσενοκοῖται n. nom. masc. pl. ἀρσενοκοίτης abuser of oneself with mankind
10 οὔτε conj. οὔτε neither, nor, nor yet, no, none
κλέπται n. nom. masc. pl. κλέπτης thief
οὔτε conj. οὔτε neither, nor, nor yet, no, none
πλεονέκται n. nom. masc. pl. πλεονέκτης covetous
οὔτε conj. οὔτε neither, nor, nor yet, no, none
μέθυσοι n. nom. masc. pl. μέθυσος drunkard
οὐ particle of negation. οὐ οὐκ οὐχ not, no, neither, none, nay, nor, never, nothing
λοίδοροι n. nom. masc. pl. λοίδορος railer, reviler
οὐχ particle of negation. οὐ οὐκ οὐχ not, no, neither, none, nay, nor, never, nothing
ἅρπαγες adj. nom. masc. pl. ἅρπαξ extortioner, ravening
βασιλείαν n. acc. fem. sg. βασιλεία kingdom, reign
Θεοῦ n. gen. masc. sg. θεός God, god
οὐ particle of negation. οὐ οὐκ οὐχ not, no, neither, none, nay, nor, never, nothing
11 καὶ conj. καί and, even, also, but
ταῦτά demo. pron. nom. neut. pl. οὗτος αὕτη τοῦτο this, the same, this same, he, she, it
τινες indefinite pron. nom. masc. pl. τὶς certain, some, any man, one, any thing
ἀλλὰ conj. ἀλλά but, yea, yet, nevertheless, howbeit, nay, therefore
ἀλλὰ conj. ἀλλά but, yea, yet, nevertheless, howbeit, nay, therefore
ἀλλ' conj. ἀλλά but, yea, yet, nevertheless, howbeit, nay, therefore
ἐν prep. ἐν (+dat) in, by, with, among, at, on, through, to, within, into, of, for
τῷ art. dat. neut. sg. ὁ ἡ τό the, this, that, he, she, it
ὀνόματι n. dat. neut. sg. ὄνομα name, call, surname
τοῦ art. gen. masc. sg. ὁ ἡ τό the, this, that, he, she, it
Κυρίου n. gen. masc. sg. κύριος Lord, lord, master, sir, LORD, God, Master, owner

Ἰησοῦ n. gen. masc. sg. Ἰησοῦς Jesus
καὶ conj. καί and, even, also, but
ἐν prep. ἐν (+dat) in, by, with, among, at, on, through, to, within, into, of, for
τῷ art. dat. neut. sg. ὁ ἡ τό the, this, that, he, she, it
Πνεύματι n. dat. neut. sg. πνεῦμα spirit, Spirit, Ghost, ghost, life. of the spirit, wind
τοῦ art. gen. masc. sg. ὁ ἡ τό the, this, that, he, she, it
Θεοῦ n. gen. masc. sg. θεός God, god
ἡμῶν pron. gen. 1p. pl. ἐγώ I
12 Πάντα adj. nom. neut. pl. πᾶς πᾶσα πᾶν all, every, whosoever, every one, no, whole, any
μοι pron. dat. 1p. sg. ἐγώ I
ἀλλ' conj. ἀλλά but, yea, yet, nevertheless, howbeit, nay, therefore
οὐ particle of negation. οὐ οὐκ οὐχ not, no, neither, none, nay, nor, never, nothing
πάντα adj. nom. neut. pl. πᾶς πᾶσα πᾶν all, every, whosoever, every one, no, whole, any
μοι pron. dat. 1p. sg. ἐγώ I
ἀλλ' conj. ἀλλά but, yea, yet, nevertheless, howbeit, nay, therefore
οὐκ particle of negation. οὐ οὐκ οὐχ not, no, neither, none, nay, nor, never, nothing
ἐγὼ pron. nom. 1p. sg. ἐγώ I
ὑπό prep. ὑπό (+gen) of, by, with, from, among, (+acc) under
τινος indefinite pron. gen. neut. sg. τὶς certain, some, any man, one, any thing
13 τὰ art. nom. neut. pl. ὁ ἡ τό the, this, that, he, she, it
βρώματα n. nom. neut. pl. βρῶμα victual, meat, food
τῇ art. dat. fem. sg. ὁ ἡ τό the, this, that, he, she, it
κοιλίᾳ n. dat. fem. sg. κοιλία belly, womb
καὶ conj. καί and, even, also, but
ἡ art. nom. fem. sg. ὁ ἡ τό the, this, that, he, she, it
κοιλία n. nom. fem. sg. κοιλία belly, womb
τοῖς art. dat. neut. pl. ὁ ἡ τό the, this, that, he, she, it
βρώμασιν n. dat. neut. pl. βρῶμα victual, meat, food
ὁ art. nom. masc. sg. ὁ ἡ τό the, this, that, he, she, it
δὲ conj. δέ but, and, now, also, to the contrary, rather, then
Θεὸς n. nom. masc. sg. θεός God, god
καὶ conj. καί and, even, also, but
ταύτην demo. pron. acc. fem. sg. οὗτος αὕτη τοῦτο this, the same, this same, he, she, it
καὶ conj. καί and, even, also, but
ταῦτα demo. pron. acc. neut. pl. οὗτος αὕτη τοῦτο this, the same, this same, he, she, it
τὸ art. nom. neut. sg. ὁ ἡ τό the, this, that, he, she, it
δὲ conj. δέ but, and, now, also, to the contrary, rather, then
σῶμα n. nom. neut. sg. σῶμα body, bodily, slave
οὐ particle of negation. οὐ οὐκ οὐχ not, no, neither, none, nay, nor, never, nothing
τῇ art. dat. fem. sg. ὁ ἡ τό the, this, that, he, she, it
πορνείᾳ n. dat. fem. sg. πορνεία fornication
ἀλλὰ conj. ἀλλά but, yea, yet, nevertheless, howbeit, nay, therefore
τῷ art. dat. masc. sg. ὁ ἡ τό the, this, that, he, she, it
Κυρίῳ n. dat. masc. sg. κύριος Lord, lord, master, sir, LORD, God, Master, owner
καὶ conj. καί and, even, also, but
ὁ art. nom. masc. sg. ὁ ἡ τό the, this, that, he, she, it
Κύριος n. nom. masc. sg. κύριος Lord, lord, master, sir, LORD, God, Master, owner
τῷ art. dat. neut. sg. ὁ ἡ τό the, this, that, he, she, it
σώματι n. dat. neut. sg. σῶμα body, bodily, slave
14 ὁ art. nom. masc. sg. ὁ ἡ τό the, this, that, he, she, it
δὲ conj. δέ but, and, now, also, to the contrary, rather, then
Θεὸς n. nom. masc. sg. θεός God, god
καὶ conj. καί and, even, also, but
τὸν art. acc. masc. sg. ὁ ἡ τό the, this, that, he, she, it
Κύριον n. acc. masc. sg. κύριος Lord, lord, master, sir, LORD, God, Master, owner

καὶ conj. καί and, even, also, but
ἡμᾶς pron. acc. 1p. pl. ἐγώ I
διὰ prep. διά (+gen) by, through, with, in, of, (+acc) for, because of, for a cause
τῆς art. gen. fem. sg. ὁ ἡ τό the, this, that, he, she, it
δυνάμεως n. gen. fem. sg. δύναμις power, mighty work, miracle, strength, might
αὐτοῦ pron. gen. masc. 3p. sg. αὐτός ή ό self, of oneself, even, very, the same, he, she, it
15 οὐκ particle of negation. οὐ οὐκ οὐχ not, no, neither, none, nay, nor, never, nothing
ὅτι conj. ὅτι that, for, because, how that, how, because that, for that, though
τὰ art. nom. neut. pl. ὁ ἡ τό the, this, that, he, she, it
σώματα n. nom. neut. pl. σῶμα body, bodily, slave
ὑμῶν pron. gen. 2p. pl. σύ thou, you
μέλη n. nom. neut. pl. μέλος member
Χριστοῦ n. gen. masc. sg. Χριστός Christ
οὖν conj. οὖν therefore, then, so, and, now, wherefore
τὰ art. acc. neut. pl. ὁ ἡ τό the, this, that, he, she, it
μέλη n. acc. neut. pl. μέλος member
τοῦ art. gen. masc. sg. ὁ ἡ τό the, this, that, he, she, it
Χριστοῦ n. gen. masc. sg. Χριστός Christ
πόρνης n. gen. fem. sg. πόρνη harlot, whore
μέλη n. acc. neut. pl. μέλος member
μὴ particle of negation. μή not, no, lest, neither, none, nothing, nor, never, without
16 ἢ particle. ἤ or, than, either, nor, or else, and, rather than
οὐκ particle of negation. οὐ οὐκ οὐχ not, no, neither, none, nay, nor, never, nothing
ὅτι conj. ὅτι that, for, because, how that, how, because that, for that, though
ὁ art. nom. masc. sg. ὁ ἡ τό the, this, that, he, she, it
τῇ art. dat. fem. sg. ὁ ἡ τό the, this, that, he, she, it
πόρνῃ n. dat. fem. sg. πόρνη harlot, whore
ἓν num. nom. neut. sg. εἷς or ἕν one, other, some, any, only, a certain
σῶμά n. nom. neut. sg. σῶμα body, bodily, slave
γάρ conj. γάρ for, and, because, but, indeed
οἱ art. nom. masc. pl. ὁ ἡ τό the, this, that, he, she, it
δύο num. nom. masc. pl. δύο two, twain, both
εἰς prep. εἰς (+acc) into, to, unto, for, in, on, toward, against, upon, at, among
σάρκα n. acc. fem. sg. σάρξ flesh, carnal
μίαν num. acc. fem. sg. εἷς or ἕν one, other, some, any, only, a certain
17 ὁ art. nom. masc. sg. ὁ ἡ τό the, this, that, he, she, it
δὲ conj. δέ but, and, now, also, to the contrary, rather, then
τῷ art. dat. masc. sg. ὁ ἡ τό the, this, that, he, she, it
Κυρίῳ n. dat. masc. sg. κύριος Lord, lord, master, sir, LORD, God, Master, owner
ἓν num. nom. neut. sg. εἷς or ἕν one, other, some, any, only, a certain
πνεῦμά n. nom. neut. sg. πνεῦμα spirit, Spirit, Ghost, ghost, life. of the spirit, wind
18 τὴν art. acc. fem. sg. ὁ ἡ τό the, this, that, he, she, it
πορνείαν n. acc. fem. sg. πορνεία fornication
πᾶν adj. nom. neut. sg. πᾶς πᾶσα πᾶν all, every, whosoever, every one, no, whole, any
ἁμάρτημα n. nom. neut. sg. ἁμάρτημα sin
ὃ relative pron. acc. neut. sg. ὅς ἥ ὅ who, which, what, that
ἐὰν conj. ἐάν if, soever, except, though, and if, but, whether, if so, so
ἄνθρωπος n. nom. masc. sg. ἄνθρωπος man, human being, person, one, certain
ἐκτὸς prep. ἐκτός except, out of, other than, outside, unless, without
τοῦ art. gen. neut. sg. ὁ ἡ τό the, this, that, he, she, it
σώματός n. gen. neut. sg. σῶμα body, bodily, slave
ὁ art. nom. masc. sg. ὁ ἡ τό the, this, that, he, she, it
δὲ conj. δέ but, and, now, also, to the contrary, rather, then
εἰς prep. εἰς (+acc) into, to, unto, for, in, on, toward, against, upon, at, among
τὸ art. acc. neut. sg. ὁ ἡ τό the, this, that, he, she, it

ἴδιον adj. acc. neut. sg. ἴδιος one's own, one's, privately
σῶμα n. acc. neut. sg. σῶμα body, bodily, slave
19 ἢ particle. ἤ or, than, either, nor, or else, and, rather than
οὐκ particle of negation. οὐ οὐκ οὐχ not, no, neither, none, nay, nor, never, nothing
ὅτι conj. ὅτι that, for, because, how that, how, because that, for that, though
τὸ art. nom. neut. sg. ὁ ἡ τό the, this, that, he, she, it
σῶμα n. nom. neut. sg. σῶμα body, bodily, slave
ὑμῶν pron. gen. 2p. pl. σύ thou, you
ναὸς n. nom. masc. sg. ναός temple, shrine
τοῦ art. gen. neut. sg. ὁ ἡ τό the, this, that, he, she, it
ἐν prep. ἐν (+dat) in, by, with, among, at, on, through, to, within, into, of, for
ὑμῖν pron. dat. 2p. pl. σύ thou, you
Ἁγίου adj. gen. neut. sg. ἅγιος Holy, holy, saint, Holy One, holy thing, most holy
Πνεύματός n. gen. neut. sg. πνεῦμα spirit, Spirit, Ghost, ghost, life. of the spirit, wind
οὗ relative pron. gen. masc. sg. ὅς ἥ ὅ who, which, what, that
ἀπὸ prep. ἀπό (+gen) from, of, out of, since, for, off, at, by, in, on
Θεοῦ n. gen. masc. sg. θεός God, god
καὶ conj. καί and, even, also, but
οὐκ particle of negation. οὐ οὐκ οὐχ not, no, neither, none, nay, nor, never, nothing
ἑαυτῶν reflexive pron. gen. masc. 3p. pl. ἑαυτοῦ himself, herself, itself, yourself, ourselves
20 γὰρ conj. γάρ for, and, because, but, indeed
τιμῆς n. gen. fem. sg. τιμή honour, price, preciousness, sum
δὴ particle. δή also, and, doubtless, now, therefore
τὸν art. acc. masc. sg. ὁ ἡ τό the, this, that, he, she, it
Θεὸν n. acc. masc. sg. θεός God, god
ἐν prep. ἐν (+dat) in, by, with, among, at, on, through, to, within, into, of, for
τῷ art. dat. neut. sg. ὁ ἡ τό the, this, that, he, she, it
σώματι n. dat. neut. sg. σῶμα body, bodily, slave
ὑμῶν pron. gen. 2p. pl. σύ thou, you
καὶ conj. καί and, even, also, but
ἐν prep. ἐν (+dat) in, by, with, among, at, on, through, to, within, into, of, for
τῷ art. dat. neut. sg. ὁ ἡ τό the, this, that, he, she, it
πνεύματι n. dat. neut. sg. πνεῦμα spirit, Spirit, Ghost, ghost, life. of the spirit, wind
ὑμῶν pron. gen. 2p. pl. σύ thou, you
ἅτινά relative pron. nom. neut. pl. ὅστις which, who, whosoever, that, whatsoever
τοῦ art. gen. masc. sg. ὁ ἡ τό the, this, that, he, she, it
Θεοῦ n. gen. masc. sg. θεός God, god

7

1 Περὶ prep. περί (+gen) of, for, concerning, (+acc) about, concerning, in
δὲ conj. δέ but, and, now, also, to the contrary, rather, then
ὧν relative pron. gen. neut. pl. ὅς ἥ ὅ who, which, what, that
μοι pron. dat. 1p. sg. ἐγώ I
καλὸν adj. nom. neut. sg. καλός good, better, goodly, meet, honest, fair, well, worthy
ἀνθρώπῳ n. dat. masc. sg. ἄνθρωπος man, human being, person, one, certain
γυναικὸς n. gen. fem. sg. γυνή woman, wife
μὴ particle of negation. μή not, no, lest, neither, none, nothing, nor, never, without
2 διὰ prep. διά (+gen) by, through, with, in, of, (+acc) for, because of, for a cause
δὲ conj. δέ but, and, now, also, to the contrary, rather, then
τὰς art. acc. fem. pl. ὁ ἡ τό the, this, that, he, she, it
πορνείας n. acc. fem. pl. πορνεία fornication
ἕκαστος adj. nom. masc. sg. ἕκαστος every man, every, every one, any man, each
τὴν art. acc. fem. sg. ὁ ἡ τό the, this, that, he, she, it
ἑαυτοῦ reflexive pron. gen. masc. 3p. sg. ἑαυτοῦ himself, herself, itself, yourself, ourselves

γυναῖκα n. acc. fem. sg. γυνή woman, wife
καὶ conj. καί and, even, also, but
ἑκάστη adj. nom. fem. sg. ἕκαστος every man, every, every one, any man, each
τὸν art. acc. masc. sg. ὁ ἡ τό the, this, that, he, she, it
ἴδιον adj. acc. masc. sg. ἴδιος one's own, one's, privately
ἄνδρα n. acc. masc. sg. ἀνήρ man, husband, sir
3 τῇ art. dat. fem. sg. ὁ ἡ τό the, this, that, he, she, it
γυναικὶ n. dat. fem. sg. γυνή woman, wife
ὁ art. nom. masc. sg. ὁ ἡ τό the, this, that, he, she, it
ἀνὴρ n. nom. masc. sg. ἀνήρ man, husband, sir
τὴν art. acc. fem. sg. ὁ ἡ τό the, this, that, he, she, it
εὔνοιαν n. acc. fem. sg. εὔνοια benevolence, good will
ὁμοίως adv. ὁμοίως likewise, so
δὲ conj. δέ but, and, now, also, to the contrary, rather, then
καὶ conj. καί and, even, also, but
ἡ art. nom. fem. sg. ὁ ἡ τό the, this, that, he, she, it
γυνὴ n. nom. fem. sg. γυνή woman, wife
τῷ art. dat. masc. sg. ὁ ἡ τό the, this, that, he, she, it
ἀνδρί n. dat. masc. sg. ἀνήρ man, husband, sir
4 ἡ art. nom. fem. sg. ὁ ἡ τό the, this, that, he, she, it
γυνὴ n. nom. fem. sg. γυνή woman, wife
τοῦ art. gen. neut. sg. ὁ ἡ τό the, this, that, he, she, it
ἰδίου adj. gen. neut. sg. ἴδιος one's own, one's, privately
σώματος n. gen. neut. sg. σῶμα body, bodily, slave
οὐκ particle of negation. οὐ οὐκ οὐχ not, no, neither, none, nay, nor, never, nothing
ἀλλ' conj. ἀλλά but, yea, yet, nevertheless, howbeit, nay, therefore
ὁ art. nom. masc. sg. ὁ ἡ τό the, this, that, he, she, it
ἀνήρ n. nom. masc. sg. ἀνήρ man, husband, sir
ὁμοίως adv. ὁμοίως likewise, so
δὲ conj. δέ but, and, now, also, to the contrary, rather, then
καὶ conj. καί and, even, also, but
ὁ art. nom. masc. sg. ὁ ἡ τό the, this, that, he, she, it
ἀνήρ n. nom. masc. sg. ἀνήρ man, husband, sir
τοῦ art. gen. neut. sg. ὁ ἡ τό the, this, that, he, she, it
ἰδίου adj. gen. neut. sg. ἴδιος one's own, one's, privately
σώματος n. gen. neut. sg. σῶμα body, bodily, slave
οὐκ particle of negation. οὐ οὐκ οὐχ not, no, neither, none, nay, nor, never, nothing
ἀλλ' conj. ἀλλά but, yea, yet, nevertheless, howbeit, nay, therefore
ἡ art. nom. fem. sg. ὁ ἡ τό the, this, that, he, she, it
γυνὴ n. nom. fem. sg. γυνή woman, wife
5 μὴ particle of negation. μή not, no, lest, neither, none, nothing, nor, never, without
ἀλλήλους pron. acc. masc. 2p. pl. ἀλλήλων one another, themselves, together, mutual
εἰ conj. εἰ if, whether, that, though, forasmuch
μὴ particle of negation. μή not, no, lest, neither, none, nothing, nor, never, without
τι indefinite pron. nom. neut. sg. τὶς certain, some, any man, one, any thing
ἂν particle. ἄν Indicating contingency. No English translation.
ἐκ prep. ἐκ ἐξ (+gen) of, from, out of, by, on, with, in, among, through
συμφώνου adj. gen. neut. sg. σύμφωνος consent
πρὸς prep. πρός (+gen) for, (+dat) at, (+acc) unto, to, with, for, against
καιρόν n. acc. masc. sg. καιρός time, season, due time, opportunity
ἵνα conj. ἵνα that, to, lest, for to, so that, albeit, because, for, so as
τῇ art. dat. fem. sg. ὁ ἡ τό the, this, that, he, she, it
νηστείᾳ n. dat. fem. sg. νηστεία fasting, fast
καὶ conj. καί and, even, also, but
τῇ art. dat. fem. sg. ὁ ἡ τό the, this, that, he, she, it

προσευχῇ n. dat. fem. sg. προσευχή prayer
καὶ conj. καί and, even, also, but
πάλιν adv. πάλιν again
ἐπὶ prep. ἐπί (+gen) on, in, upon, (+dat) in, at, for, upon, (+acc) on, upon, unto, to, against
τὸ art. acc. neut. sg. ὁ ἡ τό the, this, that, he, she, it
αὐτὸ pron. acc. neut. 3p. sg. αὐτός ἡ ὁ self, of oneself, even, very, the same, he, she, it
ἵνα conj. ἵνα that, to, lest, for to, so that, albeit, because, for, so as
μὴ particle of negation. μή not, no, lest, neither, none, nothing, nor, never, without
ὑμᾶς pron. acc. 2p. pl. σύ thou, you
ὁ art. nom. masc. sg. ὁ ἡ τό the, this, that, he, she, it
Σατανᾶς n. nom. masc. sg. Σατανᾶς Satan
διὰ prep. διά (+gen) by, through, with, in, of, (+acc) for, because of, for a cause
τὴν art. acc. fem. sg. ὁ ἡ τό the, this, that, he, she, it
ἀκρασίαν n. acc. fem. sg. ἀκρασία excess. incontinence
ὑμῶν pron. gen. 2p. pl. σύ thou, you
6 τοῦτο demo. pron. acc. neut. sg. οὗτος αὕτη τοῦτο this, the same, this same, he, she, it
δὲ conj. δέ but, and, now, also, to the contrary, rather, then
κατὰ prep. κατά (+gen) against, by, throughout, down, (+acc) according to, after, with
συγγνώμην n. acc. fem. sg. συγγνώμη permission
οὐ particle of negation. οὐ οὐκ οὐχ not, no, neither, none, nay, nor, never, nothing
κατ' prep. κατά (+gen) against, by, throughout, down, (+acc) according to, after, with
ἐπιταγήν n. acc. fem. sg. ἐπιταγή commandment, authority
7 γὰρ conj. γάρ for, and, because, but, indeed
πάντας adj. acc. masc. pl. πᾶς πᾶσα πᾶν all, every, whosoever, every one, no, whole, any
ἀνθρώπους n. acc. masc. pl. ἄνθρωπος man, human being, person, one, certain
ὡς adv. ὡς as, when, as it were, how, about, like, as soon as, even as, while
καὶ conj. καί and, even, also, but
ἐμαυτόν pron. acc. masc. 1p. sg. ἐμαυτοῦ myself, me
ἀλλ' conj. ἀλλά but, yea, yet, nevertheless, howbeit, nay, therefore
ἕκαστος adj. nom. masc. sg. ἕκαστος every man, every, every one, any man, each
ἴδιον adj. acc. neut. sg. ἴδιος one's own, one's, privately
χάρισμα n. acc. neut. sg. χάρισμα gift, free gift
ἐκ prep. ἐκ ἐξ (+gen) of, from, out of, by, on, with, in, among, through
Θεοῦ n. gen. masc. sg. θεός God, god
ὃς relative pron. nom. masc. sg. ὅς ἥ ὅ who, which, what, that
μὲν conj. μέν indeed, verily, truly, even, so, some
οὕτως adv. οὕτω οὕτως so, even so, thus, on this wise, likewise, after this manner
ὃς relative pron. nom. masc. sg. ὅς ἥ ὅ who, which, what, that
δὲ conj. δέ but, and, now, also, to the contrary, rather, then
οὕτως adv. οὕτω οὕτως so, even so, thus, on this wise, likewise, after this manner
8 δὲ conj. δέ but, and, now, also, to the contrary, rather, then
τοῖς art. dat. masc. pl. ὁ ἡ τό the, this, that, he, she, it
ἀγάμοις n. dat. masc. pl. ἄγαμος unmarried
καὶ conj. καί and, even, also, but
ταῖς art. dat. fem. pl. ὁ ἡ τό the, this, that, he, she, it
χήραις adj. dat. fem. pl. χήρα widow
καλὸν adj. nom. neut. sg. καλός good, better, goodly, meet, honest, fair, well, worthy
αὐτοῖς pron. dat. masc. 3p. pl. αὐτός ἡ ὁ self, of oneself, even, very, the same, he, she, it
ἐὰν conj. ἐάν if, soever, except, though, and if, but, whether, if so, so
ὡς adv. ὡς as, when, as it were, how, about, like, as soon as, even as, while
κἀγώ pron. nom. 1p. sg. κἀγώ and I, I also, so I, even as I
9 εἰ conj. εἰ if, whether, that, though, forasmuch
δὲ conj. δέ but, and, now, also, to the contrary, rather, then
οὐκ particle of negation. οὐ οὐκ οὐχ not, no, neither, none, nay, nor, never, nothing
κρεῖσσον compar. adj. nom. neut. sg. κρείσσων better

γάρ conj. γάρ for, and, because, but, indeed
ἤ particle. ἤ or, than, either, nor, or else, and, rather than
10 τοῖς art. dat. masc. pl. ὁ ἡ τό the, this, that, he, she, it
δὲ conj. δέ but, and, now, also, to the contrary, rather, then
οὐκ particle of negation. οὐ οὐκ οὐχ not, no, neither, none, nay, nor, never, nothing
ἐγὼ pron. nom. 1p. sg. ἐγώ I
ἀλλ' conj. ἀλλά but, yea, yet, nevertheless, howbeit, nay, therefore
ὁ art. nom. masc. sg. ὁ ἡ τό the, this, that, he, she, it
Κύριος n. nom. masc. sg. κύριος Lord, lord, master, sir, LORD, God, Master, owner
γυναῖκα n. acc. fem. sg. γυνή woman, wife
ἀπὸ prep. ἀπό (+gen) from, of, out of, since, for, off, at, by, in, on
ἀνδρὸς n. gen. masc. sg. ἀνήρ man, husband, sir
μὴ particle of negation. μή not, no, lest, neither, none, nothing, nor, never, without
11 ἐὰν conj. ἐάν if, soever, except, though, and if, but, whether, if so, so
δὲ conj. δέ but, and, now, also, to the contrary, rather, then
καὶ conj. καί and, even, also, but
ἄγαμος n. nom. fem. sg. ἄγαμος unmarried
ἢ particle. ἤ or, than, either, nor, or else, and, rather than
τῷ art. dat. masc. sg. ὁ ἡ τό the, this, that, he, she, it
ἀνδρὶ n. dat. masc. sg. ἀνήρ man, husband, sir
καὶ conj. καί and, even, also, but
ἄνδρα n. acc. masc. sg. ἀνήρ man, husband, sir
γυναῖκα n. acc. fem. sg. γυνή woman, wife
μὴ particle of negation. μή not, no, lest, neither, none, nothing, nor, never, without
12 τοῖς art. dat. masc. pl. ὁ ἡ τό the, this, that, he, she, it
δὲ conj. δέ but, and, now, also, to the contrary, rather, then
λοιποῖς adj. dat. masc. pl. λοιπός other, rest, remnant, residue, which remain
ἐγὼ pron. nom. 1p. sg. ἐγώ I
οὐχ particle of negation. οὐ οὐκ οὐχ not, no, neither, none, nay, nor, never, nothing
ὁ art. nom. masc. sg. ὁ ἡ τό the, this, that, he, she, it
Κύριος n. nom. masc. sg. κύριος Lord, lord, master, sir, LORD, God, Master, owner
εἴ conj. εἰ if, whether, that, though, forasmuch
τις indefinite pron. nom. masc. sg. τὶς certain, some, any man, one, any thing
ἀδελφὸς n. nom. masc. sg. ἀδελφός brother
γυναῖκα n. acc. fem. sg. γυνή woman, wife
ἄπιστον adj. acc. fem. sg. ἄπιστος faithless, unbelieving, infidel, thing incredible
καὶ conj. καί and, even, also, but
αὕτη demo. pron. nom. fem. sg. οὗτος αὕτη τοῦτο this, the same, this same, he, she, it
μετ' prep. μετά (+gen) with, among, against, (+acc) after
αὐτοῦ pron. gen. masc. 3p. sg. αὐτός ἡ ὁ self, of oneself, even, very, the same, he, she, it
μὴ particle of negation. μή not, no, lest, neither, none, nothing, nor, never, without
αὐτήν pron. acc. fem. 3p. sg. αὐτός ἡ ὁ self, of oneself, even, very, the same, he, she, it
13 καὶ conj. καί and, even, also, but
γυνὴ n. nom. fem. sg. γυνή woman, wife
ἥτις relative pron. nom. fem. sg. ὅστις which, who, whosoever, that, whatsoever
ἄνδρα n. acc. masc. sg. ἀνήρ man, husband, sir
ἄπιστον adj. acc. masc. sg. ἄπιστος faithless, unbelieving, infidel, thing incredible
καὶ conj. καί and, even, also, but
αὐτὸς pron. nom. masc. 3p. sg. αὐτός ἡ ὁ self, of oneself, even, very, the same, he, she, it
μετ' prep. μετά (+gen) with, among, against, (+acc) after
αὐτῆς pron. gen. fem. 3p. sg. αὐτός ἡ ὁ self, of oneself, even, very, the same, he, she, it
μὴ particle of negation. μή not, no, lest, neither, none, nothing, nor, never, without
αὐτόν pron. acc. masc. 3p. sg. αὐτός ἡ ὁ self, of oneself, even, very, the same, he, she, it
14 γὰρ conj. γάρ for, and, because, but, indeed
ὁ art. nom. masc. sg. ὁ ἡ τό the, this, that, he, she, it

ἀνὴρ n. nom. masc. sg. ἀνήρ man, husband, sir
ἄπιστος adj. nom. masc. sg. ἄπιστος faithless, unbelieving, infidel, thing incredible
ἐν prep. ἐν (+dat) in, by, with, among, at, on, through, to, within, into, of, for
τῇ art. dat. fem. sg. ὁ ἡ τό the, this, that, he, she, it
γυναικὶ n. dat. fem. sg. γυνή woman, wife
καὶ conj. καί and, even, also, but
ἡ art. nom. fem. sg. ὁ ἡ τό the, this, that, he, she, it
γυνὴ n. nom. fem. sg. γυνή woman, wife
ἡ art. nom. fem. sg. ὁ ἡ τό the, this, that, he, she, it
ἄπιστος adj. nom. fem. sg. ἄπιστος faithless, unbelieving, infidel, thing incredible
ἐν prep. ἐν (+dat) in, by, with, among, at, on, through, to, within, into, of, for
τῷ art. dat. masc. sg. ὁ ἡ τό the, this, that, he, she, it
ἀνδρί n. dat. masc. sg. ἀνήρ man, husband, sir
ἐπεὶ conj. ἐπεί because, otherwise, seeing, else, for then, for as much as, for, since
ἄρα conj. ἄρα then, therefore, haply, wherefore, perhaps, manner, no doubt, truly
τὰ art. nom. neut. pl. ὁ ἡ τό the, this, that, he, she, it
τέκνα n. nom. neut. pl. τέκνον child, son, daughter
ὑμῶν pron. gen. 2p. pl. σύ thou, you
ἀκάθαρτά adj. nom. neut. pl. ἀκάθαρτος unclean, foul
νῦν adv. νῦν now, henceforth, present, this time
δὲ conj. δέ but, and, now, also, to the contrary, rather, then
ἅγιά adj. nom. neut. pl. ἅγιος Holy, holy, saint, Holy One, holy thing, most holy
15 εἰ conj. εἰ if, whether, that, though, forasmuch
δὲ conj. δέ but, and, now, also, to the contrary, rather, then
ὁ art. nom. masc. sg. ὁ ἡ τό the, this, that, he, she, it
ἄπιστος adj. nom. masc. sg. ἄπιστος faithless, unbelieving, infidel, thing incredible
οὐ particle of negation. οὐ οὐκ οὐχ not, no, neither, none, nay, nor, never, nothing
ὁ art. nom. masc. sg. ὁ ἡ τό the, this, that, he, she, it
ἀδελφὸς n. nom. masc. sg. ἀδελφός brother
ἢ particle. ἤ or, than, either, nor, or else, and, rather than
ἡ art. nom. fem. sg. ὁ ἡ τό the, this, that, he, she, it
ἀδελφὴ n. nom. fem. sg. ἀδελφή sister
ἐν prep. ἐν (+dat) in, by, with, among, at, on, through, to, within, into, of, for
τοῖς art. dat. neut. pl. ὁ ἡ τό the, this, that, he, she, it
τοιούτοις demo. pron. dat. neut. pl. τοιοῦτος such, like
ἐν prep. ἐν (+dat) in, by, with, among, at, on, through, to, within, into, of, for
δὲ conj. δέ but, and, now, also, to the contrary, rather, then
εἰρήνῃ n. dat. fem. sg. εἰρήνη peace, quietness, rest
ἡμᾶς pron. acc. 1p. pl. ἐγώ I
ὁ art. nom. masc. sg. ὁ ἡ τό the, this, that, he, she, it
Θεός n. nom. masc. sg. θεός God, god
16 τί interrog. pron. acc. neut. sg. τίς what, who, why, where, which, how
γὰρ conj. γάρ for, and, because, but, indeed
γύναι n. voc. fem. sg. γυνή woman, wife
εἰ conj. εἰ if, whether, that, though, forasmuch
τὸν art. acc. masc. sg. ὁ ἡ τό the, this, that, he, she, it
ἄνδρα n. acc. masc. sg. ἀνήρ man, husband, sir
ἢ particle. ἤ or, than, either, nor, or else, and, rather than
τί interrog. pron. acc. neut. sg. τίς what, who, why, where, which, how
ἄνερ n. voc. masc. sg. ἀνήρ man, husband, sir
εἰ conj. εἰ if, whether, that, though, forasmuch
τὴν art. acc. fem. sg. ὁ ἡ τό the, this, that, he, she, it
γυναῖκα n. acc. fem. sg. γυνή woman, wife
17 εἰ conj. εἰ if, whether, that, though, forasmuch
μὴ particle of negation. μή not, no, lest, neither, none, nothing, nor, never, without

ἑκάστῳ adj. dat. masc. sg. ἕκαστος every man, every, every one, any man, each
ὡς adv. ὡς as, when, as it were, how, about, like, as soon as, even as, while
ὁ art. nom. masc. sg. ὁ ἡ τό the, this, that, he, she, it
Θεός n. nom. masc. sg. θεός God, god
ἕκαστον adj. acc. masc. sg. ἕκαστος every man, every, every one, any man, each
ὡς adv. ὡς as, when, as it were, how, about, like, as soon as, even as, while
ὁ art. nom. masc. sg. ὁ ἡ τό the, this, that, he, she, it
Κύριος n. nom. masc. sg. κύριος Lord, lord, master, sir, LORD, God, Master, owner
οὕτω adv. οὕτω οὕτως so, even so, thus, on this wise, likewise, after this manner
καὶ conj. καί and, even, also, but
οὕτως adv. οὕτω οὕτως so, even so, thus, on this wise, likewise, after this manner
ἐν prep. ἐν (+dat) in, by, with, among, at, on, through, to, within, into, of, for
ταῖς art. dat. fem. pl. ὁ ἡ τό the, this, that, he, she, it
ἐκκλησίαις n. dat. fem. pl. ἐκκλησία church, assembly
πάσαις adj. dat. fem. pl. πᾶς πᾶσα πᾶν all, every, whosoever, every one, no, whole, any
18 τις indefinite pron. nom. masc. sg. τὶς certain, some, any man, one, any thing
μὴ particle of negation. μή not, no, lest, neither, none, nothing, nor, never, without
ἐν prep. ἐν (+dat) in, by, with, among, at, on, through, to, within, into, of, for
ἀκροβυστίᾳ n. dat. fem. sg. ἀκροβυστία uncircumcised, uncircumcision
τις indefinite pron. nom. masc. sg. τὶς certain, some, any man, one, any thing
μὴ particle of negation. μή not, no, lest, neither, none, nothing, nor, never, without
19 ἡ art. nom. fem. sg. ὁ ἡ τό the, this, that, he, she, it
περιτομὴ n. nom. fem. sg. περιτομή circumcision
οὐδέν num. nom. neut. sg. οὐδείς no man, nothing, no, none, neither, not, nought
καὶ conj. καί and, even, also, but
ἡ art. nom. fem. sg. ὁ ἡ τό the, this, that, he, she, it
ἀκροβυστία n. nom. fem. sg. ἀκροβυστία uncircumcised, uncircumcision
οὐδέν num. nom. neut. sg. οὐδείς no man, nothing, no, none, neither, not, nought
ἀλλὰ conj. ἀλλά but, yea, yet, nevertheless, howbeit, nay, therefore
τήρησις n. nom. fem. sg. τήρησις hold, keeping, prison
ἐντολῶν n. gen. fem. pl. ἐντολή commandment, precept
Θεοῦ n. gen. masc. sg. θεός God, god
20 ἕκαστος adj. nom. masc. sg. ἕκαστος every man, every, every one, any man, each
ἐν prep. ἐν (+dat) in, by, with, among, at, on, through, to, within, into, of, for
τῇ art. dat. fem. sg. ὁ ἡ τό the, this, that, he, she, it
κλήσει n. dat. fem. sg. κλῆσις calling, vocation
ᾗ relative pron. dat. fem. sg. ὅς ἥ ὅ who, which, what, that
ἐν prep. ἐν (+dat) in, by, with, among, at, on, through, to, within, into, of, for
ταύτῃ demo. pron. dat. fem. sg. οὗτος αὕτη τοῦτο this, the same, this same, he, she, it
21 δοῦλος n. nom. masc. sg. δοῦλος servant, bondman, bond, slave
μὴ particle of negation. μή not, no, lest, neither, none, nothing, nor, never, without
σοι pron. dat. 2p. sg. σύ thou, you
ἀλλ' conj. ἀλλά but, yea, yet, nevertheless, howbeit, nay, therefore
εἰ conj. εἰ if, whether, that, though, forasmuch
καὶ conj. καί and, even, also, but
ἐλεύθερος adj. nom. masc. sg. ἐλεύθερος free, freewoman, at liberty, freeman
μᾶλλον adv. μᾶλλον rather, more, more and more, better, much, much the more
22 ὁ art. nom. masc. sg. ὁ ἡ τό the, this, that, he, she, it
γὰρ conj. γάρ for, and, because, but, indeed
ἐν prep. ἐν (+dat) in, by, with, among, at, on, through, to, within, into, of, for
Κυρίῳ n. dat. masc. sg. κύριος Lord, lord, master, sir, LORD, God, Master, owner
δοῦλος n. nom. masc. sg. δοῦλος servant, bondman, bond, slave
ἀπελεύθερος n. nom. masc. sg. ἀπελεύθερος freeman
Κυρίου n. gen. masc. sg. κύριος Lord, lord, master, sir, LORD, God, Master, owner
ὁμοίως adv. ὁμοίως likewise, so

καὶ conj. καί and, even, also, but
ὁ art. nom. masc. sg. ὁ ἡ τό the, this, that, he, she, it
ἐλεύθερος adj. nom. masc. sg. ἐλεύθερος free, freewoman, at liberty, freeman
δοῦλος n. nom. masc. sg. δοῦλος servant, bondman, bond, slave
Χριστοῦ n. gen. masc. sg. Χριστός Christ
23 τιμῆς n. gen. fem. sg. τιμή honour, price, preciousness, sum
μὴ particle of negation. μή not, no, lest, neither, none, nothing, nor, never, without
δοῦλοι n. nom. masc. pl. δοῦλος servant, bondman, bond, slave
ἀνθρώπων n. gen. masc. pl. ἄνθρωπος man, human being, person, one, certain
24 ἕκαστος adj. nom. masc. sg. ἕκαστος every man, every, every one, any man, each
ἐν prep. ἐν (+dat) in, by, with, among, at, on, through, to, within, into, of, for
ᾧ relative pron. dat. neut. sg. ὅς ἥ ὅ who, which, what, that
ἀδελφοί n. voc. masc. pl. ἀδελφός brother
ἐν prep. ἐν (+dat) in, by, with, among, at, on, through, to, within, into, of, for
τούτῳ demo. pron. dat. neut. sg. οὗτος αὕτη τοῦτο this, the same, this same, he, she, it
παρὰ prep. παρά (+gen) of, from, (+dat) with, for, (+acc) beside, at, by, above, against
τῷ art. dat. masc. sg. ὁ ἡ τό the, this, that, he, she, it
Θεῷ n. dat. masc. sg. θεός God, god
25 Περὶ prep. περί (+gen) of, for, concerning, (+acc) about, concerning, in
δὲ conj. δέ but, and, now, also, to the contrary, rather, then
τῶν art. gen. fem. pl. ὁ ἡ τό the, this, that, he, she, it
παρθένων n. gen. fem. pl. παρθένος virgin
ἐπιταγὴν n. acc. fem. sg. ἐπιταγή commandment, authority
Κυρίου n. gen. masc. sg. κύριος Lord, lord, master, sir, LORD, God, Master, owner
οὐκ particle of negation. οὐ οὐκ οὐχ not, no, neither, none, nay, nor, never, nothing
γνώμην n. acc. fem. sg. γνώμη judgement, mind, advice, purpose, will
δὲ conj. δέ but, and, now, also, to the contrary, rather, then
ὡς adv. ὡς as, when, as it were, how, about, like, as soon as, even as, while
ὑπὸ prep. ὑπό (+gen) of, by, with, from, among, (+acc) under
Κυρίου n. gen. masc. sg. κύριος Lord, lord, master, sir, LORD, God, Master, owner
πιστὸς adj. nom. masc. sg. πιστός faithful, believing, true, sure
26 οὖν conj. οὖν therefore, then, so, and, now, wherefore
τοῦτο demo. pron. acc. neut. sg. οὗτος αὕτη τοῦτο this, the same, this same, he, she, it
καλὸν adj. acc. neut. sg. καλός good, better, goodly, meet, honest, fair, well, worthy
διὰ prep. διά (+gen) by, through, with, in, of, (+acc) for, because of, for a cause
τὴν art. acc. fem. sg. ὁ ἡ τό the, this, that, he, she, it
ἀνάγκην n. acc. fem. sg. ἀνάγκη must needs, necessity, distress, inevitable
ὅτι conj. ὅτι that, for, because, how that, how, because that, for that, though
καλὸν adj. nom. neut. sg. καλός good, better, goodly, meet, honest, fair, well, worthy
ἀνθρώπῳ n. dat. masc. sg. ἄνθρωπος man, human being, person, one, certain
τὸ art. nom. neut. sg. ὁ ἡ τό the, this, that, he, she, it
οὕτως adv. οὕτω οὕτως so, even so, thus, on this wise, likewise, after this manner
27 γυναικί n. dat. fem. sg. γυνή woman, wife
μὴ particle of negation. μή not, no, lest, neither, none, nothing, nor, never, without
λύσιν n. acc. fem. sg. λύσις to be loosed
ἀπὸ prep. ἀπό (+gen) from, of, out of, since, for, off, at, by, in, on
γυναικός n. gen. fem. sg. γυνή woman, wife
μὴ particle of negation. μή not, no, lest, neither, none, nothing, nor, never, without
γυναῖκα n. acc. fem. sg. γυνή woman, wife
28 ἐὰν conj. ἐάν if, soever, except, though, and if, but, whether, if so, so
δὲ conj. δέ but, and, now, also, to the contrary, rather, then
καὶ conj. καί and, even, also, but
οὐχ particle of negation. οὐ οὐκ οὐχ not, no, neither, none, nay, nor, never, nothing
καὶ conj. καί and, even, also, but
ἐὰν conj. ἐάν if, soever, except, though, and if, but, whether, if so, so

ἡ art. nom. fem. sg. ὁ ἡ τό the, this, that, he, she, it
παρθένος n. nom. fem. sg. παρθένος virgin
οὐχ particle of negation. οὐ οὐκ οὐχ not, no, neither, none, nay, nor, never, nothing
θλῖψιν n. acc. fem. sg. θλῖψις tribulation, affliction, anguish, persecution
δὲ conj. δέ but, and, now, also, to the contrary, rather, then
τῇ art. dat. fem. sg. ὁ ἡ τό the, this, that, he, she, it
σαρκὶ n. dat. fem. sg. σάρξ flesh, carnal
οἱ art. nom. masc. pl. ὁ ἡ τό the, this, that, he, she, it
τοιοῦτοι demo. pron. nom. masc. pl. τοιοῦτος such, like
ἐγὼ pron. nom. 1p. sg. ἐγώ I
δὲ conj. δέ but, and, now, also, to the contrary, rather, then
ὑμῶν pron. gen. 2p. pl. σύ thou, you
29 τοῦτο demo. pron. acc. neut. sg. οὗτος αὕτη τοῦτο this, the same, this same, he, she, it
δέ conj. δέ but, and, now, also, to the contrary, rather, then
ἀδελφοί n. voc. masc. pl. ἀδελφός brother
ὅτι conj. ὅτι that, for, because, how that, how, because that, for that, though
ὁ art. nom. masc. sg. ὁ ἡ τό the, this, that, he, she, it
καιρὸς n. nom. masc. sg. καιρός time, season, due time, opportunity
τὸ art. acc. neut. sg. ὁ ἡ τό the, this, that, he, she, it
λοιπόν adv. λοιπόν finally, henceforth, now, besides, furthermore, moreover, then
ἵνα conj. ἵνα that, to, lest, for to, so that, albeit, because, for, so as
καὶ conj. καί and, even, also, but
οἱ art. nom. masc. pl. ὁ ἡ τό the, this, that, he, she, it
γυναῖκας n. acc. fem. pl. γυνή woman, wife
ὡς adv. ὡς as, when, as it were, how, about, like, as soon as, even as, while
μὴ particle of negation. μή not, no, lest, neither, none, nothing, nor, never, without
30 καὶ conj. καί and, even, also, but
οἱ art. nom. masc. pl. ὁ ἡ τό the, this, that, he, she, it
ὡς adv. ὡς as, when, as it were, how, about, like, as soon as, even as, while
μὴ particle of negation. μή not, no, lest, neither, none, nothing, nor, never, without
καὶ conj. καί and, even, also, but
οἱ art. nom. masc. pl. ὁ ἡ τό the, this, that, he, she, it
ὡς adv. ὡς as, when, as it were, how, about, like, as soon as, even as, while
μὴ particle of negation. μή not, no, lest, neither, none, nothing, nor, never, without
καὶ conj. καί and, even, also, but
οἱ art. nom. masc. pl. ὁ ἡ τό the, this, that, he, she, it
ὡς adv. ὡς as, when, as it were, how, about, like, as soon as, even as, while
μὴ particle of negation. μή not, no, lest, neither, none, nothing, nor, never, without
31 καὶ conj. καί and, even, also, but
οἱ art. nom. masc. pl. ὁ ἡ τό the, this, that, he, she, it
τῷ art. dat. masc. sg. ὁ ἡ τό the, this, that, he, she, it
κόσμῳ n. dat. masc. sg. κόσμος world, adorning
τούτῳ demo. pron. dat. masc. sg. οὗτος αὕτη τοῦτο this, the same, this same, he, she, it
ὡς adv. ὡς as, when, as it were, how, about, like, as soon as, even as, while
μὴ particle of negation. μή not, no, lest, neither, none, nothing, nor, never, without
γὰρ conj. γάρ for, and, because, but, indeed
τὸ art. nom. neut. sg. ὁ ἡ τό the, this, that, he, she, it
σχῆμα n. nom. neut. sg. σχῆμα fashion
τοῦ art. gen. masc. sg. ὁ ἡ τό the, this, that, he, she, it
κόσμου n. gen. masc. sg. κόσμος world, adorning
τούτου demo. pron. gen. masc. sg. οὗτος αὕτη τοῦτο this, the same, this same, he, she, it
32 δὲ conj. δέ but, and, now, also, to the contrary, rather, then
ὑμᾶς pron. acc. 2p. pl. σύ thou, you
ἀμερίμνους adj. acc. masc. pl. ἀμέριμνος secure, without care, without carefulness
ὁ art. nom. masc. sg. ὁ ἡ τό the, this, that, he, she, it

ἄγαμος n. nom. masc. sg. ἄγαμος unmarried
τὰ art. acc. neut. pl. ὁ ἡ τό the, this, that, he, she, it
τοῦ art. gen. masc. sg. ὁ ἡ τό the, this, that, he, she, it
Κυρίου n. gen. masc. sg. κύριος Lord, lord, master, sir, LORD, God, Master, owner
πῶς adv. πῶς how, by what means, after what manner
τῷ art. dat. masc. sg. ὁ ἡ τό the, this, that, he, she, it
Κυρίῳ n. dat. masc. sg. κύριος Lord, lord, master, sir, LORD, God, Master, owner
33 ὁ art. nom. masc. sg. ὁ ἡ τό the, this, that, he, she, it
δὲ conj. δέ but, and, now, also, to the contrary, rather, then
τὰ art. acc. neut. pl. ὁ ἡ τό the, this, that, he, she, it
τοῦ art. gen. masc. sg. ὁ ἡ τό the, this, that, he, she, it
κόσμου n. gen. masc. sg. κόσμος world, adorning
πῶς adv. πῶς how, by what means, after what manner
τῇ art. dat. fem. sg. ὁ ἡ τό the, this, that, he, she, it
γυναικί n. dat. fem. sg. γυνή woman, wife
34 ἡ art. nom. fem. sg. ὁ ἡ τό the, this, that, he, she, it
γυνὴ n. nom. fem. sg. γυνή woman, wife
καὶ conj. καί and, even, also, but
ἡ art. nom. fem. sg. ὁ ἡ τό the, this, that, he, she, it
παρθένος n. nom. fem. sg. παρθένος virgin
ἡ art. nom. fem. sg. ὁ ἡ τό the, this, that, he, she, it
ἄγαμος n. nom. fem. sg. ἄγαμος unmarried
τὰ art. acc. neut. pl. ὁ ἡ τό the, this, that, he, she, it
τοῦ art. gen. masc. sg. ὁ ἡ τό the, this, that, he, she, it
Κυρίου n. gen. masc. sg. κύριος Lord, lord, master, sir, LORD, God, Master, owner
ἵνα conj. ἵνα that, to, lest, for to, so that, albeit, because, for, so as
ἁγία adj. nom. fem. sg. ἅγιος Holy, holy, saint, Holy One, holy thing, most holy
καὶ conj. καί and, even, also, but
σώματι n. dat. neut. sg. σῶμα body, bodily, slave
καὶ conj. καί and, even, also, but
πνεύματι n. dat. neut. sg. πνεῦμα spirit, Spirit, Ghost, ghost, life. of the spirit, wind
ἡ art. nom. fem. sg. ὁ ἡ τό the, this, that, he, she, it
δὲ conj. δέ but, and, now, also, to the contrary, rather, then
τὰ art. acc. neut. pl. ὁ ἡ τό the, this, that, he, she, it
τοῦ art. gen. masc. sg. ὁ ἡ τό the, this, that, he, she, it
κόσμου n. gen. masc. sg. κόσμος world, adorning
πῶς adv. πῶς how, by what means, after what manner
τῷ art. dat. masc. sg. ὁ ἡ τό the, this, that, he, she, it
ἀνδρί n. dat. masc. sg. ἀνήρ man, husband, sir
35 τοῦτο demo. pron. acc. neut. sg. οὗτος αὕτη τοῦτο this, the same, this same, he, she, it
δὲ conj. δέ but, and, now, also, to the contrary, rather, then
πρὸς prep. πρός (+gen) for, (+dat) at, (+acc) unto, to, with, for, against
τὸ art. acc. neut. sg. ὁ ἡ τό the, this, that, he, she, it
ὑμῶν pron. gen. 2p. pl. σύ thou, you
αὐτῶν pron. gen. masc. 3p. pl. αὐτός ἡ ὁ self, of oneself, even, very, the same, he, she, it
οὐχ particle of negation. οὐ οὐκ οὐχ not, no, neither, none, nay, nor, never, nothing
ἵνα conj. ἵνα that, to, lest, for to, so that, albeit, because, for, so as
βρόχον n. acc. masc. sg. βρόχος snare
ὑμῖν pron. dat. 2p. pl. σύ thou, you
ἀλλὰ conj. ἀλλά but, yea, yet, nevertheless, howbeit, nay, therefore
πρὸς prep. πρός (+gen) for, (+dat) at, (+acc) unto, to, with, for, against
τὸ art. acc. neut. sg. ὁ ἡ τό the, this, that, he, she, it
εὔσχημον adj. acc. neut. sg. εὐσχήμων honourable, comely
καὶ conj. καί and, even, also, but
εὐπρόσεδρον adj. acc. neut. sg. εὐπρόσεδρος attend upon

τῷ art. dat. masc. sg. ὁ ἡ τό the, this, that, he, she, it
Κυρίῳ n. dat. masc. sg. κύριος Lord, lord, master, sir, LORD, God, Master, owner
ἀπερισπάστως adv. ἀπερισπάστως without distraction
36 εἰ conj. εἰ if, whether, that, though, forasmuch
δέ conj. δέ but, and, now, also, to the contrary, rather, then
τις indefinite pron. nom. masc. sg. τὶς certain, some, any man, one, any thing
ἐπὶ prep. ἐπί (+gen) on, in, upon, (+dat) in, at, for, upon, (+acc) on, upon, unto, to, against
τὴν art. acc. fem. sg. ὁ ἡ τό the, this, that, he, she, it
παρθένον n. acc. fem. sg. παρθένος virgin
αὐτοῦ pron. gen. masc. 3p. sg. αὐτός ἡ ὁ self, of oneself, even, very, the same, he, she, it
ἐὰν conj. ἐάν if, soever, except, though, and if, but, whether, if so, so
ὑπέρακμος adj. nom. masc. sg. ὑπέρακμος pass the flower of her age, past prime
καὶ conj. καί and, even, also, but
οὕτως adv. οὕτω οὕτως so, even so, thus, on this wise, likewise, after this manner
ὃ relative pron. acc. neut. sg. ὅς ἥ ὅ who, which, what, that
οὐχ particle of negation. οὐ οὐκ οὐχ not, no, neither, none, nay, nor, never, nothing
37 ὃς relative pron. nom. masc. sg. ὅς ἥ ὅ who, which, what, that
δὲ conj. δέ but, and, now, also, to the contrary, rather, then
ἑδραῖος adj. nom. masc. sg. ἑδραῖος stedfast, settled
ἐν prep. ἐν (+dat) in, by, with, among, at, on, through, to, within, into, of, for
τῇ art. dat. fem. sg. ὁ ἡ τό the, this, that, he, she, it
καρδίᾳ n. dat. fem. sg. καρδία heart
μὴ particle of negation. μή not, no, lest, neither, none, nothing, nor, never, without
ἀνάγκην n. acc. fem. sg. ἀνάγκη must needs, necessity, distress, inevitable
ἐξουσίαν n. acc. fem. sg. ἐξουσία power, authority, right, strength, jurisdiction
δὲ conj. δέ but, and, now, also, to the contrary, rather, then
περὶ prep. περί (+gen) of, for, concerning, (+acc) about, concerning, in
τοῦ art. gen. neut. sg. ὁ ἡ τό the, this, that, he, she, it
ἰδίου adj. gen. neut. sg. ἴδιος one's own, one's, privately
θελήματος n. gen. neut. sg. θέλημα will, desire, pleasure
καὶ conj. καί and, even, also, but
τοῦτο demo. pron. acc. neut. sg. οὗτος αὕτη τοῦτο this, the same, this same, he, she, it
ἐν prep. ἐν (+dat) in, by, with, among, at, on, through, to, within, into, of, for
τῇ art. dat. fem. sg. ὁ ἡ τό the, this, that, he, she, it
καρδίᾳ n. dat. fem. sg. καρδία heart
αὐτοῦ pron. gen. masc. 3p. sg. αὐτός ἡ ὁ self, of oneself, even, very, the same, he, she, it
τοῦ art. gen. masc. sg. ὁ ἡ τό the, this, that, he, she, it
τὴν art. acc. fem. sg. ὁ ἡ τό the, this, that, he, she, it
ἑαυτοῦ reflexive pron. gen. masc. 3p. sg. ἑαυτοῦ himself, herself, itself, yourself, ourselves
παρθένον n. acc. fem. sg. παρθένος virgin
καλῶς adv. καλῶς good, well, full well
38 ὥστε conj. ὥστε so that, wherefore, insomuch that, therefore, that, so then
καὶ conj. καί and, even, also, but
ὁ art. nom. masc. sg. ὁ ἡ τό the, this, that, he, she, it
καλῶς adv. καλῶς good, well, full well
ὁ art. nom. masc. sg. ὁ ἡ τό the, this, that, he, she, it
δὲ conj. δέ but, and, now, also, to the contrary, rather, then
μὴ particle of negation. μή not, no, lest, neither, none, nothing, nor, never, without
κρεῖσσον compar. adj. acc. neut. sg. κρείσσων better
39 γυνὴ n. nom. fem. sg. γυνή woman, wife
νόμῳ n. dat. masc. sg. νόμος law, the law
ἐφ' prep. ἐπί (+gen) on, in, upon, (+dat) in, at, for, upon, (+acc) on, upon, unto, to, against
ὅσον relative pron. acc. masc. sg. ὅσος as many as, whatsoever, that, as long as, how much
χρόνον n. acc. masc. sg. χρόνος time, season, space
ὁ art. nom. masc. sg. ὁ ἡ τό the, this, that, he, she, it

ἀνὴρ n. nom. masc. sg. ἀνήρ man, husband, sir
αὐτῆς pron. gen. fem. 3p. sg. αὐτός ἡ ὁ self, of oneself, even, very, the same, he, she, it
ἐὰν conj. ἐάν if, soever, except, though, and if, but, whether, if so, so
δὲ conj. δέ but, and, now, also, to the contrary, rather, then
ὁ art. nom. masc. sg. ὁ ἡ τό the, this, that, he, she, it
ἀνὴρ n. nom. masc. sg. ἀνήρ man, husband, sir
αὐτῆς pron. gen. fem. 3p. sg. αὐτός ἡ ὁ self, of oneself, even, very, the same, he, she, it
ἐλευθέρα adj. nom. fem. sg. ἐλεύθερος free, freewoman, at liberty, freeman
ᾧ relative pron. dat. masc. sg. ὅς ἥ ὅ who, which, what, that
μόνον adv. μόνος only, alone, by oneself
ἐν prep. ἐν (+dat) in, by, with, among, at, on, through, to, within, into, of, for
Κυρίῳ n. dat. masc. sg. κύριος Lord, lord, master, sir, LORD, God, Master, owner
40 μακαριωτέρα compar. adj. nom. fem. sg. μακάριος blessed, happy, happier
δέ conj. δέ but, and, now, also, to the contrary, rather, then
ἐὰν conj. ἐάν if, soever, except, though, and if, but, whether, if so, so
οὕτω adv. οὕτω οὕτως so, even so, thus, on this wise, likewise, after this manner
κατὰ prep. κατά (+gen) against, by, throughout, down, (+acc) according to, after, with
τὴν art. acc. fem. sg. ὁ ἡ τό the, this, that, he, she, it
ἐμὴν poss. pron. acc. fem. 1p. sg. ἐμός my, mine, mine own, of me
γνώμην n. acc. fem. sg. γνώμη judgement, mind, advice, purpose, will
δέ conj. δέ but, and, now, also, to the contrary, rather, then
κἀγὼ pron. nom. 1p. sg. κἀγώ and I, I also, so I, even as I
Πνεῦμα n. acc. neut. sg. πνεῦμα spirit, Spirit, Ghost, ghost, life. of the spirit, wind
Θεοῦ n. gen. masc. sg. θεός God, god

8

1 Περὶ prep. περί (+gen) of, for, concerning, (+acc) about, concerning, in
δὲ conj. δέ but, and, now, also, to the contrary, rather, then
τῶν art. gen. neut. pl. ὁ ἡ τό the, this, that, he, she, it
εἰδωλοθύτων adj. gen. neut. pl. εἰδωλόθυτον thing offered in sacrifice unto idols
ὅτι conj. ὅτι that, for, because, how that, how, because that, for that, though
πάντες adj. nom. masc. pl. πᾶς πᾶσα πᾶν all, every, whosoever, every one, no, whole, any
γνῶσιν n. acc. fem. sg. γνῶσις knowledge, science
ἡ art. nom. fem. sg. ὁ ἡ τό the, this, that, he, she, it
γνῶσις n. nom. fem. sg. γνῶσις knowledge, science
ἡ art. nom. fem. sg. ὁ ἡ τό the, this, that, he, she, it
δὲ conj. δέ but, and, now, also, to the contrary, rather, then
ἀγάπη n. nom. fem. sg. ἀγάπη love, charity, feast of charity
2 εἰ conj. εἰ if, whether, that, though, forasmuch
δὲ conj. δέ but, and, now, also, to the contrary, rather, then
τις indefinite pron. nom. masc. sg. τὶς certain, some, any man, one, any thing
τι indefinite pron. acc. neut. sg. τὶς certain, some, any man, one, any thing
οὐδέπω adv. οὐδέπω never before, never yet, as yet not, not yet, yet
οὐδὲν num. nom. neut. sg. οὐδείς no man, nothing, no, none, neither, not, nought
καθὼς adv. καθώς as, even as, according as, according to
3 εἰ conj. εἰ if, whether, that, though, forasmuch
δέ conj. δέ but, and, now, also, to the contrary, rather, then
τις indefinite pron. nom. masc. sg. τὶς certain, some, any man, one, any thing
τὸν art. acc. masc. sg. ὁ ἡ τό the, this, that, he, she, it
Θεόν n. acc. masc. sg. θεός God, god
οὗτος demo. pron. nom. masc. sg. οὗτος αὕτη τοῦτο this, the same, this same, he, she, it
ὑπ' prep. ὑπό (+gen) of, by, with, from, among, (+acc) under
αὐτοῦ pron. gen. masc. 3p. sg. αὐτός ἡ ὁ self, of oneself, even, very, the same, he, she, it
4 περὶ prep. περί (+gen) of, for, concerning, (+acc) about, concerning, in

τῆς art. gen. fem. sg. ὁ ἡ τό the, this, that, he, she, it
βρώσεως n. gen. fem. sg. βρῶσις rust, meat, eating, food, morsel of meat
οὖν conj. οὖν therefore, then, so, and, now, wherefore
τῶν art. gen. neut. pl. ὁ ἡ τό the, this, that, he, she, it
εἰδωλοθύτων adj. gen. neut. pl. εἰδωλόθυτον thing offered in sacrifice unto idols
ὅτι conj. ὅτι that, for, because, how that, how, because that, for that, though
οὐδὲν num. nom. neut. sg. οὐδείς no man, nothing, no, none, neither, not, nought
εἴδωλον n. nom. neut. sg. εἴδωλον idol
ἐν prep. ἐν (+dat) in, by, with, among, at, on, through, to, within, into, of, for
κόσμῳ n. dat. masc. sg. κόσμος world, adorning
καὶ conj. καί and, even, also, but
ὅτι conj. ὅτι that, for, because, how that, how, because that, for that, though
οὐδεὶς num. nom. masc. sg. οὐδείς no man, nothing, no, none, neither, not, nought
Θεὸς n. nom. masc. sg. θεός God, god
ἕτερος adj. nom. masc. sg. ἕτερος another, other, else, strange
εἰ conj. εἰ if, whether, that, though, forasmuch
μὴ particle of negation. μή not, no, lest, neither, none, nothing, nor, never, without
εἷς num. nom. masc. sg. εἷς or ἕν one, other, some, any, only, a certain
5 καὶ conj. καί and, even, also, but
γὰρ conj. γάρ for, and, because, but, indeed
εἴπερ conj. εἴπερ if it be so that, if indeed, since indeed, since, although indeed
θεοὶ n. nom. masc. pl. θεός God, god
εἴτε conj. εἴτε whether
ἐν prep. ἐν (+dat) in, by, with, among, at, on, through, to, within, into, of, for
οὐρανῷ n. dat. masc. sg. οὐρανός heaven, air, sky
εἴτε conj. εἴτε whether
ἐπὶ prep. ἐπί (+gen) on, in, upon, (+dat) in, at, for, upon, (+acc) on, upon, unto, to, against
τῆς art. gen. fem. sg. ὁ ἡ τό the, this, that, he, she, it
γῆς n. gen. fem. sg. γῆ earth, land, ground, country
ὥσπερ adv. ὥσπερ as, even as, like as
θεοὶ n. nom. masc. pl. θεός God, god
πολλοὶ adj. nom. masc. pl. πολύς many, great, much, long, abundant
καὶ conj. καί and, even, also, but
κύριοι n. nom. masc. pl. κύριος Lord, lord, master, sir, LORD, God, Master, owner
πολλοὶ adj. nom. masc. pl. πολύς many, great, much, long, abundant
6 ἀλλ’ conj. ἀλλά but, yea, yet, nevertheless, howbeit, nay, therefore
ἡμῖν pron. dat. 1p. pl. ἐγώ I
εἷς num. nom. masc. sg. εἷς or ἕν one, other, some, any, only, a certain
Θεὸς n. nom. masc. sg. θεός God, god
ὁ art. nom. masc. sg. ὁ ἡ τό the, this, that, he, she, it
πατὴρ n. nom. masc. sg. πατήρ Father, father, parent
ἐξ prep. ἐκ ἐξ (+gen) of, from, out of, by, on, with, in, among, through
οὗ relative pron. gen. masc. sg. ὅς ἥ ὅ who, which, what, that
τὰ art. nom. neut. pl. ὁ ἡ τό the, this, that, he, she, it
πάντα adj. nom. neut. pl. πᾶς πᾶσα πᾶν all, every, whosoever, every one, no, whole, any
καὶ conj. καί and, even, also, but
ἡμεῖς pron. nom. 1p. pl. ἐγώ I
εἰς prep. εἰς (+acc) into, to, unto, for, in, on, toward, against, upon, at, among
αὐτόν pron. acc. masc. 3p. sg. αὐτός ή ό self, of oneself, even, very, the same, he, she, it
καὶ conj. καί and, even, also, but
εἷς num. nom. masc. sg. εἷς or ἕν one, other, some, any, only, a certain
Κύριος n. nom. masc. sg. κύριος Lord, lord, master, sir, LORD, God, Master, owner
Ἰησοῦς n. nom. masc. sg. Ἰησοῦς Jesus
Χριστὸς n. nom. masc. sg. Χριστός Christ
δι’ prep. διά (+gen) by, through, with, in, of, (+acc) for, because of, for a cause

οὗ relative pron. gen. masc. sg. ὅς ἥ ὅ who, which, what, that
τὰ art. nom. neut. pl. ὁ ἡ τό the, this, that, he, she, it
πάντα adj. nom. neut. pl. πᾶς πᾶσα πᾶν all, every, whosoever, every one, no, whole, any
καὶ conj. καί and, even, also, but
ἡμεῖς pron. nom. 1p. pl. ἐγώ I
δι' prep. διά (+gen) by, through, with, in, of, (+acc) for, because of, for a cause
αὐτοῦ pron. gen. masc. 3p. sg. αὐτός ή ό self, of oneself, even, very, the same, he, she, it
7 ἀλλ' conj. ἀλλά but, yea, yet, nevertheless, howbeit, nay, therefore
οὐκ particle of negation. οὐ οὐκ οὐχ not, no, neither, none, nay, nor, never, nothing
ἐν prep. ἐν (+dat) in, by, with, among, at, on, through, to, within, into, of, for
πᾶσιν adj. dat. masc. pl. πᾶς πᾶσα πᾶν all, every, whosoever, every one, no, whole, any
ἡ art. nom. fem. sg. ὁ ἡ τό the, this, that, he, she, it
γνῶσις n. nom. fem. sg. γνῶσις knowledge, science
τινὲς indefinite pron. nom. masc. pl. τὶς certain, some, any man, one, any thing
δὲ conj. δέ but, and, now, also, to the contrary, rather, then
τῇ art. dat. fem. sg. ὁ ἡ τό the, this, that, he, she, it
συνειδήσει n. dat. fem. sg. συνείδησις conscience
τοῦ art. gen. neut. sg. ὁ ἡ τό the, this, that, he, she, it
εἰδώλου n. gen. neut. sg. εἴδωλον idol
ἕως conj. ἕως till, until, unto, until when, while, as far as, even, until now
ἄρτι adv. ἄρτι now, hence, here, hither, even now, present
ὡς adv. ὡς as, when, as it were, how, about, like, as soon as, even as, while
εἰδωλόθυτον adj. acc. neut. sg. εἰδωλόθυτον thing offered in sacrifice unto idols
καὶ conj. καί and, even, also, but
ἡ art. nom. fem. sg. ὁ ἡ τό the, this, that, he, she, it
συνείδησις n. nom. fem. sg. συνείδησις conscience
αὐτῶν pron. gen. masc. 3p. pl. αὐτός ή ό self, of oneself, even, very, the same, he, she, it
ἀσθενὴς adj. nom. fem. sg. ἀσθενής weak, sick, impotent, more feeble
8 βρῶμα n. nom. neut. sg. βρῶμα victual, meat, food
δὲ conj. δέ but, and, now, also, to the contrary, rather, then
ἡμᾶς pron. acc. 1p. pl. ἐγώ I
οὐ particle of negation. οὐ οὐκ οὐχ not, no, neither, none, nay, nor, never, nothing
τῷ art. dat. masc. sg. ὁ ἡ τό the, this, that, he, she, it
Θεῷ n. dat. masc. sg. θεός God, god
οὔτε conj. οὔτε neither, nor, nor yet, no, none
γὰρ conj. γάρ for, and, because, but, indeed
ἐὰν conj. ἐάν if, soever, except, though, and if, but, whether, if so, so
οὔτε conj. οὔτε neither, nor, nor yet, no, none
ἐὰν conj. ἐάν if, soever, except, though, and if, but, whether, if so, so
μὴ particle of negation. μή not, no, lest, neither, none, nothing, nor, never, without
9 δὲ conj. δέ but, and, now, also, to the contrary, rather, then
μήπως conj. μήπως lest, lest by any means, lest by some means, lest haply
ἡ art. nom. fem. sg. ὁ ἡ τό the, this, that, he, she, it
ἐξουσία n. nom. fem. sg. ἐξουσία power, authority, right, strength, jurisdiction
ὑμῶν pron. gen. 2p. pl. σύ thou, you
αὕτη demo. pron. nom. fem. sg. οὗτος αὕτη τοῦτο this, the same, this same, he, she, it
πρόσκομμα n. nom. neut. sg. πρόσκομμα stumbling, offence
τοῖς art. dat. masc. pl. ὁ ἡ τό the, this, that, he, she, it
10 ἐὰν conj. ἐάν if, soever, except, though, and if, but, whether, if so, so
γάρ conj. γάρ for, and, because, but, indeed
τις indefinite pron. nom. masc. sg. τὶς certain, some, any man, one, any thing
σὲ pron. acc. 2p. sg. σύ thou, you
τὸν art. acc. masc. sg. ὁ ἡ τό the, this, that, he, she, it
γνῶσιν n. acc. fem. sg. γνῶσις knowledge, science
ἐν prep. ἐν (+dat) in, by, with, among, at, on, through, to, within, into, of, for

εἰδωλείῳ n. dat. neut. sg. εἰδωλεῖον idol's temple
οὐχὶ adv. οὐχί not, nay
ἡ art. nom. fem. sg. ὁ ἡ τό the, this, that, he, she, it
συνείδησις n. nom. fem. sg. συνείδησις conscience
αὐτοῦ pron. gen. masc. 3p. sg. αὐτός ἡ ὁ self, of oneself, even, very, the same, he, she, it
ἀσθενοῦς adj. gen. masc. sg. ἀσθενής weak, sick, impotent, more feeble
εἰς prep. εἰς (+acc) into, to, unto, for, in, on, toward, against, upon, at, among
τὸ art. acc. neut. sg. ὁ ἡ τό the, this, that, he, she, it
τὰ art. acc. neut. pl. ὁ ἡ τό the, this, that, he, she, it
εἰδωλόθυτα adj. acc. neut. pl. εἰδωλόθυτον thing offered in sacrifice unto idols
11 καὶ conj. καί and, even, also, but
ὁ art. nom. masc. sg. ὁ ἡ τό the, this, that, he, she, it
ἀδελφὸς n. nom. masc. sg. ἀδελφός brother
ἐπὶ prep. ἐπί (+gen) on, in, upon, (+dat) in, at, for, upon, (+acc) on, upon, unto, to, against
τῇ art. dat. fem. sg. ὁ ἡ τό the, this, that, he, she, it
σῇ poss. pron. dat. fem. 2p. sg. σός thy, thine, thine own
γνώσει n. dat. fem. sg. γνῶσις knowledge, science
δι' prep. διά (+gen) by, through, with, in, of, (+acc) for, because of, for a cause
ὃν relative pron. acc. masc. sg. ὅς ἥ ὅ who, which, what, that
Χριστὸς n. nom. masc. sg. Χριστός Christ
12 οὕτω adv. οὕτω οὕτως so, even so, thus, on this wise, likewise, after this manner
δὲ conj. δέ but, and, now, also, to the contrary, rather, then
εἰς prep. εἰς (+acc) into, to, unto, for, in, on, toward, against, upon, at, among
τοὺς art. acc. masc. pl. ὁ ἡ τό the, this, that, he, she, it
ἀδελφοὺς n. acc. masc. pl. ἀδελφός brother
καὶ conj. καί and, even, also, but
αὐτῶν pron. gen. masc. 3p. pl. αὐτός ἡ ὁ self, of oneself, even, very, the same, he, she, it
τὴν art. acc. fem. sg. ὁ ἡ τό the, this, that, he, she, it
συνείδησιν n. acc. fem. sg. συνείδησις conscience
εἰς prep. εἰς (+acc) into, to, unto, for, in, on, toward, against, upon, at, among
Χριστὸν n. acc. masc. sg. Χριστός Christ
13 διόπερ conj. διόπερ wherefore
εἰ conj. εἰ if, whether, that, though, forasmuch
βρῶμα n. nom. neut. sg. βρῶμα victual, meat, food
τὸν art. acc. masc. sg. ὁ ἡ τό the, this, that, he, she, it
ἀδελφόν n. acc. masc. sg. ἀδελφός brother
μου pron. gen. 1p. sg. ἐγώ I
οὐ particle of negation. οὐ οὐκ οὐχ not, no, neither, none, nay, nor, never, nothing
μὴ particle of negation. μή not, no, lest, neither, none, nothing, nor, never, without
κρέα n. acc. neut. pl. κρέας flesh
εἰς prep. εἰς (+acc) into, to, unto, for, in, on, toward, against, upon, at, among
τὸν art. acc. masc. sg. ὁ ἡ τό the, this, that, he, she, it
αἰῶνα n. acc. masc. sg. αἰών ever, ever and ever, evermore, age, eternal, world
ἵνα conj. ἵνα that, to, lest, for to, so that, albeit, because, for, so as
μὴ particle of negation. μή not, no, lest, neither, none, nothing, nor, never, without
τὸν art. acc. masc. sg. ὁ ἡ τό the, this, that, he, she, it
ἀδελφόν n. acc. masc. sg. ἀδελφός brother
μου pron. gen. 1p. sg. ἐγώ I

9

1 Οὐκ particle of negation. οὐ οὐκ οὐχ not, no, neither, none, nay, nor, never, nothing
ἀπόστολος n. nom. masc. sg. ἀπόστολος apostle, messenger, he that is sent
οὐκ particle of negation. οὐ οὐκ οὐχ not, no, neither, none, nay, nor, never, nothing
ἐλεύθερος adj. nom. masc. sg. ἐλεύθερος free, freewoman, at liberty, freeman

οὐχὶ adv. οὐχί not, nay
Ἰησοῦν n. acc. masc. sg. Ἰησοῦς Jesus
Χριστὸν n. acc. masc. sg. Χριστός Christ
τὸν art. acc. masc. sg. ὁ ἡ τό the, this, that, he, she, it
Κύριον n. acc. masc. sg. κύριος Lord, lord, master, sir, LORD, God, Master, owner
ἡμῶν pron. gen. 1p. pl. ἐγώ I
οὐ particle of negation. οὐ οὐκ οὐχ not, no, neither, none, nay, nor, never, nothing
τὸ art. nom. neut. sg. ὁ ἡ τό the, this, that, he, she, it
ἔργον n. nom. neut. sg. ἔργον work, deed, doing labour
μου pron. gen. 1p. sg. ἐγώ I
ὑμεῖς pron. nom. 2p. pl. σύ thou, you
ἐν prep. ἐν (+dat) in, by, with, among, at, on, through, to, within, into, of, for
Κυρίῳ n. dat. masc. sg. κύριος Lord, lord, master, sir, LORD, God, Master, owner
2 εἰ conj. εἰ if, whether, that, though, forasmuch
ἄλλοις adj. dat. masc. pl. ἄλλος other, another, some, one, more, otherwise
οὐκ particle of negation. οὐ οὐκ οὐχ not, no, neither, none, nay, nor, never, nothing
ἀπόστολος n. nom. masc. sg. ἀπόστολος apostle, messenger, he that is sent
ἀλλά conj. ἀλλά but, yea, yet, nevertheless, howbeit, nay, therefore
γε particle. γέ yet, and beside, at least, doubtless
ὑμῖν pron. dat. 2p. pl. σύ thou, you
ἡ art. nom. fem. sg. ὁ ἡ τό the, this, that, he, she, it
γὰρ conj. γάρ for, and, because, but, indeed
σφραγίς n. nom. fem. sg. σφραγίς seal
τῆς art. gen. fem. sg. ὁ ἡ τό the, this, that, he, she, it
ἐμῆς poss. pron. gen. fem. 1p. sg. ἐμός my, mine, mine own, of me
ἀποστολῆς n. gen. fem. sg. ἀποστολή apostleship
ὑμεῖς pron. nom. 2p. pl. σύ thou, you
ἐν prep. ἐν (+dat) in, by, with, among, at, on, through, to, within, into, of, for
Κυρίῳ n. dat. masc. sg. κύριος Lord, lord, master, sir, LORD, God, Master, owner
3 ἡ art. nom. fem. sg. ὁ ἡ τό the, this, that, he, she, it
ἐμὴ poss. pron. nom. fem. 1p. sg. ἐμός my, mine, mine own, of me
ἀπολογία n. nom. fem. sg. ἀπολογία defence, answer, answer for oneself, clear oneself
τοῖς art. dat. masc. pl. ὁ ἡ τό the, this, that, he, she, it
ἐμὲ pron. acc. 1p. sg. ἐγώ I
αὕτη demo. pron. nom. fem. sg. οὗτος αὕτη τοῦτο this, the same, this same, he, she, it
4 μὴ particle of negation. μή not, no, lest, neither, none, nothing, nor, never, without
οὐκ particle of negation. οὐ οὐκ οὐχ not, no, neither, none, nay, nor, never, nothing
ἐξουσίαν n. acc. fem. sg. ἐξουσία power, authority, right, strength, jurisdiction
καὶ conj. καί and, even, also, but
5 μὴ particle of negation. μή not, no, lest, neither, none, nothing, nor, never, without
οὐκ particle of negation. οὐ οὐκ οὐχ not, no, neither, none, nay, nor, never, nothing
ἐξουσίαν n. acc. fem. sg. ἐξουσία power, authority, right, strength, jurisdiction
ἀδελφὴν n. acc. fem. sg. ἀδελφή sister
γυναῖκα n. acc. fem. sg. γυνή woman, wife
ὡς adv. ὡς as, when, as it were, how, about, like, as soon as, even as, while
καὶ conj. καί and, even, also, but
οἱ art. nom. masc. pl. ὁ ἡ τό the, this, that, he, she, it
λοιποὶ adj. nom. masc. pl. λοιπός other, rest, remnant, residue, which remain
ἀπόστολοι n. nom. masc. pl. ἀπόστολος apostle, messenger, he that is sent
καὶ conj. καί and, even, also, but
οἱ art. nom. masc. pl. ὁ ἡ τό the, this, that, he, she, it
ἀδελφοὶ n. nom. masc. pl. ἀδελφός brother
τοῦ art. gen. masc. sg. ὁ ἡ τό the, this, that, he, she, it
Κυρίου n. gen. masc. sg. κύριος Lord, lord, master, sir, LORD, God, Master, owner
καὶ conj. καί and, even, also, but

Κηφᾶς n. nom. masc. sg. Κηφᾶς Cephas
6 ἢ particle. ἤ or, than, either, nor, or else, and, rather than
μόνος adj. nom. masc. sg. μόνος only, alone, by oneself
ἐγὼ pron. nom. 1p. sg. ἐγώ I
καὶ conj. καί and, even, also, but
Βαρναβᾶς n. nom. masc. sg. Βαρναβᾶς Barnabas
οὐκ particle of negation. οὐ οὐκ οὐχ not, no, neither, none, nay, nor, never, nothing
ἐξουσίαν n. acc. fem. sg. ἐξουσία power, authority, right, strength, jurisdiction
τοῦ art. gen. masc. sg. ὁ ἡ τό the, this, that, he, she, it
μὴ particle of negation. μή not, no, lest, neither, none, nothing, nor, never, without
7 τίς interrog. pron. nom. masc. sg. τίς what, who, why, where, which, how
ἰδίοις adj. dat. neut. pl. ἴδιος one's own, one's, privately
ὀψωνίοις n. dat. neut. pl. ὀψώνιον wage, charge
ποτέ adv. ποτέ in time past, at any time, sometimes, in old time, once, when
τίς interrog. pron. nom. masc. sg. τίς what, who, why, where, which, how
ἀμπελῶνα n. acc. masc. sg. ἀμπελών vineyard
καὶ conj. καί and, even, also, but
ἐκ prep. ἐκ ἐξ (+gen) of, from, out of, by, on, with, in, among, through
τοῦ art. gen. masc. sg. ὁ ἡ τό the, this, that, he, she, it
καρποῦ n. gen. masc. sg. καρπός fruit
αὐτοῦ pron. gen. masc. 3p. sg. αὐτός ἡ ὁ self, of oneself, even, very, the same, he, she, it
οὐκ particle of negation. οὐ οὐκ οὐχ not, no, neither, none, nay, nor, never, nothing
ἢ particle. ἤ or, than, either, nor, or else, and, rather than
τίς interrog. pron. nom. masc. sg. τίς what, who, why, where, which, how
ποίμνην n. acc. fem. sg. ποίμνη flock, fold
καὶ conj. καί and, even, also, but
ἐκ prep. ἐκ ἐξ (+gen) of, from, out of, by, on, with, in, among, through
τοῦ art. gen. neut. sg. ὁ ἡ τό the, this, that, he, she, it
γάλακτος n. gen. neut. sg. γάλα milk
τῆς art. gen. fem. sg. ὁ ἡ τό the, this, that, he, she, it
ποίμνης n. gen. fem. sg. ποίμνη flock, fold
οὐκ particle of negation. οὐ οὐκ οὐχ not, no, neither, none, nay, nor, never, nothing
8 μὴ particle of negation. μή not, no, lest, neither, none, nothing, nor, never, without
κατὰ prep. κατά (+gen) against, by, throughout, down, (+acc) according to, after, with
ἄνθρωπον n. acc. masc. sg. ἄνθρωπος man, human being, person, one, certain
ταῦτα demo. pron. acc. neut. pl. οὗτος αὕτη τοῦτο this, the same, this same, he, she, it
ἢ particle. ἤ or, than, either, nor, or else, and, rather than
οὐχὶ particle of negation. οὐχί not, nay
καὶ conj. καί and, even, also, but
ὁ art. nom. masc. sg. ὁ ἡ τό the, this, that, he, she, it
νόμος n. nom. masc. sg. νόμος law, the law
ταῦτα demo. pron. acc. neut. pl. οὗτος αὕτη τοῦτο this, the same, this same, he, she, it
9 ἐν prep. ἐν (+dat) in, by, with, among, at, on, through, to, within, into, of, for
γὰρ conj. γάρ for, and, because, but, indeed
τῷ art. dat. masc. sg. ὁ ἡ τό the, this, that, he, she, it
Μωσέως n. gen. masc. sg. Μωσῆς Moses
νόμῳ n. dat. masc. sg. νόμος law, the law
Οὐ particle of negation. οὐ οὐκ οὐχ not, no, neither, none, nay, nor, never, nothing
βοῦν n. acc. masc. sg. βοῦς ox
μὴ particle of negation. μή not, no, lest, neither, none, nothing, nor, never, without
τῶν art. gen. masc. pl. ὁ ἡ τό the, this, that, he, she, it
βοῶν n. gen. masc. pl. βοῦς ox
τῷ art. dat. masc. sg. ὁ ἡ τό the, this, that, he, she, it
Θεῷ n. dat. masc. sg. θεός God, god
10 ἢ particle. ἤ or, than, either, nor, or else, and, rather than

δι' prep. διά (+gen) by, through, with, in, of, (+acc) for, because of, for a cause
ἡμᾶς pron. acc. 1p. pl. ἐγώ I
πάντως adv. πάντως surely, altogether, by all means, at all, needs, no doubt
δι' prep. διά (+gen) by, through, with, in, of, (+acc) for, because of, for a cause
ἡμᾶς pron. acc. 1p. pl. ἐγώ I
γὰρ conj. γάρ for, and, because, but, indeed
ὅτι conj. ὅτι that, for, because, how that, how, because that, for that, though
ἐπ' prep. ἐπί (+gen) on, in, upon, (+dat) in, at, for, upon, (+acc) on, upon, unto, to, against
ἐλπίδι n. dat. fem. sg. ἐλπίς hope, faith
ὁ art. nom. masc. sg. ὁ ἡ τό the, this, that, he, she, it
καὶ conj. καί and, even, also, but
ὁ art. nom. masc. sg. ὁ ἡ τό the, this, that, he, she, it
τῆς art. gen. fem. sg. ὁ ἡ τό the, this, that, he, she, it
ἐλπίδος n. gen. fem. sg. ἐλπίς hope, faith
αὐτοῦ pron. gen. neut. 3p. sg. αὐτός ἡ ὁ self, of oneself, even, very, the same, he, she, it
ἐπ' prep. ἐπί (+gen) on, in, upon, (+dat) in, at, for, upon, (+acc) on, upon, unto, to, against
ἐλπίδι n. dat. fem. sg. ἐλπίς hope, faith
11 εἰ conj. εἰ if, whether, that, though, forasmuch
ἡμεῖς pron. nom. 1p. pl. ἐγώ I
ὑμῖν pron. dat. 2p. pl. σύ thou, you
τὰ art. acc. neut. pl. ὁ ἡ τό the, this, that, he, she, it
πνευματικὰ adj. acc. neut. pl. πνευματικός spiritual
μέγα adj. nom. neut. sg. μέγας great, loud, greatest, high, large, mighty, strong
εἰ conj. εἰ if, whether, that, though, forasmuch
ἡμεῖς pron. nom. 1p. pl. ἐγώ I
ὑμῖν pron. dat. 2p. pl. σύ thou, you
τὰ art. acc. neut. pl. ὁ ἡ τό the, this, that, he, she, it
σαρκικὰ adj. acc. neut. pl. σαρκικός carnal, fleshly
12 εἰ conj. εἰ if, whether, that, though, forasmuch
ἄλλοι adj. nom. masc. pl. ἄλλος other, another, some, one, more, otherwise
τῆς art. gen. fem. sg. ὁ ἡ τό the, this, that, he, she, it
ἐξουσίας n. gen. fem. sg. ἐξουσία power, authority, right, strength, jurisdiction
ὑμῶν pron. gen. 2p. pl. σύ thou, you
οὐ particle of negation. οὐ οὐκ οὐχ not, no, neither, none, nay, nor, never, nothing
μᾶλλον adv. μᾶλλον rather, more, more and more, better, much, much the more
ἡμεῖς pron. nom. 1p. pl. ἐγώ I
ἀλλ' conj. ἀλλά but, yea, yet, nevertheless, howbeit, nay, therefore
οὐκ particle of negation. οὐ οὐκ οὐχ not, no, neither, none, nay, nor, never, nothing
τῇ art. dat. fem. sg. ὁ ἡ τό the, this, that, he, she, it
ἐξουσίᾳ n. dat. fem. sg. ἐξουσία power, authority, right, strength, jurisdiction
ταύτῃ demo. pron. dat. fem. sg. οὗτος αὕτη τοῦτο this, the same, this same, he, she, it
ἀλλὰ conj. ἀλλά but, yea, yet, nevertheless, howbeit, nay, therefore
πάντα adj. acc. neut. pl. πᾶς πᾶσa πᾶν all, every, whosoever, every one, no, whole, any
ἵνα conj. ἵνα that, to, lest, for to, so that, albeit, because, for, so as
μὴ particle of negation. μή not, no, lest, neither, none, nothing, nor, never, without
ἐγκοπὴν n. acc. fem. sg. ἐγκοπή hinder, hindrance
τινα indefinite pron. acc. fem. sg. τὶς certain, some, any man, one, any thing
τῷ art. dat. neut. sg. ὁ ἡ τό the, this, that, he, she, it
εὐαγγελίῳ n. dat. neut. sg. εὐαγγέλιον gospel
τοῦ art. gen. masc. sg. ὁ ἡ τό the, this, that, he, she, it
Χριστοῦ n. gen. masc. sg. Χριστός Christ
13 οὐκ particle of negation. οὐ οὐκ οὐχ not, no, neither, none, nay, nor, never, nothing
ὅτι conj. ὅτι that, for, because, how that, how, because that, for that, though
οἱ art. nom. masc. pl. ὁ ἡ τό the, this, that, he, she, it
τὰ art. acc. neut. pl. ὁ ἡ τό the, this, that, he, she, it

ἱερὰ adj. acc. neut. pl. ἱερός holy, hallowed, divine
ἐκ prep. ἐκ ἐξ (+gen) of, from, out of, by, on, with, in, among, through
τοῦ art. gen. neut. sg. ὁ ἡ τό the, this, that, he, she, it
ἱεροῦ n. gen. neut. sg. ἱερόν temple
οἱ art. nom. masc. pl. ὁ ἡ τό the, this, that, he, she, it
τῷ art. dat. neut. sg. ὁ ἡ τό the, this, that, he, she, it
θυσιαστηρίῳ n. dat. neut. sg. θυσιαστήριον altar
τῷ art. dat. neut. sg. ὁ ἡ τό the, this, that, he, she, it
θυσιαστηρίῳ n. dat. neut. sg. θυσιαστήριον altar
14 οὕτω adv. οὕτω οὕτως so, even so, thus, on this wise, likewise, after this manner
καὶ conj. καί and, even, also, but
ὁ art. nom. masc. sg. ὁ ἡ τό the, this, that, he, she, it
Κύριος n. nom. masc. sg. κύριος Lord, lord, master, sir, LORD, God, Master, owner
τοῖς art. dat. masc. pl. ὁ ἡ τό the, this, that, he, she, it
τὸ art. acc. neut. sg. ὁ ἡ τό the, this, that, he, she, it
εὐαγγέλιον n. acc. neut. sg. εὐαγγέλιον gospel
ἐκ prep. ἐκ ἐξ (+gen) of, from, out of, by, on, with, in, among, through
τοῦ art. gen. neut. sg. ὁ ἡ τό the, this, that, he, she, it
εὐαγγελίου n. gen. neut. sg. εὐαγγέλιον gospel
15 ἐγὼ pron. nom. 1p. sg. ἐγώ I
δὲ conj. δέ but, and, now, also, to the contrary, rather, then
οὐδενὶ num. dat. masc. sg. οὐδείς no man, nothing, no, none, neither, not, nought
τούτων demo. pron. gen. neut. pl. οὗτος αὕτη τοῦτο this, the same, this same, he, she, it
οὐκ particle of negation. οὐ οὐκ οὐχ not, no, neither, none, nay, nor, never, nothing
δὲ conj. δέ but, and, now, also, to the contrary, rather, then
ταῦτα demo. pron. acc. neut. pl. οὗτος αὕτη τοῦτο this, the same, this same, he, she, it
ἵνα conj. ἵνα that, to, lest, for to, so that, albeit, because, for, so as
οὕτω adv. οὕτω οὕτως so, even so, thus, on this wise, likewise, after this manner
ἐν prep. ἐν (+dat) in, by, with, among, at, on, through, to, within, into, of, for
ἐμοί pron. dat. 1p. sg. ἐγώ I
καλὸν adj. nom. neut. sg. καλός good, better, goodly, meet, honest, fair, well, worthy
γάρ conj. γάρ for, and, because, but, indeed
μοι pron. dat. 1p. sg. ἐγώ I
μᾶλλον adv. μᾶλλον rather, more, more and more, better, much, much the more
ἢ particle. ἤ or, than, either, nor, or else, and, rather than
τὸ art. acc. neut. sg. ὁ ἡ τό the, this, that, he, she, it
καύχημά n. acc. neut. sg. καύχημα whereof to glory, rejoicing, glorying, boasting
μου pron. gen. 1p. sg. ἐγώ I
ἵνα conj. ἵνα that, to, lest, for to, so that, albeit, because, for, so as
τις indefinite pron. nom. masc. sg. τὶς certain, some, any man, one, any thing
16 ἐὰν conj. ἐάν if, soever, except, though, and if, but, whether, if so, so
γὰρ conj. γάρ for, and, because, but, indeed
οὐκ particle of negation. οὐ οὐκ οὐχ not, no, neither, none, nay, nor, never, nothing
μοι pron. dat. 1p. sg. ἐγώ I
καύχημα n. nom. neut. sg. καύχημα whereof to glory, rejoicing, glorying, boasting
ἀνάγκη n. nom. fem. sg. ἀνάγκη must needs, necessity, distress, inevitable
γὰρ conj. γάρ for, and, because, but, indeed
μοι pron. dat. 1p. sg. ἐγώ I
οὐαὶ particle. οὐαί woe, alas
δὲ conj. δέ but, and, now, also, to the contrary, rather, then
μοι pron. dat. 1p. sg. ἐγώ I
ἐὰν conj. ἐάν if, soever, except, though, and if, but, whether, if so, so
μὴ particle of negation. μή not, no, lest, neither, none, nothing, nor, never, without
17 εἰ conj. εἰ if, whether, that, though, forasmuch
γὰρ conj. γάρ for, and, because, but, indeed

ἑκὼν adj. nom. masc. sg. ἑκών willingly, willing
τοῦτο demo. pron. acc. neut. sg. οὗτος αὕτη τοῦτο this, the same, this same, he, she, it
μισθὸν n. acc. masc. sg. μισθός reward, hire, wage
εἰ conj. εἰ if, whether, that, though, forasmuch
δὲ conj. δέ but, and, now, also, to the contrary, rather, then
ἄκων adj. nom. masc. sg. ἄκων against will, unwilling
οἰκονομίαν n. acc. fem. sg. οἰκονομία dispensation, stewardship, edifying
18 τίς interrog. pron. nom. masc. sg. τίς what, who, why, where, which, how
οὖν conj. οὖν therefore, then, so, and, now, wherefore
μοι pron. dat. 1p. sg. ἐγώ I
ὁ art. nom. masc. sg. ὁ ἡ τό the, this, that, he, she, it
μισθός n. nom. masc. sg. μισθός reward, hire, wage
ἵνα conj. ἵνα that, to, lest, for to, so that, albeit, because, for, so as
ἀδάπανον adj. acc. neut. sg. ἀδάπανος without charge
τὸ art. acc. neut. sg. ὁ ἡ τό the, this, that, he, she, it
εὐαγγέλιον n. acc. neut. sg. εὐαγγέλιον gospel
τοῦ art. gen. masc. sg. ὁ ἡ τό the, this, that, he, she, it
Χριστοῦ n. gen. masc. sg. Χριστός Christ
εἰς prep. εἰς (+acc) into, to, unto, for, in, on, toward, against, upon, at, among
τὸ art. acc. neut. sg. ὁ ἡ τό the, this, that, he, she, it
μὴ particle of negation. μή not, no, lest, neither, none, nothing, nor, never, without
τῇ art. dat. fem. sg. ὁ ἡ τό the, this, that, he, she, it
ἐξουσίᾳ n. dat. fem. sg. ἐξουσία power, authority, right, strength, jurisdiction
μου pron. gen. 1p. sg. ἐγώ I
ἐν prep. ἐν (+dat) in, by, with, among, at, on, through, to, within, into, of, for
τῷ art. dat. neut. sg. ὁ ἡ τό the, this, that, he, she, it
εὐαγγελίῳ n. dat. neut. sg. εὐαγγέλιον gospel
19 ἐλεύθερος adj. nom. masc. sg. ἐλεύθερος free, freewoman, at liberty, freeman
γὰρ conj. γάρ for, and, because, but, indeed
ἐκ prep. ἐκ ἐξ (+gen) of, from, out of, by, on, with, in, among, through
πάντων adj. gen. masc. pl. πᾶς πᾶσα πᾶν all, every, whosoever, every one, no, whole, any
πᾶσιν adj. dat. masc. pl. πᾶς πᾶσα πᾶν all, every, whosoever, every one, no, whole, any
ἐμαυτὸν pron. acc. masc. 1p. sg. ἐμαυτοῦ myself, me
ἵνα conj. ἵνα that, to, lest, for to, so that, albeit, because, for, so as
τοὺς art. acc. masc. pl. ὁ ἡ τό the, this, that, he, she, it
πλείονας compar. adj. acc. masc. pl. πολύς many, great, much, long, abundant
20 καὶ conj. καί and, even, also, but
τοῖς art. dat. masc. pl. ὁ ἡ τό the, this, that, he, she, it
Ἰουδαίοις adj. dat. masc. pl. Ἰουδαῖος Jew, Jewess
ὡς adv. ὡς as, when, as it were, how, about, like, as soon as, even as, while
Ἰουδαῖος adj. nom. masc. sg. Ἰουδαῖος Jew, Jewess
ἵνα conj. ἵνα that, to, lest, for to, so that, albeit, because, for, so as
Ἰουδαίους adj. acc. masc. pl. Ἰουδαῖος Jew, Jewess
τοῖς art. dat. masc. pl. ὁ ἡ τό the, this, that, he, she, it
ὑπὸ prep. ὑπό (+gen) of, by, with, from, among, (+acc) under
νόμον n. acc. masc. sg. νόμος law, the law
ὡς adv. ὡς as, when, as it were, how, about, like, as soon as, even as, while
ὑπὸ prep. ὑπό (+gen) of, by, with, from, among, (+acc) under
νόμον n. acc. masc. sg. νόμος law, the law
ἵνα conj. ἵνα that, to, lest, for to, so that, albeit, because, for, so as
τοὺς art. acc. masc. pl. ὁ ἡ τό the, this, that, he, she, it
ὑπὸ prep. ὑπό (+gen) of, by, with, from, among, (+acc) under
νόμον n. acc. masc. sg. νόμος law, the law
21 τοῖς art. dat. masc. pl. ὁ ἡ τό the, this, that, he, she, it
ἀνόμοις adj. dat. masc. pl. ἄνομος without law, transgressor, wicked, lawless, unlawful

ὡς adv. ὡς as, when, as it were, how, about, like, as soon as, even as, while
ἄνομος adj. nom. masc. sg. ἄνομος without law, transgressor, wicked, lawless, unlawful
μὴ particle of negation. μή not, no, lest, neither, none, nothing, nor, never, without
ἄνομος adj. nom. masc. sg. ἄνομος without law, transgressor, wicked, lawless, unlawful
Θεῷ n. dat. masc. sg. θεός God, god
ἀλλ' conj. ἀλλά but, yea, yet, nevertheless, howbeit, nay, therefore
ἔννομος adj. nom. masc. sg. ἔννομος lawful, under law
Χριστῷ n. dat. masc. sg. Χριστός Christ
ἵνα conj. ἵνα that, to, lest, for to, so that, albeit, because, for, so as
ἀνόμους adj. acc. masc. pl. ἄνομος without law, transgressor, wicked, lawless, unlawful
22 τοῖς art. dat. masc. pl. ὁ ἡ τό the, this, that, he, she, it
ἀσθενέσιν adj. dat. masc. pl. ἀσθενής weak, sick, impotent, more feeble
ὡς adv. ὡς as, when, as it were, how, about, like, as soon as, even as, while
ἀσθενής adj. nom. masc. sg. ἀσθενής weak, sick, impotent, more feeble
ἵνα conj. ἵνα that, to, lest, for to, so that, albeit, because, for, so as
τοὺς art. acc. masc. pl. ὁ ἡ τό the, this, that, he, she, it
ἀσθενεῖς adj. acc. masc. pl. ἀσθενής weak, sick, impotent, more feeble
τοῖς art. dat. masc. pl. ὁ ἡ τό the, this, that, he, she, it
πᾶσι adj. dat. masc. pl. πᾶς πᾶσα πᾶν all, every, whosoever, every one, no, whole, any
τὰ art. nom. neut. pl. ὁ ἡ τό the, this, that, he, she, it
πάντα adj. nom. neut. pl. πᾶς πᾶσα πᾶν all, every, whosoever, every one, no, whole, any
ἵνα conj. ἵνα that, to, lest, for to, so that, albeit, because, for, so as
πάντως adv. πάντως surely, altogether, by all means, at all, needs, no doubt
τινὰς indefinite pron. acc. masc. pl. τὶς certain, some, any man, one, any thing
23 τοῦτο demo. pron. acc. neut. sg. οὗτος αὕτη τοῦτο this, the same, this same, he, she, it
δὲ conj. δέ but, and, now, also, to the contrary, rather, then
διὰ prep. διά (+gen) by, through, with, in, of, (+acc) for, because of, for a cause
τὸ art. acc. neut. sg. ὁ ἡ τό the, this, that, he, she, it
εὐαγγέλιον n. acc. neut. sg. εὐαγγέλιον gospel
ἵνα conj. ἵνα that, to, lest, for to, so that, albeit, because, for, so as
συγκοινωνὸς n. nom. masc. sg. συγκοινωνός companion, partake with, partaker
αὐτοῦ pron. gen. neut. 3p. sg. αὐτός ἡ ὁ self, of oneself, even, very, the same, he, she, it
24 οὐκ particle of negation. οὐ οὐκ οὐχ not, no, neither, none, nay, nor, never, nothing
ὅτι conj. ὅτι that, for, because, how that, how, because that, for that, though
οἱ art. nom. masc. pl. ὁ ἡ τό the, this, that, he, she, it
ἐν prep. ἐν (+dat) in, by, with, among, at, on, through, to, within, into, of, for
σταδίῳ n. dat. neut. sg. στάδιον furlong, stadium, race
πάντες adj. nom. masc. pl. πᾶς πᾶσα πᾶν all, every, whosoever, every one, no, whole, any
μὲν conj. μέν indeed, verily, truly, even, so, some
εἷς num. nom. masc. sg. εἷς or ἕν one, other, some, any, only, a certain
δὲ conj. δέ but, and, now, also, to the contrary, rather, then
τὸ art. acc. neut. sg. ὁ ἡ τό the, this, that, he, she, it
βραβεῖον n. acc. neut. sg. βραβεῖον prize
οὕτω adv. οὕτω οὕτως so, even so, thus, on this wise, likewise, after this manner
ἵνα conj. ἵνα that, to, lest, for to, so that, albeit, because, for, so as
25 πᾶς adj. nom. masc. sg. πᾶς πᾶσα πᾶν all, every, whosoever, every one, no, whole, any
δὲ conj. δέ but, and, now, also, to the contrary, rather, then
ὁ art. nom. masc. sg. ὁ ἡ τό the, this, that, he, she, it
πάντα adj. acc. neut. pl. πᾶς πᾶσα πᾶν all, every, whosoever, every one, no, whole, any
ἐκεῖνοι demo. pron. nom. masc. pl. ἐκεῖνος that, he, the same, that same
μὲν conj. μέν indeed, verily, truly, even, so, some
οὖν conj. οὖν therefore, then, so, and, now, wherefore
ἵνα conj. ἵνα that, to, lest, for to, so that, albeit, because, for, so as
φθαρτὸν adj. acc. masc. sg. φθαρτός corruptible
στέφανον n. acc. masc. sg. στέφανος crown

ἡμεῖς pron. nom. 1p. pl. ἐγώ I
δὲ conj. δέ but, and, now, also, to the contrary, rather, then
ἄφθαρτον adj. acc. masc. sg. ἄφθαρτος uncorruptible, incorruptible, immortal, not corruptible
26 ἐγὼ pron. nom. 1p. sg. ἐγώ I
τοίνυν conj. τοίνυν therefore, then
οὕτω adv. οὕτω οὕτως so, even so, thus, on this wise, likewise, after this manner
ὡς adv. ὡς as, when, as it were, how, about, like, as soon as, even as, while
οὐκ particle of negation. οὐ οὐκ οὐχ not, no, neither, none, nay, nor, never, nothing
ἀδήλως adv. ἀδήλως uncertainly
οὕτω adv. οὕτω οὕτως so, even so, thus, on this wise, likewise, after this manner
ὡς adv. ὡς as, when, as it were, how, about, like, as soon as, even as, while
οὐκ particle of negation. οὐ οὐκ οὐχ not, no, neither, none, nay, nor, never, nothing
ἀέρα n. acc. masc. sg. ἀήρ air
27 ἀλλ' conj. ἀλλά but, yea, yet, nevertheless, howbeit, nay, therefore
μου pron. gen. 1p. sg. ἐγώ I
τὸ art. acc. neut. sg. ὁ ἡ τό the, this, that, he, she, it
σῶμα n. acc. neut. sg. σῶμα body, bodily, slave
καὶ conj. καί and, even, also, but
μήπως conj. μήπως lest, lest by any means, lest by some means, lest haply
ἄλλοις adj. dat. masc. pl. ἄλλος other, another, some, one, more, otherwise
αὐτὸς pron. nom. masc. 3p. sg. αὐτός ή ό self, of oneself, even, very, the same, he, she, it
ἀδόκιμος adj. nom. masc. sg. ἀδόκιμος reprobate, castaway, rejected

10

1 Οὐ particle of negation. οὐ οὐκ οὐχ not, no, neither, none, nay, nor, never, nothing
δὲ conj. δέ but, and, now, also, to the contrary, rather, then
ὑμᾶς pron. acc. 2p. pl. σύ thou, you
ἀδελφοί n. voc. masc. pl. ἀδελφός brother
ὅτι conj. ὅτι that, for, because, how that, how, because that, for that, though
οἱ art. nom. masc. pl. ὁ ἡ τό the, this, that, he, she, it
πατέρες n. nom. masc. pl. πατήρ Father, father, parent
ἡμῶν pron. gen. 1p. pl. ἐγώ I
πάντες adj. nom. masc. pl. πᾶς πᾶσα πᾶν all, every, whosoever, every one, no, whole, any
ὑπὸ prep. ὑπό (+gen) of, by, with, from, among, (+acc) under
τὴν art. acc. fem. sg. ὁ ἡ τό the, this, that, he, she, it
νεφέλην n. acc. fem. sg. νεφέλη cloud
καὶ conj. καί and, even, also, but
πάντες adj. nom. masc. pl. πᾶς πᾶσα πᾶν all, every, whosoever, every one, no, whole, any
διὰ prep. διά (+gen) by, through, with, in, of, (+acc) for, because of, for a cause
τῆς art. gen. fem. sg. ὁ ἡ τό the, this, that, he, she, it
θαλάσσης n. gen. fem. sg. θάλασσα sea
2 καὶ conj. καί and, even, also, but
πάντες adj. nom. masc. pl. πᾶς πᾶσα πᾶν all, every, whosoever, every one, no, whole, any
εἰς prep. εἰς (+acc) into, to, unto, for, in, on, toward, against, upon, at, among
τὸν art. acc. masc. sg. ὁ ἡ τό the, this, that, he, she, it
Μωσῆν n. acc. masc. sg. Μωσῆς Moses
ἐν prep. ἐν (+dat) in, by, with, among, at, on, through, to, within, into, of, for
τῇ art. dat. fem. sg. ὁ ἡ τό the, this, that, he, she, it
νεφέλῃ n. dat. fem. sg. νεφέλη cloud
καὶ conj. καί and, even, also, but
ἐν prep. ἐν (+dat) in, by, with, among, at, on, through, to, within, into, of, for
τῇ art. dat. fem. sg. ὁ ἡ τό the, this, that, he, she, it
θαλάσσῃ n. dat. fem. sg. θάλασσα sea
3 καὶ conj. καί and, even, also, but

πάντες adj. nom. masc. pl. πᾶς πᾶσα πᾶν all, every, whosoever, every one, no, whole, any
τὸ art. acc. neut. sg. ὁ ἡ τό the, this, that, he, she, it
αὐτὸ pron. acc. neut. 3p. sg. αὐτός ή ό self, of oneself, even, very, the same, he, she, it
βρῶμα n. acc. neut. sg. βρῶμα victual, meat, food
πνευματικὸν adj. acc. neut. sg. πνευματικός spiritual
4 καὶ conj. καί and, even, also, but
πάντες adj. nom. masc. pl. πᾶς πᾶσα πᾶν all, every, whosoever, every one, no, whole, any
τὸ art. acc. neut. sg. ὁ ἡ τό the, this, that, he, she, it
αὐτὸ pron. acc. neut. 3p. sg. αὐτός ή ό self, of oneself, even, very, the same, he, she, it
πόμα n. acc. neut. sg. πόμα drink
πνευματικὸν adj. acc. neut. sg. πνευματικός spiritual
γὰρ conj. γάρ for, and, because, but, indeed
ἐκ prep. ἐκ ἐξ (+gen) of, from, out of, by, on, with, in, among, through
πνευματικῆς adj. gen. fem. sg. πνευματικός spiritual
πέτρας n. gen. fem. sg. πέτρα rock
ἡ art. nom. fem. sg. ὁ ἡ τό the, this, that, he, she, it
δὲ conj. δέ but, and, now, also, to the contrary, rather, then
πέτρα n. nom. fem. sg. πέτρα rock
ὁ art. nom. masc. sg. ὁ ἡ τό the, this, that, he, she, it
Χριστός n. nom. masc. sg. Χριστός Christ
5 ἀλλ' conj. ἀλλά but, yea, yet, nevertheless, howbeit, nay, therefore
οὐκ particle of negation. οὐ οὐκ οὐχ not, no, neither, none, nay, nor, never, nothing
ἐν prep. ἐν (+dat) in, by, with, among, at, on, through, to, within, into, of, for
τοῖς art. dat. masc. pl. ὁ ἡ τό the, this, that, he, she, it
πλείοσιν compar. adj. dat. masc. pl. πολύς many, great, much, long, abundant
αὐτῶν pron. gen. masc. 3p. pl. αὐτός ή ό self, of oneself, even, very, the same, he, she, it
ὁ art. nom. masc. sg. ὁ ἡ τό the, this, that, he, she, it
Θεός n. nom. masc. sg. θεός God, god
γὰρ conj. γάρ for, and, because, but, indeed
ἐν prep. ἐν (+dat) in, by, with, among, at, on, through, to, within, into, of, for
τῇ art. dat. fem. sg. ὁ ἡ τό the, this, that, he, she, it
ἐρήμῳ adj. dat. fem. sg. ἔρημος wilderness, desert
6 ταῦτα demo. pron. nom. neut. pl. οὗτος αὕτη τοῦτο this, the same, this same, he, she, it
δὲ conj. δέ but, and, now, also, to the contrary, rather, then
τύποι n. nom. masc. pl. τύπος ensample, example, pattern, print, figure, fashion
ἡμῶν pron. gen. 1p. pl. ἐγώ I
εἰς prep. εἰς (+acc) into, to, unto, for, in, on, toward, against, upon, at, among
τὸ art. acc. neut. sg. ὁ ἡ τό the, this, that, he, she, it
μὴ particle of negation. μή not, no, lest, neither, none, nothing, nor, never, without
ἡμᾶς pron. acc. 1p. pl. ἐγώ I
ἐπιθυμητὰς n. acc. masc. pl. ἐπιθυμητής lust after
κακῶν adj. gen. neut. pl. κακός evil, evil thing, noisome, wicked
καθὼς adv. καθώς as, even as, according as, according to
κἀκεῖνοι demo. pron. nom. masc. pl. κἀκεῖνος and he, he also, and the other, even he
7 μηδὲ conj. μηδέ neither, nor, not, no not, nor yet, not once, not so much as
εἰδωλολάτραι n. nom. masc. pl. εἰδωλολάτρης idolater
καθώς adv. καθώς as, even as, according as, according to
τινες indefinite pron. nom. masc. pl. τὶς certain, some, any man, one, any thing
αὐτῶν pron. gen. masc. 3p. pl. αὐτός ή ό self, of oneself, even, very, the same, he, she, it
ὡς adv. ὡς as, when, as it were, how, about, like, as soon as, even as, while
ὁ art. nom. masc. sg. ὁ ἡ τό the, this, that, he, she, it
λαὸς n. nom. masc. sg. λαός people
καὶ conj. καί and, even, also, but
καὶ conj. καί and, even, also, but
8 μηδὲ conj. μηδέ neither, nor, not, no not, nor yet, not once, not so much as

καθὼς adv. καθώς as, even as, according as, according to
τινες indefinite pron. nom. masc. pl. τὶς certain, some, any man, one, any thing
αὐτῶν pron. gen. masc. 3p. pl. αὐτός ἡ ὁ self, of oneself, even, very, the same, he, she, it
καὶ conj. καί and, even, also, but
ἐν prep. ἐν (+dat) in, by, with, among, at, on, through, to, within, into, of, for
μιᾷ num. dat. fem. sg. εἷς or ἕν one, other, some, any, only, a certain
ἡμέρᾳ n. dat. fem. sg. ἡμέρα day, time, year, while, age, day time
εἰκοσιτρεῖς num. nom. fem. pl. εἴκοσιτρεῖς twenty-three
χιλιάδες n. nom. fem. pl. χιλιάς thousand
9 μηδὲ conj. μηδέ neither, nor, not, no not, nor yet, not once, not so much as
τὸν art. acc. masc. sg. ὁ ἡ τό the, this, that, he, she, it
Χριστόν n. acc. masc. sg. Χριστός Christ
καθὼς adv. καθώς as, even as, according as, according to
καὶ conj. καί and, even, also, but
τινες indefinite pron. nom. masc. pl. τὶς certain, some, any man, one, any thing
αὐτῶν pron. gen. masc. 3p. pl. αὐτός ἡ ὁ self, of oneself, even, very, the same, he, she, it
καὶ conj. καί and, even, also, but
ὑπὸ prep. ὑπό (+gen) of, by, with, from, among, (+acc) under
τῶν art. gen. masc. pl. ὁ ἡ τό the, this, that, he, she, it
ὄφεων n. gen. masc. pl. ὄφις serpent
10 μηδὲ conj. μηδέ neither, nor, not, no not, nor yet, not once, not so much as
καθὼς adv. καθώς as, even as, according as, according to
καὶ conj. καί and, even, also, but
τινὲς indefinite pron. nom. masc. pl. τὶς certain, some, any man, one, any thing
αὐτῶν pron. gen. masc. 3p. pl. αὐτός ἡ ὁ self, of oneself, even, very, the same, he, she, it
καὶ conj. καί and, even, also, but
ὑπὸ prep. ὑπό (+gen) of, by, with, from, among, (+acc) under
τοῦ art. gen. masc. sg. ὁ ἡ τό the, this, that, he, she, it
ὀλοθρευτοῦ n. gen. masc. sg. ὀλοθρευτής destroyer
11 ταῦτα demo. pron. nom. neut. pl. οὗτος αὕτη τοῦτο this, the same, this same, he, she, it
δὲ conj. δέ but, and, now, also, to the contrary, rather, then
πάντα adj. nom. neut. pl. πᾶς πᾶσα πᾶν all, every, whosoever, every one, no, whole, any
τύποι n. nom. masc. pl. τύπος ensample, example, pattern, print, figure, fashion
ἐκείνοις demo. pron. dat. masc. pl. ἐκεῖνος that, he, the same, that same
δὲ conj. δέ but, and, now, also, to the contrary, rather, then
πρὸς prep. πρός (+gen) for, (+dat) at, (+acc) unto, to, with, for, against
νουθεσίαν n. acc. fem. sg. νουθεσία admonition
ἡμῶν pron. gen. 1p. pl. ἐγώ I
εἰς prep. εἰς (+acc) into, to, unto, for, in, on, toward, against, upon, at, among
οὓς relative pron. acc. masc. pl. ὅς ἥ ὅ who, which, what, that
τὰ art. nom. neut. pl. ὁ ἡ τό the, this, that, he, she, it
τέλη n. nom. neut. pl. τέλος end, custom, ending, finally, uttermost
τῶν art. gen. masc. pl. ὁ ἡ τό the, this, that, he, she, it
αἰώνων n. gen. masc. pl. αἰών ever, ever and ever, evermore, age, eternal, world
12 ὥστε conj. ὥστε so that, wherefore, insomuch that, therefore, that, so then
ὁ art. nom. masc. sg. ὁ ἡ τό the, this, that, he, she, it
μή particle of negation. μή not, no, lest, neither, none, nothing, nor, never, without
13 πειρασμὸς n. nom. masc. sg. πειρασμός temptation, trial
ὑμᾶς pron. acc. 2p. pl. σύ thou, you
οὐκ particle of negation. οὐ οὐκ οὐχ not, no, neither, none, nay, nor, never, nothing
εἰ conj. εἰ if, whether, that, though, forasmuch
μὴ particle of negation. μή not, no, lest, neither, none, nothing, nor, never, without
ἀνθρώπινος adj. nom. masc. sg. ἀνθρώπινος man, common to man
πιστὸς adj. nom. masc. sg. πιστός faithful, believing, true, sure
δὲ conj. δέ but, and, now, also, to the contrary, rather, then

ὁ art. nom. masc. sg. ὁ ἡ τό the, this, that, he, she, it
Θεός n. nom. masc. sg. θεός God, god
ὅς relative pron. nom. masc. sg. ὅς ἥ ὅ who, which, what, that
οὐκ particle of negation. οὐ οὐκ οὐχ not, no, neither, none, nay, nor, never, nothing
ὑμᾶς pron. acc. 2p. pl. σύ thou, you
ὑπὲρ prep. ὑπέρ (+gen) for, of, for the sake of, (+acc) above, more than
ὃ relative pron. acc. neut. sg. ὅς ἥ ὅ who, which, what, that
ἀλλὰ conj. ἀλλά but, yea, yet, nevertheless, howbeit, nay, therefore
σὺν prep. σύν (+dat) with, beside
τῷ art. dat. masc. sg. ὁ ἡ τό the, this, that, he, she, it
πειρασμῷ n. dat. masc. sg. πειρασμός temptation, trial
καὶ conj. καί and, even, also, but
τὴν art. acc. fem. sg. ὁ ἡ τό the, this, that, he, she, it
ἔκβασιν n. acc. fem. sg. ἔκβασις way to escape, end
τοῦ art. gen. neut. sg. ὁ ἡ τό the, this, that, he, she, it
ὑμᾶς pron. acc. 2p. pl. σύ thou, you
14 Διόπερ conj. διόπερ wherefore
ἀγαπητοί adj. voc. masc. pl. ἀγαπητός beloved, dearly beloved, dear, wellbeloved
μου pron. gen. 1p. sg. ἐγώ I
ἀπὸ prep. ἀπό (+gen) from, of, out of, since, for, off, at, by, in, on
τῆς art. gen. fem. sg. ὁ ἡ τό the, this, that, he, she, it
εἰδωλολατρείας n. gen. fem. sg. εἰδωλολατρεία idolatry
15 ὡς adv. ὡς as, when, as it were, how, about, like, as soon as, even as, while
φρονίμοις adj. dat. masc. pl. φρόνιμος wise, wiser
ὑμεῖς pron. nom. 2p. pl. σύ thou, you
ὅ relative pron. acc. neut. sg. ὅς ἥ ὅ who, which, what, that
16 τὸ art. nom. neut. sg. ὁ ἡ τό the, this, that, he, she, it
ποτήριον n. nom. neut. sg. ποτήριον cup
τῆς art. gen. fem. sg. ὁ ἡ τό the, this, that, he, she, it
εὐλογίας n. gen. fem. sg. εὐλογία blessing, bounty, matter of bounty, fair speech
ὃ relative pron. acc. neut. sg. ὅς ἥ ὅ who, which, what, that
οὐχὶ adv. οὐχί not, nay
κοινωνία n. nom. fem. sg. κοινωνία fellowship, communion, contribution, distribution
τοῦ art. gen. neut. sg. ὁ ἡ τό the, this, that, he, she, it
αἵματος n. gen. neut. sg. αἷμα blood
τοῦ art. gen. masc. sg. ὁ ἡ τό the, this, that, he, she, it
Χριστοῦ n. gen. masc. sg. Χριστός Christ
τὸν art. acc. masc. sg. ὁ ἡ τό the, this, that, he, she, it
ἄρτον n. acc. masc. sg. ἄρτος bread, loaf
ὃν relative pron. acc. masc. sg. ὅς ἥ ὅ who, which, what, that
οὐχὶ adv. οὐχί not, nay
κοινωνία n. nom. fem. sg. κοινωνία fellowship, communion, contribution, distribution
τοῦ art. gen. neut. sg. ὁ ἡ τό the, this, that, he, she, it
σώματος n. gen. neut. sg. σῶμα body, bodily, slave
τοῦ art. gen. masc. sg. ὁ ἡ τό the, this, that, he, she, it
Χριστοῦ n. gen. masc. sg. Χριστός Christ
17 ὅτι conj. ὅτι that, for, because, how that, how, because that, for that, though
εἷς num. nom. masc. sg. εἷς or ἕν one, other, some, any, only, a certain
ἄρτος n. nom. masc. sg. ἄρτος bread, loaf
ἓν num. nom. neut. sg. εἷς or ἕν one, other, some, any, only, a certain
σῶμα n. nom. neut. sg. σῶμα body, bodily, slave
οἱ art. nom. masc. pl. ὁ ἡ τό the, this, that, he, she, it
πολλοί adj. nom. masc. pl. πολύς many, great, much, long, abundant
οἱ art. nom. masc. pl. ὁ ἡ τό the, this, that, he, she, it
γὰρ conj. γάρ for, and, because, but, indeed

πάντες adj. nom. masc. pl. πᾶς πᾶσα πᾶν all, every, whosoever, every one, no, whole, any
ἐκ prep. ἐκ ἐξ (+gen) of, from, out of, by, on, with, in, among, through
τοῦ art. gen. masc. sg. ὁ ἡ τό the, this, that, he, she, it
ἑνὸς num. gen. masc. sg. εἷς or ἕν one, other, some, any, only, a certain
ἄρτου n. gen. masc. sg. ἄρτος bread, loaf
18 τὸν art. acc. masc. sg. ὁ ἡ τό the, this, that, he, she, it
Ἰσραὴλ pron. name. masc. inde. Ἰσραήλ Israel
κατὰ prep. κατά (+gen) against, by, throughout, down, (+acc) according to, after, with
σάρκα n. acc. fem. sg. σάρξ flesh, carnal
οὐχί adv. οὐχί not, nay
οἱ art. nom. masc. pl. ὁ ἡ τό the, this, that, he, she, it
τὰς art. acc. fem. pl. ὁ ἡ τό the, this, that, he, she, it
θυσίας n. acc. fem. pl. θυσία sacrifice
κοινωνοὶ n. nom. masc. pl. κοινωνός partaker, partner, companion, fellowship
τοῦ art. gen. neut. sg. ὁ ἡ τό the, this, that, he, she, it
θυσιαστηρίου n. gen. neut. sg. θυσιαστήριον altar
19 τί interrog. pron. acc. neut. sg. τίς what, who, why, where, which, how
οὖν conj. οὖν therefore, then, so, and, now, wherefore
ὅτι conj. ὅτι that, for, because, how that, how, because that, for that, though
εἴδωλόν n. nom. neut. sg. εἴδωλον idol
τί indefinite pron. nom. neut. sg. τὶς certain, some, any man, one, any thing
ἢ particle. ἤ or, than, either, nor, or else, and, rather than
ὅτι conj. ὅτι that, for, because, how that, how, because that, for that, though
εἰδωλόθυτόν adj. nom. neut. sg. εἰδωλόθυτον thing offered in sacrifice unto idols
τί indefinite pron. nom. neut. sg. τὶς certain, some, any man, one, any thing
20 ἀλλ' conj. ἀλλά but, yea, yet, nevertheless, howbeit, nay, therefore
ὅτι conj. ὅτι that, for, because, how that, how, because that, for that, though
ἃ relative pron. acc. neut. pl. ὅς ἥ ὅ who, which, what, that
τὰ art. nom. neut. pl. ὁ ἡ τό the, this, that, he, she, it
ἔθνη n. nom. neut. pl. ἔθνος Gentile, nation, heathen, people
δαιμονίοις n. dat. neut. pl. δαιμόνιον devil, demon, god
καὶ conj. καί and, even, also, but
οὐ particle of negation. οὐ οὐκ οὐχ not, no, neither, none, nay, nor, never, nothing
Θεῷ n. dat. masc. sg. θεός God, god
οὐ particle of negation. οὐ οὐκ οὐχ not, no, neither, none, nay, nor, never, nothing
δὲ conj. δέ but, and, now, also, to the contrary, rather, then
ὑμᾶς pron. acc. 2p. pl. σύ thou, you
κοινωνοὺς n. acc. masc. pl. κοινωνός partaker, partner, companion, fellowship
τῶν art. gen. neut. pl. ὁ ἡ τό the, this, that, he, she, it
δαιμονίων n. gen. neut. pl. δαιμόνιον devil, demon, god
21 οὐ particle of negation. οὐ οὐκ οὐχ not, no, neither, none, nay, nor, never, nothing
ποτήριον n. acc. neut. sg. ποτήριον cup
Κυρίου n. gen. masc. sg. κύριος Lord, lord, master, sir, LORD, God, Master, owner
καὶ conj. καί and, even, also, but
ποτήριον n. acc. neut. sg. ποτήριον cup
δαιμονίων n. gen. neut. pl. δαιμόνιον devil, demon, god
οὐ particle of negation. οὐ οὐκ οὐχ not, no, neither, none, nay, nor, never, nothing
τραπέζης n. gen. fem. sg. τράπεζα table
Κυρίου n. gen. masc. sg. κύριος Lord, lord, master, sir, LORD, God, Master, owner
καὶ conj. καί and, even, also, but
τραπέζης n. gen. fem. sg. τράπεζα table
δαιμονίων n. gen. neut. pl. δαιμόνιον devil, demon, god
22 ἢ particle. ἤ or, than, either, nor, or else, and, rather than
τὸν art. acc. masc. sg. ὁ ἡ τό the, this, that, he, she, it
Κύριον n. acc. masc. sg. κύριος Lord, lord, master, sir, LORD, God, Master, owner

μὴ particle of negation. μή not, no, lest, neither, none, nothing, nor, never, without
ἰσχυρότεροι compar. adj. nom. masc. pl. ἰσχυρός mighty, strong, mightier, stronger
αὐτοῦ pron. gen. masc. 3p. sg. αὐτός ἡ ὁ self, of oneself, even, very, the same, he, she, it
23 Πάντα adj. nom. neut. pl. πᾶς πᾶσα πᾶν all, every, whosoever, every one, no, whole, any
μοι pron. dat. 1p. sg. ἐγώ I
ἀλλ' conj. ἀλλά but, yea, yet, nevertheless, howbeit, nay, therefore
οὐ particle of negation. οὐ οὐκ οὐχ not, no, neither, none, nay, nor, never, nothing
πάντα adj. nom. neut. pl. πᾶς πᾶσα πᾶν all, every, whosoever, every one, no, whole, any
πάντα adj. nom. neut. pl. πᾶς πᾶσα πᾶν all, every, whosoever, every one, no, whole, any
μοι pron. dat. 1p. sg. ἐγώ I
ἀλλ' conj. ἀλλά but, yea, yet, nevertheless, howbeit, nay, therefore
οὐ particle of negation. οὐ οὐκ οὐχ not, no, neither, none, nay, nor, never, nothing
πάντα adj. nom. neut. pl. πᾶς πᾶσα πᾶν all, every, whosoever, every one, no, whole, any
24 μηδεὶς num. nom. masc. sg. μηδείς μηδεμία μηδέν no man, nothing, no, none, not at all
τὸ art. acc. neut. sg. ὁ ἡ τό the, this, that, he, she, it
ἑαυτοῦ reflexive pron. gen. masc. 3p. sg. ἑαυτοῦ himself, herself, itself, yourself, ourselves
ἀλλὰ conj. ἀλλά but, yea, yet, nevertheless, howbeit, nay, therefore
τὸ art. acc. neut. sg. ὁ ἡ τό the, this, that, he, she, it
τοῦ art. gen. masc. sg. ὁ ἡ τό the, this, that, he, she, it
ἑτέρου adj. gen. masc. sg. ἕτερος another, other, else, strange
ἕκαστος adj. nom. masc. sg. ἕκαστος every man, every, every one, any man, each
25 πᾶν adj. acc. neut. sg. πᾶς πᾶσα πᾶν all, every, whosoever, every one, no, whole, any
τὸ art. acc. neut. sg. ὁ ἡ τό the, this, that, he, she, it
ἐν prep. ἐν (+dat) in, by, with, among, at, on, through, to, within, into, of, for
μακέλλῳ n. dat. neut. sg. μάκελλον shamble
μηδὲν num. acc. neut. sg. μηδείς μηδεμία μηδέν no man, nothing, no, none, not at all
διὰ prep. διά (+gen) by, through, with, in, of, (+acc) for, because of, for a cause
τὴν art. acc. fem. sg. ὁ ἡ τό the, this, that, he, she, it
συνείδησιν n. acc. fem. sg. συνείδησις conscience
26 τοῦ art. gen. masc. sg. ὁ ἡ τό the, this, that, he, she, it
γὰρ conj. γάρ for, and, because, but, indeed
Κυρίου n. gen. masc. sg. κύριος Lord, lord, master, sir, LORD, God, Master, owner
ἡ art. nom. fem. sg. ὁ ἡ τό the, this, that, he, she, it
γῆ n. nom. fem. sg. γῆ earth, land, ground, country
καὶ conj. καί and, even, also, but
τὸ art. nom. neut. sg. ὁ ἡ τό the, this, that, he, she, it
πλήρωμα n. nom. neut. sg. πλήρωμα fullness, fulfilling, full
αὐτῆς pron. gen. fem. 3p. sg. αὐτός ἡ ὁ self, of oneself, even, very, the same, he, she, it
27 εἰ conj. εἰ if, whether, that, though, forasmuch
δὲ conj. δέ but, and, now, also, to the contrary, rather, then
τις indefinite pron. nom. masc. sg. τὶς certain, some, any man, one, any thing
ὑμᾶς pron. acc. 2p. pl. σύ thou, you
τῶν art. gen. masc. pl. ὁ ἡ τό the, this, that, he, she, it
ἀπίστων adj. gen. masc. pl. ἄπιστος faithless, unbelieving, infidel, thing incredible
καὶ conj. καί and, even, also, but
πᾶν adj. acc. neut. sg. πᾶς πᾶσα πᾶν all, every, whosoever, every one, no, whole, any
τὸ art. acc. neut. sg. ὁ ἡ τό the, this, that, he, she, it
ὑμῖν pron. dat. 2p. pl. σύ thou, you
μηδὲν num. acc. neut. sg. μηδείς μηδεμία μηδέν no man, nothing, no, none, not at all
διὰ prep. διά (+gen) by, through, with, in, of, (+acc) for, because of, for a cause
τὴν art. acc. fem. sg. ὁ ἡ τό the, this, that, he, she, it
συνείδησιν n. acc. fem. sg. συνείδησις conscience
28 ἐὰν conj. ἐάν if, soever, except, though, and if, but, whether, if so, so
δέ conj. δέ but, and, now, also, to the contrary, rather, then
τις indefinite pron. nom. masc. sg. τὶς certain, some, any man, one, any thing

ὑμῖν pron. dat. 2p. pl. σύ thou, you
Τοῦτο demo. pron. nom. neut. sg. οὗτος αὕτη τοῦτο this, the same, this same, he, she, it
εἰδωλόθυτόν adj. nom. neut. sg. εἰδωλόθυτον thing offered in sacrifice unto idols
μὴ particle of negation. μή not, no, lest, neither, none, nothing, nor, never, without
δι' prep. διά (+gen) by, through, with, in, of, (+acc) for, because of, for a cause
ἐκεῖνον demo. pron. acc. masc. sg. ἐκεῖνος that, he, the same, that same
τὸν art. acc. masc. sg. ὁ ἡ τό the, this, that, he, she, it
καὶ conj. καί and, even, also, but
τὴν art. acc. fem. sg. ὁ ἡ τό the, this, that, he, she, it
συνείδησιν n. acc. fem. sg. συνείδησις conscience
τοῦ art. gen. masc. sg. ὁ ἡ τό the, this, that, he, she, it
γὰρ conj. γάρ for, and, because, but, indeed
Κυρίου n. gen. masc. sg. κύριος Lord, lord, master, sir, LORD, God, Master, owner
ἡ art. nom. fem. sg. ὁ ἡ τό the, this, that, he, she, it
γῆ n. nom. fem. sg. γῆ earth, land, ground, country
καὶ conj. καί and, even, also, but
τὸ art. nom. neut. sg. ὁ ἡ τό the, this, that, he, she, it
πλήρωμα n. nom. neut. sg. πλήρωμα fullness, fulfilling, full
αὐτῆς pron. gen. fem. 3p. sg. αὐτός ἡ ὁ self, of oneself, even, very, the same, he, she, it
29 συνείδησιν n. acc. fem. sg. συνείδησις conscience
δὲ conj. δέ but, and, now, also, to the contrary, rather, then
οὐχὶ adv. οὐχί not, nay
τὴν art. acc. fem. sg. ὁ ἡ τό the, this, that, he, she, it
ἑαυτοῦ reflexive pron. gen. masc. 3p. sg. ἑαυτοῦ himself, herself, itself, yourself, ourselves
ἀλλὰ conj. ἀλλά but, yea, yet, nevertheless, howbeit, nay, therefore
τὴν art. acc. fem. sg. ὁ ἡ τό the, this, that, he, she, it
τοῦ art. gen. masc. sg. ὁ ἡ τό the, this, that, he, she, it
ἑτέρου adj. gen. masc. sg. ἕτερος another, other, else, strange
ἱνατί adv. ἱνατί or ἵνα τί why, wherefore
γὰρ conj. γάρ for, and, because, but, indeed
ἡ art. nom. fem. sg. ὁ ἡ τό the, this, that, he, she, it
ἐλευθερία n. nom. fem. sg. ἐλευθερία liberty
μου pron. gen. 1p. sg. ἐγώ I
ὑπὸ prep. ὑπό (+gen) of, by, with, from, among, (+acc) under
ἄλλης adj. gen. fem. sg. ἄλλος other, another, some, one, more, otherwise
συνειδήσεως n. gen. fem. sg. συνείδησις conscience
30 εἰ conj. εἰ if, whether, that, though, forasmuch
δὲ conj. δέ but, and, now, also, to the contrary, rather, then
ἐγὼ pron. nom. 1p. sg. ἐγώ I
χάριτι n. dat. fem. sg. χάρις grace, thank, favour, pleasure
τί interrog. pron. acc. neut. sg. τίς what, who, why, where, which, how
ὑπὲρ prep. ὑπέρ (+gen) for, of, for the sake of, (+acc) above, more than
οὗ relative pron. gen. neut. sg. ὅς ἥ ὅ who, which, what, that
ἐγὼ pron. nom. 1p. sg. ἐγώ I
31 εἴτε conj. εἴτε whether
οὖν conj. οὖν therefore, then, so, and, now, wherefore
εἴτε conj. εἴτε whether
εἴτε conj. εἴτε whether
τι indefinite pron. acc. neut. sg. τὶς certain, some, any man, one, any thing
πάντα adj. acc. neut. pl. πᾶς πᾶσα πᾶν all, every, whosoever, every one, no, whole, any
εἰς prep. εἰς (+acc) into, to, unto, for, in, on, toward, against, upon, at, among
δόξαν n. acc. fem. sg. δόξα glory, honour, praise, dignity, worship
Θεοῦ n. gen. masc. sg. θεός God, god
32 ἀπρόσκοποι adj. nom. masc. pl. ἀπρόσκοπος void of offence, none offence
καὶ conj. καί and, even, also, but

Ἰουδαίοις adj. dat. masc. pl. Ἰουδαῖος Jew, Jewess
καὶ conj. καί and, even, also, but
Ἕλλησιν n. dat. masc. pl. Ἕλλην Greek, Gentile
καὶ conj. καί and, even, also, but
τῇ art. dat. fem. sg. ὁ ἡ τό the, this, that, he, she, it
ἐκκλησίᾳ n. dat. fem. sg. ἐκκλησία church, assembly
τοῦ art. gen. masc. sg. ὁ ἡ τό the, this, that, he, she, it
Θεοῦ n. gen. masc. sg. θεός God, god
33 καθὼς adv. καθώς as, even as, according as, according to
κἀγὼ pron. nom. 1p. sg. κἀγώ and I, I also, so I, even as I
πάντα adj. acc. neut. pl. πᾶς πᾶσα πᾶν all, every, whosoever, every one, no, whole, any
πᾶσιν adj. dat. masc. pl. πᾶς πᾶσα πᾶν all, every, whosoever, every one, no, whole, any
μὴ particle of negation. μή not, no, lest, neither, none, nothing, nor, never, without
τὸ art. acc. neut. sg. ὁ ἡ τό the, this, that, he, she, it
ἐμαυτοῦ pron. gen. masc. 1p. sg. ἐμαυτοῦ myself, me
ἀλλὰ conj. ἀλλά but, yea, yet, nevertheless, howbeit, nay, therefore
τὸ art. acc. neut. sg. ὁ ἡ τό the, this, that, he, she, it
τῶν art. gen. masc. pl. ὁ ἡ τό the, this, that, he, she, it
πολλῶν adj. gen. masc. pl. πολύς many, great, much, long, abundant
ἵνα conj. ἵνα that, to, lest, for to, so that, albeit, because, for, so as

11

1 μιμηταί n. nom. masc. pl. μιμητής follower
μου pron. gen. 1p. sg. ἐγώ I
καθὼς adv. καθώς as, even as, according as, according to
κἀγὼ pron. nom. 1p. sg. κἀγώ and I, I also, so I, even as I
Χριστοῦ n. gen. masc. sg. Χριστός Christ
2 δὲ conj. δέ but, and, now, also, to the contrary, rather, then
ὑμᾶς pron. acc. 2p. pl. σύ thou, you
ἀδελφοί n. voc. masc. pl. ἀδελφός brother
ὅτι conj. ὅτι that, for, because, how that, how, because that, for that, though
πάντα adj. acc. neut. pl. πᾶς πᾶσα πᾶν all, every, whosoever, every one, no, whole, any
μου pron. gen. 1p. sg. ἐγώ I
καί conj. καί and, even, also, but
καθὼς adv. καθώς as, even as, according as, according to
ὑμῖν pron. dat. 2p. pl. σύ thou, you
τὰς art. acc. fem. pl. ὁ ἡ τό the, this, that, he, she, it
παραδόσεις n. acc. fem. pl. παράδοσις tradition, ordinance
3 δὲ conj. δέ but, and, now, also, to the contrary, rather, then
ὑμᾶς pron. acc. 2p. pl. σύ thou, you
ὅτι conj. ὅτι that, for, because, how that, how, because that, for that, though
παντὸς adj. gen. masc. sg. πᾶς πᾶσα πᾶν all, every, whosoever, every one, no, whole, any
ἀνδρὸς n. gen. masc. sg. ἀνήρ man, husband, sir
ἡ art. nom. fem. sg. ὁ ἡ τό the, this, that, he, she, it
κεφαλὴ n. nom. fem. sg. κεφαλή head
ὁ art. nom. masc. sg. ὁ ἡ τό the, this, that, he, she, it
Χριστός n. nom. masc. sg. Χριστός Christ
κεφαλὴ n. nom. fem. sg. κεφαλή head
δὲ conj. δέ but, and, now, also, to the contrary, rather, then
γυναικὸς n. gen. fem. sg. γυνή woman, wife
ὁ art. nom. masc. sg. ὁ ἡ τό the, this, that, he, she, it
ἀνήρ n. nom. masc. sg. ἀνήρ man, husband, sir
κεφαλὴ n. nom. fem. sg. κεφαλή head
δὲ conj. δέ but, and, now, also, to the contrary, rather, then

Χριστοῦ n. gen. masc. sg. Χριστός Christ
ὁ art. nom. masc. sg. ὁ ἡ τό the, this, that, he, she, it
Θεός n. nom. masc. sg. θεός God, god
4 πᾶς adj. nom. masc. sg. πᾶς πᾶσα πᾶν all, every, whosoever, every one, no, whole, any
ἀνὴρ n. nom. masc. sg. ἀνήρ man, husband, sir
ἢ particle. ἤ or, than, either, nor, or else, and, rather than
κατὰ prep. κατά (+gen) against, by, throughout, down, (+acc) according to, after, with
κεφαλῆς n. gen. fem. sg. κεφαλή head
τὴν art. acc. fem. sg. ὁ ἡ τό the, this, that, he, she, it
κεφαλὴν n. acc. fem. sg. κεφαλή head
αὐτοῦ pron. gen. masc. 3p. sg. αὐτός ή ό self, of oneself, even, very, the same, he, she, it
5 πᾶσα adj. nom. fem. sg. πᾶς πᾶσα πᾶν all, every, whosoever, every one, no, whole, any
δὲ conj. δέ but, and, now, also, to the contrary, rather, then
γυνὴ n. nom. fem. sg. γυνή woman, wife
ἢ particle. ἤ or, than, either, nor, or else, and, rather than
ἀκατακαλύπτῳ adj. dat. fem. sg. ἀκατακάλυπτος uncovered
τῇ art. dat. fem. sg. ὁ ἡ τό the, this, that, he, she, it
κεφαλῇ n. dat. fem. sg. κεφαλή head
τὴν art. acc. fem. sg. ὁ ἡ τό the, this, that, he, she, it
κεφαλὴν n. acc. fem. sg. κεφαλή head
ἑαυτῆς reflexive pron. gen. fem. 3p. sg. ἑαυτοῦ himself, herself, itself, yourself, ourselves
ἓν num. nom. neut. sg. εἷς or ἕν one, other, some, any, only, a certain
γάρ conj. γάρ for, and, because, but, indeed
καὶ conj. καί and, even, also, but
τὸ art. nom. neut. sg. ὁ ἡ τό the, this, that, he, she, it
αὐτὸ pron. acc. neut. 3p. sg. αὐτός ή ό self, of oneself, even, very, the same, he, she, it
τῇ art. dat. fem. sg. ὁ ἡ τό the, this, that, he, she, it
6 εἰ conj. εἰ if, whether, that, though, forasmuch
γὰρ conj. γάρ for, and, because, but, indeed
οὐ particle of negation. οὐ οὐκ οὐχ not, no, neither, none, nay, nor, never, nothing
γυνή n. nom. fem. sg. γυνή woman, wife
καὶ conj. καί and, even, also, but
εἰ conj. εἰ if, whether, that, though, forasmuch
δὲ conj. δέ but, and, now, also, to the contrary, rather, then
αἰσχρὸν adj. nom. neut. sg. αἰσχρός shame
γυναικὶ n. dat. fem. sg. γυνή woman, wife
τὸ art. nom. neut. sg. ὁ ἡ τό the, this, that, he, she, it
ἢ particle. ἤ or, than, either, nor, or else, and, rather than
7 ἀνὴρ n. nom. masc. sg. ἀνήρ man, husband, sir
μὲν conj. μέν indeed, verily, truly, even, so, some
γὰρ conj. γάρ for, and, because, but, indeed
οὐκ particle of negation. οὐ οὐκ οὐχ not, no, neither, none, nay, nor, never, nothing
τὴν art. acc. fem. sg. ὁ ἡ τό the, this, that, he, she, it
κεφαλὴν n. acc. fem. sg. κεφαλή head
εἰκὼν n. nom. fem. sg. εἰκών image
καὶ conj. καί and, even, also, but
δόξα n. nom. fem. sg. δόξα glory, honour, praise, dignity, worship
Θεοῦ n. gen. masc. sg. θεός God, god
γυνὴ n. nom. fem. sg. γυνή woman, wife
δὲ conj. δέ but, and, now, also, to the contrary, rather, then
δόξα n. nom. fem. sg. δόξα glory, honour, praise, dignity, worship
ἀνδρός n. gen. masc. sg. ἀνήρ man, husband, sir
8 οὐ particle of negation. οὐ οὐκ οὐχ not, no, neither, none, nay, nor, never, nothing
γάρ conj. γάρ for, and, because, but, indeed
ἀνὴρ n. nom. masc. sg. ἀνήρ man, husband, sir

ἐκ prep. ἐκ ἐξ (+gen) of, from, out of, by, on, with, in, among, through
γυναικὸς n. gen. fem. sg. γυνή woman, wife
ἀλλὰ conj. ἀλλά but, yea, yet, nevertheless, howbeit, nay, therefore
γυνὴ n. nom. fem. sg. γυνή woman, wife
ἐξ prep. ἐκ ἐξ (+gen) of, from, out of, by, on, with, in, among, through
ἀνδρός n. gen. masc. sg. ἀνήρ man, husband, sir
9 καὶ conj. καί and, even, also, but
γὰρ conj. γάρ for, and, because, but, indeed
οὐκ particle of negation. οὐ οὐκ οὐχ not, no, neither, none, nay, nor, never, nothing
ἀνὴρ n. nom. masc. sg. ἀνήρ man, husband, sir
διὰ prep. διά (+gen) by, through, with, in, of, (+acc) for, because of, for a cause
τὴν art. acc. fem. sg. ὁ ἡ τό the, this, that, he, she, it
γυναῖκα n. acc. fem. sg. γυνή woman, wife
ἀλλὰ conj. ἀλλά but, yea, yet, nevertheless, howbeit, nay, therefore
γυνὴ n. nom. fem. sg. γυνή woman, wife
διὰ prep. διά (+gen) by, through, with, in, of, (+acc) for, because of, for a cause
τὸν art. acc. masc. sg. ὁ ἡ τό the, this, that, he, she, it
ἄνδρα n. acc. masc. sg. ἀνήρ man, husband, sir
10 διὰ prep. διά (+gen) by, through, with, in, of, (+acc) for, because of, for a cause
τοῦτο demo. pron. acc. neut. sg. οὗτος αὕτη τοῦτο this, the same, this same, he, she, it
ἡ art. nom. fem. sg. ὁ ἡ τό the, this, that, he, she, it
γυνὴ n. nom. fem. sg. γυνή woman, wife
ἐξουσίαν n. acc. fem. sg. ἐξουσία power, authority, right, strength, jurisdiction
ἐπὶ prep. ἐπί (+gen) on, in, upon, (+dat) in, at, for, upon, (+acc) on, upon, unto, to, against
τῆς art. gen. fem. sg. ὁ ἡ τό the, this, that, he, she, it
κεφαλῆς n. gen. fem. sg. κεφαλή head
διὰ prep. διά (+gen) by, through, with, in, of, (+acc) for, because of, for a cause
τοὺς art. acc. masc. pl. ὁ ἡ τό the, this, that, he, she, it
ἀγγέλους n. acc. masc. pl. ἄγγελος angel, messenger
11 πλὴν adv. πλήν but, nevertheless, but rather, notwithstanding, except, than
οὔτε conj. οὔτε neither, nor, nor yet, no, none
ἀνὴρ n. nom. masc. sg. ἀνήρ man, husband, sir
χωρὶς prep. χωρίς (+gen) without, beside. (adv.) by itself, apart, separately
γυναικὸς n. gen. fem. sg. γυνή woman, wife
γυνὴ n. nom. fem. sg. γυνή woman, wife
χωρὶς prep. χωρίς (+gen) without, beside. (adv.) by itself, apart, separately
ἀνδρὸς n. gen. masc. sg. ἀνήρ man, husband, sir
ἐν prep. ἐν (+dat) in, by, with, among, at, on, through, to, within, into, of, for
Κυρίῳ n. dat. masc. sg. κύριος Lord, lord, master, sir, LORD, God, Master, owner
12 ὥσπερ adv. ὥσπερ as, even as, like as
γὰρ conj. γάρ for, and, because, but, indeed
ἡ art. nom. fem. sg. ὁ ἡ τό the, this, that, he, she, it
γυνὴ n. nom. fem. sg. γυνή woman, wife
ἐκ prep. ἐκ ἐξ (+gen) of, from, out of, by, on, with, in, among, through
τοῦ art. gen. masc. sg. ὁ ἡ τό the, this, that, he, she, it
ἀνδρός n. gen. masc. sg. ἀνήρ man, husband, sir
οὕτω adv. οὕτω οὕτως so, even so, thus, on this wise, likewise, after this manner
καὶ conj. καί and, even, also, but
ὁ art. nom. masc. sg. ὁ ἡ τό the, this, that, he, she, it
ἀνὴρ n. nom. masc. sg. ἀνήρ man, husband, sir
διὰ prep. διά (+gen) by, through, with, in, of, (+acc) for, because of, for a cause
τῆς art. gen. fem. sg. ὁ ἡ τό the, this, that, he, she, it
γυναικός n. gen. fem. sg. γυνή woman, wife
τὰ art. nom. neut. pl. ὁ ἡ τό the, this, that, he, she, it
δὲ conj. δέ but, and, now, also, to the contrary, rather, then

πάντα adj. nom. neut. pl. πᾶς πᾶσα πᾶν all, every, whosoever, every one, no, whole, any
ἐκ prep. ἐκ ἐξ (+gen) of, from, out of, by, on, with, in, among, through
τοῦ art. gen. masc. sg. ὁ ἡ τό the, this, that, he, she, it
Θεοῦ n. gen. masc. sg. θεός God, god
13 ἐν prep. ἐν (+dat) in, by, with, among, at, on, through, to, within, into, of, for
ὑμῖν pron. dat. 2p. pl. σύ thou, you
αὐτοῖς pron. dat. masc. 2p. pl. αὐτός ἡ ὁ self, of oneself, even, very, the same, he, she, it
γυναῖκα n. acc. fem. sg. γυνή woman, wife
ἀκατακάλυπτον adj. acc. fem. sg. ἀκατακάλυπτος uncovered
τῷ art. dat. masc. sg. ὁ ἡ τό the, this, that, he, she, it
Θεῷ n. dat. masc. sg. θεός God, god
14 ἢ particle. ἤ or, than, either, nor, or else, and, rather than
οὐδὲ adv. οὐδέ neither, nor, not, no, not even, never, not yet
αὐτὴ pron. nom. fem. 3p. sg. αὐτός ἡ ὁ self, of oneself, even, very, the same, he, she, it
ἡ art. nom. fem. sg. ὁ ἡ τό the, this, that, he, she, it
φύσις n. nom. fem. sg. φύσις nature
ὑμᾶς pron. acc. 2p. pl. σύ thou, you
ὅτι conj. ὅτι that, for, because, how that, how, because that, for that, though
ἀνὴρ n. nom. masc. sg. ἀνήρ man, husband, sir
μὲν conj. μέν indeed, verily, truly, even, so, some
ἐὰν conj. ἐάν if, soever, except, though, and if, but, whether, if so, so
ἀτιμία n. nom. fem. sg. ἀτιμία vile, dishonour, reproach, shame
αὐτῷ pron. dat. masc. 3p. sg. αὐτός ἡ ὁ self, of oneself, even, very, the same, he, she, it
15 γυνὴ n. nom. fem. sg. γυνή woman, wife
δὲ conj. δέ but, and, now, also, to the contrary, rather, then
ἐὰν conj. ἐάν if, soever, except, though, and if, but, whether, if so, so
δόξα n. nom. fem. sg. δόξα glory, honour, praise, dignity, worship
αὐτῇ pron. dat. fem. 3p. sg. αὐτός ἡ ὁ self, of oneself, even, very, the same, he, she, it
ὅτι conj. ὅτι that, for, because, how that, how, because that, for that, though
ἡ art. nom. fem. sg. ὁ ἡ τό the, this, that, he, she, it
κόμη n. nom. fem. sg. κόμη hair
ἀντὶ prep. ἀντί (+gen) for, because, in the room
περιβολαίου n. gen. neut. sg. περιβόλαιον covering, vesture
αὐτῇ pron. dat. fem. 3p. sg. αὐτός ἡ ὁ self, of oneself, even, very, the same, he, she, it
16 εἰ conj. εἰ if, whether, that, though, forasmuch
δέ conj. δέ but, and, now, also, to the contrary, rather, then
τις indefinite pron. nom. masc. sg. τὶς certain, some, any man, one, any thing
φιλόνεικος adj. nom. masc. sg. φιλόνεικος contentious
ἡμεῖς pron. nom. 1p. pl. ἐγώ I
τοιαύτην demo. pron. acc. fem. sg. τοιοῦτος such, like
συνήθειαν n. acc. fem. sg. συνήθεια custom
οὐκ particle of negation. οὐ οὐκ οὐχ not, no, neither, none, nay, nor, never, nothing
οὐδὲ adv. οὐδέ neither, nor, not, no, not even, never, not yet
αἱ art. nom. fem. pl. ὁ ἡ τό the, this, that, he, she, it
ἐκκλησίαι n. nom. fem. pl. ἐκκλησία church, assembly
τοῦ art. gen. masc. sg. ὁ ἡ τό the, this, that, he, she, it
Θεοῦ n. gen. masc. sg. θεός God, god
17 Τοῦτο demo. pron. acc. neut. sg. οὗτος αὕτη τοῦτο this, the same, this same, he, she, it
δὲ conj. δέ but, and, now, also, to the contrary, rather, then
οὐκ particle of negation. οὐ οὐκ οὐχ not, no, neither, none, nay, nor, never, nothing
ὅτι conj. ὅτι that, for, because, how that, how, because that, for that, though
οὐκ particle of negation. οὐ οὐκ οὐχ not, no, neither, none, nay, nor, never, nothing
εἰς prep. εἰς (+acc) into, to, unto, for, in, on, toward, against, upon, at, among
τὸ art. acc. neut. sg. ὁ ἡ τό the, this, that, he, she, it
κρεῖττον compar. adj. acc. neut. sg. κρείττων better

ἀλλ' conj. ἀλλά but, yea, yet, nevertheless, howbeit, nay, therefore
εἰς prep. εἰς (+acc) into, to, unto, for, in, on, toward, against, upon, at, among
τὸ art. acc. neut. sg. ὁ ἡ τό the, this, that, he, she, it
ἧττον compar. adj. acc. neut. sg. ἧττον worse, less
18 πρῶτον adv. πρῶτον first, at the first, first of all, at first, at the beginning, before, chiefly
μὲν conj. μέν indeed, verily, truly, even, so, some
γὰρ conj. γάρ for, and, because, but, indeed
ὑμῶν pron. gen. 2p. pl. σύ thou, you
ἐν prep. ἐν (+dat) in, by, with, among, at, on, through, to, within, into, of, for
τῇ art. dat. fem. sg. ὁ ἡ τό the, this, that, he, she, it
ἐκκλησίᾳ n. dat. fem. sg. ἐκκλησία church, assembly
σχίσματα n. acc. neut. pl. σχίσμα rent, division, schism
ἐν prep. ἐν (+dat) in, by, with, among, at, on, through, to, within, into, of, for
ὑμῖν pron. dat. 2p. pl. σύ thou, you
καὶ conj. καί and, even, also, but
μέρος n. acc. neut. sg. μέρος part, coast, portion, behalf, respect, piece, side
τι indefinite pron. acc. neut. sg. τὶς certain, some, any man, one, any thing
19 γὰρ conj. γάρ for, and, because, but, indeed
καὶ conj. καί and, even, also, but
αἱρέσεις n. acc. fem. pl. αἵρεσις sect, heresy
ἐν prep. ἐν (+dat) in, by, with, among, at, on, through, to, within, into, of, for
ὑμῖν pron. dat. 2p. pl. σύ thou, you
ἵνα conj. ἵνα that, to, lest, for to, so that, albeit, because, for, so as
οἱ art. nom. masc. pl. ὁ ἡ τό the, this, that, he, she, it
δόκιμοι adj. nom. masc. pl. δόκιμος approved, tried
φανεροὶ adj. nom. masc. pl. φανερός manifest, abroad, open, known, outward, appear
ἐν prep. ἐν (+dat) in, by, with, among, at, on, through, to, within, into, of, for
ὑμῖν pron. dat. 2p. pl. σύ thou, you
20 οὖν conj. οὖν therefore, then, so, and, now, wherefore
ὑμῶν pron. gen. 2p. pl. σύ thou, you
ἐπὶ prep. ἐπί (+gen) on, in, upon, (+dat) in, at, for, upon, (+acc) on, upon, unto, to, against
τὸ art. acc. neut. sg. ὁ ἡ τό the, this, that, he, she, it
αὐτὸ pron. acc. neut. 3p. sg. αὐτός ἡ ὁ self, of oneself, even, very, the same, he, she, it
οὐκ particle of negation. οὐ οὐκ οὐχ not, no, neither, none, nay, nor, never, nothing
Κυριακὸν adj. acc. neut. sg. κυριακός Lord's
δεῖπνον n. acc. neut. sg. δεῖπνον supper, feast
21 ἕκαστος adj. nom. masc. sg. ἕκαστος every man, every, every one, any man, each
γὰρ conj. γάρ for, and, because, but, indeed
τὸ art. acc. neut. sg. ὁ ἡ τό the, this, that, he, she, it
ἴδιον adj. acc. neut. sg. ἴδιος one's own, one's, privately
δεῖπνον n. acc. neut. sg. δεῖπνον supper, feast
ἐν prep. ἐν (+dat) in, by, with, among, at, on, through, to, within, into, of, for
τῷ art. dat. neut. sg. ὁ ἡ τό the, this, that, he, she, it
καὶ conj. καί and, even, also, but
ὃς relative pron. nom. masc. sg. ὅς ἥ ὅ who, which, what, that
μὲν conj. μέν indeed, verily, truly, even, so, some
ὃς relative pron. nom. masc. sg. ὅς ἥ ὅ who, which, what, that
δὲ conj. δέ but, and, now, also, to the contrary, rather, then
22 μὴ particle of negation. μή not, no, lest, neither, none, nothing, nor, never, without
γὰρ conj. γάρ for, and, because, but, indeed
οἰκίας n. acc. fem. pl. οἰκία house, home, household
οὐκ particle of negation. οὐ οὐκ οὐχ not, no, neither, none, nay, nor, never, nothing
εἰς prep. εἰς (+acc) into, to, unto, for, in, on, toward, against, upon, at, among
τὸ art. acc. neut. sg. ὁ ἡ τό the, this, that, he, she, it
καὶ conj. καί and, even, also, but

ἢ particle. ἤ or, than, either, nor, or else, and, rather than
τῆς art. gen. fem. sg. ὁ ἡ τό the, this, that, he, she, it
ἐκκλησίας n. gen. fem. sg. ἐκκλησία church, assembly
τοῦ art. gen. masc. sg. ὁ ἡ τό the, this, that, he, she, it
Θεοῦ n. gen. masc. sg. θεός God, god
καὶ conj. καί and, even, also, but
τοὺς art. acc. masc. pl. ὁ ἡ τό the, this, that, he, she, it
μὴ particle of negation. μή not, no, lest, neither, none, nothing, nor, never, without
τί interrog. pron. acc. neut. sg. τίς what, who, why, where, which, how
ὑμῖν pron. dat. 2p. pl. σύ thou, you
ὑμᾶς pron. acc. 2p. pl. σύ thou, you
ἐν prep. ἐν (+dat) in, by, with, among, at, on, through, to, within, into, of, for
τούτῳ demo. pron. dat. neut. sg. οὗτος αὕτη τοῦτο this, the same, this same, he, she, it
οὐκ particle of negation. οὐ οὐκ οὐχ not, no, neither, none, nay, nor, never, nothing
23 ἐγὼ pron. nom. 1p. sg. ἐγώ I
γὰρ conj. γάρ for, and, because, but, indeed
ἀπὸ prep. ἀπό (+gen) from, of, out of, since, for, off, at, by, in, on
τοῦ art. gen. masc. sg. ὁ ἡ τό the, this, that, he, she, it
Κυρίου n. gen. masc. sg. κύριος Lord, lord, master, sir, LORD, God, Master, owner
ὃ relative pron. acc. neut. sg. ὅς ἥ ὅ who, which, what, that
καὶ conj. καί and, even, also, but
ὑμῖν pron. dat. 2p. pl. σύ thou, you
ὅτι conj. ὅτι that, for, because, how that, how, because that, for that, though
ὁ art. nom. masc. sg. ὁ ἡ τό the, this, that, he, she, it
Κύριος n. nom. masc. sg. κύριος Lord, lord, master, sir, LORD, God, Master, owner
Ἰησοῦς n. nom. masc. sg. Ἰησοῦς Jesus
ἐν prep. ἐν (+dat) in, by, with, among, at, on, through, to, within, into, of, for
τῇ art. dat. fem. sg. ὁ ἡ τό the, this, that, he, she, it
νυκτὶ n. dat. fem. sg. νύξ night
ᾗ relative pron. dat. fem. sg. ὅς ἥ ὅ who, which, what, that
ἄρτον n. acc. masc. sg. ἄρτος bread, loaf
24 καὶ conj. καί and, even, also, but
καὶ conj. καί and, even, also, but
τοῦτό demo. pron. nom. neut. sg. οὗτος αὕτη τοῦτο this, the same, this same, he, she, it
μού pron. gen. 1p. sg. ἐγώ I
τὸ art. nom. neut. sg. ὁ ἡ τό the, this, that, he, she, it
σῶμα n. nom. neut. sg. σῶμα body, bodily, slave
τὸ art. nom. neut. sg. ὁ ἡ τό the, this, that, he, she, it
ὑπὲρ prep. ὑπέρ (+gen) for, of, for the sake of, (+acc) above, more than
ὑμῶν pron. gen. 2p. pl. σύ thou, you
τοῦτο demo. pron. acc. neut. sg. οὗτος αὕτη τοῦτο this, the same, this same, he, she, it
εἰς prep. εἰς (+acc) into, to, unto, for, in, on, toward, against, upon, at, among
τὴν art. acc. fem. sg. ὁ ἡ τό the, this, that, he, she, it
ἐμὴν poss. pron. acc. fem. 1p. sg. ἐμός my, mine, mine own, of me
ἀνάμνησιν n. acc. fem. sg. ἀνάμνησις remembrance, remembrance again
25 ὡσαύτως adv. ὡσαύτως likewise, in like manner, after the same manner, even so
καὶ conj. καί and, even, also, but
τὸ art. acc. neut. sg. ὁ ἡ τό the, this, that, he, she, it
ποτήριον n. acc. neut. sg. ποτήριον cup
μετὰ prep. μετά (+gen) with, among, against, (+acc) after
τὸ art. acc. neut. sg. ὁ ἡ τό the, this, that, he, she, it
Τοῦτο demo. pron. nom. neut. sg. οὗτος αὕτη τοῦτο this, the same, this same, he, she, it
τὸ art. nom. neut. sg. ὁ ἡ τό the, this, that, he, she, it
ποτήριον n. nom. neut. sg. ποτήριον cup
ἡ art. nom. fem. sg. ὁ ἡ τό the, this, that, he, she, it

καινὴ adj. nom. fem. sg. καινός new
διαθήκη n. nom. fem. sg. διαθήκη testament, covenant
ἐν prep. ἐν (+dat) in, by, with, among, at, on, through, to, within, into, of, for
τῷ art. dat. neut. sg. ὁ ἡ τό the, this, that, he, she, it
ἐμῷ poss. pron. dat. neut. 1p. sg. ἐμός my, mine, mine own, of me
αἵματι n. dat. neut. sg. αἷμα blood
τοῦτο demo. pron. acc. neut. sg. οὗτος αὕτη τοῦτο this, the same, this same, he, she, it
ὁσάκις adv. ὁσάκις as oft as, as often as
ἂν particle. ἄν Indicating contingency. No English translation.
εἰς prep. εἰς (+acc) into, to, unto, for, in, on, toward, against, upon, at, among
τὴν art. acc. fem. sg. ὁ ἡ τό the, this, that, he, she, it
ἐμὴν poss. pron. acc. fem. 1p. sg. ἐμός my, mine, mine own, of me
ἀνάμνησιν n. acc. fem. sg. ἀνάμνησις remembrance, remembrance again
26 ὁσάκις adv. ὁσάκις as oft as, as often as
γὰρ conj. γάρ for, and, because, but, indeed
ἂν particle. ἄν Indicating contingency. No English translation.
τὸν art. acc. masc. sg. ὁ ἡ τό the, this, that, he, she, it
ἄρτον n. acc. masc. sg. ἄρτος bread, loaf
τοῦτον demo. pron. acc. masc. sg. οὗτος αὕτη τοῦτο this, the same, this same, he, she, it
καὶ conj. καί and, even, also, but
τὸ art. acc. neut. sg. ὁ ἡ τό the, this, that, he, she, it
ποτήριον n. acc. neut. sg. ποτήριον cup
τοῦτο demo. pron. acc. neut. sg. οὗτος αὕτη τοῦτο this, the same, this same, he, she, it
τὸν art. acc. masc. sg. ὁ ἡ τό the, this, that, he, she, it
θάνατον n. acc. masc. sg. θάνατος death
τοῦ art. gen. masc. sg. ὁ ἡ τό the, this, that, he, she, it
Κυρίου n. gen. masc. sg. κύριος Lord, lord, master, sir, LORD, God, Master, owner
ἄχρις prep. ἄχρι or ἄχρις (+gen) until, unto, till, even to, as far as, while, into
οὗ relative pron. gen. masc. sg. ὅς ἥ ὅ who, which, what, that
ἂν particle. ἄν Indicating contingency. No English translation.
27 ὥστε conj. ὥστε so that, wherefore, insomuch that, therefore, that, so then
ὅς relative pron. nom. masc. sg. ὅς ἥ ὅ who, which, what, that
ἂν particle. ἄν Indicating contingency. No English translation.
τὸν art. acc. masc. sg. ὁ ἡ τό the, this, that, he, she, it
ἄρτον n. acc. masc. sg. ἄρτος bread, loaf
τοῦτον demo. pron. acc. masc. sg. οὗτος αὕτη τοῦτο this, the same, this same, he, she, it
ἢ particle. ἤ or, than, either, nor, or else, and, rather than
τὸ art. acc. neut. sg. ὁ ἡ τό the, this, that, he, she, it
ποτήριον n. acc. neut. sg. ποτήριον cup
τοῦ art. gen. masc. sg. ὁ ἡ τό the, this, that, he, she, it
Κυρίου n. gen. masc. sg. κύριος Lord, lord, master, sir, LORD, God, Master, owner
ἀναξίως adv. ἀναξίως unworthily
ἔνοχος adj. nom. masc. sg. ἔνοχος in danger of, guilty of, subject to
τοῦ art. gen. neut. sg. ὁ ἡ τό the, this, that, he, she, it
σώματος n. gen. neut. sg. σῶμα body, bodily, slave
καὶ conj. καί and, even, also, but
αἵματος n. gen. neut. sg. αἷμα blood
τοῦ art. gen. masc. sg. ὁ ἡ τό the, this, that, he, she, it
Κυρίου n. gen. masc. sg. κύριος Lord, lord, master, sir, LORD, God, Master, owner
28 δὲ conj. δέ but, and, now, also, to the contrary, rather, then
ἄνθρωπος n. nom. masc. sg. ἄνθρωπος man, human being, person, one, certain
ἑαυτὸν reflexive pron. acc. masc. 3p. sg. ἑαυτοῦ himself, herself, itself, yourself, ourselves
καὶ conj. καί and, even, also, but
οὕτως adv. οὕτω οὕτως so, even so, thus, on this wise, likewise, after this manner
ἐκ prep. ἐκ ἐξ (+gen) of, from, out of, by, on, with, in, among, through

τοῦ art. gen. masc. sg. ὁ ἡ τό the, this, that, he, she, it
ἄρτου n. gen. masc. sg. ἄρτος bread, loaf
καὶ conj. καί and, even, also, but
ἐκ prep. ἐκ ἐξ (+gen) of, from, out of, by, on, with, in, among, through
τοῦ art. gen. neut. sg. ὁ ἡ τό the, this, that, he, she, it
ποτηρίου n. gen. neut. sg. ποτήριον cup
29 ὁ art. nom. masc. sg. ὁ ἡ τό the, this, that, he, she, it
γὰρ conj. γάρ for, and, because, but, indeed
καὶ conj. καί and, even, also, but
ἀναξίως adv. ἀναξίως unworthily
κρίμα n. acc. neut. sg. κρίμα judgment, damnation, condemnation
ἑαυτῷ reflexive pron. dat. masc. 3p. sg. ἑαυτοῦ himself, herself, itself, yourself, ourselves
καὶ conj. καί and, even, also, but
μὴ particle of negation. μή not, no, lest, neither, none, nothing, nor, never, without
τὸ art. acc. neut. sg. ὁ ἡ τό the, this, that, he, she, it
σῶμα n. acc. neut. sg. σῶμα body, bodily, slave
τοῦ art. gen. masc. sg. ὁ ἡ τό the, this, that, he, she, it
Κυρίου n. gen. masc. sg. κύριος Lord, lord, master, sir, LORD, God, Master, owner
30 διὰ prep. διά (+gen) by, through, with, in, of, (+acc) for, because of, for a cause
τοῦτο demo. pron. acc. neut. sg. οὗτος αὕτη τοῦτο this, the same, this same, he, she, it
ἐν prep. ἐν (+dat) in, by, with, among, at, on, through, to, within, into, of, for
ὑμῖν pron. dat. 2p. pl. σύ thou, you
πολλοὶ adj. nom. masc. pl. πολύς many, great, much, long, abundant
ἀσθενεῖς adj. nom. masc. pl. ἀσθενής weak, sick, impotent, more feeble
καὶ conj. καί and, even, also, but
ἄρρωστοι adj. nom. masc. pl. ἄρρωστος sick, sick folk, sickly, that is sick
καὶ conj. καί and, even, also, but
ἱκανοί adj. nom. masc. pl. ἱκανός many, much, long, worthy, sufficient, great, able
31 εἰ conj. εἰ if, whether, that, though, forasmuch
γὰρ conj. γάρ for, and, because, but, indeed
ἑαυτοὺς reflexive pron. acc. masc. 3p. pl. ἑαυτοῦ himself, herself, itself, yourself, ourselves
οὐκ particle of negation. οὐ οὐκ οὐχ not, no, neither, none, nay, nor, never, nothing
ἂν particle. ἄν Indicating contingency. No English translation.
32 δὲ conj. δέ but, and, now, also, to the contrary, rather, then
ὑπὸ prep. ὑπό (+gen) of, by, with, from, among, (+acc) under
Κυρίου n. gen. masc. sg. κύριος Lord, lord, master, sir, LORD, God, Master, owner
ἵνα conj. ἵνα that, to, lest, for to, so that, albeit, because, for, so as
μὴ particle of negation. μή not, no, lest, neither, none, nothing, nor, never, without
σὺν prep. σύν (+dat) with, beside
τῷ art. dat. masc. sg. ὁ ἡ τό the, this, that, he, she, it
κόσμῳ n. dat. masc. sg. κόσμος world, adorning
33 ὥστε conj. ὥστε so that, wherefore, insomuch that, therefore, that, so then
ἀδελφοί n. voc. masc. pl. ἀδελφός brother
μου pron. gen. 1p. sg. ἐγώ I
εἰς prep. εἰς (+acc) into, to, unto, for, in, on, toward, against, upon, at, among
τὸ art. acc. neut. sg. ὁ ἡ τό the, this, that, he, she, it
ἀλλήλους pron. acc. masc. 2p. pl. ἀλλήλων one another, themselves, together, mutual
34 εἴ conj. εἰ if, whether, that, though, forasmuch
δὲ conj. δέ but, and, now, also, to the contrary, rather, then
τις indefinite pron. nom. masc. sg. τὶς certain, some, any man, one, any thing
ἐν prep. ἐν (+dat) in, by, with, among, at, on, through, to, within, into, of, for
οἴκῳ n. dat. masc. sg. οἶκος house, home, household
ἵνα conj. ἵνα that, to, lest, for to, so that, albeit, because, for, so as
μὴ particle of negation. μή not, no, lest, neither, none, nothing, nor, never, without
εἰς prep. εἰς (+acc) into, to, unto, for, in, on, toward, against, upon, at, among

κρίμα n. acc. neut. sg. κρίμα judgment, damnation, condemnation
τὰ art. acc. neut. pl. ὁ ἡ τό the, this, that, he, she, it
δὲ conj. δέ but, and, now, also, to the contrary, rather, then
λοιπὰ adj. acc. neut. pl. λοιπός other, rest, remnant, residue, which remain
ὡς adv. ὡς as, when, as it were, how, about, like, as soon as, even as, while
ἂν particle. ἄν Indicating contingency. No English translation.

12

1 Περὶ prep. περί (+gen) of, for, concerning, (+acc) about, concerning, in
δὲ conj. δέ but, and, now, also, to the contrary, rather, then
τῶν art. gen. neut. pl. ὁ ἡ τό the, this, that, he, she, it
πνευματικῶν adj. gen. neut. pl. πνευματικός spiritual
ἀδελφοί n. voc. masc. pl. ἀδελφός brother
οὐ particle of negation. οὐ οὐκ οὐχ not, no, neither, none, nay, nor, never, nothing
ὑμᾶς pron. acc. 2p. pl. σύ thou, you
2 ὅτι conj. ὅτι that, for, because, how that, how, because that, for that, though
ἔθνη n. nom. neut. pl. ἔθνος Gentile, nation, heathen, people
πρὸς prep. πρός (+gen) for, (+dat) at, (+acc) unto, to, with, for, against
τὰ art. acc. neut. pl. ὁ ἡ τό the, this, that, he, she, it
εἴδωλα n. acc. neut. pl. εἴδωλον idol
τὰ art. acc. neut. pl. ὁ ἡ τό the, this, that, he, she, it
ἄφωνα adj. acc. neut. pl. ἄφωνος dumb, without signification
ὡς adv. ὡς as, when, as it were, how, about, like, as soon as, even as, while
ἂν particle. ἄν Indicating contingency. No English translation.
3 διὸ conj. διό wherefore, therefore, for which cause
ὑμῖν pron. dat. 2p. pl. σύ thou, you
ὅτι conj. ὅτι that, for, because, how that, how, because that, for that, though
οὐδεὶς num. nom. masc. sg. οὐδείς no man, nothing, no, none, neither, not, nought
ἐν prep. ἐν (+dat) in, by, with, among, at, on, through, to, within, into, of, for
Πνεύματι n. dat. neut. sg. πνεῦμα spirit, Spirit, Ghost, ghost, life. of the spirit, wind
Θεοῦ n. gen. masc. sg. θεός God, god
ἀνάθεμα n. nom. neut. sg. ἀνάθεμα accursed, Anathema, great course
Ἰησοῦν n. acc. masc. sg. Ἰησοῦς Jesus
καὶ conj. καί and, even, also, but
οὐδεὶς num. nom. masc. sg. οὐδείς no man, nothing, no, none, neither, not, nought
Κύριον n. acc. masc. sg. κύριος Lord, lord, master, sir, LORD, God, Master, owner
Ἰησοῦν n. acc. masc. sg. Ἰησοῦς Jesus
εἰ conj. εἰ if, whether, that, though, forasmuch
μὴ particle of negation. μή not, no, lest, neither, none, nothing, nor, never, without
ἐν prep. ἐν (+dat) in, by, with, among, at, on, through, to, within, into, of, for
Πνεύματι n. dat. neut. sg. πνεῦμα spirit, Spirit, Ghost, ghost, life. of the spirit, wind
Ἁγίῳ adj. dat. neut. sg. ἅγιος Holy, holy, saint, Holy One, holy thing, most holy
4 Διαιρέσεις n. nom. fem. pl. διαίρεσις diversity, difference
δὲ conj. δέ but, and, now, also, to the contrary, rather, then
χαρισμάτων n. gen. neut. pl. χάρισμα gift, free gift
τὸ art. nom. neut. sg. ὁ ἡ τό the, this, that, he, she, it
δὲ conj. δέ but, and, now, also, to the contrary, rather, then
αὐτὸ pron. acc. neut. 3p. sg. αὐτός ἡ ὁ self, of oneself, even, very, the same, he, she, it
Πνεῦμα n. nom. neut. sg. πνεῦμα spirit, Spirit, Ghost, ghost, life. of the spirit, wind
5 καὶ conj. καί and, even, also, but
διαιρέσεις n. nom. fem. pl. διαίρεσις diversity, difference
διακονιῶν n. gen. fem. pl. διακονία ministry, administration, service, office, relief
καὶ conj. καί and, even, also, but
ὁ art. nom. masc. sg. ὁ ἡ τό the, this, that, he, she, it

αὐτὸς pron. nom. masc. 3p. sg. αὐτός ή ό self, of oneself, even, very, the same, he, she, it
Κύριος n. nom. masc. sg. κύριος Lord, lord, master, sir, LORD, God, Master, owner
6 καὶ conj. καί and, even, also, but
διαιρέσεις n. nom. fem. pl. διαίρεσις diversity, difference
ἐνεργημάτων n. gen. neut. pl. ἐνέργημα operation, working
ὁ art. nom. masc. sg. ὁ ἡ τό the, this, that, he, she, it
δὲ conj. δέ but, and, now, also, to the contrary, rather, then
αὐτὸς pron. nom. masc. 3p. sg. αὐτός ή ό self, of oneself, even, very, the same, he, she, it
Θεὸς n. nom. masc. sg. θεός God, god
ὁ art. nom. masc. sg. ὁ ἡ τό the, this, that, he, she, it
τὰ art. acc. neut. pl. ὁ ἡ τό the, this, that, he, she, it
πάντα adj. acc. neut. pl. πᾶς πᾶσα πᾶν all, every, whosoever, every one, no, whole, any
ἐν prep. ἐν (+dat) in, by, with, among, at, on, through, to, within, into, of, for
πᾶσιν adj. dat. masc. pl. πᾶς πᾶσα πᾶν all, every, whosoever, every one, no, whole, any
7 ἑκάστῳ adj. dat. masc. sg. ἕκαστος every man, every, every one, any man, each
δὲ conj. δέ but, and, now, also, to the contrary, rather, then
ἡ art. nom. fem. sg. ὁ ἡ τό the, this, that, he, she, it
φανέρωσις n. nom. fem. sg. φανέρωσις manifestation
τοῦ art. gen. neut. sg. ὁ ἡ τό the, this, that, he, she, it
Πνεύματος n. gen. neut. sg. πνεῦμα spirit, Spirit, Ghost, ghost, life. of the spirit, wind
πρὸς prep. πρός (+gen) for, (+dat) at, (+acc) unto, to, with, for, against
τὸ art. acc. neut. sg. ὁ ἡ τό the, this, that, he, she, it
8 ᾧ relative pron. dat. masc. sg. ὅς ἥ ὅ who, which, what, that
μὲν conj. μέν indeed, verily, truly, even, so, some
γὰρ conj. γάρ for, and, because, but, indeed
διὰ prep. διά (+gen) by, through, with, in, of, (+acc) for, because of, for a cause
τοῦ art. gen. neut. sg. ὁ ἡ τό the, this, that, he, she, it
Πνεύματος n. gen. neut. sg. πνεῦμα spirit, Spirit, Ghost, ghost, life. of the spirit, wind
λόγος n. nom. masc. sg. λόγος word, saying, account, speech, thing, matter
σοφίας n. gen. fem. sg. σοφία wisdom
ἄλλῳ adj. dat. masc. sg. ἄλλος other, another, some, one, more, otherwise
δὲ conj. δέ but, and, now, also, to the contrary, rather, then
λόγος n. nom. masc. sg. λόγος word, saying, account, speech, thing, matter
γνώσεως n. gen. fem. sg. γνῶσις knowledge, science
κατὰ prep. κατά (+gen) against, by, throughout, down, (+acc) according to, after, with
τὸ art. acc. neut. sg. ὁ ἡ τό the, this, that, he, she, it
αὐτὸ pron. acc. neut. 3p. sg. αὐτός ή ό self, of oneself, even, very, the same, he, she, it
Πνεῦμα n. acc. neut. sg. πνεῦμα spirit, Spirit, Ghost, ghost, life. of the spirit, wind
9 ἑτέρῳ adj. dat. masc. sg. ἕτερος another, other, else, strange
δὲ conj. δέ but, and, now, also, to the contrary, rather, then
πίστις n. nom. fem. sg. πίστις faith, assurance, belief, fidelity
ἐν prep. ἐν (+dat) in, by, with, among, at, on, through, to, within, into, of, for
τῷ art. dat. neut. sg. ὁ ἡ τό the, this, that, he, she, it
αὐτῷ adj. dat. neut. sg. αὐτός ή ό self, of oneself, even, very, the same, he, she, it
Πνεύματι n. dat. neut. sg. πνεῦμα spirit, Spirit, Ghost, ghost, life. of the spirit, wind
ἄλλῳ adj. dat. masc. sg. ἄλλος other, another, some, one, more, otherwise
δὲ conj. δέ but, and, now, also, to the contrary, rather, then
χαρίσματα n. nom. neut. pl. χάρισμα gift, free gift
ἰαμάτων n. gen. neut. pl. ἴαμα healing
ἐν prep. ἐν (+dat) in, by, with, among, at, on, through, to, within, into, of, for
τῷ art. dat. neut. sg. ὁ ἡ τό the, this, that, he, she, it
αὐτῷ adj. dat. neut. sg. αὐτός ή ό self, of oneself, even, very, the same, he, she, it
Πνεύματι n. dat. neut. sg. πνεῦμα spirit, Spirit, Ghost, ghost, life. of the spirit, wind
10 ἄλλῳ adj. dat. masc. sg. ἄλλος other, another, some, one, more, otherwise
δὲ conj. δέ but, and, now, also, to the contrary, rather, then

ἐνεργήματα n. nom. neut. pl. ἐνέργημα operation, working
δυνάμεων n. gen. fem. pl. δύναμις power, mighty work, miracle, strength, might
ἄλλῳ adj. dat. masc. sg. ἄλλος other, another, some, one, more, otherwise
δὲ conj. δέ but, and, now, also, to the contrary, rather, then
προφητεία n. nom. fem. sg. προφητεία prophecy, prophesying
ἄλλῳ adj. dat. masc. sg. ἄλλος other, another, some, one, more, otherwise
δὲ conj. δέ but, and, now, also, to the contrary, rather, then
διακρίσεις n. nom. fem. pl. διάκρισις disputations, discern, discerning
πνευμάτων n. gen. neut. pl. πνεῦμα spirit, Spirit, Ghost, ghost, life. of the spirit, wind
ἑτέρῳ adj. dat. masc. sg. ἕτερος another, other, else, strange
δὲ conj. δέ but, and, now, also, to the contrary, rather, then
γένη n. nom. neut. pl. γένος kind, kindred, offspring, nation, countrymen
γλωσσῶν n. gen. fem. pl. γλῶσσα tongue
ἄλλῳ adj. dat. masc. sg. ἄλλος other, another, some, one, more, otherwise
δὲ conj. δέ but, and, now, also, to the contrary, rather, then
ἑρμηνεία n. nom. fem. sg. ἑρμηνεία interpretation
γλωσσῶν n. gen. fem. pl. γλῶσσα tongue
11 πάντα adj. acc. neut. pl. πᾶς πᾶσα πᾶν all, every, whosoever, every one, no, whole, any
δὲ conj. δέ but, and, now, also, to the contrary, rather, then
ταῦτα demo. pron. acc. neut. pl. οὗτος αὕτη τοῦτο this, the same, this same, he, she, it
τὸ art. nom. neut. sg. ὁ ἡ τό the, this, that, he, she, it
ἓν num. nom. neut. sg. εἷς or ἕν one, other, some, any, only, a certain
καὶ conj. καί and, even, also, but
τὸ art. nom. neut. sg. ὁ ἡ τό the, this, that, he, she, it
αὐτὸ pron. acc. neut. 3p. sg. αὐτός ή ό self, of oneself, even, very, the same, he, she, it
Πνεῦμα n. nom. neut. sg. πνεῦμα spirit, Spirit, Ghost, ghost, life. of the spirit, wind
ἰδίᾳ adj. dat. fem. sg. ἴδιος one's own, one's, privately
ἑκάστῳ adj. dat. masc. sg. ἕκαστος every man, every, every one, any man, each
καθὼς adv. καθώς as, even as, according as, according to
12 Καθάπερ adv. καθάπερ even as, as, as well as
γὰρ conj. γάρ for, and, because, but, indeed
τὸ art. nom. neut. sg. ὁ ἡ τό the, this, that, he, she, it
σῶμα n. nom. neut. sg. σῶμα body, bodily, slave
ἕν num. nom. neut. sg. εἷς or ἕν one, other, some, any, only, a certain
καὶ conj. καί and, even, also, but
μέλη n. acc. neut. pl. μέλος member
πολλὰ adj. acc. neut. pl. πολύς many, great, much, long, abundant
πάντα adj. nom. neut. pl. πᾶς πᾶσα πᾶν all, every, whosoever, every one, no, whole, any
δὲ conj. δέ but, and, now, also, to the contrary, rather, then
τὰ art. nom. neut. pl. ὁ ἡ τό the, this, that, he, she, it
μέλη n. nom. neut. pl. μέλος member
τοῦ art. gen. neut. sg. ὁ ἡ τό the, this, that, he, she, it
σώματος n. gen. neut. sg. σῶμα body, bodily, slave
τοῦ art. gen. neut. sg. ὁ ἡ τό the, this, that, he, she, it
ἑνός num. gen. neut. sg. εἷς or ἕν one, other, some, any, only, a certain
πολλὰ adj. nom. neut. pl. πολύς many, great, much, long, abundant
ἕν num. nom. neut. sg. εἷς or ἕν one, other, some, any, only, a certain
σῶμα n. nom. neut. sg. σῶμα body, bodily, slave
οὕτω adv. οὕτω οὕτως so, even so, thus, on this wise, likewise, after this manner
καὶ conj. καί and, even, also, but
ὁ art. nom. masc. sg. ὁ ἡ τό the, this, that, he, she, it
Χριστός n. nom. masc. sg. Χριστός Christ
13 καὶ conj. καί and, even, also, but
γὰρ conj. γάρ for, and, because, but, indeed
ἐν prep. ἐν (+dat) in, by, with, among, at, on, through, to, within, into, of, for

ἑνὶ num. dat. neut. sg. εἷς or ἕν one, other, some, any, only, a certain
Πνεύματι n. dat. neut. sg. πνεῦμα spirit, Spirit, Ghost, ghost, life. of the spirit, wind
ἡμεῖς pron. nom. 1p. pl. ἐγώ I
πάντες adj. nom. masc. pl. πᾶς πᾶσα πᾶν all, every, whosoever, every one, no, whole, any
εἰς prep. εἰς (+acc) into, to, unto, for, in, on, toward, against, upon, at, among
ἓν num. acc. neut. sg. εἷς or ἕν one, other, some, any, only, a certain
σῶμα n. acc. neut. sg. σῶμα body, bodily, slave
εἴτε conj. εἴτε whether
Ἰουδαῖοι adj. nom. masc. pl. Ἰουδαῖος Jew, Jewess
εἴτε conj. εἴτε whether
Ἕλληνες n. nom. masc. pl. Ἕλλην Greek, Gentile
εἴτε conj. εἴτε whether
δοῦλοι n. nom. masc. pl. δοῦλος servant, bondman, bond, slave
εἴτε conj. εἴτε whether
ἐλεύθεροι adj. nom. masc. pl. ἐλεύθερος free, freewoman, at liberty, freeman
καὶ conj. καί and, even, also, but
πάντες adj. nom. masc. pl. πᾶς πᾶσα πᾶν all, every, whosoever, every one, no, whole, any
εἰς prep. εἰς (+acc) into, to, unto, for, in, on, toward, against, upon, at, among
ἓν num. acc. neut. sg. εἷς or ἕν one, other, some, any, only, a certain
Πνεῦμα n. acc. neut. sg. πνεῦμα spirit, Spirit, Ghost, ghost, life. of the spirit, wind
14 καὶ conj. καί and, even, also, but
γὰρ conj. γάρ for, and, because, but, indeed
τὸ art. nom. neut. sg. ὁ ἡ τό the, this, that, he, she, it
σῶμα n. nom. neut. sg. σῶμα body, bodily, slave
οὐκ particle of negation. οὐ οὐκ οὐχ not, no, neither, none, nay, nor, never, nothing
ἓν num. nom. neut. sg. εἷς or ἕν one, other, some, any, only, a certain
μέλος n. nom. neut. sg. μέλος member
ἀλλὰ conj. ἀλλά but, yea, yet, nevertheless, howbeit, nay, therefore
πολλά adj. nom. neut. pl. πολύς many, great, much, long, abundant
15 ἐὰν conj. ἐάν if, soever, except, though, and if, but, whether, if so, so
ὁ art. nom. masc. sg. ὁ ἡ τό the, this, that, he, she, it
πούς n. nom. masc. sg. πούς foot
Ὅτι conj. ὅτι that, for, because, how that, how, because that, for that, though
οὐκ particle of negation. οὐ οὐκ οὐχ not, no, neither, none, nay, nor, never, nothing
χείρ n. nom. fem. sg. χείρ hand
οὐκ particle of negation. οὐ οὐκ οὐχ not, no, neither, none, nay, nor, never, nothing
ἐκ prep. ἐκ ἐξ (+gen) of, from, out of, by, on, with, in, among, through
τοῦ art. gen. neut. sg. ὁ ἡ τό the, this, that, he, she, it
σώματος n. gen. neut. sg. σῶμα body, bodily, slave
οὐ particle of negation. οὐ οὐκ οὐχ not, no, neither, none, nay, nor, never, nothing
παρὰ prep. παρά (+gen) of, from, (+dat) with, for, (+acc) beside, at, by, above, against
τοῦτο demo. pron. acc. neut. sg. οὗτος αὕτη τοῦτο this, the same, this same, he, she, it
οὐκ particle of negation. οὐ οὐκ οὐχ not, no, neither, none, nay, nor, never, nothing
ἐκ prep. ἐκ ἐξ (+gen) of, from, out of, by, on, with, in, among, through
τοῦ art. gen. neut. sg. ὁ ἡ τό the, this, that, he, she, it
σώματος n. gen. neut. sg. σῶμα body, bodily, slave
16 καὶ conj. καί and, even, also, but
ἐὰν conj. ἐάν if, soever, except, though, and if, but, whether, if so, so
τὸ art. nom. neut. sg. ὁ ἡ τό the, this, that, he, she, it
οὖς n. nom. neut. sg. οὖς ear
Ὅτι conj. ὅτι that, for, because, how that, how, because that, for that, though
οὐκ particle of negation. οὐ οὐκ οὐχ not, no, neither, none, nay, nor, never, nothing
ὀφθαλμός n. nom. masc. sg. ὀφθαλμός eye, sight
οὐκ particle of negation. οὐ οὐκ οὐχ not, no, neither, none, nay, nor, never, nothing
ἐκ prep. ἐκ ἐξ (+gen) of, from, out of, by, on, with, in, among, through

τοῦ art. gen. neut. sg. ὁ ἡ τό the, this, that, he, she, it
σώματος n. gen. neut. sg. σῶμα body, bodily, slave
οὐ particle of negation. οὐ οὐκ οὐχ not, no, neither, none, nay, nor, never, nothing
παρὰ prep. παρά (+gen) of, from, (+dat) with, for, (+acc) beside, at, by, above, against
τοῦτο demo. pron. acc. neut. sg. οὗτος αὕτη τοῦτο this, the same, this same, he, she, it
οὐκ particle of negation. οὐ οὐκ οὐχ not, no, neither, none, nay, nor, never, nothing
ἐκ prep. ἐκ ἐξ (+gen) of, from, out of, by, on, with, in, among, through
τοῦ art. gen. neut. sg. ὁ ἡ τό the, this, that, he, she, it
σώματος n. gen. neut. sg. σῶμα body, bodily, slave
17 εἰ conj. εἰ if, whether, that, though, forasmuch
ὅλον adj. nom. neut. sg. ὅλος all, whole, every whit, altogether
τὸ art. nom. neut. sg. ὁ ἡ τό the, this, that, he, she, it
σῶμα n. nom. neut. sg. σῶμα body, bodily, slave
ὀφθαλμός n. nom. masc. sg. ὀφθαλμός eye, sight
ποῦ particle of place. ποῦ where, whither
ἡ art. nom. fem. sg. ὁ ἡ τό the, this, that, he, she, it
ἀκοή n. nom. fem. sg. ἀκοή hearing, ear, fame, report, rumour, which one heard
εἰ conj. εἰ if, whether, that, though, forasmuch
ὅλον adj. nom. neut. sg. ὅλος all, whole, every whit, altogether
ἀκοή n. nom. fem. sg. ἀκοή hearing, ear, fame, report, rumour, which one heard
ποῦ particle of place. ποῦ where, whither
ἡ art. nom. fem. sg. ὁ ἡ τό the, this, that, he, she, it
ὄσφρησις n. nom. fem. sg. ὄσφρησις smelling
18 νυνὶ adv. νυνί now
δὲ conj. δέ but, and, now, also, to the contrary, rather, then
ὁ art. nom. masc. sg. ὁ ἡ τό the, this, that, he, she, it
Θεὸς n. nom. masc. sg. θεός God, god
τὰ art. acc. neut. pl. ὁ ἡ τό the, this, that, he, she, it
μέλη n. acc. neut. pl. μέλος member
ἓν num. acc. neut. sg. εἷς or ἕν one, other, some, any, only, a certain
ἕκαστον adj. acc. neut. sg. ἕκαστος every man, every, every one, any man, each
αὐτῶν pron. gen. neut. 3p. pl. αὐτός ἡ ὁ self, of oneself, even, very, the same, he, she, it
ἐν prep. ἐν (+dat) in, by, with, among, at, on, through, to, within, into, of, for
τῷ art. dat. neut. sg. ὁ ἡ τό the, this, that, he, she, it
σώματι n. dat. neut. sg. σῶμα body, bodily, slave
καθὼς adv. καθώς as, even as, according as, according to
19 εἰ conj. εἰ if, whether, that, though, forasmuch
δὲ conj. δέ but, and, now, also, to the contrary, rather, then
τὰ art. nom. neut. pl. ὁ ἡ τό the, this, that, he, she, it
πάντα adj. nom. neut. pl. πᾶς πᾶσα πᾶν all, every, whosoever, every one, no, whole, any
ἓν num. nom. neut. sg. εἷς or ἕν one, other, some, any, only, a certain
μέλος n. nom. neut. sg. μέλος member
ποῦ particle of place. ποῦ where, whither
τὸ art. nom. neut. sg. ὁ ἡ τό the, this, that, he, she, it
σῶμα n. nom. neut. sg. σῶμα body, bodily, slave
20 νῦν adv. νῦν now, henceforth, present, this time
δὲ conj. δέ but, and, now, also, to the contrary, rather, then
πολλὰ adj. nom. neut. pl. πολύς many, great, much, long, abundant
μὲν conj. μέν indeed, verily, truly, even, so, some
μέλη n. nom. neut. pl. μέλος member
ἓν num. nom. neut. sg. εἷς or ἕν one, other, some, any, only, a certain
δὲ conj. δέ but, and, now, also, to the contrary, rather, then
σῶμα n. nom. neut. sg. σῶμα body, bodily, slave
21 οὐ particle of negation. οὐ οὐκ οὐχ not, no, neither, none, nay, nor, never, nothing
δὲ conj. δέ but, and, now, also, to the contrary, rather, then

ὀφθαλμὸς n. nom. masc. sg. ὀφθαλμός eye, sight
τῇ art. dat. fem. sg. ὁ ἡ τό the, this, that, he, she, it
χειρί n. dat. fem. sg. χείρ hand
Χρείαν n. acc. fem. sg. χρεία need, necessity, lack, want
σου pron. gen. 2p. sg. σύ thou, you
οὐκ particle of negation. οὐ οὐκ οὐχ not, no, neither, none, nay, nor, never, nothing
ἢ particle. ἤ or, than, either, nor, or else, and, rather than
πάλιν adv. πάλιν again
ἡ art. nom. fem. sg. ὁ ἡ τό the, this, that, he, she, it
κεφαλὴ n. nom. fem. sg. κεφαλή head
τοῖς art. dat. masc. pl. ὁ ἡ τό the, this, that, he, she, it
ποσί n. dat. masc. pl. πούς foot
Χρείαν n. acc. fem. sg. χρεία need, necessity, lack, want
ὑμῶν pron. gen. 2p. pl. σύ thou, you
οὐκ particle of negation. οὐ οὐκ οὐχ not, no, neither, none, nay, nor, never, nothing
22 ἀλλὰ conj. ἀλλά but, yea, yet, nevertheless, howbeit, nay, therefore
πολλῷ adj. dat. neut. sg. πολύς many, great, much, long, abundant
μᾶλλον adv. μᾶλλον rather, more, more and more, better, much, much the more
τὰ art. nom. neut. pl. ὁ ἡ τό the, this, that, he, she, it
μέλη n. nom. neut. pl. μέλος member
τοῦ art. gen. neut. sg. ὁ ἡ τό the, this, that, he, she, it
σώματος n. gen. neut. sg. σῶμα body, bodily, slave
ἀσθενέστερα compar. adj. nom. neut. pl. ἀσθενής weak, sick, impotent, more feeble
ἀναγκαῖά adj. nom. neut. pl. ἀναγκαῖος near, necessary, more needful, of necessity
23 καὶ conj. καί and, even, also, but
ἃ relative pron. acc. neut. pl. ὅς ἥ ὅ who, which, what, that
ἀτιμότερα compar. adj. acc. neut. pl. ἄτιμος without honour, despised, less honourable
τοῦ art. gen. neut. sg. ὁ ἡ τό the, this, that, he, she, it
σώματος n. gen. neut. sg. σῶμα body, bodily, slave
τούτοις demo. pron. dat. neut. pl. οὗτος αὕτη τοῦτο this, the same, this same, he, she, it
τιμὴν n. acc. fem. sg. τιμή honour, price, preciousness, sum
περισσοτέραν compar. adj. acc. fem. sg. περισσός more, beyond measure, advantage
καὶ conj. καί and, even, also, but
τὰ art. nom. neut. pl. ὁ ἡ τό the, this, that, he, she, it
ἀσχήμονα adj. nom. neut. pl. ἀσχήμων uncomely
ἡμῶν pron. gen. 1p. pl. ἐγώ I
εὐσχημοσύνην n. acc. fem. sg. εὐσχημοσύνη comeliness
περισσοτέραν compar. adj. acc. fem. sg. περισσός more, beyond measure, advantage
24 τὰ art. nom. neut. pl. ὁ ἡ τό the, this, that, he, she, it
δὲ conj. δέ but, and, now, also, to the contrary, rather, then
εὐσχήμονα adj. nom. neut. pl. εὐσχήμων honourable, comely
ἡμῶν pron. gen. 1p. pl. ἐγώ I
οὐ particle of negation. οὐ οὐκ οὐχ not, no, neither, none, nay, nor, never, nothing
χρείαν n. acc. fem. sg. χρεία need, necessity, lack, want
ἀλλ' conj. ἀλλά but, yea, yet, nevertheless, howbeit, nay, therefore
ὁ art. nom. masc. sg. ὁ ἡ τό the, this, that, he, she, it
Θεὸς n. nom. masc. sg. θεός God, god
τὸ art. acc. neut. sg. ὁ ἡ τό the, this, that, he, she, it
σῶμα n. acc. neut. sg. σῶμα body, bodily, slave
τῷ art. dat. neut. sg. ὁ ἡ τό the, this, that, he, she, it
περισσοτέραν compar. adj. acc. fem. sg. περισσός more, beyond measure, advantage
τιμήν n. acc. fem. sg. τιμή honour, price, preciousness, sum
25 ἵνα conj. ἵνα that, to, lest, for to, so that, albeit, because, for, so as
μὴ particle of negation. μή not, no, lest, neither, none, nothing, nor, never, without
σχίσμα n. nom. neut. sg. σχίσμα rent, division, schism

ἐν prep. ἐν (+dat) in, by, with, among, at, on, through, to, within, into, of, for
τῷ art. dat. neut. sg. ὁ ἡ τό the, this, that, he, she, it
σώματι n. dat. neut. sg. σῶμα body, bodily, slave
ἀλλὰ conj. ἀλλά but, yea, yet, nevertheless, howbeit, nay, therefore
τὸ art. acc. neut. sg. ὁ ἡ τό the, this, that, he, she, it
αὐτὸ pron. acc. neut. 3p. sg. αὐτός ἡ ό self, of oneself, even, very, the same, he, she, it
ὑπὲρ prep. ὑπέρ (+gen) for, of, for the sake of, (+acc) above, more than
ἀλλήλων pron. gen. masc. pl. ἀλλήλων one another, themselves, together, mutual
τὰ art. nom. neut. pl. ὁ ἡ τό the, this, that, he, she, it
μέλη n. nom. neut. pl. μέλος member
26 καὶ conj. καί and, even, also, but
εἴτε conj. εἴτε whether
ἓν num. nom. neut. sg. εἷς or ἕν one, other, some, any, only, a certain
μέλος n. nom. neut. sg. μέλος member
πάντα adj. nom. neut. pl. πᾶς πᾶsα πᾶν all, every, whosoever, every one, no, whole, any
τὰ art. nom. neut. pl. ὁ ἡ τό the, this, that, he, she, it
μέλη n. nom. neut. pl. μέλος member
εἴτε conj. εἴτε whether
ἓν num. nom. neut. sg. εἷς or ἕν one, other, some, any, only, a certain
μέλος n. nom. neut. sg. μέλος member
πάντα adj. nom. neut. pl. πᾶς πᾶsα πᾶν all, every, whosoever, every one, no, whole, any
τὰ art. nom. neut. pl. ὁ ἡ τό the, this, that, he, she, it
μέλη n. nom. neut. pl. μέλος member
27 ὑμεῖς pron. nom. 2p. pl. σύ thou, you
δέ conj. δέ but, and, now, also, to the contrary, rather, then
σῶμα n. nom. neut. sg. σῶμα body, bodily, slave
Χριστοῦ n. gen. masc. sg. Χριστός Christ
καὶ conj. καί and, even, also, but
μέλη n. nom. neut. pl. μέλος member
ἐκ prep. ἐκ ἐξ (+gen) of, from, out of, by, on, with, in, among, through
μέρους n. gen. neut. sg. μέρος part, coast, portion, behalf, respect, piece, side
28 καὶ conj. καί and, even, also, but
οὓς relative pron. acc. masc. pl. ὅς ἥ ὅ who, which, what, that
μὲν conj. μέν indeed, verily, truly, even, so, some
ὁ art. nom. masc. sg. ὁ ἡ τό the, this, that, he, she, it
Θεὸς n. nom. masc. sg. θεός God, god
ἐν prep. ἐν (+dat) in, by, with, among, at, on, through, to, within, into, of, for
τῇ art. dat. fem. sg. ὁ ἡ τό the, this, that, he, she, it
ἐκκλησίᾳ n. dat. fem. sg. ἐκκλησία church, assembly
πρῶτον adv. πρῶτον first, at the first, first of all, at first, at the beginning, before, chiefly
ἀποστόλους n. acc. masc. pl. ἀπόστολος apostle, messenger, he that is sent
δεύτερον ordinal. adj. acc. neut. sg. δεύτερος second, second time, again, afterward
προφήτας n. acc. masc. pl. προφήτης prophet
τρίτον adv. τρίτος thirdly
διδασκάλους n. acc. masc. pl. διδάσκαλος teacher, master, doctor
ἔπειτα adv. ἔπειτα then, after that, afterward
δυνάμεις n. acc. fem. pl. δύναμις power, mighty work, miracle, strength, might
εἶτα adv. εἶτα afterward, then, after that, furthermore
χαρίσματα n. acc. neut. pl. χάρισμα gift, free gift
ἰαμάτων n. gen. neut. pl. ἴαμα healing
ἀντιλήψεις n. acc. fem. pl. ἀντιλήμψεις help
κυβερνήσεις n. acc. fem. pl. κυβέρνησις government
γένη n. acc. neut. pl. γένος kind, kindred, offspring, nation, countrymen
γλωσσῶν n. gen. fem. pl. γλῶσσα tongue
29 μὴ particle of negation. μή not, no, lest, neither, none, nothing, nor, never, without

πάντες adj. nom. masc. pl. πᾶς πᾶσα πᾶν all, every, whosoever, every one, no, whole, any
ἀπόστολοι n. nom. masc. pl. ἀπόστολος apostle, messenger, he that is sent
μὴ particle of negation. μή not, no, lest, neither, none, nothing, nor, never, without
πάντες adj. nom. masc. pl. πᾶς πᾶσα πᾶν all, every, whosoever, every one, no, whole, any
προφῆται n. nom. masc. pl. προφήτης prophet
μὴ particle of negation. μή not, no, lest, neither, none, nothing, nor, never, without
πάντες adj. nom. masc. pl. πᾶς πᾶσα πᾶν all, every, whosoever, every one, no, whole, any
διδάσκαλοι n. nom. masc. pl. διδάσκαλος teacher, master, doctor
μὴ particle of negation. μή not, no, lest, neither, none, nothing, nor, never, without
πάντες adj. nom. masc. pl. πᾶς πᾶσα πᾶν all, every, whosoever, every one, no, whole, any
δυνάμεις n. nom. fem. pl. δύναμις power, mighty work, miracle, strength, might
30 μὴ particle of negation. μή not, no, lest, neither, none, nothing, nor, never, without
πάντες adj. nom. masc. pl. πᾶς πᾶσα πᾶν all, every, whosoever, every one, no, whole, any
χαρίσματα n. acc. neut. pl. χάρισμα gift, free gift
ἰαμάτων n. gen. neut. pl. ἴαμα healing
μὴ particle of negation. μή not, no, lest, neither, none, nothing, nor, never, without
πάντες adj. nom. masc. pl. πᾶς πᾶσα πᾶν all, every, whosoever, every one, no, whole, any
γλώσσαις n. dat. fem. pl. γλῶσσα tongue
μὴ particle of negation. μή not, no, lest, neither, none, nothing, nor, never, without
πάντες adj. nom. masc. pl. πᾶς πᾶσα πᾶν all, every, whosoever, every one, no, whole, any
31 δὲ conj. δέ but, and, now, also, to the contrary, rather, then
τὰ art. acc. neut. pl. ὁ ἡ τό the, this, that, he, she, it
χαρίσματα n. acc. neut. pl. χάρισμα gift, free gift
τὰ art. acc. neut. pl. ὁ ἡ τό the, this, that, he, she, it
κρείττονα compar. adj. acc. neut. pl. κρείττων better
καὶ conj. καί and, even, also, but
ἔτι adv. ἔτι yet, more, any more, further, still, moreover
καθ' prep. κατά (+gen) against, by, throughout, down, (+acc) according to, after, with
ὑπερβολὴν n. acc. fem. sg. ὑπερβολή abundance, beyond measure, exceeding, excellency
ὁδὸν n. acc. fem. sg. ὁδός way, journey, highway
ὑμῖν pron. dat. 2p. pl. σύ thou, you

13

1 Ἐὰν conj. ἐάν if, soever, except, though, and if, but, whether, if so, so
ταῖς art. dat. fem. pl. ὁ ἡ τό the, this, that, he, she, it
γλώσσαις n. dat. fem. pl. γλῶσσα tongue
τῶν art. gen. masc. pl. ὁ ἡ τό the, this, that, he, she, it
ἀνθρώπων n. gen. masc. pl. ἄνθρωπος man, human being, person, one, certain
καὶ conj. καί and, even, also, but
τῶν art. gen. masc. pl. ὁ ἡ τό the, this, that, he, she, it
ἀγγέλων n. gen. masc. pl. ἄγγελος angel, messenger
ἀγάπην n. acc. fem. sg. ἀγάπη love, charity, feast of charity
δὲ conj. δέ but, and, now, also, to the contrary, rather, then
μὴ particle of negation. μή not, no, lest, neither, none, nothing, nor, never, without
χαλκὸς n. nom. masc. sg. χαλκός brass, money
ἢ particle. ἤ or, than, either, nor, or else, and, rather than
κύμβαλον n. nom. neut. sg. κύμβαλον cymbal
2 καὶ conj. καί and, even, also, but
ἐὰν conj. ἐάν if, soever, except, though, and if, but, whether, if so, so
προφητείαν n. acc. fem. sg. προφητεία prophecy, prophesying
καὶ conj. καί and, even, also, but
τὰ art. acc. neut. pl. ὁ ἡ τό the, this, that, he, she, it
μυστήρια n. acc. neut. pl. μυστήριον mystery
πάντα adj. acc. neut. pl. πᾶς πᾶσα πᾶν all, every, whosoever, every one, no, whole, any

καὶ conj. καί and, even, also, but
πᾶσαν adj. acc. fem. sg. πᾶς πᾶσα πᾶν all, every, whosoever, every one, no, whole, any
τὴν art. acc. fem. sg. ὁ ἡ τό the, this, that, he, she, it
γνῶσιν n. acc. fem. sg. γνῶσις knowledge, science
καὶ conj. καί and, even, also, but
ἐὰν conj. ἐάν if, soever, except, though, and if, but, whether, if so, so
πᾶσαν adj. acc. fem. sg. πᾶς πᾶσα πᾶν all, every, whosoever, every one, no, whole, any
τὴν art. acc. fem. sg. ὁ ἡ τό the, this, that, he, she, it
πίστιν n. acc. fem. sg. πίστις faith, assurance, belief, fidelity
ὥστε conj. ὥστε so that, wherefore, insomuch that, therefore, that, so then
ὄρη n. acc. neut. pl. ὄρος mountain, mount, hill
ἀγάπην n. acc. fem. sg. ἀγάπη love, charity, feast of charity
δὲ conj. δέ but, and, now, also, to the contrary, rather, then
μὴ particle of negation. μή not, no, lest, neither, none, nothing, nor, never, without
οὐδέν num. nom. neut. sg. οὐδείς no man, nothing, no, none, neither, not, nought
3 καὶ conj. καί and, even, also, but
ἐὰν conj. ἐάν if, soever, except, though, and if, but, whether, if so, so
πάντα adj. acc. neut. pl. πᾶς πᾶσα πᾶν all, every, whosoever, every one, no, whole, any
τὰ art. acc. neut. pl. ὁ ἡ τό the, this, that, he, she, it
μου pron. gen. 1p. sg. ἐγώ I
καὶ conj. καί and, even, also, but
ἐὰν conj. ἐάν if, soever, except, though, and if, but, whether, if so, so
τὸ art. acc. neut. sg. ὁ ἡ τό the, this, that, he, she, it
σῶμά n. acc. neut. sg. σῶμα body, bodily, slave
μου pron. gen. 1p. sg. ἐγώ I
ἵνα conj. ἵνα that, to, lest, for to, so that, albeit, because, for, so as
ἀγάπην n. acc. fem. sg. ἀγάπη love, charity, feast of charity
δὲ conj. δέ but, and, now, also, to the contrary, rather, then
μὴ particle of negation. μή not, no, lest, neither, none, nothing, nor, never, without
οὐδὲν num. acc. neut. sg. οὐδείς no man, nothing, no, none, neither, not, nought
4 ἡ art. nom. fem. sg. ὁ ἡ τό the, this, that, he, she, it
ἀγάπη n. nom. fem. sg. ἀγάπη love, charity, feast of charity
ἡ art. nom. fem. sg. ὁ ἡ τό the, this, that, he, she, it
ἀγάπη n. nom. fem. sg. ἀγάπη love, charity, feast of charity
οὐ particle of negation. οὐ οὐκ οὐχ not, no, neither, none, nay, nor, never, nothing
ἡ art. nom. fem. sg. ὁ ἡ τό the, this, that, he, she, it
ἀγάπη n. nom. fem. sg. ἀγάπη love, charity, feast of charity
οὐ particle of negation. οὐ οὐκ οὐχ not, no, neither, none, nay, nor, never, nothing
οὐ particle of negation. οὐ οὐκ οὐχ not, no, neither, none, nay, nor, never, nothing
5 οὐκ particle of negation. οὐ οὐκ οὐχ not, no, neither, none, nay, nor, never, nothing
οὐ particle of negation. οὐ οὐκ οὐχ not, no, neither, none, nay, nor, never, nothing
τὰ art. acc. neut. pl. ὁ ἡ τό the, this, that, he, she, it
ἑαυτῆς reflexive pron. gen. fem. 3p. sg. ἑαυτοῦ himself, herself, itself, yourself, ourselves
οὐ particle of negation. οὐ οὐκ οὐχ not, no, neither, none, nay, nor, never, nothing
οὐ particle of negation. οὐ οὐκ οὐχ not, no, neither, none, nay, nor, never, nothing
τὸ art. acc. neut. sg. ὁ ἡ τό the, this, that, he, she, it
κακόν adj. acc. neut. sg. κακός evil, evil thing, noisome, wicked
6 οὐ particle of negation. οὐ οὐκ οὐχ not, no, neither, none, nay, nor, never, nothing
ἐπὶ prep. ἐπί (+gen) on, in, upon, (+dat) in, at, for, upon, (+acc) on, upon, unto, to, against
τῇ art. dat. fem. sg. ὁ ἡ τό the, this, that, he, she, it
ἀδικίᾳ n. dat. fem. sg. ἀδικία iniquity, unrighteousness, unjust, wrong
δὲ conj. δέ but, and, now, also, to the contrary, rather, then
τῇ art. dat. fem. sg. ὁ ἡ τό the, this, that, he, she, it
ἀληθείᾳ n. dat. fem. sg. ἀλήθεια truth, verity
7 πάντα adj. acc. neut. pl. πᾶς πᾶσα πᾶν all, every, whosoever, every one, no, whole, any

πάντα adj. acc. neut. pl. πᾶς πᾶςα πᾶν all, every, whosoever, every one, no, whole, any
πάντα adj. acc. neut. pl. πᾶς πᾶςα πᾶν all, every, whosoever, every one, no, whole, any
πάντα adj. acc. neut. pl. πᾶς πᾶςα πᾶν all, every, whosoever, every one, no, whole, any
8 ἡ art. nom. fem. sg. ὁ ἡ τό the, this, that, he, she, it
ἀγάπη n. nom. fem. sg. ἀγάπη love, charity, feast of charity
οὐδέποτε adv. οὐδέποτε never, neither at any time, no at any time
εἴτε conj. εἴτε whether
δὲ conj. δέ but, and, now, also, to the contrary, rather, then
προφητεῖαι n. nom. fem. pl. προφητεία prophecy, prophesying
εἴτε conj. εἴτε whether
γλῶσσαι n. nom. fem. pl. γλῶσσα tongue
εἴτε conj. εἴτε whether
γνῶσις n. nom. fem. sg. γνῶσις knowledge, science
9 ἐκ prep. ἐκ ἐξ (+gen) of, from, out of, by, on, with, in, among, through
μέρους n. gen. neut. sg. μέρος part, coast, portion, behalf, respect, piece, side
γὰρ conj. γάρ for, and, because, but, indeed
καὶ conj. καί and, even, also, but
ἐκ prep. ἐκ ἐξ (+gen) of, from, out of, by, on, with, in, among, through
μέρους n. gen. neut. sg. μέρος part, coast, portion, behalf, respect, piece, side
10 ὅταν conj. ὅταν when, as soon as, as long as, that, whensoever, while
δὲ conj. δέ but, and, now, also, to the contrary, rather, then
τὸ art. nom. neut. sg. ὁ ἡ τό the, this, that, he, she, it
τέλειον adj. nom. neut. sg. τέλειος perfect, of full age
τότε adv. τότε then, that time
τὸ art. nom. neut. sg. ὁ ἡ τό the, this, that, he, she, it
ἐκ prep. ἐκ ἐξ (+gen) of, from, out of, by, on, with, in, among, through
μέρους n. gen. neut. sg. μέρος part, coast, portion, behalf, respect, piece, side
11 ὅτε adv. ὅτε when, after that, as soon as, while, after
νήπιος adj. nom. masc. sg. νήπιος babe, child, childish
ὡς adv. ὡς as, when, as it were, how, about, like, as soon as, even as, while
νήπιος adj. nom. masc. sg. νήπιος babe, child, childish
ὡς adv. ὡς as, when, as it were, how, about, like, as soon as, even as, while
νήπιος adj. nom. masc. sg. νήπιος babe, child, childish
ὡς adv. ὡς as, when, as it were, how, about, like, as soon as, even as, while
νήπιος adj. nom. masc. sg. νήπιος babe, child, childish
ὅτε adv. ὅτε when, after that, as soon as, while, after
δὲ conj. δέ but, and, now, also, to the contrary, rather, then
ἀνήρ n. nom. masc. sg. ἀνήρ man, husband, sir
τὰ art. acc. neut. pl. ὁ ἡ τό the, this, that, he, she, it
τοῦ art. gen. masc. sg. ὁ ἡ τό the, this, that, he, she, it
νηπίου adj. gen. masc. sg. νήπιος babe, child, childish
12 γὰρ conj. γάρ for, and, because, but, indeed
ἄρτι adv. ἄρτι now, hence, here, hither, even now, present
δι' prep. διά (+gen) by, through, with, in, of, (+acc) for, because of, for a cause
ἐσόπτρου n. gen. neut. sg. ἔσοπτρον glass
ἐν prep. ἐν (+dat) in, by, with, among, at, on, through, to, within, into, of, for五
αἰνίγματι n. dat. neut. sg. αἴνιγμα darkly
τότε adv. τότε then, that time
δὲ conj. δέ but, and, now, also, to the contrary, rather, then
πρόσωπον n. acc. neut. sg. πρόσωπον face, presence, person, countenance
πρὸς prep. πρός (+gen) for, (+dat) at, (+acc) unto, to, with, for, against
πρόσωπον n. acc. neut. sg. πρόσωπον face, presence, person, countenance
ἄρτι adv. ἄρτι now, hence, here, hither, even now, present
ἐκ prep. ἐκ ἐξ (+gen) of, from, out of, by, on, with, in, among, through
μέρους n. gen. neut. sg. μέρος part, coast, portion, behalf, respect, piece, side

τότε adv. τότε then, that time
δὲ conj. δέ but, and, now, also, to the contrary, rather, then
καθὼς adv. καθώς as, even as, according as, according to
καὶ conj. καί and, even, also, but
13 νυνὶ adv. νυνί now
δὲ conj. δέ but, and, now, also, to the contrary, rather, then
πίστις n. nom. fem. sg. πίστις faith, assurance, belief, fidelity
ἐλπίς n. nom. fem. sg. ἐλπίς hope, faith
ἀγάπη n. nom. fem. sg. ἀγάπη love, charity, feast of charity
τὰ art. nom. neut. pl. ὁ ἡ τό the, this, that, he, she, it
τρία num. nom. neut. pl. τρεῖς three
ταῦτα demo. pron. nom. neut. pl. οὗτος αὕτη τοῦτο this, the same, this same, he, she, it
μείζων compar. adj. nom. fem. sg. μέγας great, loud, greatest, high, large, mighty, strong
δὲ conj. δέ but, and, now, also, to the contrary, rather, then
τούτων demo. pron. gen. neut. pl. οὗτος αὕτη τοῦτο this, the same, this same, he, she, it
ἡ art. nom. fem. sg. ὁ ἡ τό the, this, that, he, she, it
ἀγάπη n. nom. fem. sg. ἀγάπη love, charity, feast of charity

14

1 τὴν art. acc. fem. sg. ὁ ἡ τό the, this, that, he, she, it
ἀγάπην n. acc. fem. sg. ἀγάπη love, charity, feast of charity
δὲ conj. δέ but, and, now, also, to the contrary, rather, then
τὰ art. acc. neut. pl. ὁ ἡ τό the, this, that, he, she, it
πνευματικά adj. acc. neut. pl. πνευματικός spiritual
μᾶλλον adv. μᾶλλον rather, more, more and more, better, much, much the more
δὲ conj. δέ but, and, now, also, to the contrary, rather, then
ἵνα conj. ἵνα that, to, lest, for to, so that, albeit, because, for, so as
2 ὁ art. nom. masc. sg. ὁ ἡ τό the, this, that, he, she, it
γὰρ conj. γάρ for, and, because, but, indeed
γλώσσῃ n. dat. fem. sg. γλῶσσα tongue
οὐκ particle of negation. οὐ οὐκ οὐχ not, no, neither, none, nay, nor, never, nothing
ἀνθρώποις n. dat. masc. pl. ἄνθρωπος man, human being, person, one, certain
ἀλλὰ conj. ἀλλά but, yea, yet, nevertheless, howbeit, nay, therefore
τῷ art. dat. masc. sg. ὁ ἡ τό the, this, that, he, she, it
Θεῷ n. dat. masc. sg. θεός God, god
οὐδεὶς num. nom. masc. sg. οὐδείς no man, nothing, no, none, neither, not, nought
γὰρ conj. γάρ for, and, because, but, indeed
πνεύματι n. dat. neut. sg. πνεῦμα spirit, Spirit, Ghost, ghost, life. of the spirit, wind
δὲ conj. δέ but, and, now, also, to the contrary, rather, then
μυστήρια n. acc. neut. pl. μυστήριον mystery
3 ὁ art. nom. masc. sg. ὁ ἡ τό the, this, that, he, she, it
δὲ conj. δέ but, and, now, also, to the contrary, rather, then
ἀνθρώποις n. dat. masc. pl. ἄνθρωπος man, human being, person, one, certain
οἰκοδομὴν n. acc. fem. sg. οἰκοδομή building, edifying, edification
καὶ conj. καί and, even, also, but
παράκλησιν n. acc. fem. sg. παράκλησις consolation, exhortation, comfort
καὶ conj. καί and, even, also, but
παραμυθίαν n. acc. fem. sg. παραμυθία comfort
4 ὁ art. nom. masc. sg. ὁ ἡ τό the, this, that, he, she, it
γλώσσῃ n. dat. fem. sg. γλῶσσα tongue
ἑαυτὸν reflexive pron. acc. masc. 3p. sg. ἑαυτοῦ himself, herself, itself, yourself, ourselves
ὁ art. nom. masc. sg. ὁ ἡ τό the, this, that, he, she, it
δὲ conj. δέ but, and, now, also, to the contrary, rather, then
ἐκκλησίαν n. acc. fem. sg. ἐκκλησία church, assembly

5 δὲ conj. δέ but, and, now, also, to the contrary, rather, then
πάντας adj. acc. masc. pl. πᾶς πᾶσα πᾶν all, every, whosoever, every one, no, whole, any
ὑμᾶς pron. acc. 2p. pl. σύ thou, you
γλώσσαις n. dat. fem. pl. γλῶσσα tongue
μᾶλλον adv. μᾶλλον rather, more, more and more, better, much, much the more
δὲ conj. δέ but, and, now, also, to the contrary, rather, then
ἵνα conj. ἵνα that, to, lest, for to, so that, albeit, because, for, so as
μείζων compar. adj. nom. masc. sg. μέγας great, loud, greatest, high, large, mighty, strong
γὰρ conj. γάρ for, and, because, but, indeed
ὁ art. nom. masc. sg. ὁ ἡ τό the, this, that, he, she, it
ἢ particle. ἤ or, than, either, nor, or else, and, rather than
ὁ art. nom. masc. sg. ὁ ἡ τό the, this, that, he, she, it
γλώσσαις n. dat. fem. pl. γλῶσσα tongue
ἐκτὸς adv. ἐκτός except, out of, other than, outside, unless, without
εἰ conj. εἰ if, whether, that, though, forasmuch
μὴ particle of negation. μή not, no, lest, neither, none, nothing, nor, never, without
ἵνα conj. ἵνα that, to, lest, for to, so that, albeit, because, for, so as
ἡ art. nom. fem. sg. ὁ ἡ τό the, this, that, he, she, it
ἐκκλησία n. nom. fem. sg. ἐκκλησία church, assembly
οἰκοδομὴν n. acc. fem. sg. οἰκοδομή building, edifying, edification
6 νυνὶ adv. νυνί now
δέ conj. δέ but, and, now, also, to the contrary, rather, then
ἀδελφοί n. voc. masc. pl. ἀδελφός brother
ἐὰν conj. ἐάν if, soever, except, though, and if, but, whether, if so, so
πρὸς prep. πρός (+gen) for, (+dat) at, (+acc) unto, to, with, for, against
ὑμᾶς pron. acc. 2p. pl. σύ thou, you
γλώσσαις n. dat. fem. pl. γλῶσσα tongue
τί interrog. pron. acc. neut. sg. τίς what, who, why, where, which, how
ὑμᾶς pron. acc. 2p. pl. σύ thou, you
ἐὰν conj. ἐάν if, soever, except, though, and if, but, whether, if so, so
μὴ particle of negation. μή not, no, lest, neither, none, nothing, nor, never, without
ὑμῖν pron. dat. 2p. pl. σύ thou, you
ἢ particle. ἤ or, than, either, nor, or else, and, rather than
ἐν prep. ἐν (+dat) in, by, with, among, at, on, through, to, within, into, of, for
ἀποκαλύψει n. dat. fem. sg. ἀποκάλυψις revelation, appearing, coming, manifestation
ἢ particle. ἤ or, than, either, nor, or else, and, rather than
ἐν prep. ἐν (+dat) in, by, with, among, at, on, through, to, within, into, of, for
γνώσει n. dat. fem. sg. γνῶσις knowledge, science
ἢ particle. ἤ or, than, either, nor, or else, and, rather than
ἐν prep. ἐν (+dat) in, by, with, among, at, on, through, to, within, into, of, for
προφητείᾳ n. dat. fem. sg. προφητεία prophecy, prophesying
ἢ particle. ἤ or, than, either, nor, or else, and, rather than
ἐν prep. ἐν (+dat) in, by, with, among, at, on, through, to, within, into, of, for
διδαχῇ n. dat. fem. sg. διδαχή doctrine, teaching
7 ὅμως adv. ὅμως nevertheless, and even
τὰ art. nom. neut. pl. ὁ ἡ τό the, this, that, he, she, it
ἄψυχα adj. nom. neut. pl. ἄψυχος without life
φωνὴν n. acc. fem. sg. φωνή voice, sound, noise
εἴτε conj. εἴτε whether
αὐλὸς n. nom. masc. sg. αὐλός pipe
εἴτε conj. εἴτε whether
κιθάρα n. nom. fem. sg. κιθάρα harp
ἐὰν conj. ἐάν if, soever, except, though, and if, but, whether, if so, so
διαστολὴν n. acc. fem. sg. διαστολή difference, distinction
τοῖς art. dat. masc. pl. ὁ ἡ τό the, this, that, he, she, it

φθόγγοις n. dat. masc. pl. φθόγγος sound
μὴ particle of negation. μή not, no, lest, neither, none, nothing, nor, never, without
πῶς adv. πῶς how, by what means, after what manner
τὸ art. nom. neut. sg. ὁ ἡ τό the, this, that, he, she, it
ἢ particle. ἤ or, than, either, nor, or else, and, rather than
τὸ art. nom. neut. sg. ὁ ἡ τό the, this, that, he, she, it
8 καὶ conj. καί and, even, also, but
γὰρ conj. γάρ for, and, because, but, indeed
ἐὰν conj. ἐάν if, soever, except, though, and if, but, whether, if so, so
ἄδηλον adj. acc. fem. sg. ἄδηλος appear not, uncertain
φωνὴν n. acc. fem. sg. φωνή voice, sound, noise
σάλπιγξ n. nom. fem. sg. σάλπιγξ trumpet, trump
τίς interrog. pron. nom. masc. sg. τίς what, who, why, where, which, how
εἰς prep. εἰς (+acc) into, to, unto, for, in, on, toward, against, upon, at, among
πόλεμον n. acc. masc. sg. πόλεμος war, battle, fight
9 οὕτω adv. οὕτω οὕτως so, even so, thus, on this wise, likewise, after this manner
καὶ conj. καί and, even, also, but
ὑμεῖς pron. nom. 2p. pl. σύ thou, you
διὰ prep. διά (+gen) by, through, with, in, of, (+acc) for, because of, for a cause
τῆς art. gen. fem. sg. ὁ ἡ τό the, this, that, he, she, it
γλώσσης n. gen. fem. sg. γλῶσσα tongue
ἐὰν conj. ἐάν if, soever, except, though, and if, but, whether, if so, so
μὴ particle of negation. μή not, no, lest, neither, none, nothing, nor, never, without
εὔσημον adj. acc. masc. sg. εὔσημος easy to be understood
λόγον n. acc. masc. sg. λόγος word, saying, account, speech, thing, matter
πῶς adv. πῶς how, by what means, after what manner
τὸ art. nom. neut. sg. ὁ ἡ τό the, this, that, he, she, it
γὰρ conj. γάρ for, and, because, but, indeed
εἰς prep. εἰς (+acc) into, to, unto, for, in, on, toward, against, upon, at, among
ἀέρα n. acc. masc. sg. ἀήρ air
10 τοσαῦτα demo. pron. nom. neut. pl. τοσοῦτος so much, so great, so many, so long
εἰ conj. εἰ if, whether, that, though, forasmuch
γένη n. nom. neut. pl. γένος kind, kindred, offspring, nation, countrymen
φωνῶν n. gen. fem. pl. φωνή voice, sound, noise
ἐν prep. ἐν (+dat) in, by, with, among, at, on, through, to, within, into, of, for
κόσμῳ n. dat. masc. sg. κόσμος world, adorning
καὶ conj. καί and, even, also, but
οὐδὲν num. nom. neut. sg. οὐδείς no man, nothing, no, none, neither, not, nought
ἄφωνον adj. nom. neut. sg. ἄφωνος dumb, without signification
11 ἐὰν conj. ἐάν if, soever, except, though, and if, but, whether, if so, so
οὖν conj. οὖν therefore, then, so, and, now, wherefore
μὴ particle of negation. μή not, no, lest, neither, none, nothing, nor, never, without
τὴν art. acc. fem. sg. ὁ ἡ τό the, this, that, he, she, it
δύναμιν n. acc. fem. sg. δύναμις power, mighty work, miracle, strength, might
τῆς art. gen. fem. sg. ὁ ἡ τό the, this, that, he, she, it
φωνῆς n. gen. fem. sg. φωνή voice, sound, noise
τῷ art. dat. masc. sg. ὁ ἡ τό the, this, that, he, she, it
βάρβαρος adj. nom. masc. sg. βάρβαρος barbarous, barbarian
καὶ conj. καί and, even, also, but
ὁ art. nom. masc. sg. ὁ ἡ τό the, this, that, he, she, it
ἐν prep. ἐν (+dat) in, by, with, among, at, on, through, to, within, into, of, for
ἐμοὶ pron. dat. 1p. sg. ἐγώ I
βάρβαρος adj. nom. masc. sg. βάρβαρος barbarous, barbarian
12 οὕτω adv. οὕτω οὕτως so, even so, thus, on this wise, likewise, after this manner
καὶ conj. καί and, even, also, but

ὑμεῖς pron. nom. 2p. pl. σύ thou, you
ἐπεὶ conj. ἐπεί because, otherwise, seeing, else, for then, for as much as, for, since
ζηλωταί n. nom. masc. pl. ζηλωτής zealous
πνευμάτων n. gen. neut. pl. πνεῦμα spirit, Spirit, Ghost, ghost, life. of the spirit, wind
πρὸς prep. πρός (+gen) for, (+dat) at, (+acc) unto, to, with, for, against
τὴν art. acc. fem. sg. ὁ ἡ τό the, this, that, he, she, it
οἰκοδομὴν n. acc. fem. sg. οἰκοδομή building, edifying, edification
τῆς art. gen. fem. sg. ὁ ἡ τό the, this, that, he, she, it
ἐκκλησίας n. gen. fem. sg. ἐκκλησία church, assembly
ἵνα conj. ἵνα that, to, lest, for to, so that, albeit, because, for, so as
13 διόπερ conj. διόπερ wherefore
ὁ art. nom. masc. sg. ὁ ἡ τό the, this, that, he, she, it
γλώσσῃ n. dat. fem. sg. γλῶσσα tongue
ἵνα conj. ἵνα that, to, lest, for to, so that, albeit, because, for, so as
14 ἐὰν conj. ἐάν if, soever, except, though, and if, but, whether, if so, so
γὰρ conj. γάρ for, and, because, but, indeed
γλώσσῃ n. dat. fem. sg. γλῶσσα tongue
τὸ art. nom. neut. sg. ὁ ἡ τό the, this, that, he, she, it
πνεῦμά n. nom. neut. sg. πνεῦμα spirit, Spirit, Ghost, ghost, life. of the spirit, wind
μου pron. gen. 1p. sg. ἐγώ I
ὁ art. nom. masc. sg. ὁ ἡ τό the, this, that, he, she, it
δὲ conj. δέ but, and, now, also, to the contrary, rather, then
νοῦς n. nom. masc. sg. νοῦς understanding, mind
μου pron. gen. 1p. sg. ἐγώ I
ἄκαρπός adj. nom. masc. sg. καρπός fruit
15 τί interrog. pron. nom. neut. sg. τίς what, who, why, where, which, how
οὖν conj. οὖν therefore, then, so, and, now, wherefore
τῷ art. dat. neut. sg. ὁ ἡ τό the, this, that, he, she, it
πνεύματι n. dat. neut. sg. πνεῦμα spirit, Spirit, Ghost, ghost, life. of the spirit, wind
δὲ conj. δέ but, and, now, also, to the contrary, rather, then
καὶ conj. καί and, even, also, but
τῷ art. dat. masc. sg. ὁ ἡ τό the, this, that, he, she, it
νοΐ n. dat. masc. sg. νοῦς understanding, mind
τῷ art. dat. neut. sg. ὁ ἡ τό the, this, that, he, she, it
πνεύματι n. dat. neut. sg. πνεῦμα spirit, Spirit, Ghost, ghost, life. of the spirit, wind
δὲ conj. δέ but, and, now, also, to the contrary, rather, then
καὶ conj. καί and, even, also, but
τῷ art. dat. masc. sg. ὁ ἡ τό the, this, that, he, she, it
νοΐ n. dat. masc. sg. νοῦς understanding, mind
16 ἐπεὶ conj. ἐπεί because, otherwise, seeing, else, for then, for as much as, for, since
ἐὰν conj. ἐάν if, soever, except, though, and if, but, whether, if so, so
τῷ art. dat. neut. sg. ὁ ἡ τό the, this, that, he, she, it
πνεύματι n. dat. neut. sg. πνεῦμα spirit, Spirit, Ghost, ghost, life. of the spirit, wind
ὁ art. nom. masc. sg. ὁ ἡ τό the, this, that, he, she, it
τὸν art. acc. masc. sg. ὁ ἡ τό the, this, that, he, she, it
τόπον n. acc. masc. sg. τόπος place, room, quarter
τοῦ art. gen. masc. sg. ὁ ἡ τό the, this, that, he, she, it
ἰδιώτου n. gen. masc. sg. ἰδιώτης ignorant, unlearned, rude
πῶς adv. πῶς how, by what means, after what manner
τὸ art. acc. neut. sg. ὁ ἡ τό the, this, that, he, she, it
ἀμὴν particle. ἀμήν amen, verily
ἐπὶ prep. ἐπί (+gen) on, in, upon, (+dat) in, at, for, upon, (+acc) on, upon, unto, to, against
τῇ art. dat. fem. sg. ὁ ἡ τό the, this, that, he, she, it
σῇ poss. pron. dat. fem. 2p. sg. σός thy, thine, thine own
εὐχαριστίᾳ n. dat. fem. sg. εὐχαριστία thankfulness, thanksgiving, giving of thanks

ἐπειδὴ conj. ἐπειδή because, for, after that, for that, for as much as, since
τί interrog. pron. acc. neut. sg. τίς what, who, why, where, which, how
οὐκ particle of negation. οὐ οὐκ οὐχ not, no, neither, none, nay, nor, never, nothing
17 σὺ pron. nom. 2p. sg. σύ thou, you
μὲν conj. μέν indeed, verily, truly, even, so, some
γὰρ conj. γάρ for, and, because, but, indeed
καλῶς adv. καλῶς good, well, full well
ἀλλ' conj. ἀλλά but, yea, yet, nevertheless, howbeit, nay, therefore
ὁ art. nom. masc. sg. ὁ ἡ τό the, this, that, he, she, it
ἕτερος adj. nom. masc. sg. ἕτερος another, other, else, strange
οὐκ particle of negation. οὐ οὐκ οὐχ not, no, neither, none, nay, nor, never, nothing
18 τῷ art. dat. masc. sg. ὁ ἡ τό the, this, that, he, she, it
Θεῷ n. dat. masc. sg. θεός God, god
μου pron. gen. 1p. sg. ἐγώ I
πάντων adj. gen. masc. pl. πᾶς πᾶσα πᾶν all, every, whosoever, every one, no, whole, any
ὑμῶν pron. gen. 2p. pl. σύ thou, you
μᾶλλον adv. μᾶλλον rather, more, more and more, better, much, much the more
γλώσσαις n. dat. fem. pl. γλῶσσα tongue
19 ἀλλ' conj. ἀλλά but, yea, yet, nevertheless, howbeit, nay, therefore
ἐν prep. ἐν (+dat) in, by, with, among, at, on, through, to, within, into, of, for
ἐκκλησίᾳ n. dat. fem. sg. ἐκκλησία church, assembly
πέντε num. acc. masc. pl. πέντε five
λόγους n. acc. masc. pl. λόγος word, saying, account, speech, thing, matter
διὰ prep. διά (+gen) by, through, with, in, of, (+acc) for, because of, for a cause
τοῦ art. gen. masc. sg. ὁ ἡ τό the, this, that, he, she, it
νοός n. gen. masc. sg. νοῦς understanding, mind
μου pron. gen. 1p. sg. ἐγώ I
ἵνα conj. ἵνα that, to, lest, for to, so that, albeit, because, for, so as
καὶ conj. καί and, even, also, but
ἄλλους adj. acc. masc. pl. ἄλλος other, another, some, one, more, otherwise
ἢ particle. ἤ or, than, either, nor, or else, and, rather than
μυρίους adj. acc. masc. pl. μύριοι ten thousand
λόγους n. acc. masc. pl. λόγος word, saying, account, speech, thing, matter
ἐν prep. ἐν (+dat) in, by, with, among, at, on, through, to, within, into, of, for
γλώσσῃ n. dat. fem. sg. γλῶσσα tongue
20 Ἀδελφοί n. voc. masc. pl. ἀδελφός brother
μὴ particle of negation. μή not, no, lest, neither, none, nothing, nor, never, without
παιδία n. nom. neut. pl. παιδίον child, little child, damsel
ταῖς art. dat. fem. pl. ὁ ἡ τό the, this, that, he, she, it
φρεσὶν n. dat. fem. pl. φρήν understanding, thinking, mind, intellect
ἀλλὰ conj. ἀλλά but, yea, yet, nevertheless, howbeit, nay, therefore
τῇ art. dat. fem. sg. ὁ ἡ τό the, this, that, he, she, it
κακίᾳ n. dat. fem. sg. κακία malice, maliciousness, evil, naughtiness, wickedness
ταῖς art. dat. fem. pl. ὁ ἡ τό the, this, that, he, she, it
δὲ conj. δέ but, and, now, also, to the contrary, rather, then
φρεσὶ n. dat. fem. pl. φρήν understanding, thinking, mind, intellect
τέλειοι adj. nom. masc. pl. τέλειος perfect, of full age
21 ἐν prep. ἐν (+dat) in, by, with, among, at, on, through, to, within, into, of, for
τῷ art. dat. masc. sg. ὁ ἡ τό the, this, that, he, she, it
νόμῳ n. dat. masc. sg. νόμος law, the law
ὅτι conj. ὅτι that, for, because, how that, how, because that, for that, though
Ἐν prep. ἐν (+dat) in, by, with, among, at, on, through, to, within, into, of, for
ἑτερογλώσσοις adj. dat. masc. pl. ἑτερόγλωσσος man of other tongues
καὶ conj. καί and, even, also, but
ἐν prep. ἐν (+dat) in, by, with, among, at, on, through, to, within, into, of, for

χείλεσιν n. dat. neut. pl. χεῖλος lip, shore
ἑτέροις adj. dat. masc. pl. ἕτερος another, other, else, strange
τῷ art. dat. masc. sg. ὁ ἡ τό the, this, that, he, she, it
λαῷ n. dat. masc. sg. λαός people
τούτῳ demo. pron. dat. masc. sg. οὗτος αὕτη τοῦτο this, the same, this same, he, she, it
καὶ conj. καί and, even, also, but
οὐδ' adv. οὐδέ neither, nor, not, no, not even, never, not yet
οὕτως adv. οὕτω οὕτως so, even so, thus, on this wise, likewise, after this manner
μου pron. gen. 1p. sg. ἐγώ I
Κύριος n. nom. masc. sg. κύριος Lord, lord, master, sir, LORD, God, Master, owner
22 ὥστε conj. ὥστε so that, wherefore, insomuch that, therefore, that, so then
αἱ art. nom. fem. pl. ὁ ἡ τό the, this, that, he, she, it
γλῶσσαι n. nom. fem. pl. γλῶσσα tongue
εἰς prep. εἰς (+acc) into, to, unto, for, in, on, toward, against, upon, at, among
σημεῖόν n. acc. neut. sg. σημεῖον sign, miracle, wonder, token
οὐ particle of negation. οὐ οὐκ οὐχ not, no, neither, none, nay, nor, never, nothing
τοῖς art. dat. masc. pl. ὁ ἡ τό the, this, that, he, she, it
ἀλλὰ conj. ἀλλά but, yea, yet, nevertheless, howbeit, nay, therefore
τοῖς art. dat. masc. pl. ὁ ἡ τό the, this, that, he, she, it
ἀπίστοις adj. dat. masc. pl. ἄπιστος faithless, unbelieving, infidel, thing incredible
ἡ art. nom. fem. sg. ὁ ἡ τό the, this, that, he, she, it
δὲ conj. δέ but, and, now, also, to the contrary, rather, then
προφητεία n. nom. fem. sg. προφητεία prophecy, prophesying
οὐ particle of negation. οὐ οὐκ οὐχ not, no, neither, none, nay, nor, never, nothing
τοῖς art. dat. masc. pl. ὁ ἡ τό the, this, that, he, she, it
ἀπίστοις adj. dat. masc. pl. ἄπιστος faithless, unbelieving, infidel, thing incredible
ἀλλὰ conj. ἀλλά but, yea, yet, nevertheless, howbeit, nay, therefore
τοῖς art. dat. masc. pl. ὁ ἡ τό the, this, that, he, she, it
23 ἐὰν conj. ἐάν if, soever, except, though, and if, but, whether, if so, so
οὖν conj. οὖν therefore, then, so, and, now, wherefore
ἡ art. nom. fem. sg. ὁ ἡ τό the, this, that, he, she, it
ἐκκλησία n. nom. fem. sg. ἐκκλησία church, assembly
ὅλη adj. nom. fem. sg. ὅλος all, whole, every whit, altogether
ἐπὶ prep. ἐπί (+gen) on, in, upon, (+dat) in, at, for, upon, (+acc) on, upon, unto, to, against
τὸ art. acc. neut. sg. ὁ ἡ τό the, this, that, he, she, it
αὐτὸ pron. acc. neut. 3p. sg. αὐτός ἡ ὁ self, of oneself, even, very, the same, he, she, it
καὶ conj. καί and, even, also, but
πάντες adj. nom. masc. pl. πᾶς πᾶσα πᾶν all, every, whosoever, every one, no, whole, any
γλώσσαις n. dat. fem. pl. γλῶσσα tongue
δὲ conj. δέ but, and, now, also, to the contrary, rather, then
ἰδιῶται n. nom. masc. pl. ἰδιώτης ignorant, unlearned, rude
ἢ particle. ἤ or, than, either, nor, or else, and, rather than
ἄπιστοι adj. nom. masc. pl. ἄπιστος faithless, unbelieving, infidel, thing incredible
οὐκ particle of negation. οὐ οὐκ οὐχ not, no, neither, none, nay, nor, never, nothing
ὅτι conj. ὅτι that, for, because, how that, how, because that, for that, though
24 ἐὰν conj. ἐάν if, soever, except, though, and if, but, whether, if so, so
δὲ conj. δέ but, and, now, also, to the contrary, rather, then
πάντες adj. nom. masc. pl. πᾶς πᾶσα πᾶν all, every, whosoever, every one, no, whole, any
δὲ conj. δέ but, and, now, also, to the contrary, rather, then
τις indefinite pron. nom. masc. sg. τὶς certain, some, any man, one, any thing
ἄπιστος adj. nom. masc. sg. ἄπιστος faithless, unbelieving, infidel, thing incredible
ἢ particle. ἤ or, than, either, nor, or else, and, rather than
ἰδιώτης n. nom. masc. sg. ἰδιώτης ignorant, unlearned, rude
ὑπὸ prep. ὑπό (+gen) of, by, with, from, among, (+acc) under
πάντων adj. gen. masc. pl. πᾶς πᾶσα πᾶν all, every, whosoever, every one, no, whole, any

ὑπὸ prep. ὑπό (+gen) of, by, with, from, among, (+acc) under
πάντων adj. gen. masc. pl. πᾶς πᾶσα πᾶν all, every, whosoever, every one, no, whole, any
25 καὶ conj. καί and, even, also, but
οὕτω adv. οὕτω οὕτως so, even so, thus, on this wise, likewise, after this manner
τὰ art. nom. neut. pl. ὁ ἡ τό the, this, that, he, she, it
κρυπτὰ adj. nom. neut. pl. κρυπτός secret, hid, hidden, inwardly
τῆς art. gen. fem. sg. ὁ ἡ τό the, this, that, he, she, it
καρδίας n. gen. fem. sg. καρδία heart
αὐτοῦ pron. gen. masc. 3p. sg. αὐτός ἡ ὁ self, of oneself, even, very, the same, he, she, it
φανερὰ adj. nom. neut. pl. φανερός manifest, abroad, open, known, outward, appear
καὶ conj. καί and, even, also, but
οὕτω adv. οὕτω οὕτως so, even so, thus, on this wise, likewise, after this manner
ἐπὶ prep. ἐπί (+gen) on, in, upon, (+dat) in, at, for, upon, (+acc) on, upon, unto, to, against
πρόσωπον n. acc. neut. sg. πρόσωπον face, presence, person, countenance
τῷ art. dat. masc. sg. ὁ ἡ τό the, this, that, he, she, it
Θεῷ n. dat. masc. sg. θεός God, god
ὅτι conj. ὅτι that, for, because, how that, how, because that, for that, though
ὁ art. nom. masc. sg. ὁ ἡ τό the, this, that, he, she, it
Θεὸς n. nom. masc. sg. θεός God, god
ὄντως adv. ὄντως indeed, certainly, clean, of a truth, verily
ἐν prep. ἐν (+dat) in, by, with, among, at, on, through, to, within, into, of, for
ὑμῖν pron. dat. 2p. pl. σύ thou, you
26 Τί interrog. pron. nom. neut. sg. τίς what, who, why, where, which, how
οὖν conj. οὖν therefore, then, so, and, now, wherefore
ἀδελφοί n. voc. masc. pl. ἀδελφός brother
ὅταν conj. ὅταν when, as soon as, as long as, that, whensoever, while
ἕκαστος adj. nom. masc. sg. ἕκαστος every man, every, every one, any man, each
ὑμῶν pron. gen. 2p. pl. σύ thou, you
ψαλμὸν n. acc. masc. sg. ψαλμός Psalm, psalm
διδαχὴν n. acc. fem. sg. διδαχή doctrine, teaching
γλῶσσαν n. acc. fem. sg. γλῶσσα tongue
ἀποκάλυψιν n. acc. fem. sg. ἀποκάλυψις revelation, appearing, coming, manifestation
ἑρμηνείαν n. acc. fem. sg. ἑρμηνεία interpretation
πάντα adj. nom. neut. pl. πᾶς πᾶσα πᾶν all, every, whosoever, every one, no, whole, any
πρὸς prep. πρός (+gen) for, (+dat) at, (+acc) unto, to, with, for, against
οἰκοδομὴν n. acc. fem. sg. οἰκοδομή building, edifying, edification
27 εἴτε conj. εἴτε whether
γλώσσῃ n. dat. fem. sg. γλῶσσα tongue
τις indefinite pron. nom. masc. sg. τὶς certain, some, any man, one, any thing
κατὰ prep. κατά (+gen) against, by, throughout, down, (+acc) according to, after, with
δύο num. acc. masc. pl. δύο two, twain, both
ἢ particle. ἤ or, than, either, nor, or else, and, rather than
τὸ art. acc. neut. sg. ὁ ἡ τό the, this, that, he, she, it
πλεῖστον superl. adj. acc. neut. sg. πολύς many, great, much, long, abundant
τρεῖς num. acc. masc. pl. τρεῖς three
καὶ conj. καί and, even, also, but
ἀνὰ prep. ἀνά (+acc) by, in, through, among, between. (adv.) apiece, every man, each
μέρος n. acc. neut. sg. μέρος part, coast, portion, behalf, respect, piece, side
καὶ conj. καί and, even, also, but
εἷς num. nom. masc. sg. εἷς or ἕν one, other, some, any, only, a certain
28 ἐὰν conj. ἐάν if, soever, except, though, and if, but, whether, if so, so
δὲ conj. δέ but, and, now, also, to the contrary, rather, then
μὴ particle of negation. μή not, no, lest, neither, none, nothing, nor, never, without
διερμηνευτής n. nom. masc. sg. διερμηνευτής interpreter
ἐν prep. ἐν (+dat) in, by, with, among, at, on, through, to, within, into, of, for

ἐκκλησίᾳ n. dat. fem. sg. ἐκκλησία church, assembly
ἑαυτῷ reflexive pron. dat. masc. 3p. sg. ἑαυτοῦ himself, herself, itself, yourself, ourselves
δὲ conj. δέ but, and, now, also, to the contrary, rather, then
καὶ conj. καί and, even, also, but
τῷ art. dat. masc. sg. ὁ ἡ τό the, this, that, he, she, it
Θεῷ n. dat. masc. sg. θεός God, god
29 προφῆται n. nom. masc. pl. προφήτης prophet
δὲ conj. δέ but, and, now, also, to the contrary, rather, then
δύο num. nom. masc. pl. δύο two, twain, both
ἢ particle. ἤ or, than, either, nor, or else, and, rather than
τρεῖς num. nom. masc. pl. τρεῖς three
καὶ conj. καί and, even, also, but
οἱ art. nom. masc. pl. ὁ ἡ τό the, this, that, he, she, it
ἄλλοι adj. nom. masc. pl. ἄλλος other, another, some, one, more, otherwise
30 ἐὰν conj. ἐάν if, soever, except, though, and if, but, whether, if so, so
δὲ conj. δέ but, and, now, also, to the contrary, rather, then
ἄλλῳ adj. dat. masc. sg. ἄλλος other, another, some, one, more, otherwise
ὁ art. nom. masc. sg. ὁ ἡ τό the, this, that, he, she, it
πρῶτος ordinal. adj. nom. masc. sg. πρῶτος first, chief, first of all, chiefest, best
31 γὰρ conj. γάρ for, and, because, but, indeed
καθ' prep. κατά (+gen) against, by, throughout, down, (+acc) according to, after, with
ἕνα num. acc. masc. sg. εἷς or ἕν one, other, some, any, only, a certain
πάντες adj. nom. masc. pl. πᾶς πᾶσα πᾶν all, every, whosoever, every one, no, whole, any
ἵνα conj. ἵνα that, to, lest, for to, so that, albeit, because, for, so as
πάντες adj. nom. masc. pl. πᾶς πᾶσα πᾶν all, every, whosoever, every one, no, whole, any
καὶ conj. καί and, even, also, but
πάντες adj. nom. masc. pl. πᾶς πᾶσα πᾶν all, every, whosoever, every one, no, whole, any
32 καὶ conj. καί and, even, also, but
πνεύματα n. nom. neut. pl. πνεῦμα spirit, Spirit, Ghost, ghost, life. of the spirit, wind
προφητῶν n. gen. masc. pl. προφήτης prophet
προφήταις n. dat. masc. pl. προφήτης prophet
33 οὐ particle of negation. οὐ οὐκ οὐχ not, no, neither, none, nay, nor, never, nothing
γάρ conj. γάρ for, and, because, but, indeed
ἀκαταστασίας n. gen. fem. sg. ἀκαταστασία commotion, confusion, tumult
ὁ art. nom. masc. sg. ὁ ἡ τό the, this, that, he, she, it
Θεὸς n. nom. masc. sg. θεός God, god
ἀλλ' conj. ἀλλά but, yea, yet, nevertheless, howbeit, nay, therefore
εἰρήνης n. gen. fem. sg. εἰρήνη peace, quietness, rest
ὡς adv. ὡς as, when, as it were, how, about, like, as soon as, even as, while
ἐν prep. ἐν (+dat) in, by, with, among, at, on, through, to, within, into, of, for
πάσαις adj. dat. fem. pl. πᾶς πᾶσα πᾶν all, every, whosoever, every one, no, whole, any
ταῖς art. dat. fem. pl. ὁ ἡ τό the, this, that, he, she, it
ἐκκλησίαις n. dat. fem. pl. ἐκκλησία church, assembly
τῶν art. gen. masc. pl. ὁ ἡ τό the, this, that, he, she, it
ἁγίων adj. gen. masc. pl. ἅγιος Holy, holy, saint, Holy One, holy thing, most holy
34 Αἱ art. nom. fem. pl. ὁ ἡ τό the, this, that, he, she, it
γυναῖκες n. nom. fem. pl. γυνή woman, wife
ὑμῶν pron. gen. 2p. pl. σύ thou, you
ἐν prep. ἐν (+dat) in, by, with, among, at, on, through, to, within, into, of, for
ταῖς art. dat. fem. pl. ὁ ἡ τό the, this, that, he, she, it
ἐκκλησίαις n. dat. fem. pl. ἐκκλησία church, assembly
οὐ particle of negation. οὐ οὐκ οὐχ not, no, neither, none, nay, nor, never, nothing
γὰρ conj. γάρ for, and, because, but, indeed
αὐταῖς pron. dat. fem. 3p. pl. αὐτός ἡ ὁ self, of oneself, even, very, the same, he, she, it
ἀλλ' conj. ἀλλά but, yea, yet, nevertheless, howbeit, nay, therefore

καθὼς adv. καθώς as, even as, according as, according to
καὶ conj. καί and, even, also, but
ὁ art. nom. masc. sg. ὁ ἡ τό the, this, that, he, she, it
νόμος n. nom. masc. sg. νόμος law, the law
35 εἰ conj. εἰ if, whether, that, though, forasmuch
δέ conj. δέ but, and, now, also, to the contrary, rather, then
τι indefinite pron. acc. neut. sg. τὶς certain, some, any man, one, any thing
ἐν prep. ἐν (+dat) in, by, with, among, at, on, through, to, within, into, of, for
οἴκῳ n. dat. masc. sg. οἶκος house, home, household
τοὺς art. acc. masc. pl. ὁ ἡ τό the, this, that, he, she, it
ἰδίους adj. acc. masc. pl. ἴδιος one's own, one's, privately
ἄνδρας n. acc. masc. pl. ἀνήρ man, husband, sir
αἰσχρὸν adj. nom. neut. sg. αἰσχρός shame
γάρ conj. γάρ for, and, because, but, indeed
γυναιξὶν n. dat. fem. pl. γυνή woman, wife
ἐν prep. ἐν (+dat) in, by, with, among, at, on, through, to, within, into, of, for
ἐκκλησίᾳ n. dat. fem. sg. ἐκκλησία church, assembly
36 ἢ particle. ἤ or, than, either, nor, or else, and, rather than
ἀφ' prep. ἀπό (+gen) from, of, out of, since, for, off, at, by, in, on
ὑμῶν pron. gen. 2p. pl. σύ thou, you
ὁ art. nom. masc. sg. ὁ ἡ τό the, this, that, he, she, it
λόγος n. nom. masc. sg. λόγος word, saying, account, speech, thing, matter
τοῦ art. gen. masc. sg. ὁ ἡ τό the, this, that, he, she, it
Θεοῦ n. gen. masc. sg. θεός God, god
ἢ particle. ἤ or, than, either, nor, or else, and, rather than
εἰς prep. εἰς (+acc) into, to, unto, for, in, on, toward, against, upon, at, among
ὑμᾶς pron. acc. 2p. pl. σύ thou, you
μόνους adj. acc. masc. pl. μόνος only, alone, by oneself
37 Εἴ conj. εἰ if, whether, that, though, forasmuch
τις indefinite pron. nom. masc. sg. τὶς certain, some, any man, one, any thing
προφήτης n. nom. masc. sg. προφήτης prophet
ἢ particle. ἤ or, than, either, nor, or else, and, rather than
πνευματικός adj. nom. masc. sg. πνευματικός spiritual
ἃ relative pron. acc. neut. pl. ὅς ἥ ὅ who, which, what, that
ὑμῖν pron. dat. 2p. pl. σύ thou, you
ὅτι conj. ὅτι that, for, because, how that, how, because that, for that, though
τοῦ art. gen. masc. sg. ὁ ἡ τό the, this, that, he, she, it
Κυρίου n. gen. masc. sg. κύριος Lord, lord, master, sir, LORD, God, Master, owner
ἐντολαί n. nom. fem. pl. ἐντολή commandment, precept
38 εἰ conj. εἰ if, whether, that, though, forasmuch
δέ conj. δέ but, and, now, also, to the contrary, rather, then
τις indefinite pron. nom. masc. sg. τὶς certain, some, any man, one, any thing
39 Ὥστε conj. ὥστε so that, wherefore, insomuch that, therefore, that, so then
ἀδελφοί n. voc. masc. pl. ἀδελφός brother
τὸ art. acc. neut. sg. ὁ ἡ τό the, this, that, he, she, it
καὶ conj. καί and, even, also, but
τὸ art. acc. neut. sg. ὁ ἡ τό the, this, that, he, she, it
γλώσσαις n. dat. fem. pl. γλῶσσα tongue
μὴ particle of negation. μή not, no, lest, neither, none, nothing, nor, never, without
40 πάντα adj. nom. neut. pl. πᾶς πᾶσa πᾶν all, every, whosoever, every one, no, whole, any
εὐσχημόνως adv. εὐσχημόνως honestly, decently
καὶ conj. καί and, even, also, but
κατὰ prep. κατά (+gen) against, by, throughout, down, (+acc) according to, after, with
τάξιν n. acc. fem. sg. τάξις order

15

1 δὲ conj. δέ but, and, now, also, to the contrary, rather, then
ὑμῖν pron. dat. 2p. pl. σύ thou, you
ἀδελφοί n. voc. masc. pl. ἀδελφός brother
τὸ art. acc. neut. sg. ὁ ἡ τό the, this, that, he, she, it
εὐαγγέλιον n. acc. neut. sg. εὐαγγέλιον gospel
ὃ relative pron. acc. neut. sg. ὅς ἥ ὅ who, which, what, that
ὑμῖν pron. dat. 2p. pl. σύ thou, you
ὃ relative pron. acc. neut. sg. ὅς ἥ ὅ who, which, what, that
καὶ conj. καί and, even, also, but
ἐν prep. ἐν (+dat) in, by, with, among, at, on, through, to, within, into, of, for
ᾧ relative pron. dat. neut. sg. ὅς ἥ ὅ who, which, what, that
καὶ conj. καί and, even, also, but
2 δι' prep. διά (+gen) by, through, with, in, of, (+acc) for, because of, for a cause
οὗ relative pron. gen. neut. sg. ὅς ἥ ὅ who, which, what, that
καὶ conj. καί and, even, also, but
τίνι interrog. pron. dat. masc. sg. τίς what, who, why, where, which, how
λόγῳ n. dat. masc. sg. λόγος word, saying, account, speech, thing, matter
ὑμῖν pron. dat. 2p. pl. σύ thou, you
εἰ conj. εἰ if, whether, that, though, forasmuch
ἐκτὸς adv. ἐκτός except, out of, other than, outside, unless, without
εἰ conj. εἰ if, whether, that, though, forasmuch
μὴ particle of negation. μή not, no, lest, neither, none, nothing, nor, never, without
εἰκῇ adv. εἰκῇ in vain, vainly, without a cause
3 γὰρ conj. γάρ for, and, because, but, indeed
ὑμῖν pron. dat. 2p. pl. σύ thou, you
ἐν prep. ἐν (+dat) in, by, with, among, at, on, through, to, within, into, of, for
πρώτοις ordinal. adj. dat. neut. pl. πρῶτος first, chief, first of all, chiefest, best
ὃ relative pron. acc. neut. sg. ὅς ἥ ὅ who, which, what, that
καὶ conj. καί and, even, also, but
ὅτι conj. ὅτι that, for, because, how that, how, because that, for that, though
Χριστὸς n. nom. masc. sg. Χριστός Christ
ὑπὲρ prep. ὑπέρ (+gen) for, of, for the sake of, (+acc) above, more than
τῶν art. gen. fem. pl. ὁ ἡ τό the, this, that, he, she, it
ἁμαρτιῶν n. gen. fem. pl. ἁμαρτία sin, offence, sinful
ἡμῶν pron. gen. 1p. pl. ἐγώ I
κατὰ prep. κατά (+gen) against, by, throughout, down, (+acc) according to, after, with
τὰς art. acc. fem. pl. ὁ ἡ τό the, this, that, he, she, it
γραφὰς n. acc. fem. pl. γραφή scripture
4 καὶ conj. καί and, even, also, but
ὅτι conj. ὅτι that, for, because, how that, how, because that, for that, though
καὶ conj. καί and, even, also, but
ὅτι conj. ὅτι that, for, because, how that, how, because that, for that, though
τῇ art. dat. fem. sg. ὁ ἡ τό the, this, that, he, she, it
τρίτῃ ordinal. adj. dat. fem. sg. τρίτος third
ἡμέρᾳ n. dat. fem. sg. ἡμέρα day, time, year, while, age, day time
κατὰ prep. κατά (+gen) against, by, throughout, down, (+acc) according to, after, with
τὰς art. acc. fem. pl. ὁ ἡ τό the, this, that, he, she, it
γραφὰς n. acc. fem. pl. γραφή scripture
5 καὶ conj. καί and, even, also, but
ὅτι conj. ὅτι that, for, because, how that, how, because that, for that, though
Κηφᾷ n. dat. masc. sg. Κηφᾶς Cephas
εἶτα adv. εἶτα afterward, then, after that, furthermore
τοῖς art. dat. masc. pl. ὁ ἡ τό the, this, that, he, she, it

δώδεκα num. dat. masc. pl. δώδεκα twelve
6 ἔπειτα adv. ἔπειτα then, after that, afterward
ἐπάνω adv. ἐπάνω on, over, above, upon, more than
πεντακοσίοις num. dat. masc. pl. πεντακόσιοι five hundred
ἀδελφοῖς n. dat. masc. pl. ἀδελφός brother
ἐφάπαξ adv. ἐφάπαξ once, once for all
ἐξ prep. ἐκ ἐξ (+gen) of, from, out of, by, on, with, in, among, through
ὧν relative pron. gen. masc. pl. ὅς ἥ ὅ who, which, what, that
οἱ art. nom. masc. pl. ὁ ἡ τό the, this, that, he, she, it
πλείους compar. adj. nom. masc. pl. πλείων more, many, greater, further, more part
ἕως conj. ἕως till, until, unto, until when, while, as far as, even, until now
ἄρτι adv. ἄρτι now, hence, here, hither, even now, present
τινὲς indefinite pron. nom. masc. pl. τὶς certain, some, any man, one, any thing
δὲ conj. δέ but, and, now, also, to the contrary, rather, then
καὶ conj. καί and, even, also, but
7 ἔπειτα adv. ἔπειτα then, after that, afterward
Ἰακώβῳ n. dat. masc. sg. Ἰάκωβος James
εἶτα adv. εἶτα afterward, then, after that, furthermore
τοῖς art. dat. masc. pl. ὁ ἡ τό the, this, that, he, she, it
ἀποστόλοις n. dat. masc. pl. ἀπόστολος apostle, messenger, he that is sent
πᾶσιν adj. dat. masc. pl. πᾶς πᾶσα πᾶν all, every, whosoever, every one, no, whole, any
8 ἔσχατον adv. ἔσχατος last, lowest, uttermost, uttermost part
δὲ conj. δέ but, and, now, also, to the contrary, rather, then
πάντων adj. gen. neut. pl. πᾶς πᾶσα πᾶν all, every, whosoever, every one, no, whole, any
ὡσπερεὶ adv. ὡσπερεί as
τῷ art. dat. neut. sg. ὁ ἡ τό the, this, that, he, she, it
ἐκτρώματι n. dat. neut. sg. ἔκτρωμα born out of due time
κἀμοί pron. dat. 1p. sg. κἀγώ and I, I also, so I, even as I
9 ἐγὼ pron. nom. 1p. sg. ἐγώ I
γάρ conj. γάρ for, and, because, but, indeed
ὁ art. nom. masc. sg. ὁ ἡ τό the, this, that, he, she, it
ἐλάχιστος superl. adj. nom. masc. sg. ἐλάχιστος least, very small, smallest, very little
τῶν art. gen. masc. pl. ὁ ἡ τό the, this, that, he, she, it
ἀποστόλων n. gen. masc. pl. ἀπόστολος apostle, messenger, he that is sent
ὃς relative pron. nom. masc. sg. ὅς ἥ ὅ who, which, what, that
οὐκ particle of negation. οὐ οὐκ οὐχ not, no, neither, none, nay, nor, never, nothing
ἱκανὸς adj. nom. masc. sg. ἱκανός many, much, long, worthy, sufficient, great, able
ἀπόστολος n. nom. masc. sg. ἀπόστολος apostle, messenger, he that is sent
διότι conj. διότι for, because, because that, therefore
τὴν art. acc. fem. sg. ὁ ἡ τό the, this, that, he, she, it
ἐκκλησίαν n. acc. fem. sg. ἐκκλησία church, assembly
τοῦ art. gen. masc. sg. ὁ ἡ τό the, this, that, he, she, it
Θεοῦ n. gen. masc. sg. θεός God, god
10 χάριτι n. dat. fem. sg. χάρις grace, thank, favour, pleasure
δὲ conj. δέ but, and, now, also, to the contrary, rather, then
Θεοῦ n. gen. masc. sg. θεός God, god
ὅ relative pron. nom. neut. sg. ὅς ἥ ὅ who, which, what, that
καὶ conj. καί and, even, also, but
ἡ art. nom. fem. sg. ὁ ἡ τό the, this, that, he, she, it
χάρις n. nom. fem. sg. χάρις grace, thank, favour, pleasure
αὐτοῦ pron. gen. masc. 3p. sg. αὐτός ἡ ὁ self, of oneself, even, very, the same, he, she, it
ἡ art. nom. fem. sg. ὁ ἡ τό the, this, that, he, she, it
εἰς prep. εἰς (+acc) into, to, unto, for, in, on, toward, against, upon, at, among
ἐμὲ pron. acc. 1p. sg. ἐγώ I
οὐ particle of negation. οὐ οὐκ οὐχ not, no, neither, none, nay, nor, never, nothing

κενὴ adj. nom. fem. sg. κενός empty, vain, in vain
ἀλλὰ conj. ἀλλά but, yea, yet, nevertheless, howbeit, nay, therefore
περισσότερον compar. adj. acc. masc. sg. περισσός more, beyond measure, advantage
αὐτῶν pron. gen. masc. 3p. pl. αὐτός ή ό self, of oneself, even, very, the same, he, she, it
πάντων adj. gen. masc. pl. πᾶς πᾶσα πᾶν all, every, whosoever, every one, no, whole, any
οὐκ particle of negation. οὐ οὐκ οὐχ not, no, neither, none, nay, nor, never, nothing
ἐγὼ pron. nom. 1p. sg. ἐγώ I
δὲ conj. δέ but, and, now, also, to the contrary, rather, then
ἀλλ' conj. ἀλλά but, yea, yet, nevertheless, howbeit, nay, therefore
ἡ art. nom. fem. sg. ὁ ἡ τό the, this, that, he, she, it
χάρις n. nom. fem. sg. χάρις grace, thank, favour, pleasure
τοῦ art. gen. masc. sg. ὁ ἡ τό the, this, that, he, she, it
Θεοῦ n. gen. masc. sg. θεός God, god
ἡ art. nom. fem. sg. ὁ ἡ τό the, this, that, he, she, it
σὺν prep. σύν (+dat) with, beside
ἐμοί pron. dat. 1p. sg. ἐγώ I
11 εἴτε conj. εἴτε whether
οὖν conj. οὖν therefore, then, so, and, now, wherefore
ἐγὼ pron. nom. 1p. sg. ἐγώ I
εἴτε conj. εἴτε whether
ἐκεῖνοι demo. pron. nom. masc. pl. ἐκεῖνος that, he, the same, that same
οὕτω adv. οὕτω οὕτως so, even so, thus, on this wise, likewise, after this manner
καὶ conj. καί and, even, also, but
οὕτως adv. οὕτω οὕτως so, even so, thus, on this wise, likewise, after this manner
12 Εἰ conj. εἰ if, whether, that, though, forasmuch
δὲ conj. δέ but, and, now, also, to the contrary, rather, then
Χριστὸς n. nom. masc. sg. Χριστός Christ
ὅτι conj. ὅτι that, for, because, how that, how, because that, for that, though
ἐκ prep. ἐκ ἐξ (+gen) of, from, out of, by, on, with, in, among, through
νεκρῶν adj. gen. masc. pl. νεκρός dead
πῶς adv. πῶς how, by what means, after what manner
τινες indefinite pron. nom. masc. pl. τὶς certain, some, any man, one, any thing
ἐν prep. ἐν (+dat) in, by, with, among, at, on, through, to, within, into, of, for
ὑμῖν pron. dat. 2p. pl. σύ thou, you
ὅτι conj. ὅτι that, for, because, how that, how, because that, for that, though
ἀνάστασις n. nom. fem. sg. ἀνάστασις resurrection, rising again
νεκρῶν adj. gen. masc. pl. νεκρός dead
οὐκ particle of negation. οὐ οὐκ οὐχ not, no, neither, none, nay, nor, never, nothing
13 εἰ conj. εἰ if, whether, that, though, forasmuch
δὲ conj. δέ but, and, now, also, to the contrary, rather, then
ἀνάστασις n. nom. fem. sg. ἀνάστασις resurrection, rising again
νεκρῶν adj. gen. masc. pl. νεκρός dead
οὐκ particle of negation. οὐ οὐκ οὐχ not, no, neither, none, nay, nor, never, nothing
οὐδὲ adv. οὐδέ neither, nor, not, no, not even, never, not yet
Χριστὸς n. nom. masc. sg. Χριστός Christ
14 εἰ conj. εἰ if, whether, that, though, forasmuch
δὲ conj. δέ but, and, now, also, to the contrary, rather, then
Χριστὸς n. nom. masc. sg. Χριστός Christ
οὐκ particle of negation. οὐ οὐκ οὐχ not, no, neither, none, nay, nor, never, nothing
κενὸν adj. nom. neut. sg. κενός empty, vain, in vain
ἄρα conj. ἄρα then, therefore, haply, wherefore, perhaps, manner, no doubt, truly
τὸ art. nom. neut. sg. ὁ ἡ τό the, this, that, he, she, it
κήρυγμα n. nom. neut. sg. κήρυγμα preaching
ἡμῶν pron. gen. 1p. pl. ἐγώ I
κενὴ adj. nom. fem. sg. κενός empty, vain, in vain

δὲ conj. δέ but, and, now, also, to the contrary, rather, then
καὶ conj. καί and, even, also, but
ἡ art. nom. fem. sg. ὁ ἡ τό the, this, that, he, she, it
πίστις n. nom. fem. sg. πίστις faith, assurance, belief, fidelity
ὑμῶν pron. gen. 2p. pl. σύ thou, you
15 δὲ conj. δέ but, and, now, also, to the contrary, rather, then
καὶ conj. καί and, even, also, but
ψευδομάρτυρες n. nom. masc. pl. ψευδομάρτυς false witness
τοῦ art. gen. masc. sg. ὁ ἡ τό the, this, that, he, she, it
Θεοῦ n. gen. masc. sg. θεός God, god
ὅτι conj. ὅτι that, for, because, how that, how, because that, for that, though
κατὰ prep. κατά (+gen) against, by, throughout, down, (+acc) according to, after, with
τοῦ art. gen. masc. sg. ὁ ἡ τό the, this, that, he, she, it
Θεοῦ n. gen. masc. sg. θεός God, god
ὅτι conj. ὅτι that, for, because, how that, how, because that, for that, though
τὸν art. acc. masc. sg. ὁ ἡ τό the, this, that, he, she, it
Χριστόν n. acc. masc. sg. Χριστός Christ
ὃν relative pron. acc. masc. sg. ὅς ἥ ὅ who, which, what, that
οὐκ particle of negation. οὐ οὐκ οὐχ not, no, neither, none, nay, nor, never, nothing
εἴπερ conj. εἴπερ if it be so that, if indeed, since indeed, since, although indeed
ἄρα conj. ἄρα then, therefore, haply, wherefore, perhaps, manner, no doubt, truly
νεκροὶ adj. nom. masc. pl. νεκρός dead
οὐκ particle of negation. οὐ οὐκ οὐχ not, no, neither, none, nay, nor, never, nothing
16 εἰ conj. εἰ if, whether, that, though, forasmuch
γὰρ conj. γάρ for, and, because, but, indeed
νεκροὶ adj. nom. masc. pl. νεκρός dead
οὐκ particle of negation. οὐ οὐκ οὐχ not, no, neither, none, nay, nor, never, nothing
οὐδὲ adv. οὐδέ neither, nor, not, no, not even, never, not yet
Χριστὸς n. nom. masc. sg. Χριστός Christ
17 εἰ conj. εἰ if, whether, that, though, forasmuch
δὲ conj. δέ but, and, now, also, to the contrary, rather, then
Χριστὸς n. nom. masc. sg. Χριστός Christ
οὐκ particle of negation. οὐ οὐκ οὐχ not, no, neither, none, nay, nor, never, nothing
ματαία adj. nom. fem. sg. μάταιος vanity, vain
ἡ art. nom. fem. sg. ὁ ἡ τό the, this, that, he, she, it
πίστις n. nom. fem. sg. πίστις faith, assurance, belief, fidelity
ὑμῶν pron. gen. 2p. pl. σύ thou, you
ἔτι adv. ἔτι yet, more, any more, further, still, moreover
ἐν prep. ἐν (+dat) in, by, with, among, at, on, through, to, within, into, of, for
ταῖς art. dat. fem. pl. ὁ ἡ τό the, this, that, he, she, it
ἁμαρτίαις n. dat. fem. pl. ἁμαρτία sin, offence, sinful
ὑμῶν pron. gen. 2p. pl. σύ thou, you
18 ἄρα conj. ἄρα then, therefore, haply, wherefore, perhaps, manner, no doubt, truly
καὶ conj. καί and, even, also, but
οἱ art. nom. masc. pl. ὁ ἡ τό the, this, that, he, she, it
ἐν prep. ἐν (+dat) in, by, with, among, at, on, through, to, within, into, of, for
Χριστῷ n. dat. masc. sg. Χριστός Christ
19 εἰ conj. εἰ if, whether, that, though, forasmuch
ἐν prep. ἐν (+dat) in, by, with, among, at, on, through, to, within, into, of, for
τῇ art. dat. fem. sg. ὁ ἡ τό the, this, that, he, she, it
ζωῇ n. dat. fem. sg. ζωή life, lifetime
ταύτῃ demo. pron. dat. fem. sg. οὗτος αὕτη τοῦτο this, the same, this same, he, she, it
ἐν prep. ἐν (+dat) in, by, with, among, at, on, through, to, within, into, of, for
Χριστῷ n. dat. masc. sg. Χριστός Christ
μόνον adv. μόνος only, alone, by oneself

ἐλεεινότεροι compar. adj. nom. masc. pl. ἐλεεινός miserable, most miserable
πάντων adj. gen. masc. pl. πᾶς πᾶσα πᾶν all, every, whosoever, every one, no, whole, any
ἀνθρώπων n. gen. masc. pl. ἄνθρωπος man, human being, person, one, certain
20 Νυνὶ adv. νυνί now
δὲ conj. δέ but, and, now, also, to the contrary, rather, then
Χριστὸς n. nom. masc. sg. Χριστός Christ
ἐκ prep. ἐκ ἐξ (+gen) of, from, out of, by, on, with, in, among, through
νεκρῶν adj. gen. masc. pl. νεκρός dead
ἀπαρχὴ n. nom. fem. sg. ἀπαρχή firstfruit
τῶν art. gen. masc. pl. ὁ ἡ τό the, this, that, he, she, it
21 ἐπειδὴ conj. ἐπειδή because, for, after that, for that, for as much as, since
γὰρ conj. γάρ for, and, because, but, indeed
δι' prep. διά (+gen) by, through, with, in, of, (+acc) for, because of, for a cause
ἀνθρώπου n. gen. masc. sg. ἄνθρωπος man, human being, person, one, certain
ὁ art. nom. masc. sg. ὁ ἡ τό the, this, that, he, she, it
θάνατος n. nom. masc. sg. θάνατος death
καὶ conj. καί and, even, also, but
δι' prep. διά (+gen) by, through, with, in, of, (+acc) for, because of, for a cause
ἀνθρώπου n. gen. masc. sg. ἄνθρωπος man, human being, person, one, certain
ἀνάστασις n. nom. fem. sg. ἀνάστασις resurrection, rising again
νεκρῶν adj. gen. masc. pl. νεκρός dead
22 ὥσπερ adv. ὥσπερ as, even as, like as
γὰρ conj. γάρ for, and, because, but, indeed
ἐν prep. ἐν (+dat) in, by, with, among, at, on, through, to, within, into, of, for
τῷ art. dat. masc. sg. ὁ ἡ τό the, this, that, he, she, it
'Αδὰμ n. dat. masc. sg. 'Αδάμ Adam
πάντες adj. nom. masc. pl. πᾶς πᾶσα πᾶν all, every, whosoever, every one, no, whole, any
οὕτω adv. οὕτω οὕτως so, even so, thus, on this wise, likewise, after this manner
καὶ conj. καί and, even, also, but
ἐν prep. ἐν (+dat) in, by, with, among, at, on, through, to, within, into, of, for
τῷ art. dat. masc. sg. ὁ ἡ τό the, this, that, he, she, it
Χριστῷ n. dat. masc. sg. Χριστός Christ
πάντες adj. nom. masc. pl. πᾶς πᾶσα πᾶν all, every, whosoever, every one, no, whole, any
23 ἕκαστος adj. nom. masc. sg. ἕκαστος every man, every, every one, any man, each
δὲ conj. δέ but, and, now, also, to the contrary, rather, then
ἐν prep. ἐν (+dat) in, by, with, among, at, on, through, to, within, into, of, for
τῷ art. dat. neut. sg. ὁ ἡ τό the, this, that, he, she, it
ἰδίῳ adj. dat. neut. sg. ἴδιος one's own, one's, privately
τάγματι n. dat. neut. sg. τάγμα order
ἀπαρχὴ n. nom. fem. sg. ἀπαρχή firstfruit
Χριστός n. nom. masc. sg. Χριστός Christ
ἔπειτα adv. ἔπειτα then, after that, afterward
οἱ art. nom. masc. pl. ὁ ἡ τό the, this, that, he, she, it
Χριστοῦ n. gen. masc. sg. Χριστός Christ
ἐν prep. ἐν (+dat) in, by, with, among, at, on, through, to, within, into, of, for
τῇ art. dat. fem. sg. ὁ ἡ τό the, this, that, he, she, it
παρουσίᾳ n. dat. fem. sg. παρουσία coming, presence
αὐτοῦ pron. gen. masc. 3p. sg. αὐτός ή ό self, of oneself, even, very, the same, he, she, it
24 εἶτα adv. εἶτα afterward, then, after that, furthermore
τὸ art. nom. neut. sg. ὁ ἡ τό the, this, that, he, she, it
τέλος n. nom. neut. sg. τέλος end, custom, ending, finally, uttermost
ὅταν conj. ὅταν when, as soon as, as long as, that, whensoever, while
τὴν art. acc. fem. sg. ὁ ἡ τό the, this, that, he, she, it
βασιλείαν n. acc. fem. sg. βασιλεία kingdom, reign
τῷ art. dat. masc. sg. ὁ ἡ τό the, this, that, he, she, it

Θεῷ n. dat. masc. sg. θεός God, god
καὶ conj. καί and, even, also, but
πατρί n. dat. masc. sg. πατήρ Father, father, parent
ὅταν conj. ὅταν when, as soon as, as long as, that, whensoever, while
πᾶσαν adj. acc. fem. sg. πᾶς πᾶσα πᾶν all, every, whosoever, every one, no, whole, any
ἀρχὴν n. acc. fem. sg. ἀρχή beginning, principality, corner, first, magistrate, rule
καὶ conj. καί and, even, also, but
πᾶσαν adj. acc. fem. sg. πᾶς πᾶσα πᾶν all, every, whosoever, every one, no, whole, any
ἐξουσίαν n. acc. fem. sg. ἐξουσία power, authority, right, strength, jurisdiction
καὶ conj. καί and, even, also, but
δύναμιν n. acc. fem. sg. δύναμις power, mighty work, miracle, strength, might
25 γὰρ conj. γάρ for, and, because, but, indeed
αὐτὸν pron. acc. masc. 3p. sg. αὐτός ή ό self, of oneself, even, very, the same, he, she, it
ἄχρις prep. ἄχρι or ἄχρις (+gen) until, unto, till, even to, as far as, while, into
οὗ relative pron. gen. masc. sg. ὅς ἥ ὅ who, which, what, that
ἂν particle. ἄν Indicating contingency. No English translation.
πάντας adj. acc. masc. pl. πᾶς πᾶσα πᾶν all, every, whosoever, every one, no, whole, any
τοὺς art. acc. masc. pl. ὁ ἡ τό the, this, that, he, she, it
ἐχθροὺς adj. acc. masc. pl. ἐχθρός enemy, foe
ὑπὸ prep. ὑπό (+gen) of, by, with, from, among, (+acc) under
τοὺς art. acc. masc. pl. ὁ ἡ τό the, this, that, he, she, it
πόδας n. acc. masc. pl. πούς foot
αὐτοῦ pron. gen. masc. 3p. sg. αὐτός ή ό self, of oneself, even, very, the same, he, she, it
26 ἔσχατος adj. nom. masc. sg. ἔσχατος last, lowest, uttermost, uttermost part
ἐχθρὸς adj. nom. masc. sg. ἐχθρός enemy, foe
ὁ art. nom. masc. sg. ὁ ἡ τό the, this, that, he, she, it
θάνατος n. nom. masc. sg. θάνατος death
27 πάντα adj. acc. neut. pl. πᾶς πᾶσα πᾶν all, every, whosoever, every one, no, whole, any
γὰρ conj. γάρ for, and, because, but, indeed
ὑπὸ prep. ὑπό (+gen) of, by, with, from, among, (+acc) under
τοὺς art. acc. masc. pl. ὁ ἡ τό the, this, that, he, she, it
πόδας n. acc. masc. pl. πούς foot
αὐτοῦ pron. gen. masc. 3p. sg. αὐτός ή ό self, of oneself, even, very, the same, he, she, it
ὅταν conj. ὅταν when, as soon as, as long as, that, whensoever, while
δὲ conj. δέ but, and, now, also, to the contrary, rather, then
ὅτι conj. ὅτι that, for, because, how that, how, because that, for that, though
Πάντα adj. nom. neut. pl. πᾶς πᾶσα πᾶν all, every, whosoever, every one, no, whole, any
δῆλον adj. nom. neut. sg. δῆλος bewray, certain, evident, manifest
ὅτι conj. ὅτι that, for, because, how that, how, because that, for that, though
ἐκτὸς prep. ἐκτός except, out of, other than, outside, unless, without
τοῦ art. gen. masc. sg. ὁ ἡ τό the, this, that, he, she, it
αὐτῷ pron. dat. masc. 3p. sg. αὐτός ή ό self, of oneself, even, very, the same, he, she, it
τὰ art. acc. neut. pl. ὁ ἡ τό the, this, that, he, she, it
πάντα adj. acc. neut. pl. πᾶς πᾶσα πᾶν all, every, whosoever, every one, no, whole, any
28 ὅταν conj. ὅταν when, as soon as, as long as, that, whensoever, while
δὲ conj. δέ but, and, now, also, to the contrary, rather, then
αὐτῷ pron. dat. masc. 3p. sg. αὐτός ή ό self, of oneself, even, very, the same, he, she, it
τὰ art. nom. neut. pl. ὁ ἡ τό the, this, that, he, she, it
πάντα adj. nom. neut. pl. πᾶς πᾶσα πᾶν all, every, whosoever, every one, no, whole, any
τότε adv. τότε then, that time
καὶ conj. καί and, even, also, but
αὐτὸς pron. nom. masc. 3p. sg. αὐτός ή ό self, of oneself, even, very, the same, he, she, it
ὁ art. nom. masc. sg. ὁ ἡ τό the, this, that, he, she, it
υἱὸς n. nom. masc. sg. υἱός son, child, descendant, offspring, heir
τῷ art. dat. masc. sg. ὁ ἡ τό the, this, that, he, she, it

αὐτῷ pron. dat. masc. 3p. sg. αὐτός ή ό self, of oneself, even, very, the same, he, she, it
τὰ art. acc. neut. pl. ό ή τό the, this, that, he, she, it
πάντα adj. acc. neut. pl. πᾶς πᾶsα πᾶν all, every, whosoever, every one, no, whole, any
ἵνα conj. ἵνα that, to, lest, for to, so that, albeit, because, for, so as
ὁ art. nom. masc. sg. ό ή τό the, this, that, he, she, it
Θεὸς n. nom. masc. sg. θεός God, god
τὰ art. nom. neut. pl. ό ή τό the, this, that, he, she, it
πάντα adj. nom. neut. pl. πᾶς πᾶsα πᾶν all, every, whosoever, every one, no, whole, any
ἐν prep. ἐν (+dat) in, by, with, among, at, on, through, to, within, into, of, for
πᾶσιν adj. dat. neut. pl. πᾶς πᾶsα πᾶν all, every, whosoever, every one, no, whole, any
29 Ἐπεὶ conj. ἐπεί because, otherwise, seeing, else, for then, for as much as, for, since
τί interrog. pron. acc. neut. sg. τίς what, who, why, where, which, how
οἱ art. nom. masc. pl. ό ή τό the, this, that, he, she, it
ὑπὲρ prep. ὑπέρ (+gen) for, of, for the sake of, (+acc) above, more than
τῶν art. gen. masc. pl. ό ή τό the, this, that, he, she, it
νεκρῶν adj. gen. masc. pl. νεκρός dead
εἰ conj. εἰ if, whether, that, though, forasmuch
ὅλως adv. ὅλως at all, commonly, utterly
νεκροὶ adj. nom. masc. pl. νεκρός dead
οὐκ particle of negation. οὐ οὐκ οὐχ not, no, neither, none, nay, nor, never, nothing
τί interrog. pron. acc. neut. sg. τίς what, who, why, where, which, how
καὶ conj. καί and, even, also, but
ὑπὲρ prep. ὑπέρ (+gen) for, of, for the sake of, (+acc) above, more than
τῶν art. gen. masc. pl. ό ή τό the, this, that, he, she, it
νεκρῶν adj. gen. masc. pl. νεκρός dead
30 τί interrog. pron. acc. neut. sg. τίς what, who, why, where, which, how
καὶ conj. καί and, even, also, but
ἡμεῖς pron. nom. 1p. pl. ἐγώ I
πᾶσαν adj. acc. fem. sg. πᾶς πᾶsα πᾶν all, every, whosoever, every one, no, whole, any
ὥραν n. acc. fem. sg. ὥρα hour, time, season
31 καθ' prep. κατά (+gen) against, by, throughout, down, (+acc) according to, after, with
ἡμέραν n. acc. fem. sg. ἡμέρα day, time, year, while, age, day time
νὴ particle. νή I protest by
τὴν art. acc. fem. sg. ό ή τό the, this, that, he, she, it
ὑμετέραν poss. pron. acc. fem. 2p. sg. ὑμέτερος your, yours, your own
καύχησιν n. acc. fem. sg. καύχησις boasting, rejoicing, glorying
ἣν relative pron. acc. fem. sg. ὅς ἥ ὅ who, which, what, that
ἐν prep. ἐν (+dat) in, by, with, among, at, on, through, to, within, into, of, for
Χριστῷ n. dat. masc. sg. Χριστός Christ
Ἰησοῦ n. dat. masc. sg. Ἰησοῦς Jesus
τῷ art. dat. masc. sg. ό ή τό the, this, that, he, she, it
Κυρίῳ n. dat. masc. sg. κύριος Lord, lord, master, sir, LORD, God, Master, owner
ἡμῶν pron. gen. 1p. pl. ἐγώ I
32 εἰ conj. εἰ if, whether, that, though, forasmuch
κατὰ prep. κατά (+gen) against, by, throughout, down, (+acc) according to, after, with
ἄνθρωπον n. acc. masc. sg. ἄνθρωπος man, human being, person, one, certain
ἐν prep. ἐν (+dat) in, by, with, among, at, on, through, to, within, into, of, for
Ἐφέσῳ n. dat. fem. sg. Ἔφεσος Ephesus
τί interrog. pron. nom. neut. sg. τίς what, who, why, where, which, how
μοι pron. dat. 1p. sg. ἐγώ I
τὸ art. nom. neut. sg. ό ή τό the, this, that, he, she, it
ὄφελος n. nom. neut. sg. ὄφελος advantage, profit
εἰ conj. εἰ if, whether, that, though, forasmuch
νεκροὶ adj. nom. masc. pl. νεκρός dead
οὐκ particle of negation. οὐ οὐκ οὐχ not, no, neither, none, nay, nor, never, nothing

καὶ conj. καί and, even, also, but
αὔριον adv. αὔριον tomorrow, morrow, next day
γὰρ conj. γάρ for, and, because, but, indeed
33 μὴ particle of negation. μή not, no, lest, neither, none, nothing, nor, never, without
ἤθη n. acc. neut. pl. ἦθος manner
χρήσθ' adj. acc. neut. pl. χρηστός easy, kind, better, good, gracious, goodness
ὁμιλίαι n. nom. fem. pl. ὁμιλία communication
κακαί adj. nom. fem. pl. κακός evil, evil thing, noisome, wicked
34 δικαίως adv. δικαίως justly, righteously
καὶ conj. καί and, even, also, but
μὴ particle of negation. μή not, no, lest, neither, none, nothing, nor, never, without
ἀγνωσίαν n. acc. fem. sg. ἀγνωσία not the knowledge, ignorance
γὰρ conj. γάρ for, and, because, but, indeed
Θεοῦ n. gen. masc. sg. θεός God, god
τινες indefinite pron. nom. masc. pl. τὶς certain, some, any man, one, any thing
πρὸς prep. πρός (+gen) for, (+dat) at, (+acc) unto, to, with, for, against
ἐντροπὴν n. acc. fem. sg. ἐντροπή shame
ὑμῖν pron. dat. 2p. pl. σύ thou, you
35 'Αλλ' conj. ἀλλά but, yea, yet, nevertheless, howbeit, nay, therefore
τις indefinite pron. nom. masc. sg. τὶς certain, some, any man, one, any thing
Πῶς adv. πῶς how, by what means, after what manner
οἱ art. nom. masc. pl. ὁ ἡ τό the, this, that, he, she, it
νεκροί adj. nom. masc. pl. νεκρός dead
ποίῳ interrog. pron. dat. neut. sg. ποῖος what, which, what manner of
δὲ conj. δέ but, and, now, also, to the contrary, rather, then
σώματι n. dat. neut. sg. σῶμα body, bodily, slave
36 ἄφρον adj. voc. masc. sg. ἄφρων fool, foolish, unwise
σὺ pron. nom. 2p. sg. σύ thou, you
ὃ relative pron. acc. neut. sg. ὅς ἥ ὅ who, which, what, that
οὐ particle of negation. οὐ οὐκ οὐχ not, no, neither, none, nay, nor, never, nothing
ἐὰν conj. ἐάν if, soever, except, though, and if, but, whether, if so, so
μὴ particle of negation. μή not, no, lest, neither, none, nothing, nor, never, without
37 καὶ conj. καί and, even, also, but
ὃ relative pron. acc. neut. sg. ὅς ἥ ὅ who, which, what, that
οὐ adv. οὐ οὐκ οὐχ not, no, neither, none, nay, nor, never, nothing
τὸ art. acc. neut. sg. ὁ ἡ τό the, this, that, he, she, it
σῶμα n. acc. neut. sg. σῶμα body, bodily, slave
τὸ art. acc. neut. sg. ὁ ἡ τό the, this, that, he, she, it
ἀλλὰ conj. ἀλλά but, yea, yet, nevertheless, howbeit, nay, therefore
γυμνὸν adj. acc. masc. sg. γυμνός naked, bare
κόκκον n. acc. masc. sg. κόκκος grain, corn
εἰ conj. εἰ if, whether, that, though, forasmuch
σίτου n. gen. masc. sg. σῖτος wheat, corn
ἢ conj. ἤ or, than, either, nor, or else, and, rather than
τινος indefinite pron. gen. neut. sg. τὶς certain, some, any man, one, any thing
τῶν art. gen. neut. pl. ὁ ἡ τό the, this, that, he, she, it
λοιπῶν adj. gen. neut. pl. λοιπός other, rest, remnant, residue, which remain
38 ὁ art. nom. masc. sg. ὁ ἡ τό the, this, that, he, she, it
δὲ conj. δέ but, and, now, also, to the contrary, rather, then
Θεὸς n. nom. masc. sg. θεός God, god
αὐτῷ pron. dat. masc. 3p. sg. αὐτός ἡ ὁ self, of oneself, even, very, the same, he, she, it
σῶμα n. acc. neut. sg. σῶμα body, bodily, slave
καθὼς adv. καθώς as, even as, according as, according to
καὶ conj. καί and, even, also, but
ἑκάστῳ adj. dat. masc. sg. ἕκαστος every man, every, every one, any man, each

τῶν art. gen. neut. pl. ὁ ἡ τό the, this, that, he, she, it
σπερμάτων n. gen. neut. pl. σπέρμα seed, issue
τὸ art. acc. neut. sg. ὁ ἡ τό the, this, that, he, she, it
ἴδιον adj. acc. neut. sg. ἴδιος one's own, one's, privately
σῶμα n. acc. neut. sg. σῶμα body, bodily, slave
39 οὐ particle of negation. οὐ οὐκ οὐχ not, no, neither, none, nay, nor, never, nothing
πᾶσα adj. nom. fem. sg. πᾶς πᾶσα πᾶν all, every, whosoever, every one, no, whole, any
σὰρξ n. nom. fem. sg. σάρξ flesh, carnal
ἡ art. nom. fem. sg. ὁ ἡ τό the, this, that, he, she, it
αὐτὴ adj. nom. fem. sg. αὐτός ή ό self, of oneself, even, very, the same, he, she, it
σὰρξ n. nom. fem. sg. σάρξ flesh, carnal
ἀλλὰ conj. ἀλλά but, yea, yet, nevertheless, howbeit, nay, therefore
ἄλλη adj. nom. fem. sg. ἄλλος other, another, some, one, more, otherwise
μὲν conj. μέν indeed, verily, truly, even, so, some
σὰρξ n. nom. fem. sg. σάρξ flesh, carnal
ἀνθρώπων n. gen. masc. pl. ἄνθρωπος man, human being, person, one, certain
ἄλλη adj. nom. fem. sg. ἄλλος other, another, some, one, more, otherwise
δὲ conj. δέ but, and, now, also, to the contrary, rather, then
σὰρξ n. nom. fem. sg. σάρξ flesh, carnal
κτηνῶν n. gen. neut. pl. κτῆνος beast
ἄλλη adj. nom. fem. sg. ἄλλος other, another, some, one, more, otherwise
δὲ conj. δέ but, and, now, also, to the contrary, rather, then
ἰχθύων n. gen. masc. pl. ἰχθύς fish
ἄλλη adj. nom. fem. sg. ἄλλος other, another, some, one, more, otherwise
δὲ conj. δέ but, and, now, also, to the contrary, rather, then
πτηνῶν adj. gen. neut. pl. πτηνόν bird
40 καὶ conj. καί and, even, also, but
σώματα n. nom. neut. pl. σῶμα body, bodily, slave
ἐπουράνια adj. nom. neut. pl. ἐπουράνιος heavenly, celestial, high, in heaven
καὶ conj. καί and, even, also, but
σώματα n. nom. neut. pl. σῶμα body, bodily, slave
ἐπίγεια adj. nom. neut. pl. ἐπίγειος earthly, terrestrial, in earth
ἀλλὰ conj. ἀλλά but, yea, yet, nevertheless, howbeit, nay, therefore
ἑτέρα adj. nom. fem. sg. ἕτερος another, other, else, strange
μὲν conj. μέν indeed, verily, truly, even, so, some
ἡ art. nom. fem. sg. ὁ ἡ τό the, this, that, he, she, it
τῶν art. gen. neut. pl. ὁ ἡ τό the, this, that, he, she, it
ἐπουρανίων adj. gen. neut. pl. ἐπουράνιος heavenly, celestial, high, in heaven
δόξα n. nom. fem. sg. δόξα glory, honour, praise, dignity, worship
ἑτέρα adj. nom. fem. sg. ἕτερος another, other, else, strange
δὲ conj. δέ but, and, now, also, to the contrary, rather, then
ἡ art. nom. fem. sg. ὁ ἡ τό the, this, that, he, she, it
τῶν art. gen. neut. pl. ὁ ἡ τό the, this, that, he, she, it
ἐπιγείων adj. gen. neut. pl. ἐπίγειος earthly, terrestrial, in earth
41 ἄλλη adj. nom. fem. sg. ἄλλος other, another, some, one, more, otherwise
δόξα n. nom. fem. sg. δόξα glory, honour, praise, dignity, worship
ἡλίου n. gen. masc. sg. ἥλιος sun, east
καὶ conj. καί and, even, also, but
ἄλλη adj. nom. fem. sg. ἄλλος other, another, some, one, more, otherwise
δόξα n. nom. fem. sg. δόξα glory, honour, praise, dignity, worship
σελήνης n. gen. fem. sg. σελήνη moon
καὶ conj. καί and, even, also, but
ἄλλη adj. nom. fem. sg. ἄλλος other, another, some, one, more, otherwise
δόξα n. nom. fem. sg. δόξα glory, honour, praise, dignity, worship
ἀστέρων n. gen. masc. pl. ἀστήρ star

ἀστὴρ n. nom. masc. sg. ἀστήρ star
γὰρ conj. γάρ for, and, because, but, indeed
ἀστέρος n. gen. masc. sg. ἀστήρ star
ἐν prep. ἐν (+dat) in, by, with, among, at, on, through, to, within, into, of, for
δόξῃ n. dat. fem. sg. δόξα glory, honour, praise, dignity, worship
42 οὕτω adv. οὕτω οὕτως so, even so, thus, on this wise, likewise, after this manner
καὶ conj. καί and, even, also, but
ἡ art. nom. fem. sg. ὁ ἡ τό the, this, that, he, she, it
ἀνάστασις n. nom. fem. sg. ἀνάστασις resurrection, rising again
τῶν art. gen. masc. pl. ὁ ἡ τό the, this, that, he, she, it
νεκρῶν adj. gen. masc. pl. νεκρός dead
ἐν prep. ἐν (+dat) in, by, with, among, at, on, through, to, within, into, of, for
φθορᾷ n. dat. fem. sg. φθορά corruption, destroy, perish
ἐν prep. ἐν (+dat) in, by, with, among, at, on, through, to, within, into, of, for
ἀφθαρσίᾳ n. dat. fem. sg. ἀφθαρσία immortality, incorruption, sincerity
43 ἐν prep. ἐν (+dat) in, by, with, among, at, on, through, to, within, into, of, for
ἀτιμίᾳ n. dat. fem. sg. ἀτιμία vile, dishonour, reproach, shame
ἐν prep. ἐν (+dat) in, by, with, among, at, on, through, to, within, into, of, for
δόξῃ n. dat. fem. sg. δόξα glory, honour, praise, dignity, worship
ἐν prep. ἐν (+dat) in, by, with, among, at, on, through, to, within, into, of, for
ἀσθενείᾳ n. dat. fem. sg. ἀσθένεια infirmity, weakness, disease, sickness
ἐν prep. ἐν (+dat) in, by, with, among, at, on, through, to, within, into, of, for
δυνάμει n. dat. fem. sg. δύναμις power, mighty work, miracle, strength, might
44 σῶμα n. nom. neut. sg. σῶμα body, bodily, slave
ψυχικόν adj. nom. neut. sg. ψυχικός natural, sensual
σῶμα n. nom. neut. sg. σῶμα body, bodily, slave
πνευματικόν adj. nom. neut. sg. πνευματικός spiritual
σῶμα n. nom. neut. sg. σῶμα body, bodily, slave
ψυχικόν adj. nom. neut. sg. ψυχικός natural, sensual
καὶ conj. καί and, even, also, but
σῶμα n. nom. neut. sg. σῶμα body, bodily, slave
πνευματικόν adj. nom. neut. sg. πνευματικός spiritual
45 οὕτω adv. οὕτω οὕτως so, even so, thus, on this wise, likewise, after this manner
καὶ conj. καί and, even, also, but
ὁ art. nom. masc. sg. ὁ ἡ τό the, this, that, he, she, it
πρῶτος ordinal. adj. nom. masc. sg. πρῶτος first, chief, first of all, chiefest, best
ἄνθρωπος n. nom. masc. sg. ἄνθρωπος man, human being, person, one, certain
'Αδὰμ n. nom. masc. sg. 'Αδάμ Adam
εἰς prep. εἰς (+acc) into, to, unto, for, in, on, toward, against, upon, at, among
ψυχὴν n. acc. fem. sg. ψυχή life, soul, mind, heart
ὁ art. nom. masc. sg. ὁ ἡ τό the, this, that, he, she, it
ἔσχατος adj. nom. masc. sg. ἔσχατος last, lowest, uttermost, uttermost part
'Αδὰμ n. nom. masc. sg. 'Αδάμ Adam
εἰς prep. εἰς (+acc) into, to, unto, for, in, on, toward, against, upon, at, among
πνεῦμα n. acc. neut. sg. πνεῦμα spirit, Spirit, Ghost, ghost, life. of the spirit, wind
46 ἀλλ' conj. ἀλλά but, yea, yet, nevertheless, howbeit, nay, therefore
οὐ particle of negation. οὐ οὐκ οὐχ not, no, neither, none, nay, nor, never, nothing
πρῶτον adv. πρῶτον first, at the first, first of all, at first, at the beginning, before, chiefly
τὸ art. nom. neut. sg. ὁ ἡ τό the, this, that, he, she, it
πνευματικὸν adj. nom. neut. sg. πνευματικός spiritual
ἀλλὰ conj. ἀλλά but, yea, yet, nevertheless, howbeit, nay, therefore
τὸ art. nom. neut. sg. ὁ ἡ τό the, this, that, he, she, it
ψυχικόν adj. nom. neut. sg. ψυχικός natural, sensual
ἔπειτα adv. ἔπειτα then, after that, afterward
τὸ art. nom. neut. sg. ὁ ἡ τό the, this, that, he, she, it

πνευματικὸν adj. nom. neut. sg. πνευματικός spiritual
47 ὁ art. nom. masc. sg. ὁ ἡ τό the, this, that, he, she, it
πρῶτος ordinal. adj. nom. masc. sg. πρῶτος first, chief, first of all, chiefest, best
ἄνθρωπος n. nom. masc. sg. ἄνθρωπος man, human being, person, one, certain
ἐκ prep. ἐκ ἐξ (+gen) of, from, out of, by, on, with, in, among, through
γῆς n. gen. fem. sg. γῆ earth, land, ground, country
χοϊκός adj. nom. masc. sg. χοϊκός earthy
ὁ art. nom. masc. sg. ὁ ἡ τό the, this, that, he, she, it
δεύτερος ordinal. adj. nom. masc. sg. δεύτερος second, second time, again, afterward
ἄνθρωπος n. nom. masc. sg. ἄνθρωπος man, human being, person, one, certain
ὁ art. nom. masc. sg. ὁ ἡ τό the, this, that, he, she, it
Κύριος n. nom. masc. sg. κύριος Lord, lord, master, sir, LORD, God, Master, owner
ἐξ prep. ἐκ ἐξ (+gen) of, from, out of, by, on, with, in, among, through
οὐρανοῦ. n. gen. masc. sg. οὐρανός heaven, air, sky
48 οἷος relative pron. nom. masc. sg. οἷος what manner of, such as, as, which, what, so as
ὁ art. nom. masc. sg. ὁ ἡ τό the, this, that, he, she, it
χοϊκός adj. nom. masc. sg. χοϊκός earthy
τοιοῦτοι demo. pron. nom. masc. pl. τοιοῦτος such, like
καὶ conj. καί and, even, also, but
οἱ art. nom. masc. pl. ὁ ἡ τό the, this, that, he, she, it
χοϊκοί adj. nom. masc. pl. χοϊκός earthy
καὶ conj. καί and, even, also, but
οἷος relative pron. nom. masc. sg. οἷος what manner of, such as, as, which, what, so as
ὁ art. nom. masc. sg. ὁ ἡ τό the, this, that, he, she, it
ἐπουράνιος adj. nom. masc. sg. ἐπουράνιος heavenly, celestial, high, in heaven
τοιοῦτοι demo. pron. nom. masc. pl. τοιοῦτος such, like
καὶ conj. καί and, even, also, but
οἱ art. nom. masc. pl. ὁ ἡ τό the, this, that, he, she, it
ἐπουράνιοι adj. nom. masc. pl. ἐπουράνιος heavenly, celestial, high, in heaven
49 καὶ conj. καί and, even, also, but
καθὼς adv. καθώς as, even as, according as, according to
τὴν art. acc. fem. sg. ὁ ἡ τό the, this, that, he, she, it
εἰκόνα n. acc. fem. sg. εἰκών image
τοῦ art. gen. masc. sg. ὁ ἡ τό the, this, that, he, she, it
χοϊκοῦ adj. gen. masc. sg. χοϊκός earthy
καὶ conj. καί and, even, also, but
τὴν art. acc. fem. sg. ὁ ἡ τό the, this, that, he, she, it
εἰκόνα n. acc. fem. sg. εἰκών image
τοῦ art. gen. masc. sg. ὁ ἡ τό the, this, that, he, she, it
ἐπουρανίου adj. gen. masc. sg. ἐπουράνιος heavenly, celestial, high, in heaven
50 Τοῦτο demo. pron. acc. neut. sg. οὗτος αὕτη τοῦτο this, the same, this same, he, she, it
δέ conj. δέ but, and, now, also, to the contrary, rather, then
ἀδελφοί n. voc. masc. pl. ἀδελφός brother
ὅτι conj. ὅτι that, for, because, how that, how, because that, for that, though
σὰρξ n. nom. fem. sg. σάρξ flesh, carnal
καὶ conj. καί and, even, also, but
αἷμα n. nom. neut. sg. αἷμα blood
βασιλείαν n. acc. fem. sg. βασιλεία kingdom, reign
Θεοῦ n. gen. masc. sg. θεός God, god
οὐ particle of negation. οὐ οὐκ οὐχ not, no, neither, none, nay, nor, never, nothing
οὐδὲ adv. οὐδέ neither, nor, not, no, not even, never, not yet
ἡ art. nom. fem. sg. ὁ ἡ τό the, this, that, he, she, it
φθορὰ n. nom. fem. sg. φθορά corruption, destroy, perish
τὴν art. acc. fem. sg. ὁ ἡ τό the, this, that, he, she, it
ἀφθαρσίαν n. acc. fem. sg. ἀφθαρσία immortality, incorruption, sincerity

51 μυστήριον n. acc. neut. sg. μυστήριον mystery
ὑμῖν pron. dat. 2p. pl. σύ thou, you
Πάντες adj. nom. masc. pl. πᾶς πᾶσα πᾶν all, every, whosoever, every one, no, whole, any
μὲν conj. μέν indeed, verily, truly, even, so, some
οὐ particle of negation. οὐ οὐκ οὐχ not, no, neither, none, nay, nor, never, nothing
πάντες adj. nom. masc. pl. πᾶς πᾶσα πᾶν all, every, whosoever, every one, no, whole, any
δὲ conj. δέ but, and, now, also, to the contrary, rather, then
52 ἐν prep. ἐν (+dat) in, by, with, among, at, on, through, to, within, into, of, for
ἀτόμῳ adj. dat. neut. sg. ἄτομος moment
ἐν prep. ἐν (+dat) in, by, with, among, at, on, through, to, within, into, of, for
ῥιπῇ n. dat. fem. sg. ῥιπή twinkling
ὀφθαλμοῦ n. gen. masc. sg. ὀφθαλμός eye, sight
ἐν prep. ἐν (+dat) in, by, with, among, at, on, through, to, within, into, of, for
τῇ art. dat. fem. sg. ὁ ἡ τό the, this, that, he, she, it
ἐσχάτῃ adj. dat. fem. sg. ἔσχατος last, lowest, uttermost, uttermost part
σάλπιγγι n. dat. fem. sg. σάλπιγξ trumpet, trump
γὰρ conj. γάρ for, and, because, but, indeed
καὶ conj. καί and, even, also, but
οἱ art. nom. masc. pl. ὁ ἡ τό the, this, that, he, she, it
νεκροὶ adj. nom. masc. pl. νεκρός dead
ἄφθαρτοι adj. nom. masc. pl. ἄφθαρτος uncorruptible, incorruptible, immortal, not corruptible
καὶ conj. καί and, even, also, but
ἡμεῖς pron. nom. 1p. pl. ἐγώ I
53 γὰρ conj. γάρ for, and, because, but, indeed
τὸ art. acc. neut. sg. ὁ ἡ τό the, this, that, he, she, it
φθαρτὸν adj. acc. neut. sg. φθαρτός corruptible
τοῦτο demo. pron. acc. neut. sg. οὗτος αὕτη τοῦτο this, the same, this same, he, she, it
ἀφθαρσίαν n. acc. fem. sg. ἀφθαρσία immortality, incorruption, sincerity
καὶ conj. καί and, even, also, but
τὸ art. acc. neut. sg. ὁ ἡ τό the, this, that, he, she, it
θνητὸν adj. acc. neut. sg. θνητός mortal, mortality
τοῦτο demo. pron. acc. neut. sg. οὗτος αὕτη τοῦτο this, the same, this same, he, she, it
ἀθανασίαν n. acc. fem. sg. ἀθανασία immortality
54 ὅταν conj. ὅταν when, as soon as, as long as, that, whensoever, while
δὲ conj. δέ but, and, now, also, to the contrary, rather, then
τὸ art. nom. neut. sg. ὁ ἡ τό the, this, that, he, she, it
φθαρτὸν adj. nom. neut. sg. φθαρτός corruptible
τοῦτο demo. pron. nom. neut. sg. οὗτος αὕτη τοῦτο this, the same, this same, he, she, it
ἀφθαρσίαν n. acc. fem. sg. ἀφθαρσία immortality, incorruption, sincerity
καὶ conj. καί and, even, also, but
τὸ art. nom. neut. sg. ὁ ἡ τό the, this, that, he, she, it
θνητὸν adj. nom. neut. sg. θνητός mortal, mortality
τοῦτο demo. pron. nom. neut. sg. οὗτος αὕτη τοῦτο this, the same, this same, he, she, it
ἀθανασίαν n. acc. fem. sg. ἀθανασία immortality
τότε adv. τότε then, that time
ὁ art. nom. masc. sg. ὁ ἡ τό the, this, that, he, she, it
λόγος n. nom. masc. sg. λόγος word, saying, account, speech, thing, matter
ὁ art. nom. masc. sg. ὁ ἡ τό the, this, that, he, she, it
ὁ art. nom. masc. sg. ὁ ἡ τό the, this, that, he, she, it
θάνατος n. nom. masc. sg. θάνατος death
εἰς prep. εἰς (+acc) into, to, unto, for, in, on, toward, against, upon, at, among
νῖκος n. acc. neut. sg. νῖκος victory
55 Ποῦ particle of place. ποῦ where, whither
σου pron. gen. 2p. sg. σύ thou, you
θάνατε n. voc. masc. sg. θάνατος death

τὸ art. nom. neut. sg. ὁ ἡ τό the, this, that, he, she, it
κέντρον n. nom. neut. sg. κέντρον sting, prick
ποῦ particle of place. ποῦ where, whither
σου pron. gen. 2p. sg. σύ thou, you
ᾅδη n. voc. masc. sg. ᾅδης hell, grave
τὸ art. nom. neut. sg. ὁ ἡ τό the, this, that, he, she, it
νῖκος n. nom. neut. sg. νῖκος victory
56 τὸ art. nom. neut. sg. ὁ ἡ τό the, this, that, he, she, it
δὲ conj. δέ but, and, now, also, to the contrary, rather, then
κέντρον n. nom. neut. sg. κέντρον sting, prick
τοῦ art. gen. masc. sg. ὁ ἡ τό the, this, that, he, she, it
θανάτου n. gen. masc. sg. θάνατος death
ἡ art. nom. fem. sg. ὁ ἡ τό the, this, that, he, she, it
ἁμαρτία n. nom. fem. sg. ἁμαρτία sin, offence, sinful
ἡ art. nom. fem. sg. ὁ ἡ τό the, this, that, he, she, it
δὲ conj. δέ but, and, now, also, to the contrary, rather, then
δύναμις n. nom. fem. sg. δύναμις power, mighty work, miracle, strength, might
τῆς art. gen. fem. sg. ὁ ἡ τό the, this, that, he, she, it
ἁμαρτίας n. gen. fem. sg. ἁμαρτία sin, offence, sinful
ὁ art. nom. masc. sg. ὁ ἡ τό the, this, that, he, she, it
νόμος n. nom. masc. sg. νόμος law, the law
57 τῷ art. dat. masc. sg. ὁ ἡ τό the, this, that, he, she, it
δὲ conj. δέ but, and, now, also, to the contrary, rather, then
Θεῷ n. dat. masc. sg. θεός God, god
χάρις n. nom. fem. sg. χάρις grace, thank, favour, pleasure
τῷ art. dat. masc. sg. ὁ ἡ τό the, this, that, he, she, it
ἡμῖν pron. dat. 1p. pl. ἐγώ I
τὸ art. acc. neut. sg. ὁ ἡ τό the, this, that, he, she, it
νῖκος n. acc. neut. sg. νῖκος victory
διὰ prep. διά (+gen) by, through, with, in, of, (+acc) for, because of, for a cause
τοῦ art. gen. masc. sg. ὁ ἡ τό the, this, that, he, she, it
Κυρίου n. gen. masc. sg. κύριος Lord, lord, master, sir, LORD, God, Master, owner
ἡμῶν pron. gen. 1p. pl. ἐγώ I
Ἰησοῦ n. gen. masc. sg. Ἰησοῦς Jesus
Χριστοῦ n. gen. masc. sg. Χριστός Christ
58 ὥστε conj. ὥστε so that, wherefore, insomuch that, therefore, that, so then
ἀδελφοί n. voc. masc. pl. ἀδελφός brother
μου pron. gen. 1p. sg. ἐγώ I
ἀγαπητοί adj. voc. masc. pl. ἀγαπητός beloved, dearly beloved, dear, wellbeloved
ἑδραῖοι adj. nom. masc. pl. ἑδραῖος stedfast, settled
ἀμετακίνητοι adj. nom. masc. pl. ἀμετακίνητος unmoveable
ἐν prep. ἐν (+dat) in, by, with, among, at, on, through, to, within, into, of, for
τῷ art. dat. neut. sg. ὁ ἡ τό the, this, that, he, she, it
ἔργῳ n. dat. neut. sg. ἔργον work, deed, doing labour
τοῦ art. gen. masc. sg. ὁ ἡ τό the, this, that, he, she, it
Κυρίου n. gen. masc. sg. κύριος Lord, lord, master, sir, LORD, God, Master, owner
πάντοτε adv. πάντοτε always, ever, always, evermore
ὅτι conj. ὅτι that, for, because, how that, how, because that, for that, though
ὁ art. nom. masc. sg. ὁ ἡ τό the, this, that, he, she, it
κόπος n. nom. masc. sg. κόπος labour, trouble, weariness
ὑμῶν pron. gen. 2p. pl. σύ thou, you
οὐκ particle of negation. οὐ οὐκ οὐχ not, no, neither, none, nay, nor, never, nothing
κενὸς adj. nom. masc. sg. κενός empty, vain, in vain
ἐν prep. ἐν (+dat) in, by, with, among, at, on, through, to, within, into, of, for
Κυρίῳ n. dat. masc. sg. κύριος Lord, lord, master, sir, LORD, God, Master, owner

16

1 Περὶ prep. περί (+gen) of, for, concerning, (+acc) about, concerning, in
δὲ conj. δέ but, and, now, also, to the contrary, rather, then
τῆς art. gen. fem. sg. ὁ ἡ τό the, this, that, he, she, it
λογίας n. gen. fem. sg. λογία collection, gathering
εἰς prep. εἰς (+acc) into, to, unto, for, in, on, toward, against, upon, at, among
τοὺς art. acc. masc. pl. ὁ ἡ τό the, this, that, he, she, it
ἁγίους adj. acc. masc. pl. ἅγιος Holy, holy, saint, Holy One, holy thing, most holy
ὥσπερ adv. ὥσπερ as, even as, like as
ταῖς art. dat. fem. pl. ὁ ἡ τό the, this, that, he, she, it
ἐκκλησίαις n. dat. fem. pl. ἐκκλησία church, assembly
Γαλατίας n. gen. fem. sg. Γαλατία Galatia
οὕτω adv. οὕτω οὕτως so, even so, thus, on this wise, likewise, after this manner
καὶ conj. καί and, even, also, but
ὑμεῖς pron. nom. 2p. pl. σύ thou, you
2 κατὰ prep. κατά (+gen) against, by, throughout, down, (+acc) according to, after, with
μίαν num. acc. fem. sg. εἷς or ἕν one, other, some, any, only, a certain
σαββάτων n. gen. neut. pl. σάββατον sabbath day, sabbath, week
ἕκαστος adj. nom. masc. sg. ἕκαστος every man, every, every one, any man, each
ὑμῶν pron. gen. 2p. pl. σύ thou, you
παρ' prep. παρά (+gen) of, from, (+dat) with, for, (+acc) beside, at, by, above, against
ἑαυτῷ reflexive pron. dat. masc. 3p. sg. ἑαυτοῦ himself, herself, itself, yourself, ourselves
ὅ relative pron. acc. neut. sg. ὅς ἥ ὅ who, which, what, that
τι indefinite pron. acc. neut. sg. τὶς certain, some, any man, one, any thing
ἂν particle. ἄν Indicating contingency. No English translation.
ἵνα conj. ἵνα that, to, lest, for to, so that, albeit, because, for, so as
μὴ particle of negation. μή not, no, lest, neither, none, nothing, nor, never, without
ὅταν conj. ὅταν when, as soon as, as long as, that, whensoever, while
τότε adv. τότε then, that time
λογίαι n. nom. fem. pl. λογία collection, gathering
3 ὅταν conj. ὅταν when, as soon as, as long as, that, whensoever, while
δὲ conj. δέ but, and, now, also, to the contrary, rather, then
οὓς relative pron. acc. masc. pl. ὅς ἥ ὅ who, which, what, that
ἐὰν conj. ἐάν if, soever, except, though, and if, but, whether, if so, so
δι' prep. διά (+gen) by, through, with, in, of, (+acc) for, because of, for a cause
ἐπιστολῶν n. gen. fem. pl. ἐπιστολή letter, epistle
τούτους demo. pron. acc. masc. pl. οὗτος αὕτη τοῦτο this, the same, this same, he, she, it
τὴν art. acc. fem. sg. ὁ ἡ τό the, this, that, he, she, it
χάριν n. acc. fem. sg. χάρις grace, thank, favour, pleasure
ὑμῶν pron. gen. 2p. pl. σύ thou, you
εἰς prep. εἰς (+acc) into, to, unto, for, in, on, toward, against, upon, at, among
Ἰερουσαλήμ pron. name. fem. inde. Ἰερουσαλήμ Jerusalem
4 ἐὰν conj. ἐάν if, soever, except, though, and if, but, whether, if so, so
δὲ conj. δέ but, and, now, also, to the contrary, rather, then
ἄξιον adj. nom. neut. sg. ἄξιος worthy, meet, due reward
τοῦ art. gen. neut. sg. ὁ ἡ τό the, this, that, he, she, it
κἀμὲ pron. acc. 1p. sg. κἀγώ and I, I also, so I, even as I
σὺν prep. σύν (+dat) with, beside
ἐμοὶ pron. dat. 1p. sg. ἐγώ I
5 δὲ conj. δέ but, and, now, also, to the contrary, rather, then
πρὸς prep. πρός (+gen) for, (+dat) at, (+acc) unto, to, with, for, against
ὑμᾶς pron. acc. 2p. pl. σύ thou, you
ὅταν conj. ὅταν when, as soon as, as long as, that, whensoever, while

Μακεδονίαν n. acc. fem. sg. Μακεδονία Macedonia
Μακεδονίαν n. acc. fem. sg. Μακεδονία Macedonia
γὰρ conj. γάρ for, and, because, but, indeed
6 πρὸς prep. πρός (+gen) for, (+dat) at, (+acc) unto, to, with, for, against
ὑμᾶς pron. acc. 2p. pl. σύ thou, you
δὲ conj. δέ but, and, now, also, to the contrary, rather, then
ἢ particle. ἤ or, than, either, nor, or else, and, rather than
καὶ conj. καί and, even, also, but
ἵνα conj. ἵνα that, to, lest, for to, so that, albeit, because, for, so as
ὑμεῖς pron. nom. 2p. pl. σύ thou, you
με pron. acc. 1p. sg. ἐγώ I
οὗ adv. οὗ where, whither, wherein
ἐὰν conj. ἐάν if, soever, except, though, and if, but, whether, if so, so
7 οὐ particle of negation. οὐ οὐκ οὐχ not, no, neither, none, nay, nor, never, nothing
γὰρ conj. γάρ for, and, because, but, indeed
ὑμᾶς pron. acc. 2p. pl. σύ thou, you
ἄρτι adv. ἄρτι now, hence, here, hither, even now, present
ἐν prep. ἐν (+dat) in, by, with, among, at, on, through, to, within, into, of, for
παρόδῳ n. dat. fem. sg. πάροδος way
δὲ conj. δέ but, and, now, also, to the contrary, rather, then
χρόνον n. acc. masc. sg. χρόνος time, season, space
τινὰ indefinite pron. acc. masc. sg. τὶς certain, some, any man, one, any thing
πρὸς prep. πρός (+gen) for, (+dat) at, (+acc) unto, to, with, for, against
ὑμᾶς pron. acc. 2p. pl. σύ thou, you
ἐὰν conj. ἐάν if, soever, except, though, and if, but, whether, if so, so
ὁ art. nom. masc. sg. ὁ ἡ τό the, this, that, he, she, it
Κύριος n. nom. masc. sg. κύριος Lord, lord, master, sir, LORD, God, Master, owner
8 δὲ conj. δέ but, and, now, also, to the contrary, rather, then
ἐν prep. ἐν (+dat) in, by, with, among, at, on, through, to, within, into, of, for
Ἐφέσῳ n. dat. fem. sg. Ἔφεσος Ephesus
ἕως conj. ἕως till, until, unto, until when, while, as far as, even, until now
τῆς art. gen. fem. sg. ὁ ἡ τό the, this, that, he, she, it
Πεντηκοστῆς n. gen. fem. sg. πεντηκοστή Pentecost
9 θύρα n. nom. fem. sg. θύρα door, gate
γάρ conj. γάρ for, and, because, but, indeed
μοι pron. dat. 1p. sg. ἐγώ I
μεγάλη adj. nom. fem. sg. μέγας great, loud, greatest, high, large, mighty, strong
καὶ conj. καί and, even, also, but
ἐνεργής adj. nom. fem. sg. ἐνεργής effectual, powerful
καὶ conj. καί and, even, also, but
πολλοί adj. nom. masc. pl. πολύς many, great, much, long, abundant
10 Ἐὰν conj. ἐάν if, soever, except, though, and if, but, whether, if so, so
δὲ conj. δέ but, and, now, also, to the contrary, rather, then
Τιμόθεος n. nom. masc. sg. Τιμόθεος Timotheus, Timothy
ἵνα conj. ἵνα that, to, lest, for to, so that, albeit, because, for, so as
ἀφόβως adv. ἀφόβως without fear
πρὸς prep. πρός (+gen) for, (+dat) at, (+acc) unto, to, with, for, against
ὑμᾶς pron. acc. 2p. pl. σύ thou, you
τὸ art. acc. neut. sg. ὁ ἡ τό the, this, that, he, she, it
γὰρ conj. γάρ for, and, because, but, indeed
ἔργον n. acc. neut. sg. ἔργον work, deed, doing labour
Κυρίου n. gen. masc. sg. κύριος Lord, lord, master, sir, LORD, God, Master, owner
ὡς adv. ὡς as, when, as it were, how, about, like, as soon as, even as, while
καὶ conj. καί and, even, also, but
ἐγώ pron. nom. 1p. sg. ἐγώ I

11 μὴ particle of negation. μή not, no, lest, neither, none, nothing, nor, never, without
τις indefinite pron. nom. masc. sg. τὶς certain, some, any man, one, any thing
οὖν conj. οὖν therefore, then, so, and, now, wherefore
αὐτὸν pron. acc. masc. 3p. sg. αὐτός ή ό self, of oneself, even, very, the same, he, she, it
δὲ conj. δέ but, and, now, also, to the contrary, rather, then
αὐτὸν pron. acc. masc. 3p. sg. αὐτός ή ό self, of oneself, even, very, the same, he, she, it
ἐν prep. ἐν (+dat) in, by, with, among, at, on, through, to, within, into, of, for
εἰρήνῃ n. dat. fem. sg. εἰρήνη peace, quietness, rest
ἵνα conj. ἵνα that, to, lest, for to, so that, albeit, because, for, so as
πρός prep. πρός (+gen) for, (+dat) at, (+acc) unto, to, with, for, against
με pron. acc. 1p. sg. ἐγώ I
γὰρ conj. γάρ for, and, because, but, indeed
αὐτὸν pron. acc. masc. 3p. sg. αὐτός ή ό self, of oneself, even, very, the same, he, she, it
μετὰ prep. μετά (+gen) with, among, against, (+acc) after
τῶν art. gen. masc. pl. ὁ ἡ τό the, this, that, he, she, it
ἀδελφῶν n. gen. masc. pl. ἀδελφός brother
12 περὶ prep. περί (+gen) of, for, concerning, (+acc) about, concerning, in
δὲ conj. δέ but, and, now, also, to the contrary, rather, then
Ἀπολλῶ n. gen. masc. sg. Ἀπολλώς Apollos
τοῦ art. gen. masc. sg. ὁ ἡ τό the, this, that, he, she, it
ἀδελφοῦ n. gen. masc. sg. ἀδελφός brother
πολλὰ adv. πολύς many, great, much, long, abundant
αὐτόν pron. acc. masc. 3p. sg. αὐτός ή ό self, of oneself, even, very, the same, he, she, it
ἵνα conj. ἵνα that, to, lest, for to, so that, albeit, because, for, so as
πρὸς prep. πρός (+gen) for, (+dat) at, (+acc) unto, to, with, for, against
ὑμᾶς pron. acc. 2p. pl. σύ thou, you
μετὰ prep. μετά (+gen) with, among, against, (+acc) after
τῶν art. gen. masc. pl. ὁ ἡ τό the, this, that, he, she, it
ἀδελφῶν n. gen. masc. pl. ἀδελφός brother
καὶ conj. καί and, even, also, but
πάντως adv. πάντως surely, altogether, by all means, at all, needs, no doubt
οὐκ particle of negation. οὐ οὐκ οὐχ not, no, neither, none, nay, nor, never, nothing
θέλημα n. nom. neut. sg. θέλημα will, desire, pleasure
ἵνα conj. ἵνα that, to, lest, for to, so that, albeit, because, for, so as
νῦν adv. νῦν now, henceforth, present, this time
δὲ conj. δέ but, and, now, also, to the contrary, rather, then
ὅταν conj. ὅταν when, as soon as, as long as, that, whensoever, while
13 ἐν prep. ἐν (+dat) in, by, with, among, at, on, through, to, within, into, of, for
τῇ art. dat. fem. sg. ὁ ἡ τό the, this, that, he, she, it
πίστει n. dat. fem. sg. πίστις faith, assurance, belief, fidelity
14 πάντα adj. nom. neut. pl. πᾶς πᾶσα πᾶν all, every, whosoever, every one, no, whole, any
ὑμῶν pron. gen. 2p. pl. σύ thou, you
ἐν prep. ἐν (+dat) in, by, with, among, at, on, through, to, within, into, of, for
ἀγάπῃ n. dat. fem. sg. ἀγάπη love, charity, feast of charity
15 δὲ conj. δέ but, and, now, also, to the contrary, rather, then
ὑμᾶς pron. acc. 2p. pl. σύ thou, you
ἀδελφοί n. voc. masc. pl. ἀδελφός brother
τὴν art. acc. fem. sg. ὁ ἡ τό the, this, that, he, she, it
οἰκίαν n. acc. fem. sg. οἰκία house, home, household
Στεφανᾶ n. gen. masc. sg. Στεφανᾶς Stephanas
ὅτι conj. ὅτι that, for, because, how that, how, because that, for that, though
ἀπαρχὴ n. nom. fem. sg. ἀπαρχή firstfruit
τῆς art. gen. fem. sg. ὁ ἡ τό the, this, that, he, she, it
Ἀχαΐας n. gen. fem. sg. Ἀχαΐα Achaia
καὶ conj. καί and, even, also, but

εἰς prep. εἰς (+acc) into, to, unto, for, in, on, toward, against, upon, at, among
διακονίαν n. acc. fem. sg. διακονία ministry, administration, service, office, relief
τοῖς art. dat. masc. pl. ὁ ἡ τό the, this, that, he, she, it
ἁγίοις adj. dat. masc. pl. ἅγιος Holy, holy, saint, Holy One, holy thing, most holy
ἑαυτούς reflexive pron. acc. masc. 3p. pl. ἑαυτοῦ himself, herself, itself, yourself, ourselves
16 ἵνα conj. ἵνα that, to, lest, for to, so that, albeit, because, for, so as
καὶ conj. καί and, even, also, but
ὑμεῖς pron. nom. 2p. pl. σύ thou, you
τοῖς art. dat. masc. pl. ὁ ἡ τό the, this, that, he, she, it
τοιούτοις demo. pron. dat. masc. pl. τοιοῦτος such, like
καὶ conj. καί and, even, also, but
παντὶ adj. dat. masc. sg. πᾶς πᾶσα πᾶν all, every, whosoever, every one, no, whole, any
τῷ art. dat. masc. sg. ὁ ἡ τό the, this, that, he, she, it
καὶ conj. καί and, even, also, but
17 δὲ conj. δέ but, and, now, also, to the contrary, rather, then
ἐπὶ prep. ἐπί (+gen) on, in, upon, (+dat) in, at, for, upon, (+acc) on, upon, unto, to, against
τῇ art. dat. fem. sg. ὁ ἡ τό the, this, that, he, she, it
παρουσίᾳ n. dat. fem. sg. παρουσία coming, presence
Στεφανᾶ n. gen. masc. sg. Στεφανᾶς Stephanas
καὶ conj. καί and, even, also, but
Φουρτουνάτου n. gen. masc. sg. Φορτουνᾶτος Fortunatus
καὶ conj. καί and, even, also, but
Ἀχαϊκοῦ n. gen. masc. sg. Ἀχαϊκός Achaicus
ὅτι conj. ὅτι that, for, because, how that, how, because that, for that, though
τὸ art. acc. neut. sg. ὁ ἡ τό the, this, that, he, she, it
ὑμῶν pron. gen. 2p. pl. σύ thou, you
ὑστέρημα n. acc. neut. sg. ὑστέρημα penury, that which is lacking, want, lack
οὗτοι demo. pron. nom. masc. pl. οὗτος αὕτη τοῦτο this, the same, this same, he, she, it
18 γὰρ conj. γάρ for, and, because, but, indeed
τὸ art. acc. neut. sg. ὁ ἡ τό the, this, that, he, she, it
ἐμὸν poss. pron. acc. neut. 1p. sg. ἐμός my, mine, mine own, of me
πνεῦμα n. acc. neut. sg. πνεῦμα spirit, Spirit, Ghost, ghost, life. of the spirit, wind
καὶ conj. καί and, even, also, but
τὸ art. acc. neut. sg. ὁ ἡ τό the, this, that, he, she, it
ὑμῶν pron. gen. 2p. pl. σύ thou, you
οὖν conj. οὖν therefore, then, so, and, now, wherefore
τοὺς art. acc. masc. pl. ὁ ἡ τό the, this, that, he, she, it
τοιούτους demo. pron. acc. masc. pl. τοιοῦτος such, like
19 ὑμᾶς pron. acc. 2p. pl. σύ thou, you
αἱ art. nom. fem. pl. ὁ ἡ τό the, this, that, he, she, it
ἐκκλησίαι n. nom. fem. pl. ἐκκλησία church, assembly
τῆς art. gen. fem. sg. ὁ ἡ τό the, this, that, he, she, it
Ἀσίας n. gen. fem. sg. Ἀσία Asia
ὑμᾶς pron. acc. 2p. pl. σύ thou, you
ἐν prep. ἐν (+dat) in, by, with, among, at, on, through, to, within, into, of, for
Κυρίῳ n. dat. masc. sg. κύριος Lord, lord, master, sir, LORD, God, Master, owner
πολλὰ adv. πολύς many, great, much, long, abundant
Ἀκύλας n. nom. masc. sg. Ἀκύλας Aquila
καὶ conj. καί and, even, also, but
Πρίσκιλλα n. nom. fem. sg. Πρίσκιλλα Priscilla
σὺν prep. σύν (+dat) with, beside
τῇ art. dat. fem. sg. ὁ ἡ τό the, this, that, he, she, it
κατ' prep. κατά (+gen) against, by, throughout, down, (+acc) according to, after, with
οἶκον n. acc. masc. sg. οἶκος house, home, household
αὐτῶν pron. gen. masc. 3p. pl. αὐτός ἡ ὁ self, of oneself, even, very, the same, he, she, it

ἐκκλησίᾳ n. dat. fem. sg. ἐκκλησία church, assembly
20 ὑμᾶς pron. acc. 2p. pl. σύ thou, you
οἱ art. nom. masc. pl. ὁ ἡ τό the, this, that, he, she, it
ἀδελφοὶ n. nom. masc. pl. ἀδελφός brother
πάντες adj. nom. masc. pl. πᾶς πᾶσα πᾶν all, every, whosoever, every one, no, whole, any
ἀλλήλους pron. acc. masc. 2p. pl. ἀλλήλων one another, themselves, together, mutual
ἐν prep. ἐν (+dat) in, by, with, among, at, on, through, to, within, into, of, for
φιλήματι n. dat. neut. sg. φίλημα kiss
ἁγίῳ adj. dat. neut. sg. ἅγιος Holy, holy, saint, Holy One, holy thing, most holy
21 Ὁ art. nom. masc. sg. ὁ ἡ τό the, this, that, he, she, it
ἀσπασμὸς n. nom. masc. sg. ἀσπασμός greeting, salutation
τῇ art. dat. fem. sg. ὁ ἡ τό the, this, that, he, she, it
ἐμῇ poss. pron. dat. fem. 1p. sg. ἐμός my, mine, mine own, of me
χειρὶ n. dat. fem. sg. χείρ hand
Παύλου n. gen. masc. sg. Παῦλος Paul, Paulus
22 εἴ conj. εἰ if, whether, that, though, forasmuch
τις indefinite pron. nom. masc. sg. τὶς certain, some, any man, one, any thing
οὐ particle of negation. οὐ οὐκ οὐχ not, no, neither, none, nay, nor, never, nothing
τὸν art. acc. masc. sg. ὁ ἡ τό the, this, that, he, she, it
Κύριον n. acc. masc. sg. κύριος Lord, lord, master, sir, LORD, God, Master, owner
Ἰησοῦν n. acc. masc. sg. Ἰησοῦς Jesus
Χριστὸν n. acc. masc. sg. Χριστός Christ
ἀνάθεμα n. nom. neut. sg. ἀνάθεμα accursed, Anathema, great course
Μαραν ἀθα Aramaic μαράνα ἀθα Maran-atha, the Lord cometh
23 ἡ art. nom. fem. sg. ὁ ἡ τό the, this, that, he, she, it
χάρις n. nom. fem. sg. χάρις grace, thank, favour, pleasure
τοῦ art. gen. masc. sg. ὁ ἡ τό the, this, that, he, she, it
Κυρίου n. gen. masc. sg. κύριος Lord, lord, master, sir, LORD, God, Master, owner
Ἰησοῦ n. gen. masc. sg. Ἰησοῦς Jesus
Χριστοῦ n. gen. masc. sg. Χριστός Christ
μεθ' prep. μετά (+gen) with, among, against, (+acc) after
ὑμῶν pron. gen. 2p. pl. σύ thou, you
24 ἡ art. nom. fem. sg. ὁ ἡ τό the, this, that, he, she, it
ἀγάπη n. nom. fem. sg. ἀγάπη love, charity, feast of charity
μου pron. gen. 1p. sg. ἐγώ I
μετὰ prep. μετά (+gen) with, among, against, (+acc) after
πάντων adj. gen. masc. pl. πᾶς πᾶσα πᾶν all, every, whosoever, every one, no, whole, any
ὑμῶν pron. gen. 2p. pl. σύ thou, you
ἐν prep. ἐν (+dat) in, by, with, among, at, on, through, to, within, into, of, for
Χριστῷ n. dat. masc. sg. Χριστός Christ
Ἰησοῦ n. dat. masc. sg. Ἰησοῦς Jesus
ἀμήν particle. ἀμήν amen, verily

ΠΑΥΛΟΥ ΤΟΥ ΑΠΟΣΤΟΛΟΥ
Η ΠΡΟΣ
ΚΟΡΙΝΘΙΟΥΣ
ΕΠΙΣΤΟΛΗ ΔΕΥΤΕΡΑ

1

1 Παῦλος n. nom. masc. sg. Παῦλος Paul, Paulus
ἀπόστολος n. nom. masc. sg. ἀπόστολος apostle, messenger, he that is sent
Ἰησοῦ n. gen. masc. sg. Ἰησοῦς Jesus
Χριστοῦ n. gen. masc. sg. Χριστός Christ
διὰ prep. διά (+gen) by, through, with, in, of, (+acc) for, because of, for a cause
θελήματος n. gen. neut. sg. θέλημα will, desire, pleasure
Θεοῦ n. gen. masc. sg. θεός God, god
καὶ conj. καί and, even, also, but
Τιμόθεος n. nom. masc. sg. Τιμόθεος Timotheus, Timothy
ὁ art. nom. masc. sg. ὁ ἡ τό the, this, that, he, she, it
ἀδελφὸς n. nom. masc. sg. ἀδελφός brother
τῇ art. dat. fem. sg. ὁ ἡ τό the, this, that, he, she, it
ἐκκλησίᾳ n. dat. fem. sg. ἐκκλησία church, assembly
τοῦ art. gen. masc. sg. ὁ ἡ τό the, this, that, he, she, it
Θεοῦ n. gen. masc. sg. θεός God, god
τῇ art. dat. fem. sg. ὁ ἡ τό the, this, that, he, she, it
ἐν prep. ἐν (+dat) in, by, with, among, at, on, through, to, within, into, of, for
Κορίνθῳ n. dat. fem. sg. Κόρινθος Corinth
σὺν prep. σύν (+dat) with, beside
τοῖς art. dat. masc. pl. ὁ ἡ τό the, this, that, he, she, it
ἁγίοις adj. dat. masc. pl. ἅγιος Holy, holy, saint, Holy One, holy thing, most holy
πᾶσι adj. dat. masc. pl. πᾶς πᾶσα πᾶν all, every, whosoever, every one, no, whole, any
τοῖς art. dat. masc. pl. ὁ ἡ τό the, this, that, he, she, it
ἐν prep. ἐν (+dat) in, by, with, among, at, on, through, to, within, into, of, for
ὅλῃ adj. dat. fem. sg. ὅλος all, whole, every whit, altogether
τῇ art. dat. fem. sg. ὁ ἡ τό the, this, that, he, she, it
Ἀχαΐᾳ n. dat. fem. sg. Ἀχαΐα Achaia
2 χάρις n. nom. fem. sg. χάρις grace, thank, favour, pleasure
ὑμῖν pron. dat. 2p. pl. σύ thou, you
καὶ conj. καί and, even, also, but
εἰρήνη n. nom. fem. sg. εἰρήνη peace, quietness, rest
ἀπὸ prep. ἀπό (+gen) from, of, out of, since, for, off, at, by, in, on
Θεοῦ n. gen. masc. sg. θεός God, god
πατρὸς n. gen. masc. sg. πατήρ Father, father, parent
ἡμῶν pron. gen. 1p. pl. ἐγώ I
καὶ conj. καί and, even, also, but
Κυρίου n. gen. masc. sg. κύριος Lord, lord, master, sir, LORD, God, Master, owner
Ἰησοῦ n. gen. masc. sg. Ἰησοῦς Jesus
Χριστοῦ n. gen. masc. sg. Χριστός Christ
3 Εὐλογητὸς adj. nom. masc. sg. εὐλογητός blessed
ὁ art. nom. masc. sg. ὁ ἡ τό the, this, that, he, she, it
πατὴρ n. nom. masc. sg. πατήρ Father, father, parent
τοῦ art. gen. masc. sg. ὁ ἡ τό the, this, that, he, she, it
Κυρίου n. gen. masc. sg. κύριος Lord, lord, master, sir, LORD, God, Master, owner
ἡμῶν pron. gen. 1p. pl. ἐγώ I
Ἰησοῦ n. gen. masc. sg. Ἰησοῦς Jesus

Χριστοῦ n. gen. masc. sg. Χριστός Christ
ὁ art. nom. masc. sg. ὁ ἡ τό the, this, that, he, she, it
πατὴρ n. nom. masc. sg. πατήρ Father, father, parent
τῶν art. gen. masc. pl. ὁ ἡ τό the, this, that, he, she, it
οἰκτιρμῶν n. gen. masc. pl. οἰκτιρμός mercy
καὶ conj. καί and, even, also, but
Θεὸς n. nom. masc. sg. θεός God, god
πάσης adj. gen. fem. sg. πᾶς πᾶσα πᾶν all, every, whosoever, every one, no, whole, any
παρακλήσεως n. gen. fem. sg. παράκλησις consolation, exhortation, comfort
4 ὁ art. nom. masc. sg. ὁ ἡ τό the, this, that, he, she, it
ἡμᾶς pron. acc. 1p. pl. ἐγώ I
ἐπὶ prep. ἐπί (+gen) on, in, upon, (+dat) in, at, for, upon, (+acc) on, upon, unto, to, against
πάσῃ adj. dat. fem. sg. πᾶς πᾶσα πᾶν all, every, whosoever, every one, no, whole, any
τῇ art. dat. fem. sg. ὁ ἡ τό the, this, that, he, she, it
θλίψει n. dat. fem. sg. θλῖψις tribulation, affliction, anguish, persecution
ἡμῶν pron. gen. 1p. pl. ἐγώ I
εἰς prep. εἰς (+acc) into, to, unto, for, in, on, toward, against, upon, at, among
τὸ art. acc. neut. sg. ὁ ἡ τό the, this, that, he, she, it
ἡμᾶς pron. acc. 1p. pl. ἐγώ I
τοὺς art. acc. masc. pl. ὁ ἡ τό the, this, that, he, she, it
ἐν prep. ἐν (+dat) in, by, with, among, at, on, through, to, within, into, of, for
πάσῃ adj. dat. fem. sg. πᾶς πᾶσα πᾶν all, every, whosoever, every one, no, whole, any
θλίψει n. dat. fem. sg. θλῖψις tribulation, affliction, anguish, persecution
διὰ prep. διά (+gen) by, through, with, in, of, (+acc) for, because of, for a cause
τῆς art. gen. fem. sg. ὁ ἡ τό the, this, that, he, she, it
παρακλήσεως n. gen. fem. sg. παράκλησις consolation, exhortation, comfort
ἧς relative pron. gen. fem. sg. ὅς ἥ ὅ who, which, what, that
αὐτοὶ pron. nom. masc. 3p. pl. αὐτός ἡ ὁ self, of oneself, even, very, the same, he, she, it
ὑπὸ prep. ὑπό (+gen) of, by, with, from, among, (+acc) under
τοῦ art. gen. masc. sg. ὁ ἡ τό the, this, that, he, she, it
Θεοῦ n. gen. masc. sg. θεός God, god
5 ὅτι conj. ὅτι that, for, because, how that, how, because that, for that, though
καθὼς adv. καθώς as, even as, according as, according to
τὰ art. nom. neut. pl. ὁ ἡ τό the, this, that, he, she, it
παθήματα n. nom. neut. pl. πάθημα suffering, affliction, affection, motion
τοῦ art. gen. masc. sg. ὁ ἡ τό the, this, that, he, she, it
Χριστοῦ n. gen. masc. sg. Χριστός Christ
εἰς prep. εἰς (+acc) into, to, unto, for, in, on, toward, against, upon, at, among
ἡμᾶς pron. acc. 1p. pl. ἐγώ I
οὕτω adv. οὕτω οὕτως so, even so, thus, on this wise, likewise, after this manner
διὰ prep. διά (+gen) by, through, with, in, of, (+acc) for, because of, for a cause
Χριστοῦ n. gen. masc. sg. Χριστός Christ
καὶ conj. καί and, even, also, but
ἡ art. nom. fem. sg. ὁ ἡ τό the, this, that, he, she, it
παράκλησις n. nom. fem. sg. παράκλησις consolation, exhortation, comfort
ἡμῶν pron. gen. 1p. pl. ἐγώ I
6 εἴτε conj. εἴτε whether
δὲ conj. δέ but, and, now, also, to the contrary, rather, then
ὑπὲρ prep. ὑπέρ (+gen) for, of, for the sake of, (+acc) above, more than
τῆς art. gen. fem. sg. ὁ ἡ τό the, this, that, he, she, it
ὑμῶν pron. gen. 2p. pl. σύ thou, you
παρακλήσεως n. gen. fem. sg. παράκλησις consolation, exhortation, comfort
καὶ conj. καί and, even, also, but
σωτηρίας n. gen. fem. sg. σωτηρία salvation, deliver, health, saving
τῆς art. gen. fem. sg. ὁ ἡ τό the, this, that, he, she, it

ἐν prep. ἐν (+dat) in, by, with, among, at, on, through, to, within, into, of, for
ὑπομονῇ n. dat. fem. sg. ὑπομονή patience, enduring
τῶν art. gen. neut. pl. ὁ ἡ τό the, this, that, he, she, it
αὐτῶν adj. gen. neut. pl. αὐτός ή ό self, of oneself, even, very, the same, he, she, it
παθημάτων n. gen. neut. pl. πάθημα suffering, affliction, affection, motion
ὧν relative pron. gen. neut. pl. ὅς ἥ ὅ who, which, what, that
καὶ conj. καί and, even, also, but
ἡμεῖς pron. nom. 1p. pl. ἐγώ I
εἴτε conj. εἴτε whether
ὑπὲρ prep. ὑπέρ (+gen) for, of, for the sake of, (+acc) above, more than
τῆς art. gen. fem. sg. ὁ ἡ τό the, this, that, he, she, it
ὑμῶν pron. gen. 2p. pl. σύ thou, you
παρακλήσεως n. gen. fem. sg. παράκλησις consolation, exhortation, comfort
καὶ conj. καί and, even, also, but
σωτηρίας n. gen. fem. sg. σωτηρία salvation, deliver, health, saving
7 καὶ conj. καί and, even, also, but
ἡ art. nom. fem. sg. ὁ ἡ τό the, this, that, he, she, it
ἐλπὶς n. nom. fem. sg. ἐλπίς hope, faith
ἡμῶν pron. gen. 1p. pl. ἐγώ I
βεβαία adj. nom. fem. sg. βέβαιος sure, stedfast, firm, more sure, of force
ὑπὲρ prep. ὑπέρ (+gen) for, of, for the sake of, (+acc) above, more than
ὑμῶν pron. gen. 2p. pl. σύ thou, you
ὅτι conj. ὅτι that, for, because, how that, how, because that, for that, though
ὥσπερ adv. ὥσπερ as, even as, like as
κοινωνοί n. nom. masc. pl. κοινωνός partaker, partner, companion, fellowship
τῶν art. gen. neut. pl. ὁ ἡ τό the, this, that, he, she, it
παθημάτων n. gen. neut. pl. πάθημα suffering, affliction, affection, motion
οὕτω adv. οὕτω οὕτως so, even so, thus, on this wise, likewise, after this manner
καὶ conj. καί and, even, also, but
τῆς art. gen. fem. sg. ὁ ἡ τό the, this, that, he, she, it
παρακλήσεως n. gen. fem. sg. παράκλησις consolation, exhortation, comfort
8 οὐ particle of negation. οὐ οὐκ οὐχ not, no, neither, none, nay, nor, never, nothing
γὰρ conj. γάρ for, and, because, but, indeed
ὑμᾶς pron. acc. 2p. pl. σύ thou, you
ἀδελφοί n. voc. masc. pl. ἀδελφός brother
ὑπὲρ prep. ὑπέρ (+gen) for, of, for the sake of, (+acc) above, more than
τῆς art. gen. fem. sg. ὁ ἡ τό the, this, that, he, she, it
θλίψεως n. gen. fem. sg. θλῖψις tribulation, affliction, anguish, persecution
ἡμῶν pron. gen. 1p. pl. ἐγώ I
τῆς art. gen. fem. sg. ὁ ἡ τό the, this, that, he, she, it
ἡμῖν pron. dat. 1p. pl. ἐγώ I
ἐν prep. ἐν (+dat) in, by, with, among, at, on, through, to, within, into, of, for
τῇ art. dat. fem. sg. ὁ ἡ τό the, this, that, he, she, it
'Ασίᾳ n. dat. fem. sg. 'Ασία Asia
ὅτι conj. ὅτι that, for, because, how that, how, because that, for that, though
καθ' prep. κατά (+gen) against, by, throughout, down, (+acc) according to, after, with
ὑπερβολὴν n. acc. fem. sg. ὑπερβολή abundance, beyond measure, exceeding, excellency
ὑπὲρ prep. ὑπέρ (+gen) for, of, for the sake of, (+acc) above, more than
δύναμιν n. acc. fem. sg. δύναμις power, mighty work, miracle, strength, might
ὥστε conj. ὥστε so that, wherefore, insomuch that, therefore, that, so then
ἡμᾶς pron. acc. 1p. pl. ἐγώ I
καὶ conj. καί and, even, also, but
τοῦ art. gen. neut. sg. ὁ ἡ τό the, this, that, he, she, it
9 ἀλλὰ conj. ἀλλά but, yea, yet, nevertheless, howbeit, nay, therefore
αὐτοὶ pron. nom. masc. 3p. pl. αὐτός ή ό self, of oneself, even, very, the same, he, she, it

ἐν prep. ἐν (+dat) in, by, with, among, at, on, through, to, within, into, of, for
ἑαυτοῖς reflexive pron. dat. masc. 3p. pl. ἑαυτοῦ himself, herself, itself, yourself, ourselves
τὸ art. acc. neut. sg. ὁ ἡ τό the, this, that, he, she, it
ἀπόκριμα n. acc. neut. sg. ἀπόκριμα sentence
τοῦ art. gen. masc. sg. ὁ ἡ τό the, this, that, he, she, it
θανάτου n. gen. masc. sg. θάνατος death
ἵνα conj. ἵνα that, to, lest, for to, so that, albeit, because, for, so as
μὴ particle of negation. μή not, no, lest, neither, none, nothing, nor, never, without
ἐφ' prep. ἐπί (+gen) on, in, upon, (+dat) in, at, for, upon, (+acc) on, upon, unto, to, against
ἑαυτοῖς reflexive pron. dat. masc. 3p. pl. ἑαυτοῦ himself, herself, itself, yourself, ourselves
ἀλλ' conj. ἀλλά but, yea, yet, nevertheless, howbeit, nay, therefore
ἐπὶ prep. ἐπί (+gen) on, in, upon, (+dat) in, at, for, upon, (+acc) on, upon, unto, to, against
τῷ art. dat. masc. sg. ὁ ἡ τό the, this, that, he, she, it
Θεῷ n. dat. masc. sg. θεός God, god
τῷ art. dat. masc. sg. ὁ ἡ τό the, this, that, he, she, it
τοὺς art. acc. masc. pl. ὁ ἡ τό the, this, that, he, she, it
νεκρούς adj. acc. masc. pl. νεκρός dead
10 ὃς relative pron. nom. masc. sg. ὅς ἥ ὅ who, which, what, that
ἐκ prep. ἐκ ἐξ (+gen) of, from, out of, by, on, with, in, among, through
τηλικούτου demo. pron. gen. masc. sg. τηλικοῦτος so great, so mighty
θανάτου n. gen. masc. sg. θάνατος death
ἡμᾶς pron. acc. 1p. pl. ἐγώ I
καὶ conj. καί and, even, also, but
εἰς prep. εἰς (+acc) into, to, unto, for, in, on, toward, against, upon, at, among
ὃν relative pron. acc. masc. sg. ὅς ἥ ὅ who, which, what, that
ὅτι conj. ὅτι that, for, because, how that, how, because that, for that, though
καὶ conj. καί and, even, also, but
ἔτι adv. ἔτι yet, more, any more, further, still, moreover
11 καὶ conj. καί and, even, also, but
ὑμῶν pron. gen. 2p. pl. σύ thou, you
ὑπὲρ prep. ὑπέρ (+gen) for, of, for the sake of, (+acc) above, more than
ἡμῶν pron. gen. 1p. pl. ἐγώ I
τῇ art. dat. fem. sg. ὁ ἡ τό the, this, that, he, she, it
δεήσει n. dat. fem. sg. δέησις prayer, supplication, request
ἵνα conj. ἵνα that, to, lest, for to, so that, albeit, because, for, so as
ἐκ prep. ἐκ ἐξ (+gen) of, from, out of, by, on, with, in, among, through
πολλῶν adj. gen. neut. pl. πολύς many, great, much, long, abundant
προσώπων n. gen. neut. pl. πρόσωπον face, presence, person, countenance
τὸ art. nom. neut. sg. ὁ ἡ τό the, this, that, he, she, it
εἰς prep. εἰς (+acc) into, to, unto, for, in, on, toward, against, upon, at, among
ἡμᾶς pron. acc. 1p. pl. ἐγώ I
χάρισμα n. nom. neut. sg. χάρισμα gift, free gift
διὰ prep. διά (+gen) by, through, with, in, of, (+acc) for, because of, for a cause
πολλῶν adj. gen. masc. pl. πολύς many, great, much, long, abundant
ὑπὲρ prep. ὑπέρ (+gen) for, of, for the sake of, (+acc) above, more than
ἡμῶν pron. gen. 1p. pl. ἐγώ I
12 Ἡ art. nom. fem. sg. ὁ ἡ τό the, this, that, he, she, it
γὰρ conj. γάρ for, and, because, but, indeed
καύχησις n. nom. fem. sg. καύχησις boasting, rejoicing, glorying
ἡμῶν pron. gen. 1p. pl. ἐγώ I
αὕτη demo. pron. nom. fem. sg. οὗτος αὕτη τοῦτο this, the same, this same, he, she, it
τὸ art. nom. neut. sg. ὁ ἡ τό the, this, that, he, she, it
μαρτύριον n. nom. neut. sg. μαρτύριον testimony, witness
τῆς art. gen. fem. sg. ὁ ἡ τό the, this, that, he, she, it
συνειδήσεως n. gen. fem. sg. συνείδησις conscience

ἡμῶν pron. gen. 1p. pl. ἐγώ I
ὅτι conj. ὅτι that, for, because, how that, how, because that, for that, though
ἐν prep. ἐν (+dat) in, by, with, among, at, on, through, to, within, into, of, for
ἁπλότητι n. dat. fem. sg. ἁπλότης simplicity, singleness, bountifulness, liberal, liberality
καὶ conj. καί and, even, also, but
εἰλικρινείᾳ n. dat. fem. sg. εἰλικρίνεια sincerity
Θεοῦ n. gen. masc. sg. θεός God, god
οὐκ particle of negation. οὐ οὐκ οὐχ not, no, neither, none, nay, nor, never, nothing
ἐν prep. ἐν (+dat) in, by, with, among, at, on, through, to, within, into, of, for
σοφίᾳ n. dat. fem. sg. σοφία wisdom
σαρκικῇ adj. dat. fem. sg. σαρκικός carnal, fleshly
ἀλλ' conj. ἀλλά but, yea, yet, nevertheless, howbeit, nay, therefore
ἐν prep. ἐν (+dat) in, by, with, among, at, on, through, to, within, into, of, for
χάριτι n. dat. fem. sg. χάρις grace, thank, favour, pleasure
Θεοῦ n. gen. masc. sg. θεός God, god
ἐν prep. ἐν (+dat) in, by, with, among, at, on, through, to, within, into, of, for
τῷ art. dat. masc. sg. ὁ ἡ τό the, this, that, he, she, it
κόσμῳ n. dat. masc. sg. κόσμος world, adorning
περισσοτέρως adv. περισσοτέρως more exceedingly, more abundantly, more frequent
δὲ conj. δέ but, and, now, also, to the contrary, rather, then
πρὸς prep. πρός (+gen) for, (+dat) at, (+acc) unto, to, with, for, against
ὑμᾶς pron. acc. 2p. pl. σύ thou, you
13 οὐ particle of negation. οὐ οὐκ οὐχ not, no, neither, none, nay, nor, never, nothing
γὰρ conj. γάρ for, and, because, but, indeed
ἄλλα adj. acc. neut. pl. ἄλλος other, another, some, one, more, otherwise
ὑμῖν pron. dat. 2p. pl. σύ thou, you
ἀλλ' adj. acc. neut. pl. ἀλλά but, yea, yet, nevertheless, howbeit, nay, therefore
ἢ particle. ἤ or, than, either, nor, or else, and, rather than
ἃ relative pron. acc. neut. pl. ὅς ἥ ὅ who, which, what, that
ἢ particle. ἤ or, than, either, nor, or else, and, rather than
καὶ conj. καί and, even, also, but
δὲ conj. δέ but, and, now, also, to the contrary, rather, then
ὅτι conj. ὅτι that, for, because, how that, how, because that, for that, though
καὶ conj. καί and, even, also, but
ἕως conj. ἕως till, until, unto, until when, while, as far as, even, until now
τέλους n. gen. neut. sg. τέλος end, custom, ending, finally, uttermost
14 καθὼς adv. καθώς as, even as, according as, according to
καὶ conj. καί and, even, also, but
ἡμᾶς pron. acc. 1p. pl. ἐγώ I
ἀπὸ prep. ἀπό (+gen) from, of, out of, since, for, off, at, by, in, on
μέρους n. gen. neut. sg. μέρος part, coast, portion, behalf, respect, piece, side
ὅτι conj. ὅτι that, for, because, how that, how, because that, for that, though
καύχημα n. nom. neut. sg. καύχημα whereof to glory, rejoicing, glorying, boasting
ὑμῶν pron. gen. 2p. pl. σύ thou, you
καθάπερ adv. καθάπερ even as, as, as well as
καὶ conj. καί and, even, also, but
ὑμεῖς pron. nom. 2p. pl. σύ thou, you
ἡμῶν pron. gen. 1p. pl. ἐγώ I
ἐν prep. ἐν (+dat) in, by, with, among, at, on, through, to, within, into, of, for
τῇ art. dat. fem. sg. ὁ ἡ τό the, this, that, he, she, it
ἡμέρᾳ n. dat. fem. sg. ἡμέρα day, time, year, while, age, day time
τοῦ art. gen. masc. sg. ὁ ἡ τό the, this, that, he, she, it
Κυρίου n. gen. masc. sg. κύριος Lord, lord, master, sir, LORD, God, Master, owner
Ἰησοῦ n. gen. masc. sg. Ἰησοῦς Jesus
15 Καὶ conj. καί and, even, also, but

ταύτῃ demo. pron. dat. fem. sg. οὗτος αὕτη τοῦτο this, the same, this same, he, she, it
τῇ art. dat. fem. sg. ὁ ἡ τό the, this, that, he, she, it
πεποιθήσει n. dat. fem. sg. πεποίθησις confidence, trust
πρὸς prep. πρός (+gen) for, (+dat) at, (+acc) unto, to, with, for, against
ὑμᾶς pron. acc. 2p. pl. σύ thou, you
πρότερον adv. πρότερον before, first, former, at the first
ἵνα conj. ἵνα that, to, lest, for to, so that, albeit, because, for, so as
δευτέραν ordinal. adj. acc. fem. sg. δεύτερος second, second time, again, afterward
χάριν n. acc. fem. sg. χάρις grace, thank, favour, pleasure
16 καὶ conj. καί and, even, also, but
δι' prep. διά (+gen) by, through, with, in, of, (+acc) for, because of, for a cause
ὑμῶν pron. gen. 2p. pl. σύ thou, you
εἰς prep. εἰς (+acc) into, to, unto, for, in, on, toward, against, upon, at, among
Μακεδονίαν n. acc. fem. sg. Μακεδονία Macedonia
καὶ conj. καί and, even, also, but
πάλιν adv. πάλιν again
ἀπὸ prep. ἀπό (+gen) from, of, out of, since, for, off, at, by, in, on
Μακεδονίας n. gen. fem. sg. Μακεδονία Macedonia
πρὸς prep. πρός (+gen) for, (+dat) at, (+acc) unto, to, with, for, against
ὑμᾶς pron. acc. 2p. pl. σύ thou, you
καὶ conj. καί and, even, also, but
ὑφ' prep. ὑπό (+gen) of, by, with, from, among, (+acc) under
ὑμῶν pron. gen. 2p. pl. σύ thou, you
εἰς prep. εἰς (+acc) into, to, unto, for, in, on, toward, against, upon, at, among
τὴν art. acc. fem. sg. ὁ ἡ τό the, this, that, he, she, it
Ἰουδαίαν n. acc. fem. sg. Ἰουδαία Judaea, Jewry
17 τοῦτο demo. pron. acc. neut. sg. οὗτος αὕτη τοῦτο this, the same, this same, he, she, it
οὖν conj. οὖν therefore, then, so, and, now, wherefore
μή particle of negation. μή not, no, lest, neither, none, nothing, nor, never, without
τι indefinite pron. acc. neut. sg. τὶς certain, some, any man, one, any thing
ἄρα conj. ἄρα then, therefore, haply, wherefore, perhaps, manner, no doubt, truly
τῇ art. dat. fem. sg. ὁ ἡ τό the, this, that, he, she, it
ἐλαφρίᾳ n. dat. fem. sg. ἐλαφρία lightness
ἢ particle. ἤ or, than, either, nor, or else, and, rather than
ἃ relative pron. acc. neut. pl. ὅς ἥ ὅ who, which, what, that
κατὰ prep. κατά (+gen) against, by, throughout, down, (+acc) according to, after, with
σάρκα n. acc. fem. sg. σάρξ flesh, carnal
ἵνα conj. ἵνα that, to, lest, for to, so that, albeit, because, for, so as
παρ' prep. παρά (+gen) of, from, (+dat) with, for, (+acc) beside, at, by, above, against
ἐμοὶ pron. dat. 1p. sg. ἐγώ I
τὸ art. nom. neut. sg. ὁ ἡ τό the, this, that, he, she, it
ναὶ particle. ναί yea, even so, yes, surely, truth, verily
ναὶ particle. ναί yea, even so, yes, surely, truth, verily
καὶ conj. καί and, even, also, but
τὸ art. nom. neut. sg. ὁ ἡ τό the, this, that, he, she, it
οὔ particle. οὐ οὐκ οὐχ not, no, neither, none, nay, nor, never, nothing
οὔ particle. οὐ οὐκ οὐχ not, no, neither, none, nay, nor, never, nothing
18 πιστὸς adj. nom. masc. sg. πιστός faithful, believing, true, sure
δὲ conj. δέ but, and, now, also, to the contrary, rather, then
ὁ art. nom. masc. sg. ὁ ἡ τό the, this, that, he, she, it
Θεὸς n. nom. masc. sg. θεός God, god
ὅτι conj. ὅτι that, for, because, how that, how, because that, for that, though
ὁ art. nom. masc. sg. ὁ ἡ τό the, this, that, he, she, it
λόγος n. nom. masc. sg. λόγος word, saying, account, speech, thing, matter
ἡμῶν pron. gen. 1p. pl. ἐγώ I

ὁ art. nom. masc. sg. ὁ ἡ τό the, this, that, he, she, it
πρὸς prep. πρός (+gen) for, (+dat) at, (+acc) unto, to, with, for, against
ὑμᾶς pron. acc. 2p. pl. σύ thou, you
οὐκ particle of negation. οὐ οὐκ οὐχ not, no, neither, none, nay, nor, never, nothing
ναὶ particle. ναί yea, even so, yes, surely, truth, verily
ναὶ particle. ναί yea, even so, yes, surely, truth, verily
καὶ conj. καί and, even, also, but
οὔ particle. οὐ οὐκ οὐχ not, no, neither, none, nay, nor, never, nothing
οὔ particle. οὐ οὐκ οὐχ not, no, neither, none, nay, nor, never, nothing
19 ὁ art. nom. masc. sg. ὁ ἡ τό the, this, that, he, she, it
γὰρ conj. γάρ for, and, because, but, indeed
τοῦ art. gen. masc. sg. ὁ ἡ τό the, this, that, he, she, it
Θεοῦ n. gen. masc. sg. θεός God, god
υἱὸς n. nom. masc. sg. υἱός son, child, descendant, offspring, heir
Ἰησοῦς n. nom. masc. sg. Ἰησοῦς Jesus
Χριστὸς n. nom. masc. sg. Χριστός Christ
ὁ art. nom. masc. sg. ὁ ἡ τό the, this, that, he, she, it
ἐν prep. ἐν (+dat) in, by, with, among, at, on, through, to, within, into, of, for
ὑμῖν pron. dat. 2p. pl. σύ thou, you
δι' prep. διά (+gen) by, through, with, in, of, (+acc) for, because of, for a cause
ἡμῶν pron. gen. 1p. pl. ἐγώ I
δι' prep. διά (+gen) by, through, with, in, of, (+acc) for, because of, for a cause
ἐμοῦ pron. gen. 1p. sg. ἐγώ I
καὶ conj. καί and, even, also, but
Σιλουανοῦ n. gen. masc. sg. Σιλουανός Silvanus
καὶ conj. καί and, even, also, but
Τιμοθέου n. gen. masc. sg. Τιμόθεος Timotheus, Timothy
οὐκ particle of negation. οὐ οὐκ οὐχ not, no, neither, none, nay, nor, never, nothing
ναὶ particle. ναί yea, even so, yes, surely, truth, verily
καὶ conj. καί and, even, also, but
οὔ particle. οὐ οὐκ οὐχ not, no, neither, none, nay, nor, never, nothing
ἀλλὰ conj. ἀλλά but, yea, yet, nevertheless, howbeit, nay, therefore
ναὶ particle. ναί yea, even so, yes, surely, truth, verily
ἐν prep. ἐν (+dat) in, by, with, among, at, on, through, to, within, into, of, for
αὐτῷ pron. dat. masc. 3p. sg. αὐτός ή ό self, of oneself, even, very, the same, he, she, it
20 ὅσαι relative pron. nom. fem. pl. ὅσος as many as, whatsoever, that, as long as, how much
γὰρ conj. γάρ for, and, because, but, indeed
ἐπαγγελίαι n. nom. fem. pl. ἐπαγγελία promise, message
Θεοῦ n. gen. masc. sg. θεός God, god
ἐν prep. ἐν (+dat) in, by, with, among, at, on, through, to, within, into, of, for
αὐτῷ pron. dat. masc. 3p. sg. αὐτός ή ό self, of oneself, even, very, the same, he, she, it
τὸ art. nom. neut. sg. ὁ ἡ τό the, this, that, he, she, it
ναί particle. ναί yea, even so, yes, surely, truth, verily
καὶ conj. καί and, even, also, but
ἐν prep. ἐν (+dat) in, by, with, among, at, on, through, to, within, into, of, for
αὐτῷ pron. dat. masc. 3p. sg. αὐτός ή ό self, of oneself, even, very, the same, he, she, it
τὸ art. nom. neut. sg. ὁ ἡ τό the, this, that, he, she, it
ἀμήν particle. ἀμήν amen, verily
τῷ art. dat. masc. sg. ὁ ἡ τό the, this, that, he, she, it
Θεῷ n. dat. masc. sg. θεός God, god
πρὸς prep. πρός (+gen) for, (+dat) at, (+acc) unto, to, with, for, against
δόξαν n. acc. fem. sg. δόξα glory, honour, praise, dignity, worship
δι' prep. διά (+gen) by, through, with, in, of, (+acc) for, because of, for a cause
ἡμῶν pron. gen. 1p. pl. ἐγώ I
21 ὁ art. nom. masc. sg. ὁ ἡ τό the, this, that, he, she, it

δὲ conj. δέ but, and, now, also, to the contrary, rather, then
ἡμᾶς pron. acc. 1p. pl. ἐγώ I
σὺν prep. σύν (+dat) with, beside
ὑμῖν pron. dat. 2p. pl. σύ thou, you
εἰς prep. εἰς (+acc) into, to, unto, for, in, on, toward, against, upon, at, among
Χριστὸν n. acc. masc. sg. Χριστός Christ
καὶ conj. καί and, even, also, but
ἡμᾶς pron. acc. 1p. pl. ἐγώ I
Θεός n. nom. masc. sg. θεός God, god
22 ὁ art. nom. masc. sg. ὁ ἡ τό the, this, that, he, she, it
καὶ conj. καί and, even, also, but
ἡμᾶς pron. acc. 1p. pl. ἐγώ I
καὶ conj. καί and, even, also, but
τὸν art. acc. masc. sg. ὁ ἡ τό the, this, that, he, she, it
ἀρραβῶνα n. acc. masc. sg. ἀρραβών earnest
τοῦ art. gen. neut. sg. ὁ ἡ τό the, this, that, he, she, it
Πνεύματος n. gen. neut. sg. πνεῦμα spirit, Spirit, Ghost, ghost, life. of the spirit, wind
ἐν prep. ἐν (+dat) in, by, with, among, at, on, through, to, within, into, of, for
ταῖς art. dat. fem. pl. ὁ ἡ τό the, this, that, he, she, it
καρδίαις n. dat. fem. pl. καρδία heart
ἡμῶν pron. gen. 1p. pl. ἐγώ I
23 Ἐγὼ pron. nom. 1p. sg. ἐγώ I
δὲ conj. δέ but, and, now, also, to the contrary, rather, then
μάρτυρα n. acc. masc. sg. μάρτυς or μάρτυρ witness, martyr, record
τὸν art. acc. masc. sg. ὁ ἡ τό the, this, that, he, she, it
Θεὸν n. acc. masc. sg. θεός God, god
ἐπὶ prep. ἐπί (+gen) on, in, upon, (+dat) in, at, for, upon, (+acc) on, upon, unto, to, against
τὴν art. acc. fem. sg. ὁ ἡ τό the, this, that, he, she, it
ἐμὴν poss. pron. acc. fem. 1p. sg. ἐμός my, mine, mine own, of me
ψυχήν n. acc. fem. sg. ψυχή life, soul, mind, heart
ὅτι conj. ὅτι that, for, because, how that, how, because that, for that, though
ὑμῶν pron. gen. 2p. pl. σύ thou, you
οὐκέτι adv. οὐκέτι or οὐκ έτι no more, no longer, not any more
εἰς prep. εἰς (+acc) into, to, unto, for, in, on, toward, against, upon, at, among
Κόρινθον n. acc. fem. sg. Κόρινθος Corinth
24 οὐχ particle of negation. οὐ οὐκ οὐχ not, no, neither, none, nay, nor, never, nothing
ὅτι conj. ὅτι that, for, because, how that, how, because that, for that, though
ὑμῶν pron. gen. 2p. pl. σύ thou, you
τῆς art. gen. fem. sg. ὁ ἡ τό the, this, that, he, she, it
πίστεως n. gen. fem. sg. πίστις faith, assurance, belief, fidelity
ἀλλὰ conj. ἀλλά but, yea, yet, nevertheless, howbeit, nay, therefore
συνεργοί adj. nom. masc. pl. συνεργός fellowlabourer, fellowhelper, fellowworker
τῆς art. gen. fem. sg. ὁ ἡ τό the, this, that, he, she, it
χαρᾶς n. gen. fem. sg. χαρά joy, gladness, joyfulness
ὑμῶν pron. gen. 2p. pl. σύ thou, you
τῇ art. dat. fem. sg. ὁ ἡ τό the, this, that, he, she, it
γὰρ conj. γάρ for, and, because, but, indeed
πίστει n. dat. fem. sg. πίστις faith, assurance, belief, fidelity

2

1 δὲ conj. δέ but, and, now, also, to the contrary, rather, then
ἐμαυτῷ pron. dat. masc. 1p. sg. ἐμαυτοῦ myself, me
τοῦτο demo. pron. acc. neut. sg. οὗτος αὕτη τοῦτο this, the same, this same, he, she, it
τὸ art. acc. neut. sg. ὁ ἡ τό the, this, that, he, she, it

μὴ particle of negation. μή not, no, lest, neither, none, nothing, nor, never, without
πάλιν adv. πάλιν again
ἐν prep. ἐν (+dat) in, by, with, among, at, on, through, to, within, into, of, for
λύπῃ n. dat. fem. sg. λύπη sorrow, heaviness, grief, grievous, grudgingly
πρὸς prep. πρός (+gen) for, (+dat) at, (+acc) unto, to, with, for, against
ὑμᾶς pron. acc. 2p. pl. σύ thou, you
2 εἰ conj. εἰ if, whether, that, though, forasmuch
γὰρ conj. γάρ for, and, because, but, indeed
ἐγὼ pron. nom. 1p. sg. ἐγώ I
ὑμᾶς pron. acc. 2p. pl. σύ thou, you
καὶ conj. καί and, even, also, but
τίς interrog. pron. nom. masc. sg. τίς what, who, why, where, which, how
ὁ art. nom. masc. sg. ὁ ἡ τό the, this, that, he, she, it
με pron. acc. 1p. sg. ἐγώ I
εἰ conj. εἰ if, whether, that, though, forasmuch
μὴ particle of negation. μή not, no, lest, neither, none, nothing, nor, never, without
ὁ art. nom. masc. sg. ὁ ἡ τό the, this, that, he, she, it
ἐξ prep. ἐκ ἐξ (+gen) of, from, out of, by, on, with, in, among, through
ἐμοῦ pron. gen. 1p. sg. ἐγώ I
3 καὶ conj. καί and, even, also, but
ὑμῖν pron. dat. 2p. pl. σύ thou, you
τοῦτο demo. pron. acc. neut. sg. οὗτος αὕτη τοῦτο this, the same, this same, he, she, it
αὐτό adj. acc. neut. sg. αὐτός ή ό self, of oneself, even, very, the same, he, she, it
ἵνα conj. ἵνα that, to, lest, for to, so that, albeit, because, for, so as
μὴ particle of negation. μή not, no, lest, neither, none, nothing, nor, never, without
λύπην n. acc. fem. sg. λύπη sorrow, heaviness, grief, grievous, grudgingly
ἀφ' prep. ἀπό (+gen) from, of, out of, since, for, off, at, by, in, on
ὧν relative pron. gen. masc. pl. ὅς ἥ ὅ who, which, what, that
με pron. acc. 1p. sg. ἐγώ I
ἐπὶ prep. ἐπί (+gen) on, in, upon, (+dat) in, at, for, upon, (+acc) on, upon, unto, to, against
πάντας adj. acc. masc. pl. πᾶς πᾶσα πᾶν all, every, whosoever, every one, no, whole, any
ὑμᾶς pron. acc. 2p. pl. σύ thou, you
ὅτι conj. ὅτι that, for, because, how that, how, because that, for that, though
ἡ art. nom. fem. sg. ὁ ἡ τό the, this, that, he, she, it
ἐμὴ poss. pron. nom. fem. 1p. sg. ἐμός my, mine, mine own, of me
χαρὰ n. nom. fem. sg. χαρά joy, gladness, joyfulness
πάντων adj. gen. masc. pl. πᾶς πᾶσα πᾶν all, every, whosoever, every one, no, whole, any
ὑμῶν pron. gen. 2p. pl. σύ thou, you
4 ἐκ prep. ἐκ ἐξ (+gen) of, from, out of, by, on, with, in, among, through
γὰρ conj. γάρ for, and, because, but, indeed
πολλῆς adj. gen. fem. sg. πολύς many, great, much, long, abundant
θλίψεως n. gen. fem. sg. θλῖψις tribulation, affliction, anguish, persecution
καὶ conj. καί and, even, also, but
συνοχῆς n. gen. fem. sg. συνοχή distress, anguish
καρδίας n. gen. fem. sg. καρδία heart
ὑμῖν pron. dat. 2p. pl. σύ thou, you
διὰ prep. διά (+gen) by, through, with, in, of, (+acc) for, because of, for a cause
πολλῶν adj. gen. neut. pl. πολύς many, great, much, long, abundant
δακρύων n. gen. neut. pl. δάκρυον tears
οὐχ particle of negation. οὐ οὐκ οὐχ not, no, neither, none, nay, nor, never, nothing
ἵνα conj. ἵνα that, to, lest, for to, so that, albeit, because, for, so as
ἀλλὰ conj. ἀλλά but, yea, yet, nevertheless, howbeit, nay, therefore
τὴν art. acc. fem. sg. ὁ ἡ τό the, this, that, he, she, it
ἀγάπην n. acc. fem. sg. ἀγάπη love, charity, feast of charity
ἵνα conj. ἵνα that, to, lest, for to, so that, albeit, because, for, so as

ἣν relative pron. acc. fem. sg. ὅς ἥ ὅ who, which, what, that
περισσοτέρως adv. περισσοτέρως more exceedingly, more abundantly, more frequent
εἰς prep. εἰς (+acc) into, to, unto, for, in, on, toward, against, upon, at, among
ὑμᾶς pron. acc. 2p. pl. σύ thou, you
5 Εἰ conj. εἰ if, whether, that, though, forasmuch
δέ conj. δέ but, and, now, also, to the contrary, rather, then
τις indefinite pron. nom. masc. sg. τὶς certain, some, any man, one, any thing
οὐκ particle of negation. οὐ οὐκ οὐχ not, no, neither, none, nay, nor, never, nothing
ἐμὲ pron. acc. 1p. sg. ἐγώ I
ἀλλ' conj. ἀλλά but, yea, yet, nevertheless, howbeit, nay, therefore
ἀπὸ prep. ἀπό (+gen) from, of, out of, since, for, off, at, by, in, on
μέρους n. gen. neut. sg. μέρος part, coast, portion, behalf, respect, piece, side
ἵνα conj. ἵνα that, to, lest, for to, so that, albeit, because, for, so as
μὴ particle of negation. μή not, no, lest, neither, none, nothing, nor, never, without
πάντας adj. acc. masc. pl. πᾶς πᾶσα πᾶν all, every, whosoever, every one, no, whole, any
ὑμᾶς pron. acc. 2p. pl. σύ thou, you
6 ἱκανὸν adj. nom. neut. sg. ἱκανός many, much, long, worthy, sufficient, great, able
τῷ art. dat. masc. sg. ὁ ἡ τό the, this, that, he, she, it
τοιούτῳ demo. pron. dat. masc. sg. τοιοῦτος such, like
ἡ art. nom. fem. sg. ὁ ἡ τό the, this, that, he, she, it
ἐπιτιμία n. nom. fem. sg. ἐπιτιμία punishment
αὕτη demo. pron. nom. fem. sg. οὗτος αὕτη τοῦτο this, the same, this same, he, she, it
ἡ art. nom. fem. sg. ὁ ἡ τό the, this, that, he, she, it
ὑπὸ prep. ὑπό (+gen) of, by, with, from, among, (+acc) under
τῶν art. gen. masc. pl. ὁ ἡ τό the, this, that, he, she, it
πλειόνων compar. adj. gen. masc. pl. πολύς many, great, much, long, abundant
7 ὥστε conj. ὥστε so that, wherefore, insomuch that, therefore, that, so then
τοὐναντίον adv. τοὐναντίον contrariwise
μᾶλλον adv. μᾶλλον rather, more, more and more, better, much, much the more
ὑμᾶς pron. acc. 2p. pl. σύ thou, you
καὶ conj. καί and, even, also, but
μή particle of negation. μή not, no, lest, neither, none, nothing, nor, never, without
πως particle. πώς by any means, by some means, haply, perhaps
τῇ art. dat. fem. sg. ὁ ἡ τό the, this, that, he, she, it
περισσοτέρᾳ compar. adj. dat. fem. sg. περισσός more, beyond measure, advantage
λύπῃ n. dat. fem. sg. λύπη sorrow, heaviness, grief, grievous, grudgingly
ὁ art. nom. masc. sg. ὁ ἡ τό the, this, that, he, she, it
τοιοῦτος demo. pron. nom. masc. sg. τοιοῦτος such, like
8 διὸ conj. διό wherefore, therefore, for which cause
ὑμᾶς pron. acc. 2p. pl. σύ thou, you
εἰς prep. εἰς (+acc) into, to, unto, for, in, on, toward, against, upon, at, among
αὐτὸν pron. acc. masc. 3p. sg. αὐτός ἡ ὁ self, of oneself, even, very, the same, he, she, it
ἀγάπην n. acc. fem. sg. ἀγάπη love, charity, feast of charity
9 εἰς prep. εἰς (+acc) into, to, unto, for, in, on, toward, against, upon, at, among
τοῦτο demo. pron. acc. neut. sg. οὗτος αὕτη τοῦτο this, the same, this same, he, she, it
γὰρ conj. γάρ for, and, because, but, indeed
καὶ conj. καί and, even, also, but
ἵνα conj. ἵνα that, to, lest, for to, so that, albeit, because, for, so as
τὴν art. acc. fem. sg. ὁ ἡ τό the, this, that, he, she, it
δοκιμὴν n. acc. fem. sg. δοκιμή experience, proof, experiment, trial
ὑμῶν pron. gen. 2p. pl. σύ thou, you
εἰ conj. εἰ if, whether, that, though, forasmuch
εἰς prep. εἰς (+acc) into, to, unto, for, in, on, toward, against, upon, at, among
πάντα adj. acc. neut. pl. πᾶς πᾶσα πᾶν all, every, whosoever, every one, no, whole, any
ὑπήκοοί adj. nom. masc. pl. ὑπήκοος obedient

10 ᾧ relative pron. dat. masc. sg. ὅς ἥ ὅ who, which, what, that
δέ conj. δέ but, and, now, also, to the contrary, rather, then
τι indefinite pron. acc. neut. sg. τὶς certain, some, any man, one, any thing
καὶ conj. καί and, even, also, but
ἐγώ pron. nom. 1p. sg. ἐγώ I
καὶ conj. καί and, even, also, but
γὰρ conj. γάρ for, and, because, but, indeed
ἐγώ pron. nom. 1p. sg. ἐγώ I
εἴ conj. εἰ if, whether, that, though, forasmuch
τι indefinite pron. acc. neut. sg. τὶς certain, some, any man, one, any thing
ᾧ relative pron. dat. masc. sg. ὅς ἥ ὅ who, which, what, that
δι' prep. διά (+gen) by, through, with, in, of, (+acc) for, because of, for a cause
ὑμᾶς pron. acc. 2p. pl. σύ thou, you
ἐν prep. ἐν (+dat) in, by, with, among, at, on, through, to, within, into, of, for
προσώπῳ n. dat. neut. sg. πρόσωπον face, presence, person, countenance
Χριστοῦ n. gen. masc. sg. Χριστός Christ
11 ἵνα conj. ἵνα that, to, lest, for to, so that, albeit, because, for, so as
μὴ particle of negation. μή not, no, lest, neither, none, nothing, nor, never, without
ὑπὸ prep. ὑπό (+gen) of, by, with, from, among, (+acc) under
τοῦ art. gen. masc. sg. ὁ ἡ τό the, this, that, he, she, it
Σατανᾶ n. gen. masc. sg. Σατανᾶς Satan
οὐ particle of negation. οὐ οὐκ οὐχ not, no, neither, none, nay, nor, never, nothing
γὰρ conj. γάρ for, and, because, but, indeed
αὐτοῦ pron. gen. masc. 3p. sg. αὐτός ή ό self, of oneself, even, very, the same, he, she, it
τὰ art. acc. neut. pl. ὁ ἡ τό the, this, that, he, she, it
νοήματα n. acc. neut. pl. νόημα mind, device, thought
12 δὲ conj. δέ but, and, now, also, to the contrary, rather, then
εἰς prep. εἰς (+acc) into, to, unto, for, in, on, toward, against, upon, at, among
τὴν art. acc. fem. sg. ὁ ἡ τό the, this, that, he, she, it
Τρῳάδα n. acc. fem. sg. Τρῳάς Troas
εἰς prep. εἰς (+acc) into, to, unto, for, in, on, toward, against, upon, at, among
τὸ art. acc. neut. sg. ὁ ἡ τό the, this, that, he, she, it
εὐαγγέλιον n. acc. neut. sg. εὐαγγέλιον gospel
τοῦ art. gen. masc. sg. ὁ ἡ τό the, this, that, he, she, it
Χριστοῦ n. gen. masc. sg. Χριστός Christ
καὶ conj. καί and, even, also, but
θύρας n. gen. fem. sg. θύρα door, gate
μοι pron. dat. 1p. sg. ἐγώ I
ἐν prep. ἐν (+dat) in, by, with, among, at, on, through, to, within, into, of, for
Κυρίῳ n. dat. masc. sg. κύριος Lord, lord, master, sir, LORD, God, Master, owner
13 οὐκ particle of negation. οὐ οὐκ οὐχ not, no, neither, none, nay, nor, never, nothing
ἄνεσιν n. acc. fem. sg. ἄνεσις liberty, rest, eased
τῷ art. dat. neut. sg. ὁ ἡ τό the, this, that, he, she, it
πνεύματί n. dat. neut. sg. πνεῦμα spirit, Spirit, Ghost, ghost, life. of the spirit, wind
μου pron. gen. 1p. sg. ἐγώ I
τῷ art. dat. neut. sg. ὁ ἡ τό the, this, that, he, she, it
μὴ particle of negation. μή not, no, lest, neither, none, nothing, nor, never, without
με pron. acc. 1p. sg. ἐγώ I
Τίτον n. acc. masc. sg. Τίτος Titus
τὸν art. acc. masc. sg. ὁ ἡ τό the, this, that, he, she, it
ἀδελφόν n. acc. masc. sg. ἀδελφός brother
μου pron. gen. 1p. sg. ἐγώ I
ἀλλὰ conj. ἀλλά but, yea, yet, nevertheless, howbeit, nay, therefore
αὐτοῖς pron. dat. masc. 3p. pl. αὐτός ή ό self, of oneself, even, very, the same, he, she, it
εἰς prep. εἰς (+acc) into, to, unto, for, in, on, toward, against, upon, at, among

Μακεδονίαν n. acc. fem. sg. Μακεδονία Macedonia
14 τῷ art. dat. masc. sg. ὁ ἡ τό the, this, that, he, she, it
δὲ conj. δέ but, and, now, also, to the contrary, rather, then
Θεῷ n. dat. masc. sg. θεός God, god
χάρις n. nom. fem. sg. χάρις grace, thank, favour, pleasure
τῷ art. dat. masc. sg. ὁ ἡ τό the, this, that, he, she, it
πάντοτε adv. πάντοτε always, ever, always, evermore
ἡμᾶς pron. acc. 1p. pl. ἐγώ I
ἐν prep. ἐν (+dat) in, by, with, among, at, on, through, to, within, into, of, for
τῷ art. dat. masc. sg. ὁ ἡ τό the, this, that, he, she, it
Χριστῷ n. dat. masc. sg. Χριστός Christ
καὶ conj. καί and, even, also, but
τὴν art. acc. fem. sg. ὁ ἡ τό the, this, that, he, she, it
ὀσμὴν n. acc. fem. sg. ὀσμή odour, savour
τῆς art. gen. fem. sg. ὁ ἡ τό the, this, that, he, she, it
γνώσεως n. gen. fem. sg. γνῶσις knowledge, science
αὐτοῦ pron. gen. masc. 3p. sg. αὐτός ή ό self, of oneself, even, very, the same, he, she, it
δι' prep. διά (+gen) by, through, with, in, of, (+acc) for, because of, for a cause
ἡμῶν pron. gen. 1p. pl. ἐγώ I
ἐν prep. ἐν (+dat) in, by, with, among, at, on, through, to, within, into, of, for
παντὶ adj. dat. masc. sg. πᾶς πᾶσα πᾶν all, every, whosoever, every one, no, whole, any
τόπῳ n. dat. masc. sg. τόπος place, room, quarter
15 ὅτι conj. ὅτι that, for, because, how that, how, because that, for that, though
Χριστοῦ n. gen. masc. sg. Χριστός Christ
εὐωδία n. nom. fem. sg. εὐωδία sweet savour, sweet smell, sweetsmelling
τῷ art. dat. masc. sg. ὁ ἡ τό the, this, that, he, she, it
Θεῷ n. dat. masc. sg. θεός God, god
ἐν prep. ἐν (+dat) in, by, with, among, at, on, through, to, within, into, of, for
τοῖς art. dat. masc. pl. ὁ ἡ τό the, this, that, he, she, it
καὶ conj. καί and, even, also, but
ἐν prep. ἐν (+dat) in, by, with, among, at, on, through, to, within, into, of, for
τοῖς art. dat. masc. pl. ὁ ἡ τό the, this, that, he, she, it
16 οἷς relative pron. dat. masc. pl. ὅς ἥ ὅ who, which, what, that
μὲν conj. μέν indeed, verily, truly, even, so, some
ὀσμὴ n. nom. fem. sg. ὀσμή odour, savour
θανάτου n. gen. masc. sg. θάνατος death
εἰς prep. εἰς (+acc) into, to, unto, for, in, on, toward, against, upon, at, among
θάνατον n. acc. masc. sg. θάνατος death
οἷς relative pron. dat. masc. pl. ὅς ἥ ὅ who, which, what, that
δὲ conj. δέ but, and, now, also, to the contrary, rather, then
ὀσμὴ n. nom. fem. sg. ὀσμή odour, savour
ζωῆς n. gen. fem. sg. ζωή life, lifetime
εἰς prep. εἰς (+acc) into, to, unto, for, in, on, toward, against, upon, at, among
ζωήν n. acc. fem. sg. ζωή life, lifetime
καὶ conj. καί and, even, also, but
πρὸς prep. πρός (+gen) for, (+dat) at, (+acc) unto, to, with, for, against
ταῦτα demo. pron. acc. neut. pl. οὗτος αὕτη τοῦτο this, the same, this same, he, she, it
τίς interrog. pron. nom. masc. sg. τίς what, who, why, where, which, how
ἱκανός adj. nom. masc. sg. ἱκανός many, much, long, worthy, sufficient, great, able
17 οὐ particle of negation. οὐ οὐκ οὐχ not, no, neither, none, nay, nor, never, nothing
γάρ conj. γάρ for, and, because, but, indeed
ὡς adv. ὡς as, when, as it were, how, about, like, as soon as, even as, while
οἱ art. nom. masc. pl. ὁ ἡ τό the, this, that, he, she, it
πολλοὶ adj. nom. masc. pl. πολύς many, great, much, long, abundant
τὸν art. acc. masc. sg. ὁ ἡ τό the, this, that, he, she, it

λόγον n. acc. masc. sg. λόγος word, saying, account, speech, thing, matter
τοῦ art. gen. masc. sg. ὁ ἡ τό the, this, that, he, she, it
Θεοῦ n. gen. masc. sg. θεός God, god
ἀλλ' conj. ἀλλά but, yea, yet, nevertheless, howbeit, nay, therefore
ὡς adv. ὡς as, when, as it were, how, about, like, as soon as, even as, while
ἐξ prep. ἐκ ἐξ (+gen) of, from, out of, by, on, with, in, among, through
εἰλικρινείας n. gen. fem. sg. εἰλικρίνεια sincerity
ἀλλ' conj. ἀλλά but, yea, yet, nevertheless, howbeit, nay, therefore
ὡς adv. ὡς as, when, as it were, how, about, like, as soon as, even as, while
ἐκ prep. ἐκ ἐξ (+gen) of, from, out of, by, on, with, in, among, through
Θεοῦ n. gen. masc. sg. θεός God, god
κατενώπιον prep. κατενώπιον (+gen) before, before the presence, in the sight, in sight
τοῦ art. gen. masc. sg. ὁ ἡ τό the, this, that, he, she, it
Θεοῦ n. gen. masc. sg. θεός God, god
ἐν prep. ἐν (+dat) in, by, with, among, at, on, through, to, within, into, of, for
Χριστῷ n. dat. masc. sg. Χριστός Christ

3

1 πάλιν adv. πάλιν again
ἑαυτοὺς reflexive pron. acc. masc. 3p. pl. ἑαυτοῦ himself, herself, itself, yourself, ourselves
ἢ particle. ἤ or, than, either, nor, or else, and, rather than
μὴ particle of negation. μή not, no, lest, neither, none, nothing, nor, never, without
ὥς adv. ὡς as, when, as it were, how, about, like, as soon as, even as, while
τινες indefinite pron. nom. masc. pl. τὶς certain, some, any man, one, any thing
συστατικῶν adj. gen. fem. pl. συστατικός of commendation
ἐπιστολῶν n. gen. fem. pl. ἐπιστολή letter, epistle
πρὸς prep. πρός (+gen) for, (+dat) at, (+acc) unto, to, with, for, against
ὑμᾶς pron. acc. 2p. pl. σύ thou, you
ἢ particle. ἤ or, than, either, nor, or else, and, rather than
ἐξ prep. ἐκ ἐξ (+gen) of, from, out of, by, on, with, in, among, through
ὑμῶν pron. gen. 2p. pl. σύ thou, you
συστατικῶν adj. gen. fem. pl. συστατικός of commendation
2 ἡ art. nom. fem. sg. ὁ ἡ τό the, this, that, he, she, it
ἐπιστολὴ n. nom. fem. sg. ἐπιστολή letter, epistle
ἡμῶν pron. gen. 1p. pl. ἐγώ I
ὑμεῖς pron. nom. 2p. pl. σύ thou, you
ἐν prep. ἐν (+dat) in, by, with, among, at, on, through, to, within, into, of, for
ταῖς art. dat. fem. pl. ὁ ἡ τό the, this, that, he, she, it
καρδίαις n. dat. fem. pl. καρδία heart
ἡμῶν pron. gen. 1p. pl. ἐγώ I
καὶ conj. καί and, even, also, but
ὑπὸ prep. ὑπό (+gen) of, by, with, from, among, (+acc) under
πάντων adj. gen. masc. pl. πᾶς πᾶσα πᾶν all, every, whosoever, every one, no, whole, any
ἀνθρώπων n. gen. masc. pl. ἄνθρωπος man, human being, person, one, certain
3 ὅτι conj. ὅτι that, for, because, how that, how, because that, for that, though
ἐπιστολὴ n. nom. fem. sg. ἐπιστολή letter, epistle
Χριστοῦ n. gen. masc. sg. Χριστός Christ
ὑφ' prep. ὑπό (+gen) of, by, with, from, among, (+acc) under
ἡμῶν pron. gen. 1p. pl. ἐγώ I
οὐ particle of negation. οὐ οὐκ οὐχ not, no, neither, none, nay, nor, never, nothing
μέλανι adj. dat. neut. sg. μέλας black
ἀλλὰ conj. ἀλλά but, yea, yet, nevertheless, howbeit, nay, therefore
Πνεύματι n. dat. neut. sg. πνεῦμα spirit, Spirit, Ghost, ghost, life. of the spirit, wind
Θεοῦ n. gen. masc. sg. θεός God, god

οὐκ particle of negation. οὐ οὐκ οὐχ not, no, neither, none, nay, nor, never, nothing
ἐν prep. ἐν (+dat) in, by, with, among, at, on, through, to, within, into, of, for
πλαξὶ n. dat. fem. pl. πλάξ table
λιθίναις adj. dat. fem. pl. λίθινος of stone
ἀλλ' conj. ἀλλά but, yea, yet, nevertheless, howbeit, nay, therefore
ἐν prep. ἐν (+dat) in, by, with, among, at, on, through, to, within, into, of, for
πλαξὶ n. dat. fem. pl. πλάξ table
καρδίας n. acc. fem. pl. καρδία heart
σαρκίναις adj. dat. fem. pl. σάρκινος fleshy
4 πεποίθησιν n. acc. fem. sg. πεποίθησις confidence, trust
δὲ conj. δέ but, and, now, also, to the contrary, rather, then
τοιαύτην demo. pron. acc. fem. sg. τοιοῦτος such, like
διὰ prep. διά (+gen) by, through, with, in, of, (+acc) for, because of, for a cause
τοῦ art. gen. masc. sg. ὁ ἡ τό the, this, that, he, she, it
Χριστοῦ n. gen. masc. sg. Χριστός Christ
πρὸς prep. πρός (+gen) for, (+dat) at, (+acc) unto, to, with, for, against
τὸν art. acc. masc. sg. ὁ ἡ τό the, this, that, he, she, it
Θεόν n. acc. masc. sg. θεός God, god
5 οὐχ particle of negation. οὐ οὐκ οὐχ not, no, neither, none, nay, nor, never, nothing
ὅτι conj. ὅτι that, for, because, how that, how, because that, for that, though
ἱκανοί adj. nom. masc. pl. ἱκανός many, much, long, worthy, sufficient, great, able
ἀφ' prep. ἀπό (+gen) from, of, out of, since, for, off, at, by, in, on
ἑαυτῶν reflexive pron. gen. masc. 3p. pl. ἑαυτοῦ himself, herself, itself, yourself, ourselves
τι indefinite pron. acc. neut. sg. τὶς certain, some, any man, one, any thing
ὡς adv. ὡς as, when, as it were, how, about, like, as soon as, even as, while
ἐξ prep. ἐκ ἐξ (+gen) of, from, out of, by, on, with, in, among, through
ἑαυτῶν reflexive pron. gen. masc. 3p. pl. ἑαυτοῦ himself, herself, itself, yourself, ourselves
ἀλλ' conj. ἀλλά but, yea, yet, nevertheless, howbeit, nay, therefore
ἡ art. nom. fem. sg. ὁ ἡ τό the, this, that, he, she, it
ἱκανότης n. nom. fem. sg. ἱκανότης sufficiency
ἡμῶν pron. gen. 1p. pl. ἐγώ I
ἐκ prep. ἐκ ἐξ (+gen) of, from, out of, by, on, with, in, among, through
τοῦ art. gen. masc. sg. ὁ ἡ τό the, this, that, he, she, it
Θεοῦ n. gen. masc. sg. θεός God, god
6 ὃς relative pron. nom. masc. sg. ὅς ἥ ὅ who, which, what, that
καὶ conj. καί and, even, also, but
ἡμᾶς pron. acc. 1p. pl. ἐγώ I
διακόνους n. acc. masc. pl. διάκονος minister, servant, deacon
καινῆς adj. gen. fem. sg. καινός new
διαθήκης n. gen. fem. sg. διαθήκη testament, covenant
οὐ particle of negation. οὐ οὐκ οὐχ not, no, neither, none, nay, nor, never, nothing
γράμματος n. gen. neut. sg. γράμμα letter, bill, learning, scripture, writing
ἀλλὰ conj. ἀλλά but, yea, yet, nevertheless, howbeit, nay, therefore
πνεύματος n. gen. neut. sg. πνεῦμα spirit, Spirit, Ghost, ghost, life. of the spirit, wind
τὸ art. nom. neut. sg. ὁ ἡ τό the, this, that, he, she, it
γὰρ conj. γάρ for, and, because, but, indeed
γράμμα n. nom. neut. sg. γράμμα letter, bill, learning, scripture, writing
τὸ art. nom. neut. sg. ὁ ἡ τό the, this, that, he, she, it
δὲ conj. δέ but, and, now, also, to the contrary, rather, then
πνεῦμα n. nom. neut. sg. πνεῦμα spirit, Spirit, Ghost, ghost, life. of the spirit, wind
7 εἰ conj. εἰ if, whether, that, though, forasmuch
δὲ conj. δέ but, and, now, also, to the contrary, rather, then
ἡ art. nom. fem. sg. ὁ ἡ τό the, this, that, he, she, it
διακονία n. nom. fem. sg. διακονία ministry, administration, service, office, relief
τοῦ art. gen. masc. sg. ὁ ἡ τό the, this, that, he, she, it

θανάτου n. gen. masc. sg. θάνατος death
ἐν prep. ἐν (+dat) in, by, with, among, at, on, through, to, within, into, of, for
γράμμασιν n. dat. neut. pl. γράμμα letter, bill, learning, scripture, writing
ἐν prep. ἐν (+dat) in, by, with, among, at, on, through, to, within, into, of, for
λίθοις n. dat. masc. pl. λίθος stone
ἐν prep. ἐν (+dat) in, by, with, among, at, on, through, to, within, into, of, for
δόξῃ n. dat. fem. sg. δόξα glory, honour, praise, dignity, worship
ὥστε conj. ὥστε so that, wherefore, insomuch that, therefore, that, so then
μὴ particle of negation. μή not, no, lest, neither, none, nothing, nor, never, without
τοὺς art. acc. masc. pl. ὁ ἡ τό the, this, that, he, she, it
υἱοὺς n. acc. masc. pl. υἱός son, child, descendant, offspring, heir
Ἰσραὴλ pron. name. masc. inde. Ἰσραήλ Israel
εἰς prep. εἰς (+acc) into, to, unto, for, in, on, toward, against, upon, at, among
τὸ art. acc. neut. sg. ὁ ἡ τό the, this, that, he, she, it
πρόσωπον n. acc. neut. sg. πρόσωπον face, presence, person, countenance
Μωσέως n. gen. masc. sg. Μωσῆς Moses
διὰ prep. διά (+gen) by, through, with, in, of, (+acc) for, because of, for a cause
τὴν art. acc. fem. sg. ὁ ἡ τό the, this, that, he, she, it
δόξαν n. acc. fem. sg. δόξα glory, honour, praise, dignity, worship
τοῦ art. gen. neut. sg. ὁ ἡ τό the, this, that, he, she, it
προσώπου n. gen. neut. sg. πρόσωπον face, presence, person, countenance
αὐτοῦ pron. gen. masc. 3p. sg. αὐτός ἡ ὁ self, of oneself, even, very, the same, he, she, it
τὴν art. acc. fem. sg. ὁ ἡ τό the, this, that, he, she, it
8 πῶς adv. πῶς how, by what means, after what manner
οὐχὶ adv. οὐχί not, nay
μᾶλλον adv. μᾶλλον rather, more, more and more, better, much, much the more
ἡ art. nom. fem. sg. ὁ ἡ τό the, this, that, he, she, it
διακονία n. nom. fem. sg. διακονία ministry, administration, service, office, relief
τοῦ art. gen. neut. sg. ὁ ἡ τό the, this, that, he, she, it
πνεύματος n. gen. neut. sg. πνεῦμα spirit, Spirit, Ghost, ghost, life. of the spirit, wind
ἐν prep. ἐν (+dat) in, by, with, among, at, on, through, to, within, into, of, for
δόξῃ n. dat. fem. sg. δόξα glory, honour, praise, dignity, worship
9 εἰ conj. εἰ if, whether, that, though, forasmuch
γὰρ conj. γάρ for, and, because, but, indeed
ἡ art. nom. fem. sg. ὁ ἡ τό the, this, that, he, she, it
διακονία n. nom. fem. sg. διακονία ministry, administration, service, office, relief
τῆς art. gen. fem. sg. ὁ ἡ τό the, this, that, he, she, it
κατακρίσεως n. gen. fem. sg. κατάκρισις condemnation, condemn
δόξα n. nom. fem. sg. δόξα glory, honour, praise, dignity, worship
πολλῷ adj. dat. neut. sg. πολύς many, great, much, long, abundant
μᾶλλον adv. μᾶλλον rather, more, more and more, better, much, much the more
ἡ art. nom. fem. sg. ὁ ἡ τό the, this, that, he, she, it
διακονία n. nom. fem. sg. διακονία ministry, administration, service, office, relief
τῆς art. gen. fem. sg. ὁ ἡ τό the, this, that, he, she, it
δικαιοσύνης n. gen. fem. sg. δικαιοσύνη righteousness
ἐν prep. ἐν (+dat) in, by, with, among, at, on, through, to, within, into, of, for
δόξῃ n. dat. fem. sg. δόξα glory, honour, praise, dignity, worship
10 καὶ conj. καί and, even, also, but
γὰρ conj. γάρ for, and, because, but, indeed
οὐδὲ adv. οὐδέ neither, nor, not, no, not even, never, not yet
τὸ art. nom. neut. sg. ὁ ἡ τό the, this, that, he, she, it
ἐν prep. ἐν (+dat) in, by, with, among, at, on, through, to, within, into, of, for
τούτῳ demo. pron. dat. neut. sg. οὗτος αὕτη τοῦτο this, the same, this same, he, she, it
τῷ art. dat. neut. sg. ὁ ἡ τό the, this, that, he, she, it
μέρει n. dat. neut. sg. μέρος part, coast, portion, behalf, respect, piece, side

ἕνεκεν prep. ἕνεκα, ἕνεκεν or εἵνεκεν (+gen) for the sake, for a cause, for, by reason of
τῆς art. gen. fem. sg. ὁ ἡ τό the, this, that, he, she, it
δόξης n. gen. fem. sg. δόξα glory, honour, praise, dignity, worship
11 εἰ conj. εἰ if, whether, that, though, forasmuch
γὰρ conj. γάρ for, and, because, but, indeed
τὸ art. nom. neut. sg. ὁ ἡ τό the, this, that, he, she, it
διὰ prep. διά (+gen) by, through, with, in, of, (+acc) for, because of, for a cause
δόξης n. gen. fem. sg. δόξα glory, honour, praise, dignity, worship
πολλῷ adj. dat. neut. sg. πολύς many, great, much, long, abundant
μᾶλλον adv. μᾶλλον rather, more, more and more, better, much, much the more
τὸ art. nom. neut. sg. ὁ ἡ τό the, this, that, he, she, it
ἐν prep. ἐν (+dat) in, by, with, among, at, on, through, to, within, into, of, for
δόξῃ n. dat. fem. sg. δόξα glory, honour, praise, dignity, worship
12 οὖν conj. οὖν therefore, then, so, and, now, wherefore
τοιαύτην demo. pron. acc. fem. sg. τοιοῦτος such, like
ἐλπίδα n. acc. fem. sg. ἐλπίς hope, faith
πολλῇ adj. dat. fem. sg. πολύς many, great, much, long, abundant
παρρησίᾳ n. dat. fem. sg. παρρησία boldness, confidence, openly, plainly, freely
13 καὶ conj. καί and, even, also, but
οὐ particle of negation. οὐ οὐκ οὐχ not, no, neither, none, nay, nor, never, nothing
καθάπερ adv. καθάπερ even as, as, as well as
Μωσῆς n. nom. masc. sg. Μωσῆς Moses
κάλυμμα n. acc. neut. sg. κάλυμμα vail
ἐπὶ prep. ἐπί (+gen) on, in, upon, (+dat) in, at, for, upon, (+acc) on, upon, unto, to, against
τὸ art. acc. neut. sg. ὁ ἡ τό the, this, that, he, she, it
πρόσωπον n. acc. neut. sg. πρόσωπον face, presence, person, countenance
ἑαυτοῦ reflexive pron. gen. masc. 3p. sg. ἑαυτοῦ himself, herself, itself, yourself, ourselves
πρὸς prep. πρός (+gen) for, (+dat) at, (+acc) unto, to, with, for, against
τὸ art. acc. neut. sg. ὁ ἡ τό the, this, that, he, she, it
μὴ particle of negation. μή not, no, lest, neither, none, nothing, nor, never, without
τοὺς art. acc. masc. pl. ὁ ἡ τό the, this, that, he, she, it
υἱοὺς n. acc. masc. pl. υἱός son, child, descendant, offspring, heir
Ἰσραὴλ pron. name. masc. inde. Ἰσραήλ Israel
εἰς prep. εἰς (+acc) into, to, unto, for, in, on, toward, against, upon, at, among
τὸ art. acc. neut. sg. ὁ ἡ τό the, this, that, he, she, it
τέλος n. acc. neut. sg. τέλος end, custom, ending, finally, uttermost
τοῦ art. gen. neut. sg. ὁ ἡ τό the, this, that, he, she, it
14 ἀλλ' conj. ἀλλά but, yea, yet, nevertheless, howbeit, nay, therefore
τὰ art. nom. neut. pl. ὁ ἡ τό the, this, that, he, she, it
νοήματα n. nom. neut. pl. νόημα mind, device, thought
αὐτῶν pron. gen. masc. 3p. pl. αὐτός ἡ ὁ self, of oneself, even, very, the same, he, she, it
ἄχρι prep. ἄχρι or ἄχρις (+gen) until, unto, till, even to, as far as, while, into
γὰρ conj. γάρ for, and, because, but, indeed
τῆς art. gen. fem. sg. ὁ ἡ τό the, this, that, he, she, it
σήμερον adv. σήμερον this day, today
τὸ art. nom. neut. sg. ὁ ἡ τό the, this, that, he, she, it
αὐτὸ pron. acc. neut. 3p. sg. αὐτός ἡ ὁ self, of oneself, even, very, the same, he, she, it
κάλυμμα n. nom. neut. sg. κάλυμμα vail
ἐπὶ prep. ἐπί (+gen) on, in, upon, (+dat) in, at, for, upon, (+acc) on, upon, unto, to, against
τῇ art. dat. fem. sg. ὁ ἡ τό the, this, that, he, she, it
ἀναγνώσει n. dat. fem. sg. ἀνάγνωσις reading
τῆς art. gen. fem. sg. ὁ ἡ τό the, this, that, he, she, it
παλαιᾶς adj. gen. fem. sg. παλαιός old
διαθήκης n. gen. fem. sg. διαθήκη testament, covenant
μὴ particle of negation. μή not, no, lest, neither, none, nothing, nor, never, without

ὅ art. nom. masc. sg. ὁ ἡ τό the, this, that, he, she, it
τι indefinite pron. nom. neut. sg. τὶς certain, some, any man, one, any thing
ἐν prep. ἐν (+dat) in, by, with, among, at, on, through, to, within, into, of, for
Χριστῷ n. dat. masc. sg. Χριστός Christ
15 ἀλλ' conj. ἀλλά but, yea, yet, nevertheless, howbeit, nay, therefore
ἕως conj. ἕως till, until, unto, until when, while, as far as, even, until now
σήμερον adv. σήμερον this day, today
ἡνίκα adv. ἡνίκα when
Μωσῆς n. nom. masc. sg. Μωσῆς Moses
κάλυμμα n. nom. neut. sg. κάλυμμα vail
ἐπὶ prep. ἐπί (+gen) on, in, upon, (+dat) in, at, for, upon, (+acc) on, upon, unto, to, against
τὴν art. acc. fem. sg. ὁ ἡ τό the, this, that, he, she, it
καρδίαν n. acc. fem. sg. καρδία heart
αὐτῶν pron. gen. masc. 3p. pl. αὐτός ή ό self, of oneself, even, very, the same, he, she, it
16 ἡνίκα adv. ἡνίκα when
δ' conj. δέ but, and, now, also, to the contrary, rather, then
ἂν particle. ἄν Indicating contingency. No English translation.
πρὸς prep. πρός (+gen) for, (+dat) at, (+acc) unto, to, with, for, against
Κύριον n. acc. masc. sg. κύριος Lord, lord, master, sir, LORD, God, Master, owner
τὸ art. nom. neut. sg. ὁ ἡ τό the, this, that, he, she, it
κάλυμμα n. nom. neut. sg. κάλυμμα vail
17 ὁ art. nom. masc. sg. ὁ ἡ τό the, this, that, he, she, it
δὲ conj. δέ but, and, now, also, to the contrary, rather, then
Κύριος n. nom. masc. sg. κύριος Lord, lord, master, sir, LORD, God, Master, owner
τὸ art. nom. neut. sg. ὁ ἡ τό the, this, that, he, she, it
Πνεῦμά n. nom. neut. sg. πνεῦμα spirit, Spirit, Ghost, ghost, life. of the spirit, wind
οὗ adv. οὗ where, whither, wherein
δὲ conj. δέ but, and, now, also, to the contrary, rather, then
τὸ art. nom. neut. sg. ὁ ἡ τό the, this, that, he, she, it
Πνεῦμά n. nom. neut. sg. πνεῦμα spirit, Spirit, Ghost, ghost, life. of the spirit, wind
Κυρίου n. gen. masc. sg. κύριος Lord, lord, master, sir, LORD, God, Master, owner
ἐκεῖ adv. ἐκεῖ there, thither, thitherward, yonder, yonder place
ἐλευθερία n. nom. fem. sg. ἐλευθερία liberty
18 ἡμεῖς pron. nom. 1p. pl. ἐγώ I
δὲ conj. δέ but, and, now, also, to the contrary, rather, then
πάντες adj. nom. masc. pl. πᾶς πᾶσα πᾶν all, every, whosoever, every one, no, whole, any
προσώπῳ n. dat. neut. sg. πρόσωπον face, presence, person, countenance
τὴν art. acc. fem. sg. ὁ ἡ τό the, this, that, he, she, it
δόξαν n. acc. fem. sg. δόξα glory, honour, praise, dignity, worship
Κυρίου n. gen. masc. sg. κύριος Lord, lord, master, sir, LORD, God, Master, owner
τὴν art. acc. fem. sg. ὁ ἡ τό the, this, that, he, she, it
αὐτὴν adj. acc. fem. sg. αὐτός ή ό self, of oneself, even, very, the same, he, she, it
εἰκόνα n. acc. fem. sg. εἰκών image
ἀπὸ prep. ἀπό (+gen) from, of, out of, since, for, off, at, by, in, on
δόξης n. gen. fem. sg. δόξα glory, honour, praise, dignity, worship
εἰς prep. εἰς (+acc) into, to, unto, for, in, on, toward, against, upon, at, among
δόξαν n. acc. fem. sg. δόξα glory, honour, praise, dignity, worship
καθάπερ adv. καθάπερ even as, as, as well as
ἀπὸ prep. ἀπό (+gen) from, of, out of, since, for, off, at, by, in, on
Κυρίου n. gen. masc. sg. κύριος Lord, lord, master, sir, LORD, God, Master, owner
Πνεύματος n. gen. neut. sg. πνεῦμα spirit, Spirit, Ghost, ghost, life. of the spirit, wind

4

1 Διὰ prep. διά (+gen) by, through, with, in, of, (+acc) for, because of, for a cause

τοῦτο demo. pron. acc. neut. sg. οὗτος αὕτη τοῦτο this, the same, this same, he, she, it
τὴν art. acc. fem. sg. ὁ ἡ τό the, this, that, he, she, it
διακονίαν n. acc. fem. sg. διακονία ministry, administration, service, office, relief
ταύτην demo. pron. acc. fem. sg. οὗτος αὕτη τοῦτο this, the same, this same, he, she, it
καθὼς adv. καθώς as, even as, according as, according to
οὐκ particle of negation. οὐ οὐκ οὐχ not, no, neither, none, nay, nor, never, nothing
2 ἀλλ' conj. ἀλλά but, yea, yet, nevertheless, howbeit, nay, therefore
τὰ art. acc. neut. pl. ὁ ἡ τό the, this, that, he, she, it
κρυπτὰ adj. acc. neut. pl. κρυπτός secret, hid, hidden, inwardly
τῆς art. gen. fem. sg. ὁ ἡ τό the, this, that, he, she, it
αἰσχύνης n. gen. fem. sg. αἰσχύνη shame, dishonesty
μὴ particle of negation. μή not, no, lest, neither, none, nothing, nor, never, without
ἐν prep. ἐν (+dat) in, by, with, among, at, on, through, to, within, into, of, for
πανουργίᾳ n. dat. fem. sg. πανουργία craftiness, cunning craftiness, subtilty
μηδὲ conj. μηδέ neither, nor, not, no not, nor yet, not once, not so much as
τὸν art. acc. masc. sg. ὁ ἡ τό the, this, that, he, she, it
λόγον n. acc. masc. sg. λόγος word, saying, account, speech, thing, matter
τοῦ art. gen. masc. sg. ὁ ἡ τό the, this, that, he, she, it
Θεοῦ n. gen. masc. sg. θεός God, god
ἀλλὰ conj. ἀλλά but, yea, yet, nevertheless, howbeit, nay, therefore
τῇ art. dat. fem. sg. ὁ ἡ τό the, this, that, he, she, it
φανερώσει n. dat. fem. sg. φανέρωσις manifestation
τῆς art. gen. fem. sg. ὁ ἡ τό the, this, that, he, she, it
ἀληθείας n. gen. fem. sg. ἀλήθεια truth, verity
ἑαυτοὺς reflexive pron. acc. masc. 3p. pl. ἑαυτοῦ himself, herself, itself, yourself, ourselves
πρὸς prep. πρός (+gen) for, (+dat) at, (+acc) unto, to, with, for, against
πᾶσαν adj. acc. fem. sg. πᾶς πᾶςα πᾶν all, every, whosoever, every one, no, whole, any
συνείδησιν n. acc. fem. sg. συνείδησις conscience
ἀνθρώπων n. gen. masc. pl. ἄνθρωπος man, human being, person, one, certain
ἐνώπιον prep. ἐνώπιον (+gen) before, in the sight of, in the presence of. (adv.) before
τοῦ art. gen. masc. sg. ὁ ἡ τό the, this, that, he, she, it
Θεοῦ n. gen. masc. sg. θεός God, god
3 εἰ conj. εἰ if, whether, that, though, forasmuch
δὲ conj. δέ but, and, now, also, to the contrary, rather, then
καὶ conj. καί and, even, also, but
τὸ art. nom. neut. sg. ὁ ἡ τό the, this, that, he, she, it
εὐαγγέλιον n. nom. neut. sg. εὐαγγέλιον gospel
ἡμῶν pron. gen. 1p. pl. ἐγώ I
ἐν prep. ἐν (+dat) in, by, with, among, at, on, through, to, within, into, of, for
τοῖς art. dat. masc. pl. ὁ ἡ τό the, this, that, he, she, it
4 ἐν prep. ἐν (+dat) in, by, with, among, at, on, through, to, within, into, of, for
οἷς relative pron. dat. masc. pl. ὅς ἥ ὅ who, which, what, that
ὁ art. nom. masc. sg. ὁ ἡ τό the, this, that, he, she, it
Θεὸς n. nom. masc. sg. θεός God, god
τοῦ art. gen. masc. sg. ὁ ἡ τό the, this, that, he, she, it
αἰῶνος n. gen. masc. sg. αἰών ever, ever and ever, evermore, age, eternal, world
τούτου demo. pron. gen. masc. sg. οὗτος αὕτη τοῦτο this, the same, this same, he, she, it
τὰ art. acc. neut. pl. ὁ ἡ τό the, this, that, he, she, it
νοήματα n. acc. neut. pl. νόημα mind, device, thought
τῶν art. gen. masc. pl. ὁ ἡ τό the, this, that, he, she, it
ἀπίστων adj. gen. masc. pl. ἄπιστος faithless, unbelieving, infidel, thing incredible
εἰς prep. εἰς (+acc) into, to, unto, for, in, on, toward, against, upon, at, among
τὸ art. acc. neut. sg. ὁ ἡ τό the, this, that, he, she, it
μὴ particle of negation. μή not, no, lest, neither, none, nothing, nor, never, without
αὐτοῖς pron. dat. masc. 3p. pl. αὐτός ή ό self, of oneself, even, very, the same, he, she, it

τὸν art. acc. masc. sg. ὁ ἡ τό the, this, that, he, she, it
φωτισμὸν n. acc. masc. sg. φωτισμός light
τοῦ art. gen. neut. sg. ὁ ἡ τό the, this, that, he, she, it
εὐαγγελίου n. gen. neut. sg. εὐαγγέλιον gospel
τῆς art. gen. fem. sg. ὁ ἡ τό the, this, that, he, she, it
δόξης n. gen. fem. sg. δόξα glory, honour, praise, dignity, worship
τοῦ art. gen. neut. sg. ὁ ἡ τό the, this, that, he, she, it
Χριστοῦ n. gen. masc. sg. Χριστός Christ
ὅς relative pron. nom. masc. sg. ὅς ἥ ὅ who, which, what, that
εἰκὼν n. nom. fem. sg. εἰκών image
τοῦ art. gen. neut. sg. ὁ ἡ τό the, this, that, he, she, it
Θεοῦ n. gen. masc. sg. θεός God, god
5 οὐ particle of negation. οὐ οὐκ οὐχ not, no, neither, none, nay, nor, never, nothing
γὰρ conj. γάρ for, and, because, but, indeed
ἑαυτοὺς reflexive pron. acc. masc. 3p. pl. ἑαυτοῦ himself, herself, itself, yourself, ourselves
ἀλλὰ conj. ἀλλά but, yea, yet, nevertheless, howbeit, nay, therefore
Χριστὸν n. acc. masc. sg. Χριστός Christ
Ἰησοῦν n. acc. masc. sg. Ἰησοῦς Jesus
Κύριον n. acc. masc. sg. κύριος Lord, lord, master, sir, LORD, God, Master, owner
ἑαυτοὺς reflexive pron. acc. masc. 3p. pl. ἑαυτοῦ himself, herself, itself, yourself, ourselves
δὲ conj. δέ but, and, now, also, to the contrary, rather, then
δούλους n. acc. masc. pl. δοῦλος servant, bondman, bond, slave
ὑμῶν pron. gen. 2p. pl. σύ thou, you
διὰ prep. διά (+gen) by, through, with, in, of, (+acc) for, because of, for a cause
Ἰησοῦν n. acc. masc. sg. Ἰησοῦς Jesus
6 ὅτι conj. ὅτι that, for, because, how that, how, because that, for that, though
ὁ art. nom. masc. sg. ὁ ἡ τό the, this, that, he, she, it
Θεὸς n. nom. masc. sg. θεός God, god
ὁ art. nom. masc. sg. ὁ ἡ τό the, this, that, he, she, it
ἐκ prep. ἐκ ἐξ (+gen) of, from, out of, by, on, with, in, among, through
σκότους n. gen. neut. sg. σκότος darkness
φῶς n. nom. neut. sg. φῶς light, fire
ὅς relative pron. nom. masc. sg. ὅς ἥ ὅ who, which, what, that
ἐν prep. ἐν (+dat) in, by, with, among, at, on, through, to, within, into, of, for
ταῖς art. dat. fem. pl. ὁ ἡ τό the, this, that, he, she, it
καρδίαις n. dat. fem. pl. καρδία heart
ἡμῶν pron. gen. 1p. pl. ἐγώ I
πρὸς prep. πρός (+gen) for, (+dat) at, (+acc) unto, to, with, for, against
φωτισμὸν n. acc. masc. sg. φωτισμός light
τῆς art. gen. fem. sg. ὁ ἡ τό the, this, that, he, she, it
γνώσεως n. gen. fem. sg. γνῶσις knowledge, science
τῆς art. gen. fem. sg. ὁ ἡ τό the, this, that, he, she, it
δόξης n. gen. fem. sg. δόξα glory, honour, praise, dignity, worship
τοῦ art. gen. masc. sg. ὁ ἡ τό the, this, that, he, she, it
Θεοῦ n. gen. masc. sg. θεός God, god
ἐν prep. ἐν (+dat) in, by, with, among, at, on, through, to, within, into, of, for
προσώπῳ n. dat. neut. sg. πρόσωπον face, presence, person, countenance
Ἰησοῦ n. gen. masc. sg. Ἰησοῦς Jesus
Χριστοῦ n. gen. masc. sg. Χριστός Christ
7 δὲ conj. δέ but, and, now, also, to the contrary, rather, then
τὸν art. acc. masc. sg. ὁ ἡ τό the, this, that, he, she, it
θησαυρὸν n. acc. masc. sg. θησαυρός treasure
τοῦτον demo. pron. acc. masc. sg. οὗτος αὕτη τοῦτο this, the same, this same, he, she, it
ἐν prep. ἐν (+dat) in, by, with, among, at, on, through, to, within, into, of, for
ὀστρακίνοις adj. dat. neut. pl. ὀστράκινος earthen, of earth

σκεύεσιν n. dat. neut. pl. σκεῦος vessel, good, sail, stuff
ἵνα conj. ἵνα that, to, lest, for to, so that, albeit, because, for, so as
ἡ art. nom. fem. sg. ὁ ἡ τό the, this, that, he, she, it
ὑπερβολὴ n. nom. fem. sg. ὑπερβολή abundance, beyond measure, exceeding, excellency
τῆς art. gen. fem. sg. ὁ ἡ τό the, this, that, he, she, it
δυνάμεως n. gen. fem. sg. δύναμις power, mighty work, miracle, strength, might
τοῦ art. gen. masc. sg. ὁ ἡ τό the, this, that, he, she, it
Θεοῦ n. gen. masc. sg. θεός God, god
καὶ conj. καί and, even, also, but
μὴ particle of negation. μή not, no, lest, neither, none, nothing, nor, never, without
ἐξ prep. ἐκ ἐξ (+gen) of, from, out of, by, on, with, in, among, through
ἡμῶν pron. gen. 1p. pl. ἐγώ I
8 ἐν prep. ἐν (+dat) in, by, with, among, at, on, through, to, within, into, of, for
παντὶ adj. dat. neut. sg. πᾶς πᾶσα πᾶν all, every, whosoever, every one, no, whole, any
ἀλλ' conj. ἀλλά but, yea, yet, nevertheless, howbeit, nay, therefore
οὐ particle of negation. οὐ οὐκ οὐχ not, no, neither, none, nay, nor, never, nothing
ἀλλ' conj. ἀλλά but, yea, yet, nevertheless, howbeit, nay, therefore
οὐκ particle of negation. οὐ οὐκ οὐχ not, no, neither, none, nay, nor, never, nothing
9 ἀλλ' conj. ἀλλά but, yea, yet, nevertheless, howbeit, nay, therefore
οὐκ particle of negation. οὐ οὐκ οὐχ not, no, neither, none, nay, nor, never, nothing
ἀλλ' conj. ἀλλά but, yea, yet, nevertheless, howbeit, nay, therefore
οὐκ particle of negation. οὐ οὐκ οὐχ not, no, neither, none, nay, nor, never, nothing
10 πάντοτε adv. πάντοτε always, ever, always, evermore
τὴν art. acc. fem. sg. ὁ ἡ τό the, this, that, he, she, it
νέκρωσιν n. acc. fem. sg. νέκρωσις deadness, dying
τοῦ art. gen. masc. sg. ὁ ἡ τό the, this, that, he, she, it
Κυρίου n. gen. masc. sg. κύριος Lord, lord, master, sir, LORD, God, Master, owner
'Ιησοῦ n. gen. masc. sg. 'Ιησοῦς Jesus
ἐν prep. ἐν (+dat) in, by, with, among, at, on, through, to, within, into, of, for
τῷ art. dat. neut. sg. ὁ ἡ τό the, this, that, he, she, it
σώματι n. dat. neut. sg. σῶμα body, bodily, slave
ἵνα conj. ἵνα that, to, lest, for to, so that, albeit, because, for, so as
καὶ conj. καί and, even, also, but
ἡ art. nom. fem. sg. ὁ ἡ τό the, this, that, he, she, it
ζωὴ n. nom. fem. sg. ζωή life, lifetime
τοῦ art. gen. masc. sg. ὁ ἡ τό the, this, that, he, she, it
'Ιησοῦ n. gen. masc. sg. 'Ιησοῦς Jesus
ἐν prep. ἐν (+dat) in, by, with, among, at, on, through, to, within, into, of, for
τῷ art. dat. neut. sg. ὁ ἡ τό the, this, that, he, she, it
σώματι n. dat. neut. sg. σῶμα body, bodily, slave
ἡμῶν pron. gen. 1p. pl. ἐγώ I
11 ἀεὶ adv. ἀεί always, always, ever
γὰρ conj. γάρ for, and, because, but, indeed
ἡμεῖς pron. nom. 1p. pl. ἐγώ I
οἱ art. nom. masc. pl. ὁ ἡ τό the, this, that, he, she, it
εἰς prep. εἰς (+acc) into, to, unto, for, in, on, toward, against, upon, at, among
θάνατον n. acc. masc. sg. θάνατος death
διὰ prep. διά (+gen) by, through, with, in, of, (+acc) for, because of, for a cause
'Ιησοῦν n. acc. masc. sg. 'Ιησοῦς Jesus
ἵνα conj. ἵνα that, to, lest, for to, so that, albeit, because, for, so as
καὶ conj. καί and, even, also, but
ἡ art. nom. fem. sg. ὁ ἡ τό the, this, that, he, she, it
ζωὴ n. nom. fem. sg. ζωή life, lifetime
τοῦ art. gen. masc. sg. ὁ ἡ τό the, this, that, he, she, it
'Ιησοῦ n. gen. masc. sg. 'Ιησοῦς Jesus

ἐν prep. ἐν (+dat) in, by, with, among, at, on, through, to, within, into, of, for
τῇ art. dat. fem. sg. ὁ ἡ τό the, this, that, he, she, it
θνητῇ adj. dat. fem. sg. θνητός mortal, mortality
σαρκὶ n. dat. fem. sg. σάρξ flesh, carnal
ἡμῶν pron. gen. 1p. pl. ἐγώ I
12 ὥστε conj. ὥστε so that, wherefore, insomuch that, therefore, that, so then
ὁ art. nom. masc. sg. ὁ ἡ τό the, this, that, he, she, it
μὲν conj. μέν indeed, verily, truly, even, so, some
θάνατος n. nom. masc. sg. θάνατος death
ἐν prep. ἐν (+dat) in, by, with, among, at, on, through, to, within, into, of, for
ἡμῖν pron. dat. 1p. pl. ἐγώ I
ἡ art. nom. fem. sg. ὁ ἡ τό the, this, that, he, she, it
δὲ conj. δέ but, and, now, also, to the contrary, rather, then
ζωὴ n. nom. fem. sg. ζωή life, lifetime
ἐν prep. ἐν (+dat) in, by, with, among, at, on, through, to, within, into, of, for
ὑμῖν pron. dat. 2p. pl. σύ thou, you
13 δὲ conj. δέ but, and, now, also, to the contrary, rather, then
τὸ art. acc. neut. sg. ὁ ἡ τό the, this, that, he, she, it
αὐτὸ pron. acc. neut. 3p. sg. αὐτός ἡ ὁ self, of oneself, even, very, the same, he, she, it
πνεῦμα n. acc. neut. sg. πνεῦμα spirit, Spirit, Ghost, ghost, life. of the spirit, wind
τῆς art. gen. fem. sg. ὁ ἡ τό the, this, that, he, she, it
πίστεως n. gen. fem. sg. πίστις faith, assurance, belief, fidelity
κατὰ prep. κατά (+gen) against, by, throughout, down, (+acc) according to, after, with
τὸ art. acc. neut. sg. ὁ ἡ τό the, this, that, he, she, it
διὸ conj. διό wherefore, therefore, for which cause
καὶ conj. καί and, even, also, but
ἡμεῖς pron. nom. 1p. pl. ἐγώ I
διὸ conj. διό wherefore, therefore, for which cause
καὶ conj. καί and, even, also, but
14 ὅτι conj. ὅτι that, for, because, how that, how, because that, for that, though
ὁ art. nom. masc. sg. ὁ ἡ τό the, this, that, he, she, it
τὸν art. acc. masc. sg. ὁ ἡ τό the, this, that, he, she, it
Κύριον n. acc. masc. sg. κύριος Lord, lord, master, sir, LORD, God, Master, owner
Ἰησοῦν n. acc. masc. sg. Ἰησοῦς Jesus
καὶ conj. καί and, even, also, but
ἡμᾶς pron. acc. 1p. pl. ἐγώ I
διὰ prep. διά (+gen) by, through, with, in, of, (+acc) for, because of, for a cause
Ἰησοῦ n. dat. masc. sg. Ἰησοῦς Jesus
καὶ conj. καί and, even, also, but
σὺν prep. σύν (+dat) with, beside
ὑμῖν pron. dat. 2p. pl. σύ thou, you
15 τὰ art. nom. neut. pl. ὁ ἡ τό the, this, that, he, she, it
γὰρ conj. γάρ for, and, because, but, indeed
πάντα adj. nom. neut. pl. πᾶς πᾶσα πᾶν all, every, whosoever, every one, no, whole, any
δι' prep. διά (+gen) by, through, with, in, of, (+acc) for, because of, for a cause
ὑμᾶς pron. acc. 2p. pl. σύ thou, you
ἵνα conj. ἵνα that, to, lest, for to, so that, albeit, because, for, so as
ἡ art. nom. fem. sg. ὁ ἡ τό the, this, that, he, she, it
χάρις n. nom. fem. sg. χάρις grace, thank, favour, pleasure
διὰ prep. διά (+gen) by, through, with, in, of, (+acc) for, because of, for a cause
τῶν art. gen. masc. pl. ὁ ἡ τό the, this, that, he, she, it
πλειόνων compar. adj. gen. masc. pl. πολύς many, great, much, long, abundant
τὴν art. acc. fem. sg. ὁ ἡ τό the, this, that, he, she, it
εὐχαριστίαν n. acc. fem. sg. εὐχαριστία thankfulness, thanksgiving, giving of thanks
εἰς prep. εἰς (+acc) into, to, unto, for, in, on, toward, against, upon, at, among

τὴν art. acc. fem. sg. ὁ ἡ τό the, this, that, he, she, it
δόξαν n. acc. fem. sg. δόξα glory, honour, praise, dignity, worship
τοῦ art. gen. masc. sg. ὁ ἡ τό the, this, that, he, she, it
Θεοῦ n. gen. masc. sg. θεός God, god
16 Διὸ conj. διό wherefore, therefore, for which cause
οὐκ particle of negation. οὐ οὐκ οὐχ not, no, neither, none, nay, nor, never, nothing
ἀλλ' conj. ἀλλά but, yea, yet, nevertheless, howbeit, nay, therefore
εἰ conj. εἰ if, whether, that, though, forasmuch
καὶ conj. καί and, even, also, but
ὁ art. nom. masc. sg. ὁ ἡ τό the, this, that, he, she, it
ἔξω adv. ἔξω out, without, out of, forth, away, outward
ἡμῶν pron. gen. 1p. pl. ἐγώ I
ἄνθρωπος n. nom. masc. sg. ἄνθρωπος man, human being, person, one, certain
ἀλλ' conj. ἀλλά but, yea, yet, nevertheless, howbeit, nay, therefore
ὁ art. nom. masc. sg. ὁ ἡ τό the, this, that, he, she, it
ἔσωθεν adv. ἔσωθεν within, from within, inward, inwardly
ἡμέρᾳ n. dat. fem. sg. ἡμέρα day, time, year, while, age, day time
καὶ conj. καί and, even, also, but
ἡμέρᾳ n. dat. fem. sg. ἡμέρα day, time, year, while, age, day time
17 τὸ art. nom. neut. sg. ὁ ἡ τό the, this, that, he, she, it
γὰρ conj. γάρ for, and, because, but, indeed
παραυτίκα adv. παραυτίκα momentary, instantly, immediately
ἐλαφρὸν adj. nom. neut. sg. ἐλαφρός light
τῆς art. gen. fem. sg. ὁ ἡ τό the, this, that, he, she, it
θλίψεως n. gen. fem. sg. θλῖψις tribulation, affliction, anguish, persecution
ἡμῶν pron. gen. 1p. pl. ἐγώ I
καθ' prep. κατά (+gen) against, by, throughout, down, (+acc) according to, after, with
ὑπερβολὴν n. acc. fem. sg. ὑπερβολή abundance, beyond measure, exceeding, excellency
εἰς prep. εἰς (+acc) into, to, unto, for, in, on, toward, against, upon, at, among
ὑπερβολὴν n. acc. fem. sg. ὑπερβολή abundance, beyond measure, exceeding, excellency
αἰώνιον adj. acc. neut. sg. αἰώνιος eternal, everlasting, world, for ever
βάρος n. acc. neut. sg. βάρος burden, burdensome, weight
δόξης n. gen. fem. sg. δόξα glory, honour, praise, dignity, worship
ἡμῖν pron. dat. 1p. pl. ἐγώ I
18 μὴ particle of negation. μή not, no, lest, neither, none, nothing, nor, never, without
ἡμῶν pron. gen. 1p. pl. ἐγώ I
τὰ art. acc. neut. pl. ὁ ἡ τό the, this, that, he, she, it
ἀλλὰ conj. ἀλλά but, yea, yet, nevertheless, howbeit, nay, therefore
τὰ art. acc. neut. pl. ὁ ἡ τό the, this, that, he, she, it
μὴ particle of negation. μή not, no, lest, neither, none, nothing, nor, never, without
τὰ art. nom. neut. pl. ὁ ἡ τό the, this, that, he, she, it
γὰρ conj. γάρ for, and, because, but, indeed
πρόσκαιρα adj. nom. neut. pl. πρόσκαιρος endure but for a time, for a season, temporal
τὰ art. nom. neut. pl. ὁ ἡ τό the, this, that, he, she, it
δὲ conj. δέ but, and, now, also, to the contrary, rather, then
μὴ particle of negation. μή not, no, lest, neither, none, nothing, nor, never, without
αἰώνια adj. nom. neut. pl. αἰώνιος eternal, everlasting, world, for ever

5

1 γὰρ conj. γάρ for, and, because, but, indeed
ὅτι conj. ὅτι that, for, because, how that, how, because that, for that, though
ἐὰν conj. ἐάν if, soever, except, though, and if, but, whether, if so, so
ἡ art. nom. fem. sg. ὁ ἡ τό the, this, that, he, she, it
ἐπίγειος adj. nom. fem. sg. ἐπίγειος earthly, terrestrial, in earth

ἡμῶν pron. gen. 1p. pl. ἐγώ I
οἰκία n. nom. fem. sg. οἰκία house, home, household
τοῦ art. gen. neut. sg. ὁ ἡ τό the, this, that, he, she, it
σκήνους n. gen. neut. sg. σκῆνος tabernacle
οἰκοδομὴν n. acc. fem. sg. οἰκοδομή building, edifying, edification
ἐκ prep. ἐκ ἐξ (+gen) of, from, out of, by, on, with, in, among, through
Θεοῦ n. gen. masc. sg. θεός God, god
οἰκίαν n. acc. fem. sg. οἰκία house, home, household
ἀχειροποίητον adj. acc. fem. sg. ἀχειροποίητος made without hands
αἰώνιον adj. acc. fem. sg. αἰώνιος eternal, everlasting, world, for ever
ἐν prep. ἐν (+dat) in, by, with, among, at, on, through, to, within, into, of, for
τοῖς art. dat. masc. pl. ὁ ἡ τό the, this, that, he, she, it
οὐρανοῖς n. dat. masc. pl. οὐρανός heaven, air, sky
2 καὶ conj. καί and, even, also, but
γὰρ conj. γάρ for, and, because, but, indeed
ἐν prep. ἐν (+dat) in, by, with, among, at, on, through, to, within, into, of, for
τούτῳ demo. pron. dat. neut. sg. οὗτος αὕτη τοῦτο this, the same, this same, he, she, it
τὸ art. acc. neut. sg. ὁ ἡ τό the, this, that, he, she, it
οἰκητήριον n. acc. neut. sg. οἰκητήριον house, habitation
ἡμῶν pron. gen. 1p. pl. ἐγώ I
τὸ art. acc. neut. sg. ὁ ἡ τό the, this, that, he, she, it
ἐξ prep. ἐκ ἐξ (+gen) of, from, out of, by, on, with, in, among, through
οὐρανοῦ n. gen. masc. sg. οὐρανός heaven, air, sky
3 εἴ conj. εἰ if, whether, that, though, forasmuch
γε particle. γέ yet, and beside, at least, doubtless
καὶ conj. καί and, even, also, but
οὐ particle of negation. οὐ οὐκ οὐχ not, no, neither, none, nay, nor, never, nothing
γυμνοὶ adj. nom. masc. pl. γυμνός naked, bare
4 καὶ conj. καί and, even, also, but
γὰρ conj. γάρ for, and, because, but, indeed
οἱ art. nom. masc. pl. ὁ ἡ τό the, this, that, he, she, it
ἐν prep. ἐν (+dat) in, by, with, among, at, on, through, to, within, into, of, for
τῷ art. dat. neut. sg. ὁ ἡ τό the, this, that, he, she, it
σκήνει n. dat. neut. sg. σκῆνος tabernacle
ἐφ' prep. ἐπί (+gen) on, in, upon, (+dat) in, at, for, upon, (+acc) on, upon, unto, to, against
ᾧ relative pron. dat. neut. sg. ὅς ἥ ὅ who, which, what, that
οὐ particle of negation. οὐ οὐκ οὐχ not, no, neither, none, nay, nor, never, nothing
ἀλλ' conj. ἀλλά but, yea, yet, nevertheless, howbeit, nay, therefore
ἵνα conj. ἵνα that, to, lest, for to, so that, albeit, because, for, so as
τὸ art. nom. neut. sg. ὁ ἡ τό the, this, that, he, she, it
θνητὸν adj. nom. neut. sg. θνητός mortal, mortality
ὑπὸ prep. ὑπό (+gen) of, by, with, from, among, (+acc) under
τῆς art. gen. fem. sg. ὁ ἡ τό the, this, that, he, she, it
ζωῆς n. gen. fem. sg. ζωή life, lifetime
5 ὁ art. nom. masc. sg. ὁ ἡ τό the, this, that, he, she, it
δὲ conj. δέ but, and, now, also, to the contrary, rather, then
ἡμᾶς pron. acc. 1p. pl. ἐγώ I
εἰς prep. εἰς (+acc) into, to, unto, for, in, on, toward, against, upon, at, among
αὐτὸ pron. acc. neut. 3p. sg. αὐτός ἡ ὁ self, of oneself, even, very, the same, he, she, it
τοῦτο demo. pron. acc. neut. sg. οὗτος αὕτη τοῦτο this, the same, this same, he, she, it
Θεός n. nom. masc. sg. θεός God, god
ὁ art. nom. masc. sg. ὁ ἡ τό the, this, that, he, she, it
καὶ conj. καί and, even, also, but
ἡμῖν pron. dat. 1p. pl. ἐγώ I
τὸν art. acc. masc. sg. ὁ ἡ τό the, this, that, he, she, it

ἀρραβῶνα n. acc. masc. sg. ἀρραβών earnest
τοῦ art. gen. neut. sg. ὁ ἡ τό the, this, that, he, she, it
Πνεύματος n. gen. neut. sg. πνεῦμα spirit, Spirit, Ghost, ghost, life. of the spirit, wind
6 οὖν conj. οὖν therefore, then, so, and, now, wherefore
πάντοτε adv. πάντοτε always, ever, always, evermore
καὶ conj. καί and, even, also, but
ὅτι conj. ὅτι that, for, because, how that, how, because that, for that, though
ἐν prep. ἐν (+dat) in, by, with, among, at, on, through, to, within, into, of, for
τῷ art. dat. neut. sg. ὁ ἡ τό the, this, that, he, she, it
σώματι n. dat. neut. sg. σῶμα body, bodily, slave
ἀπὸ prep. ἀπό (+gen) from, of, out of, since, for, off, at, by, in, on
τοῦ art. gen. masc. sg. ὁ ἡ τό the, this, that, he, she, it
Κυρίου n. gen. masc. sg. κύριος Lord, lord, master, sir, LORD, God, Master, owner
7 διὰ prep. διά (+gen) by, through, with, in, of, (+acc) for, because of, for a cause
πίστεως n. gen. fem. sg. πίστις faith, assurance, belief, fidelity
γὰρ conj. γάρ for, and, because, but, indeed
οὐ particle of negation. οὐ οὐκ οὐχ not, no, neither, none, nay, nor, never, nothing
διὰ prep. διά (+gen) by, through, with, in, of, (+acc) for, because of, for a cause
εἴδους n. gen. neut. sg. εἶδος shape, appearance, fashion, sight
8 δὲ conj. δέ but, and, now, also, to the contrary, rather, then
καὶ conj. καί and, even, also, but
μᾶλλον adv. μᾶλλον rather, more, more and more, better, much, much the more
ἐκ prep. ἐκ ἐξ (+gen) of, from, out of, by, on, with, in, among, through
τοῦ art. gen. neut. sg. ὁ ἡ τό the, this, that, he, she, it
σώματος n. gen. neut. sg. σῶμα body, bodily, slave
καὶ conj. καί and, even, also, but
πρὸς prep. πρός (+gen) for, (+dat) at, (+acc) unto, to, with, for, against
τὸν art. acc. masc. sg. ὁ ἡ τό the, this, that, he, she, it
Κύριον n. acc. masc. sg. κύριος Lord, lord, master, sir, LORD, God, Master, owner
9 διὸ conj. διό wherefore, therefore, for which cause
καὶ conj. καί and, even, also, but
εἴτε conj. εἴτε whether
εἴτε conj. εἴτε whether
εὐάρεστοι adj. nom. masc. pl. εὐάρεστος acceptable, wellpleasing, accepted, please well
αὐτῷ pron. dat. masc. 3p. sg. αὐτός ή ό self, of oneself, even, very, the same, he, she, it
10 τοὺς art. acc. masc. pl. ὁ ἡ τό the, this, that, he, she, it
γὰρ conj. γάρ for, and, because, but, indeed
πάντας adj. acc. masc. pl. πᾶς πᾶσα πᾶν all, every, whosoever, every one, no, whole, any
ἡμᾶς pron. acc. 1p. pl. ἐγώ I
ἔμπροσθεν prep. ἔμπροσθεν (+gen) before, in the sight of, in the presence of
τοῦ art. gen. neut. sg. ὁ ἡ τό the, this, that, he, she, it
βήματος n. gen. neut. sg. βῆμα judgment seat, throne
τοῦ art. gen. masc. sg. ὁ ἡ τό the, this, that, he, she, it
Χριστοῦ n. gen. masc. sg. Χριστός Christ
ἵνα conj. ἵνα that, to, lest, for to, so that, albeit, because, for, so as
ἕκαστος adj. nom. masc. sg. ἕκαστος every man, every, every one, any man, each
τὰ art. acc. neut. pl. ὁ ἡ τό the, this, that, he, she, it
διὰ prep. διά (+gen) by, through, with, in, of, (+acc) for, because of, for a cause
τοῦ art. gen. neut. sg. ὁ ἡ τό the, this, that, he, she, it
σώματος n. gen. neut. sg. σῶμα body, bodily, slave
πρὸς prep. πρός (+gen) for, (+dat) at, (+acc) unto, to, with, for, against
ἃ relative pron. acc. neut. pl. ὅς ἥ ὅ who, which, what, that
εἴτε conj. εἴτε whether
ἀγαθὸν adj. acc. neut. sg. ἀγαθός good, good thing, that which is good, well
εἴτε conj. εἴτε whether

κακόν adj. acc. neut. sg. κακός evil, evil thing, noisome, wicked
11 οὖν conj. οὖν therefore, then, so, and, now, wherefore
τὸν art. acc. masc. sg. ὁ ἡ τό the, this, that, he, she, it
φόβον n. acc. masc. sg. φόβος fear, terror, sore afraid
τοῦ art. gen. masc. sg. ὁ ἡ τό the, this, that, he, she, it
Κυρίου n. gen. masc. sg. κύριος Lord, lord, master, sir, LORD, God, Master, owner
ἀνθρώπους n. acc. masc. pl. ἄνθρωπος man, human being, person, one, certain
Θεῷ n. dat. masc. sg. θεός God, god
δὲ conj. δέ but, and, now, also, to the contrary, rather, then
δὲ conj. δέ but, and, now, also, to the contrary, rather, then
καὶ conj. καί and, even, also, but
ἐν prep. ἐν (+dat) in, by, with, among, at, on, through, to, within, into, of, for
ταῖς art. dat. fem. pl. ὁ ἡ τό the, this, that, he, she, it
συνειδήσεσιν n. dat. fem. pl. συνείδησις conscience
ὑμῶν pron. gen. 2p. pl. σύ thou, you
12 οὐ particle of negation. οὐ οὐκ οὐχ not, no, neither, none, nay, nor, never, nothing
γὰρ conj. γάρ for, and, because, but, indeed
πάλιν adv. πάλιν again
ἑαυτοὺς reflexive pron. acc. masc. 3p. pl. ἑαυτοῦ himself, herself, itself, yourself, ourselves
ὑμῖν pron. dat. 2p. pl. σύ thou, you
ἀλλὰ conj. ἀλλά but, yea, yet, nevertheless, howbeit, nay, therefore
ἀφορμὴν n. acc. fem. sg. ἀφορμή occasion
ὑμῖν pron. dat. 2p. pl. σύ thou, you
καυχήματος n. gen. neut. sg. καύχημα whereof to glory, rejoicing, glorying, boasting
ὑπὲρ prep. ὑπέρ (+gen) for, of, for the sake of, (+acc) above, more than
ἡμῶν pron. gen. 1p. pl. ἐγώ I
ἵνα conj. ἵνα that, to, lest, for to, so that, albeit, because, for, so as
πρὸς prep. πρός (+gen) for, (+dat) at, (+acc) unto, to, with, for, against
τοὺς art. acc. masc. pl. ὁ ἡ τό the, this, that, he, she, it
ἐν prep. ἐν (+dat) in, by, with, among, at, on, through, to, within, into, of, for
προσώπῳ n. dat. neut. sg. πρόσωπον face, presence, person, countenance
καὶ conj. καί and, even, also, but
οὐ particle of negation. οὐ οὐκ οὐχ not, no, neither, none, nay, nor, never, nothing
καρδίᾳ n. dat. fem. sg. καρδία heart
13 εἴτε conj. εἴτε whether
γὰρ conj. γάρ for, and, because, but, indeed
Θεῷ n. dat. masc. sg. θεός God, god
εἴτε conj. εἴτε whether
ὑμῖν pron. dat. 2p. pl. σύ thou, you
14 ἡ art. nom. fem. sg. ὁ ἡ τό the, this, that, he, she, it
γὰρ conj. γάρ for, and, because, but, indeed
ἀγάπη n. nom. fem. sg. ἀγάπη love, charity, feast of charity
τοῦ art. gen. masc. sg. ὁ ἡ τό the, this, that, he, she, it
Χριστοῦ n. gen. masc. sg. Χριστός Christ
ἡμᾶς pron. acc. 1p. pl. ἐγώ I
τοῦτο demo. pron. acc. neut. sg. οὗτος αὕτη τοῦτο this, the same, this same, he, she, it
ὅτι conj. ὅτι that, for, because, how that, how, because that, for that, though
εἰ conj. εἰ if, whether, that, though, forasmuch
εἷς num. nom. masc. sg. εἷς or ἕν one, other, some, any, only, a certain
ὑπὲρ prep. ὑπέρ (+gen) for, of, for the sake of, (+acc) above, more than
πάντων adj. gen. masc. pl. πᾶς πᾶςa πᾶν all, every, whosoever, every one, no, whole, any
ἄρα conj. ἄρα then, therefore, haply, wherefore, perhaps, manner, no doubt, truly
οἱ art. nom. masc. pl. ὁ ἡ τό the, this, that, he, she, it
πάντες adj. nom. masc. pl. πᾶς πᾶςa πᾶν all, every, whosoever, every one, no, whole, any
15 καὶ conj. καί and, even, also, but

ὑπὲρ prep. ὑπέρ (+gen) for, of, for the sake of, (+acc) above, more than
πάντων adj. gen. masc. pl. πᾶς πᾶσα πᾶν all, every, whosoever, every one, no, whole, any
ἵνα conj. ἵνα that, to, lest, for to, so that, albeit, because, for, so as
οἱ art. nom. masc. pl. ὁ ἡ τό the, this, that, he, she, it
μηκέτι adv. μηκέτι no more, no longer, not any more, not henceforth, not henceforward
ἑαυτοῖς reflexive pron. dat. masc. 3p. pl. ἑαυτοῦ himself, herself, itself, yourself, ourselves
ἀλλὰ conj. ἀλλά but, yea, yet, nevertheless, howbeit, nay, therefore
τῷ art. dat. masc. sg. ὁ ἡ τό the, this, that, he, she, it
ὑπὲρ prep. ὑπέρ (+gen) for, of, for the sake of, (+acc) above, more than
αὐτῶν pron. gen. masc. 3p. pl. αὐτός ἡ ὁ self, of oneself, even, very, the same, he, she, it
καὶ conj. καί and, even, also, but
16 ὥστε conj. ὥστε so that, wherefore, insomuch that, therefore, that, so then
ἡμεῖς pron. nom. 1p. pl. ἐγώ I
ἀπὸ prep. ἀπό (+gen) from, of, out of, since, for, off, at, by, in, on
τοῦ art. gen. masc. sg. ὁ ἡ τό the, this, that, he, she, it
νῦν adv. νῦν now, henceforth, present, this time
οὐδένα num. acc. masc. sg. οὐδείς no man, nothing, no, none, neither, not, nought
κατὰ prep. κατά (+gen) against, by, throughout, down, (+acc) according to, after, with
σάρκα n. acc. fem. sg. σάρξ flesh, carnal
εἰ conj. εἰ if, whether, that, though, forasmuch
δὲ conj. δέ but, and, now, also, to the contrary, rather, then
καὶ conj. καί and, even, also, but
κατὰ prep. κατά (+gen) against, by, throughout, down, (+acc) according to, after, with
σάρκα n. acc. fem. sg. σάρξ flesh, carnal
Χριστόν n. acc. masc. sg. Χριστός Christ
ἀλλὰ conj. ἀλλά but, yea, yet, nevertheless, howbeit, nay, therefore
νῦν adv. νῦν now, henceforth, present, this time
οὐκέτι adv. οὐκέτι or οὐκ ἔτι no more, no longer, not any more
17 ὥστε conj. ὥστε so that, wherefore, insomuch that, therefore, that, so then
εἴ conj. εἰ if, whether, that, though, forasmuch
τις indefinite pron. nom. masc. sg. τὶς certain, some, any man, one, any thing
ἐν prep. ἐν (+dat) in, by, with, among, at, on, through, to, within, into, of, for
Χριστῷ n. dat. masc. sg. Χριστός Christ
καινὴ adj. nom. fem. sg. καινός new
κτίσις n. nom. fem. sg. κτίσις creature, creation, building, ordinance
τὰ art. nom. neut. pl. ὁ ἡ τό the, this, that, he, she, it
ἀρχαῖα adj. nom. neut. pl. ἀρχαῖος old, one of old time
καινά adj. nom. neut. pl. καινός new
τὰ art. nom. neut. pl. ὁ ἡ τό the, this, that, he, she, it
πάντα adj. nom. neut. pl. πᾶς πᾶσα πᾶν all, every, whosoever, every one, no, whole, any
18 τὰ art. nom. neut. pl. ὁ ἡ τό the, this, that, he, she, it
δὲ conj. δέ but, and, now, also, to the contrary, rather, then
πάντα adj. nom. neut. pl. πᾶς πᾶσα πᾶν all, every, whosoever, every one, no, whole, any
ἐκ prep. ἐκ ἐξ (+gen) of, from, out of, by, on, with, in, among, through
τοῦ art. gen. masc. sg. ὁ ἡ τό the, this, that, he, she, it
Θεοῦ n. gen. masc. sg. θεός God, god
τοῦ art. gen. masc. sg. ὁ ἡ τό the, this, that, he, she, it
ἡμᾶς pron. acc. 1p. pl. ἐγώ I
ἑαυτῷ reflexive pron. dat. masc. 3p. sg. ἑαυτοῦ himself, herself, itself, yourself, ourselves
διὰ prep. διά (+gen) by, through, with, in, of, (+acc) for, because of, for a cause
Ἰησοῦ n. gen. masc. sg. Ἰησοῦς Jesus
Χριστοῦ n. gen. masc. sg. Χριστός Christ
καὶ conj. καί and, even, also, but
ἡμῖν pron. dat. 1p. pl. ἐγώ I
τὴν art. acc. fem. sg. ὁ ἡ τό the, this, that, he, she, it

διακονίαν n. acc. fem. sg. διακονία ministry, administration, service, office, relief
τῆς art. gen. fem. sg. ὁ ἡ τό the, this, that, he, she, it
καταλλαγῆς n. gen. fem. sg. καταλλαγή reconciliation, atonement, reconciling
19 ὡς adv. ὡς as, when, as it were, how, about, like, as soon as, even as, while
ὅτι conj. ὅτι that, for, because, how that, how, because that, for that, though
Θεὸς n. nom. masc. sg. θεός God, god
ἐν prep. ἐν (+dat) in, by, with, among, at, on, through, to, within, into, of, for
Χριστῷ n. dat. masc. sg. Χριστός Christ
κόσμον n. acc. masc. sg. κόσμος world, adorning
ἑαυτῷ reflexive pron. dat. masc. 3p. sg. ἑαυτοῦ himself, herself, itself, yourself, ourselves
μὴ particle of negation. μή not, no, lest, neither, none, nothing, nor, never, without
αὐτοῖς pron. dat. masc. 3p. pl. αὐτός ή ό self, of oneself, even, very, the same, he, she, it
τὰ art. acc. neut. pl. ὁ ἡ τό the, this, that, he, she, it
παραπτώματα n. acc. neut. pl. παράπτωμα trespass, offence, sin, fall, fault
αὐτῶν pron. gen. masc. 3p. pl. αὐτός ή ό self, of oneself, even, very, the same, he, she, it
καὶ conj. καί and, even, also, but
ἐν prep. ἐν (+dat) in, by, with, among, at, on, through, to, within, into, of, for
ἡμῖν pron. dat. 1p. pl. ἐγώ I
τὸν art. acc. masc. sg. ὁ ἡ τό the, this, that, he, she, it
λόγον n. acc. masc. sg. λόγος word, saying, account, speech, thing, matter
τῆς art. gen. fem. sg. ὁ ἡ τό the, this, that, he, she, it
καταλλαγῆς n. gen. fem. sg. καταλλαγή reconciliation, atonement, reconciling
20 Ὑπὲρ prep. ὑπέρ (+gen) for, of, for the sake of, (+acc) above, more than
Χριστοῦ n. gen. masc. sg. Χριστός Christ
οὖν conj. οὖν therefore, then, so, and, now, wherefore
ὡς adv. ὡς as, when, as it were, how, about, like, as soon as, even as, while
τοῦ art. gen. masc. sg. ὁ ἡ τό the, this, that, he, she, it
Θεοῦ n. gen. masc. sg. θεός God, god
δι' prep. διά (+gen) by, through, with, in, of, (+acc) for, because of, for a cause
ἡμῶν pron. gen. 1p. pl. ἐγώ I
ὑπὲρ prep. ὑπέρ (+gen) for, of, for the sake of, (+acc) above, more than
Χριστοῦ n. gen. masc. sg. Χριστός Christ
τῷ art. dat. masc. sg. ὁ ἡ τό the, this, that, he, she, it
Θεῷ n. dat. masc. sg. θεός God, god
21 τὸν art. acc. masc. sg. ὁ ἡ τό the, this, that, he, she, it
γὰρ conj. γάρ for, and, because, but, indeed
μὴ particle of negation. μή not, no, lest, neither, none, nothing, nor, never, without
ἁμαρτίαν n. acc. fem. sg. ἁμαρτία sin, offence, sinful
ὑπὲρ prep. ὑπέρ (+gen) for, of, for the sake of, (+acc) above, more than
ἡμῶν pron. gen. 1p. pl. ἐγώ I
ἁμαρτίαν n. acc. fem. sg. ἁμαρτία sin, offence, sinful
ἵνα conj. ἵνα that, to, lest, for to, so that, albeit, because, for, so as
ἡμεῖς pron. nom. 1p. pl. ἐγώ I
δικαιοσύνη n. nom. fem. sg. δικαιοσύνη righteousness
Θεοῦ n. gen. masc. sg. θεός God, god
ἐν prep. ἐν (+dat) in, by, with, among, at, on, through, to, within, into, of, for
αὐτῷ pron. dat. masc. 3p. sg. αὐτός ή ό self, of oneself, even, very, the same, he, she, it

6

1 δὲ conj. δέ but, and, now, also, to the contrary, rather, then
καὶ conj. καί and, even, also, but
μὴ particle of negation. μή not, no, lest, neither, none, nothing, nor, never, without
εἰς prep. εἰς (+acc) into, to, unto, for, in, on, toward, against, upon, at, among
κενὸν adj. acc. neut. sg. κενός empty, vain, in vain

τὴν art. acc. fem. sg. ὁ ἡ τό the, this, that, he, she, it
χάριν n. acc. fem. sg. χάρις grace, thank, favour, pleasure
τοῦ art. gen. masc. sg. ὁ ἡ τό the, this, that, he, she, it
Θεοῦ n. gen. masc. sg. θεός God, god
ὑμᾶς pron. acc. 2p. pl. σύ thou, you
2 γάρ conj. γάρ for, and, because, but, indeed
Καιρῷ n. dat. masc. sg. καιρός time, season, due time, opportunity
δεκτῷ adj. dat. masc. sg. δεκτός acceptable, accepted
σου pron. gen. 2p. sg. σύ thou, you
καὶ conj. καί and, even, also, but
ἐν prep. ἐν (+dat) in, by, with, among, at, on, through, to, within, into, of, for
ἡμέρᾳ n. dat. fem. sg. ἡμέρα day, time, year, while, age, day time
σωτηρίας n. gen. fem. sg. σωτηρία salvation, deliver, health, saving
σοι pron. dat. 2p. sg. σύ thou, you
νῦν adv. νῦν now, henceforth, present, this time
καιρὸς n. nom. masc. sg. καιρός time, season, due time, opportunity
εὐπρόσδεκτος adj. nom. masc. sg. εὐπρόσδεκτος acceptable, accepted
νῦν adv. νῦν now, henceforth, present, this time
ἡμέρα n. nom. fem. sg. ἡμέρα day, time, year, while, age, day time
σωτηρίας n. gen. fem. sg. σωτηρία salvation, deliver, health, saving
3 μηδεμίαν num. acc. fem. sg. μηδείς μηδεμία μηδέν no man, nothing, no, none, not at all
ἐν prep. ἐν (+dat) in, by, with, among, at, on, through, to, within, into, of, for
μηδενὶ num. dat. masc. sg. μηδείς μηδεμία μηδέν no man, nothing, no, none, not at all
προσκοπήν n. acc. fem. sg. προσκοπή offence
ἵνα conj. ἵνα that, to, lest, for to, so that, albeit, because, for, so as
μὴ particle of negation. μή not, no, lest, neither, none, nothing, nor, never, without
ἡ art. nom. fem. sg. ὁ ἡ τό the, this, that, he, she, it
διακονία n. nom. fem. sg. διακονία ministry, administration, service, office, relief
4 ἀλλ' conj. ἀλλά but, yea, yet, nevertheless, howbeit, nay, therefore
ἐν prep. ἐν (+dat) in, by, with, among, at, on, through, to, within, into, of, for
παντὶ adj. dat. neut. sg. πᾶς πᾶσα πᾶν all, every, whosoever, every one, no, whole, any
ἑαυτοὺς reflexive pron. acc. masc. 3p. pl. ἑαυτοῦ himself, herself, itself, yourself, ourselves
ὡς adv. ὡς as, when, as it were, how, about, like, as soon as, even as, while
Θεοῦ n. gen. masc. sg. θεός God, god
διάκονοι n. nom. masc. pl. διάκονος minister, servant, deacon
ἐν prep. ἐν (+dat) in, by, with, among, at, on, through, to, within, into, of, for
ὑπομονῇ n. dat. fem. sg. ὑπομονή patience, enduring
πολλῇ adj. dat. fem. sg. πολύς many, great, much, long, abundant
ἐν prep. ἐν (+dat) in, by, with, among, at, on, through, to, within, into, of, for
θλίψεσιν n. dat. fem. pl. θλῖψις tribulation, affliction, anguish, persecution
ἐν prep. ἐν (+dat) in, by, with, among, at, on, through, to, within, into, of, for
ἀνάγκαις n. dat. fem. pl. ἀνάγκη must needs, necessity, distress, inevitable
ἐν prep. ἐν (+dat) in, by, with, among, at, on, through, to, within, into, of, for
στενοχωρίαις n. dat. fem. pl. στενοχωρία anguish, distress
5 ἐν prep. ἐν (+dat) in, by, with, among, at, on, through, to, within, into, of, for
πληγαῖς n. dat. fem. pl. πληγή wound, plague, stripe
ἐν prep. ἐν (+dat) in, by, with, among, at, on, through, to, within, into, of, for
φυλακαῖς n. dat. fem. pl. φυλακή prison, watch, imprisonment, cage, hold, ward
ἐν prep. ἐν (+dat) in, by, with, among, at, on, through, to, within, into, of, for
ἀκαταστασίαις n. dat. fem. pl. ἀκαταστασία commotion, confusion, tumult
ἐν prep. ἐν (+dat) in, by, with, among, at, on, through, to, within, into, of, for
κόποις n. dat. masc. pl. κόπος labour, trouble, weariness
ἐν prep. ἐν (+dat) in, by, with, among, at, on, through, to, within, into, of, for
ἀγρυπνίαις n. dat. fem. pl. ἀγρυπνία watching, sleeplessness
ἐν prep. ἐν (+dat) in, by, with, among, at, on, through, to, within, into, of, for

νηστείαις n. dat. fem. pl. νηστεία fasting, fast
6 ἐν prep. ἐν (+dat) in, by, with, among, at, on, through, to, within, into, of, for
ἁγνότητι n. dat. fem. sg. ἁγνότης pureness
ἐν prep. ἐν (+dat) in, by, with, among, at, on, through, to, within, into, of, for
γνώσει n. dat. fem. sg. γνῶσις knowledge, science
ἐν prep. ἐν (+dat) in, by, with, among, at, on, through, to, within, into, of, for
μακροθυμίᾳ n. dat. fem. sg. μακροθυμία longsuffering, patience
ἐν prep. ἐν (+dat) in, by, with, among, at, on, through, to, within, into, of, for
χρηστότητι n. dat. fem. sg. χρηστότης goodness, kindness, gentleness, good
ἐν prep. ἐν (+dat) in, by, with, among, at, on, through, to, within, into, of, for
Πνεύματι n. dat. neut. sg. πνεῦμα spirit, Spirit, Ghost, ghost, life. of the spirit, wind
Ἁγίῳ adj. dat. neut. sg. ἅγιος Holy, holy, saint, Holy One, holy thing, most holy
ἐν prep. ἐν (+dat) in, by, with, among, at, on, through, to, within, into, of, for
ἀγάπῃ n. dat. fem. sg. ἀγάπη love, charity, feast of charity
ἀνυποκρίτῳ adj. dat. fem. sg. ἀνυπόκριτος unfeigned, without dissimulation
7 ἐν prep. ἐν (+dat) in, by, with, among, at, on, through, to, within, into, of, for
λόγῳ n. dat. masc. sg. λόγος word, saying, account, speech, thing, matter
ἀληθείας n. gen. fem. sg. ἀλήθεια truth, verity
ἐν prep. ἐν (+dat) in, by, with, among, at, on, through, to, within, into, of, for
δυνάμει n. dat. fem. sg. δύναμις power, mighty work, miracle, strength, might
Θεοῦ n. gen. masc. sg. θεός God, god
διὰ prep. διά (+gen) by, through, with, in, of, (+acc) for, because of, for a cause
τῶν art. gen. neut. pl. ὁ ἡ τό the, this, that, he, she, it
ὅπλων n. gen. neut. pl. ὅπλον instrument, armour, weapon
τῆς art. gen. fem. sg. ὁ ἡ τό the, this, that, he, she, it
δικαιοσύνης n. gen. fem. sg. δικαιοσύνη righteousness
τῶν art. gen. neut. pl. ὁ ἡ τό the, this, that, he, she, it
δεξιῶν adj. gen. neut. pl. δεξιός right, right hand, right side
καὶ conj. καί and, even, also, but
ἀριστερῶν adj. gen. neut. pl. ἀριστερός left, left hand
8 διὰ prep. διά (+gen) by, through, with, in, of, (+acc) for, because of, for a cause
δόξης n. gen. fem. sg. δόξα glory, honour, praise, dignity, worship
καὶ conj. καί and, even, also, but
ἀτιμίας n. gen. fem. sg. ἀτιμία vile, dishonour, reproach, shame
διὰ prep. διά (+gen) by, through, with, in, of, (+acc) for, because of, for a cause
δυσφημίας n. gen. fem. sg. δυσφημία evil report
καὶ conj. καί and, even, also, but
εὐφημίας n. gen. fem. sg. εὐφημία good report
ὡς adv. ὡς as, when, as it were, how, about, like, as soon as, even as, while
πλάνοι adj. nom. masc. pl. πλάνος deceiver, seducing
καὶ conj. καί and, even, also, but
ἀληθεῖς adj. nom. masc. pl. ἀληθής true, truly, truth
9 ὡς adv. ὡς as, when, as it were, how, about, like, as soon as, even as, while
καὶ conj. καί and, even, also, but
ὡς adv. ὡς as, when, as it were, how, about, like, as soon as, even as, while
καὶ conj. καί and, even, also, but
ὡς adv. ὡς as, when, as it were, how, about, like, as soon as, even as, while
καὶ conj. καί and, even, also, but
μὴ particle of negation. μή not, no, lest, neither, none, nothing, nor, never, without
10 ὡς adv. ὡς as, when, as it were, how, about, like, as soon as, even as, while
ἀεὶ adv. ἀεί always, always, ever
δὲ conj. δέ but, and, now, also, to the contrary, rather, then
ὡς adv. ὡς as, when, as it were, how, about, like, as soon as, even as, while
πτωχοὶ adj. nom. masc. pl. πτωχός poor, beggar, beggarly
πολλοὺς adj. acc. masc. pl. πολύς many, great, much, long, abundant

δὲ conj. δέ but, and, now, also, to the contrary, rather, then
ὡς adv. ὡς as, when, as it were, how, about, like, as soon as, even as, while
μηδὲν num. acc. neut. sg. μηδείς μηδεμία μηδέν no man, nothing, no, none, not at all
καὶ conj. καί and, even, also, but
πάντα adj. acc. neut. pl. πᾶς πᾶσα πᾶν all, every, whosoever, every one, no, whole, any
11 Τὸ art. nom. neut. sg. ὁ ἡ τό the, this, that, he, she, it
στόμα n. nom. neut. sg. στόμα mouth, face, edge
ἡμῶν pron. gen. 1p. pl. ἐγώ I
πρὸς prep. πρός (+gen) for, (+dat) at, (+acc) unto, to, with, for, against
ὑμᾶς pron. acc. 2p. pl. σύ thou, you
Κορίνθιοι n. voc. masc. pl. Κορίνθιος Corinthian
ἡ art. nom. fem. sg. ὁ ἡ τό the, this, that, he, she, it
καρδία n. nom. fem. sg. καρδία heart
ἡμῶν pron. gen. 1p. pl. ἐγώ I
12 οὐ particle of negation. οὐ οὐκ οὐχ not, no, neither, none, nay, nor, never, nothing
ἐν prep. ἐν (+dat) in, by, with, among, at, on, through, to, within, into, of, for
ἡμῖν pron. dat. 1p. pl. ἐγώ I
δὲ conj. δέ but, and, now, also, to the contrary, rather, then
ἐν prep. ἐν (+dat) in, by, with, among, at, on, through, to, within, into, of, for
τοῖς art. dat. neut. pl. ὁ ἡ τό the, this, that, he, she, it
σπλάγχνοις n. dat. neut. pl. σπλάγχνον tender, bowels, inward affection
ὑμῶν pron. gen. 2p. pl. σύ thou, you
13 τὴν art. acc. fem. sg. ὁ ἡ τό the, this, that, he, she, it
δὲ conj. δέ but, and, now, also, to the contrary, rather, then
αὐτὴν adj. acc. fem. sg. αὐτός ή ό self, of oneself, even, very, the same, he, she, it
ἀντιμισθίαν n. acc. fem. sg. ἀντιμισθία recompence
ὡς adv. ὡς as, when, as it were, how, about, like, as soon as, even as, while
τέκνοις n. dat. neut. pl. τέκνον child, son, daughter
καὶ conj. καί and, even, also, but
ὑμεῖς pron. nom. 2p. pl. σύ thou, you
14 Μὴ particle of negation. μή not, no, lest, neither, none, nothing, nor, never, without
ἀπίστοις adj. dat. masc. pl. ἄπιστος faithless, unbelieving, infidel, thing incredible
τίς interrog. pron. nom. fem. sg. τίς what, who, why, where, which, how
γὰρ conj. γάρ for, and, because, but, indeed
μετοχὴ n. nom. fem. sg. μετοχή fellowship
δικαιοσύνῃ n. dat. fem. sg. δικαιοσύνη righteousness
καὶ conj. καί and, even, also, but
ἀνομίᾳ n. dat. fem. sg. ἀνομία iniquity, transgression of the law, lawlessness
τίς interrog. pron. nom. fem. sg. τίς what, who, why, where, which, how
δὲ conj. δέ but, and, now, also, to the contrary, rather, then
κοινωνία n. nom. fem. sg. κοινωνία fellowship, communion, contribution, distribution
φωτὶ n. dat. neut. sg. φῶς light, fire
πρὸς prep. πρός (+gen) for, (+dat) at, (+acc) unto, to, with, for, against
σκότος n. acc. neut. sg. σκότος darkness
15 τίς interrog. pron. nom. fem. sg. τίς what, who, why, where, which, how
δὲ conj. δέ but, and, now, also, to the contrary, rather, then
συμφώνησις n. nom. fem. sg. συμφώνησις concord
Χριστῷ n. dat. masc. sg. Χριστός Christ
πρὸς prep. πρός (+gen) for, (+dat) at, (+acc) unto, to, with, for, against
Βελιάλ n. acc. masc. sg. Βελίαλ Belial
ἢ particle. ἤ or, than, either, nor, or else, and, rather than
τίς interrog. pron. nom. fem. sg. τίς what, who, why, where, which, how
μερὶς n. nom. fem. sg. μερίς part, share
πιστῷ adj. dat. masc. sg. πιστός faithful, believing, true, sure
μετὰ prep. μετά (+gen) with, among, against, (+acc) after

ἀπίστου adj. gen. masc. sg. ἄπιστος faithless, unbelieving, infidel, thing incredible
16 τίς interrog. pron. nom. fem. sg. τίς what, who, why, where, which, how
δὲ conj. δέ but, and, now, also, to the contrary, rather, then
συγκατάθεσις n. nom. fem. sg. συγκατάθεσις agreement
ναῷ n. dat. masc. sg. ναός temple, shrine
Θεοῦ n. gen. masc. sg. θεός God, god
μετὰ prep. μετά (+gen) with, among, against, (+acc) after
εἰδώλων n. gen. neut. pl. εἴδωλον idol
ὑμεῖς pron. nom. 2p. pl. σύ thou, you
γὰρ conj. γάρ for, and, because, but, indeed
ναὸς n. nom. masc. sg. ναός temple, shrine
Θεοῦ n. gen. masc. sg. θεός God, god
καθὼς adv. καθώς as, even as, according as, according to
ὁ art. nom. masc. sg. ὁ ἡ τό the, this, that, he, she, it
Θεὸς n. nom. masc. sg. θεός God, god
ὅτι conj. ὅτι that, for, because, how that, how, because that, for that, though
ἐν prep. ἐν (+dat) in, by, with, among, at, on, through, to, within, into, of, for
αὐτοῖς pron. dat. masc. 3p. pl. αὐτός ή ό self, of oneself, even, very, the same, he, she, it
καὶ conj. καί and, even, also, but
καὶ conj. καί and, even, also, but
αὐτῶν pron. gen. masc. 3p. pl. αὐτός ή ό self, of oneself, even, very, the same, he, she, it
Θεὸς n. nom. masc. sg. θεός God, god
καὶ conj. καί and, even, also, but
αὐτοὶ pron. nom. masc. 3p. pl. αὐτός ή ό self, of oneself, even, very, the same, he, she, it
μοι pron. dat. 1p. sg. ἐγώ I
λαός n. nom. masc. sg. λαός people
17 διὸ conj. διό wherefore, therefore, for which cause
ἐκ prep. ἐκ ἐξ (+gen) of, from, out of, by, on, with, in, among, through
μέσου adj. gen. neut. sg. μέσος midst, among, mid, between
αὐτῶν pron. gen. masc. 3p. pl. αὐτός ή ό self, of oneself, even, very, the same, he, she, it
καὶ conj. καί and, even, also, but
Κύριος n. nom. masc. sg. κύριος Lord, lord, master, sir, LORD, God, Master, owner
καὶ conj. καί and, even, also, but
ἀκαθάρτου adj. gen. neut. sg. ἀκάθαρτος unclean, foul
μὴ particle of negation. μή not, no, lest, neither, none, nothing, nor, never, without
κἀγὼ pron. nom. 1p. sg. κἀγώ and I, I also, so I, even as I
ὑμᾶς pron. acc. 2p. pl. σύ thou, you
18 καὶ conj. καί and, even, also, but
ὑμῖν pron. dat. 2p. pl. σύ thou, you
εἰς prep. εἰς (+acc) into, to, unto, for, in, on, toward, against, upon, at, among
πατέρα n. acc. masc. sg. πατήρ Father, father, parent
καὶ conj. καί and, even, also, but
ὑμεῖς pron. nom. 2p. pl. σύ thou, you
μοι pron. dat. 1p. sg. ἐγώ I
εἰς prep. εἰς (+acc) into, to, unto, for, in, on, toward, against, upon, at, among
υἱοὺς n. acc. masc. pl. υἱός son, child, descendant, offspring, heir
καὶ conj. καί and, even, also, but
θυγατέρας n. acc. fem. pl. θυγάτηρ daughter
Κύριος n. nom. masc. sg. κύριος Lord, lord, master, sir, LORD, God, Master, owner
παντοκράτωρ n. nom. masc. sg. παντοκράτωρ Almighty, omnipotent

7

1 ταύτας demo. pron. acc. fem. pl. οὗτος αὕτη τοῦτο this, the same, this same, he, she, it
οὖν conj. οὖν therefore, then, so, and, now, wherefore

τὰς art. acc. fem. pl. ὁ ἡ τό the, this, that, he, she, it
ἐπαγγελίας n. acc. fem. pl. ἐπαγγελία promise, message
ἀγαπητοί adj. voc. masc. pl. ἀγαπητός beloved, dearly beloved, dear, wellbeloved
ἑαυτοὺς reflexive pron. acc. masc. 3p. pl. ἑαυτοῦ himself, herself, itself, yourself, ourselves
ἀπὸ prep. ἀπό (+gen) from, of, out of, since, for, off, at, by, in, on
παντὸς adj. gen. masc. sg. πᾶς πᾶσα πᾶν all, every, whosoever, every one, no, whole, any
μολυσμοῦ n. gen. masc. sg. μολυσμός filthiness
σαρκὸς n. gen. fem. sg. σάρξ flesh, carnal
καὶ conj. καί and, even, also, but
πνεύματος n. gen. neut. sg. πνεῦμα spirit, Spirit, Ghost, ghost, life. of the spirit, wind
ἁγιωσύνην n. acc. fem. sg. ἁγιωσύνη holiness
ἐν prep. ἐν (+dat) in, by, with, among, at, on, through, to, within, into, of, for
φόβῳ n. dat. masc. sg. φόβος fear, terror, sore afraid
Θεοῦ n. gen. masc. sg. θεός God, god
2 ἡμᾶς pron. acc. 1p. pl. ἐγώ I
οὐδένα num. acc. masc. sg. οὐδείς no man, nothing, no, none, neither, not, nought
οὐδένα num. acc. masc. sg. οὐδείς no man, nothing, no, none, neither, not, nought
οὐδένα num. acc. masc. sg. οὐδείς no man, nothing, no, none, neither, not, nought
3 οὐ particle of negation. οὐ οὐκ οὐχ not, no, neither, none, nay, nor, never, nothing
πρὸς prep. πρός (+gen) for, (+dat) at, (+acc) unto, to, with, for, against
κατάκρισιν n. acc. fem. sg. κατάκρισις condemnation, condemn
γὰρ conj. γάρ for, and, because, but, indeed
ὅτι conj. ὅτι that, for, because, how that, how, because that, for that, though
ἐν prep. ἐν (+dat) in, by, with, among, at, on, through, to, within, into, of, for
ταῖς art. dat. fem. pl. ὁ ἡ τό the, this, that, he, she, it
καρδίαις n. dat. fem. pl. καρδία heart
ἡμῶν pron. gen. 1p. pl. ἐγώ I
εἰς prep. εἰς (+acc) into, to, unto, for, in, on, toward, against, upon, at, among
τὸ art. acc. neut. sg. ὁ ἡ τό the, this, that, he, she, it
καὶ conj. καί and, even, also, but
4 πολλή adj. nom. fem. sg. πολύς many, great, much, long, abundant
μοι pron. dat. 1p. sg. ἐγώ I
παρρησία n. nom. fem. sg. παρρησία boldness, confidence, openly, plainly, freely
πρὸς prep. πρός (+gen) for, (+dat) at, (+acc) unto, to, with, for, against
ὑμᾶς pron. acc. 2p. pl. σύ thou, you
πολλή adj. nom. fem. sg. πολύς many, great, much, long, abundant
μοι pron. dat. 1p. sg. ἐγώ I
καύχησις n. nom. fem. sg. καύχησις boasting, rejoicing, glorying
ὑπὲρ prep. ὑπέρ (+gen) for, of, for the sake of, (+acc) above, more than
ὑμῶν pron. gen. 2p. pl. σύ thou, you
τῇ art. dat. fem. sg. ὁ ἡ τό the, this, that, he, she, it
παρακλήσει n. dat. fem. sg. παράκλησις consolation, exhortation, comfort
τῇ art. dat. fem. sg. ὁ ἡ τό the, this, that, he, she, it
χαρᾷ n. dat. fem. sg. χαρά joy, gladness, joyfulness
ἐπὶ prep. ἐπί (+gen) on, in, upon, (+dat) in, at, for, upon, (+acc) on, upon, unto, to, against
πάσῃ adj. dat. fem. sg. πᾶς πᾶσα πᾶν all, every, whosoever, every one, no, whole, any
τῇ art. dat. fem. sg. ὁ ἡ τό the, this, that, he, she, it
θλίψει n. dat. fem. sg. θλῖψις tribulation, affliction, anguish, persecution
ἡμῶν pron. gen. 1p. pl. ἐγώ I
5 Καὶ conj. καί and, even, also, but
γὰρ conj. γάρ for, and, because, but, indeed
ἡμῶν pron. gen. 1p. pl. ἐγώ I
εἰς prep. εἰς (+acc) into, to, unto, for, in, on, toward, against, upon, at, among
Μακεδονίαν n. acc. fem. sg. Μακεδονία Macedonia
οὐδεμίαν num. acc. fem. sg. οὐδείς no man, nothing, no, none, neither, not, nought

ἄνεσιν n. acc. fem. sg. ἄνεσις liberty, rest, eased
ἡ art. nom. fem. sg. ὁ ἡ τό the, this, that, he, she, it
σὰρξ n. nom. fem. sg. σάρξ flesh, carnal
ἡμῶν pron. gen. 1p. pl. ἐγώ I
ἀλλ' conj. ἀλλά but, yea, yet, nevertheless, howbeit, nay, therefore
ἐν prep. ἐν (+dat) in, by, with, among, at, on, through, to, within, into, of, for
παντὶ adj. dat. neut. sg. πᾶς πᾶσα πᾶν all, every, whosoever, every one, no, whole, any
ἔξωθεν adv. ἔξωθεν without, from without, outside, outward, outwardly
μάχαι n. nom. fem. pl. μάχη fighting, strife, striving
ἔσωθεν adv. ἔσωθεν within, from within, inward, inwardly
φόβοι n. nom. masc. pl. φόβος fear, terror, sore afraid
6 ἀλλ' conj. ἀλλά but, yea, yet, nevertheless, howbeit, nay, therefore
ὁ art. nom. masc. sg. ὁ ἡ τό the, this, that, he, she, it
τοὺς art. acc. masc. pl. ὁ ἡ τό the, this, that, he, she, it
ταπεινοὺς adj. acc. masc. pl. ταπεινός humble, of low degree, base, cast down, lowly
ἡμᾶς pron. acc. 1p. pl. ἐγώ I
ὁ art. nom. masc. sg. ὁ ἡ τό the, this, that, he, she, it
Θεὸς n. nom. masc. sg. θεός God, god
ἐν prep. ἐν (+dat) in, by, with, among, at, on, through, to, within, into, of, for
τῇ art. dat. fem. sg. ὁ ἡ τό the, this, that, he, she, it
παρουσίᾳ n. dat. fem. sg. παρουσία coming, presence
Τίτου n. gen. masc. sg. Τίτος Titus
7 οὐ particle of negation. οὐ οὐκ οὐχ not, no, neither, none, nay, nor, never, nothing
μόνον adv. μόνος only, alone, by oneself
δὲ conj. δέ but, and, now, also, to the contrary, rather, then
ἐν prep. ἐν (+dat) in, by, with, among, at, on, through, to, within, into, of, for
τῇ art. dat. fem. sg. ὁ ἡ τό the, this, that, he, she, it
παρουσίᾳ n. dat. fem. sg. παρουσία coming, presence
αὐτοῦ pron. gen. masc. 3p. sg. αὐτός ἡ ὁ self, of oneself, even, very, the same, he, she, it
ἀλλὰ conj. ἀλλά but, yea, yet, nevertheless, howbeit, nay, therefore
καὶ conj. καί and, even, also, but
ἐν prep. ἐν (+dat) in, by, with, among, at, on, through, to, within, into, of, for
τῇ art. dat. fem. sg. ὁ ἡ τό the, this, that, he, she, it
παρακλήσει n. dat. fem. sg. παράκλησις consolation, exhortation, comfort
ᾗ relative pron. dat. fem. sg. ὅς ἥ ὅ who, which, what, that
ἐφ' prep. ἐπί (+gen) on, in, upon, (+dat) in, at, for, upon, (+acc) on, upon, unto, to, against
ὑμῖν pron. dat. 2p. pl. σύ thou, you
ἡμῖν pron. dat. 1p. pl. ἐγώ I
τὴν art. acc. fem. sg. ὁ ἡ τό the, this, that, he, she, it
ὑμῶν pron. gen. 2p. pl. σύ thou, you
ἐπιπόθησιν n. acc. fem. sg. ἐπιπόθησις earnest desire, vehement desire
τὸν art. acc. masc. sg. ὁ ἡ τό the, this, that, he, she, it
ὑμῶν pron. gen. 2p. pl. σύ thou, you
ὀδυρμόν n. acc. masc. sg. ὀδυρμός mourning
τὸν art. acc. masc. sg. ὁ ἡ τό the, this, that, he, she, it
ὑμῶν pron. gen. 2p. pl. σύ thou, you
ζῆλον n. acc. masc. sg. ζῆλος zeal, envying, indignation, emulation, jealousy
ὑπὲρ prep. ὑπέρ (+gen) for, of, for the sake of, (+acc) above, more than
ἐμοῦ pron. gen. 1p. sg. ἐγώ I
ὥστε conj. ὥστε so that, wherefore, insomuch that, therefore, that, so then
με pron. acc. 1p. sg. ἐγώ I
μᾶλλον adv. μᾶλλον rather, more, more and more, better, much, much the more
8 ὅτι conj. ὅτι that, for, because, how that, how, because that, for that, though
εἰ conj. εἰ if, whether, that, though, forasmuch
καὶ conj. καί and, even, also, but

ὑμᾶς pron. acc. 2p. pl. σύ thou, you
ἐν prep. ἐν (+dat) in, by, with, among, at, on, through, to, within, into, of, for
τῇ art. dat. fem. sg. ὁ ἡ τό the, this, that, he, she, it
ἐπιστολῇ n. dat. fem. sg. ἐπιστολή letter, epistle
οὐ particle of negation. οὐ οὐκ οὐχ not, no, neither, none, nay, nor, never, nothing
εἰ conj. εἰ if, whether, that, though, forasmuch
καὶ conj. καί and, even, also, but
γὰρ conj. γάρ for, and, because, but, indeed
ὅτι conj. ὅτι that, for, because, how that, how, because that, for that, though
ἡ art. nom. fem. sg. ὁ ἡ τό the, this, that, he, she, it
ἐπιστολὴ n. nom. fem. sg. ἐπιστολή letter, epistle
ἐκείνη demo. pron. nom. fem. sg. ἐκεῖνος that, he, the same, that same
ὅτι conj. ὅτι that, for, because, how that, how, because that, for that, though
πρὸς prep. πρός (+gen) for, (+dat) at, (+acc) unto, to, with, for, against
ὥραν n. acc. fem. sg. ὥρα hour, time, season
ὑμᾶς pron. acc. 2p. pl. σύ thou, you
9 νῦν adv. νῦν now, henceforth, present, this time
οὐχ particle of negation. οὐ οὐκ οὐχ not, no, neither, none, nay, nor, never, nothing
ὅτι conj. ὅτι that, for, because, how that, how, because that, for that, though
ἀλλ' conj. ἀλλά but, yea, yet, nevertheless, howbeit, nay, therefore
ὅτι conj. ὅτι that, for, because, how that, how, because that, for that, though
εἰς prep. εἰς (+acc) into, to, unto, for, in, on, toward, against, upon, at, among
μετάνοιαν n. acc. fem. sg. μετάνοια repentance
γὰρ conj. γάρ for, and, because, but, indeed
κατὰ prep. κατά (+gen) against, by, throughout, down, (+acc) according to, after, with
Θεόν n. acc. masc. sg. θεός God, god
ἵνα conj. ἵνα that, to, lest, for to, so that, albeit, because, for, so as
ἐν prep. ἐν (+dat) in, by, with, among, at, on, through, to, within, into, of, for
μηδενὶ num. dat. neut. sg. μηδείς μηδεμία μηδέν no man, nothing, no, none, not at all
ἐξ prep. ἐκ ἐξ (+gen) of, from, out of, by, on, with, in, among, through
ἡμῶν pron. gen. 1p. pl. ἐγώ I
10 ἡ art. nom. fem. sg. ὁ ἡ τό the, this, that, he, she, it
γὰρ conj. γάρ for, and, because, but, indeed
κατὰ prep. κατά (+gen) against, by, throughout, down, (+acc) according to, after, with
Θεὸν n. acc. masc. sg. θεός God, god
λύπη n. nom. fem. sg. λύπη sorrow, heaviness, grief, grievous, grudgingly
μετάνοιαν n. acc. fem. sg. μετάνοια repentance
εἰς prep. εἰς (+acc) into, to, unto, for, in, on, toward, against, upon, at, among
σωτηρίαν n. acc. fem. sg. σωτηρία salvation, deliver, health, saving
ἀμεταμέλητον adj. acc. fem. sg. ἀμεταμέλητος without repentance, not to be repented of
ἡ art. nom. fem. sg. ὁ ἡ τό the, this, that, he, she, it
δὲ conj. δέ but, and, now, also, to the contrary, rather, then
τοῦ art. gen. masc. sg. ὁ ἡ τό the, this, that, he, she, it
κόσμου n. gen. masc. sg. κόσμος world, adorning
λύπη n. nom. fem. sg. λύπη sorrow, heaviness, grief, grievous, grudgingly
θάνατον n. acc. masc. sg. θάνατος death
11 γὰρ conj. γάρ for, and, because, but, indeed
αὐτὸ pron. acc. neut. 3p. sg. αὐτός ἡ ό self, of oneself, even, very, the same, he, she, it
τοῦτο demo. pron. nom. neut. sg. οὗτος αὕτη τοῦτο this, the same, this same, he, she, it
τὸ art. nom. neut. sg. ὁ ἡ τό the, this, that, he, she, it
κατὰ prep. κατά (+gen) against, by, throughout, down, (+acc) according to, after, with
Θεὸν n. acc. masc. sg. θεός God, god
ὑμᾶς pron. acc. 2p. pl. σύ thou, you
πόσην interrog. pron. acc. fem. sg. πόσος how much, how many, how great, how long
ὑμῖν pron. dat. 2p. pl. σύ thou, you

σπουδήν n. acc. fem. sg. σπουδή diligence, haste, business, care, carefulness
ἀλλὰ conj. ἀλλά but, yea, yet, nevertheless, howbeit, nay, therefore
ἀπολογίαν n. acc. fem. sg. ἀπολογία defence, answer, answer for oneself, clear oneself
ἀλλὰ conj. ἀλλά but, yea, yet, nevertheless, howbeit, nay, therefore
ἀγανάκτησιν n. acc. fem. sg. ἀγανάκτησις indignation
ἀλλὰ conj. ἀλλά but, yea, yet, nevertheless, howbeit, nay, therefore
φόβον n. acc. masc. sg. φόβος fear, terror, sore afraid
ἀλλὰ conj. ἀλλά but, yea, yet, nevertheless, howbeit, nay, therefore
ἐπιπόθησιν n. acc. fem. sg. ἐπιπόθησις earnest desire, vehement desire
ἀλλὰ conj. ἀλλά but, yea, yet, nevertheless, howbeit, nay, therefore
ζῆλον n. acc. masc. sg. ζῆλος zeal, envying, indignation, emulation, jealousy
ἀλλ' conj. ἀλλά but, yea, yet, nevertheless, howbeit, nay, therefore
ἐκδίκησιν n. acc. fem. sg. ἐκδίκησις vengeance, punishment, revenge
ἐν prep. ἐν (+dat) in, by, with, among, at, on, through, to, within, into, of, for
παντὶ adj. dat. neut. sg. πᾶς πᾶσα πᾶν all, every, whosoever, every one, no, whole, any
ἑαυτοὺς reflexive pron. acc. masc. 3p. pl. ἑαυτοῦ himself, herself, itself, yourself, ourselves
ἁγνοὺς adj. acc. masc. pl. ἁγνός clear, pure, chaste
ἐν prep. ἐν (+dat) in, by, with, among, at, on, through, to, within, into, of, for
τῷ art. dat. neut. sg. ὁ ἡ τό the, this, that, he, she, it
πράγματι n. dat. neut. sg. πρᾶγμα thing, matter, business, work
12 ἄρα conj. ἄρα then, therefore, haply, wherefore, perhaps, manner, no doubt, truly
εἰ conj. εἰ if, whether, that, though, forasmuch
καὶ conj. καί and, even, also, but
ὑμῖν pron. dat. 2p. pl. σύ thou, you
οὐχ particle of negation. οὐ οὐκ οὐχ not, no, neither, none, nay, nor, never, nothing
εἵνεκεν adv. ἕνεκα, ἕνεκεν or εἵνεκεν (+gen) for the sake, for a cause, for, by reason of
τοῦ art. gen. masc. sg. ὁ ἡ τό the, this, that, he, she, it
οὐδὲ adv. οὐδέ neither, nor, not, no, not even, never, not yet
εἵνεκεν adv. ἕνεκα, ἕνεκεν or εἵνεκεν (+gen) for the sake, for a cause, for, by reason of
τοῦ art. gen. masc. sg. ὁ ἡ τό the, this, that, he, she, it
ἀλλ' conj. ἀλλά but, yea, yet, nevertheless, howbeit, nay, therefore
εἵνεκεν adv. ἕνεκα, ἕνεκεν or εἵνεκεν (+gen) for the sake, for a cause, for, by reason of
τοῦ art. gen. masc. sg. ὁ ἡ τό the, this, that, he, she, it
τὴν art. acc. fem. sg. ὁ ἡ τό the, this, that, he, she, it
σπουδὴν n. acc. fem. sg. σπουδή diligence, haste, business, care, carefulness
ἡμῶν pron. gen. 1p. pl. ἐγώ I
τὴν art. acc. fem. sg. ὁ ἡ τό the, this, that, he, she, it
ὑπὲρ prep. ὑπέρ (+gen) for, of, for the sake of, (+acc) above, more than
ὑμῶν pron. gen. 2p. pl. σύ thou, you
πρὸς prep. πρός (+gen) for, (+dat) at, (+acc) unto, to, with, for, against
ὑμᾶς pron. acc. 2p. pl. σύ thou, you
ἐνώπιον prep. ἐνώπιον (+gen) before, in the sight of, in the presence of. (adv.) before
τοῦ art. gen. masc. sg. ὁ ἡ τό the, this, that, he, she, it
Θεοῦ n. gen. masc. sg. θεός God, god
13 διὰ prep. διά (+gen) by, through, with, in, of, (+acc) for, because of, for a cause
τοῦτο demo. pron. acc. neut. sg. οὗτος αὕτη τοῦτο this, the same, this same, he, she, it
ἐπὶ prep. ἐπί (+gen) on, in, upon, (+dat) in, at, for, upon, (+acc) on, upon, unto, to, against
τῇ art. dat. fem. sg. ὁ ἡ τό the, this, that, he, she, it
παρακλήσει n. dat. fem. sg. παράκλησις consolation, exhortation, comfort
ὑμῶν pron. gen. 2p. pl. σύ thou, you
περισσοτέρως adv. περισσοτέρως more exceedingly, more abundantly, more frequent
δὲ conj. δέ but, and, now, also, to the contrary, rather, then
μᾶλλον adv. μᾶλλον rather, more, more and more, better, much, much the more
ἐπὶ prep. ἐπί (+gen) on, in, upon, (+dat) in, at, for, upon, (+acc) on, upon, unto, to, against
τῇ art. dat. fem. sg. ὁ ἡ τό the, this, that, he, she, it

χαρᾷ n. dat. fem. sg. χαρά joy, gladness, joyfulness
Τίτου n. gen. masc. sg. Τίτος Titus
ὅτι conj. ὅτι that, for, because, how that, how, because that, for that, though
τὸ art. nom. neut. sg. ὁ ἡ τό the, this, that, he, she, it
πνεῦμα n. nom. neut. sg. πνεῦμα spirit, Spirit, Ghost, ghost, life. of the spirit, wind
αὐτοῦ pron. gen. masc. 3p. sg. αὐτός ἡ ὁ self, of oneself, even, very, the same, he, she, it
ἀπὸ prep. ἀπό (+gen) from, of, out of, since, for, off, at, by, in, on
πάντων adj. gen. masc. pl. πᾶς πᾶσα πᾶν all, every, whosoever, every one, no, whole, any
ὑμῶν pron. gen. 2p. pl. σύ thou, you
14 ὅτι conj. ὅτι that, for, because, how that, how, because that, for that, though
εἴ conj. εἰ if, whether, that, though, forasmuch
τι indefinite pron. acc. neut. sg. τὶς certain, some, any man, one, any thing
αὐτῷ pron. dat. masc. 3p. sg. αὐτός ἡ ὁ self, of oneself, even, very, the same, he, she, it
ὑπὲρ prep. ὑπέρ (+gen) for, of, for the sake of, (+acc) above, more than
ὑμῶν pron. gen. 2p. pl. σύ thou, you
οὐ particle of negation. οὐ οὐκ οὐχ not, no, neither, none, nay, nor, never, nothing
ἀλλ' conj. ἀλλά but, yea, yet, nevertheless, howbeit, nay, therefore
ὡς adv. ὡς as, when, as it were, how, about, like, as soon as, even as, while
πάντα adj. acc. neut. pl. πᾶς πᾶσα πᾶν all, every, whosoever, every one, no, whole, any
ἐν prep. ἐν (+dat) in, by, with, among, at, on, through, to, within, into, of, for
ἀληθείᾳ n. dat. fem. sg. ἀλήθεια truth, verity
ὑμῖν pron. dat. 2p. pl. σύ thou, you
οὕτω adv. οὕτω οὕτως so, even so, thus, on this wise, likewise, after this manner
καὶ conj. καί and, even, also, but
ἡ art. nom. fem. sg. ὁ ἡ τό the, this, that, he, she, it
καύχησις n. nom. fem. sg. καύχησις boasting, rejoicing, glorying
ἡμῶν pron. gen. 1p. pl. ἐγώ I
ἡ art. nom. fem. sg. ὁ ἡ τό the, this, that, he, she, it
ἐπὶ prep. ἐπί (+gen) on, in, upon, (+dat) in, at, for, upon, (+acc) on, upon, unto, to, against
Τίτου n. gen. masc. sg. Τίτος Titus
ἀλήθεια n. nom. fem. sg. ἀλήθεια truth, verity
15 καὶ conj. καί and, even, also, but
τὰ art. nom. neut. pl. ὁ ἡ τό the, this, that, he, she, it
σπλάγχνα n. nom. neut. pl. σπλάγχνον tender, bowels, inward affection
αὐτοῦ pron. gen. masc. 3p. sg. αὐτός ἡ ὁ self, of oneself, even, very, the same, he, she, it
περισσοτέρως adv. περισσοτέρως more exceedingly, more abundantly, more frequent
εἰς prep. εἰς (+acc) into, to, unto, for, in, on, toward, against, upon, at, among
ὑμᾶς pron. acc. 2p. pl. σύ thou, you
τὴν art. acc. fem. sg. ὁ ἡ τό the, this, that, he, she, it
πάντων adj. gen. masc. pl. πᾶς πᾶσα πᾶν all, every, whosoever, every one, no, whole, any
ὑμῶν pron. gen. 2p. pl. σύ thou, you
ὑπακοήν n. acc. fem. sg. ὑπακοή obedience, obey, make obedient, obedient
ὡς adv. ὡς as, when, as it were, how, about, like, as soon as, even as, while
μετὰ prep. μετά (+gen) with, among, against, (+acc) after
φόβου n. gen. masc. sg. φόβος fear, terror, sore afraid
καὶ conj. καί and, even, also, but
τρόμου n. gen. masc. sg. τρόμος trembling, tremble
αὐτόν pron. acc. masc. 3p. sg. αὐτός ἡ ὁ self, of oneself, even, very, the same, he, she, it
16 οὖν conj. οὖν therefore, then, so, and, now, wherefore
ὅτι conj. ὅτι that, for, because, how that, how, because that, for that, though
ἐν prep. ἐν (+dat) in, by, with, among, at, on, through, to, within, into, of, for
παντὶ adj. dat. neut. sg. πᾶς πᾶσα πᾶν all, every, whosoever, every one, no, whole, any
ἐν prep. ἐν (+dat) in, by, with, among, at, on, through, to, within, into, of, for
ὑμῖν pron. dat. 2p. pl. σύ thou, you

8

1 δὲ conj. δέ but, and, now, also, to the contrary, rather, then
ὑμῖν pron. dat. 2p. pl. σύ thou, you
ἀδελφοί n. voc. masc. pl. ἀδελφός brother
τὴν art. acc. fem. sg. ὁ ἡ τό the, this, that, he, she, it
χάριν n. acc. fem. sg. χάρις grace, thank, favour, pleasure
τοῦ art. gen. masc. sg. ὁ ἡ τό the, this, that, he, she, it
Θεοῦ n. gen. masc. sg. θεός God, god
τὴν art. acc. fem. sg. ὁ ἡ τό the, this, that, he, she, it
ἐν prep. ἐν (+dat) in, by, with, among, at, on, through, to, within, into, of, for
ταῖς art. dat. fem. pl. ὁ ἡ τό the, this, that, he, she, it
ἐκκλησίαις n. dat. fem. pl. ἐκκλησία church, assembly
τῆς art. gen. fem. sg. ὁ ἡ τό the, this, that, he, she, it
Μακεδονίας n. gen. fem. sg. Μακεδονία Macedonia
2 ὅτι conj. ὅτι that, for, because, how that, how, because that, for that, though
ἐν prep. ἐν (+dat) in, by, with, among, at, on, through, to, within, into, of, for
πολλῇ adj. dat. fem. sg. πολύς many, great, much, long, abundant
δοκιμῇ n. dat. fem. sg. δοκιμή experience, proof, experiment, trial
θλίψεως n. gen. fem. sg. θλῖψις tribulation, affliction, anguish, persecution
ἡ art. nom. fem. sg. ὁ ἡ τό the, this, that, he, she, it
περισσεία n. nom. fem. sg. περισσεία abundance, abundant, superfluity
τῆς art. gen. fem. sg. ὁ ἡ τό the, this, that, he, she, it
χαρᾶς n. gen. fem. sg. χαρά joy, gladness, joyfulness
αὐτῶν pron. gen. masc. 3p. pl. αὐτός ή ό self, of oneself, even, very, the same, he, she, it
καὶ conj. καί and, even, also, but
ἡ art. nom. fem. sg. ὁ ἡ τό the, this, that, he, she, it
κατὰ prep. κατά (+gen) against, by, throughout, down, (+acc) according to, after, with
βάθους n. gen. neut. sg. βάθος deepness, depth, deep, deep thing
πτωχεία n. nom. fem. sg. πτωχεία poverty
αὐτῶν pron. gen. masc. 3p. pl. αὐτός ή ό self, of oneself, even, very, the same, he, she, it
εἰς prep. εἰς (+acc) into, to, unto, for, in, on, toward, against, upon, at, among
τὸν art. acc. masc. sg. ὁ ἡ τό the, this, that, he, she, it
πλοῦτον n. acc. masc. sg. πλοῦτος riches
τῆς art. gen. fem. sg. ὁ ἡ τό the, this, that, he, she, it
ἁπλότητος n. gen. fem. sg. ἁπλότης simplicity, singleness, bountifulness, liberal
αὐτῶν pron. gen. masc. 3p. pl. αὐτός ή ό self, of oneself, even, very, the same, he, she, it
3 ὅτι conj. ὅτι that, for, because, how that, how, because that, for that, though
κατὰ prep. κατά (+gen) against, by, throughout, down, (+acc) according to, after, with
δύναμιν n. acc. fem. sg. δύναμις power, mighty work, miracle, strength, might
καὶ conj. καί and, even, also, but
ὑπὲρ prep. ὑπέρ (+gen) for, of, for the sake of, (+acc) above, more than
δύναμιν n. acc. fem. sg. δύναμις power, mighty work, miracle, strength, might
αὐθαίρετοι adj. nom. masc. pl. αὐθαίρετος willing of oneself, of own accord
4 μετὰ prep. μετά (+gen) with, among, against, (+acc) after
πολλῆς adj. gen. fem. sg. πολύς many, great, much, long, abundant
παρακλήσεως n. gen. fem. sg. παράκλησις consolation, exhortation, comfort
ἡμῶν pron. gen. 1p. pl. ἐγώ I
τὴν art. acc. fem. sg. ὁ ἡ τό the, this, that, he, she, it
χάριν n. acc. fem. sg. χάρις grace, thank, favour, pleasure
καὶ conj. καί and, even, also, but
τὴν art. acc. fem. sg. ὁ ἡ τό the, this, that, he, she, it
κοινωνίαν n. acc. fem. sg. κοινωνία fellowship, communion, contribution, distribution
τῆς art. gen. fem. sg. ὁ ἡ τό the, this, that, he, she, it
διακονίας n. gen. fem. sg. διακονία ministry, administration, service, office, relief

τῆς art. gen. fem. sg. ὁ ἡ τό the, this, that, he, she, it
εἰς prep. εἰς (+acc) into, to, unto, for, in, on, toward, against, upon, at, among
τοὺς art. acc. masc. pl. ὁ ἡ τό the, this, that, he, she, it
ἁγίους adj. acc. masc. pl. ἅγιος Holy, holy, saint, Holy One, holy thing, most holy
ἡμᾶς pron. acc. 1p. pl. ἐγώ I
5 καὶ conj. καί and, even, also, but
οὐ particle of negation. οὐ οὐκ οὐχ not, no, neither, none, nay, nor, never, nothing
καθὼς adv. καθώς as, even as, according as, according to
ἀλλ' conj. ἀλλά but, yea, yet, nevertheless, howbeit, nay, therefore
ἑαυτοὺς reflexive pron. acc. masc. 3p. pl. ἑαυτοῦ himself, herself, itself, yourself, ourselves
πρῶτον adv. πρῶτον first, at the first, first of all, at first, at the beginning, before, chiefly
τῷ art. dat. masc. sg. ὁ ἡ τό the, this, that, he, she, it
Κυρίῳ n. dat. masc. sg. κύριος Lord, lord, master, sir, LORD, God, Master, owner
καὶ conj. καί and, even, also, but
ἡμῖν pron. dat. 1p. pl. ἐγώ I
διὰ prep. διά (+gen) by, through, with, in, of, (+acc) for, because of, for a cause
θελήματος n. gen. neut. sg. θέλημα will, desire, pleasure
Θεοῦ n. gen. masc. sg. θεός God, god
6 εἰς prep. εἰς (+acc) into, to, unto, for, in, on, toward, against, upon, at, among
τὸ art. acc. neut. sg. ὁ ἡ τό the, this, that, he, she, it
ἡμᾶς pron. acc. 1p. pl. ἐγώ I
Τίτον n. acc. masc. sg. Τίτος Titus
ἵνα conj. ἵνα that, to, lest, for to, so that, albeit, because, for, so as
καθὼς adv. καθώς as, even as, according as, according to
οὕτω adv. οὕτω οὕτως so, even so, thus, on this wise, likewise, after this manner
καὶ conj. καί and, even, also, but
εἰς prep. εἰς (+acc) into, to, unto, for, in, on, toward, against, upon, at, among
ὑμᾶς pron. acc. 2p. pl. σύ thou, you
καὶ conj. καί and, even, also, but
τὴν art. acc. fem. sg. ὁ ἡ τό the, this, that, he, she, it
χάριν n. acc. fem. sg. χάρις grace, thank, favour, pleasure
ταύτην demo. pron. acc. fem. sg. οὗτος αὕτη τοῦτο this, the same, this same, he, she, it
7 ἀλλ' conj. ἀλλά but, yea, yet, nevertheless, howbeit, nay, therefore
ὥσπερ adv. ὥσπερ as, even as, like as
ἐν prep. ἐν (+dat) in, by, with, among, at, on, through, to, within, into, of, for
παντὶ adj. dat. neut. sg. πᾶς πᾶσα πᾶν all, every, whosoever, every one, no, whole, any
πίστει n. dat. fem. sg. πίστις faith, assurance, belief, fidelity
καὶ conj. καί and, even, also, but
λόγῳ n. dat. masc. sg. λόγος word, saying, account, speech, thing, matter
καὶ conj. καί and, even, also, but
γνώσει n. dat. fem. sg. γνῶσις knowledge, science
καὶ conj. καί and, even, also, but
πάσῃ adj. dat. fem. sg. πᾶς πᾶσα πᾶν all, every, whosoever, every one, no, whole, any
σπουδῇ n. dat. fem. sg. σπουδή diligence, haste, business, care, carefulness
καὶ conj. καί and, even, also, but
τῇ art. dat. fem. sg. ὁ ἡ τό the, this, that, he, she, it
ἐξ prep. ἐκ ἐξ (+gen) of, from, out of, by, on, with, in, among, through
ὑμῶν pron. gen. 2p. pl. σύ thou, you
ἐν prep. ἐν (+dat) in, by, with, among, at, on, through, to, within, into, of, for
ἡμῖν pron. dat. 1p. pl. ἐγώ I
ἀγάπῃ n. dat. fem. sg. ἀγάπη love, charity, feast of charity
ἵνα conj. ἵνα that, to, lest, for to, so that, albeit, because, for, so as
καὶ conj. καί and, even, also, but
ἐν prep. ἐν (+dat) in, by, with, among, at, on, through, to, within, into, of, for
ταύτῃ demo. pron. dat. fem. sg. οὗτος αὕτη τοῦτο this, the same, this same, he, she, it

τῇ art. dat. fem. sg. ὁ ἡ τό the, this, that, he, she, it
χάριτι n. dat. fem. sg. χάρις grace, thank, favour, pleasure
8 οὐ particle of negation. οὐ οὐκ οὐχ not, no, neither, none, nay, nor, never, nothing
κατ' prep. κατά (+gen) against, by, throughout, down, (+acc) according to, after, with
ἐπιταγὴν n. acc. fem. sg. ἐπιταγή commandment, authority
ἀλλὰ conj. ἀλλά but, yea, yet, nevertheless, howbeit, nay, therefore
διὰ prep. διά (+gen) by, through, with, in, of, (+acc) for, because of, for a cause
τῆς art. gen. fem. sg. ὁ ἡ τό the, this, that, he, she, it
ἑτέρων adj. gen. masc. pl. ἕτερος another, other, else, strange
σπουδῆς n. gen. fem. sg. σπουδή diligence, haste, business, care, carefulness
καὶ conj. καί and, even, also, but
τὸ art. acc. neut. sg. ὁ ἡ τό the, this, that, he, she, it
τῆς art. gen. fem. sg. ὁ ἡ τό the, this, that, he, she, it
ὑμετέρας poss. pron. gen. fem. 2p. sg. ὑμέτερος your, yours, your own
ἀγάπης n. gen. fem. sg. ἀγάπη love, charity, feast of charity
γνήσιον adj. acc. neut. sg. γνήσιος sincerity, own, true
9 γὰρ conj. γάρ for, and, because, but, indeed
τὴν art. acc. fem. sg. ὁ ἡ τό the, this, that, he, she, it
χάριν n. acc. fem. sg. χάρις grace, thank, favour, pleasure
τοῦ art. gen. masc. sg. ὁ ἡ τό the, this, that, he, she, it
Κυρίου n. gen. masc. sg. κύριος Lord, lord, master, sir, LORD, God, Master, owner
ἡμῶν pron. gen. 1p. pl. ἐγώ I
'Ιησοῦ n. gen. masc. sg. 'Ιησοῦς Jesus
Χριστοῦ n. gen. masc. sg. Χριστός Christ
ὅτι conj. ὅτι that, for, because, how that, how, because that, for that, though
δι' prep. διά (+gen) by, through, with, in, of, (+acc) for, because of, for a cause
ὑμᾶς pron. acc. 2p. pl. σύ thou, you
πλούσιος adj. nom. masc. sg. πλούσιος rich
ἵνα conj. ἵνα that, to, lest, for to, so that, albeit, because, for, so as
ὑμεῖς pron. nom. 2p. pl. σύ thou, you
τῇ art. dat. fem. sg. ὁ ἡ τό the, this, that, he, she, it
ἐκείνου demo. pron. gen. masc. sg. ἐκεῖνος that, he, the same, that same
πτωχείᾳ n. dat. fem. sg. πτωχεία poverty
10 καὶ conj. καί and, even, also, but
γνώμην n. acc. fem. sg. γνώμη judgement, mind, advice, purpose, will
ἐν prep. ἐν (+dat) in, by, with, among, at, on, through, to, within, into, of, for
τούτῳ demo. pron. dat. neut. sg. οὗτος αὕτη τοῦτο this, the same, this same, he, she, it
τοῦτο demo. pron. nom. neut. sg. οὗτος αὕτη τοῦτο this, the same, this same, he, she, it
γὰρ conj. γάρ for, and, because, but, indeed
ὑμῖν pron. dat. 2p. pl. σύ thou, you
οἵτινες relative pron. nom. masc. pl. ὅστις which, who, whosoever, that, whatsoever
οὐ particle of negation. οὐ οὐκ οὐχ not, no, neither, none, nay, nor, never, nothing
μόνον adv. μόνος only, alone, by oneself
τὸ art. acc. neut. sg. ὁ ἡ τό the, this, that, he, she, it
ἀλλὰ conj. ἀλλά but, yea, yet, nevertheless, howbeit, nay, therefore
καὶ conj. καί and, even, also, but
τὸ art. acc. neut. sg. ὁ ἡ τό the, this, that, he, she, it
ἀπὸ prep. ἀπό (+gen) from, of, out of, since, for, off, at, by, in, on
πέρυσι adv. πέρυσι a year ago, last year
11 νυνὶ adv. νυνί now
δὲ conj. δέ but, and, now, also, to the contrary, rather, then
καὶ conj. καί and, even, also, but
τὸ art. acc. neut. sg. ὁ ἡ τό the, this, that, he, she, it
ὅπως adv. ὅπως that, how, to, because, so that, when
καθάπερ adv. καθάπερ even as, as, as well as

ἡ art. nom. fem. sg. ὁ ἡ τό the, this, that, he, she, it
προθυμία n. nom. fem. sg. προθυμία readiness of mind, forwardness of mind
τοῦ art. gen. neut. sg. ὁ ἡ τό the, this, that, he, she, it
οὕτω adv. οὕτω οὕτως so, even so, thus, on this wise, likewise, after this manner
καὶ conj. καί and, even, also, but
τὸ art. nom. neut. sg. ὁ ἡ τό the, this, that, he, she, it
ἐκ prep. ἐκ ἐξ (+gen) of, from, out of, by, on, with, in, among, through
τοῦ art. gen. neut. sg. ὁ ἡ τό the, this, that, he, she, it
12 εἰ conj. εἰ if, whether, that, though, forasmuch
γὰρ conj. γάρ for, and, because, but, indeed
ἡ art. nom. fem. sg. ὁ ἡ τό the, this, that, he, she, it
προθυμία n. nom. fem. sg. προθυμία readiness of mind, forwardness of mind
καθὸ adv. καθό as, according to that, inasmuch as
ἐὰν conj. ἐάν if, soever, except, though, and if, but, whether, if so, so
τις indefinite pron. nom. masc. sg. τὶς certain, some, any man, one, any thing
εὐπρόσδεκτος adj. nom. fem. sg. εὐπρόσδεκτος acceptable, accepted
οὐ particle of negation. οὐ οὐκ οὐχ not, no, neither, none, nay, nor, never, nothing
καθὸ adv. καθό as, according to that, inasmuch as
οὐκ particle of negation. οὐ οὐκ οὐχ not, no, neither, none, nay, nor, never, nothing
13 οὐ particle of negation. οὐ οὐκ οὐχ not, no, neither, none, nay, nor, never, nothing
γὰρ conj. γάρ for, and, because, but, indeed
ἵνα conj. ἵνα that, to, lest, for to, so that, albeit, because, for, so as
ἄλλοις adj. dat. masc. pl. ἄλλος other, another, some, one, more, otherwise
ἄνεσις n. nom. fem. sg. ἄνεσις liberty, rest, eased
ὑμῖν pron. dat. 2p. pl. σύ thou, you
δὲ conj. δέ but, and, now, also, to the contrary, rather, then
θλῖψις n. nom. fem. sg. θλῖψις tribulation, affliction, anguish, persecution
14 ἀλλ' conj. ἀλλά but, yea, yet, nevertheless, howbeit, nay, therefore
ἐξ prep. ἐκ ἐξ (+gen) of, from, out of, by, on, with, in, among, through
ἰσότητος n. gen. fem. sg. ἰσότης equality, equal, equity
ἐν prep. ἐν (+dat) in, by, with, among, at, on, through, to, within, into, of, for
τῷ art. dat. masc. sg. ὁ ἡ τό the, this, that, he, she, it
νῦν adv. νῦν now, henceforth, present, this time
καιρῷ n. dat. masc. sg. καιρός time, season, due time, opportunity
τὸ art. nom. neut. sg. ὁ ἡ τό the, this, that, he, she, it
ὑμῶν pron. gen. 2p. pl. σύ thou, you
περίσσευμα n. nom. neut. sg. περίσσευμα abundance, that is left
εἰς prep. εἰς (+acc) into, to, unto, for, in, on, toward, against, upon, at, among
τὸ art. acc. neut. sg. ὁ ἡ τό the, this, that, he, she, it
ἐκείνων demo. pron. gen. masc. pl. ἐκεῖνος that, he, the same, that same
ὑστέρημα n. acc. neut. sg. ὑστέρημα penury, that which is lacking, want, lack
ἵνα conj. ἵνα that, to, lest, for to, so that, albeit, because, for, so as
καὶ conj. καί and, even, also, but
τὸ art. nom. neut. sg. ὁ ἡ τό the, this, that, he, she, it
ὑμῶν pron. gen. 2p. pl. σύ thou, you
ὑστέρημα n. acc. neut. sg. ὑστέρημα penury, that which is lacking, want, lack
ὅπως adv. ὅπως that, how, to, because, so that, when
ἰσότης n. nom. fem. sg. ἰσότης equality, equal, equity
15 καθὼς adv. καθώς as, even as, according as, according to
Ὁ art. nom. masc. sg. ὁ ἡ τό the, this, that, he, she, it
τὸ art. acc. neut. sg. ὁ ἡ τό the, this, that, he, she, it
πολὺ adj. acc. neut. sg. πολύς many, great, much, long, abundant
οὐκ particle of negation. οὐ οὐκ οὐχ not, no, neither, none, nay, nor, never, nothing
καὶ conj. καί and, even, also, but
ὁ art. nom. masc. sg. ὁ ἡ τό the, this, that, he, she, it

τὸ art. acc. neut. sg. ὁ ἡ τό the, this, that, he, she, it
ὀλίγον adj. acc. neut. sg. ὀλίγος few, little, small, a while, brief, short, short space
οὐκ particle of negation. οὐ οὐκ οὐχ not, no, neither, none, nay, nor, never, nothing
16 Χάρις n. nom. fem. sg. χάρις grace, thank, favour, pleasure
δὲ conj. δέ but, and, now, also, to the contrary, rather, then
τῷ art. dat. masc. sg. ὁ ἡ τό the, this, that, he, she, it
Θεῷ n. dat. masc. sg. θεός God, god
τῷ art. dat. masc. sg. ὁ ἡ τό the, this, that, he, she, it
τὴν art. acc. fem. sg. ὁ ἡ τό the, this, that, he, she, it
αὐτὴν adj. acc. fem. sg. αὐτός ή ό self, of oneself, even, very, the same, he, she, it
σπουδὴν n. acc. fem. sg. σπουδή diligence, haste, business, care, carefulness
ὑπὲρ prep. ὑπέρ (+gen) for, of, for the sake of, (+acc) above, more than
ὑμῶν pron. gen. 2p. pl. σύ thou, you
ἐν prep. ἐν (+dat) in, by, with, among, at, on, through, to, within, into, of, for
τῇ art. dat. fem. sg. ὁ ἡ τό the, this, that, he, she, it
καρδίᾳ n. dat. fem. sg. καρδία heart
Τίτου n. gen. masc. sg. Τίτος Titus
17 ὅτι conj. ὅτι that, for, because, how that, how, because that, for that, though
τὴν art. acc. fem. sg. ὁ ἡ τό the, this, that, he, she, it
μὲν conj. μέν indeed, verily, truly, even, so, some
παράκλησιν n. acc. fem. sg. παράκλησις consolation, exhortation, comfort
σπουδαιότερος compar. adj. nom. masc. sg. σπουδαῖος more forward
δὲ conj. δέ but, and, now, also, to the contrary, rather, then
αὐθαίρετος adj. nom. masc. sg. αὐθαίρετος willing of oneself, of own accord
πρὸς prep. πρός (+gen) for, (+dat) at, (+acc) unto, to, with, for, against
ὑμᾶς pron. acc. 2p. pl. σύ thou, you
18 δὲ conj. δέ but, and, now, also, to the contrary, rather, then
μετ' prep. μετά (+gen) with, among, against, (+acc) after
αὐτοῦ pron. gen. masc. 3p. sg. αὐτός ἡ ὁ self, of oneself, even, very, the same, he, she, it
τὸν art. acc. masc. sg. ὁ ἡ τό the, this, that, he, she, it
ἀδελφὸν n. acc. masc. sg. ἀδελφός brother
οὗ relative pron. gen. masc. sg. ὅς ἥ ὅ who, which, what, that
ὁ art. nom. masc. sg. ὁ ἡ τό the, this, that, he, she, it
ἔπαινος n. nom. masc. sg. ἔπαινος praise
ἐν prep. ἐν (+dat) in, by, with, among, at, on, through, to, within, into, of, for
τῷ art. dat. neut. sg. ὁ ἡ τό the, this, that, he, she, it
εὐαγγελίῳ n. dat. neut. sg. εὐαγγέλιον gospel
διὰ prep. διά (+gen) by, through, with, in, of, (+acc) for, because of, for a cause
πασῶν adj. gen. fem. pl. πᾶς πᾶσα πᾶν all, every, whosoever, every one, no, whole, any
τῶν art. gen. fem. pl. ὁ ἡ τό the, this, that, he, she, it
ἐκκλησιῶν n. gen. fem. pl. ἐκκλησία church, assembly
19 οὐ particle of negation. οὐ οὐκ οὐχ not, no, neither, none, nay, nor, never, nothing
μόνον adv. μόνος only, alone, by oneself
δέ conj. δέ but, and, now, also, to the contrary, rather, then
ἀλλὰ conj. ἀλλά but, yea, yet, nevertheless, howbeit, nay, therefore
καὶ conj. καί and, even, also, but
ὑπὸ prep. ὑπό (+gen) of, by, with, from, among, (+acc) under
τῶν art. gen. fem. pl. ὁ ἡ τό the, this, that, he, she, it
ἐκκλησιῶν n. gen. fem. pl. ἐκκλησία church, assembly
συνέκδημος n. nom. masc. sg. συνέκδημος companion in travel, travel with
ἡμῶν pron. gen. 1p. pl. ἐγώ I
σὺν prep. σύν (+dat) with, beside
τῇ art. dat. fem. sg. ὁ ἡ τό the, this, that, he, she, it
χάριτι n. dat. fem. sg. χάρις grace, thank, favour, pleasure
ταύτῃ demo. pron. dat. fem. sg. οὗτος αὕτη τοῦτο this, the same, this same, he, she, it

τῇ art. dat. fem. sg. ὁ ἡ τό the, this, that, he, she, it
ὑφ' prep. ὑπό (+gen) of, by, with, from, among, (+acc) under
ἡμῶν pron. gen. 1p. pl. ἐγώ I
πρὸς prep. πρός (+gen) for, (+dat) at, (+acc) unto, to, with, for, against
τὴν art. acc. fem. sg. ὁ ἡ τό the, this, that, he, she, it
αὐτοῦ pron. gen. masc. 3p. sg. αὐτός ή ό self, of oneself, even, very, the same, he, she, it
τοῦ art. gen. masc. sg. ὁ ἡ τό the, this, that, he, she, it
Κυρίου n. gen. masc. sg. κύριος Lord, lord, master, sir, LORD, God, Master, owner
δόξαν n. acc. fem. sg. δόξα glory, honour, praise, dignity, worship
καὶ conj. καί and, even, also, but
προθυμίαν n. acc. fem. sg. προθυμία readiness of mind, forwardness of mind
ὑμῶν pron. gen. 2p. pl. σύ thou, you
20 τοῦτο demo. pron. acc. neut. sg. οὗτος αὕτη τοῦτο this, the same, this same, he, she, it
μή particle of negation. μή not, no, lest, neither, none, nothing, nor, never, without
τις indefinite pron. nom. masc. sg. τὶς certain, some, any man, one, any thing
ἡμᾶς pron. acc. 1p. pl. ἐγώ I
ἐν prep. ἐν (+dat) in, by, with, among, at, on, through, to, within, into, of, for
τῇ art. dat. fem. sg. ὁ ἡ τό the, this, that, he, she, it
ἁδρότητι n. dat. fem. sg. ἁδρότης abundance
ταύτῃ demo. pron. dat. fem. sg. οὗτος αὕτη τοῦτο this, the same, this same, he, she, it
τῇ art. dat. fem. sg. ὁ ἡ τό the, this, that, he, she, it
ὑφ' prep. ὑπό (+gen) of, by, with, from, among, (+acc) under
ἡμῶν pron. gen. 1p. pl. ἐγώ I
21 καλὰ adj. acc. neut. pl. καλός good, better, goodly, meet, honest, fair, well, worthy
οὐ particle of negation. οὐ οὐκ οὐχ not, no, neither, none, nay, nor, never, nothing
μόνον adv. μόνος only, alone, by oneself
ἐνώπιον prep. ἐνώπιον (+gen) before, in the sight of, in the presence of. (adv.) before
Κυρίου n. gen. masc. sg. κύριος Lord, lord, master, sir, LORD, God, Master, owner
ἀλλὰ conj. ἀλλά but, yea, yet, nevertheless, howbeit, nay, therefore
καὶ conj. καί and, even, also, but
ἐνώπιον prep. ἐνώπιον (+gen) before, in the sight of, in the presence of. (adv.) before
ἀνθρώπων n. gen. masc. pl. ἄνθρωπος man, human being, person, one, certain
22 δὲ conj. δέ but, and, now, also, to the contrary, rather, then
αὐτοῖς pron. dat. masc. 3p. pl. αὐτός ή ό self, of oneself, even, very, the same, he, she, it
τὸν art. acc. masc. sg. ὁ ἡ τό the, this, that, he, she, it
ἀδελφὸν n. acc. masc. sg. ἀδελφός brother
ἡμῶν pron. gen. 1p. pl. ἐγώ I
ὃν relative pron. acc. masc. sg. ὅς ἥ ὅ who, which, what, that
ἐν prep. ἐν (+dat) in, by, with, among, at, on, through, to, within, into, of, for
πολλοῖς adj. dat. neut. pl. πολύς many, great, much, long, abundant
πολλάκις adv. πολλάκις often, ofttimes, oft
σπουδαῖον adj. acc. masc. sg. σπουδαῖος diligent
νυνὶ adv. νυνί now
δὲ conj. δέ but, and, now, also, to the contrary, rather, then
πολὺ adv. πολύς many, great, much, long, abundant
σπουδαιότερον compar. adj. acc. masc. sg. σπουδαῖος more diligent
πεποιθήσει n. dat. fem. sg. πεποίθησις confidence, trust
πολλῇ adj. dat. fem. sg. πολύς many, great, much, long, abundant
τῇ art. dat. fem. sg. ὁ ἡ τό the, this, that, he, she, it
εἰς prep. εἰς (+acc) into, to, unto, for, in, on, toward, against, upon, at, among
ὑμᾶς pron. acc. 2p. pl. σύ thou, you
23 εἴτε conj. εἴτε whether
ὑπὲρ prep. ὑπέρ (+gen) for, of, for the sake of, (+acc) above, more than
Τίτου n. gen. masc. sg. Τίτος Titus
κοινωνὸς n. nom. masc. sg. κοινωνός partaker, partner, companion, fellowship

ἐμὸς poss. pron. nom. masc. 1p. sg. ἐμός my, mine, mine own, of me
καὶ conj. καί and, even, also, but
εἰς prep. εἰς (+acc) into, to, unto, for, in, on, toward, against, upon, at, among
ὑμᾶς pron. acc. 2p. pl. σύ thou, you
συνεργός adj. nom. masc. sg. συνεργός fellowlabourer, fellowhelper, fellowworker
εἴτε conj. εἴτε whether
ἀδελφοὶ n. nom. masc. pl. ἀδελφός brother
ἡμῶν pron. gen. 1p. pl. ἐγώ I
ἀπόστολοι n. nom. masc. pl. ἀπόστολος apostle, messenger, he that is sent
ἐκκλησιῶν n. gen. fem. pl. ἐκκλησία church, assembly
δόξα n. nom. fem. sg. δόξα glory, honour, praise, dignity, worship
Χριστοῦ n. gen. masc. sg. Χριστός Christ
24 τὴν art. acc. fem. sg. ὁ ἡ τό the, this, that, he, she, it
οὖν conj. οὖν therefore, then, so, and, now, wherefore
ἔνδειξιν n. acc. fem. sg. ἔνδειξις declare, evident token, proof
τῆς art. gen. fem. sg. ὁ ἡ τό the, this, that, he, she, it
ἀγάπης n. gen. fem. sg. ἀγάπη love, charity, feast of charity
ὑμῶν pron. gen. 2p. pl. σύ thou, you
καὶ conj. καί and, even, also, but
ἡμῶν pron. gen. 1p. pl. ἐγώ I
καυχήσεως n. gen. fem. sg. καύχησις boasting, rejoicing, glorying
ὑπὲρ prep. ὑπέρ (+gen) for, of, for the sake of, (+acc) above, more than
ὑμῶν pron. gen. 2p. pl. σύ thou, you
εἰς prep. εἰς (+acc) into, to, unto, for, in, on, toward, against, upon, at, among
αὐτοὺς pron. acc. masc. 3p. pl. αὐτός ἡ ὁ self, of oneself, even, very, the same, he, she, it
καὶ conj. καί and, even, also, but
εἰς prep. εἰς (+acc) into, to, unto, for, in, on, toward, against, upon, at, among
πρόσωπον n. acc. neut. sg. πρόσωπον face, presence, person, countenance
τῶν art. gen. fem. pl. ὁ ἡ τό the, this, that, he, she, it
ἐκκλησιῶν n. gen. fem. pl. ἐκκλησία church, assembly

9

1 Περὶ prep. περί (+gen) of, for, concerning, (+acc) about, concerning, in
μὲν conj. μέν indeed, verily, truly, even, so, some
γὰρ conj. γάρ for, and, because, but, indeed
τῆς art. gen. fem. sg. ὁ ἡ τό the, this, that, he, she, it
διακονίας n. gen. fem. sg. διακονία ministry, administration, service, office, relief
τῆς art. gen. fem. sg. ὁ ἡ τό the, this, that, he, she, it
εἰς prep. εἰς (+acc) into, to, unto, for, in, on, toward, against, upon, at, among
τοὺς art. acc. masc. pl. ὁ ἡ τό the, this, that, he, she, it
ἁγίους adj. acc. masc. pl. ἅγιος Holy, holy, saint, Holy One, holy thing, most holy
περισσόν adj. nom. neut. sg. περισσός more, beyond measure, advantage, exceedingly
μοί pron. dat. 1p. sg. ἐγώ I
τὸ art. nom. neut. sg. ὁ ἡ τό the, this, that, he, she, it
ὑμῖν pron. dat. 2p. pl. σύ thou, you
2 γὰρ conj. γάρ for, and, because, but, indeed
τὴν art. acc. fem. sg. ὁ ἡ τό the, this, that, he, she, it
προθυμίαν n. acc. fem. sg. προθυμία readiness of mind, forwardness of mind
ὑμῶν pron. gen. 2p. pl. σύ thou, you
ἣν relative pron. acc. fem. sg. ὅς ἥ ὅ who, which, what, that
ὑπὲρ prep. ὑπέρ (+gen) for, of, for the sake of, (+acc) above, more than
ὑμῶν pron. gen. 2p. pl. σύ thou, you
Μακεδόσιν n. dat. masc. pl. Μακεδών of Macedonia, Macedonian
ὅτι conj. ὅτι that, for, because, how that, how, because that, for that, though

Ἀχαΐα n. nom. fem. sg. Ἀχαΐα Achaia
ἀπὸ prep. ἀπό (+gen) from, of, out of, since, for, off, at, by, in, on
πέρυσι adv. πέρυσι a year ago, last year
καὶ conj. καί and, even, also, but
ὁ art. nom. masc. sg. ὁ ἡ τό the, this, that, he, she, it
ἐξ prep. ἐκ ἐξ (+gen) of, from, out of, by, on, with, in, among, through
ὑμῶν pron. gen. 2p. pl. σύ thou, you
ζῆλος n. nom. masc. sg. ζῆλος zeal, envying, indignation, emulation, jealousy
τοὺς art. acc. masc. pl. ὁ ἡ τό the, this, that, he, she, it
πλείονας compar. adj. acc. masc. pl. πολύς many, great, much, long, abundant
3 δὲ conj. δέ but, and, now, also, to the contrary, rather, then
τοὺς art. acc. masc. pl. ὁ ἡ τό the, this, that, he, she, it
ἀδελφούς n. acc. masc. pl. ἀδελφός brother
ἵνα conj. ἵνα that, to, lest, for to, so that, albeit, because, for, so as
μὴ particle of negation. μή not, no, lest, neither, none, nothing, nor, never, without
τὸ art. nom. neut. sg. ὁ ἡ τό the, this, that, he, she, it
καύχημα n. nom. neut. sg. καύχημα whereof to glory, rejoicing, glorying, boasting
ἡμῶν pron. gen. 1p. pl. ἐγώ I
τὸ art. nom. neut. sg. ὁ ἡ τό the, this, that, he, she, it
ὑπὲρ prep. ὑπέρ (+gen) for, of, for the sake of, (+acc) above, more than
ὑμῶν pron. gen. 2p. pl. σύ thou, you
ἐν prep. ἐν (+dat) in, by, with, among, at, on, through, to, within, into, of, for
τῷ art. dat. neut. sg. ὁ ἡ τό the, this, that, he, she, it
μέρει n. dat. neut. sg. μέρος part, coast, portion, behalf, respect, piece, side
τούτῳ demo. pron. dat. neut. sg. οὗτος αὕτη τοῦτο this, the same, this same, he, she, it
ἵνα conj. ἵνα that, to, lest, for to, so that, albeit, because, for, so as
καθὼς adv. καθώς as, even as, according as, according to
4 μή particle of negation. μή not, no, lest, neither, none, nothing, nor, never, without
πως particle. πώς by any means, by some means, haply, perhaps
ἐὰν conj. ἐάν if, soever, except, though, and if, but, whether, if so, so
σὺν prep. σύν (+dat) with, beside
ἐμοὶ pron. dat. 1p. sg. ἐγώ I
Μακεδόνες n. nom. masc. pl. Μακεδών of Macedonia, Macedonian
καὶ conj. καί and, even, also, but
ὑμᾶς pron. acc. 2p. pl. σύ thou, you
ἀπαρασκευάστους adj. acc. masc. pl. ἀπαρασκεύαστος unprepared
ἡμεῖς pron. nom. 1p. pl. ἐγώ I
ἵνα conj. ἵνα that, to, lest, for to, so that, albeit, because, for, so as
μὴ particle of negation. μή not, no, lest, neither, none, nothing, nor, never, without
ὑμεῖς pron. nom. 2p. pl. σύ thou, you
ἐν prep. ἐν (+dat) in, by, with, among, at, on, through, to, within, into, of, for
τῇ art. dat. fem. sg. ὁ ἡ τό the, this, that, he, she, it
ὑποστάσει n. dat. fem. sg. ὑπόστασις confident, confidence, substance, person, nature
ταύτῃ demo. pron. dat. fem. sg. οὗτος αὕτη τοῦτο this, the same, this same, he, she, it
τῆς art. gen. fem. sg. ὁ ἡ τό the, this, that, he, she, it
καυχήσεως n. gen. fem. sg. καύχησις boasting, rejoicing, glorying
5 ἀναγκαῖον adj. nom. neut. sg. ἀναγκαῖος near, necessary, more needful, of necessity
οὖν conj. οὖν therefore, then, so, and, now, wherefore
τοὺς art. acc. masc. pl. ὁ ἡ τό the, this, that, he, she, it
ἀδελφοὺς n. acc. masc. pl. ἀδελφός brother
ἵνα conj. ἵνα that, to, lest, for to, so that, albeit, because, for, so as
εἰς prep. εἰς (+acc) into, to, unto, for, in, on, toward, against, upon, at, among
ὑμᾶς pron. acc. 2p. pl. σύ thou, you
καὶ conj. καί and, even, also, but
τὴν art. acc. fem. sg. ὁ ἡ τό the, this, that, he, she, it

εὐλογίαν n. acc. fem. sg. εὐλογία blessing, bounty, matter of bounty, fair speech
ὑμῶν pron. gen. 2p. pl. σύ thou, you
ταύτην demo. pron. acc. fem. sg. οὗτος αὕτη τοῦτο this, the same, this same, he, she, it
ἑτοίμην adj. acc. fem. sg. ἕτοιμος ready, prepared, readiness
οὕτως adv. οὕτω οὕτως so, even so, thus, on this wise, likewise, after this manner
ὡς adv. ὡς as, when, as it were, how, about, like, as soon as, even as, while
εὐλογίαν n. acc. fem. sg. εὐλογία blessing, bounty, matter of bounty, fair speech
καὶ conj. καί and, even, also, but
μὴ particle of negation. μή not, no, lest, neither, none, nothing, nor, never, without
ὥσπερ adv. ὥσπερ as, even as, like as
πλεονεξίαν n. acc. fem. sg. πλεονεξία covetousness, covetous practice, greediness
6 Τοῦτο demo. pron. nom. neut. sg. οὗτος αὕτη τοῦτο this, the same, this same, he, she, it
δέ conj. δέ but, and, now, also, to the contrary, rather, then
ὁ art. nom. masc. sg. ὁ ἡ τό the, this, that, he, she, it
φειδομένως adv. φειδομένως sparingly
φειδομένως adv. φειδομένως sparingly
καὶ conj. καί and, even, also, but
καὶ conj. καί and, even, also, but
ὁ art. nom. masc. sg. ὁ ἡ τό the, this, that, he, she, it
ἐπ' prep. ἐπί (+gen) on, in, upon, (+dat) in, at, for, upon, (+acc) on, upon, unto, to, against
εὐλογίαις n. dat. fem. pl. εὐλογία blessing, bounty, matter of bounty, fair speech
ἐπ' prep. ἐπί (+gen) on, in, upon, (+dat) in, at, for, upon, (+acc) on, upon, unto, to, against
εὐλογίαις n. dat. fem. pl. εὐλογία blessing, bounty, matter of bounty, fair speech
καὶ conj. καί and, even, also, but
7 ἕκαστος adj. nom. masc. sg. ἕκαστος every man, every, every one, any man, each
καθὼς adv. καθώς as, even as, according as, according to
τῇ art. dat. fem. sg. ὁ ἡ τό the, this, that, he, she, it
καρδίᾳ n. dat. fem. sg. καρδία heart
μὴ particle of negation. μή not, no, lest, neither, none, nothing, nor, never, without
ἐκ prep. ἐκ ἐξ (+gen) of, from, out of, by, on, with, in, among, through
λύπης n. gen. fem. sg. λύπη sorrow, heaviness, grief, grievous, grudgingly
ἢ particle. ἤ or, than, either, nor, or else, and, rather than
ἐξ prep. ἐκ ἐξ (+gen) of, from, out of, by, on, with, in, among, through
ἀνάγκης n. gen. fem. sg. ἀνάγκη must needs, necessity, distress, inevitable
ἱλαρὸν adj. acc. masc. sg. ἱλαρός cheerful
γὰρ conj. γάρ for, and, because, but, indeed
δότην n. acc. masc. sg. δότης giver
ὁ art. nom. masc. sg. ὁ ἡ τό the, this, that, he, she, it
Θεός n. nom. masc. sg. θεός God, god
8 δυνατὸς adj. nom. masc. sg. δυνατός able, possible, mighty, strong
δὲ conj. δέ but, and, now, also, to the contrary, rather, then
ὁ art. nom. masc. sg. ὁ ἡ τό the, this, that, he, she, it
Θεὸς n. nom. masc. sg. θεός God, god
πᾶσαν adj. acc. fem. sg. πᾶς πᾶσα πᾶν all, every, whosoever, every one, no, whole, any
χάριν n. acc. fem. sg. χάρις grace, thank, favour, pleasure
εἰς prep. εἰς (+acc) into, to, unto, for, in, on, toward, against, upon, at, among
ὑμᾶς pron. acc. 2p. pl. σύ thou, you
ἵνα conj. ἵνα that, to, lest, for to, so that, albeit, because, for, so as
ἐν prep. ἐν (+dat) in, by, with, among, at, on, through, to, within, into, of, for
παντὶ adj. dat. neut. sg. πᾶς πᾶσα πᾶν all, every, whosoever, every one, no, whole, any
πάντοτε adv. πάντοτε always, ever, always, evermore
πᾶσαν adj. acc. fem. sg. πᾶς πᾶσα πᾶν all, every, whosoever, every one, no, whole, any
αὐτάρκειαν n. acc. fem. sg. αὐτάρκεια sufficiency, contentment
εἰς prep. εἰς (+acc) into, to, unto, for, in, on, toward, against, upon, at, among
πᾶν adj. acc. neut. sg. πᾶς πᾶσα πᾶν all, every, whosoever, every one, no, whole, any

ἔργον n. acc. neut. sg. ἔργον work, deed, doing labour
ἀγαθόν adj. acc. neut. sg. ἀγαθός good, good thing, that which is good, well
9 καθὼς adv. καθώς as, even as, according as, according to
τοῖς art. dat. masc. pl. ὁ ἡ τό the, this, that, he, she, it
πένησιν adj. dat. masc. pl. πένης poor
ἡ art. nom. fem. sg. ὁ ἡ τό the, this, that, he, she, it
δικαιοσύνη n. nom. fem. sg. δικαιοσύνη righteousness
αὐτοῦ pron. gen. masc. 3p. sg. αὐτός ἡ ὁ self, of oneself, even, very, the same, he, she, it
εἰς prep. εἰς (+acc) into, to, unto, for, in, on, toward, against, upon, at, among
τὸν art. acc. masc. sg. ὁ ἡ τό the, this, that, he, she, it
αἰῶνα n. acc. masc. sg. αἰών ever, ever and ever, evermore, age, eternal, world
10 ὁ art. nom. masc. sg. ὁ ἡ τό the, this, that, he, she, it
δὲ conj. δέ but, and, now, also, to the contrary, rather, then
σπέρμα n. acc. neut. sg. σπέρμα seed, issue
τῷ art. dat. masc. sg. ὁ ἡ τό the, this, that, he, she, it
καὶ conj. καί and, even, also, but
ἄρτον n. acc. masc. sg. ἄρτος bread, loaf
εἰς prep. εἰς (+acc) into, to, unto, for, in, on, toward, against, upon, at, among
βρῶσιν n. acc. fem. sg. βρῶσις rust, meat, eating, food, morsel of meat
καὶ conj. καί and, even, also, but
τὸν art. acc. masc. sg. ὁ ἡ τό the, this, that, he, she, it
σπόρον n. acc. masc. sg. σπόρος seed, seed sown
ὑμῶν pron. gen. 2p. pl. σύ thou, you
καὶ conj. καί and, even, also, but
τὰ art. acc. neut. pl. ὁ ἡ τό the, this, that, he, she, it
γεννήματα n. acc. neut. pl. γέννημα generation, fruit
τῆς art. gen. fem. sg. ὁ ἡ τό the, this, that, he, she, it
δικαιοσύνης n. gen. fem. sg. δικαιοσύνη righteousness
ὑμῶν pron. gen. 2p. pl. σύ thou, you
11 ἐν prep. ἐν (+dat) in, by, with, among, at, on, through, to, within, into, of, for
παντὶ adj. dat. neut. sg. πᾶς πᾶσα πᾶν all, every, whosoever, every one, no, whole, any
εἰς prep. εἰς (+acc) into, to, unto, for, in, on, toward, against, upon, at, among
πᾶσαν adj. acc. fem. sg. πᾶς πᾶσα πᾶν all, every, whosoever, every one, no, whole, any
ἁπλότητα n. acc. fem. sg. ἁπλότης simplicity, singleness, bountifulness, liberal
ἥτις relative pron. nom. fem. sg. ὅστις which, who, whosoever, that, whatsoever
δι' prep. διά (+gen) by, through, with, in, of, (+acc) for, because of, for a cause
ἡμῶν pron. gen. 1p. pl. ἐγώ I
εὐχαριστίαν n. acc. fem. sg. εὐχαριστία thankfulness, thanksgiving, giving of thanks
τῷ art. dat. masc. sg. ὁ ἡ τό the, this, that, he, she, it
Θεῷ n. dat. masc. sg. θεός God, god
12 ὅτι conj. ὅτι that, for, because, how that, how, because that, for that, though
ἡ art. nom. fem. sg. ὁ ἡ τό the, this, that, he, she, it
διακονία n. nom. fem. sg. διακονία ministry, administration, service, office, relief
τῆς art. gen. fem. sg. ὁ ἡ τό the, this, that, he, she, it
λειτουργίας n. gen. fem. sg. λειτουργία ministration, service, ministry
ταύτης demo. pron. gen. fem. sg. οὗτος αὕτη τοῦτο this, the same, this same, he, she, it
οὐ particle of negation. οὐ οὐκ οὐχ not, no, neither, none, nay, nor, never, nothing
μόνον adv. μόνος only, alone, by oneself
τὰ art. acc. neut. pl. ὁ ἡ τό the, this, that, he, she, it
ὑστερήματα n. acc. neut. pl. ὑστέρημα penury, that which is lacking, want, lack
τῶν art. gen. masc. pl. ὁ ἡ τό the, this, that, he, she, it
ἁγίων adj. gen. masc. pl. ἅγιος Holy, holy, saint, Holy One, holy thing, most holy
ἀλλὰ conj. ἀλλά but, yea, yet, nevertheless, howbeit, nay, therefore
καὶ conj. καί and, even, also, but
διὰ prep. διά (+gen) by, through, with, in, of, (+acc) for, because of, for a cause

πολλῶν adj. gen. fem. pl. πολύς many, great, much, long, abundant
εὐχαριστιῶν n. gen. fem. pl. εὐχαριστία thankfulness, thanksgiving, giving of thanks
τῷ art. dat. masc. sg. ὁ ἡ τό the, this, that, he, she, it
Θεῷ n. dat. masc. sg. θεός God, god
13 διὰ prep. διά (+gen) by, through, with, in, of, (+acc) for, because of, for a cause
τῆς art. gen. fem. sg. ὁ ἡ τό the, this, that, he, she, it
δοκιμῆς n. gen. fem. sg. δοκιμή experience, proof, experiment, trial
διακονίας n. gen. fem. sg. διακονία ministry, administration, service, office, relief
ταύτης demo. pron. gen. fem. sg. οὗτος αὕτη τοῦτο this, the same, this same, he, she, it
τὸν art. acc. masc. sg. ὁ ἡ τό the, this, that, he, she, it
Θεὸν n. acc. masc. sg. θεός God, god
ἐπὶ prep. ἐπί (+gen) on, in, upon, (+dat) in, at, for, upon, (+acc) on, upon, unto, to, against
τῇ art. dat. fem. sg. ὁ ἡ τό the, this, that, he, she, it
ὑποταγῇ n. dat. fem. sg. ὑποταγή subjection
τῆς art. gen. fem. sg. ὁ ἡ τό the, this, that, he, she, it
ὁμολογίας n. gen. fem. sg. ὁμολογία profession, confession, profess
ὑμῶν pron. gen. 2p. pl. σύ thou, you
εἰς prep. εἰς (+acc) into, to, unto, for, in, on, toward, against, upon, at, among
τὸ art. acc. neut. sg. ὁ ἡ τό the, this, that, he, she, it
εὐαγγέλιον n. acc. neut. sg. εὐαγγέλιον gospel
τοῦ art. gen. masc. sg. ὁ ἡ τό the, this, that, he, she, it
Χριστοῦ n. gen. masc. sg. Χριστός Christ
καὶ conj. καί and, even, also, but
ἁπλότητι n. dat. fem. sg. ἁπλότης simplicity, singleness, bountifulness, liberal, liberality
τῆς art. gen. fem. sg. ὁ ἡ τό the, this, that, he, she, it
κοινωνίας n. gen. fem. sg. κοινωνία fellowship, communion, contribution, distribution
εἰς prep. εἰς (+acc) into, to, unto, for, in, on, toward, against, upon, at, among
αὐτοὺς pron. acc. masc. 3p. pl. αὐτός ή ό self, of oneself, even, very, the same, he, she, it
καὶ conj. καί and, even, also, but
εἰς prep. εἰς (+acc) into, to, unto, for, in, on, toward, against, upon, at, among
πάντας adj. acc. masc. pl. πᾶς πᾶσα πᾶν all, every, whosoever, every one, no, whole, any
14 καὶ conj. καί and, even, also, but
αὐτῶν pron. gen. masc. 3p. pl. αὐτός ή ό self, of oneself, even, very, the same, he, she, it
δεήσει n. dat. fem. sg. δέησις prayer, supplication, request
ὑπὲρ prep. ὑπέρ (+gen) for, of, for the sake of, (+acc) above, more than
ὑμῶν pron. gen. 2p. pl. σύ thou, you
ὑμᾶς pron. acc. 2p. pl. σύ thou, you
διὰ prep. διά (+gen) by, through, with, in, of, (+acc) for, because of, for a cause
τὴν art. acc. fem. sg. ὁ ἡ τό the, this, that, he, she, it
χάριν n. acc. fem. sg. χάρις grace, thank, favour, pleasure
τοῦ art. gen. masc. sg. ὁ ἡ τό the, this, that, he, she, it
Θεοῦ n. gen. masc. sg. θεός God, god
ἐφ' prep. ἐπί (+gen) on, in, upon, (+dat) in, at, for, upon, (+acc) on, upon, unto, to, against
ὑμῖν pron. dat. 2p. pl. σύ thou, you
15 χάρις n. nom. fem. sg. χάρις grace, thank, favour, pleasure
δὲ conj. δέ but, and, now, also, to the contrary, rather, then
τῷ art. dat. masc. sg. ὁ ἡ τό the, this, that, he, she, it
Θεῷ n. dat. masc. sg. θεός God, god
ἐπὶ prep. ἐπί (+gen) on, in, upon, (+dat) in, at, for, upon, (+acc) on, upon, unto, to, against
τῇ art. dat. fem. sg. ὁ ἡ τό the, this, that, he, she, it
ἀνεκδιηγήτῳ adj. dat. fem. sg. ἀνεκδιήγητος unspeakable
αὐτοῦ pron. gen. masc. 3p. sg. αὐτός ή ό self, of oneself, even, very, the same, he, she, it
δωρεᾷ n. dat. fem. sg. δωρεά gift

10

1 Αὐτὸς pron. nom. masc. 3p. sg. αὐτός ή ό self, of oneself, even, very, the same, he, she, it
δὲ conj. δέ but, and, now, also, to the contrary, rather, then
ἐγὼ pron. nom. 1p. sg. ἐγώ I
Παῦλος n. nom. masc. sg. Παῦλος Paul, Paulus
ὑμᾶς pron. acc. 2p. pl. σύ thou, you
διὰ prep. διά (+gen) by, through, with, in, of, (+acc) for, because of, for a cause
τῆς art. gen. fem. sg. ὁ ἡ τό the, this, that, he, she, it
πρᾳότητος n. gen. fem. sg. πρᾳότης meekness
καὶ conj. καί and, even, also, but
ἐπιεικείας n. gen. fem. sg. ἐπιείκεια clemency, gentleness
τοῦ art. gen. masc. sg. ὁ ἡ τό the, this, that, he, she, it
Χριστοῦ n. gen. masc. sg. Χριστός Christ
ὃς relative pron. nom. masc. sg. ὅς ἥ ὅ who, which, what, that
κατὰ prep. κατά (+gen) against, by, throughout, down, (+acc) according to, after, with
πρόσωπον n. acc. neut. sg. πρόσωπον face, presence, person, countenance
μὲν conj. μέν indeed, verily, truly, even, so, some
ταπεινὸς adj. nom. masc. sg. ταπεινός humble, of low degree, base, cast down, lowly
ἐν prep. ἐν (+dat) in, by, with, among, at, on, through, to, within, into, of, for
ὑμῖν pron. dat. 2p. pl. σύ thou, you
δὲ conj. δέ but, and, now, also, to the contrary, rather, then
εἰς prep. εἰς (+acc) into, to, unto, for, in, on, toward, against, upon, at, among
ὑμᾶς pron. acc. 2p. pl. σύ thou, you
2 δὲ conj. δέ but, and, now, also, to the contrary, rather, then
τὸ art. acc. neut. sg. ὁ ἡ τό the, this, that, he, she, it
μὴ particle of negation. μή not, no, lest, neither, none, nothing, nor, never, without
τῇ art. dat. fem. sg. ὁ ἡ τό the, this, that, he, she, it
πεποιθήσει n. dat. fem. sg. πεποίθησις confidence, trust
ᾗ relative pron. dat. fem. sg. ὅς ἥ ὅ who, which, what, that
ἐπί prep. ἐπί (+gen) on, in, upon, (+dat) in, at, for, upon, (+acc) on, upon, unto, to, against
τινας indefinite pron. acc. masc. pl. τὶς certain, some, any man, one, any thing
τοὺς art. acc. masc. pl. ὁ ἡ τό the, this, that, he, she, it
ἡμᾶς pron. acc. 1p. pl. ἐγώ I
ὡς adv. ὡς as, when, as it were, how, about, like, as soon as, even as, while
κατὰ prep. κατά (+gen) against, by, throughout, down, (+acc) according to, after, with
σάρκα n. acc. fem. sg. σάρξ flesh, carnal
3 ἐν prep. ἐν (+dat) in, by, with, among, at, on, through, to, within, into, of, for
σαρκὶ n. dat. fem. sg. σάρξ flesh, carnal
γὰρ conj. γάρ for, and, because, but, indeed
οὐ particle of negation. οὐ οὐκ οὐχ not, no, neither, none, nay, nor, never, nothing
κατὰ prep. κατά (+gen) against, by, throughout, down, (+acc) according to, after, with
σάρκα n. acc. fem. sg. σάρξ flesh, carnal
4 τὰ art. nom. neut. pl. ὁ ἡ τό the, this, that, he, she, it
γὰρ conj. γάρ for, and, because, but, indeed
ὅπλα n. nom. neut. pl. ὅπλον instrument, armour, weapon
τῆς art. gen. fem. sg. ὁ ἡ τό the, this, that, he, she, it
στρατείας n. gen. fem. sg. στρατεία warfare
ἡμῶν pron. gen. 1p. pl. ἐγώ I
οὐ particle of negation. οὐ οὐκ οὐχ not, no, neither, none, nay, nor, never, nothing
σαρκικὰ adj. nom. neut. pl. σαρκικός carnal, fleshly
ἀλλὰ conj. ἀλλά but, yea, yet, nevertheless, howbeit, nay, therefore
δυνατὰ adj. nom. neut. pl. δυνατός able, possible, mighty, strong
τῷ art. dat. masc. sg. ὁ ἡ τό the, this, that, he, she, it
Θεῷ n. dat. masc. sg. θεός God, god

πρὸς prep. πρός (+gen) for, (+dat) at, (+acc) unto, to, with, for, against
καθαίρεσιν n. acc. fem. sg. καθαίρεσις pulling down, destruction
ὀχυρωμάτων n. gen. neut. pl. ὀχύρωμα strong hold
λογισμοὺς n. acc. masc. pl. λογισμός thought, imagination
5 καὶ conj. καί and, even, also, but
πᾶν adj. acc. neut. sg. πᾶς πᾶσα πᾶν all, every, whosoever, every one, no, whole, any
ὕψωμα n. acc. neut. sg. ὕψωμα height, high thing
κατὰ prep. κατά (+gen) against, by, throughout, down, (+acc) according to, after, with
τῆς art. gen. fem. sg. ὁ ἡ τό the, this, that, he, she, it
γνώσεως n. gen. fem. sg. γνῶσις knowledge, science
τοῦ art. gen. masc. sg. ὁ ἡ τό the, this, that, he, she, it
Θεοῦ n. gen. masc. sg. θεός God, god
καὶ conj. καί and, even, also, but
πᾶν adj. acc. neut. sg. πᾶς πᾶσα πᾶν all, every, whosoever, every one, no, whole, any
νόημα n. acc. neut. sg. νόημα mind, device, thought
εἰς prep. εἰς (+acc) into, to, unto, for, in, on, toward, against, upon, at, among
τὴν art. acc. fem. sg. ὁ ἡ τό the, this, that, he, she, it
ὑπακοὴν n. acc. fem. sg. ὑπακοή obedience, obey, make obedient, obedient
τοῦ art. gen. masc. sg. ὁ ἡ τό the, this, that, he, she, it
Χριστοῦ n. gen. masc. sg. Χριστός Christ
6 καὶ conj. καί and, even, also, but
ἐν prep. ἐν (+dat) in, by, with, among, at, on, through, to, within, into, of, for
ἑτοίμῳ adj. dat. neut. sg. ἕτοιμος ready, prepared, readiness
πᾶσαν adj. acc. fem. sg. πᾶς πᾶσα πᾶν all, every, whosoever, every one, no, whole, any
παρακοήν n. acc. fem. sg. παρακοή disobedience
ὅταν conj. ὅταν when, as soon as, as long as, that, whensoever, while
ὑμῶν pron. gen. 2p. pl. σύ thou, you
ἡ art. nom. fem. sg. ὁ ἡ τό the, this, that, he, she, it
ὑπακοή n. nom. fem. sg. ὑπακοή obedience, obey, make obedient, obedient
7 τὰ art. acc. neut. pl. ὁ ἡ τό the, this, that, he, she, it
κατὰ prep. κατά (+gen) against, by, throughout, down, (+acc) according to, after, with
πρόσωπον n. acc. neut. sg. πρόσωπον face, presence, person, countenance
εἴ conj. εἰ if, whether, that, though, forasmuch
τις indefinite pron. nom. masc. sg. τὶς certain, some, any man, one, any thing
ἑαυτῷ reflexive pron. dat. masc. 3p. sg. ἑαυτοῦ himself, herself, itself, yourself, ourselves
Χριστοῦ n. gen. masc. sg. Χριστός Christ
τοῦτο demo. pron. acc. neut. sg. οὗτος αὕτη τοῦτο this, the same, this same, he, she, it
πάλιν adv. πάλιν again
ἀφ' prep. ἀπό (+gen) from, of, out of, since, for, off, at, by, in, on
ἑαυτοῦ reflexive pron. gen. masc. 3p. sg. ἑαυτοῦ himself, herself, itself, yourself, ourselves
ὅτι conj. ὅτι that, for, because, how that, how, because that, for that, though
καθὼς adv. καθώς as, even as, according as, according to
αὐτὸς pron. nom. masc. 3p. sg. αὐτός ή ό self, of oneself, even, very, the same, he, she, it
Χριστοῦ n. gen. masc. sg. Χριστός Christ
οὕτω adv. οὕτω οὕτως so, even so, thus, on this wise, likewise, after this manner
καὶ conj. καί and, even, also, but
ἡμεῖς pron. nom. 1p. pl. ἐγώ I
Χριστοῦ n. gen. masc. sg. Χριστός Christ
8 ἐάν conj. ἐάν if, soever, except, though, and if, but, whether, if so, so
τε conj. τέ and, both, also
γὰρ conj. γάρ for, and, because, but, indeed
καὶ conj. καί and, even, also, but
περισσότερόν compar. adj. acc. neut. sg. περισσός more, beyond measure, advantage
τι indefinite pron. acc. neut. sg. τὶς certain, some, any man, one, any thing
περὶ prep. περί (+gen) of, for, concerning, (+acc) about, concerning, in

τῆς art. gen. fem. sg. ὁ ἡ τό the, this, that, he, she, it
ἐξουσίας n. gen. fem. sg. ἐξουσία power, authority, right, strength, jurisdiction
ἡμῶν pron. gen. 1p. pl. ἐγώ I
ἧς relative pron. gen. fem. sg. ὅς ἥ ὅ who, which, what, that
ὁ art. nom. masc. sg. ὁ ἡ τό the, this, that, he, she, it
Κύριος n. nom. masc. sg. κύριος Lord, lord, master, sir, LORD, God, Master, owner
ἡμῖν pron. dat. 1p. pl. ἐγώ I
εἰς prep. εἰς (+acc) into, to, unto, for, in, on, toward, against, upon, at, among
οἰκοδομὴν n. acc. fem. sg. οἰκοδομή building, edifying, edification
καὶ conj. καί and, even, also, but
οὐκ particle of negation. οὐ οὐκ οὐχ not, no, neither, none, nay, nor, never, nothing
εἰς prep. εἰς (+acc) into, to, unto, for, in, on, toward, against, upon, at, among
καθαίρεσιν n. acc. fem. sg. καθαίρεσις pulling down, destruction
ὑμῶν pron. gen. 2p. pl. σύ thou, you
οὐκ particle of negation. οὐ οὐκ οὐχ not, no, neither, none, nay, nor, never, nothing
9 ἵνα conj. ἵνα that, to, lest, for to, so that, albeit, because, for, so as
μὴ particle of negation. μή not, no, lest, neither, none, nothing, nor, never, without
ὡς adv. ὡς as, when, as it were, how, about, like, as soon as, even as, while
ἂν particle. ἄν Indicating contingency. No English translation.
ὑμᾶς pron. acc. 2p. pl. σύ thou, you
διὰ prep. διά (+gen) by, through, with, in, of, (+acc) for, because of, for a cause
τῶν art. gen. fem. pl. ὁ ἡ τό the, this, that, he, she, it
ἐπιστολῶν n. gen. fem. pl. ἐπιστολή letter, epistle
10 ὅτι conj. ὅτι that, for, because, how that, how, because that, for that, though
Αἱ art. nom. fem. pl. ὁ ἡ τό the, this, that, he, she, it
μέν conj. μέν indeed, verily, truly, even, so, some
ἐπιστολαὶ n. nom. fem. pl. ἐπιστολή letter, epistle
βαρεῖαι adj. nom. fem. pl. βαρύς grievous, heavy, weightier, weighty
καὶ conj. καί and, even, also, but
ἰσχυραί adj. nom. fem. pl. ἰσχυρός mighty, strong, mightier, stronger
ἡ art. nom. fem. sg. ὁ ἡ τό the, this, that, he, she, it
δὲ conj. δέ but, and, now, also, to the contrary, rather, then
παρουσία n. nom. fem. sg. παρουσία coming, presence
τοῦ art. gen. neut. sg. ὁ ἡ τό the, this, that, he, she, it
σώματος n. gen. neut. sg. σῶμα body, bodily, slave
ἀσθενὴς adj. nom. fem. sg. ἀσθενής weak, sick, impotent, more feeble
καὶ conj. καί and, even, also, but
ὁ art. nom. masc. sg. ὁ ἡ τό the, this, that, he, she, it
λόγος n. nom. masc. sg. λόγος word, saying, account, speech, thing, matter
11 τοῦτο demo. pron. acc. neut. sg. οὗτος αὕτη τοῦτο this, the same, this same, he, she, it
ὁ art. nom. masc. sg. ὁ ἡ τό the, this, that, he, she, it
τοιοῦτος demo. pron. nom. masc. sg. τοιοῦτος such, like
ὅτι conj. ὅτι that, for, because, how that, how, because that, for that, though
οἷοί relative pron. nom. masc. pl. οἷος what manner of, such as, as, which, what, so as
τῷ art. dat. masc. sg. ὁ ἡ τό the, this, that, he, she, it
λόγῳ n. dat. masc. sg. λόγος word, saying, account, speech, thing, matter
δι' prep. διά (+gen) by, through, with, in, of, (+acc) for, because of, for a cause
ἐπιστολῶν n. gen. fem. pl. ἐπιστολή letter, epistle
τοιοῦτοι demo. pron. nom. masc. pl. τοιοῦτος such, like
καὶ conj. καί and, even, also, but
τῷ art. dat. neut. sg. ὁ ἡ τό the, this, that, he, she, it
ἔργῳ n. dat. neut. sg. ἔργον work, deed, doing labour
12 οὐ particle of negation. οὐ οὐκ οὐχ not, no, neither, none, nay, nor, never, nothing
γὰρ conj. γάρ for, and, because, but, indeed
ἢ particle. ἤ or, than, either, nor, or else, and, rather than

ἑαυτούς reflexive pron. acc. masc. 3p. pl. ἑαυτοῦ himself, herself, itself, yourself, ourselves
τισι indefinite pron. dat. masc. pl. τὶς certain, some, any man, one, any thing
τῶν art. gen. masc. pl. ὁ ἡ τό the, this, that, he, she, it
ἑαυτούς reflexive pron. acc. masc. 3p. pl. ἑαυτοῦ himself, herself, itself, yourself, ourselves
ἀλλὰ conj. ἀλλά but, yea, yet, nevertheless, howbeit, nay, therefore
αὐτοὶ pron. nom. masc. 3p. pl. αὐτός ή ό self, of oneself, even, very, the same, he, she, it
ἐν prep. ἐν (+dat) in, by, with, among, at, on, through, to, within, into, of, for
ἑαυτοῖς reflexive pron. dat. masc. 3p. pl. ἑαυτοῦ himself, herself, itself, yourself, ourselves
ἑαυτούς reflexive pron. acc. masc. 3p. pl. ἑαυτοῦ himself, herself, itself, yourself, ourselves
καὶ conj. καί and, even, also, but
ἑαυτούς reflexive pron. acc. masc. 3p. pl. ἑαυτοῦ himself, herself, itself, yourself, ourselves
ἑαυτοῖς reflexive pron. dat. masc. 3p. pl. ἑαυτοῦ himself, herself, itself, yourself, ourselves
οὐ particle of negation. οὐ οὐκ οὐχ not, no, neither, none, nay, nor, never, nothing
13 ἡμεῖς pron. nom. 1p. pl. ἐγώ I
δὲ conj. δέ but, and, now, also, to the contrary, rather, then
οὐχὶ adv. οὐχί not, nay
εἰς prep. εἰς (+acc) into, to, unto, for, in, on, toward, against, upon, at, among
τὰ art. acc. neut. pl. ὁ ἡ τό the, this, that, he, she, it
ἄμετρα adj. acc. neut. pl. ἄμετρος thing without measure
ἀλλὰ conj. ἀλλά but, yea, yet, nevertheless, howbeit, nay, therefore
κατὰ prep. κατά (+gen) against, by, throughout, down, (+acc) according to, after, with
τὸ art. acc. neut. sg. ὁ ἡ τό the, this, that, he, she, it
μέτρον n. acc. neut. sg. μέτρον measure
τοῦ art. gen. masc. sg. ὁ ἡ τό the, this, that, he, she, it
κανόνος n. gen. masc. sg. κανών rule, line
οὗ relative pron. gen. masc. sg. ὅς ἥ ὅ who, which, what, that
ἡμῖν pron. dat. 1p. pl. ἐγώ I
ὁ art. nom. masc. sg. ὁ ἡ τό the, this, that, he, she, it
Θεὸς n. nom. masc. sg. θεός God, god
μέτρου n. gen. neut. sg. μέτρον measure
ἄχρι prep. ἄχρι or ἄχρις (+gen) until, unto, till, even to, as far as, while, into
καὶ conj. καί and, even, also, but
ὑμῶν pron. gen. 2p. pl. σύ thou, you
14 οὐ particle of negation. οὐ οὐκ οὐχ not, no, neither, none, nay, nor, never, nothing
γὰρ conj. γάρ for, and, because, but, indeed
ὡς adv. ὡς as, when, as it were, how, about, like, as soon as, even as, while
μὴ particle of negation. μή not, no, lest, neither, none, nothing, nor, never, without
εἰς prep. εἰς (+acc) into, to, unto, for, in, on, toward, against, upon, at, among
ὑμᾶς pron. acc. 2p. pl. σύ thou, you
ἑαυτούς reflexive pron. acc. masc. 3p. pl. ἑαυτοῦ himself, herself, itself, yourself, ourselves
ἄχρι prep. ἄχρι or ἄχρις (+gen) until, unto, till, even to, as far as, while, into
γὰρ conj. γάρ for, and, because, but, indeed
καὶ conj. καί and, even, also, but
ὑμῶν pron. gen. 2p. pl. σύ thou, you
ἐν prep. ἐν (+dat) in, by, with, among, at, on, through, to, within, into, of, for
τῷ art. dat. neut. sg. ὁ ἡ τό the, this, that, he, she, it
εὐαγγελίῳ n. dat. neut. sg. εὐαγγέλιον gospel
τοῦ art. gen. masc. sg. ὁ ἡ τό the, this, that, he, she, it
Χριστοῦ n. gen. masc. sg. Χριστός Christ
15 οὐκ particle of negation. οὐ οὐκ οὐχ not, no, neither, none, nay, nor, never, nothing
εἰς prep. εἰς (+acc) into, to, unto, for, in, on, toward, against, upon, at, among
τὰ art. acc. neut. pl. ὁ ἡ τό the, this, that, he, she, it
ἄμετρα adj. acc. neut. pl. ἄμετρος thing without measure
ἐν prep. ἐν (+dat) in, by, with, among, at, on, through, to, within, into, of, for
ἀλλοτρίοις adj. dat. masc. pl. ἀλλότριος stranger, another man, alien, strange

κόποις n. dat. masc. pl. κόπος labour, trouble, weariness
ἐλπίδα n. acc. fem. sg. ἐλπίς hope, faith
δὲ conj. δέ but, and, now, also, to the contrary, rather, then
τῆς art. gen. fem. sg. ὁ ἡ τό the, this, that, he, she, it
πίστεως n. gen. fem. sg. πίστις faith, assurance, belief, fidelity
ὑμῶν pron. gen. 2p. pl. σύ thou, you
ἐν prep. ἐν (+dat) in, by, with, among, at, on, through, to, within, into, of, for
ὑμῖν pron. dat. 2p. pl. σύ thou, you
κατὰ prep. κατά (+gen) against, by, throughout, down, (+acc) according to, after, with
τὸν art. acc. masc. sg. ὁ ἡ τό the, this, that, he, she, it
κανόνα n. acc. masc. sg. κανών rule, line
ἡμῶν pron. gen. 1p. pl. ἐγώ I
εἰς prep. εἰς (+acc) into, to, unto, for, in, on, toward, against, upon, at, among
περισσείαν n. acc. fem. sg. περισσεία abundance, abundant, superfluity
16 εἰς prep. εἰς (+acc) into, to, unto, for, in, on, toward, against, upon, at, among
τὰ art. acc. neut. pl. ὁ ἡ τό the, this, that, he, she, it
ὑπερέκεινα prep. ὑπερέκεινα beyond
ὑμῶν pron. gen. 2p. pl. σύ thou, you
οὐκ particle of negation. οὐ οὐκ οὐχ not, no, neither, none, nay, nor, never, nothing
ἐν prep. ἐν (+dat) in, by, with, among, at, on, through, to, within, into, of, for
ἀλλοτρίῳ adj. dat. masc. sg. ἀλλότριος stranger, another man, alien, strange
κανόνι n. dat. masc. sg. κανών rule, line
εἰς prep. εἰς (+acc) into, to, unto, for, in, on, toward, against, upon, at, among
τὰ art. acc. neut. pl. ὁ ἡ τό the, this, that, he, she, it
ἕτοιμα adj. acc. neut. pl. ἕτοιμος ready, prepared, readiness
17 ὁ art. nom. masc. sg. ὁ ἡ τό the, this, that, he, she, it
δὲ conj. δέ but, and, now, also, to the contrary, rather, then
ἐν prep. ἐν (+dat) in, by, with, among, at, on, through, to, within, into, of, for
Κυρίῳ n. dat. masc. sg. κύριος Lord, lord, master, sir, LORD, God, Master, owner
18 οὐ particle of negation. οὐ οὐκ οὐχ not, no, neither, none, nay, nor, never, nothing
γὰρ conj. γάρ for, and, because, but, indeed
ὁ art. nom. masc. sg. ὁ ἡ τό the, this, that, he, she, it
ἑαυτὸν reflexive pron. acc. masc. 3p. sg. ἑαυτοῦ himself, herself, itself, yourself, ourselves
ἐκεῖνός demo. pron. nom. masc. sg. ἐκεῖνος that, he, the same, that same
δόκιμος adj. nom. masc. sg. δόκιμος approved, tried
ἀλλ' conj. ἀλλά but, yea, yet, nevertheless, howbeit, nay, therefore
ὃν relative pron. acc. masc. sg. ὅς ἥ ὅ who, which, what, that
ὁ art. nom. masc. sg. ὁ ἡ τό the, this, that, he, she, it
Κύριος n. nom. masc. sg. κύριος Lord, lord, master, sir, LORD, God, Master, owner

11

1 μου pron. gen. 1p. sg. ἐγώ I
μικρόν adj. acc. neut. sg. μικρός little, small, least, less
τῇ art. dat. fem. sg. ὁ ἡ τό the, this, that, he, she, it
ἀφροσύνῃ n. dat. fem. sg. ἀφροσύνη foolishness, foolishly, folly
ἀλλὰ conj. ἀλλά but, yea, yet, nevertheless, howbeit, nay, therefore
καὶ conj. καί and, even, also, but
μου pron. gen. 1p. sg. ἐγώ I
2 γὰρ conj. γάρ for, and, because, but, indeed
ὑμᾶς pron. acc. 2p. pl. σύ thou, you
Θεοῦ n. gen. masc. sg. θεός God, god
ζήλῳ n. dat. masc. sg. ζῆλος zeal, envying, indignation, emulation, jealousy
γὰρ conj. γάρ for, and, because, but, indeed
ὑμᾶς pron. acc. 2p. pl. σύ thou, you

ἑνὶ num. dat. masc. sg. εἷς or ἕν one, other, some, any, only, a certain
ἀνδρὶ n. dat. masc. sg. ἀνήρ man, husband, sir
παρθένον n. acc. fem. sg. παρθένος virgin
ἁγνὴν adj. acc. fem. sg. ἁγνός clear, pure, chaste
τῷ art. dat. masc. sg. ὁ ἡ τό the, this, that, he, she, it
Χριστῷ n. dat. masc. sg. Χριστός Christ
3 δὲ conj. δέ but, and, now, also, to the contrary, rather, then
μή particle of negation. μή not, no, lest, neither, none, nothing, nor, never, without
πως particle. πώς by any means, by some means, haply, perhaps
ὡς adv. ὡς as, when, as it were, how, about, like, as soon as, even as, while
ὁ art. nom. masc. sg. ὁ ἡ τό the, this, that, he, she, it
ὄφις n. nom. masc. sg. ὄφις serpent
Εὔαν n. acc. fem. sg. Εὔα Eve
ἐν prep. ἐν (+dat) in, by, with, among, at, on, through, to, within, into, of, for
τῇ art. dat. fem. sg. ὁ ἡ τό the, this, that, he, she, it
πανουργίᾳ n. dat. fem. sg. πανουργία craftiness, cunning craftiness, subtilty
αὐτοῦ pron. gen. masc. 3p. sg. αὐτός ή ό self, of oneself, even, very, the same, he, she, it
οὕτω adv. οὕτω οὕτως so, even so, thus, on this wise, likewise, after this manner
τὰ art. nom. neut. pl. ὁ ἡ τό the, this, that, he, she, it
νοήματα n. nom. neut. pl. νόημα mind, device, thought
ὑμῶν pron. gen. 2p. pl. σύ thou, you
ἀπὸ prep. ἀπό (+gen) from, of, out of, since, for, off, at, by, in, on
τῆς art. gen. fem. sg. ὁ ἡ τό the, this, that, he, she, it
ἁπλότητος n. gen. fem. sg. ἁπλότης simplicity, singleness, bountifulness, liberality
τῆς art. gen. fem. sg. ὁ ἡ τό the, this, that, he, she, it
εἰς prep. εἰς (+acc) into, to, unto, for, in, on, toward, against, upon, at, among
τὸν art. acc. masc. sg. ὁ ἡ τό the, this, that, he, she, it
Χριστόν n. acc. masc. sg. Χριστός Christ
4 εἰ conj. εἰ if, whether, that, though, forasmuch
μὲν conj. μέν indeed, verily, truly, even, so, some
γὰρ conj. γάρ for, and, because, but, indeed
ὁ art. nom. masc. sg. ὁ ἡ τό the, this, that, he, she, it
ἄλλον adj. acc. masc. sg. ἄλλος other, another, some, one, more, otherwise
Ἰησοῦν n. acc. masc. sg. Ἰησοῦς Jesus
ὃν relative pron. acc. masc. sg. ὅς ἥ ὅ who, which, what, that
οὐκ particle of negation. οὐ οὐκ οὐχ not, no, neither, none, nay, nor, never, nothing
ἢ particle. ἤ or, than, either, nor, or else, and, rather than
πνεῦμα n. acc. neut. sg. πνεῦμα spirit, Spirit, Ghost, ghost, life. of the spirit, wind
ἕτερον adj. acc. neut. sg. ἕτερος another, other, else, strange
ὃ relative pron. acc. neut. sg. ὅς ἥ ὅ who, which, what, that
οὐκ particle of negation. οὐ οὐκ οὐχ not, no, neither, none, nay, nor, never, nothing
ἢ particle. ἤ or, than, either, nor, or else, and, rather than
εὐαγγέλιον n. acc. neut. sg. εὐαγγέλιον gospel
ἕτερον adj. acc. neut. sg. ἕτερος another, other, else, strange
ὃ relative pron. acc. neut. sg. ὅς ἥ ὅ who, which, what, that
οὐκ particle of negation. οὐ οὐκ οὐχ not, no, neither, none, nay, nor, never, nothing
καλῶς adv. καλῶς good, well, full well
5 γὰρ conj. γάρ for, and, because, but, indeed
μηδὲν num. acc. neut. sg. μηδείς μηδεμία μηδέν no man, nothing, no, none, not at all
τῶν art. gen. masc. pl. ὁ ἡ τό the, this, that, he, she, it
ὑπερ adv. ὑπέρ (+gen) for, of, for the sake of, (+acc) above, more than
λίαν adv. λίαν exceeding, greatly, very, great sore
ἀποστόλων n. gen. masc. pl. ἀπόστολος apostle, messenger, he that is sent
6 εἰ conj. εἰ if, whether, that, though, forasmuch
δὲ conj. δέ but, and, now, also, to the contrary, rather, then

καὶ conj. καί and, even, also, but
ἰδιώτης n. nom. masc. sg. ἰδιώτης ignorant, unlearned, rude
τῷ art. dat. masc. sg. ὁ ἡ τό the, this, that, he, she, it
λόγῳ n. dat. masc. sg. λόγος word, saying, account, speech, thing, matter
ἀλλ' conj. ἀλλά but, yea, yet, nevertheless, howbeit, nay, therefore
οὐ particle of negation. οὐ οὐκ οὐχ not, no, neither, none, nay, nor, never, nothing
τῇ art. dat. fem. sg. ὁ ἡ τό the, this, that, he, she, it
γνώσει n. dat. fem. sg. γνῶσις knowledge, science
ἀλλ' conj. ἀλλά but, yea, yet, nevertheless, howbeit, nay, therefore
ἐν prep. ἐν (+dat) in, by, with, among, at, on, through, to, within, into, of, for
παντὶ adj. dat. neut. sg. πᾶς πᾶσα πᾶν all, every, whosoever, every one, no, whole, any
ἐν prep. ἐν (+dat) in, by, with, among, at, on, through, to, within, into, of, for
πᾶσιν adj. dat. neut. pl. πᾶς πᾶσα πᾶν all, every, whosoever, every one, no, whole, any
εἰς prep. εἰς (+acc) into, to, unto, for, in, on, toward, against, upon, at, among
ὑμᾶς pron. acc. 2p. pl. σύ thou, you
7 ἢ particle. ἤ or, than, either, nor, or else, and, rather than
ἁμαρτίαν n. acc. fem. sg. ἁμαρτία sin, offence, sinful
ἐμαυτὸν pron. acc. masc. 1p. sg. ἐμαυτοῦ myself, me
ἵνα conj. ἵνα that, to, lest, for to, so that, albeit, because, for, so as
ὑμεῖς pron. nom. 2p. pl. σύ thou, you
ὅτι conj. ὅτι that, for, because, how that, how, because that, for that, though
δωρεὰν adv. δωρεάν freely, for nought, in vain, without a cause
τὸ art. acc. neut. sg. ὁ ἡ τό the, this, that, he, she, it
τοῦ art. gen. masc. sg. ὁ ἡ τό the, this, that, he, she, it
Θεοῦ n. gen. masc. sg. θεός God, god
εὐαγγέλιον n. acc. neut. sg. εὐαγγέλιον gospel
ὑμῖν pron. dat. 2p. pl. σύ thou, you
8 ἄλλας adj. acc. fem. pl. ἄλλος other, another, some, one, more, otherwise
ἐκκλησίας n. acc. fem. pl. ἐκκλησία church, assembly
ὀψώνιον n. acc. neut. sg. ὀψώνιον wage, charge
πρὸς prep. πρός (+gen) for, (+dat) at, (+acc) unto, to, with, for, against
τὴν art. acc. fem. sg. ὁ ἡ τό the, this, that, he, she, it
ὑμῶν pron. gen. 2p. pl. σύ thou, you
διακονίαν n. acc. fem. sg. διακονία ministry, administration, service, office, relief
9 καὶ conj. καί and, even, also, but
πρὸς prep. πρός (+gen) for, (+dat) at, (+acc) unto, to, with, for, against
ὑμᾶς pron. acc. 2p. pl. σύ thou, you
καὶ conj. καί and, even, also, but
οὐ particle of negation. οὐ οὐκ οὐχ not, no, neither, none, nay, nor, never, nothing
οὐθενός num. gen. masc. sg. οὐδείς no man, nothing, no, none, neither, not, nought
τὸ art. acc. neut. sg. ὁ ἡ τό the, this, that, he, she, it
γὰρ conj. γάρ for, and, because, but, indeed
ὑστέρημά n. acc. neut. sg. ὑστέρημα penury, that which is lacking, want, lack
μου pron. gen. 1p. sg. ἐγώ I
οἱ art. nom. masc. pl. ὁ ἡ τό the, this, that, he, she, it
ἀδελφοὶ n. nom. masc. pl. ἀδελφός brother
ἀπὸ prep. ἀπό (+gen) from, of, out of, since, for, off, at, by, in, on
Μακεδονίας n. gen. fem. sg. Μακεδονία Macedonia
καὶ conj. καί and, even, also, but
ἐν prep. ἐν (+dat) in, by, with, among, at, on, through, to, within, into, of, for
παντὶ adj. dat. neut. sg. πᾶς πᾶσα πᾶν all, every, whosoever, every one, no, whole, any
ἀβαρῆ adj. acc. masc. sg. ἀβαρής from being burdensome
ὑμῖν pron. dat. 2p. pl. σύ thou, you
ἐμαυτὸν pron. acc. masc. 1p. sg. ἐμαυτοῦ myself, me
καὶ conj. καί and, even, also, but

10 ἀλήθεια n. nom. fem. sg. ἀλήθεια truth, verity
Χριστοῦ n. gen. masc. sg. Χριστός Christ
ἐν prep. ἐν (+dat) in, by, with, among, at, on, through, to, within, into, of, for
ἐμοὶ pron. dat. 1p. sg. ἐγώ I
ὅτι conj. ὅτι that, for, because, how that, how, because that, for that, though
ἡ art. nom. fem. sg. ὁ ἡ τό the, this, that, he, she, it
καύχησις n. nom. fem. sg. καύχησις boasting, rejoicing, glorying
αὕτη demo. pron. nom. fem. sg. οὗτος αὕτη τοῦτο this, the same, this same, he, she, it
οὐ particle of negation. οὐ οὐκ οὐχ not, no, neither, none, nay, nor, never, nothing
εἰς prep. εἰς (+acc) into, to, unto, for, in, on, toward, against, upon, at, among
ἐμὲ pron. acc. 1p. sg. ἐγώ I
ἐν prep. ἐν (+dat) in, by, with, among, at, on, through, to, within, into, of, for
τοῖς art. dat. neut. pl. ὁ ἡ τό the, this, that, he, she, it
κλίμασιν n. dat. neut. pl. κλίμα region, part
τῆς art. gen. fem. sg. ὁ ἡ τό the, this, that, he, she, it
Ἀχαΐας n. gen. fem. sg. Ἀχαΐα Achaia
11 διατί adv. διατί why, for what, wherefore
ὅτι conj. ὅτι that, for, because, how that, how, because that, for that, though
οὐκ particle of negation. οὐ οὐκ οὐχ not, no, neither, none, nay, nor, never, nothing
ὑμᾶς pron. acc. 2p. pl. σύ thou, you
ὁ art. nom. masc. sg. ὁ ἡ τό the, this, that, he, she, it
Θεὸς n. nom. masc. sg. θεός God, god
12 ὃ relative pron. acc. neut. sg. ὅς ἥ ὅ who, which, what, that
δὲ conj. δέ but, and, now, also, to the contrary, rather, then
καὶ conj. καί and, even, also, but
ἵνα conj. ἵνα that, to, lest, for to, so that, albeit, because, for, so as
τὴν art. acc. fem. sg. ὁ ἡ τό the, this, that, he, she, it
ἀφορμὴν n. acc. fem. sg. ἀφορμή occasion
τῶν art. gen. masc. pl. ὁ ἡ τό the, this, that, he, she, it
ἀφορμήν n. acc. fem. sg. ἀφορμή occasion
ἵνα conj. ἵνα that, to, lest, for to, so that, albeit, because, for, so as
ἐν prep. ἐν (+dat) in, by, with, among, at, on, through, to, within, into, of, for
ᾧ relative pron. dat. neut. sg. ὅς ἥ ὅ who, which, what, that
καθὼς adv. καθώς as, even as, according as, according to
καὶ conj. καί and, even, also, but
ἡμεῖς pron. nom. 1p. pl. ἐγώ I
13 οἱ art. nom. masc. pl. ὁ ἡ τό the, this, that, he, she, it
γὰρ conj. γάρ for, and, because, but, indeed
τοιοῦτοι demo. pron. nom. masc. pl. τοιοῦτος such, like
ψευδαπόστολοι n. nom. masc. pl. ψευδαπόστολος false apostle
ἐργάται n. nom. masc. pl. ἐργάτης labourer, worker, workman
δόλιοι adj. nom. masc. pl. δόλιος deceitful
εἰς prep. εἰς (+acc) into, to, unto, for, in, on, toward, against, upon, at, among
ἀποστόλους n. acc. masc. pl. ἀπόστολος apostle, messenger, he that is sent
Χριστοῦ n. gen. masc. sg. Χριστός Christ
14 καὶ conj. καί and, even, also, but
οὐ particle of negation. οὐ οὐκ οὐχ not, no, neither, none, nay, nor, never, nothing
θαυμαστόν adj. nom. neut. sg. θαυμαστός marvellous, marvel
αὐτὸς pron. nom. masc. 3p. sg. αὐτός ἡ ὁ self, of oneself, even, very, the same, he, she, it
γὰρ conj. γάρ for, and, because, but, indeed
ὁ art. nom. masc. sg. ὁ ἡ τό the, this, that, he, she, it
Σατανᾶς n. nom. masc. sg. Σατανᾶς Satan
εἰς prep. εἰς (+acc) into, to, unto, for, in, on, toward, against, upon, at, among
ἄγγελον n. acc. masc. sg. ἄγγελος angel, messenger
φωτός n. gen. neut. sg. φῶς light, fire

15 οὐ particle of negation. οὐ οὐκ οὐχ not, no, neither, none, nay, nor, never, nothing
μέγα adj. nom. neut. sg. μέγας great, loud, greatest, high, large, mighty, strong
οὖν conj. οὖν therefore, then, so, and, now, wherefore
εἰ conj. εἰ if, whether, that, though, forasmuch
καὶ conj. καί and, even, also, but
οἱ art. nom. masc. pl. ὁ ἡ τό the, this, that, he, she, it
διάκονοι n. nom. masc. pl. διάκονος minister, servant, deacon
αὐτοῦ pron. gen. masc. 3p. sg. αὐτός ή ό self, of oneself, even, very, the same, he, she, it
ὡς adv. ὡς as, when, as it were, how, about, like, as soon as, even as, while
διάκονοι n. nom. masc. pl. διάκονος minister, servant, deacon
δικαιοσύνης n. gen. fem. sg. δικαιοσύνη righteousness
ὧν relative pron. gen. masc. pl. ὅς ἥ ὅ who, which, what, that
τὸ art. nom. neut. sg. ὁ ἡ τό the, this, that, he, she, it
τέλος n. nom. neut. sg. τέλος end, custom, ending, finally, uttermost
κατὰ prep. κατά (+gen) against, by, throughout, down, (+acc) according to, after, with
τὰ art. acc. neut. pl. ὁ ἡ τό the, this, that, he, she, it
ἔργα n. acc. neut. pl. ἔργον work, deed, doing labour
αὐτῶν pron. gen. masc. 3p. pl. αὐτός ή ό self, of oneself, even, very, the same, he, she, it
16 Πάλιν adv. πάλιν again
μή particle of negation. μή not, no, lest, neither, none, nothing, nor, never, without
τις indefinite pron. nom. masc. sg. τὶς certain, some, any man, one, any thing
με pron. acc. 1p. sg. ἐγώ I
ἄφρονα adj. acc. masc. sg. ἄφρων fool, foolish, unwise
εἰ conj. εἰ if, whether, that, though, forasmuch
δὲ conj. δέ but, and, now, also, to the contrary, rather, then
μή particle of negation. μή not, no, lest, neither, none, nothing, nor, never, without
γε particle. γέ yet, and beside, at least, doubtless
κἂν conj. κἄν though, and if, if but, also if, and if so much, at the least, yet as
ὡς adv. ὡς as, when, as it were, how, about, like, as soon as, even as, while
ἄφρονα adj. acc. masc. sg. ἄφρων fool, foolish, unwise
με pron. acc. 1p. sg. ἐγώ I
ἵνα conj. ἵνα that, to, lest, for to, so that, albeit, because, for, so as
μικρόν adj. acc. neut. sg. μικρός little, small, least, less
τι indefinite pron. acc. neut. sg. τὶς certain, some, any man, one, any thing
κἀγὼ pron. nom. 1p. sg. κἀγώ and I, I also, so I, even as I
17 ὃ relative pron. acc. neut. sg. ὅς ἥ ὅ who, which, what, that
οὐ particle of negation. οὐ οὐκ οὐχ not, no, neither, none, nay, nor, never, nothing
κατὰ prep. κατά (+gen) against, by, throughout, down, (+acc) according to, after, with
Κύριον n. acc. masc. sg. κύριος Lord, lord, master, sir, LORD, God, Master, owner
ἀλλ' conj. ἀλλά but, yea, yet, nevertheless, howbeit, nay, therefore
ὡς adv. ὡς as, when, as it were, how, about, like, as soon as, even as, while
ἐν prep. ἐν (+dat) in, by, with, among, at, on, through, to, within, into, of, for
ἀφροσύνῃ n. dat. fem. sg. ἀφροσύνη foolishness, foolishly, folly
ἐν prep. ἐν (+dat) in, by, with, among, at, on, through, to, within, into, of, for
ταύτῃ demo. pron. dat. fem. sg. οὗτος αὕτη τοῦτο this, the same, this same, he, she, it
τῇ art. dat. fem. sg. ὁ ἡ τό the, this, that, he, she, it
ὑποστάσει n. dat. fem. sg. ὑπόστασις confident, confidence, substance, person, nature
τῆς art. gen. fem. sg. ὁ ἡ τό the, this, that, he, she, it
καυχήσεως n. gen. fem. sg. καύχησις boasting, rejoicing, glorying
18 ἐπεὶ conj. ἐπεί because, otherwise, seeing, else, for then, for as much as, for, since
πολλοὶ adj. nom. masc. pl. πολύς many, great, much, long, abundant
κατὰ prep. κατά (+gen) against, by, throughout, down, (+acc) according to, after, with
τὴν art. acc. fem. sg. ὁ ἡ τό the, this, that, he, she, it
σάρκα n. acc. fem. sg. σάρξ flesh, carnal
κἀγὼ pron. nom. 1p. sg. κἀγώ and I, I also, so I, even as I

19 ἡδέως adv. ἡδέως gladly
γὰρ conj. γάρ for, and, because, but, indeed
τῶν art. gen. masc. pl. ὁ ἡ τό the, this, that, he, she, it
ἀφρόνων adj. gen. masc. pl. ἄφρων fool, foolish, unwise
φρόνιμοι adj. nom. masc. pl. φρόνιμος wise, wiser
20 γὰρ conj. γάρ for, and, because, but, indeed
εἴ conj. εἰ if, whether, that, though, forasmuch
τις indefinite pron. nom. masc. sg. τὶς certain, some, any man, one, any thing
ὑμᾶς pron. acc. 2p. pl. σύ thou, you
εἴ conj. εἰ if, whether, that, though, forasmuch
τις indefinite pron. nom. masc. sg. τὶς certain, some, any man, one, any thing
εἴ conj. εἰ if, whether, that, though, forasmuch
τις indefinite pron. nom. masc. sg. τὶς certain, some, any man, one, any thing
εἴ conj. εἰ if, whether, that, though, forasmuch
τις indefinite pron. nom. masc. sg. τὶς certain, some, any man, one, any thing
εἴ conj. εἰ if, whether, that, though, forasmuch
τις indefinite pron. nom. masc. sg. τὶς certain, some, any man, one, any thing
ὑμᾶς pron. acc. 2p. pl. σύ thou, you
εἰς prep. εἰς (+acc) into, to, unto, for, in, on, toward, against, upon, at, among
πρόσωπον n. acc. neut. sg. πρόσωπον face, presence, person, countenance
21 κατὰ prep. κατά (+gen) against, by, throughout, down, (+acc) according to, after, with
ἀτιμίαν n. acc. fem. sg. ἀτιμία vile, dishonour, reproach, shame
ὡς adv. ὡς as, when, as it were, how, about, like, as soon as, even as, while
ὅτι conj. ὅτι that, for, because, how that, how, because that, for that, though
ἡμεῖς pron. nom. 1p. pl. ἐγώ I
ἐν prep. ἐν (+dat) in, by, with, among, at, on, through, to, within, into, of, for
ᾧ relative pron. dat. neut. sg. ὅς ἥ ὅ who, which, what, that
δ' conj. δέ but, and, now, also, to the contrary, rather, then
ἄν particle. ἄν Indicating contingency. No English translation.
τις indefinite pron. nom. masc. sg. τὶς certain, some, any man, one, any thing
ἐν prep. ἐν (+dat) in, by, with, among, at, on, through, to, within, into, of, for
ἀφροσύνῃ n. dat. fem. sg. ἀφροσύνη foolishness, foolishly, folly
κἀγώ pron. nom. 1p. sg. κἀγώ and I, I also, so I, even as I
22 Ἑβραῖοί n. nom. masc. pl. Ἑβραῖος Hebrew
κἀγώ pron. nom. 1p. sg. κἀγώ and I, I also, so I, even as I
Ἰσραηλῖταί n. nom. masc. pl. Ἰσραηλίτης Israelite, Israel
κἀγώ pron. nom. 1p. sg. κἀγώ and I, I also, so I, even as I
σπέρμα n. nom. neut. sg. σπέρμα seed, issue
Ἀβραάμ n. gen. masc. sg. Ἀβραάμ Abraham
κἀγώ pron. nom. 1p. sg. κἀγώ and I, I also, so I, even as I
23 διάκονοι n. nom. masc. pl. διάκονος minister, servant, deacon
Χριστοῦ n. gen. masc. sg. Χριστός Christ
ὑπὲρ adv. ὑπέρ (+gen) for, of, for the sake of, (+acc) above, more than
ἐγώ pron. nom. 1p. sg. ἐγώ I
ἐν prep. ἐν (+dat) in, by, with, among, at, on, through, to, within, into, of, for
κόποις n. dat. masc. pl. κόπος labour, trouble, weariness
περισσοτέρως adv. περισσοτέρως more exceedingly, more abundantly, more frequent
ἐν prep. ἐν (+dat) in, by, with, among, at, on, through, to, within, into, of, for
πληγαῖς n. dat. fem. pl. πληγή wound, plague, stripe
ὑπερβαλλόντως adv. ὑπερβαλλόντως above measure
ἐν prep. ἐν (+dat) in, by, with, among, at, on, through, to, within, into, of, for
φυλακαῖς n. dat. fem. pl. φυλακή prison, watch, imprisonment, cage, hold, ward
περισσοτέρως adv. περισσοτέρως more exceedingly, more abundantly, more frequent
ἐν prep. ἐν (+dat) in, by, with, among, at, on, through, to, within, into, of, for
θανάτοις n. dat. masc. pl. θάνατος death

πολλάκις adv. πολλάκις often, ofttimes, oft
24 ὑπὸ prep. ὑπό (+gen) of, by, with, from, among, (+acc) under
Ἰουδαίων adj. gen. masc. pl. Ἰουδαῖος Jew, Jewess
πεντάκις adv. πεντάκις five times
τεσσαράκοντα num. acc. fem. pl. τεσσαράκοντα forty
παρὰ prep. παρά (+gen) of, from, (+dat) with, for, (+acc) beside, at, by, above, against
μίαν num. acc. fem. sg. εἷς or ἕν one, other, some, any, only, a certain
25 τρὶς adv. τρίς thrice, three times
ἅπαξ adv. ἅπαξ once
τρὶς adv. τρίς thrice, three times
νυχθήμερον n. acc. neut. sg. νυχθήμερον a night and a day
ἐν prep. ἐν (+dat) in, by, with, among, at, on, through, to, within, into, of, for
τῷ art. dat. masc. sg. ὁ ἡ τό the, this, that, he, she, it
βυθῷ n. dat. masc. sg. βυθός deep
26 ὁδοιπορίαις n. dat. fem. pl. ὁδοιπορία journey, journeying
πολλάκις adv. πολλάκις often, ofttimes, oft
κινδύνοις n. dat. masc. pl. κίνδυνος peril
ποταμῶν n. gen. masc. pl. ποταμός river, flood , stream, water
κινδύνοις n. dat. masc. pl. κίνδυνος peril
λῃστῶν n. gen. masc. pl. λῃστής thief, robber
κινδύνοις n. dat. masc. pl. κίνδυνος peril
ἐκ prep. ἐκ ἐξ (+gen) of, from, out of, by, on, with, in, among, through
γένους n. gen. neut. sg. γένος kind, kindred, offspring, nation, countrymen
κινδύνοις n. dat. masc. pl. κίνδυνος peril
ἐξ prep. ἐκ ἐξ (+gen) of, from, out of, by, on, with, in, among, through
ἐθνῶν n. gen. neut. pl. ἔθνος Gentile, nation, heathen, people
κινδύνοις n. dat. masc. pl. κίνδυνος peril
ἐν prep. ἐν (+dat) in, by, with, among, at, on, through, to, within, into, of, for
πόλει n. dat. fem. sg. πόλις city
κινδύνοις n. dat. masc. pl. κίνδυνος peril
ἐν prep. ἐν (+dat) in, by, with, among, at, on, through, to, within, into, of, for
ἐρημίᾳ n. dat. fem. sg. ἐρημία wilderness, desert
κινδύνοις n. dat. masc. pl. κίνδυνος peril
ἐν prep. ἐν (+dat) in, by, with, among, at, on, through, to, within, into, of, for
θαλάσσῃ n. dat. fem. sg. θάλασσα sea
κινδύνοις n. dat. masc. pl. κίνδυνος peril
ἐν prep. ἐν (+dat) in, by, with, among, at, on, through, to, within, into, of, for
ψευδαδέλφοις n. dat. masc. pl. ψευδάδελφος false brether
27 ἐν prep. ἐν (+dat) in, by, with, among, at, on, through, to, within, into, of, for
κόπῳ n. dat. masc. sg. κόπος labour, trouble, weariness
καὶ conj. καί and, even, also, but
μόχθῳ n. dat. masc. sg. μόχθος painfulness, travail
ἐν prep. ἐν (+dat) in, by, with, among, at, on, through, to, within, into, of, for
ἀγρυπνίαις n. dat. fem. pl. ἀγρυπνία watching, sleeplessness
πολλάκις adv. πολλάκις often, ofttimes, oft
ἐν prep. ἐν (+dat) in, by, with, among, at, on, through, to, within, into, of, for
λιμῷ n. dat. masc. sg. λιμός famine, hunger, dearth
καὶ conj. καί and, even, also, but
δίψει n. dat. neut. sg. δίψος thirst
ἐν prep. ἐν (+dat) in, by, with, among, at, on, through, to, within, into, of, for
νηστείαις n. dat. fem. pl. νηστεία fasting, fast
πολλάκις adv. πολλάκις often, ofttimes, oft
ἐν prep. ἐν (+dat) in, by, with, among, at, on, through, to, within, into, of, for
ψύχει n. dat. neut. sg. ψύχος cold
καὶ conj. καί and, even, also, but

γυμνότητι n. dat. fem. sg. γυμνότης nakedness
28 χωρὶς prep. χωρίς (+gen) without, beside. (adv.) by itself, apart, separately
τῶν art. gen. neut. pl. ὁ ἡ τό the, this, that, he, she, it
παρεκτὸς adv. παρεκτός (+gen) except, saving. (adv.) without, besides
ἡ art. nom. fem. sg. ὁ ἡ τό the, this, that, he, she, it
ἐπισύστασίς n. nom. fem. sg. ἐπισύστασις raising up the people, that which comes upon
μου pron. gen. 1p. sg. ἐγώ I
ἡ art. nom. fem. sg. ὁ ἡ τό the, this, that, he, she, it
καθ' prep. κατά (+gen) against, by, throughout, down, (+acc) according to, after, with
ἡμέραν n. acc. fem. sg. ἡμέρα day, time, year, while, age, day time
ἡ art. nom. fem. sg. ὁ ἡ τό the, this, that, he, she, it
μέριμνα n. nom. fem. sg. μέριμνα care
πασῶν adj. gen. fem. pl. πᾶς πᾶσα πᾶν all, every, whosoever, every one, no, whole, any
τῶν art. gen. fem. pl. ὁ ἡ τό the, this, that, he, she, it
ἐκκλησιῶν n. gen. fem. pl. ἐκκλησία church, assembly
29 τίς interrog. pron. nom. masc. sg. τίς what, who, why, where, which, how
καὶ conj. καί and, even, also, but
οὐκ particle of negation. οὐ οὐκ οὐχ not, no, neither, none, nay, nor, never, nothing
τίς interrog. pron. nom. masc. sg. τίς what, who, why, where, which, how
καὶ conj. καί and, even, also, but
οὐκ particle of negation. οὐ οὐκ οὐχ not, no, neither, none, nay, nor, never, nothing
ἐγὼ pron. nom. 1p. sg. ἐγώ I
30 εἰ conj. εἰ if, whether, that, though, forasmuch
τὰ art. acc. neut. pl. ὁ ἡ τό the, this, that, he, she, it
τῆς art. gen. fem. sg. ὁ ἡ τό the, this, that, he, she, it
ἀσθενείας n. gen. fem. sg. ἀσθένεια infirmity, weakness, disease, sickness
μου pron. gen. 1p. sg. ἐγώ I
31 ὁ art. nom. masc. sg. ὁ ἡ τό the, this, that, he, she, it
Θεὸς n. nom. masc. sg. θεός God, god
καὶ conj. καί and, even, also, but
πατὴρ n. nom. masc. sg. πατήρ Father, father, parent
τοῦ art. gen. masc. sg. ὁ ἡ τό the, this, that, he, she, it
Κυρίου n. gen. masc. sg. κύριος Lord, lord, master, sir, LORD, God, Master, owner
ἡμῶν pron. gen. 1p. pl. ἐγώ I
Ἰησοῦ n. gen. masc. sg. Ἰησοῦς Jesus
Χριστοῦ n. gen. masc. sg. Χριστός Christ
ὁ art. nom. masc. sg. ὁ ἡ τό the, this, that, he, she, it
εὐλογητὸς adj. nom. masc. sg. εὐλογητός blessed
εἰς prep. εἰς (+acc) into, to, unto, for, in, on, toward, against, upon, at, among
τοὺς art. acc. masc. pl. ὁ ἡ τό the, this, that, he, she, it
αἰῶνας n. acc. masc. pl. αἰών ever, ever and ever, evermore, age, eternal, world
ὅτι conj. ὅτι that, for, because, how that, how, because that, for that, though
οὐ particle of negation. οὐ οὐκ οὐχ not, no, neither, none, nay, nor, never, nothing
32 ἐν prep. ἐν (+dat) in, by, with, among, at, on, through, to, within, into, of, for
Δαμασκῷ n. dat. fem. sg. Δαμασκός Damascus
ὁ art. nom. masc. sg. ὁ ἡ τό the, this, that, he, she, it
ἐθνάρχης n. nom. masc. sg. ἐθνάρχης governor, ethnarch
Ἀρέτα n. gen. masc. sg. Ἀρέτας Aretas
τοῦ art. gen. masc. sg. ὁ ἡ τό the, this, that, he, she, it
βασιλέως n. gen. masc. sg. βασιλεύς king
τὴν art. acc. fem. sg. ὁ ἡ τό the, this, that, he, she, it
Δαμασκηνῶν adj. gen. masc. pl. Δαμασκηνός Damascene
πόλιν n. acc. fem. sg. πόλις city
με pron. acc. 1p. sg. ἐγώ I
33 καὶ conj. καί and, even, also, but

διὰ prep. διά (+gen) by, through, with, in, of, (+acc) for, because of, for a cause
θυρίδος n. gen. fem. sg. θυρίς window
ἐν prep. ἐν (+dat) in, by, with, among, at, on, through, to, within, into, of, for
σαργάνῃ n. dat. fem. sg. σαργάνη basket
διὰ prep. διά (+gen) by, through, with, in, of, (+acc) for, because of, for a cause
τοῦ art. gen. neut. sg. ὁ ἡ τό the, this, that, he, she, it
τείχους n. gen. neut. sg. τεῖχος wall
καὶ conj. καί and, even, also, but
τὰς art. acc. fem. pl. ὁ ἡ τό the, this, that, he, she, it
χεῖρας n. acc. fem. pl. χείρ hand
αὐτοῦ pron. gen. masc. 3p. sg. αὐτός ή ό self, of oneself, even, very, the same, he, she, it

12

1 δὴ particle. δή also, and, doubtless, now, therefore
οὐ particle of negation. οὐ οὐκ οὐχ not, no, neither, none, nay, nor, never, nothing
μοι pron. dat. 1p. sg. ἐγώ I
γὰρ conj. γάρ for, and, because, but, indeed
εἰς prep. εἰς (+acc) into, to, unto, for, in, on, toward, against, upon, at, among
ὀπτασίας n. acc. fem. pl. ὀπτασία vision
καὶ conj. καί and, even, also, but
ἀποκαλύψεις n. acc. fem. pl. ἀποκάλυψις revelation, appearing, coming, manifestation
Κυρίου n. gen. masc. sg. κύριος Lord, lord, master, sir, LORD, God, Master, owner
2 ἄνθρωπον n. acc. masc. sg. ἄνθρωπος man, human being, person, one, certain
ἐν prep. ἐν (+dat) in, by, with, among, at, on, through, to, within, into, of, for
Χριστῷ n. dat. masc. sg. Χριστός Christ
πρὸ prep. πρό (+gen) before, above
ἐτῶν n. gen. neut. pl. ἔτος year
δεκατεσσάρων num. gen. neut. pl. δεκατέσσαρες fourteen
εἴτε conj. εἴτε whether
ἐν prep. ἐν (+dat) in, by, with, among, at, on, through, to, within, into, of, for
σώματι n. dat. neut. sg. σῶμα body, bodily, slave
οὐκ particle of negation. οὐ οὐκ οὐχ not, no, neither, none, nay, nor, never, nothing
εἴτε conj. εἴτε whether
ἐκτὸς prep. ἐκτός except, out of, other than, outside, unless, without
τοῦ art. gen. neut. sg. ὁ ἡ τό the, this, that, he, she, it
σώματος n. gen. neut. sg. σῶμα body, bodily, slave
οὐκ particle of negation. οὐ οὐκ οὐχ not, no, neither, none, nay, nor, never, nothing
ὁ art. nom. masc. sg. ὁ ἡ τό the, this, that, he, she, it
Θεὸς n. nom. masc. sg. θεός God, god
τὸν art. acc. masc. sg. ὁ ἡ τό the, this, that, he, she, it
τοιοῦτον demo. pron. acc. masc. sg. τοιοῦτος such, like
ἕως conj. ἕως till, until, unto, until when, while, as far as, even, until now
τρίτου ordinal. adj. gen. masc. sg. τρίτος third
οὐρανοῦ n. gen. masc. sg. οὐρανός heaven, air, sky
3 καὶ conj. καί and, even, also, but
τὸν art. acc. masc. sg. ὁ ἡ τό the, this, that, he, she, it
τοιοῦτον demo. pron. acc. masc. sg. τοιοῦτος such, like
ἄνθρωπον n. acc. masc. sg. ἄνθρωπος man, human being, person, one, certain
εἴτε conj. εἴτε whether
ἐν prep. ἐν (+dat) in, by, with, among, at, on, through, to, within, into, of, for
σώματι n. dat. neut. sg. σῶμα body, bodily, slave
εἴτε conj. εἴτε whether
ἐκτὸς adv. ἐκτός except, out of, other than, outside, unless, without
τοῦ art. gen. neut. sg. ὁ ἡ τό the, this, that, he, she, it

σώματος n. gen. neut. sg. σῶμα body, bodily, slave
οὐκ particle of negation. οὐ οὐκ οὐχ not, no, neither, none, nay, nor, never, nothing
ὁ art. nom. masc. sg. ὁ ἡ τό the, this, that, he, she, it
Θεὸς n. nom. masc. sg. θεός God, god
4 ὅτι conj. ὅτι that, for, because, how that, how, because that, for that, though
εἰς prep. εἰς (+acc) into, to, unto, for, in, on, toward, against, upon, at, among
τὸν art. acc. masc. sg. ὁ ἡ τό the, this, that, he, she, it
παράδεισον n. acc. masc. sg. παράδεισος paradise
καὶ conj. καί and, even, also, but
ἄρρητα adj. acc. neut. pl. ἄρρητος unspeakable
ῥήματα n. acc. neut. pl. ῥῆμα word, saying, thing
ἃ relative pron. acc. neut. pl. ὅς ἥ ὅ who, which, what, that
οὐκ particle of negation. οὐ οὐκ οὐχ not, no, neither, none, nay, nor, never, nothing
ἀνθρώπῳ n. dat. masc. sg. ἄνθρωπος man, human being, person, one, certain
5 ὑπὲρ prep. ὑπέρ (+gen) for, of, for the sake of, (+acc) above, more than
τοῦ art. gen. masc. sg. ὁ ἡ τό the, this, that, he, she, it
τοιούτου demo. pron. gen. masc. sg. τοιοῦτος such, like
ὑπὲρ prep. ὑπέρ (+gen) for, of, for the sake of, (+acc) above, more than
δὲ conj. δέ but, and, now, also, to the contrary, rather, then
ἐμαυτοῦ pron. gen. masc. 1p. sg. ἐμαυτοῦ myself, me
οὐ particle of negation. οὐ οὐκ οὐχ not, no, neither, none, nay, nor, never, nothing
εἰ conj. εἰ if, whether, that, though, forasmuch
μὴ particle of negation. μή not, no, lest, neither, none, nothing, nor, never, without
ἐν prep. ἐν (+dat) in, by, with, among, at, on, through, to, within, into, of, for
ταῖς art. dat. fem. pl. ὁ ἡ τό the, this, that, he, she, it
ἀσθενείαις n. dat. fem. pl. ἀσθένεια infirmity, weakness, disease, sickness
μου pron. gen. 1p. sg. ἐγώ I
6 ἐὰν conj. ἐάν if, soever, except, though, and if, but, whether, if so, so
γὰρ conj. γάρ for, and, because, but, indeed
οὐκ particle of negation. οὐ οὐκ οὐχ not, no, neither, none, nay, nor, never, nothing
ἄφρων adj. nom. masc. sg. ἄφρων fool, foolish, unwise
ἀλήθειαν n. acc. fem. sg. ἀλήθεια truth, verity
γὰρ conj. γάρ for, and, because, but, indeed
δέ conj. δέ but, and, now, also, to the contrary, rather, then
μή particle of negation. μή not, no, lest, neither, none, nothing, nor, never, without
τις indefinite pron. nom. masc. sg. τὶς certain, some, any man, one, any thing
εἰς prep. εἰς (+acc) into, to, unto, for, in, on, toward, against, upon, at, among
ἐμὲ pron. acc. 1p. sg. ἐγώ I
ὑπὲρ prep. ὑπέρ (+gen) for, of, for the sake of, (+acc) above, more than
ὃ relative pron. acc. neut. sg. ὅς ἥ ὅ who, which, what, that
με pron. acc. 1p. sg. ἐγώ I
ἢ particle. ἤ or, than, either, nor, or else, and, rather than
τι indefinite pron. acc. neut. sg. τὶς certain, some, any man, one, any thing
ἐξ prep. ἐκ ἐξ (+gen) of, from, out of, by, on, with, in, among, through
ἐμοῦ pron. gen. 1p. sg. ἐγώ I
7 καὶ conj. καί and, even, also, but
τῇ art. dat. fem. sg. ὁ ἡ τό the, this, that, he, she, it
ὑπερβολῇ n. dat. fem. sg. ὑπερβολή abundance, beyond measure, exceeding, excellency
τῶν art. gen. fem. pl. ὁ ἡ τό the, this, that, he, she, it
ἀποκαλύψεων n. gen. fem. pl. ἀποκάλυψις revelation, appearing, coming, manifestation
ἵνα conj. ἵνα that, to, lest, for to, so that, albeit, because, for, so as
μὴ particle of negation. μή not, no, lest, neither, none, nothing, nor, never, without
μοι pron. dat. 1p. sg. ἐγώ I
σκόλοψ n. nom. masc. sg. σκόλοψ thorn
τῇ art. dat. fem. sg. ὁ ἡ τό the, this, that, he, she, it

σαρκί n. dat. fem. sg. σάρξ flesh, carnal
ἄγγελος n. nom. masc. sg. ἄγγελος angel, messenger
Σατανᾶ n. gen. masc. sg. Σατανᾶς Satan
ἵνα conj. ἵνα that, to, lest, for to, so that, albeit, because, for, so as
με pron. acc. 1p. sg. ἐγώ I
ἵνα conj. ἵνα that, to, lest, for to, so that, albeit, because, for, so as
μὴ particle of negation. μή not, no, lest, neither, none, nothing, nor, never, without
8 ὑπὲρ prep. ὑπέρ (+gen) for, of, for the sake of, (+acc) above, more than
τούτου demo. pron. gen. neut. sg. οὗτος αὕτη τοῦτο this, the same, this same, he, she, it
τρὶς adv. τρίς thrice, three times
τὸν art. acc. masc. sg. ὁ ἡ τό the, this, that, he, she, it
Κύριον n. acc. masc. sg. κύριος Lord, lord, master, sir, LORD, God, Master, owner
ἵνα conj. ἵνα that, to, lest, for to, so that, albeit, because, for, so as
ἀπ' prep. ἀπό (+gen) from, of, out of, since, for, off, at, by, in, on
ἐμοῦ pron. gen. 1p. sg. ἐγώ I
9 καὶ conj. καί and, even, also, but
μοι pron. dat. 1p. sg. ἐγώ I
σοι pron. dat. 2p. sg. σύ thou, you
ἡ art. nom. fem. sg. ὁ ἡ τό the, this, that, he, she, it
χάρις n. nom. fem. sg. χάρις grace, thank, favour, pleasure
μου pron. gen. 1p. sg. ἐγώ I
ἡ art. nom. fem. sg. ὁ ἡ τό the, this, that, he, she, it
γὰρ conj. γάρ for, and, because, but, indeed
δύναμις n. nom. fem. sg. δύναμις power, mighty work, miracle, strength, might
μου pron. gen. 1p. sg. ἐγώ I
ἐν prep. ἐν (+dat) in, by, with, among, at, on, through, to, within, into, of, for
ἀσθενείᾳ n. dat. fem. sg. ἀσθένεια infirmity, weakness, disease, sickness
ἥδιστα adv. ἥδιστα most gladly, with the greatest pleasure
οὖν conj. οὖν therefore, then, so, and, now, wherefore
μᾶλλον adv. μᾶλλον rather, more, more and more, better, much, much the more
ἐν prep. ἐν (+dat) in, by, with, among, at, on, through, to, within, into, of, for
ταῖς art. dat. fem. pl. ὁ ἡ τό the, this, that, he, she, it
ἀσθενείαις n. dat. fem. pl. ἀσθένεια infirmity, weakness, disease, sickness
μου pron. gen. 1p. sg. ἐγώ I
ἵνα conj. ἵνα that, to, lest, for to, so that, albeit, because, for, so as
ἐπ' prep. ἐπί (+gen) on, in, upon, (+dat) in, at, for, upon, (+acc) on, upon, unto, to, against
ἐμὲ pron. acc. 1p. sg. ἐγώ I
ἡ art. nom. fem. sg. ὁ ἡ τό the, this, that, he, she, it
δύναμις n. nom. fem. sg. δύναμις power, mighty work, miracle, strength, might
τοῦ art. gen. masc. sg. ὁ ἡ τό the, this, that, he, she, it
Χριστοῦ n. gen. masc. sg. Χριστός Christ
10 διὸ conj. διό wherefore, therefore, for which cause
ἐν prep. ἐν (+dat) in, by, with, among, at, on, through, to, within, into, of, for
ἀσθενείαις n. dat. fem. pl. ἀσθένεια infirmity, weakness, disease, sickness
ἐν prep. ἐν (+dat) in, by, with, among, at, on, through, to, within, into, of, for
ὕβρεσιν n. dat. fem. pl. ὕβρις hurt, harm, reproach
ἐν prep. ἐν (+dat) in, by, with, among, at, on, through, to, within, into, of, for
ἀνάγκαις n. dat. fem. pl. ἀνάγκη must needs, necessity, distress, inevitable
ἐν prep. ἐν (+dat) in, by, with, among, at, on, through, to, within, into, of, for
διωγμοῖς n. dat. masc. pl. διωγμός persecution
ἐν prep. ἐν (+dat) in, by, with, among, at, on, through, to, within, into, of, for
στενοχωρίαις n. dat. fem. pl. στενοχωρία anguish, distress
ὑπὲρ prep. ὑπέρ (+gen) for, of, for the sake of, (+acc) above, more than
Χριστοῦ n. gen. masc. sg. Χριστός Christ
ὅταν conj. ὅταν when, as soon as, as long as, that, whensoever, while

γὰρ conj. γάρ for, and, because, but, indeed
τότε adv. τότε then, that time
δυνατός adj. nom. masc. sg. δυνατός able, possible, mighty, strong
11 ἄφρων adj. nom. masc. sg. ἄφρων fool, foolish, unwise
ὑμεῖς pron. nom. 2p. pl. σύ thou, you
με pron. acc. 1p. sg. ἐγώ I
ἐγὼ pron. nom. 1p. sg. ἐγώ I
γὰρ conj. γάρ for, and, because, but, indeed
ὑφ' prep. ὑπό (+gen) of, by, with, from, among, (+acc) under
ὑμῶν pron. gen. 2p. pl. σύ thou, you
οὐδὲν num. acc. neut. sg. οὐδείς no man, nothing, no, none, neither, not, nought
γὰρ conj. γάρ for, and, because, but, indeed
τῶν art. gen. masc. pl. ὁ ἡ τό the, this, that, he, she, it
ὑπερ adv. ὑπέρ (+gen) for, of, for the sake of, (+acc) above, more than
λίαν adv. λίαν exceeding, greatly, very, great sore
ἀποστόλων n. gen. masc. pl. ἀπόστολος apostle, messenger, he that is sent
εἰ conj. εἰ if, whether, that, though, forasmuch
καὶ conj. καί and, even, also, but
οὐδὲν num. acc. neut. sg. οὐδείς no man, nothing, no, none, neither, not, nought
12 τὰ art. nom. neut. pl. ὁ ἡ τό the, this, that, he, she, it
μὲν conj. μέν indeed, verily, truly, even, so, some
σημεῖα n. nom. neut. pl. σημεῖον sign, miracle, wonder, token
τοῦ art. gen. masc. sg. ὁ ἡ τό the, this, that, he, she, it
ἀποστόλου n. gen. masc. sg. ἀπόστολος apostle, messenger, he that is sent
ἐν prep. ἐν (+dat) in, by, with, among, at, on, through, to, within, into, of, for
ὑμῖν pron. dat. 2p. pl. σύ thou, you
ἐν prep. ἐν (+dat) in, by, with, among, at, on, through, to, within, into, of, for
πάσῃ adj. dat. fem. sg. πᾶς πᾶσα πᾶν all, every, whosoever, every one, no, whole, any
ὑπομονῇ n. dat. fem. sg. ὑπομονή patience, enduring
ἐν prep. ἐν (+dat) in, by, with, among, at, on, through, to, within, into, of, for
σημείοις n. dat. neut. pl. σημεῖον sign, miracle, wonder, token
καὶ conj. καί and, even, also, but
τέρασι n. dat. neut. pl. τέρας wonder
καὶ conj. καί and, even, also, but
δυνάμεσιν n. dat. fem. pl. δύναμις power, mighty work, miracle, strength, might
13 τί interrog. pron. nom. neut. sg. τίς what, who, why, where, which, how
γάρ conj. γάρ for, and, because, but, indeed
ὃ relative pron. acc. neut. sg. ὅς ἥ ὅ who, which, what, that
ὑπὲρ prep. ὑπέρ (+gen) for, of, for the sake of, (+acc) above, more than
τὰς art. acc. fem. pl. ὁ ἡ τό the, this, that, he, she, it
λοιπὰς adj. acc. fem. pl. λοιπός other, rest, remnant, residue, which remain
ἐκκλησίας n. acc. fem. pl. ἐκκλησία church, assembly
εἰ conj. εἰ if, whether, that, though, forasmuch
μὴ particle of negation. μή not, no, lest, neither, none, nothing, nor, never, without
ὅτι conj. ὅτι that, for, because, how that, how, because that, for that, though
αὐτὸς pron. nom. masc. 3p. sg. αὐτός ή ό self, of oneself, even, very, the same, he, she, it
ἐγὼ pron. nom. 1p. sg. ἐγώ I
οὐ particle of negation. οὐ οὐκ οὐχ not, no, neither, none, nay, nor, never, nothing
ὑμῶν pron. gen. 2p. pl. σύ thou, you
μοι pron. dat. 1p. sg. ἐγώ I
τὴν art. acc. fem. sg. ὁ ἡ τό the, this, that, he, she, it
ἀδικίαν n. acc. fem. sg. ἀδικία iniquity, unrighteousness, unjust, wrong
ταύτην demo. pron. acc. fem. sg. οὗτος αὕτη τοῦτο this, the same, this same, he, she, it
14 τρίτον ordinal. adj. acc. neut. sg. τρίτος third
ἑτοίμως adv. ἑτοίμως ready

πρὸς prep. πρός (+gen) for, (+dat) at, (+acc) unto, to, with, for, against
ὑμᾶς pron. acc. 2p. sg. σύ thou, you
καὶ conj. καί and, even, also, but
οὐ particle of negation. οὐ οὐκ οὐχ not, no, neither, none, nay, nor, never, nothing
ὑμῶν pron. gen. 2p. pl. σύ thou, you
οὐ particle of negation. οὐ οὐκ οὐχ not, no, neither, none, nay, nor, never, nothing
γὰρ conj. γάρ for, and, because, but, indeed
τὰ art. acc. neut. pl. ὁ ἡ τό the, this, that, he, she, it
ὑμῶν pron. gen. 2p. pl. σύ thou, you
ἀλλ' conj. ἀλλά but, yea, yet, nevertheless, howbeit, nay, therefore
ὑμᾶς pron. acc. 2p. sg. σύ thou, you
οὐ particle of negation. οὐ οὐκ οὐχ not, no, neither, none, nay, nor, never, nothing
γὰρ conj. γάρ for, and, because, but, indeed
τὰ art. nom. neut. pl. ὁ ἡ τό the, this, that, he, she, it
τέκνα n. nom. neut. pl. τέκνον child, son, daughter
τοῖς art. dat. masc. pl. ὁ ἡ τό the, this, that, he, she, it
γονεῦσι n. dat. masc. pl. γονεύς father, (pl.) parents
ἀλλ' conj. ἀλλά but, yea, yet, nevertheless, howbeit, nay, therefore
οἱ art. nom. masc. pl. ὁ ἡ τό the, this, that, he, she, it
γονεῖς n. nom. masc. pl. γονεύς father, (pl.) parents
τοῖς art. dat. neut. pl. ὁ ἡ τό the, this, that, he, she, it
τέκνοις n. dat. neut. pl. τέκνον child, son, daughter
15 ἐγὼ pron. nom. 1p. sg. ἐγώ I
δὲ conj. δέ but, and, now, also, to the contrary, rather, then
ἥδιστα adv. ἥδιστα most gladly, with the greatest pleasure
καὶ conj. καί and, even, also, but
ὑπὲρ prep. ὑπέρ (+gen) for, of, for the sake of, (+acc) above, more than
τῶν art. gen. fem. pl. ὁ ἡ τό the, this, that, he, she, it
ψυχῶν n. gen. fem. pl. ψυχή life, soul, mind, heart
ὑμῶν pron. gen. 2p. pl. σύ thou, you
εἰ conj. εἰ if, whether, that, though, forasmuch
καὶ conj. καί and, even, also, but
περισσοτέρως adv. περισσοτέρως more exceedingly, more abundantly, more frequent
ὑμᾶς pron. acc. 2p. pl. σύ thou, you
ἧττον compar. adj. acc. neut. sg. ἧττον worse, less
16 δέ conj. δέ but, and, now, also, to the contrary, rather, then
ἐγὼ pron. nom. 1p. sg. ἐγώ I
οὐ particle of negation. οὐ οὐκ οὐχ not, no, neither, none, nay, nor, never, nothing
ὑμᾶς pron. acc. 2p. pl. σύ thou, you
ἀλλ' conj. ἀλλά but, yea, yet, nevertheless, howbeit, nay, therefore
πανοῦργος adj. nom. masc. sg. πανοῦργος crafty
δόλῳ n. dat. masc. sg. δόλος guile, deceit, subtilty, craft
ὑμᾶς pron. acc. 2p. pl. σύ thou, you
17 μὴ particle of negation. μή not, no, lest, neither, none, nothing, nor, never, without
τινα indefinite pron. acc. masc. sg. τὶς certain, some, any man, one, any thing
ὧν relative pron. gen. masc. pl. ὅς ἥ ὅ who, which, what, that
πρὸς prep. πρός (+gen) for, (+dat) at, (+acc) unto, to, with, for, against
ὑμᾶς pron. acc. 2p. pl. σύ thou, you
δι' prep. διά (+gen) by, through, with, in, of, (+acc) for, because of, for a cause
αὐτοῦ pron. gen. masc. 3p. sg. αὐτός ἥ ὅ self, of oneself, even, very, the same, he, she, it
ὑμᾶς pron. acc. 2p. pl. σύ thou, you
18 Τίτον n. acc. masc. sg. Τίτος Titus
καὶ conj. καί and, even, also, but
τὸν art. acc. masc. sg. ὁ ἡ τό the, this, that, he, she, it
ἀδελφόν n. acc. masc. sg. ἀδελφός brother

μή particle of negation. μή not, no, lest, neither, none, nothing, nor, never, without
τι indefinite pron. acc. neut. sg. τὶς certain, some, any man, one, any thing
ὑμᾶς pron. acc. 2p. pl. σύ thou, you
Τίτος n. nom. masc. sg. Τίτος Titus
οὐ particle of negation. οὐ οὐκ οὐχ not, no, neither, none, nay, nor, never, nothing
τῷ art. dat. neut. sg. ὁ ἡ τό the, this, that, he, she, it
αὐτῷ adj. dat. neut. sg. αὐτός ή ό self, of oneself, even, very, the same, he, she, it
Πνεύματι n. dat. neut. sg. πνεῦμα spirit, Spirit, Ghost, ghost, life. of the spirit, wind
οὐ particle of negation. οὐ οὐκ οὐχ not, no, neither, none, nay, nor, never, nothing
τοῖς art. dat. neut. pl. ὁ ἡ τό the, this, that, he, she, it
αὐτοῖς adj. dat. neut. pl. αὐτός ή ό self, of oneself, even, very, the same, he, she, it
ἴχνεσι n. dat. neut. pl. ἴχνος step
19 Πάλιν adv. πάλιν again
ὅτι conj. ὅτι that, for, because, how that, how, because that, for that, though
ὑμῖν pron. dat. 2p. pl. σύ thou, you
κατενώπιον prep. κατενώπιον (+gen) before, before the presence, in the sight, in sight
τοῦ art. gen. masc. sg. ὁ ἡ τό the, this, that, he, she, it
Θεοῦ n. gen. masc. sg. θεός God, god
ἐν prep. ἐν (+dat) in, by, with, among, at, on, through, to, within, into, of, for
Χριστῷ n. dat. masc. sg. Χριστός Christ
τὰ art. nom. neut. pl. ὁ ἡ τό the, this, that, he, she, it
δὲ conj. δέ but, and, now, also, to the contrary, rather, then
πάντα adj. nom. neut. pl. πᾶς πᾶsα πᾶν all, every, whosoever, every one, no, whole, any
ἀγαπητοί adj. voc. masc. pl. ἀγαπητός beloved, dearly beloved, dear, wellbeloved
ὑπὲρ prep. ὑπέρ (+gen) for, of, for the sake of, (+acc) above, more than
τῆς art. gen. fem. sg. ὁ ἡ τό the, this, that, he, she, it
ὑμῶν pron. gen. 2p. pl. σύ thou, you
οἰκοδομῆς n. gen. fem. sg. οἰκοδομή building, edifying, edification
20 γὰρ conj. γάρ for, and, because, but, indeed
μή particle of negation. μή not, no, lest, neither, none, nothing, nor, never, without
πως particle. πώς by any means, by some means, haply, perhaps
οὐχ particle of negation. οὐ οὐκ οὐχ not, no, neither, none, nay, nor, never, nothing
οἵους relative pron. acc. masc. pl. οἷος what manner of, such as, as, which, what, so as
ὑμᾶς pron. acc. 2p. pl. σύ thou, you
κἀγὼ pron. nom. 1p. sg. κἀγώ and I, I also, so I, even as I
ὑμῖν pron. dat. 2p. pl. σύ thou, you
οἷον relative pron. acc. masc. sg. οἷος what manner of, such as, as, which, what, so as
οὐ particle of negation. οὐ οὐκ οὐχ not, no, neither, none, nay, nor, never, nothing
μή particle of negation. μή not, no, lest, neither, none, nothing, nor, never, without
πως particle. πώς by any means, by some means, haply, perhaps
ἔρεις n. nom. fem. pl. ἔρις debate, strife, contention, variance
ζῆλοι n. nom. masc. pl. ζῆλος zeal, envying, indignation, emulation, jealousy
θυμοί n. nom. masc. pl. θυμός wrath, fierceness, indignation
ἐριθεῖαι n. nom. fem. pl. ἐριθεία strife, contention, contentious
καταλαλιαί n. nom. fem. pl. καταλαλιά backbiting, evil speaking
ψιθυρισμοί n. nom. masc. pl. ψιθυρισμός whispering
φυσιώσεις n. nom. fem. pl. φυσίωσις swelling
ἀκαταστασίαι n. nom. fem. pl. ἀκαταστασία commotion, confusion, tumult
21 μή particle of negation. μή not, no, lest, neither, none, nothing, nor, never, without
πάλιν adv. πάλιν again
με pron. acc. 1p. sg. ἐγώ I
ὁ art. nom. masc. sg. ὁ ἡ τό the, this, that, he, she, it
Θεός n. nom. masc. sg. θεός God, god
μου pron. gen. 1p. sg. ἐγώ I
πρὸς prep. πρός (+gen) for, (+dat) at, (+acc) unto, to, with, for, against

ὑμᾶς pron. acc. 2p. pl. σύ thou, you
καὶ conj. καί and, even, also, but
πολλοὺς adj. acc. masc. pl. πολύς many, great, much, long, abundant
τῶν art. gen. masc. pl. ὁ ἡ τό the, this, that, he, she, it
καὶ conj. καί and, even, also, but
μὴ particle of negation. μή not, no, lest, neither, none, nothing, nor, never, without
ἐπὶ prep. ἐπί (+gen) on, in, upon, (+dat) in, at, for, upon, (+acc) on, upon, unto, to, against
τῇ art. dat. fem. sg. ὁ ἡ τό the, this, that, he, she, it
ἀκαθαρσίᾳ n. dat. fem. sg. ἀκαθαρσία uncleanness
καὶ conj. καί and, even, also, but
πορνείᾳ n. dat. fem. sg. πορνεία fornication
καὶ conj. καί and, even, also, but
ἀσελγείᾳ n. dat. fem. sg. ἀσέλγεια lasciviousness, wantonness, filthy
ᾗ relative pron. dat. fem. sg. ὅς ἥ ὅ who, which, what, that

13

1 Τρίτον ordinal. adj. acc. neut. sg. τρίτος third
τοῦτο demo. pron. acc. neut. sg. οὗτος αὕτη τοῦτο this, the same, this same, he, she, it
πρὸς prep. πρός (+gen) for, (+dat) at, (+acc) unto, to, with, for, against
ὑμᾶς pron. acc. 2p. pl. σύ thou, you
ἐπὶ prep. ἐπί (+gen) on, in, upon, (+dat) in, at, for, upon, (+acc) on, upon, unto, to, against
στόματος n. gen. neut. sg. στόμα mouth, face, edge
δύο num. gen. masc. pl. δύο two, twain, both
μαρτύρων n. gen. masc. pl. μάρτυς or μάρτυρ witness, martyr, record
καὶ conj. καί and, even, also, but
τριῶν num. gen. masc. pl. τρεῖς three
πᾶν adj. nom. neut. sg. πᾶς πᾶσα πᾶν all, every, whosoever, every one, no, whole, any
ῥῆμα n. nom. neut. sg. ῥῆμα word, saying, thing
2 καὶ conj. καί and, even, also, but
ὡς adv. ὡς as, when, as it were, how, about, like, as soon as, even as, while
τὸ art. acc. neut. sg. ὁ ἡ τό the, this, that, he, she, it
δεύτερον ordinal. adj. acc. neut. sg. δεύτερος second, second time, again, afterward
καὶ conj. καί and, even, also, but
νῦν adv. νῦν now, henceforth, present, this time
τοῖς art. dat. masc. pl. ὁ ἡ τό the, this, that, he, she, it
καὶ conj. καί and, even, also, but
τοῖς art. dat. masc. pl. ὁ ἡ τό the, this, that, he, she, it
λοιποῖς adj. dat. masc. pl. λοιπός other, rest, remnant, residue, which remain
πᾶσιν adj. dat. masc. pl. πᾶς πᾶσα πᾶν all, every, whosoever, every one, no, whole, any
ὅτι conj. ὅτι that, for, because, how that, how, because that, for that, though
ἐὰν conj. ἐάν if, soever, except, though, and if, but, whether, if so, so
εἰς prep. εἰς (+acc) into, to, unto, for, in, on, toward, against, upon, at, among
τὸ art. acc. neut. sg. ὁ ἡ τό the, this, that, he, she, it
πάλιν adv. πάλιν again
οὐ particle of negation. οὐ οὐκ οὐχ not, no, neither, none, nay, nor, never, nothing
3 ἐπεὶ conj. ἐπεί because, otherwise, seeing, else, for then, for as much as, for, since
δοκιμὴν n. acc. fem. sg. δοκιμή experience, proof, experiment, trial
τοῦ art. gen. masc. sg. ὁ ἡ τό the, this, that, he, she, it
ἐν prep. ἐν (+dat) in, by, with, among, at, on, through, to, within, into, of, for
ἐμοὶ pron. dat. 1p. sg. ἐγώ I
Χριστοῦ n. gen. masc. sg. Χριστός Christ
ὃς relative pron. nom. masc. sg. ὅς ἥ ὅ who, which, what, that
εἰς prep. εἰς (+acc) into, to, unto, for, in, on, toward, against, upon, at, among
ὑμᾶς pron. acc. 2p. pl. σύ thou, you

οὐκ particle of negation. οὐ οὐκ οὐχ not, no, neither, none, nay, nor, never, nothing
ἀλλὰ conj. ἀλλά but, yea, yet, nevertheless, howbeit, nay, therefore
ἐν prep. ἐν (+dat) in, by, with, among, at, on, through, to, within, into, of, for
ὑμῖν pron. dat. 2p. pl. σύ thou, you
4 καὶ conj. καί and, even, also, but
γὰρ conj. γάρ for, and, because, but, indeed
εἰ conj. εἰ if, whether, that, though, forasmuch
ἐξ prep. ἐκ ἐξ (+gen) of, from, out of, by, on, with, in, among, through
ἀσθενείας n. gen. fem. sg. ἀσθένεια infirmity, weakness, disease, sickness
ἀλλὰ conj. ἀλλά but, yea, yet, nevertheless, howbeit, nay, therefore
ἐκ prep. ἐκ ἐξ (+gen) of, from, out of, by, on, with, in, among, through
δυνάμεως n. gen. fem. sg. δύναμις power, mighty work, miracle, strength, might
Θεοῦ n. gen. masc. sg. θεός God, god
καὶ conj. καί and, even, also, but
γὰρ conj. γάρ for, and, because, but, indeed
καὶ conj. καί and, even, also, but
ἡμεῖς pron. nom. 1p. pl. ἐγώ I
ἐν prep. ἐν (+dat) in, by, with, among, at, on, through, to, within, into, of, for
αὐτῷ pron. dat. masc. 3p. sg. αὐτός ή ό self, of oneself, even, very, the same, he, she, it
ἀλλὰ conj. ἀλλά but, yea, yet, nevertheless, howbeit, nay, therefore
σὺν prep. σύν (+dat) with, beside
αὐτῷ pron. dat. masc. 3p. sg. αὐτός ή ό self, of oneself, even, very, the same, he, she, it
ἐκ prep. ἐκ ἐξ (+gen) of, from, out of, by, on, with, in, among, through
δυνάμεως n. gen. fem. sg. δύναμις power, mighty work, miracle, strength, might
Θεοῦ n. gen. masc. sg. θεός God, god
εἰς prep. εἰς (+acc) into, to, unto, for, in, on, toward, against, upon, at, among
ὑμᾶς pron. acc. 2p. pl. σύ thou, you
5 ἑαυτοὺς reflexive pron. acc. masc. 3p. pl. ἑαυτοῦ himself, herself, itself, yourself, ourselves
εἰ conj. εἰ if, whether, that, though, forasmuch
ἐν prep. ἐν (+dat) in, by, with, among, at, on, through, to, within, into, of, for
τῇ art. dat. fem. sg. ὁ ἡ τό the, this, that, he, she, it
πίστει n. dat. fem. sg. πίστις faith, assurance, belief, fidelity
ἑαυτοὺς reflexive pron. acc. masc. 3p. pl. ἑαυτοῦ himself, herself, itself, yourself, ourselves
ἢ particle. ἤ or, than, either, nor, or else, and, rather than
οὐκ particle of negation. οὐ οὐκ οὐχ not, no, neither, none, nay, nor, never, nothing
ἑαυτοὺς reflexive pron. acc. masc. 3p. pl. ἑαυτοῦ himself, herself, itself, yourself, ourselves
ὅτι conj. ὅτι that, for, because, how that, how, because that, for that, though
Ἰησοῦς n. nom. masc. sg. Ἰησοῦς Jesus
Χριστὸς n. nom. masc. sg. Χριστός Christ
ἐν prep. ἐν (+dat) in, by, with, among, at, on, through, to, within, into, of, for
ὑμῖν pron. dat. 2p. pl. σύ thou, you
εἰ conj. εἰ if, whether, that, though, forasmuch
μή particle of negation. μή not, no, lest, neither, none, nothing, nor, never, without
τι indefinite pron. acc. neut. sg. τὶς certain, some, any man, one, any thing
ἀδόκιμοί adj. nom. masc. pl. ἀδόκιμος reprobate, castaway, rejected
6 δὲ conj. δέ but, and, now, also, to the contrary, rather, then
ὅτι conj. ὅτι that, for, because, how that, how, because that, for that, though
ὅτι conj. ὅτι that, for, because, how that, how, because that, for that, though
ἡμεῖς pron. nom. 1p. pl. ἐγώ I
οὐκ particle of negation. οὐ οὐκ οὐχ not, no, neither, none, nay, nor, never, nothing
ἀδόκιμοι adj. nom. masc. pl. ἀδόκιμος reprobate, castaway, rejected
7 δὲ conj. δέ but, and, now, also, to the contrary, rather, then
πρὸς prep. πρός (+gen) for, (+dat) at, (+acc) unto, to, with, for, against
τὸν art. acc. masc. sg. ὁ ἡ τό the, this, that, he, she, it
Θεὸν n. acc. masc. sg. θεός God, god

μὴ particle of negation. μή not, no, lest, neither, none, nothing, nor, never, without
ὑμᾶς pron. acc. 2p. pl. σύ thou, you
κακὸν adj. acc. neut. sg. κακός evil, evil thing, noisome, wicked
μηδέν num. acc. neut. sg. μηδείς μηδεμία μηδέν no man, nothing, no, none, not at all
οὐχ particle of negation. οὐ οὐκ οὐχ not, no, neither, none, nay, nor, never, nothing
ἵνα conj. ἵνα that, to, lest, for to, so that, albeit, because, for, so as
ἡμεῖς pron. nom. 1p. pl. ἐγώ I
δόκιμοι adj. nom. masc. pl. δόκιμος approved, tried
ἀλλ' conj. ἀλλά but, yea, yet, nevertheless, howbeit, nay, therefore
ἵνα conj. ἵνα that, to, lest, for to, so that, albeit, because, for, so as
ὑμεῖς pron. nom. 2p. pl. σύ thou, you
τὸ art. acc. neut. sg. ὁ ἡ τό the, this, that, he, she, it
καλὸν adj. acc. neut. sg. καλός good, better, goodly, meet, honest, fair, well, worthy
ἡμεῖς pron. nom. 1p. pl. ἐγώ I
δὲ conj. δέ but, and, now, also, to the contrary, rather, then
ὡς adv. ὡς as, when, as it were, how, about, like, as soon as, even as, while
ἀδόκιμοι adj. nom. masc. pl. ἀδόκιμος reprobate, castaway, rejected
8 οὐ particle of negation. οὐ οὐκ οὐχ not, no, neither, none, nay, nor, never, nothing
γὰρ conj. γάρ for, and, because, but, indeed
τι indefinite pron. acc. neut. sg. τὶς certain, some, any man, one, any thing
κατὰ prep. κατά (+gen) against, by, throughout, down, (+acc) according to, after, with
τῆς art. gen. fem. sg. ὁ ἡ τό the, this, that, he, she, it
ἀληθείας n. gen. fem. sg. ἀλήθεια truth, verity
ἀλλ' conj. ἀλλά but, yea, yet, nevertheless, howbeit, nay, therefore
ὑπὲρ prep. ὑπέρ (+gen) for, of, for the sake of, (+acc) above, more than
τῆς art. gen. fem. sg. ὁ ἡ τό the, this, that, he, she, it
ἀληθείας n. gen. fem. sg. ἀλήθεια truth, verity
9 γὰρ conj. γάρ for, and, because, but, indeed
ὅταν conj. ὅταν when, as soon as, as long as, that, whensoever, while
ἡμεῖς pron. nom. 1p. pl. ἐγώ I
ὑμεῖς pron. nom. 2p. pl. σύ thou, you
δὲ conj. δέ but, and, now, also, to the contrary, rather, then
δυνατοὶ adj. nom. masc. pl. δυνατός able, possible, mighty, strong
τοῦτο demo. pron. acc. neut. sg. οὗτος αὕτη τοῦτο this, the same, this same, he, she, it
δὲ conj. δέ but, and, now, also, to the contrary, rather, then
καὶ conj. καί and, even, also, but
τὴν art. acc. fem. sg. ὁ ἡ τό the, this, that, he, she, it
ὑμῶν pron. gen. 2p. pl. σύ thou, you
κατάρτισιν n. acc. fem. sg. κατάρτισις perfection
10 διὰ prep. διά (+gen) by, through, with, in, of, (+acc) for, because of, for a cause
τοῦτο demo. pron. acc. neut. sg. οὗτος αὕτη τοῦτο this, the same, this same, he, she, it
ταῦτα demo. pron. acc. neut. pl. οὗτος αὕτη τοῦτο this, the same, this same, he, she, it
ἵνα conj. ἵνα that, to, lest, for to, so that, albeit, because, for, so as
μὴ particle of negation. μή not, no, lest, neither, none, nothing, nor, never, without
ἀποτόμως adv. ἀποτόμως sharpness, sharply
κατὰ prep. κατά (+gen) against, by, throughout, down, (+acc) according to, after, with
τὴν art. acc. fem. sg. ὁ ἡ τό the, this, that, he, she, it
ἐξουσίαν n. acc. fem. sg. ἐξουσία power, authority, right, strength, jurisdiction
ἣν relative pron. acc. fem. sg. ὅς ἥ ὅ who, which, what, that
μοι pron. dat. 1p. sg. ἐγώ I
ὁ art. nom. masc. sg. ὁ ἡ τό the, this, that, he, she, it
Κύριος n. nom. masc. sg. κύριος Lord, lord, master, sir, LORD, God, Master, owner
εἰς prep. εἰς (+acc) into, to, unto, for, in, on, toward, against, upon, at, among
οἰκοδομὴν n. acc. fem. sg. οἰκοδομή building, edifying, edification
καὶ conj. καί and, even, also, but

οὐκ particle of negation. οὐ οὐκ οὐχ not, no, neither, none, nay, nor, never, nothing
εἰς prep. εἰς (+acc) into, to, unto, for, in, on, toward, against, upon, at, among
καθαίρεσιν n. acc. fem. sg. καθαίρεσις pulling down, destruction
11 Λοιπόν adv. λοιπόν finally, henceforth, now, besides, furthermore, moreover, then
ἀδελφοί n. voc. masc. pl. ἀδελφός brother
τὸ art. acc. neut. sg. ὁ ἡ τό the, this, that, he, she, it
αὐτὸ pron. acc. neut. 3p. sg. αὐτός ή ό self, of oneself, even, very, the same, he, she, it
καὶ conj. καί and, even, also, but
ὁ art. nom. masc. sg. ὁ ἡ τό the, this, that, he, she, it
Θεὸς n. nom. masc. sg. θεός God, god
τῆς art. gen. fem. sg. ὁ ἡ τό the, this, that, he, she, it
ἀγάπης n. gen. fem. sg. ἀγάπη love, charity, feast of charity
καὶ conj. καί and, even, also, but
εἰρήνης n. gen. fem. sg. εἰρήνη peace, quietness, rest
μεθ' prep. μετά (+gen) with, among, against, (+acc) after
ὑμῶν pron. gen. 2p. pl. σύ thou, you
12 ἀλλήλους pron. acc. masc. 2p. pl. ἀλλήλων one another, themselves, together, mutual
ἐν prep. ἐν (+dat) in, by, with, among, at, on, through, to, within, into, of, for
ἁγίῳ adj. dat. neut. sg. ἅγιος Holy, holy, saint, Holy One, holy thing, most holy
φιλήματι n. dat. neut. sg. φίλημα kiss
13 ὑμᾶς pron. acc. 2p. pl. σύ thou, you
οἱ art. nom. masc. pl. ὁ ἡ τό the, this, that, he, she, it
ἅγιοι adj. nom. masc. pl. ἅγιος Holy, holy, saint, Holy One, holy thing, most holy
πάντες adj. nom. masc. pl. πᾶς πᾶσα πᾶν all, every, whosoever, every one, no, whole, any
14 Ἡ art. nom. fem. sg. ὁ ἡ τό the, this, that, he, she, it
χάρις n. nom. fem. sg. χάρις grace, thank, favour, pleasure
τοῦ art. gen. masc. sg. ὁ ἡ τό the, this, that, he, she, it
Κυρίου n. gen. masc. sg. κύριος Lord, lord, master, sir, LORD, God, Master, owner
Ἰησοῦ n. gen. masc. sg. Ἰησοῦς Jesus
Χριστοῦ n. gen. masc. sg. Χριστός Christ
καὶ conj. καί and, even, also, but
ἡ art. nom. fem. sg. ὁ ἡ τό the, this, that, he, she, it
ἀγάπη n. nom. fem. sg. ἀγάπη love, charity, feast of charity
τοῦ art. gen. masc. sg. ὁ ἡ τό the, this, that, he, she, it
Θεοῦ n. gen. masc. sg. θεός God, god
καὶ conj. καί and, even, also, but
ἡ art. nom. fem. sg. ὁ ἡ τό the, this, that, he, she, it
κοινωνία n. nom. fem. sg. κοινωνία fellowship, communion, contribution, distribution
τοῦ art. gen. neut. sg. ὁ ἡ τό the, this, that, he, she, it
Ἁγίου adj. gen. neut. sg. ἅγιος Holy, holy, saint, Holy One, holy thing, most holy
Πνεύματος n. gen. neut. sg. πνεῦμα spirit, Spirit, Ghost, ghost, life. of the spirit, wind
μετὰ prep. μετά (+gen) with, among, against, (+acc) after
πάντων adj. gen. masc. pl. πᾶς πᾶσα πᾶν all, every, whosoever, every one, no, whole, any
ὑμῶν pron. gen. 2p. pl. σύ thou, you
ἀμήν particle. ἀμήν amen, verily

ΠΑΥΛΟΥ
Η ΠΡΟΣ
ΓΑΛΑΤΑΣ ΕΠΙΣΤΟΛΗ

1

1 Παῦλος n. nom. masc. sg. Παῦλος Paul, Paulus
ἀπόστολος n. nom. masc. sg. ἀπόστολος apostle, messenger, he that is sent
οὐκ particle of negation. οὐ οὐκ οὐχ not, no, neither, none, nay, nor, never, nothing
ἀπ' prep. ἀπό (+gen) from, of, out of, since, for, off, at, by, in, on
ἀνθρώπων n. gen. masc. pl. ἄνθρωπος man, human being, person, one, certain
οὐδὲ adv. οὐδέ neither, nor, not, no, not even, never, not yet
δι' prep. διά (+gen) by, through, with, in, of, (+acc) for, because of, for a cause
ἀνθρώπου n. gen. masc. sg. ἄνθρωπος man, human being, person, one, certain
ἀλλὰ conj. ἀλλά but, yea, yet, nevertheless, howbeit, nay, therefore
διὰ prep. διά (+gen) by, through, with, in, of, (+acc) for, because of, for a cause
Ἰησοῦ n. gen. masc. sg. Ἰησοῦς Jesus
Χριστοῦ n. gen. masc. sg. Χριστός Christ
καὶ conj. καί and, even, also, but
Θεοῦ n. gen. masc. sg. θεός God, god
πατρὸς n. gen. masc. sg. πατήρ Father, father, parent
τοῦ art. gen. masc. sg. ὁ ἡ τό the, this, that, he, she, it
αὐτὸν pron. acc. masc. 3p. sg. αὐτός ή ό self, of oneself, even, very, the same, he, she, it
ἐκ prep. ἐκ ἐξ (+gen) of, from, out of, by, on, with, in, among, through
νεκρῶν adj. gen. masc. pl. νεκρός dead
2 καὶ conj. καί and, even, also, but
οἱ art. nom. masc. pl. ὁ ἡ τό the, this, that, he, she, it
σὺν prep. σύν (+dat) with, beside
ἐμοὶ pron. dat. 1p. sg. ἐγώ I
πάντες adj. nom. masc. pl. πᾶς πᾶσα πᾶν all, every, whosoever, every one, no, whole, any
ἀδελφοὶ n. nom. masc. pl. ἀδελφός brother
ταῖς art. dat. fem. pl. ὁ ἡ τό the, this, that, he, she, it
ἐκκλησίαις n. dat. fem. pl. ἐκκλησία church, assembly
τῆς art. gen. fem. sg. ὁ ἡ τό the, this, that, he, she, it
Γαλατίας n. gen. fem. sg. Γαλατία Galatia
3 χάρις n. nom. fem. sg. χάρις grace, thank, favour, pleasure
ὑμῖν pron. dat. 2p. pl. σύ thou, you
καὶ conj. καί and, even, also, but
εἰρήνη n. nom. fem. sg. εἰρήνη peace, quietness, rest
ἀπὸ prep. ἀπό (+gen) from, of, out of, since, for, off, at, by, in, on
Θεοῦ n. gen. masc. sg. θεός God, god
πατρὸς n. gen. masc. sg. πατήρ Father, father, parent
καὶ conj. καί and, even, also, but
Κυρίου n. gen. masc. sg. κύριος Lord, lord, master, sir, LORD, God, Master, owner
ἡμῶν pron. gen. 1p. pl. ἐγώ I
Ἰησοῦ n. gen. masc. sg. Ἰησοῦς Jesus
Χριστοῦ n. gen. masc. sg. Χριστός Christ
4 τοῦ art. gen. masc. sg. ὁ ἡ τό the, this, that, he, she, it
ἑαυτὸν reflexive pron. acc. masc. 3p. sg. ἑαυτοῦ himself, herself, itself, yourself, ourselves
ὑπὲρ prep. ὑπέρ (+gen) for, of, for the sake of, (+acc) above, more than
τῶν art. gen. fem. pl. ὁ ἡ τό the, this, that, he, she, it
ἁμαρτιῶν n. gen. fem. pl. ἁμαρτία sin, offence, sinful
ἡμῶν pron. gen. 1p. pl. ἐγώ I

ὅπως adv. ὅπως that, how, to, because, so that, when
ἡμᾶς pron. acc. 1p. pl. ἐγώ I
ἐκ prep. ἐκ ἐξ (+gen) of, from, out of, by, on, with, in, among, through
τοῦ art. gen. masc. sg. ὁ ἡ τό the, this, that, he, she, it
αἰῶνος n. gen. masc. sg. αἰών ever, ever and ever, evermore, age, eternal, world
πονηροῦ adj. gen. masc. sg. πονηρός evil, wicked, bad
κατὰ prep. κατά (+gen) against, by, throughout, down, (+acc) according to, after, with
τὸ art. acc. neut. sg. ὁ ἡ τό the, this, that, he, she, it
θέλημα n. acc. neut. sg. θέλημα will, desire, pleasure
τοῦ art. gen. masc. sg. ὁ ἡ τό the, this, that, he, she, it
Θεοῦ n. gen. masc. sg. θεός God, god
καὶ conj. καί and, even, also, but
πατρὸς n. gen. masc. sg. πατήρ Father, father, parent
ἡμῶν pron. gen. 1p. pl. ἐγώ I
5 ᾧ relative pron. dat. masc. sg. ὅς ἥ ὅ who, which, what, that
ἡ art. nom. fem. sg. ὁ ἡ τό the, this, that, he, she, it
δόξα n. nom. fem. sg. δόξα glory, honour, praise, dignity, worship
εἰς prep. εἰς (+acc) into, to, unto, for, in, on, toward, against, upon, at, among
τοὺς art. acc. masc. pl. ὁ ἡ τό the, this, that, he, she, it
αἰῶνας n. acc. masc. pl. αἰών ever, ever and ever, evermore, age, eternal, world
τῶν art. gen. masc. pl. ὁ ἡ τό the, this, that, he, she, it
αἰώνων n. gen. masc. pl. αἰών ever, ever and ever, evermore, age, eternal, world
ἀμήν particle. ἀμήν amen, verily
6 ὅτι conj. ὅτι that, for, because, how that, how, because that, for that, though
οὕτω adv. οὕτω οὕτως so, even so, thus, on this wise, likewise, after this manner
ταχέως adv. ταχέως sortly, quickly, soon, hastily, suddenly
ἀπὸ prep. ἀπό (+gen) from, of, out of, since, for, off, at, by, in, on
τοῦ art. gen. masc. sg. ὁ ἡ τό the, this, that, he, she, it
ὑμᾶς pron. acc. 2p. pl. σύ thou, you
ἐν prep. ἐν (+dat) in, by, with, among, at, on, through, to, within, into, of, for
χάριτι n. dat. fem. sg. χάρις grace, thank, favour, pleasure
χριστοῦ n. gen. masc. sg. Χριστός Christ
εἰς prep. εἰς (+acc) into, to, unto, for, in, on, toward, against, upon, at, among
ἕτερον adj. acc. neut. sg. ἕτερος another, other, else, strange
εὐαγγέλιον n. acc. neut. sg. εὐαγγέλιον gospel
7 ὃ relative pron. nom. neut. sg. ὅς ἥ ὅ who, which, what, that
οὐκ particle of negation. οὐ οὐκ οὐχ not, no, neither, none, nay, nor, never, nothing
ἄλλο adj. nom. neut. sg. ἄλλος other, another, some, one, more, otherwise
εἰ conj. εἰ if, whether, that, though, forasmuch
μὴ particle of negation. μή not, no, lest, neither, none, nothing, nor, never, without
τινές indefinite pron. nom. masc. pl. τὶς certain, some, any man, one, any thing
οἱ art. nom. masc. pl. ὁ ἡ τό the, this, that, he, she, it
ὑμᾶς pron. acc. 2p. pl. σύ thou, you
καὶ conj. καί and, even, also, but
τὸ art. acc. neut. sg. ὁ ἡ τό the, this, that, he, she, it
εὐαγγέλιον n. acc. neut. sg. εὐαγγέλιον gospel
τοῦ art. gen. masc. sg. ὁ ἡ τό the, this, that, he, she, it
Χριστοῦ n. gen. masc. sg. Χριστός Christ
8 ἀλλὰ conj. ἀλλά but, yea, yet, nevertheless, howbeit, nay, therefore
καὶ conj. καί and, even, also, but
ἐὰν conj. ἐάν if, soever, except, though, and if, but, whether, if so, so
ἡμεῖς pron. nom. 1p. pl. ἐγώ I
ἢ particle. ἤ or, than, either, nor, or else, and, rather than
ἄγγελος n. nom. masc. sg. ἄγγελος angel, messenger
ἐξ prep. ἐκ ἐξ (+gen) of, from, out of, by, on, with, in, among, through

οὐρανοῦ n. gen. masc. sg. οὐρανός heaven, air, sky
ὑμῖν pron. dat. 2p. pl. σύ thou, you
παρ' prep. παρά (+gen) of, from, (+dat) with, for, (+acc) beside, at, by, above, against
ὃ relative pron. acc. neut. sg. ὅς ἥ ὅ who, which, what, that
ὑμῖν pron. dat. 2p. pl. σύ thou, you
ἀνάθεμα n. nom. neut. sg. ἀνάθεμα accursed, Anathema, great course
9 ὡς adv. ὡς as, when, as it were, how, about, like, as soon as, even as, while
καὶ conj. καί and, even, also, but
ἄρτι adv. ἄρτι now, hence, here, hither, even now, present
πάλιν adv. πάλιν again
εἴ conj. εἰ if, whether, that, though, forasmuch
τις indefinite pron. nom. masc. sg. τὶς certain, some, any man, one, any thing
ὑμᾶς pron. acc. 2p. pl. σύ thou, you
παρ' prep. παρά (+gen) of, from, (+dat) with, for, (+acc) beside, at, by, above, against
ὃ relative pron. acc. neut. sg. ὅς ἥ ὅ who, which, what, that
ἀνάθεμα n. nom. neut. sg. ἀνάθεμα accursed, Anathema, great course
10 ἄρτι adv. ἄρτι now, hence, here, hither, even now, present
γὰρ conj. γάρ for, and, because, but, indeed
ἀνθρώπους n. acc. masc. pl. ἄνθρωπος man, human being, person, one, certain
ἢ particle. ἤ or, than, either, nor, or else, and, rather than
τὸν art. acc. masc. sg. ὁ ἡ τό the, this, that, he, she, it
Θεόν n. acc. masc. sg. θεός God, god
ἢ particle. ἤ or, than, either, nor, or else, and, rather than
ἀνθρώποις n. dat. masc. pl. ἄνθρωπος man, human being, person, one, certain
εἰ conj. εἰ if, whether, that, though, forasmuch
γὰρ conj. γάρ for, and, because, but, indeed
ἔτι adv. ἔτι yet, more, any more, further, still, moreover
ἀνθρώποις n. dat. masc. pl. ἄνθρωπος man, human being, person, one, certain
Χριστοῦ n. gen. masc. sg. Χριστός Christ
δοῦλος n. nom. masc. sg. δοῦλος servant, bondman, bond, slave
οὐκ particle of negation. οὐ οὐκ οὐχ not, no, neither, none, nay, nor, never, nothing
ἂν particle. ἄν Indicating contingency. No English translation.
11 δὲ conj. δέ but, and, now, also, to the contrary, rather, then
ὑμῖν pron. dat. 2p. pl. σύ thou, you
ἀδελφοί n. voc. masc. pl. ἀδελφός brother
τὸ art. acc. neut. sg. ὁ ἡ τό the, this, that, he, she, it
εὐαγγέλιον n. acc. neut. sg. εὐαγγέλιον gospel
τὸ art. acc. neut. sg. ὁ ἡ τό the, this, that, he, she, it
ὑπ' prep. ὑπό (+gen) of, by, with, from, among, (+acc) under
ἐμοῦ pron. gen. 1p. sg. ἐγώ I
ὅτι conj. ὅτι that, for, because, how that, how, because that, for that, though
οὐκ particle of negation. οὐ οὐκ οὐχ not, no, neither, none, nay, nor, never, nothing
κατὰ prep. κατά (+gen) against, by, throughout, down, (+acc) according to, after, with
ἄνθρωπον n. acc. masc. sg. ἄνθρωπος man, human being, person, one, certain
12 οὐδὲ adv. οὐδέ neither, nor, not, no, not even, never, not yet
γὰρ conj. γάρ for, and, because, but, indeed
ἐγὼ pron. nom. 1p. sg. ἐγώ I
παρὰ prep. παρά (+gen) of, from, (+dat) with, for, (+acc) beside, at, by, above, against
ἀνθρώπου n. gen. masc. sg. ἄνθρωπος man, human being, person, one, certain
αὐτὸ pron. acc. neut. 3p. sg. αὐτός ή ό self, of oneself, even, very, the same, he, she, it
οὔτε conj. οὔτε neither, nor, nor yet, no, none
ἀλλὰ conj. ἀλλά but, yea, yet, nevertheless, howbeit, nay, therefore
δι' prep. διά (+gen) by, through, with, in, of, (+acc) for, because of, for a cause
ἀποκαλύψεως n. gen. fem. sg. ἀποκάλυψις revelation, appearing, coming, manifestation
Ἰησοῦ n. gen. masc. sg. Ἰησοῦς Jesus

Χριστοῦ n. gen. masc. sg. Χριστός Christ
13 γὰρ conj. γάρ for, and, because, but, indeed
τὴν art. acc. fem. sg. ὁ ἡ τό the, this, that, he, she, it
ἐμὴν poss. pron. acc. fem. 1p. sg. ἐμός my, mine, mine own, of me
ἀναστροφήν n. acc. fem. sg. ἀναστροφή conversation
ποτε adv. ποτέ in time past, at any time, sometimes, in old time, once, when
ἐν prep. ἐν (+dat) in, by, with, among, at, on, through, to, within, into, of, for
τῷ art. dat. masc. sg. ὁ ἡ τό the, this, that, he, she, it
Ἰουδαϊσμῷ n. dat. masc. sg. Ἰουδαϊσμός Jews' religion
ὅτι conj. ὅτι that, for, because, how that, how, because that, for that, though
καθ' prep. κατά (+gen) against, by, throughout, down, (+acc) according to, after, with
ὑπερβολὴν n. acc. fem. sg. ὑπερβολή abundance, beyond measure, exceeding, excellency
τὴν art. acc. fem. sg. ὁ ἡ τό the, this, that, he, she, it
ἐκκλησίαν n. acc. fem. sg. ἐκκλησία church, assembly
τοῦ art. gen. masc. sg. ὁ ἡ τό the, this, that, he, she, it
Θεοῦ n. gen. masc. sg. θεός God, god
καὶ conj. καί and, even, also, but
αὐτήν pron. acc. fem. 3p. sg. αὐτός ἡ ὁ self, of oneself, even, very, the same, he, she, it
14 καὶ conj. καί and, even, also, but
ἐν prep. ἐν (+dat) in, by, with, among, at, on, through, to, within, into, of, for
τῷ art. dat. masc. sg. ὁ ἡ τό the, this, that, he, she, it
Ἰουδαϊσμῷ n. dat. masc. sg. Ἰουδαϊσμός Jews' religion
ὑπὲρ prep. ὑπέρ (+gen) for, of, for the sake of, (+acc) above, more than
πολλοὺς adj. acc. masc. pl. πολύς many, great, much, long, abundant
συνηλικιώτας n. acc. masc. pl. συνηλικιώτης equal
ἐν prep. ἐν (+dat) in, by, with, among, at, on, through, to, within, into, of, for
τῷ art. dat. neut. sg. ὁ ἡ τό the, this, that, he, she, it
γένει n. dat. neut. sg. γένος kind, kindred, offspring, nation, countrymen
μου pron. gen. 1p. sg. ἐγώ I
περισσοτέρως adv. περισσοτέρως more exceedingly, more abundantly, more frequent
ζηλωτὴς n. nom. masc. sg. ζηλωτής zealous
τῶν art. gen. masc. pl. ὁ ἡ τό the, this, that, he, she, it
πατρικῶν adj. gen. masc. pl. πατρικός of father
μου pron. gen. 1p. sg. ἐγώ I
παραδόσεων n. gen. fem. pl. παράδοσις tradition, ordinance
15 ὅτε adv. ὅτε when, after that, as soon as, while, after
δὲ conj. δέ but, and, now, also, to the contrary, rather, then
ὁ art. nom. masc. sg. ὁ ἡ τό the, this, that, he, she, it
Θεὸς n. nom. masc. sg. θεός God, god
ὁ art. nom. masc. sg. ὁ ἡ τό the, this, that, he, she, it
με pron. acc. 1p. sg. ἐγώ I
ἐκ prep. ἐκ ἐξ (+gen) of, from, out of, by, on, with, in, among, through
κοιλίας n. gen. fem. sg. κοιλία belly, womb
μητρός n. gen. fem. sg. μήτηρ mother
μου pron. gen. 1p. sg. ἐγώ I
καὶ conj. καί and, even, also, but
διὰ prep. διά (+gen) by, through, with, in, of, (+acc) for, because of, for a cause
τῆς art. gen. fem. sg. ὁ ἡ τό the, this, that, he, she, it
χάριτος n. gen. fem. sg. χάρις grace, thank, favour, pleasure
αὐτοῦ pron. gen. masc. 3p. sg. αὐτός ἡ ὁ self, of oneself, even, very, the same, he, she, it
16 τὸν art. acc. masc. sg. ὁ ἡ τό the, this, that, he, she, it
υἱὸν n. acc. masc. sg. υἱός son, child, descendant, offspring, heir
αὐτοῦ pron. gen. masc. 3p. sg. αὐτός ἡ ὁ self, of oneself, even, very, the same, he, she, it
ἐν prep. ἐν (+dat) in, by, with, among, at, on, through, to, within, into, of, for
ἐμοί pron. dat. 1p. sg. ἐγώ I

ἵνα conj. ἵνα that, to, lest, for to, so that, albeit, because, for, so as
αὐτὸν pron. acc. masc. 3p. sg. αὐτός ἡ ὁ self, of oneself, even, very, the same, he, she, it
ἐν prep. ἐν (+dat) in, by, with, among, at, on, through, to, within, into, of, for
τοῖς art. dat. neut. pl. ὁ ἡ τό the, this, that, he, she, it
ἔθνεσιν n. dat. neut. pl. ἔθνος Gentile, nation, heathen, people
εὐθέως adv. εὐθέως immediately, straightway, forthwith, as soon as, by and by, shortly
οὐ particle of negation. οὐ οὐκ οὐχ not, no, neither, none, nay, nor, never, nothing
σαρκὶ n. dat. fem. sg. σάρξ flesh, carnal
καὶ conj. καί and, even, also, but
αἵματι n. dat. neut. sg. αἷμα blood
17 οὐδὲ adv. οὐδέ neither, nor, not, no, not even, never, not yet
εἰς prep. εἰς (+acc) into, to, unto, for, in, on, toward, against, upon, at, among
Ἱεροσόλυμα n. acc. neut. pl. Ἱεροσόλυμα Jerusalem
πρὸς prep. πρός (+gen) for, (+dat) at, (+acc) unto, to, with, for, against
τοὺς art. acc. masc. pl. ὁ ἡ τό the, this, that, he, she, it
πρὸ prep. πρό (+gen) before, above
ἐμοῦ pron. gen. 1p. sg. ἐγώ I
ἀποστόλους n. acc. masc. pl. ἀπόστολος apostle, messenger, he that is sent
ἀλλ' conj. ἀλλά but, yea, yet, nevertheless, howbeit, nay, therefore
εἰς prep. εἰς (+acc) into, to, unto, for, in, on, toward, against, upon, at, among
Ἀραβίαν n. acc. fem. sg. Ἀραβία Arabia
καὶ conj. καί and, even, also, but
πάλιν adv. πάλιν again
εἰς prep. εἰς (+acc) into, to, unto, for, in, on, toward, against, upon, at, among
Δαμασκόν n. acc. fem. sg. Δαμασκός Damascus
18 Ἔπειτα adv. ἔπειτα then, after that, afterward
μετὰ prep. μετά (+gen) with, among, against, (+acc) after
ἔτη n. acc. neut. pl. ἔτος year
τρία num. acc. neut. pl. τρεῖς three
εἰς prep. εἰς (+acc) into, to, unto, for, in, on, toward, against, upon, at, among
Ἱεροσόλυμα n. acc. neut. pl. Ἱεροσόλυμα Jerusalem
Πέτρον n. acc. masc. sg. Πέτρος Peter
καὶ conj. καί and, even, also, but
πρὸς prep. πρός (+gen) for, (+dat) at, (+acc) unto, to, with, for, against
αὐτὸν pron. acc. masc. 3p. sg. αὐτός ἡ ὁ self, of oneself, even, very, the same, he, she, it
ἡμέρας n. acc. fem. pl. ἡμέρα day, time, year, while, age, day time
δεκαπέντε num. acc. fem. pl. δεκαπέντε fifteen
19 ἕτερον adj. acc. masc. sg. ἕτερος another, other, else, strange
δὲ conj. δέ but, and, now, also, to the contrary, rather, then
τῶν art. gen. masc. pl. ὁ ἡ τό the, this, that, he, she, it
ἀποστόλων n. gen. masc. pl. ἀπόστολος apostle, messenger, he that is sent
οὐκ particle of negation. οὐ οὐκ οὐχ not, no, neither, none, nay, nor, never, nothing
εἰ conj. εἰ if, whether, that, though, forasmuch
μὴ particle of negation. μή not, no, lest, neither, none, nothing, nor, never, without
Ἰάκωβον n. acc. masc. sg. Ἰάκωβος James
τὸν art. acc. masc. sg. ὁ ἡ τό the, this, that, he, she, it
ἀδελφὸν n. acc. masc. sg. ἀδελφός brother
τοῦ art. gen. masc. sg. ὁ ἡ τό the, this, that, he, she, it
Κυρίου n. gen. masc. sg. κύριος Lord, lord, master, sir, LORD, God, Master, owner
20 ἃ relative pron. acc. neut. pl. ὅς ἥ ὅ who, which, what, that
δὲ conj. δέ but, and, now, also, to the contrary, rather, then
ὑμῖν pron. dat. 2p. pl. σύ thou, you
ἐνώπιον prep. ἐνώπιον (+gen) before, in the sight of, in the presence of. (adv.) before
τοῦ art. gen. masc. sg. ὁ ἡ τό the, this, that, he, she, it
Θεοῦ n. gen. masc. sg. θεός God, god

ὅτι conj. ὅτι that, for, because, how that, how, because that, for that, though
οὐ particle of negation. οὐ οὐκ οὐχ not, no, neither, none, nay, nor, never, nothing
21 ἔπειτα adv. ἔπειτα then, after that, afterward
εἰς prep. εἰς (+acc) into, to, unto, for, in, on, toward, against, upon, at, among
τὰ art. acc. neut. pl. ὁ ἡ τό the, this, that, he, she, it
κλίματα n. acc. neut. pl. κλίμα region, part
τῆς art. gen. fem. sg. ὁ ἡ τό the, this, that, he, she, it
Συρίας n. gen. fem. sg. Συρία Syria
καὶ conj. καί and, even, also, but
τῆς art. gen. fem. sg. ὁ ἡ τό the, this, that, he, she, it
Κιλικίας n. gen. fem. sg. Κιλικία Cilicia
22 δὲ conj. δέ but, and, now, also, to the contrary, rather, then
τῷ art. dat. neut. sg. ὁ ἡ τό the, this, that, he, she, it
προσώπῳ n. dat. neut. sg. πρόσωπον face, presence, person, countenance
ταῖς art. dat. fem. pl. ὁ ἡ τό the, this, that, he, she, it
ἐκκλησίαις n. dat. fem. pl. ἐκκλησία church, assembly
τῆς art. gen. fem. sg. ὁ ἡ τό the, this, that, he, she, it
Ἰουδαίας n. gen. fem. sg. Ἰουδαία Judaea, Jewry
ταῖς art. dat. fem. pl. ὁ ἡ τό the, this, that, he, she, it
ἐν prep. ἐν (+dat) in, by, with, among, at, on, through, to, within, into, of, for
Χριστῷ n. dat. masc. sg. Χριστός Christ
23 μόνον adv. μόνος only, alone, by oneself
δὲ conj. δέ but, and, now, also, to the contrary, rather, then
ὅτι conj. ὅτι that, for, because, how that, how, because that, for that, though
Ὁ art. nom. masc. sg. ὁ ἡ τό the, this, that, he, she, it
ἡμᾶς pron. acc. 1p. pl. ἐγώ I
ποτε adv. ποτέ in time past, at any time, sometimes, in old time, once, when
νῦν adv. νῦν now, henceforth, present, this time
τὴν art. acc. fem. sg. ὁ ἡ τό the, this, that, he, she, it
πίστιν n. acc. fem. sg. πίστις faith, assurance, belief, fidelity
ἥν relative pron. acc. fem. sg. ὅς ἥ ὅ who, which, what, that
ποτε adv. ποτέ in time past, at any time, sometimes, in old time, once, when
24 καὶ conj. καί and, even, also, but
ἐν prep. ἐν (+dat) in, by, with, among, at, on, through, to, within, into, of, for
ἐμοὶ pron. dat. 1p. sg. ἐγώ I
τὸν art. acc. masc. sg. ὁ ἡ τό the, this, that, he, she, it
Θεόν n. acc. masc. sg. θεός God, god

2

1 Ἔπειτα adv. ἔπειτα then, after that, afterward
διὰ prep. διά (+gen) by, through, with, in, of, (+acc) for, because of, for a cause
δεκατεσσάρων num. gen. neut. pl. δεκατέσσαρες fourteen
ἐτῶν n. gen. neut. pl. ἔτος year
πάλιν adv. πάλιν again
εἰς prep. εἰς (+acc) into, to, unto, for, in, on, toward, against, upon, at, among
Ἱεροσόλυμα n. acc. neut. pl. Ἱεροσόλυμα Jerusalem
μετὰ prep. μετά (+gen) with, among, against, (+acc) after
Βαρναβᾶ n. gen. masc. sg. Βαρναβᾶς Barnabas
καὶ conj. καί and, even, also, but
Τίτον n. acc. masc. sg. Τίτος Titus
2 δὲ conj. δέ but, and, now, also, to the contrary, rather, then
κατὰ prep. κατά (+gen) against, by, throughout, down, (+acc) according to, after, with
ἀποκάλυψιν n. acc. fem. sg. ἀποκάλυψις revelation, appearing, coming, manifestation
καὶ conj. καί and, even, also, but

αὐτοῖς pron. dat. masc. 3p. pl. αὐτός ἡ ὁ self, of oneself, even, very, the same, he, she, it
τὸ art. acc. neut. sg. ὁ ἡ τό the, this, that, he, she, it
εὐαγγέλιον n. acc. neut. sg. εὐαγγέλιον gospel
ὃ relative pron. acc. neut. sg. ὅς ἥ ὅ who, which, what, that
ἐν prep. ἐν (+dat) in, by, with, among, at, on, through, to, within, into, of, for
τοῖς art. dat. neut. pl. ὁ ἡ τό the, this, that, he, she, it
ἔθνεσι n. dat. neut. pl. ἔθνος Gentile, nation, heathen, people
κατ' prep. κατά (+gen) against, by, throughout, down, (+acc) according to, after, with
ἰδίαν adj. acc. fem. sg. ἴδιος one's own, one's, privately
δὲ conj. δέ but, and, now, also, to the contrary, rather, then
τοῖς art. dat. masc. pl. ὁ ἡ τό the, this, that, he, she, it
μή particle of negation. μή not, no, lest, neither, none, nothing, nor, never, without
πως particle. πώς by any means, by some means, haply, perhaps
εἰς prep. εἰς (+acc) into, to, unto, for, in, on, toward, against, upon, at, among
κενὸν adj. acc. neut. sg. κενός empty, vain, in vain
ἢ particle. ἤ or, than, either, nor, or else, and, rather than
3 ἀλλ' conj. ἀλλά but, yea, yet, nevertheless, howbeit, nay, therefore
οὐδὲ adv. οὐδέ neither, nor, not, no, not even, never, not yet
Τίτος n. nom. masc. sg. Τίτος Titus
ὁ art. nom. masc. sg. ὁ ἡ τό the, this, that, he, she, it
σὺν prep. σύν (+dat) with, beside
ἐμοί pron. dat. 1p. sg. ἐγώ I
Ἕλλην n. nom. masc. sg. Ἕλλην Greek, Gentile
4 διὰ prep. διά (+gen) by, through, with, in, of, (+acc) for, because of, for a cause
δὲ conj. δέ but, and, now, also, to the contrary, rather, then
τοὺς art. acc. masc. pl. ὁ ἡ τό the, this, that, he, she, it
παρεισάκτους adj. acc. masc. pl. παρείσακτος bring in unawares
ψευδαδέλφους n. acc. masc. pl. ψευδάδελφος false brother
οἵτινες relative pron. nom. masc. pl. ὅστις which, who, whosoever, that, whatsoever
τὴν art. acc. fem. sg. ὁ ἡ τό the, this, that, he, she, it
ἐλευθερίαν n. acc. fem. sg. ἐλευθερία liberty
ἡμῶν pron. gen. 1p. pl. ἐγώ I
ἣν relative pron. acc. fem. sg. ὅς ἥ ὅ who, which, what, that
ἐν prep. ἐν (+dat) in, by, with, among, at, on, through, to, within, into, of, for
Χριστῷ n. dat. masc. sg. Χριστός Christ
Ἰησοῦ n. dat. masc. sg. Ἰησοῦς Jesus
ἵνα conj. ἵνα that, to, lest, for to, so that, albeit, because, for, so as
ἡμᾶς pron. acc. 1p. pl. ἐγώ I
5 οἷς relative pron. dat. masc. pl. ὅς ἥ ὅ who, which, what, that
οὐδὲ adv. οὐδέ neither, nor, not, no, not even, never, not yet
πρὸς prep. πρός (+gen) for, (+dat) at, (+acc) unto, to, with, for, against
ὥραν n. acc. fem. sg. ὥρα hour, time, season
τῇ art. dat. fem. sg. ὁ ἡ τό the, this, that, he, she, it
ὑποταγῇ n. dat. fem. sg. ὑποταγή subjection
ἵνα conj. ἵνα that, to, lest, for to, so that, albeit, because, for, so as
ἡ art. nom. fem. sg. ὁ ἡ τό the, this, that, he, she, it
ἀλήθεια n. nom. fem. sg. ἀλήθεια truth, verity
τοῦ art. gen. neut. sg. ὁ ἡ τό the, this, that, he, she, it
εὐαγγελίου n. gen. neut. sg. εὐαγγέλιον gospel
πρὸς prep. πρός (+gen) for, (+dat) at, (+acc) unto, to, with, for, against
ὑμᾶς pron. acc. 2p. pl. σύ thou, you
6 ἀπὸ prep. ἀπό (+gen) from, of, out of, since, for, off, at, by, in, on
δὲ conj. δέ but, and, now, also, to the contrary, rather, then
τῶν art. gen. masc. pl. ὁ ἡ τό the, this, that, he, she, it
τι indefinite pron. acc. neut. sg. τὶς certain, some, any man, one, any thing

ὁποῖοί interrog. pron. nom. masc. pl. ὁποῖος what manner of, as, whatsoever
ποτε adv. ποτέ in time past, at any time, sometimes, in old time, once, when
οὐδέν num. acc. neut. sg. οὐδείς no man, nothing, no, none, neither, not, nought
μοι pron. dat. 1p. sg. ἐγώ I
πρόσωπον n. acc. neut. sg. πρόσωπον face, presence, person, countenance
Θεὸς n. nom. masc. sg. θεός God, god
ἀνθρώπου n. gen. masc. sg. ἄνθρωπος man, human being, person, one, certain
οὐ particle of negation. οὐ οὐκ οὐχ not, no, neither, none, nay, nor, never, nothing
ἐμοὶ pron. dat. 1p. sg. ἐγώ I
γὰρ conj. γάρ for, and, because, but, indeed
οἱ art. nom. masc. pl. ὁ ἡ τό the, this, that, he, she, it
οὐδέν num. acc. neut. sg. οὐδείς no man, nothing, no, none, neither, not, nought
7 ἀλλὰ conj. ἀλλά but, yea, yet, nevertheless, howbeit, nay, therefore
τοὐναντίον adv. τοὐναντίον contrariwise
ὅτι conj. ὅτι that, for, because, how that, how, because that, for that, though
τὸ art. acc. neut. sg. ὁ ἡ τό the, this, that, he, she, it
εὐαγγέλιον n. acc. neut. sg. εὐαγγέλιον gospel
τῆς art. gen. fem. sg. ὁ ἡ τό the, this, that, he, she, it
ἀκροβυστίας n. gen. fem. sg. ἀκροβυστία uncircumcised, uncircumcision
καθὼς adv. καθώς as, even as, according as, according to
Πέτρος n. nom. masc. sg. Πέτρος Peter
τῆς art. gen. fem. sg. ὁ ἡ τό the, this, that, he, she, it
περιτομῆς n. gen. fem. sg. περιτομή circumcision
8 ὁ art. nom. masc. sg. ὁ ἡ τό the, this, that, he, she, it
γὰρ conj. γάρ for, and, because, but, indeed
Πέτρῳ n. dat. masc. sg. Πέτρος Peter
εἰς prep. εἰς (+acc) into, to, unto, for, in, on, toward, against, upon, at, among
ἀποστολὴν n. acc. fem. sg. ἀποστολή apostleship
τῆς art. gen. fem. sg. ὁ ἡ τό the, this, that, he, she, it
περιτομῆς n. gen. fem. sg. περιτομή circumcision
καὶ conj. καί and, even, also, but
ἐμοὶ pron. dat. 1p. sg. ἐγώ I
εἰς prep. εἰς (+acc) into, to, unto, for, in, on, toward, against, upon, at, among
τὰ art. acc. neut. pl. ὁ ἡ τό the, this, that, he, she, it
ἔθνη n. acc. neut. pl. ἔθνος Gentile, nation, heathen, people
9 καὶ conj. καί and, even, also, but
τὴν art. acc. fem. sg. ὁ ἡ τό the, this, that, he, she, it
χάριν n. acc. fem. sg. χάρις grace, thank, favour, pleasure
τὴν art. acc. fem. sg. ὁ ἡ τό the, this, that, he, she, it
μοι pron. dat. 1p. sg. ἐγώ I
Ἰάκωβος n. nom. masc. sg. Ἰάκωβος James
καὶ conj. καί and, even, also, but
Κηφᾶς n. nom. masc. sg. Κηφᾶς Cephas
καὶ conj. καί and, even, also, but
Ἰωάννης n. nom. masc. sg. Ἰωάννης John
οἱ art. nom. masc. pl. ὁ ἡ τό the, this, that, he, she, it
στῦλοι n. nom. masc. pl. στῦλος pillar
δεξιὰς adj. acc. fem. pl. δεξιός right, right hand, right side
ἐμοὶ pron. dat. 1p. sg. ἐγώ I
καὶ conj. καί and, even, also, but
Βαρναβᾷ n. dat. masc. sg. Βαρναβᾶς Barnabas
κοινωνίας n. gen. fem. sg. κοινωνία fellowship, communion, contribution, distribution
ἵνα conj. ἵνα that, to, lest, for to, so that, albeit, because, for, so as
ἡμεῖς pron. nom. 1p. pl. ἐγώ I
εἰς prep. εἰς (+acc) into, to, unto, for, in, on, toward, against, upon, at, among

τὰ art. acc. neut. pl. ὁ ἡ τό the, this, that, he, she, it
ἔθνη n. acc. neut. pl. ἔθνος Gentile, nation, heathen, people
αὐτοὶ pron. nom. masc. 3p. pl. αὐτός ή ό self, of oneself, even, very, the same, he, she, it
δὲ conj. δέ but, and, now, also, to the contrary, rather, then
εἰς prep. εἰς (+acc) into, to, unto, for, in, on, toward, against, upon, at, among
τὴν art. acc. fem. sg. ὁ ἡ τό the, this, that, he, she, it
περιτομήν n. acc. fem. sg. περιτομή circumcision
10 μόνον adv. μόνος only, alone, by oneself
τῶν art. gen. masc. pl. ὁ ἡ τό the, this, that, he, she, it
πτωχῶν adj. gen. masc. pl. πτωχός poor, beggar, beggarly
ἵνα conj. ἵνα that, to, lest, for to, so that, albeit, because, for, so as
ὃ relative pron. acc. neut. sg. ὅς ἥ ὅ who, which, what, that
καὶ conj. καί and, even, also, but
αὐτὸ pron. acc. neut. 3p. sg. αὐτός ή ό self, of oneself, even, very, the same, he, she, it
τοῦτο demo. pron. acc. neut. sg. οὗτος αὕτη τοῦτο this, the same, this same, he, she, it
11 Ὅτε adv. ὅτε when, after that, as soon as, while, after
δὲ conj. δέ but, and, now, also, to the contrary, rather, then
Πέτρος n. nom. masc. sg. Πέτρος Peter
εἰς prep. εἰς (+acc) into, to, unto, for, in, on, toward, against, upon, at, among
Ἀντιόχειαν n. acc. fem. sg. Ἀντιόχεια Antioch
κατὰ prep. κατά (+gen) against, by, throughout, down, (+acc) according to, after, with
πρόσωπον n. acc. neut. sg. πρόσωπον face, presence, person, countenance
αὐτῷ pron. dat. masc. 3p. sg. αὐτός ή ό self, of oneself, even, very, the same, he, she, it
ὅτι conj. ὅτι that, for, because, how that, how, because that, for that, though
12 πρὸ prep. πρό (+gen) before, above
τοῦ art. gen. neut. sg. ὁ ἡ τό the, this, that, he, she, it
γὰρ conj. γάρ for, and, because, but, indeed
τινὰς indefinite pron. acc. masc. pl. τὶς certain, some, any man, one, any thing
ἀπὸ prep. ἀπό (+gen) from, of, out of, since, for, off, at, by, in, on
Ἰακώβου n. gen. masc. sg. Ἰάκωβος James
μετὰ prep. μετά (+gen) with, among, against, (+acc) after
τῶν art. gen. neut. pl. ὁ ἡ τό the, this, that, he, she, it
ἐθνῶν n. gen. neut. pl. ἔθνος Gentile, nation, heathen, people
ὅτε adv. ὅτε when, after that, as soon as, while, after
δὲ conj. δέ but, and, now, also, to the contrary, rather, then
καὶ conj. καί and, even, also, but
ἑαυτόν reflexive pron. acc. masc. 3p. sg. ἑαυτοῦ himself, herself, itself, yourself, ourselves
τοὺς art. acc. masc. pl. ὁ ἡ τό the, this, that, he, she, it
ἐκ prep. ἐκ ἐξ (+gen) of, from, out of, by, on, with, in, among, through
περιτομῆς n. gen. fem. sg. περιτομή circumcision
13 καὶ conj. καί and, even, also, but
αὐτῷ pron. dat. masc. 3p. sg. αὐτός ή ό self, of oneself, even, very, the same, he, she, it
καὶ conj. καί and, even, also, but
οἱ art. nom. masc. pl. ὁ ἡ τό the, this, that, he, she, it
λοιποὶ adj. nom. masc. pl. λοιπός other, rest, remnant, residue, which remain
Ἰουδαῖοι adj. nom. masc. pl. Ἰουδαῖος Jew, Jewess
ὥστε conj. ὥστε so that, wherefore, insomuch that, therefore, that, so then
καὶ conj. καί and, even, also, but
Βαρναβᾶς n. nom. masc. sg. Βαρναβᾶς Barnabas
αὐτῶν pron. gen. masc. 3p. pl. αὐτός ή ό self, of oneself, even, very, the same, he, she, it
τῇ art. dat. fem. sg. ὁ ἡ τό the, this, that, he, she, it
ὑποκρίσει n. dat. fem. sg. ὑπόκρισις hypocrisy, condemnation, dissimulation
14 ἀλλ’ conj. ἀλλά but, yea, yet, nevertheless, howbeit, nay, therefore
ὅτε adv. ὅτε when, after that, as soon as, while, after
ὅτι conj. ὅτι that, for, because, how that, how, because that, for that, though

οὐκ particle of negation. οὐ οὐκ οὐχ not, no, neither, none, nay, nor, never, nothing
πρὸς prep. πρός (+gen) for, (+dat) at, (+acc) unto, to, with, for, against
τὴν art. acc. fem. sg. ὁ ἡ τό the, this, that, he, she, it
ἀλήθειαν n. acc. fem. sg. ἀλήθεια truth, verity
τοῦ art. gen. neut. sg. ὁ ἡ τό the, this, that, he, she, it
εὐαγγελίου n. gen. neut. sg. εὐαγγέλιον gospel
τῷ art. dat. masc. sg. ὁ ἡ τό the, this, that, he, she, it
Πέτρῳ n. dat. masc. sg. Πέτρος Peter
ἔμπροσθεν prep. ἔμπροσθεν (+gen) before, in the sight of, in the presence of
πάντων adj. gen. masc. pl. πᾶς πᾶσα πᾶν all, every, whosoever, every one, no, whole, any
Εἰ conj. εἰ if, whether, that, though, forasmuch
σὺ pron. nom. 2p. sg. σύ thou, you
Ἰουδαῖος adj. nom. masc. sg. Ἰουδαῖος Jew, Jewess
ἐθνικῶς adv. ἐθνικῶς after the manner of Gentiles
καὶ conj. καί and, even, also, but
οὐκ particle of negation. οὐ οὐκ οὐχ not, no, neither, none, nay, nor, never, nothing
Ἰουδαϊκῶς adv. Ἰουδαϊκῶς as do the Jews
τί interrog. pron. acc. neut. sg. τίς what, who, why, where, which, how
τὰ art. acc. neut. pl. ὁ ἡ τό the, this, that, he, she, it
ἔθνη n. acc. neut. pl. ἔθνος Gentile, nation, heathen, people
15 ἡμεῖς pron. nom. 1p. pl. ἐγώ I
φύσει n. dat. fem. sg. φύσις nature
Ἰουδαῖοι adj. nom. masc. pl. Ἰουδαῖος Jew, Jewess
καὶ conj. καί and, even, also, but
οὐκ particle of negation. οὐ οὐκ οὐχ not, no, neither, none, nay, nor, never, nothing
ἐξ prep. ἐκ ἐξ (+gen) of, from, out of, by, on, with, in, among, through
ἐθνῶν n. gen. neut. pl. ἔθνος Gentile, nation, heathen, people
ἁμαρτωλοί adj. nom. masc. pl. ἁμαρτωλός sinner, sinful
16 ὅτι conj. ὅτι that, for, because, how that, how, because that, for that, though
οὐ particle of negation. οὐ οὐκ οὐχ not, no, neither, none, nay, nor, never, nothing
ἄνθρωπος n. nom. masc. sg. ἄνθρωπος man, human being, person, one, certain
ἐξ prep. ἐκ ἐξ (+gen) of, from, out of, by, on, with, in, among, through
ἔργων n. gen. neut. pl. ἔργον work, deed, doing labour
νόμου n. gen. masc. sg. νόμος law, the law
ἐὰν conj. ἐάν if, soever, except, though, and if, but, whether, if so, so
μὴ particle of negation. μή not, no, lest, neither, none, nothing, nor, never, without
διὰ prep. διά (+gen) by, through, with, in, of, (+acc) for, because of, for a cause
πίστεως n. gen. fem. sg. πίστις faith, assurance, belief, fidelity
Ἰησοῦ n. gen. masc. sg. Ἰησοῦς Jesus
Χριστοῦ n. gen. masc. sg. Χριστός Christ
καὶ conj. καί and, even, also, but
ἡμεῖς pron. nom. 1p. pl. ἐγώ I
εἰς prep. εἰς (+acc) into, to, unto, for, in, on, toward, against, upon, at, among
Χριστὸν n. acc. masc. sg. Χριστός Christ
Ἰησοῦν n. acc. masc. sg. Ἰησοῦς Jesus
ἵνα conj. ἵνα that, to, lest, for to, so that, albeit, because, for, so as
ἐκ prep. ἐκ ἐξ (+gen) of, from, out of, by, on, with, in, among, through
πίστεως n. gen. fem. sg. πίστις faith, assurance, belief, fidelity
Χριστοῦ n. gen. masc. sg. Χριστός Christ
καὶ conj. καί and, even, also, but
οὐκ particle of negation. οὐ οὐκ οὐχ not, no, neither, none, nay, nor, never, nothing
ἐξ prep. ἐκ ἐξ (+gen) of, from, out of, by, on, with, in, among, through
ἔργων n. gen. neut. pl. ἔργον work, deed, doing labour
νόμου n. gen. masc. sg. νόμος law, the law
διότι conj. διότι for, because, because that, therefore

οὐ particle of negation. οὐ οὐκ οὐχ not, no, neither, none, nay, nor, never, nothing
ἐξ prep. ἐκ ἐξ (+gen) of, from, out of, by, on, with, in, among, through
ἔργων n. gen. neut. pl. ἔργον work, deed, doing labour
νόμου n. gen. masc. sg. νόμος law, the law
πᾶσα adj. nom. fem. sg. πᾶς πᾶσα πᾶν all, every, whosoever, every one, no, whole, any
σάρξ n. nom. fem. sg. σάρξ flesh, carnal
17 εἰ conj. εἰ if, whether, that, though, forasmuch
δὲ conj. δέ but, and, now, also, to the contrary, rather, then
ἐν prep. ἐν (+dat) in, by, with, among, at, on, through, to, within, into, of, for
Χριστῷ n. dat. masc. sg. Χριστός Christ
καὶ conj. καί and, even, also, but
αὐτοὶ pron. nom. masc. 3p. pl. αὐτός ή ό self, of oneself, even, very, the same, he, she, it
ἁμαρτωλοί adj. nom. masc. pl. ἁμαρτωλός sinner, sinful
ἆρα adv. ἆρα therefore
Χριστὸς n. nom. masc. sg. Χριστός Christ
ἁμαρτίας n. gen. fem. sg. ἁμαρτία sin, offence, sinful
διάκονος n. nom. masc. sg. διάκονος minister, servant, deacon
μὴ particle of negation. μή not, no, lest, neither, none, nothing, nor, never, without
18 εἰ conj. εἰ if, whether, that, though, forasmuch
γὰρ conj. γάρ for, and, because, but, indeed
ἃ relative pron. acc. neut. pl. ὅς ἥ ὅ who, which, what, that
ταῦτα demo. pron. acc. neut. pl. οὗτος αὕτη τοῦτο this, the same, this same, he, she, it
πάλιν adv. πάλιν again
παραβάτην n. acc. masc. sg. παραβάτης breaker, transgressor
ἐμαυτὸν pron. acc. masc. 1p. sg. ἐμαυτοῦ myself, me
19 ἐγὼ pron. nom. 1p. sg. ἐγώ I
γὰρ conj. γάρ for, and, because, but, indeed
διὰ prep. διά (+gen) by, through, with, in, of, (+acc) for, because of, for a cause
νόμου n. gen. masc. sg. νόμος law, the law
νόμῳ n. dat. masc. sg. νόμος law, the law
ἵνα conj. ἵνα that, to, lest, for to, so that, albeit, because, for, so as
Θεῷ n. dat. masc. sg. θεός God, god
20 Χριστῷ n. dat. masc. sg. Χριστός Christ
δὲ conj. δέ but, and, now, also, to the contrary, rather, then
οὐκέτι adv. οὐκέτι or οὐκ έτι no more, no longer, not any more
ἐγώ pron. nom. 1p. sg. ἐγώ I
δὲ conj. δέ but, and, now, also, to the contrary, rather, then
ἐν prep. ἐν (+dat) in, by, with, among, at, on, through, to, within, into, of, for
ἐμοὶ pron. dat. 1p. sg. ἐγώ I
Χριστός n. nom. masc. sg. Χριστός Christ
ὃ relative pron. acc. neut. sg. ὅς ἥ ὅ who, which, what, that
δὲ conj. δέ but, and, now, also, to the contrary, rather, then
νῦν adv. νῦν now, henceforth, present, this time
ἐν prep. ἐν (+dat) in, by, with, among, at, on, through, to, within, into, of, for
σαρκί n. dat. fem. sg. σάρξ flesh, carnal
ἐν prep. ἐν (+dat) in, by, with, among, at, on, through, to, within, into, of, for
πίστει n. dat. fem. sg. πίστις faith, assurance, belief, fidelity
τῇ art. dat. fem. sg. ὁ ἡ τό the, this, that, he, she, it
τοῦ art. gen. masc. sg. ὁ ἡ τό the, this, that, he, she, it
υἱοῦ n. gen. masc. sg. υἱός son, child, descendant, offspring, heir
τοῦ art. gen. masc. sg. ὁ ἡ τό the, this, that, he, she, it
Θεοῦ n. gen. masc. sg. θεός God, god
τοῦ art. gen. masc. sg. ὁ ἡ τό the, this, that, he, she, it
με pron. acc. 1p. sg. ἐγώ I
καὶ conj. καί and, even, also, but

ἑαυτὸν reflexive pron. acc. masc. 3p. sg. ἑαυτοῦ himself, herself, itself, yourself, ourselves
ὑπὲρ prep. ὑπέρ (+gen) for, of, for the sake of, (+acc) above, more than
ἐμοῦ pron. gen. 1p. sg. ἐγώ I
21 οὐκ particle of negation. οὐ οὐκ οὐχ not, no, neither, none, nay, nor, never, nothing
τὴν art. acc. fem. sg. ὁ ἡ τό the, this, that, he, she, it
χάριν n. acc. fem. sg. χάρις grace, thank, favour, pleasure
τοῦ art. gen. masc. sg. ὁ ἡ τό the, this, that, he, she, it
Θεοῦ n. gen. masc. sg. θεός God, god
εἰ conj. εἰ if, whether, that, though, forasmuch
γὰρ conj. γάρ for, and, because, but, indeed
διὰ prep. διά (+gen) by, through, with, in, of, (+acc) for, because of, for a cause
νόμου n. gen. masc. sg. νόμος law, the law
δικαιοσύνη n. nom. fem. sg. δικαιοσύνη righteousness
ἄρα conj. ἄρα then, therefore, haply, wherefore, perhaps, manner, no doubt, truly
Χριστὸς n. nom. masc. sg. Χριστός Christ
δωρεὰν adv. δωρεάν freely, for nought, in vain, without a cause

3

1 Ὦ interjection. ὦ O
ἀνόητοι adj. voc. masc. pl. ἀνόητος fool, foolish, unwise
Γαλάται n. voc. masc. pl. Γαλάτης (pl.) Galatians
τίς interrog. pron. nom. masc. sg. τίς what, who, why, where, which, how
ὑμᾶς pron. acc. 2p. pl. σύ thou, you
τῇ art. dat. fem. sg. ὁ ἡ τό the, this, that, he, she, it
ἀληθείᾳ n. dat. fem. sg. ἀλήθεια truth, verity
μὴ particle of negation. μή not, no, lest, neither, none, nothing, nor, never, without
οἷς relative pron. dat. neut. pl. ὅς ἥ ὅ who, which, what, that
κατ' prep. κατά (+gen) against, by, throughout, down, (+acc) according to, after, with
ὀφθαλμοὺς n. acc. masc. pl. ὀφθαλμός eye, sight
Ἰησοῦς n. nom. masc. sg. Ἰησοῦς Jesus
Χριστὸς n. nom. masc. sg. Χριστός Christ
ἐν prep. ἐν (+dat) in, by, with, among, at, on, through, to, within, into, of, for
ὑμῖν pron. dat. 2p. pl. σύ thou, you
2 τοῦτο demo. pron. acc. neut. sg. οὗτος αὕτη τοῦτο this, the same, this same, he, she, it
μόνον adj. acc. neut. sg. μόνος only, alone, by oneself
ἀφ' prep. ἀπό (+gen) from, of, out of, since, for, off, at, by, in, on
ὑμῶν pron. gen. 2p. pl. σύ thou, you
ἐξ prep. ἐκ ἐξ (+gen) of, from, out of, by, on, with, in, among, through
ἔργων n. gen. neut. pl. ἔργον work, deed, doing labour
νόμου n. gen. masc. sg. νόμος law, the law
τὸ art. acc. neut. sg. ὁ ἡ τό the, this, that, he, she, it
Πνεῦμα n. acc. neut. sg. πνεῦμα spirit, Spirit, Ghost, ghost, life. of the spirit, wind
ἢ particle. ἤ or, than, either, nor, or else, and, rather than
ἐξ prep. ἐκ ἐξ (+gen) of, from, out of, by, on, with, in, among, through
ἀκοῆς n. gen. fem. sg. ἀκοή hearing, ear, fame, report, rumour, which one heard
πίστεως n. gen. fem. sg. πίστις faith, assurance, belief, fidelity
3 οὕτως adv. οὕτω οὕτως so, even so, thus, on this wise, likewise, after this manner
ἀνόητοί adj. nom. masc. pl. ἀνόητος fool, foolish, unwise
Πνεύματι n. dat. neut. sg. πνεῦμα spirit, Spirit, Ghost, ghost, life. of the spirit, wind
νῦν adv. νῦν now, henceforth, present, this time
σαρκὶ n. dat. fem. sg. σάρξ flesh, carnal
4 τοσαῦτα demo. pron. acc. neut. pl. τοσοῦτος so much, so great, so many, so long
εἰκῇ adv. εἰκῇ in vain, vainly, without a cause
εἴ conj. εἰ if, whether, that, though, forasmuch

γε particle. γέ yet, and beside, at least, doubtless
καὶ conj. καί and, even, also, but
εἰκῇ adv. εἰκῇ in vain, vainly, without a cause
5 ὁ art. nom. masc. sg. ὁ ἡ τό the, this, that, he, she, it
οὖν conj. οὖν therefore, then, so, and, now, wherefore
ὑμῖν pron. dat. 2p. pl. σύ thou, you
τὸ art. acc. neut. sg. ὁ ἡ τό the, this, that, he, she, it
Πνεῦμα n. acc. neut. sg. πνεῦμα spirit, Spirit, Ghost, ghost, life. of the spirit, wind
καὶ conj. καί and, even, also, but
δυνάμεις n. acc. fem. pl. δύναμις power, mighty work, miracle, strength, might
ἐν prep. ἐν (+dat) in, by, with, among, at, on, through, to, within, into, of, for
ὑμῖν pron. dat. 2p. pl. σύ thou, you
ἐξ prep. ἐκ ἐξ (+gen) of, from, out of, by, on, with, in, among, through
ἔργων n. gen. neut. pl. ἔργον work, deed, doing labour
νόμου n. gen. masc. sg. νόμος law, the law
ἢ particle. ἤ or, than, either, nor, or else, and, rather than
ἐξ prep. ἐκ ἐξ (+gen) of, from, out of, by, on, with, in, among, through
ἀκοῆς n. gen. fem. sg. ἀκοή hearing, ear, fame, report, rumour, which one heard
πίστεως n. gen. fem. sg. πίστις faith, assurance, belief, fidelity
6 καθὼς adv. καθώς as, even as, according as, according to
Ἀβραὰμ n. nom. masc. sg. Ἀβραάμ Abraham
τῷ art. dat. masc. sg. ὁ ἡ τό the, this, that, he, she, it
Θεῷ n. dat. masc. sg. θεός God, god
καὶ conj. καί and, even, also, but
αὐτῷ pron. dat. masc. 3p. sg. αὐτός ἡ ό self, of oneself, even, very, the same, he, she, it
εἰς prep. εἰς (+acc) into, to, unto, for, in, on, toward, against, upon, at, among
δικαιοσύνην n. acc. fem. sg. δικαιοσύνη righteousness
7 ἄρα conj. ἄρα then, therefore, haply, wherefore, perhaps, manner, no doubt, truly
ὅτι conj. ὅτι that, for, because, how that, how, because that, for that, though
οἱ art. nom. masc. pl. ὁ ἡ τό the, this, that, he, she, it
ἐκ prep. ἐκ ἐξ (+gen) of, from, out of, by, on, with, in, among, through
πίστεως n. gen. fem. sg. πίστις faith, assurance, belief, fidelity
οὗτοι demo. pron. nom. masc. pl. οὗτος αὕτη τοῦτο this, the same, this same, he, she, it
υἱοί n. nom. masc. pl. υἱός son, child, descendant, offspring, heir
Ἀβραάμ n. gen. masc. sg. Ἀβραάμ Abraham
8 δὲ conj. δέ but, and, now, also, to the contrary, rather, then
ἡ art. nom. fem. sg. ὁ ἡ τό the, this, that, he, she, it
γραφὴ n. nom. fem. sg. γραφή scripture
ὅτι conj. ὅτι that, for, because, how that, how, because that, for that, though
ἐκ prep. ἐκ ἐξ (+gen) of, from, out of, by, on, with, in, among, through
πίστεως n. gen. fem. sg. πίστις faith, assurance, belief, fidelity
τὰ art. acc. neut. pl. ὁ ἡ τό the, this, that, he, she, it
ἔθνη n. acc. neut. pl. ἔθνος Gentile, nation, heathen, people
ὁ art. nom. masc. sg. ὁ ἡ τό the, this, that, he, she, it
Θεὸς n. nom. masc. sg. θεός God, god
τῷ art. dat. masc. sg. ὁ ἡ τό the, this, that, he, she, it
Ἀβραὰμ n. dat. masc. sg. Ἀβραάμ Abraham
ὅτι conj. ὅτι that, for, because, how that, how, because that, for that, though
ἐν prep. ἐν (+dat) in, by, with, among, at, on, through, to, within, into, of, for
σοὶ pron. dat. 2p. sg. σύ thou, you
πάντα adj. nom. neut. pl. πᾶς πᾶσα πᾶν all, every, whosoever, every one, no, whole, any
τὰ art. nom. neut. pl. ὁ ἡ τό the, this, that, he, she, it
ἔθνη n. nom. neut. pl. ἔθνος Gentile, nation, heathen, people
9 ὥστε conj. ὥστε so that, wherefore, insomuch that, therefore, that, so then
οἱ art. nom. masc. pl. ὁ ἡ τό the, this, that, he, she, it

ἐκ prep. ἐκ ἐξ (+gen) of, from, out of, by, on, with, in, among, through
πίστεως n. gen. fem. sg. πίστις faith, assurance, belief, fidelity
σὺν prep. σύν (+dat) with, beside
τῷ art. dat. masc. sg. ὁ ἡ τό the, this, that, he, she, it
πιστῷ adj. dat. masc. sg. πιστός faithful, believing, true, sure
Ἀβραάμ n. dat. masc. sg. Ἀβραάμ Abraham
10 ὅσοι relative pron. nom. masc. pl. ὅσος as many as, whatsoever, that, as long as, how much
γὰρ conj. γάρ for, and, because, but, indeed
ἐξ prep. ἐκ ἐξ (+gen) of, from, out of, by, on, with, in, among, through
ἔργων n. gen. neut. pl. ἔργον work, deed, doing labour
νόμου n. gen. masc. sg. νόμος law, the law
ὑπὸ prep. ὑπό (+gen) of, by, with, from, among, (+acc) under
κατάραν n. acc. fem. sg. κατάρα curse, cursing, cursed
γὰρ conj. γάρ for, and, because, but, indeed
Ἐπικατάρατος adj. nom. masc. sg. ἐπικατάρατος cursed
πᾶς adj. nom. masc. sg. πᾶς πᾶσα πᾶν all, every, whosoever, every one, no, whole, any
ὃς relative pron. nom. masc. sg. ὅς ἥ ὅ who, which, what, that
οὐκ particle of negation. οὐ οὐκ οὐχ not, no, neither, none, nay, nor, never, nothing
ἐν prep. ἐν (+dat) in, by, with, among, at, on, through, to, within, into, of, for
πᾶσι adj. dat. neut. pl. πᾶς πᾶσα πᾶν all, every, whosoever, every one, no, whole, any
τοῖς art. dat. neut. pl. ὁ ἡ τό the, this, that, he, she, it
ἐν prep. ἐν (+dat) in, by, with, among, at, on, through, to, within, into, of, for
τῷ art. dat. neut. sg. ὁ ἡ τό the, this, that, he, she, it
βιβλίῳ n. dat. neut. sg. βιβλίον book, bill, scroll, writing
τοῦ art. gen. masc. sg. ὁ ἡ τό the, this, that, he, she, it
νόμου n. gen. masc. sg. νόμος law, the law
τοῦ art. gen. masc. sg. ὁ ἡ τό the, this, that, he, she, it
αὐτά pron. acc. neut. 3p. pl. αὐτός ἡ ὁ self, of oneself, even, very, the same, he, she, it
11 ὅτι conj. ὅτι that, for, because, how that, how, because that, for that, though
δὲ conj. δέ but, and, now, also, to the contrary, rather, then
ἐν prep. ἐν (+dat) in, by, with, among, at, on, through, to, within, into, of, for
νόμῳ n. dat. masc. sg. νόμος law, the law
οὐδεὶς num. nom. masc. sg. οὐδείς no man, nothing, no, none, neither, not, nought
παρὰ prep. παρά (+gen) of, from, (+dat) with, for, (+acc) beside, at, by, above, against
τῷ art. dat. masc. sg. ὁ ἡ τό the, this, that, he, she, it
Θεῷ n. dat. masc. sg. θεός God, god
δῆλον adj. nom. neut. sg. δῆλος bewray, certain, evident, manifest
ὅτι conj. ὅτι that, for, because, how that, how, because that, for that, though
Ὁ art. nom. masc. sg. ὁ ἡ τό the, this, that, he, she, it
δίκαιος adj. nom. masc. sg. δίκαιος righteous, just, meet, right
ἐκ prep. ἐκ ἐξ (+gen) of, from, out of, by, on, with, in, among, through
πίστεως n. gen. fem. sg. πίστις faith, assurance, belief, fidelity
12 ὁ art. nom. masc. sg. ὁ ἡ τό the, this, that, he, she, it
δὲ conj. δέ but, and, now, also, to the contrary, rather, then
νόμος n. nom. masc. sg. νόμος law, the law
οὐκ particle of negation. οὐ οὐκ οὐχ not, no, neither, none, nay, nor, never, nothing
ἐκ prep. ἐκ ἐξ (+gen) of, from, out of, by, on, with, in, among, through
πίστεως n. gen. fem. sg. πίστις faith, assurance, belief, fidelity
ἀλλ' conj. ἀλλά but, yea, yet, nevertheless, howbeit, nay, therefore
Ὁ art. nom. masc. sg. ὁ ἡ τό the, this, that, he, she, it
αὐτὰ pron. acc. neut. 3p. pl. αὐτός ἡ ὁ self, of oneself, even, very, the same, he, she, it
ἄνθρωπος n. nom. masc. sg. ἄνθρωπος man, human being, person, one, certain
ἐν prep. ἐν (+dat) in, by, with, among, at, on, through, to, within, into, of, for
αὐτοῖς pron. dat. neut. 3p. pl. αὐτός ἡ ὁ self, of oneself, even, very, the same, he, she, it
13 Χριστὸς n. nom. masc. sg. Χριστός Christ

ἡμᾶς pron. acc. 1p. pl. ἐγώ I
ἐκ prep. ἐκ ἐξ (+gen) of, from, out of, by, on, with, in, among, through
τῆς art. gen. fem. sg. ὁ ἡ τό the, this, that, he, she, it
κατάρας n. gen. fem. sg. κατάρα curse, cursing, cursed
τοῦ art. gen. masc. sg. ὁ ἡ τό the, this, that, he, she, it
νόμου n. gen. masc. sg. νόμος law, the law
ὑπὲρ prep. ὑπέρ (+gen) for, of, for the sake of, (+acc) above, more than
ἡμῶν pron. gen. 1p. pl. ἐγώ I
κατάρα n. nom. fem. sg. κατάρα curse
γὰρ conj. γάρ for, and, because, but, indeed
Ἐπικατάρατος adj. nom. masc. sg. ἐπικατάρατος cursed
πᾶς adj. nom. masc. sg. πᾶς πᾶσα πᾶν all, every, whosoever, every one, no, whole, any
ὁ art. nom. masc. sg. ὁ ἡ τό the, this, that, he, she, it
ἐπὶ prep. ἐπί (+gen) on, in, upon, (+dat) in, at, for, upon, (+acc) on, upon, unto, to, against
ξύλου n. gen. neut. sg. ξύλον tree, stave, wood, the stocks
14 ἵνα conj. ἵνα that, to, lest, for to, so that, albeit, because, for, so as
εἰς prep. εἰς (+acc) into, to, unto, for, in, on, toward, against, upon, at, among
τὰ art. acc. neut. pl. ὁ ἡ τό the, this, that, he, she, it
ἔθνη n. acc. neut. pl. ἔθνος Gentile, nation, heathen, people
ἡ art. nom. fem. sg. ὁ ἡ τό the, this, that, he, she, it
εὐλογία n. nom. fem. sg. εὐλογία blessing, bounty, matter of bounty, fair speech
τοῦ art. gen. masc. sg. ὁ ἡ τό the, this, that, he, she, it
Ἀβραὰμ n. gen. masc. sg. Ἀβραάμ Abraham
ἐν prep. ἐν (+dat) in, by, with, among, at, on, through, to, within, into, of, for
Χριστῷ n. dat. masc. sg. Χριστός Christ
Ἰησοῦ n. dat. masc. sg. Ἰησοῦς Jesus
ἵνα conj. ἵνα that, to, lest, for to, so that, albeit, because, for, so as
τὴν art. acc. fem. sg. ὁ ἡ τό the, this, that, he, she, it
ἐπαγγελίαν n. acc. fem. sg. ἐπαγγελία promise, message
τοῦ art. gen. neut. sg. ὁ ἡ τό the, this, that, he, she, it
Πνεύματος n. gen. neut. sg. πνεῦμα spirit, Spirit, Ghost, ghost, life. of the spirit, wind
διὰ prep. διά (+gen) by, through, with, in, of, (+acc) for, because of, for a cause
τῆς art. gen. fem. sg. ὁ ἡ τό the, this, that, he, she, it
πίστεως n. gen. fem. sg. πίστις faith, assurance, belief, fidelity
15 Ἀδελφοί n. voc. masc. pl. ἀδελφός brother
κατὰ prep. κατά (+gen) against, by, throughout, down, (+acc) according to, after, with
ἄνθρωπον n. acc. masc. sg. ἄνθρωπος man, human being, person, one, certain
ὅμως adv. ὅμως nevertheless, and even
ἀνθρώπου n. gen. masc. sg. ἄνθρωπος man, human being, person, one, certain
διαθήκην n. acc. fem. sg. διαθήκη testament, covenant
οὐδεὶς num. nom. masc. sg. οὐδείς no man, nothing, no, none, neither, not, nought
ἢ particle. ἤ or, than, either, nor, or else, and, rather than
16 τῷ art. dat. masc. sg. ὁ ἡ τό the, this, that, he, she, it
δὲ conj. δέ but, and, now, also, to the contrary, rather, then
Ἀβραὰμ n. dat. masc. sg. Ἀβραάμ Abraham
αἱ art. nom. fem. pl. ὁ ἡ τό the, this, that, he, she, it
ἐπαγγελίαι n. nom. fem. pl. ἐπαγγελία promise, message
καὶ conj. καί and, even, also, but
τῷ art. dat. neut. sg. ὁ ἡ τό the, this, that, he, she, it
σπέρματι n. dat. neut. sg. σπέρμα seed, issue
αὐτοῦ pron. gen. masc. 3p. sg. αὐτός ἡ ὁ self, of oneself, even, very, the same, he, she, it
οὐ particle of negation. οὐ οὐκ οὐχ not, no, neither, none, nay, nor, never, nothing
Καὶ conj. καί and, even, also, but
τοῖς art. dat. neut. pl. ὁ ἡ τό the, this, that, he, she, it
σπέρμασιν n. dat. neut. pl. σπέρμα seed, issue

ὡς adv. ὡς as, when, as it were, how, about, like, as soon as, even as, while
ἐπὶ prep. ἐπί (+gen) on, in, upon, (+dat) in, at, for, upon, (+acc) on, upon, unto, to, against
πολλῶν adj. gen. neut. pl. πολύς many, great, much, long, abundant
ἀλλ' conj. ἀλλά but, yea, yet, nevertheless, howbeit, nay, therefore
ὡς adv. ὡς as, when, as it were, how, about, like, as soon as, even as, while
ἐφ' prep. ἐπί (+gen) on, in, upon, (+dat) in, at, for, upon, (+acc) on, upon, unto, to, against
ἑνός num. gen. neut. sg. εἷς or ἕν one, other, some, any, only, a certain
Καὶ conj. καί and, even, also, but
τῷ art. dat. neut. sg. ὁ ἡ τό the, this, that, he, she, it
σπέρματι n. dat. neut. sg. σπέρμα seed, issue
σου pron. gen. 2p. sg. σύ thou, you
ὅς relative pron. nom. masc. sg. ὅς ἥ ὅ who, which, what, that
Χριστός n. nom. masc. sg. Χριστός Christ
17 τοῦτο demo. pron. acc. neut. sg. οὗτος αὕτη τοῦτο this, the same, this same, he, she, it
δὲ conj. δέ but, and, now, also, to the contrary, rather, then
διαθήκην n. acc. fem. sg. διαθήκη testament, covenant
ὑπὸ prep. ὑπό (+gen) of, by, with, from, among, (+acc) under
τοῦ art. gen. masc. sg. ὁ ἡ τό the, this, that, he, she, it
Θεοῦ n. gen. masc. sg. θεός God, god
εἰς prep. εἰς (+acc) into, to, unto, for, in, on, toward, against, upon, at, among
Χριστὸν n. acc. masc. sg. Χριστός Christ
ὁ art. nom. masc. sg. ὁ ἡ τό the, this, that, he, she, it
μετὰ prep. μετά (+gen) with, among, against, (+acc) after
ἔτη n. acc. neut. pl. ἔτος year
τετρακόσια num. acc. neut. pl. τετρακόσιοι four hundred
καὶ conj. καί and, even, also, but
τριάκοντα num. acc. neut. pl. τριάκοντα thirty, thirtyfold
νόμος n. nom. masc. sg. νόμος law, the law
οὐκ particle of negation. οὐ οὐκ οὐχ not, no, neither, none, nay, nor, never, nothing
εἰς prep. εἰς (+acc) into, to, unto, for, in, on, toward, against, upon, at, among
τὸ art. acc. neut. sg. ὁ ἡ τό the, this, that, he, she, it
τὴν art. acc. fem. sg. ὁ ἡ τό the, this, that, he, she, it
ἐπαγγελίαν n. acc. fem. sg. ἐπαγγελία promise, message
18 εἰ conj. εἰ if, whether, that, though, forasmuch
γὰρ conj. γάρ for, and, because, but, indeed
ἐκ prep. ἐκ ἐξ (+gen) of, from, out of, by, on, with, in, among, through
νόμου n. gen. masc. sg. νόμος law, the law
ἡ art. nom. fem. sg. ὁ ἡ τό the, this, that, he, she, it
κληρονομία n. nom. fem. sg. κληρονομία inheritance
οὐκέτι adv. οὐκέτι or οὐκ ἔτι no more, no longer, not any more
ἐξ prep. ἐκ ἐξ (+gen) of, from, out of, by, on, with, in, among, through
ἐπαγγελίας n. gen. fem. sg. ἐπαγγελία promise, message
τῷ art. dat. masc. sg. ὁ ἡ τό the, this, that, he, she, it
δὲ conj. δέ but, and, now, also, to the contrary, rather, then
'Αβραὰμ n. dat. masc. sg. 'Αβραάμ Abraham
δι' prep. διά (+gen) by, through, with, in, of, (+acc) for, because of, for a cause
ἐπαγγελίας n. gen. fem. sg. ἐπαγγελία promise, message
ὁ art. nom. masc. sg. ὁ ἡ τό the, this, that, he, she, it
Θεός n. nom. masc. sg. θεός God, god
19 τί interrog. pron. nom. neut. sg. τίς what, who, why, where, which, how
οὖν conj. οὖν therefore, then, so, and, now, wherefore
ὁ art. nom. masc. sg. ὁ ἡ τό the, this, that, he, she, it
νόμος n. nom. masc. sg. νόμος law, the law
τῶν art. gen. fem. pl. ὁ ἡ τό the, this, that, he, she, it
παραβάσεων n. gen. fem. pl. παράβασις breaking, transgression

χάριν adv. χάριν for a cause, because of, for sake
ἄχρις prep. ἄχρι or ἄχρις (+gen) until, unto, till, even to, as far as, while, into
οὗ relative pron. gen. masc. sg. ὅς ἥ ὅ who, which, what, that
τὸ art. nom. neut. sg. ὁ ἡ τό the, this, that, he, she, it
σπέρμα n. nom. neut. sg. σπέρμα seed, issue
ᾧ relative pron. dat. neut. sg. ὅς ἥ ὅ who, which, what, that
δι' prep. διά (+gen) by, through, with, in, of, (+acc) for, because of, for a cause
ἀγγέλων n. gen. masc. pl. ἄγγελος angel, messenger
ἐν prep. ἐν (+dat) in, by, with, among, at, on, through, to, within, into, of, for
χειρὶ n. dat. fem. sg. χείρ hand
μεσίτου n. gen. masc. sg. μεσίτης mediator
20 ὁ art. nom. masc. sg. ὁ ἡ τό the, this, that, he, she, it
δὲ conj. δέ but, and, now, also, to the contrary, rather, then
μεσίτης n. nom. masc. sg. μεσίτης mediator
ἑνὸς num. gen. masc. sg. εἷς or ἕν one, other, some, any, only, a certain
οὐκ particle of negation. οὐ οὐκ οὐχ not, no, neither, none, nay, nor, never, nothing
ὁ art. nom. masc. sg. ὁ ἡ τό the, this, that, he, she, it
δὲ conj. δέ but, and, now, also, to the contrary, rather, then
Θεὸς n. nom. masc. sg. θεός God, god
εἷς num. nom. masc. sg. εἷς or ἕν one, other, some, any, only, a certain
21 ὁ art. nom. masc. sg. ὁ ἡ τό the, this, that, he, she, it
οὖν conj. οὖν therefore, then, so, and, now, wherefore
νόμος n. nom. masc. sg. νόμος law, the law
κατὰ prep. κατά (+gen) against, by, throughout, down, (+acc) according to, after, with
τῶν art. gen. fem. pl. ὁ ἡ τό the, this, that, he, she, it
ἐπαγγελιῶν n. gen. fem. pl. ἐπαγγελία promise, message
τοῦ art. gen. masc. sg. ὁ ἡ τό the, this, that, he, she, it
Θεοῦ n. gen. masc. sg. θεός God, god
μὴ particle of negation. μή not, no, lest, neither, none, nothing, nor, never, without
εἰ conj. εἰ if, whether, that, though, forasmuch
γὰρ conj. γάρ for, and, because, but, indeed
νόμος n. nom. masc. sg. νόμος law, the law
ὁ art. nom. masc. sg. ὁ ἡ τό the, this, that, he, she, it
ὄντως adv. ὄντως indeed, certainly, clean, of a truth, verily
ἂν particle. ἄν Indicating contingency. No English translation.
ἐκ prep. ἐκ ἐξ (+gen) of, from, out of, by, on, with, in, among, through
νόμου n. gen. masc. sg. νόμος law, the law
ἡ art. nom. fem. sg. ὁ ἡ τό the, this, that, he, she, it
δικαιοσύνη n. nom. fem. sg. δικαιοσύνη righteousness
22 ἀλλὰ conj. ἀλλά but, yea, yet, nevertheless, howbeit, nay, therefore
ἡ art. nom. fem. sg. ὁ ἡ τό the, this, that, he, she, it
γραφὴ n. nom. fem. sg. γραφή scripture
τὰ art. acc. neut. pl. ὁ ἡ τό the, this, that, he, she, it
πάντα adj. acc. neut. pl. πᾶς πᾶσα πᾶν all, every, whosoever, every one, no, whole, any
ὑπὸ prep. ὑπό (+gen) of, by, with, from, among, (+acc) under
ἁμαρτίαν n. acc. fem. sg. ἁμαρτία sin, offence, sinful
ἵνα conj. ἵνα that, to, lest, for to, so that, albeit, because, for, so as
ἡ art. nom. fem. sg. ὁ ἡ τό the, this, that, he, she, it
ἐπαγγελία n. nom. fem. sg. ἐπαγγελία promise, message
ἐκ prep. ἐκ ἐξ (+gen) of, from, out of, by, on, with, in, among, through
πίστεως n. gen. fem. sg. πίστις faith, assurance, belief, fidelity
Ἰησοῦ n. gen. masc. sg. Ἰησοῦς Jesus
Χριστοῦ n. gen. masc. sg. Χριστός Christ
τοῖς art. dat. masc. pl. ὁ ἡ τό the, this, that, he, she, it
23 Πρὸ prep. πρό (+gen) before, above

χρόνου n. gen. masc. sg. χρόνος time, season, space
ὁ art. nom. masc. sg. ὁ ἡ τό the, this, that, he, she, it
Θεὸς n. nom. masc. sg. θεός God, god
τὸν art. acc. masc. sg. ὁ ἡ τό the, this, that, he, she, it
υἱὸν n. acc. masc. sg. υἱός son, child, descendant, offspring, heir
αὐτοῦ pron. gen. masc. 3p. sg. αὐτός ἡ ὁ self, of oneself, even, very, the same, he, she, it
ἐκ prep. ἐκ ἐξ (+gen) of, from, out of, by, on, with, in, among, through
γυναικός n. gen. fem. sg. γυνή woman, wife
ὑπὸ prep. ὑπό (+gen) of, by, with, from, among, (+acc) under
νόμον n. acc. masc. sg. νόμος law, the law
5 ἵνα conj. ἵνα that, to, lest, for to, so that, albeit, because, for, so as
τοὺς art. acc. masc. pl. ὁ ἡ τό the, this, that, he, she, it
ὑπὸ prep. ὑπό (+gen) of, by, with, from, among, (+acc) under
νόμον n. acc. masc. sg. νόμος law, the law
ἵνα conj. ἵνα that, to, lest, for to, so that, albeit, because, for, so as
τὴν art. acc. fem. sg. ὁ ἡ τό the, this, that, he, she, it
υἱοθεσίαν n. acc. fem. sg. υἱοθεσία adoption, adoption of children, adoption of sons
6 ὅτι conj. ὅτι that, for, because, how that, how, because that, for that, though
δέ conj. δέ but, and, now, also, to the contrary, rather, then
υἱοί n. nom. masc. pl. υἱός son, child, descendant, offspring, heir
ὁ art. nom. masc. sg. ὁ ἡ τό the, this, that, he, she, it
Θεὸς n. nom. masc. sg. θεός God, god
τὸ art. acc. neut. sg. ὁ ἡ τό the, this, that, he, she, it
Πνεῦμα n. acc. neut. sg. πνεῦμα spirit, Spirit, Ghost, ghost, life. of the spirit, wind
τοῦ art. gen. masc. sg. ὁ ἡ τό the, this, that, he, she, it
υἱοῦ n. gen. masc. sg. υἱός son, child, descendant, offspring, heir
αὐτοῦ pron. gen. masc. 3p. sg. αὐτός ἡ ὁ self, of oneself, even, very, the same, he, she, it
εἰς prep. εἰς (+acc) into, to, unto, for, in, on, toward, against, upon, at, among
τὰς art. acc. fem. pl. ὁ ἡ τό the, this, that, he, she, it
καρδίας n. acc. fem. pl. καρδία heart
ὑμῶν pron. gen. 2p. pl. σύ thou, you
'Αββᾶ n. voc. masc. sg. 'Αββᾶ Abba
ὁ art. nom. masc. sg. ὁ ἡ τό the, this, that, he, she, it
πατήρ n. nom. masc. sg. πατήρ Father, father, parent
7 ὥστε conj. ὥστε so that, wherefore, insomuch that, therefore, that, so then
οὐκέτι adv. οὐκέτι or οὐκ ἔτι no more, no longer, not any more
δοῦλος n. nom. masc. sg. δοῦλος servant, bondman, bond, slave
ἀλλὰ conj. ἀλλά but, yea, yet, nevertheless, howbeit, nay, therefore
υἱός n. nom. masc. sg. υἱός son, child, descendant, offspring, heir
εἰ conj. εἰ if, whether, that, though, forasmuch
δὲ conj. δέ but, and, now, also, to the contrary, rather, then
υἱός n. nom. masc. sg. υἱός son, child, descendant, offspring, heir
καὶ conj. καί and, even, also, but
κληρονόμος n. nom. masc. sg. κληρονόμος heir
Θεοῦ n. gen. masc. sg. θεός God, god
διὰ prep. διά (+gen) by, through, with, in, of, (+acc) for, because of, for a cause
Χριστοῦ n. gen. masc. sg. Χριστός Christ
8 'Αλλὰ conj. ἀλλά but, yea, yet, nevertheless, howbeit, nay, therefore
τότε adv. τότε then, that time
μὲν conj. μέν indeed, verily, truly, even, so, some
οὐκ particle of negation. οὐ οὐκ οὐχ not, no, neither, none, nay, nor, never, nothing
Θεὸν n. acc. masc. sg. θεός God, god
τοῖς art. dat. masc. pl. ὁ ἡ τό the, this, that, he, she, it
μὴ particle of negation. μή not, no, lest, neither, none, nothing, nor, never, without
φύσει n. dat. fem. sg. φύσις nature

θεοῖς n. dat. masc. pl. θεός God, god
9 νῦν adv. νῦν now, henceforth, present, this time
δὲ conj. δέ but, and, now, also, to the contrary, rather, then
Θεόν n. acc. masc. sg. θεός God, god
μᾶλλον adv. μᾶλλον rather, more, more and more, better, much, much the more
δὲ conj. δέ but, and, now, also, to the contrary, rather, then
ὑπὸ prep. ὑπό (+gen) of, by, with, from, among, (+acc) under
Θεοῦ n. gen. masc. sg. θεός God, god
πῶς adv. πῶς how, by what means, after what manner
πάλιν adv. πάλιν again
ἐπὶ prep. ἐπί (+gen) on, in, upon, (+dat) in, at, for, upon, (+acc) on, upon, unto, to, against
τὰ art. acc. neut. pl. ὁ ἡ τό the, this, that, he, she, it
ἀσθενῆ adj. acc. neut. pl. ἀσθενής weak, sick, impotent, more feeble
καὶ conj. καί and, even, also, but
πτωχὰ adj. acc. neut. pl. πτωχός poor, beggar, beggarly
στοιχεῖα n. acc. neut. pl. στοιχεῖον element, rudiment, principle
οἷς relative pron. dat. neut. pl. ὅς ἥ ὅ who, which, what, that
πάλιν adv. πάλιν again
ἄνωθεν adv. ἄνωθεν from above, again, the top, from the beginning, from the very first
10 ἡμέρας n. acc. fem. pl. ἡμέρα day, time, year, while, age, day time
καὶ conj. καί and, even, also, but
μῆνας n. acc. masc. pl. μήν month
καὶ conj. καί and, even, also, but
καιροὺς n. acc. masc. pl. καιρός time, season, due time, opportunity
καὶ conj. καί and, even, also, but
ἐνιαυτούς n. acc. masc. pl. ἐνιαυτός year
11 ὑμᾶς pron. acc. 2p. pl. σύ thou, you
μή particle of negation. μή not, no, lest, neither, none, nothing, nor, never, without
πως particle. πώς by any means, by some means, haply, perhaps
εἰκῆ adv. εἰκῆ in vain, vainly, without a cause
εἰς prep. εἰς (+acc) into, to, unto, for, in, on, toward, against, upon, at, among
ὑμᾶς pron. acc. 2p. pl. σύ thou, you
12 ὡς adv. ὡς as, when, as it were, how, about, like, as soon as, even as, while
ἐγώ pron. nom. 1p. sg. ἐγώ I
ὅτι conj. ὅτι that, for, because, how that, how, because that, for that, though
κἀγὼ pron. nom. 1p. sg. κἀγώ and I, I also, so I, even as I
ὡς adv. ὡς as, when, as it were, how, about, like, as soon as, even as, while
ὑμεῖς pron. nom. 2p. pl. σύ thou, you
ἀδελφοί n. voc. masc. pl. ἀδελφός brother
ὑμῶν pron. gen. 2p. pl. σύ thou, you
οὐδέν num. acc. neut. sg. οὐδείς no man, nothing, no, none, neither, not, nought
με pron. acc. 1p. sg. ἐγώ I
13 δὲ conj. δέ but, and, now, also, to the contrary, rather, then
ὅτι conj. ὅτι that, for, because, how that, how, because that, for that, though
δι' prep. διά (+gen) by, through, with, in, of, (+acc) for, because of, for a cause
ἀσθένειαν n. acc. fem. sg. ἀσθένεια infirmity, weakness, disease, sickness
τῆς art. gen. fem. sg. ὁ ἡ τό the, this, that, he, she, it
σαρκὸς n. gen. fem. sg. σάρξ flesh, carnal
ὑμῖν pron. dat. 2p. pl. σύ thou, you
τὸ art. acc. neut. sg. ὁ ἡ τό the, this, that, he, she, it
πρότερον adv. πρότερον before, first, former, at the first
14 καὶ conj. καί and, even, also, but
τὸν art. acc. masc. sg. ὁ ἡ τό the, this, that, he, she, it
πειρασμὸν n. acc. masc. sg. πειρασμός temptation, trial
μου pron. gen. 1p. sg. ἐγώ I

τὸν art. acc. masc. sg. ὁ ἡ τό the, this, that, he, she, it
ἐν prep. ἐν (+dat) in, by, with, among, at, on, through, to, within, into, of, for
τῇ art. dat. fem. sg. ὁ ἡ τό the, this, that, he, she, it
σαρκί n. dat. fem. sg. σάρξ flesh, carnal
μου pron. gen. 1p. sg. ἐγώ I
οὐκ particle of negation. οὐ οὐκ οὐχ not, no, neither, none, nay, nor, never, nothing
οὐδὲ adv. οὐδέ neither, nor, not, no, not even, never, not yet
ἀλλ' conj. ἀλλά but, yea, yet, nevertheless, howbeit, nay, therefore
ὡς adv. ὡς as, when, as it were, how, about, like, as soon as, even as, while
ἄγγελον n. acc. masc. sg. ἄγγελος angel, messenger
Θεοῦ n. gen. masc. sg. θεός God, god
με pron. acc. 1p. sg. ἐγώ I
ὡς adv. ὡς as, when, as it were, how, about, like, as soon as, even as, while
Χριστὸν n. acc. masc. sg. Χριστός Christ
Ἰησοῦν n. acc. masc. sg. Ἰησοῦς Jesus
15 τίς interrog. pron. nom. masc. sg. τίς what, who, why, where, which, how
οὖν conj. οὖν therefore, then, so, and, now, wherefore
ὁ art. nom. masc. sg. ὁ ἡ τό the, this, that, he, she, it
μακαρισμὸς n. nom. masc. sg. μακαρισμός blessedness
ὑμῶν pron. gen. 2p. pl. σύ thou, you
γὰρ conj. γάρ for, and, because, but, indeed
ὑμῖν pron. dat. 2p. pl. σύ thou, you
ὅτι conj. ὅτι that, for, because, how that, how, because that, for that, though
εἰ conj. εἰ if, whether, that, though, forasmuch
δυνατὸν adj. nom. neut. sg. δυνατός able, possible, mighty, strong
τοὺς art. acc. masc. pl. ὁ ἡ τό the, this, that, he, she, it
ὀφθαλμοὺς n. acc. masc. pl. ὀφθαλμός eye, sight
ὑμῶν pron. gen. 2p. pl. σύ thou, you
ἂν particle. ἄν Indicating contingency. No English translation.
μοι pron. dat. 1p. sg. ἐγώ I
16 ὥστε conj. ὥστε so that, wherefore, insomuch that, therefore, that, so then
ἐχθρὸς adj. nom. masc. sg. ἐχθρός enemy, foe
ὑμῶν pron. gen. 2p. pl. σύ thou, you
ὑμῖν pron. dat. 2p. pl. σύ thou, you
17 ὑμᾶς pron. acc. 2p. pl. σύ thou, you
οὐ particle of negation. οὐ οὐκ οὐχ not, no, neither, none, nay, nor, never, nothing
καλῶς adv. καλῶς good, well, full well
ἀλλὰ conj. ἀλλά but, yea, yet, nevertheless, howbeit, nay, therefore
ὑμᾶς pron. acc. 2p. pl. σύ thou, you
ἵνα conj. ἵνα that, to, lest, for to, so that, albeit, because, for, so as
αὐτοὺς pron. acc. masc. 3p. pl. αὐτός ἡ ὁ self, of oneself, even, very, the same, he, she, it
18 καλὸν adj. nom. neut. sg. καλός good, better, goodly, meet, honest, fair, well, worthy
δὲ conj. δέ but, and, now, also, to the contrary, rather, then
τὸ art. nom. neut. sg. ὁ ἡ τό the, this, that, he, she, it
ἐν prep. ἐν (+dat) in, by, with, among, at, on, through, to, within, into, of, for
καλῷ adj. dat. neut. sg. καλός good, better, goodly, meet, honest, fair, well, worthy
πάντοτε adv. πάντοτε always, ever, always, evermore
καὶ conj. καί and, even, also, but
μὴ particle of negation. μή not, no, lest, neither, none, nothing, nor, never, without
μόνον adv. μόνος only, alone, by oneself
ἐν prep. ἐν (+dat) in, by, with, among, at, on, through, to, within, into, of, for
τῷ art. dat. neut. sg. ὁ ἡ τό the, this, that, he, she, it
με pron. acc. 1p. sg. ἐγώ I
πρὸς prep. πρός (+gen) for, (+dat) at, (+acc) unto, to, with, for, against
ὑμᾶς pron. acc. 2p. pl. σύ thou, you

19 τεκνία n. voc. neut. pl. τεκνίον little child
μου pron. gen. 1p. sg. ἐγώ I
οὓς relative pron. acc. masc. pl. ὅς ἥ ὅ who, which, what, that
πάλιν adv. πάλιν again
ἄχρις prep. ἄχρι or ἄχρις (+gen) until, unto, till, even to, as far as, while, into
οὗ relative pron. gen. masc. sg. ὅς ἥ ὅ who, which, what, that
Χριστὸς n. nom. masc. sg. Χριστός Christ
ἐν prep. ἐν (+dat) in, by, with, among, at, on, through, to, within, into, of, for
ὑμῖν pron. dat. 2p. pl. σύ thou, you
20 δὲ conj. δέ but, and, now, also, to the contrary, rather, then
πρὸς prep. πρός (+gen) for, (+dat) at, (+acc) unto, to, with, for, against
ὑμᾶς pron. acc. 2p. pl. σύ thou, you
ἄρτι adv. ἄρτι now, hence, here, hither, even now, present
καὶ conj. καί and, even, also, but
τὴν art. acc. fem. sg. ὁ ἡ τό the, this, that, he, she, it
φωνήν n. acc. fem. sg. φωνή voice, sound, noise
μου pron. gen. 1p. sg. ἐγώ I
ὅτι conj. ὅτι that, for, because, how that, how, because that, for that, though
ἐν prep. ἐν (+dat) in, by, with, among, at, on, through, to, within, into, of, for
ὑμῖν pron. dat. 2p. pl. σύ thou, you
21 μοι pron. dat. 1p. sg. ἐγώ I
οἱ art. nom. masc. pl. ὁ ἡ τό the, this, that, he, she, it
ὑπὸ prep. ὑπό (+gen) of, by, with, from, among, (+acc) under
νόμον n. acc. masc. sg. νόμος law, the law
τὸν art. acc. masc. sg. ὁ ἡ τό the, this, that, he, she, it
νόμον n. acc. masc. sg. νόμος law, the law
οὐκ particle of negation. οὐ οὐκ οὐχ not, no, neither, none, nay, nor, never, nothing
22 γὰρ conj. γάρ for, and, because, but, indeed
ὅτι conj. ὅτι that, for, because, how that, how, because that, for that, though
Ἀβραὰμ n. nom. masc. sg. Ἀβραάμ Abraham
δύο num. acc. masc. pl. δύο two, twain, both
υἱοὺς n. acc. masc. pl. υἱός son, child, descendant, offspring, heir
ἕνα num. acc. masc. sg. εἶς or ἕν one, other, some, any, only, a certain
ἐκ prep. ἐκ ἐξ (+gen) of, from, out of, by, on, with, in, among, through
τῆς art. gen. fem. sg. ὁ ἡ τό the, this, that, he, she, it
παιδίσκης n. gen. fem. sg. παιδίσκη damsel, bondwoman, maid, bondmaid, maiden
καὶ conj. καί and, even, also, but
ἕνα num. acc. masc. sg. εἶς or ἕν one, other, some, any, only, a certain
ἐκ prep. ἐκ ἐξ (+gen) of, from, out of, by, on, with, in, among, through
τῆς art. gen. fem. sg. ὁ ἡ τό the, this, that, he, she, it
ἐλευθέρας adj. gen. fem. sg. ἐλεύθερος free, freewoman, at liberty, freeman
23 ἀλλ' conj. ἀλλά but, yea, yet, nevertheless, howbeit, nay, therefore
ὁ art. nom. masc. sg. ὁ ἡ τό the, this, that, he, she, it
μὲν conj. μέν indeed, verily, truly, even, so, some
ἐκ prep. ἐκ ἐξ (+gen) of, from, out of, by, on, with, in, among, through
τῆς art. gen. fem. sg. ὁ ἡ τό the, this, that, he, she, it
παιδίσκης n. gen. fem. sg. παιδίσκη damsel, bondwoman, maid, bondmaid, maiden
κατὰ prep. κατά (+gen) against, by, throughout, down, (+acc) according to, after, with
σάρκα n. acc. fem. sg. σάρξ flesh, carnal
ὁ art. nom. masc. sg. ὁ ἡ τό the, this, that, he, she, it
δὲ conj. δέ but, and, now, also, to the contrary, rather, then
ἐκ prep. ἐκ ἐξ (+gen) of, from, out of, by, on, with, in, among, through
τῆς art. gen. fem. sg. ὁ ἡ τό the, this, that, he, she, it
ἐλευθέρας adj. gen. fem. sg. ἐλεύθερος free, freewoman, at liberty, freeman
διὰ prep. διά (+gen) by, through, with, in, of, (+acc) for, because of, for a cause

τῆς art. gen. fem. sg. ὁ ἡ τό the, this, that, he, she, it
ἐπαγγελίας n. gen. fem. sg. ἐπαγγελία promise, message
24 ἅτινά relative pron. nom. neut. pl. ὅστις which, who, whosoever, that, whatsoever
αὗται demo. pron. nom. fem. pl. οὗτος αὕτη τοῦτο this, the same, this same, he, she, it
γάρ conj. γάρ for, and, because, but, indeed
αἱ art. nom. fem. pl. ὁ ἡ τό the, this, that, he, she, it
δύο num. nom. fem. pl. δύο two, twain, both
διαθῆκαι n. nom. fem. pl. διαθήκη testament, covenant
μία num. nom. fem. sg. εἷς or ἕν one, other, some, any, only, a certain
μὲν conj. μέν indeed, verily, truly, even, so, some
ἀπὸ prep. ἀπό (+gen) from, of, out of, since, for, off, at, by, in, on
ὄρους n. gen. neut. sg. ὄρος mountain, mount, hill
Σινᾶ n. gen. neut. sg. Σινᾶ Sina, Sinai
εἰς prep. εἰς (+acc) into, to, unto, for, in, on, toward, against, upon, at, among
δουλείαν n. acc. fem. sg. δουλεία bondage
ἥτις relative pron. nom. fem. sg. ὅστις which, who, whosoever, that, whatsoever
Ἁγάρ n. nom. fem. sg. Ἁγάρ Agar
25 τὸ art. nom. neut. sg. ὁ ἡ τό the, this, that, he, she, it
γάρ conj. γάρ for, and, because, but, indeed
Ἁγάρ n. nom. fem. sg. Ἁγάρ Agar
Σινᾶ n. nom. neut. sg. Σινᾶ Sina, Sinai
ὄρος n. nom. neut. sg. ὄρος mountain, mount, hill
ἐν prep. ἐν (+dat) in, by, with, among, at, on, through, to, within, into, of, for
τῇ art. dat. fem. sg. ὁ ἡ τό the, this, that, he, she, it
Ἀραβίᾳ n. dat. fem. sg. Ἀραβία Arabia
δὲ conj. δέ but, and, now, also, to the contrary, rather, then
τῇ art. dat. fem. sg. ὁ ἡ τό the, this, that, he, she, it
νῦν adv. νῦν now, henceforth, present, this time
Ἱερουσαλήμ pron. name. fem. inde. Ἱερουσαλήμ Jerusalem
δὲ conj. δέ but, and, now, also, to the contrary, rather, then
μετὰ prep. μετά (+gen) with, among, against, (+acc) after
τῶν art. gen. neut. pl. ὁ ἡ τό the, this, that, he, she, it
τέκνων n. gen. neut. pl. τέκνον child, son, daughter
αὐτῆς pron. gen. fem. 3p. sg. αὐτός ή ό self, of oneself, even, very, the same, he, she, it
26 ἡ art. nom. fem. sg. ὁ ἡ τό the, this, that, he, she, it
δὲ conj. δέ but, and, now, also, to the contrary, rather, then
ἄνω adv. ἄνω above, up, high, the brim
Ἰερουσαλὴμ pron. name. fem. inde. Ἱερουσαλήμ Jerusalem
ἐλευθέρα adj. nom. fem. sg. ἐλεύθερος free, freewoman, at liberty, freeman
ἥτις relative pron. nom. fem. sg. ὅστις which, who, whosoever, that, whatsoever
μήτηρ n. nom. fem. sg. μήτηρ mother
πάντων adj. gen. masc. pl. πᾶς πᾶσα πᾶν all, every, whosoever, every one, no, whole, any
ἡμῶν pron. gen. 1p. pl. ἐγώ I
27 γάρ conj. γάρ for, and, because, but, indeed
στεῖρα n. voc. fem. sg. στεῖρα barren
ἡ art. nom. fem. sg. ὁ ἡ τό the, this, that, he, she, it
οὐ particle of negation. οὐ οὐκ οὐχ not, no, neither, none, nay, nor, never, nothing
καὶ conj. καί and, even, also, but
ἡ art. nom. fem. sg. ὁ ἡ τό the, this, that, he, she, it
οὐκ particle of negation. οὐοὐ οὐκ οὐχ not, no, neither, none, nay, nor, never, nothing
ὅτι conj. ὅτι that, for, because, how that, how, because that, for that, though
πολλὰ adj. nom. neut. pl. πολύς many, great, much, long, abundant
τὰ art. nom. neut. pl. ὁ ἡ τό the, this, that, he, she, it
τέκνα n. nom. neut. pl. τέκνον child, son, daughter
τῆς art. gen. fem. sg. ὁ ἡ τό the, this, that, he, she, it

ἐρήμου adj. gen. fem. sg. ἔρημος wilderness, desert
μᾶλλον adv. μᾶλλον rather, more, more and more, better, much, much the more
ἤ particle. ἤ or, than, either, nor, or else, and, rather than
τῆς art. gen. fem. sg. ὁ ἡ τό the, this, that, he, she, it
τὸν art. acc. masc. sg. ὁ ἡ τό the, this, that, he, she, it
ἄνδρα n. acc. masc. sg. ἀνήρ man, husband, sir
28 ἡμεῖς pron. nom. 1p. pl. ἐγώ I
δέ conj. δέ but, and, now, also, to the contrary, rather, then
ἀδελφοί n. voc. masc. pl. ἀδελφός brother
κατὰ prep. κατά (+gen) against, by, throughout, down, (+acc) according to, after, with
Ἰσαὰκ n. acc. masc. sg. Ἰσαάκ Isaac
ἐπαγγελίας n. gen. fem. sg. ἐπαγγελία promise, message
τέκνα n. nom. neut. pl. τέκνον child, son, daughter
29 ἀλλ᾽ conj. ἀλλά but, yea, yet, nevertheless, howbeit, nay, therefore
ὥσπερ adv. ὥσπερ as, even as, like as
τότε adv. τότε then, that time
ὁ art. nom. masc. sg. ὁ ἡ τό the, this, that, he, she, it
κατὰ prep. κατά (+gen) against, by, throughout, down, (+acc) according to, after, with
σάρκα n. acc. fem. sg. σάρξ flesh, carnal
τὸν art. acc. masc. sg. ὁ ἡ τό the, this, that, he, she, it
κατὰ prep. κατά (+gen) against, by, throughout, down, (+acc) according to, after, with
Πνεῦμα n. acc. neut. sg. πνεῦμα spirit, Spirit, Ghost, ghost, life. of the spirit, wind
οὕτω adv. οὕτω οὕτως so, even so, thus, on this wise, likewise, after this manner
καὶ conj. καί and, even, also, but
νῦν adv. νῦν now, henceforth, present, this time
30 ἀλλὰ conj. ἀλλά but, yea, yet, nevertheless, howbeit, nay, therefore
τί interrog. pron. acc. neut. sg. τίς what, who, why, where, which, how
ἡ art. nom. fem. sg. ὁ ἡ τό the, this, that, he, she, it
γραφή n. nom. fem. sg. γραφή scripture
τὴν art. acc. fem. sg. ὁ ἡ τό the, this, that, he, she, it
παιδίσκην n. acc. fem. sg. παιδίσκη damsel, bondwoman, maid, bondmaid, maiden
καὶ conj. καί and, even, also, but
τὸν art. acc. masc. sg. ὁ ἡ τό the, this, that, he, she, it
υἱὸν n. acc. masc. sg. υἱός son, child, descendant, offspring, heir
αὐτῆς pron. gen. fem. 3p. sg. αὐτός ἡ ὁ self, of oneself, even, very, the same, he, she, it
οὐ particle of negation. οὐ οὐκ οὐχ not, no, neither, none, nay, nor, never, nothing
γὰρ conj. γάρ for, and, because, but, indeed
μὴ particle of negation. μή not, no, lest, neither, none, nothing, nor, never, without
ὁ art. nom. masc. sg. ὁ ἡ τό the, this, that, he, she, it
υἱὸς n. nom. masc. sg. υἱός son, child, descendant, offspring, heir
τῆς art. gen. fem. sg. ὁ ἡ τό the, this, that, he, she, it
παιδίσκης n. gen. fem. sg. παιδίσκη damsel, bondwoman, maid, bondmaid, maiden
μετὰ prep. μετά (+gen) with, among, against, (+acc) after
τοῦ art. gen. masc. sg. ὁ ἡ τό the, this, that, he, she, it
υἱοῦ n. gen. masc. sg. υἱός son, child, descendant, offspring, heir
τῆς art. gen. fem. sg. ὁ ἡ τό the, this, that, he, she, it
ἐλευθέρας adj. gen. fem. sg. ἐλεύθερος free, freewoman, at liberty, freeman
31 ἄρα conj. ἄρα then, therefore, haply, wherefore, perhaps, manner, no doubt, truly
ἀδελφοί n. voc. masc. pl. ἀδελφός brother
οὐκ particle of negation. οὐ οὐκ οὐχ not, no, neither, none, nay, nor, never, nothing
παιδίσκης n. gen. fem. sg. παιδίσκη damsel, bondwoman, maid, bondmaid, maiden
τέκνα n. nom. neut. pl. τέκνον child, son, daughter
ἀλλὰ conj. ἀλλά but, yea, yet, nevertheless, howbeit, nay, therefore
τῆς art. gen. fem. sg. ὁ ἡ τό the, this, that, he, she, it
ἐλευθέρας adj. gen. fem. sg. ἐλεύθερος free, freewoman, at liberty, freeman

5

1 τῇ art. dat. fem. sg. ὁ ἡ τό the, this, that, he, she, it
ἐλευθερίᾳ n. dat. fem. sg. ἐλευθερία liberty
οὖν conj. οὖν therefore, then, so, and, now, wherefore
ᾗ relative pron. dat. fem. sg. ὅς ἥ ὅ who, which, what, that
Χριστὸς n. nom. masc. sg. Χριστός Christ
ἡμᾶς pron. acc. 1p. pl. ἐγώ I
καὶ conj. καί and, even, also, but
μὴ particle of negation. μή not, no, lest, neither, none, nothing, nor, never, without
πάλιν adv. πάλιν again
ζυγῷ n. dat. masc. sg. ζυγός yoke, pair of balances
δουλείας n. gen. fem. sg. δουλεία bondage
2 ἐγὼ pron. nom. 1p. sg. ἐγώ I
Παῦλος n. nom. masc. sg. Παῦλος Paul, Paulus
ὑμῖν pron. dat. 2p. pl. σύ thou, you
ὅτι conj. ὅτι that, for, because, how that, how, because that, for that, though
ἐὰν conj. ἐάν if, soever, except, though, and if, but, whether, if so, so
Χριστὸς n. nom. masc. sg. Χριστός Christ
ὑμᾶς pron. acc. 2p. pl. σύ thou, you
οὐδὲν num. acc. neut. sg. οὐδείς no man, nothing, no, none, neither, not, nought
3 δὲ conj. δέ but, and, now, also, to the contrary, rather, then
πάλιν adv. πάλιν again
παντὶ adj. dat. masc. sg. πᾶς πᾶσα πᾶν all, every, whosoever, every one, no, whole, any
ἀνθρώπῳ n. dat. masc. sg. ἄνθρωπος man, human being, person, one, certain
ὅτι conj. ὅτι that, for, because, how that, how, because that, for that, though
ὀφειλέτης n. nom. masc. sg. ὀφειλέτης debtor, sinner, owe
ὅλον adj. acc. masc. sg. ὅλος all, whole, every whit, altogether
τὸν art. acc. masc. sg. ὁ ἡ τό the, this, that, he, she, it
νόμον n. acc. masc. sg. νόμος law, the law
4 ἀπὸ prep. ἀπό (+gen) from, of, out of, since, for, off, at, by, in, on
τοῦ art. gen. masc. sg. ὁ ἡ τό the, this, that, he, she, it
Χριστοῦ n. gen. masc. sg. Χριστός Christ
οἵτινες relative pron. nom. masc. pl. ὅστις which, who, whosoever, that, whatsoever
ἐν prep. ἐν (+dat) in, by, with, among, at, on, through, to, within, into, of, for
νόμῳ n. dat. masc. sg. νόμος law, the law
τῆς art. gen. fem. sg. ὁ ἡ τό the, this, that, he, she, it
χάριτος n. gen. fem. sg. χάρις grace, thank, favour, pleasure
5 ἡμεῖς pron. nom. 1p. pl. ἐγώ I
γὰρ conj. γάρ for, and, because, but, indeed
Πνεύματι n. dat. neut. sg. πνεῦμα spirit, Spirit, Ghost, ghost, life. of the spirit, wind
ἐκ prep. ἐκ ἐξ (+gen) of, from, out of, by, on, with, in, among, through
πίστεως n. gen. fem. sg. πίστις faith, assurance, belief, fidelity
ἐλπίδα n. acc. fem. sg. ἐλπίς hope, faith
δικαιοσύνης n. gen. fem. sg. δικαιοσύνη righteousness
6 ἐν prep. ἐν (+dat) in, by, with, among, at, on, through, to, within, into, of, for
γὰρ conj. γάρ for, and, because, but, indeed
Χριστῷ n. dat. masc. sg. Χριστός Christ
Ἰησοῦ n. dat. masc. sg. Ἰησοῦς Jesus
οὔτε conj. οὔτε neither, nor, nor yet, no, none
περιτομή n. nom. fem. sg. περιτομή circumcision
τι indefinite pron. acc. neut. sg. τὶς certain, some, any man, one, any thing
οὔτε conj. οὔτε neither, nor, nor yet, no, none
ἀκροβυστία n. nom. fem. sg. ἀκροβυστία uncircumcised, uncircumcision

ἀλλὰ conj. ἀλλά but, yea, yet, nevertheless, howbeit, nay, therefore
πίστις n. nom. fem. sg. πίστις faith, assurance, belief, fidelity
δι' prep. διά (+gen) by, through, with, in, of, (+acc) for, because of, for a cause
ἀγάπης n. gen. fem. sg. ἀγάπη love, charity, feast of charity
7 καλῶς adv. καλῶς good, well, full well
τίς interrog. pron. nom. masc. sg. τίς what, who, why, where, which, how
ὑμᾶς pron. acc. 2p. pl. σύ thou, you
τῇ art. dat. fem. sg. ὁ ἡ τό the, this, that, he, she, it
ἀληθείᾳ n. dat. fem. sg. ἀλήθεια truth, verity
μὴ particle of negation. μή not, no, lest, neither, none, nothing, nor, never, without
8 ἡ art. nom. fem. sg. ὁ ἡ τό the, this, that, he, she, it
πεισμονὴ n. nom. fem. sg. πεισμονή persuasion
οὐκ particle of negation. οὐ οὐκ οὐχ not, no, neither, none, nay, nor, never, nothing
ἐκ prep. ἐκ ἐξ (+gen) of, from, out of, by, on, with, in, among, through
τοῦ art. gen. masc. sg. ὁ ἡ τό the, this, that, he, she, it
ὑμᾶς pron. acc. 2p. pl. σύ thou, you
9 μικρὰ adj. nom. fem. sg. μικρός little, small, least, less
ζύμη n. nom. fem. sg. ζύμη leaven
ὅλον adj. acc. neut. sg. ὅλος all, whole, every whit, altogether
τὸ art. acc. neut. sg. ὁ ἡ τό the, this, that, he, she, it
φύραμα n. acc. neut. sg. φύραμα lump
10 ἐγὼ pron. nom. 1p. sg. ἐγώ I
εἰς prep. εἰς (+acc) into, to, unto, for, in, on, toward, against, upon, at, among
ὑμᾶς pron. acc. 2p. pl. σύ thou, you
ἐν prep. ἐν (+dat) in, by, with, among, at, on, through, to, within, into, of, for
Κυρίῳ n. dat. masc. sg. κύριος Lord, lord, master, sir, LORD, God, Master, owner
ὅτι conj. ὅτι that, for, because, how that, how, because that, for that, though
οὐδὲν num. acc. neut. sg. οὐδείς no man, nothing, no, none, neither, not, nought
ἄλλο adj. acc. neut. sg. ἄλλος other, another, some, one, more, otherwise
ὁ art. nom. masc. sg. ὁ ἡ τό the, this, that, he, she, it
δὲ conj. δέ but, and, now, also, to the contrary, rather, then
ὑμᾶς pron. acc. 2p. pl. σύ thou, you
τὸ art. acc. neut. sg. ὁ ἡ τό the, this, that, he, she, it
κρίμα n. acc. neut. sg. κρίμα judgment, damnation, condemnation
ὅστις relative pron. nom. masc. sg. ὅστις which, who, whosoever, that, whatsoever
ἂν particle. ἄν Indicating contingency. No English translation.
11 ἐγὼ pron. nom. 1p. sg. ἐγώ I
δέ conj. δέ but, and, now, also, to the contrary, rather, then
ἀδελφοί n. voc. masc. pl. ἀδελφός brother
εἰ conj. εἰ if, whether, that, though, forasmuch
περιτομὴν n. acc. fem. sg. περιτομή circumcision
ἔτι adv. ἔτι yet, more, any more, further, still, moreover
τί interrog. pron. acc. neut. sg. τίς what, who, why, where, which, how
ἔτι adv. ἔτι yet, more, any more, further, still, moreover
ἄρα conj. ἄρα then, therefore, haply, wherefore, perhaps, manner, no doubt, truly
τὸ art. nom. neut. sg. ὁ ἡ τό the, this, that, he, she, it
σκάνδαλον n. nom. neut. sg. σκάνδαλον offence, stumblingblock, thing that offend
τοῦ art. gen. masc. sg. ὁ ἡ τό the, this, that, he, she, it
σταυροῦ n. gen. masc. sg. σταυρός cross
12 ὄφελον interj. ὄφελον O that! Would that!
καὶ conj. καί and, even, also, but
οἱ art. nom. masc. pl. ὁ ἡ τό the, this, that, he, she, it
ὑμᾶς pron. acc. 2p. pl. σύ thou, you
13 Ὑμεῖς pron. nom. 2p. pl. σύ thou, you
γὰρ conj. γάρ for, and, because, but, indeed

ἐπ' prep. ἐπί (+gen) on, in, upon, (+dat) in, at, for, upon, (+acc) on, upon, unto, to, against
ἐλευθερίᾳ n. dat. fem. sg. ἐλευθερία liberty
ἀδελφοί n. voc. masc. pl. ἀδελφός brother
μόνον adv. μόνος only, alone, by oneself
μὴ particle of negation. μή not, no, lest, neither, none, nothing, nor, never, without
τὴν art. acc. fem. sg. ὁ ἡ τό the, this, that, he, she, it
ἐλευθερίαν n. acc. fem. sg. ἐλευθερία liberty
εἰς prep. εἰς (+acc) into, to, unto, for, in, on, toward, against, upon, at, among
ἀφορμὴν n. acc. fem. sg. ἀφορμή occasion
τῇ art. dat. fem. sg. ὁ ἡ τό the, this, that, he, she, it
σαρκί n. dat. fem. sg. σάρξ flesh, carnal
ἀλλὰ conj. ἀλλά but, yea, yet, nevertheless, howbeit, nay, therefore
διὰ prep. διά (+gen) by, through, with, in, of, (+acc) for, because of, for a cause
τῆς art. gen. fem. sg. ὁ ἡ τό the, this, that, he, she, it
ἀγάπης n. gen. fem. sg. ἀγάπη love, charity, feast of charity
ἀλλήλοις pron. dat. masc. 2p. pl. ἀλλήλων one another, themselves, together, mutual
14 ὁ art. nom. masc. sg. ὁ ἡ τό the, this, that, he, she, it
γὰρ conj. γάρ for, and, because, but, indeed
πᾶς adj. nom. masc. sg. πᾶς πᾶςα πᾶν all, every, whosoever, every one, no, whole, any
νόμος n. nom. masc. sg. νόμος law, the law
ἐν prep. ἐν (+dat) in, by, with, among, at, on, through, to, within, into, of, for
ἑνὶ num. dat. masc. sg. εἷς or ἕν one, other, some, any, only, a certain
λόγῳ n. dat. masc. sg. λόγος word, saying, account, speech, thing, matter
ἐν prep. ἐν (+dat) in, by, with, among, at, on, through, to, within, into, of, for
τῷ art. dat. masc. sg. ὁ ἡ τό the, this, that, he, she, it
τὸν art. acc. masc. sg. ὁ ἡ τό the, this, that, he, she, it
πλησίον adv. πλησίον neighbour, near
σου pron. gen. 2p. sg. σύ thou, you
ὡς adv. ὡς as, when, as it were, how, about, like, as soon as, even as, while
ἑαυτόν reflexive pron. acc. masc. 3p. sg. ἑαυτοῦ himself, herself, itself, yourself, ourselves
15 εἰ conj. εἰ if, whether, that, though, forasmuch
δὲ conj. δέ but, and, now, also, to the contrary, rather, then
ἀλλήλους pron. acc. masc. 2p. pl. ἀλλήλων one another, themselves, together, mutual
καὶ conj. καί and, even, also, but
μή particle of negation. μή not, no, lest, neither, none, nothing, nor, never, without
ὑπὸ prep. ὑπό (+gen) of, by, with, from, among, (+acc) under
ἀλλήλων pron. gen. masc. pl. ἀλλήλων one another, themselves, together, mutual
16 δέ conj. δέ but, and, now, also, to the contrary, rather, then
Πνεύματι n. dat. neut. sg. πνεῦμα spirit, Spirit, Ghost, ghost, life. of the spirit, wind
καὶ conj. καί and, even, also, but
ἐπιθυμίαν n. acc. fem. sg. ἐπιθυμία lust, concupiscence, desire
σαρκὸς n. gen. fem. sg. σάρξ flesh, carnal
οὐ particle of negation. οὐ οὐκ οὐχ not, no, neither, none, nay, nor, never, nothing
μὴ particle of negation. μή not, no, lest, neither, none, nothing, nor, never, without
17 ἡ art. nom. fem. sg. ὁ ἡ τό the, this, that, he, she, it
γὰρ conj. γάρ for, and, because, but, indeed
σὰρξ n. nom. fem. sg. σάρξ flesh, carnal
κατὰ prep. κατά (+gen) against, by, throughout, down, (+acc) according to, after, with
τοῦ art. gen. neut. sg. ὁ ἡ τό the, this, that, he, she, it
Πνεύματος n. gen. neut. sg. πνεῦμα spirit, Spirit, Ghost, ghost, life. of the spirit, wind
τὸ art. nom. neut. sg. ὁ ἡ τό the, this, that, he, she, it
δέ conj. δέ but, and, now, also, to the contrary, rather, then
Πνεῦμα n. nom. neut. sg. πνεῦμα spirit, Spirit, Ghost, ghost, life. of the spirit, wind
κατὰ prep. κατά (+gen) against, by, throughout, down, (+acc) according to, after, with
τῆς art. gen. fem. sg. ὁ ἡ τό the, this, that, he, she, it

σαρκός n. gen. fem. sg. σάρξ flesh, carnal
ταῦτα demo. pron. nom. neut. pl. οὗτος αὕτη τοῦτο this, the same, this same, he, she, it
δέ conj. δέ but, and, now, also, to the contrary, rather, then
ἀλλήλοις pron. dat. neut. pl. ἀλλήλων one another, themselves, together, mutual
ἵνα conj. ἵνα that, to, lest, for to, so that, albeit, because, for, so as
μὴ particle of negation. μή not, no, lest, neither, none, nothing, nor, never, without
ἃ relative pron. acc. neut. pl. ὅς ἥ ὅ who, which, what, that
ἂν particle. ἄν Indicating contingency. No English translation.
ταῦτα demo. pron. nom. neut. pl. οὗτος αὕτη τοῦτο this, the same, this same, he, she, it
18 εἰ conj. εἰ if, whether, that, though, forasmuch
δὲ conj. δέ but, and, now, also, to the contrary, rather, then
Πνεύματι n. dat. neut. sg. πνεῦμα spirit, Spirit, Ghost, ghost, life. of the spirit, wind
οὐκ particle of negation. οὐ οὐκ οὐχ not, no, neither, none, nay, nor, never, nothing
ὑπὸ prep. ὑπό (+gen) of, by, with, from, among, (+acc) under
νόμον n. acc. masc. sg. νόμος law, the law
19 φανερὰ adj. nom. neut. pl. φανερός manifest, abroad, open, known, outward, appear
δέ conj. δέ but, and, now, also, to the contrary, rather, then
τὰ art. nom. neut. pl. ὁ ἡ τό the, this, that, he, she, it
ἔργα n. nom. neut. pl. ἔργον work, deed, doing labour
τῆς art. gen. fem. sg. ὁ ἡ τό the, this, that, he, she, it
σαρκός n. gen. fem. sg. σάρξ flesh, carnal
ἅτινά relative pron. nom. neut. pl. ὅστις which, who, whosoever, that, whatsoever
μοιχεία n. nom. fem. sg. μοιχεία adultery
πορνεία n. nom. fem. sg. πορνεία fornication
ἀκαθαρσία n. nom. fem. sg. ἀκαθαρσία uncleanness
ἀσέλγεια n. nom. fem. sg. ἀσέλγεια lasciviousness, wantonness, filthy
20 εἰδωλολατρεία n. nom. fem. sg. εἰδωλολατρεία idolatry
φαρμακεία n. nom. fem. sg. φαρμακεία witchcraft, sorcery
ἔχθραι n. nom. fem. pl. ἔχθρα enmity, hatred
ἔρεις n. nom. fem. pl. ἔρις debate, strife, contention, variance
ζῆλοι n. nom. masc. pl. ζῆλος zeal, envying, indignation, emulation, jealousy
θυμοί n. nom. masc. pl. θυμός wrath, fierceness, indignation
ἐριθεῖαι n. nom. fem. pl. ἐριθεία strife, contention, contentious
διχοστασίαι n. nom. fem. pl. διχοστασία division, sedition
αἱρέσεις n. nom. fem. pl. αἵρεσις sect, heresy
21 φθόνοι n. nom. masc. pl. φθόνος envy, envying
φόνοι n. nom. masc. pl. φόνος murder, slaughter
μέθαι n. nom. fem. pl. μέθη drunkenness
κῶμοι n. nom. masc. pl. κῶμος rioting, revelling
καὶ conj. καί and, even, also, but
τὰ art. nom. neut. pl. ὁ ἡ τό the, this, that, he, she, it
ὅμοια adj. nom. neut. pl. ὅμοιος like
τούτοις demo. pron. dat. neut. pl. οὗτος αὕτη τοῦτο this, the same, this same, he, she, it
ἃ relative pron. acc. neut. pl. ὅς ἥ ὅ who, which, what, that
ὑμῖν pron. dat. 2p. pl. σύ thou, you
καθὼς adv. καθώς as, even as, according as, according to
καὶ conj. καί and, even, also, but
ὅτι conj. ὅτι that, for, because, how that, how, because that, for that, though
οἱ art. nom. masc. pl. ὁ ἡ τό the, this, that, he, she, it
τὰ art. acc. neut. pl. ὁ ἡ τό the, this, that, he, she, it
τοιαῦτα demo. pron. acc. neut. pl. τοιοῦτος such, like
βασιλείαν n. gen. masc. sg. βασιλεία kingdom, reign
Θεοῦ n. gen. masc. sg. θεός God, god
οὐ particle of negation. οὐ οὐκ οὐχ not, no, neither, none, nay, nor, never, nothing
22 ὁ art. nom. masc. sg. ὁ ἡ τό the, this, that, he, she, it

δὲ conj. δέ but, and, now, also, to the contrary, rather, then
καρπὸς n. nom. masc. sg. καρπός fruit
τοῦ art. gen. neut. sg. ὁ ἡ τό the, this, that, he, she, it
Πνεύματός n. gen. neut. sg. πνεῦμα spirit, Spirit, Ghost, ghost, life. of the spirit, wind
ἀγάπη n. nom. fem. sg. ἀγάπη love, charity, feast of charity
χαρὰ n. nom. fem. sg. χαρά joy, gladness, joyfulness
εἰρήνη n. nom. fem. sg. εἰρήνη peace, quietness, rest
μακροθυμία n. nom. fem. sg. μακροθυμία longsuffering, patience
χρηστότης n. nom. fem. sg. χρηστότης goodness, kindness, gentleness, good
ἀγαθωσύνη n. nom. fem. sg. ἀγαθωσύνη goodness
πίστις n. nom. fem. sg. πίστις faith, assurance, belief, fidelity
23 πρᾳότης n. nom. fem. sg. πρᾳότης meekness
ἐγκράτεια n. nom. fem. sg. ἐγκράτεια temperance
κατὰ prep. κατά (+gen) against, by, throughout, down, (+acc) according to, after, with
τῶν art. gen. neut. pl. ὁ ἡ τό the, this, that, he, she, it
τοιούτων demo. pron. gen. neut. pl. τοιοῦτος such, like
οὐκ particle of negation. οὐ οὐκ οὐχ not, no, neither, none, nay, nor, never, nothing
νόμος n. nom. masc. sg. νόμος law, the law
24 οἱ art. nom. masc. pl. ὁ ἡ τό the, this, that, he, she, it
δὲ conj. δέ but, and, now, also, to the contrary, rather, then
τοῦ art. gen. masc. sg. ὁ ἡ τό the, this, that, he, she, it
Χριστοῦ n. gen. masc. sg. Χριστός Christ
τὴν art. acc. fem. sg. ὁ ἡ τό the, this, that, he, she, it
σάρκα n. acc. fem. sg. σάρξ flesh, carnal
σὺν prep. σύν (+dat) with, beside
τοῖς art. dat. neut. pl. ὁ ἡ τό the, this, that, he, she, it
παθήμασι n. dat. neut. pl. πάθημα suffering, affliction, affection, motion
καὶ conj. καί and, even, also, but
ταῖς art. dat. fem. pl. ὁ ἡ τό the, this, that, he, she, it
ἐπιθυμίαις n. dat. fem. pl. ἐπιθυμία lust, concupiscence, desire
25 Εἰ conj. εἰ if, whether, that, though, forasmuch
Πνεύματι n. dat. neut. sg. πνεῦμα spirit, Spirit, Ghost, ghost, life. of the spirit, wind
Πνεύματι n. dat. neut. sg. πνεῦμα spirit, Spirit, Ghost, ghost, life. of the spirit, wind
καὶ conj. καί and, even, also, but
26 μὴ particle of negation. μή not, no, lest, neither, none, nothing, nor, never, without
κενόδοξοι adj. nom. masc. pl. κενόδοξος desirous of vain glory
ἀλλήλους pron. acc. masc. pl. ἀλλήλων one another, themselves, together, mutual
ἀλλήλοις pron. dat. masc. pl. ἀλλήλων one another, themselves, together, mutual

6

1 Ἀδελφοί n. voc. masc. pl. ἀδελφός brother
ἐὰν conj. ἐάν if, soever, except, though, and if, but, whether, if so, so
καὶ conj. καί and, even, also, but
ἄνθρωπος n. nom. masc. sg. ἄνθρωπος man, human being, person, one, certain
ἐν prep. ἐν (+dat) in, by, with, among, at, on, through, to, within, into, of, for
τινι relative pron. nom. neut. pl. τὶς certain, some, any man, one, any thing
παραπτώματι n. dat. neut. sg. παράπτωμα trespass, offence, sin, fall, fault
ὑμεῖς pron. nom. 2p. pl. σύ thou, you
οἱ art. nom. masc. pl. ὁ ἡ τό the, this, that, he, she, it
πνευματικοὶ adj. nom. masc. pl. πνευματικός spiritual
τὸν art. acc. masc. sg. ὁ ἡ τό the, this, that, he, she, it
τοιοῦτον demo. pron. acc. masc. sg. τοιοῦτος such, like
ἐν prep. ἐν (+dat) in, by, with, among, at, on, through, to, within, into, of, for
πνεύματι n. dat. neut. sg. πνεῦμα spirit, Spirit, Ghost, ghost, life. of the spirit, wind

πρᾳότητος n. gen. fem. sg. πρᾳότης meekness
σεαυτὸν pron. acc. masc. 2p. sg. σεαυτοῦ σεαυτῷ σεαυτόν thyself, thine own self
μή particle of negation. μή not, no, lest, neither, none, nothing, nor, never, without
καὶ conj. καί and, even, also, but
σὺ pron. nom. 2p. sg. σύ thou, you
2 ἀλλήλων pron. gen. masc. pl. ἀλλήλων one another, themselves, together, mutual
τὰ art. acc. neut. pl. ὁ ἡ τό the, this, that, he, she, it
βάρη n. acc. neut. pl. βάρος burden, burdensome, weight
καὶ conj. καί and, even, also, but
οὕτως adv. οὕτω οὕτως so, even so, thus, on this wise, likewise, after this manner
τὸν art. acc. masc. sg. ὁ ἡ τό the, this, that, he, she, it
νόμον n. acc. masc. sg. νόμος law, the law
τοῦ art. gen. masc. sg. ὁ ἡ τό the, this, that, he, she, it
Χριστοῦ n. gen. masc. sg. Χριστός Christ
3 εἰ conj. εἰ if, whether, that, though, forasmuch
γὰρ conj. γάρ for, and, because, but, indeed
τις indefinite pron. nom. masc. sg. τὶς certain, some, any man, one, any thing
τι indefinite pron. nom. neut. sg. τὶς certain, some, any man, one, any thing
μηδὲν num. nom. neut. sg. μηδείς μηδεμία μηδέν no man, nothing, no, none, not at all
ἑαυτόν reflexive pron. acc. masc. 3p. sg. ἑαυτοῦ himself, herself, itself, yourself, ourselves
4 τὸ art. acc. neut. sg. ὁ ἡ τό the, this, that, he, she, it
δὲ conj. δέ but, and, now, also, to the contrary, rather, then
ἔργον n. acc. neut. sg. ἔργον work, deed, doing labour
ἑαυτοῦ reflexive pron. gen. masc. 3p. sg. ἑαυτοῦ himself, herself, itself, yourself, ourselves
ἕκαστος adj. nom. masc. sg. ἕκαστος every man, every, every one, any man, each
καὶ conj. καί and, even, also, but
τότε adv. τότε then, that time
εἰς prep. εἰς (+acc) into, to, unto, for, in, on, toward, against, upon, at, among
ἑαυτὸν reflexive pron. acc. masc. 3p. sg. ἑαυτοῦ himself, herself, itself, yourself, ourselves
μόνον adj. acc. masc. sg. μόνος only, alone, by oneself
τὸ art. acc. neut. sg. ὁ ἡ τό the, this, that, he, she, it
καύχημα n. acc. neut. sg. καύχημα whereof to glory, rejoicing, glorying, boasting
καὶ conj. καί and, even, also, but
οὐκ particle of negation. οὐ οὐκ οὐχ not, no, neither, none, nay, nor, never, nothing
εἰς prep. εἰς (+acc) into, to, unto, for, in, on, toward, against, upon, at, among
τὸν art. acc. masc. sg. ὁ ἡ τό the, this, that, he, she, it
ἕτερον adj. acc. masc. sg. ἕτερος another, other, else, strange
5 ἕκαστος adj. nom. masc. sg. ἕκαστος every man, every, every one, any man, each
γὰρ conj. γάρ for, and, because, but, indeed
τὸ art. acc. neut. sg. ὁ ἡ τό the, this, that, he, she, it
ἴδιον adj. acc. neut. sg. ἴδιος one's own, one's, privately
φορτίον n. acc. neut. sg. φορτίον burden
6 δὲ conj. δέ but, and, now, also, to the contrary, rather, then
ὁ art. nom. masc. sg. ὁ ἡ τό the, this, that, he, she, it
τὸν art. acc. masc. sg. ὁ ἡ τό the, this, that, he, she, it
λόγον n. acc. masc. sg. λόγος word, saying, account, speech, thing, matter
τῷ art. dat. masc. sg. ὁ ἡ τό the, this, that, he, she, it
ἐν prep. ἐν (+dat) in, by, with, among, at, on, through, to, within, into, of, for
πᾶσιν adj. dat. neut. pl. πᾶς πᾶσα πᾶν all, every, whosoever, every one, no, whole, any
ἀγαθοῖς adj. dat. neut. pl. ἀγαθός good, good thing, that which is good, well
7 μὴ particle of negation. μή not, no, lest, neither, none, nothing, nor, never, without
Θεὸς n. nom. masc. sg. θεός God, god
οὐ particle of negation. οὐ οὐκ οὐχ not, no, neither, none, nay, nor, never, nothing
ὃ relative pron. acc. neut. sg. ὅς ἥ ὅ who, which, what, that
γὰρ conj. γάρ for, and, because, but, indeed

ἐὰν conj. ἐάν if, soever, except, though, and if, but, whether, if so, so
ἄνθρωπος n. nom. masc. sg. ἄνθρωπος man, human being, person, one, certain
τοῦτο demo. pron. acc. neut. sg. οὗτος αὕτη τοῦτο this, the same, this same, he, she, it
καὶ conj. καί and, even, also, but
8 ὅτι conj. ὅτι that, for, because, how that, how, because that, for that, though
ὁ art. nom. masc. sg. ὁ ἡ τό the, this, that, he, she, it
εἰς prep. εἰς (+acc) into, to, unto, for, in, on, toward, against, upon, at, among
τὴν art. acc. fem. sg. ὁ ἡ τό the, this, that, he, she, it
σάρκα n. acc. fem. sg. σάρξ flesh, carnal
ἑαυτοῦ reflexive pron. gen. masc. 3p. sg. ἑαυτοῦ himself, herself, itself, yourself, ourselves
ἐκ prep. ἐκ ἐξ (+gen) of, from, out of, by, on, with, in, among, through
τῆς art. gen. fem. sg. ὁ ἡ τό the, this, that, he, she, it
σαρκὸς n. gen. fem. sg. σάρξ flesh, carnal
φθοράν n. acc. fem. sg. φθορά corruption, destroy, perish
ὁ art. nom. masc. sg. ὁ ἡ τό the, this, that, he, she, it
δὲ conj. δέ but, and, now, also, to the contrary, rather, then
εἰς prep. εἰς (+acc) into, to, unto, for, in, on, toward, against, upon, at, among
τὸ art. acc. neut. sg. ὁ ἡ τό the, this, that, he, she, it
Πνεῦμα n. acc. neut. sg. πνεῦμα spirit, Spirit, Ghost, ghost, life. of the spirit, wind
ἐκ prep. ἐκ ἐξ (+gen) of, from, out of, by, on, with, in, among, through
τοῦ art. gen. neut. sg. ὁ ἡ τό the, this, that, he, she, it
Πνεύματος n. gen. neut. sg. πνεῦμα spirit, Spirit, Ghost, ghost, life. of the spirit, wind
ζωὴν n. acc. fem. sg. ζωή life, lifetime
αἰώνιον adj. acc. fem. sg. αἰώνιος eternal, everlasting, world, for ever
9 τὸ art. acc. neut. sg. ὁ ἡ τό the, this, that, he, she, it
δὲ conj. δέ but, and, now, also, to the contrary, rather, then
καλὸν adj. acc. neut. sg. καλός good, better, goodly, meet, honest, fair, well, worthy
μὴ particle of negation. μή not, no, lest, neither, none, nothing, nor, never, without
καιρῷ n. dat. masc. sg. καιρός time, season, due time, opportunity
γὰρ conj. γάρ for, and, because, but, indeed
ἰδίῳ adj. dat. masc. sg. ἴδιος one's own, one's, privately
μὴ particle of negation. μή not, no, lest, neither, none, nothing, nor, never, without
10 ἄρα conj. ἄρα then, therefore, haply, wherefore, perhaps, manner, no doubt, truly
οὖν conj. οὖν therefore, then, so, and, now, wherefore
ὡς adv. ὡς as, when, as it were, how, about, like, as soon as, even as, while
καιρὸν n. acc. masc. sg. καιρός time, season, due time, opportunity
τὸ art. acc. neut. sg. ὁ ἡ τό the, this, that, he, she, it
ἀγαθὸν adj. acc. neut. sg. ἀγαθός good, good thing, that which is good, well
πρὸς prep. πρός (+gen) for, (+dat) at, (+acc) unto, to, with, for, against
πάντας adj. acc. masc. pl. πᾶς πᾶσα πᾶν all, every, whosoever, every one, no, whole, any
μάλιστα adv. μάλιστα specially, especially, chiefly, most of all
δὲ conj. δέ but, and, now, also, to the contrary, rather, then
πρὸς prep. πρός (+gen) for, (+dat) at, (+acc) unto, to, with, for, against
τοὺς art. acc. masc. pl. ὁ ἡ τό the, this, that, he, she, it
οἰκείους adj. acc. masc. pl. οἰκεῖος of the household, one of one's own house
τῆς art. gen. fem. sg. ὁ ἡ τό the, this, that, he, she, it
πίστεως n. gen. fem. sg. πίστις faith, assurance, belief, fidelity
11 πηλίκοις interrog. pron. dat. neut. pl. πηλίκος how large, how great
ὑμῖν pron. dat. 2p. pl. σύ thou, you
γράμμασιν n. dat. neut. pl. γράμμα letter, bill, learning, scripture, writing
τῇ art. dat. fem. sg. ὁ ἡ τό the, this, that, he, she, it
ἐμῇ poss. pron. dat. fem. 1p. sg. ἐμός my, mine, mine own, of me
χειρί n. dat. fem. sg. χείρ hand
12 ὅσοι relative pron. nom. masc. pl. ὅσος as many as, whatsoever, that, as long as, how much
ἐν prep. ἐν (+dat) in, by, with, among, at, on, through, to, within, into, of, for

σαρκί n. dat. fem. sg. σάρξ flesh, carnal
οὗτοι demo. pron. nom. masc. pl. οὗτος αὕτη τοῦτο this, the same, this same, he, she, it
ὑμᾶς pron. acc. 2p. pl. σύ thou, you
μόνον adv. μόνος only, alone, by oneself
ἵνα conj. ἵνα that, to, lest, for to, so that, albeit, because, for, so as
μὴ particle of negation. μή not, no, lest, neither, none, nothing, nor, never, without
τῷ art. dat. masc. sg. ὁ ἡ τό the, this, that, he, she, it
σταυρῷ n. dat. masc. sg. σταυρός cross
τοῦ art. gen. masc. sg. ὁ ἡ τό the, this, that, he, she, it
Χριστοῦ n. gen. masc. sg. Χριστός Christ
13 οὐδὲ adv. οὐδέ neither, nor, not, no, not even, never, not yet
γὰρ conj. γάρ for, and, because, but, indeed
οἱ art. nom. masc. pl. ὁ ἡ τό the, this, that, he, she, it
αὐτοὶ pron. nom. masc. 3p. pl. αὐτός ἡ ό self, of oneself, even, very, the same, he, she, it
νόμον n. acc. masc. sg. νόμος law, the law
ἀλλὰ conj. ἀλλά but, yea, yet, nevertheless, howbeit, nay, therefore
ὑμᾶς pron. acc. 2p. pl. σύ thou, you
ἵνα conj. ἵνα that, to, lest, for to, so that, albeit, because, for, so as
ἐν prep. ἐν (+dat) in, by, with, among, at, on, through, to, within, into, of, for
τῇ art. dat. fem. sg. ὁ ἡ τό the, this, that, he, she, it
ὑμετέρᾳ poss. pron. dat. fem. 2p. sg. ὑμέτερος your, yours, your own
σαρκὶ n. dat. fem. sg. σάρξ flesh, carnal
14 ἐμοὶ pron. dat. 1p. sg. ἐγώ I
δὲ conj. δέ but, and, now, also, to the contrary, rather, then
μὴ particle of negation. μή not, no, lest, neither, none, nothing, nor, never, without
εἰ conj. εἰ if, whether, that, though, forasmuch
μὴ particle of negation. μή not, no, lest, neither, none, nothing, nor, never, without
ἐν prep. ἐν (+dat) in, by, with, among, at, on, through, to, within, into, of, for
τῷ art. dat. masc. sg. ὁ ἡ τό the, this, that, he, she, it
σταυρῷ n. dat. masc. sg. σταυρός cross
τοῦ art. gen. masc. sg. ὁ ἡ τό the, this, that, he, she, it
Κυρίου n. gen. masc. sg. κύριος Lord, lord, master, sir, LORD, God, Master, owner
ἡμῶν pron. gen. 1p. pl. ἐγώ I
Ἰησοῦ n. gen. masc. sg. Ἰησοῦς Jesus
Χριστοῦ n. gen. masc. sg. Χριστός Christ
δι' prep. διά (+gen) by, through, with, in, of, (+acc) for, because of, for a cause
οὗ relative pron. gen. masc. sg. ὅς ἥ ὅ who, which, what, that
ἐμοὶ pron. dat. 1p. sg. ἐγώ I
κόσμος n. nom. masc. sg. κόσμος world, adorning
κἀγὼ pron. nom. 1p. sg. κἀγώ and I, I also, so I, even as I
τῷ art. dat. masc. sg. ὁ ἡ τό the, this, that, he, she, it
κόσμῳ n. dat. masc. sg. κόσμος world, adorning
15 ἐν prep. ἐν (+dat) in, by, with, among, at, on, through, to, within, into, of, for
γὰρ conj. γάρ for, and, because, but, indeed
Χριστῷ n. dat. masc. sg. Χριστός Christ
Ἰησοῦ n. dat. masc. sg. Ἰησοῦς Jesus
οὔτε conj. οὔτε neither, nor, nor yet, no, none
περιτομή n. nom. fem. sg. περιτομή circumcision
τί indefinite pron. nom. neut. sg. τὶς certain, some, any man, one, any thing
οὔτε conj. οὔτε neither, nor, nor yet, no, none
ἀκροβυστία n. nom. fem. sg. ἀκροβυστία uncircumcised, uncircumcision
ἀλλὰ conj. ἀλλά but, yea, yet, nevertheless, howbeit, nay, therefore
καινὴ adj. nom. fem. sg. καινός new
κτίσις n. nom. fem. sg. κτίσις creature, creation, building, ordinance
16 καὶ conj. καί and, even, also, but

ὅσοι relative pron. nom. masc. pl. ὅσος as many as, whatsoever, that, as long as, how much
τῷ art. dat. masc. sg. ὁ ἡ τό the, this, that, he, she, it
κανόνι n. dat. masc. sg. κανών rule, line
τούτῳ demo. pron. dat. masc. sg. οὗτος αὕτη τοῦτο this, the same, this same, he, she, it
εἰρήνη n. nom. fem. sg. εἰρήνη peace, quietness, rest
ἐπ' prep. ἐπί (+gen) on, in, upon, (+dat) in, at, for, upon, (+acc) on, upon, unto, to, against
αὐτοὺς pron. acc. masc. 3p. pl. αὐτός ή ό self, of oneself, even, very, the same, he, she, it
καὶ conj. καί and, even, also, but
ἔλεος n. nom. masc. sg. ἔλεος mercy
καὶ conj. καί and, even, also, but
ἐπὶ prep. ἐπί (+gen) on, in, upon, (+dat) in, at, for, upon, (+acc) on, upon, unto, to, against
τὸν art. acc. masc. sg. ὁ ἡ τό the, this, that, he, she, it
Ἰσραὴλ pron. name. masc. inde. Ἰσραήλ Israel
τοῦ art. gen. masc. sg. ὁ ἡ τό the, this, that, he, she, it
Θεοῦ n. gen. masc. sg. θεός God, god
17 Τοῦ art. gen. neut. sg. ὁ ἡ τό the, this, that, he, she, it
λοιποῦ adj. gen. neut. sg. λοιπός other, rest, remnant, residue, which remain
κόπους n. acc. masc. pl. κόπος labour, trouble, weariness
μοι pron. dat. 1p. sg. ἐγώ I
μηδεὶς num. nom. masc. sg. μηδείς μηδεμία μηδέν no man, nothing, no, none, not at all
ἐγὼ pron. nom. 1p. sg. ἐγώ I
γὰρ conj. γάρ for, and, because, but, indeed
τὰ art. acc. neut. pl. ὁ ἡ τό the, this, that, he, she, it
στίγματα n. acc. neut. pl. στίγμα mark
τοῦ art. gen. masc. sg. ὁ ἡ τό the, this, that, he, she, it
Κυρίου n. gen. masc. sg. κύριος Lord, lord, master, sir, LORD, God, Master, owner
Ἰησοῦ n. gen. masc. sg. Ἰησοῦς Jesus
ἐν prep. ἐν (+dat) in, by, with, among, at, on, through, to, within, into, of, for
τῷ art. dat. neut. sg. ὁ ἡ τό the, this, that, he, she, it
σώματί n. dat. neut. sg. σῶμα body, bodily, slave
μου pron. gen. 1p. sg. ἐγώ I
18 Ἡ art. nom. fem. sg. ὁ ἡ τό the, this, that, he, she, it
χάρις n. nom. fem. sg. χάρις grace, thank, favour, pleasure
τοῦ art. gen. masc. sg. ὁ ἡ τό the, this, that, he, she, it
Κυρίου n. gen. masc. sg. κύριος Lord, lord, master, sir, LORD, God, Master, owner
ἡμῶν pron. gen. 1p. pl. ἐγώ I
Ἰησοῦ n. gen. masc. sg. Ἰησοῦς Jesus
Χριστοῦ n. gen. masc. sg. Χριστός Christ
μετὰ prep. μετά (+gen) with, among, against, (+acc) after
τοῦ art. gen. neut. sg. ὁ ἡ τό the, this, that, he, she, it
πνεύματος n. gen. neut. sg. πνεῦμα spirit, Spirit, Ghost, ghost, life. of the spirit, wind
ὑμῶν pron. gen. 2p. pl. σύ thou, you
ἀδελφοί n. voc. masc. pl. ἀδελφός brother
ἀμήν. particle. ἀμήν amen, verily

ΠΑΥΛΟΥ ΤΟΥ ΑΠΟΣΤΟΛΟΥ
Η ΠΡΟΣ
ΕΦΕΣΙΟΥΣ ΕΠΙΣΤΟΛΗ

1

1 Παῦλος n. nom. masc. sg. Παῦλος Paul, Paulus
ἀπόστολος n. nom. masc. sg. ἀπόστολος apostle, messenger, he that is sent
Ἰησοῦ n. gen. masc. sg. Ἰησοῦς Jesus
Χριστοῦ n. gen. masc. sg. Χριστός Christ
διὰ prep. διά (+gen) by, through, with, in, of, (+acc) for, because of, for a cause
θελήματος n. gen. neut. sg. θέλημα will, desire, pleasure
Θεοῦ n. gen. masc. sg. θεός God, god
τοῖς art. dat. masc. pl. ὁ ἡ τό the, this, that, he, she, it
ἁγίοις adj. dat. masc. pl. ἅγιος Holy, holy, saint, Holy One, holy thing, most holy
τοῖς art. dat. masc. pl. ὁ ἡ τό the, this, that, he, she, it
ἐν prep. ἐν (+dat) in, by, with, among, at, on, through, to, within, into, of, for
Ἐφέσῳ n. dat. fem. sg. Ἔφεσος Ephesus
καὶ conj. καί and, even, also, but
πιστοῖς adj. dat. masc. pl. πιστός faithful, believing, true, sure
ἐν prep. ἐν (+dat) in, by, with, among, at, on, through, to, within, into, of, for
Χριστῷ n. dat. masc. sg. Χριστός Christ
Ἰησοῦ n. dat. masc. sg. Ἰησοῦς Jesus
2 χάρις n. nom. fem. sg. χάρις grace, thank, favour, pleasure
ὑμῖν pron. dat. 2p. pl. σύ thou, you
καὶ conj. καί and, even, also, but
εἰρήνη n. nom. fem. sg. εἰρήνη peace, quietness, rest
ἀπὸ prep. ἀπό (+gen) from, of, out of, since, for, off, at, by, in, on
Θεοῦ n. gen. masc. sg. θεός God, god
πατρὸς n. gen. masc. sg. πατήρ Father, father, parent
ἡμῶν pron. gen. 1p. pl. ἐγώ I
καὶ conj. καί and, even, also, but
Κυρίου n. gen. masc. sg. κύριος Lord, lord, master, sir, LORD, God, Master, owner
Ἰησοῦ n. gen. masc. sg. Ἰησοῦς Jesus
Χριστοῦ n. gen. masc. sg. Χριστός Christ
3 Εὐλογητὸς adj. nom. masc. sg. εὐλογητός blessed
ὁ art. nom. masc. sg. ὁ ἡ τό the, this, that, he, she, it
Θεὸς n. nom. masc. sg. θεός God, god
καὶ conj. καί and, even, also, but
πατὴρ n. nom. masc. sg. πατήρ Father, father, parent
τοῦ art. gen. masc. sg. ὁ ἡ τό the, this, that, he, she, it
Κυρίου n. gen. masc. sg. κύριος Lord, lord, master, sir, LORD, God, Master, owner
ἡμῶν pron. gen. 1p. pl. ἐγώ I
Ἰησοῦ n. gen. masc. sg. Ἰησοῦς Jesus
Χριστοῦ n. gen. masc. sg. Χριστός Christ
ὁ art. nom. masc. sg. ὁ ἡ τό the, this, that, he, she, it
ἡμᾶς pron. acc. 1p. pl. ἐγώ I
ἐν prep. ἐν (+dat) in, by, with, among, at, on, through, to, within, into, of, for
πάσῃ adj. dat. fem. sg. πᾶς πᾶσα πᾶν all, every, whosoever, every one, no, whole, any
εὐλογίᾳ n. dat. fem. sg. εὐλογία blessing, bounty, matter of bounty, fair speech
πνευματικῇ adj. dat. fem. sg. πνευματικός spiritual
ἐν prep. ἐν (+dat) in, by, with, among, at, on, through, to, within, into, of, for
τοῖς art. dat. neut. pl. ὁ ἡ τό the, this, that, he, she, it

ἐπουρανίοις adj. dat. neut. pl. ἐπουράνιος heavenly, celestial, high, in heaven
ἐν prep. ἐν (+dat) in, by, with, among, at, on, through, to, within, into, of, for
Χριστῷ n. dat. masc. sg. Χριστός Christ
4 καθὼς adv. καθώς as, even as, according as, according to
ἡμᾶς pron. acc. 1p. pl. ἐγώ I
ἐν prep. ἐν (+dat) in, by, with, among, at, on, through, to, within, into, of, for
αὐτῷ pron. dat. masc. 3p. sg. αὐτός ή ό self, of oneself, even, very, the same, he, she, it
πρὸ prep. πρό (+gen) before, above
καταβολῆς n. gen. fem. sg. καταβολή foundation
κόσμου n. gen. masc. sg. κόσμος world, adorning
ἡμᾶς pron. acc. 1p. pl. ἐγώ I
ἁγίους adj. acc. masc. pl. ἅγιος Holy, holy, saint, Holy One, holy thing, most holy
καὶ conj. καί and, even, also, but
ἀμώμους adj. acc. masc. pl. ἄμωμος without blame, without fault, without spot
κατενώπιον prep. κατενώπιον (+gen) before, before the presence, in the sight, in sight
αὐτοῦ pron. gen. masc. 3p. sg. αὐτός ή ό self, of oneself, even, very, the same, he, she, it
ἐν prep. ἐν (+dat) in, by, with, among, at, on, through, to, within, into, of, for
ἀγάπῃ n. dat. fem. sg. ἀγάπη love, charity, feast of charity
5 ἡμᾶς pron. acc. 1p. pl. ἐγώ I
εἰς prep. εἰς (+acc) into, to, unto, for, in, on, toward, against, upon, at, among
υἱοθεσίαν n. acc. fem. sg. υἱοθεσία adoption, adoption of children, adoption of sons
διὰ prep. διά (+gen) by, through, with, in, of, (+acc) for, because of, for a cause
Ἰησοῦ n. gen. masc. sg. Ἰησοῦς Jesus
Χριστοῦ n. gen. masc. sg. Χριστός Christ
εἰς prep. εἰς (+acc) into, to, unto, for, in, on, toward, against, upon, at, among
αὐτόν pron. acc. masc. 3p. sg. αὐτός ή ό self, of oneself, even, very, the same, he, she, it
κατὰ prep. κατά (+gen) against, by, throughout, down, (+acc) according to, after, with
τὴν art. acc. fem. sg. ὁ ἡ τό the, this, that, he, she, it
εὐδοκίαν n. acc. fem. sg. εὐδοκία good pleasure, good will, desire
τοῦ art. gen. neut. sg. ὁ ἡ τό the, this, that, he, she, it
θελήματος n. gen. neut. sg. θέλημα will, desire, pleasure
αὐτοῦ pron. gen. masc. 3p. sg. αὐτός ή ό self, of oneself, even, very, the same, he, she, it
6 εἰς prep. εἰς (+acc) into, to, unto, for, in, on, toward, against, upon, at, among
ἔπαινον n. acc. masc. sg. ἔπαινος praise
δόξης n. gen. fem. sg. δόξα glory, honour, praise, dignity, worship
τῆς art. gen. fem. sg. ὁ ἡ τό the, this, that, he, she, it
χάριτος n. gen. fem. sg. χάρις grace, thank, favour, pleasure
αὐτοῦ pron. gen. masc. 3p. sg. αὐτός ή ό self, of oneself, even, very, the same, he, she, it
ἐν prep. ἐν (+dat) in, by, with, among, at, on, through, to, within, into, of, for
ᾗ relative pron. dat. fem. sg. ὅς ἥ ὅ who, which, what, that
ἡμᾶς pron. acc. 1p. pl. ἐγώ I
ἐν prep. ἐν (+dat) in, by, with, among, at, on, through, to, within, into, of, for
τῷ art. dat. masc. sg. ὁ ἡ τό the, this, that, he, she, it
7 ἐν prep. ἐν (+dat) in, by, with, among, at, on, through, to, within, into, of, for
ᾧ relative pron. dat. masc. sg. ὅς ἥ ὅ who, which, what, that
τὴν art. acc. fem. sg. ὁ ἡ τό the, this, that, he, she, it
ἀπολύτρωσιν n. acc. fem. sg. ἀπολύτρωσις redemption, deliverance
διὰ prep. διά (+gen) by, through, with, in, of, (+acc) for, because of, for a cause
τοῦ art. gen. neut. sg. ὁ ἡ τό the, this, that, he, she, it
αἵματος n. gen. neut. sg. αἷμα blood
αὐτοῦ pron. gen. masc. 3p. sg. αὐτός ή ό self, of oneself, even, very, the same, he, she, it
τὴν art. acc. fem. sg. ὁ ἡ τό the, this, that, he, she, it
ἄφεσιν n. acc. fem. sg. ἄφεσις remission, forgiveness, deliverance, liberty
τῶν art. gen. neut. pl. ὁ ἡ τό the, this, that, he, she, it
παραπτωμάτων n. gen. neut. pl. παράπτωμα trespass, offence, sin, fall, fault

κατὰ prep. κατά (+gen) against, by, throughout, down, (+acc) according to, after, with
τὸν art. acc. masc. sg. ὁ ἡ τό the, this, that, he, she, it
πλοῦτον n. acc. masc. sg. πλοῦτος riches
τῆς art. gen. fem. sg. ὁ ἡ τό the, this, that, he, she, it
χάριτος n. gen. fem. sg. χάρις grace, thank, favour, pleasure
αὐτοῦ pron. gen. masc. 3p. sg. αὐτός ή ό self, of oneself, even, very, the same, he, she, it
8 ἧς relative pron. gen. fem. sg. ὅς ἥ ὅ who, which, what, that
εἰς prep. εἰς (+acc) into, to, unto, for, in, on, toward, against, upon, at, among
ἡμᾶς pron. acc. 1p. pl. ἐγώ I
ἐν prep. ἐν (+dat) in, by, with, among, at, on, through, to, within, into, of, for
πάσῃ adj. dat. fem. sg. πᾶς πᾶσα πᾶν all, every, whosoever, every one, no, whole, any
σοφίᾳ n. dat. fem. sg. σοφία wisdom
καὶ conj. καί and, even, also, but
φρονήσει n. dat. fem. sg. φρόνησις prudence, wisdom
9 ἡμῖν pron. dat. 1p. pl. ἐγώ I
τὸ art. acc. neut. sg. ὁ ἡ τό the, this, that, he, she, it
μυστήριον n. acc. neut. sg. μυστήριον mystery
τοῦ art. gen. neut. sg. ὁ ἡ τό the, this, that, he, she, it
θελήματος n. gen. neut. sg. θέλημα will, desire, pleasure
αὐτοῦ pron. gen. masc. 3p. sg. αὐτός ή ό self, of oneself, even, very, the same, he, she, it
κατὰ prep. κατά (+gen) against, by, throughout, down, (+acc) according to, after, with
τὴν art. acc. fem. sg. ὁ ἡ τό the, this, that, he, she, it
εὐδοκίαν n. acc. fem. sg. εὐδοκία good pleasure, good will, desire
αὐτοῦ pron. gen. masc. 3p. sg. αὐτός ή ό self, of oneself, even, very, the same, he, she, it
ἣν relative pron. acc. fem. sg. ὅς ἥ ὅ who, which, what, that
προέθετο 2aor. mid. ind. 3p. sg. προτίθημι purpose, set forth
ἐν prep. ἐν (+dat) in, by, with, among, at, on, through, to, within, into, of, for
αὐτῷ pron. dat. masc. 3p. sg. αὐτός ή ό self, of oneself, even, very, the same, he, she, it
10 εἰς prep. εἰς (+acc) into, to, unto, for, in, on, toward, against, upon, at, among
οἰκονομίαν n. acc. fem. sg. οἰκονομία dispensation, stewardship, edifying
τοῦ art. gen. neut. sg. ὁ ἡ τό the, this, that, he, she, it
πληρώματος n. gen. neut. sg. πλήρωμα fullness, fulfilling, full
τῶν art. gen. masc. pl. ὁ ἡ τό the, this, that, he, she, it
καιρῶν n. gen. masc. pl. καιρός time, season, due time, opportunity
τὰ art. acc. neut. pl. ὁ ἡ τό the, this, that, he, she, it
πάντα adj. acc. neut. pl. πᾶς πᾶσα πᾶν all, every, whosoever, every one, no, whole, any
ἐν prep. ἐν (+dat) in, by, with, among, at, on, through, to, within, into, of, for
τῷ art. dat. masc. sg. ὁ ἡ τό the, this, that, he, she, it
Χριστῷ n. dat. masc. sg. Χριστός Christ
τά art. acc. neut. pl. ὁ ἡ τό the, this, that, he, she, it
τε conj. τέ and, both, also
ἐν prep. ἐν (+dat) in, by, with, among, at, on, through, to, within, into, of, for
τοῖς art. dat. masc. pl. ὁ ἡ τό the, this, that, he, she, it
οὐρανοῖς n. dat. masc. pl. οὐρανός heaven, air, sky
καὶ conj. καί and, even, also, but
τὰ art. acc. neut. pl. ὁ ἡ τό the, this, that, he, she, it
ἐπὶ prep. ἐπί (+gen) on, in, upon, (+dat) in, at, for, upon, (+acc) on, upon, unto, to, against
τῆς art. gen. fem. sg. ὁ ἡ τό the, this, that, he, she, it
γῆς n. gen. fem. sg. γῆ earth, land, ground, country
ἐν prep. ἐν (+dat) in, by, with, among, at, on, through, to, within, into, of, for
αὐτῷ pron. dat. masc. 3p. sg. αὐτός ή ό self, of oneself, even, very, the same, he, she, it
11 ἐν prep. ἐν (+dat) in, by, with, among, at, on, through, to, within, into, of, for
ᾧ relative pron. dat. masc. sg. ὅς ἥ ὅ who, which, what, that
καὶ conj. καί and, even, also, but
κατὰ prep. κατά (+gen) against, by, throughout, down, (+acc) according to, after, with

πρόθεσιν n. acc. fem. sg. πρόθεσις purpose, shew, shewbread
τοῦ art. gen. masc. sg. ὁ ἡ τό the, this, that, he, she, it
τὰ art. acc. neut. pl. ὁ ἡ τό the, this, that, he, she, it
πάντα adj. acc. neut. pl. πᾶς πᾶσα πᾶν all, every, whosoever, every one, no, whole, any
κατὰ prep. κατά (+gen) against, by, throughout, down, (+acc) according to, after, with
τὴν art. acc. fem. sg. ὁ ἡ τό the, this, that, he, she, it
βουλὴν n. acc. fem. sg. βουλή counsel, advise, will
τοῦ art. gen. neut. sg. ὁ ἡ τό the, this, that, he, she, it
θελήματος n. gen. neut. sg. θέλημα will, desire, pleasure
αὐτοῦ pron. gen. masc. 3p. sg. αὐτός ή ό self, of oneself, even, very, the same, he, she, it
12 εἰς prep. εἰς (+acc) into, to, unto, for, in, on, toward, against, upon, at, among
τὸ art. acc. neut. sg. ὁ ἡ τό the, this, that, he, she, it
ἡμᾶς pron. acc. 1p. pl. ἐγώ I
εἰς prep. εἰς (+acc) into, to, unto, for, in, on, toward, against, upon, at, among
ἔπαινον n. acc. masc. sg. ἔπαινος praise
τῆς art. gen. fem. sg. ὁ ἡ τό the, this, that, he, she, it
δόξης n. gen. fem. sg. δόξα glory, honour, praise, dignity, worship
αὐτοῦ pron. gen. masc. 3p. sg. αὐτός ή ό self, of oneself, even, very, the same, he, she, it
τοὺς art. acc. masc. pl. ὁ ἡ τό the, this, that, he, she, it
ἐν prep. ἐν (+dat) in, by, with, among, at, on, through, to, within, into, of, for
τῷ art. dat. masc. sg. ὁ ἡ τό the, this, that, he, she, it
Χριστῷ n. dat. masc. sg. Χριστός Christ
13 ἐν prep. ἐν (+dat) in, by, with, among, at, on, through, to, within, into, of, for
ᾧ relative pron. dat. masc. sg. ὅς ἥ ὅ who, which, what, that
καὶ conj. καί and, even, also, but
ὑμεῖς pron. nom. 2p. pl. σύ thou, you
τὸν art. acc. masc. sg. ὁ ἡ τό the, this, that, he, she, it
λόγον n. acc. masc. sg. λόγος word, saying, account, speech, thing, matter
τῆς art. gen. fem. sg. ὁ ἡ τό the, this, that, he, she, it
ἀληθείας n. gen. fem. sg. ἀλήθεια truth, verity
τὸ art. acc. neut. sg. ὁ ἡ τό the, this, that, he, she, it
εὐαγγέλιον n. acc. neut. sg. εὐαγγέλιον gospel
τῆς art. gen. fem. sg. ὁ ἡ τό the, this, that, he, she, it
σωτηρίας n. gen. fem. sg. σωτηρία salvation, deliver, health, saving
ὑμῶν pron. gen. 2p. pl. σύ thou, you
ἐν prep. ἐν (+dat) in, by, with, among, at, on, through, to, within, into, of, for
ᾧ relative pron. dat. masc. sg. ὅς ἥ ὅ who, which, what, that
καὶ conj. καί and, even, also, but
τῷ art. dat. neut. sg. ὁ ἡ τό the, this, that, he, she, it
Πνεύματι n. dat. neut. sg. πνεῦμα spirit, Spirit, Ghost, ghost, life. of the spirit, wind
τῆς art. gen. fem. sg. ὁ ἡ τό the, this, that, he, she, it
ἐπαγγελίας n. gen. fem. sg. ἐπαγγελία promise, message
τῷ art. dat. neut. sg. ὁ ἡ τό the, this, that, he, she, it
Ἁγίῳ adj. dat. neut. sg. ἅγιος Holy, holy, saint, Holy One, holy thing, most holy
14 ὅς relative pron. nom. masc. sg. ὅς ἥ ὅ who, which, what, that
ἀρραβὼν n. nom. masc. sg. ἀρραβών earnest
τῆς art. gen. fem. sg. ὁ ἡ τό the, this, that, he, she, it
κληρονομίας n. gen. fem. sg. κληρονομία inheritance
ἡμῶν pron. gen. 1p. pl. ἐγώ I
εἰς prep. εἰς (+acc) into, to, unto, for, in, on, toward, against, upon, at, among
ἀπολύτρωσιν n. acc. fem. sg. ἀπολύτρωσις redemption, deliverance
τῆς art. gen. fem. sg. ὁ ἡ τό the, this, that, he, she, it
περιποιήσεως n. gen. fem. sg. περιποίησις obtain, obtaining, purchased possession
εἰς prep. εἰς (+acc) into, to, unto, for, in, on, toward, against, upon, at, among
ἔπαινον n. acc. masc. sg. ἔπαινος praise

τῆς art. gen. fem. sg. ὁ ἡ τό the, this, that, he, she, it
δόξης n. gen. fem. sg. δόξα glory, honour, praise, dignity, worship
αὐτοῦ pron. gen. masc. 3p. sg. αὐτός ἡ ὁ self, of oneself, even, very, the same, he, she, it
15 Διὰ prep. διά (+gen) by, through, with, in, of, (+acc) for, because of, for a cause
τοῦτο demo. pron. acc. neut. sg. οὗτος αὕτη τοῦτο this, the same, this same, he, she, it
κἀγὼ pron. nom. 1p. sg. κἀγώ and I, I also, so I, even as I
τὴν art. acc. fem. sg. ὁ ἡ τό the, this, that, he, she, it
καθ' prep. κατά (+gen) against, by, throughout, down, (+acc) according to, after, with
ὑμᾶς pron. acc. 2p. pl. σύ thou, you
πίστιν n. acc. fem. sg. πίστις faith, assurance, belief, fidelity
ἐν prep. ἐν (+dat) in, by, with, among, at, on, through, to, within, into, of, for
τῷ art. dat. masc. sg. ὁ ἡ τό the, this, that, he, she, it
Κυρίῳ n. dat. masc. sg. κύριος Lord, lord, master, sir, LORD, God, Master, owner
'Ιησοῦ n. dat. masc. sg. 'Ιησοῦς Jesus
καὶ conj. καί and, even, also, but
τὴν art. acc. fem. sg. ὁ ἡ τό the, this, that, he, she, it
ἀγάπην n. acc. fem. sg. ἀγάπη love, charity, feast of charity
τὴν art. acc. fem. sg. ὁ ἡ τό the, this, that, he, she, it
εἰς prep. εἰς (+acc) into, to, unto, for, in, on, toward, against, upon, at, among
πάντας adj. acc. masc. pl. πᾶς πᾶσα πᾶν all, every, whosoever, every one, no, whole, any
τοὺς art. acc. masc. pl. ὁ ἡ τό the, this, that, he, she, it
ἁγίους adj. acc. masc. pl. ἅγιος Holy, holy, saint, Holy One, holy thing, most holy
16 οὐ particle of negation. οὐ οὐκ οὐχ not, no, neither, none, nay, nor, never, nothing
ὑπὲρ prep. ὑπέρ (+gen) for, of, for the sake of, (+acc) above, more than
ὑμῶν pron. gen. 2p. pl. σύ thou, you
μνείαν n. acc. fem. sg. μνεία mention, remembrance
ὑμῶν pron. gen. 2p. pl. σύ thou, you
ἐπὶ prep. ἐπί (+gen) on, in, upon, (+dat) in, at, for, upon, (+acc) on, upon, unto, to, against
τῶν art. gen. fem. pl. ὁ ἡ τό the, this, that, he, she, it
προσευχῶν n. gen. fem. pl. προσευχή prayer
μου pron. gen. 1p. sg. ἐγώ I
17 ἵνα conj. ἵνα that, to, lest, for to, so that, albeit, because, for, so as
ὁ art. nom. masc. sg. ὁ ἡ τό the, this, that, he, she, it
Θεὸς n. nom. masc. sg. θεός God, god
τοῦ art. gen. masc. sg. ὁ ἡ τό the, this, that, he, she, it
Κυρίου n. gen. masc. sg. κύριος Lord, lord, master, sir, LORD, God, Master, owner
ἡμῶν pron. gen. 1p. pl. ἐγώ I
'Ιησοῦ n. gen. masc. sg. 'Ιησοῦς Jesus
Χριστοῦ n. gen. masc. sg. Χριστός Christ
ὁ art. nom. masc. sg. ὁ ἡ τό the, this, that, he, she, it
πατὴρ n. nom. masc. sg. πατήρ Father, father, parent
τῆς art. gen. fem. sg. ὁ ἡ τό the, this, that, he, she, it
δόξης n. gen. fem. sg. δόξα glory, honour, praise, dignity, worship
ὑμῖν pron. dat. 2p. pl. σύ thou, you
πνεῦμα n. acc. neut. sg. πνεῦμα spirit, Spirit, Ghost, ghost, life. of the spirit, wind
σοφίας n. gen. fem. sg. σοφία wisdom
καὶ conj. καί and, even, also, but
ἀποκαλύψεως n. gen. fem. sg. ἀποκάλυψις revelation, appearing, coming, manifestation
ἐν prep. ἐν (+dat) in, by, with, among, at, on, through, to, within, into, of, for
ἐπιγνώσει n. dat. fem. sg. ἐπίγνωσις knowledge, acknowledging, acknowledgement
αὐτοῦ pron. gen. masc. 3p. sg. αὐτός ἡ ὁ self, of oneself, even, very, the same, he, she, it
18 τοὺς art. acc. masc. pl. ὁ ἡ τό the, this, that, he, she, it
ὀφθαλμοὺς n. acc. masc. pl. ὀφθαλμός eye, sighteye, sight
τῆς art. gen. fem. sg. ὁ ἡ τό the, this, that, he, she, it
διανοίας n. gen. fem. sg. διάνοια mind, understanding, imagination

ὑμῶν pron. gen. 2p. pl. σύ thou, you
εἰς prep. εἰς (+acc) into, to, unto, for, in, on, toward, against, upon, at, among
τὸ art. acc. neut. sg. ὁ ἡ τό the, this, that, he, she, it
ὑμᾶς pron. acc. 2p. pl. σύ thou, you
τίς interrog. pron. nom. fem. sg. τίς what, who, why, where, which, how
ἡ art. nom. fem. sg. ὁ ἡ τό the, this, that, he, she, it
ἐλπὶς n. nom. fem. sg. ἐλπίς hope, faith
τῆς art. gen. fem. sg. ὁ ἡ τό the, this, that, he, she, it
κλήσεως n. gen. fem. sg. κλῆσις calling, vocation
αὐτοῦ pron. gen. masc. 3p. sg. αὐτός ή ό self, of oneself, even, very, the same, he, she, it
καὶ conj. καί and, even, also, but
τίς interrog. pron. nom. masc. sg. τίς what, who, why, where, which, how
ὁ art. nom. masc. sg. ὁ ἡ τό the, this, that, he, she, it
πλοῦτος n. nom. masc. sg. πλοῦτος riches
τῆς art. gen. fem. sg. ὁ ἡ τό the, this, that, he, she, it
δόξης n. gen. fem. sg. δόξα glory, honour, praise, dignity, worship
τῆς art. gen. fem. sg. ὁ ἡ τό the, this, that, he, she, it
κληρονομίας n. gen. fem. sg. κληρονομία inheritance
αὐτοῦ pron. gen. masc. 3p. sg. αὐτός ή ό self, of oneself, even, very, the same, he, she, it
ἐν prep. ἐν (+dat) in, by, with, among, at, on, through, to, within, into, of, for
τοῖς art. dat. masc. pl. ὁ ἡ τό the, this, that, he, she, it
ἁγίοις adj. dat. masc. pl. ἅγιος Holy, holy, saint, Holy One, holy thing, most holy
19 καὶ conj. καί and, even, also, but
τί interrog. pron. nom. neut. sg. τίς what, who, why, where, which, how
τὸ art. nom. neut. sg. ὁ ἡ τό the, this, that, he, she, it
μέγεθος n. nom. neut. sg. μέγεθος greatness
τῆς art. gen. fem. sg. ὁ ἡ τό the, this, that, he, she, it
δυνάμεως n. gen. fem. sg. δύναμις power, mighty work, miracle, strength, might
αὐτοῦ pron. gen. masc. 3p. sg. αὐτός ή ό self, of oneself, even, very, the same, he, she, it
εἰς prep. εἰς (+acc) into, to, unto, for, in, on, toward, against, upon, at, among
ἡμᾶς pron. acc. 1p. pl. ἐγώ I
τοὺς art. acc. masc. pl. ὁ ἡ τό the, this, that, he, she, it
κατὰ prep. κατά (+gen) against, by, throughout, down, (+acc) according to, after, with
τὴν art. acc. fem. sg. ὁ ἡ τό the, this, that, he, she, it
ἐνέργειαν n. acc. fem. sg. ἐνέργεια working, effectual working, operation
τοῦ art. gen. neut. sg. ὁ ἡ τό the, this, that, he, she, it
κράτους n. gen. neut. sg. κράτος power, dominion, might, strength
τῆς art. gen. fem. sg. ὁ ἡ τό the, this, that, he, she, it
ἰσχύος n. gen. fem. sg. ἰσχύς strength, might, power, ability
αὐτοῦ pron. gen. masc. 3p. sg. αὐτός ή ό self, of oneself, even, very, the same, he, she, it
20 ἣν relative pron. acc. fem. sg. ὅς ἥ ὅ who, which, what, that
ἐν prep. ἐν (+dat) in, by, with, among, at, on, through, to, within, into, of, for
τῷ art. dat. masc. sg. ὁ ἡ τό the, this, that, he, she, it
Χριστῷ n. dat. masc. sg. Χριστός Christ
αὐτὸν pron. acc. masc. 3p. sg. αὐτός ή ό self, of oneself, even, very, the same, he, she, it
ἐκ prep. ἐκ ἐκ ἐξ (+gen) of, from, out of, by, on, with, in, among, through
νεκρῶν adj. gen. masc. pl. νεκρός dead
καὶ conj. καί and, even, also, but
ἐν prep. ἐν (+dat) in, by, with, among, at, on, through, to, within, into, of, for
δεξιᾷ adj. dat. fem. sg. δεξιός right, right hand, right side
αὐτοῦ pron. gen. masc. 3p. sg. αὐτός ή ό self, of oneself, even, very, the same, he, she, it
ἐν prep. ἐν (+dat) in, by, with, among, at, on, through, to, within, into, of, for
τοῖς art. dat. neut. pl. ὁ ἡ τό the, this, that, he, she, it
ἐπουρανίοις adj. dat. neut. pl. ἐπουράνιος heavenly, celestial, high, in heaven
21 ὑπεράνω prep. ὑπεράνω (+gen) far above, over, above

πάσης adj. gen. fem. sg. πᾶς πᾶσα πᾶν all, every, whosoever, every one, no, whole, any
ἀρχῆς n. gen. fem. sg. ἀρχή beginning, principality, corner, first, magistrate, rule
καὶ conj. καί and, even, also, but
ἐξουσίας n. gen. fem. sg. ἐξουσία power, authority, right, strength, jurisdiction
καὶ conj. καί and, even, also, but
δυνάμεως n. gen. fem. sg. δύναμις power, mighty work, miracle, strength, might
καὶ conj. καί and, even, also, but
κυριότητος n. gen. fem. sg. κυριότης dominion, government
καὶ conj. καί and, even, also, but
παντὸς adj. gen. neut. sg. πᾶς πᾶσα πᾶν all, every, whosoever, every one, no, whole, any
ὀνόματος n. gen. neut. sg. ὄνομα name, call, surname
οὐ particle of negation. οὐ οὐκ οὐχ not, no, neither, none, nay, nor, never, nothing
μόνον adv. μόνος only, alone, by oneself
ἐν prep. ἐν (+dat) in, by, with, among, at, on, through, to, within, into, of, for
τῷ art. dat. masc. sg. ὁ ἡ τό the, this, that, he, she, it
αἰῶνι n. dat. masc. sg. αἰών world, ever, ever and ever, evermore, age, eternal
τούτῳ demo. pron. dat. masc. sg. οὗτος αὕτη τοῦτο this, the same, this same, he, she, it
ἀλλὰ conj. ἀλλά but, yea, yet, nevertheless, howbeit, nay, therefore
καὶ conj. καί and, even, also, but
ἐν prep. ἐν (+dat) in, by, with, among, at, on, through, to, within, into, of, for
τῷ art. dat. masc. sg. ὁ ἡ τό the, this, that, he, she, it
22 καὶ conj. καί and, even, also, but
πάντα adj. acc. neut. pl. πᾶς πᾶσα πᾶν all, every, whosoever, every one, no, whole, any
ὑπὸ prep. ὑπό (+gen) of, by, with, from, among, (+acc) under
τοὺς art. acc. masc. pl. ὁ ἡ τό the, this, that, he, she, it
πόδας n. acc. masc. pl. πούς foot
αὐτοῦ pron. gen. masc. 3p. sg. αὐτός ἡ ὁ self, of oneself, even, very, the same, he, she, it
καὶ conj. καί and, even, also, but
αὐτὸν pron. acc. masc. 3p. sg. αὐτός ἡ ὁ self, of oneself, even, very, the same, he, she, it
κεφαλὴν n. acc. fem. sg. κεφαλή head
ὑπὲρ prep. ὑπέρ (+gen) for, of, for the sake of, (+acc) above, more than
πάντα adj. acc. neut. pl. πᾶς πᾶσα πᾶν all, every, whosoever, every one, no, whole, any
τῇ art. dat. fem. sg. ὁ ἡ τό the, this, that, he, she, it
ἐκκλησίᾳ n. dat. fem. sg. ἐκκλησία church, assembly
23 ἥτις relative pron. nom. fem. sg. ὅστις which, who, whosoever, that, whatsoever
τὸ art. nom. neut. sg. ὁ ἡ τό the, this, that, he, she, it
σῶμα n. nom. neut. sg. σῶμα body, bodily, slave
αὐτοῦ pron. gen. masc. 3p. sg. αὐτός ἡ ὁ self, of oneself, even, very, the same, he, she, it
τὸ art. nom. neut. sg. ὁ ἡ τό the, this, that, he, she, it
πλήρωμα n. nom. neut. sg. πλήρωμα fullness, fulfilling, full
τοῦ art. gen. masc. sg. ὁ ἡ τό the, this, that, he, she, it
πάντα adj. acc. neut. pl. πᾶς πᾶσα πᾶν all, every, whosoever, every one, no, whole, any
ἐν prep. ἐν (+dat) in, by, with, among, at, on, through, to, within, into, of, for
πᾶσι adj. dat. neut. pl. πᾶς πᾶσα πᾶν all, every, whosoever, every one, no, whole, any

2

1 Καὶ conj. καί and, even, also, but
ὑμᾶς pron. acc. 2p. pl. σύ thou, you
νεκροὺς adj. acc. masc. pl. νεκρός dead
τοῖς art. dat. neut. pl. ὁ ἡ τό the, this, that, he, she, it
παραπτώμασι n. dat. neut. pl. παράπτωμα trespass, offence, sin, fall, fault
καὶ conj. καί and, even, also, but
ταῖς art. dat. fem. pl. ὁ ἡ τό the, this, that, he, she, it
ἁμαρτίαις n. dat. fem. pl. ἁμαρτία sin, offence, sinful

2 ἐν prep. ἐν (+dat) in, by, with, among, at, on, through, to, within, into, of, for
αἷς relative pron. dat. fem. pl. ὅς ἥ ὅ who, which, what, that
ποτε adv. ποτέ in time past, at any time, sometimes, in old time, once, when
κατὰ prep. κατά (+gen) against, by, throughout, down, (+acc) according to, after, with
τὸν art. acc. masc. sg. ὁ ἡ τό the, this, that, he, she, it
αἰῶνα n. acc. masc. sg. αἰών ever, ever and ever, evermore, age, eternal, world
τοῦ art. gen. masc. sg. ὁ ἡ τό the, this, that, he, she, it
κόσμου n. gen. masc. sg. κόσμος world, adorning
τούτου demo. pron. gen. masc. sg. οὗτος αὕτη τοῦτο this, the same, this same, he, she, it
κατὰ prep. κατά (+gen) against, by, throughout, down, (+acc) according to, after, with
τὸν art. acc. masc. sg. ὁ ἡ τό the, this, that, he, she, it
ἄρχοντα n. acc. masc. sg. ἄρχων ruler, prince, chief, magistrate, chief ruler
τῆς art. gen. fem. sg. ὁ ἡ τό the, this, that, he, she, it
ἐξουσίας n. gen. fem. sg. ἐξουσία power, authority, right, strength, jurisdiction
τοῦ art. gen. masc. sg. ὁ ἡ τό the, this, that, he, she, it
ἀέρος n. gen. masc. sg. ἀήρ air
τοῦ art. gen. neut. sg. ὁ ἡ τό the, this, that, he, she, it
πνεύματος n. gen. neut. sg. πνεῦμα spirit, Spirit, Ghost, ghost, life. of the spirit, wind
τοῦ art. gen. masc. sg. ὁ ἡ τό the, this, that, he, she, it
νῦν adv. νῦν now, henceforth, present, this time
ἐν prep. ἐν (+dat) in, by, with, among, at, on, through, to, within, into, of, for
τοῖς art. dat. masc. pl. ὁ ἡ τό the, this, that, he, she, it
υἱοῖς n. dat. masc. pl. υἱός son, child, descendant, offspring, heir
τῆς art. gen. fem. sg. ὁ ἡ τό the, this, that, he, she, it
ἀπειθείας n. gen. fem. sg. ἀπείθεια unbelief, disobedience
3 ἐν prep. ἐν (+dat) in, by, with, among, at, on, through, to, within, into, of, for
οἷς relative pron. dat. masc. pl. ὅς ἥ ὅ who, which, what, that
καὶ conj. καί and, even, also, but
ἡμεῖς pron. nom. 1p. pl. ἐγώ I
πάντες adj. nom. masc. pl. πᾶς πᾶσα πᾶν all, every, whosoever, every one, no, whole, any
ποτε adv. ποτέ in time past, at any time, sometimes, in old time, once, when
ἐν prep. ἐν (+dat) in, by, with, among, at, on, through, to, within, into, of, for
ταῖς art. dat. fem. pl. ὁ ἡ τό the, this, that, he, she, it
ἐπιθυμίαις n. dat. fem. pl. ἐπιθυμία lust, concupiscence, desire
τῆς art. gen. fem. sg. ὁ ἡ τό the, this, that, he, she, it
σαρκὸς n. gen. fem. sg. σάρξ flesh, carnal
ἡμῶν pron. gen. 1p. pl. ἐγώ I
τὰ art. acc. neut. pl. ὁ ἡ τό the, this, that, he, she, it
θελήματα n. acc. neut. pl. θέλημα will, desire, pleasure
τῆς art. gen. fem. sg. ὁ ἡ τό the, this, that, he, she, it
σαρκὸς n. gen. fem. sg. σάρξ flesh, carnal
καὶ conj. καί and, even, also, but
τῶν art. gen. fem. pl. ὁ ἡ τό the, this, that, he, she, it
διανοιῶν n. gen. fem. pl. διάνοια mind, understanding, imagination
καὶ conj. καί and, even, also, but
τέκνα n. nom. neut. pl. τέκνον child, son, daughter
φύσει n. dat. fem. sg. φύσις nature
ὀργῆς n. gen. fem. sg. ὀργή wrath, anger, indignation, vengeance
ὡς adv. ὡς as, when, as it were, how, about, like, as soon as, even as, while
καὶ conj. καί and, even, also, but
οἱ art. nom. masc. pl. ὁ ἡ τό the, this, that, he, she, it
λοιποί adj. nom. masc. pl. λοιπός other, rest, remnant, residue, which remain
4 ὁ art. nom. masc. sg. ὁ ἡ τό the, this, that, he, she, it
δὲ conj. δέ but, and, now, also, to the contrary, rather, then
Θεὸς n. nom. masc. sg. θεός God, god

πλούσιος adj. nom. masc. sg. πλούσιος rich
ἐν prep. ἐν (+dat) in, by, with, among, at, on, through, to, within, into, of, for
ἐλέει n. dat. neut. sg. ἔλεος mercy
διὰ prep. διά (+gen) by, through, with, in, of, (+acc) for, because of, for a cause
τὴν art. acc. fem. sg. ὁ ἡ τό the, this, that, he, she, it
πολλὴν adj. acc. fem. sg. πολύς many, great, much, long, abundant
ἀγάπην n. acc. fem. sg. ἀγάπη love, charity, feast of charity
αὐτοῦ pron. gen. masc. 3p. sg. αὐτός ή ό self, of oneself, even, very, the same, he, she, it
ἣν relative pron. acc. fem. sg. ὅς ἥ ὅ who, which, what, that
ἡμᾶς pron. acc. 1p. pl. ἐγώ I
5 καὶ conj. καί and, even, also, but
ἡμᾶς pron. acc. 1p. pl. ἐγώ I
νεκροὺς adj. acc. masc. pl. νεκρός dead
τοῖς art. dat. neut. pl. ὁ ἡ τό the, this, that, he, she, it
παραπτώμασι n. dat. neut. pl. παράπτωμα trespass, offence, sin, fall, fault
τῷ art. dat. masc. sg. ὁ ἡ τό the, this, that, he, she, it
Χριστῷ n. dat. masc. sg. Χριστός Christ
χάριτί n. dat. fem. sg. χάρις grace, thank, favour, pleasure
6 καὶ conj. καί and, even, also, but
καὶ conj. καί and, even, also, but
ἐν prep. ἐν (+dat) in, by, with, among, at, on, through, to, within, into, of, for
τοῖς art. dat. neut. pl. ὁ ἡ τό the, this, that, he, she, it
ἐπουρανίοις adj. dat. neut. pl. ἐπουράνιος heavenly, celestial, high, in heaven
ἐν prep. ἐν (+dat) in, by, with, among, at, on, through, to, within, into, of, for
Χριστῷ n. dat. masc. sg. Χριστός Christ
Ἰησοῦ n. dat. masc. sg. Ἰησοῦς Jesus
7 ἵνα conj. ἵνα that, to, lest, for to, so that, albeit, because, for, so as
ἐν prep. ἐν (+dat) in, by, with, among, at, on, through, to, within, into, of, for
τοῖς art. dat. masc. pl. ὁ ἡ τό the, this, that, he, she, it
αἰῶσι n. dat. masc. pl. αἰών ever, ever and ever, evermore, age, eternal, world
τοῖς art. dat. masc. pl. ὁ ἡ τό the, this, that, he, she, it
τὸν art. acc. masc. sg. ὁ ἡ τό the, this, that, he, she, it
πλοῦτον n. acc. masc. sg. πλοῦτος riches
τῆς art. gen. fem. sg. ὁ ἡ τό the, this, that, he, she, it
χάριτος n. gen. fem. sg. χάρις grace, thank, favour, pleasure
αὐτοῦ pron. gen. masc. 3p. sg. αὐτός ή ό self, of oneself, even, very, the same, he, she, it
ἐν prep. ἐν (+dat) in, by, with, among, at, on, through, to, within, into, of, for
χρηστότητι n. dat. fem. sg. χρηστότης goodness, kindness, gentleness, good
ἐφ' prep. ἐπί (+gen) on, in, upon, (+dat) in, at, for, upon, (+acc) on, upon, unto, to, against
ἡμᾶς pron. acc. 1p. pl. ἐγώ I
ἐν prep. ἐν (+dat) in, by, with, among, at, on, through, to, within, into, of, for
Χριστῷ n. dat. masc. sg. Χριστός Christ
Ἰησοῦ n. dat. masc. sg. Ἰησοῦς Jesus
8 τῇ art. dat. fem. sg. ὁ ἡ τό the, this, that, he, she, it
γὰρ conj. γάρ for, and, because, but, indeed
χάριτί n. dat. fem. sg. χάρις grace, thank, favour, pleasure
διὰ prep. διά (+gen) by, through, with, in, of, (+acc) for, because of, for a cause
τῆς art. gen. fem. sg. ὁ ἡ τό the, this, that, he, she, it
πίστεως n. gen. fem. sg. πίστις faith, assurance, belief, fidelity
καὶ conj. καί and, even, also, but
τοῦτο demo. pron. nom. neut. sg. οὗτος αὕτη τοῦτο this, the same, this same, he, she, it
οὐκ particle of negation. οὐ οὐκ οὐχ not, no, neither, none, nay, nor, never, nothing
ἐξ prep. ἐκ ἐξ (+gen) of, from, out of, by, on, with, in, among, through
ὑμῶν pron. gen. 2p. pl. σύ thou, you
Θεοῦ n. gen. masc. sg. θεός God, god

τὸ art. nom. neut. sg. ὁ ἡ τό the, this, that, he, she, it
δῶρον n. nom. neut. sg. δῶρον gift, offering
9 οὐκ particle of negation. οὐ οὐκ οὐχ not, no, neither, none, nay, nor, never, nothing
ἐξ prep. ἐκ ἐξ (+gen) of, from, out of, by, on, with, in, among, through
ἔργων n. gen. neut. pl. ἔργον work, deed, doing labour
ἵνα conj. ἵνα that, to, lest, for to, so that, albeit, because, for, so as
μὴ particle of negation. μή not, no, lest, neither, none, nothing, nor, never, without
τις indefinite pron. nom. masc. sg. τὶς certain, some, any man, one, any thing
10 αὐτοῦ pron. gen. masc. 3p. sg. αὐτός ή ό self, of oneself, even, very, the same, he, she, it
γάρ conj. γάρ for, and, because, but, indeed
ποίημα n. nom. neut. sg. ποίημα thing that are made, workmanship
ἐν prep. ἐν (+dat) in, by, with, among, at, on, through, to, within, into, of, for
Χριστῷ n. dat. masc. sg. Χριστός Christ
Ἰησοῦ n. dat. masc. sg. Ἰησοῦς Jesus
ἐπὶ prep. ἐπί (+gen) on, in, upon, (+dat) in, at, for, upon, (+acc) on, upon, unto, to, against
ἔργοις n. dat. neut. pl. ἔργον work, deed, doing labour
ἀγαθοῖς adj. dat. neut. pl. ἀγαθός good, good thing, that which is good, well
οἷς relative pron. dat. neut. pl. ὅς ἥ ὅ who, which, what, that
ὁ art. nom. masc. sg. ὁ ἡ τό the, this, that, he, she, it
Θεὸς n. nom. masc. sg. θεός God, god
ἵνα conj. ἵνα that, to, lest, for to, so that, albeit, because, for, so as
ἐν prep. ἐν (+dat) in, by, with, among, at, on, through, to, within, into, of, for
αὐτοῖς pron. dat. neut. 3p. pl. αὐτός ή ό self, of oneself, even, very, the same, he, she, it
11 Διὸ conj. διό wherefore, therefore, for which cause
ὅτι conj. ὅτι that, for, because, how that, how, because that, for that, though
ὑμεῖς pron. nom. 2p. pl. σύ thou, you
ποτὲ adv. ποτέ in time past, at any time, sometimes, in old time, once, when
τὰ art. nom. neut. pl. ὁ ἡ τό the, this, that, he, she, it
ἔθνη n. nom. neut. pl. ἔθνος Gentile, nation, heathen, people
ἐν prep. ἐν (+dat) in, by, with, among, at, on, through, to, within, into, of, for
σαρκί n. dat. fem. sg. σάρξ flesh, carnal
οἱ art. nom. masc. pl. ὁ ἡ τό the, this, that, he, she, it
ἀκροβυστία n. nom. fem. sg. ἀκροβυστία uncircumcised, uncircumcision
ὑπὸ prep. ὑπό (+gen) of, by, with, from, among, (+acc) under
τῆς art. gen. fem. sg. ὁ ἡ τό the, this, that, he, she, it
περιτομῆς n. gen. fem. sg. περιτομή circumcision
ἐν prep. ἐν (+dat) in, by, with, among, at, on, through, to, within, into, of, for
σαρκί n. dat. fem. sg. σάρξ flesh, carnal
χειροποιήτου adj. gen. fem. sg. χειροποίητος made with hands, made by hands
12 ὅτι conj. ὅτι that, for, because, how that, how, because that, for that, though
ἐν prep. ἐν (+dat) in, by, with, among, at, on, through, to, within, into, of, for
τῷ art. dat. masc. sg. ὁ ἡ τό the, this, that, he, she, it
καιρῷ n. dat. masc. sg. καιρός time, season, due time, opportunity
ἐκείνῳ demo. pron. dat. masc. sg. ἐκεῖνος that, he, the same, that same
χωρὶς prep. χωρίς (+gen) without, beside. (adv.) by itself, apart, separately
Χριστοῦ n. gen. masc. sg. Χριστός Christ
τῆς art. gen. fem. sg. ὁ ἡ τό the, this, that, he, she, it
πολιτείας n. gen. fem. sg. πολιτεία freedom, citizenship, commonwealth, polity
τοῦ art. gen. masc. sg. ὁ ἡ τό the, this, that, he, she, it
Ἰσραὴλ pron. name. masc. inde. Ἰσραήλ Israel
καὶ conj. καί and, even, also, but
ξένοι adj. nom. masc. pl. ξένος stranger, strange, host
τῶν art. gen. fem. pl. ὁ ἡ τό the, this, that, he, she, it
διαθηκῶν n. gen. fem. pl. διαθήκη testament, covenant
τῆς art. gen. fem. sg. ὁ ἡ τό the, this, that, he, she, it

ἐπαγγελίας n. gen. fem. sg. ἐπαγγελία promise, message
ἐλπίδα n. acc. fem. sg. ἐλπίς hope, faith
μὴ particle of negation. μή not, no, lest, neither, none, nothing, nor, never, without
καὶ conj. καί and, even, also, but
ἄθεοι adj. nom. masc. pl. ἄθεος without God
ἐν prep. ἐν (+dat) in, by, with, among, at, on, through, to, within, into, of, for
τῷ art. dat. masc. sg. ὁ ἡ τό the, this, that, he, she, it
κόσμῳ n. dat. masc. sg. κόσμος world, adorning
13 νυνὶ adv. νυνί now
δὲ conj. δέ but, and, now, also, to the contrary, rather, then
ἐν prep. ἐν (+dat) in, by, with, among, at, on, through, to, within, into, of, for
Χριστῷ n. dat. masc. sg. Χριστός Christ
Ἰησοῦ n. dat. masc. sg. Ἰησοῦς Jesus
ὑμεῖς pron. nom. 2p. pl. σύ thou, you
οἵ art. nom. masc. pl. ὁ ἡ τό the, this, that, he, she, it
ποτε adv. ποτέ in time past, at any time, sometimes, in old time, once, when
μακρὰν adv. μακράν far, afar off, far off, good way off, great way off
ἐγγὺς adv. ἐγγύς nigh, at hand, near, nigh at hand, ready, nigh unto
ἐν prep. ἐν (+dat) in, by, with, among, at, on, through, to, within, into, of, for
τῷ art. dat. neut. sg. ὁ ἡ τό the, this, that, he, she, it
αἵματι n. dat. neut. sg. αἷμα blood
τοῦ art. gen. masc. sg. ὁ ἡ τό the, this, that, he, she, it
Χριστοῦ n. gen. masc. sg. Χριστός Christ
14 αὐτὸς pron. nom. masc. 3p. sg. αὐτός ἡ ὁ self, of oneself, even, very, the same, he, she, it
γάρ conj. γάρ for, and, because, but, indeed
ἡ art. nom. fem. sg. ὁ ἡ τό the, this, that, he, she, it
εἰρήνη n. nom. fem. sg. εἰρήνη peace, quietness, rest
ἡμῶν pron. gen. 1p. pl. ἐγώ I
ὁ art. nom. masc. sg. ὁ ἡ τό the, this, that, he, she, it
τὰ art. acc. neut. pl. ὁ ἡ τό the, this, that, he, she, it
ἀμφότερα adj. acc. neut. pl. ἀμφότερος both
ἓν num. acc. neut. sg. εἷς or ἕν one, other, some, any, only, a certain
καὶ conj. καί and, even, also, but
τὸ art. acc. neut. sg. ὁ ἡ τό the, this, that, he, she, it
μεσότοιχον n. acc. neut. sg. μεσότοιχον middle wall
τοῦ art. gen. masc. sg. ὁ ἡ τό the, this, that, he, she, it
φραγμοῦ n. gen. masc. sg. φραγμός hedge, partition
τὴν art. acc. fem. sg. ὁ ἡ τό the, this, that, he, she, it
ἔχθραν n. acc. fem. sg. ἔχθρα enmity, hatred
ἐν prep. ἐν (+dat) in, by, with, among, at, on, through, to, within, into, of, for
τῇ art. dat. fem. sg. ὁ ἡ τό the, this, that, he, she, it
σαρκὶ n. dat. fem. sg. σάρξ flesh, carnal
αὐτοῦ pron. gen. masc. 3p. sg. αὐτός ἡ ὁ self, of oneself, even, very, the same, he, she, it
15 τὸν art. acc. masc. sg. ὁ ἡ τό the, this, that, he, she, it
νόμον n. acc. masc. sg. νόμος law, the law
τῶν art. gen. fem. pl. ὁ ἡ τό the, this, that, he, she, it
ἐντολῶν n. gen. fem. pl. ἐντολή commandment, precept
ἐν prep. ἐν (+dat) in, by, with, among, at, on, through, to, within, into, of, for
δόγμασιν n. dat. neut. pl. δόγμα decree, ordinance
ἵνα conj. ἵνα that, to, lest, for to, so that, albeit, because, for, so as
τοὺς art. acc. masc. pl. ὁ ἡ τό the, this, that, he, she, it
δύο num. acc. masc. pl. δύο two, twain, both
ἐν prep. ἐν (+dat) in, by, with, among, at, on, through, to, within, into, of, for
ἑαυτῷ reflexive pron. dat. masc. 3p. sg. ἑαυτοῦ himself, herself, itself, yourself, ourselves
εἰς prep. εἰς (+acc) into, to, unto, for, in, on, toward, against, upon, at, among

ἕνα num. acc. masc. sg. εἷς or ἕν one, other, some, any, only, a certain
καινὸν adj. acc. masc. sg. καινός new
ἄνθρωπον n. acc. masc. sg. ἄνθρωπος man, human being, person, one, certain
εἰρήνην n. acc. fem. sg. εἰρήνη peace, quietness, rest
16 καὶ conj. καί and, even, also, but
τοὺς art. acc. masc. pl. ὁ ἡ τό the, this, that, he, she, it
ἀμφοτέρους adj. acc. masc. pl. ἀμφότερος both
ἐν prep. ἐν (+dat) in, by, with, among, at, on, through, to, within, into, of, for
ἑνὶ num. dat. neut. sg. εἷς or ἕν one, other, some, any, only, a certain
σώματι n. dat. neut. sg. σῶμα body, bodily, slave
τῷ art. dat. masc. sg. ὁ ἡ τό the, this, that, he, she, it
Θεῷ n. dat. masc. sg. θεός God, god
διὰ prep. διά (+gen) by, through, with, in, of, (+acc) for, because of, for a cause
τοῦ art. gen. masc. sg. ὁ ἡ τό the, this, that, he, she, it
σταυροῦ n. gen. masc. sg. σταυρός cross
τὴν art. acc. fem. sg. ὁ ἡ τό the, this, that, he, she, it
ἔχθραν n. acc. fem. sg. ἔχθρα enmity, hatred
ἐν prep. ἐν (+dat) in, by, with, among, at, on, through, to, within, into, of, for
αὐτῷ pron. dat. masc. 3p. sg. αὐτός ή ό self, of oneself, even, very, the same, he, she, it
17 καὶ conj. καί and, even, also, but
εἰρήνην n. acc. fem. sg. εἰρήνη peace, quietness, rest
ὑμῖν pron. dat. 2p. pl. σύ thou, you
τοῖς art. dat. masc. pl. ὁ ἡ τό the, this, that, he, she, it
μακρὰν adv. μακράν far, afar off, far off, good way off, great way off
καὶ conj. καί and, even, also, but
τοῖς art. dat. masc. pl. ὁ ἡ τό the, this, that, he, she, it
ἐγγύς adv. ἐγγύς nigh, at hand, near, nigh at hand, ready, nigh unto
18 ὅτι conj. ὅτι that, for, because, how that, how, because that, for that, though
δι' prep. διά (+gen) by, through, with, in, of, (+acc) for, because of, for a cause
αὐτοῦ pron. gen. masc. 3p. sg. αὐτός ή ό self, of oneself, even, very, the same, he, she, it
τὴν art. acc. fem. sg. ὁ ἡ τό the, this, that, he, she, it
προσαγωγὴν n. acc. fem. sg. προσαγωγή access
οἱ art. nom. masc. pl. ὁ ἡ τό the, this, that, he, she, it
ἀμφότεροι adj. nom. masc. pl. ἀμφότερος both
ἐν prep. ἐν (+dat) in, by, with, among, at, on, through, to, within, into, of, for
ἑνὶ num. dat. neut. sg. εἷς or ἕν one, other, some, any, only, a certain
Πνεύματι n. dat. neut. sg. πνεῦμα spirit, Spirit, Ghost, ghost, life. of the spirit, wind
πρὸς prep. πρός (+gen) for, (+dat) at, (+acc) unto, to, with, for, against
τὸν art. acc. masc. sg. ὁ ἡ τό the, this, that, he, she, it
πατέρα n. acc. masc. sg. πατήρ Father, father, parent
19 ἄρα conj. ἄρα then, therefore, haply, wherefore, perhaps, manner, no doubt, truly
οὖν conj. οὖν therefore, then, so, and, now, wherefore
οὐκέτι adv. οὐκέτι or οὐκ έτι no more, no longer, not any more
ξένοι adj. nom. masc. pl. ξένος stranger, strange, host
καὶ conj. καί and, even, also, but
πάροικοι adj. nom. masc. pl. πάροικος sojourn, stranger, foreigner
ἀλλὰ conj. ἀλλά but, yea, yet, nevertheless, howbeit, nay, therefore
συμπολῖται n. nom. masc. pl. συμπολίτης fellowcitizen
τῶν art. gen. masc. pl. ὁ ἡ τό the, this, that, he, she, it
ἁγίων adj. gen. masc. pl. ἅγιος Holy, holy, saint, Holy One, holy thing, most holy
καὶ conj. καί and, even, also, but
οἰκεῖοι adj. nom. masc. pl. οἰκεῖος of the household, one of one's own house
τοῦ art. gen. masc. sg. ὁ ἡ τό the, this, that, he, she, it
Θεοῦ n. gen. masc. sg. θεός God, god
20 ἐπὶ prep. ἐπί (+gen) on, in, upon, (+dat) in, at, for, upon, (+acc) on, upon, unto, to, against

τῷ art. dat. masc. sg. ὁ ἡ τό the, this, that, he, she, it
θεμελίῳ n. dat. masc. sg. θεμέλιος foundation
τῶν art. gen. masc. pl. ὁ ἡ τό the, this, that, he, she, it
ἀποστόλων n. gen. masc. pl. ἀπόστολος apostle, messenger, he that is sent
καὶ conj. καί and, even, also, but
προφητῶν n. gen. masc. pl. προφήτης prophet
ἀκρογωνιαίου adj. gen. masc. sg. ἀκρογωνιαῖος chief corner
αὐτοῦ pron. gen. masc. 3p. sg. αὐτός ή ό self, of oneself, even, very, the same, he, she, it
Ἰησοῦ n. gen. masc. sg. Ἰησοῦς Jesus
Χριστοῦ n. gen. masc. sg. Χριστός Christ
21 ἐν prep. ἐν (+dat) in, by, with, among, at, on, through, to, within, into, of, for
ᾧ relative pron. dat. masc. sg. ὅς ἥ ὅ who, which, what, that
πᾶσα adj. nom. fem. sg. πᾶς πᾶsα πᾶν all, every, whosoever, every one, no, whole, any
ἡ art. nom. fem. sg. ὁ ἡ τό the, this, that, he, she, it
οἰκοδομὴ n. nom. fem. sg. οἰκοδομή building, edifying, edification
εἰς prep. εἰς (+acc) into, to, unto, for, in, on, toward, against, upon, at, among
ναὸν n. acc. masc. sg. ναός temple, shrine
ἅγιον adj. acc. masc. sg. ἅγιος Holy, holy, saint, Holy One, holy thing, most holy
ἐν prep. ἐν (+dat) in, by, with, among, at, on, through, to, within, into, of, for
Κυρίῳ n. dat. masc. sg. κύριος Lord, lord, master, sir, LORD, God, Master, owner
22 ἐν prep. ἐν (+dat) in, by, with, among, at, on, through, to, within, into, of, for
ᾧ relative pron. dat. masc. sg. ὅς ἥ ὅ who, which, what, that
καὶ conj. καί and, even, also, but
ὑμεῖς pron. nom. 2p. pl. σύ thou, you
εἰς prep. εἰς (+acc) into, to, unto, for, in, on, toward, against, upon, at, among
κατοικητήριον n. acc. neut. sg. κατοικητήριον habitation into a dwelling
τοῦ art. gen. masc. sg. ὁ ἡ τό the, this, that, he, she, it
Θεοῦ n. gen. masc. sg. θεός God, god
ἐν prep. ἐν (+dat) in, by, with, among, at, on, through, to, within, into, of, for
Πνεύματι n. dat. neut. sg. πνεῦμα spirit, Spirit, Ghost, ghost, life. of the spirit, wind

3

1 Τούτου demo. pron. gen. neut. sg. οὗτος αὕτη τοῦτο this, the same, this same, he, she, it
χάριν adv. χάριν for a cause, because of, for sake
ἐγὼ pron. nom. 1p. sg. ἐγώ I
Παῦλος n. nom. masc. sg. Παῦλος Paul, Paulus
ὁ art. nom. masc. sg. ὁ ἡ τό the, this, that, he, she, it
δέσμιος n. nom. masc. sg. δέσμιος prisoner, in bonds, that is in bond
τοῦ art. gen. masc. sg. ὁ ἡ τό the, this, that, he, she, it
Χριστοῦ n. gen. masc. sg. Χριστός Christ
Ἰησοῦ n. gen. masc. sg. Ἰησοῦς Jesus
ὑπὲρ prep. ὑπέρ (+gen) for, of, for the sake of, (+acc) above, more than
ὑμῶν pron. gen. 2p. pl. σύ thou, you
τῶν art. gen. neut. pl. ὁ ἡ τό the, this, that, he, she, it
ἐθνῶν n. gen. neut. pl. ἔθνος Gentile, nation, heathen, people
2 εἴγε conj. εἴγε if so be that, if, if yet
τὴν art. acc. fem. sg. ὁ ἡ τό the, this, that, he, she, it
οἰκονομίαν n. acc. fem. sg. οἰκονομία dispensation, stewardship, edifying
τῆς art. gen. fem. sg. ὁ ἡ τό the, this, that, he, she, it
χάριτος n. gen. fem. sg. χάρις grace, thank, favour, pleasure
τοῦ art. gen. masc. sg. ὁ ἡ τό the, this, that, he, she, it
Θεοῦ n. gen. masc. sg. θεός God, god
τῆς art. gen. fem. sg. ὁ ἡ τό the, this, that, he, she, it
μοι pron. dat. 1p. sg. ἐγώ I

εἰς prep. εἰς (+acc) into, to, unto, for, in, on, toward, against, upon, at, among
ὑμᾶς pron. acc. 2p. pl. σύ thou, you
3 ὅτι conj. ὅτι that, for, because, how that, how, because that, for that, though
κατὰ prep. κατά (+gen) against, by, throughout, down, (+acc) according to, after, with
ἀποκάλυψιν n. acc. fem. sg. ἀποκάλυψις revelation, appearing, coming, manifestation
μοι pron. dat. 1p. sg. ἐγώ I
τὸ art. nom. neut. sg. ὁ ἡ τό the, this, that, he, she, it
μυστήριον n. nom. neut. sg. μυστήριον mystery
καθὼς adv. καθώς as, even as, according as, according to
ἐν prep. ἐν (+dat) in, by, with, among, at, on, through, to, within, into, of, for
ὀλίγῳ adj. dat. neut. sg. ὀλίγος few, little, small, a while, brief, short, short space
4 πρὸς prep. πρός (+gen) for, (+dat) at, (+acc) unto, to, with, for, against
ὃ relative pron. acc. neut. sg. ὅς ἥ ὅ who, which, what, that
τὴν art. acc. fem. sg. ὁ ἡ τό the, this, that, he, she, it
σύνεσίν n. acc. fem. sg. σύνεσις understanding, knowledge
μου pron. gen. 1p. sg. ἐγώ I
ἐν prep. ἐν (+dat) in, by, with, among, at, on, through, to, within, into, of, for
τῷ art. dat. neut. sg. ὁ ἡ τό the, this, that, he, she, it
μυστηρίῳ n. dat. neut. sg. μυστήριον mystery
τοῦ art. gen. masc. sg. ὁ ἡ τό the, this, that, he, she, it
Χριστοῦ n. gen. masc. sg. Χριστός Christ
5 ὃ relative pron. nom. neut. sg. ὅς ἥ ὅ who, which, what, that
ἐν prep. ἐν (+dat) in, by, with, among, at, on, through, to, within, into, of, for
ἑτέραις adj. dat. fem. pl. ἕτερος another, other, else, strange
γενεαῖς n. dat. fem. pl. γενεά generation, age, time, nation
οὐκ particle of negation. οὐ οὐκ οὐχ not, no, neither, none, nay, nor, never, nothing
τοῖς art. dat. masc. pl. ὁ ἡ τό the, this, that, he, she, it
υἱοῖς n. dat. masc. pl. υἱός son, child, descendant, offspring, heir
τῶν art. gen. masc. pl. ὁ ἡ τό the, this, that, he, she, it
ἀνθρώπων n. gen. masc. pl. ἄνθρωπος man, human being, person, one, certain
ὡς adv. ὡς as, when, as it were, how, about, like, as soon as, even as, while
νῦν adv. νῦν now, henceforth, present, this time
τοῖς art. dat. masc. pl. ὁ ἡ τό the, this, that, he, she, it
ἁγίοις adj. dat. masc. pl. ἅγιος Holy, holy, saint, Holy One, holy thing, most holy
ἀποστόλοις n. dat. masc. pl. ἀπόστολος apostle, messenger, he that is sent
αὐτοῦ pron. gen. masc. 3p. sg. αὐτός ή ό self, of oneself, even, very, the same, he, she, it
καὶ conj. καί and, even, also, but
προφήταις n. dat. masc. pl. προφήτης prophet
ἐν prep. ἐν (+dat) in, by, with, among, at, on, through, to, within, into, of, for
Πνεύματι n. dat. neut. sg. πνεῦμα spirit, Spirit, Ghost, ghost, life. of the spirit, wind
6 τὰ art. acc. neut. pl. ὁ ἡ τό the, this, that, he, she, it
ἔθνη n. acc. neut. pl. ἔθνος Gentile, nation, heathen, people
συγκληρονόμα adj. acc. neut. pl. συγκληρονόμος joint-heir, fellowheir, heir together
καὶ conj. καί and, even, also, but
σύσσωμα adj. acc. neut. pl. σύσσωμος of the same body
καὶ conj. καί and, even, also, but
συμμέτοχα adj. acc. neut. pl. συμμέτοχος partaker
τῆς art. gen. fem. sg. ὁ ἡ τό the, this, that, he, she, it
ἐπαγγελίας n. gen. fem. sg. ἐπαγγελία promise, message
αὐτοῦ pron. gen. masc. 3p. sg. αὐτός ή ό self, of oneself, even, very, the same, he, she, it
ἐν prep. ἐν (+dat) in, by, with, among, at, on, through, to, within, into, of, for
τῷ art. dat. masc. sg. ὁ ἡ τό the, this, that, he, she, it
Χριστῷ n. dat. masc. sg. Χριστός Christ
διὰ prep. διά (+gen) by, through, with, in, of, (+acc) for, because of, for a cause
τοῦ art. gen. neut. sg. ὁ ἡ τό the, this, that, he, she, it

εὐαγγελίου n. gen. neut. sg. εὐαγγέλιον gospel
7 οὗ relative pron. gen. neut. sg. ὅς ἥ ὅ who, which, what, that
διάκονος n. nom. masc. sg. διάκονος minister, servant, deacon
κατὰ prep. κατά (+gen) against, by, throughout, down, (+acc) according to, after, with
τὴν art. acc. fem. sg. ὁ ἡ τό the, this, that, he, she, it
δωρεὰν n. acc. fem. sg. δωρεά gift
τῆς art. gen. fem. sg. ὁ ἡ τό the, this, that, he, she, it
χάριτος n. gen. fem. sg. χάρις grace, thank, favour, pleasure
τοῦ art. gen. masc. sg. ὁ ἡ τό the, this, that, he, she, it
Θεοῦ n. gen. masc. sg. θεός God, god
τὴν art. acc. fem. sg. ὁ ἡ τό the, this, that, he, she, it
μοι pron. dat. 1p. sg. ἐγώ I
κατὰ prep. κατά (+gen) against, by, throughout, down, (+acc) according to, after, with
τὴν art. acc. fem. sg. ὁ ἡ τό the, this, that, he, she, it
ἐνέργειαν n. acc. fem. sg. ἐνέργεια working, effectual working, operation
τῆς art. gen. fem. sg. ὁ ἡ τό the, this, that, he, she, it
δυνάμεως n. gen. fem. sg. δύναμις power, mighty work, miracle, strength, might
αὐτοῦ pron. gen. masc. 3p. sg. αὐτός ή ό self, of oneself, even, very, the same, he, she, it
8 ἐμοὶ pron. dat. 1p. sg. ἐγώ I
τῷ art. dat. masc. sg. ὁ ἡ τό the, this, that, he, she, it
ἐλαχιστοτέρῳ compar. adj. dat. masc. sg. ἐλάχιστος least, very small, smallest, very little
πάντων adj. gen. masc. pl. πᾶς πᾶσα πᾶν all, every, whosoever, every one, no, whole, any
τῶν art. gen. masc. pl. ὁ ἡ τό the, this, that, he, she, it
ἁγίων adj. gen. masc. pl. ἅγιος Holy, holy, saint, Holy One, holy thing, most holy
ἡ art. nom. fem. sg. ὁ ἡ τό the, this, that, he, she, it
χάρις n. nom. fem. sg. χάρις grace, thank, favour, pleasure
αὕτη demo. pron. nom. fem. sg. οὗτος αὕτη τοῦτο this, the same, this same, he, she, it
ἐν prep. ἐν (+dat) in, by, with, among, at, on, through, to, within, into, of, for
τοῖς art. dat. neut. pl. ὁ ἡ τό the, this, that, he, she, it
ἔθνεσιν n. dat. neut. pl. ἔθνος Gentile, nation, heathen, people
τὸν art. acc. masc. sg. ὁ ἡ τό the, this, that, he, she, it
ἀνεξιχνίαστον adj. acc. masc. sg. ἀνεξιχνίαστος past finding out, unsearchable
πλοῦτον n. acc. masc. sg. πλοῦτος riches
τοῦ art. gen. masc. sg. ὁ ἡ τό the, this, that, he, she, it
Χριστοῦ n. gen. masc. sg. Χριστός Christ
9 καὶ conj. καί and, even, also, but
πάντας adj. acc. masc. pl. πᾶς πᾶσα πᾶν all, every, whosoever, every one, no, whole, any
τίς interrog. pron. nom. fem. sg. τίς what, who, why, where, which, how
ἡ art. nom. fem. sg. ὁ ἡ τό the, this, that, he, she, it
κοινωνία n. nom. fem. sg. κοινωνία fellowship, communion, contribution, distribution
τοῦ art. gen. neut. sg. ὁ ἡ τό the, this, that, he, she, it
μυστηρίου n. gen. neut. sg. μυστήριον mystery
τοῦ art. gen. neut. sg. ὁ ἡ τό the, this, that, he, she, it
ἀπὸ prep. ἀπό (+gen) from, of, out of, since, for, off, at, by, in, on
τῶν art. gen. masc. pl. ὁ ἡ τό the, this, that, he, she, it
αἰώνων n. gen. masc. pl. αἰών ever, ever and ever, evermore, age, eternal, world
ἐν prep. ἐν (+dat) in, by, with, among, at, on, through, to, within, into, of, for
τῷ art. dat. masc. sg. ὁ ἡ τό the, this, that, he, she, it
Θεῷ n. dat. masc. sg. θεός God, god
τῷ art. dat. masc. sg. ὁ ἡ τό the, this, that, he, she, it
τὰ art. acc. neut. pl. ὁ ἡ τό the, this, that, he, she, it
πάντα adj. acc. neut. pl. πᾶς πᾶσα πᾶν all, every, whosoever, every one, no, whole, any
διὰ prep. διά (+gen) by, through, with, in, of, (+acc) for, because of, for a cause
Ἰησοῦ n. gen. masc. sg. Ἰησοῦς Jesus
Χριστοῦ n. gen. masc. sg. Χριστός Christ

10 ἵνα conj. ἵνα that, to, lest, for to, so that, albeit, because, for, so as
νῦν adv. νῦν now, henceforth, present, this time
ταῖς art. dat. fem. pl. ὁ ἡ τό the, this, that, he, she, it
ἀρχαῖς n. dat. fem. pl. ἀρχή beginning, principality, corner, first, magistrate, rule
καὶ conj. καί and, even, also, but
ταῖς art. dat. fem. pl. ὁ ἡ τό the, this, that, he, she, it
ἐξουσίαις n. dat. fem. pl. ἐξουσία power, authority, right, strength, jurisdiction
ἐν prep. ἐν (+dat) in, by, with, among, at, on, through, to, within, into, of, for
τοῖς art. dat. neut. pl. ὁ ἡ τό the, this, that, he, she, it
ἐπουρανίοις adj. dat. neut. pl. ἐπουράνιος heavenly, celestial, high, in heaven
διὰ prep. διά (+gen) by, through, with, in, of, (+acc) for, because of, for a cause
τῆς art. gen. fem. sg. ὁ ἡ τό the, this, that, he, she, it
ἐκκλησίας n. gen. fem. sg. ἐκκλησία church, assembly
ἡ art. nom. fem. sg. ὁ ἡ τό the, this, that, he, she, it
πολυποίκιλος adj. nom. fem. sg. πολυποίκιλος manifold
σοφία n. nom. fem. sg. σοφία wisdom
τοῦ art. gen. masc. sg. ὁ ἡ τό the, this, that, he, she, it
Θεοῦ n. gen. masc. sg. θεός God, god
11 κατὰ prep. κατά (+gen) against, by, throughout, down, (+acc) according to, after, with
πρόθεσιν n. acc. fem. sg. πρόθεσις purpose, shew, shewbread
τῶν art. gen. masc. pl. ὁ ἡ τό the, this, that, he, she, it
αἰώνων n. gen. masc. pl. αἰών ever, ever and ever, evermore, age, eternal, world
ἣν relative pron. acc. fem. sg. ὅς ἥ ὅ who, which, what, that
ἐν prep. ἐν (+dat) in, by, with, among, at, on, through, to, within, into, of, for
Χριστῷ n. dat. masc. sg. Χριστός Christ
Ἰησοῦ n. dat. masc. sg. Ἰησοῦς Jesus
τῷ art. dat. masc. sg. ὁ ἡ τό the, this, that, he, she, it
Κυρίῳ n. dat. masc. sg. κύριος Lord, lord, master, sir, LORD, God, Master, owner
ἡμῶν pron. gen. 1p. pl. ἐγώ I
12 ἐν prep. ἐν (+dat) in, by, with, among, at, on, through, to, within, into, of, for
ᾧ relative pron. dat. masc. sg. ὅς ἥ ὅ who, which, what, that
τὴν art. acc. fem. sg. ὁ ἡ τό the, this, that, he, she, it
παρρησίαν n. acc. fem. sg. παρρησία boldness, confidence, openly, plainly, freely
καὶ conj. καί and, even, also, but
τὴν art. acc. fem. sg. ὁ ἡ τό the, this, that, he, she, it
προσαγωγὴν n. acc. fem. sg. προσαγωγή access
ἐν prep. ἐν (+dat) in, by, with, among, at, on, through, to, within, into, of, for
πεποιθήσει n. dat. fem. sg. πεποίθησις confidence, trust
διὰ prep. διά (+gen) by, through, with, in, of, (+acc) for, because of, for a cause
τῆς art. gen. fem. sg. ὁ ἡ τό the, this, that, he, she, it
πίστεως n. gen. fem. sg. πίστις faith, assurance, belief, fidelity
αὐτοῦ pron. gen. masc. 3p. sg. αὐτός ή ό self, of oneself, even, very, the same, he, she, it
13 διὸ conj. διό wherefore, therefore, for which cause
μὴ particle of negation. μή not, no, lest, neither, none, nothing, nor, never, without
ἐν prep. ἐν (+dat) in, by, with, among, at, on, through, to, within, into, of, for
ταῖς art. dat. fem. pl. ὁ ἡ τό the, this, that, he, she, it
θλίψεσίν n. dat. fem. pl. θλῖψις tribulation, affliction, anguish, persecution
μου pron. gen. 1p. sg. ἐγώ I
ὑπὲρ prep. ὑπέρ (+gen) for, of, for the sake of, (+acc) above, more than
ὑμῶν pron. gen. 2p. pl. σύ thou, you
ἥτις relative pron. nom. fem. sg. ὅστις which, who, whosoever, that, whatsoever
δόξα n. nom. fem. sg. δόξα glory, honour, praise, dignity, worship
ὑμῶν pron. gen. 2p. pl. σύ thou, you
14 Τούτου demo. pron. gen. neut. sg. οὗτος αὕτη τοῦτο this, the same, this same, he, she, it
χάριν adv. χάριν for a cause, because of, for sake

τὰ art. acc. neut. pl. ὁ ἡ τό the, this, that, he, she, it
γόνατά n. acc. neut. pl. γόνυ knee, kneel
μου pron. gen. 1p. sg. ἐγώ I
πρὸς prep. πρός (+gen) for, (+dat) at, (+acc) unto, to, with, for, against
τὸν art. acc. masc. sg. ὁ ἡ τό the, this, that, he, she, it
πατέρα n. acc. masc. sg. πατήρ Father, father, parent
τοῦ art. gen. masc. sg. ὁ ἡ τό the, this, that, he, she, it
Κυρίου n. gen. masc. sg. κύριος Lord, lord, master, sir, LORD, God, Master, owner
ἡμῶν pron. gen. 1p. pl. ἐγώ I
Ἰησοῦ n. gen. masc. sg. Ἰησοῦς Jesus
Χριστοῦ n. gen. masc. sg. Χριστός Christ
15 ἐξ prep. ἐκ ἐξ (+gen) of, from, out of, by, on, with, in, among, through
οὗ relative pron. gen. masc. sg. ὅς ἥ ὅ who, which, what, that
πᾶσα adj. nom. fem. sg. πᾶς πᾶσα πᾶν all, every, whosoever, every one, no, whole, any
πατριὰ n. nom. fem. sg. πατριά lineage, family, kindred
ἐν prep. ἐν (+dat) in, by, with, among, at, on, through, to, within, into, of, for
οὐρανοῖς n. dat. masc. pl. οὐρανός heaven, air, sky
καὶ conj. καί and, even, also, but
ἐπὶ prep. ἐπί (+gen) on, in, upon, (+dat) in, at, for, upon, (+acc) on, upon, unto, to, against
γῆς n. gen. fem. sg. γῆ earth, land, ground, country
16 ἵνα conj. ἵνα that, to, lest, for to, so that, albeit, because, for, so as
ὑμῖν pron. dat. 2p. pl. σύ thou, you
κατὰ prep. κατά (+gen) against, by, throughout, down, (+acc) according to, after, with
τὸν art. acc. masc. sg. ὁ ἡ τό the, this, that, he, she, it
πλοῦτον n. acc. masc. sg. πλοῦτος riches
τῆς art. gen. fem. sg. ὁ ἡ τό the, this, that, he, she, it
δόξης n. gen. fem. sg. δόξα glory, honour, praise, dignity, worship
αὐτοῦ pron. gen. masc. 3p. sg. αὐτός ή ό self, of oneself, even, very, the same, he, she, it
δυνάμει n. dat. fem. sg. δύναμις power, mighty work, miracle, strength, might
διὰ prep. διά (+gen) by, through, with, in, of, (+acc) for, because of, for a cause
τοῦ art. gen. neut. sg. ὁ ἡ τό the, this, that, he, she, it
Πνεύματος n. gen. neut. sg. πνεῦμα spirit, Spirit, Ghost, ghost, life. of the spirit, wind
αὐτοῦ pron. gen. masc. 3p. sg. αὐτός ή ό self, of oneself, even, very, the same, he, she, it
εἰς prep. εἰς (+acc) into, to, unto, for, in, on, toward, against, upon, at, among
τὸν art. acc. masc. sg. ὁ ἡ τό the, this, that, he, she, it
ἔσω adv. ἔσω within, in, inner, into, inward
ἄνθρωπον n. acc. masc. sg. ἄνθρωπος man, human being, person, one, certain
17 τὸν art. acc. masc. sg. ὁ ἡ τό the, this, that, he, she, it
Χριστὸν n. acc. masc. sg. Χριστός Christ
διὰ prep. διά (+gen) by, through, with, in, of, (+acc) for, because of, for a cause
τῆς art. gen. fem. sg. ὁ ἡ τό the, this, that, he, she, it
πίστεως n. gen. fem. sg. πίστις faith, assurance, belief, fidelity
ἐν prep. ἐν (+dat) in, by, with, among, at, on, through, to, within, into, of, for
ταῖς art. dat. fem. pl. ὁ ἡ τό the, this, that, he, she, it
καρδίαις n. dat. fem. pl. καρδία heart
ὑμῶν pron. gen. 2p. pl. σύ thou, you
ἐν prep. ἐν (+dat) in, by, with, among, at, on, through, to, within, into, of, for
ἀγάπῃ n. dat. fem. sg. ἀγάπη love, charity, feast of charity
καὶ conj. καί and, even, also, but
18 ἵνα conj. ἵνα that, to, lest, for to, so that, albeit, because, for, so as
σὺν prep. σύν (+dat) with, beside
πᾶσι adj. dat. masc. pl. πᾶς πᾶσα πᾶν all, every, whosoever, every one, no, whole, any
τοῖς art. dat. masc. pl. ὁ ἡ τό the, this, that, he, she, it
ἁγίοις adj. dat. masc. pl. ἅγιος Holy, holy, saint, Holy One, holy thing, most holy
τί interrog. pron. nom. neut. sg. τίς what, who, why, where, which, how

τὸ art. nom. neut. sg. ὁ ἡ τό the, this, that, he, she, it
πλάτος n. nom. neut. sg. πλάτος breadth
καὶ conj. καί and, even, also, but
μῆκος n. nom. neut. sg. μῆκος length
καὶ conj. καί and, even, also, but
βάθος n. nom. neut. sg. βάθος deepness, depth, deep, deep thing
καὶ conj. καί and, even, also, but
ὕψος n. nom. neut. sg. ὕψος on high, height, exalt, in exaltation
19 τε conj. τέ and, both, also
τὴν art. acc. fem. sg. ὁ ἡ τό the, this, that, he, she, it
τῆς art. gen. fem. sg. ὁ ἡ τό the, this, that, he, she, it
γνώσεως n. gen. fem. sg. γνῶσις knowledge, science
ἀγάπην n. acc. fem. sg. ἀγάπη love, charity, feast of charity
τοῦ art. gen. masc. sg. ὁ ἡ τό the, this, that, he, she, it
Χριστοῦ n. gen. masc. sg. Χριστός Christ
ἵνα conj. ἵνα that, to, lest, for to, so that, albeit, because, for, so as
εἰς prep. εἰς (+acc) into, to, unto, for, in, on, toward, against, upon, at, among
πᾶν adj. acc. neut. sg. πᾶς πᾶσα πᾶν all, every, whosoever, every one, no, whole, any
τὸ art. acc. neut. sg. ὁ ἡ τό the, this, that, he, she, it
πλήρωμα n. acc. neut. sg. πλήρωμα fullness, fulfilling, full
τοῦ art. gen. masc. sg. ὁ ἡ τό the, this, that, he, she, it
Θεοῦ n. gen. masc. sg. θεός God, god
20 Τῷ art. dat. masc. sg. ὁ ἡ τό the, this, that, he, she, it
δὲ conj. δέ but, and, now, also, to the contrary, rather, then
ὑπὲρ prep. ὑπέρ (+gen) for, of, for the sake of, (+acc) above, more than
πάντα adj. acc. neut. pl. πᾶς πᾶσα πᾶν all, every, whosoever, every one, no, whole, any
ὑπὲρ prep. ὑπέρ (+gen) for, of, for the sake of, (+acc) above, more than
ἐκ prep. ἐκ ἐξ (+gen) of, from, out of, by, on, with, in, among, through
περισσοῦ adj. gen. neut. sg. περισσός more, beyond measure, advantage, exceedingly
ὧν relative pron. gen. neut. pl. ὅς ἥ ὅ who, which, what, that
ἢ particle. ἤ or, than, either, nor, or else, and, rather than
κατὰ prep. κατά (+gen) against, by, throughout, down, (+acc) according to, after, with
τὴν art. acc. fem. sg. ὁ ἡ τό the, this, that, he, she, it
δύναμιν n. acc. fem. sg. δύναμις power, mighty work, miracle, strength, might
τὴν art. acc. fem. sg. ὁ ἡ τό the, this, that, he, she, it
ἐν prep. ἐν (+dat) in, by, with, among, at, on, through, to, within, into, of, for
ἡμῖν pron. dat. 1p. pl. ἐγώ I
21 αὐτῷ pron. dat. masc. 3p. sg. αὐτός ἡ ό self, of oneself, even, very, the same, he, she, it
ἡ art. nom. fem. sg. ὁ ἡ τό the, this, that, he, she, it
δόξα n. nom. fem. sg. δόξα glory, honour, praise, dignity, worship
ἐν prep. ἐν (+dat) in, by, with, among, at, on, through, to, within, into, of, for
τῇ art. dat. fem. sg. ὁ ἡ τό the, this, that, he, she, it
ἐκκλησίᾳ n. dat. fem. sg. ἐκκλησία church, assembly
ἐν prep. ἐν (+dat) in, by, with, among, at, on, through, to, within, into, of, for
Χριστῷ n. dat. masc. sg. Χριστός Christ
Ἰησοῦ n. dat. masc. sg. Ἰησοῦς Jesus
εἰς prep. εἰς (+acc) into, to, unto, for, in, on, toward, against, upon, at, among
πάσας adj. acc. fem. pl. πᾶς πᾶσα πᾶν all, every, whosoever, every one, no, whole, any
τὰς art. acc. fem. pl. ὁ ἡ τό the, this, that, he, she, it
γενεὰς n. acc. fem. pl. γενεά generation, age, time, nation
τοῦ art. gen. masc. sg. ὁ ἡ τό the, this, that, he, she, it
αἰῶνος n. gen. masc. sg. αἰών ever, ever and ever, evermore, age, eternal, world
τῶν art. gen. masc. pl. ὁ ἡ τό the, this, that, he, she, it
αἰώνων n. gen. masc. pl. αἰών ever, ever and ever, evermore, age, eternal, world
ἀμήν particle. ἀμήν amen, verily

4

1 οὖν conj. οὖν therefore, then, so, and, now, wherefore
ὑμᾶς pron. acc. 2p. pl. σύ thou, you
ἐγὼ pron. nom. 1p. sg. ἐγώ I
ὁ art. nom. masc. sg. ὁ ἡ τό the, this, that, he, she, it
δέσμιος n. nom. masc. sg. δέσμιος prisoner, in bonds, that is in bond
ἐν prep. ἐν (+dat) in, by, with, among, at, on, through, to, within, into, of, for
Κυρίῳ n. dat. masc. sg. κύριος Lord, lord, master, sir, LORD, God, Master, owner
ἀξίως adv. ἀξίως worthy, as become, after a godly sort
τῆς art. gen. fem. sg. ὁ ἡ τό the, this, that, he, she, it
κλήσεως n. gen. fem. sg. κλῆσις calling, vocation
ἧς relative pron. gen. fem. sg. ὅς ἥ ὅ who, which, what, that
2 μετὰ prep. μετά (+gen) with, among, against, (+acc) after
πάσης adj. gen. fem. sg. πᾶς πᾶσα πᾶν all, every, whosoever, every one, no, whole, any
ταπεινοφροσύνης n. gen. fem. sg. ταπεινοφροσύνη humility of mind, humility, lowliness
καὶ conj. καί and, even, also, but
πρᾳότητος n. gen. fem. sg. πρᾳότης meekness
μετὰ prep. μετά (+gen) with, among, against, (+acc) after
μακροθυμίας n. gen. fem. sg. μακροθυμία longsuffering, patience
ἀλλήλων pron. gen. masc. pl. ἀλλήλων one another, themselves, together, mutual
ἐν prep. ἐν (+dat) in, by, with, among, at, on, through, to, within, into, of, for
ἀγάπῃ n. dat. fem. sg. ἀγάπη love, charity, feast of charity
3 τὴν art. acc. fem. sg. ὁ ἡ τό the, this, that, he, she, it
ἑνότητα n. acc. fem. sg. ἑνότης unity
τοῦ art. gen. neut. sg. ὁ ἡ τό the, this, that, he, she, it
Πνεύματος n. gen. neut. sg. πνεῦμα spirit, Spirit, Ghost, ghost, life. of the spirit, wind
ἐν prep. ἐν (+dat) in, by, with, among, at, on, through, to, within, into, of, for
τῷ art. dat. masc. sg. ὁ ἡ τό the, this, that, he, she, it
συνδέσμῳ n. dat. masc. sg. σύνδεσμος bond, band
τῆς art. gen. fem. sg. ὁ ἡ τό the, this, that, he, she, it
εἰρήνης n. gen. fem. sg. εἰρήνη peace, quietness, rest
4 ἓν num. nom. neut. sg. εἷς or ἕν one, other, some, any, only, a certain
σῶμα n. nom. neut. sg. σῶμα body, bodily, slave
καὶ conj. καί and, even, also, but
ἓν num. nom. neut. sg. εἷς or ἕν one, other, some, any, only, a certain
Πνεῦμα n. nom. neut. sg. πνεῦμα spirit, Spirit, Ghost, ghost, life. of the spirit, wind
καθὼς adv. καθώς as, even as, according as, according to
καὶ conj. καί and, even, also, but
ἐν prep. ἐν (+dat) in, by, with, among, at, on, through, to, within, into, of, for
μιᾷ num. dat. fem. sg. εἷς or ἕν one, other, some, any, only, a certain
ἐλπίδι n. dat. fem. sg. ἐλπίς hope, faith
τῆς art. gen. fem. sg. ὁ ἡ τό the, this, that, he, she, it
κλήσεως n. gen. fem. sg. κλῆσις calling, vocation
ὑμῶν pron. gen. 2p. pl. σύ thou, you
5 εἷς num. nom. masc. sg. εἷς or ἕν one, other, some, any, only, a certain
Κύριος n. nom. masc. sg. κύριος Lord, lord, master, sir, LORD, God, Master, owner
μία num. nom. fem. sg. εἷς or ἕν one, other, some, any, only, a certain
πίστις n. nom. fem. sg. πίστις faith, assurance, belief, fidelity
ἓν num. nom. neut. sg. εἷς or ἕν one, other, some, any, only, a certain
βάπτισμα n. nom. neut. sg. βάπτισμα baptism
6 εἷς num. nom. masc. sg. εἷς or ἕν one, other, some, any, only, a certain
Θεὸς n. nom. masc. sg. θεός God, god
καὶ conj. καί and, even, also, but

πατὴρ n. nom. masc. sg. πατήρ Father, father, parent
πάντων adj. gen. masc. pl. πᾶς πᾶσα πᾶν all, every, whosoever, every one, no, whole, any
ὁ art. nom. masc. sg. ὁ ἡ τό the, this, that, he, she, it
ἐπὶ prep. ἐπί (+gen) on, in, upon, (+dat) in, at, for, upon, (+acc) on, upon, unto, to, against
πάντων adj. gen. masc. pl. πᾶς πᾶσα πᾶν all, every, whosoever, every one, no, whole, any
καὶ conj. καί and, even, also, but
διὰ prep. διά (+gen) by, through, with, in, of, (+acc) for, because of, for a cause
πάντων adj. gen. masc. pl. πᾶς πᾶσα πᾶν all, every, whosoever, every one, no, whole, any
καὶ conj. καί and, even, also, but
ἐν prep. ἐν (+dat) in, by, with, among, at, on, through, to, within, into, of, for
πᾶσιν adj. dat. masc. pl. πᾶς πᾶσα πᾶν all, every, whosoever, every one, no, whole, any
ὑμῖν pron. dat. 2p. pl. σύ thou, you
7 ἑνὶ num. dat. masc. sg. εἷς or ἕν one, other, some, any, only, a certain
δὲ conj. δέ but, and, now, also, to the contrary, rather, then
ἑκάστῳ adj. dat. masc. sg. ἕκαστος every man, every, every one, any man, each
ἡμῶν pron. gen. 1p. pl. ἐγώ I
ἡ art. nom. fem. sg. ὁ ἡ τό the, this, that, he, she, it
χάρις n. nom. fem. sg. χάρις grace, thank, favour, pleasure
κατὰ prep. κατά (+gen) against, by, throughout, down, (+acc) according to, after, with
τὸ art. acc. neut. sg. ὁ ἡ τό the, this, that, he, she, it
μέτρον n. acc. neut. sg. μέτρον measure
τῆς art. gen. fem. sg. ὁ ἡ τό the, this, that, he, she, it
δωρεᾶς n. gen. fem. sg. δωρεά gift
τοῦ art. gen. masc. sg. ὁ ἡ τό the, this, that, he, she, it
Χριστοῦ n. gen. masc. sg. Χριστός Christ
8 διὸ conj. διό wherefore, therefore, for which cause
εἰς prep. εἰς (+acc) into, to, unto, for, in, on, toward, against, upon, at, among
ὕψος n. acc. neut. sg. ὕψος on high, height, exalt, in exaltation
αἰχμαλωσίαν n. acc. fem. sg. αἰχμαλωσία captivity
καὶ conj. καί and, even, also, but
δόματα n. acc. neut. pl. δόμα gift
τοῖς art. dat. masc. pl. ὁ ἡ τό the, this, that, he, she, it
ἀνθρώποις n. dat. masc. pl. ἄνθρωπος man, human being, person, one, certain
9 τὸ art. nom. neut. sg. ὁ ἡ τό the, this, that, he, she, it
δὲ conj. δέ but, and, now, also, to the contrary, rather, then
τί interrog. pron. nom. neut. sg. τίς what, who, why, where, which, how
εἰ conj. εἰ if, whether, that, though, forasmuch
μὴ particle of negation. μή not, no, lest, neither, none, nothing, nor, never, without
ὅτι conj. ὅτι that, for, because, how that, how, because that, for that, though
καὶ conj. καί and, even, also, but
πρῶτον adv. πρῶτον first, at the first, first of all, at first, at the beginning, before, chiefly
εἰς prep. εἰς (+acc) into, to, unto, for, in, on, toward, against, upon, at, among
τὰ art. acc. neut. pl. ὁ ἡ τό the, this, that, he, she, it
κατώτερα compar. adj. acc. neut. pl. κατώτερος lower
μέρη n. acc. neut. pl. μέρος part, coast, portion, behalf, respect, piece, side
τῆς art. gen. fem. sg. ὁ ἡ τό the, this, that, he, she, it
γῆς n. gen. fem. sg. γῆ earth, land, ground, country
10 ὁ art. nom. masc. sg. ὁ ἡ τό the, this, that, he, she, it
αὐτός pron. nom. masc. 3p. sg. αὐτός ή ό self, of oneself, even, very, the same, he, she, it
καὶ conj. καί and, even, also, but
ὁ art. nom. masc. sg. ὁ ἡ τό the, this, that, he, she, it
ὑπεράνω prep. ὑπεράνω (+gen) far above, over, above
πάντων adj. gen. masc. pl. πᾶς πᾶσα πᾶν all, every, whosoever, every one, no, whole, any
τῶν art. gen. masc. pl. ὁ ἡ τό the, this, that, he, she, it
οὐρανῶν n. gen. masc. pl. οὐρανός heaven, air, sky

ἵνα conj. ἵνα that, to, lest, for to, so that, albeit, because, for, so as
τὰ art. acc. neut. pl. ὁ ἡ τό the, this, that, he, she, it
πάντα adj. acc. neut. pl. πᾶς πᾶσα πᾶν all, every, whosoever, every one, no, whole, any
11 καὶ conj. καί and, even, also, but
αὐτὸς pron. nom. masc. 3p. sg. αὐτός ἡ ὁ self, of oneself, even, very, the same, he, she, it
τοὺς art. acc. masc. pl. ὁ ἡ τό the, this, that, he, she, it
μὲν conj. μέν indeed, verily, truly, even, so, some
ἀποστόλους n. acc. masc. pl. ἀπόστολος apostle, messenger, he that is sent
τοὺς art. acc. masc. pl. ὁ ἡ τό the, this, that, he, she, it
δὲ conj. δέ but, and, now, also, to the contrary, rather, then
προφήτας n. acc. masc. pl. προφήτης prophet
τοὺς art. acc. masc. pl. ὁ ἡ τό the, this, that, he, she, it
δὲ conj. δέ but, and, now, also, to the contrary, rather, then
εὐαγγελιστάς n. acc. masc. pl. εὐαγγελιστής evangelist
τοὺς art. acc. masc. pl. ὁ ἡ τό the, this, that, he, she, it
δὲ conj. δέ but, and, now, also, to the contrary, rather, then
ποιμένας n. acc. masc. pl. ποιμήν shepherd, pastor
καὶ conj. καί and, even, also, but
διδασκάλους n. acc. masc. pl. διδάσκαλος teacher, master, doctor
12 πρὸς prep. πρός (+gen) for, (+dat) at, (+acc) unto, to, with, for, against
τὸν art. acc. masc. sg. ὁ ἡ τό the, this, that, he, she, it
καταρτισμὸν n. acc. masc. sg. καταρτισμός perfecting
τῶν art. gen. masc. pl. ὁ ἡ τό the, this, that, he, she, it
ἁγίων adj. gen. masc. pl. ἅγιος Holy, holy, saint, Holy One, holy thing, most holy
εἰς prep. εἰς (+acc) into, to, unto, for, in, on, toward, against, upon, at, among
ἔργον n. acc. neut. sg. ἔργον work, deed, doing labour
διακονίας n. gen. fem. sg. διακονία ministry, administration, service, office, relief
εἰς prep. εἰς (+acc) into, to, unto, for, in, on, toward, against, upon, at, among
οἰκοδομὴν n. acc. fem. sg. οἰκοδομή building, edifying, edification
τοῦ art. gen. neut. sg. ὁ ἡ τό the, this, that, he, she, it
σώματος n. gen. neut. sg. σῶμα body, bodily, slave
τοῦ art. gen. masc. sg. ὁ ἡ τό the, this, that, he, she, it
Χριστοῦ n. gen. masc. sg. Χριστός Christ
13 μέχρι adv. μέχρι until, unto, till, to
οἱ art. nom. masc. pl. ὁ ἡ τό the, this, that, he, she, it
πάντες adj. nom. masc. pl. πᾶς πᾶσα πᾶν all, every, whosoever, every one, no, whole, any
εἰς prep. εἰς (+acc) into, to, unto, for, in, on, toward, against, upon, at, among
τὴν art. acc. fem. sg. ὁ ἡ τό the, this, that, he, she, it
ἑνότητα n. acc. fem. sg. ἑνότης unity
τῆς art. gen. fem. sg. ὁ ἡ τό the, this, that, he, she, it
πίστεως n. gen. fem. sg. πίστις faith, assurance, belief, fidelity
καὶ conj. καί and, even, also, but
τῆς art. gen. fem. sg. ὁ ἡ τό the, this, that, he, she, it
ἐπιγνώσεως n. gen. fem. sg. ἐπίγνωσις knowledge, acknowledging, acknowledgement
τοῦ art. gen. masc. sg. ὁ ἡ τό the, this, that, he, she, it
υἱοῦ n. gen. masc. sg. υἱός son, child, descendant, offspring, heir
τοῦ art. gen. masc. sg. ὁ ἡ τό the, this, that, he, she, it
Θεοῦ n. gen. masc. sg. θεός God, god
εἰς prep. εἰς (+acc) into, to, unto, for, in, on, toward, against, upon, at, among
ἄνδρα n. acc. masc. sg. ἀνήρ man, husband, sir
τέλειον adj. acc. masc. sg. τέλειος perfect, of full age
εἰς prep. εἰς (+acc) into, to, unto, for, in, on, toward, against, upon, at, among
μέτρον n. acc. neut. sg. μέτρον measure
ἡλικίας n. gen. fem. sg. ἡλικία stature, age
τοῦ art. gen. neut. sg. ὁ ἡ τό the, this, that, he, she, it

πληρώματος n. gen. neut. sg. πλήρωμα fullness, fulfilling, full
τοῦ art. gen. neut. sg. ὁ ἡ τό the, this, that, he, she, it
Χριστοῦ n. gen. masc. sg. Χριστός Christ
14 ἵνα conj. ἵνα that, to, lest, for to, so that, albeit, because, for, so as
μηκέτι adv. μηκέτι no more, no longer, not any more, not henceforth, not henceforward
νήπιοι adj. nom. masc. pl. νήπιος babe, child, childish
καὶ conj. καί and, even, also, but
παντὶ adj. dat. masc. sg. πᾶς πᾶσα πᾶν all, every, whosoever, every one, no, whole, any
ἀνέμῳ n. dat. masc. sg. ἄνεμος wind
τῆς art. gen. fem. sg. ὁ ἡ τό the, this, that, he, she, it
διδασκαλίας n. gen. fem. sg. διδασκαλία doctrine, learning, teaching
ἐν prep. ἐν (+dat) in, by, with, among, at, on, through, to, within, into, of, for
τῇ art. dat. fem. sg. ὁ ἡ τό the, this, that, he, she, it
κυβείᾳ n. dat. fem. sg. κυβεία sleight
τῶν art. gen. masc. pl. ὁ ἡ τό the, this, that, he, she, it
ἀνθρώπων n. gen. masc. pl. ἄνθρωπος man, human being, person, one, certain
ἐν prep. ἐν (+dat) in, by, with, among, at, on, through, to, within, into, of, for
πανουργίᾳ n. dat. fem. sg. πανουργία craftiness, cunning craftiness, subtilty
πρὸς prep. πρός (+gen) for, (+dat) at, (+acc) unto, to, with, for, against
τὴν art. acc. fem. sg. ὁ ἡ τό the, this, that, he, she, it
μεθοδείαν n. acc. fem. sg. μεθοδεία wile, circumvention
τῆς art. gen. fem. sg. ὁ ἡ τό the, this, that, he, she, it
πλάνης n. gen. fem. sg. πλάνη error, deception, deceit, delusion
15 δὲ conj. δέ but, and, now, also, to the contrary, rather, then
ἐν prep. ἐν (+dat) in, by, with, among, at, on, through, to, within, into, of, for
ἀγάπῃ n. dat. fem. sg. ἀγάπη love, charity, feast of charity
εἰς prep. εἰς (+acc) into, to, unto, for, in, on, toward, against, upon, at, among
αὐτὸν pron. acc. masc. 3p. sg. αὐτός ή ό self, of oneself, even, very, the same, he, she, it
τὰ art. acc. neut. pl. ὁ ἡ τό the, this, that, he, she, it
πάντα adj. acc. neut. pl. πᾶς πᾶσα πᾶν all, every, whosoever, every one, no, whole, any
ὅς relative pron. nom. masc. sg. ὅς ἥ ὅ who, which, what, that
ἡ art. nom. fem. sg. ὁ ἡ τό the, this, that, he, she, it
κεφαλή n. nom. fem. sg. κεφαλή head
ὁ art. nom. masc. sg. ὁ ἡ τό the, this, that, he, she, it
Χριστός n. nom. masc. sg. Χριστός Christ
16 ἐξ prep. ἐκ ἐξ (+gen) of, from, out of, by, on, with, in, among, through
οὗ relative pron. gen. masc. sg. ὅς ἥ ὅ who, which, what, that
πᾶν adj. nom. neut. sg. πᾶς πᾶσα πᾶν all, every, whosoever, every one, no, whole, any
τὸ art. nom. neut. sg. ὁ ἡ τό the, this, that, he, she, it
σῶμα n. nom. neut. sg. σῶμα body, bodily, slave
καὶ conj. καί and, even, also, but
διὰ prep. διά (+gen) by, through, with, in, of, (+acc) for, because of, for a cause
πάσης adj. gen. fem. sg. πᾶς πᾶσα πᾶν all, every, whosoever, every one, no, whole, any
ἁφῆς n. gen. fem. sg. ἁφή joint
τῆς art. gen. fem. sg. ὁ ἡ τό the, this, that, he, she, it
ἐπιχορηγίας n. gen. fem. sg. ἐπιχορηγία supply
κατ' prep. κατά (+gen) against, by, throughout, down, (+acc) according to, after, with
ἐνέργειαν n. acc. fem. sg. ἐνέργεια working, effectual working, operation
ἐν prep. ἐν (+dat) in, by, with, among, at, on, through, to, within, into, of, for
μέτρῳ n. dat. neut. sg. μέτρον measure
ἑνὸς num. gen. neut. sg. εἷς or ἕν one, other, some, any, only, a certain
ἑκάστου adj. gen. neut. sg. ἕκαστος every man, every, every one, any man, each
μέρους n. gen. neut. sg. μέρος part, coast, portion, behalf, respect, piece, side
τὴν art. acc. fem. sg. ὁ ἡ τό the, this, that, he, she, it
αὔξησιν n. acc. fem. sg. αὔξησις increase

τοῦ art. gen. neut. sg. ὁ ἡ τό the, this, that, he, she, it
σώματος n. gen. neut. sg. σῶμα body, bodily, slave
εἰς prep. εἰς (+acc) into, to, unto, for, in, on, toward, against, upon, at, among
οἰκοδομὴν n. acc. fem. sg. οἰκοδομή building, edifying, edification
ἑαυτοῦ reflexive pron. gen. neut. 3p. sg. ἑαυτοῦ himself, herself, itself, yourself, ourselves
ἐν prep. ἐν (+dat) in, by, with, among, at, on, through, to, within, into, of, for
ἀγάπῃ n. dat. fem. sg. ἀγάπη love, charity, feast of charity
17 Τοῦτο demo. pron. acc. neut. sg. οὗτος αὕτη τοῦτο this, the same, this same, he, she, it
οὖν conj. οὖν therefore, then, so, and, now, wherefore
καὶ conj. καί and, even, also, but
ἐν prep. ἐν (+dat) in, by, with, among, at, on, through, to, within, into, of, for
Κυρίῳ n. dat. masc. sg. κύριος Lord, lord, master, sir, LORD, God, Master, owner
μηκέτι adv. μηκέτι no more, no longer, not any more, not henceforth, not henceforward
ὑμᾶς pron. acc. 2p. pl. σύ thou, you
καθὼς adv. καθώς as, even as, according as, according to
καὶ conj. καί and, even, also, but
τὰ art. nom. neut. pl. ὁ ἡ τό the, this, that, he, she, it
λοιπὰ adj. nom. neut. pl. λοιπός other, rest, remnant, residue, which remain
ἔθνη n. nom. neut. pl. ἔθνος Gentile, nation, heathen, people
ἐν prep. ἐν (+dat) in, by, with, among, at, on, through, to, within, into, of, for
ματαιότητι n. dat. fem. sg. ματαιότης vanity
τοῦ art. gen. masc. sg. ὁ ἡ τό the, this, that, he, she, it
νοὸς n. gen. masc. sg. νοῦς understanding, mind
αὐτῶν pron. gen. neut. 3p. pl. αὐτός ἡ ὁ self, of oneself, even, very, the same, he, she, it
18 τῇ art. dat. fem. sg. ὁ ἡ τό the, this, that, he, she, it
διανοίᾳ n. dat. fem. sg. διάνοια mind, understanding, imagination
τῆς art. gen. fem. sg. ὁ ἡ τό the, this, that, he, she, it
ζωῆς n. gen. fem. sg. ζωή life, lifetime
τοῦ art. gen. masc. sg. ὁ ἡ τό the, this, that, he, she, it
Θεοῦ n. gen. masc. sg. θεός God, god
διὰ prep. διά (+gen) by, through, with, in, of, (+acc) for, because of, for a cause
τὴν art. acc. fem. sg. ὁ ἡ τό the, this, that, he, she, it
ἄγνοιαν n. acc. fem. sg. ἄγνοια ignorance
τὴν art. acc. fem. sg. ὁ ἡ τό the, this, that, he, she, it
ἐν prep. ἐν (+dat) in, by, with, among, at, on, through, to, within, into, of, for
αὐτοῖς pron. dat. neut. 3p. pl. αὐτός ἡ ὁ self, of oneself, even, very, the same, he, she, it
διὰ prep. διά (+gen) by, through, with, in, of, (+acc) for, because of, for a cause
τὴν art. acc. fem. sg. ὁ ἡ τό the, this, that, he, she, it
πώρωσιν n. acc. fem. sg. πώρωσις hardness, blindness
τῆς art. gen. fem. sg. ὁ ἡ τό the, this, that, he, she, it
καρδίας n. gen. fem. sg. καρδία heart
αὐτῶν pron. gen. neut. 3p. pl. αὐτός ἡ ὁ self, of oneself, even, very, the same, he, she, it
19 οἵτινες relative pron. nom. masc. pl. ὅστις which, who, whosoever, that, whatsoever
ἑαυτοὺς reflexive pron. acc. masc. 3p. pl. ἑαυτοῦ himself, herself, itself, yourself, ourselves
τῇ art. dat. fem. sg. ὁ ἡ τό the, this, that, he, she, it
ἀσελγείᾳ n. dat. fem. sg. ἀσέλγεια lasciviousness, wantonness, filthy
εἰς prep. εἰς (+acc) into, to, unto, for, in, on, toward, against, upon, at, among
ἐργασίαν n. acc. fem. sg. ἐργασία diligence, working, gain, craft
ἀκαθαρσίας n. gen. fem. sg. ἀκαθαρσία uncleanness
πάσης adj. gen. fem. sg. πᾶς πᾶσα πᾶν all, every, whosoever, every one, no, whole, any
ἐν prep. ἐν (+dat) in, by, with, among, at, on, through, to, within, into, of, for
πλεονεξίᾳ n. dat. fem. sg. πλεονεξία covetousness, covetous practice, greediness
20 ὑμεῖς pron. nom. 2p. pl. σύ thou, you
δὲ conj. δέ but, and, now, also, to the contrary, rather, then
οὐχ particle of negation. οὐ οὐκ οὐχ not, no, neither, none, nay, nor, never, nothing

οὕτως adv. οὕτω οὕτως so, even so, thus, on this wise, likewise, after this manner
τὸν art. acc. masc. sg. ὁ ἡ τό the, this, that, he, she, it
Χριστόν n. acc. masc. sg. Χριστός Christ
21 εἴγε conj. εἴγε if so be that, if, if yet
αὐτὸν pron. acc. masc. 3p. sg. αὐτός ή ὁ self, of oneself, even, very, the same, he, she, it
καὶ conj. καί and, even, also, but
ἐν prep. ἐν (+dat) in, by, with, among, at, on, through, to, within, into, of, for
αὐτῷ pron. dat. masc. 3p. sg. αὐτός ή ὁ self, of oneself, even, very, the same, he, she, it
καθώς adv. καθώς as, even as, according as, according to
ἀλήθεια n. nom. fem. sg. ἀλήθεια truth, verity
ἐν prep. ἐν (+dat) in, by, with, among, at, on, through, to, within, into, of, for
τῷ art. dat. masc. sg. ὁ ἡ τό the, this, that, he, she, it
Ἰησοῦ n. dat. masc. sg. Ἰησοῦς Jesus
22 ὑμᾶς pron. acc. 2p. pl. σύ thou, you
κατὰ prep. κατά (+gen) against, by, throughout, down, (+acc) according to, after, with
τὴν art. acc. fem. sg. ὁ ἡ τό the, this, that, he, she, it
προτέραν compar. adj. acc. fem. sg. πρότερος former
ἀναστροφὴν n. acc. fem. sg. ἀναστροφή conversation
τὸν art. acc. masc. sg. ὁ ἡ τό the, this, that, he, she, it
παλαιὸν adj. acc. masc. sg. παλαιός old
ἄνθρωπον n. acc. masc. sg. ἄνθρωπος man, human being, person, one, certain
τὸν art. acc. masc. sg. ὁ ἡ τό the, this, that, he, she, it
κατὰ prep. κατά (+gen) against, by, throughout, down, (+acc) according to, after, with
τὰς art. acc. fem. pl. ὁ ἡ τό the, this, that, he, she, it
ἐπιθυμίας n. acc. fem. pl. ἐπιθυμία lust, concupiscence, desire
τῆς art. gen. fem. sg. ὁ ἡ τό the, this, that, he, she, it
ἀπάτης n. gen. fem. sg. ἀπάτη deceitfulness, deceit
23 δὲ conj. δέ but, and, now, also, to the contrary, rather, then
τῷ art. dat. neut. sg. ὁ ἡ τό the, this, that, he, she, it
πνεύματι n. dat. neut. sg. πνεῦμα spirit, Spirit, Ghost, ghost, life. of the spirit, wind
τοῦ art. gen. masc. sg. ὁ ἡ τό the, this, that, he, she, it
νοὸς n. gen. masc. sg. νοῦς understanding, mind
ὑμῶν pron. gen. 2p. pl. σύ thou, you
24 καὶ conj. καί and, even, also, but
τὸν art. acc. masc. sg. ὁ ἡ τό the, this, that, he, she, it
καινὸν adj. acc. masc. sg. καινός new
ἄνθρωπον n. acc. masc. sg. ἄνθρωπος man, human being, person, one, certain
τὸν art. acc. masc. sg. ὁ ἡ τό the, this, that, he, she, it
κατὰ prep. κατά (+gen) against, by, throughout, down, (+acc) according to, after, with
Θεὸν n. acc. masc. sg. θεός God, god
ἐν prep. ἐν (+dat) in, by, with, among, at, on, through, to, within, into, of, for
δικαιοσύνῃ n. dat. fem. sg. δικαιοσύνη righteousness
καὶ conj. καί and, even, also, but
ὁσιότητι n. dat. fem. sg. ὁσιότης holiness
τῆς art. gen. fem. sg. ὁ ἡ τό the, this, that, he, she, it
ἀληθείας n. gen. fem. sg. ἀλήθεια truth, verity
25 Διὸ conj. διό wherefore, therefore, for which cause
τὸ art. acc. neut. sg. ὁ ἡ τό the, this, that, he, she, it
ψεῦδος n. acc. neut. sg. ψεῦδος lie, lying
ἀλήθειαν n. acc. fem. sg. ἀλήθεια truth, verity
ἕκαστος adj. nom. masc. sg. ἕκαστος every man, every, every one, any man, each
μετὰ prep. μετά (+gen) with, among, against, (+acc) after
τοῦ art. gen. masc. sg. ὁ ἡ τό the, this, that, he, she, it
πλησίον adv. πλησίον neighbour, near
αὐτοῦ pron. gen. masc. 3p. sg. αὐτός ή ὁ self, of oneself, even, very, the same, he, she, it

ὅτι conj. ὅτι that, for, because, how that, how, because that, for that, though
ἀλλήλων pron. gen. masc. pl. ἀλλήλων one another, themselves, together, mutual
μέλη n. nom. neut. pl. μέλος member
26 καὶ conj. καί and, even, also, but
μὴ particle of negation. μή not, no, lest, neither, none, nothing, nor, never, without
ὁ art. nom. masc. sg. ὁ ἡ τό the, this, that, he, she, it
ἥλιος n. nom. masc. sg. ἥλιος sun, east
μὴ particle of negation. μή not, no, lest, neither, none, nothing, nor, never, without
ἐπὶ prep. ἐπί (+gen) on, in, upon, (+dat) in, at, for, upon, (+acc) on, upon, unto, to, against
τῷ art. dat. masc. sg. ὁ ἡ τό the, this, that, he, she, it
παροργισμῷ n. dat. masc. sg. παροργισμός wrath
ὑμῶν pron. gen. 2p. pl. σύ thou, you
27 μήτε conj. μήτε neither, nor, so much as, or
τόπον n. acc. masc. sg. τόπος place, room, quarter
τῷ art. dat. masc. sg. ὁ ἡ τό the, this, that, he, she, it
διαβόλῳ adj. dat. masc. sg. διάβολος devil, false accuser, Devil, slanderer
28 ὁ art. nom. masc. sg. ὁ ἡ τό the, this, that, he, she, it
μηκέτι adv. μηκέτι no more, no longer, not any more, not henceforth, not henceforward
μᾶλλον adv. μᾶλλον rather, more, more and more, better, much, much the more
δὲ conj. δέ but, and, now, also, to the contrary, rather, then
τὸ art. acc. neut. sg. ὁ ἡ τό the, this, that, he, she, it
ἀγαθόν adj. acc. neut. sg. ἀγαθός good, good thing, that which is good, well
ταῖς art. dat. fem. pl. ὁ ἡ τό the, this, that, he, she, it
χερσὶν n. dat. fem. pl. χείρ hand
ἵνα conj. ἵνα that, to, lest, for to, so that, albeit, because, for, so as
τῷ art. dat. masc. sg. ὁ ἡ τό the, this, that, he, she, it
χρείαν n. acc. fem. sg. χρεία need, necessity, lack, want
29 πᾶς adj. nom. masc. sg. πᾶς πᾶσα πᾶν all, every, whosoever, every one, no, whole, any
λόγος n. nom. masc. sg. λόγος word, saying, account, speech, thing, matter
σαπρὸς adj. nom. masc. sg. σαπρός corrupt, bad
ἐκ prep. ἐκ ἐξ (+gen) of, from, out of, by, on, with, in, among, through
τοῦ art. gen. neut. sg. ὁ ἡ τό the, this, that, he, she, it
στόματος n. gen. neut. sg. στόμα mouth, face, edge
ὑμῶν pron. gen. 2p. pl. σύ thou, you
μὴ particle of negation. μή not, no, lest, neither, none, nothing, nor, never, without
ἀλλ' conj. ἀλλά but, yea, yet, nevertheless, howbeit, nay, therefore
εἴ conj. εἰ if, whether, that, though, forasmuch
τις indefinite pron. nom. masc. sg. τὶς certain, some, any man, one, any thing
ἀγαθὸς adj. nom. masc. sg. ἀγαθός good, good thing, that which is good, well
πρὸς prep. πρός (+gen) for, (+dat) at, (+acc) unto, to, with, for, against
οἰκοδομὴν n. acc. fem. sg. οἰκοδομή building, edifying, edification
τῆς art. gen. fem. sg. ὁ ἡ τό the, this, that, he, she, it
χρείας n. gen. fem. sg. χρεία need, necessity, lack, want
ἵνα conj. ἵνα that, to, lest, for to, so that, albeit, because, for, so as
χάριν n. acc. fem. sg. χάρις grace, thank, favour, pleasure
τοῖς art. dat. masc. pl. ὁ ἡ τό the, this, that, he, she, it
30 καὶ conj. καί and, even, also, but
μὴ particle of negation. μή not, no, lest, neither, none, nothing, nor, never, without
τὸ art. acc. neut. sg. ὁ ἡ τό the, this, that, he, she, it
Πνεῦμα n. acc. neut. sg. πνεῦμα spirit, Spirit, Ghost, ghost, life. of the spirit, wind
τὸ art. acc. neut. sg. ὁ ἡ τό the, this, that, he, she, it
Ἅγιον adj. acc. neut. sg. ἅγιος Holy, holy, saint, Holy One, holy thing, most holy
τοῦ art. gen. masc. sg. ὁ ἡ τό the, this, that, he, she, it
Θεοῦ n. gen. masc. sg. θεός God, god
ἐν prep. ἐν (+dat) in, by, with, among, at, on, through, to, within, into, of, for

ᾧ relative pron. dat. neut. sg. ὅς ἥ ὅ who, which, what, that
εἰς prep. εἰς (+acc) into, to, unto, for, in, on, toward, against, upon, at, among
ἡμέραν n. acc. fem. sg. ἡμέρα day, time, year, while, age, day time
ἀπολυτρώσεως n. gen. fem. sg. ἀπολύτρωσις redemption, deliverance
31 πᾶσα adj. nom. fem. sg. πᾶς πᾶσα πᾶν all, every, whosoever, every one, no, whole, any
πικρία n. nom. fem. sg. πικρία bitterness
καὶ conj. καί and, even, also, but
θυμὸς n. nom. masc. sg. θυμός wrath, fierceness, indignation
καὶ conj. καί and, even, also, but
ὀργὴ n. nom. fem. sg. ὀργή wrath, anger, indignation, vengeance
καὶ conj. καί and, even, also, but
κραυγὴ n. nom. fem. sg. κραυγή cry, crying, clamour
καὶ conj. καί and, even, also, but
βλασφημία n. nom. fem. sg. βλασφημία blasphemy, railing, evil speaking
ἀφ' prep. ἀπό (+gen) from, of, out of, since, for, off, at, by, in, on
ὑμῶν pron. gen. 2p. pl. σύ thou, you
σὺν prep. σύν (+dat) with, beside
πάσῃ adj. dat. fem. sg. πᾶς πᾶσα πᾶν all, every, whosoever, every one, no, whole, any
κακίᾳ n. dat. fem. sg. κακία malice, maliciousness, evil, naughtiness, wickedness
32 δὲ conj. δέ but, and, now, also, to the contrary, rather, then
εἰς prep. εἰς (+acc) into, to, unto, for, in, on, toward, against, upon, at, among
ἀλλήλους pron. acc. masc. pl. ἀλλήλων one another, themselves, together, mutual
χρηστοί adj. nom. masc. pl. χρηστός easy, kind, better, good, gracious, goodness
εὔσπλαγχνοι adj. nom. masc. pl. εὔσπλαγχνος tenderhearted, pitiful
ἑαυτοῖς reflexive pron. dat. masc. 3p. pl. ἑαυτοῦ himself, herself, itself, yourself, ourselves
καθὼς adv. καθώς as, even as, according as, according to
καὶ conj. καί and, even, also, but
ὁ art. nom. masc. sg. ὁ ἡ τό the, this, that, he, she, it
Θεὸς n. nom. masc. sg. θεός God, god
ἐν prep. ἐν (+dat) in, by, with, among, at, on, through, to, within, into, of, for
Χριστῷ n. dat. masc. sg. Χριστός Christ
ὑμῖν pron. dat. 2p. pl. σύ thou, you

5

1 οὖν conj. οὖν therefore, then, so, and, now, wherefore
μιμηταὶ n. nom. masc. pl. μιμητής follower
τοῦ art. gen. masc. sg. ὁ ἡ τό the, this, that, he, she, it
Θεοῦ n. gen. masc. sg. θεός God, god
ὡς adv. ὡς as, when, as it were, how, about, like, as soon as, even as, while
τέκνα n. nom. neut. pl. τέκνον child, son, daughter
ἀγαπητὰ adj. nom. neut. pl. ἀγαπητός beloved, dearly beloved, dear, wellbeloved
2 καὶ conj. καί and, even, also, but
ἐν prep. ἐν (+dat) in, by, with, among, at, on, through, to, within, into, of, for
ἀγάπῃ n. dat. fem. sg. ἀγάπη love, charity, feast of charity
καθὼς adv. καθώς as, even as, according as, according to
καὶ conj. καί and, even, also, but
ὁ art. nom. masc. sg. ὁ ἡ τό the, this, that, he, she, it
Χριστὸς n. nom. masc. sg. Χριστός Christ
ἡμᾶς pron. acc. 1p. pl. ἐγώ I
καὶ conj. καί and, even, also, but
ἑαυτὸν reflexive pron. acc. masc. 3p. sg. ἑαυτοῦ himself, herself, itself, yourself, ourselves
ὑπὲρ prep. ὑπέρ (+gen) for, of, for the sake of, (+acc) above, more than
ἡμῶν pron. gen. 1p. pl. ἐγώ I
προσφορὰν n. acc. fem. sg. προσφορά offering, offering up

καὶ conj. καί and, even, also, but
θυσίαν n. acc. fem. sg. θυσία sacrifice
τῷ art. dat. masc. sg. ὁ ἡ τό the, this, that, he, she, it
Θεῷ n. dat. masc. sg. θεός God, god
εἰς prep. εἰς (+acc) into, to, unto, for, in, on, toward, against, upon, at, among
ὀσμὴν n. acc. fem. sg. ὀσμή odour, savour
εὐωδίας n. gen. fem. sg. εὐωδία sweet savour, sweet smell, sweetsmelling
3 πορνεία n. nom. fem. sg. πορνεία fornication
δὲ conj. δέ but, and, now, also, to the contrary, rather, then
καὶ conj. καί and, even, also, but
πᾶσα adj. nom. fem. sg. πᾶς πᾶσα πᾶν all, every, whosoever, every one, no, whole, any
ἀκαθαρσία n. nom. fem. sg. ἀκαθαρσία uncleanness
ἢ particle. ἤ or, than, either, nor, or else, and, rather than
πλεονεξία n. nom. fem. sg. πλεονεξία covetousness, covetous practice, greediness
μηδὲ adv. μηδέ neither, nor, not, no not, nor yet, not once, not so much as
ἐν prep. ἐν (+dat) in, by, with, among, at, on, through, to, within, into, of, for
ὑμῖν pron. dat. 2p. pl. σύ thou, you
καθὼς adv. καθώς as, even as, according as, according to
ἁγίοις adj. dat. masc. pl. ἅγιος Holy, holy, saint, Holy One, holy thing, most holy
4 καὶ conj. καί and, even, also, but
αἰσχρότης n. nom. fem. sg. αἰσχρότης filthiness
καὶ conj. καί and, even, also, but
μωρολογία n. nom. fem. sg. μωρολογία foolish talking
ἢ particle. ἤ or, than, either, nor, or else, and, rather than
εὐτραπελία n. nom. fem. sg. εὐτραπελία jesting
τὰ art. nom. neut. pl. ὁ ἡ τό the, this, that, he, she, it
οὐκ particle of negation. οὐ οὐκ οὐχ not, no, neither, none, nay, nor, never, nothing
ἀλλὰ conj. ἀλλά but, yea, yet, nevertheless, howbeit, nay, therefore
μᾶλλον adv. μᾶλλον rather, more, more and more, better, much, much the more
εὐχαριστία n. nom. fem. sg. εὐχαριστία thankfulness, thanksgiving, giving of thanks
5 τοῦτο demo. pron. acc. neut. sg. οὗτος αὕτη τοῦτο this, the same, this same, he, she, it
γὰρ conj. γάρ for, and, because, but, indeed
ὅτι conj. ὅτι that, for, because, how that, how, because that, for that, though
πᾶς adj. nom. masc. sg. πᾶς πᾶσα πᾶν all, every, whosoever, every one, no, whole, any
πόρνος n. nom. masc. sg. πόρνος fornicator
ἢ particle. ἤ or, than, either, nor, or else, and, rather than
ἀκάθαρτος adj. nom. masc. sg. ἀκάθαρτος unclean, foul
ἢ particle. ἤ or, than, either, nor, or else, and, rather than
πλεονέκτης n. nom. masc. sg. πλεονέκτης covetous
ὅς relative pron. nom. masc. sg. ὅς ἥ ὅ who, which, what, that
εἰδωλολάτρης n. nom. masc. sg. εἰδωλολάτρης idolater
οὐκ particle of negation. οὐ οὐκ οὐχ not, no, neither, none, nay, nor, never, nothing
κληρονομίαν n. acc. fem. sg. κληρονομία inheritance
ἐν prep. ἐν (+dat) in, by, with, among, at, on, through, to, within, into, of, for
τῇ art. dat. fem. sg. ὁ ἡ τό the, this, that, he, she, it
βασιλείᾳ n. dat. fem. sg. βασιλεία kingdom, reign
τοῦ art. gen. masc. sg. ὁ ἡ τό the, this, that, he, she, it
Χριστοῦ n. gen. masc. sg. Χριστός Christ
καὶ conj. καί and, even, also, but
Θεοῦ n. gen. masc. sg. θεός God, god
6 μηδεὶς num. nom. masc. sg. μηδείς μηδεμία μηδέν no man, nothing, no, none, not at all
ὑμᾶς pron. acc. 2p. pl. σύ thou, you
κενοῖς adj. dat. masc. pl. κενός empty, vain, in vain
λόγοις n. dat. masc. pl. λόγος word, saying, account, speech, thing, matter
διὰ prep. διά (+gen) by, through, with, in, of, (+acc) for, because of, for a cause

ταῦτα demo. pron. acc. neut. pl. οὗτος αὕτη τοῦτο this, the same, this same, he, she, it
γὰρ conj. γάρ for, and, because, but, indeed
ἡ art. nom. fem. sg. ὁ ἡ τό the, this, that, he, she, it
ὀργὴ n. nom. fem. sg. ὀργή wrath, anger, indignation, vengeance
τοῦ art. gen. masc. sg. ὁ ἡ τό the, this, that, he, she, it
Θεοῦ n. gen. masc. sg. θεός God, god
ἐπὶ prep. ἐπί (+gen) on, in, upon, (+dat) in, at, for, upon, (+acc) on, upon, unto, to, against
τοὺς art. acc. masc. pl. ὁ ἡ τό the, this, that, he, she, it
υἱοὺς n. acc. masc. pl. υἱός son, child, descendant, offspring, heir
τῆς art. gen. fem. sg. ὁ ἡ τό the, this, that, he, she, it
ἀπειθείας n. gen. fem. sg. ἀπείθεια unbelief, disobedience
7 μὴ particle of negation. μή not, no, lest, neither, none, nothing, nor, never, without
οὖν conj. οὖν therefore, then, so, and, now, wherefore
συμμέτοχοι adj. nom. masc. pl. συμμέτοχος partaker
αὐτῶν pron. gen. masc. 3p. pl. αὐτός ή ό self, of oneself, even, very, the same, he, she, it
8 γάρ conj. γάρ for, and, because, but, indeed
ποτε adv. ποτέ in time past, at any time, sometimes, in old time, once, when
σκότος n. nom. neut. sg. σκότος darkness
νῦν adv. νῦν now, henceforth, present, this time
δὲ conj. δέ but, and, now, also, to the contrary, rather, then
φῶς n. nom. neut. sg. φῶς light, fire
ἐν prep. ἐν (+dat) in, by, with, among, at, on, through, to, within, into, of, for
Κυρίῳ n. dat. masc. sg. κύριος Lord, lord, master, sir, LORD, God, Master, owner
ὡς adv. ὡς as, when, as it were, how, about, like, as soon as, even as, while
τέκνα n. nom. neut. pl. τέκνον child, son, daughter
φωτὸς n. gen. neut. sg. φῶς light, fire
9 ὁ art. nom. masc. sg. ὁ ἡ τό the, this, that, he, she, it
γὰρ conj. γάρ for, and, because, but, indeed
καρπὸς n. nom. masc. sg. καρπός fruit
τοῦ art. gen. neut. sg. ὁ ἡ τό the, this, that, he, she, it
Πνεύματος n. gen. neut. sg. πνεῦμα spirit, Spirit, Ghost, ghost, life. of the spirit, wind
ἐν prep. ἐν (+dat) in, by, with, among, at, on, through, to, within, into, of, for
πάσῃ adj. dat. fem. sg. πᾶς πᾶσα πᾶν all, every, whosoever, every one, no, whole, any
ἀγαθωσύνῃ n. dat. fem. sg. ἀγαθωσύνη goodness
καὶ conj. καί and, even, also, but
δικαιοσύνῃ n. dat. fem. sg. δικαιοσύνη righteousness
καὶ conj. καί and, even, also, but
ἀληθείᾳ n. dat. fem. sg. ἀλήθεια truth, verity
10 τί interrog. pron. nom. neut. sg. τίς what, who, why, where, which, how
εὐάρεστον adj. nom. neut. sg. εὐάρεστος acceptable, wellpleasing, accepted, please well
τῷ art. dat. masc. sg. ὁ ἡ τό the, this, that, he, she, it
Κυρίῳ n. dat. masc. sg. κύριος Lord, lord, master, sir, LORD, God, Master, owner
11 καὶ conj. καί and, even, also, but
μὴ particle of negation. μή not, no, lest, neither, none, nothing, nor, never, without
τοῖς art. dat. neut. pl. ὁ ἡ τό the, this, that, he, she, it
ἔργοις n. dat. neut. pl. ἔργον work, deed, doing labour
τοῖς art. dat. neut. pl. ὁ ἡ τό the, this, that, he, she, it
ἀκάρποις adj. dat. neut. pl. ἄκαρπος unfruitful, without fruit
τοῦ art. gen. neut. sg. ὁ ἡ τό the, this, that, he, she, it
σκότους n. gen. neut. sg. σκότος darkness
μᾶλλον adv. μᾶλλον rather, more, more and more, better, much, much the more
δὲ conj. δέ but, and, now, also, to the contrary, rather, then
καὶ conj. καί and, even, also, but
12 τὰ art. acc. neut. pl. ὁ ἡ τό the, this, that, he, she, it
γὰρ conj. γάρ for, and, because, but, indeed

κρυφῇ adv. κρυφῇ in secret
ὑπ' prep. ὑπό (+gen) of, by, with, from, among, (+acc) under
αὐτῶν pron. gen. masc. 3p. pl. αὐτός ή ό self, of oneself, even, very, the same, he, she, it
αἰσχρόν adj. nom. neut. sg. αἰσχρός shame
καὶ conj. καί and, even, also, but
13 τὰ art. nom. neut. pl. ὁ ἡ τό the, this, that, he, she, it
δὲ conj. δέ but, and, now, also, to the contrary, rather, then
πάντα adj. nom. neut. pl. πᾶς πᾶσα πᾶν all, every, whosoever, every one, no, whole, any
ὑπὸ prep. ὑπό (+gen) of, by, with, from, among, (+acc) under
τοῦ art. gen. neut. sg. ὁ ἡ τό the, this, that, he, she, it
φωτὸς n. gen. neut. sg. φῶς light, fire
14 πᾶν adj. nom. neut. sg. πᾶς πᾶσα πᾶν all, every, whosoever, every one, no, whole, any
γὰρ conj. γάρ for, and, because, but, indeed
τὸ art. nom. neut. sg. ὁ ἡ τό the, this, that, he, she, it
φῶς n. nom. neut. sg. φῶς light, fire
διὸ conj. διό wherefore, therefore, for which cause
ὁ art. nom. masc. sg. ὁ ἡ τό the, this, that, he, she, it
καὶ conj. καί and, even, also, but
ἐκ prep. ἐκ ἐξ (+gen) of, from, out of, by, on, with, in, among, through
τῶν art. gen. masc. pl. ὁ ἡ τό the, this, that, he, she, it
νεκρῶν adj. gen. masc. pl. νεκρός dead
καὶ conj. καί and, even, also, but
σοι pron. dat. 2p. sg. σύ thou, you
ὁ art. nom. masc. sg. ὁ ἡ τό the, this, that, he, she, it
Χριστός n. nom. masc. sg. Χριστός Christ
15 οὖν conj. οὖν therefore, then, so, and, now, wherefore
πῶς adv. πῶς how, by what means, after what manner
ἀκριβῶς adv. ἀκριβῶς diligently, circumspectly, perfect, perfectly
μὴ particle of negation. μή not, no, lest, neither, none, nothing, nor, never, without
ὡς adv. ὡς as, when, as it were, how, about, like, as soon as, even as, while
ἄσοφοι adj. nom. masc. pl. ἄσοφος fool
ἀλλ' conj. ἀλλά but, yea, yet, nevertheless, howbeit, nay, therefore
ὡς adv. ὡς as, when, as it were, how, about, like, as soon as, even as, while
σοφοί adj. nom. masc. pl. σοφός wise, wiser
16 τὸν art. acc. masc. sg. ὁ ἡ τό the, this, that, he, she, it
καιρόν n. acc. masc. sg. καιρός time, season, due time, opportunity
ὅτι conj. ὅτι that, for, because, how that, how, because that, for that, though
αἱ art. nom. fem. pl. ὁ ἡ τό the, this, that, he, she, it
ἡμέραι n. nom. fem. pl. ἡμέρα day, time, year, while, age, day time
πονηραί adj. nom. fem. pl. πονηρός evil, wicked, bad
17 διὰ prep. διά (+gen) by, through, with, in, of, (+acc) for, because of, for a cause
τοῦτο demo. pron. acc. neut. sg. οὗτος αὕτη τοῦτο this, the same, this same, he, she, it
μὴ particle of negation. μή not, no, lest, neither, none, nothing, nor, never, without
ἄφρονες adj. nom. masc. pl. ἄφρων fool, foolish, unwise
ἀλλὰ conj. ἀλλά but, yea, yet, nevertheless, howbeit, nay, therefore
τί interrog. pron. nom. neut. sg. τίς what, who, why, where, which, how
τὸ art. nom. neut. sg. ὁ ἡ τό the, this, that, he, she, it
θέλημα n. nom. neut. sg. θέλημα will, desire, pleasure
τοῦ art. gen. masc. sg. ὁ ἡ τό the, this, that, he, she, it
Κυρίου n. gen. masc. sg. κύριος Lord, lord, master, sir, LORD, God, Master, owner
18 καὶ conj. καί and, even, also, but
μὴ particle of negation. μή not, no, lest, neither, none, nothing, nor, never, without
οἴνῳ n. dat. masc. sg. οἶνος wine
ἐν prep. ἐν (+dat) in, by, with, among, at, on, through, to, within, into, of, for
ᾧ relative pron. dat. masc. sg. ὅς ἥ ὅ who, which, what, that

ἀσωτία n. nom. fem. sg. ἀσωτία excess, riot
ἀλλὰ conj. ἀλλά but, yea, yet, nevertheless, howbeit, nay, therefore
ἐν prep. ἐν (+dat) in, by, with, among, at, on, through, to, within, into, of, for
Πνεύματι n. dat. neut. sg. πνεῦμα spirit, Spirit, Ghost, ghost, life. of the spirit, wind
19 ἑαυτοῖς reflexive pron. dat. masc. 3p. pl. ἑαυτοῦ himself, herself, itself, yourself, ourselves
ψαλμοῖς n. dat. masc. pl. ψαλμός Psalm, psalm
καὶ conj. καί and, even, also, but
ὕμνοις n. dat. masc. pl. ὕμνος hymn
καὶ conj. καί and, even, also, but
ᾠδαῖς n. dat. fem. pl. ᾠδή song
πνευματικαῖς adj. dat. fem. pl. πνευματικός spiritual
καὶ conj. καί and, even, also, but
ἐν prep. ἐν (+dat) in, by, with, among, at, on, through, to, within, into, of, for
τῇ art. dat. fem. sg. ὁ ἡ τό the, this, that, he, she, it
καρδίᾳ n. dat. fem. sg. καρδία heart
ὑμῶν pron. gen. 2p. pl. σύ thou, you
τῷ art. dat. masc. sg. ὁ ἡ τό the, this, that, he, she, it
Κυρίῳ n. dat. masc. sg. κύριος Lord, lord, master, sir, LORD, God, Master, owner
20 πάντοτε adv. πάντοτε always, ever, always, evermore
ὑπὲρ prep. ὑπέρ (+gen) for, of, for the sake of, (+acc) above, more than
πάντων adj. gen. neut. pl. πᾶς πᾶσα πᾶν all, every, whosoever, every one, no, whole, any
ἐν prep. ἐν (+dat) in, by, with, among, at, on, through, to, within, into, of, for
ὀνόματι n. dat. neut. sg. ὄνομα name, call, surname
τοῦ art. gen. masc. sg. ὁ ἡ τό the, this, that, he, she, it
Κυρίου n. gen. masc. sg. κύριος Lord, lord, master, sir, LORD, God, Master, owner
ἡμῶν pron. gen. 1p. pl. ἐγώ I
Ἰησοῦ n. gen. masc. sg. Ἰησοῦς Jesus
Χριστοῦ n. gen. masc. sg. Χριστός Christ
τῷ art. dat. masc. sg. ὁ ἡ τό the, this, that, he, she, it
Θεῷ n. dat. masc. sg. θεός God, god
καὶ conj. καί and, even, also, but
πατρί n. dat. masc. sg. πατήρ Father, father, parent
21 ἀλλήλοις pron. dat. masc. pl. ἀλλήλων one another, themselves, together, mutual
ἐν prep. ἐν (+dat) in, by, with, among, at, on, through, to, within, into, of, for
φόβῳ n. dat. masc. sg. φόβος fear, terror, sore afraid
Θεοῦ n. gen. masc. sg. θεός God, god
22 Αἱ art. voc. fem. pl. ὁ ἡ τό the, this, that, he, she, it
γυναῖκες n. voc. fem. pl. γυνή woman, wife
τοῖς art. dat. masc. pl. ὁ ἡ τό the, this, that, he, she, it
ἰδίοις adj. dat. masc. pl. ἴδιος one's own, one's, privately
ἀνδράσιν n. dat. masc. pl. ἀνήρ man, husband, sir
ὡς adv. ὡς as, when, as it were, how, about, like, as soon as, even as, while
τῷ art. dat. masc. sg. ὁ ἡ τό the, this, that, he, she, it
Κυρίῳ n. dat. masc. sg. κύριος Lord, lord, master, sir, LORD, God, Master, owner
23 ὅτι conj. ὅτι that, for, because, how that, how, because that, for that, though
ὁ art. nom. masc. sg. ὁ ἡ τό the, this, that, he, she, it
ἀνήρ n. nom. masc. sg. ἀνήρ man, husband, sir
κεφαλὴ n. nom. fem. sg. κεφαλή head
τῆς art. gen. fem. sg. ὁ ἡ τό the, this, that, he, she, it
γυναικὸς n. gen. fem. sg. γυνή woman, wife
ὡς adv. ὡς as, when, as it were, how, about, like, as soon as, even as, while
καὶ conj. καί and, even, also, but
ὁ art. nom. masc. sg. ὁ ἡ τό the, this, that, he, she, it
Χριστὸς n. nom. masc. sg. Χριστός Christ
κεφαλὴ n. nom. fem. sg. κεφαλή head

τῆς art. gen. fem. sg. ὁ ἡ τό the, this, that, he, she, it
ἐκκλησίας n. gen. fem. sg. ἐκκλησία church, assembly
καὶ conj. καί and, even, also, but
αὐτὸς pron. nom. masc. 3p. sg. αὐτός ή ό self, of oneself, even, very, the same, he, she, it
σωτὴρ n. nom. masc. sg. σωτήρ Saviour, saviour
τοῦ art. gen. neut. sg. ὁ ἡ τό the, this, that, he, she, it
σώματος n. gen. neut. sg. σῶμα body, bodily, slave
24 ἀλλ' conj. ἀλλά but, yea, yet, nevertheless, howbeit, nay, therefore
ὥσπερ adv. ὥσπερ as, even as, like as
ἡ art. nom. fem. sg. ὁ ἡ τό the, this, that, he, she, it
ἐκκλησία n. nom. fem. sg. ἐκκλησία church, assembly
τῷ art. dat. masc. sg. ὁ ἡ τό the, this, that, he, she, it
Χριστῷ n. dat. masc. sg. Χριστός Christ
οὕτω adv. οὕτω οὕτως so, even so, thus, on this wise, likewise, after this manner
καὶ conj. καί and, even, also, but
αἱ art. nom. fem. pl. ὁ ἡ τό the, this, that, he, she, it
γυναῖκες n. nom. fem. pl. γυνή woman, wife
τοῖς art. dat. masc. pl. ὁ ἡ τό the, this, that, he, she, it
ἰδίοις adj. dat. masc. pl. ἴδιος one's own, one's, privately
ἀνδράσιν n. dat. masc. pl. ἀνήρ man, husband, sir
ἐν prep. ἐν (+dat) in, by, with, among, at, on, through, to, within, into, of, for
παντί adj. dat. neut. sg. πᾶς πᾶσα πᾶν all, every, whosoever, every one, no, whole, any
25 οἱ art. voc. masc. pl. ὁ ἡ τό the, this, that, he, she, it
ἄνδρες n. voc. masc. pl. ἀνήρ man, husband, sir
τὰς art. acc. fem. pl. ὁ ἡ τό the, this, that, he, she, it
γυναῖκας n. acc. fem. pl. γυνή woman, wife
ἑαυτῶν reflexive pron. gen. masc. 3p. pl. ἑαυτοῦ himself, herself, itself, yourself, ourselves
καθὼς adv. καθώς as, even as, according as, according to
καὶ conj. καί and, even, also, but
ὁ art. nom. masc. sg. ὁ ἡ τό the, this, that, he, she, it
Χριστὸς n. nom. masc. sg. Χριστός Christ
τὴν art. acc. fem. sg. ὁ ἡ τό the, this, that, he, she, it
ἐκκλησίαν n. acc. fem. sg. ἐκκλησία church, assembly
καὶ conj. καί and, even, also, but
ἑαυτὸν reflexive pron. acc. masc. 3p. sg. ἑαυτοῦ himself, herself, itself, yourself, ourselves
ὑπὲρ prep. ὑπέρ (+gen) for, of, for the sake of, (+acc) above, more than
αὐτῆς pron. gen. fem. 3p. sg. αὐτός ή ό self, of oneself, even, very, the same, he, she, it
26 ἵνα conj. ἵνα that, to, lest, for to, so that, albeit, because, for, so as
αὐτὴν pron. acc. fem. 3p. sg. αὐτός ή ό self, of oneself, even, very, the same, he, she, it
τῷ art. dat. neut. sg. ὁ ἡ τό the, this, that, he, she, it
λουτρῷ n. dat. neut. sg. λουτρόν washing
τοῦ art. gen. neut. sg. ὁ ἡ τό the, this, that, he, she, it
ὕδατος n. gen. neut. sg. ὕδωρ water
ἐν prep. ἐν (+dat) in, by, with, among, at, on, through, to, within, into, of, for
ῥήματι n. dat. neut. sg. ῥῆμα word, saying, thing
27 ἵνα conj. ἵνα that, to, lest, for to, so that, albeit, because, for, so as
αὐτὴν pron. acc. fem. 3p. sg. αὐτός ή ό self, of oneself, even, very, the same, he, she, it
ἑαυτῷ reflexive pron. dat. masc. 3p. sg. ἑαυτοῦ himself, herself, itself, yourself, ourselves
ἔνδοξον adj. acc. fem. sg. ἔνδοξος glorious, gorgeously, honourably
τὴν art. acc. fem. sg. ὁ ἡ τό the, this, that, he, she, it
ἐκκλησίαν n. acc. fem. sg. ἐκκλησία church, assembly
μὴ particle of negation. μή not, no, lest, neither, none, nothing, nor, never, without
σπίλον n. acc. masc. sg. σπίλος spot
ἤ particle. ἤ or, than, either, nor, or else, and, rather than
ῥυτίδα n. acc. fem. sg. ῥυτίς wrinkle

ἢ particle. ἤ or, than, either, nor, or else, and, rather than
τι indefinite pron. acc. neut. sg. τὶς certain, some, any man, one, any thing
τῶν art. gen. neut. pl. ὁ ἡ τό the, this, that, he, she, it
τοιούτων demo. pron. gen. neut. pl. τοιοῦτος such, like
ἀλλ' conj. ἀλλά but, yea, yet, nevertheless, howbeit, nay, therefore
ἵνα conj. ἵνα that, to, lest, for to, so that, albeit, because, for, so as
ἁγία adj. nom. fem. sg. ἅγιος Holy, holy, saint, Holy One, holy thing, most holy
καὶ conj. καί and, even, also, but
ἄμωμος adj. nom. fem. sg. ἄμωμος without blame, without fault, without spot
28 οὕτως adv. οὕτω οὕτως so, even so, thus, on this wise, likewise, after this manner
οἱ art. nom. masc. pl. ὁ ἡ τό the, this, that, he, she, it
ἄνδρες n. nom. masc. pl. ἀνήρ man, husband, sir
τὰς art. acc. fem. pl. ὁ ἡ τό the, this, that, he, she, it
ἑαυτῶν reflexive pron. gen. masc. 3p. pl. ἑαυτοῦ himself, herself, itself, yourself, ourselves
γυναῖκας n. acc. fem. pl. γυνή woman, wife
ὡς adv. ὡς as, when, as it were, how, about, like, as soon as, even as, while
τὰ art. acc. neut. pl. ὁ ἡ τό the, this, that, he, she, it
ἑαυτῶν reflexive pron. gen. masc. 3p. pl. ἑαυτοῦ himself, herself, itself, yourself, ourselves
σώματα n. acc. neut. pl. σῶμα body, bodily, slave
ὁ art. nom. masc. sg. ὁ ἡ τό the, this, that, he, she, it
τὴν art. acc. fem. sg. ὁ ἡ τό the, this, that, he, she, it
ἑαυτοῦ reflexive pron. gen. masc. 3p. sg. ἑαυτοῦ himself, herself, itself, yourself, ourselves
γυναῖκα n. acc. fem. sg. γυνή woman, wife
ἑαυτὸν reflexive pron. acc. masc. 3p. sg. ἑαυτοῦ himself, herself, itself, yourself, ourselves
29 οὐδεὶς num. nom. masc. sg. οὐδείς no man, nothing, no, none, neither, not, nought
γάρ conj. γάρ for, and, because, but, indeed
ποτε adv. ποτέ in time past, at any time, sometimes, in old time, once, when
τὴν art. acc. fem. sg. ὁ ἡ τό the, this, that, he, she, it
ἑαυτοῦ reflexive pron. gen. masc. 3p. sg. ἑαυτοῦ himself, herself, itself, yourself, ourselves
σάρκα n. acc. fem. sg. σάρξ flesh, carnal
ἀλλ' conj. ἀλλά but, yea, yet, nevertheless, howbeit, nay, therefore
καὶ conj. καί and, even, also, but
αὐτήν pron. acc. fem. 3p. sg. αὐτός ή ό self, of oneself, even, very, the same, he, she, it
καθὼς adv. καθώς as, even as, according as, according to
καὶ conj. καί and, even, also, but
ὁ art. nom. masc. sg. ὁ ἡ τό the, this, that, he, she, it
Κύριος n. nom. masc. sg. κύριος Lord, lord, master, sir, LORD, God, Master, owner
τὴν art. acc. fem. sg. ὁ ἡ τό the, this, that, he, she, it
ἐκκλησίαν n. acc. fem. sg. ἐκκλησία church, assembly
30 ὅτι conj. ὅτι that, for, because, how that, how, because that, for that, though
μέλη n. nom. neut. pl. μέλος member
τοῦ art. gen. neut. sg. ὁ ἡ τό the, this, that, he, she, it
σώματος n. gen. neut. sg. σῶμα body, bodily, slave
αὐτοῦ pron. gen. masc. 3p. sg. αὐτός ή ό self, of oneself, even, very, the same, he, she, it
ἐκ prep. ἐκ ἐξ (+gen) of, from, out of, by, on, with, in, among, through
τῆς art. gen. fem. sg. ὁ ἡ τό the, this, that, he, she, it
σαρκός n. gen. fem. sg. σάρξ flesh, carnal
αὐτοῦ pron. gen. masc. 3p. sg. αὐτός ή ό self, of oneself, even, very, the same, he, she, it
καὶ conj. καί and, even, also, but
τῶν art. gen. neut. pl. ὁ ἡ τό the, this, that, he, she, it
ὀστέων n. gen. neut. pl. ὀστέον bone
αὐτοῦ pron. gen. masc. 3p. sg. αὐτός ή ό self, of oneself, even, very, the same, he, she, it
31 'Αντὶ prep. ἀντί (+gen) for, because, in the room
τούτου demo. pron. gen. neut. sg. οὗτος αὕτη τοῦτο this, the same, this same, he, she, it
ἄνθρωπος n. nom. masc. sg. ἄνθρωπος man, human being, person, one, certain

τὸν art. acc. masc. sg. ὁ ἡ τό the, this, that, he, she, it
πατέρα n. acc. masc. sg. πατήρ Father, father, parent
αὐτοῦ pron. gen. masc. 3p. sg. αὐτός ἡ ὁ self, of oneself, even, very, the same, he, she, it
καὶ conj. καί and, even, also, but
τὴν art. acc. fem. sg. ὁ ἡ τό the, this, that, he, she, it
μητέρα n. acc. fem. sg. μήτηρ mother
καὶ conj. καί and, even, also, but
πρὸς prep. πρός (+gen) for, (+dat) at, (+acc) unto, to, with, for, against
τὴν art. acc. fem. sg. ὁ ἡ τό the, this, that, he, she, it
γυναῖκα n. acc. fem. sg. γυνή woman, wife
αὐτοῦ pron. gen. masc. 3p. sg. αὐτός ἡ ὁ self, of oneself, even, very, the same, he, she, it
καὶ conj. καί and, even, also, but
οἱ art. nom. masc. pl. ὁ ἡ τό the, this, that, he, she, it
δύο num. nom. masc. pl. δύο two, twain, both
εἰς prep. εἰς (+acc) into, to, unto, for, in, on, toward, against, upon, at, among
σάρκα n. acc. fem. sg. σάρξ flesh, carnal
μίαν num. acc. fem. sg. εἷς or ἕν one, other, some, any, only, a certain
32 τὸ art. nom. neut. sg. ὁ ἡ τό the, this, that, he, she, it
μυστήριον n. nom. neut. sg. μυστήριον mystery
τοῦτο demo. pron. nom. neut. sg. οὗτος αὕτη τοῦτο this, the same, this same, he, she, it
μέγα adj. nom. neut. sg. μέγας great, loud, greatest, high, large, mighty, strong
ἐγὼ pron. nom. 1p. sg. ἐγώ I
δὲ conj. δέ but, and, now, also, to the contrary, rather, then
εἰς prep. εἰς (+acc) into, to, unto, for, in, on, toward, against, upon, at, among
Χριστὸν n. acc. masc. sg. Χριστός Christ
καὶ conj. καί and, even, also, but
εἰς prep. εἰς (+acc) into, to, unto, for, in, on, toward, against, upon, at, among
τὴν art. acc. fem. sg. ὁ ἡ τό the, this, that, he, she, it
ἐκκλησίαν n. acc. fem. sg. ἐκκλησία church, assembly
33 πλὴν adv. πλήν but, nevertheless, but rather, notwithstanding, except, than
καὶ conj. καί and, even, also, but
ὑμεῖς pron. nom. 2p. pl. σύ thou, you
οἱ art. nom. masc. pl. ὁ ἡ τό the, this, that, he, she, it
καθ' prep. κατά (+gen) against, by, throughout, down, (+acc) according to, after, with
ἕνα num. acc. masc. sg. εἷς or ἕν one, other, some, any, only, a certain
ἕκαστος adj. nom. masc. sg. ἕκαστος every man, every, every one, any man, each
τὴν art. acc. fem. sg. ὁ ἡ τό the, this, that, he, she, it
ἑαυτοῦ reflexive pron. gen. masc. 3p. sg. ἑαυτοῦ himself, herself, itself, yourself, ourselves
γυναῖκα n. acc. fem. sg. γυνή woman, wife
οὕτως adv. οὕτω οὕτως so, even so, thus, on this wise, likewise, after this manner
ὡς adv. ὡς as, when, as it were, how, about, like, as soon as, even as, while
ἑαυτόν reflexive pron. acc. masc. 3p. sg. ἑαυτοῦ himself, herself, itself, yourself, ourselves
ἡ art. nom. fem. sg. ὁ ἡ τό the, this, that, he, she, it
δὲ conj. δέ but, and, now, also, to the contrary, rather, then
γυνὴ n. nom. fem. sg. γυνή woman, wife
ἵνα conj. ἵνα that, to, lest, for to, so that, albeit, because, for, so as
τὸν art. acc. masc. sg. ὁ ἡ τό the, this, that, he, she, it
ἄνδρα n. acc. masc. sg. ἀνήρ man, husband, sir

6

1 Τὰ art. voc. neut. pl. ὁ ἡ τό the, this, that, he, she, it
τέκνα n. voc. neut. pl. τέκνον child, son, daughter
τοῖς art. dat. masc. pl. ὁ ἡ τό the, this, that, he, she, it
γονεῦσιν n. dat. masc. pl. γονεύς father, (pl.) parents

ὑμῶν pron. gen. 2p. pl. σύ thou, you
ἐν prep. ἐν (+dat) in, by, with, among, at, on, through, to, within, into, of, for
Κυρίῳ n. dat. masc. sg. κύριος Lord, lord, master, sir, LORD, God, Master, owner
τοῦτο demo. pron. nom. neut. sg. οὗτος αὕτη τοῦτο this, the same, this same, he, she, it
γάρ conj. γάρ for, and, because, but, indeed
δίκαιον adj. nom. neut. sg. δίκαιος righteous, just, meet, right
2 τὸν art. acc. masc. sg. ὁ ἡ τό the, this, that, he, she, it
πατέρα n. acc. masc. sg. πατήρ Father, father, parent
σου pron. gen. 2p. sg. σύ thou, you
καὶ conj. καί and, even, also, but
τὴν art. acc. fem. sg. ὁ ἡ τό the, this, that, he, she, it
μητέρα n. acc. fem. sg. μήτηρ mother
ἥτις relative pron. nom. fem. sg. ὅστις which, who, whosoever, that, whatsoever
ἐντολὴ n. nom. fem. sg. ἐντολή commandment, precept
πρώτη ordinal. adj. nom. fem. sg. πρῶτος first, chief, first of all, chiefest, best
ἐν prep. ἐν (+dat) in, by, with, among, at, on, through, to, within, into, of, for
ἐπαγγελίᾳ n. dat. fem. sg. ἐπαγγελία promise, message
3 ἵνα conj. ἵνα that, to, lest, for to, so that, albeit, because, for, so as
εὖ adv. εὖ well, well done, good
σοι pron. dat. 2p. sg. σύ thou, you
καὶ conj. καί and, even, also, but
μακροχρόνιος adj. nom. masc. sg. μακροχρόνιος live long
ἐπὶ prep. ἐπί (+gen) on, in, upon, (+dat) in, at, for, upon, (+acc) on, upon, unto, to, against
τῆς art. gen. fem. sg. ὁ ἡ τό the, this, that, he, she, it
γῆς n. gen. fem. sg. γῆ earth, land, ground, country
4 καὶ conj. καί and, even, also, but
οἱ art. voc. masc. pl. ὁ ἡ τό the, this, that, he, she, it
πατέρες n. voc. masc. pl. πατήρ Father, father, parent
μὴ particle of negation. μή not, no, lest, neither, none, nothing, nor, never, without
τὰ art. acc. neut. pl. ὁ ἡ τό the, this, that, he, she, it
τέκνα n. acc. neut. pl. τέκνον child, son, daughter
ὑμῶν pron. gen. 2p. pl. σύ thou, you
ἀλλὰ conj. ἀλλά but, yea, yet, nevertheless, howbeit, nay, therefore
αὐτὰ pron. acc. neut. 3p. pl. αὐτός ή ό self, of oneself, even, very, the same, he, she, it
ἐν prep. ἐν (+dat) in, by, with, among, at, on, through, to, within, into, of, for
παιδείᾳ n. dat. fem. sg. παιδεία nurture, instruction, chastening, chastisement
καὶ conj. καί and, even, also, but
νουθεσίᾳ n. dat. fem. sg. νουθεσία admonition
Κυρίου n. gen. masc. sg. κύριος Lord, lord, master, sir, LORD, God, Master, owner
5 Οἱ art. voc. masc. pl. ὁ ἡ τό the, this, that, he, she, it
δοῦλοι n. voc. masc. pl. δοῦλος servant, bondman, bond, slave
τοῖς art. dat. masc. pl. ὁ ἡ τό the, this, that, he, she, it
κυρίοις n. dat. masc. pl. κύριος Lord, lord, master, sir, LORD, God, Master, owner
κατὰ prep. κατά (+gen) against, by, throughout, down, (+acc) according to, after, with
σάρκα n. acc. fem. sg. σάρξ flesh, carnal
μετὰ prep. μετά (+gen) with, among, against, (+acc) after
φόβου n. gen. masc. sg. φόβος fear, terror, sore afraid
καὶ conj. καί and, even, also, but
τρόμου n. gen. masc. sg. τρόμος trembling, tremble
ἐν prep. ἐν (+dat) in, by, with, among, at, on, through, to, within, into, of, for
ἁπλότητι n. dat. fem. sg. ἁπλότης simplicity, singleness, bountifulness, liberal, liberality
τῆς art. gen. fem. sg. ὁ ἡ τό the, this, that, he, she, it
καρδίας n. gen. fem. sg. καρδία heart
ὑμῶν pron. gen. 2p. pl. σύ thou, you
ὡς adv. ὡς as, when, as it were, how, about, like, as soon as, even as, while

τῷ art. dat. masc. sg. ὁ ἡ τό the, this, that, he, she, it
Χριστῷ n. dat. masc. sg. Χριστός Christ
6 μὴ particle of negation. μή not, no, lest, neither, none, nothing, nor, never, without
κατ' prep. κατά (+gen) against, by, throughout, down, (+acc) according to, after, with
ὀφθαλμοδουλείαν n. acc. fem. sg. ὀφθαλμοδουλεία eyeservice
ὡς adv. ὡς as, when, as it were, how, about, like, as soon as, even as, while
ἀνθρωπάρεσκοι adj. nom. masc. pl. ἀνθρωπάρεσκος menpleaser
ἀλλ' conj. ἀλλά but, yea, yet, nevertheless, howbeit, nay, therefore
ὡς adv. ὡς as, when, as it were, how, about, like, as soon as, even as, while
δοῦλοι n. nom. masc. pl. δοῦλος servant, bondman, bond, slave
τοῦ art. gen. masc. sg. ὁ ἡ τό the, this, that, he, she, it
Χριστοῦ n. gen. masc. sg. Χριστός Christ
τὸ art. acc. neut. sg. ὁ ἡ τό the, this, that, he, she, it
θέλημα n. acc. neut. sg. θέλημα will, desire, pleasure
τοῦ art. gen. masc. sg. ὁ ἡ τό the, this, that, he, she, it
Θεοῦ n. gen. masc. sg. θεός God, god
ἐκ prep. ἐκ ἐξ (+gen) of, from, out of, by, on, with, in, among, through
ψυχῆς n. gen. fem. sg. ψυχή life, soul, mind, heart
7 μετ' prep. μετά (+gen) with, among, against, (+acc) after
εὐνοίας n. gen. fem. sg. εὔνοια benevolence, good will
ὡς adv. ὡς as, when, as it were, how, about, like, as soon as, even as, while
τῷ art. dat. masc. sg. ὁ ἡ τό the, this, that, he, she, it
Κυρίῳ n. dat. masc. sg. κύριος Lord, lord, master, sir, LORD, God, Master, owner
καὶ conj. καί and, even, also, but
οὐκ particle of negation. οὐ οὐκ οὐχ not, no, neither, none, nay, nor, never, nothing
ἀνθρώποις n. dat. masc. pl. ἄνθρωπος man, human being, person, one, certain
8 ὅτι conj. ὅτι that, for, because, how that, how, because that, for that, though
ὃ relative pron. acc. neut. sg. ὅς ἥ ὅ who, which, what, that
ἐάν conj. ἐάν if, soever, except, though, and if, but, whether, if so, so
τι indefinite pron. acc. neut. sg. τὶς certain, some, any man, one, any thing
ἕκαστος adj. nom. masc. sg. ἕκαστος every man, every, every one, any man, each
ἀγαθόν adj. acc. neut. sg. ἀγαθός good, good thing, that which is good, well
τοῦτο demo. pron. acc. neut. sg. οὗτος αὕτη τοῦτο this, the same, this same, he, she, it
παρὰ prep. παρά (+gen) of, from, (+dat) with, for, (+acc) beside, at, by, above, against
τοῦ art. gen. masc. sg. ὁ ἡ τό the, this, that, he, she, it
Κυρίου n. gen. masc. sg. κύριος Lord, lord, master, sir, LORD, God, Master, owner
εἴτε conj. εἴτε whether
δοῦλος n. nom. masc. sg. δοῦλος servant, bondman, bond, slave
εἴτε conj. εἴτε whether
ἐλεύθερος adj. nom. masc. sg. ἐλεύθερος free, freewoman, at liberty, freeman
9 καὶ conj. καί and, even, also, but
οἱ art. voc. masc. pl. ὁ ἡ τό the, this, that, he, she, it
κύριοι n. voc. masc. pl. κύριος Lord, lord, master, sir, LORD, God, Master, owner
τὰ art. acc. neut. pl. ὁ ἡ τό the, this, that, he, she, it
αὐτὰ adj. acc. neut. pl. αὐτός ή ό self, of oneself, even, very, the same, he, she, it
πρὸς prep. πρός (+gen) for, (+dat) at, (+acc) unto, to, with, for, against
αὐτούς pron. acc. masc. 3p. pl. αὐτός ή ό self, of oneself, even, very, the same, he, she, it
τὴν art. acc. fem. sg. ὁ ἡ τό the, this, that, he, she, it
ἀπειλήν n. acc. fem. sg. ἀπειλή threatening
ὅτι conj. ὅτι that, for, because, how that, how, because that, for that, though
καὶ conj. καί and, even, also, but
ὑμῶν pron. gen. 2p. pl. σύ thou, you
αὐτῶν pron. gen. masc. 3p. pl. αὐτός ή ό self, of oneself, even, very, the same, he, she, it
ὁ art. nom. masc. sg. ὁ ἡ τό the, this, that, he, she, it
Κύριός n. nom. masc. sg. κύριος Lord, lord, master, sir, LORD, God, Master, owner

ἐν prep. ἐν (+dat) in, by, with, among, at, on, through, to, within, into, of, for
οὐρανοῖς n. dat. masc. pl. οὐρανός heaven, air, sky
καὶ conj. καί and, even, also, but
προσωποληψία n. nom. fem. sg. προσωποληψία respect of persons
οὐκ particle of negation. οὐ οὐκ οὐχ not, no, neither, none, nay, nor, never, nothing
παρ' prep. παρά (+gen) of, from, (+dat) with, for, (+acc) beside, at, by, above, against
αὐτῷ pron. dat. masc. 3p. sg. αὐτός ή ό self, of oneself, even, very, the same, he, she, it
10 Τὸ art. acc. neut. sg. ὁ ἡ τό the, this, that, he, she, it
λοιπόν adv. λοιπόν finally, henceforth, now, besides, furthermore, moreover, then
ἀδελφοί n. voc. masc. pl. ἀδελφός brother
μου pron. gen. 1p. sg. ἐγώ I
ἐν prep. ἐν (+dat) in, by, with, among, at, on, through, to, within, into, of, for
Κυρίῳ n. dat. masc. sg. κύριος Lord, lord, master, sir, LORD, God, Master, owner
καὶ conj. καί and, even, also, but
ἐν prep. ἐν (+dat) in, by, with, among, at, on, through, to, within, into, of, for
τῷ art. dat. neut. sg. ὁ ἡ τό the, this, that, he, she, it
κράτει n. dat. neut. sg. κράτος power, dominion, might, strength
τῆς art. gen. fem. sg. ὁ ἡ τό the, this, that, he, she, it
ἰσχύος n. gen. fem. sg. ἰσχύς strength, might, power, ability
αὐτοῦ pron. gen. masc. 3p. sg. αὐτός ή ό self, of oneself, even, very, the same, he, she, it
11 τὴν art. acc. fem. sg. ὁ ἡ τό the, this, that, he, she, it
πανοπλίαν n. acc. fem. sg. πανοπλία whole armour, all armour
τοῦ art. gen. masc. sg. ὁ ἡ τό the, this, that, he, she, it
Θεοῦ n. gen. masc. sg. θεός God, god
πρὸς prep. πρός (+gen) for, (+dat) at, (+acc) unto, to, with, for, against
τὸ art. acc. neut. sg. ὁ ἡ τό the, this, that, he, she, it
ὑμᾶς pron. acc. 2p. pl. σύ thou, you
πρὸς prep. πρός (+gen) for, (+dat) at, (+acc) unto, to, with, for, against
τὰς art. acc. fem. pl. ὁ ἡ τό the, this, that, he, she, it
μεθοδείας n. acc. fem. pl. μεθοδεία wile, circumvention
τοῦ art. gen. masc. sg. ὁ ἡ τό the, this, that, he, she, it
διαβόλου adj. gen. masc. sg. διάβολος devil, false accuser, Devil, slanderer
12 ὅτι conj. ὅτι that, for, because, how that, how, because that, for that, though
οὐκ particle of negation. οὐ οὐκ οὐχ not, no, neither, none, nay, nor, never, nothing
ἡμῖν pron. dat. 1p. pl. ἐγώ I
ἡ art. nom. fem. sg. ὁ ἡ τό the, this, that, he, she, it
πάλη n. nom. fem. sg. πάλη wrestle, wrestling
πρὸς prep. πρός (+gen) for, (+dat) at, (+acc) unto, to, with, for, against
αἷμα n. acc. neut. sg. αἷμα blood
καὶ conj. καί and, even, also, but
σάρκα n. acc. fem. sg. σάρξ flesh, carnal
ἀλλὰ conj. ἀλλά but, yea, yet, nevertheless, howbeit, nay, therefore
πρὸς prep. πρός (+gen) for, (+dat) at, (+acc) unto, to, with, for, against
τὰς art. acc. fem. pl. ὁ ἡ τό the, this, that, he, she, it
ἀρχάς n. acc. fem. pl. ἀρχή beginning, principality, corner, first, magistrate, rule
πρὸς prep. πρός (+gen) for, (+dat) at, (+acc) unto, to, with, for, against
τὰς art. acc. fem. pl. ὁ ἡ τό the, this, that, he, she, it
ἐξουσίας n. acc. fem. pl. ἐξουσία power, authority, right, strength, jurisdiction
πρὸς prep. πρός (+gen) for, (+dat) at, (+acc) unto, to, with, for, against
τοὺς art. acc. masc. pl. ὁ ἡ τό the, this, that, he, she, it
κοσμοκράτορας n. acc. masc. pl. κοσμοκράτωρ world-ruler
τοῦ art. gen. neut. sg. ὁ ἡ τό the, this, that, he, she, it
σκότους n. gen. neut. sg. σκότος darkness
τοῦ art. gen. masc. sg. ὁ ἡ τό the, this, that, he, she, it
αἰῶνος n. gen. masc. sg. αἰών ever, ever and ever, evermore, age, eternal, world

τούτου demo. pron. gen. neut. sg. οὗτος αὕτη τοῦτο this, the same, this same, he, she, it
πρὸς prep. πρός (+gen) for, (+dat) at, (+acc) unto, to, with, for, against
τὰ art. acc. neut. pl. ὁ ἡ τό the, this, that, he, she, it
πνευματικὰ adj. acc. neut. pl. πνευματικός spiritual
τῆς art. gen. fem. sg. ὁ ἡ τό the, this, that, he, she, it
πονηρίας n. gen. fem. sg. πονηρία wickedness, iniquity
ἐν prep. ἐν (+dat) in, by, with, among, at, on, through, to, within, into, of, for
τοῖς art. dat. neut. pl. ὁ ἡ τό the, this, that, he, she, it
ἐπουρανίοις adj. dat. neut. pl. ἐπουράνιος heavenly, celestial, high, in heaven
13 διὰ prep. διά (+gen) by, through, with, in, of, (+acc) for, because of, for a cause
τοῦτο demo. pron. acc. neut. sg. οὗτος αὕτη τοῦτο this, the same, this same, he, she, it
τὴν art. acc. fem. sg. ὁ ἡ τό the, this, that, he, she, it
πανοπλίαν n. acc. fem. sg. πανοπλία whole armour, all armour
τοῦ art. gen. masc. sg. ὁ ἡ τό the, this, that, he, she, it
Θεοῦ n. gen. masc. sg. θεός God, god
ἵνα conj. ἵνα that, to, lest, for to, so that, albeit, because, for, so as
ἐν prep. ἐν (+dat) in, by, with, among, at, on, through, to, within, into, of, for
τῇ art. dat. fem. sg. ὁ ἡ τό the, this, that, he, she, it
ἡμέρᾳ n. dat. fem. sg. ἡμέρα day, time, year, while, age, day time
τῇ art. dat. fem. sg. ὁ ἡ τό the, this, that, he, she, it
πονηρᾷ adj. dat. fem. sg. πονηρός evil, wicked, bad
καὶ conj. καί and, even, also, but
ἅπαντα adj. acc. neut. pl. ἅπας all, whole, all things, every, everyone
14 οὖν conj. οὖν therefore, then, so, and, now, wherefore
τὴν art. acc. fem. sg. ὁ ἡ τό the, this, that, he, she, it
ὀσφὺν n. acc. fem. sg. ὀσφύς loins
ὑμῶν pron. gen. 2p. pl. σύ thou, you
ἐν prep. ἐν (+dat) in, by, with, among, at, on, through, to, within, into, of, for
ἀληθείᾳ n. dat. fem. sg. ἀλήθεια truth, verity
καὶ conj. καί and, even, also, but
τὸν art. acc. masc. sg. ὁ ἡ τό the, this, that, he, she, it
θώρακα n. acc. masc. sg. θώραξ breastplate
τῆς art. gen. fem. sg. ὁ ἡ τό the, this, that, he, she, it
δικαιοσύνης n. gen. fem. sg. δικαιοσύνη righteousness
15 καὶ conj. καί and, even, also, but
τοὺς art. acc. masc. pl. ὁ ἡ τό the, this, that, he, she, it
πόδας n. acc. masc. pl. πούς foot
ἐν prep. ἐν (+dat) in, by, with, among, at, on, through, to, within, into, of, for
ἑτοιμασίᾳ n. dat. fem. sg. ἑτοιμασία preparation
τοῦ art. gen. neut. sg. ὁ ἡ τό the, this, that, he, she, it
εὐαγγελίου n. gen. neut. sg. εὐαγγέλιον gospel
τῆς art. gen. fem. sg. ὁ ἡ τό the, this, that, he, she, it
εἰρήνης n. gen. fem. sg. εἰρήνη peace, quietness, rest
16 ἐπὶ prep. ἐπί (+gen) on, in, upon, (+dat) in, at, for, upon, (+acc) on, upon, unto, to, against
πᾶσιν adj. dat. neut. pl. πᾶς πᾶσα πᾶν all, every, whosoever, every one, no, whole, any
τὸν art. acc. masc. sg. ὁ ἡ τό the, this, that, he, she, it
θυρεὸν n. acc. masc. sg. θυρεός shield
τῆς art. gen. fem. sg. ὁ ἡ τό the, this, that, he, she, it
πίστεως n. gen. fem. sg. πίστις faith, assurance, belief, fidelity
ἐν prep. ἐν (+dat) in, by, with, among, at, on, through, to, within, into, of, for
ᾧ relative pron. dat. masc. sg. ὅς ἥ ὅ who, which, what, that
πάντα adj. acc. neut. pl. πᾶς πᾶσα πᾶν all, every, whosoever, every one, no, whole, any
τὰ art. acc. neut. pl. ὁ ἡ τό the, this, that, he, she, it
βέλη n. acc. neut. pl. βέλος dart
τοῦ art. gen. masc. sg. ὁ ἡ τό the, this, that, he, she, it

πονηροῦ adj. gen. masc. sg. πονηρός evil, wicked, bad
τὰ art. acc. neut. pl. ὁ ἡ τό the, this, that, he, she, it
17 καὶ conj. καί and, even, also, but
τὴν art. acc. fem. sg. ὁ ἡ τό the, this, that, he, she, it
περικεφαλαίαν n. acc. fem. sg. περικεφαλαία helmet
τοῦ art. gen. neut. sg. ὁ ἡ τό the, this, that, he, she, it
σωτηρίου adj. gen. neut. sg. σωτήριον salvation
καὶ conj. καί and, even, also, but
τὴν art. acc. fem. sg. ὁ ἡ τό the, this, that, he, she, it
μάχαιραν n. acc. fem. sg. μάχαιρα sword
τοῦ art. gen. neut. sg. ὁ ἡ τό the, this, that, he, she, it
Πνεύματος n. gen. neut. sg. πνεῦμα spirit, Spirit, Ghost, ghost, life. of the spirit, wind
ὅ relative pron. nom. neut. sg. ὅς ἥ ὅ who, which, what, that
ῥῆμα n. nom. neut. sg. ῥῆμα word, saying, thing
Θεοῦ n. gen. masc. sg. θεός God, god
18 διὰ prep. διά (+gen) by, through, with, in, of, (+acc) for, because of, for a cause
πάσης adj. gen. fem. sg. πᾶς πᾶσα πᾶν all, every, whosoever, every one, no, whole, any
προσευχῆς n. gen. fem. sg. προσευχή prayer
καὶ conj. καί and, even, also, but
δεήσεως n. gen. fem. sg. δέησις prayer, supplication, request
ἐν prep. ἐν (+dat) in, by, with, among, at, on, through, to, within, into, of, for
παντὶ adj. dat. masc. sg. πᾶς πᾶσα πᾶν all, every, whosoever, every one, no, whole, any
καιρῷ n. dat. masc. sg. καιρός time, season, due time, opportunity
ἐν prep. ἐν (+dat) in, by, with, among, at, on, through, to, within, into, of, for
Πνεύματι n. dat. neut. sg. πνεῦμα spirit, Spirit, Ghost, ghost, life. of the spirit, wind
καὶ conj. καί and, even, also, but
εἰς prep. εἰς (+acc) into, to, unto, for, in, on, toward, against, upon, at, among
αὐτὸ pron. acc. neut. 3p. sg. αὐτός ή ό self, of oneself, even, very, the same, he, she, it
τοῦτο demo. pron. acc. neut. sg. οὗτος αὕτη τοῦτο this, the same, this same, he, she, it
ἐν prep. ἐν (+dat) in, by, with, among, at, on, through, to, within, into, of, for
πάσῃ adj. dat. fem. sg. πᾶς πᾶσα πᾶν all, every, whosoever, every one, no, whole, any
προσκαρτερήσει n. dat. fem. sg. προσκαρτέρησις perseverance
καὶ conj. καί and, even, also, but
δεήσει n. dat. fem. sg. δέησις prayer, supplication, request
περὶ prep. περί (+gen) of, for, concerning, (+acc) about, concerning, in
πάντων adj. gen. masc. pl. πᾶς πᾶσα πᾶν all, every, whosoever, every one, no, whole, any
τῶν art. gen. masc. pl. ὁ ἡ τό the, this, that, he, she, it
ἁγίων adj. gen. masc. pl. ἅγιος Holy, holy, saint, Holy One, holy thing, most holy
19 καὶ conj. καί and, even, also, but
ὑπὲρ prep. ὑπέρ (+gen) for, of, for the sake of, (+acc) above, more than
ἐμοῦ pron. gen. 1p. sg. ἐγώ I
ἵνα conj. ἵνα that, to, lest, for to, so that, albeit, because, for, so as
μοι pron. dat. 1p. sg. ἐγώ I
λόγος n. nom. masc. sg. λόγος word, saying, account, speech, thing, matter
ἐν prep. ἐν (+dat) in, by, with, among, at, on, through, to, within, into, of, for
ἀνοίξει n. dat. fem. sg. ἄνοιξις open, opening
τοῦ art. gen. neut. sg. ὁ ἡ τό the, this, that, he, she, it
στόματός n. gen. neut. sg. στόμα mouth, face, edge
μου pron. gen. 1p. sg. ἐγώ I
ἐν prep. ἐν (+dat) in, by, with, among, at, on, through, to, within, into, of, for
παρρησίᾳ n. dat. fem. sg. παρρησία boldness, confidence, openly, plainly, freely
τὸ art. acc. neut. sg. ὁ ἡ τό the, this, that, he, she, it
μυστήριον n. acc. neut. sg. μυστήριον mystery
τοῦ art. gen. neut. sg. ὁ ἡ τό the, this, that, he, she, it
εὐαγγελίου n. gen. neut. sg. εὐαγγέλιον gospel

20 ὑπὲρ prep. ὑπέρ (+gen) for, of, for the sake of, (+acc) above, more than
οὗ relative pron. gen. neut. sg. ὅς ἥ ὅ who, which, what, that
ἐν prep. ἐν (+dat) in, by, with, among, at, on, through, to, within, into, of, for
ἁλύσει n. dat. fem. sg. ἅλυσις chain, bond
ἵνα conj. ἵνα that, to, lest, for to, so that, albeit, because, for, so as
ἐν prep. ἐν (+dat) in, by, with, among, at, on, through, to, within, into, of, for
αὐτῷ pron. dat. neut. 3p. sg. αὐτός ή ό self, of oneself, even, very, the same, he, she, it
ὡς adv. ὡς as, when, as it were, how, about, like, as soon as, even as, while
με pron. acc. 1p. sg. ἐγώ I
21 Ἵνα conj. ἵνα that, to, lest, for to, so that, albeit, because, for, so as
δὲ conj. δέ but, and, now, also, to the contrary, rather, then
καὶ conj. καί and, even, also, but
ὑμεῖς pron. nom. 2p. pl. σύ thou, you
τὰ art. acc. neut. pl. ὁ ἡ τό the, this, that, he, she, it
κατ' prep. κατά (+gen) against, by, throughout, down, (+acc) according to, after, with
ἐμέ pron. acc. 1p. sg. ἐγώ I
τί interrog. pron. acc. neut. sg. τίς what, who, why, where, which, how
πάντα adj. acc. neut. pl. πᾶς πᾶσα πᾶν all, every, whosoever, every one, no, whole, any
ὑμῖν pron. dat. 2p. pl. σύ thou, you
Τύχικος n. nom. masc. sg. Τυχικός Tychicus
ὁ art. nom. masc. sg. ὁ ἡ τό the, this, that, he, she, it
ἀγαπητὸς adj. nom. masc. sg. ἀγαπητός beloved, dearly beloved, dear, wellbeloved
ἀδελφὸς n. nom. masc. sg. ἀδελφός brother
καὶ conj. καί and, even, also, but
πιστὸς adj. nom. masc. sg. πιστός faithful, believing, true, sure
διάκονος n. nom. masc. sg. διάκονος minister, servant, deacon
ἐν prep. ἐν (+dat) in, by, with, among, at, on, through, to, within, into, of, for
Κυρίῳ n. dat. masc. sg. κύριος Lord, lord, master, sir, LORD, God, Master, owner
22 ὃν relative pron. acc. masc. sg. ὅς ἥ ὅ who, which, what, that
πρὸς prep. πρός (+gen) for, (+dat) at, (+acc) unto, to, with, for, against
ὑμᾶς pron. acc. 2p. pl. σύ thou, you
εἰς prep. εἰς (+acc) into, to, unto, for, in, on, toward, against, upon, at, among
αὐτὸ pron. acc. neut. 3p. sg. αὐτός ή ό self, of oneself, even, very, the same, he, she, it
τοῦτο demo. pron. acc. neut. sg. οὗτος αὕτη τοῦτο this, the same, this same, he, she, it
ἵνα conj. ἵνα that, to, lest, for to, so that, albeit, because, for, so as
τὰ art. acc. neut. pl. ὁ ἡ τό the, this, that, he, she, it
περὶ prep. περί (+gen) of, for, concerning, (+acc) about, concerning, in
ἡμῶν pron. gen. 1p. pl. ἐγώ I
καὶ conj. καί and, even, also, but
τὰς art. acc. fem. pl. ὁ ἡ τό the, this, that, he, she, it
καρδίας n. acc. fem. pl. καρδία heart
ὑμῶν pron. gen. 2p. pl. σύ thou, you
23 Εἰρήνη n. nom. fem. sg. εἰρήνη peace, quietness, rest
τοῖς art. dat. masc. pl. ὁ ἡ τό the, this, that, he, she, it
ἀδελφοῖς n. dat. masc. pl. ἀδελφός brother
καὶ conj. καί and, even, also, but
ἀγάπη n. nom. fem. sg. ἀγάπη love, charity, feast of charity
μετὰ prep. μετά (+gen) with, among, against, (+acc) after
πίστεως n. gen. fem. sg. πίστις faith, assurance, belief, fidelity
ἀπὸ prep. ἀπό (+gen) from, of, out of, since, for, off, at, by, in, on
Θεοῦ n. gen. masc. sg. θεός God, god
πατρὸς n. gen. masc. sg. πατήρ Father, father, parent
καὶ conj. καί and, even, also, but
Κυρίου n. gen. masc. sg. κύριος Lord, lord, master, sir, LORD, God, Master, owner
Ἰησοῦ n. gen. masc. sg. Ἰησοῦς Jesus

Χριστοῦ n. gen. masc. sg. Χριστός Christ
24 ἡ art. nom. fem. sg. ὁ ἡ τό the, this, that, he, she, it
χάρις n. nom. fem. sg. χάρις grace, thank, favour, pleasure
μετὰ prep. μετά (+gen) with, among, against, (+acc) after
πάντων adj. gen. masc. pl. πᾶς πᾶσα πᾶν all, every, whosoever, every one, no, whole, any
τῶν art. gen. masc. pl. ὁ ἡ τό the, this, that, he, she, it
τὸν art. acc. masc. sg. ὁ ἡ τό the, this, that, he, she, it
Κύριον n. acc. masc. sg. κύριος Lord, lord, master, sir, LORD, God, Master, owner
ἡμῶν pron. gen. 1p. pl. ἐγώ I
Ἰησοῦν n. acc. masc. sg. Ἰησοῦς Jesus
Χριστὸν n. acc. masc. sg. Χριστός Christ
ἐν prep. ἐν (+dat) in, by, with, among, at, on, through, to, within, into, of, for
ἀφθαρσίᾳ n. dat. fem. sg. ἀφθαρσία immortality, incorruption, sincerity

ΠΑΥΛΟΥ ΤΟΥ ΑΠΟΣΤΟΛΟΥ
Η ΠΡΟΣ
ΦΙΛΙΠΠΗΣΙΟΥΣ ΕΠΙΣΤΟΛΗ

1

1 Παῦλος n. nom. masc. sg. Παῦλος Paul, Paulus
καὶ conj. καί and, even, also, but
Τιμόθεος n. nom. masc. sg. Τιμόθεος Timotheus, Timothy
δοῦλοι n. nom. masc. pl. δοῦλος servant, bondman, bond, slave
Ἰησοῦ n. gen. masc. sg. Ἰησοῦς Jesus
Χριστοῦ n. gen. masc. sg. Χριστός Christ
πᾶσιν adj. dat. masc. pl. πᾶς πᾶσα πᾶν all, every, whosoever, every one, no, whole, any
τοῖς art. dat. masc. pl. ὁ ἡ τό the, this, that, he, she, it
ἁγίοις adj. dat. masc. pl. ἅγιος Holy, holy, saint, Holy One, holy thing, most holy
ἐν prep. ἐν (+dat) in, by, with, among, at, on, through, to, within, into, of, for
Χριστῷ n. dat. masc. sg. Χριστός Christ
Ἰησοῦ n. dat. masc. sg. Ἰησοῦς Jesus
τοῖς art. dat. masc. pl. ὁ ἡ τό the, this, that, he, she, it
Φιλίπποις n. dat. masc. pl. Φίλιπποι Philippi
ἐν prep. ἐν (+dat) in, by, with, among, at, on, through, to, within, into, of, for
σὺν prep. σύν (+dat) with, beside
ἐπισκόποις n. dat. masc. pl. ἐπίσκοπος overseer, bishop
καὶ conj. καί and, even, also, but
διακόνοις n. dat. masc. pl. διάκονος minister, servant, deacon
2 χάρις n. nom. fem. sg. χάρις grace, thank, favour, pleasure
ὑμῖν pron. dat. 2p. pl. σύ thou, you
καὶ conj. καί and, even, also, but
εἰρήνη n. nom. fem. sg. εἰρήνη peace, quietness, rest
ἀπὸ prep. ἀπό (+gen) from, of, out of, since, for, off, at, by, in, on
Θεοῦ n. gen. masc. sg. θεός God, god
πατρὸς n. gen. masc. sg. πατήρ Father, father, parent
ἡμῶν pron. gen. 1p. pl. ἐγώ I
καὶ conj. καί and, even, also, but
Κυρίου n. gen. masc. sg. κύριος Lord, lord, master, sir, LORD, God, Master, owner
Ἰησοῦ n. gen. masc. sg. Ἰησοῦς Jesus
Χριστοῦ n. gen. masc. sg. Χριστός Christ
3 τῷ art. dat. masc. sg. ὁ ἡ τό the, this, that, he, she, it
Θεῷ n. dat. masc. sg. θεός God, god
μου pron. gen. 1p. sg. ἐγώ I
ἐπὶ prep. ἐπί (+gen) on, in, upon, (+dat) in, at, for, upon, (+acc) on, upon, unto, to, against
πάσῃ adj. dat. fem. sg. πᾶς πᾶσα πᾶν all, every, whosoever, every one, no, whole, any
τῇ art. dat. fem. sg. ὁ ἡ τό the, this, that, he, she, it
μνείᾳ n. dat. fem. sg. μνεία mention, remembrance
ὑμῶν pron. gen. 2p. pl. σύ thou, you
4 πάντοτε adv. πάντοτε always, ever, always, evermore
ἐν prep. ἐν (+dat) in, by, with, among, at, on, through, to, within, into, of, for
πάσῃ adj. dat. fem. sg. πᾶς πᾶσα πᾶν all, every, whosoever, every one, no, whole, any
δεήσει n. dat. fem. sg. δέησις prayer, supplication, request
μου pron. gen. 1p. sg. ἐγώ I
ὑπὲρ prep. ὑπέρ (+gen) for, of, for the sake of, (+acc) above, more than
πάντων adj. gen. masc. pl. πᾶς πᾶσα πᾶν all, every, whosoever, every one, no, whole, any
ὑμῶν pron. gen. 2p. pl. σύ thou, you

μετὰ prep. μετά (+gen) with, among, against, (+acc) after
χαρᾶς n. gen. fem. sg. χαρά joy, gladness, joyfulness
τὴν art. acc. fem. sg. ὁ ἡ τό the, this, that, he, she, it
δέησιν n. acc. fem. sg. δέησις prayer, supplication, request
5 ἐπὶ prep. ἐπί (+gen) on, in, upon, (+dat) in, at, for, upon, (+acc) on, upon, unto, to, against
τῇ art. dat. fem. sg. ὁ ἡ τό the, this, that, he, she, it
κοινωνίᾳ n. dat. fem. sg. κοινωνία fellowship, communion, contribution, distribution
ὑμῶν pron. gen. 2p. pl. σύ thou, you
εἰς prep. εἰς (+acc) into, to, unto, for, in, on, toward, against, upon, at, among
τὸ art. acc. neut. sg. ὁ ἡ τό the, this, that, he, she, it
εὐαγγέλιον n. acc. neut. sg. εὐαγγέλιον gospel
ἀπὸ prep. ἀπό (+gen) from, of, out of, since, for, off, at, by, in, on
πρώτης ordinal. adj. gen. fem. sg. πρῶτος first, chief, first of all, chiefest, best
ἡμέρας n. gen. fem. sg. ἡμέρα day, time, year, while, age, day time
ἄχρι prep. ἄχρι or ἄχρις (+gen) until, unto, till, even to, as far as, while, into
τοῦ art. gen. masc. sg. ὁ ἡ τό the, this, that, he, she, it
νῦν adv. νῦν now, henceforth, present, this time
6 αὐτὸ pron. acc. neut. 3p. sg. αὐτός ή ό self, of oneself, even, very, the same, he, she, it
τοῦτο demo. pron. acc. neut. sg. οὗτος αὕτη τοῦτο this, the same, this same, he, she, it
ὅτι conj. ὅτι that, for, because, how that, how, because that, for that, though
ὁ art. nom. masc. sg. ὁ ἡ τό the, this, that, he, she, it
ἐν prep. ἐν (+dat) in, by, with, among, at, on, through, to, within, into, of, for
ὑμῖν pron. dat. 2p. pl. σύ thou, you
ἔργον n. acc. neut. sg. ἔργον work, deed, doing labour
ἀγαθὸν adj. acc. neut. sg. ἀγαθός good, good thing, that which is good, well
ἄχρις prep. ἄχρι or ἄχρις (+gen) until, unto, till, even to, as far as, while, into
ἡμέρας n. gen. fem. sg. ἡμέρα day, time, year, while, age, day time
Ἰησοῦ n. gen. masc. sg. Ἰησοῦς Jesus
Χριστοῦ n. gen. masc. sg. Χριστός Christ
7 καθώς adv. καθώς as, even as, according as, according to
δίκαιον adj. nom. neut. sg. δίκαιος righteous, just, meet, right
ἐμοὶ pron. dat. 1p. sg. ἐγώ I
τοῦτο demo. pron. acc. neut. sg. οὗτος αὕτη τοῦτο this, the same, this same, he, she, it
ὑπὲρ prep. ὑπέρ (+gen) for, of, for the sake of, (+acc) above, more than
πάντων adj. gen. masc. pl. πᾶς πᾶsa πᾶν all, every, whosoever, every one, no, whole, any
ὑμῶν pron. gen. 2p. pl. σύ thou, you
διὰ prep. διά (+gen) by, through, with, in, of, (+acc) for, because of, for a cause
τὸ art. acc. neut. sg. ὁ ἡ τό the, this, that, he, she, it
με pron. acc. 1p. sg. ἐγώ I
ἐν prep. ἐν (+dat) in, by, with, among, at, on, through, to, within, into, of, for
τῇ art. dat. fem. sg. ὁ ἡ τό the, this, that, he, she, it
καρδίᾳ n. dat. fem. sg. καρδία heart
ὑμᾶς pron. acc. 2p. pl. σύ thou, you
ἔν prep. ἐν (+dat) in, by, with, among, at, on, through, to, within, into, of, for
τε conj. τέ and, both, also
τοῖς art. dat. masc. pl. ὁ ἡ τό the, this, that, he, she, it
δεσμοῖς n. dat. masc. pl. δεσμός bond, band, chain, string
μου pron. gen. 1p. sg. ἐγώ I
καὶ conj. καί and, even, also, but
τῇ art. dat. fem. sg. ὁ ἡ τό the, this, that, he, she, it
ἀπολογίᾳ n. dat. fem. sg. ἀπολογία defence, answer, answer for oneself, clear oneself
καὶ conj. καί and, even, also, but
βεβαιώσει n. dat. fem. sg. βεβαίωσις confirmation
τοῦ art. gen. neut. sg. ὁ ἡ τό the, this, that, he, she, it
εὐαγγελίου n. gen. neut. sg. εὐαγγέλιον gospel

συγκοινωνούς n. acc. masc. pl. συγκοινωνός companion, partake with, partaker
μου pron. gen. 1p. sg. ἐγώ I
τῆς art. gen. fem. sg. ὁ ἡ τό the, this, that, he, she, it
άριτος n. gen. fem. sg. χάρις grace, thank, favour, pleasure
πάντας adj. acc. masc. pl. πᾶς πᾶσα πᾶν all, every, whosoever, every one, no, whole, any
ὑμᾶς pron. acc. 2p. pl. σύ thou, you
8 μάρτυς n. nom. masc. sg. μάρτυς or μάρτυρ witness, martyr, record
γάρ conj. γάρ for, and, because, but, indeed
μου pron. gen. 1p. sg. ἐγώ I
ὁ art. nom. masc. sg. ὁ ἡ τό the, this, that, he, she, it
Θεός n. nom. masc. sg. θεός God, god
ὡς adv. ὡς as, when, as it were, how, about, like, as soon as, even as, while
πάντας adj. acc. masc. pl. πᾶς πᾶσα πᾶν all, every, whosoever, every one, no, whole, any
ὑμᾶς pron. acc. 2p. pl. σύ thou, you
ἐν prep. ἐν (+dat) in, by, with, among, at, on, through, to, within, into, of, for
σπλάγχνοις n. dat. neut. pl. σπλάγχνον tender, bowels, inward affection
Ἰησοῦ n. gen. masc. sg. Ἰησοῦς Jesus
Χριστοῦ n. gen. masc. sg. Χριστός Christ
9 καὶ conj. καί and, even, also, but
τοῦτο demo. pron. acc. neut. sg. οὗτος αὕτη τοῦτο this, the same, this same, he, she, it
ἵνα conj. ἵνα that, to, lest, for to, so that, albeit, because, for, so as
ἡ art. nom. fem. sg. ὁ ἡ τό the, this, that, he, she, it
ἀγάπη n. nom. fem. sg. ἀγάπη love, charity, feast of charity
ὑμῶν pron. gen. 2p. pl. σύ thou, you
ἔτι adv. ἔτι yet, more, any more, further, still, moreover
μᾶλλον adv. μᾶλλον rather, more, more and more, better, much, much the more
καὶ conj. καί and, even, also, but
μᾶλλον adv. μᾶλλον rather, more, more and more, better, much, much the more
ἐν prep. ἐν (+dat) in, by, with, among, at, on, through, to, within, into, of, for
ἐπιγνώσει n. dat. fem. sg. ἐπίγνωσις knowledge, acknowledging, acknowledgement
καὶ conj. καί and, even, also, but
πάσῃ adj. dat. fem. sg. πᾶς πᾶσα πᾶν all, every, whosoever, every one, no, whole, any
αἰσθήσει n. dat. fem. sg. αἴσθησις judgment, discernment, understanding, preception
10 εἰς prep. εἰς (+acc) into, to, unto, for, in, on, toward, against, upon, at, among
τὸ art. acc. neut. sg. ὁ ἡ τό the, this, that, he, she, it
ὑμᾶς pron. acc. 2p. pl. σύ thou, you
τὰ art. acc. neut. pl. ὁ ἡ τό the, this, that, he, she, it
ἵνα conj. ἵνα that, to, lest, for to, so that, albeit, because, for, so as
εἰλικρινεῖς adj. nom. masc. pl. εἰλικρινής sincere, pure
καὶ conj. καί and, even, also, but
ἀπρόσκοποι adj. nom. masc. pl. ἀπρόσκοπος none offence, without offence
ἡμέραν n. acc. fem. sg. ἡμέρα day, time, year, while, age, day time
Χριστοῦ n. gen. masc. sg. Χριστός Christ
11 καρπῶν n. gen. masc. pl. καρπός fruit
δικαιοσύνης n. gen. fem. sg. δικαιοσύνη righteousness
τῶν art. gen. masc. pl. ὁ ἡ τό the, this, that, he, she, it
διὰ prep. διά (+gen) by, through, with, in, of, (+acc) for, because of, for a cause
Ἰησοῦ n. gen. masc. sg. Ἰησοῦς Jesus
Χριστοῦ n. gen. masc. sg. Χριστός Christ
εἰς prep. εἰς (+acc) into, to, unto, for, in, on, toward, against, upon, at, among
δόξαν n. acc. fem. sg. δόξα glory, honour, praise, dignity, worship
καὶ conj. καί and, even, also, but
ἔπαινον n. acc. masc. sg. ἔπαινος praise
Θεοῦ n. gen. masc. sg. θεός God, god
12 δὲ conj. δέ but, and, now, also, to the contrary, rather, then

ὑμᾶς pron. acc. 2p. pl. σύ thou, you
ἀδελφοί n. voc. masc. pl. ἀδελφός brother
ὅτι conj. ὅτι that, for, because, how that, how, because that, for that, though
τὰ art. nom. neut. pl. ὁ ἡ τό the, this, that, he, she, it
κατ' prep. κατά (+gen) against, by, throughout, down, (+acc) according to, after, with
ἐμὲ pron. acc. 1p. sg. ἐγώ I
μᾶλλον adv. μᾶλλον rather, more, more and more, better, much, much the more
εἰς prep. εἰς (+acc) into, to, unto, for, in, on, toward, against, upon, at, among
προκοπὴν n. acc. fem. sg. προκοπή furtherance, profiting
τοῦ art. gen. neut. sg. ὁ ἡ τό the, this, that, he, she, it
εὐαγγελίου n. gen. neut. sg. εὐαγγέλιον gospel
13 ὥστε conj. ὥστε so that, wherefore, insomuch that, therefore, that, so then
τοὺς art. acc. masc. pl. ὁ ἡ τό the, this, that, he, she, it
δεσμούς n. acc. masc. pl. δεσμός bond, band, chain, string
μου pron. gen. 1p. sg. ἐγώ I
φανεροὺς adj. acc. masc. pl. φανερός manifest, abroad, open, known, outward, appear
ἐν prep. ἐν (+dat) in, by, with, among, at, on, through, to, within, into, of, for
Χριστῷ n. dat. masc. sg. Χριστός Christ
ἐν prep. ἐν (+dat) in, by, with, among, at, on, through, to, within, into, of, for
ὅλῳ adj. dat. neut. sg. ὅλος all, whole, every whit, altogether
τῷ art. dat. neut. sg. ὁ ἡ τό the, this, that, he, she, it
πραιτωρίῳ n. dat. neut. sg. πραιτώριον judgement hall, common hall, palace, Praetorium
καὶ conj. καί and, even, also, but
τοῖς art. dat. masc. pl. ὁ ἡ τό the, this, that, he, she, it
λοιποῖς adj. dat. masc. pl. λοιπός other, rest, remnant, residue, which remain
πάσι adj. dat. masc. pl. πᾶς πᾶsa πᾶν all, every, whosoever, every one, no, whole, any
14 καὶ conj. καί and, even, also, but
τοὺς art. acc. masc. pl. ὁ ἡ τό the, this, that, he, she, it
πλείονας compar. adj. acc. masc. pl. πολύς many, great, much, long, abundant
τῶν art. gen. masc. pl. ὁ ἡ τό the, this, that, he, she, it
ἀδελφῶν n. gen. masc. pl. ἀδελφός brother
ἐν prep. ἐν (+dat) in, by, with, among, at, on, through, to, within, into, of, for
Κυρίῳ n. dat. masc. sg. κύριος Lord, lord, master, sir, LORD, God, Master, owner
τοῖς art. dat. masc. pl. ὁ ἡ τό the, this, that, he, she, it
δεσμοῖς n. dat. masc. pl. δεσμός bond, band, chain, string
μου pron. gen. 1p. sg. ἐγώ I
περισσοτέρως adv. περισσοτέρως more exceedingly, more abundantly, more frequent
ἀφόβως adv. ἀφόβως without fear
τὸν art. acc. masc. sg. ὁ ἡ τό the, this, that, he, she, it
λόγον n. acc. masc. sg. λόγος word, saying, account, speech, thing, matter
15 τινὲς indefinite pron. nom. masc. pl. τὶς certain, some, any man, one, any thing
μὲν conj. μέν indeed, verily, truly, even, so, some
καὶ conj. καί and, even, also, but
διὰ prep. διά (+gen) by, through, with, in, of, (+acc) for, because of, for a cause
φθόνον n. acc. masc. sg. φθόνος envy, envying
καὶ conj. καί and, even, also, but
ἔριν n. acc. fem. sg. ἔρις debate, strife, contention, variance
τινὲς indefinite pron. nom. masc. pl. τὶς certain, some, any man, one, any thing
δὲ conj. δέ but, and, now, also, to the contrary, rather, then
καὶ conj. καί and, even, also, but
δι' prep. διά (+gen) by, through, with, in, of, (+acc) for, because of, for a cause
εὐδοκίαν n. acc. fem. sg. εὐδοκία good pleasure, good will, desire
τὸν art. acc. masc. sg. ὁ ἡ τό the, this, that, he, she, it
Χριστὸν n. acc. masc. sg. Χριστός Christ
16 οἱ art. nom. masc. pl. ὁ ἡ τό the, this, that, he, she, it

μὲν conj. μέν indeed, verily, truly, even, so, some
ἐξ prep. ἐκ ἐξ (+gen) of, from, out of, by, on, with, in, among, through
ἐριθείας n. gen. fem. sg. ἐριθεία strife, contention, contentious
τὸν art. acc. masc. sg. ὁ ἡ τό the, this, that, he, she, it
Χριστὸν n. acc. masc. sg. Χριστός Christ
οὐχ particle of negation. οὐ οὐκ οὐχ not, no, neither, none, nay, nor, never, nothing
ἁγνῶς adv. ἁγνῶς sincerely
θλῖψιν n. acc. fem. sg. θλῖψις tribulation, affliction, anguish, persecution
τοῖς art. dat. masc. pl. ὁ ἡ τό the, this, that, he, she, it
δεσμοῖς n. dat. masc. pl. δεσμός bond, band, chain, string
μου pron. gen. 1p. sg. ἐγώ I
17 οἱ art. nom. masc. pl. ὁ ἡ τό the, this, that, he, she, it
δὲ conj. δέ but, and, now, also, to the contrary, rather, then
ἐξ prep. ἐκ ἐξ (+gen) of, from, out of, by, on, with, in, among, through
ἀγάπης n. gen. fem. sg. ἀγάπη love, charity, feast of charity
ὅτι conj. ὅτι that, for, because, how that, how, because that, for that, though
εἰς prep. εἰς (+acc) into, to, unto, for, in, on, toward, against, upon, at, among
ἀπολογίαν n. acc. fem. sg. ἀπολογία defence, answer, answer for oneself, clear oneself
τοῦ art. gen. neut. sg. ὁ ἡ τό the, this, that, he, she, it
εὐαγγελίου n. gen. neut. sg. εὐαγγέλιον gospel
18 τί interrog. pron. nom. neut. sg. τίς what, who, why, where, which, how
γάρ particle. γάρ for, and, because, but, indeed
πλὴν adv. πλήν but, nevertheless, but rather, notwithstanding, except, than
παντὶ adj. dat. masc. sg. πᾶς πᾶσα πᾶν all, every, whosoever, every one, no, whole, any
τρόπῳ n. dat. masc. sg. τρόπος as, manner, means, way, conversation
εἴτε conj. εἴτε whether
προφάσει n. dat. fem. sg. πρόφασις pretence, cloke, colour, show
εἴτε conj. εἴτε whether
ἀληθείᾳ n. dat. fem. sg. ἀλήθεια truth, verity
Χριστὸς n. nom. masc. sg. Χριστός Christ
καὶ conj. καί and, even, also, but
ἐν prep. ἐν (+dat) in, by, with, among, at, on, through, to, within, into, of, for
τούτῳ demo. pron. dat. neut. sg. οὗτος αὕτη τοῦτο this, the same, this same, he, she, it
ἀλλὰ conj. ἀλλά but, yea, yet, nevertheless, howbeit, nay, therefore
καὶ conj. καί and, even, also, but
19 γὰρ conj. γάρ for, and, because, but, indeed
ὅτι conj. ὅτι that, for, because, how that, how, because that, for that, though
τοῦτό demo. pron. nom. neut. sg. οὗτος αὕτη τοῦτο this, the same, this same, he, she, it
μοι pron. dat. 1p. sg. ἐγώ I
εἰς prep. εἰς (+acc) into, to, unto, for, in, on, toward, against, upon, at, among
σωτηρίαν n. acc. fem. sg. σωτηρία salvation, deliver, health, saving
διὰ prep. διά (+gen) by, through, with, in, of, (+acc) for, because of, for a cause
τῆς art. gen. fem. sg. ὁ ἡ τό the, this, that, he, she, it
ὑμῶν pron. gen. 2p. pl. σύ thou, you
δεήσεως n. gen. fem. sg. δέησις prayer, supplication, request
καὶ conj. καί and, even, also, but
ἐπιχορηγίας n. gen. fem. sg. ἐπιχορηγία supply
τοῦ art. gen. neut. sg. ὁ ἡ τό the, this, that, he, she, it
Πνεύματος n. gen. neut. sg. πνεῦμα spirit, Spirit, Ghost, ghost, life. of the spirit, wind
Ἰησοῦ n. gen. masc. sg. Ἰησοῦς Jesus
Χριστοῦ n. gen. masc. sg. Χριστός Christ
20 κατὰ prep. κατά (+gen) against, by, throughout, down, (+acc) according to, after, with
τὴν art. acc. fem. sg. ὁ ἡ τό the, this, that, he, she, it
ἀποκαραδοκίαν n. acc. fem. sg. ἀποκαραδοκία earnest expectation
καὶ conj. καί and, even, also, but

ἐλπίδα n. acc. fem. sg. ἐλπίς hope, faith
μου pron. gen. 1p. sg. ἐγώ I
ὅτι conj. ὅτι that, for, because, how that, how, because that, for that, though
ἐν prep. ἐν (+dat) in, by, with, among, at, on, through, to, within, into, of, for
οὐδενὶ num. dat. neut. sg. οὐδείς no man, nothing, no, none, neither, not, nought
ἀλλ' conj. ἀλλά but, yea, yet, nevertheless, howbeit, nay, therefore
ἐν prep. ἐν (+dat) in, by, with, among, at, on, through, to, within, into, of, for
πάσῃ adj. dat. fem. sg. πᾶς πᾶσα πᾶν all, every, whosoever, every one, no, whole, any
παρρησίᾳ n. dat. fem. sg. παρρησία boldness, confidence, openly, plainly, freely
ὡς adv. ὡς as, when, as it were, how, about, like, as soon as, even as, while
πάντοτε adv. πάντοτε always, ever, always, evermore
καὶ conj. καί and, even, also, but
νῦν adv. νῦν now, henceforth, present, this time
Χριστὸς n. nom. masc. sg. Χριστός Christ
ἐν prep. ἐν (+dat) in, by, with, among, at, on, through, to, within, into, of, for
τῷ art. dat. neut. sg. ὁ ἡ τό the, this, that, he, she, it
σώματί n. dat. neut. sg. σῶμα body, bodily, slave
μου pron. gen. 1p. sg. ἐγώ I
εἴτε conj. εἴτε whether
διὰ prep. διά (+gen) by, through, with, in, of, (+acc) for, because of, for a cause
ζωῆς n. gen. fem. sg. ζωή life, lifetime
εἴτε conj. εἴτε whether
διὰ prep. διά (+gen) by, through, with, in, of, (+acc) for, because of, for a cause
θανάτου n. gen. masc. sg. θάνατος death
21 ἐμοὶ pron. dat. 1p. sg. ἐγώ I
γὰρ conj. γάρ for, and, because, but, indeed
τὸ art. nom. neut. sg. ὁ ἡ τό the, this, that, he, she, it
Χριστὸς n. nom. masc. sg. Χριστός Christ
καὶ conj. καί and, even, also, but
τὸ art. nom. neut. sg. ὁ ἡ τό the, this, that, he, she, it
κέρδος n. nom. neut. sg. κέρδος gain, lucre
22 εἰ conj. εἰ if, whether, that, though, forasmuch
δὲ conj. δέ but, and, now, also, to the contrary, rather, then
τὸ art. nom. neut. sg. ὁ ἡ τό the, this, that, he, she, it
ἐν prep. ἐν (+dat) in, by, with, among, at, on, through, to, within, into, of, for
σαρκί n. dat. fem. sg. σάρξ flesh, carnal
τοῦτό demo. pron. nom. neut. sg. οὗτος αὕτη τοῦτο this, the same, this same, he, she, it
μοι pron. dat. 1p. sg. ἐγώ I
καρπὸς n. nom. masc. sg. καρπός fruit
ἔργου n. gen. neut. sg. ἔργον work, deed, doing labour
καὶ conj. καί and, even, also, but
τί interrog. pron. acc. neut. sg. τίς what, who, why, where, which, how
οὐ particle of negation. οὐ οὐκ οὐχ not, no, neither, none, nay, nor, never, nothing
23 γὰρ conj. γάρ for, and, because, but, indeed
ἐκ prep. ἐκ ἐξ (+gen) of, from, out of, by, on, with, in, among, through
τῶν art. gen. neut. pl. ὁ ἡ τό the, this, that, he, she, it
δύο num. gen. neut. pl. δύο two, twain, both
τὴν art. acc. fem. sg. ὁ ἡ τό the, this, that, he, she, it
ἐπιθυμίαν n. acc. fem. sg. ἐπιθυμία lust, concupiscence, desire
εἰς prep. εἰς (+acc) into, to, unto, for, in, on, toward, against, upon, at, among
τὸ art. acc. neut. sg. ὁ ἡ τό the, this, that, he, she, it
καὶ conj. καί and, even, also, but
σὺν prep. σύν (+dat) with, beside
Χριστῷ n. dat. masc. sg. Χριστός Christ
πολλῷ adj. dat. neut. sg. πολύς many, great, much, long, abundant

μᾶλλον adv. μᾶλλον rather, more, more and more, better, much, much the more
κρεῖσσον compar. adj. nom. neut. sg. κρείσσων better
24 τὸ art. nom. neut. sg. ὁ ἡ τό the, this, that, he, she, it
δὲ conj. δέ but, and, now, also, to the contrary, rather, then
ἐν prep. ἐν (+dat) in, by, with, among, at, on, through, to, within, into, of, for
τῇ art. dat. fem. sg. ὁ ἡ τό the, this, that, he, she, it
σαρκὶ n. dat. fem. sg. σάρξ flesh, carnal
ἀναγκαιότερον compar. adj. nom. neut. sg. ἀναγκαῖος near, necessary, more needful
δι' prep. διά (+gen) by, through, with, in, of, (+acc) for, because of, for a cause
ὑμᾶς pron. acc. 2p. pl. σύ thou, you
25 καὶ conj. καί and, even, also, but
τοῦτο demo. pron. acc. neut. sg. οὗτος αὕτη τοῦτο this, the same, this same, he, she, it
ὅτι conj. ὅτι that, for, because, how that, how, because that, for that, though
καὶ conj. καί and, even, also, but
πᾶσιν adj. dat. masc. pl. πᾶς πᾶσα πᾶν all, every, whosoever, every one, no, whole, any
ὑμῖν pron. dat. 2p. pl. σύ thou, you
εἰς prep. εἰς (+acc) into, to, unto, for, in, on, toward, against, upon, at, among
τὴν art. acc. fem. sg. ὁ ἡ τό the, this, that, he, she, it
ὑμῶν pron. gen. 2p. pl. σύ thou, you
προκοπὴν n. acc. fem. sg. προκοπή furtherance, profiting
καὶ conj. καί and, even, also, but
χαρὰν n. acc. fem. sg. χαρά joy, gladness, joyfulness
τῆς art. gen. fem. sg. ὁ ἡ τό the, this, that, he, she, it
πίστεως n. gen. fem. sg. πίστις faith, assurance, belief, fidelity
26 ἵνα conj. ἵνα that, to, lest, for to, so that, albeit, because, for, so as
τὸ art. nom. neut. sg. ὁ ἡ τό the, this, that, he, she, it
καύχημα n. nom. neut. sg. καύχημα whereof to glory, rejoicing, glorying, boasting
ὑμῶν pron. gen. 2p. pl. σύ thou, you
ἐν prep. ἐν (+dat) in, by, with, among, at, on, through, to, within, into, of, for
Χριστῷ n. dat. masc. sg. Χριστός Christ
Ἰησοῦ n. dat. masc. sg. Ἰησοῦς Jesus
ἐν prep. ἐν (+dat) in, by, with, among, at, on, through, to, within, into, of, for
ἐμοὶ pron. dat. 1p. sg. ἐγώ I
διὰ prep. διά (+gen) by, through, with, in, of, (+acc) for, because of, for a cause
τῆς art. gen. fem. sg. ὁ ἡ τό the, this, that, he, she, it
ἐμῆς poss. pron. gen. fem. 1p. sg. ἐμός my, mine, mine own, of me
παρουσίας n. gen. fem. sg. παρουσία coming, presence
πάλιν adv. πάλιν again
πρὸς prep. πρός (+gen) for, (+dat) at, (+acc) unto, to, with, for, against
ὑμᾶς pron. acc. 2p. pl. σύ thou, you
27 μόνον adv. μόνος only, alone, by oneself
ἀξίως adv. ἀξίως worthy, as become, after a godly sort
τοῦ art. gen. neut. sg. ὁ ἡ τό the, this, that, he, she, it
εὐαγγελίου n. gen. neut. sg. εὐαγγέλιον gospel
τοῦ art. gen. masc. sg. ὁ ἡ τό the, this, that, he, she, it
Χριστοῦ n. gen. masc. sg. Χριστός Christ
ἵνα conj. ἵνα that, to, lest, for to, so that, albeit, because, for, so as
εἴτε conj. εἴτε whether
καὶ conj. καί and, even, also, but
ὑμᾶς pron. acc. 2p. pl. σύ thou, you
εἴτε conj. εἴτε whether
τὰ art. acc. neut. pl. ὁ ἡ τό the, this, that, he, she, it
περὶ prep. περί (+gen) of, for, concerning, (+acc) about, concerning, in
ὑμῶν pron. gen. 2p. pl. σύ thou, you
ὅτι conj. ὅτι that, for, because, how that, how, because that, for that, though

ἐν prep. ἐν (+dat) in, by, with, among, at, on, through, to, within, into, of, for
ἑνὶ num. dat. neut. sg. εἷς or ἕν one, other, some, any, only, a certain
πνεύματι n. dat. neut. sg. πνεῦμα spirit, Spirit, Ghost, ghost, life. of the spirit, wind
μιᾷ num. dat. fem. sg. εἷς or ἕν one, other, some, any, only, a certain
ψυχῇ n. dat. fem. sg. ψυχή life, soul, mind, heart
τῇ art. dat. fem. sg. ὁ ἡ τό the, this, that, he, she, it
πίστει n. dat. fem. sg. πίστις faith, assurance, belief, fidelity
τοῦ art. gen. masc. sg. ὁ ἡ τό the, this, that, he, she, it
εὐαγγελίου n. gen. neut. sg. εὐαγγέλιον gospel
28 καὶ conj. καί and, even, also, but
μὴ particle of negation. μή not, no, lest, neither, none, nothing, nor, never, without
ἐν prep. ἐν (+dat) in, by, with, among, at, on, through, to, within, into, of, for
μηδενὶ num. dat. neut. sg. μηδείς μηδεμία μηδέν no man, nothing, no, none, not at all
ὑπὸ prep. ὑπό (+gen) of, by, with, from, among, (+acc) under
τῶν art. gen. masc. pl. ὁ ἡ τό the, this, that, he, she, it
ἥτις relative pron. nom. fem. sg. ὅστις which, who, whosoever, that, whatsoever
αὐτοῖς pron. dat. masc. 3p. pl. αὐτός ή ό self, of oneself, even, very, the same, he, she, it
μέν conj. μέν indeed, verily, truly, even, so, some
ἔνδειξις n. nom. fem. sg. ἔνδειξις declare, evident token, proof
ἀπωλείας n. gen. fem. sg. ἀπώλεια destruction, perdition, waste, damnation
ὑμῖν pron. dat. 2p. pl. σύ thou, you
δὲ conj. δέ but, and, now, also, to the contrary, rather, then
σωτηρίας n. gen. fem. sg. σωτηρία salvation, deliver, health, saving
καὶ conj. καί and, even, also, but
τοῦτο demo. pron. nom. neut. sg. οὗτος αὕτη τοῦτο this, the same, this same, he, she, it
ἀπὸ prep. ἀπό (+gen) from, of, out of, since, for, off, at, by, in, on
Θεοῦ n. gen. masc. sg. θεός God, god
29 ὅτι conj. ὅτι that, for, because, how that, how, because that, for that, though
ὑμῖν pron. dat. 2p. pl. σύ thou, you
τὸ art. nom. neut. sg. ὁ ἡ τό the, this, that, he, she, it
ὑπὲρ prep. ὑπέρ (+gen) for, of, for the sake of, (+acc) above, more than
Χριστοῦ n. gen. masc. sg. Χριστός Christ
οὐ particle of negation. οὐ οὐκ οὐχ not, no, neither, none, nay, nor, never, nothing
μόνον adv. μόνος only, alone, by oneself
τὸ art. nom. neut. sg. ὁ ἡ τό the, this, that, he, she, it
εἰς prep. εἰς (+acc) into, to, unto, for, in, on, toward, against, upon, at, among
αὐτὸν pron. acc. masc. 3p. sg. αὐτός ή ό self, of oneself, even, very, the same, he, she, it
ἀλλὰ conj. ἀλλά but, yea, yet, nevertheless, howbeit, nay, therefore
καὶ conj. καί and, even, also, but
τὸ art. nom. neut. sg. ὁ ἡ τό the, this, that, he, she, it
ὑπὲρ prep. ὑπέρ (+gen) for, of, for the sake of, (+acc) above, more than
αὐτοῦ pron. gen. masc. 3p. sg. αὐτός ή ό self, of oneself, even, very, the same, he, she, it
30 τὸν art. acc. masc. sg. ὁ ἡ τό the, this, that, he, she, it
αὐτὸν adj. acc. masc. sg. αὐτός ή ό self, of oneself, even, very, the same, he, she, it
ἀγῶνα n. acc. masc. sg. ἀγών conflict, fight, contention, race
οἷον relative pron. acc. masc. sg. οἷος what manner of, such as, as, which, what, so as
ἐν prep. ἐν (+dat) in, by, with, among, at, on, through, to, within, into, of, for
ἐμοὶ pron. dat. 1p. sg. ἐγώ I
καὶ conj. καί and, even, also, but
νῦν adv. νῦν now, henceforth, present, this time
ἐν prep. ἐν (+dat) in, by, with, among, at, on, through, to, within, into, of, for
ἐμοὶ pron. dat. 1p. sg. ἐγώ I

2

1 Εἴ conj. εἰ if, whether, that, though, forasmuch
τις indefinite pron. nom. fem. sg. τὶς certain, some, any man, one, any thing
οὖν conj. οὖν therefore, then, so, and, now, wherefore
παράκλησις n. nom. fem. sg. παράκλησις consolation, exhortation, comfort
ἐν prep. ἐν (+dat) in, by, with, among, at, on, through, to, within, into, of, for
Χριστῷ n. dat. masc. sg. Χριστός Christ
εἴ conj. εἰ if, whether, that, though, forasmuch
τι indefinite pron. nom. neut. sg. τὶς certain, some, any man, one, any thing
παραμύθιον n. nom. neut. sg. παραμύθιον comfort
ἀγάπης n. gen. fem. sg. ἀγάπη love, charity, feast of charity
εἴ conj. εἰ if, whether, that, though, forasmuch
τις indefinite pron. nom. fem. sg. τὶς certain, some, any man, one, any thing
κοινωνία n. nom. fem. sg. κοινωνία fellowship, communion, contribution, distribution
Πνεύματος n. gen. neut. sg. πνεῦμα spirit, Spirit, Ghost, ghost, life. of the spirit, wind
εἴ conj. εἰ if, whether, that, though, forasmuch
τινα indefinite pron. nom. neut. pl. τὶς certain, some, any man, one, any thing
σπλάγχνα n. nom. neut. pl. σπλάγχνον tender, bowels, inward affection
καὶ conj. καί and, even, also, but
οἰκτιρμοί n. nom. masc. pl. οἰκτιρμός mercy
2 μου pron. gen. 1p. sg. ἐγώ I
τὴν art. acc. fem. sg. ὁ ἡ τό the, this, that, he, she, it
χαρὰν n. acc. fem. sg. χαρά joy, gladness, joyfulness
ἵνα conj. ἵνα that, to, lest, for to, so that, albeit, because, for, so as
τὸ art. acc. neut. sg. ὁ ἡ τό the, this, that, he, she, it
αὐτὸ pron. acc. neut. 3p. sg. αὐτός ἡ ὁ self, of oneself, even, very, the same, he, she, it
τὴν art. acc. fem. sg. ὁ ἡ τό the, this, that, he, she, it
αὐτὴν adj. acc. fem. sg. αὐτός ἡ ὁ self, of oneself, even, very, the same, he, she, it
ἀγάπην n. acc. fem. sg. ἀγάπη love, charity, feast of charity
σύμψυχοι adj. nom. masc. pl. σύμψυχος of one accord
τὸ art. acc. neut. sg. ὁ ἡ τό the, this, that, he, she, it
ἓν num. acc. neut. sg. εἷς or ἕν one, other, some, any, only, a certain
3 μηδὲν num. acc. neut. sg. μηδείς μηδεμία μηδέν no man, nothing, no, none, not at all
κατὰ prep. κατά (+gen) against, by, throughout, down, (+acc) according to, after, with
ἐριθείαν n. acc. fem. sg. ἐριθεία strife, contention, contentious
ἢ particle. ἤ or, than, either, nor, or else, and, rather than
κενοδοξίαν n. acc. fem. sg. κενοδοξία vainglory
ἀλλὰ conj. ἀλλά but, yea, yet, nevertheless, howbeit, nay, therefore
τῇ art. dat. fem. sg. ὁ ἡ τό the, this, that, he, she, it
ταπεινοφροσύνῃ n. dat. fem. sg. ταπεινοφροσύνη humility of mind, humility, lowliness
ἀλλήλους pron. acc. masc. pl. ἀλλήλων one another, themselves, together, mutual
ἑαυτῶν reflexive pron. gen. masc. 3p. pl. ἑαυτοῦ himself, herself, itself, yourself, ourselves
4 μὴ particle of negation. μή not, no, lest, neither, none, nothing, nor, never, without
τὰ art. acc. neut. pl. ὁ ἡ τό the, this, that, he, she, it
ἑαυτῶν reflexive pron. gen. masc. 3p. pl. ἑαυτοῦ himself, herself, itself, yourself, ourselves
ἕκαστος adj. nom. masc. sg. ἕκαστος every man, every, every one, any man, each
ἀλλὰ conj. ἀλλά but, yea, yet, nevertheless, howbeit, nay, therefore
καὶ conj. καί and, even, also, but
τὰ art. acc. neut. pl. ὁ ἡ τό the, this, that, he, she, it
ἑτέρων adj. gen. masc. pl. ἕτερος another, other, else, strange
ἕκαστος adj. nom. masc. sg. ἕκαστος every man, every, every one, any man, each
5 τοῦτο demo. pron. acc. neut. sg. οὗτος αὕτη τοῦτο this, the same, this same, he, she, it
γὰρ conj. γάρ for, and, because, but, indeed
ἐν prep. ἐν (+dat) in, by, with, among, at, on, through, to, within, into, of, for

ὑμῖν pron. dat. 2p. pl. σύ thou, you
ὃ relative pron. nom. neut. sg. ὅς ἥ ὅ who, which, what, that
καὶ conj. καί and, even, also, but
Χριστῷ n. dat. masc. sg. Χριστός Christ
Ἰησοῦ n. dat. masc. sg. Ἰησοῦς Jesus
6 ὃς relative pron. nom. masc. sg. ὅς ἥ ὅ who, which, what, that
ἐν prep. ἐν (+dat) in, by, with, among, at, on, through, to, within, into, of, for
μορφῇ n. dat. fem. sg. μορφή form
Θεοῦ n. gen. masc. sg. θεός God, god
οὐχ particle of negation. οὐ οὐκ οὐχ not, no, neither, none, nay, nor, never, nothing
ἁρπαγμὸν n. acc. masc. sg. ἁρπαγμός robbery
τὸ art. acc. neut. sg. ὁ ἡ τό the, this, that, he, she, it
ἴσα adj. nom. neut. pl. ἴσος equal, as much, like
Θεῷ n. dat. masc. sg. θεός God, god
7 ἀλλ' conj. ἀλλά but, yea, yet, nevertheless, howbeit, nay, therefore
ἑαυτὸν reflexive pron. acc. masc. 3p. sg. ἑαυτοῦ himself, herself, itself, yourself, ourselves
μορφὴν n. acc. fem. sg. μορφή form
δούλου n. gen. masc. sg. δοῦλος servant, bondman, bond, slave
ἐν prep. ἐν (+dat) in, by, with, among, at, on, through, to, within, into, of, for
ὁμοιώματι n. dat. neut. sg. ὁμοίωμα likeness, made like to, shape, similitude
ἀνθρώπων n. gen. masc. pl. ἄνθρωπος man, human being, person, one, certain
8 καὶ conj. καί and, even, also, but
σχήματι n. dat. neut. sg. σχῆμα fashion
ὡς adv. ὡς as, when, as it were, how, about, like, as soon as, even as, while
ἄνθρωπος n. nom. masc. sg. ἄνθρωπος man, human being, person, one, certain
ἑαυτὸν reflexive pron. acc. masc. 3p. sg. ἑαυτοῦ himself, herself, itself, yourself, ourselves
ὑπήκοος adj. nom. masc. sg. ὑπήκοος obedient
μέχρι prep. μέχρι until, unto, till, to
θανάτου n. gen. masc. sg. θάνατος death
θανάτου n. gen. masc. sg. θάνατος death
δὲ conj. δέ but, and, now, also, to the contrary, rather, then
σταυροῦ n. gen. masc. sg. σταυρός cross
9 διὸ conj. διό wherefore, therefore, for which cause
καὶ conj. καί and, even, also, but
ὁ art. nom. masc. sg. ὁ ἡ τό the, this, that, he, she, it
Θεὸς n. nom. masc. sg. θεός God, god
αὐτὸν pron. acc. masc. 3p. sg. αὐτός ή ό self, of oneself, even, very, the same, he, she, it
καὶ conj. καί and, even, also, but
αὐτῷ pron. dat. masc. 3p. sg. αὐτός ή ό self, of oneself, even, very, the same, he, she, it
ὄνομα n. acc. neut. sg. ὄνομα name, call, surname
τὸ art. acc. neut. sg. ὁ ἡ τό the, this, that, he, she, it
ὑπὲρ prep. ὑπέρ (+gen) for, of, for the sake of, (+acc) above, more than
πᾶν adj. acc. neut. sg. πᾶς πᾶσα πᾶν all, every, whosoever, every one, no, whole, any
ὄνομα n. acc. neut. sg. ὄνομα name, call, surname
10 ἵνα conj. ἵνα that, to, lest, for to, so that, albeit, because, for, so as
ἐν prep. ἐν (+dat) in, by, with, among, at, on, through, to, within, into, of, for
τῷ art. dat. neut. sg. ὁ ἡ τό the, this, that, he, she, it
ὀνόματι n. dat. neut. sg. ὄνομα name, call, surname
Ἰησοῦ n. gen. masc. sg. Ἰησοῦς Jesus
πᾶν adj. nom. neut. sg. πᾶς πᾶσα πᾶν all, every, whosoever, every one, no, whole, any
γόνυ n. nom. neut. sg. γόνυ knee, kneel
ἐπουρανίων adj. gen. masc. pl. ἐπουράνιος heavenly, celestial, high, in heaven
καὶ conj. καί and, even, also, but
ἐπιγείων adj. gen. masc. pl. ἐπίγειος earthly, terrestrial, in earth
καὶ conj. καί and, even, also, but

καταχθονίων adj. gen. masc. pl. καταχθόνιος under the earth
11 καὶ conj. καί and, even, also, but
πᾶσα adj. nom. fem. sg. πᾶς πᾶσα πᾶν all, every, whosoever, every one, no, whole, any
γλῶσσα n. nom. fem. sg. γλῶσσα tongue
ὅτι conj. ὅτι that, for, because, how that, how, because that, for that, though
Κύριος n. nom. masc. sg. κύριος Lord, lord, master, sir, LORD, God, Master, owner
Ἰησοῦς n. nom. masc. sg. Ἰησοῦς Jesus
Χριστὸς n. nom. masc. sg. Χριστός Christ
εἰς prep. εἰς (+acc) into, to, unto, for, in, on, toward, against, upon, at, among
δόξαν n. acc. fem. sg. δόξα glory, honour, praise, dignity, worship
Θεοῦ n. gen. masc. sg. θεός God, god
πατρός n. gen. masc. sg. πατήρ Father, father, parent
12 Ὥστε conj. ὥστε so that, wherefore, insomuch that, therefore, that, so then
ἀγαπητοί adj. voc. masc. pl. ἀγαπητός beloved, dearly beloved, dear, wellbeloved
μου pron. gen. 1p. sg. ἐγώ I
καθὼς adv. καθώς as, even as, according as, according to
πάντοτε adv. πάντοτε always, ever, always, evermore
μὴ particle of negation. μή not, no, lest, neither, none, nothing, nor, never, without
ὡς adv. ὡς as, when, as it were, how, about, like, as soon as, even as, while
ἐν prep. ἐν (+dat) in, by, with, among, at, on, through, to, within, into, of, for
τῇ art. dat. fem. sg. ὁ ἡ τό the, this, that, he, she, it
παρουσίᾳ n. dat. fem. sg. παρουσία coming, presence
μου pron. gen. 1p. sg. ἐγώ I
μόνον adv. μόνος only, alone, by oneself
ἀλλὰ conj. ἀλλά but, yea, yet, nevertheless, howbeit, nay, therefore
νῦν adv. νῦν now, henceforth, present, this time
πολλῷ adj. dat. neut. sg. πολύς many, great, much, long, abundant
μᾶλλον adv. μᾶλλον rather, more, more and more, better, much, much the more
ἐν prep. ἐν (+dat) in, by, with, among, at, on, through, to, within, into, of, for
τῇ art. dat. fem. sg. ὁ ἡ τό the, this, that, he, she, it
ἀπουσίᾳ n. dat. fem. sg. ἀπουσία absence
μου pron. gen. 1p. sg. ἐγώ I
μετὰ prep. μετά (+gen) with, among, against, (+acc) after
φόβου n. gen. masc. sg. φόβος fear, terror, sore afraid
καὶ conj. καί and, even, also, but
τρόμου n. gen. masc. sg. τρόμος trembling, tremble
τὴν art. acc. fem. sg. ὁ ἡ τό the, this, that, he, she, it
ἑαυτῶν reflexive pron. gen. masc. 3p. pl. ἑαυτοῦ himself, herself, itself, yourself, ourselves
σωτηρίαν n. acc. fem. sg. σωτηρία salvation, deliver, health, saving
13 ὁ art. nom. masc. sg. ὁ ἡ τό the, this, that, he, she, it
Θεὸς n. nom. masc. sg. θεός God, god
γάρ conj. γάρ for, and, because, but, indeed
ὁ art. nom. masc. sg. ὁ ἡ τό the, this, that, he, she, it
ἐν prep. ἐν (+dat) in, by, with, among, at, on, through, to, within, into, of, for
ὑμῖν pron. dat. 2p. pl. σύ thou, you
καὶ conj. καί and, even, also, but
τὸ art. acc. neut. sg. ὁ ἡ τό the, this, that, he, she, it
καὶ conj. καί and, even, also, but
τὸ art. acc. neut. sg. ὁ ἡ τό the, this, that, he, she, it
ὑπὲρ prep. ὑπέρ (+gen) for, of, for the sake of, (+acc) above, more than
τῆς art. gen. fem. sg. ὁ ἡ τό the, this, that, he, she, it
εὐδοκίας n. gen. fem. sg. εὐδοκία good pleasure, good will, desire
14 πάντα adj. acc. neut. pl. πᾶς πᾶσα πᾶν all, every, whosoever, every one, no, whole, any
χωρὶς prep. χωρίς (+gen) without, beside. (adv.) by itself, apart, separately
γογγυσμῶν n. gen. masc. pl. γογγυσμός murmuring, grudging

καὶ conj. καί and, even, also, but
διαλογισμῶν n. gen. masc. pl. διαλογισμός thought, reasoning, imagination, disputing
15 ἵνα conj. ἵνα that, to, lest, for to, so that, albeit, because, for, so as
ἄμεμπτοι adj. nom. masc. pl. ἄμεμπτος blameless, faultless, unblamable
καὶ conj. καί and, even, also, but
ἀκέραιοι adj. nom. masc. pl. ἀκέραιος harmless, innocent, simple
τέκνα n. nom. neut. pl. τέκνον child, son, daughter
Θεοῦ n. gen. masc. sg. θεός God, god
ἀμώμητα adj. nom. neut. pl. ἀμώμητος without rebuke, blameless
ἐν prep. ἐν (+dat) in, by, with, among, at, on, through, to, within, into, of, for
μέσῳ adj. dat. neut. sg. μέσος midst, among, mid, between
γενεᾶς n. gen. fem. sg. γενεά generation, age, time, nation
σκολιᾶς adj. gen. fem. sg. σκολιός crooked, froward, untoward
καὶ conj. καί and, even, also, but
ἐν prep. ἐν (+dat) in, by, with, among, at, on, through, to, within, into, of, for
οἷς relative pron. dat. masc. pl. ὅς ἥ ὅ who, which, what, that
ὡς adv. ὡς as, when, as it were, how, about, like, as soon as, even as, while
φωστῆρες n. nom. masc. pl. φωστήρ light
ἐν prep. ἐν (+dat) in, by, with, among, at, on, through, to, within, into, of, for
κόσμῳ n. dat. masc. sg. κόσμος world, adorning
16 λόγον n. acc. masc. sg. λόγος word, saying, account, speech, thing, matter
ζωῆς n. gen. fem. sg. ζωή life, lifetime
εἰς prep. εἰς (+acc) into, to, unto, for, in, on, toward, against, upon, at, among
καύχημα n. acc. neut. sg. καύχημα whereof to glory, rejoicing, glorying, boasting
ἐμοὶ pron. dat. 1p. sg. ἐγώ I
εἰς prep. εἰς (+acc) into, to, unto, for, in, on, toward, against, upon, at, among
ἡμέραν n. acc. fem. sg. ἡμέρα day, time, year, while, age, day time
Χριστοῦ n. gen. masc. sg. Χριστός Christ
ὅτι conj. ὅτι that, for, because, how that, how, because that, for that, though
οὐκ particle of negation. οὐ οὐκ οὐχ not, no, neither, none, nay, nor, never, nothing
εἰς prep. εἰς (+acc) into, to, unto, for, in, on, toward, against, upon, at, among
κενὸν adj. acc. neut. sg. κενός empty, vain, in vain
οὐδὲ adv. οὐδέ neither, nor, not, no, not even, never, not yet
εἰς prep. εἰς (+acc) into, to, unto, for, in, on, toward, against, upon, at, among
κενὸν adj. acc. neut. sg. κενός empty, vain, in vain
17 ἀλλ' conj. ἀλλά but, yea, yet, nevertheless, howbeit, nay, therefore
εἰ conj. εἰ if, whether, that, though, forasmuch
καὶ conj. καί and, even, also, but
ἐπὶ prep. ἐπί (+gen) on, in, upon, (+dat) in, at, for, upon, (+acc) on, upon, unto, to, against
τῇ art. dat. fem. sg. ὁ ἡ τό the, this, that, he, she, it
θυσίᾳ n. dat. fem. sg. θυσία sacrifice
καὶ conj. καί and, even, also, but
λειτουργίᾳ n. dat. fem. sg. λειτουργία ministration, service, ministry
τῆς art. gen. fem. sg. ὁ ἡ τό the, this, that, he, she, it
πίστεως n. gen. fem. sg. πίστις faith, assurance, belief, fidelity
ὑμῶν pron. gen. 2p. pl. σύ thou, you
καὶ conj. καί and, even, also, but
πᾶσιν adj. dat. masc. pl. πᾶς πᾶσα πᾶν all, every, whosoever, every one, no, whole, any
ὑμῖν pron. dat. 2p. pl. σύ thou, you
18 τὸ art. acc. neut. sg. ὁ ἡ τό the, this, that, he, she, it
δ' conj. δέ but, and, now, also, to the contrary, rather, then
αὐτὸ pron. acc. neut. 3p. sg. αὐτός ἡ ὁ self, of oneself, even, very, the same, he, she, it
καὶ conj. καί and, even, also, but
ὑμεῖς pron. nom. 2p. pl. σύ thou, you
καὶ conj. καί and, even, also, but

μοι pron. dat. 1p. sg. ἐγώ I
19 δὲ conj. δέ but, and, now, also, to the contrary, rather, then
ἐν prep. ἐν (+dat) in, by, with, among, at, on, through, to, within, into, of, for
Κυρίῳ n. dat. masc. sg. κύριος Lord, lord, master, sir, LORD, God, Master, owner
Ἰησοῦ n. dat. masc. sg. Ἰησοῦς Jesus
Τιμόθεον n. acc. masc. sg. Τιμόθεος Timotheus, Timothy
ταχέως adv. ταχέως sortly, quickly, soon, hastily, suddenly
ὑμῖν pron. dat. 2p. pl. σύ thou, you
ἵνα conj. ἵνα that, to, lest, for to, so that, albeit, because, for, so as
κἀγὼ pron. nom. 1p. sg. κἀγώ and I, I also, so I, even as I
τὰ art. acc. neut. pl. ὁ ἡ τό the, this, that, he, she, it
περὶ prep. περί (+gen) of, for, concerning, (+acc) about, concerning, in
ὑμῶν pron. gen. 2p. pl. σύ thou, you
20 οὐδένα num. acc. masc. sg. οὐδείς no man, nothing, no, none, neither, not, nought
γὰρ conj. γάρ for, and, because, but, indeed
ἰσόψυχον adj. acc. masc. sg. ἰσόψυχος likeminded
ὅστις relative pron. nom. masc. sg. ὅστις which, who, whosoever, that, whatsoever
γνησίως adv. γνησίως naturally, sincerely, truly
τὰ art. acc. neut. pl. ὁ ἡ τό the, this, that, he, she, it
περὶ prep. περί (+gen) of, for, concerning, (+acc) about, concerning, in
ὑμῶν pron. gen. 2p. pl. σύ thou, you
21 οἱ art. nom. masc. pl. ὁ ἡ τό the, this, that, he, she, it
πάντες adj. nom. masc. pl. πᾶς πᾶσα πᾶν all, every, whosoever, every one, no, whole, any
γὰρ conj. γάρ for, and, because, but, indeed
τὰ art. acc. neut. pl. ὁ ἡ τό the, this, that, he, she, it
ἑαυτῶν reflexive pron. gen. masc. 3p. pl. ἑαυτοῦ himself, herself, itself, yourself, ourselves
οὐ particle of negation. οὐ οὐκ οὐχ not, no, neither, none, nay, nor, never, nothing
τὰ art. acc. neut. pl. ὁ ἡ τό the, this, that, he, she, it
τοῦ art. gen. masc. sg. ὁ ἡ τό the, this, that, he, she, it
Χριστοῦ n. gen. masc. sg. Χριστός Christ
Ἰησοῦ n. gen. masc. sg. Ἰησοῦς Jesus
22 τὴν art. acc. fem. sg. ὁ ἡ τό the, this, that, he, she, it
δὲ conj. δέ but, and, now, also, to the contrary, rather, then
δοκιμὴν n. acc. fem. sg. δοκιμή experience, proof, experiment, trial
αὐτοῦ pron. gen. masc. 3p. sg. αὐτός ἡ ὁ self, of oneself, even, very, the same, he, she, it
ὅτι conj. ὅτι that, for, because, how that, how, because that, for that, though
ὡς adv. ὡς as, when, as it were, how, about, like, as soon as, even as, while
πατρὶ n. dat. masc. sg. πατήρ Father, father, parent
τέκνον n. nom. neut. sg. τέκνον child, son, daughter
σὺν prep. σύν (+dat) with, beside
ἐμοὶ pron. dat. 1p. sg. ἐγώ I
εἰς prep. εἰς (+acc) into, to, unto, for, in, on, toward, against, upon, at, among
τὸ art. acc. neut. sg. ὁ ἡ τό the, this, that, he, she, it
εὐαγγέλιον n. acc. neut. sg. εὐαγγέλιον gospel
23 τοῦτον demo. pron. acc. masc. sg. οὗτος αὕτη τοῦτο this, the same, this same, he, she, it
μὲν conj. μέν indeed, verily, truly, even, so, some
οὖν conj. οὖν therefore, then, so, and, now, wherefore
ὡς adv. ὡς as, when, as it were, how, about, like, as soon as, even as, while
ἂν particle. ἄν Indicating contingency. No English translation.
τὰ art. acc. neut. pl. ὁ ἡ τό the, this, that, he, she, it
περὶ prep. περί (+gen) of, for, concerning, (+acc) about, concerning, in
ἐμὲ pron. acc. 1p. sg. ἐγώ I
ἐξαυτῆς adv. ἐξαυτῆς immediately, by and by, presently, straightway
24 δὲ conj. δέ but, and, now, also, to the contrary, rather, then
ἐν prep. ἐν (+dat) in, by, with, among, at, on, through, to, within, into, of, for

Κυρίῳ n. dat. masc. sg. κύριος Lord, lord, master, sir, LORD, God, Master, owner
ὅτι conj. ὅτι that, for, because, how that, how, because that, for that, though
καὶ conj. καί and, even, also, but
αὐτὸς pron. nom. masc. 3p. sg. αὐτός ή ό self, of oneself, even, very, the same, he, she, it
ταχέως adv. ταχέως sortly, quickly, soon, hastily, suddenly
25 ἀναγκαῖον adj. nom. neut. sg. ἀναγκαῖος near, necessary, more needful, of necessity
δὲ conj. δέ but, and, now, also, to the contrary, rather, then
Ἐπαφρόδιτον n. acc. masc. sg. Ἐπαφρόδιτος Epaphroditus
τὸν art. acc. masc. sg. ὁ ἡ τό the, this, that, he, she, it
ἀδελφὸν n. acc. masc. sg. ἀδελφός brother
καὶ conj. καί and, even, also, but
συνεργὸν adj. acc. masc. sg. συνεργός fellowlabourer, fellowhelper, fellowworker
καὶ conj. καί and, even, also, but
συστρατιώτην n. acc. masc. sg. συστρατιώτης fellowsoldier
μου pron. gen. 1p. sg. ἐγώ I
ὑμῶν pron. gen. 2p. pl. σύ thou, you
δὲ conj. δέ but, and, now, also, to the contrary, rather, then
ἀπόστολον n. acc. masc. sg. ἀπόστολος apostle, messenger, he that is sent
καὶ conj. καί and, even, also, but
λειτουργὸν n. acc. masc. sg. λειτουργός minister, he that minister
τῆς art. gen. fem. sg. ὁ ἡ τό the, this, that, he, she, it
χρείας n. gen. fem. sg. χρεία need, necessity, lack, want
μου pron. gen. 1p. sg. ἐγώ I
πρὸς prep. πρός (+gen) for, (+dat) at, (+acc) unto, to, with, for, against
ὑμᾶς pron. acc. 2p. pl. σύ thou, you
26 ἐπειδὴ conj. ἐπειδή because, for, after that, for that, for as much as, since
πάντας adj. acc. masc. pl. πᾶς πᾶσα πᾶν all, every, whosoever, every one, no, whole, any
ὑμᾶς pron. acc. 2p. pl. σύ thou, you
καὶ conj. καί and, even, also, but
διότι conj. διότι for, because, because that, therefore
ὅτι conj. ὅτι that, for, because, how that, how, because that, for that, though
27 καὶ conj. καί and, even, also, but
γὰρ conj. γάρ for, and, because, but, indeed
παραπλήσιον adv. παραπλήσιον nigh unto
θανάτῳ n. dat. masc. sg. θάνατος death
ἀλλ' conj. ἀλλά but, yea, yet, nevertheless, howbeit, nay, therefore
ὁ art. nom. masc. sg. ὁ ἡ τό the, this, that, he, she, it
Θεὸς n. nom. masc. sg. θεός God, god
αὐτόν pron. acc. masc. 3p. sg. αὐτός ή ό self, of oneself, even, very, the same, he, she, it
οὐκ particle of negation. οὐ οὐκ οὐχ not, no, neither, none, nay, nor, never, nothing
αὐτὸν pron. acc. masc. 3p. sg. αὐτός ή ό self, of oneself, even, very, the same, he, she, it
δὲ conj. δέ but, and, now, also, to the contrary, rather, then
μόνον adj. acc. masc. sg. μόνος only, alone, by oneself
ἀλλὰ conj. ἀλλά but, yea, yet, nevertheless, howbeit, nay, therefore
καὶ conj. καί and, even, also, but
ἐμέ pron. acc. 1p. sg. ἐγώ I
ἵνα conj. ἵνα that, to, lest, for to, so that, albeit, because, for, so as
μὴ particle of negation. μή not, no, lest, neither, none, nothing, nor, never, without
λύπην n. acc. fem. sg. λύπη sorrow, heaviness, grief, grievous, grudgingly
ἐπὶ prep. ἐπί (+gen) on, in, upon, (+dat) in, at, for, upon, (+acc) on, upon, unto, to, against
λύπῃ n. dat. fem. sg. λύπη sorrow, heaviness, grief, grievous, grudgingly
28 σπουδαιοτέρως compar. adv. σπουδαίως diligently, instantly
οὖν conj. οὖν therefore, then, so, and, now, wherefore
αὐτόν pron. acc. masc. 3p. sg. αὐτός ή ό self, of oneself, even, very, the same, he, she, it
ἵνα conj. ἵνα that, to, lest, for to, so that, albeit, because, for, so as

αὐτόν pron. acc. masc. 3p. sg. αὐτός ή ό self, of oneself, even, very, the same, he, she, it
πάλιν adv. πάλιν again
κἀγὼ pron. nom. 1p. sg. κἀγώ and I, I also, so I, even as I
ἀλυπότερος compar. adj. nom. masc. sg. ἀλυπότερος less sorrowful
29 οὖν conj. οὖν therefore, then, so, and, now, wherefore
αὐτὸν pron. acc. masc. 3p. sg. αὐτός ή ό self, of oneself, even, very, the same, he, she, it
ἐν prep. ἐν (+dat) in, by, with, among, at, on, through, to, within, into, of, for
Κυρίῳ n. dat. masc. sg. κύριος Lord, lord, master, sir, LORD, God, Master, owner
μετὰ prep. μετά (+gen) with, among, against, (+acc) after
πάσης adj. gen. fem. sg. πᾶς πᾶσα πᾶν all, every, whosoever, every one, no, whole, any
χαρᾶς n. gen. fem. sg. χαρά joy, gladness, joyfulness
καὶ conj. καί and, even, also, but
τοὺς art. acc. masc. pl. ὁ ἡ τό the, this, that, he, she, it
τοιούτους demo. pron. acc. masc. pl. τοιοῦτος such, like
ἐντίμους adj. acc. masc. pl. ἔντιμος dear, precious, in reputation, more honourable
30 ὅτι conj. ὅτι that, for, because, how that, how, because that, for that, though
διὰ prep. διά (+gen) by, through, with, in, of, (+acc) for, because of, for a cause
τὸ art. acc. neut. sg. ὁ ἡ τό the, this, that, he, she, it
ἔργον n. acc. neut. sg. ἔργον work, deed, doing labour
τοῦ art. gen. masc. sg. ὁ ἡ τό the, this, that, he, she, it
Χριστοῦ n. gen. masc. sg. Χριστός Christ
μέχρι prep. μέχρι until, unto, till, to
θανάτου n. gen. masc. sg. θάνατος death
τῇ art. dat. fem. sg. ὁ ἡ τό the, this, that, he, she, it
ψυχῇ n. dat. fem. sg. ψυχή life, soul, mind, heart
ἵνα conj. ἵνα that, to, lest, for to, so that, albeit, because, for, so as
τὸ art. acc. neut. sg. ὁ ἡ τό the, this, that, he, she, it
ὑμῶν pron. gen. 2p. pl. σύ thou, you
ὑστέρημα n. acc. neut. sg. ὑστέρημα penury, that which is lacking, want, lack
τῆς art. gen. fem. sg. ὁ ἡ τό the, this, that, he, she, it
πρός prep. πρός (+gen) for, (+dat) at, (+acc) unto, to, with, for, against
με pron. acc. 1p. sg. ἐγώ I
λειτουργίας n. gen. fem. sg. λειτουργία ministration, service, ministry

3

1 Τὸ art. acc. neut. sg. ὁ ἡ τό the, this, that, he, she, it
λοιπόν adv. λοιπόν finally, henceforth, now, besides, furthermore, moreover, then
ἀδελφοί n. voc. masc. pl. ἀδελφός brother
μου pron. gen. 1p. sg. ἐγώ I
ἐν prep. ἐν (+dat) in, by, with, among, at, on, through, to, within, into, of, for
Κυρίῳ n. dat. masc. sg. κύριος Lord, lord, master, sir, LORD, God, Master, owner
τὰ art. acc. neut. pl. ὁ ἡ τό the, this, that, he, she, it
αὐτὰ adj. acc. neut. pl. αὐτός ή ό self, of oneself, even, very, the same, he, she, it
ὑμῖν pron. dat. 2p. pl. σύ thou, you
ἐμοὶ pron. dat. 1p. sg. ἐγώ I
μὲν conj. μέν indeed, verily, truly, even, so, some
οὐκ particle of negation. οὐ οὐκ οὐχ not, no, neither, none, nay, nor, never, nothing
ὀκνηρόν adj. nom. neut. sg. ὀκνηρός slothful, grievous
ὑμῖν pron. dat. 2p. pl. σύ thou, you
δὲ conj. δέ but, and, now, also, to the contrary, rather, then
ἀσφαλές adj. nom. neut. sg. ἀσφαλής certainty, certain, safe, sure
2 τοὺς art. acc. masc. pl. ὁ ἡ τό the, this, that, he, she, it
κύνας n. acc. masc. pl. κύων dog
τοὺς art. acc. masc. pl. ὁ ἡ τό the, this, that, he, she, it

κακοὺς adj. acc. masc. pl. κακός evil, evil thing, noisome, wicked
ἐργάτας n. acc. masc. pl. ἐργάτης labourer, worker, workman
τὴν art. acc. fem. sg. ὁ ἡ τό the, this, that, he, she, it
κατατομήν n. acc. fem. sg. κατατομή concision
3 ἡμεῖς pron. nom. 1p. pl. ἐγώ I
γάρ conj. γάρ for, and, because, but, indeed
ἡ art. nom. fem. sg. ὁ ἡ τό the, this, that, he, she, it
περιτομή n. nom. fem. sg. περιτομή circumcision
οἱ art. nom. masc. pl. ὁ ἡ τό the, this, that, he, she, it
πνεύματι n. dat. neut. sg. πνεῦμα spirit, Spirit, Ghost, ghost, life. of the spirit, wind
Θεῷ n. dat. masc. sg. θεός God, god
καὶ conj. καί and, even, also, but
ἐν prep. ἐν (+dat) in, by, with, among, at, on, through, to, within, into, of, for
Χριστῷ n. dat. masc. sg. Χριστός Christ
Ἰησοῦ n. dat. masc. sg. Ἰησοῦς Jesus
καὶ conj. καί and, even, also, but
οὐκ particle of negation. οὐ οὐκ οὐχ not, no, neither, none, nay, nor, never, nothing
σαρκὶ n. dat. fem. sg. σάρξ flesh, carnal
4 καίπερ conj. καίπερ though, and yet
ἐγὼ pron. nom. 1p. sg. ἐγώ I
πεποίθησιν n. acc. fem. sg. πεποίθησις confidence, trust
καὶ conj. καί and, even, also, but
ἐν prep. ἐν (+dat) in, by, with, among, at, on, through, to, within, into, of, for
σαρκί n. dat. fem. sg. σάρξ flesh, carnal
εἴ conj. εἰ if, whether, that, though, forasmuch
τις indefinite pron. nom. masc. sg. τὶς certain, some, any man, one, any thing
ἄλλος adj. nom. masc. sg. ἄλλος other, another, some, one, more, otherwise
ἐν prep. ἐν (+dat) in, by, with, among, at, on, through, to, within, into, of, for
σαρκί n. dat. fem. sg. σάρξ flesh, carnal
ἐγὼ pron. nom. 1p. sg. ἐγώ I
μᾶλλον adv. μᾶλλον rather, more, more and more, better, much, much the more
5 περιτομὴ n. nom. fem. sg. περιτομή circumcision
ὀκταήμερος adj. nom. masc. sg. ὀκταήμερος the eighth day
ἐκ prep. ἐκ ἐξ (+gen) of, from, out of, by, on, with, in, among, through
γένους n. gen. neut. sg. γένος kind, kindred, offspring, nation, countrymen
Ἰσραήλ pron. name. masc. inde. Ἰσραήλ Israel
φυλῆς n. gen. fem. sg. φυλή tribe, kindred
Βενιαμίν n. gen. masc. sg. Βενιαμίν Benjamin
Ἑβραῖος n. nom. masc. sg. Ἑβραῖος Hebrew
ἐξ prep. ἐκ ἐξ (+gen) of, from, out of, by, on, with, in, among, through
Ἑβραίων n. gen. masc. pl. Ἑβραῖος Hebrew
κατὰ prep. κατά (+gen) against, by, throughout, down, (+acc) according to, after, with
νόμον n. acc. masc. sg. νόμος law, the law
Φαρισαῖος n. nom. masc. sg. Φαρισαῖος Pharisee
6 κατὰ prep. κατά (+gen) against, by, throughout, down, (+acc) according to, after, with
ζῆλον n. acc. masc. sg. ζῆλος zeal, envying, indignation, emulation, jealousy
τὴν art. acc. fem. sg. ὁ ἡ τό the, this, that, he, she, it
ἐκκλησίαν n. acc. fem. sg. ἐκκλησία church, assembly
κατὰ prep. κατά (+gen) against, by, throughout, down, (+acc) according to, after, with
δικαιοσύνην n. acc. fem. sg. δικαιοσύνη righteousness
τὴν art. acc. fem. sg. ὁ ἡ τό the, this, that, he, she, it
ἐν prep. ἐν (+dat) in, by, with, among, at, on, through, to, within, into, of, for
νόμῳ n. dat. masc. sg. νόμος law, the law
ἄμεμπτος adj. nom. masc. sg. ἄμεμπτος blameless, faultless, unblamable
7 ἀλλ' conj. ἀλλά but, yea, yet, nevertheless, howbeit, nay, therefore

ἅτινα relative pron. nom. neut. pl. ὅστις which, who, whosoever, that, whatsoever
μοι pron. dat. 1p. sg. ἐγώ I
κέρδη n. nom. neut. pl. κέρδος gain, lucre
ταῦτα demo. pron. acc. neut. pl. οὗτος αὕτη τοῦτο this, the same, this same, he, she, it
διὰ prep. διά (+gen) by, through, with, in, of, (+acc) for, because of, for a cause
τὸν art. acc. masc. sg. ὁ ἡ τό the, this, that, he, she, it
Χριστὸν n. acc. masc. sg. Χριστός Christ
ζημίαν n. acc. fem. sg. ζημία damage, loss
8 ἀλλὰ conj. ἀλλά but, yea, yet, nevertheless, howbeit, nay, therefore
μενοῦνγε particle. μενοῦνγε yea rather, nay but, yea doubtless
καὶ conj. καί and, even, also, but
πάντα adj. acc. neut. pl. πᾶς πᾶσα πᾶν all, every, whosoever, every one, no, whole, any
ζημίαν n. acc. fem. sg. ζημία damage, loss
διὰ prep. διά (+gen) by, through, with, in, of, (+acc) for, because of, for a cause
τὸ art. acc. neut. sg. ὁ ἡ τό the, this, that, he, she, it
τῆς art. gen. fem. sg. ὁ ἡ τό the, this, that, he, she, it
γνώσεως n. gen. fem. sg. γνῶσις knowledge, science
Χριστοῦ n. gen. masc. sg. Χριστός Christ
Ἰησοῦ n. gen. masc. sg. Ἰησοῦς Jesus
τοῦ art. gen. masc. sg. ὁ ἡ τό the, this, that, he, she, it
Κυρίου n. gen. masc. sg. κύριος Lord, lord, master, sir, LORD, God, Master, owner
μου pron. gen. 1p. sg. ἐγώ I
δι' prep. διά (+gen) by, through, with, in, of, (+acc) for, because of, for a cause
ὃν relative pron. acc. masc. sg. ὅς ἥ ὅ who, which, what, that
τὰ art. acc. neut. pl. ὁ ἡ τό the, this, that, he, she, it
πάντα adj. acc. neut. pl. πᾶς πᾶσα πᾶν all, every, whosoever, every one, no, whole, any
καὶ conj. καί and, even, also, but
σκύβαλα n. acc. neut. pl. σκύβαλον dung
ἵνα conj. ἵνα that, to, lest, for to, so that, albeit, because, for, so as
Χριστὸν n. acc. masc. sg. Χριστός Christ
9 καὶ conj. καί and, even, also, but
ἐν prep. ἐν (+dat) in, by, with, among, at, on, through, to, within, into, of, for
αὐτῷ pron. dat. masc. 3p. sg. αὐτός ή ό self, of oneself, even, very, the same, he, she, it
μὴ particle of negation. μή not, no, lest, neither, none, nothing, nor, never, without
ἐμὴν poss. pron. acc. fem. 1p. sg. ἐμός my, mine, mine own, of me
δικαιοσύνην n. acc. fem. sg. δικαιοσύνη righteousness
τὴν art. acc. fem. sg. ὁ ἡ τό the, this, that, he, she, it
ἐκ prep. ἐκ ἐξ (+gen) of, from, out of, by, on, with, in, among, through
νόμου n. gen. masc. sg. νόμος law, the law
ἀλλὰ conj. ἀλλά but, yea, yet, nevertheless, howbeit, nay, therefore
τὴν art. acc. fem. sg. ὁ ἡ τό the, this, that, he, she, it
διὰ prep. διά (+gen) by, through, with, in, of, (+acc) for, because of, for a cause
πίστεως n. gen. fem. sg. πίστις faith, assurance, belief, fidelity
Χριστοῦ n. gen. masc. sg. Χριστός Christ
τὴν art. acc. fem. sg. ὁ ἡ τό the, this, that, he, she, it
ἐκ prep. ἐκ ἐξ (+gen) of, from, out of, by, on, with, in, among, through
Θεοῦ n. gen. masc. sg. θεός God, god
δικαιοσύνην n. acc. fem. sg. δικαιοσύνη righteousness
ἐπὶ prep. ἐπί (+gen) on, in, upon, (+dat) in, at, for, upon, (+acc) on, upon, unto, to, against
τῇ art. dat. fem. sg. ὁ ἡ τό the, this, that, he, she, it
πίστει n. dat. fem. sg. πίστις faith, assurance, belief, fidelity
10 τοῦ art. gen. neut. sg. ὁ ἡ τό the, this, that, he, she, it
αὐτὸν pron. acc. masc. 3p. sg. αὐτός ή ό self, of oneself, even, very, the same, he, she, it
καὶ conj. καί and, even, also, but
τὴν art. acc. fem. sg. ὁ ἡ τό the, this, that, he, she, it

δύναμιν n. acc. fem. sg. δύναμις power, mighty work, miracle, strength, might
τῆς art. gen. fem. sg. ὁ ἡ τό the, this, that, he, she, it
ἀναστάσεως n. gen. fem. sg. ἀνάστασις resurrection, rising again
αὐτοῦ pron. gen. masc. 3p. sg. αὐτός ή ό self, of oneself, even, very, the same, he, she, it
καὶ conj. καί and, even, also, but
τὴν art. acc. fem. sg. ὁ ἡ τό the, this, that, he, she, it
κοινωνίαν n. acc. fem. sg. κοινωνία fellowship, communion, contribution, distribution
τῶν art. gen. neut. pl. ὁ ἡ τό the, this, that, he, she, it
παθημάτων n. gen. neut. pl. πάθημα suffering, affliction, affection, motion
αὐτοῦ pron. gen. masc. 3p. sg. αὐτός ή ό self, of oneself, even, very, the same, he, she, it
τῷ art. dat. masc. sg. ὁ ἡ τό the, this, that, he, she, it
θανάτῳ n. dat. masc. sg. θάνατος death
αὐτοῦ pron. gen. masc. 3p. sg. αὐτός ή ό self, of oneself, even, very, the same, he, she, it
11 εἴ conj. εἰ if, whether, that, though, forasmuch
πως particle. πώς by any means, by some means, haply, perhaps
εἰς prep. εἰς (+acc) into, to, unto, for, in, on, toward, against, upon, at, among
τὴν art. acc. fem. sg. ὁ ἡ τό the, this, that, he, she, it
ἐξανάστασιν n. acc. fem. sg. ἐξανάστασις resurrection
τῶν art. gen. masc. pl. ὁ ἡ τό the, this, that, he, she, it
νεκρῶν adj. gen. masc. pl. νεκρός dead
12 οὐχ particle of negation. οὐ οὐκ οὐχ not, no, neither, none, nay, nor, never, nothing
ὅτι conj. ὅτι that, for, because, how that, how, because that, for that, though
ἤδη adv. ἤδη now, already, yet, by this time, even now, now already
ἢ particle. ἤ or, than, either, nor, or else, and, rather than
ἤδη adv. ἤδη now, already, yet, by this time, even now, now already
δὲ conj. δέ but, and, now, also, to the contrary, rather, then
εἰ conj. εἰ if, whether, that, though, forasmuch
καὶ conj. καί and, even, also, but
ἐφ' prep. ἐπί (+gen) on, in, upon, (+dat) in, at, for, upon, (+acc) on, upon, unto, to, against
ᾧ relative pron. dat. neut. sg. ὅς ἥ ὅ who, which, what, that
καὶ conj. καί and, even, also, but
ὑπὸ prep. ὑπό (+gen) of, by, with, from, among, (+acc) under
τοῦ art. gen. masc. sg. ὁ ἡ τό the, this, that, he, she, it
Χριστοῦ n. gen. masc. sg. Χριστός Christ
Ἰησοῦ n. gen. masc. sg. Ἰησοῦς Jesus
13 ἀδελφοί n. voc. masc. pl. ἀδελφός brother
ἐγὼ pron. nom. 1p. sg. ἐγώ I
ἐμαυτὸν pron. acc. masc. 1p. sg. ἐμαυτοῦ myself, me
οὐ particle of negation. οὐ οὐκ οὐχ not, no, neither, none, nay, nor, never, nothing
ἓν num. acc. neut. sg. εἷς or ἕν one, other, some, any, only, a certain
δέ conj. δέ but, and, now, also, to the contrary, rather, then
τὰ art. acc. neut. pl. ὁ ἡ τό the, this, that, he, she, it
μὲν conj. μέν indeed, verily, truly, even, so, some
ὀπίσω adv. ὀπίσω (+gen) after. (adv.) back, behind
τοῖς art. dat. neut. pl. ὁ ἡ τό the, this, that, he, she, it
δέ conj. δέ but, and, now, also, to the contrary, rather, then
ἔμπροσθεν adv. ἔμπροσθεν (+gen) before, in the sight of, in the presence of
14 κατὰ prep. κατά (+gen) against, by, throughout, down, (+acc) according to, after, with
σκοπὸν n. acc. masc. sg. σκοπός mark
ἐπὶ prep. ἐπί (+gen) on, in, upon, (+dat) in, at, for, upon, (+acc) on, upon, unto, to, against
τὸ art. acc. neut. sg. ὁ ἡ τό the, this, that, he, she, it
βραβεῖον n. acc. neut. sg. βραβεῖον prize
τῆς art. gen. fem. sg. ὁ ἡ τό the, this, that, he, she, it
ἄνω adv. ἄνω above, up, high, the brim
κλήσεως n. gen. fem. sg. κλῆσις calling, vocation

τοῦ art. gen. masc. sg. ὁ ἡ τό the, this, that, he, she, it
Θεοῦ n. gen. masc. sg. θεός God, god
ἐν prep. ἐν (+dat) in, by, with, among, at, on, through, to, within, into, of, for
Χριστῷ n. dat. masc. sg. Χριστός Christ
Ἰησοῦ n. dat. masc. sg. Ἰησοῦς Jesus
15 ὅσοι relative pron. nom. masc. pl. ὅσος as many as, whatsoever, that, as long as, how much
οὖν conj. οὖν therefore, then, so, and, now, wherefore
τέλειοι adj. nom. masc. pl. τέλειος perfect, of full age
τοῦτο demo. pron. acc. neut. sg. οὗτος αὕτη τοῦτο this, the same, this same, he, she, it
καὶ conj. καί and, even, also, but
εἴ conj. εἰ if, whether, that, though, forasmuch
τι indefinite pron. acc. neut. sg. τὶς certain, some, any man, one, any thing
ἑτέρως adv. ἑτέρως otherwise
καὶ conj. καί and, even, also, but
τοῦτο demo. pron. acc. neut. sg. οὗτος αὕτη τοῦτο this, the same, this same, he, she, it
ὁ art. nom. masc. sg. ὁ ἡ τό the, this, that, he, she, it
Θεὸς n. nom. masc. sg. θεός God, god
ὑμῖν pron. dat. 2p. pl. σύ thou, you
16 πλὴν adv. πλήν but, nevertheless, but rather, notwithstanding, except, than
εἰς prep. εἰς (+acc) into, to, unto, for, in, on, toward, against, upon, at, among
ὃ relative pron. acc. neut. sg. ὅς ἥ ὅ who, which, what, that
τῷ art. dat. neut. sg. ὁ ἡ τό the, this, that, he, she, it
αὐτῷ adj. dat. neut. sg. αὐτός ή ό self, of oneself, even, very, the same, he, she, it
κανόνι n. dat. masc. sg. κανών rule, line
τὸ art. acc. neut. sg. ὁ ἡ τό the, this, that, he, she, it
αὐτὸ pron. acc. neut. 3p. sg. αὐτός ή ό self, of oneself, even, very, the same, he, she, it
17 Συμμιμηταί n. nom. masc. pl. συμμιμητής follower together
μου pron. gen. 1p. sg. ἐγώ I
ἀδελφοί n. voc. masc. pl. ἀδελφός brother
καὶ conj. καί and, even, also, but
τοὺς art. acc. masc. pl. ὁ ἡ τό the, this, that, he, she, it
οὕτω adv. οὕτω οὕτως so, even so, thus, on this wise, likewise, after this manner
καθὼς adv. καθώς as, even as, according as, according to
τύπον n. acc. masc. sg. τύπος ensample, example, pattern, print, figure, fashion
ἡμᾶς pron. acc. 1p. pl. ἐγώ I
18 πολλοὶ adj. nom. masc. pl. πολύς many, great, much, long, abundant
γὰρ conj. γάρ for, and, because, but, indeed
οὓς relative pron. acc. masc. pl. ὅς ἥ ὅ who, which, what, that
πολλάκις adv. πολλάκις often, ofttimes, oft
ὑμῖν pron. dat. 2p. pl. σύ thou, you
νῦν adv. νῦν now, henceforth, present, this time
δὲ conj. δέ but, and, now, also, to the contrary, rather, then
καὶ conj. καί and, even, also, but
τοὺς art. acc. masc. pl. ὁ ἡ τό the, this, that, he, she, it
ἐχθροὺς adj. acc. masc. pl. ἐχθρός enemy, foe
τοῦ art. gen. masc. sg. ὁ ἡ τό the, this, that, he, she, it
σταυροῦ n. gen. masc. sg. σταυρός cross
τοῦ art. gen. masc. sg. ὁ ἡ τό the, this, that, he, she, it
Χριστοῦ n. gen. masc. sg. Χριστός Christ
19 ὧν relative pron. gen. masc. pl. ὅς ἥ ὅ who, which, what, that
τὸ art. nom. neut. sg. ὁ ἡ τό the, this, that, he, she, it
τέλος n. nom. neut. sg. τέλος end, custom, ending, finally, uttermost
ἀπώλεια n. nom. fem. sg. ἀπώλεια destruction, perdition, waste, damnation
ὧν relative pron. gen. masc. pl. ὅς ἥ ὅ who, which, what, that
ὁ art. nom. masc. sg. ὁ ἡ τό the, this, that, he, she, it

θεὸς n. nom. masc. sg. θεός God, god
ἡ art. nom. fem. sg. ὁ ἡ τό the, this, that, he, she, it
κοιλία n. nom. fem. sg. κοιλία belly, womb
καὶ conj. καί and, even, also, but
ἡ art. nom. fem. sg. ὁ ἡ τό the, this, that, he, she, it
δόξα n. nom. fem. sg. δόξα glory, honour, praise, dignity, worship
ἐν prep. ἐν (+dat) in, by, with, among, at, on, through, to, within, into, of, for
τῇ art. dat. fem. sg. ὁ ἡ τό the, this, that, he, she, it
αἰσχύνῃ n. dat. fem. sg. αἰσχύνη shame, dishonesty
αὐτῶν pron. gen. masc. 3p. pl. αὐτός ἡ ὁ self, of oneself, even, very, the same, he, she, it
οἱ art. nom. masc. pl. ὁ ἡ τό the, this, that, he, she, it
τὰ art. acc. neut. pl. ὁ ἡ τό the, this, that, he, she, it
ἐπίγεια adj. acc. neut. pl. ἐπίγειος earthly, terrestrial, in earth
20 ἡμῶν pron. gen. 1p. pl. ἐγώ I
γὰρ conj. γάρ for, and, because, but, indeed
τὸ art. nom. neut. sg. ὁ ἡ τό the, this, that, he, she, it
πολίτευμα n. nom. neut. sg. πολίτευμα conversation, citizenship
ἐν prep. ἐν (+dat) in, by, with, among, at, on, through, to, within, into, of, for
οὐρανοῖς n. dat. masc. pl. οὐρανός heaven, air, sky
ἐξ prep. ἐκ ἐξ (+gen) of, from, out of, by, on, with, in, among, through
οὗ relative pron. gen. masc. sg. ὅς ἥ ὅ who, which, what, that
καὶ conj. καί and, even, also, but
Σωτῆρα n. acc. masc. sg. σωτήρ Saviour, saviour
Κύριον n. acc. masc. sg. κύριος Lord, lord, master, sir, LORD, God, Master, owner
Ἰησοῦν n. acc. masc. sg. Ἰησοῦς Jesus
Χριστόν n. acc. masc. sg. Χριστός Christ
21 ὃς relative pron. nom. masc. sg. ὅς ἥ ὅ who, which, what, that
τὸ art. acc. neut. sg. ὁ ἡ τό the, this, that, he, she, it
σῶμα n. acc. neut. sg. σῶμα body, bodily, slave
τῆς art. gen. fem. sg. ὁ ἡ τό the, this, that, he, she, it
ταπεινώσεως n. gen. fem. sg. ταπείνωσις low estate, humiliation, that is made low
ἡμῶν pron. gen. 1p. pl. ἐγώ I
εἰς prep. εἰς (+acc) into, to, unto, for, in, on, toward, against, upon, at, among
τὸ art. acc. neut. sg. ὁ ἡ τό the, this, that, he, she, it
αὐτὸ pron. acc. neut. 3p. sg. αὐτός ἡ ὁ self, of oneself, even, very, the same, he, she, it
σύμμορφον adj. acc. neut. sg. σύμμορφος conformed to, fashioned like unto
τῷ art. dat. neut. sg. ὁ ἡ τό the, this, that, he, she, it
σώματι n. dat. neut. sg. σῶμα body, bodily, slave
τῆς art. gen. fem. sg. ὁ ἡ τό the, this, that, he, she, it
δόξης n. gen. fem. sg. δόξα glory, honour, praise, dignity, worship
αὐτοῦ pron. gen. masc. 3p. sg. αὐτός ἡ ὁ self, of oneself, even, very, the same, he, she, it
κατὰ prep. κατά (+gen) against, by, throughout, down, (+acc) according to, after, with
τὴν art. acc. fem. sg. ὁ ἡ τό the, this, that, he, she, it
ἐνέργειαν n. acc. fem. sg. ἐνέργεια working, effectual working, operation
τοῦ art. gen. neut. sg. ὁ ἡ τό the, this, that, he, she, it
αὐτὸν pron. acc. masc. 3p. sg. αὐτός ἡ ὁ self, of oneself, even, very, the same, he, she, it
καὶ conj. καί and, even, also, but
ἑαυτῷ reflexive pron. dat. masc. 3p. sg. ἑαυτοῦ himself, herself, itself, yourself, ourselves
τὰ art. acc. neut. pl. ὁ ἡ τό the, this, that, he, she, it
πάντα adj. acc. neut. pl. πᾶς πᾶσα πᾶν all, every, whosoever, every one, no, whole, any

4

1 Ὥστε conj. ὥστε so that, wherefore, insomuch that, therefore, that, so then
ἀδελφοί n. voc. masc. pl. ἀδελφός brother

μου pron. gen. 1p. sg. ἐγώ I
ἀγαπητοὶ adj. nom. masc. pl. ἀγαπητός beloved, dearly beloved, dear, wellbeloved
καὶ conj. καί and, even, also, but
ἐπιπόθητοι adj. nom. masc. pl. ἐπιπόθητος longed for
χαρὰ n. nom. fem. sg. χαρά joy, gladness, joyfulness
καὶ conj. καί and, even, also, but
στέφανός n. nom. masc. sg. στέφανος crown
μου pron. gen. 1p. sg. ἐγώ I
οὕτω adv. οὕτω οὕτως so, even so, thus, on this wise, likewise, after this manner
ἐν prep. ἐν (+dat) in, by, with, among, at, on, through, to, within, into, of, for
Κυρίῳ n. dat. masc. sg. κύριος Lord, lord, master, sir, LORD, God, Master, owner
ἀγαπητοί adj. voc. masc. pl. ἀγαπητός beloved, dearly beloved, dear, wellbeloved
2 Εὐοδίαν n. acc. fem. sg. Εὐοδία Euodias
καὶ conj. καί and, even, also, but
Συντύχην n. acc. fem. sg. Συντύχη Syntyche
τὸ art. acc. neut. sg. ὁ ἡ τό the, this, that, he, she, it
αὐτὸ pron. acc. neut. 3p. sg. αὐτός ή ό self, of oneself, even, very, the same, he, she, it
ἐν prep. ἐν (+dat) in, by, with, among, at, on, through, to, within, into, of, for
Κυρίῳ n. dat. masc. sg. κύριος Lord, lord, master, sir, LORD, God, Master, owner
3 καὶ conj. καί and, even, also, but
καὶ conj. καί and, even, also, but
σέ pron. acc. 2p. sg. σύ thou, you
σύζυγε adj. voc. masc. sg. σύζυγος yokefellow
γνήσιε adj. voc. masc. sg. γνήσιος sincerity, own, true
αὐταῖς pron. dat. fem. 3p. pl. αὐτός ή ό self, of oneself, even, very, the same, he, she, it
αἵτινες relative pron. nom. fem. pl. ὅστις which, who, whosoever, that, whatsoever
ἐν prep. ἐν (+dat) in, by, with, among, at, on, through, to, within, into, of, for
τῷ art. dat. neut. sg. ὁ ἡ τό the, this, that, he, she, it
εὐαγγελίῳ n. dat. neut. sg. εὐαγγέλιον gospel
μοι pron. dat. 1p. sg. ἐγώ I
μετὰ prep. μετά (+gen) with, among, against, (+acc) after
καὶ conj. καί and, even, also, but
Κλήμεντος n. gen. masc. sg. Κλήμης Clement
καὶ conj. καί and, even, also, but
τῶν art. gen. masc. pl. ὁ ἡ τό the, this, that, he, she, it
λοιπῶν adj. gen. masc. pl. λοιπός other, rest, remnant, residue, which remain
συνεργῶν adj. gen. masc. pl. συνεργός fellowlabourer, fellowhelper, fellowworker
μου pron. gen. 1p. sg. ἐγώ I
ὧν relative pron. gen. masc. pl. ὅς ἥ ὅ who, which, what, that
τὰ art. nom. neut. pl. ὁ ἡ τό the, this, that, he, she, it
ὀνόματα n. nom. neut. pl. ὄνομα name, call, surname
ἐν prep. ἐν (+dat) in, by, with, among, at, on, through, to, within, into, of, for
βίβλῳ n. dat. fem. sg. βίβλος book, record
ζωῆς n. gen. fem. sg. ζωή life, lifetime
4 ἐν prep. ἐν (+dat) in, by, with, among, at, on, through, to, within, into, of, for
Κυρίῳ n. dat. masc. sg. κύριος Lord, lord, master, sir, LORD, God, Master, owner
πάντοτε adv. πάντοτε always, ever, always, evermore
πάλιν adv. πάλιν again
5 τὸ art. nom. neut. sg. ὁ ἡ τό the, this, that, he, she, it
ἐπιεικὲς adj. nom. neut. sg. ἐπιεικής moderation, gentle, patient
ὑμῶν pron. gen. 2p. pl. σύ thou, you
πᾶσιν adj. dat. masc. pl. πᾶς πᾶσα πᾶν all, every, whosoever, every one, no, whole, any
ἀνθρώποις n. dat. masc. pl. ἄνθρωπος man, human being, person, one, certain
ὁ art. nom. masc. sg. ὁ ἡ τό the, this, that, he, she, it
Κύριος n. nom. masc. sg. κύριος Lord, lord, master, sir, LORD, God, Master, owner

ἐγγύς adv. ἐγγύς nigh, at hand, near, nigh at hand, ready, nigh unto
6 μηδὲν num. acc. neut. sg. μηδείς μηδεμία μηδέν no man, nothing, no, none, not at all
ἀλλ' conj. ἀλλά but, yea, yet, nevertheless, howbeit, nay, therefore
ἐν prep. ἐν (+dat) in, by, with, among, at, on, through, to, within, into, of, for
παντὶ adj. dat. neut. sg. πᾶς πᾶσα πᾶν all, every, whosoever, every one, no, whole, any
τῇ art. dat. fem. sg. ὁ ἡ τό the, this, that, he, she, it
προσευχῇ n. dat. fem. sg. προσευχή prayer
καὶ conj. καί and, even, also, but
τῇ art. dat. fem. sg. ὁ ἡ τό the, this, that, he, she, it
δεήσει n. dat. fem. sg. δέησις prayer, supplication, request
μετὰ prep. μετά (+gen) with, among, against, (+acc) after
εὐχαριστίας n. gen. fem. sg. εὐχαριστία thankfulness, thanksgiving, giving of thanks
τὰ art. nom. neut. pl. ὁ ἡ τό the, this, that, he, she, it
αἰτήματα n. nom. neut. pl. αἴτημα request, petition
ὑμῶν pron. gen. 2p. pl. σύ thou, you
πρὸς prep. πρός (+gen) for, (+dat) at, (+acc) unto, to, with, for, against
τὸν art. acc. masc. sg. ὁ ἡ τό the, this, that, he, she, it
Θεόν n. acc. masc. sg. θεός God, god
7 καὶ conj. καί and, even, also, but
ἡ art. nom. fem. sg. ὁ ἡ τό the, this, that, he, she, it
εἰρήνη n. nom. fem. sg. εἰρήνη peace, quietness, rest
τοῦ art. gen. masc. sg. ὁ ἡ τό the, this, that, he, she, it
Θεοῦ n. gen. masc. sg. θεός God, god
ἡ art. nom. fem. sg. ὁ ἡ τό the, this, that, he, she, it
πάντα adj. acc. masc. sg. πᾶς πᾶσα πᾶν all, every, whosoever, every one, no, whole, any
νοῦν n. acc. masc. sg. νοῦς understanding, mind
τὰς art. acc. fem. pl. ὁ ἡ τό the, this, that, he, she, it
καρδίας n. acc. fem. pl. καρδία heart
ὑμῶν pron. gen. 2p. pl. σύ thou, you
καὶ conj. καί and, even, also, but
τὰ art. acc. neut. pl. ὁ ἡ τό the, this, that, he, she, it
νοήματα n. acc. neut. pl. νόημα mind, device, thought
ὑμῶν pron. gen. 2p. pl. σύ thou, you
ἐν prep. ἐν (+dat) in, by, with, among, at, on, through, to, within, into, of, for
Χριστῷ n. dat. masc. sg. Χριστός Christ
Ἰησοῦ n. dat. masc. sg. Ἰησοῦς Jesus
8 Τὸ art. acc. neut. sg. ὁ ἡ τό the, this, that, he, she, it
λοιπόν adv. λοιπόν finally, henceforth, now, besides, furthermore, moreover, then
ἀδελφοί n. voc. masc. pl. ἀδελφός brother
ὅσα relative pron. nom. neut. pl. ὅσος as many as, whatsoever, that, as long as, how much
ἀληθῆ adj. nom. neut. pl. ἀληθής true, truly, truth
ὅσα relative pron. nom. neut. pl. ὅσος as many as, whatsoever, that, as long as, how much
σεμνά adj. nom. neut. pl. σεμνός honest, grave
ὅσα relative pron. nom. neut. pl. ὅσος as many as, whatsoever, that, as long as, how much
δίκαια adj. nom. neut. pl. δίκαιος righteous, just, meet, right
ὅσα relative pron. nom. neut. pl. ὅσος as many as, whatsoever, that, as long as, how much
ἁγνά adj. nom. neut. pl. ἁγνός clear, pure, chaste
ὅσα relative pron. nom. neut. pl. ὅσος as many as, whatsoever, that, as long as, how much
προσφιλῆ adj. nom. neut. pl. προσφιλής lovely
ὅσα relative pron. nom. neut. pl. ὅσος as many as, whatsoever, that, as long as, how much
εὔφημα adj. nom. neut. pl. εὔφημος good report
εἴ conj. εἰ if, whether, that, though, forasmuch
τις indefinite pron. nom. fem. sg. τὶς certain, some, any man, one, any thing
ἀρετὴ n. nom. fem. sg. ἀρετή virtue, praise
καὶ conj. καί and, even, also, but

εἴ conj. εἰ if, whether, that, though, forasmuch
τις indefinite pron. nom. masc. sg. τὶς certain, some, any man, one, any thing
ἔπαινος n. nom. masc. sg. ἔπαινος praise
ταῦτα demo. pron. acc. neut. pl. οὗτος αὕτη τοῦτο this, the same, this same, he, she, it
9 ἃ relative pron. acc. neut. pl. ὅς ἥ ὅ who, which, what, that
καὶ conj. καί and, even, also, but
καὶ conj. καί and, even, also, but
καὶ conj. καί and, even, also, but
καὶ conj. καί and, even, also, but
ἐν prep. ἐν (+dat) in, by, with, among, at, on, through, to, within, into, of, for
ἐμοί pron. dat. 1p. sg. ἐγώ I
ταῦτα demo. pron. acc. neut. pl. οὗτος αὕτη τοῦτο this, the same, this same, he, she, it
καὶ conj. καί and, even, also, but
ὁ art. nom. masc. sg. ὁ ἡ τό the, this, that, he, she, it
Θεὸς n. nom. masc. sg. θεός God, god
τῆς art. gen. fem. sg. ὁ ἡ τό the, this, that, he, she, it
εἰρήνης n. gen. fem. sg. εἰρήνη peace, quietness, rest
μεθ' prep. μετά (+gen) with, among, against, (+acc) after
ὑμῶν pron. gen. 2p. pl. σύ thou, you
10 δὲ conj. δέ but, and, now, also, to the contrary, rather, then
ἐν prep. ἐν (+dat) in, by, with, among, at, on, through, to, within, into, of, for
Κυρίῳ n. dat. masc. sg. κύριος Lord, lord, master, sir, LORD, God, Master, owner
μεγάλως adv. μεγάλως greatly
ὅτι conj. ὅτι that, for, because, how that, how, because that, for that, though
ἤδη adv. ἤδη now, already, yet, by this time, even now, now already
ποτὲ adv. ποτέ in time past, at any time, sometimes, in old time, once, when
τὸ art. acc. neut. sg. ὁ ἡ τό the, this, that, he, she, it
ὑπὲρ prep. ὑπέρ (+gen) for, of, for the sake of, (+acc) above, more than
ἐμοῦ pron. gen. 1p. sg. ἐγώ I
ἐφ' prep. ἐπί (+gen) on, in, upon, (+dat) in, at, for, upon, (+acc) on, upon, unto, to, against
ᾧ relative pron. dat. neut. sg. ὅς ἥ ὅ who, which, what, that
καὶ conj. καί and, even, also, but
δὲ conj. δέ but, and, now, also, to the contrary, rather, then
11 οὐχ particle of negation. οὐ οὐκ οὐχ not, no, neither, none, nay, nor, never, nothing
ὅτι conj. ὅτι that, for, because, how that, how, because that, for that, though
καθ' prep. κατά (+gen) against, by, throughout, down, (+acc) according to, after, with
ὑστέρησιν n. acc. fem. sg. ὑστέρησις want
ἐγὼ pron. nom. 1p. sg. ἐγώ I
γὰρ conj. γάρ for, and, because, but, indeed
ἐν prep. ἐν (+dat) in, by, with, among, at, on, through, to, within, into, of, for
οἷς relative pron. dat. neut. pl. ὅς ἥ ὅ who, which, what, that
αὐτάρκης adj. nom. masc. sg. αὐτάρκης content
12 καὶ conj. καί and, even, also, but
καὶ conj. καί and, even, also, but
ἐν prep. ἐν (+dat) in, by, with, among, at, on, through, to, within, into, of, for
παντὶ adj. dat. neut. sg. πᾶς πᾶσα πᾶν all, every, whosoever, every one, no, whole, any
καὶ conj. καί and, even, also, but
ἐν prep. ἐν (+dat) in, by, with, among, at, on, through, to, within, into, of, for
πᾶσι adj. dat. neut. pl. πᾶς πᾶσα πᾶν all, every, whosoever, every one, no, whole, any
καὶ conj. καί and, even, also, but
καὶ conj. καί and, even, also, but
καὶ conj. καί and, even, also, but
καὶ conj. καί and, even, also, but
13 πάντα adj. acc. neut. pl. πᾶς πᾶσα πᾶν all, every, whosoever, every one, no, whole, any
ἐν prep. ἐν (+dat) in, by, with, among, at, on, through, to, within, into, of, for

τῷ art. dat. masc. sg. ὁ ἡ τό the, this, that, he, she, it
με pron. acc. 1p. sg. ἐγώ I
Χριστῷ n. dat. masc. sg. Χριστός Christ
14 πλὴν conj. πλήν but, nevertheless, but rather, notwithstanding, except, than
καλῶς adv. καλῶς good, well, full well
μου pron. gen. 1p. sg. ἐγώ I
τῇ art. dat. fem. sg. ὁ ἡ τό the, this, that, he, she, it
θλίψει n. dat. fem. sg. θλῖψις tribulation, affliction, anguish, persecution
15 δὲ conj. δέ but, and, now, also, to the contrary, rather, then
καὶ conj. καί and, even, also, but
ὑμεῖς pron. nom. 2p. pl. σύ thou, you
Φιλιππήσιοι n. voc. masc. pl. Φιλιππήσιος Philippian
ὅτι conj. ὅτι that, for, because, how that, how, because that, for that, though
ἐν prep. ἐν (+dat) in, by, with, among, at, on, through, to, within, into, of, for
ἀρχῇ n. dat. fem. sg. ἀρχή beginning, principality, corner, first, magistrate, rule
τοῦ art. gen. neut. sg. ὁ ἡ τό the, this, that, he, she, it
εὐαγγελίου n. gen. neut. sg. εὐαγγέλιον gospel
ὅτε adv. ὅτε when, after that, as soon as, while, after
ἀπὸ prep. ἀπό (+gen) from, of, out of, since, for, off, at, by, in, on
Μακεδονίας n. gen. fem. sg. Μακεδονία Macedonia
οὐδεμία num. nom. fem. sg. οὐδείς no man, nothing, no, none, neither, not, nought
μοι pron. dat. 1p. sg. ἐγώ I
ἐκκλησία n. nom. fem. sg. ἐκκλησία church, assembly
εἰς prep. εἰς (+acc) into, to, unto, for, in, on, toward, against, upon, at, among
λόγον n. acc. masc. sg. λόγος word, saying, account, speech, thing, matter
δόσεως n. gen. fem. sg. δόσις giving, gift
καὶ conj. καί and, even, also, but
λήψεως n. gen. fem. sg. λῃστής thief, robber
εἰ conj. εἰ if, whether, that, though, forasmuch
μὴ particle of negation. μή not, no, lest, neither, none, nothing, nor, never, without
ὑμεῖς pron. nom. 2p. pl. σύ thou, you
μόνοι adj. nom. masc. pl. μόνος only, alone, by oneself
16 ὅτι conj. ὅτι that, for, because, how that, how, because that, for that, though
καὶ conj. καί and, even, also, but
ἐν prep. ἐν (+dat) in, by, with, among, at, on, through, to, within, into, of, for
Θεσσαλονίκῃ n. dat. fem. sg. Θεσσαλονίκη Thessalonica
καὶ conj. καί and, even, also, but
ἅπαξ adv. ἅπαξ once
καὶ conj. καί and, even, also, but
δὶς adv. δίς twice, again
εἰς prep. εἰς (+acc) into, to, unto, for, in, on, toward, against, upon, at, among
τὴν art. acc. fem. sg. ὁ ἡ τό the, this, that, he, she, it
χρείαν n. acc. fem. sg. χρεία need, necessity, lack, want
μοι pron. dat. 1p. sg. ἐγώ I
17 οὐχ particle of negation. οὐ οὐκ οὐχ not, no, neither, none, nay, nor, never, nothing
ὅτι conj. ὅτι that, for, because, how that, how, because that, for that, though
τὸ art. acc. neut. sg. ὁ ἡ τό the, this, that, he, she, it
δόμα n. acc. neut. sg. δόμα gift
ἀλλ' conj. ἀλλά but, yea, yet, nevertheless, howbeit, nay, therefore
τὸν art. acc. masc. sg. ὁ ἡ τό the, this, that, he, she, it
καρπὸν n. acc. masc. sg. καρπός fruit
τὸν art. acc. masc. sg. ὁ ἡ τό the, this, that, he, she, it
εἰς prep. εἰς (+acc) into, to, unto, for, in, on, toward, against, upon, at, among
λόγον n. acc. masc. sg. λόγος word, saying, account, speech, thing, matter
ὑμῶν pron. gen. 2p. pl. σύ thou, you

18 δὲ conj. δέ but, and, now, also, to the contrary, rather, then
πάντα adj. acc. neut. pl. πᾶς πᾶσα πᾶν all, every, whosoever, every one, no, whole, any
καὶ conj. καί and, even, also, but
παρὰ prep. παρά (+gen) of, from, (+dat) with, for, (+acc) beside, at, by, above, against
Ἐπαφροδίτου n. gen. masc. sg. Ἐπαφρόδιτος Epaphroditus
τὰ art. acc. neut. pl. ὁ ἡ τό the, this, that, he, she, it
παρ' prep. παρά (+gen) of, from, (+dat) with, for, (+acc) beside, at, by, above, against
ὑμῶν pron. gen. 2p. pl. σύ thou, you
ὀσμὴν n. acc. fem. sg. ὀσμή odour, savour
εὐωδίας n. gen. fem. sg. εὐωδία sweet savour, sweet smell, sweetsmelling
θυσίαν n. acc. fem. sg. θυσία sacrifice
δεκτήν adj. acc. fem. sg. δεκτός acceptable, accepted
εὐάρεστον adj. acc. fem. sg. εὐάρεστος acceptable, wellpleasing, accepted, please well
τῷ art. dat. masc. sg. ὁ ἡ τό the, this, that, he, she, it
Θεῷ n. dat. masc. sg. θεός God, god
19 ὁ art. nom. masc. sg. ὁ ἡ τό the, this, that, he, she, it
δὲ conj. δέ but, and, now, also, to the contrary, rather, then
Θεός n. nom. masc. sg. θεός God, god
μου pron. gen. 1p. sg. ἐγώ I
πᾶσαν adj. acc. fem. sg. πᾶς πᾶσα πᾶν all, every, whosoever, every one, no, whole, any
χρείαν n. acc. fem. sg. χρεία need, necessity, lack, want
ὑμῶν pron. gen. 2p. pl. σύ thou, you
κατὰ prep. κατά (+gen) against, by, throughout, down, (+acc) according to, after, with
τὸν art. acc. masc. sg. ὁ ἡ τό the, this, that, he, she, it
πλοῦτον n. acc. masc. sg. πλοῦτος riches
αὐτοῦ pron. gen. masc. 3p. sg. αὐτός ἡ ὁ self, of oneself, even, very, the same, he, she, it
ἐν prep. ἐν (+dat) in, by, with, among, at, on, through, to, within, into, of, for
δόξῃ n. dat. fem. sg. δόξα glory, honour, praise, dignity, worship
ἐν prep. ἐν (+dat) in, by, with, among, at, on, through, to, within, into, of, for
Χριστῷ n. dat. masc. sg. Χριστός Christ
Ἰησοῦ n. dat. masc. sg. Ἰησοῦς Jesus
20 τῷ art. dat. masc. sg. ὁ ἡ τό the, this, that, he, she, it
δὲ conj. δέ but, and, now, also, to the contrary, rather, then
Θεῷ n. dat. masc. sg. θεός God, god
καὶ conj. καί and, even, also, but
πατρὶ n. dat. masc. sg. πατήρ Father, father, parent
ἡμῶν pron. gen. 1p. pl. ἐγώ I
ἡ art. nom. fem. sg. ὁ ἡ τό the, this, that, he, she, it
δόξα n. nom. fem. sg. δόξα glory, honour, praise, dignity, worship
εἰς prep. εἰς (+acc) into, to, unto, for, in, on, toward, against, upon, at, among
τοὺς art. acc. masc. pl. ὁ ἡ τό the, this, that, he, she, it
αἰῶνας n. acc. masc. pl. αἰών ever, ever and ever, evermore, age, eternal, world
τῶν art. gen. masc. pl. ὁ ἡ τό the, this, that, he, she, it
αἰώνων n. gen. masc. pl. αἰών ever, ever and ever, evermore, age, eternal, world
ἀμήν particle. ἀμήν amen, verily
21 πάντα adj. acc. masc. sg. πᾶς πᾶσα πᾶν all, every, whosoever, every one, no, whole, any
ἅγιον adj. acc. masc. sg. ἅγιος Holy, holy, saint, Holy One, holy thing, most holy
ἐν prep. ἐν (+dat) in, by, with, among, at, on, through, to, within, into, of, for
Χριστῷ n. dat. masc. sg. Χριστός Christ
Ἰησοῦ n. dat. masc. sg. Ἰησοῦς Jesus
ὑμᾶς pron. acc. 2p. pl. σύ thou, you
οἱ art. nom. masc. pl. ὁ ἡ τό the, this, that, he, she, it
σὺν prep. σύν (+dat) with, beside
ἐμοὶ pron. dat. 1p. sg. ἐγώ I
ἀδελφοί n. nom. masc. pl. ἀδελφός brother

22 ὑμᾶς pron. acc. 2p. pl. σύ thou, you
πάντες adj. nom. masc. pl. πᾶς πᾶσα πᾶν all, every, whosoever, every one, no, whole, any
οἱ art. nom. masc. pl. ὁ ἡ τό the, this, that, he, she, it
ἅγιοι adj. nom. masc. pl. ἅγιος Holy, holy, saint, Holy One, holy thing, most holy
μάλιστα adv. μάλιστα specially, especially, chiefly, most of all
δὲ conj. δέ but, and, now, also, to the contrary, rather, then
οἱ art. nom. masc. pl. ὁ ἡ τό the, this, that, he, she, it
ἐκ prep. ἐκ ἐξ (+gen) of, from, out of, by, on, with, in, among, through
τῆς art. gen. fem. sg. ὁ ἡ τό the, this, that, he, she, it
Καίσαρος n. gen. masc. sg. Καῖσαρ Caesar
οἰκίας n. gen. fem. sg. οἰκία house, home, household
23 Ἡ art. nom. fem. sg. ὁ ἡ τό the, this, that, he, she, it
χάρις n. nom. fem. sg. χάρις grace, thank, favour, pleasure
τοῦ art. gen. masc. sg. ὁ ἡ τό the, this, that, he, she, it
Κυρίου n. gen. masc. sg. κύριος Lord, lord, master, sir, LORD, God, Master, owner
ἡμῶν pron. gen. 1p. pl. ἐγώ I
Ἰησοῦ n. gen. masc. sg. Ἰησοῦς Jesus
Χριστοῦ n. gen. masc. sg. Χριστός Christ
μετὰ prep. μετά (+gen) with, among, against, (+acc) after
πάντων adj. gen. masc. pl. πᾶς πᾶσα πᾶν all, every, whosoever, every one, no, whole, any
ὑμῶν pron. gen. 2p. pl. σύ thou, you
ἀμήν particle. ἀμήν amen, verily

ΠΑΥΛΟΥ ΤΟΥ ΑΠΟΣΤΟΛΟΥ
Η ΠΡΟΣ
ΚΟΛΟΣΣΑΕΙΣ ΕΠΙΣΤΟΛΗ

1

1 Παῦλος n. nom. masc. sg. Παῦλος Paul, Paulus
ἀπόστολος n. nom. masc. sg. ἀπόστολος apostle, messenger, he that is sent
Ἰησοῦ n. gen. masc. sg. Ἰησοῦς Jesus
Χριστοῦ n. gen. masc. sg. Χριστός Christ
διὰ prep. διά (+gen) by, through, with, in, of, (+acc) for, because of, for a cause
θελήματος n. gen. neut. sg. θέλημα will, desire, pleasure
Θεοῦ n. gen. masc. sg. θεός God, god
καὶ conj. καί and, even, also, but
Τιμόθεος n. nom. masc. sg. Τιμόθεος Timotheus, Timothy
ὁ art. nom. masc. sg. ὁ ἡ τό the, this, that, he, she, it
ἀδελφὸς n. nom. masc. sg. ἀδελφός brother
2 τοῖς art. dat. masc. pl. ὁ ἡ τό the, this, that, he, she, it
ἐν prep. ἐν (+dat) in, by, with, among, at, on, through, to, within, into, of, for
Κολοσσαῖς n. dat. fem. pl. Κολοσσαί Colosse
ἁγίοις adj. dat. masc. pl. ἅγιος Holy, holy, saint, Holy One, holy thing, most holy
καὶ conj. καί and, even, also, but
πιστοῖς adj. dat. masc. pl. πιστός faithful, believing, true, sure
ἀδελφοῖς n. dat. masc. pl. ἀδελφός brother
ἐν prep. ἐν (+dat) in, by, with, among, at, on, through, to, within, into, of, for
Χριστῷ n. dat. masc. sg. Χριστός Christ
χάρις n. nom. fem. sg. χάρις grace, thank, favour, pleasure
ὑμῖν pron. dat. 2p. pl. σύ thou, you
καὶ conj. καί and, even, also, but
εἰρήνη n. nom. fem. sg. εἰρήνη peace, quietness, rest
ἀπὸ prep. ἀπό (+gen) from, of, out of, since, for, off, at, by, in, on
Θεοῦ n. gen. masc. sg. θεός God, god
πατρὸς n. gen. masc. sg. πατήρ Father, father, parent
ἡμῶν pron. gen. 1p. pl. ἐγώ I
καὶ conj. καί and, even, also, but
Κυρίου n. gen. masc. sg. κύριος Lord, lord, master, sir, LORD, God, Master, owner
Ἰησοῦ n. gen. masc. sg. Ἰησοῦς Jesus
Χριστοῦ n. gen. masc. sg. Χριστός Christ
3 τῷ art. dat. masc. sg. ὁ ἡ τό the, this, that, he, she, it
Θεῷ n. dat. masc. sg. θεός God, god
καὶ conj. καί and, even, also, but
πατρὶ n. dat. masc. sg. πατήρ Father, father, parent
τοῦ art. gen. masc. sg. ὁ ἡ τό the, this, that, he, she, it
Κυρίου n. gen. masc. sg. κύριος Lord, lord, master, sir, LORD, God, Master, owner
ἡμῶν pron. gen. 1p. pl. ἐγώ I
Ἰησοῦ n. gen. masc. sg. Ἰησοῦς Jesus
Χριστοῦ n. gen. masc. sg. Χριστός Christ
πάντοτε adv. πάντοτε always, ever, always, evermore
περὶ prep. περί (+gen) of, for, concerning, (+acc) about, concerning, in
ὑμῶν pron. gen. 2p. pl. σύ thou, you
4 τὴν art. acc. fem. sg. ὁ ἡ τό the, this, that, he, she, it
πίστιν n. acc. fem. sg. πίστις faith, assurance, belief, fidelity
ὑμῶν pron. gen. 2p. pl. σύ thou, you

ἐν prep. ἐν (+dat) in, by, with, among, at, on, through, to, within, into, of, for
Χριστῷ n. dat. masc. sg. Χριστός Christ
Ἰησοῦ n. dat. masc. sg. Ἰησοῦς Jesus
καὶ conj. καί and, even, also, but
τὴν art. acc. fem. sg. ὁ ἡ τό the, this, that, he, she, it
ἀγάπην n. acc. fem. sg. ἀγάπη love, charity, feast of charity
τὴν art. acc. fem. sg. ὁ ἡ τό the, this, that, he, she, it
εἰς prep. εἰς (+acc) into, to, unto, for, in, on, toward, against, upon, at, among
πάντας adj. acc. masc. pl. πᾶς πᾶσα πᾶν all, every, whosoever, every one, no, whole, any
τοὺς art. acc. masc. pl. ὁ ἡ τό the, this, that, he, she, it
ἁγίους adj. acc. masc. pl. ἅγιος Holy, holy, saint, Holy One, holy thing, most holy
5 διὰ prep. διά (+gen) by, through, with, in, of, (+acc) for, because of, for a cause
τὴν art. acc. fem. sg. ὁ ἡ τό the, this, that, he, she, it
ἐλπίδα n. acc. fem. sg. ἐλπίς hope, faith
τὴν art. acc. fem. sg. ὁ ἡ τό the, this, that, he, she, it
ὑμῖν pron. dat. 2p. pl. σύ thou, you
ἐν prep. ἐν (+dat) in, by, with, among, at, on, through, to, within, into, of, for
τοῖς art. dat. masc. pl. ὁ ἡ τό the, this, that, he, she, it
οὐρανοῖς n. dat. masc. pl. οὐρανός heaven, air, sky
ἣν relative pron. acc. fem. sg. ὅς ἥ ὅ who, which, what, that
ἐν prep. ἐν (+dat) in, by, with, among, at, on, through, to, within, into, of, for
τῷ art. dat. masc. sg. ὁ ἡ τό the, this, that, he, she, it
λόγῳ n. dat. masc. sg. λόγος word, saying, account, speech, thing, matter
τῆς art. gen. fem. sg. ὁ ἡ τό the, this, that, he, she, it
ἀληθείας n. gen. fem. sg. ἀλήθεια truth, verity
τοῦ art. gen. neut. sg. ὁ ἡ τό the, this, that, he, she, it
εὐαγγελίου n. gen. neut. sg. εὐαγγέλιον gospel
6 τοῦ art. gen. neut. sg. ὁ ἡ τό the, this, that, he, she, it
εἰς prep. εἰς (+acc) into, to, unto, for, in, on, toward, against, upon, at, among
ὑμᾶς pron. acc. 2p. pl. σύ thou, you
καθὼς adv. καθώς as, even as, according as, according to
καὶ conj. καί and, even, also, but
ἐν prep. ἐν (+dat) in, by, with, among, at, on, through, to, within, into, of, for
παντὶ adj. dat. masc. sg. πᾶς πᾶσα πᾶν all, every, whosoever, every one, no, whole, any
τῷ art. dat. masc. sg. ὁ ἡ τό the, this, that, he, she, it
κόσμῳ n. dat. masc. sg. κόσμος world, adorning
καὶ conj. καί and, even, also, but
καθὼς adv. καθώς as, even as, according as, according to
καὶ conj. καί and, even, also, but
ἐν prep. ἐν (+dat) in, by, with, among, at, on, through, to, within, into, of, for
ὑμῖν pron. dat. 2p. pl. σύ thou, you
ἀφ' prep. ἀπό (+gen) from, of, out of, since, for, off, at, by, in, on
ἧς relative pron. gen. fem. sg. ὅς ἥ ὅ who, which, what, that
ἡμέρας n. gen. fem. sg. ἡμέρα day, time, year, while, age, day time
καὶ conj. καί and, even, also, but
τὴν art. acc. fem. sg. ὁ ἡ τό the, this, that, he, she, it
χάριν n. acc. fem. sg. χάρις grace, thank, favour, pleasure
τοῦ art. gen. masc. sg. ὁ ἡ τό the, this, that, he, she, it
Θεοῦ n. gen. masc. sg. θεός God, god
ἐν prep. ἐν (+dat) in, by, with, among, at, on, through, to, within, into, of, for
ἀληθείᾳ n. dat. fem. sg. ἀλήθεια truth, verity
7 καθὼς adv. καθώς as, even as, according as, according to
καὶ conj. καί and, even, also, but
ἀπὸ prep. ἀπό (+gen) from, of, out of, since, for, off, at, by, in, on
Ἐπαφρᾶ n. gen. masc. sg. Ἐπαφρᾶς Epaphras

τοῦ art. gen. masc. sg. ὁ ἡ τό the, this, that, he, she, it
ἀγαπητοῦ adj. gen. masc. sg. ἀγαπητός beloved, dearly beloved, dear, wellbeloved
συνδούλου n. gen. masc. sg. σύνδουλος fellowservant
ἡμῶν pron. gen. 1p. pl. ἐγώ I
ὅς relative pron. nom. masc. sg. ὅς ἥ ὅ who, which, what, that
πιστὸς adj. nom. masc. sg. πιστός faithful, believing, true, sure
ὑπὲρ prep. ὑπέρ (+gen) for, of, for the sake of, (+acc) above, more than
ὑμῶν pron. gen. 2p. pl. σύ thou, you
διάκονος n. nom. masc. sg. διάκονος minister, servant, deacon
τοῦ art. gen. masc. sg. ὁ ἡ τό the, this, that, he, she, it
Χριστοῦ n. gen. masc. sg. Χριστός Christ
8 ὁ art. nom. masc. sg. ὁ ἡ τό the, this, that, he, she, it
καὶ conj. καί and, even, also, but
ἡμῖν pron. dat. 1p. pl. ἐγώ I
τὴν art. acc. fem. sg. ὁ ἡ τό the, this, that, he, she, it
ὑμῶν pron. gen. 2p. pl. σύ thou, you
ἀγάπην n. acc. fem. sg. ἀγάπη love, charity, feast of charity
ἐν prep. ἐν (+dat) in, by, with, among, at, on, through, to, within, into, of, for
Πνεύματι n. dat. neut. sg. πνεῦμα spirit, Spirit, Ghost, ghost, life. of the spirit, wind
9 Διὰ prep. διά (+gen) by, through, with, in, of, (+acc) for, because of, for a cause
τοῦτο demo. pron. acc. neut. sg. οὗτος αὕτη τοῦτο this, the same, this same, he, she, it
καὶ conj. καί and, even, also, but
ἡμεῖς pron. nom. 1p. pl. ἐγώ I
ἀφ' prep. ἀπό (+gen) from, of, out of, since, for, off, at, by, in, on
ἧς relative pron. gen. fem. sg. ὅς ἥ ὅ who, which, what, that
ἡμέρας n. gen. fem. sg. ἡμέρα day, time, year, while, age, day time
οὐ particle of negation. οὐ οὐκ οὐχ not, no, neither, none, nay, nor, never, nothing
ὑπὲρ prep. ὑπέρ (+gen) for, of, for the sake of, (+acc) above, more than
ὑμῶν pron. gen. 2p. pl. σύ thou, you
καὶ conj. καί and, even, also, but
ἵνα conj. ἵνα that, to, lest, for to, so that, albeit, because, for, so as
τὴν art. acc. fem. sg. ὁ ἡ τό the, this, that, he, she, it
ἐπίγνωσιν n. acc. fem. sg. ἐπίγνωσις knowledge, acknowledging, acknowledgement
τοῦ art. gen. neut. sg. ὁ ἡ τό the, this, that, he, she, it
θελήματος n. gen. neut. sg. θέλημα will, desire, pleasure
αὐτοῦ pron. gen. masc. 3p. sg. αὐτός ή ό self, of oneself, even, very, the same, he, she, it
ἐν prep. ἐν (+dat) in, by, with, among, at, on, through, to, within, into, of, for
πάσῃ adj. dat. fem. sg. πᾶς πᾶσα πᾶν all, every, whosoever, every one, no, whole, any
σοφίᾳ n. dat. fem. sg. σοφία wisdom
καὶ conj. καί and, even, also, but
συνέσει n. dat. fem. sg. σύνεσις understanding, knowledge
πνευματικῇ adj. dat. fem. sg. πνευματικός spiritual
10 ὑμᾶς pron. acc. 2p. pl. σύ thou, you
ἀξίως adv. ἀξίως worthy, as become, after a godly sort
τοῦ art. gen. masc. sg. ὁ ἡ τό the, this, that, he, she, it
Κυρίου n. gen. masc. sg. κύριος Lord, lord, master, sir, LORD, God, Master, owner
εἰς prep. εἰς (+acc) into, to, unto, for, in, on, toward, against, upon, at, among
πᾶσαν adj. acc. fem. sg. πᾶς πᾶσα πᾶν all, every, whosoever, every one, no, whole, any
ἀρεσκείαν n. acc. fem. sg. ἀρεσκεία pleasing
ἐν prep. ἐν (+dat) in, by, with, among, at, on, through, to, within, into, of, for
παντὶ adj. dat. neut. sg. πᾶς πᾶσα πᾶν all, every, whosoever, every one, no, whole, any
ἔργῳ n. dat. neut. sg. ἔργον work, deed, doing labour
ἀγαθῷ adj. dat. neut. sg. ἀγαθός good, good thing, that which is good, well
καὶ conj. καί and, even, also, but
εἰς prep. εἰς (+acc) into, to, unto, for, in, on, toward, against, upon, at, among

τὴν art. acc. fem. sg. ὁ ἡ τό the, this, that, he, she, it
ἐπίγνωσιν n. acc. fem. sg. ἐπίγνωσις knowledge, acknowledging, acknowledgement
τοῦ art. gen. masc. sg. ὁ ἡ τό the, this, that, he, she, it
Θεοῦ n. gen. masc. sg. θεός God, god
11 ἐν prep. ἐν (+dat) in, by, with, among, at, on, through, to, within, into, of, for
πάσῃ adj. dat. fem. sg. πᾶς πᾶσα πᾶν all, every, whosoever, every one, no, whole, any
δυνάμει n. dat. fem. sg. δύναμις power, mighty work, miracle, strength, might
κατὰ prep. κατά (+gen) against, by, throughout, down, (+acc) according to, after, with
τὸ art. acc. neut. sg. ὁ ἡ τό the, this, that, he, she, it
κράτος n. acc. neut. sg. κράτος power, dominion, might, strength
τῆς art. gen. fem. sg. ὁ ἡ τό the, this, that, he, she, it
δόξης n. gen. fem. sg. δόξα glory, honour, praise, dignity, worship
αὐτοῦ pron. gen. masc. 3p. sg. αὐτός ή ό self, of oneself, even, very, the same, he, she, it
εἰς prep. εἰς (+acc) into, to, unto, for, in, on, toward, against, upon, at, among
πᾶσαν adj. acc. fem. sg. πᾶς πᾶσα πᾶν all, every, whosoever, every one, no, whole, any
ὑπομονὴν n. acc. fem. sg. ὑπομονή patience, enduring
καὶ conj. καί and, even, also, but
μακροθυμίαν n. acc. fem. sg. μακροθυμία longsuffering, patience
μετὰ prep. μετά (+gen) with, among, against, (+acc) after
χαρᾶς n. gen. fem. sg. χαρά joy, gladness, joyfulness
12 τῷ art. dat. masc. sg. ὁ ἡ τό the, this, that, he, she, it
πατρὶ n. dat. masc. sg. πατήρ Father, father, parent
τῷ art. dat. masc. sg. ὁ ἡ τό the, this, that, he, she, it
ἡμᾶς pron. acc. 1p. pl. ἐγώ I
εἰς prep. εἰς (+acc) into, to, unto, for, in, on, toward, against, upon, at, among
τὴν art. acc. fem. sg. ὁ ἡ τό the, this, that, he, she, it
μερίδα n. acc. fem. sg. μερίς part, share
τοῦ art. gen. masc. sg. ὁ ἡ τό the, this, that, he, she, it
κλήρου n. gen. masc. sg. κλῆρος lot, inheritance, part, heritage
τῶν art. gen. masc. pl. ὁ ἡ τό the, this, that, he, she, it
ἁγίων adj. gen. masc. pl. ἅγιος Holy, holy, saint, Holy One, holy thing, most holy
ἐν prep. ἐν (+dat) in, by, with, among, at, on, through, to, within, into, of, for
τῷ art. dat. neut. sg. ὁ ἡ τό the, this, that, he, she, it
φωτί n. dat. neut. sg. φῶς light, fire
13 ὃς relative pron. nom. masc. sg. ὅς ἥ ὅ who, which, what, that
ἡμᾶς pron. acc. 1p. pl. ἐγώ I
ἐκ prep. ἐκ ἐξ (+gen) of, from, out of, by, on, with, in, among, through
τῆς art. gen. fem. sg. ὁ ἡ τό the, this, that, he, she, it
ἐξουσίας n. gen. fem. sg. ἐξουσία power, authority, right, strength, jurisdiction
τοῦ art. gen. neut. sg. ὁ ἡ τό the, this, that, he, she, it
σκότους n. gen. neut. sg. σκότος darkness
καὶ conj. καί and, even, also, but
εἰς prep. εἰς (+acc) into, to, unto, for, in, on, toward, against, upon, at, among
τὴν art. acc. fem. sg. ὁ ἡ τό the, this, that, he, she, it
βασιλείαν n. acc. fem. sg. βασιλεία kingdom, reign
τοῦ art. gen. masc. sg. ὁ ἡ τό the, this, that, he, she, it
υἱοῦ n. gen. masc. sg. υἱός son, child, descendant, offspring, heir
τῆς art. gen. fem. sg. ὁ ἡ τό the, this, that, he, she, it
ἀγάπης n. gen. fem. sg. ἀγάπη love, charity, feast of charity
αὐτοῦ pron. gen. masc. 3p. sg. αὐτός ή ό self, of oneself, even, very, the same, he, she, it
14 ἐν prep. ἐν (+dat) in, by, with, among, at, on, through, to, within, into, of, for
ᾧ relative pron. dat. masc. sg. ὅς ἥ ὅ who, which, what, that
τὴν art. acc. fem. sg. ὁ ἡ τό the, this, that, he, she, it
ἀπολύτρωσιν n. acc. fem. sg. ἀπολύτρωσις redemption, deliverance
διὰ prep. διά (+gen) by, through, with, in, of, (+acc) for, because of, for a cause

τοῦ art. gen. neut. sg. ὁ ἡ τό the, this, that, he, she, it
αἵματος n. gen. neut. sg. αἷμα blood
αὐτοῦ pron. gen. masc. 3p. sg. αὐτός ή ό self, of oneself, even, very, the same, he, she, it
τὴν art. acc. fem. sg. ὁ ἡ τό the, this, that, he, she, it
ἄφεσιν n. acc. fem. sg. ἄφεσις remission, forgiveness, deliverance, liberty
τῶν art. gen. fem. pl. ὁ ἡ τό the, this, that, he, she, it
ἁμαρτιῶν n. gen. fem. pl. ἁμαρτία sin, offence, sinful
15 ὅς relative pron. nom. masc. sg. ὅς ἥ ὅ who, which, what, that
εἰκὼν n. nom. fem. sg. εἰκών image
τοῦ art. gen. masc. sg. ὁ ἡ τό the, this, that, he, she, it
Θεοῦ n. gen. masc. sg. θεός God, god
τοῦ art. gen. masc. sg. ὁ ἡ τό the, this, that, he, she, it
ἀοράτου adj. gen. masc. sg. ἀόρατος invisible, invisible thing
πρωτότοκος adj. nom. masc. sg. πρωτότοκος firstborn, first begotten
πάσης adj. gen. fem. sg. πᾶς πᾶσα πᾶν all, every, whosoever, every one, no, whole, any
κτίσεως n. gen. fem. sg. κτίσις creature, creation, building, ordinance
16 ὅτι conj. ὅτι that, for, because, how that, how, because that, for that, though
ἐν prep. ἐν (+dat) in, by, with, among, at, on, through, to, within, into, of, for
αὐτῷ pron. dat. masc. 3p. sg. αὐτός ή ό self, of oneself, even, very, the same, he, she, it
τὰ art. nom. neut. pl. ὁ ἡ τό the, this, that, he, she, it
πάντα adj. nom. neut. pl. πᾶς πᾶσα πᾶν all, every, whosoever, every one, no, whole, any
τὰ art. nom. neut. pl. ὁ ἡ τό the, this, that, he, she, it
ἐν prep. ἐν (+dat) in, by, with, among, at, on, through, to, within, into, of, for
τοῖς art. dat. masc. pl. ὁ ἡ τό the, this, that, he, she, it
οὐρανοῖς n. dat. masc. pl. οὐρανός heaven, air, sky
καὶ conj. καί and, even, also, but
τὰ art. nom. neut. pl. ὁ ἡ τό the, this, that, he, she, it
ἐπὶ prep. ἐπί (+gen) on, in, upon, (+dat) in, at, for, upon, (+acc) on, upon, unto, to, against
τῆς art. gen. fem. sg. ὁ ἡ τό the, this, that, he, she, it
γῆς n. gen. fem. sg. γῆ earth, land, ground, country
τὰ art. nom. neut. pl. ὁ ἡ τό the, this, that, he, she, it
ὁρατὰ adj. nom. neut. pl. ὁρατός visible
καὶ conj. καί and, even, also, but
τὰ art. nom. neut. pl. ὁ ἡ τό the, this, that, he, she, it
ἀόρατα adj. nom. neut. pl. ἀόρατος invisible, invisible thing
εἴτε conj. εἴτε whether
θρόνοι n. nom. masc. pl. θρόνος throne, seat
εἴτε conj. εἴτε whether
κυριότητες n. nom. fem. pl. κυριότης dominion, government
εἴτε conj. εἴτε whether
ἀρχαὶ n. nom. fem. pl. ἀρχή beginning, principality, corner, first, magistrate, rule
εἴτε conj. εἴτε whether
ἐξουσίαι n. nom. fem. pl. ἐξουσία power, authority, right, strength, jurisdiction
τὰ art. nom. neut. pl. ὁ ἡ τό the, this, that, he, she, it
πάντα adj. nom. neut. pl. πᾶς πᾶσα πᾶν all, every, whosoever, every one, no, whole, any
δι' prep. διά (+gen) by, through, with, in, of, (+acc) for, because of, for a cause
αὐτοῦ pron. gen. masc. 3p. sg. αὐτός ή ό self, of oneself, even, very, the same, he, she, it
καὶ conj. καί and, even, also, but
εἰς prep. εἰς (+acc) into, to, unto, for, in, on, toward, against, upon, at, among
αὐτὸν pron. acc. masc. 3p. sg. αὐτός ή ό self, of oneself, even, very, the same, he, she, it
17 καὶ conj. καί and, even, also, but
αὐτός pron. nom. masc. 3p. sg. αὐτός ή ό self, of oneself, even, very, the same, he, she, it
πρὸ prep. πρό (+gen) before, above
πάντων adj. gen. neut. pl. πᾶς πᾶσα πᾶν all, every, whosoever, every one, no, whole, any
καὶ conj. καί and, even, also, but

τὰ art. nom. neut. pl. ὁ ἡ τό the, this, that, he, she, it
πάντα adj. nom. neut. pl. πᾶς πᾶσα πᾶν all, every, whosoever, every one, no, whole, any
ἐν prep. ἐν (+dat) in, by, with, among, at, on, through, to, within, into, of, for
αὐτῷ pron. dat. masc. 3p. sg. αὐτός ή ό self, of oneself, even, very, the same, he, she, it
18 καὶ conj. καί and, even, also, but
αὐτός pron. nom. masc. 3p. sg. αὐτός ή ό self, of oneself, even, very, the same, he, she, it
ἡ art. nom. fem. sg. ὁ ἡ τό the, this, that, he, she, it
κεφαλὴ n. nom. fem. sg. κεφαλή head
τοῦ art. gen. neut. sg. ὁ ἡ τό the, this, that, he, she, it
σώματος n. gen. neut. sg. σῶμα body, bodily, slave
τῆς art. gen. fem. sg. ὁ ἡ τό the, this, that, he, she, it
ἐκκλησίας n. gen. fem. sg. ἐκκλησία church, assembly
ὅς relative pron. nom. masc. sg. ὅς ἥ ὅ who, which, what, that
ἀρχή n. nom. fem. sg. ἀρχή beginning, principality, corner, first, magistrate, rule
πρωτότοκος adj. nom. masc. sg. πρωτότοκος firstborn, first begotten
ἐκ prep. ἐκ ἐξ (+gen) of, from, out of, by, on, with, in, among, through
τῶν art. gen. masc. pl. ὁ ἡ τό the, this, that, he, she, it
νεκρῶν adj. gen. masc. pl. νεκρός dead
ἵνα conj. ἵνα that, to, lest, for to, so that, albeit, because, for, so as
ἐν prep. ἐν (+dat) in, by, with, among, at, on, through, to, within, into, of, for
πᾶσιν adj. dat. neut. pl. πᾶς πᾶσα πᾶν all, every, whosoever, every one, no, whole, any
αὐτός pron. nom. masc. 3p. sg. αὐτός ή ό self, of oneself, even, very, the same, he, she, it
19 ὅτι conj. ὅτι that, for, because, how that, how, because that, for that, though
ἐν prep. ἐν (+dat) in, by, with, among, at, on, through, to, within, into, of, for
αὐτῷ pron. dat. masc. 3p. sg. αὐτός ή ό self, of oneself, even, very, the same, he, she, it
πᾶν adj. acc. neut. sg. πᾶς πᾶσα πᾶν all, every, whosoever, every one, no, whole, any
τὸ art. acc. neut. sg. ὁ ἡ τό the, this, that, he, she, it
πλήρωμα n. acc. neut. sg. πλήρωμα fullness, fulfilling, full
20 καὶ conj. καί and, even, also, but
δι' prep. διά (+gen) by, through, with, in, of, (+acc) for, because of, for a cause
αὐτοῦ pron. gen. masc. 3p. sg. αὐτός ή ό self, of oneself, even, very, the same, he, she, it
τὰ art. acc. neut. pl. ὁ ἡ τό the, this, that, he, she, it
πάντα adj. acc. neut. pl. πᾶς πᾶσα πᾶν all, every, whosoever, every one, no, whole, any
εἰς prep. εἰς (+acc) into, to, unto, for, in, on, toward, against, upon, at, among
αὐτόν pron. acc. masc. 3p. sg. αὐτός ή ό self, of oneself, even, very, the same, he, she, it
διὰ prep. διά (+gen) by, through, with, in, of, (+acc) for, because of, for a cause
τοῦ art. gen. neut. sg. ὁ ἡ τό the, this, that, he, she, it
αἵματος n. gen. neut. sg. αἷμα blood
τοῦ art. gen. masc. sg. ὁ ἡ τό the, this, that, he, she, it
σταυροῦ n. gen. masc. sg. σταυρός cross
αὐτοῦ pron. gen. masc. 3p. sg. αὐτός ή ό self, of oneself, even, very, the same, he, she, it
δι' prep. διά (+gen) by, through, with, in, of, (+acc) for, because of, for a cause
αὐτοῦ pron. gen. masc. 3p. sg. αὐτός ή ό self, of oneself, even, very, the same, he, she, it
εἴτε conj. εἴτε whether
τὰ art. acc. neut. pl. ὁ ἡ τό the, this, that, he, she, it
ἐπὶ prep. ἐπί (+gen) on, in, upon, (+dat) in, at, for, upon, (+acc) on, upon, unto, to, against
τῆς art. gen. fem. sg. ὁ ἡ τό the, this, that, he, she, it
γῆς n. gen. fem. sg. γῆ earth, land, ground, country
εἴτε conj. εἴτε whether
τὰ art. acc. neut. pl. ὁ ἡ τό the, this, that, he, she, it
ἐν prep. ἐν (+dat) in, by, with, among, at, on, through, to, within, into, of, for
τοῖς art. dat. masc. pl. ὁ ἡ τό the, this, that, he, she, it
οὐρανοῖς n. dat. masc. pl. οὐρανός heaven, air, sky
21 καὶ conj. καί and, even, also, but
ὑμᾶς pron. acc. 2p. pl. σύ thou, you

ποτε adv. ποτέ in time past, at any time, sometimes, in old time, once, when
καὶ conj. καί and, even, also, but
ἐχθροὺς adj. acc. masc. pl. ἐχθρός enemy, foe
τῇ art. dat. fem. sg. ὁ ἡ τό the, this, that, he, she, it
διανοίᾳ n. dat. fem. sg. διάνοια mind, understanding, imagination
ἐν prep. ἐν (+dat) in, by, with, among, at, on, through, to, within, into, of, for
τοῖς art. dat. neut. pl. ὁ ἡ τό the, this, that, he, she, it
ἔργοις n. dat. neut. pl. ἔργον work, deed, doing labour
τοῖς art. dat. neut. pl. ὁ ἡ τό the, this, that, he, she, it
πονηροῖς adj. dat. neut. pl. πονηρός evil, wicked, bad
22 νυνὶ adv. νυνί now
δὲ conj. δέ but, and, now, also, to the contrary, rather, then
ἐν prep. ἐν (+dat) in, by, with, among, at, on, through, to, within, into, of, for
τῷ art. dat. neut. sg. ὁ ἡ τό the, this, that, he, she, it
σώματι n. dat. neut. sg. σῶμα body, bodily, slave
τῆς art. gen. fem. sg. ὁ ἡ τό the, this, that, he, she, it
σαρκὸς n. gen. fem. sg. σάρξ flesh, carnal
αὐτοῦ pron. gen. masc. 3p. sg. αὐτός ή ὁ self, of oneself, even, very, the same, he, she, it
διὰ prep. διά (+gen) by, through, with, in, of, (+acc) for, because of, for a cause
τοῦ art. gen. masc. sg. ὁ ἡ τό the, this, that, he, she, it
θανάτου n. gen. masc. sg. θάνατος death
ὑμᾶς pron. acc. 2p. pl. σύ thou, you
ἁγίους adj. acc. masc. pl. ἅγιος Holy, holy, saint, Holy One, holy thing, most holy
καὶ conj. καί and, even, also, but
ἀμώμους adj. acc. masc. pl. ἄμωμος without blame, without fault, without spot
καὶ conj. καί and, even, also, but
ἀνεγκλήτους adj. acc. masc. pl. ἀνέγκλητος blameless, unreprovable
κατενώπιον prep. κατενώπιον (+gen) before, before the presence, in the sight, in sight
αὐτοῦ pron. gen. masc. 3p. sg. αὐτός ή ὁ self, of oneself, even, very, the same, he, she, it
23 εἴγε conj. εἴγε if so be that, if, if yet
τῇ art. dat. fem. sg. ὁ ἡ τό the, this, that, he, she, it
πίστει n. dat. fem. sg. πίστις faith, assurance, belief, fidelity
καὶ conj. καί and, even, also, but
ἑδραῖοι adj. nom. masc. pl. ἑδραῖος stedfast, settled
καὶ conj. καί and, even, also, but
μὴ particle of negation. μή not, no, lest, neither, none, nothing, nor, never, without
ἀπὸ prep. ἀπό (+gen) from, of, out of, since, for, off, at, by, in, on
τῆς art. gen. fem. sg. ὁ ἡ τό the, this, that, he, she, it
ἐλπίδος n. gen. fem. sg. ἐλπίς hope, faith
τοῦ art. gen. neut. sg. ὁ ἡ τό the, this, that, he, she, it
εὐαγγελίου n. gen. neut. sg. εὐαγγέλιον gospel
οὗ relative pron. gen. neut. sg. ὅς ἥ ὅ who, which, what, that
τοῦ art. gen. neut. sg. ὁ ἡ τό the, this, that, he, she, it
ἐν prep. ἐν (+dat) in, by, with, among, at, on, through, to, within, into, of, for
πάσῃ adj. dat. fem. sg. πᾶς πᾶσα πᾶν all, every, whosoever, every one, no, whole, any
τῇ art. dat. fem. sg. ὁ ἡ τό the, this, that, he, she, it
κτίσει n. dat. fem. sg. κτίσις creature, creation, building, ordinance
τῇ art. dat. fem. sg. ὁ ἡ τό the, this, that, he, she, it
ὑπὸ prep. ὑπό (+gen) of, by, with, from, among, (+acc) under
τὸν art. acc. masc. sg. ὁ ἡ τό the, this, that, he, she, it
οὐρανόν n. acc. masc. sg. οὐρανός heaven, air, sky
οὗ relative pron. gen. neut. sg. ὅς ἥ ὅ who, which, what, that
ἐγὼ pron. nom. 1p. sg. ἐγώ I
Παῦλος n. nom. masc. sg. Παῦλος Paul, Paulus
διάκονος n. nom. masc. sg. διάκονος minister, servant, deacon

24 Ὅς relative pron. nom. masc. sg. ὅς ἥ ὅ who, which, what, that
νῦν adv. νῦν now, henceforth, present, this time
ἐν prep. ἐν (+dat) in, by, with, among, at, on, through, to, within, into, of, for
τοῖς art. dat. neut. pl. ὁ ἡ τό the, this, that, he, she, it
παθήμασί n. dat. neut. pl. πάθημα suffering, affliction, affection, motion
μου pron. gen. 1p. sg. ἐγώ I
ὑπὲρ prep. ὑπέρ (+gen) for, of, for the sake of, (+acc) above, more than
ὑμῶν pron. gen. 2p. pl. σύ thou, you
καὶ conj. καί and, even, also, but
τὰ art. acc. neut. pl. ὁ ἡ τό the, this, that, he, she, it
ὑστερήματα n. acc. neut. pl. ὑστέρημα penury, that which is lacking, want, lack
τῶν art. gen. fem. pl. ὁ ἡ τό the, this, that, he, she, it
θλίψεων n. gen. fem. pl. θλῖψις tribulation, affliction, anguish, persecution
τοῦ art. gen. masc. sg. ὁ ἡ τό the, this, that, he, she, it
Χριστοῦ n. gen. masc. sg. Χριστός Christ
ἐν prep. ἐν (+dat) in, by, with, among, at, on, through, to, within, into, of, for
τῇ art. dat. fem. sg. ὁ ἡ τό the, this, that, he, she, it
σαρκί n. dat. fem. sg. σάρξ flesh, carnal
μου pron. gen. 1p. sg. ἐγώ I
ὑπὲρ prep. ὑπέρ (+gen) for, of, for the sake of, (+acc) above, more than
τοῦ art. gen. neut. sg. ὁ ἡ τό the, this, that, he, she, it
σώματος n. gen. neut. sg. σῶμα body, bodily, slave
αὐτοῦ pron. gen. masc. 3p. sg. αὐτός ἡ ὁ self, of oneself, even, very, the same, he, she, it
ὅ relative pron. nom. neut. sg. ὅς ἥ ὅ who, which, what, that
ἡ art. nom. fem. sg. ὁ ἡ τό the, this, that, he, she, it
ἐκκλησία n. nom. fem. sg. ἐκκλησία church, assembly
25 ἧς relative pron. gen. fem. sg. ὅς ἥ ὅ who, which, what, that
ἐγὼ pron. nom. 1p. sg. ἐγώ I
διάκονος n. nom. masc. sg. διάκονος minister, servant, deacon
κατὰ prep. κατά (+gen) against, by, throughout, down, (+acc) according to, after, with
τὴν art. acc. fem. sg. ὁ ἡ τό the, this, that, he, she, it
οἰκονομίαν n. acc. fem. sg. οἰκονομία dispensation, stewardship, edifying
τοῦ art. gen. masc. sg. ὁ ἡ τό the, this, that, he, she, it
Θεοῦ n. gen. masc. sg. θεός God, god
τὴν art. acc. fem. sg. ὁ ἡ τό the, this, that, he, she, it
μοι pron. dat. 1p. sg. ἐγώ I
εἰς prep. εἰς (+acc) into, to, unto, for, in, on, toward, against, upon, at, among
ὑμᾶς pron. acc. 2p. pl. σύ thou, you
τὸν art. acc. masc. sg. ὁ ἡ τό the, this, that, he, she, it
λόγον n. acc. masc. sg. λόγος word, saying, account, speech, thing, matter
τοῦ art. gen. masc. sg. ὁ ἡ τό the, this, that, he, she, it
Θεοῦ n. gen. masc. sg. θεός God, god
26 τὸ art. acc. neut. sg. ὁ ἡ τό the, this, that, he, she, it
μυστήριον n. acc. neut. sg. μυστήριον mystery
τὸ art. acc. neut. sg. ὁ ἡ τό the, this, that, he, she, it
ἀπὸ prep. ἀπό (+gen) from, of, out of, since, for, off, at, by, in, on
τῶν art. gen. masc. pl. ὁ ἡ τό the, this, that, he, she, it
αἰώνων n. gen. masc. pl. αἰών ever, ever and ever, evermore, age, eternal, world
καὶ conj. καί and, even, also, but
ἀπὸ prep. ἀπό (+gen) from, of, out of, since, for, off, at, by, in, on
τῶν art. gen. fem. pl. ὁ ἡ τό the, this, that, he, she, it
γενεῶν n. gen. fem. pl. γενεά generation, age, time, nation
νυνὶ adv. νυνί now
δὲ conj. δέ but, and, now, also, to the contrary, rather, then
τοῖς art. dat. masc. pl. ὁ ἡ τό the, this, that, he, she, it

ἁγίοις adj. dat. masc. pl. ἅγιος Holy, holy, saint, Holy One, holy thing, most holy
αὐτοῦ pron. gen. masc. 3p. sg. αὐτός ἡ ὁ self, of oneself, even, very, the same, he, she, it
27 οἷς relative pron. dat. masc. pl. ὅς ἥ ὅ who, which, what, that
ὁ art. nom. masc. sg. ὁ ἡ τό the, this, that, he, she, it
Θεὸς n. nom. masc. sg. θεός God, god
τίς interrog. pron. nom. masc. sg. τίς what, who, why, where, which, how
ὁ art. nom. masc. sg. ὁ ἡ τό the, this, that, he, she, it
πλοῦτος n. nom. masc. sg. πλοῦτος riches
τῆς art. gen. fem. sg. ὁ ἡ τό the, this, that, he, she, it
δόξης n. gen. fem. sg. δόξα glory, honour, praise, dignity, worship
τοῦ art. gen. neut. sg. ὁ ἡ τό the, this, that, he, she, it
μυστηρίου n. gen. neut. sg. μυστήριον mystery
τούτου demo. pron. gen. neut. sg. οὗτος αὕτη τοῦτο this, the same, this same, he, she, it
ἐν prep. ἐν (+dat) in, by, with, among, at, on, through, to, within, into, of, for
τοῖς art. dat. neut. pl. ὁ ἡ τό the, this, that, he, she, it
ἔθνεσιν n. dat. neut. pl. ἔθνος Gentile, nation, heathen, people
ὅς relative pron. nom. masc. sg. ὅς ἥ ὅ who, which, what, that
Χριστὸς n. nom. masc. sg. Χριστός Christ
ἐν prep. ἐν (+dat) in, by, with, among, at, on, through, to, within, into, of, for
ὑμῖν pron. dat. 2p. pl. σύ thou, you
ἡ art. nom. fem. sg. ὁ ἡ τό the, this, that, he, she, it
ἐλπὶς n. nom. fem. sg. ἐλπίς hope, faith
τῆς art. gen. fem. sg. ὁ ἡ τό the, this, that, he, she, it
δόξης n. gen. fem. sg. δόξα glory, honour, praise, dignity, worship
28 ὃν relative pron. acc. masc. sg. ὅς ἥ ὅ who, which, what, that
ἡμεῖς pron. nom. 1p. pl. ἐγώ I
πάντα adj. acc. masc. sg. πᾶς πᾶσα πᾶν all, every, whosoever, every one, no, whole, any
ἄνθρωπον n. acc. masc. sg. ἄνθρωπος man, human being, person, one, certain
καὶ conj. καί and, even, also, but
πάντα adj. acc. masc. sg. πᾶς πᾶσα πᾶν all, every, whosoever, every one, no, whole, any
ἄνθρωπον n. acc. masc. sg. ἄνθρωπος man, human being, person, one, certain
ἐν prep. ἐν (+dat) in, by, with, among, at, on, through, to, within, into, of, for
πάσῃ adj. dat. fem. sg. πᾶς πᾶσα πᾶν all, every, whosoever, every one, no, whole, any
σοφίᾳ n. dat. fem. sg. σοφία wisdom
ἵνα conj. ἵνα that, to, lest, for to, so that, albeit, because, for, so as
πάντα adj. acc. masc. sg. πᾶς πᾶσα πᾶν all, every, whosoever, every one, no, whole, any
ἄνθρωπον n. acc. masc. sg. ἄνθρωπος man, human being, person, one, certain
τέλειον adj. acc. masc. sg. τέλειος perfect, of full age
ἐν prep. ἐν (+dat) in, by, with, among, at, on, through, to, within, into, of, for
Χριστῷ n. dat. masc. sg. Χριστός Christ
Ἰησοῦ n. dat. masc. sg. Ἰησοῦς Jesus
29 εἰς prep. εἰς (+acc) into, to, unto, for, in, on, toward, against, upon, at, among
ὃ relative pron. acc. neut. sg. ὅς ἥ ὅ who, which, what, that
καὶ conj. καί and, even, also, but
κατὰ prep. κατά (+gen) against, by, throughout, down, (+acc) according to, after, with
τὴν art. acc. fem. sg. ὁ ἡ τό the, this, that, he, she, it
ἐνέργειαν n. acc. fem. sg. ἐνέργεια working, effectual working, operation
αὐτοῦ pron. gen. masc. 3p. sg. αὐτός ἡ ὁ self, of oneself, even, very, the same, he, she, it
τὴν art. acc. fem. sg. ὁ ἡ τό the, this, that, he, she, it
ἐν prep. ἐν (+dat) in, by, with, among, at, on, through, to, within, into, of, for
ἐμοὶ pron. dat. 1p. sg. ἐγώ I
ἐν prep. ἐν (+dat) in, by, with, among, at, on, through, to, within, into, of, for
δυνάμει n. dat. fem. sg. δύναμις power, mighty work, miracle, strength, might

2

1 γὰρ conj. γάρ for, and, because, but, indeed
ὑμᾶς pron. acc. 2p. pl. σύ thou, you
ἡλίκον interrog. pron. acc. masc. sg. ἡλίκος how great
ἀγῶνα n. acc. masc. sg. ἀγών conflict, fight, contention, race
περὶ prep. περί (+gen) of, for, concerning, (+acc) about, concerning, in
ὑμῶν pron. gen. 2p. pl. σύ thou, you
καὶ conj. καί and, even, also, but
τῶν art. gen. masc. pl. ὁ ἡ τό the, this, that, he, she, it
ἐν prep. ἐν (+dat) in, by, with, among, at, on, through, to, within, into, of, for
Λαοδικείᾳ n. dat. fem. sg. Λαοδίκεια Laodicea
καὶ conj. καί and, even, also, but
ὅσοι relative pron. nom. masc. pl. ὅσος as many as, whatsoever, that, as long as, how much
οὐχ particle of negation. οὐ οὐκ οὐχ not, no, neither, none, nay, nor, never, nothing
τὸ art. acc. neut. sg. ὁ ἡ τό the, this, that, he, she, it
πρόσωπόν n. acc. neut. sg. πρόσωπον face, presence, person, countenance
μου pron. gen. 1p. sg. ἐγώ I
ἐν prep. ἐν (+dat) in, by, with, among, at, on, through, to, within, into, of, for
σαρκί n. dat. fem. sg. σάρξ flesh, carnal
2 ἵνα conj. ἵνα that, to, lest, for to, so that, albeit, because, for, so as
αἱ art. nom. fem. pl. ὁ ἡ τό the, this, that, he, she, it
καρδίαι n. nom. fem. pl. καρδία heart
αὐτῶν pron. gen. masc. 3p. pl. αὐτός ή ό self, of oneself, even, very, the same, he, she, it
ἐν prep. ἐν (+dat) in, by, with, among, at, on, through, to, within, into, of, for
ἀγάπῃ n. dat. fem. sg. ἀγάπη love, charity, feast of charity
καὶ conj. καί and, even, also, but
εἰς prep. εἰς (+acc) into, to, unto, for, in, on, toward, against, upon, at, among
πάντα adj. acc. masc. sg. πᾶς πᾶsa πᾶν all, every, whosoever, every one, no, whole, any
πλοῦτον n. acc. masc. sg. πλοῦτος riches
τῆς art. gen. fem. sg. ὁ ἡ τό the, this, that, he, she, it
πληροφορίας n. gen. fem. sg. πληροφορία full assurance, assurance
τῆς art. gen. fem. sg. ὁ ἡ τό the, this, that, he, she, it
συνέσεως n. gen. fem. sg. σύνεσις understanding, knowledge
εἰς prep. εἰς (+acc) into, to, unto, for, in, on, toward, against, upon, at, among
ἐπίγνωσιν n. acc. fem. sg. ἐπίγνωσις knowledge, acknowledging, acknowledgement
τοῦ art. gen. neut. sg. ὁ ἡ τό the, this, that, he, she, it
μυστηρίου n. gen. neut. sg. μυστήριον mystery
τοῦ art. gen. neut. sg. ὁ ἡ τό the, this, that, he, she, it
Θεοῦ n. gen. masc. sg. θεός God, god
καὶ conj. καί and, even, also, but
πατρὸς n. gen. masc. sg. πατήρ Father, father, parent
καὶ conj. καί and, even, also, but
τοῦ art. gen. neut. sg. ὁ ἡ τό the, this, that, he, she, it
Χριστοῦ n. gen. masc. sg. Χριστός Christ
3 ἐν prep. ἐν (+dat) in, by, with, among, at, on, through, to, within, into, of, for
ᾧ relative pron. dat. masc. sg. ὅς ἥ ὅ who, which, what, that
πάντες adj. nom. masc. pl. πᾶς πᾶsa πᾶν all, every, whosoever, every one, no, whole, any
οἱ art. nom. masc. pl. ὁ ἡ τό the, this, that, he, she, it
θησαυροὶ n. nom. masc. pl. θησαυρός treasure
τῆς art. gen. fem. sg. ὁ ἡ τό the, this, that, he, she, it
σοφίας n. gen. fem. sg. σοφία wisdom
καὶ conj. καί and, even, also, but
τῆς art. gen. fem. sg. ὁ ἡ τό the, this, that, he, she, it
γνώσεως n. gen. fem. sg. γνῶσις knowledge, science

ἀπόκρυφοι adj. nom. masc. pl. ἀπόκρυφος secret, hid
4 τοῦτο demo. pron. acc. neut. sg. οὗτος αὕτη τοῦτο this, the same, this same, he, she, it
δὲ conj. δέ but, and, now, also, to the contrary, rather, then
ἵνα conj. ἵνα that, to, lest, for to, so that, albeit, because, for, so as
μή particle of negation. μή not, no, lest, neither, none, nothing, nor, never, without
τις indefinite pron. nom. masc. sg. τὶς certain, some, any man, one, any thing
ὑμᾶς pron. acc. 2p. pl. σύ thou, you
ἐν prep. ἐν (+dat) in, by, with, among, at, on, through, to, within, into, of, for
πιθανολογίᾳ n. dat. fem. sg. πιθανολογία enticing word
5 εἰ conj. εἰ if, whether, that, though, forasmuch
γὰρ conj. γάρ for, and, because, but, indeed
καὶ conj. καί and, even, also, but
τῇ art. dat. fem. sg. ὁ ἡ τό the, this, that, he, she, it
σαρκὶ n. dat. fem. sg. σάρξ flesh, carnal
ἀλλὰ conj. ἀλλά but, yea, yet, nevertheless, howbeit, nay, therefore
τῷ art. dat. neut. sg. ὁ ἡ τό the, this, that, he, she, it
πνεύματι n. dat. neut. sg. πνεῦμα spirit, Spirit, Ghost, ghost, life. of the spirit, wind
σὺν prep. σύν (+dat) with, beside
ὑμῖν pron. dat. 2p. pl. σύ thou, you
καὶ conj. καί and, even, also, but
ὑμῶν pron. gen. 2p. pl. σύ thou, you
τὴν art. acc. fem. sg. ὁ ἡ τό the, this, that, he, she, it
τάξιν n. acc. fem. sg. τάξις order
καὶ conj. καί and, even, also, but
τὸ art. acc. neut. sg. ὁ ἡ τό the, this, that, he, she, it
στερέωμα n. acc. neut. sg. στερέωμα stedfastness
τῆς art. gen. fem. sg. ὁ ἡ τό the, this, that, he, she, it
εἰς prep. εἰς (+acc) into, to, unto, for, in, on, toward, against, upon, at, among
Χριστὸν n. acc. masc. sg. Χριστός Christ
πίστεως n. gen. fem. sg. πίστις faith, assurance, belief, fidelity
ὑμῶν pron. gen. 2p. pl. σύ thou, you
6 Ὡς adv. ὡς as, when, as it were, how, about, like, as soon as, even as, while
οὖν conj. οὖν therefore, then, so, and, now, wherefore
τὸν art. acc. masc. sg. ὁ ἡ τό the, this, that, he, she, it
Χριστὸν n. acc. masc. sg. Χριστός Christ
Ἰησοῦν n. acc. masc. sg. Ἰησοῦς Jesus
τὸν art. acc. masc. sg. ὁ ἡ τό the, this, that, he, she, it
Κύριον n. acc. masc. sg. κύριος Lord, lord, master, sir, LORD, God, Master, owner
ἐν prep. ἐν (+dat) in, by, with, among, at, on, through, to, within, into, of, for
αὐτῷ pron. dat. masc. 3p. sg. αὐτός ἡ ὁ self, of oneself, even, very, the same, he, she, it
7 καὶ conj. καί and, even, also, but
ἐν prep. ἐν (+dat) in, by, with, among, at, on, through, to, within, into, of, for
αὐτῷ pron. dat. masc. 3p. sg. αὐτός ἡ ὁ self, of oneself, even, very, the same, he, she, it
καὶ conj. καί and, even, also, but
ἐν prep. ἐν (+dat) in, by, with, among, at, on, through, to, within, into, of, for
τῇ art. dat. fem. sg. ὁ ἡ τό the, this, that, he, she, it
πίστει n. dat. fem. sg. πίστις faith, assurance, belief, fidelity
καθὼς adv. καθώς as, even as, according as, according to
ἐν prep. ἐν (+dat) in, by, with, among, at, on, through, to, within, into, of, for
αὐτῇ pron. dat. fem. 3p. sg. αὐτός ἡ ὁ self, of oneself, even, very, the same, he, she, it
ἐν prep. ἐν (+dat) in, by, with, among, at, on, through, to, within, into, of, for
εὐχαριστίᾳ n. dat. fem. sg. εὐχαριστία thankfulness, thanksgiving, giving of thanks
8 μή particle of negation. μή not, no, lest, neither, none, nothing, nor, never, without
τις indefinite pron. nom. masc. sg. τὶς certain, some, any man, one, any thing
ὑμᾶς pron. acc. 2p. pl. σύ thou, you

ὁ art. nom. masc. sg. ὁ ἡ τό the, this, that, he, she, it
διὰ prep. διά (+gen) by, through, with, in, of, (+acc) for, because of, for a cause
τῆς art. gen. fem. sg. ὁ ἡ τό the, this, that, he, she, it
φιλοσοφίας n. gen. fem. sg. φιλοσοφία philosophy
καὶ conj. καί and, even, also, but
κενῆς adj. gen. fem. sg. κενός empty, vain, in vain
ἀπάτης n. gen. fem. sg. ἀπάτη deceitfulness, deceit
κατὰ prep. κατά (+gen) against, by, throughout, down, (+acc) according to, after, with
τὴν art. acc. fem. sg. ὁ ἡ τό the, this, that, he, she, it
παράδοσιν n. acc. fem. sg. παράδοσις tradition, ordinance
τῶν art. gen. masc. pl. ὁ ἡ τό the, this, that, he, she, it
ἀνθρώπων n. gen. masc. pl. ἄνθρωπος man, human being, person, one, certain
κατὰ prep. κατά (+gen) against, by, throughout, down, (+acc) according to, after, with
τὰ art. acc. neut. pl. ὁ ἡ τό the, this, that, he, she, it
στοιχεῖα n. acc. neut. pl. στοιχεῖον element, rudiment, principle
τοῦ art. gen. masc. sg. ὁ ἡ τό the, this, that, he, she, it
κόσμου n. gen. masc. sg. κόσμος world, adorning
οὐ particle of negation. οὐ οὐκ οὐχ not, no, neither, none, nay, nor, never, nothing
καὶ conj. καί and, even, also, but
οὐ particle of negation. οὐ οὐκ οὐχ not, no, neither, none, nay, nor, never, nothing
κατὰ prep. κατά (+gen) against, by, throughout, down, (+acc) according to, after, with
Χριστόν n. acc. masc. sg. Χριστός Christ
9 ὅτι conj. ὅτι that, for, because, how that, how, because that, for that, though
ἐν prep. ἐν (+dat) in, by, with, among, at, on, through, to, within, into, of, for
αὐτῷ pron. dat. masc. 3p. sg. αὐτός ή ό self, of oneself, even, very, the same, he, she, it
πᾶν adj. nom. neut. sg. πᾶς πᾶσα πᾶν all, every, whosoever, every one, no, whole, any
τὸ art. nom. neut. sg. ὁ ἡ τό the, this, that, he, she, it
πλήρωμα n. nom. neut. sg. πλήρωμα fullness, fulfilling, full
τῆς art. gen. fem. sg. ὁ ἡ τό the, this, that, he, she, it
θεότητος n. gen. fem. sg. θεότης Godhead
σωματικῶς adv. σωματικῶς bodily
10 καὶ conj. καί and, even, also, but
ἐν prep. ἐν (+dat) in, by, with, among, at, on, through, to, within, into, of, for
αὐτῷ pron. dat. masc. 3p. sg. αὐτός ή ό self, of oneself, even, very, the same, he, she, it
ὅς relative pron. nom. masc. sg. ὅς ἥ ὅ who, which, what, that
ἡ art. nom. fem. sg. ὁ ἡ τό the, this, that, he, she, it
κεφαλὴ n. nom. fem. sg. κεφαλή head
πάσης adj. gen. fem. sg. πᾶς πᾶσα πᾶν all, every, whosoever, every one, no, whole, any
ἀρχῆς n. gen. fem. sg. ἀρχή beginning, principality, corner, first, magistrate, rule
καὶ conj. καί and, even, also, but
ἐξουσίας n. gen. fem. sg. ἐξουσία power, authority, right, strength, jurisdiction
11 ἐν prep. ἐν (+dat) in, by, with, among, at, on, through, to, within, into, of, for
ᾧ relative pron. dat. masc. sg. ὅς ἥ ὅ who, which, what, that
καὶ conj. καί and, even, also, but
περιτομῇ n. dat. fem. sg. περιτομή circumcision
ἀχειροποιήτῳ adj. dat. fem. sg. ἀχειροποίητος made without hands
ἐν prep. ἐν (+dat) in, by, with, among, at, on, through, to, within, into, of, for
τῇ art. dat. fem. sg. ὁ ἡ τό the, this, that, he, she, it
ἀπεκδύσει n. dat. fem. sg. ἀπέκδυσις putting off
τοῦ art. gen. neut. sg. ὁ ἡ τό the, this, that, he, she, it
σώματος n. gen. neut. sg. σῶμα body, bodily, slave
τῶν art. gen. fem. pl. ὁ ἡ τό the, this, that, he, she, it
ἁμαρτιῶν n. gen. fem. pl. ἁμαρτία sin, offence, sinful
τῆς art. gen. fem. sg. ὁ ἡ τό the, this, that, he, she, it
σαρκός n. gen. fem. sg. σάρξ flesh, carnal

ἐν prep. ἐν (+dat) in, by, with, among, at, on, through, to, within, into, of, for
τῇ art. dat. fem. sg. ὁ ἡ τό the, this, that, he, she, it
περιτομῇ n. dat. fem. sg. περιτομή circumcision
τοῦ art. gen. masc. sg. ὁ ἡ τό the, this, that, he, she, it
Χριστοῦ n. gen. masc. sg. Χριστός Christ
12 αὐτῷ pron. dat. masc. 3p. sg. αὐτός ἡ ὁ self, of oneself, even, very, the same, he, she, it
ἐν prep. ἐν (+dat) in, by, with, among, at, on, through, to, within, into, of, for
τῷ art. dat. masc. sg. ὁ ἡ τό the, this, that, he, she, it
βαπτίσματι n. dat. neut. sg. βάπτισμα baptism
ἐν prep. ἐν (+dat) in, by, with, among, at, on, through, to, within, into, of, for
ᾧ relative pron. dat. masc. sg. ὅς ἥ ὅ who, which, what, that
καὶ conj. καί and, even, also, but
διὰ prep. διά (+gen) by, through, with, in, of, (+acc) for, because of, for a cause
τῆς art. gen. fem. sg. ὁ ἡ τό the, this, that, he, she, it
πίστεως n. gen. fem. sg. πίστις faith, assurance, belief, fidelity
τῆς art. gen. fem. sg. ὁ ἡ τό the, this, that, he, she, it
ἐνεργείας n. gen. fem. sg. ἐνέργεια working, effectual working, operation
τοῦ art. gen. masc. sg. ὁ ἡ τό the, this, that, he, she, it
Θεοῦ n. gen. masc. sg. θεός God, god
τοῦ art. gen. masc. sg. ὁ ἡ τό the, this, that, he, she, it
αὐτὸν pron. acc. masc. 3p. sg. αὐτός ἡ ὁ self, of oneself, even, very, the same, he, she, it
ἐκ prep. ἐκ ἐξ (+gen) of, from, out of, by, on, with, in, among, through
τῶν art. gen. fem. pl. ὁ ἡ τό the, this, that, he, she, it
νεκρῶν adj. gen. masc. pl. νεκρός dead
13 καὶ conj. καί and, even, also, but
ὑμᾶς pron. acc. 2p. pl. σύ thou, you
νεκροὺς adj. acc. masc. pl. νεκρός dead
ἐν prep. ἐν (+dat) in, by, with, among, at, on, through, to, within, into, of, for
τοῖς art. dat. neut. pl. ὁ ἡ τό the, this, that, he, she, it
παραπτώμασι n. dat. neut. pl. παράπτωμα trespass, offence, sin, fall, fault
καὶ conj. καί and, even, also, but
τῇ art. dat. fem. sg. ὁ ἡ τό the, this, that, he, she, it
ἀκροβυστίᾳ n. dat. fem. sg. ἀκροβυστία uncircumcised, uncircumcision
τῆς art. gen. fem. sg. ὁ ἡ τό the, this, that, he, she, it
σαρκὸς n. gen. fem. sg. σάρξ flesh, carnal
ὑμῶν pron. gen. 2p. pl. σύ thou, you
σὺν prep. σύν (+dat) with, beside
αὐτῷ pron. dat. masc. 3p. sg. αὐτός ἡ ὁ self, of oneself, even, very, the same, he, she, it
ὑμῖν pron. dat. 2p. pl. σύ thou, you
πάντα adj. acc. neut. pl. πᾶς πᾶσα πᾶν all, every, whosoever, every one, no, whole, any
τὰ art. acc. neut. pl. ὁ ἡ τό the, this, that, he, she, it
παραπτώματα n. acc. neut. pl. παράπτωμα trespass, offence, sin, fall, fault
14 τὸ art. acc. neut. sg. ὁ ἡ τό the, this, that, he, she, it
καθ' prep. κατά (+gen) against, by, throughout, down, (+acc) according to, after, with
ἡμῶν pron. gen. 1p. pl. ἐγώ I
χειρόγραφον n. acc. neut. sg. χειρόγραφον handwriting
τοῖς art. dat. neut. pl. ὁ ἡ τό the, this, that, he, she, it
δόγμασιν n. dat. neut. pl. δόγμα decree, ordinance
ὃ relative pron. nom. neut. sg. ὅς ἥ ὅ who, which, what, that
ὑπεναντίον adj. nom. neut. sg. ὑπεναντίος contrary, adversary
ἡμῖν pron. dat. 1p. pl. ἐγώ I
καὶ conj. καί and, even, also, but
αὐτὸ pron. acc. neut. 3p. sg. αὐτός ἡ ὁ self, of oneself, even, very, the same, he, she, it
ἐκ prep. ἐκ ἐξ (+gen) of, from, out of, by, on, with, in, among, through
τοῦ art. gen. neut. sg. ὁ ἡ τό the, this, that, he, she, it

μέσου adj. gen. neut. sg. μέσος midst, among, mid, between
αὐτὸ pron. acc. neut. 3p. sg. αὐτός ή ό self, of oneself, even, very, the same, he, she, it
τῷ art. dat. masc. sg. ὁ ἡ τό the, this, that, he, she, it
σταυρῷ n. dat. masc. sg. σταυρός cross
15 τὰς art. acc. fem. pl. ὁ ἡ τό the, this, that, he, she, it
ἀρχὰς n. acc. fem. pl. ἀρχή beginning, principality, corner, first, magistrate, rule
καὶ conj. καί and, even, also, but
τὰς art. acc. fem. pl. ὁ ἡ τό the, this, that, he, she, it
ἐξουσίας n. acc. fem. pl. ἐξουσία power, authority, right, strength, jurisdiction
ἐν prep. ἐν (+dat) in, by, with, among, at, on, through, to, within, into, of, for
παρρησίᾳ n. dat. fem. sg. παρρησία boldness, confidence, openly, plainly, freely
αὐτοὺς pron. acc. masc. 3p. pl. αὐτός ή ό self, of oneself, even, very, the same, he, she, it
ἐν prep. ἐν (+dat) in, by, with, among, at, on, through, to, within, into, of, for
αὐτῷ pron. dat. masc. 3p. sg. αὐτός ή ό self, of oneself, even, very, the same, he, she, it
16 Μὴ particle of negation. μή not, no, lest, neither, none, nothing, nor, never, without
οὖν conj. οὖν therefore, then, so, and, now, wherefore
τις indefinite pron. nom. masc. sg. τὶς certain, some, any man, one, any thing
ὑμᾶς pron. acc. 2p. pl. σύ thou, you
ἐν prep. ἐν (+dat) in, by, with, among, at, on, through, to, within, into, of, for
βρώσει n. dat. fem. sg. βρῶσις rust, meat, eating, food, morsel of meat
ἢ particle. ἤ or, than, either, nor, or else, and, rather than
ἐν prep. ἐν (+dat) in, by, with, among, at, on, through, to, within, into, of, for
πόσει n. dat. fem. sg. πόσις drink
ἢ particle. ἤ or, than, either, nor, or else, and, rather than
ἐν prep. ἐν (+dat) in, by, with, among, at, on, through, to, within, into, of, for
μέρει n. dat. neut. sg. μέρος part, coast, portion, behalf, respect, piece, side
ἑορτῆς n. gen. fem. sg. ἑορτή feast, holyday
ἢ particle. ἤ or, than, either, nor, or else, and, rather than
νουμηνίας n. gen. fem. sg. νουμηνία new moon
ἢ particle. ἤ or, than, either, nor, or else, and, rather than
σαββάτων n. gen. neut. pl. σάββατον sabbath day, sabbath, week
17 ἅ relative pron. nom. neut. pl. ὅς ἥ ὅ who, which, what, that
σκιὰ n. nom. fem. sg. σκιά shadow
τῶν art. gen. neut. pl. ὁ ἡ τό the, this, that, he, she, it
τὸ art. nom. neut. sg. ὁ ἡ τό the, this, that, he, she, it
δὲ conj. δέ but, and, now, also, to the contrary, rather, then
σῶμα n. nom. neut. sg. σῶμα body, bodily, slave
τοῦ art. gen. masc. sg. ὁ ἡ τό the, this, that, he, she, it
Χριστοῦ n. gen. masc. sg. Χριστός Christ
18 μηδεὶς num. nom. masc. sg. μηδείς μηδεμία μηδέν no man, nothing, no, none, not at all
ὑμᾶς pron. acc. 2p. pl. σύ thou, you
ἐν prep. ἐν (+dat) in, by, with, among, at, on, through, to, within, into, of, for
ταπεινοφροσύνῃ n. dat. fem. sg. ταπεινοφροσύνη humility of mind, humility, lowliness
καὶ conj. καί and, even, also, but
θρησκείᾳ n. dat. fem. sg. θρησκεία religion, worshipping
τῶν art. gen. masc. pl. ὁ ἡ τό the, this, that, he, she, it
ἀγγέλων n. gen. masc. pl. ἄγγελος angel, messenger
ἃ relative pron. acc. neut. pl. ὅς ἥ ὅ who, which, what, that
μὴ particle of negation. μή not, no, lest, neither, none, nothing, nor, never, without
εἰκῇ adv. εἰκῇ in vain, vainly, without a cause
ὑπὸ prep. ὑπό (+gen) of, by, with, from, among, (+acc) under
τοῦ art. gen. masc. sg. ὁ ἡ τό the, this, that, he, she, it
νοὸς n. gen. masc. sg. νοῦς understanding, mind
τῆς art. gen. fem. sg. ὁ ἡ τό the, this, that, he, she, it
σαρκὸς n. gen. fem. sg. σάρξ flesh, carnal

αὐτοῦ pron. gen. masc. 3p. sg. αὐτός ή ό self, of oneself, even, very, the same, he, she, it
19 καὶ conj. καί and, even, also, but
οὐ particle of negation. οὐ οὐκ οὐχ not, no, neither, none, nay, nor, never, nothing
τὴν art. acc. fem. sg. ὁ ἡ τό the, this, that, he, she, it
κεφαλήν n. acc. fem. sg. κεφαλή head
ἐξ prep. ἐκ ἐξ (+gen) of, from, out of, by, on, with, in, among, through
οὗ relative pron. gen. masc. sg. ὅς ἥ ὅ who, which, what, that
πᾶν adj. nom. neut. sg. πᾶς πᾶσα πᾶν all, every, whosoever, every one, no, whole, any
τὸ art. nom. neut. sg. ὁ ἡ τό the, this, that, he, she, it
σῶμα n. nom. neut. sg. σῶμα body, bodily, slave
διὰ prep. διά (+gen) by, through, with, in, of, (+acc) for, because of, for a cause
τῶν art. gen. fem. pl. ὁ ἡ τό the, this, that, he, she, it
ἁφῶν n. gen. fem. pl. ἁφή joint
καὶ conj. καί and, even, also, but
συνδέσμων n. gen. masc. pl. σύνδεσμος bond, band
καὶ conj. καί and, even, also, but
τὴν art. acc. fem. sg. ὁ ἡ τό the, this, that, he, she, it
αὔξησιν n. acc. fem. sg. αὔξησις increase
τοῦ art. gen. masc. sg. ὁ ἡ τό the, this, that, he, she, it
Θεοῦ n. gen. masc. sg. θεός God, god
20 Εἰ conj. εἰ if, whether, that, though, forasmuch
οὖν conj. οὖν therefore, then, so, and, now, wherefore
σὺν prep. οὖν therefore, then, so, and, now, wherefore
τῷ art. dat. masc. sg. ὁ ἡ τό the, this, that, he, she, it
Χριστῷ n. dat. masc. sg. Χριστός Christ
ἀπὸ prep. ἀπό (+gen) from, of, out of, since, for, off, at, by, in, on
τῶν art. gen. neut. pl. ὁ ἡ τό the, this, that, he, she, it
στοιχείων n. gen. neut. pl. στοιχεῖον element, rudiment, principle
τοῦ art. gen. masc. sg. ὁ ἡ τό the, this, that, he, she, it
κόσμου n. gen. masc. sg. κόσμος world, adorning
τί interrog. pron. acc. neut. sg. τίς what, who, why, where, which, how
ὡς adv. ὡς as, when, as it were, how, about, like, as soon as, even as, while
ἐν prep. ἐν (+dat) in, by, with, among, at, on, through, to, within, into, of, for
κόσμῳ n. dat. masc. sg. κόσμος world, adorning
21 Μὴ particle of negation. μή not, no, lest, neither, none, nothing, nor, never, without
μηδὲ conj. μηδέ neither, nor, not, no not, nor yet, not once, not so much as
μηδὲ conj. μηδέ neither, nor, not, no not, nor yet, not once, not so much as
22 ἅ relative pron. nom. neut. pl. ὅς ἥ ὅ who, which, what, that
πάντα adj. nom. neut. pl. πᾶς πᾶςα πᾶν all, every, whosoever, every one, no, whole, any
εἰς prep. εἰς (+acc) into, to, unto, for, in, on, toward, against, upon, at, among
φθορὰν n. acc. fem. sg. φθορά corruption, destroy, perish
τῇ art. dat. fem. sg. ὁ ἡ τό the, this, that, he, she, it
ἀποχρήσει n. dat. fem. sg. ἀπόχρησις using
κατὰ prep. κατά (+gen) against, by, throughout, down, (+acc) according to, after, with
τὰ art. acc. neut. pl. ὁ ἡ τό the, this, that, he, she, it
ἐντάλματα n. acc. neut. pl. ἔνταλμα commandment
καὶ conj. καί and, even, also, but
διδασκαλίας n. acc. fem. pl. διδασκαλία doctrine, learning, teaching
τῶν art. gen. masc. pl. ὁ ἡ τό the, this, that, he, she, it
ἀνθρώπων n. gen. masc. pl. ἄνθρωπος man, human being, person, one, certain
23 ἅτινά relative pron. nom. neut. pl. ὅστις which, who, whosoever, that, whatsoever
λόγον n. acc. masc. sg. λόγος word, saying, account, speech, thing, matter
μὲν conj. μέν indeed, verily, truly, even, so, some
σοφίας n. gen. fem. sg. σοφία wisdom
ἐν prep. ἐν (+dat) in, by, with, among, at, on, through, to, within, into, of, for

ἐθελοθρησκείᾳ n. dat. fem. sg. ἐθελοθρησκία will worship, self-made religion
καὶ conj. καί and, even, also, but
ταπεινοφροσύνῃ n. dat. fem. sg. ταπεινοφροσύνη humility of mind, humility, lowliness
καὶ conj. καί and, even, also, but
ἀφειδίᾳ n. dat. fem. sg. ἀφειδία neglect
σώματος n. gen. neut. sg. σῶμα body, bodily, slave
οὐκ particle of negation. οὐ οὐκ οὐχ not, no, neither, none, nay, nor, never, nothing
ἐν prep. ἐν (+dat) in, by, with, among, at, on, through, to, within, into, of, for
τιμῇ n. dat. fem. sg. τιμή honour, price, preciousness, sum
τινι indefinite pron. dat. fem. sg. τὶς certain, some, any man, one, any thing
πρὸς prep. πρός (+gen) for, (+dat) at, (+acc) unto, to, with, for, against
πλησμονὴν n. acc. fem. sg. πλησμονή satisfying
τῆς art. gen. fem. sg. ὁ ἡ τό the, this, that, he, she, it
σαρκός n. gen. fem. sg. σάρξ flesh, carnal

3

1 Εἰ conj. εἰ if, whether, that, though, forasmuch
οὖν conj. οὖν therefore, then, so, and, now, wherefore
τῷ art. dat. masc. sg. ὁ ἡ τό the, this, that, he, she, it
Χριστῷ n. dat. masc. sg. Χριστός Christ
τὰ art. acc. neut. pl. ὁ ἡ τό the, this, that, he, she, it
ἄνω adv. ἄνω above, up, high, the brim
οὗ adv. οὗ where, whither, wherein
ὁ art. nom. masc. sg. ὁ ἡ τό the, this, that, he, she, it
Χριστός n. nom. masc. sg. Χριστός Christ
ἐν prep. ἐν (+dat) in, by, with, among, at, on, through, to, within, into, of, for
δεξιᾷ adj. dat. fem. sg. δεξιός right, right hand, right side
τοῦ art. gen. masc. sg. ὁ ἡ τό the, this, that, he, she, it
Θεοῦ n. gen. masc. sg. θεός God, god
2 τὰ art. acc. neut. pl. ὁ ἡ τό the, this, that, he, she, it
ἄνω adv. ἄνω above, up, high, the brim
μὴ particle of negation. μή not, no, lest, neither, none, nothing, nor, never, without
τὰ art. acc. neut. pl. ὁ ἡ τό the, this, that, he, she, it
ἐπὶ prep. ἐπί (+gen) on, in, upon, (+dat) in, at, for, upon, (+acc) on, upon, unto, to, against
τῆς art. gen. fem. sg. ὁ ἡ τό the, this, that, he, she, it
γῆς n. gen. fem. sg. γῆ earth, land, ground, country
3 γὰρ conj. γάρ for, and, because, but, indeed
καὶ conj. καί and, even, also, but
ἡ art. nom. fem. sg. ὁ ἡ τό the, this, that, he, she, it
ζωὴ n. nom. fem. sg. ζωή life, lifetime
ὑμῶν pron. gen. 2p. pl. σύ thou, you
σὺν prep. σύν (+dat) with, beside
τῷ art. dat. masc. sg. ὁ ἡ τό the, this, that, he, she, it
Χριστῷ n. dat. masc. sg. Χριστός Christ
ἐν prep. ἐν (+dat) in, by, with, among, at, on, through, to, within, into, of, for
τῷ art. dat. masc. sg. ὁ ἡ τό the, this, that, he, she, it
Θεῷ n. dat. masc. sg. θεός God, god
4 ὅταν conj. ὅταν when, as soon as, as long as, that, whensoever, while
ὁ art. nom. masc. sg. ὁ ἡ τό the, this, that, he, she, it
Χριστὸς n. nom. masc. sg. Χριστός Christ
ἡ art. nom. fem. sg. ὁ ἡ τό the, this, that, he, she, it
ζωὴ n. nom. fem. sg. ζωή life, lifetime
ἡμῶν pron. gen. 1p. pl. ἐγώ I
τότε adv. τότε then, that time

καὶ conj. καί and, even, also, but
ὑμεῖς pron. nom. 2p. pl. σύ thou, you
σὺν prep. σύν (+dat) with, beside
αὐτῷ pron. dat. masc. 3p. sg. αὐτός ή ό self, of oneself, even, very, the same, he, she, it
ἐν prep. ἐν (+dat) in, by, with, among, at, on, through, to, within, into, of, for
δόξῃ n. dat. fem. sg. δόξα glory, honour, praise, dignity, worship
5 οὖν conj. οὖν therefore, then, so, and, now, wherefore
τὰ art. acc. neut. pl. ὁ ἡ τό the, this, that, he, she, it
μέλη n. acc. neut. pl. μέλος member
ὑμῶν pron. gen. 2p. pl. σύ thou, you
τὰ art. acc. neut. pl. ὁ ἡ τό the, this, that, he, she, it
ἐπὶ prep. ἐπί (+gen) on, in, upon, (+dat) in, at, for, upon, (+acc) on, upon, unto, to, against
τῆς art. gen. fem. sg. ὁ ἡ τό the, this, that, he, she, it
γῆς n. gen. fem. sg. γῆ earth, land, ground, country
πορνείαν n. acc. fem. sg. πορνεία fornication
ἀκαθαρσίαν n. acc. fem. sg. ἀκαθαρσία uncleanness
πάθος n. acc. neut. sg. πάθος affection, inordinate affection, lust
ἐπιθυμίαν n. acc. fem. sg. ἐπιθυμία lust, concupiscence, desire
κακήν adj. acc. fem. sg. κακός evil, evil thing, noisome, wicked
καὶ conj. καί and, even, also, but
τὴν art. acc. fem. sg. ὁ ἡ τό the, this, that, he, she, it
πλεονεξίαν n. acc. fem. sg. πλεονεξία covetousness, covetous practice, greediness
ἥτις relative pron. nom. fem. sg. ὅστις which, who, whosoever, that, whatsoever
εἰδωλολατρεία n. nom. fem. sg. εἰδωλολατρεία idolatry
6 δι' prep. διά (+gen) by, through, with, in, of, (+acc) for, because of, for a cause
ἃ relative pron. acc. neut. pl. ὅς ἥ ὅ who, which, what, that
ἡ art. nom. fem. sg. ὁ ἡ τό the, this, that, he, she, it
ὀργὴ n. nom. fem. sg. ὀργή wrath, anger, indignation, vengeance
τοῦ art. gen. masc. sg. ὁ ἡ τό the, this, that, he, she, it
Θεοῦ n. gen. masc. sg. θεός God, god
ἐπὶ prep. ἐπί (+gen) on, in, upon, (+dat) in, at, for, upon, (+acc) on, upon, unto, to, against
τοὺς art. acc. masc. pl. ὁ ἡ τό the, this, that, he, she, it
υἱοὺς n. acc. masc. pl. υἱός son, child, descendant, offspring, heir
τῆς art. gen. fem. sg. ὁ ἡ τό the, this, that, he, she, it
ἀπειθείας n. gen. fem. sg. ἀπείθεια unbelief, disobedience
7 ἐν prep. ἐν (+dat) in, by, with, among, at, on, through, to, within, into, of, for
οἷς relative pron. dat. neut. pl. ὅς ἥ ὅ who, which, what, that
καὶ conj. καί and, even, also, but
ὑμεῖς pron. nom. 2p. pl. σύ thou, you
ποτε adv. ποτέ in time past, at any time, sometimes, in old time, once, when
ὅτε adv. ὅτε when, after that, as soon as, while, after
ἐν prep. ἐν (+dat) in, by, with, among, at, on, through, to, within, into, of, for
αὐτοῖς pron. dat. neut. 3p. pl. αὐτός ή ό self, of oneself, even, very, the same, he, she, it
8 νυνὶ adv. νυνί now
δὲ conj. δέ but, and, now, also, to the contrary, rather, then
καὶ conj. καί and, even, also, but
ὑμεῖς pron. nom. 2p. pl. σύ thou, you
τὰ art. acc. neut. pl. ὁ ἡ τό the, this, that, he, she, it
πάντα adj. acc. neut. pl. πᾶς πᾶσα πᾶν all, every, whosoever, every one, no, whole, any
ὀργήν n. acc. fem. sg. ὀργή wrath, anger, indignation, vengeance
θυμόν n. acc. masc. sg. θυμός wrath, fierceness, indignation
κακίαν n. acc. fem. sg. κακία malice, maliciousness, evil, naughtiness, wickedness
βλασφημίαν n. acc. fem. sg. βλασφημία blasphemy, railing, evil speaking
αἰσχρολογίαν n. acc. fem. sg. αἰσχρολογία filthy communication
ἐκ prep. ἐκ ἐξ (+gen) of, from, out of, by, on, with, in, among, through

τοῦ art. gen. neut. sg. ὁ ἡ τό the, this, that, he, she, it
στόματος n. gen. neut. sg. στόμα mouth, face, edge
ὑμῶν pron. gen. 2p. pl. σύ thou, you
9 μὴ particle of negation. μή not, no, lest, neither, none, nothing, nor, never, without
εἰς prep. εἰς (+acc) into, to, unto, for, in, on, toward, against, upon, at, among
ἀλλήλους pron. acc. masc. pl. ἀλλήλων one another, themselves, together, mutual
τὸν art. acc. masc. sg. ὁ ἡ τό the, this, that, he, she, it
παλαιὸν adj. acc. masc. sg. παλαιός old
ἄνθρωπον n. acc. masc. sg. ἄνθρωπος man, human being, person, one, certain
σὺν prep. σύν (+dat) with, beside
ταῖς art. dat. fem. pl. ὁ ἡ τό the, this, that, he, she, it
πράξεσιν n. dat. fem. pl. πρᾶξις deed, office, acting
αὐτοῦ pron. gen. masc. 3p. sg. αὐτός ή ό self, of oneself, even, very, the same, he, she, it
10 καὶ conj. καί and, even, also, but
τὸν art. acc. masc. sg. ὁ ἡ τό the, this, that, he, she, it
νέον adj. acc. masc. sg. νέος new
τὸν art. acc. masc. sg. ὁ ἡ τό the, this, that, he, she, it
εἰς prep. εἰς (+acc) into, to, unto, for, in, on, toward, against, upon, at, among
ἐπίγνωσιν n. acc. fem. sg. ἐπίγνωσις knowledge, acknowledging, acknowledgement
κατ' prep. κατά (+gen) against, by, throughout, down, (+acc) according to, after, with
εἰκόνα n. acc. fem. sg. εἰκών image
τοῦ art. gen. masc. sg. ὁ ἡ τό the, this, that, he, she, it
αὐτόν pron. acc. masc. 3p. sg. αὐτός ή ό self, of oneself, even, very, the same, he, she, it
11 ὅπου adv. ὅπου where, whither, whereas, in what place, wheresoever
οὐκ particle of negation. οὐ οὐκ οὐχ not, no, neither, none, nay, nor, never, nothing
Ἕλλην n. nom. masc. sg. Ἕλλην Greek, Gentile
καὶ conj. καί and, even, also, but
Ἰουδαῖος adj. nom. masc. sg. Ἰουδαῖος Jew, Jewess
περιτομὴ n. nom. fem. sg. περιτομή circumcision
καὶ conj. καί and, even, also, but
ἀκροβυστία n. nom. fem. sg. ἀκροβυστία uncircumcised, uncircumcision
βάρβαρος adj. nom. masc. sg. βάρβαρος barbarous, barbarian
Σκύθης n. nom. masc. sg. Σκύθης Scythian
δοῦλος n. nom. masc. sg. δοῦλος servant, bondman, bond, slave
ἐλεύθερος adj. nom. masc. sg. ἐλεύθερος free, freewoman, at liberty, freeman
ἀλλὰ conj. ἀλλά but, yea, yet, nevertheless, howbeit, nay, therefore
τὰ art. nom. neut. pl. ὁ ἡ τό the, this, that, he, she, it
πάντα adj. nom. neut. pl. πᾶς πᾶσα πᾶν all, every, whosoever, every one, no, whole, any
καὶ conj. καί and, even, also, but
ἐν prep. ἐν (+dat) in, by, with, among, at, on, through, to, within, into, of, for
πᾶσι adj. dat. neut. pl. πᾶς πᾶσα πᾶν all, every, whosoever, every one, no, whole, any
Χριστός n. nom. masc. sg. Χριστός Christ
12 οὖν conj. οὖν therefore, then, so, and, now, wherefore
ὡς adv. ὡς as, when, as it were, how, about, like, as soon as, even as, while
ἐκλεκτοὶ adj. nom. masc. pl. ἐκλεκτός elect, chosen
τοῦ art. gen. masc. sg. ὁ ἡ τό the, this, that, he, she, it
Θεοῦ n. gen. masc. sg. θεός God, god
ἅγιοι adj. nom. masc. pl. ἅγιος Holy, holy, saint, Holy One, holy thing, most holy
καὶ conj. καί and, even, also, but
σπλάγχνα n. acc. neut. pl. σπλάγχνον tender, bowels, inward affection
οἰκτιρμῶν n. gen. masc. pl. οἰκτιρμός mercy
χρηστότητα n. acc. fem. sg. χρηστότης goodness, kindness, gentleness, good
ταπεινοφροσύνην n. acc. fem. sg. ταπεινοφροσύνη humility of mind, humility, lowliness
πρᾳότητα n. acc. fem. sg. πρᾳότης meekness
μακροθυμίαν n. acc. fem. sg. μακροθυμία longsuffering, patience

13 ἀλλήλων pron. gen. masc. pl. ἀλλήλων one another, themselves, together, mutual
καὶ conj. καί and, even, also, but
ἑαυτοῖς reflexive pron. dat. masc. 3p. pl. ἑαυτοῦ himself, herself, itself, yourself, ourselves
ἐάν conj. ἐάν if, soever, except, though, and if, but, whether, if so, so
τις indefinite pron. nom. masc. sg. τὶς certain, some, any man, one, any thing
πρός prep. πρός (+gen) for, (+dat) at, (+acc) unto, to, with, for, against
τινα indefinite pron. acc. masc. sg. τὶς certain, some, any man, one, any thing
μομφήν n. acc. fem. sg. μομφή quarrel
καθὼς adv. καθώς as, even as, according as, according to
καὶ conj. καί and, even, also, but
ὁ art. nom. masc. sg. ὁ ἡ τό the, this, that, he, she, it
Χριστὸς n. nom. masc. sg. Χριστός Christ
ὑμῖν pron. dat. 2p. pl. σύ thou, you
οὕτω adv. οὕτω οὕτως so, even so, thus, on this wise, likewise, after this manner
καὶ conj. καί and, even, also, but
ὑμεῖς pron. nom. 2p. pl. σύ thou, you
14 ἐπὶ prep. ἐπί (+gen) on, in, upon, (+dat) in, at, for, upon, (+acc) on, upon, unto, to, against
πᾶσιν adj. dat. neut. pl. πᾶς πᾶσα πᾶν all, every, whosoever, every one, no, whole, any
δὲ conj. δέ but, and, now, also, to the contrary, rather, then
τούτοις demo. pron. dat. neut. pl. οὗτος αὕτη τοῦτο this, the same, this same, he, she, it
τὴν art. acc. fem. sg. ὁ ἡ τό the, this, that, he, she, it
ἀγάπην n. acc. fem. sg. ἀγάπη love, charity, feast of charity
ἥτις relative pron. nom. fem. sg. ὅστις which, who, whosoever, that, whatsoever
σύνδεσμος n. nom. masc. sg. σύνδεσμος bond, band
τῆς art. gen. fem. sg. ὁ ἡ τό the, this, that, he, she, it
τελειότητος n. gen. fem. sg. τελειότης perfectness, perfection
15 καὶ conj. καί and, even, also, but
ἡ art. nom. fem. sg. ὁ ἡ τό the, this, that, he, she, it
εἰρήνη n. nom. fem. sg. εἰρήνη peace, quietness, rest
τοῦ art. gen. masc. sg. ὁ ἡ τό the, this, that, he, she, it
Θεοῦ n. gen. masc. sg. θεός God, god
ἐν prep. ἐν (+dat) in, by, with, among, at, on, through, to, within, into, of, for
ταῖς art. dat. fem. pl. ὁ ἡ τό the, this, that, he, she, it
καρδίαις n. dat. fem. pl. καρδία heart
ὑμῶν pron. gen. 2p. pl. σύ thou, you
εἰς prep. εἰς (+acc) into, to, unto, for, in, on, toward, against, upon, at, among
ἣν relative pron. acc. fem. sg. ὅς ἥ ὅ who, which, what, that
καὶ conj. καί and, even, also, but
ἐν prep. ἐν (+dat) in, by, with, among, at, on, through, to, within, into, of, for
ἑνὶ num. dat. neut. sg. εἷς or ἕν one, other, some, any, only, a certain
σώματι n. dat. neut. sg. σῶμα body, bodily, slave
καὶ conj. καί and, even, also, but
εὐχάριστοι adj. nom. masc. pl. εὐχάριστος thankful
16 ὁ art. nom. masc. sg. ὁ ἡ τό the, this, that, he, she, it
λόγος n. nom. masc. sg. λόγος word, saying, account, speech, thing, matter
τοῦ art. gen. masc. sg. ὁ ἡ τό the, this, that, he, she, it
Χριστοῦ n. gen. masc. sg. Χριστός Christ
ἐν prep. ἐν (+dat) in, by, with, among, at, on, through, to, within, into, of, for
ὑμῖν pron. dat. 2p. pl. σύ thou, you
πλουσίως adv. πλουσίως richly, abundantly
ἐν prep. ἐν (+dat) in, by, with, among, at, on, through, to, within, into, of, for
πάσῃ adj. dat. fem. sg. πᾶς πᾶσα πᾶν all, every, whosoever, every one, no, whole, any
σοφίᾳ n. dat. fem. sg. σοφία wisdom
καὶ conj. καί and, even, also, but
ἑαυτούς reflexive pron. acc. masc. 3p. pl. ἑαυτοῦ himself, herself, itself, yourself, ourselves

ψαλμοῖς n. dat. masc. pl. ψαλμός Psalm, psalm
καὶ conj. καί and, even, also, but
ὕμνοις n. dat. masc. pl. ὕμνος hymn
καὶ conj. καί and, even, also, but
ᾠδαῖς n. dat. fem. pl. ᾠδή song
πνευματικαῖς adj. dat. fem. pl. πνευματικός spiritual
ἐν prep. ἐν (+dat) in, by, with, among, at, on, through, to, within, into, of, for
χάριτι n. dat. fem. sg. χάρις grace, thank, favour, pleasure
ἐν prep. ἐν (+dat) in, by, with, among, at, on, through, to, within, into, of, for
τῇ art. dat. fem. sg. ὁ ἡ τό the, this, that, he, she, it
καρδίᾳ n. dat. fem. sg. καρδία heart
ὑμῶν pron. gen. 2p. pl. σύ thou, you
τῷ art. dat. masc. sg. ὁ ἡ τό the, this, that, he, she, it
Κυρίῳ n. dat. masc. sg. κύριος Lord, lord, master, sir, LORD, God, Master, owner
17 καὶ conj. καί and, even, also, but
πᾶν adj. acc. neut. sg. πᾶς πᾶσα πᾶν all, every, whosoever, every one, no, whole, any
ὃ relative pron. acc. neut. sg. ὅς ἥ ὅ who, which, what, that
τι indefinite pron. acc. neut. sg. τὶς certain, some, any man, one, any thing
ἂν particle. ἄν Indicating contingency. No English translation.
ἐν prep. ἐν (+dat) in, by, with, among, at, on, through, to, within, into, of, for
λόγῳ n. dat. masc. sg. λόγος word, saying, account, speech, thing, matter
ἢ particle. ἤ or, than, either, nor, or else, and, rather than
ἐν prep. ἐν (+dat) in, by, with, among, at, on, through, to, within, into, of, for
ἔργῳ n. dat. neut. sg. ἔργον work, deed, doing labour
πάντα adj. acc. neut. pl. πᾶς πᾶσα πᾶν all, every, whosoever, every one, no, whole, any
ἐν prep. ἐν (+dat) in, by, with, among, at, on, through, to, within, into, of, for
ὀνόματι n. dat. neut. sg. ὄνομα name, call, surname
Κυρίου n. gen. masc. sg. κύριος Lord, lord, master, sir, LORD, God, Master, owner
Ἰησοῦ n. gen. masc. sg. Ἰησοῦς Jesus
τῷ art. dat. masc. sg. ὁ ἡ τό the, this, that, he, she, it
Θεῷ n. dat. masc. sg. θεός God, god
καὶ conj. καί and, even, also, but
πατρὶ n. dat. masc. sg. πατήρ Father, father, parent
δι' prep. διά (+gen) by, through, with, in, of, (+acc) for, because of, for a cause
αὐτοῦ pron. gen. masc. 3p. sg. αὐτός ή ό self, of oneself, even, very, the same, he, she, it
18 Αἱ art. nom. fem. pl. ὁ ἡ τό the, this, that, he, she, it
γυναῖκες n. nom. fem. pl. γυνή woman, wife
τοῖς art. dat. masc. pl. ὁ ἡ τό the, this, that, he, she, it
ἰδίοις adj. dat. masc. pl. ἴδιος one's own, one's, privately
ἀνδράσιν n. dat. masc. pl. ἀνήρ man, husband, sir
ὡς adv. ὡς as, when, as it were, how, about, like, as soon as, even as, while
ἐν prep. ἐν (+dat) in, by, with, among, at, on, through, to, within, into, of, for
Κυρίῳ n. dat. masc. sg. κύριος Lord, lord, master, sir, LORD, God, Master, owner
19 οἱ art. nom. masc. pl. ὁ ἡ τό the, this, that, he, she, it
ἄνδρες n. nom. masc. pl. ἀνήρ man, husband, sir
τὰς art. acc. fem. pl. ὁ ἡ τό the, this, that, he, she, it
γυναῖκας n. acc. fem. pl. γυνή woman, wife
καὶ conj. καί and, even, also, but
μὴ particle of negation. μή not, no, lest, neither, none, nothing, nor, never, without
πρὸς prep. πρός (+gen) for, (+dat) at, (+acc) unto, to, with, for, against
αὐτάς pron. acc. fem. 3p. pl. αὐτός ή ό self, of oneself, even, very, the same, he, she, it
20 τὰ art. nom. neut. pl. ὁ ἡ τό the, this, that, he, she, it
τέκνα, n. nom. neut. pl. τέκνον child, son, daughter
τοῖς art. dat. masc. pl. ὁ ἡ τό the, this, that, he, she, it
γονεῦσι n. dat. masc. pl. γονεύς father, (pl.) parents

κατὰ prep. κατά (+gen) against, by, throughout, down, (+acc) according to, after, with
πάντα adj. acc. neut. pl. πᾶς πᾶσα πᾶν all, every, whosoever, every one, no, whole, any
τοῦτο demo. pron. nom. neut. sg. οὗτος αὕτη τοῦτο this, the same, this same, he, she, it
γὰρ conj. γάρ for, and, because, but, indeed
εὐάρεστόν adj. nom. neut. sg. εὐάρεστος acceptable, wellpleasing, accepted, please well
τῷ art. dat. masc. sg. ὁ ἡ τό the, this, that, he, she, it
Κυρίῳ n. dat. masc. sg. κύριος Lord, lord, master, sir, LORD, God, Master, owner
21 οἱ art. nom. masc. pl. ὁ ἡ τό the, this, that, he, she, it
πατέρες n. nom. masc. pl. πατήρ Father, father, parent
μὴ particle of negation. μή not, no, lest, neither, none, nothing, nor, never, without
τὰ art. acc. neut. pl. ὁ ἡ τό the, this, that, he, she, it
τέκνα n. acc. neut. pl. τέκνον child, son, daughter
ὑμῶν pron. gen. 2p. pl. σύ thou, you
ἵνα conj. ἵνα that, to, lest, for to, so that, albeit, because, for, so as
μὴ particle of negation. μή not, no, lest, neither, none, nothing, nor, never, without
22 οἱ art. nom. masc. pl. ὁ ἡ τό the, this, that, he, she, it
δοῦλοι n. nom. masc. pl. δοῦλος servant, bondman, bond, slave
κατὰ prep. κατά (+gen) against, by, throughout, down, (+acc) according to, after, with
πάντα adj. acc. neut. pl. πᾶς πᾶσα πᾶν all, every, whosoever, every one, no, whole, any
τοῖς art. dat. masc. pl. ὁ ἡ τό the, this, that, he, she, it
κατὰ prep. κατά (+gen) against, by, throughout, down, (+acc) according to, after, with
σάρκα n. acc. fem. sg. σάρξ flesh, carnal
κυρίοις n. dat. masc. pl. κύριος Lord, lord, master, sir, LORD, God, Master, owner
μὴ particle of negation. μή not, no, lest, neither, none, nothing, nor, never, without
ἐν prep. ἐν (+dat) in, by, with, among, at, on, through, to, within, into, of, for
ὀφθαλμοδουλείαις n. dat. fem. pl. ὀφθαλμοδουλεία eyeservice
ὡς adv. ὡς as, when, as it were, how, about, like, as soon as, even as, while
ἀνθρωπάρεσκοι adj. nom. masc. pl. ἀνθρωπάρεσκος menpleaser
ἀλλ' conj. ἀλλά but, yea, yet, nevertheless, howbeit, nay, therefore
ἐν prep. ἐν (+dat) in, by, with, among, at, on, through, to, within, into, of, for
ἁπλότητι n. dat. fem. sg. ἁπλότης simplicity, singleness, bountifulness, liberal, liberality
καρδίας n. gen. fem. sg. καρδία heart
τὸν art. acc. masc. sg. ὁ ἡ τό the, this, that, he, she, it
Θεόν n. acc. masc. sg. θεός God, god
23 καὶ conj. καί and, even, also, but
πᾶν adj. acc. neut. sg. πᾶς πᾶσα πᾶν all, every, whosoever, every one, no, whole, any
ὃ relative pron. acc. neut. sg. ὅς ἥ ὅ who, which, what, that
τι indefinite pron. acc. neut. sg. τὶς certain, some, any man, one, any thing
ἐὰν conj. ἐάν if, soever, except, though, and if, but, whether, if so, so
ἐκ prep. ἐκ ἐξ (+gen) of, from, out of, by, on, with, in, among, through
ψυχῆς n. gen. fem. sg. ψυχή life, soul, mind, heart
ὡς adv. ὡς as, when, as it were, how, about, like, as soon as, even as, while
τῷ art. dat. masc. sg. ὁ ἡ τό the, this, that, he, she, it
Κυρίῳ n. dat. masc. sg. κύριος Lord, lord, master, sir, LORD, God, Master, owner
καὶ conj. καί and, even, also, but
οὐκ particle of negation. οὐ οὐκ οὐχ not, no, neither, none, nay, nor, never, nothing
ἀνθρώποις n. dat. masc. pl. ἄνθρωπος man, human being, person, one, certain
24 ὅτι conj. ὅτι that, for, because, how that, how, because that, for that, though
ἀπὸ prep. ἀπό (+gen) from, of, out of, since, for, off, at, by, in, on
Κυρίου n. gen. masc. sg. κύριος Lord, lord, master, sir, LORD, God, Master, owner
τὴν art. acc. fem. sg. ὁ ἡ τό the, this, that, he, she, it
ἀνταπόδοσιν n. acc. fem. sg. ἀνταπόδοσις reward
τῆς art. gen. fem. sg. ὁ ἡ τό the, this, that, he, she, it
κληρονομίας n. gen. fem. sg. κληρονομία inheritance
τῷ art. dat. masc. sg. ὁ ἡ τό the, this, that, he, she, it

γὰρ conj. γάρ for, and, because, but, indeed
Κυρίῳ n. dat. masc. sg. κύριος Lord, lord, master, sir, LORD, God, Master, owner
Χριστῷ n. dat. masc. sg. Χριστός Christ
25 ὁ art. nom. masc. sg. ὁ ἡ τό the, this, that, he, she, it
δὲ conj. δέ but, and, now, also, to the contrary, rather, then
ὃ relative pron. acc. neut. sg. ὅς ἥ ὅ who, which, what, that
καὶ conj. καί and, even, also, but
οὐκ particle of negation. οὐ οὐκ οὐχ not, no, neither, none, nay, nor, never, nothing
προσωποληψία n. nom. fem. sg. προσωποληψία respect of persons

4

1 οἱ art. nom. masc. pl. ὁ ἡ τό the, this, that, he, she, it
κύριοι n. nom. masc. pl. κύριος Lord, lord, master, sir, LORD, God, Master, owner
τὸ art. acc. neut. sg. ὁ ἡ τό the, this, that, he, she, it
δίκαιον adj. acc. neut. sg. δίκαιος righteous, just, meet, right
καὶ conj. καί and, even, also, but
τὴν art. acc. fem. sg. ὁ ἡ τό the, this, that, he, she, it
ἰσότητα n. acc. fem. sg. ἰσότης equality, equal, equity
τοῖς art. dat. masc. pl. ὁ ἡ τό the, this, that, he, she, it
δούλοις n. dat. masc. pl. δοῦλος servant, bondman, bond, slave
ὅτι conj. ὅτι that, for, because, how that, how, because that, for that, though
καὶ conj. καί and, even, also, but
ὑμεῖς pron. nom. 2p. pl. σύ thou, you
Κύριον n. acc. masc. sg. κύριος Lord, lord, master, sir, LORD, God, Master, owner
ἐν prep. ἐν (+dat) in, by, with, among, at, on, through, to, within, into, of, for
οὐρανοῖς n. dat. masc. pl. οὐρανός heaven, air, sky
2 Τῇ art. dat. fem. sg. ὁ ἡ τό the, this, that, he, she, it
προσευχῇ n. dat. fem. sg. προσευχή prayer
ἐν prep. ἐν (+dat) in, by, with, among, at, on, through, to, within, into, of, for
αὐτῇ pron. dat. fem. 3p. sg. αὐτός ἡ ὁ self, of oneself, even, very, the same, he, she, it
ἐν prep. ἐν (+dat) in, by, with, among, at, on, through, to, within, into, of, for
εὐχαριστίᾳ n. dat. fem. sg. εὐχαριστία thankfulness, thanksgiving, giving of thanks
3 ἅμα adv. ἅμα (+dat) together, with, also. (adv.) at the same time, together
καὶ conj. καί and, even, also, but
περὶ prep. περί (+gen) of, for, concerning, (+acc) about, concerning, in
ἡμῶν pron. gen. 1p. pl. ἐγώ I
ἵνα conj. ἵνα that, to, lest, for to, so that, albeit, because, for, so as
ὁ art. nom. masc. sg. ὁ ἡ τό the, this, that, he, she, it
Θεὸς n. nom. masc. sg. θεός God, god
ἡμῖν pron. dat. 1p. pl. ἐγώ I
θύραν n. acc. fem. sg. θύρα door, gate
τοῦ art. gen. masc. sg. ὁ ἡ τό the, this, that, he, she, it
λόγου n. gen. masc. sg. λόγος word, saying, account, speech, thing, matter
τὸ art. acc. neut. sg. ὁ ἡ τό the, this, that, he, she, it
μυστήριον n. acc. neut. sg. μυστήριον mystery
τοῦ art. gen. masc. sg. ὁ ἡ τό the, this, that, he, she, it
Χριστοῦ n. gen. masc. sg. Χριστός Christ
δι' prep. διά (+gen) by, through, with, in, of, (+acc) for, because of, for a cause
ὃ relative pron. acc. neut. sg. ὅς ἥ ὅ who, which, what, that
καὶ conj. καί and, even, also, but
4 ἵνα conj. ἵνα that, to, lest, for to, so that, albeit, because, for, so as
αὐτὸ pron. acc. neut. 3p. sg. αὐτός ἡ ὁ self, of oneself, even, very, the same, he, she, it
ὡς adv. ὡς as, when, as it were, how, about, like, as soon as, even as, while
με pron. acc. 1p. sg. ἐγώ I

5 ἐν prep. ἐν (+dat) in, by, with, among, at, on, through, to, within, into, of, for
σοφίᾳ n. dat. fem. sg. σοφία wisdom
πρὸς prep. πρός (+gen) for, (+dat) at, (+acc) unto, to, with, for, against
τοὺς art. acc. masc. pl. ὁ ἡ τό the, this, that, he, she, it
ἔξω adv. ἔξω out, without, out of, forth, away, outward
τὸν art. acc. masc. sg. ὁ ἡ τό the, this, that, he, she, it
καιρὸν n. acc. masc. sg. καιρός time, season, due time, opportunity
6 ὁ art. nom. masc. sg. ὁ ἡ τό the, this, that, he, she, it
λόγος n. nom. masc. sg. λόγος word, saying, account, speech, thing, matter
ὑμῶν pron. gen. 2p. pl. σύ thou, you
πάντοτε adv. πάντοτε always, ever, always, evermore
ἐν prep. ἐν (+dat) in, by, with, among, at, on, through, to, within, into, of, for
χάριτι n. dat. fem. sg. χάρις grace, thank, favour, pleasure
ἅλατι n. dat. neut. sg. ἅλας salt
πῶς adv. πῶς how, by what means, after what manner
ὑμᾶς pron. acc. 2p. pl. σύ thou, you
ἑνὶ num. dat. masc. sg. εἷς or ἕν one, other, some, any, only, a certain
ἑκάστῳ adj. dat. masc. sg. ἕκαστος every man, every, every one, any man, each
7 Τὰ art. acc. neut. pl. ὁ ἡ τό the, this, that, he, she, it
κατ' prep. κατά (+gen) against, by, throughout, down, (+acc) according to, after, with
ἐμὲ pron. acc. 1p. sg. ἐγώ I
πάντα adj. acc. neut. pl. πᾶς πᾶσα πᾶν all, every, whosoever, every one, no, whole, any
ὑμῖν pron. dat. 2p. pl. σύ thou, you
Τύχικος n. nom. masc. sg. Τυχικός Tychicus
ὁ art. nom. masc. sg. ὁ ἡ τό the, this, that, he, she, it
ἀγαπητὸς adj. nom. masc. sg. ἀγαπητός beloved, dearly beloved, dear, wellbeloved
ἀδελφὸς n. nom. masc. sg. ἀδελφός brother
καὶ conj. καί and, even, also, but
πιστὸς adj. nom. masc. sg. πιστός faithful, believing, true, sure
διάκονος n. nom. masc. sg. διάκονος minister, servant, deacon
καὶ conj. καί and, even, also, but
σύνδουλος n. nom. masc. sg. σύνδουλος fellowservant
ἐν prep. ἐν (+dat) in, by, with, among, at, on, through, to, within, into, of, for
Κυρίῳ n. dat. masc. sg. κύριος Lord, lord, master, sir, LORD, God, Master, owner
8 ὃν relative pron. acc. masc. sg. ὅς ἥ ὅ who, which, what, that
πρὸς prep. πρός (+gen) for, (+dat) at, (+acc) unto, to, with, for, against
ὑμᾶς pron. acc. 2p. pl. σύ thou, you
εἰς prep. εἰς (+acc) into, to, unto, for, in, on, toward, against, upon, at, among
αὐτὸ pron. acc. neut. 3p. sg. αὐτός ἡ ὁ self, of oneself, even, very, the same, he, she, it
τοῦτο demo. pron. acc. neut. sg. οὗτος αὕτη τοῦτο this, the same, this same, he, she, it
ἵνα conj. ἵνα that, to, lest, for to, so that, albeit, because, for, so as
τὰ art. acc. neut. pl. ὁ ἡ τό the, this, that, he, she, it
περὶ prep. περί (+gen) of, for, concerning, (+acc) about, concerning, in
ὑμῶν pron. gen. 2p. pl. σύ thou, you
καὶ conj. καί and, even, also, but
τὰς art. acc. fem. pl. ὁ ἡ τό the, this, that, he, she, it
καρδίας n. acc. fem. pl. καρδία heart
ὑμῶν pron. gen. 2p. pl. σύ thou, you
9 σὺν prep. σύν (+dat) with, beside
Ὀνησίμῳ n. dat. masc. sg. Ὀνήσιμος Onesimus
τῷ art. dat. masc. sg. ὁ ἡ τό the, this, that, he, she, it
πιστῷ adj. dat. masc. sg. πιστός faithful, believing, true, sure
καὶ conj. καί and, even, also, but
ἀγαπητῷ adj. dat. masc. sg. ἀγαπητός beloved, dearly beloved, dear, wellbeloved
ἀδελφῷ n. dat. masc. sg. ἀδελφός brother

ὅς relative pron. nom. masc. sg. ὅς ἥ ὅ who, which, what, that
ἐξ prep. ἐκ ἐξ (+gen) of, from, out of, by, on, with, in, among, through
ὑμῶν pron. gen. 2p. pl. σύ thou, you
πάντα adj. acc. neut. pl. πᾶς πᾶσα πᾶν all, every, whosoever, every one, no, whole, any
ὑμῖν pron. dat. 2p. pl. σύ thou, you
τὰ art. acc. neut. pl. ὁ ἡ τό the, this, that, he, she, it
ὧδε adv. ὧδε here, hither, in this place, there, this place
10 ὑμᾶς pron. acc. 2p. pl. σύ thou, you
Ἀρίσταρχος n. nom. masc. sg. Ἀρίσταρχος Aristarchus
ὁ art. nom. masc. sg. ὁ ἡ τό the, this, that, he, she, it
συναιχμάλωτός n. nom. masc. sg. συναιχμάλωτος fellowprisoner
μου pron. gen. 1p. sg. ἐγώ I
καὶ conj. καί and, even, also, but
Μᾶρκος n. nom. masc. sg. Μᾶρκος Mark, Marcus
ἀνεψιὸς n. nom. masc. sg. ἀνεψιός sister's son
Βαρνάβᾳ n. dat. masc. sg. Βαρναβᾶς Barnabas
περὶ prep. περί (+gen) of, for, concerning, (+acc) about, concerning, in
οὗ relative pron. gen. masc. sg. ὅς ἥ ὅ who, which, what, that
ἐντολάς n. acc. fem. pl. ἐντολή commandment, precept
ἐὰν conj. ἐάν if, soever, except, though, and if, but, whether, if so, so
πρὸς prep. πρός (+gen) for, (+dat) at, (+acc) unto, to, with, for, against
ὑμᾶς pron. acc. 2p. pl. σύ thou, you
αὐτόν pron. acc. masc. 3p. sg. αὐτός ή ό self, of oneself, even, very, the same, he, she, it
11 καὶ conj. καί and, even, also, but
Ἰησοῦς n. nom. masc. sg. Ἰησοῦς Jesus
ὁ art. nom. masc. sg. ὁ ἡ τό the, this, that, he, she, it
Ἰοῦστος n. nom. masc. sg. Ἰοῦστος Justus
οἱ art. nom. masc. pl. ὁ ἡ τό the, this, that, he, she, it
ἐκ prep. ἐκ ἐξ (+gen) of, from, out of, by, on, with, in, among, through
περιτομῆς n. gen. fem. sg. περιτομή circumcision
οὗτοι demo. pron. nom. masc. pl. οὗτος αὕτη τοῦτο this, the same, this same, he, she, it
μόνοι adj. nom. masc. pl. μόνος only, alone, by oneself
συνεργοὶ adj. nom. masc. pl. συνεργός fellowlabourer, fellowhelper, fellowworker
εἰς prep. εἰς (+acc) into, to, unto, for, in, on, toward, against, upon, at, among
τὴν art. acc. fem. sg. ὁ ἡ τό the, this, that, he, she, it
βασιλείαν n. acc. fem. sg. βασιλεία kingdom, reign
τοῦ art. gen. masc. sg. ὁ ἡ τό the, this, that, he, she, it
Θεοῦ n. gen. masc. sg. θεός God, god
οἵτινες relative pron. nom. masc. pl. ὅστις which, who, whosoever, that, whatsoever
μοι pron. dat. 1p. sg. ἐγώ I
παρηγορία n. nom. fem. sg. παρηγορία comfort
12 ὑμᾶς pron. acc. 2p. pl. σύ thou, you
Ἐπαφρᾶς n. nom. masc. sg. Ἐπαφρᾶς Epaphras
ὁ art. nom. masc. sg. ὁ ἡ τό the, this, that, he, she, it
ἐξ prep. ἐκ ἐξ (+gen) of, from, out of, by, on, with, in, among, through
ὑμῶν pron. gen. 2p. pl. σύ thou, you
δοῦλος n. nom. masc. sg. δοῦλος servant, bondman, bond, slave
Χριστοῦ n. gen. masc. sg. Χριστός Christ
πάντοτε adv. πάντοτε always, ever, always, evermore
ὑπὲρ prep. ὑπέρ (+gen) for, of, for the sake of, (+acc) above, more than
ὑμῶν pron. gen. 2p. pl. σύ thou, you
ἐν prep. ἐν (+dat) in, by, with, among, at, on, through, to, within, into, of, for
ταῖς art. dat. fem. pl. ὁ ἡ τό the, this, that, he, she, it
προσευχαῖς n. dat. fem. pl. προσευχή prayer
ἵνα conj. ἵνα that, to, lest, for to, so that, albeit, because, for, so as

τέλειοι adj. nom. masc. pl. τέλειος perfect, of full age
καὶ conj. καί and, even, also, but
ἐν prep. ἐν (+dat) in, by, with, among, at, on, through, to, within, into, of, for
παντὶ adj. dat. neut. sg. πᾶς πᾶσα πᾶν all, every, whosoever, every one, no, whole, any
θελήματι n. dat. neut. sg. θέλημα will, desire, pleasure
τοῦ art. gen. masc. sg. ὁ ἡ τό the, this, that, he, she, it
Θεοῦ n. gen. masc. sg. θεός God, god
13 γὰρ conj. γάρ for, and, because, but, indeed
αὐτῷ pron. dat. masc. 3p. sg. αὐτός ή ό self, of oneself, even, very, the same, he, she, it
ὅτι conj. ὅτι that, for, because, how that, how, because that, for that, though
ζῆλον n. acc. masc. sg. ζῆλος zeal, envying, indignation, emulation, jealousy
πολὺν adj. acc. masc. sg. πολύς many, great, much, long, abundant
ὑπὲρ prep. ὑπέρ (+gen) for, of, for the sake of, (+acc) above, more than
ὑμῶν pron. gen. 2p. pl. σύ thou, you
καὶ conj. καί and, even, also, but
τῶν art. gen. masc. pl. ὁ ἡ τό the, this, that, he, she, it
ἐν prep. ἐν (+dat) in, by, with, among, at, on, through, to, within, into, of, for
Λαοδικείᾳ n. dat. fem. sg. Λαοδίκεια Laodicea
καὶ conj. καί and, even, also, but
τῶν art. gen. masc. pl. ὁ ἡ τό the, this, that, he, she, it
ἐν prep. ἐν (+dat) in, by, with, among, at, on, through, to, within, into, of, for
Ἱεραπόλει n. dat. fem. sg. Ἱεράπολις Hierapolis
14 ὑμᾶς pron. acc. 2p. pl. σύ thou, you
Λουκᾶς n. nom. masc. sg. Λουκᾶς Luke, Lucas
ὁ art. nom. masc. sg. ὁ ἡ τό the, this, that, he, she, it
ἰατρὸς n. nom. masc. sg. ἰατρός physician
ὁ art. nom. masc. sg. ὁ ἡ τό the, this, that, he, she, it
ἀγαπητὸς adj. nom. masc. sg. ἀγαπητός beloved, dearly beloved, dear, wellbeloved
καὶ conj. καί and, even, also, but
Δημᾶς n. nom. masc. sg. Δημᾶς Demas
15 τοὺς art. acc. masc. pl. ὁ ἡ τό the, this, that, he, she, it
ἐν prep. ἐν (+dat) in, by, with, among, at, on, through, to, within, into, of, for
Λαοδικείᾳ n. dat. fem. sg. Λαοδίκεια Laodicea
ἀδελφοὺς n. acc. masc. pl. ἀδελφός brother
καὶ conj. καί and, even, also, but
Νυμφᾶν n. acc. masc. sg. Νυμφᾶς Nymphas
καὶ conj. καί and, even, also, but
τὴν art. acc. fem. sg. ὁ ἡ τό the, this, that, he, she, it
κατ’ prep. κατά (+gen) against, by, throughout, down, (+acc) according to, after, with
οἶκον n. acc. masc. sg. οἶκος house, home, household
αὐτοῦ pron. gen. masc. 3p. sg. αὐτός ή ό self, of oneself, even, very, the same, he, she, it
ἐκκλησίαν n. acc. fem. sg. ἐκκλησία church, assembly
16 καὶ conj. καί and, even, also, but
ὅταν conj. ὅταν when, as soon as, as long as, that, whensoever, while
παρ’ prep. παρά (+gen) of, from, (+dat) with, for, (+acc) beside, at, by, above, against
ὑμῖν pron. dat. 2p. pl. σύ thou, you
ἡ art. nom. fem. sg. ὁ ἡ τό the, this, that, he, she, it
ἐπιστολή n. nom. fem. sg. ἐπιστολή letter, epistle
ἵνα conj. ἵνα that, to, lest, for to, so that, albeit, because, for, so as
καὶ conj. καί and, even, also, but
ἐν prep. ἐν (+dat) in, by, with, among, at, on, through, to, within, into, of, for
τῇ art. dat. fem. sg. ὁ ἡ τό the, this, that, he, she, it
Λαοδικέων n. gen. masc. pl. Λαοδικεύς Laodicean
ἐκκλησίᾳ n. dat. fem. sg. ἐκκλησία church, assembly
καὶ conj. καί and, even, also, but

τὴν art. acc. fem. sg. ὁ ἡ τό the, this, that, he, she, it
ἐκ prep. ἐκ ἐξ (+gen) of, from, out of, by, on, with, in, among, through
Λαοδικείας n. gen. fem. sg. Λαοδίκεια Laodicea
ἵνα conj. ἵνα that, to, lest, for to, so that, albeit, because, for, so as
καὶ conj. καί and, even, also, but
ὑμεῖς pron. nom. 2p. pl. σύ thou, you
17 καὶ conj. καί and, even, also, but
Ἀρχίππῳ n. dat. masc. sg. Ἄρχιππος Archippus
τὴν art. acc. fem. sg. ὁ ἡ τό the, this, that, he, she, it
διακονίαν n. acc. fem. sg. διακονία ministry, administration, service, office, relief
ἣν relative pron. acc. fem. sg. ὅς ἥ ὅ who, which, what, that
ἐν prep. ἐν (+dat) in, by, with, among, at, on, through, to, within, into, of, for
Κυρίῳ n. dat. masc. sg. κύριος Lord, lord, master, sir, LORD, God, Master, owner
ἵνα conj. ἵνα that, to, lest, for to, so that, albeit, because, for, so as
αὐτὴν pron. acc. fem. 3p. sg. αὐτός ή ό self, of oneself, even, very, the same, he, she, it
18 Ὁ art. nom. masc. sg. ὁ ἡ τό the, this, that, he, she, it
ἀσπασμὸς n. nom. masc. sg. ἀσπασμός greeting, salutation
τῇ art. dat. fem. sg. ὁ ἡ τό the, this, that, he, she, it
ἐμῇ poss. pron. dat. fem. 1p. sg. ἐμός my, mine, mine own, of me
χειρὶ n. dat. fem. sg. χείρ hand
Παύλου n. gen. masc. sg. Παῦλος Paul, Paulus
μου pron. gen. 1p. sg. ἐγώ I
τῶν art. gen. masc. pl. ὁ ἡ τό the, this, that, he, she, it
δεσμῶν n. gen. masc. pl. δεσμός bond, band, chain, string
ἡ art. nom. fem. sg. ὁ ἡ τό the, this, that, he, she, it
χάρις n. nom. fem. sg. χάρις grace, thank, favour, pleasure
μεθ' prep. μετά (+gen) with, among, against, (+acc) after
ὑμῶν pron. gen. 2p. pl. σύ thou, you
ἀμήν particle. ἀμήν amen, verily

ΠΑΥΛΟΥ ΤΟΥ ΑΠΟΣΤΟΛΟΥ
Η ΠΡΟΣ
ΘΕΣΣΑΛΟΝΙΚΕΙΣ
ΕΠΙΣΤΟΛΗ ΠΡΩΤΗ

1

1 Παῦλος n. nom. masc. sg. Παῦλος Paul, Paulus
καὶ conj. καί and, even, also, but
Σιλουανὸς n. nom. masc. sg. Σιλουανός Silvanus
καὶ conj. καί and, even, also, but
Τιμόθεος n. nom. masc. sg. Τιμόθεος Timotheus, Timothy
τῇ art. dat. fem. sg. ὁ ἡ τό the, this, that, he, she, it
ἐκκλησίᾳ n. dat. fem. sg. ἐκκλησία church, assembly
Θεσσαλονικέων n. gen. masc. pl. Θεσσαλονικεύς Thessalonian, of Thessalonica
ἐν prep. ἐν (+dat) in, by, with, among, at, on, through, to, within, into, of, for
Θεῷ n. dat. masc. sg. θεός God, god
πατρὶ n. dat. masc. sg. πατήρ Father, father, parent
καὶ conj. καί and, even, also, but
Κυρίῳ n. dat. masc. sg. κύριος Lord, lord, master, sir, LORD, God, Master, owner
Ἰησοῦ n. dat. masc. sg. Ἰησοῦς Jesus
Χριστῷ n. dat. masc. sg. Χριστός Christ
χάρις n. nom. fem. sg. χάρις grace, thank, favour, pleasure
ὑμῖν pron. dat. 2p. pl. σύ thou, you
καὶ conj. καί and, even, also, but
εἰρήνη n. nom. fem. sg. εἰρήνη peace, quietness, rest
ἀπὸ prep. ἀπό (+gen) from, of, out of, since, for, off, at, by, in, on
Θεοῦ n. gen. masc. sg. θεός God, god
πατρὸς n. gen. masc. sg. πατήρ Father, father, parent
ἡμῶν pron. gen. 1p. pl. ἐγώ I
καὶ conj. καί and, even, also, but
Κυρίου n. gen. masc. sg. κύριος Lord, lord, master, sir, LORD, God, Master, owner
Ἰησοῦ n. gen. masc. sg. Ἰησοῦς Jesus
Χριστοῦ n. gen. masc. sg. Χριστός Christ
2 τῷ art. dat. masc. sg. ὁ ἡ τό the, this, that, he, she, it
Θεῷ n. dat. masc. sg. θεός God, god
πάντοτε adv. πάντοτε always, ever, always, evermore
περὶ prep. περί (+gen) of, for, concerning, (+acc) about, concerning, in
πάντων adj. gen. masc. pl. πᾶς πᾶσα πᾶν all, every, whosoever, every one, no, whole, any
ὑμῶν pron. gen. 2p. pl. σύ thou, you
μνείαν n. acc. fem. sg. μνεία mention, remembrance
ὑμῶν pron. gen. 2p. pl. σύ thou, you
ἐπὶ prep. ἐπί (+gen) on, in, upon, (+dat) in, at, for, upon, (+acc) on, upon, unto, to, against
τῶν art. gen. fem. pl. ὁ ἡ τό the, this, that, he, she, it
προσευχῶν n. gen. fem. pl. προσευχή prayer
ἡμῶν pron. gen. 1p. pl. ἐγώ I
ἀδιαλείπτως adv. ἀδιαλείπτως without ceasing
3 ὑμῶν pron. gen. 2p. pl. σύ thou, you
τοῦ art. gen. neut. sg. ὁ ἡ τό the, this, that, he, she, it
ἔργου n. gen. neut. sg. ἔργον work, deed, doing labour
τῆς art. gen. fem. sg. ὁ ἡ τό the, this, that, he, she, it
πίστεως n. gen. fem. sg. πίστις faith, assurance, belief, fidelity
καὶ conj. καί and, even, also, but

τοῦ art. gen. masc. sg. ὁ ἡ τό the, this, that, he, she, it
κόπου n. gen. masc. sg. κόπος labour, trouble, weariness
τῆς art. gen. fem. sg. ὁ ἡ τό the, this, that, he, she, it
ἀγάπης n. gen. fem. sg. ἀγάπη love, charity, feast of charity
καὶ conj. καί and, even, also, but
τῆς art. gen. fem. sg. ὁ ἡ τό the, this, that, he, she, it
ὑπομονῆς n. gen. fem. sg. ὑπομονή patience, enduring
τῆς art. gen. fem. sg. ὁ ἡ τό the, this, that, he, she, it
ἐλπίδος n. gen. fem. sg. ἐλπίς hope, faith
τοῦ art. gen. masc. sg. ὁ ἡ τό the, this, that, he, she, it
Κυρίου n. gen. masc. sg. κύριος Lord, lord, master, sir, LORD, God, Master, owner
ἡμῶν pron. gen. 1p. pl. ἐγώ I
Ἰησοῦ n. gen. masc. sg. Ἰησοῦς Jesus
Χριστοῦ n. gen. masc. sg. Χριστός Christ
ἔμπροσθεν prep. ἔμπροσθεν (+gen) before, in the sight of, in the presence of
τοῦ art. gen. masc. sg. ὁ ἡ τό the, this, that, he, she, it
Θεοῦ n. gen. masc. sg. θεός God, god
καὶ conj. καί and, even, also, but
πατρὸς n. gen. masc. sg. πατήρ Father, father, parent
ἡμῶν pron. gen. 1p. pl. ἐγώ I
4 ἀδελφοὶ n. voc. masc. pl. ἀδελφός brother
ὑπὸ prep. ὑπό (+gen) from, of, out of, since, for, off, at, by, in, on
Θεοῦ n. gen. masc. sg. θεός God, god
τὴν art. acc. fem. sg. ὁ ἡ τό the, this, that, he, she, it
ἐκλογὴν n. acc. fem. sg. ἐκλογή election, chosen
ὑμῶν pron. gen. 2p. pl. σύ thou, you
5 ὅτι conj. ὅτι that, for, because, how that, how, because that, for that, though
τὸ art. nom. neut. sg. ὁ ἡ τό the, this, that, he, she, it
εὐαγγέλιον n. nom. neut. sg. εὐαγγέλιον gospel
ἡμῶν pron. gen. 1p. pl. ἐγώ I
οὐκ particle of negation. οὐ οὐκ οὐχ not, no, neither, none, nay, nor, never, nothing
εἰς prep. εἰς (+acc) into, to, unto, for, in, on, toward, against, upon, at, among
ὑμᾶς pron. acc. 2p. pl. σύ thou, you
ἐν prep. ἐν (+dat) in, by, with, among, at, on, through, to, within, into, of, for
λόγῳ n. dat. masc. sg. λόγος word, saying, account, speech, thing, matter
μόνον adv. μόνος only, alone, by oneself
ἀλλὰ conj. ἀλλά but, yea, yet, nevertheless, howbeit, nay, therefore
καὶ conj. καί and, even, also, but
ἐν prep. ἐν (+dat) in, by, with, among, at, on, through, to, within, into, of, for
δυνάμει n. dat. fem. sg. δύναμις power, mighty work, miracle, strength, might
καὶ conj. καί and, even, also, but
ἐν prep. ἐν (+dat) in, by, with, among, at, on, through, to, within, into, of, for
Πνεύματι n. dat. neut. sg. πνεῦμα spirit, Spirit, Ghost, ghost, life. of the spirit, wind
Ἁγίῳ adj. dat. neut. sg. ἅγιος Holy, holy, saint, Holy One, holy thing, most holy
καὶ conj. καί and, even, also, but
ἐν prep. ἐν (+dat) in, by, with, among, at, on, through, to, within, into, of, for
πληροφορίᾳ n. dat. fem. sg. πληροφορία full assurance, assurance
πολλῇ adj. dat. fem. sg. πολύς many, great, much, long, abundant
καθὼς adv. καθώς as, even as, according as, according to
οἷοι relative pron. nom. masc. pl. οἷος what manner of, such as, as, which, what, so as
ἐν prep. ἐν (+dat) in, by, with, among, at, on, through, to, within, into, of, for
ὑμῖν pron. dat. 2p. pl. σύ thou, you
δι' prep. διά (+gen) by, through, with, in, of, (+acc) for, because of, for a cause
ὑμᾶς pron. acc. 2p. pl. σύ thou, you
6 καὶ conj. καί and, even, also, but

ὑμεῖς pron. nom. 2p. pl. σύ thou, you
μιμηταὶ n. nom. masc. pl. μιμητής follower
ἡμῶν pron. gen. 1p. pl. ἐγώ I
καὶ conj. καί and, even, also, but
τοῦ art. gen. masc. sg. ὁ ἡ τό the, this, that, he, she, it
Κυρίου n. gen. masc. sg. κύριος Lord, lord, master, sir, LORD, God, Master, owner
τὸν art. acc. masc. sg. ὁ ἡ τό the, this, that, he, she, it
λόγον n. acc. masc. sg. λόγος word, saying, account, speech, thing, matter
ἐν prep. ἐν (+dat) in, by, with, among, at, on, through, to, within, into, of, for
θλίψει n. dat. fem. sg. θλῖψις tribulation, affliction, anguish, persecution
πολλῇ adj. dat. fem. sg. πολύς many, great, much, long, abundant
μετὰ prep. μετά (+gen) with, among, against, (+acc) after
χαρᾶς n. gen. fem. sg. χαρά joy, gladness, joyfulness
Πνεύματος n. gen. neut. sg. πνεῦμα spirit, Spirit, Ghost, ghost, life. of the spirit, wind
Ἁγίου adj. gen. neut. sg. ἅγιος Holy, holy, saint, Holy One, holy thing, most holy
7 ὥστε conj. ὥστε so that, wherefore, insomuch that, therefore, that, so then
ὑμᾶς pron. acc. 2p. pl. σύ thou, you
τύπους n. acc. masc. pl. τύπος ensample, example, pattern, print, figure, fashion
πᾶσι adj. dat. masc. pl. πᾶς πᾶσα πᾶν all, every, whosoever, every one, no, whole, any
τοῖς art. dat. masc. pl. ὁ ἡ τό the, this, that, he, she, it
ἐν prep. ἐν (+dat) in, by, with, among, at, on, through, to, within, into, of, for
τῇ art. dat. fem. sg. ὁ ἡ τό the, this, that, he, she, it
Μακεδονίᾳ n. dat. fem. sg. Μακεδονία Macedonia
καὶ conj. καί and, even, also, but
τῇ art. dat. fem. sg. ὁ ἡ τό the, this, that, he, she, it
Ἀχαΐᾳ n. dat. fem. sg. Ἀχαΐα Achaia
8 ἀφ' prep. ἀπό (+gen) from, of, out of, since, for, off, at, by, in, on
ὑμῶν pron. gen. 2p. pl. σύ thou, you
γὰρ conj. γάρ for, and, because, but, indeed
ὁ art. nom. masc. sg. ὁ ἡ τό the, this, that, he, she, it
λόγος n. nom. masc. sg. λόγος word, saying, account, speech, thing, matter
τοῦ art. gen. masc. sg. ὁ ἡ τό the, this, that, he, she, it
Κυρίου n. gen. masc. sg. κύριος Lord, lord, master, sir, LORD, God, Master, owner
οὐ particle of negation. οὐ οὐκ οὐχ not, no, neither, none, nay, nor, never, nothing
μόνον adv. μόνος only, alone, by oneself
ἐν prep. ἐν (+dat) in, by, with, among, at, on, through, to, within, into, of, for
τῇ art. dat. fem. sg. ὁ ἡ τό the, this, that, he, she, it
Μακεδονίᾳ n. dat. fem. sg. Μακεδονία Macedonia
καὶ conj. καί and, even, also, but
Ἀχαΐᾳ n. dat. fem. sg. Ἀχαΐα Achaia
ἀλλὰ conj. ἀλλά but, yea, yet, nevertheless, howbeit, nay, therefore
καὶ conj. καί and, even, also, but
ἐν prep. ἐν (+dat) in, by, with, among, at, on, through, to, within, into, of, for
παντὶ adj. dat. masc. sg. πᾶς πᾶσα πᾶν all, every, whosoever, every one, no, whole, any
τόπῳ n. dat. masc. sg. τόπος place, room, quarterplace, room, quarter
ἡ art. nom. fem. sg. ὁ ἡ τό the, this, that, he, she, it
πίστις n. nom. fem. sg. πίστις faith, assurance, belief, fidelity
ὑμῶν pron. gen. 2p. pl. σύ thou, you
ἡ art. nom. fem. sg. ὁ ἡ τό the, this, that, he, she, it
πρὸς prep. πρός (+gen) for, (+dat) at, (+acc) unto, to, with, for, against
τὸν art. acc. masc. sg. ὁ ἡ τό the, this, that, he, she, it
Θεὸν n. acc. masc. sg. θεός God, god
ὥστε conj. ὥστε so that, wherefore, insomuch that, therefore, that, so then
μὴ particle of negation. μή not, no, lest, neither, none, nothing, nor, never, without
χρείαν n. acc. fem. sg. χρεία need, necessity, lack, want

ἡμᾶς pron. acc. 1p. pl. ἐγώ I
τι indefinite pron. acc. neut. sg. τὶς certain, some, any man, one, any thing
9 αὐτοὶ pron. nom. masc. 3p. pl. αὐτός ἡ ὁ self, of oneself, even, very, the same, he, she, it
γὰρ conj. γάρ for, and, because, but, indeed
περὶ prep. περί (+gen) of, for, concerning, (+acc) about, concerning, in
ἡμῶν pron. gen. 1p. pl. ἐγώ I
ὁποίαν interrog. pron. acc. fem. sg. ὁποῖος what manner of, as, of what sort, whatsoever
εἴσοδον n. acc. fem. sg. εἴσοδος coming, entrance into, entering in
πρὸς prep. πρός (+gen) for, (+dat) at, (+acc) unto, to, with, for, against
ὑμᾶς pron. acc. 2p. pl. σύ thou, you
καὶ conj. καί and, even, also, but
πῶς adv. πῶς how, by what means, after what manner
πρὸς prep. πρός (+gen) for, (+dat) at, (+acc) unto, to, with, for, against
τὸν art. acc. masc. sg. ὁ ἡ τό the, this, that, he, she, it
Θεὸν n. acc. masc. sg. θεός God, god
ἀπὸ prep. ἀπό (+gen) from, of, out of, since, for, off, at, by, in, on
τῶν art. gen. neut. pl. ὁ ἡ τό the, this, that, he, she, it
εἰδώλων n. gen. neut. pl. εἴδωλον idol
Θεῷ n. dat. masc. sg. θεός God, god
καὶ conj. καί and, even, also, but
ἀληθινῷ adj. dat. masc. sg. ἀληθινός true
10 καὶ conj. καί and, even, also, but
τὸν art. acc. masc. sg. ὁ ἡ τό the, this, that, he, she, it
υἱὸν n. acc. masc. sg. υἱός son, child, descendant, offspring, heir
αὐτοῦ pron. gen. masc. 3p. sg. αὐτός ἡ ὁ self, of oneself, even, very, the same, he, she, it
ἐκ prep. ἐκ ἐξ (+gen) of, from, out of, by, on, with, in, among, through
τῶν art. gen. masc. pl. ὁ ἡ τό the, this, that, he, she, it
οὐρανῶν n. gen. masc. pl. οὐρανός heaven, air, sky
ὃν relative pron. acc. masc. sg. ὅς ἥ ὅ who, which, what, that
ἐκ prep. ἐκ ἐξ (+gen) of, from, out of, by, on, with, in, among, through
νεκρῶν adj. gen. masc. pl. νεκρός dead
Ἰησοῦν n. acc. masc. sg. Ἰησοῦς Jesus
τὸν art. acc. masc. sg. ὁ ἡ τό the, this, that, he, she, it
ἡμᾶς pron. acc. 1p. pl. ἐγώ I
ἀπὸ prep. ἀπό (+gen) from, of, out of, since, for, off, at, by, in, on
τῆς art. gen. fem. sg. ὁ ἡ τό the, this, that, he, she, it
ὀργῆς n. gen. fem. sg. ὀργή wrath, anger, indignation, vengeance
τῆς art. gen. fem. sg. ὁ ἡ τό the, this, that, he, she, it

2

1 Αὐτοὶ pron. nom. masc. 3p. pl. αὐτός ἡ ὁ self, of oneself, even, very, the same, he, she, it
γὰρ conj. γάρ for, and, because, but, indeed
ἀδελφοί n. voc. masc. pl. ἀδελφός brother
τὴν art. acc. fem. sg. ὁ ἡ τό the, this, that, he, she, it
εἴσοδον n. acc. fem. sg. εἴσοδος coming, entrance into, entering in
ἡμῶν pron. gen. 1p. pl. ἐγώ I
τὴν art. acc. fem. sg. ὁ ἡ τό the, this, that, he, she, it
πρὸς prep. πρός (+gen) for, (+dat) at, (+acc) unto, to, with, for, against
ὑμᾶς pron. acc. 2p. pl. σύ thou, you
ὅτι conj. ὅτι that, for, because, how that, how, because that, for that, though
οὐ particle of negation. οὐ οὐκ οὐχ not, no, neither, none, nay, nor, never, nothing
κενὴ adj. nom. fem. sg. κενός empty, vain, in vain
2 ἀλλὰ conj. ἀλλά but, yea, yet, nevertheless, howbeit, nay, therefore
καὶ conj. καί and, even, also, but

καὶ conj. καί and, even, also, but
καθὼς adv. καθώς as, even as, according as, according to
ἐν prep. ἐν (+dat) in, by, with, among, at, on, through, to, within, into, of, for
Φιλίπποις n. dat. masc. pl. Φίλιπποι Philippi
ἐν prep. ἐν (+dat) in, by, with, among, at, on, through, to, within, into, of, for
τῷ art. dat. masc. sg. ὁ ἡ τό the, this, that, he, she, it
Θεῷ n. dat. masc. sg. θεός God, god
ἡμῶν pron. gen. 1p. pl. ἐγώ I
πρὸς prep. πρός (+gen) for, (+dat) at, (+acc) unto, to, with, for, against
ὑμᾶς pron. acc. 2p. pl. σύ thou, you
τὸ art. acc. neut. sg. ὁ ἡ τό the, this, that, he, she, it
εὐαγγέλιον n. acc. neut. sg. εὐαγγέλιον gospel
τοῦ art. gen. masc. sg. ὁ ἡ τό the, this, that, he, she, it
Θεοῦ n. gen. masc. sg. θεός God, god
ἐν prep. ἐν (+dat) in, by, with, among, at, on, through, to, within, into, of, for
πολλῷ adj. dat. masc. sg. πολύς many, great, much, long, abundant
ἀγῶνι n. dat. masc. sg. ἀγών conflict, fight, contention, race
3 ἡ art. nom. fem. sg. ὁ ἡ τό the, this, that, he, she, it
γὰρ conj. γάρ for, and, because, but, indeed
παράκλησις n. nom. fem. sg. παράκλησις consolation, exhortation, comfort
ἡμῶν pron. gen. 1p. pl. ἐγώ I
οὐκ particle of negation. οὐ οὐκ οὐχ not, no, neither, none, nay, nor, never, nothing
ἐκ prep. ἐκ ἐξ (+gen) of, from, out of, by, on, with, in, among, through
πλάνης n. gen. fem. sg. πλάνη error, deception, deceit, delusion
οὐδὲ adv. οὐδέ neither, nor, not, no, not even, never, not yet
ἐξ prep. ἐκ ἐξ (+gen) of, from, out of, by, on, with, in, among, through
ἀκαθαρσίας n. gen. fem. sg. ἀκαθαρσία uncleanness
οὔτε conj. οὔτε neither, nor, nor yet, no, none
ἐν prep. ἐν (+dat) in, by, with, among, at, on, through, to, within, into, of, for
δόλῳ n. dat. masc. sg. δόλος guile, deceit, subtilty, craft
4 ἀλλὰ conj. ἀλλά but, yea, yet, nevertheless, howbeit, nay, therefore
καθὼς adv. καθώς as, even as, according as, according to
ὑπὸ prep. ὑπό (+gen) of, by, with, from, among, (+acc) under
τοῦ art. gen. masc. sg. ὁ ἡ τό the, this, that, he, she, it
Θεοῦ n. gen. masc. sg. θεός God, god
τὸ art. acc. neut. sg. ὁ ἡ τό the, this, that, he, she, it
εὐαγγέλιον n. acc. neut. sg. εὐαγγέλιον gospel
οὕτω adv. οὕτω οὕτως so, even so, thus, on this wise, likewise, after this manner
οὐχ particle of negation. οὐ οὐκ οὐχ not, no, neither, none, nay, nor, never, nothing
ὡς adv. ὡς as, when, as it were, how, about, like, as soon as, even as, while
ἀνθρώποις n. dat. masc. pl. ἄνθρωπος man, human being, person, one, certain
ἀλλὰ conj. ἀλλά but, yea, yet, nevertheless, howbeit, nay, therefore
τῷ art. dat. masc. sg. ὁ ἡ τό the, this, that, he, she, it
Θεῷ n. dat. masc. sg. θεός God, god
τῷ art. dat. masc. sg. ὁ ἡ τό the, this, that, he, she, it
τὰς art. acc. fem. pl. ὁ ἡ τό the, this, that, he, she, it
καρδίας n. acc. fem. pl. καρδία heart
ἡμῶν pron. gen. 1p. pl. ἐγώ I
5 οὔτε conj. οὔτε neither, nor, nor yet, no, none
γάρ conj. γάρ for, and, because, but, indeed
ποτε adv. ποτέ in time past, at any time, sometimes, in old time, once, when
ἐν prep. ἐν (+dat) in, by, with, among, at, on, through, to, within, into, of, for
λόγῳ n. dat. masc. sg. λόγος word, saying, account, speech, thing, matter
κολακείας n. gen. fem. sg. κολακεία flattering
καθὼς adv. καθώς as, even as, according as, according to

οὔτε conj. οὔτε neither, nor, nor yet, no, none
ἐν prep. ἐν (+dat) in, by, with, among, at, on, through, to, within, into, of, for
προφάσει n. dat. fem. sg. πρόφασις pretence, cloke, colour, show
πλεονεξίας n. gen. fem. sg. πλεονεξία covetousness, covetous practice, greediness
Θεὸς n. nom. masc. sg. θεός God, god
μάρτυς n. nom. masc. sg. μάρτυς or μάρτυρ witness, martyr, record
6 οὔτε conj. οὔτε neither, nor, nor yet, no, none
ἐξ prep. ἐκ ἐξ (+gen) of, from, out of, by, on, with, in, among, through
ἀνθρώπων n. gen. masc. pl. ἄνθρωπος man, human being, person, one, certain
δόξαν n. acc. fem. sg. δόξα glory, honour, praise, dignity, worship
οὔτε conj. οὔτε neither, nor, nor yet, no, none
ἀφ' prep. ἀπό (+gen) from, of, out of, since, for, off, at, by, in, on
ὑμῶν pron. gen. 2p. pl. σύ thou, you
οὔτε conj. οὔτε neither, nor, nor yet, no, none
ἀπ' prep. ἀπό (+gen) from, of, out of, since, for, off, at, by, in, on
ἄλλων adj. gen. masc. pl. ἄλλος other, another, some, one, more, otherwise
ἐν prep. ἐν (+dat) in, by, with, among, at, on, through, to, within, into, of, for
βάρει n. dat. neut. sg. βάρος burden, burdensome, weight
ὡς adv. ὡς as, when, as it were, how, about, like, as soon as, even as, while
Χριστοῦ n. gen. masc. sg. Χριστός Christ
ἀπόστολοι n. nom. masc. pl. ἀπόστολος apostle, messenger, he that is sent
7 ἀλλ' conj. ἀλλά but, yea, yet, nevertheless, howbeit, nay, therefore
ἤπιοι adj. nom. masc. pl. ἤπιος gentle
ἐν prep. ἐν (+dat) in, by, with, among, at, on, through, to, within, into, of, for
μέσῳ adj. dat. neut. sg. μέσος midst, among, mid, between
ὑμῶν pron. gen. 2p. pl. σύ thou, you
ὡς adv. ὡς as, when, as it were, how, about, like, as soon as, even as, while
ἂν particle. ἄν Indicating contingency. No English translation.
τροφὸς n. nom. fem. sg. τροφός nurse
τὰ art. acc. neut. pl. ὁ ἡ τό the, this, that, he, she, it
ἑαυτῆς reflexive pron. gen. fem. 3p. sg. ἑαυτοῦ himself, herself, itself, yourself, ourselves
τέκνα n. acc. neut. pl. τέκνον child, son, daughter
8 οὕτως adv. οὕτω οὕτως so, even so, thus, on this wise, likewise, after this manner
ὑμῶν pron. gen. 2p. pl. σύ thou, you
ὑμῖν pron. dat. 2p. pl. σύ thou, you
οὐ particle of negation. οὐ οὐκ οὐχ not, no, neither, none, nay, nor, never, nothing
μόνον adv. μόνος only, alone, by oneself
τὸ art. acc. neut. sg. ὁ ἡ τό the, this, that, he, she, it
εὐαγγέλιον n. acc. neut. sg. εὐαγγέλιον gospel
τοῦ art. gen. masc. sg. ὁ ἡ τό the, this, that, he, she, it
Θεοῦ n. gen. masc. sg. θεός God, god
ἀλλὰ conj. ἀλλά but, yea, yet, nevertheless, howbeit, nay, therefore
καὶ conj. καί and, even, also, but
τὰς art. acc. fem. pl. ὁ ἡ τό the, this, that, he, she, it
ἑαυτῶν reflexive pron. gen. masc. 3p. pl. ἑαυτοῦ himself, herself, itself, yourself, ourselves
ψυχάς n. acc. fem. pl. ψυχή life, soul, mind, heart
διότι conj. διότι for, because, because that, therefore
ἀγαπητοὶ adj. nom. masc. pl. ἀγαπητός beloved, dearly beloved, dear, wellbeloved
ἡμῖν pron. dat. 1p. pl. ἐγώ I
9 γάρ conj. γάρ for, and, because, but, indeed
ἀδελφοί n. voc. masc. pl. ἀδελφός brother
τὸν art. acc. masc. sg. ὁ ἡ τό the, this, that, he, she, it
κόπον n. acc. masc. sg. κόπος labour, trouble, weariness
ἡμῶν pron. gen. 1p. pl. ἐγώ I
καὶ conj. καί and, even, also, but

τὸν art. acc. masc. sg. ὁ ἡ τό the, this, that, he, she, it
μόχθον n. acc. masc. sg. μόχθος painfulness, travail
νυκτὸς n. gen. fem. sg. νύξ night
γάρ conj. γάρ for, and, because, but, indeed
καὶ conj. καί and, even, also, but
ἡμέρας n. gen. fem. sg. ἡμέρα day, time, year, while, age, day time
πρὸς prep. πρός (+gen) for, (+dat) at, (+acc) unto, to, with, for, against
τὸ art. acc. neut. sg. ὁ ἡ τό the, this, that, he, she, it
μὴ particle of negation. μή not, no, lest, neither, none, nothing, nor, never, without
τινα indefinite pron. acc. masc. sg. τὶς certain, some, any man, one, any thing
ὑμῶν pron. gen. 2p. pl. σύ thou, you
εἰς prep. εἰς (+acc) into, to, unto, for, in, on, toward, against, upon, at, among
ὑμᾶς pron. acc. 2p. pl. σύ thou, you
τὸ art. acc. neut. sg. ὁ ἡ τό the, this, that, he, she, it
εὐαγγέλιον n. acc. neut. sg. εὐαγγέλιον gospel
τοῦ art. gen. masc. sg. ὁ ἡ τό the, this, that, he, she, it
Θεοῦ n. gen. masc. sg. θεός God, god
10 ὑμεῖς pron. nom. 2p. pl. σύ thou, you
μάρτυρες n. nom. masc. pl. μάρτυς or μάρτυρ witness, martyr, record
καὶ conj. καί and, even, also, but
ὁ art. nom. masc. sg. ὁ ἡ τό the, this, that, he, she, it
Θεός n. nom. masc. sg. θεός God, god
ὡς adv. ὡς as, when, as it were, how, about, like, as soon as, even as, while
ὁσίως adv. ὁσίως holily
καὶ conj. καί and, even, also, but
δικαίως adv. δικαίως justly, righteously
καὶ conj. καί and, even, also, but
ἀμέμπτως adv. ἀμέμπτως unblameably, blameless
ὑμῖν pron. dat. 2p. pl. σύ thou, you
τοῖς art. dat. masc. pl. ὁ ἡ τό the, this, that, he, she, it
11 καθάπερ adv. καθάπερ even as, as, as well as
ὡς adv. ὡς as, when, as it were, how, about, like, as soon as, even as, while
ἕνα num. acc. masc. sg. εἷς or ἕν one, other, some, any, only, a certain
ἕκαστον adj. acc. masc. sg. ἕκαστος every man, every, every one, any man, each
ὑμῶν pron. gen. 2p. pl. σύ thou, you
ὡς adv. ὡς as, when, as it were, how, about, like, as soon as, even as, while
πατὴρ n. nom. masc. sg. πατήρ Father, father, parent
τέκνα n. acc. neut. pl. τέκνον child, son, daughter
ἑαυτοῦ reflexive pron. gen. masc. 3p. sg. ἑαυτοῦ himself, herself, itself, yourself, ourselves
ὑμᾶς pron. acc. 2p. pl. σύ thou, you
καὶ conj. καί and, even, also, but
καὶ conj. καί and, even, also, but
12 εἰς prep. εἰς (+acc) into, to, unto, for, in, on, toward, against, upon, at, among
τὸ art. acc. neut. sg. ὁ ἡ τό the, this, that, he, she, it
ὑμᾶς pron. acc. 2p. pl. σύ thou, you
ἀξίως adv. ἀξίως worthy, as become, after a godly sort
τοῦ art. gen. masc. sg. ὁ ἡ τό the, this, that, he, she, it
Θεοῦ n. gen. masc. sg. θεός God, god
τοῦ art. gen. masc. sg. ὁ ἡ τό the, this, that, he, she, it
ὑμᾶς pron. acc. 2p. pl. σύ thou, you
εἰς prep. εἰς (+acc) into, to, unto, for, in, on, toward, against, upon, at, among
τὴν art. acc. fem. sg. ὁ ἡ τό the, this, that, he, she, it
ἑαυτοῦ reflexive pron. gen. masc. 3p. sg. ἑαυτοῦ himself, herself, itself, yourself, ourselves
βασιλείαν n. acc. fem. sg. βασιλεία kingdom, reign
καὶ conj. καί and, even, also, but

δόξαν n. acc. fem. sg. δόξα glory, honour, praise, dignity, worship
13 Διὰ prep. διά (+gen) by, through, with, in, of, (+acc) for, because of, for a cause
τοῦτο demo. pron. acc. neut. sg. οὗτος αὕτη τοῦτο this, the same, this same, he, she, it
καὶ conj. καί and, even, also, but
ἡμεῖς pron. nom. 1p. pl. ἐγώ I
τῷ art. dat. masc. sg. ὁ ἡ τό the, this, that, he, she, it
Θεῷ n. dat. masc. sg. θεός God, god
ἀδιαλείπτως adv. ἀδιαλείπτως without ceasing
ὅτι conj. ὅτι that, for, because, how that, how, because that, for that, though
λόγον n. acc. masc. sg. λόγος word, saying, account, speech, thing, matter
ἀκοῆς n. gen. fem. sg. ἀκοή hearing, ear, fame, report, rumour, which one heard
παρ' prep. παρά (+gen) of, from, (+dat) with, for, (+acc) beside, at, by, above, against
ἡμῶν pron. gen. 1p. pl. ἐγώ I
τοῦ art. gen. masc. sg. ὁ ἡ τό the, this, that, he, she, it
Θεοῦ n. gen. masc. sg. θεός God, god
οὐ particle of negation. οὐ οὐκ οὐχ not, no, neither, none, nay, nor, never, nothing
λόγον n. acc. masc. sg. λόγος word, saying, account, speech, thing, matter
ἀνθρώπων n. gen. masc. pl. ἄνθρωπος man, human being, person, one, certain
ἀλλὰ conj. ἀλλά but, yea, yet, nevertheless, howbeit, nay, therefore
καθώς adv. καθώς as, even as, according as, according to
ἀληθῶς adv. ἀληθῶς indeed, of a truth, surely, truly, in truth, of a surety, verily, very
λόγον n. acc. masc. sg. λόγος word, saying, account, speech, thing, matter
Θεοῦ n. gen. masc. sg. θεός God, god
ὃς relative pron. nom. masc. sg. ὅς ἥ ὅ who, which, what, that
καὶ conj. καί and, even, also, but
ἐν prep. ἐν (+dat) in, by, with, among, at, on, through, to, within, into, of, for
ὑμῖν pron. dat. 2p. pl. σύ thou, you
τοῖς art. dat. masc. pl. ὁ ἡ τό the, this, that, he, she, it
14 ὑμεῖς pron. nom. 2p. pl. σύ thou, you
γὰρ conj. γάρ for, and, because, but, indeed
μιμηταὶ n. nom. masc. pl. μιμητής follower
ἀδελφοί n. voc. masc. pl. ἀδελφός brother
τῶν art. gen. fem. pl. ὁ ἡ τό the, this, that, he, she, it
ἐκκλησιῶν n. gen. fem. pl. ἐκκλησία church, assembly
τοῦ art. gen. masc. sg. ὁ ἡ τό the, this, that, he, she, it
Θεοῦ n. gen. masc. sg. θεός God, god
τῶν art. gen. fem. pl. ὁ ἡ τό the, this, that, he, she, it
ἐν prep. ἐν (+dat) in, by, with, among, at, on, through, to, within, into, of, for
τῇ art. dat. fem. sg. ὁ ἡ τό the, this, that, he, she, it
Ἰουδαίᾳ n. dat. fem. sg. Ἰουδαία Judaea, Jewry
ἐν prep. ἐν (+dat) in, by, with, among, at, on, through, to, within, into, of, for
Χριστῷ n. dat. masc. sg. Χριστός Christ
Ἰησοῦ n. dat. masc. sg. Ἰησοῦς Jesus
ὅτι conj. ὅτι that, for, because, how that, how, because that, for that, though
ταυτὰ crasis for τὰ αὐτά ταὐτά like, even thus, so, like manner
καὶ conj. καί and, even, also, but
ὑμεῖς pron. nom. 2p. pl. σύ thou, you
ὑπὸ prep. ὑπό (+gen) of, by, with, from, among, (+acc) under
τῶν art. gen. masc. pl. ὁ ἡ τό the, this, that, he, she, it
ἰδίων adj. gen. masc. pl. ἴδιος one's own, one's, privately
συμφυλετῶν n. gen. masc. pl. συμφυλέτης countryman
καθὼς adv. καθώς as, even as, according as, according to
καὶ conj. καί and, even, also, but
αὐτοὶ pron. nom. masc. 3p. pl. αὐτός ή ό self, of oneself, even, very, the same, he, she, it
ὑπὸ prep. ὑπό (+gen) of, by, with, from, among, (+acc) under

τῶν art. gen. masc. pl. ὁ ἡ τό the, this, that, he, she, it
Ἰουδαίων adj. gen. masc. pl. Ἰουδαῖος Jew, Jewess
15 τῶν art. gen. masc. pl. ὁ ἡ τό the, this, that, he, she, it
καὶ conj. καί and, even, also, but
τὸν art. acc. masc. sg. ὁ ἡ τό the, this, that, he, she, it
Κύριον n. acc. masc. sg. κύριος Lord, lord, master, sir, LORD, God, Master, owner
Ἰησοῦν n. acc. masc. sg. Ἰησοῦς Jesus
καὶ conj. καί and, even, also, but
τοὺς art. acc. masc. pl. ὁ ἡ τό the, this, that, he, she, it
ἰδίους adj. acc. masc. pl. ἴδιος one's own, one's, privately
προφήτας n. acc. masc. pl. προφήτης prophet
καὶ conj. καί and, even, also, but
ἡμᾶς pron. acc. 1p. pl. ἐγώ I
καὶ conj. καί and, even, also, but
Θεῷ n. dat. masc. sg. θεός God, god
μὴ particle of negation. μή not, no, lest, neither, none, nothing, nor, never, without
καὶ conj. καί and, even, also, but
πᾶσιν adj. dat. masc. pl. πᾶς πᾶσα πᾶν all, every, whosoever, every one, no, whole, any
ἀνθρώποις n. dat. masc. pl. ἄνθρωπος man, human being, person, one, certain
ἐναντίων adj. gen. masc. pl. ἐναντίος contrary, against, over against
16 ἡμᾶς pron. acc. 1p. pl. ἐγώ I
τοῖς art. dat. neut. pl. ὁ ἡ τό the, this, that, he, she, it
ἔθνεσι n. dat. neut. pl. ἔθνος Gentile, nation, heathen, people
ἵνα conj. ἵνα that, to, lest, for to, so that, albeit, because, for, so as
εἰς prep. εἰς (+acc) into, to, unto, for, in, on, toward, against, upon, at, among
τὸ art. acc. neut. sg. ὁ ἡ τό the, this, that, he, she, it
αὐτῶν pron. gen. masc. 3p. pl. αὐτός ή ό self, of oneself, even, very, the same, he, she, it
τὰς art. acc. fem. pl. ὁ ἡ τό the, this, that, he, she, it
ἁμαρτίας n. acc. fem. pl. ἁμαρτία sin, offence, sinful
πάντοτε adv. πάντοτε always, ever, always, evermore
δὲ conj. δέ but, and, now, also, to the contrary, rather, then
ἐπ' prep. ἐπί (+gen) on, in, upon, (+dat) in, at, for, upon, (+acc) on, upon, unto, to, against
αὐτοὺς pron. acc. masc. 3p. pl. αὐτός ή ό self, of oneself, even, very, the same, he, she, it
ἡ art. nom. fem. sg. ὁ ἡ τό the, this, that, he, she, it
ὀργὴ n. nom. fem. sg. ὀργή wrath, anger, indignation, vengeance
εἰς prep. εἰς (+acc) into, to, unto, for, in, on, toward, against, upon, at, among
τέλος n. acc. neut. sg. τέλος end, custom, ending, finally, uttermost
17 Ἡμεῖς pron. nom. 1p. pl. ἐγώ I
δέ conj. δέ but, and, now, also, to the contrary, rather, then
ἀδελφοί n. voc. masc. pl. ἀδελφός brother
ἀφ' prep. ἀπό (+gen) from, of, out of, since, for, off, at, by, in, on
ὑμῶν pron. gen. 2p. pl. σύ thou, you
πρὸς prep. πρός (+gen) for, (+dat) at, (+acc) unto, to, with, for, against
καιρὸν n. acc. masc. sg. καιρός time, season, due time, opportunity
ὥρας n. gen. fem. sg. ὥρα hour, time, season
προσώπῳ n. dat. neut. sg. πρόσωπον face, presence, person, countenance
οὐ particle of negation. οὐ οὐκ οὐχ not, no, neither, none, nay, nor, never, nothing
καρδίᾳ n. dat. fem. sg. καρδία heart
περισσοτέρως adv. περισσοτέρως more exceedingly, more abundantly, more frequent
τὸ art. acc. neut. sg. ὁ ἡ τό the, this, that, he, she, it
πρόσωπον n. acc. neut. sg. πρόσωπον face, presence, person, countenance
ὑμῶν pron. gen. 2p. pl. σύ thou, you
ἐν prep. ἐν (+dat) in, by, with, among, at, on, through, to, within, into, of, for
πολλῇ adj. dat. fem. sg. πολύς many, great, much, long, abundant
ἐπιθυμίᾳ n. dat. fem. sg. ἐπιθυμία lust, concupiscence, desire

18 διὸ conj. διό wherefore, therefore, for which cause
πρὸς prep. πρός (+gen) for, (+dat) at, (+acc) unto, to, with, for, against
ὑμᾶς pron. acc. 2p. pl. σύ thou, you
ἐγὼ pron. nom. 1p. sg. ἐγώ I
μὲν conj. μέν indeed, verily, truly, even, so, some
Παῦλος n. nom. masc. sg. Παῦλος Paul, Paulus
καὶ conj. καί and, even, also, but
ἅπαξ adv. ἅπαξ once
καὶ conj. καί and, even, also, but
δίς adv. δίς twice, again
καὶ conj. καί and, even, also, but
ἡμᾶς pron. acc. 1p. pl. ἐγώ I
ὁ art. nom. masc. sg. ὁ ἡ τό the, this, that, he, she, it
Σατανᾶς n. nom. masc. sg. Σατανᾶς Satan
19 τίς interrog. pron. nom. fem. sg. τίς what, who, why, where, which, how
γὰρ conj. γάρ for, and, because, but, indeed
ἡμῶν pron. gen. 1p. pl. ἐγώ I
ἐλπὶς n. nom. fem. sg. ἐλπίς hope, faith
ἢ particle. ἤ or, than, either, nor, or else, and, rather than
χαρὰ n. nom. fem. sg. χαρά joy, gladness, joyfulness
ἢ particle. ἤ or, than, either, nor, or else, and, rather than
στέφανος n. nom. masc. sg. στέφανος crown
καυχήσεως n. gen. fem. sg. καύχησις boasting, rejoicing, glorying
ἢ particle. ἤ or, than, either, nor, or else, and, rather than
οὐχὶ adv. οὐχί not, nay
καὶ conj. καί and, even, also, but
ὑμεῖς pron. nom. 2p. pl. σύ thou, you
ἔμπροσθεν prep. ἔμπροσθεν (+gen) before, in the sight of, in the presence of
τοῦ art. gen. masc. sg. ὁ ἡ τό the, this, that, he, she, it
Κυρίου n. gen. masc. sg. κύριος Lord, lord, master, sir, LORD, God, Master, owner
ἡμῶν pron. gen. 1p. pl. ἐγώ I
Ἰησοῦ n. gen. masc. sg. Ἰησοῦς Jesus
Χριστοῦ n. gen. masc. sg. Χριστός Christ
ἐν prep. ἐν (+dat) in, by, with, among, at, on, through, to, within, into, of, for
τῇ art. dat. fem. sg. ὁ ἡ τό the, this, that, he, she, it
αὐτοῦ pron. gen. masc. 3p. sg. αὐτός ἡ ὁ self, of oneself, even, very, the same, he, she, it
παρουσίᾳ n. dat. fem. sg. παρουσία coming, presence
20 ὑμεῖς pron. nom. 2p. pl. σύ thou, you
γάρ conj. γάρ for, and, because, but, indeed
ἡ art. nom. fem. sg. ὁ ἡ τό the, this, that, he, she, it
δόξα n. nom. fem. sg. δόξα glory, honour, praise, dignity, worship
ἡμῶν pron. gen. 1p. pl. ἐγώ I
καὶ conj. καί and, even, also, but
ἡ art. nom. fem. sg. ὁ ἡ τό the, this, that, he, she, it
χαρά n. nom. fem. sg. χαρά joy, gladness, joyfulness

3

1 Διὸ conj. διό wherefore, therefore, for which cause
μηκέτι adv. μηκέτι no more, no longer, not any more, not henceforth, not henceforward
ἐν prep. ἐν (+dat) in, by, with, among, at, on, through, to, within, into, of, for
Ἀθήναις n. dat. fem. pl. Ἀθῆναι Athens
μόνοι adj. nom. masc. pl. μόνος only, alone, by oneself
2 καὶ conj. καί and, even, also, but
Τιμόθεον n. acc. masc. sg. Τιμόθεος Timotheus, Timothy

τὸν art. acc. masc. sg. ὁ ἡ τό the, this, that, he, she, it
ἀδελφὸν n. acc. masc. sg. ἀδελφός brother
ἡμῶν pron. gen. 1p. pl. ἐγώ I
καὶ conj. καί and, even, also, but
διάκονον n. acc. masc. sg. διάκονος minister, servant, deacon
τοῦ art. gen. masc. sg. ὁ ἡ τό the, this, that, he, she, it
Θεοῦ n. gen. masc. sg. θεός God, god
καὶ conj. καί and, even, also, but
συνεργὸν adj. acc. masc. sg. συνεργός fellowlabourer, fellowhelper, fellowworker
ἡμῶν pron. gen. 1p. pl. ἐγώ I
ἐν prep. ἐν (+dat) in, by, with, among, at, on, through, to, within, into, of, for
τῷ art. dat. neut. sg. ὁ ἡ τό the, this, that, he, she, it
εὐαγγελίῳ n. dat. neut. sg. εὐαγγέλιον gospel
τοῦ art. gen. masc. sg. ὁ ἡ τό the, this, that, he, she, it
Χριστοῦ n. gen. masc. sg. Χριστός Christ
εἰς prep. εἰς (+acc) into, to, unto, for, in, on, toward, against, upon, at, among
τὸ art. acc. neut. sg. ὁ ἡ τό the, this, that, he, she, it
ὑμᾶς pron. acc. 2p. pl. σύ thou, you
καὶ conj. καί and, even, also, but
ὑμᾶς pron. acc. 2p. pl. σύ thou, you
περὶ prep. περί (+gen) of, for, concerning, (+acc) about, concerning, in
τῆς art. gen. fem. sg. ὁ ἡ τό the, this, that, he, she, it
πίστεως n. gen. fem. sg. πίστις faith, assurance, belief, fidelity
ὑμῶν pron. gen. 2p. pl. σύ thou, you
3 τῷ art. dat. masc. sg. ὁ ἡ τό the, this, that, he, she, it
μηδένα num. acc. masc. sg. μηδείς μηδεμία μηδέν no man, nothing, no, none, not at all
ἐν prep. ἐν (+dat) in, by, with, among, at, on, through, to, within, into, of, for
ταῖς art. dat. fem. pl. ὁ ἡ τό the, this, that, he, she, it
θλίψεσι n. dat. fem. pl. θλῖψις tribulation, affliction, anguish, persecution
ταύταις demo. pron. dat. fem. pl. οὗτος αὕτη τοῦτο this, the same, this same, he, she, it
αὐτοὶ pron. nom. masc. 3p. pl. αὐτός ή ό self, of oneself, even, very, the same, he, she, it
γὰρ conj. γάρ for, and, because, but, indeed
ὅτι conj. ὅτι that, for, because, how that, how, because that, for that, though
εἰς prep. εἰς (+acc) into, to, unto, for, in, on, toward, against, upon, at, among
τοῦτο demo. pron. acc. neut. sg. οὗτος αὕτη τοῦτο this, the same, this same, he, she, it
4 καὶ conj. καί and, even, also, but
γὰρ conj. γάρ for, and, because, but, indeed
ὅτε adv. ὅτε when, after that, as soon as, while, after
πρὸς prep. πρός (+gen) for, (+dat) at, (+acc) unto, to, with, for, against
ὑμᾶς pron. acc. 2p. pl. σύ thou, you
ὑμῖν pron. dat. 2p. pl. σύ thou, you
ὅτι conj. ὅτι that, for, because, how that, how, because that, for that, though
καθὼς adv. καθώς as, even as, according as, according to
καὶ conj. καί and, even, also, but
καὶ conj. καί and, even, also, but
5 διὰ prep. διά (+gen) by, through, with, in, of, (+acc) for, because of, for a cause
τοῦτο demo. pron. acc. neut. sg. οὗτος αὕτη τοῦτο this, the same, this same, he, she, it
κἀγὼ pron. nom. 1p. sg. κἀγώ and I, I also, so I, even as I
μηκέτι adv. μηκέτι no more, no longer, not any more, not henceforth, not henceforward
εἰς prep. εἰς (+acc) into, to, unto, for, in, on, toward, against, upon, at, among
τὸ art. acc. neut. sg. ὁ ἡ τό the, this, that, he, she, it
τὴν art. acc. fem. sg. ὁ ἡ τό the, this, that, he, she, it
πίστιν n. acc. fem. sg. πίστις faith, assurance, belief, fidelity
ὑμῶν pron. gen. 2p. pl. σύ thou, you
μή particle of negation. μή not, no, lest, neither, none, nothing, nor, never, without

πως particle. πώς by any means, by some means, haply, perhaps
ὑμᾶς pron. acc. 2p. pl. σύ thou, you
ὁ art. nom. masc. sg. ὁ ἡ τό the, this, that, he, she, it
καὶ conj. καί and, even, also, but
εἰς prep. εἰς (+acc) into, to, unto, for, in, on, toward, against, upon, at, among
κενὸν adj. acc. neut. sg. κενός empty, vain, in vain
ὁ art. nom. masc. sg. ὁ ἡ τό the, this, that, he, she, it
κόπος n. nom. masc. sg. κόπος labour, trouble, weariness
ἡμῶν pron. gen. 1p. pl. ἐγώ I
6 ἄρτι adv. ἄρτι now, hence, here, hither, even now, present
δὲ conj. δέ but, and, now, also, to the contrary, rather, then
Τιμοθέου n. gen. masc. sg. Τιμόθεος Timotheus, Timothy
πρὸς prep. πρός (+gen) for, (+dat) at, (+acc) unto, to, with, for, against
ἡμᾶς pron. acc. 1p. pl. ἐγώ I
ἀφ' prep. ἀπό (+gen) from, of, out of, since, for, off, at, by, in, on
ὑμῶν pron. gen. 2p. pl. σύ thou, you
καὶ conj. καί and, even, also, but
ἡμῖν pron. dat. 1p. pl. ἐγώ I
τὴν art. acc. fem. sg. ὁ ἡ τό the, this, that, he, she, it
πίστιν n. acc. fem. sg. πίστις faith, assurance, belief, fidelity
καὶ conj. καί and, even, also, but
τὴν art. acc. fem. sg. ὁ ἡ τό the, this, that, he, she, it
ἀγάπην n. acc. fem. sg. ἀγάπη love, charity, feast of charity
ὑμῶν pron. gen. 2p. pl. σύ thou, you
καὶ conj. καί and, even, also, but
ὅτι conj. ὅτι that, for, because, how that, how, because that, for that, though
μνείαν n. acc. fem. sg. μνεία mention, remembrance
ἡμῶν pron. gen. 1p. pl. ἐγώ I
ἀγαθὴν adj. acc. fem. sg. ἀγαθός good, good thing, that which is good, well
πάντοτε adv. πάντοτε always, ever, always, evermore
καθάπερ adv. καθάπερ even as, as, as well as
ἡμᾶς pron. acc. 1p. pl. ἐγώ I
καθάπερ adv. καθάπερ even as, as, as well as
καὶ conj. καί and, even, also, but
ἡμεῖς pron. nom. 1p. pl. ἐγώ I
ὑμᾶς pron. acc. 2p. pl. σύ thou, you
7 διὰ prep. διά (+gen) by, through, with, in, of, (+acc) for, because of, for a cause
τοῦτο demo. pron. acc. neut. sg. οὗτος αὕτη τοῦτο this, the same, this same, he, she, it
ἀδελφοί n. voc. masc. pl. ἀδελφός brother
ἐφ' prep. ἐπί (+gen) on, in, upon, (+dat) in, at, for, upon, (+acc) on, upon, unto, to, against
ὑμῖν pron. dat. 2p. pl. σύ thou, you
ἐπὶ prep. ἐπί (+gen) on, in, upon, (+dat) in, at, for, upon, (+acc) on, upon, unto, to, against
πάσῃ adj. dat. fem. sg. πᾶς πᾶσα πᾶν all, every, whosoever, every one, no, whole, any
τῇ art. dat. fem. sg. ὁ ἡ τό the, this, that, he, she, it
θλίψει n. dat. fem. sg. θλῖψις tribulation, affliction, anguish, persecution
καὶ conj. καί and, even, also, but
ἀνάγκῃ n. dat. fem. sg. ἀνάγκη must needs, necessity, distress, inevitable
ἡμῶν pron. gen. 1p. pl. ἐγώ I
διὰ prep. διά (+gen) by, through, with, in, of, (+acc) for, because of, for a cause
τῆς art. gen. fem. sg. ὁ ἡ τό the, this, that, he, she, it
ὑμῶν pron. gen. 2p. pl. σύ thou, you
πίστεως n. gen. fem. sg. πίστις faith, assurance, belief, fidelity
8 ὅτι conj. ὅτι that, for, because, how that, how, because that, for that, though
νῦν adv. νῦν now, henceforth, present, this time
ἐὰν conj. ἐάν if, soever, except, though, and if, but, whether, if so, so

ὑμεῖς pron. nom. 2p. pl. σύ thou, you
ἐν prep. ἐν (+dat) in, by, with, among, at, on, through, to, within, into, of, for
Κυρίῳ n. dat. masc. sg. κύριος Lord, lord, master, sir, LORD, God, Master, owner
9 τίνα interrog. pron. acc. fem. sg. τίς what, who, why, where, which, how
γὰρ conj. γάρ for, and, because, but, indeed
εὐχαριστίαν n. acc. fem. sg. εὐχαριστία thankfulness, thanksgiving, giving of thanks
τῷ art. dat. masc. sg. ὁ ἡ τό the, this, that, he, she, it
Θεῷ n. dat. masc. sg. θεός God, god
περὶ prep. περί (+gen) of, for, concerning, (+acc) about, concerning, in
ὑμῶν pron. gen. 2p. pl. σύ thou, you
ἐπὶ prep. ἐπί (+gen) on, in, upon, (+dat) in, at, for, upon, (+acc) on, upon, unto, to, against
πάσῃ adj. dat. fem. sg. πᾶς πᾶσα πᾶν all, every, whosoever, every one, no, whole, any
τῇ art. dat. fem. sg. ὁ ἡ τό the, this, that, he, she, it
χαρᾷ n. dat. fem. sg. χαρά joy, gladness, joyfulness
ᾗ relative pron. dat. fem. sg. ὅς ἥ ὅ who, which, what, that
δι’ prep. διά (+gen) by, through, with, in, of, (+acc) for, because of, for a cause
ὑμᾶς pron. acc. 2p. pl. σύ thou, you
ἔμπροσθεν prep. ἔμπροσθεν (+gen) before, in the sight of, in the presence of
τοῦ art. gen. masc. sg. ὁ ἡ τό the, this, that, he, she, it
Θεοῦ n. gen. masc. sg. θεός God, god
ἡμῶν pron. gen. 1p. pl. ἐγώ I
10 νυκτὸς n. gen. fem. sg. νύξ night
καὶ conj. καί and, even, also, but
ἡμέρας n. gen. fem. sg. ἡμέρα day, time, year, while, age, day time
ὑπὲρ prep. ὑπέρ (+gen) for, of, for the sake of, (+acc) above, more than
ἐκ prep. ἐκ ἐξ (+gen) of, from, out of, by, on, with, in, among, through
περισσοῦ adj. gen. neut. sg. περισσός more, beyond measure, advantage, exceedingly
εἰς prep. εἰς (+acc) into, to, unto, for, in, on, toward, against, upon, at, among
τὸ art. acc. neut. sg. ὁ ἡ τό the, this, that, he, she, it
ὑμῶν pron. gen. 2p. pl. σύ thou, you
τὸ art. acc. neut. sg. ὁ ἡ τό the, this, that, he, she, it
πρόσωπον n. acc. neut. sg. πρόσωπον face, presence, person, countenance
καὶ conj. καί and, even, also, but
τὰ art. acc. neut. pl. ὁ ἡ τό the, this, that, he, she, it
ὑστερήματα n. acc. neut. pl. ὑστέρημα penury, that which is lacking, want, lack
τῆς art. gen. fem. sg. ὁ ἡ τό the, this, that, he, she, it
πίστεως n. gen. fem. sg. πίστις faith, assurance, belief, fidelity
ὑμῶν pron. gen. 2p. pl. σύ thou, you
11 Αὐτὸς pron. nom. masc. 3p. sg. αὐτός ἡ ὁ self, of oneself, even, very, the same, he, she, it
δὲ conj. δέ but, and, now, also, to the contrary, rather, then
ὁ art. nom. masc. sg. ὁ ἡ τό the, this, that, he, she, it
Θεὸς n. nom. masc. sg. θεός God, god
καὶ conj. καί and, even, also, but
πατὴρ n. nom. masc. sg. πατήρ Father, father, parent
ἡμῶν pron. gen. 1p. pl. ἐγώ I
καὶ conj. καί and, even, also, but
ὁ art. nom. masc. sg. ὁ ἡ τό the, this, that, he, she, it
Κύριος n. nom. masc. sg. κύριος Lord, lord, master, sir, LORD, God, Master, owner
ἡμῶν pron. gen. 1p. pl. ἐγώ I
Ἰησοῦς n. nom. masc. sg. Ἰησοῦς Jesus
Χριστός n. nom. masc. sg. Χριστός Christ
τὴν art. acc. fem. sg. ὁ ἡ τό the, this, that, he, she, it
ὁδὸν n. acc. fem. sg. ὁδός way, journey, highway
ἡμῶν pron. gen. 1p. pl. ἐγώ I
πρὸς prep. πρός (+gen) for, (+dat) at, (+acc) unto, to, with, for, against

ὑμᾶς pron. acc. 2p. pl. σύ thou, you
12 ὑμᾶς pron. acc. 2p. pl. σύ thou, you
δὲ conj. δέ but, and, now, also, to the contrary, rather, then
ὁ art. nom. masc. sg. ὁ ἡ τό the, this, that, he, she, it
Κύριος n. nom. masc. sg. κύριος Lord, lord, master, sir, LORD, God, Master, owner
καὶ conj. καί and, even, also, but
τῇ art. dat. fem. sg. ὁ ἡ τό the, this, that, he, she, it
ἀγάπῃ n. dat. fem. sg. ἀγάπη love, charity, feast of charity
εἰς prep. εἰς (+acc) into, to, unto, for, in, on, toward, against, upon, at, among
ἀλλήλους pron. acc. masc. pl. ἀλλήλων one another, themselves, together, mutual
καὶ conj. καί and, even, also, but
εἰς prep. εἰς (+acc) into, to, unto, for, in, on, toward, against, upon, at, among
πάντας adj. acc. masc. pl. πᾶς πᾶσα πᾶν all, every, whosoever, every one, no, whole, any
καθάπερ adv. καθάπερ even as, as, as well as
καὶ conj. καί and, even, also, but
ἡμεῖς pron. nom. 1p. pl. ἐγώ I
εἰς prep. εἰς (+acc) into, to, unto, for, in, on, toward, against, upon, at, among
ὑμᾶς pron. acc. 2p. pl. σύ thou, you
13 εἰς prep. εἰς (+acc) into, to, unto, for, in, on, toward, against, upon, at, among
τὸ art. acc. neut. sg. ὁ ἡ τό the, this, that, he, she, it
ὑμῶν pron. gen. 2p. pl. σύ thou, you
τὰς art. acc. fem. pl. ὁ ἡ τό the, this, that, he, she, it
καρδίας n. acc. fem. pl. καρδία heart
ἀμέμπτους adj. acc. fem. pl. ἄμεμπτος blameless, faultless, unblamable
ἐν prep. ἐν (+dat) in, by, with, among, at, on, through, to, within, into, of, for
ἁγιωσύνῃ n. dat. fem. sg. ἁγιωσύνη holiness
ἔμπροσθεν prep. ἔμπροσθεν (+gen) before, in the sight of, in the presence of
τοῦ art. gen. masc. sg. ὁ ἡ τό the, this, that, he, she, it
Θεοῦ n. gen. masc. sg. θεός God, god
καὶ conj. καί and, even, also, but
πατρὸς n. gen. masc. sg. πατήρ Father, father, parent
ἡμῶν pron. gen. 1p. pl. ἐγώ I
ἐν prep. ἐν (+dat) in, by, with, among, at, on, through, to, within, into, of, for
τῇ art. dat. fem. sg. ὁ ἡ τό the, this, that, he, she, it
παρουσίᾳ n. dat. fem. sg. παρουσία coming, presence
τοῦ art. gen. masc. sg. ὁ ἡ τό the, this, that, he, she, it
Κυρίου n. gen. masc. sg. κύριος Lord, lord, master, sir, LORD, God, Master, owner
ἡμῶν pron. gen. 1p. pl. ἐγώ I
Ἰησοῦ n. gen. masc. sg. Ἰησοῦς Jesus
Χριστοῦ n. gen. masc. sg. Χριστός Christ
μετὰ prep. μετά (+gen) with, among, against, (+acc) after
πάντων adj. gen. masc. pl. πᾶς πᾶσα πᾶν all, every, whosoever, every one, no, whole, any
τῶν art. gen. masc. pl. ὁ ἡ τό the, this, that, he, she, it
ἁγίων adj. gen. masc. pl. ἅγιος Holy, holy, saint, Holy One, holy thing, most holy
αὐτοῦ pron. gen. masc. 3p. sg. αὐτός ἡ ό self, of oneself, even, very, the same, he, she, it

4

1 Τὸ art. acc. neut. sg. ὁ ἡ τό the, this, that, he, she, it
λοιπὸν adv. λοιπόν finally, henceforth, now, besides, furthermore, moreover, then
οὖν conj. οὖν therefore, then, so, and, now, wherefore
ἀδελφοί n. voc. masc. pl. ἀδελφός brother
ὑμᾶς pron. acc. 2p. pl. σύ thou, you
καὶ conj. καί and, even, also, but
ἐν prep. ἐν (+dat) in, by, with, among, at, on, through, to, within, into, of, for

Κυρίῳ n. dat. masc. sg. κύριος Lord, lord, master, sir, LORD, God, Master, owner
Ἰησοῦ n. dat. masc. sg. Ἰησοῦς Jesus
καθὼς adv. καθώς as, even as, according as, according to
παρ' prep. παρά (+gen) of, from, (+dat) with, for, (+acc) beside, at, by, above, against
ἡμῶν pron. gen. 1p. pl. ἐγώ I
τὸ art. acc. neut. sg. ὁ ἡ τό the, this, that, he, she, it
πῶς adv. πῶς how, by what means, after what manner
ὑμᾶς pron. acc. 2p. pl. σύ thou, you
καὶ conj. καί and, even, also, but
Θεῷ n. dat. masc. sg. θεός God, god
ἵνα conj. ἵνα that, to, lest, for to, so that, albeit, because, for, so as
μᾶλλον adv. μᾶλλον rather, more, more and more, better, much, much the more
2 γὰρ conj. γάρ for, and, because, but, indeed
τίνας interrog. pron. acc. fem. pl. τίς what, who, why, where, which, how
παραγγελίας n. acc. fem. pl. παραγγελία charge, commandment
ὑμῖν pron. dat. 2p. pl. σύ thou, you
διὰ prep. διά (+gen) by, through, with, in, of, (+acc) for, because of, for a cause
τοῦ art. gen. masc. sg. ὁ ἡ τό the, this, that, he, she, it
Κυρίου n. gen. masc. sg. κύριος Lord, lord, master, sir, LORD, God, Master, owner
Ἰησοῦ n. gen. masc. sg. Ἰησοῦς Jesus
3 τοῦτο demo. pron. nom. neut. sg. οὗτος αὕτη τοῦτο this, the same, this same, he, she, it
γάρ conj. γάρ for, and, because, but, indeed
θέλημα n. nom. neut. sg. θέλημα will, desire, pleasure
τοῦ art. gen. masc. sg. ὁ ἡ τό the, this, that, he, she, it
Θεοῦ n. gen. masc. sg. θεός God, god
ὁ art. nom. masc. sg. ὁ ἡ τό the, this, that, he, she, it
ἁγιασμὸς n. nom. masc. sg. ἁγιασμός holiness, sanctification
ὑμῶν pron. gen. 2p. pl. σύ thou, you
ὑμᾶς pron. acc. 2p. pl. σύ thou, you
ἀπὸ prep. ἀπό (+gen) from, of, out of, since, for, off, at, by, in, on
τῆς art. gen. fem. sg. ὁ ἡ τό the, this, that, he, she, it
πορνείας n. gen. fem. sg. πορνεία fornication
4 ἕκαστον adj. acc. masc. sg. ἕκαστος every man, every, every one, any man, each
ὑμῶν pron. gen. 2p. pl. σύ thou, you
τὸ art. acc. neut. sg. ὁ ἡ τό the, this, that, he, she, it
ἑαυτοῦ reflexive pron. gen. masc. 3p. sg. ἑαυτοῦ himself, herself, itself, yourself, ourselves
σκεῦος n. acc. neut. sg. σκεῦος vessel, good, sail, stuff
ἐν prep. ἐν (+dat) in, by, with, among, at, on, through, to, within, into, of, for
ἁγιασμῷ n. dat. masc. sg. ἁγιασμός holiness, sanctification
καὶ conj. καί and, even, also, but
τιμῇ n. dat. fem. sg. τιμή honour, price, preciousness, sum
5 μὴ particle of negation. μή not, no, lest, neither, none, nothing, nor, never, without
ἐν prep. ἐν (+dat) in, by, with, among, at, on, through, to, within, into, of, for
πάθει n. dat. neut. sg. πάθος affection, inordinate affection, lust
ἐπιθυμίας n. gen. fem. sg. ἐπιθυμία lust, concupiscence, desire
καθάπερ adv. καθάπερ even as, as, as well as
καὶ conj. καί and, even, also, but
τὰ art. nom. neut. pl. ὁ ἡ τό the, this, that, he, she, it
ἔθνη n. nom. neut. pl. ἔθνος Gentile, nation, heathen, people
τὰ art. nom. neut. pl. ὁ ἡ τό the, this, that, he, she, it
μὴ particle of negation. μή not, no, lest, neither, none, nothing, nor, never, without
τὸν art. acc. masc. sg. ὁ ἡ τό the, this, that, he, she, it
Θεόν n. acc. masc. sg. θεός God, god
6 τὸ art. acc. neut. sg. ὁ ἡ τό the, this, that, he, she, it
μὴ particle of negation. μή not, no, lest, neither, none, nothing, nor, never, without

καὶ conj. καί and, even, also, but
ἐν prep. ἐν (+dat) in, by, with, among, at, on, through, to, within, into, of, for
τῷ art. dat. neut. sg. ὁ ἡ τό the, this, that, he, she, it
πράγματι n. dat. neut. sg. πρᾶγμα thing, matter, business, work
τὸν art. acc. masc. sg. ὁ ἡ τό the, this, that, he, she, it
ἀδελφὸν n. acc. masc. sg. ἀδελφός brother
αὐτοῦ pron. gen. masc. 3p. sg. αὐτός ἡ ὁ self, of oneself, even, very, the same, he, she, it
διότι conj. διότι for, because, because that, therefore
ἔκδικος adj. nom. masc. sg. ἔκδικος revenger, avenger
ὁ art. nom. masc. sg. ὁ ἡ τό the, this, that, he, she, it
Κύριος n. nom. masc. sg. κύριος Lord, lord, master, sir, LORD, God, Master, owner
περὶ prep. περί (+gen) of, for, concerning, (+acc) about, concerning, in
πάντων adj. gen. neut. pl. πᾶς πᾶσα πᾶν all, every, whosoever, every one, no, whole, any
τούτων demo. pron. gen. neut. pl. οὗτος αὕτη τοῦτο this, the same, this same, he, she, it
καθὼς adv. καθώς as, even as, according as, according to
καὶ conj. καί and, even, also, but
ὑμῖν pron. dat. 2p. pl. σύ thou, you
καὶ conj. καί and, even, also, but
7 οὐ particle of negation. οὐ οὐκ οὐχ not, no, neither, none, nay, nor, never, nothing
γὰρ conj. γάρ for, and, because, but, indeed
ἡμᾶς pron. acc. 1p. pl. ἐγώ I
ὁ art. nom. masc. sg. ὁ ἡ τό the, this, that, he, she, it
Θεὸς n. nom. masc. sg. θεός God, god
ἐπὶ prep. ἐπί (+gen) on, in, upon, (+dat) in, at, for, upon, (+acc) on, upon, unto, to, against
ἀκαθαρσίᾳ n. dat. fem. sg. ἀκαθαρσία uncleanness
ἀλλ’ conj. ἀλλά but, yea, yet, nevertheless, howbeit, nay, therefore
ἐν prep. ἐν (+dat) in, by, with, among, at, on, through, to, within, into, of, for
ἁγιασμῷ n. dat. masc. sg. ἁγιασμός holiness, sanctification
8 τοιγαροῦν particle. τοιγαροῦν therefore, wherefore
ὁ art. nom. masc. sg. ὁ ἡ τό the, this, that, he, she, it
οὐκ particle of negation. οὐ οὐκ οὐχ not, no, neither, none, nay, nor, never, nothing
ἄνθρωπον n. acc. masc. sg. ἄνθρωπος man, human being, person, one, certain
ἀλλὰ conj. ἀλλά but, yea, yet, nevertheless, howbeit, nay, therefore
τὸν art. acc. masc. sg. ὁ ἡ τό the, this, that, he, she, it
Θεὸν n. acc. masc. sg. θεός God, god
τὸν art. acc. masc. sg. ὁ ἡ τό the, this, that, he, she, it
καὶ conj. καί and, even, also, but
τὸ art. acc. neut. sg. ὁ ἡ τό the, this, that, he, she, it
Πνεῦμα n. acc. neut. sg. πνεῦμα spirit, Spirit, Ghost, ghost, life. of the spirit, wind
αὐτοῦ pron. gen. masc. 3p. sg. αὐτός ἡ ὁ self, of oneself, even, very, the same, he, she, it
τὸ art. acc. neut. sg. ὁ ἡ τό the, this, that, he, she, it
Ἅγιον adj. acc. neut. sg. ἅγιος Holy, holy, saint, Holy One, holy thing, most holy
εἰς prep. εἰς (+acc) into, to, unto, for, in, on, toward, against, upon, at, among
ἡμᾶς pron. acc. 1p. pl. ἐγώ I
9 Περὶ prep. περί (+gen) of, for, concerning, (+acc) about, concerning, in
δὲ conj. δέ but, and, now, also, to the contrary, rather, then
τῆς art. gen. fem. sg. ὁ ἡ τό the, this, that, he, she, it
φιλαδελφίας n. gen. fem. sg. φιλαδελφία brotherly love, brotherly kindness
οὐ particle of negation. οὐ οὐκ οὐχ not, no, neither, none, nay, nor, never, nothing
χρείαν n. acc. fem. sg. χρεία need, necessity, lack, want
ὑμῖν pron. dat. 2p. pl. σύ thou, you
αὐτοὶ pron. nom. masc. 2p. pl. αὐτός ἡ ὁ self, of oneself, even, very, the same, he, she, it
γὰρ conj. γάρ for, and, because, but, indeed
ὑμεῖς pron. nom. 2p. pl. σύ thou, you
θεοδίδακτοί adj. nom. masc. pl. θεοδίδακτος taught of God

εἰς prep. εἰς (+acc) into, to, unto, for, in, on, toward, against, upon, at, among
τὸ art. acc. neut. sg. ὁ ἡ τό the, this, that, he, she, it
ἀλλήλους pron. acc. masc. pl. ἀλλήλων one another, themselves, together, mutual
10 καὶ conj. καί and, even, also, but
γὰρ conj. γάρ for, and, because, but, indeed
αὐτὸ pron. acc. neut. 3p. sg. αὐτός ή ό self, of oneself, even, very, the same, he, she, it
εἰς prep. εἰς (+acc) into, to, unto, for, in, on, toward, against, upon, at, among
πάντας adj. acc. masc. pl. πᾶς πᾶσα πᾶν all, every, whosoever, every one, no, whole, any
τοὺς art. acc. masc. pl. ὁ ἡ τό the, this, that, he, she, it
ἀδελφοὺς n. acc. masc. pl. ἀδελφός brother
τοὺς art. acc. masc. pl. ὁ ἡ τό the, this, that, he, she, it
ἐν prep. ἐν (+dat) in, by, with, among, at, on, through, to, within, into, of, for
ὅλῃ adj. dat. fem. sg. ὅλος all, whole, every whit, altogether
τῇ art. dat. fem. sg. ὁ ἡ τό the, this, that, he, she, it
Μακεδονίᾳ. n. dat. fem. sg. Μακεδονία Macedonia
δὲ conj. δέ but, and, now, also, to the contrary, rather, then
ὑμᾶς pron. acc. 2p. pl. σύ thou, you
ἀδελφοί n. voc. masc. pl. ἀδελφός brother
μᾶλλον adv. μᾶλλον rather, more, more and more, better, much, much the more
11 καὶ conj. καί and, even, also, but
καὶ conj. καί and, even, also, but
τὰ art. acc. neut. pl. ὁ ἡ τό the, this, that, he, she, it
ἴδια adj. acc. neut. pl. ἴδιος one's own, one's, privately
καὶ conj. καί and, even, also, but
ταῖς art. dat. fem. pl. ὁ ἡ τό the, this, that, he, she, it
ἰδίαις adj. dat. fem. pl. ἴδιος one's own, one's, privately
χερσὶν n. dat. fem. pl. χείρ hand
ὑμῶν pron. gen. 2p. pl. σύ thou, you
καθὼς adv. καθώς as, even as, according as, according to
ὑμῖν pron. dat. 2p. pl. σύ thou, you
12 ἵνα conj. ἵνα that, to, lest, for to, so that, albeit, because, for, so as
εὐσχημόνως adv. εὐσχημόνως honestly, decently
πρὸς prep. πρός (+gen) for, (+dat) at, (+acc) unto, to, with, for, against
τοὺς art. acc. masc. pl. ὁ ἡ τό the, this, that, he, she, it
ἔξω adv. ἔξω out, without, out of, forth, away, outward
καὶ conj. καί and, even, also, but
μηδενὸς num. gen. neut. sg. μηδείς μηδεμία μηδέν no man, nothing, no, none, not at all
χρείαν n. acc. fem. sg. χρεία need, necessity, lack, want
13 Οὐ particle of negation. οὐ οὐκ οὐχ not, no, neither, none, nay, nor, never, nothing
δὲ conj. δέ but, and, now, also, to the contrary, rather, then
ὑμᾶς pron. acc. 2p. pl. σύ thou, you
ἀδελφοί n. voc. masc. pl. ἀδελφός brother
περὶ prep. περί (+gen) of, for, concerning, (+acc) about, concerning, in
τῶν art. gen. masc. pl. ὁ ἡ τό the, this, that, he, she, it
ἵνα conj. ἵνα that, to, lest, for to, so that, albeit, because, for, so as
μὴ particle of negation. μή not, no, lest, neither, none, nothing, nor, never, without
καθὼς adv. καθώς as, even as, according as, according to
καὶ conj. καί and, even, also, but
οἱ art. nom. masc. pl. ὁ ἡ τό the, this, that, he, she, it
λοιποὶ adj. nom. masc. pl. λοιπός other, rest, remnant, residue, which remain
οἱ art. nom. masc. pl. ὁ ἡ τό the, this, that, he, she, it
μὴ particle of negation. μή not, no, lest, neither, none, nothing, nor, never, without
ἐλπίδα n. acc. fem. sg. ἐλπίς hope, faith
14 εἰ conj. εἰ if, whether, that, though, forasmuch
γὰρ conj. γάρ for, and, because, but, indeed

ὅτι conj. ὅτι that, for, because, how that, how, because that, for that, though
Ἰησοῦς n. nom. masc. sg. Ἰησοῦς Jesus
καὶ conj. καί and, even, also, but
οὕτω adv. οὕτω οὕτως so, even so, thus, on this wise, likewise, after this manner
καὶ conj. καί and, even, also, but
ὁ art. nom. masc. sg. ὁ ἡ τό the, this, that, he, she, it
Θεὸς n. nom. masc. sg. θεός God, god
τοὺς art. acc. masc. pl. ὁ ἡ τό the, this, that, he, she, it
διὰ prep. διά (+gen) by, through, with, in, of, (+acc) for, because of, for a cause
τοῦ art. gen. masc. sg. ὁ ἡ τό the, this, that, he, she, it
Ἰησοῦ n. gen. masc. sg. Ἰησοῦς Jesus
σὺν prep. σύν (+dat) with, beside
αὐτῷ pron. dat. masc. 3p. sg. αὐτός ή ό self, of oneself, even, very, the same, he, she, it
15 τοῦτο demo. pron. acc. neut. sg. οὗτος αὕτη τοῦτο this, the same, this same, he, she, it
γὰρ conj. γάρ for, and, because, but, indeed
ὑμῖν pron. dat. 2p. pl. σύ thou, you
ἐν prep. ἐν (+dat) in, by, with, among, at, on, through, to, within, into, of, for
λόγῳ n. dat. masc. sg. λόγος word, saying, account, speech, thing, matter
Κυρίου n. gen. masc. sg. κύριος Lord, lord, master, sir, LORD, God, Master, owner
ὅτι conj. ὅτι that, for, because, how that, how, because that, for that, though
ἡμεῖς pron. nom. 1p. pl. ἐγώ I
οἱ art. nom. masc. pl. ὁ ἡ τό the, this, that, he, she, it
οἱ art. nom. masc. pl. ὁ ἡ τό the, this, that, he, she, it
εἰς prep. εἰς (+acc) into, to, unto, for, in, on, toward, against, upon, at, among
τὴν art. acc. fem. sg. ὁ ἡ τό the, this, that, he, she, it
παρουσίαν n. acc. fem. sg. παρουσία coming, presence
τοῦ art. gen. masc. sg. ὁ ἡ τό the, this, that, he, she, it
Κυρίου n. gen. masc. sg. κύριος Lord, lord, master, sir, LORD, God, Master, owner
οὐ particle of negation. οὐ οὐκ οὐχ not, no, neither, none, nay, nor, never, nothing
μὴ particle of negation. μή not, no, lest, neither, none, nothing, nor, never, without
τοὺς art. acc. masc. pl. ὁ ἡ τό the, this, that, he, she, it
16 ὅτι conj. ὅτι that, for, because, how that, how, because that, for that, though
αὐτὸς pron. nom. masc. 3p. sg. αὐτός ή ό self, of oneself, even, very, the same, he, she, it
ὁ art. nom. masc. sg. ὁ ἡ τό the, this, that, he, she, it
Κύριος n. nom. masc. sg. κύριος Lord, lord, master, sir, LORD, God, Master, owner
ἐν prep. ἐν (+dat) in, by, with, among, at, on, through, to, within, into, of, for
κελεύσματι n. dat. neut. sg. κέλευσμα shout
ἐν prep. ἐν (+dat) in, by, with, among, at, on, through, to, within, into, of, for
φωνῇ n. dat. fem. sg. φωνή voice, sound, noise
ἀρχαγγέλου n. gen. masc. sg. ἀρχάγγελος archangel
καὶ conj. καί and, even, also, but
ἐν prep. ἐν (+dat) in, by, with, among, at, on, through, to, within, into, of, for
σάλπιγγι n. dat. fem. sg. σάλπιγξ trumpet, trump
Θεοῦ n. gen. masc. sg. θεός God, god
ἀπ' prep. ἀπό (+gen) from, of, out of, since, for, off, at, by, in, on
οὐρανοῦ n. gen. masc. sg. οὐρανός heaven, air, sky
καὶ conj. καί and, even, also, but
οἱ art. nom. masc. pl. ὁ ἡ τό the, this, that, he, she, it
νεκροὶ adj. nom. masc. pl. νεκρός dead
ἐν prep. ἐν (+dat) in, by, with, among, at, on, through, to, within, into, of, for
Χριστῷ n. dat. masc. sg. Χριστός Christ
πρῶτον adv. πρῶτον first, at the first, first of all, at first, at the beginning, before, chiefly
17 ἔπειτα adv. ἔπειτα then, after that, afterward
ἡμεῖς pron. nom. 1p. pl. ἐγώ I
οἱ art. nom. masc. pl. ὁ ἡ τό the, this, that, he, she, it

οἱ art. nom. masc. pl. ὁ ἡ τό the, this, that, he, she, it
ἅμα adv. ἅμα (+dat) together, with, also. (adv.) at the same time, together
σὺν prep. σύν (+dat) with, beside
αὐτοῖς pron. dat. masc. 3p. pl. αὐτός ή ό self, of oneself, even, very, the same, he, she, it
ἐν prep. ἐν (+dat) in, by, with, among, at, on, through, to, within, into, of, for
νεφέλαις n. dat. fem. pl. νεφέλη cloud
εἰς prep. εἰς (+acc) into, to, unto, for, in, on, toward, against, upon, at, among
ἀπάντησιν n. acc. fem. sg. ἀπάντησις meet, encounter
τοῦ art. gen. masc. sg. ὁ ἡ τό the, this, that, he, she, it
Κυρίου n. gen. masc. sg. κύριος Lord, lord, master, sir, LORD, God, Master, owner
εἰς prep. εἰς (+acc) into, to, unto, for, in, on, toward, against, upon, at, among
ἀέρα n. acc. masc. sg. ἀήρ air
καὶ conj. καί and, even, also, butand
οὕτω adv. οὕτω οὕτως so, even so, thus, on this wise, likewise, after this manner
πάντοτε adv. πάντοτε always, ever, always, evermore
σὺν prep. σύν (+dat) with, beside
Κυρίῳ n. dat. masc. sg. κύριος Lord, lord, master, sir, LORD, God, Master, owner
18 ὥστε conj. ὥστε so that, wherefore, insomuch that, therefore, that, so then
ἀλλήλους pron. acc. masc. pl. ἀλλήλων one another, themselves, together, mutual
ἐν prep. ἐν (+dat) in, by, with, among, at, on, through, to, within, into, of, for
τοῖς art. dat. masc. pl. ὁ ἡ τό the, this, that, he, she, it
λόγοις n. dat. masc. pl. λόγος word, saying, account, speech, thing, matter
τούτοις demo. pron. dat. masc. pl. οὗτος αὕτη τοῦτο this, the same, this same, he, she, it

5

1 Περὶ prep. περί (+gen) of, for, concerning, (+acc) about, concerning, in
δὲ conj. δέ but, and, now, also, to the contrary, rather, then
τῶν art. gen. masc. pl. ὁ ἡ τό the, this, that, he, she, it
χρόνων n. gen. masc. pl. χρόνος time, season, space
καὶ conj. καί and, even, also, but
τῶν art. gen. masc. pl. ὁ ἡ τό the, this, that, he, she, it
καιρῶν n. gen. masc. pl. καιρός time, season, due time, opportunity
ἀδελφοί n. voc. masc. pl. ἀδελφός brother
οὐ particle of negation. οὐ οὐκ οὐχ not, no, neither, none, nay, nor, never, nothing
χρείαν n. acc. fem. sg. χρεία need, necessity, lack, want
ὑμῖν pron. dat. 2p. pl. σύ thou, you
2 αὐτοὶ pron. nom. masc. 3p. pl. αὐτός ή ό self, of oneself, even, very, the same, he, she, it
γὰρ conj. γάρ for, and, because, but, indeed
ἀκριβῶς adv. ἀκριβῶς diligently, circumspectly, perfect, perfectly
ὅτι conj. ὅτι that, for, because, how that, how, because that, for that, though
ἡ art. nom. fem. sg. ὁ ἡ τό the, this, that, he, she, it
ἡμέρα n. nom. fem. sg. ἡμέρα day, time, year, while, age, day time
Κυρίου n. gen. masc. sg. κύριος Lord, lord, master, sir, LORD, God, Master, owner
ὡς adv. ὡς as, when, as it were, how, about, like, as soon as, even as, while
κλέπτης n. nom. masc. sg. κλέπτης thief
ἐν prep. ἐν (+dat) in, by, with, among, at, on, through, to, within, into, of, for
νυκτὶ n. dat. fem. sg. νύξ night
οὕτως adv. οὕτω οὕτως so, even so, thus, on this wise, likewise, after this manner
3 ὅταν conj. ὅταν when, as soon as, as long as, that, whensoever, while
γὰρ conj. γάρ for, and, because, but, indeed
Εἰρήνη n. nom. fem. sg. εἰρήνη peace, quietness, rest
καὶ conj. καί and, even, also, but
ἀσφάλεια n. nom. fem. sg. ἀσφάλεια certainty, safety
τότε adv. τότε then, that time

αἰφνίδιος adj. nom. masc. sg. αἰφνίδιος unawares, sudden
αὐτοῖς pron. dat. masc. 3p. pl. αὐτός ή ό self, of oneself, even, very, the same, he, she, it
ὄλεθρος n. nom. masc. sg. ὄλεθρος destruction
ὥσπερ adv. ὥσπερ as, even as, like as
ἡ art. nom. fem. sg. ὁ ἡ τό the, this, that, he, she, it
ὠδὶν n. nom. fem. sg. ὠδίν sorrow, pain, travail
τῇ art. dat. fem. sg. ὁ ἡ τό the, this, that, he, she, it
ἐν prep. ἐν (+dat) in, by, with, among, at, on, through, to, within, into, of, for
γαστρὶ n. dat. fem. sg. γαστήρ having in the womb, with child, belly, womb
καὶ conj. καί and, even, also, but
οὐ particle of negation. οὐ οὐκ οὐχ not, no, neither, none, nay, nor, never, nothing
μὴ particle of negation. μή not, no, lest, neither, none, nothing, nor, never, without
4 ὑμεῖς pron. nom. 2p. pl. σύ thou, you
δέ conj. δέ but, and, now, also, to the contrary, rather, then
ἀδελφοί n. voc. masc. pl. ἀδελφός brother
οὐκ particle of negation. οὐ οὐκ οὐχ not, no, neither, none, nay, nor, never, nothing
ἐν prep. ἐν (+dat) in, by, with, among, at, on, through, to, within, into, of, for
σκότει n. dat. neut. sg. σκότος darkness
ἵνα conj. ἵνα that, to, lest, for to, so that, albeit, because, for, so as
ἡ art. nom. fem. sg. ὁ ἡ τό the, this, that, he, she, it
ἡμέρα n. nom. fem. sg. ἡμέρα day, time, year, while, age, day time
ὑμᾶς pron. acc. 2p. pl. σύ thou, you
ὡς adv. ὡς as, when, as it were, how, about, like, as soon as, even as, while
κλέπτης n. nom. masc. sg. κλέπτης thief
5 πάντες adj. nom. masc. pl. πᾶς πᾶσα πᾶν all, every, whosoever, every one, no, whole, any
ὑμεῖς pron. nom. 2p. pl. σύ thou, you
υἱοὶ n. nom. masc. pl. υἱός son, child, descendant, offspring, heir
φωτός n. gen. neut. sg. φῶς light, fire
καὶ conj. καί and, even, also, but
υἱοὶ n. nom. masc. pl. υἱός son, child, descendant, offspring, heir
ἡμέρας n. gen. fem. sg. ἡμέρα day, time, year, while, age, day time
οὐκ particle of negation. οὐ οὐκ οὐχ not, no, neither, none, nay, nor, never, nothing
νυκτὸς n. gen. fem. sg. νύξ night
οὐδὲ adv. οὐδέ neither, nor, not, no, not even, never, not yet
σκότους n. gen. neut. sg. σκότος darkness
6 ἄρα conj. ἄρα then, therefore, haply, wherefore, perhaps, manner, no doubt, truly
οὖν conj. οὖν therefore, then, so, and, now, wherefore
μὴ particle of negation. μή not, no, lest, neither, none, nothing, nor, never, without
ὡς adv. ὡς as, when, as it were, how, about, like, as soon as, even as, while
καὶ conj. καί and, even, also, but
οἱ art. nom. masc. pl. ὁ ἡ τό the, this, that, he, she, it
λοιποί adj. nom. masc. pl. λοιπός other, rest, remnant, residue, which remain
ἀλλὰ conj. ἀλλά but, yea, yet, nevertheless, howbeit, nay, therefore
καὶ conj. καί and, even, also, but
7 οἱ art. nom. masc. pl. ὁ ἡ τό the, this, that, he, she, it
γὰρ conj. γάρ for, and, because, but, indeed
νυκτὸς n. gen. fem. sg. νύξ night
καὶ conj. καί and, even, also, but
οἱ art. nom. masc. pl. ὁ ἡ τό the, this, that, he, she, it
νυκτὸς n. gen. fem. sg. νύξ night
8 ἡμεῖς pron. nom. 1p. pl. ἐγώ I
δὲ conj. δέ but, and, now, also, to the contrary, rather, then
ἡμέρας n. gen. fem. sg. ἡμέρα day, time, year, while, age, day time
θώρακα n. acc. masc. sg. θώραξ breastplate
πίστεως n. gen. fem. sg. πίστις faith, assurance, belief, fidelity

καὶ conj. καί and, even, also, but
ἀγάπης n. gen. fem. sg. ἀγάπη love, charity, feast of charity
καὶ conj. καί and, even, also, but
περικεφαλαίαν n. acc. fem. sg. περικεφαλαία helmet
ἐλπίδα n. acc. fem. sg. ἐλπίς hope, faith
σωτηρίας n. gen. fem. sg. σωτηρία salvation, deliver, health, saving
9 ὅτι conj. ὅτι that, for, because, how that, how, because that, for that, though
οὐκ particle of negation. οὐ οὐκ οὐχ not, no, neither, none, nay, nor, never, nothing
ἡμᾶς pron. acc. 1p. pl. ἐγώ I
ὁ art. nom. masc. sg. ὁ ἡ τό the, this, that, he, she, it
Θεὸς n. nom. masc. sg. θεός God, god
εἰς prep. εἰς (+acc) into, to, unto, for, in, on, toward, against, upon, at, among
ὀργὴν n. acc. fem. sg. ὀργή wrath, anger, indignation, vengeance
ἀλλ' conj. ἀλλά but, yea, yet, nevertheless, howbeit, nay, therefore
εἰς prep. εἰς (+acc) into, to, unto, for, in, on, toward, against, upon, at, among
περιποίησιν n. acc. fem. sg. περιποίησις obtain, obtaining, purchased possession
σωτηρίας n. gen. fem. sg. σωτηρία salvation, deliver, health, saving
διὰ prep. διά (+gen) by, through, with, in, of, (+acc) for, because of, for a cause
τοῦ art. gen. masc. sg. ὁ ἡ τό the, this, that, he, she, it
Κυρίου n. gen. masc. sg. κύριος Lord, lord, master, sir, LORD, God, Master, owner
ἡμῶν pron. gen. 1p. pl. ἐγώ I
Ἰησοῦ n. gen. masc. sg. Ἰησοῦς Jesus
Χριστοῦ n. gen. masc. sg. Χριστός Christ
10 τοῦ art. gen. masc. sg. ὁ ἡ τό the, this, that, he, she, it
ὑπὲρ prep. ὑπέρ (+gen) for, of, for the sake of, (+acc) above, more than
ἡμῶν pron. gen. 1p. pl. ἐγώ I
ἵνα conj. ἵνα that, to, lest, for to, so that, albeit, because, for, so as
εἴτε conj. εἴτε whether
εἴτε conj. εἴτε whether
ἅμα adv. ἅμα (+dat) together, with, also. (adv.) at the same time, together
σὺν prep. σύν (+dat) with, beside
αὐτῷ pron. dat. masc. 3p. sg. αὐτός ή ό self, of oneself, even, very, the same, he, she, it
11 διὸ conj. διό wherefore, therefore, for which cause
ἀλλήλους pron. acc. masc. pl. ἀλλήλων one another, themselves, together, mutual
καὶ conj. καί and, even, also, but
εἷς num. nom. masc. sg. εἷς or ἕν one, other, some, any, only, a certain
τὸν art. acc. masc. sg. ὁ ἡ τό the, this, that, he, she, it
ἕνα num. acc. masc. sg. εἷς or ἕν one, other, some, any, only, a certain
καθὼς adv. καθώς as, even as, according as, according to
καὶ conj. καί and, even, also, but
12 δὲ conj. δέ but, and, now, also, to the contrary, rather, then
ὑμᾶς pron. acc. 2p. pl. σύ thou, you
ἀδελφοί n. voc. masc. pl. ἀδελφός brother
τοὺς art. acc. masc. pl. ὁ ἡ τό the, this, that, he, she, it
ἐν prep. ἐν (+dat) in, by, with, among, at, on, through, to, within, into, of, for
ὑμῖν pron. dat. 2p. pl. σύ thou, you
καὶ conj. καί and, even, also, but
ὑμῶν pron. gen. 2p. pl. σύ thou, you
ἐν prep. ἐν (+dat) in, by, with, among, at, on, through, to, within, into, of, for
Κυρίῳ n. dat. masc. sg. κύριος Lord, lord, master, sir, LORD, God, Master, owner
καὶ conj. καί and, even, also, but
ὑμᾶς pron. acc. 2p. pl. σύ thou, you
13 καὶ conj. καί and, even, also, but
αὐτοὺς pron. acc. masc. 3p. pl. αὐτός ή ό self, of oneself, even, very, the same, he, she, it
ὑπὲρ prep. ὑπέρ (+gen) for, of, for the sake of, (+acc) above, more than

ἐκ prep. ἐκ ἐξ (+gen) of, from, out of, by, on, with, in, among, through
περισσοῦ adj. gen. neut. sg. περισσός more, beyond measure, advantage, exceedingly
ἐν prep. ἐν (+dat) in, by, with, among, at, on, through, to, within, into, of, for
ἀγάπῃ n. dat. fem. sg. ἀγάπη love, charity, feast of charity
διὰ prep. διά (+gen) by, through, with, in, of, (+acc) for, because of, for a cause
τὸ art. acc. neut. sg. ὁ ἡ τό the, this, that, he, she, it
ἔργον n. acc. neut. sg. ἔργον work, deed, doing labour
αὐτῶν pron. gen. masc. 3p. pl. αὐτός ἡ ὁ self, of oneself, even, very, the same, he, she, it
ἐν prep. ἐν (+dat) in, by, with, among, at, on, through, to, within, into, of, for
ἑαυτοῖς reflexive pron. dat. masc. 3p. pl. ἑαυτοῦ himself, herself, itself, yourself, ourselves
14 δὲ conj. δέ but, and, now, also, to the contrary, rather, then
ὑμᾶς pron. acc. 2p. pl. σύ thou, you
ἀδελφοί n. voc. masc. pl. ἀδελφός brother
τοὺς art. acc. masc. pl. ὁ ἡ τό the, this, that, he, she, it
ἀτάκτους adj. acc. masc. pl. ἄτακτος unruly
τοὺς art. acc. masc. pl. ὁ ἡ τό the, this, that, he, she, it
ὀλιγοψύχους adj. acc. masc. pl. ὀλιγόψυχος feebleminded
τῶν art. gen. masc. pl. ὁ ἡ τό the, this, that, he, she, it
ἀσθενῶν adj. gen. masc. pl. ἀσθενής weak, sick, impotent, more feeble
πρὸς prep. πρός (+gen) for, (+dat) at, (+acc) unto, to, with, for, against
πάντας adj. acc. masc. pl. πᾶς πᾶσα πᾶν all, every, whosoever, every one, no, whole, any
15 μή particle of negation. μή not, no, lest, neither, none, nothing, nor, never, without
τις indefinite pron. nom. masc. sg. τὶς certain, some, any man, one, any thing
κακὸν adj. acc. neut. sg. κακός evil, evil thing, noisome, wicked
ἀντὶ prep. ἀντί (+gen) for, because, in the room
κακοῦ adj. gen. neut. sg. κακός evil, evil thing, noisome, wicked
τινι indefinite pron. dat. masc. sg. τὶς certain, some, any man, one, any thing
ἀλλὰ conj. ἀλλά but, yea, yet, nevertheless, howbeit, nay, therefore
πάντοτε adv. πάντοτε always, ever, always, evermore
τὸ art. acc. neut. sg. ὁ ἡ τό the, this, that, he, she, it
ἀγαθὸν adj. acc. neut. sg. ἀγαθός good, good thing, that which is good, well
καὶ conj. καί and, even, also, but
εἰς prep. εἰς (+acc) into, to, unto, for, in, on, toward, against, upon, at, among
ἀλλήλους pron. acc. masc. pl. ἀλλήλων one another, themselves, together, mutual
καὶ conj. καί and, even, also, but
εἰς prep. εἰς (+acc) into, to, unto, for, in, on, toward, against, upon, at, among
πάντας adj. acc. masc. pl. πᾶς πᾶσα πᾶν all, every, whosoever, every one, no, whole, any
16 πάντοτε adv. πάντοτε always, ever, always, evermore
17 ἀδιαλείπτως adv. ἀδιαλείπτως without ceasing
18 ἐν prep. ἐν (+dat) in, by, with, among, at, on, through, to, within, into, of, for
παντὶ adj. dat. neut. sg. πᾶς πᾶσα πᾶν all, every, whosoever, every one, no, whole, any
τοῦτο demo. pron. nom. neut. sg. οὗτος αὕτη τοῦτο this, the same, this same, he, she, it
γὰρ conj. γάρ for, and, because, but, indeed
θέλημα n. nom. neut. sg. θέλημα will, desire, pleasure
Θεοῦ n. gen. masc. sg. θεός God, god
ἐν prep. ἐν (+dat) in, by, with, among, at, on, through, to, within, into, of, for
Χριστῷ n. dat. masc. sg. Χριστός Christ
Ἰησοῦ n. dat. masc. sg. Ἰησοῦς Jesus
εἰς prep. εἰς (+acc) into, to, unto, for, in, on, toward, against, upon, at, among
ὑμᾶς pron. acc. 2p. pl. σύ thou, you
19 τὸ art. acc. neut. sg. ὁ ἡ τό the, this, that, he, she, it
Πνεῦμα n. acc. neut. sg. πνεῦμα spirit, Spirit, Ghost, ghost, life. of the spirit, wind
μὴ particle of negation. μή not, no, lest, neither, none, nothing, nor, never, without
20 προφητείας n. acc. fem. pl. προφητεία prophecy, prophesying
μὴ particle of negation. μή not, no, lest, neither, none, nothing, nor, never, without

21 πάντα adj. acc. neut. pl. πᾶς πᾶσα πᾶν all, every, whosoever, every one, no, whole, any
τὸ art. acc. neut. sg. ὁ ἡ τό the, this, that, he, she, it
καλὸν adj. acc. neut. sg. καλός good, better, goodly, meet, honest, fair, well, worthy
22 ἀπὸ prep. ἀπό (+gen) from, of, out of, since, for, off, at, by, in, on
παντὸς adj. gen. neut. sg. πᾶς πᾶσα πᾶν all, every, whosoever, every one, no, whole, any
εἴδους n. gen. neut. sg. εἶδος shape, appearance, fashion, sight
πονηροῦ adj. gen. neut. sg. πονηρός evil, wicked, bad
23 Αὐτὸς pron. nom. masc. 3p. sg. αὐτός ή ό self, of oneself, even, very, the same, he, she, it
δὲ conj. δέ but, and, now, also, to the contrary, rather, then
ὁ art. nom. masc. sg. ὁ ἡ τό the, this, that, he, she, it
Θεὸς n. nom. masc. sg. θεός God, god
τῆς art. gen. fem. sg. ὁ ἡ τό the, this, that, he, she, it
εἰρήνης n. gen. fem. sg. εἰρήνη peace, quietness, rest
ὑμᾶς pron. acc. 2p. pl. σύ thou, you
ὁλοτελεῖς adj. acc. masc. pl. ὁλοτελής wholly
καὶ conj. καί and, even, also, but
ὁλόκληρον adj. nom. neut. sg. ὁλόκληρος whole, entire
ὑμῶν pron. gen. 2p. pl. σύ thou, you
τὸ art. nom. neut. sg. ὁ ἡ τό the, this, that, he, she, it
πνεῦμα n. nom. neut. sg. πνεῦμα spirit, Spirit, Ghost, ghost, life. of the spirit, wind
καὶ conj. καί and, even, also, but
ἡ art. nom. fem. sg. ὁ ἡ τό the, this, that, he, she, it
ψυχὴ n. nom. fem. sg. ψυχή life, soul, mind, heart
καὶ conj. καί and, even, also, but
τὸ art. nom. neut. sg. ὁ ἡ τό the, this, that, he, she, it
σῶμα n. nom. neut. sg. σῶμα body, bodily, slave
ἀμέμπτως adv. ἀμέμπτως unblameably, blameless
ἐν prep. ἐν (+dat) in, by, with, among, at, on, through, to, within, into, of, for
τῇ art. dat. fem. sg. ὁ ἡ τό the, this, that, he, she, it
παρουσίᾳ n. dat. fem. sg. παρουσία coming, presence
τοῦ art. gen. masc. sg. ὁ ἡ τό the, this, that, he, she, it
Κυρίου n. gen. masc. sg. κύριος Lord, lord, master, sir, LORD, God, Master, owner
ἡμῶν pron. gen. 1p. pl. ἐγώ I
Ἰησοῦ n. gen. masc. sg. Ἰησοῦς Jesus
Χριστοῦ n. gen. masc. sg. Χριστός Christ
24 πιστὸς adj. nom. masc. sg. πιστός faithful, believing, true, sure
ὁ art. nom. masc. sg. ὁ ἡ τό the, this, that, he, she, it
ὑμᾶς pron. acc. 2p. pl. σύ thou, you
ὃς relative pron. nom. masc. sg. ὅς ἥ ὅ who, which, what, that
καὶ conj. καί and, even, also, but
25 Ἀδελφοί n. voc. masc. pl. ἀδελφός brother
περὶ prep. περί (+gen) of, for, concerning, (+acc) about, concerning, in
ἡμῶν pron. gen. 1p. pl. ἐγώ I
26 τοὺς art. acc. masc. pl. ὁ ἡ τό the, this, that, he, she, it
ἀδελφοὺς n. acc. masc. pl. ἀδελφός brother
πάντας adj. acc. masc. pl. πᾶς πᾶσα πᾶν all, every, whosoever, every one, no, whole, any
ἐν prep. ἐν (+dat) in, by, with, among, at, on, through, to, within, into, of, for
φιλήματι n. dat. neut. sg. φίλημα kiss
ἁγίῳ adj. dat. neut. sg. ἅγιος Holy, holy, saint, Holy One, holy thing, most holy
27 ὑμᾶς pron. acc. 2p. pl. σύ thou, you
τὸν art. acc. masc. sg. ὁ ἡ τό the, this, that, he, she, it
Κύριον n. acc. masc. sg. κύριος Lord, lord, master, sir, LORD, God, Master, owner
τὴν art. acc. fem. sg. ὁ ἡ τό the, this, that, he, she, it
ἐπιστολὴν n. acc. fem. sg. ἐπιστολή letter, epistle
πᾶσι adj. dat. masc. pl. πᾶς πᾶσα πᾶν all, every, whosoever, every one, no, whole, any

τοῖς art. dat. masc. pl. ὁ ἡ τό the, this, that, he, she, it
ἁγίοις adj. dat. masc. pl. ἅγιος Holy, holy, saint, Holy One, holy thing, most holy
ἀδελφοῖς n. dat. masc. pl. ἀδελφός brother
28 Ἡ art. nom. fem. sg. ὁ ἡ τό the, this, that, he, she, it
χάρις n. nom. fem. sg. χάρις grace, thank, favour, pleasure
τοῦ art. gen. masc. sg. ὁ ἡ τό the, this, that, he, she, it
Κυρίου n. gen. masc. sg. κύριος Lord, lord, master, sir, LORD, God, Master, owner
ἡμῶν pron. gen. 1p. pl. ἐγώ I
Ἰησοῦ n. gen. masc. sg. Ἰησοῦς Jesus
Χριστοῦ n. gen. masc. sg. Χριστός Christ
μεθ' prep. μετά (+gen) with, among, against, (+acc) after
ὑμῶν pron. gen. 2p. pl. σύ thou, you
ἀμήν particle. ἀμήν amen, verily

ΠΑΥΛΟΥ ΤΟΥ ΑΠΟΣΤΟΛΟΥ
Η ΠΡΟΣ
ΘΕΣΣΑΛΟΝΙΚΕΙΣ
ΕΠΙΣΤΟΛΗ ΔΕΥΤΕΡΑ

1

1 Παῦλος n. nom. masc. sg. Παῦλος Paul, Paulus
καὶ conj. καί and, even, also, but
Σιλουανὸς n. nom. masc. sg. Σιλουανός Silvanus
καὶ conj. καί and, even, also, but
Τιμόθεος n. nom. masc. sg. Τιμόθεος Timotheus, Timothy
τῇ art. dat. fem. sg. ὁ ἡ τό the, this, that, he, she, it
ἐκκλησίᾳ n. dat. fem. sg. ἐκκλησία church, assembly
Θεσσαλονικέων n. gen. masc. pl. Θεσσαλονικεύς Thessalonian, of Thessalonica
ἐν prep. ἐν (+dat) in, by, with, among, at, on, through, to, within, into, of, for
Θεῷ n. dat. masc. sg. θεός God, god
πατρὶ n. dat. masc. sg. πατήρ Father, father, parent
ἡμῶν pron. gen. 1p. pl. ἐγώ I
καὶ conj. καί and, even, also, but
Κυρίῳ n. dat. masc. sg. κύριος Lord, lord, master, sir, LORD, God, Master, owner
Ἰησοῦ n. dat. masc. sg. Ἰησοῦς Jesus
Χριστῷ n. dat. masc. sg. Χριστός Christ
2 χάρις n. nom. fem. sg. χάρις grace, thank, favour, pleasure
ὑμῖν pron. dat. 2p. pl. σύ thou, you
καὶ conj. καί and, even, also, but
εἰρήνη n. nom. fem. sg. εἰρήνη peace, quietness, rest
ἀπὸ prep. ἀπό (+gen) from, of, out of, since, for, off, at, by, in, on
Θεοῦ n. gen. masc. sg. θεός God, god
πατρὸς n. gen. masc. sg. πατήρ Father, father, parent
ἡμῶν pron. gen. 1p. pl. ἐγώ I
καὶ conj. καί and, even, also, but
Κυρίου n. gen. masc. sg. κύριος Lord, lord, master, sir, LORD, God, Master, owner
Ἰησοῦ n. gen. masc. sg. Ἰησοῦς Jesus
Χριστοῦ n. gen. masc. sg. Χριστός Christ
3 τῷ art. dat. masc. sg. ὁ ἡ τό the, this, that, he, she, it
Θεῷ n. dat. masc. sg. θεός God, god
πάντοτε adv. πάντοτε always, ever, always, evermore
περὶ prep. περί (+gen) of, for, concerning, (+acc) about, concerning, in
ὑμῶν pron. gen. 2p. pl. σύ thou, you
ἀδελφοί n. voc. masc. pl. ἀδελφός brother
καθὼς adv. καθώς as, even as, according as, according to
ἄξιόν adj. nom. neut. sg. ἄξιος worthy, meet, due reward
ὅτι conj. ὅτι that, for, because, how that, how, because that, for that, though
ἡ art. nom. fem. sg. ὁ ἡ τό the, this, that, he, she, it
πίστις n. nom. fem. sg. πίστις faith, assurance, belief, fidelity
ὑμῶν pron. gen. 2p. pl. σύ thou, you
καὶ conj. καί and, even, also, but
ἡ art. nom. fem. sg. ὁ ἡ τό the, this, that, he, she, it
ἀγάπη n. nom. fem. sg. ἀγάπη love, charity, feast of charity
ἑνὸς num. gen. masc. sg. εἷς or ἕν one, other, some, any, only, a certain
ἑκάστου adj. gen. masc. sg. ἕκαστος every man, every, every one, any man, each
πάντων adj. gen. masc. pl. πᾶς πᾶσα πᾶν all, every, whosoever, every one, no, whole, any

ὑμῶν pron. gen. 2p. pl. σύ thou, you
εἰς prep. εἰς (+acc) into, to, unto, for, in, on, toward, against, upon, at, among
ἀλλήλους pron. acc. masc. pl. ἀλλήλων one another, themselves, together, mutual
4 ὥστε conj. ὥστε so that, wherefore, insomuch that, therefore, that, so then
ἡμᾶς pron. acc. 1p. pl. ἐγώ I
αὐτοὺς pron. acc. masc. 1p. pl. αὐτός ἡ ὁ self, of oneself, even, very, the same, he, she, it
ἐν prep. ἐν (+dat) in, by, with, among, at, on, through, to, within, into, of, for
ὑμῖν pron. dat. 2p. pl. σύ thou, you
ἐν prep. ἐν (+dat) in, by, with, among, at, on, through, to, within, into, of, for
ταῖς art. dat. fem. pl. ὁ ἡ τό the, this, that, he, she, it
ἐκκλησίαις n. dat. fem. pl. ἐκκλησία church, assembly
τοῦ art. gen. masc. sg. ὁ ἡ τό the, this, that, he, she, it
Θεοῦ n. gen. masc. sg. θεός God, god
ὑπὲρ prep. ὑπέρ (+gen) for, of, for the sake of, (+acc) above, more than
τῆς art. gen. fem. sg. ὁ ἡ τό the, this, that, he, she, it
ὑπομονῆς n. gen. fem. sg. ὑπομονή patience, enduring
ὑμῶν pron. gen. 2p. pl. σύ thou, you
καὶ conj. καί and, even, also, but
πίστεως n. gen. fem. sg. πίστις faith, assurance, belief, fidelity
ἐν prep. ἐν (+dat) in, by, with, among, at, on, through, to, within, into, of, for
πᾶσι adj. dat. masc. pl. πᾶς πᾶσα πᾶν all, every, whosoever, every one, no, whole, any
τοῖς art. dat. masc. pl. ὁ ἡ τό the, this, that, he, she, it
διωγμοῖς n. dat. masc. pl. διωγμός persecution
ὑμῶν pron. gen. 2p. pl. σύ thou, you
καὶ conj. καί and, even, also, but
ταῖς art. dat. fem. pl. ὁ ἡ τό the, this, that, he, she, it
θλίψεσιν n. dat. fem. pl. θλῖψις tribulation, affliction, anguish, persecution
αἷς relative pron. dat. fem. pl. ὅς ἥ ὅ who, which, what, that
5 ἔνδειγμα n. nom. neut. sg. ἔνδειγμα manifest token
τῆς art. gen. fem. sg. ὁ ἡ τό the, this, that, he, she, it
δικαίας adj. gen. fem. sg. δίκαιος righteous, just, meet, right
κρίσεως n. gen. fem. sg. κρίσις judgment, damnation, accusation, condemnation
τοῦ art. gen. masc. sg. ὁ ἡ τό the, this, that, he, she, it
Θεοῦ n. gen. masc. sg. θεός God, god
εἰς prep. εἰς (+acc) into, to, unto, for, in, on, toward, against, upon, at, among
τὸ art. acc. neut. sg. ὁ ἡ τό the, this, that, he, she, it
ὑμᾶς pron. acc. 2p. pl. σύ thou, you
τῆς art. gen. fem. sg. ὁ ἡ τό the, this, that, he, she, it
βασιλείας n. gen. fem. sg. βασιλεία kingdom, reign
τοῦ art. gen. masc. sg. ὁ ἡ τό the, this, that, he, she, it
Θεοῦ n. gen. masc. sg. θεός God, god
ὑπὲρ prep. ὑπέρ (+gen) for, of, for the sake of, (+acc) above, more than
ἧς relative pron. gen. fem. sg. ὅς ἥ ὅ who, which, what, that
καὶ conj. καί and, even, also, but
6 εἴπερ conj. εἴπερ if it be so that, if indeed, since indeed, since, although indeed
δίκαιον adj. nom. neut. sg. δίκαιος righteous, just, meet, right
παρὰ prep. παρά (+gen) of, from, (+dat) with, for, (+acc) beside, at, by, above, against
Θεῷ n. dat. masc. sg. θεός God, god
τοῖς art. dat. masc. pl. ὁ ἡ τό the, this, that, he, she, it
ὑμᾶς pron. acc. 2p. pl. σύ thou, you
θλῖψιν n. acc. fem. sg. θλῖψις tribulation, affliction, anguish, persecution
7 καὶ conj. καί and, even, also, but
ὑμῖν pron. dat. 2p. pl. σύ thou, you
τοῖς art. dat. masc. pl. ὁ ἡ τό the, this, that, he, she, it
ἄνεσιν n. acc. fem. sg. ἄνεσις liberty, rest, eased

μεθ' prep. μετά (+gen) with, among, against, (+acc) after
ἡμῶν pron. gen. 1p. pl. ἐγώ I
ἐν prep. ἐν (+dat) in, by, with, among, at, on, through, to, within, into, of, for
τῇ art. dat. fem. sg. ὁ ἡ τό the, this, that, he, she, it
ἀποκαλύψει n. dat. fem. sg. ἀποκάλυψις revelation, appearing, coming, manifestation
τοῦ art. gen. masc. sg. ὁ ἡ τό the, this, that, he, she, it
Κυρίου n. gen. masc. sg. κύριος Lord, lord, master, sir, LORD, God, Master, owner
Ἰησοῦ n. gen. masc. sg. Ἰησοῦς Jesus
ἀπ' prep. ἀπό (+gen) from, of, out of, since, for, off, at, by, in, on
οὐρανοῦ n. gen. masc. sg. οὐρανός heaven, air, sky
μετ' prep. μετά (+gen) with, among, against, (+acc) after
ἀγγέλων n. gen. masc. pl. ἄγγελος angel, messenger
δυνάμεως n. gen. fem. sg. δύναμις power, mighty work, miracle, strength, might
αὐτοῦ pron. gen. masc. 3p. sg. αὐτός ἡ ὁ self, of oneself, even, very, the same, he, she, it
8 ἐν prep. ἐν (+dat) in, by, with, among, at, on, through, to, within, into, of, for
πυρὶ n. dat. neut. sg. πῦρ fire, fiery
φλογός n. gen. fem. sg. φλόξ flame, flaming
ἐκδίκησιν n. acc. fem. sg. ἐκδίκησις vengeance, punishment, revenge
τοῖς art. dat. masc. pl. ὁ ἡ τό the, this, that, he, she, it
μὴ particle of negation. μή not, no, lest, neither, none, nothing, nor, never, without
Θεὸν n. acc. masc. sg. θεός God, god
καὶ conj. καί and, even, also, but
τοῖς art. dat. masc. pl. ὁ ἡ τό the, this, that, he, she, it
μὴ particle of negation. μή not, no, lest, neither, none, nothing, nor, never, without
τῷ art. dat. neut. sg. ὁ ἡ τό the, this, that, he, she, it
εὐαγγελίῳ n. dat. neut. sg. εὐαγγέλιον gospel
τοῦ art. gen. masc. sg. ὁ ἡ τό the, this, that, he, she, it
Κυρίου n. gen. masc. sg. κύριος Lord, lord, master, sir, LORD, God, Master, owner
ἡμῶν pron. gen. 1p. pl. ἐγώ I
Ἰησοῦ n. gen. masc. sg. Ἰησοῦς Jesus
Χριστοῦ n. gen. masc. sg. Χριστός Christ
9 οἵτινες relative pron. nom. masc. pl. ὅστις which, who, whosoever, that, whatsoever
δίκην n. acc. fem. sg. δίκη judgment, vengeance, punish
ὄλεθρον n. acc. masc. sg. ὄλεθρος destruction
αἰώνιον adj. acc. masc. sg. αἰώνιος eternal, everlasting, world, for ever
ἀπὸ prep. ἀπό (+gen) from, of, out of, since, for, off, at, by, in, on
προσώπου n. gen. neut. sg. πρόσωπον face, presence, person, countenance
τοῦ art. gen. masc. sg. ὁ ἡ τό the, this, that, he, she, it
Κυρίου n. gen. masc. sg. κύριος Lord, lord, master, sir, LORD, God, Master, owner
καὶ conj. καί and, even, also, but
ἀπὸ prep. ἀπό (+gen) from, of, out of, since, for, off, at, by, in, on
τῆς art. gen. fem. sg. ὁ ἡ τό the, this, that, he, she, it
δόξης n. gen. fem. sg. δόξα glory, honour, praise, dignity, worship
τῆς art. gen. fem. sg. ὁ ἡ τό the, this, that, he, she, it
ἰσχύος n. gen. fem. sg. ἰσχύς strength, might, power, ability
αὐτοῦ pron. gen. masc. 3p. sg. αὐτός ἡ ὁ self, of oneself, even, very, the same, he, she, it
10 ὅταν conj. ὅταν when, as soon as, as long as, that, whensoever, while
ἐν prep. ἐν (+dat) in, by, with, among, at, on, through, to, within, into, of, for
τοῖς art. dat. masc. pl. ὁ ἡ τό the, this, that, he, she, it
ἁγίοις adj. dat. masc. pl. ἅγιος Holy, holy, saint, Holy One, holy thing, most holy
αὐτοῦ pron. gen. masc. 3p. sg. αὐτός ἡ ὁ self, of oneself, even, very, the same, he, she, it
καὶ conj. καί and, even, also, but
ἐν prep. ἐν (+dat) in, by, with, among, at, on, through, to, within, into, of, for
πᾶσι adj. dat. masc. pl. πᾶς πᾶσα πᾶν all, every, whosoever, every one, no, whole, any
τοῖς art. dat. masc. pl. ὁ ἡ τό the, this, that, he, she, it

ὅτι conj. ὅτι that, for, because, how that, how, because that, for that, though
τὸ art. nom. neut. sg. ὁ ἡ τό the, this, that, he, she, it
μαρτύριον n. nom. neut. sg. μαρτύριον testimony, witness
ἡμῶν pron. gen. 1p. pl. ἐγώ I
ἐφ' prep. ἐπί (+gen) on, in, upon, (+dat) in, at, for, upon, (+acc) on, upon, unto, to, against
ὑμᾶς pron. acc. 2p. pl. σύ thou, you
ἐν prep. ἐν (+dat) in, by, with, among, at, on, through, to, within, into, of, for
τῇ art. dat. fem. sg. ὁ ἡ τό the, this, that, he, she, it
ἡμέρᾳ n. dat. fem. sg. ἡμέρα day, time, year, while, age, day time
ἐκείνῃ demo. pron. dat. fem. sg. ἐκεῖνος that, he, the same, that same
11 εἰς prep. εἰς (+acc) into, to, unto, for, in, on, toward, against, upon, at, among
ὃ relative pron. acc. neut. sg. ὅς ἥ ὅ who, which, what, that
καὶ conj. καί and, even, also, but
πάντοτε adv. πάντοτε always, ever, always, evermore
περὶ prep. περί (+gen) of, for, concerning, (+acc) about, concerning, in
ὑμῶν pron. gen. 2p. pl. σύ thou, you
ἵνα conj. ἵνα that, to, lest, for to, so that, albeit, because, for, so as
ὑμᾶς pron. acc. 2p. pl. σύ thou, you
τῆς art. gen. fem. sg. ὁ ἡ τό the, this, that, he, she, it
κλήσεως n. gen. fem. sg. κλῆσις calling, vocation
ὁ art. nom. masc. sg. ὁ ἡ τό the, this, that, he, she, it
Θεὸς n. nom. masc. sg. θεός God, god
ἡμῶν pron. gen. 1p. pl. ἐγώ I
καὶ conj. καί and, even, also, but
πᾶσαν adj. acc. fem. sg. πᾶς πᾶσα πᾶν all, every, whosoever, every one, no, whole, any
εὐδοκίαν n. acc. fem. sg. εὐδοκία good pleasure, good will, desire
ἀγαθωσύνης n. gen. fem. sg. ἀγαθωσύνη goodness
καὶ conj. καί and, even, also, but
ἔργον n. acc. neut. sg. ἔργον work, deed, doing labour
πίστεως n. gen. fem. sg. πίστις faith, assurance, belief, fidelity
ἐν prep. ἐν (+dat) in, by, with, among, at, on, through, to, within, into, of, for
δυνάμει n. dat. fem. sg. δύναμις power, mighty work, miracle, strength, might
12 ὅπως adv. ὅπως that, how, to, because, so that, when
τὸ art. nom. neut. sg. ὁ ἡ τό the, this, that, he, she, it
ὄνομα n. nom. neut. sg. ὄνομα name, call, surname
τοῦ art. gen. masc. sg. ὁ ἡ τό the, this, that, he, she, it
Κυρίου n. gen. masc. sg. κύριος Lord, lord, master, sir, LORD, God, Master, owner
ἡμῶν pron. gen. 1p. pl. ἐγώ I
Ἰησοῦ n. gen. masc. sg. Ἰησοῦς Jesus
Χριστοῦ n. gen. masc. sg. Χριστός Christ
ἐν prep. ἐν (+dat) in, by, with, among, at, on, through, to, within, into, of, for
ὑμῖν pron. dat. 2p. pl. σύ thou, you
καὶ conj. καί and, even, also, but
ὑμεῖς pron. nom. 2p. pl. σύ thou, you
ἐν prep. ἐν (+dat) in, by, with, among, at, on, through, to, within, into, of, for
αὐτῷ pron. dat. masc. 3p. sg. αὐτός ή ό self, of oneself, even, very, the same, he, she, it
κατὰ prep. κατά (+gen) against, by, throughout, down, (+acc) according to, after, with
τὴν art. acc. fem. sg. ὁ ἡ τό the, this, that, he, she, it
χάριν n. acc. fem. sg. χάρις grace, thank, favour, pleasure
τοῦ art. gen. masc. sg. ὁ ἡ τό the, this, that, he, she, it
Θεοῦ n. gen. masc. sg. θεός God, god
ἡμῶν pron. gen. 1p. pl. ἐγώ I
καὶ conj. καί and, even, also, but
Κυρίου n. gen. masc. sg. κύριος Lord, lord, master, sir, LORD, God, Master, owner
Ἰησοῦ n. gen. masc. sg. Ἰησοῦς Jesus

Χριστοῦ n. gen. masc. sg. Χριστός Christ

2

1 δὲ conj. δέ but, and, now, also, to the contrary, rather, then
ὑμᾶς pron. acc. 2p. pl. σύ thou, you
ἀδελφοί n. voc. masc. pl. ἀδελφός brother
ὑπὲρ prep. ὑπέρ (+gen) for, of, for the sake of, (+acc) above, more than
τῆς art. gen. fem. sg. ὁ ἡ τό the, this, that, he, she, it
παρουσίας n. gen. fem. sg. παρουσία coming, presence
τοῦ art. gen. masc. sg. ὁ ἡ τό the, this, that, he, she, it
Κυρίου n. gen. masc. sg. κύριος Lord, lord, master, sir, LORD, God, Master, owner
ἡμῶν pron. gen. 1p. pl. ἐγώ I
Ἰησοῦ n. gen. masc. sg. Ἰησοῦς Jesus
Χριστοῦ n. gen. masc. sg. Χριστός Christ
καὶ conj. καί and, even, also, but
ἡμῶν pron. gen. 1p. pl. ἐγώ I
ἐπισυναγωγῆς n. gen. fem. sg. ἐπισυναγωγή gathering together, assembling together
ἐπ' prep. ἐπί (+gen) on, in, upon, (+dat) in, at, for, upon, (+acc) on, upon, unto, to, against
αὐτὸν pron. acc. masc. 3p. sg. αὐτός ή ό self, of oneself, even, very, the same, he, she, it
2 εἰς prep. εἰς (+acc) into, to, unto, for, in, on, toward, against, upon, at, among
τὸ art. acc. neut. sg. ὁ ἡ τό the, this, that, he, she, it
μὴ particle of negation. μή not, no, lest, neither, none, nothing, nor, never, without
ταχέως adv. ταχέως sortly, quickly, soon, hastily, suddenly
ὑμᾶς pron. acc. 2p. pl. σύ thou, you
ἀπὸ prep. ἀπό (+gen) from, of, out of, since, for, off, at, by, in, on
τοῦ art. gen. masc. sg. ὁ ἡ τό the, this, that, he, she, it
νοὸς n. gen. masc. sg. νοῦς understanding, mind
μήτε conj. μήτε neither, nor, so much as, or
μήτε conj. μήτε neither, nor, so much as, or
διὰ prep. διά (+gen) by, through, with, in, of, (+acc) for, because of, for a cause
πνεύματος n. gen. neut. sg. πνεῦμα spirit, Spirit, Ghost, ghost, life. of the spirit, wind
μήτε conj. μήτε neither, nor, so much as, or
διὰ prep. διά (+gen) by, through, with, in, of, (+acc) for, because of, for a cause
λόγου n. gen. masc. sg. λόγος word, saying, account, speech, thing, matter
μήτε conj. μήτε neither, nor, so much as, or
δι' prep. διά (+gen) by, through, with, in, of, (+acc) for, because of, for a cause
ἐπιστολῆς n. gen. fem. sg. ἐπιστολή letter, epistle
ὡς adv. ὡς as, when, as it were, how, about, like, as soon as, even as, while
δι' prep. διά (+gen) by, through, with, in, of, (+acc) for, because of, for a cause
ἡμῶν pron. gen. 1p. pl. ἐγώ I
ὡς adv. ὡς as, when, as it were, how, about, like, as soon as, even as, while
ὅτι conj. ὅτι that, for, because, how that, how, because that, for that, though
ἡ art. nom. fem. sg. ὁ ἡ τό the, this, that, he, she, it
ἡμέρα n. nom. fem. sg. ἡμέρα day, time, year, while, age, day time
τοῦ art. gen. masc. sg. ὁ ἡ τό the, this, that, he, she, it
Χριστοῦ n. gen. masc. sg. Χριστός Christ
3 μὴ particle of negation. μή not, no, lest, neither, none, nothing, nor, never, without
τις indefinite pron. nom. masc. sg. τὶς certain, some, any man, one, any thing
ὑμᾶς pron. acc. 2p. pl. σύ thou, you
κατὰ prep. κατά (+gen) against, by, throughout, down, (+acc) according to, after, with
μηδένα num. acc. masc. sg. μηδείς μηδεμία μηδέν no man, nothing, no, none, not at all
τρόπον n. acc. masc. sg. τρόπος as, manner, means, way, conversation
ὅτι conj. ὅτι that, for, because, how that, how, because that, for that, though
ἐὰν conj. ἐάν if, soever, except, though, and if, but, whether, if so, so

μὴ particle of negation. μή not, no, lest, neither, none, nothing, nor, never, without
ἡ art. nom. fem. sg. ὁ ἡ τό the, this, that, he, she, it
ἀποστασία n. nom. fem. sg. ἀποστασία falling away, apostasy, forsake
πρῶτον adv. πρῶτον first, at the first, first of all, at first, at the beginning, before, chiefly
καὶ conj. καί and, even, also, but
ὁ art. nom. masc. sg. ὁ ἡ τό the, this, that, he, she, it
ἄνθρωπος n. nom. masc. sg. ἄνθρωπος man, human being, person, one, certain
τῆς art. gen. fem. sg. ὁ ἡ τό the, this, that, he, she, it
ἁμαρτίας n. gen. fem. sg. ἁμαρτία sin, offence, sinful
ὁ art. nom. masc. sg. ὁ ἡ τό the, this, that, he, she, it
υἱὸς n. nom. masc. sg. υἱός son, child, descendant, offspring, heir
τῆς art. gen. fem. sg. ὁ ἡ τό the, this, that, he, she, it
ἀπωλείας n. gen. fem. sg. ἀπώλεια destruction, perdition, waste, damnation
4 ὁ art. nom. masc. sg. ὁ ἡ τό the, this, that, he, she, it
καὶ conj. καί and, even, also, but
ἐπὶ prep. ἐπί (+gen) on, in, upon, (+dat) in, at, for, upon, (+acc) on, upon, unto, to, against
πᾶν adj. acc. neut. sg. πᾶς πᾶσα πᾶν all, every, whosoever, every one, no, whole, any
τὸ art. acc. neut. sg. ὁ ἡ τό the, this, that, he, she, it
Θεὸν n. acc. masc. sg. θεός God, god
ἢ particle. ἤ or, than, either, nor, or else, and, rather than
σέβασμα n. acc. neut. sg. σέβασμα devotion, that is worshipped
ὥστε conj. ὥστε so that, wherefore, insomuch that, therefore, that, so then
αὐτὸν pron. acc. masc. 3p. sg. αὐτός ή ό self, of oneself, even, very, the same, he, she, it
εἰς prep. εἰς (+acc) into, to, unto, for, in, on, toward, against, upon, at, among
τὸν art. acc. masc. sg. ὁ ἡ τό the, this, that, he, she, it
ναὸν n. acc. masc. sg. ναός temple, shrine
τοῦ art. gen. masc. sg. ὁ ἡ τό the, this, that, he, she, it
Θεοῦ n. gen. masc. sg. θεός God, god
ὡς adv. ὡς as, when, as it were, how, about, like, as soon as, even as, while
Θεὸν n. acc. masc. sg. θεός God, god
ἑαυτὸν reflexive pron. acc. masc. 3p. sg. ἑαυτοῦ himself, herself, itself, yourself, ourselves
ὅτι conj. ὅτι that, for, because, how that, how, because that, for that, though
Θεός n. nom. masc. sg. θεός God, god
5 οὐ particle of negation. οὐ οὐκ οὐχ not, no, neither, none, nay, nor, never, nothing
ὅτι conj. ὅτι that, for, because, how that, how, because that, for that, though
ἔτι adv. ἔτι yet, more, any more, further, still, moreover
πρὸς prep. πρός (+gen) for, (+dat) at, (+acc) unto, to, with, for, against
ὑμᾶς pron. acc. 2p. pl. σύ thou, you
ταῦτα demo. pron. acc. neut. pl. οὗτος αὕτη τοῦτο this, the same, this same, he, she, it
ὑμῖν pron. dat. 2p. pl. σύ thou, you
6 καὶ conj. καί and, even, also, but
νῦν adv. νῦν now, henceforth, present, this time
τὸ art. acc. neut. sg. ὁ ἡ τό the, this, that, he, she, it
εἰς prep. εἰς (+acc) into, to, unto, for, in, on, toward, against, upon, at, among
τὸ art. acc. neut. sg. ὁ ἡ τό the, this, that, he, she, it
αὐτὸν pron. acc. masc. 3p. sg. αὐτός ή ό self, of oneself, even, very, the same, he, she, it
ἐν prep. ἐν (+dat) in, by, with, among, at, on, through, to, within, into, of, for
τῷ art. dat. masc. sg. ὁ ἡ τό the, this, that, he, she, it
ἑαυτοῦ reflexive pron. gen. masc. 3p. sg. ἑαυτοῦ himself, herself, itself, yourself, ourselves
καιρῷ n. dat. masc. sg. καιρός time, season, due time, opportunity
7 τὸ art. nom. neut. sg. ὁ ἡ τό the, this, that, he, she, it
γὰρ conj. γάρ for, and, because, but, indeed
μυστήριον n. nom. neut. sg. μυστήριον mystery
ἤδη adv. ἤδη now, already, yet, by this time, even now, now already
τῆς art. gen. fem. sg. ὁ ἡ τό the, this, that, he, she, it

ἀνομίας n. gen. fem. sg. ἀνομία iniquity, transgression of the law, lawlessness
μόνον adv. μόνος only, alone, by oneself
ὁ art. nom. masc. sg. ὁ ἡ τό the, this, that, he, she, it
ἄρτι adv. ἄρτι now, hence, here, hither, even now, present
ἕως conj. ἕως till, until, unto, until when, while, as far as, even, until now
ἐκ prep. ἐκ ἐξ (+gen) of, from, out of, by, on, with, in, among, through
μέσου adj. gen. neut. sg. μέσος midst, among, mid, between
8 καὶ conj. καί and, even, also, but
τότε adv. τότε then, that time
ὁ art. nom. masc. sg. ὁ ἡ τό the, this, that, he, she, it
ἄνομος adj. nom. masc. sg. ἄνομος without law, transgressor, wicked, lawless, unlawful
ὃν relative pron. acc. masc. sg. ὅς ἥ ὅ who, which, what, that
ὁ art. nom. masc. sg. ὁ ἡ τό the, this, that, he, she, it
Κύριος n. nom. masc. sg. κύριος Lord, lord, master, sir, LORD, God, Master, owner
τῷ art. dat. neut. sg. ὁ ἡ τό the, this, that, he, she, it
πνεύματι n. dat. neut. sg. πνεῦμα spirit, Spirit, Ghost, ghost, life. of the spirit, wind
τοῦ art. gen. neut. sg. ὁ ἡ τό the, this, that, he, she, it
στόματος n. gen. neut. sg. στόμα mouth, face, edge
αὐτοῦ pron. gen. masc. 3p. sg. αὐτός ή ό self, of oneself, even, very, the same, he, she, it
καὶ conj. καί and, even, also, but
τῇ art. dat. fem. sg. ὁ ἡ τό the, this, that, he, she, it
ἐπιφανείᾳ n. dat. fem. sg. ἐπιφάνεια appearing, brightness
τῆς art. gen. fem. sg. ὁ ἡ τό the, this, that, he, she, it
παρουσίας n. gen. fem. sg. παρουσία coming, presence
αὐτοῦ pron. gen. masc. 3p. sg. αὐτός ή ό self, of oneself, even, very, the same, he, she, it
9 οὗ relative pron. gen. masc. sg. ὅς ἥ ὅ who, which, what, that
ἡ art. nom. fem. sg. ὁ ἡ τό the, this, that, he, she, it
παρουσία n. nom. fem. sg. παρουσία coming, presence
κατ' prep. κατά (+gen) against, by, throughout, down, (+acc) according to, after, with
ἐνέργειαν n. acc. fem. sg. ἐνέργεια working, effectual working, operation
τοῦ art. gen. masc. sg. ὁ ἡ τό the, this, that, he, she, it
Σατανᾶ n. gen. masc. sg. Σατανᾶς Satan
ἐν prep. ἐν (+dat) in, by, with, among, at, on, through, to, within, into, of, for
πάσῃ adj. dat. fem. sg. πᾶς πᾶσα πᾶν all, every, whosoever, every one, no, whole, any
δυνάμει n. dat. fem. sg. δύναμις power, mighty work, miracle, strength, might
καὶ conj. καί and, even, also, but
σημείοις n. dat. neut. pl. σημεῖον sign, miracle, wonder, token
καὶ conj. καί and, even, also, but
τέρασιν n. dat. neut. pl. τέρας wonder
ψεύδους n. gen. neut. sg. ψεῦδος lie, lying
10 καὶ conj. καί and, even, also, but
ἐν prep. ἐν (+dat) in, by, with, among, at, on, through, to, within, into, of, for
πάσῃ adj. dat. fem. sg. πᾶς πᾶσα πᾶν all, every, whosoever, every one, no, whole, any
ἀπάτῃ n. dat. fem. sg. ἀπάτη deceitfulness, deceit
τῆς art. gen. fem. sg. ὁ ἡ τό the, this, that, he, she, it
ἀδικίας n. gen. fem. sg. ἀδικία iniquity, unrighteousness, unjust, wrong
ἐν prep. ἐν (+dat) in, by, with, among, at, on, through, to, within, into, of, for
τοῖς art. dat. masc. pl. ὁ ἡ τό the, this, that, he, she, it
ἀνθ' prep. ἀντί (+gen) for, because, in the room
ὧν relative pron. gen. masc. pl. ὅς ἥ ὅ who, which, what, that
τὴν art. acc. fem. sg. ὁ ἡ τό the, this, that, he, she, it
ἀγάπην n. acc. fem. sg. ἀγάπη love, charity, feast of charity
τῆς art. gen. fem. sg. ὁ ἡ τό the, this, that, he, she, it
ἀληθείας n. gen. fem. sg. ἀλήθεια truth, verity
οὐκ particle of negation. οὐ οὐκ οὐχ not, no, neither, none, nay, nor, never, nothing

εἰς prep. εἰς (+acc) into, to, unto, for, in, on, toward, against, upon, at, among
τὸ art. acc. neut. sg. ὁ ἡ τό the, this, that, he, she, it
αὐτούς pron. acc. masc. 3p. pl. αὐτός ή ό self, of oneself, even, very, the same, he, she, it
11 καὶ conj. καί and, even, also, but
διὰ prep. διά (+gen) by, through, with, in, of, (+acc) for, because of, for a cause
τοῦτο demo. pron. acc. neut. sg. οὗτος αὕτη τοῦτο this, the same, this same, he, she, it
αὐτοῖς pron. dat. masc. 3p. pl. αὐτός ή ό self, of oneself, even, very, the same, he, she, it
ὁ art. nom. masc. sg. ὁ ἡ τό the, this, that, he, she, it
Θεὸς n. nom. masc. sg. θεός God, god
ἐνέργειαν n. acc. fem. sg. ἐνέργεια working, effectual working, operation
πλάνης n. gen. fem. sg. πλάνη error, deception, deceit, delusion
εἰς prep. εἰς (+acc) into, to, unto, for, in, on, toward, against, upon, at, among
τὸ art. acc. neut. sg. ὁ ἡ τό the, this, that, he, she, it
αὐτοὺς pron. acc. masc. 3p. pl. αὐτός ή ό self, of oneself, even, very, the same, he, she, it
τῷ art. dat. neut. sg. ὁ ἡ τό the, this, that, he, she, it
ψεύδει n. dat. neut. sg. ψεῦδος lie, lying
12 ἵνα conj. ἵνα that, to, lest, for to, so that, albeit, because, for, so as
πάντες adj. nom. masc. pl. πᾶς πᾶσα πᾶν all, every, whosoever, every one, no, whole, any
οἱ art. nom. masc. pl. ὁ ἡ τό the, this, that, he, she, it
μὴ particle of negation. μή not, no, lest, neither, none, nothing, nor, never, without
τῇ art. dat. fem. sg. ὁ ἡ τό the, this, that, he, she, it
ἀληθείᾳ n. dat. fem. sg. ἀλήθεια truth, verity
ἀλλ᾽ conj. ἀλλά but, yea, yet, nevertheless, howbeit, nay, therefore
ἐν prep. ἐν (+dat) in, by, with, among, at, on, through, to, within, into, of, for
τῇ art. dat. fem. sg. ὁ ἡ τό the, this, that, he, she, it
ἀδικίᾳ n. dat. fem. sg. ἀδικία iniquity, unrighteousness, unjust, wrong
13 Ἡμεῖς pron. nom. 1p. pl. ἐγώ I
δὲ conj. δέ but, and, now, also, to the contrary, rather, then
τῷ art. dat. masc. sg. ὁ ἡ τό the, this, that, he, she, it
Θεῷ n. dat. masc. sg. θεός God, god
πάντοτε adv. πάντοτε always, ever, always, evermore
περὶ prep. περί (+gen) of, for, concerning, (+acc) about, concerning, in
ὑμῶν pron. gen. 2p. pl. σύ thou, you
ἀδελφοὶ n. voc. masc. pl. ἀδελφός brother
ὑπὸ prep. ὑπό (+gen) of, by, with, from, among, (+acc) under
Κυρίου n. gen. masc. sg. κύριος Lord, lord, master, sir, LORD, God, Master, owner
ὅτι conj. ὅτι that, for, because, how that, how, because that, for that, though
ὑμᾶς pron. acc. 2p. pl. σύ thou, you
ὁ art. nom. masc. sg. ὁ ἡ τό the, this, that, he, she, it
Θεὸς n. nom. masc. sg. θεός God, god
ἀπ᾽ prep. ἀπό (+gen) from, of, out of, since, for, off, at, by, in, on
ἀρχῆς n. gen. fem. sg. ἀρχή beginning, principality, corner, first, magistrate, rule
εἰς prep. εἰς (+acc) into, to, unto, for, in, on, toward, against, upon, at, among
σωτηρίαν n. acc. fem. sg. σωτηρία salvation, deliver, health, saving
ἐν prep. ἐν (+dat) in, by, with, among, at, on, through, to, within, into, of, for
ἁγιασμῷ n. dat. masc. sg. ἁγιασμός holiness, sanctification
Πνεύματος n. gen. neut. sg. πνεῦμα spirit, Spirit, Ghost, ghost, life. of the spirit, wind
καὶ conj. καί and, even, also, but
πίστει n. dat. fem. sg. πίστις faith, assurance, belief, fidelity
ἀληθείας n. gen. fem. sg. ἀλήθεια truth, verity
14 εἰς prep. εἰς (+acc) into, to, unto, for, in, on, toward, against, upon, at, among
ὃ relative pron. acc. neut. sg. ὅς ἥ ὅ who, which, what, that
ὑμᾶς pron. acc. 2p. pl. σύ thou, you
διὰ prep. διά (+gen) by, through, with, in, of, (+acc) for, because of, for a cause
τοῦ art. gen. neut. sg. ὁ ἡ τό the, this, that, he, she, it

εὐαγγελίου n. gen. neut. sg. εὐαγγέλιον gospel
ἡμῶν pron. gen. 1p. pl. ἐγώ I
εἰς prep. εἰς (+acc) into, to, unto, for, in, on, toward, against, upon, at, among
περιποίησιν n. acc. fem. sg. περιποίησις obtain, obtaining, purchased possession
δόξης n. gen. fem. sg. δόξα glory, honour, praise, dignity, worship
τοῦ art. gen. masc. sg. ὁ ἡ τό the, this, that, he, she, it
Κυρίου n. gen. masc. sg. κύριος Lord, lord, master, sir, LORD, God, Master, owner
ἡμῶν pron. gen. 1p. pl. ἐγώ I
Ἰησοῦ n. gen. masc. sg. Ἰησοῦς Jesus
Χριστοῦ n. gen. masc. sg. Χριστός Christ
15 ἄρα conj. ἄρα then, therefore, haply, wherefore, perhaps, manner, no doubt, truly
οὖν conj. οὖν therefore, then, so, and, now, wherefore
ἀδελφοί n. voc. masc. pl. ἀδελφός brother
καὶ conj. καί and, even, also, but
τὰς art. acc. fem. pl. ὁ ἡ τό the, this, that, he, she, it
παραδόσεις n. acc. fem. pl. παράδοσις tradition, ordinance
ἃς relative pron. acc. fem. pl. ὅς ἥ ὅ who, which, what, that
εἴτε conj. εἴτε whether
διὰ prep. διά (+gen) by, through, with, in, of, (+acc) for, because of, for a cause
λόγου n. gen. masc. sg. λόγος word, saying, account, speech, thing, matter
εἴτε conj. εἴτε whether
δι' prep. διά (+gen) by, through, with, in, of, (+acc) for, because of, for a cause
ἐπιστολῆς n. gen. fem. sg. ἐπιστολή letter, epistle
ἡμῶν pron. gen. 1p. pl. ἐγώ I
16 Αὐτὸς pron. nom. masc. 3p. sg. αὐτός ή ό self, of oneself, even, very, the same, he, she, it
δὲ conj. δέ but, and, now, also, to the contrary, rather, then
ὁ art. nom. masc. sg. ὁ ἡ τό the, this, that, he, she, it
Κύριος n. nom. masc. sg. κύριος Lord, lord, master, sir, LORD, God, Master, owner
ἡμῶν pron. gen. 1p. pl. ἐγώ I
Ἰησοῦς n. nom. masc. sg. Ἰησοῦς Jesus
Χριστὸς n. nom. masc. sg. Χριστός Christ
καὶ conj. καί and, even, also, but
ὁ art. nom. masc. sg. ὁ ἡ τό the, this, that, he, she, it
Θεὸς n. nom. masc. sg. θεός God, god
καὶ conj. καί and, even, also, but
πατὴρ n. nom. masc. sg. πατήρ Father, father, parent
ἡμῶν pron. gen. 1p. pl. ἐγώ I
ὁ art. nom. masc. sg. ὁ ἡ τό the, this, that, he, she, it
ἡμᾶς pron. acc. 1p. pl. ἐγώ I
καὶ conj. καί and, even, also, but
παράκλησιν n. acc. fem. sg. παράκλησις consolation, exhortation, comfort
αἰωνίαν adj. acc. fem. sg. αἰώνιος eternal, everlasting, world, for ever
καὶ conj. καί and, even, also, but
ἐλπίδα n. acc. fem. sg. ἐλπίς hope, faith
ἀγαθὴν adj. acc. fem. sg. ἀγαθός good, good thing, that which is good, well
ἐν prep. ἐν (+dat) in, by, with, among, at, on, through, to, within, into, of, for
χάριτι n. dat. fem. sg. χάρις grace, thank, favour, pleasure
17 ὑμῶν pron. gen. 2p. pl. σύ thou, you
τὰς art. acc. fem. pl. ὁ ἡ τό the, this, that, he, she, it
καρδίας n. acc. fem. pl. καρδία heart
καὶ conj. καί and, even, also, but
ὑμᾶς pron. acc. 2p. pl. σύ thou, you
ἐν prep. ἐν (+dat) in, by, with, among, at, on, through, to, within, into, of, for
παντὶ adj. dat. neut. sg. πᾶς πᾶσα πᾶν all, every, whosoever, every one, no, whole, any
λόγῳ n. dat. masc. sg. λόγος word, saying, account, speech, thing, matter

καὶ conj. καί and, even, also, but
ἔργῳ n. dat. neut. sg. ἔργον work, deed, doing labour
ἀγαθῷ adj. dat. masc. sg. ἀγαθός good, good thing, that which is good, well

3

1 Τὸ art. acc. neut. sg. ὁ ἡ τό the, this, that, he, she, it
λοιπὸν adj. acc. neut. sg. λοιπός other, rest, remnant, residue, which remain
ἀδελφοί n. voc. masc. pl. ἀδελφός brother
περὶ prep. περί (+gen) of, for, concerning, (+acc) about, concerning, in
ἡμῶν pron. gen. 1p. pl. ἐγώ I
ἵνα conj. ἵνα that, to, lest, for to, so that, albeit, because, for, so as
ὁ art. nom. masc. sg. ὁ ἡ τό the, this, that, he, she, it
λόγος n. nom. masc. sg. λόγος word, saying, account, speech, thing, matter
τοῦ art. gen. masc. sg. ὁ ἡ τό the, this, that, he, she, it
Κυρίου n. gen. masc. sg. κύριος Lord, lord, master, sir, LORD, God, Master, owner
καὶ conj. καί and, even, also, but
καθὼς adv. καθώς as, even as, according as, according to
καὶ conj. καί and, even, also, but
πρὸς prep. πρός (+gen) for, (+dat) at, (+acc) unto, to, with, for, against
ὑμᾶς pron. acc. 2p. pl. σύ thou, you
2 καὶ conj. καί and, even, also, but
ἵνα conj. ἵνα that, to, lest, for to, so that, albeit, because, for, so as
ἀπὸ prep. ἀπό (+gen) from, of, out of, since, for, off, at, by, in, on
τῶν art. gen. masc. pl. ὁ ἡ τό the, this, that, he, she, it
ἀτόπων adj. gen. masc. pl. ἄτοπος amiss, harm, unreasonable
καὶ conj. καί and, even, also, but
πονηρῶν adj. gen. masc. pl. πονηρός evil, wicked, bad
ἀνθρώπων n. gen. masc. pl. ἄνθρωπος man, human being, person, one, certain
οὐ particle of negation. οὐ οὐκ οὐχ not, no, neither, none, nay, nor, never, nothing
γὰρ conj. γάρ for, and, because, but, indeed
πάντων adj. gen. masc. pl. πᾶς πᾶσα πᾶν all, every, whosoever, every one, no, whole, any
ἡ art. nom. fem. sg. ὁ ἡ τό the, this, that, he, she, it
πίστις n. nom. fem. sg. πίστις faith, assurance, belief, fidelity
3 πιστὸς adj. nom. masc. sg. πιστός faithful, believing, true, sure
δέ conj. δέ but, and, now, also, to the contrary, rather, then
ὁ art. nom. masc. sg. ὁ ἡ τό the, this, that, he, she, it
Κύριος n. nom. masc. sg. κύριος Lord, lord, master, sir, LORD, God, Master, owner
ὃς relative pron. nom. masc. sg. ὅς ἥ ὅ who, which, what, that
ὑμᾶς pron. acc. 2p. pl. σύ thou, you
καὶ conj. καί and, even, also, but
ἀπὸ prep. ἀπό (+gen) from, of, out of, since, for, off, at, by, in, on
τοῦ art. gen. masc. sg. ὁ ἡ τό the, this, that, he, she, it
πονηροῦ adj. gen. masc. sg. πονηρός evil, wicked, bad
4 δὲ conj. δέ but, and, now, also, to the contrary, rather, then
ἐν prep. ἐν (+dat) in, by, with, among, at, on, through, to, within, into, of, for
Κυρίῳ n. dat. masc. sg. κύριος Lord, lord, master, sir, LORD, God, Master, owner
ἐφ' prep. ἐπί (+gen) on, in, upon, (+dat) in, at, for, upon, (+acc) on, upon, unto, to, against
ὑμᾶς pron. acc. 2p. pl. σύ thou, you
ὅτι conj. ὅτι that, for, because, how that, how, because that, for that, though
ἃ relative pron. acc. neut. pl. ὅς ἥ ὅ who, which, what, that
ὑμῖν pron. dat. 2p. pl. σύ thou, you
καὶ conj. καί and, even, also, but
καὶ conj. καί and, even, also, but
5 ὁ art. nom. masc. sg. ὁ ἡ τό the, this, that, he, she, it

δὲ conj. δέ but, and, now, also, to the contrary, rather, then
Κύριος n. nom. masc. sg. κύριος Lord, lord, master, sir, LORD, God, Master, owner
ὑμῶν pron. gen. 2p. pl. σύ thou, you
τὰς art. acc. fem. pl. ὁ ἡ τό the, this, that, he, she, it
καρδίας n. acc. fem. pl. καρδία heart
εἰς prep. εἰς (+acc) into, to, unto, for, in, on, toward, against, upon, at, among
τὴν art. acc. fem. sg. ὁ ἡ τό the, this, that, he, she, it
ἀγάπην n. acc. fem. sg. ἀγάπη love, charity, feast of charity
τοῦ art. gen. masc. sg. ὁ ἡ τό the, this, that, he, she, it
Θεοῦ n. gen. masc. sg. θεός God, god
καὶ conj. καί and, even, also, but
εἰς prep. εἰς (+acc) into, to, unto, for, in, on, toward, against, upon, at, among
τὴν art. acc. fem. sg. ὁ ἡ τό the, this, that, he, she, it
ὑπομονὴν n. acc. fem. sg. ὑπομονή patience, enduring
τοῦ art. gen. masc. sg. ὁ ἡ τό the, this, that, he, she, it
Χριστοῦ n. gen. masc. sg. Χριστός Christ
6 δὲ conj. δέ but, and, now, also, to the contrary, rather, then
ὑμῖν pron. dat. 2p. pl. σύ thou, you
ἀδελφοί n. voc. masc. pl. ἀδελφός brother
ἐν prep. ἐν (+dat) in, by, with, among, at, on, through, to, within, into, of, for
ὀνόματι n. dat. neut. sg. ὄνομα name, call, surname
τοῦ art. gen. masc. sg. ὁ ἡ τό the, this, that, he, she, it
Κυρίου n. gen. masc. sg. κύριος Lord, lord, master, sir, LORD, God, Master, owner
ἡμῶν pron. gen. 1p. pl. ἐγώ I
Ἰησοῦ n. gen. masc. sg. Ἰησοῦς Jesus
Χριστοῦ n. gen. masc. sg. Χριστός Christ
ὑμᾶς pron. acc. 2p. pl. σύ thou, you
ἀπὸ prep. ἀπό (+gen) from, of, out of, since, for, off, at, by, in, on
παντὸς adj. gen. masc. sg. πᾶς πᾶσα πᾶν all, every, whosoever, every one, no, whole, any
ἀδελφοῦ n. gen. masc. sg. ἀδελφός brother
ἀτάκτως adv. ἀτάκτως disorderly
καὶ conj. καί and, even, also, but
μὴ particle of negation. μή not, no, lest, neither, none, nothing, nor, never, without
κατὰ prep. κατά (+gen) against, by, throughout, down, (+acc) according to, after, with
τὴν art. acc. fem. sg. ὁ ἡ τό the, this, that, he, she, it
παράδοσιν n. acc. fem. sg. παράδοσις tradition, ordinance
ἣν relative pron. acc. fem. sg. ὅς ἥ ὅ who, which, what, that
παρ' prep. παρά (+gen) of, from, (+dat) with, for, (+acc) beside, at, by, above, against
ἡμῶν pron. gen. 1p. pl. ἐγώ I
7 αὐτοὶ pron. nom. masc. 2p. pl. αὐτός ή ό self, of oneself, even, very, the same, he, she, it
γὰρ conj. γάρ for, and, because, but, indeed
πῶς adv. πῶς how, by what means, after what manner
ἡμᾶς pron. acc. 1p. pl. ἐγώ I
ὅτι conj. ὅτι that, for, because, how that, how, because that, for that, though
οὐκ particle of negation. οὐ οὐκ οὐχ not, no, neither, none, nay, nor, never, nothing
ἐν prep. ἐν (+dat) in, by, with, among, at, on, through, to, within, into, of, for
ὑμῖν pron. dat. 2p. pl. σύ thou, you
8 οὐδὲ adv. οὐδέ neither, nor, not, no, not even, never, not yet
δωρεὰν adv. δωρεάν freely, for nought, in vain, without a cause
ἄρτον n. acc. masc. sg. ἄρτος bread, loaf
παρά prep. παρά (+gen) of, from, (+dat) with, for, (+acc) beside, at, by, above, against
τινος indefinite pron. gen. masc. sg. τὶς certain, some, any man, one, any thing
ἀλλ' conj. ἀλλά but, yea, yet, nevertheless, howbeit, nay, therefore
ἐν prep. ἐν (+dat) in, by, with, among, at, on, through, to, within, into, of, for
κόπῳ n. dat. masc. sg. κόπος labour, trouble, weariness

καὶ conj. καί and, even, also, but
μόχθῳ n. dat. masc. sg. μόχθος painfulness, travail
νύκτα n. acc. fem. sg. νύξ night
καὶ conj. καί and, even, also, but
ἡμέραν n. acc. fem. sg. ἡμέρα day, time, year, while, age, day time
πρὸς prep. πρός (+gen) for, (+dat) at, (+acc) unto, to, with, for, against
τὸ art. acc. neut. sg. ὁ ἡ τό the, this, that, he, she, it
μὴ particle of negation. μή not, no, lest, neither, none, nothing, nor, never, without
τινα indefinite pron. acc. masc. sg. τὶς certain, some, any man, one, any thing
ὑμῶν pron. gen. 2p. pl. σύ thou, you
9 οὐχ particle of negation. οὐ οὐκ οὐχ not, no, neither, none, nay, nor, never, nothing
ὅτι conj. ὅτι that, for, because, how that, how, because that, for that, though
οὐκ particle of negation. οὐ οὐκ οὐχ not, no, neither, none, nay, nor, never, nothing
ἐξουσίαν n. acc. fem. sg. ἐξουσία power, authority, right, strength, jurisdiction
ἀλλ' conj. ἀλλά but, yea, yet, nevertheless, howbeit, nay, therefore
ἵνα conj. ἵνα that, to, lest, for to, so that, albeit, because, for, so as
ἑαυτοὺς reflexive pron. acc. masc. 3p. pl. ἑαυτοῦ himself, herself, itself, yourself, ourselves
τύπον n. acc. masc. sg. τύπος ensample, example, pattern, print, figure, fashion
ὑμῖν pron. dat. 2p. pl. σύ thou, you
εἰς prep. εἰς (+acc) into, to, unto, for, in, on, toward, against, upon, at, among
τὸ art. acc. neut. sg. ὁ ἡ τό the, this, that, he, she, it
ἡμᾶς pron. acc. 1p. pl. ἐγώ I
10 καὶ conj. καί and, even, also, but
γὰρ conj. γάρ for, and, because, but, indeed
ὅτε adv. ὅτε when, after that, as soon as, while, after
πρὸς prep. πρός (+gen) for, (+dat) at, (+acc) unto, to, with, for, against
ὑμᾶς pron. acc. 2p. pl. σύ thou, you
τοῦτο demo. pron. acc. neut. sg. οὗτος αὕτη τοῦτο this, the same, this same, he, she, it
ὑμῖν pron. dat. 2p. pl. σύ thou, you
ὅτι conj. ὅτι that, for, because, how that, how, because that, for that, though
Εἴ conj. εἰ if, whether, that, though, forasmuch
τις indefinite pron. nom. masc. sg. τὶς certain, some, any man, one, any thing
οὐ particle of negation. οὐ οὐκ οὐχ not, no, neither, none, nay, nor, never, nothing
μηδὲ adv. μηδέ neither, nor, not, no not, nor yet, not once, not so much as
11 γάρ conj. γάρ for, and, because, but, indeed
τινας indefinite pron. acc. masc. pl. τὶς certain, some, any man, one, any thing
ἐν prep. ἐν (+dat) in, by, with, among, at, on, through, to, within, into, of, for
ὑμῖν pron. dat. 2p. pl. σύ thou, you
ἀτάκτως adv. ἀτάκτως disorderly
μηδὲν num. acc. neut. sg. μηδείς μηδεμία μηδέν no man, nothing, no, none, not at all
ἀλλὰ conj. ἀλλά but, yea, yet, nevertheless, howbeit, nay, therefore
12 τοῖς art. dat. masc. pl. ὁ ἡ τό the, this, that, he, she, it
δὲ conj. δέ but, and, now, also, to the contrary, rather, then
τοιούτοις demo. pron. dat. masc. pl. τοιοῦτος such, like
καὶ conj. καί and, even, also, but
διὰ prep. διά (+gen) by, through, with, in, of, (+acc) for, because of, for a cause
τοῦ art. gen. masc. sg. ὁ ἡ τό the, this, that, he, she, it
Κυρίου n. gen. masc. sg. κύριος Lord, lord, master, sir, LORD, God, Master, owner
ἡμῶν pron. gen. 1p. pl. ἐγώ I
'Ιησοῦ n. gen. masc. sg. 'Ιησοῦς Jesus
Χριστοῦ n. gen. masc. sg. Χριστός Christ
ἵνα conj. ἵνα that, to, lest, for to, so that, albeit, because, for, so as
μετὰ prep. μετά (+gen) with, among, against, (+acc) after
ἡσυχίας n. gen. fem. sg. ἡσυχία silence, quietness
τὸν art. acc. masc. sg. ὁ ἡ τό the, this, that, he, she, it

ἑαυτῶν reflexive pron. gen. masc. 3p. pl. ἑαυτοῦ himself, herself, itself, yourself, ourselves
ἄρτον n. acc. masc. sg. ἄρτος bread, loaf
13 ὑμεῖς pron. nom. 2p. pl. σύ thou, you
δέ conj. δέ but, and, now, also, to the contrary, rather, then
ἀδελφοί n. voc. masc. pl. ἀδελφός brother
μὴ particle of negation. μή not, no, lest, neither, none, nothing, nor, never, without
14 εἰ conj. εἰ if, whether, that, though, forasmuch
δέ conj. δέ but, and, now, also, to the contrary, rather, then
τις indefinite pron. nom. masc. sg. τὶς certain, some, any man, one, any thing
οὐχ particle of negation. οὐ οὐκ οὐχ not, no, neither, none, nay, nor, never, nothing
τῷ art. dat. masc. sg. ὁ ἡ τό the, this, that, he, she, it
λόγῳ n. dat. masc. sg. λόγος word, saying, account, speech, thing, matter
ἡμῶν pron. gen. 1p. pl. ἐγώ I
διὰ prep. διά (+gen) by, through, with, in, of, (+acc) for, because of, for a cause
τῆς art. gen. fem. sg. ὁ ἡ τό the, this, that, he, she, it
ἐπιστολῆς n. gen. fem. sg. ἐπιστολή letter, epistle
τοῦτον demo. pron. acc. masc. sg. οὗτος αὕτη τοῦτο this, the same, this same, he, she, it
καὶ conj. καί and, even, also, but
μὴ particle of negation. μή not, no, lest, neither, none, nothing, nor, never, without
αὐτῷ pron. dat. masc. 3p. sg. αὐτός ή ό self, of oneself, even, very, the same, he, she, it
ἵνα conj. ἵνα that, to, lest, for to, so that, albeit, because, for, so as
15 καὶ conj. καί and, even, also, but
μὴ particle of negation. μή not, no, lest, neither, none, nothing, nor, never, without
ὡς adv. ὡς as, when, as it were, how, about, like, as soon as, even as, while
ἐχθρὸν adj. acc. masc. sg. ἐχθρός enemy, foe
ἀλλὰ conj. ἀλλά but, yea, yet, nevertheless, howbeit, nay, therefore
ὡς adv. ὡς as, when, as it were, how, about, like, as soon as, even as, while
ἀδελφόν n. acc. masc. sg. ἀδελφός brother
16 Αὐτὸς pron. nom. masc. 3p. sg. αὐτός ή ό self, of oneself, even, very, the same, he, she, it
δὲ conj. δέ but, and, now, also, to the contrary, rather, then
ὁ art. nom. masc. sg. ὁ ἡ τό the, this, that, he, she, it
Κύριος n. nom. masc. sg. κύριος Lord, lord, master, sir, LORD, God, Master, owner
τῆς art. gen. fem. sg. ὁ ἡ τό the, this, that, he, she, it
εἰρήνης n. gen. fem. sg. εἰρήνη peace, quietness, rest
ὑμῖν pron. dat. 2p. pl. σύ thou, you
τὴν art. acc. fem. sg. ὁ ἡ τό the, this, that, he, she, it
εἰρήνην n. acc. fem. sg. εἰρήνη peace, quietness, rest
διὰ prep. διά (+gen) by, through, with, in, of, (+acc) for, because of, for a cause
παντὸς adj. gen. neut. sg. πᾶς πᾶσα πᾶν all, every, whosoever, every one, no, whole, any
ἐν prep. ἐν (+dat) in, by, with, among, at, on, through, to, within, into, of, for
παντὶ adj. dat. masc. sg. πᾶς πᾶσα πᾶν all, every, whosoever, every one, no, whole, any
τρόπῳ n. dat. masc. sg. τρόπος as, manner, means, way, conversation
ὁ art. nom. masc. sg. ὁ ἡ τό the, this, that, he, she, it
Κύριος n. nom. masc. sg. κύριος Lord, lord, master, sir, LORD, God, Master, owner
μετὰ prep. μετά (+gen) with, among, against, (+acc) after
πάντων adj. gen. masc. pl. πᾶς πᾶσα πᾶν all, every, whosoever, every one, no, whole, any
ὑμῶν pron. gen. 2p. pl. σύ thou, you
17 Ὁ art. nom. masc. sg. ὁ ἡ τό the, this, that, he, she, it
ἀσπασμὸς n. nom. masc. sg. ἀσπασμός greeting, salutation
τῇ art. dat. fem. sg. ὁ ἡ τό the, this, that, he, she, it
ἐμῇ poss. pron. dat. fem. 1p. sg. ἐμός my, mine, mine own, of me
χειρὶ n. dat. fem. sg. χείρ hand
Παύλου n. gen. masc. sg. Παῦλος Paul, Paulus
ὅ relative pron. nom. neut. sg. ὅς ἥ ὅ who, which, what, that
σημεῖον n. nom. neut. sg. σημεῖον sign, miracle, wonder, token

ἐν prep. ἐν (+dat) in, by, with, among, at, on, through, to, within, into, of, for
πάσῃ adj. dat. fem. sg. πᾶς πᾶσα πᾶν all, every, whosoever, every one, no, whole, any
ἐπιστολῇ n. dat. fem. sg. ἐπιστολή letter, epistle
οὕτω adv. οὕτω οὕτως so, even so, thus, on this wise, likewise, after this manner
18 ἡ art. nom. fem. sg. ὁ ἡ τό the, this, that, he, she, it
χάρις n. nom. fem. sg. χάρις grace, thank, favour, pleasure
τοῦ art. gen. masc. sg. ὁ ἡ τό the, this, that, he, she, it
Κυρίου n. gen. masc. sg. κύριος Lord, lord, master, sir, LORD, God, Master, owner
ἡμῶν pron. gen. 1p. pl. ἐγώ I
Ἰησοῦ n. gen. masc. sg. Ἰησοῦς Jesus
Χριστοῦ n. gen. masc. sg. Χριστός Christ
μετὰ prep. μετά (+gen) with, among, against, (+acc) after
πάντων adj. gen. masc. pl. πᾶς πᾶσα πᾶν all, every, whosoever, every one, no, whole, any
ὑμῶν pron. gen. 2p. pl. σύ thou, you
ἀμήν particle. ἀμήν amen, verily

ΠΑΥΛΟΥ ΤΟΥ ΑΠΟΣΤΟΛΟΥ
Η ΠΡΟΣ
ΤΙΜΟΘΕΟΝ
ΕΠΙΣΤΟΛΗ ΠΡΩΤΗ

1

1 Παῦλος n. nom. masc. sg. Παῦλος Paul, Paulus
ἀπόστολος n. nom. masc. sg. ἀπόστολος apostle, messenger, he that is sent
Ἰησοῦ n. gen. masc. sg. Ἰησοῦς Jesus
Χριστοῦ n. gen. masc. sg. Χριστός Christ
κατ' prep. κατά (+gen) against, by, throughout, down, (+acc) according to, after, with
ἐπιταγὴν n. acc. fem. sg. ἐπιταγή commandment, authority
Θεοῦ n. gen. masc. sg. θεός God, god
σωτῆρος n. gen. masc. sg. σωτήρ Saviour, saviour
ἡμῶν pron. gen. 1p. pl. ἐγώ I
καὶ conj. καί and, even, also, but
Κυρίου n. gen. masc. sg. κύριος Lord, lord, master, sir, LORD, God, Master, owner
Ἰησοῦ n. gen. masc. sg. Ἰησοῦς Jesus
Χριστοῦ n. gen. masc. sg. Χριστός Christ
τῆς art. gen. fem. sg. ὁ ἡ τό the, this, that, he, she, it
ἐλπίδος n. gen. fem. sg. ἐλπίς hope, faith
ἡμῶν pron. gen. 1p. pl. ἐγώ I
2 Τιμοθέῳ n. dat. masc. sg. Τιμόθεος Timotheus, Timothy
γνησίῳ adj. dat. neut. sg. γνήσιος sincerity, own, true
τέκνῳ n. dat. neut. sg. τέκνον child, son, daughter
ἐν prep. ἐν (+dat) in, by, with, among, at, on, through, to, within, into, of, for
πίστει n. dat. fem. sg. πίστις faith, assurance, belief, fidelity
χάρις n. nom. fem. sg. χάρις grace, thank, favour, pleasure
ἔλεος n. nom. masc. sg. ἔλεος mercy
εἰρήνη n. nom. fem. sg. εἰρήνη peace, quietness, rest
ἀπὸ prep. ἀπό (+gen) from, of, out of, since, for, off, at, by, in, on
Θεοῦ n. gen. masc. sg. θεός God, god
πατρὸς n. gen. masc. sg. πατήρ Father, father, parent
ἡμῶν pron. gen. 1p. pl. ἐγώ I
καὶ conj. καί and, even, also, but
Ἰησοῦ n. gen. masc. sg. Ἰησοῦς Jesus
Χριστοῦ n. gen. masc. sg. Χριστός Christ
τοῦ art. gen. masc. sg. ὁ ἡ τό the, this, that, he, she, it
Κυρίου n. gen. masc. sg. κύριος Lord, lord, master, sir, LORD, God, Master, owner
ἡμῶν pron. gen. 1p. pl. ἐγώ I
3 Καθὼς adv. καθώς as, even as, according as, according to
σε pron. acc. 2p. sg. σύ thou, you
ἐν prep. ἐν (+dat) in, by, with, among, at, on, through, to, within, into, of, for
Ἐφέσῳ n. dat. fem. sg. Ἔφεσος Ephesus
εἰς prep. εἰς (+acc) into, to, unto, for, in, on, toward, against, upon, at, among
Μακεδονίαν n. acc. fem. sg. Μακεδονία Macedonia
ἵνα conj. ἵνα that, to, lest, for to, so that, albeit, because, for, so as
τισὶ indefinite pron. dat. masc. pl. τὶς certain, some, any man, one, any thing
μὴ particle of negation. μή not, no, lest, neither, none, nothing, nor, never, without
4 μηδὲ conj. μηδέ neither, nor, not, no not, nor yet, not once, not so much as
μύθοις n. dat. masc. pl. μῦθος fable, myth
καὶ conj. καί and, even, also, but

γενεαλογίαις n. dat. fem. pl. γενεαλογία genealogy
ἀπεράντοις adj. dat. fem. pl. ἀπέραντος endless
αἵτινες relative pron. nom. fem. pl. ὅστις which, who, whosoever, that, whatsoever
ζητήσεις n. acc. fem. pl. ζήτησις question
μᾶλλον adv. μᾶλλον rather, more, more and more, better, much, much the more
ἢ particle. ἤ or, than, either, nor, or else, and, rather than
οἰκονομίαν n. acc. fem. sg. οἰκονομία dispensation, stewardship, edifying
Θεοῦ n. gen. masc. sg. θεός God, god
τὴν art. acc. fem. sg. ὁ ἡ τό the, this, that, he, she, it
ἐν prep. ἐν (+dat) in, by, with, among, at, on, through, to, within, into, of, for
πίστει n. dat. fem. sg. πίστις faith, assurance, belief, fidelity
5 τὸ art. nom. neut. sg. ὁ ἡ τό the, this, that, he, she, it
δὲ conj. δέ but, and, now, also, to the contrary, rather, then
τέλος n. nom. neut. sg. τέλος end, custom, ending, finally, uttermost
τῆς art. gen. fem. sg. ὁ ἡ τό the, this, that, he, she, it
παραγγελίας n. gen. fem. sg. παραγγελία charge, commandment
ἀγάπη n. nom. fem. sg. ἀγάπη love, charity, feast of charity
ἐκ prep. ἐκ ἐξ (+gen) of, from, out of, by, on, with, in, among, through
καθαρᾶς adj. gen. fem. sg. καθαρός pure, clean, clear
καρδίας n. gen. fem. sg. καρδία heart
καὶ conj. καί and, even, also, but
συνειδήσεως n. gen. fem. sg. συνείδησις conscience
ἀγαθῆς adj. gen. fem. sg. ἀγαθός good, good thing, that which is good, well
καὶ conj. καί and, even, also, but
πίστεως n. gen. fem. sg. πίστις faith, assurance, belief, fidelity
ἀνυποκρίτου adj. gen. fem. sg. ἀνυπόκριτος unfeigned, without dissimulation
6 ὧν relative pron. gen. fem. pl. ὅς ἥ ὅ who, which, what, that
τινες indefinite pron. nom. masc. pl. τὶς certain, some, any man, one, any thing
εἰς prep. εἰς (+acc) into, to, unto, for, in, on, toward, against, upon, at, among
ματαιολογίαν n. acc. fem. sg. ματαιολογία vain jangling
7 νομοδιδάσκαλοι n. nom. masc. pl. νομοδιδάσκαλος doctor of the law, teacher of the law
μὴ particle of negation. μή not, no, lest, neither, none, nothing, nor, never, without
μήτε conj. μήτε neither, nor, so much as, or
ἃ relative pron. acc. neut. pl. ὅς ἥ ὅ who, which, what, that
μήτε conj. μήτε neither, nor, so much as, or
περὶ prep. περί (+gen) of, for, concerning, (+acc) about, concerning, in
τίνων interrog. pron. gen. neut. pl. τίς what, who, why, where, which, how
8 δὲ conj. δέ but, and, now, also, to the contrary, rather, then
ὅτι conj. ὅτι that, for, because, how that, how, because that, for that, though
καλὸς adj. nom. masc. sg. καλός good, better, goodly, meet, honest, fair, well, worthy
ὁ art. nom. masc. sg. ὁ ἡ τό the, this, that, he, she, it
νόμος n. nom. masc. sg. νόμος law, the law
ἐάν conj. ἐάν if, soever, except, though, and if, but, whether, if so, so
τις indefinite pron. nom. masc. sg. τὶς certain, some, any man, one, any thing
αὐτῷ pron. dat. masc. 3p. sg. αὐτός ἡ ὁ self, of oneself, even, very, the same, he, she, it
νομίμως adv. νομίμως lawfully
9 τοῦτο demo. pron. acc. neut. sg. οὗτος αὕτη τοῦτο this, the same, this same, he, she, it
ὅτι conj. ὅτι that, for, because, how that, how, because that, for that, though
δικαίῳ adj. dat. masc. sg. δίκαιος righteous, just, meet, right
νόμος n. nom. masc. sg. νόμος law, the law
οὐ particle of negation. οὐ οὐκ οὐχ not, no, neither, none, nay, nor, never, nothing
ἀνόμοις adj. dat. masc. pl. ἄνομος without law, transgressor, wicked, lawless, unlawful
δὲ conj. δέ but, and, now, also, to the contrary, rather, then
καὶ conj. καί and, even, also, but
ἀνυποτάκτοις adj. dat. masc. pl. ἀνυπότακτος disobedient, unruly, that is not put under

ἀσεβέσι adj. dat. masc. pl. ἀσεβής ungodly, ungodly man
καὶ conj. καί and, even, also, but
ἁμαρτωλοῖς adj. dat. masc. pl. ἁμαρτωλός sinner, sinful
ἀνοσίοις adj. dat. masc. pl. ἀνόσιος unholy
καὶ conj. καί and, even, also, but
βεβήλοις adj. dat. masc. pl. βέβηλος profane, profane person
πατραλῴαις n. dat. masc. pl. πατραλῴας or πατραλῴης murderer of father
καὶ conj. καί and, even, also, but
μητραλῴαις n. dat. masc. pl. μητρολῴας or μητρολῴης murderer of mother
ἀνδροφόνοις n. dat. masc. pl. ἀνδροφόνος manslayer
10 πόρνοις n. dat. masc. pl. πόρνος fornicator
ἀρσενοκοίταις n. dat. masc. pl. ἀρσενοκοίτης that defile oneself with mankind
ἀνδραποδισταῖς n. dat. masc. pl. ἀνδραποδιστής menstealer
ψεύσταις n. dat. masc. pl. ψεύστης liar
ἐπιόρκοις adj. dat. masc. pl. ἐπίορκος perjured person
καὶ conj. καί and, even, also, but
εἴ conj. εἰ if, whether, that, though, forasmuch
τι indefinite pron. nom. neut. sg. τὶς certain, some, any man, one, any thing
ἕτερον adj. nom. neut. sg. ἕτερος another, other, else, strange
τῇ art. dat. fem. sg. ὁ ἡ τό the, this, that, he, she, it
διδασκαλίᾳ n. dat. fem. sg. διδασκαλία doctrine, learning, teaching
11 κατὰ prep. κατά (+gen) against, by, throughout, down, (+acc) according to, after, with
τὸ art. acc. neut. sg. ὁ ἡ τό the, this, that, he, she, it
εὐαγγέλιον n. acc. neut. sg. εὐαγγέλιον gospel
τῆς art. gen. fem. sg. ὁ ἡ τό the, this, that, he, she, it
δόξης n. gen. fem. sg. δόξα glory, honour, praise, dignity, worship
τοῦ art. gen. masc. sg. ὁ ἡ τό the, this, that, he, she, it
μακαρίου adj. gen. masc. sg. μακάριος blessed, happy
Θεοῦ n. gen. masc. sg. θεός God, god
ὃ relative pron. acc. neut. sg. ὅς ἥ ὅ who, which, what, that
ἐγώ pron. nom. 1p. sg. ἐγώ I
12 Καὶ conj. καί and, even, also, but
χάριν n. acc. fem. sg. χάρις grace, thank, favour, pleasure
τῷ art. dat. masc. sg. ὁ ἡ τό the, this, that, he, she, it
με pron. acc. 1p. sg. ἐγώ I
Χριστῷ n. dat. masc. sg. Χριστός Christ
Ἰησοῦ n. dat. masc. sg. Ἰησοῦς Jesus
τῷ art. dat. masc. sg. ὁ ἡ τό the, this, that, he, she, it
Κυρίῳ n. dat. masc. sg. κύριος Lord, lord, master, sir, LORD, God, Master, owner
ἡμῶν pron. gen. 1p. pl. ἐγώ I
ὅτι conj. ὅτι that, for, because, how that, how, because that, for that, though
πιστόν adj. acc. masc. sg. πιστός faithful, believing, true, sure
με pron. acc. 1p. sg. ἐγώ I
εἰς prep. εἰς (+acc) into, to, unto, for, in, on, toward, against, upon, at, among
διακονίαν n. acc. fem. sg. διακονία ministry, administration, service, office, relief
13 τὸν art. acc. masc. sg. ὁ ἡ τό the, this, that, he, she, it
πρότερον adv. πρότερον before, first, former, at the first
βλάσφημον adj. acc. masc. sg. βλάσφημος blasphemous, blasphemer, railing
καὶ conj. καί and, even, also, but
διώκτην n. acc. masc. sg. διώκτης persecutor
καὶ conj. καί and, even, also, but
ὑβριστήν n. acc. masc. sg. ὑβριστής despiteful, injurious
ἀλλ' conj. ἀλλά but, yea, yet, nevertheless, howbeit, nay, therefore
ὅτι conj. ὅτι that, for, because, how that, how, because that, for that, though
ἐν prep. ἐν (+dat) in, by, with, among, at, on, through, to, within, into, of, for

ἀπιστίᾳ n. dat. fem. sg. ἀπιστία unbelief
14 δὲ conj. δέ but, and, now, also, to the contrary, rather, then
ἡ art. nom. fem. sg. ὁ ἡ τό the, this, that, he, she, it
χάρις n. nom. fem. sg. χάρις grace, thank, favour, pleasure
τοῦ art. gen. masc. sg. ὁ ἡ τό the, this, that, he, she, it
Κυρίου n. gen. masc. sg. κύριος Lord, lord, master, sir, LORD, God, Master, owner
ἡμῶν pron. gen. 1p. pl. ἐγώ I
μετὰ prep. μετά (+gen) with, among, against, (+acc) after
πίστεως n. gen. fem. sg. πίστις faith, assurance, belief, fidelity
καὶ conj. καί and, even, also, but
ἀγάπης n. gen. fem. sg. ἀγάπη love, charity, feast of charity
τῆς art. gen. fem. sg. ὁ ἡ τό the, this, that, he, she, it
ἐν prep. ἐν (+dat) in, by, with, among, at, on, through, to, within, into, of, for
Χριστῷ n. dat. masc. sg. Χριστός Christ
Ἰησοῦ n. dat. masc. sg. Ἰησοῦς Jesus
15 πιστὸς adj. nom. masc. sg. πιστός faithful, believing, true, sure
ὁ art. nom. masc. sg. ὁ ἡ τό the, this, that, he, she, it
λόγος n. nom. masc. sg. λόγος word, saying, account, speech, thing, matter
καὶ conj. καί and, even, also, but
πάσης adj. gen. fem. sg. πᾶς πᾶσα πᾶν all, every, whosoever, every one, no, whole, any
ἀποδοχῆς n. gen. fem. sg. ἀποδοχή acceptation
ἄξιος adj. nom. masc. sg. ἄξιος worthy, meet, due reward
ὅτι conj. ὅτι that, for, because, how that, how, because that, for that, though
Χριστὸς n. nom. masc. sg. Χριστός Christ
Ἰησοῦς n. nom. masc. sg. Ἰησοῦς Jesus
εἰς prep. εἰς (+acc) into, to, unto, for, in, on, toward, against, upon, at, among
τὸν art. acc. masc. sg. ὁ ἡ τό the, this, that, he, she, it
κόσμον n. acc. masc. sg. κόσμος world, adorning
ἁμαρτωλοὺς adj. acc. masc. pl. ἁμαρτωλός sinner, sinful
ὧν relative pron. gen. masc. pl. ὅς ἥ ὅ who, which, what, that
πρῶτός ordinal. adj. nom. masc. sg. πρῶτος first, chief, first of all, chiefest, best
ἐγώ pron. nom. 1p. sg. ἐγώ I
16 ἀλλὰ conj. ἀλλά but, yea, yet, nevertheless, howbeit, nay, therefore
διὰ prep. διά (+gen) by, through, with, in, of, (+acc) for, because of, for a cause
τοῦτο demo. pron. acc. neut. sg. οὗτος αὕτη τοῦτο this, the same, this same, he, she, it
ἵνα conj. ἵνα that, to, lest, for to, so that, albeit, because, for, so as
ἐν prep. ἐν (+dat) in, by, with, among, at, on, through, to, within, into, of, for
ἐμοὶ pron. dat. 1p. sg. ἐγώ I
πρώτῳ ordinal. adj. dat. masc. sg. πρῶτος first, chief, first of all, chiefest, best
Ἰησοῦς n. nom. masc. sg. Ἰησοῦς Jesus
Χριστὸς n. nom. masc. sg. Χριστός Christ
τὴν art. acc. fem. sg. ὁ ἡ τό the, this, that, he, she, it
πᾶσαν adj. acc. fem. sg. πᾶς πᾶσα πᾶν all, every, whosoever, every one, no, whole, any
μακροθυμίαν n. acc. fem. sg. μακροθυμία longsuffering, patience
πρὸς prep. πρός (+gen) for, (+dat) at, (+acc) unto, to, with, for, against
ὑποτύπωσιν n. acc. fem. sg. ὑποτύπωσις form, pattern
τῶν art. gen. masc. pl. ὁ ἡ τό the, this, that, he, she, it
ἐπ' prep. ἐπί (+gen) on, in, upon, (+dat) in, at, for, upon, (+acc) on, upon, unto, to, against
αὐτῷ pron. dat. masc. 3p. sg. αὐτός ἡ ὁ self, of oneself, even, very, the same, he, she, it
εἰς prep. εἰς (+acc) into, to, unto, for, in, on, toward, against, upon, at, among
ζωὴν n. acc. fem. sg. ζωή life, lifetime
αἰώνιον adj. acc. fem. sg. αἰώνιος eternal, everlasting, world, for ever
17 τῷ art. dat. masc. sg. ὁ ἡ τό the, this, that, he, she, it
δὲ conj. δέ but, and, now, also, to the contrary, rather, then
βασιλεῖ n. dat. masc. sg. βασιλεύς king

τῶν art. gen. masc. pl. ὁ ἡ τό the, this, that, he, she, it
αἰώνων n. gen. masc. pl. αἰών ever, ever and ever, evermore, age, eternal, world
ἀφθάρτῳ adj. dat. masc. sg. ἄφθαρτος uncorruptible, incorruptible, immortal, not corruptible
ἀοράτῳ adj. dat. masc. sg. ἀόρατος invisible, invisible thing
μόνῳ adj. dat. masc. sg. μόνος only, alone, by oneself
σοφῷ adj. dat. masc. sg. σοφός wise, wiser
Θεῷ n. dat. masc. sg. θεός God, god
τιμὴ n. nom. fem. sg. τιμή honour, price, preciousness, sum
καὶ conj. καί and, even, also, but
δόξα n. nom. fem. sg. δόξα glory, honour, praise, dignity, worship
εἰς prep. εἰς (+acc) into, to, unto, for, in, on, toward, against, upon, at, among
τοὺς art. acc. masc. pl. ὁ ἡ τό the, this, that, he, she, it
αἰῶνας n. acc. masc. pl. αἰών ever, ever and ever, evermore, age, eternal, world
τῶν art. gen. masc. pl. ὁ ἡ τό the, this, that, he, she, it
αἰώνων n. gen. masc. pl. αἰών ever, ever and ever, evermore, age, eternal, world
ἀμήν particle. ἀμήν amen, verily
18 Ταύτην demo. pron. acc. fem. sg. οὗτος αὕτη τοῦτο this, the same, this same, he, she, it
τὴν art. acc. fem. sg. ὁ ἡ τό the, this, that, he, she, it
παραγγελίαν n. acc. fem. sg. παραγγελία charge, commandment
σοι pron. dat. 2p. sg. σύ thou, you
τέκνον n. voc. neut. sg. τέκνον child, son, daughter
Τιμόθεε n. voc. masc. sg. Τιμόθεος Timotheus, Timothy
κατὰ prep. κατά (+gen) against, by, throughout, down, (+acc) according to, after, with
τὰς art. acc. fem. pl. ὁ ἡ τό the, this, that, he, she, it
ἐπὶ prep. ἐπί (+gen) on, in, upon, (+dat) in, at, for, upon, (+acc) on, upon, unto, to, against
σὲ pron. acc. 2p. sg. σύ thou, you
προφητείας n. acc. fem. pl. προφητεία prophecy, prophesying
ἵνα conj. ἵνα that, to, lest, for to, so that, albeit, because, for, so as
ἐν prep. ἐν (+dat) in, by, with, among, at, on, through, to, within, into, of, for
αὐταῖς pron. dat. fem. 3p. pl. αὐτός ἡ ὁ self, of oneself, even, very, the same, he, she, it
τὴν art. acc. fem. sg. ὁ ἡ τό the, this, that, he, she, it
καλὴν adj. acc. fem. sg. καλός good, better, goodly, meet, honest, fair, well, worthy
στρατείαν n. acc. fem. sg. στρατεία warfare
19 πίστιν n. acc. fem. sg. πίστις faith, assurance, belief, fidelity
καὶ conj. καί and, even, also, but
ἀγαθὴν adj. acc. fem. sg. ἀγαθός good, good thing, that which is good, well
συνείδησιν n. acc. fem. sg. συνείδησις conscience
ἥν relative pron. acc. fem. sg. ὅς ἥ ὅ who, which, what, that
τινες indefinite pron. nom. masc. pl. τὶς certain, some, any man, one, any thing
περὶ prep. περί (+gen) of, for, concerning, (+acc) about, concerning, in
τὴν art. acc. fem. sg. ὁ ἡ τό the, this, that, he, she, it
πίστιν n. acc. fem. sg. πίστις faith, assurance, belief, fidelity
20 ὧν relative pron. gen. masc. pl. ὅς ἥ ὅ who, which, what, that
Ὑμέναιος n. nom. masc. sg. Ὑμέναιος Hymenaeus
καὶ conj. καί and, even, also, but
Ἀλέξανδρος n. nom. masc. sg. Ἀλέξανδρος Alexander
οὓς relative pron. acc. masc. pl. ὅς ἥ ὅ who, which, what, that
τῷ art. dat. masc. sg. ὁ ἡ τό the, this, that, he, she, it
Σατανᾷ n. dat. masc. sg. Σατανᾶς Satan
ἵνα conj. ἵνα that, to, lest, for to, so that, albeit, because, for, so as
μὴ particle of negation. μή not, no, lest, neither, none, nothing, nor, never, without

2

1 οὖν conj. οὖν therefore, then, so, and, now, wherefore

πρῶτον adv. πρῶτον first, at the first, first of all, at first, at the beginning, before, chiefly
πάντων adj. gen. neut. pl. πᾶς πᾶσα πᾶν all, every, whosoever, every one, no, whole, any
δεήσεις n. acc. fem. pl. δέησις prayer, supplication, request
προσευχὰς n. acc. fem. pl. προσευχή prayer
ἐντεύξεις n. acc. fem. pl. ἔντευξις intercession, prayer
εὐχαριστίας n. acc. fem. pl. εὐχαριστία thankfulness, thanksgiving, giving of thanks
ὑπὲρ prep. ὑπέρ (+gen) for, of, for the sake of, (+acc) above, more than
πάντων adj. gen. masc. pl. πᾶς πᾶσα πᾶν all, every, whosoever, every one, no, whole, any
ἀνθρώπων n. gen. masc. pl. ἄνθρωπος man, human being, person, one, certain
2 ὑπὲρ prep. ὑπέρ (+gen) for, of, for the sake of, (+acc) above, more than
βασιλέων n. gen. masc. pl. βασιλεύς king
καὶ conj. καί and, even, also, but
πάντων adj. gen. masc. pl. πᾶς πᾶσα πᾶν all, every, whosoever, every one, no, whole, any
τῶν art. gen. masc. pl. ὁ ἡ τό the, this, that, he, she, it
ἐν prep. ἐν (+dat) in, by, with, among, at, on, through, to, within, into, of, for
ὑπεροχῇ n. dat. fem. sg. ὑπεροχή excellency, authority
ἵνα conj. ἵνα that, to, lest, for to, so that, albeit, because, for, so as
ἤρεμον adj. acc. masc. sg. ἤρεμος quiet
καὶ conj. καί and, even, also, but
ἡσύχιον adj. acc. masc. sg. ἡσύχιος peaceable, quiet
βίον n. acc. masc. sg. βίος life, living, good
ἐν prep. ἐν (+dat) in, by, with, among, at, on, through, to, within, into, of, for
πάσῃ adj. dat. fem. sg. πᾶς πᾶσα πᾶν all, every, whosoever, every one, no, whole, any
εὐσεβείᾳ n. dat. fem. sg. εὐσέβεια godliness, holiness
καὶ conj. καί and, even, also, but
σεμνότητι n. dat. fem. sg. σεμνότης honesty, gravity
3 τοῦτο demo. pron. nom. neut. sg. οὗτος αὕτη τοῦτο this, the same, this same, he, she, it
γὰρ conj. γάρ for, and, because, but, indeed
καλὸν adj. nom. neut. sg. καλός good, better, goodly, meet, honest, fair, well, worthy
καὶ conj. καί and, even, also, but
ἀπόδεκτον adj. nom. neut. sg. ἀπόδεκτος acceptable
ἐνώπιον prep. ἐνώπιον (+gen) before, in the sight of, in the presence of. (adv.) before
τοῦ art. gen. masc. sg. ὁ ἡ τό the, this, that, he, she, it
σωτῆρος n. gen. masc. sg. σωτήρ Saviour, saviour
ἡμῶν pron. gen. 1p. pl. ἐγώ I
Θεοῦ n. gen. masc. sg. θεός God, god
4 ὃς relative pron. nom. masc. sg. ὅς ἥ ὅ who, which, what, that
πάντας adj. acc. masc. pl. πᾶς πᾶσα πᾶν all, every, whosoever, every one, no, whole, any
ἀνθρώπους n. acc. masc. pl. ἄνθρωπος man, human being, person, one, certain
καὶ conj. καί and, even, also, but
εἰς prep. εἰς (+acc) into, to, unto, for, in, on, toward, against, upon, at, among
ἐπίγνωσιν n. acc. fem. sg. ἐπίγνωσις knowledge, acknowledging, acknowledgement
ἀληθείας n. gen. fem. sg. ἀλήθεια truth, verity
5 εἷς num. nom. masc. sg. εἷς or ἕν one, other, some, any, only, a certain
γὰρ conj. γάρ for, and, because, but, indeed
Θεός n. nom. masc. sg. θεός God, god
εἷς num. nom. masc. sg. εἷς or ἕν one, other, some, any, only, a certain
καὶ conj. καί and, even, also, but
μεσίτης n. nom. masc. sg. μεσίτης mediator
Θεοῦ n. gen. masc. sg. θεός God, god
καὶ conj. καί and, even, also, but
ἀνθρώπων n. gen. masc. pl. ἄνθρωπος man, human being, person, one, certain
ἄνθρωπος n. nom. masc. sg. ἄνθρωπος man, human being, person, one, certain
Χριστὸς n. nom. masc. sg. Χριστός Christ
Ἰησοῦς n. nom. masc. sg. Ἰησοῦς Jesus

6 ὁ art. nom. masc. sg. ὁ ἡ τό the, this, that, he, she, it
ἑαυτὸν reflexive pron. acc. masc. 3p. sg. ἑαυτοῦ himself, herself, itself, yourself, ourselves
ἀντίλυτρον n. acc. neut. sg. ἀντίλυτρον ransom
ὑπὲρ prep. ὑπέρ (+gen) for, of, for the sake of, (+acc) above, more than
πάντων adj. gen. masc. pl. πᾶς πᾶςα πᾶν all, every, whosoever, every one, no, whole, any
τὸ art. nom. neut. sg. ὁ ἡ τό the, this, that, he, she, it
μαρτύριον n. nom. neut. sg. μαρτύριον testimony, witness
καιροῖς n. dat. masc. pl. καιρός time, season, due time, opportunity
ἰδίοις adj. dat. masc. pl. ἴδιος one's own, one's, privately
7 εἰς prep. εἰς (+acc) into, to, unto, for, in, on, toward, against, upon, at, among
ὃ relative pron. acc. neut. sg. ὅς ἥ ὅ who, which, what, that
ἐγὼ pron. nom. 1p. sg. ἐγώ I
κῆρυξ n. nom. masc. sg. κῆρυξ preacher
καὶ conj. καί and, even, also, but
ἀπόστολος n. nom. masc. sg. ἀπόστολος apostle, messenger, he that is sent
ἀλήθειαν n. acc. fem. sg. ἀλήθεια truth, verity
ἐν prep. ἐν (+dat) in, by, with, among, at, on, through, to, within, into, of, for
Χριστῷ n. dat. masc. sg. Χριστός Christ
οὐ particle of negation. οὐ οὐκ οὐχ not, no, neither, none, nay, nor, never, nothing
διδάσκαλος n. nom. masc. sg. διδάσκαλος teacher, master, doctor
ἐθνῶν n. gen. neut. pl. ἔθνος Gentile, nation, heathen, people
ἐν prep. ἐν (+dat) in, by, with, among, at, on, through, to, within, into, of, for
πίστει n. dat. fem. sg. πίστις faith, assurance, belief, fidelity
καὶ conj. καί and, even, also, but
ἀληθείᾳ n. dat. fem. sg. ἀλήθεια truth, verity
8 οὖν conj. οὖν therefore, then, so, and, now, wherefore
τοὺς art. acc. masc. pl. ὁ ἡ τό the, this, that, he, she, it
ἄνδρας n. acc. masc. pl. ἀνήρ man, husband, sir
ἐν prep. ἐν (+dat) in, by, with, among, at, on, through, to, within, into, of, for
παντὶ adj. dat. masc. sg. πᾶς πᾶςα πᾶν all, every, whosoever, every one, no, whole, any
τόπῳ n. dat. masc. sg. τόπος place, room, quarter
ὁσίους adj. acc. fem. pl. ὅσιος holy, Holy, mercy
χεῖρας n. acc. fem. pl. χείρ hand
χωρὶς prep. χωρίς (+gen) without, beside. (adv.) by itself, apart, separately
ὀργῆς n. gen. fem. sg. ὀργή wrath, anger, indignation, vengeance
καὶ conj. καί and, even, also, but
διαλογισμοῦ n. gen. masc. sg. διαλογισμός thought, reasoning, imagination, disputing
9 ὡσαύτως adv. ὡσαύτως likewise, in like manner, after the same manner, even so
καὶ χonj. καί and, even, also, but
τὰς art. acc. fem. pl. ὁ ἡ τό the, this, that, he, she, it
γυναῖκας n. acc. fem. pl. γυνή woman, wife
ἐν prep. ἐν (+dat) in, by, with, among, at, on, through, to, within, into, of, for
καταστολῇ n. dat. fem. sg. καταστολή apparel
κοσμίῳ adj. dat. fem. sg. κόσμιος modest, of good behaviour
μετὰ prep. μετά (+gen) with, among, against, (+acc) after
αἰδοῦς n. gen. fem. sg. αἰδώς shamefacedness, reverence
καὶ χonj. καί and, even, also, but
σωφροσύνης n. gen. fem. sg. σωφροσύνη soberness, sobriety
ἑαυτάς reflexive pron. acc. fem. 3p. pl. ἑαυτοῦ himself, herself, itself, yourself, ourselves
μὴ particle of negation. μή not, no, lest, neither, none, nothing, nor, never, without
ἐν prep. ἐν (+dat) in, by, with, among, at, on, through, to, within, into, of, for
πλέγμασιν n. dat. neut. pl. πλέγμα broided hair, braid of hair
ἢ particle. ἤ or, than, either, nor, or else, and, rather than
χρυσῷ n. dat. masc. sg. χρυσός gold
ἢ particle. ἤ or, than, either, nor, or else, and, rather than

μαργαρίταις n. dat. masc. pl. μαργαρίτης pearl
ἢ particle. ἤ or, than, either, nor, or else, and, rather than
ἱματισμῷ n. dat. masc. sg. ἱματισμός apparel, array, raiment, vesture
πολυτελεῖ adj. dat. masc. sg. πολυτελής very precious, costly, of great price
10 ἀλλ' conj. ἀλλά but, yea, yet, nevertheless, howbeit, nay, therefore
ὃ relative pron. nom. neut. sg. ὅς ἥ ὅ who, which, what, that
γυναιξὶν n. dat. fem. pl. γυνή woman, wife
θεοσέβειαν n. acc. fem. sg. θεοσέβεια godliness
δι' prep. διά (+gen) by, through, with, in, of, (+acc) for, because of, for a cause
ἔργων n. gen. neut. pl. ἔργον work, deed, doing labour
ἀγαθῶν adj. gen. neut. pl. ἀγαθός good, good thing, that which is good, well
11 γυνὴ n. nom. fem. sg. γυνή woman, wife
ἐν prep. ἐν (+dat) in, by, with, among, at, on, through, to, within, into, of, for
ἡσυχίᾳ n. dat. fem. sg. ἡσυχία silence, quietness
ἐν prep. ἐν (+dat) in, by, with, among, at, on, through, to, within, into, of, for
πάσῃ adj. dat. fem. sg. πᾶς πᾶσα πᾶν all, every, whosoever, every one, no, whole, any
ὑποταγῇ n. dat. fem. sg. ὑποταγή subjection
12 γυναικὶ n. dat. fem. sg. γυνή woman, wife
δὲ conj. δέ but, and, now, also, to the contrary, rather, then
οὐκ particle of negation. οὐ οὐκ οὐχ not, no, neither, none, nay, nor, never, nothing
οὐδὲ adv. οὐδέ neither, nor, not, no, not even, never, not yet
ἀνδρός n. gen. masc. sg. ἀνήρ man, husband, sir
ἀλλ' conj. ἀλλά but, yea, yet, nevertheless, howbeit, nay, therefore
ἐν prep. ἐν (+dat) in, by, with, among, at, on, through, to, within, into, of, for
ἡσυχίᾳ n. dat. fem. sg. ἡσυχία silence, quietness
13 Ἀδὰμ n. nom. masc. sg. Ἀδάμ Adam
γὰρ conj. γάρ for, and, because, but, indeed
πρῶτος ordinal. adj. nom. masc. sg. πρῶτος first, chief, first of all, chiefest, best
εἶτα adv. εἶτα afterward, then, after that, furthermore
Εὔα n. nom. fem. sg. Εὔα Eve
14 καὶ conj. καί and, even, also, but
Ἀδὰμ n. nom. masc. sg. Ἀδάμ Adam
οὐκ particle of negation. οὐ οὐκ οὐχ not, no, neither, none, nay, nor, never, nothing
ἡ art. nom. fem. sg. ὁ ἡ τό the, this, that, he, she, it
δὲ conj. δέ but, and, now, also, to the contrary, rather, then
γυνὴ n. nom. fem. sg. γυνή woman, wife
ἐν prep. ἐν (+dat) in, by, with, among, at, on, through, to, within, into, of, for
παραβάσει n. dat. fem. sg. παράβασις breaking, transgression
15 δὲ conj. δέ but, and, now, also, to the contrary, rather, then
διὰ prep. διά (+gen) by, through, with, in, of, (+acc) for, because of, for a cause
τῆς art. gen. fem. sg. ὁ ἡ τό the, this, that, he, she, it
τεκνογονίας n. gen. fem. sg. τεκνογονία child bearing
ἐὰν conj. ἐάν if, soever, except, though, and if, but, whether, if so, so
ἐν prep. ἐν (+dat) in, by, with, among, at, on, through, to, within, into, of, for
πίστει n. dat. fem. sg. πίστις faith, assurance, belief, fidelity
καὶ conj. καί and, even, also, but
ἀγάπῃ n. dat. fem. sg. ἀγάπη love, charity, feast of charity
καὶ conj. καί and, even, also, but
ἁγιασμῷ n. dat. masc. sg. ἁγιασμός holiness, sanctification
μετὰ prep. μετά (+gen) with, among, against, (+acc) after
σωφροσύνης n. gen. fem. sg. σωφροσύνη soberness, sobriety

3

1 πιστὸς adj. nom. masc. sg. πιστός faithful, believing, true, sure

ὁ art. nom. masc. sg. ὁ ἡ τό the, this, that, he, she, it
λόγος n. nom. masc. sg. λόγος word, saying, account, speech, thing, matter
Εἴ conj. εἰ if, whether, that, though, forasmuch
τις indefinite pron. nom. masc. sg. τὶς certain, some, any man, one, any thing
ἐπισκοπῆς n. gen. fem. sg. ἐπισκοπή bishoprick, visitation, the office of a bishop
καλοῦ adj. gen. neut. sg. καλός good, better, goodly, meet, honest, fair, well, worthy
ἔργου n. gen. neut. sg. ἔργον work, deed, doing labour
2 οὖν conj. οὖν therefore, then, so, and, now, wherefore
τὸν art. acc. masc. sg. ὁ ἡ τό the, this, that, he, she, it
ἐπίσκοπον n. acc. masc. sg. ἐπίσκοπος overseer, bishop
ἀνεπίληπτον adj. acc. masc. sg. ἀνεπίληπτος blameless, unrebukeable
μιᾶς num. gen. fem. sg. εἶς or ἕν one, other, some, any, only, a certain
γυναικὸς n. gen. fem. sg. γυνή woman, wife
ἄνδρα n. acc. masc. sg. ἀνήρ man, husband, sir
νηφάλιον adj. acc. masc. sg. νηφάλιος vigilant, sober
σώφρονα adj. acc. masc. sg. σώφρων sober, discreet, temperate
κόσμιον adj. acc. masc. sg. κόσμιος modest, of good behaviour
φιλόξενον adj. acc. masc. sg. φιλόξενος given to hospitality, lover of hospitality
διδακτικόν adj. acc. masc. sg. διδακτικός apt to teach
3 μὴ particle of negation. μή not, no, lest, neither, none, nothing, nor, never, without
πάροινον adj. acc. masc. sg. πάροινος given to wine
μὴ particle of negation. μή not, no, lest, neither, none, nothing, nor, never, without
πλήκτην n. acc. masc. sg. πλήκτης striker
μὴ particle of negation. μή not, no, lest, neither, none, nothing, nor, never, without
αἰσχροκερδῆ adj. acc. masc. sg. αἰσχροκερδής greedy of filthy lucre
ἀλλ' conj. ἀλλά but, yea, yet, nevertheless, howbeit, nay, therefore
ἐπιεικῆ adj. acc. masc. sg. ἐπιεικής moderation, gentle, patient
ἄμαχον adj. acc. masc. sg. ἄμαχος not a brawler
ἀφιλάργυρον adj. acc. masc. sg. ἀφιλάργυρος not covetous, without covetousness
4 τοῦ art. gen. masc. sg. ὁ ἡ τό the, this, that, he, she, it
ἰδίου adj. gen. masc. sg. ἴδιος one's own, one's, privately
οἴκου n. gen. masc. sg. οἶκος house, home, household
καλῶς adv. καλῶς good, well, full well
τέκνα n. acc. neut. pl. τέκνον child, son, daughter
ἐν prep. ἐν (+dat) in, by, with, among, at, on, through, to, within, into, of, for
ὑποταγῇ n. dat. fem. sg. ὑποταγή subjection
μετὰ prep. μετά (+gen) with, among, against, (+acc) after
πάσης adj. gen. fem. sg. πᾶς πᾶσα πᾶν all, every, whosoever, every one, no, whole, any
σεμνότητος n. gen. fem. sg. σεμνότης honesty, gravity
5 εἰ conj. εἰ if, whether, that, though, forasmuch
δέ conj. δέ but, and, now, also, to the contrary, rather, then
τις indefinite pron. nom. masc. sg. τὶς certain, some, any man, one, any thing
τοῦ art. gen. masc. sg. ὁ ἡ τό the, this, that, he, she, it
ἰδίου adj. gen. masc. sg. ἴδιος one's own, one's, privately
οἴκου n. gen. masc. sg. οἶκος house, home, household
οὐκ particle of negation. οὐ οὐκ οὐχ not, no, neither, none, nay, nor, never, nothing
πῶς adv. πῶς how, by what means, after what manner
ἐκκλησίας n. gen. fem. sg. ἐκκλησία church, assembly
Θεοῦ n. gen. masc. sg. θεός God, god
6 μὴ particle of negation. μή not, no, lest, neither, none, nothing, nor, never, without
νεόφυτον adj. acc. masc. sg. νεόφυτος novice
ἵνα conj. ἵνα that, to, lest, for to, so that, albeit, because, for, so as
μὴ particle of negation. μή not, no, lest, neither, none, nothing, nor, never, without
εἰς prep. εἰς (+acc) into, to, unto, for, in, on, toward, against, upon, at, among
κρίμα n. acc. neut. sg. κρίμα judgment, damnation, condemnation

τοῦ art. gen. masc. sg. ὁ ἡ τό the, this, that, he, she, it
διαβόλου adj. gen. masc. sg. διάβολος devil, false accuser, Devil, slanderer
7 δὲ conj. δέ but, and, now, also, to the contrary, rather, then
αὐτὸν pron. acc. masc. 3p. sg. αὐτός ἡ ὁ self, of oneself, even, very, the same, he, she, it
καὶ conj. καί and, even, also, but
μαρτυρίαν n. acc. fem. sg. μαρτυρία testimony, witness, record, report
καλὴν adj. acc. fem. sg. καλός good, better, goodly, meet, honest, fair, well, worthy
ἀπὸ prep. ἀπό (+gen) from, of, out of, since, for, off, at, by, in, on
τῶν art. gen. masc. pl. ὁ ἡ τό the, this, that, he, she, it
ἔξωθεν adv. ἔξωθεν without, from without, outside, outward, outwardly
ἵνα conj. ἵνα that, to, lest, for to, so that, albeit, because, for, so as
μὴ particle of negation. μή not, no, lest, neither, none, nothing, nor, never, without
εἰς prep. εἰς (+acc) into, to, unto, for, in, on, toward, against, upon, at, among
ὀνειδισμὸν n. acc. masc. sg. ὀνειδισμός reproach
καὶ conj. καί and, even, also, but
παγίδα n. acc. fem. sg. παγίς snare
τοῦ art. gen. masc. sg. ὁ ἡ τό the, this, that, he, she, it
διαβόλου adj. gen. masc. sg. διάβολος devil, false accuser, Devil, slanderer
8 διακόνους n. acc. masc. pl. διάκονος minister, servant, deacon
ὡσαύτως adv. ὡσαύτως likewise, in like manner, after the same manner, even so
σεμνούς adj. acc. masc. pl. σεμνός honest, grave
μὴ particle of negation. μή not, no, lest, neither, none, nothing, nor, never, without
διλόγους adj. acc. masc. pl. δίλογος doubletongued
μὴ particle of negation. μή not, no, lest, neither, none, nothing, nor, never, without
οἴνῳ n. dat. masc. sg. οἶνος wine
πολλῷ adj. dat. masc. sg. πολύς many, great, much, long, abundant
μὴ particle of negation. μή not, no, lest, neither, none, nothing, nor, never, without
αἰσχροκερδεῖς adj. acc. masc. pl. αἰσχροκερδής greedy of filthy lucre
9 τὸ art. acc. neut. sg. ὁ ἡ τό the, this, that, he, she, it
μυστήριον n. acc. neut. sg. μυστήριον mystery
τῆς art. gen. fem. sg. ὁ ἡ τό the, this, that, he, she, it
πίστεως n. gen. fem. sg. πίστις faith, assurance, belief, fidelity
ἐν prep. ἐν (+dat) in, by, with, among, at, on, through, to, within, into, of, for
καθαρᾷ adj. dat. fem. sg. καθαρός pure, clean, clear
συνειδήσει n. dat. fem. sg. συνείδησις conscience
10 καὶ conj. καί and, even, also, but
οὗτοι demo. pron. nom. masc. pl. οὗτος αὕτη τοῦτο this, the same, this same, he, she, it
δὲ conj. δέ but, and, now, also, to the contrary, rather, then
πρῶτον adv. πρῶτον first, at the first, first of all, at first, at the beginning, before, chiefly
εἶτα adv. εἶτα afterward, then, after that, furthermore
ἀνέγκλητοι adj. nom. masc. pl. ἀνέγκλητος blameless, unreprovable
11 γυναῖκας n. acc. fem. pl. γυνή woman, wife
ὡσαύτως adv. ὡσαύτως likewise, in like manner, after the same manner, even so
σεμνάς adj. acc. fem. pl. σεμνός honest, grave
μὴ particle of negation. μή not, no, lest, neither, none, nothing, nor, never, without
διαβόλους adj. acc. fem. pl. διάβολος devil, false accuser, Devil, slanderer
νηφαλίους adj. acc. fem. pl. νηφάλιος vigilant, sober
πιστὰς adj. acc. fem. pl. πιστός faithful, believing, true, sure
ἐν prep. ἐν (+dat) in, by, with, among, at, on, through, to, within, into, of, for
πᾶσι adj. dat. neut. pl. πᾶς πᾶσα πᾶν all, every, whosoever, every one, no, whole, any
12 διάκονοι n. nom. masc. pl. διάκονος minister, servant, deacon
μιᾶς num. gen. fem. sg. εἷς or ἕν one, other, some, any, only, a certain
γυναικὸς n. gen. fem. sg. γυνή woman, wife
ἄνδρες n. nom. masc. pl. ἀνήρ man, husband, sir
τέκνων n. gen. neut. pl. τέκνον child, son, daughter

καλῶς adv. καλῶς good, well, full well
καὶ conj. καί and, even, also, but
τῶν art. gen. masc. pl. ὁ ἡ τό the, this, that, he, she, it
ἰδίων adj. gen. masc. pl. ἴδιος one's own, one's, privately
οἴκων n. gen. masc. pl. οἶκος house, home, household
13 οἱ art. nom. masc. pl. ὁ ἡ τό the, this, that, he, she, it
γὰρ conj. γάρ for, and, because, but, indeed
καλῶς adv. καλῶς good, well, full well
βαθμὸν n. acc. masc. sg. βαθμός degree
ἑαυτοῖς reflexive pron. dat. masc. 3p. pl. ἑαυτοῦ himself, herself, itself, yourself, ourselves
καλὸν adj. acc. masc. sg. καλός good, better, goodly, meet, honest, fair, well, worthy
καὶ conj. καί and, even, also, but
πολλὴν adj. acc. fem. sg. πολύς many, great, much, long, abundant
παρρησίαν n. acc. fem. sg. παρρησία boldness, confidence, openly, plainly, freely
ἐν prep. ἐν (+dat) in, by, with, among, at, on, through, to, within, into, of, for
πίστει n. dat. fem. sg. πίστις faith, assurance, belief, fidelity
τῇ art. dat. fem. sg. ὁ ἡ τό the, this, that, he, she, it
ἐν prep. ἐν (+dat) in, by, with, among, at, on, through, to, within, into, of, for
Χριστῷ n. dat. masc. sg. Χριστός Christ
Ἰησοῦ n. dat. masc. sg. Ἰησοῦς Jesus
14 Ταῦτά demo. pron. acc. neut. pl. οὗτος αὕτη τοῦτο this, the same, this same, he, she, it
σοι pron. dat. 2p. sg. σύ thou, you
πρὸς prep. πρός (+gen) for, (+dat) at, (+acc) unto, to, with, for, against
σὲ pron. acc. 2p. sg. σύ thou, you
τάχιον adv. τάχιον sortly, quickly, sooner
15 ἐὰν conj. ἐάν if, soever, except, though, and if, but, whether, if so, so
δὲ conj. δέ but, and, now, also, to the contrary, rather, then
ἵνα conj. ἵνα that, to, lest, for to, so that, albeit, because, for, so as
πῶς adv. πῶς how, by what means, after what manner
ἐν prep. ἐν (+dat) in, by, with, among, at, on, through, to, within, into, of, for
οἴκῳ n. dat. masc. sg. οἶκος house, home, household
Θεοῦ n. gen. masc. sg. θεός God, god
ἥτις relative pron. nom. fem. sg. ὅστις which, who, whosoever, that, whatsoever
ἐκκλησία n. nom. fem. sg. ἐκκλησία church, assembly
Θεοῦ n. gen. masc. sg. θεός God, god
στῦλος n. nom. masc. sg. στῦλος pillar
καὶ conj. καί and, even, also, but
ἑδραίωμα n. nom. neut. sg. ἑδραίωμα ground
τῆς art. gen. fem. sg. ὁ ἡ τό the, this, that, he, she, it
ἀληθείας n. gen. fem. sg. ἀλήθεια truth, verity
16 καὶ conj. καί and, even, also, but
ὁμολογουμένως adv. ὁμολογουμένως without controversy
μέγα adj. nom. neut. sg. μέγας great, loud, greatest, high, large, mighty, strong
τὸ art. nom. neut. sg. ὁ ἡ τό the, this, that, he, she, it
τῆς art. gen. fem. sg. ὁ ἡ τό the, this, that, he, she, it
εὐσεβείας n. gen. fem. sg. εὐσέβεια godliness, holiness
μυστήριον n. nom. neut. sg. μυστήριον mystery
Θεὸς n. nom. masc. sg. θεός God, god
ἐν prep. ἐν (+dat) in, by, with, among, at, on, through, to, within, into, of, for
σαρκί n. dat. fem. sg. σάρξ flesh, carnal
ἐν prep. ἐν (+dat) in, by, with, among, at, on, through, to, within, into, of, for
πνεύματι n. dat. neut. sg. πνεῦμα spirit, Spirit, Ghost, ghost, life. of the spirit, wind
ἀγγέλοις n. dat. masc. pl. ἄγγελος angel, messenger
ἐν prep. ἐν (+dat) in, by, with, among, at, on, through, to, within, into, of, for
ἔθνεσιν n. dat. neut. pl. ἔθνος Gentile, nation, heathen, people

ἐν prep. ἐν (+dat) in, by, with, among, at, on, through, to, within, into, of, for
κόσμῳ n. dat. masc. sg. κόσμος world, adorning
ἐν prep. ἐν (+dat) in, by, with, among, at, on, through, to, within, into, of, for
δόξῃ n. dat. fem. sg. δόξα glory, honour, praise, dignity, worship

4

1 Τὸ art. nom. neut. sg. ὁ ἡ τό the, this, that, he, she, it
δὲ conj. δέ but, and, now, also, to the contrary, rather, then
Πνεῦμα n. nom. neut. sg. πνεῦμα spirit, Spirit, Ghost, ghost, life. of the spirit, wind
ῥητῶς adv. ῥητῶς expressly
ὅτι conj. ὅτι that, for, because, how that, how, because that, for that, though
ἐν prep. ἐν (+dat) in, by, with, among, at, on, through, to, within, into, of, for
ὑστέροις compar. adj. dat. masc. pl. ὕστερος latter
καιροῖς n. dat. masc. pl. καιρός time, season, due time, opportunity
τινες indefinite pron. nom. masc. pl. τὶς certain, some, any man, one, any thing
τῆς art. gen. fem. sg. ὁ ἡ τό the, this, that, he, she, it
πίστεως n. gen. fem. sg. πίστις faith, assurance, belief, fidelity
πνεύμασι n. dat. neut. pl. πνεῦμα spirit, Spirit, Ghost, ghost, life. of the spirit, wind
πλάνοις adj. dat. neut. pl. πλάνος deceiver, seducing
καὶ conj. καί and, even, also, but
διδασκαλίαις n. dat. fem. pl. διδασκαλία doctrine, learning, teaching
δαιμονίων n. gen. neut. pl. δαιμόνιον devil, demon, god
2 ἐν prep. ἐν (+dat) in, by, with, among, at, on, through, to, within, into, of, for
ὑποκρίσει n. dat. fem. sg. ὑπόκρισις hypocrisy, condemnation, dissimulation
ψευδολόγων adj. gen. masc. pl. ψευδολόγος speaking lies
τὴν art. acc. fem. sg. ὁ ἡ τό the, this, that, he, she, it
ἰδίαν adj. acc. fem. sg. ἴδιος one's own, one's, privately
συνείδησιν n. acc. fem. sg. συνείδησις conscience
3 βρωμάτων n. gen. neut. pl. βρῶμα victual, meat, food
ἃ relative pron. acc. neut. pl. ὅς ἥ ὅ who, which, what, that
ὁ art. nom. masc. sg. ὁ ἡ τό the, this, that, he, she, it
Θεὸς n. nom. masc. sg. θεός God, god
εἰς prep. εἰς (+acc) into, to, unto, for, in, on, toward, against, upon, at, among
μετάληψιν n. acc. fem. sg. μετάληψις be received
μετὰ prep. μετά (+gen) with, among, against, (+acc) after
εὐχαριστίας n. gen. fem. sg. εὐχαριστία thankfulness, thanksgiving, giving of thanks
τοῖς art. dat. masc. pl. ὁ ἡ τό the, this, that, he, she, it
πιστοῖς adj. dat. masc. pl. πιστός faithful, believing, true, sure
καὶ conj. καί and, even, also, but
τὴν art. acc. fem. sg. ὁ ἡ τό the, this, that, he, she, it
ἀλήθειαν n. acc. fem. sg. ἀλήθεια truth, verity
4 ὅτι conj. ὅτι that, for, because, how that, how, because that, for that, though
πᾶν adj. nom. neut. sg. πᾶς πᾶσa πᾶν all, every, whosoever, every one, no, whole, any
κτίσμα n. nom. neut. sg. κτίσμα creature
Θεοῦ n. gen. masc. sg. θεός God, god
καλὸν adj. nom. neut. sg. καλός good, better, goodly, meet, honest, fair, well, worthy
καὶ conj. καί and, even, also, but
οὐδὲν num. nom. neut. sg. οὐδείς no man, nothing, no, none, neither, not, nought
ἀπόβλητον adj. nom. neut. sg. ἀπόβλητος be refused
μετὰ prep. μετά (+gen) with, among, against, (+acc) after
εὐχαριστίας n. gen. fem. sg. εὐχαριστία thankfulness, thanksgiving, giving of thanks
5 γὰρ conj. γάρ for, and, because, but, indeed
διὰ prep. διά (+gen) by, through, with, in, of, (+acc) for, because of, for a cause
λόγου n. gen. masc. sg. λόγος word, saying, account, speech, thing, matter

Θεοῦ n. gen. masc. sg. θεός God, god
καὶ conj. καί and, even, also, but
ἐντεύξεως n. gen. fem. sg. ἔντευξις intercession, prayer
6 Ταῦτα demo. pron. acc. neut. pl. οὗτος αὕτη τοῦτο this, the same, this same, he, she, it
τοῖς art. dat. masc. pl. ὁ ἡ τό the, this, that, he, she, it
ἀδελφοῖς n. dat. masc. pl. ἀδελφός brother
καλὸς adj. nom. masc. sg. καλός good, better, goodly, meet, honest, fair, well, worthy
διάκονος n. nom. masc. sg. διάκονος minister, servant, deacon
Ἰησοῦ n. gen. masc. sg. Ἰησοῦς Jesus
Χριστοῦ n. gen. masc. sg. Χριστός Christ
τοῖς art. dat. masc. pl. ὁ ἡ τό the, this, that, he, she, it
λόγοις n. dat. masc. pl. λόγος word, saying, account, speech, thing, matter
τῆς art. gen. fem. sg. ὁ ἡ τό the, this, that, he, she, it
πίστεως n. gen. fem. sg. πίστις faith, assurance, belief, fidelity
καὶ conj. καί and, even, also, but
τῆς art. gen. fem. sg. ὁ ἡ τό the, this, that, he, she, it
καλῆς adj. gen. fem. sg. καλός good, better, goodly, meet, honest, fair, well, worthy
διδασκαλίας n. gen. fem. sg. διδασκαλία doctrine, learning, teaching
ᾗ relative pron. dat. fem. sg. ὅς ἥ ὅ who, which, what, that
7 τοὺς art. acc. masc. pl. ὁ ἡ τό the, this, that, he, she, it
δὲ conj. δέ but, and, now, also, to the contrary, rather, then
βεβήλους adj. acc. masc. pl. βέβηλος profane, profane person
καὶ conj. καί and, even, also, but
γραώδεις adj. acc. masc. pl. γραώδης old wife
μύθους n. acc. masc. pl. μῦθος fable, myth
δὲ conj. δέ but, and, now, also, to the contrary, rather, then
σεαυτὸν pron. acc. masc. 2p. sg. σεαυτοῦ σεαυτῷ σεαυτόν thyself, thine own self
πρὸς prep. πρός (+gen) for, (+dat) at, (+acc) unto, to, with, for, against
εὐσέβειαν n. acc. fem. sg. εὐσέβεια godliness, holiness
8 ἡ art. nom. fem. sg. ὁ ἡ τό the, this, that, he, she, it
γὰρ conj. γάρ for, and, because, but, indeed
σωματικὴ adj. nom. fem. sg. σωματικός bodily
γυμνασία n. nom. fem. sg. γυμνασία exercise
πρὸς prep. πρός (+gen) for, (+dat) at, (+acc) unto, to, with, for, against
ὀλίγον adj. acc. masc. sg. ὀλίγος few, little, small, a while, brief, short, short space
ὠφέλιμος adj. nom. fem. sg. ὠφέλιμος profitable, profit
ἡ art. nom. fem. sg. ὁ ἡ τό the, this, that, he, she, it
δὲ conj. δέ but, and, now, also, to the contrary, rather, then
εὐσέβεια n. nom. fem. sg. εὐσέβεια godliness, holiness
πρὸς prep. πρός (+gen) for, (+dat) at, (+acc) unto, to, with, for, against
πάντα adj. acc. neut. pl. πᾶς πᾶσα πᾶν all, every, whosoever, every one, no, whole, any
ὠφέλιμός adj. nom. fem. sg. ὠφέλιμος profitable, profit
ἐπαγγελίαν n. acc. fem. sg. ἐπαγγελία promise, message
ζωῆς n. gen. fem. sg. ζωή life, lifetime
τῆς art. gen. fem. sg. ὁ ἡ τό the, this, that, he, she, it
νῦν adv. νῦν now, henceforth, present, this time
καὶ conj. καί and, even, also, but
τῆς art. gen. fem. sg. ὁ ἡ τό the, this, that, he, she, it
9 πιστὸς adj. nom. masc. sg. πιστός faithful, believing, true, sure
ὁ art. nom. masc. sg. ὁ ἡ τό the, this, that, he, she, it
λόγος n. nom. masc. sg. λόγος word, saying, account, speech, thing, matter
καὶ conj. καί and, even, also, but
πάσης adj. gen. fem. sg. πᾶς πᾶσα πᾶν all, every, whosoever, every one, no, whole, any
ἀποδοχῆς n. gen. fem. sg. ἀποδοχή acceptation
ἄξιος adj. nom. masc. sg. ἄξιος worthy, meet, due reward

10 εἰς prep. εἰς (+acc) into, to, unto, for, in, on, toward, against, upon, at, among
τοῦτο demo. pron. acc. neut. sg. οὗτος αὕτη τοῦτο this, the same, this same, he, she, it
γὰρ conj. γάρ for, and, because, but, indeed
καὶ conj. καί and, even, also, but
καὶ conj. καί and, even, also, but
ὅτι conj. ὅτι that, for, because, how that, how, because that, for that, though
ἐπὶ prep. ἐπί (+gen) on, in, upon, (+dat) in, at, for, upon, (+acc) on, upon, unto, to, against
Θεῷ n. dat. masc. sg. θεός God, god
ὅς relative pron. nom. masc. sg. ὅς ἥ ὅ who, which, what, that
σωτὴρ n. nom. masc. sg. σωτήρ Saviour, saviour
πάντων adj. gen. masc. pl. πᾶς πᾶσα πᾶν all, every, whosoever, every one, no, whole, any
ἀνθρώπων n. gen. masc. pl. ἄνθρωπος man, human being, person, one, certain
μάλιστα adv. μάλιστα specially, especially, chiefly, most of all
πιστῶν adj. gen. masc. pl. πιστός faithful, believing, true, sure
11 ταῦτα demo. pron. acc. neut. pl. οὗτος αὕτη τοῦτο this, the same, this same, he, she, it
καὶ conj. καί and, even, also, but
12 μηδείς num. nom. masc. sg. μηδείς μηδεμία μηδέν no man, nothing, no, none, not at all
σου pron. gen. 2p. sg. σύ thou, you
τῆς art. gen. fem. sg. ὁ ἡ τό the, this, that, he, she, it
νεότητος n. gen. fem. sg. νεότης youth
ἀλλὰ conj. ἀλλά but, yea, yet, nevertheless, howbeit, nay, therefore
τύπος n. nom. masc. sg. τύπος ensample, example, pattern, print, figure, fashion
τῶν art. gen. masc. pl. ὁ ἡ τό the, this, that, he, she, it
πιστῶν adj. gen. masc. pl. πιστός faithful, believing, true, sure
ἐν prep. ἐν (+dat) in, by, with, among, at, on, through, to, within, into, of, for
λόγῳ n. dat. masc. sg. λόγος word, saying, account, speech, thing, matter
ἐν prep. ἐν (+dat) in, by, with, among, at, on, through, to, within, into, of, for
ἀναστροφῇ n. dat. fem. sg. ἀναστροφή conversation
ἐν prep. ἐν (+dat) in, by, with, among, at, on, through, to, within, into, of, for
ἀγάπῃ n. dat. fem. sg. ἀγάπη love, charity, feast of charity
ἐν prep. ἐν (+dat) in, by, with, among, at, on, through, to, within, into, of, for
πνεύματι n. dat. neut. sg. πνεῦμα spirit, Spirit, Ghost, ghost, life. of the spirit, wind
ἐν prep. ἐν (+dat) in, by, with, among, at, on, through, to, within, into, of, for
πίστει n. dat. fem. sg. πίστις faith, assurance, belief, fidelity
ἐν prep. ἐν (+dat) in, by, with, among, at, on, through, to, within, into, of, for
ἁγνείᾳ n. dat. fem. sg. ἁγνεία purity
13 ἕως conj. ἕως till, until, unto, until when, while, as far as, even, until now
τῇ art. dat. fem. sg. ὁ ἡ τό the, this, that, he, she, it
ἀναγνώσει n. dat. fem. sg. ἀνάγνωσις reading
τῇ art. dat. fem. sg. ὁ ἡ τό the, this, that, he, she, it
παρακλήσει n. dat. fem. sg. παράκλησις consolation, exhortation, comfort
τῇ art. dat. fem. sg. ὁ ἡ τό the, this, that, he, she, it
διδασκαλίᾳ n. dat. fem. sg. διδασκαλία doctrine, learning, teaching
14 μὴ particle of negation. μή not, no, lest, neither, none, nothing, nor, never, without
τοῦ art. gen. neut. sg. ὁ ἡ τό the, this, that, he, she, it
ἐν prep. ἐν (+dat) in, by, with, among, at, on, through, to, within, into, of, for
σοὶ pron. dat. 2p. sg. σύ thou, you
χαρίσματος n. gen. neut. sg. χάρισμα gift, free gift
ὃ relative pron. nom. neut. sg. ὅς ἥ ὅ who, which, what, that
σοὶ pron. dat. 2p. sg. σύ thou, you
διὰ prep. διά (+gen) by, through, with, in, of, (+acc) for, because of, for a cause
προφητείας n. gen. fem. sg. προφητεία prophecy, prophesying
μετὰ prep. μετά (+gen) with, among, against, (+acc) after
ἐπιθέσεως n. gen. fem. sg. ἐπίθεσις putting on, laying on
τῶν art. gen. fem. pl. ὁ ἡ τό the, this, that, he, she, it

χειρῶν n. gen. fem. pl. χείρ hand
τοῦ art. gen. neut. sg. ὁ ἡ τό the, this, that, he, she, it
πρεσβυτερίου n. gen. neut. sg. πρεσβυτέριον elder, estate of an elder, presbytery
15 ταῦτα demo. pron. acc. neut. pl. οὗτος αὕτη τοῦτο this, the same, this same, he, she, it
ἐν prep. ἐν (+dat) in, by, with, among, at, on, through, to, within, into, of, for
τούτοις demo. pron. dat. neut. pl. οὗτος αὕτη τοῦτο this, the same, this same, he, she, it
ἵνα conj. ἵνα that, to, lest, for to, so that, albeit, because, for, so as
σου pron. gen. 2p. sg. σύ thou, you
ἡ art. nom. fem. sg. ὁ ἡ τό the, this, that, he, she, it
προκοπὴ n. nom. fem. sg. προκοπή furtherance, profiting
φανερὰ adj. nom. fem. sg. φανερός manifest, abroad, open, known, outward, appear
ἐν prep. ἐν (+dat) in, by, with, among, at, on, through, to, within, into, of, for
πᾶσιν adj. dat. masc. pl. πᾶς πᾶσα πᾶν all, every, whosoever, every one, no, whole, any
16 σεαυτῷ pron. dat. masc. 2p. sg. σεαυτοῦ σεαυτῷ σεαυτόν thyself, thine own self
καὶ conj. καί and, even, also, but
τῇ art. dat. fem. sg. ὁ ἡ τό the, this, that, he, she, it
διδασκαλίᾳ n. dat. fem. sg. διδασκαλία doctrine, learning, teaching
αὐτοῖς pron. dat. neut. 3p. pl. αὐτός ή ό self, of oneself, even, very, the same, he, she, it
τοῦτο demo. pron. acc. neut. sg. οὗτος αὕτη τοῦτο this, the same, this same, he, she, it
γὰρ conj. γάρ for, and, because, but, indeed
καὶ conj. καί and, even, also, but
σεαυτὸν pron. acc. masc. 2p. sg. σεαυτοῦ σεαυτῷ σεαυτόν thyself, thine own self
καὶ conj. καί and, even, also, but
τοὺς art. acc. masc. pl. ὁ ἡ τό the, this, that, he, she, it
σου pron. gen. 2p. sg. σύ thou, you

5

1 Πρεσβυτέρῳ compar. adj. dat. masc. sg. πρεσβύτερος elder, elder woman, eldest, old man
μὴ particle of negation. μή not, no, lest, neither, none, nothing, nor, never, without
ἀλλὰ conj. ἀλλά but, yea, yet, nevertheless, howbeit, nay, therefore
ὡς adv. ὡς as, when, as it were, how, about, like, as soon as, even as, while
πατέρα n. acc. masc. sg. πατήρ Father, father, parent
νεωτέρους compar. adj. acc. masc. pl. νέος new
ὡς adv. ὡς as, when, as it were, how, about, like, as soon as, even as, while
ἀδελφούς n. acc. masc. pl. ἀδελφός brother
2 πρεσβυτέρας compar. adj. acc. fem. pl. πρεσβύτερος elder, elder woman, eldest, old man
ὡς adv. ὡς as, when, as it were, how, about, like, as soon as, even as, while
μητέρας n. acc. fem. pl. μήτηρ mother
νεωτέρας compar. adj. acc. fem. pl. νέος new
ὡς adv. ὡς as, when, as it were, how, about, like, as soon as, even as, while
ἀδελφὰς n. acc. fem. pl. ἀδελφή sister
ἐν prep. ἐν (+dat) in, by, with, among, at, on, through, to, within, into, of, for
πάσῃ adj. dat. fem. sg. πᾶς πᾶσα πᾶν all, every, whosoever, every one, no, whole, any
ἁγνείᾳ n. dat. fem. sg. ἁγνεία purity
3 χήρας adj. acc. fem. pl. χήρα widow
τὰς art. acc. fem. pl. ὁ ἡ τό the, this, that, he, she, it
ὄντως adv. ὄντως indeed, certainly, clean, of a truth, verily
χήρας adj. acc. fem. pl. χήρα widow
4 εἰ conj. εἰ if, whether, that, though, forasmuch
δέ conj. δέ but, and, now, also, to the contrary, rather, then
τις indefinite pron. nom. fem. sg. τὶς certain, some, any man, one, any thing
χήρα adj. nom. fem. sg. χήρα widow
τέκνα n. acc. neut. pl. τέκνον child, son, daughter
ἢ particle. ἤ or, than, either, nor, or else, and, rather than

ἔκγονα adj. acc. neut. pl. ἔκγονος nephew, descendant
πρῶτον adv. πρῶτον first, at the first, first of all, at first, at the beginning, before, chiefly
τὸν art. acc. masc. sg. ὁ ἡ τό the, this, that, he, she, it
ἴδιον adj. acc. masc. sg. ἴδιος one's own, one's, privately
οἶκον n. acc. masc. sg. οἶκος house, home, household
καὶ conj. καί and, even, also, but
ἀμοιβὰς n. acc. fem. pl. ἀμοιβή requite
τοῖς art. dat. masc. pl. ὁ ἡ τό the, this, that, he, she, it
προγόνοις adj. dat. masc. pl. πρόγονος forefather, parent
τοῦτο demo. pron. nom. neut. sg. οὗτος αὕτη τοῦτο this, the same, this same, he, she, it
γάρ conj. γάρ for, and, because, but, indeed
καλὸν adj. nom. neut. sg. καλός good, better, goodly, meet, honest, fair, well, worthy
καὶ conj. καί and, even, also, but
ἀπόδεκτον adj. nom. neut. sg. ἀπόδεκτος acceptable
ἐνώπιον prep. ἐνώπιον (+gen) before, in the sight of, in the presence of. (adv.) before
τοῦ art. gen. masc. sg. ὁ ἡ τό the, this, that, he, she, it
Θεοῦ n. gen. masc. sg. θεός God, god
5 ἡ art. nom. fem. sg. ὁ ἡ τό the, this, that, he, she, it
δὲ conj. δέ but, and, now, also, to the contrary, rather, then
ὄντως adv. ὄντως indeed, certainly, clean, of a truth, verily
χήρα adj. nom. fem. sg. χήρα widow
καὶ conj. καί and, even, also, but
ἐπὶ prep. ἐπί (+gen) on, in, upon, (+dat) in, at, for, upon, (+acc) on, upon, unto, to, against
τὸν art. acc. masc. sg. ὁ ἡ τό the, this, that, he, she, it
Θεὸν n. acc. masc. sg. θεός God, god
καὶ conj. καί and, even, also, but
ταῖς art. dat. fem. pl. ὁ ἡ τό the, this, that, he, she, it
δεήσεσι n. dat. fem. pl. δέησις prayer, supplication, request
καὶ conj. καί and, even, also, but
ταῖς art. dat. fem. pl. ὁ ἡ τό the, this, that, he, she, it
προσευχαῖς n. dat. fem. pl. προσευχή prayer
νυκτὸς n. gen. fem. sg. νύξ night
καὶ conj. καί and, even, also, but
ἡμέρας n. gen. fem. sg. ἡμέρα day, time, year, while, age, day time
6 ἡ art. nom. fem. sg. ὁ ἡ τό the, this, that, he, she, it
δὲ conj. δέ but, and, now, also, to the contrary, rather, then
7 καὶ conj. καί and, even, also, but
ταῦτα demo. pron. acc. neut. pl. οὗτος αὕτη τοῦτο this, the same, this same, he, she, it
ἵνα conj. ἵνα that, to, lest, for to, so that, albeit, because, for, so as
ἀνεπίληπτοι adj. nom. masc. pl. ἀνεπίληπτος blameless, unrebukeable
8 εἰ conj. εἰ if, whether, that, though, forasmuch
δέ conj. δέ but, and, now, also, to the contrary, rather, then
τις indefinite pron. nom. masc. sg. τὶς certain, some, any man, one, any thing
τῶν art. gen. masc. pl. ὁ ἡ τό the, this, that, he, she, it
ἰδίων adj. gen. masc. pl. ἴδιος one's own, one's, privately
καὶ conj. καί and, even, also, but
μάλιστα adv. μάλιστα specially, especially, chiefly, most of all
τῶν art. gen. masc. pl. ὁ ἡ τό the, this, that, he, she, it
οἰκείων adj. gen. masc. pl. οἰκεῖος of the household, one of one's own house
οὐ particle of negation. οὐ οὐκ οὐχ not, no, neither, none, nay, nor, never, nothing
τὴν art. acc. fem. sg. ὁ ἡ τό the, this, that, he, she, it
πίστιν n. acc. fem. sg. πίστις faith, assurance, belief, fidelity
καὶ conj. καί and, even, also, but
ἀπίστου adj. gen. masc. sg. ἄπιστος faithless, unbelieving, infidel, thing incredible
χείρων compar. adj. nom. masc. sg. χείρων worse, sorer, worse and worse

9 χήρα adj. nom. fem. sg. χήρα widow
μὴ particle of negation. μή not, no, lest, neither, none, nothing, nor, never, without
ἔλαττον compar. adj. nom. neut. sg. ἐλάττων worse, younger
ἐτῶν n. gen. neut. pl. ἔτος year
ἑξήκοντα num. gen. neut. pl. ἑξήκοντα threescore, sixty, sixtyfold
ἑνὸς num. gen. masc. sg. εἶς or ἕν one, other, some, any, only, a certain
ἀνδρὸς n. gen. masc. sg. ἀνήρ man, husband, sir
γυνή n. nom. fem. sg. γυνή woman, wife
10 ἐν prep. ἐν (+dat) in, by, with, among, at, on, through, to, within, into, of, for
ἔργοις n. dat. neut. pl. ἔργον work, deed, doing labour
καλοῖς adj. dat. neut. pl. καλός good, better, goodly, meet, honest, fair, well, worthy
εἰ conj. εἰ if, whether, that, though, forasmuch
εἰ conj. εἰ if, whether, that, though, forasmuch
εἰ conj. εἰ if, whether, that, though, forasmuch
ἁγίων adj. gen. masc. pl. ἅγιος Holy, holy, saint, Holy One, holy thing, most holy
πόδας n. acc. masc. pl. πούς foot
εἰ conj. εἰ if, whether, that, though, forasmuch
εἰ conj. εἰ if, whether, that, though, forasmuch
παντὶ adj. dat. neut. sg. πᾶς πᾶσα πᾶν all, every, whosoever, every one, no, whole, any
ἔργῳ n. dat. neut. sg. ἔργον work, deed, doing labour
ἀγαθῷ adj. dat. neut. sg. ἀγαθός good, good thing, that which is good, well
11 νεωτέρας compar. adj. acc. fem. pl. νέος new
δὲ conj. δέ but, and, now, also, to the contrary, rather, then
χήρας adj. acc. fem. pl. χήρα widow
ὅταν conj. ὅταν when, as soon as, as long as, that, whensoever, while
γὰρ conj. γάρ for, and, because, but, indeed
τοῦ art. gen. masc. sg. ὁ ἡ τό the, this, that, he, she, it
Χριστοῦ n. gen. masc. sg. Χριστός Christ
12 κρίμα n. acc. neut. sg. κρίμα judgment, damnation, condemnation
ὅτι conj. ὅτι that, for, because, how that, how, because that, for that, though
τὴν art. acc. fem. sg. ὁ ἡ τό the, this, that, he, she, it
πρώτην ordinal. adj. acc. fem. sg. πρῶτος first, chief, first of all, chiefest, best
πίστιν n. acc. fem. sg. πίστις faith, assurance, belief, fidelity
13 ἅμα adv. ἅμα (+dat) together, with, also. (adv.) at the same time, together
δὲ conj. δέ but, and, now, also, to the contrary, rather, then
καὶ conj. καί and, even, also, but
ἀργαὶ adj. nom. fem. pl. ἀργός idle, barren, slow
τὰς art. acc. fem. pl. ὁ ἡ τό the, this, that, he, she, it
οἰκίας n. acc. fem. pl. οἰκία house, home, household
οὐ particle of negation. οὐ οὐκ οὐχ not, no, neither, none, nay, nor, never, nothing
μόνον adv. μόνος only, alone, by oneself
δὲ conj. δέ but, and, now, also, to the contrary, rather, then
ἀργαὶ adj. nom. fem. pl. ἀργός idle, barren, slow
ἀλλὰ conj. ἀλλά but, yea, yet, nevertheless, howbeit, nay, therefore
καὶ conj. καί and, even, also, but
φλύαροι adj. nom. fem. pl. φλύαρος tattler
καὶ conj. καί and, even, also, but
περίεργοι adj. nom. fem. pl. περίεργος curious, busy, sorcery
τὰ art. acc. neut. pl. ὁ ἡ τό the, this, that, he, she, it
μὴ particle of negation. μή not, no, lest, neither, none, nothing, nor, never, without
14 οὖν conj. οὖν therefore, then, so, and, now, wherefore
νεωτέρας compar. adj. acc. fem. pl. νέος new
μηδεμίαν num. acc. fem. sg. μηδείς μηδεμία μηδέν no man, nothing, no, none, not at all
ἀφορμὴν n. acc. fem. sg. ἀφορμή occasion
τῷ art. dat. masc. sg. ὁ ἡ τό the, this, that, he, she, it

λοιδορίας n. gen. fem. sg. λοιδορία reproach, railing
χάριν adv. χάριν for a cause, because of, for sake
15 ἤδη adv. ἤδη now, already, yet, by this time, even now, now already
γάρ conj. γάρ for, and, because, but, indeed
τινες indefinite pron. nom. masc. pl. τὶς certain, some, any man, one, any thing
ὀπίσω prep. ὀπίσω (+gen) after. (adv.) back, behind
τοῦ art. gen. masc. sg. ὁ ἡ τό the, this, that, he, she, it
Σατανᾶ n. gen. masc. sg. Σατανᾶς Satan
16 εἴ conj. εἰ if, whether, that, though, forasmuch
τις indefinite pron. nom. fem. sg. τὶς certain, some, any man, one, any thing
πιστὸς adj. nom. masc. sg. πιστός faithful, believing, true, sure
ἢ particle. ἤ or, than, either, nor, or else, and, rather than
πιστὴ adj. nom. fem. sg. πιστός faithful, believing, true, sure
χήρας adj. acc. fem. pl. χήρα widow
αὐταῖς pron. dat. fem. 3p. pl. αὐτός ἡ ὁ self, of oneself, even, very, the same, he, she, it
καὶ conj. καί and, even, also, but
μὴ particle of negation. μή not, no, lest, neither, none, nothing, nor, never, without
ἡ art. nom. fem. sg. ὁ ἡ τό the, this, that, he, she, it
ἐκκλησία n. nom. fem. sg. ἐκκλησία church, assembly
ἵνα conj. ἵνα that, to, lest, for to, so that, albeit, because, for, so as
ταῖς art. dat. fem. pl. ὁ ἡ τό the, this, that, he, she, it
ὄντως adv. ὄντως indeed, certainly, clean, of a truth, verily
χήραις adj. dat. fem. pl. χήρα widow
17 Οἱ art. nom. masc. pl. ὁ ἡ τό the, this, that, he, she, it
καλῶς adv. καλῶς good, well, full well
πρεσβύτεροι adj. nom. masc. pl. πρεσβύτερος elder, elder woman, eldest, old man
διπλῆς adj. gen. fem. sg. διπλοῦς twofold more, double
τιμῆς n. gen. fem. sg. τιμή honour, price, preciousness, sum
μάλιστα adv. μάλιστα specially, especially, chiefly, most of all
οἱ art. nom. masc. pl. ὁ ἡ τό the, this, that, he, she, it
ἐν prep. ἐν (+dat) in, by, with, among, at, on, through, to, within, into, of, for
λόγῳ n. dat. masc. sg. λόγος word, saying, account, speech, thing, matter
καὶ conj. καί and, even, also, but
διδασκαλίᾳ n. dat. fem. sg. διδασκαλία doctrine, learning, teaching
18 γὰρ conj. γάρ for, and, because, but, indeed
ἡ art. nom. fem. sg. ὁ ἡ τό the, this, that, he, she, it
γραφή n. nom. fem. sg. γραφή scripture
Βοῦν n. acc. masc. sg. βοῦς ox
οὐ particle of negation. οὐ οὐκ οὐχ not, no, neither, none, nay, nor, never, nothing
καί conj. καί and, even, also, but
Ἄξιος adj. nom. masc. sg. ἄξιος worthy, meet, due reward
ὁ art. nom. masc. sg. ὁ ἡ τό the, this, that, he, she, it
ἐργάτης n. nom. masc. sg. ἐργάτης labourer, worker, workman
τοῦ art. gen. masc. sg. ὁ ἡ τό the, this, that, he, she, it
μισθοῦ n. gen. masc. sg. μισθός reward, hire, wage
αὐτοῦ pron. gen. masc. 3p. sg. αὐτός ἡ ὁ self, of oneself, even, very, the same, he, she, it
19 κατὰ prep. κατά (+gen) against, by, throughout, down, (+acc) according to, after, with
πρεσβυτέρου adj. gen. masc. sg. πρεσβύτερος elder, elder woman, eldest, old man
κατηγορίαν n. acc. fem. sg. κατηγορία accusation, accuse
μὴ particle of negation. μή not, no, lest, neither, none, nothing, nor, never, without
ἐκτὸς adv. ἐκτός except, out of, other than, outside, unless, without
εἰ conj. εἰ if, whether, that, though, forasmuch
μὴ particle of negation. μή not, no, lest, neither, none, nothing, nor, never, without
ἐπὶ prep. ἐπί (+gen) on, in, upon, (+dat) in, at, for, upon, (+acc) on, upon, unto, to, against
δύο num. gen. masc. pl. δύο two, twain, both

ἢ particle. ἤ or, than, either, nor, or else, and, rather than
τριῶν num. gen. masc. pl. τρεῖς three
μαρτύρων n. gen. masc. pl. μάρτυς or μάρτυρ witness, martyr, record
20 τοὺς art. acc. masc. pl. ὁ ἡ τό the, this, that, he, she, it
ἐνώπιον prep. ἐνώπιον (+gen) before, in the sight of, in the presence of. (adv.) before
πάντων adj. gen. masc. pl. πᾶς πᾶσα πᾶν all, every, whosoever, every one, no, whole, any
ἵνα conj. ἵνα that, to, lest, for to, so that, albeit, because, for, so as
καὶ conj. καί and, even, also, but
οἱ art. nom. masc. pl. ὁ ἡ τό the, this, that, he, she, it
λοιποὶ adj. nom. masc. pl. λοιπός other, rest, remnant, residue, which remain
φόβον n. acc. masc. sg. φόβος fear, terror, sore afraid
21 ἐνώπιον prep. ἐνώπιον (+gen) before, in the sight of, in the presence of. (adv.) before
τοῦ art. gen. masc. sg. ὁ ἡ τό the, this, that, he, she, it
Θεοῦ n. gen. masc. sg. θεός God, god
καὶ conj. καί and, even, also, but
Κυρίου n. gen. masc. sg. κύριος Lord, lord, master, sir, LORD, God, Master, owner
Ἰησοῦ n. gen. masc. sg. Ἰησοῦς Jesus
Χριστοῦ n. gen. masc. sg. Χριστός Christ
καὶ conj. καί and, even, also, but
τῶν art. gen. masc. pl. ὁ ἡ τό the, this, that, he, she, it
ἐκλεκτῶν adj. gen. masc. pl. ἐκλεκτός elect, chosen
ἀγγέλων n. gen. masc. pl. ἄγγελος angel, messenger
ἵνα conj. ἵνα that, to, lest, for to, so that, albeit, because, for, so as
ταῦτα demo. pron. acc. neut. pl. οὗτος αὕτη τοῦτο this, the same, this same, he, she, it
χωρὶς prep. χωρίς (+gen) without, beside. (adv.) by itself, apart, separately
προκρίματος n. gen. neut. sg. πρόκριμα preferring one before another
μηδὲν num. acc. neut. sg. μηδείς μηδεμία μηδέν no man, nothing, no, none, not at all
κατὰ prep. κατά (+gen) against, by, throughout, down, (+acc) according to, after, with
πρόσκλισιν n. acc. fem. sg. πρόσκλισις partiality
22 χεῖρας n. acc. fem. pl. χείρ hand
ταχέως adv. ταχέως sortly, quickly, soon, hastily, suddenly
μηδενὶ num. dat. masc. sg. μηδείς μηδεμία μηδέν no man, nothing, no, none, not at all
μηδὲ conj. μηδέ neither, nor, not, no not, nor yet, not once, not so much as
ἁμαρτίαις n. dat. fem. pl. ἁμαρτία sin, offence, sinful
ἀλλοτρίαις adj. dat. fem. pl. ἀλλότριος stranger, another man, alien, strange
σεαυτὸν pron. acc. masc. 2p. sg. σεαυτοῦ σεαυτῷ σεαυτόν thyself, thine own self
ἁγνὸν adj. acc. masc. sg. ἁγνός clear, pure, chaste
23 μηκέτι adv. μηκέτι no more, no longer, not any more, not henceforth, not henceforward
ἀλλ᾽ conj. ἀλλά but, yea, yet, nevertheless, howbeit, nay, therefore
οἴνῳ n. dat. masc. sg. οἶνος wine
ὀλίγῳ adj. dat. masc. sg. ὀλίγος few, little, small, a while, brief, short, short space
διὰ prep. διά (+gen) by, through, with, in, of, (+acc) for, because of, for a cause
τὸν art. acc. masc. sg. ὁ ἡ τό the, this, that, he, she, it
στόμαχον n. acc. masc. sg. στόμαχος stomach
σου pron. gen. 2p. sg. σύ thou, you
καὶ conj. καί and, even, also, but
τὰς art. acc. fem. pl. ὁ ἡ τό the, this, that, he, she, it
πυκνάς adj. acc. fem. pl. πυκνός often, frequently
σου pron. gen. 2p. sg. σύ thou, you
ἀσθενείας n. acc. fem. pl. ἀσθένεια infirmity, weakness, disease, sickness
24 τινῶν indefinite pron. gen. masc. pl. τὶς certain, some, any man, one, any thing
ἀνθρώπων n. gen. masc. pl. ἄνθρωπος man, human being, person, one, certain
αἱ art. nom. fem. pl. ὁ ἡ τό the, this, that, he, she, it
ἁμαρτίαι n. nom. fem. pl. ἁμαρτία sin, offence, sinful
πρόδηλοί adj. nom. fem. pl. πρόδηλος open beforehand, manifest beforehand, evident

εἰς prep. εἰς (+acc) into, to, unto, for, in, on, toward, against, upon, at, among
κρίσιν n. acc. fem. sg. κρίσις judgment, damnation, accusation, condemnation
τισὶ indefinite pron. dat. masc. pl. τὶς certain, some, any man, one, any thing
δὲ conj. δέ but, and, now, also, to the contrary, rather, then
καὶ conj. καί and, even, also, but
25 ὡσαύτως adv. ὡσαύτως likewise, in like manner, after the same manner, even so
καὶ conj. καί and, even, also, but
τὰ art. nom. neut. pl. ὁ ἡ τό the, this, that, he, she, it
καλὰ adj. nom. neut. pl. καλός good, better, goodly, meet, honest, fair, well, worthy
ἔργα n. nom. neut. pl. ἔργον work, deed, doing labour
πρόδηλα adj. nom. neut. pl. πρόδηλος open beforehand, manifest beforehand, evident
καὶ conj. καί and, even, also, but
τὰ art. nom. neut. pl. ὁ ἡ τό the, this, that, he, she, it
ἄλλως adv. ἄλλως otherwise
οὐ particle of negation. οὐ οὐκ οὐχ not, no, neither, none, nay, nor, never, nothing

6

1 Ὅσοι relative pron. nom. masc. pl. ὅσος as many as, whatsoever, that, as long as, how much
ὑπὸ prep. ὑπό (+gen) of, by, with, from, among, (+acc) under
ζυγὸν n. acc. masc. sg. ζυγός yoke, pair of balances
δοῦλοι n. nom. masc. pl. δοῦλος servant, bondman, bond, slave
τοὺς art. acc. masc. pl. ὁ ἡ τό the, this, that, he, she, it
ἰδίους adj. acc. masc. pl. ἴδιος one's own, one's, privately
δεσπότας n. acc. masc. pl. δεσπότης Lord, master
πάσης adj. gen. fem. sg. πᾶς πᾶσα πᾶν all, every, whosoever, every one, no, whole, any
τιμῆς n. gen. fem. sg. τιμή honour, price, preciousness, sum
ἀξίους adj. acc. masc. pl. ἄξιος worthy, meet, due reward
ἵνα conj. ἵνα that, to, lest, for to, so that, albeit, because, for, so as
μὴ particle of negation. μή not, no, lest, neither, none, nothing, nor, never, without
τὸ art. nom. neut. sg. ὁ ἡ τό the, this, that, he, she, it
ὄνομα n. nom. neut. sg. ὄνομα name, call, surname
τοῦ art. gen. masc. sg. ὁ ἡ τό the, this, that, he, she, it
Θεοῦ n. gen. masc. sg. θεός God, god
καὶ conj. καί and, even, also, but
ἡ art. nom. fem. sg. ὁ ἡ τό the, this, that, he, she, it
διδασκαλία n. nom. fem. sg. διδασκαλία doctrine, learning, teaching
2 οἱ art. nom. masc. pl. ὁ ἡ τό the, this, that, he, she, it
δὲ conj. δέ but, and, now, also, to the contrary, rather, then
πιστοὺς adj. acc. masc. pl. πιστός faithful, believing, true, sure
δεσπότας n. acc. masc. pl. δεσπότης Lord, master
μὴ particle of negation. μή not, no, lest, neither, none, nothing, nor, never, without
ὅτι conj. ὅτι that, for, because, how that, how, because that, for that, though
ἀδελφοί n. nom. masc. pl. ἀδελφός brother
ἀλλὰ conj. ἀλλά but, yea, yet, nevertheless, howbeit, nay, therefore
μᾶλλον adv. μᾶλλον rather, more, more and more, better, much, much the more
ὅτι conj. ὅτι that, for, because, how that, how, because that, for that, though
πιστοί adj. nom. masc. pl. πιστός faithful, believing, true, sure
καὶ conj. καί and, even, also, but
ἀγαπητοὶ adj. nom. masc. pl. ἀγαπητός beloved, dearly beloved, dear, wellbeloved
οἱ art. nom. masc. pl. ὁ ἡ τό the, this, that, he, she, it
τῆς art. gen. fem. sg. ὁ ἡ τό the, this, that, he, she, it
εὐεργεσίας n. gen. fem. sg. εὐεργεσία good deed done, benefit
ταῦτα demo. pron. acc. neut. pl. οὗτος αὕτη τοῦτο this, the same, this same, he, she, it
καὶ conj. καί and, even, also, but

3 Εἴ conj. εἰ if, whether, that, though, forasmuch
τις indefinite pron. nom. masc. sg. τὶς certain, some, any man, one, any thing
καὶ conj. καί and, even, also, but
μὴ particle of negation. μή not, no, lest, neither, none, nothing, nor, never, without
λόγοις n. dat. masc. pl. λόγος word, saying, account, speech, thing, matter
τοῖς art. dat. masc. pl. ὁ ἡ τό the, this, that, he, she, it
τοῦ art. gen. masc. sg. ὁ ἡ τό the, this, that, he, she, it
Κυρίου n. gen. masc. sg. κύριος Lord, lord, master, sir, LORD, God, Master, owner
ἡμῶν pron. gen. 1p. pl. ἐγώ I
Ἰησοῦ n. gen. masc. sg. Ἰησοῦς Jesus
Χριστοῦ n. gen. masc. sg. Χριστός Christ
καὶ conj. καί and, even, also, but
τῇ art. dat. fem. sg. ὁ ἡ τό the, this, that, he, she, it
κατ' prep. κατά (+gen) against, by, throughout, down, (+acc) according to, after, with
εὐσέβειαν n. acc. fem. sg. εὐσέβεια godliness, holiness
διδασκαλίᾳ n. dat. fem. sg. διδασκαλία doctrine, learning, teaching
4 μηδὲν num. acc. neut. sg. μηδείς μηδεμία μηδέν no man, nothing, no, none, not at all
ἀλλὰ conj. ἀλλά but, yea, yet, nevertheless, howbeit, nay, therefore
περὶ prep. περί (+gen) of, for, concerning, (+acc) about, concerning, in
ζητήσεις n. acc. fem. pl. ζήτησις question
καὶ conj. καί and, even, also, but
λογομαχίας n. acc. fem. pl. λογομαχία strife of words
ἐξ prep. ἐκ ἐξ (+gen) of, from, out of, by, on, with, in, among, through
ὧν relative pron. gen. fem. pl. ὅς ἥ ὅ who, which, what, that
φθόνος n. nom. masc. sg. φθόνος envy, envying
ἔρις n. nom. fem. sg. ἔρις debate, strife, contention, variance
βλασφημίαι n. nom. fem. pl. βλασφημία blasphemy, railing, evil speaking
ὑπόνοιαι n. nom. fem. pl. ὑπόνοια surmising
πονηραί adj. nom. fem. pl. πονηρός evil, wicked, bad
5 παραδιατριβαὶ n. nom. fem. pl. παραδιατριβή perverse disputing
ἀνθρώπων n. gen. masc. pl. ἄνθρωπος man, human being, person, one, certain
τὸν art. acc. masc. sg. ὁ ἡ τό the, this, that, he, she, it
νοῦν n. acc. masc. sg. νοῦς understanding, mind
καὶ conj. καί and, even, also, but
τῆς art. gen. fem. sg. ὁ ἡ τό the, this, that, he, she, it
ἀληθείας n. gen. fem. sg. ἀλήθεια truth, verity
πορισμὸν n. acc. masc. sg. πορισμός gain
τὴν art. acc. fem. sg. ὁ ἡ τό the, this, that, he, she, it
εὐσέβειαν n. acc. fem. sg. εὐσέβεια godliness, holiness
ἀπὸ prep. ἀπό (+gen) from, of, out of, since, for, off, at, by, in, on
τῶν art. gen. masc. pl. ὁ ἡ τό the, this, that, he, she, it
τοιούτων demo. pron. gen. masc. pl. τοιοῦτος such, like
6 δὲ conj. δέ but, and, now, also, to the contrary, rather, then
πορισμὸς n. nom. masc. sg. πορισμός gain
μέγας adj. nom. masc. sg. μέγας great, loud, greatest, high, large, mighty, strong
ἡ art. nom. fem. sg. ὁ ἡ τό the, this, that, he, she, it
εὐσέβεια n. nom. fem. sg. εὐσέβεια godliness, holiness
μετὰ prep. μετά (+gen) with, among, against, (+acc) after
αὐταρκείας n. gen. fem. sg. αὐτάρκεια contentment
7 οὐδὲν num. acc. neut. sg. οὐδείς no man, nothing, no, none, neither, not, nought
γὰρ conj. γάρ for, and, because, but, indeed
εἰς prep. εἰς (+acc) into, to, unto, for, in, on, toward, against, upon, at, among
τὸν art. acc. masc. sg. ὁ ἡ τό the, this, that, he, she, it
κόσμον n. acc. masc. sg. κόσμος world, adorning
δῆλον adj. nom. neut. sg. δῆλος bewray, certain, evident, manifest

ὅτι conj. ὅτι that, for, because, how that, how, because that, for that, though
οὐδὲ adv. οὐδέ neither, nor, not, no, not even, never, not yet
τι indefinite pron. acc. neut. sg. τὶς certain, some, any man, one, any thing
8 δὲ conj. δέ but, and, now, also, to the contrary, rather, then
διατροφὰς n. acc. fem. pl. διατροφή food
καὶ conj. καί and, even, also, but
σκεπάσματα n. acc. neut. pl. σκέπασμα raiment
τούτοις demo. pron. dat. neut. pl. οὗτος αὕτη τοῦτο this, the same, this same, he, she, it
9 οἱ art. nom. masc. pl. ὁ ἡ τό the, this, that, he, she, it
δὲ conj. δέ but, and, now, also, to the contrary, rather, then
εἰς prep. εἰς (+acc) into, to, unto, for, in, on, toward, against, upon, at, among
πειρασμὸν n. acc. masc. sg. πειρασμός temptation, trial
καὶ conj. καί and, even, also, but
παγίδα n. acc. fem. sg. παγίς snare
καὶ conj. καί and, even, also, but
ἐπιθυμίας n. acc. fem. pl. ἐπιθυμία lust, concupiscence, desire
πολλὰς adj. acc. fem. pl. πολύς many, great, much, long, abundant
ἀνοήτους adj. acc. fem. pl. ἀνόητος fool, foolish, unwise
καὶ conj. καί and, even, also, but
βλαβεράς adj. acc. fem. pl. βλαβερός hurtful
αἵτινες relative pron. nom. fem. pl. ὅστις which, who, whosoever, that, whatsoever
τοὺς art. acc. masc. pl. ὁ ἡ τό the, this, that, he, she, it
ἀνθρώπους n. acc. masc. pl. ἄνθρωπος man, human being, person, one, certain
εἰς prep. εἰς (+acc) into, to, unto, for, in, on, toward, against, upon, at, among
ὄλεθρον n. acc. masc. sg. ὄλεθρος destruction
καὶ conj. καί and, even, also, but
ἀπώλειαν n. acc. fem. sg. ἀπώλεια destruction, perdition, waste, damnation
10 ῥίζα n. nom. fem. sg. ῥίζα root
γὰρ conj. γάρ for, and, because, but, indeed
πάντων adj. gen. neut. pl. πᾶς πᾶσα πᾶν all, every, whosoever, every one, no, whole, any
τῶν art. gen. neut. pl. ὁ ἡ τό the, this, that, he, she, it
κακῶν adj. gen. neut. pl. κακός evil, evil thing, noisome, wicked
ἡ art. nom. fem. sg. ὁ ἡ τό the, this, that, he, she, it
φιλαργυρία n. nom. fem. sg. φιλαργυρία love of money
ἧς relative pron. gen. fem. sg. ὅς ἥ ὅ who, which, what, that
τινες indefinite pron. nom. masc. pl. τὶς certain, some, any man, one, any thing
ἀπὸ prep. ἀπό (+gen) from, of, out of, since, for, off, at, by, in, on
τῆς art. gen. fem. sg. ὁ ἡ τό the, this, that, he, she, it
πίστεως n. gen. fem. sg. πίστις faith, assurance, belief, fidelity
καὶ conj. καί and, even, also, but
ἑαυτοὺς reflexive pron. acc. masc. 3p. pl. ἑαυτοῦ himself, herself, itself, yourself, ourselves
ὀδύναις n. dat. fem. pl. ὀδύνη sorrow
πολλαῖς adj. dat. fem. pl. πολύς many, great, much, long, abundant
11 Σὺ pron. nom. 2p. sg. σύ thou, you
δέ conj. δέ but, and, now, also, to the contrary, rather, then
ὦ interjection. ὦ O
ἄνθρωπε n. voc. masc. sg. ἄνθρωπος man, human being, person, one, certain
τοῦ art. gen. masc. sg. ὁ ἡ τό the, this, that, he, she, it
Θεοῦ n. gen. masc. sg. θεός God, god
ταῦτα demo. pron. acc. neut. pl. οὗτος αὕτη τοῦτο this, the same, this same, he, she, it
δέ conj. δέ but, and, now, also, to the contrary, rather, then
δικαιοσύνην n. acc. fem. sg. δικαιοσύνη righteousness
εὐσέβειαν n. acc. fem. sg. εὐσέβεια godliness, holiness
πίστιν n. acc. fem. sg. πίστις faith, assurance, belief, fidelity
ἀγάπην n. acc. fem. sg. ἀγάπη love, charity, feast of charity

ὑπομονὴν n. acc. fem. sg. ὑπομονή patience, enduring
πρᾳότητα n. acc. fem. sg. πρᾳότης meekness
12 τὸν art. acc. masc. sg. ὁ ἡ τό the, this, that, he, she, it
καλὸν adj. acc. masc. sg. καλός good, better, goodly, meet, honest, fair, well, worthy
ἀγῶνα n. acc. masc. sg. ἀγών conflict, fight, contention, race
τῆς art. gen. fem. sg. ὁ ἡ τό the, this, that, he, she, it
πίστεως n. gen. fem. sg. πίστις faith, assurance, belief, fidelity
αἰωνίου adj. gen. fem. sg. αἰώνιος eternal, everlasting, world, for ever
ζωῆς n. gen. fem. sg. ζωή life, lifetime
εἰς prep. εἰς (+acc) into, to, unto, for, in, on, toward, against, upon, at, among
ἣν relative pron. acc. fem. sg. ὅς ἥ ὅ who, which, what, that
καὶ conj. καί and, even, also, but
καὶ conj. καί and, even, also, but
τὴν art. acc. fem. sg. ὁ ἡ τό the, this, that, he, she, it
καλὴν adj. acc. fem. sg. καλός good, better, goodly, meet, honest, fair, well, worthy
ὁμολογίαν n. acc. fem. sg. ὁμολογία profession, confession, profess
ἐνώπιον prep. ἐνώπιον (+gen) before, in the sight of, in the presence of. (adv.) before
πολλῶν adj. gen. masc. pl. πολύς many, great, much, long, abundant
μαρτύρων n. gen. masc. pl. μάρτυς or μάρτυρ witness, martyr, record
13 σοι pron. dat. 2p. sg. σύ thou, you
ἐνώπιον prep. ἐνώπιον (+gen) before, in the sight of, in the presence of. (adv.) before
τοῦ art. gen. masc. sg. ὁ ἡ τό the, this, that, he, she, it
Θεοῦ n. gen. masc. sg. θεός God, god
τοῦ art. gen. masc. sg. ὁ ἡ τό the, this, that, he, she, it
τὰ art. acc. neut. pl. ὁ ἡ τό the, this, that, he, she, it
πάντα adj. acc. neut. pl. πᾶς πᾶσα πᾶν all, every, whosoever, every one, no, whole, any
καὶ conj. καί and, even, also, but
Χριστοῦ n. gen. masc. sg. Χριστός Christ
Ἰησοῦ n. gen. masc. sg. Ἰησοῦς Jesus
τοῦ art. gen. masc. sg. ὁ ἡ τό the, this, that, he, she, it
ἐπὶ prep. ἐπί (+gen) on, in, upon, (+dat) in, at, for, upon, (+acc) on, upon, unto, to, against
Ποντίου n. gen. masc. sg. Πόντιος Pontius
Πιλάτου n. gen. masc. sg. Πιλᾶτος Pilate
τὴν art. acc. fem. sg. ὁ ἡ τό the, this, that, he, she, it
καλὴν adj. acc. fem. sg. καλός good, better, goodly, meet, honest, fair, well, worthy
ὁμολογίαν n. acc. fem. sg. ὁμολογία profession, confession, profess
14 σε pron. acc. 2p. sg. σύ thou, you
τὴν art. acc. fem. sg. ὁ ἡ τό the, this, that, he, she, it
ἐντολὴν n. acc. fem. sg. ἐντολή commandment, precept
ἄσπιλον adj. acc. fem. sg. ἄσπιλος without spot, unspotted
ἀνεπίλημπτον adj. acc. fem. sg. ἀνεπίλημπτος blameless, unrebukeable
μέχρι prep. μέχρι until, unto, till, to
τῆς art. gen. fem. sg. ὁ ἡ τό the, this, that, he, she, it
ἐπιφανείας n. gen. fem. sg. ἐπιφάνεια appearing, brightness
τοῦ art. gen. masc. sg. ὁ ἡ τό the, this, that, he, she, it
Κυρίου n. gen. masc. sg. κύριος Lord, lord, master, sir, LORD, God, Master, owner
ἡμῶν pron. gen. 1p. pl. ἐγώ I
Ἰησοῦ n. gen. masc. sg. Ἰησοῦς Jesus
Χριστοῦ n. gen. masc. sg. Χριστός Christ
15 ἣν relative pron. acc. fem. sg. ὅς ἥ ὅ who, which, what, that
καιροῖς n. dat. masc. pl. καιρός time, season, due time, opportunity
ἰδίοις adj. dat. masc. pl. ἴδιος one's own, one's, privately
ὁ art. nom. masc. sg. ὁ ἡ τό the, this, that, he, she, it
μακάριος adj. nom. masc. sg. μακάριος blessed, happy
καὶ conj. καί and, even, also, but

μόνος adj. nom. masc. sg. μόνος only, alone, by oneself
δυνάστης n. nom. masc. sg. δυνάστης mighty, of great authority, Potentate
ὁ art. nom. masc. sg. ὁ ἡ τό the, this, that, he, she, it
Βασιλεὺς n. nom. masc. sg. βασιλεύς king
τῶν art. gen. masc. pl. ὁ ἡ τό the, this, that, he, she, it
καὶ conj. καί and, even, also, but
Κύριος n. nom. masc. sg. κύριος Lord, lord, master, sir, LORD, God, Master, owner
τῶν art. gen. masc. pl. ὁ ἡ τό the, this, that, he, she, it
16 ὁ art. nom. masc. sg. ὁ ἡ τό the, this, that, he, she, it
μόνος adj. nom. masc. sg. μόνος only, alone, by oneself
ἀθανασίαν n. acc. fem. sg. ἀθανασία immortality
φῶς n. acc. neut. sg. φῶς light, fire
ἀπρόσιτον adj. acc. neut. sg. ἀπρόσιτος which no man can approach
ὃν relative pron. acc. masc. sg. ὅς ἥ ὅ who, which, what, that
οὐδεὶς num. nom. masc. sg. οὐδείς no man, nothing, no, none, neither, not, nought
ἀνθρώπων n. gen. masc. pl. ἄνθρωπος man, human being, person, one, certain
οὐδὲ adv. οὐδέ neither, nor, not, no, not even, never, not yet
ᾧ relative pron. dat. masc. sg. ὅς ἥ ὅ who, which, what, that
τιμὴ n. nom. fem. sg. τιμή honour, price, preciousness, sum
καὶ conj. καί and, even, also, but
κράτος n. nom. neut. sg. κράτος power, dominion, might, strength
αἰώνιον adj. nom. neut. sg. αἰώνιος eternal, everlasting, world, for ever
ἀμήν particle. ἀμήν amen, verily
17 Τοῖς art. dat. masc. pl. ὁ ἡ τό the, this, that, he, she, it
πλουσίοις adj. dat. masc. pl. πλούσιος rich
ἐν prep. ἐν (+dat) in, by, with, among, at, on, through, to, within, into, of, for
τῷ art. dat. masc. sg. ὁ ἡ τό the, this, that, he, she, it
νῦν adv. νῦν now, henceforth, present, this time
αἰῶνι n. dat. masc. sg. αἰών ever, ever and ever, evermore, age, eternal, world
μὴ particle of negation. μή not, no, lest, neither, none, nothing, nor, never, without
μηδὲ conj. μηδέ neither, nor, not, no not, nor yet, not once, not so much as
ἐπὶ prep. ἐπί (+gen) on, in, upon, (+dat) in, at, for, upon, (+acc) on, upon, unto, to, against
πλούτου n. gen. masc. sg. πλοῦτος riches
ἀδηλότητι n. dat. fem. sg. ἀδηλότης uncertain
ἀλλ' conj. ἀλλά but, yea, yet, nevertheless, howbeit, nay, therefore
ἐν prep. ἐν (+dat) in, by, with, among, at, on, through, to, within, into, of, for
τῷ art. dat. masc. sg. ὁ ἡ τό the, this, that, he, she, it
Θεῷ n. dat. masc. sg. θεός God, god
τῷ art. dat. masc. sg. ὁ ἡ τό the, this, that, he, she, it
τῷ art. dat. masc. sg. ὁ ἡ τό the, this, that, he, she, it
ἡμῖν pron. dat. 1p. pl. ἐγώ I
πλουσίως adv. πλουσίως richly, abundantly
πάντα adj. acc. neut. pl. πᾶς πᾶσα πᾶν all, every, whosoever, every one, no, whole, any
εἰς prep. εἰς (+acc) into, to, unto, for, in, on, toward, against, upon, at, among
ἀπόλαυσιν n. acc. fem. sg. ἀπόλαυσις enjoy
18 ἐν prep. ἐν (+dat) in, by, with, among, at, on, through, to, within, into, of, for
ἔργοις n. dat. neut. pl. ἔργον work, deed, doing labour
καλοῖς adj. dat. neut. pl. καλός good, better, goodly, meet, honest, fair, well, worthy
εὐμεταδότους adj. acc. masc. pl. εὐμετάδοτος ready to distribute
κοινωνικούς adj. acc. masc. pl. κοινωνικός willing to communicate
19 ἑαυτοῖς reflexive pron. dat. masc. 3p. pl. ἑαυτοῦ himself, herself, itself, yourself, ourselves
θεμέλιον n. acc. masc. sg. θεμέλιος foundation
καλὸν adj. acc. masc. sg. καλός good, better, goodly, meet, honest, fair, well, worthy
εἰς prep. εἰς (+acc) into, to, unto, for, in, on, toward, against, upon, at, among
τὸ art. acc. neut. sg. ὁ ἡ τό the, this, that, he, she, it

ἵνα conj. ἵνα that, to, lest, for to, so that, albeit, because, for, so as
τῆς art. gen. fem. sg. ὁ ἡ τό the, this, that, he, she, it
αἰωνίου adj. gen. fem. sg. αἰώνιος eternal, everlasting, world, for ever
ζωῆς n. gen. fem. sg. ζωή life, lifetime
20 Ὦ interjection. ὦ O
Τιμόθεε n. voc. masc. sg. Τιμόθεος Timotheus, Timothy
τὴν art. acc. fem. sg. ὁ ἡ τό the, this, that, he, she, it
παρακαταθήκην n. acc. fem. sg. παρακαταθήκη that which is committed to one's trust
τὰς art. acc. fem. pl. ὁ ἡ τό the, this, that, he, she, it
βεβήλους adj. acc. fem. pl. βέβηλος profane, profane person
κενοφωνίας n. acc. fem. pl. κενοφωνία vain babbling
καὶ conj. καί and, even, also, but
ἀντιθέσεις n. acc. fem. pl. ἀντίθεσις opposition
τῆς art. gen. fem. sg. ὁ ἡ τό the, this, that, he, she, it
ψευδωνύμου adj. gen. fem. sg. ψευδώνυμος falsely so called
γνώσεως n. gen. fem. sg. γνῶσις knowledge, science
21 ἥν relative pron. acc. fem. sg. ὅς ἥ ὅ who, which, what, that
τινες indefinite pron. nom. masc. pl. τὶς certain, some, any man, one, any thing
περὶ prep. περί (+gen) of, for, concerning, (+acc) about, concerning, in
τὴν art. acc. fem. sg. ὁ ἡ τό the, this, that, he, she, it
πίστιν n. acc. fem. sg. πίστις faith, assurance, belief, fidelity
Ἡ art. nom. fem. sg. ὁ ἡ τό the, this, that, he, she, it
χάρις n. nom. fem. sg. χάρις grace, thank, favour, pleasure
μετὰ prep. μετά (+gen) with, among, against, (+acc) after
σοῦ pron. gen. 2p. sg. σύ thou, you
ἀμήν particle. ἀμήν amen, verily

ΠΑΥΛΟΥ ΤΟΥ ΑΠΟΣΤΟΛΟΥ
Η ΠΡΟΣ
ΤΙΜΟΘΕΟΝ
ΕΠΙΣΤΟΛΗ ΔΕΥΤΕΡΑ

1

1 Παῦλος n. nom. masc. sg. Παῦλος Paul, Paulus
ἀπόστολος n. nom. masc. sg. ἀπόστολος apostle, messenger, he that is sent
Ἰησοῦ n. gen. masc. sg. Ἰησοῦς Jesus
Χριστοῦ n. gen. masc. sg. Χριστός Christ
διὰ prep. διά (+gen) by, through, with, in, of, (+acc) for, because of, for a cause
θελήματος n. gen. neut. sg. θέλημα will, desire, pleasure
Θεοῦ n. gen. masc. sg. θεός God, god
κατ' prep. κατά (+gen) against, by, throughout, down, (+acc) according to, after, with
ἐπαγγελίαν n. acc. fem. sg. ἐπαγγελία promise, message
ζωῆς n. gen. fem. sg. ζωή life, lifetime
τῆς art. gen. fem. sg. ὁ ἡ τό the, this, that, he, she, it
ἐν prep. ἐν (+dat) in, by, with, among, at, on, through, to, within, into, of, for
Χριστῷ n. dat. masc. sg. Χριστός Christ
Ἰησοῦ n. dat. masc. sg. Ἰησοῦς Jesus
2 Τιμοθέῳ n. dat. masc. sg. Τιμόθεος Timotheus, Timothy
ἀγαπητῷ adj. dat. neut. sg. ἀγαπητός beloved, dearly beloved, dear, wellbeloved
τέκνῳ n. dat. neut. sg. τέκνον child, son, daughter
χάρις n. nom. fem. sg. χάρις grace, thank, favour, pleasure
ἔλεος n. nom. masc. sg. ἔλεος mercy
εἰρήνη n. nom. fem. sg. εἰρήνη peace, quietness, rest
ἀπὸ prep. ἀπό (+gen) from, of, out of, since, for, off, at, by, in, on
Θεοῦ n. gen. masc. sg. θεός God, god
πατρὸς n. gen. masc. sg. πατήρ Father, father, parent
καὶ conj. καί and, even, also, but
Χριστοῦ n. gen. masc. sg. Χριστός Christ
Ἰησοῦ n. gen. masc. sg. Ἰησοῦς Jesus
τοῦ art. gen. masc. sg. ὁ ἡ τό the, this, that, he, she, it
Κυρίου n. gen. masc. sg. κύριος Lord, lord, master, sir, LORD, God, Master, owner
ἡμῶν pron. gen. 1p. pl. ἐγώ I
3 Χάριν n. acc. fem. sg. χάρις grace, thank, favour, pleasure
τῷ art. dat. masc. sg. ὁ ἡ τό the, this, that, he, she, it
Θεῷ n. dat. masc. sg. θεός God, god
ᾧ relative pron. dat. masc. sg. ὅς ἥ ὅ who, which, what, that
ἀπὸ prep. ἀπό (+gen) from, of, out of, since, for, off, at, by, in, on
προγόνων adj. gen. masc. pl. πρόγονος forefather, parent
ἐν prep. ἐν (+dat) in, by, with, among, at, on, through, to, within, into, of, for
καθαρᾷ adj. dat. fem. sg. καθαρός pure, clean, clear
συνειδήσει n. dat. fem. sg. συνείδησις conscience
ὡς adv. ὡς as, when, as it were, how, about, like, as soon as, even as, while
ἀδιάλειπτον adj. acc. fem. sg. ἀδιάλειπτος without ceasing, continual
τὴν art. acc. fem. sg. ὁ ἡ τό the, this, that, he, she, it
περὶ prep. περί (+gen) of, for, concerning, (+acc) about, concerning, in
σοῦ pron. gen. 2p. sg. σύ thou, you
μνείαν n. acc. fem. sg. μνεία mention, remembrance

ἐν prep. ἐν (+dat) in, by, with, among, at, on, through, to, within, into, of, for
ταῖς art. dat. fem. pl. ὁ ἡ τό the, this, that, he, she, it
δεήσεσί n. dat. fem. pl. δέησις prayer, supplication, request
μου pron. gen. 1p. sg. ἐγώ I
νυκτὸς n. gen. fem. sg. νύξ night
καὶ conj. καί and, even, also, but
ἡμέρας n. gen. fem. sg. ἡμέρα day, time, year, while, age, day time
4 σε pron. acc. 2p. sg. σύ thou, you
ἰδεῖν 2aor. act. inf. εἰδέω εἰδῶ οἶδα know, see, behold
σου pron. gen. 2p. sg. σύ thou, you
τῶν art. gen. neut. pl. ὁ ἡ τό the, this, that, he, she, it
δακρύων n. gen. neut. pl. δάκρυον tears
ἵνα conj. ἵνα that, to, lest, for to, so that, albeit, because, for, so as
χαρᾶς n. gen. fem. sg. χαρά joy, gladness, joyfulness
5 ὑπόμνησιν n. acc. fem. sg. ὑπόμνησις remembrance, putting in remembrance
τῆς art. gen. fem. sg. ὁ ἡ τό the, this, that, he, she, it
ἐν prep. ἐν (+dat) in, by, with, among, at, on, through, to, within, into, of, for
σοὶ pron. dat. 2p. sg. σύ thou, you
ἀνυποκρίτου adj. gen. fem. sg. ἀνυπόκριτος unfeigned, without dissimulation
πίστεως n. gen. fem. sg. πίστις faith, assurance, belief, fidelity
ἥτις relative pron. nom. fem. sg. ὅστις which, who, whosoever, that, whatsoever
πρῶτον adv. πρῶτον first, at the first, first of all, at first, at the beginning, before, chiefly
ἐν prep. ἐν (+dat) in, by, with, among, at, on, through, to, within, into, of, for
τῇ art. dat. fem. sg. ὁ ἡ τό the, this, that, he, she, it
μάμμῃ n. dat. fem. sg. μάμμη grandmother
σου pron. gen. 2p. sg. σύ thou, you
Λωΐδι n. dat. fem. sg. Λωΐς Lois
καὶ conj. καί and, even, also, but
τῇ art. dat. fem. sg. ὁ ἡ τό the, this, that, he, she, it
μητρί n. dat. fem. sg. μήτηρ mother
σου pron. gen. 2p. sg. σύ thou, you
Εὐνίκῃ n. dat. fem. sg. Εὐνίκη Eunice
δὲ conj. δέ but, and, now, also, to the contrary, rather, then
ὅτι conj. ὅτι that, for, because, how that, how, because that, for that, though
καὶ conj. καί and, even, also, but
ἐν prep. ἐν (+dat) in, by, with, among, at, on, through, to, within, into, of, for
σοὶ pron. dat. 2p. sg. σύ thou, you
6 δι' prep. διά (+gen) by, through, with, in, of, (+acc) for, because of, for a cause
ἣν relative pron. acc. fem. sg. ὅς ἥ ὅ who, which, what, that
αἰτίαν n. acc. fem. sg. αἰτία cause, reason, accusation, fault
σε pron. acc. 2p. sg. σύ thou, you
τὸ art. acc. neut. sg. ὁ ἡ τό the, this, that, he, she, it
χάρισμα n. acc. neut. sg. χάρισμα gift, free gift
τοῦ art. gen. masc. sg. ὁ ἡ τό the, this, that, he, she, it
Θεοῦ n. gen. masc. sg. θεός God, god
ὅ relative pron. nom. neut. sg. ὅς ἥ ὅ who, which, what, that
ἐν prep. ἐν (+dat) in, by, with, among, at, on, through, to, within, into, of, for
σοὶ pron. dat. 2p. sg. σύ thou, you
διὰ prep. διά (+gen) by, through, with, in, of, (+acc) for, because of, for a cause
τῆς art. gen. fem. sg. ὁ ἡ τό the, this, that, he, she, it
ἐπιθέσεως n. gen. fem. sg. ἐπίθεσις putting on, laying on
τῶν art. gen. fem. pl. ὁ ἡ τό the, this, that, he, she, it
χειρῶν n. gen. fem. pl. χείρ hand
μου pron. gen. 1p. sg. ἐγώ I
7 οὐ particle of negation. οὐ οὐκ οὐχ not, no, neither, none, nay, nor, never, nothing

γὰρ conj. γάρ for, and, because, but, indeed
ἡμῖν pron. dat. 1p. pl. ἐγώ I
ὁ art. nom. masc. sg. ὁ ἡ τό the, this, that, he, she, it
Θεὸς n. nom. masc. sg. θεός God, god
πνεῦμα n. acc. neut. sg. πνεῦμα spirit, Spirit, Ghost, ghost, life. of the spirit, wind
δειλίας n. gen. fem. sg. δειλία fear
ἀλλὰ conj. ἀλλά but, yea, yet, nevertheless, howbeit, nay, therefore
δυνάμεως n. gen. fem. sg. δύναμις power, mighty work, miracle, strength, might
καὶ conj. καί and, even, also, but
ἀγάπης n. gen. fem. sg. ἀγάπη love, charity, feast of charity
καὶ conj. καί and, even, also, but
σωφρονισμοῦ n. gen. masc. sg. σωφρονισμός sound mind
8 μὴ particle of negation. μή not, no, lest, neither, none, nothing, nor, never, without
οὖν conj. οὖν therefore, then, so, and, now, wherefore
τὸ art. acc. neut. sg. ὁ ἡ τό the, this, that, he, she, it
μαρτύριον n. acc. neut. sg. μαρτύριον testimony, witness
τοῦ art. gen. masc. sg. ὁ ἡ τό the, this, that, he, she, it
Κυρίου n. gen. masc. sg. κύριος Lord, lord, master, sir, LORD, God, Master, owner
ἡμῶν pron. gen. 1p. pl. ἐγώ I
μηδὲ conj. μηδέ neither, nor, not, no not, nor yet, not once, not so much as
ἐμὲ pron. acc. 1p. sg. ἐγώ I
τὸν art. acc. masc. sg. ὁ ἡ τό the, this, that, he, she, it
δέσμιον n. acc. masc. sg. δέσμιος prisoner, in bonds, that is in bond
αὐτοῦ pron. gen. masc. 3p. sg. αὐτός ἡ ὁ self, of oneself, even, very, the same, he, she, it
ἀλλὰ conj. ἀλλά but, yea, yet, nevertheless, howbeit, nay, therefore
τῷ art. dat. neut. sg. ὁ ἡ τό the, this, that, he, she, it
εὐαγγελίῳ n. dat. neut. sg. εὐαγγέλιον gospel
κατὰ prep. κατά (+gen) against, by, throughout, down, (+acc) according to, after, with
δύναμιν n. acc. fem. sg. δύναμις power, mighty work, miracle, strength, might
Θεοῦ n. gen. masc. sg. θεός God, god
9 τοῦ art. gen. masc. sg. ὁ ἡ τό the, this, that, he, she, it
ἡμᾶς pron. acc. 1p. pl. ἐγώ I
καὶ conj. καί and, even, also, but
κλήσει n. dat. fem. sg. κλῆσις calling, vocation
ἁγίᾳ adj. dat. fem. sg. ἅγιος Holy, holy, saint, Holy One, holy thing, most holy
οὐ particle of negation. οὐ οὐκ οὐχ not, no, neither, none, nay, nor, never, nothing
κατὰ prep. κατά (+gen) against, by, throughout, down, (+acc) according to, after, with
τὰ art. acc. neut. pl. ὁ ἡ τό the, this, that, he, she, it
ἔργα n. acc. neut. pl. ἔργον work, deed, doing labour
ἡμῶν pron. gen. 1p. pl. ἐγώ I
ἀλλὰ conj. ἀλλά but, yea, yet, nevertheless, howbeit, nay, therefore
κατ' prep. κατά (+gen) against, by, throughout, down, (+acc) according to, after, with
ἰδίαν adj. acc. fem. sg. ἴδιος one's own, one's, privately
πρόθεσιν n. acc. fem. sg. πρόθεσις purpose, shew, shewbread
καὶ conj. καί and, even, also, but
χάριν n. acc. fem. sg. χάρις grace, thank, favour, pleasure
τὴν art. acc. fem. sg. ὁ ἡ τό the, this, that, he, she, it
ἡμῖν pron. dat. 1p. pl. ἐγώ I
ἐν prep. ἐν (+dat) in, by, with, among, at, on, through, to, within, into, of, for
Χριστῷ n. dat. masc. sg. Χριστός Christ
'Ιησοῦ n. dat. masc. sg. 'Ιησοῦς Jesus
πρὸ prep. πρό (+gen) before, above
χρόνων n. gen. masc. pl. χρόνος time, season, space
αἰωνίων adj. gen. masc. pl. αἰώνιος eternal, everlasting, world, for ever
10 δὲ conj. δέ but, and, now, also, to the contrary, rather, then

νῦν adv. νῦν now, henceforth, present, this time
διὰ prep. διά (+gen) by, through, with, in, of, (+acc) for, because of, for a cause
τῆς art. gen. fem. sg. ὁ ἡ τό the, this, that, he, she, it
ἐπιφανείας n. gen. fem. sg. ἐπιφάνεια appearing, brightness
τοῦ art. gen. masc. sg. ὁ ἡ τό the, this, that, he, she, it
σωτῆρος n. gen. masc. sg. σωτήρ Saviour, saviour
ἡμῶν pron. gen. 1p. pl. ἐγώ I
Ἰησοῦ n. gen. masc. sg. Ἰησοῦς Jesus
Χριστοῦ n. gen. masc. sg. Χριστός Christ
μὲν conj. μέν indeed, verily, truly, even, so, some
τὸν art. acc. masc. sg. ὁ ἡ τό the, this, that, he, she, it
θάνατον n. acc. masc. sg. θάνατος death
δὲ conj. δέ but, and, now, also, to the contrary, rather, then
ζωὴν n. acc. fem. sg. ζωή life, lifetime
καὶ conj. καί and, even, also, but
ἀφθαρσίαν n. acc. fem. sg. ἀφθαρσία immortality, incorruption, sincerity
διὰ prep. διά (+gen) by, through, with, in, of, (+acc) for, because of, for a cause
τοῦ art. gen. neut. sg. ὁ ἡ τό the, this, that, he, she, it
εὐαγγελίου n. gen. neut. sg. εὐαγγέλιον gospel
11 εἰς prep. εἰς (+acc) into, to, unto, for, in, on, toward, against, upon, at, among
ὃ relative pron. acc. neut. sg. ὅς ἥ ὅ who, which, what, that
ἐγὼ pron. nom. 1p. sg. ἐγώ I
κῆρυξ n. nom. masc. sg. κήρυξ preacher
καὶ conj. καί and, even, also, but
ἀπόστολος n. nom. masc. sg. ἀπόστολος apostle, messenger, he that is sent
καὶ conj. καί and, even, also, but
διδάσκαλος n. nom. masc. sg. διδάσκαλος teacher, master, doctor
ἐθνῶν n. gen. neut. pl. ἔθνος Gentile, nation, heathen, people
12 δι' prep. διά (+gen) by, through, with, in, of, (+acc) for, because of, for a cause
ἣν relative pron. acc. fem. sg. ὅς ἥ ὅ who, which, what, that
αἰτίαν n. acc. fem. sg. αἰτία cause, reason, accusation, fault
καὶ conj. καί and, even, also, but
ταῦτα demo. pron. acc. neut. pl. οὗτος αὕτη τοῦτο this, the same, this same, he, she, it
ἀλλ' conj. ἀλλά but, yea, yet, nevertheless, howbeit, nay, therefore
οὐκ particle of negation. οὐ οὐκ οὐχ not, no, neither, none, nay, nor, never, nothing
γὰρ conj. γάρ for, and, because, but, indeed
ᾧ relative pron. dat. masc. sg. ὅς ἥ ὅ who, which, what, that
καὶ conj. καί and, even, also, but
ὅτι conj. ὅτι that, for, because, how that, how, because that, for that, though
δυνατός adj. nom. masc. sg. δυνατός able, possible, mighty, strong
τὴν art. acc. fem. sg. ὁ ἡ τό the, this, that, he, she, it
παραθήκην n. acc. fem. sg. παραθήκη commit unto
μου pron. gen. 1p. sg. ἐγώ I
εἰς prep. εἰς (+acc) into, to, unto, for, in, on, toward, against, upon, at, among
ἐκείνην demo. pron. acc. fem. sg. ἐκεῖνος that, he, the same, that same
τὴν art. acc. fem. sg. ὁ ἡ τό the, this, that, he, she, it
ἡμέραν n. acc. fem. sg. ἡμέρα day, time, year, while, age, day time
13 ὑποτύπωσιν n. acc. fem. sg. ὑποτύπωσις form, pattern
λόγων n. gen. masc. pl. λόγος word, saying, account, speech, thing, matter
ὧν relative pron. gen. masc. pl. ὅς ἥ ὅ who, which, what, that
παρ' prep. παρά (+gen) of, from, (+dat) with, for, (+acc) beside, at, by, above, against
ἐμοῦ pron. gen. 1p. sg. ἐγώ I
ἐν prep. ἐν (+dat) in, by, with, among, at, on, through, to, within, into, of, for
πίστει n. dat. fem. sg. πίστις faith, assurance, belief, fidelity
καὶ conj. καί and, even, also, but

ἀγάπῃ n. dat. fem. sg. ἀγάπη love, charity, feast of charity
τῇ art. dat. fem. sg. ὁ ἡ τό the, this, that, he, she, it
ἐν prep. ἐν (+dat) in, by, with, among, at, on, through, to, within, into, of, for
Χριστῷ n. dat. masc. sg. Χριστός Christ
Ἰησοῦ n. dat. masc. sg. Ἰησοῦς Jesus
14 τὴν art. acc. fem. sg. ὁ ἡ τό the, this, that, he, she, it
καλὴν adj. acc. fem. sg. καλός good, better, goodly, meet, honest, fair, well, worthy
παρακαταθήκην n. acc. fem. sg. παρακαταθήκη that thing which was committed unto
διὰ prep. διά (+gen) by, through, with, in, of, (+acc) for, because of, for a cause
Πνεύματος n. gen. neut. sg. πνεῦμα spirit, Spirit, Ghost, ghost, life. of the spirit, wind
Ἁγίου adj. gen. neut. sg. ἅγιος Holy, holy, saint, Holy One, holy thing, most holy
τοῦ art. gen. neut. sg. ὁ ἡ τό the, this, that, he, she, it
ἐν prep. ἐν (+dat) in, by, with, among, at, on, through, to, within, into, of, for
ἡμῖν pron. dat. 1p. pl. ἐγώ I
15 τοῦτο demo. pron. acc. neut. sg. οὗτος αὕτη τοῦτο this, the same, this same, he, she, it
ὅτι conj. ὅτι that, for, because, how that, how, because that, for that, though
με pron. acc. 1p. sg. ἐγώ I
πάντες adj. nom. masc. pl. πᾶς πᾶσα πᾶν all, every, whosoever, every one, no, whole, any
οἱ art. nom. masc. pl. ὁ ἡ τό the, this, that, he, she, it
ἐν prep. ἐν (+dat) in, by, with, among, at, on, through, to, within, into, of, for
τῇ art. dat. fem. sg. ὁ ἡ τό the, this, that, he, she, it
Ἀσίᾳ n. dat. fem. sg. Ἀσία Asia
ὧν relative pron. gen. masc. pl. ὅς ἥ ὅ who, which, what, that
Φύγελλος n. nom. masc. sg. Φύγελλος Phygellus
καὶ conj. καί and, even, also, but
Ἑρμογένης n. nom. masc. sg. Ἑρμογένης Hermogenes
16 ἔλεος n. acc. neut. sg. ἔλεος mercy
ὁ art. nom. masc. sg. ὁ ἡ τό the, this, that, he, she, it
Κύριος n. nom. masc. sg. κύριος Lord, lord, master, sir, LORD, God, Master, owner
τῷ art. dat. masc. sg. ὁ ἡ τό the, this, that, he, she, it
Ὀνησιφόρου n. gen. masc. sg. Ὀνησίφορος Onesiphorus
οἴκῳ n. dat. masc. sg. οἶκος house, home, household
ὅτι conj. ὅτι that, for, because, how that, how, because that, for that, though
πολλάκις adv. πολλάκις often, ofttimes, oft
με pron. acc. 1p. sg. ἐγώ I
καὶ conj. καί and, even, also, but
τὴν art. acc. fem. sg. ὁ ἡ τό the, this, that, he, she, it
ἅλυσίν n. acc. fem. sg. ἅλυσις chain, bond
μου pron. gen. 1p. sg. ἐγώ I
οὐκ particle of negation. οὐ οὐκ οὐχ not, no, neither, none, nay, nor, never, nothing
17 ἀλλὰ conj. ἀλλά but, yea, yet, nevertheless, howbeit, nay, therefore
ἐν prep. ἐν (+dat) in, by, with, among, at, on, through, to, within, into, of, for
Ῥώμῃ n. dat. fem. sg. Ῥώμη Rome
σπουδαιότερον compar. adj. acc. masc. sg. σπουδαῖος diligently, instantly
με pron. acc. 1p. sg. ἐγώ I
καὶ conj. καί and, even, also, but
18 αὐτῷ pron. dat. masc. 3p. sg. αὐτός ἡ ὁ self, of oneself, even, very, the same, he, she, it
ὁ art. nom. masc. sg. ὁ ἡ τό the, this, that, he, she, it
Κύριος n. nom. masc. sg. κύριος Lord, lord, master, sir, LORD, God, Master, owner
ἔλεος n. acc. neut. sg. ἔλεος mercy
παρὰ prep. παρά (+gen) of, from, (+dat) with, for, (+acc) beside, at, by, above, against
Κυρίου n. gen. masc. sg. κύριος Lord, lord, master, sir, LORD, God, Master, owner
ἐν prep. ἐν (+dat) in, by, with, among, at, on, through, to, within, into, of, for
ἐκείνῃ demo. pron. dat. fem. sg. ἐκεῖνος that, he, the same, that same
τῇ art. dat. fem. sg. ὁ ἡ τό the, this, that, he, she, it

ἡμέρᾳ n. dat. fem. sg. ἡμέρα day, time, year, while, age, day time
καὶ conj. καί and, even, also, but
ὅσα relative pron. acc. neut. pl. ὅσος as many as, whatsoever, that, as long as, how much
ἐν prep. ἐν (+dat) in, by, with, among, at, on, through, to, within, into, of, for
Ἐφέσῳ n. dat. fem. sg. Ἔφεσος Ephesus
βέλτιον n. acc. neut. sg. βελτίων very well
σὺ pron. nom. 2p. sg. σύ thou, you

2

1 Σὺ pron. nom. 2p. sg. σύ thou, you
οὖν conj. οὖν therefore, then, so, and, now, wherefore
τέκνον n. voc. neut. sg. τέκνον child, son, daughter
μου pron. gen. 1p. sg. ἐγώ I
ἐν prep. ἐν (+dat) in, by, with, among, at, on, through, to, within, into, of, for
τῇ art. dat. fem. sg. ὁ ἡ τό the, this, that, he, she, it
χάριτι n. dat. fem. sg. χάρις grace, thank, favour, pleasure
τῇ art. dat. fem. sg. ὁ ἡ τό the, this, that, he, she, it
ἐν prep. ἐν (+dat) in, by, with, among, at, on, through, to, within, into, of, for
Χριστῷ n. dat. masc. sg. Χριστός Christ
Ἰησοῦ n. dat. masc. sg. Ἰησοῦς Jesus
2 καὶ conj. καί and, even, also, but
ἃ relative pron. acc. neut. pl. ὅς ἥ ὅ who, which, what, that
παρ' prep. παρά (+gen) of, from, (+dat) with, for, (+acc) beside, at, by, above, against
ἐμοῦ pron. gen. 1p. sg. ἐγώ I
διὰ prep. διά (+gen) by, through, with, in, of, (+acc) for, because of, for a cause
πολλῶν adj. gen. masc. pl. πολύς many, great, much, long, abundant
μαρτύρων n. gen. masc. pl. μάρτυς or μάρτυρ witness, martyr, record
ταῦτα demo. pron. acc. neut. pl. οὗτος αὕτη τοῦτο this, the same, this same, he, she, it
πιστοῖς adj. dat. masc. pl. πιστός faithful, believing, true, sure
ἀνθρώποις n. dat. masc. pl. ἄνθρωπος man, human being, person, one, certain
οἵτινες relative pron. nom. masc. pl. ὅστις which, who, whosoever, that, whatsoever
ἱκανοὶ adj. nom. masc. pl. ἱκανός many, much, long, worthy, sufficient, great, able
καὶ conj. καί and, even, also, but
ἑτέρους adj. acc. masc. pl. ἕτερος another, other, else, strange
3 σὺ pron. nom. 2p. sg. σύ thou, you
οὖν conj. οὖν therefore, then, so, and, now, wherefore
ὡς adv. ὡς as, when, as it were, how, about, like, as soon as, even as, while
καλὸς adj. nom. masc. sg. καλός good, better, goodly, meet, honest, fair, well, worthy
στρατιώτης n. nom. masc. sg. στρατιώτης soldier
Ἰησοῦ n. gen. masc. sg. Ἰησοῦς Jesus
Χριστοῦ n. gen. masc. sg. Χριστός Christ
4 οὐδεὶς num. nom. masc. sg. οὐδείς no man, nothing, no, none, neither, not, nought
ταῖς art. dat. fem. pl. ὁ ἡ τό the, this, that, he, she, it
τοῦ art. gen. masc. sg. ὁ ἡ τό the, this, that, he, she, it
βίου n. gen. masc. sg. βίος life, living, good
πραγματείαις n. dat. fem. pl. πραγματεία affair
ἵνα conj. ἵνα that, to, lest, for to, so that, albeit, because, for, so as
τῷ art. dat. masc. sg. ὁ ἡ τό the, this, that, he, she, it
5 ἐὰν conj. ἐάν if, soever, except, though, and if, but, whether, if so, so
δὲ conj. δέ but, and, now, also, to the contrary, rather, then
καὶ conj. καί and, even, also, but
τις indefinite pron. nom. masc. sg. τὶς certain, some, any man, one, any thing
οὐ particle of negation. οὐ οὐκ οὐχ not, no, neither, none, nay, nor, never, nothing
ἐὰν conj. ἐάν if, soever, except, though, and if, but, whether, if so, so

μὴ particle of negation. μή not, no, lest, neither, none, nothing, nor, never, without
νομίμως adv. νομίμως lawfully
6 τὸν art. acc. masc. sg. ὁ ἡ τό the, this, that, he, she, it
γεωργὸν n. acc. masc. sg. γεωργός husbandmen
πρῶτον adv. πρῶτον first, at the first, first of all, at first, at the beginning, before, chiefly
τῶν art. gen. masc. pl. ὁ ἡ τό the, this, that, he, she, it
καρπῶν n. gen. masc. pl. καρπός fruit
7 ἃ relative pron. acc. neut. pl. ὅς ἥ ὅ who, which, what, that
γάρ conj. γάρ for, and, because, but, indeed
σοι pron. dat. 2p. sg. σύ thou, you
ὁ art. nom. masc. sg. ὁ ἡ τό the, this, that, he, she, it
Κύριος n. nom. masc. sg. κύριος Lord, lord, master, sir, LORD, God, Master, owner
σύνεσιν n. acc. fem. sg. σύνεσις understanding, knowledge
ἐν prep. ἐν (+dat) in, by, with, among, at, on, through, to, within, into, of, for
πᾶσι adj. dat. neut. pl. πᾶς πᾶσα πᾶν all, every, whosoever, every one, no, whole, any
8 Ἰησοῦν n. acc. masc. sg. Ἰησοῦς Jesus
Χριστὸν n. acc. masc. sg. Χριστός Christ
ἐκ prep. ἐκ ἐξ (+gen) of, from, out of, by, on, with, in, among, through
νεκρῶν adj. gen. masc. pl. νεκρός dead
ἐκ prep. ἐκ ἐξ (+gen) of, from, out of, by, on, with, in, among, through
σπέρματος n. gen. neut. sg. σπέρμα seed, issue
Δαβίδ n. gen. masc. sg. Δαβίδ David
κατὰ prep. κατά (+gen) against, by, throughout, down, (+acc) according to, after, with
τὸ art. acc. neut. sg. ὁ ἡ τό the, this, that, he, she, it
εὐαγγέλιόν n. acc. neut. sg. εὐαγγέλιον gospel
μου pron. gen. 1p. sg. ἐγώ I
9 ἐν prep. ἐν (+dat) in, by, with, among, at, on, through, to, within, into, of, for
ᾧ relative pron. dat. neut. sg. ὅς ἥ ὅ who, which, what, that
μέχρι prep. μέχρι until, unto, till, to
δεσμῶν n. gen. masc. pl. δεσμός bond, band, chain, string
ὡς adv. ὡς as, when, as it were, how, about, like, as soon as, even as, while
κακοῦργος adj. nom. masc. sg. κακοῦργος malefactor, evil doer
ἀλλ' conj. ἀλλά but, yea, yet, nevertheless, howbeit, nay, therefore
ὁ art. nom. masc. sg. ὁ ἡ τό the, this, that, he, she, it
λόγος n. nom. masc. sg. λόγος word, saying, account, speech, thing, matter
τοῦ art. gen. masc. sg. ὁ ἡ τό the, this, that, he, she, it
Θεοῦ n. gen. masc. sg. θεός God, god
οὐ particle of negation. οὐ οὐκ οὐχ not, no, neither, none, nay, nor, never, nothing
10 διὰ prep. διά (+gen) by, through, with, in, of, (+acc) for, because of, for a cause
τοῦτο demo. pron. acc. neut. sg. οὗτος αὕτη τοῦτο this, the same, this same, he, she, it
πάντα adj. acc. neut. pl. πᾶς πᾶσα πᾶν all, every, whosoever, every one, no, whole, any
διὰ prep. διά (+gen) by, through, with, in, of, (+acc) for, because of, for a cause
τοὺς art. acc. masc. pl. ὁ ἡ τό the, this, that, he, she, it
ἐκλεκτούς adj. acc. masc. pl. ἐκλεκτός elect, chosen
ἵνα conj. ἵνα that, to, lest, for to, so that, albeit, because, for, so as
καὶ conj. καί and, even, also, but
αὐτοὶ pron. nom. masc. 3p. pl. αὐτός ἡ ὁ self, of oneself, even, very, the same, he, she, it
σωτηρίας n. gen. fem. sg. σωτηρία salvation, deliver, health, saving
τῆς art. gen. fem. sg. ὁ ἡ τό the, this, that, he, she, it
ἐν prep. ἐν (+dat) in, by, with, among, at, on, through, to, within, into, of, for
Χριστῷ n. dat. masc. sg. Χριστός Christ
Ἰησοῦ n. dat. masc. sg. Ἰησοῦς Jesus
μετὰ prep. μετά (+gen) with, among, against, (+acc) after
δόξης n. gen. fem. sg. δόξα glory, honour, praise, dignity, worship
αἰωνίου adj. gen. fem. sg. αἰώνιος eternal, everlasting, world, for ever

11 πιστὸς adj. nom. masc. sg. πιστός faithful, believing, true, sure
ὁ art. nom. masc. sg. ὁ ἡ τό the, this, that, he, she, it
λόγος n. nom. masc. sg. λόγος word, saying, account, speech, thing, matter
Εἰ conj. εἰ if, whether, that, though, forasmuch
γὰρ conj. γάρ for, and, because, but, indeed
καὶ conj. καί and, even, also, but
12 εἰ conj. εἰ if, whether, that, though, forasmuch
καὶ conj. καί and, even, also, but
εἰ conj. εἰ if, whether, that, though, forasmuch
κἀκεῖνος demo. pron. nom. masc. sg. κἀκεῖνος and he, he also, and the other, even he
ἡμᾶς pron. acc. 1p. pl. ἐγώ I
13 εἰ conj. εἰ if, whether, that, though, forasmuch
ἐκεῖνος demo. pron. nom. masc. sg. ἐκεῖνος that, he, the same, that same
πιστὸς adj. nom. masc. sg. πιστός faithful, believing, true, sure
ἑαυτὸν reflexive pron. acc. masc. 3p. sg. ἑαυτοῦ himself, herself, itself, yourself, ourselves
οὐ particle of negation. οὐ οὐκ οὐχ not, no, neither, none, nay, nor, never, nothing
14 Ταῦτα demo. pron. acc. neut. pl. οὗτος αὕτη τοῦτο this, the same, this same, he, she, it
ἐνώπιον prep. ἐνώπιον (+gen) before, in the sight of, in the presence of. (adv.) before
τοῦ art. gen. masc. sg. ὁ ἡ τό the, this, that, he, she, it
Κυρίου n. gen. masc. sg. κύριος Lord, lord, master, sir, LORD, God, Master, owner
μὴ particle of negation. μή not, no, lest, neither, none, nothing, nor, never, without
εἰς prep. εἰς (+acc) into, to, unto, for, in, on, toward, against, upon, at, among
οὐδὲν num. acc. neut. sg. οὐδείς no man, nothing, no, none, neither, not, nought
χρήσιμον adj. acc. neut. sg. χρήσιμος profit
ἐπὶ prep. ἐπί (+gen) on, in, upon, (+dat) in, at, for, upon, (+acc) on, upon, unto, to, against
καταστροφῇ n. dat. fem. sg. καταστροφή subverting, overthrow
τῶν art. gen. masc. pl. ὁ ἡ τό the, this, that, he, she, it
15 σεαυτὸν pron. acc. masc. 2p. sg. σεαυτοῦ σεαυτῷ σεαυτόν thyself, thine own self
δόκιμον adj. acc. masc. sg. δόκιμος approved, tried
τῷ art. dat. masc. sg. ὁ ἡ τό the, this, that, he, she, it
Θεῷ n. dat. masc. sg. θεός God, god
ἐργάτην n. acc. masc. sg. ἐργάτης labourer, worker, workman
ἀνεπαίσχυντον adj. acc. masc. sg. ἀνεπαίσχυντος that needeth not to be ashamed
τὸν art. acc. masc. sg. ὁ ἡ τό the, this, that, he, she, it
λόγον n. acc. masc. sg. λόγος word, saying, account, speech, thing, matter
τῆς art. gen. fem. sg. ὁ ἡ τό the, this, that, he, she, it
ἀληθείας n. gen. fem. sg. ἀλήθεια truth, verity
16 τὰς art. acc. fem. pl. ὁ ἡ τό the, this, that, he, she, it
δὲ conj. δέ but, and, now, also, to the contrary, rather, then
βεβήλους adj. acc. fem. pl. βέβηλος profane, profane person
κενοφωνίας n. acc. fem. pl. κενοφωνία vain babbling
ἐπὶ prep. ἐπί (+gen) on, in, upon, (+dat) in, at, for, upon, (+acc) on, upon, unto, to, against
πλεῖον compar. adj. acc. neut. sg. πολύς many, great, much, long, abundant
γὰρ conj. γάρ for, and, because, but, indeed
ἀσεβείας n. gen. fem. sg. ἀσέβεια ungodliness, ungodly
17 καὶ conj. καί and, even, also, but
ὁ art. nom. masc. sg. ὁ ἡ τό the, this, that, he, she, it
λόγος n. nom. masc. sg. λόγος word, saying, account, speech, thing, matter
αὐτῶν pron. gen. masc. 3p. pl. αὐτός ἡ ὁ self, of oneself, even, very, the same, he, she, it
ὡς adv. ὡς as, when, as it were, how, about, like, as soon as, even as, while
γάγγραινα n. nom. fem. sg. γάγγραινα canker, gangrene
νομὴν n. acc. fem. sg. νομή pasture, eat
ὧν relative pron. gen. masc. pl. ὅς ἥ ὅ who, which, what, that
Ὑμέναιος n. nom. masc. sg. Ὑμέναιος Hymenaeus
καὶ conj. καί and, even, also, but

Φίλητος n. nom. masc. sg. Φίλητος Philetus
18 οἵτινες relative pron. nom. masc. pl. ὅστις which, who, whosoever, that, whatsoever
περὶ prep. περί (+gen) of, for, concerning, (+acc) about, concerning, in
τὴν art. acc. fem. sg. ὁ ἡ τό the, this, that, he, she, it
ἀλήθειαν n. acc. fem. sg. ἀλήθεια truth, verity
τὴν art. acc. fem. sg. ὁ ἡ τό the, this, that, he, she, it
ἀνάστασιν n. acc. fem. sg. ἀνάστασις resurrection, rising again
ἤδη adv. ἤδη now, already, yet, by this time, even now, now already
καὶ conj. καί and, even, also, but
τὴν art. acc. fem. sg. ὁ ἡ τό the, this, that, he, she, it
τινων indefinite pron. gen. masc. pl. τὶς certain, some, any man, one, any thing
πίστιν n. acc. fem. sg. πίστις faith, assurance, belief, fidelity
19 ὁ art. nom. masc. sg. ὁ ἡ τό the, this, that, he, she, it
μέντοι conj. μέντοι yet, nevertheless, but, howbeit, likewise
στερεὸς adj. nom. masc. sg. στερεός sure, stedfast, strong, solid
θεμέλιος n. nom. masc. sg. θεμέλιος foundation
τοῦ art. gen. masc. sg. ὁ ἡ τό the, this, that, he, she, it
Θεοῦ n. gen. masc. sg. θεός God, god
τὴν art. acc. fem. sg. ὁ ἡ τό the, this, that, he, she, it
σφραγῖδα n. acc. fem. sg. σφραγίς seal
ταύτην demo. pron. acc. fem. sg. οὗτος αὕτη τοῦτο this, the same, this same, he, she, it
Κύριος n. nom. masc. sg. κύριος Lord, lord, master, sir, LORD, God, Master, owner
τοὺς art. acc. masc. pl. ὁ ἡ τό the, this, that, he, she, it
αὐτοῦ pron. gen. masc. 3p. sg. αὐτός ή ό self, of oneself, even, very, the same, he, she, it
καί conj. καί and, even, also, but
ἀπὸ prep. ἀπό (+gen) from, of, out of, since, for, off, at, by, in, on
ἀδικίας n. gen. fem. sg. ἀδικία iniquity, unrighteousness, unjust, wrong
πᾶς adj. nom. masc. sg. πᾶς πᾶσα πᾶν all, every, whosoever, every one, no, whole, any
ὁ art. nom. masc. sg. ὁ ἡ τό the, this, that, he, she, it
τὸ art. acc. neut. sg. ὁ ἡ τό the, this, that, he, she, it
ὄνομα n. acc. neut. sg. ὄνομα name, call, surname
Χριστοῦ n. gen. masc. sg. Χριστός Christ
20 ἐν prep. ἐν (+dat) in, by, with, among, at, on, through, to, within, into, of, for
μεγάλῃ adj. dat. fem. sg. μέγας great, loud, greatest, high, large, mighty, strong
δὲ conj. δέ but, and, now, also, to the contrary, rather, then
οἰκίᾳ n. dat. fem. sg. οἰκία house, home, household
οὐκ particle of negation. οὐ οὐκ οὐχ not, no, neither, none, nay, nor, never, nothing
μόνον adv. μόνος only, alone, by oneself
σκεύη n. nom. neut. pl. σκεῦος vessel, good, sail, stuff
χρυσᾶ adj. nom. neut. pl. χρύσεος golden, of gold
καὶ conj. καί and, even, also, but
ἀργυρᾶ adj. nom. neut. pl. ἀργύρεος of silver
ἀλλὰ conj. ἀλλά but, yea, yet, nevertheless, howbeit, nay, therefore
καὶ conj. καί and, even, also, but
ξύλινα adj. nom. neut. pl. ξύλινος of wood
καὶ conj. καί and, even, also, but
ὀστράκινα adj. nom. neut. pl. ὀστράκινος earthen, of earth
καὶ conj. καί and, even, also, but
ἃ relative pron. nom. neut. pl. ὅς ἥ ὅ who, which, what, that
μὲν conj. μέν indeed, verily, truly, even, so, some
εἰς prep. εἰς (+acc) into, to, unto, for, in, on, toward, against, upon, at, among
τιμὴν n. acc. fem. sg. τιμή honour, price, preciousness, sum
ἃ relative pron. nom. neut. pl. ὅς ἥ ὅ who, which, what, that
δὲ conj. δέ but, and, now, also, to the contrary, rather, then
εἰς prep. εἰς (+acc) into, to, unto, for, in, on, toward, against, upon, at, among

ἀτιμίαν n. acc. fem. sg. ἀτιμία vile, dishonour, reproach, shame
21 ἐὰν conj. ἐάν if, soever, except, though, and if, but, whether, if so, so
οὖν conj. οὖν therefore, then, so, and, now, wherefore
τις indefinite pron. nom. masc. sg. τὶς certain, some, any man, one, any thing
ἑαυτὸν reflexive pron. acc. masc. 3p. sg. ἑαυτοῦ himself, herself, itself, yourself, ourselves
ἀπὸ prep. ἀπό (+gen) from, of, out of, since, for, off, at, by, in, on
τούτων demo. pron. gen. neut. pl. οὗτος αὕτη τοῦτο this, the same, this same, he, she, it
σκεῦος n. nom. neut. sg. σκεῦος vessel, good, sail, stuff
εἰς prep. εἰς (+acc) into, to, unto, for, in, on, toward, against, upon, at, among
τιμήν n. acc. fem. sg. τιμή honour, price, preciousness, sum
καὶ conj. καί and, even, also, but
εὔχρηστον adj. nom. neut. sg. εὔχρηστος meet for use, profitable
τῷ art. dat. masc. sg. ὁ ἡ τό the, this, that, he, she, it
δεσπότῃ n. dat. masc. sg. δεσπότης Lord, master
εἰς prep. εἰς (+acc) into, to, unto, for, in, on, toward, against, upon, at, among
πᾶν adj. acc. neut. sg. πᾶς πᾶσα πᾶν all, every, whosoever, every one, no, whole, any
ἔργον n. acc. neut. sg. ἔργον work, deed, doing labour
ἀγαθὸν adj. acc. neut. sg. ἀγαθός good, good thing, that which is good, well
22 τὰς art. acc. fem. pl. ὁ ἡ τό the, this, that, he, she, it
δὲ conj. δέ but, and, now, also, to the contrary, rather, then
νεωτερικὰς adj. acc. fem. pl. νεωτερικός youthful
ἐπιθυμίας n. acc. fem. pl. ἐπιθυμία lust, concupiscence, desire
δὲ conj. δέ but, and, now, also, to the contrary, rather, then
δικαιοσύνην n. acc. fem. sg. δικαιοσύνη righteousness
πίστιν n. acc. fem. sg. πίστις faith, assurance, belief, fidelity
ἀγάπην n. acc. fem. sg. ἀγάπη love, charity, feast of charity
εἰρήνην n. acc. fem. sg. εἰρήνη peace, quietness, rest
μετὰ prep. μετά (+gen) with, among, against, (+acc) after
τῶν art. gen. masc. pl. ὁ ἡ τό the, this, that, he, she, it
τὸν art. acc. masc. sg. ὁ ἡ τό the, this, that, he, she, it
Κύριον n. acc. masc. sg. κύριος Lord, lord, master, sir, LORD, God, Master, owner
ἐκ prep. ἐκ ἐξ (+gen) of, from, out of, by, on, with, in, among, through
καθαρᾶς adj. gen. fem. sg. καθαρός pure, clean, clear
καρδίας n. gen. fem. sg. καρδία heart
23 τὰς art. acc. fem. pl. ὁ ἡ τό the, this, that, he, she, it
δὲ conj. δέ but, and, now, also, to the contrary, rather, then
μωρὰς adj. acc. fem. pl. μωρός fool, foolish
καὶ conj. καί and, even, also, but
ἀπαιδεύτους adj. acc. fem. pl. ἀπαίδευτος unlearned
ζητήσεις n. acc. fem. pl. ζήτησις question
ὅτι conj. ὅτι that, for, because, how that, how, because that, for that, though
μάχας n. acc. fem. pl. μάχη fighting, strife, striving
24 δοῦλον n. acc. masc. sg. δοῦλος servant, bondman, bond, slave
δὲ conj. δέ but, and, now, also, to the contrary, rather, then
Κυρίου n. gen. masc. sg. κύριος Lord, lord, master, sir, LORD, God, Master, owner
οὐ particle of negation. οὐ οὐκ οὐχ not, no, neither, none, nay, nor, never, nothing
ἀλλ' conj. ἀλλά but, yea, yet, nevertheless, howbeit, nay, therefore
ἤπιον adj. acc. masc. sg. ἤπιος gentle
πρὸς prep. πρός (+gen) for, (+dat) at, (+acc) unto, to, with, for, against
πάντας adj. acc. masc. pl. πᾶς πᾶσα πᾶν all, every, whosoever, every one, no, whole, any
διδακτικόν adj. acc. masc. sg. διδακτικός apt to teach
ἀνεξίκακον adj. acc. masc. sg. ἀνεξίκακος patient
25 ἐν prep. ἐν (+dat) in, by, with, among, at, on, through, to, within, into, of, for
πρᾳότητι n. dat. fem. sg. πρᾳότης meekness
τοὺς art. acc. masc. pl. ὁ ἡ τό the, this, that, he, she, it

μήποτε adv. μήποτε lest, lest at any time, lest haply
αὐτοῖς pron. dat. masc. 3p. pl. αὐτός ή ό self, of oneself, even, very, the same, he, she, it
ὁ art. nom. masc. sg. ὁ ἡ τό the, this, that, he, she, it
Θεὸς n. nom. masc. sg. θεός God, god
μετάνοιαν n. acc. fem. sg. μετάνοια repentance
εἰς prep. εἰς (+acc) into, to, unto, for, in, on, toward, against, upon, at, among
ἐπίγνωσιν n. acc. fem. sg. ἐπίγνωσις knowledge, acknowledging, acknowledgement
ἀληθείας n. gen. fem. sg. ἀλήθεια truth, verity
26 καὶ conj. καί and, even, also, but
ἐκ prep. ἐκ ἐξ (+gen) of, from, out of, by, on, with, in, among, through
τῆς art. gen. fem. sg. ὁ ἡ τό the, this, that, he, she, it
τοῦ art. gen. masc. sg. ὁ ἡ τό the, this, that, he, she, it
διαβόλου adj. gen. masc. sg. διάβολος devil, false accuser, Devil, slanderer
παγίδος n. gen. fem. sg. παγίς snare
ὑπ' prep. ὑπό (+gen) of, by, with, from, among, (+acc) under
αὐτοῦ pron. gen. masc. 3p. sg. αὐτός ή ό self, of oneself, even, very, the same, he, she, it
εἰς prep. εἰς (+acc) into, to, unto, for, in, on, toward, against, upon, at, among
τὸ art. acc. neut. sg. ὁ ἡ τό the, this, that, he, she, it
ἐκείνου demo. pron. gen. masc. sg. ἐκεῖνος that, he, the same, that same
θέλημα n. acc. neut. sg. θέλημα will, desire, pleasure

3

1 Τοῦτο demo. pron. acc. neut. sg. οὗτος αὕτη τοῦτο this, the same, this same, he, she, it
δὲ conj. δέ but, and, now, also, to the contrary, rather, then
ὅτι conj. ὅτι that, for, because, how that, how, because that, for that, though
ἐν prep. ἐν (+dat) in, by, with, among, at, on, through, to, within, into, of, for
ἐσχάταις adj. dat. fem. pl. ἔσχατος last, lowest, uttermost, uttermost part
ἡμέραις n. dat. fem. pl. ἡμέρα day, time, year, while, age, day time
καιροὶ n. nom. masc. pl. καιρός time, season, due time, opportunity
χαλεποί adj. nom. masc. pl. χαλεπός fierce, perilous
2 γὰρ conj. γάρ for, and, because, but, indeed
οἱ art. nom. masc. pl. ὁ ἡ τό the, this, that, he, she, it
ἄνθρωποι n. nom. masc. pl. ἄνθρωπος man, human being, person, one, certain
φίλαυτοι adj. nom. masc. pl. φίλαυτος lover of one's own self
φιλάργυροι adj. nom. masc. pl. φιλάργυρος covetous
ἀλαζόνες n. nom. masc. pl. ἀλαζών boaster
ὑπερήφανοι adj. nom. masc. pl. ὑπερήφανος proud
βλάσφημοι adj. nom. masc. pl. βλάσφημος blasphemous, blasphemer, railing
γονεῦσιν n. dat. masc. pl. γονεύς father, (pl.) parents
ἀπειθεῖς adj. nom. masc. pl. ἀπειθής disobedient
ἀχάριστοι adj. nom. masc. pl. ἀχάριστος unthankful
ἀνόσιοι adj. nom. masc. pl. ἀνόσιος unholy
3 ἄστοργοι adj. nom. masc. pl. ἄστοργος without natural affection
ἄσπονδοι adj. nom. masc. pl. ἄσπονδος implacable, trucebreaker
διάβολοι adj. nom. masc. pl. διάβολος devil, false accuser, Devil, slanderer
ἀκρατεῖς adj. nom. masc. pl. ἀκρατής incontinent
ἀνήμεροι adj. nom. masc. pl. ἀνήμερος fierce
ἀφιλάγαθοι adj. nom. masc. pl. ἀφιλάγαθος despiser of those that are good
4 προδόται n. nom. masc. pl. προδότης traitor, betrayer
προπετεῖς adj. nom. masc. pl. προπετής rashly, heady
φιλήδονοι adj. nom. masc. pl. φιλήδονος lover of pleasures
μᾶλλον adv. μᾶλλον rather, more, more and more, better, much, much the more
ἢ particle. ἤ or, than, either, nor, or else, and, rather than
φιλόθεοι adj. nom. masc. pl. φιλόθεος lover of God

5 μόρφωσιν n. acc. fem. sg. μόρφωσις form
εὐσεβείας n. gen. fem. sg. εὐσέβεια godliness, holiness
τὴν art. acc. fem. sg. ὁ ἡ τό the, this, that, he, she, it
δὲ conj. δέ but, and, now, also, to the contrary, rather, then
δύναμιν n. acc. fem. sg. δύναμις power, mighty work, miracle, strength, might
αὐτῆς pron. gen. fem. 3p. sg. αὐτός ή ό self, of oneself, even, very, the same, he, she, it
καὶ conj. καί and, even, also, but
τούτους demo. pron. acc. masc. pl. οὗτος αὕτη τοῦτο this, the same, this same, he, she, it
6 ἐκ prep. ἐκ ἐξ (+gen) of, from, out of, by, on, with, in, among, through
τούτων demo. pron. gen. masc. pl. οὗτος αὕτη τοῦτο this, the same, this same, he, she, it
γάρ conj. γάρ for, and, because, but, indeed
οἱ art. nom. masc. pl. ὁ ἡ τό the, this, that, he, she, it
εἰς prep. εἰς (+acc) into, to, unto, for, in, on, toward, against, upon, at, among
τὰς art. acc. fem. pl. ὁ ἡ τό the, this, that, he, she, it
οἰκίας n. acc. fem. pl. οἰκία house, home, household
καὶ conj. καί and, even, also, but
τὰ art. acc. neut. pl. ὁ ἡ τό the, this, that, he, she, it
γυναικάρια n. acc. neut. pl. γυναικάριον silly woman
ἁμαρτίαις n. dat. fem. pl. ἁμαρτία sin, offence, sinful
ἐπιθυμίαις n. dat. fem. pl. ἐπιθυμία lust, concupiscence, desire
ποικίλαις adj. dat. fem. pl. ποικίλος divers, manifold
7 πάντοτε adv. πάντοτε always, ever, always, evermore
καὶ conj. καί and, even, also, but
μηδέποτε adv. μηδέποτε never
εἰς prep. εἰς (+acc) into, to, unto, for, in, on, toward, against, upon, at, among
ἐπίγνωσιν n. acc. fem. sg. ἐπίγνωσις knowledge, acknowledging, acknowledgement
ἀληθείας n. gen. fem. sg. ἀλήθεια truth, verity
8 ὃν relative pron. acc. masc. sg. ὅς ἥ ὅ who, which, what, that
τρόπον n. acc. masc. sg. τρόπος as, manner, means, way, conversation
δὲ conj. δέ but, and, now, also, to the contrary, rather, then
Ἰάννης n. nom. masc. sg. Ἰάννης Jannes
καὶ conj. καί and, even, also, but
Ἰαμβρῆς n. nom. masc. sg. Ἰαμβρῆς Jambres
Μωϋσεῖ n. dat. masc. sg. Μωϋσεύς Moses
οὕτω adv. οὕτω οὕτως so, even so, thus, on this wise, likewise, after this manner
καὶ conj. καί and, even, also, but
οὗτοι demo. pron. nom. masc. pl. οὗτος αὕτη τοῦτο this, the same, this same, he, she, it
τῇ art. dat. fem. sg. ὁ ἡ τό the, this, that, he, she, it
ἀληθείᾳ n. dat. fem. sg. ἀλήθεια truth, verity
ἄνθρωποι n. nom. masc. pl. ἄνθρωπος man, human being, person, one, certain
τὸν art. acc. masc. sg. ὁ ἡ τό the, this, that, he, she, it
νοῦν n. acc. masc. sg. νοῦς understanding, mind
ἀδόκιμοι adj. nom. masc. pl. ἀδόκιμος reprobate, castaway, rejected
περὶ prep. περί (+gen) of, for, concerning, (+acc) about, concerning, in
τὴν art. acc. fem. sg. ὁ ἡ τό the, this, that, he, she, it
πίστιν n. acc. fem. sg. πίστις faith, assurance, belief, fidelity
9 ἀλλ' conj. ἀλλά but, yea, yet, nevertheless, howbeit, nay, therefore
οὐ particle of negation. οὐ οὐκ οὐχ not, no, neither, none, nay, nor, never, nothing
ἐπὶ prep. ἐπί (+gen) on, in, upon, (+dat) in, at, for, upon, (+acc) on, upon, unto, to, against
πλεῖον compar. adj. acc. neut. sg. πολύς many, great, much, long, abundant
ἡ art. nom. fem. sg. ὁ ἡ τό the, this, that, he, she, it
γὰρ conj. γάρ for, and, because, but, indeed
ἄνοια n. nom. fem. sg. ἄνοια madness, folly
αὐτῶν pron. gen. masc. 3p. pl. αὐτός ή ό self, of oneself, even, very, the same, he, she, it
ἔκδηλος adj. nom. fem. sg. ἔκδηλος manifest

πᾶσιν adj. dat. masc. pl. πᾶς πᾶσα πᾶν all, every, whosoever, every one, no, whole, any
ὡς adv. ὡς as, when, as it were, how, about, like, as soon as, even as, while
καὶ conj. καί and, even, also, but
ἡ art. nom. fem. sg. ὁ ἡ τό the, this, that, he, she, it
ἐκείνων demo. pron. gen. masc. pl. ἐκεῖνος that, he, the same, that same
10 σὺ pron. nom. 2p. sg. σύ thou, you
δὲ conj. δέ but, and, now, also, to the contrary, rather, then
μου pron. gen. 1p. sg. ἐγώ I
τῇ art. dat. fem. sg. ὁ ἡ τό the, this, that, he, she, it
διδασκαλίᾳ n. dat. fem. sg. διδασκαλία doctrine, learning, teaching
τῇ art. dat. fem. sg. ὁ ἡ τό the, this, that, he, she, it
ἀγωγῇ n. dat. fem. sg. ἀγωγή manner of life
τῇ art. dat. fem. sg. ὁ ἡ τό the, this, that, he, she, it
προθέσει n. dat. fem. sg. πρόθεσις purpose, shew, shewbread
τῇ art. dat. fem. sg. ὁ ἡ τό the, this, that, he, she, it
πίστει n. dat. fem. sg. πίστις faith, assurance, belief, fidelity
τῇ art. dat. fem. sg. ὁ ἡ τό the, this, that, he, she, it
μακροθυμίᾳ n. dat. fem. sg. μακροθυμία longsuffering, patience
τῇ art. dat. fem. sg. ὁ ἡ τό the, this, that, he, she, it
ἀγάπῃ n. dat. fem. sg. ἀγάπη love, charity, feast of charity
τῇ art. dat. fem. sg. ὁ ἡ τό the, this, that, he, she, it
ὑπομονῇ n. dat. fem. sg. ὑπομονή patience, enduring
11 τοῖς art. dat. masc. pl. ὁ ἡ τό the, this, that, he, she, it
διωγμοῖς n. dat. masc. pl. διωγμός persecution
τοῖς art. dat. neut. pl. ὁ ἡ τό the, this, that, he, she, it
παθήμασιν n. dat. neut. pl. πάθημα suffering, affliction, affection, motion
οἷά relative pron. nom. neut. pl. οἷος what manner of, such as, as, which, what, so as
μοι pron. dat. 1p. sg. ἐγώ I
ἐν prep. ἐν (+dat) in, by, with, among, at, on, through, to, within, into, of, for
Ἀντιοχείᾳ n. dat. fem. sg. Ἀντιόχεια Antioch
ἐν prep. ἐν (+dat) in, by, with, among, at, on, through, to, within, into, of, for
Ἰκονίῳ n. dat. neut. sg. Ἰκόνιον Iconium
ἐν prep. ἐν (+dat) in, by, with, among, at, on, through, to, within, into, of, for
Λύστροις n. dat. neut. pl. Λύστρα Lystra
οἵους relative pron. acc. masc. pl. οἷος what manner of, such as, as, which, what, so as
διωγμοὺς n. acc. masc. pl. διωγμός persecution
καὶ conj. καί and, even, also, but
ἐκ prep. ἐκ ἐξ (+gen) of, from, out of, by, on, with, in, among, through
πάντων adj. gen. neut. pl. πᾶς πᾶσα πᾶν all, every, whosoever, every one, no, whole, any
με pron. acc. 1p. sg. ἐγώ I
ὁ art. nom. masc. sg. ὁ ἡ τό the, this, that, he, she, it
Κύριος ν. nom. masc. sg. κύριος Lord, lord, master, sir, LORD, God, Master, owner
12 καὶ conj. καί and, even, also, but
πάντες adj. nom. masc. pl. πᾶς πᾶσα πᾶν all, every, whosoever, every one, no, whole, any
δὲ conj. δέ but, and, now, also, to the contrary, rather, then
οἱ art. nom. masc. pl. ὁ ἡ τό the, this, that, he, she, it
εὐσεβῶς adv. εὐσεβῶς godly
ἐν prep. ἐν (+dat) in, by, with, among, at, on, through, to, within, into, of, for
Χριστῷ n. dat. masc. sg. Χριστός Christ
Ἰησοῦ n. dat. masc. sg. Ἰησοῦς Jesus
13 πονηροὶ adj. nom. masc. pl. πονηρός evil, wicked, bad
δὲ conj. δέ but, and, now, also, to the contrary, rather, then
ἄνθρωποι n. nom. masc. pl. ἄνθρωπος man, human being, person, one, certain
καὶ conj. καί and, even, also, but
γόητες n. nom. masc. pl. γόης seducer

ἐπὶ prep. ἐπί (+gen) on, in, upon, (+dat) in, at, for, upon, (+acc) on, upon, unto, to, against
τὸ art. acc. neut. sg. ὁ ἡ τό the, this, that, he, she, it
χεῖρον compar. adj. acc. neut. sg. χείρων worse, sorer, worse and worse
καὶ conj. καί and, even, also, but
14 σὺ pron. nom. 2p. sg. σύ thou, you
δὲ conj. δέ but, and, now, also, to the contrary, rather, then
ἐν prep. ἐν (+dat) in, by, with, among, at, on, through, to, within, into, of, for
οἷς relative pron. dat. neut. pl. ὅς ἥ ὅ who, which, what, that
καὶ conj. καί and, even, also, but
παρὰ prep. παρά (+gen) of, from, (+dat) with, for, (+acc) beside, at, by, above, against
τίνος interrog. pron. gen. masc. sg. τίς what, who, why, where, which, how
15 καὶ conj. καί and, even, also, but
ὅτι conj. ὅτι that, for, because, how that, how, because that, for that, though
ἀπὸ prep. ἀπό (+gen) from, of, out of, since, for, off, at, by, in, on
βρέφους n. gen. neut. sg. βρέφος babe, child, infant, young child
τὰ art. acc. neut. pl. ὁ ἡ τό the, this, that, he, she, it
ἱερὰ adj. acc. neut. pl. ἱερός holy, hallowed, divine
γράμματα n. acc. neut. pl. γράμμα letter, bill, learning, scripture, writing
τὰ art. acc. neut. pl. ὁ ἡ τό the, this, that, he, she, it
σε pron. acc. 2p. sg. σύ thou, you
εἰς prep. εἰς (+acc) into, to, unto, for, in, on, toward, against, upon, at, among
σωτηρίαν n. acc. fem. sg. σωτηρία salvation, deliver, health, saving
διὰ prep. διά (+gen) by, through, with, in, of, (+acc) for, because of, for a cause
πίστεως n. gen. fem. sg. πίστις faith, assurance, belief, fidelity
τῆς art. gen. fem. sg. ὁ ἡ τό the, this, that, he, she, it
ἐν prep. ἐν (+dat) in, by, with, among, at, on, through, to, within, into, of, for
Χριστῷ n. dat. masc. sg. Χριστός Christ
Ἰησοῦ n. dat. masc. sg. Ἰησοῦς Jesus
16 πᾶσα adj. nom. fem. sg. πᾶς πᾶσα πᾶν all, every, whosoever, every one, no, whole, any
γραφὴ n. nom. fem. sg. γραφή scripture
θεόπνευστος adj. nom. fem. sg. given by inspiration of God
καὶ conj. καί and, even, also, but
ὠφέλιμος adj. nom. fem. sg. ὠφέλιμος profitable, profit
πρὸς prep. πρός (+gen) for, (+dat) at, (+acc) unto, to, with, for, against
διδασκαλίαν n. acc. fem. sg. διδασκαλία doctrine, learning, teaching
πρὸς prep. πρός (+gen) for, (+dat) at, (+acc) unto, to, with, for, against
ἔλεγχον n. acc. masc. sg. ἔλεγχος reproof, evidence
πρὸς prep. πρός (+gen) for, (+dat) at, (+acc) unto, to, with, for, against
ἐπανόρθωσιν n. acc. fem. sg. ἐπανόρθωσις correction
πρὸς prep. πρός (+gen) for, (+dat) at, (+acc) unto, to, with, for, against
παιδείαν n. acc. fem. sg. παιδεία nurture, instruction, chastening, chastisement
τὴν art. acc. fem. sg. ὁ ἡ τό the, this, that, he, she, it
ἐν prep. ἐν (+dat) in, by, with, among, at, on, through, to, within, into, of, for
δικαιοσύνῃ n. dat. fem. sg. δικαιοσύνη righteousness
17 ἵνα conj. ἵνα that, to, lest, for to, so that, albeit, because, for, so as
ἄρτιος adj. nom. masc. sg. ἄρτιος perfect
ὁ art. nom. masc. sg. ὁ ἡ τό the, this, that, he, she, it
τοῦ art. gen. masc. sg. ὁ ἡ τό the, this, that, he, she, it
Θεοῦ n. gen. masc. sg. θεός God, god
ἄνθρωπος n. nom. masc. sg. ἄνθρωπος man, human being, person, one, certain
πρὸς prep. πρός (+gen) for, (+dat) at, (+acc) unto, to, with, for, against
πᾶν adj. acc. neut. sg. πᾶς πᾶσα πᾶν all, every, whosoever, every one, no, whole, any
ἔργον n. acc. neut. sg. ἔργον work, deed, doing labour
ἀγαθὸν adj. acc. neut. sg. ἀγαθός good, good thing, that which is good, well

4

1 οὖν conj. οὖν therefore, then, so, and, now, wherefore
ἐγὼ pron. nom. 1p. sg. ἐγώ I
ἐνώπιον prep. ἐνώπιον (+gen) before, in the sight of, in the presence of. (adv.) before
τοῦ art. gen. masc. sg. ὁ ἡ τό the, this, that, he, she, it
Θεοῦ n. gen. masc. sg. θεός God, god
καὶ conj. καί and, even, also, but
τοῦ art. gen. masc. sg. ὁ ἡ τό the, this, that, he, she, it
Κυρίου n. gen. masc. sg. κύριος Lord, lord, master, sir, LORD, God, Master, owner
Ἰησοῦ n. gen. masc. sg. Ἰησοῦς Jesus
Χριστοῦ n. gen. masc. sg. Χριστός Christ
τοῦ art. gen. masc. sg. ὁ ἡ τό the, this, that, he, she, it
καὶ conj. καί and, even, also, but
νεκρούς adj. acc. masc. pl. νεκρός dead
κατὰ prep. κατά (+gen) against, by, throughout, down, (+acc) according to, after, with
τὴν art. acc. fem. sg. ὁ ἡ τό the, this, that, he, she, it
ἐπιφάνειαν n. acc. fem. sg. ἐπιφάνεια appearing, brightness
αὐτοῦ pron. gen. masc. 3p. sg. αὐτός ή ό self, of oneself, even, very, the same, he, she, it
καὶ conj. καί and, even, also, but
τὴν art. acc. fem. sg. ὁ ἡ τό the, this, that, he, she, it
βασιλείαν n. acc. fem. sg. βασιλεία kingdom, reign
αὐτοῦ pron. gen. masc. 3p. sg. αὐτός ή ό self, of oneself, even, very, the same, he, she, it
2 τὸν art. acc. masc. sg. ὁ ἡ τό the, this, that, he, she, it
λόγον n. acc. masc. sg. λόγος word, saying, account, speech, thing, matter
εὐκαίρως adv. εὐκαίρως conveniently, in season
ἀκαίρως adv. ἀκαίρως out of season
ἐν prep. ἐν (+dat) in, by, with, among, at, on, through, to, within, into, of, for
πάσῃ adj. dat. fem. sg. πᾶς πᾶσα πᾶν all, every, whosoever, every one, no, whole, any
μακροθυμίᾳ n. dat. fem. sg. μακροθυμία longsuffering, patience
καὶ conj. καί and, even, also, but
διδαχῇ n. dat. fem. sg. διδαχή doctrine, teaching
3 γὰρ conj. γάρ for, and, because, but, indeed
καιρὸς n. nom. masc. sg. καιρός time, season, due time, opportunity
ὅτε adv. ὅτε when, after that, as soon as, while, after
τῆς art. gen. fem. sg. ὁ ἡ τό the, this, that, he, she, it
διδασκαλίας n. gen. fem. sg. διδασκαλία doctrine, learning, teaching
οὐκ particle of negation. οὐ οὐκ οὐχ not, no, neither, none, nay, nor, never, nothing
ἀλλὰ conj. ἀλλά but, yea, yet, nevertheless, howbeit, nay, therefore
κατὰ prep. κατά (+gen) against, by, throughout, down, (+acc) according to, after, with
τὰς art. acc. fem. pl. ὁ ἡ τό the, this, that, he, she, it
ἐπιθυμίας n. acc. fem. pl. ἐπιθυμία lust, concupiscence, desire
τὰς art. acc. fem. pl. ὁ ἡ τό the, this, that, he, she, it
ἰδίας adj. acc. fem. pl. ἴδιος one's own, one's, privately
ἑαυτοῖς reflexive pron. dat. masc. 3p. pl. ἑαυτοῦ himself, herself, itself, yourself, ourselves
διδασκάλους n. acc. masc. pl. διδάσκαλος teacher, master, doctor
τὴν art. acc. fem. sg. ὁ ἡ τό the, this, that, he, she, it
ἀκοὴν n. acc. fem. sg. ἀκοή hearing, ear, fame, report, rumour, which one heard
4 καὶ conj. καί and, even, also, but
ἀπὸ prep. ἀπό (+gen) from, of, out of, since, for, off, at, by, in, on
μὲν conj. μέν indeed, verily, truly, even, so, some
τῆς art. gen. fem. sg. ὁ ἡ τό the, this, that, he, she, it
ἀληθείας n. gen. fem. sg. ἀλήθεια truth, verity
τὴν art. acc. fem. sg. ὁ ἡ τό the, this, that, he, she, it
ἀκοὴν n. acc. fem. sg. ἀκοή hearing, ear, fame, report, rumour, which one heard

ἐπὶ prep. ἐπί (+gen) on, in, upon, (+dat) in, at, for, upon, (+acc) on, upon, unto, to, against
δὲ conj. δέ but, and, now, also, to the contrary, rather, then
τοὺς art. acc. masc. pl. ὁ ἡ τό the, this, that, he, she, it
μύθους n. acc. masc. pl. μῦθος fable, myth
5 σὺ pron. nom. 2p. sg. σύ thou, you
δὲ conj. δέ but, and, now, also, to the contrary, rather, then
ἐν prep. ἐν (+dat) in, by, with, among, at, on, through, to, within, into, of, for
πᾶσι adj. dat. neut. pl. πᾶς πᾶσα πᾶν all, every, whosoever, every one, no, whole, any
ἔργον n. acc. neut. sg. ἔργον work, deed, doing labour
εὐαγγελιστοῦ n. gen. masc. sg. εὐαγγελιστής evangelist
τὴν art. acc. fem. sg. ὁ ἡ τό the, this, that, he, she, it
διακονίαν n. acc. fem. sg. διακονία ministry, administration, service, office, relief
σου pron. gen. 2p. sg. σύ thou, you
6 ἐγὼ pron. nom. 1p. sg. ἐγώ I
γὰρ conj. γάρ for, and, because, but, indeed
ἤδη adv. ἤδη now, already, yet, by this time, even now, now already
καὶ conj. καί and, even, also, but
ὁ art. nom. masc. sg. ὁ ἡ τό the, this, that, he, she, it
καιρὸς n. nom. masc. sg. καιρός time, season, due time, opportunity
τῆς art. gen. fem. sg. ὁ ἡ τό the, this, that, he, she, it
ἐμῆς poss. pron. gen. fem. 1p. sg. ἐμός my, mine, mine own, of me
ἀναλύσεώς n. gen. fem. sg. ἀνάλυσις departure
7 τὸν art. acc. masc. sg. ὁ ἡ τό the, this, that, he, she, it
ἀγῶνα n. acc. masc. sg. ἀγών conflict, fight, contention, race
τὸν art. acc. masc. sg. ὁ ἡ τό the, this, that, he, she, it
καλὸν adj. acc. masc. sg. καλός good, better, goodly, meet, honest, fair, well, worthy
τὸν art. acc. masc. sg. ὁ ἡ τό the, this, that, he, she, it
δρόμον n. acc. masc. sg. δρόμος course
τὴν art. acc. fem. sg. ὁ ἡ τό the, this, that, he, she, it
πίστιν n. acc. fem. sg. πίστις faith, assurance, belief, fidelity
8 λοιπὸν adv. λοιπόν finally, henceforth, now, besides, furthermore, moreover, then
μοι pron. dat. 1p. sg. ἐγώ I
ὁ art. nom. masc. sg. ὁ ἡ τό the, this, that, he, she, it
τῆς art. gen. fem. sg. ὁ ἡ τό the, this, that, he, she, it
δικαιοσύνης n. gen. fem. sg. δικαιοσύνη righteousness
στέφανος n. nom. masc. sg. στέφανος crown
ὃν relative pron. acc. masc. sg. ὅς ἥ ὅ who, which, what, that
μοι pron. dat. 1p. sg. ἐγώ I
ὁ art. nom. masc. sg. ὁ ἡ τό the, this, that, he, she, it
Κύριος n. nom. masc. sg. κύριος Lord, lord, master, sir, LORD, God, Master, owner
ἐν prep. ἐν (+dat) in, by, with, among, at, on, through, to, within, into, of, for
ἐκείνῃ demo. pron. dat. fem. sg. ἐκεῖνος that, he, the same, that same
τῇ art. dat. fem. sg. ὁ ἡ τό the, this, that, he, she, it
ἡμέρᾳ n. dat. fem. sg. ἡμέρα day, time, year, while, age, day time
ὁ art. nom. masc. sg. ὁ ἡ τό the, this, that, he, she, it
δίκαιος adj. nom. masc. sg. δίκαιος righteous, just, meet, right
κριτής n. nom. masc. sg. κριτής judge
οὐ particle of negation. οὐ οὐκ οὐχ not, no, neither, none, nay, nor, never, nothing
μόνον adv. μόνος only, alone, by oneself
δὲ conj. δέ but, and, now, also, to the contrary, rather, then
ἐμοὶ pron. dat. 1p. sg. ἐγώ I
ἀλλὰ conj. ἀλλά but, yea, yet, nevertheless, howbeit, nay, therefore
καὶ conj. καί and, even, also, but
πᾶσι adj. dat. masc. pl. πᾶς πᾶσα πᾶν all, every, whosoever, every one, no, whole, any
τοῖς art. dat. masc. pl. ὁ ἡ τό the, this, that, he, she, it

τὴν art. acc. fem. sg. ὁ ἡ τό the, this, that, he, she, it
ἐπιφάνειαν n. acc. fem. sg. ἐπιφάνεια appearing, brightness
αὐτοῦ pron. gen. masc. 3p. sg. αὐτός ή ό self, of oneself, even, very, the same, he, she, it
9 πρός prep. πρός (+gen) for, (+dat) at, (+acc) unto, to, with, for, against
με pron. acc. 1p. sg. ἐγώ I
ταχέως adv. ταχέως sortly, quickly, soon, hastily, suddenly
10 Δημᾶς n. nom. masc. sg. Δημᾶς Demas
γάρ conj. γάρ for, and, because, but, indeed
με pron. acc. 1p. sg. ἐγώ I
τὸν art. acc. masc. sg. ὁ ἡ τό the, this, that, he, she, it
νῦν adv. νῦν now, henceforth, present, this time
αἰῶνα n. acc. masc. sg. αἰών ever, ever and ever, evermore, age, eternal, world
καὶ conj. καί and, even, also, but
εἰς prep. εἰς (+acc) into, to, unto, for, in, on, toward, against, upon, at, among
Θεσσαλονίκην n. acc. fem. sg. Θεσσαλονίκη Thessalonica
Κρήσκης n. nom. masc. sg. Κρήσκης Crescens
εἰς prep. εἰς (+acc) into, to, unto, for, in, on, toward, against, upon, at, among
Γαλατίαν n. acc. fem. sg. Γαλατία Galatia
Τίτος n. nom. masc. sg. Τίτος Titus
εἰς prep. εἰς (+acc) into, to, unto, for, in, on, toward, against, upon, at, among
Δαλματίαν n. acc. fem. sg. Δαλματία Dalmatia
11 Λουκᾶς n. nom. masc. sg. Λουκᾶς Luke, Lucas
μόνος adj. nom. masc. sg. μόνος only, alone, by oneself
μετ' prep. μετά (+gen) with, among, against, (+acc) after
ἐμοῦ pron. gen. 1p. sg. ἐγώ I
Μᾶρκον n. acc. masc. sg. Μᾶρκος Mark, Marcus
μετὰ prep. μετά (+gen) with, among, against, (+acc) after
σεαυτοῦ pron. gen. masc. 2p. sg. σεαυτοῦ σεαυτῷ σεαυτόν thyself, thine own self
γάρ conj. γάρ for, and, because, but, indeed
μοι pron. dat. 1p. sg. ἐγώ I
εὔχρηστος adj. nom. masc. sg. εὔχρηστος meet for use, profitable
εἰς prep. εἰς (+acc) into, to, unto, for, in, on, toward, against, upon, at, among
διακονίαν n. acc. fem. sg. διακονία ministry, administration, service, office, relief
12 Τύχικον n. acc. masc. sg. Τυχικός Tychicus
δὲ conj. δέ but, and, now, also, to the contrary, rather, then
εἰς prep. εἰς (+acc) into, to, unto, for, in, on, toward, against, upon, at, among
Ἔφεσον n. acc. fem. sg. Ἔφεσος Ephesus
13 τὸν art. acc. masc. sg. ὁ ἡ τό the, this, that, he, she, it
φελόνην n. acc. masc. sg. φελόνης cloke, thick cloak for travelling with a hood
ὃν relative pron. acc. masc. sg. ὅς ἥ ὅ who, which, what, that
ἐν prep. ἐν (+dat) in, by, with, among, at, on, through, to, within, into, of, for
Τρῳάδι n. dat. fem. sg. Τρῳάς Troas
παρὰ prep. παρά (+gen) of, from, (+dat) with, for, (+acc) beside, at, by, above, against
Κάρπῳ n. dat. masc. sg. Κάρπος Carpus
καὶ conj. καί and, even, also, but
τὰ art. acc. neut. pl. ὁ ἡ τό the, this, that, he, she, it
βιβλία n. acc. neut. pl. βιβλίον book, bill, scroll, writing
μάλιστα adv. μάλιστα specially, especially, chiefly, most of all
τὰς art. acc. fem. pl. ὁ ἡ τό the, this, that, he, she, it
μεμβράνας n. acc. fem. pl. μεμβράνα parchment
14 Ἀλέξανδρος n. nom. masc. sg. Ἀλέξανδρος Alexander
ὁ art. nom. masc. sg. ὁ ἡ τό the, this, that, he, she, it
χαλκεὺς n. nom. masc. sg. χαλκεύς coppersmith
πολλά adj. acc. neut. pl. πολύς many, great, much, long, abundant
μοι pron. dat. 1p. sg. ἐγώ I

κακὰ adj. acc. neut. pl. κακός evil, evil thing, noisome, wicked
αὐτῷ pron. dat. masc. 3p. sg. αὐτός ή ό self, of oneself, even, very, the same, he, she, it
ὁ art. nom. masc. sg. ὁ ἡ τό the, this, that, he, she, it
Κύριος n. nom. masc. sg. κύριος Lord, lord, master, sir, LORD, God, Master, owner
κακὰ adj. acc. neut. pl. κακός evil, evil thing, noisome, wicked
τὰ art. acc. neut. pl. ὁ ἡ τό the, this, that, he, she, it
ἔργα n. acc. neut. pl. ἔργον work, deed, doing labour
αὐτοῦ pron. gen. masc. 3p. sg. αὐτός ή ό self, of oneself, even, very, the same, he, she, it
15 ὃν relative pron. acc. masc. sg. ὅς ἥ ὅ who, which, what, that
καὶ conj. καί and, even, also, but
σὺ pron. nom. 2p. sg. σύ thou, you
λίαν adv. λίαν exceeding, greatly, very, great sore
γὰρ conj. γάρ for, and, because, but, indeed
τοῖς art. dat. masc. pl. ὁ ἡ τό the, this, that, he, she, it
ἡμετέροις poss. pron. dat. masc. 1p. pl. ἡμέτερος our
λόγοις n. dat. masc. pl. λόγος word, saying, account, speech, thing, matter
16 ἐν prep. ἐν (+dat) in, by, with, among, at, on, through, to, within, into, of, for
τῇ art. dat. fem. sg. ὁ ἡ τό the, this, that, he, she, it
πρώτῃ ordinal. adj. dat. fem. sg. πρῶτος first, chief, first of all, chiefest, best
μου pron. gen. 1p. sg. ἐγώ I
ἀπολογίᾳ n. dat. fem. sg. ἀπολογία defence, answer, answer for oneself, clear oneself
οὐδείς num. nom. masc. sg. οὐδείς no man, nothing, no, none, neither, not, nought
μοι pron. dat. 1p. sg. ἐγώ I
ἀλλὰ conj. ἀλλά but, yea, yet, nevertheless, howbeit, nay, therefore
πάντες adj. nom. masc. pl. πᾶς πᾶσα πᾶν all, every, whosoever, every one, no, whole, any
με pron. acc. 1p. sg. ἐγώ I
μὴ particle of negation. μή not, no, lest, neither, none, nothing, nor, never, without
αὐτοῖς pron. dat. masc. 3p. pl. αὐτός ή ό self, of oneself, even, very, the same, he, she, it
17 ὁ art. nom. masc. sg. ὁ ἡ τό the, this, that, he, she, it
δὲ conj. δέ but, and, now, also, to the contrary, rather, then
Κύριός n. nom. masc. sg. κύριος Lord, lord, master, sir, LORD, God, Master, owner
μοι pron. dat. 1p. sg. ἐγώ I
καὶ conj. καί and, even, also, but
με pron. acc. 1p. sg. ἐγώ I
ἵνα conj. ἵνα that, to, lest, for to, so that, albeit, because, for, so as
δι' prep. διά (+gen) by, through, with, in, of, (+acc) for, because of, for a cause
ἐμοῦ pron. gen. 1p. sg. ἐγώ I
τὸ art. nom. neut. sg. ὁ ἡ τό the, this, that, he, she, it
κήρυγμα n. nom. neut. sg. κήρυγμα preaching
καὶ conj. καί and, even, also, but
πάντα adj. nom. neut. pl. πᾶς πᾶσα πᾶν all, every, whosoever, every one, no, whole, any
τὰ art. nom. neut. pl. ὁ ἡ τό the, this, that, he, she, it
ἔθνη n. nom. neut. pl. ἔθνος Gentile, nation, heathen, people
καὶ conj. καί and, even, also, but
ἐκ prep. ἐκ ἐξ (+gen) of, from, out of, by, on, with, in, among, through
στόματος n. gen. neut. sg. στόμα mouth, face, edge
λέοντος n. gen. masc. sg. λέων lion
18 καὶ conj. καί and, even, also, but
με pron. acc. 1p. sg. ἐγώ I
ὁ art. nom. masc. sg. ὁ ἡ τό the, this, that, he, she, it
Κύριος n. nom. masc. sg. κύριος Lord, lord, master, sir, LORD, God, Master, owner
ἀπὸ prep. ἀπό (+gen) from, of, out of, since, for, off, at, by, in, on
παντὸς adj. gen. neut. sg. πᾶς πᾶσα πᾶν all, every, whosoever, every one, no, whole, any
ἔργου n. gen. neut. sg. ἔργον work, deed, doing labour
πονηροῦ adj. gen. neut. sg. πονηρός evil, wicked, bad
καὶ conj. καί and, even, also, but

εἰς prep. εἰς (+acc) into, to, unto, for, in, on, toward, against, upon, at, among
τὴν art. acc. fem. sg. ὁ ἡ τό the, this, that, he, she, it
βασιλείαν n. acc. fem. sg. βασιλεία kingdom, reign
αὐτοῦ pron. gen. masc. 3p. sg. αὐτός ἡ ὁ self, of oneself, even, very, the same, he, she, it
τὴν art. acc. fem. sg. ὁ ἡ τό the, this, that, he, she, it
ἐπουράνιον adj. acc. fem. sg. ἐπουράνιος heavenly, celestial, high, in heaven
ᾧ relative pron. dat. masc. sg. ὅς ἥ ὅ who, which, what, that
ἡ art. nom. fem. sg. ὁ ἡ τό the, this, that, he, she, it
δόξα n. nom. fem. sg. δόξα glory, honour, praise, dignity, worship
εἰς prep. εἰς (+acc) into, to, unto, for, in, on, toward, against, upon, at, among
τοὺς art. acc. masc. pl. ὁ ἡ τό the, this, that, he, she, it
αἰῶνας n. acc. masc. pl. αἰών ever, ever and ever, evermore, age, eternal, world
τῶν art. gen. masc. pl. ὁ ἡ τό the, this, that, he, she, it
αἰώνων n. gen. masc. pl. αἰών ever, ever and ever, evermore, age, eternal, world
ἀμήν particle. ἀμήν amen, verily
19 Πρίσκαν n. acc. fem. sg. Πρίσκιλλα Priscilla
καὶ conj. καί and, even, also, but
᾿Ακύλαν n. acc. masc. sg. ᾿Ακύλας Aquila
καὶ conj. καί and, even, also, but
τὸν art. acc. masc. sg. ὁ ἡ τό the, this, that, he, she, it
᾿Ονησιφόρου n. gen. masc. sg. ᾿Ονησίφορος Onesiphorus
οἶκον n. acc. masc. sg. οἶκος house, home, household
20 Ἔραστος n. nom. masc. sg. Ἔραστος Erastus
ἐν prep. ἐν (+dat) in, by, with, among, at, on, through, to, within, into, of, for
Κορίνθῳ n. dat. fem. sg. Κόρινθος Corinth
Τρόφιμον n. acc. masc. sg. Τρόφιμος Trophimus
δὲ conj. δέ but, and, now, also, to the contrary, rather, then
ἐν prep. ἐν (+dat) in, by, with, among, at, on, through, to, within, into, of, for
Μιλήτῳ n. dat. fem. sg. Μίλητος Miletus, Miletum
21 πρὸ prep. πρό (+gen) before, above
χειμῶνος n. gen. masc. sg. χειμών foul weather, winter, tempest
σε pron. acc. 2p. sg. σύ thou, you
Εὔβουλος n. nom. masc. sg. Εὔβουλος Eubulus
καὶ conj. καί and, even, also, but
Πούδης n. nom. masc. sg. Πούδης Pudens
καὶ conj. καί and, even, also, but
Λῖνος n. nom. masc. sg. Λῖνος Linus
καὶ conj. καί and, even, also, but
Κλαυδία n. nom. fem. sg. Κλαυδία Claudia
καὶ conj. καί and, even, also, but
οἱ art. nom. masc. pl. ὁ ἡ τό the, this, that, he, she, it
ἀδελφοὶ n. nom. masc. pl. ἀδελφός brother
πάντες adj. nom. masc. pl. πᾶς πᾶσα πᾶν all, every, whosoever, every one, no, whole, any
22 Ὁ art. nom. masc. sg. ὁ ἡ τό the, this, that, he, she, it
Κύριος n. nom. masc. sg. κύριος Lord, lord, master, sir, LORD, God, Master, owner
᾿Ιησοῦς n. nom. masc. sg. ᾿Ιησοῦς Jesus
Χριστὸς n. nom. masc. sg. Χριστός Christ
μετὰ prep. μετά (+gen) with, among, against, (+acc) after
τοῦ art. gen. neut. sg. ὁ ἡ τό the, this, that, he, she, it
πνεύματός n. gen. neut. sg. πνεῦμα spirit, Spirit, Ghost, ghost, life. of the spirit, wind
σου pron. gen. 2p. sg. σύ thou, you
ἡ art. nom. fem. sg. ὁ ἡ τό the, this, that, he, she, it
χάρις n. nom. fem. sg. χάρις grace, thank, favour, pleasure
μεθ' prep. μετά (+gen) with, among, against, (+acc) after
ὑμῶν pron. gen. 2p. pl. σύ thou, you
ἀμήν particle. ἀμήν amen, verily

ΠΑΥΛΟΥ
Η ΠΡΟΣ
ΤΙΤΟΝ ΕΠΙΣΤΟΛΗ

1

1 Παῦλος n. nom. masc. sg. Παῦλος Paul, Paulus
δοῦλος n. nom. masc. sg. δοῦλος servant, bondman, bond, slave
Θεοῦ n. gen. masc. sg. θεός God, god
ἀπόστολος n. nom. masc. sg. ἀπόστολος apostle, messenger, he that is sent
δὲ conj. δέ but, and, now, also, to the contrary, rather, then
Ἰησοῦ n. gen. masc. sg. Ἰησοῦς Jesus
Χριστοῦ n. gen. masc. sg. Χριστός Christ
κατὰ prep. κατά (+gen) against, by, throughout, down, (+acc) according to, after, with
πίστιν n. acc. fem. sg. πίστις faith, assurance, belief, fidelity
ἐκλεκτῶν adj. gen. masc. pl. ἐκλεκτός elect, chosen
Θεοῦ n. gen. masc. sg. θεός God, god
καὶ conj. καί and, even, also, but
ἐπίγνωσιν n. acc. fem. sg. ἐπίγνωσις knowledge, acknowledging, acknowledgement
ἀληθείας n. gen. fem. sg. ἀλήθεια truth, verity
τῆς art. gen. fem. sg. ὁ ἡ τό the, this, that, he, she, it
κατ' prep. κατά (+gen) against, by, throughout, down, (+acc) according to, after, with
εὐσέβειαν n. acc. fem. sg. εὐσέβεια godliness, holiness
2 ἐπ' prep. ἐπί (+gen) on, in, upon, (+dat) in, at, for, upon, (+acc) on, upon, unto, to, against
ἐλπίδι n. dat. fem. sg. ἐλπίς hope, faith
ζωῆς n. gen. fem. sg. ζωή life, lifetime
αἰωνίου adj. gen. fem. sg. αἰώνιος eternal, everlasting, world, for ever
ἣν relative pron. acc. fem. sg. ὅς ἥ ὅ who, which, what, that
ὁ art. nom. masc. sg. ὁ ἡ τό the, this, that, he, she, it
ἀψευδὴς adj. nom. masc. sg. ἀψευδής that cannot lie
Θεὸς n. nom. masc. sg. θεός God, god
πρὸ prep. πρό (+gen) before, above
χρόνων n. gen. masc. pl. χρόνος time, season, space
αἰωνίων adj. gen. masc. pl. αἰώνιος eternal, everlasting, world, for ever
3 δὲ conj. δέ but, and, now, also, to the contrary, rather, then
καιροῖς n. dat. masc. pl. καιρός time, season, due time, opportunity
ἰδίοις adj. dat. masc. pl. ἴδιος one's own, one's, privately
τὸν art. acc. masc. sg. ὁ ἡ τό the, this, that, he, she, it
λόγον n. acc. masc. sg. λόγος word, saying, account, speech, thing, matter
αὐτοῦ pron. gen. masc. 3p. sg. αὐτός ή ό self, of oneself, even, very, the same, he, she, it
ἐν prep. ἐν (+dat) in, by, with, among, at, on, through, to, within, into, of, for
κηρύγματι n. dat. neut. sg. κήρυγμα preaching
ὃ relative pron. acc. neut. sg. ὅς ἥ ὅ who, which, what, that
ἐγὼ pron. nom. 1p. sg. ἐγώ I
κατ' prep. κατά (+gen) against, by, throughout, down, (+acc) according to, after, with
ἐπιταγὴν n. acc. fem. sg. ἐπιταγή commandment, authority
τοῦ art. gen. masc. sg. ὁ ἡ τό the, this, that, he, she, it
σωτῆρος n. gen. masc. sg. σωτήρ Saviour, saviour
ἡμῶν pron. gen. 1p. pl. ἐγώ I
Θεοῦ n. gen. masc. sg. θεός God, god
4 Τίτῳ n. dat. masc. sg. Τίτος Titus
γνησίῳ adj. dat. neut. sg. γνήσιος sincerity, own, true
τέκνῳ n. dat. neut. sg. τέκνον child, son, daughter

κατὰ prep. κατά (+gen) against, by, throughout, down, (+acc) according to, after, with
κοινὴν adj. acc. fem. sg. κοινός common, unclean, defiled, unholy
πίστιν n. acc. fem. sg. πίστις faith, assurance, belief, fidelity
χάρις n. nom. fem. sg. χάρις grace, thank, favour, pleasure
ἔλεος n. acc. masc. sg. ἔλεος mercy
εἰρήνη n. nom. fem. sg. εἰρήνη peace, quietness, rest
ἀπὸ prep. ἀπό (+gen) from, of, out of, since, for, off, at, by, in, on
Θεοῦ n. gen. masc. sg. θεός God, god
πατρὸς n. gen. masc. sg. πατήρ Father, father, parent
καὶ conj. καί and, even, also, but
Κυρίου n. gen. masc. sg. κύριος Lord, lord, master, sir, LORD, God, Master, owner
Ἰησοῦ n. gen. masc. sg. Ἰησοῦς Jesus
Χριστοῦ n. gen. masc. sg. Χριστός Christ
τοῦ art. gen. masc. sg. ὁ ἡ τό the, this, that, he, she, it
σωτῆρος n. gen. masc. sg. σωτήρ Saviour, saviour
ἡμῶν pron. gen. 1p. pl. ἐγώ I
5 Τούτου demo. pron. gen. neut. sg. οὗτος αὕτη τοῦτο this, the same, this same, he, she, it
χάριν adv. χάριν for a cause, because of, for sake
σε pron. acc. 2p. sg. σύ thou, you
ἐν prep. ἐν (+dat) in, by, with, among, at, on, through, to, within, into, of, for
Κρήτῃ n. dat. fem. sg. Κρήτη Crete
ἵνα conj. ἵνα that, to, lest, for to, so that, albeit, because, for, so as
τὰ art. acc. neut. pl. ὁ ἡ τό the, this, that, he, she, it
καὶ conj. καί and, even, also, but
κατὰ prep. κατά (+gen) against, by, throughout, down, (+acc) according to, after, with
πόλιν n. acc. fem. sg. πόλις city
πρεσβυτέρους adj. acc. masc. pl. πρεσβύτερος elder, elder woman, eldest, old man
ὡς adv. ὡς as, when, as it were, how, about, like, as soon as, even as, while
ἐγώ pron. nom. 1p. sg. ἐγώ I
σοι pron. dat. 2p. sg. σύ thou, you
6 εἴ conj. εἰ if, whether, that, though, forasmuch
τίς indefinite pron. nom. masc. sg. τὶς certain, some, any man, one, any thing
ἀνέγκλητος adj. nom. masc. sg. ἀνέγκλητος blameless, unreprovable
μιᾶς num. gen. fem. sg. εἷς or ἓν one, other, some, any, only, a certain
γυναικὸς n. gen. fem. sg. γυνή woman, wife
ἀνήρ n. nom. masc. sg. ἀνήρ man, husband, sir
τέκνα n. acc. neut. pl. τέκνον child, son, daughter
πιστά adj. acc. neut. pl. πιστός faithful, believing, true, sure
μὴ particle of negation. μή not, no, lest, neither, none, nothing, nor, never, without
ἐν prep. ἐν (+dat) in, by, with, among, at, on, through, to, within, into, of, for
κατηγορίᾳ n. dat. fem. sg. κατηγορία accusation, accuse
ἀσωτίας n. gen. fem. sg. ἀσωτία excess, riot
ἢ particle. ἤ or, than, either, nor, or else, and, rather than
ἀνυπότακτα adj. acc. neut. pl. ἀνυπότακτος disobedient, unruly, that is not put under
7 γὰρ conj. γάρ for, and, because, but, indeed
τὸν art. acc. masc. sg. ὁ ἡ τό the, this, that, he, she, it
ἐπίσκοπον n. acc. masc. sg. ἐπίσκοπος overseer, bishop
ἀνέγκλητον adj. acc. masc. sg. ἀνέγκλητος blameless, unreprovable
ὡς adv. ὡς as, when, as it were, how, about, like, as soon as, even as, while
Θεοῦ n. gen. masc. sg. θεός God, god
οἰκονόμον n. acc. masc. sg. οἰκονόμος steward, chamberlain, governor
μὴ particle of negation. μή not, no, lest, neither, none, nothing, nor, never, without
αὐθάδη adj. acc. masc. sg. αὐθάδης selfwilled
μὴ particle of negation. μή not, no, lest, neither, none, nothing, nor, never, without
ὀργίλον adj. acc. masc. sg. ὀργίλος soon angry

μὴ particle of negation. μή not, no, lest, neither, none, nothing, nor, never, without
πάροινον adj. acc. masc. sg. πάροινος given to wine
μὴ particle of negation. μή not, no, lest, neither, none, nothing, nor, never, without
πλήκτην n. acc. masc. sg. πλήκτης striker
μὴ particle of negation. μή not, no, lest, neither, none, nothing, nor, never, without
αἰσχροκερδῆ adj. acc. masc. sg. αἰσχροκερδής given to filthy lucre
8 ἀλλὰ conj. ἀλλά but, yea, yet, nevertheless, howbeit, nay, therefore
φιλόξενον adj. acc. masc. sg. φιλόξενος given to hospitality, lover of hospitality
φιλάγαθον adj. acc. masc. sg. φιλάγαθος lover of good men, lover of goodness
σώφρονα adj. acc. masc. sg. σώφρων sober, discreet, temperate
δίκαιον adj. acc. masc. sg. δίκαιος righteous, just, meet, right
ὅσιον adj. acc. masc. sg. ὅσιος holy, Holy, mercy
ἐγκρατῆ adj. acc. masc. sg. ἐγκρατής temperate
9 τοῦ art. gen. masc. sg. ὁ ἡ τό the, this, that, he, she, it
κατὰ prep. κατά (+gen) against, by, throughout, down, (+acc) according to, after, with
τὴν art. acc. fem. sg. ὁ ἡ τό the, this, that, he, she, it
διδαχὴν n. acc. fem. sg. διδαχή doctrine, teaching
πιστοῦ adj. gen. masc. sg. πιστός faithful, believing, true, sure
λόγου n. gen. masc. sg. λόγος word, saying, account, speech, thing, matter
ἵνα conj. ἵνα that, to, lest, for to, so that, albeit, because, for, so as
δυνατὸς adj. nom. masc. sg. δυνατός able, possible, mighty, strong
καὶ conj. καί and, even, also, but
ἐν prep. ἐν (+dat) in, by, with, among, at, on, through, to, within, into, of, for
τῇ art. dat. fem. sg. ὁ ἡ τό the, this, that, he, she, it
διδασκαλίᾳ n. dat. fem. sg. διδασκαλία doctrine, learning, teaching
τῇ art. dat. fem. sg. ὁ ἡ τό the, this, that, he, she, it
καὶ conj. καί and, even, also, but
τοὺς art. acc. masc. pl. ὁ ἡ τό the, this, that, he, she, it
10 γὰρ conj. γάρ for, and, because, but, indeed
πολλοὶ adj. nom. masc. pl. πολύς many, great, much, long, abundant
καὶ conj. καί and, even, also, but
ἀνυπότακτοι adj. nom. masc. pl. ἀνυπότακτος disobedient, unruly, that is not put under
ματαιολόγοι adj. nom. masc. pl. ματαιολόγος vain talker
καὶ conj. καί and, even, also, but
φρεναπάται n. nom. masc. pl. φρεναπάτης deceiver
μάλιστα adv. μάλιστα specially, especially, chiefly, most of all
οἱ art. nom. masc. pl. ὁ ἡ τό the, this, that, he, she, it
ἐκ prep. ἐκ ἐξ (+gen) of, from, out of, by, on, with, in, among, through
περιτομῆς n. gen. fem. sg. περιτομή circumcision
11 οὓς relative pron. acc. masc. pl. ὅς ἥ ὅ who, which, what, that
οἵτινες relative pron. nom. masc. pl. ὅστις which, who, whosoever, that, whatsoever
ὅλους adj. acc. masc. pl. ὅλος all, whole, every whit, altogether
οἴκους n. acc. masc. pl. οἶκος house, home, household
ἃ relative pron. acc. neut. pl. ὅς ἥ ὅ who, which, what, that
μὴ particle of negation. μή not, no, lest, neither, none, nothing, nor, never, without
αἰσχροῦ adj. gen. neut. sg. αἰσχρός filthy
κέρδους n. gen. neut. sg. κέρδος gain, lucre
χάριν adv. χάριν for a cause, because of, for sake
12 τις indefinite pron. nom. masc. sg. τὶς certain, some, any man, one, any thing
ἐξ prep. ἐκ ἐξ (+gen) of, from, out of, by, on, with, in, among, through
αὐτῶν pron. gen. masc. 3p. pl. αὐτός ἥ ὁ self, of oneself, even, very, the same, he, she, it
ἴδιος adj. nom. masc. sg. ἴδιος one's own, one's, privately
αὐτῶν pron. gen. masc. 3p. pl. αὐτός ἥ ὁ self, of oneself, even, very, the same, he, she, it
προφήτης n. nom. masc. sg. προφήτης prophet
Κρῆτες n. nom. masc. pl. Κρής (pl.) Cretes, Cretians

ἀεὶ adv. ἀεί always, always, ever
ψεῦσται n. nom. masc. pl. ψεύστης liar
κακὰ adj. nom. neut. pl. κακός evil, evil thing, noisome, wicked
θηρία n. nom. neut. pl. θηρίον beast, wild beast, venomous beast
γαστέρες n. nom. fem. pl. γαστήρ having in the womb, with child, belly, womb
ἀργαί adj. nom. fem. pl. ἀργός idle, barren, slow
13 ἡ art. nom. fem. sg. ὁ ἡ τό the, this, that, he, she, it
μαρτυρία n. nom. fem. sg. μαρτυρία testimony, witness, record, report
αὕτη demo. pron. nom. fem. sg. οὗτος αὕτη τοῦτο this, the same, this same, he, she, it
ἀληθής adj. nom. fem. sg. ἀληθής true, truly, truth
δι' prep. διά (+gen) by, through, with, in, of, (+acc) for, because of, for a cause
ἣν relative pron. acc. fem. sg. ὅς ἥ ὅ who, which, what, that
αἰτίαν n. acc. fem. sg. αἰτία cause, reason, accusation, fault
αὐτοὺς pron. acc. masc. 3p. pl. αὐτός ή ό self, of oneself, even, very, the same, he, she, it
ἀποτόμως adv. ἀποτόμως sharpness, sharply
ἵνα conj. ἵνα that, to, lest, for to, so that, albeit, because, for, so as
ἐν prep. ἐν (+dat) in, by, with, among, at, on, through, to, within, into, of, for
τῇ art. dat. fem. sg. ὁ ἡ τό the, this, that, he, she, it
πίστει n. dat. fem. sg. πίστις faith, assurance, belief, fidelity
14 μὴ particle of negation. μή not, no, lest, neither, none, nothing, nor, never, without
Ἰουδαϊκοῖς adj. dat. masc. pl. Ἰουδαϊκός Jewish
μύθοις n. dat. masc. pl. μῦθος fable, myth
καὶ conj. καί and, even, also, but
ἐντολαῖς n. dat. fem. pl. ἐντολή commandment, precept
ἀνθρώπων n. gen. masc. pl. ἄνθρωπος man, human being, person, one, certain
τὴν art. acc. fem. sg. ὁ ἡ τό the, this, that, he, she, it
ἀλήθειαν n. acc. fem. sg. ἀλήθεια truth, verity
15 πάντα adj. nom. neut. pl. πᾶς πᾶσα πᾶν all, every, whosoever, every one, no, whole, any
μὲν conj. μέν indeed, verily, truly, even, so, some
καθαρὰ adj. nom. neut. pl. καθαρός pure, clean, clear
τοῖς art. dat. masc. pl. ὁ ἡ τό the, this, that, he, she, it
καθαροῖς adj. dat. masc. pl. καθαρός pure, clean, clear
τοῖς art. dat. masc. pl. ὁ ἡ τό the, this, that, he, she, it
δὲ conj. δέ but, and, now, also, to the contrary, rather, then
καὶ conj. καί and, even, also, but
ἀπίστοις adj. dat. masc. pl. ἄπιστος faithless, unbelieving, infidel, thing incredible
οὐδὲν num. nom. neut. sg. οὐδείς no man, nothing, no, none, neither, not, nought
καθαρόν adj. nom. neut. sg. καθαρός pure, clean, clear
ἀλλὰ conj. ἀλλά but, yea, yet, nevertheless, howbeit, nay, therefore
αὐτῶν pron. gen. masc. 3p. pl. αὐτός ή ό self, of oneself, even, very, the same, he, she, it
καὶ conj. καί and, even, also, but
ὁ art. nom. masc. sg. ὁ ἡ τό the, this, that, he, she, it
νοῦς n. nom. masc. sg. νοῦς understanding, mind
καὶ conj. καί and, even, also, but
ἡ art. nom. fem. sg. ὁ ἡ τό the, this, that, he, she, it
συνείδησις n. nom. fem. sg. συνείδησις conscience
16 Θεὸν n. acc. masc. sg. θεός God, god
τοῖς art. dat. neut. pl. ὁ ἡ τό the, this, that, he, she, it
δὲ conj. δέ but, and, now, also, to the contrary, rather, then
ἔργοις n. dat. neut. pl. ἔργον work, deed, doing labour
βδελυκτοὶ adj. nom. masc. pl. βδελυκτός abominable
καὶ conj. καί and, even, also, but
ἀπειθεῖς adj. nom. masc. pl. ἀπειθής disobedient
καὶ conj. καί and, even, also, but
πρὸς prep. πρός (+gen) for, (+dat) at, (+acc) unto, to, with, for, against

πᾶν adj. acc. neut. sg. πᾶς πᾶσα πᾶν all, every, whosoever, every one, no, whole, any
ἔργον n. acc. neut. sg. ἔργον work, deed, doing labour
ἀγαθὸν adj. acc. neut. sg. ἀγαθός good, good thing, that which is good, well
ἀδόκιμοι adj. nom. masc. pl. ἀδόκιμος reprobate, castaway, rejected

2

1 Σὺ pron. nom. 2p. sg. σύ thou, you
δὲ conj. δέ but, and, now, also, to the contrary, rather, then
ἃ relative pron. nom. neut. pl. ὅς ἥ ὅ who, which, what, that
τῇ art. dat. fem. sg. ὁ ἡ τό the, this, that, he, she, it
διδασκαλίᾳ n. dat. fem. sg. διδασκαλία doctrine, learning, teaching
2 πρεσβύτας n. acc. masc. pl. πρεσβύτης old man, aged, aged man
νηφαλίους adj. acc. masc. pl. νηφάλιος vigilant, sober
σεμνούς adj. acc. masc. pl. σεμνός honest, grave
σώφρονας adj. acc. masc. pl. σώφρων sober, discreet, temperate
τῇ art. dat. fem. sg. ὁ ἡ τό the, this, that, he, she, it
πίστει n. dat. fem. sg. πίστις faith, assurance, belief, fidelity
τῇ art. dat. fem. sg. ὁ ἡ τό the, this, that, he, she, it
ἀγάπῃ n. dat. fem. sg. ἀγάπη love, charity, feast of charity
τῇ art. dat. fem. sg. ὁ ἡ τό the, this, that, he, she, it
ὑπομονῇ n. dat. fem. sg. ὑπομονή patience, enduring
3 πρεσβύτιδας n. acc. fem. pl. πρεσβῦτις aged woman
ὡσαύτως adv. ὡσαύτως likewise, in like manner, after the same manner, even so
ἐν prep. ἐν (+dat) in, by, with, among, at, on, through, to, within, into, of, for
καταστήματι n. dat. neut. sg. κατάστημα behaviour
ἱεροπρεπεῖς adj. acc. fem. pl. ἱεροπρεπής as becometh holiness
μὴ particle of negation. μή not, no, lest, neither, none, nothing, nor, never, without
διαβόλους adj. acc. fem. pl. διάβολος devil, false accuser, Devil, slanderer
μὴ particle of negation. μή not, no, lest, neither, none, nothing, nor, never, without
οἴνῳ n. dat. masc. sg. οἶνος wine
πολλῷ adj. dat. masc. sg. πολύς many, great, much, long, abundant
καλοδιδασκάλους adj. acc. fem. pl. καλοδιδάσκαλος teacher of good things
4 ἵνα conj. ἵνα that, to, lest, for to, so that, albeit, because, for, so as
τὰς art. acc. fem. pl. ὁ ἡ τό the, this, that, he, she, it
νέας adj. acc. fem. pl. νέος new
φιλάνδρους adj. acc. fem. pl. φίλανδρος love one's husband
φιλοτέκνους adj. acc. fem. pl. φιλότεκνος love one's children
5 σώφρονας adj. acc. fem. pl. σώφρων sober, discreet, temperate
ἁγνὰς adj. acc. fem. pl. ἁγνός clear, pure, chaste
οἰκουροὺς adj. acc. fem. pl. οἰκουρός keeper at home
ἀγαθάς adj. acc. fem. pl. ἀγαθός good, good thing, that which is good, well
τοῖς art. dat. masc. pl. ὁ ἡ τό the, this, that, he, she, it
ἰδίοις adj. dat. masc. pl. ἴδιος one's own, one's, privately
ἀνδράσιν n. dat. masc. pl. ἀνήρ man, husband, sir
ἵνα conj. ἵνα that, to, lest, for to, so that, albeit, because, for, so as
μὴ particle of negation. μή not, no, lest, neither, none, nothing, nor, never, without
ὁ art. nom. masc. sg. ὁ ἡ τό the, this, that, he, she, it
λόγος n. nom. masc. sg. λόγος word, saying, account, speech, thing, matter
τοῦ art. gen. masc. sg. ὁ ἡ τό the, this, that, he, she, it
Θεοῦ n. gen. masc. sg. θεός God, god
6 τοὺς art. acc. masc. pl. ὁ ἡ τό the, this, that, he, she, it
νεωτέρους compar. adj. acc. masc. pl. νέος new
ὡσαύτως adv. ὡσαύτως likewise, in like manner, after the same manner, even so
7 περὶ prep. περί (+gen) of, for, concerning, (+acc) about, concerning, in
πάντα adj. acc. neut. pl. πᾶς πᾶσα πᾶν all, every, whosoever, every one, no, whole, any

σεαυτὸν pron. acc. masc. 2p. sg. σεαυτοῦ σεαυτῷ σεαυτόν thyself, thine own self
τύπον n. acc. masc. sg. τύπος ensample, example, pattern, print, figure, fashion
καλῶν adj. gen. neut. pl. καλός good, better, goodly, meet, honest, fair, well, worthy
ἔργων n. gen. neut. pl. ἔργον work, deed, doing labour
ἐν prep. ἐν (+dat) in, by, with, among, at, on, through, to, within, into, of, for
τῇ art. dat. fem. sg. ὁ ἡ τό the, this, that, he, she, it
διδασκαλίᾳ n. dat. fem. sg. διδασκαλία doctrine, learning, teaching
ἀδιάφθορίαν n. acc. fem. sg. ἀδιαφθορία uncorruptness
σεμνότητα n. acc. fem. sg. σεμνότης honesty, gravity
ἀφθαρσιαν n. acc. fem. sg. ἀφθαρσία immortality, incorruption, sincerity
8 λόγον n. acc. masc. sg. λόγος word, saying, account, speech, thing, matter
ὑγιῆ adj. acc. masc. sg. ὑγιής whole, sound
ἀκατάγνωστον adj. acc. masc. sg. ἀκατάγνωστος that cannot be condemned
ἵνα conj. ἵνα that, to, lest, for to, so that, albeit, because, for, so as
ὁ art. nom. masc. pl. ὁ ἡ τό the, this, that, he, she, it
ἐξ prep. ἐκ ἐξ (+gen) of, from, out of, by, on, with, in, among, through
ἐναντίας adj. gen. fem. sg. ἐναντίος contrary, against, over against
μηδὲν num. acc. neut. sg. μηδείς μηδεμία μηδέν no man, nothing, no, none, not at all
περὶ prep. περί (+gen) of, for, concerning, (+acc) about, concerning, in
ὑμῶν pron. gen. 2p. pl. σύ thou, you
φαῦλον adj. acc. neut. sg. φαῦλος evil
9 δούλους n. acc. masc. pl. δοῦλος servant, bondman, bond, slave
ἰδίοις adj. dat. masc. pl. ἴδιος one's own, one's, privately
δεσπόταις n. dat. masc. pl. δεσπότης Lord, master
ἐν prep. ἐν (+dat) in, by, with, among, at, on, through, to, within, into, of, for
πᾶσιν adj. dat. neut. pl. πᾶς πᾶσα πᾶν all, every, whosoever, every one, no, whole, any
εὐαρέστους adj. acc. masc. pl. εὐάρεστος acceptable, wellpleasing, accepted, please well
μὴ particle of negation. μή not, no, lest, neither, none, nothing, nor, never, without
10 μὴ particle of negation. μή not, no, lest, neither, none, nothing, nor, never, without
ἀλλὰ conj. ἀλλά but, yea, yet, nevertheless, howbeit, nay, therefore
πίστιν n. acc. fem. sg. πίστις faith, assurance, belief, fidelity
πᾶσαν adj. acc. fem. sg. πᾶς πᾶσα πᾶν all, every, whosoever, every one, no, whole, any
ἀγαθήν adj. acc. fem. sg. ἀγαθός good, good thing, that which is good, well
ἵνα conj. ἵνα that, to, lest, for to, so that, albeit, because, for, so as
τὴν art. acc. fem. sg. ὁ ἡ τό the, this, that, he, she, it
διδασκαλίαν n. acc. fem. sg. διδασκαλία doctrine, learning, teaching
τοῦ art. gen. masc. sg. ὁ ἡ τό the, this, that, he, she, it
σωτῆρος n. gen. masc. sg. σωτήρ Saviour, saviour
ἡμῶν pron. gen. 1p. pl. ἐγώ I
Θεοῦ n. gen. masc. sg. θεός God, god
ἐν prep. ἐν (+dat) in, by, with, among, at, on, through, to, within, into, of, for
πᾶσιν adj. dat. neut. pl. πᾶς πᾶσα πᾶν all, every, whosoever, every one, no, whole, any
11 γὰρ conj. γάρ for, and, because, but, indeed
ἡ art. nom. fem. sg. ὁ ἡ τό the, this, that, he, she, it
χάρις n. nom. fem. sg. χάρις grace, thank, favour, pleasure
τοῦ art. gen. masc. sg. ὁ ἡ τό the, this, that, he, she, it
Θεοῦ n. gen. masc. sg. θεός God, god
ἡ art. nom. fem. sg. ὁ ἡ τό the, this, that, he, she, it
σωτήριος adj. nom. fem. sg. σωτήριον salvation
πᾶσιν adj. dat. masc. pl. πᾶς πᾶσα πᾶν all, every, whosoever, every one, no, whole, any
ἀνθρώποις n. dat. masc. pl. ἄνθρωπος man, human being, person, one, certain
12 ἡμᾶς pron. acc. 1p. pl. ἐγώ I
ἵνα conj. ἵνα that, to, lest, for to, so that, albeit, because, for, so as
τὴν art. acc. fem. sg. ὁ ἡ τό the, this, that, he, she, it
ἀσέβειαν n. acc. fem. sg. ἀσέβεια ungodliness, ungodly

καὶ conj. καί and, even, also, but
τὰς art. acc. fem. pl. ὁ ἡ τό the, this, that, he, she, it
κοσμικὰς adj. acc. fem. pl. κοσμικός worldly
ἐπιθυμίας n. acc. fem. pl. ἐπιθυμία lust, concupiscence, desire
σωφρόνως adv. σωφρόνως soberly
καὶ conj. καί and, even, also, but
δικαίως adv. δικαίως justly, righteously
καὶ conj. καί and, even, also, but
εὐσεβῶς adv. εὐσεβῶς godly
ἐν prep. ἐν (+dat) in, by, with, among, at, on, through, to, within, into, of, for
τῷ art. dat. masc. sg. ὁ ἡ τό the, this, that, he, she, it
νῦν adv. νῦν now, henceforth, present, this time
αἰῶνι n. dat. masc. sg. αἰών ever, ever and ever, evermore, age, eternal, world
13 τὴν art. acc. fem. sg. ὁ ἡ τό the, this, that, he, she, it
μακαρίαν adj. acc. fem. sg. μακάριος blessed, happy
ἐλπίδα n. acc. fem. sg. ἐλπίς hope, faith
καὶ conj. καί and, even, also, but
ἐπιφάνειαν n. acc. fem. sg. ἐπιφάνεια appearing, brightness
τῆς art. gen. fem. sg. ὁ ἡ τό the, this, that, he, she, it
δόξης n. gen. fem. sg. δόξα glory, honour, praise, dignity, worship
τοῦ art. gen. masc. sg. ὁ ἡ τό the, this, that, he, she, it
μεγάλου adj. gen. masc. sg. μέγας great, loud, greatest, high, large, mighty, strong
Θεοῦ n. gen. masc. sg. θεός God, god
καὶ conj. καί and, even, also, but
σωτῆρος n. gen. masc. sg. σωτήρ Saviour, saviour
ἡμῶν pron. gen. 1p. pl. ἐγώ I
Ἰησοῦ n. gen. masc. sg. Ἰησοῦς Jesus
Χριστοῦ n. gen. masc. sg. Χριστός Christ
14 ὃς relative pron. nom. masc. sg. ὅς ἥ ὅ who, which, what, that
ἑαυτὸν reflexive pron. acc. masc. 3p. sg. ἑαυτοῦ himself, herself, itself, yourself, ourselves
ὑπὲρ prep. ὑπέρ (+gen) for, of, for the sake of, (+acc) above, more than
ἡμῶν pron. gen. 1p. pl. ἐγώ I
ἵνα conj. ἵνα that, to, lest, for to, so that, albeit, because, for, so as
ἡμᾶς pron. acc. 1p. pl. ἐγώ I
ἀπὸ prep. ἀπό (+gen) from, of, out of, since, for, off, at, by, in, on
πάσης adj. gen. fem. sg. πᾶς πᾶσα πᾶν all, every, whosoever, every one, no, whole, any
ἀνομίας n. gen. fem. sg. ἀνομία iniquity, transgression of the law, lawlessness
καὶ conj. καί and, even, also, but
ἑαυτῷ reflexive pron. dat. masc. 3p. sg. ἑαυτοῦ himself, herself, itself, yourself, ourselves
λαὸν n. acc. masc. sg. λαός people
περιούσιον adj. acc. masc. sg. περιούσιος peculiar
ζηλωτὴν n. acc. masc. sg. ζηλωτής zealous
καλῶν adj. gen. neut. pl. καλός good, better, goodly, meet, honest, fair, well, worthy
ἔργων n. gen. neut. pl. ἔργον work, deed, doing labour
15 Ταῦτα demo. pron. acc. neut. pl. οὗτος αὕτη τοῦτο this, the same, this same, he, she, it
καὶ conj. καί and, even, also, but
καὶ conj. καί and, even, also, but
μετὰ prep. μετά (+gen) with, among, against, (+acc) after
πάσης adj. gen. fem. sg. πᾶς πᾶσα πᾶν all, every, whosoever, every one, no, whole, any
ἐπιταγῆς n. gen. fem. sg. ἐπιταγή commandment, authority
μηδείς num. nom. masc. sg. μηδείς μηδεμία μηδέν no man, nothing, no, none, not at all
σου pron. gen. 2p. sg. σύ thou, you

3

1 αὐτοὺς pron. acc. masc. 3p. pl. αὐτός ή ό self, of oneself, even, very, the same, he, she, it
ἀρχαῖς n. dat. fem. pl. ἀρχή beginning, principality, corner, first, magistrate, rule
καὶ conj. καί and, even, also, but
ἐξουσίαις n. dat. fem. pl. ἐξουσία power, authority, right, strength, jurisdiction
πρὸς prep. πρός (+gen) for, (+dat) at, (+acc) unto, to, with, for, against
πᾶν adj. acc. neut. sg. πᾶς πᾶσα πᾶν all, every, whosoever, every one, no, whole, any
ἔργον n. acc. neut. sg. ἔργον work, deed, doing labour
ἀγαθὸν adj. acc. neut. sg. ἀγαθός good, good thing, that which is good, well
ἑτοίμους adj. acc. masc. pl. ἕτοιμος ready, prepared, readiness
2 μηδένα num. acc. masc. sg. μηδείς μηδεμία μηδέν no man, nothing, no, none, not at all
ἀμάχους adj. acc. masc. pl. ἄμαχος not a brawler
ἐπιεικεῖς adj. acc. masc. pl. ἐπιεικής moderation, gentle, patient
πᾶσαν adj. acc. fem. sg. πᾶς πᾶσα πᾶν all, every, whosoever, every one, no, whole, any
πρᾳότητα n. acc. fem. sg. πρᾳότης meekness
πρὸς prep. πρός (+gen) for, (+dat) at, (+acc) unto, to, with, for, against
πάντας adj. acc. masc. pl. πᾶς πᾶσα πᾶν all, every, whosoever, every one, no, whole, any
ἀνθρώπους n. acc. masc. pl. ἄνθρωπος man, human being, person, one, certain
3 γάρ conj. γάρ for, and, because, but, indeed
ποτε adv. ποτέ in time past, at any time, sometimes, in old time, once, when
καὶ conj. καί and, even, also, but
ἡμεῖς pron. nom. 1p. pl. ἐγώ I
ἀνόητοι adj. nom. masc. pl. ἀνόητος fool, foolish, unwise
ἀπειθεῖς adj. nom. masc. pl. ἀπειθής disobedient
ἐπιθυμίαις n. dat. fem. pl. ἐπιθυμία lust, concupiscence, desire
καὶ conj. καί and, even, also, but
ἡδοναῖς n. dat. fem. pl. ἡδονή pleasure, lust
ποικίλαις adj. dat. fem. pl. ποικίλος divers, manifold
ἐν prep. ἐν (+dat) in, by, with, among, at, on, through, to, within, into, of, for
κακίᾳ n. dat. fem. sg. κακία malice, maliciousness, evil, naughtiness, wickedness
καὶ conj. καί and, even, also, but
φθόνῳ n. dat. masc. sg. φθόνος envy, envying
στυγητοί adj. nom. masc. pl. στυγνητός hateful
ἀλλήλους pron. acc. masc. pl. ἀλλήλων one another, themselves, together, mutual
4 ὅτε adv. ὅτε when, after that, as soon as, while, after
δὲ conj. δέ but, and, now, also, to the contrary, rather, then
ἡ art. nom. fem. sg. ὁ ἡ τό the, this, that, he, she, it
χρηστότης n. nom. fem. sg. χρηστότης goodness, kindness, gentleness, good
καὶ conj. καί and, even, also, but
ἡ art. nom. fem. sg. ὁ ἡ τό the, this, that, he, she, it
φιλανθρωπία n. nom. fem. sg. φιλανθρωπία kindness, love toward man
τοῦ art. gen. masc. sg. ὁ ἡ τό the, this, that, he, she, it
σωτῆρος n. gen. masc. sg. σωτήρ Saviour, saviour
ἡμῶν pron. gen. 1p. pl. ἐγώ I
Θεοῦ n. gen. masc. sg. θεός God, god
5 οὐκ particle of negation. οὐ οὐκ οὐχ not, no, neither, none, nay, nor, never, nothing
ἐξ prep. ἐκ ἐξ (+gen) of, from, out of, by, on, with, in, among, through
ἔργων n. gen. neut. pl. ἔργον work, deed, doing labour
τῶν art. gen. neut. pl. ὁ ἡ τό the, this, that, he, she, it
ἐν prep. ἐν (+dat) in, by, with, among, at, on, through, to, within, into, of, for
δικαιοσύνῃ n. dat. fem. sg. δικαιοσύνη righteousness
ὧν relative pron. gen. neut. pl. ὅς ἥ ὅ who, which, what, that
ἡμεῖς pron. nom. 1p. pl. ἐγώ I
ἀλλὰ conj. ἀλλά but, yea, yet, nevertheless, howbeit, nay, therefore

κατὰ prep. κατά (+gen) against, by, throughout, down, (+acc) according to, after, with
τὸν art. acc. masc. sg. ὁ ἡ τό the, this, that, he, she, it
αὐτοῦ pron. gen. masc. 3p. sg. αὐτός ή ό self, of oneself, even, very, the same, he, she, it
ἔλεον n. acc. masc. sg. ἔλεος mercy
ἡμᾶς pron. acc. 1p. pl. ἐγώ I
διὰ prep. διά (+gen) by, through, with, in, of, (+acc) for, because of, for a cause
λουτροῦ n. gen. neut. sg. λουτρόν washing
παλιγγενεσίας n. gen. fem. sg. παλιγγενεσία regeneration
καὶ conj. καί and, even, also, but
ἀνακαινώσεως n. gen. fem. sg. ἀνακαίνωσις renewing
Πνεύματος n. gen. neut. sg. πνεῦμα spirit, Spirit, Ghost, ghost, life. of the spirit, wind
Ἁγίου adj. gen. neut. sg. ἅγιος Holy, holy, saint, Holy One, holy thing, most holy
6 οὗ relative pron. gen. neut. sg. ὅς ἥ ὅ who, which, what, that
ἐφ' prep. ἐπί (+gen) on, in, upon, (+dat) in, at, for, upon, (+acc) on, upon, unto, to, against
ἡμᾶς pron. acc. 1p. pl. ἐγώ I
πλουσίως adv. πλουσίως richly, abundantly
διὰ prep. διά (+gen) by, through, with, in, of, (+acc) for, because of, for a cause
Ἰησοῦ n. gen. masc. sg. Ἰησοῦς Jesus
Χριστοῦ n. gen. masc. sg. Χριστός Christ
τοῦ art. gen. masc. sg. ὁ ἡ τό the, this, that, he, she, it
σωτῆρος n. gen. masc. sg. σωτήρ Saviour, saviour
ἡμῶν pron. gen. 1p. pl. ἐγώ I
7 ἵνα conj. ἵνα that, to, lest, for to, so that, albeit, because, for, so as
τῇ art. dat. fem. sg. ὁ ἡ τό the, this, that, he, she, it
ἐκείνου demo. pron. gen. masc. sg. ἐκεῖνος that, he, the same, that same
χάριτι n. dat. fem. sg. χάρις grace, thank, favour, pleasure
κληρονόμοι n. nom. masc. pl. κληρονόμος heir
κατ' prep. κατά (+gen) against, by, throughout, down, (+acc) according to, after, with
ἐλπίδα n. acc. fem. sg. ἐλπίς hope, faith
ζωῆς n. gen. fem. sg. ζωή life, lifetime
αἰωνίου adj. gen. fem. sg. αἰώνιος eternal, everlasting, world, for ever
8 πιστὸς adj. nom. masc. sg. πιστός faithful, believing, true, sure
ὁ art. nom. masc. sg. ὁ ἡ τό the, this, that, he, she, it
λόγος n. nom. masc. sg. λόγος word, saying, account, speech, thing, matter
καὶ conj. καί and, even, also, but
περὶ prep. περί (+gen) of, for, concerning, (+acc) about, concerning, in
τούτων demo. pron. gen. neut. pl. οὗτος αὕτη τοῦτο this, the same, this same, he, she, it
σε pron. acc. 2p. sg. σύ thou, you
ἵνα conj. ἵνα that, to, lest, for to, so that, albeit, because, for, so as
καλῶν adj. gen. neut. pl. καλός good, better, goodly, meet, honest, fair, well, worthy
ἔργων n. gen. neut. pl. ἔργον work, deed, doing labour
οἱ art. nom. masc. pl. ὁ ἡ τό the, this, that, he, she, it
τῷ art. dat. masc. sg. ὁ ἡ τό the, this, that, he, she, it
Θεῷ n. dat. masc. sg. θεός God, god
ταῦτά demo. pron. nom. neut. pl. οὗτος αὕτη τοῦτο this, the same, this same, he, she, it
τὰ art. nom. neut. pl. ὁ ἡ τό the, this, that, he, she, it
καλὰ adj. nom. neut. pl. καλός good, better, goodly, meet, honest, fair, well, worthy
καὶ conj. καί and, even, also, but
ὠφέλιμα adj. nom. neut. pl. ὠφέλιμος profitable, profit
τοῖς art. dat. masc. pl. ὁ ἡ τό the, this, that, he, she, it
ἀνθρώποις n. dat. masc. pl. ἄνθρωπος man, human being, person, one, certain
9 μωρὰς adj. acc. fem. pl. μωρός fool, foolish
δὲ conj. δέ but, and, now, also, to the contrary, rather, then
ζητήσεις n. acc. fem. pl. ζήτησις question
καὶ conj. καί and, even, also, but

γενεαλογίας n. acc. fem. pl. γενεαλογία genealogy
καὶ conj. καί and, even, also, but
ἔρεις n. acc. fem. pl. ἔρις debate, strife, contention, variance
καὶ conj. καί and, even, also, but
μάχας n. acc. fem. pl. μάχη fighting, strife, striving
νομικὰς adj. acc. fem. pl. νομικός lawyer, about the law
γὰρ conj. γάρ for, and, because, but, indeed
ἀνωφελεῖς adj. nom. fem. pl. ἀνωφελής unprofitable, unprofitableness
καὶ conj. καί and, even, also, but
μάταιοι adj. nom. fem. pl. μάταιος vanity, vain
10 αἱρετικὸν adj. acc. masc. sg. αἱρετικός heretick
ἄνθρωπον n. acc. masc. sg. ἄνθρωπος man, human being, person, one, certain
μετὰ prep. μετά (+gen) with, among, against, (+acc) after
μίαν num. acc. fem. sg. εἷς or ἕν one, other, some, any, only, a certain
καὶ conj. καί and, even, also, but
δευτέραν ordinal. adj. acc. fem. sg. δεύτερος second, second time, again, afterward
νουθεσίαν n. acc. fem. sg. νουθεσία admonition
11 ὅτι conj. ὅτι that, for, because, how that, how, because that, for that, though
ὁ art. nom. masc. sg. ὁ ἡ τό the, this, that, he, she, it
τοιοῦτος demo. pron. nom. masc. sg. τοιοῦτος such, like
καὶ conj. καί and, even, also, but
αὐτοκατάκριτος adj. nom. masc. sg. αὐτοκατάκριτος condemned of oneself
12 Ὅταν conj. ὅταν when, as soon as, as long as, that, whensoever, while
Ἀρτεμᾶν n. acc. masc. sg. Ἀρτεμᾶς Artemas
πρὸς prep. πρός (+gen) for, (+dat) at, (+acc) unto, to, with, for, against
σὲ pron. acc. 2p. sg. σύ thou, you
ἢ particle. ἤ or, than, either, nor, or else, and, rather than
Τύχικον n. acc. masc. sg. Τυχικός Tychicus
πρός prep. πρός (+gen) for, (+dat) at, (+acc) unto, to, with, for, against
με pron. acc. 1p. sg. ἐγώ I
εἰς prep. εἰς (+acc) into, to, unto, for, in, on, toward, against, upon, at, among
Νικόπολιν n. acc. fem. sg. Νικόπολις Nicopolis
ἐκεῖ adv. ἐκεῖ there, thither, thitherward, yonder, yonder place
γὰρ conj. γάρ for, and, because, but, indeed
13 Ζηνᾶν n. acc. masc. sg. Ζηνᾶς Zenas
τὸν art. acc. masc. sg. ὁ ἡ τό the, this, that, he, she, it
νομικὸν adj. acc. masc. sg. νομικός lawyer, about the law
καὶ conj. καί and, even, also, but
Ἀπολλῶ n. acc. masc. sg. Ἀπολλῶς Apollos
σπουδαίως adv. σπουδαίως diligently, instantly
ἵνα conj. ἵνα that, to, lest, for to, so that, albeit, because, for, so as
μηδὲν num. nom. neut. sg. μηδείς μηδεμία μηδέν no man, nothing, no, none, not at all
αὐτοῖς pron. dat. masc. 3p. pl. αὐτός ή ό self, of oneself, even, very, the same, he, she, it
14 δὲ conj. δέ but, and, now, also, to the contrary, rather, then
καὶ conj. καί and, even, also, but
οἱ art. nom. masc. pl. ὁ ἡ τό the, this, that, he, she, it
ἡμέτεροι poss. pron. nom. masc. 1p. pl. ἡμέτερος our
καλῶν adj. gen. neut. pl. καλός good, better, goodly, meet, honest, fair, well, worthy
ἔργων n. gen. neut. pl. ἔργον work, deed, doing labour
εἰς prep. εἰς (+acc) into, to, unto, for, in, on, toward, against, upon, at, among
τὰς art. acc. fem. pl. ὁ ἡ τό the, this, that, he, she, it
ἀναγκαίας adj. acc. fem. pl. ἀναγκαῖος near, necessary, more needful, of necessity
χρείας n. acc. fem. pl. χρεία need, necessity, lack, want
ἵνα conj. ἵνα that, to, lest, for to, so that, albeit, because, for, so as
μὴ particle of negation. μή not, no, lest, neither, none, nothing, nor, never, without

ἄκαρποι adj. nom. masc. pl. ἄκαρπος unfruitful, without fruit
15 σε pron. acc. 2p. sg. σύ thou, you
οἱ art. nom. masc. pl. ὁ ἡ τό the, this, that, he, she, it
μετ' prep. μετά (+gen) with, among, against, (+acc) after
ἐμοῦ pron. gen. 1p. sg. ἐγώ I
πάντες adj. nom. masc. pl. πᾶς πᾶσα πᾶν all, every, whosoever, every one, no, whole, any
τοὺς art. acc. masc. pl. ὁ ἡ τό the, this, that, he, she, it
ἡμᾶς pron. acc. 1p. pl. ἐγώ I
ἐν prep. ἐν (+dat) in, by, with, among, at, on, through, to, within, into, of, for
πίστει n. dat. fem. sg. πίστις faith, assurance, belief, fidelity
Ἡ art. nom. fem. sg. ὁ ἡ τό the, this, that, he, she, it
χάρις n. nom. fem. sg. χάρις grace, thank, favour, pleasure
μετὰ prep. μετά (+gen) with, among, against, (+acc) after
πάντων adj. gen. masc. pl. πᾶς πᾶσα πᾶν all, every, whosoever, every one, no, whole, any
ὑμῶν pron. gen. 2p. pl. σύ thou, you
ἀμήν particle. ἀμήν amen, verily

ΠΑΥΛΟΥ
Η ΠΡΟΣ
ΦΙΛΗΜΟΝΑ ΕΠΙΣΤΟΛΗ

1

1 Παῦλος n. nom. masc. sg. Παῦλος Paul, Paulus
δέσμιος n. nom. masc. sg. δέσμιος prisoner, in bonds, that is in bond
Χριστοῦ n. gen. masc. sg. Χριστός Christ
Ἰησοῦ n. gen. masc. sg. Ἰησοῦς Jesus
καὶ conj. καί and, even, also, but
Τιμόθεος n. nom. masc. sg. Τιμόθεος Timotheus, Timothy
ὁ art. nom. masc. sg. ὁ ἡ τό the, this, that, he, she, it
ἀδελφὸς n. nom. masc. sg. ἀδελφός brother
Φιλήμονι n. dat. masc. sg. Φιλήμων Philemon
τῷ art. dat. masc. sg. ὁ ἡ τό the, this, that, he, she, it
ἀγαπητῷ adj. dat. masc. sg. ἀγαπητός beloved, dearly beloved, dear, wellbeloved
καὶ conj. καί and, even, also, but
συνεργῷ adj. dat. masc. sg. συνεργός fellowlabourer, fellowhelper, fellowworker
ἡμῶν pron. gen. 1p. pl. ἐγώ I
2 καὶ conj. καί and, even, also, but
Ἀπφίᾳ n. dat. fem. sg. Ἀπφία Apphia
τῇ art. dat. fem. sg. ὁ ἡ τό the, this, that, he, she, it
ἀγαπητῇ adj. dat. fem. sg. ἀγαπητός beloved, dearly beloved, dear, wellbeloved
καὶ conj. καί and, even, also, but
Ἀρχίππῳ n. dat. masc. sg. Ἄρχιππος Archippus
τῷ art. dat. masc. sg. ὁ ἡ τό the, this, that, he, she, it
συστρατιώτῃ n. dat. masc. sg. συστρατιώτης fellowsoldier
ἡμῶν pron. gen. 1p. pl. ἐγώ I
καὶ conj. καί and, even, also, but
τῇ art. dat. fem. sg. ὁ ἡ τό the, this, that, he, she, it
κατ᾽ prep. κατά (+gen) against, by, throughout, down, (+acc) according to, after, with
οἶκον n. acc. masc. sg. οἶκος house, home, household
σου pron. gen. 2p. sg. σύ thou, you
ἐκκλησίᾳ n. dat. fem. sg. ἐκκλησία church, assembly
3 χάρις n. nom. fem. sg. χάρις grace, thank, favour, pleasure
ὑμῖν pron. dat. 2p. pl. σύ thou, you
καὶ conj. καί and, even, also, but
εἰρήνη n. nom. fem. sg. εἰρήνη peace, quietness, rest
ἀπὸ prep. ἀπό (+gen) from, of, out of, since, for, off, at, by, in, on
Θεοῦ n. gen. masc. sg. θεός God, god
πατρὸς n. gen. masc. sg. πατήρ Father, father, parent
ἡμῶν pron. gen. 1p. pl. ἐγώ I
καὶ conj. καί and, even, also, but
Κυρίου n. gen. masc. sg. κύριος Lord, lord, master, sir, LORD, God, Master, owner
Ἰησοῦ n. gen. masc. sg. Ἰησοῦς Jesus
Χριστοῦ n. gen. masc. sg. Χριστός Christ
4 τῷ art. dat. masc. sg. ὁ ἡ τό the, this, that, he, she, it
Θεῷ n. dat. masc. sg. θεός God, god
μου pron. gen. 1p. sg. ἐγώ I
πάντοτε adv. πάντοτε always, ever, always, evermore
μνείαν n. acc. fem. sg. μνεία mention, remembrance
σου pron. gen. 2p. sg. σύ thou, you

ἐπὶ prep. ἐπί (+gen) on, in, upon, (+dat) in, at, for, upon, (+acc) on, upon, unto, to, against
τῶν art. gen. fem. pl. ὁ ἡ τό the, this, that, he, she, it
προσευχῶν n. gen. fem. pl. προσευχή prayer
μου pron. gen. 1p. sg. ἐγώ I
5 σου pron. gen. 2p. sg. σύ thou, you
τὴν art. acc. fem. sg. ὁ ἡ τό the, this, that, he, she, it
ἀγάπην n. acc. fem. sg. ἀγάπη love, charity, feast of charity
καὶ conj. καί and, even, also, but
τὴν art. acc. fem. sg. ὁ ἡ τό the, this, that, he, she, it
πίστιν n. acc. fem. sg. πίστις faith, assurance, belief, fidelity
ἣν relative pron. acc. fem. sg. ὅς ἥ ὅ who, which, what, that
πρὸς prep. πρός (+gen) for, (+dat) at, (+acc) unto, to, with, for, against
τὸν art. acc. masc. sg. ὁ ἡ τό the, this, that, he, she, it
Κύριον n. acc. masc. sg. κύριος Lord, lord, master, sir, LORD, God, Master, owner
Ἰησοῦν n. acc. masc. sg. Ἰησοῦς Jesus
καὶ conj. καί and, even, also, but
εἰς prep. εἰς (+acc) into, to, unto, for, in, on, toward, against, upon, at, among
πάντας adj. acc. masc. pl. πᾶς πᾶσα πᾶν all, every, whosoever, every one, no, whole, any
τοὺς art. acc. masc. pl. ὁ ἡ τό the, this, that, he, she, it
ἁγίους adj. acc. masc. pl. ἅγιος Holy, holy, saint, Holy One, holy thing, most holy
6 ὅπως adv. ὅπως that, how, to, because, so that, when
ἡ art. nom. fem. sg. ὁ ἡ τό the, this, that, he, she, it
κοινωνία n. nom. fem. sg. κοινωνία fellowship, communion, contribution, distribution
τῆς art. gen. fem. sg. ὁ ἡ τό the, this, that, he, she, it
πίστεώς n. gen. fem. sg. πίστις faith, assurance, belief, fidelity
σου pron. gen. 2p. sg. σύ thou, you
ἐνεργὴς adj. nom. fem. sg. ἐνεργής effectual, powerful
ἐν prep. ἐν (+dat) in, by, with, among, at, on, through, to, within, into, of, for
ἐπιγνώσει n. dat. fem. sg. ἐπίγνωσις knowledge, acknowledging, acknowledgement
παντὸς adj. gen. neut. sg. πᾶς πᾶσα πᾶν all, every, whosoever, every one, no, whole, any
ἀγαθοῦ adj. gen. neut. sg. ἀγαθός good, good thing, that which is good, well
τοῦ art. gen. neut. sg. ὁ ἡ τό the, this, that, he, she, it
ἐν prep. ἐν (+dat) in, by, with, among, at, on, through, to, within, into, of, for
ὑμῖν pron. dat. 2p. pl. σύ thou, you
εἰς prep. εἰς (+acc) into, to, unto, for, in, on, toward, against, upon, at, among
Χριστόν n. acc. masc. sg. Χριστός Christ
Ἰησοῦν n. acc. masc. sg. Ἰησοῦς Jesus
7 χαρὰν n. acc. fem. sg. χαρά joy, gladness, joyfulness
γὰρ conj. γάρ for, and, because, but, indeed
πολλὴν adj. acc. fem. sg. πολύς many, great, much, long, abundant
καὶ conj. καί and, even, also, but
παράκλησιν n. acc. fem. sg. παράκλησις consolation, exhortation, comfort
ἐπὶ prep. ἐπί (+gen) on, in, upon, (+dat) in, at, for, upon, (+acc) on, upon, unto, to, against
τῇ art. dat. fem. sg. ὁ ἡ τό the, this, that, he, she, it
ἀγάπῃ n. dat. fem. sg. ἀγάπη love, charity, feast of charity
σου pron. gen. 2p. sg. σύ thou, you
ὅτι conj. ὅτι that, for, because, how that, how, because that, for that, though
τὰ art. nom. neut. pl. ὁ ἡ τό the, this, that, he, she, it
σπλάγχνα n. nom. neut. pl. σπλάγχνον tender, bowels, inward affection
τῶν art. gen. masc. pl. ὁ ἡ τό the, this, that, he, she, it
ἁγίων adj. gen. masc. pl. ἅγιος Holy, holy, saint, Holy One, holy thing, most holy
διὰ prep. διά (+gen) by, through, with, in, of, (+acc) for, because of, for a cause
σοῦ pron. gen. 2p. sg. σύ thou, you
ἀδελφέ n. voc. masc. sg. ἀδελφός brother
8 Διὸ conj. διό wherefore, therefore, for which cause

πολλὴν adj. acc. fem. sg. πολύς many, great, much, long, abundant
ἐν prep. ἐν (+dat) in, by, with, among, at, on, through, to, within, into, of, for
Χριστῷ n. dat. masc. sg. Χριστός Christ
παρρησίαν n. acc. fem. sg. παρρησία boldness, confidence, openly, plainly, freely
σοι pron. dat. 2p. sg. σύ thou, you
τὸ art. acc. neut. sg. ὁ ἡ τό the, this, that, he, she, it
9 διὰ prep. διά (+gen) by, through, with, in, of, (+acc) for, because of, for a cause
τὴν art. acc. fem. sg. ὁ ἡ τό the, this, that, he, she, it
ἀγάπην n. acc. fem. sg. ἀγάπη love, charity, feast of charity
μᾶλλον adv. μᾶλλον rather, more, more and more, better, much, much the more
τοιοῦτος demo. pron. nom. masc. sg. τοιοῦτος such, like
ὡς adv. ὡς as, when, as it were, how, about, like, as soon as, even as, while
Παῦλος n. nom. masc. sg. Παῦλος Paul, Paulus
πρεσβύτης n. nom. masc. sg. πρεσβύτης old man, aged, aged man
νυνὶ adv. νυνί now
δὲ conj. δέ but, and, now, also, to the contrary, rather, then
καὶ conj. καί and, even, also, but
δέσμιος n. nom. masc. sg. δέσμιος prisoner, in bonds, that is in bond
Ἰησοῦ n. gen. masc. sg. Ἰησοῦς Jesus
Χριστοῦ n. gen. masc. sg. Χριστός Christ
10 σε pron. acc. 2p. sg. σύ thou, you
περὶ prep. περί (+gen) of, for, concerning, (+acc) about, concerning, in
τοῦ art. gen. neut. sg. ὁ ἡ τό the, this, that, he, she, it
ἐμοῦ poss. pron. gen. neut. 1p. sg. ἐμός my, mine, mine own, of me
τέκνου n. gen. neut. sg. τέκνον child, son, daughter
ὃν relative pron. acc. masc. sg. ὅς ἥ ὅ who, which, what, that
ἐν prep. ἐν (+dat) in, by, with, among, at, on, through, to, within, into, of, for
τοῖς art. dat. masc. pl. ὁ ἡ τό the, this, that, he, she, it
δεσμοῖς n. dat. masc. pl. δεσμός bond, band, chain, string
μου pron. gen. 1p. sg. ἐγώ I
Ὀνήσιμον n. acc. masc. sg. Ὀνήσιμος Onesimus
11 τόν art. acc. masc. sg. ὁ ἡ τό the, this, that, he, she, it
ποτέ adv. ποτέ in time past, at any time, sometimes, in old time, once, when
σοι pron. dat. 2p. sg. σύ thou, you
ἄχρηστον adj. acc. masc. sg. ἄχρηστος unprofitable
νυνὶ adv. νυνί now
δὲ conj. δέ but, and, now, also, to the contrary, rather, then
σοι pron. dat. 2p. sg. σύ thou, you
καὶ conj. καί and, even, also, but
ἐμοὶ pron. dat. 1p. sg. ἐγώ I
εὔχρηστον adj. acc. masc. sg. εὔχρηστος profitable, meet for use
12 ὃν relative pron. acc. masc. sg. ὅς ἥ ὅ who, which, what, that
σὺ pron. nom. 2p. sg. σύ thou, you
δὲ conj. δέ but, and, now, also, to the contrary, rather, then
αὐτόν pron. acc. masc. 3p. sg. αὐτός ή ό self, of oneself, even, very, the same, he, she, it
τοῦτ' demo. pron. nom. neut. sg. οὗτος αὕτη τοῦτο this, the same, this same, he, she, it
τὰ art. acc. neut. pl. ὁ ἡ τό the, this, that, he, she, it
ἐμὰ poss. pron. acc. neut. 1p. pl. ἐμός my, mine, mine own, of me
σπλάγχνα n. acc. neut. pl. σπλάγχνον tender, bowels, inward affection
13 ὃν relative pron. acc. masc. sg. ὅς ἥ ὅ who, which, what, that
ἐγὼ pron. nom. 1p. sg. ἐγώ I
πρὸς prep. πρός (+gen) for, (+dat) at, (+acc) unto, to, with, for, against
ἐμαυτὸν pron. acc. masc. 1p. sg. ἐμαυτοῦ myself, me
ἵνα conj. ἵνα that, to, lest, for to, so that, albeit, because, for, so as
ὑπὲρ prep. ὑπέρ (+gen) for, of, for the sake of, (+acc) above, more than

σοῦ pron. gen. 2p. sg. σύ thou, you
μοι pron. dat. 1p. sg. ἐγώ I
ἐν prep. ἐν (+dat) in, by, with, among, at, on, through, to, within, into, of, for
τοῖς art. dat. masc. pl. ὁ ἡ τό the, this, that, he, she, it
δεσμοῖς n. dat. masc. pl. δεσμός bond, band, chain, string
τοῦ art. gen. neut. sg. ὁ ἡ τό the, this, that, he, she, it
εὐαγγελίου n. gen. neut. sg. εὐαγγέλιον gospel
14 χωρὶς prep. χωρίς (+gen) without, beside. (adv.) by itself, apart, separately
δὲ conj. δέ but, and, now, also, to the contrary, rather, then
τῆς art. gen. fem. sg. ὁ ἡ τό the, this, that, he, she, it
σῆς poss. pron. gen. fem. 2p. sg. σός thy, thine, thine own
γνώμης n. gen. fem. sg. γνώμη judgement, mind, advice, purpose, will
οὐδὲν num. acc. neut. sg. οὐδείς no man, nothing, no, none, neither, not, nought
ἵνα conj. ἵνα that, to, lest, for to, so that, albeit, because, for, so as
μὴ particle of negation. μή not, no, lest, neither, none, nothing, nor, never, without
ὡς adv. ὡς as, when, as it were, how, about, like, as soon as, even as, while
κατὰ prep. κατά (+gen) against, by, throughout, down, (+acc) according to, after, with
ἀνάγκην n. acc. fem. sg. ἀνάγκη must needs, necessity, distress, inevitable
τὸ art. nom. neut. sg. ὁ ἡ τό the, this, that, he, she, it
ἀγαθόν adj. nom. neut. sg. ἀγαθός good, good thing, that which is good, well
σου pron. gen. 2p. sg. σύ thou, you
ἀλλὰ conj. ἀλλά but, yea, yet, nevertheless, howbeit, nay, therefore
κατὰ prep. κατά (+gen) against, by, throughout, down, (+acc) according to, after, with
ἑκούσιον adj. acc. neut. sg. ἑκούσιος willingly
15 τάχα adv. τάχα peradventure, perhaps
γὰρ conj. γάρ for, and, because, but, indeed
διὰ prep. διά (+gen) by, through, with, in, of, (+acc) for, because of, for a cause
τοῦτο demo. pron. acc. neut. sg. οὗτος αὕτη τοῦτο this, the same, this same, he, she, it
πρὸς prep. πρός (+gen) for, (+dat) at, (+acc) unto, to, with, for, against
ὥραν n. acc. fem. sg. ὥρα hour, time, season
ἵνα conj. ἵνα that, to, lest, for to, so that, albeit, because, for, so as
αἰώνιον adj. acc. masc. sg. αἰώνιος eternal, everlasting, world, for ever
αὐτὸν pron. acc. masc. 3p. sg. αὐτός ἡ ὁ self, of oneself, even, very, the same, he, she, it
16 οὐκέτι adv. οὐκέτι or οὐκ ἔτι no more, no longer, not any more
ὡς adv. ὡς as, when, as it were, how, about, like, as soon as, even as, while
δοῦλον n. acc. masc. sg. δοῦλος servant, bondman, bond, slave
ἀλλ' conj. ἀλλά but, yea, yet, nevertheless, howbeit, nay, therefore
ὑπὲρ prep. ὑπέρ (+gen) for, of, for the sake of, (+acc) above, more than
δοῦλον n. acc. masc. sg. δοῦλος servant, bondman, bond, slave
ἀδελφὸν n. acc. masc. sg. ἀδελφός brother
ἀγαπητόν adj. acc. masc. sg. ἀγαπητός beloved, dearly beloved, dear, wellbeloved
μάλιστα adv. μάλιστα specially, especially, chiefly, most of all
ἐμοί pron. dat. 1p. sg. ἐγώ I
πόσῳ interrog. pron. dat. neut. sg. πόσος how much, how many, how great, how long
δὲ conj. δέ but, and, now, also, to the contrary, rather, then
μᾶλλον adv. μᾶλλον rather, more, more and more, better, much, much the more
σοὶ pron. dat. 2p. sg. σύ thou, you
καὶ conj. καί and, even, also, but
ἐν prep. ἐν (+dat) in, by, with, among, at, on, through, to, within, into, of, for
σαρκὶ n. dat. fem. sg. σάρξ flesh, carnal
καὶ conj. καί and, even, also, but
ἐν prep. ἐν (+dat) in, by, with, among, at, on, through, to, within, into, of, for
Κυρίῳ n. dat. masc. sg. κύριος Lord, lord, master, sir, LORD, God, Master, owner
17 εἰ conj. εἰ if, whether, that, though, forasmuch
οὖν conj. οὖν therefore, then, so, and, now, wherefore

ἐμὲ pron. acc. 1p. sg. ἐγώ I
κοινωνόν n. acc. masc. sg. κοινωνός partaker, partner, companion, fellowship
αὐτὸν pron. acc. masc. 3p. sg. αὐτός ή ό self, of oneself, even, very, the same, he, she, it
ὡς adv. ὡς as, when, as it were, how, about, like, as soon as, even as, while
ἐμέ pron. acc. 1p. sg. ἐγώ I
18 εἰ conj. εἰ if, whether, that, though, forasmuch
δέ conj. δέ but, and, now, also, to the contrary, rather, then
τι indefinite pron. acc. neut. sg. τὶς certain, some, any man, one, any thing
σε pron. acc. 2p. sg. σύ thou, you
ἢ particle. ἤ or, than, either, nor, or else, and, rather than
τοῦτο demo. pron. acc. neut. sg. οὗτος αὕτη τοῦτο this, the same, this same, he, she, it
ἐμοὶ pron. dat. 1p. sg. ἐγώ I
19 ἐγὼ pron. nom. 1p. sg. ἐγώ I
Παῦλος n. nom. masc. sg. Παῦλος Paul, Paulus
τῇ art. dat. fem. sg. ὁ ἡ τό the, this, that, he, she, it
ἐμῇ poss. pron. dat. fem. 1p. sg. ἐμός my, mine, mine own, of me
χειρί n. dat. fem. sg. χείρ hand
ἐγὼ pron. nom. 1p. sg. ἐγώ I
ἵνα conj. ἵνα that, to, lest, for to, so that, albeit, because, for, so as
μὴ particle of negation. μή not, no, lest, neither, none, nothing, nor, never, without
σοι pron. dat. 2p. sg. σύ thou, you
ὅτι conj. ὅτι that, for, because, how that, how, because that, for that, though
καὶ conj. καί and, even, also, but
σεαυτόν pron. acc. masc. 2p. sg. σεαυτοῦ σεαυτῷ σεαυτόν thyself, thine own self
μοι pron. dat. 1p. sg. ἐγώ I
20 ναὶ particle. ναί yea, even so, yes, surely, truth, verily
ἀδελφέ n. voc. masc. sg. ἀδελφός brother
ἐγώ pron. nom. 1p. sg. ἐγώ I
σου pron. gen. 2p. sg. σύ thou, you
ἐν prep. ἐν (+dat) in, by, with, among, at, on, through, to, within, into, of, for
Κυρίῳ n. dat. masc. sg. κύριος Lord, lord, master, sir, LORD, God, Master, owner
μου pron. gen. 1p. sg. ἐγώ I
τὰ art. acc. neut. pl. ὁ ἡ τό the, this, that, he, she, it
σπλάγχνα n. acc. neut. pl. σπλάγχνον tender, bowels, inward affection
ἐν prep. ἐν (+dat) in, by, with, among, at, on, through, to, within, into, of, for
Κυρίῳ n. dat. masc. sg. κύριος Lord, lord, master, sir, LORD, God, Master, owner
21 τῇ art. dat. fem. sg. ὁ ἡ τό the, this, that, he, she, it
ὑπακοῇ n. dat. fem. sg. ὑπακοή obedience, obey, make obedient, obedient
σου pron. gen. 2p. sg. σύ thou, you
σοι pron. dat. 2p. sg. σύ thou, you
ὅτι conj. ὅτι that, for, because, how that, how, because that, for that, though
καὶ conj. καί and, even, also, but
ὑπὲρ prep. ὑπέρ (+gen) for, of, for the sake of, (+acc) above, more than
ὃ relative pron. acc. neut. sg. ὅς ἥ ὅ who, which, what, that
22 ἅμα adv. ἅμα (+dat) together, with, also. (adv.) at the same time, together
δὲ conj. δέ but, and, now, also, to the contrary, rather, then
καὶ conj. καί and, even, also, but
μοι pron. dat. 1p. sg. ἐγώ I
ξενίαν n. acc. fem. sg. ξενία lodging
γὰρ conj. γάρ for, and, because, but, indeed
ὅτι conj. ὅτι that, for, because, how that, how, because that, for that, though
διὰ prep. διά (+gen) by, through, with, in, of, (+acc) for, because of, for a cause
τῶν art. gen. fem. pl. ὁ ἡ τό the, this, that, he, she, it
προσευχῶν n. gen. fem. pl. προσευχή prayer
ὑμῶν pron. gen. 2p. pl. σύ thou, you

ὑμῖν pron. dat. 2p. pl. σύ thou, you
23 σε pron. acc. 2p. sg. σύ thou, you
Ἐπαφρᾶς n. nom. masc. sg. Ἐπαφρᾶς Epaphras
ὁ art. nom. masc. sg. ὁ ἡ τό the, this, that, he, she, it
συναιχμάλωτός n. nom. masc. sg. συναιχμάλωτος fellowprisoner
μου pron. gen. 1p. sg. ἐγώ I
ἐν prep. ἐν (+dat) in, by, with, among, at, on, through, to, within, into, of, for
Χριστῷ n. dat. masc. sg. Χριστός Christ
Ἰησοῦ n. dat. masc. sg. Ἰησοῦς Jesus
24 Μᾶρκος n. nom. masc. sg. Μᾶρκος Mark, Marcus
Ἀρίσταρχος n. nom. masc. sg. Ἀρίσταρχος Aristarchus
Δημᾶς n. nom. masc. sg. Δημᾶς Demas
Λουκᾶς n. nom. masc. sg. Λουκᾶς Luke, Lucas
οἱ art. nom. masc. pl. ὁ ἡ τό the, this, that, he, she, it
συνεργοί adj. nom. masc. pl. συνεργός fellowlabourer, fellowhelper, fellowworker
μου pron. gen. 1p. sg. ἐγώ I
25 Ἡ art. nom. fem. sg. ὁ ἡ τό the, this, that, he, she, it
χάρις n. nom. fem. sg. χάρις grace, thank, favour, pleasure
τοῦ art. gen. masc. sg. ὁ ἡ τό the, this, that, he, she, it
Κυρίου n. gen. masc. sg. κύριος Lord, lord, master, sir, LORD, God, Master, owner
ἡμῶν pron. gen. 1p. pl. ἐγώ I
Ἰησοῦ n. gen. masc. sg. Ἰησοῦς Jesus
Χριστοῦ n. gen. masc. sg. Χριστός Christ
μετὰ prep. μετά (+gen) with, among, against, (+acc) after
τοῦ art. gen. neut. sg. ὁ ἡ τό the, this, that, he, she, it
πνεύματος n. gen. neut. sg. πνεῦμα spirit, Spirit, Ghost, ghost, life. of the spirit, wind
ὑμῶν pron. gen. 2p. pl. σύ thou, you
ἀμήν particle. ἀμήν amen, verily

ΠΑΥΛΟΥ ΤΟΥ ΑΠΟΣΤΟΛΟΥ
Η ΠΡΟΣ
ΕΒΡΑΙΟΥΣ ΕΠΙΣΤΟΛΗ

1

1 Πολυμερῶς adv. πολυμερῶς at sundry times, by many portions
καὶ conj. καί and, even, also, but
πολυτρόπως adv. πολυτρόπως in divers manners
πάλαι adv. πάλαι long age, a great while ago, any while, in time past, old, of old
ὁ art. nom. masc. sg. ὁ ἡ τό the, this, that, he, she, it
Θεὸς n. nom. masc. sg. θεός God, god
τοῖς art. dat. masc. pl. ὁ ἡ τό the, this, that, he, she, it
πατράσιν n. dat. masc. pl. πατήρ Father, father, parent
ἐν prep. ἐν (+dat) in, by, with, among, at, on, through, to, within, into, of, for
τοῖς art. dat. masc. pl. ὁ ἡ τό the, this, that, he, she, it
προφήταις n. dat. masc. pl. προφήτης prophet
2 ἐπ' prep. ἐπί (+gen) on, in, upon, (+dat) in, at, for, upon, (+acc) on, upon, unto, to, against
ἐσχάτων adj. gen. fem. pl. ἔσχατος last, lowest, uttermost, uttermost part
τῶν art. gen. fem. pl. ὁ ἡ τό the, this, that, he, she, it
ἡμερῶν n. gen. fem. pl. ἡμέρα day, time, year, while, age, day time
τούτων demo. pron. gen. fem. pl. οὗτος αὕτη τοῦτο this, the same, this same, he, she, it
ἡμῖν pron. dat. 1p. pl. ἐγώ I
ἐν prep. ἐν (+dat) in, by, with, among, at, on, through, to, within, into, of, for
υἱῷ n. dat. masc. sg. υἱός son, child, descendant, offspring, heir
ὃν relative pron. acc. masc. sg. ὅς ἥ ὅ who, which, what, that
κληρονόμον n. acc. masc. sg. κληρονόμος heir
πάντων adj. gen. neut. pl. πᾶς πᾶσα πᾶν all, every, whosoever, every one, no, whole, any
δι' prep. διά (+gen) by, through, with, in, of, (+acc) for, because of, for a cause
οὗ relative pron. gen. masc. sg. ὅς ἥ ὅ who, which, what, that
καὶ conj. καί and, even, also, but
τοὺς art. acc. masc. pl. ὁ ἡ τό the, this, that, he, she, it
αἰῶνας n. acc. masc. pl. αἰών ever, ever and ever, evermore, age, eternal, world
3 ὃς relative pron. nom. masc. sg. ὅς ἥ ὅ who, which, what, that
ἀπαύγασμα n. nom. neut. sg. ἀπαύγασμα brightness
τῆς art. gen. fem. sg. ὁ ἡ τό the, this, that, he, she, it
δόξης n. gen. fem. sg. δόξα glory, honour, praise, dignity, worship
καὶ conj. καί and, even, also, but
χαρακτὴρ n. nom. masc. sg. χαρακτήρ express image
τῆς art. gen. fem. sg. ὁ ἡ τό the, this, that, he, she, it
ὑποστάσεως n. gen. fem. sg. ὑπόστασις confidence, substance, person, nature
αὐτοῦ pron. gen. masc. 3p. sg. αὐτός ή ό self, of oneself, even, very, the same, he, she, it
τε conj. τέ and, both, also
τὰ art. acc. neut. pl. ὁ ἡ τό the, this, that, he, she, it
πάντα adj. acc. neut. pl. πᾶς πᾶσα πᾶν all, every, whosoever, every one, no, whole, any
τῷ art. dat. neut. sg. ὁ ἡ τό the, this, that, he, she, it
ῥήματι n. dat. neut. sg. ῥῆμα word, saying, thing
τῆς art. gen. fem. sg. ὁ ἡ τό the, this, that, he, she, it
δυνάμεως n. gen. fem. sg. δύναμις power, mighty work, miracle, strength, might
αὐτοῦ pron. gen. masc. 3p. sg. αὐτός ή ό self, of oneself, even, very, the same, he, she, it
δι' prep. διά (+gen) by, through, with, in, of, (+acc) for, because of, for a cause
ἑαυτοῦ reflexive pron. gen. masc. 3p. sg. ἑαυτοῦ himself, herself, itself, yourself, ourselves
καθαρισμὸν n. acc. masc. sg. καθαρισμός cleansing, purge, purifying, purification

τῶν art. gen. fem. pl. ὁ ἡ τό the, this, that, he, she, it
ἁμαρτιῶν n. gen. fem. pl. ἁμαρτία sin, offence, sinful
ἡμῶν pron. gen. 1p. pl. ἐγώ I
ἐν prep. ἐν (+dat) in, by, with, among, at, on, through, to, within, into, of, for
δεξιᾷ adj. dat. fem. sg. δεξιός right, right hand, right side
τῆς art. gen. fem. sg. ὁ ἡ τό the, this, that, he, she, it
μεγαλωσύνης n. gen. fem. sg. μεγαλωσύνη Majesty
ἐν prep. ἐν (+dat) in, by, with, among, at, on, through, to, within, into, of, for
ὑψηλοῖς adj. dat. neut. pl. ὑψηλός high, higher, highly esteemed
4 τοσούτῳ demo. pron. dat. neut. sg. τοσοῦτος so much, so great, so many, so long
κρείττων compar. adj. nom. masc. sg. κρείττων better
τῶν art. gen. masc. pl. ὁ ἡ τό the, this, that, he, she, it
ἀγγέλων n. gen. masc. pl. ἄγγελος angel, messenger
ὅσῳ relative pron. dat. neut. sg. ὅσος as many as, whatsoever, that, as long as, how much
διαφορώτερον compar. adj. acc. neut. sg. διάφορος differing, more excellent, divers
παρ' prep. παρά (+gen) of, from, (+dat) with, for, (+acc) beside, at, by, above, against
αὐτοὺς pron. acc. masc. 3p. pl. αὐτός ἡ ὁ self, of oneself, even, very, the same, he, she, it
ὄνομα n. acc. neut. sg. ὄνομα name, call, surname
5 τίνι interrog. pron. dat. masc. sg. τίς what, who, why, where, which, how
γὰρ conj. γάρ for, and, because, but, indeed
ποτε adv. ποτέ in time past, at any time, sometimes, in old time, once, when
τῶν art. gen. masc. pl. ὁ ἡ τό the, this, that, he, she, it
ἀγγέλων n. gen. masc. pl. ἄγγελος angel, messenger
Υἱός n. nom. masc. sg. υἱός son, child, descendant, offspring, heir
μου pron. gen. 1p. sg. ἐγώ I
σύ pron. nom. 2p. sg. σύ thou, you
ἐγὼ pron. nom. 1p. sg. ἐγώ I
σήμερον adv. σήμερον this day, today
σε pron. acc. 2p. sg. σύ thou, you
καὶ conj. καί and, even, also, but
πάλιν adv. πάλιν again
Ἐγὼ pron. nom. 1p. sg. ἐγώ I
αὐτῷ pron. dat. masc. 3p. sg. αὐτός ἡ ὁ self, of oneself, even, very, the same, he, she, it
εἰς prep. εἰς (+acc) into, to, unto, for, in, on, toward, against, upon, at, among
πατέρα n. acc. masc. sg. πατήρ Father, father, parent
καὶ conj. καί and, even, also, but
αὐτὸς pron. nom. masc. 3p. sg. αὐτός ἡ ὁ self, of oneself, even, very, the same, he, she, it
μοι pron. dat. 1p. sg. ἐγώ I
εἰς prep. εἰς (+acc) into, to, unto, for, in, on, toward, against, upon, at, among
υἱόν n. acc. masc. sg. υἱός son, child, descendant, offspring, heir
6 ὅταν conj. ὅταν when, as soon as, as long as, that, whensoever, while
δὲ conj. δέ but, and, now, also, to the contrary, rather, then
πάλιν adv. πάλιν again
τὸν art. acc. masc. sg. ὁ ἡ τό the, this, that, he, she, it
πρωτότοκον adj. acc. masc. sg. πρωτότοκος firstborn, first begotten
εἰς prep. εἰς (+acc) into, to, unto, for, in, on, toward, against, upon, at, among
τὴν art. acc. fem. sg. ὁ ἡ τό the, this, that, he, she, it
οἰκουμένην n. acc. fem. sg. οἰκουμένη world, earth
Καὶ conj. καί and, even, also, but
αὐτῷ pron. dat. masc. 3p. sg. αὐτός ἡ ὁ self, of oneself, even, very, the same, he, she, it
πάντες adj. nom. masc. pl. πᾶς πᾶσα πᾶν all, every, whosoever, every one, no, whole, any
ἄγγελοι n. nom. masc. pl. ἄγγελος angel, messenger
Θεοῦ n. gen. masc. sg. θεός God, god
7 καὶ conj. καί and, even, also, but
πρὸς prep. πρός (+gen) for, (+dat) at, (+acc) unto, to, with, for, against

μὲν conj. μέν indeed, verily, truly, even, so, some
τοὺς art. acc. masc. pl. ὁ ἡ τό the, this, that, he, she, it
ἀγγέλους n. acc. masc. pl. ἄγγελος angel, messenger
Ὁ art. nom. masc. sg. ὁ ἡ τό the, this, that, he, she, it
τοὺς art. acc. masc. pl. ὁ ἡ τό the, this, that, he, she, it
ἀγγέλους n. acc. masc. pl. ἄγγελος angel, messenger
αὐτοῦ pron. gen. masc. 3p. sg. αὐτός ή ό self, of oneself, even, very, the same, he, she, it
πνεύματα n. acc. neut. pl. πνεῦμα spirit, Spirit, Ghost, ghost, life. of the spirit, wind
καὶ conj. καί and, even, also, but
τοὺς art. acc. masc. pl. ὁ ἡ τό the, this, that, he, she, it
λειτουργοὺς n. acc. masc. pl. λειτουργός minister, he that minister
αὐτοῦ pron. gen. masc. 3p. sg. αὐτός ή ό self, of oneself, even, very, the same, he, she, it
πυρὸς n. gen. neut. sg. πῦρ fire, fiery
φλόγα n. acc. fem. sg. φλόξ flame, flaming
8 πρὸς prep. πρός (+gen) for, (+dat) at, (+acc) unto, to, with, for, against
δὲ conj. δέ but, and, now, also, to the contrary, rather, then
τὸν art. acc. masc. sg. ὁ ἡ τό the, this, that, he, she, it
υἱόν n. acc. masc. sg. υἱός son, child, descendant, offspring, heir
Ὁ art. nom. masc. sg. ὁ ἡ τό the, this, that, he, she, it
θρόνος n. nom. masc. sg. θρόνος throne, seat
σου pron. gen. 2p. sg. σύ thou, you
ὁ art. nom. masc. sg. ὁ ἡ τό the, this, that, he, she, it
Θεός n. nom. masc. sg. θεός God, god
εἰς prep. εἰς (+acc) into, to, unto, for, in, on, toward, against, upon, at, among
τὸν art. acc. masc. sg. ὁ ἡ τό the, this, that, he, she, it
αἰῶνα n. acc. masc. sg. αἰών ever, ever and ever, evermore, age, eternal, world
τοῦ art. gen. masc. sg. ὁ ἡ τό the, this, that, he, she, it
αἰῶνος n. gen. masc. sg. αἰών ever, ever and ever, evermore, age, eternal, world
ῥάβδος n. nom. fem. sg. ῥάβδος rod, sceptre, stave, staff
εὐθύτητος n. gen. fem. sg. εὐθύτης righteousness
ἡ art. nom. fem. sg. ὁ ἡ τό the, this, that, he, she, it
ῥάβδος n. nom. fem. sg. ῥάβδος rod, sceptre, stave, staff
τῆς art. gen. fem. sg. ὁ ἡ τό the, this, that, he, she, it
βασιλείας n. gen. fem. sg. βασιλεία kingdom, reign
σου pron. gen. 2p. sg. σύ thou, you
9 δικαιοσύνην n. acc. fem. sg. δικαιοσύνη righteousness
καὶ conj. καί and, even, also, but
ἀνομίαν n. acc. fem. sg. ἀνομία iniquity, transgression of the law, lawlessness
διὰ prep. διά (+gen) by, through, with, in, of, (+acc) for, because of, for a cause
τοῦτο demo. pron. acc. neut. sg. οὗτος αὕτη τοῦτο this, the same, this same, he, she, it
σε pron. acc. 2p. sg. σύ thou, you
ὁ art. nom. masc. sg. ὁ ἡ τό the, this, that, he, she, it
Θεός n. nom. masc. sg. θεός God, god
ὁ art. nom. masc. sg. ὁ ἡ τό the, this, that, he, she, it
Θεός n. nom. masc. sg. θεός God, god
σου pron. gen. 2p. sg. σύ thou, you
ἔλαιον n. acc. neut. sg. ἔλαιον oil
ἀγαλλιάσεως n. gen. fem. sg. ἀγαλλίασις gladness, exceeding joy, joy
παρὰ prep. παρά (+gen) of, from, (+dat) with, for, (+acc) beside, at, by, above, against
τοὺς art. acc. masc. pl. ὁ ἡ τό the, this, that, he, she, it
μετόχους adj. acc. masc. pl. μέτοχος partner, partaker, fellow
σου pron. gen. 2p. sg. σύ thou, you
10 καί conj. καί and, even, also, but
Σὺ pron. nom. 2p. sg. σύ thou, you
κατ᾽ prep. κατά (+gen) against, by, throughout, down, (+acc) according to, after, with

ἀρχάς n. acc. fem. pl. ἀρχή beginning, principality, corner, first, magistrate, rule
Κύριε n. voc. masc. sg. κύριος Lord, lord, master, sir, LORD, God, Master, owner
τὴν art. acc. fem. sg. ὁ ἡ τό the, this, that, he, she, it
γῆν n. acc. fem. sg. γῆ earth, land, ground, country
καί conj. καί and, even, also, but
ἔργα n. nom. neut. pl. ἔργον work, deed, doing labour
τῶν art. gen. fem. pl. ὁ ἡ τό the, this, that, he, she, it
χειρῶν n. gen. fem. pl. χείρ hand
σού pron. gen. 2p. sg. σύ thou, you
οἱ art. nom. masc. pl. ὁ ἡ τό the, this, that, he, she, it
οὐρανοί n. nom. masc. pl. οὐρανός heaven, air, sky
11 αὐτοὶ pron. nom. masc. 3p. pl. αὐτός ἡ ὁ self, of oneself, even, very, the same, he, she, it
σὺ pron. nom. 2p. sg. σύ thou, you
δὲ conj. δέ but, and, now, also, to the contrary, rather, then
καὶ conj. καί and, even, also, but
πάντες adj. nom. masc. pl. πᾶς πᾶσα πᾶν all, every, whosoever, every one, no, whole, any
ὡς adv. ὡς as, when, as it were, how, about, like, as soon as, even as, while
ἱμάτιον n. nom. neut. sg. ἱμάτιον cloke, garment, clothes, raiment, robe, vesture
12 καὶ conj. καί and, even, also, but
ὡσεὶ adv. ὡσεί about, as, like, as it had been, as it were, like as
περιβόλαιον n. acc. neut. sg. περιβόλαιον covering, vesture
αὐτούς pron. acc. masc. 3p. pl. αὐτός ἡ ὁ self, of oneself, even, very, the same, he, she, it
καί conj. καί and, even, also, but
σὺ pron. nom. 2p. sg. σύ thou, you
δὲ conj. δέ but, and, now, also, to the contrary, rather, then
ὁ art. nom. masc. sg. ὁ ἡ τό the, this, that, he, she, it
αὐτὸς pron. nom. masc. 3p. sg. αὐτός ἡ ὁ self, of oneself, even, very, the same, he, she, it
καί conj. καί and, even, also, but
τὰ art. nom. neut. pl. ὁ ἡ τό the, this, that, he, she, it
ἔτη n. nom. neut. pl. ἔτος year
σου pron. gen. 2p. sg. σύ thou, you
οὐκ particle of negation. οὐ οὐκ οὐχ not, no, neither, none, nay, nor, never, nothing
13 πρὸς prep. πρός (+gen) for, (+dat) at, (+acc) unto, to, with, for, against
τίνα interrog. pron. acc. masc. sg. τίς what, who, why, where, which, how
δὲ conj. δέ but, and, now, also, to the contrary, rather, then
τῶν art. gen. masc. pl. ὁ ἡ τό the, this, that, he, she, it
ἀγγέλων n. gen. masc. pl. ἄγγελος angel, messenger
ποτε adv. ποτέ in time past, at any time, sometimes, in old time, once, when
ἐκ prep. ἐκ ἐξ (+gen) of, from, out of, by, on, with, in, among, through
δεξιῶν adj. gen. neut. pl. δεξιός right, right hand, right side
μου pron. gen. 1p. sg. ἐγώ I
ἕως conj. ἕως till, until, unto, until when, while, as far as, even, until now
ἂν particle. ἄν Indicating contingency. No English translation.
τοὺς art. acc. masc. pl. ὁ ἡ τό the, this, that, he, she, it
ἐχθρούς adj. acc. masc. pl. ἐχθρός enemy, foe
σου pron. gen. 2p. sg. σύ thou, you
ὑποπόδιον n. acc. neut. sg. ὑποπόδιον footstool
τῶν art. gen. masc. pl. ὁ ἡ τό the, this, that, he, she, it
ποδῶν n. gen. masc. pl. πούς foot
σου pron. gen. 2p. sg. σύ thou, you
14 οὐχὶ adv. οὐχί not, nay
πάντες adj. nom. masc. pl. πᾶς πᾶσα πᾶν all, every, whosoever, every one, no, whole, any
λειτουργικὰ adj. nom. neut. pl. λειτουργικός ministering
πνεύματα n. nom. neut. pl. πνεῦμα spirit, Spirit, Ghost, ghost, life. of the spirit, wind
εἰς prep. εἰς (+acc) into, to, unto, for, in, on, toward, against, upon, at, among

διακονίαν n. acc. fem. sg. διακονία ministry, administration, service, office, relief
διὰ prep. διά (+gen) by, through, with, in, of, (+acc) for, because of, for a cause
τοὺς art. acc. masc. pl. ὁ ἡ τό the, this, that, he, she, it
σωτηρίαν n. acc. fem. sg. σωτηρία salvation, deliver, health, saving

2

1 Διὰ prep. διά (+gen) by, through, with, in, of, (+acc) for, because of, for a cause
τοῦτο demo. pron. acc. neut. sg. οὗτος αὕτη τοῦτο this, the same, this same, he, she, it
περισσοτέρως adv. περισσοτέρως more exceedingly, more abundantly, more frequent
ἡμᾶς pron. acc. 1p. pl. ἐγώ I
τοῖς art. dat. neut. pl. ὁ ἡ τό the, this, that, he, she, it
μή particle of negation. μή not, no, lest, neither, none, nothing, nor, never, without
ποτε adv. ποτέ in time past, at any time, sometimes, in old time, once, when
2 εἰ conj. εἰ if, whether, that, though, forasmuch
γὰρ conj. γάρ for, and, because, but, indeed
ὁ art. nom. masc. sg. ὁ ἡ τό the, this, that, he, she, it
δι' prep. διά (+gen) by, through, with, in, of, (+acc) for, because of, for a cause
ἀγγέλων n. gen. masc. pl. ἄγγελος angel, messenger
λόγος n. nom. masc. sg. λόγος word, saying, account, speech, thing, matter
βέβαιος adj. nom. masc. sg. βέβαιος sure, stedfast, firm, more sure, of force
καὶ conj. καί and, even, also, but
πᾶσα adj. nom. fem. sg. πᾶς πᾶσα πᾶν all, every, whosoever, every one, no, whole, any
παράβασις n. nom. fem. sg. παράβασις breaking, transgression
καὶ conj. καί and, even, also, but
παρακοὴ n. nom. fem. sg. παρακοή disobedience
ἔνδικον adj. acc. fem. sg. ἔνδικος just
μισθαποδοσίαν n. acc. fem. sg. μισθαποδοσία recompence of reward
3 πῶς adv. πῶς how, by what means, after what manner
ἡμεῖς pron. nom. 1p. pl. ἐγώ I
τηλικαύτης demo. pron. gen. fem. sg. τηλικοῦτος so great, so mighty
σωτηρίας n. gen. fem. sg. σωτηρία salvation, deliver, health, saving
ἥτις relative pron. nom. fem. sg. ὅστις which, who, whosoever, that, whatsoever
ἀρχὴν n. acc. fem. sg. ἀρχή beginning, principality, corner, first, magistrate, rule
διὰ prep. διά (+gen) by, through, with, in, of, (+acc) for, because of, for a cause
τοῦ art. gen. masc. sg. ὁ ἡ τό the, this, that, he, she, it
Κυρίου n. gen. masc. sg. κύριος Lord, lord, master, sir, LORD, God, Master, owner
ὑπὸ prep. ὑπό (+gen) of, by, with, from, among, (+acc) under
τῶν art. gen. masc. pl. ὁ ἡ τό the, this, that, he, she, it
εἰς prep. εἰς (+acc) into, to, unto, for, in, on, toward, against, upon, at, among
ἡμᾶς pron. acc. 1p. pl. ἐγώ I
4 τοῦ art. gen. masc. sg. ὁ ἡ τό the, this, that, he, she, it
Θεοῦ n. gen. masc. sg. θεός God, god
σημείοις n. dat. neut. pl. σημεῖον sign, miracle, wonder, token
τε conj. τέ and, both, also
καὶ conj. καί and, even, also, but
τέρασιν n. dat. neut. pl. τέρας wonder
καὶ conj. καί and, even, also, but
ποικίλαις adj. dat. fem. pl. ποικίλος divers, manifold
δυνάμεσι n. dat. fem. pl. δύναμις power, mighty work, miracle, strength, might
καὶ conj. καί and, even, also, but
Πνεύματος n. gen. neut. sg. πνεῦμα spirit, Spirit, Ghost, ghost, life. of the spirit, wind
'Αγίου adj. gen. neut. sg. ἅγιος Holy, holy, saint, Holy One, holy thing, most holy
μερισμοῖς n. dat. masc. pl. μερισμός gift, dividing asunder
κατὰ prep. κατά (+gen) against, by, throughout, down, (+acc) according to, after, with

τὴν art. acc. fem. sg. ὁ ἡ τό the, this, that, he, she, it
αὐτοῦ pron. gen. masc. 3p. sg. αὐτός ή ό self, of oneself, even, very, the same, he, she, it
θέλησιν n. acc. fem. sg. θέλησις will
5 Οὐ particle of negation. οὐ οὐκ οὐχ not, no, neither, none, nay, nor, never, nothing
γὰρ conj. γάρ for, and, because, but, indeed
ἀγγέλοις n. dat. masc. pl. ἄγγελος angel, messenger
τὴν art. acc. fem. sg. ὁ ἡ τό the, this, that, he, she, it
οἰκουμένην n. acc. fem. sg. οἰκουμένη world, earth
τὴν art. acc. fem. sg. ὁ ἡ τό the, this, that, he, she, it
περὶ prep. περί (+gen) of, for, concerning, (+acc) about, concerning, in
ἧς relative pron. gen. fem. sg. ὅς ἥ ὅ who, which, what, that
6 δέ conj. δέ but, and, now, also, to the contrary, rather, then
πού particle. πού about, in a certain place
τις indefinite pron. nom. masc. sg. τὶς certain, some, any man, one, any thing
Τί interrog. pron. nom. neut. sg. τίς what, who, why, where, which, how
ἄνθρωπος n. nom. masc. sg. ἄνθρωπος man, human being, person, one, certain
ὅτι conj. ὅτι that, for, because, how that, how, because that, for that, though
αὐτοῦ pron. gen. masc. 3p. sg. αὐτός ή ό self, of oneself, even, very, the same, he, she, it
ἢ particle. ἤ or, than, either, nor, or else, and, rather than
υἱὸς n. nom. masc. sg. υἱός son, child, descendant, offspring, heir
ἀνθρώπου n. gen. masc. sg. ἄνθρωπος man, human being, person, one, certain
ὅτι conj. ὅτι that, for, because, how that, how, because that, for that, though
αὐτόν pron. acc. masc. 3p. sg. αὐτός ή ό self, of oneself, even, very, the same, he, she, it
7 αὐτὸν pron. acc. masc. 3p. sg. αὐτός ή ό self, of oneself, even, very, the same, he, she, it
βραχύ adj. acc. neut. sg. βραχύς little while, little, few words, little space
τι indefinite pron. acc. neut. sg. τὶς certain, some, any man, one, any thing
παρ' prep. παρά (+gen) of, from, (+dat) with, for, (+acc) beside, at, by, above, against
ἀγγέλους n. acc. masc. pl. ἄγγελος angel, messenger
δόξῃ n. dat. fem. sg. δόξα glory, honour, praise, dignity, worship
καὶ conj. καί and, even, also, but
τιμῇ n. dat. fem. sg. τιμή honour, price, preciousness, sum
αὐτόν pron. acc. masc. 3p. sg. αὐτός ή ό self, of oneself, even, very, the same, he, she, it
καὶ conj. καί and, even, also, but
αὐτόν pron. acc. masc. 3p. sg. αὐτός ή ό self, of oneself, even, very, the same, he, she, it
ἐπὶ prep. ἐπί (+gen) on, in, upon, (+dat) in, at, for, upon, (+acc) on, upon, unto, to, against
τὰ art. acc. neut. pl. ὁ ἡ τό the, this, that, he, she, it
ἔργα n. acc. neut. pl. ἔργον work, deed, doing labour
τῶν art. gen. fem. pl. ὁ ἡ τό the, this, that, he, she, it
χειρῶν n. gen. fem. pl. χείρ hand
σου pron. gen. 2p. sg. σύ thou, you
8 πάντα adj. acc. neut. pl. πᾶς πᾶσα πᾶν all, every, whosoever, every one, no, whole, any
ὑποκάτω adv. ὑποκάτω under
τῶν art. gen. masc. pl. ὁ ἡ τό the, this, that, he, she, it
ποδῶν n. gen. masc. pl. πούς foot
αὐτοῦ pron. gen. masc. 3p. sg. αὐτός ή ό self, of oneself, even, very, the same, he, she, it
ἐν prep. ἐν (+dat) in, by, with, among, at, on, through, to, within, into, of, for
γὰρ conj. γάρ for, and, because, but, indeed
τῷ art. dat. neut. sg. ὁ ἡ τό the, this, that, he, she, it
αὐτῷ pron. dat. masc. 3p. sg. αὐτός ή ό self, of oneself, even, very, the same, he, she, it
τὰ art. acc. neut. pl. ὁ ἡ τό the, this, that, he, she, it
πάντα adj. acc. neut. pl. πᾶς πᾶσα πᾶν all, every, whosoever, every one, no, whole, any
οὐδὲν num. acc. neut. sg. οὐδείς no man, nothing, no, none, neither, not, nought
αὐτῷ pron. dat. masc. 3p. sg. αὐτός ή ό self, of oneself, even, very, the same, he, she, it
ἀνυπότακτον adj. acc. neut. sg. ἀνυπότακτος disobedient, unruly, that is not put under
νῦν adv. νῦν now, henceforth, present, this time

δὲ conj. δέ but, and, now, also, to the contrary, rather, then
οὔπω adv. οὔπω not yet
αὐτῷ pron. dat. masc. 3p. sg. αὐτός ή ό self, of oneself, even, very, the same, he, she, it
τὰ art. acc. neut. pl. ὁ ἡ τό the, this, that, he, she, it
πάντα adj. acc. neut. pl. πᾶς πᾶσα πᾶν all, every, whosoever, every one, no, whole, any
9 τὸν art. acc. masc. sg. ὁ ἡ τό the, this, that, he, she, it
δὲ conj. δέ but, and, now, also, to the contrary, rather, then
βραχύ adj. acc. neut. sg. βραχύς little while, little, few words, little space
τι indefinite pron. acc. neut. sg. τὶς certain, some, any man, one, any thing
παρ' prep. παρά (+gen) of, from, (+dat) with, for, (+acc) beside, at, by, above, against
ἀγγέλους n. acc. masc. pl. ἄγγελος angel, messenger
'Ιησοῦν n. acc. masc. sg. 'Ιησοῦς Jesus
διὰ prep. διά (+gen) by, through, with, in, of, (+acc) for, because of, for a cause
τὸ art. acc. neut. sg. ὁ ἡ τό the, this, that, he, she, it
πάθημα n. acc. neut. sg. πάθημα suffering, affliction, affection, motion
τοῦ art. gen. masc. sg. ὁ ἡ τό the, this, that, he, she, it
θανάτου n. gen. masc. sg. θάνατος death
δόξῃ n. dat. fem. sg. δόξα glory, honour, praise, dignity, worship
καὶ conj. καί and, even, also, but
τιμῇ n. dat. fem. sg. τιμή honour, price, preciousness, sum
ὅπως adv. ὅπως that, how, to, because, so that, when
χάριτι n. dat. fem. sg. χάρις grace, thank, favour, pleasure
Θεοῦ n. gen. masc. sg. θεός God, god
ὑπὲρ prep. ὑπέρ (+gen) for, of, for the sake of, (+acc) above, more than
παντὸς adj. gen. masc. sg. πᾶς πᾶσα πᾶν all, every, whosoever, every one, no, whole, any
θανάτου n. gen. masc. sg. θάνατος death
10 γὰρ conj. γάρ for, and, because, but, indeed
αὐτῷ pron. dat. masc. 3p. sg. αὐτός ή ό self, of oneself, even, very, the same, he, she, it
δι' prep. διά (+gen) by, through, with, in, of, (+acc) for, because of, for a cause
ὃν relative pron. acc. masc. sg. ὅς ἥ ὅ who, which, what, that
τὰ art. nom. neut. pl. ὁ ἡ τό the, this, that, he, she, it
πάντα adj. nom. neut. pl. πᾶς πᾶσα πᾶν all, every, whosoever, every one, no, whole, any
καὶ conj. καί and, even, also, but
δι' prep. διά (+gen) by, through, with, in, of, (+acc) for, because of, for a cause
οὗ relative pron. gen. masc. sg. ὅς ἥ ὅ who, which, what, that
τὰ art. nom. neut. pl. ὁ ἡ τό the, this, that, he, she, it
πάντα adj. nom. neut. pl. πᾶς πᾶσα πᾶν all, every, whosoever, every one, no, whole, any
πολλοὺς adj. acc. masc. pl. πολύς many, great, much, long, abundant
υἱοὺς n. acc. masc. pl. υἱός son, child, descendant, offspring, heir
εἰς prep. εἰς (+acc) into, to, unto, for, in, on, toward, against, upon, at, among
δόξαν n. acc. fem. sg. δόξα glory, honour, praise, dignity, worship
τὸν art. acc. masc. sg. ὁ ἡ τό the, this, that, he, she, it
ἀρχηγὸν n. acc. masc. sg. ἀρχηγός Prince, author, captain
τῆς art. gen. fem. sg. ὁ ἡ τό the, this, that, he, she, it
σωτηρίας n. gen. fem. sg. σωτηρία salvation, deliver, health, saving
αὐτῶν pron. gen. masc. 3p. pl. αὐτός ή ό self, of oneself, even, very, the same, he, she, it
διὰ prep. διά (+gen) by, through, with, in, of, (+acc) for, because of, for a cause
παθημάτων n. gen. neut. pl. πάθημα suffering, affliction, affection, motion
11 ὅ art. nom. masc. sg. ὁ ἡ τό the, this, that, he, she, it
τε conj. τέ and, both, also
γὰρ conj. γάρ for, and, because, but, indeed
καὶ conj. καί and, even, also, but
οἱ art. nom. masc. pl. ὁ ἡ τό the, this, that, he, she, it
ἐξ prep. ἐκ ἐξ (+gen) of, from, out of, by, on, with, in, among, through
ἑνὸς num. gen. masc. sg. εἷς or ἕν one, other, some, any, only, a certain

πάντες adj. nom. masc. pl. πᾶς πᾶσα πᾶν all, every, whosoever, every one, no, whole, any
δι' prep. διά (+gen) by, through, with, in, of, (+acc) for, because of, for a cause
ἣν relative pron. acc. fem. sg. ὅς ἥ ὅ who, which, what, that
αἰτίαν n. acc. fem. sg. αἰτία cause, reason, accusation, fault
οὐκ particle of negation. οὐ οὐκ οὐχ not, no, neither, none, nay, nor, never, nothing
ἀδελφοὺς n. acc. masc. pl. ἀδελφός brother
αὐτοὺς pron. acc. masc. 3p. pl. αὐτός ή ό self, of oneself, even, very, the same, he, she, it
12 τὸ art. acc. neut. sg. ὁ ἡ τό the, this, that, he, she, it
ὄνομά n. acc. neut. sg. ὄνομα name, call, surname
σου pron. gen. 2p. sg. σύ thou, you
τοῖς art. dat. masc. pl. ὁ ἡ τό the, this, that, he, she, it
ἀδελφοῖς n. dat. masc. pl. ἀδελφός brother
μου pron. gen. 1p. sg. ἐγώ I
ἐν prep. ἐν (+dat) in, by, with, among, at, on, through, to, within, into, of, for
μέσῳ adj. dat. neut. sg. μέσος midst, among, mid, between
ἐκκλησίας n. gen. fem. sg. ἐκκλησία church, assembly
σε pron. acc. 2p. sg. σύ thou, you
13 καὶ conj. καί and, even, also, but
πάλιν adv. πάλιν again
Ἐγὼ pron. nom. 1p. sg. ἐγώ I
ἐπ' prep. ἐπί (+gen) on, in, upon, (+dat) in, at, for, upon, (+acc) on, upon, unto, to, against
αὐτῷ pron. dat. masc. 3p. sg. αὐτός ή ό self, of oneself, even, very, the same, he, she, it
καὶ conj. καί and, even, also, but
πάλιν adv. πάλιν again
ἐγὼ pron. nom. 1p. sg. ἐγώ I
καὶ conj. καί and, even, also, but
τὰ art. nom. neut. pl. ὁ ἡ τό the, this, that, he, she, it
παιδία n. nom. neut. pl. παιδίον child, little child, damsel
ἅ relative pron. acc. neut. pl. ὅς ἥ ὅ who, which, what, that
μοι pron. dat. 1p. sg. ἐγώ I
ὁ art. nom. masc. sg. ὁ ἡ τό the, this, that, he, she, it
Θεός n. nom. masc. sg. θεός God, god
14 ἐπεὶ conj. ἐπεί because, otherwise, seeing, else, for then, for as much as, for, since
οὖν conj. οὖν therefore, then, so, and, now, wherefore
τὰ art. nom. neut. pl. ὁ ἡ τό the, this, that, he, she, it
παιδία n. nom. neut. pl. παιδίον child, little child, damsel
σαρκός n. gen. fem. sg. σάρξ flesh, carnal
καὶ conj. καί and, even, also, but
αἵματος n. gen. neut. sg. αἷμα blood
καὶ conj. καί and, even, also, but
αὐτὸς pron. nom. masc. 3p. sg. αὐτός ή ό self, of oneself, even, very, the same, he, she, it
παραπλησίως adv. παραπλησίως likewise
τῶν art. gen. neut. pl. ὁ ἡ τό the, this, that, he, she, it
αὐτῶν adj. gen. neut. pl. αὐτός ή ό self, of oneself, even, very, the same, he, she, it
ἵνα conj. ἵνα that, to, lest, for to, so that, albeit, because, for, so as
διὰ prep. διά (+gen) by, through, with, in, of, (+acc) for, because of, for a cause
τοῦ art. gen. masc. sg. ὁ ἡ τό the, this, that, he, she, it
θανάτου n. gen. masc. sg. θάνατος death
τὸν art. acc. masc. sg. ὁ ἡ τό the, this, that, he, she, it
τὸ art. acc. neut. sg. ὁ ἡ τό the, this, that, he, she, it
κράτος n. acc. neut. sg. κράτος power, dominion, might, strength
τοῦ art. gen. masc. sg. ὁ ἡ τό the, this, that, he, she, it
θανάτου n. gen. masc. sg. θάνατος death
τοῦτ' demo. pron. nom. neut. sg. οὗτος αὕτη τοῦτο this, the same, this same, he, she, it
τὸν art. acc. masc. sg. ὁ ἡ τό the, this, that, he, she, it

διάβολον adj. acc. masc. sg. διάβολος devil, false accuser, Devil, slanderer
15 καὶ conj. καί and, even, also, but
τούτους demo. pron. acc. masc. pl. οὗτος αὕτη τοῦτο this, the same, this same, he, she, it
ὅσοι relative pron. nom. masc. pl. ὅσος as many as, whatsoever, that, as long as, how much
φόβῳ n. dat. masc. sg. φόβος fear, terror, sore afraid
θανάτου n. gen. masc. sg. θάνατος death
διὰ prep. διά (+gen) by, through, with, in, of, (+acc) for, because of, for a cause
παντὸς adj. gen. neut. sg. πᾶς πᾶσα πᾶν all, every, whosoever, every one, no, whole, any
τοῦ art. gen. neut. sg. ὁ ἡ τό the, this, that, he, she, it
ἔνοχοι adj. nom. masc. pl. ἔνοχος in danger of, guilty of, subject to
δουλείας n. gen. fem. sg. δουλεία bondage
16 οὐ particle of negation. οὐ οὐκ οὐχ not, no, neither, none, nay, nor, never, nothing
γὰρ conj. γάρ for, and, because, but, indeed
δήπου particle. δήπου verily
ἀγγέλων n. gen. masc. pl. ἄγγελος angel, messenger
ἀλλὰ conj. ἀλλά but, yea, yet, nevertheless, howbeit, nay, therefore
σπέρματος n. gen. neut. sg. σπέρμα seed, issue
Ἀβραὰμ n. gen. masc. sg. Ἀβραάμ Abraham
17 ὅθεν adv. ὅθεν wherefore, from whence, whereupon, where, from thence, whence
κατὰ prep. κατά (+gen) against, by, throughout, down, (+acc) according to, after, with
πάντα adj. acc. neut. pl. πᾶς πᾶσα πᾶν all, every, whosoever, every one, no, whole, any
τοῖς art. dat. masc. pl. ὁ ἡ τό the, this, that, he, she, it
ἀδελφοῖς n. dat. masc. pl. ἀδελφός brother
ἵνα conj. ἵνα that, to, lest, for to, so that, albeit, because, for, so as
ἐλεήμων adj. nom. masc. sg. ἐλεήμων merciful
καὶ conj. καί and, even, also, but
πιστὸς adj. nom. masc. sg. πιστός faithful, believing, true, sure
ἀρχιερεὺς n. nom. masc. sg. ἀρχιερεύς chief priest, high priest
τὰ art. acc. neut. pl. ὁ ἡ τό the, this, that, he, she, it
πρὸς prep. πρός (+gen) for, (+dat) at, (+acc) unto, to, with, for, against
τὸν art. acc. masc. sg. ὁ ἡ τό the, this, that, he, she, it
Θεὸν n. acc. masc. sg. θεός God, god
εἰς prep. εἰς (+acc) into, to, unto, for, in, on, toward, against, upon, at, among
τὸ art. acc. neut. sg. ὁ ἡ τό the, this, that, he, she, it
τὰς art. acc. fem. pl. ὁ ἡ τό the, this, that, he, she, it
ἁμαρτίας n. acc. fem. pl. ἁμαρτία sin, offence, sinful
τοῦ art. gen. masc. sg. ὁ ἡ τό the, this, that, he, she, it
λαοῦ n. gen. masc. sg. λαός people
18 ἐν prep. ἐν (+dat) in, by, with, among, at, on, through, to, within, into, of, for
ᾧ relative pron. dat. neut. sg. ὅς ἥ ὅ who, which, what, that
γὰρ conj. γάρ for, and, because, but, indeed
αὐτὸς pron. nom. masc. 3p. sg. αὐτός ἡ ὁ self, of oneself, even, very, the same, he, she, it
τοῖς art. dat. masc. pl. ὁ ἡ τό the, this, that, he, she, it

3

1 Ὅθεν adv. ὅθεν wherefore, from whence, whereupon, where, from thence, whence
ἀδελφοὶ n. voc. masc. pl. ἀδελφός brother
ἅγιοι adj. voc. masc. pl. ἅγιος Holy, holy, saint, Holy One, holy thing, most holy
κλήσεως n. gen. fem. sg. κλῆσις calling, vocation
ἐπουρανίου adj. gen. fem. sg. ἐπουράνιος heavenly, celestial, high, in heaven
μέτοχοι adj. nom. masc. pl. μέτοχος partner, partaker, fellow
τὸν art. acc. masc. sg. ὁ ἡ τό the, this, that, he, she, it
ἀπόστολον n. acc. masc. sg. ἀπόστολος apostle, messenger, he that is sent
καὶ conj. καί and, even, also, but

ἀρχιερέα n. acc. masc. sg. ἀρχιερεύς chief priest, high priest
τῆς art. gen. fem. sg. ὁ ἡ τό the, this, that, he, she, it
ὁμολογίας n. gen. fem. sg. ὁμολογία profession, confession, profess
ἡμῶν pron. gen. 1p. pl. ἐγώ I
Χριστὸν n. acc. masc. sg. Χριστός Christ
Ἰησοῦν n. acc. masc. sg. Ἰησοῦς Jesus
2 πιστὸν adj. acc. masc. sg. πιστός faithful, believing, true, sure
τῷ art. dat. masc. sg. ὁ ἡ τό the, this, that, he, she, it
αὐτὸν pron. acc. masc. 3p. sg. αὐτός ή ό self, of oneself, even, very, the same, he, she, it
ὡς adv. ὡς as, when, as it were, how, about, like, as soon as, even as, while
καὶ conj. καί and, even, also, but
Μωσῆς n. nom. masc. sg. Μωσῆς Moses
ἐν prep. ἐν (+dat) in, by, with, among, at, on, through, to, within, into, of, for
ὅλῳ adj. dat. masc. sg. ὅλος all, whole, every whit, altogether
τῷ art. dat. masc. sg. ὁ ἡ τό the, this, that, he, she, it
οἴκῳ n. dat. masc. sg. οἶκος house, home, household
αὐτοῦ pron. gen. masc. 3p. sg. αὐτός ή ό self, of oneself, even, very, the same, he, she, it
3 πλείονος compar. adj. gen. fem. sg. πολύς many, great, much, long, abundant
γὰρ conj. γάρ for, and, because, but, indeed
δόξης n. gen. fem. sg. δόξα glory, honour, praise, dignity, worship
οὗτος demo. pron. nom. masc. sg. οὗτος αὕτη τοῦτο this, the same, this same, he, she, it
παρὰ prep. παρά (+gen) of, from, (+dat) with, for, (+acc) beside, at, by, above, against
Μωσῆν n. acc. masc. sg. Μωσῆς Moses
καθ' prep. κατά (+gen) against, by, throughout, down, (+acc) according to, after, with
ὅσον relative pron. acc. neut. sg. ὅσος as many as, whatsoever, that, as long as, how much
πλείονα compar. adj. acc. fem. sg. πολύς many, great, much, long, abundant
τιμὴν n. acc. fem. sg. τιμή honour, price, preciousness, sum
τοῦ art. gen. masc. sg. ὁ ἡ τό the, this, that, he, she, it
οἴκου n. gen. masc. sg. οἶκος house, home, household
ὁ art. nom. masc. sg. ὁ ἡ τό the, this, that, he, she, it
αὐτόν pron. acc. masc. 3p. sg. αὐτός ή ό self, of oneself, even, very, the same, he, she, it
4 πᾶς adj. nom. masc. sg. πᾶς πᾶσα πᾶν all, every, whosoever, every one, no, whole, any
γὰρ conj. γάρ for, and, because, but, indeed
οἶκος n. nom. masc. sg. οἶκος house, home, household
ὑπό prep. ὑπό (+gen) of, by, with, from, among, (+acc) under
τινος indefinite pron. gen. masc. sg. τὶς certain, some, any man, one, any thing
ὁ art. nom. masc. sg. ὁ ἡ τό the, this, that, he, she, it
δὲ conj. δέ but, and, now, also, to the contrary, rather, then
τὰ art. acc. neut. pl. ὁ ἡ τό the, this, that, he, she, it
πάντα adj. acc. neut. pl. πᾶς πᾶσα πᾶν all, every, whosoever, every one, no, whole, any
Θεός n. nom. masc. sg. θεός God, god
5 καὶ conj. καί and, even, also, but
Μωσῆς n. nom. masc. sg. Μωσῆς Moses
μὲν conj. μέν indeed, verily, truly, even, so, some
πιστὸς adj. nom. masc. sg. πιστός faithful, believing, true, sure
ἐν prep. ἐν (+dat) in, by, with, among, at, on, through, to, within, into, of, for
ὅλῳ adj. dat. masc. sg. ὅλος all, whole, every whit, altogether
τῷ art. dat. masc. sg. ὁ ἡ τό the, this, that, he, she, it
οἴκῳ n. dat. masc. sg. οἶκος house, home, household
αὐτοῦ pron. gen. masc. 3p. sg. αὐτός ή ό self, of oneself, even, very, the same, he, she, it
ὡς adv. ὡς as, when, as it were, how, about, like, as soon as, even as, while
θεράπων n. nom. masc. sg. θεράπων servant
εἰς prep. εἰς (+acc) into, to, unto, for, in, on, toward, against, upon, at, among
μαρτύριον n. acc. neut. sg. μαρτύριον testimony, witness
τῶν art. gen. neut. pl. ὁ ἡ τό the, this, that, he, she, it

6 Χριστὸς n. nom. masc. sg. Χριστός Christ
δὲ conj. δέ but, and, now, also, to the contrary, rather, then
ὡς adv. ὡς as, when, as it were, how, about, like, as soon as, even as, while
υἱὸς n. nom. masc. sg. υἱός son, child, descendant, offspring, heir
ἐπὶ prep. ἐπί (+gen) on, in, upon, (+dat) in, at, for, upon, (+acc) on, upon, unto, to, against
τὸν art. acc. masc. sg. ὁ ἡ τό the, this, that, he, she, it
οἶκον n. acc. masc. sg. οἶκος house, home, household
αὐτοῦ pron. gen. masc. 3p. sg. αὐτός ἡ ὁ self, of oneself, even, very, the same, he, she, it
οὗ relative pron. gen. masc. sg. ὅς ἥ ὅ who, which, what, that
οἶκός n. nom. masc. sg. οἶκος house, home, household
ἡμεῖς pron. nom. 1p. pl. ἐγώ I
ἐάνπερ conj. ἐάνπερ if it be that, if at all events
τὴν art. acc. fem. sg. ὁ ἡ τό the, this, that, he, she, it
παρρησίαν n. acc. fem. sg. παρρησία boldness, confidence, openly, plainly, freely
καὶ conj. καί and, even, also, but
τὸ art. acc. neut. sg. ὁ ἡ τό the, this, that, he, she, it
καύχημα n. acc. neut. sg. καύχημα whereof to glory, rejoicing, glorying, boasting
τῆς art. gen. fem. sg. ὁ ἡ τό the, this, that, he, she, it
ἐλπίδος n. gen. fem. sg. ἐλπίς hope, faith
μέχρι prep. μέχρι until, unto, till, to
τέλους n. gen. neut. sg. τέλος end, custom, ending, finally, uttermost
βεβαίαν adj. acc. fem. sg. βέβαιος sure, stedfast, firm, more sure, of force
7 διό conj. διό wherefore, therefore, for which cause
καθὼς adv. καθώς as, even as, according as, according to
τὸ art. nom. neut. sg. ὁ ἡ τό the, this, that, he, she, it
Πνεῦμα n. nom. neut. sg. πνεῦμα spirit, Spirit, Ghost, ghost, life. of the spirit, wind
τὸ art. nom. neut. sg. ὁ ἡ τό the, this, that, he, she, it
Ἅγιον adj. nom. neut. sg. ἅγιος Holy, holy, saint, Holy One, holy thing, most holy
Σήμερον adv. σήμερον this day, today
ἐὰν conj. ἐάν if, soever, except, though, and if, but, whether, if so, so
τῆς art. gen. fem. sg. ὁ ἡ τό the, this, that, he, she, it
φωνῆς n. gen. fem. sg. φωνή voice, sound, noise
αὐτοῦ pron. gen. masc. 3p. sg. αὐτός ἡ ὁ self, of oneself, even, very, the same, he, she, it
8 μὴ particle of negation. μή not, no, lest, neither, none, nothing, nor, never, without
τὰς art. acc. fem. pl. ὁ ἡ τό the, this, that, he, she, it
καρδίας n. acc. fem. pl. καρδία heart
ὑμῶν pron. gen. 2p. pl. σύ thou, you
ὡς adv. ὡς as, when, as it were, how, about, like, as soon as, even as, while
ἐν prep. ἐν (+dat) in, by, with, among, at, on, through, to, within, into, of, for
τῷ art. dat. masc. sg. ὁ ἡ τό the, this, that, he, she, it
παραπικρασμῷ n. dat. masc. sg. παραπικρασμός provocation
κατὰ prep. κατά (+gen) against, by, throughout, down, (+acc) according to, after, with
τὴν art. acc. fem. sg. ὁ ἡ τό the, this, that, he, she, it
ἡμέραν n. acc. fem. sg. ἡμέρα day, time, year, while, age, day time
τοῦ art. gen. masc. sg. ὁ ἡ τό the, this, that, he, she, it
πειρασμοῦ n. gen. masc. sg. πειρασμός temptation, trial
ἐν prep. ἐν (+dat) in, by, with, among, at, on, through, to, within, into, of, for
τῇ art. dat. fem. sg. ὁ ἡ τό the, this, that, he, she, it
ἐρήμῳ adj. dat. fem. sg. ἔρημος wilderness, desert
9 οὗ adv. οὗ where, whither, wherein
με pron. acc. 1p. sg. ἐγώ I
οἱ art. nom. masc. pl. ὁ ἡ τό the, this, that, he, she, it
πατέρες n. nom. masc. pl. πατήρ Father, father, parent
ὑμῶν pron. gen. 2p. pl. σύ thou, you
με pron. acc. 1p. sg. ἐγώ I

καὶ conj. καί and, even, also, but
τὰ art. acc. neut. pl. ὁ ἡ τό the, this, that, he, she, it
ἔργα n. acc. neut. pl. ἔργον work, deed, doing labour
μου pron. gen. 1p. sg. ἐγώ I
τεσσαράκοντα num. acc. neut. pl. τεσσαράκοντα forty
ἔτη n. acc. neut. pl. ἔτος year
10 διὸ conj. διό wherefore, therefore, for which cause
τῇ art. dat. fem. sg. ὁ ἡ τό the, this, that, he, she, it
γενεᾷ n. dat. fem. sg. γενεά generation, age, time, nation
ἐκείνῃ demo. pron. dat. fem. sg. ἐκεῖνος that, he, the same, that same
καὶ conj. καί and, even, also, but
'Αεὶ adv. ἀεί always, always, ever
τῇ art. dat. fem. sg. ὁ ἡ τό the, this, that, he, she, it
καρδίᾳ n. dat. fem. sg. καρδία heart
αὐτοὶ pron. nom. masc. 3p. pl. αὐτός ή ό self, of oneself, even, very, the same, he, she, it
δὲ conj. δέ but, and, now, also, to the contrary, rather, then
οὐκ particle of negation. οὐ οὐκ οὐχ not, no, neither, none, nay, nor, never, nothing
τὰς art. acc. fem. pl. ὁ ἡ τό the, this, that, he, she, it
ὁδούς n. acc. fem. pl. ὁδός way, journey, highway
μου pron. gen. 1p. sg. ἐγώ I
11 ὡς adv. ὡς as, when, as it were, how, about, like, as soon as, even as, while
ἐν prep. ἐν (+dat) in, by, with, among, at, on, through, to, within, into, of, for
τῇ art. dat. fem. sg. ὁ ἡ τό the, this, that, he, she, it
ὀργῇ n. dat. fem. sg. ὀργή wrath, anger, indignation, vengeance
μου pron. gen. 1p. sg. ἐγώ I
Εἰ conj. εἰ if, whether, that, though, forasmuch
εἰς prep. εἰς (+acc) into, to, unto, for, in, on, toward, against, upon, at, among
τὴν art. acc. fem. sg. ὁ ἡ τό the, this, that, he, she, it
κατάπαυσίν n. acc. fem. sg. κατάπαυσις rest
μου pron. gen. 1p. sg. ἐγώ I
12 ἀδελφοί n. voc. masc. pl. ἀδελφός brother
μή particle of negation. μή not, no, lest, neither, none, nothing, nor, never, without
ποτε adv. ποτέ in time past, at any time, sometimes, in old time, once, when
ἔν prep. ἐν (+dat) in, by, with, among, at, on, through, to, within, into, of, for
τινι indefinite pron. dat. masc. sg. τὶς certain, some, any man, one, any thing
ὑμῶν pron. gen. 2p. pl. σύ thou, you
καρδία n. nom. fem. sg. καρδία heart
πονηρὰ adj. nom. fem. sg. πονηρός evil, wicked, bad
ἀπιστίας n. gen. fem. sg. ἀπιστία unbelief
ἔν prep. ἐν (+dat) in, by, with, among, at, on, through, to, within, into, of, for
τῷ art. dat. neut. sg. ὁ ἡ τό the, this, that, he, she, it
ἀπὸ prep. ἀπό (+gen) from, of, out of, since, for, off, at, by, in, on
Θεοῦ n. gen. masc. sg. θεός God, god
13 ἀλλὰ conj. ἀλλά but, yea, yet, nevertheless, howbeit, nay, therefore
ἑαυτοὺς reflexive pron. acc. masc. 3p. pl. ἑαυτοῦ himself, herself, itself, yourself, ourselves
καθ' prep. κατά (+gen) against, by, throughout, down, (+acc) according to, after, with
ἑκάστην adj. acc. fem. sg. ἕκαστος every man, every, every one, any man, each
ἡμέραν n. acc. fem. sg. ἡμέρα day, time, year, while, age, day time
ἄχρις prep. ἄχρι or ἄχρις (+gen) until, unto, till, even to, as far as, while, into
οὗ relative pron. gen. masc. sg. ὅς ἥ ὅ who, which, what, that
τὸ art. nom. neut. sg. ὁ ἡ τό the, this, that, he, she, it
σήμερον adv. σήμερον this day, today
ἵνα conj. ἵνα that, to, lest, for to, so that, albeit, because, for, so as
μὴ particle of negation. μή not, no, lest, neither, none, nothing, nor, never, without
τις indefinite pron. nom. masc. sg. τὶς certain, some, any man, one, any thing

ἐξ prep. ἐκ ἐξ (+gen) of, from, out of, by, on, with, in, among, through
ὑμῶν pron. gen. 2p. pl. σύ thou, you
ἀπάτῃ n. dat. fem. sg. ἀπάτη deceitfulness, deceit
τῆς art. gen. fem. sg. ὁ ἡ τό the, this, that, he, she, it
ἁμαρτίας n. gen. fem. sg. ἁμαρτία sin, offence, sinful
14 μέτοχοι adj. nom. masc. pl. μέτοχος partner, partaker, fellow
γὰρ conj. γάρ for, and, because, but, indeed
τοῦ art. gen. masc. sg. ὁ ἡ τό the, this, that, he, she, it
Χριστοῦ n. gen. masc. sg. Χριστός Christ
ἐάνπερ conj. ἐάνπερ if it be that, if at all events
τὴν art. acc. fem. sg. ὁ ἡ τό the, this, that, he, she, it
ἀρχὴν n. acc. fem. sg. ἀρχή beginning, principality, corner, first, magistrate, rule
τῆς art. gen. fem. sg. ὁ ἡ τό the, this, that, he, she, it
ὑποστάσεως n. gen. fem. sg. ὑπόστασις confidence, substance, person, nature
μέχρι prep. μέχρι until, unto, till, to
τέλους n. gen. neut. sg. τέλος end, custom, ending, finally, uttermost
βεβαίαν adj. acc. fem. sg. βέβαιος sure, stedfast, firm, more sure, of force
15 ἐν prep. ἐν (+dat) in, by, with, among, at, on, through, to, within, into, of, for
τῷ art. dat. neut. sg. ὁ ἡ τό the, this, that, he, she, it
Σήμερον adv. σήμερον this day, today
ἐὰν conj. ἐάν if, soever, except, though, and if, but, whether, if so, so
τῆς art. gen. fem. sg. ὁ ἡ τό the, this, that, he, she, it
φωνῆς n. gen. fem. sg. φωνή voice, sound, noise
αὐτοῦ pron. gen. masc. 3p. sg. αὐτός ή ό self, of oneself, even, very, the same, he, she, it
μὴ particle of negation. μή not, no, lest, neither, none, nothing, nor, never, without
τὰς art. acc. fem. pl. ὁ ἡ τό the, this, that, he, she, it
καρδίας n. acc. fem. pl. καρδία heart
ὑμῶν pron. gen. 2p. pl. σύ thou, you
ὡς adv. ὡς as, when, as it were, how, about, like, as soon as, even as, while
ἐν prep. ἐν (+dat) in, by, with, among, at, on, through, to, within, into, of, for
τῷ art. dat. masc. sg. ὁ ἡ τό the, this, that, he, she, it
παραπικρασμῷ n. dat. masc. sg. παραπικρασμός provocation
16 τίνες interrog. pron. nom. masc. pl. τίς what, who, why, where, which, how
γὰρ conj. γάρ for, and, because, but, indeed
ἀλλ’ conj. ἀλλά but, yea, yet, nevertheless, howbeit, nay, therefore
οὐ particle of negation. οὐ οὐκ οὐχ not, no, neither, none, nay, nor, never, nothing
πάντες adj. nom. masc. pl. πᾶς πᾶσα πᾶν all, every, whosoever, every one, no, whole, any
οἱ art. nom. masc. pl. ὁ ἡ τό the, this, that, he, she, it
ἐξ prep. ἐκ ἐξ (+gen) of, from, out of, by, on, with, in, among, through
Αἰγύπτου n. gen. fem. sg. Αἴγυπτος Egypt
διὰ prep. διά (+gen) by, through, with, in, of, (+acc) for, because of, for a cause
Μωσέως n. gen. masc. sg. Μωσῆς Moses
17 τίσι interrog. pron. dat. masc. pl. τίς what, who, why, where, which, how
δὲ conj. δέ but, and, now, also, to the contrary, rather, then
τεσσαράκοντα num. acc. neut. pl. τεσσαράκοντα forty
ἔτη n. acc. neut. pl. ἔτος year
οὐχὶ adv. οὐχί not, nay
τοῖς art. dat. masc. pl. ὁ ἡ τό the, this, that, he, she, it
ὧν relative pron. gen. masc. pl. ὅς ἥ ὅ who, which, what, that
τὰ art. nom. neut. pl. ὁ ἡ τό the, this, that, he, she, it
κῶλα n. nom. neut. pl. κῶλον carcass
ἐν prep. ἐν (+dat) in, by, with, among, at, on, through, to, within, into, of, for
τῇ art. dat. fem. sg. ὁ ἡ τό the, this, that, he, she, it
ἐρήμῳ adj. dat. fem. sg. ἔρημος wilderness, desert
18 τίσι interrog. pron. dat. masc. pl. τίς what, who, why, where, which, how

δὲ conj. δέ but, and, now, also, to the contrary, rather, then
μὴ particle of negation. μή not, no, lest, neither, none, nothing, nor, never, without
εἰς prep. εἰς (+acc) into, to, unto, for, in, on, toward, against, upon, at, among
τὴν art. acc. fem. sg. ὁ ἡ τό the, this, that, he, she, it
κατάπαυσιν n. acc. fem. sg. κατάπαυσις rest
αὐτοῦ pron. gen. masc. 3p. sg. αὐτός ή ὁ self, of oneself, even, very, the same, he, she, it
εἰ conj. εἰ if, whether, that, though, forasmuch
μὴ particle of negation. μή not, no, lest, neither, none, nothing, nor, never, without
τοῖς art. dat. masc. pl. ὁ ἡ τό the, this, that, he, she, it
19 καὶ conj. καί and, even, also, but
ὅτι conj. ὅτι that, for, because, how that, how, because that, for that, though
οὐκ particle of negation. οὐ οὐκ οὐχ not, no, neither, none, nay, nor, never, nothing
δι' prep. διά (+gen) by, through, with, in, of, (+acc) for, because of, for a cause
ἀπιστίαν n. acc. fem. sg. ἀπιστία unbelief

4

1 οὖν conj. οὖν therefore, then, so, and, now, wherefore
μή particle of negation. μή not, no, lest, neither, none, nothing, nor, never, without
ποτε adv. ποτέ in time past, at any time, sometimes, in old time, once, when
ἐπαγγελίας n. gen. fem. sg. ἐπαγγελία promise, message
εἰς prep. εἰς (+acc) into, to, unto, for, in, on, toward, against, upon, at, among
τὴν art. acc. fem. sg. ὁ ἡ τό the, this, that, he, she, it
κατάπαυσιν n. acc. fem. sg. κατάπαυσις rest
αὐτοῦ pron. gen. masc. 3p. sg. αὐτός ή ὁ self, of oneself, even, very, the same, he, she, it
τις indefinite pron. nom. masc. sg. τὶς certain, some, any man, one, any thing
ἐξ prep. ἐκ ἐξ (+gen) of, from, out of, by, on, with, in, among, through
ὑμῶν pron. gen. 2p. pl. σύ thou, you
2 καὶ conj. καί and, even, also, but
γάρ conj. γάρ for, and, because, but, indeed
καθάπερ adv. καθάπερ even as, as, as well as
κἀκεῖνοι demo. pron. nom. masc. pl. κἀκεῖνος and he, he also, and the other, even he
ἀλλ' conj. ἀλλά but, yea, yet, nevertheless, howbeit, nay, therefore
οὐκ particle of negation. οὐ οὐκ οὐχ not, no, neither, none, nay, nor, never, nothing
ὁ art. nom. masc. sg. ὁ ἡ τό the, this, that, he, she, it
λόγος n. nom. masc. sg. λόγος word, saying, account, speech, thing, matter
τῆς art. gen. fem. sg. ὁ ἡ τό the, this, that, he, she, it
ἀκοῆς n. gen. fem. sg. ἀκοή hearing, ear, fame, report, rumour, which one heard
ἐκείνους demo. pron. acc. masc. pl. ἐκεῖνος that, he, the same, that same
μὴ particle of negation. μή not, no, lest, neither, none, nothing, nor, never, without
τῇ art. dat. fem. sg. ὁ ἡ τό the, this, that, he, she, it
πίστει n. dat. fem. sg. πίστις faith, assurance, belief, fidelity
τοῖς art. dat. masc. pl. ὁ ἡ τό the, this, that, he, she, it
3 γὰρ conj. γάρ for, and, because, but, indeed
εἰς prep. εἰς (+acc) into, to, unto, for, in, on, toward, against, upon, at, among
τὴν art. acc. fem. sg. ὁ ἡ τό the, this, that, he, she, it
κατάπαυσιν n. acc. fem. sg. κατάπαυσις rest
οἱ art. nom. masc. pl. ὁ ἡ τό the, this, that, he, she, it
καθὼς adv. καθώς as, even as, according as, according to
Ὡς adv. ὡς as, when, as it were, how, about, like, as soon as, even as, while
ἐν prep. ἐν (+dat) in, by, with, among, at, on, through, to, within, into, of, for
τῇ art. dat. fem. sg. ὁ ἡ τό the, this, that, he, she, it
ὀργῇ n. dat. fem. sg. ὀργή wrath, anger, indignation, vengeance
μου pron. gen. 1p. sg. ἐγώ I
Εἰ conj. εἰ if, whether, that, though, forasmuch

εἰς prep. εἰς (+acc) into, to, unto, for, in, on, toward, against, upon, at, among
τὴν art. acc. fem. sg. ὁ ἡ τό the, this, that, he, she, it
κατάπαυσιν n. acc. fem. sg. κατάπαυσις rest
μου pron. gen. 1p. sg. ἐγώ I
καίτοι conj. καίτοι although
τῶν art. gen. neut. pl. ὁ ἡ τό the, this, that, he, she, it
ἔργων n. gen. neut. pl. ἔργον work, deed, doing labour
ἀπὸ prep. ἀπό (+gen) from, of, out of, since, for, off, at, by, in, on
καταβολῆς n. gen. fem. sg. καταβολή foundation
κόσμου n. gen. masc. sg. κόσμος world, adorning
4 γάρ conj. γάρ for, and, because, but, indeed
που particle. πού about, in a certain place
περὶ prep. περί (+gen) of, for, concerning, (+acc) about, concerning, in
τῆς art. gen. fem. sg. ὁ ἡ τό the, this, that, he, she, it
ἑβδόμης ordinal. adj. gen. fem. sg. ἕβδομος seventh
οὕτω adv. οὕτω οὕτως so, even so, thus, on this wise, likewise, after this manner
Καὶ conj. καί and, even, also, but
ὁ art. nom. masc. sg. ὁ ἡ τό the, this, that, he, she, it
Θεὸς n. nom. masc. sg. θεός God, god
ἐν prep. ἐν (+dat) in, by, with, among, at, on, through, to, within, into, of, for
τῇ art. dat. fem. sg. ὁ ἡ τό the, this, that, he, she, it
ἡμέρᾳ n. dat. fem. sg. ἡμέρα day, time, year, while, age, day time
τῇ art. dat. fem. sg. ὁ ἡ τό the, this, that, he, she, it
ἑβδόμῃ ordinal. adj. dat. fem. sg. ἕβδομος seventh
ἀπὸ prep. ἀπό (+gen) from, of, out of, since, for, off, at, by, in, on
πάντων adj. gen. neut. pl. πᾶς πᾶσα πᾶν all, every, whosoever, every one, no, whole, any
τῶν art. gen. neut. pl. ὁ ἡ τό the, this, that, he, she, it
ἔργων n. gen. neut. pl. ἔργον work, deed, doing labour
αὐτοῦ pron. gen. masc. 3p. sg. αὐτός ή ό self, of oneself, even, very, the same, he, she, it
5 καὶ conj. καί and, even, also, but
ἐν prep. ἐν (+dat) in, by, with, among, at, on, through, to, within, into, of, for
τούτῳ demo. pron. dat. masc. sg. οὗτος αὕτη τοῦτο this, the same, this same, he, she, it
πάλιν adv. πάλιν again
Εἰ conj. εἰ if, whether, that, though, forasmuch
εἰς prep. εἰς (+acc) into, to, unto, for, in, on, toward, against, upon, at, among
τὴν art. acc. fem. sg. ὁ ἡ τό the, this, that, he, she, it
κατάπαυσίν n. acc. fem. sg. κατάπαυσις rest
μου pron. gen. 1p. sg. ἐγώ I
6 ἐπεὶ conj. ἐπεί because, otherwise, seeing, else, for then, for as much as, for, since
οὖν conj. οὖν therefore, then, so, and, now, wherefore
τινὰς indefinite pron. acc. masc. pl. τὶς certain, some, any man, one, any thing
εἰς prep. εἰς (+acc) into, to, unto, for, in, on, toward, against, upon, at, among
αὐτήν pron. acc. fem. 3p. sg. αὐτός ή ό self, of oneself, even, very, the same, he, she, it
καὶ conj. καί and, even, also, but
οἱ art. nom. masc. pl. ὁ ἡ τό the, this, that, he, she, it
πρότερον adv. πρότερον before, first, former, at the first
οὐκ particle of negation. οὐ οὐκ οὐχ not, no, neither, none, nay, nor, never, nothing
δι' prep. διά (+gen) by, through, with, in, of, (+acc) for, because of, for a cause
ἀπείθειαν n. acc. fem. sg. ἀπείθεια unbelief, disobedience
7 πάλιν adv. πάλιν again
τινὰ indefinite pron. acc. fem. sg. τὶς certain, some, any man, one, any thing
ἡμέραν n. acc. fem. sg. ἡμέρα day, time, year, while, age, day time
Σήμερον adv. σήμερον this day, today
ἐν prep. ἐν (+dat) in, by, with, among, at, on, through, to, within, into, of, for
Δαβὶδ n. dat. masc. sg. Δαβίδ David

μετὰ prep. μετά (+gen) with, among, against, (+acc) after
τοσοῦτον demo. pron. acc. masc. sg. τοσοῦτος so much, so great, so many, so long
χρόνον n. acc. masc. sg. χρόνος time, season, space
καθὼς adv. καθώς as, even as, according as, according to
Σήμερον adv. σήμερον this day, today
ἐὰν conj. ἐάν if, soever, except, though, and if, but, whether, if so, so
τῆς art. gen. fem. sg. ὁ ἡ τό the, this, that, he, she, it
φωνῆς n. gen. fem. sg. φωνή voice, sound, noise
αὐτοῦ pron. gen. masc. 3p. sg. αὐτός ή ό self, of oneself, even, very, the same, he, she, it
μὴ particle of negation. μή not, no, lest, neither, none, nothing, nor, never, without
τὰς art. acc. fem. pl. ὁ ἡ τό the, this, that, he, she, it
καρδίας n. acc. fem. pl. καρδία heart
ὑμῶν pron. gen. 2p. pl. σύ thou, you
8 εἰ conj. εἰ if, whether, that, though, forasmuch
γὰρ conj. γάρ for, and, because, but, indeed
αὐτοὺς pron. acc. masc. 3p. pl. αὐτός ή ό self, of oneself, even, very, the same, he, she, it
Ἰησοῦς n. nom. masc. sg. Ἰησοῦς Jesus, Joshua
οὐκ particle of negation. οὐ οὐκ οὐχ not, no, neither, none, nay, nor, never, nothing
ἂν particle. ἄν Indicating contingency. No English translation.
περὶ prep. περί (+gen) of, for, concerning, (+acc) about, concerning, in
ἄλλης adj. gen. fem. sg. ἄλλος other, another, some, one, more, otherwise
μετὰ prep. μετά (+gen) with, among, against, (+acc) after
ταῦτα demo. pron. acc. neut. pl. οὗτος αὕτη τοῦτο this, the same, this same, he, she, it
ἡμέρας n. gen. fem. sg. ἡμέρα day, time, year, while, age, day time
9 ἄρα conj. ἄρα then, therefore, haply, wherefore, perhaps, manner, no doubt, truly
σαββατισμὸς n. nom. masc. sg. σαββατισμός rest
τῷ art. dat. masc. sg. ὁ ἡ τό the, this, that, he, she, it
λαῷ n. dat. masc. sg. λαός people
τοῦ art. gen. masc. sg. ὁ ἡ τό the, this, that, he, she, it
Θεοῦ n. gen. masc. sg. θεός God, god
10 ὁ art. nom. masc. sg. ὁ ἡ τό the, this, that, he, she, it
γὰρ conj. γάρ for, and, because, but, indeed
εἰς prep. εἰς (+acc) into, to, unto, for, in, on, toward, against, upon, at, among
τὴν art. acc. fem. sg. ὁ ἡ τό the, this, that, he, she, it
κατάπαυσιν n. acc. fem. sg. κατάπαυσις rest
αὐτοῦ pron. gen. masc. 3p. sg. αὐτός ή ό self, of oneself, even, very, the same, he, she, it
καὶ conj. καί and, even, also, but
αὐτὸς pron. nom. masc. 3p. sg. αὐτός ή ό self, of oneself, even, very, the same, he, she, it
ἀπὸ prep. ἀπό (+gen) from, of, out of, since, for, off, at, by, in, on
τῶν art. gen. neut. pl. ὁ ἡ τό the, this, that, he, she, it
ἔργων n. gen. neut. pl. ἔργον work, deed, doing labour
αὐτοῦ pron. gen. masc. 3p. sg. αὐτός ή ό self, of oneself, even, very, the same, he, she, it
ὥσπερ adv. ὥσπερ as, even as, like as
ἀπὸ prep. ἀπό (+gen) from, of, out of, since, for, off, at, by, in, on
τῶν art. gen. neut. pl. ὁ ἡ τό the, this, that, he, she, it
ἰδίων adj. gen. neut. pl. ἴδιος one's own, one's, privately
ὁ art. nom. masc. sg. ὁ ἡ τό the, this, that, he, she, it
Θεός n. nom. masc. sg. θεός God, god
11 οὖν conj. οὖν therefore, then, so, and, now, wherefore
εἰς prep. εἰς (+acc) into, to, unto, for, in, on, toward, against, upon, at, among
ἐκείνην demo. pron. acc. fem. sg. ἐκεῖνος that, he, the same, that same
τὴν art. acc. fem. sg. ὁ ἡ τό the, this, that, he, she, it
κατάπαυσιν n. acc. fem. sg. κατάπαυσις rest
ἵνα conj. ἵνα that, to, lest, for to, so that, albeit, because, for, so as
μὴ particle of negation. μή not, no, lest, neither, none, nothing, nor, never, without

ἐν prep. ἐν (+dat) in, by, with, among, at, on, through, to, within, into, of, for
τῷ art. dat. neut. sg. ὁ ἡ τό the, this, that, he, she, it
αὐτῷ adj. dat. neut. sg. αὐτός ἡ ὁ self, of oneself, even, very, the same, he, she, it
τις indefinite pron. nom. masc. sg. τὶς certain, some, any man, one, any thing
ὑποδείγματι n. dat. neut. sg. ὑπόδειγμα example, ensample, pattern
τῆς art. gen. fem. sg. ὁ ἡ τό the, this, that, he, she, it
ἀπειθείας n. gen. fem. sg. ἀπείθεια unbelief, disobedience
12 γὰρ conj. γάρ for, and, because, but, indeed
ὁ art. nom. masc. sg. ὁ ἡ τό the, this, that, he, she, it
λόγος n. nom. masc. sg. λόγος word, saying, account, speech, thing, matter
τοῦ art. gen. masc. sg. ὁ ἡ τό the, this, that, he, she, it
Θεοῦ n. gen. masc. sg. θεός God, god
καὶ conj. καί and, even, also, but
ἐνεργὴς adj. nom. masc. sg. ἐνεργής effectual, powerful
καὶ conj. καί and, even, also, but
τομώτερος compar. adj. nom. masc. sg. τομώτερος sharper
ὑπὲρ prep. ὑπέρ (+gen) for, of, for the sake of, (+acc) above, more than
πᾶσαν adj. acc. fem. sg. πᾶς πᾶσα πᾶν all, every, whosoever, every one, no, whole, any
μάχαιραν n. acc. fem. sg. μάχαιρα sword
δίστομον adj. acc. fem. sg. δίστομος twoedged, with two edges
καὶ conj. καί and, even, also, but
ἄχρι prep. ἄχρι or ἄχρις (+gen) until, unto, till, even to, as far as, while, into
μερισμοῦ n. gen. masc. sg. μερισμός gift, dividing asunder
ψυχῆς n. gen. fem. sg. ψυχή life, soul, mind, heart
τε conj. τέ and, both, also
καὶ conj. καί and, even, also, but
πνεύματος n. gen. neut. sg. πνεῦμα spirit, Spirit, Ghost, ghost, life. of the spirit, wind
ἁρμῶν n. gen. masc. pl. ἁρμός joint
τε conj. τέ and, both, also
καὶ conj. καί and, even, also, but
μυελῶν n. gen. masc. pl. μυελός marrow
καὶ conj. καί and, even, also, but
κριτικὸς adj. nom. masc. sg. κριτικός discerner
ἐνθυμήσεων n. gen. fem. pl. ἐνθύμησις thought, device
καὶ conj. καί and, even, also, but
ἐννοιῶν n. gen. fem. pl. ἔννοια intent, mind
καρδίας n. gen. fem. sg. καρδία heart
13 καὶ conj. καί and, even, also, but
οὐκ particle of negation. οὐ οὐκ οὐχ not, no, neither, none, nay, nor, never, nothing
κτίσις n. nom. fem. sg. κτίσις creature, creation, building, ordinance
ἀφανὴς adj. nom. fem. sg. ἀφανής that is not manifest
ἐνώπιον prep. ἐνώπιον (+gen) before, in the sight of, in the presence of. (adv.) before
αὐτοῦ pron. gen. masc. 3p. sg. αὐτός ἡ ὁ self, of oneself, even, very, the same, he, she, it
πάντα adj. nom. neut. pl. πᾶς πᾶσα πᾶν all, every, whosoever, every one, no, whole, any
δὲ conj. δέ but, and, now, also, to the contrary, rather, then
γυμνὰ adj. nom. neut. pl. γυμνός naked, bare
καὶ conj. καί and, even, also, but
τοῖς art. dat. masc. pl. ὁ ἡ τό the, this, that, he, she, it
ὀφθαλμοῖς n. dat. masc. pl. ὀφθαλμός eye, sight
αὐτοῦ pron. gen. masc. 3p. sg. αὐτός ἡ ὁ self, of oneself, even, very, the same, he, she, it
πρὸς prep. πρός (+gen) for, (+dat) at, (+acc) unto, to, with, for, against
ὃν relative pron. acc. masc. sg. ὅς ἥ ὅ who, which, what, that
ἡμῖν pron. dat. 1p. pl. ἐγώ I
ὁ art. nom. masc. sg. ὁ ἡ τό the, this, that, he, she, it
λόγος n. nom. masc. sg. λόγος word, saying, account, speech, thing, matter

14 οὖν conj. οὖν therefore, then, so, and, now, wherefore
ἀρχιερέα n. acc. masc. sg. ἀρχιερεύς chief priest, high priest
μέγαν adj. acc. masc. sg. μέγας great, loud, greatest, high, large, mighty, strong
τοὺς art. acc. masc. pl. ὁ ἡ τό the, this, that, he, she, it
οὐρανούς n. acc. masc. pl. οὐρανός heaven, air, sky
Ἰησοῦν n. acc. masc. sg. Ἰησοῦς Jesus
τὸν art. acc. masc. sg. ὁ ἡ τό the, this, that, he, she, it
υἱὸν n. acc. masc. sg. υἱός son, child, descendant, offspring, heir
τοῦ art. gen. masc. sg. ὁ ἡ τό the, this, that, he, she, it
Θεοῦ n. gen. masc. sg. θεός God, god
τῆς art. gen. fem. sg. ὁ ἡ τό the, this, that, he, she, it
ὁμολογίας n. gen. fem. sg. ὁμολογία profession, confession, profess
15 οὐ particle of negation. οὐ οὐκ οὐχ not, no, neither, none, nay, nor, never, nothing
γὰρ conj. γάρ for, and, because, but, indeed
ἀρχιερέα n. acc. masc. sg. ἀρχιερεύς chief priest, high priest
μὴ particle of negation. μή not, no, lest, neither, none, nothing, nor, never, without
ταῖς art. dat. fem. pl. ὁ ἡ τό the, this, that, he, she, it
ἀσθενείαις n. dat. fem. pl. ἀσθένεια infirmity, weakness, disease, sickness
ἡμῶν pron. gen. 1p. pl. ἐγώ I
δὲ conj. δέ but, and, now, also, to the contrary, rather, then
κατὰ prep. κατά (+gen) against, by, throughout, down, (+acc) according to, after, with
πάντα adj. acc. neut. pl. πᾶς πᾶσα πᾶν all, every, whosoever, every one, no, whole, any
καθ' prep. κατά (+gen) against, by, throughout, down, (+acc) according to, after, with
ὁμοιότητα n. acc. fem. sg. ὁμοιότης like, similitude
χωρὶς prep. χωρίς (+gen) without, beside. (adv.) by itself, apart, separately
ἁμαρτίας n. gen. fem. sg. ἁμαρτία sin, offence, sinful
16 οὖν conj. οὖν therefore, then, so, and, now, wherefore
μετὰ prep. μετά (+gen) with, among, against, (+acc) after
παρρησίας n. gen. fem. sg. παρρησία boldness, confidence, openly, plainly, freely
τῷ art. dat. masc. sg. ὁ ἡ τό the, this, that, he, she, it
θρόνῳ n. dat. masc. sg. θρόνος throne, seat
τῆς art. gen. fem. sg. ὁ ἡ τό the, this, that, he, she, it
χάριτος n. gen. fem. sg. χάρις grace, thank, favour, pleasure
ἵνα conj. ἵνα that, to, lest, for to, so that, albeit, because, for, so as
ἔλεον n. acc. masc. sg. ἔλεος mercy
καὶ conj. καί and, even, also, but
χάριν n. acc. fem. sg. χάρις grace, thank, favour, pleasure
εἰς prep. εἰς (+acc) into, to, unto, for, in, on, toward, against, upon, at, among
εὔκαιρον adj. acc. fem. sg. εὔκαιρος convenient, in time of, seasonable
βοήθειαν n. acc. fem. sg. βοήθεια help, need

5

1 Πᾶς adj. nom. masc. sg. πᾶς πᾶσα πᾶν all, every, whosoever, every one, no, whole, any
γὰρ conj. γάρ for, and, because, but, indeed
ἀρχιερεὺς n. nom. masc. sg. ἀρχιερεύς chief priest, high priest
ἐξ prep. ἐκ ἐξ (+gen) of, from, out of, by, on, with, in, among, through
ἀνθρώπων n. gen. masc. pl. ἄνθρωπος man, human being, person, one, certain
ὑπὲρ prep. ὑπέρ (+gen) for, of, for the sake of, (+acc) above, more than
ἀνθρώπων n. gen. masc. pl. ἄνθρωπος man, human being, person, one, certain
τὰ art. acc. neut. pl. ὁ ἡ τό the, this, that, he, she, it
πρὸς prep. πρός (+gen) for, (+dat) at, (+acc) unto, to, with, for, against
τὸν art. acc. masc. sg. ὁ ἡ τό the, this, that, he, she, it
Θεόν n. acc. masc. sg. θεός God, god
ἵνα conj. ἵνα that, to, lest, for to, so that, albeit, because, for, so as

δῶρά n. acc. neut. pl. δῶρον gift, offering
τε conj. τέ and, both, also
καὶ conj. καί and, even, also, but
θυσίας n. acc. fem. pl. θυσία sacrifice
ὑπὲρ prep. ὑπέρ (+gen) for, of, for the sake of, (+acc) above, more than
ἁμαρτιῶν n. gen. fem. pl. ἁμαρτία sin, offence, sinful
2 τοῖς art. dat. masc. pl. ὁ ἡ τό the, this, that, he, she, it
καὶ conj. καί and, even, also, but
ἐπεὶ conj. ἐπεί because, otherwise, seeing, else, for then, for as much as, for, since
καὶ conj. καί and, even, also, but
αὐτὸς pron. nom. masc. 3p. sg. αὐτός ἡ ὁ self, of oneself, even, very, the same, he, she, it
ἀσθένειαν n. acc. fem. sg. ἀσθένεια infirmity, weakness, disease, sickness
3 καὶ conj. καί and, even, also, but
διὰ prep. διά (+gen) by, through, with, in, of, (+acc) for, because of, for a cause
ταύτην demo. pron. acc. fem. sg. οὗτος αὕτη τοῦτο this, the same, this same, he, she, it
καθὼς adv. καθώς as, even as, according as, according to
περὶ prep. περί (+gen) of, for, concerning, (+acc) about, concerning, in
τοῦ art. gen. masc. sg. ὁ ἡ τό the, this, that, he, she, it
λαοῦ n. gen. masc. sg. λαός people
οὕτω adv. οὕτω οὕτως so, even so, thus, on this wise, likewise, after this manner
καὶ conj. καί and, even, also, but
περὶ prep. περί (+gen) of, for, concerning, (+acc) about, concerning, in
ἑαυτοῦ reflexive pron. gen. masc. 3p. sg. ἑαυτοῦ himself, herself, itself, yourself, ourselves
ὑπὲρ prep. ὑπέρ (+gen) for, of, for the sake of, (+acc) above, more than
ἁμαρτιῶν n. gen. fem. pl. ἁμαρτία sin, offence, sinful
4 καὶ conj. καί and, even, also, but
οὐχ particle of negation. οὐ οὐκ οὐχ not, no, neither, none, nay, nor, never, nothing
ἑαυτῷ reflexive pron. dat. masc. 3p. sg. ἑαυτοῦ himself, herself, itself, yourself, ourselves
τις indefinite pron. nom. masc. sg. τὶς certain, some, any man, one, any thing
τὴν art. acc. fem. sg. ὁ ἡ τό the, this, that, he, she, it
τιμὴν n. acc. fem. sg. τιμή honour, price, preciousness, sum
ἀλλὰ conj. ἀλλά but, yea, yet, nevertheless, howbeit, nay, therefore
ὁ art. nom. masc. sg. ὁ ἡ τό the, this, that, he, she, it
ὑπὸ prep. ὑπό (+gen) of, by, with, from, among, (+acc) under
τοῦ art. gen. masc. sg. ὁ ἡ τό the, this, that, he, she, it
Θεοῦ n. gen. masc. sg. θεός God, god
καθάπερ adv. καθάπερ even as, as, as well as
καὶ conj. καί and, even, also, but
ὁ art. nom. masc. sg. ὁ ἡ τό the, this, that, he, she, it
Ἀαρών n. nom. masc. sg. Ἀαρών Aaron
5 οὕτω adv. οὕτω οὕτως so, even so, thus, on this wise, likewise, after this manner
καὶ conj. καί and, even, also, but
ὁ art. nom. masc. sg. ὁ ἡ τό the, this, that, he, she, it
Χριστὸς n. nom. masc. sg. Χριστός Christ
οὐχ particle of negation. οὐ οὐκ οὐχ not, no, neither, none, nay, nor, never, nothing
ἑαυτὸν reflexive pron. acc. masc. 3p. sg. ἑαυτοῦ himself, herself, itself, yourself, ourselves
ἀρχιερέα n. acc. masc. sg. ἀρχιερεύς chief priest, high priest
ἀλλ' conj. ἀλλά but, yea, yet, nevertheless, howbeit, nay, therefore
ὁ art. nom. masc. sg. ὁ ἡ τό the, this, that, he, she, it
πρὸς prep. πρός (+gen) for, (+dat) at, (+acc) unto, to, with, for, against
αὐτόν pron. acc. masc. 3p. sg. αὐτός ἡ ὁ self, of oneself, even, very, the same, he, she, it
Υἱός n. nom. masc. sg. υἱός son, child, descendant, offspring, heir
μου pron. gen. 1p. sg. ἐγώ I
σύ pron. nom. 2p. sg. σύ thou, you
ἐγὼ pron. nom. 1p. sg. ἐγώ I

σήμερον adv. σήμερον this day, today
σε pron. acc. 2p. sg. σύ thou, you
6 καθὼς adv. καθώς as, even as, according as, according to
καὶ conj. καί and, even, also, but
ἐν prep. ἐν (+dat) in, by, with, among, at, on, through, to, within, into, of, for
ἑτέρῳ adj. dat. masc. sg. ἕτερος another, other, else, strange
Σὺ pron. nom. 2p. sg. σύ thou, you
ἱερεὺς n. nom. masc. sg. ἱερεύς priest
εἰς prep. εἰς (+acc) into, to, unto, for, in, on, toward, against, upon, at, among
τὸν art. acc. masc. sg. ὁ ἡ τό the, this, that, he, she, it
αἰῶνα n. acc. masc. sg. αἰών ever, ever and ever, evermore, age, eternal, world
κατὰ prep. κατά (+gen) against, by, throughout, down, (+acc) according to, after, with
τὴν art. acc. fem. sg. ὁ ἡ τό the, this, that, he, she, it
τάξιν n. acc. fem. sg. τάξις order
Μελχισέδεκ n. gen. masc. sg. Μελχισέδεκ Melchisedec
7 ὃς relative pron. nom. masc. sg. ὅς ἥ ὅ who, which, what, that
ἐν prep. ἐν (+dat) in, by, with, among, at, on, through, to, within, into, of, for
ταῖς art. dat. fem. pl. ὁ ἡ τό the, this, that, he, she, it
ἡμέραις n. dat. fem. pl. ἡμέρα day, time, year, while, age, day time
τῆς art. gen. fem. sg. ὁ ἡ τό the, this, that, he, she, it
σαρκὸς n. gen. fem. sg. σάρξ flesh, carnal
αὐτοῦ pron. gen. masc. 3p. sg. αὐτός ή ό self, of oneself, even, very, the same, he, she, it
δεήσεις n. acc. fem. pl. δέησις prayer, supplication, request
τε conj. τέ and, both, also
καὶ conj. καί and, even, also, but
ἱκετηρίας n. acc. fem. pl. ἱκετηρία supplication
πρὸς prep. πρός (+gen) for, (+dat) at, (+acc) unto, to, with, for, against
τὸν art. acc. masc. sg. ὁ ἡ τό the, this, that, he, she, it
αὐτὸν pron. acc. masc. 3p. sg. αὐτός ή ό self, of oneself, even, very, the same, he, she, it
ἐκ prep. ἐκ ἐξ (+gen) of, from, out of, by, on, with, in, among, through
θανάτου n. gen. masc. sg. θάνατος death
μετὰ prep. μετά (+gen) with, among, against, (+acc) after
κραυγῆς n. gen. fem. sg. κραυγή cry, crying, clamour
ἰσχυρᾶς adj. gen. fem. sg. ἰσχυρός mighty, strong, mightier, stronger
καὶ conj. καί and, even, also, but
δακρύων n. gen. neut. pl. δάκρυον tears
καὶ conj. καί and, even, also, but
ἀπὸ prep. ἀπό (+gen) from, of, out of, since, for, off, at, by, in, on
τῆς art. gen. fem. sg. ὁ ἡ τό the, this, that, he, she, it
εὐλαβείας n. gen. fem. sg. εὐλάβεια fear, fearing, godly fear
8 καίπερ conj. καίπερ though, and yet
υἱός n. nom. masc. sg. υἱός son, child, descendant, offspring, heir
ἀφ' prep. ἀπό (+gen) from, of, out of, since, for, off, at, by, in, on
ὧν relative pron. gen. neut. pl. ὅς ἥ ὅ who, which, what, that
τὴν art. acc. fem. sg. ὁ ἡ τό the, this, that, he, she, it
ὑπακοήν n. acc. fem. sg. ὑπακοή obedience, obey, make obedient, obedient
9 καὶ conj. καί and, even, also, but
τοῖς art. dat. masc. pl. ὁ ἡ τό the, this, that, he, she, it
αὐτῷ pron. dat. masc. 3p. sg. αὐτός ή ό self, of oneself, even, very, the same, he, she, it
πᾶσιν adj. dat. masc. pl. πᾶς πᾶσα πᾶν all, every, whosoever, every one, no, whole, any
αἴτιος adj. nom. masc. sg. αἴτιος cause, fault, author
σωτηρίας n. gen. fem. sg. σωτηρία salvation, deliver, health, saving
αἰωνίου adj. gen. fem. sg. αἰώνιος eternal, everlasting, world, for ever
10 ὑπὸ prep. ὑπό (+gen) of, by, with, from, among, (+acc) under
τοῦ art. gen. masc. sg. ὁ ἡ τό the, this, that, he, she, it

Θεοῦ n. gen. masc. sg. θεός God, god
ἀρχιερεὺς n. nom. masc. sg. ἀρχιερεύς chief priest, high priest
κατὰ prep. κατά (+gen) against, by, throughout, down, (+acc) according to, after, with
τὴν art. acc. fem. sg. ὁ ἡ τό the, this, that, he, she, it
τάξιν n. acc. fem. sg. τάξις order
Μελχισέδεκ n. gen. masc. sg. Μελχισέδεκ Melchisedec
11 Περὶ prep. περί (+gen) of, for, concerning, (+acc) about, concerning, in
οὗ relative pron. gen. masc. sg. ὅς ἥ ὅ who, which, what, that
πολὺς adj. nom. masc. sg. πολύς many, great, much, long, abundant
ἡμῖν pron. dat. 1p. pl. ἐγώ I
ὁ art. nom. masc. sg. ὁ ἡ τό the, this, that, he, she, it
λόγος n. nom. masc. sg. λόγος word, saying, account, speech, thing, matter
καὶ conj. καί and, even, also, but
δυσερμήνευτος adj. nom. masc. sg. δυσερμήνευτος hard to be uttered
ἐπεὶ conj. ἐπεί because, otherwise, seeing, else, for then, for as much as, for, since
νωθροὶ adj. nom. masc. pl. νωθρός dull, slothful
ταῖς art. dat. fem. pl. ὁ ἡ τό the, this, that, he, she, it
ἀκοαῖς n. dat. fem. pl. ἀκοή hearing, ear, fame, report, rumour, which one heard
12 καὶ conj. καί and, even, also, but
γὰρ conj. γάρ for, and, because, but, indeed
διδάσκαλοι n. nom. masc. pl. διδάσκαλος teacher, master, doctor
διὰ prep. διά (+gen) by, through, with, in, of, (+acc) for, because of, for a cause
τὸν art. acc. masc. sg. ὁ ἡ τό the, this, that, he, she, it
χρόνον n. acc. masc. sg. χρόνος time, season, space
πάλιν adv. πάλιν again
χρείαν n. acc. fem. sg. χρεία need, necessity, lack, want
τοῦ art. gen. neut. sg. ὁ ἡ τό the, this, that, he, she, it
ὑμᾶς pron. acc. 2p. pl. σύ thou, you
τινὰ indefinite pron. acc. masc. sg. τὶς certain, some, any man, one, any thing
τὰ art. acc. neut. pl. ὁ ἡ τό the, this, that, he, she, it
στοιχεῖα n. acc. neut. pl. στοιχεῖον element, rudiment, principle
τῆς art. gen. fem. sg. ὁ ἡ τό the, this, that, he, she, it
ἀρχῆς n. gen. fem. sg. ἀρχή beginning, principality, corner, first, magistrate, rule
τῶν art. gen. neut. pl. ὁ ἡ τό the, this, that, he, she, it
λογίων n. gen. neut. pl. λόγιον oracle
τοῦ art. gen. masc. sg. ὁ ἡ τό the, this, that, he, she, it
Θεοῦ n. gen. masc. sg. θεός God, god
καὶ conj. καί and, even, also, but
χρείαν n. acc. fem. sg. χρεία need, necessity, lack, want
γάλακτος n. gen. neut. sg. γάλα milk
καὶ conj. καί and, even, also, but
οὐ particle of negation. οὐ οὐκ οὐχ not, no, neither, none, nay, nor, never, nothing
στερεᾶς adj. gen. fem. sg. στερεός sure, stedfast, strong, solid
τροφῆς n. gen. fem. sg. τροφή meat, food
13 πᾶς adj. nom. masc. sg. πᾶς πᾶσα πᾶν all, every, whosoever, every one, no, whole, any
γὰρ conj. γάρ for, and, because, but, indeed
ὁ art. nom. masc. sg. ὁ ἡ τό the, this, that, he, she, it
γάλακτος n. gen. neut. sg. γάλα milk
ἄπειρος adj. nom. masc. sg. ἄπειρος unskilful
λόγου n. gen. masc. sg. λόγος word, saying, account, speech, thing, matter
δικαιοσύνης n. gen. fem. sg. δικαιοσύνη righteousness
νήπιος adj. nom. masc. sg. νήπιος babe, child, childish
γὰρ conj. γάρ for, and, because, but, indeed
14 τελείων adj. gen. masc. pl. τέλειος perfect, of full age
δέ conj. δέ but, and, now, also, to the contrary, rather, then

ἡ art. nom. fem. sg. ὁ ἡ τό the, this, that, he, she, it
στερεὰ adj. nom. fem. sg. στερεός sure, stedfast, strong, solid
τροφή n. nom. fem. sg. τροφή meat, food
τῶν art. gen. masc. pl. ὁ ἡ τό the, this, that, he, she, it
διὰ prep. διά (+gen) by, through, with, in, of, (+acc) for, because of, for a cause
τὴν art. acc. fem. sg. ὁ ἡ τό the, this, that, he, she, it
ἕξιν n. acc. fem. sg. ἕξις use
τὰ art. acc. neut. pl. ὁ ἡ τό the, this, that, he, she, it
αἰσθητήρια n. acc. neut. pl. αἰσθητήριον sense
πρὸς prep. πρός (+gen) for, (+dat) at, (+acc) unto, to, with, for, against
διάκρισιν n. acc. fem. sg. διάκρισις disputations, discern, discerning
καλοῦ adj. gen. neut. sg. καλός good, better, goodly, meet, honest, fair, well, worthy
τε conj. τέ and, both, also
καὶ conj. καί and, even, also, but
κακοῦ adj. gen. neut. sg. κακός evil, evil thing, noisome, wicked

6

1 Διὸ conj. διό wherefore, therefore, for which cause
τὸν art. acc. masc. sg. ὁ ἡ τό the, this, that, he, she, it
τῆς art. gen. fem. sg. ὁ ἡ τό the, this, that, he, she, it
ἀρχῆς n. gen. fem. sg. ἀρχή beginning, principality, corner, first, magistrate, rule
τοῦ art. gen. masc. sg. ὁ ἡ τό the, this, that, he, she, it
Χριστοῦ n. gen. masc. sg. Χριστός Christ
λόγον n. acc. masc. sg. λόγος word, saying, account, speech, thing, matter
ἐπὶ prep. ἐπί (+gen) on, in, upon, (+dat) in, at, for, upon, (+acc) on, upon, unto, to, against
τὴν art. acc. fem. sg. ὁ ἡ τό the, this, that, he, she, it
τελειότητα n. acc. fem. sg. τελειότης perfectness, perfection
μὴ particle of negation. μή not, no, lest, neither, none, nothing, nor, never, without
πάλιν adv. πάλιν again
θεμέλιον n. acc. masc. sg. θεμέλιος foundation
μετανοίας n. gen. fem. sg. μετάνοια repentance
ἀπὸ prep. ἀπό (+gen) from, of, out of, since, for, off, at, by, in, on
νεκρῶν adj. gen. neut. pl. νεκρός dead
ἔργων n. gen. neut. pl. ἔργον work, deed, doing labour
καὶ conj. καί and, even, also, but
πίστεως n. gen. fem. sg. πίστις faith, assurance, belief, fidelity
ἐπὶ prep. ἐπί (+gen) on, in, upon, (+dat) in, at, for, upon, (+acc) on, upon, unto, to, against
Θεόν n. acc. masc. sg. θεός God, god
2 βαπτισμῶν n. gen. masc. pl. βαπτισμός washing, baptism
διδαχῆς n. gen. fem. sg. διδαχή doctrine, teaching
ἐπιθέσεώς n. gen. fem. sg. ἐπίθεσις putting on, laying on
τε conj. τέ and, both, also
χειρῶν n. gen. fem. pl. χείρ hand
ἀναστάσεώς n. gen. fem. sg. ἀνάστασις resurrection, rising again
τε conj. τέ and, both, also
νεκρῶν adj. gen. masc. pl. νεκρός dead
καὶ conj. καί and, even, also, but
κρίματος n. gen. neut. sg. κρίμα judgment, damnation, condemnation
αἰωνίου adj. gen. neut. sg. αἰώνιος eternal, everlasting, world, for ever
3 καὶ conj. καί and, even, also, but
τοῦτο demo. pron. acc. neut. sg. οὗτος αὕτη τοῦτο this, the same, this same, he, she, it
ἐάνπερ conj. ἐάνπερ if it be that, if at all events
ὁ art. nom. masc. sg. ὁ ἡ τό the, this, that, he, she, it
Θεός n. nom. masc. sg. θεός God, god

4 ἀδύνατον adj. nom. neut. sg. ἀδύνατος impossible, not possible, cannot do
γὰρ conj. γάρ for, and, because, but, indeed
τοὺς art. acc. masc. pl. ὁ ἡ τό the, this, that, he, she, it
ἅπαξ adv. ἅπαξ once
τε conj. τέ and, both, also
τῆς art. gen. fem. sg. ὁ ἡ τό the, this, that, he, she, it
δωρεᾶς n. gen. fem. sg. δωρεά gift
τῆς art. gen. fem. sg. ὁ ἡ τό the, this, that, he, she, it
ἐπουρανίου adj. gen. fem. sg. ἐπουράνιος heavenly, celestial, high, in heaven
καὶ conj. καί and, even, also, but
μετόχους adj. acc. masc. pl. μέτοχος partner, partaker, fellow
Πνεύματος n. gen. neut. sg. πνεῦμα spirit, Spirit, Ghost, ghost, life. of the spirit, wind
Ἁγίου adj. gen. neut. sg. ἅγιος Holy, holy, saint, Holy One, holy thing, most holy
5 καὶ conj. καί and, even, also, but
καλὸν adj. acc. neut. sg. καλός good, better, goodly, meet, honest, fair, well, worthy
Θεοῦ n. gen. masc. sg. θεός God, god
ῥῆμα n. acc. neut. sg. ῥῆμα word, saying, thing
δυνάμεις n. acc. fem. pl. δύναμις power, mighty work, miracle, strength, might
τε conj. τέ and, both, also
αἰῶνος n. gen. masc. sg. αἰών ever, ever and ever, evermore, age, eternal, world
6 καὶ conj. καί and, even, also, but
πάλιν adv. πάλιν again
εἰς prep. εἰς (+acc) into, to, unto, for, in, on, toward, against, upon, at, among
μετάνοιαν n. acc. fem. sg. μετάνοια repentance
ἑαυτοῖς reflexive pron. dat. masc. 3p. pl. ἑαυτοῦ himself, herself, itself, yourself, ourselves
τὸν art. acc. masc. sg. ὁ ἡ τό the, this, that, he, she, it
υἱὸν n. acc. masc. sg. υἱός son, child, descendant, offspring, heir
τοῦ art. gen. masc. sg. ὁ ἡ τό the, this, that, he, she, it
Θεοῦ n. gen. masc. sg. θεός God, god
καὶ conj. καί and, even, also, but
7 γῆ n. nom. fem. sg. γῆ earth, land, ground, country
γὰρ conj. γάρ for, and, because, but, indeed
ἡ art. nom. fem. sg. ὁ ἡ τό the, this, that, he, she, it
τὸν art. acc. masc. sg. ὁ ἡ τό the, this, that, he, she, it
ἐπ' prep. ἐπί (+gen) on, in, upon, (+dat) in, at, for, upon, (+acc) on, upon, unto, to, against
αὐτῆς pron. gen. fem. 3p. sg. αὐτός ἡ ὁ self, of oneself, even, very, the same, he, she, it
πολλάκις adv. πολλάκις often, ofttimes, oft
ὑετὸν n. acc. masc. sg. ὑετός rain
καὶ conj. καί and, even, also, but
βοτάνην n. acc. fem. sg. βοτάνη herb
εὔθετον adj. acc. fem. sg. εὔθετος fit, meet
ἐκείνοις demo. pron. dat. masc. pl. ἐκεῖνος that, he, the same, that same
δι' prep. διά (+gen) by, through, with, in, of, (+acc) for, because of, for a cause
οὓς relative pron. acc. masc. pl. ὅς ἥ ὅ who, which, what, that
καὶ conj. καί and, even, also, but
εὐλογίας n. gen. fem. sg. εὐλογία blessing, bounty, matter of bounty, fair speech
ἀπὸ prep. ἀπό (+gen) from, of, out of, since, for, off, at, by, in, on
τοῦ art. gen. masc. sg. ὁ ἡ τό the, this, that, he, she, it
Θεοῦ n. gen. masc. sg. θεός God, god
8 δὲ conj. δέ but, and, now, also, to the contrary, rather, then
ἀκάνθας n. acc. fem. pl. ἄκανθα thorn
καὶ conj. καί and, even, also, but
τριβόλους n. acc. masc. pl. τρίβολος thistle, brier
ἀδόκιμος adj. nom. fem. sg. ἀδόκιμος reprobate, castaway, rejected
καὶ conj. καί and, even, also, but

κατάρας n. gen. fem. sg. κατάρα curse, cursing, cursed
ἐγγύς adv. ἐγγύς nigh, at hand, near, nigh at hand, ready, nigh unto
ἧς relative pron. gen. fem. sg. ὅς ἥ ὅ who, which, what, that
τὸ art. nom. neut. sg. ὁ ἡ τό the, this, that, he, she, it
τέλος n. nom. neut. sg. τέλος end, custom, ending, finally, uttermost
εἰς prep. εἰς (+acc) into, to, unto, for, in, on, toward, against, upon, at, among
καῦσιν n. acc. fem. sg. καῦσις being burned, burning
9 δὲ conj. δέ but, and, now, also, to the contrary, rather, then
περὶ prep. περί (+gen) of, for, concerning, (+acc) about, concerning, in
ὑμῶν pron. gen. 2p. pl. σύ thou, you
ἀγαπητοί adj. voc. masc. pl. ἀγαπητός beloved, dearly beloved, dear, wellbeloved
τὰ art. acc. neut. pl. ὁ ἡ τό the, this, that, he, she, it
κρείσσονα compar. adj. acc. neut. pl. κρείσσων better
καὶ conj. καί and, even, also, but
σωτηρίας n. gen. fem. sg. σωτηρία salvation, deliver, health, saving
εἰ conj. εἰ if, whether, that, though, forasmuch
καὶ conj. καί and, even, also, but
οὕτω adv. οὕτω οὕτως so, even so, thus, on this wise, likewise, after this manner
10 οὐ particle of negation. οὐ οὐκ οὐχ not, no, neither, none, nay, nor, never, nothing
γὰρ conj. γάρ for, and, because, but, indeed
ἄδικος adj. nom. masc. sg. ἄδικος unjust, unrighteous
ὁ art. nom. masc. sg. ὁ ἡ τό the, this, that, he, she, it
Θεὸς n. nom. masc. sg. θεός God, god
τοῦ art. gen. neut. sg. ὁ ἡ τό the, this, that, he, she, it
ἔργου n. gen. neut. sg. ἔργον work, deed, doing labour
ὑμῶν pron. gen. 2p. pl. σύ thou, you
καὶ conj. καί and, even, also, but
τοῦ art. gen. masc. sg. ὁ ἡ τό the, this, that, he, she, it
κόπου n. gen. masc. sg. κόπος labour, trouble, weariness
τῆς art. gen. fem. sg. ὁ ἡ τό the, this, that, he, she, it
ἀγάπης n. gen. fem. sg. ἀγάπη love, charity, feast of charity
ἧς relative pron. gen. fem. sg. ὅς ἥ ὅ who, which, what, that
εἰς prep. εἰς (+acc) into, to, unto, for, in, on, toward, against, upon, at, among
τὸ art. acc. neut. sg. ὁ ἡ τό the, this, that, he, she, it
ὄνομα n. acc. neut. sg. ὄνομα name, call, surname
αὐτοῦ pron. gen. masc. 3p. sg. αὐτός ή ό self, of oneself, even, very, the same, he, she, it
τοῖς art. dat. masc. pl. ὁ ἡ τό the, this, that, he, she, it
ἁγίοις adj. dat. masc. pl. ἅγιος Holy, holy, saint, Holy One, holy thing, most holy
καὶ conj. καί and, even, also, but
11 δὲ conj. δέ but, and, now, also, to the contrary, rather, then
ἕκαστον adj. acc. masc. sg. ἕκαστος every man, every, every one, any man, each
ὑμῶν pron. gen. 2p. pl. σύ thou, you
τὴν art. acc. fem. sg. ὁ ἡ τό the, this, that, he, she, it
αὐτὴν adj. acc. fem. sg. αὐτός ή ό self, of oneself, even, very, the same, he, she, it
σπουδὴν n. acc. fem. sg. σπουδή diligence, haste, business, care, carefulness
πρὸς prep. πρός (+gen) for, (+dat) at, (+acc) unto, to, with, for, against
τὴν art. acc. fem. sg. ὁ ἡ τό the, this, that, he, she, it
πληροφορίαν n. acc. fem. sg. πληροφορία full assurance, assurance
τῆς art. gen. fem. sg. ὁ ἡ τό the, this, that, he, she, it
ἐλπίδος n. gen. fem. sg. ἐλπίς hope, faith
ἄχρι prep. ἄχρι or ἄχρις (+gen) until, unto, till, even to, as far as, while, into
τέλους n. gen. neut. sg. τέλος end, custom, ending, finally, uttermost
12 ἵνα conj. ἵνα that, to, lest, for to, so that, albeit, because, for, so as
μὴ particle of negation. μή not, no, lest, neither, none, nothing, nor, never, without
νωθροὶ adj. nom. masc. pl. νωθρός dull, slothful

μιμηταὶ n. nom. masc. pl. μιμητής follower
δὲ conj. δέ but, and, now, also, to the contrary, rather, then
τῶν art. gen. masc. pl. ὁ ἡ τό the, this, that, he, she, it
διὰ prep. διά (+gen) by, through, with, in, of, (+acc) for, because of, for a cause
πίστεως n. gen. fem. sg. πίστις faith, assurance, belief, fidelity
καὶ conj. καί and, even, also, but
μακροθυμίας n. gen. fem. sg. μακροθυμία longsuffering, patience
τὰς art. acc. fem. pl. ὁ ἡ τό the, this, that, he, she, it
ἐπαγγελίας n. acc. fem. pl. ἐπαγγελία promise, message
13 Τῷ art. dat. masc. sg. ὁ ἡ τό the, this, that, he, she, it
γὰρ conj. γάρ for, and, because, but, indeed
'Αβραὰμ n. dat. masc. sg. 'Αβραάμ Abraham
ὁ art. nom. masc. sg. ὁ ἡ τό the, this, that, he, she, it
Θεός n. nom. masc. sg. θεός God, god
ἐπεὶ conj. ἐπεί because, otherwise, seeing, else, for then, for as much as, for, since
κατ' prep. κατά (+gen) against, by, throughout, down, (+acc) according to, after, with
οὐδενὸς num. gen. masc. sg. οὐδείς no man, nothing, no, none, neither, not, nought
μείζονος compar. adj. gen. masc. sg. μέγας great, loud, greatest, high, large, mighty, strong
καθ' prep. κατά (+gen) against, by, throughout, down, (+acc) according to, after, with
ἑαυτοῦ reflexive pron. gen. masc. 3p. sg. ἑαυτοῦ himself, herself, itself, yourself, ourselves
14 Ἦ μὴν particle. ἦ μήν surely
σε pron. acc. 2p. sg. σύ thou, you
καὶ conj. καί and, even, also, but
σε pron. acc. 2p. sg. σύ thou, you
15 καὶ conj. καί and, even, also, but
οὕτω adv. οὕτω οὕτως so, even so, thus, on this wise, likewise, after this manner
τῆς art. gen. fem. sg. ὁ ἡ τό the, this, that, he, she, it
ἐπαγγελίας n. gen. fem. sg. ἐπαγγελία promise, message
16 ἄνθρωποι n. nom. masc. pl. ἄνθρωπος man, human being, person, one, certain
μὲν conj. μέν indeed, verily, truly, even, so, some
γὰρ conj. γάρ for, and, because, but, indeed
κατὰ prep. κατά (+gen) against, by, throughout, down, (+acc) according to, after, with
τοῦ art. gen. masc. sg. ὁ ἡ τό the, this, that, he, she, it
μείζονος compar. adj. gen. masc. sg. μέγας great, loud, greatest, high, large, mighty, strong
καὶ conj. καί and, even, also, but
πάσης adj. gen. fem. sg. πᾶς πᾶσα πᾶν all, every, whosoever, every one, no, whole, any
αὐτοῖς pron. dat. masc. 3p. pl. αὐτός ή ό self, of oneself, even, very, the same, he, she, it
ἀντιλογίας n. gen. fem. sg. ἀντιλογία strife, contradiction, gainsaying
πέρας n. nom. neut. sg. πέρας uttermost parts, utmost part, end
εἰς prep. εἰς (+acc) into, to, unto, for, in, on, toward, against, upon, at, among
βεβαίωσιν n. acc. fem. sg. βεβαίωσις confirmation
ὁ art. nom. masc. sg. ὁ ἡ τό the, this, that, he, she, it
ὅρκος n. nom. masc. sg. ὅρκος oath
17 ἐν prep. ἐν (+dat) in, by, with, among, at, on, through, to, within, into, of, for
ᾧ relative pron. dat. masc. sg. ὅς ἥ ὅ who, which, what, that
περισσότερον compar. adj. nom. neut. sg. περισσός more, beyond measure, advantage
ὁ art. nom. masc. sg. ὁ ἡ τό the, this, that, he, she, it
Θεὸς n. nom. masc. sg. θεός God, god
τοῖς art. dat. masc. pl. ὁ ἡ τό the, this, that, he, she, it
κληρονόμοις n. dat. masc. pl. κληρονόμος heir
τῆς art. gen. fem. sg. ὁ ἡ τό the, this, that, he, she, it
ἐπαγγελίας n. gen. fem. sg. ἐπαγγελία promise, message
τὸ art. acc. neut. sg. ὁ ἡ τό the, this, that, he, she, it
ἀμετάθετον adj. acc. neut. sg. ἀμετάθετος immutability, immutable
τῆς art. gen. fem. sg. ὁ ἡ τό the, this, that, he, she, it

βουλῆς n. gen. fem. sg. βουλή counsel, advise, will
αὐτοῦ pron. gen. masc. 3p. sg. αὐτός ἡ ὁ self, of oneself, even, very, the same, he, she, it
ὅρκῳ n. dat. masc. sg. ὅρκος oath
18 ἵνα conj. ἵνα that, to, lest, for to, so that, albeit, because, for, so as
διὰ prep. διά (+gen) by, through, with, in, of, (+acc) for, because of, for a cause
δύο num. gen. neut. pl. δύο two, twain, both
πραγμάτων n. gen. neut. pl. πρᾶγμα thing, matter, business, work
ἀμεταθέτων adj. gen. neut. pl. ἀμετάθετος immutability, immutable
ἐν prep. ἐν (+dat) in, by, with, among, at, on, through, to, within, into, of, for
οἷς relative pron. dat. neut. pl. ὅς ἥ ὅ who, which, what, that
ἀδύνατον adj. nom. neut. sg. ἀδύνατος impossible, not possible, cannot do
Θεόν n. acc. masc. sg. θεός God, god
ἰσχυρὰν adj. acc. fem. sg. ἰσχυρός mighty, strong, mightier, stronger
παράκλησιν n. acc. fem. sg. παράκλησις consolation, exhortation, comfort
οἱ art. nom. masc. pl. ὁ ἡ τό the, this, that, he, she, it
τῆς art. gen. fem. sg. ὁ ἡ τό the, this, that, he, she, it
ἐλπίδος n. gen. fem. sg. ἐλπίς hope, faith
19 ἣν relative pron. acc. fem. sg. ὅς ἥ ὅ who, which, what, that
ὡς adv. ὡς as, when, as it were, how, about, like, as soon as, even as, while
ἄγκυραν n. acc. fem. sg. ἄγκυρα anchor
τῆς art. gen. fem. sg. ὁ ἡ τό the, this, that, he, she, it
ψυχῆς n. gen. fem. sg. ψυχή life, soul, mind, heart
ἀσφαλῆ adj. acc. fem. sg. ἀσφαλής certainty, certain, safe, sure
τε conj. τέ and, both, also
καὶ conj. καί and, even, also, but
βεβαίαν adj. acc. fem. sg. βέβαιος sure, stedfast, firm, more sure, of force
καὶ conj. καί and, even, also, but
εἰς prep. εἰς (+acc) into, to, unto, for, in, on, toward, against, upon, at, among
τὸ art. acc. neut. sg. ὁ ἡ τό the, this, that, he, she, it
ἐσώτερον adj. acc. neut. sg. ἐσώτερος inner, within
τοῦ art. gen. neut. sg. ὁ ἡ τό the, this, that, he, she, it
καταπετάσματος n. gen. neut. sg. καταπέτασμα veil
20 ὅπου adv. ὅπου where, whither, whereas, in what place, wheresoever
πρόδρομος adj. nom. masc. sg. πρόδρομος forerunner
ὑπὲρ prep. ὑπέρ (+gen) for, of, for the sake of, (+acc) above, more than
ἡμῶν pron. gen. 1p. pl. ἐγώ I
Ἰησοῦς n. nom. masc. sg. Ἰησοῦς Jesus
κατὰ prep. κατά (+gen) against, by, throughout, down, (+acc) according to, after, with
τὴν art. acc. fem. sg. ὁ ἡ τό the, this, that, he, she, it
τάξιν n. acc. fem. sg. τάξις order
Μελχισέδεκ n. gen. masc. sg. Μελχισέδεκ Melchisedec
ἀρχιερεὺς n. nom. masc. sg. ἀρχιερεύς chief priest, high priest
εἰς prep. εἰς (+acc) into, to, unto, for, in, on, toward, against, upon, at, among
τὸν art. acc. masc. sg. ὁ ἡ τό the, this, that, he, she, it
αἰῶνα n. acc. masc. sg. αἰών ever, ever and ever, evermore, age, eternal, world

7

1 Οὗτος demo. pron. nom. masc. sg. οὗτος αὕτη τοῦτο this, the same, this same, he, she, it
γὰρ conj. γάρ for, and, because, but, indeed
ὁ art. nom. masc. sg. ὁ ἡ τό the, this, that, he, she, it
Μελχισέδεκ n. nom. masc. sg. Μελχισέδεκ Melchisedec
βασιλεὺς n. nom. masc. sg. βασιλεύς king
Σαλήμ n. gen. fem. sg. Σαλήμ Salem
ἱερεὺς n. nom. masc. sg. ἱερεύς priest

τοῦ art. gen. masc. sg. ὁ ἡ τό the, this, that, he, she, it
Θεοῦ n. gen. masc. sg. θεός God, god
τοῦ art. gen. masc. sg. ὁ ἡ τό the, this, that, he, she, it
ὑψίστου superl. adj. gen. masc. sg. ὕψιστος highest, Highest, most high, most High
ὁ art. nom. masc. sg. ὁ ἡ τό the, this, that, he, she, it
'Αβραὰμ n. dat. masc. sg. 'Αβραάμ Abraham
ἀπὸ prep. ἀπό (+gen) from, of, out of, since, for, off, at, by, in, on
τῆς art. gen. fem. sg. ὁ ἡ τό the, this, that, he, she, it
κοπῆς n. gen. fem. sg. κοπή slaughter
τῶν art. gen. masc. pl. ὁ ἡ τό the, this, that, he, she, it
βασιλέων n. gen. masc. pl. βασιλεύς king
καὶ conj. καί and, even, also, but
αὐτόν pron. acc. masc. 3p. sg. αὐτός ή ό self, of oneself, even, very, the same, he, she, it
2 ᾧ relative pron. dat. masc. sg. ὅς ἥ ὅ who, which, what, that
καὶ conj. καί and, even, also, but
δεκάτην ordinal. adj. acc. fem. sg. δέκατος tenth
ἀπὸ prep. ἀπό (+gen) from, of, out of, since, for, off, at, by, in, on
πάντων adj. gen. neut. pl. πᾶς πᾶσα πᾶν all, every, whosoever, every one, no, whole, any
'Αβραάμ n. nom. masc. sg. 'Αβραάμ Abraham
πρῶτον adv. πρῶτον first, at the first, first of all, at first, at the beginning, before, chiefly
μὲν conj. μέν indeed, verily, truly, even, so, some
βασιλεὺς n. nom. masc. sg. βασιλεύς king
δικαιοσύνης n. gen. fem. sg. δικαιοσύνη righteousness
ἔπειτα adv. ἔπειτα then, after that, afterward
δὲ conj. δέ but, and, now, also, to the contrary, rather, then
καὶ conj. καί and, even, also, but
βασιλεὺς n. nom. masc. sg. βασιλεύς king
Σαλήμ n. gen. fem. sg. Σαλήμ Salem
ὅ relative pron. nom. neut. sg. ὅς ἥ ὅ who, which, what, that
βασιλεὺς n. nom. masc. sg. βασιλεύς king
εἰρήνης n. gen. fem. sg. εἰρήνη peace, quietness, rest
3 ἀπάτωρ adj. nom. masc. sg. ἀπάτωρ without father
ἀμήτωρ adj. nom. masc. sg. ἀμήτωρ without mother
ἀγενεαλόγητος adj. nom. masc. sg. ἀγενεαλόγητος without descent
μήτε conj. μήτε neither, nor, so much as, or
ἀρχὴν n. acc. fem. sg. ἀρχή beginning, principality, corner, first, magistrate, rule
ἡμερῶν n. gen. fem. pl. ἡμέρα day, time, year, while, age, day time
μήτε conj. μήτε neither, nor, so much as, or
ζωῆς n. gen. fem. sg. ζωή life, lifetime
τέλος n. acc. neut. sg. τέλος end, custom, ending, finally, uttermost
δὲ conj. δέ but, and, now, also, to the contrary, rather, then
τῷ art. dat. masc. sg. ὁ ἡ τό the, this, that, he, she, it
υἱῷ n. dat. masc. sg. υἱός son, child, descendant, offspring, heir
τοῦ art. gen. masc. sg. ὁ ἡ τό the, this, that, he, she, it
Θεοῦ n. gen. masc. sg. θεός God, god
ἱερεὺς n. nom. masc. sg. ἱερεύς priest
εἰς prep. εἰς (+acc) into, to, unto, for, in, on, toward, against, upon, at, among
τὸ art. acc. neut. sg. ὁ ἡ τό the, this, that, he, she, it
διηνεκές adj. acc. neut. sg. διηνεκής continually, for ever
4 δὲ conj. δέ but, and, now, also, to the contrary, rather, then
πηλίκος interrog. pron. nom. masc. sg. πηλίκος how large, how great
οὗτος demo. pron. nom. masc. sg. οὗτος αὕτη τοῦτο this, the same, this same, he, she, it
ᾧ relative pron. dat. masc. sg. ὅς ἥ ὅ who, which, what, that
καὶ conj. καί and, even, also, but
δεκάτην ordinal. adj. acc. fem. sg. δέκατος tenth

'Αβραὰμ n. nom. masc. sg. 'Αβραάμ Abraham
ἐκ prep. ἐκ ἐξ (+gen) of, from, out of, by, on, with, in, among, through
τῶν art. gen. neut. pl. ὁ ἡ τό the, this, that, he, she, it
ἀκροθινίων n. gen. neut. pl. ἀκροθίνιον spoil
ὁ art. nom. masc. sg. ὁ ἡ τό the, this, that, he, she, it
πατριάρχης n. nom. masc. sg. πατριάρχης patriarch
5 καὶ conj. καί and, even, also, but
οἱ art. nom. masc. pl. ὁ ἡ τό the, this, that, he, she, it
μὲν conj. μέν indeed, verily, truly, even, so, some
ἐκ prep. ἐκ ἐξ (+gen) of, from, out of, by, on, with, in, among, through
τῶν art. gen. masc. pl. ὁ ἡ τό the, this, that, he, she, it
υἱῶν n. gen. masc. pl. υἱός son, child, descendant, offspring, heir
Λευὶ n. gen. masc. sg. Λευί Levi
τὴν art. acc. fem. sg. ὁ ἡ τό the, this, that, he, she, it
ἱερατείαν n. acc. fem. sg. ἱερατεία priest's office, office of the priesthood
ἐντολὴν n. acc. fem. sg. ἐντολή commandment, precept
τὸν art. acc. masc. sg. ὁ ἡ τό the, this, that, he, she, it
λαὸν n. acc. masc. sg. λαός people
κατὰ prep. κατά (+gen) against, by, throughout, down, (+acc) according to, after, with
τὸν art. acc. masc. sg. ὁ ἡ τό the, this, that, he, she, it
νόμον n. acc. masc. sg. νόμος law, the law
τοῦτ' demo. pron. nom. neut. sg. οὗτος αὕτη τοῦτο this, the same, this same, he, she, it
τοὺς art. acc. masc. pl. ὁ ἡ τό the, this, that, he, she, it
ἀδελφοὺς n. acc. masc. pl. ἀδελφός brother
αὐτῶν pron. gen. masc. 3p. pl. αὐτός ἡ ὁ self, of oneself, even, very, the same, he, she, it
καίπερ conj. καίπερ though, and yet
ἐκ prep. ἐκ ἐξ (+gen) of, from, out of, by, on, with, in, among, through
τῆς art. gen. fem. sg. ὁ ἡ τό the, this, that, he, she, it
ὀσφύος n. gen. fem. sg. ὀσφύς loins
'Αβραάμ n. gen. masc. sg. 'Αβραάμ Abraham
6 ὁ art. nom. masc. sg. ὁ ἡ τό the, this, that, he, she, it
δὲ conj. δέ but, and, now, also, to the contrary, rather, then
μὴ particle of negation. μή not, no, lest, neither, none, nothing, nor, never, without
ἐξ prep. ἐκ ἐξ (+gen) of, from, out of, by, on, with, in, among, through
αὐτῶν pron. gen. masc. 3p. pl. αὐτός ἡ ὁ self, of oneself, even, very, the same, he, she, it
τὸν art. acc. masc. sg. ὁ ἡ τό the, this, that, he, she, it
'Αβραὰμ n. acc. masc. sg. 'Αβραάμ Abraham
καὶ conj. καί and, even, also, but
τὸν art. acc. masc. sg. ὁ ἡ τό the, this, that, he, she, it
τὰς art. acc. fem. pl. ὁ ἡ τό the, this, that, he, she, it
ἐπαγγελίας n. acc. fem. pl. ἐπαγγελία promise, message
7 χωρὶς prep. χωρίς (+gen) without, beside. (adv.) by itself, apart, separately
δὲ conj. δέ but, and, now, also, to the contrary, rather, then
πάσης adj. gen. fem. sg. πᾶς πᾶσα πᾶν all, every, whosoever, every one, no, whole, any
ἀντιλογίας n. gen. fem. sg. ἀντιλογία strife, contradiction, gainsaying
τὸ art. nom. neut. sg. ὁ ἡ τό the, this, that, he, she, it
ἔλαττον compar. adj. nom. neut. sg. ἐλάττων worse, younger
ὑπὸ prep. ὑπό (+gen) of, by, with, from, among, (+acc) under
τοῦ art. gen. masc. sg. ὁ ἡ τό the, this, that, he, she, it
κρείττονος compar. adj. gen. masc. sg. κρείττων better
8 καὶ conj. καί and, even, also, but
ὧδε adv. ὧδε here, hither, in this place, there, this place
μὲν conj. μέν indeed, verily, truly, even, so, some
δεκάτας ordinal. adj. acc. fem. pl. δέκατος tenth
ἄνθρωποι n. nom. masc. pl. ἄνθρωπος man, human being, person, one, certain

ἐκεῖ adv. ἐκεῖ there, thither, thitherward, yonder, yonder place
δὲ conj. δέ but, and, now, also, to the contrary, rather, then
ὅτι conj. ὅτι that, for, because, how that, how, because that, for that, though
9 καὶ conj. καί and, even, also, but
ὡς adv. ὡς as, when, as it were, how, about, like, as soon as, even as, while
ἔπος n. acc. neut. sg. ἔπος word
διὰ prep. διά (+gen) by, through, with, in, of, (+acc) for, because of, for a cause
Ἀβραὰμ n. gen. masc. sg. Ἀβραάμ Abraham
καὶ conj. καί and, even, also, but
Λευῒ n. nom. masc. sg. Λευΐ Levi
ὁ art. nom. masc. sg. ὁ ἡ τό the, this, that, he, she, it
δεκάτας ordinal. adj. acc. fem. pl. δέκατος tenth
10 ἔτι adv. ἔτι yet, more, any more, further, still, moreover
γὰρ conj. γάρ for, and, because, but, indeed
ἐν prep. ἐν (+dat) in, by, with, among, at, on, through, to, within, into, of, for
τῇ art. dat. fem. sg. ὁ ἡ τό the, this, that, he, she, it
ὀσφύϊ n. dat. fem. sg. ὀσφύς loins
τοῦ art. gen. masc. sg. ὁ ἡ τό the, this, that, he, she, it
πατρὸς n. gen. masc. sg. πατήρ Father, father, parent
ὅτε adv. ὅτε when, after that, as soon as, while, after
αὐτῷ pron. dat. masc. 3p. sg. αὐτός ή ό self, of oneself, even, very, the same, he, she, it
ὁ art. nom. masc. sg. ὁ ἡ τό the, this, that, he, she, it
Μελχισέδεκ n. nom. masc. sg. Μελχισέδεκ Melchisedec
11 Εἰ conj. εἰ if, whether, that, though, forasmuch
μὲν conj. μέν indeed, verily, truly, even, so, some
οὖν conj. οὖν therefore, then, so, and, now, wherefore
τελείωσις n. nom. fem. sg. τελείωσις performance, perfection
διὰ prep. διά (+gen) by, through, with, in, of, (+acc) for, because of, for a cause
τῆς art. gen. fem. sg. ὁ ἡ τό the, this, that, he, she, it
Λευϊτικῆς adj. gen. fem. sg. Λευϊτικός Levitical
ἱερωσύνης n. gen. fem. sg. ἱερωσύνη priesthood
ὁ art. nom. masc. sg. ὁ ἡ τό the, this, that, he, she, it
λαὸς n. nom. masc. sg. λαός people
γὰρ conj. γάρ for, and, because, but, indeed
ἐπ' prep. ἐπί (+gen) on, in, upon, (+dat) in, at, for, upon, (+acc) on, upon, unto, to, against
αὐτῇ pron. dat. fem. 3p. sg. αὐτός ή ό self, of oneself, even, very, the same, he, she, it
τίς interrog. pron. nom. fem. sg. τίς what, who, why, where, which, how
ἔτι adv. ἔτι yet, more, any more, further, still, moreover
χρεία n. nom. fem. sg. χρεία need, necessity, lack, want
κατὰ prep. κατά (+gen) against, by, throughout, down, (+acc) according to, after, with
τὴν art. acc. fem. sg. ὁ ἡ τό the, this, that, he, she, it
τάξιν n. acc. fem. sg. τάξις order
Μελχισέδεκ n. gen. masc. sg. Μελχισέδεκ Melchisedec
ἕτερον adj. acc. masc. sg. ἕτερος another, other, else, strange
ἱερέα n. acc. masc. sg. ἱερεύς priest
καὶ conj. καί and, even, also, but
οὐ particle of negation. οὐ οὐκ οὐχ not, no, neither, none, nay, nor, never, nothing
κατὰ prep. κατά (+gen) against, by, throughout, down, (+acc) according to, after, with
τὴν art. acc. fem. sg. ὁ ἡ τό the, this, that, he, she, it
τάξιν n. acc. fem. sg. τάξις order
Ἀαρὼν n. gen. masc. sg. Ἀαρών Aaron
12 γὰρ conj. γάρ for, and, because, but, indeed
τῆς art. gen. fem. sg. ὁ ἡ τό the, this, that, he, she, it
ἱερωσύνης n. gen. fem. sg. ἱερωσύνη priesthood
ἐξ prep. ἐκ ἐξ (+gen) of, from, out of, by, on, with, in, among, through

ἀνάγκης n. gen. fem. sg. ἀνάγκη must needs, necessity, distress, inevitable
καὶ conj. καί and, even, also, but
νόμου n. gen. masc. sg. νόμος law, the law
μετάθεσις n. nom. fem. sg. μετάθεσις change, removing, translation
13 ἐφ' prep. ἐπί (+gen) on, in, upon, (+dat) in, at, for, upon, (+acc) on, upon, unto, to, against
ὃν relative pron. acc. masc. sg. ὅς ἥ ὅ who, which, what, that
γὰρ conj. γάρ for, and, because, but, indeed
ταῦτα demo. pron. nom. neut. pl. οὗτος αὕτη τοῦτο this, the same, this same, he, she, it
φυλῆς n. gen. fem. sg. φυλή tribe, kindred
ἑτέρας adj. gen. fem. sg. ἕτερος another, other, else, strange
ἀφ' prep. ἀπό (+gen) from, of, out of, since, for, off, at, by, in, on
ἧς relative pron. gen. fem. sg. ὅς ἥ ὅ who, which, what, that
οὐδεὶς num. nom. masc. sg. οὐδείς no man, nothing, no, none, neither, not, nought
τῷ art. dat. neut. sg. ὁ ἡ τό the, this, that, he, she, it
θυσιαστηρίῳ n. dat. neut. sg. θυσιαστήριον altar
14 πρόδηλον adj. nom. neut. sg. πρόδηλος open beforehand, manifest beforehand, evident
γὰρ conj. γάρ for, and, because, but, indeed
ὅτι conj. ὅτι that, for, because, how that, how, because that, for that, though
ἐξ prep. ἐκ ἐξ (+gen) of, from, out of, by, on, with, in, among, through
Ἰούδα n. gen. masc. sg. Ἰούδας Judas, Juda, Judah, Jude
ὁ art. nom. masc. sg. ὁ ἡ τό the, this, that, he, she, it
Κύριος n. nom. masc. sg. κύριος Lord, lord, master, sir, LORD, God, Master, owner
ἡμῶν pron. gen. 1p. pl. ἐγώ I
εἰς prep. εἰς (+acc) into, to, unto, for, in, on, toward, against, upon, at, among
ἣν relative pron. acc. fem. sg. ὅς ἥ ὅ who, which, what, that
φυλὴν n. acc. fem. sg. φυλή tribe, kindred
οὐδὲν num. acc. neut. sg. οὐδείς no man, nothing, no, none, neither, not, nought
περὶ prep. περί (+gen) of, for, concerning, (+acc) about, concerning, in
ἱερωσυνής n. gen. fem. sg. ἱερωσύνη priesthood
Μωσῆς n. nom. masc. sg. Μωσῆς Moses
15 καὶ conj. καί and, even, also, but
περισσότερον compar. adj. nom. neut. sg. περισσός more, beyond measure, advantage
ἔτι adv. ἔτι yet, more, any more, further, still, moreover
κατάδηλόν adj. nom. neut. sg. κατάδηλος evident
εἰ conj. εἰ if, whether, that, though, forasmuch
κατὰ prep. κατά (+gen) against, by, throughout, down, (+acc) according to, after, with
τὴν art. acc. fem. sg. ὁ ἡ τό the, this, that, he, she, it
ὁμοιότητα n. acc. fem. sg. ὁμοιότης like, similitude
Μελχισέδεκ n. gen. masc. sg. Μελχισέδεκ Melchisedec
ἱερεὺς n. nom. masc. sg. ἱερεύς priest
ἕτερος adj. nom. masc. sg. ἕτερος another, other, else, strange
16 ὃς relative pron. nom. masc. sg. ὅς ἥ ὅ who, which, what, that
οὐ particle of negation. οὐ οὐκ οὐχ not, no, neither, none, nay, nor, never, nothing
κατὰ prep. κατά (+gen) against, by, throughout, down, (+acc) according to, after, with
νόμον n. acc. masc. sg. νόμος law, the law
ἐντολῆς n. gen. fem. sg. ἐντολή commandment, precept
σαρκικῆς adj. gen. fem. sg. σαρκικός carnal, fleshly
ἀλλὰ conj. ἀλλά but, yea, yet, nevertheless, howbeit, nay, therefore
κατὰ prep. κατά (+gen) against, by, throughout, down, (+acc) according to, after, with
δύναμιν n. acc. fem. sg. δύναμις power, mighty work, miracle, strength, might
ζωῆς n. gen. fem. sg. ζωή life, lifetime
ἀκαταλύτου adj. gen. fem. sg. ἀκατάλυτος endless
17 γὰρ conj. γάρ for, and, because, but, indeed
ὅτι conj. ὅτι that, for, because, how that, how, because that, for that, though
Σὺ pron. nom. 2p. sg. σύ thou, you

ἱερεὺς n. nom. masc. sg. ἱερεύς priest
εἰς prep. εἰς (+acc) into, to, unto, for, in, on, toward, against, upon, at, among
τὸν art. acc. masc. sg. ὁ ἡ τό the, this, that, he, she, it
αἰῶνα n. acc. masc. sg. αἰών ever, ever and ever, evermore, age, eternal, world
κατὰ prep. κατά (+gen) against, by, throughout, down, (+acc) according to, after, with
τὴν art. acc. fem. sg. ὁ ἡ τό the, this, that, he, she, it
τάξιν n. acc. fem. sg. τάξις order
Μελχισέδεκ n. gen. masc. sg. Μελχισέδεκ Melchisedec
18 ἀθέτησις n. nom. fem. sg. ἀθέτησις put away, disannulling
μὲν conj. μέν indeed, verily, truly, even, so, some
γὰρ conj. γάρ for, and, because, but, indeed
ἐντολῆς n. gen. fem. sg. ἐντολή commandment, precept
διὰ prep. διά (+gen) by, through, with, in, of, (+acc) for, because of, for a cause
τὸ art. acc. neut. sg. ὁ ἡ τό the, this, that, he, she, it
αὐτῆς pron. gen. fem. 3p. sg. αὐτός ή ό self, of oneself, even, very, the same, he, she, it
ἀσθενὲς adj. acc. neut. sg. ἀσθενής weak, sick, impotent, more feeble
καὶ conj. καί and, even, also, but
ἀνωφελές adj. acc. neut. sg. ἀνωφελής unprofitable, unprofitableness
19 οὐδὲν num. acc. neut. sg. οὐδείς no man, nothing, no, none, neither, not, nought
γὰρ conj. γάρ for, and, because, but, indeed
ὁ art. nom. masc. sg. ὁ ἡ τό the, this, that, he, she, it
νόμος n. nom. masc. sg. νόμος law, the law
ἐπεισαγωγὴ n. nom. fem. sg. ἐπεισαγωγή bringing in
δὲ conj. δέ but, and, now, also, to the contrary, rather, then
κρείττονος compar. adj. gen. fem. sg. κρείττων better
ἐλπίδος n. gen. fem. sg. ἐλπίς hope, faith
δι' prep. διά (+gen) by, through, with, in, of, (+acc) for, because of, for a cause
ἧς relative pron. gen. fem. sg. ὅς ἥ ὅ who, which, what, that
τῷ art. dat. masc. sg. ὁ ἡ τό the, this, that, he, she, it
Θεῷ n. dat. masc. sg. θεός God, god
20 καὶ conj. καί and, even, also, but
καθ' prep. κατά (+gen) against, by, throughout, down, (+acc) according to, after, with
ὅσον relative pron. acc. neut. sg. ὅσος as many as, whatsoever, that, as long as, how much
οὐ particle of negation. οὐ οὐκ οὐχ not, no, neither, none, nay, nor, never, nothing
χωρὶς prep. χωρίς (+gen) without, beside. (adv.) by itself, apart, separately
ὁρκωμοσίας n. gen. fem. sg. ὁρκωμοσία oath
21 οἱ art. nom. masc. pl. ὁ ἡ τό the, this, that, he, she, it
μὲν conj. μέν indeed, verily, truly, even, so, some
γὰρ conj. γάρ for, and, because, but, indeed
χωρὶς prep. χωρίς (+gen) without, beside. (adv.) by itself, apart, separately
ὁρκωμοσίας n. gen. fem. sg. ὁρκωμοσία oath
ἱερεῖς n. nom. masc. pl. ἱερεύς priest
ὁ art. nom. masc. sg. ὁ ἡ τό the, this, that, he, she, it
δὲ conj. δέ but, and, now, also, to the contrary, rather, then
μετὰ prep. μετά (+gen) with, among, against, (+acc) after
ὁρκωμοσίας n. gen. fem. sg. ὁρκωμοσία oath
διὰ prep. διά (+gen) by, through, with, in, of, (+acc) for, because of, for a cause
τοῦ art. gen. masc. sg. ὁ ἡ τό the, this, that, he, she, it
πρὸς prep. πρός (+gen) for, (+dat) at, (+acc) unto, to, with, for, against
αὐτόν pron. acc. masc. 3p. sg. αὐτός ή ό self, of oneself, even, very, the same, he, she, it
Κύριος n. nom. masc. sg. κύριος Lord, lord, master, sir, LORD, God, Master, owner
καὶ conj. καί and, even, also, but
οὐ particle of negation. οὐ οὐκ οὐχ not, no, neither, none, nay, nor, never, nothing
Σὺ pron. nom. 2p. sg. σύ thou, you
ἱερεὺς n. nom. masc. sg. ἱερεύς priest

εἰς prep. εἰς (+acc) into, to, unto, for, in, on, toward, against, upon, at, among
τὸν art. acc. masc. sg. ὁ ἡ τό the, this, that, he, she, it
αἰῶνα n. acc. masc. sg. αἰών ever, ever and ever, evermore, age, eternal, world
κατὰ prep. κατά (+gen) against, by, throughout, down, (+acc) according to, after, with
τὴν art. acc. fem. sg. ὁ ἡ τό the, this, that, he, she, it
τάξιν n. acc. fem. sg. τάξις order
Μελχισέδεκ n. gen. masc. sg. Μελχισέδεκ Melchisedec
22 κατὰ prep. κατά (+gen) against, by, throughout, down, (+acc) according to, after, with
τοσοῦτον demo. pron. acc. neut. sg. τοσοῦτος so much, so great, so many, so long
κρείττονος compar. adj. gen. fem. sg. κρείττων better
διαθήκης n. gen. fem. sg. διαθήκη testament, covenant
ἔγγυος adj. nom. masc. sg. ἔγγυος surety
Ἰησοῦς n. nom. masc. sg. Ἰησοῦς Jesus
23 καὶ conj. καί and, even, also, but
οἱ art. nom. masc. pl. ὁ ἡ τό the, this, that, he, she, it
μὲν conj. μέν indeed, verily, truly, even, so, some
πλείονές compar. adj. nom. masc. pl. πολύς many, great, much, long, abundant
ἱερεῖς n. nom. masc. pl. ἱερεύς priest
διὰ prep. διά (+gen) by, through, with, in, of, (+acc) for, because of, for a cause
τὸ art. acc. neut. sg. ὁ ἡ τό the, this, that, he, she, it
θανάτῳ n. dat. masc. sg. θάνατος death
24 ὁ art. nom. masc. sg. ὁ ἡ τό the, this, that, he, she, it
δὲ conj. δέ but, and, now, also, to the contrary, rather, then
διὰ prep. διά (+gen) by, through, with, in, of, (+acc) for, because of, for a cause
τὸ art. acc. neut. sg. ὁ ἡ τό the, this, that, he, she, it
αὐτὸν pron. acc. masc. 3p. sg. αὐτός ή ό self, of oneself, even, very, the same, he, she, it
εἰς prep. εἰς (+acc) into, to, unto, for, in, on, toward, against, upon, at, among
τὸν art. acc. masc. sg. ὁ ἡ τό the, this, that, he, she, it
αἰῶνα n. acc. masc. sg. αἰών ever, ever and ever, evermore, age, eternal, world
ἀπαράβατον adj. acc. fem. sg. ἀπαράβατος unchangeable
τὴν art. acc. fem. sg. ὁ ἡ τό the, this, that, he, she, it
ἱερωσύνην n. acc. fem. sg. ἱερωσύνη priesthood
25 ὅθεν adv. ὅθεν wherefore, from whence, whereupon, where, from thence, whence
καὶ conj. καί and, even, also, but
εἰς prep. εἰς (+acc) into, to, unto, for, in, on, toward, against, upon, at, among
τὸ art. acc. neut. sg. ὁ ἡ τό the, this, that, he, she, it
παντελὲς adj. acc. neut. sg. παντελής in no wise, uttermost
τοὺς art. acc. masc. pl. ὁ ἡ τό the, this, that, he, she, it
δι' prep. διά (+gen) by, through, with, in, of, (+acc) for, because of, for a cause
αὐτοῦ pron. gen. masc. 3p. sg. αὐτός ή ό self, of oneself, even, very, the same, he, she, it
τῷ art. dat. masc. sg. ὁ ἡ τό the, this, that, he, she, it
Θεῷ n. dat. masc. sg. θεός God, god
πάντοτε adv. πάντοτε always, ever, always, evermore
εἰς prep. εἰς (+acc) into, to, unto, for, in, on, toward, against, upon, at, among
τὸ art. acc. neut. sg. ὁ ἡ τό the, this, that, he, she, it
ὑπὲρ prep. ὑπέρ (+gen) for, of, for the sake of, (+acc) above, more than
αὐτῶν pron. gen. masc. 3p. pl. αὐτός ή ό self, of oneself, even, very, the same, he, she, it
26 Τοιοῦτος demo. pron. nom. masc. sg. τοιοῦτος such, like
γὰρ conj. γάρ for, and, because, but, indeed
ἡμῖν pron. dat. 1p. pl. ἐγώ I
ἀρχιερεύς n. nom. masc. sg. ἀρχιερεύς chief priest, high priest
ὅσιος adj. nom. masc. sg. ὅσιος holy, Holy, mercy
ἄκακος adj. nom. masc. sg. ἄκακος simple, harmless
ἀμίαντος adj. nom. masc. sg. ἀμίαντος undefiled
ἀπὸ prep. ἀπό (+gen) from, of, out of, since, for, off, at, by, in, on

τῶν art. gen. masc. pl. ὁ ἡ τό the, this, that, he, she, it
ἁμαρτωλῶν adj. gen. masc. pl. ἁμαρτωλός sinner, sinful
καὶ conj. καί and, even, also, but
ὑψηλότερος compar. adj. nom. masc. sg. ὑψηλός high, higher, highly esteemed
τῶν art. gen. masc. pl. ὁ ἡ τό the, this, that, he, she, it
οὐρανῶν n. gen. masc. pl. οὐρανός heaven, air, sky
27 ὃς relative pron. nom. masc. sg. ὅς ἥ ὅ who, which, what, that
οὐκ particle of negation. οὐ οὐκ οὐχ not, no, neither, none, nay, nor, never, nothing
καθ' prep. κατά (+gen) against, by, throughout, down, (+acc) according to, after, with
ἡμέραν n. acc. fem. sg. ἡμέρα day, time, year, while, age, day time
ἀνάγκην n. acc. fem. sg. ἀνάγκη must needs, necessity, distress, inevitable
ὥσπερ adv. ὥσπερ as, even as, like as
οἱ art. nom. masc. pl. ὁ ἡ τό the, this, that, he, she, it
ἀρχιερεῖς n. nom. masc. pl. ἀρχιερεύς chief priest, high priest
πρότερον adv. πρότερον before, first, former, at the first
ὑπὲρ prep. ὑπέρ (+gen) for, of, for the sake of, (+acc) above, more than
τῶν art. gen. fem. pl. ὁ ἡ τό the, this, that, he, she, it
ἰδίων adj. gen. fem. pl. ἴδιος one's own, one's, privately
ἁμαρτιῶν n. gen. fem. pl. ἁμαρτία sin, offence, sinful
θυσίας n. acc. fem. pl. θυσία sacrifice
ἔπειτα adv. ἔπειτα then, after that, afterward
τῶν art. gen. fem. pl. ὁ ἡ τό the, this, that, he, she, it
τοῦ art. gen. masc. sg. ὁ ἡ τό the, this, that, he, she, it
λαοῦ n. gen. masc. sg. λαός people
τοῦτο demo. pron. acc. neut. sg. οὗτος αὕτη τοῦτο this, the same, this same, he, she, it
γὰρ conj. γάρ for, and, because, but, indeed
ἐφάπαξ adv. ἐφάπαξ once, once for all
ἑαυτὸν reflexive pron. acc. masc. 3p. sg. ἑαυτοῦ himself, herself, itself, yourself, ourselves
28 ὁ art. nom. masc. sg. ὁ ἡ τό the, this, that, he, she, it
νόμος n. nom. masc. sg. νόμος law, the law
γὰρ conj. γάρ for, and, because, but, indeed
ἀνθρώπους n. acc. masc. pl. ἄνθρωπος man, human being, person, one, certain
ἀρχιερεῖς n. acc. masc. pl. ἀρχιερεύς chief priest, high priest
ἀσθένειαν n. acc. fem. sg. ἀσθένεια infirmity, weakness, disease, sickness
ὁ art. nom. masc. sg. ὁ ἡ τό the, this, that, he, she, it
λόγος n. nom. masc. sg. λόγος word, saying, account, speech, thing, matter
δὲ conj. δέ but, and, now, also, to the contrary, rather, then
τῆς art. gen. fem. sg. ὁ ἡ τό the, this, that, he, she, it
ὁρκωμοσίας n. gen. fem. sg. ὁρκωμοσία oath
τῆς art. gen. fem. sg. ὁ ἡ τό the, this, that, he, she, it
μετὰ prep. μετά (+gen) with, among, against, (+acc) after
τὸν art. acc. masc. sg. ὁ ἡ τό the, this, that, he, she, it
νόμον n. acc. masc. sg. νόμος law, the law
υἱὸν n. acc. masc. sg. υἱός son, child, descendant, offspring, heir
εἰς prep. εἰς (+acc) into, to, unto, for, in, on, toward, against, upon, at, among
τὸν art. acc. masc. sg. ὁ ἡ τό the, this, that, he, she, it
αἰῶνα n. acc. masc. sg. αἰών ever, ever and ever, evermore, age, eternal, world

8

1 Κεφάλαιον n. nom. neut. sg. κεφάλαιον sum
δὲ conj. δέ but, and, now, also, to the contrary, rather, then
ἐπὶ prep. ἐπί (+gen) on, in, upon, (+dat) in, at, for, upon, (+acc) on, upon, unto, to, against
τοῖς art. dat. neut. pl. ὁ ἡ τό the, this, that, he, she, it
τοιοῦτον demo. pron. acc. masc. sg. τοιοῦτος such, like

ἀρχιερέα n. acc. masc. sg. ἀρχιερεύς chief priest, high priest
ὃς relative pron. nom. masc. sg. ὅς ἥ ὅ who, which, what, that
ἐν prep. ἐν (+dat) in, by, with, among, at, on, through, to, within, into, of, for
δεξιᾷ adj. dat. fem. sg. δεξιός right, right hand, right side
τοῦ art. gen. masc. sg. ὁ ἡ τό the, this, that, he, she, it
θρόνου n. gen. masc. sg. θρόνος throne, seat
τῆς art. gen. fem. sg. ὁ ἡ τό the, this, that, he, she, it
μεγαλωσύνης n. gen. fem. sg. μεγαλωσύνη Majesty
ἐν prep. ἐν (+dat) in, by, with, among, at, on, through, to, within, into, of, for
τοῖς art. dat. masc. pl. ὁ ἡ τό the, this, that, he, she, it
οὐρανοῖς n. dat. masc. pl. οὐρανός heaven, air, sky
2 τῶν art. gen. neut. pl. ὁ ἡ τό the, this, that, he, she, it
ἁγίων adj. gen. neut. pl. ἅγιος Holy, holy, saint, Holy One, holy thing, most holy
λειτουργὸς n. nom. masc. sg. λειτουργός minister, he that minister
καὶ conj. καί and, even, also, but
τῆς art. gen. fem. sg. ὁ ἡ τό the, this, that, he, she, it
σκηνῆς n. gen. fem. sg. σκηνή tabernacle, habitation
τῆς art. gen. fem. sg. ὁ ἡ τό the, this, that, he, she, it
ἀληθινῆς adj. gen. fem. sg. ἀληθινός true
ἣν relative pron. acc. fem. sg. ὅς ἥ ὅ who, which, what, that
ὁ art. nom. masc. sg. ὁ ἡ τό the, this, that, he, she, it
Κύριος n. nom. masc. sg. κύριος Lord, lord, master, sir, LORD, God, Master, owner
καὶ conj. καί and, even, also, but
οὐκ particle of negation. οὐ οὐκ οὐχ not, no, neither, none, nay, nor, never, nothing
ἄνθρωπος n. nom. masc. sg. ἄνθρωπος man, human being, person, one, certain
3 πᾶς adj. nom. masc. sg. πᾶς πᾶσα πᾶν all, every, whosoever, every one, no, whole, any
γὰρ conj. γάρ for, and, because, but, indeed
ἀρχιερεὺς n. nom. masc. sg. ἀρχιερεύς chief priest, high priest
εἰς prep. εἰς (+acc) into, to, unto, for, in, on, toward, against, upon, at, among
τὸ art. acc. neut. sg. ὁ ἡ τό the, this, that, he, she, it
δῶρά n. acc. neut. pl. δῶρον gift, offering
τε conj. τέ and, both, also
καὶ conj. καί and, even, also, but
θυσίας n. acc. fem. pl. θυσία sacrifice
ὅθεν adv. ὅθεν wherefore, from whence, whereupon, where, from thence, whence
ἀναγκαῖον adj. nom. neut. sg. ἀναγκαῖος near, necessary, more needful, of necessity
τι indefinite pron. acc. neut. sg. τὶς certain, some, any man, one, any thing
καὶ conj. καί and, even, also, but
τοῦτον demo. pron. acc. masc. sg. οὗτος αὕτη τοῦτο this, the same, this same, he, she, it
ὃ relative pron. acc. neut. sg. ὅς ἥ ὅ who, which, what, that
4 εἰ conj. εἰ if, whether, that, though, forasmuch
μὲν conj. μέν indeed, verily, truly, even, so, some
γὰρ conj. γάρ for, and, because, but, indeed
ἐπὶ prep. ἐπί (+gen) on, in, upon, (+dat) in, at, for, upon, (+acc) on, upon, unto, to, against
γῆς n. gen. fem. sg. γῆ earth, land, ground, country
οὐδ' adv. οὐδέ neither, nor, not, no, not even, never, not yet
ἂν particle. ἄν Indicating contingency. No English translation.
ἱερεύς n. nom. masc. sg. ἱερεύς priest
τῶν art. gen. masc. pl. ὁ ἡ τό the, this, that, he, she, it
ἱερέων n. gen. masc. pl. ἱερεύς priest
τῶν art. gen. masc. pl. ὁ ἡ τό the, this, that, he, she, it
κατὰ prep. κατά (+gen) against, by, throughout, down, (+acc) according to, after, with
τὸν art. acc. masc. sg. ὁ ἡ τό the, this, that, he, she, it
νόμον n. acc. masc. sg. νόμος law, the law
τὰ art. acc. neut. pl. ὁ ἡ τό the, this, that, he, she, it

δῶρα n. acc. neut. pl. δῶρον gift, offering
5 οἵτινες relative pron. nom. masc. pl. ὅστις which, who, whosoever, that, whatsoever
ὑποδείγματι n. dat. neut. sg. ὑπόδειγμα example, ensample, pattern
καὶ conj. καί and, even, also, but
σκιᾷ n. dat. fem. sg. σκιά shadow
τῶν art. gen. neut. pl. ὁ ἡ τό the, this, that, he, she, it
ἐπουρανίων adj. gen. neut. pl. ἐπουράνιος heavenly, celestial, high, in heaven
καθὼς adv. καθώς as, even as, according as, according to
Μωσῆς n. nom. masc. sg. Μωσῆς Moses
τὴν art. acc. fem. sg. ὁ ἡ τό the, this, that, he, she, it
σκηνήν n. acc. fem. sg. σκηνή tabernacle, habitation
γάρ conj. γάρ for, and, because, but, indeed
πάντα adj. acc. neut. pl. πᾶς πᾶσα πᾶν all, every, whosoever, every one, no, whole, any
κατὰ prep. κατά (+gen) against, by, throughout, down, (+acc) according to, after, with
τὸν art. acc. masc. sg. ὁ ἡ τό the, this, that, he, she, it
τύπον n. acc. masc. sg. τύπος ensample, example, pattern, print, figure, fashion
τὸν art. acc. masc. sg. ὁ ἡ τό the, this, that, he, she, it
σοι pron. dat. 2p. sg. σύ thou, you
ἐν prep. ἐν (+dat) in, by, with, among, at, on, through, to, within, into, of, for
τῷ art. dat. neut. sg. ὁ ἡ τό the, this, that, he, she, it
ὄρει n. dat. neut. sg. ὄρος mountain, mount, hill
6 νυνὶ adv. νυνί now
δὲ conj. δέ but, and, now, also, to the contrary, rather, then
διαφορωτέρας compar. adj. gen. fem. sg. διάφορος differing, more excellent, divers
λειτουργίας n. gen. fem. sg. λειτουργία ministration, service, ministry
ὅσῳ relative pron. dat. neut. sg. ὅσος as many as, whatsoever, that, as long as, how much
καὶ conj. καί and, even, also, but
κρείττονός compar. adj. gen. fem. sg. κρείττων better
διαθήκης n. gen. fem. sg. διαθήκη testament, covenant
μεσίτης n. nom. masc. sg. μεσίτης mediator
ἥτις relative pron. nom. fem. sg. ὅστις which, who, whosoever, that, whatsoever
ἐπὶ prep. ἐπί (+gen) on, in, upon, (+dat) in, at, for, upon, (+acc) on, upon, unto, to, against
κρείττοσιν compar. adj. dat. fem. pl. κρείττων better
ἐπαγγελίαις n. dat. fem. pl. ἐπαγγελία promise, message
7 εἰ conj. εἰ if, whether, that, though, forasmuch
γὰρ conj. γάρ for, and, because, but, indeed
ἡ art. nom. fem. sg. ὁ ἡ τό the, this, that, he, she, it
πρώτη ordinal. adj. nom. fem. sg. πρῶτος first, chief, first of all, chiefest, best
ἐκείνη demo. pron. nom. fem. sg. ἐκεῖνος that, he, the same, that same
ἄμεμπτος adj. nom. fem. sg. ἄμεμπτος blameless, faultless, unblamable
οὐκ particle of negation. οὐ οὐκ οὐχ not, no, neither, none, nay, nor, never, nothing
ἂν particle. ἄν Indicating contingency. No English translation.
δευτέρας ordinal. adj. gen. fem. sg. δεύτερος second, second time, again, afterward
τόπος n. nom. masc. sg. τόπος place, room, quarter
8 γὰρ conj. γάρ for, and, because, but, indeed
αὐτοῖς pron. dat. masc. 3p. pl. αὐτός ἡ ὁ self, of oneself, even, very, the same, he, she, it
ἡμέραι n. nom. fem. pl. ἡμέρα day, time, year, while, age, day time
Κύριος n. nom. masc. sg. κύριος Lord, lord, master, sir, LORD, God, Master, owner
καὶ conj. καί and, even, also, but
ἐπὶ prep. ἐπί (+gen) on, in, upon, (+dat) in, at, for, upon, (+acc) on, upon, unto, to, against
τὸν art. acc. masc. sg. ὁ ἡ τό the, this, that, he, she, it
οἶκον n. acc. masc. sg. οἶκος house, home, household
Ἰσραὴλ pron. name. masc. inde. Ἰσραήλ Israel
καὶ conj. καί and, even, also, but
ἐπὶ prep. ἐπί (+gen) on, in, upon, (+dat) in, at, for, upon, (+acc) on, upon, unto, to, against

τὸν art. acc. masc. sg. ὁ ἡ τό the, this, that, he, she, it
οἶκον n. acc. masc. sg. οἶκος house, home, household
Ἰούδα n. gen. masc. sg. Ἰούδας Judas, Juda, Judah, Jude
διαθήκην n. acc. fem. sg. διαθήκη testament, covenant
καινήν adj. acc. fem. sg. καινός new
9 οὐ particle of negation. οὐ οὐκ οὐχ not, no, neither, none, nay, nor, never, nothing
κατὰ prep. κατά (+gen) against, by, throughout, down, (+acc) according to, after, with
τὴν art. acc. fem. sg. ὁ ἡ τό the, this, that, he, she, it
διαθήκην n. acc. fem. sg. διαθήκη testament, covenant
ἣν relative pron. acc. fem. sg. ὅς ἥ ὅ who, which, what, that
τοῖς art. dat. masc. pl. ὁ ἡ τό the, this, that, he, she, it
πατράσιν n. dat. masc. pl. πατήρ Father, father, parent
αὐτῶν pron. gen. masc. 3p. pl. αὐτός ή ό self, of oneself, even, very, the same, he, she, it
ἐν prep. ἐν (+dat) in, by, with, among, at, on, through, to, within, into, of, for
ἡμέρᾳ n. dat. fem. sg. ἡμέρα day, time, year, while, age, day time
μου pron. gen. 1p. sg. ἐγώ I
τῆς art. gen. fem. sg. ὁ ἡ τό the, this, that, he, she, it
χειρὸς n. gen. fem. sg. χείρ hand
αὐτῶν pron. gen. masc. 3p. pl. αὐτός ή ό self, of oneself, even, very, the same, he, she, it
αὐτοὺς pron. acc. masc. 3p. pl. αὐτός ή ό self, of oneself, even, very, the same, he, she, it
ἐκ prep. ἐκ ἐξ (+gen) of, from, out of, by, on, with, in, among, through
γῆς n. gen. fem. sg. γῆ earth, land, ground, country
Αἰγύπτου n. gen. fem. sg. Αἴγυπτος Egypt
ὅτι conj. ὅτι that, for, because, how that, how, because that, for that, though
αὐτοὶ pron. nom. masc. 3p. pl. αὐτός ή ό self, of oneself, even, very, the same, he, she, it
οὐκ particle of negation. οὐ οὐκ οὐχ not, no, neither, none, nay, nor, never, nothing
ἐν prep. ἐν (+dat) in, by, with, among, at, on, through, to, within, into, of, for
τῇ art. dat. fem. sg. ὁ ἡ τό the, this, that, he, she, it
διαθήκῃ n. dat. fem. sg. διαθήκη testament, covenant
μου pron. gen. 1p. sg. ἐγώ I
κἀγὼ pron. nom. 1p. sg. κἀγώ and I, I also, so I, even as I
αὐτῶν pron. gen. masc. 3p. pl. αὐτός ή ό self, of oneself, even, very, the same, he, she, it
Κύριος n. nom. masc. sg. κύριος Lord, lord, master, sir, LORD, God, Master, owner
10 ὅτι conj. ὅτι that, for, because, how that, how, because that, for that, though
αὕτη demo. pron. nom. fem. sg. οὗτος αὕτη τοῦτο this, the same, this same, he, she, it
ἡ art. nom. fem. sg. ὁ ἡ τό the, this, that, he, she, it
διαθήκη n. nom. fem. sg. διαθήκη testament, covenant
ἣν relative pron. acc. fem. sg. ὅς ἥ ὅ who, which, what, that
τῷ art. dat. masc. sg. ὁ ἡ τό the, this, that, he, she, it
οἴκῳ n. dat. masc. sg. οἶκος house, home, household
Ἰσραὴλ pron. name. masc. inde. Ἰσραήλ Israel
μετὰ prep. μετά (+gen) with, among, against, (+acc) after
τὰς art. acc. fem. pl. ὁ ἡ τό the, this, that, he, she, it
ἡμέρας n. acc. fem. pl. ἡμέρα day, time, year, while, age, day time
ἐκείνας demo. pron. acc. fem. pl. ἐκεῖνος that, he, the same, that same
Κύριος n. nom. masc. sg. κύριος Lord, lord, master, sir, LORD, God, Master, owner
νόμους n. acc. masc. pl. νόμος law, the law
μου pron. gen. 1p. sg. ἐγώ I
εἰς prep. εἰς (+acc) into, to, unto, for, in, on, toward, against, upon, at, among
τὴν art. acc. fem. sg. ὁ ἡ τό the, this, that, he, she, it
διάνοιαν n. acc. fem. sg. διάνοια mind, understanding, imagination
αὐτῶν pron. gen. masc. 3p. pl. αὐτός ή ό self, of oneself, even, very, the same, he, she, it
καὶ conj. καί and, even, also, but
ἐπὶ prep. ἐπί (+gen) on, in, upon, (+dat) in, at, for, upon, (+acc) on, upon, unto, to, against
καρδίας n. acc. fem. pl. καρδία heart

αὐτῶν pron. gen. masc. 3p. pl. αὐτός ή ό self, of oneself, even, very, the same, he, she, it
αὐτούς pron. acc. masc. 3p. pl. αὐτός ή ό self, of oneself, even, very, the same, he, she, it
καὶ conj. καί and, even, also, but
αὐτοῖς pron. dat. masc. 3p. pl. αὐτός ή ό self, of oneself, even, very, the same, he, she, it
εἰς prep. εἰς (+acc) into, to, unto, for, in, on, toward, against, upon, at, among
Θεόν n. acc. masc. sg. θεός God, god
καὶ conj. καί and, even, also, but
αὐτοὶ pron. nom. masc. 3p. pl. αὐτός ή ό self, of oneself, even, very, the same, he, she, it
μοι pron. dat. 1p. sg. ἐγώ I
εἰς prep. εἰς (+acc) into, to, unto, for, in, on, toward, against, upon, at, among
λαόν n. acc. masc. sg. λαός people
11 καὶ conj. καί and, even, also, but
οὐ particle of negation. οὐ οὐκ οὐχ not, no, neither, none, nay, nor, never, nothing
μὴ particle of negation. μή not, no, lest, neither, none, nothing, nor, never, without
ἕκαστος adj. nom. masc. sg. ἕκαστος every man, every, every one, any man, each
τὸν art. acc. masc. sg. ὁ ἡ τό the, this, that, he, she, it
πλησίον adv. πλησίον neighbour, near
αὐτοῦ pron. gen. masc. 3p. sg. αὐτός ή ό self, of oneself, even, very, the same, he, she, it
καὶ conj. καί and, even, also, but
ἕκαστος adj. nom. masc. sg. ἕκαστος every man, every, every one, any man, each
τὸν art. acc. masc. sg. ὁ ἡ τό the, this, that, he, she, it
ἀδελφὸν n. acc. masc. sg. ἀδελφός brother
αὐτοῦ pron. gen. masc. 3p. sg. αὐτός ή ό self, of oneself, even, very, the same, he, she, it
τὸν art. acc. masc. sg. ὁ ἡ τό the, this, that, he, she, it
Κύριον n. acc. masc. sg. κύριος Lord, lord, master, sir, LORD, God, Master, owner
ὅτι conj. ὅτι that, for, because, how that, how, because that, for that, though
πάντες adj. nom. masc. pl. πᾶς πᾶσα πᾶν all, every, whosoever, every one, no, whole, any
με pron. acc. 1p. sg. ἐγώ I
ἀπὸ prep. ἀπό (+gen) from, of, out of, since, for, off, at, by, in, on
μικροῦ adj. gen. masc. sg. μικρός little, small, least, less
αὐτῶν pron. gen. masc. 3p. pl. αὐτός ή ό self, of oneself, even, very, the same, he, she, it
ἕως conj. ἕως till, until, unto, until when, while, as far as, even, until now
μεγάλου adj. gen. masc. sg. μέγας great, loud, greatest, high, large, mighty, strong
αὐτῶν pron. gen. masc. 3p. pl. αὐτός ή ό self, of oneself, even, very, the same, he, she, it
12 ὅτι conj. ὅτι that, for, because, how that, how, because that, for that, though
ἵλεως adj. nom. masc. sg. ἵλεως be it far, merciful
ταῖς art. dat. fem. pl. ὁ ἡ τό the, this, that, he, she, it
ἀδικίαις n. dat. fem. pl. ἀδικία iniquity, unrighteousness, unjust, wrong
αὐτῶν pron. gen. masc. 3p. pl. αὐτός ή ό self, of oneself, even, very, the same, he, she, it
καὶ conj. καί and, even, also, but
τῶν art. gen. fem. pl. ὁ ἡ τό the, this, that, he, she, it
ἁμαρτιῶν n. gen. fem. pl. ἁμαρτία sin, offence, sinful
αὐτῶν pron. gen. masc. 3p. pl. αὐτός ή ό self, of oneself, even, very, the same, he, she, it
καὶ conj. καί and, even, also, but
τῶν art. gen. fem. pl. ὁ ἡ τό the, this, that, he, she, it
ἀνομιῶν n. gen. fem. pl. ἀνομία iniquity, transgression of the law, lawlessness
αὐτῶν pron. gen. masc. 3p. pl. αὐτός ή ό self, of oneself, even, very, the same, he, she, it
οὐ particle of negation. οὐ οὐκ οὐχ not, no, neither, none, nay, nor, never, nothing
μὴ particle of negation. μή not, no, lest, neither, none, nothing, nor, never, without
ἔτι adv. ἔτι yet, more, any more, further, still, moreover
13 ἐν prep. ἐν (+dat) in, by, with, among, at, on, through, to, within, into, of, for
τῷ art. dat. neut. sg. ὁ ἡ τό the, this, that, he, she, it
Καινὴν adj. acc. fem. sg. καινός new
τὴν art. acc. fem. sg. ὁ ἡ τό the, this, that, he, she, it
πρώτην ordinal. adj. acc. fem. sg. πρῶτος first, chief, first of all, chiefest, best

τὸ art. nom. neut. sg. ὁ ἡ τό the, this, that, he, she, it
δὲ conj. δέ but, and, now, also, to the contrary, rather, then
καὶ conj. καί and, even, also, but
ἐγγὺς adv. ἐγγύς nigh, at hand, near, nigh at hand, ready, nigh unto
ἀφανισμοῦ n. gen. masc. sg. ἀφανισμός vanishing away

9

1 μὲν conj. μέν indeed, verily, truly, even, so, some
οὖν conj. οὖν therefore, then, so, and, now, wherefore
καὶ conj. καί and, even, also, but
ἡ art. nom. fem. sg. ὁ ἡ τό the, this, that, he, she, it
πρώτη ordinal. adj. nom. fem. sg. πρῶτος first, chief, first of all, chiefest, best
δικαιώματα n. acc. neut. pl. δικαίωμα ordinance, righteousness, judgement, justification
λατρείας n. gen. fem. sg. λατρεία service, divine service
τό art. acc. neut. sg. ὁ ἡ τό the, this, that, he, she, it
τε conj. τέ and, both, also
ἅγιον adj. acc. neut. sg. ἅγιος Holy, holy, saint, Holy One, holy thing, most holy
κοσμικόν adj. acc. neut. sg. κοσμικός worldly
2 σκηνὴ n. nom. fem. sg. σκηνή tabernacle, habitation
γὰρ conj. γάρ for, and, because, but, indeed
ἡ art. nom. fem. sg. ὁ ἡ τό the, this, that, he, she, it
πρώτη ordinal. adj. nom. fem. sg. πρῶτος first, chief, first of all, chiefest, best
ἐν prep. ἐν (+dat) in, by, with, among, at, on, through, to, within, into, of, for
ᾗ relative pron. dat. fem. sg. ὅς ἥ ὅ who, which, what, that
ἥ art. nom. fem. sg. ὁ ἡ τό the, this, that, he, she, it
τε conj. τέ and, both, also
λυχνία n. nom. fem. sg. λυχνία candlestick, lampstand
καὶ conj. καί and, even, also, but
ἡ art. nom. fem. sg. ὁ ἡ τό the, this, that, he, she, it
τράπεζα n. nom. fem. sg. τράπεζα table
καὶ conj. καί and, even, also, but
ἡ art. nom. fem. sg. ὁ ἡ τό the, this, that, he, she, it
πρόθεσις n. nom. fem. sg. πρόθεσις purpose, shew, shewbread
τῶν art. gen. masc. pl. ὁ ἡ τό the, this, that, he, she, it
ἄρτων n. gen. masc. pl. ἄρτος bread, loaf
ἥτις relative pron. nom. fem. sg. ὅστις which, who, whosoever, that, whatsoever
ἅγια adj. nom. neut. pl. ἅγιος Holy, holy, saint, Holy One, holy thing, most holy
3 μετὰ prep. μετά (+gen) with, among, against, (+acc) after
δὲ conj. δέ but, and, now, also, to the contrary, rather, then
τὸ art. acc. neut. sg. ὁ ἡ τό the, this, that, he, she, it
δεύτερον ordinal. adj. acc. neut. sg. δεύτερος second, second time, again, afterward
καταπέτασμα n. acc. neut. sg. καταπέτασμα veil
σκηνὴ n. nom. fem. sg. σκηνή tabernacle, habitation
ἡ art. nom. fem. sg. ὁ ἡ τό the, this, that, he, she, it
ἅγια adj. nom. neut. pl. ἅγιος Holy, holy, saint, Holy One, holy thing, most holy
ἁγίων adj. gen. neut. pl. ἅγιος Holy, holy, saint, Holy One, holy thing, most holy
4 χρυσοῦν adj. acc. neut. sg. χρύσεος golden, of gold
θυμιατήριον n. acc. neut. sg. θυμιατήριον censer
καὶ conj. καί and, even, also, but
τὴν art. acc. fem. sg. ὁ ἡ τό the, this, that, he, she, it
κιβωτὸν n. acc. fem. sg. κιβωτός ark
τῆς art. gen. fem. sg. ὁ ἡ τό the, this, that, he, she, it
διαθήκης n. gen. fem. sg. διαθήκη testament, covenant
πάντοθεν adv. πάντοθεν on every side, round about

χρυσίῳ n. dat. neut. sg. χρυσίον gold
ἐν prep. ἐν (+dat) in, by, with, among, at, on, through, to, within, into, of, for
ᾗ relative pron. dat. fem. sg. ὅς ἥ ὅ who, which, what, that
στάμνος n. nom. fem. sg. στάμνος pot
χρυσῆ adj. nom. fem. sg. χρύσεος golden, of gold
τὸ art. acc. neut. sg. ὁ ἡ τό the, this, that, he, she, it
μάννα n. acc. neut. sg. μάννα manna
καὶ conj. καί and, even, also, but
ἡ art. nom. fem. sg. ὁ ἡ τό the, this, that, he, she, it
ῥάβδος n. nom. fem. sg. ῥάβδος rod, sceptre, stave, staff
'Ααρὼν n. gen. masc. sg. 'Ααρών Aaron
ἡ art. nom. fem. sg. ὁ ἡ τό the, this, that, he, she, it
καὶ conj. καί and, even, also, but
αἱ art. nom. fem. pl. ὁ ἡ τό the, this, that, he, she, it
πλάκες n. nom. fem. pl. πλάξ table
τῆς art. gen. fem. sg. ὁ ἡ τό the, this, that, he, she, it
διαθήκης n. gen. fem. sg. διαθήκη testament, covenant
5 ὑπεράνω prep. ὑπεράνω (+gen) far above, over, above
δὲ conj. δέ but, and, now, also, to the contrary, rather, then
αὐτῆς pron. gen. fem. 3p. sg. αὐτός ή ό self, of oneself, even, very, the same, he, she, it
Χερουβὶμ n. nom. neut. pl. Χερουβίμ cherubim
δόξης n. gen. fem. sg. δόξα glory, honour, praise, dignity, worship
τὸ art. acc. neut. sg. ὁ ἡ τό the, this, that, he, she, it
ἱλαστήριον adj. acc. neut. sg. ἱλαστήριον propitiation, mercyseat
περὶ prep. περί (+gen) of, for, concerning, (+acc) about, concerning, in
ὧν relative pron. gen. neut. pl. ὅς ἥ ὅ who, which, what, that
οὐκ particle of negation. οὐ οὐκ οὐχ not, no, neither, none, nay, nor, never, nothing
νῦν adv. νῦν now, henceforth, present, this time
κατὰ prep. κατά (+gen) against, by, throughout, down, (+acc) according to, after, with
μέρος n. acc. neut. sg. μέρος part, coast, portion, behalf, respect, piece, side
6 τούτων demo. pron. gen. neut. pl. οὗτος αὕτη τοῦτο this, the same, this same, he, she, it
δὲ conj. δέ but, and, now, also, to the contrary, rather, then
οὕτω adv. οὕτω οὕτως so, even so, thus, on this wise, likewise, after this manner
εἰς prep. εἰς (+acc) into, to, unto, for, in, on, toward, against, upon, at, among
μὲν conj. μέν indeed, verily, truly, even, so, some
τὴν art. acc. fem. sg. ὁ ἡ τό the, this, that, he, she, it
πρώτην ordinal. adj. acc. fem. sg. πρῶτος first, chief, first of all, chiefest, best
σκηνὴν n. acc. fem. sg. σκηνή tabernacle, habitation
διὰ prep. διά (+gen) by, through, with, in, of, (+acc) for, because of, for a cause
παντὸς adj. gen. neut. sg. πᾶς πᾶσα πᾶν all, every, whosoever, every one, no, whole, any
οἱ art. nom. masc. pl. ὁ ἡ τό the, this, that, he, she, it
ἱερεῖς n. nom. masc. pl. ἱερεύς priest
τὰς art. acc. fem. pl. ὁ ἡ τό the, this, that, he, she, it
λατρείας n. acc. fem. pl. λατρεία service, divine service
7 εἰς prep. εἰς (+acc) into, to, unto, for, in, on, toward, against, upon, at, among
δὲ conj. δέ but, and, now, also, to the contrary, rather, then
τὴν art. acc. fem. sg. ὁ ἡ τό the, this, that, he, she, it
δευτέραν ordinal. adj. acc. fem. sg. δεύτερος second, second time, again, afterward
ἅπαξ adv. ἅπαξ once
τοῦ art. gen. masc. sg. ὁ ἡ τό the, this, that, he, she, it
ἐνιαυτοῦ n. gen. masc. sg. ἐνιαυτός year
μόνος adj. nom. masc. sg. μόνος only, alone, by oneself
ὁ art. nom. masc. sg. ὁ ἡ τό the, this, that, he, she, it
ἀρχιερεύς n. nom. masc. sg. ἀρχιερεύς chief priest, high priest
οὐ particle of negation. οὐ οὐκ οὐχ not, no, neither, none, nay, nor, never, nothing

χωρὶς prep. χωρίς (+gen) without, beside. (adv.) by itself, apart, separately
αἵματος n. gen. neut. sg. αἷμα blood
ὃ relative pron. acc. neut. sg. ὅς ἥ ὅ who, which, what, that
ὑπὲρ prep. ὑπέρ (+gen) for, of, for the sake of, (+acc) above, more than
ἑαυτοῦ reflexive pron. gen. masc. 3p. sg. ἑαυτοῦ himself, herself, itself, yourself, ourselves
καὶ conj. καί and, even, also, but
τῶν art. gen. neut. pl. ὁ ἡ τό the, this, that, he, she, it
τοῦ art. gen. masc. sg. ὁ ἡ τό the, this, that, he, she, it
λαοῦ n. gen. masc. sg. λαός people
ἀγνοημάτων n. gen. neut. pl. ἀγνόημα error
8 τοῦτο demo. pron. acc. neut. sg. οὗτος αὕτη τοῦτο this, the same, this same, he, she, it
τοῦ art. gen. neut. sg. ὁ ἡ τό the, this, that, he, she, it
Πνεύματος n. gen. neut. sg. πνεῦμα spirit, Spirit, Ghost, ghost, life. of the spirit, wind
τοῦ art. gen. neut. sg. ὁ ἡ τό the, this, that, he, she, it
Ἁγίου adj. gen. neut. sg. ἅγιος Holy, holy, saint, Holy One, holy thing, most holy
μήπω adv. μήπω not yet
τὴν art. acc. fem. sg. ὁ ἡ τό the, this, that, he, she, it
τῶν art. gen. neut. pl. ὁ ἡ τό the, this, that, he, she, it
ἁγίων adj. gen. neut. pl. ἅγιος Holy, holy, saint, Holy One, holy thing, most holy
ὁδὸν n. acc. fem. sg. ὁδός way, journey, highway
ἔτι adv. ἔτι yet, more, any more, further, still, moreover
τῆς art. gen. fem. sg. ὁ ἡ τό the, this, that, he, she, it
πρώτης ordinal. adj. gen. fem. sg. πρῶτος first, chief, first of all, chiefest, best
σκηνῆς n. gen. fem. sg. σκηνή tabernacle, habitation
στάσιν n. acc. fem. sg. στάσις dissension, sedition, insurrection, standing, uproar
9 ἥτις relative pron. nom. fem. sg. ὅστις which, who, whosoever, that, whatsoever
παραβολὴ n. nom. fem. sg. παραβολή parable, figure, comparison, proverb
εἰς prep. εἰς (+acc) into, to, unto, for, in, on, toward, against, upon, at, among
τὸν art. acc. masc. sg. ὁ ἡ τό the, this, that, he, she, it
καιρὸν n. acc. masc. sg. καιρός time, season, due time, opportunity
τὸν art. acc. masc. sg. ὁ ἡ τό the, this, that, he, she, it
καθ' prep. κατά (+gen) against, by, throughout, down, (+acc) according to, after, with
ὃν relative pron. acc. masc. sg. ὅς ἥ ὅ who, which, what, that
δῶρά n. nom. neut. pl. δῶρον gift, offering
τε conj. τέ and, both, also
καὶ conj. καί and, even, also, but
θυσίαι n. nom. fem. pl. θυσία sacrifice
μὴ particle of negation. μή not, no, lest, neither, none, nothing, nor, never, without
κατὰ prep. κατά (+gen) against, by, throughout, down, (+acc) according to, after, with
συνείδησιν n. acc. fem. sg. συνείδησις conscience
τὸν art. acc. masc. sg. ὁ ἡ τό the, this, that, he, she, it
10 μόνον adv. μόνος only, alone, by oneself
ἐπὶ prep. ἐπί (+gen) on, in, upon, (+dat) in, at, for, upon, (+acc) on, upon, unto, to, against
βρώμασι n. dat. neut. pl. βρῶμα victual, meat, food
καὶ conj. καί and, even, also, but
πόμασι n. dat. neut. pl. πόμα drink
καὶ conj. καί and, even, also, but
διαφόροις adj. dat. masc. pl. διάφορος differing, more excellent, divers
βαπτισμοῖς n. dat. masc. pl. βαπτισμός washing, baptism
καὶ conj. καί and, even, also, but
δικαιώμασι n. dat. neut. pl. δικαίωμα ordinance, righteousness, judgement, justification
σαρκὸς n. gen. fem. sg. σάρξ flesh, carnal
μέχρι prep. μέχρι until, unto, till, to
καιροῦ n. gen. masc. sg. καιρός time, season, due time, opportunity
διορθώσεως n. gen. fem. sg. διόρθωσις reformation

11 Χριστὸς n. nom. masc. sg. Χριστός Christ
δὲ conj. δέ but, and, now, also, to the contrary, rather, then
ἀρχιερεὺς n. nom. masc. sg. ἀρχιερεύς chief priest, high priest
τῶν art. gen. neut. pl. ὁ ἡ τό the, this, that, he, she, it
ἀγαθῶν adj. gen. neut. pl. ἀγαθός good, good thing, that which is good, well
διὰ prep. διά (+gen) by, through, with, in, of, (+acc) for, because of, for a cause
τῆς art. gen. fem. sg. ὁ ἡ τό the, this, that, he, she, it
μείζονος compar. adj. gen. fem. sg. μέγας great, loud, greatest, high, large, mighty, strong
καὶ conj. καί and, even, also, but
τελειοτέρας compar. adj. gen. fem. sg. τέλειος perfect, of full age
σκηνῆς n. gen. fem. sg. σκηνή tabernacle, habitation
οὐ particle of negation. οὐ οὐκ οὐχ not, no, neither, none, nay, nor, never, nothing
χειροποιήτου adj. gen. fem. sg. χειροποίητος made with hands, made by hands
τοῦτ' demo. pron. nom. neut. sg. οὗτος αὕτη τοῦτο this, the same, this same, he, she, it
οὐ particle of negation. οὐ οὐκ οὐχ not, no, neither, none, nay, nor, never, nothing
ταύτης demo. pron. gen. fem. sg. οὗτος αὕτη τοῦτο this, the same, this same, he, she, it
τῆς art. gen. fem. sg. ὁ ἡ τό the, this, that, he, she, it
κτίσεως n. gen. fem. sg. κτίσις creature, creation, building, ordinance
12 οὐδὲ adv. οὐδέ neither, nor, not, no, not even, never, not yet
δι' prep. διά (+gen) by, through, with, in, of, (+acc) for, because of, for a cause
αἵματος n. gen. neut. sg. αἷμα blood
τράγων n. gen. masc. pl. τράγος goat
καὶ conj. καί and, even, also, but
μόσχων n. gen. masc. pl. μόσχος calf
διὰ prep. διά (+gen) by, through, with, in, of, (+acc) for, because of, for a cause
δὲ conj. δέ but, and, now, also, to the contrary, rather, then
τοῦ art. gen. neut. sg. ὁ ἡ τό the, this, that, he, she, it
ἰδίου adj. gen. neut. sg. ἴδιος one's own, one's, privately
αἵματος n. gen. neut. sg. αἷμα blood
ἐφάπαξ adv. ἐφάπαξ once, once for all
εἰς prep. εἰς (+acc) into, to, unto, for, in, on, toward, against, upon, at, among
τὰ art. acc. neut. pl. ὁ ἡ τό the, this, that, he, she, it
ἅγια adj. acc. neut. pl. ἅγιος Holy, holy, saint, Holy One, holy thing, most holy
αἰωνίαν adj. acc. fem. sg. αἰώνιος eternal, everlasting, world, for ever
λύτρωσιν n. acc. fem. sg. λύτρωσις redeem, redemption
13 εἰ conj. εἰ if, whether, that, though, forasmuch
γὰρ conj. γάρ for, and, because, but, indeed
τὸ art. nom. neut. sg. ὁ ἡ τό the, this, that, he, she, it
αἷμα n. nom. neut. sg. αἷμα blood
ταύρων n. gen. masc. pl. ταῦρος oxen, bull
καὶ conj. καί and, even, also, but
τράγων n. gen. masc. pl. τράγος goat
καὶ conj. καί and, even, also, but
σποδὸς n. nom. fem. sg. σποδός ashes
δαμάλεως n. gen. fem. sg. δάμαλις heifer
τοὺς art. acc. masc. pl. ὁ ἡ τό the, this, that, he, she, it
πρὸς prep. πρός (+gen) for, (+dat) at, (+acc) unto, to, with, for, against
τὴν art. acc. fem. sg. ὁ ἡ τό the, this, that, he, she, it
τῆς art. gen. fem. sg. ὁ ἡ τό the, this, that, he, she, it
σαρκὸς n. gen. fem. sg. σάρξ flesh, carnal
καθαρότητα n. acc. fem. sg. καθαρότης purifying
14 πόσῳ interrog. pron. dat. neut. sg. πόσος how much, how many, how great, how long
μᾶλλον adv. μᾶλλον rather, more, more and more, better, much, much the more
τὸ art. nom. neut. sg. ὁ ἡ τό the, this, that, he, she, it
αἷμα n. nom. neut. sg. αἷμα blood

τοῦ art. gen. masc. sg. ὁ ἡ τό the, this, that, he, she, it
Χριστοῦ n. gen. masc. sg. Χριστός Christ
ὃς relative pron. nom. masc. sg. ὅς ἥ ὅ who, which, what, that
διὰ prep. διά (+gen) by, through, with, in, of, (+acc) for, because of, for a cause
Πνεύματος n. gen. neut. sg. πνεῦμα spirit, Spirit, Ghost, ghost, life. of the spirit, wind
αἰωνίου adj. gen. neut. sg. αἰώνιος eternal, everlasting, world, for ever
ἑαυτὸν reflexive pron. acc. masc. 3p. sg. ἑαυτοῦ himself, herself, itself, yourself, ourselves
ἄμωμον adj. acc. masc. sg. ἄμωμος without blame, without fault, without spot
τῷ art. dat. masc. sg. ὁ ἡ τό the, this, that, he, she, it
Θεῷ n. dat. masc. sg. θεός God, god
τὴν art. acc. fem. sg. ὁ ἡ τό the, this, that, he, she, it
συνείδησιν n. acc. fem. sg. συνείδησις conscience
ὑμῶν pron. gen. 2p. pl. σύ thou, you
ἀπὸ prep. ἀπό (+gen) from, of, out of, since, for, off, at, by, in, on
νεκρῶν adj. gen. neut. pl. νεκρός dead
ἔργων n. gen. neut. pl. ἔργον work, deed, doing labour
εἰς prep. εἰς (+acc) into, to, unto, for, in, on, toward, against, upon, at, among
τὸ art. acc. neut. sg. ὁ ἡ τό the, this, that, he, she, it
Θεῷ n. dat. masc. sg. θεός God, god
15 καὶ conj. καί and, even, also, but
διὰ prep. διά (+gen) by, through, with, in, of, (+acc) for, because of, for a cause
τοῦτο demo. pron. acc. neut. sg. οὗτος αὕτη τοῦτο this, the same, this same, he, she, it
διαθήκης n. gen. fem. sg. διαθήκη testament, covenant
καινῆς adj. gen. fem. sg. καινός new
μεσίτης n. nom. masc. sg. μεσίτης mediator
ὅπως adv. ὅπως that, how, to, because, so that, when
θανάτου n. gen. masc. sg. θάνατος death
εἰς prep. εἰς (+acc) into, to, unto, for, in, on, toward, against, upon, at, among
ἀπολύτρωσιν n. acc. fem. sg. ἀπολύτρωσις redemption, deliverance
τῶν art. gen. fem. pl. ὁ ἡ τό the, this, that, he, she, it
ἐπὶ prep. ἐπί (+gen) on, in, upon, (+dat) in, at, for, upon, (+acc) on, upon, unto, to, against
τῇ art. dat. fem. sg. ὁ ἡ τό the, this, that, he, she, it
πρώτῃ ordinal. adj. dat. fem. sg. πρῶτος first, chief, first of all, chiefest, best
διαθήκῃ n. dat. fem. sg. διαθήκη testament, covenant
παραβάσεων n. gen. fem. pl. παράβασις breaking, transgression
τὴν art. acc. fem. sg. ὁ ἡ τό the, this, that, he, she, it
ἐπαγγελίαν n. acc. fem. sg. ἐπαγγελία promise, message
οἱ art. nom. masc. pl. ὁ ἡ τό the, this, that, he, she, it
τῆς art. gen. fem. sg. ὁ ἡ τό the, this, that, he, she, it
αἰωνίου adj. gen. fem. sg. αἰώνιος eternal, everlasting, world, for ever
κληρονομίας n. gen. fem. sg. κληρονομία inheritance
16 ὅπου adv. ὅπου where, whither, whereas, in what place, wheresoever
γὰρ conj. γάρ for, and, because, but, indeed
διαθήκη n. nom. fem. sg. διαθήκη testament, covenant
θάνατον n. acc. masc. sg. θάνατος death
ἀνάγκη n. nom. fem. sg. ἀνάγκη must needs, necessity, distress, inevitable
τοῦ art. gen. masc. sg. ὁ ἡ τό the, this, that, he, she, it
17 διαθήκη n. nom. fem. sg. διαθήκη testament, covenant
γὰρ conj. γάρ for, and, because, but, indeed
ἐπὶ prep. ἐπί (+gen) on, in, upon, (+dat) in, at, for, upon, (+acc) on, upon, unto, to, against
νεκροῖς adj. dat. masc. pl. νεκρός dead
βεβαία adj. nom. fem. sg. βέβαιος sure, stedfast, firm, more sure, of force
ἐπεὶ conj. ἐπεί because, otherwise, seeing, else, for then, for as much as, for, since
μή particle of negation. μή not, no, lest, neither, none, nothing, nor, never, without
ποτε adv. ποτέ in time past, at any time, sometimes, in old time, once, when

ὅτε adv. ὅτε when, after that, as soon as, while, after
ὁ art. nom. masc. sg. ὁ ἡ τό the, this, that, he, she, it
18 ὅθεν adv. ὅθεν wherefore, from whence, whereupon, where, from thence, whence
οὐδ' adv. οὐδέ neither, nor, not, no, not even, never, not yet
ἡ art. nom. fem. sg. ὁ ἡ τό the, this, that, he, she, it
πρώτη ordinal. adj. nom. fem. sg. πρῶτος first, chief, first of all, chiefest, best
χωρὶς prep. χωρίς (+gen) without, beside. (adv.) by itself, apart, separately
αἵματος n. gen. neut. sg. αἷμα blood
19 γὰρ conj. γάρ for, and, because, but, indeed
πάσης adj. gen. fem. sg. πᾶς πᾶσα πᾶν all, every, whosoever, every one, no, whole, any
ἐντολῆς n. gen. fem. sg. ἐντολή commandment, precept
κατὰ prep. κατά (+gen) against, by, throughout, down, (+acc) according to, after, with
νόμον n. acc. masc. sg. νόμος law, the law
ὑπὸ prep. ὑπό (+gen) of, by, with, from, among, (+acc) under
Μωϋσέως n. gen. masc. sg. Μωϋσεύς Moses
παντὶ adj. dat. masc. sg. πᾶς πᾶσα πᾶν all, every, whosoever, every one, no, whole, any
τῷ art. dat. masc. sg. ὁ ἡ τό the, this, that, he, she, it
λαῷ n. dat. masc. sg. λαός people
τὸ art. acc. neut. sg. ὁ ἡ τό the, this, that, he, she, it
αἷμα n. acc. neut. sg. αἷμα blood
τῶν art. gen. masc. pl. ὁ ἡ τό the, this, that, he, she, it
μόσχων n. gen. masc. pl. μόσχος calf
καὶ conj. καί and, even, also, but
τράγων n. gen. masc. pl. τράγος goat
μετὰ prep. μετά (+gen) with, among, against, (+acc) after
ὕδατος n. gen. neut. sg. ὕδωρ water
καὶ conj. καί and, even, also, but
ἐρίου n. gen. neut. sg. ἔριον wool
κοκκίνου adj. gen. neut. sg. κόκκινος scarlet, scarlet colour, scarlet coloured
καὶ conj. καί and, even, also, but
ὑσσώπου n. gen. masc. sg. ὕσσωπος hyssop
αὐτό pron. acc. neut. 3p. sg. αὐτός ή ό self, of oneself, even, very, the same, he, she, it
τε conj. τέ and, both, also
τὸ art. acc. neut. sg. ὁ ἡ τό the, this, that, he, she, it
βιβλίον n. acc. neut. sg. βιβλίον book, bill, scroll, writing
καὶ conj. καί and, even, also, but
πάντα adj. acc. masc. sg. πᾶς πᾶσα πᾶν all, every, whosoever, every one, no, whole, any
τὸν art. acc. masc. sg. ὁ ἡ τό the, this, that, he, she, it
λαὸν n. acc. masc. sg. λαός people
20 Τοῦτο demo. pron. nom. neut. sg. οὗτος αὕτη τοῦτο this, the same, this same, he, she, it
τὸ art. nom. neut. sg. ὁ ἡ τό the, this, that, he, she, it
αἷμα n. nom. neut. sg. αἷμα blood
τῆς art. gen. fem. sg. ὁ ἡ τό the, this, that, he, she, it
διαθήκης n. gen. fem. sg. διαθήκη testament, covenant
ἧς relative pron. gen. fem. sg. ὅς ἥ ὅ who, which, what, that
πρὸς prep. πρός (+gen) for, (+dat) at, (+acc) unto, to, with, for, against
ὑμᾶς pron. acc. 2p. pl. σύ thou, you
ὁ art. nom. masc. sg. ὁ ἡ τό the, this, that, he, she, it
Θεός n. nom. masc. sg. θεός God, god
21 καὶ conj. καί and, even, also, but
τὴν art. acc. fem. sg. ὁ ἡ τό the, this, that, he, she, it
σκηνὴν n. acc. fem. sg. σκηνή tabernacle, habitation
δὲ conj. δέ but, and, now, also, to the contrary, rather, then
καὶ conj. καί and, even, also, but
πάντα adj. acc. neut. pl. πᾶς πᾶσα πᾶν all, every, whosoever, every one, no, whole, any

τὰ art. acc. neut. pl. ὁ ἡ τό the, this, that, he, she, it
σκεύη n. acc. neut. pl. σκεῦος vessel, good, sail, stuff
τῆς art. gen. fem. sg. ὁ ἡ τό the, this, that, he, she, it
λειτουργίας n. gen. fem. sg. λειτουργία ministration, service, ministry
τῷ art. dat. neut. sg. ὁ ἡ τό the, this, that, he, she, it
αἵματι n. dat. neut. sg. αἷμα blood
ὁμοίως adv. ὁμοίως likewise, so
22 καὶ conj. καί and, even, also, but
σχεδὸν adv. σχεδόν almost
ἐν prep. ἐν (+dat) in, by, with, among, at, on, through, to, within, into, of, for
αἵματι n. dat. neut. sg. αἷμα blood
πάντα adj. nom. neut. pl. πᾶς πᾶσα πᾶν all, every, whosoever, every one, no, whole, any
κατὰ prep. κατά (+gen) against, by, throughout, down, (+acc) according to, after, with
τὸν art. acc. masc. sg. ὁ ἡ τό the, this, that, he, she, it
νόμον n. acc. masc. sg. νόμος law, the law
καὶ conj. καί and, even, also, but
χωρὶς prep. χωρίς (+gen) without, beside. (adv.) by itself, apart, separately
αἱματεκχυσίας n. gen. fem. sg. αἱματεκχυσία shedding of blood
οὐ particle of negation. οὐ οὐκ οὐχ not, no, neither, none, nay, nor, never, nothing
ἄφεσις n. nom. fem. sg. ἄφεσις remission, forgiveness, deliverance, liberty
23 Ἀνάγκη n. nom. fem. sg. ἀνάγκη must needs, necessity, distress, inevitable
οὖν conj. οὖν therefore, then, so, and, now, wherefore
τὰ art. acc. neut. pl. ὁ ἡ τό the, this, that, he, she, it
μὲν conj. μέν indeed, verily, truly, even, so, some
ὑποδείγματα n. acc. neut. pl. ὑπόδειγμα example, ensample, pattern
τῶν art. gen. neut. pl. ὁ ἡ τό the, this, that, he, she, it
ἐν prep. ἐν (+dat) in, by, with, among, at, on, through, to, within, into, of, for
τοῖς art. dat. masc. pl. ὁ ἡ τό the, this, that, he, she, it
οὐρανοῖς n. dat. masc. pl. οὐρανός heaven, air, sky
τούτοις demo. pron. dat. neut. pl. οὗτος αὕτη τοῦτο this, the same, this same, he, she, it
αὐτὰ pron. acc. neut. 3p. pl. αὐτός ή ό self, of oneself, even, very, the same, he, she, it
δὲ conj. δέ but, and, now, also, to the contrary, rather, then
τὰ art. acc. neut. pl. ὁ ἡ τό the, this, that, he, she, it
ἐπουράνια adj. acc. neut. pl. ἐπουράνιος heavenly, celestial, high, in heaven
κρείττοσιν compar. adj. dat. fem. pl. κρείττων better
θυσίαις n. dat. fem. pl. θυσία sacrifice
παρὰ prep. παρά (+gen) of, from, (+dat) with, for, (+acc) beside, at, by, above, against
ταύτας demo. pron. acc. fem. pl. οὗτος αὕτη τοῦτο this, the same, this same, he, she, it
24 οὐ particle of negation. οὐ οὐκ οὐχ not, no, neither, none, nay, nor, never, nothing
γὰρ conj. γάρ for, and, because, but, indeed
εἰς prep. εἰς (+acc) into, to, unto, for, in, on, toward, against, upon, at, among
χειροποίητα adj. acc. neut. pl. χειροποίητος made with hands, made by hands
ἅγια adj. acc. neut. pl. ἅγιος Holy, holy, saint, Holy One, holy thing, most holy
ὁ art. nom. masc. sg. ὁ ἡ τό the, this, that, he, she, it
Χριστός n. nom. masc. sg. Χριστός Christ
ἀντίτυπα adj. acc. neut. pl. ἀντίτυπος figure, like figure whereunto
τῶν art. gen. neut. pl. ὁ ἡ τό the, this, that, he, she, it
ἀληθινῶν adj. gen. neut. pl. ἀληθινός true
ἀλλ' conj. ἀλλά but, yea, yet, nevertheless, howbeit, nay, therefore
εἰς prep. εἰς (+acc) into, to, unto, for, in, on, toward, against, upon, at, among
αὐτὸν pron. acc. masc. 3p. sg. αὐτός ή ό self, of oneself, even, very, the same, he, she, it
τὸν art. acc. masc. sg. ὁ ἡ τό the, this, that, he, she, it
οὐρανόν n. acc. masc. sg. οὐρανός heaven, air, sky
νῦν adv. νῦν now, henceforth, present, this time
τῷ art. dat. neut. sg. ὁ ἡ τό the, this, that, he, she, it

προσώπῳ n. dat. neut. sg. πρόσωπον face, presence, person, countenance
τοῦ art. gen. masc. sg. ὁ ἡ τό the, this, that, he, she, it
Θεοῦ n. gen. masc. sg. θεός God, god
ὑπὲρ prep. ὑπέρ (+gen) for, of, for the sake of, (+acc) above, more than
ἡμῶν pron. gen. 1p. pl. ἐγώ I
25 οὐδ' adv. οὐδέ neither, nor, not, no, not even, never, not yet
ἵνα conj. ἵνα that, to, lest, for to, so that, albeit, because, for, so as
πολλάκις adv. πολλάκις often, ofttimes, oft
ἑαυτόν reflexive pron. acc. masc. 3p. sg. ἑαυτοῦ himself, herself, itself, yourself, ourselves
ὥσπερ adv. ὥσπερ as, even as, like as
ὁ art. nom. masc. sg. ὁ ἡ τό the, this, that, he, she, it
ἀρχιερεὺς n. nom. masc. sg. ἀρχιερεύς chief priest, high priest
εἰς prep. εἰς (+acc) into, to, unto, for, in, on, toward, against, upon, at, among
τὰ art. acc. neut. pl. ὁ ἡ τό the, this, that, he, she, it
ἅγια adj. acc. neut. pl. ἅγιος Holy, holy, saint, Holy One, holy thing, most holy
κατ' prep. κατά (+gen) against, by, throughout, down, (+acc) according to, after, with
ἐνιαυτὸν n. acc. masc. sg. ἐνιαυτός year
ἐν prep. ἐν (+dat) in, by, with, among, at, on, through, to, within, into, of, for
αἵματι n. dat. neut. sg. αἷμα blood
ἀλλοτρίῳ adj. dat. neut. sg. ἀλλότριος stranger, another man, alien, strange
26 ἐπεὶ conj. ἐπεί because, otherwise, seeing, else, for then, for as much as, for, since
αὐτὸν pron. acc. masc. 3p. sg. αὐτός ή ό self, of oneself, even, very, the same, he, she, it
πολλάκις adv. πολλάκις often, ofttimes, oft
ἀπὸ prep. ἀπό (+gen) from, of, out of, since, for, off, at, by, in, on
καταβολῆς n. gen. fem. sg. καταβολή foundation
κόσμου n. gen. masc. sg. κόσμος world, adorning
νῦν adv. νῦν now, henceforth, present, this time
δὲ conj. δέ but, and, now, also, to the contrary, rather, then
ἅπαξ adv. ἅπαξ once
ἐπὶ prep. ἐπί (+gen) on, in, upon, (+dat) in, at, for, upon, (+acc) on, upon, unto, to, against
συντελείᾳ n. dat. fem. sg. συντέλεια end
τῶν art. gen. masc. pl. ὁ ἡ τό the, this, that, he, she, it
αἰώνων n. gen. masc. pl. αἰών ever, ever and ever, evermore, age, eternal, world
εἰς prep. εἰς (+acc) into, to, unto, for, in, on, toward, against, upon, at, among
ἀθέτησιν n. acc. fem. sg. ἀθέτησις put away, disannulling
ἁμαρτίας n. gen. fem. sg. ἁμαρτία sin, offence, sinful
διὰ prep. διά (+gen) by, through, with, in, of, (+acc) for, because of, for a cause
τῆς art. gen. fem. sg. ὁ ἡ τό the, this, that, he, she, it
θυσίας n. gen. fem. sg. θυσία sacrifice
αὐτοῦ pron. gen. masc. 3p. sg. αὐτός ή ό self, of oneself, even, very, the same, he, she, it
27 καὶ conj. καί and, even, also, but
καθ' prep. κατά (+gen) against, by, throughout, down, (+acc) according to, after, with
ὅσον relative pron. acc. neut. sg. ὅσος as many as, whatsoever, that, as long as, how much
τοῖς art. dat. masc. pl. ὁ ἡ τό the, this, that, he, she, it
ἀνθρώποις n. dat. masc. pl. ἄνθρωπος man, human being, person, one, certain
ἅπαξ adv. ἅπαξ once
μετὰ prep. μετά (+gen) with, among, against, (+acc) after
δὲ conj. δέ but, and, now, also, to the contrary, rather, then
τοῦτο demo. pron. acc. neut. sg. οὗτος αὕτη τοῦτο this, the same, this same, he, she, it
κρίσις n. nom. fem. sg. κρίσις judgment, damnation, accusation, condemnation
28 οὕτως adv. οὕτω οὕτως so, even so, thus, on this wise, likewise, after this manner
ὁ art. nom. masc. sg. ὁ ἡ τό the, this, that, he, she, it
Χριστὸς n. nom. masc. sg. Χριστός Christ
ἅπαξ adv. ἅπαξ once
εἰς prep. εἰς (+acc) into, to, unto, for, in, on, toward, against, upon, at, among

τὸ art. acc. neut. sg. ὁ ἡ τό the, this, that, he, she, it
πολλῶν adj. gen. masc. pl. πολύς many, great, much, long, abundant
ἁμαρτίας n. acc. fem. pl. ἁμαρτία sin, offence, sinful
ἐκ prep. ἐκ ἐξ (+gen) of, from, out of, by, on, with, in, among, through
δευτέρου ordinal. adj. gen. masc. sg. δεύτερος second, second time, again, afterward
χωρὶς prep. χωρίς (+gen) without, beside. (adv.) by itself, apart, separately
ἁμαρτίας n. gen. fem. sg. ἁμαρτία sin, offence, sinful
τοῖς art. dat. masc. pl. ὁ ἡ τό the, this, that, he, she, it
αὐτὸν pron. acc. masc. 3p. sg. αὐτός ἡ ὁ self, of oneself, even, very, the same, he, she, it
εἰς prep. εἰς (+acc) into, to, unto, for, in, on, toward, against, upon, at, among
σωτηρίαν n. acc. fem. sg. σωτηρία salvation, deliver, health, saving

10

1 Σκιὰν n. acc. fem. sg. σκιά shadow
γὰρ conj. γάρ for, and, because, but, indeed
ὁ art. nom. masc. sg. ὁ ἡ τό the, this, that, he, she, it
νόμος n. nom. masc. sg. νόμος law, the law
τῶν art. gen. neut. pl. ὁ ἡ τό the, this, that, he, she, it
ἀγαθῶν adj. gen. neut. pl. ἀγαθός good, good thing, that which is good, well
οὐκ particle of negation. οὐ οὐκ οὐχ not, no, neither, none, nay, nor, never, nothing
αὐτὴν pron. acc. fem. 3p. sg. αὐτός ἡ ὁ self, of oneself, even, very, the same, he, she, it
τὴν art. acc. fem. sg. ὁ ἡ τό the, this, that, he, she, it
εἰκόνα n. acc. fem. sg. εἰκών image
τῶν art. gen. neut. pl. ὁ ἡ τό the, this, that, he, she, it
πραγμάτων n. gen. neut. pl. πρᾶγμα thing, matter, business, work
κατ' prep. κατά (+gen) against, by, throughout, down, (+acc) according to, after, with
ἐνιαυτὸν n. acc. masc. sg. ἐνιαυτός year
ταῖς art. dat. fem. pl. ὁ ἡ τό the, this, that, he, she, it
αὐταῖς adj. dat. fem. pl. αὐτός ἡ ὁ self, of oneself, even, very, the same, he, she, it
θυσίαις n. dat. fem. pl. θυσία sacrifice
ἃς relative pron. acc. fem. pl. ὅς ἥ ὅ who, which, what, that
εἰς prep. εἰς (+acc) into, to, unto, for, in, on, toward, against, upon, at, among
τὸ art. acc. neut. sg. ὁ ἡ τό the, this, that, he, she, it
διηνεκὲς adj. acc. neut. sg. διηνεκής continually, for ever
οὐδέποτε adv. οὐδέποτε never, neither at any time, no at any time
τοὺς art. acc. masc. pl. ὁ ἡ τό the, this, that, he, she, it
2 ἐπεὶ conj. ἐπεί because, otherwise, seeing, else, for then, for as much as, for, since
οὐκ particle of negation. οὐ οὐκ οὐχ not, no, neither, none, nay, nor, never, nothing
ἂν particle. ἄν Indicating contingency. No English translation.
διὰ prep. διά (+gen) by, through, with, in, of, (+acc) for, because of, for a cause
τὸ art. acc. neut. sg. ὁ ἡ τό the, this, that, he, she, it
μηδεμίαν num. acc. fem. sg. μηδείς μηδεμία μηδέν no man, nothing, no, none, not at all
ἔτι adv. ἔτι yet, more, any more, further, still, moreover
συνείδησιν n. acc. fem. sg. συνείδησις conscience
ἁμαρτιῶν n. gen. fem. pl. ἁμαρτία sin, offence, sinful
τοὺς art. acc. masc. pl. ὁ ἡ τό the, this, that, he, she, it
ἅπαξ adv. ἅπαξ once
3 ἀλλ' conj. ἀλλά but, yea, yet, nevertheless, howbeit, nay, therefore
ἐν prep. ἐν (+dat) in, by, with, among, at, on, through, to, within, into, of, for
αὐταῖς pron. dat. fem. 3p. pl. αὐτός ἡ ὁ self, of oneself, even, very, the same, he, she, it
ἀνάμνησις n. nom. fem. sg. ἀνάμνησις remembrance, remembrance again
ἁμαρτιῶν n. gen. fem. pl. ἁμαρτία sin, offence, sinful
κατ' prep. κατά (+gen) against, by, throughout, down, (+acc) according to, after, with
ἐνιαυτόν n. acc. masc. sg. ἐνιαυτός year

4 ἀδύνατον adj. nom. neut. sg. ἀδύνατος impossible, not possible, cannot do
γὰρ conj. γάρ for, and, because, but, indeed
αἷμα n. acc. neut. sg. αἷμα blood
ταύρων n. gen. masc. pl. ταῦρος oxen, bull
καὶ conj. καί and, even, also, but
τράγων n. gen. masc. pl. τράγος goat
ἁμαρτίας n. acc. fem. pl. ἁμαρτία sin, offence, sinful
5 διὸ conj. διό wherefore, therefore, for which cause
εἰς prep. εἰς (+acc) into, to, unto, for, in, on, toward, against, upon, at, among
τὸν art. acc. masc. sg. ὁ ἡ τό the, this, that, he, she, it
κόσμον n. acc. masc. sg. κόσμος world, adorning
Θυσίαν n. acc. fem. sg. θυσία sacrifice
καὶ conj. καί and, even, also, but
προσφορὰν n. acc. fem. sg. προσφορά offering, offering up
οὐκ particle of negation. οὐ οὐκ οὐχ not, no, neither, none, nay, nor, never, nothing
σῶμα n. acc. neut. sg. σῶμα body, bodily, slave
δὲ conj. δέ but, and, now, also, to the contrary, rather, then
μοι pron. dat. 1p. sg. ἐγώ I
6 ὁλοκαυτώματα n. acc. neut. pl. ὁλοκαύτωμα whole burnt offering, burnt offering
καὶ conj. καί and, even, also, but
περὶ prep. περί (+gen) of, for, concerning, (+acc) about, concerning, in
ἁμαρτίας n. gen. fem. sg. ἁμαρτία sin, offence, sinful
οὐκ particle of negation. οὐ οὐκ οὐχ not, no, neither, none, nay, nor, never, nothing
7 τότε adv. τότε then, that time
ἐν prep. ἐν (+dat) in, by, with, among, at, on, through, to, within, into, of, for
κεφαλίδι n. dat. fem. sg. κεφαλίς volume
βιβλίου n. gen. neut. sg. βιβλίον book, bill, scroll, writing
περὶ prep. περί (+gen) of, for, concerning, (+acc) about, concerning, in
ἐμοῦ pron. gen. 1p. sg. ἐγώ I
τοῦ art. gen. neut. sg. ὁ ἡ τό the, this, that, he, she, it
ὁ art. nom. masc. sg. ὁ ἡ τό the, this, that, he, she, it
Θεὸς n. nom. masc. sg. θεός God, god
τὸ art. acc. neut. sg. ὁ ἡ τό the, this, that, he, she, it
θέλημά n. acc. neut. sg. θέλημα will, desire, pleasure
σου pron. gen. 2p. sg. σύ thou, you
8 ἀνώτερον adj. acc. neut. sg. ἀνώτερος higher, above
ὅτι conj. ὅτι that, for, because, how that, how, because that, for that, though
Θυσίαν n. acc. fem. sg. θυσία sacrifice
καὶ conj. καί and, even, also, but
προσφορὰν n. acc. fem. sg. προσφορά offering, offering up
καὶ conj. καί and, even, also, but
ὁλοκαυτώματα n. acc. neut. pl. ὁλοκαύτωμα whole burnt offering, burnt offering
καὶ conj. καί and, even, also, but
περὶ prep. περί (+gen) of, for, concerning, (+acc) about, concerning, in
ἁμαρτίας n. gen. fem. sg. ἁμαρτία sin, offence, sinful
οὐκ particle of negation. οὐ οὐκ οὐχ not, no, neither, none, nay, nor, never, nothing
οὐδὲ adv. οὐδέ neither, nor, not, no, not even, never, not yet
αἵτινες relative pron. nom. fem. pl. ὅστις which, who, whosoever, that, whatsoever
κατὰ prep. κατά (+gen) against, by, throughout, down, (+acc) according to, after, with
τὸν art. acc. masc. sg. ὁ ἡ τό the, this, that, he, she, it
νόμον n. acc. masc. sg. νόμος law, the law
9 τότε adv. τότε then, that time
τοῦ art. gen. neut. sg. ὁ ἡ τό the, this, that, he, she, it
ὁ art. nom. masc. sg. ὁ ἡ τό the, this, that, he, she, it
Θεός n. nom. masc. sg. θεός God, god

τὸ art. acc. neut. sg. ὁ ἡ τό the, this, that, he, she, it
θέλημά n. acc. neut. sg. θέλημα will, desire, pleasure
σου pron. gen. 2p. sg. σύ thou, you
τὸ art. acc. neut. sg. ὁ ἡ τό the, this, that, he, she, it
πρῶτον ordinal. adj. acc. neut. sg. πρῶτος first, chief, first of all, chiefest, best
ἵνα conj. ἵνα that, to, lest, for to, so that, albeit, because, for, so as
τὸ art. acc. neut. sg. ὁ ἡ τό the, this, that, he, she, it
δεύτερον ordinal. adj. acc. neut. sg. δεύτερος second, second time, again, afterward
10 ἐν prep. ἐν (+dat) in, by, with, among, at, on, through, to, within, into, of, for
ᾧ relative pron. dat. neut. sg. ὅς ἥ ὅ who, which, what, that
θελήματι n. dat. neut. sg. θέλημα will, desire, pleasure
διὰ prep. διά (+gen) by, through, with, in, of, (+acc) for, because of, for a cause
τῆς art. gen. fem. sg. ὁ ἡ τό the, this, that, he, she, it
προσφορᾶς n. gen. fem. sg. προσφορά offering, offering up
τοῦ art. gen. neut. sg. ὁ ἡ τό the, this, that, he, she, it
σώματος n. gen. neut. sg. σῶμα body, bodily, slave
τοῦ art. gen. masc. sg. ὁ ἡ τό the, this, that, he, she, it
Ἰησοῦ n. gen. masc. sg. Ἰησοῦς Jesus
Χριστοῦ n. gen. masc. sg. Χριστός Christ
ἐφάπαξ adv. ἐφάπαξ once, once for all
11 καὶ conj. καί and, even, also, but
πᾶς adj. nom. masc. sg. πᾶς πᾶσα πᾶν all, every, whosoever, every one, no, whole, any
μὲν conj. μέν indeed, verily, truly, even, so, some
ἱερεὺς n. nom. masc. sg. ἱερεύς priest
καθ' prep. κατά (+gen) against, by, throughout, down, (+acc) according to, after, with
ἡμέραν n. acc. fem. sg. ἡμέρα day, time, year, while, age, day time
καὶ conj. καί and, even, also, but
τὰς art. acc. fem. pl. ὁ ἡ τό the, this, that, he, she, it
αὐτὰς adj. acc. fem. pl. αὐτός ή ό self, of oneself, even, very, the same, he, she, it
πολλάκις adv. πολλάκις often, ofttimes, oft
θυσίας n. acc. fem. pl. θυσία sacrifice
αἵτινες relative pron. nom. fem. pl. ὅστις which, who, whosoever, that, whatsoever
οὐδέποτε adv. οὐδέποτε never, neither at any time, no at any time
ἁμαρτίας n. acc. fem. pl. ἁμαρτία sin, offence, sinful
12 αὐτὸς pron. nom. masc. 3p. sg. αὐτός ή ό self, of oneself, even, very, the same, he, she, it
δὲ conj. δέ but, and, now, also, to the contrary, rather, then
μίαν num. acc. fem. sg. εἷς or ἕν one, other, some, any, only, a certain
ὑπὲρ prep. ὑπέρ (+gen) for, of, for the sake of, (+acc) above, more than
ἁμαρτιῶν n. gen. fem. pl. ἁμαρτία sin, offence, sinful
θυσίαν n. acc. fem. sg. θυσία sacrifice
εἰς prep. εἰς (+acc) into, to, unto, for, in, on, toward, against, upon, at, among
τὸ art. acc. neut. sg. ὁ ἡ τό the, this, that, he, she, it
διηνεκὲς adj. acc. neut. sg. διηνεκής continually, for ever
ἐν prep. ἐν (+dat) in, by, with, among, at, on, through, to, within, into, of, for
δεξιᾷ adj. dat. fem. sg. δεξιός right, right hand, right side
τοῦ art. gen. masc. sg. ὁ ἡ τό the, this, that, he, she, it
Θεοῦ n. gen. masc. sg. θεός God, god
13 τὸ art. acc. neut. sg. ὁ ἡ τό the, this, that, he, she, it
λοιπὸν adv. λοιπόν finally, henceforth, now, besides, furthermore, moreover, then
ἕως conj. ἕως till, until, unto, until when, while, as far as, even, until now
οἱ art. nom. masc. pl. ὁ ἡ τό the, this, that, he, she, it
ἐχθροὶ adj. nom. masc. pl. ἐχθρός enemy, foe
αὐτοῦ pron. gen. masc. 3p. sg. αὐτός ή ό self, of oneself, even, very, the same, he, she, it
ὑποπόδιον n. nom. neut. sg. ὑποπόδιον footstool
τῶν art. gen. masc. pl. ὁ ἡ τό the, this, that, he, she, it

ποδῶν n. gen. masc. pl. πούς foot
αὐτοῦ pron. gen. masc. 3p. sg. αὐτός ή ὁ self, of oneself, even, very, the same, he, she, it
14 μιᾷ num. dat. fem. sg. εἷς or ἕν one, other, some, any, only, a certain
γὰρ conj. γάρ for, and, because, but, indeed
προσφορᾷ n. dat. fem. sg. προσφορά offering, offering up
εἰς prep. εἰς (+acc) into, to, unto, for, in, on, toward, against, upon, at, among
τὸ art. acc. neut. sg. ὁ ἡ τό the, this, that, he, she, it
διηνεκὲς adj. acc. neut. sg. διηνεκής continually, for ever
τοὺς art. acc. masc. pl. ὁ ἡ τό the, this, that, he, she, it
15 δὲ conj. δέ but, and, now, also, to the contrary, rather, then
ἡμῖν pron. dat. 1p. pl. ἐγώ I
καὶ conj. καί and, even, also, but
τὸ art. nom. neut. sg. ὁ ἡ τό the, this, that, he, she, it
Πνεῦμα n. nom. neut. sg. πνεῦμα spirit, Spirit, Ghost, ghost, life. of the spirit, wind
τὸ art. nom. neut. sg. ὁ ἡ τό the, this, that, he, she, it
῞Αγιον adj. nom. neut. sg. ἅγιος Holy, holy, saint, Holy One, holy thing, most holy
μετὰ prep. μετά (+gen) with, among, against, (+acc) after
γὰρ conj. γάρ for, and, because, but, indeed
τὸ art. acc. neut. sg. ὁ ἡ τό the, this, that, he, she, it
16 Αὕτη demo. pron. nom. fem. sg. οὗτος αὕτη τοῦτο this, the same, this same, he, she, it
ἡ art. nom. fem. sg. ὁ ἡ τό the, this, that, he, she, it
διαθήκη n. nom. fem. sg. διαθήκη testament, covenant
ἣν relative pron. acc. fem. sg. ὅς ἥ ὅ who, which, what, that
πρὸς prep. πρός (+gen) for, (+dat) at, (+acc) unto, to, with, for, against
αὐτοὺς pron. acc. masc. 3p. pl. αὐτός ἡ ὁ self, of oneself, even, very, the same, he, she, it
μετὰ prep. μετά (+gen) with, among, against, (+acc) after
τὰς art. acc. fem. pl. ὁ ἡ τό the, this, that, he, she, it
ἡμέρας n. acc. fem. pl. ἡμέρα day, time, year, while, age, day time
ἐκείνας demo. pron. acc. fem. pl. ἐκεῖνος that, he, the same, that same
Κύριος n. nom. masc. sg. κύριος Lord, lord, master, sir, LORD, God, Master, owner
νόμους n. acc. masc. pl. νόμος law, the law
μου pron. gen. 1p. sg. ἐγώ I
ἐπὶ prep. ἐπί (+gen) on, in, upon, (+dat) in, at, for, upon, (+acc) on, upon, unto, to, against
καρδίας n. acc. fem. pl. καρδία heart
αὐτῶν pron. gen. masc. 3p. pl. αὐτός ἡ ὁ self, of oneself, even, very, the same, he, she, it
καὶ conj. καί and, even, also, but
ἐπὶ prep. ἐπί (+gen) on, in, upon, (+dat) in, at, for, upon, (+acc) on, upon, unto, to, against
τῶν art. gen. fem. pl. ὁ ἡ τό the, this, that, he, she, it
διανοιῶν n. gen. fem. pl. διάνοια mind, understanding, imagination
αὐτῶν pron. gen. masc. 3p. pl. αὐτός ἡ ὁ self, of oneself, even, very, the same, he, she, it
αὐτούς pron. acc. masc. 3p. pl. αὐτός ἡ ὁ self, of oneself, even, very, the same, he, she, it
17 καὶ conj. καί and, even, also, but
τῶν art. gen. fem. pl. ὁ ἡ τό the, this, that, he, she, it
ἁμαρτιῶν n. gen. fem. pl. ἁμαρτία sin, offence, sinful
αὐτῶν pron. gen. masc. 3p. pl. αὐτός ἡ ὁ self, of oneself, even, very, the same, he, she, it
καὶ conj. καί and, even, also, but
τῶν art. gen. fem. pl. ὁ ἡ τό the, this, that, he, she, it
ἀνομιῶν n. gen. fem. pl. ἀνομία iniquity, transgression of the law, lawlessness
αὐτῶν pron. gen. masc. 3p. pl. αὐτός ἡ ὁ self, of oneself, even, very, the same, he, she, it
οὐ particle of negation. οὐ οὐκ οὐχ not, no, neither, none, nay, nor, never, nothing
μὴ particle of negation. μή not, no, lest, neither, none, nothing, nor, never, without
ἔτι adv. ἔτι yet, more, any more, further, still, moreover
18 ὅπου adv. ὅπου where, whither, whereas, in what place, wheresoever
δὲ conj. δέ but, and, now, also, to the contrary, rather, then
ἄφεσις n. nom. fem. sg. ἄφεσις remission, forgiveness, deliverance, liberty

τούτων demo. pron. gen. fem. pl. οὗτος αὕτη τοῦτο this, the same, this same, he, she, it
οὐκέτι adv. οὐκέτι or οὐκ ἔτι no more, no longer, not any more
προσφορὰ n. nom. fem. sg. προσφορά offering, offering up
περὶ prep. περί (+gen) of, for, concerning, (+acc) about, concerning, in
ἁμαρτίας n. gen. fem. sg. ἁμαρτία sin, offence, sinful
19 οὖν conj. οὖν therefore, then, so, and, now, wherefore
ἀδελφοί n. voc. masc. pl. ἀδελφός brother
παρρησίαν n. acc. fem. sg. παρρησία boldness, confidence, openly, plainly, freely
εἰς prep. εἰς (+acc) into, to, unto, for, in, on, toward, against, upon, at, among
τὴν art. acc. fem. sg. ὁ ἡ τό the, this, that, he, she, it
εἴσοδον n. acc. fem. sg. εἴσοδος coming, entrance into, entering in
τῶν art. gen. neut. pl. ὁ ἡ τό the, this, that, he, she, it
ἁγίων adj. gen. neut. pl. ἅγιος Holy, holy, saint, Holy One, holy thing, most holy
ἐν prep. ἐν (+dat) in, by, with, among, at, on, through, to, within, into, of, for
τῷ art. dat. neut. sg. ὁ ἡ τό the, this, that, he, she, it
αἵματι n. dat. neut. sg. αἷμα blood
Ἰησοῦ n. gen. masc. sg. Ἰησοῦς Jesus
20 ἣν relative pron. acc. fem. sg. ὅς ἥ ὅ who, which, what, that
ἡμῖν pron. dat. 1p. pl. ἐγώ I
ὁδὸν n. acc. fem. sg. ὁδός way, journey, highway
πρόσφατον adj. acc. fem. sg. πρόσφατος new
καὶ conj. καί and, even, also, but
διὰ prep. διά (+gen) by, through, with, in, of, (+acc) for, because of, for a cause
τοῦ art. gen. neut. sg. ὁ ἡ τό the, this, that, he, she, it
καταπετάσματος n. gen. neut. sg. καταπέτασμα veil
τοῦτ' demo. pron. nom. neut. sg. οὗτος αὕτη τοῦτο this, the same, this same, he, she, it
τῆς art. gen. fem. sg. ὁ ἡ τό the, this, that, he, she, it
σαρκὸς n. gen. fem. sg. σάρξ flesh, carnal
αὐτοῦ pron. gen. masc. 3p. sg. αὐτός ή ό self, of oneself, even, very, the same, he, she, it
21 καὶ conj. καί and, even, also, but
ἱερέα n. acc. masc. sg. ἱερεύς priest
μέγαν adj. acc. masc. sg. μέγας great, loud, greatest, high, large, mighty, strong
ἐπὶ prep. ἐπί (+gen) on, in, upon, (+dat) in, at, for, upon, (+acc) on, upon, unto, to, against
τὸν art. acc. masc. sg. ὁ ἡ τό the, this, that, he, she, it
οἶκον n. acc. masc. sg. οἶκος house, home, household
τοῦ art. gen. masc. sg. ὁ ἡ τό the, this, that, he, she, it
Θεοῦ n. gen. masc. sg. θεός God, god
22 μετὰ prep. μετά (+gen) with, among, against, (+acc) after
ἀληθινῆς adj. gen. fem. sg. ἀληθινός true
καρδίας n. gen. fem. sg. καρδία heart
ἐν prep. ἐν (+dat) in, by, with, among, at, on, through, to, within, into, of, for
πληροφορίᾳ n. dat. fem. sg. πληροφορία full assurance, assurance
πίστεως n. gen. fem. sg. πίστις faith, assurance, belief, fidelity
τὰς art. acc. fem. pl. ὁ ἡ τό the, this, that, he, she, it
καρδίας n. acc. fem. pl. καρδία heart
ἀπὸ prep. ἀπό (+gen) from, of, out of, since, for, off, at, by, in, on
συνειδήσεως n. gen. fem. sg. συνείδησις conscience
πονηρᾶς adj. gen. fem. sg. πονηρός evil, wicked, bad
καὶ conj. καί and, even, also, but
τὸ art. acc. neut. sg. ὁ ἡ τό the, this, that, he, she, it
σῶμα n. acc. neut. sg. σῶμα body, bodily, slave
ὕδατι n. dat. neut. sg. ὕδωρ water
καθαρῷ adj. dat. neut. sg. καθαρός pure, clean, clear
23 τὴν art. acc. fem. sg. ὁ ἡ τό the, this, that, he, she, it
ὁμολογίαν n. acc. fem. sg. ὁμολογία profession, confession, profess

τῆς art. gen. fem. sg. ὁ ἡ τό the, this, that, he, she, it
ἐλπίδος n. gen. fem. sg. ἐλπίς hope, faith
ἀκλινῆ adj. acc. fem. sg. ἀκλινής without wavering
πιστὸς adj. nom. masc. sg. πιστός faithful, believing, true, sure
γὰρ conj. γάρ for, and, because, but, indeed
ὁ art. nom. masc. sg. ὁ ἡ τό the, this, that, he, she, it
24 καὶ conj. καί and, even, also, but
ἀλλήλους pron. acc. masc. pl. ἀλλήλων one another, themselves, together, mutual
εἰς prep. εἰς (+acc) into, to, unto, for, in, on, toward, against, upon, at, among
παροξυσμὸν n. acc. masc. sg. παροξυσμός contention so sharp, to provoke unto
ἀγάπης n. gen. fem. sg. ἀγάπη love, charity, feast of charity
καὶ conj. καί and, even, also, but
καλῶν adj. gen. neut. pl. καλός good, better, goodly, meet, honest, fair, well, worthy
ἔργων n. gen. neut. pl. ἔργον work, deed, doing labour
25 μὴ particle of negation. μή not, no, lest, neither, none, nothing, nor, never, without
τὴν art. acc. fem. sg. ὁ ἡ τό the, this, that, he, she, it
ἐπισυναγωγὴν n. acc. fem. sg. ἐπισυναγωγή gathering together, assembling together
ἑαυτῶν reflexive pron. gen. masc. 3p. pl. ἑαυτοῦ himself, herself, itself, yourself, ourselves
καθὼς adv. καθώς as, even as, according as, according to
ἔθος n. nom. neut. sg. ἔθος custom, manner, be wont
τισίν indefinite pron. dat. masc. pl. τὶς certain, some, any man, one, any thing
ἀλλὰ conj. ἀλλά but, yea, yet, nevertheless, howbeit, nay, therefore
καὶ conj. καί and, even, also, but
τοσούτῳ demo. pron. dat. neut. sg. τοσοῦτος so much, so great, so many, so long
μᾶλλον adv. μᾶλλον rather, more, more and more, better, much, much the more
ὅσῳ relative pron. dat. neut. sg. ὅσος as many as, whatsoever, that, as long as, how much
τὴν art. acc. fem. sg. ὁ ἡ τό the, this, that, he, she, it
ἡμέραν n. acc. fem. sg. ἡμέρα day, time, year, while, age, day time
26 Ἑκουσίως adv. ἑκουσίως wilfully, willingly
γὰρ conj. γάρ for, and, because, but, indeed
ἡμῶν pron. gen. 1p. pl. ἐγώ I
μετὰ prep. μετά (+gen) with, among, against, (+acc) after
τὸ art. acc. neut. sg. ὁ ἡ τό the, this, that, he, she, it
τὴν art. acc. fem. sg. ὁ ἡ τό the, this, that, he, she, it
ἐπίγνωσιν n. acc. fem. sg. ἐπίγνωσις knowledge, acknowledging, acknowledgement
τῆς art. gen. fem. sg. ὁ ἡ τό the, this, that, he, she, it
ἀληθείας n. gen. fem. sg. ἀλήθεια truth, verity
οὐκέτι adv. οὐκέτι or οὐκ ἔτι no more, no longer, not any more
περὶ prep. περί (+gen) of, for, concerning, (+acc) about, concerning, in
ἁμαρτιῶν n. gen. fem. pl. ἁμαρτία sin, offence, sinful
θυσία n. nom. fem. sg. θυσία sacrifice
27 φοβερὰ adj. nom. fem. sg. φοβερός fearful, terrible
δέ conj. δέ but, and, now, also, to the contrary, rather, then
τις indefinite pron. nom. fem. sg. τὶς certain, some, any man, one, any thing
ἐκδοχὴ n. nom. fem. sg. ἐκδοχή looking for
κρίσεως n. gen. fem. sg. κρίσις judgment, damnation, accusation, condemnation
καὶ conj. καί and, even, also, but
πυρὸς n. gen. neut. sg. πῦρ fire, fiery
ζῆλος n. nom. neut. sg. ζῆλος zeal, envying, indignation, emulation, jealousy
τοὺς art. acc. masc. pl. ὁ ἡ τό the, this, that, he, she, it
ὑπεναντίους adj. acc. masc. pl. ὑπεναντίος contrary, adversary
28 τις indefinite pron. nom. masc. sg. τὶς certain, some, any man, one, any thing
νόμον n. acc. masc. sg. νόμος law, the law
Μωσέως n. gen. masc. sg. Μωσῆς Moses
χωρὶς prep. χωρίς (+gen) without, beside. (adv.) by itself, apart, separately

οἰκτιρμῶν n. gen. masc. pl. οἰκτιρμός mercy
ἐπὶ prep. ἐπί (+gen) on, in, upon, (+dat) in, at, for, upon, (+acc) on, upon, unto, to, against
δυσὶν num. dat. masc. pl. δύο two, twain, both
ἢ particle. ἤ or, than, either, nor, or else, and, rather than
τρισὶν num. dat. masc. pl. τρεῖς three
μάρτυσιν n. dat. masc. pl. μάρτυς or μάρτυρ witness, martyr, record
29 πόσῳ interrog. pron. dat. neut. sg. πόσος how much, how many, how great, how long
χείρονος compar. adj. gen. fem. sg. χείρων worse, sorer, worse and worse
τιμωρίας n. gen. fem. sg. τιμωρία punishment
ὁ art. nom. masc. sg. ὁ ἡ τό the, this, that, he, she, it
τὸν art. acc. masc. sg. ὁ ἡ τό the, this, that, he, she, it
υἱὸν n. acc. masc. sg. υἱός son, child, descendant, offspring, heir
τοῦ art. gen. masc. sg. ὁ ἡ τό the, this, that, he, she, it
Θεοῦ n. gen. masc. sg. θεός God, god
καὶ conj. καί and, even, also, but
τὸ art. acc. neut. sg. ὁ ἡ τό the, this, that, he, she, it
αἷμα n. acc. neut. sg. αἷμα blood
τῆς art. gen. fem. sg. ὁ ἡ τό the, this, that, he, she, it
διαθήκης n. gen. fem. sg. διαθήκη testament, covenant
κοινὸν adj. acc. neut. sg. κοινός common, unclean, defiled, unholy
ἐν prep. ἐν (+dat) in, by, with, among, at, on, through, to, within, into, of, for
ᾧ relative pron. dat. neut. sg. ὅς ἥ ὅ who, which, what, that
καὶ conj. καί and, even, also, but
τὸ art. acc. neut. sg. ὁ ἡ τό the, this, that, he, she, it
Πνεῦμα n. acc. neut. sg. πνεῦμα spirit, Spirit, Ghost, ghost, life. of the spirit, wind
τῆς art. gen. fem. sg. ὁ ἡ τό the, this, that, he, she, it
χάριτος n. gen. fem. sg. χάρις grace, thank, favour, pleasure
30 γὰρ conj. γάρ for, and, because, but, indeed
τὸν art. acc. masc. sg. ὁ ἡ τό the, this, that, he, she, it
Ἐμοὶ pron. dat. 1p. sg. ἐγώ I
ἐκδίκησις n. nom. fem. sg. ἐκδίκησις vengeance, punishment, revenge
ἐγὼ pron. nom. 1p. sg. ἐγώ I
Κύριος n. nom. masc. sg. κύριος Lord, lord, master, sir, LORD, God, Master, owner
καὶ conj. καί and, even, also, but
πάλιν adv. πάλιν again
Κύριος n. nom. masc. sg. κύριος Lord, lord, master, sir, LORD, God, Master, owner
τὸν art. acc. masc. sg. ὁ ἡ τό the, this, that, he, she, it
λαὸν n. acc. masc. sg. λαός people
αὐτοῦ pron. gen. masc. 3p. sg. αὐτός ἡ ὁ self, of oneself, even, very, the same, he, she, it
31 φοβερὸν adj. nom. neut. sg. φοβερός fearful, terrible
τὸ art. nom. neut. sg. ὁ ἡ τό the, this, that, he, she, it
εἰς prep. εἰς (+acc) into, to, unto, for, in, on, toward, against, upon, at, among
χεῖρας n. acc. fem. pl. χείρ hand
Θεοῦ n. gen. masc. sg. θεός God, god
32 δὲ conj. δέ but, and, now, also, to the contrary, rather, then
τὰς art. acc. fem. pl. ὁ ἡ τό the, this, that, he, she, it
πρότερον adv. πρότερον before, first, former, at the first
ἡμέρας n. acc. fem. pl. ἡμέρα day, time, year, while, age, day time
ἐν prep. ἐν (+dat) in, by, with, among, at, on, through, to, within, into, of, for
αἷς relative pron. dat. fem. pl. ὅς ἥ ὅ who, which, what, that
πολλὴν adj. acc. fem. sg. πολύς many, great, much, long, abundant
ἄθλησιν n. acc. fem. sg. ἄθλησις fight
παθημάτων n. gen. neut. pl. πάθημα suffering, affliction, affection, motion
33 τοῦτο demo. pron. acc. neut. sg. οὗτος αὕτη τοῦτο this, the same, this same, he, she, it
μὲν conj. μέν indeed, verily, truly, even, so, some

ὀνειδισμοῖς n. dat. masc. pl. ὀνειδισμός reproach
τε conj. τέ and, both, also
καὶ conj. καί and, even, also, but
θλίψεσι n. dat. fem. pl. θλῖψις tribulation, affliction, anguish, persecution
τοῦτο demo. pron. acc. neut. sg. οὗτος αὕτη τοῦτο this, the same, this same, he, she, it
δὲ conj. δέ but, and, now, also, to the contrary, rather, then
κοινωνοὶ n. nom. masc. pl. κοινωνός partaker, partner, companion, fellowship
τῶν art. gen. masc. pl. ὁ ἡ τό the, this, that, he, she, it
οὕτως adv. οὕτω οὕτως so, even so, thus, on this wise, likewise, after this manner
34 καὶ conj. καί and, even, also, but
γὰρ conj. γάρ for, and, because, but, indeed
τοῖς art. dat. masc. pl. ὁ ἡ τό the, this, that, he, she, it
δεσμοῖς n. dat. masc. pl. δεσμός bond, band, chain, string
μου pron. gen. 1p. sg. ἐγώ I
καὶ conj. καί and, even, also, but
τὴν art. acc. fem. sg. ὁ ἡ τό the, this, that, he, she, it
ἁρπαγὴν n. acc. fem. sg. ἁρπαγή extortion, ravening, spoiling
τῶν art. gen. neut. pl. ὁ ἡ τό the, this, that, he, she, it
ὑμῶν pron. gen. 2p. pl. σύ thou, you
μετὰ prep. μετά (+gen) with, among, against, (+acc) after
χαρᾶς n. gen. fem. sg. χαρά joy, gladness, joyfulness
ἐν prep. ἐν (+dat) in, by, with, among, at, on, through, to, within, into, of, for
ἑαυτοῖς reflexive pron. dat. masc. 3p. pl. ἑαυτοῦ himself, herself, itself, yourself, ourselves
κρείττονα compar. adj. acc. fem. sg. κρείττων better
ὕπαρξιν n. acc. fem. sg. ὕπαρξις goods, substance
ἐν prep. ἐν (+dat) in, by, with, among, at, on, through, to, within, into, of, for
οὐρανοῖς n. dat. masc. pl. οὐρανός heaven, air, sky
καὶ conj. καί and, even, also, but
35 μὴ particle of negation. μή not, no, lest, neither, none, nothing, nor, never, without
οὖν conj. οὖν therefore, then, so, and, now, wherefore
τὴν art. acc. fem. sg. ὁ ἡ τό the, this, that, he, she, it
παρρησίαν n. acc. fem. sg. παρρησία boldness, confidence, openly, plainly, freely
ὑμῶν pron. gen. 2p. pl. σύ thou, you
ἥτις relative pron. nom. fem. sg. ὅστις which, who, whosoever, that, whatsoever
μισθαποδοσίαν n. acc. fem. sg. μισθαποδοσία recompence of reward
μεγάλην adj. acc. fem. sg. μέγας great, loud, greatest, high, large, mighty, strong
36 ὑπομονῆς n. gen. fem. sg. ὑπομονή patience, enduring
γὰρ conj. γάρ for, and, because, but, indeed
χρείαν n. acc. fem. sg. χρεία need, necessity, lack, want
ἵνα conj. ἵνα that, to, lest, for to, so that, albeit, because, for, so as
τὸ art. acc. neut. sg. ὁ ἡ τό the, this, that, he, she, it
θέλημα n. acc. neut. sg. θέλημα will, desire, pleasure
τοῦ art. gen. masc. sg. ὁ ἡ τό the, this, that, he, she, it
Θεοῦ n. gen. masc. sg. θεός God, god
τὴν art. acc. fem. sg. ὁ ἡ τό the, this, that, he, she, it
ἐπαγγελίαν n. acc. fem. sg. ἐπαγγελία promise, message
37 ἔτι adv. ἔτι yet, more, any more, further, still, moreover
γὰρ conj. γάρ for, and, because, but, indeed
μικρὸν adj. acc. masc. sg. μικρός little, small, least, less
ὅσον relative pron. acc. masc. sg. ὅσος as many as, whatsoever, that, as long as, how much
ὅσον relative pron. acc. masc. sg. ὅσος as many as, whatsoever, that, as long as, how much
Ὁ art. nom. masc. sg. ὁ ἡ τό the, this, that, he, she, it
καὶ conj. καί and, even, also, but
οὐ particle of negation. οὐ οὐκ οὐχ not, no, neither, none, nay, nor, never, nothing
38 ὁ art. nom. masc. sg. ὁ ἡ τό the, this, that, he, she, it

δὲ conj. δέ but, and, now, also, to the contrary, rather, then
δίκαιός adj. nom. masc. sg. δίκαιος righteous, just, meet, right
ἐκ prep. ἐκ ἐξ (+gen) of, from, out of, by, on, with, in, among, through
πίστεως n. gen. fem. sg. πίστις faith, assurance, belief, fidelity
καὶ conj. καί and, even, also, but
ἐὰν conj. ἐάν if, soever, except, though, and if, but, whether, if so, so
οὐκ particle of negation. οὐ οὐκ οὐχ not, no, neither, none, nay, nor, never, nothing
ἡ art. nom. fem. sg. ὁ ἡ τό the, this, that, he, she, it
ψυχή n. nom. fem. sg. ψυχή life, soul, mind, heart
μου pron. gen. 1p. sg. ἐγώ I
ἐν prep. ἐν (+dat) in, by, with, among, at, on, through, to, within, into, of, for
αὐτῷ pron. dat. masc. 3p. sg. αὐτός ή ό self, of oneself, even, very, the same, he, she, it
39 ἡμεῖς pron. nom. 1p. pl. ἐγώ I
δὲ conj. δέ but, and, now, also, to the contrary, rather, then
οὐκ particle of negation. οὐ οὐκ οὐχ not, no, neither, none, nay, nor, never, nothing
ὑποστολῆς n. gen. fem. sg. ὑποστολή drawing back
εἰς prep. εἰς (+acc) into, to, unto, for, in, on, toward, against, upon, at, among
ἀπώλειαν n. acc. fem. sg. ἀπώλεια destruction, perdition, waste, damnation
ἀλλὰ conj. ἀλλά but, yea, yet, nevertheless, howbeit, nay, therefore
πίστεως n. gen. fem. sg. πίστις faith, assurance, belief, fidelity
εἰς prep. εἰς (+acc) into, to, unto, for, in, on, toward, against, upon, at, among
περιποίησιν n. acc. fem. sg. περιποίησις saving, obtain, obtaining, peculiar
ψυχῆς n. gen. fem. sg. ψυχή life, soul, mind, heart

11

1 δὲ conj. δέ but, and, now, also, to the contrary, rather, then
πίστις n. nom. fem. sg. πίστις faith, assurance, belief, fidelity
ὑπόστασις n. nom. fem. sg. ὑπόστασις confidence, substance, person, nature
πραγμάτων n. gen. neut. pl. πρᾶγμα thing, matter, business, work
ἔλεγχος n. nom. masc. sg. ἔλεγχος reproof, evidence
οὐ particle of negation. οὐ οὐκ οὐχ not, no, neither, none, nay, nor, never, nothing
2 ἐν prep. ἐν (+dat) in, by, with, among, at, on, through, to, within, into, of, for
ταύτῃ demo. pron. dat. fem. sg. οὗτος αὕτη τοῦτο this, the same, this same, he, she, it
γὰρ conj. γάρ for, and, because, but, indeed
οἱ art. nom. masc. pl. ὁ ἡ τό the, this, that, he, she, it
πρεσβύτεροι adj. nom. masc. pl. πρεσβύτερος elder, elder woman, eldest, old man
3 πίστει n. dat. fem. sg. πίστις faith, assurance, belief, fidelity
τοὺς art. acc. masc. pl. ὁ ἡ τό the, this, that, he, she, it
αἰῶνας n. acc. masc. pl. αἰών ever, ever and ever, evermore, age, eternal, world
ῥήματι n. dat. neut. sg. ῥῆμα word, saying, thing
Θεοῦ n. gen. masc. sg. θεός God, god
εἰς prep. εἰς (+acc) into, to, unto, for, in, on, toward, against, upon, at, among
τὰ art. nom. neut. pl. ὁ ἡ τό the, this, that, he, she, it
μὴ particle of negation. μή not, no, lest, neither, none, nothing, nor, never, without
ἐκ prep. ἐκ ἐξ (+gen) of, from, out of, by, on, with, in, among, through
τὰ art. nom. neut. pl. ὁ ἡ τό the, this, that, he, she, it
4 πίστει n. dat. fem. sg. πίστις faith, assurance, belief, fidelity
πλείονα compar. adj. acc. fem. sg. πολύς many, great, much, long, abundant
θυσίαν n. acc. fem. sg. θυσία sacrifice
῎Αβελ n. nom. masc. sg. ῎Αβελ Abel
παρὰ prep. παρά (+gen) of, from, (+dat) with, for, (+acc) beside, at, by, above, against
Κάϊν n. acc. masc. sg. Κάϊν Cain
τῷ art. dat. masc. sg. ὁ ἡ τό the, this, that, he, she, it
Θεῷ n. dat. masc. sg. θεός God, god

δι' prep. διά (+gen) by, through, with, in, of, (+acc) for, because of, for a cause
ἧς relative pron. gen. fem. sg. ὅς ἥ ὅ who, which, what, that
δίκαιος adj. nom. masc. sg. δίκαιος righteous, just, meet, right
ἐπὶ prep. ἐπί (+gen) on, in, upon, (+dat) in, at, for, upon, (+acc) on, upon, unto, to, against
τοῖς art. dat. neut. pl. ὁ ἡ τό the, this, that, he, she, it
δώροις n. dat. neut. pl. δῶρον gift, offering
αὐτοῦ pron. gen. masc. 3p. sg. αὐτός ή ό self, of oneself, even, very, the same, he, she, it
τοῦ art. gen. masc. sg. ὁ ἡ τό the, this, that, he, she, it
Θεοῦ n. gen. masc. sg. θεός God, god
καὶ conj. καί and, even, also, but
δι' prep. διά (+gen) by, through, with, in, of, (+acc) for, because of, for a cause
αὐτῆς pron. gen. fem. 3p. sg. αὐτός ή ό self, of oneself, even, very, the same, he, she, it
ἔτι adv. ἔτι yet, more, any more, further, still, moreover
5 πίστει n. dat. fem. sg. πίστις faith, assurance, belief, fidelity
Ἑνὼχ n. nom. masc. sg. Ἐνώχ Enoch
τοῦ art. gen. neut. sg. ὁ ἡ τό the, this, that, he, she, it
μὴ particle of negation. μή not, no, lest, neither, none, nothing, nor, never, without
θάνατον n. acc. masc. sg. θάνατος death
καὶ conj. καί and, even, also, but
οὐχ particle of negation. οὐ οὐκ οὐχ not, no, neither, none, nay, nor, never, nothing
διότι conj. διότι for, because, because that, therefore
αὐτὸν pron. acc. masc. 3p. sg. αὐτός ή ό self, of oneself, even, very, the same, he, she, it
ὁ art. nom. masc. sg. ὁ ἡ τό the, this, that, he, she, it
Θεός n. nom. masc. sg. θεός God, god
πρὸ prep. πρό (+gen) before, above
γὰρ conj. γάρ for, and, because, but, indeed
τῆς art. gen. fem. sg. ὁ ἡ τό the, this, that, he, she, it
μεταθέσεως n. gen. fem. sg. μετάθεσις change, removing, translation
αὐτοῦ pron. gen. masc. 3p. sg. αὐτός ή ό self, of oneself, even, very, the same, he, she, it
τῷ art. dat. masc. sg. ὁ ἡ τό the, this, that, he, she, it
Θεῷ n. dat. masc. sg. θεός God, god
6 χωρὶς prep. χωρίς (+gen) without, beside. (adv.) by itself, apart, separately
δὲ conj. δέ but, and, now, also, to the contrary, rather, then
πίστεως n. gen. fem. sg. πίστις faith, assurance, belief, fidelity
ἀδύνατον adj. nom. neut. sg. ἀδύνατος impossible, not possible, cannot do
γὰρ conj. γάρ for, and, because, but, indeed
τὸν art. acc. masc. sg. ὁ ἡ τό the, this, that, he, she, it
τῷ art. dat. masc. sg. ὁ ἡ τό the, this, that, he, she, it
Θεῷ n. dat. masc. sg. θεός God, god
ὅτι conj. ὅτι that, for, because, how that, how, because that, for that, though
καὶ conj. καί and, even, also, but
τοῖς art. dat. masc. pl. ὁ ἡ τό the, this, that, he, she, it
αὐτὸν pron. acc. masc. 3p. sg. αὐτός ή ό self, of oneself, even, very, the same, he, she, it
μισθαποδότης n. nom. masc. sg. μισθαποδότης rewarder
7 πίστει n. dat. fem. sg. πίστις faith, assurance, belief, fidelity
Νῶε n. nom. masc. sg. Νῶε Noe, Noah
περὶ prep. περί (+gen) of, for, concerning, (+acc) about, concerning, in
τῶν art. gen. neut. pl. ὁ ἡ τό the, this, that, he, she, it
μηδέπω adv. μηδέπω not as yet
κιβωτὸν n. acc. fem. sg. κιβωτός ark
εἰς prep. εἰς (+acc) into, to, unto, for, in, on, toward, against, upon, at, among
σωτηρίαν n. acc. fem. sg. σωτηρία salvation, deliver, health, saving
τοῦ art. gen. masc. sg. ὁ ἡ τό the, this, that, he, she, it
οἴκου n. gen. masc. sg. οἶκος house, home, household
αὐτοῦ pron. gen. masc. 3p. sg. αὐτός ή ό self, of oneself, even, very, the same, he, she, it

δι' prep. διά (+gen) by, through, with, in, of, (+acc) for, because of, for a cause
ἧς relative pron. gen. fem. sg. ὅς ἥ ὅ who, which, what, that
τὸν art. acc. masc. sg. ὁ ἡ τό the, this, that, he, she, it
κόσμον n. acc. masc. sg. κόσμος world, adorning
καὶ conj. καί and, even, also, but
τῆς art. gen. fem. sg. ὁ ἡ τό the, this, that, he, she, it
κατὰ prep. κατά (+gen) against, by, throughout, down, (+acc) according to, after, with
πίστιν n. acc. fem. sg. πίστις faith, assurance, belief, fidelity
δικαιοσύνης n. gen. fem. sg. δικαιοσύνη righteousness
κληρονόμος n. nom. masc. sg. κληρονόμος heir
8 πίστει n. dat. fem. sg. πίστις faith, assurance, belief, fidelity
Ἀβραὰμ n. nom. masc. sg. Ἀβραάμ Abraham
εἰς prep. εἰς (+acc) into, to, unto, for, in, on, toward, against, upon, at, among
τὸν art. acc. masc. sg. ὁ ἡ τό the, this, that, he, she, it
τόπον n. acc. masc. sg. τόπος place, room, quarter
ὃν relative pron. acc. masc. sg. ὅς ἥ ὅ who, which, what, that
εἰς prep. εἰς (+acc) into, to, unto, for, in, on, toward, against, upon, at, among
κληρονομίαν n. acc. fem. sg. κληρονομία inheritance
καὶ conj. καί and, even, also, but
μὴ particle of negation. μή not, no, lest, neither, none, nothing, nor, never, without
ποῦ particle of place. ποῦ where, whither
9 πίστει n. dat. fem. sg. πίστις faith, assurance, belief, fidelity
εἰς prep. εἰς (+acc) into, to, unto, for, in, on, toward, against, upon, at, among
τὴν art. acc. fem. sg. ὁ ἡ τό the, this, that, he, she, it
γῆν n. acc. fem. sg. γῆ earth, land, ground, country
τῆς art. gen. fem. sg. ὁ ἡ τό the, this, that, he, she, it
ἐπαγγελίας n. gen. fem. sg. ἐπαγγελία promise, message
ὡς adv. ὡς as, when, as it were, how, about, like, as soon as, even as, while
ἀλλοτρίαν adj. acc. fem. sg. ἀλλότριος stranger, another man, alien, strange
ἐν prep. ἐν (+dat) in, by, with, among, at, on, through, to, within, into, of, for
σκηναῖς n. dat. fem. pl. σκηνή tabernacle, habitation
μετὰ prep. μετά (+gen) with, among, against, (+acc) after
Ἰσαὰκ n. gen. masc. sg. Ἰσαάκ Isaac
καὶ conj. καί and, even, also, but
Ἰακὼβ n. gen. masc. sg. Ἰακώβ Jacob
τῶν art. gen. masc. pl. ὁ ἡ τό the, this, that, he, she, it
συγκληρονόμων adj. gen. masc. pl. συγκληρονόμος joint-heir, fellowheir, heir together
τῆς art. gen. fem. sg. ὁ ἡ τό the, this, that, he, she, it
ἐπαγγελίας n. gen. fem. sg. ἐπαγγελία promise, message
τῆς art. gen. fem. sg. ὁ ἡ τό the, this, that, he, she, it
αὐτῆς adj. gen. fem. sg. αὐτός ή ό self, of oneself, even, very, the same, he, she, it
10 γὰρ conj. γάρ for, and, because, but, indeed
τὴν art. acc. fem. sg. ὁ ἡ τό the, this, that, he, she, it
τοὺς art. acc. masc. pl. ὁ ἡ τό the, this, that, he, she, it
θεμελίους n. acc. masc. pl. θεμέλιος foundation
πόλιν n. acc. fem. sg. πόλις city
ἧς relative pron. gen. fem. sg. ὅς ἥ ὅ who, which, what, that
τεχνίτης n. nom. masc. sg. τεχνίτης craftsmen, builder
καὶ conj. καί and, even, also, but
δημιουργὸς n. nom. masc. sg. δημιουργός maker
ὁ art. nom. masc. sg. ὁ ἡ τό the, this, that, he, she, it
Θεός n. nom. masc. sg. θεός God, god
11 πίστει n. dat. fem. sg. πίστις faith, assurance, belief, fidelity
καὶ conj. καί and, even, also, but
αὐτὴ pron. nom. fem. 3p. sg. αὐτός ή ό self, of oneself, even, very, the same, he, she, it

Σάρρα n. nom. fem. sg. Σάρρα Sara, Sarah
δύναμιν n. acc. fem. sg. δύναμις power, mighty work, miracle, strength, might
εἰς prep. εἰς (+acc) into, to, unto, for, in, on, toward, against, upon, at, among
καταβολὴν n. acc. fem. sg. καταβολή foundation
σπέρματος n. gen. neut. sg. σπέρμα seed, issue
καὶ conj. καί and, even, also, but
παρὰ prep. παρά (+gen) of, from, (+dat) with, for, (+acc) beside, at, by, above, against
καιρὸν n. acc. masc. sg. καιρός time, season, due time, opportunity
ἡλικίας n. gen. fem. sg. ἡλικία stature, age
ἐπεὶ conj. ἐπεί because, otherwise, seeing, else, for then, for as much as, for, since
πιστὸν adj. acc. masc. sg. πιστός faithful, believing, true, sure
τὸν art. acc. masc. sg. ὁ ἡ τό the, this, that, he, she, it
12 διὸ conj. διό wherefore, therefore, for which cause
καὶ conj. καί and, even, also, but
ἀφ' prep. ἀπό (+gen) from, of, out of, since, for, off, at, by, in, on
ἑνὸς num. gen. masc. sg. εἷς or ἕν one, other, some, any, only, a certain
καὶ conj. καί and, even, also, but
ταῦτα demo. pron. acc. neut. pl. οὗτος αὕτη τοῦτο this, the same, this same, he, she, it
καθὼς adv. καθώς as, even as, according as, according to
τὰ art. nom. neut. pl. ὁ ἡ τό the, this, that, he, she, it
ἄστρα n. nom. neut. pl. ἄστρον star
τοῦ art. gen. masc. sg. ὁ ἡ τό the, this, that, he, she, it
οὐρανοῦ n. gen. masc. sg. οὐρανός heaven, air, sky
τῷ art. dat. neut. sg. ὁ ἡ τό the, this, that, he, she, it
πλήθει n. dat. neut. sg. πλῆθος multitude, bundle, company
καὶ conj. καί and, even, also, but
ὡσεὶ adv. ὡσεί about, as, like, as it had been, as it were, like as
ἄμμος n. nom. fem. sg. ἄμμος sand
ἡ art. nom. fem. sg. ὁ ἡ τό the, this, that, he, she, it
παρὰ prep. παρά (+gen) of, from, (+dat) with, for, (+acc) beside, at, by, above, against
τὸ art. acc. neut. sg. ὁ ἡ τό the, this, that, he, she, it
χεῖλος n. acc. neut. sg. χεῖλος lip, shore
τῆς art. gen. fem. sg. ὁ ἡ τό the, this, that, he, she, it
θαλάσσης n. gen. fem. sg. θάλασσα sea
ἡ art. nom. fem. sg. ὁ ἡ τό the, this, that, he, she, it
ἀναρίθμητος adj. nom. fem. sg. ἀναρίθμητος innumerable
13 Κατὰ prep. κατά (+gen) against, by, throughout, down, (+acc) according to, after, with
πίστιν n. acc. fem. sg. πίστις faith, assurance, belief, fidelity
οὗτοι demo. pron. nom. masc. pl. οὗτος αὕτη τοῦτο this, the same, this same, he, she, it
πάντες adj. nom. masc. pl. πᾶς πᾶσα πᾶν all, every, whosoever, every one, no, whole, any
μὴ particle of negation. μή not, no, lest, neither, none, nothing, nor, never, without
τὰς art. acc. fem. pl. ὁ ἡ τό the, this, that, he, she, it
ἐπαγγελίας n. acc. fem. pl. ἐπαγγελία promise, message
ἀλλὰ conj. ἀλλά but, yea, yet, nevertheless, howbeit, nay, therefore
πόρρωθεν adv. πόρρωθεν afar off
αὐτὰς pron. acc. fem. 3p. pl. αὐτός ή ό self, of oneself, even, very, the same, he, she, it
καὶ conj. καί and, even, also, but
καὶ conj. καί and, even, also, but
καὶ conj. καί and, even, also, but
ὅτι conj. ὅτι that, for, because, how that, how, because that, for that, though
ξένοι adj. nom. masc. pl. ξένος stranger, strange, host
καὶ conj. καί and, even, also, but
παρεπίδημοί adj. nom. masc. pl. παρεπίδημος pilgrim
ἐπὶ prep. ἐπί (+gen) on, in, upon, (+dat) in, at, for, upon, (+acc) on, upon, unto, to, against
τῆς art. gen. fem. sg. ὁ ἡ τό the, this, that, he, she, it

γῆς n. gen. fem. sg. γῆ earth, land, ground, country
14 οἱ art. nom. masc. pl. ὁ ἡ τό the, this, that, he, she, it
γὰρ conj. γάρ for, and, because, but, indeed
τοιαῦτα demo. pron. acc. neut. pl. τοιοῦτος such, like
ὅτι conj. ὅτι that, for, because, how that, how, because that, for that, though
πατρίδα n. acc. fem. sg. πατρίς country, own country
15 καὶ conj. καί and, even, also, but
εἰ conj. εἰ if, whether, that, though, forasmuch
μὲν conj. μέν indeed, verily, truly, even, so, some
ἐκείνης demo. pron. gen. fem. sg. ἐκεῖνος that, he, the same, that same
ἀφ' prep. ἀπό (+gen) from, of, out of, since, for, off, at, by, in, on
ἧς relative pron. gen. fem. sg. ὅς ἥ ὅ who, which, what, that
ἂν particle. ἄν Indicating contingency. No English translation.
καιρὸν n. acc. masc. sg. καιρός time, season, due time, opportunity
16 νυνὶ adv. νυνί now
δὲ conj. δέ but, and, now, also, to the contrary, rather, then
κρείττονος compar. adj. gen. fem. sg. κρείττων better
τοῦτ' demo. pron. nom. neut. sg. οὗτος αὕτη τοῦτο this, the same, this same, he, she, it
ἐπουρανίου adj. gen. fem. sg. ἐπουράνιος heavenly, celestial, high, in heaven
διὸ conj. διό wherefore, therefore, for which cause
οὐκ particle of negation. οὐ οὐκ οὐχ not, no, neither, none, nay, nor, never, nothing
αὐτοὺς pron. acc. masc. 3p. pl. αὐτός ή ό self, of oneself, even, very, the same, he, she, it
ὁ art. nom. masc. sg. ὁ ἡ τό the, this, that, he, she, it
Θεὸς n. nom. masc. sg. θεός God, god
Θεὸς n. nom. masc. sg. θεός God, god
αὐτῶν pron. gen. masc. 3p. pl. αὐτός ή ό self, of oneself, even, very, the same, he, she, it
γὰρ conj. γάρ for, and, because, but, indeed
αὐτοῖς pron. dat. masc. 3p. pl. αὐτός ή ό self, of oneself, even, very, the same, he, she, it
πόλιν n. acc. fem. sg. πόλις city
17 Πίστει n. dat. fem. sg. πίστις faith, assurance, belief, fidelity
Ἀβραὰμ n. nom. masc. sg. Ἀβραάμ Abraham
τὸν art. acc. masc. sg. ὁ ἡ τό the, this, that, he, she, it
Ἰσαὰκ n. acc. masc. sg. Ἰσαάκ Isaac
καὶ conj. καί and, even, also, but
τὸν art. acc. masc. sg. ὁ ἡ τό the, this, that, he, she, it
μονογενῆ adj. acc. masc. sg. μονογενής only begotten, only, only child
ὁ art. nom. masc. sg. ὁ ἡ τό the, this, that, he, she, it
τὰς art. acc. fem. pl. ὁ ἡ τό the, this, that, he, she, it
ἐπαγγελίας n. acc. fem. pl. ἐπαγγελία promise, message
18 πρὸς prep. πρός (+gen) for, (+dat) at, (+acc) unto, to, with, for, against
ὃν relative pron. acc. masc. sg. ὅς ἥ ὅ who, which, what, that
ὅτι conj. ὅτι that, for, because, how that, how, because that, for that, though
Ἐν prep. ἐν (+dat) in, by, with, among, at, on, through, to, within, into, of, for
Ἰσαὰκ n. dat. masc. sg. Ἰσαάκ Isaac
σοι pron. dat. 2p. sg. σύ thou, you
σπέρμα n. nom. neut. sg. σπέρμα seed, issue
19 ὅτι conj. ὅτι that, for, because, how that, how, because that, for that, though
καὶ conj. καί and, even, also, but
ἐκ prep. ἐκ ἐξ (+gen) of, from, out of, by, on, with, in, among, through
νεκρῶν adj. gen. masc. pl. νεκρός dead
δυνατὸς adj. nom. masc. sg. δυνατός able, possible, mighty, strong
ὁ art. nom. masc. sg. ὁ ἡ τό the, this, that, he, she, it
Θεός n. nom. masc. sg. θεός God, god
ὅθεν adv. ὅθεν wherefore, from whence, whereupon, where, from thence, whence
αὐτὸν pron. acc. masc. 3p. sg. αὐτός ή ό self, of oneself, even, very, the same, he, she, it

καὶ conj. καί and, even, also, but
ἐν prep. ἐν (+dat) in, by, with, among, at, on, through, to, within, into, of, for
παραβολῇ n. dat. fem. sg. παραβολή parable, figure, comparison, proverb
20 πίστει n. dat. fem. sg. πίστις faith, assurance, belief, fidelity
περὶ prep. περί (+gen) of, for, concerning, (+acc) about, concerning, in
Ἰσαὰκ n. nom. masc. sg. Ἰσαάκ Isaac
τὸν art. acc. masc. sg. ὁ ἡ τό the, this, that, he, she, it
Ἰακὼβ n. acc. masc. sg. Ἰακώβ Jacob
καὶ conj. καί and, even, also, but
τὸν art. acc. masc. sg. ὁ ἡ τό the, this, that, he, she, it
Ἠσαῦ n. acc. masc. sg. Ἠσαῦ Esau
21 πίστει n. dat. fem. sg. πίστις faith, assurance, belief, fidelity
Ἰακὼβ n. nom. masc. sg. Ἰακώβ Jacob
ἕκαστον adj. acc. masc. sg. ἕκαστος every man, every, every one, any man, each
τῶν art. gen. masc. pl. ὁ ἡ τό the, this, that, he, she, it
υἱῶν n. gen. masc. pl. υἱός son, child, descendant, offspring, heir
Ἰωσὴφ n. gen. masc. sg. Ἰωσήφ Joseph
καὶ conj. καί and, even, also, but
ἐπὶ prep. ἐπί (+gen) on, in, upon, (+dat) in, at, for, upon, (+acc) on, upon, unto, to, against
τὸ art. acc. neut. sg. ὁ ἡ τό the, this, that, he, she, it
ἄκρον n. acc. neut. sg. ἄκρον one end, uttermost part, tip, top
τῆς art. gen. fem. sg. ὁ ἡ τό the, this, that, he, she, it
ῥάβδου n. gen. fem. sg. ῥάβδος rod, sceptre, stave, staff
αὐτοῦ pron. gen. masc. 3p. sg. αὐτός ἡ ὁ self, of oneself, even, very, the same, he, she, it
22 πίστει n. dat. fem. sg. πίστις faith, assurance, belief, fidelity
Ἰωσὴφ n. nom. masc. sg. Ἰωσήφ Joseph
περὶ prep. περί (+gen) of, for, concerning, (+acc) about, concerning, in
τῆς art. gen. fem. sg. ὁ ἡ τό the, this, that, he, she, it
ἐξόδου n. gen. fem. sg. ἔξοδος decease, departing
τῶν art. gen. masc. pl. ὁ ἡ τό the, this, that, he, she, it
υἱῶν n. gen. masc. pl. υἱός son, child, descendant, offspring, heir
Ἰσραὴλ pron. name. masc. inde. Ἰσραήλ Israel
καὶ conj. καί and, even, also, but
περὶ prep. περί (+gen) of, for, concerning, (+acc) about, concerning, in
τῶν art. gen. neut. pl. ὁ ἡ τό the, this, that, he, she, it
ὀστέων n. gen. neut. pl. ὀστέον bone
αὐτοῦ pron. gen. masc. 3p. sg. αὐτός ἡ ὁ self, of oneself, even, very, the same, he, she, it
23 πίστει n. dat. fem. sg. πίστις faith, assurance, belief, fidelity
Μωσῆς n. nom. masc. sg. Μωσῆς Moses
τρίμηνον adj. acc. neut. sg. τρίμηνον three months
ὑπὸ prep. ὑπό (+gen) of, by, with, from, among, (+acc) under
τῶν art. gen. masc. pl. ὁ ἡ τό the, this, that, he, she, it
πατέρων n. gen. masc. pl. πατήρ Father, father, parent
αὐτοῦ pron. gen. masc. 3p. sg. αὐτός ἡ ὁ self, of oneself, even, very, the same, he, she, it
διότι conj. διότι for, because, because that, therefore
ἀστεῖον adj. acc. neut. sg. ἀστεῖος fair, proper
τὸ art. acc. neut. sg. ὁ ἡ τό the, this, that, he, she, it
παιδίον n. acc. neut. sg. παιδίον child, little child, damsel
καὶ conj. καί and, even, also, but
οὐκ particle of negation. οὐ οὐκ οὐχ not, no, neither, none, nay, nor, never, nothing
τὸ art. acc. neut. sg. ὁ ἡ τό the, this, that, he, she, it
διάταγμα n. acc. neut. sg. διάταγμα commandment
τοῦ art. gen. masc. sg. ὁ ἡ τό the, this, that, he, she, it
βασιλέως n. gen. masc. sg. βασιλεύς king
24 πίστει n. dat. fem. sg. πίστις faith, assurance, belief, fidelity

Μωσῆς n. nom. masc. sg. Μωσῆς Moses
μέγας adj. nom. masc. sg. μέγας great, loud, greatest, high, large, mighty, strong
υἱὸς n. nom. masc. sg. υἱός son, child, descendant, offspring, heir
θυγατρὸς n. gen. fem. sg. θυγάτηρ daughter
Φαραώ n. gen. masc. sg. Φαραώ Pharaoh
25 μᾶλλον adv. μᾶλλον rather, more, more and more, better, much, much the more
τῷ art. dat. masc. sg. ὁ ἡ τό the, this, that, he, she, it
λαῷ n. dat. masc. sg. λαός people
τοῦ art. gen. masc. sg. ὁ ἡ τό the, this, that, he, she, it
Θεοῦ n. gen. masc. sg. θεός God, god
ἢ particle. ἤ or, than, either, nor, or else, and, rather than
πρόσκαιρον adj. acc. fem. sg. πρόσκαιρος endure but for a time, for a season, temporal
ἁμαρτίας n. gen. fem. sg. ἁμαρτία sin, offence, sinful
ἀπόλαυσιν n. acc. fem. sg. ἀπόλαυσις enjoy
26 μείζονα compar. adj. acc. masc. sg. μέγας great, loud, greatest, high, large, mighty, strong
πλοῦτον n. acc. masc. sg. πλοῦτος riches
τῶν art. gen. masc. pl. ὁ ἡ τό the, this, that, he, she, it
ἐν prep. ἐν (+dat) in, by, with, among, at, on, through, to, within, into, of, for
Αἰγύπτῳ n. dat. fem. sg. Αἴγυπτος Egypt
θησαυρῶν n. gen. masc. pl. θησαυρός treasure
τὸν art. acc. masc. sg. ὁ ἡ τό the, this, that, he, she, it
ὀνειδισμὸν n. acc. masc. sg. ὀνειδισμός reproach
τοῦ art. gen. masc. sg. ὁ ἡ τό the, this, that, he, she, it
Χριστοῦ n. gen. masc. sg. Χριστός Christ
γὰρ conj. γάρ for, and, because, but, indeed
εἰς prep. εἰς (+acc) into, to, unto, for, in, on, toward, against, upon, at, among
τὴν art. acc. fem. sg. ὁ ἡ τό the, this, that, he, she, it
μισθαποδοσίαν n. acc. fem. sg. μισθαποδοσία recompence of the reward
27 πίστει n. dat. fem. sg. πίστις faith, assurance, belief, fidelity
Αἴγυπτον n. acc. fem. sg. Αἴγυπτος Egypt
μὴ particle of negation. μή not, no, lest, neither, none, nothing, nor, never, without
τὸν art. acc. masc. sg. ὁ ἡ τό the, this, that, he, she, it
θυμὸν n. acc. masc. sg. θυμός wrath, fierceness, indignation
τοῦ art. gen. masc. sg. ὁ ἡ τό the, this, that, he, she, it
βασιλέως n. gen. masc. sg. βασιλεύς king
τὸν art. acc. masc. sg. ὁ ἡ τό the, this, that, he, she, it
γὰρ conj. γάρ for, and, because, but, indeed
ἀόρατον adj. acc. masc. sg. ἀόρατος invisible, invisible thing
ὡς adv. ὡς as, when, as it were, how, about, like, as soon as, even as, while
28 πίστει n. dat. fem. sg. πίστις faith, assurance, belief, fidelity
τὸ art. acc. neut. sg. ὁ ἡ τό the, this, that, he, she, it
πάσχα n. acc. neut. sg. πάσχα passover, Easter
καὶ conj. καί and, even, also, but
τὴν art. acc. fem. sg. ὁ ἡ τό the, this, that, he, she, it
πρόσχυσιν n. acc. fem. sg. πρόσχυσις sprinkling
τοῦ art. gen. neut. sg. ὁ ἡ τό the, this, that, he, she, it
αἵματος n. gen. neut. sg. αἷμα blood
ἵνα conj. ἵνα that, to, lest, for to, so that, albeit, because, for, so as
μὴ particle of negation. μή not, no, lest, neither, none, nothing, nor, never, without
ὁ art. nom. masc. sg. ὁ ἡ τό the, this, that, he, she, it
τὰ art. acc. neut. pl. ὁ ἡ τό the, this, that, he, she, it
πρωτότοκα adj. acc. neut. pl. πρωτότοκος firstborn, first begotten
αὐτῶν pron. gen. masc. 3p. pl. αὐτός ἡ ὁ self, of oneself, even, very, the same, he, she, it
29 πίστει n. dat. fem. sg. πίστις faith, assurance, belief, fidelity
τὴν art. acc. fem. sg. ὁ ἡ τό the, this, that, he, she, it

ἐρυθρὰν adj. acc. fem. sg. ἐρυθρός Red
θάλασσαν n. acc. fem. sg. θάλασσα sea
ὡς adv. ὡς as, when, as it were, how, about, like, as soon as, even as, while
διὰ prep. διά (+gen) by, through, with, in, of, (+acc) for, because of, for a cause
ξηρᾶς adj. gen. fem. sg. ξηρός withered, dry
ἧς relative pron. gen. fem. sg. ὅς ἥ ὅ who, which, what, that
πεῖραν n. acc. fem. sg. πεῖρα trial
οἱ art. nom. masc. pl. ὁ ἡ τό the, this, that, he, she, it
Αἰγύπτιοι adj. nom. masc. pl. Αἰγύπτιος Egyptian
30 πίστει n. dat. fem. sg. πίστις faith, assurance, belief, fidelity
τὰ art. nom. neut. pl. ὁ ἡ τό the, this, that, he, she, it
τείχη n. nom. neut. pl. τεῖχος wall
Ἰεριχὼ n. gen. fem. sg. Ἰεριχώ Jericho
ἐπὶ prep. ἐπί (+gen) on, in, upon, (+dat) in, at, for, upon, (+acc) on, upon, unto, to, against
ἑπτὰ num. acc. fem. pl. ἑπτά seven, seventh
ἡμέρας n. acc. fem. pl. ἡμέρα day, time, year, while, age, day time
31 πίστει n. dat. fem. sg. πίστις faith, assurance, belief, fidelity
Ῥαὰβ n. nom. fem. sg. Ῥαάβ Rahab
ἡ art. nom. fem. sg. ὁ ἡ τό the, this, that, he, she, it
πόρνη n. nom. fem. sg. πόρνη harlot, whore
οὐ particle of negation. οὐ οὐκ οὐχ not, no, neither, none, nay, nor, never, nothing
τοῖς art. dat. masc. pl. ὁ ἡ τό the, this, that, he, she, it
τοὺς art. acc. masc. pl. ὁ ἡ τό the, this, that, he, she, it
κατασκόπους n. acc. masc. pl. κατάσκοπος spy
μετ' prep. μετά (+gen) with, among, against, (+acc) after
εἰρήνης n. gen. fem. sg. εἰρήνη peace, quietness, rest
32 καὶ conj. καί and, even, also, but
τί interrog. pron. acc. neut. sg. τίς what, who, why, where, which, how
ἔτι adv. ἔτι yet, more, any more, further, still, moreover
γὰρ conj. γάρ for, and, because, but, indeed
με pron. acc. 1p. sg. ἐγώ I
ὁ art. nom. masc. sg. ὁ ἡ τό the, this, that, he, she, it
χρόνος n. nom. masc. sg. χρόνος time, season, space
περὶ prep. περί (+gen) of, for, concerning, (+acc) about, concerning, in
Γεδεών n. gen. masc. sg. Γεδεών Gedeon
Βαράκ n. gen. masc. sg. Βαράκ Barak
τε conj. τέ and, both, also
καὶ conj. καί and, even, also, but
Σαμψών n. gen. masc. sg. Σαμψών Samson
καὶ conj. καί and, even, also, but
Ἰεφθάε n. gen. masc. sg. Ἰεφθάε Jephthae
Δαβίδ n. gen. masc. sg. Δαβίδ David
τε conj. τέ and, both, also
καὶ conj. καί and, even, also, but
Σαμουὴλ n. gen. masc. sg. Σαμουήλ Samuel
καὶ conj. καί and, even, also, but
τῶν art. gen. masc. pl. ὁ ἡ τό the, this, that, he, she, it
προφητῶν n. gen. masc. pl. προφήτης prophet
33 οἳ relative pron. nom. masc. pl. ὅς ἥ ὅ who, which, what, that
διὰ prep. διά (+gen) by, through, with, in, of, (+acc) for, because of, for a cause
πίστεως n. gen. fem. sg. πίστις faith, assurance, belief, fidelity
βασιλείας n. acc. fem. pl. βασιλεία kingdom, reign
δικαιοσύνην n. acc. fem. sg. δικαιοσύνη righteousness
ἐπαγγελιῶν n. gen. fem. pl. ἐπαγγελία promise, message
στόματα n. acc. neut. pl. στόμα mouth, face, edge

λεόντων n. gen. masc. pl. λέων lion
34 δύναμιν n. acc. fem. sg. δύναμις power, mighty work, miracle, strength, might
πυρός n. gen. neut. sg. πῦρ fire, fiery
στόματα n. acc. neut. pl. στόμα mouth, face, edge
μαχαίρης n. gen. fem. sg. μάχαιρα sword
μαχαίρας n. gen. fem. sg. μάχαιρα sword
ἀπὸ prep. ἀπό (+gen) from, of, out of, since, for, off, at, by, in, on
ἀσθενείας n. gen. fem. sg. ἀσθένεια infirmity, weakness, disease, sickness
ἰσχυροὶ adj. nom. masc. pl. ἰσχυρός mighty, strong, mightier, stronger
ἐν prep. ἐν (+dat) in, by, with, among, at, on, through, to, within, into, of, for
πολέμῳ n. dat. masc. sg. πόλεμος war, battle, fight
παρεμβολὰς n. acc. fem. pl. παρεμβολή castle, camp, army
ἀλλοτρίων adj. gen. masc. pl. ἀλλότριος stranger, another man, alien, strange
35 γυναῖκες n. nom. fem. pl. γυνή woman, wife
ἐξ prep. ἐκ ἐξ (+gen) of, from, out of, by, on, with, in, among, through
ἀναστάσεως n. gen. fem. sg. ἀνάστασις resurrection, rising again
τοὺς art. acc. masc. pl. ὁ ἡ τό the, this, that, he, she, it
νεκροὺς adj. acc. masc. pl. νεκρός dead
αὐτῶν pron. gen. fem. 3p. pl. αὐτός ή ό self, of oneself, even, very, the same, he, she, it
ἄλλοι adj. nom. masc. pl. ἄλλος other, another, some, one, more, otherwise
δὲ conj. δέ but, and, now, also, to the contrary, rather, then
οὐ particle of negation. οὐ οὐκ οὐχ not, no, neither, none, nay, nor, never, nothing
τὴν art. acc. fem. sg. ὁ ἡ τό the, this, that, he, she, it
ἀπολύτρωσιν n. acc. fem. sg. ἀπολύτρωσις redemption, deliverance
ἵνα conj. ἵνα that, to, lest, for to, so that, albeit, because, for, so as
κρείττονος compar. adj. gen. fem. sg. κρείττων better
ἀναστάσεως n. gen. fem. sg. ἀνάστασις resurrection, rising again
36 ἕτεροι adj. nom. masc. pl. ἕτερος another, other, else, strange
δὲ conj. δέ but, and, now, also, to the contrary, rather, then
ἐμπαιγμῶν n. gen. masc. pl. ἐμπαιγμός mocking
καὶ conj. καί and, even, also, but
μαστίγων n. gen. fem. pl. μάστιξ plague, scourging
πεῖραν n. acc. fem. sg. πεῖρα trial
ἔτι adv. ἔτι yet, more, any more, further, still, moreover
δὲ conj. δέ but, and, now, also, to the contrary, rather, then
δεσμῶν n. gen. masc. pl. δεσμός bond, band, chain, string
καὶ conj. καί and, even, also, but
φυλακῆς n. gen. fem. sg. φυλακή prison, watch, imprisonment, cage, hold, ward
37 ἐν prep. ἐν (+dat) in, by, with, among, at, on, through, to, within, into, of, for
φόνῳ n. dat. masc. sg. φόνος murder, slaughter
μαχαίρας n. gen. fem. sg. μάχαιρα sword
ἐν prep. ἐν (+dat) in, by, with, among, at, on, through, to, within, into, of, for
μηλωταῖς n. dat. fem. pl. μηλωτή sheepskin
ἐν prep. ἐν (+dat) in, by, with, among, at, on, through, to, within, into, of, for
αἰγείοις adj. dat. neut. pl. αἴγειος of goat
δέρμασιν n. dat. neut. pl. δέρμα skin
38 ὧν relative pron. gen. masc. pl. ὅς ἥ ὅ who, which, what, that
οὐκ particle of negation. οὐ οὐκ οὐχ not, no, neither, none, nay, nor, never, nothing
ἄξιος adj. nom. masc. sg. ἄξιος worthy, meet, due reward
ὁ art. nom. masc. sg. ὁ ἡ τό the, this, that, he, she, it
κόσμος n. nom. masc. sg. κόσμος world, adorning
ἐν prep. ἐν (+dat) in, by, with, among, at, on, through, to, within, into, of, for
ἐρημίαις n. dat. fem. pl. ἐρημία wilderness, desert
καὶ conj. καί and, even, also, but
ὄρεσι n. dat. neut. pl. ὄρος mountain, mount, hill

καὶ conj. καί and, even, also, but
σπηλαίοις n. dat. neut. pl. σπήλαιον den, cave
καὶ conj. καί and, even, also, but
ταῖς art. dat. fem. pl. ὁ ἡ τό the, this, that, he, she, it
ὀπαῖς n. dat. fem. pl. ὀπή cave, place
τῆς art. gen. fem. sg. ὁ ἡ τό the, this, that, he, she, it
γῆς n. gen. fem. sg. γῆ earth, land, ground, country
39 καὶ conj. καί and, even, also, but
οὗτοι demo. pron. nom. masc. pl. οὗτος αὕτη τοῦτο this, the same, this same, he, she, it
πάντες adj. nom. masc. pl. πᾶς πᾶσα πᾶν all, every, whosoever, every one, no, whole, any
διὰ prep. διά (+gen) by, through, with, in, of, (+acc) for, because of, for a cause
τῆς art. gen. fem. sg. ὁ ἡ τό the, this, that, he, she, it
πίστεως n. gen. fem. sg. πίστις faith, assurance, belief, fidelity
οὐκ particle of negation. οὐ οὐκ οὐχ not, no, neither, none, nay, nor, never, nothing
τὴν art. acc. fem. sg. ὁ ἡ τό the, this, that, he, she, it
ἐπαγγελίαν n. acc. fem. sg. ἐπαγγελία promise, message
40 τοῦ art. gen. masc. sg. ὁ ἡ τό the, this, that, he, she, it
Θεοῦ n. gen. masc. sg. θεός God, god
περὶ prep. περί (+gen) of, for, concerning, (+acc) about, concerning, in
ἡμῶν pron. gen. 1p. pl. ἐγώ I
κρεῖττόν compar. adj. acc. neut. sg. κρείττων better
τι indefinite pron. acc. neut. sg. τὶς certain, some, any man, one, any thing
ἵνα conj. ἵνα that, to, lest, for to, so that, albeit, because, for, so as
μὴ particle of negation. μή not, no, lest, neither, none, nothing, nor, never, without
χωρὶς prep. χωρίς (+gen) without, beside. (adv.) by itself, apart, separately
ἡμῶν pron. gen. 1p. pl. ἐγώ I

12

1 Τοιγαροῦν particle. τοιγαροῦν therefore, wherefore
καὶ conj. καί and, even, also, but
ἡμεῖς pron. nom. 1p. pl. ἐγώ I
τοσοῦτον demo. pron. acc. neut. sg. τοσοῦτος so much, so great, so many, so long
ἡμῖν pron. dat. 1p. pl. ἐγώ I
νέφος n. acc. neut. sg. νέφος cloud
μαρτύρων n. gen. masc. pl. μάρτυς or μάρτυρ witness, martyr, record
ὄγκον n. acc. masc. sg. ὄγκος weight
πάντα adj. acc. masc. sg. πᾶς πᾶσα πᾶν all, every, whosoever, every one, no, whole, any
καὶ conj. καί and, even, also, but
τὴν art. acc. fem. sg. ὁ ἡ τό the, this, that, he, she, it
εὐπερίστατον adj. acc. fem. sg. εὐπερίστατος which doth so easily beset
ἁμαρτίαν n. acc. fem. sg. ἁμαρτία sin, offence, sinful
δι' prep. διά (+gen) by, through, with, in, of, (+acc) for, because of, for a cause
ὑπομονῆς n. gen. fem. sg. ὑπομονή patience, enduring
τὸν art. acc. masc. sg. ὁ ἡ τό the, this, that, he, she, it
ἡμῖν pron. dat. 1p. pl. ἐγώ I
ἀγῶνα n. acc. masc. sg. ἀγών conflict, fight, contention, race
2 εἰς prep. εἰς (+acc) into, to, unto, for, in, on, toward, against, upon, at, among
τὸν art. acc. masc. sg. ὁ ἡ τό the, this, that, he, she, it
τῆς art. gen. fem. sg. ὁ ἡ τό the, this, that, he, she, it
πίστεως n. gen. fem. sg. πίστις faith, assurance, belief, fidelity
ἀρχηγὸν n. acc. masc. sg. ἀρχηγός Prince, author, captain
καὶ conj. καί and, even, also, but
τελειωτὴν n. acc. masc. sg. τελειωτής finisher
Ἰησοῦν n. acc. masc. sg. Ἰησοῦς Jesus

ὃς relative pron. nom. masc. sg. ὅς ἥ ὅ who, which, what, that
ἀντὶ prep. ἀντί (+gen) for, because, in the room
τῆς art. gen. fem. sg. ὁ ἡ τό the, this, that, he, she, it
αὐτῷ pron. dat. masc. 3p. sg. αὐτός ή ό self, of oneself, even, very, the same, he, she, it
χαρᾶς n. gen. fem. sg. χαρά joy, gladness, joyfulness
σταυρὸν n. acc. masc. sg. σταυρός cross
αἰσχύνης n. gen. fem. sg. αἰσχύνη shame, dishonesty
ἐν prep. ἐν (+dat) in, by, with, among, at, on, through, to, within, into, of, for
δεξιᾷ adj. dat. fem. sg. δεξιός right, right hand, right side
τε conj. τέ and, both, also
τοῦ art. gen. masc. sg. ὁ ἡ τό the, this, that, he, she, it
θρόνου n. gen. masc. sg. θρόνος throne, seat
τοῦ art. gen. masc. sg. ὁ ἡ τό the, this, that, he, she, it
Θεοῦ n. gen. masc. sg. θεός God, god
3 γὰρ conj. γάρ for, and, because, but, indeed
τὸν art. acc. masc. sg. ὁ ἡ τό the, this, that, he, she, it
τοιαύτην demo. pron. acc. fem. sg. τοιοῦτος such, like
ὑπὸ prep. ὑπό (+gen) of, by, with, from, among, (+acc) under
τῶν art. gen. masc. pl. ὁ ἡ τό the, this, that, he, she, it
ἁμαρτωλῶν adj. gen. masc. pl. ἁμαρτωλός sinner, sinful
εἰς prep. εἰς (+acc) into, to, unto, for, in, on, toward, against, upon, at, among
αὐτὸν pron. acc. masc. 3p. sg. αὐτός ή ό self, of oneself, even, very, the same, he, she, it
ἀντιλογίαν n. acc. fem. sg. ἀντιλογία strife, contradiction, gainsaying
ἵνα conj. ἵνα that, to, lest, for to, so that, albeit, because, for, so as
μὴ particle of negation. μή not, no, lest, neither, none, nothing, nor, never, without
ταῖς art. dat. fem. pl. ὁ ἡ τό the, this, that, he, she, it
ψυχαῖς n. dat. fem. pl. ψυχή life, soul, mind, heart
ὑμῶν pron. gen. 2p. pl. σύ thou, you
4 οὔπω adv. οὔπω not yet
μέχρις prep. μέχρι until, unto, till, to
αἵματος n. gen. neut. sg. αἷμα blood
πρὸς prep. πρός (+gen) for, (+dat) at, (+acc) unto, to, with, for, against
τὴν art. acc. fem. sg. ὁ ἡ τό the, this, that, he, she, it
ἁμαρτίαν n. acc. fem. sg. ἁμαρτία sin, offence, sinful
5 καὶ conj. καί and, even, also, but
τῆς art. gen. fem. sg. ὁ ἡ τό the, this, that, he, she, it
παρακλήσεως n. gen. fem. sg. παράκλησις consolation, exhortation, comfort
ἥτις relative pron. nom. fem. sg. ὅστις which, who, whosoever, that, whatsoever
ὑμῖν pron. dat. 2p. pl. σύ thou, you
ὡς adv. ὡς as, when, as it were, how, about, like, as soon as, even as, while
υἱοῖς n. dat. masc. pl. υἱός son, child, descendant, offspring, heir
Υἱέ n. voc. masc. sg. υἱός son, child, descendant, offspring, heir
μου pron. gen. 1p. sg. ἐγώ I
μὴ particle of negation. μή not, no, lest, neither, none, nothing, nor, never, without
παιδείας n. gen. fem. sg. παιδεία nurture, instruction, chastening, chastisement
Κυρίου n. gen. masc. sg. κύριος Lord, lord, master, sir, LORD, God, Master, owner
μηδὲ conj. μηδέ neither, nor, not, no not, nor yet, not once, not so much as
ὑπ' prep. ὑπό (+gen) of, by, with, from, among, (+acc) under
αὐτοῦ pron. gen. masc. 3p. sg. αὐτός ή ό self, of oneself, even, very, the same, he, she, it
6 ὃν relative pron. acc. masc. sg. ὅς ἥ ὅ who, which, what, that
γὰρ conj. γάρ for, and, because, but, indeed
Κύριος n. nom. masc. sg. κύριος Lord, lord, master, sir, LORD, God, Master, owner
δὲ conj. δέ but, and, now, also, to the contrary, rather, then
πάντα adj. acc. masc. sg. πᾶς πᾶσα πᾶν all, every, whosoever, every one, no, whole, any
υἱὸν n. acc. masc. sg. υἱός son, child, descendant, offspring, heir

ὃν relative pron. acc. masc. sg. ὅς ἥ ὅ who, which, what, that
7 εἰ conj. εἰ if, whether, that, though, forasmuch
παιδείαν n. acc. fem. sg. παιδεία nurture, instruction, chastening, chastisement
ὡς adv. ὡς as, when, as it were, how, about, like, as soon as, even as, while
υἱοῖς n. dat. masc. pl. υἱός son, child, descendant, offspring, heir
ὑμῖν pron. dat. 2p. pl. σύ thou, you
ὁ art. nom. masc. sg. ὁ ἡ τό the, this, that, he, she, it
Θεός n. nom. masc. sg. θεός God, god
τίς interrog. pron. nom. masc. sg. τίς what, who, why, where, which, how
γὰρ conj. γάρ for, and, because, but, indeed
υἱὸς n. nom. masc. sg. υἱός son, child, descendant, offspring, heir
ὃν relative pron. acc. masc. sg. ὅς ἥ ὅ who, which, what, that
οὐ particle of negation. οὐ οὐκ οὐχ not, no, neither, none, nay, nor, never, nothing
πατὴρ n. nom. masc. sg. πατήρ Father, father, parent
8 εἰ conj. εἰ if, whether, that, though, forasmuch
δὲ conj. δέ but, and, now, also, to the contrary, rather, then
χωρίς prep. χωρίς (+gen) without, beside. (adv.) by itself, apart, separately
παιδείας n. gen. fem. sg. παιδεία nurture, instruction, chastening, chastisement
ἧς relative pron. gen. fem. sg. ὅς ἥ ὅ who, which, what, that
μέτοχοι adj. nom. masc. pl. μέτοχος partner, partaker, fellow
πάντες adj. nom. masc. pl. πᾶς πᾶσα πᾶν all, every, whosoever, every one, no, whole, any
ἄρα conj. ἄρα then, therefore, haply, wherefore, perhaps, manner, no doubt, truly
νόθοι adj. nom. masc. pl. νόθος bastard
καὶ conj. καί and, even, also, but
οὐχ particle of negation. οὐ οὐκ οὐχ not, no, neither, none, nay, nor, never, nothing
υἱοί n. nom. masc. pl. υἱός son, child, descendant, offspring, heir
9 εἶτα adv. εἶτα afterward, then, after that, furthermore
τοὺς art. acc. masc. pl. ὁ ἡ τό the, this, that, he, she, it
μὲν conj. μέν indeed, verily, truly, even, so, some
τῆς art. gen. fem. sg. ὁ ἡ τό the, this, that, he, she, it
σαρκὸς n. gen. fem. sg. σάρξ flesh, carnal
ἡμῶν pron. gen. 1p. pl. ἐγώ I
πατέρας n. acc. masc. pl. πατήρ Father, father, parent
παιδευτὰς n. acc. masc. pl. παιδευτής instructor, correct
καὶ conj. καί and, even, also, but
οὐ particle of negation. οὐ οὐκ οὐχ not, no, neither, none, nay, nor, never, nothing
πολλῷ adj. dat. neut. sg. πολύς many, great, much, long, abundant
μᾶλλον adv. μᾶλλον rather, more, more and more, better, much, much the more
τῷ art. dat. masc. sg. ὁ ἡ τό the, this, that, he, she, it
πατρὶ n. dat. masc. sg. πατήρ Father, father, parent
τῶν art. gen. neut. pl. ὁ ἡ τό the, this, that, he, she, it
πνευμάτων n. gen. neut. pl. πνεῦμα spirit, Spirit, Ghost, ghost, life. of the spirit, wind
καὶ conj. καί and, even, also, but
10 οἱ art. nom. masc. pl. ὁ ἡ τό the, this, that, he, she, it
μὲν conj. μέν indeed, verily, truly, even, so, some
γὰρ conj. γάρ for, and, because, but, indeed
πρὸς prep. πρός (+gen) for, (+dat) at, (+acc) unto, to, with, for, against
ὀλίγας adj. acc. fem. pl. ὀλίγος few, little, small, a while, brief, short, short space
ἡμέρας n. acc. fem. pl. ἡμέρα day, time, year, while, age, day time
κατὰ prep. κατά (+gen) against, by, throughout, down, (+acc) according to, after, with
τὸ art. acc. neut. sg. ὁ ἡ τό the, this, that, he, she, it
αὐτοῖς pron. dat. masc. 3p. pl. αὐτός ἡ ὁ self, of oneself, even, very, the same, he, she, it
ὁ art. nom. masc. sg. ὁ ἡ τό the, this, that, he, she, it
δὲ conj. δέ but, and, now, also, to the contrary, rather, then
ἐπὶ prep. ἐπί (+gen) on, in, upon, (+dat) in, at, for, upon, (+acc) on, upon, unto, to, against

τὸ art. acc. neut. sg. ὁ ἡ τό the, this, that, he, she, it
εἰς prep. εἰς (+acc) into, to, unto, for, in, on, toward, against, upon, at, among
τὸ art. acc. neut. sg. ὁ ἡ τό the, this, that, he, she, it
τῆς art. gen. fem. sg. ὁ ἡ τό the, this, that, he, she, it
ἁγιότητος n. gen. fem. sg. ἁγιότης holiness
αὐτοῦ pron. gen. masc. 3p. sg. αὐτός ή ό self, of oneself, even, very, the same, he, she, it
11 πᾶσα adj. nom. fem. sg. πᾶς πᾶσα πᾶν all, every, whosoever, every one, no, whole, any
δὲ conj. δέ but, and, now, also, to the contrary, rather, then
παιδεία n. nom. fem. sg. παιδεία nurture, instruction, chastening, chastisement
πρὸς prep. πρός (+gen) for, (+dat) at, (+acc) unto, to, with, for, against
μὲν conj. μέν indeed, verily, truly, even, so, some
τὸ art. acc. neut. sg. ὁ ἡ τό the, this, that, he, she, it
οὐ particle of negation. οὐ οὐκ οὐχ not, no, neither, none, nay, nor, never, nothing
χαρᾶς n. gen. fem. sg. χαρά joy, gladness, joyfulness
ἀλλὰ conj. ἀλλά but, yea, yet, nevertheless, howbeit, nay, therefore
λύπης n. gen. fem. sg. λύπη sorrow, heaviness, grief, grievous, grudgingly
ὕστερον adv. ὕστερον afterward, last, at the last, last of all
δὲ conj. δέ but, and, now, also, to the contrary, rather, then
καρπὸν n. acc. masc. sg. καρπός fruit
εἰρηνικὸν adj. acc. masc. sg. εἰρηνικός peaceable
τοῖς art. dat. masc. pl. ὁ ἡ τό the, this, that, he, she, it
δι' prep. διά (+gen) by, through, with, in, of, (+acc) for, because of, for a cause
αὐτῆς pron. gen. fem. 3p. sg. αὐτός ή ό self, of oneself, even, very, the same, he, she, it
δικαιοσύνης n. gen. fem. sg. δικαιοσύνη righteousness
12 διὸ conj. διό wherefore, therefore, for which cause
τὰς art. acc. fem. pl. ὁ ἡ τό the, this, that, he, she, it
χεῖρας n. acc. fem. pl. χείρ hand
καὶ conj. καί and, even, also, but
τὰ art. acc. neut. pl. ὁ ἡ τό the, this, that, he, she, it
γόνατα n. acc. neut. pl. γόνυ knee, kneel
13 καὶ conj. καί and, even, also, but
τροχιὰς n. acc. fem. pl. τροχιά path
ὀρθὰς adj. acc. fem. pl. ὀρθός upright, straight
τοῖς art. dat. masc. pl. ὁ ἡ τό the, this, that, he, she, it
ποσὶν n. dat. masc. pl. πούς foot
ὑμῶν pron. gen. 2p. pl. σύ thou, you
ἵνα conj. ἵνα that, to, lest, for to, so that, albeit, because, for, so as
μὴ particle of negation. μή not, no, lest, neither, none, nothing, nor, never, without
τὸ art. nom. neut. sg. ὁ ἡ τό the, this, that, he, she, it
χωλὸν adj. nom. neut. sg. χωλός lame, halt, cripple
δὲ conj. δέ but, and, now, also, to the contrary, rather, then
μᾶλλον adv. μᾶλλον rather, more, more and more, better, much, much the more
14 Εἰρήνην n. acc. fem. sg. εἰρήνη peace, quietness, rest
μετὰ prep. μετά (+gen) with, among, against, (+acc) after
πάντων adj. gen. masc. pl. πᾶς πᾶσα πᾶν all, every, whosoever, every one, no, whole, any
καὶ conj. καί and, even, also, but
τὸν art. acc. masc. sg. ὁ ἡ τό the, this, that, he, she, it
ἁγιασμόν n. acc. masc. sg. ἁγιασμός holiness, sanctification
οὗ relative pron. gen. masc. sg. ὅς ἥ ὅ who, which, what, that
χωρὶς prep. χωρίς (+gen) without, beside. (adv.) by itself, apart, separately
οὐδεὶς num. nom. masc. sg. οὐδείς no man, nothing, no, none, neither, not, nought
τὸν art. acc. masc. sg. ὁ ἡ τό the, this, that, he, she, it
Κύριον n. acc. masc. sg. κύριος Lord, lord, master, sir, LORD, God, Master, owner
15 μή particle of negation. μή not, no, lest, neither, none, nothing, nor, never, without
τις indefinite pron. nom. masc. sg. τὶς certain, some, any man, one, any thing

ἀπὸ prep. ἀπό (+gen) from, of, out of, since, for, off, at, by, in, on
τῆς art. gen. fem. sg. ὁ ἡ τό the, this, that, he, she, it
χάριτος n. gen. fem. sg. χάρις grace, thank, favour, pleasure
τοῦ art. gen. masc. sg. ὁ ἡ τό the, this, that, he, she, it
Θεοῦ n. gen. masc. sg. θεός God, god
μή particle of negation. μή not, no, lest, neither, none, nothing, nor, never, without
τις indefinite pron. nom. masc. sg. τὶς certain, some, any man, one, any thing
ῥίζα n. nom. fem. sg. ῥίζα root
πικρίας n. gen. fem. sg. πικρία bitterness
ἄνω adv. ἄνω above, up, high, the brim
καὶ conj. καί and, even, also, but
διὰ prep. διά (+gen) by, through, with, in, of, (+acc) for, because of, for a cause
ταύτης demo. pron. gen. fem. sg. οὗτος αὕτη τοῦτο this, the same, this same, he, she, it
πολλοί adj. nom. masc. pl. πολύς many, great, much, long, abundant
16 μή particle of negation. μή not, no, lest, neither, none, nothing, nor, never, without
τις indefinite pron. nom. masc. sg. τὶς certain, some, any man, one, any thing
πόρνος n. nom. masc. sg. πόρνος fornicator
ἤ particle. ἤ or, than, either, nor, or else, and, rather than
βέβηλος adj. nom. masc. sg. βέβηλος profane, profane person
ὡς adv. ὡς as, when, as it were, how, about, like, as soon as, even as, while
Ἠσαῦ n. nom. masc. sg. Ἠσαῦ Esau
ὃς relative pron. nom. masc. sg. ὅς ἥ ὅ who, which, what, that
ἀντὶ prep. ἀντί (+gen) for, because, in the room
βρώσεως n. gen. fem. sg. βρῶσις rust, meat, eating, food, morsel of meat
μιᾶς num. gen. fem. sg. εἷς or ἕν one, other, some, any, only, a certain
τὰ art. acc. neut. pl. ὁ ἡ τό the, this, that, he, she, it
πρωτοτόκια n. acc. neut. pl. πρωτοτόκια birthright
αὐτοῦ pron. gen. masc. 3p. sg. αὐτός ή ό self, of oneself, even, very, the same, he, she, it
17 γὰρ conj. γάρ for, and, because, but, indeed
ὅτι conj. ὅτι that, for, because, how that, how, because that, for that, though
καὶ conj. καί and, even, also, but
μετέπειτα adv. μετέπειτα afterward
τὴν art. acc. fem. sg. ὁ ἡ τό the, this, that, he, she, it
εὐλογίαν n. acc. fem. sg. εὐλογία blessing, bounty, matter of bounty, fair speech
μετανοίας n. gen. fem. sg. μετάνοια repentance
γὰρ conj. γάρ for, and, because, but, indeed
τόπον n. acc. masc. sg. τόπος place, room, quarter
οὐχ particle of negation. οὐ οὐκ οὐχ not, no, neither, none, nay, nor, never, nothing
καίπερ conj. καίπερ though, and yet
μετὰ prep. μετά (+gen) with, among, against, (+acc) after
δακρύων n. gen. neut. pl. δάκρυον tears
αὐτήν pron. acc. fem. 3p. sg. αὐτός ή ό self, of oneself, even, very, the same, he, she, it
18 Οὐ particle of negation. οὐ οὐκ οὐχ not, no, neither, none, nay, nor, never, nothing
γὰρ conj. γάρ for, and, because, but, indeed
ὄρει n. dat. neut. sg. ὄρος mountain, mount, hill
καὶ conj. καί and, even, also, but
πυρὶ n. dat. neut. sg. πῦρ fire, fiery
καὶ conj. καί and, even, also, but
γνόφῳ n. dat. masc. sg. γνόφος blackness
καὶ conj. καί and, even, also, but
σκότῳ n. dat. masc. sg. σκότος darkness
καὶ conj. καί and, even, also, but
θυέλλῃ n. dat. fem. sg. θύελλα tempest
19 καὶ conj. καί and, even, also, but
σάλπιγγος n. gen. fem. sg. σάλπιγξ trumpet, trump

ἤχῳ n. dat. masc. sg. ἦχος fame, sound
καὶ conj. καί and, even, also, but
φωνῇ n. dat. fem. sg. φωνή voice, sound, noise
ῥημάτων n. gen. neut. pl. ῥῆμα word, saying, thing
ἧς relative pron. gen. fem. sg. ὅς ἥ ὅ who, which, what, that
οἱ art. nom. masc. pl. ὁ ἡ τό the, this, that, he, she, it
μὴ particle of negation. μή not, no, lest, neither, none, nothing, nor, never, without
αὐτοῖς pron. dat. masc. 3p. pl. αὐτός ή ό self, of oneself, even, very, the same, he, she, it
λόγον n. acc. masc. sg. λόγος word, saying, account, speech, thing, matter
20 οὐκ particle of negation. οὐ οὐκ οὐχ not, no, neither, none, nay, nor, never, nothing
γὰρ conj. γάρ for, and, because, but, indeed
τὸ art. acc. neut. sg. ὁ ἡ τό the, this, that, he, she, it
Κἂν conj. κἄν though, and if, if but, also if, and if so much, at the least, yet as
θηρίον n. nom. neut. sg. θηρίον beast, wild beast, venomous beast
τοῦ art. gen. neut. sg. ὁ ἡ τό the, this, that, he, she, it
ὄρους n. gen. neut. sg. ὄρος mountain, mount, hill
ἢ particle. ἤ or, than, either, nor, or else, and, rather than
βολίδι n. dat. fem. sg. βολίς dart
21 καί conj. καί and, even, also, but
οὕτω adv. οὕτω οὕτως so, even so, thus, on this wise, likewise, after this manner
φοβερὸν adj. nom. neut. sg. φοβερός fearful, terrible
τὸ art. nom. neut. sg. ὁ ἡ τό the, this, that, he, she, it
Μωσῆς n. nom. masc. sg. Μωσῆς Moses
Ἔκφοβός adj. nom. masc. sg. ἔκφοβος sore afraid, exceedingly fear, exceedingly fearful
καί conj. καί and, even, also, but
ἔντρομος adj. nom. masc. sg. ἔντρομος trembling, quaking
22 ἀλλὰ conj. ἀλλά but, yea, yet, nevertheless, howbeit, nay, therefore
Σιὼν n. dat. fem. sg. Σιών Sion
ὄρει n. dat. neut. sg. ὄρος mountain, mount, hill
καὶ conj. καί and, even, also, but
πόλει n. dat. fem. sg. πόλις city
Θεοῦ n. gen. masc. sg. θεός God, god
Ἰερουσαλὴμ pron. name. fem. inde. Ἱερουσαλήμ Jerusalem
ἐπουρανίῳ adj. dat. fem. sg. ἐπουράνιος heavenly, celestial, high, in heaven
καὶ conj. καί and, even, also, but
μυριάσιν n. dat. fem. pl. μυριάς innumerable multitude, myriad, innumerable company
ἀγγέλων n. gen. masc. pl. ἄγγελος angel, messenger
πανηγύρει n. dat. fem. sg. πανήγυρις general assembly
23 καὶ conj. καί and, even, also, but
ἐκκλησίᾳ n. dat. fem. sg. ἐκκλησία church, assembly
πρωτοτόκων adj. gen. masc. pl. πρωτότοκος firstborn, first begotten
ἐν prep. ἐν (+dat) in, by, with, among, at, on, through, to, within, into, of, for
οὐρανοῖς n. dat. masc. pl. οὐρανός heaven, air, sky
καὶ conj. καί and, even, also, but
κριτῇ n. dat. masc. sg. κριτής judge
Θεῷ n. dat. masc. sg. θεός God, god
πάντων adj. gen. masc. pl. πᾶς πᾶσα πᾶν all, every, whosoever, every one, no, whole, any
καὶ conj. καί and, even, also, but
πνεύμασι n. dat. neut. pl. πνεῦμα spirit, Spirit, Ghost, ghost, life. of the spirit, wind
δικαίων adj. gen. masc. pl. δίκαιος righteous, just, meet, right
24 καὶ conj. καί and, even, also, but
διαθήκης n. gen. fem. sg. διαθήκη testament, covenant
νέας adj. gen. fem. sg. νέος new
μεσίτῃ n. dat. masc. sg. μεσίτης mediator
Ἰησοῦ n. dat. masc. sg. Ἰησοῦς Jesus

καὶ conj. καί and, even, also, but
αἵματι n. dat. neut. sg. αἷμα blood
ῥαντισμοῦ n. gen. masc. sg. ῥαντισμός sprinkling
κρείττονα compar. adj. acc. neut. pl. κρείττων better
παρὰ prep. παρά (+gen) of, from, (+dat) with, for, (+acc) beside, at, by, above, against
τὸ art. acc. neut. sg. ὁ ἡ τό the, this, that, he, she, it
Ἄβελ n. gen. masc. sg. Ἄβελ Abel
25 μὴ particle of negation. μή not, no, lest, neither, none, nothing, nor, never, without
τὸν art. acc. masc. sg. ὁ ἡ τό the, this, that, he, she, it
εἰ conj. εἰ if, whether, that, though, forasmuch
γὰρ conj. γάρ for, and, because, but, indeed
ἐκεῖνοι demo. pron. nom. masc. pl. ἐκεῖνος that, he, the same, that same
οὐκ particle of negation. οὐ οὐκ οὐχ not, no, neither, none, nay, nor, never, nothing
τὸν art. acc. masc. sg. ὁ ἡ τό the, this, that, he, she, it
ἐπὶ prep. ἐπί (+gen) on, in, upon, (+dat) in, at, for, upon, (+acc) on, upon, unto, to, against
τῆς art. gen. fem. sg. ὁ ἡ τό the, this, that, he, she, it
γῆς n. gen. fem. sg. γῆ earth, land, ground, country
πολλῷ adj. dat. neut. sg. πολύς many, great, much, long, abundant
μᾶλλον adv. μᾶλλον rather, more, more and more, better, much, much the more
ἡμεῖς pron. nom. 1p. pl. ἐγώ I
οἱ art. nom. masc. pl. ὁ ἡ τό the, this, that, he, she, it
τὸν art. acc. masc. sg. ὁ ἡ τό the, this, that, he, she, it
ἀπ' prep. ἀπό (+gen) from, of, out of, since, for, off, at, by, in, on
οὐρανῶν n. gen. masc. pl. οὐρανός heaven, air, sky
26 οὗ relative pron. gen. masc. sg. ὅς ἥ ὅ who, which, what, that
ἡ art. nom. fem. sg. ὁ ἡ τό the, this, that, he, she, it
φωνὴ n. nom. fem. sg. φωνή voice, sound, noise
τὴν art. acc. fem. sg. ὁ ἡ τό the, this, that, he, she, it
γῆν n. acc. fem. sg. γῆ earth, land, ground, country
τότε adv. τότε then, that time
νῦν adv. νῦν now, henceforth, present, this time
δὲ conj. δέ but, and, now, also, to the contrary, rather, then
Ἔτι adv. ἔτι yet, more, any more, further, still, moreover
ἅπαξ adv. ἅπαξ once
ἐγὼ pron. nom. 1p. sg. ἐγώ I
οὐ particle of negation. οὐ οὐκ οὐχ not, no, neither, none, nay, nor, never, nothing
μόνον adv. μόνος only, alone, by oneself
τὴν art. acc. fem. sg. ὁ ἡ τό the, this, that, he, she, it
γῆν n. acc. fem. sg. γῆ earth, land, ground, country
ἀλλὰ conj. ἀλλά but, yea, yet, nevertheless, howbeit, nay, therefore
καὶ conj. καί and, even, also, but
τὸν art. acc. masc. sg. ὁ ἡ τό the, this, that, he, she, it
οὐρανόν n. acc. masc. sg. οὐρανός heaven, air, sky
27 τὸ art. nom. neut. sg. ὁ ἡ τό the, this, that, he, she, it
δὲ conj. δέ but, and, now, also, to the contrary, rather, then
Ἔτι adv. ἔτι yet, more, any more, further, still, moreover
ἅπαξ adv. ἅπαξ once
τῶν art. gen. neut. pl. ὁ ἡ τό the, this, that, he, she, it
τὴν art. acc. fem. sg. ὁ ἡ τό the, this, that, he, she, it
μετάθεσιν n. acc. fem. sg. μετάθεσις change, removing, translation
ὡς adv. ὡς as, when, as it were, how, about, like, as soon as, even as, while
ἵνα conj. ἵνα that, to, lest, for to, so that, albeit, because, for, so as
τὰ art. nom. neut. pl. ὁ ἡ τό the, this, that, he, she, it
μὴ particle of negation. μή not, no, lest, neither, none, nothing, nor, never, without
28 διὸ conj. διό wherefore, therefore, for which cause

βασιλείαν n. acc. fem. sg. βασιλεία kingdom, reign
ἀσάλευτον adj. acc. fem. sg. ἀσάλευτος unmoveable, which cannot be moved
χάριν n. acc. fem. sg. χάρις grace, thank, favour, pleasure
δι' prep. διά (+gen) by, through, with, in, of, (+acc) for, because of, for a cause
ἧς relative pron. gen. fem. sg. ὅς ἥ ὅ who, which, what, that
εὐαρέστως adv. εὐαρέστως acceptably
τῷ art. dat. masc. sg. ὁ ἡ τό the, this, that, he, she, it
Θεῷ n. dat. masc. sg. θεός God, god
μετὰ prep. μετά (+gen) with, among, against, (+acc) after
αἰδοῦς n. gen. fem. sg. αἰδώς shamefacedness, reverence
καὶ conj. καί and, even, also, but
εὐλαβείας n. gen. fem. sg. εὐλάβεια fear, fearing, godly fear
29 καὶ conj. καί and, even, also, but
γὰρ conj. γάρ for, and, because, but, indeed
ὁ art. nom. masc. sg. ὁ ἡ τό the, this, that, he, she, it
Θεὸς n. nom. masc. sg. θεός God, god
ἡμῶν pron. gen. 1p. pl. ἐγώ I
πῦρ n. nom. neut. sg. πῦρ fire, fiery

13

1 Ἡ art. nom. fem. sg. ὁ ἡ τό the, this, that, he, she, it
φιλαδελφία n. nom. fem. sg. φιλαδελφία brotherly love, brotherly kindness
2 τῆς art. gen. fem. sg. ὁ ἡ τό the, this, that, he, she, it
φιλοξενίας n. gen. fem. sg. φιλοξενία hospitality
μὴ particle of negation. μή not, no, lest, neither, none, nothing, nor, never, without
διὰ prep. διά (+gen) by, through, with, in, of, (+acc) for, because of, for a cause
ταύτης demo. pron. gen. fem. sg. οὗτος αὕτη τοῦτο this, the same, this same, he, she, it
γὰρ conj. γάρ for, and, because, but, indeed
τινες indefinite pron. nom. masc. pl. τὶς certain, some, any man, one, any thing
ἀγγέλους n. acc. masc. pl. ἄγγελος angel, messenger
3 τῶν art. gen. masc. pl. ὁ ἡ τό the, this, that, he, she, it
δεσμίων n. gen. masc. pl. δέσμιος prisoner, in bonds, that is in bond
ὡς adv. ὡς as, when, as it were, how, about, like, as soon as, even as, while
τῶν art. gen. masc. pl. ὁ ἡ τό the, this, that, he, she, it
ὡς adv. ὡς as, when, as it were, how, about, like, as soon as, even as, while
καὶ conj. καί and, even, also, but
αὐτοὶ pron. nom. masc. 2p. pl. αὐτός ή ό self, of oneself, even, very, the same, he, she, it
ἐν prep. ἐν (+dat) in, by, with, among, at, on, through, to, within, into, of, for
σώματι n. dat. neut. sg. σῶμα body, bodily, slave
4 τίμιος adj. nom. masc. sg. τίμιος precious, dear, has in reputation, honourable
ὁ art. nom. masc. sg. ὁ ἡ τό the, this, that, he, she, it
γάμος n. nom. masc. sg. γάμος marriage, wedding
ἐν prep. ἐν (+dat) in, by, with, among, at, on, through, to, within, into, of, for
πᾶσι adj. dat. neut. pl. πᾶς πᾶσα πᾶν all, every, whosoever, every one, no, whole, any
καὶ conj. καί and, even, also, but
ἡ art. nom. fem. sg. ὁ ἡ τό the, this, that, he, she, it
κοίτη n. nom. fem. sg. κοίτη bed, chambering
ἀμίαντος adj. nom. fem. sg. ἀμίαντος undefiled
πόρνους n. acc. masc. pl. πόρνος fornicator
δὲ conj. δέ but, and, now, also, to the contrary, rather, then
καὶ conj. καί and, even, also, but
μοιχοὺς n. acc. masc. pl. μοιχός adulterer
ὁ art. nom. masc. sg. ὁ ἡ τό the, this, that, he, she, it
Θεός n. nom. masc. sg. θεός God, god

5 ἀφιλάργυρος adj. nom. masc. sg. ἀφιλάργυρος not covetous, without covetousness
ὁ art. nom. masc. sg. ὁ ἡ τό the, this, that, he, she, it
τρόπος n. nom. masc. sg. τρόπος as, manner, means, way, conversation
τοῖς art. dat. neut. pl. ὁ ἡ τό the, this, that, he, she, it
αὐτὸς pron. nom. masc. 3p. sg. αὐτός ή ό self, of oneself, even, very, the same, he, she, it
γὰρ conj. γάρ for, and, because, but, indeed
Οὐ particle of negation. οὐ οὐκ οὐχ not, no, neither, none, nay, nor, never, nothing
μὴ particle of negation. μή not, no, lest, neither, none, nothing, nor, never, without
σε pron. acc. 2p. sg. σύ thou, you
οὐδ' adv. οὐδέ neither, nor, not, no, not even, never, not yet
οὐ particle of negation. οὐ οὐκ οὐχ not, no, neither, none, nay, nor, never, nothing
μὴ particle of negation. μή not, no, lest, neither, none, nothing, nor, never, without
σε pron. acc. 2p. sg. σύ thou, you
6 ὥστε conj. ὥστε so that, wherefore, insomuch that, therefore, that, so then
ἡμᾶς pron. acc. 1p. pl. ἐγώ I
Κύριος n. nom. masc. sg. κύριος Lord, lord, master, sir, LORD, God, Master, owner
ἐμοὶ pron. dat. 1p. sg. ἐγώ I
βοηθός adj. nom. masc. sg. βοηθός helper
καὶ conj. καί and, even, also, but
οὐ particle of negation. οὐ οὐκ οὐχ not, no, neither, none, nay, nor, never, nothing
τί interrog. pron. acc. neut. sg. τίς what, who, why, where, which, how
μοι pron. dat. 1p. sg. ἐγώ I
ἄνθρωπος n. nom. masc. sg. ἄνθρωπος man, human being, person, one, certain
7 τῶν art. gen. masc. pl. ὁ ἡ τό the, this, that, he, she, it
ὑμῶν pron. gen. 2p. pl. σύ thou, you
οἵτινες relative pron. nom. masc. pl. ὅστις which, who, whosoever, that, whatsoever
ὑμῖν pron. dat. 2p. pl. σύ thou, you
τὸν art. acc. masc. sg. ὁ ἡ τό the, this, that, he, she, it
λόγον n. acc. masc. sg. λόγος word, saying, account, speech, thing, matter
τοῦ art. gen. masc. sg. ὁ ἡ τό the, this, that, he, she, it
Θεοῦ n. gen. masc. sg. θεός God, god
ὧν relative pron. gen. masc. pl. ὅς ἥ ὅ who, which, what, that
τὴν art. acc. fem. sg. ὁ ἡ τό the, this, that, he, she, it
ἔκβασιν n. acc. fem. sg. ἔκβασις way to escape, end
τῆς art. gen. fem. sg. ὁ ἡ τό the, this, that, he, she, it
ἀναστροφῆς n. gen. fem. sg. ἀναστροφή conversation
τὴν art. acc. fem. sg. ὁ ἡ τό the, this, that, he, she, it
πίστιν n. acc. fem. sg. πίστις faith, assurance, belief, fidelity
8 Ἰησοῦς n. nom. masc. sg. Ἰησοῦς Jesus
Χριστὸς n. nom. masc. sg. Χριστός Christ
χθὲς adv. χθές yesterday
καὶ conj. καί and, even, also, but
σήμερον adv. σήμερον this day, today
ὁ art. nom. masc. sg. ὁ ἡ τό the, this, that, he, she, it
αὐτὸς pron. nom. masc. 3p. sg. αὐτός ή ό self, of oneself, even, very, the same, he, she, it
καὶ conj. καί and, even, also, but
εἰς prep. εἰς (+acc) into, to, unto, for, in, on, toward, against, upon, at, among
τοὺς art. acc. masc. pl. ὁ ἡ τό the, this, that, he, she, it
αἰῶνας n. acc. masc. pl. αἰών ever, ever and ever, evermore, age, eternal, world
9 διδαχαῖς n. dat. fem. pl. διδαχή doctrine, teaching
ποικίλαις adj. dat. fem. pl. ποικίλος divers, manifold
καὶ conj. καί and, even, also, but
ξέναις adj. dat. fem. pl. ξένος stranger, strange, host
μὴ particle of negation. μή not, no, lest, neither, none, nothing, nor, never, without
καλὸν adj. nom. neut. sg. καλός good, better, goodly, meet, honest, fair, well, worthy

γὰρ conj. γάρ for, and, because, but, indeed
χάριτι n. dat. fem. sg. χάρις grace, thank, favour, pleasure
τὴν art. acc. fem. sg. ὁ ἡ τό the, this, that, he, she, it
καρδίαν n. acc. fem. sg. καρδία heart
οὐ particle of negation. οὐ οὐκ οὐχ not, no, neither, none, nay, nor, never, nothing
βρώμασιν n. dat. neut. pl. βρῶμα victual, meat, food
ἐν prep. ἐν (+dat) in, by, with, among, at, on, through, to, within, into, of, for
οἷς relative pron. dat. neut. pl. ὅς ἥ ὅ who, which, what, that
οὐκ particle of negation. οὐ οὐκ οὐχ not, no, neither, none, nay, nor, never, nothing
οἱ art. nom. masc. pl. ὁ ἡ τό the, this, that, he, she, it
10 θυσιαστήριον n. acc. neut. sg. θυσιαστήριον altar
ἐξ prep. ἐκ ἐξ (+gen) of, from, out of, by, on, with, in, among, through
οὗ relative pron. gen. neut. sg. ὅς ἥ ὅ who, which, what, that
οὐκ particle of negation. οὐ οὐκ οὐχ not, no, neither, none, nay, nor, never, nothing
ἐξουσίαν n. acc. fem. sg. ἐξουσία power, authority, right, strength, jurisdiction
οἱ art. nom. masc. pl. ὁ ἡ τό the, this, that, he, she, it
τῇ art. dat. fem. sg. ὁ ἡ τό the, this, that, he, she, it
σκηνῇ n. dat. fem. sg. σκηνή tabernacle, habitation
11 ὧν relative pron. gen. neut. pl. ὅς ἥ ὅ who, which, what, that
γὰρ conj. γάρ for, and, because, but, indeed
ζώων n. gen. neut. pl. ζῶον beast
τὸ art. nom. neut. sg. ὁ ἡ τό the, this, that, he, she, it
αἷμα n. nom. neut. sg. αἷμα blood
περὶ prep. περί (+gen) of, for, concerning, (+acc) about, concerning, in
ἁμαρτίας n. gen. fem. sg. ἁμαρτία sin, offence, sinful
εἰς prep. εἰς (+acc) into, to, unto, for, in, on, toward, against, upon, at, among
τὰ art. acc. neut. pl. ὁ ἡ τό the, this, that, he, she, it
ἅγια adj. acc. neut. pl. ἅγιος Holy, holy, saint, Holy One, holy thing, most holy
διὰ prep. διά (+gen) by, through, with, in, of, (+acc) for, because of, for a cause
τοῦ art. gen. masc. sg. ὁ ἡ τό the, this, that, he, she, it
ἀρχιερέως n. gen. masc. sg. ἀρχιερεύς chief priest, high priest
τούτων demo. pron. gen. neut. pl. οὗτος αὕτη τοῦτο this, the same, this same, he, she, it
τὰ art. nom. neut. pl. ὁ ἡ τό the, this, that, he, she, it
σώματα n. nom. neut. pl. σῶμα body, bodily, slave
ἔξω prep. ἔξω out, without, out of, forth, away, outward
τῆς art. gen. fem. sg. ὁ ἡ τό the, this, that, he, she, it
παρεμβολῆς n. gen. fem. sg. παρεμβολή castle, camp, army
12 διὸ conj. διό wherefore, therefore, for which cause
καὶ conj. καί and, even, also, but
Ἰησοῦς n. nom. masc. sg. Ἰησοῦς Jesus
ἵνα conj. ἵνα that, to, lest, for to, so that, albeit, because, for, so as
διὰ prep. διά (+gen) by, through, with, in, of, (+acc) for, because of, for a cause
τοῦ art. gen. neut. sg. ὁ ἡ τό the, this, that, he, she, it
ἰδίου adj. gen. neut. sg. ἴδιος one's own, one's, privately
αἵματος n. gen. neut. sg. αἷμα blood
τὸν art. acc. masc. sg. ὁ ἡ τό the, this, that, he, she, it
λαόν n. acc. masc. sg. λαός people
ἔξω prep. ἔξω out, without, out of, forth, away, outward
τῆς art. gen. fem. sg. ὁ ἡ τό the, this, that, he, she, it
πύλης n. gen. fem. sg. πύλη gate
13 τοίνυν conj. τοίνυν therefore, then
πρὸς prep. πρός (+gen) for, (+dat) at, (+acc) unto, to, with, for, against
αὐτὸν pron. acc. masc. 3p. sg. αὐτός ή ό self, of oneself, even, very, the same, he, she, it
ἔξω prep. ἔξω out, without, out of, forth, away, outward
τῆς art. gen. fem. sg. ὁ ἡ τό the, this, that, he, she, it

παρεμβολῆς n. gen. fem. sg. παρεμβολή castle, camp, army
τὸν art. acc. masc. sg. ὁ ἡ τό the, this, that, he, she, it
ὀνειδισμὸν n. acc. masc. sg. ὀνειδισμός reproach
αὐτοῦ pron. gen. masc. 3p. sg. αὐτός ή ὁ self, of oneself, even, very, the same, he, she, it
14 οὐ particle of negation. οὐ οὐκ οὐχ not, no, neither, none, nay, nor, never, nothing
γὰρ conj. γάρ for, and, because, but, indeed
ὧδε adv. ὧδε here, hither, in this place, there, this place
πόλιν n. acc. fem. sg. πόλις city
ἀλλὰ conj. ἀλλά but, yea, yet, nevertheless, howbeit, nay, therefore
τὴν art. acc. fem. sg. ὁ ἡ τό the, this, that, he, she, it
15 δι' prep. διά (+gen) by, through, with, in, of, (+acc) for, because of, for a cause
αὐτοῦ pron. gen. masc. 3p. sg. αὐτός ή ὁ self, of oneself, even, very, the same, he, she, it
οὖν conj. οὖν therefore, then, so, and, now, wherefore
θυσίαν n. acc. fem. sg. θυσία sacrifice
αἰνέσεως n. gen. fem. sg. αἴνεσις praise
διὰ prep. διά (+gen) by, through, with, in, of, (+acc) for, because of, for a cause
παντὸς adj. gen. neut. sg. πᾶς πᾶσα πᾶν all, every, whosoever, every one, no, whole, any
τῷ art. dat. masc. sg. ὁ ἡ τό the, this, that, he, she, it
Θεῷ n. dat. masc. sg. θεός God, god
τοῦτ' demo. pron. nom. neut. sg. οὗτος αὕτη τοῦτο this, the same, this same, he, she, it
καρπὸν n. acc. masc. sg. καρπός fruit
χειλέων n. gen. neut. pl. χεῖλος lip, shore
τῷ art. dat. neut. sg. ὁ ἡ τό the, this, that, he, she, it
ὀνόματι n. dat. neut. sg. ὄνομα name, call, surname
αὐτοῦ pron. gen. masc. 3p. sg. αὐτός ή ὁ self, of oneself, even, very, the same, he, she, it
16 τῆς art. gen. fem. sg. ὁ ἡ τό the, this, that, he, she, it
δὲ conj. δέ but, and, now, also, to the contrary, rather, then
εὐποιΐας n. gen. fem. sg. εὐποιΐα doing good
καὶ conj. καί and, even, also, but
κοινωνίας n. gen. fem. sg. κοινωνία fellowship, communion, contribution, distribution
μὴ particle of negation. μή not, no, lest, neither, none, nothing, nor, never, without
τοιαύταις demo. pron. dat. fem. pl. τοιοῦτος such, like
γὰρ conj. γάρ for, and, because, but, indeed
θυσίαις n. dat. fem. pl. θυσία sacrifice
ὁ art. nom. masc. sg. ὁ ἡ τό the, this, that, he, she, it
Θεός n. nom. masc. sg. θεός God, god
17 τοῖς art. dat. masc. pl. ὁ ἡ τό the, this, that, he, she, it
ὑμῶν pron. gen. 2p. pl. σύ thou, you
καὶ conj. καί and, even, also, but
αὐτοὶ pron. nom. masc. 3p. pl. αὐτός ή ὁ self, of oneself, even, very, the same, he, she, it
γὰρ conj. γάρ for, and, because, but, indeed
ὑπὲρ prep. ὑπέρ (+gen) for, of, for the sake of, (+acc) above, more than
τῶν art. gen. fem. pl. ὁ ἡ τό the, this, that, he, she, it
ψυχῶν n. gen. fem. pl. ψυχή life, soul, mind, heart
ὑμῶν pron. gen. 2p. pl. σύ thou, you
ὡς adv. ὡς as, when, as it were, how, about, like, as soon as, even as, while
λόγον n. acc. masc. sg. λόγος word, saying, account, speech, thing, matter
ἵνα conj. ἵνα that, to, lest, for to, so that, albeit, because, for, so as
μετὰ prep. μετά (+gen) with, among, against, (+acc) after
χαρᾶς n. gen. fem. sg. χαρά joy, gladness, joyfulness
τοῦτο demo. pron. acc. neut. sg. οὗτος αὕτη τοῦτο this, the same, this same, he, she, it
καὶ conj. καί and, even, also, but
μὴ particle of negation. μή not, no, lest, neither, none, nothing, nor, never, without
ἀλυσιτελὲς adj. nom. neut. sg. ἀλυσιτελής unprofitable
γὰρ conj. γάρ for, and, because, but, indeed

ὑμῖν pron. dat. 2p. pl. σύ thou, you
τοῦτο demo. pron. nom. neut. sg. οὗτος αὕτη τοῦτο this, the same, this same, he, she, it
18 περὶ prep. περί (+gen) of, for, concerning, (+acc) about, concerning, in
ἡμῶν pron. gen. 1p. pl. ἐγώ I
γὰρ conj. γάρ for, and, because, but, indeed
ὅτι conj. ὅτι that, for, because, how that, how, because that, for that, though
καλὴν adj. acc. fem. sg. καλός good, better, goodly, meet, honest, fair, well, worthy
συνείδησιν n. acc. fem. sg. συνείδησις conscience
ἐν prep. ἐν (+dat) in, by, with, among, at, on, through, to, within, into, of, for
πᾶσι adj. dat. neut. pl. πᾶς πᾶσα πᾶν all, every, whosoever, every one, no, whole, any
καλῶς adv. καλῶς good, well, full well
19 περισσοτέρως adv. περισσοτέρως more exceedingly, more abundantly, more frequent
δὲ conj. δέ but, and, now, also, to the contrary, rather, then
τοῦτο demo. pron. acc. neut. sg. οὗτος αὕτη τοῦτο this, the same, this same, he, she, it
ἵνα conj. ἵνα that, to, lest, for to, so that, albeit, because, for, so as
τάχιον adv. τάχιον sortly, quickly, sooner
ὑμῖν pron. dat. 2p. pl. σύ thou, you
20 Ὁ art. nom. masc. sg. ὁ ἡ τό the, this, that, he, she, it
δὲ conj. δέ but, and, now, also, to the contrary, rather, then
Θεὸς n. nom. masc. sg. θεός God, god
τῆς art. gen. fem. sg. ὁ ἡ τό the, this, that, he, she, it
εἰρήνης n. gen. fem. sg. εἰρήνη peace, quietness, rest
ὁ art. nom. masc. sg. ὁ ἡ τό the, this, that, he, she, it
ἐκ prep. ἐκ ἐξ (+gen) of, from, out of, by, on, with, in, among, through
νεκρῶν adj. gen. masc. pl. νεκρός dead
τὸν art. acc. masc. sg. ὁ ἡ τό the, this, that, he, she, it
ποιμένα n. acc. masc. sg. ποιμήν shepherd, pastor
τῶν art. gen. neut. pl. ὁ ἡ τό the, this, that, he, she, it
προβάτων n. gen. neut. pl. πρόβατον sheep
τὸν art. acc. masc. sg. ὁ ἡ τό the, this, that, he, she, it
μέγαν adj. acc. masc. sg. μέγας great, loud, greatest, high, large, mighty, strong
ἐν prep. ἐν (+dat) in, by, with, among, at, on, through, to, within, into, of, for
αἵματι n. dat. neut. sg. αἷμα blood
διαθήκης n. gen. fem. sg. διαθήκη testament, covenant
αἰωνίου adj. gen. fem. sg. αἰώνιος eternal, everlasting, world, for ever
τὸν art. acc. masc. sg. ὁ ἡ τό the, this, that, he, she, it
Κύριον n. acc. masc. sg. κύριος Lord, lord, master, sir, LORD, God, Master, owner
ἡμῶν pron. gen. 1p. pl. ἐγώ I
Ἰησοῦν n. acc. masc. sg. Ἰησοῦς Jesus
21 ὑμᾶς pron. acc. 2p. pl. σύ thou, you
ἐν prep. ἐν (+dat) in, by, with, among, at, on, through, to, within, into, of, for
παντὶ adj. dat. neut. sg. πᾶς πᾶσα πᾶν all, every, whosoever, every one, no, whole, any
ἔργῳ n. dat. neut. sg. ἔργον work, deed, doing labour
ἀγαθῷ adj. dat. neut. sg. ἀγαθός good, good thing, that which is good, well
εἰς prep. εἰς (+acc) into, to, unto, for, in, on, toward, against, upon, at, among
τὸ art. acc. neut. sg. ὁ ἡ τό the, this, that, he, she, it
τὸ art. acc. neut. sg. ὁ ἡ τό the, this, that, he, she, it
θέλημα n. acc. neut. sg. θέλημα will, desire, pleasure
αὐτοῦ pron. gen. masc. 3p. sg. αὐτός ή ό self, of oneself, even, very, the same, he, she, it
ἐν prep. ἐν (+dat) in, by, with, among, at, on, through, to, within, into, of, for
ὑμῖν pron. dat. 2p. pl. σύ thou, you
τὸ art. acc. neut. sg. ὁ ἡ τό the, this, that, he, she, it
εὐάρεστον adj. acc. neut. sg. εὐάρεστος acceptable, wellpleasing, accepted, please well
ἐνώπιον prep. ἐνώπιον (+gen) before, in the sight of, in the presence of. (adv.) before
αὐτοῦ pron. gen. masc. 3p. sg. αὐτός ή ό self, of oneself, even, very, the same, he, she, it

διὰ prep. διά (+gen) by, through, with, in, of, (+acc) for, because of, for a cause
Ἰησοῦ n. gen. masc. sg. Ἰησοῦς Jesus
Χριστοῦ n. gen. masc. sg. Χριστός Christ
ᾧ relative pron. dat. masc. sg. ὅς ἥ ὅ who, which, what, that
ἡ art. nom. fem. sg. ὁ ἡ τό the, this, that, he, she, it
δόξα n. nom. fem. sg. δόξα glory, honour, praise, dignity, worship
εἰς prep. εἰς (+acc) into, to, unto, for, in, on, toward, against, upon, at, among
τοὺς art. acc. masc. pl. ὁ ἡ τό the, this, that, he, she, it
αἰῶνας n. acc. masc. pl. αἰών ever, ever and ever, evermore, age, eternal, world
τῶν art. gen. masc. pl. ὁ ἡ τό the, this, that, he, she, it
αἰώνων n. gen. masc. pl. αἰών ever, ever and ever, evermore, age, eternal, world
ἀμήν particle. ἀμήν amen, verily
22 δὲ conj. δέ but, and, now, also, to the contrary, rather, then
ὑμᾶς pron. acc. 2p. pl. σύ thou, you
ἀδελφοί n. voc. masc. pl. ἀδελφός brother
τοῦ art. gen. masc. sg. ὁ ἡ τό the, this, that, he, she, it
λόγου n. gen. masc. sg. λόγος word, saying, account, speech, thing, matter
τῆς art. gen. fem. sg. ὁ ἡ τό the, this, that, he, she, it
παρακλήσεως n. gen. fem. sg. παράκλησις consolation, exhortation, comfort
καὶ conj. καί and, even, also, but
γὰρ conj. γάρ for, and, because, but, indeed
διὰ prep. διά (+gen) by, through, with, in, of, (+acc) for, because of, for a cause
βραχέων adj. gen. neut. pl. βραχύς little while, little, few words, little space
ὑμῖν pron. dat. 2p. pl. σύ thou, you
23 τὸν art. acc. masc. sg. ὁ ἡ τό the, this, that, he, she, it
ἀδελφὸν n. acc. masc. sg. ἀδελφός brother
Τιμόθεον n. acc. masc. sg. Τιμόθεος Timotheus, Timothy
μεθ' prep. μετά (+gen) with, among, against, (+acc) after
οὗ relative pron. gen. masc. sg. ὅς ἥ ὅ who, which, what, that
ἐὰν conj. ἐάν if, soever, except, though, and if, but, whether, if so, so
τάχιον adv. τάχιον sortly, quickly, sooner
ὑμᾶς pron. acc. 2p. pl. σύ thou, you
24 πάντας adj. acc. masc. pl. πᾶς πᾶσα πᾶν all, every, whosoever, every one, no, whole, any
τοὺς art. acc. masc. pl. ὁ ἡ τό the, this, that, he, she, it
ὑμῶν pron. gen. 2p. pl. σύ thou, you
καὶ conj. καί and, even, also, but
πάντας adj. acc. masc. pl. πᾶς πᾶσα πᾶν all, every, whosoever, every one, no, whole, any
τοὺς art. acc. masc. pl. ὁ ἡ τό the, this, that, he, she, it
ἁγίους adj. acc. masc. pl. ἅγιος Holy, holy, saint, Holy One, holy thing, most holy
ὑμᾶς pron. acc. 2p. pl. σύ thou, you
οἱ art. nom. masc. pl. ὁ ἡ τό the, this, that, he, she, it
ἀπὸ prep. ἀπό (+gen) from, of, out of, since, for, off, at, by, in, on
τῆς art. gen. fem. sg. ὁ ἡ τό the, this, that, he, she, it
Ἰταλίας n. gen. fem. sg. Ἰταλία Italy
25 Ἡ art. nom. fem. sg. ὁ ἡ τό the, this, that, he, she, it
χάρις n. nom. fem. sg. χάρις grace, thank, favour, pleasure
μετὰ prep. μετά (+gen) with, among, against, (+acc) after
πάντων adj. gen. masc. pl. πᾶς πᾶσα πᾶν all, every, whosoever, every one, no, whole, any
ὑμῶν pron. gen. 2p. pl. σύ thou, you
ἀμήν particle. ἀμήν amen, verily

ΙΑΚΩΒΟΥ
ΕΠΙΣΤΟΛΗ ΚΑΘΟΛΙΚΗ

1

1 Ἰάκωβος n. nom. masc. sg. Ἰάκωβος James
Θεοῦ n. gen. masc. sg. θεός God, god
καὶ conj. καί and, even, also, but
Κυρίου n. gen. masc. sg. κύριος Lord, lord, master, sir, LORD, God, Master, owner
Ἰησοῦ n. gen. masc. sg. Ἰησοῦς Jesus
Χριστοῦ n. gen. masc. sg. Χριστός Christ
δοῦλος n. nom. masc. sg. δοῦλος servant, bondman, bond, slave
ταῖς art. dat. fem. pl. ὁ ἡ τό the, this, that, he, she, it
δώδεκα num. dat. fem. pl. δώδεκα twelve
φυλαῖς n. dat. fem. pl. φυλή tribe, kindred
ταῖς art. dat. fem. pl. ὁ ἡ τό the, this, that, he, she, it
ἐν prep. ἐν (+dat) in, by, with, among, at, on, through, to, within, into, of, for
τῇ art. dat. fem. sg. ὁ ἡ τό the, this, that, he, she, it
διασπορᾷ n. dat. fem. sg. διασπορά dispersion, one who is scattered abroad
2 Πᾶσαν adj. acc. fem. sg. πᾶς πᾶσα πᾶν all, every, whosoever, every one, no, whole, any
χαρὰν n. acc. fem. sg. χαρά joy, gladness, joyfulness
ἀδελφοί n. voc. masc. pl. ἀδελφός brother
μου pron. gen. 1p. sg. ἐγώ I
ὅταν conj. ὅταν when, as soon as, as long as, that, whensoever, while
πειρασμοῖς n. dat. masc. pl. πειρασμός temptation, trial
ποικίλοις adj. dat. masc. pl. ποικίλος divers, manifold
3 ὅτι conj. ὅτι that, for, because, how that, how, because that, for that, though
τὸ art. nom. neut. sg. ὁ ἡ τό the, this, that, he, she, it
δοκίμιον n. nom. neut. sg. δοκίμιον trying, trial
ὑμῶν pron. gen. 2p. pl. σύ thou, you
τῆς art. gen. fem. sg. ὁ ἡ τό the, this, that, he, she, it
πίστεως n. gen. fem. sg. πίστις faith, assurance, belief, fidelity
ὑπομονήν n. acc. fem. sg. ὑπομονή patience, enduring
4 ἡ art. nom. fem. sg. ὁ ἡ τό the, this, that, he, she, it
δὲ conj. δέ but, and, now, also, to the contrary, rather, then
ὑπομονὴ n. nom. fem. sg. ὑπομονή patience, enduring
ἔργον n. acc. neut. sg. ἔργον work, deed, doing labour
τέλειον adj. acc. neut. sg. τέλειος perfect, of full age
ἵνα conj. ἵνα that, to, lest, for to, so that, albeit, because, for, so as
τέλειοι adj. nom. masc. pl. τέλειος perfect, of full age
καὶ conj. καί and, even, also, but
ὁλόκληροι adj. nom. masc. pl. ὁλόκληρος whole, entire
ἐν prep. ἐν (+dat) in, by, with, among, at, on, through, to, within, into, of, for
μηδενὶ num. dat. neut. sg. μηδείς μηδεμία μηδέν no man, nothing, no, none, not at all
5 Εἰ conj. εἰ if, whether, that, though, forasmuch
δέ conj. δέ but, and, now, also, to the contrary, rather, then
τις indefinite pron. nom. masc. sg. τὶς certain, some, any man, one, any thing
ὑμῶν pron. gen. 2p. pl. σύ thou, you
σοφίας n. gen. fem. sg. σοφία wisdom
παρὰ prep. παρά (+gen) of, from, (+dat) with, for, (+acc) beside, at, by, above, against
τοῦ art. gen. masc. sg. ὁ ἡ τό the, this, that, he, she, it
Θεοῦ n. gen. masc. sg. θεός God, god
πᾶσιν adj. dat. masc. pl. πᾶς πᾶσα πᾶν all, every, whosoever, every one, no, whole, any
ἁπλῶς adv. ἁπλῶς liberally

καὶ conj. καί and, even, also, but
μὴ particle of negation. μή not, no, lest, neither, none, nothing, nor, never, without
καὶ conj. καί and, even, also, but
αὐτῷ pron. dat. masc. 3p. sg. αὐτός ή ό self, of oneself, even, very, the same, he, she, it
6 δὲ conj. δέ but, and, now, also, to the contrary, rather, then
ἐν prep. ἐν (+dat) in, by, with, among, at, on, through, to, within, into, of, for
πίστει n. dat. fem. sg. πίστις faith, assurance, belief, fidelity
μηδὲν num. acc. neut. sg. μηδείς μηδεμία μηδέν no man, nothing, no, none, not at all
ὁ art. nom. masc. sg. ὁ ἡ τό the, this, that, he, she, it
γὰρ conj. γάρ for, and, because, but, indeed
κλύδωνι n. dat. masc. sg. κλύδων raging, wave
θαλάσσης n. gen. fem. sg. θάλασσα sea
καὶ conj. καί and, even, also, but
7 μὴ particle of negation. μή not, no, lest, neither, none, nothing, nor, never, without
γὰρ particle. γάρ for, and, because, but, indeed
ὁ art. nom. masc. sg. ὁ ἡ τό the, this, that, he, she, it
ἄνθρωπος n. nom. masc. sg. ἄνθρωπος man, human being, person, one, certain
ἐκεῖνος demo. pron. nom. masc. sg. ἐκεῖνος that, he, the same, that same
ὅτι conj. ὅτι that, for, because, how that, how, because that, for that, though
τι indefinite pron. acc. neut. sg. τὶς certain, some, any man, one, any thing
παρὰ prep. παρά (+gen) of, from, (+dat) with, for, (+acc) beside, at, by, above, against
τοῦ art. gen. masc. sg. ὁ ἡ τό the, this, that, he, she, it
Κυρίου n. gen. masc. sg. κύριος Lord, lord, master, sir, LORD, God, Master, owner
8 ἀνὴρ n. nom. masc. sg. ἀνήρ man, husband, sir
δίψυχος adj. nom. masc. sg. δίψυχος double minded
ἀκατάστατος adj. nom. masc. sg. ἀκατάστατος unstable
ἐν prep. ἐν (+dat) in, by, with, among, at, on, through, to, within, into, of, for
πάσαις adj. dat. fem. pl. πᾶς πᾶσα πᾶν all, every, whosoever, every one, no, whole, any
ταῖς art. dat. fem. pl. ὁ ἡ τό the, this, that, he, she, it
ὁδοῖς n. dat. fem. pl. ὁδός way, journey, highway
αὐτοῦ pron. gen. masc. 3p. sg. αὐτός ή ό self, of oneself, even, very, the same, he, she, it
9 δὲ conj. δέ but, and, now, also, to the contrary, rather, then
ὁ art. nom. masc. sg. ὁ ἡ τό the, this, that, he, she, it
ἀδελφὸς n. nom. masc. sg. ἀδελφός brother
ὁ art. nom. masc. sg. ὁ ἡ τό the, this, that, he, she, it
ταπεινὸς adj. nom. masc. sg. ταπεινός humble, of low degree, base, cast down, lowly
ἐν prep. ἐν (+dat) in, by, with, among, at, on, through, to, within, into, of, for
τῷ art. dat. neut. sg. ὁ ἡ τό the, this, that, he, she, it
ὕψει n. dat. neut. sg. ὕψος on high, height, exalt, in exaltation
αὐτοῦ pron. gen. masc. 3p. sg. αὐτός ή ό self, of oneself, even, very, the same, he, she, it
10 ὁ art. nom. masc. sg. ὁ ἡ τό the, this, that, he, she, it
δὲ conj. δέ but, and, now, also, to the contrary, rather, then
πλούσιος adj. nom. masc. sg. πλούσιος rich
ἐν prep. ἐν (+dat) in, by, with, among, at, on, through, to, within, into, of, for
τῇ art. dat. fem. sg. ὁ ἡ τό the, this, that, he, she, it
ταπεινώσει n. dat. fem. sg. ταπείνωσις low estate, humiliation, that is made low
αὐτοῦ pron. gen. masc. 3p. sg. αὐτός ή ό self, of oneself, even, very, the same, he, she, it
ὅτι conj. ὅτι that, for, because, how that, how, because that, for that, though
ὡς adv. ὡς as, when, as it were, how, about, like, as soon as, even as, while
ἄνθος n. nom. neut. sg. ἄνθος flower
χόρτου n. gen. masc. sg. χόρτος grass, blade, hay
11 γὰρ conj. γάρ for, and, because, but, indeed
ὁ art. nom. masc. sg. ὁ ἡ τό the, this, that, he, she, it
ἥλιος n. nom. masc. sg. ἥλιος sun, east
σὺν prep. σύν (+dat) with, beside

τῷ art. dat. masc. sg. ὁ ἡ τό the, this, that, he, she, it
καύσωνι n. dat. masc. sg. καύσων heat, burning heat
καὶ conj. καί and, even, also, but
τὸν art. acc. masc. sg. ὁ ἡ τό the, this, that, he, she, it
χόρτον n. acc. masc. sg. χόρτος grass, blade, hay
καὶ conj. καί and, even, also, but
τὸ art. nom. neut. sg. ὁ ἡ τό the, this, that, he, she, it
ἄνθος n. nom. neut. sg. ἄνθος flower
αὐτοῦ pron. gen. masc. 3p. sg. αὐτός ή ό self, of oneself, even, very, the same, he, she, it
καὶ conj. καί and, even, also, but
ἡ art. nom. fem. sg. ὁ ἡ τό the, this, that, he, she, it
εὐπρέπεια n. nom. fem. sg. εὐπρέπεια grace
τοῦ art. gen. neut. sg. ὁ ἡ τό the, this, that, he, she, it
προσώπου n. gen. neut. sg. πρόσωπον face, presence, person, countenance
αὐτοῦ pron. gen. masc. 3p. sg. αὐτός ή ό self, of oneself, even, very, the same, he, she, it
οὕτω adv. οὕτω οὕτως so, even so, thus, on this wise, likewise, after this manner
καὶ conj. καί and, even, also, but
ὁ art. nom. masc. sg. ὁ ἡ τό the, this, that, he, she, it
πλούσιος adj. nom. masc. sg. πλούσιος rich
ἐν prep. ἐν (+dat) in, by, with, among, at, on, through, to, within, into, of, for
ταῖς art. dat. fem. pl. ὁ ἡ τό the, this, that, he, she, it
πορείαις n. dat. fem. pl. πορεία way, journeying
αὐτοῦ pron. gen. masc. 3p. sg. αὐτός ή ό self, of oneself, even, very, the same, he, she, it
12 Μακάριος adj. nom. masc. sg. μακάριος blessed, happy
ἀνὴρ n. nom. masc. sg. ἀνήρ man, husband, sir
ὃς relative pron. nom. masc. sg. ὅς ἥ ὅ who, which, what, that
πειρασμόν n. acc. masc. sg. πειρασμός temptation, trial
ὅτι conj. ὅτι that, for, because, how that, how, because that, for that, though
δόκιμος adj. nom. masc. sg. δόκιμος approved, tried
τὸν art. acc. masc. sg. ὁ ἡ τό the, this, that, he, she, it
στέφανον n. acc. masc. sg. στέφανος crown
τῆς art. gen. fem. sg. ὁ ἡ τό the, this, that, he, she, it
ζωῆς n. gen. fem. sg. ζωή life, lifetime
ὃν relative pron. acc. masc. sg. ὅς ἥ ὅ who, which, what, that
ὁ art. nom. masc. sg. ὁ ἡ τό the, this, that, he, she, it
Κύριος n. nom. masc. sg. κύριος Lord, lord, master, sir, LORD, God, Master, owner
τοῖς art. dat. masc. pl. ὁ ἡ τό the, this, that, he, she, it
αὐτόν pron. acc. masc. 3p. sg. αὐτός ή ό self, of oneself, even, very, the same, he, she, it
13 μηδεὶς num. nom. masc. sg. μηδείς μηδεμία μηδέν no man, nothing, no, none, not at all
ὅτι conj. ὅτι that, for, because, how that, how, because that, for that, though
'Ἀπὸ prep. ἀπό (+gen) from, of, out of, since, for, off, at, by, in, on
τοῦ art. gen. masc. sg. ὁ ἡ τό the, this, that, he, she, it
Θεοῦ n. gen. masc. sg. θεός God, god
ὁ art. nom. masc. sg. ὁ ἡ τό the, this, that, he, she, it
γὰρ conj. γάρ for, and, because, but, indeed
Θεὸς n. nom. masc. sg. θεός God, god
ἀπείραστός adj. nom. masc. sg. ἀπείραστος cannot be tempted
κακῶν adj. gen. neut. pl. κακός evil, evil thing, noisome, wicked
δὲ conj. δέ but, and, now, also, to the contrary, rather, then
αὐτὸς pron. nom. masc. 3p. sg. αὐτός ή ό self, of oneself, even, very, the same, he, she, it
οὐδένα num. acc. masc. sg. οὐδείς no man, nothing, no, none, neither, not, nought
14 ἕκαστος adj. nom. masc. sg. ἕκαστος every man, every, every one, any man, each
δὲ conj. δέ but, and, now, also, to the contrary, rather, then
ὑπὸ prep. ὑπό (+gen) of, by, with, from, among, (+acc) under
τῆς art. gen. fem. sg. ὁ ἡ τό the, this, that, he, she, it

ἰδίας adj. gen. fem. sg. ἴδιος one's own, one's, privately
ἐπιθυμίας n. gen. fem. sg. ἐπιθυμία lust, concupiscence, desire
καὶ conj. καί and, even, also, but
15 εἶτα adv. εἶτα afterward, then, after that, furthermore
ἡ art. nom. fem. sg. ὁ ἡ τό the, this, that, he, she, it
ἐπιθυμία n. nom. fem. sg. ἐπιθυμία lust, concupiscence, desire
ἁμαρτίαν n. acc. fem. sg. ἁμαρτία sin, offence, sinful
ἡ art. nom. fem. sg. ὁ ἡ τό the, this, that, he, she, it
δὲ conj. δέ but, and, now, also, to the contrary, rather, then
ἁμαρτία n. nom. fem. sg. ἁμαρτία sin, offence, sinful
θάνατον n. acc. masc. sg. θάνατος death
16 μὴ particle of negation. μή not, no, lest, neither, none, nothing, nor, never, without
ἀδελφοί n. voc. masc. pl. ἀδελφός brother
μου pron. gen. 1p. sg. ἐγώ I
ἀγαπητοί adj. voc. masc. pl. ἀγαπητός beloved, dearly beloved, dear, wellbeloved
17 πᾶσα adj. nom. fem. sg. πᾶς πᾶσa πᾶν all, every, whosoever, every one, no, whole, any
δόσις n. nom. fem. sg. δόσις giving, gift
ἀγαθὴ adj. nom. fem. sg. ἀγαθός good, good thing, that which is good, well
καὶ conj. καί and, even, also, but
πᾶν adj. nom. neut. sg. πᾶς πᾶσa πᾶν all, every, whosoever, every one, no, whole, any
δώρημα n. nom. neut. sg. δώρημα gift
τέλειον adj. nom. neut. sg. τέλειος perfect, of full age
ἄνωθέν adv. ἄνωθεν from above, again, the top, from the beginning, from the very first
ἀπὸ prep. ἀπό (+gen) from, of, out of, since, for, off, at, by, in, on
τοῦ art. gen. masc. sg. ὁ ἡ τό the, this, that, he, she, it
πατρὸς n. gen. masc. sg. πατήρ Father, father, parent
τῶν art. gen. neut. pl. ὁ ἡ τό the, this, that, he, she, it
φώτων n. gen. neut. pl. φῶς light, fire
παρ' prep. παρά (+gen) of, from, (+dat) with, for, (+acc) beside, at, by, above, against
ᾧ relative pron. dat. masc. sg. ὅς ἥ ὅ who, which, what, that
οὐκ particle of negation. οὐ οὐκ οὐχ not, no, neither, none, nay, nor, never, nothing
παραλλαγὴ n. nom. fem. sg. παραλλαγή variableness
ἢ particle. ἤ or, than, either, nor, or else, and, rather than
τροπῆς n. gen. fem. sg. τροπή turning
ἀποσκίασμα n. nom. neut. sg. ἀποσκίασμα shadow
18 ἡμᾶς pron. acc. 1p. pl. ἐγώ I
λόγῳ n. dat. masc. sg. λόγος word, saying, account, speech, thing, matter
ἀληθείας n. gen. fem. sg. ἀλήθεια truth, verity
εἰς prep. εἰς (+acc) into, to, unto, for, in, on, toward, against, upon, at, among
τὸ art. acc. neut. sg. ὁ ἡ τό the, this, that, he, she, it
ἡμᾶς pron. acc. 1p. pl. ἐγώ I
ἀπαρχήν n. acc. fem. sg. ἀπαρχή firstfruit
τινα indefinite pron. acc. fem. sg. τὶς certain, some, any man, one, any thing
τῶν art. gen. neut. pl. ὁ ἡ τό the, this, that, he, she, it
αὐτοῦ pron. gen. masc. 3p. sg. αὐτός ή ό self, of oneself, even, very, the same, he, she, it
κτισμάτων n. gen. neut. pl. κτίσμα creature
19 Ὥστε conj. ὥστε so that, wherefore, insomuch that, therefore, that, so then
ἀδελφοί n. voc. masc. pl. ἀδελφός brother
μου pron. gen. 1p. sg. ἐγώ I
ἀγαπητοί adj. voc. masc. pl. ἀγαπητός beloved, dearly beloved, dear, wellbeloved
πᾶς adj. nom. masc. sg. πᾶς πᾶσa πᾶν all, every, whosoever, every one, no, whole, any
ἄνθρωπος n. nom. masc. sg. ἄνθρωπος man, human being, person, one, certain
ταχὺς adj. nom. masc. sg. ταχύς swift
εἰς prep. εἰς (+acc) into, to, unto, for, in, on, toward, against, upon, at, among
τὸ art. acc. neut. sg. ὁ ἡ τό the, this, that, he, she, it

βραδὺς adj. nom. masc. sg. βραδύς slow
εἰς prep. εἰς (+acc) into, to, unto, for, in, on, toward, against, upon, at, among
τὸ art. acc. neut. sg. ὁ ἡ τό the, this, that, he, she, it
βραδὺς adj. nom. masc. sg. βραδύς slow
εἰς prep. εἰς (+acc) into, to, unto, for, in, on, toward, against, upon, at, among
ὀργήν n. acc. fem. sg. ὀργή wrath, anger, indignation, vengeance
20 ὀργὴ n. nom. fem. sg. ὀργή wrath, anger, indignation, vengeance
γὰρ conj. γάρ for, and, because, but, indeed
ἀνδρὸς n. gen. masc. sg. ἀνήρ man, husband, sir
δικαιοσύνην n. acc. fem. sg. δικαιοσύνη righteousness
Θεοῦ n. gen. masc. sg. θεός God, god
οὐ particle of negation. οὐ οὐκ οὐχ not, no, neither, none, nay, nor, never, nothing
21 διὸ conj. διό wherefore, therefore, for which cause
πᾶσαν adj. acc. fem. sg. πᾶς πᾶσα πᾶν all, every, whosoever, every one, no, whole, any
ῥυπαρίαν n. acc. fem. sg. ῥυπαρία filthiness
καὶ conj. καί and, even, also, but
περισσείαν n. acc. fem. sg. περισσεία abundance, abundant, superfluity
κακίας n. gen. fem. sg. κακία malice, maliciousness, evil, naughtiness, wickedness
ἐν prep. ἐν (+dat) in, by, with, among, at, on, through, to, within, into, of, for
πρᾳΰτητι n. dat. fem. sg. πρᾳΰτης meekness
τὸν art. acc. masc. sg. ὁ ἡ τό the, this, that, he, she, it
ἔμφυτον adj. acc. masc. sg. ἔμφυτος engrafted
λόγον n. acc. masc. sg. λόγος word, saying, account, speech, thing, matter
τὸν art. acc. masc. sg. ὁ ἡ τό the, this, that, he, she, it
τὰς art. acc. fem. pl. ὁ ἡ τό the, this, that, he, she, it
ψυχὰς n. acc. fem. pl. ψυχή life, soul, mind, heart
ὑμῶν pron. gen. 2p. pl. σύ thou, you
22 δὲ conj. δέ but, and, now, also, to the contrary, rather, then
ποιηταὶ n. nom. masc. pl. ποιητής doer, poet
λόγου n. gen. masc. sg. λόγος word, saying, account, speech, thing, matter
καὶ conj. καί and, even, also, but
μὴ particle of negation. μή not, no, lest, neither, none, nothing, nor, never, without
μόνον adv. μόνος only, alone, by oneself
ἀκροαταὶ n. nom. masc. pl. ἀκροατής hearer
ἑαυτούς reflexive pron. acc. masc. 3p. pl. ἑαυτοῦ himself, herself, itself, yourself, ourselves
23 ὅτι conj. ὅτι that, for, because, how that, how, because that, for that, though
εἴ conj. εἰ if, whether, that, though, forasmuch
τις indefinite pron. nom. masc. sg. τὶς certain, some, any man, one, any thing
ἀκροατὴς n. nom. masc. sg. ἀκροατής hearer
λόγου n. gen. masc. sg. λόγος word, saying, account, speech, thing, matter
καὶ conj. καί and, even, also, but
οὐ particle of negation. οὐ οὐκ οὐχ not, no, neither, none, nay, nor, never, nothing
ποιητής n. nom. masc. sg. ποιητής doer, poet
οὗτος demo. pron. nom. masc. sg. οὗτος αὕτη τοῦτο this, the same, this same, he, she, it
ἀνδρὶ n. dat. masc. sg. ἀνήρ man, husband, sir
τὸ art. acc. neut. sg. ὁ ἡ τό the, this, that, he, she, it
πρόσωπον n. acc. neut. sg. πρόσωπον face, presence, person, countenance
τῆς art. gen. fem. sg. ὁ ἡ τό the, this, that, he, she, it
γενέσεως n. gen. fem. sg. γένεσις generation, birth, lineage
αὐτοῦ pron. gen. masc. 3p. sg. αὐτός ἡ ὁ self, of oneself, even, very, the same, he, she, it
ἐν prep. ἐν (+dat) in, by, with, among, at, on, through, to, within, into, of, for
ἐσόπτρῳ n. dat. neut. sg. ἔσοπτρον glass
24 γὰρ conj. γάρ for, and, because, but, indeed
ἑαυτὸν reflexive pron. acc. masc. 3p. sg. ἑαυτοῦ himself, herself, itself, yourself, ourselves
καὶ conj. καί and, even, also, but

καὶ conj. καί and, even, also, but
εὐθέως adv. εὐθέως immediately, straightway, forthwith, as soon as, by and by, shortly
ὁποῖος interrog. pron. nom. masc. sg. ὁποῖος what manner of, as, of what sort
25 ὁ art. nom. masc. sg. ὁ ἡ τό the, this, that, he, she, it
δὲ conj. δέ but, and, now, also, to the contrary, rather, then
εἰς prep. εἰς (+acc) into, to, unto, for, in, on, toward, against, upon, at, among
νόμον n. acc. masc. sg. νόμος law, the law
τέλειον adj. acc. masc. sg. τέλειος perfect, of full age
τὸν art. acc. masc. sg. ὁ ἡ τό the, this, that, he, she, it
τῆς art. gen. fem. sg. ὁ ἡ τό the, this, that, he, she, it
ἐλευθερίας n. gen. fem. sg. ἐλευθερία liberty
καὶ conj. καί and, even, also, but
οὗτος demo. pron. nom. masc. sg. οὗτος αὕτη τοῦτο this, the same, this same, he, she, it
οὐκ particle of negation. οὐ οὐκ οὐχ not, no, neither, none, nay, nor, never, nothing
ἀκροατὴς n. nom. masc. sg. ἀκροατής hearer
ἐπιλησμονῆς n. gen. fem. sg. ἐπιλησμονή forgetful, forgetfulness
ἀλλὰ conj. ἀλλά but, yea, yet, nevertheless, howbeit, nay, therefore
ποιητὴς n. nom. masc. sg. ποιητής doer, poet
ἔργου n. gen. neut. sg. ἔργον work, deed, doing labour
οὗτος demo. pron. nom. masc. sg. οὗτος αὕτη τοῦτο this, the same, this same, he, she, it
μακάριος adj. nom. masc. sg. μακάριος blessed, happy
ἐν prep. ἐν (+dat) in, by, with, among, at, on, through, to, within, into, of, for
τῇ art. dat. fem. sg. ὁ ἡ τό the, this, that, he, she, it
ποιήσει n. dat. fem. sg. ποίησις deed, doing
αὐτοῦ pron. gen. masc. 3p. sg. αὐτός ἡ ὁ self, of oneself, even, very, the same, he, she, it
26 εἴ conj. εἰ if, whether, that, though, forasmuch
τις indefinite pron. nom. masc. sg. τὶς certain, some, any man, one, any thing
θρησκὸς adj. nom. masc. sg. θρῆσκος religious
ἐν prep. ἐν (+dat) in, by, with, among, at, on, through, to, within, into, of, for
ὑμῖν pron. dat. 2p. pl. σύ thou, you
μὴ particle of negation. μή not, no, lest, neither, none, nothing, nor, never, without
γλῶσσαν n. acc. fem. sg. γλῶσσα tongue
αὐτοῦ pron. gen. masc. 3p. sg. αὐτός ἡ ὁ self, of oneself, even, very, the same, he, she, it
ἀλλ' conj. ἀλλά but, yea, yet, nevertheless, howbeit, nay, therefore
καρδίαν n. acc. fem. sg. καρδία heart
αὐτοῦ pron. gen. masc. 3p. sg. αὐτός ἡ ὁ self, of oneself, even, very, the same, he, she, it
τούτου demo. pron. gen. masc. sg. οὗτος αὕτη τοῦτο this, the same, this same, he, she, it
μάταιος adj. nom. fem. sg. μάταιος vanity, vain
ἡ art. nom. fem. sg. ὁ ἡ τό the, this, that, he, she, it
θρησκεία n. nom. fem. sg. θρησκεία religion, worshipping
27 θρησκεία n. nom. fem. sg. θρησκεία religion, worshipping
καθαρὰ adj. nom. fem. sg. καθαρός pure, clean, clear
καὶ conj. καί and, even, also, but
ἀμίαντος adj. nom. fem. sg. ἀμίαντος undefiled
παρὰ prep. παρά (+gen) of, from, (+dat) with, for, (+acc) beside, at, by, above, against
τῷ art. dat. masc. sg. ὁ ἡ τό the, this, that, he, she, it
Θεῷ n. dat. masc. sg. θεός God, god
καὶ conj. καί and, even, also, but
πατρὶ n. dat. masc. sg. πατήρ Father, father, parent
αὕτη demo. pron. nom. fem. sg. οὗτος αὕτη τοῦτο this, the same, this same, he, she, it
ὀρφανοὺς adj. acc. masc. pl. ὀρφανός comfortless, fatherless
καὶ conj. καί and, even, also, but
χήρας adj. acc. fem. pl. χήρα widow
ἐν prep. ἐν (+dat) in, by, with, among, at, on, through, to, within, into, of, for
τῇ art. dat. fem. sg. ὁ ἡ τό the, this, that, he, she, it

θλίψει n. dat. fem. sg. θλῖψις tribulation, affliction, anguish, persecution
αὐτῶν pron. gen. masc. 3p. pl. αὐτός ή ό self, of oneself, even, very, the same, he, she, it
ἄσπιλον adj. acc. masc. sg. ἄσπιλος without spot, unspotted
ἑαυτὸν reflexive pron. acc. masc. 3p. sg. ἑαυτοῦ himself, herself, itself, yourself, ourselves
ἀπὸ prep. ἀπό (+gen) from, of, out of, since, for, off, at, by, in, on
τοῦ art. gen. masc. sg. ὁ ἡ τό the, this, that, he, she, it
κόσμου n. gen. masc. sg. κόσμος world, adorning

2

1 Ἀδελφοί n. voc. masc. pl. ἀδελφός brother
μου pron. gen. 1p. sg. ἐγώ I
μὴ particle of negation. μή not, no, lest, neither, none, nothing, nor, never, without
ἐν prep. ἐν (+dat) in, by, with, among, at, on, through, to, within, into, of, for
προσωποληψίαις n. dat. fem. pl. προσωποληψία respect of persons
τὴν art. acc. fem. sg. ὁ ἡ τό the, this, that, he, she, it
πίστιν n. acc. fem. sg. πίστις faith, assurance, belief, fidelity
τοῦ art. gen. masc. sg. ὁ ἡ τό the, this, that, he, she, it
Κυρίου n. gen. masc. sg. κύριος Lord, lord, master, sir, LORD, God, Master, owner
ἡμῶν pron. gen. 1p. pl. ἐγώ I
Ἰησοῦ n. gen. masc. sg. Ἰησοῦς Jesus
Χριστοῦ n. gen. masc. sg. Χριστός Christ
τῆς art. gen. fem. sg. ὁ ἡ τό the, this, that, he, she, it
δόξης n. gen. fem. sg. δόξα glory, honour, praise, dignity, worship
2 ἐὰν conj. ἐάν if, soever, except, though, and if, but, whether, if so, so
γὰρ conj. γάρ for, and, because, but, indeed
εἰς prep. εἰς (+acc) into, to, unto, for, in, on, toward, against, upon, at, among
τὴν art. acc. fem. sg. ὁ ἡ τό the, this, that, he, she, it
συναγωγὴν n. acc. fem. sg. συναγωγή synagogue, assembly, congregation
ὑμῶν pron. gen. 2p. pl. σύ thou, you
ἀνὴρ n. nom. masc. sg. ἀνήρ man, husband, sir
χρυσοδακτύλιος adj. nom. masc. sg. χρυσοδακτύλιος with a gold ring
ἐν prep. ἐν (+dat) in, by, with, among, at, on, through, to, within, into, of, for
ἐσθῆτι n. dat. fem. sg. ἐσθής robe, apparel, clothing, raiment
λαμπρᾷ adj. dat. fem. sg. λαμπρός gorgeous, bright, goodly, white, clear
δὲ conj. δέ but, and, now, also, to the contrary, rather, then
καὶ conj. καί and, even, also, but
πτωχὸς adj. nom. masc. sg. πτωχός poor, beggar, beggarly
ἐν prep. ἐν (+dat) in, by, with, among, at, on, through, to, within, into, of, for
ῥυπαρᾷ adj. dat. fem. sg. ῥυπαρός vile
ἐσθῆτι n. dat. fem. sg. ἐσθής robe, apparel, clothing, raiment
3 καὶ conj. καί and, even, also, but
ἐπὶ prep. ἐπί (+gen) on, in, upon, (+dat) in, at, for, upon, (+acc) on, upon, unto, to, against
τὸν art. acc. masc. sg. ὁ ἡ τό the, this, that, he, she, it
τὴν art. acc. fem. sg. ὁ ἡ τό the, this, that, he, she, it
ἐσθῆτα n. acc. fem. sg. ἐσθής robe, apparel, clothing, raiment
τὴν art. acc. fem. sg. ὁ ἡ τό the, this, that, he, she, it
λαμπρὰν adj. acc. fem. sg. λαμπρός gorgeous, bright, goodly, white, clear
καὶ conj. καί and, even, also, but
αὐτῷ pron. dat. masc. 3p. sg. αὐτός ή ό self, of oneself, even, very, the same, he, she, it
Σὺ pron. nom. 2p. sg. σύ thou, you
ὧδε adv. ὧδε here, hither, in this place, there, this place
καλῶς adv. καλῶς good, well, full well
καὶ conj. καί and, even, also, but
τῷ art. dat. masc. sg. ὁ ἡ τό the, this, that, he, she, it

πτωχῷ adj. dat. masc. sg. πτωχός poor, beggar, beggarly
Σὺ pron. nom. 2p. sg. σύ thou, you
ἐκεῖ adv. ἐκεῖ there, thither, thitherward, yonder, yonder place
ἢ particle. ἤ or, than, either, nor, or else, and, rather than
ὧδε adv. ὧδε here, hither, in this place, there, this place
ὑπὸ prep. ὑπό (+gen) of, by, with, from, among, (+acc) under
τὸ art. acc. neut. sg. ὁ ἡ τό the, this, that, he, she, it
ὑποπόδιόν n. acc. neut. sg. ὑποπόδιον footstool
μου pron. gen. 1p. sg. ἐγώ I
4 καὶ conj. καί and, even, also, but
οὐ particle of negation. οὐ οὐκ οὐχ not, no, neither, none, nay, nor, never, nothing
ἐν prep. ἐν (+dat) in, by, with, among, at, on, through, to, within, into, of, for
ἑαυτοῖς reflexive pron. dat. masc. 3p. pl. ἑαυτοῦ himself, herself, itself, yourself, ourselves
καὶ conj. καί and, even, also, but
κριταὶ n. nom. masc. pl. κριτής judge
διαλογισμῶν n. gen. masc. pl. διαλογισμός thought, reasoning, imagination, disputing
πονηρῶν adj. gen. masc. pl. πονηρός evil, wicked, bad
5 ἀδελφοί n. voc. masc. pl. ἀδελφός brother
μου pron. gen. 1p. sg. ἐγώ I
ἀγαπητοί adj. voc. masc. pl. ἀγαπητός beloved, dearly beloved, dear, wellbeloved
οὐχ particle of negation. οὐ οὐκ οὐχ not, no, neither, none, nay, nor, never, nothing
ὁ art. nom. masc. sg. ὁ ἡ τό the, this, that, he, she, it
Θεὸς n. nom. masc. sg. θεός God, god
τοὺς art. acc. masc. pl. ὁ ἡ τό the, this, that, he, she, it
πτωχοὺς adj. acc. masc. pl. πτωχός poor, beggar, beggarly
τοῦ art. gen. masc. sg. ὁ ἡ τό the, this, that, he, she, it
κόσμου n. gen. masc. sg. κόσμος world, adorning
τούτου demo. pron. gen. masc. sg. οὗτος αὕτη τοῦτο this, the same, this same, he, she, it
πλουσίους adj. acc. masc. pl. πλούσιος rich
ἐν prep. ἐν (+dat) in, by, with, among, at, on, through, to, within, into, of, for
πίστει n. dat. fem. sg. πίστις faith, assurance, belief, fidelity
καὶ conj. καί and, even, also, but
κληρονόμους n. acc. masc. pl. κληρονόμος heir
τῆς art. gen. fem. sg. ὁ ἡ τό the, this, that, he, she, it
βασιλείας n. gen. fem. sg. βασιλεία kingdom, reign
ἧς relative pron. gen. fem. sg. ὅς ἥ ὅ who, which, what, that
τοῖς art. dat. masc. pl. ὁ ἡ τό the, this, that, he, she, it
αὐτόν pron. acc. masc. 3p. sg. αὐτός ή ó self, of oneself, even, very, the same, he, she, it
6 ὑμεῖς pron. nom. 2p. pl. σύ thou, you
δὲ conj. δέ but, and, now, also, to the contrary, rather, then
τὸν art. acc. masc. sg. ὁ ἡ τό the, this, that, he, she, it
πτωχόν adj. acc. masc. sg. πτωχός poor, beggar, beggarly
οὐχ particle of negation. οὐ οὐκ οὐχ not, no, neither, none, nay, nor, never, nothing
οἱ art. nom. masc. pl. ὁ ἡ τό the, this, that, he, she, it
πλούσιοι adj. nom. masc. pl. πλούσιος rich
ὑμῶν pron. gen. 2p. pl. σύ thou, you
καὶ conj. καί and, even, also, but
αὐτοὶ pron. nom. masc. 3p. pl. αὐτός ή ó self, of oneself, even, very, the same, he, she, it
ὑμᾶς pron. acc. 2p. pl. σύ thou, you
εἰς prep. εἰς (+acc) into, to, unto, for, in, on, toward, against, upon, at, among
κριτήρια n. acc. neut. pl. κριτήριον judge, judgement, judgement seat
7 οὐκ particle of negation. οὐ οὐκ οὐχ not, no, neither, none, nay, nor, never, nothing
αὐτοὶ pron. nom. masc. 3p. pl. αὐτός ή ó self, of oneself, even, very, the same, he, she, it
τὸ art. acc. neut. sg. ὁ ἡ τό the, this, that, he, she, it
καλὸν adj. acc. neut. sg. καλός good, better, goodly, meet, honest, fair, well, worthy

ὄνομα n. acc. neut. sg. ὄνομα name, call, surname
τὸ art. acc. neut. sg. ὁ ἡ τό the, this, that, he, she, it
ἐφ' prep. ἐπί (+gen) on, in, upon, (+dat) in, at, for, upon, (+acc) on, upon, unto, to, against
ὑμᾶς pron. acc. 2p. pl. σύ thou, you
8 εἰ conj. εἰ if, whether, that, though, forasmuch
μέντοι conj. μέντοι yet, nevertheless, but, howbeit, likewise
νόμον n. acc. masc. sg. νόμος law, the law
βασιλικὸν adj. acc. masc. sg. βασιλικός nobleman, royal, king
κατὰ prep. κατά (+gen) against, by, throughout, down, (+acc) according to, after, with
τὴν art. acc. fem. sg. ὁ ἡ τό the, this, that, he, she, it
γραφήν n. acc. fem. sg. γραφή scripture
τὸν art. acc. masc. sg. ὁ ἡ τό the, this, that, he, she, it
πλησίον adv. πλησίον neighbour, near
σου pron. gen. 2p. sg. σύ thou, you
ὡς adv. ὡς as, when, as it were, how, about, like, as soon as, even as, while
σεαυτόν pron. acc. masc. 2p. sg. σεαυτοῦ σεαυτῷ σεαυτόν thyself, thine own self
καλῶς adv. καλῶς good, well, full well
9 εἰ conj. εἰ if, whether, that, though, forasmuch
δὲ conj. δέ but, and, now, also, to the contrary, rather, then
ἁμαρτίαν n. acc. fem. sg. ἁμαρτία sin, offence, sinful
ὑπὸ prep. ὑπό (+gen) of, by, with, from, among, (+acc) under
τοῦ art. gen. masc. sg. ὁ ἡ τό the, this, that, he, she, it
νόμου n. gen. masc. sg. νόμος law, the law
ὡς adv. ὡς as, when, as it were, how, about, like, as soon as, even as, while
παραβάται n. nom. masc. pl. παραβάτης breaker, transgressor
10 ὅστις relative pron. nom. masc. sg. ὅστις which, who, whosoever, that, whatsoever
γὰρ conj. γάρ for, and, because, but, indeed
ὅλον adj. acc. masc. sg. ὅλος all, whole, every whit, altogether
τὸν art. acc. masc. sg. ὁ ἡ τό the, this, that, he, she, it
νόμον n. acc. masc. sg. νόμος law, the law
δὲ conj. δέ but, and, now, also, to the contrary, rather, then
ἐν prep. ἐν (+dat) in, by, with, among, at, on, through, to, within, into, of, for
ἑνί num. dat. neut. sg. εἷς or ἕν one, other, some, any, only, a certain
πάντων adj. gen. neut. pl. πᾶς πᾶσα πᾶν all, every, whosoever, every one, no, whole, any
ἔνοχος adj. nom. masc. sg. ἔνοχος in danger of, guilty of, subject to
11 ὁ art. nom. masc. sg. ὁ ἡ τό the, this, that, he, she, it
γὰρ conj. γάρ for, and, because, but, indeed
Μὴ particle of negation. μή not, no, lest, neither, none, nothing, nor, never, without
καί conj. καί and, even, also, but
Μὴ particle of negation. μή not, no, lest, neither, none, nothing, nor, never, without
εἰ conj. εἰ if, whether, that, though, forasmuch
δὲ conj. δέ but, and, now, also, to the contrary, rather, then
οὐ particle of negation. οὐ οὐκ οὐχ not, no, neither, none, nay, nor, never, nothing
δὲ conj. δέ but, and, now, also, to the contrary, rather, then
παραβάτης n. nom. masc. sg. παραβάτης breaker, transgressor
νόμου n. gen. masc. sg. νόμος law, the law
12 οὕτω adv. οὕτω οὕτως so, even so, thus, on this wise, likewise, after this manner
καὶ conj. καί and, even, also, but
οὕτω adv. οὕτω οὕτως so, even so, thus, on this wise, likewise, after this manner
ὡς adv. ὡς as, when, as it were, how, about, like, as soon as, even as, while
διὰ prep. διά (+gen) by, through, with, in, of, (+acc) for, because of, for a cause
νόμου n. gen. masc. sg. νόμος law, the law
ἐλευθερίας n. gen. fem. sg. ἐλευθερία liberty
13 ἡ art. nom. fem. sg. ὁ ἡ τό the, this, that, he, she, it
γὰρ conj. γάρ for, and, because, but, indeed

κρίσις n. nom. fem. sg. κρίσις judgment, damnation, accusation, condemnation
ἀνίλεως adj. nom. fem. sg. ἀνίλεως without mercy
τῷ art. dat. masc. sg. ὁ ἡ τό the, this, that, he, she, it
μὴ particle of negation. μή not, no, lest, neither, none, nothing, nor, never, without
ἔλεος n. acc. neut. sg. ἔλεος mercy
καὶ conj. καί and, even, also, but
ἔλεος n. nom. neut. sg. ἔλεος mercy
κρίσεως n. gen. fem. sg. κρίσις judgment, damnation, accusation, condemnation
14 Τί interrog. pron. nom. neut. sg. τίς what, who, why, where, which, how
τὸ art. nom. neut. sg. ὁ ἡ τό the, this, that, he, she, it
ὄφελος n. nom. neut. sg. ὄφελος advantage, profit
ἀδελφοί n. voc. masc. pl. ἀδελφός brother
μου pron. gen. 1p. sg. ἐγώ I
ἐὰν conj. ἐάν if, soever, except, though, and if, but, whether, if so, so
πίστιν n. acc. fem. sg. πίστις faith, assurance, belief, fidelity
τις indefinite pron. nom. masc. sg. τὶς certain, some, any man, one, any thing
ἔργα n. acc. neut. pl. ἔργον work, deed, doing labour
δὲ conj. δέ but, and, now, also, to the contrary, rather, then
μὴ particle of negation. μή not, no, lest, neither, none, nothing, nor, never, without
μη particle of negation. μή not, no, lest, neither, none, nothing, nor, never, without
ἡ art. nom. fem. sg. ὁ ἡ τό the, this, that, he, she, it
πίστις n. nom. fem. sg. πίστις faith, assurance, belief, fidelity
αὐτόν pron. acc. masc. 3p. sg. αὐτός ή ό self, of oneself, even, very, the same, he, she, it
15 ἐὰν conj. ἐάν if, soever, except, though, and if, but, whether, if so, so
δέ conj. δέ but, and, now, also, to the contrary, rather, then
ἀδελφὸς n. nom. masc. sg. ἀδελφός brother
ἢ particle. ἤ or, than, either, nor, or else, and, rather than
ἀδελφὴ n. nom. fem. sg. ἀδελφή sister
γυμνοὶ adj. nom. masc. pl. γυμνός naked, bare
καὶ conj. καί and, even, also, but
τῆς art. gen. fem. sg. ὁ ἡ τό the, this, that, he, she, it
ἐφημέρου adj. gen. fem. sg. ἐφήμερος daily
τροφῆς n. gen. fem. sg. τροφή meat, food
16 δέ conj. δέ but, and, now, also, to the contrary, rather, then
τις indefinite pron. nom. masc. sg. τὶς certain, some, any man, one, any thing
αὐτοῖς pron. dat. masc. 3p. pl. αὐτός ή ό self, of oneself, even, very, the same, he, she, it
ἐξ prep. ἐκ ἐξ (+gen) of, from, out of, by, on, with, in, among, through
ὑμῶν pron. gen. 2p. pl. σύ thou, you
ἐν prep. ἐν (+dat) in, by, with, among, at, on, through, to, within, into, of, for
εἰρήνῃ n. dat. fem. sg. εἰρήνη peace, quietness, rest
καὶ conj. καί and, even, also, but
μὴ particle of negation. μή not, no, lest, neither, none, nothing, nor, never, without
δέ conj. δέ but, and, now, also, to the contrary, rather, then
αὐτοῖς pron. dat. masc. 3p. pl. αὐτός ή ό self, of oneself, even, very, the same, he, she, it
τὰ art. acc. neut. pl. ὁ ἡ τό the, this, that, he, she, it
ἐπιτήδεια adj. acc. neut. pl. ἐπιτήδειος thing which is needful
τοῦ art. gen. neut. sg. ὁ ἡ τό the, this, that, he, she, it
σώματος n. gen. neut. sg. σῶμα body, bodily, slave
τί interrog. pron. nom. neut. sg. τίς what, who, why, where, which, how
τὸ art. nom. neut. sg. ὁ ἡ τό the, this, that, he, she, it
ὄφελος n. nom. neut. sg. ὄφελος advantage, profit
17 οὕτω adv. οὕτω οὕτως so, even so, thus, on this wise, likewise, after this manner
καὶ conj. καί and, even, also, but
ἡ art. nom. fem. sg. ὁ ἡ τό the, this, that, he, she, it
πίστις n. nom. fem. sg. πίστις faith, assurance, belief, fidelity

ἐὰν conj. ἐάν if, soever, except, though, and if, but, whether, if so, so
μὴ particle of negation. μή not, no, lest, neither, none, nothing, nor, never, without
ἔργα n. acc. neut. pl. ἔργον work, deed, doing labour
νεκρά adj. nom. fem. sg. νεκρός dead
καθ' prep. κατά (+gen) against, by, throughout, down, (+acc) according to, after, with
ἑαυτήν reflexive pron. acc. fem. 3p. sg. ἑαυτοῦ himself, herself, itself, yourself, ourselves
18 ἀλλ' conj. ἀλλά but, yea, yet, nevertheless, howbeit, nay, therefore
τις indefinite pron. nom. masc. sg. τὶς certain, some, any man, one, any thing
Σὺ pron. nom. 2p. sg. σύ thou, you
πίστιν n. acc. fem. sg. πίστις faith, assurance, belief, fidelity
κἀγὼ pron. nom. 1p. sg. κἀγώ and I, I also, so I, even as I
ἔργα n. acc. neut. pl. ἔργον work, deed, doing labour
μοι pron. dat. 1p. sg. ἐγώ I
τὴν art. acc. fem. sg. ὁ ἡ τό the, this, that, he, she, it
πίστιν n. acc. fem. sg. πίστις faith, assurance, belief, fidelity
σου pron. gen. 2p. sg. σύ thou, you
χωρὶς prep. χωρίς (+gen) without, beside. (adv.) by itself, apart, separately
τῶν art. gen. neut. pl. ὁ ἡ τό the, this, that, he, she, it
ἔργων n. gen. neut. pl. ἔργον work, deed, doing labour
σου pron. gen. 2p. sg. σύ thou, you
κἀγὼ pron. nom. 1p. sg. κἀγώ and I, I also, so I, even as I
σοι pron. dat. 2p. sg. σύ thou, you
ἐκ prep. ἐκ ἐξ (+gen) of, from, out of, by, on, with, in, among, through
τῶν art. gen. neut. pl. ὁ ἡ τό the, this, that, he, she, it
ἔργων n. gen. neut. pl. ἔργον work, deed, doing labour
μου pron. gen. 1p. sg. ἐγώ I
τὴν art. acc. fem. sg. ὁ ἡ τό the, this, that, he, she, it
πίστιν n. acc. fem. sg. πίστις faith, assurance, belief, fidelity
μου pron. gen. 1p. sg. ἐγώ I
19 σὺ pron. nom. 2p. sg. σύ thou, you
ὅτι conj. ὅτι that, for, because, how that, how, because that, for that, though
ὁ art. nom. masc. sg. ὁ ἡ τό the, this, that, he, she, it
Θεός n. nom. masc. sg. θεός God, god
εἷς num. nom. masc. sg. εἷς or ἕν one, other, some, any, only, a certain
καλῶς adv. καλῶς good, well, full well
καὶ conj. καί and, even, also, but
τὰ art. nom. neut. pl. ὁ ἡ τό the, this, that, he, she, it
δαιμόνια n. nom. neut. pl. δαιμόνιον devil, demon, god
καὶ conj. καί and, even, also, but
20 δὲ conj. δέ but, and, now, also, to the contrary, rather, then
ὦ interjection. ὦ O
ἄνθρωπε n. voc. masc. sg. ἄνθρωπος man, human being, person, one, certain
κενέ adj. voc. masc. sg. κενός empty, vain, in vain
ὅτι conj. ὅτι that, for, because, how that, how, because that, for that, though
ἡ art. nom. fem. sg. ὁ ἡ τό the, this, that, he, she, it
πίστις n. nom. fem. sg. πίστις faith, assurance, belief, fidelity
χωρὶς prep. χωρίς (+gen) without, beside. (adv.) by itself, apart, separately
τῶν art. gen. neut. pl. ὁ ἡ τό the, this, that, he, she, it
ἔργων n. gen. neut. pl. ἔργον work, deed, doing labour
νεκρά adj. nom. fem. sg. νεκρός dead
21 'Αβραὰμ n. nom. masc. sg. 'Αβραάμ Abraham
ὁ art. nom. masc. sg. ὁ ἡ τό the, this, that, he, she, it
πατὴρ n. nom. masc. sg. πατήρ Father, father, parent
ἡμῶν pron. gen. 1p. pl. ἐγώ I
οὐκ particle of negation. οὐ οὐκ οὐχ not, no, neither, none, nay, nor, never, nothing

ἐξ prep. ἐκ ἐξ (+gen) of, from, out of, by, on, with, in, among, through
ἔργων n. gen. neut. pl. ἔργον work, deed, doing labour
Ἰσαὰκ n. acc. masc. sg. Ἰσαάκ Isaac
τὸν art. acc. masc. sg. ὁ ἡ τό the, this, that, he, she, it
υἱὸν n. acc. masc. sg. υἱός son, child, descendant, offspring, heir
αὐτοῦ pron. gen. masc. 3p. sg. αὐτός ή ó self, of oneself, even, very, the same, he, she, it
ἐπὶ prep. ἐπί (+gen) on, in, upon, (+dat) in, at, for, upon, (+acc) on, upon, unto, to, against
τὸ art. acc. neut. sg. ὁ ἡ τό the, this, that, he, she, it
θυσιαστήριον n. acc. neut. sg. θυσιαστήριον altar
22 ὅτι conj. ὅτι that, for, because, how that, how, because that, for that, though
ἡ art. nom. fem. sg. ὁ ἡ τό the, this, that, he, she, it
πίστις n. nom. fem. sg. πίστις faith, assurance, belief, fidelity
τοῖς art. dat. neut. pl. ὁ ἡ τό the, this, that, he, she, it
ἔργοις n. dat. neut. pl. ἔργον work, deed, doing labour
αὐτοῦ pron. gen. masc. 3p. sg. αὐτός ή ó self, of oneself, even, very, the same, he, she, it
καὶ conj. καί and, even, also, but
ἐκ prep. ἐκ ἐξ (+gen) of, from, out of, by, on, with, in, among, through
τῶν art. gen. neut. pl. ὁ ἡ τό the, this, that, he, she, it
ἔργων n. gen. neut. pl. ἔργον work, deed, doing labour
ἡ art. nom. fem. sg. ὁ ἡ τό the, this, that, he, she, it
πίστις n. nom. fem. sg. πίστις faith, assurance, belief, fidelity
23 καὶ conj. καί and, even, also, but
ἡ art. nom. fem. sg. ὁ ἡ τό the, this, that, he, she, it
γραφὴ n. nom. fem. sg. γραφή scripture
ἡ art. nom. fem. sg. ὁ ἡ τό the, this, that, he, she, it
δὲ conj. δέ but, and, now, also, to the contrary, rather, then
Ἀβραὰμ n. nom. masc. sg. Ἀβραάμ Abraham
τῷ art. dat. masc. sg. ὁ ἡ τό the, this, that, he, she, it
Θεῷ n. dat. masc. sg. θεός God, god
καὶ conj. καί and, even, also, but
αὐτῷ pron. dat. masc. 3p. sg. αὐτός ή ó self, of oneself, even, very, the same, he, she, it
εἰς prep. εἰς (+acc) into, to, unto, for, in, on, toward, against, upon, at, among
δικαιοσύνην n. acc. fem. sg. δικαιοσύνη righteousness
καὶ conj. καί and, even, also, but
φίλος adj. nom. masc. sg. φίλος friend
Θεοῦ n. gen. masc. sg. θεός God, god
24 τοίνυν conj. τοίνυν therefore, then
ὅτι conj. ὅτι that, for, because, how that, how, because that, for that, though
ἐξ prep. ἐκ ἐξ (+gen) of, from, out of, by, on, with, in, among, through
ἔργων n. gen. neut. pl. ἔργον work, deed, doing labour
ἄνθρωπος n. nom. masc. sg. ἄνθρωπος man, human being, person, one, certain
καὶ conj. καί and, even, also, but
οὐκ particle of negation. οὐ οὐκ οὐχ not, no, neither, none, nay, nor, never, nothing
ἐκ prep. ἐκ ἐξ (+gen) of, from, out of, by, on, with, in, among, through
πίστεως n. gen. fem. sg. πίστις faith, assurance, belief, fidelity
μόνον adv. μόνος only, alone, by oneself
25 ὁμοίως adv. ὁμοίως likewise, so
δὲ conj. δέ but, and, now, also, to the contrary, rather, then
καὶ conj. καί and, even, also, but
Ῥαὰβ n. nom. fem. sg. Ῥαάβ Rahab
ἡ art. nom. fem. sg. ὁ ἡ τό the, this, that, he, she, it
πόρνη n. nom. fem. sg. πόρνη harlot, whore
οὐκ particle of negation. οὐ οὐκ οὐχ not, no, neither, none, nay, nor, never, nothing
ἐξ prep. ἐκ ἐξ (+gen) of, from, out of, by, on, with, in, among, through
ἔργων n. gen. neut. pl. ἔργον work, deed, doing labour

τοὺς art. acc. masc. pl. ὁ ἡ τό the, this, that, he, she, it
ἀγγέλους n. acc. masc. pl. ἄγγελος angel, messenger
καὶ conj. καί and, even, also, but
ἑτέρᾳ adj. dat. fem. sg. ἕτερος another, other, else, strange
ὁδῷ n. dat. fem. sg. ὁδός way, journey, highway
26 ὥσπερ adv. ὥσπερ as, even as, like as
γὰρ conj. γάρ for, and, because, but, indeed
τὸ art. nom. neut. sg. ὁ ἡ τό the, this, that, he, she, it
σῶμα n. nom. neut. sg. σῶμα body, bodily, slave
χωρὶς prep. χωρίς (+gen) without, beside. (adv.) by itself, apart, separately
πνεύματος n. gen. neut. sg. πνεῦμα spirit, Spirit, Ghost, ghost, life. of the spirit, wind
νεκρόν adj. nom. neut. sg. νεκρός dead
οὕτω adv. οὕτω οὕτως so, even so, thus, on this wise, likewise, after this manner
καὶ conj. καί and, even, also, but
ἡ art. nom. fem. sg. ὁ ἡ τό the, this, that, he, she, it
πίστις n. nom. fem. sg. πίστις faith, assurance, belief, fidelity
χωρὶς prep. χωρίς (+gen) without, beside. (adv.) by itself, apart, separately
τῶν art. gen. neut. pl. ὁ ἡ τό the, this, that, he, she, it
ἔργων n. gen. neut. pl. ἔργον work, deed, doing labour
νεκρά adj. nom. fem. sg. νεκρός dead

3

1 Μὴ particle of negation. μή not, no, lest, neither, none, nothing, nor, never, without
πολλοὶ adj. nom. masc. pl. πολύς many, great, much, long, abundant
διδάσκαλοι n. nom. masc. pl. διδάσκαλος teacher, master, doctor
ἀδελφοί n. voc. masc. pl. ἀδελφός brother
μου pron. gen. 1p. sg. ἐγώ I
ὅτι conj. ὅτι that, for, because, how that, how, because that, for that, though
μεῖζον compar. adj. acc. neut. sg. μέγας great, loud, greatest, high, large, mighty, strong
κρίμα n. acc. neut. sg. κρίμα judgment, damnation, condemnation
2 πολλὰ adj. acc. neut. pl. πολύς many, great, much, long, abundant
γὰρ conj. γάρ for, and, because, but, indeed
ἅπαντες adj. nom. masc. pl. ἅπας all, whole, all things, every, everyone
εἴ conj. εἰ if, whether, that, though, forasmuch
τις indefinite pron. nom. masc. sg. τὶς certain, some, any man, one, any thing
ἐν prep. ἐν (+dat) in, by, with, among, at, on, through, to, within, into, of, for
λόγῳ n. dat. masc. sg. λόγος word, saying, account, speech, thing, matter
οὐ particle of negation. οὐ οὐκ οὐχ not, no, neither, none, nay, nor, never, nothing
οὗτος demo. pron. nom. masc. sg. οὗτος αὕτη τοῦτο this, the same, this same, he, she, it
τέλειος adj. nom. masc. sg. τέλειος perfect, of full age
ἀνὴρ n. nom. masc. sg. ἀνήρ man, husband, sir
δυνατὸς adj. nom. masc. sg. δυνατός able, possible, mighty, strong
καὶ conj. καί and, even, also, but
ὅλον adj. acc. neut. sg. ὅλος all, whole, every whit, altogether
τὸ art. acc. neut. sg. ὁ ἡ τό the, this, that, he, she, it
σῶμα n. acc. neut. sg. σῶμα body, bodily, slave
3 τῶν art. gen. masc. pl. ὁ ἡ τό the, this, that, he, she, it
ἵππων n. gen. masc. pl. ἵππος horse
τοὺς art. acc. masc. pl. ὁ ἡ τό the, this, that, he, she, it
χαλινοὺς n. acc. masc. pl. χαλινός bit, bridle
εἰς prep. εἰς (+acc) into, to, unto, for, in, on, toward, against, upon, at, among
τὰ art. acc. neut. pl. ὁ ἡ τό the, this, that, he, she, it
στόματα n. acc. neut. pl. στόμα mouth, face, edge
πρὸς prep. πρός (+gen) for, (+dat) at, (+acc) unto, to, with, for, against

τὸ art. acc. neut. sg. ὁ ἡ τό the, this, that, he, she, it
αὐτοὺς pron. acc. masc. 3p. pl. αὐτός ή ό self, of oneself, even, very, the same, he, she, it
ἡμῖν pron. dat. 1p. pl. ἐγώ I
καὶ conj. καί and, even, also, but
ὅλον adj. acc. neut. sg. ὅλος all, whole, every whit, altogether
τὸ art. acc. neut. sg. ὁ ἡ τό the, this, that, he, she, it
σῶμα n. acc. neut. sg. σῶμα body, bodily, slave
αὐτῶν pron. gen. masc. 3p. pl. αὐτός ή ό self, of oneself, even, very, the same, he, she, it
4 καὶ conj. καί and, even, also, but
τὰ art. nom. neut. pl. ὁ ἡ τό the, this, that, he, she, it
πλοῖα n. nom. neut. pl. πλοῖον ship, boat
τηλικαῦτα demo. pron. nom. neut. pl. τηλικοῦτος so great, so mighty
καὶ conj. καί and, even, also, but
ὑπὸ prep. ὑπό (+gen) of, by, with, from, among, (+acc) under
σκληρῶν adj. gen. masc. pl. σκληρός hard, fierce
ἀνέμων n. gen. masc. pl. ἄνεμος wind
ὑπὸ prep. ὑπό (+gen) of, by, with, from, among, (+acc) under
ἐλαχίστου superl. adj. gen. neut. sg. ἐλάχιστος least, very small, smallest, very little
πηδαλίου n. gen. neut. sg. πηδάλιον rudder, helm
ὅπου adv. ὅπου where, whither, whereas, in what place, wheresoever
ἂν particle. ἄν Indicating contingency. No English translation.
ἡ art. nom. fem. sg. ὁ ἡ τό the, this, that, he, she, it
ὁρμὴ n. nom. fem. sg. ὁρμή assault, impulse
τοῦ art. gen. masc. sg. ὁ ἡ τό the, this, that, he, she, it
5 οὕτω adv. οὕτω οὕτως so, even so, thus, on this wise, likewise, after this manner
καὶ conj. καί and, even, also, but
ἡ art. nom. fem. sg. ὁ ἡ τό the, this, that, he, she, it
γλῶσσα n. nom. fem. sg. γλῶσσα tongue
μικρὸν adj. nom. neut. sg. μικρός little, small, least, less
μέλος n. nom. neut. sg. μέλος member
καὶ conj. καί and, even, also, but
ὀλίγον adj. nom. neut. sg. ὀλίγος few, little, small, a while, brief, short, short space
πῦρ n. nom. neut. sg. πῦρ fire, fiery
ἡλίκην interrog. pron. acc. fem. sg. ἡλίκος how great
ὕλην n. acc. fem. sg. ὕλη matter, material
6 καὶ conj. καί and, even, also, but
ἡ art. nom. fem. sg. ὁ ἡ τό the, this, that, he, she, it
γλῶσσα n. nom. fem. sg. γλῶσσα tongue
πῦρ n. nom. neut. sg. πῦρ fire, fiery
ὁ art. nom. masc. sg. ὁ ἡ τό the, this, that, he, she, it
κόσμος n. nom. masc. sg. κόσμος world, adorning
τῆς art. gen. fem. sg. ὁ ἡ τό the, this, that, he, she, it
ἀδικίας n. gen. fem. sg. ἀδικία iniquity, unrighteousness, unjust, wrong
οὕτως adv. οὕτω οὕτως so, even so, thus, on this wise, likewise, after this manner
ἡ art. nom. fem. sg. ὁ ἡ τό the, this, that, he, she, it
γλῶσσα n. nom. fem. sg. γλῶσσα tongue
ἐν prep. ἐν (+dat) in, by, with, among, at, on, through, to, within, into, of, for
τοῖς art. dat. neut. pl. ὁ ἡ τό the, this, that, he, she, it
μέλεσιν n. dat. neut. pl. μέλος member
ἡμῶν pron. gen. 1p. pl. ἐγώ I
ἡ art. nom. fem. sg. ὁ ἡ τό the, this, that, he, she, it
ὅλον adj. acc. neut. sg. ὅλος all, whole, every whit, altogether
τὸ art. acc. neut. sg. ὁ ἡ τό the, this, that, he, she, it
σῶμα n. acc. neut. sg. σῶμα body, bodily, slave
καὶ conj. καί and, even, also, but

τὸν art. acc. masc. sg. ὁ ἡ τό the, this, that, he, she, it
τροχὸν n. acc. masc. sg. τροχός course
τῆς art. gen. fem. sg. ὁ ἡ τό the, this, that, he, she, it
γενέσεως n. gen. fem. sg. γένεσις generation, birth, lineage
καὶ conj. καί and, even, also, but
ὑπὸ prep. ὑπό (+gen) of, by, with, from, among, (+acc) under
τῆς art. gen. fem. sg. ὁ ἡ τό the, this, that, he, she, it
γεέννης n. gen. fem. sg. γέεννα hell
7 πᾶσα adj. nom. fem. sg. πᾶς πᾶσα πᾶν all, every, whosoever, every one, no, whole, any
γὰρ conj. γάρ for, and, because, but, indeed
φύσις n. nom. fem. sg. φύσις nature
θηρίων n. gen. neut. pl. θηρίον beast, wild beast, venomous beast
τε conj. τέ and, both, also
καὶ conj. καί and, even, also, but
πετεινῶν adj. gen. neut. pl. πετεινόν fowl, bird
ἑρπετῶν n. gen. neut. pl. ἑρπετόν creeping thing, serpent
τε conj. τέ and, both, also
καὶ conj. καί and, even, also, but
ἐναλίων adj. gen. neut. pl. ἐνάλιος thing in the sea
καὶ conj. καί and, even, also, but
τῇ art. dat. fem. sg. ὁ ἡ τό the, this, that, he, she, it
φύσει n. dat. fem. sg. φύσις nature
τῇ art. dat. fem. sg. ὁ ἡ τό the, this, that, he, she, it
ἀνθρωπίνῃ adj. dat. fem. sg. ἀνθρώπινος man, after the manner of men man, human
8 τὴν art. acc. fem. sg. ὁ ἡ τό the, this, that, he, she, it
δὲ conj. δέ but, and, now, also, to the contrary, rather, then
γλῶσσαν n. acc. fem. sg. γλῶσσα tongue
οὐδεὶς num. nom. masc. sg. οὐδείς no man, nothing, no, none, neither, not, nought
ἀνθρώπων n. gen. masc. pl. ἄνθρωπος man, human being, person, one, certain
ἀκατάσχετον adj. nom. neut. sg. ἀκατάσχετος unruly
κακόν adj. nom. neut. sg. κακός evil, evil thing, noisome, wicked
μεστὴ adj. nom. fem. sg. μεστός full
ἰοῦ n. gen. masc. sg. ἰός poison, rust
θανατηφόρου adj. gen. masc. sg. θανατηφόρος deadly
9 ἐν prep. ἐν (+dat) in, by, with, among, at, on, through, to, within, into, of, for
αὐτῇ pron. dat. fem. 3p. sg. αὐτός ἡ ὁ self, of oneself, even, very, the same, he, she, it
τὸν art. acc. masc. sg. ὁ ἡ τό the, this, that, he, she, it
Θεὸν n. acc. masc. sg. θεός God, god
καὶ conj. καί and, even, also, but
πατέρα n. acc. masc. sg. πατήρ Father, father, parent
καὶ conj. καί and, even, also, but
ἐν prep. ἐν (+dat) in, by, with, among, at, on, through, to, within, into, of, for
αὐτῇ pron. dat. fem. 3p. sg. αὐτός ἡ ὁ self, of oneself, even, very, the same, he, she, it
τοὺς art. acc. masc. pl. ὁ ἡ τό the, this, that, he, she, it
ἀνθρώπους n. acc. masc. pl. ἄνθρωπος man, human being, person, one, certain
τοὺς art. acc. masc. pl. ὁ ἡ τό the, this, that, he, she, it
καθ' prep. κατά (+gen) against, by, throughout, down, (+acc) according to, after, with
ὁμοίωσιν n. acc. fem. sg. ὁμοίωσις similitude
Θεοῦ n. gen. masc. sg. θεός God, god
10 ἐκ prep. ἐκ ἐξ (+gen) of, from, out of, by, on, with, in, among, through
τοῦ art. gen. neut. sg. ὁ ἡ τό the, this, that, he, she, it
αὐτοῦ adj. gen. neut. sg. αὐτός ἡ ὁ self, of oneself, even, very, the same, he, she, it
στόματος n. gen. neut. sg. στόμα mouth, face, edge
εὐλογία n. nom. fem. sg. εὐλογία blessing, bounty, matter of bounty, fair speech
καὶ conj. καί and, even, also, but

κατάρα n. nom. fem. sg. κατάρα curse, cursing, cursed
οὐ particle of negation. οὐ οὐκ οὐχ not, no, neither, none, nay, nor, never, nothing
ἀδελφοί n. voc. masc. pl. ἀδελφός brother
μου pron. gen. 1p. sg. ἐγώ I
ταῦτα demo. pron. nom. neut. pl. οὗτος αὕτη τοῦτο this, the same, this same, he, she, it
οὕτω adv. οὕτω οὕτως so, even so, thus, on this wise, likewise, after this manner
11 μήτι interrog. particle of negation. μήτι not, how much more
ἡ art. nom. fem. sg. ὁ ἡ τό the, this, that, he, she, it
πηγὴ n. nom. fem. sg. πηγή fountain, well
ἐκ prep. ἐκ ἐξ (+gen) of, from, out of, by, on, with, in, among, through
τῆς art. gen. fem. sg. ὁ ἡ τό the, this, that, he, she, it
αὐτῆς adj. gen. fem. sg. αὐτός ή ό self, of oneself, even, very, the same, he, she, it
ὀπῆς n. gen. fem. sg. ὀπή cave, place
τὸ art. acc. neut. sg. ὁ ἡ τό the, this, that, he, she, it
γλυκὺ adj. acc. neut. sg. γλυκύς sweet, fresh
καὶ conj. καί and, even, also, but
τὸ art. acc. neut. sg. ὁ ἡ τό the, this, that, he, she, it
πικρόν adj. acc. neut. sg. πικρός bitter
12 μὴ particle of negation. μή not, no, lest, neither, none, nothing, nor, never, without
ἀδελφοί n. voc. masc. pl. ἀδελφός brother
μου pron. gen. 1p. sg. ἐγώ I
συκῆ n. nom. fem. sg. συκῆ fig tree
ἐλαίας n. acc. fem. pl. ἐλαία Olives, olive tree, olive berry
ἢ particle. ἤ or, than, either, nor, or else, and, rather than
ἄμπελος n. nom. fem. sg. ἄμπελος vine
σῦκα n. acc. neut. pl. σῦκον fig
οὕτως adv. οὕτω οὕτως so, even so, thus, on this wise, likewise, after this manner
οὐδεμία num. nom. fem. sg. οὐδείς no man, nothing, no, none, neither, not, nought
πηγὴ n. nom. fem. sg. πηγή fountain, well
ἁλυκὸν adj. acc. neut. sg. ἁλυκός salt
καὶ conj. καί and, even, also, but
γλυκὺ adj. acc. neut. sg. γλυκύς sweet, fresh
ὕδωρ n. acc. neut. sg. ὕδωρ water
13 Τίς interrog. pron. nom. masc. sg. τίς what, who, why, where, which, how
σοφὸς adj. nom. masc. sg. σοφός wise, wiser
καὶ conj. καί and, even, also, but
ἐπιστήμων adj. nom. masc. sg. ἐπιστήμων endue with knowledge
ἐν prep. ἐν (+dat) in, by, with, among, at, on, through, to, within, into, of, for
ὑμῖν pron. dat. 2p. pl. σύ thou, you
ἐκ prep. ἐκ ἐξ (+gen) of, from, out of, by, on, with, in, among, through
τῆς art. gen. fem. sg. ὁ ἡ τό the, this, that, he, she, it
καλῆς adj. gen. fem. sg. καλός good, better, goodly, meet, honest, fair, well, worthy
ἀναστροφῆς n. gen. fem. sg. ἀναστροφή conversation
τὰ art. acc. neut. pl. ὁ ἡ τό the, this, that, he, she, it
ἔργα n. acc. neut. pl. ἔργον work, deed, doing labour
αὐτοῦ pron. gen. masc. 3p. sg. αὐτός ή ό self, of oneself, even, very, the same, he, she, it
ἐν prep. ἐν (+dat) in, by, with, among, at, on, through, to, within, into, of, for
πραΰτητι n. dat. fem. sg. πραΰτης meekness
σοφίας n. gen. fem. sg. σοφία wisdom
14 εἰ conj. εἰ if, whether, that, though, forasmuch
δὲ conj. δέ but, and, now, also, to the contrary, rather, then
ζῆλον n. acc. masc. sg. ζῆλος zeal, envying, indignation, emulation, jealousy
πικρὸν adj. acc. masc. sg. πικρός bitter
καὶ conj. καί and, even, also, but
ἐριθείαν n. acc. fem. sg. ἐριθεία strife, contention, contentious

ἐν prep. ἐν (+dat) in, by, with, among, at, on, through, to, within, into, of, for
τῇ art. dat. fem. sg. ὁ ἡ τό the, this, that, he, she, it
καρδίᾳ n. dat. fem. sg. καρδία heart
ὑμῶν pron. gen. 2p. pl. σύ thou, you
μὴ particle of negation. μή not, no, lest, neither, none, nothing, nor, never, without
καὶ conj. καί and, even, also, but
κατὰ prep. κατά (+gen) against, by, throughout, down, (+acc) according to, after, with
τῆς art. gen. fem. sg. ὁ ἡ τό the, this, that, he, she, it
ἀληθείας n. gen. fem. sg. ἀλήθεια truth, verity
15 οὐκ particle of negation. οὐ οὐκ οὐχ not, no, neither, none, nay, nor, never, nothing
αὕτη demo. pron. nom. fem. sg. οὗτος αὕτη τοῦτο this, the same, this same, he, she, it
ἡ art. nom. fem. sg. ὁ ἡ τό the, this, that, he, she, it
σοφία n. nom. fem. sg. σοφία wisdom
ἄνωθεν adv. ἄνωθεν from above, again, the top, from the beginning, from the very first
ἀλλ' conj. ἀλλά but, yea, yet, nevertheless, howbeit, nay, therefore
ἐπίγειος adj. nom. fem. sg. ἐπίγειος earthly, terrestrial, in earth
ψυχική adj. nom. fem. sg. ψυχικός natural, sensual
δαιμονιώδης adj. nom. fem. sg. δαιμονιώδης devilish
16 ὅπου adv. ὅπου where, whither, whereas, in what place, wheresoever
γὰρ conj. γάρ for, and, because, but, indeed
ζῆλος n. nom. masc. sg. ζῆλος zeal, envying, indignation, emulation, jealousy
καὶ conj. καί and, even, also, but
ἐριθεία n. nom. fem. sg. ἐριθεία strife, contention, contentious
ἐκεῖ adv. ἐκεῖ there, thither, thitherward, yonder, yonder place
ἀκαταστασία n. nom. fem. sg. ἀκαταστασία commotion, confusion, tumult
καὶ conj. καί and, even, also, but
πᾶν adj. nom. neut. sg. πᾶς πᾶσα πᾶν all, every, whosoever, every one, no, whole, any
φαῦλον adj. nom. neut. sg. φαῦλος evil
πρᾶγμα n. nom. neut. sg. πρᾶγμα thing, matter, business, work
17 ἡ art. nom. fem. sg. ὁ ἡ τό the, this, that, he, she, it
δὲ conj. δέ but, and, now, also, to the contrary, rather, then
ἄνωθεν adv. ἄνωθεν from above, again, the top, from the beginning, from the very first
σοφία n. nom. fem. sg. σοφία wisdom
πρῶτον adv. πρῶτον first, at the first, first of all, at first, at the beginning, before, chiefly
μὲν conj. μέν indeed, verily, truly, even, so, some
ἁγνή adj. nom. fem. sg. ἁγνός clear, pure, chaste
ἔπειτα adv. ἔπειτα then, after that, afterward
εἰρηνική adj. nom. fem. sg. εἰρηνικός peaceable
ἐπιεικής adj. nom. fem. sg. ἐπιεικής moderation, gentle, patient
εὐπειθής adj. nom. fem. sg. εὐπειθής easy to be intreated
μεστὴ adj. nom. fem. sg. μεστός full
ἐλέους n. gen. neut. sg. ἔλεος mercy
καὶ conj. καί and, even, also, but
καρπῶν n. gen. masc. pl. καρπός fruit
ἀγαθῶν adj. gen. masc. pl. ἀγαθός good, good thing, that which is good, well
ἀδιάκριτος adj. nom. fem. sg. ἀδιάκριτος without partiality
καὶ conj. καί and, even, also, but
ἀνυπόκριτος adj. nom. fem. sg. ἀνυπόκριτος unfeigned, without hypocrisy
18 καρπὸς n. nom. masc. sg. καρπός fruit
δὲ conj. δέ but, and, now, also, to the contrary, rather, then
τῆς art. gen. fem. sg. ὁ ἡ τό the, this, that, he, she, it
δικαιοσύνης n. gen. fem. sg. δικαιοσύνη righteousness
ἐν prep. ἐν (+dat) in, by, with, among, at, on, through, to, within, into, of, for
εἰρήνῃ n. dat. fem. sg. εἰρήνη peace, quietness, rest
τοῖς art. dat. masc. pl. ὁ ἡ τό the, this, that, he, she, it

εἰρήνην n. acc. fem. sg. εἰρήνη peace, quietness, rest

4

1 Πόθεν adv. πόθεν whence, from whence
πόλεμοι n. nom. masc. pl. πόλεμος war, battle, fight
καὶ conj. καί and, even, also, but
μάχαι n. nom. fem. pl. μάχη fighting, strife, striving
ἐν prep. ἐν (+dat) in, by, with, among, at, on, through, to, within, into, of, for
ὑμῖν pron. dat. 2p. pl. σύ thou, you
οὐκ particle of negation. οὐ οὐκ οὐχ not, no, neither, none, nay, nor, never, nothing
ἐντεῦθεν adv. ἐντεῦθεν hence, from hence, on either side, from this place
ἐκ prep. ἐκ ἐξ (+gen) of, from, out of, by, on, with, in, among, through
τῶν art. gen. fem. pl. ὁ ἡ τό the, this, that, he, she, it
ἡδονῶν n. gen. fem. pl. ἡδονή pleasure, lust
ὑμῶν pron. gen. 2p. pl. σύ thou, you
τῶν art. gen. fem. pl. ὁ ἡ τό the, this, that, he, she, it
ἐν prep. ἐν (+dat) in, by, with, among, at, on, through, to, within, into, of, for
τοῖς art. dat. neut. pl. ὁ ἡ τό the, this, that, he, she, it
μέλεσιν n. dat. neut. pl. μέλος member
ὑμῶν pron. gen. 2p. pl. σύ thou, you
2 καὶ conj. καί and, even, also, but
οὐκ particle of negation. οὐ οὐκ οὐχ not, no, neither, none, nay, nor, never, nothing
καὶ conj. καί and, even, also, but
καὶ conj. καί and, even, also, but
οὐ particle of negation. οὐ οὐκ οὐχ not, no, neither, none, nay, nor, never, nothing
καὶ conj. καί and, even, also, but
οὐκ particle of negation. οὐ οὐκ οὐχ not, no, neither, none, nay, nor, never, nothing
δέ conj. δέ but, and, now, also, to the contrary, rather, then
διὰ prep. διά (+gen) by, through, with, in, of, (+acc) for, because of, for a cause
τὸ art. acc. neut. sg. ὁ ἡ τό the, this, that, he, she, it
μὴ particle of negation. μή not, no, lest, neither, none, nothing, nor, never, without
ὑμᾶς pron. acc. 2p. pl. σύ thou, you
3 καὶ conj. καί and, even, also, but
οὐ particle of negation. οὐ οὐκ οὐχ not, no, neither, none, nay, nor, never, nothing
διότι conj. διότι for, because, because that, therefore
κακῶς adv. κακῶς sick, diseased, evil, amiss, grievously, miserably, sore
ἵνα conj. ἵνα that, to, lest, for to, so that, albeit, because, for, so as
ἐν prep. ἐν (+dat) in, by, with, among, at, on, through, to, within, into, of, for
ταῖς art. dat. fem. pl. ὁ ἡ τό the, this, that, he, she, it
ἡδοναῖς n. dat. fem. pl. ἡδονή pleasure, lust
ὑμῶν pron. gen. 2p. pl. σύ thou, you
4 μοιχοὶ n. voc. masc. pl. μοιχός adulterer
καὶ conj. καί and, even, also, but
μοιχαλίδες n. voc. fem. pl. μοιχαλίς adulterous, adulteress, adultery
οὐκ particle of negation. οὐ οὐκ οὐχ not, no, neither, none, nay, nor, never, nothing
ὅτι conj. ὅτι that, for, because, how that, how, because that, for that, though
ἡ art. nom. fem. sg. ὁ ἡ τό the, this, that, he, she, it
φιλία n. nom. fem. sg. φιλία friendship
τοῦ art. gen. masc. sg. ὁ ἡ τό the, this, that, he, she, it
κόσμου n. gen. masc. sg. κόσμος world, adorning
ἔχθρα n. nom. fem. sg. ἔχθρα enmity, hatred
Θεοῦ n. gen. masc. sg. θεός God, god
ὃς relative pron. nom. masc. sg. ὅς ἥ ὅ who, which, what, that
ἂν particle. ἄν Indicating contingency. No English translation.

οὖν conj. οὖν therefore, then, so, and, now, wherefore
φίλος adj. nom. masc. sg. φίλος friend
τοῦ art. gen. masc. sg. ὁ ἡ τό the, this, that, he, she, it
κόσμου n. gen. masc. sg. κόσμος world, adorning
ἐχθρὸς adj. nom. masc. sg. ἐχθρός enemy, foe
τοῦ art. gen. masc. sg. ὁ ἡ τό the, this, that, he, she, it
Θεοῦ n. gen. masc. sg. θεός God, god
5 ἢ particle. ἤ or, than, either, nor, or else, and, rather than
ὅτι conj. ὅτι that, for, because, how that, how, because that, for that, though
κενῶς adv. κενῶς
ἡ art. nom. fem. sg. ὁ ἡ τό the, this, that, he, she, it
γραφὴ n. nom. fem. sg. γραφή scripture
Πρὸς prep. πρός (+gen) for, (+dat) at, (+acc) unto, to, with, for, against
φθόνον n. acc. masc. sg. φθόνος envy, envying
τὸ art. nom. neut. sg. ὁ ἡ τό the, this, that, he, she, it
πνεῦμα n. nom. neut. sg. πνεῦμα spirit, Spirit, Ghost, ghost, life. of the spirit, wind
ὃ relative pron. acc. neut. sg. ὅς ἥ ὅ who, which, what, that
ἐν prep. ἐν (+dat) in, by, with, among, at, on, through, to, within, into, of, for
ἡμῖν pron. dat. 1p. pl. ἐγώ I
6 μείζονα compar. adj. acc. fem. sg. μέγας great, loud, greatest, high, large, mighty, strong
δὲ conj. δέ but, and, now, also, to the contrary, rather, then
χάριν n. acc. fem. sg. χάρις grace, thank, favour, pleasure
διὸ conj. διό wherefore, therefore, for which cause
Ὁ art. nom. masc. sg. ὁ ἡ τό the, this, that, he, she, it
Θεὸς n. nom. masc. sg. θεός God, god
ὑπερηφάνοις adj. dat. masc. pl. ὑπερήφανος proud
ταπεινοῖς adj. dat. masc. pl. ταπεινός humble, of low degree, base, cast down, lowly
δὲ conj. δέ but, and, now, also, to the contrary, rather, then
χάριν n. acc. fem. sg. χάρις grace, thank, favour, pleasure
7 οὖν conj. οὖν therefore, then, so, and, now, wherefore
τῷ art. dat. masc. sg. ὁ ἡ τό the, this, that, he, she, it
Θεῷ n. dat. masc. sg. θεός God, god
τῷ art. dat. masc. sg. ὁ ἡ τό the, this, that, he, she, it
διαβόλῳ adj. dat. masc. sg. διάβολος devil, false accuser, Devil, slanderer
καὶ conj. καί and, even, also, but
ἀφ' prep. ἀπό (+gen) from, of, out of, since, for, off, at, by, in, on
ὑμῶν pron. gen. 2p. pl. σύ thou, you
8 τῷ art. dat. masc. sg. ὁ ἡ τό the, this, that, he, she, it
Θεῷ n. dat. masc. sg. θεός God, god
καὶ conj. καί and, even, also, but
ὑμῖν pron. dat. 2p. pl. σύ thou, you
χεῖρας n. acc. fem. pl. χείρ hand
ἁμαρτωλοί adj. voc. masc. pl. ἁμαρτωλός sinner, sinful
καὶ conj. καί and, even, also, but
καρδίας n. acc. fem. pl. καρδία heart
δίψυχοι adj. voc. masc. pl. δίψυχος double minded
9 καὶ conj. καί and, even, also, but
καὶ conj. καί and, even, also, but
ὁ art. nom. masc. sg. ὁ ἡ τό the, this, that, he, she, it
γέλως n. nom. masc. sg. γέλως laughter
ὑμῶν pron. gen. 2p. pl. σύ thou, you
εἰς prep. εἰς (+acc) into, to, unto, for, in, on, toward, against, upon, at, among
πένθος n. acc. neut. sg. πένθος mourning, sorrow
καὶ conj. καί and, even, also, but
ἡ art. nom. fem. sg. ὁ ἡ τό the, this, that, he, she, it

χαρὰ n. nom. fem. sg. χαρά joy, gladness, joyfulness
εἰς prep. εἰς (+acc) into, to, unto, for, in, on, toward, against, upon, at, among
κατήφειαν n. acc. fem. sg. κατήφεια heaviness
10 ἐνώπιον prep. ἐνώπιον (+gen) before, in the sight of, in the presence of. (adv.) before
τοῦ art. gen. masc. sg. ὁ ἡ τό the, this, that, he, she, it
Κυρίου n. gen. masc. sg. κύριος Lord, lord, master, sir, LORD, God, Master, owner
καὶ conj. καί and, even, also, but
ὑμᾶς pron. acc. 2p. pl. σύ thou, you
11 Μὴ particle of negation. μή not, no, lest, neither, none, nothing, nor, never, without
ἀλλήλων pron. gen. masc. pl. ἀλλήλων one another, themselves, together, mutual
ἀδελφοί n. voc. masc. pl. ἀδελφός brother
ὁ art. nom. masc. sg. ὁ ἡ τό the, this, that, he, she, it
ἀδελφοῦ n. gen. masc. sg. ἀδελφός brother
καὶ conj. καί and, even, also, but
τὸν art. acc. masc. sg. ὁ ἡ τό the, this, that, he, she, it
ἀδελφὸν n. acc. masc. sg. ἀδελφός brother
αὐτοῦ pron. gen. masc. 3p. sg. αὐτός ή ό self, of oneself, even, very, the same, he, she, it
νόμου n. gen. masc. sg. νόμος law, the law
καὶ conj. καί and, even, also, but
νόμον n. acc. masc. sg. νόμος law, the law
εἰ conj. εἰ if, whether, that, though, forasmuch
δὲ conj. δέ but, and, now, also, to the contrary, rather, then
νόμον n. acc. masc. sg. νόμος law, the law
οὐκ particle of negation. οὐ οὐκ οὐχ not, no, neither, none, nay, nor, never, nothing
ποιητὴς n. nom. masc. sg. ποιητής doer, poet
νόμου n. gen. masc. sg. νόμος law, the law
ἀλλὰ conj. ἀλλά but, yea, yet, nevertheless, howbeit, nay, therefore
κριτής n. nom. masc. sg. κριτής judge
12 εἷς num. nom. masc. sg. εἷς or ἕν one, other, some, any, only, a certain
ὁ art. nom. masc. sg. ὁ ἡ τό the, this, that, he, she, it
νομοθέτης n. nom. masc. sg. νομοθέτης lawgiver
ὁ art. nom. masc. sg. ὁ ἡ τό the, this, that, he, she, it
καὶ conj. καί and, even, also, but
σὺ pron. nom. 2p. sg. σύ thou, you
τίς interrog. pron. nom. masc. sg. τίς what, who, why, where, which, how
ὃς relative pron. nom. masc. sg. ὅς ἥ ὅ who, which, what, that
τὸν art. acc. masc. sg. ὁ ἡ τό the, this, that, he, she, it
ἕτερον adj. acc. masc. sg. ἕτερος another, other, else, strange
13 νῦν adv. νῦν now, henceforth, present, this time
οἱ art. nom. masc. pl. ὁ ἡ τό the, this, that, he, she, it
Σήμερον adv. σήμερον this day, today
ἢ particle. ἤ or, than, either, nor, or else, and, rather than
αὔριον adv. αὔριον tomorrow, morrow, next day
εἰς prep. εἰς (+acc) into, to, unto, for, in, on, toward, against, upon, at, among
τήνδε demo. pron. acc. fem. sg. ὅδε ἥδε τόδε this, he, she, such, thus
τὴν art. acc. fem. sg. ὁ ἡ τό the, this, that, he, she, it
πόλιν n. acc. fem. sg. πόλις city
καὶ conj. καί and, even, also, but
ἐκεῖ adv. ἐκεῖ there, thither, thitherward, yonder, yonder place
ἐνιαυτὸν n. acc. masc. sg. ἐνιαυτός year
ἕνα num. acc. masc. sg. εἷς or ἕν one, other, some, any, only, a certain
καὶ conj. καί and, even, also, but
καὶ conj. καί and, even, also, but
14 οἵτινες relative pron. nom. masc. pl. ὅστις which, who, whosoever, that, whatsoever
οὐκ particle of negation. οὐ οὐκ οὐχ not, no, neither, none, nay, nor, never, nothing

τὸ art. acc. neut. sg. ὁ ἡ τό the, this, that, he, she, it
τῆς art. gen. fem. sg. ὁ ἡ τό the, this, that, he, she, it
αὔριον adv. αὔριον tomorrow, morrow, next day
ποία interrog. pron. nom. fem. sg. ποῖος what, which, what manner of
γὰρ conj. γάρ for, and, because, but, indeed
ἡ art. nom. fem. sg. ὁ ἡ τό the, this, that, he, she, it
ζωὴ n. nom. fem. sg. ζωή life, lifetime
ὑμῶν pron. gen. 2p. pl. σύ thou, you
ἀτμὶς n. nom. fem. sg. ἀτμίς vapour
γὰρ conj. γάρ for, and, because, but, indeed
ἡ art. nom. fem. sg. ὁ ἡ τό the, this, that, he, she, it
πρὸς prep. πρός (+gen) for, (+dat) at, (+acc) unto, to, with, for, against
ὀλίγον adj. acc. neut. sg. ὀλίγος few, little, small, a while, brief, short, short space
ἔπειτα adv. ἔπειτα then, after that, afterward
δὲ conj. δέ but, and, now, also, to the contrary, rather, then
15 ἀντὶ prep. ἀντί (+gen) for, because, in the room
τοῦ art. gen. neut. sg. ὁ ἡ τό the, this, that, he, she, it
ὑμᾶς pron. acc. 2p. pl. σύ thou, you
Ἐὰν conj. ἐάν if, soever, except, though, and if, but, whether, if so, so
ὁ art. nom. masc. sg. ὁ ἡ τό the, this, that, he, she, it
Κύριος n. nom. masc. sg. κύριος Lord, lord, master, sir, LORD, God, Master, owner
καὶ conj. καί and, even, also, but
καὶ conj. καί and, even, also, but
τοῦτο demo. pron. acc. neut. sg. οὗτος αὕτη τοῦτο this, the same, this same, he, she, it
ἢ particle. ἤ or, than, either, nor, or else, and, rather than
ἐκεῖνο demo. pron. acc. neut. sg. ἐκεῖνος that, he, the same, that same
16 νῦν adv. νῦν now, henceforth, present, this time
δὲ conj. δέ but, and, now, also, to the contrary, rather, then
ἐν prep. ἐν (+dat) in, by, with, among, at, on, through, to, within, into, of, for
ταῖς art. dat. fem. pl. ὁ ἡ τό the, this, that, he, she, it
ἀλαζονείαις n. dat. fem. pl. ἀλαζονεία boasting, pride
ὑμῶν pron. gen. 2p. pl. σύ thou, you
πᾶσα adj. nom. fem. sg. πᾶς πᾶσα πᾶν all, every, whosoever, every one, no, whole, any
καύχησις n. nom. fem. sg. καύχησις boasting, rejoicing, glorying
τοιαύτη demo. pron. nom. fem. sg. τοιοῦτος such, like
πονηρά adj. nom. fem. sg. πονηρός evil, wicked, bad
17 οὖν conj. οὖν therefore, then, so, and, now, wherefore
καλὸν adj. acc. neut. sg. καλός good, better, goodly, meet, honest, fair, well, worthy
καὶ conj. καί and, even, also, but
μὴ particle of negation. μή not, no, lest, neither, none, nothing, nor, never, without
ἁμαρτία n. nom. fem. sg. ἁμαρτία sin, offence, sinful
αὐτῷ pron. dat. masc. 3p. sg. αὐτός ἡ ὁ self, of oneself, even, very, the same, he, she, it

5

1 νῦν adv. νῦν now, henceforth, present, this time
οἱ art. nom. masc. pl. ὁ ἡ τό the, this, that, he, she, it
πλούσιοι adj. nom. masc. pl. πλούσιος rich
ἐπὶ prep. ἐπί (+gen) on, in, upon, (+dat) in, at, for, upon, (+acc) on, upon, unto, to, against
ταῖς art. dat. fem. pl. ὁ ἡ τό the, this, that, he, she, it
ταλαιπωρίαις n. dat. fem. pl. ταλαιπωρία misery
ὑμῶν pron. gen. 2p. pl. σύ thou, you
ταῖς art. dat. fem. pl. ὁ ἡ τό the, this, that, he, she, it
2 ὁ art. nom. masc. sg. ὁ ἡ τό the, this, that, he, she, it
πλοῦτος n. nom. masc. sg. πλοῦτος riches

ὑμῶν pron. gen. 2p. pl. σύ thou, you
καὶ conj. καί and, even, also, but
τὰ art. nom. neut. pl. ὁ ἡ τό the, this, that, he, she, it
ἱμάτια n. nom. neut. pl. ἱμάτιον cloke, garment, clothes, raiment, robe, vesture
ὑμῶν pron. gen. 2p. pl. σύ thou, you
σητόβρωτα adj. nom. neut. pl. σητόβρωτος motheaten
3 ὁ art. nom. masc. sg. ὁ ἡ τό the, this, that, he, she, it
χρυσὸς n. nom. masc. sg. χρυσός gold
ὑμῶν pron. gen. 2p. pl. σύ thou, you
καὶ conj. καί and, even, also, but
ὁ art. nom. masc. sg. ὁ ἡ τό the, this, that, he, she, it
ἄργυρος n. nom. masc. sg. ἄργυρος silver
καὶ conj. καί and, even, also, but
ὁ art. nom. masc. sg. ὁ ἡ τό the, this, that, he, she, it
ἰὸς n. nom. masc. sg. ἰός poison, rust
αὐτῶν pron. gen. masc. 3p. pl. αὐτός ἡ ὁ self, of oneself, even, very, the same, he, she, it
εἰς prep. εἰς (+acc) into, to, unto, for, in, on, toward, against, upon, at, among
μαρτύριον n. acc. neut. sg. μαρτύριον testimony, witness
ὑμῖν pron. dat. 2p. pl. σύ thou, you
καὶ conj. καί and, even, also, but
τὰς art. acc. fem. pl. ὁ ἡ τό the, this, that, he, she, it
σάρκας n. acc. fem. pl. σάρξ flesh, carnal
ὑμῶν pron. gen. 2p. pl. σύ thou, you
ὡς adv. ὡς as, when, as it were, how, about, like, as soon as, even as, while
πῦρ n. nom. neut. sg. πῦρ fire, fiery
ἐν prep. ἐν (+dat) in, by, with, among, at, on, through, to, within, into, of, for
ἐσχάταις adj. dat. fem. pl. ἔσχατος last, lowest, uttermost, uttermost part
ἡμέραις n. dat. fem. pl. ἡμέρα day, time, year, while, age, day time
4 ὁ art. nom. masc. sg. ὁ ἡ τό the, this, that, he, she, it
μισθὸς n. nom. masc. sg. μισθός reward, hire, wage
τῶν art. gen. masc. pl. ὁ ἡ τό the, this, that, he, she, it
ἐργατῶν n. gen. masc. pl. ἐργάτης labourer, worker, workman
τῶν art. gen. masc. pl. ὁ ἡ τό the, this, that, he, she, it
τὰς art. acc. fem. pl. ὁ ἡ τό the, this, that, he, she, it
χώρας n. acc. fem. pl. χώρα country, region, land, field, coast, ground
ὑμῶν pron. gen. 2p. pl. σύ thou, you
ὁ art. nom. masc. sg. ὁ ἡ τό the, this, that, he, she, it
ἀφ' prep. ἀπό (+gen) from, of, out of, since, for, off, at, by, in, on
ὑμῶν pron. gen. 2p. pl. σύ thou, you
καὶ conj. καί and, even, also, but
αἱ art. nom. fem. pl. ὁ ἡ τό the, this, that, he, she, it
βοαὶ n. nom. fem. pl. βοή cry
τῶν art. gen. masc. pl. ὁ ἡ τό the, this, that, he, she, it
εἰς prep. εἰς (+acc) into, to, unto, for, in, on, toward, against, upon, at, among
τὰ art. acc. neut. pl. ὁ ἡ τό the, this, that, he, she, it
ὦτα n. acc. neut. pl. οὖς ear
Κυρίου n. gen. masc. sg. κύριος Lord, lord, master, sir, LORD, God, Master, owner
Σαβαὼθ n. gen. masc. pl. Σαβαώθ Sabaoth
5 ἐπὶ prep. ἐπί (+gen) on, in, upon, (+dat) in, at, for, upon, (+acc) on, upon, unto, to, against
τῆς art. gen. fem. sg. ὁ ἡ τό the, this, that, he, she, it
γῆς n. gen. fem. sg. γῆ earth, land, ground, country
καὶ conj. καί and, even, also, but
τὰς art. acc. fem. pl. ὁ ἡ τό the, this, that, he, she, it
καρδίας n. acc. fem. pl. καρδία heart
ὑμῶν pron. gen. 2p. pl. σύ thou, you

ὡς adv. ὡς as, when, as it were, how, about, like, as soon as, even as, while
ἐν prep. ἐν (+dat) in, by, with, among, at, on, through, to, within, into, of, for
ἡμέρᾳ n. dat. fem. sg. ἡμέρα day, time, year, while, age, day time
σφαγῆς n. gen. fem. sg. σφαγή slaughter
6 τὸν art. acc. masc. sg. ὁ ἡ τό the, this, that, he, she, it
δίκαιον adj. acc. masc. sg. δίκαιος righteous, just, meet, right
οὐκ particle of negation. οὐ οὐκ οὐχ not, no, neither, none, nay, nor, never, nothing
ὑμῖν pron. dat. 2p. pl. σύ thou, you
7 οὖν conj. οὖν therefore, then, so, and, now, wherefore
ἀδελφοί n. voc. masc. pl. ἀδελφός brother
ἕως conj. ἕως till, until, unto, until when, while, as far as, even, until now
τῆς art. gen. fem. sg. ὁ ἡ τό the, this, that, he, she, it
παρουσίας n. gen. fem. sg. παρουσία coming, presence
τοῦ art. gen. masc. sg. ὁ ἡ τό the, this, that, he, she, it
Κυρίου n. gen. masc. sg. κύριος Lord, lord, master, sir, LORD, God, Master, owner
ὁ art. nom. masc. sg. ὁ ἡ τό the, this, that, he, she, it
γεωργὸς n. nom. masc. sg. γεωργός husbandmen
τὸν art. acc. masc. sg. ὁ ἡ τό the, this, that, he, she, it
τίμιον adj. acc. masc. sg. τίμιος precious, dear, has in reputation, honourable
καρπὸν n. acc. masc. sg. καρπός fruit
τῆς art. gen. fem. sg. ὁ ἡ τό the, this, that, he, she, it
γῆς n. gen. fem. sg. γῆ earth, land, ground, country
ἐπ' prep. ἐπί (+gen) on, in, upon, (+dat) in, at, for, upon, (+acc) on, upon, unto, to, against
αὐτῷ pron. dat. masc. 3p. sg. αὐτός ἡ ό self, of oneself, even, very, the same, he, she, it
ἕως conj. ἕως till, until, unto, until when, while, as far as, even, until now
ἂν particle. ἄν Indicating contingency. No English translation.
ὑετὸν n. acc. masc. sg. ὑετός rain
πρόϊμον adj. acc. masc. sg. πρόϊμος early
καὶ conj. καί and, even, also, but
ὄψιμον adj. acc. masc. sg. ὄψιμος latter
8 καὶ conj. καί and, even, also, but
ὑμεῖς pron. nom. 2p. pl. σύ thou, you
τὰς art. acc. fem. pl. ὁ ἡ τό the, this, that, he, she, it
καρδίας n. acc. fem. pl. καρδία heart
ὑμῶν pron. gen. 2p. pl. σύ thou, you
ὅτι conj. ὅτι that, for, because, how that, how, because that, for that, though
ἡ art. nom. fem. sg. ὁ ἡ τό the, this, that, he, she, it
παρουσία n. nom. fem. sg. παρουσία coming, presence
τοῦ art. gen. masc. sg. ὁ ἡ τό the, this, that, he, she, it
Κυρίου n. gen. masc. sg. κύριος Lord, lord, master, sir, LORD, God, Master, owner
9 μὴ particle of negation. μή not, no, lest, neither, none, nothing, nor, never, without
κατ' prep. κατά (+gen) against, by, throughout, down, (+acc) according to, after, with
ἀλλήλων pron. gen. masc. pl. ἀλλήλων one another, themselves, together, mutual
ἀδελφοί n. voc. masc. pl. ἀδελφός brother
ἵνα conj. ἵνα that, to, lest, for to, so that, albeit, because, for, so as
μὴ particle of negation. μή not, no, lest, neither, none, nothing, nor, never, without
ὁ art. nom. masc. sg. ὁ ἡ τό the, this, that, he, she, it
κριτὴς n. nom. masc. sg. κριτής judge
πρὸ prep. πρό (+gen) before, above
τῶν art. gen. fem. pl. ὁ ἡ τό the, this, that, he, she, it
θυρῶν n. gen. fem. pl. θύρα door, gate
10 ὑπόδειγμα n. acc. neut. sg. ὑπόδειγμα example, ensample, pattern
τῆς art. gen. fem. sg. ὁ ἡ τό the, this, that, he, she, it
κακοπαθίας n. gen. fem. sg. κακοπάθεια suffering affliction
ἀδελφοί n. voc. masc. pl. ἀδελφός brother

μου pron. gen. 1p. sg. ἐγώ I
καὶ conj. καί and, even, also, but
τῆς art. gen. fem. sg. ὁ ἡ τό the, this, that, he, she, it
μακροθυμίας n. gen. fem. sg. μακροθυμία longsuffering, patience
τοὺς art. acc. masc. pl. ὁ ἡ τό the, this, that, he, she, it
προφήτας n. acc. masc. pl. προφήτης prophet
οἳ relative pron. nom. masc. pl. ὅς ἥ ὅ who, which, what, that
τῷ art. dat. neut. sg. ὁ ἡ τό the, this, that, he, she, it
ὀνόματι n. dat. neut. sg. ὄνομα name, call, surname
Κυρίου n. gen. masc. sg. κύριος Lord, lord, master, sir, LORD, God, Master, owner
11 τοὺς art. acc. masc. pl. ὁ ἡ τό the, this, that, he, she, it
τὴν art. acc. fem. sg. ὁ ἡ τό the, this, that, he, she, it
ὑπομονὴν n. acc. fem. sg. ὑπομονή patience, enduring
Ἰὼβ n. gen. masc. sg. Ἰώβ Job
καὶ conj. καί and, even, also, but
τὸ art. acc. neut. sg. ὁ ἡ τό the, this, that, he, she, it
τέλος n. acc. neut. sg. τέλος end, custom, ending, finally, uttermost
Κυρίου n. gen. masc. sg. κύριος Lord, lord, master, sir, LORD, God, Master, owner
ὅτι conj. ὅτι that, for, because, how that, how, because that, for that, though
πολύσπλαγχνός adj. nom. masc. sg. πολύσπλαγχνος very pitiful
ὁ art. nom. masc. sg. ὁ ἡ τό the, this, that, he, she, it
Κύριος n. nom. masc. sg. κύριος Lord, lord, master, sir, LORD, God, Master, owner
καὶ conj. καί and, even, also, but
οἰκτίρμων adj. nom. masc. sg. οἰκτίρμων merciful, of tender mercy
12 Πρὸ prep. πρό (+gen) before, above
πάντων adj. gen. neut. pl. πᾶς πᾶσα πᾶν all, every, whosoever, every one, no, whole, any
δέ conj. δέ but, and, now, also, to the contrary, rather, then
ἀδελφοί n. voc. masc. pl. ἀδελφός brother
μου pron. gen. 1p. sg. ἐγώ I
μὴ particle of negation. μή not, no, lest, neither, none, nothing, nor, never, without
μήτε conj. μήτε neither, nor, so much as, or
τὸν art. acc. masc. sg. ὁ ἡ τό the, this, that, he, she, it
οὐρανὸν n. acc. masc. sg. οὐρανός heaven, air, sky
μήτε conj. μήτε neither, nor, so much as, or
τὴν art. acc. fem. sg. ὁ ἡ τό the, this, that, he, she, it
γῆν n. acc. fem. sg. γῆ earth, land, ground, country
μήτε conj. μήτε neither, nor, so much as, or
ἄλλον adj. acc. masc. sg. ἄλλος other, another, some, one, more, otherwise
τινὰ indefinite pron. acc. masc. sg. τὶς certain, some, any man, one, any thing
ὅρκον n. acc. masc. sg. ὅρκος oath
δέ conj. δέ but, and, now, also, to the contrary, rather, then
ὑμῶν pron. gen. 2p. pl. σύ thou, you
τὸ art. nom. neut. sg. ὁ ἡ τό the, this, that, he, she, it
ναὶ particle. ναί yea, even so, yes, surely, truth, verily
ναὶ particle. ναί yea, even so, yes, surely, truth, verily
καὶ conj. καί and, even, also, but
τὸ art. nom. neut. sg. ὁ ἡ τό the, this, that, he, she, it
οὔ particle of negation. οὐ οὐκ οὐχ not, no, neither, none, nay, nor, never, nothing
οὔ particle of negation. οὐ οὐκ οὐχ not, no, neither, none, nay, nor, never, nothing
ἵνα conj. ἵνα that, to, lest, for to, so that, albeit, because, for, so as
μὴ particle of negation. μή not, no, lest, neither, none, nothing, nor, never, without
ὑπὸ prep. ὑπό (+gen) of, by, with, from, among, (+acc) under
κρίσιν n. acc. fem. sg. κρίσις judgment, damnation, accusation, condemnation
13 τις indefinite pron. nom. masc. sg. τὶς certain, some, any man, one, any thing
ἐν prep. ἐν (+dat) in, by, with, among, at, on, through, to, within, into, of, for

ὑμῖν pron. dat. 2p. pl. σύ thou, you
τις indefinite pron. nom. masc. sg. τὶς certain, some, any man, one, any thing
14 τις indefinite pron. nom. masc. sg. τὶς certain, some, any man, one, any thing
ἐν prep. ἐν (+dat) in, by, with, among, at, on, through, to, within, into, of, for
ὑμῖν pron. dat. 2p. pl. σύ thou, you
τοὺς art. acc. masc. pl. ὁ ἡ τό the, this, that, he, she, it
πρεσβυτέρους adj. acc. masc. pl. πρεσβύτερος elder, elder woman, eldest, old man
τῆς art. gen. fem. sg. ὁ ἡ τό the, this, that, he, she, it
ἐκκλησίας n. gen. fem. sg. ἐκκλησία church, assembly
καὶ conj. καί and, even, also, but
ἐπ' prep. ἐπί (+gen) on, in, upon, (+dat) in, at, for, upon, (+acc) on, upon, unto, to, against
αὐτὸν pron. acc. masc. 3p. sg. αὐτός ή ό self, of oneself, even, very, the same, he, she, it
αὐτὸν pron. acc. masc. 3p. sg. αὐτός ή ό self, of oneself, even, very, the same, he, she, it
ἐλαίῳ n. dat. neut. sg. ἔλαιον oil
ἐν prep. ἐν (+dat) in, by, with, among, at, on, through, to, within, into, of, for
τῷ art. dat. neut. sg. ὁ ἡ τό the, this, that, he, she, it
ὀνόματι n. dat. neut. sg. ὄνομα name, call, surname
τοῦ art. gen. masc. sg. ὁ ἡ τό the, this, that, he, she, it
Κυρίου n. gen. masc. sg. κύριος Lord, lord, master, sir, LORD, God, Master, owner
15 καὶ conj. καί and, even, also, but
ἡ art. nom. fem. sg. ὁ ἡ τό the, this, that, he, she, it
εὐχὴ n. nom. fem. sg. εὐχή vow, prayer
τῆς art. gen. fem. sg. ὁ ἡ τό the, this, that, he, she, it
πίστεως n. gen. fem. sg. πίστις faith, assurance, belief, fidelity
τὸν art. acc. masc. sg. ὁ ἡ τό the, this, that, he, she, it
καὶ conj. καί and, even, also, but
αὐτὸν pron. acc. masc. 3p. sg. αὐτός ή ό self, of oneself, even, very, the same, he, she, it
ὁ art. nom. masc. sg. ὁ ἡ τό the, this, that, he, she, it
Κύριος n. nom. masc. sg. κύριος Lord, lord, master, sir, LORD, God, Master, owner
κἂν conj. κἄν though, and if, if but, also if, and if so much, at the least, yet as
ἁμαρτίας n. acc. fem. pl. ἁμαρτία sin, offence, sinful
αὐτῷ pron. dat. masc. 3p. sg. αὐτός ή ό self, of oneself, even, very, the same, he, she, it
16 ἀλλήλοις pron. dat. masc. pl. ἀλλήλων one another, themselves, together, mutual
τὰ art. acc. neut. pl. ὁ ἡ τό the, this, that, he, she, it
παραπτώματα n. acc. neut. pl. παράπτωμα trespass, offence, sin, fall, fault
καὶ conj. καί and, even, also, but
ὑπὲρ prep. ὑπέρ (+gen) for, of, for the sake of, (+acc) above, more than
ἀλλήλων pron. gen. masc. pl. ἀλλήλων one another, themselves, together, mutual
ὅπως adv. ὅπως that, how, to, because, so that, when
πολὺ adv. πολύς many, great, much, long, abundant
δέησις n. nom. fem. sg. δέησις prayer, supplication, request
δικαίου adj. gen. masc. sg. δίκαιος righteous, just, meet, right
17 Ἠλίας n. nom. masc. sg. Ἠλίας Elias, Elijah
ἄνθρωπος n. nom. masc. sg. ἄνθρωπος man, human being, person, one, certain
ὁμοιοπαθὴς adj. nom. masc. sg. ὁμοιοπαθής of like passion, subject to like passion
ἡμῖν pron. dat. 1p. pl. ἐγώ I
καὶ conj. καί and, even, also, but
προσευχῇ n. dat. fem. sg. προσευχή prayer
τοῦ art. gen. neut. sg. ὁ ἡ τό the, this, that, he, she, it
μὴ particle of negation. μή not, no, lest, neither, none, nothing, nor, never, without
καὶ conj. καί and, even, also, but
οὐκ particle of negation. οὐ οὐκ οὐχ not, no, neither, none, nay, nor, never, nothing
ἐπὶ prep. ἐπί (+gen) on, in, upon, (+dat) in, at, for, upon, (+acc) on, upon, unto, to, against
τῆς art. gen. fem. sg. ὁ ἡ τό the, this, that, he, she, it
γῆς n. gen. fem. sg. γῆ earth, land, ground, country

ἐνιαυτοὺς n. acc. masc. pl. ἐνιαυτός year
τρεῖς num. acc. masc. pl. τρεῖς three
καὶ conj. καί and, even, also, but
μῆνας n. acc. masc. pl. μήν month
ἕξ num. acc. masc. pl. ἕξ six
18 καὶ conj. καί and, even, also, but
πάλιν adv. πάλιν again
καὶ conj. καί and, even, also, but
ὁ art. nom. masc. sg. ὁ ἡ τό the, this, that, he, she, it
οὐρανὸς n. nom. masc. sg. οὐρανός heaven, air, sky
ὑετὸν n. acc. masc. sg. ὑετός rain
καὶ conj. καί and, even, also, but
ἡ art. nom. fem. sg. ὁ ἡ τό the, this, that, he, she, it
γῆ n. nom. fem. sg. γῆ earth, land, ground, country
τὸν art. acc. masc. sg. ὁ ἡ τό the, this, that, he, she, it
καρπὸν n. acc. masc. sg. καρπός fruit
αὐτῆς pron. gen. fem. 3p. sg. αὐτός ή ό self, of oneself, even, very, the same, he, she, it
19 Ἀδελφοί n. voc. masc. pl. ἀδελφός brother
ἐάν conj. ἐάν if, soever, except, though, and if, but, whether, if so, so
τις indefinite pron. nom. masc. sg. τὶς certain, some, any man, one, any thing
ἐν prep. ἐν (+dat) in, by, with, among, at, on, through, to, within, into, of, for
ὑμῖν pron. dat. 2p. pl. σύ thou, you
ἀπὸ prep. ἀπό (+gen) from, of, out of, since, for, off, at, by, in, on
τῆς art. gen. fem. sg. ὁ ἡ τό the, this, that, he, she, it
ἀληθείας n. gen. fem. sg. ἀλήθεια truth, verity
καὶ conj. καί and, even, also, but
τις indefinite pron. nom. masc. sg. τὶς certain, some, any man, one, any thing
αὐτόν pron. acc. masc. 3p. sg. αὐτός ή ό self, of oneself, even, very, the same, he, she, it
20 ὅτι conj. ὅτι that, for, because, how that, how, because that, for that, though
ὁ art. nom. masc. sg. ὁ ἡ τό the, this, that, he, she, it
ἁμαρτωλὸν adj. acc. masc. sg. ἁμαρτωλός sinner, sinful
ἐκ prep. ἐκ ἐξ (+gen) of, from, out of, by, on, with, in, among, through
πλάνης n. gen. fem. sg. πλάνη error, deception, deceit, delusion
ὁδοῦ n. gen. fem. sg. ὁδός way, journey, highway
αὐτοῦ pron. gen. masc. 3p. sg. αὐτός ή ό self, of oneself, even, very, the same, he, she, it
ψυχὴν n. acc. fem. sg. ψυχή life, soul, mind, heart
ἐκ prep. ἐκ ἐξ (+gen) of, from, out of, by, on, with, in, among, through
θανάτου n. gen. masc. sg. θάνατος death
καὶ conj. καί and, even, also, but
πλῆθος n. acc. neut. sg. πλῆθος multitude, bundle, company
ἁμαρτιῶν n. gen. fem. pl. ἁμαρτία sin, offence, sinful

ΠΕΤΡΟΥ
ΕΠΙΣΤΟΛΗ ΚΑΘΟΛΙΚΗ ΠΡΩΤΗ

1

1 Πέτρος n. nom. masc. sg. Πέτρος Peter
ἀπόστολος n. nom. masc. sg. ἀπόστολος apostle, messenger, he that is sent
Ἰησοῦ n. gen. masc. sg. Ἰησοῦς Jesus
Χριστοῦ n. gen. masc. sg. Χριστός Christ
ἐκλεκτοῖς adj. dat. masc. pl. ἐκλεκτός elect, chosen
παρεπιδήμοις adj. dat. masc. pl. παρεπίδημος pilgrim
διασπορᾶς n. gen. fem. sg. διασπορά dispersion, one who is scattered abroad
Πόντου n. gen. masc. sg. Πόντος Pontus
Γαλατίας n. gen. fem. sg. Γαλατία Galatia
Καππαδοκίας n. gen. fem. sg. Καππαδοκία Cappadocia
Ἀσίας n. gen. fem. sg. Ἀσία Asia
καὶ conj. καί and, even, also, but
Βιθυνίας n. gen. fem. sg. Βιθυνία Bithynia
2 κατὰ prep. κατά (+gen) against, by, throughout, down, (+acc) according to, after, with
πρόγνωσιν n. acc. fem. sg. πρόγνωσις foreknowledge
Θεοῦ n. gen. masc. sg. θεός God, god
πατρὸς n. gen. masc. sg. πατήρ Father, father, parent
ἐν prep. ἐν (+dat) in, by, with, among, at, on, through, to, within, into, of, for
ἁγιασμῷ n. dat. masc. sg. ἁγιασμός holiness, sanctification
Πνεύματος n. gen. neut. sg. πνεῦμα spirit, Spirit, Ghost, ghost, life. of the spirit, wind
εἰς prep. εἰς (+acc) into, to, unto, for, in, on, toward, against, upon, at, among
ὑπακοὴν n. acc. fem. sg. ὑπακοή obedience, obey, make obedient, obedient
καὶ conj. καί and, even, also, but
ῥαντισμὸν n. acc. masc. sg. ῥαντισμός sprinkling
αἵματος n. gen. neut. sg. αἷμα blood
Ἰησοῦ n. gen. masc. sg. Ἰησοῦς Jesus
Χριστοῦ n. gen. masc. sg. Χριστός Christ
χάρις n. nom. fem. sg. χάρις grace, thank, favour, pleasure
ὑμῖν pron. dat. 2p. pl. σύ thou, you
καὶ conj. καί and, even, also, but
εἰρήνη n. nom. fem. sg. εἰρήνη peace, quietness, rest
3 Εὐλογητὸς adj. nom. masc. sg. εὐλογητός blessed
ὁ art. nom. masc. sg. ὁ ἡ τό the, this, that, he, she, it
Θεὸς n. nom. masc. sg. θεός God, god
καὶ conj. καί and, even, also, but
πατὴρ n. nom. masc. sg. πατήρ Father, father, parent
τοῦ art. gen. masc. sg. ὁ ἡ τό the, this, that, he, she, it
Κυρίου n. gen. masc. sg. κύριος Lord, lord, master, sir, LORD, God, Master, owner
ἡμῶν pron. gen. 1p. pl. ἐγώ I
Ἰησοῦ n. gen. masc. sg. Ἰησοῦς Jesus
Χριστοῦ n. gen. masc. sg. Χριστός Christ
ὁ art. nom. masc. sg. ὁ ἡ τό the, this, that, he, she, it
κατὰ prep. κατά (+gen) against, by, throughout, down, (+acc) according to, after, with
τὸ art. acc. neut. sg. ὁ ἡ τό the, this, that, he, she, it
πολὺ adj. acc. neut. sg. πολύς many, great, much, long, abundant
αὐτοῦ pron. gen. masc. 3p. sg. αὐτός ἡ ὁ self, of oneself, even, very, the same, he, she, it
ἔλεος n. acc. neut. sg. ἔλεος mercy
ἡμᾶς pron. acc. 1p. pl. ἐγώ I
εἰς prep. εἰς (+acc) into, to, unto, for, in, on, toward, against, upon, at, among

ἐλπίδα n. acc. fem. sg. ἐλπίς hope, faith
δι' prep. διά (+gen) by, through, with, in, of, (+acc) for, because of, for a cause
ἀναστάσεως n. gen. fem. sg. ἀνάστασις resurrection, rising again
Ἰησοῦ n. gen. masc. sg. Ἰησοῦς Jesus
Χριστοῦ n. gen. masc. sg. Χριστός Christ
ἐκ prep. ἐκ ἐξ (+gen) of, from, out of, by, on, with, in, among, through
νεκρῶν adj. gen. masc. pl. νεκρός dead
4 εἰς prep. εἰς (+acc) into, to, unto, for, in, on, toward, against, upon, at, among
κληρονομίαν n. acc. fem. sg. κληρονομία inheritance
ἄφθαρτον adj. acc. fem. sg. ἄφθαρτος uncorruptible, incorruptible, immortal, not corruptible
καὶ conj. καί and, even, also, but
ἀμίαντον adj. acc. fem. sg. ἀμίαντος undefiled
καὶ conj. καί and, even, also, but
ἀμάραντον adj. acc. fem. sg. ἀμάραντος that fadeth not away
ἐν prep. ἐν (+dat) in, by, with, among, at, on, through, to, within, into, of, for
οὐρανοῖς n. dat. masc. pl. οὐρανός heaven, air, sky
εἰς prep. εἰς (+acc) into, to, unto, for, in, on, toward, against, upon, at, among
ὑμᾶς pron. acc. 2p. pl. σύ thou, you
5 τοὺς art. acc. masc. pl. ὁ ἡ τό the, this, that, he, she, it
ἐν prep. ἐν (+dat) in, by, with, among, at, on, through, to, within, into, of, for
δυνάμει n. dat. fem. sg. δύναμις power, mighty work, miracle, strength, might
Θεοῦ n. gen. masc. sg. θεός God, god
διὰ prep. διά (+gen) by, through, with, in, of, (+acc) for, because of, for a cause
πίστεως n. gen. fem. sg. πίστις faith, assurance, belief, fidelity
εἰς prep. εἰς (+acc) into, to, unto, for, in, on, toward, against, upon, at, among
σωτηρίαν n. acc. fem. sg. σωτηρία salvation, deliver, health, saving
ἑτοίμην adj. acc. fem. sg. ἕτοιμος ready, prepared, readiness
ἐν prep. ἐν (+dat) in, by, with, among, at, on, through, to, within, into, of, for
καιρῷ n. dat. masc. sg. καιρός time, season, due time, opportunity
ἐσχάτῳ adj. dat. masc. sg. ἔσχατος last, lowest, uttermost, uttermost part
6 ἐν prep. ἐν (+dat) in, by, with, among, at, on, through, to, within, into, of, for
ᾧ relative pron. dat. neut. sg. ὅς ἥ ὅ who, which, what, that
ὀλίγον adv. ὀλίγον a little
ἄρτι adv. ἄρτι now, hence, here, hither, even now, present
εἰ conj. εἰ if, whether, that, though, forasmuch
ποικίλοις adj. dat. masc. pl. ποικίλος divers, manifold
πειρασμοῖς n. dat. masc. pl. πειρασμός temptation, trial
7 ἵνα conj. ἵνα that, to, lest, for to, so that, albeit, because, for, so as
τὸ art. nom. neut. sg. ὁ ἡ τό the, this, that, he, she, it
δοκίμιον n. nom. neut. sg. δοκίμιον trying, trial
ὑμῶν pron. gen. 2p. pl. σύ thou, you
τῆς art. gen. fem. sg. ὁ ἡ τό the, this, that, he, she, it
πίστεως n. gen. fem. sg. πίστις faith, assurance, belief, fidelity
πολὺ adj. nom. neut. sg. πολύς many, great, much, long, abundant
τιμιώτερον compar. adj. nom. neut. sg. τίμιος precious, dear, has in reputation
χρυσίου n. gen. neut. sg. χρυσίον gold
τοῦ art. gen. neut. sg. ὁ ἡ τό the, this, that, he, she, it
διὰ prep. διά (+gen) by, through, with, in, of, (+acc) for, because of, for a cause
πυρὸς n. gen. neut. sg. πῦρ fire, fiery
δὲ conj. δέ but, and, now, also, to the contrary, rather, then
εἰς prep. εἰς (+acc) into, to, unto, for, in, on, toward, against, upon, at, among
ἔπαινον n. acc. masc. sg. ἔπαινος praise
καὶ conj. καί and, even, also, but
τιμὴν n. acc. fem. sg. τιμή honour, price, preciousness, sum
καὶ conj. καί and, even, also, but

δόξαν n. acc. fem. sg. δόξα glory, honour, praise, dignity, worship
ἐν prep. ἐν (+dat) in, by, with, among, at, on, through, to, within, into, of, for
ἀποκαλύψει n. dat. fem. sg. ἀποκάλυψις revelation, appearing, coming, manifestation
Ἰησοῦ n. gen. masc. sg. Ἰησοῦς Jesus
Χριστοῦ n. gen. masc. sg. Χριστός Christ
8 ὃν relative pron. acc. masc. sg. ὅς ἥ ὅ who, which, what, that
οὐκ particle of negation. οὐ οὐκ οὐχ not, no, neither, none, nay, nor, never, nothing
εἰς prep. εἰς (+acc) into, to, unto, for, in, on, toward, against, upon, at, among
ὃν relative pron. acc. masc. sg. ὅς ἥ ὅ who, which, what, that
ἄρτι adv. ἄρτι now, hence, here, hither, even now, present
μὴ particle of negation. μή not, no, lest, neither, none, nothing, nor, never, without
δὲ conj. δέ but, and, now, also, to the contrary, rather, then
χαρᾷ n. dat. fem. sg. χαρά joy, gladness, joyfulness
ἀνεκλαλήτῳ adj. dat. fem. sg. ἀνεκλάλητος unspeakable
καὶ conj. καί and, even, also, but
9 τὸ art. acc. neut. sg. ὁ ἡ τό the, this, that, he, she, it
τέλος n. acc. neut. sg. τέλος end, custom, ending, finally, uttermost
τῆς art. gen. fem. sg. ὁ ἡ τό the, this, that, he, she, it
πίστεως n. gen. fem. sg. πίστις faith, assurance, belief, fidelity
ὑμῶν pron. gen. 2p. pl. σύ thou, you
σωτηρίαν n. acc. fem. sg. σωτηρία salvation, deliver, health, saving
ψυχῶν n. gen. fem. pl. ψυχή life, soul, mind, heart
10 περὶ prep. περί (+gen) of, for, concerning, (+acc) about, concerning, in
ἧς relative pron. gen. fem. sg. ὅς ἥ ὅ who, which, what, that
σωτηρίας n. gen. fem. sg. σωτηρία salvation, deliver, health, saving
καὶ conj. καί and, even, also, but
προφῆται n. nom. masc. pl. προφήτης prophet
οἱ art. nom. masc. pl. ὁ ἡ τό the, this, that, he, she, it
περὶ prep. περί (+gen) of, for, concerning, (+acc) about, concerning, in
τῆς art. gen. fem. sg. ὁ ἡ τό the, this, that, he, she, it
εἰς prep. εἰς (+acc) into, to, unto, for, in, on, toward, against, upon, at, among
ὑμᾶς pron. acc. 2p. pl. σύ thou, you
χάριτος n. gen. fem. sg. χάρις grace, thank, favour, pleasure
11 εἰς prep. εἰς (+acc) into, to, unto, for, in, on, toward, against, upon, at, among
τίνα interrog. pron. acc. masc. sg. τίς what, who, why, where, which, how
ἢ particle. ἤ or, than, either, nor, or else, and, rather than
ποῖον interrog. pron. acc. masc. sg. ποῖος what, which, what manner of
καιρὸν n. acc. masc. sg. καιρός time, season, due time, opportunity
τὸ art. nom. neut. sg. ὁ ἡ τό the, this, that, he, she, it
ἐν prep. ἐν (+dat) in, by, with, among, at, on, through, to, within, into, of, for
αὐτοῖς pron. dat. masc. 3p. pl. αὐτός ή ό self, of oneself, even, very, the same, he, she, it
Πνεῦμα n. nom. neut. sg. πνεῦμα spirit, Spirit, Ghost, ghost, life. of the spirit, wind
Χριστοῦ n. gen. masc. sg. Χριστός Christ
τὰ art. acc. neut. pl. ὁ ἡ τό the, this, that, he, she, it
εἰς prep. εἰς (+acc) into, to, unto, for, in, on, toward, against, upon, at, among
Χριστὸν n. acc. masc. sg. Χριστός Christ
παθήματα n. acc. neut. pl. πάθημα suffering, affliction, affection, motion
καὶ conj. καί and, even, also, but
τὰς art. acc. fem. pl. ὁ ἡ τό the, this, that, he, she, it
μετὰ prep. μετά (+gen) with, among, against, (+acc) after
ταῦτα demo. pron. acc. neut. pl. οὗτος αὕτη τοῦτο this, the same, this same, he, she, it
δόξας n. acc. fem. pl. δόξα glory, honour, praise, dignity, worship
12 οἷς relative pron. dat. masc. pl. ὅς ἥ ὅ who, which, what, that
ὅτι conj. ὅτι that, for, because, how that, how, because that, for that, though
οὐχ particle of negation. οὐ οὐκ οὐχ not, no, neither, none, nay, nor, never, nothing

ἑαυτοῖς reflexive pron. dat. masc. 3p. pl. ἑαυτοῦ himself, herself, itself, yourself, ourselves
ἡμῖν pron. dat. 1p. pl. ἐγώ I
δὲ conj. δέ but, and, now, also, to the contrary, rather, then
αὐτά pron. acc. neut. 3p. pl. αὐτός ή ό self, of oneself, even, very, the same, he, she, it
ἃ relative pron. nom. neut. pl. ὅς ἥ ὅ who, which, what, that
νῦν adv. νῦν now, henceforth, present, this time
ὑμῖν pron. dat. 2p. pl. σύ thou, you
διὰ prep. διά (+gen) by, through, with, in, of, (+acc) for, because of, for a cause
τῶν art. gen. masc. pl. ὁ ἡ τό the, this, that, he, she, it
ὑμᾶς pron. acc. 2p. pl. σύ thou, you
ἐν prep. ἐν (+dat) in, by, with, among, at, on, through, to, within, into, of, for
Πνεύματι n. dat. neut. sg. πνεῦμα spirit, Spirit, Ghost, ghost, life. of the spirit, wind
Ἁγίῳ adj. dat. neut. sg. ἅγιος Holy, holy, saint, Holy One, holy thing, most holy
ἀπ' prep. ἀπό (+gen) from, of, out of, since, for, off, at, by, in, on
οὐρανοῦ n. gen. masc. sg. οὐρανός heaven, air, sky
εἰς prep. εἰς (+acc) into, to, unto, for, in, on, toward, against, upon, at, among
ἃ relative pron. acc. neut. pl. ὅς ἥ ὅ who, which, what, that
ἄγγελοι n. nom. masc. pl. ἄγγελος angel, messenger
13 Διὸ conj. διό wherefore, therefore, for which cause
τὰς art. acc. fem. pl. ὁ ἡ τό the, this, that, he, she, it
ὀσφύας n. acc. fem. pl. ὀσφύς loins
τῆς art. gen. fem. sg. ὁ ἡ τό the, this, that, he, she, it
διανοίας n. gen. fem. sg. διάνοια mind, understanding, imagination
ὑμῶν pron. gen. 2p. pl. σύ thou, you
τελείως adv. τελείως to the end, perfectly
ἐπὶ prep. ἐπί (+gen) on, in, upon, (+dat) in, at, for, upon, (+acc) on, upon, unto, to, against
τὴν art. acc. fem. sg. ὁ ἡ τό the, this, that, he, she, it
ὑμῖν pron. dat. 2p. pl. σύ thou, you
χάριν n. acc. fem. sg. χάρις grace, thank, favour, pleasure
ἐν prep. ἐν (+dat) in, by, with, among, at, on, through, to, within, into, of, for
ἀποκαλύψει n. dat. fem. sg. ἀποκάλυψις revelation, appearing, coming, manifestation
Ἰησοῦ n. gen. masc. sg. Ἰησοῦς Jesus
Χριστοῦ n. gen. masc. sg. Χριστός Christ
14 ὡς adv. ὡς as, when, as it were, how, about, like, as soon as, even as, while
τέκνα n. nom. neut. pl. τέκνον child, son, daughter
ὑπακοῆς n. gen. fem. sg. ὑπακοή obedience, obey, make obedient, obedient
μὴ particle of negation. μή not, no, lest, neither, none, nothing, nor, never, without
ταῖς art. dat. fem. pl. ὁ ἡ τό the, this, that, he, she, it
πρότερον adv. πρότερον before, first, former, at the first
ἐν prep. ἐν (+dat) in, by, with, among, at, on, through, to, within, into, of, for
τῇ art. dat. fem. sg. ὁ ἡ τό the, this, that, he, she, it
ἀγνοίᾳ n. dat. fem. sg. ἄγνοια ignorance
ὑμῶν pron. gen. 2p. pl. σύ thou, you
ἐπιθυμίαις n. dat. fem. pl. ἐπιθυμία lust, concupiscence, desire
15 ἀλλὰ conj. ἀλλά but, yea, yet, nevertheless, howbeit, nay, therefore
κατὰ prep. κατά (+gen) against, by, throughout, down, (+acc) according to, after, with
τὸν art. acc. masc. sg. ὁ ἡ τό the, this, that, he, she, it
ὑμᾶς pron. acc. 2p. pl. σύ thou, you
ἅγιον adj. acc. masc. sg. ἅγιος Holy, holy, saint, Holy One, holy thing, most holy
καὶ conj. καί and, even, also, but
αὐτοὶ pron. nom. masc. 2p. pl. αὐτός ή ό self, of oneself, even, very, the same, he, she, it
ἅγιοι adj. nom. masc. pl. ἅγιος Holy, holy, saint, Holy One, holy thing, most holy
ἐν prep. ἐν (+dat) in, by, with, among, at, on, through, to, within, into, of, for
πάσῃ adj. dat. fem. sg. πᾶς πᾶσα πᾶν all, every, whosoever, every one, no, whole, any
ἀναστροφῇ n. dat. fem. sg. ἀναστροφή conversation

16 διότι conj. διότι for, because, because that, therefore
Ἅγιοι adj. nom. masc. pl. ἅγιος Holy, holy, saint, Holy One, holy thing, most holy
ὅτι conj. ὅτι that, for, because, how that, how, because that, for that, though
ἐγὼ pron. nom. 1p. sg. ἐγώ I
ἅγιος adj. nom. masc. sg. ἅγιος Holy, holy, saint, Holy One, holy thing, most holy
17 καὶ conj. καί and, even, also, but
εἰ conj. εἰ if, whether, that, though, forasmuch
πατέρα n. acc. masc. sg. πατήρ Father, father, parent
τὸν art. acc. masc. sg. ὁ ἡ τό the, this, that, he, she, it
ἀπροσωπολήπτως adv. ἀπροσωπολήπτως without respect of persons
κατὰ prep. κατά (+gen) against, by, throughout, down, (+acc) according to, after, with
τὸ art. acc. neut. sg. ὁ ἡ τό the, this, that, he, she, it
ἑκάστου adj. gen. masc. sg. ἕκαστος every man, every, every one, any man, each
ἔργον n. acc. neut. sg. ἔργον work, deed, doing labour
ἐν prep. ἐν (+dat) in, by, with, among, at, on, through, to, within, into, of, for
φόβῳ n. dat. masc. sg. φόβος fear, terror, sore afraid
τὸν art. acc. masc. sg. ὁ ἡ τό the, this, that, he, she, it
τῆς art. gen. fem. sg. ὁ ἡ τό the, this, that, he, she, it
παροικίας n. gen. fem. sg. παροικία sojourning
ὑμῶν pron. gen. 2p. pl. σύ thou, you
χρόνον n. acc. masc. sg. χρόνος time, season, space
18 ὅτι conj. ὅτι that, for, because, how that, how, because that, for that, though
οὐ particle of negation. οὐ οὐκ οὐχ not, no, neither, none, nay, nor, never, nothing
φθαρτοῖς adj. dat. neut. pl. φθαρτός corruptible
ἀργυρίῳ n. dat. neut. sg. ἀργύριον money, piece of silver, silver
ἢ particle. ἤ or, than, either, nor, or else, and, rather than
χρυσίῳ n. dat. neut. sg. χρυσίον gold
ἐκ prep. ἐκ ἐξ (+gen) of, from, out of, by, on, with, in, among, through
τῆς art. gen. fem. sg. ὁ ἡ τό the, this, that, he, she, it
ματαίας adj. gen. fem. sg. μάταιος vanity, vain
ὑμῶν pron. gen. 2p. pl. σύ thou, you
ἀναστροφῆς n. gen. fem. sg. ἀναστροφή conversation
πατροπαραδότου adj. gen. fem. sg. πατροπαράδοτος received by tradition from fathers
19 ἀλλὰ conj. ἀλλά but, yea, yet, nevertheless, howbeit, nay, therefore
τιμίῳ adj. dat. neut. sg. τίμιος precious, dear, has in reputation, honourable
αἵματι n. dat. neut. sg. αἷμα blood
ὡς adv. ὡς as, when, as it were, how, about, like, as soon as, even as, while
ἀμνοῦ n. gen. masc. sg. ἀμνός lamb, Lamb
ἀμώμου adj. gen. masc. sg. ἄμωμος without blame, without fault, without spot
καὶ conj. καί and, even, also, but
ἀσπίλου adj. gen. masc. sg. ἄσπιλος without spot, unspotted
Χριστοῦ n. gen. masc. sg. Χριστός Christ
20 μὲν conj. μέν indeed, verily, truly, even, so, some
πρὸ prep. πρό (+gen) before, above
καταβολῆς n. gen. fem. sg. καταβολή foundation
κόσμου n. gen. masc. sg. κόσμος world, adorning
δὲ conj. δέ but, and, now, also, to the contrary, rather, then
ἐπ' prep. ἐπί (+gen) on, in, upon, (+dat) in, at, for, upon, (+acc) on, upon, unto, to, against
ἐσχάτων adj. gen. fem. pl. ἔσχατος last, lowest, uttermost, uttermost part
τῶν art. gen. masc. pl. ὁ ἡ τό the, this, that, he, she, it
χρόνων n. gen. masc. pl. χρόνος time, season, space
δι' prep. διά (+gen) by, through, with, in, of, (+acc) for, because of, for a cause
ὑμᾶς pron. acc. 2p. pl. σύ thou, you
21 τοὺς art. acc. masc. pl. ὁ ἡ τό the, this, that, he, she, it
δι' prep. διά (+gen) by, through, with, in, of, (+acc) for, because of, for a cause

αὐτοῦ pron. gen. masc. 3p. sg. αὐτός ή ό self, of oneself, even, very, the same, he, she, it
εἰς prep. εἰς (+acc) into, to, unto, for, in, on, toward, against, upon, at, among
Θεὸν n. acc. masc. sg. θεός God, god
τὸν art. acc. masc. sg. ὁ ἡ τό the, this, that, he, she, it
αὐτὸν pron. acc. masc. 3p. sg. αὐτός ή ό self, of oneself, even, very, the same, he, she, it
ἐκ prep. ἐκ ἐξ (+gen) of, from, out of, by, on, with, in, among, through
νεκρῶν adj. gen. masc. pl. νεκρός dead
καὶ conj. καί and, even, also, but
δόξαν n. acc. fem. sg. δόξα glory, honour, praise, dignity, worship
αὐτῷ pron. dat. masc. 3p. sg. αὐτός ή ό self, of oneself, even, very, the same, he, she, it
ὥστε conj. ὥστε so that, wherefore, insomuch that, therefore, that, so then
τὴν art. acc. fem. sg. ὁ ἡ τό the, this, that, he, she, it
πίστιν n. acc. fem. sg. πίστις faith, assurance, belief, fidelity
ὑμῶν pron. gen. 2p. pl. σύ thou, you
καὶ conj. καί and, even, also, but
ἐλπίδα n. acc. fem. sg. ἐλπίς hope, faith
εἰς prep. εἰς (+acc) into, to, unto, for, in, on, toward, against, upon, at, among
Θεὸν n. acc. masc. sg. θεός God, god
22 τὰς art. acc. fem. pl. ὁ ἡ τό the, this, that, he, she, it
ψυχὰς n. acc. fem. pl. ψυχή life, soul, mind, heart
ὑμῶν pron. gen. 2p. pl. σύ thou, you
ἐν prep. ἐν (+dat) in, by, with, among, at, on, through, to, within, into, of, for
τῇ art. dat. fem. sg. ὁ ἡ τό the, this, that, he, she, it
ὑπακοῇ n. dat. fem. sg. ὑπακοή obedience, obey, make obedient, obedient
τῆς art. gen. fem. sg. ὁ ἡ τό the, this, that, he, she, it
ἀληθείας n. gen. fem. sg. ἀλήθεια truth, verity
διὰ prep. διά (+gen) by, through, with, in, of, (+acc) for, because of, for a cause
Πνεύματος n. gen. neut. sg. πνεῦμα spirit, Spirit, Ghost, ghost, life. of the spirit, wind
εἰς prep. εἰς (+acc) into, to, unto, for, in, on, toward, against, upon, at, among
φιλαδελφίαν n. acc. fem. sg. φιλαδελφία brotherly kindness, love of the brethren
ἀνυπόκριτον adj. acc. fem. sg. ἀνυπόκριτος unfeigned, without hypocrisy
ἐκ prep. ἐκ ἐξ (+gen) of, from, out of, by, on, with, in, among, through
καθαρᾶς adj. gen. fem. sg. καθαρός pure, clean, clear
καρδίας n. gen. fem. sg. καρδία heart
ἀλλήλους pron. acc. masc. pl. ἀλλήλων one another, themselves, together, mutual
ἐκτενῶς adv. ἐκτενῶς fervently
23 οὐκ particle of negation. οὐ οὐκ οὐχ not, no, neither, none, nay, nor, never, nothing
ἐκ prep. ἐκ ἐξ (+gen) of, from, out of, by, on, with, in, among, through
σπορᾶς n. gen. fem. sg. σπορά seed
φθαρτῆς adj. gen. fem. sg. φθαρτός corruptible
ἀλλὰ conj. ἀλλά but, yea, yet, nevertheless, howbeit, nay, therefore
ἀφθάρτου adj. gen. fem. sg. ἄφθαρτος uncorruptible, incorruptible, immortal, not corruptible
διὰ prep. διά (+gen) by, through, with, in, of, (+acc) for, because of, for a cause
λόγου n. gen. masc. sg. λόγος word, saying, account, speech, thing, matter
Θεοῦ n. gen. masc. sg. θεός God, god
καὶ conj. καί and, even, also, but
εἰς prep. εἰς (+acc) into, to, unto, for, in, on, toward, against, upon, at, among
τὸν art. acc. masc. sg. ὁ ἡ τό the, this, that, he, she, it
αἰῶνα n. acc. masc. sg. αἰών ever, ever and ever, evermore, age, eternal, world
24 διότι conj. διότι for, because, because that, therefore
πᾶσα adj. nom. fem. sg. πᾶς πᾶσα πᾶν all, every, whosoever, every one, no, whole, any
σὰρξ n. nom. fem. sg. σάρξ flesh, carnal
ὡς adv. ὡς as, when, as it were, how, about, like, as soon as, even as, while
χόρτος n. nom. masc. sg. χόρτος grass, blade, hay
καὶ conj. καί and, even, also, but

πᾶσα adj. nom. fem. sg. πᾶς πᾶσα πᾶν all, every, whosoever, every one, no, whole, any
δόξα n. nom. fem. sg. δόξα glory, honour, praise, dignity, worship
ἀνθρώπου n. gen. masc. sg. ἄνθρωπος man, human being, person, one, certain
ὡς adv. ὡς as, when, as it were, how, about, like, as soon as, even as, while
ἄνθος n. nom. neut. sg. ἄνθος flower
χόρτου n. gen. masc. sg. χόρτος grass, blade, hay
ὁ art. nom. masc. sg. ὁ ἡ τό the, this, that, he, she, it
χόρτος n. nom. masc. sg. χόρτος grass, blade, hay
καὶ conj. καί and, even, also, but
τὸ art. nom. neut. sg. ὁ ἡ τό the, this, that, he, she, it
ἄνθος n. nom. neut. sg. ἄνθος flower
αὐτοῦ pron. gen. masc. 3p. sg. αὐτός ἡ ὁ self, of oneself, even, very, the same, he, she, it
25 τὸ art. nom. neut. sg. ὁ ἡ τό the, this, that, he, she, it
δὲ conj. δέ but, and, now, also, to the contrary, rather, then
ῥῆμα n. nom. neut. sg. ῥῆμα word, saying, thing
Κυρίου n. gen. masc. sg. κύριος Lord, lord, master, sir, LORD, God, Master, owner
εἰς prep. εἰς (+acc) into, to, unto, for, in, on, toward, against, upon, at, among
τὸν art. acc. masc. sg. ὁ ἡ τό the, this, that, he, she, it
αἰῶνα n. acc. masc. sg. αἰών ever, ever and ever, evermore, age, eternal, world
τοῦτο demo. pron. nom. neut. sg. οὗτος αὕτη τοῦτο this, the same, this same, he, she, it
δὲ conj. δέ but, and, now, also, to the contrary, rather, then
τὸ art. nom. neut. sg. ὁ ἡ τό the, this, that, he, she, it
ῥῆμα n. nom. neut. sg. ῥῆμα word, saying, thing
τὸ art. nom. neut. sg. ὁ ἡ τό the, this, that, he, she, it
εἰς prep. εἰς (+acc) into, to, unto, for, in, on, toward, against, upon, at, among
ὑμᾶς pron. acc. 2p. pl. σύ thou, you

2

1 οὖν conj. οὖν therefore, then, so, and, now, wherefore
πᾶσαν adj. acc. fem. sg. πᾶς πᾶσα πᾶν all, every, whosoever, every one, no, whole, any
κακίαν n. acc. fem. sg. κακία malice, maliciousness, evil, naughtiness, wickedness
καὶ conj. καί and, even, also, but
πάντα adj. acc. masc. sg. πᾶς πᾶσα πᾶν all, every, whosoever, every one, no, whole, any
δόλον n. acc. masc. sg. δόλος guile, deceit, subtilty, craft
καὶ conj. καί and, even, also, but
ὑποκρίσεις n. acc. fem. pl. ὑπόκρισις hypocrisy, condemnation, dissimulation
καὶ conj. καί and, even, also, but
φθόνους n. acc. masc. pl. φθόνος envy, envying
καὶ conj. καί and, even, also, but
πάσας adj. acc. fem. pl. πᾶς πᾶσα πᾶν all, every, whosoever, every one, no, whole, any
καταλαλιάς n. acc. fem. pl. καταλαλιά backbiting, evil speaking
2 ὡς adv. ὡς as, when, as it were, how, about, like, as soon as, even as, while
ἀρτιγέννητα adj. nom. neut. pl. ἀρτιγέννητος newborn
βρέφη n. nom. neut. pl. βρέφος babe, child, infant, young child
τὸ art. acc. neut. sg. ὁ ἡ τό the, this, that, he, she, it
λογικὸν adj. acc. neut. sg. λογικός reasonable, of the word
ἄδολον adj. acc. neut. sg. ἄδολος sincere
γάλα n. acc. neut. sg. γάλα milk
ἵνα conj. ἵνα that, to, lest, for to, so that, albeit, because, for, so as
ἐν prep. ἐν (+dat) in, by, with, among, at, on, through, to, within, into, of, for
αὐτῷ pron. dat. neut. 3p. sg. αὐτός ἡ ὁ self, of oneself, even, very, the same, he, she, it
3 εἴπερ conj. εἴπερ if it be so that, if indeed, since indeed, since, although indeed
ὅτι conj. ὅτι that, for, because, how that, how, because that, for that, though
χρηστὸς adj. nom. masc. sg. χρηστός easy, kind, better, good, gracious, goodness

ὁ art. nom. masc. sg. ὁ ἡ τό the, this, that, he, she, it
Κύριος n. nom. masc. sg. κύριος Lord, lord, master, sir, LORD, God, Master, owner
4 πρὸς prep. πρός (+gen) for, (+dat) at, (+acc) unto, to, with, for, against
ὃν relative pron. acc. masc. sg. ὅς ἥ ὅ who, which, what, that
λίθον n. acc. masc. sg. λίθος stone
ὑπὸ prep. ὑπό (+gen) of, by, with, from, among, (+acc) under
ἀνθρώπων n. gen. masc. pl. ἄνθρωπος man, human being, person, one, certain
μὲν conj. μέν indeed, verily, truly, even, so, some
παρὰ prep. παρά (+gen) of, from, (+dat) with, for, (+acc) beside, at, by, above, against
δὲ conj. δέ but, and, now, also, to the contrary, rather, then
Θεῷ n. dat. masc. sg. θεός God, god
ἐκλεκτὸν adj. acc. masc. sg. ἐκλεκτός elect, chosen
ἔντιμον adj. acc. masc. sg. ἔντιμος dear, precious, in reputation, more honourable
5 καὶ conj. καί and, even, also, but
αὐτοὶ pron. nom. masc. 2p. pl. αὐτός ή ό self, of oneself, even, very, the same, he, she, it
ὡς adv. ὡς as, when, as it were, how, about, like, as soon as, even as, while
λίθοι n. nom. masc. pl. λίθος stone
οἶκος n. nom. masc. sg. οἶκος house, home, household
πνευματικὸς adj. nom. masc. sg. πνευματικός spiritual
ἱεράτευμα n. acc. neut. sg. ἱεράτευμα priesthood
ἅγιον adj. acc. neut. sg. ἅγιος Holy, holy, saint, Holy One, holy thing, most holy
πνευματικὰς adj. acc. fem. pl. πνευματικός spiritual
θυσίας n. acc. fem. pl. θυσία sacrifice
εὐπροσδέκτους adj. acc. fem. pl. εὐπρόσδεκτος acceptable, accepted
τῷ art. dat. masc. sg. ὁ ἡ τό the, this, that, he, she, it
Θεῷ n. dat. masc. sg. θεός God, god
διὰ prep. διά (+gen) by, through, with, in, of, (+acc) for, because of, for a cause
Ἰησοῦ n. gen. masc. sg. Ἰησοῦς Jesus
Χριστοῦ n. gen. masc. sg. Χριστός Christ
6 διὸ conj. διό wherefore, therefore, for which cause
καὶ conj. καί and, even, also, but
ἐν prep. ἐν (+dat) in, by, with, among, at, on, through, to, within, into, of, for
τῇ art. dat. fem. sg. ὁ ἡ τό the, this, that, he, she, it
γραφῇ n. dat. fem. sg. γραφή scripture
ἐν prep. ἐν (+dat) in, by, with, among, at, on, through, to, within, into, of, for
Σιὼν n. dat. fem. sg. Σιών Sion
λίθον n. acc. masc. sg. λίθος stone
ἀκρογωνιαῖον adj. acc. masc. sg. ἀκρογωνιαῖος chief corner
ἐκλεκτὸν adj. acc. masc. sg. ἐκλεκτός elect, chosen
ἔντιμον adj. acc. masc. sg. ἔντιμος dear, precious, in reputation, more honourable
καὶ conj. καί and, even, also, but
ὁ art. nom. masc. sg. ὁ ἡ τό the, this, that, he, she, it
ἐπ' prep. ἐπί (+gen) on, in, upon, (+dat) in, at, for, upon, (+acc) on, upon, unto, to, against
αὐτῷ pron. dat. masc. 3p. sg. αὐτός ή ό self, of oneself, even, very, the same, he, she, it
οὐ particle of negation. οὐ οὐκ οὐχ not, no, neither, none, nay, nor, never, nothing
μὴ particle of negation. μή not, no, lest, neither, none, nothing, nor, never, without
7 ὑμῖν pron. dat. 2p. pl. σύ thou, you
οὖν conj. οὖν therefore, then, so, and, now, wherefore
ἡ art. nom. fem. sg. ὁ ἡ τό the, this, that, he, she, it
τιμὴ n. nom. fem. sg. τιμή honour, price, preciousness, sum
τοῖς art. dat. masc. pl. ὁ ἡ τό the, this, that, he, she, it
δὲ conj. δέ but, and, now, also, to the contrary, rather, then
Λίθον n. acc. masc. sg. λίθος stone
ὃν relative pron. acc. masc. sg. ὅς ἥ ὅ who, which, what, that
οἱ art. nom. masc. pl. ὁ ἡ τό the, this, that, he, she, it

οὗτος demo. pron. nom. masc. sg. οὗτος αὕτη τοῦτο this, the same, this same, he, she, it
εἰς prep. εἰς (+acc) into, to, unto, for, in, on, toward, against, upon, at, among
κεφαλὴν n. acc. fem. sg. κεφαλή head
γωνίας n. gen. fem. sg. γωνία corner, quarter
8 καὶ conj. καί and, even, also, but
Λίθος n. nom. masc. sg. λίθος stone
προσκόμματος n. gen. neut. sg. πρόσκομμα stumbling, offence
καὶ conj. καί and, even, also, but
πέτρα n. nom. fem. sg. πέτρα rock
σκανδάλου n. gen. neut. sg. σκάνδαλον offence, stumblingblock, thing that offend
οἳ relative pron. nom. masc. pl. ὅς ἥ ὅ who, which, what, that
τῷ art. dat. masc. sg. ὁ ἡ τό the, this, that, he, she, it
λόγῳ n. dat. masc. sg. λόγος word, saying, account, speech, thing, matter
εἰς prep. εἰς (+acc) into, to, unto, for, in, on, toward, against, upon, at, among
ὃ relative pron. acc. neut. sg. ὅς ἥ ὅ who, which, what, that
καὶ conj. καί and, even, also, but
9 ὑμεῖς pron. nom. 2p. pl. σύ thou, you
δὲ conj. δέ but, and, now, also, to the contrary, rather, then
γένος n. nom. neut. sg. γένος kind, kindred, offspring, nation, countrymen
ἐκλεκτόν adj. nom. neut. sg. ἐκλεκτός elect, chosen
βασίλειον adj. nom. neut. sg. βασίλειος royal
ἱεράτευμα n. nom. neut. sg. ἱεράτευμα priesthood
ἔθνος n. nom. neut. sg. ἔθνος Gentile, nation, heathen, people
ἅγιον adj. nom. neut. sg. ἅγιος Holy, holy, saint, Holy One, holy thing, most holy
λαὸς n. nom. masc. sg. λαός people
εἰς prep. εἰς (+acc) into, to, unto, for, in, on, toward, against, upon, at, among
περιποίησιν n. acc. fem. sg. περιποίησις peculiar, obtain, obtaining, saving
ὅπως adv. ὅπως that, how, to, because, so that, when
τὰς art. acc. fem. pl. ὁ ἡ τό the, this, that, he, she, it
ἀρετὰς n. acc. fem. pl. ἀρετή virtue, praise
τοῦ art. gen. masc. sg. ὁ ἡ τό the, this, that, he, she, it
ἐκ prep. ἐκ ἐξ (+gen) of, from, out of, by, on, with, in, among, through
σκότους n. gen. neut. sg. σκότος darkness
ὑμᾶς pron. acc. 2p. pl. σύ thou, you
εἰς prep. εἰς (+acc) into, to, unto, for, in, on, toward, against, upon, at, among
τὸ art. acc. neut. sg. ὁ ἡ τό the, this, that, he, she, it
θαυμαστὸν adj. acc. neut. sg. θαυμαστός marvellous, marvel
αὐτοῦ pron. gen. masc. 3p. sg. αὐτός ἡ ὁ self, of oneself, even, very, the same, he, she, it
φῶς n. acc. neut. sg. φῶς light, fire
10 οἵ art. nom. masc. pl. ὁ ἡ τό the, this, that, he, she, it
ποτε adv. ποτέ in time past, at any time, sometimes, in old time, once, when
οὐ particle of negation. οὐ οὐκ οὐχ not, no, neither, none, nay, nor, never, nothing
λαὸς n. nom. masc. sg. λαός people
νῦν adv. νῦν now, henceforth, present, this time
δὲ conj. δέ but, and, now, also, to the contrary, rather, then
λαὸς n. nom. masc. sg. λαός people
Θεοῦ n. gen. masc. sg. θεός God, god
οἱ art. nom. masc. pl. ὁ ἡ τό the, this, that, he, she, it
οὐκ particle of negation. οὐ οὐκ οὐχ not, no, neither, none, nay, nor, never, nothing
νῦν adv. νῦν now, henceforth, present, this time
δὲ conj. δέ but, and, now, also, to the contrary, rather, then
11 Ἀγαπητοί adj. voc. masc. pl. ἀγαπητός beloved, dearly beloved, dear, wellbeloved
ὡς adv. ὡς as, when, as it were, how, about, like, as soon as, even as, while
παροίκους adj. acc. masc. pl. πάροικος sojourn, stranger, foreigner
καὶ conj. καί and, even, also, but

παρεπιδήμους adj. acc. masc. pl. παρεπίδημος pilgrim
τῶν art. gen. fem. pl. ὁ ἡ τό the, this, that, he, she, it
σαρκικῶν adj. gen. fem. pl. σαρκικός carnal, fleshly
ἐπιθυμιῶν n. gen. fem. pl. ἐπιθυμία lust, concupiscence, desire
αἵτινες relative pron. nom. fem. pl. ὅστις which, who, whosoever, that, whatsoever
κατὰ prep. κατά (+gen) against, by, throughout, down, (+acc) according to, after, with
τῆς art. gen. fem. sg. ὁ ἡ τό the, this, that, he, she, it
ψυχῆς n. gen. fem. sg. ψυχή life, soul, mind, heart
12 τὴν art. acc. fem. sg. ὁ ἡ τό the, this, that, he, she, it
ἀναστροφὴν n. acc. fem. sg. ἀναστροφή conversation
ὑμῶν pron. gen. 2p. pl. σύ thou, you
ἐν prep. ἐν (+dat) in, by, with, among, at, on, through, to, within, into, of, for
τοῖς art. dat. neut. pl. ὁ ἡ τό the, this, that, he, she, it
ἔθνεσιν n. dat. neut. pl. ἔθνος Gentile, nation, heathen, people
καλήν adj. acc. fem. sg. καλός good, better, goodly, meet, honest, fair, well, worthy
ἵνα conj. ἵνα that, to, lest, for to, so that, albeit, because, for, so as
ἐν prep. ἐν (+dat) in, by, with, among, at, on, through, to, within, into, of, for
ᾧ relative pron. dat. neut. sg. ὅς ἥ ὅ who, which, what, that
ὑμῶν pron. gen. 2p. pl. σύ thou, you
ὡς adv. ὡς as, when, as it were, how, about, like, as soon as, even as, while
κακοποιῶν adj. gen. masc. pl. κακοποιός evildoer, malefactor
ἐκ prep. ἐκ ἐξ (+gen) of, from, out of, by, on, with, in, among, through
τῶν art. gen. neut. pl. ὁ ἡ τό the, this, that, he, she, it
καλῶν adj. gen. neut. pl. καλός good, better, goodly, meet, honest, fair, well, worthy
ἔργων n. gen. neut. pl. ἔργον work, deed, doing labour
τὸν art. acc. masc. sg. ὁ ἡ τό the, this, that, he, she, it
Θεὸν n. acc. masc. sg. θεός God, god
ἐν prep. ἐν (+dat) in, by, with, among, at, on, through, to, within, into, of, for
ἡμέρᾳ n. dat. fem. sg. ἡμέρα day, time, year, while, age, day time
ἐπισκοπῆς n. gen. fem. sg. ἐπισκοπή bishoprick, visitation, the office of a bishop
13 οὖν conj. οὖν therefore, then, so, and, now, wherefore
πάσῃ adj. dat. fem. sg. πᾶς πᾶσα πᾶν all, every, whosoever, every one, no, whole, any
ἀνθρωπίνῃ adj. dat. fem. sg. ἀνθρώπινος man, after the manner of men man
κτίσει n. dat. fem. sg. κτίσις creature, creation, building, ordinance
διὰ prep. διά (+gen) by, through, with, in, of, (+acc) for, because of, for a cause
τὸν art. acc. masc. sg. ὁ ἡ τό the, this, that, he, she, it
Κύριον n. acc. masc. sg. κύριος Lord, lord, master, sir, LORD, God, Master, owner
εἴτε conj. εἴτε whether
βασιλεῖ n. dat. masc. sg. βασιλεύς king
ὡς adv. ὡς as, when, as it were, how, about, like, as soon as, even as, while
14 εἴτε conj. εἴτε whether
ἡγεμόσιν n. dat. masc. pl. ἡγεμών governor, ruler, prince
ὡς adv. ὡς as, when, as it were, how, about, like, as soon as, even as, while
δι' prep. διά (+gen) by, through, with, in, of, (+acc) for, because of, for a cause
αὐτοῦ pron. gen. masc. 3p. sg. αὐτός ἡ ὁ self, of oneself, even, very, the same, he, she, it
εἰς prep. εἰς (+acc) into, to, unto, for, in, on, toward, against, upon, at, among
ἐκδίκησιν n. acc. fem. sg. ἐκδίκησις vengeance, punishment, revenge
μὲν conj. μέν indeed, verily, truly, even, so, some
κακοποιῶν adj. gen. masc. pl. κακοποιός evildoer, malefactor
ἔπαινον n. acc. masc. sg. ἔπαινος praise
δὲ conj. δέ but, and, now, also, to the contrary, rather, then
ἀγαθοποιῶν adj. gen. masc. pl. ἀγαθοποιός that do well
15 ὅτι conj. ὅτι that, for, because, how that, how, because that, for that, though
οὕτως adv. οὕτω οὕτως so, even so, thus, on this wise, likewise, after this manner
τὸ art. nom. neut. sg. ὁ ἡ τό the, this, that, he, she, it

θέλημα n. nom. neut. sg. θέλημα will, desire, pleasure
τοῦ art. gen. masc. sg. ὁ ἡ τό the, this, that, he, she, it
Θεοῦ n. gen. masc. sg. θεός God, god
τὴν art. acc. fem. sg. ὁ ἡ τό the, this, that, he, she, it
τῶν art. gen. masc. pl. ὁ ἡ τό the, this, that, he, she, it
ἀφρόνων adj. gen. masc. pl. ἄφρων fool, foolish, unwise
ἀνθρώπων n. gen. masc. pl. ἄνθρωπος man, human being, person, one, certain
ἀγνωσίαν n. acc. fem. sg. ἀγνωσία not the knowledge, ignorance
16 ὡς adv. ὡς as, when, as it were, how, about, like, as soon as, even as, while
ἐλεύθεροι adj. nom. masc. pl. ἐλεύθερος free, freewoman, at liberty, freeman
καὶ conj. καί and, even, also, but
μὴ particle of negation. μή not, no, lest, neither, none, nothing, nor, never, without
ὡς adv. ὡς as, when, as it were, how, about, like, as soon as, even as, while
ἐπικάλυμμα n. acc. neut. sg. ἐπικάλυμμα cloke
τῆς art. gen. fem. sg. ὁ ἡ τό the, this, that, he, she, it
κακίας n. gen. fem. sg. κακία malice, maliciousness, evil, naughtiness, wickedness
τὴν art. acc. fem. sg. ὁ ἡ τό the, this, that, he, she, it
ἐλευθερίαν n. acc. fem. sg. ἐλευθερία liberty
ἀλλ' conj. ἀλλά but, yea, yet, nevertheless, howbeit, nay, therefore
ὡς adv. ὡς as, when, as it were, how, about, like, as soon as, even as, while
δοῦλοι n. nom. masc. pl. δοῦλος servant, bondman, bond, slave
Θεοῦ n. gen. masc. sg. θεός God, god
17 πάντας adj. acc. masc. pl. πᾶς πᾶσα πᾶν all, every, whosoever, every one, no, whole, any
τὴν art. acc. fem. sg. ὁ ἡ τό the, this, that, he, she, it
ἀδελφότητα n. acc. fem. sg. ἀδελφότης brotherhood brethren
τὸν art. acc. masc. sg. ὁ ἡ τό the, this, that, he, she, it
Θεὸν n. acc. masc. sg. θεός God, god
τὸν art. acc. masc. sg. ὁ ἡ τό the, this, that, he, she, it
βασιλέα n. acc. masc. sg. βασιλεύς king
18 Οἱ art. nom. masc. pl. ὁ ἡ τό the, this, that, he, she, it
οἰκέται n. nom. masc. pl. οἰκέτης servant, household servant
ἐν prep. ἐν (+dat) in, by, with, among, at, on, through, to, within, into, of, for
παντὶ adj. dat. masc. sg. πᾶς πᾶσα πᾶν all, every, whosoever, every one, no, whole, any
φόβῳ n. dat. masc. sg. φόβος fear, terror, sore afraid
τοῖς art. dat. masc. pl. ὁ ἡ τό the, this, that, he, she, it
δεσπόταις n. dat. masc. pl. δεσπότης Lord, master
οὐ particle of negation. οὐ οὐκ οὐχ not, no, neither, none, nay, nor, never, nothing
μόνον adv. μόνος only, alone, by oneself
τοῖς art. dat. masc. pl. ὁ ἡ τό the, this, that, he, she, it
ἀγαθοῖς adj. dat. masc. pl. ἀγαθός good, good thing, that which is good, well
καὶ conj. καί and, even, also, but
ἐπιεικέσιν adj. dat. masc. pl. ἐπιεικής moderation, gentle, patient
ἀλλὰ conj. ἀλλά but, yea, yet, nevertheless, howbeit, nay, therefore
καὶ conj. καί and, even, also, but
τοῖς art. dat. masc. pl. ὁ ἡ τό the, this, that, he, she, it
σκολιοῖς adj. dat. masc. pl. σκολιός crooked, froward, untoward
19 τοῦτο demo. pron. nom. neut. sg. οὗτος αὕτη τοῦτο this, the same, this same, he, she, it
γὰρ conj. γάρ for, and, because, but, indeed
χάρις n. nom. fem. sg. χάρις grace, thank, favour, pleasure
εἰ conj. εἰ if, whether, that, though, forasmuch
διὰ prep. διά (+gen) by, through, with, in, of, (+acc) for, because of, for a cause
συνείδησιν n. acc. fem. sg. συνείδησις conscience
Θεοῦ n. gen. masc. sg. θεός God, god
τις indefinite pron. nom. masc. sg. τὶς certain, some, any man, one, any thing
λύπας n. acc. fem. pl. λύπη sorrow, heaviness, grief, grievous, grudgingly

ἀδίκως adv. ἀδίκως wrongfully
20 ποῖον interrog. pron. nom. neut. sg. ποῖος what, which, what manner of
γὰρ conj. γάρ for, and, because, but, indeed
κλέος n. nom. neut. sg. κλέος glory
εἰ conj. εἰ if, whether, that, though, forasmuch
καὶ conj. καί and, even, also, but
ἀλλ' conj. ἀλλά but, yea, yet, nevertheless, howbeit, nay, therefore
εἰ conj. εἰ if, whether, that, though, forasmuch
καὶ conj. καί and, even, also, but
τοῦτο demo. pron. nom. neut. sg. οὗτος αὕτη τοῦτο this, the same, this same, he, she, it
χάρις n. nom. fem. sg. χάρις grace, thank, favour, pleasure
παρὰ prep. παρά (+gen) of, from, (+dat) with, for, (+acc) beside, at, by, above, against
Θεῷ n. dat. masc. sg. θεός God, god
21 εἰς prep. εἰς (+acc) into, to, unto, for, in, on, toward, against, upon, at, among
τοῦτο demo. pron. acc. neut. sg. οὗτος αὕτη τοῦτο this, the same, this same, he, she, it
γὰρ conj. γάρ for, and, because, but, indeed
ὅτι conj. ὅτι that, for, because, how that, how, because that, for that, though
καὶ conj. καί and, even, also, but
Χριστὸς n. nom. masc. sg. Χριστός Christ
ὑπὲρ prep. ὑπέρ (+gen) for, of, for the sake of, (+acc) above, more than
ἡμῶν pron. gen. 1p. pl. ἐγώ I
ἡμῖν pron. dat. 1p. pl. ἐγώ I
ὑπογραμμὸν n. acc. masc. sg. ὑπογραμμός example
ἵνα conj. ἵνα that, to, lest, for to, so that, albeit, because, for, so as
τοῖς art. dat. neut. pl. ὁ ἡ τό the, this, that, he, she, it
ἴχνεσιν n. dat. neut. pl. ἴχνος step
αὐτοῦ pron. gen. masc. 3p. sg. αὐτός ή ό self, of oneself, even, very, the same, he, she, it
22 ὃς relative pron. nom. masc. sg. ὅς ἥ ὅ who, which, what, that
ἁμαρτίαν n. acc. fem. sg. ἁμαρτία sin, offence, sinful
οὐκ particle of negation. οὐ οὐκ οὐχ not, no, neither, none, nay, nor, never, nothing
οὐδὲ adv. οὐδέ neither, nor, not, no, not even, never, not yet
δόλος n. nom. masc. sg. δόλος guile, deceit, subtilty, craft
ἐν prep. ἐν (+dat) in, by, with, among, at, on, through, to, within, into, of, for
τῷ art. dat. neut. sg. ὁ ἡ τό the, this, that, he, she, it
στόματι n. dat. neut. sg. στόμα mouth, face, edge
αὐτοῦ pron. gen. masc. 3p. sg. αὐτός ή ό self, of oneself, even, very, the same, he, she, it
23 ὃς relative pron. nom. masc. sg. ὅς ἥ ὅ who, which, what, that
οὐκ particle of negation. οὐ οὐκ οὐχ not, no, neither, none, nay, nor, never, nothing
οὐκ particle of negation. οὐ οὐκ οὐχ not, no, neither, none, nay, nor, never, nothing
δὲ conj. δέ but, and, now, also, to the contrary, rather, then
τῷ art. dat. masc. sg. ὁ ἡ τό the, this, that, he, she, it
δικαίως adv. δικαίως justly, righteously
24 ὃς relative pron. nom. masc. sg. ὅς ἥ ὅ who, which, what, that
τὰς art. acc. fem. pl. ὁ ἡ τό the, this, that, he, she, it
ἁμαρτίας n. acc. fem. pl. ἁμαρτία sin, offence, sinful
ἡμῶν pron. gen. 1p. pl. ἐγώ I
αὐτὸς pron. nom. masc. 3p. sg. αὐτός ή ό self, of oneself, even, very, the same, he, she, it
ἐν prep. ἐν (+dat) in, by, with, among, at, on, through, to, within, into, of, for
τῷ art. dat. neut. sg. ὁ ἡ τό the, this, that, he, she, it
σώματι n. dat. neut. sg. σῶμα body, bodily, slave
αὐτοῦ pron. gen. masc. 3p. sg. αὐτός ή ό self, of oneself, even, very, the same, he, she, it
ἐπὶ prep. ἐπί (+gen) on, in, upon, (+dat) in, at, for, upon, (+acc) on, upon, unto, to, against
τὸ art. acc. neut. sg. ὁ ἡ τό the, this, that, he, she, it
ξύλον n. acc. neut. sg. ξύλον tree, stave, wood, the stocks
ἵνα conj. ἵνα that, to, lest, for to, so that, albeit, because, for, so as

ταῖς art. dat. fem. pl. ὁ ἡ τό the, this, that, he, she, it
ἁμαρτίαις n. dat. fem. pl. ἁμαρτία sin, offence, sinful
τῇ art. dat. fem. sg. ὁ ἡ τό the, this, that, he, she, it
δικαιοσύνῃ n. dat. fem. sg. δικαιοσύνη righteousness
οὗ relative pron. gen. masc. sg. ὅς ἥ ὅ who, which, what, that
τῷ art. dat. masc. sg. ὁ ἡ τό the, this, that, he, she, it
μώλωπι n. dat. masc. sg. μώλωψ stripe
αὐτοῦ pron. gen. masc. 3p. sg. αὐτός ή ό self, of oneself, even, very, the same, he, she, it
25 γὰρ conj. γάρ for, and, because, but, indeed
ὡς adv. ὡς as, when, as it were, how, about, like, as soon as, even as, while
πρόβατα n. nom. neut. pl. πρόβατον sheep
ἀλλ' conj. ἀλλά but, yea, yet, nevertheless, howbeit, nay, therefore
νῦν adv. νῦν now, henceforth, present, this time
ἐπὶ prep. ἐπί (+gen) on, in, upon, (+dat) in, at, for, upon, (+acc) on, upon, unto, to, against
τὸν art. acc. masc. sg. ὁ ἡ τό the, this, that, he, she, it
ποιμένα n. acc. masc. sg. ποιμήν shepherd, pastor
καὶ conj. καί and, even, also, but
ἐπίσκοπον n. acc. masc. sg. ἐπίσκοπος overseer, bishop
τῶν art. gen. fem. pl. ὁ ἡ τό the, this, that, he, she, it
ψυχῶν n. gen. fem. pl. ψυχή life, soul, mind, heart
ὑμῶν pron. gen. 2p. pl. σύ thou, you

3

1 Ὁμοίως adv. ὁμοίως likewise, so
αἱ art. nom. fem. pl. ὁ ἡ τό the, this, that, he, she, it
γυναῖκες n. nom. fem. pl. γυνή woman, wife
τοῖς art. dat. masc. pl. ὁ ἡ τό the, this, that, he, she, it
ἰδίοις adj. dat. masc. pl. ἴδιος one's own, one's, privately
ἀνδράσιν n. dat. masc. pl. ἀνήρ man, husband, sir
ἵνα conj. ἵνα that, to, lest, for to, so that, albeit, because, for, so as
καὶ conj. καί and, even, also, but
εἴ conj. εἰ if, whether, that, though, forasmuch
τινες indefinite pron. nom. masc. pl. τὶς certain, some, any man, one, any thing
τῷ art. dat. masc. sg. ὁ ἡ τό the, this, that, he, she, it
λόγῳ n. dat. masc. sg. λόγος word, saying, account, speech, thing, matter
διὰ prep. διά (+gen) by, through, with, in, of, (+acc) for, because of, for a cause
τῆς art. gen. fem. sg. ὁ ἡ τό the, this, that, he, she, it
τῶν art. gen. fem. pl. ὁ ἡ τό the, this, that, he, she, it
γυναικῶν n. gen. fem. pl. γυνή woman, wife
ἀναστροφῆς n. gen. fem. sg. ἀναστροφή conversation
ἄνευ prep. ἄνευ without
λόγου n. gen. masc. sg. λόγος word, saying, account, speech, thing, matter
2 τὴν art. acc. fem. sg. ὁ ἡ τό the, this, that, he, she, it
ἐν prep. ἐν (+dat) in, by, with, among, at, on, through, to, within, into, of, for
φόβῳ n. dat. masc. sg. φόβος fear, terror, sore afraid
ἁγνὴν adj. acc. fem. sg. ἁγνός clear, pure, chaste
ἀναστροφὴν n. acc. fem. sg. ἀναστροφή conversation
ὑμῶν pron. gen. 2p. pl. σύ thou, you
3 ὧν relative pron. gen. fem. pl. ὅς ἥ ὅ who, which, what, that
οὐχ particle of negation. οὐ οὐκ οὐχ not, no, neither, none, nay, nor, never, nothing
ὁ art. nom. masc. sg. ὁ ἡ τό the, this, that, he, she, it
ἔξωθεν adv. ἔξωθεν without, from without, outside, outward, outwardly
ἐμπλοκῆς n. gen. fem. sg. ἐμπλοκή plaiting
τριχῶν n. gen. fem. pl. θρίξ hair

καὶ conj. καί and, even, also, but
περιθέσεως n. gen. fem. sg. περίθεσις wearing
χρυσίων n. gen. neut. pl. χρυσίον gold
ἢ particle. ἤ or, than, either, nor, or else, and, rather than
ἐνδύσεως n. gen. fem. sg. ἔνδυσις putting on
ἱματίων n. gen. neut. pl. ἱμάτιον cloke, garment, clothes, raiment, robe, vesture
κόσμος n. nom. masc. sg. κόσμος world, adorning
4 ἀλλ' conj. ἀλλά but, yea, yet, nevertheless, howbeit, nay, therefore
ὁ art. nom. masc. sg. ὁ ἡ τό the, this, that, he, she, it
κρυπτὸς adj. nom. masc. sg. κρυπτός secret, hid, hidden, inwardly
τῆς art. gen. fem. sg. ὁ ἡ τό the, this, that, he, she, it
καρδίας n. gen. fem. sg. καρδία heart
ἄνθρωπος n. nom. masc. sg. ἄνθρωπος man, human being, person, one, certain
ἐν prep. ἐν (+dat) in, by, with, among, at, on, through, to, within, into, of, for
τῷ art. dat. masc. sg. ὁ ἡ τό the, this, that, he, she, it
φθάρτῳ adj. dat. masc. sg. ἄφθαρτος uncorruptible, incorruptible, immortal, not corruptible
τοῦ art. gen. neut. sg. ὁ ἡ τό the, this, that, he, she, it
πρᾳέος adj. gen. neut. sg. πραΰς meek
καὶ conj. καί and, even, also, but
ἡσυχίου adj. gen. neut. sg. ἡσύχιος peaceable, quiet
πνεύματος n. gen. neut. sg. πνεῦμα spirit, Spirit, Ghost, ghost, life. of the spirit, wind
ὅ relative pron. nom. neut. sg. ὅς ἥ ὅ who, which, what, that
ἐνώπιον prep. ἐνώπιον (+gen) before, in the sight of, in the presence of. (adv.) before
τοῦ art. gen. masc. sg. ὁ ἡ τό the, this, that, he, she, it
Θεοῦ n. gen. masc. sg. θεός God, god
πολυτελές adj. nom. neut. sg. πολυτελής very precious, costly, of great price
5 οὕτω adv. οὕτω οὕτως so, even so, thus, on this wise, likewise, after this manner
γάρ conj. γάρ for, and, because, but, indeed
ποτε adv. ποτέ in time past, at any time, sometimes, in old time, once, when
καὶ conj. καί and, even, also, but
αἱ art. nom. fem. pl. ὁ ἡ τό the, this, that, he, she, it
ἅγιαι adj. nom. fem. pl. ἅγιος Holy, holy, saint, Holy One, holy thing, most holy
γυναῖκες n. nom. fem. pl. γυνή woman, wife
αἱ art. nom. fem. pl. ὁ ἡ τό the, this, that, he, she, it
ἐπὶ prep. ἐπί (+gen) on, in, upon, (+dat) in, at, for, upon, (+acc) on, upon, unto, to, against
τὸν art. acc. masc. sg. ὁ ἡ τό the, this, that, he, she, it
Θεὸν n. acc. masc. sg. θεός God, god
ἑαυτάς reflexive pron. acc. fem. 3p. pl. ἑαυτοῦ himself, herself, itself, yourself, ourselves
τοῖς art. dat. masc. pl. ὁ ἡ τό the, this, that, he, she, it
ἰδίοις adj. dat. masc. pl. ἴδιος one's own, one's, privately
ἀνδράσιν n. dat. masc. pl. ἀνήρ man, husband, sir
6 ὡς adv. ὡς as, when, as it were, how, about, like, as soon as, even as, while
Σάρρα n. nom. fem. sg. Σάρρα Sara, Sarah
τῷ art. dat. masc. sg. ὁ ἡ τό the, this, that, he, she, it
'Αβραάμ n. dat. masc. sg. 'Αβραάμ Abraham
κύριον n. acc. masc. sg. κύριος Lord, lord, master, sir, LORD, God, Master, owner
αὐτὸν pron. acc. masc. 3p. sg. αὐτός ἡ ὁ self, of oneself, even, very, the same, he, she, it
ἧς relative pron. gen. fem. sg. ὅς ἥ ὅ who, which, what, that
τέκνα n. nom. neut. pl. τέκνον child, son, daughter
καὶ conj. καί and, even, also, but
μὴ particle of negation. μή not, no, lest, neither, none, nothing, nor, never, without
μηδεμίαν num. acc. fem. sg. μηδείς μηδεμία μηδέν no man, nothing, no, none, not at all
πτόησιν n. acc. fem. sg. πτόησις amazement
7 Οἱ art. nom. masc. pl. ὁ ἡ τό the, this, that, he, she, it
ἄνδρες n. nom. masc. pl. ἀνήρ man, husband, sir

ὁμοίως adv. ὁμοίως likewise, so
κατὰ prep. κατά (+gen) against, by, throughout, down, (+acc) according to, after, with
γνῶσιν n. acc. fem. sg. γνῶσις knowledge, science
ὡς adv. ὡς as, when, as it were, how, about, like, as soon as, even as, while
ἀσθενεστέρῳ compar. adj. dat. neut. sg. ἀσθενής weak, sick, impotent, more feeble
σκεύει n. dat. neut. sg. σκεῦος vessel, good, sail, stuff
τῷ art. dat. neut. sg. ὁ ἡ τό the, this, that, he, she, it
γυναικείῳ adj. dat. neut. sg. γυναικεῖος wife
τιμὴν n. acc. fem. sg. τιμή honour, price, preciousness, sum
ὡς adv. ὡς as, when, as it were, how, about, like, as soon as, even as, while
καὶ conj. καί and, even, also, but
συγκληρονόμοις adj. dat. masc. pl. συγκληρονόμος joint-heir, fellowheir, heir together
χάριτος n. gen. fem. sg. χάρις grace, thank, favour, pleasure
ζωῆς n. gen. fem. sg. ζωή life, lifetime
εἰς prep. εἰς (+acc) into, to, unto, for, in, on, toward, against, upon, at, among
τὸ art. acc. neut. sg. ὁ ἡ τό the, this, that, he, she, it
μὴ particle of negation. μή not, no, lest, neither, none, nothing, nor, never, without
τὰς art. acc. fem. pl. ὁ ἡ τό the, this, that, he, she, it
προσευχὰς n. acc. fem. pl. προσευχή prayer
ὑμῶν pron. gen. 2p. pl. σύ thou, you
8 Τὸ art. acc. neut. sg. ὁ ἡ τό the, this, that, he, she, it
δὲ conj. δέ but, and, now, also, to the contrary, rather, then
τέλος n. acc. neut. sg. τέλος end, custom, ending, finally, uttermost
πάντες adj. voc. masc. pl. πᾶς πᾶσα πᾶν all, every, whosoever, every one, no, whole, any
ὁμόφρονες adj. nom. masc. pl. ὁμόφρων of one mind
συμπαθεῖς adj. nom. masc. pl. συμπαθής having compassion one of another
φιλάδελφοι adj. nom. masc. pl. φιλάδελφος love as brethren
εὔσπλαγχνοι adj. nom. masc. pl. εὔσπλαγχνος tenderhearted, pitiful
φιλόφρονες adj. nom. masc. pl. φιλόφρων courteous
9 μὴ particle of negation. μή not, no, lest, neither, none, nothing, nor, never, without
κακὸν adj. acc. neut. sg. κακός evil, evil thing, noisome, wicked
ἀντὶ prep. ἀντί (+gen) for, because, in the room
κακοῦ adj. gen. neut. sg. κακός evil, evil thing, noisome, wicked
ἢ particle. ἤ or, than, either, nor, or else, and, rather than
λοιδορίαν n. acc. fem. sg. λοιδορία reproach, railing
ἀντὶ prep. ἀντί (+gen) for, because, in the room
λοιδορίας n. gen. fem. sg. λοιδορία reproach, railing
τοὐναντίον adv. τοὐναντίον contrariwise
δὲ conj. δέ but, and, now, also, to the contrary, rather, then
ὅτι conj. ὅτι that, for, because, how that, how, because that, for that, though
εἰς prep. εἰς (+acc) into, to, unto, for, in, on, toward, against, upon, at, among
τοῦτο demo. pron. acc. neut. sg. οὗτος αὕτη τοῦτο this, the same, this same, he, she, it
ἵνα conj. ἵνα that, to, lest, for to, so that, albeit, because, for, so as
εὐλογίαν n. acc. fem. sg. εὐλογία blessing, bounty, matter of bounty, fair speech
10 Ὁ art. nom. masc. sg. ὁ ἡ τό the, this, that, he, she, it
γὰρ conj. γάρ for, and, because, but, indeed
ζωὴν n. acc. fem. sg. ζωή life, lifetime
καὶ conj. καί and, even, also, but
ἡμέρας n. acc. fem. pl. ἡμέρα day, time, year, while, age, day time
ἀγαθὰς adj. acc. fem. pl. ἀγαθός good, good thing, that which is good, well
τὴν art. acc. fem. sg. ὁ ἡ τό the, this, that, he, she, it
γλῶσσαν n. acc. fem. sg. γλῶσσα tongue
αὐτοῦ pron. gen. masc. 3p. sg. αὐτός ή ό self, of oneself, even, very, the same, he, she, it
ἀπὸ prep. ἀπό (+gen) from, of, out of, since, for, off, at, by, in, on
κακοῦ adj. gen. neut. sg. κακός evil, evil thing, noisome, wicked

καὶ conj. καί and, even, also, but
χείλη n. acc. neut. pl. χεῖλος lip, shore
αὐτοῦ pron. gen. masc. 3p. sg. αὐτός ή ό self, of oneself, even, very, the same, he, she, it
τοῦ art. gen. neut. sg. ὁ ἡ τό the, this, that, he, she, it
μὴ particle of negation. μή not, no, lest, neither, none, nothing, nor, never, without
δόλον n. acc. masc. sg. δόλος guile, deceit, subtilty, craft
11 ἀπὸ prep. ἀπό (+gen) from, of, out of, since, for, off, at, by, in, on
κακοῦ adj. gen. neut. sg. κακός evil, evil thing, noisome, wicked
καὶ conj. καί and, even, also, but
ἀγαθόν adj. acc. neut. sg. ἀγαθός good, good thing, that which is good, well
εἰρήνην n. acc. fem. sg. εἰρήνη peace, quietness, rest
καὶ conj. καί and, even, also, but
αὐτήν pron. acc. fem. 3p. sg. αὐτός ή ό self, of oneself, even, very, the same, he, she, it
12 ὅτι conj. ὅτι that, for, because, how that, how, because that, for that, though
οἱ art. nom. masc. pl. ὁ ἡ τό the, this, that, he, she, it
ὀφθαλμοὶ n. nom. masc. pl. ὀφθαλμός eye, sight
Κυρίου n. gen. masc. sg. κύριος Lord, lord, master, sir, LORD, God, Master, owner
ἐπὶ prep. ἐπί (+gen) on, in, upon, (+dat) in, at, for, upon, (+acc) on, upon, unto, to, against
δικαίους adj. acc. masc. pl. δίκαιος righteous, just, meet, right
καὶ conj. καί and, even, also, but
ὦτα n. nom. neut. pl. οὖς ear
αὐτοῦ pron. gen. masc. 3p. sg. αὐτός ή ό self, of oneself, even, very, the same, he, she, it
εἰς prep. εἰς (+acc) into, to, unto, for, in, on, toward, against, upon, at, among
δέησιν n. acc. fem. sg. δέησις prayer, supplication, request
αὐτῶν pron. gen. masc. 3p. pl. αὐτός ή ό self, of oneself, even, very, the same, he, she, it
πρόσωπον n. nom. neut. sg. πρόσωπον face, presence, person, countenance
δὲ conj. δέ but, and, now, also, to the contrary, rather, then
Κυρίου n. gen. masc. sg. κύριος Lord, lord, master, sir, LORD, God, Master, owner
ἐπὶ prep. ἐπί (+gen) on, in, upon, (+dat) in, at, for, upon, (+acc) on, upon, unto, to, against
κακά adj. acc. neut. pl. κακός evil, evil thing, noisome, wicked
13 Καὶ conj. καί and, even, also, but
τίς interrog. pron. nom. masc. sg. τίς what, who, why, where, which, how
ὁ art. nom. masc. sg. ὁ ἡ τό the, this, that, he, she, it
ὑμᾶς pron. acc. 2p. pl. σύ thou, you
ἐὰν conj. ἐάν if, soever, except, though, and if, but, whether, if so, so
τοῦ art. gen. neut. sg. ὁ ἡ τό the, this, that, he, she, it
ἀγαθοῦ adj. gen. neut. sg. ἀγαθός good, good thing, that which is good, well
μιμηταὶ n. nom. masc. pl. μιμητής follower
14 ἀλλ' conj. ἀλλά but, yea, yet, nevertheless, howbeit, nay, therefore
εἰ conj. εἰ if, whether, that, though, forasmuch
καὶ conj. καί and, even, also, but
διὰ prep. διά (+gen) by, through, with, in, of, (+acc) for, because of, for a cause
δικαιοσύνην n. acc. fem. sg. δικαιοσύνη righteousness
μακάριοι adj. nom. masc. pl. μακάριος blessed, happy
Τὸν art. acc. masc. sg. ὁ ἡ τό the, this, that, he, she, it
δὲ conj. δέ but, and, now, also, to the contrary, rather, then
φόβον n. acc. masc. sg. φόβος fear, terror, sore afraid
αὐτῶν pron. gen. masc. 3p. pl. αὐτός ή ό self, of oneself, even, very, the same, he, she, it
μὴ particle of negation. μή not, no, lest, neither, none, nothing, nor, never, without
μηδὲ conj. μηδέ neither, nor, not, no not, nor yet, not once, not so much as
15 Κύριον n. acc. masc. sg. κύριος Lord, lord, master, sir, LORD, God, Master, owner
δὲ conj. δέ but, and, now, also, to the contrary, rather, then
τὸν art. acc. masc. sg. ὁ ἡ τό the, this, that, he, she, it
Θεὸν n. acc. masc. sg. θεός God, god
ἐν prep. ἐν (+dat) in, by, with, among, at, on, through, to, within, into, of, for

ταῖς art. dat. fem. pl. ὁ ἡ τό the, this, that, he, she, it
καρδίαις n. dat. fem. pl. καρδία heart
ὑμῶν pron. gen. 2p. pl. σύ thou, you
ἕτοιμοι adj. nom. masc. pl. ἕτοιμος ready, prepared, readiness
δὲ conj. δέ but, and, now, also, to the contrary, rather, then
ἀεὶ adv. ἀεί always, always, ever
πρὸς prep. πρός (+gen) for, (+dat) at, (+acc) unto, to, with, for, against
ἀπολογίαν n. acc. fem. sg. ἀπολογία defence, answer, answer for oneself, clear oneself
παντὶ adj. dat. masc. sg. πᾶς πᾶσα πᾶν all, every, whosoever, every one, no, whole, any
τῷ art. dat. masc. sg. ὁ ἡ τό the, this, that, he, she, it
ὑμᾶς pron. acc. 2p. pl. σύ thou, you
λόγον n. acc. masc. sg. λόγος word, saying, account, speech, thing, matter
περὶ prep. περί (+gen) of, for, concerning, (+acc) about, concerning, in
τῆς art. gen. fem. sg. ὁ ἡ τό the, this, that, he, she, it
ἐν prep. ἐν (+dat) in, by, with, among, at, on, through, to, within, into, of, for
ὑμῖν pron. dat. 2p. pl. σύ thou, you
ἐλπίδος n. gen. fem. sg. ἐλπίς hope, faith
μετὰ prep. μετά (+gen) with, among, against, (+acc) after
πρᾳΰτητος n. gen. fem. sg. πρᾳΰτης meekness
καὶ conj. καί and, even, also, but
φόβου n. gen. masc. sg. φόβος fear, terror, sore afraid
16 συνείδησιν n. acc. fem. sg. συνείδησις conscience
ἀγαθήν adj. acc. fem. sg. ἀγαθός good, good thing, that which is good, well
ἵνα conj. ἵνα that, to, lest, for to, so that, albeit, because, for, so as
ἐν prep. ἐν (+dat) in, by, with, among, at, on, through, to, within, into, of, for
ᾧ relative pron. dat. neut. sg. ὅς ἥ ὅ who, which, what, that
ὑμῶν pron. gen. 2p. pl. σύ thou, you
ὡς adv. ὡς as, when, as it were, how, about, like, as soon as, even as, while
κακοποιῶν adj. gen. masc. pl. κακοποιός evildoer, malefactor
οἱ art. nom. masc. pl. ὁ ἡ τό the, this, that, he, she, it
ὑμῶν pron. gen. 2p. pl. σύ thou, you
τὴν art. acc. fem. sg. ὁ ἡ τό the, this, that, he, she, it
ἀγαθὴν adj. acc. fem. sg. ἀγαθός good, good thing, that which is good, well
ἐν prep. ἐν (+dat) in, by, with, among, at, on, through, to, within, into, of, for
Χριστῷ n. dat. masc. sg. Χριστός Christ
ἀναστροφήν n. acc. fem. sg. ἀναστροφή conversation
17 κρεῖττον compar. adj. nom. neut. sg. κρείττων better
γὰρ conj. γάρ for, and, because, but, indeed
εἰ conj. εἰ if, whether, that, though, forasmuch
τὸ art. nom. neut. sg. ὁ ἡ τό the, this, that, he, she, it
θέλημα n. nom. neut. sg. θέλημα will, desire, pleasure
τοῦ art. gen. masc. sg. ὁ ἡ τό the, this, that, he, she, it
Θεοῦ n. gen. masc. sg. θεός God, god
ἢ particle. ἤ or, than, either, nor, or else, and, rather than
18 ὅτι conj. ὅτι that, for, because, how that, how, because that, for that, though
καὶ conj. καί and, even, also, but
Χριστὸς n. nom. masc. sg. Χριστός Christ
ἅπαξ adv. ἅπαξ once
περὶ prep. περί (+gen) of, for, concerning, (+acc) about, concerning, in
ἁμαρτιῶν n. gen. fem. pl. ἁμαρτία sin, offence, sinful
δίκαιος adj. nom. masc. sg. δίκαιος righteous, just, meet, right
ὑπὲρ prep. ὑπέρ (+gen) for, of, for the sake of, (+acc) above, more than
ἀδίκων adj. gen. masc. pl. ἄδικος unjust, unrighteous
ἵνα conj. ἵνα that, to, lest, for to, so that, albeit, because, for, so as
ἡμᾶς pron. acc. 1p. pl. ἐγώ I

τῷ art. dat. masc. sg. ὁ ἡ τό the, this, that, he, she, it
Θεῷ n. dat. masc. sg. θεός God, god
μὲν conj. μέν indeed, verily, truly, even, so, some
σαρκὶ n. dat. fem. sg. σάρξ flesh, carnal
δὲ conj. δέ but, and, now, also, to the contrary, rather, then
τῷ art. dat. neut. sg. ὁ ἡ τό the, this, that, he, she, it
πνεύματι n. dat. neut. sg. πνεῦμα spirit, Spirit, Ghost, ghost, life. of the spirit, wind
19 ἐν prep. ἐν (+dat) in, by, with, among, at, on, through, to, within, into, of, for
ᾧ relative pron. dat. neut. sg. ὅς ἥ ὅ who, which, what, that
καὶ conj. καί and, even, also, but
τοῖς art. dat. neut. pl. ὁ ἡ τό the, this, that, he, she, it
ἐν prep. ἐν (+dat) in, by, with, among, at, on, through, to, within, into, of, for
φυλακῇ n. dat. fem. sg. φυλακή prison, watch, imprisonment, cage, hold, ward
πνεύμασι n. dat. neut. pl. πνεῦμα spirit, Spirit, Ghost, ghost, life. of the spirit, wind
20 ποτε adv. ποτέ in time past, at any time, sometimes, in old time, once, when
ὅτε adv. ὅτε when, after that, as soon as, while, after
ἅπαξ adv. ἅπαξ once
ἡ art. nom. fem. sg. ὁ ἡ τό the, this, that, he, she, it
τοῦ art. gen. masc. sg. ὁ ἡ τό the, this, that, he, she, it
Θεοῦ n. gen. masc. sg. θεός God, god
μακροθυμία n. nom. fem. sg. μακροθυμία longsuffering, patience
ἐν prep. ἐν (+dat) in, by, with, among, at, on, through, to, within, into, of, for
ἡμέραις n. dat. fem. pl. ἡμέρα day, time, year, while, age, day time
Νῶε n. gen. masc. sg. Νῶε Noe, Noah
κιβωτοῦ n. gen. fem. sg. κιβωτός ark
εἰς prep. εἰς (+acc) into, to, unto, for, in, on, toward, against, upon, at, among
ἣν relative pron. acc. fem. sg. ὅς ἥ ὅ who, which, what, that
ὀλίγαι adj. nom. fem. pl. ὀλίγος few, little, small, a while, brief, short, short space
τοῦτ' demo. pron. nom. neut. sg. οὗτος αὕτη τοῦτο this, the same, this same, he, she, it
ὀκτὼ num. nom. fem. pl. ὀκτώ eight
ψυχαί n. nom. fem. pl. ψυχή life, soul, mind, heart
δι' prep. διά (+gen) by, through, with, in, of, (+acc) for, because of, for a cause
ὕδατος n. gen. neut. sg. ὕδωρ water
21 ᾧ relative pron. dat. neut. sg. ὅς ἥ ὅ who, which, what, that
καὶ conj. καί and, even, also, but
ἡμᾶς pron. acc. 1p. pl. ἐγώ I
ἀντίτυπον adj. nom. neut. sg. ἀντίτυπος figure, like figure whereunto
νῦν adv. νῦν now, henceforth, present, this time
βάπτισμα n. nom. neut. sg. βάπτισμα baptism
οὐ particle of negation. οὐ οὐκ οὐχ not, no, neither, none, nay, nor, never, nothing
σαρκὸς n. gen. fem. sg. σάρξ flesh, carnal
ἀπόθεσις n. nom. fem. sg. ἀπόθεσις putting away, put off, putting off
ῥύπου n. gen. masc. sg. ῥύπος filth
ἀλλὰ conj. ἀλλά but, yea, yet, nevertheless, howbeit, nay, therefore
συνειδήσεως n. gen. fem. sg. συνείδησις conscience
ἀγαθῆς adj. gen. fem. sg. ἀγαθός good, good thing, that which is good, well
ἐπερώτημα n. nom. neut. sg. ἐπερώτημα answer
εἰς prep. εἰς (+acc) into, to, unto, for, in, on, toward, against, upon, at, among
Θεόν n. acc. masc. sg. θεός God, god
δι' prep. διά (+gen) by, through, with, in, of, (+acc) for, because of, for a cause
ἀναστάσεως n. gen. fem. sg. ἀνάστασις resurrection, rising again
Ἰησοῦ n. gen. masc. sg. Ἰησοῦς Jesus
Χριστοῦ n. gen. masc. sg. Χριστός Christ
22 ὅς relative pron. nom. masc. sg. ὅς ἥ ὅ who, which, what, that
ἐν prep. ἐν (+dat) in, by, with, among, at, on, through, to, within, into, of, for

δεξιᾷ adj. dat. fem. sg. δεξιός right, right hand, right side
τοῦ art. gen. masc. sg. ὁ ἡ τό the, this, that, he, she, it
Θεοῦ n. gen. masc. sg. θεός God, god
εἰς prep. εἰς (+acc) into, to, unto, for, in, on, toward, against, upon, at, among
οὐρανόν n. acc. masc. sg. οὐρανός heaven, air, sky
αὐτῷ pron. dat. masc. 3p. sg. αὐτός ή ό self, of oneself, even, very, the same, he, she, it
ἀγγέλων n. gen. masc. pl. ἄγγελος angel, messenger
καὶ conj. καί and, even, also, but
ἐξουσιῶν n. gen. fem. pl. ἐξουσία power, authority, right, strength, jurisdiction
καὶ conj. καί and, even, also, but
δυνάμεων n. gen. fem. pl. δύναμις power, mighty work, miracle, strength, might

4

1 Χριστοῦ n. gen. masc. sg. Χριστός Christ
οὖν conj. οὖν therefore, then, so, and, now, wherefore
ὑπὲρ prep. ὑπέρ (+gen) for, of, for the sake of, (+acc) above, more than
ἡμῶν pron. gen. 1p. pl. ἐγώ I
σαρκὶ n. dat. fem. sg. σάρξ flesh, carnal
καὶ conj. καί and, even, also, but
ὑμεῖς pron. nom. 2p. pl. σύ thou, you
τὴν art. acc. fem. sg. ὁ ἡ τό the, this, that, he, she, it
αὐτὴν adj. acc. fem. sg. αὐτός ή ό self, of oneself, even, very, the same, he, she, it
ἔννοιαν n. acc. fem. sg. ἔννοια intent, mind
ὅτι conj. ὅτι that, for, because, how that, how, because that, for that, though
ὁ art. nom. masc. sg. ὁ ἡ τό the, this, that, he, she, it
ἐν prep. ἐν (+dat) in, by, with, among, at, on, through, to, within, into, of, for
σαρκὶ n. dat. fem. sg. σάρξ flesh, carnal
ἁμαρτίας n. gen. fem. sg. ἁμαρτία sin, offence, sinful
2 εἰς prep. εἰς (+acc) into, to, unto, for, in, on, toward, against, upon, at, among
τὸ art. acc. neut. sg. ὁ ἡ τό the, this, that, he, she, it
μηκέτι adv. μηκέτι no more, no longer, not any more, not henceforth, not henceforward
ἀνθρώπων n. gen. masc. pl. ἄνθρωπος man, human being, person, one, certain
ἐπιθυμίαις n. dat. fem. pl. ἐπιθυμία lust, concupiscence, desire
ἀλλὰ conj. ἀλλά but, yea, yet, nevertheless, howbeit, nay, therefore
θελήματι n. dat. neut. sg. θέλημα will, desire, pleasure
Θεοῦ n. gen. masc. sg. θεός God, god
τὸν art. acc. masc. sg. ὁ ἡ τό the, this, that, he, she, it
ἐπίλοιπον adj. acc. masc. sg. ἐπίλοιπος rest, remaining
ἐν prep. ἐν (+dat) in, by, with, among, at, on, through, to, within, into, of, for
σαρκὶ n. dat. fem. sg. σάρξ flesh, carnal
χρόνον n. acc. masc. sg. χρόνος time, season, space
3 ἀρκετὸς adj. nom. masc. sg. ἀρκετός enough, sufficient, suffice
γὰρ conj. γάρ for, and, because, but, indeed
ἡμῖν pron. dat. 1p. pl. ἐγώ I
ὁ art. nom. masc. sg. ὁ ἡ τό the, this, that, he, she, it
χρόνος n. nom. masc. sg. χρόνος time, season, space
τοῦ art. gen. masc. sg. ὁ ἡ τό the, this, that, he, she, it
βίου n. gen. masc. sg. βίος life, living, good
τὸ art. acc. neut. sg. ὁ ἡ τό the, this, that, he, she, it
θέλημα n. acc. neut. sg. θέλημα will, desire, pleasure
τῶν art. gen. neut. pl. ὁ ἡ τό the, this, that, he, she, it
ἐθνῶν n. gen. neut. pl. ἔθνος Gentile, nation, heathen, people
ἐν prep. ἐν (+dat) in, by, with, among, at, on, through, to, within, into, of, for
ἀσελγείαις n. dat. fem. pl. ἀσέλγεια lasciviousness, wantonness, filthy

ἐπιθυμίαις n. dat. fem. pl. ἐπιθυμία lust, concupiscence, desire
οἰνοφλυγίαις n. dat. fem. pl. οἰνοφλυγία excess of wine
κώμοις n. dat. masc. pl. κῶμος rioting, revelling
πότοις n. dat. masc. pl. πότος banquetings, drinking
καὶ conj. καί and, even, also, but
ἀθεμίτοις adj. dat. fem. pl. ἀθέμιτος unlawful thing, abominable
εἰδωλολατρείαις n. dat. fem. pl. εἰδωλολατρεία idolatry
4 ἐν prep. ἐν (+dat) in, by, with, among, at, on, through, to, within, into, of, for
ᾧ relative pron. dat. neut. sg. ὅς ἥ ὅ who, which, what, that
μὴ particle of negation. μή not, no, lest, neither, none, nothing, nor, never, without
ὑμῶν pron. gen. 2p. pl. σύ thou, you
εἰς prep. εἰς (+acc) into, to, unto, for, in, on, toward, against, upon, at, among
τὴν art. acc. fem. sg. ὁ ἡ τό the, this, that, he, she, it
αὐτὴν adj. acc. fem. sg. αὐτός ή ό self, of oneself, even, very, the same, he, she, it
τῆς art. gen. fem. sg. ὁ ἡ τό the, this, that, he, she, it
ἀσωτίας n. gen. fem. sg. ἀσωτία excess, riot
ἀνάχυσιν n. acc. fem. sg. ἀνάχυσις excess
5 οἳ relative pron. nom. masc. pl. ὅς ἥ ὅ who, which, what, that
λόγον n. acc. masc. sg. λόγος word, saying, account, speech, thing, matter
τῷ art. dat. masc. sg. ὁ ἡ τό the, this, that, he, she, it
ἑτοίμως adv. ἑτοίμως ready
καὶ conj. καί and, even, also, but
νεκρούς adj. acc. masc. pl. νεκρός dead
6 εἰς prep. εἰς (+acc) into, to, unto, for, in, on, toward, against, upon, at, among
τοῦτο demo. pron. acc. neut. sg. οὗτος αὕτη τοῦτο this, the same, this same, he, she, it
γὰρ conj. γάρ for, and, because, but, indeed
καὶ conj. καί and, even, also, but
νεκροῖς adj. dat. masc. pl. νεκρός dead
ἵνα conj. ἵνα that, to, lest, for to, so that, albeit, because, for, so as
μὲν conj. μέν indeed, verily, truly, even, so, some
κατὰ prep. κατά (+gen) against, by, throughout, down, (+acc) according to, after, with
ἀνθρώπους n. acc. masc. pl. ἄνθρωπος man, human being, person, one, certain
σαρκὶ n. dat. fem. sg. σάρξ flesh, carnal
δὲ conj. δέ but, and, now, also, to the contrary, rather, then
κατὰ prep. κατά (+gen) against, by, throughout, down, (+acc) according to, after, with
Θεὸν n. acc. masc. sg. θεός God, god
πνεύματι n. dat. neut. sg. πνεῦμα spirit, Spirit, Ghost, ghost, life. of the spirit, wind
7 Πάντων adj. gen. neut. pl. πᾶς πᾶςa πᾶν all, every, whosoever, every one, no, whole, any
δὲ conj. δέ but, and, now, also, to the contrary, rather, then
τὸ art. nom. neut. sg. ὁ ἡ τό the, this, that, he, she, it
τέλος n. nom. neut. sg. τέλος end, custom, ending, finally, uttermost
οὖν conj. οὖν therefore, then, so, and, now, wherefore
καὶ conj. καί and, even, also, but
εἰς prep. εἰς (+acc) into, to, unto, for, in, on, toward, against, upon, at, among
τὰς art. acc. fem. pl. ὁ ἡ τό the, this, that, he, she, it
προσευχάς n. acc. fem. pl. προσευχή prayer
8 πρὸ prep. πρό (+gen) before, above
πάντων adj. gen. neut. pl. πᾶς πᾶςa πᾶν all, every, whosoever, every one, no, whole, any
δὲ conj. δέ but, and, now, also, to the contrary, rather, then
τὴν art. acc. fem. sg. ὁ ἡ τό the, this, that, he, she, it
εἰς prep. εἰς (+acc) into, to, unto, for, in, on, toward, against, upon, at, among
ἑαυτοὺς reflexive pron. acc. masc. 3p. pl. ἑαυτοῦ himself, herself, itself, yourself, ourselves
ἀγάπην n. acc. fem. sg. ἀγάπη love, charity, feast of charity
ἐκτενῆ adj. acc. fem. sg. ἐκτενής fervent, without ceasing, intense
ὅτι conj. ὅτι that, for, because, how that, how, because that, for that, though

ἡ art. nom. fem. sg. ὁ ἡ τό the, this, that, he, she, it
ἀγάπη n. nom. fem. sg. ἀγάπη love, charity, feast of charity
πλῆθος n. acc. neut. sg. πλῆθος multitude, bundle, company
ἁμαρτιῶν n. gen. fem. pl. ἁμαρτία sin, offence, sinful
9 φιλόξενοι adj. nom. masc. pl. φιλόξενος given to hospitality, use hospitality
εἰς prep. εἰς (+acc) into, to, unto, for, in, on, toward, against, upon, at, among
ἀλλήλους pron. acc. masc. pl. ἀλλήλων one another, themselves, together, mutual
ἄνευ prep. ἄνευ without
γογγυσμῶν n. gen. masc. pl. γογγυσμός murmuring, grudging
10 ἕκαστος adj. nom. masc. sg. ἕκαστος every man, every, every one, any man, each
καθὼς adv. καθώς as, even as, according as, according to
χάρισμα n. acc. neut. sg. χάρισμα gift, free gift
εἰς prep. εἰς (+acc) into, to, unto, for, in, on, toward, against, upon, at, among
ἑαυτοὺς reflexive pron. acc. masc. 3p. pl. ἑαυτοῦ himself, herself, itself, yourself, ourselves
αὐτὸ pron. acc. neut. 3p. sg. αὐτός ή ό self, of oneself, even, very, the same, he, she, it
ὡς adv. ὡς as, when, as it were, how, about, like, as soon as, even as, while
καλοὶ adj. nom. masc. pl. καλός good, better, goodly, meet, honest, fair, well, worthy
οἰκονόμοι n. nom. masc. pl. οἰκονόμος steward, chamberlain, governor
ποικίλης adj. gen. fem. sg. ποικίλος divers, manifold
χάριτος n. gen. fem. sg. χάρις grace, thank, favour, pleasure
Θεοῦ n. gen. masc. sg. θεός God, god
11 εἴ conj. εἰ if, whether, that, though, forasmuch
τις indefinite pron. nom. masc. sg. τὶς certain, some, any man, one, any thing
ὡς adv. ὡς as, when, as it were, how, about, like, as soon as, even as, while
λόγια n. acc. neut. pl. λόγιον oracle
Θεοῦ n. gen. masc. sg. θεός God, god
εἴ conj. εἰ if, whether, that, though, forasmuch
τις indefinite pron. nom. masc. sg. τὶς certain, some, any man, one, any thing
ὡς adv. ὡς as, when, as it were, how, about, like, as soon as, even as, while
ἐξ prep. ἐκ ἐξ (+gen) of, from, out of, by, on, with, in, among, through
ἰσχύος n. gen. fem. sg. ἰσχύς strength, might, power, ability
ἧς relative pron. gen. fem. sg. ὅς ἥ ὅ who, which, what, that
ὁ art. nom. masc. sg. ὁ ἡ τό the, this, that, he, she, it
Θεός n. nom. masc. sg. θεός God, god
ἵνα conj. ἵνα that, to, lest, for to, so that, albeit, because, for, so as
ἐν prep. ἐν (+dat) in, by, with, among, at, on, through, to, within, into, of, for
πᾶσι adj. dat. neut. pl. πᾶς πᾶσα πᾶν all, every, whosoever, every one, no, whole, any
ὁ art. nom. masc. sg. ὁ ἡ τό the, this, that, he, she, it
Θεός n. nom. masc. sg. θεός God, god
διὰ prep. διά (+gen) by, through, with, in, of, (+acc) for, because of, for a cause
Ἰησοῦ n. gen. masc. sg. Ἰησοῦς Jesus
Χριστοῦ n. gen. masc. sg. Χριστός Christ
ᾧ relative pron. dat. masc. sg. ὅς ἥ ὅ who, which, what, that
ἡ art. nom. fem. sg. ὁ ἡ τό the, this, that, he, she, it
δόξα n. nom. fem. sg. δόξα glory, honour, praise, dignity, worship
καὶ conj. καί and, even, also, but
τὸ art. nom. neut. sg. ὁ ἡ τό the, this, that, he, she, it
κράτος n. nom. neut. sg. κράτος power, dominion, might, strength
εἰς prep. εἰς (+acc) into, to, unto, for, in, on, toward, against, upon, at, among
τοὺς art. acc. masc. pl. ὁ ἡ τό the, this, that, he, she, it
αἰῶνας n. acc. masc. pl. αἰών ever, ever and ever, evermore, age, eternal, world
τῶν art. gen. masc. pl. ὁ ἡ τό the, this, that, he, she, it
αἰώνων n. gen. masc. pl. αἰών ever, ever and ever, evermore, age, eternal, world
ἀμήν particle. ἀμήν amen, verily
12 Ἀγαπητοί adj. voc. masc. pl. ἀγαπητός beloved, dearly beloved, dear, wellbeloved

μὴ particle of negation. μή not, no, lest, neither, none, nothing, nor, never, without
τῇ art. dat. fem. sg. ὁ ἡ τό the, this, that, he, she, it
ἐν prep. ἐν (+dat) in, by, with, among, at, on, through, to, within, into, of, for
ὑμῖν pron. dat. 2p. pl. σύ thou, you
πυρώσει n. dat. fem. sg. πύρωσις fiery trial, burning
πρὸς prep. πρός (+gen) for, (+dat) at, (+acc) unto, to, with, for, against
πειρασμὸν n. acc. masc. sg. πειρασμός temptation, trial
ὑμῖν pron. dat. 2p. pl. σύ thou, you
ὡς adv. ὡς as, when, as it were, how, about, like, as soon as, even as, while
ξένου adj. gen. neut. sg. ξένος stranger, strange, host
ὑμῖν pron. dat. 2p. pl. σύ thou, you
13 ἀλλὰ conj. ἀλλά but, yea, yet, nevertheless, howbeit, nay, therefore
καθὸ adv. καθό as, according to that, inasmuch as
τοῖς art. dat. neut. pl. ὁ ἡ τό the, this, that, he, she, it
τοῦ art. gen. masc. sg. ὁ ἡ τό the, this, that, he, she, it
Χριστοῦ n. gen. masc. sg. Χριστός Christ
παθήμασι n. dat. neut. pl. πάθημα suffering, affliction, affection, motion
ἵνα conj. ἵνα that, to, lest, for to, so that, albeit, because, for, so as
καὶ conj. καί and, even, also, but
ἐν prep. ἐν (+dat) in, by, with, among, at, on, through, to, within, into, of, for
τῇ art. dat. fem. sg. ὁ ἡ τό the, this, that, he, she, it
ἀποκαλύψει n. dat. fem. sg. ἀποκάλυψις revelation, appearing, coming, manifestation
τῆς art. gen. fem. sg. ὁ ἡ τό the, this, that, he, she, it
δόξης n. gen. fem. sg. δόξα glory, honour, praise, dignity, worship
αὐτοῦ pron. gen. masc. 3p. sg. αὐτός ή ό self, of oneself, even, very, the same, he, she, it
14 εἰ conj. εἰ if, whether, that, though, forasmuch
ἐν prep. ἐν (+dat) in, by, with, among, at, on, through, to, within, into, of, for
ὀνόματι n. dat. neut. sg. ὄνομα name, call, surname
Χριστοῦ n. gen. masc. sg. Χριστός Christ
μακάριοι adj. nom. masc. pl. μακάριος blessed, happy
ὅτι conj. ὅτι that, for, because, how that, how, because that, for that, though
τὸ art. nom. neut. sg. ὁ ἡ τό the, this, that, he, she, it
τῆς art. gen. fem. sg. ὁ ἡ τό the, this, that, he, she, it
δόξης n. gen. fem. sg. δόξα glory, honour, praise, dignity, worship
καὶ conj. καί and, even, also, but
τὸ art. nom. neut. sg. ὁ ἡ τό the, this, that, he, she, it
τοῦ art. gen. masc. sg. ὁ ἡ τό the, this, that, he, she, it
Θεοῦ n. gen. masc. sg. θεός God, god
Πνεῦμα n. nom. neut. sg. πνεῦμα spirit, Spirit, Ghost, ghost, life. of the spirit, wind
ἐφ' prep. ἐπί (+gen) on, in, upon, (+dat) in, at, for, upon, (+acc) on, upon, unto, to, against
ὑμᾶς pron. acc. 2p. pl. σύ thou, you
κατὰ prep. κατά (+gen) against, by, throughout, down, (+acc) according to, after, with
μὲν conj. μέν indeed, verily, truly, even, so, some
αὐτοὺς pron. acc. masc. 3p. pl. αὐτός ή ό self, of oneself, even, very, the same, he, she, it
κατὰ prep. κατά (+gen) against, by, throughout, down, (+acc) according to, after, with
δὲ conj. δέ but, and, now, also, to the contrary, rather, then
ὑμᾶς pron. acc. 2p. pl. σύ thou, you
15 μὴ particle of negation. μή not, no, lest, neither, none, nothing, nor, never, without
γάρ particle. γάρ for, and, because, but, indeed
τις indefinite pron. nom. masc. sg. τὶς certain, some, any man, one, any thing
ὑμῶν pron. gen. 2p. pl. σύ thou, you
ὡς adv. ὡς as, when, as it were, how, about, like, as soon as, even as, while
φονεὺς n. nom. masc. sg. φονεύς murderer
ἢ particle. ἤ or, than, either, nor, or else, and, rather than
κλέπτης n. nom. masc. sg. κλέπτης thief

ἢ particle. ἤ or, than, either, nor, or else, and, rather than
κακοποιὸς adj. nom. masc. sg. κακοποιός evildoer, malefactor
ἢ particle. ἤ or, than, either, nor, or else, and, rather than
ὡς adv. ὡς as, when, as it were, how, about, like, as soon as, even as, while
ἀλλοτριοεπίσκοπος n. nom. masc. sg. ἀλλοτριεπίσκοπος busybody in other men's matters
16 εἰ conj. εἰ if, whether, that, though, forasmuch
δὲ conj. δέ but, and, now, also, to the contrary, rather, then
ὡς adv. ὡς as, when, as it were, how, about, like, as soon as, even as, while
Χριστιανός n. nom. masc. sg. Χριστιανός Christian
μὴ particle of negation. μή not, no, lest, neither, none, nothing, nor, never, without
δὲ conj. δέ but, and, now, also, to the contrary, rather, then
τὸν art. acc. masc. sg. ὁ ἡ τό the, this, that, he, she, it
Θεὸν n. acc. masc. sg. θεός God, god
ἐν prep. ἐν (+dat) in, by, with, among, at, on, through, to, within, into, of, for
τῷ art. dat. neut. sg. ὁ ἡ τό the, this, that, he, she, it
μέρει n. dat. neut. sg. μέρος part, coast, portion, behalf, respect, piece, side
τούτῳ demo. pron. dat. neut. sg. οὗτος αὕτη τοῦτο this, the same, this same, he, she, it
17 ὅτι conj. ὅτι that, for, because, how that, how, because that, for that, though
ὁ art. nom. masc. sg. ὁ ἡ τό the, this, that, he, she, it
καιρὸς n. nom. masc. sg. καιρός time, season, due time, opportunity
τοῦ art. gen. neut. sg. ὁ ἡ τό the, this, that, he, she, it
τὸ art. acc. neut. sg. ὁ ἡ τό the, this, that, he, she, it
κρίμα n. acc. neut. sg. κρίμα judgment, damnation, condemnation
ἀπὸ prep. ἀπό (+gen) from, of, out of, since, for, off, at, by, in, on
τοῦ art. gen. masc. sg. ὁ ἡ τό the, this, that, he, she, it
οἴκου n. gen. masc. sg. οἶκος house, home, household
τοῦ art. gen. masc. sg. ὁ ἡ τό the, this, that, he, she, it
Θεοῦ n. gen. masc. sg. θεός God, god
εἰ conj. εἰ if, whether, that, though, forasmuch
δὲ conj. δέ but, and, now, also, to the contrary, rather, then
πρῶτον adv. πρῶτον first, at the first, first of all, at first, at the beginning, before, chiefly
ἀφ' prep. ἀπό (+gen) from, of, out of, since, for, off, at, by, in, on
ἡμῶν pron. gen. 1p. pl. ἐγώ I
τί interrog. pron. nom. neut. sg. τίς what, who, why, where, which, how
τὸ art. nom. neut. sg. ὁ ἡ τό the, this, that, he, she, it
τέλος n. nom. neut. sg. τέλος end, custom, ending, finally, uttermost
τῶν art. gen. masc. pl. ὁ ἡ τό the, this, that, he, she, it
τῷ art. dat. neut. sg. ὁ ἡ τό the, this, that, he, she, it
τοῦ art. gen. masc. sg. ὁ ἡ τό the, this, that, he, she, it
Θεοῦ n. gen. masc. sg. θεός God, god
εὐαγγελίῳ n. dat. neut. sg. εὐαγγέλιον gospel
18 καὶ conj. καί and, even, also, but
Εἰ conj. εἰ if, whether, that, though, forasmuch
ὁ art. nom. masc. sg. ὁ ἡ τό the, this, that, he, she, it
δίκαιος adj. nom. masc. sg. δίκαιος righteous, just, meet, right
μόλις adv. μόλις scarce, with difficulty, scarcely, hardly
ὁ art. nom. masc. sg. ὁ ἡ τό the, this, that, he, she, it
ἀσεβὴς adj. nom. masc. sg. ἀσεβής ungodly, ungodly man
καὶ conj. καί and, even, also, but
ἁμαρτωλὸς adj. nom. masc. sg. ἁμαρτωλός sinner, sinful
ποῦ particle of place. ποῦ where, whither
19 ὥστε conj. ὥστε so that, wherefore, insomuch that, therefore, that, so then
καὶ conj. καί and, even, also, but
οἱ art. nom. masc. pl. ὁ ἡ τό the, this, that, he, she, it
κατὰ prep. κατά (+gen) against, by, throughout, down, (+acc) according to, after, with

τὸ art. acc. neut. sg. ὁ ἡ τό the, this, that, he, she, it
θέλημα n. acc. neut. sg. θέλημα will, desire, pleasure
τοῦ art. gen. masc. sg. ὁ ἡ τό the, this, that, he, she, it
Θεοῦ n. gen. masc. sg. θεός God, god
ὡς adv. ὡς as, when, as it were, how, about, like, as soon as, even as, while
πιστῷ adj. dat. masc. sg. πιστός faithful, believing, true, sure
κτίστῃ n. dat. masc. sg. κτίστης Creator
τὰς art. acc. fem. pl. ὁ ἡ τό the, this, that, he, she, it
ψυχὰς n. acc. fem. pl. ψυχή life, soul, mind, heart
ἑαυτῶν reflexive pron. gen. masc. 3p. pl. ἑαυτοῦ himself, herself, itself, yourself, ourselves
ἐν prep. ἐν (+dat) in, by, with, among, at, on, through, to, within, into, of, for
ἀγαθοποιΐᾳ n. dat. fem. sg. ἀγαθοποιΐα well doing

5

1 Πρεσβυτέρους adj. acc. masc. pl. πρεσβύτερος elder, elder woman, eldest, old man
τοὺς art. acc. masc. pl. ὁ ἡ τό the, this, that, he, she, it
ἐν prep. ἐν (+dat) in, by, with, among, at, on, through, to, within, into, of, for
ὑμῖν pron. dat. 2p. pl. σύ thou, you
ὁ art. nom. masc. sg. ὁ ἡ τό the, this, that, he, she, it
συμπρεσβύτερος n. nom. masc. sg. πρεσβύτερος elder, elder woman, eldest, old man
καὶ conj. καί and, even, also, but
μάρτυς n. nom. masc. sg. μάρτυς or μάρτυρ witness, martyr, record
τῶν art. gen. neut. pl. ὁ ἡ τό the, this, that, he, she, it
τοῦ art. gen. masc. sg. ὁ ἡ τό the, this, that, he, she, it
Χριστοῦ n. gen. masc. sg. Χριστός Christ
παθημάτων n. gen. neut. pl. πάθημα suffering, affliction, affection, motion
ὁ art. nom. masc. sg. ὁ ἡ τό the, this, that, he, she, it
καὶ conj. καί and, even, also, but
τῆς art. gen. fem. sg. ὁ ἡ τό the, this, that, he, she, it
δόξης n. gen. fem. sg. δόξα glory, honour, praise, dignity, worship
κοινωνός n. nom. masc. sg. κοινωνός partaker, partner, companion, fellowship
2 τὸ art. acc. neut. sg. ὁ ἡ τό the, this, that, he, she, it
ἐν prep. ἐν (+dat) in, by, with, among, at, on, through, to, within, into, of, for
ὑμῖν pron. dat. 2p. pl. σύ thou, you
ποίμνιον n. acc. neut. sg. ποίμνιον flock
τοῦ art. gen. masc. sg. ὁ ἡ τό the, this, that, he, she, it
Θεοῦ n. gen. masc. sg. θεός God, god
μὴ particle of negation. μή not, no, lest, neither, none, nothing, nor, never, without
ἀναγκαστῶς adv. ἀναγκαστῶς by constraint
ἀλλ' conj. ἀλλά but, yea, yet, nevertheless, howbeit, nay, therefore
ἑκουσίως adv. ἑκουσίως wilfully, willingly
μηδὲ conj. μηδέ neither, nor, not, no not, nor yet, not once, not so much as
αἰσχροκερδῶς adv. αἰσχροκερδῶς for filthy lucre
ἀλλὰ conj. ἀλλά but, yea, yet, nevertheless, howbeit, nay, therefore
προθύμως adv. προθύμως of a ready mind
3 μηδ' conj. μηδέ neither, nor, not, no not, nor yet, not once, not so much as
ὡς adv. ὡς as, when, as it were, how, about, like, as soon as, even as, while
τῶν art. gen. masc. pl. ὁ ἡ τό the, this, that, he, she, it
κλήρων n. gen. masc. pl. κλῆρος lot, inheritance, part, heritage
ἀλλὰ conj. ἀλλά but, yea, yet, nevertheless, howbeit, nay, therefore
τύποι n. nom. masc. pl. τύπος ensample, example, pattern, print, figure, fashion
τοῦ art. gen. neut. sg. ὁ ἡ τό the, this, that, he, she, it
ποιμνίου n. gen. neut. sg. ποίμνιον flock
4 καὶ conj. καί and, even, also, but

τοῦ art. gen. masc. sg. ὁ ἡ τό the, this, that, he, she, it
ἀρχιποίμενος n. gen. masc. sg. ἀρχιποίμην chief Shepherd
τὸν art. acc. masc. sg. ὁ ἡ τό the, this, that, he, she, it
ἀμαράντινον adj. acc. masc. sg. ἀμαράντινος that fadeth not away
τῆς art. gen. fem. sg. ὁ ἡ τό the, this, that, he, she, it
δόξης n. gen. fem. sg. δόξα glory, honour, praise, dignity, worship
στέφανον n. acc. masc. sg. στέφανος crown
5 ὁμοίως adv. ὁμοίως likewise, so
νεώτεροι compar. adj. nom. masc. pl. νέος new
πρεσβυτέροις compar. adj. dat. masc. pl. πρεσβύτερος elder, elder woman, eldest, old man
πάντες adj. voc. masc. pl. πᾶς πᾶσα πᾶν all, every, whosoever, every one, no, whole, any
δὲ conj. δέ but, and, now, also, to the contrary, rather, then
ἀλλήλοις pron. dat. masc. pl. ἀλλήλων one another, themselves, together, mutual
τὴν art. acc. fem. sg. ὁ ἡ τό the, this, that, he, she, it
ταπεινοφροσύνην n. acc. fem. sg. ταπεινοφροσύνη humility of mind, humility, lowliness
ὅτι conj. ὅτι that, for, because, how that, how, because that, for that, though
ὁ art. nom. masc. sg. ὁ ἡ τό the, this, that, he, she, it
Θεὸς n. nom. masc. sg. θεός God, god
ὑπερηφάνοις adj. dat. masc. pl. ὑπερήφανος proud
ταπεινοῖς adj. dat. masc. pl. ταπεινός humble, of low degree, base, cast down, lowly
δὲ conj. δέ but, and, now, also, to the contrary, rather, then
χάριν n. acc. fem. sg. χάρις grace, thank, favour, pleasure
6 οὖν conj. οὖν therefore, then, so, and, now, wherefore
ὑπὸ prep. ὑπό (+gen) of, by, with, from, among, (+acc) under
τὴν art. acc. fem. sg. ὁ ἡ τό the, this, that, he, she, it
κραταιὰν adj. acc. fem. sg. κραταιός mighty
χεῖρα n. acc. fem. sg. χείρ hand
τοῦ art. gen. masc. sg. ὁ ἡ τό the, this, that, he, she, it
Θεοῦ n. gen. masc. sg. θεός God, god
ἵνα conj. ἵνα that, to, lest, for to, so that, albeit, because, for, so as
ὑμᾶς pron. acc. 2p. pl. σύ thou, you
ἐν prep. ἐν (+dat) in, by, with, among, at, on, through, to, within, into, of, for
καιρῷ n. dat. masc. sg. καιρός time, season, due time, opportunity
7 πᾶσαν adj. acc. fem. sg. πᾶς πᾶσα πᾶν all, every, whosoever, every one, no, whole, any
τὴν art. acc. fem. sg. ὁ ἡ τό the, this, that, he, she, it
μέριμναν n. acc. fem. sg. μέριμνα care
ὑμῶν pron. gen. 2p. pl. σύ thou, you
ἐπ' prep. ἐπί (+gen) on, in, upon, (+dat) in, at, for, upon, (+acc) on, upon, unto, to, against
αὐτόν pron. acc. masc. 3p. sg. αὐτός ἡ ό self, of oneself, even, very, the same, he, she, it
ὅτι conj. ὅτι that, for, because, how that, how, because that, for that, though
αὐτῷ pron. dat. masc. 3p. sg. αὐτός ἡ ό self, of oneself, even, very, the same, he, she, it
περὶ prep. περί (+gen) of, for, concerning, (+acc) about, concerning, in
ὑμῶν pron. gen. 2p. pl. σύ thou, you
8 ὅτι conj. οὅτι that, for, because, how that, how, because that, for that, thoughὅτι
ὁ art. nom. masc. sg. ὁ ἡ τό the, this, that, he, she, it
ἀντίδικος n. nom. masc. sg. ἀντίδικος adversary
ὑμῶν pron. gen. 2p. pl. σύ thou, you
διάβολος adj. nom. masc. sg. διάβολος devil, false accuser, Devil, slanderer
ὡς adv. ὡς as, when, as it were, how, about, like, as soon as, even as, while
λέων n. nom. masc. sg. λέων lion
τινα indefinite pron. acc. masc. sg. τὶς certain, some, any man, one, any thing
9 ᾧ relative pron. dat. masc. sg. ὅς ἥ ὅ who, which, what, that
στερεοὶ adj. nom. masc. pl. στερεός sure, stedfast, strong, solid
τῇ art. dat. fem. sg. ὁ ἡ τό the, this, that, he, she, it
πίστει n. dat. fem. sg. πίστις faith, assurance, belief, fidelity

τὰ art. acc. neut. pl. ὁ ἡ τό the, this, that, he, she, it
αὐτὰ adj. acc. neut. pl. αὐτός ἡ ὁ self, of oneself, even, very, the same, he, she, it
τῶν art. gen. neut. pl. ὁ ἡ τό the, this, that, he, she, it
παθημάτων n. gen. neut. pl. πάθημα suffering, affliction, affection, motion
τῇ art. dat. fem. sg. ὁ ἡ τό the, this, that, he, she, it
ἐν prep. ἐν (+dat) in, by, with, among, at, on, through, to, within, into, of, for
κόσμῳ n. dat. masc. sg. κόσμος world, adorning
ὑμῶν pron. gen. 2p. pl. σύ thou, you
ἀδελφότητι n. dat. fem. sg. ἀδελφότης brotherhood brethren
10 ὁ art. nom. masc. sg. ὁ ἡ τό the, this, that, he, she, it
δὲ conj. δέ but, and, now, also, to the contrary, rather, then
Θεὸς n. nom. masc. sg. θεός God, god
πάσης adj. gen. fem. sg. πᾶς πᾶσα πᾶν all, every, whosoever, every one, no, whole, any
χάριτος n. gen. fem. sg. χάρις grace, thank, favour, pleasure
ὁ art. nom. masc. sg. ὁ ἡ τό the, this, that, he, she, it
ἡμᾶς pron. acc. 1p. pl. ἐγώ I
εἰς prep. εἰς (+acc) into, to, unto, for, in, on, toward, against, upon, at, among
τὴν art. acc. fem. sg. ὁ ἡ τό the, this, that, he, she, it
αἰώνιον adj. acc. fem. sg. αἰώνιος eternal, everlasting, world, for ever
αὐτοῦ pron. gen. masc. 3p. sg. αὐτός ἡ ὁ self, of oneself, even, very, the same, he, she, it
δόξαν n. acc. fem. sg. δόξα glory, honour, praise, dignity, worship
ἐν prep. ἐν (+dat) in, by, with, among, at, on, through, to, within, into, of, for
Χριστῷ n. dat. masc. sg. Χριστός Christ
Ἰησοῦ n. dat. masc. sg. Ἰησοῦς Jesus
ὀλίγον adv. ὀλίγον a little
αὐτὸς pron. nom. masc. 3p. sg. αὐτός ἡ ὁ self, of oneself, even, very, the same, he, she, it
ὑμᾶς pron. acc. 2p. pl. σύ thou, you
11 αὐτῷ pron. dat. masc. 3p. sg. αὐτός ἡ ὁ self, of oneself, even, very, the same, he, she, it
ἡ art. nom. fem. sg. ὁ ἡ τό the, this, that, he, she, it
δόξα n. nom. fem. sg. δόξα glory, honour, praise, dignity, worship
καὶ conj. καί and, even, also, but
τὸ art. nom. neut. sg. ὁ ἡ τό the, this, that, he, she, it
κράτος n. nom. neut. sg. κράτος power, dominion, might, strength
εἰς prep. εἰς (+acc) into, to, unto, for, in, on, toward, against, upon, at, among
τοὺς art. acc. masc. pl. ὁ ἡ τό the, this, that, he, she, it
αἰῶνας n. acc. masc. pl. αἰών ever, ever and ever, evermore, age, eternal, world
τῶν art. gen. masc. pl. ὁ ἡ τό the, this, that, he, she, it
αἰώνων n. gen. masc. pl. αἰών ever, ever and ever, evermore, age, eternal, world
ἀμήν particle. ἀμήν amen, verily
12 Διὰ prep. διά (+gen) by, through, with, in, of, (+acc) for, because of, for a cause
Σιλουανοῦ n. gen. masc. sg. Σιλουανός Silvanus
ὑμῖν pron. dat. 2p. pl. σύ thou, you
τοῦ art. gen. masc. sg. ὁ ἡ τό the, this, that, he, she, it
πιστοῦ adj. gen. masc. sg. πιστός faithful, believing, true, sure
ἀδελφοῦ n. gen. masc. sg. ἀδελφός brother
ὡς adv. ὡς as, when, as it were, how, about, like, as soon as, even as, while
δι' prep. διά (+gen) by, through, with, in, of, (+acc) for, because of, for a cause
ὀλίγων adj. gen. masc. pl. ὀλίγος few, little, small, a while, brief, short, short space
καὶ conj. καί and, even, also, but
ταύτην demo. pron. acc. fem. sg. οὗτος αὕτη τοῦτο this, the same, this same, he, she, it
ἀληθῆ adj. acc. fem. sg. ἀληθής true, truly, truth
χάριν n. acc. fem. sg. χάρις grace, thank, favour, pleasure
τοῦ art. gen. masc. sg. ὁ ἡ τό the, this, that, he, she, it
Θεοῦ n. gen. masc. sg. θεός God, god
εἰς prep. εἰς (+acc) into, to, unto, for, in, on, toward, against, upon, at, among

ἥν relative pron. acc. fem. sg. ὅς ἥ ὅ who, which, what, that
13 ὑμᾶς pron. acc. 2p. pl. σύ thou, you
ἡ art. nom. fem. sg. ὁ ἡ τό the, this, that, he, she, it
ἐν prep. ἐν (+dat) in, by, with, among, at, on, through, to, within, into, of, for
Βαβυλῶνι n. dat. fem. sg. Βαβυλών Babylon
συνεκλεκτὴ adj. nom. fem. sg. συνεκλεκτός elected together with
καὶ conj. καί and, even, also, but
Μᾶρκος n. nom. masc. sg. Μᾶρκος Mark, Marcus
ὁ art. nom. masc. sg. ὁ ἡ τό the, this, that, he, she, it
υἱός n. nom. masc. sg. υἱός son, child, descendant, offspring, heir
μου pron. gen. 1p. sg. ἐγώ I
14 ἀλλήλους pron. acc. masc. pl. ἀλλήλων one another, themselves, together, mutual
ἐν prep. ἐν (+dat) in, by, with, among, at, on, through, to, within, into, of, for
φιλήματι n. dat. neut. sg. φίλημα kiss
ἀγάπης n. gen. fem. sg. ἀγάπη love, charity, feast of charity
Εἰρήνη n. nom. fem. sg. εἰρήνη peace, quietness, rest
ὑμῖν pron. dat. 2p. pl. σύ thou, you
πᾶσι adj. dat. masc. pl. πᾶς πᾶσα πᾶν all, every, whosoever, every one, no, whole, any
τοῖς art. dat. masc. pl. ὁ ἡ τό the, this, that, he, she, it
ἐν prep. ἐν (+dat) in, by, with, among, at, on, through, to, within, into, of, for
Χριστῷ n. dat. masc. sg. Χριστός Christ
Ἰησοῦ n. dat. masc. sg. Ἰησοῦς Jesus
ἀμήν particle. ἀμήν amen, verily

ΠΕΤΡΟΥ
ΕΠΙΣΤΟΛΗ ΚΑΘΟΛΙΚΗ ΔΕΥΤΕΡΑ

1

1 Σίμων n. nom. masc. sg. Σίμων Simon
Πέτρος n. nom. masc. sg. Πέτρος Peter
δοῦλος n. nom. masc. sg. δοῦλος servant, bondman, bond, slave
καὶ conj. καί and, even, also, but
ἀπόστολος n. nom. masc. sg. ἀπόστολος apostle, messenger, he that is sent
Ἰησοῦ n. gen. masc. sg. Ἰησοῦς Jesus
Χριστοῦ n. gen. masc. sg. Χριστός Christ
τοῖς art. dat. masc. pl. ὁ ἡ τό the, this, that, he, she, it
ἰσότιμον adj. acc. fem. sg. ἰσότιμος like precious
ἡμῖν pron. dat. 1p. pl. ἐγώ I
πίστιν n. acc. fem. sg. πίστις faith, assurance, belief, fidelity
ἐν prep. ἐν (+dat) in, by, with, among, at, on, through, to, within, into, of, for
δικαιοσύνῃ n. dat. fem. sg. δικαιοσύνη righteousness
τοῦ art. gen. masc. sg. ὁ ἡ τό the, this, that, he, she, it
Θεοῦ n. gen. masc. sg. θεός God, god
ἡμῶν pron. gen. 1p. pl. ἐγώ I
καὶ conj. καί and, even, also, but
σωτῆρος n. gen. masc. sg. σωτήρ Saviour, saviour
ἡμῶν pron. gen. 1p. pl. ἐγώ I
Ἰησοῦ n. gen. masc. sg. Ἰησοῦς Jesus
Χριστοῦ n. gen. masc. sg. Χριστός Christ
2 χάρις n. nom. fem. sg. χάρις grace, thank, favour, pleasure
ὑμῖν pron. dat. 2p. pl. σύ thou, you
καὶ conj. καί and, even, also, but
εἰρήνη n. nom. fem. sg. εἰρήνη peace, quietness, rest
ἐν prep. ἐν (+dat) in, by, with, among, at, on, through, to, within, into, of, for
ἐπιγνώσει n. dat. fem. sg. ἐπίγνωσις knowledge, acknowledging, acknowledgement
τοῦ art. gen. masc. sg. ὁ ἡ τό the, this, that, he, she, it
Θεοῦ n. gen. masc. sg. θεός God, god
καὶ conj. καί and, even, also, but
Ἰησοῦ n. gen. masc. sg. Ἰησοῦς Jesus
τοῦ art. gen. masc. sg. ὁ ἡ τό the, this, that, he, she, it
Κυρίου n. gen. masc. sg. κύριος Lord, lord, master, sir, LORD, God, Master, owner
ἡμῶν pron. gen. 1p. pl. ἐγώ I
3 ὡς adv. ὡς as, when, as it were, how, about, like, as soon as, even as, while
πάντα adj. acc. neut. pl. πᾶς πᾶσα πᾶν all, every, whosoever, every one, no, whole, any
ἡμῖν pron. dat. 1p. pl. ἐγώ I
τῆς art. gen. fem. sg. ὁ ἡ τό the, this, that, he, she, it
θείας adj. gen. fem. sg. θεῖος divine
δυνάμεως n. gen. fem. sg. δύναμις power, mighty work, miracle, strength, might
αὐτοῦ pron. gen. masc. 3p. sg. αὐτός ή ό self, of oneself, even, very, the same, he, she, it
τὰ art. acc. neut. pl. ὁ ἡ τό the, this, that, he, she, it
πρὸς prep. πρός (+gen) for, (+dat) at, (+acc) unto, to, with, for, against
ζωὴν n. acc. fem. sg. ζωή life, lifetime
καὶ conj. καί and, even, also, but
εὐσέβειαν n. acc. fem. sg. εὐσέβεια godliness, holiness
διὰ prep. διά (+gen) by, through, with, in, of, (+acc) for, because of, for a cause
τῆς art. gen. fem. sg. ὁ ἡ τό the, this, that, he, she, it
ἐπιγνώσεως n. gen. fem. sg. ἐπίγνωσις knowledge, acknowledging, acknowledgement

τοῦ art. gen. masc. sg. ὁ ἡ τό the, this, that, he, she, it
ἡμᾶς pron. acc. 1p. pl. ἐγώ I
διὰ prep. διά (+gen) by, through, with, in, of, (+acc) for, because of, for a cause
δόξης n. gen. fem. sg. δόξα glory, honour, praise, dignity, worship
καὶ conj. καί and, even, also, but
ἀρετῆς n. gen. fem. sg. ἀρετή virtue, praise
4 δι' prep. διά (+gen) by, through, with, in, of, (+acc) for, because of, for a cause
ὧν relative pron. gen. neut. pl. ὅς ἥ ὅ who, which, what, that
τὰ art. acc. neut. pl. ὁ ἡ τό the, this, that, he, she, it
μέγιστα superl. adj. acc. neut. pl. μέγας great, loud, greatest, high, large, mighty, strong
ἡμῖν pron. dat. 1p. pl. ἐγώ I
καὶ conj. καί and, even, also, but
τίμια adj. acc. neut. pl. τίμιος precious, dear, has in reputation, honourable
ἐπαγγέλματα n. acc. neut. pl. ἐπάγγελμα promise
ἵνα conj. ἵνα that, to, lest, for to, so that, albeit, because, for, so as
διὰ prep. διά (+gen) by, through, with, in, of, (+acc) for, because of, for a cause
τούτων demo. pron. gen. neut. pl. οὗτος αὕτη τοῦτο this, the same, this same, he, she, it
θείας adj. gen. fem. sg. θεῖος divine
κοινωνοὶ n. nom. masc. pl. κοινωνός partaker, partner, companion, fellowship
φύσεως n. gen. fem. sg. φύσις nature
τῆς art. gen. fem. sg. ὁ ἡ τό the, this, that, he, she, it
ἐν prep. ἐν (+dat) in, by, with, among, at, on, through, to, within, into, of, for
κόσμῳ n. dat. masc. sg. κόσμος world, adorning
ἐν prep. ἐν (+dat) in, by, with, among, at, on, through, to, within, into, of, for
ἐπιθυμίᾳ n. dat. fem. sg. ἐπιθυμία lust, concupiscence, desire
φθορᾶς n. gen. fem. sg. φθορά corruption, destroy, perish
5 καὶ conj. καί and, even, also, but
αὐτὸ pron. acc. neut. 3p. sg. αὐτός ἡ ὁ self, of oneself, even, very, the same, he, she, it
τοῦτο demo. pron. acc. neut. sg. οὗτος αὕτη τοῦτο this, the same, this same, he, she, it
δὲ conj. δέ but, and, now, also, to the contrary, rather, then
σπουδὴν n. acc. fem. sg. σπουδή diligence, haste, business, care, carefulness
πᾶσαν adj. acc. fem. sg. πᾶς πᾶσα πᾶν all, every, whosoever, every one, no, whole, any
ἐν prep. ἐν (+dat) in, by, with, among, at, on, through, to, within, into, of, for
τῇ art. dat. fem. sg. ὁ ἡ τό the, this, that, he, she, it
πίστει n. dat. fem. sg. πίστις faith, assurance, belief, fidelity
ὑμῶν pron. gen. 2p. pl. σύ thou, you
τὴν art. acc. fem. sg. ὁ ἡ τό the, this, that, he, she, it
ἀρετήν n. acc. fem. sg. ἀρετή virtue, praise
ἐν prep. ἐν (+dat) in, by, with, among, at, on, through, to, within, into, of, for
δὲ conj. δέ but, and, now, also, to the contrary, rather, then
τῇ art. dat. fem. sg. ὁ ἡ τό the, this, that, he, she, it
ἀρετῇ n. dat. fem. sg. ἀρετή virtue, praise
τὴν art. acc. fem. sg. ὁ ἡ τό the, this, that, he, she, it
γνῶσιν n. acc. fem. sg. γνῶσις knowledge, science
6 ἐν prep. ἐν (+dat) in, by, with, among, at, on, through, to, within, into, of, for
δὲ conj. δέ but, and, now, also, to the contrary, rather, then
τῇ art. dat. fem. sg. ὁ ἡ τό the, this, that, he, she, it
γνώσει n. dat. fem. sg. γνῶσις knowledge, science
τὴν art. acc. fem. sg. ὁ ἡ τό the, this, that, he, she, it
ἐγκράτειαν n. acc. fem. sg. ἐγκράτεια temperance
ἐν prep. ἐν (+dat) in, by, with, among, at, on, through, to, within, into, of, for
δὲ conj. δέ but, and, now, also, to the contrary, rather, then
τῇ art. dat. fem. sg. ὁ ἡ τό the, this, that, he, she, it
ἐγκρατείᾳ n. dat. fem. sg. ἐγκράτεια temperance
τὴν art. acc. fem. sg. ὁ ἡ τό the, this, that, he, she, it

ὑπομονὴν n. acc. fem. sg. ὑπομονή patience, enduring
ἐν prep. ἐν (+dat) in, by, with, among, at, on, through, to, within, into, of, for
δὲ conj. δέ but, and, now, also, to the contrary, rather, then
τῇ art. dat. fem. sg. ὁ ἡ τό the, this, that, he, she, it
ὑπομονῇ n. dat. fem. sg. ὑπομονή patience, enduring
τὴν art. acc. fem. sg. ὁ ἡ τό the, this, that, he, she, it
εὐσέβειαν n. acc. fem. sg. εὐσέβεια godliness, holiness
7 ἐν prep. ἐν (+dat) in, by, with, among, at, on, through, to, within, into, of, for
δὲ conj. δέ but, and, now, also, to the contrary, rather, then
τῇ art. dat. fem. sg. ὁ ἡ τό the, this, that, he, she, it
εὐσεβείᾳ n. dat. fem. sg. εὐσέβεια godliness, holiness
τὴν art. acc. fem. sg. ὁ ἡ τό the, this, that, he, she, it
φιλαδελφίαν n. acc. fem. sg. φιλαδελφία brotherly love, brotherly kindness
ἐν prep. ἐν (+dat) in, by, with, among, at, on, through, to, within, into, of, for
δὲ conj. δέ but, and, now, also, to the contrary, rather, then
τῇ art. dat. fem. sg. ὁ ἡ τό the, this, that, he, she, it
φιλαδελφίᾳ n. dat. fem. sg. φιλαδελφία brotherly love, brotherly kindness
τὴν art. acc. fem. sg. ὁ ἡ τό the, this, that, he, she, it
ἀγάπην n. acc. fem. sg. ἀγάπη love, charity, feast of charity
8 ταῦτα demo. pron. nom. neut. pl. οὗτος αὕτη τοῦτο this, the same, this same, he, she, it
γὰρ conj. γάρ for, and, because, but, indeed
ὑμῖν pron. dat. 2p. pl. σύ thou, you
καὶ conj. καί and, even, also, but
οὐκ particle of negation. οὐ οὐκ οὐχ not, no, neither, none, nay, nor, never, nothing
ἀργοὺς adj. acc. masc. pl. ἀργός idle, barren, slow
οὐδὲ adv. οὐδέ neither, nor, not, no, not even, never, not yet
ἀκάρπους adj. acc. masc. pl. ἄκαρπος unfruitful, without fruit
εἰς prep. εἰς (+acc) into, to, unto, for, in, on, toward, against, upon, at, among
τὴν art. acc. fem. sg. ὁ ἡ τό the, this, that, he, she, it
τοῦ art. gen. masc. sg. ὁ ἡ τό the, this, that, he, she, it
Κυρίου n. gen. masc. sg. κύριος Lord, lord, master, sir, LORD, God, Master, owner
ἡμῶν pron. gen. 1p. pl. ἐγώ I
Ἰησοῦ n. gen. masc. sg. Ἰησοῦς Jesus
Χριστοῦ n. gen. masc. sg. Χριστός Christ
ἐπίγνωσιν n. acc. fem. sg. ἐπίγνωσις knowledge, acknowledging, acknowledgement
9 ᾧ relative pron. dat. masc. sg. ὅς ἥ ὅ who, which, what, that
γὰρ conj. γάρ for, and, because, but, indeed
μὴ particle of negation. μή not, no, lest, neither, none, nothing, nor, never, without
ταῦτα demo. pron. nom. neut. pl. οὗτος αὕτη τοῦτο this, the same, this same, he, she, it
τυφλός adj. nom. masc. sg. τυφλός blind
λήθην n. acc. fem. sg. λήθη forget, forgetfulness
τοῦ art. gen. masc. sg. ὁ ἡ τό the, this, that, he, she, it
καθαρισμοῦ n. gen. masc. sg. καθαρισμός cleansing, purge, purifying, purification
τῶν art. gen. fem. pl. ὁ ἡ τό the, this, that, he, she, it
πάλαι adv. πάλαι long age, a great while ago, any while, in time past, old, of old
αὐτοῦ pron. gen. masc. 3p. sg. αὐτός ή ό self, of oneself, even, very, the same, he, she, it
ἁμαρτιῶν n. gen. fem. pl. ἁμαρτία sin, offence, sinful
10 διὸ conj. διό wherefore, therefore, for which cause
μᾶλλον adv. μᾶλλον rather, more, more and more, better, much, much the more
ἀδελφοί n. voc. masc. pl. ἀδελφός brother
βεβαίαν adj. acc. fem. sg. βέβαιος sure, stedfast, firm, more sure, of force
ὑμῶν pron. gen. 2p. pl. σύ thou, you
τὴν art. acc. fem. sg. ὁ ἡ τό the, this, that, he, she, it
κλῆσιν n. acc. fem. sg. κλῆσις calling, vocation
καὶ conj. καί and, even, also, but

ἐκλογὴν n. acc. fem. sg. ἐκλογή election, chosen
ταῦτα demo. pron. acc. neut. pl. οὗτος αὕτη τοῦτο this, the same, this same, he, she, it
γὰρ conj. γάρ for, and, because, but, indeed
οὐ particle of negation. οὐ οὐκ οὐχ not, no, neither, none, nay, nor, never, nothing
μὴ particle of negation. μή not, no, lest, neither, none, nothing, nor, never, without
ποτε adv. ποτέ in time past, at any time, sometimes, in old time, once, when
11 οὕτω adv. οὕτω οὕτως so, even so, thus, on this wise, likewise, after this manner
γὰρ conj. γάρ for, and, because, but, indeed
πλουσίως adv. πλουσίως richly, abundantly
ὑμῖν pron. dat. 2p. pl. σύ thou, you
ἡ art. nom. fem. sg. ὁ ἡ τό the, this, that, he, she, it
εἴσοδος n. nom. fem. sg. εἴσοδος coming, entrance into, entering in
εἰς prep. εἰς (+acc) into, to, unto, for, in, on, toward, against, upon, at, among
τὴν art. acc. fem. sg. ὁ ἡ τό the, this, that, he, she, it
αἰώνιον adj. acc. fem. sg. αἰώνιος eternal, everlasting, world, for ever
βασιλείαν n. acc. fem. sg. βασιλεία kingdom, reign
τοῦ art. gen. masc. sg. ὁ ἡ τό the, this, that, he, she, it
Κυρίου n. gen. masc. sg. κύριος Lord, lord, master, sir, LORD, God, Master, owner
ἡμῶν pron. gen. 1p. pl. ἐγώ I
καὶ conj. καί and, even, also, but
σωτῆρος n. gen. masc. sg. σωτήρ Saviour, saviour
Ἰησοῦ n. gen. masc. sg. Ἰησοῦς Jesus
Χριστοῦ n. gen. masc. sg. Χριστός Christ
12 Διὸ conj. διό wherefore, therefore, for which cause
οὐκ particle of negation. οὐ οὐκ οὐχ not, no, neither, none, nay, nor, never, nothing
ὑμᾶς pron. acc. 2p. pl. σύ thou, you
ἀεὶ adv. ἀεί always, always, ever
περὶ prep. περί (+gen) of, for, concerning, (+acc) about, concerning, in
τούτων demo. pron. gen. neut. pl. οὗτος αὕτη τοῦτο this, the same, this same, he, she, it
καίπερ conj. καίπερ though, and yet
καὶ conj. καί and, even, also, but
ἐν prep. ἐν (+dat) in, by, with, among, at, on, through, to, within, into, of, for
τῇ art. dat. fem. sg. ὁ ἡ τό the, this, that, he, she, it
ἀληθείᾳ n. dat. fem. sg. ἀλήθεια truth, verity
13 δίκαιον adj. acc. neut. sg. δίκαιος righteous, just, meet, right
δὲ conj. δέ but, and, now, also, to the contrary, rather, then
ἐφ' prep. ἐπί (+gen) on, in, upon, (+dat) in, at, for, upon, (+acc) on, upon, unto, to, against
ὅσον relative pron. acc. masc. sg. ὅσος as many as, whatsoever, that, as long as, how much
ἐν prep. ἐν (+dat) in, by, with, among, at, on, through, to, within, into, of, for
τούτῳ demo. pron. dat. neut. sg. οὗτος αὕτη τοῦτο this, the same, this same, he, she, it
τῷ art. dat. neut. sg. ὁ ἡ τό the, this, that, he, she, it
σκηνώματι n. dat. neut. sg. σκήνωμα tabernacle
ὑμᾶς pron. acc. 2p. pl. σύ thou, you
ἐν prep. ἐν (+dat) in, by, with, among, at, on, through, to, within, into, of, for
ὑπομνήσει n. dat. fem. sg. ὑπόμνησις remembrance, putting in remembrance
14 ὅτι conj. ὅτι that, for, because, how that, how, because that, for that, though
ταχινή adj. nom. fem. sg. ταχινός shortly, swift
ἡ art. nom. fem. sg. ὁ ἡ τό the, this, that, he, she, it
ἀπόθεσις n. nom. fem. sg. ἀπόθεσις putting away, put off, putting off
τοῦ art. gen. neut. sg. ὁ ἡ τό the, this, that, he, she, it
σκηνώματός n. gen. neut. sg. σκήνωμα tabernacle
μου pron. gen. 1p. sg. ἐγώ I
καθὼς adv. καθώς as, even as, according as, according to
καὶ conj. καί and, even, also, but
ὁ art. nom. masc. sg. ὁ ἡ τό the, this, that, he, she, it

Κύριος n. nom. masc. sg. κύριος Lord, lord, master, sir, LORD, God, Master, owner
ἡμῶν pron. gen. 1p. pl. ἐγώ I
Ἰησοῦς n. nom. masc. sg. Ἰησοῦς Jesus
Χριστὸς n. nom. masc. sg. Χριστός Christ
μοι pron. dat. 1p. sg. ἐγώ I
15 δὲ conj. δέ but, and, now, also, to the contrary, rather, then
καὶ conj. καί and, even, also, but
ἑκάστοτε adv. ἑκάστοτε always
ὑμᾶς pron. acc. 2p. pl. σύ thou, you
μετὰ prep. μετά (+gen) with, among, against, (+acc) after
τὴν art. acc. fem. sg. ὁ ἡ τό the, this, that, he, she, it
ἐμὴν poss. pron. acc. fem. 1p. sg. ἐμός my, mine, mine own, of me
ἔξοδον n. acc. fem. sg. ἔξοδος decease, departing
τὴν art. acc. fem. sg. ὁ ἡ τό the, this, that, he, she, it
τούτων demo. pron. gen. neut. pl. οὗτος αὕτη τοῦτο this, the same, this same, he, she, it
μνήμην n. acc. fem. sg. μνήμη remembrance
16 Οὐ particle of negation. οὐ οὐκ οὐχ not, no, neither, none, nay, nor, never, nothing
γὰρ conj. γάρ for, and, because, but, indeed
μύθοις n. dat. masc. pl. μῦθος fable, myth
ὑμῖν pron. dat. 2p. pl. σύ thou, you
τὴν art. acc. fem. sg. ὁ ἡ τό the, this, that, he, she, it
τοῦ art. gen. masc. sg. ὁ ἡ τό the, this, that, he, she, it
Κυρίου n. gen. masc. sg. κύριος Lord, lord, master, sir, LORD, God, Master, owner
ἡμῶν pron. gen. 1p. pl. ἐγώ I
Ἰησοῦ n. gen. masc. sg. Ἰησοῦς Jesus
Χριστοῦ n. gen. masc. sg. Χριστός Christ
δύναμιν n. acc. fem. sg. δύναμις power, mighty work, miracle, strength, might
καὶ conj. καί and, even, also, but
παρουσίαν n. acc. fem. sg. παρουσία coming, presence
ἀλλ' conj. ἀλλά but, yea, yet, nevertheless, howbeit, nay, therefore
ἐπόπται n. nom. masc. pl. ἐπόπτης eyewitness
τῆς art. gen. fem. sg. ὁ ἡ τό the, this, that, he, she, it
ἐκείνου demo. pron. gen. masc. sg. ἐκεῖνος that, he, the same, that same
μεγαλειότητος n. gen. fem. sg. μεγαλειότης mighty power, magnificence, majesty
17 γὰρ conj. γάρ for, and, because, but, indeed
παρὰ prep. παρά (+gen) of, from, (+dat) with, for, (+acc) beside, at, by, above, against
Θεοῦ n. gen. masc. sg. θεός God, god
πατρὸς n. gen. masc. sg. πατήρ Father, father, parent
τιμὴν n. acc. fem. sg. τιμή honour, price, preciousness, sum
καὶ conj. καί and, even, also, but
δόξαν n. acc. fem. sg. δόξα glory, honour, praise, dignity, worship
φωνῆς n. gen. fem. sg. φωνή voice, sound, noise
αὐτῷ pron. dat. masc. 3p. sg. αὐτός ἡ ὁ self, of oneself, even, very, the same, he, she, it
τοιᾶσδε demo. pron. gen. fem. sg. τοιόσδε such
ὑπὸ prep. ὑπό (+gen) of, by, with, from, among, (+acc) under
τῆς art. gen. fem. sg. ὁ ἡ τό the, this, that, he, she, it
μεγαλοπρεποῦς adj. gen. fem. sg. μεγαλοπρεπής excellent
δόξης n. gen. fem. sg. δόξα glory, honour, praise, dignity, worship
Οὗτός demo. pron. nom. masc. sg. οὗτος αὕτη τοῦτο this, the same, this same, he, she, it
ὁ art. nom. masc. sg. ὁ ἡ τό the, this, that, he, she, it
υἱός n. nom. masc. sg. υἱός son, child, descendant, offspring, heir
μου pron. gen. 1p. sg. ἐγώ I
ὁ art. nom. masc. sg. ὁ ἡ τό the, this, that, he, she, it
ἀγαπητός adj. nom. masc. sg. ἀγαπητός beloved, dearly beloved, dear, wellbeloved
εἰς prep. εἰς (+acc) into, to, unto, for, in, on, toward, against, upon, at, among

ὃν relative pron. acc. masc. sg. ὅς ἥ ὅ who, which, what, that
ἐγὼ pron. nom. 1p. sg. ἐγώ I
18 καὶ conj. καί and, even, also, but
ταύτην demo. pron. acc. fem. sg. οὗτος αὕτη τοῦτο this, the same, this same, he, she, it
τὴν art. acc. fem. sg. ὁ ἡ τό the, this, that, he, she, it
φωνὴν n. acc. fem. sg. φωνή voice, sound, noise
ἡμεῖς pron. nom. 1p. pl. ἐγώ I
ἐξ prep. ἐκ ἐξ (+gen) of, from, out of, by, on, with, in, among, through
οὐρανοῦ n. gen. masc. sg. οὐρανός heaven, air, sky
σὺν prep. σύν (+dat) with, beside
αὐτῷ pron. dat. masc. 3p. sg. αὐτός ή ό self, of oneself, even, very, the same, he, she, it
ἐν prep. ἐν (+dat) in, by, with, among, at, on, through, to, within, into, of, for
τῷ art. dat. neut. sg. ὁ ἡ τό the, this, that, he, she, it
ὄρει n. dat. neut. sg. ὄρος mountain, mount, hill
τῷ art. dat. neut. sg. ὁ ἡ τό the, this, that, he, she, it
ἁγίῳ adj. dat. neut. sg. ἅγιος Holy, holy, saint, Holy One, holy thing, most holy
19 καὶ conj. καί and, even, also, but
βεβαιότερον compar. adj. acc. masc. sg. βέβαιος sure, stedfast, firm, more sure, of force
τὸν art. acc. masc. sg. ὁ ἡ τό the, this, that, he, she, it
προφητικὸν adj. acc. masc. sg. προφητικός of the prophets, of prophecy
λόγον n. acc. masc. sg. λόγος word, saying, account, speech, thing, matter
ᾧ relative pron. dat. masc. sg. ὅς ἥ ὅ who, which, what, that
καλῶς adv. καλῶς good, well, full well
ὡς adv. ὡς as, when, as it were, how, about, like, as soon as, even as, while
λύχνῳ n. dat. masc. sg. λύχνος candle, light, lamp
ἐν prep. ἐν (+dat) in, by, with, among, at, on, through, to, within, into, of, for
αὐχμηρῷ adj. dat. masc. sg. αὐχμηρός dark
τόπῳ n. dat. masc. sg. τόπος place, room, quarter
ἕως conj. ἕως till, until, unto, until when, while, as far as, even, until now
οὗ relative pron. gen. masc. sg. ὅς ἥ ὅ who, which, what, that
ἡμέρα n. nom. fem. sg. ἡμέρα day, time, year, while, age, day time
καὶ conj. καί and, even, also, but
φωσφόρος adj. nom. masc. sg. φωσφόρος day star
ἐν prep. ἐν (+dat) in, by, with, among, at, on, through, to, within, into, of, for
ταῖς art. dat. fem. pl. ὁ ἡ τό the, this, that, he, she, it
καρδίαις n. dat. fem. pl. καρδία heart
ὑμῶν pron. gen. 2p. pl. σύ thou, you
20 τοῦτο demo. pron. acc. neut. sg. οὗτος αὕτη τοῦτο this, the same, this same, he, she, it
πρῶτον adv. πρῶτον first, at the first, first of all, at first, at the beginning, before, chiefly
ὅτι conj. ὅτι that, for, because, how that, how, because that, for that, though
πᾶσα adj. nom. fem. sg. πᾶς πᾶσα πᾶν all, every, whosoever, every one, no, whole, any
προφητεία n. nom. fem. sg. προφητεία prophecy, prophesying
γραφῆς n. gen. fem. sg. γραφή scripture
ἰδίας adj. gen. fem. sg. ἴδιος one's own, one's, privately
ἐπιλύσεως n. gen. fem. sg. ἐπίλυσις interpretation
οὐ particle of negation. οὐ οὐκ οὐχ not, no, neither, none, nay, nor, never, nothing
21 οὐ particle of negation. οὐ οὐκ οὐχ not, no, neither, none, nay, nor, never, nothing
γὰρ conj. γάρ for, and, because, but, indeed
θελήματι n. dat. neut. sg. θέλημα will, desire, pleasure
ἀνθρώπου n. gen. masc. sg. ἄνθρωπος man, human being, person, one, certain
ποτέ adv. ποτέ in time past, at any time, sometimes, in old time, once, when
προφητεία n. nom. fem. sg. προφητεία prophecy, prophesying
ἀλλ' conj. ἀλλά but, yea, yet, nevertheless, howbeit, nay, therefore
ὑπὸ prep. ὑπό (+gen) of, by, with, from, among, (+acc) under
Πνεύματος n. gen. neut. sg. πνεῦμα spirit, Spirit, Ghost, ghost, life. of the spirit, wind

Ἁγίου adj. gen. neut. sg. ἅγιος Holy, holy, saint, Holy One, holy thing, most holy
ἅγιοι adj. nom. masc. pl. ἅγιος Holy, holy, saint, Holy One, holy thing, most holy
Θεοῦ n. gen. masc. sg. θεός God, god
ἄνθρωποι n. nom. masc. pl. ἄνθρωπος man, human being, person, one, certain

2

1 δὲ conj. δέ but, and, now, also, to the contrary, rather, then
καὶ conj. καί and, even, also, but
ψευδοπροφῆται n. nom. masc. pl. ψευδοπροφήτης false prophet
ἐν prep. ἐν (+dat) in, by, with, among, at, on, through, to, within, into, of, for
τῷ art. dat. masc. sg. ὁ ἡ τό the, this, that, he, she, it
λαῷ n. dat. masc. sg. λαός people
ὡς adv. ὡς as, when, as it were, how, about, like, as soon as, even as, while
ὑμῖν pron. dat. 2p. pl. σύ thou, you
ἐν prep. ἐν (+dat) in, by, with, among, at, on, through, to, within, into, of, for
ὑμῖν pron. dat. 2p. pl. σύ thou, you
ψευδοδιδάσκαλοι n. nom. masc. pl. ψευδοδιδάσκαλος false teacher
οἵτινες relative pron. nom. masc. pl. ὅστις which, who, whosoever, that, whatsoever
αἱρέσεις n. acc. fem. pl. αἵρεσις sect, heresy
ἀπωλείας n. gen. fem. sg. ἀπώλεια destruction, perdition, waste, damnation
καὶ conj. καί and, even, also, but
τὸν art. acc. masc. sg. ὁ ἡ τό the, this, that, he, she, it
αὐτοὺς pron. acc. masc. 3p. pl. αὐτός ἡ ό self, of oneself, even, very, the same, he, she, it
δεσπότην n. acc. masc. sg. δεσπότης Lord, master
ἑαυτοῖς reflexive pron. dat. masc. 3p. pl. ἑαυτοῦ himself, herself, itself, yourself, ourselves
ταχινὴν adj. acc. fem. sg. ταχινός shortly, swift
ἀπώλειαν n. acc. fem. sg. ἀπώλεια destruction, perdition, waste, damnation
2 καὶ conj. καί and, even, also, but
πολλοὶ adj. nom. masc. pl. πολύς many, great, much, long, abundant
αὐτῶν pron. gen. masc. 3p. pl. αὐτός ἡ ό self, of oneself, even, very, the same, he, she, it
ταῖς art. dat. fem. pl. ὁ ἡ τό the, this, that, he, she, it
ἀπωλείαις n. dat. fem. pl. ἀπώλεια destruction, perdition, waste, damnation
δι' prep. διά (+gen) by, through, with, in, of, (+acc) for, because of, for a cause
οὓς relative pron. acc. masc. pl. ὅς ἥ ὅ who, which, what, that
ἡ art. nom. fem. sg. ὁ ἡ τό the, this, that, he, she, it
ὁδὸς n. nom. fem. sg. ὁδός way, journey, highway
τῆς art. gen. fem. sg. ὁ ἡ τό the, this, that, he, she, it
ἀληθείας n. gen. fem. sg. ἀλήθεια truth, verity
3 καὶ conj. καί and, even, also, but
ἐν prep. ἐν (+dat) in, by, with, among, at, on, through, to, within, into, of, for
πλεονεξίᾳ n. dat. fem. sg. πλεονεξία covetousness, covetous practice, greediness
πλαστοῖς adj. dat. masc. pl. πλαστός feigned
λόγοις n. dat. masc. pl. λόγος word, saying, account, speech, thing, matter
ὑμᾶς pron. acc. 2p. pl. σύ thou, you
οἷς relative pron. dat. masc. pl. ὅς ἥ ὅ who, which, what, that
τὸ art. nom. neut. sg. ὁ ἡ τό the, this, that, he, she, it
κρίμα n. nom. neut. sg. κρίμα judgment, damnation, condemnation
ἔκπαλαι adv. ἔκπαλαι of a long time, of old
οὐκ particle of negation. οὐ οὐκ οὐχ not, no, neither, none, nay, nor, never, nothing
καὶ conj. καί and, even, also, but
ἡ art. nom. fem. sg. ὁ ἡ τό the, this, that, he, she, it
ἀπώλεια n. nom. fem. sg. ἀπώλεια destruction, perdition, waste, damnation
αὐτῶν pron. gen. masc. 3p. pl. αὐτός ἡ ό self, of oneself, even, very, the same, he, she, it
οὐ particle of negation. οὐ οὐκ οὐχ not, no, neither, none, nay, nor, never, nothing

4 εἰ conj. εἰ if, whether, that, though, forasmuch
γὰρ conj. γάρ for, and, because, but, indeed
ὁ art. nom. masc. sg. ὁ ἡ τό the, this, that, he, she, it
Θεὸς n. nom. masc. sg. θεός God, god
ἀγγέλων n. gen. masc. pl. ἄγγελος angel, messenger
οὐκ particle of negation. οὐ οὐκ οὐχ not, no, neither, none, nay, nor, never, nothing
ἀλλὰ conj. ἀλλά but, yea, yet, nevertheless, howbeit, nay, therefore
σειραῖς n. dat. fem. pl. σειρά chain
ζόφου n. gen. masc. sg. ζόφος darkness, blackness, mist
εἰς prep. εἰς (+acc) into, to, unto, for, in, on, toward, against, upon, at, among
κρίσιν n. acc. fem. sg. κρίσις judgment, damnation, accusation, condemnation
5 καὶ conj. καί and, even, also, but
ἀρχαίου adj. gen. masc. sg. ἀρχαῖος old, one of old time
κόσμου n. gen. masc. sg. κόσμος world, adorning
οὐκ particle of negation. οὐ οὐκ οὐχ not, no, neither, none, nay, nor, never, nothing
ἀλλ' conj. ἀλλά but, yea, yet, nevertheless, howbeit, nay, therefore
ὄγδοον ordinal. adj. acc. masc. sg. ὄγδοος eighth
Νῶε n. acc. masc. sg. Νῶε Noe, Noah
δικαιοσύνης n. gen. fem. sg. δικαιοσύνη righteousness
κήρυκα n. acc. masc. sg. κήρυξ preacher
κατακλυσμὸν n. acc. masc. sg. κατακλυσμός flood
κόσμῳ n. dat. masc. sg. κόσμος world, adorning
ἀσεβῶν adj. gen. masc. pl. ἀσεβής ungodly, ungodly man
6 καὶ conj. καί and, even, also, but
πόλεις n. acc. fem. pl. πόλις city
Σοδόμων n. gen. neut. pl. Σόδομα Sodom, Sodoma
καὶ conj. καί and, even, also, but
Γομόρρας n. gen. fem. sg. Γόμορρα Gomorrha
καταστροφῇ n. dat. fem. sg. καταστροφή subverting, overthrow
ὑπόδειγμα n. acc. neut. sg. ὑπόδειγμα example, ensample, pattern
7 καὶ conj. καί and, even, also, but
δίκαιον adj. acc. masc. sg. δίκαιος righteous, just, meet, right
Λὼτ n. acc. masc. sg. Λώτ Lot
ὑπὸ prep. ὑπό (+gen) of, by, with, from, among, (+acc) under
τῆς art. gen. fem. sg. ὁ ἡ τό the, this, that, he, she, it
τῶν art. gen. masc. pl. ὁ ἡ τό the, this, that, he, she, it
ἀθέσμων adj. gen. masc. pl. ἄθεσμος wicked
ἐν prep. ἐν (+dat) in, by, with, among, at, on, through, to, within, into, of, for
ἀσελγείᾳ n. dat. fem. sg. ἀσέλγεια lasciviousness, wantonness, filthy
ἀναστροφῆς n. gen. fem. sg. ἀναστροφή conversation
8 βλέμματι n. dat. neut. sg. βλέμμα seeing
γὰρ conj. γάρ for, and, because, but, indeed
καὶ conj. καί and, even, also, but
ἀκοῇ n. dat. fem. sg. ἀκοή hearing, ear, fame, report, rumour, which one heard
ὁ art. nom. masc. sg. ὁ ἡ τό the, this, that, he, she, it
δίκαιος adj. nom. masc. sg. δίκαιος righteous, just, meet, right
ἐν prep. ἐν (+dat) in, by, with, among, at, on, through, to, within, into, of, for
αὐτοῖς pron. dat. masc. 3p. pl. αὐτός ή ό self, of oneself, even, very, the same, he, she, it
ἡμέραν n. acc. fem. sg. ἡμέρα day, time, year, while, age, day time
ἐξ prep. ἐκ ἐξ (+gen) of, from, out of, by, on, with, in, among, through
ἡμέρας n. gen. fem. sg. ἡμέρα day, time, year, while, age, day time
ψυχὴν n. acc. fem. sg. ψυχή life, soul, mind, heart
δικαίαν adj. acc. fem. sg. δίκαιος righteous, just, meet, right
ἀνόμοις adj. dat. neut. pl. ἄνομος without law, transgressor, wicked, lawless, unlawful
ἔργοις n. dat. neut. pl. ἔργον work, deed, doing labour

9 Κύριος n. nom. masc. sg. κύριος Lord, lord, master, sir, LORD, God, Master, owner
εὐσεβεῖς adj. acc. masc. pl. εὐσεβής devout, godly
ἐκ prep. ἐκ ἐξ (+gen) of, from, out of, by, on, with, in, among, through
πειρασμῶν n. gen. masc. pl. πειρασμός temptation, trial
ἀδίκους adj. acc. masc. pl. ἄδικος unjust, unrighteous
δὲ conj. δέ but, and, now, also, to the contrary, rather, then
εἰς prep. εἰς (+acc) into, to, unto, for, in, on, toward, against, upon, at, among
ἡμέραν n. acc. fem. sg. ἡμέρα day, time, year, while, age, day time
κρίσεως n. gen. fem. sg. κρίσις judgment, damnation, accusation, condemnation
10 μάλιστα adv. μάλιστα specially, especially, chiefly, most of all
δὲ conj. δέ but, and, now, also, to the contrary, rather, then
τοὺς art. acc. masc. pl. ὁ ἡ τό the, this, that, he, she, it
ὀπίσω prep. ὀπίσω (+gen) after. (adv.) back, behind
σαρκὸς n. gen. fem. sg. σάρξ flesh, carnal
ἐν prep. ἐν (+dat) in, by, with, among, at, on, thróugh, to, within, into, of, for
ἐπιθυμίᾳ n. dat. fem. sg. ἐπιθυμία lust, concupiscence, desire
μιασμοῦ n. gen. masc. sg. μιασμός uncleanness
καὶ conj. καί and, even, also, but
κυριότητος n. gen. fem. sg. κυριότης dominion, government
τολμηταὶ n. nom. masc. pl. τολμητής presumptuous
αὐθάδεις adj. nom. masc. pl. αὐθάδης selfwilled
δόξας n. acc. fem. pl. δόξα glory, honour, praise, dignity, worship
οὐ particle of negation. οὐ οὐκ οὐχ not, no, neither, none, nay, nor, never, nothing
11 ὅπου adv. ὅπου where, whither, whereas, in what place, wheresoever
ἄγγελοι n. nom. masc. pl. ἄγγελος angel, messenger
ἰσχύϊ n. dat. fem. sg. ἰσχύς strength, might, power, ability
καὶ conj. καί and, even, also, but
δυνάμει n. dat. fem. sg. δύναμις power, mighty work, miracle, strength, might
μείζονες compar. adj. nom. masc. pl. μέγας great, loud, greatest, high, large, mighty, strong
οὐ particle of negation. οὐ οὐκ οὐχ not, no, neither, none, nay, nor, never, nothing
κατ' prep. κατά (+gen) against, by, throughout, down, (+acc) according to, after, with
αὐτῶν pron. gen. masc. 3p. pl. αὐτός ή ό self, of oneself, even, very, the same, he, she, it
παρὰ prep. παρά (+gen) of, from, (+dat) with, for, (+acc) beside, at, by, above, against
Κυρίῳ n. dat. masc. sg. κύριος Lord, lord, master, sir, LORD, God, Master, owner
βλάσφημον adj. acc. fem. sg. βλάσφημος blasphemous, blasphemer, railing
κρίσιν n. acc. fem. sg. κρίσις judgment, damnation, accusation, condemnation
12 οὗτοι demo. pron. nom. masc. pl. οὗτος αὕτη τοῦτο this, the same, this same, he, she, it
δὲ conj. δέ but, and, now, also, to the contrary, rather, then
ὡς adv. ὡς as, when, as it were, how, about, like, as soon as, even as, while
ἄλογα adj. nom. neut. pl. ἄλογος unreasonable, brute
ζῷα n. nom. neut. pl. ζῷον beast
φυσικὰ adj. nom. neut. pl. φυσικός natural
εἰς prep. εἰς (+acc) into, to, unto, for, in, on, toward, against, upon, at, among
ἅλωσιν n. acc. fem. sg. ἅλωσις taking, catching, capture
καὶ conj. καί and, even, also, but
φθορὰν n. acc. fem. sg. φθορά corruption, destroy, perish
ἐν prep. ἐν (+dat) in, by, with, among, at, on, through, to, within, into, of, for
οἷς relative pron. dat. neut. pl. ὅς ἥ ὅ who, which, what, that
ἐν prep. ἐν (+dat) in, by, with, among, at, on, through, to, within, into, of, for
τῇ art. dat. fem. sg. ὁ ἡ τό the, this, that, he, she, it
φθορᾷ n. dat. fem. sg. φθορά corruption, destroy, perish
αὐτῶν pron. gen. masc. 3p. pl. αὐτός ή ό self, of oneself, even, very, the same, he, she, it
13 μισθὸν n. acc. masc. sg. μισθός reward, hire, wage
ἀδικίας n. gen. fem. sg. ἀδικία iniquity, unrighteousness, unjust, wrong
ἡδονὴν n. acc. fem. sg. ἡδονή pleasure, lust

τὴν art. acc. fem. sg. ὁ ἡ τό the, this, that, he, she, it
ἐν prep. ἐν (+dat) in, by, with, among, at, on, through, to, within, into, of, for
ἡμέρᾳ n. dat. fem. sg. ἡμέρα day, time, year, while, age, day time
τρυφήν n. acc. fem. sg. τρυφή riot
σπίλοι n. nom. masc. pl. σπίλος spot
καὶ conj. καί and, even, also, but
μῶμοι n. nom. masc. pl. μῶμος blemish
ἐν prep. ἐν (+dat) in, by, with, among, at, on, through, to, within, into, of, for
ταῖς art. dat. fem. pl. ὁ ἡ τό the, this, that, he, she, it
ἀπάταις n. dat. fem. pl. ἀπάτη deceitfulness, deceit
αὐτῶν pron. gen. masc. 3p. pl. αὐτός ή ό self, of oneself, even, very, the same, he, she, it
ὑμῖν pron. dat. 2p. pl. σύ thou, you
14 ὀφθαλμοὺς n. acc. masc. pl. ὀφθαλμός eye, sight
μεστοὺς adj. acc. masc. pl. μεστός full
μοιχαλίδος adj. gen. fem. sg. μοιχαλίς adulterous, adulteress, adultery
καὶ conj. καί and, even, also, but
ἀκαταπαύστους adj. acc. masc. pl. ἀκατάπαυστος that cannot cease
ἁμαρτίας n. gen. fem. sg. ἁμαρτία sin, offence, sinful
ψυχὰς n. acc. fem. pl. ψυχή life, soul, mind, heart
ἀστηρίκτους adj. acc. fem. pl. ἀστήρικτος unstable
καρδίαν n. acc. fem. sg. καρδία heart
πλεονεξίαις n. dat. fem. pl. πλεονεξία covetousness, covetous practice, greediness
κατάρας n. gen. fem. sg. κατάρα curse, cursing, cursed
τέκνα n. nom. neut. pl. τέκνον child, son, daughter
15 τὴν art. acc. fem. sg. ὁ ἡ τό the, this, that, he, she, it
εὐθεῖαν adj. acc. fem. sg. εὐθύς straight, right
ὁδὸν n. acc. fem. sg. ὁδός way, journey, highway
τῇ art. dat. fem. sg. ὁ ἡ τό the, this, that, he, she, it
ὁδῷ n. dat. fem. sg. ὁδός way, journey, highway
τοῦ art. gen. masc. sg. ὁ ἡ τό the, this, that, he, she, it
Βαλαὰμ n. gen. masc. sg. Βαλαάμ Balaam
τοῦ art. gen. masc. sg. ὁ ἡ τό the, this, that, he, she, it
Βοσόρ n. gen. masc. sg. Βοσόρ Bosor
ὃς relative pron. nom. masc. sg. ὅς ἥ ὅ who, which, what, that
μισθὸν n. acc. masc. sg. μισθός reward, hire, wage
ἀδικίας n. gen. fem. sg. ἀδικία iniquity, unrighteousness, unjust, wrong
16 ἔλεγξιν n. acc. fem. sg. ἔλεγξις rebuke
δὲ conj. δέ but, and, now, also, to the contrary, rather, then
ἰδίας adj. gen. fem. sg. ἴδιος one's own, one's, privately
παρανομίας n. gen. fem. sg. παρανομία iniquity
ὑποζύγιον n. nom. neut. sg. ὑποζύγιος ass, beast of burden, under the york
ἄφωνον adj. nom. neut. sg. ἄφωνος dumb, without signification
ἐν prep. ἐν (+dat) in, by, with, among, at, on, through, to, within, into, of, for
ἀνθρώπου n. gen. masc. sg. ἄνθρωπος man, human being, person, one, certain
φωνῇ n. dat. fem. sg. φωνή voice, sound, noise
τὴν art. acc. fem. sg. ὁ ἡ τό the, this, that, he, she, it
τοῦ art. gen. masc. sg. ὁ ἡ τό the, this, that, he, she, it
προφήτου n. gen. masc. sg. προφήτης prophet
παραφρονίαν n. acc. fem. sg. παραφρονία madness
17 οὗτοί demo. pron. nom. masc. pl. οὗτος αὕτη τοῦτο this, the same, this same, he, she, it
πηγαὶ n. nom. fem. pl. πηγή fountain, well
ἄνυδροι adj. nom. fem. pl. ἄνυδρος dry, without water
νεφέλαι n. nom. fem. pl. νεφέλη cloud
ὑπὸ prep. ὑπό (+gen) of, by, with, from, among, (+acc) under
λαίλαπος n. gen. fem. sg. λαῖλαψ storm, tempest

οἷς relative pron. dat. masc. pl. ὅς ἥ ὅ who, which, what, that
ὁ art. nom. masc. sg. ὁ ἡ τό the, this, that, he, she, it
ζόφος n. nom. masc. sg. ζόφος darkness, blackness, mist
τοῦ art. gen. neut. sg. ὁ ἡ τό the, this, that, he, she, it
σκότους n. gen. neut. sg. σκότος darkness
εἰς prep. εἰς (+acc) into, to, unto, for, in, on, toward, against, upon, at, among
αἰῶνα n. acc. masc. sg. αἰών ever, ever and ever, evermore, age, eternal, world
18 ὑπέρογκα adj. acc. neut. pl. ὑπέρογκος great swelling
γὰρ conj. γάρ for, and, because, but, indeed
ματαιότητος n. gen. fem. sg. ματαιότης vanity
ἐν prep. ἐν (+dat) in, by, with, among, at, on, through, to, within, into, of, for
ἐπιθυμίαις n. dat. fem. pl. ἐπιθυμία lust, concupiscence, desire
σαρκὸς n. gen. fem. sg. σάρξ flesh, carnal
ἐν prep. ἐν (+dat) in, by, with, among, at, on, through, to, within, into, of, for
ἀσελγείαις n. dat. fem. pl. ἀσέλγεια lasciviousness, wantonness, filthy
τοὺς art. acc. masc. pl. ὁ ἡ τό the, this, that, he, she, it
ὄντως adv. ὄντως indeed, certainly, clean, of a truth, verily
τοὺς art. acc. masc. pl. ὁ ἡ τό the, this, that, he, she, it
ἐν prep. ἐν (+dat) in, by, with, among, at, on, through, to, within, into, of, for
πλάνῃ n. dat. fem. sg. πλάνη error, deception, deceit, delusion
19 ἐλευθερίαν n. acc. fem. sg. ἐλευθερία liberty
αὐτοῖς pron. dat. masc. 3p. pl. αὐτός ἡ ὁ self, of oneself, even, very, the same, he, she, it
αὐτοὶ pron. nom. masc. 3p. pl. αὐτός ἡ ὁ self, of oneself, even, very, the same, he, she, it
δοῦλοι n. nom. masc. pl. δοῦλος servant, bondman, bond, slave
τῆς art. gen. fem. sg. ὁ ἡ τό the, this, that, he, she, it
φθορᾶς n. gen. fem. sg. φθορά corruption, destroy, perish
ᾧ relative pron. dat. masc. sg. ὅς ἥ ὅ who, which, what, that
γάρ conj. γάρ for, and, because, but, indeed
τις indefinite pron. nom. masc. sg. τὶς certain, some, any man, one, any thing
τούτῳ demo. pron. dat. masc. sg. οὗτος αὕτη τοῦτο this, the same, this same, he, she, it
καὶ conj. καί and, even, also, but
20 εἰ conj. εἰ if, whether, that, though, forasmuch
γὰρ conj. γάρ for, and, because, but, indeed
τὰ art. acc. neut. pl. ὁ ἡ τό the, this, that, he, she, it
μιάσματα n. acc. neut. pl. μίασμα pollution
τοῦ art. gen. masc. sg. ὁ ἡ τό the, this, that, he, she, it
κόσμου n. gen. masc. sg. κόσμος world, adorning
ἐν prep. ἐν (+dat) in, by, with, among, at, on, through, to, within, into, of, for
ἐπιγνώσει n. dat. fem. sg. ἐπίγνωσις knowledge, acknowledging, acknowledgement
τοῦ art. gen. masc. sg. ὁ ἡ τό the, this, that, he, she, it
Κυρίου n. gen. masc. sg. κύριος Lord, lord, master, sir, LORD, God, Master, owner
καὶ conj. καί and, even, also, but
σωτῆρος n. gen. masc. sg. σωτήρ Saviour, saviour
Ἰησοῦ n. gen. masc. sg. Ἰησοῦς Jesus
Χριστοῦ n. gen. masc. sg. Χριστός Christ
τούτοις demo. pron. dat. neut. pl. οὗτος αὕτη τοῦτο this, the same, this same, he, she, it
δὲ conj. δέ but, and, now, also, to the contrary, rather, then
πάλιν adv. πάλιν again
αὐτοῖς pron. dat. masc. 3p. pl. αὐτός ἡ ὁ self, of oneself, even, very, the same, he, she, it
τὰ art. nom. neut. pl. ὁ ἡ τό the, this, that, he, she, it
ἔσχατα adj. nom. neut. pl. ἔσχατος last, lowest, uttermost, uttermost part
χείρονα compar. adj. nom. neut. pl. χείρων worse, sorer, worse and worse
τῶν art. gen. neut. pl. ὁ ἡ τό the, this, that, he, she, it
πρώτων ordinal. adj. gen. neut. pl. πρῶτος first, chief, first of all, chiefest, best
21 κρεῖττον compar. adj. nom. neut. sg. κρείττων better

γὰρ conj. γάρ for, and, because, but, indeed
αὐτοῖς pron. dat. masc. 3p. pl. αὐτός ή ό self, of oneself, even, very, the same, he, she, it
μὴ particle of negation. μή not, no, lest, neither, none, nothing, nor, never, without
τὴν art. acc. fem. sg. ὁ ἡ τό the, this, that, he, she, it
ὁδὸν n. acc. fem. sg. ὁδός way, journey, highway
τῆς art. gen. fem. sg. ὁ ἡ τό the, this, that, he, she, it
δικαιοσύνης n. gen. fem. sg. δικαιοσύνη righteousness
ἢ particle. ἤ or, than, either, nor, or else, and, rather than
ἐκ prep. ἐκ ἐξ (+gen) of, from, out of, by, on, with, in, among, through
τῆς art. gen. fem. sg. ὁ ἡ τό the, this, that, he, she, it
αὐτοῖς pron. dat. masc. 3p. pl. αὐτός ή ό self, of oneself, even, very, the same, he, she, it
ἁγίας adj. gen. fem. sg. ἅγιος Holy, holy, saint, Holy One, holy thing, most holy
ἐντολῆς n. gen. fem. sg. ἐντολή commandment, precept
22 δὲ conj. δέ but, and, now, also, to the contrary, rather, then
αὐτοῖς pron. dat. masc. 3p. pl. αὐτός ή ό self, of oneself, even, very, the same, he, she, it
τὸ art. nom. neut. sg. ὁ ἡ τό the, this, that, he, she, it
τῆς art. gen. fem. sg. ὁ ἡ τό the, this, that, he, she, it
ἀληθοῦς adj. gen. fem. sg. ἀληθής true, truly, truth
παροιμίας n. gen. fem. sg. παροιμία proverb, parable
Κύων n. nom. masc. sg. κύων dog
ἐπὶ prep. ἐπί (+gen) on, in, upon, (+dat) in, at, for, upon, (+acc) on, upon, unto, to, against
τὸ art. acc. neut. sg. ὁ ἡ τό the, this, that, he, she, it
ἴδιον adj. acc. neut. sg. ἴδιος one's own, one's, privately
ἐξέραμα n. acc. neut. sg. ἐξέραμα vomit
καί conj. καί and, even, also, but
ὗς n. nom. fem. sg. ὗς sow
εἰς prep. εἰς (+acc) into, to, unto, for, in, on, toward, against, upon, at, among
κύλισμα n. acc. neut. sg. κύλισμα wallowing
βορβόρου n. gen. masc. sg. βόρβορος mire

3

1 Ταύτην demo. pron. acc. fem. sg. οὗτος αὕτη τοῦτο this, the same, this same, he, she, it
ἤδη adv. ἤδη now, already, yet, by this time, even now, now already
ἀγαπητοί adj. voc. masc. pl. ἀγαπητός beloved, dearly beloved, dear, wellbeloved
δευτέραν ordinal. adj. acc. fem. sg. δεύτερος second, second time, again, afterward
ὑμῖν pron. dat. 2p. pl. σύ thou, you
ἐπιστολήν n. acc. fem. sg. ἐπιστολή letter, epistle
ἐν prep. ἐν (+dat) in, by, with, among, at, on, through, to, within, into, of, for
αἷς relative pron. dat. fem. pl. ὅς ἥ ὅ who, which, what, that
ὑμῶν pron. gen. 2p. pl. σύ thou, you
ἐν prep. ἐν (+dat) in, by, with, among, at, on, through, to, within, into, of, for
ὑπομνήσει n. dat. fem. sg. ὑπόμνησις remembrance, putting in remembrance
τὴν art. acc. fem. sg. ὁ ἡ τό the, this, that, he, she, it
εἰλικρινῆ adj. acc. fem. sg. εἰλικρινής sincere, pure
διάνοιαν n. acc. fem. sg. διάνοια mind, understanding, imagination
2 τῶν art. gen. neut. pl. ὁ ἡ τό the, this, that, he, she, it
ῥημάτων n. gen. neut. pl. ῥῆμα word, saying, thing
ὑπὸ prep. ὑπό (+gen) of, by, with, from, among, (+acc) under
τῶν art. gen. masc. pl. ὁ ἡ τό the, this, that, he, she, it
ἁγίων adj. gen. masc. pl. ἅγιος Holy, holy, saint, Holy One, holy thing, most holy
προφητῶν n. gen. masc. pl. προφήτης prophet
καὶ conj. καί and, even, also, but
τῆς art. gen. fem. sg. ὁ ἡ τό the, this, that, he, she, it
τῶν art. gen. masc. pl. ὁ ἡ τό the, this, that, he, she, it

ἀποστόλων n. gen. masc. pl. ἀπόστολος apostle, messenger, he that is sent
ἡμῶν pron. gen. 1p. pl. ἐγώ I
ἐντολῆς n. gen. fem. sg. ἐντολή commandment, precept
τοῦ art. gen. masc. sg. ὁ ἡ τό the, this, that, he, she, it
Κυρίου n. gen. masc. sg. κύριος Lord, lord, master, sir, LORD, God, Master, owner
καὶ conj. καί and, even, also, but
σωτῆρος n. gen. masc. sg. σωτήρ Saviour, saviour
3 τοῦτο demo. pron. acc. neut. sg. οὗτος αὕτη τοῦτο this, the same, this same, he, she, it
πρῶτον adv. πρῶτον first, at the first, first of all, at first, at the beginning, before, chiefly
ὅτι conj. ὅτι that, for, because, how that, how, because that, for that, though
ἐπ' prep. ἐπί (+gen) on, in, upon, (+dat) in, at, for, upon, (+acc) on, upon, unto, to, against
ἐσχάτου adj. gen. neut. sg. ἔσχατος last, lowest, uttermost, uttermost part
τῶν art. gen. fem. pl. ὁ ἡ τό the, this, that, he, she, it
ἡμερῶν n. gen. fem. pl. ἡμέρα day, time, year, while, age, day time
ἐμπαῖκται n. nom. masc. pl. ἐμπαίκτης scoffer, mocker
κατὰ prep. κατά (+gen) against, by, throughout, down, (+acc) according to, after, with
τὰς art. acc. fem. pl. ὁ ἡ τό the, this, that, he, she, it
ἰδίας adj. acc. fem. pl. ἴδιος one's own, one's, privately
αὐτῶν pron. gen. masc. 3p. pl. αὐτός ή ό self, of oneself, even, very, the same, he, she, it
ἐπιθυμίας n. acc. fem. pl. ἐπιθυμία lust, concupiscence, desire
4 καὶ conj. καί and, even, also, but
Ποῦ particle of place. ποῦ where, whither
ἡ art. nom. fem. sg. ὁ ἡ τό the, this, that, he, she, it
ἐπαγγελία n. nom. fem. sg. ἐπαγγελία promise, message
τῆς art. gen. fem. sg. ὁ ἡ τό the, this, that, he, she, it
παρουσίας n. gen. fem. sg. παρουσία coming, presence
αὐτοῦ pron. gen. masc. 3p. sg. αὐτός ή ό self, of oneself, even, very, the same, he, she, it
ἀφ' prep. ἀπό (+gen) from, of, out of, since, for, off, at, by, in, on
ἧς relative pron. gen. fem. sg. ὅς ἥ ὅ who, which, what, that
γὰρ conj. γάρ for, and, because, but, indeed
οἱ art. nom. masc. pl. ὁ ἡ τό the, this, that, he, she, it
πατέρες n. nom. masc. pl. πατήρ Father, father, parent
πάντα adj. nom. neut. pl. πᾶς πᾶςα πᾶν all, every, whosoever, every one, no, whole, any
οὕτω adv. οὕτω οὕτως so, even so, thus, on this wise, likewise, after this manner
ἀπ' prep. ἀπό (+gen) from, of, out of, since, for, off, at, by, in, on
ἀρχῆς n. gen. fem. sg. ἀρχή beginning, principality, corner, first, magistrate, rule
κτίσεως n. gen. fem. sg. κτίσις creature, creation, building, ordinance
5 γὰρ conj. γάρ for, and, because, but, indeed
αὐτοὺς pron. acc. masc. 3p. pl. αὐτός ή ό self, of oneself, even, very, the same, he, she, it
τοῦτο demo. pron. nom. neut. sg. οὗτος αὕτη τοῦτο this, the same, this same, he, she, it
ὅτι conj. ὅτι that, for, because, how that, how, because that, for that, though
οὐρανοὶ n. nom. masc. pl. οὐρανός heaven, air, sky
ἔκπαλαι adv. ἔκπαλαι of a long time, of old
καὶ conj. καί and, even, also, but
γῆ n. nom. fem. sg. γῆ earth, land, ground, country
ἐξ prep. ἐκ ἐξ (+gen) of, from, out of, by, on, with, in, among, through
ὕδατος n. gen. neut. sg. ὕδωρ water
καὶ conj. καί and, even, also, but
δι' prep. διά (+gen) by, through, with, in, of, (+acc) for, because of, for a cause
ὕδατος n. gen. neut. sg. ὕδωρ water
τῷ art. dat. masc. sg. ὁ ἡ τό the, this, that, he, she, it
τοῦ art. gen. masc. sg. ὁ ἡ τό the, this, that, he, she, it
Θεοῦ n. gen. masc. sg. θεός God, god
λόγῳ n. dat. masc. sg. λόγος word, saying, account, speech, thing, matter
6 δι' prep. διά (+gen) by, through, with, in, of, (+acc) for, because of, for a cause

ὧν relative pron. gen. neut. pl. ὅς ἥ ὅ who, which, what, that
ὁ art. nom. masc. sg. ὁ ἡ τό the, this, that, he, she, it
τότε adv. τότε then, that time
κόσμος n. nom. masc. sg. κόσμος world, adorning
ὕδατι n. dat. neut. sg. ὕδωρ water
7 οἱ art. nom. masc. pl. ὁ ἡ τό the, this, that, he, she, it
δὲ conj. δέ but, and, now, also, to the contrary, rather, then
νῦν adv. νῦν now, henceforth, present, this time
οὐρανοὶ n. nom. masc. pl. οὐρανός heaven, air, sky
καὶ conj. καί and, even, also, but
ἡ art. nom. fem. sg. ὁ ἡ τό the, this, that, he, she, it
γῆ n. nom. fem. sg. γῆ earth, land, ground, country
τῷ art. dat. masc. sg. ὁ ἡ τό the, this, that, he, she, it
αὐτῷ adj. dat. masc. sg. αὐτός ή ό self, of oneself, even, very, the same, he, she, it
λόγῳ n. dat. masc. sg. λόγος word, saying, account, speech, thing, matter
πυρί n. dat. neut. sg. πῦρ fire, fiery
εἰς prep. εἰς (+acc) into, to, unto, for, in, on, toward, against, upon, at, among
ἡμέραν n. acc. fem. sg. ἡμέρα day, time, year, while, age, day time
κρίσεως n. gen. fem. sg. κρίσις judgment, damnation, accusation, condemnation
καὶ conj. καί and, even, also, but
ἀπωλείας n. gen. fem. sg. ἀπώλεια destruction, perdition, waste, damnation
τῶν art. gen. masc. pl. ὁ ἡ τό the, this, that, he, she, it
ἀσεβῶν adj. gen. masc. pl. ἀσεβής ungodly, ungodly man
ἀνθρώπων n. gen. masc. pl. ἄνθρωπος man, human being, person, one, certain
8 Ἓν num. nom. neut. sg. εἷς or ἕν one, other, some, any, only, a certain
δὲ conj. δέ but, and, now, also, to the contrary, rather, then
τοῦτο demo. pron. nom. neut. sg. οὗτος αὕτη τοῦτο this, the same, this same, he, she, it
μὴ particle of negation. μή not, no, lest, neither, none, nothing, nor, never, without
ὑμᾶς pron. acc. 2p. pl. σύ thou, you
ἀγαπητοί adj. voc. masc. pl. ἀγαπητός beloved, dearly beloved, dear, wellbeloved
ὅτι conj. ὅτι that, for, because, how that, how, because that, for that, though
μία num. nom. fem. sg. εἷς or ἕν one, other, some, any, only, a certain
ἡμέρα n. nom. fem. sg. ἡμέρα day, time, year, while, age, day time
παρὰ prep. παρά (+gen) of, from, (+dat) with, for, (+acc) beside, at, by, above, against
Κυρίῳ n. dat. masc. sg. κύριος Lord, lord, master, sir, LORD, God, Master, owner
ὡς adv. ὡς as, when, as it were, how, about, like, as soon as, even as, while
χίλια num. nom. neut. pl. χίλιοι one thousand
ἔτη n. nom. neut. pl. ἔτος year
καὶ conj. καί and, even, also, but
χίλια num. nom. neut. pl. χίλιοι one thousand
ἔτη n. nom. neut. pl. ἔτος year
ὡς adv. ὡς as, when, as it were, how, about, like, as soon as, even as, while
ἡμέρα n. nom. fem. sg. ἡμέρα day, time, year, while, age, day time
μία num. nom. fem. sg. εἷς or ἕν one, other, some, any, only, a certain
9 οὐ particle of negation. οὐ οὐκ οὐχ not, no, neither, none, nay, nor, never, nothing
ὁ art. nom. masc. sg. ὁ ἡ τό the, this, that, he, she, it
Κύριος n. nom. masc. sg. κύριος Lord, lord, master, sir, LORD, God, Master, owner
τῆς art. gen. fem. sg. ὁ ἡ τό the, this, that, he, she, it
ἐπαγγελίας n. gen. fem. sg. ἐπαγγελία promise, message
ὡς adv. ὡς as, when, as it were, how, about, like, as soon as, even as, while
τινες indefinite pron. nom. masc. pl. τὶς certain, some, any man, one, any thing
βραδύτητα n. acc. fem. sg. βραδύτης slackness
ἀλλὰ conj. ἀλλά but, yea, yet, nevertheless, howbeit, nay, therefore
εἰς prep. εἰς (+acc) into, to, unto, for, in, on, toward, against, upon, at, among
ἡμᾶς pron. acc. 1p. pl. ἐγώ I

μὴ particle of negation. μή not, no, lest, neither, none, nothing, nor, never, without
τινὰς indefinite pron. acc. masc. pl. τὶς certain, some, any man, one, any thing
ἀλλὰ conj. ἀλλά but, yea, yet, nevertheless, howbeit, nay, therefore
πάντας adj. acc. masc. pl. πᾶς πᾶσα πᾶν all, every, whosoever, every one, no, whole, any
εἰς prep. εἰς (+acc) into, to, unto, for, in, on, toward, against, upon, at, among
μετάνοιαν n. acc. fem. sg. μετάνοια repentance
10 δὲ conj. δέ but, and, now, also, to the contrary, rather, then
ἡ art. nom. fem. sg. ὁ ἡ τό the, this, that, he, she, it
ἡμέρα n. nom. fem. sg. ἡμέρα day, time, year, while, age, day time
Κυρίου n. gen. masc. sg. κύριος Lord, lord, master, sir, LORD, God, Master, owner
ὡς adv. ὡς as, when, as it were, how, about, like, as soon as, even as, while
κλέπτης n. nom. masc. sg. κλέπτης thief
ἐν prep. ἐν (+dat) in, by, with, among, at, on, through, to, within, into, of, for
νυκτὶ n. dat. fem. sg. νύξ night
ἐν prep. ἐν (+dat) in, by, with, among, at, on, through, to, within, into, of, for
ᾗ relative pron. dat. fem. sg. ὅς ἥ ὅ who, which, what, that
οἱ art. nom. masc. pl. ὁ ἡ τό the, this, that, he, she, it
οὐρανοὶ n. nom. masc. pl. οὐρανός heaven, air, sky
ῥοιζηδὸν adv. ῥοιζηδόν with a great noise
στοιχεῖα n. nom. neut. pl. στοιχεῖον element, rudiment, principle
δὲ conj. δέ but, and, now, also, to the contrary, rather, then
καὶ conj. καί and, even, also, but
γῆ n. nom. fem. sg. γῆ earth, land, ground, country
καὶ conj. καί and, even, also, but
τὰ art. nom. neut. pl. ὁ ἡ τό the, this, that, he, she, it
ἐν prep. ἐν (+dat) in, by, with, among, at, on, through, to, within, into, of, for
αὐτῇ pron. dat. fem. 3p. sg. αὐτός ή ό self, of oneself, even, very, the same, he, she, it
ἔργα n. nom. neut. pl. ἔργον work, deed, doing labour
11 τούτων demo. pron. gen. neut. pl. οὗτος αὕτη τοῦτο this, the same, this same, he, she, it
οὖν conj. οὖν therefore, then, so, and, now, wherefore
πάντων adj. gen. neut. pl. πᾶς πᾶσα πᾶν all, every, whosoever, every one, no, whole, any
ποταποὺς interrog. pron. acc. masc. pl. ποταπός what manner of, what
ὑμᾶς pron. acc. 2p. pl. σύ thou, you
ἐν prep. ἐν (+dat) in, by, with, among, at, on, through, to, within, into, of, for
ἁγίαις adj. dat. fem. pl. ἅγιος Holy, holy, saint, Holy One, holy thing, most holy
ἀναστροφαῖς n. dat. fem. pl. ἀναστροφή conversation
καὶ conj. καί and, even, also, but
εὐσεβείαις n. dat. fem. pl. εὐσέβεια godliness, holiness
12 καὶ conj. καί and, even, also, but
τὴν art. acc. fem. sg. ὁ ἡ τό the, this, that, he, she, it
παρουσίαν n. acc. fem. sg. παρουσία coming, presence
τῆς art. gen. fem. sg. ὁ ἡ τό the, this, that, he, she, it
τοῦ art. gen. masc. sg. ὁ ἡ τό the, this, that, he, she, it
Θεοῦ n. gen. masc. sg. θεός God, god
ἡμέρας n. gen. fem. sg. ἡμέρα day, time, year, while, age, day time
δι' prep. διά (+gen) by, through, with, in, of, (+acc) for, because of, for a cause
ἣν relative pron. acc. fem. sg. ὅς ἥ ὅ who, which, what, that
οὐρανοὶ n. nom. masc. pl. οὐρανός heaven, air, sky
καὶ conj. καί and, even, also, but
στοιχεῖα n. nom. neut. pl. στοιχεῖον element, rudiment, principle
13 καινοὺς adj. acc. masc. pl. καινός new
δὲ conj. δέ but, and, now, also, to the contrary, rather, then
οὐρανοὺς n. acc. masc. pl. οὐρανός heaven, air, sky
καὶ conj. καί and, even, also, but
γῆν n. acc. fem. sg. γῆ earth, land, ground, country

καινὴν adj. acc. fem. sg. καινός new
κατὰ prep. κατά (+gen) against, by, throughout, down, (+acc) according to, after, with
τὸ art. acc. neut. sg. ὁ ἡ τό the, this, that, he, she, it
ἐπάγγελμα n. acc. neut. sg. ἐπάγγελμα promise
αὐτοῦ pron. gen. masc. 3p. sg. αὐτός ή ό self, of oneself, even, very, the same, he, she, it
ἐν prep. ἐν (+dat) in, by, with, among, at, on, through, to, within, into, of, for
οἷς relative pron. dat. masc. pl. ὅς ἥ ὅ who, which, what, that
δικαιοσύνη n. nom. fem. sg. δικαιοσύνη righteousness
14 Διό conj. διό wherefore, therefore, for which cause
ἀγαπητοί adj. voc. masc. pl. ἀγαπητός beloved, dearly beloved, dear, wellbeloved
ταῦτα demo. pron. acc. neut. pl. οὗτος αὕτη τοῦτο this, the same, this same, he, she, it
ἄσπιλοι adj. nom. masc. pl. ἄσπιλος without spot, unspotted
καὶ conj. καί and, even, also, but
ἀμώμητοι adj. nom. masc. pl. ἀμώμητος without rebuke, blameless
αὐτῷ pron. dat. masc. 3p. sg. αὐτός ή ό self, of oneself, even, very, the same, he, she, it
ἐν prep. ἐν (+dat) in, by, with, among, at, on, through, to, within, into, of, for
εἰρήνῃ n. dat. fem. sg. εἰρήνη peace, quietness, rest
15 καὶ conj. καί and, even, also, but
τὴν art. acc. fem. sg. ὁ ἡ τό the, this, that, he, she, it
τοῦ art. gen. masc. sg. ὁ ἡ τό the, this, that, he, she, it
Κυρίου n. gen. masc. sg. κύριος Lord, lord, master, sir, LORD, God, Master, owner
ἡμῶν pron. gen. 1p. pl. ἐγώ I
μακροθυμίαν n. acc. fem. sg. μακροθυμία longsuffering, patience
σωτηρίαν n. acc. fem. sg. σωτηρία salvation, deliver, health, saving
καθὼς adv. καθώς as, even as, according as, according to
καὶ conj. καί and, even, also, but
ὁ art. nom. masc. sg. ὁ ἡ τό the, this, that, he, she, it
ἀγαπητὸς adj. nom. masc. sg. ἀγαπητός beloved, dearly beloved, dear, wellbeloved
ἡμῶν pron. gen. 1p. pl. ἐγώ I
ἀδελφὸς n. nom. masc. sg. ἀδελφός brother
Παῦλος n. nom. masc. sg. Παῦλος Paul, Paulus
κατὰ prep. κατά (+gen) against, by, throughout, down, (+acc) according to, after, with
τὴν art. acc. fem. sg. ὁ ἡ τό the, this, that, he, she, it
αὐτῷ pron. dat. masc. 3p. sg. αὐτός ή ό self, of oneself, even, very, the same, he, she, it
σοφίαν n. acc. fem. sg. σοφία wisdom
ὑμῖν pron. dat. 2p. pl. σύ thou, you
16 ὡς adv. ὡς as, when, as it were, how, about, like, as soon as, even as, while
καὶ conj. καί and, even, also, but
ἐν prep. ἐν (+dat) in, by, with, among, at, on, through, to, within, into, of, for
πάσαις adj. dat. fem. pl. πᾶς πᾶσα πᾶν all, every, whosoever, every one, no, whole, any
ταῖς art. dat. fem. pl. ὁ ἡ τό the, this, that, he, she, it
ἐπιστολαῖς n. dat. fem. pl. ἐπιστολή letter, epistle
ἐν prep. ἐν (+dat) in, by, with, among, at, on, through, to, within, into, of, for
αὐταῖς pron. dat. fem. 3p. pl. αὐτός ή ό self, of oneself, even, very, the same, he, she, it
περὶ prep. περί (+gen) of, for, concerning, (+acc) about, concerning, in
τούτων demo. pron. gen. neut. pl. οὗτος αὕτη τοῦτο this, the same, this same, he, she, it
ἐν prep. ἐν (+dat) in, by, with, among, at, on, through, to, within, into, of, for
οἷς relative pron. dat. masc. pl. ὅς ἥ ὅ who, which, what, that
δυσνόητά adj. nom. neut. pl. δυσνόητος hard to be understood
τινα indefinite pron. nom. neut. pl. τὶς certain, some, any man, one, any thing
ἃ relative pron. acc. neut. pl. ὅς ἥ ὅ who, which, what, that
οἱ art. nom. masc. pl. ὁ ἡ τό the, this, that, he, she, it
ἀμαθεῖς adj. nom. masc. pl. ἀμαθής unlearned
καὶ conj. καί and, even, also, but
ἀστήρικτοι adj. nom. masc. pl. ἀστήρικτος unstable

ὡς adv. ὡς as, when, as it were, how, about, like, as soon as, even as, while
καὶ conj. καί and, even, also, but
τὰς art. acc. fem. pl. ὁ ἡ τό the, this, that, he, she, it
λοιπὰς adj. acc. fem. pl. λοιπός other, rest, remnant, residue, which remain
γραφὰς n. acc. fem. pl. γραφή scripture
πρὸς prep. πρός (+gen) for, (+dat) at, (+acc) unto, to, with, for, against
τὴν art. acc. fem. sg. ὁ ἡ τό the, this, that, he, she, it
ἰδίαν adj. acc. fem. sg. ἴδιος one's own, one's, privately
αὐτῶν pron. gen. masc. 3p. pl. αὐτός ή ό self, of oneself, even, very, the same, he, she, it
ἀπώλειαν n. acc. fem. sg. ἀπώλεια destruction, perdition, waste, damnation
17 ὑμεῖς pron. nom. 2p. pl. σύ thou, you
οὖν conj. οὖν therefore, then, so, and, now, wherefore
ἀγαπητοί adj. voc. masc. pl. ἀγαπητός beloved, dearly beloved, dear, wellbeloved
ἵνα conj. ἵνα that, to, lest, for to, so that, albeit, because, for, so as
μὴ particle of negation. μή not, no, lest, neither, none, nothing, nor, never, without
τῇ art. dat. fem. sg. ὁ ἡ τό the, this, that, he, she, it
τῶν art. gen. masc. pl. ὁ ἡ τό the, this, that, he, she, it
ἀθέσμων adj. gen. masc. pl. ἄθεσμος wicked
πλάνῃ n. dat. fem. sg. πλάνη error, deception, deceit, delusion
τοῦ art. gen. masc. sg. ὁ ἡ τό the, this, that, he, she, it
ἰδίου adj. gen. masc. sg. ἴδιος one's own, one's, privately
στηριγμοῦ n. gen. masc. sg. στηριγμός stedfastness
18 δὲ conj. δέ but, and, now, also, to the contrary, rather, then
ἐν prep. ἐν (+dat) in, by, with, among, at, on, through, to, within, into, of, for
χάριτι n. dat. fem. sg. χάρις grace, thank, favour, pleasure
καὶ conj. καί and, even, also, but
γνώσει n. dat. fem. sg. γνῶσις knowledge, science
τοῦ art. gen. masc. sg. ὁ ἡ τό the, this, that, he, she, it
Κυρίου n. gen. masc. sg. κύριος Lord, lord, master, sir, LORD, God, Master, owner
ἡμῶν pron. gen. 1p. pl. ἐγώ I
καὶ conj. καί and, even, also, but
σωτῆρος n. gen. masc. sg. σωτήρ Saviour, saviour
Ἰησοῦ n. gen. masc. sg. Ἰησοῦς Jesus
Χριστοῦ n. gen. masc. sg. Χριστός Christ
αὐτῷ pron. dat. masc. 3p. sg. αὐτός ή ό self, of oneself, even, very, the same, he, she, it
ἡ art. nom. fem. sg. ὁ ἡ τό the, this, that, he, she, it
δόξα n. nom. fem. sg. δόξα glory, honour, praise, dignity, worship
καὶ conj. καί and, even, also, but
νῦν adv. νῦν now, henceforth, present, this time
καὶ conj. καί and, even, also, but
εἰς prep. εἰς (+acc) into, to, unto, for, in, on, toward, against, upon, at, among
ἡμέραν n. acc. fem. sg. ἡμέρα day, time, year, while, age, day time
αἰῶνος n. gen. masc. sg. αἰών ever, ever and ever, evermore, age, eternal, world
ἀμήν particle. ἀμήν amen, verily

ΙΩΑΝΝΟΥ
ΕΠΙΣΤΟΛΗ ΚΑΘΟΛΙΚΗ ΠΡΩΤΗ

1

1 Ὃ relative pron. nom. neut. sg. ὅς ἥ ὅ who, which, what, that
ἀπ' prep. ἀπό (+gen) from, of, out of, since, for, off, at, by, in, on
ἀρχῆς n. gen. fem. sg. ἀρχή beginning, principality, corner, first, magistrate, rule
ὃ relative pron. acc. neut. sg. ὅς ἥ ὅ who, which, what, that
ὃ relative pron. acc. neut. sg. ὅς ἥ ὅ who, which, what, that
τοῖς art. dat. masc. pl. ὁ ἡ τό the, this, that, he, she, it
ὀφθαλμοῖς n. dat. masc. pl. ὀφθαλμός eye, sight
ἡμῶν pron. gen. 1p. pl. ἐγώ I
ὃ relative pron. acc. neut. sg. ὅς ἥ ὅ who, which, what, that
καὶ conj. καί and, even, also, but
αἱ art. nom. fem. pl. ὁ ἡ τό the, this, that, he, she, it
χεῖρες n. nom. fem. pl. χείρ hand
ἡμῶν pron. gen. 1p. pl. ἐγώ I
περὶ prep. περί (+gen) of, for, concerning, (+acc) about, concerning, in
τοῦ art. gen. masc. sg. ὁ ἡ τό the, this, that, he, she, it
λόγου n. gen. masc. sg. λόγος word, saying, account, speech, thing, matter
τῆς art. gen. fem. sg. ὁ ἡ τό the, this, that, he, she, it
ζωῆς n. gen. fem. sg. ζωή life, lifetime
2 καὶ conj. καί and, even, also, but
ἡ art. nom. fem. sg. ὁ ἡ τό the, this, that, he, she, it
ζωὴ n. nom. fem. sg. ζωή life, lifetime
καὶ conj. καί and, even, also, but
καὶ conj. καί and, even, also, but
καὶ conj. καί and, even, also, but
ὑμῖν pron. dat. 2p. pl. σύ thou, you
τὴν art. acc. fem. sg. ὁ ἡ τό the, this, that, he, she, it
ζωὴν n. acc. fem. sg. ζωή life, lifetime
τὴν art. acc. fem. sg. ὁ ἡ τό the, this, that, he, she, it
αἰώνιον adj. acc. fem. sg. αἰώνιος eternal, everlasting, world, for ever
ἥτις relative pron. nom. fem. sg. ὅστις which, who, whosoever, that, whatsoever
πρὸς prep. πρός (+gen) for, (+dat) at, (+acc) unto, to, with, for, against
τὸν art. acc. masc. sg. ὁ ἡ τό the, this, that, he, she, it
πατέρα n. acc. masc. sg. πατήρ Father, father, parent
καὶ conj. καί and, even, also, but
ἡμῖν pron. dat. 1p. pl. ἐγώ I
3 ὃ relative pron. acc. neut. sg. ὅς ἥ ὅ who, which, what, that
καὶ conj. καί and, even, also, but
ὑμῖν pron. dat. 2p. pl. σύ thou, you
ἵνα conj. ἵνα that, to, lest, for to, so that, albeit, because, for, so as
καὶ conj. καί and, even, also, but
ὑμεῖς pron. nom. 2p. pl. σύ thou, you
κοινωνίαν n. acc. fem. sg. κοινωνία fellowship, communion, contribution, distribution
μεθ' prep. μετά (+gen) with, among, against, (+acc) after
ἡμῶν pron. gen. 1p. pl. ἐγώ I
καὶ conj. καί and, even, also, but
ἡ art. nom. fem. sg. ὁ ἡ τό the, this, that, he, she, it
κοινωνία n. nom. fem. sg. κοινωνία fellowship, communion, contribution, distribution
δὲ conj. δέ but, and, now, also, to the contrary, rather, then
ἡ art. nom. fem. sg. ὁ ἡ τό the, this, that, he, she, it

ἡμετέρα poss. pron. nom. fem. 1p. sg. ἡμέτερος our
μετὰ prep. μετά (+gen) with, among, against, (+acc) after
τοῦ art. gen. masc. sg. ὁ ἡ τό the, this, that, he, she, it
πατρὸς n. gen. masc. sg. πατήρ Father, father, parent
καὶ conj. καί and, even, also, but
μετὰ prep. μετά (+gen) with, among, against, (+acc) after
τοῦ art. gen. masc. sg. ὁ ἡ τό the, this, that, he, she, it
υἱοῦ n. gen. masc. sg. υἱός son, child, descendant, offspring, heir
αὐτοῦ pron. gen. masc. 3p. sg. αὐτός ἡ ὁ self, of oneself, even, very, the same, he, she, it
Ἰησοῦ n. gen. masc. sg. Ἰησοῦς Jesus
Χριστοῦ n. gen. masc. sg. Χριστός Christ
4 καὶ conj. καί and, even, also, but
ταῦτα demo. pron. acc. neut. pl. οὗτος αὕτη τοῦτο this, the same, this same, he, she, it
ὑμῖν pron. dat. 2p. pl. σύ thou, you
ἵνα conj. ἵνα that, to, lest, for to, so that, albeit, because, for, so as
ἡ art. nom. fem. sg. ὁ ἡ τό the, this, that, he, she, it
χαρὰ n. nom. fem. sg. χαρά joy, gladness, joyfulness
ὑμῶν pron. gen. 2p. pl. σύ thou, you
5 Καὶ conj. καί and, even, also, but
αὕτη demo. pron. nom. fem. sg. οὗτος αὕτη τοῦτο this, the same, this same, he, she, it
ἡ art. nom. fem. sg. ὁ ἡ τό the, this, that, he, she, it
ἀγγελία n. nom. fem. sg. ἀγγελία message
ἣν relative pron. acc. fem. sg. ὅς ἥ ὅ who, which, what, that
ἀπ' prep. ἀπό (+gen) from, of, out of, since, for, off, at, by, in, on
αὐτοῦ pron. gen. masc. 3p. sg. αὐτός ἡ ὁ self, of oneself, even, very, the same, he, she, it
καὶ conj. καί and, even, also, but
ὑμῖν pron. dat. 2p. pl. σύ thou, you
ὅτι conj. ὅτι that, for, because, how that, how, because that, for that, though
ὁ art. nom. masc. sg. ὁ ἡ τό the, this, that, he, she, it
Θεὸς n. nom. masc. sg. θεός God, god
φῶς n. nom. neut. sg. φῶς light, fire
καὶ conj. καί and, even, also, but
σκοτία n. nom. fem. sg. σκοτία darkness, dark
ἐν prep. ἐν (+dat) in, by, with, among, at, on, through, to, within, into, of, for
αὐτῷ pron. dat. masc. 3p. sg. αὐτός ἡ ὁ self, of oneself, even, very, the same, he, she, it
οὐκ particle of negation. οὐ οὐκ οὐχ not, no, neither, none, nay, nor, never, nothing
οὐδεμία num. nom. fem. sg. οὐδείς no man, nothing, no, none, neither, not, nought
6 ἐὰν conj. ἐάν if, soever, except, though, and if, but, whether, if so, so
ὅτι conj. ὅτι that, for, because, how that, how, because that, for that, though
κοινωνίαν n. acc. fem. sg. κοινωνία fellowship, communion, contribution, distribution
μετ' prep. μετά (+gen) with, among, against, (+acc) after
αὐτοῦ pron. gen. masc. 3p. sg. αὐτός ἡ ὁ self, of oneself, even, very, the same, he, she, it
καὶ conj. καί and, even, also, but
ἐν prep. ἐν (+dat) in, by, with, among, at, on, through, to, within, into, of, for
τῷ art. dat. neut. sg. ὁ ἡ τό the, this, that, he, she, it
σκότει n. dat. neut. sg. σκότος darkness
καὶ conj. καί and, even, also, but
οὐ particle of negation. οὐ οὐκ οὐχ not, no, neither, none, nay, nor, never, nothing
τὴν art. acc. fem. sg. ὁ ἡ τό the, this, that, he, she, it
ἀλήθειαν n. acc. fem. sg. ἀλήθεια truth, verity
7 ἐὰν conj. ἐάν if, soever, except, though, and if, but, whether, if so, so
δὲ conj. δέ but, and, now, also, to the contrary, rather, then
ἐν prep. ἐν (+dat) in, by, with, among, at, on, through, to, within, into, of, for
τῷ art. dat. neut. sg. ὁ ἡ τό the, this, that, he, she, it
φωτὶ n. dat. neut. sg. φῶς light, fire

ὡς adv. ὡς as, when, as it were, how, about, like, as soon as, even as, while
αὐτός pron. nom. masc. 3p. sg. αὐτός ή ό self, of oneself, even, very, the same, he, she, it
ἐν prep. ἐν (+dat) in, by, with, among, at, on, through, to, within, into, of, for
τῷ art. dat. neut. sg. ὁ ἡ τό the, this, that, he, she, it
φωτὶ n. dat. neut. sg. φῶς light, fire
κοινωνίαν n. acc. fem. sg. κοινωνία fellowship, communion, contribution, distribution
μετ' prep. μετά (+gen) with, among, against, (+acc) after
ἀλλήλων pron. gen. masc. pl. ἀλλήλων one another, themselves, together, mutual
καὶ conj. καί and, even, also, but
τὸ art. nom. neut. sg. ὁ ἡ τό the, this, that, he, she, it
αἷμα n. nom. neut. sg. αἷμα blood
Ἰησοῦ n. gen. masc. sg. Ἰησοῦς Jesus
Χριστοῦ n. gen. masc. sg. Χριστός Christ
τοῦ art. gen. masc. sg. ὁ ἡ τό the, this, that, he, she, it
υἱοῦ n. gen. masc. sg. υἱός son, child, descendant, offspring, heir
αὐτοῦ pron. gen. masc. 3p. sg. αὐτός ή ό self, of oneself, even, very, the same, he, she, it
ἡμᾶς pron. acc. 1p. pl. ἐγώ I
ἀπὸ prep. ἀπό (+gen) from, of, out of, since, for, off, at, by, in, on
πάσης adj. gen. fem. sg. πᾶς πᾶσα πᾶν all, every, whosoever, every one, no, whole, any
ἁμαρτίας n. gen. fem. sg. ἁμαρτία sin, offence, sinful
8 ἐὰν conj. ἐάν if, soever, except, though, and if, but, whether, if so, so
ὅτι conj. ὅτι that, for, because, how that, how, because that, for that, though
ἁμαρτίαν n. acc. fem. sg. ἁμαρτία sin, offence, sinful
οὐκ particle of negation. οὐ οὐκ οὐχ not, no, neither, none, nay, nor, never, nothing
ἑαυτοὺς reflexive pron. acc. masc. 3p. pl. ἑαυτοῦ himself, herself, itself, yourself, ourselves
καὶ conj. καί and, even, also, but
ἡ art. nom. fem. sg. ὁ ἡ τό the, this, that, he, she, it
ἀλήθεια n. nom. fem. sg. ἀλήθεια truth, verity
οὐκ particle of negation. οὐ οὐκ οὐχ not, no, neither, none, nay, nor, never, nothing
ἐν prep. ἐν (+dat) in, by, with, among, at, on, through, to, within, into, of, for
ἡμῖν pron. dat. 1p. pl. ἐγώ I
9 ἐὰν conj. ἐάν if, soever, except, though, and if, but, whether, if so, so
τὰς art. acc. fem. pl. ὁ ἡ τό the, this, that, he, she, it
ἁμαρτίας n. acc. fem. pl. ἁμαρτία sin, offence, sinful
ἡμῶν pron. gen. 1p. pl. ἐγώ I
πιστός adj. nom. masc. sg. πιστός faithful, believing, true, sure
καὶ conj. καί and, even, also, but
δίκαιος adj. nom. masc. sg. δίκαιος righteous, just, meet, right
ἵνα conj. ἵνα that, to, lest, for to, so that, albeit, because, for, so as
ἡμῖν pron. dat. 1p. pl. ἐγώ I
τὰς art. acc. fem. pl. ὁ ἡ τό the, this, that, he, she, it
ἁμαρτίας n. acc. fem. pl. ἁμαρτία sin, offence, sinful
καὶ conj. καί and, even, also, but
ἡμᾶς pron. acc. 1p. pl. ἐγώ I
ἀπὸ prep. ἀπό (+gen) from, of, out of, since, for, off, at, by, in, on
πάσης adj. gen. fem. sg. πᾶς πᾶσα πᾶν all, every, whosoever, every one, no, whole, any
ἀδικίας n. gen. fem. sg. ἀδικία iniquity, unrighteousness, unjust, wrong
10 ἐὰν conj. ἐάν if, soever, except, though, and if, but, whether, if so, so
ὅτι conj. ὅτι that, for, because, how that, how, because that, for that, though
οὐχ particle of negation. οὐ οὐκ οὐχ not, no, neither, none, nay, nor, never, nothing
ψεύστην n. acc. masc. sg. ψεύστης liar
αὐτὸν pron. acc. masc. 3p. sg. αὐτός ή ό self, of oneself, even, very, the same, he, she, it
καὶ conj. καί and, even, also, but
ὁ art. nom. masc. sg. ὁ ἡ τό the, this, that, he, she, it
λόγος n. nom. masc. sg. λόγος word, saying, account, speech, thing, matter

αὐτοῦ pron. gen. masc. 3p. sg. αὐτός ή ό self, of oneself, even, very, the same, he, she, it
οὐκ particle of negation. οὐ οὐκ οὐχ not, no, neither, none, nay, nor, never, nothing
ἐν prep. ἐν (+dat) in, by, with, among, at, on, through, to, within, into, of, for
ἡμῖν pron. dat. 1p. pl. ἐγώ I

2

1 Τεκνία n. voc. neut. pl. τεκνίον little child
μου pron. gen. 1p. sg. ἐγώ I
ταῦτα demo. pron. acc. neut. pl. οὗτος αὕτη τοῦτο this, the same, this same, he, she, it
ὑμῖν pron. dat. 2p. pl. σύ thou, you
ἵνα conj. ἵνα that, to, lest, for to, so that, albeit, because, for, so as
μὴ particle of negation. μή not, no, lest, neither, none, nothing, nor, never, without
καὶ conj. καί and, even, also, but
ἐάν conj. ἐάν if, soever, except, though, and if, but, whether, if so, so
τις indefinite pron. nom. masc. sg. τὶς certain, some, any man, one, any thing
παράκλητον n. acc. masc. sg. παράκλητος Comforter, advocate
πρὸς prep. πρός (+gen) for, (+dat) at, (+acc) unto, to, with, for, against
τὸν art. acc. masc. sg. ὁ ἡ τό the, this, that, he, she, it
πατέρα n. acc. masc. sg. πατήρ Father, father, parent
Ἰησοῦν n. acc. masc. sg. Ἰησοῦς Jesus
Χριστὸν n. acc. masc. sg. Χριστός Christ
δίκαιον adj. acc. masc. sg. δίκαιος righteous, just, meet, right
2 καὶ conj. καί and, even, also, but
αὐτὸς pron. nom. masc. 3p. sg. αὐτός ή ό self, of oneself, even, very, the same, he, she, it
ἱλασμός n. nom. masc. sg. ἱλασμός propitiation
περὶ prep. περί (+gen) of, for, concerning, (+acc) about, concerning, in
τῶν art. gen. fem. pl. ὁ ἡ τό the, this, that, he, she, it
ἁμαρτιῶν n. gen. fem. pl. ἁμαρτία sin, offence, sinful
ἡμῶν pron. gen. 1p. pl. ἐγώ I
οὐ particle of negation. οὐ οὐκ οὐχ not, no, neither, none, nay, nor, never, nothing
περὶ prep. περί (+gen) of, for, concerning, (+acc) about, concerning, in
τῶν art. gen. fem. pl. ὁ ἡ τό the, this, that, he, she, it
ἡμετέρων poss. pron. gen. fem. 1p. pl. ἡμέτερος our
δὲ conj. δέ but, and, now, also, to the contrary, rather, then
μόνον adv. μόνος only, alone, by oneself
ἀλλὰ conj. ἀλλά but, yea, yet, nevertheless, howbeit, nay, therefore
καὶ conj. καί and, even, also, but
περὶ prep. περί (+gen) of, for, concerning, (+acc) about, concerning, in
ὅλου adj. gen. masc. sg. ὅλος all, whole, every whit, altogether
τοῦ art. gen. masc. sg. ὁ ἡ τό the, this, that, he, she, it
κόσμου n. gen. masc. sg. κόσμος world, adorning
3 καὶ conj. καί and, even, also, but
ἐν prep. ἐν (+dat) in, by, with, among, at, on, through, to, within, into, of, for
τούτῳ demo. pron. dat. neut. sg. οὗτος αὕτη τοῦτο this, the same, this same, he, she, it
ὅτι conj. ὅτι that, for, because, how that, how, because that, for that, though
αὐτόν pron. acc. masc. 3p. sg. αὐτός ή ό self, of oneself, even, very, the same, he, she, it
ἐὰν conj. ἐάν if, soever, except, though, and if, but, whether, if so, so
τὰς art. acc. fem. pl. ὁ ἡ τό the, this, that, he, she, it
ἐντολὰς n. acc. fem. pl. ἐντολή commandment, precept
αὐτοῦ pron. gen. masc. 3p. sg. αὐτός ή ό self, of oneself, even, very, the same, he, she, it
4 ὁ art. nom. masc. sg. ὁ ἡ τό the, this, that, he, she, it
αὐτόν pron. acc. masc. 3p. sg. αὐτός ή ό self, of oneself, even, very, the same, he, she, it
καὶ conj. καί and, even, also, but
τὰς art. acc. fem. pl. ὁ ἡ τό the, this, that, he, she, it

ἐντολὰς n. acc. fem. pl. ἐντολή commandment, precept
αὐτοῦ pron. gen. masc. 3p. sg. αὐτός ή ό self, of oneself, even, very, the same, he, she, it
μὴ particle of negation. μή not, no, lest, neither, none, nothing, nor, never, without
ψεύστης n. nom. masc. sg. ψεύστης liar
καὶ conj. καί and, even, also, but
ἐν prep. ἐν (+dat) in, by, with, among, at, on, through, to, within, into, of, for
τούτῳ demo. pron. dat. masc. sg. οὗτος αὕτη τοῦτο this, the same, this same, he, she, it
ἡ art. nom. fem. sg. ὁ ἡ τό the, this, that, he, she, it
ἀλήθεια n. nom. fem. sg. ἀλήθεια truth, verity
οὐκ particle of negation. οὐ οὐκ οὐχ not, no, neither, none, nay, nor, never, nothing
5 ὃς relative pron. nom. masc. sg. ὅς ἥ ὅ who, which, what, that
δ' conj. δέ but, and, now, also, to the contrary, rather, then
ἂν particle. ἄν Indicating contingency. No English translation.
αὐτοῦ pron. gen. masc. 3p. sg. αὐτός ή ό self, of oneself, even, very, the same, he, she, it
τὸν art. acc. masc. sg. ὁ ἡ τό the, this, that, he, she, it
λόγον n. acc. masc. sg. λόγος word, saying, account, speech, thing, matter
ἀληθῶς adv. ἀληθῶς indeed, of a truth, surely, truly, in truth, of a surety, verily, very
ἐν prep. ἐν (+dat) in, by, with, among, at, on, through, to, within, into, of, for
τούτῳ demo. pron. dat. masc. sg. οὗτος αὕτη τοῦτο this, the same, this same, he, she, it
ἡ art. nom. fem. sg. ὁ ἡ τό the, this, that, he, she, it
ἀγάπη n. nom. fem. sg. ἀγάπη love, charity, feast of charity
τοῦ art. gen. masc. sg. ὁ ἡ τό the, this, that, he, she, it
Θεοῦ n. gen. masc. sg. θεός God, god
ἐν prep. ἐν (+dat) in, by, with, among, at, on, through, to, within, into, of, for
τούτῳ demo. pron. dat. neut. sg. οὗτος αὕτη τοῦτο this, the same, this same, he, she, it
ὅτι conj. ὅτι that, for, because, how that, how, because that, for that, though
ἐν prep. ἐν (+dat) in, by, with, among, at, on, through, to, within, into, of, for
αὐτῷ pron. dat. masc. 3p. sg. αὐτός ή ό self, of oneself, even, very, the same, he, she, it
6 ὁ art. nom. masc. sg. ὁ ἡ τό the, this, that, he, she, it
ἐν prep. ἐν (+dat) in, by, with, among, at, on, through, to, within, into, of, for
αὐτῷ pron. dat. masc. 3p. sg. αὐτός ή ό self, of oneself, even, very, the same, he, she, it
καθὼς adv. καθώς as, even as, according as, according to
ἐκεῖνος demo. pron. nom. masc. sg. ἐκεῖνος that, he, the same, that same
καὶ conj. καί and, even, also, but
αὐτὸς pron. nom. masc. 3p. sg. αὐτός ή ό self, of oneself, even, very, the same, he, she, it
οὕτω adv. οὕτω οὕτως so, even so, thus, on this wise, likewise, after this manner
7 'Αδελφοί n. voc. masc. pl. ἀδελφός brother
οὐκ particle of negation. οὐ οὐκ οὐχ not, no, neither, none, nay, nor, never, nothing
ἐντολὴν n. acc. fem. sg. ἐντολή commandment, precept
καινὴν adj. acc. fem. sg. καινός new
ὑμῖν pron. dat. 2p. pl. σύ thou, you
ἀλλ' conj. ἀλλά but, yea, yet, nevertheless, howbeit, nay, therefore
ἐντολὴν n. acc. fem. sg. ἐντολή commandment, precept
παλαιὰν adj. acc. fem. sg. παλαιός old
ἣν relative pron. acc. fem. sg. ὅς ἥ ὅ who, which, what, that
ἀπ' prep. ἀπό (+gen) from, of, out of, since, for, off, at, by, in, on
ἀρχῆς n. gen. fem. sg. ἀρχή beginning, principality, corner, first, magistrate, rule
ἡ art. nom. fem. sg. ὁ ἡ τό the, this, that, he, she, it
ἐντολὴ n. nom. fem. sg. ἐντολή commandment, precept
ἡ art. nom. fem. sg. ὁ ἡ τό the, this, that, he, she, it
παλαιά adj. nom. fem. sg. παλαιός old
ὁ art. nom. masc. sg. ὁ ἡ τό the, this, that, he, she, it
λόγος n. nom. masc. sg. λόγος word, saying, account, speech, thing, matter
ὃν relative pron. acc. masc. sg. ὅς ἥ ὅ who, which, what, that
ἀπ' prep. ἀπό (+gen) from, of, out of, since, for, off, at, by, in, on

ἀρχῆς n. gen. fem. sg. ἀρχή beginning, principality, corner, first, magistrate, rule
8 πάλιν adv. πάλιν again
ἐντολὴν n. acc. fem. sg. ἐντολή commandment, precept
καινὴν adj. acc. fem. sg. καινός new
ὑμῖν pron. dat. 2p. pl. σύ thou, you
ὅ relative pron. nom. neut. sg. ὅς ἥ ὅ who, which, what, that
ἀληθὲς adj. nom. neut. sg. ἀληθής true, truly, truth
ἐν prep. ἐν (+dat) in, by, with, among, at, on, through, to, within, into, of, for
αὐτῷ pron. dat. masc. 3p. sg. αὐτός ή ό self, of oneself, even, very, the same, he, she, it
καὶ conj. καί and, even, also, but
ἐν prep. ἐν (+dat) in, by, with, among, at, on, through, to, within, into, of, for
ὑμῖν pron. dat. 2p. pl. σύ thou, you
ὅτι conj. ὅτι that, for, because, how that, how, because that, for that, though
ἡ art. nom. fem. sg. ὁ ἡ τό the, this, that, he, she, it
σκοτία n. nom. fem. sg. σκοτία darkness, dark
καὶ conj. καί and, even, also, but
τὸ art. nom. neut. sg. ὁ ἡ τό the, this, that, he, she, it
φῶς n. nom. neut. sg. φῶς light, fire
τὸ art. nom. neut. sg. ὁ ἡ τό the, this, that, he, she, it
ἀληθινὸν adj. nom. neut. sg. ἀληθινός true
ἤδη adv. ἤδη now, already, yet, by this time, even now, now already
9 ὁ art. nom. masc. sg. ὁ ἡ τό the, this, that, he, she, it
ἐν prep. ἐν (+dat) in, by, with, among, at, on, through, to, within, into, of, for
τῷ art. dat. neut. sg. ὁ ἡ τό the, this, that, he, she, it
φωτὶ n. dat. neut. sg. φῶς light, fire
καὶ conj. καί and, even, also, but
τὸν art. acc. masc. sg. ὁ ἡ τό the, this, that, he, she, it
ἀδελφὸν n. acc. masc. sg. ἀδελφός brother
αὐτοῦ pron. gen. masc. 3p. sg. αὐτός ή ό self, of oneself, even, very, the same, he, she, it
ἐν prep. ἐν (+dat) in, by, with, among, at, on, through, to, within, into, of, for
τῇ art. dat. fem. sg. ὁ ἡ τό the, this, that, he, she, it
σκοτίᾳ n. dat. fem. sg. σκοτία darkness, dark
ἕως conj. ἕως till, until, unto, until when, while, as far as, even, until now
ἄρτι adv. ἄρτι now, hence, here, hither, even now, present
10 ὁ art. nom. masc. sg. ὁ ἡ τό the, this, that, he, she, it
τὸν art. acc. masc. sg. ὁ ἡ τό the, this, that, he, she, it
ἀδελφὸν n. acc. masc. sg. ἀδελφός brother
αὐτοῦ pron. gen. masc. 3p. sg. αὐτός ή ό self, of oneself, even, very, the same, he, she, it
ἐν prep. ἐν (+dat) in, by, with, among, at, on, through, to, within, into, of, for
τῷ art. dat. neut. sg. ὁ ἡ τό the, this, that, he, she, it
φωτὶ n. dat. neut. sg. φῶς light, fire
καὶ conj. καί and, even, also, but
σκάνδαλον n. nom. neut. sg. σκάνδαλον offence, stumblingblock, thing that offend
ἐν prep. ἐν (+dat) in, by, with, among, at, on, through, to, within, into, of, for
αὐτῷ pron. dat. masc. 3p. sg. αὐτός ή ό self, of oneself, even, very, the same, he, she, it
οὐκ particle of negation. οὐ οὐκ οὐχ not, no, neither, none, nay, nor, never, nothing
11 ὁ art. nom. masc. sg. ὁ ἡ τό the, this, that, he, she, it
δὲ conj. δέ but, and, now, also, to the contrary, rather, then
τὸν art. acc. masc. sg. ὁ ἡ τό the, this, that, he, she, it
ἀδελφὸν n. acc. masc. sg. ἀδελφός brother
αὐτοῦ pron. gen. masc. 3p. sg. αὐτός ή ό self, of oneself, even, very, the same, he, she, it
ἐν prep. ἐν (+dat) in, by, with, among, at, on, through, to, within, into, of, for
τῇ art. dat. fem. sg. ὁ ἡ τό the, this, that, he, she, it
σκοτίᾳ n. dat. fem. sg. σκοτία darkness, dark
καὶ conj. καί and, even, also, but

ἐν prep. ἐν (+dat) in, by, with, among, at, on, through, to, within, into, of, for
τῇ art. dat. fem. sg. ὁ ἡ τό the, this, that, he, she, it
σκοτίᾳ n. dat. fem. sg. σκοτία darkness, dark
καὶ conj. καί and, even, also, but
οὐκ particle of negation. οὐ οὐκ οὐχ not, no, neither, none, nay, nor, never, nothing
ποῦ particle of place. ποῦ where, whither
ὅτι conj. ὅτι that, for, because, how that, how, because that, for that, though
ἡ art. nom. fem. sg. ὁ ἡ τό the, this, that, he, she, it
σκοτία n. nom. fem. sg. σκοτία darkness, dark
τοὺς art. acc. masc. pl. ὁ ἡ τό the, this, that, he, she, it
ὀφθαλμοὺς n. acc. masc. pl. ὀφθαλμός eye, sight
αὐτοῦ pron. gen. masc. 3p. sg. αὐτός ή ό self, of oneself, even, very, the same, he, she, it
12 ὑμῖν pron. dat. 2p. pl. σύ thou, you
τεκνία n. voc. neut. pl. τεκνίον little child
ὅτι conj. ὅτι that, for, because, how that, how, because that, for that, though
ὑμῖν pron. dat. 2p. pl. σύ thou, you
αἱ art. nom. fem. pl. ὁ ἡ τό the, this, that, he, she, it
ἁμαρτίαι n. nom. fem. pl. ἁμαρτία sin, offence, sinful
διὰ prep. διά (+gen) by, through, with, in, of, (+acc) for, because of, for a cause
τὸ art. acc. neut. sg. ὁ ἡ τό the, this, that, he, she, it
ὄνομα n. acc. neut. sg. ὄνομα name, call, surname
αὐτοῦ pron. gen. masc. 3p. sg. αὐτός ή ό self, of oneself, even, very, the same, he, she, it
13 ὑμῖν pron. dat. 2p. pl. σύ thou, you
πατέρες n. voc. masc. pl. πατήρ Father, father, parent
ὅτι conj. ὅτι that, for, because, how that, how, because that, for that, though
τὸν art. acc. masc. sg. ὁ ἡ τό the, this, that, he, she, it
ἀπ' prep. ἀπό (+gen) from, of, out of, since, for, off, at, by, in, on
ἀρχῆς n. gen. fem. sg. ἀρχή beginning, principality, corner, first, magistrate, rule
ὑμῖν pron. dat. 2p. pl. σύ thou, you
νεανίσκοι n. voc. masc. pl. νεανίσκος young man
ὅτι conj. ὅτι that, for, because, how that, how, because that, for that, though
τὸν art. acc. masc. sg. ὁ ἡ τό the, this, that, he, she, it
πονηρόν adj. acc. masc. sg. πονηρός evil, wicked, bad
ὑμῖν pron. dat. 2p. pl. σύ thou, you
παιδία n. voc. neut. pl. παιδίον child, little child, damsel
ὅτι conj. ὅτι that, for, because, how that, how, because that, for that, though
τὸν art. acc. masc. sg. ὁ ἡ τό the, this, that, he, she, it
πατέρα n. acc. masc. sg. πατήρ Father, father, parent
14 ὑμῖν pron. dat. 2p. pl. σύ thou, you
πατέρες n. voc. masc. pl. πατήρ Father, father, parent
ὅτι conj. ὅτι that, for, because, how that, how, because that, for that, though
τὸν art. acc. masc. sg. ὁ ἡ τό the, this, that, he, she, it
ἀπ' prep. ἀπό (+gen) from, of, out of, since, for, off, at, by, in, on
ἀρχῆς n. gen. fem. sg. ἀρχή beginning, principality, corner, first, magistrate, rule
ὑμῖν pron. dat. 2p. pl. σύ thou, you
νεανίσκοι n. voc. masc. pl. νεανίσκος young man
ὅτι conj. ὅτι that, for, because, how that, how, because that, for that, though
ἰσχυροί adj. nom. masc. pl. ἰσχυρός mighty, strong, mightier, stronger
καὶ conj. καί and, even, also, but
ὁ art. nom. masc. sg. ὁ ἡ τό the, this, that, he, she, it
λόγος n. nom. masc. sg. λόγος word, saying, account, speech, thing, matter
τοῦ art. gen. masc. sg. ὁ ἡ τό the, this, that, he, she, it
Θεοῦ n. gen. masc. sg. θεός God, god
ἐν prep. ἐν (+dat) in, by, with, among, at, on, through, to, within, into, of, for
ὑμῖν pron. dat. 2p. pl. σύ thou, you

καὶ conj. καί and, even, also, but
τὸν art. acc. masc. sg. ὁ ἡ τό the, this, that, he, she, it
πονηρόν adj. acc. masc. sg. πονηρός evil, wicked, bad
15 μὴ particle of negation. μή not, no, lest, neither, none, nothing, nor, never, without
τὸν art. acc. masc. sg. ὁ ἡ τό the, this, that, he, she, it
κόσμον n. acc. masc. sg. κόσμος world, adorning
μηδὲ conj. μηδέ neither, nor, not, no not, nor yet, not once, not so much as
τὰ art. acc. neut. pl. ὁ ἡ τό the, this, that, he, she, it
ἐν prep. ἐν (+dat) in, by, with, among, at, on, through, to, within, into, of, for
τῷ art. dat. masc. sg. ὁ ἡ τό the, this, that, he, she, it
κόσμῳ n. dat. masc. sg. κόσμος world, adorning
ἐάν conj. ἐάν if, soever, except, though, and if, but, whether, if so, so
τις indefinite pron. nom. masc. sg. τὶς certain, some, any man, one, any thing
τὸν art. acc. masc. sg. ὁ ἡ τό the, this, that, he, she, it
κόσμον n. acc. masc. sg. κόσμος world, adorning
οὐκ particle of negation. οὐ οὐκ οὐχ not, no, neither, none, nay, nor, never, nothing
ἡ art. nom. fem. sg. ὁ ἡ τό the, this, that, he, she, it
ἀγάπη n. nom. fem. sg. ἀγάπη love, charity, feast of charity
τοῦ art. gen. masc. sg. ὁ ἡ τό the, this, that, he, she, it
πατρὸς n. gen. masc. sg. πατήρ Father, father, parent
ἐν prep. ἐν (+dat) in, by, with, among, at, on, through, to, within, into, of, for
αὐτῷ pron. dat. masc. 3p. sg. αὐτός ή ό self, of oneself, even, very, the same, he, she, it
16 ὅτι conj. ὅτι that, for, because, how that, how, because that, for that, though
πᾶν adj. nom. neut. sg. πᾶς πᾶσα πᾶν all, every, whosoever, every one, no, whole, any
τὸ art. nom. neut. sg. ὁ ἡ τό the, this, that, he, she, it
ἐν prep. ἐν (+dat) in, by, with, among, at, on, through, to, within, into, of, for
τῷ art. dat. masc. sg. ὁ ἡ τό the, this, that, he, she, it
κόσμῳ n. dat. masc. sg. κόσμος world, adorning
ἡ art. nom. fem. sg. ὁ ἡ τό the, this, that, he, she, it
ἐπιθυμία n. nom. fem. sg. ἐπιθυμία lust, concupiscence, desire
τῆς art. gen. fem. sg. ὁ ἡ τό the, this, that, he, she, it
σαρκὸς n. gen. fem. sg. σάρξ flesh, carnal
καὶ conj. καί and, even, also, but
ἡ art. nom. fem. sg. ὁ ἡ τό the, this, that, he, she, it
ἐπιθυμία n. nom. fem. sg. ἐπιθυμία lust, concupiscence, desire
τῶν art. gen. masc. pl. ὁ ἡ τό the, this, that, he, she, it
ὀφθαλμῶν n. gen. masc. pl. ὀφθαλμός eye, sight
καὶ conj. καί and, even, also, but
ἡ art. nom. fem. sg. ὁ ἡ τό the, this, that, he, she, it
ἀλαζονεία n. nom. fem. sg. ἀλαζονεία boasting, pride
τοῦ art. gen. masc. sg. ὁ ἡ τό the, this, that, he, she, it
βίου n. gen. masc. sg. βίος life, living, good
οὐκ particle of negation. οὐ οὐκ οὐχ not, no, neither, none, nay, nor, never, nothing
ἐκ prep. ἐκ ἐξ (+gen) of, from, out of, by, on, with, in, among, through
τοῦ art. gen. masc. sg. ὁ ἡ τό the, this, that, he, she, it
πατρὸς n. gen. masc. sg. πατήρ Father, father, parent
ἀλλ' conj. ἀλλά but, yea, yet, nevertheless, howbeit, nay, therefore
ἐκ prep. ἐκ ἐξ (+gen) of, from, out of, by, on, with, in, among, through
τοῦ art. gen. masc. sg. ὁ ἡ τό the, this, that, he, she, it
κόσμου n. gen. masc. sg. κόσμος world, adorning
17 καὶ conj. καί and, even, also, but
ὁ art. nom. masc. sg. ὁ ἡ τό the, this, that, he, she, it
κόσμος n. nom. masc. sg. κόσμος world, adorning
καὶ conj. καί and, even, also, but
ἡ art. nom. fem. sg. ὁ ἡ τό the, this, that, he, she, it

ἐπιθυμία n. nom. fem. sg. ἐπιθυμία lust, concupiscence, desire
αὐτοῦ pron. gen. masc. 3p. sg. αὐτός ή ό self, of oneself, even, very, the same, he, she, it
ὁ art. nom. masc. sg. ὁ ἡ τό the, this, that, he, she, it
δὲ conj. δέ but, and, now, also, to the contrary, rather, then
τὸ art. acc. neut. sg. ὁ ἡ τό the, this, that, he, she, it
θέλημα n. acc. neut. sg. θέλημα will, desire, pleasure
τοῦ art. gen. masc. sg. ὁ ἡ τό the, this, that, he, she, it
Θεοῦ n. gen. masc. sg. θεός God, god
εἰς prep. εἰς (+acc) into, to, unto, for, in, on, toward, against, upon, at, among
τὸν art. acc. masc. sg. ὁ ἡ τό the, this, that, he, she, it
αἰῶνα n. acc. masc. sg. αἰών ever, ever and ever, evermore, age, eternal, world
18 Παιδία n. voc. neut. pl. παιδίον child, little child, damsel
ἐσχάτη adj. nom. fem. sg. ἔσχατος last, lowest, uttermost, uttermost part
ὥρα n. nom. fem. sg. ὥρα hour, time, season
καὶ conj. καί and, even, also, but
καθὼς adv. καθώς as, even as, according as, according to
ὅτι conj. ὅτι that, for, because, how that, how, because that, for that, though
ὁ art. nom. masc. sg. ὁ ἡ τό the, this, that, he, she, it
ἀντίχριστος n. nom. masc. sg. ἀντίχριστος antichrist
καὶ conj. καί and, even, also, but
νῦν adv. νῦν now, henceforth, present, this time
ἀντίχριστοι n. nom. masc. pl. ἀντίχριστος antichrist
πολλοὶ adj. nom. masc. pl. πολύς many, great, much, long, abundant
ὅθεν adv. ὅθεν wherefore, from whence, whereupon, where, from thence, whence
ὅτι conj. ὅτι that, for, because, how that, how, because that, for that, though
ἐσχάτη adj. nom. fem. sg. ἔσχατος last, lowest, uttermost, uttermost part
ὥρα n. nom. fem. sg. ὥρα hour, time, season
19 ἐξ prep. ἐκ ἐξ (+gen) of, from, out of, by, on, with, in, among, through
ἡμῶν pron. gen. 1p. pl. ἐγώ I
ἀλλ' conj. ἀλλά but, yea, yet, nevertheless, howbeit, nay, therefore
οὐκ particle of negation. οὐ οὐκ οὐχ not, no, neither, none, nay, nor, never, nothing
ἐξ prep. ἐκ ἐξ (+gen) of, from, out of, by, on, with, in, among, through
ἡμῶν pron. gen. 1p. pl. ἐγώ I
εἰ conj. εἰ if, whether, that, though, forasmuch
γὰρ conj. γάρ for, and, because, but, indeed
ἐξ prep. ἐκ ἐξ (+gen) of, from, out of, by, on, with, in, among, through
ἡμῶν pron. gen. 1p. pl. ἐγώ I
ἂν particle. ἄν Indicating contingency. No English translation.
μεθ' prep. μετά (+gen) with, among, against, (+acc) after
ἡμῶν pron. gen. 1p. pl. ἐγώ I
ἀλλ' conj. ἀλλά but, yea, yet, nevertheless, howbeit, nay, therefore
ἵνα conj. ἵνα that, to, lest, for to, so that, albeit, because, for, so as
ὅτι conj. ὅτι that, for, because, how that, how, because that, for that, though
οὐκ particle of negation. οὐ οὐκ οὐχ not, no, neither, none, nay, nor, never, nothing
πάντες adj. nom. masc. pl. πᾶς πᾶσα πᾶν all, every, whosoever, every one, no, whole, any
ἐξ prep. ἐκ ἐξ (+gen) of, from, out of, by, on, with, in, among, through
ἡμῶν pron. gen. 1p. pl. ἐγώ I
20 καὶ conj. καί and, even, also, but
ὑμεῖς pron. nom. 2p. pl. σύ thou, you
χρῖσμα n. acc. neut. sg. χρῖσμα unction, anointing
ἀπὸ prep. ἀπό (+gen) from, of, out of, since, for, off, at, by, in, on
τοῦ art. gen. masc. sg. ὁ ἡ τό the, this, that, he, she, it
ἁγίου adj. gen. masc. sg. ἅγιος Holy, holy, saint, Holy One, holy thing, most holy
καὶ conj. καί and, even, also, but
πάντα adj. acc. neut. pl. πᾶς πᾶσα πᾶν all, every, whosoever, every one, no, whole, any

21 οὐκ particle of negation. οὐ οὐκ οὐχ not, no, neither, none, nay, nor, never, nothing
ὑμῖν pron. dat. 2p. pl. σύ thou, you
ὅτι conj. ὅτι that, for, because, how that, how, because that, for that, though
οὐκ particle of negation. οὐ οὐκ οὐχ not, no, neither, none, nay, nor, never, nothing
τὴν art. acc. fem. sg. ὁ ἡ τό the, this, that, he, she, it
ἀλήθειαν n. acc. fem. sg. ἀλήθεια truth, verity
ἀλλ' conj. ἀλλά but, yea, yet, nevertheless, howbeit, nay, therefore
ὅτι conj. ὅτι that, for, because, how that, how, because that, for that, though
αὐτὴν pron. acc. fem. 3p. sg. αὐτός ή ό self, of oneself, even, very, the same, he, she, it
καὶ conj. καί and, even, also, but
ὅτι conj. ὅτι that, for, because, how that, how, because that, for that, though
πᾶν adj. nom. neut. sg. πᾶς πᾶςα πᾶν all, every, whosoever, every one, no, whole, any
ψεῦδος n. nom. neut. sg. ψεῦδος lie, lying
ἐκ prep. ἐκ ἐξ (+gen) of, from, out of, by, on, with, in, among, through
τῆς art. gen. fem. sg. ὁ ἡ τό the, this, that, he, she, it
ἀληθείας n. gen. fem. sg. ἀλήθεια truth, verity
οὐκ particle of negation. οὐ οὐκ οὐχ not, no, neither, none, nay, nor, never, nothing
22 τίς interrog. pron. nom. masc. sg. τίς what, who, why, where, which, how
ὁ art. nom. masc. sg. ὁ ἡ τό the, this, that, he, she, it
ψεύστης n. nom. masc. sg. ψεύστης liar
εἰ conj. εἰ if, whether, that, though, forasmuch
μὴ particle of negation. μή not, no, lest, neither, none, nothing, nor, never, without
ὁ art. nom. masc. sg. ὁ ἡ τό the, this, that, he, she, it
ὅτι conj. ὅτι that, for, because, how that, how, because that, for that, though
Ἰησοῦς n. nom. masc. sg. Ἰησοῦς Jesus
οὐκ particle of negation. οὐ οὐκ οὐχ not, no, neither, none, nay, nor, never, nothing
ὁ art. nom. masc. sg. ὁ ἡ τό the, this, that, he, she, it
Χριστός n. nom. masc. sg. Χριστός Christ
οὗτός demo. pron. nom. masc. sg. οὗτος αὕτη τοῦτο this, the same, this same, he, she, it
ὁ art. nom. masc. sg. ὁ ἡ τό the, this, that, he, she, it
ἀντίχριστος n. nom. masc. sg. ἀντίχριστος antichrist
ὁ art. nom. masc. sg. ὁ ἡ τό the, this, that, he, she, it
τὸν art. acc. masc. sg. ὁ ἡ τό the, this, that, he, she, it
πατέρα n. acc. masc. sg. πατήρ Father, father, parent
καὶ conj. καί and, even, also, but
τὸν art. acc. masc. sg. ὁ ἡ τό the, this, that, he, she, it
υἱόν n. acc. masc. sg. υἱός son, child, descendant, offspring, heir
23 πᾶς adj. nom. masc. sg. πᾶς πᾶςα πᾶν all, every, whosoever, every one, no, whole, any
ὁ art. nom. masc. sg. ὁ ἡ τό the, this, that, he, she, it
τὸν art. acc. masc. sg. ὁ ἡ τό the, this, that, he, she, it
υἱὸν n. acc. masc. sg. υἱός son, child, descendant, offspring, heir
οὐδὲ adv. οὐδέ neither, nor, not, no, not even, never, not yet
τὸν art. acc. masc. sg. ὁ ἡ τό the, this, that, he, she, it
πατέρα n. acc. masc. sg. πατήρ Father, father, parent
ὁ art. nom. masc. sg. ὁ ἡ τό the, this, that, he, she, it
τὸν art. acc. masc. sg. ὁ ἡ τό the, this, that, he, she, it
υἱὸν n. acc. masc. sg. υἱός son, child, descendant, offspring, heir
καὶ conj. καί and, even, also, but
τὸν art. acc. masc. sg. ὁ ἡ τό the, this, that, he, she, it
πατέρα n. acc. masc. sg. πατήρ Father, father, parent
24 ὑμεῖς pron. nom. 2p. pl. σύ thou, you
οὖν conj. οὖν therefore, then, so, and, now, wherefore
ὃ relative pron. acc. neut. sg. ὅς ἥ ὅ who, which, what, that
ἀπ' prep. ἀπό (+gen) from, of, out of, since, for, off, at, by, in, on
ἀρχῆς n. gen. fem. sg. ἀρχή beginning, principality, corner, first, magistrate, rule

ἐν prep. ἐν (+dat) in, by, with, among, at, on, through, to, within, into, of, for
ὑμῖν pron. dat. 2p. pl. σύ thou, you
ἐὰν conj. ἐάν if, soever, except, though, and if, but, whether, if so, so
ἐν prep. ἐν (+dat) in, by, with, among, at, on, through, to, within, into, of, for
ὑμῖν pron. dat. 2p. pl. σύ thou, you
ὃ relative pron. acc. neut. sg. ὅς ἥ ὅ who, which, what, that
ἀπ' prep. ἀπό (+gen) from, of, out of, since, for, off, at, by, in, on
ἀρχῆς n. gen. fem. sg. ἀρχή beginning, principality, corner, first, magistrate, rule
καὶ conj. καί and, even, also, but
ὑμεῖς pron. nom. 2p. pl. σύ thou, you
ἐν prep. ἐν (+dat) in, by, with, among, at, on, through, to, within, into, of, for
τῷ art. dat. masc. sg. ὁ ἡ τό the, this, that, he, she, it
υἱῷ n. dat. masc. sg. υἱός son, child, descendant, offspring, heir
καὶ conj. καί and, even, also, but
ἐν prep. ἐν (+dat) in, by, with, among, at, on, through, to, within, into, of, for
τῷ art. dat. masc. sg. ὁ ἡ τό the, this, that, he, she, it
πατρὶ n. dat. masc. sg. πατήρ Father, father, parent
25 καὶ conj. καί and, even, also, but
αὕτη demo. pron. nom. fem. sg. οὗτος αὕτη τοῦτο this, the same, this same, he, she, it
ἡ art. nom. fem. sg. ὁ ἡ τό the, this, that, he, she, it
ἐπαγγελία n. nom. fem. sg. ἐπαγγελία promise, message
ἣν relative pron. acc. fem. sg. ὅς ἥ ὅ who, which, what, that
αὐτὸς pron. nom. masc. 3p. sg. αὐτός ή ό self, of oneself, even, very, the same, he, she, it
ἡμῖν pron. dat. 1p. pl. ἐγώ I
τὴν art. acc. fem. sg. ὁ ἡ τό the, this, that, he, she, it
ζωὴν n. acc. fem. sg. ζωή life, lifetime
τὴν art. acc. fem. sg. ὁ ἡ τό the, this, that, he, she, it
αἰώνιον adj. acc. fem. sg. αἰώνιος eternal, everlasting, world, for ever
26 ταῦτα demo. pron. acc. neut. pl. οὗτος αὕτη τοῦτο this, the same, this same, he, she, it
ὑμῖν pron. dat. 2p. pl. σύ thou, you
περὶ prep. περί (+gen) of, for, concerning, (+acc) about, concerning, in
τῶν art. gen. masc. pl. ὁ ἡ τό the, this, that, he, she, it
ὑμᾶς pron. acc. 2p. pl. σύ thou, you
27 καὶ conj. καί and, even, also, but
ὑμεῖς pron. nom. 2p. pl. σύ thou, you
τὸ art. nom. neut. sg. ὁ ἡ τό the, this, that, he, she, it
χρῖσμα n. nom. neut. sg. χρῖσμα unction, anointing
ὃ relative pron. acc. neut. sg. ὅς ἥ ὅ who, which, what, that
ἀπ' prep. ἀπό (+gen) from, of, out of, since, for, off, at, by, in, on
αὐτοῦ pron. gen. masc. 3p. sg. αὐτός ή ό self, of oneself, even, very, the same, he, she, it
ἐν prep. ἐν (+dat) in, by, with, among, at, on, through, to, within, into, of, for
ὑμῖν pron. dat. 2p. pl. σύ thou, you
καὶ conj. καί and, even, also, but
οὐ particle of negation. οὐ οὐκ οὐχ not, no, neither, none, nay, nor, never, nothing
χρείαν n. acc. fem. sg. χρεία need, necessity, lack, want
ἵνα conj. ἵνα that, to, lest, for to, so that, albeit, because, for, so as
τις indefinite pron. nom. masc. sg. τὶς certain, some, any man, one, any thing
ὑμᾶς pron. acc. 2p. pl. σύ thou, you
ἀλλ' conj. ἀλλά but, yea, yet, nevertheless, howbeit, nay, therefore
ὡς adv. ὡς as, when, as it were, how, about, like, as soon as, even as, while
τὸ art. nom. neut. sg. ὁ ἡ τό the, this, that, he, she, it
αὐτὸ pron. nom. neut. 3p. sg. αὐτός ή ό self, of oneself, even, very, the same, he, she, it
χρῖσμα n. nom. neut. sg. χρῖσμα unction, anointing
ὑμᾶς pron. acc. 2p. pl. σύ thou, you
περὶ prep. περί (+gen) of, for, concerning, (+acc) about, concerning, in

πάντων adj. gen. neut. pl. πᾶς πᾶσα πᾶν all, every, whosoever, every one, no, whole, any
καὶ conj. καί and, even, also, but
ἀληθές adj. nom. neut. sg. ἀληθής true, truly, truth
καὶ conj. καί and, even, also, but
οὐκ particle of negation. οὐ οὐκ οὐχ not, no, neither, none, nay, nor, never, nothing
ψεῦδος n. nom. neut. sg. ψεῦδος lie, lying
καὶ conj. καί and, even, also, but
καθὼς adv. καθώς as, even as, according as, according to
ὑμᾶς pron. acc. 2p. pl. σύ thou, you
ἐν prep. ἐν (+dat) in, by, with, among, at, on, through, to, within, into, of, for
αὐτῷ pron. dat. masc. 3p. sg. αὐτός ή ό self, of oneself, even, very, the same, he, she, it
28 καὶ conj. καί and, even, also, but
νῦν adv. νῦν now, henceforth, present, this time
τεκνία n. voc. neut. pl. τεκνίον little child
ἐν prep. ἐν (+dat) in, by, with, among, at, on, through, to, within, into, of, for
αὐτῷ pron. dat. masc. 3p. sg. αὐτός ή ό self, of oneself, even, very, the same, he, she, it
ἵνα conj. ἵνα that, to, lest, for to, so that, albeit, because, for, so as
ὅταν conj. ὅταν when, as soon as, as long as, that, whensoever, while
παρρησίαν n. acc. fem. sg. παρρησία boldness, confidence, openly, plainly, freely
καὶ conj. καί and, even, also, but
μὴ particle of negation. μή not, no, lest, neither, none, nothing, nor, never, without
ἀπ' prep. ἀπό (+gen) from, of, out of, since, for, off, at, by, in, on
αὐτοῦ pron. gen. masc. 3p. sg. αὐτός ή ό self, of oneself, even, very, the same, he, she, it
ἐν prep. ἐν (+dat) in, by, with, among, at, on, through, to, within, into, of, for
τῇ art. dat. fem. sg. ὁ ἡ τό the, this, that, he, she, it
παρουσίᾳ n. dat. fem. sg. παρουσία coming, presence
αὐτοῦ pron. gen. masc. 3p. sg. αὐτός ή ό self, of oneself, even, very, the same, he, she, it
29 ἐὰν conj. ἐάν if, soever, except, though, and if, but, whether, if so, so
ὅτι conj. ὅτι that, for, because, how that, how, because that, for that, though
δίκαιός adj. nom. masc. sg. δίκαιος righteous, just, meet, right
ὅτι conj. ὅτι that, for, because, how that, how, because that, for that, though
πᾶς adj. nom. masc. sg. πᾶς πᾶσα πᾶν all, every, whosoever, every one, no, whole, any
ὁ art. nom. masc. sg. ὁ ἡ τό the, this, that, he, she, it
τὴν art. acc. fem. sg. ὁ ἡ τό the, this, that, he, she, it
δικαιοσύνην n. acc. fem. sg. δικαιοσύνη righteousness
ἐξ prep. ἐκ ἐξ (+gen) of, from, out of, by, on, with, in, among, through
αὐτοῦ pron. gen. masc. 3p. sg. αὐτός ή ό self, of oneself, even, very, the same, he, she, it

3

1 ποταπὴν interrog. pron. acc. fem. sg. ποταπός what manner of, what
ἀγάπην n. acc. fem. sg. ἀγάπη love, charity, feast of charity
ἡμῖν pron. dat. 1p. pl. ἐγώ I
ὁ art. nom. masc. sg. ὁ ἡ τό the, this, that, he, she, it
πατὴρ n. nom. masc. sg. πατήρ Father, father, parent
ἵνα conj. ἵνα that, to, lest, for to, so that, albeit, because, for, so as
τέκνα n. nom. neut. pl. τέκνον child, son, daughter
Θεοῦ n. gen. masc. sg. θεός God, god
διὰ prep. διά (+gen) by, through, with, in, of, (+acc) for, because of, for a cause
τοῦτο demo. pron. acc. neut. sg. οὗτος αὕτη τοῦτο this, the same, this same, he, she, it
ὁ art. nom. masc. sg. ὁ ἡ τό the, this, that, he, she, it
κόσμος n. nom. masc. sg. κόσμος world, adorning
οὐ particle of negation. οὐ οὐκ οὐχ not, no, neither, none, nay, nor, never, nothing
ἡμᾶς pron. acc. 1p. pl. ἐγώ I
ὅτι conj. ὅτι that, for, because, how that, how, because that, for that, though

οὐκ particle of negation. οὐ οὐκ οὐχ not, no, neither, none, nay, nor, never, nothing
αὐτόν pron. acc. masc. 3p. sg. αὐτός ή ό self, of oneself, even, very, the same, he, she, it
2 ἀγαπητοί adj. voc. masc. pl. ἀγαπητός beloved, dearly beloved, dear, wellbeloved
νῦν adv. νῦν now, henceforth, present, this time
τέκνα n. nom. neut. pl. τέκνον child, son, daughter
Θεοῦ n. gen. masc. sg. θεός God, god
καὶ conj. καί and, even, also, but
οὔπω adv. οὔπω not yet
τί interrog. pron. nom. neut. sg. τίς what, who, why, where, which, how
δὲ conj. δέ but, and, now, also, to the contrary, rather, then
ὅτι conj. ὅτι that, for, because, how that, how, because that, for that, though
ἐὰν conj. ἐάν if, soever, except, though, and if, but, whether, if so, so
ὅμοιοι adj. nom. masc. pl. ὅμοιος like
αὐτῷ pron. dat. masc. 3p. sg. αὐτός ή ό self, of oneself, even, very, the same, he, she, it
ὅτι conj. ὅτι that, for, because, how that, how, because that, for that, though
αὐτὸν pron. acc. masc. 3p. sg. αὐτός ή ό self, of oneself, even, very, the same, he, she, it
καθώς adv. καθώς as, even as, according as, according to
3 καὶ conj. καί and, even, also, but
πᾶς adj. nom. masc. sg. πᾶς πᾶσα πᾶν all, every, whosoever, every one, no, whole, any
ὁ art. nom. masc. sg. ὁ ἡ τό the, this, that, he, she, it
τὴν art. acc. fem. sg. ὁ ἡ τό the, this, that, he, she, it
ἐλπίδα n. acc. fem. sg. ἐλπίς hope, faith
ταύτην demo. pron. acc. fem. sg. οὗτος αὕτη τοῦτο this, the same, this same, he, she, it
ἐπ' prep. ἐπί (+gen) on, in, upon, (+dat) in, at, for, upon, (+acc) on, upon, unto, to, against
αὐτῷ pron. dat. masc. 3p. sg. αὐτός ή ό self, of oneself, even, very, the same, he, she, it
ἑαυτόν reflexive pron. acc. masc. 3p. sg. ἑαυτοῦ himself, herself, itself, yourself, ourselves
καθὼς adv. καθώς as, even as, according as, according to
ἐκεῖνος demo. pron. nom. masc. sg. ἐκεῖνος that, he, the same, that same
ἁγνός adj. nom. masc. sg. ἁγνός clear, pure, chaste
4 πᾶς adj. nom. masc. sg. πᾶς πᾶσα πᾶν all, every, whosoever, every one, no, whole, any
ὁ art. nom. masc. sg. ὁ ἡ τό the, this, that, he, she, it
τὴν art. acc. fem. sg. ὁ ἡ τό the, this, that, he, she, it
ἁμαρτίαν n. acc. fem. sg. ἁμαρτία sin, offence, sinful
καὶ conj. καί and, even, also, but
τὴν art. acc. fem. sg. ὁ ἡ τό the, this, that, he, she, it
ἀνομίαν n. acc. fem. sg. ἀνομία iniquity, transgression of the law, lawlessness
καὶ conj. καί and, even, also, but
ἡ art. nom. fem. sg. ὁ ἡ τό the, this, that, he, she, it
ἁμαρτία n. nom. fem. sg. ἁμαρτία sin, offence, sinful
ἡ art. nom. fem. sg. ὁ ἡ τό the, this, that, he, she, it
ἀνομία n. nom. fem. sg. ἀνομία iniquity, transgression of the law, lawlessness
5 καὶ conj. καί and, even, also, but
ὅτι conj. ὅτι that, for, because, how that, how, because that, for that, though
ἐκεῖνος demo. pron. nom. masc. sg. ἐκεῖνος that, he, the same, that same
ἵνα conj. ἵνα that, to, lest, for to, so that, albeit, because, for, so as
τὰς art. acc. fem. pl. ὁ ἡ τό the, this, that, he, she, it
ἁμαρτίας n. acc. fem. pl. ἁμαρτία sin, offence, sinful
ἡμῶν pron. gen. 1p. pl. ἐγώ I
καὶ conj. καί and, even, also, but
ἁμαρτία n. nom. fem. sg. ἁμαρτία sin, offence, sinful
ἐν prep. ἐν (+dat) in, by, with, among, at, on, through, to, within, into, of, for
αὐτῷ pron. dat. masc. 3p. sg. αὐτός ή ό self, of oneself, even, very, the same, he, she, it
οὐκ particle of negation. οὐ οὐκ οὐχ not, no, neither, none, nay, nor, never, nothing
6 πᾶς adj. nom. masc. sg. πᾶς πᾶσα πᾶν all, every, whosoever, every one, no, whole, any
ὁ art. nom. masc. sg. ὁ ἡ τό the, this, that, he, she, it

ἐν prep. ἐν (+dat) in, by, with, among, at, on, through, to, within, into, of, for
αὐτῷ pron. dat. masc. 3p. sg. αὐτός ή ό self, of oneself, even, very, the same, he, she, it
οὐχ particle of negation. οὐ οὐκ οὐχ not, no, neither, none, nay, nor, never, nothing
πᾶς adj. nom. masc. sg. πᾶς πᾶσα πᾶν all, every, whosoever, every one, no, whole, any
ὁ art. nom. masc. sg. ὁ ἡ τό the, this, that, he, she, it
οὐχ particle of negation. οὐ οὐκ οὐχ not, no, neither, none, nay, nor, never, nothing
αὐτὸν pron. acc. masc. 3p. sg. αὐτός ή ό self, of oneself, even, very, the same, he, she, it
οὐδὲ adv. οὐδέ neither, nor, not, no, not even, never, not yet
αὐτὸν pron. acc. masc. 3p. sg. αὐτός ή ό self, of oneself, even, very, the same, he, she, it
7 τεκνία n. voc. neut. pl. τεκνίον little child
μηδεὶς num. nom. masc. sg. μηδείς μηδεμία μηδέν no man, nothing, no, none, not at all
ὑμᾶς pron. acc. 2p. pl. σύ thou, you
ὁ art. nom. masc. sg. ὁ ἡ τό the, this, that, he, she, it
τὴν art. acc. fem. sg. ὁ ἡ τό the, this, that, he, she, it
δικαιοσύνην n. acc. fem. sg. δικαιοσύνη righteousness
δίκαιός adj. nom. masc. sg. δίκαιος righteous, just, meet, right
καθὼς adv. καθώς as, even as, according as, according to
ἐκεῖνος demo. pron. nom. masc. sg. ἐκεῖνος that, he, the same, that same
δίκαιός adj. nom. masc. sg. δίκαιος righteous, just, meet, right
8 ὁ art. nom. masc. sg. ὁ ἡ τό the, this, that, he, she, it
τὴν art. acc. fem. sg. ὁ ἡ τό the, this, that, he, she, it
ἁμαρτίαν n. acc. fem. sg. ἁμαρτία sin, offence, sinful
ἐκ prep. ἐκ ἐξ (+gen) of, from, out of, by, on, with, in, among, through
τοῦ art. gen. masc. sg. ὁ ἡ τό the, this, that, he, she, it
διαβόλου adj. gen. masc. sg. διάβολος devil, false accuser, Devil, slanderer
ὅτι conj. ὅτι that, for, because, how that, how, because that, for that, though
ἀπ' prep. ἀπό (+gen) from, of, out of, since, for, off, at, by, in, on
ἀρχῆς n. gen. fem. sg. ἀρχή beginning, principality, corner, first, magistrate, rule
ὁ art. nom. masc. sg. ὁ ἡ τό the, this, that, he, she, it
διάβολος adj. nom. masc. sg. διάβολος devil, false accuser, Devil, slanderer
εἰς prep. εἰς (+acc) into, to, unto, for, in, on, toward, against, upon, at, among
τοῦτο demo. pron. acc. neut. sg. οὗτος αὕτη τοῦτο this, the same, this same, he, she, it
ὁ art. nom. masc. sg. ὁ ἡ τό the, this, that, he, she, it
υἱὸς n. nom. masc. sg. υἱός son, child, descendant, offspring, heir
τοῦ art. gen. masc. sg. ὁ ἡ τό the, this, that, he, she, it
Θεοῦ n. gen. masc. sg. θεός God, god
ἵνα conj. ἵνα that, to, lest, for to, so that, albeit, because, for, so as
τὰ art. acc. neut. pl. ὁ ἡ τό the, this, that, he, she, it
ἔργα n. acc. neut. pl. ἔργον work, deed, doing labour
τοῦ art. gen. masc. sg. ὁ ἡ τό the, this, that, he, she, it
διαβόλου adj. gen. masc. sg. διάβολος devil, false accuser, Devil, slanderer
9 πᾶς adj. nom. masc. sg. πᾶς πᾶσα πᾶν all, every, whosoever, every one, no, whole, any
ὁ art. nom. masc. sg. ὁ ἡ τό the, this, that, he, she, it
ἐκ prep. ἐκ ἐξ (+gen) of, from, out of, by, on, with, in, among, through
τοῦ art. gen. masc. sg. ὁ ἡ τό the, this, that, he, she, it
Θεοῦ n. gen. masc. sg. θεός God, god
ἁμαρτίαν n. acc. fem. sg. ἁμαρτία sin, offence, sinful
οὐ particle of negation. οὐ οὐκ οὐχ not, no, neither, none, nay, nor, never, nothing
ὅτι conj. ὅτι that, for, because, how that, how, because that, for that, though
σπέρμα n. nom. neut. sg. σπέρμα seed, issue
αὐτοῦ pron. gen. masc. 3p. sg. αὐτός ή ό self, of oneself, even, very, the same, he, she, it
ἐν prep. ἐν (+dat) in, by, with, among, at, on, through, to, within, into, of, for
αὐτῷ pron. dat. masc. 3p. sg. αὐτός ή ό self, of oneself, even, very, the same, he, she, it
καὶ conj. καί and, even, also, but
οὐ particle of negation. οὐ οὐκ οὐχ not, no, neither, none, nay, nor, never, nothing

ὅτι conj. ὅτι that, for, because, how that, how, because that, for that, though
ἐκ prep. ἐκ ἐξ (+gen) of, from, out of, by, on, with, in, among, through
τοῦ art. gen. masc. sg. ὁ ἡ τό the, this, that, he, she, it
Θεοῦ n. gen. masc. sg. θεός God, god
10 ἐν prep. ἐν (+dat) in, by, with, among, at, on, through, to, within, into, of, for
τούτῳ demo. pron. dat. neut. sg. οὗτος αὕτη τοῦτο this, the same, this same, he, she, it
φανερά adj. nom. neut. pl. φανερός manifest, abroad, open, known, outward, appear
τὰ art. nom. neut. pl. ὁ ἡ τό the, this, that, he, she, it
τέκνα n. nom. neut. pl. τέκνον child, son, daughter
τοῦ art. gen. masc. sg. ὁ ἡ τό the, this, that, he, she, it
Θεοῦ n. gen. masc. sg. θεός God, god
καὶ conj. καί and, even, also, but
τὰ art. nom. neut. pl. ὁ ἡ τό the, this, that, he, she, it
τέκνα n. nom. neut. pl. τέκνον child, son, daughter
τοῦ art. gen. masc. sg. ὁ ἡ τό the, this, that, he, she, it
διαβόλου adj. gen. masc. sg. διάβολος devil, false accuser, Devil, slanderer
πᾶς adj. nom. masc. sg. πᾶς πᾶσα πᾶν all, every, whosoever, every one, no, whole, any
ὁ art. nom. masc. sg. ὁ ἡ τό the, this, that, he, she, it
μὴ particle of negation. μή not, no, lest, neither, none, nothing, nor, never, without
δικαιοσύνην n. acc. fem. sg. δικαιοσύνη righteousness
οὐκ particle of negation. οὐ οὐκ οὐχ not, no, neither, none, nay, nor, never, nothing
ἐκ prep. ἐκ ἐξ (+gen) of, from, out of, by, on, with, in, among, through
τοῦ art. gen. masc. sg. ὁ ἡ τό the, this, that, he, she, it
Θεοῦ n. gen. masc. sg. θεός God, god
καὶ conj. καί and, even, also, but
ὁ art. nom. masc. sg. ὁ ἡ τό the, this, that, he, she, it
μὴ particle of negation. μή not, no, lest, neither, none, nothing, nor, never, without
τὸν art. acc. masc. sg. ὁ ἡ τό the, this, that, he, she, it
ἀδελφὸν n. acc. masc. sg. ἀδελφός brother
αὐτοῦ pron. gen. masc. 3p. sg. αὐτός ή ό self, of oneself, even, very, the same, he, she, it
11 ὅτι conj. ὅτι that, for, because, how that, how, because that, for that, though
αὕτη demo. pron. nom. fem. sg. οὗτος αὕτη τοῦτο this, the same, this same, he, she, it
ἡ art. nom. fem. sg. ὁ ἡ τό the, this, that, he, she, it
ἀγγελία n. nom. fem. sg. ἀγγελία message
ἣν relative pron. acc. fem. sg. ὅς ἥ ὅ who, which, what, that
ἀπ' prep. ἀπό (+gen) from, of, out of, since, for, off, at, by, in, on
ἀρχῆς n. gen. fem. sg. ἀρχή beginning, principality, corner, first, magistrate, rule
ἵνα conj. ἵνα that, to, lest, for to, so that, albeit, because, for, so as
ἀλλήλους pron. acc. masc. pl. ἀλλήλων one another, themselves, together, mutual
12 οὐ particle of negation. οὐ οὐκ οὐχ not, no, neither, none, nay, nor, never, nothing
καθὼς adv. καθώς as, even as, according as, according to
Κάϊν n. nom. masc. sg. Κάϊν Cain
ἐκ prep. ἐκ ἐξ (+gen) of, from, out of, by, on, with, in, among, through
τοῦ art. gen. masc. sg. ὁ ἡ τό the, this, that, he, she, it
πονηροῦ adj. gen. masc. sg. πονηρός evil, wicked, bad
καὶ conj. καί and, even, also, but
τὸν art. acc. masc. sg. ὁ ἡ τό the, this, that, he, she, it
ἀδελφὸν n. acc. masc. sg. ἀδελφός brother
αὐτοῦ pron. gen. masc. 3p. sg. αὐτός ή ό self, of oneself, even, very, the same, he, she, it
καὶ conj. καί and, even, also, but
χάριν adv. χάριν for a cause, because of, for sake
τίνος interrog. pron. gen. neut. sg. τίς what, who, why, where, which, how
αὐτόν pron. acc. masc. 3p. sg. αὐτός ή ό self, of oneself, even, very, the same, he, she, it
ὅτι conj. ὅτι that, for, because, how that, how, because that, for that, though
τὰ art. nom. neut. pl. ὁ ἡ τό the, this, that, he, she, it

ἔργα n. nom. neut. pl. ἔργον work, deed, doing labour
αὐτοῦ pron. gen. masc. 3p. sg. αὐτός ή ό self, of oneself, even, very, the same, he, she, it
πονηρὰ adj. nom. neut. pl. πονηρός evil, wicked, bad
τὰ art. nom. neut. pl. ὁ ἡ τό the, this, that, he, she, it
δὲ conj. δέ but, and, now, also, to the contrary, rather, then
τοῦ art. gen. masc. sg. ὁ ἡ τό the, this, that, he, she, it
ἀδελφοῦ n. gen. masc. sg. ἀδελφός brother
αὐτοῦ pron. gen. masc. 3p. sg. αὐτός ή ό self, of oneself, even, very, the same, he, she, it
δίκαια adj. nom. neut. pl. δίκαιος righteous, just, meet, right
13 Μὴ particle of negation. μή not, no, lest, neither, none, nothing, nor, never, without
ἀδελφοί n. voc. masc. pl. ἀδελφός brother
μου pron. gen. 1p. sg. ἐγώ I
εἰ conj. εἰ if, whether, that, though, forasmuch
ὑμᾶς pron. acc. 2p. pl. σύ thou, you
ὁ art. nom. masc. sg. ὁ ἡ τό the, this, that, he, she, it
κόσμος n. nom. masc. sg. κόσμος world, adorning
14 ἡμεῖς pron. nom. 1p. pl. ἐγώ I
ὅτι conj. ὅτι that, for, because, how that, how, because that, for that, though
ἐκ prep. ἐκ ἐξ (+gen) of, from, out of, by, on, with, in, among, through
τοῦ art. gen. masc. sg. ὁ ἡ τό the, this, that, he, she, it
θανάτου n. gen. masc. sg. θάνατος death
εἰς prep. εἰς (+acc) into, to, unto, for, in, on, toward, against, upon, at, among
τὴν art. acc. fem. sg. ὁ ἡ τό the, this, that, he, she, it
ζωήν n. acc. fem. sg. ζωή life, lifetime
ὅτι conj. ὅτι that, for, because, how that, how, because that, for that, though
τοὺς art. acc. masc. pl. ὁ ἡ τό the, this, that, he, she, it
ἀδελφούς n. acc. masc. pl. ἀδελφός brother
ὁ art. nom. masc. sg. ὁ ἡ τό the, this, that, he, she, it
μὴ particle of negation. μή not, no, lest, neither, none, nothing, nor, never, without
τὸν art. acc. masc. sg. ὁ ἡ τό the, this, that, he, she, it
ἀδελφόν n. acc. masc. sg. ἀδελφός brother
ἐν prep. ἐν (+dat) in, by, with, among, at, on, through, to, within, into, of, for
τῷ art. dat. masc. sg. ὁ ἡ τό the, this, that, he, she, it
θανάτῳ n. dat. masc. sg. θάνατος death
15 πᾶς adj. nom. masc. sg. πᾶς πᾶσα πᾶν all, every, whosoever, every one, no, whole, any
ὁ art. nom. masc. sg. ὁ ἡ τό the, this, that, he, she, it
τὸν art. acc. masc. sg. ὁ ἡ τό the, this, that, he, she, it
ἀδελφὸν n. acc. masc. sg. ἀδελφός brother
αὐτοῦ pron. gen. masc. 3p. sg. αὐτός ή ό self, of oneself, even, very, the same, he, she, it
ἀνθρωποκτόνος n. nom. masc. sg. ἀνθρωποκτόνος murderer
καὶ conj. καί and, even, also, but
ὅτι conj. ὅτι that, for, because, how that, how, because that, for that, though
πᾶς adj. nom. masc. sg. πᾶς πᾶσα πᾶν all, every, whosoever, every one, no, whole, any
ἀνθρωποκτόνος n. nom. masc. sg. ἀνθρωποκτόνος murderer
οὐκ particle of negation. οὐ οὐκ οὐχ not, no, neither, none, nay, nor, never, nothing
ζωὴν n. acc. fem. sg. ζωή life, lifetime
αἰώνιον adj. acc. fem. sg. αἰώνιος eternal, everlasting, world, for ever
ἐν prep. ἐν (+dat) in, by, with, among, at, on, through, to, within, into, of, for
αὐτῷ pron. dat. masc. 3p. sg. αὐτός ή ό self, of oneself, even, very, the same, he, she, it
16 ἐν prep. ἐν (+dat) in, by, with, among, at, on, through, to, within, into, of, for
τούτῳ demo. pron. dat. neut. sg. οὗτος αὕτη τοῦτο this, the same, this same, he, she, it
τὴν art. acc. fem. sg. ὁ ἡ τό the, this, that, he, she, it
ἀγάπην n. acc. fem. sg. ἀγάπη love, charity, feast of charity
τοῦ art. gen. masc. sg. ὁ ἡ τό the, this, that, he, she, it
Θεοῦ n. gen. masc. sg. θεός God, god

ὅτι conj. ὅτι that, for, because, how that, how, because that, for that, though
ἐκεῖνος demo. pron. nom. masc. sg. ἐκεῖνος that, he, the same, that same
ὑπὲρ prep. ὑπέρ (+gen) for, of, for the sake of, (+acc) above, more than
ἡμῶν pron. gen. 1p. pl. ἐγώ I
τὴν art. acc. fem. sg. ὁ ἡ τό the, this, that, he, she, it
ψυχὴν n. acc. fem. sg. ψυχή life, soul, mind, heart
αὐτοῦ pron. gen. masc. 3p. sg. αὐτός ή ό self, of oneself, even, very, the same, he, she, it
καὶ conj. καί and, even, also, but
ἡμεῖς pron. nom. 1p. pl. ἐγώ I
ὑπὲρ prep. ὑπέρ (+gen) for, of, for the sake of, (+acc) above, more than
τῶν art. gen. masc. pl. ὁ ἡ τό the, this, that, he, she, it
ἀδελφῶν n. gen. masc. pl. ἀδελφός brother
τὰς art. acc. fem. pl. ὁ ἡ τό the, this, that, he, she, it
ψυχὰς n. acc. fem. pl. ψυχή life, soul, mind, heart
17 ὃς relative pron. nom. masc. sg. ὅς ἥ ὅ who, which, what, that
δ' conj. δέ but, and, now, also, to the contrary, rather, then
ἂν particle. ἄν Indicating contingency. No English translation.
τὸν art. acc. masc. sg. ὁ ἡ τό the, this, that, he, she, it
βίον n. acc. masc. sg. βίος life, living, good
τοῦ art. gen. masc. sg. ὁ ἡ τό the, this, that, he, she, it
κόσμου n. gen. masc. sg. κόσμος world, adorning
καὶ conj. καί and, even, also, but
τὸν art. acc. masc. sg. ὁ ἡ τό the, this, that, he, she, it
ἀδελφὸν n. acc. masc. sg. ἀδελφός brother
αὐτοῦ pron. gen. masc. 3p. sg. αὐτός ή ό self, of oneself, even, very, the same, he, she, it
χρείαν n. acc. fem. sg. χρεία need, necessity, lack, want
καὶ conj. καί and, even, also, but
τὰ art. acc. neut. pl. ὁ ἡ τό the, this, that, he, she, it
σπλάγχνα n. acc. neut. pl. σπλάγχνον tender, bowels, inward affection
αὐτοῦ pron. gen. masc. 3p. sg. αὐτός ή ό self, of oneself, even, very, the same, he, she, it
ἀπ' prep. ἀπό (+gen) from, of, out of, since, for, off, at, by, in, on
αὐτοῦ pron. gen. masc. 3p. sg. αὐτός ή ό self, of oneself, even, very, the same, he, she, it
πῶς adv. πῶς how, by what means, after what manner
ἡ art. nom. fem. sg. ὁ ἡ τό the, this, that, he, she, it
ἀγάπη n. nom. fem. sg. ἀγάπη love, charity, feast of charity
τοῦ art. gen. masc. sg. ὁ ἡ τό the, this, that, he, she, it
Θεοῦ n. gen. masc. sg. θεός God, god
ἐν prep. ἐν (+dat) in, by, with, among, at, on, through, to, within, into, of, for
αὐτῷ pron. dat. masc. 3p. sg. αὐτός ή ό self, of oneself, even, very, the same, he, she, it
18 τεκνία n. voc. neut. pl. τεκνίον little child
μου pron. gen. 1p. sg. ἐγώ I
μὴ particle of negation. μή not, no, lest, neither, none, nothing, nor, never, without
λόγῳ n. dat. masc. sg. λόγος word, saying, account, speech, thing, matter
μηδὲ conj. μηδέ neither, nor, not, no not, nor yet, not once, not so much as
γλώσσῃ n. dat. fem. sg. γλῶσσα tongue
ἀλλ' conj. ἀλλά but, yea, yet, nevertheless, howbeit, nay, therefore
ἔργῳ n. dat. neut. sg. ἔργον work, deed, doing labour
καὶ conj. καί and, even, also, but
ἀληθείᾳ n. dat. fem. sg. ἀλήθεια truth, verity
19 καὶ conj. καί and, even, also, but
ἐν prep. ἐν (+dat) in, by, with, among, at, on, through, to, within, into, of, for
τούτῳ demo. pron. dat. neut. sg. οὗτος αὕτη τοῦτο this, the same, this same, he, she, it
ὅτι conj. ὅτι that, for, because, how that, how, because that, for that, though
ἐκ prep. ἐκ ἐξ (+gen) of, from, out of, by, on, with, in, among, through
τῆς art. gen. fem. sg. ὁ ἡ τό the, this, that, he, she, it

ἀληθείας n. gen. fem. sg. ἀλήθεια truth, verity
καὶ conj. καί and, even, also, but
ἔμπροσθεν prep. ἔμπροσθεν (+gen) before, in the sight of, in the presence of
αὐτοῦ pron. gen. masc. 3p. sg. αὐτός ή ό self, of oneself, even, very, the same, he, she, it
τὰς art. acc. fem. pl. ὁ ἡ τό the, this, that, he, she, it
καρδίας n. acc. fem. pl. καρδία heart
ἡμῶν pron. gen. 1p. pl. ἐγώ I
20 ὅτι conj. ὅτι that, for, because, how that, how, because that, for that, though
ἐὰν conj. ἐάν if, soever, except, though, and if, but, whether, if so, so
ἡμῶν pron. gen. 1p. pl. ἐγώ I
ἡ art. nom. fem. sg. ὁ ἡ τό the, this, that, he, she, it
καρδία n. nom. fem. sg. καρδία heart
ὅτι conj. ὅτι that, for, because, how that, how, because that, for that, though
μείζων compar. adj. nom. masc. sg. μέγας great, loud, greatest, high, large, mighty, strong
ὁ art. nom. masc. sg. ὁ ἡ τό the, this, that, he, she, it
Θεὸς n. nom. masc. sg. θεός God, god
τῆς art. gen. fem. sg. ὁ ἡ τό the, this, that, he, she, it
καρδίας n. gen. fem. sg. καρδία heart
ἡμῶν pron. gen. 1p. pl. ἐγώ I
καὶ conj. καί and, even, also, but
πάντα adj. acc. neut. pl. πᾶς πᾶσα πᾶν all, every, whosoever, every one, no, whole, any
21 ἀγαπητοί adj. voc. masc. pl. ἀγαπητός beloved, dearly beloved, dear, wellbeloved
ἐὰν conj. ἐάν if, soever, except, though, and if, but, whether, if so, so
ἡ art. nom. fem. sg. ὁ ἡ τό the, this, that, he, she, it
καρδία n. nom. fem. sg. καρδία heart
ἡμῶν pron. gen. 1p. pl. ἐγώ I
μὴ particle of negation. μή not, no, lest, neither, none, nothing, nor, never, without
ἡμῶν pron. gen. 1p. pl. ἐγώ I
παρρησίαν n. acc. fem. sg. παρρησία boldness, confidence, openly, plainly, freely
πρὸς prep. πρός (+gen) for, (+dat) at, (+acc) unto, to, with, for, against
τὸν art. acc. masc. sg. ὁ ἡ τό the, this, that, he, she, it
Θεόν n. acc. masc. sg. θεός God, god
22 καὶ conj. καί and, even, also, but
ὃ relative pron. acc. neut. sg. ὅς ἥ ὅ who, which, what, that
ἐὰν conj. ἐάν if, soever, except, though, and if, but, whether, if so, so
παρ' prep. παρά (+gen) of, from, (+dat) with, for, (+acc) beside, at, by, above, against
αὐτοῦ pron. gen. masc. 3p. sg. αὐτός ή ό self, of oneself, even, very, the same, he, she, it
ὅτι conj. ὅτι that, for, because, how that, how, because that, for that, though
τὰς art. acc. fem. pl. ὁ ἡ τό the, this, that, he, she, it
ἐντολὰς n. acc. fem. pl. ἐντολή commandment, precept
αὐτοῦ pron. gen. masc. 3p. sg. αὐτός ή ό self, of oneself, even, very, the same, he, she, it
καὶ conj. καί and, even, also, but
τὰ art. acc. neut. pl. ὁ ἡ τό the, this, that, he, she, it
ἀρεστὰ adj. acc. neut. pl. ἀρεστός thing that please, please, reason
ἐνώπιον prep. ἐνώπιον (+gen) before, in the sight of, in the presence of. (adv.) before
αὐτοῦ pron. gen. masc. 3p. sg. αὐτός ή ό self, of oneself, even, very, the same, he, she, it
23 καὶ conj. καί and, even, also, but
αὕτη demo. pron. nom. fem. sg. οὗτος αὕτη τοῦτο this, the same, this same, he, she, it
ἡ art. nom. fem. sg. ὁ ἡ τό the, this, that, he, she, it
ἐντολὴ n. nom. fem. sg. ἐντολή commandment, precept
αὐτοῦ pron. gen. masc. 3p. sg. αὐτός ή ό self, of oneself, even, very, the same, he, she, it
ἵνα conj. ἵνα that, to, lest, for to, so that, albeit, because, for, so as
τῷ art. dat. neut. sg. ὁ ἡ τό the, this, that, he, she, it
ὀνόματι n. dat. neut. sg. ὄνομα name, call, surname
τοῦ art. gen. masc. sg. ὁ ἡ τό the, this, that, he, she, it

υἱοῦ n. gen. masc. sg. υἱός son, child, descendant, offspring, heir
αὐτοῦ pron. gen. masc. 3p. sg. αὐτός ή ό self, of oneself, even, very, the same, he, she, it
Ἰησοῦ n. gen. masc. sg. Ἰησοῦς Jesus
Χριστοῦ n. gen. masc. sg. Χριστός Christ
καὶ conj. καί and, even, also, but
ἀλλήλους pron. acc. masc. pl. ἀλλήλων one another, themselves, together, mutual
καθὼς adv. καθώς as, even as, according as, according to
ἐντολὴν n. acc. fem. sg. ἐντολή commandment, precept
ἡμῖν pron. dat. 1p. pl. ἐγώ I
24 καὶ conj. καί and, even, also, but
ὁ art. nom. masc. sg. ὁ ἡ τό the, this, that, he, she, it
τὰς art. acc. fem. pl. ὁ ἡ τό the, this, that, he, she, it
ἐντολὰς n. acc. fem. pl. ἐντολή commandment, precept
αὐτοῦ pron. gen. masc. 3p. sg. αὐτός ή ό self, of oneself, even, very, the same, he, she, it
ἐν prep. ἐν (+dat) in, by, with, among, at, on, through, to, within, into, of, for
αὐτῷ pron. dat. masc. 3p. sg. αὐτός ή ό self, of oneself, even, very, the same, he, she, it
καὶ conj. καί and, even, also, but
αὐτὸς pron. nom. masc. 3p. sg. αὐτός ή ό self, of oneself, even, very, the same, he, she, it
ἐν prep. ἐν (+dat) in, by, with, among, at, on, through, to, within, into, of, for
αὐτῷ pron. dat. masc. 3p. sg. αὐτός ή ό self, of oneself, even, very, the same, he, she, it
καὶ conj. καί and, even, also, but
ἐν prep. ἐν (+dat) in, by, with, among, at, on, through, to, within, into, of, for
τούτῳ demo. pron. dat. neut. sg. οὗτος αὕτη τοῦτο this, the same, this same, he, she, it
ὅτι conj. ὅτι that, for, because, how that, how, because that, for that, though
ἐν prep. ἐν (+dat) in, by, with, among, at, on, through, to, within, into, of, for
ἡμῖν pron. dat. 1p. pl. ἐγώ I
ἐκ prep. ἐκ ἐξ (+gen) of, from, out of, by, on, with, in, among, through
τοῦ art. gen. neut. sg. ὁ ἡ τό the, this, that, he, she, it
Πνεύματος n. gen. neut. sg. πνεῦμα spirit, Spirit, Ghost, ghost, life. of the spirit, wind
οὗ relative pron. gen. neut. sg. ὅς ἥ ὅ who, which, what, that
ἡμῖν pron. dat. 1p. pl. ἐγώ I

4

1 Ἀγαπητοί adj. voc. masc. pl. ἀγαπητός beloved, dearly beloved, dear, wellbeloved
μὴ particle of negation. μή not, no, lest, neither, none, nothing, nor, never, without
παντὶ adj. dat. neut. sg. πᾶς πᾶσα πᾶν all, every, whosoever, every one, no, whole, any
πνεύματι n. dat. neut. sg. πνεῦμα spirit, Spirit, Ghost, ghost, life. of the spirit, wind
ἀλλὰ conj. ἀλλά but, yea, yet, nevertheless, howbeit, nay, therefore
τὰ art. acc. neut. pl. ὁ ἡ τό the, this, that, he, she, it
πνεύματα n. acc. neut. pl. πνεῦμα spirit, Spirit, Ghost, ghost, life. of the spirit, wind
εἰ conj. εἰ if, whether, that, though, forasmuch
ἐκ prep. ἐκ ἐξ (+gen) of, from, out of, by, on, with, in, among, through
τοῦ art. gen. masc. sg. ὁ ἡ τό the, this, that, he, she, it
Θεοῦ n. gen. masc. sg. θεός God, god
ὅτι conj. ὅτι that, for, because, how that, how, because that, for that, though
πολλοὶ adj. nom. masc. pl. πολύς many, great, much, long, abundant
ψευδοπροφῆται n. nom. masc. pl. ψευδοπροφήτης false prophet
εἰς prep. εἰς (+acc) into, to, unto, for, in, on, toward, against, upon, at, among
τὸν art. acc. masc. sg. ὁ ἡ τό the, this, that, he, she, it
κόσμον n. acc. masc. sg. κόσμος world, adorning
2 ἐν prep. ἐν (+dat) in, by, with, among, at, on, through, to, within, into, of, for
τούτῳ demo. pron. dat. neut. sg. οὗτος αὕτη τοῦτο this, the same, this same, he, she, it
τὸ art. acc. neut. sg. ὁ ἡ τό the, this, that, he, she, it
Πνεῦμα n. acc. neut. sg. πνεῦμα spirit, Spirit, Ghost, ghost, life. of the spirit, wind

τοῦ art. gen. masc. sg. ὁ ἡ τό the, this, that, he, she, it
Θεοῦ n. gen. masc. sg. θεός God, god
πᾶν adj. nom. neut. sg. πᾶς πᾶσa πᾶν all, every, whosoever, every one, no, whole, any
πνεῦμα n. nom. neut. sg. πνεῦμα spirit, Spirit, Ghost, ghost, life. of the spirit, wind
ὃ relative pron. nom. neut. sg. ὅς ἥ ὅ who, which, what, that
Ἰησοῦν n. acc. masc. sg. Ἰησοῦς Jesus
Χριστὸν n. acc. masc. sg. Χριστός Christ
ἐν prep. ἐν (+dat) in, by, with, among, at, on, through, to, within, into, of, for
σαρκὶ n. dat. fem. sg. σάρξ flesh, carnal
ἐκ prep. ἐκ ἐξ (+gen) of, from, out of, by, on, with, in, among, through
τοῦ art. gen. masc. sg. ὁ ἡ τό the, this, that, he, she, it
Θεοῦ n. gen. masc. sg. θεός God, god
3 καὶ conj. καί and, even, also, but
πᾶν adj. nom. neut. sg. πᾶς πᾶσa πᾶν all, every, whosoever, every one, no, whole, any
πνεῦμα n. nom. neut. sg. πνεῦμα spirit, Spirit, Ghost, ghost, life. of the spirit, wind
ὃ relative pron. nom. neut. sg. ὅς ἥ ὅ who, which, what, that
μὴ particle of negation. μή not, no, lest, neither, none, nothing, nor, never, without
τὸν art. acc. masc. sg. ὁ ἡ τό the, this, that, he, she, it
Ἰησοῦν n. acc. masc. sg. Ἰησοῦς Jesus
Χριστὸν n. acc. masc. sg. Χριστός Christ
ἐν prep. ἐν (+dat) in, by, with, among, at, on, through, to, within, into, of, for
σαρκὶ n. dat. fem. sg. σάρξ flesh, carnal
ἐκ prep. ἐκ ἐξ (+gen) of, from, out of, by, on, with, in, among, through
τοῦ art. gen. masc. sg. ὁ ἡ τό the, this, that, he, she, it
Θεοῦ n. gen. masc. sg. θεός God, god
οὐκ particle of negation. οὐ οὐκ οὐχ not, no, neither, none, nay, nor, never, nothing
καὶ conj. καί and, even, also, but
τοῦτό demo. pron. nom. neut. sg. οὗτος αὕτη τοῦτο this, the same, this same, he, she, it
τὸ art. nom. neut. sg. ὁ ἡ τό the, this, that, he, she, it
τοῦ art. gen. masc. sg. ὁ ἡ τό the, this, that, he, she, it
ἀντιχρίστου n. gen. masc. sg. ἀντίχριστος antichrist
ὃ relative pron. acc. neut. sg. ὅς ἥ ὅ who, which, what, that
ὅτι conj. ὅτι that, for, because, how that, how, because that, for that, though
καὶ conj. καί and, even, also, but
νῦν adv. νῦν now, henceforth, present, this time
ἐν prep. ἐν (+dat) in, by, with, among, at, on, through, to, within, into, of, for
τῷ art. dat. masc. sg. ὁ ἡ τό the, this, that, he, she, it
κόσμῳ n. dat. masc. sg. κόσμος world, adorning
ἤδη adv. ἤδη now, already, yet, by this time, even now, now already
4 ὑμεῖς pron. nom. 2p. pl. σύ thou, you
ἐκ prep. ἐκ ἐξ (+gen) of, from, out of, by, on, with, in, among, through
τοῦ art. gen. masc. sg. ὁ ἡ τό the, this, that, he, she, it
Θεοῦ n. gen. masc. sg. θεός God, god
τεκνία n. voc. neut. pl. τεκνίον little child
καὶ conj. καί and, even, also, but
αὐτούς pron. acc. masc. 3p. pl. αὐτός ή ό self, of oneself, even, very, the same, he, she, it
ὅτι conj. ὅτι that, for, because, how that, how, because that, for that, though
μείζων compar. adj. nom. masc. sg. μέγας great, loud, greatest, high, large, mighty, strong
ὁ art. nom. masc. sg. ὁ ἡ τό the, this, that, he, she, it
ἐν prep. ἐν (+dat) in, by, with, among, at, on, through, to, within, into, of, for
ὑμῖν pron. dat. 2p. pl. σύ thou, you
ἢ particle. ἤ or, than, either, nor, or else, and, rather than
ὁ art. nom. masc. sg. ὁ ἡ τό the, this, that, he, she, it
ἐν prep. ἐν (+dat) in, by, with, among, at, on, through, to, within, into, of, for
τῷ art. dat. masc. sg. ὁ ἡ τό the, this, that, he, she, it

κόσμῳ n. dat. masc. sg. κόσμος world, adorning
5 αὐτοὶ pron. nom. masc. 3p. pl. αὐτός ή ό self, of oneself, even, very, the same, he, she, it
ἐκ prep. ἐκ ἐξ (+gen) of, from, out of, by, on, with, in, among, through
τοῦ art. gen. masc. sg. ὁ ἡ τό the, this, that, he, she, it
κόσμου n. gen. masc. sg. κόσμος world, adorning
διὰ prep. διά (+gen) by, through, with, in, of, (+acc) for, because of, for a cause
τοῦτο demo. pron. acc. neut. sg. οὗτος αὕτη τοῦτο this, the same, this same, he, she, it
ἐκ prep. ἐκ ἐξ (+gen) of, from, out of, by, on, with, in, among, through
τοῦ art. gen. masc. sg. ὁ ἡ τό the, this, that, he, she, it
κόσμου n. gen. masc. sg. κόσμος world, adorning
καὶ conj. καί and, even, also, but
ὁ art. nom. masc. sg. ὁ ἡ τό the, this, that, he, she, it
κόσμος n. nom. masc. sg. κόσμος world, adorning
αὐτῶν pron. gen. masc. 3p. pl. αὐτός ή ό self, of oneself, even, very, the same, he, she, it
6 ἡμεῖς pron. nom. 1p. pl. ἐγώ I
ἐκ prep. ἐκ ἐξ (+gen) of, from, out of, by, on, with, in, among, through
τοῦ art. gen. masc. sg. ὁ ἡ τό the, this, that, he, she, it
Θεοῦ n. gen. masc. sg. θεός God, god
ὁ art. nom. masc. sg. ὁ ἡ τό the, this, that, he, she, it
τὸν art. acc. masc. sg. ὁ ἡ τό the, this, that, he, she, it
Θεὸν n. acc. masc. sg. θεός God, god
ἡμῶν pron. gen. 1p. pl. ἐγώ I
ὅς relative pron. nom. masc. sg. ὅς ἥ ὅ who, which, what, that
οὐκ particle of negation. οὐ οὐκ οὐχ not, no, neither, none, nay, nor, never, nothing
ἐκ prep. ἐκ ἐξ (+gen) of, from, out of, by, on, with, in, among, through
τοῦ art. gen. masc. sg. ὁ ἡ τό the, this, that, he, she, it
Θεοῦ n. gen. masc. sg. θεός God, god
οὐκ particle of negation. οὐ οὐκ οὐχ not, no, neither, none, nay, nor, never, nothing
ἡμῶν pron. gen. 1p. pl. ἐγώ I
ἐκ prep. ἐκ ἐξ (+gen) of, from, out of, by, on, with, in, among, through
τούτου demo. pron. gen. neut. sg. οὗτος αὕτη τοῦτο this, the same, this same, he, she, it
τὸ art. acc. neut. sg. ὁ ἡ τό the, this, that, he, she, it
πνεῦμα n. acc. neut. sg. πνεῦμα spirit, Spirit, Ghost, ghost, life. of the spirit, wind
τῆς art. gen. fem. sg. ὁ ἡ τό the, this, that, he, she, it
ἀληθείας n. gen. fem. sg. ἀλήθεια truth, verity
καὶ conj. καί and, even, also, but
τὸ art. acc. neut. sg. ὁ ἡ τό the, this, that, he, she, it
πνεῦμα n. acc. neut. sg. πνεῦμα spirit, Spirit, Ghost, ghost, life. of the spirit, wind
τῆς art. gen. fem. sg. ὁ ἡ τό the, this, that, he, she, it
πλάνης n. gen. fem. sg. πλάνη error, deception, deceit, delusion
7 Ἀγαπητοί adj. voc. masc. pl. ἀγαπητός beloved, dearly beloved, dear, wellbeloved
ἀλλήλους pron. acc. masc. pl. ἀλλήλων one another, themselves, together, mutual
ὅτι conj. ὅτι that, for, because, how that, how, because that, for that, though
ἡ art. nom. fem. sg. ὁ ἡ τό the, this, that, he, she, it
ἀγάπη n. nom. fem. sg. ἀγάπη love, charity, feast of charity
ἐκ prep. ἐκ ἐξ (+gen) of, from, out of, by, on, with, in, among, through
τοῦ art. gen. masc. sg. ὁ ἡ τό the, this, that, he, she, it
Θεοῦ n. gen. masc. sg. θεός God, god
καὶ conj. καί and, even, also, but
πᾶς adj. nom. masc. sg. πᾶς πᾶσα πᾶν all, every, whosoever, every one, no, whole, any
ὁ art. nom. masc. sg. ὁ ἡ τό the, this, that, he, she, it
ἐκ prep. ἐκ ἐξ (+gen) of, from, out of, by, on, with, in, among, through
τοῦ art. gen. masc. sg. ὁ ἡ τό the, this, that, he, she, it
Θεοῦ n. gen. masc. sg. θεός God, god
καὶ conj. καί and, even, also, but

τὸν art. acc. masc. sg. ὁ ἡ τό the, this, that, he, she, it
Θεόν n. acc. masc. sg. θεός God, god
8 ὁ art. nom. masc. sg. ὁ ἡ τό the, this, that, he, she, it
μὴ particle of negation. μή not, no, lest, neither, none, nothing, nor, never, without
οὐκ particle of negation. οὐ οὐκ οὐχ not, no, neither, none, nay, nor, never, nothing
τὸν art. acc. masc. sg. ὁ ἡ τό the, this, that, he, she, it
Θεόν n. acc. masc. sg. θεός God, god
ὅτι conj. ὅτι that, for, because, how that, how, because that, for that, though
ὁ art. nom. masc. sg. ὁ ἡ τό the, this, that, he, she, it
Θεὸς n. nom. masc. sg. θεός God, god
ἀγάπη n. nom. fem. sg. ἀγάπη love, charity, feast of charity
9 ἐν prep. ἐν (+dat) in, by, with, among, at, on, through, to, within, into, of, for
τούτῳ demo. pron. dat. neut. sg. οὗτος αὕτη τοῦτο this, the same, this same, he, she, it
ἡ art. nom. fem. sg. ὁ ἡ τό the, this, that, he, she, it
ἀγάπη n. nom. fem. sg. ἀγάπη love, charity, feast of charity
τοῦ art. gen. masc. sg. ὁ ἡ τό the, this, that, he, she, it
Θεοῦ n. gen. masc. sg. θεός God, god
ἐν prep. ἐν (+dat) in, by, with, among, at, on, through, to, within, into, of, for
ἡμῖν pron. dat. 1p. pl. ἐγώ I
ὅτι conj. ὅτι that, for, because, how that, how, because that, for that, though
τὸν art. acc. masc. sg. ὁ ἡ τό the, this, that, he, she, it
υἱὸν n. acc. masc. sg. υἱός son, child, descendant, offspring, heir
αὐτοῦ pron. gen. masc. 3p. sg. αὐτός ή ό self, of oneself, even, very, the same, he, she, it
τὸν art. acc. masc. sg. ὁ ἡ τό the, this, that, he, she, it
μονογενῆ adj. acc. masc. sg. μονογενής only begotten, only, only child
ὁ art. nom. masc. sg. ὁ ἡ τό the, this, that, he, she, it
Θεὸς n. nom. masc. sg. θεός God, god
εἰς prep. εἰς (+acc) into, to, unto, for, in, on, toward, against, upon, at, among
τὸν art. acc. masc. sg. ὁ ἡ τό the, this, that, he, she, it
κόσμον n. acc. masc. sg. κόσμος world, adorning
ἵνα conj. ἵνα that, to, lest, for to, so that, albeit, because, for, so as
δι' prep. διά (+gen) by, through, with, in, of, (+acc) for, because of, for a cause
αὐτοῦ pron. gen. masc. 3p. sg. αὐτός ή ό self, of oneself, even, very, the same, he, she, it
10 ἐν prep. ἐν (+dat) in, by, with, among, at, on, through, to, within, into, of, for
τούτῳ demo. pron. dat. neut. sg. οὗτος αὕτη τοῦτο this, the same, this same, he, she, it
ἡ art. nom. fem. sg. ὁ ἡ τό the, this, that, he, she, it
ἀγάπη n. nom. fem. sg. ἀγάπη love, charity, feast of charity
οὐχ particle of negation. οὐ οὐκ οὐχ not, no, neither, none, nay, nor, never, nothing
ὅτι conj. ὅτι that, for, because, how that, how, because that, for that, though
ἡμεῖς pron. nom. 1p. pl. ἐγώ I
τὸν art. acc. masc. sg. ὁ ἡ τό the, this, that, he, she, it
Θεὸν n. acc. masc. sg. θεός God, god
ἀλλ' conj. ἀλλά but, yea, yet, nevertheless, howbeit, nay, therefore
ὅτι conj. ὅτι that, for, because, how that, how, because that, for that, though
αὐτὸς pron. nom. masc. 3p. sg. αὐτός ή ό self, of oneself, even, very, the same, he, she, it
ἡμᾶς pron. acc. 1p. pl. ἐγώ I
καὶ conj. καί and, even, also, but
τὸν art. acc. masc. sg. ὁ ἡ τό the, this, that, he, she, it
υἱὸν n. acc. masc. sg. υἱός son, child, descendant, offspring, heir
αὐτοῦ pron. gen. masc. 3p. sg. αὐτός ή ό self, of oneself, even, very, the same, he, she, it
ἱλασμὸν n. acc. masc. sg. ἱλασμός propitiation
περὶ prep. περί (+gen) of, for, concerning, (+acc) about, concerning, in
τῶν art. gen. fem. pl. ὁ ἡ τό the, this, that, he, she, it
ἁμαρτιῶν n. gen. fem. pl. ἁμαρτία sin, offence, sinful
ἡμῶν pron. gen. 1p. pl. ἐγώ I

11 ἀγαπητοί adj. voc. masc. pl. ἀγαπητός beloved, dearly beloved, dear, wellbeloved
εἰ conj. εἰ if, whether, that, though, forasmuch
οὕτως adv. οὕτω οὕτως so, even so, thus, on this wise, likewise, after this manner
ὁ art. nom. masc. sg. ὁ ἡ τό the, this, that, he, she, it
Θεὸς n. nom. masc. sg. θεός God, god
ἡμᾶς pron. acc. 1p. pl. ἐγώ I
καὶ conj. καί and, even, also, but
ἡμεῖς pron. nom. 1p. pl. ἐγώ I
ἀλλήλους pron. acc. masc. pl. ἀλλήλων one another, themselves, together, mutual
12 Θεὸν n. acc. masc. sg. θεός God, god
οὐδεὶς num. nom. masc. sg. οὐδείς no man, nothing, no, none, neither, not, nought
πώποτε adv. πώποτε at any time, never
ἐὰν conj. ἐάν if, soever, except, though, and if, but, whether, if so, so
ἀλλήλους pron. acc. masc. pl. ἀλλήλων one another, themselves, together, mutual
ὁ art. nom. masc. sg. ὁ ἡ τό the, this, that, he, she, it
Θεὸς n. nom. masc. sg. θεός God, god
ἐν prep. ἐν (+dat) in, by, with, among, at, on, through, to, within, into, of, for
ἡμῖν pron. dat. 1p. pl. ἐγώ I
καὶ conj. καί and, even, also, but
ἡ art. nom. fem. sg. ὁ ἡ τό the, this, that, he, she, it
ἀγάπη n. nom. fem. sg. ἀγάπη love, charity, feast of charity
αὐτοῦ pron. gen. masc. 3p. sg. αὐτός ή ό self, of oneself, even, very, the same, he, she, it
ἐν prep. ἐν (+dat) in, by, with, among, at, on, through, to, within, into, of, for
ἡμῖν pron. dat. 1p. pl. ἐγώ I
13 ἐν prep. ἐν (+dat) in, by, with, among, at, on, through, to, within, into, of, for
τούτῳ demo. pron. dat. neut. sg. οὗτος αὕτη τοῦτο this, the same, this same, he, she, it
ὅτι conj. ὅτι that, for, because, how that, how, because that, for that, though
ἐν prep. ἐν (+dat) in, by, with, among, at, on, through, to, within, into, of, for
αὐτῷ pron. dat. masc. 3p. sg. αὐτός ή ό self, of oneself, even, very, the same, he, she, it
καὶ conj. καί and, even, also, but
αὐτὸς pron. nom. masc. 3p. sg. αὐτός ή ό self, of oneself, even, very, the same, he, she, it
ἐν prep. ἐν (+dat) in, by, with, among, at, on, through, to, within, into, of, for
ἡμῖν pron. dat. 1p. pl. ἐγώ I
ὅτι conj. ὅτι that, for, because, how that, how, because that, for that, though
ἐκ prep. ἐκ ἐξ (+gen) of, from, out of, by, on, with, in, among, through
τοῦ art. gen. neut. sg. ὁ ἡ τό the, this, that, he, she, it
Πνεύματος n. gen. neut. sg. πνεῦμα spirit, Spirit, Ghost, ghost, life. of the spirit, wind
αὐτοῦ pron. gen. masc. 3p. sg. αὐτός ή ό self, of oneself, even, very, the same, he, she, it
ἡμῖν pron. dat. 1p. pl. ἐγώ I
14 καὶ conj. καί and, even, also, but
ἡμεῖς pron. nom. 1p. pl. ἐγώ I
καὶ conj. καί and, even, also, but
ὅτι conj. ὅτι that, for, because, how that, how, because that, for that, though
ὁ art. nom. masc. sg. ὁ ἡ τό the, this, that, he, she, it
πατὴρ n. nom. masc. sg. πατήρ Father, father, parent
τὸν art. acc. masc. sg. ὁ ἡ τό the, this, that, he, she, it
υἱὸν n. acc. masc. sg. υἱός son, child, descendant, offspring, heir
σωτῆρα n. acc. masc. sg. σωτήρ Saviour, saviour
τοῦ art. gen. masc. sg. ὁ ἡ τό the, this, that, he, she, it
κόσμου n. gen. masc. sg. κόσμος world, adorning
15 ὃς relative pron. nom. masc. sg. ὅς ἥ ὅ who, which, what, that
ἂν particle. ἄν Indicating contingency. No English translation.
ὅτι conj. ὅτι that, for, because, how that, how, because that, for that, though
Ἰησοῦς n. nom. masc. sg. Ἰησοῦς Jesus
ὁ art. nom. masc. sg. ὁ ἡ τό the, this, that, he, she, it

υἱὸς n. nom. masc. sg. υἱός son, child, descendant, offspring, heir
τοῦ art. gen. masc. sg. ὁ ἡ τό the, this, that, he, she, it
Θεοῦ n. gen. masc. sg. θεός God, god
ὁ art. nom. masc. sg. ὁ ἡ τό the, this, that, he, she, it
Θεὸς n. nom. masc. sg. θεός God, god
ἐν prep. ἐν (+dat) in, by, with, among, at, on, through, to, within, into, of, for
αὐτῷ pron. dat. masc. 3p. sg. αὐτός ή ό self, of oneself, even, very, the same, he, she, it
καὶ conj. καί and, even, also, but
αὐτὸς pron. nom. masc. 3p. sg. αὐτός ή ό self, of oneself, even, very, the same, he, she, it
ἐν prep. ἐν (+dat) in, by, with, among, at, on, through, to, within, into, of, for
τῷ art. dat. masc. sg. ὁ ἡ τό the, this, that, he, she, it
Θεῷ n. dat. masc. sg. θεός God, god
16 καὶ conj. καί and, even, also, but
ἡμεῖς pron. nom. 1p. pl. ἐγώ I
καὶ conj. καί and, even, also, but
τὴν art. acc. fem. sg. ὁ ἡ τό the, this, that, he, she, it
ἀγάπην n. acc. fem. sg. ἀγάπη love, charity, feast of charity
ἣν relative pron. acc. fem. sg. ὅς ἥ ὅ who, which, what, that
ὁ art. nom. masc. sg. ὁ ἡ τό the, this, that, he, she, it
Θεὸς n. nom. masc. sg. θεός God, god
ἐν prep. ἐν (+dat) in, by, with, among, at, on, through, to, within, into, of, for
ἡμῖν pron. dat. 1p. pl. ἐγώ I
ὁ art. nom. masc. sg. ὁ ἡ τό the, this, that, he, she, it
Θεὸς n. nom. masc. sg. θεός God, god
ἀγάπη n. nom. fem. sg. ἀγάπη love, charity, feast of charity
καὶ conj. καί and, even, also, but
ὁ art. nom. masc. sg. ὁ ἡ τό the, this, that, he, she, it
ἐν prep. ἐν (+dat) in, by, with, among, at, on, through, to, within, into, of, for
τῇ art. dat. fem. sg. ὁ ἡ τό the, this, that, he, she, it
ἀγάπῃ n. dat. fem. sg. ἀγάπη love, charity, feast of charity
ἐν prep. ἐν (+dat) in, by, with, among, at, on, through, to, within, into, of, for
τῷ art. dat. masc. sg. ὁ ἡ τό the, this, that, he, she, it
Θεῷ n. dat. masc. sg. θεός God, god
καὶ conj. καί and, even, also, but
ὁ art. nom. masc. sg. ὁ ἡ τό the, this, that, he, she, it
Θεὸς n. nom. masc. sg. θεός God, god
ἐν prep. ἐν (+dat) in, by, with, among, at, on, through, to, within, into, of, for
αὐτῷ pron. dat. masc. 3p. sg. αὐτός ή ό self, of oneself, even, very, the same, he, she, it
17 ἐν prep. ἐν (+dat) in, by, with, among, at, on, through, to, within, into, of, for
τούτῳ demo. pron. dat. neut. sg. οὗτος αὕτη τοῦτο this, the same, this same, he, she, it
ἡ art. nom. fem. sg. ὁ ἡ τό the, this, that, he, she, it
ἀγάπη n. nom. fem. sg. ἀγάπη love, charity, feast of charity
μεθ' prep. μετά (+gen) with, among, against, (+acc) after
ἡμῶν pron. gen. 1p. pl. ἐγώ I
ἵνα conj. ἵνα that, to, lest, for to, so that, albeit, because, for, so as
παρρησίαν n. acc. fem. sg. παρρησία boldness, confidence, openly, plainly, freely
ἐν prep. ἐν (+dat) in, by, with, among, at, on, through, to, within, into, of, for
τῇ art. dat. fem. sg. ὁ ἡ τό the, this, that, he, she, it
ἡμέρᾳ n. dat. fem. sg. ἡμέρα day, time, year, while, age, day time
τῆς art. gen. fem. sg. ὁ ἡ τό the, this, that, he, she, it
κρίσεως n. gen. fem. sg. κρίσις judgment, damnation, accusation, condemnation
ὅτι conj. ὅτι that, for, because, how that, how, because that, for that, though
καθὼς adv. καθώς as, even as, according as, according to
ἐκεῖνός demo. pron. nom. masc. sg. ἐκεῖνος that, he, the same, that same
καὶ conj. καί and, even, also, but

ἡμεῖς pron. nom. 1p. pl. ἐγώ I
ἐν prep. ἐν (+dat) in, by, with, among, at, on, through, to, within, into, of, for
τῷ art. dat. masc. sg. ὁ ἡ τό the, this, that, he, she, it
κόσμῳ n. dat. masc. sg. κόσμος world, adorning
τούτῳ demo. pron. dat. masc. sg. οὗτος αὕτη τοῦτο this, the same, this same, he, she, it
18 φόβος n. nom. masc. sg. φόβος fear, terror, sore afraid
οὐκ particle of negation. οὐ οὐκ οὐχ not, no, neither, none, nay, nor, never, nothing
ἐν prep. ἐν (+dat) in, by, with, among, at, on, through, to, within, into, of, for
τῇ art. dat. fem. sg. ὁ ἡ τό the, this, that, he, she, it
ἀγάπῃ n. dat. fem. sg. ἀγάπη love, charity, feast of charity
ἀλλ' conj. ἀλλά but, yea, yet, nevertheless, howbeit, nay, therefore
ἡ art. nom. fem. sg. ὁ ἡ τό the, this, that, he, she, it
τελεία adj. nom. fem. sg. τέλειος perfect, of full age
ἀγάπη n. nom. fem. sg. ἀγάπη love, charity, feast of charity
ἔξω adv. ἔξω out, without, out of, forth, away, outward
τὸν art. acc. masc. sg. ὁ ἡ τό the, this, that, he, she, it
φόβον n. acc. masc. sg. φόβος fear, terror, sore afraid
ὅτι conj. ὅτι that, for, because, how that, how, because that, for that, though
ὁ art. nom. masc. sg. ὁ ἡ τό the, this, that, he, she, it
φόβος n. nom. masc. sg. φόβος fear, terror, sore afraid
κόλασιν n. acc. fem. sg. κόλασις punishment, torment
ὁ art. nom. masc. sg. ὁ ἡ τό the, this, that, he, she, it
δὲ conj. δέ but, and, now, also, to the contrary, rather, then
οὐ particle of negation. οὐ οὐκ οὐχ not, no, neither, none, nay, nor, never, nothing
ἐν prep. ἐν (+dat) in, by, with, among, at, on, through, to, within, into, of, for
τῇ art. dat. fem. sg. ὁ ἡ τό the, this, that, he, she, it
ἀγάπῃ n. dat. fem. sg. ἀγάπη love, charity, feast of charity
19 ἡμεῖς pron. nom. 1p. pl. ἐγώ I
αὐτόν pron. acc. masc. 3p. sg. αὐτός ή ό self, of oneself, even, very, the same, he, she, it
ὅτι conj. ὅτι that, for, because, how that, how, because that, for that, though
αὐτὸς pron. nom. masc. 3p. sg. αὐτός ή ό self, of oneself, even, very, the same, he, she, it
πρῶτος ordinal. adj. nom. masc. sg. πρῶτος first, chief, first of all, chiefest, best
ἡμᾶς pron. acc. 1p. pl. ἐγώ I
20 ἐάν conj. ἐάν if, soever, except, though, and if, but, whether, if so, so
τις indefinite pron. nom. masc. sg. τὶς certain, some, any man, one, any thing
ὅτι conj. ὅτι that, for, because, how that, how, because that, for that, though
τὸν art. acc. masc. sg. ὁ ἡ τό the, this, that, he, she, it
Θεὸν n. acc. masc. sg. θεός God, god
καὶ conj. καί and, even, also, but
τὸν art. acc. masc. sg. ὁ ἡ τό the, this, that, he, she, it
ἀδελφὸν n. acc. masc. sg. ἀδελφός brother
αὐτοῦ pron. gen. masc. 3p. sg. αὐτός ή ό self, of oneself, even, very, the same, he, she, it
ψεύστης n. nom. masc. sg. ψεύστης liar
ὁ art. nom. masc. sg. ὁ ἡ τό the, this, that, he, she, it
γὰρ conj. γάρ for, and, because, but, indeed
μὴ particle of negation. μή not, no, lest, neither, none, nothing, nor, never, without
τὸν art. acc. masc. sg. ὁ ἡ τό the, this, that, he, she, it
ἀδελφὸν n. acc. masc. sg. ἀδελφός brother
αὐτοῦ pron. gen. masc. 3p. sg. αὐτός ή ό self, of oneself, even, very, the same, he, she, it
ὃν relative pron. acc. masc. sg. ὅς ἥ ὅ who, which, what, that
τὸν art. acc. masc. sg. ὁ ἡ τό the, this, that, he, she, it
Θεὸν n. acc. masc. sg. θεός God, god
ὃν relative pron. acc. masc. sg. ὅς ἥ ὅ who, which, what, that
οὐχ particle of negation. οὐ οὐκ οὐχ not, no, neither, none, nay, nor, never, nothing
πῶς adv. πῶς how, by what means, after what manner

21 καὶ conj. καί and, even, also, but
ταύτην demo. pron. acc. fem. sg. οὗτος αὕτη τοῦτο this, the same, this same, he, she, it
τὴν art. acc. fem. sg. ὁ ἡ τό the, this, that, he, she, it
ἐντολὴν n. acc. fem. sg. ἐντολή commandment, precept
ἀπ' prep. ἀπό (+gen) from, of, out of, since, for, off, at, by, in, on
αὐτοῦ pron. gen. masc. 3p. sg. αὐτός ἡ ὁ self, of oneself, even, very, the same, he, she, it
ἵνα conj. ἵνα that, to, lest, for to, so that, albeit, because, for, so as
ὁ art. nom. masc. sg. ὁ ἡ τό the, this, that, he, she, it
τὸν art. acc. masc. sg. ὁ ἡ τό the, this, that, he, she, it
Θεὸν n. acc. masc. sg. θεός God, god
καὶ conj. καί and, even, also, but
τὸν art. acc. masc. sg. ὁ ἡ τό the, this, that, he, she, it
ἀδελφὸν n. acc. masc. sg. ἀδελφός brother
αὐτοῦ pron. gen. masc. 3p. sg. αὐτός ἡ ὁ self, of oneself, even, very, the same, he, she, it

5

1 Πᾶς adj. nom. masc. sg. πᾶς πᾶσα πᾶν all, every, whosoever, every one, no, whole, any
ὁ art. nom. masc. sg. ὁ ἡ τό the, this, that, he, she, it
ὅτι conj. ὅτι that, for, because, how that, how, because that, for that, though
Ἰησοῦς n. nom. masc. sg. Ἰησοῦς Jesus
ὁ art. nom. masc. sg. ὁ ἡ τό the, this, that, he, she, it
Χριστὸς n. nom. masc. sg. Χριστός Christ
ἐκ prep. ἐκ ἐξ (+gen) of, from, out of, by, on, with, in, among, through
τοῦ art. gen. masc. sg. ὁ ἡ τό the, this, that, he, she, it
Θεοῦ n. gen. masc. sg. θεός God, god
καὶ conj. καί and, even, also, but
πᾶς adj. nom. masc. sg. πᾶς πᾶσα πᾶν all, every, whosoever, every one, no, whole, any
ὁ art. nom. masc. sg. ὁ ἡ τό the, this, that, he, she, it
τὸν art. acc. masc. sg. ὁ ἡ τό the, this, that, he, she, it
καὶ conj. καί and, even, also, but
τὸν art. acc. masc. sg. ὁ ἡ τό the, this, that, he, she, it
ἐξ prep. ἐκ ἐξ (+gen) of, from, out of, by, on, with, in, among, through
αὐτοῦ pron. gen. masc. 3p. sg. αὐτός ἡ ὁ self, of oneself, even, very, the same, he, she, it
2 ἐν prep. ἐν (+dat) in, by, with, among, at, on, through, to, within, into, of, for
τούτῳ demo. pron. dat. neut. sg. οὗτος αὕτη τοῦτο this, the same, this same, he, she, it
ὅτι conj. ὅτι that, for, because, how that, how, because that, for that, though
τὰ art. acc. neut. pl. ὁ ἡ τό the, this, that, he, she, it
τέκνα n. acc. neut. pl. τέκνον child, son, daughter
τοῦ art. gen. masc. sg. ὁ ἡ τό the, this, that, he, she, it
Θεοῦ n. gen. masc. sg. θεός God, god
ὅταν conj. ὅταν when, as soon as, as long as, that, whensoever, while
τὸν art. acc. masc. sg. ὁ ἡ τό the, this, that, he, she, it
Θεὸν n. acc. masc. sg. θεός God, god
καὶ conj. καί and, even, also, but
τὰς art. acc. fem. pl. ὁ ἡ τό the, this, that, he, she, it
ἐντολὰς n. acc. fem. pl. ἐντολή commandment, precept
αὐτοῦ pron. gen. masc. 3p. sg. αὐτός ἡ ὁ self, of oneself, even, very, the same, he, she, it
3 αὕτη demo. pron. nom. fem. sg. οὗτος αὕτη τοῦτο this, the same, this same, he, she, it
γάρ conj. γάρ for, and, because, but, indeed
ἡ art. nom. fem. sg. ὁ ἡ τό the, this, that, he, she, it
ἀγάπη n. nom. fem. sg. ἀγάπη love, charity, feast of charity
τοῦ art. gen. masc. sg. ὁ ἡ τό the, this, that, he, she, it
Θεοῦ n. gen. masc. sg. θεός God, god
ἵνα conj. ἵνα that, to, lest, for to, so that, albeit, because, for, so as

τὰς art. acc. fem. pl. ὁ ἡ τό the, this, that, he, she, it
ἐντολὰς n. acc. fem. pl. ἐντολή commandment, precept
αὐτοῦ pron. gen. masc. 3p. sg. αὐτός ή ό self, of oneself, even, very, the same, he, she, it
καὶ conj. καί and, even, also, but
αἱ art. nom. fem. pl. ὁ ἡ τό the, this, that, he, she, it
ἐντολαὶ n. nom. fem. pl. ἐντολή commandment, precept
αὐτοῦ pron. gen. masc. 3p. sg. αὐτός ή ό self, of oneself, even, very, the same, he, she, it
βαρεῖαι adj. nom. fem. pl. βαρύς grievous, heavy, weightier, weighty
οὐκ particle of negation. οὐ οὐκ οὐχ not, no, neither, none, nay, nor, never, nothing
4 ὅτι conj. ὅτι that, for, because, how that, how, because that, for that, though
πᾶν adj. nom. neut. sg. πᾶς πᾶσα πᾶν all, every, whosoever, every one, no, whole, any
τὸ art. nom. neut. sg. ὁ ἡ τό the, this, that, he, she, it
ἐκ prep. ἐκ ἐξ (+gen) of, from, out of, by, on, with, in, among, through
τοῦ art. gen. masc. sg. ὁ ἡ τό the, this, that, he, she, it
Θεοῦ n. gen. masc. sg. θεός God, god
τὸν art. acc. masc. sg. ὁ ἡ τό the, this, that, he, she, it
κόσμον n. acc. masc. sg. κόσμος world, adorning
καὶ conj. καί and, even, also, but
αὕτη demo. pron. nom. fem. sg. οὗτος αὕτη τοῦτο this, the same, this same, he, she, it
ἡ art. nom. fem. sg. ὁ ἡ τό the, this, that, he, she, it
νίκη n. nom. fem. sg. νίκη victory
ἡ art. nom. fem. sg. ὁ ἡ τό the, this, that, he, she, it
τὸν art. acc. masc. sg. ὁ ἡ τό the, this, that, he, she, it
κόσμον n. acc. masc. sg. κόσμος world, adorning
ἡ art. nom. fem. sg. ὁ ἡ τό the, this, that, he, she, it
πίστις n. nom. fem. sg. πίστις faith, assurance, belief, fidelity
ἡμῶν pron. gen. 1p. pl. ἐγώ I
5 τίς interrog. pron. nom. masc. sg. τίς what, who, why, where, which, how
ὁ art. nom. masc. sg. ὁ ἡ τό the, this, that, he, she, it
τὸν art. acc. masc. sg. ὁ ἡ τό the, this, that, he, she, it
κόσμον n. acc. masc. sg. κόσμος world, adorning
εἰ conj. εἰ if, whether, that, though, forasmuch
μὴ particle of negation. μή not, no, lest, neither, none, nothing, nor, never, without
ὁ art. nom. masc. sg. ὁ ἡ τό the, this, that, he, she, it
ὅτι conj. ὅτι that, for, because, how that, how, because that, for that, though
Ἰησοῦς n. nom. masc. sg. Ἰησοῦς Jesus
ὁ art. nom. masc. sg. ὁ ἡ τό the, this, that, he, she, it
υἱὸς n. nom. masc. sg. υἱός son, child, descendant, offspring, heir
τοῦ art. gen. masc. sg. ὁ ἡ τό the, this, that, he, she, it
Θεοῦ n. gen. masc. sg. θεός God, god
6 οὗτός demo. pron. nom. masc. sg. οὗτος αὕτη τοῦτο this, the same, this same, he, she, it
ὁ art. nom. masc. sg. ὁ ἡ τό the, this, that, he, she, it
δι' prep. διά (+gen) by, through, with, in, of, (+acc) for, because of, for a cause
ὕδατος n. gen. neut. sg. ὕδωρ water
καὶ conj. καί and, even, also, but
αἵματος n. gen. neut. sg. αἷμα blood
Ἰησοῦς n. nom. masc. sg. Ἰησοῦς Jesus
ὁ art. nom. masc. sg. ὁ ἡ τό the, this, that, he, she, it
Χριστός n. nom. masc. sg. Χριστός Christ
οὐκ particle of negation. οὐ οὐκ οὐχ not, no, neither, none, nay, nor, never, nothing
ἐν prep. ἐν (+dat) in, by, with, among, at, on, through, to, within, into, of, for
τῷ art. dat. neut. sg. ὁ ἡ τό the, this, that, he, she, it
ὕδατι n. dat. neut. sg. ὕδωρ water
μόνον adv. μόνος only, alone, by oneself
ἀλλ' conj. ἀλλά but, yea, yet, nevertheless, howbeit, nay, therefore

ἐν prep. ἐν (+dat) in, by, with, among, at, on, through, to, within, into, of, for
τῷ art. dat. neut. sg. ὁ ἡ τό the, this, that, he, she, it
ὕδατι n. dat. neut. sg. ὕδωρ water
καὶ conj. καί and, even, also, but
τῷ art. dat. neut. sg. ὁ ἡ τό the, this, that, he, she, it
αἵματι n. dat. neut. sg. αἷμα blood
καὶ conj. καί and, even, also, but
τὸ art. nom. neut. sg. ὁ ἡ τό the, this, that, he, she, it
Πνεῦμά n. nom. neut. sg. πνεῦμα spirit, Spirit, Ghost, ghost, life. of the spirit, wind
τὸ art. nom. neut. sg. ὁ ἡ τό the, this, that, he, she, it
ὅτι conj. ὅτι that, for, because, how that, how, because that, for that, though
τὸ art. nom. neut. sg. ὁ ἡ τό the, this, that, he, she, it
Πνεῦμά n. nom. neut. sg. πνεῦμα spirit, Spirit, Ghost, ghost, life. of the spirit, wind
ἡ art. nom. fem. sg. ὁ ἡ τό the, this, that, he, she, it
ἀλήθεια n. nom. fem. sg. ἀλήθεια truth, verity
7 ὅτι conj. ὅτι that, for, because, how that, how, because that, for that, though
τρεῖς num. nom. masc. pl. τρεῖς three
οἱ art. nom. masc. pl. ὁ ἡ τό the, this, that, he, she, it
ἐν prep. ἐν (+dat) in, by, with, among, at, on, through, to, within, into, of, for
τῷ art. dat. masc. sg. ὁ ἡ τό the, this, that, he, she, it
οὐρανῷ n. dat. masc. sg. οὐρανός heaven, air, sky
ὁ art. nom. masc. sg. ὁ ἡ τό the, this, that, he, she, it
πατήρ n. nom. masc. sg. πατήρ Father, father, parent
ὁ art. nom. masc. sg. ὁ ἡ τό the, this, that, he, she, it
λόγος n. nom. masc. sg. λόγος word, saying, account, speech, thing, matter
καὶ conj. καί and, even, also, but
τὸ art. nom. neut. sg. ὁ ἡ τό the, this, that, he, she, it
Ἅγιον adj. nom. neut. sg. ἅγιος Holy, holy, saint, Holy One, holy thing, most holy
Πνεῦμα n. nom. neut. sg. πνεῦμα spirit, Spirit, Ghost, ghost, life. of the spirit, wind
καὶ conj. καί and, even, also, but
οὗτοι demo. pron. nom. masc. pl. οὗτος αὕτη τοῦτο this, the same, this same, he, she, it
οἱ art. nom. masc. pl. ὁ ἡ τό the, this, that, he, she, it
τρεῖς num. nom. masc. pl. τρεῖς three
ἕν num. nom. neut. sg. εἷς or ἕν one, other, some, any, only, a certain
8 καὶ conj. καί and, even, also, but
τρεῖς num. nom. masc. pl. τρεῖς three
οἱ art. nom. masc. pl. ὁ ἡ τό the, this, that, he, she, it
ἐν prep. ἐν (+dat) in, by, with, among, at, on, through, to, within, into, of, for
τῇ art. dat. fem. sg. ὁ ἡ τό the, this, that, he, she, it
γῇ n. dat. fem. sg. γῆ earth, land, ground, country
τὸ art. nom. neut. sg. ὁ ἡ τό the, this, that, he, she, it
Πνεῦμα n. nom. neut. sg. πνεῦμα spirit, Spirit, Ghost, ghost, life. of the spirit, wind
καὶ conj. καί and, even, also, but
τὸ art. nom. neut. sg. ὁ ἡ τό the, this, that, he, she, it
ὕδωρ n. nom. neut. sg. ὕδωρ water
καὶ conj. καί and, even, also, but
τὸ art. nom. neut. sg. ὁ ἡ τό the, this, that, he, she, it
αἷμα n. nom. neut. sg. αἷμα blood
καὶ conj. καί and, even, also, but
οἱ art. nom. masc. pl. ὁ ἡ τό the, this, that, he, she, it
τρεῖς num. nom. masc. pl. τρεῖς three
εἰς prep. εἰς (+acc) into, to, unto, for, in, on, toward, against, upon, at, among
τὸ art. acc. neut. sg. ὁ ἡ τό the, this, that, he, she, it
ἕν num. acc. neut. sg. εἷς or ἕν one, other, some, any, only, a certain
9 εἰ conj. εἰ if, whether, that, though, forasmuch

τὴν art. acc. fem. sg. ὁ ἡ τό the, this, that, he, she, it
μαρτυρίαν n. acc. fem. sg. μαρτυρία testimony, witness, record, report
τῶν art. gen. masc. pl. ὁ ἡ τό the, this, that, he, she, it
ἀνθρώπων n. gen. masc. pl. ἄνθρωπος man, human being, person, one, certain
ἡ art. nom. fem. sg. ὁ ἡ τό the, this, that, he, she, it
μαρτυρία n. nom. fem. sg. μαρτυρία testimony, witness, record, report
τοῦ art. gen. masc. sg. ὁ ἡ τό the, this, that, he, she, it
Θεοῦ n. gen. masc. sg. θεός God, god
μείζων compar. adj. nom. fem. sg. μέγας great, loud, greatest, high, large, mighty, strong
ὅτι conj. ὅτι that, for, because, how that, how, because that, for that, though
αὕτη demo. pron. nom. fem. sg. οὗτος αὕτη τοῦτο this, the same, this same, he, she, it
ἡ art. nom. fem. sg. ὁ ἡ τό the, this, that, he, she, it
μαρτυρία n. nom. fem. sg. μαρτυρία testimony, witness, record, report
τοῦ art. gen. masc. sg. ὁ ἡ τό the, this, that, he, she, it
Θεοῦ n. gen. masc. sg. θεός God, god
ἣν relative pron. acc. fem. sg. ὅς ἥ ὅ who, which, what, that
περὶ prep. περί (+gen) of, for, concerning, (+acc) about, concerning, in
τοῦ art. gen. masc. sg. ὁ ἡ τό the, this, that, he, she, it
υἱοῦ n. gen. masc. sg. υἱός son, child, descendant, offspring, heir
αὐτοῦ pron. gen. masc. 3p. sg. αὐτός ή ό self, of oneself, even, very, the same, he, she, it
10 ὁ art. nom. masc. sg. ὁ ἡ τό the, this, that, he, she, it
εἰς prep. εἰς (+acc) into, to, unto, for, in, on, toward, against, upon, at, among
τὸν art. acc. masc. sg. ὁ ἡ τό the, this, that, he, she, it
υἱὸν n. acc. masc. sg. υἱός son, child, descendant, offspring, heir
τοῦ art. gen. masc. sg. ὁ ἡ τό the, this, that, he, she, it
Θεοῦ n. gen. masc. sg. θεός God, god
τὴν art. acc. fem. sg. ὁ ἡ τό the, this, that, he, she, it
μαρτυρίαν n. acc. fem. sg. μαρτυρία testimony, witness, record, report
ἐν prep. ἐν (+dat) in, by, with, among, at, on, through, to, within, into, of, for
ἑαυτῷ reflexive pron. dat. masc. 3p. sg. ἑαυτοῦ himself, herself, itself, yourself, ourselves
ὁ art. nom. masc. sg. ὁ ἡ τό the, this, that, he, she, it
μὴ particle of negation. μή not, no, lest, neither, none, nothing, nor, never, without
τῷ art. dat. masc. sg. ὁ ἡ τό the, this, that, he, she, it
Θεῷ n. dat. masc. sg. θεός God, god
ψεύστην n. acc. masc. sg. ψεύστης liar
αὐτόν pron. acc. masc. 3p. sg. αὐτός ή ό self, of oneself, even, very, the same, he, she, it
ὅτι conj. ὅτι that, for, because, how that, how, because that, for that, though
οὐ particle of negation. οὐ οὐκ οὐχ not, no, neither, none, nay, nor, never, nothing
εἰς prep. εἰς (+acc) into, to, unto, for, in, on, toward, against, upon, at, among
τὴν art. acc. fem. sg. ὁ ἡ τό the, this, that, he, she, it
μαρτυρίαν n. acc. fem. sg. μαρτυρία testimony, witness, record, report
ἣν relative pron. acc. fem. sg. ὅς ἥ ὅ who, which, what, that
ὁ art. nom. masc. sg. ὁ ἡ τό the, this, that, he, she, it
Θεὸς n. nom. masc. sg. θεός God, god
περὶ prep. περί (+gen) of, for, concerning, (+acc) about, concerning, in
τοῦ art. gen. masc. sg. ὁ ἡ τό the, this, that, he, she, it
υἱοῦ n. gen. masc. sg. υἱός son, child, descendant, offspring, heir
αὐτοῦ pron. gen. masc. 3p. sg. αὐτός ή ό self, of oneself, even, very, the same, he, she, it
11 καὶ conj. καί and, even, also, but
αὕτη demo. pron. nom. fem. sg. οὗτος αὕτη τοῦτο this, the same, this same, he, she, it
ἡ art. nom. fem. sg. ὁ ἡ τό the, this, that, he, she, it
μαρτυρία n. nom. fem. sg. μαρτυρία testimony, witness, record, report
ὅτι conj. ὅτι that, for, because, how that, how, because that, for that, though
ζωὴν n. acc. fem. sg. ζωή life, lifetime
αἰώνιον adj. acc. fem. sg. αἰώνιος eternal, everlasting, world, for ever

ἡμῖν pron. dat. 1p. pl. ἐγώ I
ὁ art. nom. masc. sg. ὁ ἡ τό the, this, that, he, she, it
Θεός n. nom. masc. sg. θεός God, god
καὶ conj. καί and, even, also, but
αὕτη demo. pron. nom. fem. sg. οὗτος αὕτη τοῦτο this, the same, this same, he, she, it
ἡ art. nom. fem. sg. ὁ ἡ τό the, this, that, he, she, it
ζωὴ n. nom. fem. sg. ζωή life, lifetime
ἐν prep. ἐν (+dat) in, by, with, among, at, on, through, to, within, into, of, for
τῷ art. dat. masc. sg. ὁ ἡ τό the, this, that, he, she, it
υἱῷ n. dat. masc. sg. υἱός son, child, descendant, offspring, heir
αὐτοῦ pron. gen. masc. 3p. sg. αὐτός ή ό self, of oneself, even, very, the same, he, she, it
12 ὁ art. nom. masc. sg. ὁ ἡ τό the, this, that, he, she, it
τὸν art. acc. masc. sg. ὁ ἡ τό the, this, that, he, she, it
υἱὸν n. acc. masc. sg. υἱός son, child, descendant, offspring, heir
τὴν art. acc. fem. sg. ὁ ἡ τό the, this, that, he, she, it
ζωήν n. acc. fem. sg. ζωή life, lifetime
ὁ art. nom. masc. sg. ὁ ἡ τό the, this, that, he, she, it
μὴ particle of negation. μή not, no, lest, neither, none, nothing, nor, never, without
τὸν art. acc. masc. sg. ὁ ἡ τό the, this, that, he, she, it
υἱὸν n. acc. masc. sg. υἱός son, child, descendant, offspring, heir
τοῦ art. gen. masc. sg. ὁ ἡ τό the, this, that, he, she, it
Θεοῦ n. gen. masc. sg. θεός God, god
τὴν art. acc. fem. sg. ὁ ἡ τό the, this, that, he, she, it
ζωήν n. acc. fem. sg. ζωή life, lifetime
οὐκ particle of negation. οὐ οὐκ οὐχ not, no, neither, none, nay, nor, never, nothing
13 Ταῦτα demo. pron. acc. neut. pl. οὗτος αὕτη τοῦτο this, the same, this same, he, she, it
ὑμῖν pron. dat. 2p. pl. σύ thou, you
τοῖς art. dat. masc. pl. ὁ ἡ τό the, this, that, he, she, it
εἰς prep. εἰς (+acc) into, to, unto, for, in, on, toward, against, upon, at, among
τὸ art. acc. neut. sg. ὁ ἡ τό the, this, that, he, she, it
ὄνομα n. acc. neut. sg. ὄνομα name, call, surname
τοῦ art. gen. masc. sg. ὁ ἡ τό the, this, that, he, she, it
υἱοῦ n. gen. masc. sg. υἱός son, child, descendant, offspring, heir
τοῦ art. gen. masc. sg. ὁ ἡ τό the, this, that, he, she, it
Θεοῦ n. gen. masc. sg. θεός God, god
ἵνα conj. ἵνα that, to, lest, for to, so that, albeit, because, for, so as
ὅτι conj. ὅτι that, for, because, how that, how, because that, for that, though
ζωὴν n. acc. fem. sg. ζωή life, lifetime
αἰώνιον adj. acc. fem. sg. αἰώνιος eternal, everlasting, world, for ever
καὶ conj. καί and, even, also, but
ἵνα conj. ἵνα that, to, lest, for to, so that, albeit, because, for, so as
εἰς prep. εἰς (+acc) into, to, unto, for, in, on, toward, against, upon, at, among
τὸ art. acc. neut. sg. ὁ ἡ τό the, this, that, he, she, it
ὄνομα n. acc. neut. sg. ὄνομα name, call, surname
τοῦ art. gen. masc. sg. ὁ ἡ τό the, this, that, he, she, it
υἱοῦ n. gen. masc. sg. υἱός son, child, descendant, offspring, heir
τοῦ art. gen. masc. sg. ὁ ἡ τό the, this, that, he, she, it
Θεοῦ n. gen. masc. sg. θεός God, god
14 καὶ conj. καί and, even, also, but
αὕτη demo. pron. nom. fem. sg. οὗτος αὕτη τοῦτο this, the same, this same, he, she, it
ἡ art. nom. fem. sg. ὁ ἡ τό the, this, that, he, she, it
παρρησία n. nom. fem. sg. παρρησία boldness, confidence, openly, plainly, freely
ἣν relative pron. acc. fem. sg. ὅς ἥ ὅ who, which, what, that
πρὸς prep. πρός (+gen) for, (+dat) at, (+acc) unto, to, with, for, against
αὐτόν pron. acc. masc. 3p. sg. αὐτός ή ό self, of oneself, even, very, the same, he, she, it

ὅτι conj. ὅτι that, for, because, how that, how, because that, for that, though
ἐάν conj. ἐάν if, soever, except, though, and if, but, whether, if so, so
τι indefinite pron. acc. neut. sg. τὶς certain, some, any man, one, any thing
κατὰ prep. κατά (+gen) against, by, throughout, down, (+acc) according to, after, with
τὸ art. acc. neut. sg. ὁ ἡ τό the, this, that, he, she, it
θέλημα n. acc. neut. sg. θέλημα will, desire, pleasure
αὐτοῦ pron. gen. masc. 3p. sg. αὐτός ή ό self, of oneself, even, very, the same, he, she, it
ἡμῶν pron. gen. 1p. pl. ἐγώ I
15 καὶ conj. καί and, even, also, but
ἐὰν conj. ἐάν if, soever, except, though, and if, but, whether, if so, so
ὅτι conj. ὅτι that, for, because, how that, how, because that, for that, though
ἡμῶν pron. gen. 1p. pl. ἐγώ I
ὃ relative pron. acc. neut. sg. ὅς ἥ ὅ who, which, what, that
ἂν particle. ἄν Indicating contingency. No English translation.
ὅτι conj. ὅτι that, for, because, how that, how, because that, for that, though
τὰ art. acc. neut. pl. ὁ ἡ τό the, this, that, he, she, it
αἰτήματα n. acc. neut. pl. αἴτημα request, petition
ἃ relative pron. acc. neut. pl. ὅς ἥ ὅ who, which, what, that
παρ' prep. παρά (+gen) of, from, (+dat) with, for, (+acc) beside, at, by, above, against
αὐτοῦ pron. gen. masc. 3p. sg. αὐτός ή ό self, of oneself, even, very, the same, he, she, it
16 ἐὰν conj. ἐάν if, soever, except, though, and if, but, whether, if so, so
τις indefinite pron. nom. masc. sg. τὶς certain, some, any man, one, any thing
τὸν art. acc. masc. sg. ὁ ἡ τό the, this, that, he, she, it
ἀδελφὸν n. acc. masc. sg. ἀδελφός brother
αὐτοῦ pron. gen. masc. 3p. sg. αὐτός ή ό self, of oneself, even, very, the same, he, she, it
ἁμαρτίαν n. acc. fem. sg. ἁμαρτία sin, offence, sinful
μὴ particle of negation. μή not, no, lest, neither, none, nothing, nor, never, without
πρὸς prep. πρός (+gen) for, (+dat) at, (+acc) unto, to, with, for, against
θάνατον n. acc. masc. sg. θάνατος death
καὶ conj. καί and, even, also, but
αὐτῷ pron. dat. masc. 3p. sg. αὐτός ή ό self, of oneself, even, very, the same, he, she, it
ζωήν n. acc. fem. sg. ζωή life, lifetime
τοῖς art. dat. masc. pl. ὁ ἡ τό the, this, that, he, she, it
μὴ particle of negation. μή not, no, lest, neither, none, nothing, nor, never, without
πρὸς prep. πρός (+gen) for, (+dat) at, (+acc) unto, to, with, for, against
θάνατον n. acc. masc. sg. θάνατος death
ἁμαρτία n. nom. fem. sg. ἁμαρτία sin, offence, sinful
πρὸς prep. πρός (+gen) for, (+dat) at, (+acc) unto, to, with, for, against
θάνατον n. acc. masc. sg. θάνατος death
οὐ particle of negation. οὐ οὐκ οὐχ not, no, neither, none, nay, nor, never, nothing
περὶ prep. περί (+gen) of, for, concerning, (+acc) about, concerning, in
ἐκείνης demo. pron. gen. fem. sg. ἐκεῖνος that, he, the same, that same
ἵνα conj. ἵνα that, to, lest, for to, so that, albeit, because, for, so as
17 πᾶσα adj. nom. fem. sg. πᾶς πᾶσα πᾶν all, every, whosoever, every one, no, whole, any
ἀδικία n. nom. fem. sg. ἀδικία iniquity, unrighteousness, unjust, wrong
ἁμαρτία n. nom. fem. sg. ἁμαρτία sin, offence, sinful
καὶ conj. καί and, even, also, but
ἁμαρτία n. nom. fem. sg. ἁμαρτία sin, offence, sinful
οὐ particle of negation. οὐ οὐκ οὐχ not, no, neither, none, nay, nor, never, nothing
πρὸς prep. πρός (+gen) for, (+dat) at, (+acc) unto, to, with, for, against
θάνατον n. acc. masc. sg. θάνατος death
18 ὅτι conj. ὅτι that, for, because, how that, how, because that, for that, though
πᾶς adj. nom. masc. sg. πᾶς πᾶσα πᾶν all, every, whosoever, every one, no, whole, any
ὁ art. nom. masc. sg. ὁ ἡ τό the, this, that, he, she, it
ἐκ prep. ἐκ ἐξ (+gen) of, from, out of, by, on, with, in, among, through

τοῦ art. gen. masc. sg. ὁ ἡ τό the, this, that, he, she, it
Θεοῦ n. gen. masc. sg. θεός God, god
οὐχ particle of negation. οὐ οὐκ οὐχ not, no, neither, none, nay, nor, never, nothing
ἀλλ' conj. ἀλλά but, yea, yet, nevertheless, howbeit, nay, therefore
ὁ art. nom. masc. sg. ὁ ἡ τό the, this, that, he, she, it
ἐκ prep. ἐκ ἐξ (+gen) of, from, out of, by, on, with, in, among, through
τοῦ art. gen. masc. sg. ὁ ἡ τό the, this, that, he, she, it
Θεοῦ n. gen. masc. sg. θεός God, god
ἑαυτὸν reflexive pron. acc. masc. 3p. sg. ἑαυτοῦ himself, herself, itself, yourself, ourselves
καὶ conj. καί and, even, also, but
ὁ art. nom. masc. sg. ὁ ἡ τό the, this, that, he, she, it
πονηρὸς adj. nom. masc. sg. πονηρός evil, wicked, bad
οὐχ particle of negation. οὐ οὐκ οὐχ not, no, neither, none, nay, nor, never, nothing
αὐτοῦ pron. gen. masc. 3p. sg. αὐτός ἡ ὁ self, of oneself, even, very, the same, he, she, it
19 ὅτι conj. ὅτι that, for, because, how that, how, because that, for that, though
ἐκ prep. ἐκ ἐξ (+gen) of, from, out of, by, on, with, in, among, through
τοῦ art. gen. masc. sg. ὁ ἡ τό the, this, that, he, she, it
Θεοῦ n. gen. masc. sg. θεός God, god
καὶ conj. καί and, even, also, but
ὁ art. nom. masc. sg. ὁ ἡ τό the, this, that, he, she, it
κόσμος n. nom. masc. sg. κόσμος world, adorning
ὅλος adj. nom. masc. sg. ὅλος all, whole, every whit, altogether
ἐν prep. ἐν (+dat) in, by, with, among, at, on, through, to, within, into, of, for
τῷ art. dat. masc. sg. ὁ ἡ τό the, this, that, he, she, it
πονηρῷ adj. dat. masc. sg. πονηρός evil, wicked, bad
20 δὲ conj. δέ but, and, now, also, to the contrary, rather, then
ὅτι conj. ὅτι that, for, because, how that, how, because that, for that, though
ὁ art. nom. masc. sg. ὁ ἡ τό the, this, that, he, she, it
υἱὸς n. nom. masc. sg. υἱός son, child, descendant, offspring, heir
τοῦ art. gen. masc. sg. ὁ ἡ τό the, this, that, he, she, it
Θεοῦ n. gen. masc. sg. θεός God, god
καὶ conj. καί and, even, also, but
ἡμῖν pron. dat. 1p. pl. ἐγώ I
διάνοιαν n. acc. fem. sg. διάνοια mind, understanding, imagination
ἵνα conj. ἵνα that, to, lest, for to, so that, albeit, because, for, so as
τὸν art. acc. masc. sg. ὁ ἡ τό the, this, that, he, she, it
ἀληθινόν adj. acc. masc. sg. ἀληθινός true
καὶ conj. καί and, even, also, but
ἐν prep. ἐν (+dat) in, by, with, among, at, on, through, to, within, into, of, for
τῷ art. dat. masc. sg. ὁ ἡ τό the, this, that, he, she, it
ἀληθινῷ adj. dat. masc. sg. ἀληθινός true
ἐν prep. ἐν (+dat) in, by, with, among, at, on, through, to, within, into, of, for
τῷ art. dat. masc. sg. ὁ ἡ τό the, this, that, he, she, it
υἱῷ n. dat. masc. sg. υἱός son, child, descendant, offspring, heir
αὐτοῦ pron. gen. masc. 3p. sg. αὐτός ἡ ὁ self, of oneself, even, very, the same, he, she, it
Ἰησοῦ n. dat. masc. sg. Ἰησοῦς Jesus
Χριστῷ n. dat. masc. sg. Χριστός Christ
οὗτός demo. pron. nom. masc. sg. οὗτος αὕτη τοῦτο this, the same, this same, he, she, it
ὁ art. nom. masc. sg. ὁ ἡ τό the, this, that, he, she, it
ἀληθινὸς adj. nom. masc. sg. ἀληθινός true
Θεὸς n. nom. masc. sg. θεός God, god
καὶ conj. καί and, even, also, but
ἡ art. nom. fem. sg. ὁ ἡ τό the, this, that, he, she, it
ζωὴ n. nom. fem. sg. ζωή life, lifetime
αἰώνιος adj. nom. fem. sg. αἰώνιος eternal, everlasting, world, for ever

21 Τεκνία n. voc. neut. pl. τεκνίον little child
ἑαυτοὺς reflexive pron. acc. masc. 3p. pl. ἑαυτοῦ himself, herself, itself, yourself, ourselves
ἀπὸ prep. ἀπό (+gen) from, of, out of, since, for, off, at, by, in, on
τῶν art. gen. neut. pl. ὁ ἡ τό the, this, that, he, she, it
εἰδώλων n. gen. neut. pl. εἴδωλον idol
ἀμήν particle. ἀμήν amen, verily

ΙΩΑΝΝΟΥ
ΕΠΙΣΤΟΛΗ ΔΕΥΤΕΡΑ

1

1 Ὁ art. nom. masc. sg. ὁ ἡ τό the, this, that, he, she, it
πρεσβύτερος adj. nom. masc. sg. πρεσβύτερος elder, elder woman, eldest, old man
ἐκλεκτῇ adj. dat. fem. sg. ἐκλεκτός elect, chosen
κυρίᾳ n. dat. fem. sg. κυρία lady
καὶ conj. καί and, even, also, but
τοῖς art. dat. neut. pl. ὁ ἡ τό the, this, that, he, she, it
τέκνοις n. dat. neut. pl. τέκνον child, son, daughter
αὐτῆς pron. gen. fem. 3p. sg. αὐτός ή ό self, of oneself, even, very, the same, he, she, it
οὓς relative pron. acc. masc. pl. ὅς ἥ ὅ who, which, what, that
ἐγὼ pron. nom. 1p. sg. ἐγώ I
ἐν prep. ἐν (+dat) in, by, with, among, at, on, through, to, within, into, of, for
ἀληθείᾳ n. dat. fem. sg. ἀλήθεια truth, verity
καὶ conj. καί and, even, also, but
οὐκ particle of negation. οὐ οὐκ οὐχ not, no, neither, none, nay, nor, never, nothing
ἐγὼ pron. nom. 1p. sg. ἐγώ I
μόνος adj. nom. masc. sg. μόνος only, alone, by oneself
ἀλλὰ conj. ἀλλά but, yea, yet, nevertheless, howbeit, nay, therefore
καὶ conj. καί and, even, also, but
πάντες adj. nom. masc. pl. πᾶς πᾶσα πᾶν all, every, whosoever, every one, no, whole, any
οἱ art. nom. masc. pl. ὁ ἡ τό the, this, that, he, she, it
τὴν art. acc. fem. sg. ὁ ἡ τό the, this, that, he, she, it
ἀλήθειαν n. acc. fem. sg. ἀλήθεια truth, verity
2 διὰ prep. διά (+gen) by, through, with, in, of, (+acc) for, because of, for a cause
τὴν art. acc. fem. sg. ὁ ἡ τό the, this, that, he, she, it
ἀλήθειαν n. acc. fem. sg. ἀλήθεια truth, verity
τὴν art. acc. fem. sg. ὁ ἡ τό the, this, that, he, she, it
ἐν prep. ἐν (+dat) in, by, with, among, at, on, through, to, within, into, of, for
ἡμῖν pron. dat. 1p. pl. ἐγώ I
καὶ conj. καί and, even, also, but
μεθ' prep. μετά (+gen) with, among, against, (+acc) after
ἡμῶν pron. gen. 1p. pl. ἐγώ I
εἰς prep. εἰς (+acc) into, to, unto, for, in, on, toward, against, upon, at, among
τὸν art. acc. masc. sg. ὁ ἡ τό the, this, that, he, she, it
αἰῶνα n. acc. masc. sg. αἰών ever, ever and ever, evermore, age, eternal, world
3 μεθ' prep. μετά (+gen) with, among, against, (+acc) after
ὑμῶν pron. gen. 2p. pl. σύ thou, you
χάρις n. nom. fem. sg. χάρις grace, thank, favour, pleasure
ἔλεος n. nom. neut. sg. ἔλεος mercy
εἰρήνη n. nom. fem. sg. εἰρήνη peace, quietness, rest
παρὰ prep. παρά (+gen) of, from, (+dat) with, for, (+acc) beside, at, by, above, against
Θεοῦ n. gen. masc. sg. θεός God, god
πατρὸς n. gen. masc. sg. πατήρ Father, father, parent
καὶ conj. καί and, even, also, but
παρὰ prep. παρά (+gen) of, from, (+dat) with, for, (+acc) beside, at, by, above, against
Κυρίου n. gen. masc. sg. κύριος Lord, lord, master, sir, LORD, God, Master, owner
Ἰησοῦ n. gen. masc. sg. Ἰησοῦς Jesus
Χριστοῦ n. gen. masc. sg. Χριστός Christ
τοῦ art. gen. masc. sg. ὁ ἡ τό the, this, that, he, she, it
υἱοῦ n. gen. masc. sg. υἱός son, child, descendant, offspring, heir

τοῦ art. gen. masc. sg. ὁ ἡ τό the, this, that, he, she, it
πατρὸς n. gen. masc. sg. πατήρ Father, father, parent
ἐν prep. ἐν (+dat) in, by, with, among, at, on, through, to, within, into, of, for
ἀληθείᾳ n. dat. fem. sg. ἀλήθεια truth, verity
καὶ conj. καί and, even, also, but
ἀγάπῃ n. dat. fem. sg. ἀγάπη love, charity, feast of charity
4 λίαν adv. λίαν exceeding, greatly, very, great sore
ὅτι conj. ὅτι that, for, because, how that, how, because that, for that, though
ἐκ prep. ἐκ ἐξ (+gen) of, from, out of, by, on, with, in, among, through
τῶν art. gen. neut. pl. ὁ ἡ τό the, this, that, he, she, it
τέκνων n. gen. neut. pl. τέκνον child, son, daughter
σου pron. gen. 2p. sg. σύ thou, you
ἐν prep. ἐν (+dat) in, by, with, among, at, on, through, to, within, into, of, for
ἀληθείᾳ n. dat. fem. sg. ἀλήθεια truth, verity
καθὼς adv. καθώς as, even as, according as, according to
ἐντολὴν n. acc. fem. sg. ἐντολή commandment, precept
παρὰ prep. παρά (+gen) of, from, (+dat) with, for, (+acc) beside, at, by, above, against
τοῦ art. gen. masc. sg. ὁ ἡ τό the, this, that, he, she, it
πατρός n. gen. masc. sg. πατήρ Father, father, parent
5 καὶ conj. καί and, even, also, but
νῦν adv. νῦν now, henceforth, present, this time
σε pron. acc. 2p. sg. σύ thou, you
κυρία n. voc. fem. sg. κυρία lady
οὐχ particle of negation. οὐ οὐκ οὐχ not, no, neither, none, nay, nor, never, nothing
ὡς adv. ὡς as, when, as it were, how, about, like, as soon as, even as, while
ἐντολὴν n. acc. fem. sg. ἐντολή commandment, precept
σοι pron. dat. 2p. sg. σύ thou, you
καινὴν adj. acc. fem. sg. καινός new
ἀλλὰ conj. ἀλλά but, yea, yet, nevertheless, howbeit, nay, therefore
ἣν relative pron. acc. fem. sg. ὅς ἥ ὅ who, which, what, that
ἀπ' prep. ἀπό (+gen) from, of, out of, since, for, off, at, by, in, on
ἀρχῆς n. gen. fem. sg. ἀρχή beginning, principality, corner, first, magistrate, rule
ἵνα conj. ἵνα that, to, lest, for to, so that, albeit, because, for, so as
ἀλλήλους pron. acc. masc. pl. ἀλλήλων one another, themselves, together, mutual
6 καὶ conj. καί and, even, also, but
αὕτη demo. pron. nom. fem. sg. οὗτος αὕτη τοῦτο this, the same, this same, he, she, it
ἡ art. nom. fem. sg. ὁ ἡ τό the, this, that, he, she, it
ἀγάπη n. nom. fem. sg. ἀγάπη love, charity, feast of charity
ἵνα conj. ἵνα that, to, lest, for to, so that, albeit, because, for, so as
κατὰ prep. κατά (+gen) against, by, throughout, down, (+acc) according to, after, with
τὰς art. acc. fem. pl. ὁ ἡ τό the, this, that, he, she, it
ἐντολὰς n. acc. fem. pl. ἐντολή commandment, precept
αὐτοῦ pron. gen. masc. 3p. sg. αὐτός ἡ ὁ self, of oneself, even, very, the same, he, she, it
αὕτη demo. pron. nom. fem. sg. οὗτος αὕτη τοῦτο this, the same, this same, he, she, it
ἡ art. nom. fem. sg. ὁ ἡ τό the, this, that, he, she, it
ἐντολή n. nom. fem. sg. ἐντολή commandment, precept
καθὼς adv. καθώς as, even as, according as, according to
ἀπ' prep. ἀπό (+gen) from, of, out of, since, for, off, at, by, in, on
ἀρχῆς n. gen. fem. sg. ἀρχή beginning, principality, corner, first, magistrate, rule
ἵνα conj. ἵνα that, to, lest, for to, so that, albeit, because, for, so as
ἐν prep. ἐν (+dat) in, by, with, among, at, on, through, to, within, into, of, for
αὐτῇ pron. dat. fem. 3p. sg. αὐτός ἡ ὁ self, of oneself, even, very, the same, he, she, it
7 ὅτι conj. ὅτι that, for, because, how that, how, because that, for that, though
πολλοὶ adj. nom. masc. pl. πολύς many, great, much, long, abundant
πλάνοι adj. nom. masc. pl. πλάνος deceiver, seducing

εἰς prep. εἰς (+acc) into, to, unto, for, in, on, toward, against, upon, at, among
τὸν art. acc. masc. sg. ὁ ἡ τό the, this, that, he, she, it
κόσμον n. acc. masc. sg. κόσμος world, adorning
οἱ art. nom. masc. pl. ὁ ἡ τό the, this, that, he, she, it
μὴ particle of negation. μή not, no, lest, neither, none, nothing, nor, never, without
Ἰησοῦν n. acc. masc. sg. Ἰησοῦς Jesus
Χριστὸν n. acc. masc. sg. Χριστός Christ
ἐν prep. ἐν (+dat) in, by, with, among, at, on, through, to, within, into, of, for
σαρκί n. dat. fem. sg. σάρξ flesh, carnal
οὗτός demo. pron. nom. masc. sg. οὗτος αὕτη τοῦτο this, the same, this same, he, she, it
ὁ art. nom. masc. sg. ὁ ἡ τό the, this, that, he, she, it
πλάνος adj. nom. masc. sg. πλάνος deceiver, seducing
καὶ conj. καί and, even, also, but
ὁ art. nom. masc. sg. ὁ ἡ τό the, this, that, he, she, it
ἀντίχριστος n. nom. masc. sg. ἀντίχριστος antichrist
8 ἑαυτούς reflexive pron. acc. masc. 3p. pl. ἑαυτοῦ himself, herself, itself, yourself, ourselves
ἵνα conj. ἵνα that, to, lest, for to, so that, albeit, because, for, so as
μὴ particle of negation. μή not, no, lest, neither, none, nothing, nor, never, without
ἃ relative pron. acc. neut. pl. ὅς ἥ ὅ who, which, what, that
ἀλλὰ conj. ἀλλά but, yea, yet, nevertheless, howbeit, nay, therefore
μισθὸν n. acc. masc. sg. μισθός reward, hire, wage
πλήρη adj. acc. masc. sg. πλήρης full
9 πᾶς adj. nom. masc. sg. πᾶς πᾶσα πᾶν all, every, whosoever, every one, no, whole, any
ὁ art. nom. masc. sg. ὁ ἡ τό the, this, that, he, she, it
καὶ conj. καί and, even, also, but
μὴ particle of negation. μή not, no, lest, neither, none, nothing, nor, never, without
ἐν prep. ἐν (+dat) in, by, with, among, at, on, through, to, within, into, of, for
τῇ art. dat. fem. sg. ὁ ἡ τό the, this, that, he, she, it
διδαχῇ n. dat. fem. sg. διδαχή doctrine, teaching
τοῦ art. gen. masc. sg. ὁ ἡ τό the, this, that, he, she, it
Χριστοῦ n. gen. masc. sg. Χριστός Christ
Θεὸν n. acc. masc. sg. θεός God, god
οὐκ particle of negation. οὐ οὐκ οὐχ not, no, neither, none, nay, nor, never, nothing
ὁ art. nom. masc. sg. ὁ ἡ τό the, this, that, he, she, it
ἐν prep. ἐν (+dat) in, by, with, among, at, on, through, to, within, into, of, for
τῇ art. dat. fem. sg. ὁ ἡ τό the, this, that, he, she, it
διδαχῇ n. dat. fem. sg. διδαχή doctrine, teaching
τοῦ art. gen. masc. sg. ὁ ἡ τό the, this, that, he, she, it
Χριστοῦ n. gen. masc. sg. Χριστός Christ
οὗτος demo. pron. nom. masc. sg. οὗτος αὕτη τοῦτο this, the same, this same, he, she, it
καὶ conj. καί and, even, also, but
τὸν art. acc. masc. sg. ὁ ἡ τό the, this, that, he, she, it
πατέρα n. acc. masc. sg. πατήρ Father, father, parent
καὶ conj. καί and, even, also, but
τὸν art. acc. masc. sg. ὁ ἡ τό the, this, that, he, she, it
υἱὸν n. acc. masc. sg. υἱός son, child, descendant, offspring, heir
10 εἴ conj. εἰ if, whether, that, though, forasmuch
τις indefinite pron. nom. masc. sg. τὶς certain, some, any man, one, any thing
πρὸς prep. πρός (+gen) for, (+dat) at, (+acc) unto, to, with, for, against
ὑμᾶς pron. acc. 2p. pl. σύ thou, you
καὶ conj. καί and, even, also, but
ταύτην demo. pron. acc. fem. sg. οὗτος αὕτη τοῦτο this, the same, this same, he, she, it
τὴν art. acc. fem. sg. ὁ ἡ τό the, this, that, he, she, it
διδαχὴν n. acc. fem. sg. διδαχή doctrine, teaching
οὐ particle of negation. οὐ οὐκ οὐχ not, no, neither, none, nay, nor, never, nothing

μὴ particle of negation. μή not, no, lest, neither, none, nothing, nor, never, without
αὐτὸν pron. acc. masc. 3p. sg. αὐτός ή ό self, of oneself, even, very, the same, he, she, it
εἰς prep. εἰς (+acc) into, to, unto, for, in, on, toward, against, upon, at, among
οἰκίαν n. acc. fem. sg. οἰκία house, home, household
καὶ conj. καί and, even, also, but
αὐτῷ pron. dat. masc. 3p. sg. αὐτός ή ό self, of oneself, even, very, the same, he, she, it
μὴ particle of negation. μή not, no, lest, neither, none, nothing, nor, never, without
11 ὁ art. nom. masc. sg. ὁ ἡ τό the, this, that, he, she, it
γὰρ conj. γάρ for, and, because, but, indeed
αὐτῷ pron. dat. masc. 3p. sg. αὐτός ή ό self, of oneself, even, very, the same, he, she, it
τοῖς art. dat. neut. pl. ὁ ἡ τό the, this, that, he, she, it
ἔργοις n. dat. neut. pl. ἔργον work, deed, doing labour
αὐτοῦ pron. gen. masc. 3p. sg. αὐτός ή ό self, of oneself, even, very, the same, he, she, it
τοῖς art. dat. neut. pl. ὁ ἡ τό the, this, that, he, she, it
πονηροῖς adj. dat. neut. pl. πονηρός evil, wicked, bad
12 Πολλὰ adj. acc. neut. pl. πολύς many, great, much, long, abundant
ὑμῖν pron. dat. 2p. pl. σύ thou, you
οὐκ particle of negation. οὐ οὐκ οὐχ not, no, neither, none, nay, nor, never, nothing
διὰ prep. διά (+gen) by, through, with, in, of, (+acc) for, because of, for a cause
χάρτου n. gen. masc. sg. χάρτης paper
καὶ conj. καί and, even, also, but
μέλανος adj. gen. neut. sg. μέλας black
ἀλλὰ conj. ἀλλά but, yea, yet, nevertheless, howbeit, nay, therefore
πρὸς prep. πρός (+gen) for, (+dat) at, (+acc) unto, to, with, for, against
ὑμᾶς pron. acc. 2p. pl. σύ thou, you
καὶ conj. καί and, even, also, but
στόμα n. acc. neut. sg. στόμα mouth, face, edge
πρὸς prep. πρός (+gen) for, (+dat) at, (+acc) unto, to, with, for, against
στόμα n. acc. neut. sg. στόμα mouth, face, edge
ἵνα conj. ἵνα that, to, lest, for to, so that, albeit, because, for, so as
ἡ art. nom. fem. sg. ὁ ἡ τό the, this, that, he, she, it
χαρὰ n. nom. fem. sg. χαρά joy, gladness, joyfulness
ἡμῶν pron. gen. 1p. pl. ἐγώ I
13 σε pron. acc. 2p. sg. σύ thou, you
τὰ art. nom. neut. pl. ὁ ἡ τό the, this, that, he, she, it
τέκνα n. nom. neut. pl. τέκνον child, son, daughter
τῆς art. gen. fem. sg. ὁ ἡ τό the, this, that, he, she, it
ἀδελφῆς n. gen. fem. sg. ἀδελφή sister
σου pron. gen. 2p. sg. σύ thou, you
τῆς art. gen. fem. sg. ὁ ἡ τό the, this, that, he, she, it
ἐκλεκτῆς adj. gen. fem. sg. ἐκλεκτός elect, chosen
ἀμήν particle. ἀμήν amen, verily

ΙΩΑΝΝΟΥ
ΕΠΙΣΤΟΛΗ ΤΡΙΤΗ

1

1 Ὁ art. nom. masc. sg. ὁ ἡ τό the, this, that, he, she, it
πρεσβύτερος adj. nom. masc. sg. πρεσβύτερος elder, elder woman, eldest, old man
Γαΐῳ n. dat. masc. sg. Γάϊος Gaius
τῷ art. dat. masc. sg. ὁ ἡ τό the, this, that, he, she, it
ἀγαπητῷ adj. dat. masc. sg. ἀγαπητός beloved, dearly beloved, dear, wellbeloved
ὃν relative pron. acc. masc. sg. ὅς ἥ ὅ who, which, what, that
ἐγὼ pron. nom. 1p. sg. ἐγώ I
ἐν prep. ἐν (+dat) in, by, with, among, at, on, through, to, within, into, of, for
ἀληθείᾳ n. dat. fem. sg. ἀλήθεια truth, verity
2 Ἀγαπητέ adj. voc. masc. sg. ἀγαπητός beloved, dearly beloved, dear, wellbeloved
περὶ prep. περί (+gen) of, for, concerning, (+acc) about, concerning, in
πάντων adj. gen. neut. pl. πᾶς πᾶσα πᾶν all, every, whosoever, every one, no, whole, any
σε pron. acc. 2p. sg. σύ thou, you
καὶ conj. καί and, even, also, but
καθὼς adv. καθώς as, even as, according as, according to
σου pron. gen. 2p. sg. σύ thou, you
ἡ art. nom. fem. sg. ὁ ἡ τό the, this, that, he, she, it
ψυχή n. nom. fem. sg. ψυχή life, soul, mind, heart
3 γὰρ conj. γάρ for, and, because, but, indeed
λίαν adv. λίαν exceeding, greatly, very, great sore
ἀδελφῶν n. gen. masc. pl. ἀδελφός brother
καὶ conj. καί and, even, also, but
σου pron. gen. 2p. sg. σύ thou, you
τῇ art. dat. fem. sg. ὁ ἡ τό the, this, that, he, she, it
ἀληθείᾳ n. dat. fem. sg. ἀλήθεια truth, verity
καθὼς adv. καθώς as, even as, according as, according to
σὺ pron. nom. 2p. sg. σύ thou, you
ἐν prep. ἐν (+dat) in, by, with, among, at, on, through, to, within, into, of, for
ἀληθείᾳ n. dat. fem. sg. ἀλήθεια truth, verity
4 μειζοτέραν compar. adj. acc. fem. sg. μέγας great, loud, greatest, high, large, mighty, strong
τούτων demo. pron. gen. neut. pl. οὗτος αὕτη τοῦτο this, the same, this same, he, she, it
οὐκ particle of negation. οὐ οὐκ οὐχ not, no, neither, none, nay, nor, never, nothing
χαράν n. acc. fem. sg. χαρά joy, gladness, joyfulness
ἵνα conj. ἵνα that, to, lest, for to, so that, albeit, because, for, so as
τὰ art. acc. neut. pl. ὁ ἡ τό the, this, that, he, she, it
ἐμὰ poss. pron. acc. neut. 1p. pl. ἐμός my, mine, mine own, of me
τέκνα n. acc. neut. pl. τέκνον child, son, daughter
ἐν prep. ἐν (+dat) in, by, with, among, at, on, through, to, within, into, of, for
ἀληθείᾳ n. dat. fem. sg. ἀλήθεια truth, verity
5 Ἀγαπητέ adj. voc. masc. sg. ἀγαπητός beloved, dearly beloved, dear, wellbeloved
πιστὸν adj. acc. neut. sg. πιστός faithful, believing, true, sure
ὃ relative pron. acc. neut. sg. ὅς ἥ ὅ who, which, what, that
ἐὰν conj. ἐάν if, soever, except, though, and if, but, whether, if so, so
εἰς prep. εἰς (+acc) into, to, unto, for, in, on, toward, against, upon, at, among
τοὺς art. acc. masc. pl. ὁ ἡ τό the, this, that, he, she, it
ἀδελφοὺς n. acc. masc. pl. ἀδελφός brother
καὶ conj. καί and, even, also, but
εἰς prep. εἰς (+acc) into, to, unto, for, in, on, toward, against, upon, at, among
τοὺς art. acc. masc. pl. ὁ ἡ τό the, this, that, he, she, it

ξένους adj. acc. masc. pl. ξένος stranger, strange, host
6 οἳ relative pron. nom. masc. pl. ὅς ἥ ὅ who, which, what, that
σου pron. gen. 2p. sg. σύ thou, you
τῇ art. dat. fem. sg. ὁ ἡ τό the, this, that, he, she, it
ἀγάπῃ n. dat. fem. sg. ἀγάπη love, charity, feast of charity
ἐνώπιον prep. ἐνώπιον (+gen) before, in the sight of, in the presence of. (adv.) before
ἐκκλησίας n. gen. fem. sg. ἐκκλησία church, assembly
οὓς relative pron. acc. masc. pl. ὅς ἥ ὅ who, which, what, that
καλῶς adv. καλῶς good, well, full well
ἀξίως adv. ἀξίως worthy, as become, after a godly sort
τοῦ art. gen. masc. sg. ὁ ἡ τό the, this, that, he, she, it
Θεοῦ n. gen. masc. sg. θεός God, god
7 ὑπὲρ prep. ὑπέρ (+gen) for, of, for the sake of, (+acc) above, more than
γὰρ conj. γάρ for, and, because, but, indeed
τοῦ art. gen. neut. sg. ὁ ἡ τό the, this, that, he, she, it
ὀνόματος n. gen. neut. sg. ὄνομα name, call, surname
αὐτοῦ pron. gen. masc. 3p. sg. αὐτός ή ό self, of oneself, even, very, the same, he, she, it
μηδὲν num. acc. neut. sg. μηδείς μηδεμία μηδέν no man, nothing, no, none, not at all
ἀπὸ prep. ἀπό (+gen) from, of, out of, since, for, off, at, by, in, on
τῶν art. gen. masc. pl. ὁ ἡ τό the, this, that, he, she, it
ἐθνῶν n. gen. neut. pl. ἔθνος Gentile, nation, heathen, people
8 ἡμεῖς pron. nom. 1p. pl. ἐγώ I
οὖν conj. οὖν therefore, then, so, and, now, wherefore
τοὺς art. acc. masc. pl. ὁ ἡ τό the, this, that, he, she, it
τοιούτους demo. pron. acc. masc. pl. τοιοῦτος such, like
ἵνα conj. ἵνα that, to, lest, for to, so that, albeit, because, for, so as
συνεργοὶ adj. nom. masc. pl. συνεργός fellowlabourer, fellowhelper, fellowworker
τῇ art. dat. fem. sg. ὁ ἡ τό the, this, that, he, she, it
ἀληθείᾳ n. dat. fem. sg. ἀλήθεια truth, verity
9 τῇ art. dat. fem. sg. ὁ ἡ τό the, this, that, he, she, it
ἐκκλησίᾳ n. dat. fem. sg. ἐκκλησία church, assembly
ἀλλ' conj. ἀλλά but, yea, yet, nevertheless, howbeit, nay, therefore
ὁ art. nom. masc. sg. ὁ ἡ τό the, this, that, he, she, it
αὐτῶν pron. gen. masc. 3p. pl. αὐτός ή ό self, of oneself, even, very, the same, he, she, it
Διοτρέφης n. nom. masc. sg. Διοτρέφης Diotrephes
οὐκ particle of negation. οὐ οὐκ οὐχ not, no, neither, none, nay, nor, never, nothing
ἡμᾶς pron. acc. 1p. pl. ἐγώ I
10 διὰ prep. διά (+gen) by, through, with, in, of, (+acc) for, because of, for a cause
τοῦτο demo. pron. acc. neut. sg. οὗτος αὕτη τοῦτο this, the same, this same, he, she, it
ἐὰν conj. ἐάν if, soever, except, though, and if, but, whether, if so, so
αὐτοῦ pron. gen. masc. 3p. sg. αὐτός ή ό self, of oneself, even, very, the same, he, she, it
τὰ art. acc. neut. pl. ὁ ἡ τό the, this, that, he, she, it
ἔργα n. acc. neut. pl. ἔργον work, deed, doing labour
ἃ relative pron. acc. neut. pl. ὅς ἥ ὅ who, which, what, that
λόγοις n. dat. masc. pl. λόγος word, saying, account, speech, thing, matter
πονηροῖς adj. dat. masc. pl. πονηρός evil, wicked, bad
ἡμᾶς pron. acc. 1p. pl. ἐγώ I
καὶ conj. καί and, even, also, but
μὴ particle of negation. μή not, no, lest, neither, none, nothing, nor, never, without
ἐπὶ prep. ἐπί (+gen) on, in, upon, (+dat) in, at, for, upon, (+acc) on, upon, unto, to, against
τούτοις demo. pron. dat. masc. pl. οὗτος αὕτη τοῦτο this, the same, this same, he, she, it
οὔτε conj. οὔτε neither, nor, nor yet, no, none
αὐτὸς pron. nom. masc. 3p. sg. αὐτός ή ό self, of oneself, even, very, the same, he, she, it
τοὺς art. acc. masc. pl. ὁ ἡ τό the, this, that, he, she, it
ἀδελφοὺς n. acc. masc. pl. ἀδελφός brother

καὶ conj. καί and, even, also, but
τοὺς art. acc. masc. pl. ὁ ἡ τό the, this, that, he, she, it
καὶ conj. καί and, even, also, but
ἐκ prep. ἐκ ἐξ (+gen) of, from, out of, by, on, with, in, among, through
τῆς art. gen. fem. sg. ὁ ἡ τό the, this, that, he, she, it
ἐκκλησίας n. gen. fem. sg. ἐκκλησία church, assembly
11 ἀγαπητέ adj. voc. masc. sg. ἀγαπητός beloved, dearly beloved, dear, wellbeloved
μὴ particle of negation. μή not, no, lest, neither, none, nothing, nor, never, without
τὸ art. acc. neut. sg. ὁ ἡ τό the, this, that, he, she, it
κακὸν adj. acc. neut. sg. κακός evil, evil thing, noisome, wicked
ἀλλὰ conj. ἀλλά but, yea, yet, nevertheless, howbeit, nay, therefore
τὸ art. acc. neut. sg. ὁ ἡ τό the, this, that, he, she, it
ἀγαθόν adj. acc. neut. sg. ἀγαθός good, good thing, that which is good, well
ὁ art. nom. masc. sg. ὁ ἡ τό the, this, that, he, she, it
ἐκ prep. ἐκ ἐξ (+gen) of, from, out of, by, on, with, in, among, through
τοῦ art. gen. masc. sg. ὁ ἡ τό the, this, that, he, she, it
Θεοῦ n. gen. masc. sg. θεός God, god
ὁ art. nom. masc. sg. ὁ ἡ τό the, this, that, he, she, it
δὲ conj. δέ but, and, now, also, to the contrary, rather, then
οὐχ particle of negation. οὐ οὐκ οὐχ not, no, neither, none, nay, nor, never, nothing
τὸν art. acc. masc. sg. ὁ ἡ τό the, this, that, he, she, it
Θεόν n. acc. masc. sg. θεός God, god
12 Δημητρίῳ n. dat. masc. sg. Δημήτριος Demetrius
ὑπὸ prep. ὑπό (+gen) of, by, with, from, among, (+acc) under
πάντων adj. gen. masc. pl. πᾶς πᾶσα πᾶν all, every, whosoever, every one, no, whole, any
καὶ conj. καί and, even, also, but
ὑπ' prep. ὑπό (+gen) of, by, with, from, among, (+acc) under
αὐτῆς pron. gen. fem. 3p. sg. αὐτός ή ό self, of oneself, even, very, the same, he, she, it
τῆς art. gen. fem. sg. ὁ ἡ τό the, this, that, he, she, it
ἀληθείας n. gen. fem. sg. ἀλήθεια truth, verity
καὶ conj. καί and, even, also, but
ἡμεῖς pron. nom. 1p. pl. ἐγώ I
δὲ conj. δέ but, and, now, also, to the contrary, rather, then
καὶ conj. καί and, even, also, but
ὅτι conj. ὅτι that, for, because, how that, how, because that, for that, though
ἡ art. nom. fem. sg. ὁ ἡ τό the, this, that, he, she, it
μαρτυρία n. nom. fem. sg. μαρτυρία testimony, witness, record, report
ἡμῶν pron. gen. 1p. pl. ἐγώ I
ἀληθής adj. nom. fem. sg. ἀληθής true, truly, truth
13 Πολλὰ adj. acc. neut. pl. πολύς many, great, much, long, abundant
ἀλλ' conj. ἀλλά but, yea, yet, nevertheless, howbeit, nay, therefore
οὐ particle of negation. οὐ οὐκ οὐχ not, no, neither, none, nay, nor, never, nothing
διὰ prep. διά (+gen) by, through, with, in, of, (+acc) for, because of, for a cause
μέλανος adj. gen. neut. sg. μέλας black
καὶ conj. καί and, even, also, but
καλάμου adj. gen. masc. sg. κάλαμος reed, pen
σοι pron. dat. 2p. sg. σύ thou, you
14 δὲ conj. δέ but, and, now, also, to the contrary, rather, then
εὐθέως adv. εὐθέως immediately, straightway, forthwith, as soon as, by and by, shortly
σε pron. acc. 2p. sg. σύ thou, you
καὶ conj. καί and, even, also, but
στόμα n. nom. neut. sg. στόμα mouth, face, edge
πρὸς prep. πρός (+gen) for, (+dat) at, (+acc) unto, to, with, for, against
στόμα n. nom. neut. sg. στόμα mouth, face, edge
εἰρήνη n. nom. fem. sg. εἰρήνη peace, quietness, rest

σοι pron. dat. 2p. sg. σύ thou, you
σε pron. acc. 2p. sg. σύ thou, you
οἱ art. nom. masc. pl. ὁ ἡ τό the, this, that, he, she, it
φίλοι adj. nom. masc. pl. φίλος friend
τοὺς art. acc. masc. pl. ὁ ἡ τό the, this, that, he, she, it
φίλους adj. acc. masc. pl. φίλος friend
κατ' prep. κατά (+gen) against, by, throughout, down, (+acc) according to, after, with
ὄνομα n. acc. neut. sg. ὄνομα name, call, surname

ΙΟΥΔΑ
ΕΠΙΣΤΟΛΗ ΚΑΘΟΛΙΚΗ

1 Ἰούδας n. nom. masc. sg. Ἰούδας Judas, Juda, Judah, Jude
Ἰησοῦ n. gen. masc. sg. Ἰησοῦς Jesus
Χριστοῦ n. gen. masc. sg. Χριστός Christ
δοῦλος n. nom. masc. sg. δοῦλος servant, bondman, bond, slave
ἀδελφὸς n. nom. masc. sg. ἀδελφός brother
δὲ conj. δέ but, and, now, also, to the contrary, rather, then
Ἰακώβου n. gen. masc. sg. Ἰάκωβος James
τοῖς art. dat. masc. pl. ὁ ἡ τό the, this, that, he, she, it
ἐν prep. ἐν (+dat) in, by, with, among, at, on, through, to, within, into, of, for
Θεῷ n. dat. masc. sg. θεός God, god
πατρὶ n. dat. masc. sg. πατήρ Father, father, parent
καὶ conj. καί and, even, also, but
Ἰησοῦ n. dat. masc. sg. Ἰησοῦς Jesus
Χριστῷ n. dat. masc. sg. Χριστός Christ
κλητοῖς adj. dat. masc. pl. κλητός called
2 ἔλεος n. nom. neut. sg. ἔλεος mercy
ὑμῖν pron. dat. 2p. pl. σύ thou, you
καὶ conj. καί and, even, also, but
εἰρήνη n. nom. fem. sg. εἰρήνη peace, quietness, rest
καὶ conj. καί and, even, also, but
ἀγάπη n. nom. fem. sg. ἀγάπη love, charity, feast of charity
3 Ἀγαπητοί adj. voc. masc. pl. ἀγαπητός beloved, dearly beloved, dear, wellbeloved
πᾶσαν adj. acc. fem. sg. πᾶς πᾶσα πᾶν all, every, whosoever, every one, no, whole, any
σπουδὴν n. acc. fem. sg. σπουδή diligence, haste, business, care, carefulness
ὑμῖν pron. dat. 2p. pl. σύ thou, you
περὶ prep. περί (+gen) of, for, concerning, (+acc) about, concerning, in
τῆς art. gen. fem. sg. ὁ ἡ τό the, this, that, he, she, it
κοινῆς adj. gen. fem. sg. κοινός common, unclean, defiled, unholy
σωτηρίας n. gen. fem. sg. σωτηρία salvation, deliver, health, saving
ἀνάγκην n. acc. fem. sg. ἀνάγκη must needs, necessity, distress, inevitable
ὑμῖν pron. dat. 2p. pl. σύ thou, you
τῇ art. dat. fem. sg. ὁ ἡ τό the, this, that, he, she, it
ἅπαξ adv. ἅπαξ once
τοῖς art. dat. masc. pl. ὁ ἡ τό the, this, that, he, she, it
ἁγίοις adj. dat. masc. pl. ἅγιος Holy, holy, saint, Holy One, holy thing, most holy
πίστει n. dat. fem. sg. πίστις faith, assurance, belief, fidelity
4 γάρ conj. γάρ for, and, because, but, indeed
τινες indefinite pron. nom. masc. pl. τὶς certain, some, any man, one, any thing
ἄνθρωποι n. nom. masc. pl. ἄνθρωπος man, human being, person, one, certain
οἱ art. nom. masc. pl. ὁ ἡ τό the, this, that, he, she, it
πάλαι adv. πάλαι long age, a great while ago, any while, in time past, old, of old
εἰς prep. εἰς (+acc) into, to, unto, for, in, on, toward, against, upon, at, among
τοῦτο demo. pron. acc. neut. sg. οὗτος αὕτη τοῦτο this, the same, this same, he, she, it
τὸ art. acc. neut. sg. ὁ ἡ τό the, this, that, he, she, it
κρίμα n. acc. neut. sg. κρίμα judgment, damnation, condemnation
ἀσεβεῖς adj. nom. masc. pl. ἀσεβής ungodly, ungodly man
τὴν art. acc. fem. sg. ὁ ἡ τό the, this, that, he, she, it
τοῦ art. gen. masc. sg. ὁ ἡ τό the, this, that, he, she, it
Θεοῦ n. gen. masc. sg. θεός God, god
ἡμῶν pron. gen. 1p. pl. ἐγώ I

χάριν n. acc. fem. sg. χάρις grace, thank, favour, pleasure
εἰς prep. εἰς (+acc) into, to, unto, for, in, on, toward, against, upon, at, among
ἀσέλγειαν n. acc. fem. sg. ἀσέλγεια lasciviousness, wantonness, filthy
καὶ conj. καί and, even, also, but
τὸν art. acc. masc. sg. ὁ ἡ τό the, this, that, he, she, it
μόνον adj. acc. masc. sg. μόνος only, alone, by oneself
δεσπότην n. acc. masc. sg. δεσπότης Lord, master
Θεόν n. acc. masc. sg. θεός God, god
καὶ conj. καί and, even, also, but
Κύριον n. acc. masc. sg. κύριος Lord, lord, master, sir, LORD, God, Master, owner
ἡμῶν pron. gen. 1p. pl. ἐγώ I
Ἰησοῦν n. acc. masc. sg. Ἰησοῦς Jesus
Χριστὸν n. acc. masc. sg. Χριστός Christ
5 δὲ conj. δέ but, and, now, also, to the contrary, rather, then
ὑμᾶς pron. acc. 2p. pl. σύ thou, you
ὑμᾶς pron. acc. 2p. pl. σύ thou, you
ἅπαξ adv. ἅπαξ once
τοῦτο demo. pron. acc. neut. sg. οὗτος αὕτη τοῦτο this, the same, this same, he, she, it
ὅτι conj. ὅτι that, for, because, how that, how, because that, for that, though
ὁ art. nom. masc. sg. ὁ ἡ τό the, this, that, he, she, it
Κύριος n. nom. masc. sg. κύριος Lord, lord, master, sir, LORD, God, Master, owner
λαὸν n. acc. masc. sg. λαός people
ἐκ prep. ἐκ ἐξ (+gen) of, from, out of, by, on, with, in, among, through
γῆς n. gen. fem. sg. γῆ earth, land, ground, country
Αἰγύπτου n. gen. fem. sg. Αἴγυπτος Egypt
τὸ art. acc. neut. sg. ὁ ἡ τό the, this, that, he, she, it
δεύτερον ordinal. adj. acc. neut. sg. δεύτερος second, second time, again, afterward
τοὺς art. acc. masc. pl. ὁ ἡ τό the, this, that, he, she, it
μὴ particle of negation. μή not, no, lest, neither, none, nothing, nor, never, without
6 ἀγγέλους n. acc. masc. pl. ἄγγελος angel, messenger
τε conj. τέ and, both, also
τοὺς art. acc. masc. pl. ὁ ἡ τό the, this, that, he, she, it
μὴ particle of negation. μή not, no, lest, neither, none, nothing, nor, never, without
τὴν art. acc. fem. sg. ὁ ἡ τό the, this, that, he, she, it
ἑαυτῶν reflexive pron. gen. masc. 3p. pl. ἑαυτοῦ himself, herself, itself, yourself, ourselves
ἀρχὴν n. acc. fem. sg. ἀρχή beginning, principality, corner, first, magistrate, rule
ἀλλὰ conj. ἀλλά but, yea, yet, nevertheless, howbeit, nay, therefore
τὸ art. acc. neut. sg. ὁ ἡ τό the, this, that, he, she, it
ἴδιον adj. acc. neut. sg. ἴδιος one's own, one's, privately
οἰκητήριον n. acc. neut. sg. οἰκητήριον house, habitation
εἰς prep. εἰς (+acc) into, to, unto, for, in, on, toward, against, upon, at, among
κρίσιν n. acc. fem. sg. κρίσις judgment, damnation, accusation, condemnation
μεγάλης adj. gen. fem. sg. μέγας great, loud, greatest, high, large, mighty, strong
ἡμέρας n. gen. fem. sg. ἡμέρα day, time, year, while, age, day time
δεσμοῖς n. dat. masc. pl. δεσμός bond, band, chain, string
ἀϊδίοις adj. dat. neut. pl. ἀΐδιος eternal, everlasting
ὑπὸ prep. ὑπό (+gen) of, by, with, from, among, (+acc) under
ζόφον n. acc. masc. sg. ζόφος darkness, blackness, mist
7 ὡς adv. ὡς as, when, as it were, how, about, like, as soon as, even as, while
Σόδομα n. nom. neut. pl. Σόδομα Sodom, Sodoma
καὶ conj. καί and, even, also, but
Γόμορρα n. nom. fem. sg. Γόμορρα Gomorrha
καὶ conj. καί and, even, also, but
αἱ art. nom. fem. pl. ὁ ἡ τό the, this, that, he, she, it
περὶ prep. περί (+gen) of, for, concerning, (+acc) about, concerning, in

αὐτὰς pron. acc. fem. 3p. pl. αὐτός ἡ ὁ self, of oneself, even, very, the same, he, she, it
πόλεις n. nom. fem. pl. πόλις city
τὸν art. acc. masc. sg. ὁ ἡ τό the, this, that, he, she, it
ὅμοιον adj. acc. masc. sg. ὅμοιος like
τούτοις demo. pron. dat. masc. pl. οὗτος αὕτη τοῦτο this, the same, this same, he, she, it
τρόπον n. acc. masc. sg. τρόπος as, manner, means, way, conversation
καὶ conj. καί and, even, also, but
ὀπίσω prep. ὀπίσω (+gen) after. (adv.) back, behind
σαρκὸς n. gen. fem. sg. σάρξ flesh, carnal
ἑτέρας adj. gen. fem. sg. ἕτερος another, other, else, strange
δεῖγμα n. acc. neut. sg. δεῖγμα example
πυρὸς n. gen. neut. sg. πῦρ fire, fiery
αἰωνίου adj. gen. neut. sg. αἰώνιος eternal, everlasting, world, for ever
δίκην n. acc. fem. sg. δίκη judgment, vengeance, punish
8 ὁμοίως adv. ὁμοίως likewise, so
μέντοι conj. μέντοι yet, nevertheless, but, howbeit, likewise
καὶ conj. καί and, even, also, but
οὗτοι demo. pron. nom. masc. pl. οὗτος αὕτη τοῦτο this, the same, this same, he, she, it
σάρκα n. acc. fem. sg. σάρξ flesh, carnal
μὲν conj. μέν indeed, verily, truly, even, so, some
κυριότητα n. acc. fem. sg. κυριότης dominion, government
δὲ conj. δέ but, and, now, also, to the contrary, rather, then
δόξας n. acc. fem. pl. δόξα glory, honour, praise, dignity, worship
δὲ conj. δέ but, and, now, also, to the contrary, rather, then
9 ὁ art. nom. masc. sg. ὁ ἡ τό the, this, that, he, she, it
δὲ conj. δέ but, and, now, also, to the contrary, rather, then
Μιχαὴλ n. nom. masc. sg. Μιχαήλ Michael
ἀρχάγγελος n. nom. masc. sg. ἀρχάγγελος archangel
ὅτε adv. ὅτε when, after that, as soon as, while, after
τῷ art. dat. masc. sg. ὁ ἡ τό the, this, that, he, she, it
διαβόλῳ adj. dat. masc. sg. διάβολος devil, false accuser, Devil, slanderer
περὶ prep. περί (+gen) of, for, concerning, (+acc) about, concerning, in
τοῦ art. gen. neut. sg. ὁ ἡ τό the, this, that, he, she, it
Μωσέως n. gen. masc. sg. Μωσῆς Moses
σώματος n. gen. neut. sg. σῶμα body, bodily, slave
οὐκ particle of negation. οὐ οὐκ οὐχ not, no, neither, none, nay, nor, never, nothing
κρίσιν n. acc. fem. sg. κρίσις judgment, damnation, accusation, condemnation
βλασφημίας n. gen. fem. sg. βλασφημία blasphemy, railing, evil speaking
ἀλλ' conj. ἀλλά but, yea, yet, nevertheless, howbeit, nay, therefore
σοι pron. dat. 2p. sg. σύ thou, you
Κύριος n. nom. masc. sg. κύριος Lord, lord, master, sir, LORD, God, Master, owner
10 οὗτοι demo. pron. nom. masc. pl. οὗτος αὕτη τοῦτο this, the same, this same, he, she, it
δὲ conj. δέ but, and, now, also, to the contrary, rather, then
ὅσα relative pron. acc. neut. pl. ὅσος as many as, whatsoever, that, as long as, how much
μὲν conj. μέν indeed, verily, truly, even, so, some
οὐκ particle of negation. οὐ οὐκ οὐχ not, no, neither, none, nay, nor, never, nothing
ὅσα relative pron. acc. neut. pl. ὅσος as many as, whatsoever, that, as long as, how much
δὲ conj. δέ but, and, now, also, to the contrary, rather, then
φυσικῶς adv. φυσικῶς naturally
ὡς adv. ὡς as, when, as it were, how, about, like, as soon as, even as, while
τὰ art. nom. neut. pl. ὁ ἡ τό the, this, that, he, she, it
ἄλογα adj. nom. neut. pl. ἄλογος unreasonable, brute
ζῷα n. nom. neut. pl. ζῷον beast
ἐν prep. ἐν (+dat) in, by, with, among, at, on, through, to, within, into, of, for
τούτοις demo. pron. dat. neut. pl. οὗτος αὕτη τοῦτο this, the same, this same, he, she, it

11 οὐαὶ particle. οὐαί woe, alas
αὐτοῖς pron. dat. masc. 3p. pl. αὐτός ή ό self, of oneself, even, very, the same, he, she, it
ὅτι conj. ὅτι that, for, because, how that, how, because that, for that, though
τῇ art. dat. fem. sg. ὁ ἡ τό the, this, that, he, she, it
ὁδῷ n. dat. fem. sg. ὁδός way, journey, highway
τοῦ art. gen. masc. sg. ὁ ἡ τό the, this, that, he, she, it
Κάϊν n. gen. masc. sg. Κάϊν Cain
καὶ conj. καί and, even, also, but
τῇ art. dat. fem. sg. ὁ ἡ τό the, this, that, he, she, it
πλάνῃ n. dat. fem. sg. πλάνη error, deception, deceit, delusion
τοῦ art. gen. masc. sg. ὁ ἡ τό the, this, that, he, she, it
Βαλαὰμ n. gen. masc. sg. Βαλαάμ Balaam
μισθοῦ n. gen. masc. sg. μισθός reward, hire, wage
καὶ conj. καί and, even, also, but
τῇ art. dat. fem. sg. ὁ ἡ τό the, this, that, he, she, it
ἀντιλογίᾳ n. dat. fem. sg. ἀντιλογία strife, contradiction, gainsaying
τοῦ art. gen. masc. sg. ὁ ἡ τό the, this, that, he, she, it
Κόρε n. gen. masc. sg. Κόρε Core, Korah
12 οὗτοί demo. pron. nom. masc. pl. οὗτος αὕτη τοῦτο this, the same, this same, he, she, it
ἐν prep. ἐν (+dat) in, by, with, among, at, on, through, to, within, into, of, for
ταῖς art. dat. fem. pl. ὁ ἡ τό the, this, that, he, she, it
ἀγάπαις n. dat. fem. pl. ἀγάπη love, charity, feast of charity
ὑμῶν pron. gen. 2p. pl. σύ thou, you
σπιλάδες n. nom. fem. pl. σπιλάς spot
ὑμῖν pron. dat. 2p. pl. σύ thou, you
ἀφόβως adv. ἀφόβως without fear
ἑαυτοὺς reflexive pron. acc. masc. 3p. pl. ἑαυτοῦ himself, herself, itself, yourself, ourselves
νεφέλαι n. nom. fem. pl. νεφέλη cloud
ἄνυδροι adj. nom. fem. pl. ἄνυδρος dry, without water
ὑπὸ prep. ὑπό (+gen) of, by, with, from, among, (+acc) under
ἀνέμων n. gen. masc. pl. ἄνεμος wind
δένδρα n. nom. neut. pl. δένδρον tree
φθινοπωρινὰ adj. nom. neut. pl. φθινοπωρινός whose fruit withereth
ἄκαρπα adj. nom. neut. pl. ἄκαρπος unfruitful, without fruit
δὶς adv. δίς twice, again
13 κύματα n. nom. neut. pl. κῦμα wave
ἄγρια adj. nom. neut. pl. ἄγριος wild, raging
θαλάσσης n. gen. fem. sg. θάλασσα sea
τὰς art. acc. fem. pl. ὁ ἡ τό the, this, that, he, she, it
ἑαυτῶν reflexive pron. gen. masc. 3p. pl. ἑαυτοῦ himself, herself, itself, yourself, ourselves
αἰσχύνας n. acc. fem. pl. αἰσχύνη shame, dishonesty
ἀστέρες n. nom. masc. pl. ἀστήρ star
πλανῆται adj. nom. masc. pl. πλανήτης wandering
οἷς relative pron. dat. masc. pl. ὅς ἥ ὅ who, which, what, that
ὁ art. nom. masc. sg. ὁ ἡ τό the, this, that, he, she, it
ζόφος n. nom. masc. sg. ζόφος darkness, blackness, mist
τοῦ art. gen. neut. sg. ὁ ἡ τό the, this, that, he, she, it
σκότους n. gen. neut. sg. σκότος darkness
εἰς prep. εἰς (+acc) into, to, unto, for, in, on, toward, against, upon, at, among
τὸν art. acc. masc. sg. ὁ ἡ τό the, this, that, he, she, it
αἰῶνα n. acc. masc. sg. αἰών ever, ever and ever, evermore, age, eternal, world
14 δὲ conj. δέ but, and, now, also, to the contrary, rather, then
καὶ conj. καί and, even, also, but
τούτοις demo. pron. dat. masc. pl. οὗτος αὕτη τοῦτο this, the same, this same, he, she, it
ἕβδομος ordinal. adj. nom. masc. sg. ἕβδομος seventh

ἀπὸ prep. ἀπό (+gen) from, of, out of, since, for, off, at, by, in, on
Ἀδὰμ n. gen. masc. sg. Ἀδάμ Adam
Ἑνὼχ n. nom. masc. sg. Ἑνώχ Enoch
Κύριος n. nom. masc. sg. κύριος Lord, lord, master, sir, LORD, God, Master, owner
ἐν prep. ἐν (+dat) in, by, with, among, at, on, through, to, within, into, of, for
μυριάσιν n. dat. fem. pl. μυριάς innumerable multitude, myriad, innumerable company
ἁγίαις adj. dat. fem. pl. ἅγιος Holy, holy, saint, Holy One, holy thing, most holy
αὐτοῦ pron. gen. masc. 3p. sg. αὐτός ή ό self, of oneself, even, very, the same, he, she, it
15 κρίσιν n. acc. fem. sg. κρίσις judgment, damnation, accusation, condemnation
κατὰ prep. κατά (+gen) against, by, throughout, down, (+acc) according to, after, with
πάντων adj. gen. masc. pl. πᾶς πᾶσα πᾶν all, every, whosoever, every one, no, whole, any
καὶ conj. καί and, even, also, but
πάντας adj. acc. masc. pl. πᾶς πᾶσα πᾶν all, every, whosoever, every one, no, whole, any
τοὺς art. acc. masc. pl. ὁ ἡ τό the, this, that, he, she, it
ἀσεβεῖς adj. nom. masc. pl. ἀσεβής ungodly, ungodly man
αὐτῶν pron. gen. masc. 3p. pl. αὐτός ή ό self, of oneself, even, very, the same, he, she, it
περὶ prep. περί (+gen) of, for, concerning, (+acc) about, concerning, in
πάντων adj. gen. neut. pl. πᾶς πᾶσα πᾶν all, every, whosoever, every one, no, whole, any
τῶν art. gen. neut. pl. ὁ ἡ τό the, this, that, he, she, it
ἔργων n. gen. neut. pl. ἔργον work, deed, doing labour
ἀσεβείας n. gen. fem. sg. ἀσέβεια ungodliness, ungodly
αὐτῶν pron. gen. masc. 3p. pl. αὐτός ή ό self, of oneself, even, very, the same, he, she, it
ὧν relative pron. gen. neut. pl. ὅς ἥ ὅ who, which, what, that
σκληρῶν adj. gen. neut. pl. σκληρός hard, fierce
καὶ conj. καί and, even, also, but
περὶ prep. περί (+gen) of, for, concerning, (+acc) about, concerning, in
πάντων adj. gen. neut. pl. πᾶς πᾶσα πᾶν all, every, whosoever, every one, no, whole, any
τῶν art. gen. neut. pl. ὁ ἡ τό the, this, that, he, she, it
σκληρῶν adj. gen. neut. pl. σκληρός hard, fierce
ὧν relative pron. gen. neut. pl. ὅς ἥ ὅ who, which, what, that
κατ' prep. κατά (+gen) against, by, throughout, down, (+acc) according to, after, with
αὐτοῦ pron. gen. masc. 3p. sg. αὐτός ή ό self, of oneself, even, very, the same, he, she, it
ἁμαρτωλοὶ adj. nom. masc. pl. ἁμαρτωλός sinner, sinful
ἀσεβεῖς adj. nom. masc. pl. ἀσεβής ungodly, ungodly man
16 οὗτοί demo. pron. nom. masc. pl. οὗτος αὕτη τοῦτο this, the same, this same, he, she, it
γογγυσταὶ n. nom. masc. pl. γογγυστής murmurer
μεμψίμοιροι adj. nom. masc. pl. μεμψίμοιρος complainer
κατὰ prep. κατά (+gen) against, by, throughout, down, (+acc) according to, after, with
τὰς art. acc. fem. pl. ὁ ἡ τό the, this, that, he, she, it
ἐπιθυμίας n. acc. fem. pl. ἐπιθυμία lust, concupiscence, desire
αὐτῶν pron. gen. masc. 3p. pl. αὐτός ή ό self, of oneself, even, very, the same, he, she, it
καὶ conj. καί and, even, also, but
τὸ art. nom. neut. sg. ὁ ἡ τό the, this, that, he, she, it
στόμα n. nom. neut. sg. στόμα mouth, face, edge
αὐτῶν pron. gen. masc. 3p. pl. αὐτός ή ό self, of oneself, even, very, the same, he, she, it
ὑπέρογκα adj. acc. neut. pl. ὑπέρογκος great swelling
πρόσωπα n. acc. neut. pl. πρόσωπον face, presence, person, countenance
ὠφελείας n. gen. fem. sg. ὠφέλεια profit, advantage
χάριν adv. χάριν for a cause, because of, for sake
17 Ὑμεῖς pron. nom. 2p. pl. σύ thou, you
δέ conj. δέ but, and, now, also, to the contrary, rather, then
ἀγαπητοί adj. voc. masc. pl. ἀγαπητός beloved, dearly beloved, dear, wellbeloved
τῶν art. gen. neut. pl. ὁ ἡ τό the, this, that, he, she, it
ῥημάτων n. gen. neut. pl. ῥῆμα word, saying, thing
τῶν art. gen. neut. pl. ὁ ἡ τό the, this, that, he, she, it

ὑπὸ prep. ὑπό (+gen) of, by, with, from, among, (+acc) under
τῶν art. gen. masc. pl. ὁ ἡ τό the, this, that, he, she, it
ἀποστόλων n. gen. masc. pl. ἀπόστολος apostle, messenger, he that is sent
τοῦ art. gen. masc. sg. ὁ ἡ τό the, this, that, he, she, it
Κυρίου n. gen. masc. sg. κύριος Lord, lord, master, sir, LORD, God, Master, owner
ἡμῶν pron. gen. 1p. pl. ἐγώ I
Ἰησοῦ n. gen. masc. sg. Ἰησοῦς Jesus
Χριστοῦ n. gen. masc. sg. Χριστός Christ
18 ὅτι conj. ὅτι that, for, because, how that, how, because that, for that, though
ὑμῖν pron. dat. 2p. pl. σύ thou, you
ὅτι conj. ὅτι that, for, because, how that, how, because that, for that, though
ἐν prep. ἐν (+dat) in, by, with, among, at, on, through, to, within, into, of, for
ἐσχάτῳ adj. dat. masc. sg. ἔσχατος last, lowest, uttermost, uttermost part
χρόνῳ n. dat. masc. sg. χρόνος time, season, space
ἐμπαῖκται n. nom. masc. pl. ἐμπαίκτης scoffer, mocker
κατὰ prep. κατά (+gen) against, by, throughout, down, (+acc) according to, after, with
τὰς art. acc. fem. pl. ὁ ἡ τό the, this, that, he, she, it
ἑαυτῶν reflexive pron. gen. masc. 3p. pl. ἑαυτοῦ himself, herself, itself, yourself, ourselves
ἐπιθυμίας n. acc. fem. pl. ἐπιθυμία lust, concupiscence, desire
τῶν art. gen. fem. pl. ὁ ἡ τό the, this, that, he, she, it
ἀσεβειῶν n. gen. fem. pl. ἀσέβεια ungodliness, ungodly
19 οὗτοί demo. pron. nom. masc. pl. οὗτος αὕτη τοῦτο this, the same, this same, he, she, it
οἱ art. nom. masc. pl. ὁ ἡ τό the, this, that, he, she, it
ἑαυτούς reflexive pron. acc. masc. 3p. pl. ἑαυτοῦ himself, herself, itself, yourself, ourselves
ψυχικοί adj. nom. masc. pl. ψυχικός natural, sensual
Πνεῦμα n. acc. neut. sg. πνεῦμα spirit, Spirit, Ghost, ghost, life. of the spirit, wind
μὴ particle of negation. μή not, no, lest, neither, none, nothing, nor, never, without
20 ὑμεῖς pron. nom. 2p. pl. σύ thou, you
δέ conj. δέ but, and, now, also, to the contrary, rather, then
ἀγαπητοί adj. voc. masc. pl. ἀγαπητός beloved, dearly beloved, dear, wellbeloved
τῇ art. dat. fem. sg. ὁ ἡ τό the, this, that, he, she, it
ἁγιωτάτῃ superl. adj. dat. fem. sg. ἅγιος Holy, holy, saint, Holy One, holy thing, most holy
ὑμῶν pron. gen. 2p. pl. σύ thou, you
πίστει n. dat. fem. sg. πίστις faith, assurance, belief, fidelity
ἑαυτοὺς reflexive pron. acc. masc. 3p. pl. ἑαυτοῦ himself, herself, itself, yourself, ourselves
ἐν prep. ἐν (+dat) in, by, with, among, at, on, through, to, within, into, of, for
Πνεύματι n. dat. neut. sg. πνεῦμα spirit, Spirit, Ghost, ghost, life. of the spirit, wind
Ἁγίῳ adj. dat. neut. sg. ἅγιος Holy, holy, saint, Holy One, holy thing, most holy
21 ἑαυτοὺς reflexive pron. acc. masc. 3p. pl. ἑαυτοῦ himself, herself, itself, yourself, ourselves
ἐν prep. ἐν (+dat) in, by, with, among, at, on, through, to, within, into, of, for
ἀγάπῃ n. dat. fem. sg. ἀγάπη love, charity, feast of charity
Θεοῦ n. gen. masc. sg. θεός God, god
τὸ art. acc. neut. sg. ὁ ἡ τό the, this, that, he, she, it
ἔλεος n. acc. neut. sg. ἔλεος mercy
τοῦ art. gen. masc. sg. ὁ ἡ τό the, this, that, he, she, it
Κυρίου n. gen. masc. sg. κύριος Lord, lord, master, sir, LORD, God, Master, owner
ἡμῶν pron. gen. 1p. pl. ἐγώ I
Ἰησοῦ n. gen. masc. sg. Ἰησοῦς Jesus
Χριστοῦ n. gen. masc. sg. Χριστός Christ
εἰς prep. εἰς (+acc) into, to, unto, for, in, on, toward, against, upon, at, among
ζωὴν n. acc. fem. sg. ζωή life, lifetime
αἰώνιον adj. acc. fem. sg. αἰώνιος eternal, everlasting, world, for ever
22 καὶ conj. καί and, even, also, but
οὓς relative pron. acc. masc. pl. ὅς ἥ ὅ who, which, what, that
μὲν conj. μέν indeed, verily, truly, even, so, some

23 οὓς relative pron. acc. masc. pl. ὅς ἥ ὅ who, which, what, that
δὲ conj. δέ but, and, now, also, to the contrary, rather, then
ἐν prep. ἐν (+dat) in, by, with, among, at, on, through, to, within, into, of, for
φόβῳ n. dat. masc. sg. φόβος fear, terror, sore afraid
ἐκ prep. ἐκ ἐξ (+gen) of, from, out of, by, on, with, in, among, through
τοῦ art. gen. neut. sg. ὁ ἡ τό the, this, that, he, she, it
πυρὸς n. gen. neut. sg. πῦρ fire, fiery
καὶ conj. καί and, even, also, but
τὸν art. acc. masc. sg. ὁ ἡ τό the, this, that, he, she, it
ἀπὸ prep. ἀπό (+gen) from, of, out of, since, for, off, at, by, in, on
τῆς art. gen. fem. sg. ὁ ἡ τό the, this, that, he, she, it
σαρκὸς n. gen. fem. sg. σάρξ flesh, carnal
χιτῶνα n. acc. masc. sg. χιτών coat, clothes, garment
24 Τῷ art. dat. masc. sg. ὁ ἡ τό the, this, that, he, she, it
δὲ conj. δέ but, and, now, also, to the contrary, rather, then
ὑμᾶς pron. acc. 2p. pl. σύ thou, you
ἀπταίστους adj. acc. masc. pl. ἄπταιστος from falling
καὶ conj. καί and, even, also, but
κατενώπιον prep. κατενώπιον (+gen) before, before the presence, in the sight, in sight
τῆς art. gen. fem. sg. ὁ ἡ τό the, this, that, he, she, it
δόξης n. gen. fem. sg. δόξα glory, honour, praise, dignity, worship
αὐτοῦ pron. gen. masc. 3p. sg. αὐτός ή ό self, of oneself, even, very, the same, he, she, it
ἀμώμους adj. acc. masc. pl. ἄμωμος without blame, without fault, without spot
ἐν prep. ἐν (+dat) in, by, with, among, at, on, through, to, within, into, of, for
ἀγαλλιάσει n. dat. fem. sg. ἀγαλλίασις gladness, exceeding joy, joy
25 μόνῳ adj. dat. masc. sg. μόνος only, alone, by oneself
σοφῷ adj. dat. masc. sg. σοφός wise, wiser
Θεῷ n. dat. masc. sg. θεός God, god
σωτῆρι n. dat. masc. sg. σωτήρ Saviour, saviour
ἡμῶν pron. gen. 1p. pl. ἐγώ I
δόξα n. nom. fem. sg. δόξα glory, honour, praise, dignity, worship
καὶ conj. καί and, even, also, but
μεγαλωσύνη n. nom. fem. sg. μεγαλωσύνη majesty
κράτος n. nom. neut. sg. κράτος power, dominion, might, strength
καὶ conj. καί and, even, also, but
ἐξουσία n. nom. fem. sg. ἐξουσία power, authority, right, strength, jurisdiction
καὶ conj. καί and, even, also, but
νῦν adv. νῦν now, henceforth, present, this time
καὶ conj. καί and, even, also, but
εἰς prep. εἰς (+acc) into, to, unto, for, in, on, toward, against, upon, at, among
πάντας adj. acc. masc. pl. πᾶς πᾶσα πᾶν all, every, whosoever, every one, no, whole, any
τοὺς art. acc. masc. pl. ὁ ἡ τό the, this, that, he, she, it
αἰῶνας n. acc. masc. pl. αἰών ever, ever and ever, evermore, age, eternal, world
ἀμήν particle. ἀμήν amen, verily

ΑΠΟΚΑΛΥΨΙΣ
ΤΟΥ ΑΓΙΟΥ
ΙΩΑΝΝΟΥ ΤΟΥ ΘΕΟΛΟΓΟΥ

1

1 Ἀποκάλυψις n. nom. fem. sg. ἀποκάλυψις revelation, appearing, coming, manifestation
Ἰησοῦ n. gen. masc. sg. Ἰησοῦς Jesus
Χριστοῦ n. gen. masc. sg. Χριστός Christ
ἣν relative pron. acc. fem. sg. ὅς ἥ ὅ who, which, what, that
αὐτῷ pron. dat. masc. 3p. sg. αὐτός ή ό self, of oneself, even, very, the same, he, she, it
ὁ art. nom. masc. sg. ὁ ἡ τό the, this, that, he, she, it
Θεὸς n. nom. masc. sg. θεός God, god
τοῖς art. dat. masc. pl. ὁ ἡ τό the, this, that, he, she, it
δούλοις n. dat. masc. pl. δοῦλος servant, bondman, bond, slave
αὐτοῦ pron. gen. masc. 3p. sg. αὐτός ή ό self, of oneself, even, very, the same, he, she, it
ἃ relative pron. acc. neut. pl. ὅς ἥ ὅ who, which, what, that
ἐν prep. ἐν (+dat) in, by, with, among, at, on, through, to, within, into, of, for
τάχει n. dat. neut. sg. τάχος speedily, short, quick
καὶ conj. καί and, even, also, but
διὰ prep. διά (+gen) by, through, with, in, of, (+acc) for, because of, for a cause
τοῦ art. gen. masc. sg. ὁ ἡ τό the, this, that, he, she, it
ἀγγέλου n. gen. masc. sg. ἄγγελος angel, messenger
αὐτοῦ pron. gen. masc. 3p. sg. αὐτός ή ό self, of oneself, even, very, the same, he, she, it
τῷ art. dat. masc. sg. ὁ ἡ τό the, this, that, he, she, it
δούλῳ n. dat. masc. sg. δοῦλος servant, bondman, bond, slave
αὐτοῦ pron. gen. masc. 3p. sg. αὐτός ή ό self, of oneself, even, very, the same, he, she, it
Ἰωάννῃ n. dat. masc. sg. Ἰωάννης John
2 ὃς relative pron. nom. masc. sg. ὅς ἥ ὅ who, which, what, that
τὸν art. acc. masc. sg. ὁ ἡ τό the, this, that, he, she, it
λόγον n. acc. masc. sg. λόγος word, saying, account, speech, thing, matter
τοῦ art. gen. masc. sg. ὁ ἡ τό the, this, that, he, she, it
Θεοῦ n. gen. masc. sg. θεός God, god
καὶ conj. καί and, even, also, but
τὴν art. acc. fem. sg. ὁ ἡ τό the, this, that, he, she, it
μαρτυρίαν n. acc. fem. sg. μαρτυρία testimony, witness, record, report
Ἰησοῦ n. gen. masc. sg. Ἰησοῦς Jesus
Χριστοῦ n. gen. masc. sg. Χριστός Christ
ὅσα relative pron. acc. neut. pl. ὅσος as many as, whatsoever, that, as long as, how much
τε conj. τέ and, both, also
3 μακάριος adj. nom. masc. sg. μακάριος blessed, happy
ὁ art. nom. masc. sg. ὁ ἡ τό the, this, that, he, she, it
καὶ conj. καί and, even, also, but
οἱ art. nom. masc. pl. ὁ ἡ τό the, this, that, he, she, it
τοὺς art. acc. masc. pl. ὁ ἡ τό the, this, that, he, she, it
λόγους n. acc. masc. pl. λόγος word, saying, account, speech, thing, matter
τῆς art. gen. fem. sg. ὁ ἡ τό the, this, that, he, she, it
προφητείας n. gen. fem. sg. προφητεία prophecy, prophesying
καὶ conj. καί and, even, also, but
τὰ art. acc. neut. pl. ὁ ἡ τό the, this, that, he, she, it
ἐν prep. ἐν (+dat) in, by, with, among, at, on, through, to, within, into, of, for
αὐτῇ pron. dat. fem. 3p. sg. αὐτός ή ό self, of oneself, even, very, the same, he, she, it
ὁ art. nom. masc. sg. ὁ ἡ τό the, this, that, he, she, it

γὰρ conj. γάρ for, and, because, but, indeed
καιρὸς n. nom. masc. sg. καιρός time, season, due time, opportunity
ἐγγύς adv. ἐγγύς nigh, at hand, near, nigh at hand, ready, nigh unto
4 Ἰωάννης n. nom. masc. sg. Ἰωάννης John
ταῖς art. dat. fem. pl. ὁ ἡ τό the, this, that, he, she, it
ἑπτὰ num. dat. fem. pl. ἑπτά seven, seventh
ἐκκλησίαις n. dat. fem. pl. ἐκκλησία church, assembly
ταῖς art. dat. fem. pl. ὁ ἡ τό the, this, that, he, she, it
ἐν prep. ἐν (+dat) in, by, with, among, at, on, through, to, within, into, of, for
τῇ art. dat. fem. sg. ὁ ἡ τό the, this, that, he, she, it
Ἀσίᾳ n. dat. fem. sg. Ἀσία Asia
χάρις n. nom. fem. sg. χάρις grace, thank, favour, pleasure
ὑμῖν pron. dat. 2p. pl. σύ thou, you
καὶ conj. καί and, even, also, but
εἰρήνη n. nom. fem. sg. εἰρήνη peace, quietness, rest
ἀπὸ prep. ἀπό (+gen) from, of, out of, since, for, off, at, by, in, on
τοῦ art. gen. masc. sg. ὁ ἡ τό the, this, that, he, she, it
ὁ art. nom. masc. sg. ὁ ἡ τό the, this, that, he, she, it
καὶ conj. καί and, even, also, but
ὁ art. nom. masc. sg. ὁ ἡ τό the, this, that, he, she, it
καὶ conj. καί and, even, also, but
ὁ art. nom. masc. sg. ὁ ἡ τό the, this, that, he, she, it
καὶ conj. καί and, even, also, but
ἀπὸ prep. ἀπό (+gen) from, of, out of, since, for, off, at, by, in, on
τῶν art. gen. neut. pl. ὁ ἡ τό the, this, that, he, she, it
ἑπτὰ num. gen. neut. pl. ἑπτά seven, seventh
πνευμάτων n. gen. neut. pl. πνεῦμα spirit, Spirit, Ghost, ghost, life. of the spirit, wind
ἃ relative pron. nom. neut. pl. ὅς ἥ ὅ who, which, what, that
ἐνώπιον prep. ἐνώπιον (+gen) before, in the sight of, in the presence of. (adv.) before
τοῦ art. gen. masc. sg. ὁ ἡ τό the, this, that, he, she, it
θρόνου n. gen. masc. sg. θρόνος throne, seat
αὐτοῦ pron. gen. masc. 3p. sg. αὐτός ή ό self, of oneself, even, very, the same, he, she, it
5 καὶ conj. καί and, even, also, but
ἀπὸ prep. ἀπό (+gen) from, of, out of, since, for, off, at, by, in, on
Ἰησοῦ n. gen. masc. sg. Ἰησοῦς Jesus
Χριστοῦ n. gen. masc. sg. Χριστός Christ
ὁ art. nom. masc. sg. ὁ ἡ τό the, this, that, he, she, it
μάρτυς n. nom. masc. sg. μάρτυς or μάρτυρ witness, martyr, record
ὁ art. nom. masc. sg. ὁ ἡ τό the, this, that, he, she, it
πιστός adj. nom. masc. sg. πιστός faithful, believing, true, sure
ὁ art. nom. masc. sg. ὁ ἡ τό the, this, that, he, she, it
πρωτότοκος adj. nom. masc. sg. πρωτότοκος firstborn, first begotten
ἐκ prep. ἐκ ἐξ (+gen) of, from, out of, by, on, with, in, among, through
τῶν art. gen. masc. pl. ὁ ἡ τό the, this, that, he, she, it
νεκρῶν adj. gen. masc. pl. νεκρός dead
καὶ conj. καί and, even, also, but
ὁ art. nom. masc. sg. ὁ ἡ τό the, this, that, he, she, it
ἄρχων n. nom. masc. sg. ἄρχων ruler, prince, chief, magistrate, chief ruler
τῶν art. gen. masc. pl. ὁ ἡ τό the, this, that, he, she, it
βασιλέων n. gen. masc. pl. βασιλεύς king
τῆς art. gen. fem. sg. ὁ ἡ τό the, this, that, he, she, it
γῆς n. gen. fem. sg. γῆ earth, land, ground, country
τῷ art. dat. masc. sg. ὁ ἡ τό the, this, that, he, she, it
ἡμᾶς pron. acc. 1p. pl. ἐγώ I
καὶ conj. καί and, even, also, but

ἡμᾶς pron. acc. 1p. pl. ἐγώ I
ἀπὸ prep. ἀπό (+gen) from, of, out of, since, for, off, at, by, in, on
τῶν art. gen. fem. pl. ὁ ἡ τό the, this, that, he, she, it
ἁμαρτιῶν n. gen. fem. pl. ἁμαρτία sin, offence, sinful
ἡμῶν pron. gen. 1p. pl. ἐγώ I
ἐν prep. ἐν (+dat) in, by, with, among, at, on, through, to, within, into, of, for
τῷ art. dat. neut. sg. ὁ ἡ τό the, this, that, he, she, it
αἵματι n. dat. neut. sg. αἷμα blood
αὐτοῦ pron. gen. masc. 3p. sg. αὐτός ή ό self, of oneself, even, very, the same, he, she, it
6 καὶ conj. καί and, even, also, but
ἡμᾶς pron. acc. 1p. pl. ἐγώ I
βασιλεῖς n. acc. masc. pl. βασιλεύς king
καὶ conj. καί and, even, also, but
ἱερεῖς n. acc. masc. pl. ἱερεύς priest
τῷ art. dat. masc. sg. ὁ ἡ τό the, this, that, he, she, it
Θεῷ n. dat. masc. sg. θεός God, god
καὶ conj. καί and, even, also, but
πατρὶ n. dat. masc. sg. πατήρ Father, father, parent
αὐτοῦ pron. gen. masc. 3p. sg. αὐτός ή ό self, of oneself, even, very, the same, he, she, it
αὐτῷ pron. dat. masc. 3p. sg. αὐτός ή ό self, of oneself, even, very, the same, he, she, it
ἡ art. nom. fem. sg. ὁ ἡ τό the, this, that, he, she, it
δόξα n. nom. fem. sg. δόξα glory, honour, praise, dignity, worship
καὶ conj. καί and, even, also, but
τὸ art. nom. neut. sg. ὁ ἡ τό the, this, that, he, she, it
κράτος n. nom. neut. sg. κράτος power, dominion, might, strength
εἰς prep. εἰς (+acc) into, to, unto, for, in, on, toward, against, upon, at, among
τοὺς art. acc. masc. pl. ὁ ἡ τό the, this, that, he, she, it
αἰῶνας n. acc. masc. pl. αἰών ever, ever and ever, evermore, age, eternal, world
τῶν art. gen. masc. pl. ὁ ἡ τό the, this, that, he, she, it
αἰώνων n. gen. masc. pl. αἰών ever, ever and ever, evermore, age, eternal, world
ἀμήν particle. ἀμήν amen, verily
7 μετὰ prep. μετά (+gen) with, among, against, (+acc) after
τῶν art. gen. fem. pl. ὁ ἡ τό the, this, that, he, she, it
νεφελῶν n. gen. fem. pl. νεφέλη cloud
καὶ conj. καί and, even, also, but
αὐτὸν pron. acc. masc. 3p. sg. αὐτός ή ό self, of oneself, even, very, the same, he, she, it
πᾶς adj. nom. masc. sg. πᾶς πᾶσα πᾶν all, every, whosoever, every one, no, whole, any
ὀφθαλμὸς n. nom. masc. sg. ὀφθαλμός eye, sight
καὶ conj. καί and, even, also, but
οἵτινες relative pron. nom. masc. pl. ὅστις which, who, whosoever, that, whatsoever
αὐτὸν pron. acc. masc. 3p. sg. αὐτός ή ό self, of oneself, even, very, the same, he, she, it
καὶ conj. καί and, even, also, but
ἐπ' prep. ἐπί (+gen) on, in, upon, (+dat) in, at, for, upon, (+acc) on, upon, unto, to, against
αὐτὸν pron. acc. masc. 3p. sg. αὐτός ή ό self, of oneself, even, very, the same, he, she, it
πᾶσαι adj. nom. fem. pl. πᾶς πᾶσα πᾶν all, every, whosoever, every one, no, whole, any
αἱ art. nom. fem. pl. ὁ ἡ τό the, this, that, he, she, it
φυλαὶ n. nom. fem. pl. φυλή tribe, kindred
τῆς art. gen. fem. sg. ὁ ἡ τό the, this, that, he, she, it
γῆς n. gen. fem. sg. γῆ earth, land, ground, country
ναί particle. ναί yea, even so, yes, surely, truth, verily
ἀμήν particle. ἀμήν amen, verily
8 Ἐγώ pron. nom. 1p. sg. ἐγώ I
τὸ art. nom. neut. sg. ὁ ἡ τό the, this, that, he, she, it
Α n. nom. neut. sg. Α Alpha
καὶ conj. καί and, even, also, but

τὸ art. nom. neut. sg. ὁ ἡ τό the, this, that, he, she, it
Ω n. nom. neut. sg. Ω Omega
ἀρχὴ n. nom. fem. sg. ἀρχή beginning, principality, corner, first, magistrate, rule
καὶ conj. καί and, even, also, but
τέλος n. nom. neut. sg. τέλος end, custom, ending, finally, uttermost
ὁ art. nom. masc. sg. ὁ ἡ τό the, this, that, he, she, it
Κύριος n. nom. masc. sg. κύριος Lord, lord, master, sir, LORD, God, Master, owner
ὁ art. nom. masc. sg. ὁ ἡ τό the, this, that, he, she, it
καὶ conj. καί and, even, also, but
ὁ art. nom. masc. sg. ὁ ἡ τό the, this, that, he, she, it
καὶ conj. καί and, even, also, but
ὁ art. nom. masc. sg. ὁ ἡ τό the, this, that, he, she, it
καὶ conj. καί and, even, also, but
ὁ art. nom. masc. sg. ὁ ἡ τό the, this, that, he, she, it
ὁ art. nom. masc. sg. ὁ ἡ τό the, this, that, he, she, it
παντοκράτωρ n. nom. masc. sg. παντοκράτωρ Almighty, omnipotent
9 Ἐγὼ pron. nom. 1p. sg. ἐγώ I
Ἰωάννης n. nom. masc. sg. Ἰωάννης John
ὁ art. nom. masc. sg. ὁ ἡ τό the, this, that, he, she, it
καὶ conj. καί and, even, also, but
ἀδελφὸς n. nom. masc. sg. ἀδελφός brother
ὑμῶν pron. gen. 2p. pl. σύ thou, you
καὶ conj. καί and, even, also, but
συγκοινωνὸς n. nom. masc. sg. συγκοινωνός companion, partake with, partaker
ἐν prep. ἐν (+dat) in, by, with, among, at, on, through, to, within, into, of, for
τῇ art. dat. fem. sg. ὁ ἡ τό the, this, that, he, she, it
θλίψει n. dat. fem. sg. θλῖψις tribulation, affliction, anguish, persecution
καὶ conj. καί and, even, also, but
ἐν prep. ἐν (+dat) in, by, with, among, at, on, through, to, within, into, of, for
τῇ art. dat. fem. sg. ὁ ἡ τό the, this, that, he, she, it
βασιλείᾳ n. dat. fem. sg. βασιλεία kingdom, reign
καὶ conj. καί and, even, also, but
ὑπομονῇ n. dat. fem. sg. ὑπομονή patience, enduring
Ἰησοῦ n. gen. masc. sg. Ἰησοῦς Jesus
Χριστοῦ n. gen. masc. sg. Χριστός Christ
ἐν prep. ἐν (+dat) in, by, with, among, at, on, through, to, within, into, of, for
τῇ art. dat. fem. sg. ὁ ἡ τό the, this, that, he, she, it
νήσῳ n. dat. fem. sg. νῆσος isle, island
τῇ art. dat. fem. sg. ὁ ἡ τό the, this, that, he, she, it
Πάτμῳ n. dat. fem. sg. Πάτμος Patmos
διὰ prep. διά (+gen) by, through, with, in, of, (+acc) for, because of, for a cause
τὸν art. acc. masc. sg. ὁ ἡ τό the, this, that, he, she, it
λόγον n. acc. masc. sg. λόγος word, saying, account, speech, thing, matter
τοῦ art. gen. masc. sg. ὁ ἡ τό the, this, that, he, she, it
Θεοῦ n. gen. masc. sg. θεός God, god
καὶ conj. καί and, even, also, but
διὰ prep. διά (+gen) by, through, with, in, of, (+acc) for, because of, for a cause
τὴν art. acc. fem. sg. ὁ ἡ τό the, this, that, he, she, it
μαρτυρίαν n. acc. fem. sg. μαρτυρία testimony, witness, record, report
Ἰησοῦ n. gen. masc. sg. Ἰησοῦς Jesus
Χριστοῦ n. gen. masc. sg. Χριστός Christ
10 ἐν prep. ἐν (+dat) in, by, with, among, at, on, through, to, within, into, of, for
Πνεύματι n. dat. neut. sg. πνεῦμα spirit, Spirit, Ghost, ghost, life. of the spirit, wind
ἐν prep. ἐν (+dat) in, by, with, among, at, on, through, to, within, into, of, for
τῇ art. dat. fem. sg. ὁ ἡ τό the, this, that, he, she, it

Κυριακῇ adj. dat. fem. sg. κυριακός Lord's
ἡμέρᾳ n. dat. fem. sg. ἡμέρα day, time, year, while, age, day time
καὶ conj. καί and, even, also, but
ὀπίσω prep. ὀπίσω (+gen) after. (adv.) back, behind
μου pron. gen. 1p. sg. ἐγώ I
φωνὴν n. acc. fem. sg. φωνή voice, sound, noise
μεγάλην adj. acc. fem. sg. μέγας great, loud, greatest, high, large, mighty, strong
ὡς adv. ὡς as, when, as it were, how, about, like, as soon as, even as, while
σάλπιγγος n. gen. fem. sg. σάλπιγξ trumpet, trump
11 Ἐγώ pron. nom. 1p. sg. ἐγώ I
τὸ art. nom. neut. sg. ὁ ἡ τό the, this, that, he, she, it
Α n. nom. neut. sg. Α Alpha
καὶ conj. καί and, even, also, but
τὸ art. nom. neut. sg. ὁ ἡ τό the, this, that, he, she, it
Ω n. nom. neut. sg. Ω Omega
ὁ art. nom. masc. sg. ὁ ἡ τό the, this, that, he, she, it
πρῶτος ordinal. adj. nom. masc. sg. πρῶτος first, chief, first of all, chiefest, best
ἔσχατος adj. nom. masc. sg. ἔσχατος last, lowest, uttermost, uttermost part
καὶ conj. καί and, even, also, but
ὁ art. nom. masc. sg. ὁ ἡ τό the, this, that, he, she, it
ἔσχατος adj. nom. masc. sg. ἔσχατος last, lowest, uttermost, uttermost part
καὶ conj. καί and, even, also, but
Ὃ relative pron. acc. neut. sg. ὅς ἥ ὅ who, which, what, that
εἰς prep. εἰς (+acc) into, to, unto, for, in, on, toward, against, upon, at, among
βιβλίον n. acc. neut. sg. βιβλίον book, bill, scroll, writing
καὶ conj. καί and, even, also, but
ταῖς art. dat. fem. pl. ὁ ἡ τό the, this, that, he, she, it
ἑπτὰ num. dat. fem. pl. ἑπτά seven, seventh
ἐκκλησίαις n. dat. fem. pl. ἐκκλησία church, assembly
ταῖς art. dat. fem. pl. ὁ ἡ τό the, this, that, he, she, it
ἐν prep. ἐν (+dat) in, by, with, among, at, on, through, to, within, into, of, for
Ἀσίᾳ n. dat. fem. sg. Ἀσία Asia
εἰς prep. εἰς (+acc) into, to, unto, for, in, on, toward, against, upon, at, among
Ἔφεσον n. acc. fem. sg. Ἔφεσος Ephesus
καὶ conj. καί and, even, also, but
εἰς prep. εἰς (+acc) into, to, unto, for, in, on, toward, against, upon, at, among
Σμύρναν n. acc. fem. sg. Σμύρνα Smyrna, myrrh
καὶ conj. καί and, even, also, but
εἰς prep. εἰς (+acc) into, to, unto, for, in, on, toward, against, upon, at, among
Πέργαμον n. acc. fem. sg. Πέργαμος Pergamos
καὶ conj. καί and, even, also, but
εἰς prep. εἰς (+acc) into, to, unto, for, in, on, toward, against, upon, at, among
Θυάτειρα n. acc. neut. pl. Θυάτειρα Thyatira
καὶ conj. καί and, even, also, but
εἰς prep. εἰς (+acc) into, to, unto, for, in, on, toward, against, upon, at, among
Σάρδεις n. acc. fem. pl. Σάρδεις Sardis
καὶ conj. καί and, even, also, but
εἰς prep. εἰς (+acc) into, to, unto, for, in, on, toward, against, upon, at, among
Φιλαδέλφειαν n. acc. fem. sg. Φιλαδέλφεια Philadelphia
καὶ conj. καί and, even, also, but
εἰς prep. εἰς (+acc) into, to, unto, for, in, on, toward, against, upon, at, among
Λαοδίκειαν n. acc. fem. sg. Λαοδίκεια Laodicea
12 καὶ conj. καί and, even, also, but
τὴν art. acc. fem. sg. ὁ ἡ τό the, this, that, he, she, it
φωνὴν n. acc. fem. sg. φωνή voice, sound, noise

ἥτις relative pron. nom. fem. sg. ὅστις which, who, whosoever, that, whatsoever
μετ' prep. μετά (+gen) with, among, against, (+acc) after
ἐμοῦ pron. gen. 1p. sg. ἐγώ I
καὶ conj. καί and, even, also, but
ἑπτὰ num. acc. fem. pl. ἑπτά seven, seventh
λυχνίας n. acc. fem. pl. λυχνία candlestick, lampstand
χρυσᾶς adj. acc. fem. pl. χρύσεος golden, of gold
13 καὶ conj. καί and, even, also, but
ἐν prep. ἐν (+dat) in, by, with, among, at, on, through, to, within, into, of, for
μέσῳ adj. dat. neut. sg. μέσος midst, among, mid, between
τῶν art. gen. fem. pl. ὁ ἡ τό the, this, that, he, she, it
ἑπτὰ num. gen. fem. pl. ἑπτά seven, seventh
λυχνιῶν n. gen. fem. pl. λυχνία candlestick, lampstand
ὅμοιον adj. acc. masc. sg. ὅμοιος like
υἱῷ n. dat. masc. sg. υἱός son, child, descendant, offspring, heir
ἀνθρώπου n. gen. masc. sg. ἄνθρωπος man, human being, person, one, certain
ποδήρη adj. acc. masc. sg. ποδήρης garment down to the foot
καὶ conj. καί and, even, also, but
πρὸς prep. πρός (+gen) for, (+dat) at, (+acc) unto, to, with, for, against
τοῖς art. dat. masc. pl. ὁ ἡ τό the, this, that, he, she, it
μαστοῖς n. dat. masc. pl. μαστός pap, breast
ζώνην n. acc. fem. sg. ζώνη girdle, purse
χρυσῆν adj. acc. fem. sg. χρύσεος golden, of gold
14 ἡ art. nom. fem. sg. ὁ ἡ τό the, this, that, he, she, it
δὲ conj. δέ but, and, now, also, to the contrary, rather, then
κεφαλὴ n. nom. fem. sg. κεφαλή head
αὐτοῦ pron. gen. masc. 3p. sg. αὐτός ή ό self, of oneself, even, very, the same, he, she, it
καὶ conj. καί and, even, also, but
αἱ art. nom. fem. pl. ὁ ἡ τό the, this, that, he, she, it
τρίχες n. nom. fem. pl. θρίξ hair
λευκαὶ adj. nom. fem. pl. λευκός white
ὡσεὶ adv. ὡσεί about, as, like, as it had been, as it were, like as
ἔριον n. nom. neut. sg. ἔριον wool
λευκόν adj. nom. neut. sg. λευκός white
ὡς adv. ὡς as, when, as it were, how, about, like, as soon as, even as, while
χιὼν n. nom. fem. sg. χιών snow
καὶ conj. καί and, even, also, but
οἱ art. nom. masc. pl. ὁ ἡ τό the, this, that, he, she, it
ὀφθαλμοὶ n. nom. masc. pl. ὀφθαλμός eye, sight
αὐτοῦ pron. gen. masc. 3p. sg. αὐτός ή ό self, of oneself, even, very, the same, he, she, it
ὡς adv. ὡς as, when, as it were, how, about, like, as soon as, even as, while
φλὸξ n. nom. fem. sg. φλόξ flame, flaming
πυρὸς n. gen. neut. sg. πῦρ fire, fiery
15 καὶ conj. καί and, even, also, but
οἱ art. nom. masc. pl. ὁ ἡ τό the, this, that, he, she, it
πόδες n. nom. masc. pl. πούς foot
αὐτοῦ pron. gen. masc. 3p. sg. αὐτός ή ό self, of oneself, even, very, the same, he, she, it
ὅμοιοι adj. nom. masc. pl. ὅμοιος like
χαλκολιβάνῳ n. dat. neut. sg. χαλκολίβανον fine brass
ὡς adv. ὡς as, when, as it were, how, about, like, as soon as, even as, while
ἐν prep. ἐν (+dat) in, by, with, among, at, on, through, to, within, into, of, for
καμίνῳ n. dat. fem. sg. κάμινος furnace
καὶ conj. καί and, even, also, but
ἡ art. nom. fem. sg. ὁ ἡ τό the, this, that, he, she, it
φωνὴ n. nom. fem. sg. φωνή voice, sound, noise

αὐτοῦ pron. gen. masc. 3p. sg. αὐτός ή ό self, of oneself, even, very, the same, he, she, it
ὡς adv. ὡς as, when, as it were, how, about, like, as soon as, even as, while
φωνὴ n. nom. fem. sg. φωνή voice, sound, noise
ὑδάτων n. gen. neut. pl. ὕδωρ water
πολλῶν adj. gen. neut. pl. πολύς many, great, much, long, abundant
16 καὶ conj. καί and, even, also, but
ἐν prep. ἐν (+dat) in, by, with, among, at, on, through, to, within, into, of, for
τῇ art. dat. fem. sg. ὁ ἡ τό the, this, that, he, she, it
δεξιᾷ adj. dat. fem. sg. δεξιός right, right hand, right side
αὐτοῦ pron. gen. masc. 3p. sg. αὐτός ή ό self, of oneself, even, very, the same, he, she, it
χειρὶ n. dat. fem. sg. χείρ hand
ἀστέρας n. acc. masc. pl. ἀστήρ star
ἑπτὰ num. acc. masc. pl. ἑπτά seven, seventh
καὶ conj. καί and, even, also, but
ἐκ prep. ἐκ ἐξ (+gen) of, from, out of, by, on, with, in, among, through
τοῦ art. gen. neut. sg. ὁ ἡ τό the, this, that, he, she, it
στόματος n. gen. neut. sg. στόμα mouth, face, edge
αὐτοῦ pron. gen. masc. 3p. sg. αὐτός ή ό self, of oneself, even, very, the same, he, she, it
ῥομφαία n. nom. fem. sg. ῥομφαία sword
δίστομος adj. nom. fem. sg. δίστομος twoedged, with two edges
ὀξεῖα adj. nom. fem. sg. ὀξύς swift, sharp
καὶ conj. καί and, even, also, but
ἡ art. nom. fem. sg. ὁ ἡ τό the, this, that, he, she, it
ὄψις n. nom. fem. sg. ὄψις appearance, countenance, face
αὐτοῦ pron. gen. masc. 3p. sg. αὐτός ή ό self, of oneself, even, very, the same, he, she, it
ὡς adv. ὡς as, when, as it were, how, about, like, as soon as, even as, while
ὁ art. nom. masc. sg. ὁ ἡ τό the, this, that, he, she, it
ἥλιος n. nom. masc. sg. ἥλιος sun, east
ἐν prep. ἐν (+dat) in, by, with, among, at, on, through, to, within, into, of, for
τῇ art. dat. fem. sg. ὁ ἡ τό the, this, that, he, she, it
δυνάμει n. dat. fem. sg. δύναμις power, mighty work, miracle, strength, might
αὐτοῦ pron. gen. masc. 3p. sg. αὐτός ή ό self, of oneself, even, very, the same, he, she, it
17 καὶ conj. καί and, even, also, but
ὅτε adv. ὅτε when, after that, as soon as, while, after
αὐτόν pron. acc. masc. 3p. sg. αὐτός ή ό self, of oneself, even, very, the same, he, she, it
πρὸς prep. πρός (+gen) for, (+dat) at, (+acc) unto, to, with, for, against
τοὺς art. acc. masc. pl. ὁ ἡ τό the, this, that, he, she, it
πόδας n. acc. masc. pl. πούς foot
αὐτοῦ pron. gen. masc. 3p. sg. αὐτός ή ό self, of oneself, even, very, the same, he, she, it
ὡς adv. ὡς as, when, as it were, how, about, like, as soon as, even as, while
νεκρός adj. nom. masc. sg. νεκρός dead
καὶ conj. καί and, even, also, but
τὴν art. acc. fem. sg. ὁ ἡ τό the, this, that, he, she, it
δεξιὰν adj. acc. fem. sg. δεξιός right, right hand, right side
αὐτοῦ pron. gen. masc. 3p. sg. αὐτός ή ό self, of oneself, even, very, the same, he, she, it
χεῖρα n. acc. fem. sg. χείρ hand
ἐπ' prep. ἐπί (+gen) on, in, upon, (+dat) in, at, for, upon, (+acc) on, upon, unto, to, against
ἐμὲ pron. acc. 1p. sg. ἐγώ I
μοι pron. dat. 1p. sg. ἐγώ I
Μὴ particle of negation. μή not, no, lest, neither, none, nothing, nor, never, without
ἐγώ pron. nom. 1p. sg. ἐγώ I
ὁ art. nom. masc. sg. ὁ ἡ τό the, this, that, he, she, it
πρῶτος ordinal. adj. nom. masc. sg. πρῶτος first, chief, first of all, chiefest, best
καὶ conj. καί and, even, also, but
ὁ art. nom. masc. sg. ὁ ἡ τό the, this, that, he, she, it

ἔσχατος adj. nom. masc. sg. ἔσχατος last, lowest, uttermost, uttermost part
18 καὶ conj. καί and, even, also, but
ὁ art. nom. masc. sg. ὁ ἡ τό the, this, that, he, she, it
καὶ conj. καί and, even, also, but
νεκρὸς adj. nom. masc. sg. νεκρός dead
καὶ conj. καί and, even, also, but
εἰς prep. εἰς (+acc) into, to, unto, for, in, on, toward, against, upon, at, among
τοὺς art. acc. masc. pl. ὁ ἡ τό the, this, that, he, she, it
αἰῶνας n. acc. masc. pl. αἰών ever, ever and ever, evermore, age, eternal, world
τῶν art. gen. masc. pl. ὁ ἡ τό the, this, that, he, she, it
αἰώνων n. gen. masc. pl. αἰών ever, ever and ever, evermore, age, eternal, world
ἀμήν particle. ἀμήν amen, verily
καὶ conj. καί and, even, also, but
τὰς art. acc. fem. pl. ὁ ἡ τό the, this, that, he, she, it
κλεῖς n. acc. fem. pl. κλείς key
τοῦ art. gen. masc. sg. ὁ ἡ τό the, this, that, he, she, it
ᾅδου n. gen. masc. sg. ᾅδης hell, grave
καὶ conj. καί and, even, also, but
τοῦ art. gen. masc. sg. ὁ ἡ τό the, this, that, he, she, it
θανάτου n. gen. masc. sg. θάνατος death
19 ἃ relative pron. acc. neut. pl. ὅς ἥ ὅ who, which, what, that
καὶ conj. καί and, even, also, but
ἃ relative pron. nom. neut. pl. ὅς ἥ ὅ who, which, what, that
καὶ conj. καί and, even, also, but
ἃ relative pron. nom. neut. pl. ὅς ἥ ὅ who, which, what, that
μετὰ prep. μετά (+gen) with, among, against, (+acc) after
ταῦτα demo. pron. acc. neut. pl. οὗτος αὕτη τοῦτο this, the same, this same, he, she, it
20 τὸ art. nom. neut. sg. ὁ ἡ τό the, this, that, he, she, it
μυστήριον n. nom. neut. sg. μυστήριον mystery
τῶν art. gen. masc. pl. ὁ ἡ τό the, this, that, he, she, it
ἑπτὰ num. gen. masc. pl. ἑπτά seven, seventh
ἀστέρων n. gen. masc. pl. ἀστήρ star
ὧν relative pron. gen. masc. pl. ὅς ἥ ὅ who, which, what, that
ἐπὶ prep. ἐπί (+gen) on, in, upon, (+dat) in, at, for, upon, (+acc) on, upon, unto, to, against
τῆς art. gen. fem. sg. ὁ ἡ τό the, this, that, he, she, it
δεξιᾶς adj. gen. fem. sg. δεξιός right, right hand, right side
μου pron. gen. 1p. sg. ἐγώ I
καὶ conj. καί and, even, also, but
τὰς art. acc. fem. pl. ὁ ἡ τό the, this, that, he, she, it
ἑπτὰ num. acc. fem. pl. ἑπτά seven, seventh
λυχνίας n. acc. fem. pl. λυχνία candlestick, lampstand
τὰς art. acc. fem. pl. ὁ ἡ τό the, this, that, he, she, it
χρυσᾶς adj. acc. fem. pl. χρύσεος golden, of gold
οἱ art. nom. masc. pl. ὁ ἡ τό the, this, that, he, she, it
ἑπτὰ num. nom. masc. pl. ἑπτά seven, seventh
ἀστέρες n. nom. masc. pl. ἀστήρ star
ἄγγελοι n. nom. masc. pl. ἄγγελος angel, messenger
τῶν art. gen. fem. pl. ὁ ἡ τό the, this, that, he, she, it
ἑπτὰ num. gen. fem. pl. ἑπτά seven, seventh
ἐκκλησιῶν n. gen. fem. pl. ἐκκλησία church, assembly
καὶ conj. καί and, even, also, but
αἱ art. nom. fem. pl. ὁ ἡ τό the, this, that, he, she, it
ἑπτὰ num. nom. fem. pl. ἑπτά seven, seventh
λυχνίαι n. nom. fem. pl. λυχνία candlestick, lampstand
ἃς relative pron. acc. fem. pl. ὅς ἥ ὅ who, which, what, that

ἑπτὰ num. nom. fem. pl. ἑπτά seven, seventh
ἐκκλησίαι n. nom. fem. pl. ἐκκλησία church, assembly

2

1 Τῷ art. dat. masc. sg. ὁ ἡ τό the, this, that, he, she, it
ἀγγέλῳ n. dat. masc. sg. ἄγγελος angel, messenger
τῆς art. gen. fem. sg. ὁ ἡ τό the, this, that, he, she, it
Ἐφεσίνης n. gen. fem. sg. Ἐφεσῖνος of Ephesus
ἐκκλησίας n. gen. fem. sg. ἐκκλησία church, assembly
Τάδε demo. pron. acc. neut. pl. ὅδε ἥδε τόδε this, he, she, such, thus
ὁ art. nom. masc. sg. ὁ ἡ τό the, this, that, he, she, it
τοὺς art. acc. masc. pl. ὁ ἡ τό the, this, that, he, she, it
ἑπτὰ num. acc. masc. pl. ἑπτά seven, seventh
ἀστέρας n. acc. masc. pl. ἀστήρ star
ἐν prep. ἐν (+dat) in, by, with, among, at, on, through, to, within, into, of, for
τῇ art. dat. fem. sg. ὁ ἡ τό the, this, that, he, she, it
δεξιᾷ adj. dat. fem. sg. δεξιός right, right hand, right side
αὐτοῦ pron. gen. masc. 3p. sg. αὐτός ἡ ὁ self, of oneself, even, very, the same, he, she, it
ὁ art. nom. masc. sg. ὁ ἡ τό the, this, that, he, she, it
ἐν prep. ἐν (+dat) in, by, with, among, at, on, through, to, within, into, of, for
μέσῳ adj. dat. neut. sg. μέσος midst, among, mid, between
τῶν art. gen. fem. pl. ὁ ἡ τό the, this, that, he, she, it
ἑπτὰ num. gen. fem. pl. ἑπτά seven, seventh
λυχνιῶν n. gen. fem. pl. λυχνία candlestick, lampstand
χρυσῶν adj. gen. fem. pl. χρύσεος golden, of gold
2 τὰ art. acc. neut. pl. ὁ ἡ τό the, this, that, he, she, it
ἔργα n. acc. neut. pl. ἔργον work, deed, doing labour
σου pron. gen. 2p. sg. σύ thou, you
καὶ conj. καί and, even, also, but
τὸν art. acc. masc. sg. ὁ ἡ τό the, this, that, he, she, it
κόπον n. acc. masc. sg. κόπος labour, trouble, weariness
σου pron. gen. 2p. sg. σύ thou, you
καὶ conj. καί and, even, also, but
τὴν art. acc. fem. sg. ὁ ἡ τό the, this, that, he, she, it
ὑπομονήν n. acc. fem. sg. ὑπομονή patience, enduring
σου pron. gen. 2p. sg. σύ thou, you
καὶ conj. καί and, even, also, but
ὅτι conj. ὅτι that, for, because, how that, how, because that, for that, though
οὐ particle of negation. οὐ οὐκ οὐχ not, no, neither, none, nay, nor, never, nothing
κακούς adj. acc. masc. pl. κακός evil, evil thing, noisome, wicked
καὶ conj. καί and, even, also, but
τοὺς art. acc. masc. pl. ὁ ἡ τό the, this, that, he, she, it
ἀποστόλους n. acc. masc. pl. ἀπόστολος apostle, messenger, he that is sent
καὶ conj. καί and, even, also, but
οὐκ particle of negation. οὐ οὐκ οὐχ not, no, neither, none, nay, nor, never, nothing
καὶ conj. καί and, even, also, but
αὐτοὺς pron. acc. masc. 3p. pl. αὐτός ἡ ὁ self, of oneself, even, very, the same, he, she, it
ψευδεῖς adj. acc. masc. pl. ψευδής false, liar
3 καὶ conj. καί and, even, also, but
καὶ conj. καί and, even, also, but
ὑπομονὴν n. acc. fem. sg. ὑπομονή patience, enduring
καὶ conj. καί and, even, also, but
διὰ prep. διά (+gen) by, through, with, in, of, (+acc) for, because of, for a cause
τὸ art. acc. neut. sg. ὁ ἡ τό the, this, that, he, she, it

ὄνομά n. acc. neut. sg. ὄνομα name, call, surname
μου pron. gen. 1p. sg. ἐγώ I
καὶ conj. καί and, even, also, but
οὐ particle of negation. οὐ οὐκ οὐχ not, no, neither, none, nay, nor, never, nothing
4 ἀλλ' conj. ἀλλά but, yea, yet, nevertheless, howbeit, nay, therefore
κατὰ prep. κατά (+gen) against, by, throughout, down, (+acc) according to, after, with
σοῦ pron. gen. 2p. sg. σύ thou, you
ὅτι conj. ὅτι that, for, because, how that, how, because that, for that, though
τὴν art. acc. fem. sg. ὁ ἡ τό the, this, that, he, she, it
ἀγάπην n. acc. fem. sg. ἀγάπη love, charity, feast of charity
σοῦ pron. gen. 2p. sg. σύ thou, you
τὴν art. acc. fem. sg. ὁ ἡ τό the, this, that, he, she, it
πρώτην ordinal. adj. acc. fem. sg. πρῶτος first, chief, first of all, chiefest, best
5 οὖν conj. οὖν therefore, then, so, and, now, wherefore
πόθεν adv. πόθεν whence, from whence
καὶ conj. καί and, even, also, but
καὶ conj. καί and, even, also, but
τὰ art. acc. neut. pl. ὁ ἡ τό the, this, that, he, she, it
πρῶτα ordinal. adj. acc. neut. pl. πρῶτος first, chief, first of all, chiefest, best
ἔργα n. acc. neut. pl. ἔργον work, deed, doing labour
εἰ conj. εἰ if, whether, that, though, forasmuch
δὲ conj. δέ but, and, now, also, to the contrary, rather, then
μή particle of negation. μή not, no, lest, neither, none, nothing, nor, never, without
σοι pron. dat. 2p. sg. σύ thou, you
ταχύ adv. ταχύ quickly, lightly
καὶ conj. καί and, even, also, but
τὴν art. acc. fem. sg. ὁ ἡ τό the, this, that, he, she, it
λυχνίαν n. acc. fem. sg. λυχνία candlestick, lampstand
σου pron. gen. 2p. sg. σύ thou, you
ἐκ prep. ἐκ ἐξ (+gen) of, from, out of, by, on, with, in, among, through
τοῦ art. gen. masc. sg. ὁ ἡ τό the, this, that, he, she, it
τόπου n. gen. masc. sg. τόπος place, room, quarter
αὐτῆς pron. gen. fem. 3p. sg. αὐτός ἡ ὁ self, of oneself, even, very, the same, he, she, it
ἐὰν conj. ἐάν if, soever, except, though, and if, but, whether, if so, so
μὴ particle of negation. μή not, no, lest, neither, none, nothing, nor, never, without
6 ἀλλὰ conj. ἀλλά but, yea, yet, nevertheless, howbeit, nay, therefore
τοῦτο demo. pron. acc. neut. sg. οὗτος αὕτη τοῦτο this, the same, this same, he, she, it
ὅτι conj. ὅτι that, for, because, how that, how, because that, for that, though
τὰ art. acc. neut. pl. ὁ ἡ τό the, this, that, he, she, it
ἔργα n. acc. neut. pl. ἔργον work, deed, doing labour
τῶν art. gen. masc. pl. ὁ ἡ τό the, this, that, he, she, it
Νικολαϊτῶν n. gen. masc. pl. Νικολαΐτης Nicolaitane
ἃ relative pron. acc. neut. pl. ὅς ἥ ὅ who, which, what, that
κἀγὼ pron. nom. 1p. sg. κἀγώ and I, I also, so I, even as I
7 ὁ art. nom. masc. sg. ὁ ἡ τό the, this, that, he, she, it
οὖς n. acc. neut. sg. οὖς ear
τί interrog. pron. acc. neut. sg. τίς what, who, why, where, which, how
τὸ art. nom. neut. sg. ὁ ἡ τό the, this, that, he, she, it
Πνεῦμα n. nom. neut. sg. πνεῦμα spirit, Spirit, Ghost, ghost, life. of the spirit, wind
ταῖς art. dat. fem. pl. ὁ ἡ τό the, this, that, he, she, it
ἐκκλησίαις n. dat. fem. pl. ἐκκλησία church, assembly
τῷ art. dat. masc. sg. ὁ ἡ τό the, this, that, he, she, it
αὐτῷ pron. dat. masc. 3p. sg. αὐτός ἡ ὁ self, of oneself, even, very, the same, he, she, it
ἐκ prep. ἐκ ἐξ (+gen) of, from, out of, by, on, with, in, among, through
τοῦ art. gen. neut. sg. ὁ ἡ τό the, this, that, he, she, it

ξύλου n. gen. neut. sg. ξύλον tree, stave, wood, the stocks
τῆς art. gen. fem. sg. ὁ ἡ τό the, this, that, he, she, it
ζωῆς n. gen. fem. sg. ζωή life, lifetime
ὅ relative pron. nom. neut. sg. ὅς ἥ ὅ who, which, what, that
ἐν prep. ἐν (+dat) in, by, with, among, at, on, through, to, within, into, of, for
μέσῳ adj. dat. neut. sg. μέσος midst, among, mid, between
τοῦ art. gen. masc. sg. ὁ ἡ τό the, this, that, he, she, it
παραδείσου n. gen. masc. sg. παράδεισος paradise
τοῦ art. gen. masc. sg. ὁ ἡ τό the, this, that, he, she, it
Θεοῦ n. gen. masc. sg. θεός God, god
8 Καὶ conj. καί and, even, also, but
τῷ art. dat. masc. sg. ὁ ἡ τό the, this, that, he, she, it
ἀγγέλῳ n. dat. masc. sg. ἄγγελος angel, messenger
τῆς art. gen. fem. sg. ὁ ἡ τό the, this, that, he, she, it
ἐκκλησίας n. gen. fem. sg. ἐκκλησία church, assembly
Σμυρναίων n. dat. fem. sg. Σμυρναῖος Smyrnean
Τάδε demo. pron. acc. neut. pl. ὅδε ἥδε τόδε this, he, she, such, thus
ὁ art. nom. masc. sg. ὁ ἡ τό the, this, that, he, she, it
πρῶτος ordinal. adj. nom. masc. sg. πρῶτος first, chief, first of all, chiefest, best
καὶ conj. καί and, even, also, but
ὁ art. nom. masc. sg. ὁ ἡ τό the, this, that, he, she, it
ἔσχατος adj. nom. masc. sg. ἔσχατος last, lowest, uttermost, uttermost part
ὃς relative pron. nom. masc. sg. ὅς ἥ ὅ who, which, what, that
νεκρὸς adj. nom. masc. sg. νεκρός dead
καὶ conj. καί and, even, also, but
9 σου pron. gen. 2p. sg. σύ thou, you
τὰ art. acc. neut. pl. ὁ ἡ τό the, this, that, he, she, it
ἔργα n. acc. neut. pl. ἔργον work, deed, doing labour
καὶ conj. καί and, even, also, but
τὴν art. acc. fem. sg. ὁ ἡ τό the, this, that, he, she, it
θλῖψιν n. acc. fem. sg. θλῖψις tribulation, affliction, anguish, persecution
καὶ conj. καί and, even, also, but
τὴν art. acc. fem. sg. ὁ ἡ τό the, this, that, he, she, it
πτωχείαν n. acc. fem. sg. πτωχεία poverty
πλούσιος adj. nom. masc. sg. πλούσιος rich
δὲ conj. δέ but, and, now, also, to the contrary, rather, then
καὶ conj. καί and, even, also, but
τὴν art. acc. fem. sg. ὁ ἡ τό the, this, that, he, she, it
βλασφημίαν n. acc. fem. sg. βλασφημία blasphemy, railing, evil speaking
τῶν art. gen. masc. pl. ὁ ἡ τό the, this, that, he, she, it
Ἰουδαίους adj. acc. masc. pl. Ἰουδαῖος Jew, Jewess
ἑαυτοὺς reflexive pron. acc. masc. 3p. pl. ἑαυτοῦ himself, herself, itself, yourself, ourselves
καὶ conj. καί and, even, also, but
οὐκ particle of negation. οὐ οὐκ οὐχ not, no, neither, none, nay, nor, never, nothing
ἀλλὰ conj. ἀλλά but, yea, yet, nevertheless, howbeit, nay, therefore
συναγωγὴ n. nom. fem. sg. συναγωγή synagogue, assembly, congregation
τοῦ art. gen. masc. sg. ὁ ἡ τό the, this, that, he, she, it
Σατανᾶ n. gen. masc. sg. Σατανᾶς Satan
10 μηδὲν num. acc. neut. sg. μηδείς μηδεμία μηδέν no man, nothing, no, none, not at all
ἃ relative pron. acc. neut. pl. ὅς ἥ ὅ who, which, what, that
ἐξ prep. ἐκ ἐξ (+gen) of, from, out of, by, on, with, in, among, through
ὑμῶν pron. gen. 2p. pl. σύ thou, you
ὁ art. nom. masc. sg. ὁ ἡ τό the, this, that, he, she, it
διάβολος adj. nom. masc. sg. διάβολος devil, false accuser, Devil, slanderer
εἰς prep. εἰς (+acc) into, to, unto, for, in, on, toward, against, upon, at, among

φυλακὴν n. acc. fem. sg. φυλακή prison, watch, imprisonment, cage, hold, ward
ἵνα conj. ἵνα that, to, lest, for to, so that, albeit, because, for, so as
καὶ conj. καί and, even, also, but
θλῖψιν n. acc. fem. sg. θλῖψις tribulation, affliction, anguish, persecution
ἡμερῶν n. gen. fem. pl. ἡμέρα day, time, year, while, age, day time
δέκα num. gen. fem. pl. δέκα ten
πιστὸς adj. nom. masc. sg. πιστός faithful, believing, true, sure
ἄχρι prep. ἄχρι or ἄχρις (+gen) until, unto, till, even to, as far as, while, into
θανάτου n. gen. masc. sg. θάνατος death
καὶ conj. καί and, even, also, but
σοι pron. dat. 2p. sg. σύ thou, you
τὸν art. acc. masc. sg. ὁ ἡ τό the, this, that, he, she, it
στέφανον n. acc. masc. sg. στέφανος crown
τῆς art. gen. fem. sg. ὁ ἡ τό the, this, that, he, she, it
ζωῆς n. gen. fem. sg. ζωή life, lifetime
11 ὁ art. nom. masc. sg. ὁ ἡ τό the, this, that, he, she, it
οὖς n. acc. neut. sg. οὖς ear
τί interrog. pron. acc. neut. sg. τίς what, who, why, where, which, how
τὸ art. nom. neut. sg. ὁ ἡ τό the, this, that, he, she, it
Πνεῦμα n. nom. neut. sg. πνεῦμα spirit, Spirit, Ghost, ghost, life. of the spirit, wind
ταῖς art. dat. fem. pl. ὁ ἡ τό the, this, that, he, she, it
ἐκκλησίαις n. dat. fem. pl. ἐκκλησία church, assembly
ὁ art. nom. masc. sg. ὁ ἡ τό the, this, that, he, she, it
οὐ particle of negation. οὐ οὐκ οὐχ not, no, neither, none, nay, nor, never, nothing
μὴ particle of negation. μή not, no, lest, neither, none, nothing, nor, never, without
ἐκ prep. ἐκ ἐξ (+gen) of, from, out of, by, on, with, in, among, through
τοῦ art. gen. masc. sg. ὁ ἡ τό the, this, that, he, she, it
θανάτου n. gen. masc. sg. θάνατος death
τοῦ art. gen. masc. sg. ὁ ἡ τό the, this, that, he, she, it
δευτέρου ordinal. adj. gen. masc. sg. δεύτερος second, second time, again, afterward
12 Καὶ conj. καί and, even, also, but
τῷ art. dat. masc. sg. ὁ ἡ τό the, this, that, he, she, it
ἀγγέλῳ n. dat. masc. sg. ἄγγελος angel, messenger
τῆς art. gen. fem. sg. ὁ ἡ τό the, this, that, he, she, it
ἐν prep. ἐν (+dat) in, by, with, among, at, on, through, to, within, into, of, for
Περγάμῳ n. dat. fem. sg. Πέργαμος Pergamos
ἐκκλησίας n. gen. fem. sg. ἐκκλησία church, assembly
Τάδε demo. pron. acc. neut. pl. ὅδε ἥδε τόδε this, he, she, such, thus
ὁ art. nom. masc. sg. ὁ ἡ τό the, this, that, he, she, it
τὴν art. acc. fem. sg. ὁ ἡ τό the, this, that, he, she, it
ῥομφαίαν n. acc. fem. sg. ῥομφαία sword
τὴν art. acc. fem. sg. ὁ ἡ τό the, this, that, he, she, it
δίστομον adj. acc. fem. sg. δίστομος twoedged, with two edges
τὴν art. acc. fem. sg. ὁ ἡ τό the, this, that, he, she, it
ὀξεῖαν adj. acc. fem. sg. ὀξύς swift, sharp
13 τὰ art. acc. neut. pl. ὁ ἡ τό the, this, that, he, she, it
ἔργα n. acc. neut. pl. ἔργον work, deed, doing labour
σου pron. gen. 2p. sg. σύ thou, you
καὶ conj. καί and, even, also, but
ποῦ particle of place. ποῦ where, whither
ὅπου adv. ὅπου where, whither, whereas, in what place, wheresoever
ὁ art. nom. masc. sg. ὁ ἡ τό the, this, that, he, she, it
θρόνος n. nom. masc. sg. θρόνος throne, seat
τοῦ art. gen. masc. sg. ὁ ἡ τό the, this, that, he, she, it
Σατανᾶ n. gen. masc. sg. Σατανᾶς Satan

καὶ conj. καί and, even, also, but
τὸ art. acc. neut. sg. ὁ ἡ τό the, this, that, he, she, it
ὄνομά n. acc. neut. sg. ὄνομα name, call, surname
μου pron. gen. 1p. sg. ἐγώ I
καὶ conj. καί and, even, also, but
οὐκ particle of negation. οὐ οὐκ οὐχ not, no, neither, none, nay, nor, never, nothing
τὴν art. acc. fem. sg. ὁ ἡ τό the, this, that, he, she, it
πίστιν n. acc. fem. sg. πίστις faith, assurance, belief, fidelity
μου pron. gen. 1p. sg. ἐγώ I
καὶ conj. καί and, even, also, but
ἐν prep. ἐν (+dat) in, by, with, among, at, on, through, to, within, into, of, for
ταῖς art. dat. fem. pl. ὁ ἡ τό the, this, that, he, she, it
ἡμέραις n. dat. fem. pl. ἡμέρα day, time, year, while, age, day time
ἐν prep. ἐν (+dat) in, by, with, among, at, on, through, to, within, into, of, for
αἷς relative pron. dat. fem. pl. ὅς ἥ ὅ who, which, what, that
Ἀντιπᾶς n. nom. masc. sg. Ἀντιπᾶς Antipas
ὁ art. nom. masc. sg. ὁ ἡ τό the, this, that, he, she, it
μάρτυς n. nom. masc. sg. μάρτυς or μάρτυρ witness, martyr, record
μου pron. gen. 1p. sg. ἐγώ I
ὁ art. nom. masc. sg. ὁ ἡ τό the, this, that, he, she, it
πιστός adj. nom. masc. sg. πιστός faithful, believing, true, sure
ὃς relative pron. nom. masc. sg. ὅς ἥ ὅ who, which, what, that
παρ' prep. παρά (+gen) of, from, (+dat) with, for, (+acc) beside, at, by, above, against
ὑμῖν pron. dat. 2p. pl. σύ thou, you
ὅπου adv. ὅπου where, whither, whereas, in what place, wheresoever
ὁ art. nom. masc. sg. ὁ ἡ τό the, this, that, he, she, it
Σατανᾶς n. nom. masc. sg. Σατανᾶς Satan
14 ἀλλ' conj. ἀλλά but, yea, yet, nevertheless, howbeit, nay, therefore
κατὰ prep. κατά (+gen) against, by, throughout, down, (+acc) according to, after, with
σοῦ pron. gen. 2p. sg. σύ thou, you
ὀλίγα adj. acc. neut. pl. ὀλίγος few, little, small, a while, brief, short, short space
ὅτι conj. ὅτι that, for, because, how that, how, because that, for that, though
ἐκεῖ adv. ἐκεῖ there, thither, thitherward, yonder, yonder place
τὴν art. acc. fem. sg. ὁ ἡ τό the, this, that, he, she, it
διδαχὴν n. acc. fem. sg. διδαχή doctrine, teaching
Βαλαάμ n. gen. masc. sg. Βαλαάμ Balaam
ὃς relative pron. nom. masc. sg. ὅς ἥ ὅ who, which, what, that
τὸν art. acc. masc. sg. ὁ ἡ τό the, this, that, he, she, it
Βαλὰκ n. acc. masc. sg. Βαλάκ Balac
σκάνδαλον n. acc. neut. sg. σκάνδαλον offence, stumblingblock, thing that offend
ἐνώπιον prep. ἐνώπιον (+gen) before, in the sight of, in the presence of. (adv.) before
τῶν art. gen. masc. pl. ὁ ἡ τό the, this, that, he, she, it
υἱῶν n. gen. masc. pl. υἱός son, child, descendant, offspring, heir
Ἰσραὴλ pron. name. masc. inde. Ἰσραήλ Israel
εἰδωλόθυτα adj. acc. neut. pl. εἰδωλόθυτον thing sacrificed unto idols
καὶ conj. καί and, even, also, but
15 οὕτως adv. οὕτω οὕτως so, even so, thus, on this wise, likewise, after this manner
καὶ conj. καί and, even, also, but
σὺ pron. nom. 2p. sg. σύ thou, you
τὴν art. acc. fem. sg. ὁ ἡ τό the, this, that, he, she, it
διδαχὴν n. acc. fem. sg. διδαχή doctrine, teaching
τῶν art. gen. masc. pl. ὁ ἡ τό the, this, that, he, she, it
Νικολαϊτῶν n. gen. masc. pl. Νικολαΐτης Nicolaitane
ὃ relative pron. acc. neut. sg. ὅς ἥ ὅ who, which, what, that
16 εἰ conj. εἰ if, whether, that, though, forasmuch

δὲ conj. δέ but, and, now, also, to the contrary, rather, then
μή particle of negation. μή not, no, lest, neither, none, nothing, nor, never, without
σοι pron. dat. 2p. sg. σύ thou, you
ταχύ adv. ταχύ quickly, lightly
καὶ conj. καί and, even, also, but
μετ' prep. μετά (+gen) with, among, against, (+acc) after
αὐτῶν pron. gen. masc. 3p. pl. αὐτός ή ό self, of oneself, even, very, the same, he, she, it
ἐν prep. ἐν (+dat) in, by, with, among, at, on, through, to, within, into, of, for
τῇ art. dat. fem. sg. ὁ ἡ τό the, this, that, he, she, it
ῥομφαίᾳ n. dat. fem. sg. ῥομφαία sword
τοῦ art. gen. neut. sg. ὁ ἡ τό the, this, that, he, she, it
στόματός n. gen. neut. sg. στόμα mouth, face, edge
μου pron. gen. 1p. sg. ἐγώ I
17 ὁ art. nom. masc. sg. ὁ ἡ τό the, this, that, he, she, it
οὖς n. acc. neut. sg. οὖς ear
τί interrog. pron. acc. neut. sg. τίς what, who, why, where, which, how
τὸ art. nom. neut. sg. ὁ ἡ τό the, this, that, he, she, it
Πνεῦμα n. nom. neut. sg. πνεῦμα spirit, Spirit, Ghost, ghost, life. of the spirit, wind
ταῖς art. dat. fem. pl. ὁ ἡ τό the, this, that, he, she, it
ἐκκλησίαις n. dat. fem. pl. ἐκκλησία church, assembly
τῷ art. dat. masc. sg. ὁ ἡ τό the, this, that, he, she, it
αὐτῷ pron. dat. masc. 3p. sg. αὐτός ή ό self, of oneself, even, very, the same, he, she, it
ἀπὸ prep. ἀπό (+gen) from, of, out of, since, for, off, at, by, in, on
τοῦ art. gen. neut. sg. ὁ ἡ τό the, this, that, he, she, it
μάννα n. gen. neut. sg. μάννα manna
τοῦ art. gen. neut. sg. ὁ ἡ τό the, this, that, he, she, it
καὶ conj. καί and, even, also, but
αὐτῷ pron. dat. masc. 3p. sg. αὐτός ή ό self, of oneself, even, very, the same, he, she, it
ψῆφον n. acc. fem. sg. ψῆφος voice, pebble of voting, stone
λευκήν adj. acc. fem. sg. λευκός white
καὶ conj. καί and, even, also, but
ἐπὶ prep. ἐπί (+gen) on, in, upon, (+dat) in, at, for, upon, (+acc) on, upon, unto, to, against
τὴν art. acc. fem. sg. ὁ ἡ τό the, this, that, he, she, it
ψῆφον n. acc. fem. sg. ψῆφος voice, pebble of voting, stone
ὄνομα n. acc. neut. sg. ὄνομα name, call, surname
καινὸν adj. acc. neut. sg. καινός new
ὃ relative pron. acc. neut. sg. ὅς ἥ ὅ who, which, what, that
οὐδεὶς num. nom. masc. sg. οὐδείς no man, nothing, no, none, neither, not, nought
εἰ conj. εἰ if, whether, that, though, forasmuch
μὴ particle of negation. μή not, no, lest, neither, none, nothing, nor, never, without
ὁ art. nom. masc. sg. ὁ ἡ τό the, this, that, he, she, it
18 Καὶ conj. καί and, even, also, but
τῷ art. dat. masc. sg. ὁ ἡ τό the, this, that, he, she, it
ἀγγέλῳ n. dat. masc. sg. ἄγγελος angel, messenger
τῆς art. gen. fem. sg. ὁ ἡ τό the, this, that, he, she, it
ἐν prep. ἐν (+dat) in, by, with, among, at, on, through, to, within, into, of, for
Θυατείροις n. dat. neut. pl. Θυάτειρα Thyatira
ἐκκλησίας n. gen. fem. sg. ἐκκλησία church, assembly
Τάδε demo. pron. acc. neut. pl. ὅδε ἥδε τόδε this, he, she, such, thus
ὁ art. nom. masc. sg. ὁ ἡ τό the, this, that, he, she, it
υἱὸς n. nom. masc. sg. υἱός son, child, descendant, offspring, heir
τοῦ art. gen. masc. sg. ὁ ἡ τό the, this, that, he, she, it
Θεοῦ n. gen. masc. sg. θεός God, god
ὁ art. nom. masc. sg. ὁ ἡ τό the, this, that, he, she, it
τοὺς art. acc. masc. pl. ὁ ἡ τό the, this, that, he, she, it

ὀφθαλμοὺς n. acc. masc. pl. ὀφθαλμός eye, sight
αὐτοῦ pron. gen. masc. 3p. sg. αὐτός ή ό self, of oneself, even, very, the same, he, she, it
ὡς adv. ὡς as, when, as it were, how, about, like, as soon as, even as, while
φλόγα n. acc. fem. sg. φλόξ flame, flaming
πυρὸς n. gen. neut. sg. πῦρ fire, fiery
καὶ conj. καί and, even, also, but
οἱ art. nom. masc. pl. ὁ ἡ τό the, this, that, he, she, it
πόδες n. nom. masc. pl. πούς foot
αὐτοῦ pron. gen. masc. 3p. sg. αὐτός ή ό self, of oneself, even, very, the same, he, she, it
ὅμοιοι adj. nom. masc. pl. ὅμοιος like
χαλκολιβάνῳ n. dat. neut. sg. χαλκολίβανον fine brass
19 σου pron. gen. 2p. sg. σύ thou, you
τὰ art. acc. neut. pl. ὁ ἡ τό the, this, that, he, she, it
ἔργα n. acc. neut. pl. ἔργον work, deed, doing labour
καὶ conj. καί and, even, also, but
τὴν art. acc. fem. sg. ὁ ἡ τό the, this, that, he, she, it
ἀγάπην n. acc. fem. sg. ἀγάπη love, charity, feast of charity
καὶ conj. καί and, even, also, but
τὴν art. acc. fem. sg. ὁ ἡ τό the, this, that, he, she, it
διακονίαν n. acc. fem. sg. διακονία ministry, administration, service, office, relief
καὶ conj. καί and, even, also, but
τὴν art. acc. fem. sg. ὁ ἡ τό the, this, that, he, she, it
πίστιν n. acc. fem. sg. πίστις faith, assurance, belief, fidelity
καὶ conj. καί and, even, also, but
τὴν art. acc. fem. sg. ὁ ἡ τό the, this, that, he, she, it
ὑπομονήν n. acc. fem. sg. ὑπομονή patience, enduring
σου pron. gen. 2p. sg. σύ thou, you
καὶ conj. καί and, even, also, but
τὰ art. acc. neut. pl. ὁ ἡ τό the, this, that, he, she, it
ἔργα n. acc. neut. pl. ἔργον work, deed, doing labour
σου pron. gen. 2p. sg. σύ thou, you
καὶ conj. καί and, even, also, but
τὰ art. acc. neut. pl. ὁ ἡ τό the, this, that, he, she, it
ἔσχατα adj. acc. neut. pl. ἔσχατος last, lowest, uttermost, uttermost part
πλείονα compar. adj. acc. neut. pl. πολύς many, great, much, long, abundant
τῶν art. gen. neut. pl. ὁ ἡ τό the, this, that, he, she, it
πρώτων ordinal. adj. gen. neut. pl. πρῶτος first, chief, first of all, chiefest, best
20 ἀλλ' conj. ἀλλά but, yea, yet, nevertheless, howbeit, nay, therefore
κατὰ prep. κατά (+gen) against, by, throughout, down, (+acc) according to, after, with
σοῦ pron. gen. 2p. sg. σύ thou, you
ὀλίγα adj. acc. neut. pl. ὀλίγος few, little, small, a while, brief, short, short space
ὅτι conj. ὅτι that, for, because, how that, how, because that, for that, though
τὴν art. acc. fem. sg. ὁ ἡ τό the, this, that, he, she, it
γυναῖκα n. acc. fem. sg. γυνή woman, wife
Ἰεζαβήλ n. acc. fem. sg. Ἰεζάβελ Jezebel
τὴν art. acc. fem. sg. ὁ ἡ τό the, this, that, he, she, it
ἑαυτὴν reflexive pron. acc. fem. 3p. sg. ἑαυτοῦ himself, herself, itself, yourself, ourselves
προφῆτιν n. acc. fem. sg. προφῆτις prophetess
καὶ conj. καί and, even, also, but
ἐμοὺς poss. pron. acc. masc. 1p. pl. ἐμός my, mine, mine own, of me
δούλους n. acc. masc. pl. δοῦλος servant, bondman, bond, slave
καὶ conj. καί and, even, also, but
εἰδωλόθυτα adj. acc. neut. pl. εἰδωλόθυτον thing sacrificed unto idols
21 καὶ conj. καί and, even, also, but
αὐτῇ pron. dat. fem. 3p. sg. αὐτός ή ό self, of oneself, even, very, the same, he, she, it

χρόνον n. acc. masc. sg. χρόνος time, season, space
ἵνα conj. ἵνα that, to, lest, for to, so that, albeit, because, for, so as
ἐκ prep. ἐκ ἐξ (+gen) of, from, out of, by, on, with, in, among, through
τῆς art. gen. fem. sg. ὁ ἡ τό the, this, that, he, she, it
πορνείας n. gen. fem. sg. πορνεία fornication
αὐτῆς pron. gen. fem. 3p. sg. αὐτός ή ό self, of oneself, even, very, the same, he, she, it
καὶ conj. καί and, even, also, but
οὐ particle of negation. οὐ οὐκ οὐχ not, no, neither, none, nay, nor, never, nothing
22 ἐγὼ pron. nom. 1p. sg. ἐγώ I
αὐτὴν pron. acc. fem. 3p. sg. αὐτός ή ό self, of oneself, even, very, the same, he, she, it
εἰς prep. εἰς (+acc) into, to, unto, for, in, on, toward, against, upon, at, among
κλίνην n. acc. fem. sg. κλίνη bed, table
καὶ conj. καί and, even, also, but
τοὺς art. acc. masc. pl. ὁ ἡ τό the, this, that, he, she, it
μετ' prep. μετά (+gen) with, among, against, (+acc) after
αὐτῆς pron. gen. fem. 3p. sg. αὐτός ή ό self, of oneself, even, very, the same, he, she, it
εἰς prep. εἰς (+acc) into, to, unto, for, in, on, toward, against, upon, at, among
θλῖψιν n. acc. fem. sg. θλῖψις tribulation, affliction, anguish, persecution
μεγάλην adj. acc. fem. sg. μέγας great, loud, greatest, high, large, mighty, strong
ἐὰν conj. ἐάν if, soever, except, though, and if, but, whether, if so, so
μὴ particle of negation. μή not, no, lest, neither, none, nothing, nor, never, without
ἐκ prep. ἐκ ἐξ (+gen) of, from, out of, by, on, with, in, among, through
τῶν art. gen. neut. pl. ὁ ἡ τό the, this, that, he, she, it
ἔργων n. gen. neut. pl. ἔργον work, deed, doing labour
αὐτῶν pron. gen. masc. 3p. pl. αὐτός ή ό self, of oneself, even, very, the same, he, she, it
23 καὶ conj. καί and, even, also, but
τὰ art. acc. neut. pl. ὁ ἡ τό the, this, that, he, she, it
τέκνα n. acc. neut. pl. τέκνον child, son, daughter
αὐτῆς pron. gen. fem. 3p. sg. αὐτός ή ό self, of oneself, even, very, the same, he, she, it
ἐν prep. ἐν (+dat) in, by, with, among, at, on, through, to, within, into, of, for
θανάτῳ n. dat. masc. sg. θάνατος death
καὶ conj. καί and, even, also, but
πᾶσαι adj. nom. fem. pl. πᾶς πᾶσα πᾶν all, every, whosoever, every one, no, whole, any
αἱ art. nom. fem. pl. ὁ ἡ τό the, this, that, he, she, it
ἐκκλησίαι n. nom. fem. pl. ἐκκλησία church, assembly
ὅτι conj. ὅτι that, for, because, how that, how, because that, for that, though
ἐγώ pron. nom. 1p. sg. ἐγώ I
ὁ art. nom. masc. sg. ὁ ἡ τό the, this, that, he, she, it
νεφροὺς n. acc. masc. pl. νεφρός (pl.) reins, kidneys
καὶ conj. καί and, even, also, but
καρδίας n. acc. fem. pl. καρδία heart
καὶ conj. καί and, even, also, but
ὑμῖν pron. dat. 2p. pl. σύ thou, you
ἑκάστῳ adj. dat. masc. sg. ἕκαστος every man, every, every one, any man, each
κατὰ prep. κατά (+gen) against, by, throughout, down, (+acc) according to, after, with
τὰ art. acc. neut. pl. ὁ ἡ τό the, this, that, he, she, it
ἔργα n. acc. neut. pl. ἔργον work, deed, doing labour
ὑμῶν pron. gen. 2p. pl. σύ thou, you
24 ὑμῖν pron. dat. 2p. pl. σύ thou, you
δὲ conj. δέ but, and, now, also, to the contrary, rather, then
καὶ conj. καί and, even, also, but
τοῖς art. dat. masc. pl. ὁ ἡ τό the, this, that, he, she, it
λοιποῖς adj. dat. masc. pl. λοιπός other, rest, remnant, residue, which remain
τοῖς art. dat. masc. pl. ὁ ἡ τό the, this, that, he, she, it
ἐν prep. ἐν (+dat) in, by, with, among, at, on, through, to, within, into, of, for

Θυατείροις n. dat. neut. pl. Θυάτειρα Thyatira
ὅσοι relative pron. nom. masc. pl. ὅσος as many as, whatsoever, that, as long as, how much
οὐκ particle of negation. οὐ οὐκ οὐχ not, no, neither, none, nay, nor, never, nothing
τὴν art. acc. fem. sg. ὁ ἡ τό the, this, that, he, she, it
διδαχὴν n. acc. fem. sg. διδαχή doctrine, teaching
ταύτην demo. pron. acc. fem. sg. οὗτος αὕτη τοῦτο this, the same, this same, he, she, it
καὶ conj. καί and, even, also, but
οἵτινες relative pron. nom. masc. pl. ὅστις which, who, whosoever, that, whatsoever
οὐκ particle of negation. οὐ οὐκ οὐχ not, no, neither, none, nay, nor, never, nothing
τὰ art. acc. neut. pl. ὁ ἡ τό the, this, that, he, she, it
βάθη n. acc. neut. pl. βάθος deepness, depth, deep, deep thing
τοῦ art. gen. masc. sg. ὁ ἡ τό the, this, that, he, she, it
Σατανᾶ n. gen. masc. sg. Σατανᾶς Satan
ὡς adv. ὡς as, when, as it were, how, about, like, as soon as, even as, while
Οὐ particle of negation. οὐ οὐκ οὐχ not, no, neither, none, nay, nor, never, nothing
ἐφ' prep. ἐπί (+gen) on, in, upon, (+dat) in, at, for, upon, (+acc) on, upon, unto, to, against
ὑμᾶς pron. acc. 2p. pl. σύ thou, you
ἄλλο adj. acc. neut. sg. ἄλλος other, another, some, one, more, otherwise
βάρος n. acc. neut. sg. βάρος burden, burdensome, weight
25 πλὴν conj. πλήν but, nevertheless, but rather, notwithstanding, except, than
ὃ relative pron. acc. neut. sg. ὅς ἥ ὅ who, which, what, that
ἄχρις prep. ἄχρι or ἄχρις (+gen) until, unto, till, even to, as far as, while, into
οὗ relative pron. gen. masc. sg. ὅς ἥ ὅ who, which, what, that
ἂν particle. ἄν Indicating contingency. No English translation.
26 καὶ conj. καί and, even, also, but
ὁ art. nom. masc. sg. ὁ ἡ τό the, this, that, he, she, it
καὶ conj. καί and, even, also, but
ὁ art. nom. masc. sg. ὁ ἡ τό the, this, that, he, she, it
ἄχρι prep. ἄχρι or ἄχρις (+gen) until, unto, till, even to, as far as, while, into
τέλους n. gen. neut. sg. τέλος end, custom, ending, finally, uttermost
τὰ art. acc. neut. pl. ὁ ἡ τό the, this, that, he, she, it
ἔργα n. acc. neut. pl. ἔργον work, deed, doing labour
μου pron. gen. 1p. sg. ἐγώ I
αὐτῷ pron. dat. masc. 3p. sg. αὐτός ἡ ὁ self, of oneself, even, very, the same, he, she, it
ἐξουσίαν n. acc. fem. sg. ἐξουσία power, authority, right, strength, jurisdiction
ἐπὶ prep. ἐπί (+gen) on, in, upon, (+dat) in, at, for, upon, (+acc) on, upon, unto, to, against
τῶν art. gen. neut. pl. ὁ ἡ τό the, this, that, he, she, it
ἐθνῶν n. gen. neut. pl. ἔθνος Gentile, nation, heathen, people
27 καὶ conj. καί and, even, also, but
αὐτοὺς pron. acc. masc. 3p. pl. αὐτός ἡ ὁ self, of oneself, even, very, the same, he, she, it
ἐν prep. ἐν (+dat) in, by, with, among, at, on, through, to, within, into, of, for
ῥάβδῳ n. dat. fem. sg. ῥάβδος rod, sceptre, stave, staff
σιδηρᾷ adj. dat. fem. sg. σιδήρεος iron, of iron
ὡς adv. ὡς as, when, as it were, how, about, like, as soon as, even as, while
τὰ art. nom. neut. pl. ὁ ἡ τό the, this, that, he, she, it
σκεύη n. nom. neut. pl. σκεῦος vessel, good, sail, stuff
τὰ art. nom. neut. pl. ὁ ἡ τό the, this, that, he, she, it
κεραμικὰ adj. nom. neut. pl. κεραμικός of a potter
ὡς adv. ὡς as, when, as it were, how, about, like, as soon as, even as, while
κἀγὼ pron. nom. 1p. sg. κἀγώ and I, I also, so I, even as I
παρὰ prep. παρά (+gen) of, from, (+dat) with, for, (+acc) beside, at, by, above, against
τοῦ art. gen. masc. sg. ὁ ἡ τό the, this, that, he, she, it
πατρός n. gen. masc. sg. πατήρ Father, father, parent
μου pron. gen. 1p. sg. ἐγώ I
28 καὶ conj. καί and, even, also, but

αὐτῷ pron. dat. masc. 3p. sg. αὐτός ή ό self, of oneself, even, very, the same, he, she, it
τὸν art. acc. masc. sg. ὁ ἡ τό the, this, that, he, she, it
ἀστέρα n. acc. masc. sg. ἀστήρ star
τὸν art. acc. masc. sg. ὁ ἡ τό the, this, that, he, she, it
πρωϊνόν adj. acc. masc. sg. πρωϊνός morning
29 ὁ art. nom. masc. sg. ὁ ἡ τό the, this, that, he, she, it
οὖς n. acc. neut. sg. οὖς ear
τί interrog. pron. acc. neut. sg. τίς what, who, why, where, which, how
τὸ art. nom. neut. sg. ὁ ἡ τό the, this, that, he, she, it
Πνεῦμα n. nom. neut. sg. πνεῦμα spirit, Spirit, Ghost, ghost, life. of the spirit, wind
ταῖς art. dat. fem. pl. ὁ ἡ τό the, this, that, he, she, it
ἐκκλησίαις n. dat. fem. pl. ἐκκλησία church, assembly

3

1 Καὶ conj. καί and, even, also, but
τῷ art. dat. masc. sg. ὁ ἡ τό the, this, that, he, she, it
ἀγγέλῳ n. dat. masc. sg. ἄγγελος angel, messenger
τῆς art. gen. fem. sg. ὁ ἡ τό the, this, that, he, she, it
ἐν prep. ἐν (+dat) in, by, with, among, at, on, through, to, within, into, of, for
Σάρδεσιν n. dat. fem. pl. Σάρδεις Sardis
ἐκκλησίας n. gen. fem. sg. ἐκκλησία church, assembly
Τάδε demo. pron. acc. neut. pl. ὅδε ἥδε τόδε this, he, she, such, thus
ὁ art. nom. masc. sg. ὁ ἡ τό the, this, that, he, she, it
τὰ art. acc. neut. pl. ὁ ἡ τό the, this, that, he, she, it
ἑπτὰ num. acc. neut. pl. ἑπτά seven, seventh
πνεύματα n. acc. neut. pl. πνεῦμα spirit, Spirit, Ghost, ghost, life. of the spirit, wind
τοῦ art. gen. masc. sg. ὁ ἡ τό the, this, that, he, she, it
Θεοῦ n. gen. masc. sg. θεός God, god
καὶ conj. καί and, even, also, but
τοὺς art. acc. masc. pl. ὁ ἡ τό the, this, that, he, she, it
ἑπτὰ num. acc. masc. pl. ἑπτά seven, seventh
ἀστέρας n. acc. masc. pl. ἀστήρ star
σου pron. gen. 2p. sg. σύ thou, you
τὰ art. acc. neut. pl. ὁ ἡ τό the, this, that, he, she, it
ἔργα n. acc. neut. pl. ἔργον work, deed, doing labour
ὅτι conj. ὅτι that, for, because, how that, how, because that, for that, though
τὸ art. acc. neut. sg. ὁ ἡ τό the, this, that, he, she, it
ὄνομα n. acc. neut. sg. ὄνομα name, call, surname
ὅτι conj. ὅτι that, for, because, how that, how, because that, for that, though
καὶ conj. καί and, even, also, but
νεκρὸς adj. nom. masc. sg. νεκρός dead
2 καὶ conj. καί and, even, also, but
τὰ art. acc. neut. pl. ὁ ἡ τό the, this, that, he, she, it
λοιπὰ adj. acc. neut. pl. λοιπός other, rest, remnant, residue, which remain
ἃ relative pron. nom. neut. pl. ὅς ἥ ὅ who, which, what, that
οὐ particle of negation. οὐ οὐκ οὐχ not, no, neither, none, nay, nor, never, nothing
γὰρ conj. γάρ for, and, because, but, indeed
σου pron. gen. 2p. sg. σύ thou, you
τὰ art. acc. neut. pl. ὁ ἡ τό the, this, that, he, she, it
ἔργα n. acc. neut. pl. ἔργον work, deed, doing labour
ἐνώπιον prep. ἐνώπιον (+gen) before, in the sight of, in the presence of. (adv.) before
τοῦ art. gen. masc. sg. ὁ ἡ τό the, this, that, he, she, it
Θεοῦ n. gen. masc. sg. θεός God, god
3 οὖν conj. οὖν therefore, then, so, and, now, wherefore

πῶς adv. πῶς how, by what means, after what manner
καὶ conj. καί and, even, also, but
καὶ conj. καί and, even, also, but
καὶ conj. καί and, even, also, but
ἐὰν conj. ἐάν if, soever, except, though, and if, but, whether, if so, so
οὖν conj. οὖν therefore, then, so, and, now, wherefore
μὴ particle of negation. μή not, no, lest, neither, none, nothing, nor, never, without
ἐπὶ prep. ἐπί (+gen) on, in, upon, (+dat) in, at, for, upon, (+acc) on, upon, unto, to, against
σε pron. acc. 2p. sg. σύ thou, you
ὡς adv. ὡς as, when, as it were, how, about, like, as soon as, even as, while
κλέπτης n. nom. masc. sg. κλέπτης thief
καὶ conj. καί and, even, also, but
οὐ particle of negation. οὐ οὐκ οὐχ not, no, neither, none, nay, nor, never, nothing
μὴ particle of negation. μή not, no, lest, neither, none, nothing, nor, never, without
ποίαν interrog. pron. acc. fem. sg. ποῖος what, which, what manner of
ὥραν n. acc. fem. sg. ὥρα hour, time, season
ἐπὶ prep. ἐπί (+gen) on, in, upon, (+dat) in, at, for, upon, (+acc) on, upon, unto, to, against
σε pron. acc. 2p. sg. σύ thou, you
4 ὀλίγα adj. acc. neut. pl. ὀλίγος few, little, small, a while, brief, short, short space
ὀνόματα n. acc. neut. pl. ὄνομα name, call, surname
καὶ conj. καί and, even, also, but
ἐν prep. ἐν (+dat) in, by, with, among, at, on, through, to, within, into, of, for
Σάρδεσιν n. dat. fem. pl. Σάρδεις Sardis
ἃ relative pron. nom. neut. pl. ὅς ἥ ὅ who, which, what, that
οὐκ particle of negation. οὐ οὐκ οὐχ not, no, neither, none, nay, nor, never, nothing
τὰ art. acc. neut. pl. ὁ ἡ τό the, this, that, he, she, it
ἱμάτια n. acc. neut. pl. ἱμάτιον cloke, garment, clothes, raiment, robe, vesture
αὐτῶν pron. gen. neut. 3p. pl. αὐτός ἡ ὁ self, of oneself, even, very, the same, he, she, it
καὶ conj. καί and, even, also, but
μετ' prep. μετά (+gen) with, among, against, (+acc) after
ἐμοῦ pron. gen. 1p. sg. ἐγώ I
ἐν prep. ἐν (+dat) in, by, with, among, at, on, through, to, within, into, of, for
λευκοῖς adj. dat. neut. pl. λευκός white
ὅτι conj. ὅτι that, for, because, how that, how, because that, for that, though
ἄξιοί adj. nom. masc. pl. ἄξιος worthy, meet, due reward
5 ὁ art. nom. masc. sg. ὁ ἡ τό the, this, that, he, she, it
οὗτος demo. pron. nom. masc. sg. οὗτος αὕτη τοῦτο this, the same, this same, he, she, it
ἐν prep. ἐν (+dat) in, by, with, among, at, on, through, to, within, into, of, for
ἱματίοις n. dat. neut. pl. ἱμάτιον cloke, garment, clothes, raiment, robe, vesture
λευκοῖς adj. dat. neut. pl. λευκός white
καὶ conj. καί and, even, also, but
οὐ particle of negation. οὐ οὐκ οὐχ not, no, neither, none, nay, nor, never, nothing
μὴ particle of negation. μή not, no, lest, neither, none, nothing, nor, never, without
τὸ art. acc. neut. sg. ὁ ἡ τό the, this, that, he, she, it
ὄνομα n. acc. neut. sg. ὄνομα name, call, surname
αὐτοῦ pron. gen. masc. 3p. sg. αὐτός ἡ ὁ self, of oneself, even, very, the same, he, she, it
ἐκ prep. ἐκ ἐξ (+gen) of, from, out of, by, on, with, in, among, through
τῆς art. gen. fem. sg. ὁ ἡ τό the, this, that, he, she, it
βίβλου n. gen. fem. sg. βίβλος book, record
τῆς art. gen. fem. sg. ὁ ἡ τό the, this, that, he, she, it
ζωῆς n. gen. fem. sg. ζωή life, lifetime
καὶ conj. καί and, even, also, but
τὸ art. acc. neut. sg. ὁ ἡ τό the, this, that, he, she, it
ὄνομα n. acc. neut. sg. ὄνομα name, call, surname
αὐτοῦ pron. gen. masc. 3p. sg. αὐτός ἡ ὁ self, of oneself, even, very, the same, he, she, it

ἐνώπιον prep. ἐνώπιον (+gen) before, in the sight of, in the presence of. (adv.) before
τοῦ art. gen. masc. sg. ὁ ἡ τό the, this, that, he, she, it
πατρός n. gen. masc. sg. πατήρ Father, father, parent
μου pron. gen. 1p. sg. ἐγώ I
τὸ art. acc. neut. sg. ὁ ἡ τό the, this, that, he, she, it
ὄνομα n. acc. neut. sg. ὄνομα name, call, surname
αὐτοῦ pron. gen. masc. 3p. sg. αὐτός ή ό self, of oneself, even, very, the same, he, she, it
ἐνώπιον prep. ἐνώπιον (+gen) before, in the sight of, in the presence of. (adv.) before
τῶν art. gen. masc. pl. ὁ ἡ τό the, this, that, he, she, it
ἀγγέλων n. gen. masc. pl. ἄγγελος angel, messenger
αὐτοῦ pron. gen. masc. 3p. sg. αὐτός ή ό self, of oneself, even, very, the same, he, she, it
6 ὁ art. nom. masc. sg. ὁ ἡ τό the, this, that, he, she, it
οὖς n. acc. neut. sg. οὖς ear
τί interrog. pron. acc. neut. sg. τίς what, who, why, where, which, how
τὸ art. nom. neut. sg. ὁ ἡ τό the, this, that, he, she, it
Πνεῦμα n. nom. neut. sg. πνεῦμα spirit, Spirit, Ghost, ghost, life. of the spirit, wind
ταῖς art. dat. fem. pl. ὁ ἡ τό the, this, that, he, she, it
ἐκκλησίαις n. dat. fem. pl. ἐκκλησία church, assembly
7 Καὶ conj. καί and, even, also, but
τῷ art. dat. masc. sg. ὁ ἡ τό the, this, that, he, she, it
ἀγγέλῳ n. dat. masc. sg. ἄγγελος angel, messenger
τῆς art. gen. fem. sg. ὁ ἡ τό the, this, that, he, she, it
ἐν prep. ἐν (+dat) in, by, with, among, at, on, through, to, within, into, of, for
Φιλαδελφείᾳ n. dat. fem. sg. Φιλαδέλφεια Philadelphia
ἐκκλησίας n. gen. fem. sg. ἐκκλησία church, assembly
Τάδε demo. pron. acc. neut. pl. ὅδε ἥδε τόδε this, he, she, such, thus
ὁ art. nom. masc. sg. ὁ ἡ τό the, this, that, he, she, it
ἅγιος adj. nom. masc. sg. ἅγιος Holy, holy, saint, Holy One, holy thing, most holy
ὁ art. nom. masc. sg. ὁ ἡ τό the, this, that, he, she, it
ἀληθινός adj. nom. masc. sg. ἀληθινός true
ὁ art. nom. masc. sg. ὁ ἡ τό the, this, that, he, she, it
τὴν art. acc. fem. sg. ὁ ἡ τό the, this, that, he, she, it
κλεῖδα n. acc. fem. sg. κλείς key
τοῦ art. gen. masc. sg. ὁ ἡ τό the, this, that, he, she, it
Δαβίδ n. gen. masc. sg. Δαβίδ David
ὁ art. nom. masc. sg. ὁ ἡ τό the, this, that, he, she, it
καὶ conj. καί and, even, also, but
οὐδεὶς num. nom. masc. sg. οὐδείς no man, nothing, no, none, neither, not, nought
καὶ conj. καί and, even, also, but
καὶ conj. καί and, even, also, but
οὐδεὶς num. nom. masc. sg. οὐδείς no man, nothing, no, none, neither, not, nought
8 σου pron. gen. 2p. sg. σύ thou, you
τὰ art. acc. neut. pl. ὁ ἡ τό the, this, that, he, she, it
ἔργα n. acc. neut. pl. ἔργον work, deed, doing labour
ἐνώπιόν prep. ἐνώπιον (+gen) before, in the sight of, in the presence of. (adv.) before
σου pron. gen. 2p. sg. σύ thou, you
θύραν n. acc. fem. sg. θύρα door, gate
καὶ conj. καί and, even, also, but
οὐδεὶς num. nom. masc. sg. οὐδείς no man, nothing, no, none, neither, not, nought
αὐτήν pron. acc. fem. 3p. sg. αὐτός ή ό self, of oneself, even, very, the same, he, she, it
ὅτι conj. ὅτι that, for, because, how that, how, because that, for that, though
μικρὰν adj. acc. fem. sg. μικρός little, small, least, less
δύναμιν n. acc. fem. sg. δύναμις power, mighty work, miracle, strength, might
καὶ conj. καί and, even, also, but
μου pron. gen. 1p. sg. ἐγώ I

τὸν art. acc. masc. sg. ὁ ἡ τό the, this, that, he, she, it
λόγον n. acc. masc. sg. λόγος word, saying, account, speech, thing, matter
καὶ conj. καί and, even, also, but
οὐκ particle of negation. οὐ οὐκ οὐχ not, no, neither, none, nay, nor, never, nothing
τὸ art. acc. neut. sg. ὁ ἡ τό the, this, that, he, she, it
ὄνομά n. acc. neut. sg. ὄνομα name, call, surname
μου pron. gen. 1p. sg. ἐγώ I
9 ἐκ prep. ἐκ ἐξ (+gen) of, from, out of, by, on, with, in, among, through
τῆς art. gen. fem. sg. ὁ ἡ τό the, this, that, he, she, it
συναγωγῆς n. gen. fem. sg. συναγωγή synagogue, assembly, congregation
τοῦ art. gen. masc. sg. ὁ ἡ τό the, this, that, he, she, it
Σατανᾶ n. gen. masc. sg. Σατανᾶς Satan
τῶν art. gen. masc. pl. ὁ ἡ τό the, this, that, he, she, it
ἑαυτοὺς reflexive pron. acc. masc. 3p. pl. ἑαυτοῦ himself, herself, itself, yourself, ourselves
Ἰουδαίους adj. acc. masc. pl. Ἰουδαῖος Jew, Jewess
καὶ conj. καί and, even, also, but
οὐκ particle of negation. οὐ οὐκ οὐχ not, no, neither, none, nay, nor, never, nothing
ἀλλὰ conj. ἀλλά but, yea, yet, nevertheless, howbeit, nay, therefore
αὐτοὺς pron. acc. masc. 3p. pl. αὐτός ή ό self, of oneself, even, very, the same, he, she, it
ἵνα conj. ἵνα that, to, lest, for to, so that, albeit, because, for, so as
καὶ conj. καί and, even, also, but
ἐνώπιον prep. ἐνώπιον (+gen) before, in the sight of, in the presence of. (adv.) before
τῶν art. gen. masc. pl. ὁ ἡ τό the, this, that, he, she, it
ποδῶν n. gen. masc. pl. πούς foot
σου pron. gen. 2p. sg. σύ thou, you
καὶ conj. καί and, even, also, but
ὅτι conj. ὅτι that, for, because, how that, how, because that, for that, though
ἐγὼ pron. nom. 1p. sg. ἐγώ I
σε pron. acc. 2p. sg. σύ thou, you
10 ὅτι conj. ὅτι that, for, because, how that, how, because that, for that, though
τὸν art. acc. masc. sg. ὁ ἡ τό the, this, that, he, she, it
λόγον n. acc. masc. sg. λόγος word, saying, account, speech, thing, matter
τῆς art. gen. fem. sg. ὁ ἡ τό the, this, that, he, she, it
ὑπομονῆς n. gen. fem. sg. ὑπομονή patience, enduring
μου pron. gen. 1p. sg. ἐγώ I
κἀγώ pron. nom. 1p. sg. κἀγώ and I, I also, so I, even as I
σε pron. acc. 2p. sg. σύ thou, you
ἐκ prep. ἐκ ἐξ (+gen) of, from, out of, by, on, with, in, among, through
τῆς art. gen. fem. sg. ὁ ἡ τό the, this, that, he, she, it
ὥρας n. gen. fem. sg. ὥρα hour, time, season
τοῦ art. gen. masc. sg. ὁ ἡ τό the, this, that, he, she, it
πειρασμοῦ n. gen. masc. sg. πειρασμός temptation, trial
τῆς art. gen. fem. sg. ὁ ἡ τό the, this, that, he, she, it
ἐπὶ prep. ἐπί (+gen) on, in, upon, (+dat) in, at, for, upon, (+acc) on, upon, unto, to, against
τῆς art. gen. fem. sg. ὁ ἡ τό the, this, that, he, she, it
οἰκουμένης n. gen. fem. sg. οἰκουμένη world, earth
ὅλης adj. gen. fem. sg. ὅλος all, whole, every whit, altogether
τοὺς art. acc. masc. pl. ὁ ἡ τό the, this, that, he, she, it
ἐπὶ prep. ἐπί (+gen) on, in, upon, (+dat) in, at, for, upon, (+acc) on, upon, unto, to, against
τῆς art. gen. fem. sg. ὁ ἡ τό the, this, that, he, she, it
γῆς n. gen. fem. sg. γῆ earth, land, ground, country
11 ταχύ adv. ταχύ quickly, lightly
ὃ relative pron. acc. neut. sg. ὅς ἥ ὅ who, which, what, that
ἵνα conj. ἵνα that, to, lest, for to, so that, albeit, because, for, so as
μηδεὶς num. nom. masc. sg. μηδείς μηδεμία μηδέν no man, nothing, no, none, not at all

τὸν art. acc. masc. sg. ὁ ἡ τό the, this, that, he, she, it
στέφανόν n. acc. masc. sg. στέφανος crown
σου pron. gen. 2p. sg. σύ thou, you
12 ὁ art. nom. masc. sg. ὁ ἡ τό the, this, that, he, she, it
αὐτὸν pron. acc. masc. 3p. sg. αὐτός ἡ ὁ self, of oneself, even, very, the same, he, she, it
στῦλον n. acc. masc. sg. στῦλος pillar
ἐν prep. ἐν (+dat) in, by, with, among, at, on, through, to, within, into, of, for
τῷ art. dat. masc. sg. ὁ ἡ τό the, this, that, he, she, it
ναῷ n. dat. masc. sg. ναός temple, shrine
τοῦ art. gen. masc. sg. ὁ ἡ τό the, this, that, he, she, it
Θεοῦ n. gen. masc. sg. θεός God, god
μου pron. gen. 1p. sg. ἐγώ I
καὶ conj. καί and, even, also, but
ἔξω adv. ἔξω out, without, out of, forth, away, outward
οὐ particle of negation. οὐ οὐκ οὐχ not, no, neither, none, nay, nor, never, nothing
μὴ particle of negation. μή not, no, lest, neither, none, nothing, nor, never, without
ἔτι adv. ἔτι yet, more, any more, further, still, moreover
καὶ conj. καί and, even, also, but
ἐπ' prep. ἐπί (+gen) on, in, upon, (+dat) in, at, for, upon, (+acc) on, upon, unto, to, against
αὐτὸν pron. acc. masc. 3p. sg. αὐτός ἡ ὁ self, of oneself, even, very, the same, he, she, it
τὸ art. acc. neut. sg. ὁ ἡ τό the, this, that, he, she, it
ὄνομα n. acc. neut. sg. ὄνομα name, call, surname
τοῦ art. gen. masc. sg. ὁ ἡ τό the, this, that, he, she, it
Θεοῦ n. gen. masc. sg. θεός God, god
μου pron. gen. 1p. sg. ἐγώ I
καὶ conj. καί and, even, also, but
τὸ art. acc. neut. sg. ὁ ἡ τό the, this, that, he, she, it
ὄνομα n. acc. neut. sg. ὄνομα name, call, surname
τῆς art. gen. fem. sg. ὁ ἡ τό the, this, that, he, she, it
πόλεως n. gen. fem. sg. πόλις city
τοῦ art. gen. masc. sg. ὁ ἡ τό the, this, that, he, she, it
Θεοῦ n. gen. masc. sg. θεός God, god
μου pron. gen. 1p. sg. ἐγώ I
τῆς art. gen. fem. sg. ὁ ἡ τό the, this, that, he, she, it
καινῆς adj. gen. fem. sg. καινός new
Ἱερουσαλήμ pron. name. fem. inde. Ἱερουσαλήμ Jerusalem
ἡ art. nom. fem. sg. ὁ ἡ τό the, this, that, he, she, it
ἐκ prep. ἐκ ἐξ (+gen) of, from, out of, by, on, with, in, among, through
τοῦ art. gen. masc. sg. ὁ ἡ τό the, this, that, he, she, it
οὐρανοῦ n. gen. masc. sg. οὐρανός heaven, air, sky
ἀπὸ prep. ἀπό (+gen) from, of, out of, since, for, off, at, by, in, on
τοῦ art. gen. masc. sg. ὁ ἡ τό the, this, that, he, she, it
Θεοῦ n. gen. masc. sg. θεός God, god
μου pron. gen. 1p. sg. ἐγώ I
καὶ conj. καί and, even, also, but
τὸ art. acc. neut. sg. ὁ ἡ τό the, this, that, he, she, it
ὄνομα n. acc. neut. sg. ὄνομα name, call, surname
μου pron. gen. 1p. sg. ἐγώ I
τὸ art. acc. neut. sg. ὁ ἡ τό the, this, that, he, she, it
καινόν adj. acc. neut. sg. καινός new
13 ὁ art. nom. masc. sg. ὁ ἡ τό the, this, that, he, she, it
οὖς n. acc. neut. sg. οὖς ear
τί interrog. pron. acc. neut. sg. τίς what, who, why, where, which, how
τὸ art. nom. neut. sg. ὁ ἡ τό the, this, that, he, she, it
Πνεῦμα n. nom. neut. sg. πνεῦμα spirit, Spirit, Ghost, ghost, life. of the spirit, wind

ταῖς art. dat. fem. pl. ὁ ἡ τό the, this, that, he, she, it
ἐκκλησίαις n. dat. fem. pl. ἐκκλησία church, assembly
14 Καὶ conj. καί and, even, also, but
τῷ art. dat. masc. sg. ὁ ἡ τό the, this, that, he, she, it
ἀγγέλῳ n. dat. masc. sg. ἄγγελος angel, messenger
τῆς art. gen. fem. sg. ὁ ἡ τό the, this, that, he, she, it
ἐκκλησίας n. gen. fem. sg. ἐκκλησία church, assembly
Λαοδικέων n. gen. masc. pl. Λαοδικεύς Laodicean
Τάδε demo. pron. acc. neut. pl. ὅδε ἥδε τόδε this, he, she, such, thus
ὁ art. nom. masc. sg. ὁ ἡ τό the, this, that, he, she, it
'Αμήν particle. ἀμήν amen, verily
ὁ art. nom. masc. sg. ὁ ἡ τό the, this, that, he, she, it
μάρτυς n. nom. masc. sg. μάρτυς or μάρτυρ witness, martyr, record
ὁ art. nom. masc. sg. ὁ ἡ τό the, this, that, he, she, it
πιστὸς adj. nom. masc. sg. πιστός faithful, believing, true, sure
καὶ conj. καί and, even, also, but
ἀληθινός adj. nom. masc. sg. ἀληθινός true
ἡ art. nom. fem. sg. ὁ ἡ τό the, this, that, he, she, it
ἀρχὴ n. nom. fem. sg. ἀρχή beginning, principality, corner, first, magistrate, rule
τῆς art. gen. fem. sg. ὁ ἡ τό the, this, that, he, she, it
κτίσεως n. gen. fem. sg. κτίσις creature, creation, building, ordinance
τοῦ art. gen. masc. sg. ὁ ἡ τό the, this, that, he, she, it
Θεοῦ n. gen. masc. sg. θεός God, god
15 σου pron. gen. 2p. sg. σύ thou, you
τὰ art. acc. neut. pl. ὁ ἡ τό the, this, that, he, she, it
ἔργα n. acc. neut. pl. ἔργον work, deed, doing labour
ὅτι conj. ὅτι that, for, because, how that, how, because that, for that, though
οὔτε conj. οὔτε neither, nor, nor yet, no, none
ψυχρὸς adj. nom. masc. sg. ψυχρός cold
οὔτε conj. οὔτε neither, nor, nor yet, no, none
ζεστός adj. nom. masc. sg. ζεστός hot
ὄφελον interj. ὄφελον O that! Would that!
ψυχρὸς adj. nom. masc. sg. ψυχρός cold
ἢ particle. ἤ or, than, either, nor, or else, and, rather than
ζεστός adj. nom. masc. sg. ζεστός hot
16 οὕτως adv. οὕτω οὕτως so, even so, thus, on this wise, likewise, after this manner
ὅτι conj. ὅτι that, for, because, how that, how, because that, for that, though
χλιαρὸς adj. nom. masc. sg. χλιαρός lukewarm
καὶ conj. καί and, even, also, but
οὔτε conj. οὔτε neither, nor, nor yet, no, none
ψυχρός adj. nom. masc. sg. ψυχρός cold
οὔτε conj. οὔτε neither, nor, nor yet, no, none
ζεστὸς adj. nom. masc. sg. ζεστός hot
σε pron. acc. 2p. sg. σύ thou, you
ἐκ prep. ἐκ ἐξ (+gen) of, from, out of, by, on, with, in, among, through
τοῦ art. gen. neut. sg. ὁ ἡ τό the, this, that, he, she, it
στόματός n. gen. neut. sg. στόμα mouth, face, edge
μου pron. gen. 1p. sg. ἐγώ
17 ὅτι conj. ὅτι that, for, because, how that, how, because that, for that, though
ὅτι conj. ὅτι that, for, because, how that, how, because that, for that, though
Πλούσιός adj. nom. masc. sg. πλούσιος rich
καὶ conj. καί and, even, also, but
καὶ conj. καί and, even, also, but
οὐδενὸς num. gen. neut. sg. οὐδείς no man, nothing, no, none, neither, not, nought
χρείαν n. acc. fem. sg. χρεία need, necessity, lack, want

καὶ conj. καί and, even, also, but
οὐκ particle of negation. οὐ οὐκ οὐχ not, no, neither, none, nay, nor, never, nothing
ὅτι conj. ὅτι that, for, because, how that, how, because that, for that, though
σὺ pron. nom. 2p. sg. σύ thou, you
ὁ art. nom. masc. sg. ὁ ἡ τό the, this, that, he, she, it
ταλαίπωρος adj. nom. masc. sg. ταλαίπωρος wretched
καὶ conj. καί and, even, also, but
ἐλεεινὸς adj. nom. masc. sg. ἐλεεινός miserable, most miserable
καὶ conj. καί and, even, also, but
πτωχὸς adj. nom. masc. sg. πτωχός poor, beggar, beggarly
καὶ conj. καί and, even, also, but
τυφλὸς adj. nom. masc. sg. τυφλός blind
καὶ conj. καί and, even, also, but
γυμνός adj. nom. masc. sg. γυμνός naked, bare
18 σοι pron. dat. 2p. sg. σύ thou, you
παρ' prep. παρά (+gen) of, from, (+dat) with, for, (+acc) beside, at, by, above, against
ἐμοῦ pron. gen. 1p. sg. ἐγώ I
χρυσίον n. acc. neut. sg. χρυσίον gold
ἐκ prep. ἐκ ἐξ (+gen) of, from, out of, by, on, with, in, among, through
πυρὸς n. gen. neut. sg. πῦρ fire, fiery
ἵνα conj. ἵνα that, to, lest, for to, so that, albeit, because, for, so as
καὶ conj. καί and, even, also, but
ἱμάτια n. acc. neut. pl. ἱμάτιον cloke, garment, clothes, raiment, robe, vesture
λευκὰ adj. acc. neut. pl. λευκός white
ἵνα conj. ἵνα that, to, lest, for to, so that, albeit, because, for, so as
καὶ conj. καί and, even, also, but
μὴ particle of negation. μή not, no, lest, neither, none, nothing, nor, never, without
ἡ art. nom. fem. sg. ὁ ἡ τό the, this, that, he, she, it
αἰσχύνη n. nom. fem. sg. αἰσχύνη shame, dishonesty
τῆς art. gen. fem. sg. ὁ ἡ τό the, this, that, he, she, it
γυμνότητός n. gen. fem. sg. γυμνότης nakedness
σου pron. gen. 2p. sg. σύ thou, you
καὶ conj. καί and, even, also, but
κολλούριον n. acc. neut. sg. κολλούριον eyesalve
τοὺς art. acc. masc. pl. ὁ ἡ τό the, this, that, he, she, it
ὀφθαλμούς n. acc. masc. pl. ὀφθαλμός eye, sight
σου pron. gen. 2p. sg. σύ thou, you
ἵνα conj. ἵνα that, to, lest, for to, so that, albeit, because, for, so as
19 ἐγὼ pron. nom. 1p. sg. ἐγώ I
ὅσους relative pron. acc. masc. pl. ὅσος as many as, whatsoever, that, as long as, how much
ἐὰν conj. ἐάν if, soever, except, though, and if, but, whether, if so, so
καὶ conj. καί and, even, also, but
οὖν conj. οὖν therefore, then, so, and, now, wherefore
καὶ conj. καί and, even, also, but
20 ἐπὶ prep. ἐπί (+gen) on, in, upon, (+dat) in, at, for, upon, (+acc) on, upon, unto, to, against
τὴν art. acc. fem. sg. ὁ ἡ τό the, this, that, he, she, it
θύραν n. acc. fem. sg. θύρα door, gate
καὶ conj. καί and, even, also, but
ἐάν conj. ἐάν if, soever, except, though, and if, but, whether, if so, so
τις indefinite pron. nom. masc. sg. τὶς certain, some, any man, one, any thing
τῆς art. gen. fem. sg. ὁ ἡ τό the, this, that, he, she, it
φωνῆς n. gen. fem. sg. φωνή voice, sound, noise
μου pron. gen. 1p. sg. ἐγώ I
καὶ conj. καί and, even, also, but
τὴν art. acc. fem. sg. ὁ ἡ τό the, this, that, he, she, it

θύραν n. acc. fem. sg. θύρα door, gate
πρὸς prep. πρός (+gen) for, (+dat) at, (+acc) unto, to, with, for, against
αὐτὸν pron. acc. masc. 3p. sg. αὐτός ή ό self, of oneself, even, very, the same, he, she, it
καὶ conj. καί and, even, also, but
μετ' prep. μετά (+gen) with, among, against, (+acc) after
αὐτοῦ pron. gen. masc. 3p. sg. αὐτός ή ό self, of oneself, even, very, the same, he, she, it
καὶ conj. καί and, even, also, but
αὐτὸς pron. nom. masc. 3p. sg. αὐτός ή ό self, of oneself, even, very, the same, he, she, it
μετ' prep. μετά (+gen) with, among, against, (+acc) after
ἐμοῦ pron. gen. 1p. sg. ἐγώ I
21 ὁ art. nom. masc. sg. ὁ ἡ τό the, this, that, he, she, it
αὐτῷ pron. dat. masc. 3p. sg. αὐτός ή ό self, of oneself, even, very, the same, he, she, it
μετ' prep. μετά (+gen) with, among, against, (+acc) after
ἐμοῦ pron. gen. 1p. sg. ἐγώ I
ἐν prep. ἐν (+dat) in, by, with, among, at, on, through, to, within, into, of, for
τῷ art. dat. masc. sg. ὁ ἡ τό the, this, that, he, she, it
θρόνῳ n. dat. masc. sg. θρόνος throne, seat
μου pron. gen. 1p. sg. ἐγώ I
ὡς adv. ὡς as, when, as it were, how, about, like, as soon as, even as, while
κἀγὼ pron. nom. 1p. sg. κἀγώ and I, I also, so I, even as I
καὶ conj. καί and, even, also, but
μετὰ prep. μετά (+gen) with, among, against, (+acc) after
τοῦ art. gen. masc. sg. ὁ ἡ τό the, this, that, he, she, it
πατρός n. gen. masc. sg. πατήρ Father, father, parent
μου pron. gen. 1p. sg. ἐγώ I
ἐν prep. ἐν (+dat) in, by, with, among, at, on, through, to, within, into, of, for
τῷ art. dat. masc. sg. ὁ ἡ τό the, this, that, he, she, it
θρόνῳ n. dat. masc. sg. θρόνος throne, seat
αὐτοῦ pron. gen. masc. 3p. sg. αὐτός ή ό self, of oneself, even, very, the same, he, she, it
22 ὁ art. nom. masc. sg. ὁ ἡ τό the, this, that, he, she, it
οὖς n. acc. neut. sg. οὖς ear
τί interrog. pron. acc. neut. sg. τίς what, who, why, where, which, how
τὸ art. nom. neut. sg. ὁ ἡ τό the, this, that, he, she, it
Πνεῦμα n. nom. neut. sg. πνεῦμα spirit, Spirit, Ghost, ghost, life. of the spirit, wind
ταῖς art. dat. fem. pl. ὁ ἡ τό the, this, that, he, she, it
ἐκκλησίαις n. dat. fem. pl. ἐκκλησία church, assembly

4

1 Μετὰ prep. μετά (+gen) with, among, against, (+acc) after
ταῦτα demo. pron. acc. neut. pl. οὗτος αὕτη τοῦτο this, the same, this same, he, she, it
καὶ conj. καί and, even, also, but
θύρα n. nom. fem. sg. θύρα door, gate
ἐν prep. ἐν (+dat) in, by, with, among, at, on, through, to, within, into, of, for
τῷ art. dat. masc. sg. ὁ ἡ τό the, this, that, he, she, it
οὐρανῷ n. dat. masc. sg. οὐρανός heaven, air, sky
καὶ conj. καί and, even, also, but
ἡ art. nom. fem. sg. ὁ ἡ τό the, this, that, he, she, it
φωνὴ n. nom. fem. sg. φωνή voice, sound, noise
ἡ art. nom. fem. sg. ὁ ἡ τό the, this, that, he, she, it
πρώτη ordinal. adj. nom. fem. sg. πρῶτος first, chief, first of all, chiefest, best
ἣν relative pron. acc. fem. sg. ὅς ἥ ὅ who, which, what, that
ὡς adv. ὡς as, when, as it were, how, about, like, as soon as, even as, while
σάλπιγγος n. gen. fem. sg. σάλπιγξ trumpet, trump
μετ' prep. μετά (+gen) with, among, against, (+acc) after

ἐμοῦ pron. gen. 1p. sg. ἐγώ I
ὧδε adv. ὧδε here, hither, in this place, there, this place
καὶ conj. καί and, even, also, but
σοι pron. dat. 2p. sg. σύ thou, you
ἃ relative pron. acc. neut. pl. ὅς ἥ ὅ who, which, what, that
μετὰ prep. μετά (+gen) with, among, against, (+acc) after
ταῦτα demo. pron. acc. neut. pl. οὗτος αὕτη τοῦτο this, the same, this same, he, she, it
2 καὶ conj. καί and, even, also, but
εὐθέως adv. εὐθέως immediately, straightway, forthwith, as soon as, by and by, shortly
ἐν prep. ἐν (+dat) in, by, with, among, at, on, through, to, within, into, of, for
πνεύματι n. dat. neut. sg. πνεῦμα spirit, Spirit, Ghost, ghost, life. of the spirit, wind
καὶ conj. καί and, even, also, but
θρόνος n. nom. masc. sg. θρόνος throne, seat
ἐν prep. ἐν (+dat) in, by, with, among, at, on, through, to, within, into, of, for
τῷ art. dat. masc. sg. ὁ ἡ τό the, this, that, he, she, it
οὐρανῷ n. dat. masc. sg. οὐρανός heaven, air, sky
καὶ conj. καί and, even, also, but
ἐπὶ prep. ἐπί (+gen) on, in, upon, (+dat) in, at, for, upon, (+acc) on, upon, unto, to, against
τοῦ art. gen. masc. sg. ὁ ἡ τό the, this, that, he, she, it
θρόνου n. gen. masc. sg. θρόνος throne, seat
3 καὶ conj. καί and, even, also, but
ὁ art. nom. masc. sg. ὁ ἡ τό the, this, that, he, she, it
ὅμοιος adj. nom. masc. sg. ὅμοιος like
ὁράσει n. dat. fem. sg. ὅρασις vision, to look upon, in sight
λίθῳ n. dat. masc. sg. λίθος stone
ἰάσπιδι n. dat. fem. sg. ἴασπις jasper, a precious stone of various colours
καὶ conj. καί and, even, also, but
σαρδίνῳ n. dat. neut. sg. σάρδινος sardine, a precious stone of a blood-red colour
καὶ conj. καί and, even, also, but
ἶρις n. nom. fem. sg. ἶρις rainbow
κυκλόθεν prep. κυκλόθεν round about, about
τοῦ art. gen. masc. sg. ὁ ἡ τό the, this, that, he, she, it
θρόνου n. gen. masc. sg. θρόνος throne, seat
ὁμοία adj. nom. fem. sg. ὅμοιος like
ὁράσει n. dat. fem. sg. ὅρασις vision, to look upon, in sight
σμαραγδίνῳ adj. dat. masc. sg. σμαράγδινος emerald, of smaragdus
4 καὶ conj. καί and, even, also, but
κυκλόθεν prep. κυκλόθεν round about, about
τοῦ art. gen. masc. sg. ὁ ἡ τό the, this, that, he, she, it
θρόνου n. gen. masc. sg. θρόνος throne, seat
θρόνοι n. nom. masc. pl. θρόνος throne, seat
εἴκοσι num. nom. masc. pl. εἴκοσι twenty
καὶ conj. καί and, even, also, but
τέσσαρες num. nom. masc. pl. τέσσαρες four
καὶ conj. καί and, even, also, but
ἐπὶ prep. ἐπί (+gen) on, in, upon, (+dat) in, at, for, upon, (+acc) on, upon, unto, to, against
τοὺς art. acc. masc. pl. ὁ ἡ τό the, this, that, he, she, it
θρόνους n. acc. masc. pl. θρόνος throne, seat
τοὺς art. acc. masc. pl. ὁ ἡ τό the, this, that, he, she, it
εἴκοσι num. acc. masc. pl. εἴκοσι twenty
καὶ conj. καί and, even, also, but
τέσσαρας num. acc. masc. pl. τέσσαρες four
πρεσβυτέρους adj. acc. masc. pl. πρεσβύτερος elder, elder woman, eldest, old man
ἐν prep. ἐν (+dat) in, by, with, among, at, on, through, to, within, into, of, for
ἱματίοις n. dat. neut. pl. ἱμάτιον cloke, garment, clothes, raiment, robe, vesture

λευκοῖς adj. dat. neut. pl. λευκός white
καὶ conj. καί and, even, also, but
ἐπὶ prep. ἐπί (+gen) on, in, upon, (+dat) in, at, for, upon, (+acc) on, upon, unto, to, against
τὰς art. acc. fem. pl. ὁ ἡ τό the, this, that, he, she, it
κεφαλὰς n. acc. fem. pl. κεφαλή head
αὐτῶν pron. gen. masc. 3p. pl. αὐτός ή ό self, of oneself, even, very, the same, he, she, it
στεφάνους n. acc. masc. pl. στέφανος crown
χρυσοῦς adj. acc. masc. pl. χρύσεος golden, of gold
5 καὶ conj. καί and, even, also, but
ἐκ prep. ἐκ ἐξ (+gen) of, from, out of, by, on, with, in, among, through
τοῦ art. gen. masc. sg. ὁ ἡ τό the, this, that, he, she, it
θρόνου n. gen. masc. sg. θρόνος throne, seat
ἀστραπαὶ n. nom. fem. pl. ἀστραπή lightning, bright shining
καὶ conj. καί and, even, also, but
βρονταί n. nom. fem. pl. βροντή thunder, thundering
καὶ conj. καί and, even, also, but
φωναὶ n. nom. fem. pl. φωνή voice, sound, noise
καὶ conj. καί and, even, also, but
ἑπτὰ num. nom. fem. pl. ἑπτά seven, seventh
λαμπάδες n. nom. fem. pl. λαμπάς lamp, light, torch
πυρὸς n. gen. neut. sg. πῦρ fire, fiery
ἐνώπιον prep. ἐνώπιον (+gen) before, in the sight of, in the presence of. (adv.) before
τοῦ art. gen. masc. sg. ὁ ἡ τό the, this, that, he, she, it
θρόνου n. gen. masc. sg. θρόνος throne, seat
αἵ relative pron. nom. fem. pl. ὅς ἥ ὅ who, which, what, that
τὰ art. nom. neut. pl. ὁ ἡ τό the, this, that, he, she, it
ἑπτὰ num. nom. neut. pl. ἑπτά seven, seventh
πνεύματα n. nom. neut. pl. πνεῦμα spirit, Spirit, Ghost, ghost, life. of the spirit, wind
τοῦ art. gen. masc. sg. ὁ ἡ τό the, this, that, he, she, it
Θεοῦ n. gen. masc. sg. θεός God, god
6 καὶ conj. καί and, even, also, but
ἐνώπιον prep. ἐνώπιον (+gen) before, in the sight of, in the presence of. (adv.) before
τοῦ art. gen. masc. sg. ὁ ἡ τό the, this, that, he, she, it
θρόνου n. gen. masc. sg. θρόνος throne, seat
θάλασσα n. nom. fem. sg. θάλασσα sea
ὑαλίνη adj. nom. fem. sg. ὑάλινος of glass
ὁμοία adj. nom. fem. sg. ὅμοιος like
κρυστάλλῳ n. dat. masc. sg. κρύσταλλος crystal
καὶ conj. καί and, even, also, but
ἐν prep. ἐν (+dat) in, by, with, among, at, on, through, to, within, into, of, for
μέσῳ adj. dat. neut. sg. μέσος midst, among, mid, between
τοῦ art. gen. masc. sg. ὁ ἡ τό the, this, that, he, she, it
θρόνου n. gen. masc. sg. θρόνος throne, seat
καὶ conj. καί and, even, also, but
κύκλῳ prep. κύκλῳ round about, round
τοῦ art. gen. masc. sg. ὁ ἡ τό the, this, that, he, she, it
θρόνου n. gen. masc. sg. θρόνος throne, seat
τέσσαρα num. nom. neut. pl. τέσσαρες four
ζῷα n. nom. neut. pl. ζῷον beast
ὀφθαλμῶν n. gen. masc. pl. ὀφθαλμός eye, sight
ἔμπροσθεν adv. ἔμπροσθεν (+gen) before, in the sight of, in the presence of
καὶ conj. καί and, even, also, but
ὄπισθεν adv. ὄπισθεν behind, after, backside
7 καὶ conj. καί and, even, also, but
τὸ art. nom. neut. sg. ὁ ἡ τό the, this, that, he, she, it

ζῶον n. nom. neut. sg. ζῶον beast
τὸ art. nom. neut. sg. ὁ ἡ τό the, this, that, he, she, it
πρῶτον ordinal. adj. nom. neut. sg. πρῶτος first, chief, first of all, chiefest, best
ὅμοιον adj. nom. neut. sg. ὅμοιος like
λέοντι n. dat. masc. sg. λέων lion
καὶ conj. καί and, even, also, but
τὸ art. nom. neut. sg. ὁ ἡ τό the, this, that, he, she, it
δεύτερον ordinal. adj. nom. neut. sg. δεύτερος second, second time, again, afterward
ζῶον n. nom. neut. sg. ζῶον beast
ὅμοιον adj. nom. neut. sg. ὅμοιος like
μόσχῳ n. dat. masc. sg. μόσχος calf
καὶ conj. καί and, even, also, but
τὸ art. nom. neut. sg. ὁ ἡ τό the, this, that, he, she, it
τρίτον ordinal. adj. nom. neut. sg. τρίτος third
ζῶον n. nom. neut. sg. ζῶον beast
τὸ art. acc. neut. sg. ὁ ἡ τό the, this, that, he, she, it
πρόσωπον n. acc. neut. sg. πρόσωπον face, presence, person, countenance
ὡς adv. ὡς as, when, as it were, how, about, like, as soon as, even as, while
ἄνθρωπος n. nom. masc. sg. ἄνθρωπος man, human being, person, one, certain
καὶ conj. καί and, even, also, but
τὸ art. nom. neut. sg. ὁ ἡ τό the, this, that, he, she, it
τέταρτον ordinal. adj. nom. neut. sg. τέταρτος fourth, four
ζῶον n. nom. neut. sg. ζῶον beast
ὅμοιον adj. nom. neut. sg. ὅμοιος like
ἀετῷ n. dat. masc. sg. ἀετός eagle
8 καὶ conj. καί and, even, also, but
τέσσαρα num. nom. neut. pl. τέσσαρες four
ζῶα n. nom. neut. pl. ζῶον beast
ἓν num. nom. neut. sg. εἷς or ἕν one, other, some, any, only, a certain
καθ' prep. κατά (+gen) against, by, throughout, down, (+acc) according to, after, with
ἑαυτὸ reflexive pron. acc. neut. 3p. sg. ἑαυτοῦ himself, herself, itself, yourself, ourselves
ἀνὰ adv. ἀνά (+acc) by, in, through, among, between. (adv.) apiece, every man, each
πτέρυγας n. acc. fem. pl. πτέρυξ wing
ἓξ num. acc. fem. pl. ἕξ six
κυκλόθεν adv. κυκλόθεν round about, about
καὶ conj. καί and, even, also, but
ἔσωθεν adv. ἔσωθεν within, from within, inward, inwardly
ὀφθαλμῶν n. gen. masc. pl. ὀφθαλμός eye, sight
καὶ conj. καί and, even, also, but
ἀνάπαυσιν n. acc. fem. sg. ἀνάπαυσις rest
οὐκ particle of negation. οὐ οὐκ οὐχ not, no, neither, none, nay, nor, never, nothing
ἡμέρας n. gen. fem. sg. ἡμέρα day, time, year, while, age, day time
καὶ conj. καί and, even, also, but
νυκτὸς n. gen. fem. sg. νύξ night
Ἅγιος adj. nom. masc. sg. ἅγιος Holy, holy, saint, Holy One, holy thing, most holy
ἅγιος adj. nom. masc. sg. ἅγιος Holy, holy, saint, Holy One, holy thing, most holy
ἅγιος adj. nom. masc. sg. ἅγιος Holy, holy, saint, Holy One, holy thing, most holy
Κύριος n. nom. masc. sg. κύριος Lord, lord, master, sir, LORD, God, Master, owner
ὁ art. nom. masc. sg. ὁ ἡ τό the, this, that, he, she, it
Θεὸς n. nom. masc. sg. θεός God, god
ὁ art. nom. masc. sg. ὁ ἡ τό the, this, that, he, she, it
παντοκράτωρ n. nom. masc. sg. παντοκράτωρ Almighty, omnipotent
ὁ art. nom. masc. sg. ὁ ἡ τό the, this, that, he, she, it
καὶ conj. καί and, even, also, but
ὁ art. nom. masc. sg. ὁ ἡ τό the, this, that, he, she, it

καὶ conj. καί and, even, also, but
ὁ art. nom. masc. sg. ὁ ἡ τό the, this, that, he, she, it
9 καὶ conj. καί and, even, also, but
ὅταν conj. ὅταν when, as soon as, as long as, that, whensoever, while
τὰ art. nom. neut. pl. ὁ ἡ τό the, this, that, he, she, it
ζῷα n. nom. neut. pl. ζῷον beast
δόξαν n. acc. fem. sg. δόξα glory, honour, praise, dignity, worship
καὶ conj. καί and, even, also, but
τιμὴν n. acc. fem. sg. τιμή honour, price, preciousness, sum
καὶ conj. καί and, even, also, but
εὐχαριστίαν n. acc. fem. sg. εὐχαριστία thankfulness, thanksgiving, giving of thanks
τῷ art. dat. masc. sg. ὁ ἡ τό the, this, that, he, she, it
ἐπὶ prep. ἐπί (+gen) on, in, upon, (+dat) in, at, for, upon, (+acc) on, upon, unto, to, against
τοῦ art. gen. masc. sg. ὁ ἡ τό the, this, that, he, she, it
θρόνου n. gen. masc. sg. θρόνος throne, seat
τῷ art. dat. masc. sg. ὁ ἡ τό the, this, that, he, she, it
εἰς prep. εἰς (+acc) into, to, unto, for, in, on, toward, against, upon, at, among
τοὺς art. acc. masc. pl. ὁ ἡ τό the, this, that, he, she, it
αἰῶνας n. acc. masc. pl. αἰών ever, ever and ever, evermore, age, eternal, world
τῶν art. gen. masc. pl. ὁ ἡ τό the, this, that, he, she, it
αἰώνων n. gen. masc. pl. αἰών ever, ever and ever, evermore, age, eternal, world
10 οἱ art. nom. masc. pl. ὁ ἡ τό the, this, that, he, she, it
εἴκοσι num. nom. masc. pl. εἴκοσι twenty
καὶ conj. καί and, even, also, but
τέσσαρες num. nom. masc. pl. τέσσαρες four
πρεσβύτεροι adj. nom. masc. pl. πρεσβύτερος elder, elder woman, eldest, old man
ἐνώπιον prep. ἐνώπιον (+gen) before, in the sight of, in the presence of. (adv.) before
τοῦ art. gen. masc. sg. ὁ ἡ τό the, this, that, he, she, it
ἐπὶ prep. ἐπί (+gen) on, in, upon, (+dat) in, at, for, upon, (+acc) on, upon, unto, to, against
τοῦ art. gen. masc. sg. ὁ ἡ τό the, this, that, he, she, it
θρόνου n. gen. masc. sg. θρόνος throne, seat
καὶ conj. καί and, even, also, but
τῷ art. dat. masc. sg. ὁ ἡ τό the, this, that, he, she, it
εἰς prep. εἰς (+acc) into, to, unto, for, in, on, toward, against, upon, at, among
τοὺς art. acc. masc. pl. ὁ ἡ τό the, this, that, he, she, it
αἰῶνας n. acc. masc. pl. αἰών ever, ever and ever, evermore, age, eternal, world
τῶν art. gen. masc. pl. ὁ ἡ τό the, this, that, he, she, it
αἰώνων n. gen. masc. pl. αἰών ever, ever and ever, evermore, age, eternal, world
καὶ conj. καί and, even, also, but
τοὺς art. acc. masc. pl. ὁ ἡ τό the, this, that, he, she, it
στεφάνους n. acc. masc. pl. στέφανος crown
αὐτῶν pron. gen. masc. 3p. pl. αὐτός ἡ ὁ self, of oneself, even, very, the same, he, she, it
ἐνώπιον prep. ἐνώπιον (+gen) before, in the sight of, in the presence of. (adv.) before
τοῦ art. gen. masc. sg. ὁ ἡ τό the, this, that, he, she, it
θρόνου n. gen. masc. sg. θρόνος throne, seat
11 Ἄξιος adj. nom. masc. sg. ἄξιος worthy, meet, due reward
Κύριε n. voc. masc. sg. κύριος Lord, lord, master, sir, LORD, God, Master, owner
τὴν art. acc. fem. sg. ὁ ἡ τό the, this, that, he, she, it
δόξαν n. acc. fem. sg. δόξα glory, honour, praise, dignity, worship
καὶ conj. καί and, even, also, but
τὴν art. acc. fem. sg. ὁ ἡ τό the, this, that, he, she, it
τιμὴν n. acc. fem. sg. τιμή honour, price, preciousness, sum
καὶ conj. καί and, even, also, but
τὴν art. acc. fem. sg. ὁ ἡ τό the, this, that, he, she, it
δύναμιν n. acc. fem. sg. δύναμις power, mighty work, miracle, strength, might

ὅτι conj. ὅτι that, for, because, how that, how, because that, for that, though
σὺ pron. nom. 2p. sg. σύ thou, you
τὰ art. acc. neut. pl. ὁ ἡ τό the, this, that, he, she, it
πάντα adj. acc. neut. pl. πᾶς πᾶσα πᾶν all, every, whosoever, every one, no, whole, any
καὶ conj. καί and, even, also, but
διὰ prep. διά (+gen) by, through, with, in, of, (+acc) for, because of, for a cause
τὸ art. acc. neut. sg. ὁ ἡ τό the, this, that, he, she, it
θέλημά n. acc. neut. sg. θέλημα will, desire, pleasure
σου pron. gen. 2p. sg. σύ thou, you
καὶ conj. καί and, even, also, but

5

1 Καὶ conj. καί and, even, also, but
ἐπὶ prep. ἐπί (+gen) on, in, upon, (+dat) in, at, for, upon, (+acc) on, upon, unto, to, against
τὴν art. acc. fem. sg. ὁ ἡ τό the, this, that, he, she, it
δεξιὰν adj. acc. fem. sg. δεξιός right, right hand, right side
τοῦ art. gen. masc. sg. ὁ ἡ τό the, this, that, he, she, it
ἐπὶ prep. ἐπί (+gen) on, in, upon, (+dat) in, at, for, upon, (+acc) on, upon, unto, to, against
τοῦ art. gen. masc. sg. ὁ ἡ τό the, this, that, he, she, it
θρόνου n. gen. masc. sg. θρόνος throne, seat
βιβλίον n. acc. neut. sg. βιβλίον book, bill, scroll, writing
ἔσωθεν adv. ἔσωθεν within, from within, inward, inwardly
καὶ conj. καί and, even, also, but
ὄπισθεν adv. ὄπισθεν behind, after, backside
σφραγῖσιν n. dat. fem. pl. σφραγίς seal
ἑπτά num. dat. fem. pl. ἑπτά seven, seventh
2 καὶ conj. καί and, even, also, but
ἄγγελον n. acc. masc. sg. ἄγγελος angel, messenger
ἰσχυρὸν adj. acc. masc. sg. ἰσχυρός mighty, strong, mightier, stronger
φωνῇ n. dat. fem. sg. φωνή voice, sound, noise
μεγάλῃ adj. dat. fem. sg. μέγας great, loud, greatest, high, large, mighty, strong
Τίς interrog. pron. nom. masc. sg. τίς what, who, why, where, which, how
ἄξιος adj. nom. masc. sg. ἄξιος worthy, meet, due reward
τὸ art. acc. neut. sg. ὁ ἡ τό the, this, that, he, she, it
βιβλίον n. acc. neut. sg. βιβλίον book, bill, scroll, writing
καὶ conj. καί and, even, also, but
τὰς art. acc. fem. pl. ὁ ἡ τό the, this, that, he, she, it
σφραγῖδας n. acc. fem. pl. σφραγίς seal
αὐτοῦ pron. gen. neut. 3p. sg. αὐτός ή ό self, of oneself, even, very, the same, he, she, it
3 καὶ conj. καί and, even, also, but
οὐδεὶς num. nom. masc. sg. οὐδείς no man, nothing, no, none, neither, not, nought
ἐν prep. ἐν (+dat) in, by, with, among, at, on, through, to, within, into, of, for
τῷ art. dat. masc. sg. ὁ ἡ τό the, this, that, he, she, it
οὐρανῷ n. dat. masc. sg. οὐρανός heaven, air, sky
οὐδὲ adv. οὐδέ neither, nor, not, no, not even, never, not yet
ἐπὶ prep. ἐπί (+gen) on, in, upon, (+dat) in, at, for, upon, (+acc) on, upon, unto, to, against
τῆς art. gen. fem. sg. ὁ ἡ τό the, this, that, he, she, it
γῆς n. gen. fem. sg. γῆ earth, land, ground, country
οὐδὲ adv. οὐδέ neither, nor, not, no, not even, never, not yet
ὑποκάτω adv. ὑποκάτω under
τῆς art. gen. fem. sg. ὁ ἡ τό the, this, that, he, she, it
γῆς n. gen. fem. sg. γῆ earth, land, ground, country
τὸ art. acc. neut. sg. ὁ ἡ τό the, this, that, he, she, it
βιβλίον n. acc. neut. sg. βιβλίον book, bill, scroll, writing

οὐδὲ adv. οὐδέ neither, nor, not, no, not even, never, not yet
αὐτό pron. acc. neut. 3p. sg. αὐτός ή ό self, of oneself, even, very, the same, he, she, it
4 καὶ conj. καί and, even, also, but
ἐγὼ pron. nom. 1p. sg. ἐγώ I
πολλά adj. acc. neut. pl. πολύς many, great, much, long, abundant
ὅτι conj. ὅτι that, for, because, how that, how, because that, for that, though
οὐδεὶς num. nom. masc. sg. οὐδείς no man, nothing, no, none, neither, not, nought
ἄξιος adj. nom. masc. sg. ἄξιος worthy, meet, due reward
καὶ conj. καί and, even, also, but
τὸ art. acc. neut. sg. ὁ ἡ τό the, this, that, he, she, it
βιβλίον n. acc. neut. sg. βιβλίον book, bill, scroll, writing
οὔτε conj. οὔτε neither, nor, nor yet, no, none
αὐτό pron. acc. neut. 3p. sg. αὐτός ή ό self, of oneself, even, very, the same, he, she, it
5 καὶ conj. καί and, even, also, but
εἷς num. nom. masc. sg. εἷς or ἕν one, other, some, any, only, a certain
ἐκ prep. ἐκ ἐξ (+gen) of, from, out of, by, on, with, in, among, through
τῶν art. gen. masc. pl. ὁ ἡ τό the, this, that, he, she, it
πρεσβυτέρων adj. gen. masc. pl. πρεσβύτερος elder, elder woman, eldest, old man
μοι pron. dat. 1p. sg. ἐγώ I
Μὴ particle of negation. μή not, no, lest, neither, none, nothing, nor, never, without
ὁ art. nom. masc. sg. ὁ ἡ τό the, this, that, he, she, it
λέων n. nom. masc. sg. λέων lion
ὁ art. nom. masc. sg. ὁ ἡ τό the, this, that, he, she, it
ἐκ prep. ἐκ ἐξ (+gen) of, from, out of, by, on, with, in, among, through
τῆς art. gen. fem. sg. ὁ ἡ τό the, this, that, he, she, it
φυλῆς n. gen. fem. sg. φυλή tribe, kindred
Ἰούδα n. gen. masc. sg. Ἰούδας Judas, Juda, Judah, Jude
ἡ art. nom. fem. sg. ὁ ἡ τό the, this, that, he, she, it
ῥίζα n. nom. fem. sg. ῥίζα root
Δαβίδ n. gen. masc. sg. Δαβίδ David
τὸ art. acc. neut. sg. ὁ ἡ τό the, this, that, he, she, it
βιβλίον n. acc. neut. sg. βιβλίον book, bill, scroll, writing
καὶ conj. καί and, even, also, but
τὰς art. acc. fem. pl. ὁ ἡ τό the, this, that, he, she, it
ἑπτὰ num. acc. fem. pl. ἑπτά seven, seventh
σφραγῖδας n. acc. fem. pl. σφραγίς seal
αὐτοῦ pron. gen. neut. 3p. sg. αὐτός ή ό self, of oneself, even, very, the same, he, she, it
6 καὶ conj. καί and, even, also, but
καὶ conj. καί and, even, also, but
ἐν prep. ἐν (+dat) in, by, with, among, at, on, through, to, within, into, of, for
μέσῳ adj. dat. neut. sg. μέσος midst, among, mid, between
τοῦ art. gen. masc. sg. ὁ ἡ τό the, this, that, he, she, it
θρόνου n. gen. masc. sg. θρόνος throne, seat
καὶ conj. καί and, even, also, but
τῶν art. gen. neut. pl. ὁ ἡ τό the, this, that, he, she, it
τεσσάρων num. gen. neut. pl. τέσσαρες four
ζώων n. gen. neut. pl. ζῷον beast
καὶ conj. καί and, even, also, but
ἐν prep. ἐν (+dat) in, by, with, among, at, on, through, to, within, into, of, for
μέσῳ adj. dat. neut. sg. μέσος midst, among, mid, between
τῶν art. gen. masc. pl. ὁ ἡ τό the, this, that, he, she, it
πρεσβυτέρων adj. gen. masc. pl. πρεσβύτερος elder, elder woman, eldest, old man
ἀρνίον n. nom. neut. sg. ἀρνίον Lamb, lamb
ὡς adv. ὡς as, when, as it were, how, about, like, as soon as, even as, while
κέρατα n. acc. neut. pl. κέρας horn

ἑπτὰ num. acc. neut. pl. ἑπτά seven, seventh
καὶ conj. καί and, even, also, but
ὀφθαλμοὺς n. acc. masc. pl. ὀφθαλμός eye, sight
ἑπτὰ num. acc. masc. pl. ἑπτά seven, seventh
οἵ relative pron. nom. masc. pl. ὅς ἥ ὅ who, which, what, that
τὰ art. nom. neut. pl. ὁ ἡ τό the, this, that, he, she, it
ἑπτὰ num. nom. neut. pl. ἑπτά seven, seventh
τοῦ art. gen. masc. sg. ὁ ἡ τό the, this, that, he, she, it
Θεοῦ n. gen. masc. sg. θεός God, god
πνεύματα n. nom. neut. pl. πνεῦμα spirit, Spirit, Ghost, ghost, life. of the spirit, wind
τὰ art. nom. neut. pl. ὁ ἡ τό the, this, that, he, she, it
εἰς prep. εἰς (+acc) into, to, unto, for, in, on, toward, against, upon, at, among
πᾶσαν adj. acc. fem. sg. πᾶς πᾶsα πᾶν all, every, whosoever, every one, no, whole, any
τὴν art. acc. fem. sg. ὁ ἡ τό the, this, that, he, she, it
γῆν n. acc. fem. sg. γῆ earth, land, ground, country
7 καὶ conj. καί and, even, also, but
καὶ conj. καί and, even, also, but
τὸ art. acc. neut. sg. ὁ ἡ τό the, this, that, he, she, it
βιβλίον n. acc. neut. sg. βιβλίον book, bill, scroll, writing
ἐκ prep. ἐκ ἐξ (+gen) of, from, out of, by, on, with, in, among, through
τῆς art. gen. fem. sg. ὁ ἡ τό the, this, that, he, she, it
δεξιᾶς adj. gen. fem. sg. δεξιός right, right hand, right side
τοῦ art. gen. masc. sg. ὁ ἡ τό the, this, that, he, she, it
ἐπὶ prep. ἐπί (+gen) on, in, upon, (+dat) in, at, for, upon, (+acc) on, upon, unto, to, against
τοῦ art. gen. masc. sg. ὁ ἡ τό the, this, that, he, she, it
θρόνου n. gen. masc. sg. θρόνος throne, seat
8 καὶ conj. καί and, even, also, but
ὅτε adv. ὅτε when, after that, as soon as, while, after
τὸ art. acc. neut. sg. ὁ ἡ τό the, this, that, he, she, it
βιβλίον n. acc. neut. sg. βιβλίον book, bill, scroll, writing
τὰ art. nom. neut. pl. ὁ ἡ τό the, this, that, he, she, it
τέσσαρα num. nom. neut. pl. τέσσαρες four
ζῷα n. nom. neut. pl. ζῷον beast
καὶ conj. καί and, even, also, but
οἱ art. nom. masc. pl. ὁ ἡ τό the, this, that, he, she, it
εἰκοσιτέσσαρες num. nom. masc. pl. εἰκοσιτέσσαρες twenty-four
πρεσβύτεροι adj. nom. masc. pl. πρεσβύτερος elder, elder woman, eldest, old man
ἐνώπιον prep. ἐνώπιον (+gen) before, in the sight of, in the presence of. (adv.) before
τοῦ art. gen. neut. sg. ὁ ἡ τό the, this, that, he, she, it
ἀρνίου n. gen. neut. sg. ἀρνίον Lamb, lamb
ἕκαστος adj. nom. masc. sg. ἕκαστος every man, every, every one, any man, each
κιθάρας n. acc. fem. pl. κιθάρα harp
καὶ conj. καί and, even, also, but
φιάλας n. acc. fem. pl. φιάλη vial
χρυσᾶς adj. acc. fem. pl. χρύσεος golden, of gold
θυμιαμάτων n. gen. neut. pl. θυμίαμα incense, odour
αἵ relative pron. nom. fem. pl. ὅς ἥ ὅ who, which, what, that
αἱ art. nom. fem. pl. ὁ ἡ τό the, this, that, he, she, it
προσευχαὶ n. nom. fem. pl. προσευχή prayer
τῶν art. gen. masc. pl. ὁ ἡ τό the, this, that, he, she, it
ἁγίων adj. gen. masc. pl. ἅγιος Holy, holy, saint, Holy One, holy thing, most holy
9 καὶ conj. καί and, even, also, but
ᾠδὴν n. acc. fem. sg. ᾠδή song
καινὴν adj. acc. fem. sg. καινός new
Ἄξιος adj. nom. masc. sg. ἄξιος worthy, meet, due reward

τὸ art. acc. neut. sg. ὁ ἡ τό the, this, that, he, she, it
βιβλίον n. acc. neut. sg. βιβλίον book, bill, scroll, writing
καὶ conj. καί and, even, also, but
τὰς art. acc. fem. pl. ὁ ἡ τό the, this, that, he, she, it
σφραγῖδας n. acc. fem. pl. σφραγίς seal
αὐτοῦ pron. gen. neut. 3p. sg. αὐτός ή ό self, of oneself, even, very, the same, he, she, it
ὅτι conj. ὅτι that, for, because, how that, how, because that, for that, though
καὶ conj. καί and, even, also, but
τῷ art. dat. masc. sg. ὁ ἡ τό the, this, that, he, she, it
Θεῷ n. dat. masc. sg. θεός God, god
ἡμᾶς pron. acc. 1p. pl. ἐγώ I
ἐν prep. ἐν (+dat) in, by, with, among, at, on, through, to, within, into, of, for
τῷ art. dat. neut. sg. ὁ ἡ τό the, this, that, he, she, it
αἵματι n. dat. neut. sg. αἷμα blood
σου pron. gen. 2p. sg. σύ thou, you
ἐκ prep. ἐκ ἐξ (+gen) of, from, out of, by, on, with, in, among, through
πάσης adj. gen. fem. sg. πᾶς πᾶςα πᾶν all, every, whosoever, every one, no, whole, any
φυλῆς n. gen. fem. sg. φυλή tribe, kindred
καὶ conj. καί and, even, also, but
γλώσσης n. gen. fem. sg. γλῶσσα tongue
καὶ conj. καί and, even, also, but
λαοῦ n. gen. masc. sg. λαός people
καὶ conj. καί and, even, also, but
ἔθνους n. gen. neut. sg. ἔθνος Gentile, nation, heathen, people
10 καὶ conj. καί and, even, also, but
ἡμᾶς pron. acc. 1p. pl. ἐγώ I
τῷ art. dat. masc. sg. ὁ ἡ τό the, this, that, he, she, it
Θεῷ n. dat. masc. sg. θεός God, god
ἡμῶν pron. gen. 1p. pl. ἐγώ I
βασιλεῖς n. acc. masc. pl. βασιλεύς king
καὶ conj. καί and, even, also, but
ἱερεῖς n. acc. masc. pl. ἱερεύς priest
καὶ conj. καί and, even, also, but
ἐπὶ prep. ἐπί (+gen) on, in, upon, (+dat) in, at, for, upon, (+acc) on, upon, unto, to, against
τῆς art. gen. fem. sg. ὁ ἡ τό the, this, that, he, she, it
γῆς n. gen. fem. sg. γῆ earth, land, ground, country
11 καὶ conj. καί and, even, also, but
καὶ conj. καί and, even, also, but
φωνὴν n. acc. fem. sg. φωνή voice, sound, noise
ἀγγέλων n. gen. masc. pl. ἄγγελος angel, messenger
πολλῶν adj. gen. masc. pl. πολύς many, great, much, long, abundant
κυκλόθεν adv. κυκλόθεν round about, about
τοῦ art. gen. masc. sg. ὁ ἡ τό the, this, that, he, she, it
θρόνου n. gen. masc. sg. θρόνος throne, seat
καὶ conj. καί and, even, also, but
τῶν art. gen. neut. pl. ὁ ἡ τό the, this, that, he, she, it
ζώων n. gen. neut. pl. ζῶον beast
καὶ conj. καί and, even, also, but
τῶν art. gen. masc. pl. ὁ ἡ τό the, this, that, he, she, it
πρεσβυτέρων adj. gen. masc. pl. πρεσβύτερος elder, elder woman, eldest, old man
καὶ conj. καί and, even, also, but
ὁ art. nom. masc. sg. ὁ ἡ τό the, this, that, he, she, it
ἀριθμὸς n. nom. masc. sg. ἀριθμός number
αὐτῶν pron. gen. masc. 3p. pl. αὐτός ή ό self, of oneself, even, very, the same, he, she, it
μυριάδες n. nom. masc. pl. μυριάς innumerable multitude, myriad, innumerable company

μυριάδων n. gen. masc. pl. μυριάς innumerable multitude, ten thousand, myriad
καὶ conj. καί and, even, also, but
χιλιάδες n. nom. fem. pl. χιλιάς thousand
χιλιάδων n. gen. fem. pl. χιλιάς thousand
12 φωνῇ n. dat. fem. sg. φωνή voice, sound, noise
μεγάλῃ adj. dat. fem. sg. μέγας great, loud, greatest, high, large, mighty, strong
Ἄξιόν adj. nom. neut. sg. ἄξιος worthy, meet, due reward
τὸ art. nom. neut. sg. ὁ ἡ τό the, this, that, he, she, it
ἀρνίον n. nom. neut. sg. ἀρνίον Lamb, lamb
τὸ art. nom. neut. sg. ὁ ἡ τό the, this, that, he, she, it
τὴν art. acc. fem. sg. ὁ ἡ τό the, this, that, he, she, it
δύναμιν n. acc. fem. sg. δύναμις power, mighty work, miracle, strength, might
καὶ conj. καί and, even, also, but
πλοῦτον n. acc. masc. sg. πλοῦτος riches
καὶ conj. καί and, even, also, but
σοφίαν n. acc. fem. sg. σοφία wisdom
καὶ conj. καί and, even, also, but
ἰσχὺν n. acc. fem. sg. ἰσχύς strength, might, power, ability
καὶ conj. καί and, even, also, but
τιμὴν n. acc. fem. sg. τιμή honour, price, preciousness, sum
καὶ conj. καί and, even, also, but
δόξαν n. acc. fem. sg. δόξα glory, honour, praise, dignity, worship
καὶ conj. καί and, even, also, but
εὐλογίαν n. acc. fem. sg. εὐλογία blessing, bounty, matter of bounty, fair speech
13 καὶ conj. καί and, even, also, but
πᾶν adj. acc. neut. sg. πᾶς πᾶσα πᾶν all, every, whosoever, every one, no, whole, any
κτίσμα n. acc. neut. sg. κτίσμα creature
ὃ relative pron. nom. neut. sg. ὅς ἥ ὅ who, which, what, that
ἐν prep. ἐν (+dat) in, by, with, among, at, on, through, to, within, into, of, for
τῷ art. dat. masc. sg. ὁ ἡ τό the, this, that, he, she, it
οὐρανῷ n. dat. masc. sg. οὐρανός heaven, air, sky
καὶ conj. καί and, even, also, but
ἐν prep. ἐν (+dat) in, by, with, among, at, on, through, to, within, into, of, for
τῇ art. dat. fem. sg. ὁ ἡ τό the, this, that, he, she, it
γῇ n. dat. fem. sg. γῆ earth, land, ground, country
καὶ conj. καί and, even, also, but
ὑποκάτω adv. ὑποκάτω under
τῆς art. gen. fem. sg. ὁ ἡ τό the, this, that, he, she, it
γῆς n. gen. fem. sg. γῆ earth, land, ground, country
καὶ conj. καί and, even, also, but
ἐπὶ prep. ἐπί (+gen) on, in, upon, (+dat) in, at, for, upon, (+acc) on, upon, unto, to, against
τῆς art. gen. fem. sg. ὁ ἡ τό the, this, that, he, she, it
θαλάσσης n. gen. fem. sg. θάλασσα sea
ἅ relative pron. nom. neut. pl. ὅς ἥ ὅ who, which, what, that
καὶ conj. καί and, even, also, but
τὰ art. acc. neut. pl. ὁ ἡ τό the, this, that, he, she, it
ἐν prep. ἐν (+dat) in, by, with, among, at, on, through, to, within, into, of, for
αὐτοῖς pron. dat. neut. 3p. pl. αὐτός ή ό self, of oneself, even, very, the same, he, she, it
πάντα adj. acc. neut. pl. πᾶς πᾶσα πᾶν all, every, whosoever, every one, no, whole, any
Τῷ art. dat. masc. sg. ὁ ἡ τό the, this, that, he, she, it
ἐπὶ prep. ἐπί (+gen) on, in, upon, (+dat) in, at, for, upon, (+acc) on, upon, unto, to, against
τοῦ art. gen. masc. sg. ὁ ἡ τό the, this, that, he, she, it
θρόνου n. gen. masc. sg. θρόνος throne, seat
καὶ conj. καί and, even, also, but
τῷ art. dat. neut. sg. ὁ ἡ τό the, this, that, he, she, it

ἀρνίῳ n. dat. neut. sg. ἀρνίον Lamb, lamb
ἡ art. nom. fem. sg. ὁ ἡ τό the, this, that, he, she, it
εὐλογία n. nom. fem. sg. εὐλογία blessing, bounty, matter of bounty, fair speech
καὶ conj. καί and, even, also, but
ἡ art. nom. fem. sg. ὁ ἡ τό the, this, that, he, she, it
τιμὴ n. nom. fem. sg. τιμή honour, price, preciousness, sum
καὶ conj. καί and, even, also, but
ἡ art. nom. fem. sg. ὁ ἡ τό the, this, that, he, she, it
δόξα n. nom. fem. sg. δόξα glory, honour, praise, dignity, worship
καὶ conj. καί and, even, also, but
τὸ art. nom. neut. sg. ὁ ἡ τό the, this, that, he, she, it
κράτος n. nom. neut. sg. κράτος power, dominion, might, strength
εἰς prep. εἰς (+acc) into, to, unto, for, in, on, toward, against, upon, at, among
τοὺς art. acc. masc. pl. ὁ ἡ τό the, this, that, he, she, it
αἰῶνας n. acc. masc. pl. αἰών ever, ever and ever, evermore, age, eternal, world
τῶν art. gen. masc. pl. ὁ ἡ τό the, this, that, he, she, it
αἰώνων n. gen. masc. pl. αἰών ever, ever and ever, evermore, age, eternal, world
14 καὶ conj. καί and, even, also, but
τὰ art. nom. neut. pl. ὁ ἡ τό the, this, that, he, she, it
τέσσαρα num. nom. neut. pl. τέσσαρες four
ζῷα n. nom. neut. pl. ζῷον beast
Ἀμήν particle. ἀμήν amen, verily
καὶ conj. καί and, even, also, but
οἱ art. nom. masc. pl. ὁ ἡ τό the, this, that, he, she, it
εἰκοσιτέσσαρες num. nom. masc. pl. εἰκοσιτέσσαρες twenty-four
πρεσβύτεροι adj. nom. masc. pl. πρεσβύτερος elder, elder woman, eldest, old man
καὶ conj. καί and, even, also, but
εἰς prep. εἰς (+acc) into, to, unto, for, in, on, toward, against, upon, at, among
τοὺς art. acc. masc. pl. ὁ ἡ τό the, this, that, he, she, it
αἰῶνας n. acc. masc. pl. αἰών ever, ever and ever, evermore, age, eternal, world
τῶν art. gen. masc. pl. ὁ ἡ τό the, this, that, he, she, it
αἰώνων n. gen. masc. pl. αἰών ever, ever and ever, evermore, age, eternal, world

6

1 Καὶ conj. καί and, even, also, but
ὅτε adv. ὅτε when, after that, as soon as, while, after
τὸ art. nom. neut. sg. ὁ ἡ τό the, this, that, he, she, it
ἀρνίον n. nom. neut. sg. ἀρνίον Lamb, lamb
μίαν num. acc. fem. sg. εἷς or ἕν one, other, some, any, only, a certain
ἐκ prep. ἐκ ἐξ (+gen) of, from, out of, by, on, with, in, among, through
τῶν art. gen. fem. pl. ὁ ἡ τό the, this, that, he, she, it
σφραγίδων n. gen. fem. pl. σφραγίς seal
καὶ conj. καί and, even, also, but
ἑνὸς num. gen. neut. sg. εἷς or ἕν one, other, some, any, only, a certain
ἐκ prep. ἐκ ἐξ (+gen) of, from, out of, by, on, with, in, among, through
τῶν art. gen. neut. pl. ὁ ἡ τό the, this, that, he, she, it
τεσσάρων num. gen. neut. pl. τέσσαρες four
ζῴων n. gen. neut. pl. ζῷον beast
ὡς adv. ὡς as, when, as it were, how, about, like, as soon as, even as, while
φωνῆς n. gen. fem. sg. φωνή voice, sound, noise
βροντῆς n. gen. fem. sg. βροντή thunder, thundering
καὶ conj. καί and, even, also, but
2 καὶ conj. καί and, even, also, but
καὶ conj. καί and, even, also, but

ἵππος n. nom. masc. sg. ἵππος horse
λευκός adj. nom. masc. sg. λευκός white
καὶ conj. καί and, even, also, but
ὁ art. nom. masc. sg. ὁ ἡ τό the, this, that, he, she, it
ἐπ' prep. ἐπί (+gen) on, in, upon, (+dat) in, at, for, upon, (+acc) on, upon, unto, to, against
αὐτῷ pron. dat. masc. 3p. sg. αὐτός ἡ ὁ self, of oneself, even, very, the same, he, she, it
τόξον n. acc. neut. sg. τόξον bow
καὶ conj. καί and, even, also, but
αὐτῷ pron. dat. masc. 3p. sg. αὐτός ἡ ὁ self, of oneself, even, very, the same, he, she, it
στέφανος n. nom. masc. sg. στέφανος crown
καὶ conj. καί and, even, also, but
καὶ conj. καί and, even, also, but
ἵνα conj. ἵνα that, to, lest, for to, so that, albeit, because, for, so as
3 Καὶ conj. καί and, even, also, but
ὅτε adv. ὅτε when, after that, as soon as, while, after
τὴν art. acc. fem. sg. ὁ ἡ τό the, this, that, he, she, it
δευτέραν ordinal. adj. acc. fem. sg. δεύτερος second, second time, again, afterward
σφραγῖδα n. acc. fem. sg. σφραγίς seal
τοῦ art. gen. neut. sg. ὁ ἡ τό the, this, that, he, she, it
δευτέρου ordinal. adj. gen. neut. sg. δεύτερος second, second time, again, afterward
ζώου n. gen. neut. sg. ζῶον beast
καὶ conj. καί and, even, also, but
4 καὶ conj. καί and, even, also, but
ἄλλος adj. nom. masc. sg. ἄλλος other, another, some, one, more, otherwise
ἵππος n. nom. masc. sg. ἵππος horse
πυρρός adj. nom. masc. sg. πυρρός red
καὶ conj. καί and, even, also, but
τῷ art. dat. masc. sg. ὁ ἡ τό the, this, that, he, she, it
ἐπ' prep. ἐπί (+gen) on, in, upon, (+dat) in, at, for, upon, (+acc) on, upon, unto, to, against
αὐτῷ pron. dat. masc. 3p. sg. αὐτός ἡ ὁ self, of oneself, even, very, the same, he, she, it
αὐτῷ pron. dat. masc. 3p. sg. αὐτός ἡ ὁ self, of oneself, even, very, the same, he, she, it
τὴν art. acc. fem. sg. ὁ ἡ τό the, this, that, he, she, it
εἰρήνην n. acc. fem. sg. εἰρήνη peace, quietness, rest
ἀπὸ prep. ἀπό (+gen) from, of, out of, since, for, off, at, by, in, on
τῆς art. gen. fem. sg. ὁ ἡ τό the, this, that, he, she, it
γῆς n. gen. fem. sg. γῆ earth, land, ground, country
καὶ conj. καί and, even, also, but
ἵνα conj. ἵνα that, to, lest, for to, so that, albeit, because, for, so as
ἀλλήλους pron. acc. masc. pl. ἀλλήλων one another, themselves, together, mutual
καὶ conj. καί and, even, also, but
αὐτῷ pron. dat. masc. 3p. sg. αὐτός ἡ ὁ self, of oneself, even, very, the same, he, she, it
μάχαιρα n. nom. fem. sg. μάχαιρα sword
μεγάλη adj. nom. fem. sg. μέγας great, loud, greatest, high, large, mighty, strong
5 Καὶ conj. καί and, even, also, but
ὅτε adv. ὅτε when, after that, as soon as, while, after
τὴν art. acc. fem. sg. ὁ ἡ τό the, this, that, he, she, it
τρίτην ordinal. adj. acc. fem. sg. τρίτος third
σφραγῖδα n. acc. fem. sg. σφραγίς seal
τοῦ art. gen. neut. sg. ὁ ἡ τό the, this, that, he, she, it
τρίτου ordinal. adj. gen. neut. sg. τρίτος third
ζώου n. gen. neut. sg. ζῶον beast
καὶ conj. καί and, even, also, but
καὶ conj. καί and, even, also, but
καὶ conj. καί and, even, also, but
ἵππος n. nom. masc. sg. ἵππος horse

μέλας adj. nom. masc. sg. μέλας black
καὶ conj. καί and, even, also, but
ὁ art. nom. masc. sg. ὁ ἡ τό the, this, that, he, she, it
ἐπ' prep. ἐπί (+gen) on, in, upon, (+dat) in, at, for, upon, (+acc) on, upon, unto, to, against
αὐτῷ pron. dat. masc. 3p. sg. αὐτός ή ό self, of oneself, even, very, the same, he, she, it
ζυγὸν n. acc. masc. sg. ζυγός yoke, pair of balances
ἐν prep. ἐν (+dat) in, by, with, among, at, on, through, to, within, into, of, for
τῇ art. dat. fem. sg. ὁ ἡ τό the, this, that, he, she, it
χειρὶ n. dat. fem. sg. χείρ hand
αὐτοῦ pron. gen. masc. 3p. sg. αὐτός ή ό self, of oneself, even, very, the same, he, she, it
6 καὶ conj. καί and, even, also, but
φωνὴν n. acc. fem. sg. φωνή voice, sound, noise
ἐν prep. ἐν (+dat) in, by, with, among, at, on, through, to, within, into, of, for
μέσῳ adj. dat. neut. sg. μέσος midst, among, mid, between
τῶν art. gen. neut. pl. ὁ ἡ τό the, this, that, he, she, it
τεσσάρων num. gen. neut. pl. τέσσαρες four
ζώων n. gen. neut. pl. ζῶον beast
Χοῖνιξ n. nom. fem. sg. χοῖνιξ measure
σίτου n. gen. masc. sg. σῖτος wheat, corn
δηναρίου n. gen. neut. sg. δηνάριον pence, penny, denarius
καὶ conj. καί and, even, also, but
τρεῖς num. nom. fem. pl. τρεῖς three
χοίνικες n. nom. fem. pl. χοῖνιξ measure
κριθῆς n. gen. fem. sg. κριθή barley
δηναρίου n. gen. neut. sg. δηνάριον pence, penny, denarius
καὶ conj. καί and, even, also, but
τὸ art. acc. neut. sg. ὁ ἡ τό the, this, that, he, she, it
ἔλαιον n. acc. neut. sg. ἔλαιον oil
καὶ conj. καί and, even, also, but
τὸν art. acc. masc. sg. ὁ ἡ τό the, this, that, he, she, it
οἶνον n. acc. masc. sg. οἶνος wine
μὴ particle of negation. μή not, no, lest, neither, none, nothing, nor, never, without
7 Καὶ conj. καί and, even, also, but
ὅτε adv. ὅτε when, after that, as soon as, while, after
τὴν art. acc. fem. sg. ὁ ἡ τό the, this, that, he, she, it
σφραγῖδα n. acc. fem. sg. σφραγίς seal
τὴν art. acc. fem. sg. ὁ ἡ τό the, this, that, he, she, it
τετάρτην ordinal. adj. acc. fem. sg. τέταρτος fourth, four
φωνὴν n. acc. fem. sg. φωνή voice, sound, noise
τοῦ art. gen. neut. sg. ὁ ἡ τό the, this, that, he, she, it
τετάρτου ordinal. adj. gen. neut. sg. τέταρτος fourth, four
ζώου n. gen. neut. sg. ζῶον beast
καὶ conj. καί and, even, also, but
8 καὶ conj. καί and, even, also, but
καὶ conj. καί and, even, also, but
ἵππος n. nom. masc. sg. ἵππος horse
χλωρός adj. nom. masc. sg. χλωρός green, pale
καὶ conj. καί and, even, also, but
ὁ art. nom. masc. sg. ὁ ἡ τό the, this, that, he, she, it
ἐπάνω prep. ἐπάνω (+gen) on, over, above, upon, more than
αὐτοῦ pron. gen. masc. 3p. sg. αὐτός ή ό self, of oneself, even, very, the same, he, she, it
ὄνομα n. nom. neut. sg. ὄνομα name, call, surname
αὐτῷ pron. dat. masc. 3p. sg. αὐτός ή ό self, of oneself, even, very, the same, he, she, it
ὁ art. nom. masc. sg. ὁ ἡ τό the, this, that, he, she, it
Θάνατος n. nom. masc. sg. θάνατος death

καὶ conj. καί and, even, also, but
ὁ art. nom. masc. sg. ὁ ἡ τό the, this, that, he, she, it
ᾅδης n. nom. masc. sg. ᾅδης hell, grave
μετ' prep. μετά (+gen) with, among, against, (+acc) after
αὐτοῦ pron. gen. masc. 3p. sg. αὐτός ή ό self, of oneself, even, very, the same, he, she, it
καὶ conj. καί and, even, also, but
αὐτοῖς pron. dat. masc. 3p. pl. αὐτός ή ό self, of oneself, even, very, the same, he, she, it
ἐξουσία n. nom. fem. sg. ἐξουσία power, authority, right, strength, jurisdiction
ἐπὶ prep. ἐπί (+gen) on, in, upon, (+dat) in, at, for, upon, (+acc) on, upon, unto, to, against
τὸ art. acc. neut. sg. ὁ ἡ τό the, this, that, he, she, it
τέταρτον ordinal. adj. acc. neut. sg. τέταρτος fourth, four
τῆς art. gen. fem. sg. ὁ ἡ τό the, this, that, he, she, it
γῆς n. gen. fem. sg. γῆ earth, land, ground, country
ἐν prep. ἐν (+dat) in, by, with, among, at, on, through, to, within, into, of, for
ῥομφαίᾳ n. dat. fem. sg. ῥομφαία sword
καὶ conj. καί and, even, also, but
ἐν prep. ἐν (+dat) in, by, with, among, at, on, through, to, within, into, of, for
λιμῷ n. dat. masc. sg. λιμός famine, hunger, dearth
καὶ conj. καί and, even, also, but
ἐν prep. ἐν (+dat) in, by, with, among, at, on, through, to, within, into, of, for
θανάτῳ n. dat. masc. sg. θάνατος death
καὶ conj. καί and, even, also, but
ὑπὸ prep. ὑπό (+gen) of, by, with, from, among, (+acc) under
τῶν art. gen. neut. pl. ὁ ἡ τό the, this, that, he, she, it
θηρίων n. gen. neut. pl. θηρίον beast, wild beast, venomous beast
τῆς art. gen. fem. sg. ὁ ἡ τό the, this, that, he, she, it
γῆς n. gen. fem. sg. γῆ earth, land, ground, country
9 Καὶ conj. καί and, even, also, but
ὅτε adv. ὅτε when, after that, as soon as, while, after
τὴν art. acc. fem. sg. ὁ ἡ τό the, this, that, he, she, it
πέμπτην ordinal. adj. acc. fem. sg. πέμπτος fifth
σφραγῖδα n. acc. fem. sg. σφραγίς seal
ὑποκάτω adv. ὑποκάτω under
τοῦ art. gen. neut. sg. ὁ ἡ τό the, this, that, he, she, it
θυσιαστηρίου n. gen. neut. sg. θυσιαστήριον altar
τὰς art. acc. fem. pl. ὁ ἡ τό the, this, that, he, she, it
ψυχὰς n. acc. fem. pl. ψυχή life, soul, mind, heart
τῶν art. gen. masc. pl. ὁ ἡ τό the, this, that, he, she, it
διὰ prep. διά (+gen) by, through, with, in, of, (+acc) for, because of, for a cause
τὸν art. acc. masc. sg. ὁ ἡ τό the, this, that, he, she, it
λόγον n. acc. masc. sg. λόγος word, saying, account, speech, thing, matter
τοῦ art. gen. masc. sg. ὁ ἡ τό the, this, that, he, she, it
Θεοῦ n. gen. masc. sg. θεός God, god
καὶ conj. καί and, even, also, but
διὰ prep. διά (+gen) by, through, with, in, of, (+acc) for, because of, for a cause
τὴν art. acc. fem. sg. ὁ ἡ τό the, this, that, he, she, it
μαρτυρίαν n. acc. fem. sg. μαρτυρία testimony, witness, record, report
ἣν relative pron. acc. fem. sg. ὅς ἥ ὅ who, which, what, that
10 καὶ conj. καί and, even, also, but
φωνῇ n. dat. fem. sg. φωνή voice, sound, noise
μεγάλῃ adj. dat. fem. sg. μέγας great, loud, greatest, high, large, mighty, strong
Ἕως conj. ἕως till, until, unto, until when, while, as far as, even, until now
πότε interrogative particle. πότε when, how long
ὁ art. nom. masc. sg. ὁ ἡ τό the, this, that, he, she, it
δεσπότης n. nom. masc. sg. δεσπότης Lord, master

ὁ art. nom. masc. sg. ὁ ἡ τό the, this, that, he, she, it
ἅγιος adj. nom. masc. sg. ἅγιος Holy, holy, saint, Holy One, holy thing, most holy
καὶ conj. καί and, even, also, but
ὁ art. nom. masc. sg. ὁ ἡ τό the, this, that, he, she, it
ἀληθινός adj. nom. masc. sg. ἀληθινός true
οὐ particle of negation. οὐ οὐκ οὐχ not, no, neither, none, nay, nor, never, nothing
καὶ conj. καί and, even, also, but
τὸ art. acc. neut. sg. ὁ ἡ τό the, this, that, he, she, it
αἷμα n. acc. neut. sg. αἷμα blood
ἡμῶν pron. gen. 1p. pl. ἐγώ I
ἀπὸ prep. ἀπό (+gen) from, of, out of, since, for, off, at, by, in, on
τῶν art. gen. masc. pl. ὁ ἡ τό the, this, that, he, she, it
ἐπὶ prep. ἐπί (+gen) on, in, upon, (+dat) in, at, for, upon, (+acc) on, upon, unto, to, against
τῆς art. gen. fem. sg. ὁ ἡ τό the, this, that, he, she, it
γῆς n. gen. fem. sg. γῆ earth, land, ground, country
11 καὶ conj. καί and, even, also, but
ἑκάστοις adj. dat. masc. pl. ἕκαστος every man, every, every one, any man, each
στολαὶ n. nom. fem. pl. στολή robe, long clothing, long garment, long robe
λευκαί adj. nom. fem. pl. λευκός white
καὶ conj. καί and, even, also, but
αὐτοῖς pron. dat. masc. 3p. pl. αὐτός ή ό self, of oneself, even, very, the same, he, she, it
ἵνα conj. ἵνα that, to, lest, for to, so that, albeit, because, for, so as
ἔτι adv. ἔτι yet, more, any more, further, still, moreover
χρόνον n. acc. masc. sg. χρόνος time, season, space
μικρόν adj. acc. masc. sg. μικρός little, small, least, less
ἕως conj. ἕως till, until, unto, until when, while, as far as, even, until now
οὗ relative pron. gen. masc. sg. ὅς ἥ ὅ who, which, what, that
καὶ conj. καί and, even, also, but
οἱ art. nom. masc. pl. ὁ ἡ τό the, this, that, he, she, it
σύνδουλοι n. nom. masc. pl. σύνδουλος fellowservant
αὐτῶν pron. gen. masc. 3p. pl. αὐτός ή ό self, of oneself, even, very, the same, he, she, it
καὶ conj. καί and, even, also, but
οἱ art. nom. masc. pl. ὁ ἡ τό the, this, that, he, she, it
ἀδελφοὶ n. nom. masc. pl. ἀδελφός brother
αὐτῶν pron. gen. masc. 3p. pl. αὐτός ή ό self, of oneself, even, very, the same, he, she, it
οἱ art. nom. masc. pl. ὁ ἡ τό the, this, that, he, she, it
ὡς adv. ὡς as, when, as it were, how, about, like, as soon as, even as, while
καὶ conj. καί and, even, also, but
αὐτοί pron. nom. masc. 3p. pl. αὐτός ή ό self, of oneself, even, very, the same, he, she, it
12 Καὶ conj. καί and, even, also, but
ὅτε adv. ὅτε when, after that, as soon as, while, after
τὴν art. acc. fem. sg. ὁ ἡ τό the, this, that, he, she, it
σφραγῖδα n. acc. fem. sg. σφραγίς seal
τὴν art. acc. fem. sg. ὁ ἡ τό the, this, that, he, she, it
ἕκτην ordinal. adj. acc. fem. sg. ἕκτος sixth
καὶ conj. καί and, even, also, but
σεισμὸς n. nom. masc. sg. σεισμός earthquake, tempest
μέγας adj. nom. masc. sg. μέγας great, loud, greatest, high, large, mighty, strong
καὶ conj. καί and, even, also, but
ὁ art. nom. masc. sg. ὁ ἡ τό the, this, that, he, she, it
ἥλιος n. nom. masc. sg. ἥλιος sun, east
μέλας adj. nom. masc. sg. μέλας black
ὡς adv. ὡς as, when, as it were, how, about, like, as soon as, even as, while
σάκκος n. nom. masc. sg. σάκκος sackcloth
τρίχινος adj. nom. masc. sg. τρίχινος of hair

καὶ conj. καί and, even, also, but
ἡ art. nom. fem. sg. ὁ ἡ τό the, this, that, he, she, it
σελήνη n. nom. fem. sg. σελήνη moon
ὡς adv. ὡς as, when, as it were, how, about, like, as soon as, even as, while
αἷμα n. nom. neut. sg. αἷμα blood
13 καὶ conj. καί and, even, also, but
οἱ art. nom. masc. pl. ὁ ἡ τό the, this, that, he, she, it
ἀστέρες n. nom. masc. pl. ἀστήρ star
τοῦ art. gen. masc. sg. ὁ ἡ τό the, this, that, he, she, it
οὐρανοῦ n. gen. masc. sg. οὐρανός heaven, air, sky
εἰς prep. εἰς (+acc) into, to, unto, for, in, on, toward, against, upon, at, among
τὴν art. acc. fem. sg. ὁ ἡ τό the, this, that, he, she, it
γῆν n. acc. fem. sg. γῆ earth, land, ground, country
ὡς adv. ὡς as, when, as it were, how, about, like, as soon as, even as, while
συκῆ n. nom. fem. sg. συκῆ fig tree
τοὺς art. acc. masc. pl. ὁ ἡ τό the, this, that, he, she, it
ὀλύνθους n. acc. masc. pl. ὄλυνθος untimely fig
αὐτῆς pron. gen. fem. 3p. sg. αὐτός ἡ ὁ self, of oneself, even, very, the same, he, she, it
ὑπὸ prep. ὑπό (+gen) of, by, with, from, among, (+acc) under
μεγάλου adj. gen. masc. sg. μέγας great, loud, greatest, high, large, mighty, strong
ἀνέμου n. gen. masc. sg. ἄνεμος wind
14 καὶ conj. καί and, even, also, but
οὐρανὸς n. nom. masc. sg. οὐρανός heaven, air, sky
ὡς adv. ὡς as, when, as it were, how, about, like, as soon as, even as, while
βιβλίον n. nom. neut. sg. βιβλίον book, bill, scroll, writing
καὶ conj. καί and, even, also, but
πᾶν adj. nom. neut. sg. πᾶς πᾶσα πᾶν all, every, whosoever, every one, no, whole, any
ὄρος n. nom. neut. sg. ὄρος mountain, mount, hill
καὶ conj. καί and, even, also, but
νῆσος n. nom. fem. sg. νῆσος isle, island
ἐκ prep. ἐκ ἐξ (+gen) of, from, out of, by, on, with, in, among, through
τῶν art. gen. masc. pl. ὁ ἡ τό the, this, that, he, she, it
τόπων n. gen. masc. pl. τόπος place, room, quarter
αὐτῶν pron. gen. neut. 3p. pl. αὐτός ἡ ὁ self, of oneself, even, very, the same, he, she, it
15 καὶ conj. καί and, even, also, but
οἱ art. nom. masc. pl. ὁ ἡ τό the, this, that, he, she, it
βασιλεῖς n. nom. masc. pl. βασιλεύς king
τῆς art. gen. fem. sg. ὁ ἡ τό the, this, that, he, she, it
γῆς n. gen. fem. sg. γῆ earth, land, ground, country
καὶ conj. καί and, even, also, but
οἱ art. nom. masc. pl. ὁ ἡ τό the, this, that, he, she, it
μεγιστᾶνες n. nom. masc. pl. μεγιστάνες great men, lords
καὶ conj. καί and, even, also, but
οἱ art. nom. masc. pl. ὁ ἡ τό the, this, that, he, she, it
πλούσιοι adj. nom. masc. pl. πλούσιος rich
καὶ conj. καί and, even, also, but
οἱ art. nom. masc. pl. ὁ ἡ τό the, this, that, he, she, it
χιλίαρχοι n. nom. masc. pl. χιλίαρχος high captain, chief captain, captain
καὶ conj. καί and, even, also, but
οἱ art. nom. masc. pl. ὁ ἡ τό the, this, that, he, she, it
δυνατοί adj. nom. masc. pl. δυνατός able, possible, mighty, strong
καὶ conj. καί and, even, also, but
πᾶς adj. nom. masc. sg. πᾶς πᾶσα πᾶν all, every, whosoever, every one, no, whole, any
δοῦλος n. nom. masc. sg. δοῦλος servant, bondman, bond, slave
καὶ conj. καί and, even, also, but

πᾶς adj. nom. masc. sg. πᾶς πᾶσα πᾶν all, every, whosoever, every one, no, whole, any
ἐλεύθερος adj. nom. masc. sg. ἐλεύθερος free, freewoman, at liberty, freeman
ἑαυτοὺς reflexive pron. acc. masc. 3p. pl. ἑαυτοῦ himself, herself, itself, yourself, ourselves
εἰς prep. εἰς (+acc) into, to, unto, for, in, on, toward, against, upon, at, among
τὰ art. acc. neut. pl. ὁ ἡ τό the, this, that, he, she, it
σπήλαια n. acc. neut. pl. σπήλαιον den, cave
καὶ conj. καί and, even, also, but
εἰς prep. εἰς (+acc) into, to, unto, for, in, on, toward, against, upon, at, among
τὰς art. acc. fem. pl. ὁ ἡ τό the, this, that, he, she, it
πέτρας n. acc. fem. pl. πέτρα rock
τῶν art. gen. neut. pl. ὁ ἡ τό the, this, that, he, she, it
ὀρέων n. gen. neut. pl. ὄρος mountain, mount, hill
16 καὶ conj. καί and, even, also, but
τοῖς art. dat. neut. pl. ὁ ἡ τό the, this, that, he, she, it
ὄρεσι n. dat. neut. pl. ὄρος mountain, mount, hill
καὶ conj. καί and, even, also, but
ταῖς art. dat. fem. pl. ὁ ἡ τό the, this, that, he, she, it
πέτραις n. dat. fem. pl. πέτρα rock
ἐφ' prep. ἐπί (+gen) on, in, upon, (+dat) in, at, for, upon, (+acc) on, upon, unto, to, against
ἡμᾶς pron. acc. 1p. pl. ἐγώ I
καὶ conj. καί and, even, also, but
ἡμᾶς pron. acc. 1p. pl. ἐγώ I
ἀπὸ prep. ἀπό (+gen) from, of, out of, since, for, off, at, by, in, on
προσώπου n. gen. neut. sg. πρόσωπον face, presence, person, countenance
τοῦ art. gen. masc. sg. ὁ ἡ τό the, this, that, he, she, it
ἐπὶ prep. ἐπί (+gen) on, in, upon, (+dat) in, at, for, upon, (+acc) on, upon, unto, to, against
τοῦ art. gen. masc. sg. ὁ ἡ τό the, this, that, he, she, it
θρόνου n. gen. masc. sg. θρόνος throne, seat
καὶ conj. καί and, even, also, but
ἀπὸ prep. ἀπό (+gen) from, of, out of, since, for, off, at, by, in, on
τῆς art. gen. fem. sg. ὁ ἡ τό the, this, that, he, she, it
ὀργῆς n. gen. fem. sg. ὀργή wrath, anger, indignation, vengeance
τοῦ art. gen. neut. sg. ὁ ἡ τό the, this, that, he, she, it
ἀρνίου n. gen. neut. sg. ἀρνίον Lamb, lamb
17 ὅτι conj. ὅτι that, for, because, how that, how, because that, for that, though
ἡ art. nom. fem. sg. ὁ ἡ τό the, this, that, he, she, it
ἡμέρα n. nom. fem. sg. ἡμέρα day, time, year, while, age, day time
ἡ art. nom. fem. sg. ὁ ἡ τό the, this, that, he, she, it
μεγάλη adj. nom. fem. sg. μέγας great, loud, greatest, high, large, mighty, strong
τῆς art. gen. fem. sg. ὁ ἡ τό the, this, that, he, she, it
ὀργῆς n. gen. fem. sg. ὀργή wrath, anger, indignation, vengeance
αὐτοῦ pron. gen. masc. 3p. sg. αὐτός ἡ ὁ self, of oneself, even, very, the same, he, she, it
καὶ conj. καί and, even, also, but
τίς interrog. pron. nom. masc. sg. τίς what, who, why, where, which, how

7

1 Καὶ conj. καί and, even, also, but
μετὰ prep. μετά (+gen) with, among, against, (+acc) after
ταῦτα demo. pron. acc. neut. pl. οὗτος αὕτη τοῦτο this, the same, this same, he, she, it
τέσσαρας num. acc. masc. pl. τέσσαρες four
ἀγγέλους n. acc. masc. pl. ἄγγελος angel, messenger
ἐπὶ prep. ἐπί (+gen) on, in, upon, (+dat) in, at, for, upon, (+acc) on, upon, unto, to, against
τὰς art. acc. fem. pl. ὁ ἡ τό the, this, that, he, she, it
τέσσαρας num. acc. fem. pl. τέσσαρες four

γωνίας n. acc. fem. pl. γωνία corner, quarter
τῆς art. gen. fem. sg. ὁ ἡ τό the, this, that, he, she, it
γῆς n. gen. fem. sg. γῆ earth, land, ground, country
τοὺς art. acc. masc. pl. ὁ ἡ τό the, this, that, he, she, it
τέσσαρας num. acc. masc. pl. τέσσαρες four
ἀνέμους n. acc. masc. pl. ἄνεμος wind
τῆς art. gen. fem. sg. ὁ ἡ τό the, this, that, he, she, it
γῆς n. gen. fem. sg. γῆ earth, land, ground, country
ἵνα conj. ἵνα that, to, lest, for to, so that, albeit, because, for, so as
μὴ particle of negation. μή not, no, lest, neither, none, nothing, nor, never, without
ἄνεμος n. nom. masc. sg. ἄνεμος wind
ἐπὶ prep. ἐπί (+gen) on, in, upon, (+dat) in, at, for, upon, (+acc) on, upon, unto, to, against
τῆς art. gen. fem. sg. ὁ ἡ τό the, this, that, he, she, it
γῆς n. gen. fem. sg. γῆ earth, land, ground, country
μήτε conj. μήτε neither, nor, so much as, or
ἐπὶ prep. ἐπί (+gen) on, in, upon, (+dat) in, at, for, upon, (+acc) on, upon, unto, to, against
τῆς art. gen. fem. sg. ὁ ἡ τό the, this, that, he, she, it
θαλάσσης n. gen. fem. sg. θάλασσα sea
μήτε conj. μήτε neither, nor, so much as, or
ἐπὶ prep. ἐπί (+gen) on, in, upon, (+dat) in, at, for, upon, (+acc) on, upon, unto, to, against
πᾶν adj. acc. neut. sg. πᾶς πᾶσα πᾶν all, every, whosoever, every one, no, whole, any
δένδρον n. acc. neut. sg. δένδρον tree
2 καὶ conj. καί and, even, also, but
ἄλλον adj. acc. masc. sg. ἄλλος other, another, some, one, more, otherwise
ἄγγελον n. acc. masc. sg. ἄγγελος angel, messenger
ἀπὸ prep. ἀπό (+gen) from, of, out of, since, for, off, at, by, in, on
ἀνατολῆς n. gen. fem. sg. ἀνατολή east, rising of the sun, dayspring
ἡλίου n. gen. masc. sg. ἥλιος sun, east
σφραγῖδα n. acc. fem. sg. σφραγίς seal
Θεοῦ n. gen. masc. sg. θεός God, god
καὶ conj. καί and, even, also, but
φωνῇ n. dat. fem. sg. φωνή voice, sound, noise
μεγάλῃ adj. dat. fem. sg. μέγας great, loud, greatest, high, large, mighty, strong
τοῖς art. dat. masc. pl. ὁ ἡ τό the, this, that, he, she, it
τέσσαρσιν num. dat. masc. pl. τέσσαρες four
ἀγγέλοις n. dat. masc. pl. ἄγγελος angel, messenger
οἷς relative pron. dat. masc. pl. ὅς ἥ ὅ who, which, what, that
αὐτοῖς pron. dat. masc. 3p. pl. αὐτός ή ό self, of oneself, even, very, the same, he, she, it
τὴν art. acc. fem. sg. ὁ ἡ τό the, this, that, he, she, it
γῆν n. acc. fem. sg. γῆ earth, land, ground, country
καὶ conj. καί and, even, also, but
τὴν art. acc. fem. sg. ὁ ἡ τό the, this, that, he, she, it
θάλασσαν n. acc. fem. sg. θάλασσα sea
3 Μὴ particle of negation. μή not, no, lest, neither, none, nothing, nor, never, without
τὴν art. acc. fem. sg. ὁ ἡ τό the, this, that, he, she, it
γῆν n. acc. fem. sg. γῆ earth, land, ground, country
μήτε conj. μήτε neither, nor, so much as, or
γῆν n. acc. fem. sg. γῆ earth, land, ground, country
θάλασσαν n. acc. fem. sg. θάλασσα sea
μήτε conj. μήτε neither, nor, so much as, or
τὰ art. acc. neut. pl. ὁ ἡ τό the, this, that, he, she, it
δένδρα n. acc. neut. pl. δένδρον tree
ἄχρις prep. ἄχρι or ἄχρις (+gen) until, unto, till, even to, as far as, while, into
οὗ relative pron. gen. masc. sg. ὅς ἥ ὅ who, which, what, that
τοὺς art. acc. masc. pl. ὁ ἡ τό the, this, that, he, she, it

δούλους n. acc. masc. pl. δοῦλος servant, bondman, bond, slave
τοῦ art. gen. masc. sg. ὁ ἡ τό the, this, that, he, she, it
Θεοῦ n. gen. masc. sg. θεός God, god
ἡμῶν pron. gen. 1p. pl. ἐγώ I
ἐπὶ prep. ἐπί (+gen) on, in, upon, (+dat) in, at, for, upon, (+acc) on, upon, unto, to, against
τῶν art. gen. neut. pl. ὁ ἡ τό the, this, that, he, she, it
μετώπων n. gen. neut. pl. μέτωπον forehead
αὐτῶν pron. gen. masc. 3p. pl. αὐτός ή ό self, of oneself, even, very, the same, he, she, it
4 καὶ conj. καί and, even, also, but
τὸν art. acc. masc. sg. ὁ ἡ τό the, this, that, he, she, it
ἀριθμὸν n. acc. masc. sg. ἀριθμός number
τῶν art. gen. masc. pl. ὁ ἡ τό the, this, that, he, she, it
ρμδ´ abbreviated numeral. ρμδ´ one hundred forty four
χιλιάδες n. nom. fem. pl. χιλιάς thousand
ἐκ prep. ἐκ ἐξ (+gen) of, from, out of, by, on, with, in, among, through
πάσης adj. gen. fem. sg. πᾶς πᾶσα πᾶν all, every, whosoever, every one, no, whole, any
φυλῆς n. gen. fem. sg. φυλή tribe, kindred
υἱῶν n. gen. masc. pl. υἱός son, child, descendant, offspring, heir
Ἰσραήλ pron. name. masc. inde. Ἰσραήλ Israel
5 Ἐκ prep. ἐκ ἐξ (+gen) of, from, out of, by, on, with, in, among, through
φυλῆς n. gen. fem. sg. φυλή tribe, kindred
Ἰούδα n. gen. masc. sg. Ἰούδας Judas, Juda, Judah, Jude
ιβ´ abbreviated numeral. ιβ´ twelve
χιλιάδες n. nom. fem. pl. χιλιάς thousand
Ἐκ prep. ἐκ ἐξ (+gen) of, from, out of, by, on, with, in, among, through
φυλῆς n. gen. fem. sg. φυλή tribe, kindred
Ῥουβὴν n. gen. masc. sg. Ῥουβήν Reuben
ιβ´ abbreviated numeral. ιβ´ twelve
χιλιάδες n. nom. fem. pl. χιλιάς thousand
Ἐκ prep. ἐκ ἐξ (+gen) of, from, out of, by, on, with, in, among, through
φυλῆς n. gen. fem. sg. φυλή tribe, kindred
Γὰδ n. gen. masc. sg. Γάδ Gad
ιβ´ abbreviated numeral. ιβ´ twelve
χιλιάδες n. nom. fem. pl. χιλιάς thousand
6 Ἐκ prep. ἐκ ἐξ (+gen) of, from, out of, by, on, with, in, among, through
φυλῆς n. gen. fem. sg. φυλή tribe, kindred
Ἀσὴρ n. gen. masc. sg. Ἀσήρ Aser, Asher
ιβ´ abbreviated numeral. ιβ´ twelve
χιλιάδες n. nom. fem. pl. χιλιάς thousand
Ἐκ prep. ἐκ ἐξ (+gen) of, from, out of, by, on, with, in, among, through
φυλῆς n. gen. fem. sg. φυλή tribe, kindred
Νεφθαλείμ n. gen. masc. sg. Νεφθαλείμ Nephthalim
ιβ´ abbreviated numeral. ιβ´ twelve
χιλιάδες n. nom. fem. pl. χιλιάς thousand
Ἐκ prep. ἐκ ἐξ (+gen) of, from, out of, by, on, with, in, among, through
φυλῆς n. gen. fem. sg. φυλή tribe, kindred
Μανασσῆ n. gen. masc. sg. Μανασσῆς Manasses
ιβ´ abbreviated numeral. ιβ´ twelve
χιλιάδες n. nom. fem. pl. χιλιάς thousand
7 Ἐκ prep. ἐκ ἐξ (+gen) of, from, out of, by, on, with, in, among, through
φυλῆς n. gen. fem. sg. φυλή tribe, kindred
Συμεὼν n. gen. masc. sg. Συμεών Simeon, Simon
ιβ´ abbreviated numeral. ιβ´ twelve
χιλιάδες n. nom. fem. pl. χιλιάς thousand
Ἐκ prep. ἐκ ἐξ (+gen) of, from, out of, by, on, with, in, among, through

φυλῆς n. gen. fem. sg. φυλή tribe, kindred
Λευί n. gen. masc. sg. Λευί Levi
ιβ´ abbreviated numeral. ιβ´ twelve
χιλιάδες n. nom. fem. pl. χιλιάς thousand
Ἐκ prep. ἐκ ἐξ (+gen) of, from, out of, by, on, with, in, among, through
φυλῆς n. gen. fem. sg. φυλή tribe, kindred
Ἰσαχὰρ n. gen. masc. sg. Ἰσαχάρ Issachar
ιβ´ abbreviated numeral. ιβ´ twelve
χιλιάδες n. nom. fem. pl. χιλιάς thousand
8 Ἐκ prep. ἐκ ἐξ (+gen) of, from, out of, by, on, with, in, among, through
φυλῆς n. gen. fem. sg. φυλή tribe, kindred
Ζαβουλὼν n. gen. masc. sg. Ζαβουλών Zabulon
ιβ´ abbreviated numeral. ιβ´ twelve
χιλιάδες n. nom. fem. pl. χιλιάς thousand
Ἐκ prep. ἐκ ἐξ (+gen) of, from, out of, by, on, with, in, among, through
φυλῆς n. gen. fem. sg. φυλή tribe, kindred
Ἰωσὴφ n. gen. masc. sg. Ἰωσήφ Joseph
ιβ´ abbreviated numeral. ιβ´ twelve
χιλιάδες n. nom. fem. pl. χιλιάς thousand
Ἐκ prep. ἐκ ἐξ (+gen) of, from, out of, by, on, with, in, among, through
φυλῆς n. gen. fem. sg. φυλή tribe, kindred
Βενιαμὶν n. gen. masc. sg. Βενιαμίν Benjamin
ιβ´ abbreviated numeral. ιβ´ twelve
χιλιάδες n. nom. fem. pl. χιλιάς thousand
9 Μετὰ prep. μετά (+gen) with, among, against, (+acc) after
ταῦτα demo. pron. acc. neut. pl. οὗτος αὕτη τοῦτο this, the same, this same, he, she, it
καὶ conj. καί and, even, also, but
ὄχλος n. nom. masc. sg. ὄχλος people, multitude, company, press, number
πολύς adj. nom. masc. sg. πολύς many, great, much, long, abundant
ὃν relative pron. acc. masc. sg. ὅς ἥ ὅ who, which, what, that
αὐτὸν pron. acc. masc. 3p. sg. αὐτός ή ό self, of oneself, even, very, the same, he, she, it
οὐδεὶς num. nom. masc. sg. οὐδείς no man, nothing, no, none, neither, not, nought
ἐκ prep. ἐκ ἐξ (+gen) of, from, out of, by, on, with, in, among, through
παντὸς adj. gen. neut. sg. πᾶς πᾶσα πᾶν all, every, whosoever, every one, no, whole, any
ἔθνους n. gen. neut. sg. ἔθνος Gentile, nation, heathen, people
καὶ conj. καί and, even, also, but
φυλῶν n. gen. fem. pl. φυλή tribe, kindred
καὶ conj. καί and, even, also, but
λαῶν n. gen. masc. pl. λαός people
καὶ conj. καί and, even, also, but
γλωσσῶν n. gen. fem. pl. γλῶσσα tongue
ἐνώπιον prep. ἐνώπιον (+gen) before, in the sight of, in the presence of. (adv.) before
τοῦ art. gen. masc. sg. ὁ ἡ τό the, this, that, he, she, it
θρόνου n. gen. masc. sg. θρόνος throne, seat
καὶ conj. καί and, even, also, but
ἐνώπιον prep. ἐνώπιον (+gen) before, in the sight of, in the presence of. (adv.) before
τοῦ art. gen. neut. sg. ὁ ἡ τό the, this, that, he, she, it
ἀρνίου n. gen. neut. sg. ἀρνίον Lamb, lamb
στολὰς n. acc. fem. pl. στολή robe, long clothing, long garment, long robe
λευκὰς adj. acc. fem. pl. λευκός white
καὶ conj. καί and, even, also, but
φοίνικες n. nom. masc. pl. φοῖνιξ palm-tree
ἐν prep. ἐν (+dat) in, by, with, among, at, on, through, to, within, into, of, for
ταῖς art. dat. fem. pl. ὁ ἡ τό the, this, that, he, she, it
χερσὶν n. dat. fem. pl. χείρ hand

αὐτῶν pron. gen. masc. 3p. pl. αὐτός ἡ ὁ self, of oneself, even, very, the same, he, she, it
10 καὶ conj. καί and, even, also, but
φωνῇ n. dat. fem. sg. φωνή voice, sound, noise
μεγάλῃ adj. dat. fem. sg. μέγας great, loud, greatest, high, large, mighty, strong
Ἡ art. nom. fem. sg. ὁ ἡ τό the, this, that, he, she, it
σωτηρία n. nom. fem. sg. σωτηρία salvation, deliver, health, saving
τῷ art. dat. masc. sg. ὁ ἡ τό the, this, that, he, she, it
Θεῷ n. dat. masc. sg. θεός God, god
ἡμῶν pron. gen. 1p. pl. ἐγώ I
τῷ art. dat. masc. sg. ὁ ἡ τό the, this, that, he, she, it
ἐπὶ prep. ἐπί (+gen) on, in, upon, (+dat) in, at, for, upon, (+acc) on, upon, unto, to, against
τοῦ art. gen. masc. sg. ὁ ἡ τό the, this, that, he, she, it
θρόνου n. gen. masc. sg. θρόνος throne, seat
καὶ conj. καί and, even, also, but
τῷ art. dat. neut. sg. ὁ ἡ τό the, this, that, he, she, it
ἀρνίῳ n. dat. neut. sg. ἀρνίον Lamb, lamb
11 καὶ conj. καί and, even, also, but
πάντες adj. nom. masc. pl. πᾶς πᾶσα πᾶν all, every, whosoever, every one, no, whole, any
οἱ art. nom. masc. pl. ὁ ἡ τό the, this, that, he, she, it
ἄγγελοι n. nom. masc. pl. ἄγγελος angel, messenger
κύκλῳ adv. κύκλῳ round about, round
τοῦ art. gen. masc. sg. ὁ ἡ τό the, this, that, he, she, itό
θρόνου n. gen. masc. sg. θρόνος throne, seat
καὶ conj. καί and, even, also, but
τῶν art. gen. masc. pl. ὁ ἡ τό the, this, that, he, she, it
πρεσβυτέρων adj. gen. masc. pl. πρεσβύτερος elder, elder woman, eldest, old man
καὶ conj. καί and, even, also, but
τῶν art. gen. neut. pl. ὁ ἡ τό the, this, that, he, she, it
τεσσάρων num. gen. neut. pl. τέσσαρες four
ζώων n. gen. neut. pl. ζῶον beast
καὶ conj. καί and, even, also, but
ἐνώπιον prep. ἐνώπιον (+gen) before, in the sight of, in the presence of. (adv.) before
τοῦ art. gen. masc. sg. ὁ ἡ τό the, this, that, he, she, itό
θρόνου n. gen. masc. sg. θρόνος throne, seat
ἐπὶ prep. ἐπί (+gen) on, in, upon, (+dat) in, at, for, upon, (+acc) on, upon, unto, to, against
πρόσωπον n. acc. neut. sg. πρόσωπον face, presence, person, countenance
αὐτῶν pron. gen. masc. 3p. pl. αὐτός ἡ ὁ self, of oneself, even, very, the same, he, she, it
καὶ conj. καί and, even, also, but
τῷ art. dat. masc. sg. ὁ ἡ τό the, this, that, he, she, it
Θεῷ n. dat. masc. sg. θεός God, god
12 Ἀμήν particle. ἀμήν amen, verily
ἡ art. nom. fem. sg. ὁ ἡ τό the, this, that, he, she, it
εὐλογία n. nom. fem. sg. εὐλογία blessing, bounty, matter of bounty, fair speech
καὶ conj. καί and, even, also, but
ἡ art. nom. fem. sg. ὁ ἡ τό the, this, that, he, she, it
δόξα n. nom. fem. sg. δόξα glory, honour, praise, dignity, worship
καὶ conj. καί and, even, also, but
ἡ art. nom. fem. sg. ὁ ἡ τό the, this, that, he, she, it
σοφία n. nom. fem. sg. σοφία wisdom
καὶ conj. καί and, even, also, but
ἡ art. nom. fem. sg. ὁ ἡ τό the, this, that, he, she, it
εὐχαριστία n. nom. fem. sg. εὐχαριστία thankfulness, thanksgiving, giving of thanks
καὶ conj. καί and, even, also, but
ἡ art. nom. fem. sg. ὁ ἡ τό the, this, that, he, she, it
τιμὴ n. nom. fem. sg. τιμή honour, price, preciousness, sum

καὶ conj. καί and, even, also, but
ἡ art. nom. fem. sg. ὁ ἡ τό the, this, that, he, she, it
δύναμις n. nom. fem. sg. δύναμις power, mighty work, miracle, strength, might
καὶ conj. καί and, even, also, but
ἡ art. nom. fem. sg. ὁ ἡ τό the, this, that, he, she, it
ἰσχὺς n. nom. fem. sg. ἰσχύς strength, might, power, ability
τῷ art. dat. masc. sg. ὁ ἡ τό the, this, that, he, she, it
Θεῷ n. dat. masc. sg. θεός God, god
ἡμῶν pron. gen. 1p. pl. ἐγώ I
εἰς prep. εἰς (+acc) into, to, unto, for, in, on, toward, against, upon, at, among
τοὺς art. acc. masc. pl. ὁ ἡ τό the, this, that, he, she, it
αἰῶνας n. acc. masc. pl. αἰών ever, ever and ever, evermore, age, eternal, world
τῶν art. gen. masc. pl. ὁ ἡ τό the, this, that, he, she, it
αἰώνων n. gen. masc. pl. αἰών ever, ever and ever, evermore, age, eternal, world
ἀμήν particle. ἀμήν amen, verily
13 καὶ conj. καί and, even, also, but
εἷς num. nom. masc. sg. εἷς or ἕν one, other, some, any, only, a certain
ἐκ prep. ἐκ ἐξ (+gen) of, from, out of, by, on, with, in, among, through
τῶν art. gen. masc. pl. ὁ ἡ τό the, this, that, he, she, it
πρεσβυτέρων adj. gen. masc. pl. πρεσβύτερος elder, elder woman, eldest, old man
μοι pron. dat. 1p. sg. ἐγώ I
Οὗτοι demo. pron. nom. masc. pl. οὗτος αὕτη τοῦτο this, the same, this same, he, she, it
οἱ art. nom. masc. pl. ὁ ἡ τό the, this, that, he, she, it
τὰς art. acc. fem. pl. ὁ ἡ τό the, this, that, he, she, it
στολὰς n. acc. fem. pl. στολή robe, long clothing, long garment, long robe
τὰς art. acc. fem. pl. ὁ ἡ τό the, this, that, he, she, it
λευκὰς adj. acc. fem. pl. λευκός white
τίνες interrog. pron. nom. masc. pl. τίς what, who, why, where, which, how
καὶ conj. καί and, even, also, but
πόθεν adv. πόθεν whence, from whence
14 καὶ conj. καί and, even, also, but
αὐτῷ pron. dat. masc. 3p. sg. αὐτός ή ό self, of oneself, even, very, the same, he, she, it
Κύριέ n. voc. masc. sg. κύριος Lord, lord, master, sir, LORD, God, Master, owner
σὺ pron. nom. 2p. sg. σύ thou, you
καὶ conj. καί and, even, also, but
μοι pron. dat. 1p. sg. ἐγώ I
Οὗτοί demo. pron. nom. masc. pl. οὗτος αὕτη τοῦτο this, the same, this same, he, she, it
οἱ art. nom. masc. pl. ὁ ἡ τό the, this, that, he, she, it
ἐκ prep. ἐκ ἐξ (+gen) of, from, out of, by, on, with, in, among, through
τῆς art. gen. fem. sg. ὁ ἡ τό the, this, that, he, she, it
θλίψεως n. gen. fem. sg. θλῖψις tribulation, affliction, anguish, persecution
τῆς art. gen. fem. sg. ὁ ἡ τό the, this, that, he, she, it
μεγάλης adj. gen. fem. sg. μέγας great, loud, greatest, high, large, mighty, strong
καὶ conj. καί and, even, also, but
τὰς art. acc. fem. pl. ὁ ἡ τό the, this, that, he, she, it
στολὰς n. acc. fem. pl. στολή robe, long clothing, long garment, long robe
αὐτῶν pron. gen. masc. 3p. pl. αὐτός ή ό self, of oneself, even, very, the same, he, she, it
καὶ conj. καί and, even, also, but
αὐτὰς pron. acc. fem. 3p. pl. αὐτός ή ό self, of oneself, even, very, the same, he, she, it
ἐν prep. ἐν (+dat) in, by, with, among, at, on, through, to, within, into, of, for
τῷ art. dat. neut. sg. ὁ ἡ τό the, this, that, he, she, it
αἵματι n. dat. neut. sg. αἷμα blood
τοῦ art. gen. neut. sg. ὁ ἡ τό the, this, that, he, she, it
ἀρνίου n. gen. neut. sg. ἀρνίον Lamb, lamb
15 διὰ prep. διά (+gen) by, through, with, in, of, (+acc) for, because of, for a cause

τοῦτό demo. pron. acc. neut. sg. οὗτος αὕτη τοῦτο this, the same, this same, he, she, it
ἐνώπιον prep. ἐνώπιον (+gen) before, in the sight of, in the presence of. (adv.) before
τοῦ art. gen. masc. sg. ὁ ἡ τό the, this, that, he, she, it
θρόνου n. gen. masc. sg. θρόνος throne, seat
τοῦ art. gen. masc. sg. ὁ ἡ τό the, this, that, he, she, it
Θεοῦ n. gen. masc. sg. θεός God, god
καὶ conj. καί and, even, also, but
αὐτῷ pron. dat. masc. 3p. sg. αὐτός ἡ ό self, of oneself, even, very, the same, he, she, it
ἡμέρας n. gen. fem. sg. ἡμέρα day, time, year, while, age, day time
καὶ conj. καί and, even, also, but
νυκτὸς n. gen. fem. sg. νύξ night
ἐν prep. ἐν (+dat) in, by, with, among, at, on, through, to, within, into, of, for
τῷ art. dat. masc. sg. ὁ ἡ τό the, this, that, he, she, it
ναῷ n. dat. masc. sg. ναός temple, shrine
αὐτοῦ pron. gen. masc. 3p. sg. αὐτός ἡ ὁ self, of oneself, even, very, the same, he, she, it
καὶ conj. καί and, even, also, but
ὁ art. nom. masc. sg. ὁ ἡ τό the, this, that, he, she, it
ἐπὶ prep. ἐπί (+gen) on, in, upon, (+dat) in, at, for, upon, (+acc) on, upon, unto, to, against
τοῦ art. gen. masc. sg. ὁ ἡ τό the, this, that, he, she, it
θρόνου n. gen. masc. sg. θρόνος throne, seat
ἐπ' prep. ἐπί (+gen) on, in, upon, (+dat) in, at, for, upon, (+acc) on, upon, unto, to, against
αὐτούς pron. acc. masc. 3p. pl. αὐτός ἡ ὁ self, of oneself, even, very, the same, he, she, it
16 οὐ particle of negation. οὐ οὐκ οὐχ not, no, neither, none, nay, nor, never, nothing
ἔτι adv. ἔτι yet, more, any more, further, still, moreover
οὐδὲ adv. οὐδέ neither, nor, not, no, not even, never, not yet
ἔτι adv. ἔτι yet, more, any more, further, still, moreover
οὐδὲ adv. οὐδέ neither, nor, not, no, not even, never, not yet
μὴ particle of negation. μή not, no, lest, neither, none, nothing, nor, never, without
ἐπ' prep. ἐπί (+gen) on, in, upon, (+dat) in, at, for, upon, (+acc) on, upon, unto, to, against
αὐτοὺς pron. acc. masc. 3p. pl. αὐτός ἡ ὁ self, of oneself, even, very, the same, he, she, it
ὁ art. nom. masc. sg. ὁ ἡ τό the, this, that, he, she, it
ἥλιος n. nom. masc. sg. ἥλιος sun, east
οὐδὲ adv. οὐδέ neither, nor, not, no, not even, never, not yet
πᾶν adj. nom. neut. sg. πᾶς πᾶσα πᾶν all, every, whosoever, every one, no, whole, any
καῦμα n. nom. neut. sg. καῦμα heat
17 ὅτι conj. ὅτι that, for, because, how that, how, because that, for that, though
τὸ art. nom. neut. sg. ὁ ἡ τό the, this, that, he, she, it
ἀρνίον n. nom. neut. sg. ἀρνίον Lamb, lamb
τὸ art. nom. neut. sg. ὁ ἡ τό the, this, that, he, she, it
ἀνὰ prep. ἀνά (+acc) by, in, through, among, between. (adv.) apiece, every man, each
μέσον adj. acc. neut. sg. μέσος midst, among, mid, between
τοῦ art. gen. masc. sg. ὁ ἡ τό the, this, that, he, she, it
θρόνου n. gen. masc. sg. θρόνος throne, seat
αὐτοὺς pron. acc. masc. 3p. pl. αὐτός ἡ ὁ self, of oneself, even, very, the same, he, she, it
καὶ conj. καί and, even, also, but
αὐτοὺς pron. acc. masc. 3p. pl. αὐτός ἡ ὁ self, of oneself, even, very, the same, he, she, it
ἐπὶ prep. ἐπί (+gen) on, in, upon, (+dat) in, at, for, upon, (+acc) on, upon, unto, to, against
πηγὰς n. acc. fem. pl. πηγή fountain, well
ὑδάτων n. gen. neut. pl. ὕδωρ water
καὶ conj. καί and, even, also, but
ὁ art. nom. masc. sg. ὁ ἡ τό the, this, that, he, she, it
Θεὸς n. nom. masc. sg. θεός God, god
πᾶν adj. acc. neut. sg. πᾶς πᾶσα πᾶν all, every, whosoever, every one, no, whole, any
δάκρυον n. acc. neut. sg. δάκρυον tears
ἀπὸ prep. ἀπό (+gen) from, of, out of, since, for, off, at, by, in, on

τῶν art. gen. masc. pl. ὁ ἡ τό the, this, that, he, she, it
ὀφθαλμῶν n. gen. masc. pl. ὀφθαλμός eye, sight
αὐτῶν pron. gen. masc. 3p. pl. αὐτός ἡ ὁ self, of oneself, even, very, the same, he, she, it

8

1 Καὶ conj. καί and, even, also, but
ὅτε adv. ὅτε when, after that, as soon as, while, after
τὴν art. acc. fem. sg. ὁ ἡ τό the, this, that, he, she, it
σφραγῖδα n. acc. fem. sg. σφραγίς seal
τὴν art. acc. fem. sg. ὁ ἡ τό the, this, that, he, she, it
ἑβδόμην ordinal. adj. acc. fem. sg. ἕβδομος seventh
σιγὴ n. nom. fem. sg. σιγή silence
ἐν prep. ἐν (+dat) in, by, with, among, at, on, through, to, within, into, of, for
τῷ art. dat. masc. sg. ὁ ἡ τό the, this, that, he, she, it
οὐρανῷ n. dat. masc. sg. οὐρανός heaven, air, sky
ὡς adv. ὡς as, when, as it were, how, about, like, as soon as, even as, while
ἡμιώριον n. acc. neut. sg. ἡμιώριον half an hour
2 καὶ conj. καί and, even, also, but
τοὺς art. acc. masc. pl. ὁ ἡ τό the, this, that, he, she, it
ἑπτὰ num. acc. masc. pl. ἑπτά seven, seventh
ἀγγέλους n. acc. masc. pl. ἄγγελος angel, messenger
οἳ relative pron. nom. masc. pl. ὅς ἥ ὅ who, which, what, that
ἐνώπιον prep. ἐνώπιον (+gen) before, in the sight of, in the presence of. (adv.) before
τοῦ art. gen. masc. sg. ὁ ἡ τό the, this, that, he, she, it
Θεοῦ n. gen. masc. sg. θεός God, god
καὶ conj. καί and, even, also, but
αὐτοῖς pron. dat. masc. 3p. pl. αὐτός ἡ ὁ self, of oneself, even, very, the same, he, she, it
ἑπτὰ num. nom. fem. pl. ἑπτά seven, seventh
σάλπιγγες n. nom. fem. pl. σάλπιγξ trumpet, trump
3 Καὶ conj. καί and, even, also, but
ἄλλος adj. nom. masc. sg. ἄλλος other, another, some, one, more, otherwise
ἄγγελος n. nom. masc. sg. ἄγγελος angel, messenger
καὶ conj. καί and, even, also, but
ἐπὶ prep. ἐπί (+gen) on, in, upon, (+dat) in, at, for, upon, (+acc) on, upon, unto, to, against
τὸ art. acc. neut. sg. ὁ ἡ τό the, this, that, he, she, it
θυσιαστήριον n. acc. neut. sg. θυσιαστήριον altar
τοῦ art. gen. neut. sg. ὁ ἡ τό the, this, that, he, she, it
θυσιαστηρίου n. gen. neut. sg. θυσιαστήριον altar
λιβανωτὸν n. acc. masc. sg. λιβανωτός censer
χρυσοῦν adj. acc. masc. sg. χρύσεος golden, of gold
καὶ conj. καί and, even, also, but
αὐτῷ pron. dat. masc. 3p. sg. αὐτός ἡ ὁ self, of oneself, even, very, the same, he, she, it
θυμιάματα n. nom. neut. pl. θυμίαμα incense, odour
πολλά adj. nom. neut. pl. πολύς many, great, much, long, abundant
ἵνα conj. ἵνα that, to, lest, for to, so that, albeit, because, for, so as
ταῖς art. dat. fem. pl. ὁ ἡ τό the, this, that, he, she, it
προσευχαῖς n. dat. fem. pl. προσευχή prayer
τῶν art. gen. masc. pl. ὁ ἡ τό the, this, that, he, she, it
ἁγίων adj. gen. masc. pl. ἅγιος Holy, holy, saint, Holy One, holy thing, most holy
πάντων adj. gen. masc. pl. πᾶς πᾶσα πᾶν all, every, whosoever, every one, no, whole, any
ἐπὶ prep. ἐπί (+gen) on, in, upon, (+dat) in, at, for, upon, (+acc) on, upon, unto, to, against
τὸ art. acc. neut. sg. ὁ ἡ τό the, this, that, he, she, it
θυσιαστήριον n. acc. neut. sg. θυσιαστήριον altar
τὸ art. acc. neut. sg. ὁ ἡ τό the, this, that, he, she, it

χρυσοῦν adj. acc. neut. sg. χρύσεος golden, of gold
τὸ art. acc. neut. sg. ὁ ἡ τό the, this, that, he, she, it
ἐνώπιον prep. ἐνώπιον (+gen) before, in the sight of, in the presence of. (adv.) before
τοῦ art. gen. masc. sg. ὁ ἡ τό the, this, that, he, she, it
θρόνου n. gen. masc. sg. θρόνος throne, seat
4 καὶ conj. καί and, even, also, but
ὁ art. nom. masc. sg. ὁ ἡ τό the, this, that, he, she, it
καπνὸς n. nom. masc. sg. καπνός smoke
τῶν art. gen. neut. pl. ὁ ἡ τό the, this, that, he, she, it
θυμιαμάτων n. gen. neut. pl. θυμίαμα incense, odour
ταῖς art. dat. fem. pl. ὁ ἡ τό the, this, that, he, she, it
προσευχαῖς n. dat. fem. pl. προσευχή prayer
τῶν art. gen. masc. pl. ὁ ἡ τό the, this, that, he, she, it
ἁγίων adj. gen. masc. pl. ἅγιος Holy, holy, saint, Holy One, holy thing, most holy
ἐκ prep. ἐκ ἐξ (+gen) of, from, out of, by, on, with, in, among, through
χειρὸς n. gen. fem. sg. χείρ hand
τοῦ art. gen. masc. sg. ὁ ἡ τό the, this, that, he, she, it
ἀγγέλου n. gen. masc. sg. ἄγγελος angel, messenger
ἐνώπιον prep. ἐνώπιον (+gen) before, in the sight of, in the presence of. (adv.) before
τοῦ art. gen. masc. sg. ὁ ἡ τό the, this, that, he, she, it
Θεοῦ n. gen. masc. sg. θεός God, god
5 καὶ conj. καί and, even, also, but
ὁ art. nom. masc. sg. ὁ ἡ τό the, this, that, he, she, it
ἄγγελος n. nom. masc. sg. ἄγγελος angel, messenger
τὸ art. nom. neut. sg. ὁ ἡ τό the, this, that, he, she, it
λιβανωτὸν n. acc. masc. sg. λιβανωτός censer
καὶ conj. καί and, even, also, but
αὐτὸ pron. acc. masc. 3p. sg. αὐτός ἡ ὁ self, of oneself, even, very, the same, he, she, it
ἐκ prep. ἐκ ἐξ (+gen) of, from, out of, by, on, with, in, among, through
τοῦ art. gen. neut. sg. ὁ ἡ τό the, this, that, he, she, it
πυρὸς n. gen. neut. sg. πῦρ fire, fiery
τοῦ art. gen. neut. sg. ὁ ἡ τό the, this, that, he, she, it
θυσιαστηρίου n. gen. neut. sg. θυσιαστήριον altar
καὶ conj. καί and, even, also, but
εἰς prep. εἰς (+acc) into, to, unto, for, in, on, toward, against, upon, at, among
τὴν art. acc. fem. sg. ὁ ἡ τό the, this, that, he, she, it
γῆν n. acc. fem. sg. γῆ earth, land, ground, country
καὶ conj. καί and, even, also, but
φωναὶ n. nom. fem. pl. φωνή voice, sound, noise
καὶ conj. καί and, even, also, but
βρονταὶ n. nom. fem. pl. βροντή thunder, thundering
καὶ conj. καί and, even, also, but
ἀστραπαὶ n. nom. fem. pl. ἀστραπή lightning, bright shining
καὶ conj. καί and, even, also, but
σεισμός n. nom. masc. sg. σεισμός earthquake, tempest
6 Καὶ conj. καί and, even, also, but
οἱ art. nom. masc. pl. ὁ ἡ τό the, this, that, he, she, it
ἑπτὰ num. nom. masc. pl. ἑπτά seven, seventh
ἄγγελοι n. nom. masc. pl. ἄγγελος angel, messenger
οἱ art. nom. masc. pl. ὁ ἡ τό the, this, that, he, she, it
τὰς art. acc. fem. pl. ὁ ἡ τό the, this, that, he, she, it
ἑπτὰ num. acc. fem. pl. ἑπτά seven, seventh
σάλπιγγας n. acc. fem. pl. σάλπιγξ trumpet, trump
ἑαυτοὺς reflexive pron. acc. masc. 3p. pl. ἑαυτοῦ himself, herself, itself, yourself, ourselves
ἵνα conj. ἵνα that, to, lest, for to, so that, albeit, because, for, so as

7 Καὶ conj. καί and, even, also, but
ὁ art. nom. masc. sg. ὁ ἡ τό the, this, that, he, she, it
πρῶτος ordinal. adj. nom. masc. sg. πρῶτος first, chief, first of all, chiefest, best
ἄγγελος n. nom. masc. sg. ἄγγελος angel, messenger
καὶ conj. καί and, even, also, but
χάλαζα n. nom. fem. sg. χάλαζα hail
καὶ conj. καί and, even, also, but
πῦρ n. nom. neut. sg. πῦρ fire, fiery
αἵματι n. dat. neut. sg. αἷμα blood
καὶ conj. καί and, even, also, but
εἰς prep. εἰς (+acc) into, to, unto, for, in, on, toward, against, upon, at, among
τὴν art. acc. fem. sg. ὁ ἡ τό the, this, that, he, she, it
γῆν n. acc. fem. sg. γῆ earth, land, ground, country
καὶ conj. καί and, even, also, but
τὸ art. nom. neut. sg. ὁ ἡ τό the, this, that, he, she, it
τρίτον ordinal. adj. nom. neut. sg. τρίτος third
τῶν art. gen. neut. pl. ὁ ἡ τό the, this, that, he, she, it
δένδρων n. gen. neut. pl. δένδρον tree
καὶ conj. καί and, even, also, but
πᾶς adj. nom. masc. sg. πᾶς πᾶσα πᾶν all, every, whosoever, every one, no, whole, any
χόρτος n. nom. masc. sg. χόρτος grass, blade, hay
χλωρὸς adj. nom. masc. sg. χλωρός green, pale
8 Καὶ conj. καί and, even, also, but
ὁ art. nom. masc. sg. ὁ ἡ τό the, this, that, he, she, it
δεύτερος ordinal. adj. nom. masc. sg. δεύτερος second, second time, again, afterward
ἄγγελος n. nom. masc. sg. ἄγγελος angel, messenger
καὶ conj. καί and, even, also, but
ὡς adv. ὡς as, when, as it were, how, about, like, as soon as, even as, while
ὄρος n. nom. neut. sg. ὄρος mountain, mount, hill
μέγα adj. nom. neut. sg. μέγας great, loud, greatest, high, large, mighty, strong
πυρὶ n. dat. neut. sg. πῦρ fire, fiery
εἰς prep. εἰς (+acc) into, to, unto, for, in, on, toward, against, upon, at, among
τὴν art. acc. fem. sg. ὁ ἡ τό the, this, that, he, she, it
θάλασσαν n. acc. fem. sg. θάλασσα sea
καὶ conj. καί and, even, also, but
τὸ art. nom. neut. sg. ὁ ἡ τό the, this, that, he, she, it
τρίτον ordinal. adj. nom. neut. sg. τρίτος third
τῆς art. gen. fem. sg. ὁ ἡ τό the, this, that, he, she, it
θαλάσσης n. gen. fem. sg. θάλασσα sea
αἷμα n. nom. neut. sg. αἷμα blood
9 καὶ conj. καί and, even, also, but
τὸ art. nom. neut. sg. ὁ ἡ τό the, this, that, he, she, it
τρίτον ordinal. adj. nom. neut. sg. τρίτος third
τῶν art. gen. neut. pl. ὁ ἡ τό the, this, that, he, she, it
κτισμάτων n. gen. neut. pl. κτίσμα creature
τῶν art. gen. neut. pl. ὁ ἡ τό the, this, that, he, she, it
ἐν prep. ἐν (+dat) in, by, with, among, at, on, through, to, within, into, of, for
τῇ art. dat. fem. sg. ὁ ἡ τό the, this, that, he, she, it
θαλάσσῃ n. dat. fem. sg. θάλασσα sea
τὰ art. nom. neut. pl. ὁ ἡ τό the, this, that, he, she, it
ψυχὰς n. acc. fem. pl. ψυχή life, soul, mind, heart
καὶ conj. καί and, even, also, but
τὸ art. nom. neut. sg. ὁ ἡ τό the, this, that, he, she, it
τρίτον ordinal. adj. nom. neut. sg. τρίτος third
τῶν art. gen. neut. pl. ὁ ἡ τό the, this, that, he, she, it

πλοίων n. gen. neut. pl. πλοῖον ship, boat
10 Καὶ conj. καί and, even, also, but
ὁ art. nom. masc. sg. ὁ ἡ τό the, this, that, he, she, it
τρίτος ordinal. adj. nom. masc. sg. τρίτος third
ἄγγελος n. nom. masc. sg. ἄγγελος angel, messenger
καὶ conj. καί and, even, also, but
ἐκ prep. ἐκ ἐξ (+gen) of, from, out of, by, on, with, in, among, through
τοῦ art. gen. masc. sg. ὁ ἡ τό the, this, that, he, she, it
οὐρανοῦ n. gen. masc. sg. οὐρανός heaven, air, sky
ἀστὴρ n. nom. masc. sg. ἀστήρ star
μέγας adj. nom. masc. sg. μέγας great, loud, greatest, high, large, mighty, strong
ὡς adv. ὡς as, when, as it were, how, about, like, as soon as, even as, while
λαμπὰς n. nom. fem. sg. λαμπάς lamp, light, torch
καὶ conj. καί and, even, also, but
ἐπὶ prep. ἐπί (+gen) on, in, upon, (+dat) in, at, for, upon, (+acc) on, upon, unto, to, against
τὸ art. acc. neut. sg. ὁ ἡ τό the, this, that, he, she, it
τρίτον ordinal. adj. acc. neut. sg. τρίτος third
τῶν art. gen. masc. pl. ὁ ἡ τό the, this, that, he, she, it
ποταμῶν n. gen. masc. pl. ποταμός river, flood , stream, water
καὶ conj. καί and, even, also, but
ἐπὶ prep. ἐπί (+gen) on, in, upon, (+dat) in, at, for, upon, (+acc) on, upon, unto, to, against
τὰς art. acc. fem. pl. ὁ ἡ τό the, this, that, he, she, it
πηγὰς n. acc. fem. pl. πηγή fountain, well
ὑδάτων n. gen. neut. pl. ὕδωρ water
11 καὶ conj. καί and, even, also, but
τὸ art. nom. neut. sg. ὁ ἡ τό the, this, that, he, she, it
ὄνομα n. nom. neut. sg. ὄνομα name, call, surname
τοῦ art. gen. masc. sg. ὁ ἡ τό the, this, that, he, she, it
ἀστέρος n. gen. masc. sg. ἀστήρ star
Ἄψινθος n. nom. masc. sg. ἄψινθος Wormwood
καὶ conj. καί and, even, also, but
τὸ art. nom. neut. sg. ὁ ἡ τό the, this, that, he, she, it
τρίτον ordinal. adj. nom. neut. sg. τρίτος third
τῶν art. gen. neut. pl. ὁ ἡ τό the, this, that, he, she, it
ὑδάτων n. gen. neut. pl. ὕδωρ water
εἰς prep. εἰς (+acc) into, to, unto, for, in, on, toward, against, upon, at, among
ἄψινθον n. acc. fem. sg. ἄψινθος wormwood
καὶ conj. καί and, even, also, but
πολλοὶ adj. nom. masc. pl. πολύς many, great, much, long, abundant
ἀνθρώπων n. gen. masc. pl. ἄνθρωπος man, human being, person, one, certain
ἐκ prep. ἐκ ἐξ (+gen) of, from, out of, by, on, with, in, among, through
τῶν art. gen. neut. pl. ὁ ἡ τό the, this, that, he, she, it
ὑδάτων n. gen. neut. pl. ὕδωρ water
ὅτι conj. ὅτι that, for, because, how that, how, because that, for that, though
12 Καὶ conj. καί and, even, also, but
ὁ art. nom. masc. sg. ὁ ἡ τό the, this, that, he, she, it
τέταρτος ordinal. adj. nom. masc. sg. τέταρτος fourth, four
ἄγγελος n. nom. masc. sg. ἄγγελος angel, messenger
καὶ conj. καί and, even, also, but
τὸ art. nom. neut. sg. ὁ ἡ τό the, this, that, he, she, it
τρίτον ordinal. adj. nom. neut. sg. τρίτος third
τοῦ art. gen. masc. sg. ὁ ἡ τό the, this, that, he, she, it
ἡλίου n. gen. masc. sg. ἥλιος sun, east
καὶ conj. καί and, even, also, but
τὸ art. nom. neut. sg. ὁ ἡ τό the, this, that, he, she, it

τρίτον ordinal. adj. nom. neut. sg. τρίτος third
τῆς art. gen. fem. sg. ὁ ἡ τό the, this, that, he, she, it
σελήνης n. gen. fem. sg. σελήνη moon
καὶ conj. καί and, even, also, but
τὸ art. nom. neut. sg. ὁ ἡ τό the, this, that, he, she, it
τρίτον ordinal. adj. nom. neut. sg. τρίτος third
τῶν art. gen. masc. pl. ὁ ἡ τό the, this, that, he, she, it
ἀστέρων n. gen. masc. pl. ἀστήρ star
ἵνα conj. ἵνα that, to, lest, for to, so that, albeit, because, for, so as
τὸ art. nom. neut. sg. ὁ ἡ τό the, this, that, he, she, it
τρίτον ordinal. adj. nom. neut. sg. τρίτος third
αὐτῶν pron. gen. masc. 3p. pl. αὐτός ή ό self, of oneself, even, very, the same, he, she, it
καὶ conj. καί and, even, also, but
ἡ art. nom. fem. sg. ὁ ἡ τό the, this, that, he, she, it
ἡμέρα n. nom. fem. sg. ἡμέρα day, time, year, while, age, day time
μὴ particle of negation. μή not, no, lest, neither, none, nothing, nor, never, without
τὸ art. nom. neut. sg. ὁ ἡ τό the, this, that, he, she, it
τρίτον ordinal. adj. nom. neut. sg. τρίτος third
αὐτῆς pron. gen. fem. 3p. sg. αὐτός ή ό self, of oneself, even, very, the same, he, she, it
καὶ conj. καί and, even, also, but
ἡ art. nom. fem. sg. ὁ ἡ τό the, this, that, he, she, it
νὺξ n. nom. fem. sg. νύξ night
ὁμοίως adv. ὁμοίως likewise, so
13 Καὶ conj. καί and, even, also, but
καὶ conj. καί and, even, also, but
ἑνὸς num. gen. masc. sg. εἷς or ἕν one, other, some, any, only, a certain
ἀγγέλου n. gen. masc. sg. ἄγγελος angel, messenger
ἐν prep. ἐν (+dat) in, by, with, among, at, on, through, to, within, into, of, for
μεσουρανήματι n. dat. neut. sg. μεσουράνημα midst of heaven
φωνῇ n. dat. fem. sg. φωνή voice, sound, noise
μεγάλῃ adj. dat. fem. sg. μέγας great, loud, greatest, high, large, mighty, strong
Οὐαὶ particle. οὐαί woe, alas
οὐαὶ particle. οὐαί woe, alas
οὐαὶ particle. οὐαί woe, alas
τοῖς art. dat. masc. pl. ὁ ἡ τό the, this, that, he, she, it
ἐπὶ prep. ἐπί (+gen) on, in, upon, (+dat) in, at, for, upon, (+acc) on, upon, unto, to, against
τῆς art. gen. fem. sg. ὁ ἡ τό the, this, that, he, she, it
γῆς n. gen. fem. sg. γῆ earth, land, ground, country
ἐκ prep. ἐκ ἐξ (+gen) of, from, out of, by, on, with, in, among, through
τῶν art. gen. fem. pl. ὁ ἡ τό the, this, that, he, she, it
λοιπῶν adj. gen. fem. pl. λοιπός other, rest, remnant, residue, which remain
φωνῶν n. gen. fem. pl. φωνή voice, sound, noise
τῆς art. gen. fem. sg. ὁ ἡ τό the, this, that, he, she, it
σάλπιγγος n. gen. fem. sg. σάλπιγξ trumpet, trump
τῶν art. gen. masc. pl. ὁ ἡ τό the, this, that, he, she, it
τριῶν num. gen. masc. pl. τρεῖς three
ἀγγέλων n. gen. masc. pl. ἄγγελος angel, messenger
τῶν art. gen. masc. pl. ὁ ἡ τό the, this, that, he, she, it

9

1 Καὶ conj. καί and, even, also, but
ὁ art. nom. masc. sg. ὁ ἡ τό the, this, that, he, she, it
πέμπτος ordinal. adj. nom. masc. sg. πέμπτος fifth
ἄγγελος n. nom. masc. sg. ἄγγελος angel, messenger

καὶ conj. καί and, even, also, but
ἀστέρα n. acc. masc. sg. ἀστήρ star
ἐκ prep. ἐκ ἐξ (+gen) of, from, out of, by, on, with, in, among, through
τοῦ art. gen. masc. sg. ὁ ἡ τό the, this, that, he, she, it
οὐρανοῦ n. gen. masc. sg. οὐρανός heaven, air, sky
εἰς prep. εἰς (+acc) into, to, unto, for, in, on, toward, against, upon, at, among
τὴν art. acc. fem. sg. ὁ ἡ τό the, this, that, he, she, it
γῆν n. acc. fem. sg. γῆ earth, land, ground, country
καὶ conj. καί and, even, also, but
αὐτῷ pron. dat. masc. 3p. sg. αὐτός ή ό self, of oneself, even, very, the same, he, she, it
ἡ art. nom. fem. sg. ὁ ἡ τό the, this, that, he, she, it
κλεὶς n. nom. fem. sg. κλείς key
τοῦ art. gen. neut. sg. ὁ ἡ τό the, this, that, he, she, it
φρέατος n. gen. neut. sg. φρέαρ pit, well
τῆς art. gen. fem. sg. ὁ ἡ τό the, this, that, he, she, it
ἀβύσσου n. gen. fem. sg. ἄβυσσος deep, abyss, bottomless pit, bottomless
2 καὶ conj. καί and, even, also, but
τὸ art. acc. neut. sg. ὁ ἡ τό the, this, that, he, she, it
φρέαρ n. acc. neut. sg. φρέαρ pit, well
τῆς art. gen. fem. sg. ὁ ἡ τό the, this, that, he, she, it
ἀβύσσου n. gen. fem. sg. ἄβυσσος deep, abyss, bottomless pit, bottomless
καὶ conj. καί and, even, also, but
καπνὸς n. nom. masc. sg. καπνός smoke
ἐκ prep. ἐκ ἐξ (+gen) of, from, out of, by, on, with, in, among, through
τοῦ art. gen. neut. sg. ὁ ἡ τό the, this, that, he, she, it
φρέατος n. gen. neut. sg. φρέαρ pit, well
ὡς adv. ὡς as, when, as it were, how, about, like, as soon as, even as, while
καπνὸς n. nom. masc. sg. καπνός smoke
καμίνου n. gen. fem. sg. κάμινος furnace
μεγάλης adj. gen. fem. sg. μέγας great, loud, greatest, high, large, mighty, strong
καὶ conj. καί and, even, also, but
ὁ art. nom. masc. sg. ὁ ἡ τό the, this, that, he, she, it
ἥλιος n. nom. masc. sg. ἥλιος sun, east
καὶ conj. καί and, even, also, but
ὁ art. nom. masc. sg. ὁ ἡ τό the, this, that, he, she, it
ἀὴρ n. nom. masc. sg. ἀήρ air
ἐκ prep. ἐκ ἐξ (+gen) of, from, out of, by, on, with, in, among, through
τοῦ art. gen. masc. sg. ὁ ἡ τό the, this, that, he, she, it
καπνοῦ n. gen. masc. sg. καπνός smoke
τοῦ art. gen. neut. sg. ὁ ἡ τό the, this, that, he, she, it
φρέατος n. gen. neut. sg. φρέαρ pit, well
3 καὶ conj. καί and, even, also, but
ἐκ prep. ἐκ ἐξ (+gen) of, from, out of, by, on, with, in, among, through
τοῦ art. gen. masc. sg. ὁ ἡ τό the, this, that, he, she, it
καπνοῦ n. gen. masc. sg. καπνός smoke
ἀκρίδες n. nom. fem. pl. ἀκρίς locust
εἰς prep. εἰς (+acc) into, to, unto, for, in, on, toward, against, upon, at, among
τὴν art. acc. fem. sg. ὁ ἡ τό the, this, that, he, she, it
γῆν n. acc. fem. sg. γῆ earth, land, ground, country
καὶ conj. καί and, even, also, but
αὐταῖς pron. dat. fem. 3p. pl. αὐτός ή ό self, of oneself, even, very, the same, he, she, it
ἐξουσία n. nom. fem. sg. ἐξουσία power, authority, right, strength, jurisdiction
ὡς adv. ὡς as, when, as it were, how, about, like, as soon as, even as, while
ἐξουσίαν n. acc. fem. sg. ἐξουσία power, authority, right, strength, jurisdiction
οἱ art. nom. masc. pl. ὁ ἡ τό the, this, that, he, she, it

σκορπίοι n. nom. masc. pl. σκορπίος scorpion
τῆς art. gen. fem. sg. ὁ ἡ τό the, this, that, he, she, it
γῆς n. gen. fem. sg. γῆ earth, land, ground, country
4 καὶ conj. καί and, even, also, but
αὐταῖς pron. dat. fem. 3p. pl. αὐτός ἡ ὁ self, of oneself, even, very, the same, he, she, it
ἵνα conj. ἵνα that, to, lest, for to, so that, albeit, because, for, so as
μὴ particle of negation. μή not, no, lest, neither, none, nothing, nor, never, without
τὸν art. acc. masc. sg. ὁ ἡ τό the, this, that, he, she, it
χόρτον n. acc. masc. sg. χόρτος grass, blade, hay
τῆς art. gen. fem. sg. ὁ ἡ τό the, this, that, he, she, it
γῆς n. gen. fem. sg. γῆ earth, land, ground, country
οὐδὲ adv. οὐδέ neither, nor, not, no, not even, never, not yet
πᾶν adj. acc. neut. sg. πᾶς πᾶσα πᾶν all, every, whosoever, every one, no, whole, any
χλωρὸν adj. acc. neut. sg. χλωρός green, pale
οὐδὲ adv. οὐδέ neither, nor, not, no, not even, never, not yet
πᾶν adj. acc. neut. sg. πᾶς πᾶσα πᾶν all, every, whosoever, every one, no, whole, any
δένδρον n. acc. neut. sg. δένδρον tree
εἰ conj. εἰ if, whether, that, though, forasmuch
μὴ particle of negation. μή not, no, lest, neither, none, nothing, nor, never, without
τοὺς art. acc. masc. pl. ὁ ἡ τό the, this, that, he, she, it
ἀνθρώπους n. acc. masc. pl. ἄνθρωπος man, human being, person, one, certain
μόνους adj. acc. masc. pl. μόνος only, alone, by oneself
οἵτινες relative pron. nom. masc. pl. ὅστις which, who, whosoever, that, whatsoever
οὐκ particle of negation. οὐ οὐκ οὐχ not, no, neither, none, nay, nor, never, nothing
τὴν art. acc. fem. sg. ὁ ἡ τό the, this, that, he, she, it
σφραγῖδα n. acc. fem. sg. σφραγίς seal
τοῦ art. gen. masc. sg. ὁ ἡ τό the, this, that, he, she, it
Θεοῦ n. gen. masc. sg. θεός God, god
ἐπὶ prep. ἐπί (+gen) on, in, upon, (+dat) in, at, for, upon, (+acc) on, upon, unto, to, against
τῶν art. gen. neut. pl. ὁ ἡ τό the, this, that, he, she, it
μετώπων n. gen. neut. pl. μέτωπον forehead
αὐτῶν pron. gen. masc. 3p. pl. αὐτός ἡ ὁ self, of oneself, even, very, the same, he, she, it
5 καὶ conj. καί and, even, also, but
αὐταῖς pron. dat. fem. 3p. pl. αὐτός ἡ ὁ self, of oneself, even, very, the same, he, she, it
ἵνα conj. ἵνα that, to, lest, for to, so that, albeit, because, for, so as
μὴ particle of negation. μή not, no, lest, neither, none, nothing, nor, never, without
αὐτούς pron. acc. masc. 3p. pl. αὐτός ἡ ὁ self, of oneself, even, very, the same, he, she, it
ἀλλ' conj. ἀλλά but, yea, yet, nevertheless, howbeit, nay, therefore
ἵνα conj. ἵνα that, to, lest, for to, so that, albeit, because, for, so as
μῆνας n. acc. masc. pl. μήν month
πέντε num. acc. masc. pl. πέντε five
καὶ conj. καί and, even, also, but
ὁ art. nom. masc. sg. ὁ ἡ τό the, this, that, he, she, it
βασανισμὸς n. nom. masc. sg. βασανισμός torment
αὐτῶν pron. gen. fem. 3p. pl. αὐτός ἡ ὁ self, of oneself, even, very, the same, he, she, it
ὡς adv. ὡς as, when, as it were, how, about, like, as soon as, even as, while
βασανισμὸς n. nom. masc. sg. βασανισμός torment
σκορπίου n. gen. masc. sg. σκορπίος scorpion
ὅταν conj. ὅταν when, as soon as, as long as, that, whensoever, while
ἄνθρωπον n. acc. masc. sg. ἄνθρωπος man, human being, person, one, certain
6 καὶ conj. καί and, even, also, but
ἐν prep. ἐν (+dat) in, by, with, among, at, on, through, to, within, into, of, for
ταῖς art. dat. fem. pl. ὁ ἡ τό the, this, that, he, she, it
ἡμέραις n. dat. fem. pl. ἡμέρα day, time, year, while, age, day time
ἐκείναις demo. pron. dat. fem. pl. ἐκεῖνος that, he, the same, that same

οἱ art. nom. masc. pl. ὁ ἡ τό the, this, that, he, she, it
ἄνθρωποι n. nom. masc. pl. ἄνθρωπος man, human being, person, one, certain
τὸν art. acc. masc. sg. ὁ ἡ τό the, this, that, he, she, it
θάνατον n. acc. masc. sg. θάνατος death
καὶ conj. καί and, even, also, but
οὐχ particle of negation. οὐ οὐκ οὐχ not, no, neither, none, nay, nor, never, nothing
αὐτόν pron. acc. masc. 3p. sg. αὐτός ή ό self, of oneself, even, very, the same, he, she, it
καὶ conj. καί and, even, also, but
καὶ conj. καί and, even, also, but
ὁ art. nom. masc. sg. ὁ ἡ τό the, this, that, he, she, it
θάνατος n. nom. masc. sg. θάνατος death
ἀπ' prep. ἀπό (+gen) from, of, out of, since, for, off, at, by, in, on
αὐτῶν pron. gen. masc. 3p. pl. αὐτός ή ό self, of oneself, even, very, the same, he, she, it
7 καὶ conj. καί and, even, also, but
τὰ art. nom. neut. pl. ὁ ἡ τό the, this, that, he, she, it
ὁμοιώματα n. nom. neut. pl. ὁμοίωμα likeness, made like to, shape, similitude
τῶν art. gen. fem. pl. ὁ ἡ τό the, this, that, he, she, it
ἀκρίδων n. gen. fem. pl. ἀκρίς locust
ὅμοια adj. nom. neut. pl. ὅμοιος like
ἵπποις n. dat. masc. pl. ἵππος horse
εἰς prep. εἰς (+acc) into, to, unto, for, in, on, toward, against, upon, at, among
πόλεμον n. acc. masc. sg. πόλεμος war, battle, fight
καὶ conj. καί and, even, also, but
ἐπὶ prep. ἐπί (+gen) on, in, upon, (+dat) in, at, for, upon, (+acc) on, upon, unto, to, against
τὰς art. acc. fem. pl. ὁ ἡ τό the, this, that, he, she, it
κεφαλὰς n. acc. fem. pl. κεφαλή head
αὐτῶν pron. gen. fem. 3p. pl. αὐτός ή ό self, of oneself, even, very, the same, he, she, it
ὡς adv. ὡς as, when, as it were, how, about, like, as soon as, even as, while
στέφανοι n. nom. masc. pl. στέφανος crown
ὅμοιοι adj. nom. masc. pl. ὅμοιος like
χρυσῷ n. dat. masc. sg. χρυσός gold
καὶ conj. καί and, even, also, but
τὰ art. nom. neut. pl. ὁ ἡ τό the, this, that, he, she, it
πρόσωπα n. nom. neut. pl. πρόσωπον face, presence, person, countenance
αὐτῶν pron. gen. fem. 3p. pl. αὐτός ή ό self, of oneself, even, very, the same, he, she, it
ὡς adv. ὡς as, when, as it were, how, about, like, as soon as, even as, while
πρόσωπα n. nom. neut. pl. πρόσωπον face, presence, person, countenance
ἀνθρώπων n. gen. masc. pl. ἄνθρωπος man, human being, person, one, certain
8 καὶ conj. καί and, even, also, but
τρίχας n. acc. fem. pl. θρίξ hair
ὡς adv. ὡς as, when, as it were, how, about, like, as soon as, even as, while
τρίχας n. acc. fem. pl. θρίξ hair
γυναικῶν n. gen. fem. pl. γυνή woman, wife
καὶ conj. καί and, even, also, but
οἱ art. nom. masc. pl. ὁ ἡ τό the, this, that, he, she, it
ὀδόντες n. nom. masc. pl. ὀδούς tooth
αὐτῶν pron. gen. fem. 3p. pl. αὐτός ή ό self, of oneself, even, very, the same, he, she, it
ὡς adv. ὡς as, when, as it were, how, about, like, as soon as, even as, while
λεόντων n. gen. masc. pl. λέων lion
9 καὶ conj. καί and, even, also, but
θώρακας n. acc. masc. pl. θώραξ breastplate
ὡς adv. ὡς as, when, as it were, how, about, like, as soon as, even as, while
θώρακας n. acc. masc. pl. θώραξ breastplate
σιδηροῦς adj. acc. masc. pl. σιδήρεος iron, of iron
καὶ conj. καί and, even, also, but

ἡ art. nom. fem. sg. ὁ ἡ τό the, this, that, he, she, it
φωνὴ n. nom. fem. sg. φωνή voice, sound, noise
τῶν art. gen. fem. pl. ὁ ἡ τό the, this, that, he, she, it
πτερύγων n. gen. fem. pl. πτέρυξ wing
αὐτῶν pron. gen. fem. 3p. pl. αὐτός ή ό self, of oneself, even, very, the same, he, she, it
ὡς adv. ὡς as, when, as it were, how, about, like, as soon as, even as, while
φωνὴ n. nom. fem. sg. φωνή voice, sound, noise
ἁρμάτων n. gen. neut. pl. ἅρμα chariot
ἵππων n. gen. masc. pl. ἵππος horse
πολλῶν adj. gen. masc. pl. πολύς many, great, much, long, abundant
εἰς prep. εἰς (+acc) into, to, unto, for, in, on, toward, against, upon, at, among
πόλεμον n. acc. masc. sg. πόλεμος war, battle, fight
10 καὶ conj. καί and, even, also, but
οὐρὰς n. acc. fem. pl. οὐρά tail
ὁμοίας adj. acc. fem. pl. ὅμοιος like
σκορπίοις n. dat. masc. pl. σκορπίος scorpion
καὶ conj. καί and, even, also, but
κέντρα n. acc. neut. pl. κέντρον sting, prick
ἐν prep. ἐν (+dat) in, by, with, among, at, on, through, to, within, into, of, for
ταῖς art. dat. fem. pl. ὁ ἡ τό the, this, that, he, she, it
οὐραῖς n. dat. fem. pl. οὐρά tail
αὐτῶν pron. gen. fem. 3p. pl. αὐτός ή ό self, of oneself, even, very, the same, he, she, it
καὶ conj. καί and, even, also, but
ἡ art. nom. fem. sg. ὁ ἡ τό the, this, that, he, she, it
ἐξουσία n. nom. fem. sg. ἐξουσία power, authority, right, strength, jurisdiction
αὐτῶν pron. gen. fem. 3p. pl. αὐτός ή ό self, of oneself, even, very, the same, he, she, it
τοὺς art. acc. masc. pl. ὁ ἡ τό the, this, that, he, she, it
ἀνθρώπους n. acc. masc. pl. ἄνθρωπος man, human being, person, one, certain
μῆνας n. acc. masc. pl. μήν month
πέντε num. acc. masc. pl. πέντε five
11 καὶ conj. καί and, even, also, but
ἐπ' prep. ἐπί (+gen) on, in, upon, (+dat) in, at, for, upon, (+acc) on, upon, unto, to, against
αὐτῶν pron. gen. fem. 3p. pl. αὐτός ή ό self, of oneself, even, very, the same, he, she, it
βασιλέα n. acc. masc. sg. βασιλεύς king
τὸν art. acc. masc. sg. ὁ ἡ τό the, this, that, he, she, it
ἄγγελον n. acc. masc. sg. ἄγγελος angel, messenger
τῆς art. gen. fem. sg. ὁ ἡ τό the, this, that, he, she, it
ἀβύσσου n. gen. fem. sg. ἄβυσσος deep, abyss, bottomless pit, bottomless
ὄνομα n. nom. neut. sg. ὄνομα name, call, surname
αὐτῷ pron. dat. masc. 3p. sg. αὐτός ή ό self, of oneself, even, very, the same, he, she, it
Ἑβραϊστὶ adv. Ἑβραϊστί in the Hebrew
'Αβαδδών n. nom. masc. sg. 'Αβαδδών Abaddon
καὶ conj. καί and, even, also, but
ἐν prep. ἐν (+dat) in, by, with, among, at, on, through, to, within, into, of, for
τῇ art. dat. fem. sg. ὁ ἡ τό the, this, that, he, she, it
Ἑλληνικῇ adj. dat. fem. sg. Ἑλληνικός Greek, of Greek
ὄνομα n. nom. neut. sg. ὄνομα name, call, surname
'Απολλύων n. nom. masc. sg. 'Απολλύων Apollyon
12 Ἡ art. nom. fem. sg. ὁ ἡ τό the, this, that, he, she, it
οὐαὶ particle. οὐαί woe, alas
ἡ art. nom. fem. sg. ὁ ἡ τό the, this, that, he, she, it
μία num. nom. fem. sg. εἷς or ἕν one, other, some, any, only, a certain
ἔτι adv. ἔτι yet, more, any more, further, still, moreover
δύο num. nom. fem. pl. δύο two, twain, both
οὐαὶ particle. οὐαί woe, alas

μετὰ prep. μετά (+gen) with, among, against, (+acc) after
ταῦτα demo. pron. acc. neut. pl. οὗτος αὕτη τοῦτο this, the same, this same, he, she, it
13 Καὶ conj. καί and, even, also, but
ὁ art. nom. masc. sg. ὁ ἡ τό the, this, that, he, she, it
ἕκτος ordinal. adj. nom. masc. sg. ἕκτος sixth
ἄγγελος n. nom. masc. sg. ἄγγελος angel, messenger
καὶ conj. καί and, even, also, but
φωνὴν n. acc. fem. sg. φωνή voice, sound, noise
μίαν num. acc. fem. sg. εἷς or ἕν one, other, some, any, only, a certain
ἐκ prep. ἐκ ἐξ (+gen) of, from, out of, by, on, with, in, among, through
τῶν art. gen. neut. pl. ὁ ἡ τό the, this, that, he, she, it
τεσσάρων num. gen. neut. pl. τέσσαρες four
κεράτων n. gen. neut. pl. κέρας horn
τοῦ art. gen. neut. sg. ὁ ἡ τό the, this, that, he, she, it
θυσιαστηρίου n. gen. neut. sg. θυσιαστήριον altar
τοῦ art. gen. neut. sg. ὁ ἡ τό the, this, that, he, she, it
χρυσοῦ adj. gen. neut. sg. χρύσεος golden, of gold
τοῦ art. gen. neut. sg. ὁ ἡ τό the, this, that, he, she, it
ἐνώπιον prep. ἐνώπιον (+gen) before, in the sight of, in the presence of. (adv.) before
τοῦ art. gen. masc. sg. ὁ ἡ τό the, this, that, he, she, it
Θεοῦ n. gen. masc. sg. θεός God, god
14 τῷ art. dat. masc. sg. ὁ ἡ τό the, this, that, he, she, it
ἕκτῳ ordinal. adj. dat. masc. sg. ἕκτος sixth
ἀγγέλῳ n. dat. masc. sg. ἄγγελος angel, messenger
ὅς relative pron. nom. masc. sg. ὅς ἥ ὅ who, which, what, that
τὴν art. acc. fem. sg. ὁ ἡ τό the, this, that, he, she, it
σάλπιγγα n. acc. fem. sg. σάλπιγξ trumpet, trump
τοὺς art. acc. masc. pl. ὁ ἡ τό the, this, that, he, she, it
τέσσαρας num. acc. masc. pl. τέσσαρες four
ἀγγέλους n. acc. masc. pl. ἄγγελος angel, messenger
τοὺς art. acc. masc. pl. ὁ ἡ τό the, this, that, he, she, it
ἐπὶ prep. ἐπί (+gen) on, in, upon, (+dat) in, at, for, upon, (+acc) on, upon, unto, to, against
τῷ art. dat. masc. sg. ὁ ἡ τό the, this, that, he, she, it
ποταμῷ n. dat. masc. sg. ποταμός river, flood , stream, water
τῷ art. dat. masc. sg. ὁ ἡ τό the, this, that, he, she, it
μεγάλῳ adj. dat. masc. sg. μέγας great, loud, greatest, high, large, mighty, strong
Εὐφράτῃ n. dat. masc. sg. Εὐφράτης Euphrates
15 καὶ conj. καί and, even, also, but
οἱ art. nom. masc. pl. ὁ ἡ τό the, this, that, he, she, it
τέσσαρες num. nom. masc. pl. τέσσαρες four
ἄγγελοι n. nom. masc. pl. ἄγγελος angel, messenger
οἱ art. nom. masc. pl. ὁ ἡ τό the, this, that, he, she, it
εἰς prep. εἰς (+acc) into, to, unto, for, in, on, toward, against, upon, at, among
τὴν art. acc. fem. sg. ὁ ἡ τό the, this, that, he, she, it
ὥραν n. acc. fem. sg. ὥρα hour, time, season
καὶ conj. καί and, even, also, but
ἡμέραν n. acc. fem. sg. ἡμέρα day, time, year, while, age, day time
καὶ conj. καί and, even, also, but
μῆνα n. acc. masc. sg. μήν month
καὶ conj. καί and, even, also, but
ἐνιαυτόν n. acc. masc. sg. ἐνιαυτός year
ἵνα conj. ἵνα that, to, lest, for to, so that, albeit, because, for, so as
τὸ art. acc. neut. sg. ὁ ἡ τό the, this, that, he, she, it
τρίτον ordinal. adj. acc. neut. sg. τρίτος third
τῶν art. gen. masc. pl. ὁ ἡ τό the, this, that, he, she, it

ἀνθρώπων n. gen. masc. pl. ἄνθρωπος man, human being, person, one, certain
16 καὶ conj. καί and, even, also, but
ὁ art. nom. masc. sg. ὁ ἡ τό the, this, that, he, she, it
ἀριθμὸς n. nom. masc. sg. ἀριθμός number
στρατευμάτων n. gen. neut. pl. στράτευμα army, man of war, soldier
τοῦ art. gen. neut. sg. ὁ ἡ τό the, this, that, he, she, it
ἱππικοῦ adj. gen. neut. sg. ἱππικον horse, horseman
δύο num. nom. masc. pl. δύο two, twain, both
μυριάδες n. nom. masc. pl. μυριάς innumerable multitude, myriad, innumerable company
μυριάδων n. gen. masc. pl. μυριάς innumerable multitude, myriad, innumerable company
καὶ conj. καί and, even, also, but
τὸν art. acc. masc. sg. ὁ ἡ τό the, this, that, he, she, it
ἀριθμὸν n. acc. masc. sg. ἀριθμός number
αὐτῶν pron. gen. neut. 3p. pl. αὐτός ή ό self, of oneself, even, very, the same, he, she, it
17 καὶ conj. καί and, even, also, but
οὕτως adv. οὕτω οὕτως so, even so, thus, on this wise, likewise, after this manner
τοὺς art. acc. masc. pl. ὁ ἡ τό the, this, that, he, she, it
ἵππους n. acc. masc. pl. ἵππος horse
ἐν prep. ἐν (+dat) in, by, with, among, at, on, through, to, within, into, of, for
τῇ art. dat. fem. sg. ὁ ἡ τό the, this, that, he, she, it
ὁράσει n. dat. fem. sg. ὅρασις vision, to look upon, in sight
καὶ conj. καί and, even, also, but
τοὺς art. acc. masc. pl. ὁ ἡ τό the, this, that, he, she, it
ἐπ' prep. ἐπί (+gen) on, in, upon, (+dat) in, at, for, upon, (+acc) on, upon, unto, to, against
αὐτῶν pron. gen. masc. 3p. pl. αὐτός ή ό self, of oneself, even, very, the same, he, she, it
θώρακας n. acc. masc. pl. θώραξ breastplate
πυρίνους adj. acc. masc. pl. πύρινος of fire
καὶ conj. καί and, even, also, but
ὑακινθίνους adj. acc. masc. pl. ὑακίνθινος of jacinth, of hyacinth
καὶ conj. καί and, even, also, but
θειώδεις adj. acc. masc. pl. θειώδης brimstone
καὶ conj. καί and, even, also, but
αἱ art. nom. fem. pl. ὁ ἡ τό the, this, that, he, she, it
κεφαλαὶ n. nom. fem. pl. κεφαλή head
τῶν art. gen. masc. pl. ὁ ἡ τό the, this, that, he, she, it
ἵππων n. gen. masc. pl. ἵππος horse
ὡς adv. ὡς as, when, as it were, how, about, like, as soon as, even as, while
κεφαλαὶ n. nom. fem. pl. κεφαλή head
λεόντων n. gen. masc. pl. λέων lion
καὶ conj. καί and, even, also, but
ἐκ prep. ἐκ ἐξ (+gen) of, from, out of, by, on, with, in, among, through
τῶν art. gen. neut. pl. ὁ ἡ τό the, this, that, he, she, it
στομάτων n. gen. neut. pl. στόμα mouth, face, edge
αὐτῶν pron. gen. masc. 3p. pl. αὐτός ή ό self, of oneself, even, very, the same, he, she, it
πῦρ n. nom. neut. sg. πῦρ fire, fiery
καὶ conj. καί and, even, also, but
καπνὸς n. nom. masc. sg. καπνός smoke
καὶ conj. καί and, even, also, but
θεῖον n. nom. neut. sg. θεῖον brimstone
18 ὑπὸ prep. ὑπό (+gen) of, by, with, from, among, (+acc) under
τῶν art. gen. fem. pl. ὁ ἡ τό the, this, that, he, she, it
τριῶν num. gen. fem. pl. τρεῖς three
τούτων demo. pron. gen. fem. pl. οὗτος αὕτη τοῦτο this, the same, this same, he, she, it
τὸ art. nom. neut. sg. ὁ ἡ τό the, this, that, he, she, it
τρίτον ordinal. adj. nom. neut. sg. τρίτος third

τῶν art. gen. masc. pl. ὁ ἡ τό the, this, that, he, she, it
ἀνθρώπων n. gen. masc. pl. ἄνθρωπος man, human being, person, one, certain
ἐκ prep. ἐκ ἐξ (+gen) of, from, out of, by, on, with, in, among, through
τοῦ art. gen. neut. sg. ὁ ἡ τό the, this, that, he, she, it
πυρὸς n. gen. neut. sg. πῦρ fire, fiery
καὶ conj. καί and, even, also, but
ἐκ prep. ἐκ ἐξ (+gen) of, from, out of, by, on, with, in, among, through
τοῦ art. gen. masc. sg. ὁ ἡ τό the, this, that, he, she, it
καπνοῦ n. gen. masc. sg. καπνός smoke
καὶ conj. καί and, even, also, but
ἐκ prep. ἐκ ἐξ (+gen) of, from, out of, by, on, with, in, among, through
τοῦ art. gen. masc. sg. ὁ ἡ τό the, this, that, he, she, it
θείου n. gen. neut. sg. θεῖον brimstone
τοῦ art. gen. masc. sg. ὁ ἡ τό the, this, that, he, she, it
ἐκ prep. ἐκ ἐξ (+gen) of, from, out of, by, on, with, in, among, through
τῶν art. gen. neut. pl. ὁ ἡ τό the, this, that, he, she, it
στομάτων n. gen. neut. pl. στόμα mouth, face, edge
αὐτῶν pron. gen. masc. 3p. pl. αὐτός ή ό self, of oneself, even, very, the same, he, she, it
19 ἡ art. nom. fem. sg. ὁ ἡ τό the, this, that, he, she, it
γὰρ conj. γάρ for, and, because, but, indeed
ἐξουσία n. nom. fem. sg. ἐξουσία power, authority, right, strength, jurisdiction
αὐτῶν pron. gen. masc. 3p. pl. αὐτός ή ό self, of oneself, even, very, the same, he, she, it
ἐν prep. ἐν (+dat) in, by, with, among, at, on, through, to, within, into, of, for
τῷ art. dat. neut. sg. ὁ ἡ τό the, this, that, he, she, it
στόματι n. dat. neut. sg. στόμα mouth, face, edge
αὐτῶν pron. gen. masc. 3p. pl. αὐτός ή ό self, of oneself, even, very, the same, he, she, it
καὶ conj. καί and, even, also, but
ἐν prep. ἐν (+dat) in, by, with, among, at, on, through, to, within, into, of, for
ταῖς art. dat. fem. pl. ὁ ἡ τό the, this, that, he, she, it
οὐραῖς n. dat. fem. pl. οὐρά tail
αὐτῶν pron. gen. masc. 3p. pl. αὐτός ή ό self, of oneself, even, very, the same, he, she, it
αἱ art. nom. fem. pl. ὁ ἡ τό the, this, that, he, she, it
γὰρ conj. γάρ for, and, because, but, indeed
οὐραὶ n. nom. fem. pl. οὐρά tail
αὐτῶν pron. gen. masc. 3p. pl. αὐτός ή ό self, of oneself, even, very, the same, he, she, it
ὅμοιαι adj. nom. fem. pl. ὅμοιος like
ὄφεσιν n. dat. masc. pl. ὄφις serpent
κεφαλὰς n. acc. fem. pl. κεφαλή head
καὶ conj. καί and, even, also, but
ἐν prep. ἐν (+dat) in, by, with, among, at, on, through, to, within, into, of, for
αὐταῖς pron. dat. fem. 3p. pl. αὐτός ή ό self, of oneself, even, very, the same, he, she, it
20 καὶ conj. καί and, even, also, but
οἱ art. nom. masc. pl. ὁ ἡ τό the, this, that, he, she, it
λοιποὶ adj. nom. masc. pl. λοιπός other, rest, remnant, residue, which remain
τῶν art. gen. masc. pl. ὁ ἡ τό the, this, that, he, she, it
ἀνθρώπων n. gen. masc. pl. ἄνθρωπος man, human being, person, one, certain
οἳ relative pron. nom. masc. pl. ὅς ἥ ὅ who, which, what, that
οὐκ particle of negation. οὐ οὐκ οὐχ not, no, neither, none, nay, nor, never, nothing
ἐν prep. ἐν (+dat) in, by, with, among, at, on, through, to, within, into, of, for
ταῖς art. dat. fem. pl. ὁ ἡ τό the, this, that, he, she, it
πληγαῖς n. dat. fem. pl. πληγή wound, plague, stripe
ταύταις demo. pron. dat. fem. pl. οὗτος αὕτη τοῦτο this, the same, this same, he, she, it
οὐ particle of negation. οὐ οὐκ οὐχ not, no, neither, none, nay, nor, never, nothing
ἐκ prep. ἐκ ἐξ (+gen) of, from, out of, by, on, with, in, among, through
τῶν art. gen. neut. pl. ὁ ἡ τό the, this, that, he, she, it

ἔργων n. gen. neut. pl. ἔργον work, deed, doing labour
τῶν art. gen. fem. pl. ὁ ἡ τό the, this, that, he, she, it
χειρῶν n. gen. fem. pl. χείρ hand
αὐτῶν pron. gen. masc. 3p. pl. αὐτός ή ό self, of oneself, even, very, the same, he, she, it
ἵνα conj. ἵνα that, to, lest, for to, so that, albeit, because, for, so as
μὴ particle of negation. μή not, no, lest, neither, none, nothing, nor, never, without
τὰ art. acc. neut. pl. ὁ ἡ τό the, this, that, he, she, it
δαιμόνια n. acc. neut. pl. δαιμόνιον devil, demon, god
καὶ conj. καί and, even, also, but
εἴδωλα n. acc. neut. pl. εἴδωλον idol
τὰ art. acc. neut. pl. ὁ ἡ τό the, this, that, he, she, it
χρυσᾶ adj. acc. neut. pl. χρύσεος golden, of gold
καὶ conj. καί and, even, also, but
τὰ art. acc. neut. pl. ὁ ἡ τό the, this, that, he, she, it
ἀργυρᾶ adj. acc. neut. pl. ἀργύρεος of silver
καὶ conj. καί and, even, also, but
τὰ art. acc. neut. pl. ὁ ἡ τό the, this, that, he, she, it
χαλκᾶ adj. acc. neut. pl. χάλκεος brass
καὶ conj. καί and, even, also, but
τὰ art. acc. neut. pl. ὁ ἡ τό the, this, that, he, she, it
λίθινα adj. acc. neut. pl. λίθινος of stone
καὶ conj. καί and, even, also, but
τὰ art. acc. neut. pl. ὁ ἡ τό the, this, that, he, she, it
ξύλινα adj. acc. neut. pl. ξύλινος of wood
ἃ relative pron. nom. neut. pl. ὅς ἥ ὅ who, which, what, that
οὔτε conj. οὔτε neither, nor, nor yet, no, none
οὔτε conj. οὔτε neither, nor, nor yet, no, none
οὔτε conj. οὔτε neither, nor, nor yet, no, none
21 καὶ conj. καί and, even, also, but
οὐ particle of negation. οὐ οὐκ οὐχ not, no, neither, none, nay, nor, never, nothing
ἐκ prep. ἐκ ἐξ (+gen) of, from, out of, by, on, with, in, among, through
τῶν art. gen. masc. pl. ὁ ἡ τό the, this, that, he, she, it
φόνων n. gen. masc. pl. φόνος murder, slaughter
αὐτῶν pron. gen. masc. 3p. pl. αὐτός ή ό self, of oneself, even, very, the same, he, she, it
οὔτε conj. οὔτε neither, nor, nor yet, no, none
ἐκ prep. ἐκ ἐξ (+gen) of, from, out of, by, on, with, in, among, through
τῶν art. gen. fem. pl. ὁ ἡ τό the, this, that, he, she, it
φαρμακειῶν n. gen. fem. pl. φαρμακεία witchcraft, sorcery
αὐτῶν pron. gen. masc. 3p. pl. αὐτός ή ό self, of oneself, even, very, the same, he, she, it
οὔτε conj. οὔτε neither, nor, nor yet, no, none
ἐκ prep. ἐκ ἐξ (+gen) of, from, out of, by, on, with, in, among, through
τῆς art. gen. fem. sg. ὁ ἡ τό the, this, that, he, she, it
πορνείας n. gen. fem. sg. πορνεία fornication
αὐτῶν pron. gen. masc. 3p. pl. αὐτός ή ό self, of oneself, even, very, the same, he, she, it
οὔτε conj. οὔτε neither, nor, nor yet, no, none
ἐκ prep. ἐκ ἐξ (+gen) of, from, out of, by, on, with, in, among, through
τῶν art. gen. neut. pl. ὁ ἡ τό the, this, that, he, she, it
κλεμμάτων n. gen. neut. pl. κλέμμα theft
αὐτῶν pron. gen. masc. 3p. pl. αὐτός ή ό self, of oneself, even, very, the same, he, she, it

10

1 Καὶ conj. καί and, even, also, but
ἄλλον adj. acc. masc. sg. ἄλλος other, another, some, one, more, otherwise
ἄγγελον n. acc. masc. sg. ἄγγελος angel, messenger

ἰσχυρὸν adj. acc. masc. sg. ἰσχυρός mighty, strong, mightier, stronger
ἐκ prep. ἐκ ἐξ (+gen) of, from, out of, by, on, with, in, among, through
τοῦ art. gen. masc. sg. ὁ ἡ τό the, this, that, he, she, it
οὐρανοῦ n. gen. masc. sg. οὐρανός heaven, air, sky
νεφέλην n. acc. fem. sg. νεφέλη cloud
καὶ conj. καί and, even, also, but
ἶρις n. nom. fem. sg. ἶρις rainbow
ἐπὶ prep. ἐπί (+gen) on, in, upon, (+dat) in, at, for, upon, (+acc) on, upon, unto, to, against
τῆς art. gen. fem. sg. ὁ ἡ τό the, this, that, he, she, it
κεφαλῆς n. gen. fem. sg. κεφαλή head
καὶ conj. καί and, even, also, but
τὸ art. nom. neut. sg. ὁ ἡ τό the, this, that, he, she, it
πρόσωπον n. nom. neut. sg. πρόσωπον face, presence, person, countenance
αὐτοῦ pron. gen. masc. 3p. sg. αὐτός ή ό self, of oneself, even, very, the same, he, she, it
ὡς adv. ὡς as, when, as it were, how, about, like, as soon as, even as, while
ὁ art. nom. masc. sg. ὁ ἡ τό the, this, that, he, she, it
ἥλιος n. nom. masc. sg. ἥλιος sun, east
καὶ conj. καί and, even, also, but
οἱ art. nom. masc. pl. ὁ ἡ τό the, this, that, he, she, it
πόδες n. nom. masc. pl. πούς foot
αὐτοῦ pron. gen. masc. 3p. sg. αὐτός ή ό self, of oneself, even, very, the same, he, she, it
ὡς adv. ὡς as, when, as it were, how, about, like, as soon as, even as, while
στῦλοι n. nom. masc. pl. στῦλος pillar
πυρός n. gen. neut. sg. πῦρ fire, fiery
2 καὶ conj. καί and, even, also, but
ἐν prep. ἐν (+dat) in, by, with, among, at, on, through, to, within, into, of, for
τῇ art. dat. fem. sg. ὁ ἡ τό the, this, that, he, she, it
χειρὶ n. dat. fem. sg. χείρ hand
αὐτοῦ pron. gen. masc. 3p. sg. αὐτός ή ό self, of oneself, even, very, the same, he, she, it
βιβλαρίδιον n. acc. neut. sg. βιβλαρίδιον little book
καὶ conj. καί and, even, also, but
τὸν art. acc. masc. sg. ὁ ἡ τό the, this, that, he, she, it
πόδα n. acc. masc. sg. πούς foot
αὐτοῦ pron. gen. masc. 3p. sg. αὐτός ή ό self, of oneself, even, very, the same, he, she, it
τὸν art. acc. masc. sg. ὁ ἡ τό the, this, that, he, she, it
δεξιὸν adj. acc. masc. sg. δεξιός right, right hand, right side
ἐπὶ prep. ἐπί (+gen) on, in, upon, (+dat) in, at, for, upon, (+acc) on, upon, unto, to, against
τὴν art. acc. fem. sg. ὁ ἡ τό the, this, that, he, she, it
θάλασσαν n. acc. fem. sg. θάλασσα sea
τὸν art. acc. masc. sg. ὁ ἡ τό the, this, that, he, she, it
δὲ conj. δέ but, and, now, also, to the contrary, rather, then
εὐώνυμον adj. acc. masc. sg. εὐώνυμος left
ἐπὶ prep. ἐπί (+gen) on, in, upon, (+dat) in, at, for, upon, (+acc) on, upon, unto, to, against
τὴν art. acc. fem. sg. ὁ ἡ τό the, this, that, he, she, it
γῆν n. acc. fem. sg. γῆ earth, land, ground, country
3 καὶ conj. καί and, even, also, but
φωνῇ n. dat. fem. sg. φωνή voice, sound, noise
μεγάλῃ adj. dat. fem. sg. μέγας great, loud, greatest, high, large, mighty, strong
ὥσπερ adv. ὥσπερ as, even as, like as
λέων n. nom. masc. sg. λέων lion
καὶ conj. καί and, even, also, but
ὅτε adv. ὅτε when, after that, as soon as, while, after
αἱ art. nom. fem. pl. ὁ ἡ τό the, this, that, he, she, it
ἑπτὰ num. nom. fem. pl. ἑπτά seven, seventh
βρονταὶ n. nom. fem. pl. βροντή thunder, thundering

τὰς art. acc. fem. pl. ὁ ἡ τό the, this, that, he, she, it
ἑαυτῶν reflexive pron. gen. masc. 3p. pl. ἑαυτοῦ himself, herself, itself, yourself, ourselves
φωνάς n. acc. fem. pl. φωνή voice, sound, noise
4 καὶ conj. καί and, even, also, but
ὅτε adv. ὅτε when, after that, as soon as, while, after
αἱ art. nom. fem. pl. ὁ ἡ τό the, this, that, he, she, it
ἑπτὰ num. nom. fem. pl. ἑπτά seven, seventh
βρονταί n. nom. fem. pl. βροντή thunder, thundering
τὰς art. acc. fem. pl. ὁ ἡ τό the, this, that, he, she, it
φωνὰς n. acc. fem. pl. φωνή voice, sound, noise
ἑαυτῶν reflexive pron. gen. masc. 3p. pl. ἑαυτοῦ himself, herself, itself, yourself, ourselves
καὶ conj. καί and, even, also, but
φωνὴν n. acc. fem. sg. φωνή voice, sound, noise
ἐκ prep. ἐκ ἐξ (+gen) of, from, out of, by, on, with, in, among, through
τοῦ art. gen. masc. sg. ὁ ἡ τό the, this, that, he, she, it
οὐρανοῦ n. gen. masc. sg. οὐρανός heaven, air, sky
μοι pron. dat. 1p. sg. ἐγώ I
ἃ relative pron. acc. neut. pl. ὅς ἥ ὅ who, which, what, that
αἱ art. nom. fem. pl. ὁ ἡ τό the, this, that, he, she, it
ἑπτὰ num. nom. fem. pl. ἑπτά seven, seventh
βρονταί n. nom. fem. pl. βροντή thunder, thundering
καὶ conj. καί and, even, also, but
μὴ particle of negation. μή not, no, lest, neither, none, nothing, nor, never, without
ταῦτα demo. pron. acc. neut. pl. οὗτος αὕτη τοῦτο this, the same, this same, he, she, it
5 καὶ conj. καί and, even, also, but
ὁ art. nom. masc. sg. ὁ ἡ τό the, this, that, he, she, it
ἄγγελος n. nom. masc. sg. ἄγγελος angel, messenger
ὃν relative pron. acc. masc. sg. ὅς ἥ ὅ who, which, what, that
ἐπὶ prep. ἐπί (+gen) on, in, upon, (+dat) in, at, for, upon, (+acc) on, upon, unto, to, against
τῆς art. gen. fem. sg. ὁ ἡ τό the, this, that, he, she, it
θαλάσσης n. gen. fem. sg. θάλασσα sea
καὶ conj. καί and, even, also, but
ἐπὶ prep. ἐπί (+gen) on, in, upon, (+dat) in, at, for, upon, (+acc) on, upon, unto, to, against
τῆς art. gen. fem. sg. ὁ ἡ τό the, this, that, he, she, it
γῆς n. gen. fem. sg. γῆ earth, land, ground, country
τὴν art. acc. fem. sg. ὁ ἡ τό the, this, that, he, she, it
χεῖρα n. acc. fem. sg. χείρ hand
αὐτοῦ pron. gen. masc. 3p. sg. αὐτός ἡ ὁ self, of oneself, even, very, the same, he, she, it
εἰς prep. εἰς (+acc) into, to, unto, for, in, on, toward, against, upon, at, among
τὸν art. acc. masc. sg. ὁ ἡ τό the, this, that, he, she, it
οὐρανὸν n. acc. masc. sg. οὐρανός heaven, air, sky
6 καὶ conj. καί and, even, also, but
ἐν prep. ἐν (+dat) in, by, with, among, at, on, through, to, within, into, of, for
τῷ art. dat. masc. sg. ὁ ἡ τό the, this, that, he, she, it
εἰς prep. εἰς (+acc) into, to, unto, for, in, on, toward, against, upon, at, among
τοὺς art. acc. masc. pl. ὁ ἡ τό the, this, that, he, she, it
αἰῶνας n. acc. masc. pl. αἰών ever, ever and ever, evermore, age, eternal, world
τῶν art. gen. masc. pl. ὁ ἡ τό the, this, that, he, she, it
αἰώνων n. gen. masc. pl. αἰών ever, ever and ever, evermore, age, eternal, world
ὃς relative pron. nom. masc. sg. ὅς ἥ ὅ who, which, what, that
τὸν art. acc. masc. sg. ὁ ἡ τό the, this, that, he, she, it
οὐρανὸν n. acc. masc. sg. οὐρανός heaven, air, sky
καὶ conj. καί and, even, also, but
τὰ art. acc. neut. pl. ὁ ἡ τό the, this, that, he, she, it
ἐν prep. ἐν (+dat) in, by, with, among, at, on, through, to, within, into, of, for

αὐτῷ pron. dat. masc. 3p. sg. αὐτός ή ό self, of oneself, even, very, the same, he, she, it
καὶ conj. καί and, even, also, but
τὴν art. acc. fem. sg. ό ή τό the, this, that, he, she, it
γῆν n. acc. fem. sg. γῆ earth, land, ground, country
καὶ conj. καί and, even, also, but
τὰ art. acc. neut. pl. ό ή τό the, this, that, he, she, it
ἐν prep. ἐν (+dat) in, by, with, among, at, on, through, to, within, into, of, for
αὐτῇ pron. dat. fem. 3p. sg. αὐτός ή ό self, of oneself, even, very, the same, he, she, it
καὶ conj. καί and, even, also, but
τὴν art. acc. fem. sg. ό ή τό the, this, that, he, she, it
θάλασσαν n. acc. fem. sg. θάλασσα sea
καὶ conj. καί and, even, also, but
τὰ art. acc. neut. pl. ό ή τό the, this, that, he, she, it
ἐν prep. ἐν (+dat) in, by, with, among, at, on, through, to, within, into, of, for
αὐτῇ pron. dat. fem. 3p. sg. αὐτός ή ό self, of oneself, even, very, the same, he, she, it
ὅτι conj. ὅτι that, for, because, how that, how, because that, for that, though
χρόνος n. nom. masc. sg. χρόνος time, season, space
οὐκ particle of negation. οὐ οὐκ οὐχ not, no, neither, none, nay, nor, never, nothing
ἔτι adv. ἔτι yet, more, any more, further, still, moreover
7 ἀλλὰ conj. ἀλλά but, yea, yet, nevertheless, howbeit, nay, therefore
ἐν prep. ἐν (+dat) in, by, with, among, at, on, through, to, within, into, of, for
ταῖς art. dat. fem. pl. ό ή τό the, this, that, he, she, it
ἡμέραις n. dat. fem. pl. ἡμέρα day, time, year, while, age, day time
τῆς art. gen. fem. sg. ό ή τό the, this, that, he, she, it
φωνῆς n. gen. fem. sg. φωνή voice, sound, noise
τοῦ art. gen. masc. sg. ό ή τό the, this, that, he, she, it
ἑβδόμου ordinal. adj. gen. masc. sg. ἕβδομος seventh
ἀγγέλου n. gen. masc. sg. ἄγγελος angel, messenger
ὅταν conj. ὅταν when, as soon as, as long as, that, whensoever, while
καὶ conj. καί and, even, also, but
τὸ art. nom. neut. sg. ό ή τό the, this, that, he, she, it
μυστήριον n. nom. neut. sg. μυστήριον mystery
τοῦ art. gen. masc. sg. ό ή τό the, this, that, he, she, it
Θεοῦ n. gen. masc. sg. θεός God, god
ὡς adv. ὡς as, when, as it were, how, about, like, as soon as, even as, while
τοῖς art. dat. masc. pl. ό ή τό the, this, that, he, she, it
ἑαυτοῦ reflexive pron. gen. masc. 3p. sg. ἑαυτοῦ himself, herself, itself, yourself, ourselves
δούλοις n. dat. masc. pl. δοῦλος servant, bondman, bond, slave
τοῖς art. dat. masc. pl. ό ή τό the, this, that, he, she, it
προφήταις n. dat. masc. pl. προφήτης prophet
8 καὶ conj. καί and, even, also, but
ἡ art. nom. fem. sg. ό ή τό the, this, that, he, she, it
φωνὴ n. nom. fem. sg. φωνή voice, sound, noise
ἣν relative pron. acc. fem. sg. ὅς ἥ ὅ who, which, what, that
ἐκ prep. ἐκ ἐξ (+gen) of, from, out of, by, on, with, in, among, through
τοῦ art. gen. masc. sg. ό ή τό the, this, that, he, she, it
οὐρανοῦ n. gen. masc. sg. οὐρανός heaven, air, sky
πάλιν adv. πάλιν again
μετ' prep. μετά (+gen) with, among, against, (+acc) after
ἐμοῦ pron. gen. 1p. sg. ἐγώ I
καὶ conj. καί and, even, also, but
τὸ art. acc. neut. sg. ό ή τό the, this, that, he, she, it
βιβλαρίδιον n. acc. neut. sg. βιβλαρίδιον little book
τὸ art. acc. neut. sg. ό ή τό the, this, that, he, she, it
ἐν prep. ἐν (+dat) in, by, with, among, at, on, through, to, within, into, of, for

τῇ art. dat. fem. sg. ὁ ἡ τό the, this, that, he, she, it
χειρὶ n. dat. fem. sg. χείρ hand
ἀγγέλου n. gen. masc. sg. ἄγγελος angel, messenger
τοῦ art. gen. masc. sg. ὁ ἡ τό the, this, that, he, she, it
ἐπὶ prep. ἐπί (+gen) on, in, upon, (+dat) in, at, for, upon, (+acc) on, upon, unto, to, against
τῆς art. gen. fem. sg. ὁ ἡ τό the, this, that, he, she, it
θαλάσσης n. gen. fem. sg. θάλασσα sea
καὶ conj. καί and, even, also, but
ἐπὶ prep. ἐπί (+gen) on, in, upon, (+dat) in, at, for, upon, (+acc) on, upon, unto, to, against
τῆς art. gen. fem. sg. ὁ ἡ τό the, this, that, he, she, it
γῆς n. gen. fem. sg. γῆ earth, land, ground, country
9 καὶ conj. καί and, even, also, but
πρὸς prep. πρός (+gen) for, (+dat) at, (+acc) unto, to, with, for, against
τὸν art. acc. masc. sg. ὁ ἡ τό the, this, that, he, she, it
ἄγγελον n. acc. masc. sg. ἄγγελος angel, messenger
αὐτῷ pron. dat. masc. 3p. sg. αὐτός ή ό self, of oneself, even, very, the same, he, she, it
μοι pron. dat. 1p. sg. ἐγώ I
τὸ art. acc. neut. sg. ὁ ἡ τό the, this, that, he, she, it
βιβλαρίδιον n. acc. neut. sg. βιβλαρίδιον little book
καὶ conj. καί and, even, also, but
μοι pron. dat. 1p. sg. ἐγώ I
καὶ conj. καί and, even, also, but
αὐτό pron. acc. neut. 3p. sg. αὐτός ή ό self, of oneself, even, very, the same, he, she, it
καὶ conj. καί and, even, also, but
σου pron. gen. 2p. sg. σύ thou, you
τὴν art. acc. fem. sg. ὁ ἡ τό the, this, that, he, she, it
κοιλίαν n. acc. fem. sg. κοιλία belly, womb
ἀλλ' conj. ἀλλά but, yea, yet, nevertheless, howbeit, nay, therefore
ἐν prep. ἐν (+dat) in, by, with, among, at, on, through, to, within, into, of, for
τῷ art. dat. neut. sg. ὁ ἡ τό the, this, that, he, she, it
στόματί n. dat. neut. sg. στόμα mouth, face, edge
σου pron. gen. 2p. sg. σύ thou, you
γλυκὺ adj. nom. neut. sg. γλυκύς sweet, fresh
ὡς adv. ὡς as, when, as it were, how, about, like, as soon as, even as, while
μέλι n. nom. neut. sg. μέλι honey
10 καὶ conj. καί and, even, also, but
τὸ art. acc. neut. sg. ὁ ἡ τό the, this, that, he, she, it
βιβλαρίδιον n. acc. neut. sg. βιβλαρίδιον little book
ἐκ prep. ἐκ ἐξ (+gen) of, from, out of, by, on, with, in, among, through
τῆς art. gen. fem. sg. ὁ ἡ τό the, this, that, he, she, it
χειρὸς n. gen. fem. sg. χείρ hand
τοῦ art. gen. masc. sg. ὁ ἡ τό the, this, that, he, she, it
ἀγγέλου n. gen. masc. sg. ἄγγελος angel, messenger
καὶ conj. καί and, even, also, but
αὐτό pron. acc. neut. 3p. sg. αὐτός ή ό self, of oneself, even, very, the same, he, she, it
καὶ conj. καί and, even, also, but
ἐν prep. ἐν (+dat) in, by, with, among, at, on, through, to, within, into, of, for
τῷ art. dat. neut. sg. ὁ ἡ τό the, this, that, he, she, it
στόματί n. dat. neut. sg. στόμα mouth, face, edge
μου pron. gen. 1p. sg. ἐγώ I
ὡς adv. ὡς as, when, as it were, how, about, like, as soon as, even as, while
μέλι n. nom. neut. sg. μέλι honey
γλυκὺ adj. nom. neut. sg. γλυκύς sweet, fresh
καὶ conj. καί and, even, also, but
ὅτε adv. ὅτε when, after that, as soon as, while, after

αὐτό pron. acc. neut. 3p. sg. αὐτός ή ό self, of oneself, even, very, the same, he, she, it
ἡ art. nom. fem. sg. ὁ ἡ τό the, this, that, he, she, it
κοιλία n. nom. fem. sg. κοιλία belly, womb
μου pron. gen. 1p. sg. ἐγώ I
11 καὶ conj. καί and, even, also, but
μοι pron. dat. 1p. sg. ἐγώ I
σε pron. acc. 2p. sg. σύ thou, you
πάλιν adv. πάλιν again
ἐπὶ prep. ἐπί (+gen) on, in, upon, (+dat) in, at, for, upon, (+acc) on, upon, unto, to, against
λαοῖς n. dat. masc. pl. λαός people
καὶ conj. καί and, even, also, but
ἔθνεσιν n. dat. neut. pl. ἔθνος Gentile, nation, heathen, people
καὶ conj. καί and, even, also, but
γλώσσαις n. dat. fem. pl. γλῶσσα tongue
καὶ conj. καί and, even, also, but
βασιλεῦσιν n. dat. masc. pl. βασιλεύς king
πολλοῖς adj. dat. masc. pl. πολύς many, great, much, long, abundant

11

1 Καὶ conj. καί and, even, also, but
μοι pron. dat. 1p. sg. ἐγώ I
κάλαμος n. nom. masc. sg. κάλαμος reed, pen
ὅμοιος adj. nom. masc. sg. ὅμοιος like
ῥάβδῳ n. dat. fem. sg. ῥάβδος rod, sceptre, stave, staff
καὶ conj. καί and, even, also, but
ὁ art. nom. masc. sg. ὁ ἡ τό the, this, that, he, she, it
ἄγγελος n. nom. masc. sg. ἄγγελος angel, messenger
καὶ conj. καί and, even, also, but
τὸν art. acc. masc. sg. ὁ ἡ τό the, this, that, he, she, it
ναὸν n. acc. masc. sg. ναός temple, shrine
τοῦ art. gen. masc. sg. ὁ ἡ τό the, this, that, he, she, it
Θεοῦ n. gen. masc. sg. θεός God, god
καὶ conj. καί and, even, also, but
τὸ art. acc. neut. sg. ὁ ἡ τό the, this, that, he, she, it
θυσιαστήριον n. acc. neut. sg. θυσιαστήριον altar
καὶ conj. καί and, even, also, but
τοὺς art. acc. masc. pl. ὁ ἡ τό the, this, that, he, she, it
ἐν prep. ἐν (+dat) in, by, with, among, at, on, through, to, within, into, of, for
αὐτῷ pron. dat. masc. 3p. sg. αὐτός ή ό self, of oneself, even, very, the same, he, she, it
2 καὶ conj. καί and, even, also, but
τὴν art. acc. fem. sg. ὁ ὁ ἡ τό the, this, that, he, she, it
αὐλὴν n. acc. fem. sg. αὐλή palace, court, hall, fold
τὴν art. acc. fem. sg. ὁ ἡ τό the, this, that, he, she, it
ἔξωθεν adv. ἔξωθεν without, from without, outside, outward, outwardly
τοῦ art. gen. masc. sg. ὁ ἡ τό the, this, that, he, she, it
ναοῦ n. gen. masc. sg. ναός temple, shrine
ἔξω adv. ἔξω out, without, out of, forth, away, outward
καὶ conj. καί and, even, also, but
μὴ particle of negation. μή not, no, lest, neither, none, nothing, nor, never, without
αὐτὴν pron. acc. fem. 3p. sg. αὐτός ή ό self, of oneself, even, very, the same, he, she, it
ὅτι conj. ὅτι that, for, because, how that, how, because that, for that, though
τοῖς art. dat. neut. pl. ὁ ἡ τό the, this, that, he, she, it
ἔθνεσι n. dat. neut. pl. ἔθνος Gentile, nation, heathen, people
καὶ conj. καί and, even, also, but

τὴν art. acc. fem. sg. ὁ ὁ ἡ τό the, this, that, he, she, it
πόλιν n. acc. fem. sg. πόλις city
τὴν art. acc. fem. sg. ὁ ὁ ἡ τό the, this, that, he, she, it
ἁγίαν adj. acc. fem. sg. ἅγιος Holy, holy, saint, Holy One, holy thing, most holy
μῆνας n. acc. masc. pl. μήν month
τεσσαράκοντα num. acc. masc. pl. τεσσαράκοντα forty
δύο num. acc. masc. pl. δύο two, twain, both
3 καὶ conj. καί and, even, also, but
τοῖς art. dat. masc. pl. ὁ ἡ τό the, this, that, he, she, it
δυσὶν num. dat. masc. pl. δύο two, twain, both
μάρτυσί n. dat. masc. pl. μάρτυς or μάρτυρ witness, martyr, record
μου pron. gen. 1p. sg. ἐγώ I
καὶ conj. καί and, even, also, but
ἡμέρας n. acc. fem. pl. ἡμέρα day, time, year, while, age, day time
χιλίας num. acc. fem. pl. χίλιοι one thousand
διακοσίας num. acc. fem. pl. διακόσιοι two hundred
ἑξήκοντα num. acc. fem. pl. ἑξήκοντα threescore, sixty, sixtyfold
σάκκους n. acc. masc. pl. σάκκος sackcloth
4 οὗτοί demo. pron. nom. masc. pl. οὗτος αὕτη τοῦτο this, the same, this same, he, she, it
αἱ art. nom. fem. pl. ὁ ἡ τό the, this, that, he, she, it
δύο num. nom. fem. pl. δύο two, twain, both
ἐλαῖαι n. nom. fem. pl. ἐλαία Olives, olive tree, olive berry
καὶ conj. καί and, even, also, but
αἱ art. nom. fem. pl. ὁ ἡ τό the, this, that, he, she, it
δύο num. nom. fem. pl. δύο two, twain, both
λυχνίαι n. nom. fem. pl. λυχνία candlestick, lampstand
αἱ art. nom. fem. pl. ὁ ἡ τό the, this, that, he, she, it
ἐνώπιον prep. ἐνώπιον (+gen) before, in the sight of, in the presence of. (adv.) before
τοῦ art. gen. masc. sg. ὁ ἡ τό the, this, that, he, she, it
Θεοῦ n. gen. masc. sg. θεός God, god
τῆς art. gen. fem. sg. ὁ ἡ τό the, this, that, he, she, it
γῆς n. gen. fem. sg. γῆ earth, land, ground, country
5 καὶ conj. καί and, even, also, but
εἴ conj. εἰ if, whether, that, though, forasmuch
τις indefinite pron. nom. masc. sg. τὶς certain, some, any man, one, any thing
αὐτοὺς pron. acc. masc. 3p. pl. αὐτός ἡ ὁ self, of oneself, even, very, the same, he, she, it
πῦρ n. nom. neut. sg. πῦρ fire, fiery
ἐκ prep. ἐκ ἐξ (+gen) of, from, out of, by, on, with, in, among, through
τοῦ art. gen. neut. sg. ὁ ἡ τό the, this, that, he, she, it
στόματος n. gen. neut. sg. στόμα mouth, face, edge
αὐτῶν pron. gen. masc. 3p. pl. αὐτός ἡ ὁ self, of oneself, even, very, the same, he, she, it
καὶ conj. καί and, even, also, but
τοὺς art. acc. masc. pl. ὁ ἡ τό the, this, that, he, she, it
ἐχθροὺς adj. acc. masc. pl. ἐχθρός enemy, foe
αὐτῶν pron. gen. masc. 3p. pl. αὐτός ἡ ὁ self, of oneself, even, very, the same, he, she, it
καὶ conj. καί and, even, also, but
εἴ conj. εἰ if, whether, that, though, forasmuch
τις indefinite pron. nom. masc. sg. τὶς certain, some, any man, one, any thing
αὐτοὺς pron. acc. masc. 3p. pl. αὐτός ἡ ὁ self, of oneself, even, very, the same, he, she, it
οὕτω adv. οὕτω οὕτως so, even so, thus, on this wise, likewise, after this manner
αὐτὸν pron. acc. masc. 3p. sg. αὐτός ἡ ὁ self, of oneself, even, very, the same, he, she, it
6 οὗτοι demo. pron. nom. masc. pl. οὗτος αὕτη τοῦτο this, the same, this same, he, she, it
ἐξουσίαν n. acc. fem. sg. ἐξουσία power, authority, right, strength, jurisdiction
τὸν art. acc. masc. sg. ὁ ἡ τό the, this, that, he, she, it
οὐρανόν n. acc. masc. sg. οὐρανός heaven, air, sky

ἵνα conj. ἵνα that, to, lest, for to, so that, albeit, because, for, so as
μὴ particle of negation. μή not, no, lest, neither, none, nothing, nor, never, without
ὑετὸς n. nom. masc. sg. ὑετός rain
ἐν prep. ἐν (+dat) in, by, with, among, at, on, through, to, within, into, of, for
ἡμέραις n. dat. fem. pl. ἡμέρα day, time, year, while, age, day time
αὐτῶν pron. gen. masc. 3p. pl. αὐτός ή ό self, of oneself, even, very, the same, he, she, it
τῆς art. gen. fem. sg. ὁ ἡ τό the, this, that, he, she, it
προφητείας n. gen. fem. sg. προφητεία prophecy, prophesying
καὶ conj. καί and, even, also, but
ἐξουσίαν n. acc. fem. sg. ἐξουσία power, authority, right, strength, jurisdiction
ἐπὶ prep. ἐπί (+gen) on, in, upon, (+dat) in, at, for, upon, (+acc) on, upon, unto, to, against
τῶν art. gen. neut. pl. ὁ ἡ τό the, this, that, he, she, it
ὑδάτων n. gen. neut. pl. ὕδωρ water
αὐτὰ pron. acc. neut. 3p. pl. αὐτός ή ό self, of oneself, even, very, the same, he, she, it
εἰς prep. εἰς (+acc) into, to, unto, for, in, on, toward, against, upon, at, among
αἷμα n. acc. neut. sg. αἷμα blood
καὶ conj. καί and, even, also, but
τὴν art. acc. fem. sg. ὁ ἡ τό the, this, that, he, she, it
γῆν n. acc. fem. sg. γῆ earth, land, ground, country
πάσῃ adj. dat. fem. sg. πᾶς πᾶσα πᾶν all, every, whosoever, every one, no, whole, any
πληγῇ n. dat. fem. sg. πληγή wound, plague, stripe
ὁσάκις adv. ὁσάκις as oft as, as often as
ἐὰν conj. ἐάν if, soever, except, though, and if, but, whether, if so, so
7 καὶ conj. καί and, even, also, but
ὅταν conj. ὅταν when, as soon as, as long as, that, whensoever, while
τὴν art. acc. fem. sg. ὁ ἡ τό the, this, that, he, she, it
μαρτυρίαν n. acc. fem. sg. μαρτυρία testimony, witness, record, report
αὐτῶν pron. gen. masc. 3p. pl. αὐτός ή ό self, of oneself, even, very, the same, he, she, it
τὸ art. nom. neut. sg. ὁ ἡ τό the, this, that, he, she, it
θηρίον n. nom. neut. sg. θηρίον beast, wild beast, venomous beast
τὸ art. nom. neut. sg. ὁ ἡ τό the, this, that, he, she, it
ἐκ prep. ἐκ ἐξ (+gen) of, from, out of, by, on, with, in, among, through
τῆς art. gen. fem. sg. ὁ ἡ τό the, this, that, he, she, it
ἀβύσσου n. gen. fem. sg. ἄβυσσος deep, abyss, bottomless pit, bottomless
πόλεμον n. acc. masc. sg. πόλεμος war, battle, fight
μετ’ prep. μετά (+gen) with, among, against, (+acc) after
αὐτῶν pron. gen. masc. 3p. pl. αὐτός ή ό self, of oneself, even, very, the same, he, she, it
καὶ conj. καί and, even, also, but
αὐτοὺς pron. acc. masc. 3p. pl. αὐτός ή ό self, of oneself, even, very, the same, he, she, it
καὶ conj. καί and, even, also, but
αὐτοὺς pron. acc. masc. 3p. pl. αὐτός ή ό self, of oneself, even, very, the same, he, she, it
8 καὶ conj. καί and, even, also, but
τὰ art. acc. neut. pl. ὁ ἡ τό the, this, that, he, she, it
πτώματα n. nom. neut. pl. πτῶμα carcase, dead body, corpse
αὐτῶν pron. gen. masc. 3p. pl. αὐτός ή ό self, of oneself, even, very, the same, he, she, it
ἐπὶ prep. ἐπί (+gen) on, in, upon, (+dat) in, at, for, upon, (+acc) on, upon, unto, to, against
τῆς art. gen. fem. sg. ὁ ἡ τό the, this, that, he, she, it
πλατείας adj. gen. fem. sg. πλατύς wide, broad
πόλεως n. gen. fem. sg. πόλις city
τῆς art. gen. fem. sg. ὁ ἡ τό the, this, that, he, she, it
μεγάλης adj. gen. fem. sg. μέγας great, loud, greatest, high, large, mighty, strong
ἥτις relative pron. nom. fem. sg. ὅστις which, who, whosoever, that, whatsoever
πνευματικῶς adv. πνευματικῶς spiritually
Σόδομα n. nom. neut. pl. Σόδομα Sodom, Sodoma
καὶ conj. καί and, even, also, but

Αἴγυπτος n. nom. fem. sg. Αἴγυπτος Egypt
ὅπου adv. ὅπου where, whither, whereas, in what place, wheresoever
καὶ conj. καί and, even, also, but
ὁ art. nom. masc. sg. ὁ ἡ τό the, this, that, he, she, it
Κύριος n. nom. masc. sg. κύριος Lord, lord, master, sir, LORD, God, Master, owner
ἡμῶν pron. gen. 1p. pl. ἐγώ I
9 καὶ conj. καί and, even, also, but
ἐκ prep. ἐκ ἐξ (+gen) of, from, out of, by, on, with, in, among, through
τῶν art. gen. masc. pl. ὁ ἡ τό the, this, that, he, she, it
λαῶν n. gen. masc. pl. λαός people
καὶ conj. καί and, even, also, but
φυλῶν n. gen. fem. pl. φυλή tribe, kindred
καὶ conj. καί and, even, also, but
γλωσσῶν n. gen. fem. pl. γλῶσσα tongue
καὶ conj. καί and, even, also, but
ἐθνῶν n. gen. neut. pl. ἔθνος Gentile, nation, heathen, people
τὰ art. acc. neut. pl. ὁ ἡ τό the, this, that, he, she, it
πτώματα n. acc. neut. pl. πτῶμα carcase, dead body, corpse
αὐτῶν pron. gen. masc. 3p. pl. αὐτός ή ό self, of oneself, even, very, the same, he, she, it
ἡμέρας n. acc. fem. pl. ἡμέρα day, time, year, while, age, day time
τρεῖς num. acc. fem. pl. τρεῖς three
καὶ conj. καί and, even, also, but
ἥμισυ adj. acc. neut. sg. ἥμισυς half
καὶ conj. καί and, even, also, but
τὰ art. acc. neut. pl. ὁ ἡ τό the, this, that, he, she, it
πτώματα n. acc. neut. pl. πτῶμα carcase, dead body, corpse
αὐτῶν pron. gen. masc. 3p. pl. αὐτός ή ό self, of oneself, even, very, the same, he, she, it
οὐκ particle of negation. οὐ οὐκ οὐχ not, no, neither, none, nay, nor, never, nothing
εἰς prep. εἰς (+acc) into, to, unto, for, in, on, toward, against, upon, at, among
μνήματα n. acc. neut. pl. μνῆμα sepulchre, tomb, grave
10 καὶ conj. καί and, even, also, but
οἱ art. nom. masc. pl. ὁ ἡ τό the, this, that, he, she, it
ἐπὶ prep. ἐπί (+gen) on, in, upon, (+dat) in, at, for, upon, (+acc) on, upon, unto, to, against
τῆς art. gen. fem. sg. ὁ ἡ τό the, this, that, he, she, it
γῆς n. gen. fem. sg. γῆ earth, land, ground, country
ἐπ' prep. ἐπί (+gen) on, in, upon, (+dat) in, at, for, upon, (+acc) on, upon, unto, to, against
αὐτοῖς pron. dat. masc. 3p. pl. αὐτός ή ό self, of oneself, even, very, the same, he, she, it
καὶ conj. καί and, even, also, but
καὶ conj. καί and, even, also, but
δῶρα n. acc. neut. pl. δῶρον gift, offering
ἀλλήλοις pron. dat. masc. pl. ἀλλήλων one another, themselves, together, mutual
ὅτι conj. ὅτι that, for, because, how that, how, because that, for that, though
οὗτοι demo. pron. nom. masc. pl. οὗτος αὕτη τοῦτο this, the same, this same, he, she, it
οἱ art. nom. masc. pl. ὁ ἡ τό the, this, that, he, she, it
δύο num. nom. masc. pl. δύο two, twain, both
προφῆται n. nom. masc. pl. προφήτης prophet
τοὺς art. acc. masc. pl. ὁ ἡ τό the, this, that, he, she, it
ἐπὶ prep. ἐπί (+gen) on, in, upon, (+dat) in, at, for, upon, (+acc) on, upon, unto, to, against
τῆς art. gen. fem. sg. ὁ ἡ τό the, this, that, he, she, it
γῆς n. gen. fem. sg. γῆ earth, land, ground, country
11 καὶ conj. καί and, even, also, but
μετὰ prep. μετά (+gen) with, among, against, (+acc) after
τὰς art. acc. fem. pl. ὁ ἡ τό the, this, that, he, she, it
τρεῖς num. acc. fem. pl. τρεῖς three
ἡμέρας n. acc. fem. pl. ἡμέρα day, time, year, while, age, day time

καὶ conj. καί and, even, also, but
ἥμισυ adj. acc. neut. sg. ἥμισυς half
πνεῦμα n. nom. neut. sg. πνεῦμα spirit, Spirit, Ghost, ghost, life. of the spirit, wind
ζωῆς n. gen. fem. sg. ζωή life, lifetime
ἐκ prep. ἐκ ἐξ (+gen) of, from, out of, by, on, with, in, among, through
τοῦ art. gen. masc. sg. ὁ ἡ τό the, this, that, he, she, it
Θεοῦ n. gen. masc. sg. θεός God, god
ἐπ' prep. ἐπί (+gen) on, in, upon, (+dat) in, at, for, upon, (+acc) on, upon, unto, to, against
αὐτούς pron. acc. masc. 3p. pl. αὐτός ή ό self, of oneself, even, very, the same, he, she, it
καὶ conj. καί and, even, also, but
ἐπὶ prep. ἐπί (+gen) on, in, upon, (+dat) in, at, for, upon, (+acc) on, upon, unto, to, against
τοὺς art. acc. masc. pl. ὁ ἡ τό the, this, that, he, she, it
πόδας n. acc. masc. pl. πούς foot
αὐτῶν pron. gen. masc. 3p. pl. αὐτός ή ό self, of oneself, even, very, the same, he, she, it
καὶ conj. καί and, even, also, but
φόβος n. nom. masc. sg. φόβος fear, terror, sore afraid
μέγας adj. nom. masc. sg. μέγας great, loud, greatest, high, large, mighty, strong
ἐπὶ prep. ἐπί (+gen) on, in, upon, (+dat) in, at, for, upon, (+acc) on, upon, unto, to, against
τοὺς art. acc. masc. pl. ὁ ἡ τό the, this, that, he, she, it
αὐτούς pron. acc. masc. 3p. pl. αὐτός ή ό self, of oneself, even, very, the same, he, she, it
12 καὶ conj. καί and, even, also, but
φωνὴν n. acc. fem. sg. φωνή voice, sound, noise
μεγάλην adj. acc. fem. sg. μέγας great, loud, greatest, high, large, mighty, strong
ἐκ prep. ἐκ ἐξ (+gen) of, from, out of, by, on, with, in, among, through
τοῦ art. gen. masc. sg. ὁ ἡ τό the, this, that, he, she, it
οὐρανοῦ n. gen. masc. sg. οὐρανός heaven, air, sky
αὐτοῖς pron. dat. masc. 3p. pl. αὐτός ή ό self, of oneself, even, very, the same, he, she, it
ὧδε adv. ὧδε here, hither, in this place, there, this place
καὶ conj. καί and, even, also, but
εἰς prep. εἰς (+acc) into, to, unto, for, in, on, toward, against, upon, at, among
τὸν art. acc. masc. sg. ὁ ἡ τό the, this, that, he, she, it
οὐρανὸν n. acc. masc. sg. οὐρανός heaven, air, sky
ἐν prep. ἐν (+dat) in, by, with, among, at, on, through, to, within, into, of, for
τῇ art. dat. fem. sg. ὁ ἡ τό the, this, that, he, she, it
νεφέλῃ n. dat. fem. sg. νεφέλη cloud
καὶ conj. καί and, even, also, but
αὐτοὺς pron. acc. masc. 3p. pl. αὐτός ή ό self, of oneself, even, very, the same, he, she, it
οἱ art. nom. masc. pl. ὁ ἡ τό the, this, that, he, she, it
ἐχθροὶ adj. nom. masc. pl. ἐχθρός enemy, foe
αὐτῶν pron. gen. masc. 3p. pl. αὐτός ή ό self, of oneself, even, very, the same, he, she, it
13 καὶ conj. καί and, even, also, but
ἐν prep. ἐν (+dat) in, by, with, among, at, on, through, to, within, into, of, for
ἐκείνῃ demo. pron. dat. fem. sg. ἐκεῖνος that, he, the same, that same
τῇ art. dat. fem. sg. ὁ ἡ τό the, this, that, he, she, it
ὥρᾳ n. dat. fem. sg. ὥρα hour, time, season
σεισμὸς n. nom. masc. sg. σεισμός earthquake, tempest
μέγας adj. nom. masc. sg. μέγας great, loud, greatest, high, large, mighty, strong
καὶ conj. καί and, even, also, but
τὸ art. nom. neut. sg. ὁ ἡ τό the, this, that, he, she, it
δέκατον ordinal. adj. nom. neut. sg. δέκατος tenth
τῆς art. gen. fem. sg. ὁ ἡ τό the, this, that, he, she, it
πόλεως n. gen. fem. sg. πόλις city
καὶ conj. καί and, even, also, but
ἐν prep. ἐν (+dat) in, by, with, among, at, on, through, to, within, into, of, for
τῷ art. dat. masc. sg. ὁ ἡ τό the, this, that, he, she, it

σεισμῷ n. dat. masc. sg. σεισμός earthquake, tempest
ὀνόματα n. nom. neut. pl. ὄνομα name, call, surname
ἀνθρώπων n. gen. masc. pl. ἄνθρωπος man, human being, person, one, certain
χιλιάδες n. nom. fem. pl. χιλιάς thousand
ἑπτὰ num. nom. fem. pl. ἑπτά seven, seventh
καὶ conj. καί and, even, also, but
οἱ art. nom. masc. pl. ὁ ἡ τό the, this, that, he, she, it
λοιποὶ adj. nom. masc. pl. λοιπός other, rest, remnant, residue, which remain
ἔμφοβοι adj. nom. masc. pl. ἔμφοβος afraid, affrighted, tremble
καὶ conj. καί and, even, also, but
δόξαν n. acc. fem. sg. δόξα glory, honour, praise, dignity, worship
τῷ art. dat. masc. sg. ὁ ἡ τό the, this, that, he, she, it
Θεῷ n. dat. masc. sg. θεός God, god
τοῦ art. gen. masc. sg. ὁ ἡ τό the, this, that, he, she, it
οὐρανοῦ n. gen. masc. sg. οὐρανός heaven, air, sky
14 Ἡ art. nom. fem. sg. ὁ ἡ τό the, this, that, he, she, it
οὐαὶ particle. οὐαί woe, alas
ἡ art. nom. fem. sg. ὁ ἡ τό the, this, that, he, she, it
δευτέρα ordinal. adj. nom. fem. sg. δεύτερος second, second time, again, afterward
καὶ conj. καί and, even, also, but
ἡ art. nom. fem. sg. ὁ ἡ τό the, this, that, he, she, it
οὐαὶ particle. οὐαί woe, alas
ἡ art. nom. fem. sg. ὁ ἡ τό the, this, that, he, she, it
τρίτη ordinal. adj. nom. fem. sg. τρίτος third
ταχύ adv. ταχύ quickly, lightly
15 Καὶ conj. καί and, even, also, but
ὁ art. nom. masc. sg. ὁ ἡ τό the, this, that, he, she, it
ἕβδομος ordinal. adj. nom. masc. sg. ἕβδομος seventh
ἄγγελος n. nom. masc. sg. ἄγγελος angel, messenger
καὶ conj. καί and, even, also, but
φωναὶ n. nom. fem. pl. φωνή voice, sound, noise
μεγάλαι adj. nom. fem. pl. μέγας great, loud, greatest, high, large, mighty, strong
ἐν prep. ἐν (+dat) in, by, with, among, at, on, through, to, within, into, of, for
τῷ art. dat. masc. sg. ὁ ἡ τό the, this, that, he, she, it
οὐρανῷ n. dat. masc. sg. οὐρανός heaven, air, sky
αἱ art. nom. fem. pl. ὁ ἡ τό the, this, that, he, she, it
βασιλεῖαι n. nom. fem. pl. βασιλεία kingdom, reign
τοῦ art. gen. masc. sg. ὁ ἡ τό the, this, that, he, she, it
κόσμου n. gen. masc. sg. κόσμος world, adorning
τοῦ art. gen. masc. sg. ὁ ἡ τό the, this, that, he, she, it
Κυρίου n. gen. masc. sg. κύριος Lord, lord, master, sir, LORD, God, Master, owner
ἡμῶν pron. gen. 1p. pl. ἐγώ I
καὶ conj. καί and, even, also, but
τοῦ art. gen. masc. sg. ὁ ἡ τό the, this, that, he, she, it
Χριστοῦ n. gen. masc. sg. Χριστός Christ
αὐτοῦ pron. gen. masc. 3p. sg. αὐτός ἡ ό self, of oneself, even, very, the same, he, she, it
καὶ conj. καί and, even, also, but
εἰς prep. εἰς (+acc) into, to, unto, for, in, on, toward, against, upon, at, among
τοὺς art. acc. masc. pl. ὁ ἡ τό the, this, that, he, she, it
αἰῶνας n. acc. masc. pl. αἰών ever, ever and ever, evermore, age, eternal, world
τῶν art. gen. masc. pl. ὁ ἡ τό the, this, that, he, she, it
αἰώνων n. gen. masc. pl. αἰών ever, ever and ever, evermore, age, eternal, world
16 καὶ conj. καί and, even, also, but
οἱ art. nom. masc. pl. ὁ ἡ τό the, this, that, he, she, it
εἴκοσι num. nom. masc. pl. εἴκοσι twenty

καὶ conj. καί and, even, also, but
τέσσαρες num. nom. masc. pl. τέσσαρες four
πρεσβύτεροι adj. nom. masc. pl. πρεσβύτερος elder, elder woman, eldest, old man
οἱ art. nom. masc. pl. ὁ ἡ τό the, this, that, he, she, it
ἐνώπιον prep. ἐνώπιον (+gen) before, in the sight of, in the presence of. (adv.) before
τοῦ art. gen. masc. sg. ὁ ἡ τό the, this, that, he, she, it
Θεοῦ n. gen. masc. sg. θεός God, god
ἐπὶ prep. ἐπί (+gen) on, in, upon, (+dat) in, at, for, upon, (+acc) on, upon, unto, to, against
τοὺς art. acc. masc. pl. ὁ ἡ τό the, this, that, he, she, it
θρόνους n. acc. masc. pl. θρόνος throne, seat
αὐτῶν pron. gen. masc. 3p. pl. αὐτός ἡ ὁ self, of oneself, even, very, the same, he, she, it
ἐπὶ prep. ἐπί (+gen) on, in, upon, (+dat) in, at, for, upon, (+acc) on, upon, unto, to, against
τὰ art. acc. neut. pl. ὁ ἡ τό the, this, that, he, she, it
πρόσωπα n. acc. neut. pl. πρόσωπον face, presence, person, countenance
αὐτῶν pron. gen. masc. 3p. pl. αὐτός ἡ ὁ self, of oneself, even, very, the same, he, she, it
καὶ conj. καί and, even, also, but
τῷ art. dat. masc. sg. ὁ ἡ τό the, this, that, he, she, it
Θεῷ n. dat. masc. sg. θεός God, god
17 σοι pron. dat. 2p. sg. σύ thou, you
Κύριε n. voc. masc. sg. κύριος Lord, lord, master, sir, LORD, God, Master, owner
ὁ art. nom. masc. sg. ὁ ἡ τό the, this, that, he, she, it
Θεὸς n. nom. masc. sg. θεός God, god
ὁ art. nom. masc. sg. ὁ ἡ τό the, this, that, he, she, it
παντοκράτωρ n. nom. masc. sg. παντοκράτωρ Almighty, omnipotent
ὁ art. nom. masc. sg. ὁ ἡ τό the, this, that, he, she, it
καὶ conj. καί and, even, also, but
ὁ art. nom. masc. sg. ὁ ἡ τό the, this, that, he, she, it
καὶ conj. καί and, even, also, but
ὁ art. nom. masc. sg. ὁ ἡ τό the, this, that, he, she, it
ὅτι conj. ὅτι that, for, because, how that, how, because that, for that, though
τὴν art. acc. fem. sg. ὁ ἡ τό the, this, that, he, she, it
δύναμίν n. acc. fem. sg. δύναμις power, mighty work, miracle, strength, might
σου pron. gen. 2p. sg. σύ thou, you
τὴν art. acc. fem. sg. ὁ ἡ τό the, this, that, he, she, it
μεγάλην adj. acc. fem. sg. μέγας great, loud, greatest, high, large, mighty, strong
καὶ conj. καί and, even, also, but
18 καὶ conj. καί and, even, also, but
τὰ art. nom. neut. pl. ὁ ἡ τό the, this, that, he, she, it
ἔθνη n. nom. neut. pl. ἔθνος Gentile, nation, heathen, people
καὶ conj. καί and, even, also, but
ἡ art. nom. fem. sg. ὁ ἡ τό the, this, that, he, she, it
ὀργή n. nom. fem. sg. ὀργή wrath, anger, indignation, vengeance
σου pron. gen. 2p. sg. σύ thou, you
καὶ conj. καί and, even, also, but
ὁ art. nom. masc. sg. ὁ ἡ τό the, this, that, he, she, it
καιρὸς n. nom. masc. sg. καιρός time, season, due time, opportunity
τῶν art. gen. masc. pl. ὁ ἡ τό the, this, that, he, she, it
νεκρῶν adj. gen. masc. pl. νεκρός dead
καὶ conj. καί and, even, also, but
τὸν art. acc. masc. sg. ὁ ἡ τό the, this, that, he, she, it
μισθὸν n. acc. masc. sg. μισθός reward, hire, wage
τοῖς art. dat. masc. pl. ὁ ἡ τό the, this, that, he, she, it
δούλοις n. dat. masc. pl. δοῦλος servant, bondman, bond, slave
σου pron. gen. 2p. sg. σύ thou, you
τοῖς art. dat. masc. pl. ὁ ἡ τό the, this, that, he, she, it

προφήταις n. dat. masc. pl. προφήτης prophet
καὶ conj. καί and, even, also, but
τοῖς art. dat. masc. pl. ὁ ἡ τό the, this, that, he, she, it
ἁγίοις adj. dat. masc. pl. ἅγιος Holy, holy, saint, Holy One, holy thing, most holy
καὶ conj. καί and, even, also, but
τοῖς art. dat. masc. pl. ὁ ἡ τό the, this, that, he, she, it
τὸ art. acc. neut. sg. ὁ ἡ τό the, this, that, he, she, it
ὄνομά n. acc. neut. sg. ὄνομα name, call, surname
σου pron. gen. 2p. sg. σύ thou, you
τοῖς art. dat. masc. pl. ὁ ἡ τό the, this, that, he, she, it
μικροῖς adj. dat. masc. pl. μικρός little, small, least, less
καὶ conj. καί and, even, also, but
τοῖς art. dat. masc. pl. ὁ ἡ τό the, this, that, he, she, it
μεγάλοις adj. dat. masc. pl. μέγας great, loud, greatest, high, large, mighty, strong
καὶ conj. καί and, even, also, but
τοὺς art. acc. masc. pl. ὁ ἡ τό the, this, that, he, she, it
τὴν art. acc. fem. sg. ὁ ἡ τό the, this, that, he, she, it
γῆν n. acc. fem. sg. γῆ earth, land, ground, country
19 καὶ conj. καί and, even, also, but
ὁ art. nom. masc. sg. ὁ ἡ τό the, this, that, he, she, it
ναὸς n. nom. masc. sg. ναός temple, shrine
τοῦ art. gen. masc. sg. ὁ ἡ τό the, this, that, he, she, it
Θεοῦ n. gen. masc. sg. θεός God, god
ἐν prep. ἐν (+dat) in, by, with, among, at, on, through, to, within, into, of, for
τῷ art. dat. masc. sg. ὁ ἡ τό the, this, that, he, she, it
οὐρανῷ n. dat. masc. sg. οὐρανός heaven, air, sky
καὶ conj. καί and, even, also, but
ἡ art. nom. fem. sg. ὁ ἡ τό the, this, that, he, she, it
κιβωτὸς n. nom. fem. sg. κιβωτός ark
τῆς art. gen. fem. sg. ὁ ἡ τό the, this, that, he, she, it
διαθήκης n. gen. fem. sg. διαθήκη testament, covenant
αὐτοῦ pron. gen. masc. 3p. sg. αὐτός ή ό self, of oneself, even, very, the same, he, she, it
ἐν prep. ἐν (+dat) in, by, with, among, at, on, through, to, within, into, of, for
τῷ art. dat. masc. sg. ὁ ἡ τό the, this, that, he, she, it
ναῷ n. dat. masc. sg. ναός temple, shrine
αὐτοῦ pron. gen. masc. 3p. sg. αὐτός ή ό self, of oneself, even, very, the same, he, she, it
καὶ conj. καί and, even, also, but
ἀστραπαὶ n. nom. fem. pl. ἀστραπή lightning, bright shining
καὶ conj. καί and, even, also, but
φωναὶ n. nom. fem. pl. φωνή voice, sound, noise
καὶ conj. καί and, even, also, but
βρονταὶ n. nom. fem. pl. βροντή thunder, thundering
καὶ conj. καί and, even, also, but
σεισμὸς n. nom. masc. sg. σεισμός earthquake, tempest
καὶ conj. καί and, even, also, but
χάλαζα n. nom. fem. sg. χάλαζα hail
μεγάλη adj. nom. fem. sg. μέγας great, loud, greatest, high, large, mighty, strong

12

1 Καὶ conj. καί and, even, also, but
σημεῖον n. nom. neut. sg. σημεῖον sign, miracle, wonder, token
μέγα adj. nom. neut. sg. μέγας great, loud, greatest, high, large, mighty, strong
ἐν prep. ἐν (+dat) in, by, with, among, at, on, through, to, within, into, of, for
τῷ art. dat. masc. sg. ὁ ἡ τό the, this, that, he, she, it

οὐρανῷ n. dat. masc. sg. οὐρανός heaven, air, sky
γυνὴ n. nom. fem. sg. γυνή woman, wife
τὸν art. acc. masc. sg. ὁ ἡ τό the, this, that, he, she, it
ἥλιον n. acc. masc. sg. ἥλιος sun, east
καὶ conj. καί and, even, also, but
ἡ art. nom. fem. sg. ὁ ἡ τό the, this, that, he, she, it
σελήνη n. nom. fem. sg. σελήνη moon
ὑποκάτω adv. ὑποκάτω under
τῶν art. gen. masc. pl. ὁ ἡ τό the, this, that, he, she, it
ποδῶν n. gen. masc. pl. πούς foot
αὐτῆς pron. gen. fem. 3p. sg. αὐτός ή ό self, of oneself, even, very, the same, he, she, it
καὶ conj. καί and, even, also, but
ἐπὶ prep. ἐπί (+gen) on, in, upon, (+dat) in, at, for, upon, (+acc) on, upon, unto, to, against
τῆς art. gen. fem. sg. ὁ ἡ τό the, this, that, he, she, it
κεφαλῆς n. gen. fem. sg. κεφαλή head
αὐτῆς pron. gen. fem. 3p. sg. αὐτός ή ό self, of oneself, even, very, the same, he, she, it
στέφανος n. nom. masc. sg. στέφανος crown
ἀστέρων n. gen. masc. pl. ἀστήρ star
δώδεκα num. gen. masc. pl. δώδεκα twelve
2 καὶ conj. καί and, even, also, but
ἐν prep. ἐν (+dat) in, by, with, among, at, on, through, to, within, into, of, for
γαστρὶ n. dat. fem. sg. γαστήρ having in the womb, with child, belly, womb
καὶ conj. καί and, even, also, but
3 καὶ conj. καί and, even, also, but
ἄλλο adj. nom. neut. sg. ἄλλος other, another, some, one, more, otherwise
σημεῖον n. nom. neut. sg. σημεῖον sign, miracle, wonder, token
ἐν prep. ἐν (+dat) in, by, with, among, at, on, through, to, within, into, of, for
τῷ art. dat. masc. sg. ὁ ἡ τό the, this, that, he, she, it
οὐρανῷ n. dat. masc. sg. οὐρανός heaven, air, sky
καὶ conj. καί and, even, also, but
δράκων n. nom. masc. sg. δράκων dragon
μέγας adj. nom. masc. sg. μέγας great, loud, greatest, high, large, mighty, strong
πυρρὸς adj. nom. masc. sg. πυρρός red
κεφαλὰς n. acc. fem. pl. κεφαλή head
ἑπτὰ num. acc. fem. pl. ἑπτά seven, seventh
καὶ conj. καί and, even, also, but
κέρατα n. acc. neut. pl. κέρας horn
δέκα num. acc. neut. pl. δέκα ten
καὶ conj. καί and, even, also, but
ἐπὶ prep. ἐπί (+gen) on, in, upon, (+dat) in, at, for, upon, (+acc) on, upon, unto, to, against
τὰς art. acc. fem. pl. ὁ ἡ τό the, this, that, he, she, it
κεφαλὰς n. acc. fem. pl. κεφαλή head
αὐτοῦ pron. gen. masc. 3p. sg. αὐτός ή ό self, of oneself, even, very, the same, he, she, it
διαδήματα n. acc. neut. pl. διάδημα crown, diadem
ἑπτὰ num. acc. neut. pl. ἑπτά seven, seventh
4 καὶ conj. καί and, even, also, but
ἡ art. nom. fem. sg. ὁ ἡ τό the, this, that, he, she, it
οὐρὰ n. nom. fem. sg. οὐρά tail
αὐτοῦ pron. gen. masc. 3p. sg. αὐτός ή ό self, of oneself, even, very, the same, he, she, it
τὸ art. acc. neut. sg. ὁ ἡ τό the, this, that, he, she, it
τρίτον ordinal. adj. acc. neut. sg. τρίτος third
τῶν art. gen. masc. pl. ὁ ἡ τό the, this, that, he, she, it
ἀστέρων n. gen. masc. pl. ἀστήρ star
τοῦ art. gen. masc. sg. ὁ ἡ τό the, this, that, he, she, it
οὐρανοῦ n. gen. masc. sg. οὐρανός heaven, air, sky

καὶ conj. καί and, even, also, but
αὐτοὺς pron. acc. masc. 3p. pl. αὐτός ή ό self, of oneself, even, very, the same, he, she, it
εἰς prep. εἰς (+acc) into, to, unto, for, in, on, toward, against, upon, at, among
τὴν art. acc. fem. sg. ό ή τό the, this, that, he, she, it
γῆν n. acc. fem. sg. γῆ earth, land, ground, country
καὶ conj. καί and, even, also, but
ὁ art. nom. masc. sg. ό ή τό the, this, that, he, she, it
δράκων n. nom. masc. sg. δράκων dragon
ἐνώπιον prep. ἐνώπιον (+gen) before, in the sight of, in the presence of. (adv.) before
τῆς art. gen. fem. sg. ό ή τό the, this, that, he, she, it
γυναικὸς n. gen. fem. sg. γυνή woman, wife
τῆς art. gen. fem. sg. ό ή τό the, this, that, he, she, it
ἵνα conj. ἵνα that, to, lest, for to, so that, albeit, because, for, so as
ὅταν conj. ὅταν when, as soon as, as long as, that, whensoever, while
τὸ art. acc. neut. sg. ό ή τό the, this, that, he, she, it
τέκνον n. acc. neut. sg. τέκνον child, son, daughter
αὐτῆς pron. gen. fem. 3p. sg. αὐτός ή ό self, of oneself, even, very, the same, he, she, it
5 καὶ conj. καί and, even, also, but
υἱὸν n. acc. masc. sg. υἱός son, child, descendant, offspring, heir
ἄρρενα n. acc. masc. sg. ἄρρην man, male
ὃς relative pron. nom. masc. sg. ὅς ἥ ὅ who, which, what, that
πάντα adj. acc. neut. pl. πᾶς πᾶσα πᾶν all, every, whosoever, every one, no, whole, any
τὰ art. acc. neut. pl. ό ή τό the, this, that, he, she, it
ἔθνη n. acc. neut. pl. ἔθνος Gentile, nation, heathen, people
ἐν prep. ἐν (+dat) in, by, with, among, at, on, through, to, within, into, of, for
ῥάβδῳ n. dat. fem. sg. ῥάβδος rod, sceptre, stave, staff
σιδηρᾷ adj. dat. fem. sg. σιδήρεος iron, of iron
καὶ conj. καί and, even, also, but
τὸ art. nom. neut. sg. ό ή τό the, this, that, he, she, it
τέκνον n. nom. neut. sg. τέκνον child, son, daughter
αὐτῆς pron. gen. fem. 3p. sg. αὐτός ή ό self, of oneself, even, very, the same, he, she, it
πρὸς prep. πρός (+gen) for, (+dat) at, (+acc) unto, to, with, for, against
τὸν art. acc. masc. sg. ό ή τό the, this, that, he, she, it
Θεὸν n. acc. masc. sg. θεός God, god
καὶ conj. καί and, even, also, but
τὸν art. acc. masc. sg. ό ή τό the, this, that, he, she, it
θρόνον n. acc. masc. sg. θρόνος throne, seat
αὐτοῦ pron. gen. masc. 3p. sg. αὐτός ή ό self, of oneself, even, very, the same, he, she, it
6 καὶ conj. καί and, even, also, but
ἡ art. nom. fem. sg. ό ή τό the, this, that, he, she, it
γυνὴ n. nom. fem. sg. γυνή woman, wife
εἰς prep. εἰς (+acc) into, to, unto, for, in, on, toward, against, upon, at, among
τὴν art. acc. fem. sg. ό ή τό the, this, that, he, she, it
ἔρημον adj. acc. fem. sg. ἔρημος wilderness, desert
ὅπου adv. ὅπου where, whither, whereas, in what place, wheresoever
τόπον n. acc. masc. sg. τόπος place, room, quarter
ἀπὸ prep. ἀπό (+gen) from, of, out of, since, for, off, at, by, in, on
τοῦ art. gen. masc. sg. ό ή τό the, this, that, he, she, it
Θεοῦ n. gen. masc. sg. θεός God, god
ἵνα conj. ἵνα that, to, lest, for to, so that, albeit, because, for, so as
ἐκεῖ adv. ἐκεῖ there, thither, thitherward, yonder, yonder place
αὐτὴν pron. acc. fem. 3p. sg. αὐτός ή ό self, of oneself, even, very, the same, he, she, it
ἡμέρας n. acc. fem. pl. ἡμέρα day, time, year, while, age, day time
χιλίας num. acc. fem. pl. χίλιοι one thousand
διακοσίας num. acc. fem. pl. διακόσιοι two hundred

ἑξήκοντα num. acc. fem. pl. ἑξήκοντα threescore, sixty, sixtyfold
7 Καὶ conj. καί and, even, also, but
πόλεμος n. nom. masc. sg. πόλεμος war, battle, fight
ἐν prep. ἐν (+dat) in, by, with, among, at, on, through, to, within, into, of, for
τῷ art. dat. masc. sg. ὁ ἡ τό the, this, that, he, she, it
οὐρανῷ n. dat. masc. sg. οὐρανός heaven, air, sky
ὁ art. nom. masc. sg. ὁ ἡ τό the, this, that, he, she, it
Μιχαὴλ n. nom. masc. sg. Μιχαήλ Michael
καὶ conj. καί and, even, also, but
οἱ art. nom. masc. pl. ὁ ἡ τό the, this, that, he, she, it
ἄγγελοι n. nom. masc. pl. ἄγγελος angel, messenger
αὐτοῦ pron. gen. masc. 3p. sg. αὐτός ή ὁ self, of oneself, even, very, the same, he, she, it
κατὰ prep. κατά (+gen) against, by, throughout, down, (+acc) according to, after, with
τοῦ art. gen. masc. sg. ὁ ἡ τό the, this, that, he, she, it
δράκοντος n. gen. masc. sg. δράκων dragon
καὶ conj. καί and, even, also, but
ὁ art. nom. masc. sg. ὁ ἡ τό the, this, that, he, she, it
δράκων n. nom. masc. sg. δράκων dragon
καὶ conj. καί and, even, also, but
οἱ art. nom. masc. pl. ὁ ἡ τό the, this, that, he, she, it
ἄγγελοι n. nom. masc. pl. ἄγγελος angel, messenger
αὐτοῦ pron. gen. masc. 3p. sg. αὐτός ή ὁ self, of oneself, even, very, the same, he, she, it
8 καὶ conj. καί and, even, also, but
οὐκ particle of negation. οὐ οὐκ οὐχ not, no, neither, none, nay, nor, never, nothing
οὔτε conj. οὔτε neither, nor, nor yet, no, none
τόπος n. nom. masc. sg. τόπος place, room, quarter
αὐτῶν pron. gen. masc. 3p. pl. αὐτός ή ὁ self, of oneself, even, very, the same, he, she, it
ἔτι adv. ἔτι yet, more, any more, further, still, moreover
ἐν prep. ἐν (+dat) in, by, with, among, at, on, through, to, within, into, of, for
τῷ art. dat. masc. sg. ὁ ἡ τό the, this, that, he, she, it
οὐρανῷ n. dat. masc. sg. οὐρανός heaven, air, sky
9 καὶ conj. καί and, even, also, but
ὁ art. nom. masc. sg. ὁ ἡ τό the, this, that, he, she, it
δράκων n. nom. masc. sg. δράκων dragon
ὁ art. nom. masc. sg. ὁ ἡ τό the, this, that, he, she, it
μέγας adj. nom. masc. sg. μέγας great, loud, greatest, high, large, mighty, strong
ὁ art. nom. masc. sg. ὁ ἡ τό the, this, that, he, she, it
ὄφις n. nom. masc. sg. ὄφις serpent
ὁ art. nom. masc. sg. ὁ ἡ τό the, this, that, he, she, it
ἀρχαῖος adj. nom. masc. sg. ἀρχαῖος old, one of old time
ὁ art. nom. masc. sg. ὁ ἡ τό the, this, that, he, she, it
διάβολος adj. nom. masc. sg. διάβολος devil, false accuser, Devil, slanderer
καὶ conj. καί and, even, also, but
ὁ art. nom. masc. sg. ὁ ἡ τό the, this, that, he, she, it
Σατανᾶς n. nom. masc. sg. Σατανᾶς Satan
ὁ art. nom. masc. sg. ὁ ἡ τό the, this, that, he, she, it
τὴν art. acc. fem. sg. ὁ ἡ τό the, this, that, he, she, it
οἰκουμένην n. acc. fem. sg. οἰκουμένη world, earth
ὅλην adj. acc. fem. sg. ὅλος all, whole, every whit, altogether
εἰς prep. εἰς (+acc) into, to, unto, for, in, on, toward, against, upon, at, among
τὴν art. acc. fem. sg. ὁ ἡ τό the, this, that, he, she, it
γῆν n. acc. fem. sg. γῆ earth, land, ground, country
καὶ conj. καί and, even, also, but
οἱ art. nom. masc. pl. ὁ ἡ τό the, this, that, he, she, it
ἄγγελοι n. nom. masc. pl. ἄγγελος angel, messenger

αὐτοῦ pron. gen. masc. 3p. sg. αὐτός ή ό self, of oneself, even, very, the same, he, she, it
μετ' prep. μετά (+gen) with, among, against, (+acc) after
αὐτοῦ pron. gen. masc. 3p. sg. αὐτός ή ό self, of oneself, even, very, the same, he, she, it
10 καὶ conj. καί and, even, also, but
φωνὴν n. acc. fem. sg. φωνή voice, sound, noise
μεγάλην adj. acc. fem. sg. μέγας great, loud, greatest, high, large, mighty, strong
ἐν prep. ἐν (+dat) in, by, with, among, at, on, through, to, within, into, of, for
τῷ art. dat. masc. sg. ὁ ἡ τό the, this, that, he, she, it
οὐρανῷ n. dat. masc. sg. οὐρανός heaven, air, sky
Ἄρτι adv. ἄρτι now, hence, here, hither, even now, present
ἡ art. nom. fem. sg. ὁ ἡ τό the, this, that, he, she, it
σωτηρία n. nom. fem. sg. σωτηρία salvation, deliver, health, saving
καὶ conj. καί and, even, also, but
ἡ art. nom. fem. sg. ὁ ἡ τό the, this, that, he, she, it
δύναμις n. nom. fem. sg. δύναμις power, mighty work, miracle, strength, might
καὶ conj. καί and, even, also, but
ἡ art. nom. fem. sg. ὁ ἡ τό the, this, that, he, she, it
βασιλεία n. nom. fem. sg. βασιλεία kingdom, reign
τοῦ art. gen. masc. sg. ὁ ἡ τό the, this, that, he, she, it
Θεοῦ n. gen. masc. sg. θεός God, god
ἡμῶν pron. gen. 1p. pl. ἐγώ I
καὶ conj. καί and, even, also, but
ἡ art. nom. fem. sg. ὁ ἡ τό the, this, that, he, she, it
ἐξουσία n. nom. fem. sg. ἐξουσία power, authority, right, strength, jurisdiction
τοῦ art. gen. masc. sg. ὁ ἡ τό the, this, that, he, she, it
Χριστοῦ n. gen. masc. sg. Χριστός Christ
αὐτοῦ pron. gen. masc. 3p. sg. αὐτός ή ό self, of oneself, even, very, the same, he, she, it
ὅτι conj. ὅτι that, for, because, how that, how, because that, for that, though
ὁ art. nom. masc. sg. ὁ ἡ τό the, this, that, he, she, it
κατήγορος n. nom. masc. sg. κατήγορος accuser
τῶν art. gen. masc. pl. ὁ ἡ τό the, this, that, he, she, it
ἀδελφῶν n. gen. masc. pl. ἀδελφός brother
ἡμῶν pron. gen. 1p. pl. ἐγώ I
ὁ art. nom. masc. sg. ὁ ἡ τό the, this, that, he, she, it
αὐτῶν pron. gen. masc. 3p. pl. αὐτός ή ό self, of oneself, even, very, the same, he, she, it
ἐνώπιον prep. ἐνώπιον (+gen) before, in the sight of, in the presence of. (adv.) before
τοῦ art. gen. masc. sg. ὁ ἡ τό the, this, that, he, she, it
Θεοῦ n. gen. masc. sg. θεός God, god
ἡμῶν pron. gen. 1p. pl. ἐγώ I
ἡμέρας n. gen. fem. sg. ἡμέρα day, time, year, while, age, day time
καὶ conj. καί and, even, also, but
νυκτός n. gen. fem. sg. νύξ night
11 καὶ conj. καί and, even, also, but
αὐτοὶ pron. nom. masc. 3p. pl. αὐτός ή ό self, of oneself, even, very, the same, he, she, it
αὐτὸν pron. acc. masc. 3p. sg. αὐτός ή ό self, of oneself, even, very, the same, he, she, it
διὰ prep. διά (+gen) by, through, with, in, of, (+acc) for, because of, for a cause
τὸ art. acc. neut. sg. ὁ ἡ τό the, this, that, he, she, it
αἷμα n. acc. neut. sg. αἷμα blood
τοῦ art. gen. neut. sg. ὁ ἡ τό the, this, that, he, she, it
ἀρνίου n. gen. neut. sg. ἀρνίον Lamb, lamb
καὶ conj. καί and, even, also, but
διὰ prep. διά (+gen) by, through, with, in, of, (+acc) for, because of, for a cause
τὸν art. acc. masc. sg. ὁ ἡ τό the, this, that, he, she, it
λόγον n. acc. masc. sg. λόγος word, saying, account, speech, thing, matter
τῆς art. gen. fem. sg. ὁ ἡ τό the, this, that, he, she, it

μαρτυρίας n. gen. fem. sg. μαρτυρία testimony, witness, record, report
αὐτῶν pron. gen. masc. 3p. pl. αὐτός ή ό self, of oneself, even, very, the same, he, she, it
καὶ conj. καί and, even, also, but
οὐκ particle of negation. οὐ οὐκ οὐχ not, no, neither, none, nay, nor, never, nothing
τὴν art. acc. fem. sg. ὁ ἡ τό the, this, that, he, she, it
ψυχὴν n. acc. fem. sg. ψυχή life, soul, mind, heart
αὐτῶν pron. gen. masc. 3p. pl. αὐτός ή ό self, of oneself, even, very, the same, he, she, it
ἄχρι prep. ἄχρι or ἄχρις (+gen) until, unto, till, even to, as far as, while, into
θανάτου n. gen. masc. sg. θάνατος death
12 διὰ prep. διά (+gen) by, through, with, in, of, (+acc) for, because of, for a cause
τοῦτο demo. pron. acc. neut. sg. οὗτος αὕτη τοῦτο this, the same, this same, he, she, it
οἱ art. nom. masc. pl. ὁ ἡ τό the, this, that, he, she, it
οὐρανοὶ n. nom. masc. pl. οὐρανός heaven, air, sky
καὶ conj. καί and, even, also, but
οἱ art. nom. masc. pl. ὁ ἡ τό the, this, that, he, she, it
ἐν prep. ἐν (+dat) in, by, with, among, at, on, through, to, within, into, of, for
αὐτοῖς pron. dat. masc. 3p. pl. αὐτός ή ό self, of oneself, even, very, the same, he, she, it
οὐαὶ particle. οὐαί woe, alas
τοῖς art. dat. masc. pl. ὁ ἡ τό the, this, that, he, she, it
τὴν art. acc. fem. sg. ὁ ἡ τό the, this, that, he, she, it
γῆν n. acc. fem. sg. γῆ earth, land, ground, country
καὶ conj. καί and, even, also, but
τὴν art. acc. fem. sg. ὁ ἡ τό the, this, that, he, she, it
θάλασσαν n. acc. fem. sg. θάλασσα sea
ὅτι conj. ὅτι that, for, because, how that, how, because that, for that, though
ὁ art. nom. masc. sg. ὁ ἡ τό the, this, that, he, she, it
διάβολος adj. nom. masc. sg. διάβολος devil, false accuser, Devil, slanderer
πρὸς prep. πρός (+gen) for, (+dat) at, (+acc) unto, to, with, for, against
ὑμᾶς pron. acc. 2p. pl. σύ thou, you
θυμὸν n. acc. masc. sg. θυμός wrath, fierceness, indignation
μέγαν adj. acc. masc. sg. μέγας great, loud, greatest, high, large, mighty, strong
ὅτι conj. ὅτι that, for, because, how that, how, because that, for that, though
ὀλίγον adj. acc. masc. sg. ὀλίγος few, little, small, a while, brief, short, short space
καιρὸν n. acc. masc. sg. καιρός time, season, due time, opportunity
13 Καὶ conj. καί and, even, also, but
ὅτε adv. ὅτε when, after that, as soon as, while, after
ὁ art. nom. masc. sg. ὁ ἡ τό the, this, that, he, she, it
δράκων n. nom. masc. sg. δράκων dragon
ὅτι conj. ὅτι that, for, because, how that, how, because that, for that, though
εἰς prep. εἰς (+acc) into, to, unto, for, in, on, toward, against, upon, at, among
τὴν art. acc. fem. sg. ὁ ἡ τό the, this, that, he, she, it
γῆν n. acc. fem. sg. γῆ earth, land, ground, country
τὴν art. acc. fem. sg. ὁ ἡ τό the, this, that, he, she, it
γυναῖκα n. acc. fem. sg. γυνή woman, wife
ἥτις relative pron. nom. fem. sg. ὅστις which, who, whosoever, that, whatsoever
τὸν art. acc. masc. sg. ὁ ἡ τό the, this, that, he, she, it
ἄρρενα n. acc. masc. sg. ἄρρην man, male
14 καὶ conj. καί and, even, also, but
τῇ art. dat. fem. sg. ὁ ἡ τό the, this, that, he, she, it
γυναικὶ n. dat. fem. sg. γυνή woman, wife
δύο num. nom. fem. pl. δύο two, twain, both
πτέρυγες n. nom. fem. pl. πτέρυξ wing
τοῦ art. gen. masc. sg. ὁ ἡ τό the, this, that, he, she, it
ἀετοῦ n. gen. masc. sg. ἀετός eagle
τοῦ art. gen. masc. sg. ὁ ἡ τό the, this, that, he, she, it

μεγάλου adj. gen. masc. sg. μέγας great, loud, greatest, high, large, mighty, strong
ἵνα conj. ἵνα that, to, lest, for to, so that, albeit, because, for, so as
εἰς prep. εἰς (+acc) into, to, unto, for, in, on, toward, against, upon, at, among
τὴν art. acc. fem. sg. ὁ ἡ τό the, this, that, he, she, it
ἔρημον adj. acc. fem. sg. ἔρημος wilderness, desert
εἰς prep. εἰς (+acc) into, to, unto, for, in, on, toward, against, upon, at, among
τὸν art. acc. masc. sg. ὁ ἡ τό the, this, that, he, she, it
τόπον n. acc. masc. sg. τόπος place, room, quarter
αὐτῆς pron. gen. fem. 3p. sg. αὐτός ή ό self, of oneself, even, very, the same, he, she, it
ὅπου adv. ὅπου where, whither, whereas, in what place, wheresoever
ἐκεῖ adv. ἐκεῖ there, thither, thitherward, yonder, yonder place
καιρὸν n. acc. masc. sg. καιρός time, season, due time, opportunity
καὶ conj. καί and, even, also, but
καιροὺς n. acc. masc. pl. καιρός time, season, due time, opportunity
καὶ conj. καί and, even, also, but
ἥμισυ adj. acc. neut. sg. ἥμισυς half
καιροῦ n. gen. masc. sg. καιρός time, season, due time, opportunity
ἀπὸ prep. ἀπό (+gen) from, of, out of, since, for, off, at, by, in, on
προσώπου n. gen. neut. sg. πρόσωπον face, presence, person, countenance
τοῦ art. gen. masc. sg. ὁ ἡ τό the, this, that, he, she, it
ὄφεως n. gen. masc. sg. ὄφις serpent
15 καὶ conj. καί and, even, also, but
ὁ art. nom. masc. sg. ὁ ἡ τό the, this, that, he, she, it
ὄφις n. nom. masc. sg. ὄφις serpent
ὀπίσω prep. ὀπίσω (+gen) after. (adv.) back, behind
τῆς art. gen. fem. sg. ὁ ἡ τό the, this, that, he, she, it
γυναικὸς n. gen. fem. sg. γυνή woman, wife
ἐκ prep. ἐκ ἐξ (+gen) of, from, out of, by, on, with, in, among, through
τοῦ art. gen. neut. sg. ὁ ἡ τό the, this, that, he, she, it
στόματος n. gen. neut. sg. στόμα mouth, face, edge
αὐτοῦ pron. gen. masc. 3p. sg. αὐτός ή ό self, of oneself, even, very, the same, he, she, it
ὕδωρ n. acc. neut. sg. ὕδωρ water
ὡς adv. ὡς as, when, as it were, how, about, like, as soon as, even as, while
ποταμόν n. acc. masc. sg. ποταμός river, flood , stream, water
ἵνα conj. ἵνα that, to, lest, for to, so that, albeit, because, for, so as
ταύτην demo. pron. acc. fem. sg. οὗτος αὕτη τοῦτο this, the same, this same, he, she, it
ποταμοφόρητον adj. acc. fem. sg. ποταμοφόρητος carried away of the flood
16 καὶ conj. καί and, even, also, but
ἡ art. nom. fem. sg. ὁ ἡ τό the, this, that, he, she, it
γῆ n. nom. fem. sg. γῆ earth, land, ground, country
τῇ art. dat. fem. sg. ὁ ἡ τό the, this, that, he, she, it
γυναικὶ n. dat. fem. sg. γυνή woman, wife
καὶ conj. καί and, even, also, but
ἡ art. nom. fem. sg. ὁ ἡ τό the, this, that, he, she, it
γῆ n. nom. fem. sg. γῆ earth, land, ground, country
τὸ art. acc. neut. sg. ὁ ἡ τό the, this, that, he, she, it
στόμα n. acc. neut. sg. στόμα mouth, face, edge
αὐτῆς pron. gen. fem. 3p. sg. αὐτός ή ό self, of oneself, even, very, the same, he, she, it
καὶ conj. καί and, even, also, but
τὸν art. acc. masc. sg. ὁ ἡ τό the, this, that, he, she, it
ποταμὸν n. acc. masc. sg. ποταμός river, flood , stream, water
ὃν relative pron. acc. masc. sg. ὅς ἥ ὅ who, which, what, that
ὁ art. nom. masc. sg. ὁ ἡ τό the, this, that, he, she, it
δράκων n. nom. masc. sg. δράκων dragon
ἐκ prep. ἐκ ἐξ (+gen) of, from, out of, by, on, with, in, among, through

τοῦ art. gen. neut. sg. ὁ ἡ τό the, this, that, he, she, it
στόματος n. gen. neut. sg. στόμα mouth, face, edge
αὐτοῦ pron. gen. masc. 3p. sg. αὐτός ἡ ὁ self, of oneself, even, very, the same, he, she, it
17 καὶ conj. καί and, even, also, but
ὁ art. nom. masc. sg. ὁ ἡ τό the, this, that, he, she, it
δράκων n. nom. masc. sg. δράκων dragon
ἐπὶ prep. ἐπί (+gen) on, in, upon, (+dat) in, at, for, upon, (+acc) on, upon, unto, to, against
τῇ art. dat. fem. sg. ὁ ἡ τό the, this, that, he, she, it
γυναικί n. dat. fem. sg. γυνή woman, wife
καὶ conj. καί and, even, also, but
πόλεμον n. acc. masc. sg. πόλεμος war, battle, fight
μετὰ prep. μετά (+gen) with, among, against, (+acc) after
τῶν art. gen. neut. pl. ὁ ἡ τό the, this, that, he, she, it
λοιπῶν adj. gen. neut. pl. λοιπός other, rest, remnant, residue, which remain
τοῦ art. gen. neut. sg. ὁ ἡ τό the, this, that, he, she, it
σπέρματος n. gen. neut. sg. σπέρμα seed, issue
αὐτῆς pron. gen. fem. 3p. sg. αὐτός ἡ ὁ self, of oneself, even, very, the same, he, she, it
τῶν art. gen. masc. pl. ὁ ἡ τό the, this, that, he, she, it
τὰς art. acc. fem. pl. ὁ ἡ τό the, this, that, he, she, it
ἐντολὰς n. acc. fem. pl. ἐντολή commandment, precept
τοῦ art. gen. masc. sg. ὁ ἡ τό the, this, that, he, she, it
Θεοῦ n. gen. masc. sg. θεός God, god
καὶ conj. καί and, even, also, but
τὴν art. acc. fem. sg. ὁ ἡ τό the, this, that, he, she, it
μαρτυρίαν n. acc. fem. sg. μαρτυρία testimony, witness, record, report
τοῦ art. gen. masc. sg. ὁ ἡ τό the, this, that, he, she, it
Ἰησοῦ n. gen. masc. sg. Ἰησοῦς Jesus
Χριστοῦ n. gen. masc. sg. Χριστός Christ

13

1 καὶ conj. καί and, even, also, but
ἐπὶ prep. ἐπί (+gen) on, in, upon, (+dat) in, at, for, upon, (+acc) on, upon, unto, to, against
τὴν art. acc. fem. sg. ὁ ἡ τό the, this, that, he, she, it
ἄμμον n. acc. fem. sg. ἄμμος sand
τῆς art. gen. fem. sg. ὁ ἡ τό the, this, that, he, she, it
θαλάσσης n. gen. fem. sg. θάλασσα sea
Καὶ conj. καί and, even, also, but
ἐκ prep. ἐκ ἐξ (+gen) of, from, out of, by, on, with, in, among, through
τῆς art. gen. fem. sg. ὁ ἡ τό the, this, that, he, she, it
θηρίον n. acc. neut. sg. θηρίον beast, wild beast, venomous beast
κεφαλὰς n. acc. fem. pl. κεφαλή head
ἑπτὰ num. acc. fem. pl. ἑπτά seven, seventh
καὶ conj. καί and, even, also, but
κέρατα n. acc. neut. pl. κέρας horn
δέκα num. acc. neut. pl. δέκα ten
καὶ conj. καί and, even, also, but
ἐπὶ prep. ἐπί (+gen) on, in, upon, (+dat) in, at, for, upon, (+acc) on, upon, unto, to, against
τῶν art. gen. neut. pl. ὁ ἡ τό the, this, that, he, she, it
κεράτων n. gen. neut. pl. κέρας horn
αὐτοῦ pron. gen. neut. 3p. sg. αὐτός ἡ ὁ self, of oneself, even, very, the same, he, she, it
δέκα num. acc. neut. pl. δέκα ten
διαδήματα n. acc. neut. pl. διάδημα crown, diadem
καὶ conj. καί and, even, also, but
ἐπὶ prep. ἐπί (+gen) on, in, upon, (+dat) in, at, for, upon, (+acc) on, upon, unto, to, against

τὰς art. acc. fem. pl. ὁ ἡ τό the, this, that, he, she, it
κεφαλὰς n. acc. fem. pl. κεφαλή head
αὐτοῦ pron. gen. neut. 3p. sg. αὐτός ή ό self, of oneself, even, very, the same, he, she, it
ὀνόμα n. nom. neut. sg. ὄνομα name, call, surname
βλασφημίας n. gen. fem. sg. βλασφημία blasphemy, railing, evil speaking
2 καὶ conj. καί and, even, also, but
τὸ art. nom. neut. sg. ὁ ἡ τό the, this, that, he, she, it
θηρίον n. nom. neut. sg. θηρίον beast, wild beast, venomous beast
ὃ relative pron. acc. neut. sg. ὅς ἥ ὅ who, which, what, that
ὅμοιον adj. nom. neut. sg. ὅμοιος like
παρδάλει n. dat. fem. sg. πάρδαλις leopard
καὶ conj. καί and, even, also, but
οἱ art. nom. masc. pl. ὁ ἡ τό the, this, that, he, she, it
πόδες n. nom. masc. pl. πούς foot
αὐτοῦ pron. gen. neut. 3p. sg. αὐτός ή ό self, of oneself, even, very, the same, he, she, it
ὡς adv. ὡς as, when, as it were, how, about, like, as soon as, even as, while
ἄρκτου n. gen. fem. sg. ἄρκτος bear
καὶ conj. καί and, even, also, but
οἱ art. nom. masc. pl. ὁ ἡ τό the, this, that, he, she, it
στόμα n. nom. neut. sg. στόμα mouth, face, edge
αὐτοῦ pron. gen. neut. 3p. sg. αὐτός ή ό self, of oneself, even, very, the same, he, she, it
ὡς adv. ὡς as, when, as it were, how, about, like, as soon as, even as, while
στόμα n. nom. neut. sg. στόμα mouth, face, edge
λέοντος n. gen. masc. sg. λέων lion
καὶ conj. καί and, even, also, but
αὐτῷ pron. dat. neut. 3p. sg. αὐτός ή ό self, of oneself, even, very, the same, he, she, it
ὁ art. nom. masc. sg. ὁ ἡ τό the, this, that, he, she, it
δράκων n. nom. masc. sg. δράκων dragon
τὴν art. acc. fem. sg. ὁ ἡ τό the, this, that, he, she, it
δύναμιν n. acc. fem. sg. δύναμις power, mighty work, miracle, strength, might
αὐτοῦ pron. gen. masc. 3p. sg. αὐτός ή ό self, of oneself, even, very, the same, he, she, it
καὶ conj. καί and, even, also, but
τὸν art. acc. masc. sg. ὁ ἡ τό the, this, that, he, she, it
θρόνον n. acc. masc. sg. θρόνος throne, seat
αὐτοῦ pron. gen. neut. 3p. sg. αὐτός ή ό self, of oneself, even, very, the same, he, she, it
καὶ conj. καί and, even, also, but
ἐξουσίαν n. acc. fem. sg. ἐξουσία power, authority, right, strength, jurisdiction
μεγάλην adj. acc. fem. sg. μέγας great, loud, greatest, high, large, mighty, strong
3 καὶ conj. καί and, even, also, but
μίαν num. acc. fem. sg. εἷς or ἕν one, other, some, any, only, a certain
τῶν art. gen. fem. pl. ὁ ἡ τό the, this, that, he, she, it
κεφαλῶν n. gen. fem. pl. κεφαλή head
αὐτοῦ pron. gen. neut. 3p. sg. αὐτός ή ό self, of oneself, even, very, the same, he, she, it
ὡς adv. ὡς as, when, as it were, how, about, like, as soon as, even as, while
εἰς prep. εἰς (+acc) into, to, unto, for, in, on, toward, against, upon, at, among
θάνατον n. acc. masc. sg. θάνατος death
καὶ conj. καί and, even, also, but
ἡ art. nom. fem. sg. ὁ ἡ τό the, this, that, he, she, it
πληγὴ n. nom. fem. sg. πληγή wound, plague, stripe
τοῦ art. gen. masc. sg. ὁ ἡ τό the, this, that, he, she, it
θανάτου n. gen. masc. sg. θάνατος death
αὐτοῦ pron. gen. neut. 3p. sg. αὐτός ή ό self, of oneself, even, very, the same, he, she, it
καὶ conj. καί and, even, also, but
ὅλη adj. nom. fem. sg. ὅλος all, whole, every whit, altogether
ἡ art. nom. fem. sg. ὁ ἡ τό the, this, that, he, she, it

γῆ n. nom. fem. sg. γῆ earth, land, ground, country
ὀπίσω prep. ὀπίσω (+gen) after. (adv.) back, behind
τοῦ art. gen. neut. sg. ὁ ἡ τό the, this, that, he, she, it
θηρίου n. gen. neut. sg. θηρίον beast, wild beast, venomous beast
4 καὶ conj. καί and, even, also, but
τὸν art. acc. masc. sg. ὁ ἡ τό the, this, that, he, she, it
δράκοντα n. acc. masc. sg. δράκων dragon
ὃς relative pron. nom. masc. sg. ὅς ἥ ὅ who, which, what, that
ἐξουσίαν n. acc. fem. sg. ἐξουσία power, authority, right, strength, jurisdiction
τῷ art. dat. neut. sg. ὁ ἡ τό the, this, that, he, she, it
θηρίῳ n. dat. neut. sg. θηρίον beast, wild beast, venomous beast
καὶ conj. καί and, even, also, but
τὸ art. acc. neut. sg. ὁ ἡ τό the, this, that, he, she, it
θηρίον n. acc. neut. sg. θηρίον beast, wild beast, venomous beast
Τίς interrog. pron. nom. masc. sg. τίς what, who, why, where, which, how
ὅμοιος adj. nom. masc. sg. ὅμοιος like
τῷ art. dat. neut. sg. ὁ ἡ τό the, this, that, he, she, it
θηρίῳ n. dat. neut. sg. θηρίον beast, wild beast, venomous beast
τίς interrog. pron. nom. masc. sg. τίς what, who, why, where, which, how
μετ' prep. μετά (+gen) with, among, against, (+acc) after
αὐτοῦ pron. gen. neut. 3p. sg. αὐτός ἡ ὁ self, of oneself, even, very, the same, he, she, it
5 καὶ conj. καί and, even, also, but
αὐτῷ pron. dat. neut. 3p. sg. αὐτός ἡ ὁ self, of oneself, even, very, the same, he, she, it
στόμα n. nom. neut. sg. στόμα mouth, face, edge
μεγάλα adj. acc. neut. pl. μέγας great, loud, greatest, high, large, mighty, strong
καὶ conj. καί and, even, also, but
βλασφημίας n. acc. fem. pl. βλασφημία blasphemy, railing, evil speaking
καὶ conj. καί and, even, also, but
αὐτῷ pron. dat. neut. 3p. sg. αὐτός ἡ ὁ self, of oneself, even, very, the same, he, she, it
ἐξουσία n. nom. fem. sg. ἐξουσία power, authority, right, strength, jurisdiction
μῆνας n. acc. masc. pl. μήν month
τεσσαράκοντα num. acc. masc. pl. τεσσαράκοντα forty
δύο num. acc. masc. pl. δύο two, twain, both
6 καὶ conj. καί and, even, also, but
τὸ art. acc. neut. sg. ὁ ἡ τό the, this, that, he, she, it
στόμα n. acc. neut. sg. στόμα mouth, face, edge
αὐτοῦ pron. gen. neut. 3p. sg. αὐτός ἡ ὁ self, of oneself, even, very, the same, he, she, it
εἰς prep. εἰς (+acc) into, to, unto, for, in, on, toward, against, upon, at, among
βλασφημίαν n. acc. fem. sg. βλασφημία blasphemy, railing, evil speaking
πρὸς prep. πρός (+gen) for, (+dat) at, (+acc) unto, to, with, for, against
τὸν art. acc. masc. sg. ὁ ἡ τό the, this, that, he, she, it
Θεὸν n. acc. masc. sg. θεός God, god
τὸ art. acc. neut. sg. ὁ ἡ τό the, this, that, he, she, it
ὄνομα n. acc. neut. sg. ὄνομα name, call, surname
αὐτοῦ pron. gen. masc. 3p. sg. αὐτός ἡ ὁ self, of oneself, even, very, the same, he, she, it
καὶ conj. καί and, even, also, but
τὴν art. acc. fem. sg. ὁ ἡ τό the, this, that, he, she, it
σκηνὴν n. acc. fem. sg. σκηνή tabernacle, habitation
αὐτοῦ pron. gen. masc. 3p. sg. αὐτός ἡ ὁ self, of oneself, even, very, the same, he, she, it
καὶ conj. καί and, even, also, but
τοὺς art. acc. masc. pl. ὁ ἡ τό the, this, that, he, she, it
ἐν prep. ἐν (+dat) in, by, with, among, at, on, through, to, within, into, of, for
τῷ art. dat. masc. sg. ὁ ἡ τό the, this, that, he, she, it
οὐρανῷ n. dat. masc. sg. οὐρανός heaven, air, sky
7 καὶ conj. καί and, even, also, but

αὐτῷ pron. dat. neut. 3p. sg. αὐτός ή ό self, of oneself, even, very, the same, he, she, it
πόλεμον n. acc. masc. sg. πόλεμος war, battle, fight
μετὰ prep. μετά (+gen) with, among, against, (+acc) after
τῶν art. gen. masc. pl. ὁ ἡ τό the, this, that, he, she, it
ἁγίων adj. gen. masc. pl. ἅγιος Holy, holy, saint, Holy One, holy thing, most holy
καὶ conj. καί and, even, also, but
αὐτούς pron. acc. masc. 3p. pl. αὐτός ή ό self, of oneself, even, very, the same, he, she, it
καὶ conj. καί and, even, also, but
αὐτῷ pron. dat. neut. 3p. sg. αὐτός ή ό self, of oneself, even, very, the same, he, she, it
ἐξουσία n. nom. fem. sg. ἐξουσία power, authority, right, strength, jurisdiction
ἐπὶ prep. ἐπί (+gen) on, in, upon, (+dat) in, at, for, upon, (+acc) on, upon, unto, to, against
πᾶσαν adj. acc. fem. sg. πᾶς πᾶσα πᾶν all, every, whosoever, every one, no, whole, any
φυλὴν n. acc. fem. sg. φυλή tribe, kindred
καὶ conj. καί and, even, also, but
γλῶσσαν n. acc. fem. sg. γλῶσσα tongue
καὶ conj. καί and, even, also, but
ἔθνος n. acc. neut. sg. ἔθνος Gentile, nation, heathen, people
8 καὶ conj. καί and, even, also, but
αὐτῷ pron. dat. neut. 3p. sg. αὐτός ή ό self, of oneself, even, very, the same, he, she, it
πάντες adj. nom. masc. pl. πᾶς πᾶσα πᾶν all, every, whosoever, every one, no, whole, any
οἱ art. nom. masc. pl. ὁ ἡ τό the, this, that, he, she, it
ἐπὶ prep. ἐπί (+gen) on, in, upon, (+dat) in, at, for, upon, (+acc) on, upon, unto, to, against
τῆς art. gen. fem. sg. ὁ ἡ τό the, this, that, he, she, it
γῆς n. gen. fem. sg. γῆ earth, land, ground, country
ὧν relative pron. gen. masc. pl. ὅς ἥ ὅ who, which, what, that
οὐ particle of negation. οὐ οὐκ οὐχ not, no, neither, none, nay, nor, never, nothing
τὰ art. nom. neut. pl. ὁ ἡ τό the, this, that, he, she, it
ὀνόματα n. nom. neut. pl. ὄνομα name, call, surname
ἐν prep. ἐν (+dat) in, by, with, among, at, on, through, to, within, into, of, for
τῇ art. dat. fem. sg. ὁ ἡ τό the, this, that, he, she, it
βίβλῳ n. dat. fem. sg. βίβλος book, record
τῆς art. gen. fem. sg. ὁ ἡ τό the, this, that, he, she, it
ζωῆς n. gen. fem. sg. ζωή life, lifetime
τοῦ art. gen. neut. sg. ὁ ἡ τό the, this, that, he, she, it
ἀρνίου n. gen. neut. sg. ἀρνίον Lamb, lamb
ἀπὸ prep. ἀπό (+gen) from, of, out of, since, for, off, at, by, in, on
καταβολῆς n. gen. fem. sg. καταβολή foundation
κόσμου n. gen. masc. sg. κόσμος world, adorning
9 εἴ conj. εἰ if, whether, that, though, forasmuch
τις indefinite pron. nom. masc. sg. τὶς certain, some, any man, one, any thing
οὖς n. acc. neut. sg. οὖς ear
10 εἴ conj. εἰ if, whether, that, though, forasmuch
τις indefinite pron. nom. masc. sg. τὶς certain, some, any man, one, any thing
αἰχμαλωσίαν n. acc. fem. sg. αἰχμαλωσία captivity
εἰς prep. εἰς (+acc) into, to, unto, for, in, on, toward, against, upon, at, among
αἰχμαλωσίαν n. acc. fem. sg. αἰχμαλωσία captivity
εἴ conj. εἰ if, whether, that, though, forasmuch
τις indefinite pron. nom. masc. sg. τὶς certain, some, any man, one, any thing
ἐν prep. ἐν (+dat) in, by, with, among, at, on, through, to, within, into, of, for
μαχαίρᾳ n. dat. fem. sg. μάχαιρα sword
αὐτὸν pron. acc. masc. 3p. sg. αὐτός ή ό self, of oneself, even, very, the same, he, she, it
ἐν prep. ἐν (+dat) in, by, with, among, at, on, through, to, within, into, of, for
μαχαίρᾳ n. dat. fem. sg. μάχαιρα sword
ὧδέ adv. ὧδε here, hither, in this place, there, this place
ἡ art. nom. fem. sg. ὁ ἡ τό the, this, that, he, she, it

ὑπομονὴ n. nom. fem. sg. ὑπομονή patience, enduring
καὶ conj. καί and, even, also, but
ἡ art. nom. fem. sg. ὁ ἡ τό the, this, that, he, she, it
πίστις n. nom. fem. sg. πίστις faith, assurance, belief, fidelity
τῶν art. gen. masc. pl. ὁ ἡ τό the, this, that, he, she, it
ἁγίων adj. gen. masc. pl. ἅγιος Holy, holy, saint, Holy One, holy thing, most holy
11 Καὶ conj. καί and, even, also, but
ἄλλο adj. acc. neut. sg. ἄλλος other, another, some, one, more, otherwise
θηρίον n. acc. neut. sg. θηρίον beast, wild beast, venomous beast
ἐκ prep. ἐκ ἐξ (+gen) of, from, out of, by, on, with, in, among, through
τῆς art. gen. fem. sg. ὁ ἡ τό the, this, that, he, she, it
γῆς n. gen. fem. sg. γῆ earth, land, ground, country
καὶ conj. καί and, even, also, but
κέρατα n. acc. neut. pl. κέρας horn
δύο num. acc. neut. pl. δύο two, twain, both
ὅμοια adj. acc. neut. pl. ὅμοιος like
ἀρνίῳ n. dat. neut. sg. ἀρνίον Lamb, lamb
καὶ conj. καί and, even, also, but
ὡς adv. ὡς as, when, as it were, how, about, like, as soon as, even as, while
δράκων n. nom. masc. sg. δράκων dragon
12 καὶ conj. καί and, even, also, but
τὴν art. acc. fem. sg. ὁ ἡ τό the, this, that, he, she, it
ἐξουσίαν n. acc. fem. sg. ἐξουσία power, authority, right, strength, jurisdiction
τοῦ art. gen. neut. sg. ὁ ἡ τό the, this, that, he, she, it
πρώτου ordinal. adj. gen. neut. sg. πρῶτος first, chief, first of all, chiefest, best
θηρίου n. gen. neut. sg. θηρίον beast, wild beast, venomous beast
πᾶσαν adj. acc. fem. sg. πᾶς πᾶσα πᾶν all, every, whosoever, every one, no, whole, any
ἐνώπιον prep. ἐνώπιον (+gen) before, in the sight of, in the presence of. (adv.) before
αὐτοῦ pron. gen. neut. 3p. sg. αὐτός ή ό self, of oneself, even, very, the same, he, she, it
καὶ conj. καί and, even, also, but
τὴν art. acc. fem. sg. ὁ ἡ τό the, this, that, he, she, it
γῆν n. acc. fem. sg. γῆ earth, land, ground, country
καὶ conj. καί and, even, also, but
τοὺς art. acc. masc. pl. ὁ ἡ τό the, this, that, he, she, it
ἐν prep. ἐν (+dat) in, by, with, among, at, on, through, to, within, into, of, for
αὐτῇ pron. dat. fem. 3p. sg. αὐτός ή ό self, of oneself, even, very, the same, he, she, it
ἵνα conj. ἵνα that, to, lest, for to, so that, albeit, because, for, so as
τὸ art. acc. neut. sg. ὁ ἡ τό the, this, that, he, she, it
θηρίον n. acc. neut. sg. θηρίον beast, wild beast, venomous beast
τὸ art. acc. neut. sg. ὁ ἡ τό the, this, that, he, she, it
πρῶτον ordinal. adj. acc. neut. sg. πρῶτος first, chief, first of all, chiefest, best
οὗ relative pron. gen. neut. sg. ὅς ἥ ὅ who, which, what, that
ἡ art. nom. fem. sg. ὁ ἡ τό the, this, that, he, she, it
πληγὴ n. nom. fem. sg. πληγή wound, plague, stripe
τοῦ art. gen. masc. sg. ὁ ἡ τό the, this, that, he, she, it
θανάτου n. gen. masc. sg. θάνατος death
αὐτοῦ pron. gen. neut. 3p. sg. αὐτός ή ό self, of oneself, even, very, the same, he, she, it
13 καὶ conj. καί and, even, also, but
σημεῖα n. acc. neut. pl. σημεῖον sign, miracle, wonder, token
μεγάλα adj. acc. neut. pl. μέγας great, loud, greatest, high, large, mighty, strong
ἵνα conj. ἵνα that, to, lest, for to, so that, albeit, because, for, so as
καὶ conj. καί and, even, also, but
πῦρ n. acc. neut. sg. πῦρ fire, fiery
ἐκ prep. ἐκ ἐξ (+gen) of, from, out of, by, on, with, in, among, through
τοῦ art. gen. masc. sg. ὁ ἡ τό the, this, that, he, she, it

οὐρανοῦ n. gen. masc. sg. οὐρανός heaven, air, sky
εἰς prep. εἰς (+acc) into, to, unto, for, in, on, toward, against, upon, at, among
τὴν art. acc. fem. sg. ὁ ἡ τό the, this, that, he, she, it
γῆν n. acc. fem. sg. γῆ earth, land, ground, country
ἐνώπιον prep. ἐνώπιον (+gen) before, in the sight of, in the presence of. (adv.) before
τῶν art. gen. masc. pl. ὁ ἡ τό the, this, that, he, she, it
ἀνθρώπων n. gen. masc. pl. ἄνθρωπος man, human being, person, one, certain
14 καὶ conj. καί and, even, also, but
τοὺς art. acc. masc. pl. ὁ ἡ τό the, this, that, he, she, it
ἐπὶ prep. ἐπί (+gen) on, in, upon, (+dat) in, at, for, upon, (+acc) on, upon, unto, to, against
τῆς art. gen. fem. sg. ὁ ἡ τό the, this, that, he, she, it
γῆς n. gen. fem. sg. γῆ earth, land, ground, country
διὰ prep. διά (+gen) by, through, with, in, of, (+acc) for, because of, for a cause
τὰ art. acc. neut. pl. ὁ ἡ τό the, this, that, he, she, it
σημεῖα n. acc. neut. pl. σημεῖον sign, miracle, wonder, token
ἃ relative pron. nom. neut. pl. ὅς ἥ ὅ who, which, what, that
αὐτῷ pron. dat. neut. 3p. sg. αὐτός ή ό self, of oneself, even, very, the same, he, she, it
ἐνώπιον prep. ἐνώπιον (+gen) before, in the sight of, in the presence of. (adv.) before
τοῦ art. gen. neut. sg. ὁ ἡ τό the, this, that, he, she, it
θηρίου n. gen. neut. sg. θηρίον beast, wild beast, venomous beast
τοῖς art. dat. masc. pl. ὁ ἡ τό the, this, that, he, she, it
ἐπὶ prep. ἐπί (+gen) on, in, upon, (+dat) in, at, for, upon, (+acc) on, upon, unto, to, against
τῆς art. gen. fem. sg. ὁ ἡ τό the, this, that, he, she, it
γῆς n. gen. fem. sg. γῆ earth, land, ground, country
εἰκόνα n. acc. fem. sg. εἰκών image
τῷ art. dat. neut. sg. ὁ ἡ τό the, this, that, he, she, it
θηρίῳ n. dat. neut. sg. θηρίον beast, wild beast, venomous beast
ὃ relative pron. nom. neut. sg. ὅς ἥ ὅ who, which, what, that
τὴν art. acc. fem. sg. ὁ ἡ τό the, this, that, he, she, it
πληγὴν n. acc. fem. sg. πληγή wound, plague, stripe
τῆς art. gen. fem. sg. ὁ ἡ τό the, this, that, he, she, it
μαχαίρας n. gen. fem. sg. μάχαιρα sword
καὶ conj. καί and, even, also, but
15 καὶ conj. καί and, even, also, but
αὐτῷ pron. dat. neut. 3p. sg. αὐτός ή ό self, of oneself, even, very, the same, he, she, it
πνεῦμα n. acc. neut. sg. πνεῦμα spirit, Spirit, Ghost, ghost, life. of the spirit, wind
τῇ art. dat. fem. sg. ὁ ἡ τό the, this, that, he, she, it
εἰκόνι n. dat. fem. sg. εἰκών image
τοῦ art. gen. neut. sg. ὁ ἡ τό the, this, that, he, she, it
θηρίου n. gen. neut. sg. θηρίον beast, wild beast, venomous beast
ἵνα conj. ἵνα that, to, lest, for to, so that, albeit, because, for, so as
καὶ conj. καί and, even, also, but
ἡ art. nom. fem. sg. ὁ ἡ τό the, this, that, he, she, it
εἰκὼν n. nom. fem. sg. εἰκών image
τοῦ art. gen. neut. sg. ὁ ἡ τό the, this, that, he, she, it
θηρίου n. gen. neut. sg. θηρίον beast, wild beast, venomous beast
καὶ conj. καί and, even, also, but
ὅσοι relative pron. nom. masc. pl. ὅσος as many as, whatsoever, that, as long as, how much
ἂν particle. ἄν Indicating contingency. No English translation.
μὴ particle of negation. μή not, no, lest, neither, none, nothing, nor, never, without
τὴν art. acc. fem. sg. ὁ ἡ τό the, this, that, he, she, it
εἰκόνα n. acc. fem. sg. εἰκών image
τοῦ art. gen. neut. sg. ὁ ἡ τό the, this, that, he, she, it
θηρίου n. gen. neut. sg. θηρίον beast, wild beast, venomous beast
ἵνα conj. ἵνα that, to, lest, for to, so that, albeit, because, for, so as

16 καὶ conj. καί and, even, also, but
πάντας adj. acc. masc. pl. πᾶς πᾶσα πᾶν all, every, whosoever, every one, no, whole, any
τοὺς art. acc. masc. pl. ὁ ἡ τό the, this, that, he, she, it
μικροὺς adj. acc. masc. pl. μικρός little, small, least, less
καὶ conj. καί and, even, also, but
τοὺς art. acc. masc. pl. ὁ ἡ τό the, this, that, he, she, it
μεγάλους adj. acc. masc. pl. μέγας great, loud, greatest, high, large, mighty, strong
καὶ conj. καί and, even, also, but
τοὺς art. acc. masc. pl. ὁ ἡ τό the, this, that, he, she, it
πλουσίους adj. acc. masc. pl. πλούσιος rich
καὶ conj. καί and, even, also, but
τοὺς art. acc. masc. pl. ὁ ἡ τό the, this, that, he, she, it
πτωχούς adj. acc. masc. pl. πτωχός poor, beggar, beggarly
καὶ conj. καί and, even, also, but
τοὺς art. acc. masc. pl. ὁ ἡ τό the, this, that, he, she, it
ἐλευθέρους adj. acc. masc. pl. ἐλεύθερος free, freewoman, at liberty, freeman
καὶ conj. καί and, even, also, but
τοὺς art. acc. masc. pl. ὁ ἡ τό the, this, that, he, she, it
δούλους n. acc. masc. pl. δοῦλος servant, bondman, bond, slave
ἵνα conj. ἵνα that, to, lest, for to, so that, albeit, because, for, so as
αὐτοῖς pron. dat. masc. 3p. pl. αὐτός ή ό self, of oneself, even, very, the same, he, she, it
χάραγμα n. acc. neut. sg. χάραγμα mark, graven
ἐπὶ prep. ἐπί (+gen) on, in, upon, (+dat) in, at, for, upon, (+acc) on, upon, unto, to, against
τῆς art. gen. fem. sg. ὁ ἡ τό the, this, that, he, she, it
χειρὸς n. gen. fem. sg. χείρ hand
αὐτῶν pron. gen. masc. 3p. pl. αὐτός ή ό self, of oneself, even, very, the same, he, she, it
τῆς art. gen. fem. sg. ὁ ἡ τό the, this, that, he, she, it
δεξιᾶς adj. gen. fem. sg. δεξιός right, right hand, right side
ἢ particle. ἢ or, than, either, nor, or else, and, rather than
ἐπὶ prep. ἐπί (+gen) on, in, upon, (+dat) in, at, for, upon, (+acc) on, upon, unto, to, against
τῶν art. gen. neut. pl. ὁ ἡ τό the, this, that, he, she, it
μετώπων n. gen. neut. pl. μέτωπον forehead
αὐτῶν pron. gen. masc. 3p. pl. αὐτός ή ό self, of oneself, even, very, the same, he, she, it
17 καὶ conj. καί and, even, also, but
ἵνα conj. ἵνα that, to, lest, for to, so that, albeit, because, for, so as
μὴ particle of negation. μή not, no, lest, neither, none, nothing, nor, never, without
τις indefinite pron. nom. masc. sg. τὶς certain, some, any man, one, any thing
ἢ particle. ἢ or, than, either, nor, or else, and, rather than
εἰ conj. εἰ if, whether, that, though, forasmuch
μὴ particle of negation. μή not, no, lest, neither, none, nothing, nor, never, without
ὁ art. nom. masc. sg. ὁ ἡ τό the, this, that, he, she, it
τὸ art. acc. neut. sg. ὁ ἡ τό the, this, that, he, she, it
χάραγμα n. acc. neut. sg. χάραγμα mark, graven
ἢ particle. ἢ or, than, either, nor, or else, and, rather than
ὄνομα n. acc. neut. sg. ὄνομα name, call, surname
τοῦ art. gen. neut. sg. ὁ ἡ τό the, this, that, he, she, it
θηρίου n. gen. neut. sg. θηρίον beast, wild beast, venomous beast
ἢ particle. ἢ or, than, either, nor, or else, and, rather than
τὸν art. acc. masc. sg. ὁ ἡ τό the, this, that, he, she, it
ἀριθμὸν n. acc. masc. sg. ἀριθμός number
τοῦ art. gen. neut. sg. ὁ ἡ τό the, this, that, he, she, it
ὀνόματος n. gen. neut. sg. ὄνομα name, call, surname
αὐτοῦ pron. gen. neut. 3p. sg. αὐτός ή ό self, of oneself, even, very, the same, he, she, it
18 ὧδε adv. ὧδε here, hither, in this place, there, this place
ἡ art. nom. fem. sg. ὁ ἡ τό the, this, that, he, she, it

σοφία n. nom. fem. sg. σοφία wisdom
ὁ art. nom. masc. sg. ὁ ἡ τό the, this, that, he, she, it
τὸν art. acc. masc. sg. ὁ ἡ τό the, this, that, he, she, it
νοῦν n. acc. masc. sg. νοῦς understanding, mind
τὸν art. acc. masc. sg. ὁ ἡ τό the, this, that, he, she, it
ἀριθμὸν n. acc. masc. sg. ἀριθμός number
τοῦ art. gen. neut. sg. ὁ ἡ τό the, this, that, he, she, it
θηρίου n. gen. neut. sg. θηρίον beast, wild beast, venomous beast
ἀριθμὸς n. nom. masc. sg. ἀριθμός number
γὰρ conj. γάρ for, and, because, but, indeed
ἀνθρώπου n. gen. masc. sg. ἄνθρωπος man, human being, person, one, certain
καὶ conj. καί and, even, also, but
ὁ art. nom. masc. sg. ὁ ἡ τό the, this, that, he, she, it
ἀριθμὸς n. nom. masc. sg. ἀριθμός number
αὐτοῦ pron. gen. neut. 3p. sg. αὐτός ἡ ὁ self, of oneself, even, very, the same, he, she, it
χξς´ abbreviated numeral. χξς´ Six hundred threescore and six

14

1 Καὶ conj. καί and, even, also, but
καὶ conj. καί and, even, also, but
ἀρνίον n. nom. neut. sg. ἀρνίον Lamb, lamb
ἐπὶ prep. ἐπί (+gen) on, in, upon, (+dat) in, at, for, upon, (+acc) on, upon, unto, to, against
τὸ art. acc. neut. sg. ὁ ἡ τό the, this, that, he, she, it
ὄρος n. acc. neut. sg. ὄρος mountain, mount, hill
Σιὼν n. gen. fem. sg. Σιών Sion
καὶ conj. καί and, even, also, but
μετ' prep. μετά (+gen) with, among, against, (+acc) after
αὐτοῦ pron. gen. masc. 3p. sg. αὐτός ἡ ὁ self, of oneself, even, very, the same, he, she, it
ἑκατὸν num. nom. fem. pl. ἑκατόν hundred, hundredfold
τεσσαρακοντατέσσαρες num. nom. fem. pl. τεσσαρακοντατέσσαρες forty and four
χιλιάδες n. nom. fem. pl. χιλιάς thousand
τὸ art. acc. neut. sg. ὁ ἡ τό the, this, that, he, she, it
ὄνομα n. acc. neut. sg. ὄνομα name, call, surname
τοῦ art. gen. masc. sg. ὁ ἡ τό the, this, that, he, she, it
πατρὸς n. gen. masc. sg. πατήρ Father, father, parent
αὐτοῦ pron. gen. masc. 3p. sg. αὐτός ἡ ὁ self, of oneself, even, very, the same, he, she, it
ἐπὶ prep. ἐπί (+gen) on, in, upon, (+dat) in, at, for, upon, (+acc) on, upon, unto, to, against
τῶν art. gen. neut. pl. ὁ ἡ τό the, this, that, he, she, it
μετώπων n. gen. neut. pl. μέτωπον forehead
αὐτῶν pron. gen. masc. 3p. pl. αὐτός ἡ ὁ self, of oneself, even, very, the same, he, she, it
2 καὶ conj. καί and, even, also, but
φωνὴν n. acc. fem. sg. φωνή voice, sound, noise
ἐκ prep. ἐκ ἐξ (+gen) of, from, out of, by, on, with, in, among, through
τοῦ art. gen. masc. sg. ὁ ἡ τό the, this, that, he, she, it
οὐρανοῦ n. gen. masc. sg. οὐρανός heaven, air, sky
ὡς adv. ὡς as, when, as it were, how, about, like, as soon as, even as, while
φωνὴν n. acc. fem. sg. φωνή voice, sound, noise
ὑδάτων n. gen. neut. pl. ὕδωρ water
πολλῶν adj. gen. neut. pl. πολύς many, great, much, long, abundant
καὶ conj. καί and, even, also, but
ὡς adv. ὡς as, when, as it were, how, about, like, as soon as, even as, while
φωνὴν n. acc. fem. sg. φωνή voice, sound, noise
βροντῆς n. gen. fem. sg. βροντή thunder, thundering
μεγάλης adj. gen. fem. sg. μέγας great, loud, greatest, high, large, mighty, strong

καὶ conj. καί and, even, also, but
φωνὴν n. acc. fem. sg. φωνή voice, sound, noise
κιθαρῳδῶν n. gen. masc. pl. κιθαρῳδός harper
ἐν prep. ἐν (+dat) in, by, with, among, at, on, through, to, within, into, of, for
ταῖς art. dat. fem. pl. ὁ ἡ τό the, this, that, he, she, it
κιθάραις n. dat. fem. pl. κιθάρα harp
αὐτῶν pron. gen. masc. 3p. pl. αὐτός ή ό self, of oneself, even, very, the same, he, she, it
3 καὶ conj. καί and, even, also, but
ὡς adv. ώς as, when, as it were, how, about, like, as soon as, even as, while
ᾠδὴν n. acc. fem. sg. ᾠδή song
καινὴν adj. acc. fem. sg. καινός new
ἐνώπιον prep. ἐνώπιον (+gen) before, in the sight of, in the presence of. (adv.) before
τοῦ art. gen. masc. sg. ὁ ἡ τό the, this, that, he, she, it
θρόνου n. gen. masc. sg. θρόνος throne, seat
καὶ conj. καί and, even, also, but
ἐνώπιον prep. ἐνώπιον (+gen) before, in the sight of, in the presence of. (adv.) before
τῶν art. gen. neut. pl. ὁ ἡ τό the, this, that, he, she, it
τεσσάρων num. gen. neut. pl. τέσσαρες four
ζώων n. gen. neut. pl. ζῷον beast
καὶ conj. καί and, even, also, but
τῶν art. gen. masc. pl. ὁ ἡ τό the, this, that, he, she, it
πρεσβυτέρων adj. gen. masc. pl. πρεσβύτερος elder, elder woman, eldest, old man
καὶ conj. καί and, even, also, but
οὐδεὶς num. nom. masc. sg. οὐδείς no man, nothing, no, none, neither, not, nought
τὴν art. acc. fem. sg. ὁ ἡ τό the, this, that, he, she, it
ᾠδὴν n. acc. fem. sg. ᾠδή song
εἰ conj. εἰ if, whether, that, though, forasmuch
μὴ particle of negation. μή not, no, lest, neither, none, nothing, nor, never, without
αἱ art. nom. fem. pl. ὁ ἡ τό the, this, that, he, she, it
ἑκατὸν num. nom. fem. pl. ἑκατόν hundred, hundredfold
τεσσαρακοντατέσσαρες num. nom. fem. pl. τεσσαρακοντατέσσαρες forty and four
χιλιάδες n. nom. fem. pl. χιλιάς thousand
οἱ art. nom. masc. pl. ὁ ἡ τό the, this, that, he, she, it
ἀπὸ prep. ἀπό (+gen) from, of, out of, since, for, off, at, by, in, on
τῆς art. gen. fem. sg. ὁ ἡ τό the, this, that, he, she, it
γῆς n. gen. fem. sg. γῆ earth, land, ground, country
4 οὗτοί demo. pron. nom. masc. pl. οὗτος αὕτη τοῦτο this, the same, this same, he, she, it
οἳ relative pron. nom. masc. pl. ὅς ἥ ὅ who, which, what, that
μετὰ prep. μετά (+gen) with, among, against, (+acc) after
γυναικῶν n. gen. fem. pl. γυνή woman, wife
οὐκ particle of negation. οὐ οὐκ οὐχ not, no, neither, none, nay, nor, never, nothing
παρθένοι n. nom. masc. pl. παρθένος virgin
γάρ conj. γάρ for, and, because, but, indeed
οὗτοί demo. pron. nom. masc. pl. οὗτος αὕτη τοῦτο this, the same, this same, he, she, it
οἱ art. nom. masc. pl. ὁ ἡ τό the, this, that, he, she, it
τῷ art. dat. neut. sg. ὁ ἡ τό the, this, that, he, she, it
ἀρνίῳ n. dat. neut. sg. ἀρνίον Lamb, lamb
ὅπου adv. ὅπου where, whither, whereas, in what place, wheresoever
ἂν particle. ἄν Indicating contingency. No English translation.
οὗτοι demo. pron. nom. masc. pl. οὗτος αὕτη τοῦτο this, the same, this same, he, she, it
ἀπὸ prep. ἀπό (+gen) from, of, out of, since, for, off, at, by, in, on
τῶν art. gen. masc. pl. ὁ ἡ τό the, this, that, he, she, it
ἀνθρώπων n. gen. masc. pl. ἄνθρωπος man, human being, person, one, certain
ἀπαρχὴ n. nom. fem. sg. ἀπαρχή firstfruit
τῷ art. dat. masc. sg. ὁ ἡ τό the, this, that, he, she, it

Θεῷ n. dat. masc. sg. θεός God, god
καὶ conj. καί and, even, also, but
τῷ art. dat. neut. sg. ὁ ἡ τό the, this, that, he, she, it
ἀρνίῳ n. dat. neut. sg. ἀρνίον Lamb, lamb
5 καὶ conj. καί and, even, also, but
ἐν prep. ἐν (+dat) in, by, with, among, at, on, through, to, within, into, of, for
τῷ art. dat. neut. sg. ὁ ἡ τό the, this, that, he, she, it
στόματι n. dat. neut. sg. στόμα mouth, face, edge
αὐτῶν pron. gen. masc. 3p. pl. αὐτός ἡ ὁ self, of oneself, even, very, the same, he, she, it
οὐχ particle of negation. οὐ οὐκ οὐχ not, no, neither, none, nay, nor, never, nothing
δόλος n. nom. masc. sg. δόλος guile, deceit, subtilty, craft
ἄμωμοί adj. nom. masc. pl. ἄμωμος without blame, without fault, without spot
γάρ conj. γάρ for, and, because, but, indeed
ἐνώπιον prep. ἐνώπιον (+gen) before, in the sight of, in the presence of. (adv.) before
τοῦ art. gen. masc. sg. ὁ ἡ τό the, this, that, he, she, it
θρόνου n. gen. masc. sg. θρόνος throne, seat
τοῦ art. gen. masc. sg. ὁ ἡ τό the, this, that, he, she, it
Θεοῦ n. gen. masc. sg. θεός God, god
6 Καὶ conj. καί and, even, also, but
ἄλλον adj. acc. masc. sg. ἄλλος other, another, some, one, more, otherwise
ἄγγελον n. acc. masc. sg. ἄγγελος angel, messenger
ἐν prep. ἐν (+dat) in, by, with, among, at, on, through, to, within, into, of, for
μεσουρανήματι n. dat. neut. sg. μεσουράνημα midst of heaven
εὐαγγέλιον n. acc. neut. sg. εὐαγγέλιον gospel
αἰώνιον adj. acc. neut. sg. αἰώνιος eternal, everlasting, world, for ever
τοὺς art. acc. masc. pl. ὁ ἡ τό the, this, that, he, she, it
ἐπὶ prep. ἐπί (+gen) on, in, upon, (+dat) in, at, for, upon, (+acc) on, upon, unto, to, against
τῆς art. gen. fem. sg. ὁ ἡ τό the, this, that, he, she, it
γῆς n. gen. fem. sg. γῆ earth, land, ground, country
καὶ conj. καί and, even, also, but
πᾶν adj. acc. neut. sg. πᾶς πᾶσα πᾶν all, every, whosoever, every one, no, whole, any
ἔθνος n. acc. neut. sg. ἔθνος Gentile, nation, heathen, people
καὶ conj. καί and, even, also, but
φυλὴν n. acc. fem. sg. φυλή tribe, kindred
καὶ conj. καί and, even, also, but
γλῶσσαν n. acc. fem. sg. γλῶσσα tongue
καὶ conj. καί and, even, also, but
λαόν n. acc. masc. sg. λαός people
7 ἐν prep. ἐν (+dat) in, by, with, among, at, on, through, to, within, into, of, for
φωνῇ n. dat. fem. sg. φωνή voice, sound, noise
μεγάλῃ adj. dat. fem. sg. μέγας great, loud, greatest, high, large, mighty, strong
τὸν art. acc. masc. sg. ὁ ἡ τό the, this, that, he, she, it
Θεὸν n. acc. masc. sg. θεός God, god
καὶ conj. καί and, even, also, but
αὐτῷ pron. dat. masc. 3p. sg. αὐτός ἡ ὁ self, of oneself, even, very, the same, he, she, it
δόξαν n. acc. fem. sg. δόξα glory, honour, praise, dignity, worship
ὅτι conj. ὅτι that, for, because, how that, how, because that, for that, though
ἡ art. nom. fem. sg. ὁ ἡ τό the, this, that, he, she, it
ὥρα n. nom. fem. sg. ὥρα hour, time, season
τῆς art. gen. fem. sg. ὁ ἡ τό the, this, that, he, she, it
κρίσεως n. gen. fem. sg. κρίσις judgment, damnation, accusation, condemnation
αὐτοῦ pron. gen. masc. 3p. sg. αὐτός ἡ ὁ self, of oneself, even, very, the same, he, she, it
καὶ conj. καί and, even, also, but
τῷ art. dat. masc. sg. ὁ ἡ τό the, this, that, he, she, it
τὸν art. acc. masc. sg. ὁ ἡ τό the, this, that, he, she, it

οὐρανὸν n. acc. masc. sg. οὐρανός heaven, air, sky
καὶ conj. καί and, even, also, but
τὴν art. acc. fem. sg. ὁ ἡ τό the, this, that, he, she, it
γῆν n. acc. fem. sg. γῆ earth, land, ground, country
καὶ conj. καί and, even, also, but
τὴν art. acc. fem. sg. ὁ ἡ τό the, this, that, he, she, it
θάλασσαν n. acc. fem. sg. θάλασσα sea
καὶ conj. καί and, even, also, but
πηγὰς n. acc. fem. pl. πηγή fountain, well
ὑδάτων n. gen. neut. pl. ὕδωρ water
8 Καὶ conj. καί and, even, also, but
ἄλλος adj. nom. masc. sg. ἄλλος other, another, some, one, more, otherwise
ἄγγελος n. nom. masc. sg. ἄγγελος angel, messenger
Βαβυλὼν n. nom. fem. sg. Βαβυλών Babylon
ἡ art. nom. fem. sg. ὁ ἡ τό the, this, that, he, she, it
πόλις n. nom. fem. sg. πόλις city
ἡ art. nom. fem. sg. ὁ ἡ τό the, this, that, he, she, it
μεγάλη adj. nom. fem. sg. μέγας great, loud, greatest, high, large, mighty, strong
ὅτι conj. ὅτι that, for, because, how that, how, because that, for that, though
ἐκ prep. ἐκ ἐξ (+gen) of, from, out of, by, on, with, in, among, through
τοῦ art. gen. masc. sg. ὁ ἡ τό the, this, that, he, she, it
οἴνου n. gen. masc. sg. οἶνος wine
τοῦ art. gen. masc. sg. ὁ ἡ τό the, this, that, he, she, it
θυμοῦ n. gen. masc. sg. θυμός wrath, fierceness, indignation
τῆς art. gen. fem. sg. ὁ ἡ τό the, this, that, he, she, it
πορνείας n. gen. fem. sg. πορνεία fornication
αὐτῆς pron. gen. fem. 3p. sg. αὐτός ή ό self, of oneself, even, very, the same, he, she, it
πάντα adj. acc. neut. pl. πᾶς πᾶσα πᾶν all, every, whosoever, every one, no, whole, any
ἔθνη n. acc. neut. pl. ἔθνος Gentile, nation, heathen, people
9 Καὶ conj. καί and, even, also, but
τρίτος ordinal. adj. nom. masc. sg. τρίτος third
ἄγγελος n. nom. masc. sg. ἄγγελος angel, messenger
αὐτοῖς pron. dat. masc. 3p. pl. αὐτός ή ό self, of oneself, even, very, the same, he, she, it
ἐν prep. ἐν (+dat) in, by, with, among, at, on, through, to, within, into, of, for
φωνῇ n. dat. fem. sg. φωνή voice, sound, noise
μεγάλῃ adj. dat. fem. sg. μέγας great, loud, greatest, high, large, mighty, strong
Εἴ conj. εἰ if, whether, that, though, forasmuch
τις indefinite pron. nom. masc. sg. τὶς certain, some, any man, one, any thing
τὸ art. acc. neut. sg. ὁ ἡ τό the, this, that, he, she, it
θηρίον n. acc. neut. sg. θηρίον beast, wild beast, venomous beast
καὶ conj. καί and, even, also, but
τὴν art. acc. fem. sg. ὁ ἡ τό the, this, that, he, she, it
εἰκόνα n. acc. fem. sg. εἰκών image
αὐτοῦ pron. gen. neut. 3p. sg. αὐτός ή ό self, of oneself, even, very, the same, he, she, it
καὶ conj. καί and, even, also, but
χάραγμα n. acc. neut. sg. χάραγμα mark, graven
ἐπὶ prep. ἐπί (+gen) on, in, upon, (+dat) in, at, for, upon, (+acc) on, upon, unto, to, against
τοῦ art. gen. neut. sg. ὁ ἡ τό the, this, that, he, she, it
μετώπου n. gen. neut. sg. μέτωπον forehead
αὐτοῦ pron. gen. masc. 3p. sg. αὐτός ή ό self, of oneself, even, very, the same, he, she, it
ἢ particle. ἤ or, than, either, nor, or else, and, rather than
ἐπὶ prep. ἐπί (+gen) on, in, upon, (+dat) in, at, for, upon, (+acc) on, upon, unto, to, against
τὴν art. acc. fem. sg. ὁ ἡ τό the, this, that, he, she, it
χεῖρα n. acc. fem. sg. χείρ hand
αὐτοῦ pron. gen. masc. 3p. sg. αὐτός ή ό self, of oneself, even, very, the same, he, she, it

10 καὶ conj. καί and, even, also, but
αὐτὸς pron. nom. masc. 3p. sg. αὐτός ἡ ὁ self, of oneself, even, very, the same, he, she, it
ἐκ prep. ἐκ ἐξ (+gen) of, from, out of, by, on, with, in, among, through
τοῦ art. gen. masc. sg. ὁ ἡ τό the, this, that, he, she, it
οἴνου n. gen. masc. sg. οἶνος wine
τοῦ art. gen. masc. sg. ὁ ἡ τό the, this, that, he, she, it
θυμοῦ n. gen. masc. sg. θυμός wrath, fierceness, indignation
τοῦ art. gen. masc. sg. ὁ ἡ τό the, this, that, he, she, it
Θεοῦ n. gen. masc. sg. θεός God, god
τοῦ art. gen. masc. sg. ὁ ἡ τό the, this, that, he, she, it
ἀκράτου adj. gen. masc. sg. ἄκρατος without mixture
ἐν prep. ἐν (+dat) in, by, with, among, at, on, through, to, within, into, of, for
τῷ art. dat. neut. sg. ὁ ἡ τό the, this, that, he, she, it
ποτηρίῳ n. dat. neut. sg. ποτήριον cup
τῆς art. gen. fem. sg. ὁ ἡ τό the, this, that, he, she, it
ὀργῆς n. gen. fem. sg. ὀργή wrath, anger, indignation, vengeance
αὐτοῦ pron. gen. masc. 3p. sg. αὐτός ἡ ὁ self, of oneself, even, very, the same, he, she, it
πυρὶ n. dat. neut. sg. πῦρ fire, fiery
καὶ conj. καί and, even, also, but
θείῳ n. dat. neut. sg. θεῖον brimstone
ἐνώπιον prep. ἐνώπιον (+gen) before, in the sight of, in the presence of. (adv.) before
τῶν art. gen. masc. pl. ὁ ἡ τό the, this, that, he, she, it
ἁγίων adj. gen. masc. pl. ἅγιος Holy, holy, saint, Holy One, holy thing, most holy
ἀγγέλων n. gen. masc. pl. ἄγγελος angel, messenger
καὶ conj. καί and, even, also, but
ἐνώπιον prep. ἐνώπιον (+gen) before, in the sight of, in the presence of. (adv.) before
τοῦ art. gen. neut. sg. ὁ ἡ τό the, this, that, he, she, it
ἀρνίου n. gen. neut. sg. ἀρνίον Lamb, lamb
11 καὶ conj. καί and, even, also, but
ὁ art. nom. masc. sg. ὁ ἡ τό the, this, that, he, she, it
καπνὸς n. nom. masc. sg. καπνός smoke
τοῦ art. gen. masc. sg. ὁ ἡ τό the, this, that, he, she, it
βασανισμοῦ n. gen. masc. sg. βασανισμός torment
αὐτῶν pron. gen. masc. 3p. pl. αὐτός ἡ ὁ self, of oneself, even, very, the same, he, she, it
εἰς prep. εἰς (+acc) into, to, unto, for, in, on, toward, against, upon, at, among
αἰῶνας n. acc. masc. pl. αἰών ever, ever and ever, evermore, age, eternal, world
αἰώνων n. gen. masc. pl. αἰών ever, ever and ever, evermore, age, eternal, world
καὶ conj. καί and, even, also, but
οὐκ particle of negation. οὐ οὐκ οὐχ not, no, neither, none, nay, nor, never, nothing
ἀνάπαυσιν n. acc. fem. sg. ἀνάπαυσις rest
ἡμέρας n. gen. fem. sg. ἡμέρα day, time, year, while, age, day time
καὶ conj. καί and, even, also, but
νυκτὸς n. gen. fem. sg. νύξ night
οἱ art. nom. masc. pl. ὁ ἡ τό the, this, that, he, she, it
τὸ art. acc. neut. sg. ὁ ἡ τό the, this, that, he, she, it
θηρίον n. acc. neut. sg. θηρίον beast, wild beast, venomous beast
καὶ conj. καί and, even, also, but
τὴν art. acc. fem. sg. ὁ ἡ τό the, this, that, he, she, it
εἰκόνα n. acc. fem. sg. εἰκών image
αὐτοῦ pron. gen. neut. 3p. sg. αὐτός ἡ ὁ self, of oneself, even, very, the same, he, she, it
καὶ conj. καί and, even, also, but
εἴ conj. εἰ if, whether, that, though, forasmuch
τις indefinite pron. nom. masc. sg. τὶς certain, some, any man, one, any thing
τὸ art. acc. neut. sg. ὁ ἡ τό the, this, that, he, she, it
χάραγμα n. acc. neut. sg. χάραγμα mark, graven

τοῦ art. gen. neut. sg. ὁ ἡ τό the, this, that, he, she, it
ὀνόματος n. gen. neut. sg. ὄνομα name, call, surname
αὐτοῦ pron. gen. neut. 3p. sg. αὐτός ἡ ὁ self, of oneself, even, very, the same, he, she, it
12 ὧδε adv. ὧδε here, hither, in this place, there, this place
ὑπομονὴ n. nom. fem. sg. ὑπομονή patience, enduring
τῶν art. gen. masc. pl. ὁ ἡ τό the, this, that, he, she, it
ἁγίων adj. gen. masc. pl. ἅγιος Holy, holy, saint, Holy One, holy thing, most holy
ὧδε adv. ὧδε here, hither, in this place, there, this place
οἱ art. nom. masc. pl. ὁ ἡ τό the, this, that, he, she, it
τὰς art. acc. fem. pl. ὁ ἡ τό the, this, that, he, she, it
ἐντολὰς n. acc. fem. pl. ἐντολή commandment, precept
τοῦ art. gen. masc. sg. ὁ ἡ τό the, this, that, he, she, it
Θεοῦ n. gen. masc. sg. θεός God, god
καὶ conj. καί and, even, also, but
τὴν art. acc. fem. sg. ὁ ἡ τό the, this, that, he, she, it
πίστιν n. acc. fem. sg. πίστις faith, assurance, belief, fidelity
Ἰησοῦ n. gen. masc. sg. Ἰησοῦς Jesus
13 Καὶ conj. καί and, even, also, but
φωνῆς n. gen. fem. sg. φωνή voice, sound, noise
ἐκ prep. ἐκ ἐξ (+gen) of, from, out of, by, on, with, in, among, through
τοῦ art. gen. masc. sg. ὁ ἡ τό the, this, that, he, she, it
οὐρανοῦ n. gen. masc. sg. οὐρανός heaven, air, sky
μοι pron. dat. 1p. sg. ἐγώ I
Μακάριοι adj. nom. masc. pl. μακάριος blessed, happy
οἱ art. nom. masc. pl. ὁ ἡ τό the, this, that, he, she, it
νεκροὶ adj. nom. masc. pl. νεκρός dead
οἱ art. nom. masc. pl. ὁ ἡ τό the, this, that, he, she, it
ἐν prep. ἐν (+dat) in, by, with, among, at, on, through, to, within, into, of, for
Κυρίῳ n. dat. masc. sg. κύριος Lord, lord, master, sir, LORD, God, Master, owner
ἀπ' prep. ἀπό (+gen) from, of, out of, since, for, off, at, by, in, on
ἄρτι adv. ἄρτι now, hence, here, hither, even now, present
ναί particle. ναί yea, even so, yes, surely, truth, verily
τὸ art. nom. neut. sg. ὁ ἡ τό the, this, that, he, she, it
Πνεῦμα n. nom. neut. sg. πνεῦμα spirit, Spirit, Ghost, ghost, life. of the spirit, wind
ἵνα conj. ἵνα that, to, lest, for to, so that, albeit, because, for, so as
ἐκ prep. ἐκ ἐξ (+gen) of, from, out of, by, on, with, in, among, through
τῶν art. gen. masc. pl. ὁ ἡ τό the, this, that, he, she, it
κόπων n. gen. masc. pl. κόπος labour, trouble, weariness
αὐτῶν pron. gen. masc. 3p. pl. αὐτός ἡ ὁ self, of oneself, even, very, the same, he, she, it
τὰ art. nom. neut. pl. ὁ ἡ τό the, this, that, he, she, it
δὲ conj. δέ but, and, now, also, to the contrary, rather, then
ἔργα n. nom. neut. pl. ἔργον work, deed, doing labour
αὐτῶν pron. gen. masc. 3p. pl. αὐτός ἡ ὁ self, of oneself, even, very, the same, he, she, it
μετ' prep. μετά (+gen) with, among, against, (+acc) after
αὐτῶν pron. gen. masc. 3p. pl. αὐτός ἡ ὁ self, of oneself, even, very, the same, he, she, it
14 Καὶ conj. καί and, even, also, but
καὶ conj. καί and, even, also, but
νεφέλη n. nom. fem. sg. νεφέλη cloud
λευκή adj. nom. fem. sg. λευκός white
καὶ conj. καί and, even, also, but
ἐπὶ prep. ἐπί (+gen) on, in, upon, (+dat) in, at, for, upon, (+acc) on, upon, unto, to, against
τὴν art. acc. fem. sg. ὁ ἡ τό the, this, that, he, she, it
νεφέλην n. acc. fem. sg. νεφέλη cloud
ὅμοιος adj. nom. masc. sg. ὅμοιος like
υἱῷ n. dat. masc. sg. υἱός son, child, descendant, offspring, heir

ἀνθρώπου n. gen. masc. sg. ἄνθρωπος man, human being, person, one, certain
ἐπὶ prep. ἐπί (+gen) on, in, upon, (+dat) in, at, for, upon, (+acc) on, upon, unto, to, against
τῆς art. gen. fem. sg. ὁ ἡ τό the, this, that, he, she, it
κεφαλῆς n. gen. fem. sg. κεφαλή head
αὐτοῦ pron. gen. masc. 3p. sg. αὐτός ή ό self, of oneself, even, very, the same, he, she, it
στέφανον n. acc. masc. sg. στέφανος crown
χρυσοῦν adj. acc. masc. sg. χρύσεος golden, of gold
καὶ conj. καί and, even, also, but
ἐν prep. ἐν (+dat) in, by, with, among, at, on, through, to, within, into, of, for
τῇ art. dat. fem. sg. ὁ ἡ τό the, this, that, he, she, it
χειρὶ n. dat. fem. sg. χείρ hand
αὐτοῦ pron. gen. masc. 3p. sg. αὐτός ή ό self, of oneself, even, very, the same, he, she, it
δρέπανον n. acc. neut. sg. δρέπανον sickle
ὀξύ adj. acc. neut. sg. ὀξύς swift, sharp
15 καὶ conj. καί and, even, also, but
ἄλλος adj. nom. masc. sg. ἄλλος other, another, some, one, more, otherwise
ἄγγελος n. nom. masc. sg. ἄγγελος angel, messenger
ἐκ prep. ἐκ ἐξ (+gen) of, from, out of, by, on, with, in, among, through
τοῦ art. gen. masc. sg. ὁ ἡ τό the, this, that, he, she, it
ναοῦ n. gen. masc. sg. ναός temple, shrine
ἐν prep. ἐν (+dat) in, by, with, among, at, on, through, to, within, into, of, for
μεγάλῃ adj. dat. fem. sg. μέγας great, loud, greatest, high, large, mighty, strong
φωνῇ n. dat. fem. sg. φωνή voice, sound, noise
τῷ art. dat. masc. sg. ὁ ἡ τό the, this, that, he, she, it
ἐπὶ prep. ἐπί (+gen) on, in, upon, (+dat) in, at, for, upon, (+acc) on, upon, unto, to, against
τῆς art. gen. fem. sg. ὁ ἡ τό the, this, that, he, she, it
νεφέλης n. gen. fem. sg. νεφέλη cloud
τὸ art. acc. neut. sg. ὁ ἡ τό the, this, that, he, she, it
δρέπανόν n. acc. neut. sg. δρέπανον sickle
σου pron. gen. 2p. sg. σύ thou, you
καὶ conj. καί and, even, also, but
ὅτι conj. ὅτι that, for, because, how that, how, because that, for that, though
σοι pron. dat. 2p. sg. σύ thou, you
ἡ art. nom. fem. sg. ὁ ἡ τό the, this, that, he, she, it
ὥρα n. nom. fem. sg. ὥρα hour, time, season
τοῦ art. gen. masc. sg. ὁ ἡ τό the, this, that, he, she, it
ὅτι conj. ὅτι that, for, because, how that, how, because that, for that, though
ὁ art. nom. masc. sg. ὁ ἡ τό the, this, that, he, she, it
θερισμὸς n. nom. masc. sg. θερισμός harvest
τῆς art. gen. fem. sg. ὁ ἡ τό the, this, that, he, she, it
γῆς n. gen. fem. sg. γῆ earth, land, ground, country
16 καὶ conj. καί and, even, also, but
ὁ art. nom. masc. sg. ὁ ἡ τό the, this, that, he, she, it
ἐπὶ prep. ἐπί (+gen) on, in, upon, (+dat) in, at, for, upon, (+acc) on, upon, unto, to, against
τὴν art. acc. fem. sg. ὁ ἡ τό the, this, that, he, she, it
νεφέλην n. acc. fem. sg. νεφέλη cloud
τὸ art. acc. neut. sg. ὁ ἡ τό the, this, that, he, she, it
δρέπανον n. acc. neut. sg. δρέπανον sickle
αὐτοῦ pron. gen. masc. 3p. sg. αὐτός ή ό self, of oneself, even, very, the same, he, she, it
ἐπὶ prep. ἐπί (+gen) on, in, upon, (+dat) in, at, for, upon, (+acc) on, upon, unto, to, against
τὴν art. acc. fem. sg. ὁ ἡ τό the, this, that, he, she, it
γῆν n. acc. fem. sg. γῆ earth, land, ground, country
καὶ conj. καί and, even, also, but
ἡ art. nom. fem. sg. ὁ ἡ τό the, this, that, he, she, it
γῆ n. nom. fem. sg. γῆ earth, land, ground, country

17 Καὶ conj. καί and, even, also, but
ἄλλος adj. nom. masc. sg. ἄλλος other, another, some, one, more, otherwise
ἄγγελος n. nom. masc. sg. ἄγγελος angel, messenger
ἐκ prep. ἐκ ἐξ (+gen) of, from, out of, by, on, with, in, among, through
τοῦ art. gen. masc. sg. ὁ ἡ τό the, this, that, he, she, it
ναοῦ n. gen. masc. sg. ναός temple, shrine
τοῦ art. gen. masc. sg. ὁ ἡ τό the, this, that, he, she, it
ἐν prep. ἐν (+dat) in, by, with, among, at, on, through, to, within, into, of, for
τῷ art. dat. masc. sg. ὁ ἡ τό the, this, that, he, she, it
οὐρανῷ n. dat. masc. sg. οὐρανός heaven, air, sky
καὶ conj. καί and, even, also, but
αὐτὸς pron. nom. masc. 3p. sg. αὐτός ή ό self, of oneself, even, very, the same, he, she, it
δρέπανον n. acc. neut. sg. δρέπανον sickle
ὀξύ adj. acc. neut. sg. ὀξύς swift, sharp
18 καὶ conj. καί and, even, also, but
ἄλλος adj. nom. masc. sg. ἄλλος other, another, some, one, more, otherwise
ἄγγελος n. nom. masc. sg. ἄγγελος angel, messenger
ἐκ prep. ἐκ ἐξ (+gen) of, from, out of, by, on, with, in, among, through
τοῦ art. gen. neut. sg. ὁ ἡ τό the, this, that, he, she, it
θυσιαστηρίου n. gen. neut. sg. θυσιαστήριον altar
ἐξουσίαν n. acc. fem. sg. ἐξουσία power, authority, right, strength, jurisdiction
ἐπὶ prep. ἐπί (+gen) on, in, upon, (+dat) in, at, for, upon, (+acc) on, upon, unto, to, against
τοῦ art. gen. neut. sg. ὁ ἡ τό the, this, that, he, she, it
πυρός n. gen. neut. sg. πῦρ fire, fiery
καὶ conj. καί and, even, also, but
κραυγῇ n. dat. fem. sg. κραυγή cry, crying, clamour
μεγάλῃ adj. dat. fem. sg. μέγας great, loud, greatest, high, large, mighty, strong
τῷ art. dat. masc. sg. ὁ ἡ τό the, this, that, he, she, it
τὸ art. acc. neut. sg. ὁ ἡ τό the, this, that, he, she, it
δρέπανον n. acc. neut. sg. δρέπανον sickle
τὸ art. acc. neut. sg. ὁ ἡ τό the, this, that, he, she, it
ὀξὺ adj. acc. neut. sg. ὀξύς swift, sharp
σου pron. gen. 2p. sg. σύ thou, you
τὸ art. acc. neut. sg. ὁ ἡ τό the, this, that, he, she, it
δρέπανον n. acc. neut. sg. δρέπανον sickle
τὸ art. acc. neut. sg. ὁ ἡ τό the, this, that, he, she, it
ὀξὺ adj. acc. neut. sg. ὀξύς swift, sharp
καὶ conj. καί and, even, also, but
τοὺς art. acc. masc. pl. ὁ ἡ τό the, this, that, he, she, it
βότρυας n. acc. masc. pl. βότρυς cluster
τῆς art. gen. fem. sg. ὁ ἡ τό the, this, that, he, she, it
ἀμπέλου n. gen. fem. sg. ἄμπελος vine
τῆς art. gen. fem. sg. ὁ ἡ τό the, this, that, he, she, it
γῆς n. gen. fem. sg. γῆ earth, land, ground, country
ὅτι conj. ὅτι that, for, because, how that, how, because that, for that, though
αἱ art. nom. fem. pl. ὁ ἡ τό the, this, that, he, she, it
σταφυλαὶ n. nom. fem. pl. σταφυλή grape
αὐτῆς pron. gen. fem. 3p. sg. αὐτός ή ό self, of oneself, even, very, the same, he, she, it
19 καὶ conj. καί and, even, also, but
ὁ art. nom. masc. sg. ὁ ἡ τό the, this, that, he, she, it
ἄγγελος n. nom. masc. sg. ἄγγελος angel, messenger
τὸ art. acc. neut. sg. ὁ ἡ τό the, this, that, he, she, it
δρέπανον n. acc. neut. sg. δρέπανον sickle
αὐτοῦ pron. gen. masc. 3p. sg. αὐτός ή ό self, of oneself, even, very, the same, he, she, it
εἰς prep. εἰς (+acc) into, to, unto, for, in, on, toward, against, upon, at, among

τὴν art. acc. fem. sg. ὁ ἡ τό the, this, that, he, she, it
γῆν n. acc. fem. sg. γῆ earth, land, ground, country
καὶ conj. καί and, even, also, but
τὴν art. acc. fem. sg. ὁ ἡ τό the, this, that, he, she, it
ἄμπελον n. acc. fem. sg. ἄμπελος vine
τῆς art. gen. fem. sg. ὁ ἡ τό the, this, that, he, she, it
γῆς n. gen. fem. sg. γῆ earth, land, ground, country
καὶ conj. καί and, even, also, but
εἰς prep. εἰς (+acc) into, to, unto, for, in, on, toward, against, upon, at, among
τὴν art. acc. fem. sg. ὁ ἡ τό the, this, that, he, she, it
ληνὸν n. acc. fem. sg. ληνός winepress
τοῦ art. gen. masc. sg. ὁ ἡ τό the, this, that, he, she, it
θυμοῦ n. gen. masc. sg. θυμός wrath, fierceness, indignation
τοῦ art. gen. masc. sg. ὁ ἡ τό the, this, that, he, she, it
Θεοῦ n. gen. masc. sg. θεός God, god
τὴν art. acc. fem. sg. ὁ ἡ τό the, this, that, he, she, it
μέγαλην adj. acc. fem. sg. μέγας great, loud, greatest, high, large, mighty, strong
20 καὶ conj. καί and, even, also, but
ἡ art. nom. fem. sg. ὁ ἡ τό the, this, that, he, she, it
ληνὸς n. nom. fem. sg. ληνός winepress
ἔξω adv. ἔξω out, without, out of, forth, away, outward
τῆς art. gen. fem. sg. ὁ ἡ τό the, this, that, he, she, it
πόλεως n. gen. fem. sg. πόλις city
καὶ conj. καί and, even, also, but
αἷμα n. nom. neut. sg. αἷμα blood
ἐκ prep. ἐκ ἐξ (+gen) of, from, out of, by, on, with, in, among, through
τῆς art. gen. fem. sg. ὁ ἡ τό the, this, that, he, she, it
ληνοῦ n. gen. fem. sg. ληνός winepress
ἄχρι prep. ἄχρι or ἄχρις (+gen) until, unto, till, even to, as far as, while, into
τῶν art. gen. masc. pl. ὁ ἡ τό the, this, that, he, she, it
χαλινῶν n. gen. masc. pl. χαλινός bit, bridle
τῶν art. gen. masc. pl. ὁ ἡ τό the, this, that, he, she, it
ἵππων n. gen. masc. pl. ἵππος horse
ἀπὸ prep. ἀπό (+gen) from, of, out of, since, for, off, at, by, in, on
σταδίων n. gen. masc. pl. στάδιον furlong, stadium, race
χιλίων num. gen. masc. pl. χίλιοι one thousand
ἑξακοσίων num. gen. masc. pl. ἑξακόσιοι six hundred

15

1 Καὶ conj. καί and, even, also, but
ἄλλο adj. acc. neut. sg. ἄλλος other, another, some, one, more, otherwise
σημεῖον n. acc. neut. sg. σημεῖον sign, miracle, wonder, token
ἐν prep. ἐν (+dat) in, by, with, among, at, on, through, to, within, into, of, for
τῷ art. dat. masc. sg. ὁ ἡ τό the, this, that, he, she, it
οὐρανῷ n. dat. masc. sg. οὐρανός heaven, air, sky
μέγα adj. acc. neut. sg. μέγας great, loud, greatest, high, large, mighty, strong
καὶ conj. καί and, even, also, but
θαυμαστόν adj. acc. neut. sg. θαυμαστός marvellous, marvel
ἀγγέλους n. acc. masc. pl. ἄγγελος angel, messenger
ἑπτὰ num. acc. masc. pl. ἑπτά seven, seventh
πληγὰς n. acc. fem. pl. πληγή wound, plague, stripe
ἑπτὰ num. acc. fem. pl. ἑπτά seven, seventh
τὰς art. acc. fem. pl. ὁ ἡ τό the, this, that, he, she, it
ἐσχάτας adj. acc. fem. pl. ἔσχατος last, lowest, uttermost, uttermost part

ὅτι conj. ὅτι that, for, because, how that, how, because that, for that, though
ἐν prep. ἐν (+dat) in, by, with, among, at, on, through, to, within, into, of, for
αὐταῖς pron. dat. fem. 3p. pl. αὐτός ή ό self, of oneself, even, very, the same, he, she, it
ὁ art. nom. masc. sg. ὁ ἡ τό the, this, that, he, she, it
θυμὸς n. nom. masc. sg. θυμός wrath, fierceness, indignation
τοῦ art. gen. masc. sg. ὁ ἡ τό the, this, that, he, she, it
Θεοῦ n. gen. masc. sg. θεός God, god
2 Καὶ conj. καί and, even, also, but
ὡς adv. ὡς as, when, as it were, how, about, like, as soon as, even as, while
θάλασσαν n. acc. fem. sg. θάλασσα sea
ὑαλίνην adj. acc. fem. sg. ὑάλινος of glass
πυρὶ n. dat. neut. sg. πῦρ fire, fiery
καὶ conj. καί and, even, also, but
τοὺς art. acc. masc. pl. ὁ ἡ τό the, this, that, he, she, it
ἐκ prep. ἐκ ἐξ (+gen) of, from, out of, by, on, with, in, among, through
τοῦ art. gen. neut. sg. ὁ ἡ τό the, this, that, he, she, it
θηρίου n. gen. neut. sg. θηρίον beast, wild beast, venomous beast
καὶ conj. καί and, even, also, but
ἐκ prep. ἐκ ἐξ (+gen) of, from, out of, by, on, with, in, among, through
τῆς art. gen. fem. sg. ὁ ἡ τό the, this, that, he, she, it
εἰκόνος n. gen. fem. sg. εἰκών image
αὐτοῦ pron. gen. neut. 3p. sg. αὐτός ή ό self, of oneself, even, very, the same, he, she, it
καὶ conj. καί and, even, also, but
ἐκ prep. ἐκ ἐξ (+gen) of, from, out of, by, on, with, in, among, through
τοῦ art. gen. neut. sg. ὁ ἡ τό the, this, that, he, she, it
χαράγματος n. gen. neut. sg. χάραγμα mark, graven
αὐτοῦ pron. gen. neut. 3p. sg. αὐτός ή ό self, of oneself, even, very, the same, he, she, it
ἐκ prep. ἐκ ἐξ (+gen) of, from, out of, by, on, with, in, among, through
τοῦ art. gen. masc. sg. ὁ ἡ τό the, this, that, he, she, it
ἀριθμοῦ n. gen. masc. sg. ἀριθμός number
τοῦ art. gen. neut. sg. ὁ ἡ τό the, this, that, he, she, it
ὀνόματος n. gen. neut. sg. ὄνομα name, call, surname
αὐτοῦ pron. gen. neut. 3p. sg. αὐτός ή ό self, of oneself, even, very, the same, he, she, it
ἐπὶ prep. ἐπί (+gen) on, in, upon, (+dat) in, at, for, upon, (+acc) on, upon, unto, to, against
τὴν art. acc. fem. sg. ὁ ἡ τό the, this, that, he, she, it
θάλασσαν n. acc. fem. sg. θάλασσα sea
τὴν art. acc. fem. sg. ὁ ἡ τό the, this, that, he, she, it
ὑαλίνην adj. acc. fem. sg. ὑάλινος of glass
κιθάρας n. acc. fem. pl. κιθάρα harp
τοῦ art. gen. neut. sg. ὁ ἡ τό the, this, that, he, she, it
Θεοῦ n. gen. masc. sg. θεός God, god
3 καὶ conj. καί and, even, also, but
τὴν art. acc. fem. sg. ὁ ἡ τό the, this, that, he, she, it
ᾠδὴν n. acc. fem. sg. ᾠδή song
Μωσέως n. gen. masc. sg. Μωσῆς Moses
τοῦ art. gen. masc. sg. ὁ ἡ τό the, this, that, he, she, it
δούλου n. gen. masc. sg. δοῦλος servant, bondman, bond, slave
τοῦ art. gen. masc. sg. ὁ ἡ τό the, this, that, he, she, it
Θεοῦ n. gen. masc. sg. θεός God, god
καὶ conj. καί and, even, also, but
τὴν art. acc. fem. sg. ὁ ἡ τό the, this, that, he, she, it
ᾠδὴν n. acc. fem. sg. ᾠδή song
τοῦ art. gen. masc. sg. ὁ ἡ τό the, this, that, he, she, it
ἀρνίου n. gen. neut. sg. ἀρνίον Lamb, lamb
Μεγάλα adj. nom. neut. pl. μέγας great, loud, greatest, high, large, mighty, strong

καὶ conj. καί and, even, also, but
θαυμαστὰ adj. nom. neut. pl. θαυμαστός marvellous, marvel
τὰ art. nom. neut. pl. ὁ ἡ τό the, this, that, he, she, it
ἔργα n. nom. neut. pl. ἔργον work, deed, doing labour
σου pron. gen. 2p. sg. σύ thou, you
Κύριε n. voc. masc. sg. κύριος Lord, lord, master, sir, LORD, God, Master, owner
ὁ art. nom. masc. sg. ὁ ἡ τό the, this, that, he, she, it
Θεὸς n. nom. masc. sg. θεός God, god
ὁ art. nom. masc. sg. ὁ ἡ τό the, this, that, he, she, it
παντοκράτωρ n. nom. masc. sg. παντοκράτωρ Almighty, omnipotent
δίκαιαι adj. nom. fem. pl. δίκαιος righteous, just, meet, right
καὶ conj. καί and, even, also, but
ἀληθιναὶ adj. nom. fem. pl. ἀληθινός true
αἱ art. nom. fem. pl. ὁ ἡ τό the, this, that, he, she, it
ὁδοί n. nom. fem. pl. ὁδός way, journey, highway
σου pron. gen. 2p. sg. σύ thou, you
ὁ art. nom. masc. sg. ὁ ἡ τό the, this, that, he, she, it
βασιλεὺς n. nom. masc. sg. βασιλεύς king
τῶν art. gen. masc. pl. ὁ ἡ τό the, this, that, he, she, it
ἁγίων adj. gen. masc. pl. ἅγιος Holy, holy, saint, Holy One, holy thing, most holy
4 τίς interrog. pron. nom. masc. sg. τίς what, who, why, where, which, how
οὐ particle of negation. οὐ οὐκ οὐχ not, no, neither, none, nay, nor, never, nothing
μὴ particle of negation. μή not, no, lest, neither, none, nothing, nor, never, without
σε pron. acc. 2p. sg. σύ thou, you
Κύριε n. voc. masc. sg. κύριος Lord, lord, master, sir, LORD, God, Master, owner
καὶ conj. καί and, even, also, but
τὸ art. acc. neut. sg. ὁ ἡ τό the, this, that, he, she, it
ὄνομά n. acc. neut. sg. ὄνομα name, call, surname
σου pron. gen. 2p. sg. σύ thou, you
ὅτι conj. ὅτι that, for, because, how that, how, because that, for that, though
μόνος adj. nom. masc. sg. μόνος only, alone, by oneself
ὅσιος adj. nom. masc. sg. ὅσιος holy, Holy, mercy
ὅτι conj. ὅτι that, for, because, how that, how, because that, for that, though
πάντα adj. nom. neut. pl. πᾶς πᾶσα πᾶν all, every, whosoever, every one, no, whole, any
τὰ art. nom. neut. pl. ὁ ἡ τό the, this, that, he, she, it
ἔθνη n. nom. neut. pl. ἔθνος Gentile, nation, heathen, people
καὶ conj. καί and, even, also, but
ἐνώπιόν prep. ἐνώπιον (+gen) before, in the sight of, in the presence of. (adv.) before
σου pron. gen. 2p. sg. σύ thou, you
ὅτι conj. ὅτι that, for, because, how that, how, because that, for that, though
τὰ art. nom. neut. pl. ὁ ἡ τό the, this, that, he, she, it
δικαιώματά n. nom. neut. pl. δικαίωμα ordinance, righteousness, judgement, justification
σου pron. gen. 2p. sg. σύ thou, you
5 Καὶ conj. καί and, even, also, but
μετὰ prep. μετά (+gen) with, among, against, (+acc) after
ταῦτα demo. pron. acc. neut. pl. οὗτος αὕτη τοῦτο this, the same, this same, he, she, it
καὶ conj. καί and, even, also, but
ὁ art. nom. masc. sg. ὁ ἡ τό the, this, that, he, she, it
ναὸς n. nom. masc. sg. ναός temple, shrine
τῆς art. gen. fem. sg. ὁ ἡ τό the, this, that, he, she, it
σκηνῆς n. gen. fem. sg. σκηνή tabernacle, habitation
τοῦ art. gen. neut. sg. ὁ ἡ τό the, this, that, he, she, it
μαρτυρίου n. gen. neut. sg. μαρτύριον testimony, witness
ἐν prep. ἐν (+dat) in, by, with, among, at, on, through, to, within, into, of, for
τῷ art. dat. masc. sg. ὁ ἡ τό the, this, that, he, she, it

οὐρανῷ n. dat. masc. sg. οὐρανός heaven, air, sky
6 καὶ conj. καί and, even, also, but
οἱ art. nom. masc. pl. ὁ ἡ τό the, this, that, he, she, it
ἑπτὰ num. nom. masc. pl. ἑπτά seven, seventh
ἄγγελοι n. nom. masc. pl. ἄγγελος angel, messenger
τὰς art. acc. fem. pl. ὁ ἡ τό the, this, that, he, she, it
ἑπτὰ num. acc. fem. pl. ἑπτά seven, seventh
πληγὰς n. acc. fem. pl. πληγή wound, plague, stripe
ἐκ prep. ἐκ ἐξ (+gen) of, from, out of, by, on, with, in, among, through
τοῦ art. gen. masc. sg. ὁ ἡ τό the, this, that, he, she, it
ναοῦ n. gen. masc. sg. ναός temple, shrine
λίνον n. acc. neut. sg. λίνον flax, linen
καθαρὸν adj. acc. neut. sg. καθαρός pure, clean, clear
καὶ conj. καί and, even, also, but
λαμπρὸν adj. acc. neut. sg. λαμπρός gorgeous, bright, goodly, white, clear
καὶ conj. καί and, even, also, but
περὶ prep. περί (+gen) of, for, concerning, (+acc) about, concerning, in
τὰ art. acc. neut. pl. ὁ ἡ τό the, this, that, he, she, it
στήθη n. acc. neut. pl. στῆθος breast
ζώνας n. acc. fem. pl. ζώνη girdle, purse
χρυσᾶς adj. acc. fem. pl. χρύσεος golden, of gold
7 καὶ conj. καί and, even, also, but
ἓν num. nom. neut. sg. εἷς or ἕν one, other, some, any, only, a certain
ἐκ prep. ἐκ ἐξ (+gen) of, from, out of, by, on, with, in, among, through
τῶν art. gen. neut. pl. ὁ ἡ τό the, this, that, he, she, it
τεσσάρων num. gen. neut. pl. τέσσαρες four
ζώων n. gen. neut. pl. ζῶον beast
τοῖς art. dat. masc. pl. ὁ ἡ τό the, this, that, he, she, it
ἑπτὰ num. dat. masc. pl. ἑπτά seven, seventh
ἀγγέλοις n. dat. masc. pl. ἄγγελος angel, messenger
ἑπτὰ num. acc. fem. pl. ἑπτά seven, seventh
φιάλας n. acc. fem. pl. φιάλη vial
χρυσᾶς adj. acc. fem. pl. χρύσεος golden, of gold
τοῦ art. gen. masc. sg. ὁ ἡ τό the, this, that, he, she, it
θυμοῦ n. gen. masc. sg. θυμός wrath, fierceness, indignation
τοῦ art. gen. masc. sg. ὁ ἡ τό the, this, that, he, she, it
Θεοῦ n. gen. masc. sg. θεός God, god
τοῦ art. gen. masc. sg. ὁ ἡ τό the, this, that, he, she, it
εἰς prep. εἰς (+acc) into, to, unto, for, in, on, toward, against, upon, at, among
τοὺς art. acc. masc. pl. ὁ ἡ τό the, this, that, he, she, it
αἰῶνας n. acc. masc. pl. αἰών ever, ever and ever, evermore, age, eternal, world
τῶν art. gen. masc. pl. ὁ ἡ τό the, this, that, he, she, it
αἰώνων n. gen. masc. pl. αἰών ever, ever and ever, evermore, age, eternal, world
8 καὶ conj. καί and, even, also, but
ὁ art. nom. masc. sg. ὁ ἡ τό the, this, that, he, she, it
ναὸς n. nom. masc. sg. ναός temple, shrine
καπνοῦ n. gen. masc. sg. καπνός smoke
ἐκ prep. ἐκ ἐξ (+gen) of, from, out of, by, on, with, in, among, through
τῆς art. gen. fem. sg. ὁ ἡ τό the, this, that, he, she, it
δόξης n. gen. fem. sg. δόξα glory, honour, praise, dignity, worship
τοῦ art. gen. masc. sg. ὁ ἡ τό the, this, that, he, she, it
Θεοῦ n. gen. masc. sg. θεός God, god
καὶ conj. καί and, even, also, but
ἐκ prep. ἐκ ἐξ (+gen) of, from, out of, by, on, with, in, among, through
τῆς art. gen. fem. sg. ὁ ἡ τό the, this, that, he, she, it

δυνάμεως n. gen. fem. sg. δύναμις power, mighty work, miracle, strength, might
αὐτοῦ pron. gen. masc. 3p. sg. αὐτός ή ό self, of oneself, even, very, the same, he, she, it
καὶ conj. καί and, even, also, but
οὐδεὶς num. nom. masc. sg. οὐδείς no man, nothing, no, none, neither, not, nought
εἰς prep. εἰς (+acc) into, to, unto, for, in, on, toward, against, upon, at, among
τὸν art. acc. masc. sg. ὁ ἡ τό the, this, that, he, she, it
ναὸν n. acc. masc. sg. ναός temple, shrine
ἄχρι prep. ἄχρι or ἄχρις (+gen) until, unto, till, even to, as far as, while, into
αἱ art. nom. fem. pl. ὁ ἡ τό the, this, that, he, she, it
ἑπτὰ num. nom. fem. pl. ἑπτά seven, seventh
πληγαὶ n. nom. fem. pl. πληγή wound, plague, stripe
τῶν art. gen. masc. pl. ὁ ἡ τό the, this, that, he, she, it
ἑπτὰ num. gen. masc. pl. ἑπτά seven, seventh
ἀγγέλων n. gen. masc. pl. ἄγγελος angel, messenger

16

1 Καὶ conj. καί and, even, also, but
φωνῆς n. gen. fem. sg. φωνή voice, sound, noise
μεγάλης adj. gen. fem. sg. μέγας great, loud, greatest, high, large, mighty, strong
ἐκ prep. ἐκ ἐξ (+gen) of, from, out of, by, on, with, in, among, through
τοῦ art. gen. masc. sg. ὁ ἡ τό the, this, that, he, she, it
ναοῦ n. gen. masc. sg. ναός temple, shrine
τοῖς art. dat. masc. pl. ὁ ἡ τό the, this, that, he, she, it
ἑπτὰ num. dat. masc. pl. ἑπτά seven, seventh
ἀγγέλοις n. dat. masc. pl. ἄγγελος angel, messenger
καὶ conj. καί and, even, also, but
τὰς art. acc. fem. pl. ὁ ἡ τό the, this, that, he, she, it
φιάλας n. acc. fem. pl. φιάλη vial
τοῦ art. gen. masc. sg. ὁ ἡ τό the, this, that, he, she, it
θυμοῦ n. gen. masc. sg. θυμός wrath, fierceness, indignation
τοῦ art. gen. masc. sg. ὁ ἡ τό the, this, that, he, she, it
Θεοῦ n. gen. masc. sg. θεός God, god
εἰς prep. εἰς (+acc) into, to, unto, for, in, on, toward, against, upon, at, among
τὴν art. acc. fem. sg. ὁ ἡ τό the, this, that, he, she, it
γῆν n. acc. fem. sg. γῆ earth, land, ground, country
2 Καὶ conj. καί and, even, also, but
ὁ art. nom. masc. sg. ὁ ἡ τό the, this, that, he, she, it
πρῶτος ordinal. adj. nom. masc. sg. πρῶτος first, chief, first of all, chiefest, best
καὶ conj. καί and, even, also, but
τὴν art. acc. fem. sg. ὁ ὁ ἡ τό the, this, that, he, she, it
φιάλην n. acc. fem. sg. φιάλη vial
αὐτοῦ pron. gen. masc. 3p. sg. αὐτός ή ό self, of oneself, even, very, the same, he, she, it
ἐπὶ prep. ἐπί (+gen) on, in, upon, (+dat) in, at, for, upon, (+acc) on, upon, unto, to, against
τὴν art. acc. fem. sg. ὁ ὁ ἡ τό the, this, that, he, she, it
γῆν n. acc. fem. sg. γῆ earth, land, ground, country
καὶ conj. καί and, even, also, but
ἕλκος n. nom. neut. sg. ἕλκος sore
κακὸν adj. nom. neut. sg. κακός evil, evil thing, noisome, wicked
καὶ conj. καί and, even, also, but
πονηρὸν adj. nom. neut. sg. πονηρός evil, wicked, bad
εἰς prep. εἰς (+acc) into, to, unto, for, in, on, toward, against, upon, at, among
τοὺς art. acc. masc. pl. ὁ ἡ τό the, this, that, he, she, it
ἀνθρώπους n. acc. masc. pl. ἄνθρωπος man, human being, person, one, certain
τοὺς art. acc. masc. pl. ὁ ἡ τό the, this, that, he, she, it

τὸ art. acc. neut. sg. ὁ ἡ τό the, this, that, he, she, it
χάραγμα n. acc. neut. sg. χάραγμα mark, graven
τοῦ art. gen. neut. sg. ὁ ἡ τό the, this, that, he, she, it
θηρίου n. gen. neut. sg. θηρίον beast, wild beast, venomous beast
καὶ conj. καί and, even, also, but
τοὺς art. acc. masc. pl. ὁ ἡ τό the, this, that, he, she, it
τῇ art. dat. fem. sg. ὁ ἡ τό the, this, that, he, she, it
εἰκόνι n. dat. fem. sg. εἰκών image
αὐτοῦ pron. gen. masc. 3p. sg. αὐτός ἡ ὁ self, of oneself, even, very, the same, he, she, it
3 Καὶ conj. καί and, even, also, but
ὁ art. nom. masc. sg. ὁ ἡ τό the, this, that, he, she, it
δεύτερος ordinal. adj. nom. masc. sg. δεύτερος second, second time, again, afterward
ἄγγελος n. nom. masc. sg. ἄγγελος angel, messenger
τὴν art. acc. fem. sg. ὁ ἡ τό the, this, that, he, she, it
φιάλην n. acc. fem. sg. φιάλη vial
αὐτοῦ pron. gen. masc. 3p. sg. αὐτός ἡ ὁ self, of oneself, even, very, the same, he, she, it
εἰς prep. εἰς (+acc) into, to, unto, for, in, on, toward, against, upon, at, among
τὴν art. acc. fem. sg. ὁ ἡ τό the, this, that, he, she, it
θάλασσαν n. acc. fem. sg. θάλασσα sea
καὶ conj. καί and, even, also, but
αἷμα n. nom. neut. sg. αἷμα blood
ὡς adv. ὡς as, when, as it were, how, about, like, as soon as, even as, while
νεκροῦ adj. gen. masc. sg. νεκρός dead
καὶ conj. καί and, even, also, but
πᾶσα adj. nom. fem. sg. πᾶς πᾶσα πᾶν all, every, whosoever, every one, no, whole, any
ψυχὴ n. nom. fem. sg. ψυχή life, soul, mind, heart
ἐν prep. ἐν (+dat) in, by, with, among, at, on, through, to, within, into, of, for
τῇ art. dat. fem. sg. ὁ ἡ τό the, this, that, he, she, it
θαλάσσῃ n. dat. fem. sg. θάλασσα sea
4 Καὶ conj. καί and, even, also, but
ὁ art. nom. masc. sg. ὁ ἡ τό the, this, that, he, she, it
τρίτος ordinal. adj. nom. masc. sg. τρίτος third
ἄγγελος n. nom. masc. sg. ἄγγελος angel, messenger
τὴν art. acc. fem. sg. ὁ ἡ τό the, this, that, he, she, it
φιάλην n. acc. fem. sg. φιάλη vial
αὐτοῦ pron. gen. masc. 3p. sg. αὐτός ἡ ὁ self, of oneself, even, very, the same, he, she, it
εἰς prep. εἰς (+acc) into, to, unto, for, in, on, toward, against, upon, at, among
τοὺς art. acc. masc. pl. ὁ ἡ τό the, this, that, he, she, it
ποταμοὺς n. acc. masc. pl. ποταμός river, flood , stream, water
καὶ conj. καί and, even, also, but
εἰς prep. εἰς (+acc) into, to, unto, for, in, on, toward, against, upon, at, among
τὰς art. acc. fem. pl. ὁ ἡ τό the, this, that, he, she, it
πηγὰς n. acc. fem. pl. πηγή fountain, well
τῶν art. gen. neut. pl. ὁ ἡ τό the, this, that, he, she, it
ὑδάτων n. gen. neut. pl. ὕδωρ water
αἷμα n. nom. neut. sg. αἷμα blood
καὶ conj. καί and, even, also, but
5 καὶ conj. καί and, even, also, but
τοῦ art. gen. masc. sg. ὁ ἡ τό the, this, that, he, she, it
ἀγγέλου n. gen. masc. sg. ἄγγελος angel, messenger
τῶν art. gen. neut. pl. ὁ ἡ τό the, this, that, he, she, it
ὑδάτων n. gen. neut. pl. ὕδωρ water
Δίκαιος adj. nom. masc. sg. δίκαιος righteous, just, meet, right
Κύριε n. voc. masc. sg. κύριος Lord, lord, master, sir, LORD, God, Master, owner
ὁ art. nom. masc. sg. ὁ ἡ τό the, this, that, he, she, it

καὶ conj. καί and, even, also, but
ὁ art. nom. masc. sg. ὁ ἡ τό the, this, that, he, she, it
καὶ conj. καί and, even, also, but
ὁ art. nom. masc. sg. ὁ ἡ τό the, this, that, he, she, it
ὅτι conj. ὅτι that, for, because, how that, how, because that, for that, though
ταῦτα demo. pron. acc. neut. pl. οὗτος αὕτη τοῦτο this, the same, this same, he, she, it
6 ὅτι conj. ὅτι that, for, because, how that, how, because that, for that, though
αἷμα n. acc. neut. sg. αἷμα blood
ἁγίων adj. gen. masc. pl. ἅγιος Holy, holy, saint, Holy One, holy thing, most holy
καὶ conj. καί and, even, also, but
προφητῶν n. gen. masc. pl. προφήτης prophet
καὶ conj. καί and, even, also, but
αἷμα n. acc. neut. sg. αἷμα blood
αὐτοῖς pron. dat. masc. 3p. pl. αὐτός ή ό self, of oneself, even, very, the same, he, she, it
ἄξιοί adj. nom. masc. pl. ἄξιος worthy, meet, due reward
γάρ conj. γάρ for, and, because, but, indeed
7 καὶ conj. καί and, even, also, but
ἄλλου adj. gen. masc. sg. ἄλλος other, another, some, one, more, otherwise
ἐκ prep. ἐκ ἐξ (+gen) of, from, out of, by, on, with, in, among, through
τοῦ art. gen. neut. sg. ὁ ἡ τό the, this, that, he, she, it
θυσιαστηρίου n. gen. neut. sg. θυσιαστήριον altar
Ναὶ particle. ναί yea, even so, yes, surely, truth, verily
Κύριε n. voc. masc. sg. κύριος Lord, lord, master, sir, LORD, God, Master, owner
ὁ art. nom. masc. sg. ὁ ἡ τό the, this, that, he, she, it
Θεὸς n. nom. masc. sg. θεός God, god
ὁ art. nom. masc. sg. ὁ ἡ τό the, this, that, he, she, it
παντοκράτωρ n. nom. masc. sg. παντοκράτωρ Almighty, omnipotent
ἀληθιναὶ adj. nom. fem. pl. ἀληθινός true
καὶ conj. καί and, even, also, but
δίκαιαι adj. nom. fem. pl. δίκαιος righteous, just, meet, right
αἱ art. nom. fem. pl. ὁ ἡ τό the, this, that, he, she, it
κρίσεις n. nom. fem. pl. κρίσις judgment, damnation, accusation, condemnation
σου pron. gen. 2p. sg. σύ thou, you
8 Καὶ conj. καί and, even, also, but
ὁ art. nom. masc. sg. ὁ ἡ τό the, this, that, he, she, it
τέταρτος ordinal. adj. nom. masc. sg. τέταρτος fourth, four
ἄγγελος n. nom. masc. sg. ἄγγελος angel, messenger
τὴν art. acc. fem. sg. ὁ ἡ τό the, this, that, he, she, it
φιάλην n. acc. fem. sg. φιάλη vial
αὐτοῦ pron. gen. masc. 3p. sg. αὐτός ή ό self, of oneself, even, very, the same, he, she, it
ἐπὶ prep. ἐπί (+gen) on, in, upon, (+dat) in, at, for, upon, (+acc) on, upon, unto, to, against
τὸν art. acc. masc. sg. ὁ ἡ τό the, this, that, he, she, it
ἥλιον n. acc. masc. sg. ἥλιος sun, east
καὶ conj. καί and, even, also, but
αὐτῷ pron. dat. masc. 3p. sg. αὐτός ή ό self, of oneself, even, very, the same, he, she, it
τοὺς art. acc. masc. pl. ὁ ἡ τό the, this, that, he, she, it
ἀνθρώπους n. acc. masc. pl. ἄνθρωπος man, human being, person, one, certain
ἐν prep. ἐν (+dat) in, by, with, among, at, on, through, to, within, into, of, for
πυρί n. dat. neut. sg. πῦρ fire, fiery
9 καὶ conj. καί and, even, also, but
οἱ art. nom. masc. pl. ὁ ἡ τό the, this, that, he, she, it
ἄνθρωποι n. nom. masc. pl. ἄνθρωπος man, human being, person, one, certain
καῦμα n. acc. neut. sg. καῦμα heat
μέγα adj. acc. neut. sg. μέγας great, loud, greatest, high, large, mighty, strong
καὶ conj. καί and, even, also, but

τὸ art. acc. neut. sg. ὁ ἡ τό the, this, that, he, she, it
ὄνομα n. acc. neut. sg. ὄνομα name, call, surname
τοῦ art. gen. masc. sg. ὁ ἡ τό the, this, that, he, she, it
Θεοῦ n. gen. masc. sg. θεός God, god
τοῦ art. gen. masc. sg. ὁ ἡ τό the, this, that, he, she, it
ἐξουσίαν n. acc. fem. sg. ἐξουσία power, authority, right, strength, jurisdiction
ἐπὶ prep. ἐπί (+gen) on, in, upon, (+dat) in, at, for, upon, (+acc) on, upon, unto, to, against
τὰς art. acc. fem. pl. ὁ ἡ τό the, this, that, he, she, it
πληγὰς n. acc. fem. pl. πληγή wound, plague, stripe
ταύτας demo. pron. acc. fem. pl. οὗτος αὕτη τοῦτο this, the same, this same, he, she, it
καὶ conj. καί and, even, also, but
οὐ particle of negation. οὐ οὐκ οὐχ not, no, neither, none, nay, nor, never, nothing
αὐτῷ pron. dat. masc. 3p. sg. αὐτός ή ό self, of oneself, even, very, the same, he, she, it
δόξαν n. acc. fem. sg. δόξα glory, honour, praise, dignity, worship
10 Καὶ conj. καί and, even, also, but
ὁ art. nom. masc. sg. ὁ ἡ τό the, this, that, he, she, it
πέμπτος ordinal. adj. nom. masc. sg. πέμπτος fifth
ἄγγελος n. nom. masc. sg. ἄγγελος angel, messenger
τὴν art. acc. fem. sg. ὁ ἡ τό the, this, that, he, she, it
φιάλην n. acc. fem. sg. φιάλη vial
αὐτοῦ pron. gen. masc. 3p. sg. αὐτός ή ό self, of oneself, even, very, the same, he, she, it
ἐπὶ prep. ἐπί (+gen) on, in, upon, (+dat) in, at, for, upon, (+acc) on, upon, unto, to, against
τὸν art. acc. masc. sg. ὁ ἡ τό the, this, that, he, she, it
θρόνον n. acc. masc. sg. θρόνος throne, seat
τοῦ art. gen. neut. sg. ὁ ἡ τό the, this, that, he, she, it
θηρίου n. gen. neut. sg. θηρίον beast, wild beast, venomous beast
καὶ conj. καί and, even, also, but
ἡ art. nom. fem. sg. ὁ ἡ τό the, this, that, he, she, it
βασιλεία n. nom. fem. sg. βασιλεία kingdom, reign
αὐτοῦ pron. gen. neut. 3p. sg. αὐτός ή ό self, of oneself, even, very, the same, he, she, it
καὶ conj. καί and, even, also, but
τὰς art. acc. fem. pl. ὁ ἡ τό the, this, that, he, she, it
γλώσσας n. acc. fem. pl. γλῶσσα tongue
αὐτῶν pron. gen. masc. 3p. pl. αὐτός ή ό self, of oneself, even, very, the same, he, she, it
ἐκ prep. ἐκ ἐξ (+gen) of, from, out of, by, on, with, in, among, through
τοῦ art. gen. masc. sg. ὁ ἡ τό the, this, that, he, she, it
πόνου n. gen. masc. sg. πόνος pain
11 καὶ conj. καί and, even, also, but
τὸν art. acc. masc. sg. ὁ ἡ τό the, this, that, he, she, it
Θεὸν n. acc. masc. sg. θεός God, god
τοῦ art. gen. masc. sg. ὁ ἡ τό the, this, that, he, she, it
οὐρανοῦ n. gen. masc. sg. οὐρανός heaven, air, sky
ἐκ prep. ἐκ ἐξ (+gen) of, from, out of, by, on, with, in, among, through
τῶν art. gen. masc. pl. ὁ ἡ τό the, this, that, he, she, it
πόνων n. gen. masc. pl. πόνος pain
αὐτῶν pron. gen. masc. 3p. pl. αὐτός ή ό self, of oneself, even, very, the same, he, she, it
καὶ conj. καί and, even, also, but
ἐκ prep. ἐκ ἐξ (+gen) of, from, out of, by, on, with, in, among, through
τῶν art. gen. neut. pl. ὁ ἡ τό the, this, that, he, she, it
ἑλκῶν n. gen. neut. pl. ἕλκος sore
αὐτῶν pron. gen. masc. 3p. pl. αὐτός ή ό self, of oneself, even, very, the same, he, she, it
καὶ conj. καί and, even, also, but
οὐ particle of negation. οὐ οὐκ οὐχ not, no, neither, none, nay, nor, never, nothing
ἐκ prep. ἐκ ἐξ (+gen) of, from, out of, by, on, with, in, among, through
τῶν art. gen. neut. pl. ὁ ἡ τό the, this, that, he, she, it

ἔργων n. gen. neut. pl. ἔργον work, deed, doing labour
αὐτῶν pron. gen. masc. 3p. pl. αὐτός ή ό self, of oneself, even, very, the same, he, she, it
12 Καὶ conj. καί and, even, also, but
ὁ art. nom. masc. sg. ὁ ἡ τό the, this, that, he, she, it
ἕκτος ordinal. adj. nom. masc. sg. ἕκτος sixth
ἄγγελος n. nom. masc. sg. ἄγγελος angel, messenger
τὴν art. acc. fem. sg. ὁ ἡ τό the, this, that, he, she, it
φιάλην n. acc. fem. sg. φιάλη vial
αὐτοῦ pron. gen. masc. 3p. sg. αὐτός ή ό self, of oneself, even, very, the same, he, she, it
ἐπὶ prep. ἐπί (+gen) on, in, upon, (+dat) in, at, for, upon, (+acc) on, upon, unto, to, against
τὸν art. acc. masc. sg. ὁ ἡ τό the, this, that, he, she, it
ποταμὸν n. acc. masc. sg. ποταμός river, flood , stream, water
τὸν art. acc. masc. sg. ὁ ἡ τό the, this, that, he, she, it
μέγαν adj. acc. masc. sg. μέγας great, loud, greatest, high, large, mighty, strong
τὸν art. acc. masc. sg. ὁ ἡ τό the, this, that, he, she, it
Εὐφράτην n. acc. masc. sg. Εὐφράτης Euphrates
καὶ conj. καί and, even, also, but
τὸ art. nom. neut. sg. ὁ ἡ τό the, this, that, he, she, it
ὕδωρ n. nom. neut. sg. ὕδωρ water
αὐτοῦ pron. gen. masc. 3p. sg. αὐτός ή ό self, of oneself, even, very, the same, he, she, it
ἵνα conj. ἵνα that, to, lest, for to, so that, albeit, because, for, so as
ἡ art. nom. fem. sg. ὁ ἡ τό the, this, that, he, she, it
ὁδὸς n. nom. fem. sg. ὁδός way, journey, highway
τῶν art. gen. masc. pl. ὁ ἡ τό the, this, that, he, she, it
βασιλέων n. gen. masc. pl. βασιλεύς king
τῶν art. gen. masc. pl. ὁ ἡ τό the, this, that, he, she, it
ἀπὸ prep. ἀπό (+gen) from, of, out of, since, for, off, at, by, in, on
ἀνατολῶν n. gen. fem. pl. ἀνατολή east, rising of the sun, dayspring
ἡλίου n. gen. masc. sg. ἥλιος sun, east
13 καὶ conj. καί and, even, also, but
ἐκ prep. ἐκ ἐξ (+gen) of, from, out of, by, on, with, in, among, through
τοῦ art. gen. neut. sg. ὁ ἡ τό the, this, that, he, she, it
στόματος n. gen. neut. sg. στόμα mouth, face, edge
τοῦ art. gen. masc. sg. ὁ ἡ τό the, this, that, he, she, it
δράκοντος n. gen. masc. sg. δράκων dragon
καὶ conj. καί and, even, also, but
ἐκ prep. ἐκ ἐξ (+gen) of, from, out of, by, on, with, in, among, through
τοῦ art. gen. neut. sg. ὁ ἡ τό the, this, that, he, she, it
στόματος n. gen. neut. sg. στόμα mouth, face, edge
τοῦ art. gen. masc. sg. ὁ ἡ τό the, this, that, he, she, it
θηρίου n. gen. neut. sg. θηρίον beast, wild beast, venomous beast
καὶ conj. καί and, even, also, but
ἐκ prep. ἐκ ἐξ (+gen) of, from, out of, by, on, with, in, among, through
τοῦ art. gen. neut. sg. ὁ ἡ τό the, this, that, he, she, it
στόματος n. gen. neut. sg. στόμα mouth, face, edge
τοῦ art. gen. masc. sg. ὁ ἡ τό the, this, that, he, she, it
ψευδοπροφήτου n. gen. masc. sg. ψευδοπροφήτης false prophet
πνεύματα n. acc. neut. pl. πνεῦμα spirit, Spirit, Ghost, ghost, life. of the spirit, wind
τρία num. acc. neut. pl. τρεῖς three
ἀκάθαρτα adj. acc. neut. pl. ἀκάθαρτος unclean, foul
ὅμοια adj. acc. neut. pl. ὅμοιος like
βατράχοις n. dat. masc. pl. βάτραχος frog
14 γὰρ conj. γάρ for, and, because, but, indeed
πνεύματα n. nom. neut. pl. πνεῦμα spirit, Spirit, Ghost, ghost, life. of the spirit, wind
δαιμόνων n. gen. masc. pl. δαίμων devil, demon

σημεῖα n. acc. neut. pl. σημεῖον sign, miracle, wonder, token
ἃ relative pron. nom. neut. pl. ὅς ἥ ὅ who, which, what, that
ἐπὶ prep. ἐπί (+gen) on, in, upon, (+dat) in, at, for, upon, (+acc) on, upon, unto, to, against
τοὺς art. acc. masc. pl. ὁ ἡ τό the, this, that, he, she, it
βασιλεῖς n. acc. masc. pl. βασιλεύς king
τῆς art. gen. fem. sg. ὁ ἡ τό the, this, that, he, she, it
γῆς n. gen. fem. sg. γῆ earth, land, ground, country
καὶ conj. καί and, even, also, but
τῆς art. gen. fem. sg. ὁ ἡ τό the, this, that, he, she, it
οἰκουμένης n. gen. fem. sg. οἰκουμένη world, earth
ὅλης adj. gen. fem. sg. ὅλος all, whole, every whit, altogether
αὐτοὺς pron. acc. masc. 3p. pl. αὐτός ή ό self, of oneself, even, very, the same, he, she, it
εἰς prep. εἰς (+acc) into, to, unto, for, in, on, toward, against, upon, at, among
τὸν art. acc. masc. sg. ὁ ἡ τό the, this, that, he, she, it
πόλεμον n. acc. masc. sg. πόλεμος war, battle, fight
τῆς art. gen. fem. sg. ὁ ἡ τό the, this, that, he, she, it
ἡμέρας n. gen. fem. sg. ἡμέρα day, time, year, while, age, day time
ἐκείνης demo. pron. gen. fem. sg. ἐκεῖνος that, he, the same, that same
τῆς art. gen. fem. sg. ὁ ἡ τό the, this, that, he, she, it
μεγάλης adj. gen. fem. sg. μέγας great, loud, greatest, high, large, mighty, strong
τοῦ art. gen. masc. sg. ὁ ἡ τό the, this, that, he, she, it
Θεοῦ n. gen. masc. sg. θεός God, god
τοῦ art. gen. masc. sg. ὁ ἡ τό the, this, that, he, she, it
παντοκράτορος n. gen. masc. sg. παντοκράτωρ Almighty, omnipotent
15 ὡς adv. ὡς as, when, as it were, how, about, like, as soon as, even as, while
κλέπτης n. nom. masc. sg. κλέπτης thief
μακάριος adj. nom. masc. sg. μακάριος blessed, happy
ὁ art. nom. masc. sg. ὁ ἡ τό the, this, that, he, she, it
καὶ conj. καί and, even, also, but
τὰ art. acc. neut. pl. ὁ ἡ τό the, this, that, he, she, it
ἱμάτια n. acc. neut. pl. ἱμάτιον cloke, garment, clothes, raiment, robe, vesture
αὐτοῦ pron. gen. masc. 3p. sg. αὐτός ή ό self, of oneself, even, very, the same, he, she, it
ἵνα conj. ἵνα that, to, lest, for to, so that, albeit, because, for, so as
μὴ particle of negation. μή not, no, lest, neither, none, nothing, nor, never, without
γυμνὸς adj. nom. masc. sg. γυμνός naked, bare
καὶ conj. καί and, even, also, but
τὴν art. acc. fem. sg. ὁ ἡ τό the, this, that, he, she, it
ἀσχημοσύνην n. acc. fem. sg. ἀσχημοσύνη that which is unseemly, shame
αὐτοῦ pron. gen. masc. 3p. sg. αὐτός ή ό self, of oneself, even, very, the same, he, she, it
16 καὶ conj. καί and, even, also, but
αὐτοὺς pron. acc. masc. 3p. pl. αὐτός ή ό self, of oneself, even, very, the same, he, she, it
εἰς prep. εἰς (+acc) into, to, unto, for, in, on, toward, against, upon, at, among
τὸν art. acc. masc. sg. ὁ ἡ τό the, this, that, he, she, it
τόπον n. acc. masc. sg. τόπος place, room, quarter
τὸν art. acc. masc. sg. ὁ ἡ τό the, this, that, he, she, it
Ἑβραϊστὶ adv. Ἑβραϊστί in the Hebrew
Ἀρμαγεδδών n. nom. neut. sg. Ἀρμαγεδδών Armageddon
17 Καὶ conj. καί and, even, also, but
ὁ art. nom. masc. sg. ὁ ἡ τό the, this, that, he, she, it
ἕβδομος ordinal. adj. nom. masc. sg. ἕβδομος seventh
ἄγγελος n. nom. masc. sg. ἄγγελος angel, messenger
τὴν art. acc. fem. sg. ὁ ἡ τό the, this, that, he, she, it
φιάλην n. acc. fem. sg. φιάλη vial
αὐτοῦ pron. gen. masc. 3p. sg. αὐτός ή ό self, of oneself, even, very, the same, he, she, it
εἰς prep. εἰς (+acc) into, to, unto, for, in, on, toward, against, upon, at, among

τὸν art. acc. masc. sg. ὁ ἡ τό the, this, that, he, she, it
ἀέρα n. acc. masc. sg. ἀήρ air
καὶ conj. καί and, even, also, but
φωνὴ n. nom. fem. sg. φωνή voice, sound, noise
μεγάλη adj. nom. fem. sg. μέγας great, loud, greatest, high, large, mighty, strong
ἀπὸ prep. ἀπό (+gen) from, of, out of, since, for, off, at, by, in, on
τοῦ art. gen. masc. sg. ὁ ἡ τό the, this, that, he, she, it
ναοῦ n. gen. masc. sg. ναός temple, shrine
τοῦ art. gen. masc. sg. ὁ ἡ τό the, this, that, he, she, it
οὐρανοῦ n. gen. masc. sg. οὐρανός heaven, air, sky
ἀπὸ prep. ἀπό (+gen) from, of, out of, since, for, off, at, by, in, on
τοῦ art. gen. masc. sg. ὁ ἡ τό the, this, that, he, she, it
θρόνου n. gen. masc. sg. θρόνος throne, seat
18 καὶ conj. καί and, even, also, but
φωναὶ n. nom. fem. pl. φωνή voice, sound, noise
καὶ conj. καί and, even, also, but
βρονταὶ n. nom. fem. pl. βροντή thunder, thundering
καὶ conj. καί and, even, also, but
ἀστραπαὶ n. nom. fem. pl. ἀστραπή lightning, bright shining
καὶ conj. καί and, even, also, but
σεισμὸς n. nom. masc. sg. σεισμός earthquake, tempest
μέγας adj. nom. masc. sg. μέγας great, loud, greatest, high, large, mighty, strong
οἷος relative pron. nom. masc. sg. οἷος what manner of, such as, as, which, what, so as
οὐκ particle of negation. οὐ οὐκ οὐχ not, no, neither, none, nay, nor, never, nothing
ἀφ' prep. ἀπό (+gen) from, of, out of, since, for, off, at, by, in, on
οὗ relative pron. gen. masc. sg. ὅς ἥ ὅ who, which, what, that
οἱ art. nom. masc. pl. ὁ ἡ τό the, this, that, he, she, it
ἄνθρωποι n. nom. masc. pl. ἄνθρωπος man, human being, person, one, certain
ἐπὶ prep. ἐπί (+gen) on, in, upon, (+dat) in, at, for, upon, (+acc) on, upon, unto, to, against
τῆς art. gen. fem. sg. ὁ ἡ τό the, this, that, he, she, it
γῆς n. gen. fem. sg. γῆ earth, land, ground, country
τηλικοῦτος demo. pron. nom. masc. sg. τηλικοῦτος so great, so mighty
σεισμὸς n. nom. masc. sg. σεισμός earthquake, tempest
οὕτω adv. οὕτω οὕτως so, even so, thus, on this wise, likewise, after this manner
μέγας adj. nom. masc. sg. μέγας great, loud, greatest, high, large, mighty, strong
19 καὶ conj. καί and, even, also, but
ἡ art. nom. fem. sg. ὁ ἡ τό the, this, that, he, she, it
πόλις n. nom. fem. sg. πόλις city
ἡ art. nom. fem. sg. ὁ ἡ τό the, this, that, he, she, it
μεγάλη adj. nom. fem. sg. μέγας great, loud, greatest, high, large, mighty, strong
εἰς prep. εἰς (+acc) into, to, unto, for, in, on, toward, against, upon, at, among
τρία num. acc. neut. pl. τρεῖς three
μέρη n. acc. neut. pl. μέρος part, coast, portion, behalf, respect, piece, side
καὶ conj. καί and, even, also, but
αἱ art. nom. fem. pl. ὁ ἡ τό the, this, that, he, she, it
πόλεις n. nom. fem. pl. πόλις city
τῶν art. gen. neut. pl. ὁ ἡ τό the, this, that, he, she, it
ἐθνῶν n. gen. neut. pl. ἔθνος Gentile, nation, heathen, people
καὶ conj. καί and, even, also, but
Βαβυλὼν n. nom. fem. sg. Βαβυλών Babylon
ἡ art. nom. fem. sg. ὁ ἡ τό the, this, that, he, she, it
μεγάλη adj. nom. fem. sg. μέγας great, loud, greatest, high, large, mighty, strong
ἐνώπιον prep. ἐνώπιον (+gen) before, in the sight of, in the presence of. (adv.) before
τοῦ art. gen. masc. sg. ὁ ἡ τό the, this, that, he, she, it
Θεοῦ n. gen. masc. sg. θεός God, god

αὐτῇ pron. dat. fem. 3p. sg. αὐτός ή ό self, of oneself, even, very, the same, he, she, it
τὸ art. acc. neut. sg. ὁ ἡ τό the, this, that, he, she, it
ποτήριον n. acc. neut. sg. ποτήριον cup
τοῦ art. gen. masc. sg. ὁ ἡ τό the, this, that, he, she, it
οἴνου n. gen. masc. sg. οἶνος wine
τοῦ art. gen. masc. sg. ὁ ἡ τό the, this, that, he, she, it
θυμοῦ n. gen. masc. sg. θυμός wrath, fierceness, indignation
τῆς art. gen. fem. sg. ὁ ἡ τό the, this, that, he, she, it
ὀργῆς n. gen. fem. sg. ὀργή wrath, anger, indignation, vengeance
αὐτοῦ pron. gen. masc. 3p. sg. αὐτός ή ό self, of oneself, even, very, the same, he, she, it
20 καὶ conj. καί and, even, also, but
πᾶσα adj. nom. fem. sg. πᾶς πᾶσα πᾶν all, every, whosoever, every one, no, whole, any
νῆσος n. nom. fem. sg. νῆσος isle, island
καὶ conj. καί and, even, also, but
ὄρη n. nom. neut. pl. ὄρος mountain, mount, hill
οὐχ particle of negation. οὐ οὐκ οὐχ not, no, neither, none, nay, nor, never, nothing
21 καὶ conj. καί and, even, also, but
χάλαζα n. nom. fem. sg. χάλαζα hail
μεγάλη adj. nom. fem. sg. μέγας great, loud, greatest, high, large, mighty, strong
ὡς adv. ὡς as, when, as it were, how, about, like, as soon as, even as, while
ταλαντιαία adj. nom. fem. sg. ταλαντιαῖος
ἐκ prep. ἐκ ἐξ (+gen) of, from, out of, by, on, with, in, among, through
τοῦ art. gen. masc. sg. ὁ ἡ τό the, this, that, he, she, it
οὐρανοῦ n. gen. masc. sg. οὐρανός heaven, air, sky
ἐπὶ prep. ἐπί (+gen) on, in, upon, (+dat) in, at, for, upon, (+acc) on, upon, unto, to, against
τοὺς art. acc. masc. pl. ὁ ἡ τό the, this, that, he, she, it
ἀνθρώπους n. acc. masc. pl. ἄνθρωπος man, human being, person, one, certain
καὶ conj. καί and, even, also, but
οἱ art. nom. masc. pl. ὁ ἡ τό the, this, that, he, she, it
ἄνθρωποι n. nom. masc. pl. ἄνθρωπος man, human being, person, one, certain
τὸν art. acc. masc. sg. ὁ ἡ τό the, this, that, he, she, it
Θεὸν n. acc. masc. sg. θεός God, god
ἐκ prep. ἐκ ἐξ (+gen) of, from, out of, by, on, with, in, among, through
τῆς art. gen. fem. sg. ὁ ἡ τό the, this, that, he, she, it
πληγῆς n. gen. fem. sg. πληγή wound, plague, stripe
τῆς art. gen. fem. sg. ὁ ἡ τό the, this, that, he, she, it
χαλάζης n. gen. fem. sg. χάλαζα hail
ὅτι conj. ὅτι that, for, because, how that, how, because that, for that, though
μεγάλη adj. nom. fem. sg. μέγας great, loud, greatest, high, large, mighty, strong
ἡ art. nom. fem. sg. ὁ ἡ τό the, this, that, he, she, it
πληγὴ n. nom. fem. sg. πληγή wound, plague, stripe
αὐτῆς pron. gen. fem. 3p. sg. αὐτός ή ό self, of oneself, even, very, the same, he, she, it
σφόδρα adv. σφόδρα exceeding, very, greatly, exceedingly, sore

17

1 Καὶ conj. καί and, even, also, but
εἷς num. nom. masc. sg. εἷς or ἕν one, other, some, any, only, a certain
ἐκ prep. ἐκ ἐξ (+gen) of, from, out of, by, on, with, in, among, through
τῶν art. gen. masc. pl. ὁ ἡ τό the, this, that, he, she, it
ἑπτὰ num. gen. masc. pl. ἑπτά seven, seventh
ἀγγέλων n. gen. masc. pl. ἄγγελος angel, messenger
τῶν art. gen. masc. pl. ὁ ἡ τό the, this, that, he, she, it
τὰς art. acc. fem. pl. ὁ ἡ τό the, this, that, he, she, it
ἑπτὰ num. acc. fem. pl. ἑπτά seven, seventh

φιάλας n. acc. fem. pl. φιάλη vial
καὶ conj. καί and, even, also, but
μετ’ prep. μετά (+gen) with, among, against, (+acc) after
ἐμοῦ pron. gen. 1p. sg. ἐγώ I
μοι pron. dat. 1p. sg. ἐγώ I
σοι pron. dat. 2p. sg. σύ thou, you
τὸ art. acc. neut. sg. ὁ ἡ τό the, this, that, he, she, it
κρίμα n. acc. neut. sg. κρίμα judgment, damnation, condemnation
τῆς art. gen. fem. sg. ὁ ἡ τό the, this, that, he, she, it
πόρνης n. gen. fem. sg. πόρνη harlot, whore
τῆς art. gen. fem. sg. ὁ ἡ τό the, this, that, he, she, it
μεγάλης adj. gen. fem. sg. μέγας great, loud, greatest, high, large, mighty, strong
τῆς art. gen. fem. sg. ὁ ἡ τό the, this, that, he, she, it
ἐπὶ prep. ἐπί (+gen) on, in, upon, (+dat) in, at, for, upon, (+acc) on, upon, unto, to, against
τῶν art. gen. neut. pl. ὁ ἡ τό the, this, that, he, she, it
ὑδάτων n. gen. neut. pl. ὕδωρ water
τῶν art. gen. neut. pl. ὁ ἡ τό the, this, that, he, she, it
πολλῶν adj. gen. neut. pl. πολύς many, great, much, long, abundant
2 μεθ’ prep. μετά (+gen) with, among, against, (+acc) after
ἧς relative pron. gen. fem. sg. ὅς ἥ ὅ who, which, what, that
οἱ art. nom. masc. pl. ὁ ἡ τό the, this, that, he, she, it
βασιλεῖς n. nom. masc. pl. βασιλεύς king
τῆς art. gen. fem. sg. ὁ ἡ τό the, this, that, he, she, it
γῆς n. gen. fem. sg. γῆ earth, land, ground, country
καὶ conj. καί and, even, also, but
ἐκ prep. ἐκ ἐξ (+gen) of, from, out of, by, on, with, in, among, through
τοῦ art. gen. masc. sg. ὁ ἡ τό the, this, that, he, she, it
οἴνου n. gen. masc. sg. οἶνος wine
γῆς n. gen. fem. sg. γῆ earth, land, ground, country
πορνείας n. gen. fem. sg. πορνεία fornication
αὐτῆς pron. gen. fem. 3p. sg. αὐτός ή ό self, of oneself, even, very, the same, he, she, it
οἱ art. nom. masc. pl. ὁ ἡ τό the, this, that, he, she, it
τὴν art. acc. fem. sg. ὁ ἡ τό the, this, that, he, she, it
γῆν n. acc. fem. sg. γῆ earth, land, ground, country
3 καὶ conj. καί and, even, also, but
με pron. acc. 1p. sg. ἐγώ I
εἰς prep. εἰς (+acc) into, to, unto, for, in, on, toward, against, upon, at, among
ἔρημον adj. acc. fem. sg. ἔρημος wilderness, desert
ἐν prep. ἐν (+dat) in, by, with, among, at, on, through, to, within, into, of, for
Πνεύματι n. dat. neut. sg. πνεῦμα spirit, Spirit, Ghost, ghost, life. of the spirit, wind
καὶ conj. καί and, even, also, but
γυναῖκα n. acc. fem. sg. γυνή woman, wife
ἐπὶ prep. ἐπί (+gen) on, in, upon, (+dat) in, at, for, upon, (+acc) on, upon, unto, to, against
θηρίον n. acc. neut. sg. θηρίον beast, wild beast, venomous beast
κόκκινον adj. acc. neut. sg. κόκκινος scarlet, scarlet colour, scarlet coloured
ὀνομάτων n. gen. neut. pl. ὄνομα name, call, surname
βλασφημίας n. gen. fem. sg. βλασφημία blasphemy, railing, evil speaking
κεφαλὰς n. acc. fem. pl. κεφαλή head
ἑπτὰ num. acc. fem. pl. ἑπτά seven, seventh
καὶ conj. καί and, even, also, but
κέρατα n. acc. neut. pl. κέρας horn
δέκα num. acc. neut. pl. δέκα ten
4 καὶ conj. καί and, even, also, but
ἡ art. nom. fem. sg. ὁ ἡ τό the, this, that, he, she, it
γυνὴ n. nom. fem. sg. γυνή woman, wife

πορφύρᾳ n. dat. fem. sg. πορφύρα purple
καὶ conj. καί and, even, also, but
κοκκίνῳ adj. dat. neut. sg. κόκκινος scarlet, scarlet colour, scarlet coloured
καὶ conj. καί and, even, also, but
χρυσῷ n. dat. masc. sg. χρυσός gold
καὶ conj. καί and, even, also, but
λίθῳ n. dat. masc. sg. λίθος stone
τιμίῳ adj. dat. masc. sg. τίμιος precious, dear, has in reputation, honourable
καὶ conj. καί and, even, also, but
μαργαρίταις n. dat. masc. pl. μαργαρίτης pearl
χρυσοῦν adj. acc. neut. sg. χρύσεος golden, of gold
ποτήριον n. acc. neut. sg. ποτήριον cup
ἐν prep. ἐν (+dat) in, by, with, among, at, on, through, to, within, into, of, for
τῇ art. dat. fem. sg. ὁ ἡ τό the, this, that, he, she, it
χειρὶ n. dat. fem. sg. χείρ hand
αὐτῆς pron. gen. fem. 3p. sg. αὐτός ή ό self, of oneself, even, very, the same, he, she, it
βδελυγμάτων n. gen. neut. pl. βδέλυγμα abomination
καὶ conj. καί and, even, also, but
ἀκαθάρτητος n. gen. fem. sg. ἀκαθάρτης filthiness
πορνείας n. gen. fem. sg. πορνεία fornication
αὐτῆς pron. gen. fem. 3p. sg. αὐτός ή ό self, of oneself, even, very, the same, he, she, it
5 καὶ conj. καί and, even, also, but
ἐπὶ prep. ἐπί (+gen) on, in, upon, (+dat) in, at, for, upon, (+acc) on, upon, unto, to, against
τὸ art. acc. neut. sg. ὁ ἡ τό the, this, that, he, she, it
μέτωπον n. acc. neut. sg. μέτωπον forehead
αὐτῆς pron. gen. fem. 3p. sg. αὐτός ή ό self, of oneself, even, very, the same, he, she, it
ὄνομα n. nom. neut. sg. ὄνομα name, call, surname
Μυστήριον n. nom. neut. sg. μυστήριον mystery
Βαβυλὼν n. nom. fem. sg. Βαβυλών Babylon
ἡ art. nom. fem. sg. ὁ ἡ τό the, this, that, he, she, it
μεγάλη adj. nom. fem. sg. μέγας great, loud, greatest, high, large, mighty, strong
ἡ art. nom. fem. sg. ὁ ἡ τό the, this, that, he, she, it
μήτηρ n. nom. fem. sg. μήτηρ mother
τῶν art. gen. fem. pl. ὁ ἡ τό the, this, that, he, she, it
πορνῶν n. gen. fem. pl. πόρνη harlot, whore
καὶ conj. καί and, even, also, but
τῶν art. gen. neut. pl. ὁ ἡ τό the, this, that, he, she, it
βδελυγμάτων n. gen. neut. pl. βδέλυγμα abomination
τῆς art. gen. fem. sg. ὁ ἡ τό the, this, that, he, she, it
γῆς n. gen. fem. sg. γῆ earth, land, ground, country
6 καὶ conj. καί and, even, also, but
τὴν art. acc. fem. sg. ὁ ἡ τό the, this, that, he, she, it
γυναῖκα n. acc. fem. sg. γυνή woman, wife
ἐκ prep. ἐκ ἐξ (+gen) of, from, out of, by, on, with, in, among, through
τοῦ art. gen. neut. sg. ὁ ἡ τό the, this, that, he, she, it
αἵματος n. gen. neut. sg. αἷμα blood
τῶν art. gen. masc. pl. ὁ ἡ τό the, this, that, he, she, it
ἁγίων adj. gen. masc. pl. ἅγιος Holy, holy, saint, Holy One, holy thing, most holy
καὶ conj. καί and, even, also, but
ἐκ prep. ἐκ ἐξ (+gen) of, from, out of, by, on, with, in, among, through
τοῦ art. gen. neut. sg. ὁ ἡ τό the, this, that, he, she, it
αἵματος n. gen. neut. sg. αἷμα blood
τῶν art. gen. masc. pl. ὁ ἡ τό the, this, that, he, she, it
μαρτύρων n. gen. masc. pl. μάρτυς or μάρτυρ witness, martyr, record
Ἰησοῦ n. gen. masc. sg. Ἰησοῦς Jesus

καὶ conj. καί and, even, also, but
αὐτὴν pron. acc. fem. 3p. sg. αὐτός ή ό self, of oneself, even, very, the same, he, she, it
θαῦμα n. acc. neut. sg. θαῦμα admiration
μέγα adj. acc. neut. sg. μέγας great, loud, greatest, high, large, mighty, strong
7 καὶ conj. καί and, even, also, but
μοι pron. dat. 1p. sg. ἐγώ I
ὁ art. nom. masc. sg. ὁ ἡ τό the, this, that, he, she, it
ἄγγελος n. nom. masc. sg. ἄγγελος angel, messenger
Διατί adv. διατί why, for what, wherefore
ἐγὼ pron. nom. 1p. sg. ἐγώ I
σοι pron. dat. 2p. sg. σύ thou, you
τὸ art. acc. neut. sg. ὁ ἡ τό the, this, that, he, she, it
μυστήριον n. acc. neut. sg. μυστήριον mystery
τῆς art. gen. fem. sg. ὁ ἡ τό the, this, that, he, she, it
γυναικὸς n. gen. fem. sg. γυνή woman, wife
καὶ conj. καί and, even, also, but
τοῦ art. gen. neut. sg. ὁ ἡ τό the, this, that, he, she, it
θηρίου n. gen. neut. sg. θηρίον beast, wild beast, venomous beast
τοῦ art. gen. neut. sg. ὁ ἡ τό the, this, that, he, she, it
αὐτὴν pron. acc. fem. 3p. sg. αὐτός ή ό self, of oneself, even, very, the same, he, she, it
τοῦ art. gen. neut. sg. ὁ ἡ τό the, this, that, he, she, it
τὰς art. acc. fem. pl. ὁ ἡ τό the, this, that, he, she, it
ἑπτὰ num. acc. fem. pl. ἑπτά seven, seventh
κεφαλὰς n. acc. fem. pl. κεφαλή head
καὶ conj. καί and, even, also, but
τὰ art. acc. neut. pl. ὁ ἡ τό the, this, that, he, she, it
δέκα num. acc. neut. pl. δέκα ten
κέρατα n. acc. neut. pl. κέρας horn
8 τὸ art. nom. neut. sg. ὁ ἡ τό the, this, that, he, she, it
θηρίον n. nom. neut. sg. θηρίον beast, wild beast, venomous beast
ὃ relative pron. acc. neut. sg. ὅς ἥ ὅ who, which, what, that
καὶ conj. καί and, even, also, but
οὐκ particle of negation. οὐ οὐκ οὐχ not, no, neither, none, nay, nor, never, nothing
καὶ conj. καί and, even, also, but
ἐκ prep. ἐκ ἐξ (+gen) of, from, out of, by, on, with, in, among, through
τῆς art. gen. fem. sg. ὁ ἡ τό the, this, that, he, she, it
ἀβύσσου n. gen. fem. sg. ἄβυσσος deep, abyss, bottomless pit, bottomless
καὶ conj. καί and, even, also, but
εἰς prep. εἰς (+acc) into, to, unto, for, in, on, toward, against, upon, at, among
ἀπώλειαν n. acc. fem. sg. ἀπώλεια destruction, perdition, waste, damnation
καὶ conj. καί and, even, also, but
οἱ art. nom. masc. pl. ὁ ἡ τό the, this, that, he, she, it
ἐπὶ prep. ἐπί (+gen) on, in, upon, (+dat) in, at, for, upon, (+acc) on, upon, unto, to, against
τῆς art. gen. fem. sg. ὁ ἡ τό the, this, that, he, she, it
γῆς n. gen. fem. sg. γῆ earth, land, ground, country
ὧν relative pron. gen. masc. pl. ὅς ἥ ὅ who, which, what, that
οὐ particle of negation. οὐ οὐκ οὐχ not, no, neither, none, nay, nor, never, nothing
τὰ art. nom. neut. pl. ὁ ἡ τό the, this, that, he, she, it
ὀνόματα n. nom. neut. pl. ὄνομα name, call, surname
ἐπὶ prep. ἐπί (+gen) on, in, upon, (+dat) in, at, for, upon, (+acc) on, upon, unto, to, against
τὸ art. acc. neut. sg. ὁ ἡ τό the, this, that, he, she, it
βιβλίον n. acc. neut. sg. βιβλίον book, bill, scroll, writing
τῆς art. gen. fem. sg. ὁ ἡ τό the, this, that, he, she, it
ζωῆς n. gen. fem. sg. ζωή life, lifetime
ἀπὸ prep. ἀπό (+gen) from, of, out of, since, for, off, at, by, in, on

καταβολῆς n. gen. fem. sg. καταβολή foundation
κόσμου n. gen. masc. sg. κόσμος world, adorning
τὸ art. acc. neut. sg. ὁ ἡ τό the, this, that, he, she, it
θηρίον n. acc. neut. sg. θηρίον beast, wild beast, venomous beast
ὃ relative pron. nom. neut. sg. ὅς ἥ ὅ who, which, what, that
τι indefinite pron. nom. neut. sg. τὶς certain, some, any man, one, any thing
καὶ conj. καί and, even, also, but
οὐκ particle of negation. οὐ οὐκ οὐχ not, no, neither, none, nay, nor, never, nothing
καίπερ conj. καίπερ though, and yet
9 ὧδε adv. ὧδε here, hither, in this place, there, this place
ὁ art. nom. masc. sg. ὁ ἡ τό the, this, that, he, she, it
νοῦς n. nom. masc. sg. νοῦς understanding, mind
ὁ art. nom. masc. sg. ὁ ἡ τό the, this, that, he, she, it
σοφίαν n. acc. fem. sg. σοφία wisdom
αἱ art. nom. fem. pl. ὁ ἡ τό the, this, that, he, she, it
ἑπτὰ num. nom. fem. pl. ἑπτά seven, seventh
κεφαλαὶ n. nom. fem. pl. κεφαλή head
ὄρη n. nom. neut. pl. ὄρος mountain, mount, hill
ἑπτὰ num. nom. neut. pl. ἑπτά seven, seventh
ὅπου adv. ὅπου where, whither, whereas, in what place, wheresoever
ἡ art. nom. fem. sg. ὁ ἡ τό the, this, that, he, she, it
γυνὴ n. nom. fem. sg. γυνή woman, wife
ἐπ' prep. ἐπί (+gen) on, in, upon, (+dat) in, at, for, upon, (+acc) on, upon, unto, to, against
αὐτῶν pron. gen. neut. 3p. pl. αὐτός ή ό self, of oneself, even, very, the same, he, she, it
10 καὶ conj. καί and, even, also, but
βασιλεῖς n. nom. masc. pl. βασιλεύς king
ἑπτά num. nom. masc. pl. ἑπτά seven, seventh
οἱ art. nom. masc. pl. ὁ ἡ τό the, this, that, he, she, it
πέντε num. nom. masc. pl. πέντε five
καὶ conj. καί and, even, also, but
ὁ art. nom. masc. sg. ὁ ἡ τό the, this, that, he, she, it
εἷς num. nom. masc. sg. εἷς or ἕν one, other, some, any, only, a certain
ὁ art. nom. masc. sg. ὁ ἡ τό the, this, that, he, she, it
ἄλλος adj. nom. masc. sg. ἄλλος other, another, some, one, more, otherwise
οὔπω adv. οὔπω not yet
καὶ conj. καί and, even, also, but
ὅταν conj. ὅταν when, as soon as, as long as, that, whensoever, while
ὀλίγον adv. ὀλίγον a little
αὐτὸν pron. acc. masc. 3p. sg. αὐτός ή ό self, of oneself, even, very, the same, he, she, it
11 καὶ conj. καί and, even, also, but
τὸ art. nom. neut. sg. ὁ ἡ τό the, this, that, he, she, it
θηρίον n. nom. neut. sg. θηρίον beast, wild beast, venomous beast
ὃ relative pron. nom. neut. sg. ὅς ἥ ὅ who, which, what, that
καὶ conj. καί and, even, also, but
οὐκ particle of negation. οὐ οὐκ οὐχ not, no, neither, none, nay, nor, never, nothing
καὶ conj. καί and, even, also, but
αὐτὸς pron. nom. masc. 3p. sg. αὐτός ή ό self, of oneself, even, very, the same, he, she, it
ὄγδοός ordinal. adj. nom. masc. sg. ὄγδοος eighth
καὶ conj. καί and, even, also, but
ἐκ prep. ἐκ ἐξ (+gen) of, from, out of, by, on, with, in, among, through
τῶν art. gen. masc. pl. ὁ ἡ τό the, this, that, he, she, it
ἑπτά num. gen. masc. pl. ἑπτά seven, seventh
καὶ conj. καί and, even, also, but
εἰς prep. εἰς (+acc) into, to, unto, for, in, on, toward, against, upon, at, among
ἀπώλειαν n. acc. fem. sg. ἀπώλεια destruction, perdition, waste, damnation

12 καὶ conj. καί and, even, also, but
τὰ art. nom. neut. pl. ὁ ἡ τό the, this, that, he, she, it
δέκα num. nom. neut. pl. δέκα ten
κέρατα n. nom. neut. pl. κέρας horn
ἃ relative pron. acc. neut. pl. ὅς ἥ ὅ who, which, what, that
δέκα num. nom. masc. pl. δέκα ten
βασιλεῖς n. nom. masc. pl. βασιλεύς king
οἵτινες relative pron. nom. masc. pl. ὅστις which, who, whosoever, that, whatsoever
βασιλείαν n. acc. fem. sg. βασιλεία kingdom, reign
οὔπω adv. οὔπω not yet
ἀλλ' conj. ἀλλά but, yea, yet, nevertheless, howbeit, nay, therefore
ἐξουσίαν n. acc. fem. sg. ἐξουσία power, authority, right, strength, jurisdiction
ὡς adv. ὡς as, when, as it were, how, about, like, as soon as, even as, while
βασιλεῖς n. nom. masc. pl. βασιλεύς king
μίαν num. acc. fem. sg. εἷς or ἕν one, other, some, any, only, a certain
ὥραν n. acc. fem. sg. ὥρα hour, time, season
μετὰ prep. μετά (+gen) with, among, against, (+acc) after
τοῦ art. gen. neut. sg. ὁ ἡ τό the, this, that, he, she, it
θηρίου n. gen. neut. sg. θηρίον beast, wild beast, venomous beast
13 οὗτοι demo. pron. nom. masc. pl. οὗτος αὕτη τοῦτο this, the same, this same, he, she, it
μίαν num. acc. fem. sg. εἷς or ἕν one, other, some, any, only, a certain
γνώμην n. acc. fem. sg. γνώμη judgement, mind, advice, purpose, will
καὶ conj. καί and, even, also, but
τὴν art. acc. fem. sg. ὁ ἡ τό the, this, that, he, she, it
δύναμιν n. acc. fem. sg. δύναμις power, mighty work, miracle, strength, might
καὶ conj. καί and, even, also, but
τὴν art. acc. fem. sg. ὁ ἡ τό the, this, that, he, she, it
ἐξουσίαν n. acc. fem. sg. ἐξουσία power, authority, right, strength, jurisdiction
ἑαυτῶν reflexive pron. gen. masc. 3p. pl. ἑαυτοῦ himself, herself, itself, yourself, ourselves
τῷ art. dat. neut. sg. ὁ ἡ τό the, this, that, he, she, it
θηρίῳ n. dat. neut. sg. θηρίον beast, wild beast, venomous beast
14 οὗτοι demo. pron. nom. masc. pl. οὗτος αὕτη τοῦτο this, the same, this same, he, she, it
μετὰ prep. μετά (+gen) with, among, against, (+acc) after
τοῦ art. gen. neut. sg. ὁ ἡ τό the, this, that, he, she, it
ἀρνίου n. gen. neut. sg. ἀρνίον Lamb, lamb
καὶ conj. καί and, even, also, but
τὸ art. nom. neut. sg. ὁ ἡ τό the, this, that, he, she, it
ἀρνίον n. nom. neut. sg. ἀρνίον Lamb, lamb
αὐτούς pron. acc. masc. 3p. pl. αὐτός ἡ ὁ self, of oneself, even, very, the same, he, she, it
ὅτι conj. ὅτι that, for, because, how that, how, because that, for that, though
Κύριος n. nom. masc. sg. κύριος Lord, lord, master, sir, LORD, God, Master, owner
κυρίων n. gen. masc. pl. κύριος Lord, lord, master, sir, LORD, God, Master, owner
καὶ conj. καί and, even, also, but
Βασιλεὺς n. nom. masc. sg. βασιλεύς king
βασιλέων n. gen. masc. pl. βασιλεύς king
καὶ conj. καί and, even, also, but
οἱ art. nom. masc. pl. ὁ ἡ τό the, this, that, he, she, it
μετ' prep. μετά (+gen) with, among, against, (+acc) after
αὐτοῦ pron. gen. masc. 3p. sg. αὐτός ἡ ὁ self, of oneself, even, very, the same, he, she, it
κλητοὶ adj. nom. masc. pl. κλητός called
καὶ conj. καί and, even, also, but
ἐκλεκτοὶ adj. nom. masc. pl. ἐκλεκτός elect, chosen
καὶ conj. καί and, even, also, but
πιστοί adj. nom. masc. pl. πιστός faithful, believing, true, sure
15 καὶ conj. καί and, even, also, but

μοι pron. dat. 1p. sg. ἐγώ I
Τὰ art. nom. neut. pl. ὁ ἡ τό the, this, that, he, she, it
ὕδατα n. nom. neut. pl. ὕδωρ water
ἃ relative pron. acc. neut. pl. ὅς ἥ ὅ who, which, what, that
οὗ adv. οὗ where, whither, wherein
ἡ art. nom. fem. sg. ὁ ἡ τό the, this, that, he, she, it
πόρνη n. nom. fem. sg. πόρνη harlot, whore
λαοὶ n. nom. masc. pl. λαός people
καὶ conj. καί and, even, also, but
ὄχλοι n. nom. masc. pl. ὄχλος people, multitude, company, press, number
καὶ conj. καί and, even, also, but
ἔθνη n. nom. neut. pl. ἔθνος Gentile, nation, heathen, people
καὶ conj. καί and, even, also, but
γλῶσσαι n. nom. fem. pl. γλῶσσα tongue
16 καὶ conj. καί and, even, also, but
τὰ art. nom. neut. pl. ὁ ἡ τό the, this, that, he, she, it
δέκα num. nom. neut. pl. δέκα ten
κέρατα n. nom. neut. pl. κέρας horn
ἃ relative pron. acc. neut. pl. ὅς ἥ ὅ who, which, what, that
ἐπὶ prep. ἐπί (+gen) on, in, upon, (+dat) in, at, for, upon, (+acc) on, upon, unto, to, against
τὸ art. nom. neut. sg. ὁ ἡ τό the, this, that, he, she, it
θηρίον n. nom. neut. sg. θηρίον beast, wild beast, venomous beast
οὗτοι demo. pron. nom. masc. pl. οὗτος αὕτη τοῦτο this, the same, this same, he, she, it
τὴν art. acc. fem. sg. ὁ ἡ τό the, this, that, he, she, it
πόρνην n. acc. fem. sg. πόρνη harlot, whore
καὶ conj. καί and, even, also, but
αὐτὴν pron. acc. fem. 3p. sg. αὐτός ή ό self, of oneself, even, very, the same, he, she, it
καὶ conj. καί and, even, also, but
γυμνὴν adj. acc. fem. sg. γυμνός naked, bare
καὶ conj. καί and, even, also, but
τὰς art. acc. fem. pl. ὁ ἡ τό the, this, that, he, she, it
σάρκας n. acc. fem. pl. σάρξ flesh, carnal
αὐτῆς pron. gen. fem. 3p. sg. αὐτός ή ό self, of oneself, even, very, the same, he, she, it
καὶ conj. καί and, even, also, but
αὐτὴν pron. acc. fem. 3p. sg. αὐτός ή ό self, of oneself, even, very, the same, he, she, it
ἐν prep. ἐν (+dat) in, by, with, among, at, on, through, to, within, into, of, for
πυρί n. dat. neut. sg. πῦρ fire, fiery
17 ὁ art. nom. masc. sg. ὁ ἡ τό the, this, that, he, she, it
γὰρ conj. γάρ for, and, because, but, indeed
Θεὸς n. nom. masc. sg. θεός God, god
εἰς prep. εἰς (+acc) into, to, unto, for, in, on, toward, against, upon, at, among
τὰς art. acc. fem. pl. ὁ ἡ τό the, this, that, he, she, it
καρδίας n. acc. fem. pl. καρδία heart
αὐτῶν pron. gen. masc. 3p. pl. αὐτός ή ό self, of oneself, even, very, the same, he, she, it
τὴν art. acc. fem. sg. ὁ ἡ τό the, this, that, he, she, it
γνώμην n. acc. fem. sg. γνώμη judgement, mind, advice, purpose, will
αὐτοῦ pron. gen. masc. 3p. sg. αὐτός ή ό self, of oneself, even, very, the same, he, she, it
καὶ conj. καί and, even, also, but
μίαν num. acc. fem. sg. εἷς or ἕν one, other, some, any, only, a certain
γνώμην n. acc. fem. sg. γνώμη judgement, mind, advice, purpose, will
καὶ conj. καί and, even, also, but
τὴν art. acc. fem. sg. ὁ ἡ τό the, this, that, he, she, it
βασιλείαν n. acc. fem. sg. βασιλεία kingdom, reign
αὐτῶν pron. gen. masc. 3p. pl. αὐτός ή ό self, of oneself, even, very, the same, he, she, it
τῷ art. dat. neut. sg. ὁ ἡ τό the, this, that, he, she, it

θηρίῳ n. dat. neut. sg. θηρίον beast, wild beast, venomous beast
ἄχρι prep. ἄχρι or ἄχρις (+gen) until, unto, till, even to, as far as, while, into
τὰ art. nom. neut. pl. ὁ ἡ τό the, this, that, he, she, it
ῥήματα n. nom. neut. pl. ῥῆμα word, saying, thing
τοῦ art. gen. masc. sg. ὁ ἡ τό the, this, that, he, she, it
Θεοῦ n. gen. masc. sg. θεός God, god
18 καὶ conj. καί and, even, also, but
ἡ art. nom. fem. sg. ὁ ἡ τό the, this, that, he, she, it
γυνὴ n. nom. fem. sg. γυνή woman, wife
ἣν relative pron. acc. fem. sg. ὅς ἥ ὅ who, which, what, that
ἡ art. nom. fem. sg. ὁ ἡ τό the, this, that, he, she, it
πόλις n. nom. fem. sg. πόλις city
ἡ art. nom. fem. sg. ὁ ἡ τό the, this, that, he, she, it
μεγάλη adj. nom. fem. sg. μέγας great, loud, greatest, high, large, mighty, strong
ἡ art. nom. fem. sg. ὁ ἡ τό the, this, that, he, she, it
βασιλείαν n. acc. fem. sg. βασιλεία kingdom, reign
ἐπὶ prep. ἐπί (+gen) on, in, upon, (+dat) in, at, for, upon, (+acc) on, upon, unto, to, against
τῶν art. gen. masc. pl. ὁ ἡ τό the, this, that, he, she, it
βασιλέων n. gen. masc. pl. βασιλεύς king
τῆς art. gen. fem. sg. ὁ ἡ τό the, this, that, he, she, it
γῆς n. gen. fem. sg. γῆ earth, land, ground, country

18

1 Καὶ conj. καί and, even, also, but
μετὰ prep. μετά (+gen) with, among, against, (+acc) after
ταῦτα demo. pron. acc. neut. pl. οὗτος αὕτη τοῦτο this, the same, this same, he, she, it
ἄλλον adj. acc. masc. sg. ἄλλος other, another, some, one, more, otherwise
ἄγγελον n. acc. masc. sg. ἄγγελος angel, messenger
ἐκ prep. ἐκ ἐξ (+gen) of, from, out of, by, on, with, in, among, through
τοῦ art. gen. masc. sg. ὁ ἡ τό the, this, that, he, she, it
οὐρανοῦ n. gen. masc. sg. οὐρανός heaven, air, sky
ἐξουσίαν n. acc. fem. sg. ἐξουσία power, authority, right, strength, jurisdiction
μεγάλην adj. acc. fem. sg. μέγας great, loud, greatest, high, large, mighty, strong
καὶ conj. καί and, even, also, but
ἡ art. nom. fem. sg. ὁ ἡ τό the, this, that, he, she, it
γῆ n. nom. fem. sg. γῆ earth, land, ground, country
ἐκ prep. ἐκ ἐξ (+gen) of, from, out of, by, on, with, in, among, through
τῆς art. gen. fem. sg. ὁ ἡ τό the, this, that, he, she, it
δόξης n. gen. fem. sg. δόξα glory, honour, praise, dignity, worship
αὐτοῦ pron. gen. masc. 3p. sg. αὐτός ή ό self, of oneself, even, very, the same, he, she, it
2 καὶ conj. καί and, even, also, but
ἐν prep. ἐν (+dat) in, by, with, among, at, on, through, to, within, into, of, for
ἰσχύϊ n. dat. fem. sg. ἰσχύς strength, might, power, ability
φωνῇ n. dat. fem. sg. φωνή voice, sound, noise
μεγάλῃ adj. dat. fem. sg. μέγας great, loud, greatest, high, large, mighty, strong
Βαβυλὼν n. nom. fem. sg. Βαβυλών Babylon
ἡ art. nom. fem. sg. ὁ ἡ τό the, this, that, he, she, it
μεγάλη adj. nom. fem. sg. μέγας great, loud, greatest, high, large, mighty, strong
καὶ conj. καί and, even, also, but
κατοικητήριον n. nom. neut. sg. κατοικητήριον habitation into a dwelling
δαιμόνων n. gen. masc. pl. δαίμων devil, demon
καὶ conj. καί and, even, also, but
φυλακὴ n. nom. fem. sg. φυλακή prison, watch, imprisonment, cage, hold, ward
παντὸς adj. gen. neut. sg. πᾶς πᾶσα πᾶν all, every, whosoever, every one, no, whole, any

πνεύματος n. gen. neut. sg. πνεῦμα spirit, Spirit, Ghost, ghost, life. of the spirit, wind
ἀκαθάρτου adj. gen. neut. sg. ἀκάθαρτος unclean, foul
καὶ conj. καί and, even, also, but
φυλακὴ n. nom. fem. sg. φυλακή prison, watch, imprisonment, cage, hold, ward
παντὸς adj. gen. neut. sg. πᾶς πᾶσα πᾶν all, every, whosoever, every one, no, whole, any
ὀρνέου n. gen. neut. sg. ὄρνεον bird, fowl
ἀκαθάρτου adj. gen. neut. sg. ἀκάθαρτος unclean, foul
καὶ conj. καί and, even, also, but
3 ὅτι conj. ὅτι that, for, because, how that, how, because that, for that, though
ἐκ prep. ἐκ ἐξ (+gen) of, from, out of, by, on, with, in, among, through
τοῦ art. gen. masc. sg. ὁ ἡ τό the, this, that, he, she, it
οἴνου n. gen. masc. sg. οἶνος wine
τοῦ art. gen. masc. sg. ὁ ἡ τό the, this, that, he, she, it
θυμοῦ n. gen. masc. sg. θυμός wrath, fierceness, indignation
τῆς art. gen. fem. sg. ὁ ἡ τό the, this, that, he, she, it
πορνείας n. gen. fem. sg. πορνεία fornication
αὐτῆς pron. gen. fem. 3p. sg. αὐτός ή ό self, of oneself, even, very, the same, he, she, it
πάντα adj. nom. neut. pl. πᾶς πᾶσα πᾶν all, every, whosoever, every one, no, whole, any
τὰ art. nom. neut. pl. ὁ ἡ τό the, this, that, he, she, it
ἔθνη n. nom. neut. pl. ἔθνος Gentile, nation, heathen, people
καὶ conj. καί and, even, also, but
οἱ art. nom. masc. pl. ὁ ἡ τό the, this, that, he, she, it
βασιλεῖς n. nom. masc. pl. βασιλεύς king
τῆς art. gen. fem. sg. ὁ ἡ τό the, this, that, he, she, it
γῆς n. gen. fem. sg. γῆ earth, land, ground, country
μετ' prep. μετά (+gen) with, among, against, (+acc) after
αὐτῆς pron. gen. fem. 3p. sg. αὐτός ή ό self, of oneself, even, very, the same, he, she, it
καὶ conj. καί and, even, also, but
οἱ art. nom. masc. pl. ὁ ἡ τό the, this, that, he, she, it
ἔμποροι n. nom. masc. pl. ἔμπορος merchant
τῆς art. gen. fem. sg. ὁ ἡ τό the, this, that, he, she, it
γῆς n. gen. fem. sg. γῆ earth, land, ground, country
ἐκ prep. ἐκ ἐξ (+gen) of, from, out of, by, on, with, in, among, through
τῆς art. gen. fem. sg. ὁ ἡ τό the, this, that, he, she, it
δυνάμεως n. gen. fem. sg. δύναμις power, mighty work, miracle, strength, might
τοῦ art. gen. neut. sg. ὁ ἡ τό the, this, that, he, she, it
στρήνους n. gen. neut. sg. στρῆνος delicacy
αὐτῆς pron. gen. fem. 3p. sg. αὐτός ή ό self, of oneself, even, very, the same, he, she, it
4 Καὶ conj. καί and, even, also, but
ἄλλην adj. acc. fem. sg. ἄλλος other, another, some, one, more, otherwise
φωνὴν n. acc. fem. sg. φωνή voice, sound, noise
ἐκ prep. ἐκ ἐξ (+gen) of, from, out of, by, on, with, in, among, through
τοῦ art. gen. masc. sg. ὁ ἡ τό the, this, that, he, she, it
οὐρανοῦ n. gen. masc. sg. οὐρανός heaven, air, sky
ἐξ prep. ἐκ ἐξ (+gen) of, from, out of, by, on, with, in, among, through
αὐτῆς pron. gen. fem. 3p. sg. αὐτός ή ό self, of oneself, even, very, the same, he, she, it
ὁ art. nom. masc. sg. ὁ ἡ τό the, this, that, he, she, it
λαός n. nom. masc. sg. λαός people
μου pron. gen. 1p. sg. ἐγώ I
ἵνα conj. ἵνα that, to, lest, for to, so that, albeit, because, for, so as
μὴ particle of negation. μή not, no, lest, neither, none, nothing, nor, never, without
ταῖς art. dat. fem. pl. ὁ ἡ τό the, this, that, he, she, it
ἁμαρτίαις n. dat. fem. pl. ἁμαρτία sin, offence, sinful
αὐτῆς pron. gen. fem. 3p. sg. αὐτός ή ό self, of oneself, even, very, the same, he, she, it
καὶ conj. καί and, even, also, but

ἵνα conj. ἵνα that, to, lest, for to, so that, albeit, because, for, so as
μὴ particle of negation. μή not, no, lest, neither, none, nothing, nor, never, without
ἐκ prep. ἐκ ἐξ (+gen) of, from, out of, by, on, with, in, among, through
τῶν art. gen. fem. pl. ὁ ἡ τό the, this, that, he, she, it
πληγῶν n. gen. fem. pl. πληγή wound, plague, stripe
αὐτῆς pron. gen. fem. 3p. sg. αὐτός ή ό self, of oneself, even, very, the same, he, she, it
5 ὅτι conj. ὅτι that, for, because, how that, how, because that, for that, though
αὐτῆς pron. gen. fem. 3p. sg. αὐτός ή ό self, of oneself, even, very, the same, he, she, it
αἱ art. nom. fem. pl. ὁ ἡ τό the, this, that, he, she, it
ἁμαρτίαι n. nom. fem. pl. ἁμαρτία sin, offence, sinful
ἄχρι prep. ἄχρι or ἄχρις (+gen) until, unto, till, even to, as far as, while, into
τοῦ art. gen. masc. sg. ὁ ἡ τό the, this, that, he, she, it
οὐρανοῦ n. gen. masc. sg. οὐρανός heaven, air, sky
καὶ conj. καί and, even, also, but
ὁ art. nom. masc. sg. ὁ ἡ τό the, this, that, he, she, it
Θεὸς n. nom. masc. sg. θεός God, god
τὰ art. acc. neut. pl. ὁ ἡ τό the, this, that, he, she, it
ἀδικήματα n. acc. neut. pl. ἀδίκημα matter of wrong, evil doing, iniquity
αὐτῆς pron. gen. fem. 3p. sg. αὐτός ή ό self, of oneself, even, very, the same, he, she, it
6 αὐτῇ pron. dat. fem. 3p. sg. αὐτός ή ό self, of oneself, even, very, the same, he, she, it
ὡς adv. ὡς as, when, as it were, how, about, like, as soon as, even as, while
καὶ conj. καί and, even, also, but
αὐτὴ pron. nom. fem. 3p. sg. αὐτός ή ό self, of oneself, even, very, the same, he, she, it
ὑμῖν pron. dat. 2p. pl. σύ thou, you
καὶ conj. καί and, even, also, but
αὐτῇ pron. dat. fem. 3p. sg. αὐτός ή ό self, of oneself, even, very, the same, he, she, it
διπλᾶ adj. acc. neut. pl. διπλοῦς twofold more, double
κατὰ prep. κατά (+gen) against, by, throughout, down, (+acc) according to, after, with
τὰ art. acc. neut. pl. ὁ ἡ τό the, this, that, he, she, it
ἔργα n. acc. neut. pl. ἔργον work, deed, doing labour
αὐτῆς pron. gen. fem. 3p. sg. αὐτός ή ό self, of oneself, even, very, the same, he, she, it
ἐν prep. ἐν (+dat) in, by, with, among, at, on, through, to, within, into, of, for
τῷ art. dat. neut. sg. ὁ ἡ τό the, this, that, he, she, it
ποτηρίῳ n. dat. neut. sg. ποτήριον cup
ᾧ relative pron. dat. neut. sg. ὅς ἥ ὅ who, which, what, that
αὐτῇ pron. dat. fem. 3p. sg. αὐτός ή ό self, of oneself, even, very, the same, he, she, it
διπλοῦν adj. acc. neut. sg. διπλοῦς twofold more, double
7 ὅσα relative pron. acc. neut. pl. ὅσος as many as, whatsoever, that, as long as, how much
ἑαυτὴν reflexive pron. acc. fem. 3p. sg. ἑαυτοῦ himself, herself, itself, yourself, ourselves
καὶ conj. καί and, even, also, but
τοσοῦτον demo. pron. acc. masc. sg. τοσοῦτος so much, so great, so many, so long
αὐτῇ pron. dat. fem. 3p. sg. αὐτός ή ό self, of oneself, even, very, the same, he, she, it
βασανισμὸν n. acc. masc. sg. βασανισμός torment
καὶ conj. καί and, even, also, but
πένθος n. acc. neut. sg. πένθος mourning, sorrow
ὅτι conj. ὅτι that, for, because, how that, how, because that, for that, though
ἐν prep. ἐν (+dat) in, by, with, among, at, on, through, to, within, into, of, for
τῇ art. dat. fem. sg. ὁ ἡ τό the, this, that, he, she, it
καρδίᾳ n. dat. fem. sg. καρδία heart
αὐτῆς pron. gen. fem. 3p. sg. αὐτός ή ό self, of oneself, even, very, the same, he, she, it
βασίλισσα n. nom. fem. sg. βασίλισσα queen
καὶ conj. καί and, even, also, but
χήρα adj. nom. fem. sg. χήρα widow
οὐκ particle of negation. οὐ οὐκ οὐχ not, no, neither, none, nay, nor, never, nothing
καὶ conj. καί and, even, also, but

πένθος n. acc. neut. sg. πένθος mourning, sorrow
οὐ particle of negation. οὐ οὐκ οὐχ not, no, neither, none, nay, nor, never, nothing
μὴ particle of negation. μή not, no, lest, neither, none, nothing, nor, never, without
8 διὰ prep. διά (+gen) by, through, with, in, of, (+acc) for, because of, for a cause
τοῦτο demo. pron. acc. neut. sg. οὗτος αὕτη τοῦτο this, the same, this same, he, she, it
ἐν prep. ἐν (+dat) in, by, with, among, at, on, through, to, within, into, of, for
μιᾷ num. dat. fem. sg. εἷς or ἕν one, other, some, any, only, a certain
ἡμέρᾳ n. dat. fem. sg. ἡμέρα day, time, year, while, age, day time
αἱ art. nom. fem. pl. ὁ ἡ τό the, this, that, he, she, it
πληγαὶ n. nom. fem. pl. πληγή wound, plague, stripe
αὐτῆς pron. gen. fem. 3p. sg. αὐτός ή ό self, of oneself, even, very, the same, he, she, it
θάνατος n. nom. masc. sg. θάνατος death
καὶ conj. καί and, even, also, but
πένθος n. nom. neut. sg. πένθος mourning, sorrow
καὶ conj. καί and, even, also, but
λιμός n. nom. masc. sg. λιμός famine, hunger, dearth
καὶ conj. καί and, even, also, but
ἐν prep. ἐν (+dat) in, by, with, among, at, on, through, to, within, into, of, for
πυρὶ n. dat. neut. sg. πῦρ fire, fiery
ὅτι conj. ὅτι that, for, because, how that, how, because that, for that, though
ἰσχυρὸς adj. nom. masc. sg. ἰσχυρός mighty, strong, mightier, stronger
Κύριος n. nom. masc. sg. κύριος Lord, lord, master, sir, LORD, God, Master, owner
ὁ art. nom. masc. sg. ὁ ἡ τό the, this, that, he, she, it
Θεὸς n. nom. masc. sg. θεός God, god
ὁ art. nom. masc. sg. ὁ ἡ τό the, this, that, he, she, it
αὐτήν pron. acc. fem. 3p. sg. αὐτός ή ό self, of oneself, even, very, the same, he, she, it
9 καὶ conj. καί and, even, also, but
αὐτήν pron. acc. fem. 3p. sg. αὐτός ή ό self, of oneself, even, very, the same, he, she, it
καὶ conj. καί and, even, also, but
ἐπ' prep. ἐπί (+gen) on, in, upon, (+dat) in, at, for, upon, (+acc) on, upon, unto, to, against
αὐτῇ pron. dat. fem. 3p. sg. αὐτός ή ό self, of oneself, even, very, the same, he, she, it
οἱ art. nom. masc. pl. ὁ ἡ τό the, this, that, he, she, it
βασιλεῖς n. nom. masc. pl. βασιλεύς king
τῆς art. gen. fem. sg. ὁ ἡ τό the, this, that, he, she, it
γῆς n. gen. fem. sg. γῆ earth, land, ground, country
οἱ art. nom. masc. pl. ὁ ἡ τό the, this, that, he, she, it
μετ' prep. μετά (+gen) with, among, against, (+acc) after
αὐτῆς pron. gen. fem. 3p. sg. αὐτός ή ό self, of oneself, even, very, the same, he, she, it
καὶ conj. καί and, even, also, but
ὅταν conj. ὅταν when, as soon as, as long as, that, whensoever, while
τὸν art. acc. masc. sg. ὁ ἡ τό the, this, that, he, she, it
καπνὸν n. acc. masc. sg. καπνός smoke
τῆς art. gen. fem. sg. ὁ ἡ τό the, this, that, he, she, it
πυρώσεως n. gen. fem. sg. πύρωσις fiery trial, burning
αὐτῆς pron. gen. fem. 3p. sg. αὐτός ή ό self, of oneself, even, very, the same, he, she, it
10 ἀπὸ prep. ἀπό (+gen) from, of, out of, since, for, off, at, by, in, on
μακρόθεν adv. μακρόθεν afar off, from far
διὰ prep. διά (+gen) by, through, with, in, of, (+acc) for, because of, for a cause
τὸν art. acc. masc. sg. ὁ ἡ τό the, this, that, he, she, it
φόβον n. acc. masc. sg. φόβος fear, terror, sore afraid
τοῦ art. gen. masc. sg. ὁ ἡ τό the, this, that, he, she, it
βασανισμοῦ n. gen. masc. sg. βασανισμός torment
αὐτῆς pron. gen. fem. 3p. sg. αὐτός ή ό self, of oneself, even, very, the same, he, she, it
Οὐαὶ particle. οὐαί woe, alas
οὐαὶ particle. οὐαί woe, alas

ἡ art. nom. fem. sg. ὁ ἡ τό the, this, that, he, she, it
πόλις n. nom. fem. sg. πόλις city
ἡ art. nom. fem. sg. ὁ ἡ τό the, this, that, he, she, it
μεγάλη adj. nom. fem. sg. μέγας great, loud, greatest, high, large, mighty, strong
Βαβυλὼν n. nom. fem. sg. Βαβυλών Babylon
ἡ art. nom. fem. sg. ὁ ἡ τό the, this, that, he, she, it
πόλις n. nom. fem. sg. πόλις city
ἡ art. nom. fem. sg. ὁ ἡ τό the, this, that, he, she, it
ἰσχυρά adj. nom. fem. sg. ἰσχυρός mighty, strong, mightier, stronger
ὅτι conj. ὅτι that, for, because, how that, how, because that, for that, though
ἐν prep. ἐν (+dat) in, by, with, among, at, on, through, to, within, into, of, for
μιᾷ num. dat. fem. sg. εἷς or ἕν one, other, some, any, only, a certain
ὥρᾳ n. dat. fem. sg. ὥρα hour, time, season
ἡ art. nom. fem. sg. ὁ ἡ τό the, this, that, he, she, it
κρίσις n. nom. fem. sg. κρίσις judgment, damnation, accusation, condemnation
σου pron. gen. 2p. sg. σύ thou, you
11 καὶ conj. καί and, even, also, but
οἱ art. nom. masc. pl. ὁ ἡ τό the, this, that, he, she, it
ἔμποροι n. nom. masc. pl. ἔμπορος merchant
τῆς art. gen. fem. sg. ὁ ἡ τό the, this, that, he, she, it
γῆς n. gen. fem. sg. γῆ earth, land, ground, country
καὶ conj. καί and, even, also, but
ἐπ' prep. ἐπί (+gen) on, in, upon, (+dat) in, at, for, upon, (+acc) on, upon, unto, to, against
αὐτῇ pron. dat. fem. 3p. sg. αὐτός ἡ ὁ self, of oneself, even, very, the same, he, she, it
ὅτι conj. ὅτι that, for, because, how that, how, because that, for that, though
τὸν art. acc. masc. sg. ὁ ἡ τό the, this, that, he, she, it
γόμον n. acc. masc. sg. γόμος burden, merchandise
αὐτῶν pron. gen. masc. 3p. pl. αὐτός ἡ ὁ self, of oneself, even, very, the same, he, she, it
οὐδεὶς num. nom. masc. sg. οὐδείς no man, nothing, no, none, neither, not, nought
οὐκέτι adv. οὐκέτι or οὐκ ἔτι no more, no longer, not any more
12 γόμον n. acc. masc. sg. γόμος burden, merchandise
χρυσοῦ n. gen. masc. sg. χρυσός gold
καὶ conj. καί and, even, also, but
ἀργύρου n. gen. masc. sg. ἄργυρος silver
καὶ conj. καί and, even, also, but
λίθου n. gen. masc. sg. λίθος stone
τιμίου adj. gen. masc. sg. τίμιος precious, dear, has in reputation, honourable
καὶ conj. καί and, even, also, but
μαργαρίτου n. gen. masc. sg. μαργαρίτης pearl
καὶ conj. καί and, even, also, but
βύσσου n. gen. fem. sg. βύσσος fine linen
καὶ conj. καί and, even, also, but
πορφύρας n. gen. fem. sg. πορφύρα purple
καὶ conj. καί and, even, also, but
σηρικοῦ adj. gen. neut. sg. σηρικός silk
καὶ conj. καί and, even, also, but
κοκκίνου adj. gen. neut. sg. κόκκινος scarlet, scarlet colour, scarlet coloured
καὶ conj. καί and, even, also, but
πᾶν adj. acc. neut. sg. πᾶς πᾶσα πᾶν all, every, whosoever, every one, no, whole, any
ξύλον n. acc. neut. sg. ξύλον tree, stave, wood, the stocks
θύϊνον adj. acc. neut. sg. θύϊνος thyine, thyme
καὶ conj. καί and, even, also, but
πᾶν adj. acc. neut. sg. πᾶς πᾶσα πᾶν all, every, whosoever, every one, no, whole, any
σκεῦος n. acc. neut. sg. σκεῦος vessel, good, sail, stuff
ἐλεφάντινον adj. acc. neut. sg. ἐλεφάντινος ivory

καὶ conj. καί and, even, also, but
πᾶν adj. acc. neut. sg. πᾶς πᾶσα πᾶν all, every, whosoever, every one, no, whole, any
σκεῦος n. acc. neut. sg. σκεῦος vessel, good, sail, stuff
ἐκ prep. ἐκ ἐξ (+gen) of, from, out of, by, on, with, in, among, through
ξύλου n. gen. neut. sg. ξύλον tree, stave, wood, the stocks
τιμιωτάτου superl. adj. gen. neut. sg. τίμιος precious, dear, honourable
καὶ conj. καί and, even, also, but
χαλκοῦ n. gen. masc. sg. χαλκός brass, money
καὶ conj. καί and, even, also, but
σιδήρου n. gen. masc. sg. σίδηρος iron
καὶ conj. καί and, even, also, but
μαρμάρου n. gen. masc. sg. μάρμαρος marble
13 καὶ conj. καί and, even, also, but
κινάμωμον n. acc. neut. sg. κιννάμωμον cinnamon
καὶ conj. καί and, even, also, but
θυμιάματα n. acc. neut. pl. θυμίαμα incense, odour
καὶ conj. καί and, even, also, but
μύρον n. acc. neut. sg. μύρον ointment
καὶ conj. καί and, even, also, but
λίβανον n. acc. masc. sg. λίβανος frankincense
καὶ conj. καί and, even, also, but
οἶνον n. acc. masc. sg. οἶνος wine
καὶ conj. καί and, even, also, but
ἔλαιον n. acc. neut. sg. ἔλαιον oil
καὶ conj. καί and, even, also, but
σεμίδαλιν n. acc. fem. sg. σεμίδαλις fine flour
καὶ conj. καί and, even, also, but
σῖτον n. acc. masc. sg. σῖτος wheat, corn
καὶ conj. καί and, even, also, but
κτήνη n. acc. neut. pl. κτῆνος beast
καὶ conj. καί and, even, also, but
πρόβατα n. acc. neut. pl. πρόβατον sheep
καὶ conj. καί and, even, also, but
ἵππων n. gen. masc. pl. ἵππος horse
καὶ conj. καί and, even, also, but
ῥεδῶν n. gen. fem. pl. ῥέδα chariot
καὶ conj. καί and, even, also, but
σωμάτων n. gen. neut. pl. σῶμα body, bodily, slave
καὶ conj. καί and, even, also, but
ψυχὰς n. acc. fem. pl. ψυχή life, soul, mind, heart
ἀνθρώπων n. gen. masc. pl. ἄνθρωπος man, human being, person, one, certain
14 καὶ conj. καί and, even, also, but
ἡ art. nom. fem. sg. ὁ ἡ τό the, this, that, he, she, it
ὀπώρα n. nom. fem. sg. ὀπώρα fruit
τῆς art. gen. fem. sg. ὁ ἡ τό the, this, that, he, she, it
ἐπιθυμίας n. gen. fem. sg. ἐπιθυμία lust, concupiscence, desire
τῆς art. gen. fem. sg. ὁ ἡ τό the, this, that, he, she, it
ψυχῆς n. gen. fem. sg. ψυχή life, soul, mind, heart
σου pron. gen. 2p. sg. σύ thou, you
ἀπὸ prep. ἀπό (+gen) from, of, out of, since, for, off, at, by, in, on
σοῦ pron. gen. 2p. sg. σύ thou, you
καὶ conj. καί and, even, also, but
πάντα adj. nom. neut. pl. πᾶς πᾶσα πᾶν all, every, whosoever, every one, no, whole, any
τὰ art. nom. neut. pl. ὁ ἡ τό the, this, that, he, she, it
λιπαρὰ adj. nom. neut. pl. λιπαρός dainty

καὶ conj. καί and, even, also, but
τὰ art. nom. neut. pl. ὁ ἡ τό the, this, that, he, she, it
λαμπρὰ adj. nom. neut. pl. λαμπρός gorgeous, bright, goodly, white, clear
ἀπὸ prep. ἀπό (+gen) from, of, out of, since, for, off, at, by, in, on
σοῦ pron. gen. 2p. sg. σύ thou, you
καὶ conj. καί and, even, also, but
οὐκέτι adv. οὐκέτι or οὐκ ἔτι no more, no longer, not any more
οὐ particle of negation. οὐ οὐκ οὐχ not, no, neither, none, nay, nor, never, nothing
μὴ particle of negation. μή not, no, lest, neither, none, nothing, nor, never, without
αὐτὰ pron. acc. neut. 3p. pl. αὐτός ή ό self, of oneself, even, very, the same, he, she, it
15 οἱ art. nom. masc. pl. ὁ ἡ τό the, this, that, he, she, it
ἔμποροι n. nom. masc. pl. ἔμπορος merchant
τούτων demo. pron. gen. neut. pl. οὗτος αὕτη τοῦτο this, the same, this same, he, she, it
οἱ art. nom. masc. pl. ὁ ἡ τό the, this, that, he, she, it
ἀπ' prep. ἀπό (+gen) from, of, out of, since, for, off, at, by, in, on
αὐτῆς pron. gen. fem. 3p. sg. αὐτός ή ό self, of oneself, even, very, the same, he, she, it
ἀπὸ prep. ἀπό (+gen) from, of, out of, since, for, off, at, by, in, on
μακρόθεν adv. μακρόθεν afar off, from far
διὰ prep. διά (+gen) by, through, with, in, of, (+acc) for, because of, for a cause
τὸν art. acc. masc. sg. ὁ ἡ τό the, this, that, he, she, it
φόβον n. acc. masc. sg. φόβος fear, terror, sore afraid
τοῦ art. gen. masc. sg. ὁ ἡ τό the, this, that, he, she, it
βασανισμοῦ n. gen. masc. sg. βασανισμός torment
αὐτῆς pron. gen. fem. 3p. sg. αὐτός ή ό self, of oneself, even, very, the same, he, she, it
καὶ conj. καί and, even, also, but
16 καὶ conj. καί and, even, also, but
Οὐαὶ particle. οὐαί woe, alas
οὐαὶ particle. οὐαί woe, alas
ἡ art. nom. fem. sg. ὁ ἡ τό the, this, that, he, she, it
πόλις n. nom. fem. sg. πόλις city
ἡ art. nom. fem. sg. ὁ ἡ τό the, this, that, he, she, it
μεγάλη adj. nom. fem. sg. μέγας great, loud, greatest, high, large, mighty, strong
ἡ art. nom. fem. sg. ὁ ἡ τό the, this, that, he, she, it
βύσσινον adj. acc. neut. sg. βύσσινος fine linen
καὶ conj. καί and, even, also, but
πορφυροῦν adj. acc. neut. sg. πορφυροῦς purple
καὶ conj. καί and, even, also, but
κόκκινον adj. acc. neut. sg. κόκκινος scarlet, scarlet colour, scarlet coloured
καὶ conj. καί and, even, also, but
ἐν prep. ἐν (+dat) in, by, with, among, at, on, through, to, within, into, of, for
χρυσῷ n. dat. masc. sg. χρυσός gold
καὶ conj. καί and, even, also, but
λίθῳ n. dat. masc. sg. λίθος stone
τιμίῳ adj. dat. masc. sg. τίμιος precious, dear, has in reputation, honourable
καὶ conj. καί and, even, also, but
μαργαρίταις n. dat. masc. pl. μαργαρίτης pearl
17 ὅτι conj. ὅτι that, for, because, how that, how, because that, for that, though
μιᾷ num. dat. fem. sg. εἷς or ἕν one, other, some, any, only, a certain
ὥρᾳ n. dat. fem. sg. ὥρα hour, time, season
ὁ art. nom. masc. sg. ὁ ἡ τό the, this, that, he, she, it
τοσοῦτος demo. pron. nom. masc. sg. τοσοῦτος so much, so great, so many, so long
πλοῦτος n. nom. masc. sg. πλοῦτος riches
καὶ conj. καί and, even, also, but
πᾶς adj. nom. masc. sg. πᾶς πᾶσα πᾶν all, every, whosoever, every one, no, whole, any
κυβερνήτης n. nom. masc. sg. κυβερνήτης master, shipmaster

καὶ conj. καί and, even, also, but
πᾶς adj. nom. masc. sg. πᾶς πᾶσα πᾶν all, every, whosoever, every one, no, whole, any
ἐπὶ prep. ἐπί (+gen) on, in, upon, (+dat) in, at, for, upon, (+acc) on, upon, unto, to, against
τῶν art. gen. neut. pl. ὁ ἡ τό the, this, that, he, she, it
πλοίων n. gen. neut. pl. πλοῖον ship, boat
ὁ art. nom. masc. sg. ὁ ἡ τό the, this, that, he, she, it
ὅμιλος n. nom. masc. sg. ὅμιλος company
καὶ conj. καί and, even, also, but
ναῦται n. nom. masc. pl. ναύτης shipman, sailor
καὶ conj. καί and, even, also, but
ὅσοι relative pron. nom. masc. pl. ὅσος as many as, whatsoever, that, as long as, how much
τὴν art. acc. fem. sg. ὁ ἡ τό the, this, that, he, she, it
θάλασσαν n. acc. fem. sg. θάλασσα sea
ἀπὸ prep. ἀπό (+gen) from, of, out of, since, for, off, at, by, in, on
μακρόθεν adv. μακρόθεν afar off, from far
18 καὶ conj. καί and, even, also, but
τὸν art. acc. masc. sg. ὁ ἡ τό the, this, that, he, she, it
καπνὸν n. acc. masc. sg. καπνός smoke
τῆς art. gen. fem. sg. ὁ ἡ τό the, this, that, he, she, it
πυρώσεως n. gen. fem. sg. πύρωσις fiery trial, burning
αὐτῆς pron. gen. fem. 3p. sg. αὐτός ή ό self, of oneself, even, very, the same, he, she, it
Τίς interrog. pron. nom. fem. sg. τίς what, who, why, where, which, how
ὁμοία adj. nom. fem. sg. ὅμοιος like
τῇ art. dat. fem. sg. ὁ ἡ τό the, this, that, he, she, it
πόλει n. dat. fem. sg. πόλις city
τῇ art. dat. fem. sg. ὁ ἡ τό the, this, that, he, she, it
μεγάλῃ adj. dat. fem. sg. μέγας great, loud, greatest, high, large, mighty, strong
19 καὶ conj. καί and, even, also, but
χοῦν n. acc. masc. sg. χόος or χοῦς dust
ἐπὶ prep. ἐπί (+gen) on, in, upon, (+dat) in, at, for, upon, (+acc) on, upon, unto, to, against
τὰς art. acc. fem. pl. ὁ ἡ τό the, this, that, he, she, it
κεφαλὰς n. acc. fem. pl. κεφαλή head
αὐτῶν pron. gen. masc. 3p. pl. αὐτός ή ό self, of oneself, even, very, the same, he, she, it
καὶ conj. καί and, even, also, but
καὶ conj. καί and, even, also, but
Οὐαὶ particle. οὐαί woe, alas
οὐαὶ particle. οὐαί woe, alas
ἡ art. nom. fem. sg. ὁ ἡ τό the, this, that, he, she, it
πόλις n. nom. fem. sg. πόλις city
ἡ art. nom. fem. sg. ὁ ἡ τό the, this, that, he, she, it
μεγάλη adj. nom. fem. sg. μέγας great, loud, greatest, high, large, mighty, strong
ἐν prep. ἐν (+dat) in, by, with, among, at, on, through, to, within, into, of, for
ᾗ relative pron. dat. fem. sg. ὅς ἥ ὅ who, which, what, that
πάντες adj. nom. masc. pl. πᾶς πᾶσα πᾶν all, every, whosoever, every one, no, whole, any
οἱ art. nom. masc. pl. ὁ ἡ τό the, this, that, he, she, it
πλοῖα n. acc. neut. pl. πλοῖον ship, boat
ἐν prep. ἐν (+dat) in, by, with, among, at, on, through, to, within, into, of, for
τῇ art. dat. fem. sg. ὁ ἡ τό the, this, that, he, she, it
θαλάσσῃ n. dat. fem. sg. θάλασσα sea
ἐκ prep. ἐκ ἐξ (+gen) of, from, out of, by, on, with, in, among, through
τῆς art. gen. fem. sg. ὁ ἡ τό the, this, that, he, she, it
τιμιότητος n. gen. fem. sg. τιμιότης costliness
αὐτῆς pron. gen. fem. 3p. sg. αὐτός ή ό self, of oneself, even, very, the same, he, she, it
ὅτι conj. ὅτι that, for, because, how that, how, because that, for that, though
μιᾷ num. dat. fem. sg. εἷς or ἕν one, other, some, any, only, a certain

ὥρᾳ n. dat. fem. sg. ὥρα hour, time, season
20 ἐπ' prep. ἐπί (+gen) on, in, upon, (+dat) in, at, for, upon, (+acc) on, upon, unto, to, against
αὐτήν pron. acc. fem. 3p. sg. αὐτός ή ό self, of oneself, even, very, the same, he, she, it
οὐρανὲ n. voc. masc. sg. οὐρανός heaven, air, sky
καὶ conj. καί and, even, also, but
οἱ art. nom. masc. pl. ὁ ἡ τό the, this, that, he, she, it
ἅγιοι adj. nom. masc. pl. ἅγιος Holy, holy, saint, Holy One, holy thing, most holy
ἀπόστολοι n. nom. masc. pl. ἀπόστολος apostle, messenger, he that is sent
καὶ conj. καί and, even, also, but
οἱ art. nom. masc. pl. ὁ ἡ τό the, this, that, he, she, it
προφῆται n. nom. masc. pl. προφήτης prophet
ὅτι conj. ὅτι that, for, because, how that, how, because that, for that, though
ὁ art. nom. masc. sg. ὁ ἡ τό the, this, that, he, she, it
Θεὸς n. nom. masc. sg. θεός God, god
τὸ art. acc. neut. sg. ὁ ἡ τό the, this, that, he, she, it
κρίμα n. acc. neut. sg. κρίμα judgment, damnation, condemnation
ὑμῶν pron. gen. 2p. pl. σύ thou, you
ἐξ prep. ἐκ ἐξ (+gen) of, from, out of, by, on, with, in, among, through
αὐτῆς pron. gen. fem. 3p. sg. αὐτός ή ό self, of oneself, even, very, the same, he, she, it
21 Καὶ conj. καί and, even, also, but
εἷς num. nom. masc. sg. εἷς or ἕν one, other, some, any, only, a certain
ἄγγελος n. nom. masc. sg. ἄγγελος angel, messenger
ἰσχυρὸς adj. nom. masc. sg. ἰσχυρός mighty, strong, mightier, stronger
λίθον n. acc. masc. sg. λίθος stone
ὡς adv. ὡς as, when, as it were, how, about, like, as soon as, even as, while
μύλον n. acc. masc. sg. μύλος millstone
μέγαν adj. acc. masc. sg. μέγας great, loud, greatest, high, large, mighty, strong
καὶ conj. καί and, even, also, but
εἰς prep. εἰς (+acc) into, to, unto, for, in, on, toward, against, upon, at, among
τὴν art. acc. fem. sg. ὁ ἡ τό the, this, that, he, she, it
θάλασσαν n. acc. fem. sg. θάλασσα sea
Οὕτως adv. οὕτω οὕτως so, even so, thus, on this wise, likewise, after this manner
ὁρμήματι n. dat. neut. sg. ὅρμημα violence
Βαβυλὼν n. nom. fem. sg. Βαβυλών Babylon
ἡ art. nom. fem. sg. ὁ ἡ τό the, this, that, he, she, it
μεγάλη adj. nom. fem. sg. μέγας great, loud, greatest, high, large, mighty, strong
πόλις n. nom. fem. sg. πόλις city
καὶ conj. καί and, even, also, but
οὐ particle of negation. οὐ οὐκ οὐχ not, no, neither, none, nay, nor, never, nothing
μὴ particle of negation. μή not, no, lest, neither, none, nothing, nor, never, without
ἔτι adv. ἔτι yet, more, any more, further, still, moreover
22 καὶ conj. καί and, even, also, but
φωνὴ n. nom. fem. sg. φωνή voice, sound, noise
κιθαρῳδῶν n. gen. masc. pl. κιθαρῳδός harper
καὶ conj. καί and, even, also, but
μουσικῶν adj. gen. masc. pl. μουσικός musician
καὶ conj. καί and, even, also, but
αὐλητῶν n. gen. masc. pl. αὐλητής minstrel, piper
καὶ conj. καί and, even, also, but
σαλπιστῶν n. gen. masc. pl. σαλπιστής trumpeter
οὐ particle of negation. οὐ οὐκ οὐχ not, no, neither, none, nay, nor, never, nothing
μὴ particle of negation. μή not, no, lest, neither, none, nothing, nor, never, without
ἐν prep. ἐν (+dat) in, by, with, among, at, on, through, to, within, into, of, for
σοὶ pron. dat. 2p. sg. σύ thou, you
ἔτι adv. ἔτι yet, more, any more, further, still, moreover

καὶ conj. καί and, even, also, but
πᾶς adj. nom. masc. sg. πᾶς πᾶσα πᾶν all, every, whosoever, every one, no, whole, any
τεχνίτης n. nom. masc. sg. τεχνίτης craftsmen, builder
πάσης adj. gen. fem. sg. πᾶς πᾶσα πᾶν all, every, whosoever, every one, no, whole, any
τέχνης n. gen. fem. sg. τέχνη art, craft, occupation
οὐ particle of negation. οὐ οὐκ οὐχ not, no, neither, none, nay, nor, never, nothing
μὴ particle of negation. μή not, no, lest, neither, none, nothing, nor, never, without
ἐν prep. ἐν (+dat) in, by, with, among, at, on, through, to, within, into, of, for
σοὶ pron. dat. 2p. sg. σύ thou, you
ἔτι adv. ἔτι yet, more, any more, further, still, moreover
καὶ conj. καί and, even, also, but
φωνὴ n. nom. fem. sg. φωνή voice, sound, noise
μύλου n. gen. masc. sg. μύλος millstone
οὐ particle of negation. οὐ οὐκ οὐχ not, no, neither, none, nay, nor, never, nothing
μὴ particle of negation. μή not, no, lest, neither, none, nothing, nor, never, without
ἐν prep. ἐν (+dat) in, by, with, among, at, on, through, to, within, into, of, for
σοὶ pron. dat. 2p. sg. σύ thou, you
ἔτι adv. ἔτι yet, more, any more, further, still, moreover
23 καὶ conj. καί and, even, also, but
φῶς n. nom. neut. sg. φῶς light, fire
λύχνου n. gen. masc. sg. λύχνος candle, light, lamp
οὐ particle of negation. οὐ οὐκ οὐχ not, no, neither, none, nay, nor, never, nothing
μὴ particle of negation. μή not, no, lest, neither, none, nothing, nor, never, without
ἐν prep. ἐν (+dat) in, by, with, among, at, on, through, to, within, into, of, for
σοὶ pron. dat. 2p. sg. σύ thou, you
ἔτι adv. ἔτι yet, more, any more, further, still, moreover
καὶ conj. καί and, even, also, but
φωνὴ n. nom. fem. sg. φωνή voice, sound, noise
νυμφίου n. gen. masc. sg. νυμφίος bridegroom
καὶ conj. καί and, even, also, but
νύμφης n. gen. fem. sg. νύμφη bride, daughter in law
οὐ particle of negation. οὐ οὐκ οὐχ not, no, neither, none, nay, nor, never, nothing
μὴ particle of negation. μή not, no, lest, neither, none, nothing, nor, never, without
ἐν prep. ἐν (+dat) in, by, with, among, at, on, through, to, within, into, of, for
σοὶ pron. dat. 2p. sg. σύ thou, you
ἔτι adv. ἔτι yet, more, any more, further, still, moreover
ὅτι conj. ὅτι that, for, because, how that, how, because that, for that, though
οἱ art. nom. masc. pl. ὁ ἡ τό the, this, that, he, she, it
ἔμποροί n. nom. masc. pl. ἔμπορος merchant
σου pron. gen. 2p. sg. σύ thou, you
οἱ art. nom. masc. pl. ὁ ἡ τό the, this, that, he, she, it
μεγιστᾶνες n. nom. masc. pl. μεγιστάνες great men, lords
τῆς art. gen. fem. sg. ὁ ἡ τό the, this, that, he, she, it
γῆς n. gen. fem. sg. γῆ earth, land, ground, country
ὅτι conj. ὅτι that, for, because, how that, how, because that, for that, though
ἐν prep. ἐν (+dat) in, by, with, among, at, on, through, to, within, into, of, for
τῇ art. dat. fem. sg. ὁ ἡ τό the, this, that, he, she, it
φαρμακείᾳ n. dat. fem. sg. φαρμακεία witchcraft, sorcery
σου pron. gen. 2p. sg. σύ thou, you
πάντα adj. nom. neut. pl. πᾶς πᾶσα πᾶν all, every, whosoever, every one, no, whole, any
τὰ art. nom. neut. pl. ὁ ἡ τό the, this, that, he, she, it
ἔθνη n. nom. neut. pl. ἔθνος Gentile, nation, heathen, people
24 καὶ conj. καί and, even, also, but
ἐν prep. ἐν (+dat) in, by, with, among, at, on, through, to, within, into, of, for
αὐτῇ pron. dat. fem. 3p. sg. αὐτός ή ό self, of oneself, even, very, the same, he, she, it

αἷμα n. nom. neut. sg. αἷμα blood
προφητῶν n. gen. masc. pl. προφήτης prophet
καὶ conj. καί and, even, also, but
ἁγίων adj. gen. masc. pl. ἅγιος Holy, holy, saint, Holy One, holy thing, most holy
καὶ conj. καί and, even, also, but
πάντων adj. gen. masc. pl. πᾶς πᾶσα πᾶν all, every, whosoever, every one, no, whole, any
τῶν art. gen. masc. pl. ὁ ἡ τό the, this, that, he, she, it
ἐπὶ prep. ἐπί (+gen) on, in, upon, (+dat) in, at, for, upon, (+acc) on, upon, unto, to, against
τῆς art. gen. fem. sg. ὁ ἡ τό the, this, that, he, she, it
γῆς n. gen. fem. sg. γῆ earth, land, ground, country

19

1 Καὶ conj. καί and, even, also, but
μετὰ prep. μετά (+gen) with, among, against, (+acc) after
ταῦτα demo. pron. acc. neut. pl. οὗτος αὕτη τοῦτο this, the same, this same, he, she, it
φωνὴν n. acc. fem. sg. φωνή voice, sound, noise
ὄχλου n. gen. masc. sg. ὄχλος people, multitude, company, press, number
πολλοῦ adj. gen. masc. sg. πολύς many, great, much, long, abundant
μεγάλην adj. acc. fem. sg. μέγας great, loud, greatest, high, large, mighty, strong
ἐν prep. ἐν (+dat) in, by, with, among, at, on, through, to, within, into, of, for
τῷ art. dat. masc. sg. ὁ ἡ τό the, this, that, he, she, it
οὐρανῷ n. dat. masc. sg. οὐρανός heaven, air, sky
Ἀλληλούϊα particle. ἀλληλούϊα Alleluia
ἡ art. nom. fem. sg. ὁ ἡ τό the, this, that, he, she, it
σωτηρία n. nom. fem. sg. σωτηρία salvation, deliver, health, saving
καὶ conj. καί and, even, also, but
ἡ art. nom. fem. sg. ὁ ἡ τό the, this, that, he, she, it
δόξα n. nom. fem. sg. δόξα glory, honour, praise, dignity, worship
καὶ conj. καί and, even, also, but
ἡ art. nom. fem. sg. ὁ ἡ τό the, this, that, he, she, it
τιμὴ n. nom. fem. sg. τιμή honour, price, preciousness, sum
καὶ conj. καί and, even, also, but
ἡ art. nom. fem. sg. ὁ ἡ τό the, this, that, he, she, it
δύναμις n. nom. fem. sg. δύναμις power, mighty work, miracle, strength, might
Κυρίῳ n. dat. masc. sg. κύριος Lord, lord, master, sir, LORD, God, Master, owner
τῷ art. dat. masc. sg. ὁ ἡ τό the, this, that, he, she, it
Θεῷ n. dat. masc. sg. θεός God, god
ἡμῶν pron. gen. 1p. pl. ἐγώ I
2 ὅτι conj. ὅτι that, for, because, how that, how, because that, for that, though
ἀληθιναὶ adj. nom. fem. pl. ἀληθινός true
καὶ conj. καί and, even, also, but
δίκαιαι adj. nom. fem. pl. δίκαιος righteous, just, meet, right
αἱ art. nom. fem. pl. ὁ ἡ τό the, this, that, he, she, it
κρίσεις n. nom. fem. pl. κρίσις judgment, damnation, accusation, condemnation
αὐτοῦ pron. gen. masc. 3p. sg. αὐτός ή ό self, of oneself, even, very, the same, he, she, it
ὅτι conj. ὅτι that, for, because, how that, how, because that, for that, though
τὴν art. acc. fem. sg. ὁ ἡ τό the, this, that, he, she, it
πόρνην n. acc. fem. sg. πόρνη harlot, whore
τὴν art. acc. fem. sg. ὁ ἡ τό the, this, that, he, she, it
μεγάλην adj. acc. fem. sg. μέγας great, loud, greatest, high, large, mighty, strong
ἥτις relative pron. nom. fem. sg. ὅστις which, who, whosoever, that, whatsoever
τὴν art. acc. fem. sg. ὁ ἡ τό the, this, that, he, she, it
γῆν n. acc. fem. sg. γῆ earth, land, ground, country
ἐν prep. ἐν (+dat) in, by, with, among, at, on, through, to, within, into, of, for

τῇ art. dat. fem. sg. ὁ ἡ τό the, this, that, he, she, it
πορνείᾳ n. dat. fem. sg. πορνεία fornication
αὐτῆς pron. gen. fem. 3p. sg. αὐτός ή ό self, of oneself, even, very, the same, he, she, it
καὶ conj. καί and, even, also, but
τὸ art. acc. neut. sg. ὁ ἡ τό the, this, that, he, she, it
αἷμα n. acc. neut. sg. αἷμα blood
τῶν art. gen. masc. pl. ὁ ἡ τό the, this, that, he, she, it
δούλων n. gen. masc. pl. δοῦλος servant, bondman, bond, slave
αὐτοῦ pron. gen. masc. 3p. sg. αὐτός ή ό self, of oneself, even, very, the same, he, she, it
ἐκ prep. ἐκ ἐξ (+gen) of, from, out of, by, on, with, in, among, through
τῆς art. gen. fem. sg. ὁ ἡ τό the, this, that, he, she, it
χειρὸς n. gen. fem. sg. χείρ hand
αὐτῆς pron. gen. fem. 3p. sg. αὐτός ή ό self, of oneself, even, very, the same, he, she, it
3 καὶ conj. καί and, even, also, but
δεύτερον ordinal. adj. acc. neut. sg. δεύτερος second, second time, again, afterward
'Αλληλούϊα particle. ἀλληλούϊα Alleluia
καὶ conj. καί and, even, also, but
ὁ art. nom. masc. sg. ὁ ἡ τό the, this, that, he, she, it
καπνὸς n. nom. masc. sg. καπνός smoke
αὐτῆς pron. gen. fem. 3p. sg. αὐτός ή ό self, of oneself, even, very, the same, he, she, it
εἰς prep. εἰς (+acc) into, to, unto, for, in, on, toward, against, upon, at, among
τοὺς art. acc. masc. pl. ὁ ἡ τό the, this, that, he, she, it
αἰῶνας n. acc. masc. pl. αἰών ever, ever and ever, evermore, age, eternal, world
τῶν art. gen. masc. pl. ὁ ἡ τό the, this, that, he, she, it
αἰώνων n. gen. masc. pl. αἰών ever, ever and ever, evermore, age, eternal, world
4 καὶ conj. καί and, even, also, but
οἱ art. nom. masc. pl. ὁ ἡ τό the, this, that, he, she, it
πρεσβύτεροι adj. nom. masc. pl. πρεσβύτερος elder, elder woman, eldest, old man
οἱ art. nom. masc. pl. ὁ ἡ τό the, this, that, he, she, it
εἴκοσι num. nom. masc. pl. εἴκοσι twenty
τέσσαρες num. nom. masc. pl. τέσσαρες four
καὶ conj. καί and, even, also, but
τὰ art. nom. neut. pl. ὁ ἡ τό the, this, that, he, she, it
τέσσαρα num. nom. neut. pl. τέσσαρες four
ζῷα n. nom. neut. pl. ζῷον beast
καὶ conj. καί and, even, also, but
τῷ art. dat. masc. sg. ὁ ἡ τό the, this, that, he, she, it
Θεῷ n. dat. masc. sg. θεός God, god
τῷ art. dat. masc. sg. ὁ ἡ τό the, this, that, he, she, it
ἐπὶ prep. ἐπί (+gen) on, in, upon, (+dat) in, at, for, upon, (+acc) on, upon, unto, to, against
τοῦ art. gen. masc. sg. ὁ ἡ τό the, this, that, he, she, it
θρόνου n. gen. masc. sg. θρόνος throne, seat
'Αμὴν particle. ἀμήν amen, verily
'Αλληλούϊα particle. ἀλληλούϊα Alleluia
5 καὶ conj. καί and, even, also, but
φωνὴ n. nom. fem. sg. φωνή voice, sound, noise
ἐκ prep. ἐκ ἐξ (+gen) of, from, out of, by, on, with, in, among, through
τοῦ art. gen. masc. sg. ὁ ἡ τό the, this, that, he, she, it
θρόνου n. gen. masc. sg. θρόνος throne, seat
τὸν art. acc. masc. sg. ὁ ἡ τό the, this, that, he, she, it
Θεὸν n. acc. masc. sg. θεός God, god
ἡμῶν pron. gen. 1p. pl. ἐγώ I
πάντες adj. voc. masc. pl. πᾶς πᾶσα πᾶν all, every, whosoever, every one, no, whole, any
οἱ art. nom. masc. pl. ὁ ἡ τό the, this, that, he, she, it
δοῦλοι n. nom. masc. pl. δοῦλος servant, bondman, bond, slave

αὐτοῦ pron. gen. masc. 3p. sg. αὐτός ή ό self, of oneself, even, very, the same, he, she, it
καὶ conj. καί and, even, also, but
οἱ art. nom. masc. pl. ὁ ἡ τό the, this, that, he, she, it
αὐτόν pron. acc. masc. 3p. sg. αὐτός ή ό self, of oneself, even, very, the same, he, she, it
καὶ conj. καί and, even, also, but
οἱ art. nom. masc. pl. ὁ ἡ τό the, this, that, he, she, it
μικροὶ adj. nom. masc. pl. μικρός little, small, least, less
καὶ conj. καί and, even, also, but
οἱ art. nom. masc. pl. ὁ ἡ τό the, this, that, he, she, it
μεγάλοι adj. nom. masc. pl. μέγας great, loud, greatest, high, large, mighty, strong
6 καὶ conj. καί and, even, also, but
ὡς adv. ὡς as, when, as it were, how, about, like, as soon as, even as, while
φωνὴν n. acc. fem. sg. φωνή voice, sound, noise
ὄχλου n. gen. masc. sg. ὄχλος people, multitude, company, press, number
πολλοῦ adj. gen. masc. sg. πολύς many, great, much, long, abundant
καὶ conj. καί and, even, also, but
ὡς adv. ὡς as, when, as it were, how, about, like, as soon as, even as, while
φωνὴν n. acc. fem. sg. φωνή voice, sound, noise
ὑδάτων n. gen. neut. pl. ὕδωρ water
πολλῶν adj. gen. neut. pl. πολύς many, great, much, long, abundant
καὶ conj. καί and, even, also, but
ὡς adv. ὡς as, when, as it were, how, about, like, as soon as, even as, while
φωνὴν n. acc. fem. sg. φωνή voice, sound, noise
βροντῶν n. gen. fem. pl. βροντή thunder, thundering
ἰσχυρῶν adj. gen. fem. pl. ἰσχυρός mighty, strong, mightier, stronger
Ἀλληλούϊα particle. ἀλληλούϊα Alleluia
ὅτι conj. ὅτι that, for, because, how that, how, because that, for that, though
Κύριος n. nom. masc. sg. κύριος Lord, lord, master, sir, LORD, God, Master, owner
ὁ art. nom. masc. sg. ὁ ἡ τό the, this, that, he, she, it
Θεὸς n. nom. masc. sg. θεός God, god
ὁ art. nom. masc. sg. ὁ ἡ τό the, this, that, he, she, it
παντοκράτωρ n. nom. masc. sg. παντοκράτωρ Almighty, omnipotent
7 καὶ conj. καί and, even, also, but
καὶ conj. καί and, even, also, but
τὴν art. acc. fem. sg. ὁ ἡ τό the, this, that, he, she, it
δόξαν n. acc. fem. sg. δόξα glory, honour, praise, dignity, worship
αὐτῷ pron. dat. masc. 3p. sg. αὐτός ή ό self, of oneself, even, very, the same, he, she, it
ὅτι conj. ὅτι that, for, because, how that, how, because that, for that, though
ὁ art. nom. masc. sg. ὁ ἡ τό the, this, that, he, she, it
γάμος n. nom. masc. sg. γάμος marriage, wedding
τοῦ art. gen. neut. sg. ὁ ἡ τό the, this, that, he, she, it
ἀρνίου n. gen. neut. sg. ἀρνίον Lamb, lamb
καὶ conj. καί and, even, also, but
ἡ art. nom. fem. sg. ὁ ἡ τό the, this, that, he, she, it
γυνὴ n. nom. fem. sg. γυνή woman, wife
αὐτοῦ pron. gen. masc. 3p. sg. αὐτός ή ό self, of oneself, even, very, the same, he, she, it
ἑαυτὴν reflexive pron. acc. fem. 3p. sg. ἑαυτοῦ himself, herself, itself, yourself, ourselves
8 καὶ conj. καί and, even, also, but
αὐτῇ pron. dat. fem. 3p. sg. αὐτός ή ό self, of oneself, even, very, the same, he, she, it
ἵνα conj. ἵνα that, to, lest, for to, so that, albeit, because, for, so as
βύσσινον adj. acc. neut. sg. βύσσινος fine linen
καθαρόν adj. acc. neut. sg. καθαρός pure, clean, clear
καὶ conj. καί and, even, also, but
λαμπρὸν adj. acc. neut. sg. λαμπρός gorgeous, bright, goodly, white, clear
τὸ art. nom. neut. sg. ὁ ἡ τό the, this, that, he, she, it

γὰρ conj. γάρ for, and, because, but, indeed
βύσσινον adj. nom. neut. sg. βύσσινος fine linen
τὰ art. nom. neut. pl. ὁ ἡ τό the, this, that, he, she, it
δικαιώματα n. nom. neut. pl. δικαίωμα ordinance, righteousness, judgement, justification
τῶν art. gen. masc. pl. ὁ ἡ τό the, this, that, he, she, it
ἁγίων adj. gen. masc. pl. ἅγιος Holy, holy, saint, Holy One, holy thing, most holy
9 καὶ conj. καί and, even, also, but
μοι pron. dat. 1p. sg. ἐγώ I
Μακάριοι adj. nom. masc. pl. μακάριος blessed, happy
οἱ art. nom. masc. pl. ὁ ἡ τό the, this, that, he, she, it
εἰς prep. εἰς (+acc) into, to, unto, for, in, on, toward, against, upon, at, among
τὸ art. acc. neut. sg. ὁ ἡ τό the, this, that, he, she, it
δεῖπνον n. acc. neut. sg. δεῖπνον supper, feast
τοῦ art. gen. masc. sg. ὁ ἡ τό the, this, that, he, she, it
γάμου n. gen. masc. sg. γάμος marriage, wedding
τοῦ art. gen. neut. sg. ὁ ἡ τό the, this, that, he, she, it
ἀρνίου n. gen. neut. sg. ἀρνίον Lamb, lamb
καὶ conj. καί and, even, also, but
μοι pron. dat. 1p. sg. ἐγώ I
Οὗτοι demo. pron. nom. masc. pl. οὗτος αὕτη τοῦτο this, the same, this same, he, she, it
οἱ art. nom. masc. pl. ὁ ἡ τό the, this, that, he, she, it
λόγοι n. nom. masc. pl. λόγος word, saying, account, speech, thing, matter
ἀληθινοὶ adj. nom. masc. pl. ἀληθινός true
τοῦ art. gen. neut. sg. ὁ ἡ τό the, this, that, he, she, it
Θεοῦ n. gen. masc. sg. θεός God, god
10 καὶ conj. καί and, even, also, but
ἔμπροσθεν prep. ἔμπροσθεν (+gen) before, in the sight of, in the presence of
τῶν art. gen. masc. pl. ὁ ἡ τό the, this, that, he, she, it
ποδῶν n. gen. masc. pl. πούς foot
αὐτοῦ pron. gen. masc. 3p. sg. αὐτός ή ό self, of oneself, even, very, the same, he, she, it
αὐτῷ pron. dat. masc. 3p. sg. αὐτός ή ό self, of oneself, even, very, the same, he, she, it
καὶ conj. καί and, even, also, but
μοι pron. dat. 1p. sg. ἐγώ I
μή particle of negation. μή not, no, lest, neither, none, nothing, nor, never, without
σύνδουλός n. nom. masc. sg. σύνδουλος fellowservant
σου pron. gen. 2p. sg. σύ thou, you
καὶ conj. καί and, even, also, but
τῶν art. gen. masc. pl. ὁ ἡ τό the, this, that, he, she, it
ἀδελφῶν n. gen. masc. pl. ἀδελφός brother
σου pron. gen. 2p. sg. σύ thou, you
τῶν art. gen. masc. pl. ὁ ἡ τό the, this, that, he, she, it
τὴν art. acc. fem. sg. ὁ ἡ τό the, this, that, he, she, it
μαρτυρίαν n. acc. fem. sg. μαρτυρία testimony, witness, record, report
τοῦ art. gen. masc. sg. ὁ ἡ τό the, this, that, he, she, it
Ἰησοῦ n. gen. masc. sg. Ἰησοῦς Jesus
τῷ art. dat. masc. sg. ὁ ἡ τό the, this, that, he, she, it
Θεῷ n. dat. masc. sg. θεός God, god
ἡ art. nom. fem. sg. ὁ ἡ τό the, this, that, he, she, it
γὰρ conj. γάρ for, and, because, but, indeed
μαρτυρία n. nom. fem. sg. μαρτυρία testimony, witness, record, report
τοῦ art. gen. masc. sg. ὁ ἡ τό the, this, that, he, she, it
Ἰησοῦ n. gen. masc. sg. Ἰησοῦς Jesus
τὸ art. nom. neut. sg. ὁ ἡ τό the, this, that, he, she, it
πνεῦμα n. nom. neut. sg. πνεῦμα spirit, Spirit, Ghost, ghost, life. of the spirit, wind
τῆς art. gen. fem. sg. ὁ ἡ τό the, this, that, he, she, it

προφητείας n. gen. fem. sg. προφητεία prophecy, prophesying
11 Καὶ conj. καί and, even, also, but
τὸν art. acc. masc. sg. ὁ ἡ τό the, this, that, he, she, it
οὐρανὸν n. acc. masc. sg. οὐρανός heaven, air, sky
καὶ conj. καί and, even, also, but
ἵππος n. nom. masc. sg. ἵππος horse
λευκός adj. nom. masc. sg. λευκός white
καὶ conj. καί and, even, also, but
ὁ art. nom. masc. sg. ὁ ἡ τό the, this, that, he, she, it
ἐπ' prep. ἐπί (+gen) on, in, upon, (+dat) in, at, for, upon, (+acc) on, upon, unto, to, against
αὐτὸν pron. acc. masc. 3p. sg. αὐτός ή ό self, of oneself, even, very, the same, he, she, it
πιστὸς adj. nom. masc. sg. πιστός faithful, believing, true, sure
καὶ conj. καί and, even, also, but
ἀληθινός adj. nom. masc. sg. ἀληθινός true
καὶ conj. καί and, even, also, but
ἐν prep. ἐν (+dat) in, by, with, among, at, on, through, to, within, into, of, for
δικαιοσύνῃ n. dat. fem. sg. δικαιοσύνη righteousness
καὶ conj. καί and, even, also, but
12 οἱ art. nom. masc. pl. ὁ ἡ τό the, this, that, he, she, it
δὲ conj. δέ but, and, now, also, to the contrary, rather, then
ὀφθαλμοὶ n. nom. masc. pl. ὀφθαλμός eye, sight
αὐτοῦ pron. gen. masc. 3p. sg. αὐτός ή ό self, of oneself, even, very, the same, he, she, it
ὡς adv. ὡς as, when, as it were, how, about, like, as soon as, even as, while
φλὸξ n. nom. fem. sg. φλόξ flame, flaming
πυρός n. gen. neut. sg. πῦρ fire, fiery
καὶ conj. καί and, even, also, but
ἐπὶ prep. ἐπί (+gen) on, in, upon, (+dat) in, at, for, upon, (+acc) on, upon, unto, to, against
τὴν art. acc. fem. sg. ὁ ἡ τό the, this, that, he, she, it
κεφαλὴν n. acc. fem. sg. κεφαλή head
αὐτοῦ pron. gen. masc. 3p. sg. αὐτός ή ό self, of oneself, even, very, the same, he, she, it
διαδήματα n. nom. neut. pl. διάδημα crown, diadem
πολλά adj. nom. neut. pl. πολύς many, great, much, long, abundant
ὄνομα n. acc. neut. sg. ὄνομα name, call, surname
ὃ relative pron. acc. neut. sg. ὅς ἥ ὅ who, which, what, that
οὐδεὶς num. nom. masc. sg. οὐδείς no man, nothing, no, none, neither, not, nought
εἰ conj. εἰ if, whether, that, though, forasmuch
μὴ particle of negation. μή not, no, lest, neither, none, nothing, nor, never, without
αὐτός pron. nom. masc. 3p. sg. αὐτός ή ό self, of oneself, even, very, the same, he, she, it
13 καὶ conj. καί and, even, also, but
ἱμάτιον n. acc. neut. sg. ἱμάτιον cloke, garment, clothes, raiment, robe, vesture
αἵματι n. dat. neut. sg. αἷμα blood
καὶ conj. καί and, even, also, but
τὸ art. nom. neut. sg. ὁ ἡ τό the, this, that, he, she, it
ὄνομα n. nom. neut. sg. ὄνομα name, call, surname
αὐτοῦ pron. gen. masc. 3p. sg. αὐτός ή ό self, of oneself, even, very, the same, he, she, it
Ὁ art. nom. masc. sg. ὁ ἡ τό the, this, that, he, she, it
λόγος n. nom. masc. sg. λόγος word, saying, account, speech, thing, matter
τοῦ art. gen. masc. sg. ὁ ἡ τό the, this, that, he, she, it
Θεοῦ n. gen. masc. sg. θεός God, god
14 καὶ conj. καί and, even, also, but
τὰ art. nom. neut. pl. ὁ ἡ τό the, this, that, he, she, it
στρατεύματα n. nom. neut. pl. στράτευμα army, man of war, soldier
τὰ art. nom. neut. pl. ὁ ἡ τό the, this, that, he, she, it
ἐν prep. ἐν (+dat) in, by, with, among, at, on, through, to, within, into, of, for
τῷ art. dat. masc. sg. ὁ ἡ τό the, this, that, he, she, it

οὐρανῷ n. dat. masc. sg. οὐρανός heaven, air, sky
αὐτῷ pron. dat. masc. 3p. sg. αὐτός ή ό self, of oneself, even, very, the same, he, she, it
ἐφ' prep. ἐπί (+gen) on, in, upon, (+dat) in, at, for, upon, (+acc) on, upon, unto, to, against
ἵπποις n. dat. masc. pl. ἵππος horse
λευκοῖς adj. dat. masc. pl. λευκός white
βύσσινον adj. acc. neut. sg. βύσσινος fine linen
λευκὸν adj. acc. neut. sg. λευκός white
καὶ conj. καί and, even, also, but
καθαρόν adj. acc. neut. sg. καθαρός pure, clean, clear
15 καὶ conj. καί and, even, also, but
ἐκ prep. ἐκ ἐξ (+gen) of, from, out of, by, on, with, in, among, through
τοῦ art. gen. neut. sg. ὁ ἡ τό the, this, that, he, she, it
στόματος n. gen. neut. sg. στόμα mouth, face, edge
αὐτοῦ pron. gen. masc. 3p. sg. αὐτός ή ό self, of oneself, even, very, the same, he, she, it
ῥομφαία n. nom. fem. sg. ῥομφαία sword
ὀξεῖα adj. nom. fem. sg. ὀξύς swift, sharp
ἵνα conj. ἵνα that, to, lest, for to, so that, albeit, because, for, so as
ἐν prep. ἐν (+dat) in, by, with, among, at, on, through, to, within, into, of, for
αὐτῇ pron. dat. fem. 3p. sg. αὐτός ή ό self, of oneself, even, very, the same, he, she, it
τὰ art. acc. neut. pl. ὁ ἡ τό the, this, that, he, she, it
ἔθνη n. acc. neut. pl. ἔθνος Gentile, nation, heathen, people
καὶ conj. καί and, even, also, but
αὐτὸς pron. nom. masc. 3p. sg. αὐτός ή ό self, of oneself, even, very, the same, he, she, it
αὐτοὺς pron. acc. masc. 3p. pl. αὐτός ή ό self, of oneself, even, very, the same, he, she, it
ἐν prep. ἐν (+dat) in, by, with, among, at, on, through, to, within, into, of, for
ῥάβδῳ n. dat. fem. sg. ῥάβδος rod, sceptre, stave, staff
σιδηρᾷ adj. dat. fem. sg. σιδήρεος iron, of iron
καὶ conj. καί and, even, also, but
αὐτὸς pron. nom. masc. 3p. sg. αὐτός ή ό self, of oneself, even, very, the same, he, she, it
τὴν art. acc. fem. sg. ὁ ἡ τό the, this, that, he, she, it
ληνὸν n. acc. fem. sg. ληνός winepress
τοῦ art. gen. masc. sg. ὁ ἡ τό the, this, that, he, she, it
οἴνου n. gen. masc. sg. οἶνος wine
τοῦ art. gen. masc. sg. ὁ ἡ τό the, this, that, he, she, it
θυμοῦ n. gen. masc. sg. θυμός wrath, fierceness, indignation
καὶ conj. καί and, even, also, but
τῆς art. gen. fem. sg. ὁ ἡ τό the, this, that, he, she, it
ὀργῆς n. gen. fem. sg. ὀργή wrath, anger, indignation, vengeance
τοῦ art. gen. masc. sg. ὁ ἡ τό the, this, that, he, she, it
Θεοῦ n. gen. masc. sg. θεός God, god
τοῦ art. gen. masc. sg. ὁ ἡ τό the, this, that, he, she, it
παντοκράτορος n. gen. masc. sg. παντοκράτωρ Almighty, omnipotent
16 καὶ conj. καί and, even, also, but
ἐπὶ prep. ἐπί (+gen) on, in, upon, (+dat) in, at, for, upon, (+acc) on, upon, unto, to, against
τὸ art. acc. neut. sg. ὁ ἡ τό the, this, that, he, she, it
ἱμάτιον n. acc. neut. sg. ἱμάτιον cloke, garment, clothes, raiment, robe, vesture
καὶ conj. καί and, even, also, but
ἐπὶ prep. ἐπί (+gen) on, in, upon, (+dat) in, at, for, upon, (+acc) on, upon, unto, to, against
τὸν art. acc. masc. sg. ὁ ἡ τό the, this, that, he, she, it
μηρὸν n. acc. masc. sg. μηρός thigh
αὐτοῦ pron. gen. masc. 3p. sg. αὐτός ή ό self, of oneself, even, very, the same, he, she, it
ὄνομα n. acc. neut. sg. ὄνομα name, call, surname
Βασιλεὺς n. nom. masc. sg. βασιλεύς king
βασιλέων n. gen. masc. pl. βασιλεύς king
καὶ conj. καί and, even, also, but

Κύριος n. nom. masc. sg. κύριος Lord, lord, master, sir, LORD, God, Master, owner
κυρίων n. gen. masc. pl. κύριος Lord, lord, master, sir, LORD, God, Master, owner
17 Καὶ conj. καί and, even, also, but
ἕνα num. acc. masc. sg. εἷς or ἕν one, other, some, any, only, a certain
ἄγγελον n. acc. masc. sg. ἄγγελος angel, messenger
ἐν prep. ἐν (+dat) in, by, with, among, at, on, through, to, within, into, of, for
τῷ art. dat. masc. sg. ὁ ἡ τό the, this, that, he, she, it
ἡλίῳ n. dat. masc. sg. ἥλιος sun, east
καὶ conj. καί and, even, also, but
φωνῇ n. dat. fem. sg. φωνή voice, sound, noise
μεγάλῃ adj. dat. fem. sg. μέγας great, loud, greatest, high, large, mighty, strong
πᾶσι adj. dat. neut. pl. πᾶς πᾶσα πᾶν all, every, whosoever, every one, no, whole, any
τοῖς art. dat. neut. pl. ὁ ἡ τό the, this, that, he, she, it
ὀρνέοις n. dat. neut. pl. ὄρνεον bird, fowl
τοῖς art. dat. neut. pl. ὁ ἡ τό the, this, that, he, she, it
ἐν prep. ἐν (+dat) in, by, with, among, at, on, through, to, within, into, of, for
μεσουρανήματι n. dat. neut. sg. μεσουράνημα midst of heaven
Δεῦτε adv. δεῦτε come, follow
καὶ conj. καί and, even, also, but
εἰς prep. εἰς (+acc) into, to, unto, for, in, on, toward, against, upon, at, among
τὸ art. acc. neut. sg. ὁ ἡ τό the, this, that, he, she, it
δεῖπνον n. acc. neut. sg. δεῖπνον supper, feast
τοῦ art. gen. masc. sg. ὁ ἡ τό the, this, that, he, she, it
μεγάλου adj. gen. masc. sg. μέγας great, loud, greatest, high, large, mighty, strong
Θεοῦ n. gen. masc. sg. θεός God, god
18 ἵνα conj. ἵνα that, to, lest, for to, so that, albeit, because, for, so as
σάρκας n. acc. fem. pl. σάρξ flesh, carnal
βασιλέων n. gen. masc. pl. βασιλεύς king
καὶ conj. καί and, even, also, but
σάρκας n. acc. fem. pl. σάρξ flesh, carnal
χιλιάρχων n. gen. masc. pl. χιλίαρχος high captain, chief captain, captain
καὶ conj. καί and, even, also, but
σάρκας n. acc. fem. pl. σάρξ flesh, carnal
ἰσχυρῶν adj. gen. masc. pl. ἰσχυρός mighty, strong, mightier, stronger
καὶ conj. καί and, even, also, but
σάρκας n. acc. fem. pl. σάρξ flesh, carnal
ἵππων n. gen. masc. pl. ἵππος horse
καὶ conj. καί and, even, also, but
τῶν art. gen. masc. pl. ὁ ἡ τό the, this, that, he, she, it
ἐπ' prep. ἐπί (+gen) on, in, upon, (+dat) in, at, for, upon, (+acc) on, upon, unto, to, against
αὐτῶν pron. gen. masc. 3p. pl. αὐτός ή ό self, of oneself, even, very, the same, he, she, it
καὶ conj. καί and, even, also, but
σάρκας n. acc. fem. pl. σάρξ flesh, carnal
πάντων adj. gen. masc. pl. πᾶς πᾶsa πᾶν all, every, whosoever, every one, no, whole, any
ἐλευθέρων adj. gen. masc. pl. ἐλεύθερος free, freewoman, at liberty, freeman
τε conj. τέ and, both, also
καὶ conj. καί and, even, also, but
δούλων n. gen. masc. pl. δοῦλος servant, bondman, bond, slave
καὶ conj. καί and, even, also, but
μικρῶν adj. gen. masc. pl. μικρός little, small, least, less
καὶ conj. καί and, even, also, but
μεγάλων adj. gen. masc. pl. μέγας great, loud, greatest, high, large, mighty, strong
19 Καὶ conj. καί and, even, also, but
τὸ art. acc. neut. sg. ὁ ἡ τό the, this, that, he, she, it
θηρίον n. acc. neut. sg. θηρίον beast, wild beast, venomous beast

καὶ conj. καί and, even, also, but
τοὺς art. acc. masc. pl. ὁ ἡ τό the, this, that, he, she, it
βασιλεῖς n. acc. masc. pl. βασιλεύς king
τῆς art. gen. fem. sg. ὁ ἡ τό the, this, that, he, she, it
γῆς n. gen. fem. sg. γῆ earth, land, ground, country
καὶ conj. καί and, even, also, but
τὰ art. acc. neut. pl. ὁ ἡ τό the, this, that, he, she, it
στρατεύματα n. acc. neut. pl. στράτευμα army, man of war, soldier
αὐτῶν pron. gen. masc. 3p. pl. αὐτός ή ό self, of oneself, even, very, the same, he, she, it
πόλεμον n. acc. masc. sg. πόλεμος war, battle, fight
μετὰ prep. μετά (+gen) with, among, against, (+acc) after
τοῦ art. gen. masc. sg. ὁ ἡ τό the, this, that, he, she, it
ἐπὶ prep. ἐπί (+gen) on, in, upon, (+dat) in, at, for, upon, (+acc) on, upon, unto, to, against
τοῦ art. gen. masc. sg. ὁ ἡ τό the, this, that, he, she, it
ἵππου n. gen. masc. sg. ἵππος horse
καὶ conj. καί and, even, also, but
μετὰ prep. μετά (+gen) with, among, against, (+acc) after
τοῦ art. gen. masc. sg. ὁ ἡ τό the, this, that, he, she, it
στρατεύματος n. gen. neut. sg. στράτευμα army, man of war, soldier
αὐτοῦ pron. gen. masc. 3p. sg. αὐτός ή ό self, of oneself, even, very, the same, he, she, it
20 καὶ conj. καί and, even, also, but
τὸ art. nom. neut. sg. ὁ ἡ τό the, this, that, he, she, it
θηρίον n. nom. neut. sg. θηρίον beast, wild beast, venomous beast
καὶ conj. καί and, even, also, but
μετὰ prep. μετά (+gen) with, among, against, (+acc) after
τούτου demo. pron. gen. neut. sg. οὗτος αὕτη τοῦτο this, the same, this same, he, she, it
ὁ art. nom. masc. sg. ὁ ἡ τό the, this, that, he, she, it
ψευδοπροφήτης n. nom. masc. sg. ψευδοπροφήτης false prophet
ὁ art. nom. masc. sg. ὁ ἡ τό the, this, that, he, she, it
τὰ art. acc. neut. pl. ὁ ἡ τό the, this, that, he, she, it
σημεῖα n. acc. neut. pl. σημεῖον sign, miracle, wonder, token
ἐνώπιον prep. ἐνώπιον (+gen) before, in the sight of, in the presence of. (adv.) before
αὐτοῦ pron. gen. neut. 3p. sg. αὐτός ή ό self, of oneself, even, very, the same, he, she, it
ἐν prep. ἐν (+dat) in, by, with, among, at, on, through, to, within, into, of, for
οἷς relative pron. dat. neut. pl. ὅς ἥ ὅ who, which, what, that
τοὺς art. acc. masc. pl. ὁ ἡ τό the, this, that, he, she, it
τὸ art. acc. neut. sg. ὁ ἡ τό the, this, that, he, she, it
χάραγμα n. acc. neut. sg. χάραγμα mark, graven
τοῦ art. gen. neut. sg. ὁ ἡ τό the, this, that, he, she, it
θηρίου n. gen. neut. sg. θηρίον beast, wild beast, venomous beast
καὶ conj. καί and, even, also, but
τοὺς art. acc. masc. pl. ὁ ἡ τό the, this, that, he, she, it
τῇ art. dat. fem. sg. ὁ ἡ τό the, this, that, he, she, it
εἰκόνι n. dat. fem. sg. εἰκών image
αὐτοῦ pron. gen. neut. 3p. sg. αὐτός ή ό self, of oneself, even, very, the same, he, she, it
οἱ art. nom. masc. pl. ὁ ἡ τό the, this, that, he, she, it
δύο num. nom. masc. pl. δύο two, twain, both
εἰς prep. εἰς (+acc) into, to, unto, for, in, on, toward, against, upon, at, among
τὴν art. acc. fem. sg. ὁ ἡ τό the, this, that, he, she, it
λίμνην n. acc. fem. sg. λίμην lake
τοῦ art. gen. neut. sg. ὁ ἡ τό the, this, that, he, she, it
πυρὸς n. gen. neut. sg. πῦρ fire, fiery
τὴν art. acc. fem. sg. ὁ ἡ τό the, this, that, he, she, it
ἐν prep. ἐν (+dat) in, by, with, among, at, on, through, to, within, into, of, for
τῷ art. dat. neut. sg. ὁ ἡ τό the, this, that, he, she, it

θείῳ n. dat. neut. sg. θεῖον brimstone
21 καὶ conj. καί and, even, also, but
οἱ art. nom. masc. pl. ὁ ἡ τό the, this, that, he, she, it
λοιποὶ adj. nom. masc. pl. λοιπός other, rest, remnant, residue, which remain
ἐν prep. ἐν (+dat) in, by, with, among, at, on, through, to, within, into, of, for
τῇ art. dat. fem. sg. ὁ ἡ τό the, this, that, he, she, it
ῥομφαίᾳ n. dat. fem. sg. ῥομφαία sword
τοῦ art. gen. masc. sg. ὁ ἡ τό the, this, that, he, she, it
ἐπὶ prep. ἐπί (+gen) on, in, upon, (+dat) in, at, for, upon, (+acc) on, upon, unto, to, against
τοῦ art. gen. masc. sg. ὁ ἡ τό the, this, that, he, she, it
ἵππου n. gen. masc. sg. ἵππος horse
τῇ art. dat. fem. sg. ὁ ἡ τό the, this, that, he, she, it
ἐκ prep. ἐκ ἐξ (+gen) of, from, out of, by, on, with, in, among, through
τοῦ art. gen. neut. sg. ὁ ἡ τό the, this, that, he, she, it
στόματος n. gen. neut. sg. στόμα mouth, face, edge
αὐτοῦ pron. gen. masc. 3p. sg. αὐτός ή ό self, of oneself, even, very, the same, he, she, it
καὶ conj. καί and, even, also, but
πάντα adj. nom. neut. pl. πᾶς πᾶσα πᾶν all, every, whosoever, every one, no, whole, any
τὰ art. nom. neut. pl. ὁ ἡ τό the, this, that, he, she, it
ὄρνεα n. nom. neut. pl. ὄρνεον bird, fowl
ἐκ prep. ἐκ ἐξ (+gen) of, from, out of, by, on, with, in, among, through
τῶν art. gen. fem. pl. ὁ ἡ τό the, this, that, he, she, it
σαρκῶν n. gen. fem. pl. σάρξ flesh, carnal
αὐτῶν pron. gen. masc. 3p. pl. αὐτός ή ό self, of oneself, even, very, the same, he, she, it

20

1 Καὶ conj. καί and, even, also, but
ἄγγελον n. acc. masc. sg. ἄγγελος angel, messenger
ἐκ prep. ἐκ ἐξ (+gen) of, from, out of, by, on, with, in, among, through
τοῦ art. gen. masc. sg. ὁ ἡ τό the, this, that, he, she, it
οὐρανοῦ n. gen. masc. sg. οὐρανός heaven, air, sky
τὴν art. acc. fem. sg. ὁ ἡ τό the, this, that, he, she, it
κλεῖδα n. acc. fem. sg. κλείς key
τῆς art. gen. fem. sg. ὁ ἡ τό the, this, that, he, she, it
ἀβύσσου n. gen. fem. sg. ἄβυσσος deep, abyss, bottomless pit, bottomless
καὶ conj. καί and, even, also, but
ἅλυσιν n. acc. fem. sg. ἅλυσις chain, bond
μεγάλην adj. acc. fem. sg. μέγας great, loud, greatest, high, large, mighty, strong
ἐπὶ prep. ἐπί (+gen) on, in, upon, (+dat) in, at, for, upon, (+acc) on, upon, unto, to, against
τὴν art. acc. fem. sg. ὁ ἡ τό the, this, that, he, she, it
χεῖρα n. acc. fem. sg. χείρ hand
αὐτοῦ pron. gen. masc. 3p. sg. αὐτός ή ό self, of oneself, even, very, the same, he, she, it
2 καὶ conj. καί and, even, also, but
τὸν art. acc. masc. sg. ὁ ἡ τό the, this, that, he, she, it
δράκοντα n. acc. masc. sg. δράκων dragon
τὸν art. acc. masc. sg. ὁ ἡ τό the, this, that, he, she, it
ὄφιν n. acc. masc. sg. ὄφις serpent
τὸν art. acc. masc. sg. ὁ ἡ τό the, this, that, he, she, it
ἀρχαῖον adj. acc. masc. sg. ἀρχαῖος old, one of old time
ὅς relative pron. nom. masc. sg. ὅς ἥ ὅ who, which, what, that
διάβολος adj. nom. masc. sg. διάβολος devil, false accuser, Devil, slanderer
καὶ conj. καί and, even, also, but
Σατανᾶς n. nom. masc. sg. Σατανᾶς Satan
καὶ conj. καί and, even, also, but

αὐτὸν pron. acc. masc. 3p. sg. αὐτός ή ό self, of oneself, even, very, the same, he, she, it
χίλια num. acc. neut. pl. χίλιοι one thousand
ἔτη n. acc. neut. pl. ἔτος year
3 καὶ conj. καί and, even, also, but
αὐτὸν pron. acc. masc. 3p. sg. αὐτός ή ό self, of oneself, even, very, the same, he, she, it
εἰς prep. εἰς (+acc) into, to, unto, for, in, on, toward, against, upon, at, among
τὴν art. acc. fem. sg. ὁ ἡ τό the, this, that, he, she, it
ἄβυσσον n. acc. fem. sg. ἄβυσσος deep, abyss, bottomless pit, bottomless
καὶ conj. καί and, even, also, but
αὐτὸν pron. acc. masc. 3p. sg. αὐτός ή ό self, of oneself, even, very, the same, he, she, it
καὶ conj. καί and, even, also, but
ἐπάνω prep. ἐπάνω (+gen) on, over, above, upon, more than
αὐτοῦ pron. gen. masc. 3p. sg. αὐτός ή ό self, of oneself, even, very, the same, he, she, it
ἵνα conj. ἵνα that, to, lest, for to, so that, albeit, because, for, so as
μὴ particle of negation. μή not, no, lest, neither, none, nothing, nor, never, without
τὰ art. acc. neut. pl. ὁ ἡ τό the, this, that, he, she, it
ἔθνη n. acc. neut. pl. ἔθνος Gentile, nation, heathen, people
ἔτι adv. ἔτι yet, more, any more, further, still, moreover
ἄχρι prep. ἄχρι or ἄχρις (+gen) until, unto, till, even to, as far as, while, into
τὰ art. nom. neut. pl. ὁ ἡ τό the, this, that, he, she, it
χίλια num. nom. neut. pl. χίλιοι one thousand
ἔτη n. nom. neut. pl. ἔτος year
καὶ conj. καί and, even, also, but
μετὰ prep. μετά (+gen) with, among, against, (+acc) after
ταῦτα demo. pron. acc. neut. pl. οὗτος αὕτη τοῦτο this, the same, this same, he, she, it
αὐτὸν pron. acc. masc. 3p. sg. αὐτός ή ό self, of oneself, even, very, the same, he, she, it
μικρὸν adj. acc. masc. sg. μικρός little, small, least, less
χρόνον n. acc. masc. sg. χρόνος time, season, space
4 Καὶ conj. καί and, even, also, but
θρόνους n. acc. masc. pl. θρόνος throne, seat
καὶ conj. καί and, even, also, but
ἐπ' prep. ἐπί (+gen) on, in, upon, (+dat) in, at, for, upon, (+acc) on, upon, unto, to, against
αὐτοὺς pron. acc. masc. 3p. pl. αὐτός ή ό self, of oneself, even, very, the same, he, she, it
καὶ conj. καί and, even, also, but
κρίμα n. nom. neut. sg. κρίμα judgment, damnation, condemnation
αὐτοῖς pron. dat. masc. 3p. pl. αὐτός ή ό self, of oneself, even, very, the same, he, she, it
καὶ conj. καί and, even, also, but
τὰς art. acc. fem. pl. ὁ ἡ τό the, this, that, he, she, it
ψυχὰς n. acc. fem. pl. ψυχή life, soul, mind, heart
τῶν art. gen. masc. pl. ὁ ἡ τό the, this, that, he, she, it
διὰ prep. διά (+gen) by, through, with, in, of, (+acc) for, because of, for a cause
τὴν art. acc. fem. sg. ὁ ἡ τό the, this, that, he, she, it
μαρτυρίαν n. acc. fem. sg. μαρτυρία testimony, witness, record, report
Ἰησοῦ n. gen. masc. sg. Ἰησοῦς Jesus
καὶ conj. καί and, even, also, but
διὰ prep. διά (+gen) by, through, with, in, of, (+acc) for, because of, for a cause
τὸν art. acc. masc. sg. ὁ ἡ τό the, this, that, he, she, it
λόγον n. acc. masc. sg. λόγος word, saying, account, speech, thing, matter
τοῦ art. gen. masc. sg. ὁ ἡ τό the, this, that, he, she, it
Θεοῦ n. gen. masc. sg. θεός God, god
καὶ conj. καί and, even, also, but
οἵτινες relative pron. nom. masc. pl. ὅστις which, who, whosoever, that, whatsoever
οὐ particle of negation. οὐ οὐκ οὐχ not, no, neither, none, nay, nor, never, nothing
τῷ art. dat. neut. sg. ὁ ἡ τό the, this, that, he, she, it
θηριῷ n. dat. neut. sg. θηρίον beast, wild beast, venomous beast

οὔτε conj. οὔτε neither, nor, nor yet, no, none
τὴν art. acc. fem. sg. ὁ ἡ τό the, this, that, he, she, it
εἰκόνα n. acc. fem. sg. εἰκών image
αὐτοῦ pron. gen. neut. 3p. sg. αὐτός ή ὁ self, of oneself, even, very, the same, he, she, it
καὶ conj. καί and, even, also, but
οὐκ particle of negation. οὐ οὐκ οὐχ not, no, neither, none, nay, nor, never, nothing
τὸ art. acc. neut. sg. ὁ ἡ τό the, this, that, he, she, it
χάραγμα n. acc. neut. sg. χάραγμα mark, graven
ἐπὶ prep. ἐπί (+gen) on, in, upon, (+dat) in, at, for, upon, (+acc) on, upon, unto, to, against
τὸ art. acc. neut. sg. ὁ ἡ τό the, this, that, he, she, it
μέτωπον n. acc. neut. sg. μέτωπον forehead
αὐτῶν pron. gen. masc. 3p. pl. αὐτός ή ὁ self, of oneself, even, very, the same, he, she, it
καὶ conj. καί and, even, also, but
ἐπὶ prep. ἐπί (+gen) on, in, upon, (+dat) in, at, for, upon, (+acc) on, upon, unto, to, against
τὴν art. acc. fem. sg. ὁ ἡ τό the, this, that, he, she, it
χεῖρα n. acc. fem. sg. χείρ hand
αὐτῶν pron. gen. masc. 3p. pl. αὐτός ή ὁ self, of oneself, even, very, the same, he, she, it
καὶ conj. καί and, even, also, but
καὶ conj. καί and, even, also, but
μετὰ prep. μετά (+gen) with, among, against, (+acc) after
Χριστοῦ n. gen. masc. sg. Χριστός Christ
χίλια num. acc. neut. pl. χίλιοι one thousand
ἔτη n. acc. neut. pl. ἔτος year
5 οἱ art. nom. masc. pl. ὁ ἡ τό the, this, that, he, she, it
δὲ conj. δέ but, and, now, also, to the contrary, rather, then
λοιποὶ adj. nom. masc. pl. λοιπός other, rest, remnant, residue, which remain
τῶν art. gen. masc. pl. ὁ ἡ τό the, this, that, he, she, it
νεκρῶν adj. gen. masc. pl. νεκρός dead
οὐκ particle of negation. οὐ οὐκ οὐχ not, no, neither, none, nay, nor, never, nothing
ἕως conj. ἕως till, until, unto, until when, while, as far as, even, until now
τὰ art. nom. neut. pl. ὁ ἡ τό the, this, that, he, she, it
χίλια num. nom. neut. pl. χίλιοι one thousand
ἔτη n. nom. neut. pl. ἔτος year
αὕτη demo. pron. nom. fem. sg. οὗτος αὕτη τοῦτο this, the same, this same, he, she, it
ἡ art. nom. fem. sg. ὁ ἡ τό the, this, that, he, she, it
ἀνάστασις n. nom. fem. sg. ἀνάστασις resurrection, rising again
ἡ art. nom. fem. sg. ὁ ἡ τό the, this, that, he, she, it
πρώτη ordinal. adj. nom. fem. sg. πρῶτος first, chief, first of all, chiefest, best
6 μακάριος adj. nom. masc. sg. μακάριος blessed, happy
καὶ conj. καί and, even, also, but
ἅγιος adj. nom. masc. sg. ἅγιος Holy, holy, saint, Holy One, holy thing, most holy
ὁ art. nom. masc. sg. ὁ ἡ τό the, this, that, he, she, it
μέρος n. acc. neut. sg. μέρος part, coast, portion, behalf, respect, piece, side
ἐν prep. ἐν (+dat) in, by, with, among, at, on, through, to, within, into, of, for
τῇ art. dat. fem. sg. ὁ ἡ τό the, this, that, he, she, it
ἀναστάσει n. dat. fem. sg. ἀνάστασις resurrection, rising again
τῇ art. dat. fem. sg. ὁ ἡ τό the, this, that, he, she, it
πρώτῃ ordinal. adj. dat. fem. sg. πρῶτος first, chief, first of all, chiefest, best
ἐπὶ prep. ἐπί (+gen) on, in, upon, (+dat) in, at, for, upon, (+acc) on, upon, unto, to, against
τούτων demo. pron. gen. masc. pl. οὗτος αὕτη τοῦτο this, the same, this same, he, she, it
ὁ art. nom. masc. sg. ὁ ἡ τό the, this, that, he, she, it
θάνατος n. nom. masc. sg. θάνατος death
ὁ art. nom. masc. sg. ὁ ἡ τό the, this, that, he, she, it
δεύτερος ordinal. adj. nom. masc. sg. δεύτερος second, second time, again, afterward
οὐκ particle of negation. οὐ οὐκ οὐχ not, no, neither, none, nay, nor, never, nothing

ἐξουσίαν n. acc. fem. sg. ἐξουσία power, authority, right, strength, jurisdiction
ἀλλ' conj. ἀλλά but, yea, yet, nevertheless, howbeit, nay, therefore
ἱερεῖς n. nom. masc. pl. ἱερεύς priest
τοῦ art. gen. masc. sg. ὁ ἡ τό the, this, that, he, she, it
Θεοῦ n. gen. masc. sg. θεός God, god
καὶ conj. καί and, even, also, but
τοῦ art. gen. masc. sg. ὁ ἡ τό the, this, that, he, she, it
Χριστοῦ n. gen. masc. sg. Χριστός Christ
καὶ conj. καί and, even, also, but
μετ' prep. μετά (+gen) with, among, against, (+acc) after
αὐτοῦ pron. gen. masc. 3p. sg. αὐτός ή ὁ self, of oneself, even, very, the same, he, she, it
χίλια num. acc. neut. pl. χίλιοι one thousand
ἔτη n. acc. neut. pl. ἔτος year
7 Καὶ conj. καί and, even, also, but
ὅταν conj. ὅταν when, as soon as, as long as, that, whensoever, while
τὰ art. nom. neut. pl. ὁ ἡ τό the, this, that, he, she, it
χίλια num. nom. neut. pl. χίλιοι one thousand
ἔτη n. nom. neut. pl. ἔτος year
ὁ art. nom. masc. sg. ὁ ἡ τό the, this, that, he, she, it
Σατανᾶς n. nom. masc. sg. Σατανᾶς Satan
ἐκ prep. ἐκ ἐξ (+gen) of, from, out of, by, on, with, in, among, through
τῆς art. gen. fem. sg. ὁ ἡ τό the, this, that, he, she, it
φυλακῆς n. gen. fem. sg. φυλακή prison, watch, imprisonment, cage, hold, ward
αὐτοῦ pron. gen. masc. 3p. sg. αὐτός ή ὁ self, of oneself, even, very, the same, he, she, it
8 καὶ conj. καί and, even, also, but
τὰ art. acc. neut. pl. ὁ ἡ τό the, this, that, he, she, it
ἔθνη n. acc. neut. pl. ἔθνος Gentile, nation, heathen, people
τὰ art. acc. neut. pl. ὁ ἡ τό the, this, that, he, she, it
ἐν prep. ἐν (+dat) in, by, with, among, at, on, through, to, within, into, of, for
ταῖς art. dat. fem. pl. ὁ ἡ τό the, this, that, he, she, it
τέσσαρσι num. dat. fem. pl. τέσσαρες four
γωνίαις n. dat. fem. pl. γωνία corner, quarter
τῆς art. gen. fem. sg. ὁ ἡ τό the, this, that, he, she, it
γῆς n. gen. fem. sg. γῆ earth, land, ground, country
τὸν art. acc. masc. sg. ὁ ἡ τό the, this, that, he, she, it
Γὼγ n. acc. masc. sg. Γώγ Gog
καὶ conj. καί and, even, also, but
τὸν art. acc. masc. sg. ὁ ἡ τό the, this, that, he, she, it
Μαγώγ n. acc. masc. sg. Μαγώγ Magog
αὐτοὺς pron. acc. masc. 3p. pl. αὐτός ή ὁ self, of oneself, even, very, the same, he, she, it
εἰς prep. εἰς (+acc) into, to, unto, for, in, on, toward, against, upon, at, among
πόλεμον n. acc. masc. sg. πόλεμος war, battle, fight
ὧν relative pron. gen. masc. pl. ὅς ἥ ὅ who, which, what, that
ὁ art. nom. masc. sg. ὁ ἡ τό the, this, that, he, she, it
ἀριθμὸς n. nom. masc. sg. ἀριθμός number
ὡς adv. ὡς as, when, as it were, how, about, like, as soon as, even as, while
ἡ art. nom. fem. sg. ὁ ἡ τό the, this, that, he, she, it
ἄμμος n. nom. fem. sg. ἄμμος sand
τῆς art. gen. fem. sg. ὁ ἡ τό the, this, that, he, she, it
θαλάσσης n. gen. fem. sg. θάλασσα sea
9 καὶ conj. καί and, even, also, but
ἐπὶ prep. ἐπί (+gen) on, in, upon, (+dat) in, at, for, upon, (+acc) on, upon, unto, to, against
τὸ art. acc. neut. sg. ὁ ἡ τό the, this, that, he, she, it
πλάτος n. acc. neut. sg. πλάτος breadth
τῆς art. gen. fem. sg. ὁ ἡ τό the, this, that, he, she, it

γῆς n. gen. fem. sg. γῆ earth, land, ground, country
καὶ conj. καί and, even, also, but
τὴν art. acc. fem. sg. ὁ ἡ τό the, this, that, he, she, it
παρεμβολὴν n. acc. fem. sg. παρεμβολή castle, camp, army
τῶν art. gen. masc. pl. ὁ ἡ τό the, this, that, he, she, it
ἁγίων adj. gen. masc. pl. ἅγιος Holy, holy, saint, Holy One, holy thing, most holy
καὶ conj. καί and, even, also, but
τὴν art. acc. fem. sg. ὁ ἡ τό the, this, that, he, she, it
πόλιν n. acc. fem. sg. πόλις city
τὴν art. acc. fem. sg. ὁ ἡ τό the, this, that, he, she, it
καὶ conj. καί and, even, also, but
πῦρ n. nom. neut. sg. πῦρ fire, fiery
ἀπὸ prep. ἀπό (+gen) from, of, out of, since, for, off, at, by, in, on
τοῦ art. gen. masc. sg. ὁ ἡ τό the, this, that, he, she, it
Θεοῦ n. gen. masc. sg. θεός God, god
ἐκ prep. ἐκ ἐξ (+gen) of, from, out of, by, on, with, in, among, through
τοῦ art. gen. masc. sg. ὁ ἡ τό the, this, that, he, she, it
οὐρανοῦ n. gen. masc. sg. οὐρανός heaven, air, sky
καὶ conj. καί and, even, also, but
αὐτούς pron. acc. masc. 3p. pl. αὐτός ἡ ὁ self, of oneself, even, very, the same, he, she, it
10 καὶ conj. καί and, even, also, but
ὁ art. nom. masc. sg. ὁ ἡ τό the, this, that, he, she, it
διάβολος adj. nom. masc. sg. διάβολος devil, false accuser, Devil, slanderer
ὁ art. nom. masc. sg. ὁ ἡ τό the, this, that, he, she, it
αὐτοὺς pron. acc. masc. 3p. pl. αὐτός ἡ ὁ self, of oneself, even, very, the same, he, she, it
εἰς prep. εἰς (+acc) into, to, unto, for, in, on, toward, against, upon, at, among
τὴν art. acc. fem. sg. ὁ ἡ τό the, this, that, he, she, it
λίμνην n. acc. fem. sg. λίμην lake
τοῦ art. gen. neut. sg. ὁ ἡ τό the, this, that, he, she, it
πυρὸς n. gen. neut. sg. πῦρ fire, fiery
καὶ conj. καί and, even, also, but
θείου n. gen. neut. sg. θεῖον brimstone
ὅπου adv. ὅπου where, whither, whereas, in what place, wheresoever
τὸ art. nom. neut. sg. ὁ ἡ τό the, this, that, he, she, it
θηρίον n. nom. neut. sg. θηρίον beast, wild beast, venomous beast
καὶ conj. καί and, even, also, but
ὁ art. nom. masc. sg. ὁ ἡ τό the, this, that, he, she, it
ψευδοπροφήτης n. nom. masc. sg. ψευδοπροφήτης false prophet
καὶ conj. καί and, even, also, but
ἡμέρας n. gen. fem. sg. ἡμέρα day, time, year, while, age, day time
καὶ conj. καί and, even, also, but
νυκτὸς n. gen. fem. sg. νύξ night
εἰς prep. εἰς (+acc) into, to, unto, for, in, on, toward, against, upon, at, among
τοὺς art. acc. masc. pl. ὁ ἡ τό the, this, that, he, she, it
αἰῶνας n. acc. masc. pl. αἰών ever, ever and ever, evermore, age, eternal, world
τῶν art. gen. masc. pl. ὁ ἡ τό the, this, that, he, she, it
αἰώνων n. gen. masc. pl. αἰών ever, ever and ever, evermore, age, eternal, world
11 Καὶ conj. καί and, even, also, but
θρόνον n. acc. masc. sg. θρόνος throne, seat
λευκὸν adj. acc. masc. sg. λευκός white
μέγαν adj. acc. masc. sg. μέγας great, loud, greatest, high, large, mighty, strong
καὶ conj. καί and, even, also, but
τὸν art. acc. masc. sg. ὁ ἡ τό the, this, that, he, she, it
ἐπ' prep. ἐπί (+gen) on, in, upon, (+dat) in, at, for, upon, (+acc) on, upon, unto, to, against
αὐτοῦ pron. gen. masc. 3p. sg. αὐτός ἡ ὁ self, of oneself, even, very, the same, he, she, it

οὗ relative pron. gen. masc. sg. ὅς ἥ ὅ who, which, what, that
ἀπὸ prep. ἀπό (+gen) from, of, out of, since, for, off, at, by, in, on
προσώπου n. gen. neut. sg. πρόσωπον face, presence, person, countenance
ἡ art. nom. fem. sg. ὁ ἡ τό the, this, that, he, she, it
γῆ n. nom. fem. sg. γῆ earth, land, ground, countryearth, land, ground, country
καὶ conj. καί and, even, also, but
ὁ art. nom. masc. sg. ὁ ἡ τό the, this, that, he, she, it
οὐρανὸς n. nom. masc. sg. οὐρανός heaven, air, sky
καὶ conj. καί and, even, also, but
τόπος n. nom. masc. sg. τόπος place, room, quarter
οὐχ particle of negation. οὐ οὐκ οὐχ not, no, neither, none, nay, nor, never, nothing
αὐτοῖς pron. dat. neut. 3p. pl. αὐτός ἡ ὁ self, of oneself, even, very, the same, he, she, it
12 καὶ conj. καί and, even, also, but
τοὺς art. acc. masc. pl. ὁ ἡ τό the, this, that, he, she, it
νεκρούς adj. acc. masc. pl. νεκρός dead
μικρούς adj. acc. masc. pl. μικρός little, small, least, less
καὶ conj. καί and, even, also, but
μεγάλους adj. acc. masc. pl. μέγας great, loud, greatest, high, large, mighty, strong
ἐνώπιον prep. ἐνώπιον (+gen) before, in the sight of, in the presence of. (adv.) before
τοῦ art. gen. masc. sg. ὁ ἡ τό the, this, that, he, she, it
Θεοῦ n. gen. masc. sg. θεός God, god
καὶ conj. καί and, even, also, but
βιβλία n. nom. neut. pl. βιβλίον book, bill, scroll, writing
καὶ conj. καί and, even, also, but
βιβλίον n. nom. neut. sg. βιβλίον book, bill, scroll, writing
ἄλλο adj. nom. neut. sg. ἄλλος other, another, some, one, more, otherwise
ὅ relative pron. nom. neut. sg. ὅς ἥ ὅ who, which, what, that
τῆς art. gen. fem. sg. ὁ ἡ τό the, this, that, he, she, it
ζωῆς n. gen. fem. sg. ζωή life, lifetime
καὶ conj. καί and, even, also, but
οἱ art. nom. masc. pl. ὁ ἡ τό the, this, that, he, she, it
νεκροὶ adj. nom. masc. pl. νεκρός dead
ἐκ prep. ἐκ ἐξ (+gen) of, from, out of, by, on, with, in, among, through
τῶν art. gen. neut. pl. ὁ ἡ τό the, this, that, he, she, it
ἐν prep. ἐν (+dat) in, by, with, among, at, on, through, to, within, into, of, for
τοῖς art. dat. neut. pl. ὁ ἡ τό the, this, that, he, she, it
βιβλίοις n. dat. neut. pl. βιβλίον book, bill, scroll, writing
κατὰ prep. κατά (+gen) against, by, throughout, down, (+acc) according to, after, with
τὰ art. acc. neut. pl. ὁ ἡ τό the, this, that, he, she, it
ἔργα n. acc. neut. pl. ἔργον work, deed, doing labour
αὐτῶν pron. gen. masc. 3p. pl. αὐτός ἡ ὁ self, of oneself, even, very, the same, he, she, it
13 καὶ conj. καί and, even, also, but
ἡ art. nom. fem. sg. ὁ ἡ τό the, this, that, he, she, it
θάλασσα n. nom. fem. sg. θάλασσα sea
τοὺς art. acc. masc. pl. ὁ ἡ τό the, this, that, he, she, it
ἐν prep. ἐν (+dat) in, by, with, among, at, on, through, to, within, into, of, for
αὐτῇ pron. dat. fem. 3p. sg. αὐτός ἡ ὁ self, of oneself, even, very, the same, he, she, it
νεκροὺς adj. acc. masc. pl. νεκρός dead
καὶ conj. καί and, even, also, but
ὁ art. nom. masc. sg. ὁ ἡ τό the, this, that, he, she, it
θάνατος n. nom. masc. sg. θάνατος death
καὶ conj. καί and, even, also, but
ὁ art. nom. masc. sg. ὁ ἡ τό the, this, that, he, she, it
ᾅδης n. nom. masc. sg. ᾅδης hell, grave
τοὺς art. acc. masc. pl. ὁ ἡ τό the, this, that, he, she, it

ἐν prep. ἐν (+dat) in, by, with, among, at, on, through, to, within, into, of, for
αὐτοῖς pron. dat. masc. 3p. pl. αὐτός ή ό self, of oneself, even, very, the same, he, she, it
νεκροὺς adj. acc. masc. pl. νεκρός dead
καὶ conj. καί and, even, also, but
ἕκαστος adj. nom. masc. sg. ἕκαστος every man, every, every one, any man, each
κατὰ prep. κατά (+gen) against, by, throughout, down, (+acc) according to, after, with
τὰ art. acc. neut. pl. ὁ ἡ τό the, this, that, he, she, it
ἔργα n. acc. neut. pl. ἔργον work, deed, doing labour
αὐτῶν pron. gen. masc. 3p. pl. αὐτός ή ό self, of oneself, even, very, the same, he, she, it
14 καὶ conj. καί and, even, also, but
ὁ art. nom. masc. sg. ὁ ἡ τό the, this, that, he, she, it
θάνατος n. nom. masc. sg. θάνατος death
καὶ conj. καί and, even, also, but
ὁ art. nom. masc. sg. ὁ ἡ τό the, this, that, he, she, it
ᾅδης n. nom. masc. sg. ᾅδης hell, grave
εἰς prep. εἰς (+acc) into, to, unto, for, in, on, toward, against, upon, at, among
τὴν art. acc. fem. sg. ὁ ἡ τό the, this, that, he, she, it
λίμνην n. acc. fem. sg. λίμην lake
τοῦ art. gen. neut. sg. ὁ ἡ τό the, this, that, he, she, it
πυρός n. gen. neut. sg. πῦρ fire, fiery
οὗτος demo. pron. nom. masc. sg. οὗτος αὕτη τοῦτο this, the same, this same, he, she, it
ὁ art. nom. masc. sg. ὁ ἡ τό the, this, that, he, she, it
δεύτερός ordinal. adj. nom. masc. sg. δεύτερος second, second time, again, afterward
θάνατος n. nom. masc. sg. θάνατος death
15 καὶ conj. καί and, even, also, but
εἴ conj. εἰ if, whether, that, though, forasmuch
τις indefinite pron. nom. masc. sg. τὶς certain, some, any man, one, any thing
οὐχ particle of negation. οὐ οὐκ οὐχ not, no, neither, none, nay, nor, never, nothing
ἐν prep. ἐν (+dat) in, by, with, among, at, on, through, to, within, into, of, for
τῇ art. dat. fem. sg. ὁ ἡ τό the, this, that, he, she, it
βίβλῳ n. dat. fem. sg. βίβλος book, record
τῆς art. gen. fem. sg. ὁ ἡ τό the, this, that, he, she, it
ζωῆς n. gen. fem. sg. ζωή life, lifetime
εἰς prep. εἰς (+acc) into, to, unto, for, in, on, toward, against, upon, at, among
τὴν art. acc. fem. sg. ὁ ἡ τό the, this, that, he, she, it
λίμνην n. acc. fem. sg. λίμην lake
τοῦ art. gen. neut. sg. ὁ ἡ τό the, this, that, he, she, it
πυρός n. gen. neut. sg. πῦρ fire, fiery

21

1 Καὶ conj. καί and, even, also, but
οὐρανὸν n. acc. masc. sg. οὐρανός heaven, air, sky
καινὸν adj. acc. masc. sg. καινός new
καὶ conj. καί and, even, also, but
γῆν n. acc. fem. sg. γῆ earth, land, ground, country
καινήν adj. acc. fem. sg. καινός new
ὁ art. nom. masc. sg. ὁ ἡ τό the, this, that, he, she, it
γὰρ conj. γάρ for, and, because, but, indeed
πρῶτος ordinal. adj. nom. masc. sg. πρῶτος first, chief, first of all, chiefest, best
οὐρανὸς n. nom. masc. sg. οὐρανός heaven, air, sky
καὶ conj. καί and, even, also, but
ἡ art. nom. fem. sg. ὁ ἡ τό the, this, that, he, she, it
πρώτη ordinal. adj. nom. fem. sg. πρῶτος first, chief, first of all, chiefest, best
γῆ n. nom. fem. sg. γῆ earth, land, ground, country

καὶ conj. καί and, even, also, but
ἡ art. nom. fem. sg. ὁ ἡ τό the, this, that, he, she, it
θάλασσα n. nom. fem. sg. θάλασσα sea
οὐκ particle of negation. οὐ οὐκ οὐχ not, no, neither, none, nay, nor, never, nothing
ἔτι adv. ἔτι yet, more, any more, further, still, moreover
2 καὶ conj. καί and, even, also, but
ἐγὼ pron. nom. 1p. sg. ἐγώ I
Ἰωάννης n. nom. masc. sg. Ἰωάννης John
τὴν art. acc. fem. sg. ὁ ἡ τό the, this, that, he, she, it
πόλιν n. acc. fem. sg. πόλις city
τὴν art. acc. fem. sg. ὁ ἡ τό the, this, that, he, she, it
ἁγίαν adj. acc. fem. sg. ἅγιος Holy, holy, saint, Holy One, holy thing, most holy
Ἱερουσαλὴμ pron. name. fem. inde. Ἱερουσαλήμ Jerusalem
καινὴν adj. acc. fem. sg. καινός new
ἀπὸ prep. ἀπό (+gen) from, of, out of, since, for, off, at, by, in, on
τοῦ art. gen. masc. sg. ὁ ἡ τό the, this, that, he, she, it
Θεοῦ n. gen. masc. sg. θεός God, god
ἐκ prep. ἐκ ἐξ (+gen) of, from, out of, by, on, with, in, among, through
τοῦ art. gen. masc. sg. ὁ ἡ τό the, this, that, he, she, it
οὐρανοῦ n. gen. masc. sg. οὐρανός heaven, air, sky
ὡς adv. ὡς as, when, as it were, how, about, like, as soon as, even as, while
νύμφην n. acc. fem. sg. νύμφη bride, daughter in law
τῷ art. dat. masc. sg. ὁ ἡ τό the, this, that, he, she, it
ἀνδρὶ n. dat. masc. sg. ἀνήρ man, husband, sir
αὐτῆς pron. gen. fem. 3p. sg. αὐτός ή ό self, of oneself, even, very, the same, he, she, it
3 καὶ conj. καί and, even, also, but
φωνῆς n. gen. fem. sg. φωνή voice, sound, noise
μεγάλης adj. gen. fem. sg. μέγας great, loud, greatest, high, large, mighty, strong
ἐκ prep. ἐκ ἐξ (+gen) of, from, out of, by, on, with, in, among, through
τοῦ art. gen. masc. sg. ὁ ἡ τό the, this, that, he, she, it
οὐρανοῦ n. gen. masc. sg. οὐρανός heaven, air, sky
ἡ art. nom. fem. sg. ὁ ἡ τό the, this, that, he, she, it
σκηνὴ n. nom. fem. sg. σκηνή tabernacle, habitation
τοῦ art. gen. masc. sg. ὁ ἡ τό the, this, that, he, she, it
Θεοῦ n. gen. masc. sg. θεός God, god
μετὰ prep. μετά (+gen) with, among, against, (+acc) after
τῶν art. gen. masc. pl. ὁ ἡ τό the, this, that, he, she, it
ἀνθρώπων n. gen. masc. pl. ἄνθρωπος man, human being, person, one, certain
καὶ conj. καί and, even, also, but
μετ' prep. μετά (+gen) with, among, against, (+acc) after
αὐτῶν pron. gen. masc. 3p. pl. αὐτός ή ό self, of oneself, even, very, the same, he, she, it
καὶ conj. καί and, even, also, but
αὐτοὶ pron. nom. masc. 3p. pl. αὐτός ή ό self, of oneself, even, very, the same, he, she, it
λαοὶ n. nom. masc. pl. λαός people
αὐτοῦ pron. gen. masc. 3p. sg. αὐτός ή ό self, of oneself, even, very, the same, he, she, it
καὶ conj. καί and, even, also, but
αὐτὸς pron. nom. masc. 3p. sg. αὐτός ή ό self, of oneself, even, very, the same, he, she, it
ὁ art. nom. masc. sg. ὁ ἡ τό the, this, that, he, she, it
Θεὸς n. nom. masc. sg. θεός God, god
μετ' prep. μετά (+gen) with, among, against, (+acc) after
αὐτῶν pron. gen. masc. 3p. pl. αὐτός ή ό self, of oneself, even, very, the same, he, she, it
Θεὸς n. nom. masc. sg. θεός God, god
αὐτῶν pron. gen. masc. 3p. pl. αὐτός ή ό self, of oneself, even, very, the same, he, she, it
4 καὶ conj. καί and, even, also, but
ὁ art. nom. masc. sg. ὁ ἡ τό the, this, that, he, she, it

Θεὸς n. nom. masc. sg. θεός God, god
πᾶν adj. acc. neut. sg. πᾶς πᾶσα πᾶν all, every, whosoever, every one, no, whole, any
δάκρυον n. acc. neut. sg. δάκρυον tears
ἀπὸ prep. ἀπό (+gen) from, of, out of, since, for, off, at, by, in, on
τῶν art. gen. masc. pl. ὁ ἡ τό the, this, that, he, she, it
ὀφθαλμῶν n. gen. masc. pl. ὀφθαλμός eye, sight
αὐτῶν pron. gen. masc. 3p. pl. αὐτός ἡ ὁ self, of oneself, even, very, the same, he, she, it
καὶ conj. καί and, even, also, but
ὁ art. nom. masc. sg. ὁ ἡ τό the, this, that, he, she, it
θάνατος n. nom. masc. sg. θάνατος death
οὐκ particle of negation. οὐ οὐκ οὐχ not, no, neither, none, nay, nor, never, nothing
ἔτι adv. ἔτι yet, more, any more, further, still, moreover
οὔτε conj. οὔτε neither, nor, nor yet, no, none
πένθος n. nom. neut. sg. πένθος mourning, sorrow
οὔτε conj. οὔτε neither, nor, nor yet, no, none
κραυγὴ n. nom. fem. sg. κραυγή cry, crying, clamour
οὔτε conj. οὔτε neither, nor, nor yet, no, none
πόνος n. nom. masc. sg. πόνος pain
οὐκ particle of negation. οὐ οὐκ οὐχ not, no, neither, none, nay, nor, never, nothing
ἔτι adv. ἔτι yet, more, any more, further, still, moreover
ὅτι conj. ὅτι that, for, because, how that, how, because that, for that, though
τὰ art. nom. neut. pl. ὁ ἡ τό the, this, that, he, she, it
πρῶτα ordinal. adj. nom. neut. pl. πρῶτος first, chief, first of all, chiefest, best
5 καὶ conj. καί and, even, also, but
ὁ art. nom. masc. sg. ὁ ἡ τό the, this, that, he, she, it
ἐπὶ prep. ἐπί (+gen) on, in, upon, (+dat) in, at, for, upon, (+acc) on, upon, unto, to, against
τοῦ art. gen. masc. sg. ὁ ἡ τό the, this, that, he, she, it
θρόνου n. gen. masc. sg. θρόνος throne, seat
καινὰ adj. acc. neut. pl. καινός new
πάντα adj. acc. neut. pl. πᾶς πᾶσα πᾶν all, every, whosoever, every one, no, whole, any
καὶ conj. καί and, even, also, but
μοι pron. dat. 1p. sg. ἐγώ I
ὅτι conj. ὅτι that, for, because, how that, how, because that, for that, though
οὗτοι demo. pron. nom. masc. pl. οὗτος αὕτη τοῦτο this, the same, this same, he, she, it
οἱ art. nom. masc. pl. ὁ ἡ τό the, this, that, he, she, it
λόγοι n. nom. masc. pl. λόγος word, saying, account, speech, thing, matter
ἀληθινοί adj. nom. masc. pl. ἀληθινός true
καὶ conj. καί and, even, also, but
πιστοὶ adj. nom. masc. pl. πιστός faithful, believing, true, sure
6 καὶ conj. καί and, even, also, but
μοι pron. dat. 1p. sg. ἐγώ I
ἐγώ pron. nom. 1p. sg. ἐγώ I
τὸ art. nom. neut. sg. ὁ ἡ τό the, this, that, he, she, it
Α n. nom. neut. sg. Α Alpha
καὶ conj. καί and, even, also, but
τὸ art. nom. neut. sg. ὁ ἡ τό the, this, that, he, she, it
Ω n. nom. neut. sg. Ω Omega
ἡ art. nom. fem. sg. ὁ ἡ τό the, this, that, he, she, it
ἀρχὴ n. nom. fem. sg. ἀρχή beginning, principality, corner, first, magistrate, rule
καὶ conj. καί and, even, also, but
τὸ art. nom. neut. sg. ὁ ἡ τό the, this, that, he, she, it
τέλος n. nom. neut. sg. τέλος end, custom, ending, finally, uttermost
ἐγώ pron. nom. 1p. sg. ἐγώ I
τῷ art. dat. masc. sg. ὁ ἡ τό the, this, that, he, she, it
ἐκ prep. ἐκ ἐξ (+gen) of, from, out of, by, on, with, in, among, through

τῆς art. gen. fem. sg. ὁ ἡ τό the, this, that, he, she, it
πηγῆς n. gen. fem. sg. πηγή fountain, well
τοῦ art. gen. neut. sg. ὁ ἡ τό the, this, that, he, she, it
ὕδατος n. gen. neut. sg. ὕδωρ water
τῆς art. gen. fem. sg. ὁ ἡ τό the, this, that, he, she, it
ζωῆς n. gen. fem. sg. ζωή life, lifetime
δωρεάν adv. δωρεάν freely, for nought, in vain, without a cause
7 ὁ art. nom. masc. sg. ὁ ἡ τό the, this, that, he, she, it
πάντα adj. acc. neut. pl. πᾶς πᾶσα πᾶν all, every, whosoever, every one, no, whole, any
καὶ conj. καί and, even, also, but
αὐτῷ pron. dat. masc. 3p. sg. αὐτός ή ό self, of oneself, even, very, the same, he, she, it
Θεὸς n. nom. masc. sg. θεός God, god
καὶ conj. καί and, even, also, but
αὐτὸς pron. nom. masc. 3p. sg. αὐτός ή ό self, of oneself, even, very, the same, he, she, it
μοι pron. dat. 1p. sg. ἐγώ I
ὁ art. nom. masc. sg. ὁ ἡ τό the, this, that, he, she, it
υἱός n. nom. masc. sg. υἱός son, child, descendant, offspring, heir
8 δειλοῖς adj. dat. masc. pl. δειλός fearful
δὲ conj. δέ but, and, now, also, to the contrary, rather, then
καὶ conj. καί and, even, also, but
ἀπίστοις adj. dat. masc. pl. ἄπιστος faithless, unbelieving, infidel, thing incredible
καὶ conj. καί and, even, also, but
καὶ conj. καί and, even, also, but
φονεῦσιν n. dat. masc. pl. φονεύς murderer
καὶ conj. καί and, even, also, but
πόρνοις n. dat. masc. pl. πόρνος fornicator
καὶ conj. καί and, even, also, but
φαρμακεῦσι n. dat. masc. pl. φαρμακεύς
καὶ conj. καί and, even, also, but
εἰδωλολάτραις n. dat. masc. pl. εἰδωλολάτρης idolater
καὶ conj. καί and, even, also, but
πᾶσι adj. dat. masc. pl. πᾶς πᾶσα πᾶν all, every, whosoever, every one, no, whole, any
τοῖς art. dat. masc. pl. ὁ ἡ τό the, this, that, he, she, it
ψευδέσιν adj. dat. masc. pl. ψευδής false, liar
τὸ art. nom. neut. sg. ὁ ἡ τό the, this, that, he, she, it
μέρος n. nom. neut. sg. μέρος part, coast, portion, behalf, respect, piece, side
αὐτῶν pron. gen. masc. 3p. pl. αὐτός ή ό self, of oneself, even, very, the same, he, she, it
ἐν prep. ἐν (+dat) in, by, with, among, at, on, through, to, within, into, of, for
τῇ art. dat. fem. sg. ὁ ἡ τό the, this, that, he, she, it
λίμνῃ n. dat. fem. sg. λίμνη lake
τῇ art. dat. fem. sg. ὁ ἡ τό the, this, that, he, she, it
πυρὶ n. dat. neut. sg. πῦρ fire, fiery
καὶ conj. καί and, even, also, but
θείῳ n. dat. neut. sg. θεῖον brimstone
ὅ relative pron. nom. neut. sg. ὅς ἥ ὅ who, which, what, that
δεύτερος ordinal. adj. nom. masc. sg. δεύτερος second, second time, again, afterward
θάνατος n. nom. masc. sg. θάνατος death
9 Καὶ conj. καί and, even, also, but
πρὸς prep. πρός (+gen) for, (+dat) at, (+acc) unto, to, with, for, against
με pron. acc. 1p. sg. ἐγώ I
εἷς num. nom. masc. sg. εἷς or ἕν one, other, some, any, only, a certain
τῶν art. gen. masc. pl. ὁ ἡ τό the, this, that, he, she, it
ἑπτὰ num. gen. masc. pl. ἑπτά seven, seventh
ἀγγέλων n. gen. masc. pl. ἄγγελος angel, messenger
τῶν art. gen. masc. pl. ὁ ἡ τό the, this, that, he, she, it

τὰς art. acc. fem. pl. ὁ ἡ τό the, this, that, he, she, it
ἑπτὰ num. acc. fem. pl. ἑπτά seven, seventh
φιάλας n. acc. fem. pl. φιάλη vial
τὰς art. acc. fem. pl. ὁ ἡ τό the, this, that, he, she, it
τῶν art. gen. fem. pl. ὁ ἡ τό the, this, that, he, she, it
ἑπτὰ num. gen. fem. pl. ἑπτά seven, seventh
πληγῶν n. gen. fem. pl. πληγή wound, plague, stripe
τῶν art. gen. fem. pl. ὁ ἡ τό the, this, that, he, she, it
ἐσχάτων adj. gen. fem. pl. ἔσχατος last, lowest, uttermost, uttermost part
καὶ conj. καί and, even, also, but
μετ' prep. μετά (+gen) with, among, against, (+acc) after
ἐμοῦ pron. gen. 1p. sg. ἐγώ I
Δεῦρο adv. δεῦρο come, come hither
σοι pron. dat. 2p. sg. σύ thou, you
τὴν art. acc. fem. sg. ὁ ἡ τό the, this, that, he, she, it
νύμφην n. acc. fem. sg. νύμφη bride, daughter in law
τοῦ art. gen. neut. sg. ὁ ἡ τό the, this, that, he, she, it
ἀρνίου n. gen. neut. sg. ἀρνίον Lamb, lamb
τὴν art. acc. fem. sg. ὁ ἡ τό the, this, that, he, she, it
γυναῖκα n. acc. fem. sg. γυνή woman, wife
10 καὶ conj. καί and, even, also, but
με pron. acc. 1p. sg. ἐγώ I
ἐν prep. ἐν (+dat) in, by, with, among, at, on, through, to, within, into, of, for
Πνεύματι n. dat. neut. sg. πνεῦμα spirit, Spirit, Ghost, ghost, life. of the spirit, wind
ἐπ' prep. ἐπί (+gen) on, in, upon, (+dat) in, at, for, upon, (+acc) on, upon, unto, to, against
ὄρος n. acc. neut. sg. ὄρος mountain, mount, hill
μέγα adj. acc. neut. sg. μέγας great, loud, greatest, high, large, mighty, strong
καὶ conj. καί and, even, also, but
ὑψηλόν adj. acc. neut. sg. ὑψηλός high, higher, highly esteemed
καὶ conj. καί and, even, also, but
μοι pron. dat. 1p. sg. ἐγώ I
τὴν art. acc. fem. sg. ὁ ἡ τό the, this, that, he, she, it
πόλιν n. acc. fem. sg. πόλις city
τὴν art. acc. fem. sg. ὁ ἡ τό the, this, that, he, she, it
μεγάλην adj. acc. fem. sg. μέγας great, loud, greatest, high, large, mighty, strong
τὴν art. acc. fem. sg. ὁ ἡ τό the, this, that, he, she, it
ἁγίαν adj. acc. fem. sg. ἅγιος Holy, holy, saint, Holy One, holy thing, most holy
Ἱερουσαλήμ pron. name. fem. inde. Ἱερουσαλήμ Jerusalem
ἐκ prep. ἐκ ἐξ (+gen) of, from, out of, by, on, with, in, among, through
τοῦ art. gen. masc. sg. ὁ ἡ τό the, this, that, he, she, it
οὐρανοῦ n. gen. masc. sg. οὐρανός heaven, air, sky
ἀπὸ prep. ἀπό (+gen) from, of, out of, since, for, off, at, by, in, on
τοῦ art. gen. masc. sg. ὁ ἡ τό the, this, that, he, she, it
Θεοῦ n. gen. masc. sg. θεός God, god
11 τὴν art. acc. fem. sg. ὁ ἡ τό the, this, that, he, she, it
δόξαν n. acc. fem. sg. δόξα glory, honour, praise, dignity, worship
τοῦ art. gen. masc. sg. ὁ ἡ τό the, this, that, he, she, it
Θεοῦ n. gen. masc. sg. θεός God, god
καὶ conj. καί and, even, also, but
ὁ art. nom. masc. sg. ὁ ἡ τό the, this, that, he, she, it
φωστὴρ n. nom. masc. sg. φωστήρ light
αὐτῆς pron. gen. fem. 3p. sg. αὐτός ή ό self, of oneself, even, very, the same, he, she, it
ὅμοιος adj. nom. masc. sg. ὅμοιος like
λίθῳ n. dat. masc. sg. λίθος stone
τιμιωτάτῳ superl. adj. dat. masc. sg. τίμιος precious, dear, honourable

ὡς adv. ὡς as, when, as it were, how, about, like, as soon as, even as, while
λίθῳ n. dat. masc. sg. λίθος stone
ἰάσπιδι n. dat. fem. sg. ἴασπις jasper, a precious stone of various colours
12 τε conj. τέ and, both, also
τεῖχος n. acc. neut. sg. τεῖχος wall
μέγα adj. acc. neut. sg. μέγας great, loud, greatest, high, large, mighty, strong
καὶ conj. καί and, even, also, but
ὑψηλόν adj. acc. neut. sg. ὑψηλός high, higher, highly esteemed
πυλῶνας n. acc. masc. pl. πυλών gate, porch
δώδεκα num. acc. masc. pl. δώδεκα twelve
καὶ conj. καί and, even, also, but
ἐπὶ prep. ἐπί (+gen) on, in, upon, (+dat) in, at, for, upon, (+acc) on, upon, unto, to, against
τοῖς art. dat. masc. pl. ὁ ἡ τό the, this, that, he, she, it
πυλῶσιν n. dat. masc. pl. πυλών gate, porch
ἀγγέλους n. acc. masc. pl. ἄγγελος angel, messenger
δώδεκα num. acc. masc. pl. δώδεκα twelve
καὶ conj. καί and, even, also, but
ὀνόματα n. acc. neut. pl. ὄνομα name, call, surname
ἅ relative pron. nom. neut. pl. ὅς ἥ ὅ who, which, what, that
τῶν art. gen. fem. pl. ὁ ἡ τό the, this, that, he, she, it
δώδεκα num. gen. fem. pl. δώδεκα twelve
φυλῶν n. gen. fem. pl. φυλή tribe, kindred
τῶν art. gen. masc. pl. ὁ ἡ τό the, this, that, he, she, it
υἱῶν n. gen. masc. pl. υἱός son, child, descendant, offspring, heir
Ἰσραήλ pron. name. masc. inde. Ἰσραήλ Israel
13 ἀπ' prep. ἀπό (+gen) from, of, out of, since, for, off, at, by, in, on
ἀνατολῆς n. gen. fem. sg. ἀνατολή east, rising of the sun, dayspring
πυλῶνες n. nom. masc. pl. πυλών gate, porch
τρεῖς num. nom. masc. pl. τρεῖς three
ἀπὸ prep. ἀπό (+gen) from, of, out of, since, for, off, at, by, in, on
βορρᾶ n. gen. masc. sg. βορρᾶς north
πυλῶνες n. nom. masc. pl. πυλών gate, porch
τρεῖς num. nom. masc. pl. τρεῖς three
ἀπὸ prep. ἀπό (+gen) from, of, out of, since, for, off, at, by, in, on
νότου n. gen. masc. sg. νότος south, south wind
πυλῶνες n. nom. masc. pl. πυλών gate, porch
τρεῖς num. nom. masc. pl. τρεῖς three
καὶ conj. καί and, even, also, but
ἀπὸ prep. ἀπό (+gen) from, of, out of, since, for, off, at, by, in, on
δυσμῶν n. gen. fem. pl. δυσμή west
πυλῶνες n. nom. masc. pl. πυλών gate, porch
τρεῖς num. nom. masc. pl. τρεῖς three
14 καὶ conj. καί and, even, also, but
τὸ art. nom. neut. sg. ὁ ἡ τό the, this, that, he, she, it
τεῖχος n. nom. neut. sg. τεῖχος wall
τῆς art. gen. fem. sg. ὁ ἡ τό the, this, that, he, she, it
πόλεως n. gen. fem. sg. πόλις city
θεμελίους n. acc. masc. pl. θεμέλιος foundation
δώδεκα num. acc. masc. pl. δώδεκα twelve
καὶ conj. καί and, even, also, but
ἐν prep. ἐν (+dat) in, by, with, among, at, on, through, to, within, into, of, for
αὐτοῖς pron. dat. masc. 3p. pl. αὐτός ἡ ὁ self, of oneself, even, very, the same, he, she, it
ὀνόματα n. acc. neut. pl. ὄνομα name, call, surname
τῶν art. gen. masc. pl. ὁ ἡ τό the, this, that, he, she, it
δώδεκα num. gen. masc. pl. δώδεκα twelve

ἀποστόλων n. gen. masc. pl. ἀπόστολος apostle, messenger, he that is sent
τοῦ art. gen. neut. sg. ὁ ἡ τό the, this, that, he, she, it
ἀρνίου n. gen. neut. sg. ἀρνίον Lamb, lamb
15 καὶ conj. καί and, even, also, but
ὁ art. nom. masc. sg. ὁ ἡ τό the, this, that, he, she, it
μετ' prep. μετά (+gen) with, among, against, (+acc) after
ἐμοῦ pron. gen. 1p. sg. ἐγώ I
κάλαμον n. acc. masc. sg. κάλαμος reed, pen
χρυσοῦν adj. acc. neut. sg. χρύσεος golden, of gold
ἵνα conj. ἵνα that, to, lest, for to, so that, albeit, because, for, so as
τὴν art. acc. fem. sg. ὁ ἡ τό the, this, that, he, she, it
πόλιν n. acc. fem. sg. πόλις city
καὶ conj. καί and, even, also, but
τοὺς art. acc. masc. pl. ὁ ἡ τό the, this, that, he, she, it
πυλῶνας n. acc. masc. pl. πυλών gate, porch
αὐτῆς pron. gen. fem. 3p. sg. αὐτός ή ό self, of oneself, even, very, the same, he, she, it
καὶ conj. καί and, even, also, but
τὸ art. acc. neut. sg. ὁ ἡ τό the, this, that, he, she, it
τεῖχος n. acc. neut. sg. τεῖχος wall
αὐτῆς pron. gen. fem. 3p. sg. αὐτός ή ό self, of oneself, even, very, the same, he, she, it
16 καὶ conj. καί and, even, also, but
ἡ art. nom. fem. sg. ὁ ἡ τό the, this, that, he, she, it
πόλις n. nom. fem. sg. πόλις city
τετράγωνος adj. nom. fem. sg. τετράγωνος foursquare
καὶ conj. καί and, even, also, but
τὸ art. nom. neut. sg. ὁ ἡ τό the, this, that, he, she, it
μῆκος n. nom. neut. sg. μῆκος length
αὐτῆς pron. gen. fem. 3p. sg. αὐτός ή ό self, of oneself, even, very, the same, he, she, it
τοσοῦτόν demo. pron. nom. neut. sg. τοσοῦτος so much, so great, so many, so long
ὅσον relative pron. nom. neut. sg. ὅσος as many as, whatsoever, that, as long as, how much
καὶ conj. καί and, even, also, but
τὸ art. nom. neut. sg. ὁ ἡ τό the, this, that, he, she, it
πλάτος n. nom. neut. sg. πλάτος breadth
καὶ conj. καί and, even, also, but
τὴν art. acc. fem. sg. ὁ ἡ τό the, this, that, he, she, it
πόλιν n. acc. fem. sg. πόλις city
τῷ art. dat. masc. sg. ὁ ἡ τό the, this, that, he, she, it
καλάμῳ n. dat. masc. sg. κάλαμος reed, pen
ἐπὶ prep. ἐπί (+gen) on, in, upon, (+dat) in, at, for, upon, (+acc) on, upon, unto, to, against
σταδίων n. gen. masc. pl. στάδιον furlong, stadium, race
δώδεκα num. gen. neut. pl. δώδεκα twelve
χιλιάδων n. gen. fem. pl. χιλιάς thousand
τὸ art. nom. neut. sg. ὁ ἡ τό the, this, that, he, she, it
μῆκος n. nom. neut. sg. μῆκος length
καὶ conj. καί and, even, also, but
τὸ art. nom. neut. sg. ὁ ἡ τό the, this, that, he, she, it
πλάτος n. nom. neut. sg. πλάτος breadth
καὶ conj. καί and, even, also, but
τὸ art. nom. neut. sg. ὁ ἡ τό the, this, that, he, she, it
ὕψος n. nom. neut. sg. ὕψος on high, height, exalt, in exaltation
αὐτῆς pron. gen. fem. 3p. sg. αὐτός ή ό self, of oneself, even, very, the same, he, she, it
ἴσα adj. nom. neut. pl. ἴσος equal, as much, like
17 καὶ conj. καί and, even, also, but
τὸ art. acc. neut. sg. ὁ ἡ τό the, this, that, he, she, it
τεῖχος n. acc. neut. sg. τεῖχος wall

αὐτῆς pron. gen. fem. 3p. sg. αὐτός ή ό self, of oneself, even, very, the same, he, she, it
ἑκατὸν num. gen. masc. pl. ἑκατόν hundred, hundredfold
τεσσαρακοντατεσσάρων num. gen. masc. pl. τεσσαρακοντατέσσαρες forty and four
πηχῶν n. gen. masc. pl. πῆχυς cubit, forearm
μέτρον n. acc. neut. sg. μέτρον measure
ἀνθρώπου n. gen. masc. sg. ἄνθρωπος man, human being, person, one, certain
ὅ relative pron. nom. neut. sg. ὅς ἥ ὅ who, which, what, that
ἀγγέλου n. gen. masc. sg. ἄγγελος angel, messenger
18 καὶ conj. καί and, even, also, but
ἡ art. nom. fem. sg. ὁ ἡ τό the, this, that, he, she, it
ἐνδόμησις n. nom. fem. sg. ἐνδόμησις building
τοῦ art. gen. neut. sg. ὁ ἡ τό the, this, that, he, she, it
τείχους n. gen. neut. sg. τεῖχος wall
αὐτῆς pron. gen. fem. 3p. sg. αὐτός ή ό self, of oneself, even, very, the same, he, she, it
ἴασπις n. nom. fem. sg. ἰάσπις jasper, a precious stone of various colours
καὶ conj. καί and, even, also, but
ἡ art. nom. fem. sg. ὁ ἡ τό the, this, that, he, she, it
πόλις n. nom. fem. sg. πόλις city
χρυσίον n. nom. neut. sg. χρυσίον gold
καθαρὸν adj. nom. neut. sg. καθαρός pure, clean, clear
ὅμοια adj. nom. fem. sg. ὅμοιος like
ὑάλῳ n. dat. fem. sg. ὕαλος glass
καθαρῷ adj. dat. masc. sg. καθαρός pure, clean, clear
19 καὶ conj. καί and, even, also, but
οἱ art. nom. masc. pl. ὁ ἡ τό the, this, that, he, she, it
θεμέλιοι n. nom. masc. pl. θεμέλιος foundation
τοῦ art. gen. neut. sg. ὁ ἡ τό the, this, that, he, she, it
τείχους n. gen. neut. sg. τεῖχος wall
τῆς art. gen. fem. sg. ὁ ἡ τό the, this, that, he, she, it
πόλεως n. gen. fem. sg. πόλις city
παντὶ adj. dat. masc. sg. πᾶς πᾶσα πᾶν all, every, whosoever, every one, no, whole, any
λίθῳ n. dat. masc. sg. λίθος stone
τιμίῳ adj. dat. masc. sg. τίμιος precious, dear, has in reputation, honourable
ὁ art. nom. masc. sg. ὁ ἡ τό the, this, that, he, she, it
θεμέλιος n. nom. masc. sg. θεμέλιος foundation
ὁ art. nom. masc. sg. ὁ ἡ τό the, this, that, he, she, it
πρῶτος ordinal. adj. nom. masc. sg. πρῶτος first, chief, first of all, chiefest, best
ἴασπις n. nom. fem. sg. ἰάσπις jasper, a precious stone of various colours
ὁ art. nom. masc. sg. ὁ ἡ τό the, this, that, he, she, it
δεύτερος ordinal. adj. nom. masc. sg. δεύτερος second, second time, again, afterward
σάπφειρος n. nom. fem. sg. σάπφιρος sapphire
ὁ art. nom. masc. sg. ὁ ἡ τό the, this, that, he, she, it
τρίτος ordinal. adj. nom. masc. sg. τρίτος third
χαλκηδών n. nom. masc. sg. χαλκηδών chalcedony
ὁ art. nom. masc. sg. ὁ ἡ τό the, this, that, he, she, it
τέταρτος ordinal. adj. nom. masc. sg. τέταρτος fourth, four
σμάραγδος n. nom. masc. sg. σμάραγδος emerald
20 ὁ art. nom. masc. sg. ὁ ἡ τό the, this, that, he, she, it
πέμπτος ordinal. adj. nom. masc. sg. πέμπτος fifth
σαρδόνυξ n. nom. masc. sg. σαρδόνυξ sardonyx
ὁ art. nom. masc. sg. ὁ ἡ τό the, this, that, he, she, it
ἕκτος ordinal. adj. nom. masc. sg. ἕκτος sixth
σάρδιος n. nom. masc. sg. σάρδιος sardius
ὁ art. nom. masc. sg. ὁ ἡ τό the, this, that, he, she, it
ἕβδομος ordinal. adj. nom. masc. sg. ἕβδομος seventh

χρυσόλιθος n. nom. masc. sg. χρυσόλιθος chrysolite
ὁ art. nom. masc. sg. ὁ ἡ τό the, this, that, he, she, it
ὄγδοος ordinal. adj. nom. masc. sg. ὄγδοος eighth
βήρυλλος n. nom. masc. sg. βήρυλλος beryl
ὁ art. nom. masc. sg. ὁ ἡ τό the, this, that, he, she, it
ἔννατος ordinal. adj. nom. masc. sg. ἔννατος ninth
τοπάζιον n. nom. neut. sg. τοπάζιον topaz
ὁ art. nom. masc. sg. ὁ ἡ τό the, this, that, he, she, it
δέκατος ordinal. adj. nom. masc. sg. δέκατος tenth
χρυσόπρασος n. nom. masc. sg. χρυσόπρασος chrysoprasus
ὁ art. nom. masc. sg. ὁ ἡ τό the, this, that, he, she, it
ἑνδέκατος ordinal. adj. nom. masc. sg. ἑνδέκατος eleventh
ὑάκινθος n. nom. masc. sg. ὑάκινθος jacinth
ὁ art. nom. masc. sg. ὁ ἡ τό the, this, that, he, she, it
δωδέκατος ordinal. adj. nom. masc. sg. δωδέκατος twelfth
ἀμέθυστος n. nom. fem. sg. ἀμέθυστος amethyst
21 καὶ conj. καί and, even, also, but
οἱ art. nom. masc. pl. ὁ ἡ τό the, this, that, he, she, it
δώδεκα num. nom. masc. pl. δώδεκα twelve
πυλῶνες n. nom. masc. pl. πυλών gate, porch
δώδεκα num. nom. masc. pl. δώδεκα twelve
μαργαρῖται n. nom. masc. pl. μαργαρίτης pearl
ἀνὰ adv. ἀνά (+acc) by, in, through, among, between. (adv.) apiece, every man, each
εἷς num. nom. masc. sg. εἷς or ἕν one, other, some, any, only, a certain
ἕκαστος adj. nom. masc. sg. ἕκαστος every man, every, every one, any man, each
τῶν art. gen. masc. pl. ὁ ἡ τό the, this, that, he, she, it
πυλώνων n. gen. masc. pl. πυλών gate, porch
ἐξ prep. ἐκ ἐξ (+gen) of, from, out of, by, on, with, in, among, through
ἑνὸς num. gen. masc. sg. εἷς or ἕν one, other, some, any, only, a certain
μαργαρίτου n. gen. masc. sg. μαργαρίτης pearl
καὶ conj. καί and, even, also, but
ἡ art. nom. fem. sg. ὁ ἡ τό the, this, that, he, she, it
πλατεῖα adj. nom. fem. sg. πλατύς wide, broad
τῆς art. gen. fem. sg. ὁ ἡ τό the, this, that, he, she, it
πόλεως n. gen. fem. sg. πόλις city
χρυσίον n. nom. neut. sg. χρυσίον gold
καθαρὸν adj. nom. neut. sg. καθαρός pure, clean, clear
ὡς adv. ὡς as, when, as it were, how, about, like, as soon as, even as, while
ὕαλος n. nom. fem. sg. ὕαλος glass
διαφανής adj. nom. masc. sg. διαφανής transparent
22 καὶ conj. καί and, even, also, but
ναὸν n. acc. masc. sg. ναός temple, shrine
οὐκ particle of negation. οὐ οὐκ οὐχ not, no, neither, none, nay, nor, never, nothing
ἐν prep. ἐν (+dat) in, by, with, among, at, on, through, to, within, into, of, for
αὐτῇ pron. dat. fem. 3p. sg. αὐτός ή ό self, of oneself, even, very, the same, he, she, it
ὁ art. nom. masc. sg. ὁ ἡ τό the, this, that, he, she, it
γὰρ conj. γάρ for, and, because, but, indeed
Κύριος n. nom. masc. sg. κύριος Lord, lord, master, sir, LORD, God, Master, owner
ὁ art. nom. masc. sg. ὁ ἡ τό the, this, that, he, she, it
Θεὸς n. nom. masc. sg. θεός God, god
ὁ art. nom. masc. sg. ὁ ἡ τό the, this, that, he, she, it
παντοκράτωρ n. nom. masc. sg. παντοκράτωρ Almighty, omnipotent
ναὸς n. nom. masc. sg. ναός temple, shrine
αὐτῆς pron. gen. fem. 3p. sg. αὐτός ή ό self, of oneself, even, very, the same, he, she, it
καὶ conj. καί and, even, also, but

τὸ art. nom. neut. sg. ὁ ἡ τό the, this, that, he, she, it
ἀρνίον n. nom. neut. sg. ἀρνίον Lamb, lamb
23 καὶ conj. καί and, even, also, but
ἡ art. nom. fem. sg. ὁ ἡ τό the, this, that, he, she, it
πόλις n. nom. fem. sg. πόλις city
οὐ particle of negation. οὐ οὐκ οὐχ not, no, neither, none, nay, nor, never, nothing
χρείαν n. acc. fem. sg. χρεία need, necessity, lack, want
τοῦ art. gen. masc. sg. ὁ ἡ τό the, this, that, he, she, it
ἡλίου n. gen. masc. sg. ἥλιος sun, east
οὐδὲ adv. οὐδέ neither, nor, not, no, not even, never, not yet
τῆς art. gen. fem. sg. ὁ ἡ τό the, this, that, he, she, it
σελήνης n. gen. fem. sg. σελήνη moon
ἵνα conj. ἵνα that, to, lest, for to, so that, albeit, because, for, so as
ἐν prep. ἐν (+dat) in, by, with, among, at, on, through, to, within, into, of, for
αὐτῇ pron. dat. fem. 3p. sg. αὐτός ή ό self, of oneself, even, very, the same, he, she, it
ἡ art. nom. fem. sg. ὁ ἡ τό the, this, that, he, she, it
γὰρ conj. γάρ for, and, because, but, indeed
δόξα n. nom. fem. sg. δόξα glory, honour, praise, dignity, worship
τοῦ art. gen. masc. sg. ὁ ἡ τό the, this, that, he, she, it
Θεοῦ n. gen. masc. sg. θεός God, god
αὐτήν pron. acc. fem. 3p. sg. αὐτός ή ό self, of oneself, even, very, the same, he, she, it
καὶ conj. καί and, even, also, but
ὁ art. nom. masc. sg. ὁ ἡ τό the, this, that, he, she, it
λύχνος n. nom. masc. sg. λύχνος candle, light, lamp
αὐτῆς pron. gen. fem. 3p. sg. αὐτός ή ό self, of oneself, even, very, the same, he, she, it
τὸ art. nom. neut. sg. ὁ ἡ τό the, this, that, he, she, it
ἀρνίον n. nom. neut. sg. ἀρνίον Lamb, lamb
24 καὶ conj. καί and, even, also, but
τὰ art. nom. neut. pl. ὁ ἡ τό the, this, that, he, she, it
ἔθνη n. nom. neut. pl. ἔθνος Gentile, nation, heathen, people
τῶν art. gen. masc. pl. ὁ ἡ τό the, this, that, he, she, it
ἐν prep. ἐν (+dat) in, by, with, among, at, on, through, to, within, into, of, for
τῷ art. dat. neut. sg. ὁ ἡ τό the, this, that, he, she, it
φωτί n. dat. neut. sg. φῶς light, fire
αὐτῆς pron. gen. fem. 3p. sg. αὐτός ή ό self, of oneself, even, very, the same, he, she, it
καὶ conj. καί and, even, also, but
οἱ art. nom. masc. pl. ὁ ἡ τό the, this, that, he, she, it
βασιλεῖς n. nom. masc. pl. βασιλεύς king
τῆς art. gen. fem. sg. ὁ ἡ τό the, this, that, he, she, it
γῆς n. gen. fem. sg. γῆ earth, land, ground, country
τὴν art. acc. fem. sg. ὁ ἡ τό the, this, that, he, she, it
δόξαν n. acc. fem. sg. δόξα glory, honour, praise, dignity, worship
καὶ conj. καί and, even, also, but
τὴν art. acc. fem. sg. ὁ ἡ τό the, this, that, he, she, it
τιμὴν n. acc. fem. sg. τιμή honour, price, preciousness, sum
αὐτῶν pron. gen. masc. 3p. pl. αὐτός ή ό self, of oneself, even, very, the same, he, she, it
εἰς prep. εἰς (+acc) into, to, unto, for, in, on, toward, against, upon, at, among
αὐτήν pron. acc. fem. 3p. sg. αὐτός ή ό self, of oneself, even, very, the same, he, she, it
25 καὶ conj. καί and, even, also, but
οἱ art. nom. masc. pl. ὁ ἡ τό the, this, that, he, she, it
πυλῶνες n. nom. masc. pl. πυλών gate, porch
αὐτῆς pron. gen. fem. 3p. sg. αὐτός ή ό self, of oneself, even, very, the same, he, she, it
οὐ particle of negation. οὐ οὐκ οὐχ not, no, neither, none, nay, nor, never, nothing
μὴ particle of negation. μή not, no, lest, neither, none, nothing, nor, never, without
ἡμέρας n. gen. fem. sg. ἡμέρα day, time, year, while, age, day time

νὺξ n. nom. fem. sg. νύξ night
γὰρ conj. γάρ for, and, because, but, indeed
οὐκ particle of negation. οὐ οὐκ οὐχ not, no, neither, none, nay, nor, never, nothing
ἐκεῖ adv. ἐκεῖ there, thither, thitherward, yonder, yonder place
26 καὶ conj. καί and, even, also, but
τὴν art. acc. fem. sg. ὁ ἡ τό the, this, that, he, she, it
δόξαν n. acc. fem. sg. δόξα glory, honour, praise, dignity, worship
καὶ conj. καί and, even, also, but
τὴν art. acc. fem. sg. ὁ ἡ τό the, this, that, he, she, it
τιμὴν n. acc. fem. sg. τιμή honour, price, preciousness, sum
τῶν art. gen. neut. pl. ὁ ἡ τό the, this, that, he, she, it
ἐθνῶν n. gen. neut. pl. ἔθνος Gentile, nation, heathen, people
εἰς prep. εἰς (+acc) into, to, unto, for, in, on, toward, against, upon, at, among
αὐτήν pron. acc. fem. 3p. sg. αὐτός ή ό self, of oneself, even, very, the same, he, she, it
27 καὶ conj. καί and, even, also, but
οὐ particle of negation. οὐ οὐκ οὐχ not, no, neither, none, nay, nor, never, nothing
μὴ particle of negation. μή not, no, lest, neither, none, nothing, nor, never, without
εἰς prep. εἰς (+acc) into, to, unto, for, in, on, toward, against, upon, at, among
αὐτὴν pron. acc. fem. 3p. sg. αὐτός ή ό self, of oneself, even, very, the same, he, she, it
πᾶν adj. nom. neut. sg. πᾶς πᾶσα πᾶν all, every, whosoever, every one, no, whole, any
καὶ conj. καί and, even, also, but
βδέλυγμα n. acc. neut. sg. βδέλυγμα abomination
καὶ conj. καί and, even, also, but
ψεῦδος n. acc. neut. sg. ψεῦδος lie, lying
εἰ conj. εἰ if, whether, that, though, forasmuch
μὴ particle of negation. μή not, no, lest, neither, none, nothing, nor, never, without
οἱ art. nom. masc. pl. ὁ ἡ τό the, this, that, he, she, it
ἐν prep. ἐν (+dat) in, by, with, among, at, on, through, to, within, into, of, for
τῷ art. dat. neut. sg. ὁ ἡ τό the, this, that, he, she, it
βιβλίῳ n. dat. neut. sg. βιβλίον book, bill, scroll, writing
τῆς art. gen. fem. sg. ὁ ἡ τό the, this, that, he, she, it
ζωῆς n. gen. fem. sg. ζωή life, lifetime
τοῦ art. gen. neut. sg. ὁ ἡ τό the, this, that, he, she, it
ἀρνίου n. gen. neut. sg. ἀρνίον Lamb, lamb

22

1 καὶ conj. καί and, even, also, but
μοι pron. dat. 1p. sg. ἐγώ I
καθαρὸν adj. acc. masc. sg. καθαρός pure, clean, clear
ποταμὸν n. acc. masc. sg. ποταμός river, flood , stream, water
ὕδατος n. gen. neut. sg. ὕδωρ water
ζωῆς n. gen. fem. sg. ζωή life, lifetime
λαμπρὸν adj. acc. masc. sg. λαμπρός gorgeous, bright, goodly, white, clear
ὡς adv. ὡς as, when, as it were, how, about, like, as soon as, even as, while
κρύσταλλον n. acc. masc. sg. κρύσταλλος crystal
ἐκ prep. ἐκ ἐξ (+gen) of, from, out of, by, on, with, in, among, through
τοῦ art. gen. masc. sg. ὁ ἡ τό the, this, that, he, she, it
θρόνου n. gen. masc. sg. θρόνος throne, seat
τοῦ art. gen. masc. sg. ὁ ἡ τό the, this, that, he, she, it
Θεοῦ n. gen. masc. sg. θεός God, god
καὶ conj. καί and, even, also, but
τοῦ art. gen. neut. sg. ὁ ἡ τό the, this, that, he, she, it
ἀρνίου n. gen. neut. sg. ἀρνίον Lamb, lamb
2 ἐν prep. ἐν (+dat) in, by, with, among, at, on, through, to, within, into, of, for

μέσῳ adj. dat. neut. sg. μέσος midst, among, mid, between
τῆς art. gen. fem. sg. ὁ ἡ τό the, this, that, he, she, it
πλατείας adj. gen. fem. sg. πλατύς wide, broad
αὐτῆς pron. gen. fem. 3p. sg. αὐτός ή ό self, of oneself, even, very, the same, he, she, it
καὶ conj. καί and, even, also, but
τοῦ art. gen. masc. sg. ὁ ἡ τό the, this, that, he, she, it
ποταμοῦ n. gen. masc. sg. ποταμός river, flood , stream, water
ἐντεῦθεν adv. ἐντεῦθεν hence, from hence, on either side, from this place
καὶ conj. καί and, even, also, but
ἐντεῦθεν adv. ἐντεῦθεν hence, from hence, on either side, from this place
ξύλον n. nom. neut. sg. ξύλον tree, stave, wood, the stocks
ζωῆς n. gen. fem. sg. ζωή life, lifetime
καρποὺς n. acc. masc. pl. καρπός fruit
δώδεκα num. acc. masc. pl. δώδεκα twelve
κατὰ prep. κατά (+gen) against, by, throughout, down, (+acc) according to, after, with
μῆνα n. acc. masc. sg. μήν month
ἕνα num. acc. masc. sg. εἷς or ἓν one, other, some, any, only, a certain
ἕκαστον adj. acc. masc. sg. ἕκαστος every man, every, every one, any man, each
τὸν art. acc. masc. sg. ὁ ἡ τό the, this, that, he, she, it
καρπὸν n. acc. masc. sg. καρπός fruit
αὐτοῦ pron. gen. neut. 3p. sg. αὐτός ή ό self, of oneself, even, very, the same, he, she, it
καὶ conj. καί and, even, also, but
τὰ art. nom. neut. pl. ὁ ἡ τό the, this, that, he, she, it
φύλλα n. nom. neut. pl. φύλλον leaf
τοῦ art. gen. neut. sg. ὁ ἡ τό the, this, that, he, she, it
ξύλου n. gen. neut. sg. ξύλον tree, stave, wood, the stocks
εἰς prep. εἰς (+acc) into, to, unto, for, in, on, toward, against, upon, at, among
θεραπείαν n. acc. fem. sg. θεραπεία healing, service, household
τῶν art. gen. neut. pl. ὁ ἡ τό the, this, that, he, she, it
ἐθνῶν n. gen. neut. pl. ἔθνος Gentile, nation, heathen, people
3 καὶ conj. καί and, even, also, but
πᾶν adj. nom. neut. sg. πᾶς πᾶσa πᾶν all, every, whosoever, every one, no, whole, any
κατανάθεμα n. nom. neut. sg. κατανάθεμα curse
οὐκ particle of negation. οὐ οὐκ οὐχ not, no, neither, none, nay, nor, never, nothing
ἔτι adv. ἔτι yet, more, any more, further, still, moreover
καὶ conj. καί and, even, also, but
ὁ art. nom. masc. sg. ὁ ἡ τό the, this, that, he, she, it
θρόνος n. nom. masc. sg. θρόνος throne, seat
τοῦ art. gen. masc. sg. ὁ ἡ τό the, this, that, he, she, it
Θεοῦ n. gen. masc. sg. θεός God, god
καὶ conj. καί and, even, also, but
τοῦ art. gen. neut. sg. ὁ ἡ τό the, this, that, he, she, it
ἀρνίου n. gen. neut. sg. ἀρνίον Lamb, lamb
ἐν prep. ἐν (+dat) in, by, with, among, at, on, through, to, within, into, of, for
αὐτῇ pron. dat. fem. 3p. sg. αὐτός ή ό self, of oneself, even, very, the same, he, she, it
καὶ conj. καί and, even, also, but
οἱ art. nom. masc. pl. ὁ ἡ τό the, this, that, he, she, it
δοῦλοι n. nom. masc. pl. δοῦλος servant, bondman, bond, slave
αὐτοῦ pron. gen. masc. 3p. sg. αὐτός ή ό self, of oneself, even, very, the same, he, she, it
αὐτῷ pron. dat. masc. 3p. sg. αὐτός ή ό self, of oneself, even, very, the same, he, she, it
4 καὶ conj. καί and, even, also, but
τὸ art. acc. neut. sg. ὁ ἡ τό the, this, that, he, she, it
πρόσωπον n. acc. neut. sg. πρόσωπον face, presence, person, countenance
αὐτοῦ pron. gen. masc. 3p. sg. αὐτός ή ό self, of oneself, even, very, the same, he, she, it
καὶ conj. καί and, even, also, but

τὸ art. nom. neut. sg. ὁ ἡ τό the, this, that, he, she, it
ὄνομα n. nom. neut. sg. ὄνομα name, call, surname
αὐτοῦ pron. gen. masc. 3p. sg. αὐτός ή ό self, of oneself, even, very, the same, he, she, it
ἐπὶ prep. ἐπί (+gen) on, in, upon, (+dat) in, at, for, upon, (+acc) on, upon, unto, to, against
τῶν art. gen. neut. pl. ὁ ἡ τό the, this, that, he, she, it
μετώπων n. gen. neut. pl. μέτωπον forehead
αὐτῶν pron. gen. masc. 3p. pl. αὐτός ή ό self, of oneself, even, very, the same, he, she, it
5 καὶ conj. καί and, even, also, but
νὺξ n. nom. fem. sg. νύξ night
οὐκ particle of negation. οὐ οὐκ οὐχ not, no, neither, none, nay, nor, never, nothing
ἐκεῖ adv. ἐκεῖ there, thither, thitherward, yonder, yonder place
καὶ conj. καί and, even, also, but
χρείαν n. acc. fem. sg. χρεία need, necessity, lack, want
οὐκ particle of negation. οὐ οὐκ οὐχ not, no, neither, none, nay, nor, never, nothing
λύχνου n. gen. masc. sg. λύχνος candle, light, lamp
καὶ conj. καί and, even, also, but
φωτὸς n. gen. neut. sg. φῶς light, fire
ἡλίου n. gen. masc. sg. ἥλιος sun, east
ὅτι conj. ὅτι that, for, because, how that, how, because that, for that, though
Κύριος n. nom. masc. sg. κύριος Lord, lord, master, sir, LORD, God, Master, owner
ὁ art. nom. masc. sg. ὁ ἡ τό the, this, that, he, she, it
Θεὸς n. nom. masc. sg. θεός God, god
αὐτούς pron. acc. masc. 3p. pl. αὐτός ή ό self, of oneself, even, very, the same, he, she, it
καὶ conj. καί and, even, also, but
εἰς prep. εἰς (+acc) into, to, unto, for, in, on, toward, against, upon, at, among
τοὺς art. acc. masc. pl. ὁ ἡ τό the, this, that, he, she, it
αἰῶνας n. acc. masc. pl. αἰών ever, ever and ever, evermore, age, eternal, world
τῶν art. gen. masc. pl. ὁ ἡ τό the, this, that, he, she, it
αἰώνων n. gen. masc. pl. αἰών ever, ever and ever, evermore, age, eternal, world
6 Καὶ conj. καί and, even, also, but
μοι pron. dat. 1p. sg. ἐγώ I
Οὗτοι demo. pron. nom. masc. pl. οὗτος αὕτη τοῦτο this, the same, this same, he, she, it
οἱ art. nom. masc. pl. ὁ ἡ τό the, this, that, he, she, it
λόγοι n. nom. masc. pl. λόγος word, saying, account, speech, thing, matter
πιστοὶ adj. nom. masc. pl. πιστός faithful, believing, true, sure
καὶ conj. καί and, even, also, but
ἀληθινοί adj. nom. masc. pl. ἀληθινός true
καὶ conj. καί and, even, also, but
Κύριος n. nom. masc. sg. κύριος Lord, lord, master, sir, LORD, God, Master, owner
ὁ art. nom. masc. sg. ὁ ἡ τό the, this, that, he, she, it
Θεὸς n. nom. masc. sg. θεός God, god
τῶν art. gen. masc. pl. ὁ ἡ τό the, this, that, he, she, it
ἁγίων adj. gen. masc. pl. ἅγιος Holy, holy, saint, Holy One, holy thing, most holy
προφητῶν n. gen. masc. pl. προφήτης prophet
τὸν art. acc. masc. sg. ὁ ἡ τό the, this, that, he, she, it
ἄγγελον n. acc. masc. sg. ἄγγελος angel, messenger
αὐτοῦ pron. gen. masc. 3p. sg. αὐτός ή ό self, of oneself, even, very, the same, he, she, it
τοῖς art. dat. masc. pl. ὁ ἡ τό the, this, that, he, she, it
δούλοις n. dat. masc. pl. δοῦλος servant, bondman, bond, slave
αὐτοῦ pron. gen. masc. 3p. sg. αὐτός ή ό self, of oneself, even, very, the same, he, she, it
ἃ relative pron. acc. neut. pl. ὅς ἥ ὅ who, which, what, that
ἐν prep. ἐν (+dat) in, by, with, among, at, on, through, to, within, into, of, for
τάχει n. dat. neut. sg. τάχος speedily, short, quick
7 ταχύ adv. ταχύ quickly, lightly
μακάριος adj. nom. masc. sg. μακάριος blessed, happy

ὁ art. nom. masc. sg. ὁ ἡ τό the, this, that, he, she, it
τοὺς art. acc. masc. pl. ὁ ἡ τό the, this, that, he, she, it
λόγους n. acc. masc. pl. λόγος word, saying, account, speech, thing, matter
τῆς art. gen. fem. sg. ὁ ἡ τό the, this, that, he, she, it
προφητείας n. gen. fem. sg. προφητεία prophecy, prophesying
τοῦ art. gen. neut. sg. ὁ ἡ τό the, this, that, he, she, it
βιβλίου n. gen. neut. sg. βιβλίον book, bill, scroll, writing
τούτου demo. pron. gen. neut. sg. οὗτος αὕτη τοῦτο this, the same, this same, he, she, it
8 Καὶ conj. καί and, even, also, but
ἐγὼ pron. nom. 1p. sg. ἐγώ I
Ἰωάννης n. nom. masc. sg. Ἰωάννης John
ὁ art. nom. masc. sg. ὁ ἡ τό the, this, that, he, she, it
ταῦτα demo. pron. acc. neut. pl. οὗτος αὕτη τοῦτο this, the same, this same, he, she, it
καὶ conj. καί and, even, also, but
καὶ conj. καί and, even, also, but
ὅτε adv. ὅτε when, after that, as soon as, while, after
καὶ conj. καί and, even, also, but
ἔμπροσθεν prep. ἔμπροσθεν (+gen) before, in the sight of, in the presence of
τῶν art. gen. masc. pl. ὁ ἡ τό the, this, that, he, she, it
ποδῶν n. gen. masc. pl. πούς foot
τοῦ art. gen. masc. sg. ὁ ἡ τό the, this, that, he, she, it
ἀγγέλου n. gen. masc. sg. ἄγγελος angel, messenger
τοῦ art. gen. masc. sg. ὁ ἡ τό the, this, that, he, she, it
μοι pron. dat. 1p. sg. ἐγώ I
ταῦτα demo. pron. acc. neut. pl. οὗτος αὕτη τοῦτο this, the same, this same, he, she, it
9 καὶ conj. καί and, even, also, but
μοι pron. dat. 1p. sg. ἐγώ I
μή particle of negation. μή not, no, lest, neither, none, nothing, nor, never, without
σύνδουλός n. nom. masc. sg. σύνδουλος fellowservant
σού pron. gen. 2p. sg. σύ thou, you
γὰρ conj. γάρ for, and, because, but, indeed
καὶ conj. καί and, even, also, but
τῶν art. gen. masc. pl. ὁ ἡ τό the, this, that, he, she, it
ἀδελφῶν n. gen. masc. pl. ἀδελφός brother
σου pron. gen. 2p. sg. σύ thou, you
τῶν art. gen. masc. pl. ὁ ἡ τό the, this, that, he, she, it
προφητῶν n. gen. masc. pl. προφήτης prophet
καὶ conj. καί and, even, also, but
τῶν art. gen. masc. pl. ὁ ἡ τό the, this, that, he, she, it
τοὺς art. acc. masc. pl. ὁ ἡ τό the, this, that, he, she, it
λόγους n. acc. masc. pl. λόγος word, saying, account, speech, thing, matter
τοῦ art. gen. neut. sg. ὁ ἡ τό the, this, that, he, she, it
βιβλίου n. gen. neut. sg. βιβλίον book, bill, scroll, writing
τούτου demo. pron. gen. neut. sg. οὗτος αὕτη τοῦτο this, the same, this same, he, she, it
τῷ art. dat. masc. sg. ὁ ἡ τό the, this, that, he, she, it
Θεῷ n. dat. masc. sg. θεός God, god
10 Καὶ conj. καί and, even, also, but
μοι pron. dat. 1p. sg. ἐγώ I
Μὴ particle of negation. μή not, no, lest, neither, none, nothing, nor, never, without
τοὺς art. acc. masc. pl. ὁ ἡ τό the, this, that, he, she, it
λόγους n. acc. masc. pl. λόγος word, saying, account, speech, thing, matter
τῆς art. gen. fem. sg. ὁ ἡ τό the, this, that, he, she, it
προφητείας n. gen. fem. sg. προφητεία prophecy, prophesying
τοῦ art. gen. neut. sg. ὁ ἡ τό the, this, that, he, she, it
βιβλίου n. gen. neut. sg. βιβλίον book, bill, scroll, writing

τούτου demo. pron. gen. neut. sg. οὗτος αὕτη τοῦτο this, the same, this same, he, she, it
ὅτι conj. ὅτι that, for, because, how that, how, because that, for that, though
ὁ art. nom. masc. sg. ὁ ἡ τό the, this, that, he, she, it
καιρὸς n. nom. masc. sg. καιρός time, season, due time, opportunity
ἐγγύς adv. ἐγγύς nigh, at hand, near, nigh at hand, ready, nigh unto
11 ὁ art. nom. masc. sg. ὁ ἡ τό the, this, that, he, she, it
ἔτι adv. ἔτι yet, more, any more, further, still, moreover
καὶ conj. καί and, even, also, but
ὁ art. nom. masc. sg. ὁ ἡ τό the, this, that, he, she, it
ἔτι adv. ἔτι yet, more, any more, further, still, moreover
καὶ conj. καί and, even, also, but
ὁ art. nom. masc. sg. ὁ ἡ τό the, this, that, he, she, it
δίκαιος adj. nom. masc. sg. δίκαιος righteous, just, meet, right
ἔτι adv. ἔτι yet, more, any more, further, still, moreover
καὶ conj. καί and, even, also, but
ὁ art. nom. masc. sg. ὁ ἡ τό the, this, that, he, she, it
ἅγιος adj. nom. masc. sg. ἅγιος Holy, holy, saint, Holy One, holy thing, most holy
ἔτι adv. ἔτι yet, more, any more, further, still, moreover
12 καὶ conj. καί and, even, also, but
ταχύ adv. ταχύ quickly, lightly
καὶ conj. καί and, even, also, but
ὁ art. nom. masc. sg. ὁ ἡ τό the, this, that, he, she, it
μισθός n. nom. masc. sg. μισθός reward, hire, wage
μου pron. gen. 1p. sg. ἐγώ I
μετ' prep. μετά (+gen) with, among, against, (+acc) after
ἐμοῦ pron. gen. 1p. sg. ἐγώ I
ἑκάστῳ adj. dat. masc. sg. ἕκαστος every man, every, every one, any man, each
ὡς adv. ὡς as, when, as it were, how, about, like, as soon as, even as, while
τὸ art. nom. neut. sg. ὁ ἡ τό the, this, that, he, she, it
ἔργον n. nom. neut. sg. ἔργον work, deed, doing labour
αὐτοῦ pron. gen. masc. 3p. sg. αὐτός ή ό self, of oneself, even, very, the same, he, she, it
13 ἐγὼ pron. nom. 1p. sg. ἐγώ I
τὸ art. nom. neut. sg. ὁ ἡ τό the, this, that, he, she, it
Α n. nom. neut. sg. Α Alpha
καὶ conj. καί and, even, also, but
τὸ art. nom. neut. sg. ὁ ἡ τό the, this, that, he, she, it
Ω n. nom. neut. sg. Ω Omega
ἀρχὴ n. nom. fem. sg. ἀρχή beginning, principality, corner, first, magistrate, rule
καὶ conj. καί and, even, also, but
τέλος n. nom. neut. sg. τέλος end, custom, ending, finally, uttermost
ὁ art. nom. masc. sg. ὁ ἡ τό the, this, that, he, she, it
πρῶτος ordinal. adj. nom. masc. sg. πρῶτος first, chief, first of all, chiefest, best
καὶ conj. καί and, even, also, but
ὁ art. nom. masc. sg. ὁ ἡ τό the, this, that, he, she, it
ἔσχατος adj. nom. masc. sg. ἔσχατος last, lowest, uttermost, uttermost part
14 μακάριοι adj. nom. masc. pl. μακάριος blessed, happy
οἱ art. nom. masc. pl. ὁ ἡ τό the, this, that, he, she, it
τὰς art. acc. fem. pl. ὁ ἡ τό the, this, that, he, she, it
ἐντολὰς n. acc. fem. pl. ἐντολή commandment, precept
αὐτοῦ pron. gen. masc. 3p. sg. αὐτός ή ό self, of oneself, even, very, the same, he, she, it
ἵνα conj. ἵνα that, to, lest, for to, so that, albeit, because, for, so as
ἡ art. nom. fem. sg. ὁ ἡ τό the, this, that, he, she, it
ἐξουσία n. nom. fem. sg. ἐξουσία power, authority, right, strength, jurisdiction
αὐτῶν pron. gen. masc. 3p. pl. αὐτός ή ό self, of oneself, even, very, the same, he, she, it
ἐπὶ prep. ἐπί (+gen) on, in, upon, (+dat) in, at, for, upon, (+acc) on, upon, unto, to, against

τὸ art. acc. neut. sg. ὁ ἡ τό the, this, that, he, she, it
ξύλον n. acc. neut. sg. ξύλον tree, stave, wood, the stocks
τῆς art. gen. fem. sg. ὁ ἡ τό the, this, that, he, she, it
ζωῆς n. gen. fem. sg. ζωή life, lifetime
καὶ conj. καί and, even, also, but
τοῖς art. dat. masc. pl. ὁ ἡ τό the, this, that, he, she, it
πυλῶσιν n. dat. masc. pl. πυλών gate, porch
εἰς prep. εἰς (+acc) into, to, unto, for, in, on, toward, against, upon, at, among
τὴν art. acc. fem. sg. ὁ ἡ τό the, this, that, he, she, it
πόλιν n. acc. fem. sg. πόλις city
15 ἔξω adv. ἔξω out, without, out of, forth, away, outward
δὲ conj. δέ but, and, now, also, to the contrary, rather, then
οἱ art. nom. masc. pl. ὁ ἡ τό the, this, that, he, she, it
κύνες n. nom. masc. pl. κύων dog
καὶ conj. καί and, even, also, but
οἱ art. nom. masc. pl. ὁ ἡ τό the, this, that, he, she, it
φαρμακοὶ n. nom. masc. pl. φαρμακός sorcerer
καὶ conj. καί and, even, also, but
οἱ art. nom. masc. pl. ὁ ἡ τό the, this, that, he, she, it
πόρνοι n. nom. masc. pl. πόρνος fornicator
καὶ conj. καί and, even, also, but
οἱ art. nom. masc. pl. ὁ ἡ τό the, this, that, he, she, it
φονεῖς n. nom. masc. pl. φονεύς murderer
καὶ conj. καί and, even, also, but
οἱ art. nom. masc. pl. ὁ ἡ τό the, this, that, he, she, it
εἰδωλολάτραι n. nom. masc. pl. εἰδωλολάτρης idolater
καὶ conj. καί and, even, also, but
πᾶς adj. nom. masc. sg. πᾶς πᾶσα πᾶν all, every, whosoever, every one, no, whole, any
ὁ art. nom. masc. sg. ὁ ἡ τό the, this, that, he, she, it
καὶ conj. καί and, even, also, but
ψεῦδος n. acc. neut. sg. ψεῦδος lie, lying
16 Ἐγὼ pron. nom. 1p. sg. ἐγώ I
Ἰησοῦς n. nom. masc. sg. Ἰησοῦς Jesus
τὸν art. acc. masc. sg. ὁ ἡ τό the, this, that, he, she, it
ἄγγελόν n. acc. masc. sg. ἄγγελος angel, messenger
μου pron. gen. 1p. sg. ἐγώ I
ὑμῖν pron. dat. 2p. pl. σύ thou, you
ταῦτα demo. pron. acc. neut. pl. οὗτος αὕτη τοῦτο this, the same, this same, he, she, it
ἐπὶ prep. ἐπί (+gen) on, in, upon, (+dat) in, at, for, upon, (+acc) on, upon, unto, to, against
ταῖς art. dat. fem. pl. ὁ ἡ τό the, this, that, he, she, it
ἐκκλησίαις n. dat. fem. pl. ἐκκλησία church, assembly
ἐγὼ pron. nom. 1p. sg. ἐγώ I
ἡ art. nom. fem. sg. ὁ ἡ τό the, this, that, he, she, it
ῥίζα n. nom. fem. sg. ῥίζα root
καὶ conj. καί and, even, also, but
τὸ art. nom. neut. sg. ὁ ἡ τό the, this, that, he, she, it
γένος n. nom. neut. sg. γένος kind, kindred, offspring, nation, countrymen
τοῦ art. gen. masc. sg. ὁ ἡ τό the, this, that, he, she, it
Δαβίδ n. gen. masc. sg. Δαβίδ David
ὁ art. nom. masc. sg. ὁ ἡ τό the, this, that, he, she, it
ἀστὴρ n. nom. masc. sg. ἀστήρ star
ὁ art. nom. masc. sg. ὁ ἡ τό the, this, that, he, she, it
λαμπρὸς adj. nom. masc. sg. λαμπρός gorgeous, bright, goodly, white, clear
καὶ conj. καί and, even, also, but
ὀρθρινός adj. nom. masc. sg. ὀρθρινός morning

17 Καὶ conj. καί and, even, also, but
τὸ art. nom. neut. sg. ὁ ἡ τό the, this, that, he, she, it
Πνεῦμα n. nom. neut. sg. πνεῦμα spirit, Spirit, Ghost, ghost, life. of the spirit, wind
καὶ conj. καί and, even, also, but
ἡ art. nom. fem. sg. ὁ ἡ τό the, this, that, he, she, it
νύμφη n. nom. fem. sg. νύμφη bride, daughter in law
καὶ conj. καί and, even, also, but
ὁ art. nom. masc. sg. ὁ ἡ τό the, this, that, he, she, it
καὶ conj. καί and, even, also, but
ὁ art. nom. masc. sg. ὁ ἡ τό the, this, that, he, she, it
καὶ conj. καί and, even, also, but
ὁ art. nom. masc. sg. ὁ ἡ τό the, this, that, he, she, it
τὸ art. acc. neut. sg. ὁ ἡ τό the, this, that, he, she, it
ὕδωρ n. acc. neut. sg. ὕδωρ water
ζωῆς n. gen. fem. sg. ζωή life, lifetime
δωρεάν adv. δωρεάν freely, for nought, in vain, without a cause
18 γὰρ conj. γάρ for, and, because, but, indeed
παντὶ adj. dat. masc. sg. πᾶς πᾶσα πᾶν all, every, whosoever, every one, no, whole, any
τοὺς art. acc. masc. pl. ὁ ἡ τό the, this, that, he, she, it
λόγους n. acc. masc. pl. λόγος word, saying, account, speech, thing, matter
τῆς art. gen. fem. sg. ὁ ἡ τό the, this, that, he, she, it
προφητείας n. gen. fem. sg. προφητεία prophecy, prophesying
τοῦ art. gen. neut. sg. ὁ ἡ τό the, this, that, he, she, it
βιβλίου n. gen. neut. sg. βιβλίον book, bill, scroll, writing
τούτου demo. pron. gen. neut. sg. οὗτος αὕτη τοῦτο this, the same, this same, he, she, it
Ἐάν conj. ἐάν if, soever, except, though, and if, but, whether, if so, so
τις indefinite pron. nom. masc. sg. τὶς certain, some, any man, one, any thing
πρὸς prep. πρός (+gen) for, (+dat) at, (+acc) unto, to, with, for, against
ταῦτα demo. pron. acc. neut. pl. οὗτος αὕτη τοῦτο this, the same, this same, he, she, it
ὁ art. nom. masc. sg. ὁ ἡ τό the, this, that, he, she, it
Θεὸς n. nom. masc. sg. θεός God, god
ἐπ' prep. ἐπί (+gen) on, in, upon, (+dat) in, at, for, upon, (+acc) on, upon, unto, to, against
αὐτὸν pron. acc. masc. 3p. sg. αὐτός ή ό self, of oneself, even, very, the same, he, she, it
τὰς art. acc. fem. pl. ὁ ἡ τό the, this, that, he, she, it
πληγὰς n. acc. fem. pl. πληγή wound, plague, stripe
τὰς art. acc. fem. pl. ὁ ἡ τό the, this, that, he, she, it
ἐν prep. ἐν (+dat) in, by, with, among, at, on, through, to, within, into, of, for
βιβλίῳ n. dat. neut. sg. βιβλίον book, bill, scroll, writing
τούτῳ demo. pron. dat. neut. sg. οὗτος αὕτη τοῦτο this, the same, this same, he, she, it
19 καὶ conj. καί and, even, also, but
ἐάν conj. ἐάν if, soever, except, though, and if, but, whether, if so, so
τις indefinite pron. nom. masc. sg. τὶς certain, some, any man, one, any thing
ἀπὸ prep. ἀπό (+gen) from, of, out of, since, for, off, at, by, in, on
τῶν art. gen. masc. pl. ὁ ἡ τό the, this, that, he, she, it
λόγων n. gen. masc. pl. λόγος word, saying, account, speech, thing, matter
βιβλίου n. gen. neut. sg. βιβλίον book, bill, scroll, writing
τῆς art. gen. fem. sg. ὁ ἡ τό the, this, that, he, she, it
προφητείας n. gen. fem. sg. προφητεία prophecy, prophesying
ταύτης demo. pron. gen. fem. sg. οὗτος αὕτη τοῦτο this, the same, this same, he, she, it
ὁ art. nom. masc. sg. ὁ ἡ τό the, this, that, he, she, it
Θεὸς n. nom. masc. sg. θεός God, god
τὸ art. acc. neut. sg. ὁ ἡ τό the, this, that, he, she, it
μέρος n. acc. neut. sg. μέρος part, coast, portion, behalf, respect, piece, side
αὐτοῦ pron. gen. masc. 3p. sg. αὐτός ή ό self, of oneself, even, very, the same, he, she, it
ἀπὸ prep. ἀπό (+gen) from, of, out of, since, for, off, at, by, in, on

βίβλου n. gen. fem. sg. βίβλος book, record
τῆς art. gen. fem. sg. ὁ ἡ τό the, this, that, he, she, it
ζωῆς n. gen. fem. sg. ζωή life, lifetime
καὶ conj. καί and, even, also, but
ἐκ prep. ἐκ ἐξ (+gen) of, from, out of, by, on, with, in, among, through
τῆς art. gen. fem. sg. ὁ ἡ τό the, this, that, he, she, it
πόλεως n. gen. fem. sg. πόλις city
τῆς art. gen. fem. sg. ὁ ἡ τό the, this, that, he, she, it
ἁγίας adj. gen. fem. sg. ἅγιος Holy, holy, saint, Holy One, holy thing, most holy
καὶ conj. καί and, even, also, but
τῶν art. gen. neut. pl. ὁ ἡ τό the, this, that, he, she, it
ἐν prep. ἐν (+dat) in, by, with, among, at, on, through, to, within, into, of, for
βιβλίῳ n. dat. neut. sg. βιβλίον book, bill, scroll, writing
τούτῳ demo. pron. dat. neut. sg. οὗτος αὕτη τοῦτο this, the same, this same, he, she, it
20 ὁ art. nom. masc. sg. ὁ ἡ τό the, this, that, he, she, it
ταῦτα demo. pron. acc. neut. pl. οὗτος αὕτη τοῦτο this, the same, this same, he, she, it
Ναί particle. ναί yea, even so, yes, surely, truth, verily
ταχύ adv. ταχύ quickly, lightly
ἀμήν particle. ἀμήν amen, verily
Ναί particle. ναί yea, even so, yes, surely, truth, verily
Κύριε n. voc. masc. sg. κύριος Lord, lord, master, sir, LORD, God, Master, owner
Ἰησοῦ n. voc. masc. sg. Ἰησοῦς Jesus
21 Ἡ art. nom. fem. sg. ὁ ἡ τό the, this, that, he, she, it
χάρις n. nom. fem. sg. χάρις grace, thank, favour, pleasure
τοῦ art. gen. masc. sg. ὁ ἡ τό the, this, that, he, she, it
Κυρίου n. gen. masc. sg. κύριος Lord, lord, master, sir, LORD, God, Master, owner
ἡμῶν pron. gen. 1p. pl. ἐγώ I
Ἰησοῦ n. gen. masc. sg. Ἰησοῦς Jesus
Χριστοῦ n. gen. masc. sg. Χριστός Christ
μετὰ prep. μετά (+gen) with, among, against, (+acc) after
πάντων adj. gen. masc. pl. πᾶς πᾶσα πᾶν all, every, whosoever, every one, no, whole, any
ὑμῶν pron. gen. 2p. pl. σύ thou, you
ἀμήν particle. ἀμήν amen, verily

ΤΕΛΟΣ

BIBLIOGRAPHY

Bible

Η ΚΑΙΝΗ ΔΙΑΘΗΚΗ The New Testament: The Greek Text Underlying The English Authorised Version of 1611. London: Trinitarian Bible Society, n.d.

Η ΚΑΙΝΗ ΔΙΑΘΗΚΗ The New Covenant: The Greek New Testament Stephanus 1550 Received Text. London: Bibles.org.uk, 2005.

Aland, Barbara, Kurt Aland, Johannes Karavidopoulos, Carlo Maria Martini, Bruce Metzger, ed. *The Greek New Testament, Fourth Revised Edition*. Stuttgart: Deutsche Bibelgesellschaft, 1994.

Berry, George Ricker. *The Interlinear KJV Parallel New Testament In Greek And English Based on the Majority Test With Lexicon And Synonyms*. Grand Rapids: Zondervan Publishing House, n.d.

King James Version

Nestle, Erwin and Kurt Aland, ed. *Novum Testamentum Graece*, 27. revidierte Auflage. Stuttgart: Deutsche Bibelgesellschaft, 2006.

Scrivener, Frederich H. A., ed. *Scrivener's Annotated Greek New Testament: Being The Exact Greek Textus Receptus That Underlies The King James Bible*. Collingswood: Dean Burgon Society Press, 1999.

Dictionary

Gingrich, F. Wilbur and Frederick W. Danker. *A Greek-English Lexicon of the New Testament and Other Early Christian Literature, Second Edition Revised and Augmented from Walter Bauer's Fifth Edition, 1958*. Chicago: The University of Chicago Press, 1979.

Guillemette, Pierre. *The Greek New Testament Analyzed*. Scottdale: Herald Press, 1986.

Han, Nathan E. *A Parsing Guide to the Greek New Testament*. Scottdale: Herald Press, 1991.

Kubo, Sakae. *A Reader's Greek-English Lexicon of the New Testament and Beginner's Guide for the Translation of New Testament Greek*. Grand Rapids: Zondervan Publishing House, 1975.

Lau, Yeong Shoon. "A Textus Receptus–King James Version Greek–English Lexicon of the New Testament." Master's thesis, Far Eastern Bible College, 1997.

Park, Seung-Kyu. *A Declension Guide: to the Textus Receptus Greek New Testament Underlying the King James Version*. Cleveland, Georgia: the Old Paths Publications, Inc., 2014.

Park, Seung-Kyu. *A Parsing Guide to the Greek New Testament Underlying the King James Version* (Cleveland: The Old Paths Publications, Inc., 2014

Perschbacher, Wesley J. ed. *The New Analytical Greek Lexicon*. Peabody: Hendrickson Publishers, 1990.

Ra, Hyung-Tak. *Logos Bible Dictionary*. Seoul: Logos Publishing House, 2011.

Thayer, Joseph H. *Thayer's Greek-English Lexicon of the New Testament: Coded Strong's Numbering System*. Peabody, Massachusetts: Hendrickson Publisher, Inc., 2000.

Zodhiates, Spiros. *The Complete Word Study Dictionary: New Testament*. Iowa Falls, Iowa: World Bible Publishers, Inc., 1992.

Grammar

Black, David Alan. *Learn to Read New Testament Greek [1]*. Nashville: Broadman Press, 1993.

Brooks, James A. & Carlton L. Winbery, *Syntax Of New Testament Greek*. Lanham: University Press of America, Inc., 1988.

Khoo, Jeffrey. *Greek Exegesis*. Singapore: Far Eastern Bible College, 2010.

Machen, J. Gresham. *New Testament Greek For Beginners*. New York: Macmillan Publishing Company, 1823.

Wallace, Daniel B. *Greek Grammar Beyond the Basics: An Exegetical Syntax of the New Testament*. Grand Rapids, Michigan: Zondervan, 1996.

Wenham, J. W. *The Elements of the New Testament Greek*. Cambridge, UK: Cambridge University Press, 1965

Were, Nelson Noel Ng'uono. *Biblical Greek Syntax*. Singapore: Far Eastern Bible College, 2006.

Book

Burgon, John W. *The Causes of Corruption of the Traditional Text of the New Testament*. Lafayette. IN: Sovereign Grace Publishers, Inc., 1998.

Cairns, Earle E. *Christianity Through The Centuries: A History of the Christian Church*. Grand Rapids: Zondervan Publishing House, 1996.

Far Eastern Bible College. *FEBC Prospectus 2022-2026*. Singapore: Far Eastern Bible College, 2022.

Farrell, Joseph P. *God, History, and Dialectic: The Theological Foundations of the Two Europes and Their Cultural Consequences*. Digital Edition. 2016, Joseph P. Farrell.

Finkbeiner, Douglas. "An Examination of 'Make Disciples of All Nations' in Matthew 28:18-20." Calvary Baptist Theological Journal 7. Spring 1991.

Hauser, Alan J. and Duane F. Watson. *A History of Biblical Interpretation, Volume 2: The Medieval through the Reformation Periods*. Edited. Grand Rapids, Michigan: William B. Eerdmans Publishing Company, 2009.

Khoo, Jeffrey. *Kept Pure In All Ages: Recapturing the Authorised Version and the Doctrine of Providential Preservation*. Singapore: Far Eastern Bible College, 2001.

Kim, Hyo-Sung. *Problems of the New Testament Original Text*. Seoul: Old-time Faith, 2013.

Moorman, J. A. *8,000 Differences Between the N.T. Greek Words of the King James Bible and the Modern Versions*. Collingswood: The Bible for Today and The Dean Burgon Society, 2002.

Ra, Chaewon. *Verbal Plenary Preservation and Human Responsibility: The Law of Inalterability in the Bible*. Cleveland, GA: The Old Path Publications, Inc., 2022.

Skariah, George. "The Biblical Doctrine of the Perfect Preservation of the Holy Scriptures." PhD dissertation, Far Eastern Bible College, 2005.

Tow, Timothy. "The Unfinished Commission (Matt 28:18-20)." The Burning Bush (January 1999), Vol. 5 No.1. Singapore; Far Eastern Bible College, 1999.

Waite, D. A. *Defending the King James Bible: A Four-fold Superiority*. Collingswood: The Bible For Today Press, 1992.

Software and Website

Deluxe Bible International. Missionsoft. http://misoft.co.kr/.

"γραφή," Blue Letter Bible, accessed on July 21, 2022, https://www.blueletterbible.org/lexicon/g1124/kjv/tr/0-1/.

ABOUT THE AUTHORS
Dr. S. K. Park & Dr. Ra ChaeWon

Dr. S.K. Park is a missionary to Tanzania in East Africa. He earned his Doctor of Philosophy (Ph.D., History) from the KyungHee University in Seoul, South Korea in 2011, and also his Doctor of Theology (Th.D.) from the Far Eastern Bible College of Singapore in 2013. He has served as a professor and the principal of the Bible College of East Africa Tanzania since 2014.

Dr. Ra ChaeWon, his wife, earned her Doctor of Philosophy (Ph.D., Business Administration) from the Yonsei University in Seoul, South Korea in 2007. From September 2010 to December 2016, she served as an accounting professor at the Handong Global University of South Korea. Afterwards, in response to God's calling for her, she joined the Far Eastern Bible College of Singapore in 2017 for her theological studies. She earned her Master of Divinity in 2020 and her Master of Theology in 2022. She is working on her Doctor of Religious Education dissertation from the Far Eastern Bible College of Singapore. She is a missionary to Tanzania in East Africa. She has served as a professor and the Dean of Administration of the Bible College of East Africa Tanzania and as the principal of the Chemchem Kindergarten, Bible College Education Centre.

Milton Keynes UK
Ingram Content Group UK Ltd.
UKHW051833101124
450927UK00008B/83